S0-BNW-326

WADSWORTH
CENGAGE Learning

is committed to
vailable, with the support
ormat you choose.

Learning Solutions – Training & Support

We're your partner in the classroom – online and off.

CengageCourse delivers dynamic, interactive ways to teach and learn using relevant, engaging content with an accent on flexibility and reliability. When you select the **CengageCourse** solution that matches your needs, you'll discover ease and efficiency in teaching and course management.

CourseCare

CourseCare is a revolutionary program providing you with exceptional services and support to integrate your Cengage Learning Digital Solution into your course. Our dedicated team of digital solutions experts will partner with you to design and implement a program built around your course needs. We offer in-depth, one-on-one professional training of our programs and access to a 24/7 Technical Support website. **CourseCare** provides one-on-one service every step of the way—from finding the right solution for your course to training to ongoing support—helping you to drive student engagement.

For more than a decade, **TeamUP Faculty Programs** have helped faculty reach and engage students through peer-to-peer consultations, workshops, and professional development conferences. Our team of **Faculty Programs Consultants and Faculty Advisors** provide implementation training and professional development opportunities customized to your needs.

Access, Rent, Save, and Engage.

Save up to 60%

CENGAGE**brain**.com

At CengageBrain.com students will be able **to save up to 60%** on their course materials through our full spectrum of options. Students will have the option to **Rent** their textbooks, purchase print **textbooks, eTextbooks,** or individual **eChapters** and **Audio Books** all for substantial savings over average retail prices.

CengageBrain.com also includes single sign-on access to Cengage Learning's broad range of homework and study tools, and features a selection of free content.

PREVIEW

An important form of learning is *cooperative learning*, in which small groups of students work together. The four students participating in this project can learn a great deal from each other. Students engaged in cooperative learning, compared with those who receive more traditional methods of instruction, often display significantly higher performance in subjects on which they work as a group.

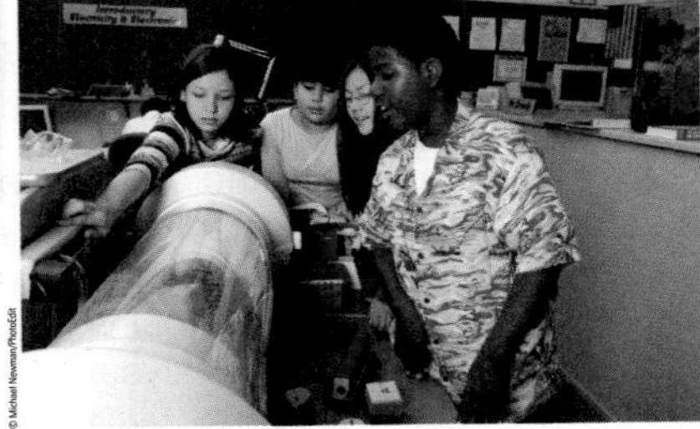

© Michael Newman/PhotoEdit

classroom and high academic performance in early adolescence (Linney & Seidman, 1989; Rutter, 1983; Rutter et al., 1979; Wentzel, 2002).

Children are able to recognize the strength of their interpersonal relationship with a teacher as early as first grade. When they perceive that teachers care about them, children have more favorable attitudes toward school (Valeski & Stipek, 2001). Moreover, teacher–child relationships that begin early in the schooling process have long-term outcomes. Bridget Hamre and Robert Pianta (2001) asked kindergarten teachers in a small community to assess their personal relationships with each of their students. Nearly 200 of these students were followed through eighth grade. Those reported to have had a negative relationship with the teacher as kindergartners, for example, showing conflict and overdependency, continued to have difficulties with school over the next eight years. However, if children who displayed behavior problems in kindergarten were able to develop positive relationships with their kindergarten teachers, it helped to counter behavioral difficulties in the later school years, a finding that has considerable implications for the importance of a young student's relationship with his or her teacher and academic success.

RISK | RESILIENCE

Cultural Differences in School Achievement

SOCIOCULTURAL INFLUENCE

The school experience is not necessarily the same for children of different racial and ethnic backgrounds. Children who attend school bring with them attitudes about school that are first nurtured within their families, as well as cultural beliefs that may be in synchrony or in conflict with the predominant belief system of the school (Gibson & Ogbu, 1991). For example, are schools a vehicle for economic and personal advancement? Cultural and ethnic groups may vary in their responses to this question. Is verbal, rational expression (which schools emphasize) the optimal means of human communication as opposed to emotional or spiritual sharing? Again, cultures sometimes differ in the extent to which they value these various skills. One of the major challenges facing educators is how to ensure the academic success of children who come from a range of cultural-ethnic backgrounds.

RISK | RESILIENCE

The Achievement Gap A concern arising from research on school achievement in the United States is that a significant number of children from some groups—for example, African American and Hispanic children—score lower than Caucasian children on measures of

380 | CHAPTER 10 | ACHIEVEMENT

◀ Chapter 10, "Achievement," now focuses on the numerous factors that research has identified as being linked to success in school.

© Marchen/Digital Vision/Jupiter Images

When mothers work, their children are less likely to hold stereotyped beliefs about gender, probably because they see both parents in multiple roles.

(see Chapter 10, "Achievement"), and higher mathematics achievement in school for the child compared with the effects when mothers did not work (Vandell & Ramanan, 1992).

In general, the clearest effect of maternal employment involves the gender-role attitudes of both sons and daughters. As we saw in Chapter 13, "Gender," when mothers work outside the home, their children are less likely than children of at-home mothers to hold stereotypical beliefs about males and females and more likely to see both sexes as competent (Hoffman & Youngblade, 1999). When both mother and father work, sons and daughters have the opportunity to see both parents in multiple roles—as powerful, competent wage earners and nurturant, warm caregivers—a factor that probably contributes to more egalitarian beliefs.

Overall, maternal employment is not a simple, "neat" variable in studying child development. Some mothers work out of sheer economic necessity, whereas others are more concerned with realizing personal or career goals, for example. As researchers point out, the impact of maternal employment is better understood through its effects on family dynamics, parental attitudes, and the alternative child care arrangements the family chooses. It is to these factors that we now turn our attention.

Maternal Employment and Parent–Child Interaction In terms of direct, one-to-one mother–child interaction, no significant differences have been found between employed and nonemployed mothers (Gottfried et al., 2002). Employed mothers often compensate for the time they miss with their children during the workweek by allocating more time for them during mornings and evenings (Ahnert, Rickert, & Lamb, 2000). In many instances, fathers assume more responsibilities for child care when the mother works, especially when parents have nonstandard work schedules and when they hold nontraditional beliefs about child care (Han, 2004; NICHD Early Child Care Research Network, 2000b). As we saw in our earlier discussion, responsive and sensitive "fathering" provides the same benefits to children as effective "mothering."

Overall, what matters more than whether the mother works is her attitude toward mothering and work and why she is working or staying home. In one study of mothers of infants, women who remained at home contrary to their preference had higher scores on tests of depression and stress than mothers who preferred to be at home and were not in the labor force and employed mothers who valued their positions in the work world (Hock & DeMeis, 1990). We saw earlier in this chapter that parental stress has been implicated as a factor in less consistent and less nurturant parenting. On the other hand, when maternal employment is the factor that produces tension, parenting practices also may suffer. Researchers have found that mothers who worked more than forty hours per week, for example, were more anxious and unhappy and had less sensitive and less animated interactions with their infants than mothers who worked less than forty hours per week (Owen & Cox, 1988). In general, family factors continue to predict child outcomes, even though, when mothers work, their children are likely to be enrolled in full-time child care. Variables such as parental child-rearing style, psychological well-being, and sensitivity are associated with children's cognitive and social development irrespective of the child's caregiving context (NICHD Early Child Care Research Group, 1998b). First and foremost, it is parents who play a primary role.

The Effects of Daycare About one-fourth of children enter child care during the first five months after birth, according to one national survey. About half begin regular child care before they turn three (Singer et al., 1998). Child care arrangements take various forms, from in-home care provided by a relative or paid caregiver to group care in a formal, organized

538 | CHAPTER 14 | THE FAMILY

New Content Highlights

Among many other topics, this edition presents new or expanded material on:

- "Developmental science," a term incorporated throughout to highlight the increasingly interdisciplinary nature of the field
- Neuroscience (Ch. 2, Ch. 11)
- Epigenetics, recent work highlighting molecular studies of genetic influences on development (Ch. 3)
- Consequences of cocaine use and effects on the newborn from drugs given during childbirth (Ch. 4)
- Brain development during adolescence, effects of sleep, determinants of body growth (Ch. 5)
- Primary mechanisms associated with language acquisition, presented in systematic discussions (Ch. 7)
- Development of self-regulation and conscience, antisocial behavior/aggression (Ch. 12)
- Effective parenting, effects of physical punishment, consequences of maternal employment on development, PTSD, gay and lesbian parenting (Ch. 14)
- Video deficits in children under 18 months, effects of relocating children in low-income families to more affluent neighborhoods, development difficulties found in children from affluent families, effects of social networks on social development (Ch. 16)

Five themes

provide coherence to the myriad details about child development

The book's key themes in development, introduced in Chapter 1 and integrated as appropriate throughout chapters, provide a framework to help students discern the importance and interrelatedness of the multitude of facts about child development. Streamlined from six themes to five (Nature and Nurture, Sociocultural Influence, Continuity/Discontinuity, Interaction among Domains, and Risk/Resilience), these pedagogical tools are also vehicles for encouraging critical analysis.

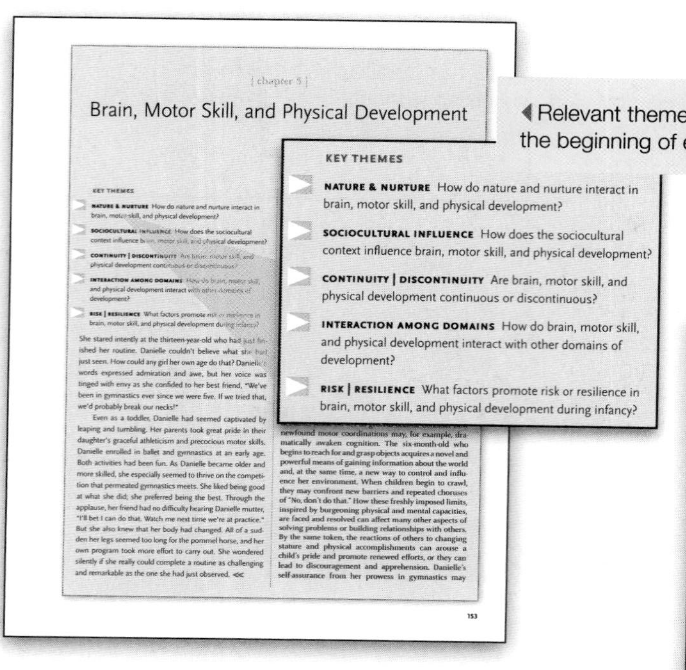

[chapter 5]

Brain, Motor Skill, and Physical Development

KEY THEMES

NATURE & NURTURE How do nature and nurture interact in brain, motor skill, and physical development?

SOCIOCULTURAL INFLUENCE How does the sociocultural context influence brain, motor skill, and physical development?

CONTINUITY | DISCONTINUITY Are brain, motor skill, and physical development continuous or discontinuous?

INTERACTION AMONG DOMAINS How do brain, motor skill, and physical development interact with other domains of development?

RISK | RESILIENCE What factors promote risk or resilience in brain, motor skill, and physical development during infancy?

She stared intently at the thirteen-year-old who had just finished her routine. Danielle couldn't believe what she had just seen. How could any girl her own age do that? Danielle's words expressed admiration and awe, but her voice was tinged with envy as she confided to her best friend, "We've been in gymnastics ever since we were five. If we tried that, we'd probably break our necks!"

Even as a toddler, Danielle had seemed captivated by leaping and tumbling. Her parents took great pride in their daughter's graceful athleticism and precocious motor skills. Danielle enrolled in ballet and gymnastics at an early age. Both activities had been fun. As Danielle became older and more skilled, she especially seemed to thrive on the competition that permeated gymnastics meets. She liked being good at what she did; she preferred being the best. Through the applause, her friend had no difficulty hearing Danielle mutter, "I'll bet I can do that. Watch me next time we're at practice." But she also knew that her body had changed. All of a sudden her legs seemed too long for the pommel horse, and her own program took more effort to carry out. She wondered silently if she really could complete a routine as challenging and remarkable as the one she had just observed. <<

newfound motor coordinations may, for example, dramatically awaken cognition. The six-month-old who begins to reach for and grasp objects acquires a novel and powerful means of gaining information about the world and, at the same time, a new way to control and influence her environment. When children begin to crawl, they may confront new barriers and repeated choruses of "No, don't do that." How these freshly imposed limits, inspired by burgeoning physical and mental capacities, are faced and resolved can affect many other aspects of solving problems or building relationships with others. By the same token, the reactions of others to changing stature and physical accomplishments can arouse a child's pride and promote renewed efforts, or they can lead to discouragement and apprehension. Danielle's self-assurance from her prowess in gymnastics may

153

◀ Relevant themes, formulated as questions, are listed at the beginning of each chapter (starting with Chapter 3).

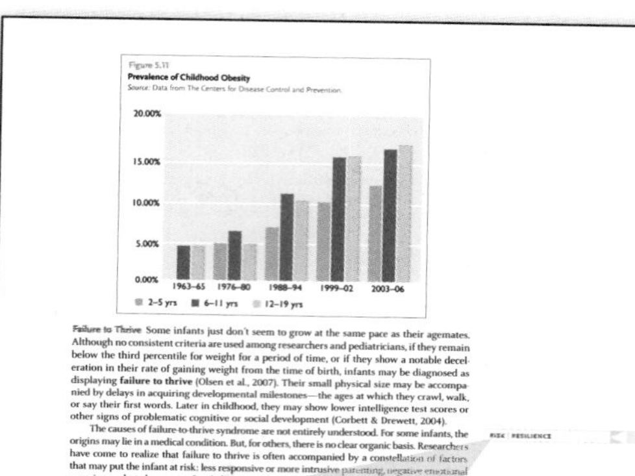

Figure 5.11

Prevalence of Childhood Obesity

Source: Data from The Centers for Disease Control and Prevention.

Failure to Thrive Some infants just don't seem to grow at the same pace as their agemates. Although no consistent criteria are used among researchers and pediatricians, if they remain below the third percentile for weight for a period of time, or if they show a notable deceleration in their rate of gaining weight from the time of birth, infants may be diagnosed as displaying **failure to thrive** (Olsen et al., 2007). Their small physical size may be accompanied by delays in acquiring developmental milestones—the ages at which they crawl, walk, or say their first words. Later in childhood, they may show lower intelligence test scores or other signs of problematic cognitive or social development (Corbett & Drewett, 2004).

The causes of failure-to-thrive syndrome are not entirely understood. For some infants, the origins may lie in a medical condition. But, for others, there is no clear organic basis. Researchers have come to realize that failure to thrive is often accompanied by a constellation of factors that may put the infant at risk: less responsive or more intrusive parenting, negative emotional experiences, but also greater familial exposure to poverty, violence, and other sources of stress.

RISK | RESILIENCE

other signs of problematic cognitive or social development (Corbett & Drewett, 2004).

The causes of failure-to-thrive syndrome are not entirely understood. For some infants, the origins may lie in a medical condition. But, for others, there is no clear organic basis. Researchers have come to realize that failure to thrive is often accompanied by a constellation of factors that may put the infant at risk: less responsive or more intrusive parenting, negative emotional experiences, but also greater familial exposure to poverty, violence, and other sources of stress.

RISK | RESILIENCE

of two- to six-year-olds growing up in urban regions in China (Luo & Hu, 2002). Fortunately, at least within the United States, the percentage of children overweight or obese appears to have stopped increasing in the last decade although the numbers continue to remain perilously high (Ogden et al., 2010).

Most estimates of obesity are measured by *body mass index (BMI)*. The BMI is determined by dividing the weight of a child or adult (in kilograms) by the square of his or her

failure to thrive Designation for a child whose growth in height or weight is below the third percentile for children of the same age.

▲ Throughout the chapter, themes are identified in the margin next to relevant discussions, serving to organize the material. The new theme concerning risk and resilience is especially relevant to the book's focus on practical applications of developmental science.

chapter recap

Summary of Developmental Themes

Nature & Nurture

How do nature and nurture interact in brain, motor skill, and physical development?

Brain development, the acquisition of motor skills, and physical development are the products of complex systems influenced by both biology and experience. For example, biological processes, both genetic and hormonal, augment the proliferation and migration of neurons. At the same time, environmental factors can have a potent effect on the way brain wiring proceeds. Although babies seem to be intrinsically motivated to exercise rudimentary motor skills, experiences such as practice and training can also encourage their acquisition. Once a child attains locomotion or other skills, she or he provokes new reactions from caregivers, which may include encouragement or restrictions of the types of behaviors the child displays. Genetic factors, brain centers that regulate growth, and hormones such as HGH, testosterone, and estrogen, among others, are biological factors that contribute to growth and physical maturity. However, adequate nutrition, stimulation, and the emotional and social support of caregivers are critical environmental factors as well.

Moreover, the reactions of others to physical development (for example, early maturity or excessive weight gain) may result in differing behavioral consequences for children, including with whom they associate or whether they engage in practices involving dieting and eating that can influence health and physical well-being.

Sociocultural Influence

How does the sociocultural context influence brain, motor skill, and physical development?

Motor skill development and physical growth are embedded within settings, resources, and beliefs promoted by the society in which the child lives. For example, the extent to which a culture encourages specific skills, such as the acquisition of motor milestones and various physical skills, or provides positive evaluations for such things as being tall or slender, affects infants' and children's efforts to achieve various competencies and physical attributes. Knowledge about safe sleeping arrangements can reduce the occurrence of SIDS, and more access to nutritional resources has produced secular trends related to many changes in physical development such as greater height and the earlier appearance of menarche. Changes in eating habits, in physical activity, and in

| CHAPTER RECAP | 193

◀ A synopsis of how the themes are illustrated in the chapter appears in the ***Chapter Recap***, reinforcing students' comprehension and retention.

Practical application of developmental science
is illuminated in boxed features

research applied to parenting | Encouraging Young Children's Compliance

Even though preschoolers are beginning to exert signs of self-control, most parents still provide their young children with a hefty dose of supervision. And with their rising independence, children are not always ready to accept it. The frequency with which conflict occurs between parents and children in American families—for example, asking the child to delay a response, slow down an activity, stop an unacceptable behavior, pay attention, or help out with an uninteresting task—is typically high, perhaps on the order of fifteen to twenty times per hour (Laible & Thompson, 2002). The commitment to complying with a "don't" uttered by caregivers appears to be acquired somewhat earlier and more rapidly by children in American families than consistency in responding to a "do." This difference may be because parents are more likely to enforce the former than the latter or because they persist more in prohibiting negative behaviors (Kochanska, 2002; Kochanska, Coy, & Murray, 2001). Can caregivers do anything to encourage the emergence of socially acceptable and compliant behaviors during early childhood? Research findings suggest that there is a link between child compliance and several characteristics of caregivers.

1. *Be supportive, responsive, accepting, sensitive, and emotionally available to children.* Researchers have found that, when mothers showed eager responsiveness to their toddlers and were generally positive in the emotions they expressed, their children often responded in kind, with cooperation and enthusiasm. When mother–child pairs displayed this *mutually responsive orientation,* the children were likely to continue to comply with mothers' requests even several years later (Kochanska & Murray, 2000).
2. *Justify the need for children to act in certain ways.* Researchers have noted that mothers who used a high level of justification when their children were thirty months old also had children who were more compliant with adult requests six months later. When caregivers make statements like "You need to eat your dinner, so that you will not be hungry later," they are helping their children to understand multiple perspectives on social conflicts, offering an opportunity for growth (Laible & Thompson, 2002).
3. *Offer a compromise or provide a benefit for alternative responses.* When caregivers show an interest in putting an end to a conflict ("I'll let you have a cookie if you eat your dinner"), children are learning an important lesson: that relationships are important and that conflict resolution skills are useful in preserving those relationships (Laible & Thompson, 2002).
4. *Emphasize behaving competently over inhibiting activities.* When mothers emphasize "do" over "don't" in their toddlers and preschoolers, fewer compliance and behavior problems arise at age five. Perhaps by encouraging children to
tasks ("Clean up") or self-care behaviors ("Ti
competence that have repercussions for the
requests (Kuczynski & Kochanska, 1995).

◀ Research Applied to Parenting/Education

These boxes are designed to identify some of the implications of research that extend beyond the laboratory, and to help students think about questions and concerns that typically affect parents and teachers in their interactions with children. New topics include reducing sensitivity to pain (Ch. 6), encouraging young children's compliance (Ch. 12), and preventing bullying (Ch. 15).

Figure 9.9
Theory of Mind in Deaf Individuals
Members of a deaf community in Nicaragua developed their own sign language. As the language evolved and included more mental state words (such as "know" on the left and "doesn't know" on the right), individuals began to use more of these words and also showed greater success on a false belief test.
Source: From Pyers, J. E., & Senghas, A. (2009). Language promotes false-belief understanding: Evidence from learners of a new sign language. *Psychological Science, 20,* 805–811.

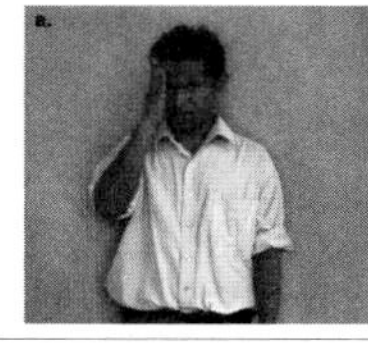

atypical development | Childhood Autism

Childhood autism is a puzzling disorder affecting about 1 in every 110 children born, according to government statistics collected in 2006 (Centers for Disease Control, 2010). The disorder, more common among boys than girls, is characterized by the child's preference to be alone, poor eye contact and general lack of social skills, often the absence of meaningful language, and a preference for sameness and elaborate routines. Some autistic children show unusual skills, such as being able to recite lengthy passages from memory, put together complex jigsaw puzzles, or create intricate drawings. Often these children show a fascination with spinning objects or repeating the speech patterns of someone else. The hallmark trait, though, is the lack of contact these children have with the social world, starting at an early age. Kanner's (1943) description of one autistic boy captures the syndrome well: "He seems almost to draw into his shell and live within himself" (p. 218).

Since Leo Kanner first identified this psychopathology, numerous causes of autism have been proposed, ranging from deprived early emotional relationships with parents to defective neurological wiring in the brain (Waterhouse, Fein, & Modahl, 1996). An intriguing more recent suggestion is that autistic children, for biological reasons, lack the ability to think about mental states; that is, they lack a "theory of mind" that most children begin to develop during the preschool years. Consider how autistic children behave in the "false belief" task described earlier. Whereas most normal four-year-olds are successful, most nine-year-old autistic children fail this problem (Baron-Cohen, Tager-Flusberg, & Cohen, 1993; Peterson, Wellman, & Liu, 2005). These results suggest that autistic children cannot conceptualize the mental state of another individual. Autistic children, the argument proceeds, have severe deficits in communication and social interaction precisely because they cannot appreciate what the contents of another person's mind might be (Frith & Happé, 1999).

Not all researchers believe that the absence of a "theory of mind" explains childhood autism. Some maintain that autistic children cannot disengage their attention from a stimulus on which they are focusing, such as the hiding location in the "false belief" task (Hughes & Russell, 1993). Others suggest that problems with memory, processing speech sounds, or executive control processes are responsible (Bennetto, Pennington, & Rogers, 1996; Carlson, Moses, & Hix, 1998; Whitehouse & Bishop, 2008). Moreover, even if autistic children lack a theory of mind, it may not be because of a neurological deficit.

| UNDERSTANDING PSYCHOLOGICAL STATES | 335

◀ Atypical Development Boxes

The authors continue to include within most chapters an ***Atypical Development*** feature to emphasize that the same processes that help to explain normal development can also help us understand development that is different from the norm.

PREVIEW

Guided opportunities to think critically
help students become educated consumers

what do you think? What Are the Consequences of Friending and Defriending?

No one doubts that technology has dramatically changed our lives over the past several decades. And those changes may also be affecting how peers relate to one another and what is meant by being a friend. Social networking and texting have become a major part of many teenagers' Internet-savvy activities. For example, 93 percent of teenagers in the United States use the Internet and 73 percent of them access social network sites (Lenhart et al., 2010).

Although considerable interest has been focused on the intellectual impact of Internet use and the potentially negative influences associated with cyberbullying and sexual communications via such media, might this activity also be changing how we develop and interact with friends? Do you think, for example, that as a result of greater use of electronic communications, children and teenagers may have fewer face-to-face interactions with their friends, a trend that has been suggested by some researchers (Subrahmanyam & Greenfield, 2008)? Does this means of maintaining contact with others provide as much emotional support and trust, a hallmark of strong friendships, as that which occurs when individuals interact with one another in person? What might be the consequences of missing the visible social cues and subtle emotional variations that are difficult to convey outside of the immediate one-to-one context that has historically served to support friendships? As a result, are children and teenagers becoming less adept at reading these cues when the opportunities arise? And what might be the impact of such communications because they are often more public, that is, possibly viewed by many others? Could texting and communicating via social networks to establish and maintain friendships then lead to more superficial interactions? Or could such activities actually make friends more available and thus permit the establishment of tighter and closer bonds with each other? Might these various means of communication, for example, help shy children and adolescents reach out to and stay in touch with others?

There are additional issues regarding the dynamics of children's friendships. Have you ever been defriended or invited someone to be a friend who failed to answer your request to become one? What do you think the reactions of children and teenagers are to this kind of "social" exchange? Is it likely to be the same as when friends have unsuccessful social interactions in person? Is it a "convenient," less emotionally difficult way of letting someone know your feelings about them or, in the case of defriending, is it likely to be communicated and then perceived as a less polite, harsher, and, as a consequence, more negative interaction than a face-to-face rejection? How do you think these newer ways of establishing, maintaining, and changing friends assist or complicate social relationships for children and teenagers?

◀ **NEW!** ***What Do You Think?*** boxes spark debate and extended discussion by combining the previous edition's *Controversy Boxes* and *What Do You Think?* questions into one feature.

New topics include "Should Child Rearing Be Regulated?" and "What Are the Consequences of Friending and Defriending?"

to which they compare themselves with celebrities or other girls in school, or even see idealized thin bodies in commercials, predicts the degree of body dissatisfaction that they report (Hargreaves & Tiggemann, 2003; Jones, 2004).

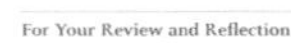

For Your Review and Reflection

- What are the consequences of poor nutrition for growth? What are the differences between marasmus and kwashiorkor?
- What is a secular trend?
- What is failure to thrive and what are some of its consequences for development?
- How may sociocultural factors be contributing to the increase in obesity observed in many nations? How are interactions among domains evident in discussions of nutrition and obesity?
- Why are dieting and eating disorders of concern? What are anorexia nervosa and bulimia, and how do they affect development?
- Do you think that media, physical activity, and the perceptions of others have had an influence on your views about what to eat and the importance of exercise? In what ways?

PHYSICAL MATURITY | 187

◀ ***For Your Review and Reflection*** items provide a series of questions designed to promote a review of the material at the end of each major section. This feature provides an active way for students to recap and verify their understanding of the topic just covered.

PREVIEW

Instructive visual chronologies
clarify and complement the narrative

Chronology Charts

Redesigned to be even more accessible and relevant, these charts (one or two in most chapters) summarize the child's specific developmental attainments at various ages. By giving students a sense of the pattern and typical timing of important events in the child's life, the charts serve as another organizing device for the material.

CHRONOLOGY Development of Self and Self-Regulation: Birth to 13+ Years

MONTHS BIRTH | YEARS BIRTH

© Jamie Grill/Tetra Images/Jupiter Images

© Radius Images/Jupiter Images

8–9 Months
- Parent initiates attempts to regulate infant's behavior.

12–15 Months
- Parent's efforts to control behavior emphasize toddler's safety, preservation of property, and avoidance of harm to others.
- Toddler shows the first signs of self-regulation.

© Marcin Balcerzak/Shutterstock.com

15–18 Months
- Recognizes self in mirror and photos.
- Parent's increased efforts at co-regulation emphasize family routines, self-care, and increased independence.

18–30 Months
- Begins to be capable of delaying gratification.

2 ½–6 Years
- Defines self by categorical judgments.
- Recognizes agency for physical and cognitive achievements.
- Exercises overt self-regulation using language.
- Recognizes increasingly effective ways to delay gratification.

6–9 Years
- Defines self by social comparisons.
- Displays global self-esteem.
- Recognizes agency for social achievements.
- Exercises self-regulation through internalized language.

10–13 Years
- Defines self in terms of social roles.
- Begins to use autonomous criteria for evaluating of self.
- Recognizes contradictory views of self.
- Shows metacognitive understanding of self-regulation.

© SW Productions/Photodisc/Jupiter Images

13+ Years
- Defines self in terms of principled values.
- Begins to accept and resolve contradictory views of self.
- Begins to address issues of identity.
- Recognizes self within the broader society.

describes the sequence in the development of understanding the self and self-regulation based on the findings of research. Children often show individual differences in ges at which they display the various developmental achievements outlined here.

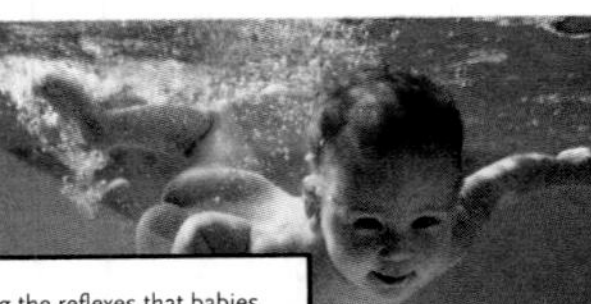

Among the reflexes that babies display is the swimming reflex. When young infants are placed in water, breathing is suspended, and they engage in swim-like movements with their arms and legs.

...compet ...more ca their new world with surprisingly adept abilities, amor reactions to touch, light, sound, and other kinds of sti exhibited even prenatally.

Reflexes are among the building blocks that soo and the acquisition of *developmental milestones*— skills. Along with breathing and swallowing, *primitiv* ing (see Table 5.1), provide nourishment for the infant's survival. Among our evolutionary ancestors, other reflexes, such as the Moro and palmar reflexes, helped to protect newborns from danger. *Postural reflexes*, including stepping, swimming, and body righting (which are surprisingly similar to later voluntary movements), appear to be designed to maintain a specific orientation to the environment. If primitive or postural reflexes are absent, are too strong or too weak, display unequal strength when normally elicited from either side of the body, or continue to be exhibited beyond certain ages, a pediatrician may begin to suspect cerebral palsy or some other neurological impairment and developmental difficulties for the baby.

Motor Milestones

Reflexes are often viewed as fixed responses to a stimulus. However, many early motor behaviors that young infants produce consist of coordinated actions. Repeated sequences of motions performed with no apparent goal such as rubbing one foot against the other, rocking back and forth, bouncing up and down, swaying side to side, striking or banging objects, mouthing and tonguing, and shaking and nodding the head may eventually be recruited and integrated into organized voluntary motor skills and activities such as grasping, crawling, and walking (Thelen, 1996). These latter motor milestones, once mastered, open up new worlds to the infant. Moreover, they lead caregivers to respond in different ways: childproofing the home to prevent accidents, allowing greater independence, expecting more mature behavior. Most gains in infant movement

reflex Involuntary reaction to touch, light, sound, and other kinds of stimulation.

166 | CHAPTER 5 | BRAIN, MOTOR SKILL, AND PHYSICAL DEVELOPMENT

Annotated Illustrations and Charts

An extensive program of illustrations, accompanied by informative captions, helps to make the material more engaging and comprehensible.

PREVIEW

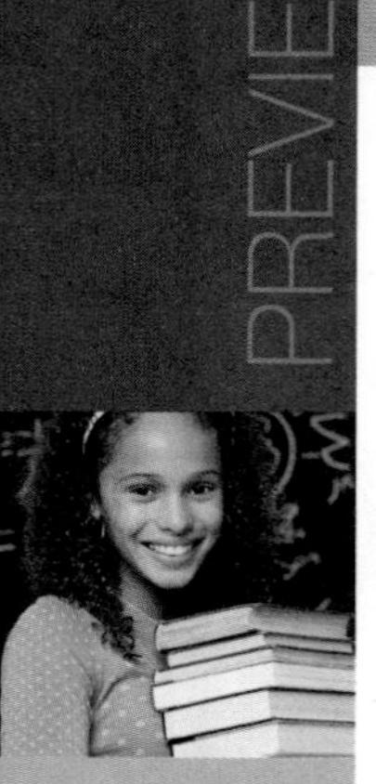

Teaching and learning resources
support instructors and students

PowerLecture™ with ExamView®
ISBN: 978-1-111-35493-0

This one-stop lecture and class preparation tool contains ready-to-use Microsoft® PowerPoint® lecture slides, art from the text, and video clips. It also includes **ExamView® Computerized Testing**, which lets you create, customize, and deliver tests and study guides (both print and online) in minutes using items from the printed Test Bank in electronic format.

Instructor's Resource Manual
ISBN: 978-0-618-60868-3

This manual contains a complete set of chapter outlines and learning objectives matching those provided in the Study Guide for students, as well as lecture topics, classroom exercises, demonstrations, handouts, and recommended readings, videos, and Internet sites.

Test Bank
ISBN: 978-0-618-62318-1

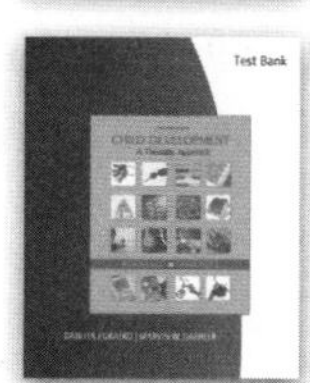

Nearly 2,000 multiple-choice items are keyed to the learning objective, section in the text where the answer can be found, type of question (Fact, Concept, or Application), and correct answer. A set of essay questions for each chapter and a concluding set of essay questions can be used to encourage students to apply their critical thinking skills.

Developmental Psychology CourseMate

Cengage Learning's **Developmental Psychology CourseMate** brings course concepts to life with interactive learning, study, and exam preparation tools that support the printed textbook. Students can read an integrated eBook, take notes, review flashcards, watch videos, and take practice quizzes online.

CengageNOW™ for Child Development: A Thematic Approach

CengageNOW™ is an online teaching and learning resource that gives you more control in less time and delivers better outcomes—NOW—with grading, quizzing, and the ability to create assignments and track student outcomes. The flexible assignments and grade book allow you to choose the options that best suit your course plan, while diagnostic *Personalized Study Plans* (based on chapter-specific tests) empower students to master concepts and prepare for exams. **CengageNOW** also includes a Cengage Learning eBook version of the text.

WebTutor™ with eBook on Blackboard® or WebCT®

Jumpstart your course with customizable, text-specific content for use within your course management system. Whether you want to web-enable your class or put an entire course online, **WebTutor™** delivers with a wide array of resources including quizzing, videos, and more.

Study Guide
ISBN: 978-0-618-61864-4

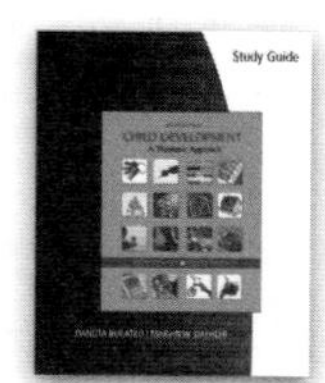

This guide contains a set of learning objectives for each chapter of the text, a detailed study outline, a key terms section, and a self-quiz consisting of 30 multiple-choice questions with an answer key.

The Wadsworth Developmental Psychology Media Library

A variety of videos from ABC News are available upon adoption—great as lecture launchers or to spark class discussion. Contact your local Cengage Learning representative for details.

Contact your local Cengage Learning representative for assistance with packaging any of the student resources described above with new texts.

[sixth edition]

Child Development
A THEMATIC APPROACH

Danuta Bukatko
College of the Holy Cross

Marvin W. Daehler
University of Massachusetts, Amherst

WADSWORTH
CENGAGE Learning™

Australia • Brazil • Japan • Korea • Mexico • Singapore • Spain • United Kingdom • United States

***Child Development: A Thematic Approach*, Sixth Edition**
Danuta Bukatko and Marvin W. Daehler

Publisher: Linda Schreiber-Ganster
Executive Editor: Jon-David Hague
Senior Editor: Jaime Perkins
Associate Development Editor: Nicolas Albert
Assistant Editor: Paige Leeds
Editorial Assistant: Jessica Alderman
Media Editor: Mary Noel
Marketing Manager: Jessica Egbert
Marketing Assistant: Anna Andersen
Marketing Communications Manager: Laura Localio
Content Project Manager: Charlene M. Carpentier
Design Director: Rob Hugel
Art Director: Vernon Boes
Print Buyer: Karen Hunt
Rights Acquisitions Specialist: Roberta Broyer
Production Service and Compositor: Integra
Text Designer: Jeanne Calabrese
Photo Researcher: Bill Smith Group
Text Researcher: Sarah D'Stair
Illustrator: Carol Zuber-Mallison
Cover Designer: Terri Wright
Cover Image: Infant keys, car keys, trike, © Photodisc, Getty Images; model house, © Judith Collins/Alamy; motorcycle, © Artostock.com/Alamy; chalkboard, © Coston Stock/Alamy; abacus, © photo division/Masterfile; all remaining images, © Masterfile

Library of Congress Control Number: 2010936205

Student Edition:

ISBN-13: 978-0-618-60865-2

ISBN-10: 0-618-60865-6

Loose-leaf Edition:

ISBN-13: 978-1-111-34534-1

ISBN-10: 1-111-34534-1

Wadsworth
20 Davis Drive
Belmont, CA 94002-3098
USA

Cengage Learning is a leading provider of customized learning solutions with office locations around the globe, including Singapore, the United Kingdom, Australia, Mexico, Brazil, and Japan. Locate your local office at: **www.cengage.com/global**

Cengage Learning products are represented in Canada by Nelson Education, Ltd.

To learn more about Wadsworth, visit **www.cengage.com/wadsworth**

Purchase any of our products at your local college store or at our preferred online store **www.cengagebrain.com.**

Printed in the United States of America
1 2 3 4 5 6 7 15 14 13 12 11

To Don, for being the most understanding and caring lifelong partner one could ask for, and who, in his own very important way, makes a difference in the lives of children. D. B.

To Nathan, Emily, and Jacob, who continually demonstrate why the study of child development is so important. M. W. D.

Brief Contents

Contents

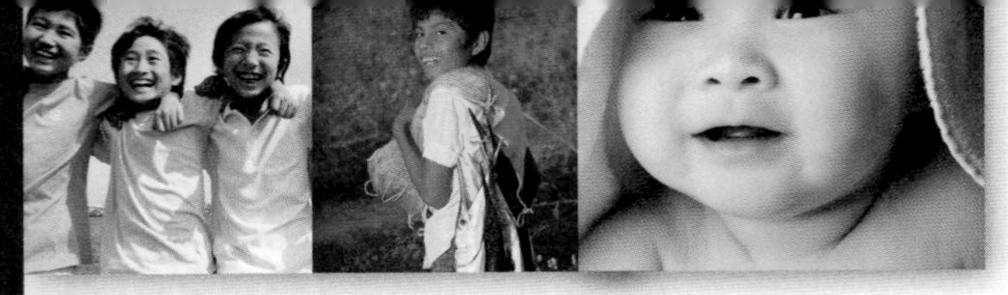

Features

What Do You Think?

Chronology Charts

Atypical Development

Research Applied to Parenting / Education

About the Authors

DANUTA BUKATKO is Professor of Psychology and the Joseph H. Maguire '58 Professor of Education at the College of the Holy Cross. She received her Ph.D. in Developmental Psychology from the University of Massachusetts at Amherst and has spent the subsequent 35 years at Holy Cross teaching courses in Child Development, Cognitive Development, Statistics and Research Methods, and Gender-Role Development. She has served as Department Chair, Assistant Dean, and Director of Women's and Gender Studies at different points in her career. She has received the Arthur J. O'Leary Faculty Recognition Award from Holy Cross for her teaching, mentoring, and service contributions to the college. She also has used several grants from the National Science Foundation and other funding agencies to promote the development of innovative teaching approaches in psychology and professional development among K–12 teachers. Her research interests include memory and representation in young children, as well as children's concepts about gender.

MARVIN DAEHLER is Emeritus Professor in the Department of Psychology at the University of Massachusetts at Amherst. He received his Ph.D. from the Institute of Child Development at the University of Minnesota and spent his professional career at the University of Massachusetts at Amherst where he continues to be active in the Developmental Area. He is a Fellow in Division 7 (Developmental Psychology) of the American Psychological Association as well as a Fellow of the Association for Psychological Science. He has been an Associate Editor for the journal *Child Development* and the *Monographs of the Society for Research in Child Development,* and a reviewer for research articles submitted to numerous other developmental publications. He also has served on grant review panels for the National Institutes of Health (NIH) and Department of Education and as Associate Chair, Director of Graduate Studies, and Director of Undergraduate Studies for various periods while a member of the Department of Psychology at the University of Massachusetts. His research activities, supported by grants from the National Science Foundation and National Institutes of Health, have been concerned with understanding the development of memory, basic representational abilities, and transfer in problem-solving in very young children.

Preface

In our first edition of this text, we identified some very explicit goals for *Child Development: A Thematic Approach.* Vast amounts of information about child development have been gathered by researchers, yet we as teachers must help students understand the most important aspects of that process. Given the tendency for researchers to hone in on very specific areas of child development, we must also give students a meaningful sense of the child as a whole person and help them to recognize the myriad of influences that affect development. These goals have become even more important to us in this sixth edition. Technology has created an information explosion whose influence is continually expanding. For example, the Internet has become a vast storehouse for material about child development. In addition, it has become increasingly common for other forms of media—television, magazines, and newspapers—to cover various topics concerning the psychological growth of children. The availability of so much information has made another teaching goal even more important. We must sharpen and help students refine their critical-thinking skills so they become educated consumers in our "information age." Thus we remain as committed as ever to presenting the story of child development from the perspective of carefully constructed theory and effectively designed research. We believe that it is important for students to be well grounded in the scientific approach to studying children, and for them to carry this approach with them as they continue to learn about children after they leave our classes.

To achieve these goals, we have been guided by a number of practices in preparing this sixth edition. We have continued to research the primary journals that publish material on child development to identify major advances in the field. As a result, the reader can feel confident that the findings, as well as the interpretations of what these findings say about child development, are not only current, but among the most important for understanding the many processes associated with child development. Five major themes are repeatedly considered throughout the various chapters to help in recognizing important aspects of development that have often guided the research efforts of scientists in the field. In many of the chapters, we have included chronologies designed to summarize the major developmental changes, many occurring over short time periods, to give readers a sense of the dramatic growth that takes place in a number of domains from conception through adolescence. Students may be taking a course in child development for a number of reasons, for example, to become a more informed parent, to work professionally in a field involving children such as a teacher, social worker, or therapist, or to simply learn more about the remarkable changes that human development undergoes from conception through adolescence. These reasons have been important in guiding the incorporation of the special features "Research Applied to Parenting/Education," "Atypical Development," and "What Do You Think?" in nearly every chapter. Additional review and reflection questions at the end of major sections in each chapter have been included to help students integrate the information provided with the major themes running throughout the chapters as well as with their own experiences of growing up.

A Thematic Approach

In this sixth edition, we have continued to uphold our commitment toward providing a comprehensive, topically organized, up-to-date picture of development from conception through adolescence. Most importantly, we draw students' attention to the themes that replay themselves throughout the course of development, the fundamental issues that resurface continually and that provide coherence to the many reported findings. These themes, we believe, can serve as frameworks to help students understand and remember the multitude of facts about child development. They can also serve as organizational ideas for lectures or for questions that instructors pose on examinations or other assignments. We highlight the following five themes throughout our discussion of child development:

- How do nature and nurture interact during development?
- How does the sociocultural context influence development?
- Is development continuous or discontinuous?
- How do the various domains of development interact?
- What factors promote risk or resilience in development?

By drawing out these themes, we hope to stimulate readers to think about the major factors that contribute to development, that is, why development proceeds as it does. We believe that when students engage in this sort of broader reflection, they will become more adept critical thinkers as they grapple with integrating the specific findings that are discussed. We also believe that they will be more likely to appreciate the ramifications of theory and research for applied issues such as parenting practices, education, and social policies for children, which are ultimately concerns for all of us. The new theme concerning risk and resilience introduced in this edition is especially relevant to these practical applications of developmental science. We anticipate that nearly all readers will have completed an introductory psychology course that puts forth many of the fundamental concepts that influence the field. Thus this text, including the themes around which it is organized, is designed to expand on that basic knowledge, highlighting those theories, methodologies, and research findings that are especially pivotal to understanding child development.

Organization of the Text

In keeping with a topical organization, our chapters are generally organized around changes from infancy through adolescence associated with a particular domain of development. Thus, after considering genetic and hereditary influences and the prenatal period and birth in Chapters 3 and 4, we focus on developmental changes in the brain, motor skills, and physical development (Chapter 5), learning and perception (Chapter 6), language (Chapter 7), cognitive development (Chapter 8), social cognition (Chapter 9), achievement (Chapter 10), emotion (Chapter 11), self and values (Chapter 12), and gender (Chapter 13). Although many contextual influences bearing on developmental changes are discussed in each of these chapters, the final three chapters specifically focus on the family (Chapter 14), peers (Chapter 15), and systems beyond family and peers, such as media, schools, and neighborhoods (Chapter 16), contexts which undoubtedly can have enormous consequences for children's development.

Why have we organized this book topically? Most child development texts are designed in one of two ways—topically, the framework used here, or chronologically, that is, focusing on the major periods of childhood: infancy, early childhood, middle childhood, and adolescence. We have preferred a topical organization because most theoretical perspectives focus on processes associated with a particular domain of development, for example, language, cognitive development, or emotions from "beginning to end." Thus, a sound pedagogical argument can be made for using a topical organization. We have included chronologies in most of the chapters, though, as a way of highlighting the fact that development may be more important in some domains during particular age periods than others. Furthermore, by pointing out places in the text where interactions between domains are important, we have provided substantial opportunities for identifying ways in which findings that bear on one aspect may have significance for another realm of development.

Major Changes and Features for the Sixth Edition

As will become apparent in the more detailed listing of changes, new and updated material has been incorporated in every chapter. However, several chapters in this edition have undergone major reorganization. The most substantial changes will be found in Chapters 8,

9, and 10. Chapter 8 (Cognition) now covers traditional theories of cognitive development (Piaget's, Vygotsky's, and information-processing theories) as well as concept development, attention, and most aspects of memory. In previous editions, this material had been distributed over two different chapters. Chapter 9 (Social Cognition) now focuses on summarizing the remarkable growth in research concerned with various topics associated with how the infant, child, and adolescent orient to the social world, understand psychological states and social groups, and the many influences on cognitive development that originate from and are fostered by social contexts. Researchers have typically ignored the interaction between the social world and cognitive development in the past, but in recent years thinking processes and representations relevant to the social world have become increasingly recognized for their importance to cognitive development. This chapter gives due recognition to this burgeoning field of research. Chapter 10 (Achievement) now focuses on the numerous factors that research has identified as being linked to success in school. Individual differences in ability continue to be addressed, but so too are factors like motivation (formerly in Chapter 12) and the roles of parents, peers, and teachers (formerly in Chapter 16).

Throughout nearly every chapter, new research findings on the brain and its relation to development in the specific domain under consideration have been added. Powerful new noninvasive procedures, many described in Chapter 2, have become available to record brain activity in infants as well as older children and to shed new light on developmental processes. The added material reflects the substantial growth in research in developmental neuroscience. Although much work remains to be done in this field of specialization, it has launched a new level of explanation for many findings concerning child development and at the same time has raised numerous interesting questions for further study. In addition, we are delighted to say that there is now more research on children from different ethnic and cultural backgrounds available. We have made a deliberate effort to include these cross-cultural studies throughout the text.

Many features that have been positively received in our previous editions have been retained for this sixth edition although substantive changes have been made to some of them. One new feature, however, is our "What Do You Think?" boxes that have been designed to encourage readers to think critically about their positions on controversial issues in the field.

What Do You Think? In previous editions we included "Controversy" boxes in which both sides of a specific issue relevant to each chapter had been discussed. However, rather than suggesting a number of potential answers to address these controversies as was done in the past, we have reorganized the manner in which the controversies are presented to motivate students to reflect on and clarify their own position relevant to the issues. Important questions about development often do not have clear-cut answers. In the real world, however, decisions must frequently be made about children and their families in the face of conflicting research findings or theoretical beliefs. Should children serve as eyewitnesses in courts of law? Should sex preselection be permitted? These controversies can serve as the foundation for debate and extended discussion in the classroom. In keeping with this objective, we have framed the "What Do You Think?" feature in a more open-ended way, incorporating many questions designed to stimulate critical thinking among students. For several chapters, new topics have been introduced for this feature to promote discussion:

Chapter 1: Should Child Rearing Be Regulated?
Chapter 8: Should Virtual Schools Be Promoted?
Chapter 12: Who Is Responsible for Moral Development?
Chapter 15: What Are the Consequences of Friending and Defriending?

Key Themes in Development In keeping with our overall goals and objectives, we have retained several features from previous editions of this book. Within each chapter, some or all of the five developmental themes previously identified serve to organize and provide coherence for the material. We see these themes as pedagogical tools designed to help students discern the importance and interrelatedness of various facts, and as vehicles for instructors to encourage critical analysis among students. The themes are highlighted for students in several ways.

1. The themes most immediately relevant to a chapter are listed at its start.
2. Indicators in the margins of the chapter point to discussions of each key theme.
3. Each chapter closes with a brief synopsis of how the key themes are illustrated in the domain explored by the chapter.

Students and instructors may, of course, find additional instances of the five themes we have identified. They may also locate new and additional themes. We encourage readers to search for additional themes to provide further integration and organization to the vast material that constitutes the scientific study of child development.

Chronology Charts From our own experience as teachers who have adopted a topical approach to child development, we know that students often get so immersed in the information on a given topic that they lose sense of the child's achievements over time. Consequently, we include one or two Chronology Charts in most chapters that summarize the child's specific developmental achievements at various ages. We caution students that these figures are meant only to give a picture of the overall trajectory of development, a loose outline of the sequence of events we expect to see in many children. Nonetheless, we believe that these guidelines will give students a sense of the patterns and typical timing of important events in the child's life and that they will serve as another organizing device for the material presented in each chapter. We have added new photos to highlight characteristics of several important developmental changes listed in each chronology and to make the chronologies more visually attractive to the reader. For comparative and review purposes, students can locate all the Chronology Charts by consulting the list on the inside front cover.

Research Applied to Parenting/Education We designed one of the most popular features in our previous editions to identify some of the implications of research that extend beyond the laboratory. In doing so, our goal was to help students think about questions and concerns that typically affect parents and teachers in their interactions with children. This feature addresses such topics as the steps that parents might take to reduce the risk of sudden infant death syndrome and the strategies teachers might follow to promote gender equity in the classroom. Each topic covered in this feature is introduced with a continuation of the chapter opening vignette and is followed by a set of points that, based on our current knowledge, leads to positive consequences for children and their development. These points, of course, should not be considered the final word on the subject, but they will help readers to understand how research has led to practical benefits for children, parents, and teachers. For a complete list of topics covered in this feature, see the inside front cover. In several chapters new topics have been introduced for this feature:

Chapter 6: Reducing Sensitivity to Pain
Chapter 12: Encouraging Young Children's Compliance
Chapter 15: Preventing Bullying

Atypical Development Rather than include a separate chapter on developmental problems, we have chosen to include a feature concerned with atypical development within most chapters. In doing so, we hope to emphasize that the same processes that help to explain normal development also can help us to understand development that is different from the norm. We believe that the reverse is also true—that understanding atypical development can illuminate the factors that guide more typical child development. Thus, we consider such topics as attention deficit hyperactivity disorder, conduct disorders, and posttraumatic stress disorder. A complete list of topics appears on the inside front cover.

For Your Review and Reflection A series of questions designed to promote a review of the material is presented at the end of major sections of the text in each chapter. These questions provide an active way for students to review and verify their understanding of the topic that they just covered. We have added two additional types of questions to most of these sections. One type of question is designed to encourage students to integrate the material with one or more of the major themes considered in that section. A second question added to each section is designed to help students relate the material to their own experience of growing up and undergoing developmental changes. These latter questions ask readers to reflect on and think about the material from a more personal perspective; they are included to help them remember and integrate the material, to "bring it home," so to speak, and as a way to promote their understanding that the topics are not abstract nor unrelated to their own development.

Study Aids The chapter outlines, chapter recaps, and marginal and end-of-text glossaries all serve to underscore important themes, terms, and concepts. We hope that students will actively utilize these aids to reinforce what they have learned in the chapter body. In addition, we employ several strategies to make the material in this text more accessible to students: vignettes to open the chapter and the "Research Applied to Parenting/Education" features, the liberal use of examples throughout the text, and an extensive program of figures, tables, and photos accompanied by instructive captions.

New to This Edition

We have already pointed out that Chapters 8, 9, and 10 have been substantially reorganized and that new material has been included within several of the features included in the text. Within each chapter, we have tried to pay attention to important emerging themes and concepts in the research literature and as a result, more than one thousand new references have been included in this sixth edition. In fact, some content has changed in every chapter in our effort to provide an up-to-date portrait of contemporary research. These changes include the following:

Chapter 1:

- The term "developmental science" incorporated into the text and defined in boldface. This label is used in many locations throughout the text to highlight the increasingly interdisciplinary nature of the field. "Developmental science" includes research activities influencing our understanding of development from disciplines as diverse as neuroscience to public policy.
- A new study and figure to highlight behavior modification to illustrate a typical example of its application and the power of social rewards to influence behavior.
- Use of the label "systems approaches" to summarize the wide range of theoretical approaches that incorporate biological, physical, and social settings in their approaches to account for behavior.

Chapter 2:

- Updated or new figures and examples illustrating meta-analysis, an experimental study, and a cross-sectional study.
- Relocation of discussion of the microgenetic approach within this chapter to highlight its importance as a strategy for assessing developmental change.
- Relocation and substantially increased discussion of neuroscience, specifically the various technologies and methods designed to assess brain functioning to further enhance understanding of developmental changes.

Chapter 3:

- New vignette to introduce issues to be considered in this chapter.
- Updated information and relocated material bearing on the estimated number of human genes.
- An introduction to the concept of "epigenetics" and its implications for the exhibition of phenotypic characteristics.
- Further discussion of recent landmark work highlighting molecular studies of genetic influences on development including implications and findings bearing on proteomics and the transcription and translation of DNA. This newer research provides support for

further emphasis on the interaction between genetic and experiential factors and its implications for individual differences in development.
- Updated information in the several tables describing various inherited genetic conditions.

Chapter 4:

- New vignette to identify issues to be considered in this chapter.
- Updated information in the chronology for prenatal development.
- New figure showing decline in rates of spina bifida and anencephaly over the last 20 years, summarizing past month cigarette use by pregnant and nonpregnant women of different ages, and HIV/AIDS transmission to infants.
- Replacement of the older concept of "alcohol-related neurodevelopmental disabilities (ARND)" with the more recently recommended classification label "Fetal Alcohol Spectrum Disorders (FASD)."
- Updated information in the various tables summarizing the consequences of a number of prescription and other frequently used drugs, as well as various maternal conditions for prenatal development.
- Replacement of the older term "illegal drugs" with the more preferred label "illicit drugs."
- Substantial revision to the text discussing the consequences of cocaine to suggest that its long-term detrimental effects may be more prevalent than some researchers have claimed.
- More information about the consequences for the newborn of drugs given during childbirth.
- New discussion of treatment programs such as the Newborn Individual Development Care and Assessment Program (NIDCAP) and updated information on massage as a procedure designed to promote development in preterm infants.

Chapter 5:

- Reorganization and substantial updating of information on brain development. Separate subsections have been added for discussion of glial cells and myelination as well as considerably more information on the development of the brain during adolescence. An updated figure shows the estimated number of synaptic connections in several regions of the brain and a new figure illustrates the myelination of neurons throughout development.
- Relocation of information on Sudden Infant Death Syndrome (SIDS) and patterns of sleep in infants to this chapter and inclusion of substantially more information about effects of sleep in adolescents.
- Extensive reorganization of the material concerned with determinants of body growth. A separate subsection now covers "Biological Determinants of Body Growth and Development" (genetic, neural, and hormonal influences).
- A new major section titled "Nutrition and Psychological Factors Associated with Body Growth." This topic now includes subsections concerned with nutrition and health (including secular trends), failure to thrive, and an expanded discussion of obesity that incorporates considerations of dieting efforts.
- New figures showing proportion of children with stunted growth in different countries, the percentage of overweight and obese children in the United States, the combined effects of meeting recommended physical activity levels and reduced media viewing on weight, and the percentage of youth dieting in various countries around the world.

Chapter 6:

- Added material on "Observational Learning" to foster thinking about the broader context in which this behavior is displayed, including discussion of new studies involving very young children's selectivity in engaging in imitative behavior.
- New section on "Other Forms of Learning" that includes material on implicit learning and information about statistical learning.
- A separate section on infants' learning about faces and explanations for this phenomenon along with a new figure illustrating infants' preferences for face-like stimuli.
- A new section titled "Auditory and Visual Perceptual Narrowing" and a new figure to demonstrate evidence supporting this perceptual phenomenon.

- Added material on infant capacities for discriminating smells, tastes, and touches.
- New information on face perception in older children, including consideration of the early institutionalization of children and how it has neurological consequences affecting processing of faces.

Chapter 7:

- Substantial reorganization so that major theoretical positions contributing to explanations of language acquisition, titled "Foundations of Language Development," appear early in the chapter.
- Extensive reorganization of empirical findings and processes in language acquisition. One major section focuses on "Language Development During Infancy," followed by another major section emphasizing "Language Development Beyond Infancy." Within each of these sections, presentation of the content has been reordered to provide a more systematic discussion of the primary mechanisms (e.g. constraints, social processes) associated with language acquisition.
- New figures showing critical periods in second language learning, statistical learning of speech sounds, taxonomic constraints in word extensions, commonalities and differences among cultures in first word learning, young children's sensitivity to syntactic information, differential brain activity in two-year-olds in response to correct and incorrect grammar, and the development of syntax.

Chapter 8:

- Three major theoretical perspectives (Piaget, Vygotsky, and information processing) now are presented at the beginning of the chapter. All three perspectives are presented more succinctly.
- New sections highlighting core knowledge and dynamic systems theories.
- New figures pertaining to young children's understanding of early concepts, spatial reasoning, elicited imitation, and developmental differences in generating retrieval cues to facilitate memory.
- Extensive reorganization of material in the section on "Concept Development."
- Discussion of "Attention," "Memory," "Problem Solving," and "The Executive Function" relocated to this chapter and considerable reorganization of material presented in these sections.
- Expanded discussion of "The Executive Function," including how it is assessed, as well as new material on judgment and decision making in adolescents.

Chapter 9:

- Relocation of the section "Detecting Animacy" and more information provided on this topic.
- New section titled "Gaze Following" and new information included under this topic.
- Many new figures to illustrate gaze following and joint attention, understanding an actor's goals, effects of experience on reaching for toys using "sticky mittens," infant reaction to a picture as if a real object, infant reactions to the same object photographed from different perspectives, interpretations given by the child to drawings, the procedure involved in using the false belief task, the relationship between mental state language and performance on theory of mind task, the theory of mind in deaf individuals, and the preference for a toy labeled by a native language speaker.
- New section titled "Social Referencing" and relocation of material related to this topic to this chapter.
- New section and material concerned with the development of "Understanding Others' Goals and Intentions."
- New discussion of infants' understanding of pictures and drawings.
- Relocation of material associated with reading maps to this chapter to further highlight the ability of children to use socially constructed representations.
- Relocation of material associated with "Understanding Psychological States" to this chapter to emphasize additional important developments in social cognition.
- New material added on children's ability to engage in deception to illustrate their burgeoning ability to promote false beliefs in others and understand theory of mind.

- Relocation of material on referential communication from the chapter on language and new information about how it is related to children's understanding of theory of mind.
- New section on "Cognition in a Social Context" and relocation of material to this chapter on the important ways sociocultural, parental, and peer processes are implemented to take advantage of the child's growing social cognitive abilities.
- Material highlighting the contributions of social factors to memory development now organized under the topic of "Memory in a Social Context."
- New section on "Understanding Social Groups" and new information on when children form social categories, form in-group preferences, and display prejudice and discrimination.

Chapter 10:

- Additional material on new versions of intelligence tests including the WISC-IV.
- Relocation of discussion of mastery motivation and stereotype threat to this chapter.
- Relocation of material on parental, peer, and teacher influences on academic achievement to this chapter.
- New material added on the role of parents in boosting children's school-related motivations.
- Revamped discussion of the achievement gap and the effects of early intervention programs.
- Relocation of material on learning sciences and mastery of academic subjects to this chapter.

Chapter 11:

- New figures illustrating differential looking times by infants to faces displaying several different emotions and brain areas associated with inhibiting a response.
- Separate sections established for "Emotions During Early and Middle Childhood" and "Emotions During Adolescence."
- New material outlining neuroscience's contributions to understanding emotion in children.
- New discussion of the development of emotional self-efficacy, internalizing and externalizing behavior, and dealing with stress during adolescence.

Chapter 12:

- Many new figures including illustration of temporo-parietal junction where processing of self information appears to occur, developmental changes in self-esteem, group self-esteem and exploration in ethnic American groups, a model of self-regulation, and differences in brain activity for adolescents with and without conduct disorders.
- Only material on "Self as Object" retained in this chapter; information on "Self as Subject" relocated to Chapter 10 on Achievement.
- Added information on Marcia's four statuses pertaining to adolescent identity.
- More extensive discussion of the development of self-regulation.
- Additional information on the development of conscience.
- New section on antisocial behavior with a focus on aggression.

Chapter 13:

- New section on "Enacting Stereotypes."
- Updated information on gender and mathematics achievement.
- New information on the development of a sexual self.
- New section on sexual harassment and its consequences.

Chapter 14:

- Updated information on the demographics of contemporary American families.
- Increased discussion of the elements of effective parenting.
- Expanded presentation on the consequences of behavioral versus psychological control among parents.
- Updated discussion of the effects of physical punishment on children.
- Expanded material on family-focused interventions designed to prevent instances of child abuse.

- Updated information on the consequences of maternal employment and child care experiences on child development.
- New information on PTSD among children exposed to trauma.
- New section on gay and lesbian parenting.

Chapter 15:

- Relocated section on "Children's Friendships" to follow discussion of "Developmental Changes in Peer Relations"
- New figures to depict percentage of rough-and-tumble play at different ages, importance of perceived status, and bullying as an international problem.
- New section on the development of romantic relationships during adolescence.
- Increased discussion of "Characteristics of Popular and Unpopular Children."
- New material incorporated within the feature "Atypical Development: Social Withdrawal."
- Substantially more information provided on the topic of bullying within the feature "Research Applied to Education: Preventing Bullying."

Chapter 16:

- New table showing amount of time children spend exposed to various media.
- Many new figures illustrating amount of time children under six spend engaged in various activities in addition to viewing television, when very young children begin to comprehend televised material, the effect sizes reported from meta-analytic studies of various kind of media content on behavior and attitudes in children, differences in brain activation patterns when watching violent versus nonviolent television programming, amount of time and types of activities young children engage in using the computer, amount of exposure to pollutants for children living in low-income compared to more affluent communities, and levels of exposure to violence.
- Extensive added discussion of whether children under 18 months of age display a video deficit, including examples of more limited learning from viewing a televised activity versus observing a live person.
- Discussion of potential attentional difficulties associated with viewing large amounts of televised material during infancy.
- Evidence for differential brain activation in children viewing aggressive versus non-aggressive content on television.
- New discussion of exposure to sexual content on television and implications for adolescent behavior.
- Added information on social networks and their consequences for social development.
- New section on "Neighborhoods, Low Income, and Children in Poverty" summarizing research findings on the effects of relocating children in low-income families to more affluent neighborhoods and differences in availability and the use of resources by children in low-income neighborhoods compared to more affluent neighborhoods.
- New discussion on children's exposure to pollutants in low-income neighborhoods.
- New section on "Affluent Neighborhoods" and consideration of some of the developmental difficulties found in children growing up in affluent families.
- New material added on children's exposure to violence and war, as a consequence of experiencing natural disasters such as Hurricane Katrina and the effects of the terrorist attack occurring on 9/11.

Road Map to the Contents of the Text

We begin the text with two chapters that set the stage for the balance of the book. Chapter 1 introduces the five developmental themes, some brief historical contributions to the field, and major theories of development. Chapter 2 considers the historical and scientific roots of developmental psychology and the research methodologies that the field typically employs today.

The next three chapters deal primarily with the biological underpinnings and physical changes that characterize child development. Chapter 3 explains the mechanisms of heredity and evaluates the role of genetics in the expression of many human traits and behaviors. Chapter 4 sketches the major features of prenatal development and focuses on how environmental factors, such as teratogens, can modify the genetic blueprint for physical and behavioral development. Chapter 5 introduces material on brain growth and differentiation, considers issues associated with sleep, and outlines the major features of physical and motor skill development and the factors that influence development in these areas.

The next group of chapters focuses on the development of children's various mental capacities. Chapter 6 reviews the literature on children's learning and development of perception. Chapter 7 describes language development, highlighting contemporary research on infant language, and the social context of language acquisition. Chapter 8 features theories of cognitive development, as well as recent research on concept formation, attention, memory, problem-solving, and executive function. Chapter 9 focuses on social cognition, including the emerging capacity to respond to social stimulation, understand psychological states in self and others, the contexts that influence social cognitive skills, and children's understanding of social groups. Chapter 10 examines the broad topic of achievement as it is influenced by individual differences in ability, concepts of self, and environmental factors such as parents, peers, and teachers.

The child's growing social and emotional achievements constitute the focus of the next group of chapters. We devote Chapter 11 to a treatment of emotional development. Chapter 12 covers self and moral and prosocial development, including some consideration of antisocial behavior. Chapter 13 discusses the most recent ideas on gender development, including substantial treatment of gender schema theory.

In the final portion of the text, we consider the most important external forces that shape the path of child development—family, peers, as well as media, computers, school environment, and the neighborhood. Chapter 14 adopts a family systems approach to emphasize how various family members continually influence one another. Chapter 15 is entirely dedicated to the influence of peers and covers the expanding research on this topic. Chapter 16 considers the special influence of technology and events beyond the family and peers – television and other media, computers, and the contexts surrounding children, their neighborhoods and the resources available in them, school, and some of the consequences of serious disruptions to daily living because of exposure to war, disasters, and terrorism.

Accompanying this book are several print and electronic ancillaries for students and instructors, enhanced for the sixth edition.

Student Ancillaries

Study Guide The Study Guide contains a set of learning objectives designed for each chapter of the text. In addition, each chapter of the Study Guide includes a detailed study outline, a key terms section, and a self-quiz with multiple-choice questions. An answer key tells students not only which response is correct but also why each of the other choices is incorrect.

Instructor Ancillaries

Instructor's Resource Manual The Instructor's Resource Manual contains a complete set of chapter outlines and learning objectives matching those provided in the Study Guide for students, as well as lecture topics, classroom exercises, demonstrations, and handouts. It also features recommended readings, videos, and Internet sites.

Test Bank The Test Bank includes nearly two thousand multiple-choice items. Each is accompanied by a key that provides the learning objective, section in the text where the answer can be found, type of question (Fact, Concept, or Application), and correct answer. Because we are committed to the idea that students should be encouraged to engage in critical thinking about child development, we have retained a set of essay questions for each chapter and a concluding set of essay questions that might constitute part of a cumulative final examination in the course.

PowerLecture

PowerLecture provides a collection of book-specific, media-rich PowerPoint lecture and class tools to enhance the educational experience.

CengageNOW™

CengageNOW™ is an online teaching and learning resource that gives the instructor more control over the course with grading, quizzing, and the ability to create assignments and track student outcomes. The flexible assignment and gradebook allow the instructor to choose the options that best suit the overall course plan, while a diagnostic Personalized Study Plan (featuring chapter-specific test, Study Plan, and post-test) empowers students to master concepts, prepare for exams, and get a better grade.

Webtutor

Webtutor provides customizable, rich, text-specific content that can be interfaced with a Course Management System.

CourseMate

To access additional course materials (including CourseMate), please visit www.cengagebrain.com. At the CengageBrain.com home page, search for the ISBN of your title (from the back cover of your book) using the search box at the top of the page. This will take you to the product page where these resources can be found.

Acknowledgments

Our current and former students at Holy Cross and the University of Massachusetts have continued to serve as the primary inspiration for our work on this text. Each time we have taught the child development course, we have seen their enthusiasm and appreciation for what we teach, but we also have found that, from them, we learn how to communicate our messages about developmental processes more effectively.

We also appreciate the insightful comments and constructive criticisms provided by the reviewers for this text. Their classroom experiences have provided a broader perspective than our own, and we believe our book has become stronger because of their valued input. We would like to express our thanks to the following individuals who served in this capacity for the fifth edition, whose influence continues to be felt:

Viktor K. Broderick, *Ferris State University*
Jeffrey T. Coldren, *Youngstown State University*
Margaret Dempsey, *Tulane University*
Michelle K. Demaray, *Northern Illinois University*
K. Laurie Dickson, *Northern Arizona University*
Rebecca Eaton, *The University of Alabama in Huntsville*
Lynn Haller, *Morehead State University*
Robert F. Rycek, *University of Nebraska at Kearney*

We would also like to thank the reviewers who helped fashion this sixth edition:

Shannon Welch, *University of Idaho*
Lisa Fozio-Thielk, *Waubonsee Community College*
Judy Watkinson, *Arizona Western College*

Eric Peterson, *University of Northern Colorado*
Belinda Blevins-Knabe, *University of Arkansas at Little Rock*
Denise L. Winsor, *University of Memphis*
Monica R. Sylvia, *Le Moyne College*

In addition, we would like to express our gratitude to colleagues at our respective institutions for reading and commenting on various chapters and just sharing ideas that were helpful in our revision. Special thanks go to Pat Kramer and Richard Schmidt at Holy Cross, who have provided important intellectual inspiration and personal support throughout the years. At the University of Massachusetts, Daniel Anderson, Neal Berthier, Richard Bogartz, Erik Cheries, Matthew Davidson, Rachel Keen, Jennifer Martin McDermott, Nancy Myers, and Lisa Scott provided a wealth of information and stimulating ideas in formal seminars and informal hallway conversations. Just as these faculty colleagues have offered insightful perspectives, so too have a spirited company of former and present graduate students at the university who have carried out research on a number of aspects of development. They are too great in number to identify individually, so they must be thanked collectively. They will, however, surely be aware of our admiration for their efforts toward enhancing our knowledge of development. One individual at the University of Massachusetts, however, Patrice Stering, must be singled out for her contributions in providing reference material for a number of the chapters.

As with previous editions, several individuals at Cengage have demonstrated their talent, dedication, and professionalism: Jaime Perkins, Senior Editor; Tali Beesley, Associate Development Editor; Nic Albert, Associate Development Editor; Paige Leeds, Assistant Editor; Jessica Alderman, Editorial Assistant; Mary Noel, Media Editor; Jessica Egbert, Marketing Manager; Talia Wise, Executive Marketing Communications Manager; Charlene Carpentier, Content Project Manager; Vernon Boes, Senior Art Director; Karen Hunt, Manufacturing Buyer; and Roberta Broyer, Permissions Acquisition Specialist. We thank them for their important contributions to this project.

Danuta Bukatko
Marvin W. Daehler

© Gavriel Jecan/Corbis

CHAPTER OUTLINE

[chapter 1]

Themes and Theories

Andrew had spent an enormous amount of time carefully aligning the beams, braces, and other equipment at just the right locations on his building project. It looked great! He was fascinated by how he could make the crane swing up and down, and how it would lift and drop the small metal pieces with the magnet. But six-year-old Andrew was so absorbed in his play that he failed to notice his one-year-old sister, Heather, rapidly crawling toward these shiny, eye-catching objects. Benjamin, at fourteen, was the oldest child in the family and had been placed in charge of watching both Andrew and Heather as their parents prepared dinner in the kitchen. Unfortunately, he had also become distracted by the challenging new computer game he had just borrowed from his friend.

As she crawled within reach of Andrew's construction set, Heather grabbed the truck on which the crane was mounted and pulled it sharply, pitching beams, equipment, and everything else into a chaotic heap. For one brief instant, Andrew froze in horror as he observed the devastation his little sister had just wrought. Then came the almost reflexive, inevitable shriek at the top of his lungs: "HEATHER! GET OUTTA HERE!" as he simultaneously swung his arm in Heather's direction in an uncontrollable burst of emotion. Andrew's shout was more than enough to produce a wail from Heather, but the sting across her back from Andrew's hand didn't help, either. Benjamin, startled by the uproar, anticipated the melee about to begin and raced to the kitchen, knowing full well that his mother and father were the only ones who would be able to reinstate tranquility after this unfortunate exchange between his little brother and sister. <<

Although the specifics may be very different, this type of exchange between siblings is probably not uncommon in families and households around the world. And it serves to introduce some of the issues central to this book. For example, consider the developmental differences displayed by Heather, Andrew, and Benjamin during this interaction. Heather, only one year of age, does not move about or handle objects in the same way as her older siblings. Perhaps even more important, Heather seems to have very little appreciation for the consequences her impulsive reach might have on both Andrew and the construction set. Her six-year-old brother displays far greater physical dexterity and more sophisticated planning and thinking about the toys that are part of his play. Andrew also has excellent verbal skills with which to express his thoughts and emotions, although he still has some difficulty regulating the latter. Yet Andrew's reasoning about his world pales in comparison with that of his older brother, Benjamin, who is captivated by a complex computer game. Moreover, at the age of fourteen, Benjamin has been given increased responsibility, such as looking after both younger siblings. Although he is not always as careful and conscientious in this task as his mother and father might like, his parents feel reasonably assured that, if things are not going well, Benjamin knows where to seek assistance.

How did these enormous developmental differences come about? That is a primary question addressed in this book. But there are other matters of interest in the sequence of events described here. How should their parents now deal with the conflict in order to bring about peace between Heather and Andrew? How would you? How should his parents respond to the angry outburst from Andrew? How might they have encouraged Benjamin to take his baby-sitting responsibilities more seriously? If you have taken on such activities, when and how did you gain the trust of your parents or other parents to act in this more adult-like fashion?

When we think about trying to answer these kinds of questions, common sense often seems like the place to start. For generations, common sense provided the wisdom by which caregivers understood and reared children. For example, when Heather, Andrew, and Benjamin could not get along with one another, their

Although intently inspecting something found in their yard, these two brothers are undoubtedly processing the object which is the center of their attention in different ways. How do differences associated with, for example, being able to talk and think about the things they find interesting come about? This question is just one of many studied by developmental scientists and discussed throughout this book.

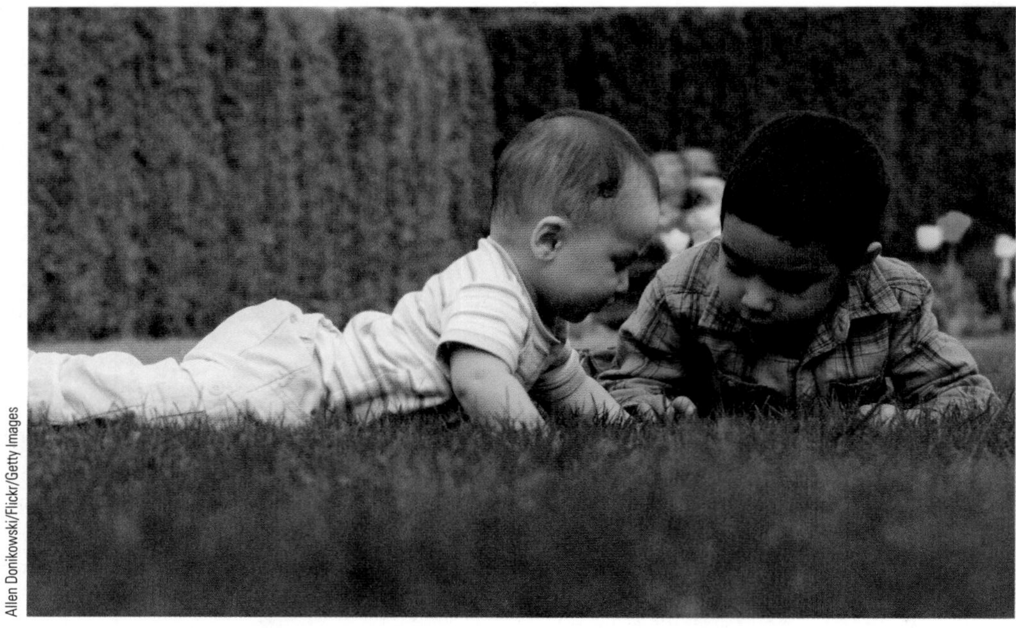

Allen Donikowski/Flickr/Getty Images

parents might have spanked the child whom they thought to be at fault. They would be following a commonly accepted approach to dealing with conflict, a method that seems to be shared in many cultures. As an illustration, among the proverbs expressed by the Ovambo of southwest Africa is the saying, "A cranky child has not been spanked," and Korean parents may say, "Treat the child you love with the rod; treat the child you hate with another cake." These expressions sound much like another you may have heard: "Spare the rod, spoil the child." Proverbs like these that encourage physical disciplining of children can be found in many cultures around the world (for instance, see Palacios, 1996).

Although common sense is important in child rearing, in some circumstances it may yield unexpected and perhaps even undesirable consequences. For example, is physical punishment an effective way of reducing unacceptable behaviors in children as caregivers in many societies often believe? Perhaps not; for example, researchers have found that the children of parents who routinely resort to physical punishment often initiate more aggressive acts than do the children of parents who rely on alternative methods of disciplining undesirable conduct (Bandura & Walters, 1959; Dodge, Pettit, & Bates, 1994). This finding has been observed in Native American (McCord, 1977) and British working-class homes (Farrington, 1991), as well as in families in the United States, Australia, Finland, Poland, and Israel (Eron, Huesmann, & Zelli, 1991). In other words, under some circumstances, physical punishment appears to encourage rather than discourage aggressive actions and may escalate into increasingly coercive interactions between parent and child. Thus, the commonsense practice of disciplining by physical punishment, a practice supported by various cultural proverbs, may need to be examined more closely. This is precisely the point at which the need for the scientific study of children and their development enters.

What Is Development?

Development, as we use the term, means all the physical and psychological changes a human being undergoes in a lifetime, from the moment of conception until death. The study of human development is, above all, the study of change (Overton, 2006). From the very moment of birth (and even before), changes are swift and impressive. Within a few short months, the newborn who looked so helpless (we will see that the true state of affairs is otherwise) comes to control his or her own body, to locomote, and to master simple tasks, such as self-feeding. In the years that follow, the child

development Physical and psychological changes in the individual over a lifetime.

begins to understand and speak a language, engages in more and more complex thinking and problem solving, displays a distinct personality, and develops the skills necessary to interact with peers and others in the community. The range and complexity of every young person's achievements in the first two decades of life can only be called extraordinary.

One of the goals of this book is to give you an overview of the most significant changes in behavior and thinking processes that occur throughout infancy, childhood, and early adolescence. In the pages that follow, we *describe* the growing child's accomplishments in many domains of development. For example, we detail the basic physical and mental capabilities in infants and children and examine the social and emotional skills children acquire as they reach out to form relationships with their family members, peers, and others.

A second important goal is to help you appreciate just how and why children develop in the specific ways they do. In other words, we also try to *explain* developmental outcomes in children. How do the genetic blueprints inherited from parents help to shape the growing child? What is the role of the environment? How does the society or culture in which the child lives influence development? Do the changes that take place occur gradually or suddenly? And how do the many facets of development influence one another?

A third important goal is to begin identifying ways in which research on children will help to *enhance* their development. Some children appear to thrive with respect to their intellectual and social accomplishments; others do not. Knowledge about factors that contribute to these different outcomes may assist parents, teachers, and others who work with children. What contributes to optimal development, sometimes even against great odds? As you may imagine, although we often seek simple answers to this question as well as those concerned with explaining development, the answers are neither simple nor always obvious (Horowitz, 2000).

Developmental psychology is the discipline concerned with the scientific study of changes in human behaviors and mental activities as they occur over a lifetime. *Developmental psychologists* rely on research to learn about growth and change in children. Researchers have not studied every important aspect of child development, and sometimes studies do not point to clear, unambiguous answers about the nature of development. Indeed, psychologists often disagree on the conclusions they draw from a given set of data. Nonetheless, scientific fact-finding has the advantage of being verifiable—that is, can be put to the test for further confirmation by other researchers—and, as a result, is also more objective and systematic than personal interpretations of children's behavior.

In the past decade or so, developmental psychology has become far more interdisciplinary in its efforts. Today research on children and their development falls under the rubric of what might more appropriately be called **developmental science** (Lerner, 2006) to reflect the fact that investigators come from many different disciplines and consider numerous factors, including biological, social, and cultural systems, in explanations of development and the contexts in which it takes place. Essential to developmental science are **theories**, sets of ideas or propositions that help to organize or explain observable phenomena. More than a personal opinion or a casual hypothesis, a scientific theory is firmly grounded in the information collected by researchers. For many, theories seem far less interesting than descriptions of the vast assortment of intellectual, linguistic, social, physical, and other behaviors and capabilities that undergo change with time. However, by describing children's accomplishments in a systematic, integrated way, theories *organize* or make sense of the enormous amount of information researchers have gleaned. Theories of development also help to *explain* our observations. Is your neighbor's little boy shy because he inherited some trait, or did his social experiences encourage him to become this way? How might both factors play a part? Did your niece's precocious mathematical skills develop from her experience with her home computer, or does she just have a natural flair for numbers? Was Andrew's angry reaction to his baby sister a biological response or something he had learned? Developmental scientists are interested in understanding the factors that contribute to the emergence of these kinds of behaviors and skills, and their theories are ways of articulating ideas about how these behaviors and skills develop in individual children.

developmental psychology Systematic and scientific study of changes in human behaviors and mental activities over time.

developmental science The interdisciplinary field of research and theories concerned with studies and explanations of human development.

theories Sets of ideas or propositions that help to organize or explain observable phenomena.

A good theory goes beyond description and explanation, however. It leads to *predictions* about behavior, predictions that are clear and easily tested. If shyness results from social experiences, for example, the withdrawn four-year-old should profit from a program that teaches social skills. If, on the other hand, shyness is a stable, unchangeable personality trait, even extensive training in sociability may have very little impact. Explaining and predicting behavior are not only gratifying but also essential for translating ideas into applications—creating meaningful programs and ways to assist parents, teachers, and others who work to enhance and promote the development of children. For example, when a theory proposes that adults are an important source of imitative learning and that parents who display aggressive behavior provide a model for responding to a frustrating situation, we can begin to understand why common proverbs like "Spare the rod and spoil the child" sometimes need to be reevaluated.

Research programs designed to identify those factors that better the lives of children have become a part of the rapidly growing interdisciplinary effort known as *applied developmental science* (Lerner, 2006; Lerner, Jacobs, & Wertlieb, 2003). Not only do parents, teachers, and others who interact with children gain from this research, but so do lawmakers, public agencies, and other groups engaged in identifying what cultural and social goals are most beneficial to children. **Social policies** are programs and plans established by local, regional, or national organizations and agencies to enhance society. These are often government programs, but businesses, private foundations, and other groups attempt to implement social policies that are designed to achieve a particular purpose with respect to the members of a community. The goals of many of these policies are geared toward alleviating social problems. Social policies may, for example, be concerned with increasing the effectiveness of education for children, encouraging healthy weight gains by increasing exercise, reducing teenage pregnancy, eliminating child abuse, preventing young people from smoking cigarettes, encouraging parents to enforce the use of seat belts, promoting self-esteem, and advocating a host of other goals. Research can help identify social problems that limit or interfere with children's development and can assist parents, educators, and policymakers in establishing programs to reduce or eliminate the factors that hinder psychological health and competence in children. You will have the opportunity to consider many social policies that are relevant to children in the chapters that follow.

In this chapter, our discussion focuses on several broad theories, and some of their historical antecedents, that have influenced explanations of children's behavior. No single theory provides a full explanation of all behavior. Some theories strive to make sense of intellectual and cognitive development; others focus on social, emotional, personality, or other aspects of development. Theories also vary in the extent to which they present formalized, testable ideas. Thus, some are more useful than others in providing explanations for behavior that can be rigorously evaluated. And they often disagree in their answers to the fundamental questions of development. Before we examine specific theories, let's consider a cluster of basic questions that all theories of development should address.

For Your Review and Reflection

- What is development?
- What is developmental science?
- What role do theories play in the scientific process?
- What role does developmental science play in the formation of social policy?
- What are your reasons for studying child development? Are you more interested in descriptions of child behavior, explanations of child behavior, or how to optimize child development? Why?
- What are some of the challenges you can predict researchers may have when attempting to describe, explain, and enhance children's development?

social policy Programs and plans established by local, regional, or national public and private organizations and agencies designed to achieve a particular social purpose or goal.

Five Major Themes in Developmental Psychology

As you read about different aspects of child development—language acquisition, peer relationships, motor skills, emergence of self-worth, and many others—you will find that certain questions about development surface again and again. We call these questions *themes in development*. Various theories provide different answers to these questions. Good theories, grounded in careful research, help us to think about and understand these major themes. What are these key questions?

How Do Nature and Nurture Interact in Development?

We have all heard expressions like "He has good genes" or "She had a great upbringing" to explain some trait or behavior. These explanations offer two very different answers to a basic question that has, since the beginnings of psychology, fueled a controversy among theorists that continues, at least in some circles, even today. Dubbed the **nature-nurture debate**, the dispute centers on whether the child's development is the result of genetic endowment or environmental influences.

Do children typically crawl at nine months and walk at twelve months of age as part of some inborn, unfolding program or because they have learned these motor responses? Do they readily acquire language because their environment demands it or because they are genetically predisposed to do so? Are boys more aggressive than girls because of cultural conditioning or biological factors? In some areas, such as the presence of early infant competencies, the development of intelligence, and the emergence of gender roles, the debate over nature versus nurture has been particularly heated.

Why all the uproar about such a question? One reason is that the answer has major implications for children's developmental outcomes, for parenting practices, for the organization of schooling, and for other practical applications of research. If, for example, experiments support the view that intelligence is guided largely by heredity, providing children with rich learning experiences may have minimal impact on their eventual levels of intellectual skill. If, on the other hand, research and theory more convincingly show that intellectual development is shaped primarily by environmental events, it becomes vital to provide children with experiences designed to optimize their intellectual growth. Answers to this type of question are likely to have an impact on social policy by affecting how funds are allocated to health, educational, and many other programs.

Psychologists and developmental scientists now recognize that much of the controversy has been unconstructive. *Both* nature and nurture are essential to all aspects of behavior. Thus, the debate has increasingly shifted away from identifying *which* or *how much* of these two factors contributes in any given situation. Instead, the question is *how* heredity and environment *influence each other* to fashion the behaviors we see in children and eventually in adults.

One thing that makes it difficult to determine how heredity and environment interact is the fact that *children are active players in the process of their own development.* That active role may be evident at two different levels. The first begins with certain attributes and qualities that children possess and exhibit, perhaps because of inborn qualities of personality or behavioral style. By virtue of being placid or active, fearful or curious, children elicit reactions from others. Thus, children are not simply passive recipients of the environment or blank slates on which it writes. Their own capacities and efforts to become immersed in their physical and social world often modify what they experience and affect their development in profound ways. A second, perhaps more fundamental, way in which children contribute to their own development comes about because they are equipped to actively construct and organize ways of thinking, feeling, and communicating to assist them in making

nature-nurture debate Historically, the theoretical controversy over whether development is the result of the child's genetic endowment or environmental influences.

sense of their world. Children formulate these conceptualizations to help them respond to and understand the rich array of physical and social events they experience.

Recent findings suggest yet another factor that makes it difficult to determine how nature and nurture interact—environmental events can sometimes have major influences on when and how genetic information affects development (Fagiolini, Jensen, & Champagne, 2009). In other words, genes and experience likely involve multiple levels of interaction that build upon one another to influence developmental outcomes (Spencer et al., 2009), an issue to which we return in Chapter 3, "Genetics and Heredity."

How Does the Sociocultural Context Influence Development?

Development is influenced by more than just the immediate environment of the family. Children grow up within a larger social community: the *sociocultural context.* The sociocultural context includes unique customs, values, and beliefs about the proper way to rear children and the ultimate goals for their development. Think back to your family and the cultural standards and values that determined how you were reared. Were you allowed to be assertive and speak your mind, or were you expected to be compliant toward adults and never challenge them? Were you encouraged to fend for yourself, or were caregivers, relatives, and even cultural institutions, such as the school, church, or some other agency, expected to assist with your needs throughout childhood, adolescence, and perhaps even into your early adult years? How was your development affected by your family's economic status and educational attainments? By your gender and ethnic identity?

Sociocultural factors affect everything from the kinds of child-rearing practices parents engage in to the level of health care and education children receive; they affect, for example, children's physical well-being, social standing, sense of self-esteem, "personality," and emotional expressiveness. As you explore the various domains of development, you will come to appreciate that many developmental outcomes are heavily influenced by the sociocultural context.

Is Development Continuous or Discontinuous?

Everyone agrees that children's behaviors and abilities change, sometimes in dramatic ways. However, there is less consensus on how best to explain these changes. On the one hand, development can be viewed as a *continuous* process in which new attainments in thinking,

Children grow up in many different cultures and families. Many experience a close and loving relationship with their parents and siblings, some do not. Some have few possessions whereas others have the latest technological gadgets. Some also engage in religious activities, have opportunities to attend challenging schools, and have ready access to many available resources in the community. How these sociocultural differences influence a child's development is a key theme guiding the research interests of many developmental scientists.

Figure 1.1

Development as a Continuous Versus a Discontinuous Process

Children display many changes in their abilities and behaviors throughout development. According to some, the best way to explain these changes is in terms of the gradual acquisition of the structures and processes that underlie growth (A). Others believe that development undergoes a series of stagelike transformations during which underlying structures and processes exhibit rapid reorganization followed by a period of relative stability (B). However, other approaches suggest that, at any given time, children may exhibit multiple ways of demonstrating some ability or capacity, as is evident in the "overlapping waves" (Siegler & Alibali, 2005) depiction of development (C). According to this view, the ability or capacity displayed by children will depend on a variety of situational and developmental factors.

Source: From EMERGING MINDS: THE PROCESS OF CHANGE IN CHILDREN'S THINKING by Robert S. Siegler. Copyright © 1996 by Oxford University Press, Inc. Used by permission of Oxford University Press, Inc.

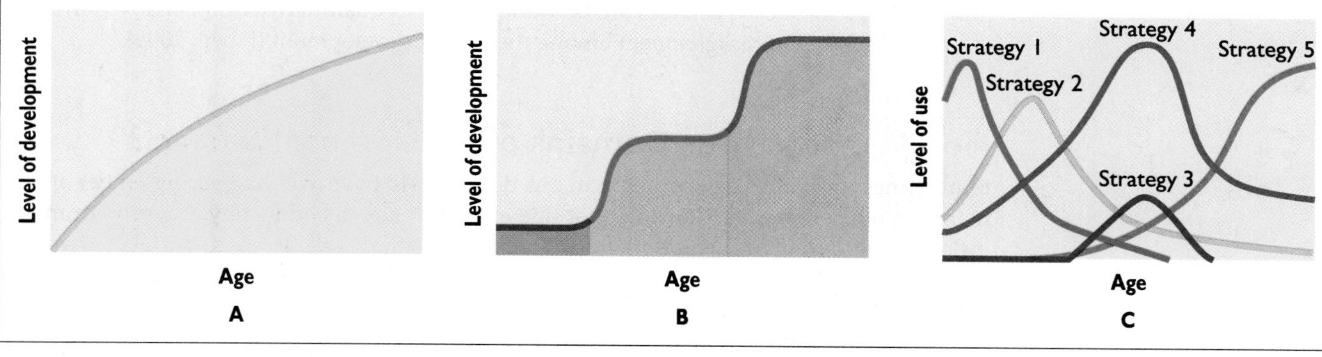

language, and social behavior are characterized by gradual, steady, small, *quantitative* advances. For example, substantial progress in reasoning or problem solving may stem from the ability to remember more and more pieces of information. Or, as neural coordination and muscle strength gradually increase, the infant may advance from crawling to walking—a progression that, by anyone's account, has substantial consequences for both child and caregiver. Thus, even though at two given points in time the child's ability to think or locomote may look very different, the transformation may arise from gradual, quantitative improvements in the speed, efficiency, or strength with which mental or physical processes are carried out, rather than from a dramatic reorganization of some underlying capacity.

Alternatively, some theories see development as *discontinuous*. They explain development in terms of the child's progress through a series of **stages**, or periods during which innovative developmental accomplishments abruptly surface, presumably because some fundamental reorganizations in thinking or other capacities underlying behavior have taken place. In this view, development undergoes rapid transitions as one stage ends and a new one begins, followed by relatively stable periods during which the child's behaviors and abilities change very little (see Figure 1.1). Abrupt or rapid changes resulting in a dramatic reorganization in how children perceive, think, feel, or behave are interpreted as *qualitative* advances in development. From this perspective, children establish new ways of thinking—for instance, during the early school years—that change problem solving, moral judgment, interactions with peers, and other activities. In adolescence, they move to yet another level of thinking that influences these various domains of behavior in still different ways.

When we try to discern if development is continuous or discontinuous, it is important to remember that there is considerable variability in individual children's skills that can complicate how we decide between these two points of view. Many ways of behaving and thinking are available to children at any given time. Which one will be expressed depends on a variety of circumstances. Robert Siegler (1996; Siegler & Alibali, 2005) has suggested that different strategies or ways of responding can best be described as "overlapping waves," because they often coexist in the child's repertoire. Some methods of responding may be exhibited more frequently at younger ages and others at older ages. Although some strategies may be discarded as the child gains more experience and as others are freshly formulated, at any particular time

stage Developmental period during which the organization of thought and behavior is qualitatively different from that of an earlier or later period.

children are likely to be able to use several competing approaches for responding to a situation. For example, when young children demonstrate the ability to add two numbers, say 4 plus 3, they may do so using several different strategies, such as counting from 1, counting beginning with the larger of the pair of numbers, comparing the problem to another whose answer is already known, or directly retrieving the information from memory. Which specific strategy a child employs will depend on how much experience the child has had with the problem, how familiar he or she is with each of the numbers, how quickly the answer must be determined, and how much effort is required to carry out the strategy, among other things.

Few, if any, aspects of human growth appear to mimic the dramatic transformations found in the life cycle of an insect as it changes from egg to larva to pupa and finally to adult—periods in which a stable physical organization is followed by rapid reorganization and emergence of a new point in the life cycle. Yet, over the months and years, children do become quite different. Whether these changes are best understood as quantitative or qualitative advances is a point of frequent disagreement among theories of development (Liben, 2008).

How Do the Various Domains of Development Interact?

Many times the child's development in one domain will have a direct bearing on her attainments in other domains. Consider just one example: how a child's physical growth might influence her social and emotional development. A child who has become taller than her peers may experience very different interactions with adults and classmates than a child who is small for his age. The taller child might be given more responsibilities by a teacher or be asked by peers to lead the group more frequently. These opportunities may instill a sense of worth and offer occasions to practice social skills that are less frequently available to the smaller child. As these social skills are exercised and become more refined and advanced, the taller child may receive still more opportunities that promote social and even cognitive development. Our ultimate aim is to understand the child as a whole individual, not just as someone who undergoes, for example, physical, perceptual, emotional, cognitive, or social development. To do so, we must keep in mind that no single component of development unfolds in isolation from the rest.

What Factors Promote Risk or Resilience in Development?

Human development may proceed along many different paths and at quite different rates from one individual to another. One especially important reason that differences emerge

Tara Moore/Riser/Getty Images

The computer may expose young children to new kinds of risks for their development not experienced by previous generations of children. Another key theme in the research carried out by many developmental scientists is understanding what factors expose children to greater risk or promote resilience in development even in the face of risk.

is that individual children are exposed to various kinds and levels of benefits and risks during their development. For example, *risk* may be a consequence of genetic or biological complications, as well as rearing or cultural events, that promote development in less than optimal ways. An accidental head injury; exposure to a disease, such as AIDS; being reared by an abusive parent; experiencing parents' divorce; attending an unstimulating daycare center; or exposure to the devastating consequences of war are just a few of the many factors that can affect the course of development and may limit healthy progress. Individual children, because of their genetic or biological makeup, or because of other resources available in their environment, respond to these risks in different ways. *Resilient* children, those who seem able to most effectively resist the negative consequences of risk, tend to have a constellation of individual qualities that include a relatively relaxed, self-confident character that permits them to adapt and respond intelligently in difficult situations and circumstances. In addition, they are likely to benefit from a close, encouraging relationship with at least one member of their family and with others beyond the family, such as a teacher or close friend, or through their membership in some supportive agency or organization, such as a club or church (Goldstein & Brooks, 2005; Luthar, Cicchetti, & Becker, 2000; Masten, Cutuli, Herbers, & Reed, 2009; Rutter, 1990; Werner, 2005).

Several points about risk and resilience are important to note. First, most researchers recognize that, when children are said to be at risk, it is usually not because of a single factor, such as poverty, exposure to disease, or attendance at a school with few resources. Rather, risk factors tend to occur in clusters. Thus, understanding child development requires an awareness of the many layers of influence that have an impact on children's lives, from family settings, to neighborhoods, to the larger society (Sameroff, 2005). Second, some researchers feel that the term *resilience* should be restricted to instances in which children are able to overcome some adversity, and that other terms (such as *promotive factors* or *assets*) are more appropriate when we are describing positive factors in development, regardless of risk (Wright & Masten, 2005). Finally, a discussion of risk and resilience usually has strong implications for interventions that might improve the lives of children who experience hardship. As a result, these topics are of special interest to developmental scientists involved in education, clinical work, and other applied fields.

In the discussions that follow concerning various historical contributions to developmental psychology and the major theoretical approaches still important in the field today, it will be apparent that answers pertaining to the themes often differ. However, these five developmental themes, summarized in Figure 1.2, will have an important influence

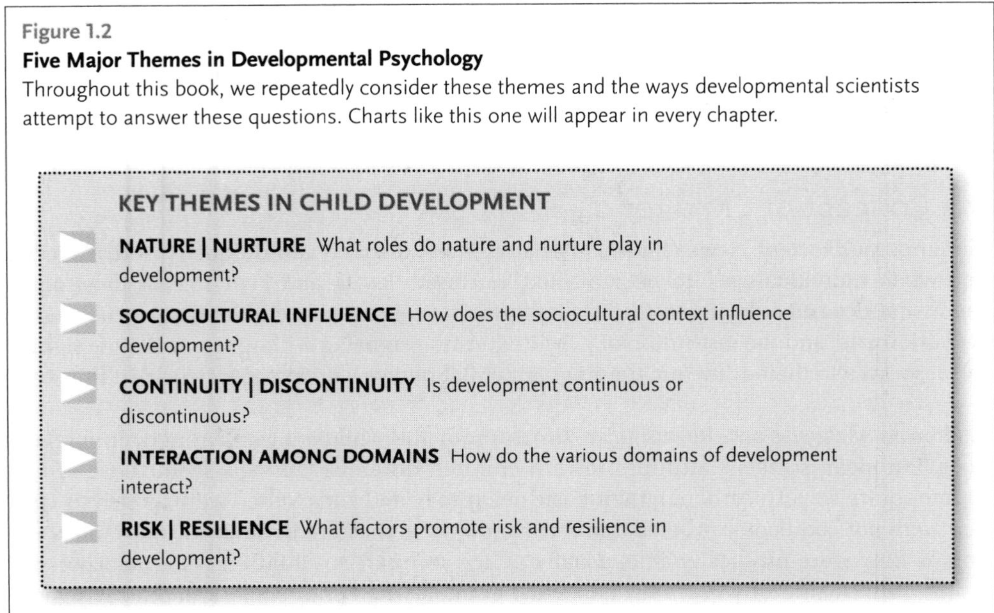

KEY THEMES IN CHILD DEVELOPMENT
NATURE | NURTURE What roles do nature and nurture play in development?
SOCIOCULTURAL INFLUENCE How does the sociocultural context influence development?
CONTINUITY | DISCONTINUITY Is development continuous or discontinuous?
INTERACTION AMONG DOMAINS How do the various domains of development interact?
RISK | RESILIENCE What factors promote risk and resilience in development?

Figure 1.2
Five Major Themes in Developmental Psychology
Throughout this book, we repeatedly consider these themes and the ways developmental scientists attempt to answer these questions. Charts like this one will appear in every chapter.

on our discussion of developmental psychology throughout this book. In nearly all the chapters that follow, we will begin by reminding you of the major themes associated with the topic being covered and you will see icons throughout the chapter identifying themes particularly relevant to the research being discussed. But as you are studying the material in each chapter, evaluate and assess how research findings not singled out by an icon also bear on or contribute to our understanding of these questions. At the end of each chapter, we will close by providing a summary of some of the most important findings bearing on these themes. One of the best ways to review them now is to take a few minutes to consider your stand on each of the themes.

For Your Review and Reflection

- Can you think of ways that nature and nurture might interact in the process of child development? Can you think of examples of how children play active roles in their own development?
- How and to what extent do you feel that society's concerns, values, and resources affect an individual's development?
- Do you find it easier to understand development in terms of continuous or discontinuous, more stagelike change?
- To what extent do you think advances or difficulties in one domain affect the child's development in other domains?
- Can you think of examples of factors that might put children's development at risk?
- What additional themes do you think should be central to studies of child development?

The Study of the Child: Historical Perspectives

Children became a focus of serious study comparatively late in the history of science, primarily within the last hundred years or so. Despite this relatively short history, developmental psychology as a science has grown at an astonishing rate, especially in recent decades, and is a thriving modern-day field of study. Each year hundreds of books and thousands of articles about children's growth are published for professionals interested in specific developmental issues and for parents or teachers. Scientists and laypersons, however, have not always had such a focused and conscious desire to understand the process of child development. In fact, societal attitudes toward childhood as a concept have shifted considerably over the last several centuries.

The Concept of Childhood

Contemporary society views childhood as a separate, distinct, and unique period, a special time when individuals are to be protected, nurtured, loved, and kept free of most adult responsibilities and obligations. Child labor laws try to ensure that children are not abused in the work world, and the institution of public education signals a willingness to devote significant resources to their academic training. But childhood was not always viewed in this way.

Children in Medieval and Renaissance Times From the Middle Ages through premodern times, European society's attitudes toward children differed strikingly from those of our contemporary society. Although their basic needs to be fed and clothed were tended to, children were not coddled or protected in the same way as they are in most societies today. As soon as they were physically able, usually at age seven or so, children were incorporated into the adult world of work; they harvested grain, learned craft skills, and otherwise contributed to the local economy. In medieval times, Western European children did not have special clothes, toys, or games. Once they were old enough to shed swaddling clothes, they wore adult fashions and pursued adult pastimes, such as archery, chess, and even gambling (Ariès, 1962).

In certain respects, however, premodern European society regarded children as vulnerable, fragile, and unable to assume the full responsibilities of adulthood. Medical writings alluded to the special illnesses of young children, and laws prohibited marriages of children under age twelve (Kroll, 1977). Religious movements of this era proclaimed the innocence of children and urged that they be educated. Children's souls, as well as adults', must be saved, said clerics, and they held that parents were morally responsible for their children's spiritual well-being. Thus, even though medieval children were incorporated quickly into the adult world, they were recognized both as different from adults and as possessing special needs.

A noticeable shift in attitudes toward children occurred in Europe during the sixteenth century. In 1545 English physician and lawyer Thomas Phayre published the first book on pediatrics. In addition, the advent of the printing press during that century made possible the wide distribution of other manuals on the care of infants and children. The first grammar schools were established to educate upper-class boys in economics and politics. Upper-class girls attended convent schools or received private instruction intended to cultivate modesty and obedience, as well as other skills thought to be useful in their future roles as wives and mothers (Shahar, 1990).

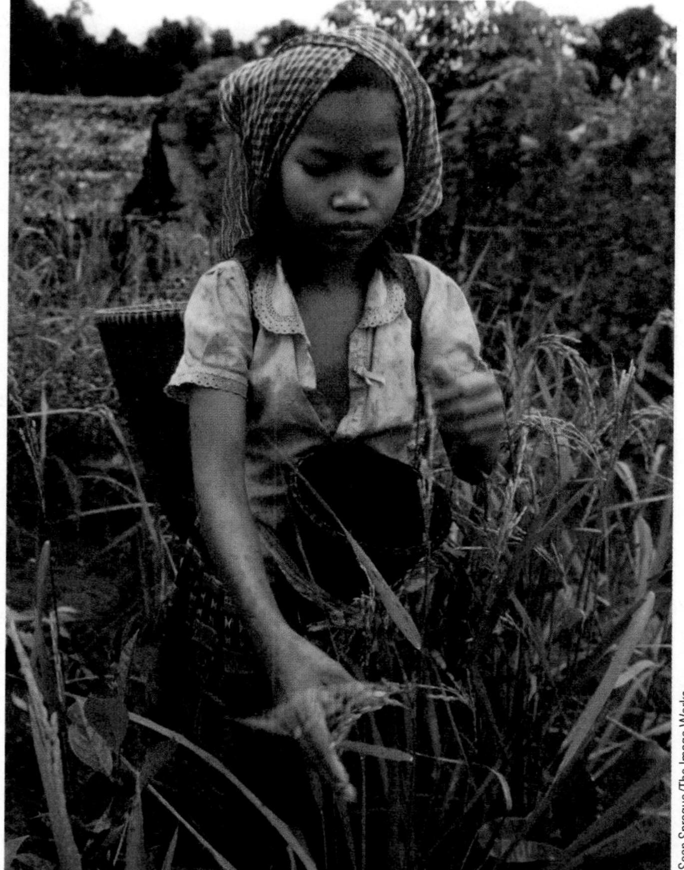
© Sean Sprague/The Image Works

In many regions of the world, children spend much of their time engaged in physical labor. This girl, helping to harvest rice in Cambodia, very likely had little opportunity to learn to read or write. Historically, and in some cultures yet today, attitudes about childhood differ greatly from those held in recent times in most Western societies.

Probably one of the most significant social changes occurred as a result of the transition from agrarian to trade-based economies in the sixteenth and seventeenth centuries, and the subsequent growth of industrialization in the eighteenth century. As people relocated from farms to towns and as the production of goods shifted outside the home, the primary role of the family in Western society changed from ensuring economic survival to the nurturing of children (Hareven, 1985). Closeness and emotional attachment increasingly became the hallmarks of parent-child relations.

The Age of Enlightenment The impact of these sweeping social changes was reflected in the writings of several key thinkers who shaped the popular understanding of childhood. In the seventeenth and eighteenth centuries, two philosophers proposed important but distinctly different ideas about the nature and education of children. In his famous treatise *An Essay Concerning Human Understanding* (1961), originally published in 1690, the British philosopher John Locke (1632–1704) described his views on the acquisition of human knowledge. Virtually no information is inborn, according to Locke. The newborn's mind is a *tabula rasa*, literally a "blank slate," on which perceptual experiences are imprinted. Locke's philosophy of **empiricism**, the idea that environmental experiences shape the individual, foreshadowed the emergence of learning theory and the modern-day psychological school of behaviorism. Locke believed that rewards and punishments from others, imitation, and the associations the child forms between events are key elements in the formation of the mind.

In a second work, *Some Thoughts Concerning Education* (1693/1964), Locke expounded further on his philosophy of training children:

> *The great mistake I have observed in people's breeding their children . . . is that the mind has not been made obedient to discipline and pliant to reason when it was most tender, most easy to be bowed. . . . He that is not used to submit his will to*

empiricism Theory that environmental experiences shape the individual; more specifically, that all knowledge is derived from sensory experiences.

Erich Lessing/Art Resource, NY

In premodern Europe, children often dressed like adults and participated in many adult activities. At the same time, though, children were seen as fragile and in need of protection.

the reason of others when he is young, will scarce hearken to submit to his own reason when he is of an age to make use of it.

Locke argued in support of the importance of early experiences and proper training, yet he maintained that child rearing and education should proceed through the use of reason rather than harsh discipline. In his view, parents must find a balance between being overly indulgent and overly restrictive as they manage their child's behavior. As we will see, many of these same themes resound in contemporary research on good parenting and represent a contrast to the strict disciplinary stance of Western society before the eighteenth century.

The second influential philosopher of the Enlightenment was Jean Jacques Rousseau (1712–1778), a French thinker who embraced the ideal of the child as a "noble savage." According to Rousseau, children are born with a propensity to act on impulses but not necessarily with the aim of wrongdoing. They require the gentle guidance of adult authority to bring their natural instincts and tendencies in line with the social order. In *Émile* (1762/1895), Rousseau set forth these beliefs about child rearing:

> *Never command him to do anything whatever, not the least thing in the world. Never allow him even to imagine that you assume to have any authority over him. Let him know merely that he is weak and that you are strong; that by virtue of his condition and your own he is necessarily at your mercy.*
>
> *. . . Do not give your scholar any sort of verbal lesson, for he is to be taught only by experience. Inflict on him no species of punishment, for he does not know what it is to be in fault.*

Rousseau emphasized the dynamic relationship between the curious and energetic child and the demands of his or her social environment as represented by adults. Adults should not stifle the child's natural development and spirit through domination. Contemporary theories that acknowledge the active role of the child in the process of development have distinct roots in Rousseau's writings.

Rousseau also advanced some radical ideas about education. Children, he held, should not be forced to learn by rote the vast amounts of information that adults perceive as important. Instead, teachers should capitalize on the natural curiosity of children and allow them to discover on their own the myriad facts and phenomena that make up the world. Rousseau's ideas on the nature of education would resonate with the twentieth-century writings of Jean Piaget.

Both Locke and Rousseau emphasized the notion of the child as a developing, as opposed to a static, being. Both challenged the supposition that children are merely passive subjects of adult authority, and both advanced the idea that children should be treated with reason and respect. Having been elevated by the efforts of these worthy thinkers to an object of intellectual interest, the child was now ready to become the subject of scientific study.

The Origins of Developmental Psychology

By the mid- to late 1800s, scholars in the natural sciences, especially biology, saw in the study of children an opportunity to support their emerging theories about the origins of human beings and their behaviors. Charles Darwin, for example, hypothesized that the similarities between the behaviors of humans and those of other species were the result of common evolutionary ancestors. Thus, he observed one of his own child's behaviors as a way to further support his theory of evolution. Similarly, Wilhelm Preyer, another biologist, was initially interested in the physiology of embryological development but soon extended his investigations to behavioral development after birth. In the United States and Europe, key researchers who participated in the birth of psychology as an academic discipline also began to show an interest in studying children. By the beginning of the twentieth century, developmental psychology was established as a legitimate area of psychological inquiry.

The Baby Biographers: Charles Darwin and Wilhelm Preyer One of the first attempts to observe a child for the purpose of scientific understanding can be found in the writings of Charles Darwin. Eager to uncover important clues about the origins of the human species, Darwin recorded in great detail his infant son's behaviors during the first three years of life. Darwin documented the presence of early reflexes, such as sucking, as well as the emergence of voluntary motor movements, language, and emotions such as fear, anger, and affection. Where he saw similarities, he linked the behaviors of the young child to those of other species, such as when he concluded that the infant's comprehension of simple words was not unlike the ability of "lower animals" to understand words spoken by humans (Darwin, 1877).

In 1882 the German biologist Wilhelm Preyer published *The Mind of the Child* (1882/1888–1889), a work that described in great detail the development of his son Axel during the first three years of life. Preyer wrote meticulously of his son's sensory development, motor accomplishments, language production, and memory, even noting indications of an emerging concept of self. Although Preyer followed in the footsteps of several previous "baby biographers," including Darwin, he was the first to insist that observations of children be conducted systematically, recorded immediately and unobtrusively, and repeated several times each day. By advocating the application of scientific techniques to the study of children, the baby biographers—Preyer, in particular—set in motion the beginnings of the child development movement in the United States.

G. Stanley Hall is considered to be the founder of modern child psychology.

G. Stanley Hall: The Founder of Modern Child Psychology The psychologist perhaps most associated with launching the new discipline of child study in the United States was G. Stanley Hall, who in 1878 became the first American to obtain a Ph.D. in psychology. Hall is also known for founding the first psychological journal in the United States in 1887 and, in 1891, the first journal of developmental psychology, *Pedagogical Seminary* (now called *The Journal of Genetic Psychology*). In addition, he founded and served as the first president of the American Psychological Association (APA).

As the first American to study in Europe with the pioneer psychologist Wilhelm Wundt, G. Stanley Hall returned to the United States in 1880 with an interest in studying the "content of children's minds." Adopting the questionnaire method he had learned about in Germany, he had teachers ask about 200 kindergarten-age children questions like "Have you ever seen a cow?" or "What are bricks made of?" The percentages of children who gave particular answers were tabulated, and comparisons were made between the responses of boys and girls, city children and country children, and children of different ethnic backgrounds (Hall, 1891). For the first time, researchers were collecting data to compare groups of children, in contrast to previous approaches that had emphasized the detailed examination of individual children.

Alfred Binet: The Study of Individual Differences The French psychologist Alfred Binet is known primarily as the developer of the first formal assessment scale of intelligence. Binet was a pioneer in the study of **individual differences**, those unique characteristics that distinguish one person from others in the larger group.

Binet's original interest lay in the general features of children's thinking, including memory and reasoning about numbers. To that end, he closely scrutinized the behaviors of his two daughters as they progressed from toddlerhood to the teenage years. He noted, in particular, how one daughter, Madeleine, was serious and reflective as she tried to solve problems, whereas the other daughter, Alice, was more impulsive and temperamental (Fancher, 1998). His studies of children's thinking had two significant outcomes: first, they demonstrated that a description of individual differences

individual differences Unique characteristics that distinguish a person from other members of a larger group.

contributed to the understanding of human development, and second, they provided the basis for more formal tests of children's mental abilities (Cairns & Cairns, 2006). In response to a request from the Ministry of Public Instruction in Paris for a tool to screen for students with learning problems, Binet and another colleague, Théodore Simon, developed a series of tasks to systematically measure motor skills, vocabulary, problem solving, and a wide range of other higher-order thought processes (Binet & Simon, 1905). This instrument could identify patterns in mental capabilities that were unique to each child.

The idea of mental testing caught on very quickly in the United States, especially among clinicians, early educators, and other professionals concerned with the practical side of dealing with children. For the first time, it was legitimate, even important, to consider variation in mental abilities from person to person.

James Mark Baldwin: Developmental Theorist Considered the founder of academic psychology in Canada (Hoff, 1992), James Mark Baldwin established a laboratory at the University of Toronto devoted to the systematic study of movement patterns, handedness, and color vision in infants (Cairns, 1992). Soon, however, his interests shifted away from gathering empirical data. He became one of the most influential developmental theorists of the early twentieth century.

One of Baldwin's most important propositions was that development is a dynamic and hierarchical process, such that "every genetic change ushers in a real advance, a progression on the part of nature to a higher mode of reality" (Baldwin, 1930, p. 86). Baldwin applied these ideas to the domain of cognitive development by suggesting that mental advances occur in a stagelike sequence in which the earliest thought is prelogical but gives way to logical and eventually hyperlogical or formal reasoning—ideas that today are often linked to Piaget.

Baldwin is also recognized for his unique perspective on social development and the formation of personality. Instead of characterizing the child as a passive recipient of the behaviors and beliefs endorsed by the larger society, he described the child's emerging self as a product of continual reciprocal interactions between the child and others. The proposition that development results from a mutual dynamic between the child and others took a long time to catch on among psychologists, but this idea, so popular today, is actually almost a century old (Cairns & Ornstein, 1979).

Sigmund Freud: The Importance of Early Experience During the early decades of the twentieth century, Sigmund Freud's theory also became extremely influential, particularly with respect to explaining emotional and personality development. Freud proposed in his psychosexual theory of development that many aspects of the individual's personality originate in an early and broad form of childhood sexuality. The fuel that powers human behavior, according to Freud, is a set of biological instincts. The psychological tension induced by these instincts, called *libido* or *libidinal energy*, gradually builds and requires eventual discharge. Under many circumstances, this energy is reduced as rapidly as possible. Sometimes, however, tensions like those associated with hunger or pain in infants cannot be eliminated immediately. Because of these delays, mental structures and behavioral responses eventually organize into more satisfactory ways of decreasing tension. For example, behavioral acts might include calling out to the caregiver as a signal to be fed or eventually learning to feed oneself, responses that normally lead to a reduction in libidinal urges by effective, rational, and socially acceptable means.

The locus of tension and the optimal ways to reduce needs change with age. Freud identified five stages of psychosexual development, periods during which libidinal energy is usually associated with a specific area of the body. During the *oral stage*, lasting until about one year of age, libidinal energy is focused around the mouth and is reduced through sucking, chewing, eating, and biting. Throughout the subsequent *anal stage*, from about one to three years of age, this energy is centered on satisfactorily expelling body wastes. The *phallic stage*, typically bridging the period between three and five years of age, is characterized as a time of desire for the opposite-sex parent and of other forms of immature gratification surrounding the genitals. A relatively long *latency* period lasts from about five years of age to adolescence and is a time in which libidinal energy is submerged or expressed, for example, through a more culturally acceptable focus on the acquisition of social or intellectual skills. During the final period, the *genital stage*, which occurs in adolescence and continues throughout adulthood, mature forms of genital satisfaction are theorized to be an important source of tension reduction.

Freud believed that the individual's progression through these stages is greatly influenced by maturation. However, the environment also plays a critical role. Lack of opportunity to meet needs adequately or to express them during a stage could lead to negative consequences in the way the child relates to others and to feelings of low self-worth. For example, the infant whose sucking efforts are not gratified may become *fixated*; that is, preoccupied with actions associated with the mouth for the rest of his or her life. A child whose toilet training is too lax may become messy, disorderly, or wasteful, whereas one whose toilet training is too strict may display a possessive, retentive (frugal and stingy) personality or show an excessive concern with cleanliness and orderliness in later adulthood.

Freud's view of development has been criticized extensively for its overemphasis on libidinal gratification, as well as for its cultural and gender limitations. So, too, has his method for arriving at his theory: asking adults to reflect on their earliest experiences. As a consequence, his contributions have often been discounted. Nevertheless, for Freud, as for many developmental psychologists today, events that occur during the earliest years of development and that involve interactions with the family were of paramount importance in understanding and explaining behavior throughout the later years of an individual's life.

The Continued Growth of Developmental Psychology in the Twentieth Century

From the beginning of the twentieth century to the mid-1940s, psychologists interested in development increasingly concentrated their efforts on gathering descriptive information about children. At what ages do most children achieve the milestones of motor development, such as sitting, crawling, and walking? When do children develop emotions, such as fear and anger? What are children's beliefs about punishment, friendship, and morality? It was during this era of intensive fact gathering that many *norms* of development—that is, the ages at which most children are able to accomplish a given developmental task—were established. For example, Arnold Gesell summarized norms for motor development during the first five years of life, guidelines that are still useful to psychologists, pediatricians, and other professionals who work with children in diagnosing developmental problems or delays (Gesell & Thompson, 1934, 1938).

Over the years, questions about norms gave way to research on the variables that cause development to occur in the way it does. For example, is maturation or experience responsible for the sequence of motor behaviors most children display? Even over seventy years ago, researchers found that the answer was not simple. Myrtle McGraw (1935, 1939), in her classic studies of the twins Johnny and Jimmy, reported that training Johnny (but not Jimmy) to reach for objects, crawl, and swim during infancy accelerated motor development, but only when he was already showing signs of physiological maturity. Similarly, do predictable sequences in language development occur because of biological influences or learning? What factors lead to the emergence of emotional ties children form with caregivers? Researchers today continue to ask questions like these, but they increasingly recognize the complexities of these influences on child development.

In her classic studies of a pair of twins, Myrtle McGraw found that both maturation and experience contributed to motor skill development.

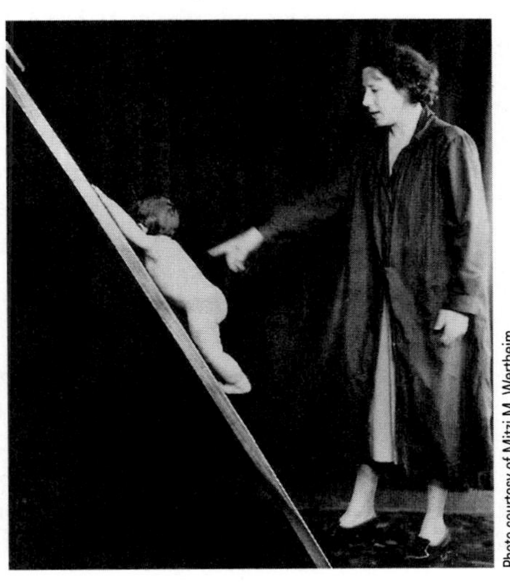
Photo courtesy of Mitzi M. Wertheim

The first half of the twentieth century also saw the founding of a number of major institutes or research centers that attracted bright young scholars who dedicated their lives to the scientific study of children. A further sign of the professionalization of the discipline was the formation of the Society for Research in Child Development (SRCD) in 1933 for scientists who wished to share their growing knowledge of child behavior and development. Today the membership of this society numbers about 5,500 professionals working with children in a variety of research, applied, and other contexts in settings such as colleges, universities, research institutes, and hospitals and who come from more than 50 different countries around the world (Society for Research in Child Development, 2010).

Scholars now inform us about child development from an assortment of disciplines beyond developmental psychology, including anthropology, sociology, education, medicine, biology, and several sub-areas of psychology (such as neuropsychology, comparative psychology, and clinical psychology). Each discipline has its own specialized emphasis on developmental processes ranging from cell biology to cultural influences. Nonetheless, the pooled knowledge that now comprises the field of developmental science offers a far more complete understanding of child development than we might expect, given that the systematic observation of children began only a little more than a century ago.

For Your Review and Reflection

- How have views of childhood changed from medieval and Renaissance times to today?
- What were John Locke's and Jean Jacques Rousseau's views of childhood? Do your ideas about development align with either of them? Looking back, do you feel your parents ascribed to either Locke or Rousseau's ideals when raising you? What differences have you noticed about how some of your friends were reared?
- How did Charles Darwin, Wilhelm Preyer, G. Stanley Hall, Alfred Binet, and James Mark Baldwin contribute to developmental psychology?
- What was Sigmund Freud's psychosexual theory of development?
- What emphases emerged in research on children during the first half of the twentieth century?
- What topics are missing in these early approaches to understanding child development? Which of the major themes were of primary interest to those who first began to observe children? Which major themes received little attention?

Theories of Development

A number of major theories influence our understanding of development today. We introduce them and briefly highlight some of the major concepts and principles associated with each in the sections that follow. However, their contributions will be a major part of our discussion in later chapters as well. In considering these theories in this first chapter, we focus in particular on where each stands with respect to the major themes in developmental psychology.

Learning Theory Approaches

Learning theorists study how principles of learning cause the individual to change and develop. **Learning**, the relatively permanent change in behavior that results from experience, undoubtedly contributes to why the infant smiles as her mother approaches, the three-year-old says a polite "Thank you" on receiving his grandmother's present, the five-year-old displays newfound skill in tying her shoes, and the adolescent expresses a clear preference for the most fashionable item of clothing to wear.

In the extreme view, some learning theorists believe, as John B. Watson did, that learning mechanisms can be exploited to create virtually any type of person.

> *Give me a dozen healthy infants, well-formed, and my own specified world to bring them up in and I'll guarantee to take any one at random and train him to become any type of specialist I might select—doctor, lawyer, artist, merchant-chief, and yes, even beggar-man and thief, regardless of his talents, penchants, tendencies, abilities, vocations, and race of his ancestors.* (Watson, 1930, p. 104)

learning Relatively permanent change in behavior as a result of such experiences as exploration, observation, and practice.

Although present-day supporters of learning theory seldom take such a radical position, they are in agreement that basic principles of learning can have a powerful influence on child development (Gewirtz & Peláez-Nogueras, 1992; Schlinger, 1992).

Behaviorism **Behaviorism** is a theoretical account of development that relies on basic principles of learning to explain developmental changes in behavior. Behaviorism has its roots in the radical learning position introduced by John B. Watson and was extended by B. F. Skinner (1953, 1974) and by others in more recent years.

Nearly a century ago, the Russian physiologist Ivan Pavlov observed that dogs would often start to salivate at the sound of a bell or some other arbitrary stimulus after the stimulus had previously been accompanied by food. In this type of learning, called *classical conditioning,* a neutral stimulus begins to elicit a response following its repeated pairing with another stimulus that already elicits that response. We learn certain behaviors and emotions as a result of classical conditioning. For example, children and adults may become anxious on entering a dental office because of its association with previous painful treatments performed by the dentist.

To understand a second basic principle of learning, consider two babies who smile as their caregivers approach. With one baby, the caregiver stops, says "Hi, baby!" and briefly rocks the cradle. With the other baby, the caregiver walks on past, preoccupied. Which baby do you think is more likely to repeat her smile when the caregiver nears again? If you reasoned that the first is more likely than the second because the behavior was followed by a positive event (attention or approval), which often increases the frequency of a behavior, you know something about the principle of operant conditioning. *Operant conditioning* (also called *instrumental conditioning*) refers to the process by which the frequency of a behavior changes depending on response consequences in the form of a desirable or undesirable outcome. Behavior analysts have used this principle to account for the emergence of such straightforward behaviors as the one-year-old's waving good-bye to far more sophisticated skills involving memory, language, social interaction, and complex problem solving.

Operant and classical conditioning have been shown to have enormous potential to change behavior. *Behavior modification*, sometimes called *applied behavior analysis,* involves the systematic application of operant conditioning to modify human activity. As an illustration, Anthony Cammilleri and Gregory Hanley (2005) investigated whether teacher attention could be used to increase the variety of activities a child would undertake in a school setting. Would a five-year-old and a seven-year-old, whom teachers noted typically worked on only a small set of skills when given choices in the classroom, be willing to undertake a greater variety of activities if given more teacher attention for doing so? During sixty-minute periods held over a number of days, each child could choose to do a variety of computer or workbook activities encouraging improvement in academic skills (e.g., grammar, math facts, reading, etc.) or more gamelike activities (e.g., an Internet computer game, block construction, etc). Each child was free to continue or switch activities at any time but every five minutes was reminded to make a choice that could be either a new activity or one in which she had already spent some time. During the baseline period, no feedback was given for a choice. However, every time the child selected a new activity during the intervention period, she was given a card that could be traded in to receive the teacher's attention for two minutes. As Figure 1.3 shows, Tina, the five-year-old, seldom changed activities during the baseline period but was far more likely to try novel activities and, in turn, complete more units of academic activity, during the intervention periods. Similar findings were obtained for the seven-year-old. The opportunity to gain increased attention from the teacher encouraged these children to sample a wider range of activities than they otherwise would, including some activities having potential academic benefits.

Applied behavior analysis has become a powerful approach used by teachers, therapists, and caregivers to bring about changes in behavior ranging from the elimination of temper tantrums and other disruptive responses to encouraging

behaviorism Learning theory perspective that explains the development of behavior according to the principles of classical and operant conditioning.

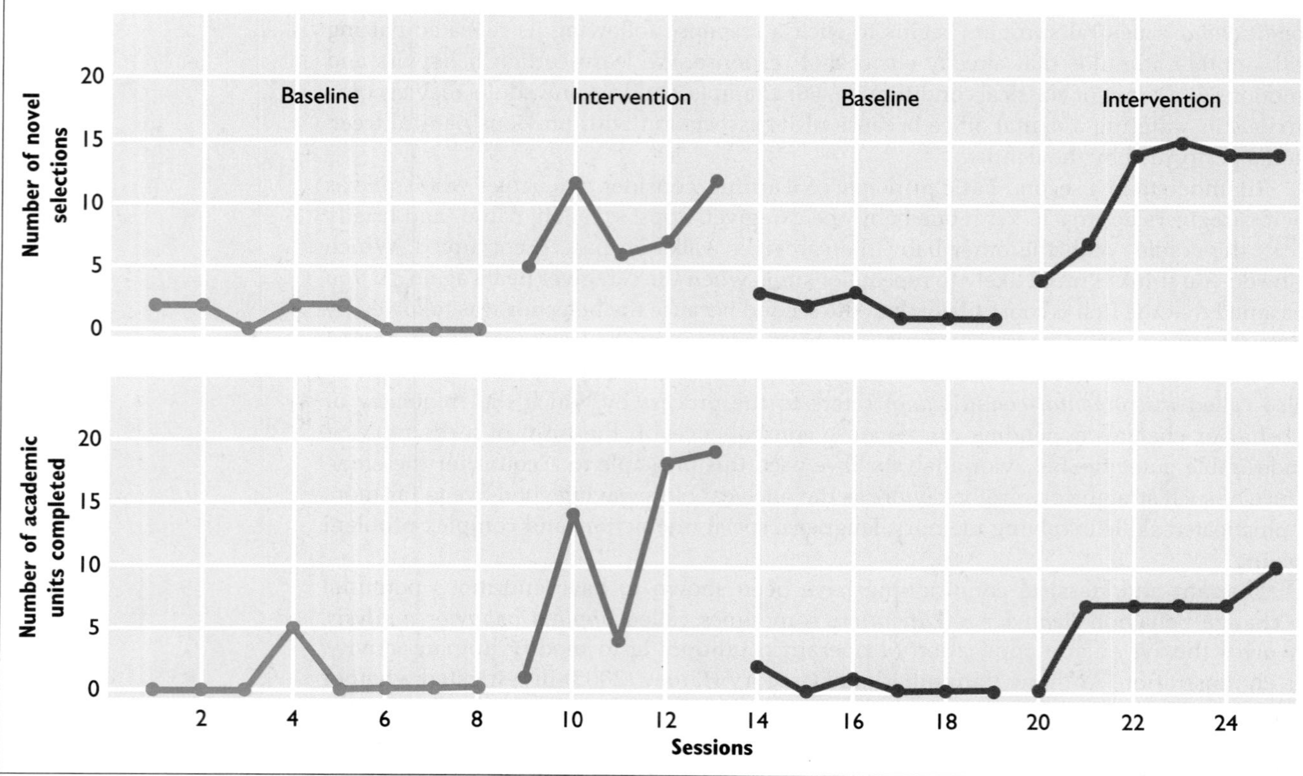

Figure 1.3

A Behavioral Approach to Increasing a Wider Variety of Task Activities

During the intervention period, when able to receive increased attention from the teacher by selecting different activities to work on, this five-year-old displayed a markedly greater variety of task choices compared with baseline periods when she did not receive teacher attention for selecting novel tasks (see top part of the figure). One benefit of this behavior modification procedure, as can be seen in the bottom portion of the figure, is that she completed more academically related tasks during the intervention periods than during the baseline periods.

Source: From Cammilleri, A. P., & Hanley, G. P. (2005). Use of a lag differential reinforcement contingency to increase varied selections of classroom activities. *Journal of Applied Behavior Analysis, 38,* 111–115. Figure 1, p. 113. Copyright © 2005. Reprinted with permission.

healthy diets and safe driving habits. Even some of its detractors have suggested that behavior analysis may have done more to benefit human welfare than any other psychological theory (Hebb, 1980). Yet behavior analysis has drawn extensive criticism. Its critics, including some learning theorists, remain unconvinced that a behavior can be understood without taking into account the child's feelings and reasons for engaging in that behavior. In other words, mental, emotional, and motivational factors also play a prominent role in how a child interprets and responds to stimulation. Among various learning perspectives, social learning theory attempts to incorporate these factors into its explanation of behavior and development.

Social Learning Theory **Social learning theory** emphasizes the importance of learning through observing and imitating the behaviors displayed by others. Thus, the socialization methods practiced and exhibited by parents and caregivers have a major impact on whether an individual will be friendly, outgoing, confident, and honest rather than shy or perhaps hostile, aggressive, and untrustworthy. Although operant and classical conditioning play a substantial role in the socialization of the child, social learning theorists underscore **observational learning**, the acquisition of behaviors from listening to and watching other people. The two-year-old who stands before a mirror pretending to shave in imitation of his father is displaying observational learning.

social learning theory Theoretical approach emphasizing the importance of learning through observation and imitation of behaviors modeled by others.

observational learning Learning that takes place by simply observing another person's behavior.

Similarly, you may have witnessed the embarrassment of a parent whose three-year-old has uttered a profanity, a behavior probably acquired by the same process.

According to Albert Bandura (1965), psychology's best-known spokesperson for social learning, a society could never effectively convey complex language, social and moral customs, or other achievements to its younger members without relying extensively on observational learning. Significant learning occurs, often completely without error, through the act of watching and imitating another person, a *model* (Bandura, 1965). For example, girls in one region of Guatemala learn to weave simply by keeping an eye on the procedures carried out by an expert, an approach to learning new skills common to the fields, homes, and shops of communities all over the world. Social learning theorists propose that many kinds of complex social activities, including the acquisition of gender roles, aggression, prosocial responses (such as willingness to assist others), resistance to temptation, and other facets of moral development, are learned primarily through observing others (Bandura & Walters, 1963).

© fStop/Alamy

Social learning theory emphasizes the important role that observation of another person's behavior plays in learning. This daughter engages in the practice of putting on make-up by observing her mother perform this activity. Social learning provides an important mechanism by which she and others acquire many customs and behaviors in their society.

In accounting for the acquisition of complex behaviors, Bandura has often referred to cognitive processes within his theory, now known as *social cognitive theory*. Bandura (1989) believes that four sets of cognitive processes are especially important in observational learning (see Figure 1.4). Attentional processes determine what information will be acquired from models, and memory processes convert these observations into stored mental representations. Production processes then transform these stored mental representations into matching behaviors, and motivational processes define which behaviors are likely to be performed. As each of these processes becomes more sophisticated, observational and other forms of learning become increasingly refined and proficient, and the child becomes more effective in regulating his or her own behavior (Grusec, 1992).

Learning Theory and Themes in Development What stance do behavior analysts and social cognitive theorists take on the five major developmental themes we introduced at the

(A) Attentional Processes

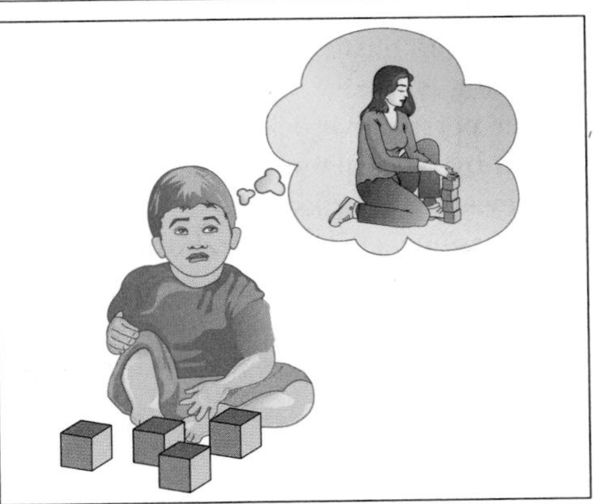

(B) Memory Processes

(C) Production Processes

(D) Motivational Processes

Figure 1.4
Bandura's Observational Learning Cognitive Processes
Albert Bandura believes these four sets of cognitive processes are especially important in observational learning.

beginning of this chapter? Keep in mind that, as our discussions of behavior analysis and social cognitive theory suggest, not all learning theorists share the same views about the prime determinants of development.

- *Nature & nurture.* Behavior analysts believe that biological and genetic factors may limit the kinds of responses that can be performed and help to define which events are reinforcing or punishing. But ultimately it is the environment that controls behavior. For behaviorists, a child's functioning is the outcome of a history of behaviors and their associated consequences. In keeping with their strong experiential emphasis, behaviorists believe the child's role in development is passive. Skinner claimed that "a person does not act upon the world, the world acts upon him" (1971, p. 211). According to Skinner, psychologists should abolish references to unobservable mental or cognitive constructs, such as motives, goals, needs, or thoughts, in their explanations of behavior. Bandura's social cognitive theory differs from behavior analysis by embracing mental and motivational constructs and processes for interpreting and understanding others as well as the self. Social cognitive theory therefore confers a much more active status on the child than does behavior analysis.
- *Sociocultural influence.* Behaviorists believe that, although societies differ in the responses viewed as desirable or unacceptable, the mechanisms of learning are universal for individuals in all cultures. Rewards and punishments delivered in the immediate environment are the key to understanding development. Social learning theorists give sociocultural context more emphasis than behaviorists do by pointing out, for example, that advances in communication technology (such as television) expand the opportunity for children and adults to acquire many novel skills and patterns of behavior through observational learning.
- *Continuity/discontinuity.* Both behavior analysts and social learning theorists consider development to be continuous rather than stagelike. Any departure from this pattern would stem from abrupt shifts in environmental circumstances, such as when the child enters school or the adolescent enters the work environment.
- *Interaction among domains.* Whereas behavior analysts explain development in all domains in terms of the basic principles of learning, social cognitive theorists stress that learning is linked to the child's physical, cognitive, and social development. Thus, this latter perspective acknowledges the interaction among different domains of development by recognizing that the child's learning is a consequence of what he or she feels, believes, and thinks.
- *Risk/resilience.* The general principles of learning apply to all individuals, whatever their situation, and can account for both risk and recovery from risk. It is important to analyze the unique kinds of experiences each person receives; for example, the specific models to which she or he is exposed or the particular behaviors rewarded by others in the environment.

Piaget's Cognitive-Developmental Theory

According to **cognitive-developmental theory**, behavior reflects the emergence of various cognitive *structures*, organized units or patterns of thinking, that influence how the child interprets experience. Cognitive-developmental theories tend to share the fundamental assumption that normal children display common intellectual, emotional, and social capacities despite widely varying experiences. Most three- and four-year-olds around the world, for example, believe that a gallon of water, when poured from one container to another of a different shape, changes in amount, an error children rarely make once they reach seven or eight years of age. Cognitive-developmental theorists explain this profound change in reasoning in terms of children's acquiring new ways of understanding their world.

cognitive-developmental theory Theoretical orientation, most frequently associated with Piaget, emphasizing the active construction of psychological structures to interpret experience.

The most extensive and best-known cognitive-developmental theory was put forward by Jean Piaget. His vigorous defense of physical and mental *action* as the basis for cognitive development (Beilin & Fireman, 1999) and his belief that intellectual capacities undergo *qualitative* reorganization at different stages of development have had a monumental impact, not only on developmental psychologists, but also on educators and other professionals working with children.

Bill Anderson/Photo Researchers, Inc.

Jean Piaget's keen observations and insights concerning the behavior of children laid the groundwork for his theory of cognitive development. Piaget's ideas about how thinking develops have influenced psychologists, educators, and many others in their attempts to understand children.

Piaget's Theory Piaget's vision of human development was based on two overriding assumptions about intelligence: (1) it is a form of biological adaptation, and (2) it becomes organized as the individual interacts with the external world (Piaget, 1971). **Adaptation** is a tendency to adjust or become more attuned to the conditions imposed by the environment. **Organization** refers to a tendency for intellectual structures and processes to become more systematic and coherent. Just as arms, eyes, lungs, heart, and other physical structures assemble and take shape to carry out biological functions, so do mental structures array themselves in ever more powerful patterns to support more complex thought. These changes, however, depend on the opportunity to look and touch, handle and play with, and construct and order the rich assortment of experiences stemming from action on the environment. From the abundant encounters provided in commonplace physical and social experiences, the child confronts unexpected and puzzling outcomes that ultimately lead to reorganizations in thought.

The basic mental structure in Piaget's theory is a **scheme**, a coordinated and systematic pattern of action or way of reasoning. A scheme is a kind of template for acting or thinking applied to similar classes of objects or situations. The infant who sucks at her mother's breast, on her favorite pacifier, and her thumb is exercising a scheme of sucking. The six-year-old who realizes that his eight Matchbox cars can be stored in an equal number of boxes regardless of how they are scattered about the floor is also exercising a scheme, this time one concerned with number. The infant's schemes are limited to patterns of action applied to objects: sucking, grasping, shaking, and so forth. The older child's schemes will often involve mental processes and be far more complex as he or she reasons about such things as classes of objects, number, or spatial relations, and, by adolescence, the meaning of life and the origins of the universe. For Piaget, earlier schemes set the stage for constructing new and more sophisticated schemes.

Piaget believed that schemes change through two complementary processes. The first, **assimilation**, refers to the process of interpreting an experience in terms of current ways of understanding things. The second, **accommodation**, refers to the modifications in behavior and thinking that take place when the old ways of understanding, the old schemes, no longer fit. To illustrate these two processes, consider the infant's first experience with sucking a pacifier. Upon feeling it in the mouth, the infant engages the already formed scheme for sucking at the mother's breast. In other words, this new experience is *assimilated* into the pre-existing scheme. But the shape and taste of the pacifier are not the same as the mother's breast. The child's scheme must *accommodate* to this new encounter. In a similar manner throughout development, the child's intellectual capacities become reshaped and reorganized as the child attempts to adjust—that is, accommodate—to new experiences.

For Piaget, assimilation and accommodation are complementary aspects of all psychological activity, processes engaged in a constant tug of war in the never-ending goal of acquiring understanding (Valsiner, 2006). Fortunately, adaptation in the form of newer and more complex schemes is the result of this continuous dynamic. The outcome of adaptation is a more effective fitting together of the many pieces of knowledge that make up the child's understanding. The process by which assimilation and accommodation bring about more organized and powerful schemes for thinking is called **equilibration**. Each new experience can cause

adaptation In Piagetian theory, the inborn tendency to adjust or become more attuned to conditions imposed by the environment; takes place through assimilation and accommodation.

organization In Piagetian theory, the inborn tendency for structures and processes to become more systematic and coherent.

scheme In Piagetian theory, the mental structure underlying a coordinated and systematic pattern of behaviors or thinking applied across similar objects or situations.

assimilation In Piagetian theory, a component of adaptation; process of interpreting an experience in terms of current ways (schemes) of understanding things.

accommodation In Piagetian theory, a component of adaptation; process of modification in thinking (schemes) that takes place when old ways of understanding something no longer fit.

equilibration In Piagetian theory, an innate self-regulatory process that, through accommodation and assimilation, results in more organized and powerful schemes for adapting to the environment.

TABLE 1.1 Piaget's Stages of Cognitive Development

Stage	Emerging Cognitive Structure (schemes)	Typical Achievements and Behaviors
Sensorimotor (birth until 1½–2 years)	Sensory and motor actions, initially reflexes, quickly differentiate by means of accommodation and coordinate to form adaptive ways of acting on the environment.	Infants suck, grasp, look, reach, and so forth, responses that become organized into complex activities such as hand-eye coordination, knowledge of space and objects, and eventually rudimentary symbols designed to solve problems and understand the physical world.
Preoperational (1½–7 years)	Symbols stand for or represent objects and events, but communication and thought remain relatively inflexible.	Children begin to acquire language and mental representations, but thought remains unidimensional and oriented around the self.
Concrete Operational (7–11 years)	Cognitive operations permit logical reasoning about concrete objects, events, and relationships.	Children are no longer fooled by appearance, and they can reason more systematically with respect to classes, number, and other characteristics of their physical and social world.
Formal Operational (11 years and above)	Operations can be performed on operations. Thought becomes abstract, and all possible outcomes can be considered.	Adolescents and adults are able to reason about hypothetical outcomes. Abstract issues (e.g., religion, morality, alternative lifestyles) are systematically evaluated.

imbalance, which can be corrected only by modification of the child's schemes. In trying to make sense of his or her world, the child develops more adaptive ways of thinking.

During some periods of development, schemes may undergo rapid and substantial modification and reorganization. The more effective levels of knowledge that emerge from these restructurings are the basis for different stages in Piaget's theory of development. Piaget proposed that development proceeds through four stages: *sensorimotor, preoperational, concrete,* and *formal.* Table 1.1 briefly identifies these stages. Each higher stage is defined by the appearance of a qualitatively different level of thinking, an increasingly more sophisticated form of knowledge through which the child displays greater intellectual balance for responding to the environment. However, each new stage does not suddenly appear full-blown; it arises from the integration and incorporation of earlier ways of thinking.

Piaget's wide range of observations, his frequently surprising findings about what infants and children can and cannot do, and his theoretical explanations and assumptions have sparked a wealth of research on cognitive, social, and moral development. Many researchers applaud his innovative conceptualizations concerning development. For example, Piaget vigorously embraced the notion of children as active participants in their own development, a viewpoint that others have widely adopted. However, the central concept of qualitative differences in thinking between children and adults, and particularly of stagelike transformations, has been less favorably received (Fischer & Bidell, 2006; Thelen & Smith, 1994).

Piaget's Theory and Themes in Development How does Piaget's theory address the five major themes of development?

- *Nature & nurture.* Piaget theorized that a number of biologically based factors contribute to cognitive development. Among them is maturation, the gradual unfolding over time of genetic programs for development. Another factor is the child's inherent tendency to act, physically or mentally, on the environment. Nevertheless, for Piaget, development is clearly the product of the interaction of these factors with experience. In Piaget's theory, knowledge is *constructed*; that is, it is created and formed by the continuous revision and reorganization of intellectual structures in conjunction with experience. Piaget's constructivist model depicts a mind actively engaged in knowing and understanding its environment.
- *Sociocultural influence.* For Piaget, children develop in much the same way in all cultures around the world because of their similar biological makeup and the common physical and social world to which all humans must adapt. Different cultural or educational opportunities, however, can affect the speed and ultimate level of achievement in cognitive development.

- *Continuity/discontinuity.* Although recognizing continuous changes, Piaget's theory focuses on the ways schemes undergo reorganization and change to form distinctive stages in development. In his later writings and conversations, Piaget began to downplay the importance of stages (Piaget, 1971; Vuyk, 1981). He believed that an overemphasis on stages had led to too much concern with describing periods of intellectual stability or equilibrium when, in fact, cognition is always undergoing development. Cognitive development, he eventually concluded, is more like a spiral in which change constantly occurs, although sometimes at faster rates than at other times (Beilin, 1989).
- *Interaction among domains.* Piaget's theory has implications for many domains of development. For example, his ideas about cognitive development have been used to explain changes in communication, moral thinking, and aspects of *social cognition,* such as how children understand the thoughts, intentions, feelings, and views of others. Nevertheless, Piaget has been criticized for paying relatively little attention to how social and emotional domains influence cognitive development.
- *Risk/resilience.* Piaget placed very little emphasis on individual differences in development. His goal was to identify the principles that applied to cognitive and other aspects of development in all children. However, in his emphasis on providing children with environmental experiences that match their biological readiness to learn, Piaget does suggest some factors that might put children at risk.

Information-Processing Approaches

Computer information processing as a metaphor for human thinking has generated so many models and theories that it is difficult to single out any one approach as a prototype (Klahr & MacWhinney, 1998). However, one common thread evident in any **information-processing** point of view is the notion that humans, like computers, have a *limited capacity* for taking in and operating on the vast amount of information available to them. Thus, changes in cognitive structures (for example, short- and long-term memory) and processes (for instance, strategies, rules, and plans associated with attending, remembering, and decision making) are an essential component in explaining how older children might process information more fully and effectively than younger children.

A feature that sets an information-processing theory apart from many other theories is its detailed effort to explain exactly how the child comes to identify the letters of the alphabet, remember the multiplication tables, recall the main ideas of a story, give a classmate directions to his or her home, or decide whether it is safe to cross the street. For example, how does a six-year-old solve addition problems? She may have practiced this activity over and over, and learned the answer to each particular problem by rote over many months of exposure to them. Or she may rely on some kind of strategy that permits her to consistently arrive at the correct answer. For example, she could start with the first number of the addition problem and then add one unit the number of times indicated by the second number. Thus, for the problem 3 + 5, she may begin at 3 and add 1 to it the necessary five times to arrive at the correct answer.

How could we tell whether one child was engaging in the first procedure, retrieving information from long-term rote memory, and another child, the second procedure of utilizing a rule to determine the answer? One clue could come from the length of time it takes to solve various addition problems. If a child is using the first technique, she can be expected to solve each problem in about the same length of time. If she uses the second technique, however, she will likely take somewhat longer to answer a problem in which the second number is very large than when it is very small. We may also see the child producing other observable behaviors, such as holding up three fingers to begin with and counting off additional fingers to arrive at the correct answer to suggest that she is using a strategy rather than rote memory.

As this example illustrates, information-processing theorists frequently attempt to describe the rules, strategies, and procedures that children employ to complete a task and that help them to remember, make inferences, and solve problems. Why has this approach become popular in

information processing Theoretical approach that views humans as having a limited ability to process information, much like computers.

developmental psychology? One reason is disenchantment with learning, Piagetian, and other perspectives for explaining behavior. For instance, although learning theories attempt to identify which abilities are learned, they have offered few insights into how the child's mind changes with age in learning these abilities. Piaget's cognitive-developmental theory is concerned with this issue, but his explanations have been difficult to translate into ideas about how the mind actually functions. Moreover, the information-processing approach can be extended to account for development in many other domains, including language acquisition, peer relationships, and even social and personality development. Not surprisingly, given their breadth of application, information-processing approaches are discussed further in a number of the chapters that follow.

Information-Processing Approaches and Themes in Development Because of the wide variety of information-processing models theorized to account for changes in development, we can draw only broad conclusions concerning their positions on the various themes in development.

- *Nature & nurture.* Information-processing models have said little about nature and nurture. Some basic capacities to perceive and process information are assumed at or before birth, and the system may be attuned to respond in certain ways, for example, to language and other kinds of information. The environment has an obvious impact on development because it provides input for processing by the mind. The implicit assumption in most models is that basic cognitive structures and processes interact with experience to produce changes in the system. Children, of course, react to the environment, but they also initiate and construct strategies and procedures that assist in processing information more effectively. From this perspective, children take an increasingly active role in controlling their own learning and development.
- *Sociocultural influence.* As in the case of learning theory, the sociocultural context of development often has been ignored by information-processing theorists. Perhaps this is because researchers have typically focused on identifying how the mind operates on specific problems rather than on how the mind is affected by the kinds of problems a culture presents to it. Nevertheless, this latter concern has become increasingly incorporated in more recent models of information processing.
- *Continuity/discontinuity.* In most information-processing models, cognitive development is theorized to undergo quantitative rather than qualitative changes. For example, children retain increasing numbers of items in both short-term and long-term memory, and interpret information and apply various strategies more efficiently and effectively with development. Similarly, the acquisition of new strategies for storing and retrieving information, new rules for problem solving, and new ways of thinking about and processing information is interpreted as shifts in ability that come about because of relatively small, continuous improvements in the capacity to process information.
- *Interaction among domains.* A notable limitation of many information-processing models is their failure to consider emotional, motivational, and other domains of behavior. How social factors, such as instructions, modeling, and the cultural context of learning, lead to developmental changes in processing information is also rarely spelled out (Klahr, 1989). However, as already noted, information-processing approaches are increasingly being extended to other domains of development, including language and social and personality development.
- *Risk/resilience.* Many information-processing theories pay little heed to the factors that might result in risks in development. However, their potential to explain such differences in terms of variations in rules, strategies, and other procedures for processing information is considerable.

Erikson's Psychosocial Approach

For the most part, the theoretical models we have examined so far have been concerned with learning and cognitive development. With *psychosocial* models, we shift to a substantially greater focus on emotions and personality. At one time, Freud's theory of personality was extremely influential in explaining emotional and personality development. However, Erik Erikson's theory gained far greater attention in subsequent years. Like Freud, Erikson theorized that personality development progresses through stages. During each stage, the child must resolve conflicts between needs or feelings and external obstacles that are unique to that particular time in the life span. The satisfactory resolution of these conflicts leads to a healthy personality and a productive lifestyle. But, in contrast to Freud, Erikson included several additional stages during adulthood, and he gave socialization and society far greater importance in his theory.

Psychosocial Theory In his classic work *Childhood and Society* (1950), Erikson outlined eight stages of development, as summarized in Table 1.2. During the first stage, Erikson theorized that *incorporation*, or taking in, is the primary mode for acting adaptively toward the world. In Erikson's view, this mode of activity extends beyond the mouth and includes other senses, such as looking and hearing, and motor systems, such as reaching and grasping, systems designed to expand the infant's resources for absorbing and responding to reality. Each subsequent stage identified another important mode for adapting to the environment.

Society, according to Erikson, plays a critical role in shaping and forming reality for the child. Communities create their own demands and set their own criteria for socializing the child. In one society, an infant may be permitted to breast-feed whenever hungry over a period of several years, whereas infants in another society may be nursed or bottle-fed on a rigid schedule and weaned within the first year of life. In another example, the timing and severity of toilet training, as well as the means by which caregivers initiate it, may differ vastly from one society to another. Cultures differ in the requirements imposed on the child, yet each child must adapt to his or her own culture's regulations. Thus, Erikson's

TABLE 1.2 Erikson's Stages of Psychosocial Development

Stage	Adaptive Mode	Significant Events and Outcomes
Basic Trust Versus Mistrust (birth to 1 year)	Incorporation — to take in (and give in return)	Babies must find consistency, predictability, and reliability in their caregivers' behaviors to gain a sense of trust and hope.
Autonomy Versus Shame and Doubt (1–3 years)	Control — to hold on and to let go	The child begins to explore and make choices in order to understand what is manageable and socially acceptable.
Initiative Versus Guilt (3–6 years)	Intrusion — to go after	The child begins to make plans, set goals, and persist in both physical and social exchanges to gain a sense of purpose and remain enthusiastic even in the face of inevitable frustration.
Industry Versus Inferiority (6 years to puberty)	Construction — to build things and relationships	The child acquires skills and performs "work" in the form of becoming educated and supporting the family in order to feel competent and attain a sense of achievement.
Identity Versus Identity Confusion (puberty to adulthood)	Integration — to be oneself (or not be oneself)	The adolescent attempts to discover his or her identity and place in society by trying out many roles in order to answer the question, "Who am I?"
Intimacy Versus Isolation (young adulthood)	Solidarity — to lose and find oneself in another	Having achieved a sense of identity, the young adult can now share himself or herself with another to avoid a sense of isolation, self-absorption, and the absence of love.
Generativity Versus Stagnation (middle adulthood)	Productivity — to make and to take care of	The adult produces things and ideas through work and creates and cares for the next generation to gain a sense of fulfillment and caring.
Integrity Versus Despair (old age)	Acceptance — to be (by having been) and to face not being	The older adult reviews and evaluates his or her life and accepts its worth, even if he or she has not reached all goals, to achieve a sense of wisdom.

Erik Homburger/Stock Montage

Erik Erikson outlined eight stages of personality development. His psychosocial theory emphasized that at each stage, individuals must successfully adapt to new forms of demands placed on them by society. He also stressed that cultures frequently differ in how they help individuals to negotiate these demands.

psychosocial theory of development highlights the child's composite need to initiate adaptive modes of functioning while meeting the variety of demands framed by the society in which he or she lives.

Erikson theorized that the individual confronts a specific crisis as society imposes new demands in each stage. The resolution of each crisis may or may not be successful, but triumphs at earlier stages lay the groundwork for the negotiation of later stages. Moreover, each society has evolved ways to help individuals meet their needs. Caregiving practices, educational programs, social organizations, occupational training, and moral and ethical instruction are examples of cultural systems established to foster healthy, productive psychosocial development.

A common theme underlying the various features of Erikson's theory is the search for **identity**, or the acceptance of both self and one's society. At each stage, this search is manifested in a specific way. The needs to develop a feeling of trust for a caregiver, acquire a sense of autonomy, initiate exchanges with the world, and learn and become competent in school and other settings are examples of how the infant and child discovers who and what she or he is and will become. During adolescence, the individual confronts the issue of identity directly. But the answer to "Who am I?" is elaborated and made clearer as the individual progresses through each psychosocial stage.

In summary, Erikson's views of personality development highlighted the practices society uses to encourage and promote healthy social and personality development. However, he painted development with a broad brush; consequently, his theory is frequently criticized for its vagueness. Still, just as Piaget identified meaningful issues in cognitive development, Erikson—regardless of the precision of his specific formulations—had a flair for targeting crucial issues in social and personality development. His work may well be seen as a forerunner to more contemporary theories with their emphasis on developmental systems and the notion that levels of influence, ranging from biological through cultural and historical, all must be considered for an adequate accounting of development.

Psychosocial Theory and Themes in Development Our discussion of Erikson's theory has already focused on a number of themes in development, but let's consider them once more.

- *Nature & nurture.* A biological contribution to behavior, extended from Freud's theory, is evident in Erikson's positions. Yet psychosocial theory must be considered interactionist, given the momentous role the presence and absence of appropriate socializing experiences play in resolving conflicts that arise at every stage. At the same time, in Erikson's theory, the emphasis on establishing an identity for self within society suggests an active role for the child in development.
- *Sociocultural influence.* The broader sociocultural context in which caregivers encourage children to master, explore, and engage in their physical and social environments, especially during the early years of life, plays a critical role in Erikson's theory of development. For Erikson, the sociocultural context is a key factor in understanding an individual's personality and social relationships.
- *Continuity/discontinuity.* Erikson identified eight stages in personality development over an individual's life span. The successful negotiation of earlier stages lays the groundwork for continued psychological growth. The individual unable to work through a crisis at one time, however, may still effectively resolve it at a later stage.
- *Interaction among domains.* Erikson links social, emotional, and cognitive development together in the individual's efforts to achieve identity. For example, a sense of trust emerges from taking in through the senses as well as the motor system; a sense of industry reflects intellectual competence as well as the ability to interact effectively with others; and discovering one's identity requires the integration of all of one's psychological skills and competencies.

psychosocial theory of development Erikson's theory that personality develops through eight stages of adaptive functioning to meet the demands framed by society.

identity In Eriksonian psychosocial theory, the acceptance of both self and society, a concept that must be achieved at every stage but is especially important during adolescence.

© Earl & Nazima Kowall/CORBIS

Systems approaches to development give recognition to the dramatic impact that broad sociocultural factors can have on children's lives. These children in Ethiopia attend an overcrowded school with few educational resources, a setting far different from classrooms in most Western countries. Schooling and work, family structure, economic resources, and many other social contexts vary tremendously for children living in different cultures. Researchers need to consider these types of broad factors affecting children's lives in order to fully understand development.

- *Risk/resilience.* The psychosocial stages are considered common to every individual in every culture. However, the success with which each stage is negotiated can vary dramatically from one individual to another and from one society to another. Although not specifically focused on risk factors in development, Erikson's theory offers many insights into how and why risks and resilience might come about.

Systems Approaches

Psychologists have long recognized that children live in vastly different circumstances and that these differences can have a dramatic influence on development. Some children grow up in households with a single parent, others with two parents, and still others with grandparents and perhaps aunts and uncles; children in foster care, on the other hand, may be shuffled frequently from one family to another. In addition, siblings within the same family may receive quite different experiences as a function of being the eldest or youngest, or of being singled out for certain kinds of treatment and expectations by family members. Number of siblings, economic resources, space and privacy, independence, and emotional atmosphere are among the vast assortment of factors that vary in the immediate surroundings of children.

Differences in the contexts of development extend far beyond a child's immediate family, however. Physical surroundings, access to schools, job opportunities, technological innovations, natural disasters, political ideologies, and war, as well as the cultural dictates of the community, influence the way children are reared. Some of these circumstances will be more supportive of development than others. Apart from the physical and sociocultural contexts in which each child lives is still another factor: the innate and species-specific predispositions, the biological context that equips the child to learn and develop.

Developmental theories usually focus on immediate experience, defined narrowly in terms of contemporary circumstances and recent events, and how it affects development. Yet culture, the historical legacy of earlier generations of a given social group, as well as the evolutionary pressures that have shaped humans to exist in their natural environment are also major factors affecting growth. Put another way, the transformation from infant to child to adult takes place within a complex, multidirectional system of influences (Gottlieb, Wahlsten, & Lickliter, 2006). **Systems views** are concerned with understanding this broad range of biological, physical, and sociocultural settings, and how they affect development.

systems views Theories of development that are concerned with the effects of a broad range of biological, physical, and sociocultural settings on the process of development.

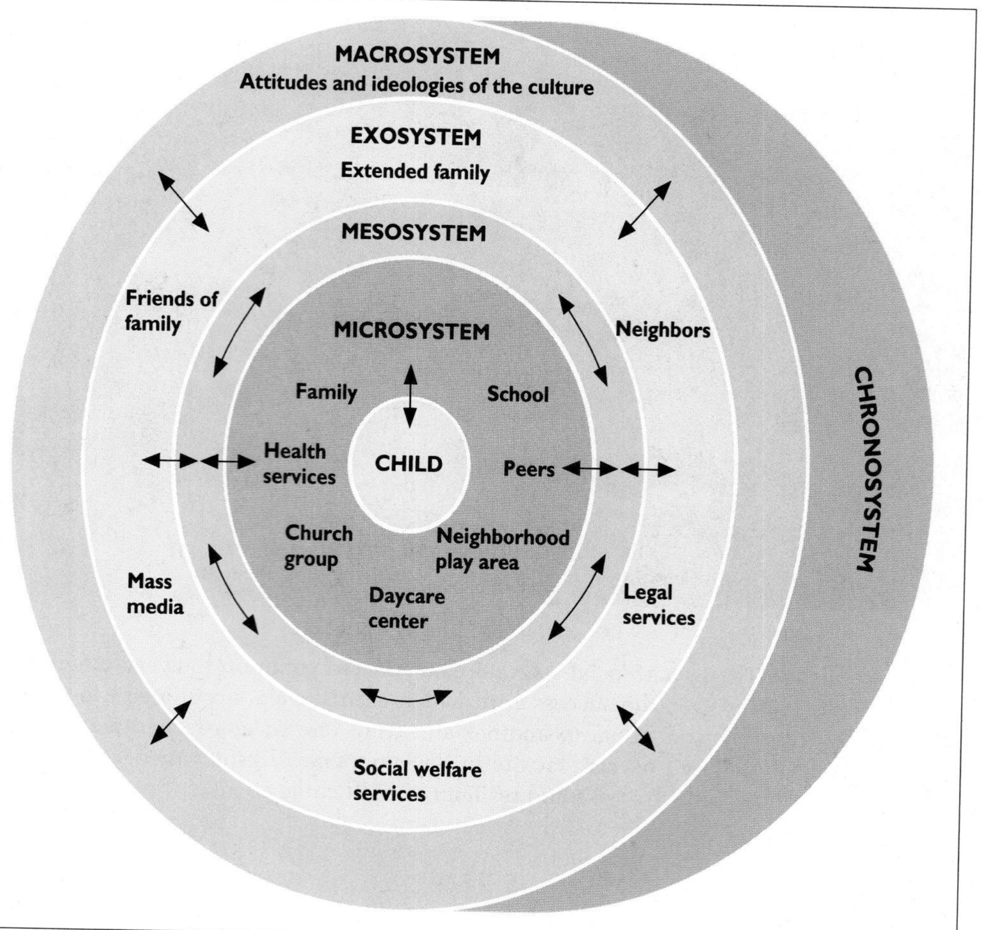

Figure 1.5
Bronfenbrenner's Bioecological Model
At the core of Bronfenbrenner's bioecological model is the child's biological and psychological makeup, based on individual genetic and developmental history. This makeup continues to be affected and modified by the child's immediate physical and social environment (microsystem), as well as interactions among the systems within this environment (mesosystem). Other broader social, political, and economic conditions (exosystem) influence the structure and availability of microsystems and the manner in which they affect the child. Social, political, and economic conditions are themselves influenced by the general beliefs and attitudes (macrosystem) shared by members of the society, and all of these systems are affected by changes that occur over time (chronosystem).
Source: From Garabino, J., Sociocultural risk: Dangers to competence. In C. Kopp and J. Krakow (Eds.), *Child Development in a Social Context.* Copyright © 1982. Used by permission of Addison-Wesley.

Ecological Systems Theory The most extensive description of the context in which development proceeds has been put forth in the **bioecological model** proposed by Urie Bronfenbrenner (1989; Bronfenbrenner & Morris, 2006). Ecological theories in general stress the need to understand development in terms of the everyday environment in which children are reared, a concern that is seldom the focus of many other theories. Commenting on the state of developmental psychology several decades ago, Bronfenbrenner claimed that "much of contemporary developmental psychology is the science of the strange behavior of children in strange situations with strange adults for the briefest possible periods of time" (Bronfenbrenner, 1977, p. 513). Development, Bronfenbrenner believes, must be studied not only in the laboratory but also in the homes, schools, neighborhoods, and communities in which it takes place.

One of Bronfenbrenner's major theoretical contributions has been his comprehensive portrait of the environment—the biological and ecological forces and systems that exist at several different but interrelated levels—and the bidirectional and reciprocal relationships that exist among them. These levels are shown in Figure 1.5. At the center is the child's biological and psychological makeup, including her cognitive capacities and socioemotional and motivational propensities (such as temperament and personality) for responding to and acting on the environment. Settings and associated proximal processes having the most immediate and direct impact on an individual's biological and psychological qualities make up the **microsystem**. These elements include the home and members of the household, social and educational circumstances (including classmates, teachers, and classroom resources), and neighborhoods (including physical layout, friends, and acquaintances).

bioecological model Bronfenbrenner's theory that development is influenced by experiences arising from broader biological, social, and cultural systems as well as a child's immediate surroundings.

microsystem In Bronfenbrenner's ecological systems theory, the immediate environment provided in such settings as the home, school, workplace, and neighborhood.

The **mesosystem** includes the many interrelationships among the various settings within the microsystem. For example, opportunities and expectations within the family, such as access to books and learning to read or an emphasis on acquiring basic academic and socialization skills, may critically influence the child's experiences and success in another microsystem, the school. As another example, a child of divorced parents living in separate neighborhoods may undergo frequent moves between the two homes. Such a living arrangement may have repercussions for the range and kinds of friendships the child can establish with peers.

Social, economic, political, religious, and other settings can affect development either directly or indirectly through their impact on those who care for the child. These wider contexts make up the **exosystem**. In many countries today, for example, the child seldom is part of either parent's work environment. Nevertheless, the parent who encounters a difficult problem at work may bring frustrations home and express them through impatient, even angry, exchanges with members of the family. Urban renewal planned at city hall may have dramatic consequences for children and their interactions with peers, hopefully for the better, but perhaps not always with that effect. Skirmishes between rival villages or countries may bring poverty if the family breadwinner is killed in fighting.

The broadest context is the **macrosystem**. The macrosystem includes the spiritual and religious values, legal and political practices, and ceremonies and customs shared by a cultural group. Cultural beliefs about child rearing, the role of schools and family in education, the importance of maintaining kinship affiliations, tolerance for different lifestyles, and the ethical and moral conventions of a society affect the child both directly (through the socialization practices of the caregivers) and indirectly (through the cultural norms and strictures defining acceptable and desirable behavior).

These four systems do not remain constant over time. Historical events like famines, wars, or other natural disasters can disrupt and devastate conventional microsystems, such as schools and neighborhoods, as well as the social, economic, political, and religious framework of a community provided by the exosystem. The arrival of a new family member, the separation of parents, the move to a new home, and the loss of a peer are examples of other changes a child may experience at different times. The **chronosystem** is Bronfenbrenner's (1995) term for this temporal dimension of influence. Change is always taking place, and these time-linked shifts and transitions may have greater or lesser impact depending on when they occur during the child's development. Thus temporal events, too, have far-reaching consequences for each individual's psychological development.

Vygotsky's Sociocultural Theory Bronfenbrenner's bioecological model highlights the many different contexts in which development proceeds. Lev Vygotsky's sociocultural theory blends these different levels into one overarching concept: culture. What is culture? It is, of course, the many facets of the environment that humans have created and continue to produce, including such physical artifacts as tools and furnishings. But, even more important, culture includes language and the practices, values, and beliefs accumulated and communicated from one generation to the next through that language system. Culture, in other words, is the human-generated, historical accumulation of one's surroundings, and it has an enormous influence on the way children are reared. Vygotsky's **sociocultural theory** emphasizes the unique collective wisdom compiled by a culture and transmitted to the child through ongoing, daily interactions with the more knowledgeable members of that society.

A central tenet of Vygotsky's sociocultural theory is that, as children become exposed to and participate in their community, they begin to internalize and adopt, often with the guidance of a skilled partner, such as a parent or teacher, the culturally based, more mature and effective methods of thinking about and solving problems (Wertsch, 1985; Wertsch & Tulviste, 1992). For example, in sitting down with and reading to the child, the caregiver demonstrates how important this activity is, so that eventually the child comes to value it

mesosystem In Bronfenbrenner's ecological systems theory, the environment provided by the interrelationships among the various settings of the microsystem.

exosystem In Bronfenbrenner's ecological systems theory, environmental settings that indirectly affect the child by influencing the various microsystems forming the child's immediate environment.

macrosystem In Bronfenbrenner's ecological systems theory, major historical events and the broad values, practices, and customs shared by a culture.

chronosystem In Bronfenbrenner's ecological systems theory, the constantly changing temporal component of the environment that can influence development.

sociocultural theory Vygotsky's developmental theory emphasizing the importance of cultural tools, symbols, and ways of thinking that the child acquires from more knowledgeable members of the community.

Lev Vygotsky's sociocultural theory emphasizes that the cultural experiences to which children are exposed become an indispensable part of their development. This woman, in teaching her child to weave, is transmitting important information to her offspring. By becoming aware of how communities convey knowledge to their younger members, we can begin to appreciate how culture influences attitudes, beliefs, and values, as well as skills that promote cognitive development.

Danita Delimont/Gallo Images/Getty Images

in her own behavior. Vygotsky believed that language is an especially important tool in this dialogue, because it, too, is internalized by the child to affect thinking and problem solving.

One quality that permeates both bioecological models and sociocultural views of development is the seamless alloy that embodies development as the child is affected by and, in turn, actively influences his or her surroundings (Sameroff, 2009). Development is dynamic, a never-ending *transaction* involving continuing, reciprocal exchanges: people and settings transform the child, who in turn affects the people and settings surrounding him, which further reshape the child in an endless progression.

Consider the baby born with low birth weight. Such an infant often displays a sharp, shrill cry and has difficulty nursing. Because of these factors and the baby's fragile appearance, a mother who might otherwise feel confident may become anxious and uncertain about her caregiving abilities. Her apprehensions may translate into inconsistent behaviors, to which the baby, in turn, responds with irregular patterns of feeding and sleeping. These difficulties further reduce the mother's confidence in her abilities and enjoyment of her baby, leading to fewer social interactions and less positive stimulation for the infant. As a consequence, achievements in other areas of development, such as language acquisition, may be delayed. But what factor, precisely, caused these delays? To answer this question, we might point to the child's low birth weight or the mother's avoidance of her infant as a proximal cause. However, these explanations fall far short of capturing the many complex elements that contributed to the mother's behaviors and the child's development.

The importance of these complex transactions becomes especially apparent when psychologists and others attempt to modify the course of development. The mother who has avoided her low-birth-weight infant because of a widening gulf of anxious reactions brought about by disappointments and unhappy exchanges will need to gain a greater understanding of the typical problems such babies face, receive support and reinforcement for her efforts to initiate confident caregiving skills, and acquire richer insights into how development is affected by experiences, only some of which she can control.

Dynamic Systems Theory It should be evident by now that systems theories champion the importance of many interacting events to account for development. **Dynamic systems theory** captures this idea and at the same time stresses the emergence over time of more advanced, complex behaviors from these many interactions (Lewis, 2000). Of particular interest in this theoretical orientation is the notion that development reflects the product of reorganizations that

dynamic systems theory Theoretical orientation that explains development as the emerging organization arising from the interaction of many different processes.

arise from the interactions of various levels of the system that could not be observed or expected from each component level by itself. One outcome of this reorganization is a stable, more adaptive way of responding (Thelen & Smith, 1994, 2006). When the right combinations of elements are present, then new, sometimes unexpected, capacities emerge.

One of the more important implications of dynamic systems theory is that development is not controlled or regulated by any one particular factor, for example, by the brain, the genes, child-rearing practices, or any other specific influence. Instead, these various components are parts of a cascading process that induces more organized and advanced behaviors or ways of thinking. Perhaps one of the best examples illustrating a dynamic systems view is learning to walk. As Thelen and Smith indicate, "Learning to walk is less a prescribed, logically inevitable process than a confluence of available states within particular contextual opportunities" (1994, p. 72). In more concrete terms, learning to walk results from a necessary combination of inherited human anatomical and neural systems, opportunities to exercise muscles, the desire to move around more effectively, the availability of acceptable surfaces and other supportive physical environments, and parenting that fosters exploration and sensorimotor development. Walking begins when the right blend of these comes together (see Figure 1.6). So, too, do new accomplishments in perception, language, cognition, and social behavior.

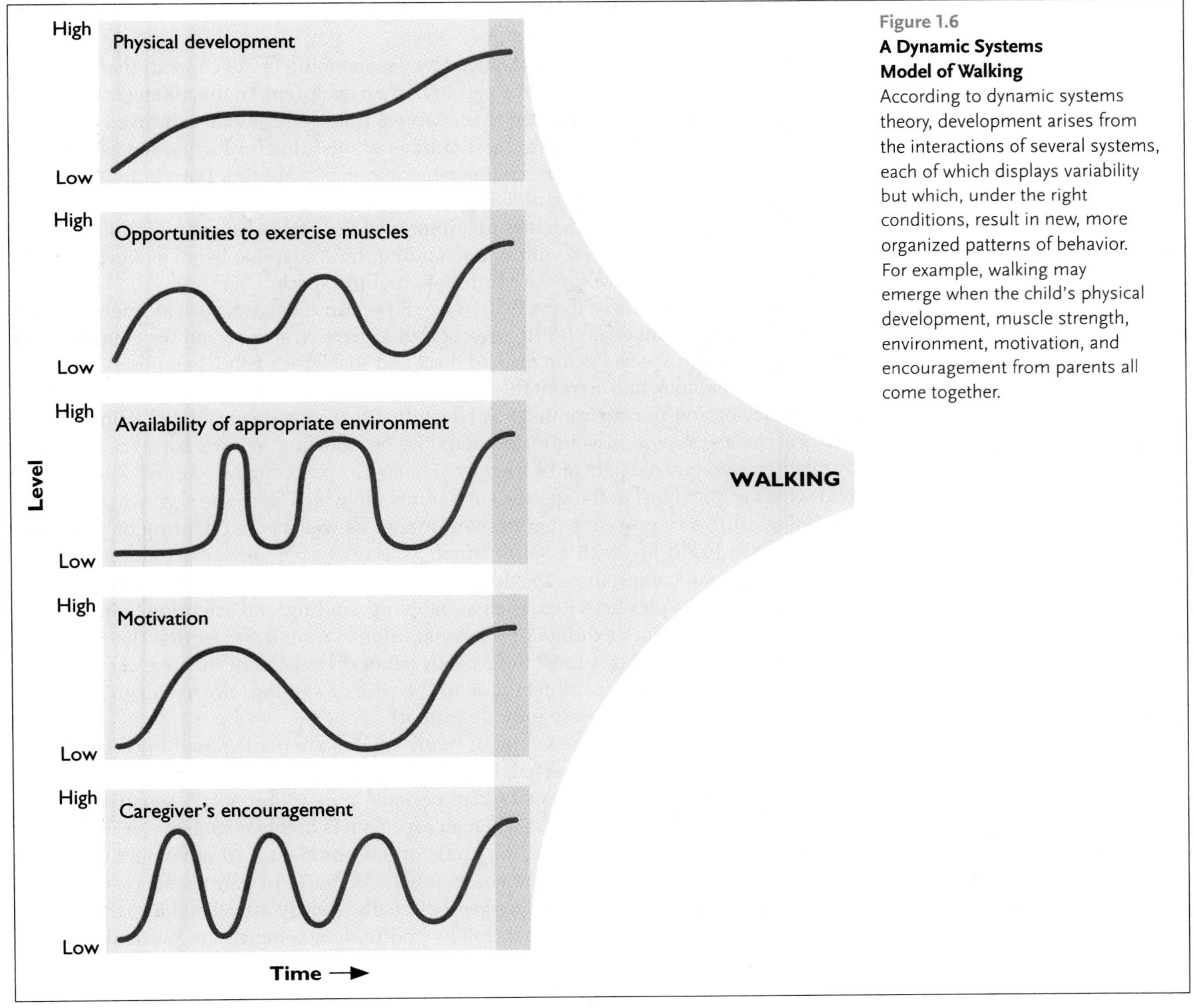

Figure 1.6
A Dynamic Systems Model of Walking
According to dynamic systems theory, development arises from the interactions of several systems, each of which displays variability but which, under the right conditions, result in new, more organized patterns of behavior. For example, walking may emerge when the child's physical development, muscle strength, environment, motivation, and encouragement from parents all come together.

Konrad Lorenz, an ethologist, is being followed by young geese who have imprinted to him. Imprinting in young animals typically occurs to other members of the same species who, under normal circumstances, are present shortly after hatching or the birth of an animal. One question posed by ethologists is whether human infants also show some form of imprinting.

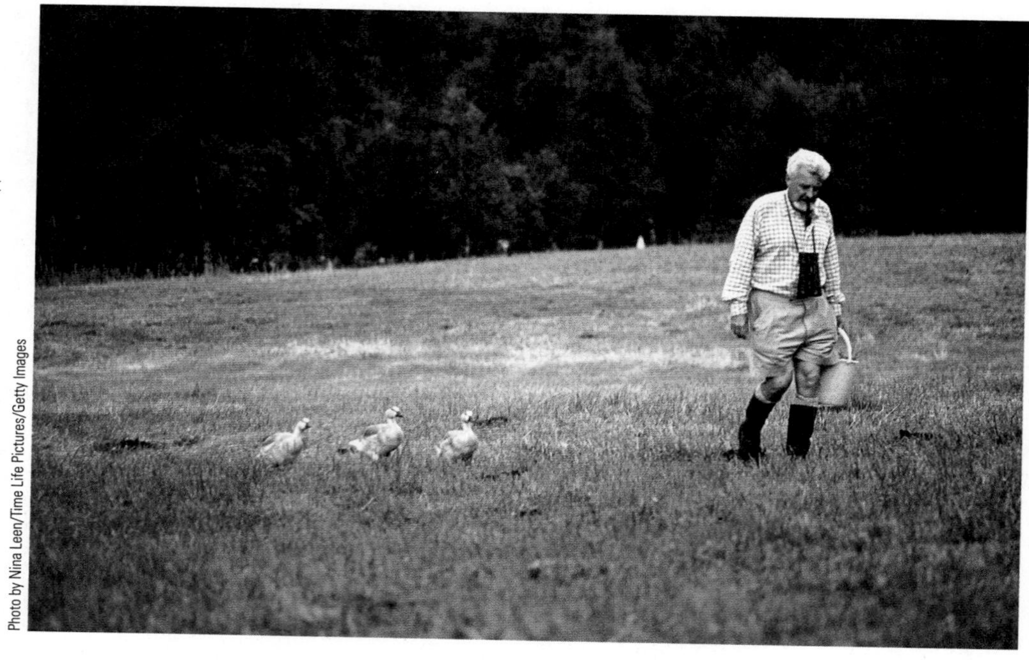

Photo by Nina Leen/Time Life Pictures/Getty Images

Ethological Theory Development is influenced by yet one more broad context: the biological history and constraints that have been a part of human evolution. In the nineteenth century, Darwin and other biologists concluded that adaptive traits—those that improved the likelihood of survival and thus ensured a greater number of offspring for further reproduction—were more likely to be found in succeeding generations of a species. Darwin hypothesized that, through *evolution*, the descent of living species from earlier species of animals, humans inherited biological traits and capacities that improved their rate of survival. **Ethology** is the discipline specifically concerned with understanding how adaptive behaviors evolved and what functions they still serve for the continuation of the species.

Ethological theory surfaced in the 1930s when European zoologists, such as Konrad Lorenz (1963/1966) and Niko Tinbergen (1951), investigated aggressive actions and the courtship and mating rituals of such species as the mallard duck and stickleback fish. Their observations led to explanations that took into account the *mutual* interchange between the inherited, biological bases of behavior and the environment in which that behavior was exhibited (Hinde, 1989). Ethological studies propose answers to questions like the following: Why do babies cry or smile? Why might the ten-year-old fight or be friendly? Ethologists point out the adaptive value of such activities for the individual in the specific environment in which he or she is growing up.

Ethological theory proposes that human infants, as well as the offspring of other species of animals, begin life with a set of innate, *species-specific* behaviors common to all members. In human babies, these include reflexes, such as sucking and grasping, and may also include more complex activities, such as babbling, smiling, and orienting to interesting sensory events—behaviors exhibited by normal infants around the world. These species-specific behaviors help infants meet their needs either directly, as in the case of sucking as a means of acquiring food, or indirectly, as in the case of smiling, a behavior that attracts caregivers and encourages them to provide support.

Besides innate behaviors, the young of many species are predisposed to certain kinds of learning that are not easily reversed, learning that may occur only during limited *sensitive* or *critical* periods in development. A **sensitive period** occurs when an organism is highly responsive or vulnerable to specific kinds of environmental stimulation. One of the best-known examples is found in various species of birds, including geese. Usually, shortly after hatching, the gosling begins to follow and prefers being near a particular object. Normally, that entity will be another goose, its mother. In displaying this tendency, the gosling not only learns about

ethology Theoretical orientation and discipline concerned with the evolutionary origins of behavior and its adaptive and survival value in animals, including humans.

sensitive period Brief period during which specific kinds of experiences have significant positive or negative consequences for development and behavior; also called *critical period.*

its species more generally but also increases the likelihood of being fed and protected. This form of learning that takes place during a brief interval early in life and is difficult to modify once established is known as **imprinting**.

Do other animals show imprinting? Mammals, such as horses and sheep, do. What about human infants? John Bowlby's (1969) theory of attachment suggests that they do, at least to some degree. Bowlby noted that the crying, babbling, and smiling behaviors of young infants signal needs and elicit supportive and protective responses from adults. These behaviors, along with following and talking in older infants, become organized and integrated with social and emotional reactions of caregivers to form the basis for attachment, a mutual system of physical, social, and emotional stimulation and support between caregiver and young. Many experts believe that the failure to form this strong emotional bond with a caregiver in infancy is linked to serious emotional and other problems that occur later in childhood, an issue that will be discussed more fully in Chapter 11 discussing emotions.

Systems Theories and Themes in Development Systems theories generally agree on many of the themes in development, and where differences exist, they are most often found in ethological theories.

- *Nature & nurture.* Systems theories differ widely in their emphasis on nature and nurture, but all recognize the importance of both to development. For ethologists, however, behaviors are closely linked to nature because they have helped, or continue to help, humans survive. Systems theories, even those having an ethological focus, tend to view the child as actively engaged with the environment. In calling for their caregivers, exploring and playing, and seeking out playmates, infants and children elicit reactions from the adults and peers around them. Both individuals and environments change in highly interdependent ways, and the relationship between the two is *bidirectional*, each influencing the other.
- *Sociocultural influence.* Perhaps more than any other theoretical orientation, systems theories are concerned with the ways broad sociocultural patterns affect development and how the larger social systems and settings in which children are reared affect their behavior and shape their minds.
- *Continuity/discontinuity.* Most systems theories place little emphasis on qualitative changes in development. Instead, such models describe the continuous ebb and flow of interactions that transpire throughout development to produce incremental change. One exception is dynamic systems theory where new, and possibly unexpected, capacities may emerge. Ethologists also often emphasize that particular periods in development are critical for establishing certain competencies. For example, infancy is considered a crucial time for forming emotional ties with caregivers.
- *Interaction among domains.* Not surprisingly, most systems theories are typically concerned with the entire fabric of human growth and claim substantial interactions among cognitive, linguistic, social, and other domains. Ethological theorists especially focus on the interrelationship between biological and other aspects of development.
- *Risk/resilience.* Aside from ethological theories, systems theories focus on the unique configuration of circumstances that foster motor, cognitive, linguistic, social, and personality development. Given the immense number of factors potentially affecting the child, individual differences are often an important aspect to be explained by such theories, including factors that promote risk and resilience. In their emphasis on the multiple layers of influences on child development and on the transactions that occur between child and caregiver, systems theories capture the complexities involved in any discussion of risk and resilience.

For Your Review and Reflection

- What is learning? What are some of its basic mechanisms? How do behavior analysis and social learning theory differ?
- What are the primary factors underlying change in Piaget's theory of cognitive development? How do schemes, assimilation, accommodation, and

imprinting Form of learning, difficult to reverse, during a sensitive period in development in which an organism tends to stay near a particular stimulus.

equilibration help to explain the increasingly adaptive and organized nature of cognition?

- What characteristics distinguish information-processing approaches from other theories of development?
- What is the focus of Erikson's theory of psychosocial development?
- What common assumptions underlie various systems approaches to development—for example, Bronfenbrenner's bioecological model, Vygotsky's sociocultural theory, dynamic systems theory, and ethological theory? How do they differ?
- How do these theoretical perspectives differ from one another? Which theoretical perspectives seem to capture best what you believe accounts for development? Why?
- Consider each of the five major themes in development introduced at the beginning of this chapter. Which of the major theoretical perspectives seem especially informative in considering each of these five themes?
- As a parent, which major theory do you think would be most useful to you? What if you are a teacher?

What Develops?

All theories of development, of course, are ultimately concerned with the simple question: What develops? As you have seen in this chapter, the answers differ. For learning theorists, what develops is a set of responses. For Piaget, it is a set of cognitive structures. For information-processing enthusiasts, it is mental structures, processes, and strategies for responding. For psychosocial theorists, it is identity and characteristics of personality. For most systems theorists, it is a pattern of mutually supportive individual and cultural relationships. For ethologists, it is adaptive behaviors.

Theories, by giving us models for observing and interpreting behavior, have had an enormous influence on the way we view children and their development. Why so many different theories? The reason is that each brings an important perspective to our understanding of development. Some remind us of the importance of emotions, others of cognitive structures. Some keep us honest about the role of our biological nature; others perform the same service for the culture in which we are born and reared. Various theories enrich and broaden our understanding of development. We will frequently draw on their contributions for interpreting the many behaviors of children. We hope that you will, too.

As we have introduced developmental theories, we have also discussed their positions on five major themes of development. Table 1.3 summarizes these positions for the major theories introduced in this chapter. As you read further, you may find yourself revising your own stand on the five themes.

what do you think? Should Child Rearing Be Regulated?

If and when the opportunity to become a parent arises, information you will have acquired from this book should be helpful, and you are very likely to supplement your knowledge by further educating yourself about child rearing. But what about many others who become parents? Every year many take on this responsibility, although some may not be very well prepared for it. Should *some* standard of competency be expected of every parent? For example, should prospective parents be asked to demonstrate knowledge of children and their development? Who would be responsible for implementing such an expectation? How would it be possible to ensure that parents become knowledgeable and effective in their rearing of children? Do we even have the necessary knowledge to encourage such a program? Would the use of financial incentives and disincentives (for example, tax deductions, access to services and programs, etc.) be an effective way to help promote such parenting knowledge? Or would some standard of parenting knowledge impinge on the rights and freedoms that every family could have in deciding what is best for their children?

TABLE 1.3 The Main Developmental Theories and Where They Stand on the Five Themes of Development

Theme	Learning Theory Approaches	Piaget's Theory	Information-Processing Approaches	Erikson's Psychosocial Theory	Systems Views
How do nature and nurture interact in development?	Emphasis on the role of the environment.	Emphasis on interaction of nature and nurture. Maturation sets limits on how rapidly development proceeds, but experience is necessary for the formation of cognitive structures.	Structures and processes presumably have an inherent emphasis, but experience is likely to be important for their operation.	Stress on an interactional position that recognizes societal demands as well as the child's biological makeup.	Major emphasis on the interaction of biological structures and environmental experiences.
How does the sociocultural context influence development?	Sociocultural factors determine which behaviors are reinforced, punished, or available from models, but the principles of learning are considered to be universal.	Cognitive structures underlying thought are universal.	Rules, strategies, and procedures acquired to perform tasks might differ from one culture to another, but these differences have received little attention.	Sociocultural context is a major component.	Culture is a critical determinant of behavior, although ethological principles are presumed to apply in all cultures.
Is development continuous or discontinuous?	Continuous. Development consists of the acquisition of a greater number of learned responses.	Discontinuous. Development proceeds in four qualitatively different stages.	Usually continuous. Development consists of the acquisition of more effective structures and processes for performing tasks.	Discontinuous. Development proceeds through eight stages.	Continuous. Development involves transactions between the child and the environment.
How do the various domains of development interact?	Universal learning processes work in many domains, but learning itself is highly situational.	Cognitive development has implications for social and moral development.	Usually concerned only with cognition, but have also been used to understand social and emotional relationship.	Failure to progress through stages may disrupt progress in many domains besides personality development.	Because of the strong interdependence between child and environment, all aspects of development are closely related.
What factors promote risk or resilience in development?	Risk and resilience can be understood in terms of reinforcements, punishments, and the types of models to which the child is exposed.	Does not place an emphasis on risk and resilience, but suggests that risks can occur if environmental experiences matching the child's biological readiness are not supplied.	Little explicit consideration of risk and resilience, although the potential is there.	Not specifically focused on risk and resilience, but failure to negotiate the stages can result in risk.	Focus on multiple factors that influence development as well as on role of child-caregiver transactions provides excellent starting point for examining risk and resilience.

chapter recap

Summary of Developmental Themes

Nature & Nurture

What roles do nature and nurture play in development?
This issue is concerned with how genetic and experiential variables interact to influence behavior. One implication of this interaction is that children play an active role in the process of development. Multiple levels of interaction between genes and experience are involved in determining developmental outcomes.

Sociocultural Influence

How does the sociocultural context influence development?
Children grow up in a social environment and cultural community that can have a tremendous impact on the behaviors that are displayed.

Continuity | Discontinuity

Is development continuous or discontinuous?
Changes in behavior may stem from quantitative, incremental developmental advances or qualitative reorganization. Children's behavior also may be influenced by multiple strategies or ways of responding.

Interaction Among Domains

How do the various domains of development interact?
Developmental scientists are concerned with the "whole" child; thus, they are interested in how skills and capacities acquired in some area affect other aspects of behavior.

Risk | Resilience

What factors promote risk or resilience in development?
Certain biological or environmental factors may be associated with a course of development that is less than optimal. Other factors may protect the child from the impact of these risks. Developmental scientists are interested in identifying the complexities of risk and resilience so that appropriate interventions can be designed.

Chapter Review

What Is Development?

Development refers to all of the physical and psychological changes that occur throughout a human's lifetime.

What are developmental psychology and developmental science?
Developmental psychology is the discipline concerned with the scientific study of changes in human behaviors and mental processes over a lifetime. *Developmental science* is now often the label given to this field of study because researchers from many different disciplines work together to consider biological, social, and other complex systems that affect human development.

What role do theories play in the scientific process?
Theories serve to organize information gathered by researchers, explain observations, and predict behaviors that should occur in future observations.

What role does developmental psychology play in the formation of social policy?
The information gathered in research should be helpful in suggesting specific actions for *social policy*, plans by government or private agencies to alleviate social problems.

Five Major Themes in Developmental Psychology

What roles do nature and nurture play in development?
Often described as the *nature-nurture debate,* this issue is concerned with how genetic and experiential variables interact to influence behavior. Research reveals that there are multiple levels of interaction involving the genes and experience.

How does the sociocultural context influence development?
Children grow up in a social environment and cultural community that can have a tremendous impact on the behaviors that are displayed.

Is development continuous or discontinuous?
Changes in behavior may stem from quantitative, incremental developmental advances or qualitative reorganization that is often described as a stage in development. However, at any one time in development behavior may be influenced by multiple strategies or ways of responding.

How do the various domains of development interact?
Developmental scientists are concerned with the "whole" child; thus, they are interested in how skills and capacities acquired in one area of development may affect other aspects of behavior.

What factors promote risk or resilience in development?
Individual differences exist in the development of behavior. Some children are able to cope with difficult biological or environmental conditions effectively; others seem less able to do so. In addition, some children are exposed to events that increase the risks associated with their development. Developmental scientists attempt to identify those factors that promote risk and those factors that promote resilience in children's abilities to respond effectively to the circumstances that influence their development.

The Study of the Child: Historical Perspectives

How have views of childhood changed from medieval and Renaissance times to today?
In medieval and premodern times, although recognized as vulnerable, children quickly became a part of adult society. By the seventeenth and eighteenth centuries, children were viewed as worthy of special attention in terms of parenting and education. By the beginning of the twentieth century, children became the objects of scientific study.

What were John Locke's and Jean Jacques Rousseau's views of childhood?
Philosophers, such as John Locke, emphasized *empiricism*, the view that experience shapes the development of the individual, whereas others, such as Jean Jacques Rousseau, wrote about the curious and active nature of the child.

How did Charles Darwin, Wilhelm Preyer, G. Stanley Hall, Alfred Binet, and James Mark Baldwin contribute to developmental psychology?
Baby biographers, such as Charles Darwin and Wilhelm Preyer, carried out the first systematic observations of individual children. G. Stanley Hall introduced the questionnaire method for studying

large groups of children. Alfred Binet initiated the movement to study *individual differences* in children's behavior and abilities. Theorist James Mark Baldwin viewed the child as a participant in his or her own cognitive and social development.

What was Sigmund Freud's psychosexual theory of development?
Freud emphasized the importance of early experience on development and posited a series of *psychosexual stages* that children must successfully negotiate in order to demonstrate normal personality development.

What emphases emerged in research on children during the first half of the twentieth century?
For much of the first half of the twentieth century, work was carried out on gathering descriptive information about children. Arnold Gesell and others focused on establishing norms of behavior. Limited research also began to be initiated to investigate the variables that might cause development.

Theories of Development

What is learning? What are some of its basic mechanisms? How do behaviorism and social learning theory differ in explaining what takes place during learning?
Learning is the permanent change in behavior that results from experience. *Behaviorism* relies on two basic forms of learning, classical and operant conditioning, to bring about behavioral change. *Social learning theory,* as outlined by Albert Bandura, adds *observational learning* as an important mechanism by which behavior is continuously modified and changed.

What are the primary factors underlying change in Piaget's theory of cognitive development? How do schemes, assimilation, accommodation, and equilibration help to explain the increasingly adaptive and organized nature of cognition?
Jean Piaget's *cognitive-developmental theory* highlights the child's construction of *schemes,* or patterns of acting on and thinking about the world. Through *assimilation* and *accommodation,* a child's schemes actively adapt to the demands of the environment by becoming more organized, conceptual, and logical. These regulatory processes of *adaptation* and *organization* result in *equilibration.* Cognitive development progresses through a series of qualitatively different stages according to Piaget's theory.

What characteristics distinguish information-processing approaches from other theories of development?
Information-processing models use the computer as a metaphor in accounting for cognitive development. Developmental differences in cognitive structures and processes, such as rules, strategies, and procedures, account for changes in attention, memory, thinking, and problem solving.

What is the focus of Erikson's theory of psychosocial development?
Erikson's *psychosocial theory of development* focuses on the sociocultural context in which behavioral needs are met. Personality development proceeds through a series of stages in which self and societal demands are resolved to construct one's *identity.* Individuals who successfully negotiate these demands become contributing members of society.

What common assumptions underlie various systems approaches to development—for example, Bronfenbrenner's bioecological model, Vygotsky's sociocultural theory, dynamic systems theory, and ethological theory? How do they differ?
Systems approaches view human development from a broad framework involving multiple, bidirectionally interacting levels of influence. Bronfenbrenner's *bioecological model* looks beyond the immediate experiences of family, peers, and friends, and considers the biological as well as the broader sociocultural contexts in which development proceeds. In particular, processes within the *microsystem, mesosystem, exosystem, macrosystem,* and *chronosystem* are considered. Vygotsky's *sociocultural theory* views culture as the historical legacy of a community and emphasizes the social interactions by which this heritage is transferred from others and adopted by the child to become part of his or her way of thinking. *Dynamic systems theory* proposes that new, complex, and sometimes qualitatively different behaviors arise from the interaction of events at many different levels in the system. *Ethology* pays special attention to the biological, evolutionary heritage each individual brings to the world as the basis for species-specific behaviors found to be adaptive in interacting with the environment. Ethologists emphasize that some experiences may be especially important during *sensitive periods* in development and further suggest that relative permanent influences on behavior may occur through the mechanism of *imprinting.*

Key Terms and Concepts

accommodation (p. 23)
adaptation (p. 23)
assimilation (p. 23)
behaviorism (p. 19)
bioecological model (p. 30)
chronosystem (p. 31)
cognitive-developmental theory (p. 22)
development (p. 4)
developmental psychology (p. 5)
developmental science (p. 5)
dynamic systems theory (p. 32)
empiricism (p. 13)
ethology (p. 34)
equilibration (p. 23)
exosystem (p. 31)
identity (p. 28)
imprinting (p. 35)
individual differences (p. 15)
information processing (p. 25)
learning (p. 18)
macrosystem (p. 31)
mesosystem (p. 31)
microsystem (p. 30)
nature-nurture debate (p. 7)
observational learning (p. 20)
organization (p. 23)
psychosocial theory of development (p. 28)
scheme (p. 23)
sensitive period (p. 34)
social learning theory (p. 20)
social policy (p. 6)
sociocultural theory (p. 31)
stage (p. 9)
systems views (p. 29)
theories (p. 5)

Media Resources

Access an integrated eBook and chapter-specific interactive learning tools, including flashcards, quizzes, videos, and more, in your Developmental Psychology CourseMate, accessed through CengageBrain.com.

© Rossario/Shutterstock.com

CHAPTER OUTLINE

[chapter 2]

Studying Child Development

To me, research is discovery: an odyssey of surprises, confirmations, and unexpected twists and turns that contribute to the excitement of a research career. . . . The excitement of a research career is that the story told by the data is always more interesting than the one you expect to confirm. In this sense, human behavior is far more interesting and provocative than even the most thoughtful theories allow, and this means that the scientist must be instructed by the lessons revealed by unexpected research findings—while maintaining humility about her or his capacity to predict the next turn in the road. (Thompson, 1996, p. 69) <<

These words, written by developmental researcher Ross Thompson, reveal the genuine enthusiasm of the scientist for the task of systematically observing and making sense of human behavior. Like investigators in many disciplines, developmental scientists are firmly committed to the idea that theories and hypotheses, such as those described in Chapter 1, "Themes and Theories," should be thoroughly and systematically tested using sound principles of science. Included in this approach is the reliance on *empirical data,* rather than personal opinions or popular beliefs, in order to draw conclusions. But, as Thompson suggests, researchers must be prepared to modify or even cast off theories if their observations suggest other truths. At first glance, this outcome may seem discouraging. But, as many researchers can attest, great rewards lie in the simple notion of discovering something new.

Part of the reason that researchers get drawn into the enterprise of developmental psychology is that they are captivated by and want to understand the fascinating, complex, and oftentimes surprising array of behaviors children display. Moreover, there is the sheer fun of being a "child watcher." As even the most casual of observers can confirm, children are simply delightful subjects of study. Research can also make a real difference in the lives of children. For example, newborn nurseries for premature infants now contain rocking chairs so that parents and nurses can rock and stimulate babies previously confined to incubators. Bilingual education programs capitalize on the ease with which young children master the complexities of language. Clinical interventions help shy children master the social skills that help them to establish positive peer relationships. The benefits of each of these approaches have been revealed through the systematic study of the child.

Collecting data about children, then, is an essential and rewarding aspect of developmental psychology as it allows us to draw scientific conclusions and, from those conclusions, derive further hypotheses about ways to understand and optimize child development. Thus, being well grounded in research techniques is important for students of the discipline. With this principle in mind, we devote this chapter to methodological issues in developmental psychology. We hope that, by alerting you to important issues in the research process, we will better equip you to think critically about the findings of the numerous studies you will encounter in subsequent chapters.

The scientific study of child development has resulted in changes in how children are treated in real-life settings. For example, because of research on the kinds of experiences that benefit premature infants, caregivers are now encouraged to touch and sensitively interact with their preterm babies.

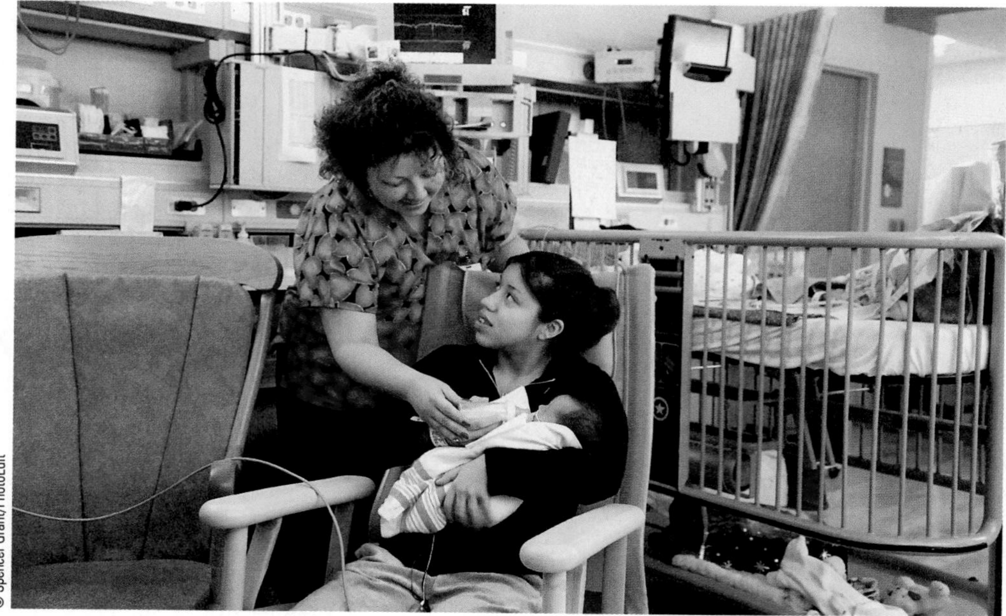

Research Methods in Developmental Psychology

Like their colleagues in all the sciences, researchers in child development seek to gather data that are objective, measurable, and capable of being replicated in controlled studies by other researchers. Their studies, in other words, are based on the **scientific method**. Frequently, they initiate research to evaluate the predictions of a specific theory (for instance, is cognitive development stagelike, as Piaget suggested?). The scientific method dictates that theories must be revised or elaborated as new observations confirm or refute them. The process of scientific fact-finding involves a constant cycle of theorizing, empirical testing of the resulting hypotheses, and revision (or even outright rejection) of theories as new data come in. Alternatively, investigators may formulate a research question to determine an application of theory to a real-world situation (for instance, can early intervention programs for preschoolers boost later school achievement?). Regardless of the motivation, the general principles of good science are as important to research in child development as they are to any other research arena. Although many of the methods child development researchers use are the very same techniques psychologists routinely employ in other specialized areas, some methodological approaches are particularly useful in studying changes in behavior or mental processes that occur over time.

Measuring Attributes and Behaviors

All researchers are interested in identifying relationships among **variables**, those factors in a given situation that have no fixed or constant value. In child development studies, the variables are individual attributes, experiences, or behaviors that differ from one time to the next or from one person to another. Ultimately, researchers are interested in determining the causal relationships among variables; that is, they wish to identify those variables directly responsible for the occurrence of other variables. Does watching television cause children to behave aggressively? Do withdrawn children have academic problems once they enroll in school? Does the way a parent interacts with a toddler raise or lower the child's later cognitive skills? In posing each of these questions, researchers are

scientific method Use of objective, measurable, and repeatable techniques to gather information.

variable Factor having no fixed or constant value in a given situation.

hypothesizing that some attribute or experience of the child is causally related to another attribute or behavior.

The first problem the researcher faces is that of **operationally defining**, or specifying in measurable terms, the variables under study. Take the case of aggression. This term can be defined as parental ratings of a child's physical hostility, the child's own reports of his or her level of violent behavior, or the number of hits and kicks recorded by an observer of the child's behavior. The key point is that variables must be defined in terms of precise measurement procedures that other researchers can use if they wish to repeat the study.

The measurement of variables must also be valid and reliable. **Validity** refers to how well an assessment procedure actually measures the variable under study. Parental reports of physical violence, for example, or even the child's own self-reports may not be the best indicators of aggression. Parents may not want a researcher to know about their child's misbehavior, or they may lack complete knowledge of how their child behaves outside the home. Children's own reports may not be very accurate because the children may wish to present themselves to adults in a certain way. If a trained observer records the number of hits or kicks the child displays during a school day, the resulting measurement of aggression is likely to be valid.

Reliability is the degree to which the same results will be obtained consistently if the measure is administered repeatedly or if several observers are viewing the same behavior episodes. In the first case, suppose a child takes an intelligence test one time and then two weeks later takes the test again. If the test has high *test-retest reliability*, she should obtain similar scores on the two testing occasions. In the second case, two or more observers viewing a child's behavior should agree about what they are seeing (for example, did the child smile in the presence of a stranger?); if they do agree, the measure has high *inter-rater reliability*. Both types of reliability are calculated mathematically and are usually reported by researchers in their published reports of experiments; both are very important factors in good scientific research. Measurements of behavior that fluctuate dramatically from one observation time to another or from one observer to another are virtually useless as data.

Methods of Collecting Data

What is the best way for researchers in developmental psychology to gather information about children? Should they simply watch children as they go about their routines in natural settings? Should children be brought into the researcher's laboratory to be observed? Should the researcher ask the child questions about the topic under study? Each approach offers advantages and disadvantages, and the choice of research tactic will often depend on the nature of the investigator's questions. If we are interested in exploring children's spontaneous tendencies to behave aggressively as they play (for instance, do boys play more aggressively than girls?), we will probably find a *naturalistic approach* most appropriate. If we want to see whether children's behavior is influenced by the presence of an aggressive model, we might use a *structured observation* to systematically expose some children to this manipulation in a laboratory setting. If we want to examine how children understand aggression, its antecedents, and its consequences, we might adopt another strategy, such as a *structured interview* or a *questionnaire*. Sometimes researchers combine two or more of these data collection methods within a study or series of studies.

Naturalistic Observation Researchers have no better way to see how children really behave than to observe them in natural settings: in their home, on the playground, at school, and in other places that are part of their everyday lives. After all, the ultimate goal of developmental science is to describe and explain changes in behavior that actually occur. **Naturalistic observations** do not involve the manipulation of variables; researchers simply observe and record behaviors of interest from the natural series of events that unfold in a real-world setting.

operational definition Specification of variables in terms of measurable properties.

validity Degree to which an assessment procedure actually measures the variable under consideration.

reliability Degree to which a measure will yield the same results if administered repeatedly.

naturalistic observation Study in which observations of naturally occurring behavior are made in real-life settings.

In naturalistic observations, researchers observe and record children's behaviors in real-life settings such as playgrounds, schools, or homes.

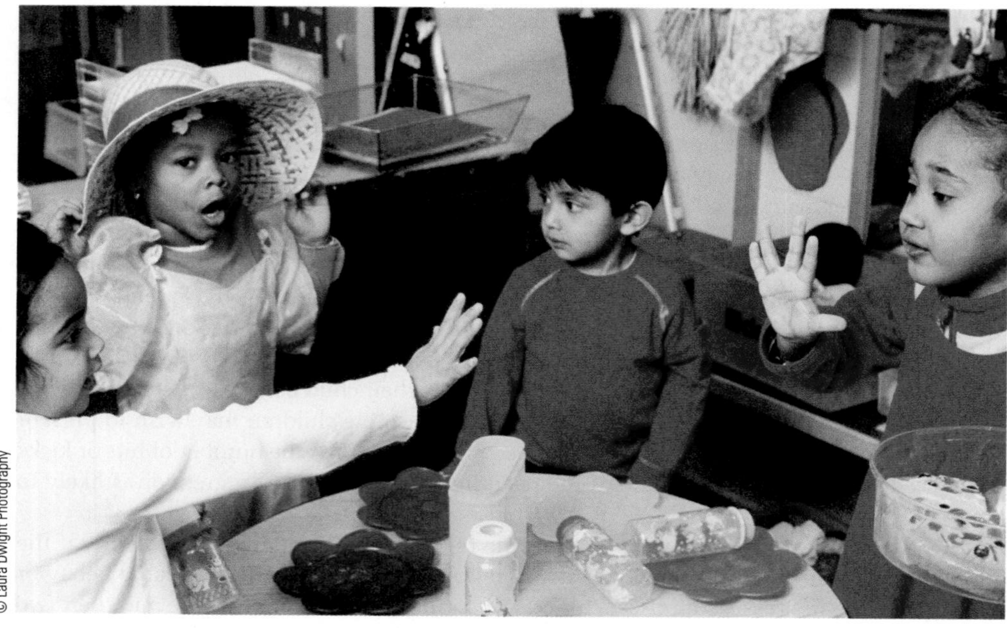

A study by Herbert Ginsburg and his colleagues (Ginsburg, Pappas, & Seo, 2001), for example, used naturalistic observations to assess the degree to which preschool-age children used mathematical concepts in their spontaneous free-play activities. The study was conducted in four childcare centers that enrolled children from different ethnic and social class backgrounds. Each of the eighty children in the study was videotaped for fifteen minutes during free-play time. Then, raters coded the videotapes for the presence of six types of mathematical activities: classification, dynamics (or transformation of objects), enumeration, magnitude comparison, spatial relations, and pattern and shape exploration. The results showed that children spent almost half of the observation period engaged in some form of mathematical activity. Furthermore, there were no gender or social class differences in the tendency to use mathematical concepts in free play.

Several methodological issues are especially relevant to naturalistic observations. First, as researchers code the stream of activities they observe, they need to use clear operational definitions of the behaviors of interest. Ginsburg and his colleagues did so by specifying the elements that constituted each particular form of mathematical activity. For example, enumeration was defined as counting, use of one-to-one correspondence, estimation of quantity, or any statement of number words. Second, researchers must be aware that children (and others) might react to the presence of an observer by behaving in atypical or "unnatural" ways. To reduce such **participant reactivity**, children in this study were acclimated to the video camera and cordless microphone they wore before the recordings began. Finally, to minimize the effects of **observer bias**, the possibility that the researcher would interpret ongoing events to be consistent with his or her prior hypotheses, pairs of independent observers coded thirty of the eighty children to ensure the reliability of the findings. Researchers usually require that at least one of the observers is unfamiliar with the purposes of the study.

An important advantage of naturalistic observations is that researchers can see the events and behaviors that precede the target behaviors they are recording; they can also note the consequences of those same target behaviors. In this way, they may be able to discern important relationships in sequences of events. Moreover, naturalistic observations give researchers powerful insights into which variables are important to study in the first place, insights they may not derive solely by observing children in the laboratory. For example, a laboratory study might not reveal the high level of unguided engagement preschoolers have with mathematical concepts. Often the trends or phenomena identified in such preliminary studies become the focus of more intensive, controlled laboratory experiments. Naturalistic observations also have the distinct advantage of examining

participant reactivity Tendency of individuals who know they are under observation to alter natural behavior.

observer bias Tendency of researchers to interpret ongoing events as being consistent with their research hypotheses.

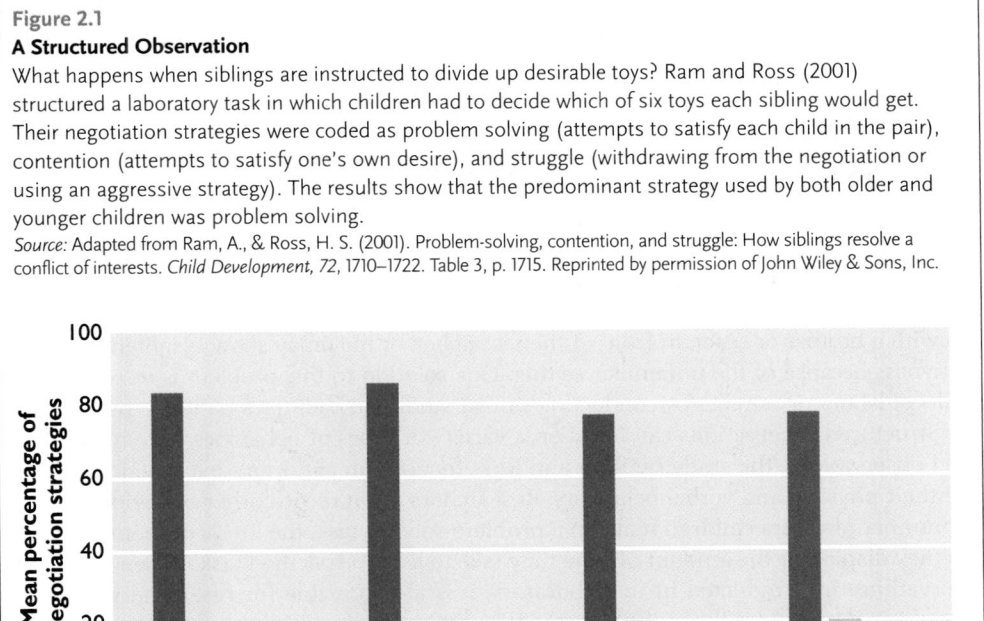

Figure 2.1
A Structured Observation
What happens when siblings are instructed to divide up desirable toys? Ram and Ross (2001) structured a laboratory task in which children had to decide which of six toys each sibling would get. Their negotiation strategies were coded as problem solving (attempts to satisfy each child in the pair), contention (attempts to satisfy one's own desire), and struggle (withdrawing from the negotiation or using an aggressive strategy). The results show that the predominant strategy used by both older and younger children was problem solving.
Source: Adapted from Ram, A., & Ross, H. S. (2001). Problem-solving, contention, and struggle: How siblings resolve a conflict of interests. *Child Development, 72*, 1710–1722. Table 3, p. 1715. Reprinted by permission of John Wiley & Sons, Inc.

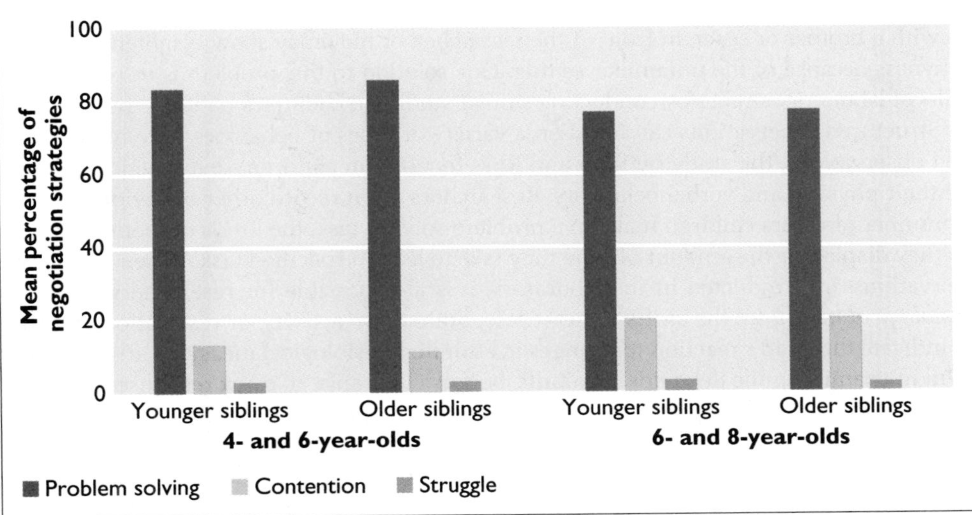

real-life behaviors as opposed to behaviors that may emerge only in response to some contrived laboratory manipulation.

Some cautions regarding this method are in order, however. A wide range of variables may influence the behaviors under observation, and it is not always possible to control them. Cause-and-effect relationships, therefore, cannot be deduced. Do preschoolers evidence mathematical thinking because they are in a "school" environment or because certain kinds of toys or materials are available to them? Or do none of these environmental circumstances matter? Answering questions like these requires the systematic manipulation of variables, a tactic that is part of other research approaches.

Structured Observation Researchers cannot always depend on a child to display behaviors of scientific interest to them during observation. Researchers who observe a child in the home, school, or other natural setting may simply not be present when vocalization, sharing, aggression, or other behaviors that they wish to study occur. Therefore, developmental scientists may choose to observe behaviors in a more structured setting, usually the laboratory, in which they devise situations to elicit behaviors of interest to them. **Structured observations** are the record of specific behaviors the child displays in a situation that the experimenter constructs. Structured observations, like naturalistic observations, are a way to collect data by looking at and recording the child's behaviors, but this form of looking takes place under highly controlled conditions.

A study of the ways in which siblings resolve potential conflicts illustrates how structured observations are typically conducted (Ram & Ross, 2001). Pairs of siblings ages four and six years and six and eight years, respectively, were brought to a laboratory. First, each child was escorted to a private room and asked to rate the quality of his or her relationship with the sibling. Each child was also asked to indicate how much he or she liked six toys that the siblings could later take home. Next, the siblings were reunited and instructed to divide up the toys between themselves. The researchers were interested in the types of negotiation strategies these children used. A portion of the results is shown in Figure 2.1. As the graph shows, the most

structured observation Study in which behaviors are recorded as they occur within a situation constructed by the experimenter, usually in the laboratory.

prevalent strategy was "problem solving," attempting to achieve a solution that satisfied both children. Least frequent was a class of behaviors the researchers called "struggle," the display of some form of overt conflict.

Although these researchers could have attempted to conduct their study of sibling interactions through naturalistic observations in the children's homes, they might have had to wait a long time for the targeted interactions to take place spontaneously. Furthermore, by conducting this study in a laboratory, the researchers were able to keep tight control over the instructions the children received and the specific toys they had to divide between themselves.

At the same time, structured observations may have limitations, especially if they are conducted in a laboratory setting. Children may not react in the same ways in the research room as they do in real life. They may be reticent to display negative behaviors, such as lack of cooperation with a brother or sister, in front of the researcher, or they may show heightened distress or shyness because of the unfamiliar setting. One solution to this problem is to confirm the results of laboratory studies by conducting similar studies in children's natural environments.

Structured observations can focus on a variety of types of behaviors. Like many structured observations, the study by Ram and Ross focused on children's overt actions, in this case their physical and verbal behaviors. Researchers often record other behaviors, such as the number of errors children make in a problem-solving task, the kinds of memory strategies they display, or the amount of time they take to learn a specified task. When structured observations are conducted in the laboratory, it is also possible for researchers to obtain *physiological measures*, the shifts in heart rate, brain wave activity, or respiration rate that can indicate the child's reaction to changes in stimuli. Physiological measures are especially useful in examining the behavior of infants, because the range of overt responses that very young children usually display is more limited than that of older children.

The Interview and the Questionnaire Sometimes the best way to glean information about what children know or how they behave is not simply to observe them but to ask them directly. Researchers have found that talking with children about their conceptions of friendship, gender roles, problem-solving skills—in fact, almost anything in the child's world—has yielded a wealth of material for analysis.

Many investigators use the technique of **structured interviews**, studies in which each participant is asked the same sequence of questions. For example, the goal of a study conducted by Mary Levitt and her colleagues (Levitt et al., 2005) was to explore the sources of social support for fourth- and sixth-grade children from different ethnic backgrounds. The researchers were also interested in the relationship of social support to psychological adjustment. A total of 691 African American, European American, and Hispanic American children were interviewed about the people most important in their lives; a second round of interviews was conducted two years later. Each child was questioned by an interviewer of the same cultural background as the child, to maximize the child's comfort with the session and the accuracy of his or her responses. Examples of the standard questions employed in this study include "Are there people who make you feel better when something bothers you or you are not sure about something?" and "Are there people who like to be with you and do fun things with you?" Using the same interview protocol allowed the researchers to make systematic comparisons among groups according to age, gender, and ethnicity. The results showed that, for all children, regardless of ethnic background, the family was an important source of social support. However, adjustment was best for children who had multiple sources of social support, either close family along with extended family or close family along with friends.

Another "asking" technique that researchers use with children is to obtain written or computer-recorded responses to a standard set of items in a **questionnaire**. Because questionnaires can be administered to large numbers of children at the same time, researchers can use this method to obtain a large set of data very quickly, especially if the questionnaire is administered online. Questionnaires can be scored quickly, particularly if the items ask participants to pick from a set of multiple-choice items or to rate items on a numerical scale. Children, however, may have difficulty understanding the items and may not be able to answer accurately without guidance from

structured interview Standardized set of questions administered orally to participants.

questionnaire Set of standardized questions administered to participants in written form.

© Corbis

Structured interviews provide a useful way to obtain information on what children know, how they feel, and how they interpret their world.

an adult. Under those conditions, oral interviews with individual children may provide more reliable and valid information about how children think and feel.

Researchers who use interviews and questionnaires to collect data from children must be careful, though. Sometimes young respondents, like their adult counterparts, will try to present themselves in the most favorable light or answer questions in the way they think the researcher expects them to. In the study of children's sources of social support, for example, participants may have said that they talked with their parents when they had problems because they knew this was the expected response. To prompt participants to answer as honestly as possible, researchers try not to react positively or negatively as the participant responds, and they also try to explain, before the start of the interview or questionnaire, the importance of answering truthfully.

The Meta-Analytic Study Sometimes researchers do not actually collect empirical data themselves but instead make a statistical analysis of a body of previously published research on a specific topic that allows them to draw some general conclusions. Instead of looking or asking, they "crunch" data; that is, they combine the results of numerous studies to assess whether the central variable common to all has an important effect. This technique, called **meta-analysis**, is particularly useful when the results of studies in the same area are inconsistent or conflict with one another.

A good example of meta-analysis is a recent study conducted by Janet Hyde and her colleagues to assess the existence of sex differences in children's mathematical skills (Hyde et al., 2008). A commonly held belief is that boys are better than girls at doing mathematics and that this ability is an inborn trait. This idea obviously has important educational implications for male and female students. But what do the data show? Hyde and her colleagues collected the results of mathematical achievement of all boys and girls in grades 2 through 11 in ten states. (This body of studies represented the participation of more than 7 million participants!) For each grade level, a statistical measure representing *effect size* was computed, a mathematical way of expressing the size of the difference in male and female scores. Hyde and her colleagues (2008) found that the average difference between males and females was exceedingly small, leading the researchers to conclude that sex differences in mathematical ability are not large enough to be of scientific significance. Conducting a meta-analysis requires the careful transcription of hundreds of statistical figures, a powerful computer, and a good deal of computational skill. Because the researcher taking this approach did not design the original studies, she or he cannot always be sure that the

meta-analysis Statistical examination of a body of research studies to assess the effect of the common central variable.

TABLE 2.1 Advantages and Disadvantages of Information-Gathering Approaches

Approach	Description	Advantages	Disadvantages
Naturalistic Observations	Observations of behaviors as they occur in children's real-life environments.	Can note antecedents and consequences of behaviors; see real-life behaviors.	Possibility of participant reactivity and observer bias; less control over variables; cause-and-effect relationships difficult to establish.
Structured Observations	Observations of behaviors in situations constructed by the experimenter.	More control over conditions that elicit behaviors.	Children may not react as they would in real life.
Interviews and Questionnaires	Asking children (or parents) about what they know or how they behave.	Quick way to assess children's knowledge or reports of their behaviors.	Children may not always respond truthfully or accurately.
Meta-analytic Studies	Statistical analysis of other researchers' findings to look for the size of a variable's effects.	Pools a large body of research findings to sort out conflicting findings; no participants are observed.	Requires careful mathematical computation; variables may not have been defined identically across all studies.

central variables have been defined in identical ways across studies. Moreover, studies that do not present their data in the form necessary for analysis may have to be eliminated from the pool; potentially valuable information may thus be lost. Despite these difficulties, the meta-analytic approach allows researchers to draw conclusions based on a large corpus of research, not just individual studies, and thereby to profit from an accumulated body of knowledge. Thus, this technique has become increasingly popular in developmental research.

From our discussion, it should be clear that there is no single right way to study children. Researchers must consider their overall goals and their available resources as they make decisions about how to construct a research study. Table 2.1 summarizes the advantages and disadvantages of the four general types of data collection just described.

Research Designs

Besides formulating their hypotheses, identifying the variables, and choosing a method of gathering information about children, investigators must select the research design they will use as part of their study. The *research design* is the overall conceptual approach that defines whether the variables will be manipulated, how many children will be studied, and the precise sequence of events as the study proceeds. Research designs may be fairly complex, and an investigator might choose more than one design for each part of a large study. Generally, however, researchers select from one of three study types: correlational designs, experimental designs, and case studies or single-case designs.

The Correlational Design Studies in which the researcher looks for systematic relationships among variables use the correlational design and are called **correlational studies**. Instead of manipulating the variables, in this design the investigator obtains measures of two or more characteristics of the participants and sees whether changes in one variable are accompanied by changes in the other. Some variables show a **positive correlation**; that is, as the values of one variable change, scores on the other variable change in the same direction. For example, if a positive correlation exists between children's television viewing and their aggression, as the number of hours of TV viewing increases, the number of aggressive acts committed increases as well. A **negative correlation** indicates that, as scores on one variable change, scores on the other variable change in the

correlational study Study that assesses whether changes in one variable are accompanied by systematic changes in another variable.

positive correlation Relationship in which changes in one variable are accompanied by systematic changes in another variable in the same direction.

negative correlation Relationship in which changes in one variable are accompanied by systematic changes in another variable in the opposite direction.

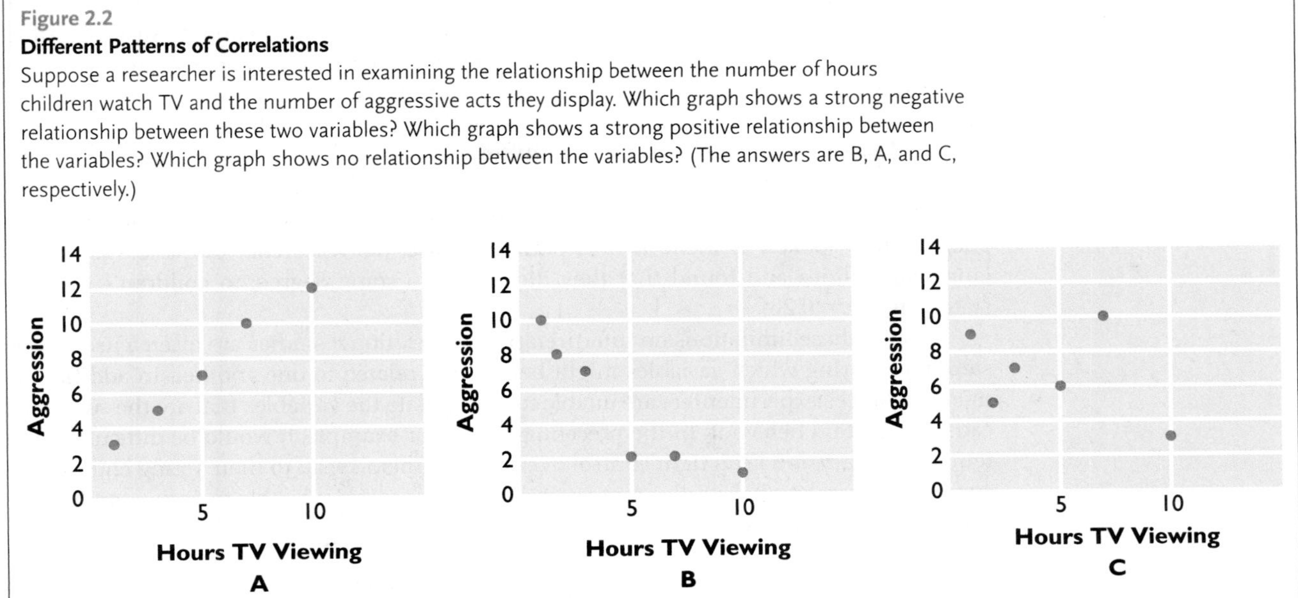

Figure 2.2
Different Patterns of Correlations
Suppose a researcher is interested in examining the relationship between the number of hours children watch TV and the number of aggressive acts they display. Which graph shows a strong negative relationship between these two variables? Which graph shows a strong positive relationship between the variables? Which graph shows no relationship between the variables? (The answers are B, A, and C, respectively.)

opposite direction. Thus, using our example, a negative relationship exists if aggression decreases as TV viewing increases.

The statistic used to describe the strength of a relationship between two variables is called the **correlation coefficient**, or *r*. Correlation coefficients may range from +1.00 (perfectly positively correlated) to –1.00 (perfectly negatively correlated). As the correlation coefficient approaches 0.00 (which signifies no relationship), the relationship between the two variables becomes weaker. A rule of thumb is that correlations of 0.70 or higher usually signify strong relationships, whereas those below 0.20 represent weak relationships. In most cases, values falling in between indicate a moderate relationship between two variables. Figure 2.2 offers the opportunity to examine some of these different patterns of outcomes.

We can use a portion of a study conducted by Qi Wang (2006b) to illustrate the key features of correlational research. A major objective of this study was to see if the way in which mothers talked with their toddlers about past shared events was related to the quality of children's memories for those events. The investigator found a statistically significant correlation of $r = 0.78$ between the number of elaborations provided by mothers ("Do you remember what we did at school yesterday?") and the number of shared memories reported by the children. Thus, the more prompts and discussion the mothers provided, the more children remembered. In contrast, children's ages correlated $r = 0.08$ with the number of shared memory reports, suggesting no relationship between those two variables. Children do not simply remember more about past events in their lives as they grow older; their autobiographical memories appear to be constructed in the context of conversations with their mothers.

A related technique, and one that has become very important to developmental researchers, is **regression analysis**. Here, researchers try to build on the information provided by correlations to make predictions about outcome variables. For example, in the study above, Wang found that the variables of child's background culture, gender, age, and language skills predicted 22 percent of the variability in children's memory reports. However, the single variable "maternal elaboration" boosted the predictive power in the study another 20 percent. Much of the effort in developmental science involves predicting eventual child outcomes from earlier events and experiences. Thus, regression analysis has become a powerful technique in the toolkit of developmental researchers.

correlation coefficient (*r*) Statistical measure, ranging from +1.00 to –1.00, that summarizes the strength and direction of the relationship between two variables; does not provide information about causation.

regression analysis A correlation-based statistical technique that allows researchers to make predictions about outcome variables based on one or more predictor variables.

Because researchers do not actively manipulate the variables in correlational (and regression) studies, they must be cautious about making statements about cause and effect when strong relationships are found. In the previous study, for example, do maternal verbalizations cause children to have richer memories? Or are children with good memories more interesting conversation partners, causing their mothers to discuss past events more frequently? Still another possibility is that some third factor (usually not measured by the researcher) influences both variables. Perhaps, for example, some children have excellent language skills, and that factor influences both their memory reports and the maternal language that is spoken to them. In this particular case, the researcher did assess children's language abilities and found that they did relate, to some degree, to children's memory statements ($r = 0.20$).

Despite these limitations on interpretation, correlational studies are often a useful first step in exploring which variables might be causally related to one another. In addition, in many instances experimenters are unable to manipulate the variables that are the suspected causes of certain behavior. In the preceding study, for example, it would be difficult to systematically vary and keep tight control over how mothers speak to their young children. In such cases, correlational studies represent the only approach available to understanding the influences on child development.

The Experimental Design The **experimental design** involves the manipulation of one or more **independent variables**—the variables that are manipulated or controlled by the investigator, often because they are the suspected cause of a behavior—to observe the effects on the **dependent variable**, the suspected outcome. One major goal of this type of study is to control for as many factors as possible that can influence the outcome, aside from the independent variables. To the extent that the researcher has been successful in doing so, the study is said to have strong **internal validity**. Experimental studies are frequently conducted in laboratory situations, in which it is possible to ensure that all participants are exposed to the same environmental conditions and the same task instructions. In addition, **random assignment** of participants to different treatment groups (in which one group is usually a *control group* that receives no treatment) helps to avoid any systematic variation aside from that precipitated by the independent variables. As a consequence, one distinct advantage of the experimental study design is that cause-and-effect relationships among variables can be identified.

To illustrate the experimental design, consider the following questions: Do adolescents engage in more risk-taking behaviors when they are with a group of peers than when they are alone? Moreover, in risk-taking situations, are adolescents more influenced by their peers than are older individuals? In one portion of a study reported by Margo Gardner and Laurence Steinberg (Gardner & Steinberg, 2005), adolescents (ages thirteen to sixteen), young adults (ages eighteen to twenty-two), and older adults (over age twenty-four) were asked to play a computer game of "Chicken." The game required participants to "drive" a car as close as possible to an abruptly appearing wall without crashing, with the appearance of the wall signaled by a yellow and then a red warning light (see Figure 2.3). Although points could be won by driving after the yellow light signal appeared, the risk of crashing into the wall was also greater. In this experiment, there were two independent variables—age of the participants and the test situation—whether the game was played alone or in the presence of two familiar peers. The dependent variable was the number of risk-taking behaviors displayed during the computer game. Risk taking was defined as the length of time participants moved the cars after the yellow warning light flashed on the screen. It also included the number of times a car was restarted and moved after the yellow light appeared.

On the surface, it may seem that the design of this study was relatively straightforward. However, individuals could vary their risk taking while playing "Chicken" for any number of reasons, such as the speed of car or the predictability of the warning signals and the appearance of the wall. Therefore, it

experimental design Research method in which one or more independent variables are manipulated to determine the effect on other, dependent variables.

independent variable Variable manipulated by the experimenter; the suspected cause.

dependent variable Behavior that is measured; suspected effect of an experimental manipulation.

internal validity The ability to draw cause-and-effect conclusions by controlling for extraneous variables in an experimental study.

random assignment Use of principles of chance to assign participants to treatment and control groups; avoids systematic bias.

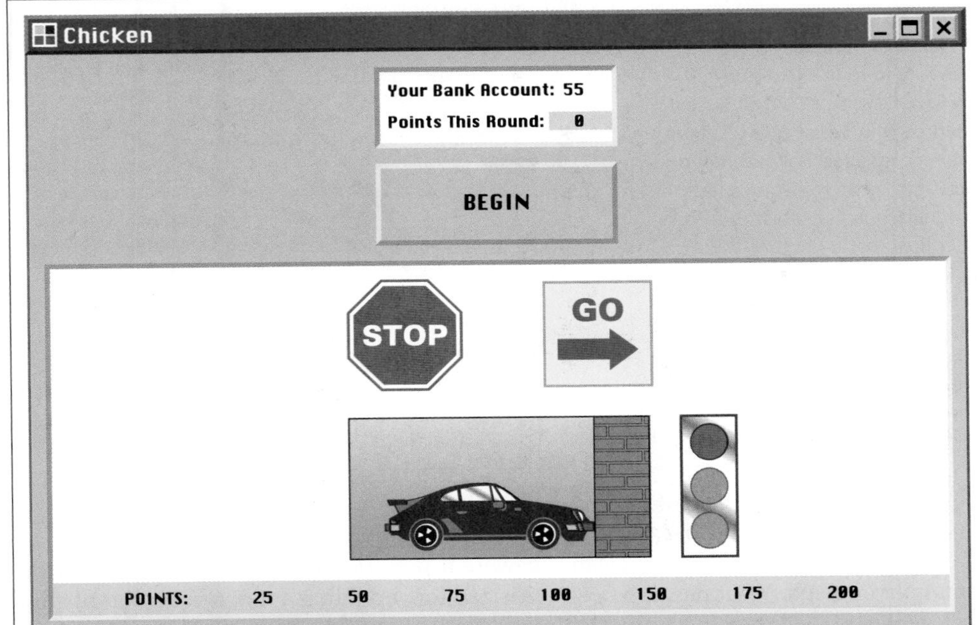

Figure 2.3
Assessing Adolescents' Risk Taking
To assess the influence of peers' presence on adolescents' risk-taking behaviors, Gardner and Steinberg (2005) asked participants to play a computer driving game. The goal of the game was to drive the car as close to a wall as possible without crashing, in order to obtain points. Yellow and red lights flashed on the screen before the wall appeared. Here, the car crashed because the driver kept the car moving when the red light appeared.
Source: Adapted from Gardner & Steinberg, 2005.

was important for the researchers to control for as many variables as possible, such that only the independent variable changed across conditions. Under such circumstances, the experimenter can be more confident that the independent variable is causing changes in the dependent variable. The experimenters took steps to address these issues. The speed of the car was kept constant across all experimental conditions, for example, and the warning signals and wall were presented at varied, predetermined times across the fifteen trials for each participant. The results of this experiment, shown in Figure 2.4, indicated that adolescents displayed significantly more risky behaviors when they were with their peers than when they were alone. In addition, the effect of the peer group on risky driving was much greater for the adolescents than for the other two age groups.

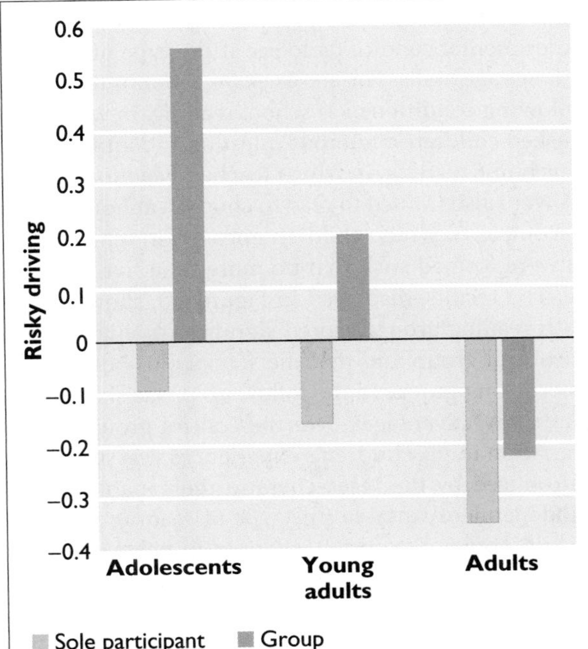

Figure 2.4
An Experimental Study
This graph shows the results of an experiment assessing adolescents', young adults', and adults' risk-taking behaviors in the computer driving game. The independent variables were the participants' age and the context of the game, playing alone or with two other peers present. The dependent variable was the amount of risk taking (a higher score represents greater risk taking). The results show that adolescents are more likely to take risks in the presence of peers than when they are alone and that the effect of peers is magnified for this age group compared with the others.
Source: Data from Gardner & Steinberg, 2005.

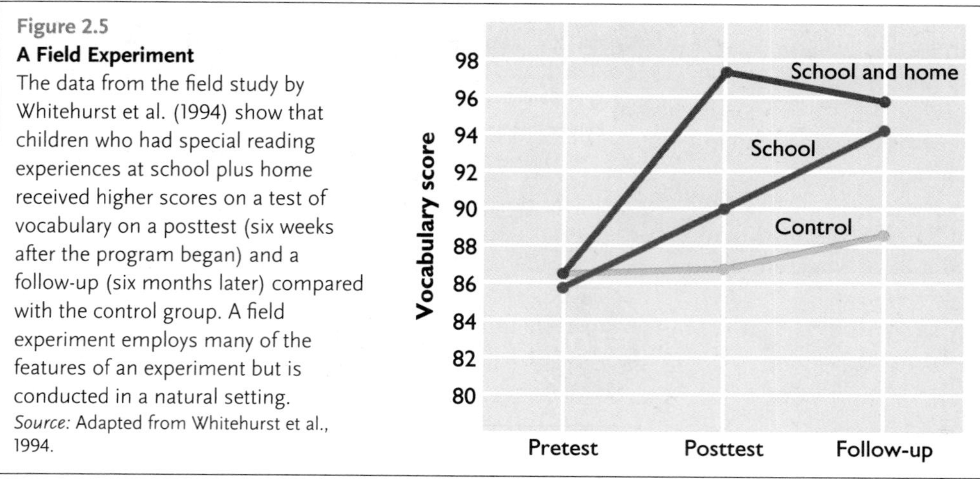

Figure 2.5
A Field Experiment
The data from the field study by Whitehurst et al. (1994) show that children who had special reading experiences at school plus home received higher scores on a test of vocabulary on a posttest (six weeks after the program began) and a follow-up (six months later) compared with the control group. A field experiment employs many of the features of an experiment but is conducted in a natural setting.
Source: Adapted from Whitehurst et al., 1994.

The experimental approach has been the traditional design choice for many developmental scientists because of the "clean" answers it provides about the causes of developmental phenomena. Yet it has also been criticized for providing a narrow portrait of child development. Development in the real world is likely to be caused by many variables; few changes are likely to be the result of a single or even a few independent variables. In that sense, experimental studies typically fail to capture the complexities of age-related changes. Moreover, we have already mentioned that children may not react normally when they are brought into the laboratory setting, where most experiments are conducted. Children may "clam up" because they are shy about being in unfamiliar surroundings with strangers and mechanical equipment. Or they may rush through the experimental task just to get it over with. Issues like these are concerned with **external validity**, our ability to generalize a study's findings across different situations and contexts, and even different groups of children.

In recognition of these problems, many researchers have tried to achieve a more homelike feeling in their laboratories, with comfortable couches, chairs, tables, and rugs instead of sterile, bare-walled rooms filled with equipment. Another tactic has been to conduct **field experiments**, in which the experimental manipulations are actually carried out in a natural setting, such as the child's home or school. In one such field experiment, Grover Whitehurst and his colleagues (Whitehurst et al., 1994) randomly assigned children attending preschool to one of three experimental conditions to see if the type of reading experiences they had influenced their language skills. For six weeks, a ten-minute period was allocated each day to one of the following conditions: (1) school reading, in which the teacher read a book and concurrently asked children numerous questions about the story and promoted discussion; (2) school plus home reading, in which teachers read to children in the same special manner, but parents were also trained to read to children at home using an active discussion approach; and (3) control, in which children engaged in ten minutes of teacher-supervised play. The groups were formed such that no more than five children participated in each at any single time. The results, displayed in Figure 2.5, showed that, at the end of six weeks, children in both reading groups scored significantly higher on a test of vocabulary compared with the control group and that the school-plus-home reading group scored higher than the school reading group. In the follow-up phase six months later, both reading groups continued to show advantages over the control group in language skills. Because the only known variation in the children's experiences was systematically introduced by the researchers in their manipulation of the independent variable (the type of reading group to which children were exposed), changes in behavior could be attributed to the type of reading program. In addition, the natural setting of this field experiment minimized the problems associated with bringing children into the artificial surroundings of a laboratory.

external validity The ability to generalize the findings of a study to other situations, contexts, or individuals.

field experiment Study in which the experimental manipulations are carried out in a natural setting.

In some instances, it is not possible for the researcher to randomly assign participants to treatment groups, because of logistical or ethical difficulties. In these cases, the researcher may take advantage of the natural separation of participants into different groups. **Quasi-experiments** are studies in which researchers investigate the effects of independent variables that they do not manipulate themselves but that occur as a result of children's natural experiences. Suppose a researcher wanted to investigate the effects of a longer school year on children's academic skills. One way to make sure that it is the length of the school year that influences performance, rather than the initial characteristics of the children, is to randomly assign children to two groups, one with a longer school year and one with a regular school year. That way, children with greater and lesser abilities, for example, would be equally likely to appear in both groups. However, it would be unethical, and also logistically very difficult, to assign children to different schools in this way. Julie Frazier and Frederick Morrison (1998) learned of one elementary school that was extending its school year from 180 to 210 days and took the opportunity to assess the impact on the achievement of kindergartners in mathematics, reading, general knowledge, and vocabulary. The researchers found that children with additional time in school during the year showed greater gains in achievement, especially in mathematics, compared with students who attended a school with a regular 180-day calendar.

The results of quasi-experimental designs must be interpreted with caution. The children who experienced an extended school year may have differed in systematic ways from children who had a regular academic year, ways that could have accounted for their better performance. For example, the former group may have had parents who were very concerned with academic achievement and spent more time teaching them at home. The investigators took great care to try to make the two groups equivalent at the outset of the study by matching them on intelligence test scores, medical history, parents' occupations, parents' expectations about school, and several other dimensions. Could other competing explanations for the outcomes be ruled out? Because the schools were in the same district, their curricula were equivalent. Most revealing, though, was the pattern of exactly at what time gains in achievement were made. Through the winter, when the two school programs still had an equivalent number of days, the students in both groups showed similar patterns of growth in achievement. However, it was during the summer, after the extended days occurred, that student achievement patterns diverged. Thus, researchers who conduct quasi-experimental studies must be very concerned with ruling out alternative explanations for their findings. Despite these methodological difficulties, quasi-experimental studies offer a way to address important questions about the complex influences on child development, questions that often have powerful real-world implications.

Case Studies and the Single-Case Design Some notable discoveries about developmental processes have come from the in-depth examination of a single child or just a few children. At times, psychologists make an intensive description of an individual child, much as the baby biographers did. Freud and Piaget both relied heavily on such **case studies** of individuals to formulate their broad theories of personality and cognitive development, respectively. Case studies can be particularly revealing when researchers discover a child with an unusual ability or disability, or an uncommon past history. The details of a child's background, cognitive skills, or behaviors can, in some cases, provide important insights about the process of development or even a critical test of a theory. For example, researchers (Fletcher-Flinn & Thompson, 2000) reported the case of a three-and-a-half-year-old child who was able to read at the level of an eight-and-a-half-year-old. Did this precocious reader focus on the sounds made by each letter in a word, a process that many reading specialists say is essential to skilled reading? Extensive tests and observations indicated that this child had little awareness of the correspondence between individual letters and their sounds, a finding that suggests that successful reading may not depend on phonics skills for all children. Although case studies can provide a rich picture of a given aspect of development, they must also be interpreted with caution. The observations reported in case studies can be subjective in nature and thus vulnerable to the phenomenon of observer bias that was discussed earlier in this chapter.

quasi-experiment Study in which researchers investigate the effects of independent variables that they do not manipulate themselves but that occur as a result of participants' natural experiences.

case study In-depth description of psychological characteristics and behaviors of an individual, often in the form of a narrative.

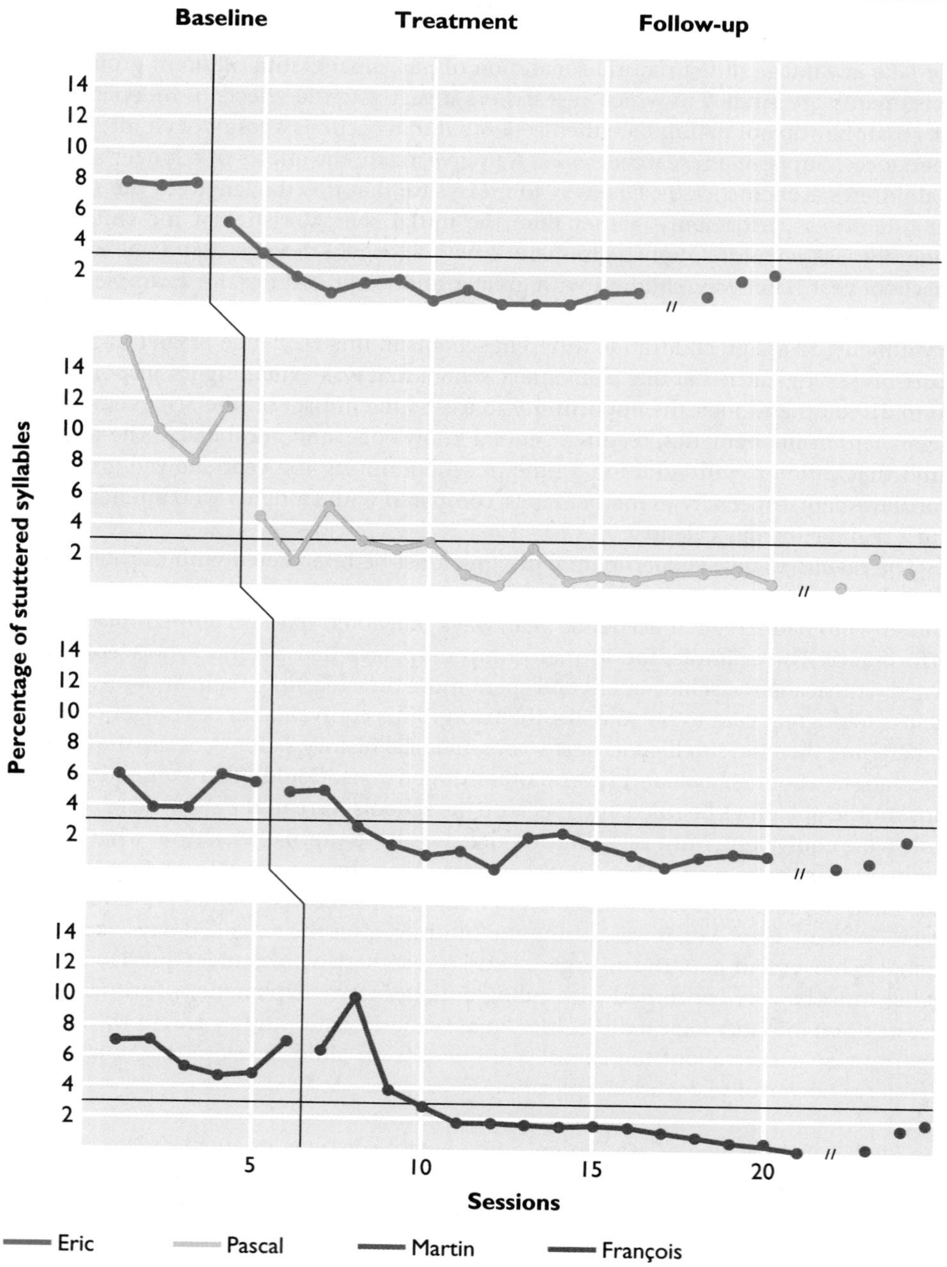

Figure 2.6
A Single-Case Design
In this example of a single-case design, four boys with stuttering problems were observed during a baseline period. Next, a program to treat their speech problems was begun. The graph shows that the percentage of stuttered syllables declined dramatically following the onset of treatment and remained low during the follow-up period. Because the four children showed similar patterns of behavior change, and because the behavior change was maintained long after the treatment ended, the researchers concluded that their treatment was effective.
Source: From Gagnon, M., & Ladouceur, R. (1992). Behavioral treatment of child stutterers: Replication and extension. *Behavior Therapy, 23*, pp. 113–129. Copyright © 1992 by the Association for Advancement of Behavior Therapy. Reprinted by permission of the publisher.

In other instances, researchers introduce experimental treatments to one or a few children and note any changes in their behavior over time. The emphasis is on the systematic collection of data, rather than on providing a detailed narrative, as is often done in case studies. Frequently the purpose of these **single-case designs** is to evaluate a clinical treatment for a problem behavior or an educational program designed to increase or decrease specific activities in the child.

Suppose we wish to evaluate the effectiveness of a treatment for stuttering in children. One team of researchers selected four boys, ages ten to eleven years, who had difficulty with stuttering (Gagnon & Ladouceur, 1992). Their first step was to record the percentage of stuttered syllables each boy spoke during the baseline period prior to the start of the treatment. Next, the treatment began. During two one-hour sessions per week, each boy received instruction on how to recognize stuttering and how to regulate breathing during stuttering. Special speaking exercises and parent information sessions were also introduced. Finally, the participants' speech was assessed

single-case design Study that follows only one or a few participants over a period of time, with an emphasis on systematic collection of data.

at one month and six months following the end of treatment. Figure 2.6 shows the decline in percentage of stuttered syllables among the children from baseline through follow-up periods. Was the treatment effective? The fact that all four participants showed similar declines in stuttering and that the stuttering remained low during follow-up several months later suggests that it was.

Single-case designs do not require large groups of children or the random assignment of participants to groups. Each participant essentially serves as his or her own control by experiencing all conditions in the experiment over a period of time. As with any study involving only one or a few individuals, however, researchers' ability to generalize to a larger group of children may be limited. Perhaps the child or children they selected for the study were particularly responsive to the treatment, a treatment that might not work as well for other children. In addition, the researcher must be aware of any other circumstances concurrent with the treatment that may have actually produced the behavior changes. For example, did the children in the stuttering study mature neurologically, and did that maturation cause the reduction in speech problems? The fact that the treatment started at different times for each of the four children and was immediately followed by a decrease in stuttering suggests that the treatment and not some other factor caused the changes.

Table 2.2 presents an overview of the strengths and weaknesses of case studies and single-case designs, as well as other research designs that we have examined briefly here.

For Your Review and Reflection

- What issues must researchers pay attention to when they measure attributes and behaviors?
- What four information-gathering techniques do developmental researchers generally have available to them? What are the advantages and disadvantages of each technique?
- What are the different research designs that researchers might employ to study child development? What are the strengths and weaknesses of each design?
- Suppose you wanted to study the relationship between parental discipline techniques and children's compliance with their parents' requests. Which information-gathering technique would you use? Why? Which research design would you use? Why?

TABLE 2.2 Strengths and Weaknesses of Research Designs

Design	Description	Strengths	Weaknesses
Correlational Design	Researcher sees if changes in one variable are accompanied by systematic changes in another variable.	Useful when conditions do not permit the manipulation of variables.	Cannot determine cause-and-effect relationships.
Experimental Design	Researcher manipulates one or more independent variables to observe the effects on the dependent variable(s).	Can isolate cause-and-effect relationships.	May not yield information about real-life behaviors.
Field Experiment	Experiment conducted in real-life, naturalistic settings.	Can isolate cause-and-effect relationships; behaviors are observed in natural settings.	Less control over treatment conditions.
Quasi-experiment	Assignment of participants to groups is determined by their natural experiences.	Takes advantage of natural separation of children into groups.	Factors other than independent variables may be causing results.
Case Study/ Single-Case Design	In-depth observation of one or a few children over a period of time.	Does not require large pool of participants.	Can be vulnerable to observer bias; ability to generalize to the larger population may be limited.

Special Issues in Developmental Research

Because of the nature of the questions that developmental researchers ask, certain research strategies take on special significance. How does some aspect of development change with age? How do individual children display transitions in how they think or behave? How do nature and nurture interact to result in a specific developmental outcome? To answer questions like these, researchers turn to an array of strategies that are especially useful when questions about child development are involved.

Strategies for Assessing Developmental Change

The developmental researcher faces a problem unique to this field: how to record the changes in behavior that occur over time. For the most part, the investigator has two choices: to observe individual children repeatedly over time or to select children of different ages to participate in one study at a given time. Each approach has its strengths and limitations, and each has contributed substantially to our understanding of child development.

The Longitudinal Study **Longitudinal studies** assess the same sample of participants repeatedly at various points in time, usually over a span of years. This approach has the longest historical tradition in developmental psychology. The early baby biographies were in essence longitudinal observations, and several major longitudinal projects that were initiated in the early 1900s continued for decades. One of the most famous is Lewis Terman's study of intellectually gifted children, begun in 1921 (Terman, 1925; Terman & Oden, 1959).

Terman identified 952 children aged two to fourteen years who had scored 140 or above on a standardized test of intelligence. He was interested in answering several questions about these exceptionally bright children. Would they become extraordinarily successful later in life? Did they possess any specific cluster of common personality traits? Did they adapt well socially? The sample was followed until most participants reached sixty years of age, and a wealth of information was collected over this long span of time. One finding was that many individuals in this sample had highly successful careers in science, academics, business, and other professions. In addition, contrary to many popular stereotypes, high intelligence was associated with greater physical and mental health and adaptive social functioning later in life.

Longitudinal research is costly and requires a substantial research effort. Participants followed over a period of years often move or become unavailable for other reasons; just keeping track of them requires constant and careful recordkeeping. In addition, one might raise questions about the characteristics of the people who remain in the study: perhaps they are less mobile, or perhaps those who agree to participate in a thirty-year study have unique qualities that can affect the interpretation of the project's results (for instance, they may be less energetic or be more curious about themselves and more introspective). Another difficulty lies in the fact that participants who are tested repeatedly often get better at the tests, not because of any changes in their abilities, but because the tests become more familiar over time. Participants who take a test of spatial skill again and again may improve due to practice with the test and not as a result of any developmental change in their abilities. If the researcher attempts to avert this outcome by designing a different version of the same test, the problem then becomes whether the two tests are similar enough!

One of the biggest methodological drawbacks of longitudinal research is the possibility of an **age-history confound.** Suppose a researcher began a twenty-year longitudinal study in 1970 and found that individuals' gender-role

longitudinal study Research in which the same participants are repeatedly tested over a period of time, usually years.

age-history confound In longitudinal studies, the co-occurrence of historical factors with changes in age; affects the ability to interpret results.

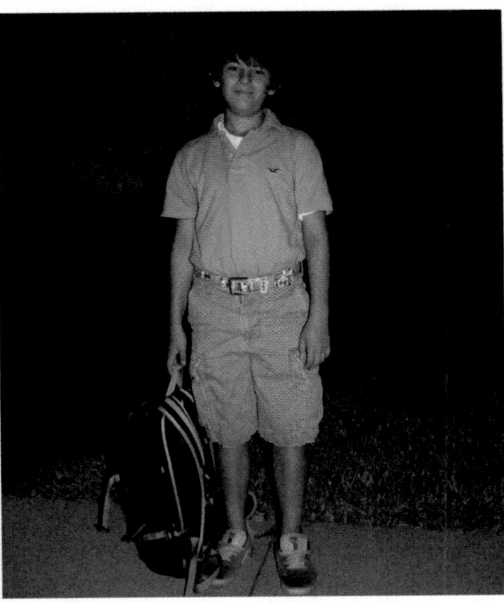

Amy Dunleavy

Longitudinal studies assess the same individuals over a span of years, sometimes ranging from infancy through adolescence. This strategy for assessing developmental change allows researchers to identify the stability of many human characteristics.

beliefs became less stereotyped as the years progressed; that is, participants were less likely to believe that females are dependent, passive, and emotional, and that males are independent, aggressive, and logical. Are these shifts in attitude associated with development? Or did some historical factor, such as the women's movement, bring about the changes in beliefs? Because participants age as cultural and historical events occur, it is often difficult to decide which factor has affected the results of a longitudinal study. Moreover, consider a twenty-year longitudinal study begun in the 1940s versus a similar study begun in the 1990s. Many of the factors that are likely to influence children's development today—television, daycare, and computers, to name a few—probably would not have been included in studies begun five decades ago.

Despite all these difficulties, the longitudinal approach has distinct advantages that no other research tactic offers; in fact, certain research questions in child development can *only* be answered longitudinally. If a researcher is interested in identifying the *stability* of human characteristics—that is, how likely it is that early attributes will be maintained later in development—the longitudinal approach is the method of choice. Only by observing the same person over time can we answer such questions as "Do passive infants become shy adults?" or "Do early experiences with peers affect the child's ability to form friendships in adolescence?" For researchers interested in understanding the process of development and the factors that precede and follow specific developmental phenomena, particularly with respect to individual differences, the longitudinal strategy remains a powerful one.

The Cross-Sectional Study Possibly the most widely used strategy for studying developmental differences is the **cross-sectional study**, in which children of varying ages are examined at the same point in time. Cross-sectional studies take less time to complete and are usually more economical than longitudinal studies.

A good example of cross-sectional research is a recent investigation of young children's understanding of whether a series of pictures portrayed real or imaginary events (Carrick & Quas, 2006). Do children understand that some events are a matter of fantasy (ducks arguing) and some are real (children arguing)? Furthermore, does the depiction of an emotion in the picture make a difference in this understanding? The responses of three-, four-, and five-year-olds to pictures that portrayed fantasy events are shown in Figure 2.7. What does the graph reveal about age differences in responding?

cross-sectional study Study in which individuals of different ages are examined at the same point in time.

Figure 2.7

A Cross-Sectional Study

In this example of a cross-sectional study, children of different ages were asked, "Can this happen in real life?" as they viewed pictures that portrayed real or fantasy events. This graph shows children's responses to fantasy events, which varied in the kinds of emotions portrayed in the pictures. Note that a higher score indicates a greater tendency to answer "No" to the experimenters' question. What developmental trends are apparent to you in this graph? Cross-sectional studies allow researchers to examine age differences in performance quickly and efficiently.

Source: Adapted from Carrick & Quas, 2006.

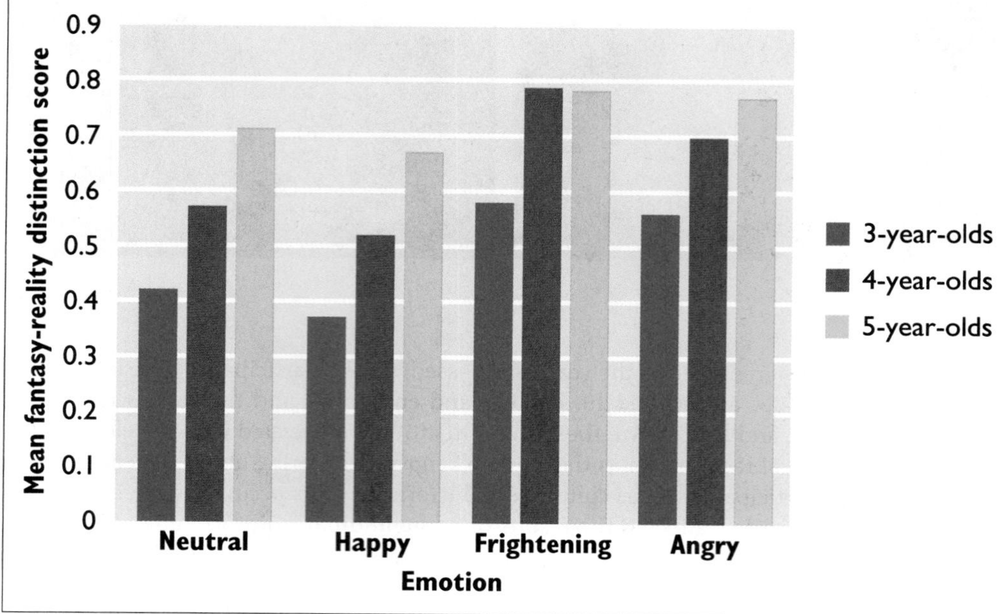

The cross-sectional approach allowed the researchers to make a rapid assessment of the children's performance without waiting for them to grow several years older. They were, however, unable to draw conclusions about individual children and about how characteristics observable at one age might be related to characteristics at another age. Would the children who were most likely to make incorrect responses at age three also be the ones who were incorrect at age five? In other words, are there some young children who cling to fantasy beliefs for long periods of time? The cross-sectional approach does not provide answers to these kinds of questions. Most cross-sectional studies involve pooling the scores of individual participants such that the average performance of an entire group of children of a specified age is reported; the average scores of two or more groups of children are then compared. The result is that information about individuals is not the focus of data analysis in this type of study.

Another difficulty with cross-sectional designs is that cohort effects may interfere with our ability to draw clear conclusions. **Cohort effects** are all the characteristics shared by children growing up in a specific social and historical context. For example, many of today's five-year-olds have had extensive peer experience through their enrollment in childcare and other preschool programs, whereas many eighteen-year-olds may not have. A researcher comparing the two groups might mistakenly conclude that younger children are more sociable than older children, but the differential exposure to agemates early in life—that is, the cohort effect—may be responsible for the findings, rather than changes in sociability with age. Cross-sectional studies are a quick means of providing descriptions of age changes in all sorts of behaviors. Where they sometimes fall short is in helping us to understand the processes underlying those age-related changes.

cohort effect All the characteristics shared by individuals growing up in a specific social and historical context.

The Sequential Study One way to combine the advantages of both longitudinal and cross-sectional approaches is the

Figure 2.8
A Sequential Study
Age differences in behavior patterns over time can be assessed with sequential studies. In a study of children's self-concepts from elementary school through high school, Cole and his colleagues (Cole et al., 2001) assessed two groups of children over a period of six years. The first was a group of third-graders. The data in the graph show changes in their academic self-concept from third through eighth grade (based on a test with the scale shown on the left y-axis). The second group was in the sixth grade at the start of the study. The data in the graph show changes in their self-concepts from sixth through eleventh grade (based on a test for older children with the scale shown on the right y-axis). Thus, information about a nine-year age span was obtained in six years. The dotted lines in this graph indicate places where the slope of the function changes, and also correspond to shifts in school settings from elementary to middle to secondary school. What do these data reveal about changes in academic self-concept over time?
Source: From Cole, D. A., Maxwell, S. E., Martin, J. M., Peeke, L. G., Seroczynski, A. D., Tram, J. M., Hoffman, K. B., Ruiz, M. D., Jacquez, F., & Maschman, T. (2001). The development of multiple domains of child and adolescent self concept: A cohort sequential longitudinal design. *Child Development*, 72, 1723–1746. Figure 3, p. 1735. Reprinted by permission of John Wiley & Sons.

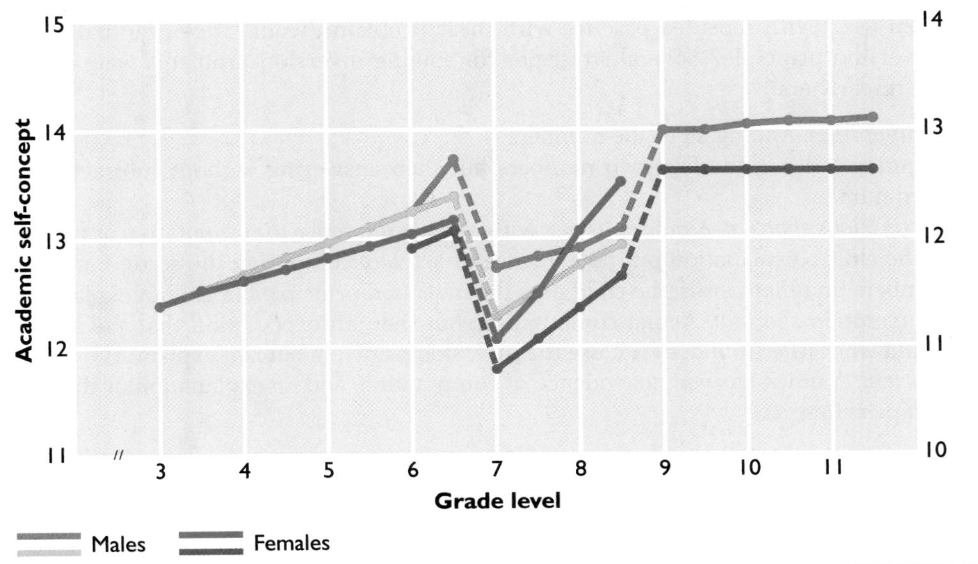

sequential study, in which groups of children of different ages are followed repeatedly but for only a few years. For example, David Cole and his colleagues (Cole et al., 2001) examined changes in children's self-concepts from the elementary to the high school years. Two groups of children—a group of third-graders and a group of sixth-graders—were followed for a period of six years. Every six months, the children took a battery of tests assessing several aspects of self-confidence, such as academic competence, social acceptance, and physical appearance. Thus, by the end of the study, data were available for children in the third through eleventh grades.

Figure 2.8 shows the results for academic competence. Both boys and girls showed gains in this domain from third through sixth grade but evidenced a decline in seventh grade, followed by increases in successive years. (Note that both groups of children were measured in sixth, seventh, and eighth grades.) Because subsets of the children were assessed repeatedly, information about the stability of self-concept for individual children was available, just as it would have been in a longitudinal study. The benefit of the sequential design was that it allowed information about a nine-year span to be obtained in six years.

Although most developmental researchers still prefer to conduct cross-sectional studies because of their expediency, the sequential study provides a convenient way to reap the advantages of both cross-sectional and longitudinal approaches to studying developmental change.

sequential study Study that examines groups of individuals of different ages over a period of time; usually shorter than a longitudinal study.

The Microgenetic Study Longitudinal, cross-sectional, and sequential studies may not reveal a complete picture of development. When researchers use these methods, they tend to focus on average differences in performance from one time to the next or from one age group to another. But this approach usually does not tell us much about the precise processes that change as the child develops. A key feature of the **microgenetic approach** is examining a child's performance while she is engaged in a specific task, making note of any changes in behaviors that occur from trial to trial. Through this close analysis of the child's progress from one level of understanding to another, we can glean important details about development and have a better sense of the mechanisms that are responsible for change (Siegler, 1997, 2006; Siegler & Crowley, 1991).

An experiment conducted by Robert Siegler and Elsbeth Stern (1998) illustrates this method. These researchers were interested in second-graders' tactics as they solved arithmetic problems that involved the principle of inversion—for example, 35 + 8 – 8. Here, it is possible to use a shortcut to arrive at the answer—the quantity (8 – 8) can be quickly discounted because the result is 0. Only children who did not know the inversion principle were selected to participate. In solving these problems, what kinds of strategies would children use? With repeated practice with these problems, would they eventually learn the inversion principle? Several strategies for solving inversion problems were defined by the researchers:

- *Computation.* Adding all of the numbers
- *Negation.* Adding the first two numbers but then answering without subtracting the third number
- *Unconscious shortcut.* A quick answer, with a vague reference to computation or negation in the child's explanation but no evidence of actually computing the second and third numbers (in other words, the child uses the inversion principle but cannot explain it)
- *Computation shortcut.* Actual computation, but then an explanation that the shortcut would work (the child does not use the inversion principle but can explain it)
- *Shortcut.* A quick answer, no evidence of computation, and an explanation of the inversion principle

The strategies in this list were presumed to increase in sophistication from top to bottom. In the experiment, one group of children received twenty inversion problems, and a second group received ten inversion problems and ten standard problems (for example, 35 + 8 – 2) over a total of six practice sessions. After each individual problem was completed, the researcher asked the child how he or she figured out the problem. The researchers noted the child's numerical answer, the time it took to solve the problem, the explanation the child provided, and any other behaviors that occurred during the trial. Figure 2.9 shows a portion of the results for children who received blocks of twenty inversion problems.

In the graph, trial 0 represents each child's first use of the best strategy, the shortcut (thus, 100 percent of the children are represented at this point). Notice that, three trials before trial 0, on trial –3, 87 percent of the children were using the unconscious shortcut, but very few were using computation or any other strategy. This pattern suggests that, right before children discover the actual shortcut, they use it without being fully aware of it or being able to verbalize it. This pattern of results, by the way, did not emerge for children who had mixed sets of inversion and standard problems. Instead, they relied more on computation shortcuts right before they discovered the inversion principle.

As you can see, fine-grained analyses of trial-to-trial changes in children's responses can provide rich information—in this case, about the way their thought processes change. However, this approach requires careful planning and the selection of tasks that are likely to reveal developmental change, as well as concentrated efforts at close observation. Despite these challenges, the microgenetic approach is increasingly becoming part of the arsenal of methods used to study developmental change.

It should be obvious from this discussion that no single research approach represents the perfect way to study development. Table 2.3 summarizes the relative benefits of each of the research strategies for assessing developmental change.

microgenetic study A research approach in which close observations are made of the individual child's behavior from one trial to the next.

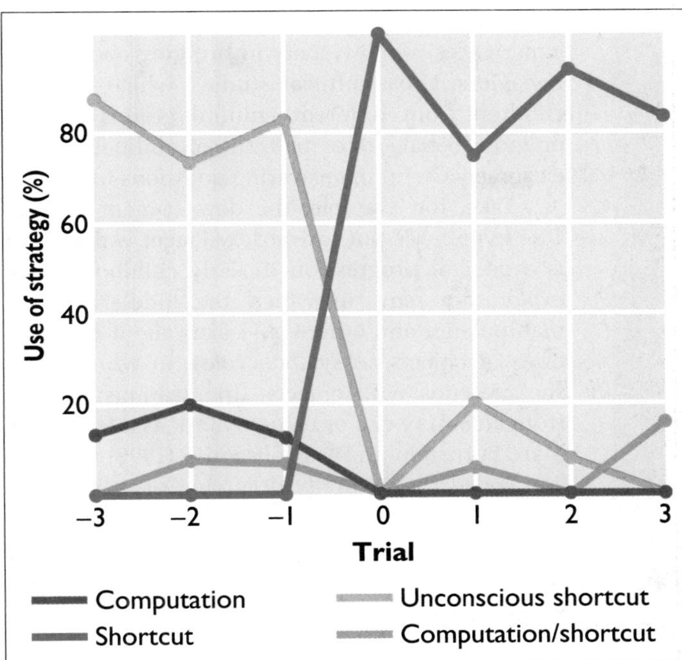

Figure 2.9
A Microgenetic Analysis of Children's Strategy Use
In Siegler and Stern's (1998) experiment, children were closely observed as they solved a series of problems involving the inversion principle. The best strategy was a shortcut (e.g., 8 – 8 = 0). Trial 0 on this graph represents the point at which each child began to use this strategy. Notice that, on previous trials (e.g., Trial –3), many children were using an unconscious shortcut, as opposed to computation, to solve the problems. (Note that in this particular portion of the study, none of the children used negation.) A microgenetic approach allows researchers to understand more of the details of the process of development.
Source: Data from Siegler & Stern, 1998.

Cross-Cultural Studies of Development

Some of the most fundamental questions about the nature of development concern the universality of the various features of psychological growth. Do all children learn language in the same way, regardless of the specific language they acquire? Does children's thinking develop in a universal sequence? Are certain emotions common to all children regardless of attitudes about the appropriateness of crying, smiling, or feeling angry in the larger social group in which they live?

If psychological development does display universal features, this circumstance has far-reaching implications. It could imply, on the one hand, that a child's behavior is largely shaped by biological and genetic factors that govern the unfolding of some human behaviors. Variations in aspects of psychological development across cultures, on the

TABLE 2.3 Strategies for Assessing Developmental Change

Approach	Description	Advantages	Disadvantages
Longitudinal Study	Repeated testing of the same group of children over an extended period of time.	Can examine the stability of characteristics.	Requires a significant investment of time and resources; problems with participant attrition; can have age-history confound.
Cross-Sectional Study	Comparison of children of different ages at the same point in time.	Requires less time; less costly than longitudinal study.	Cannot study individual patterns of development or the stability of traits; subject to cohort effects.
Sequential Study	Observation of children of two or more different ages over a shorter period of time than in longitudinal studies.	Combines the advantages of both longitudinal and cross-sectional approaches; can obtain information about stability of traits in a short period of time.	Has same problems as longitudinal studies, but to a lesser degree.
Microgenetic Study	Close observation of children's trial-by-trial performance as they are engaged with a task.	Permits the identification of the precise processes that change with development.	Requires careful selection of tasks that will reveal developmental changes, as well as close, careful observations.

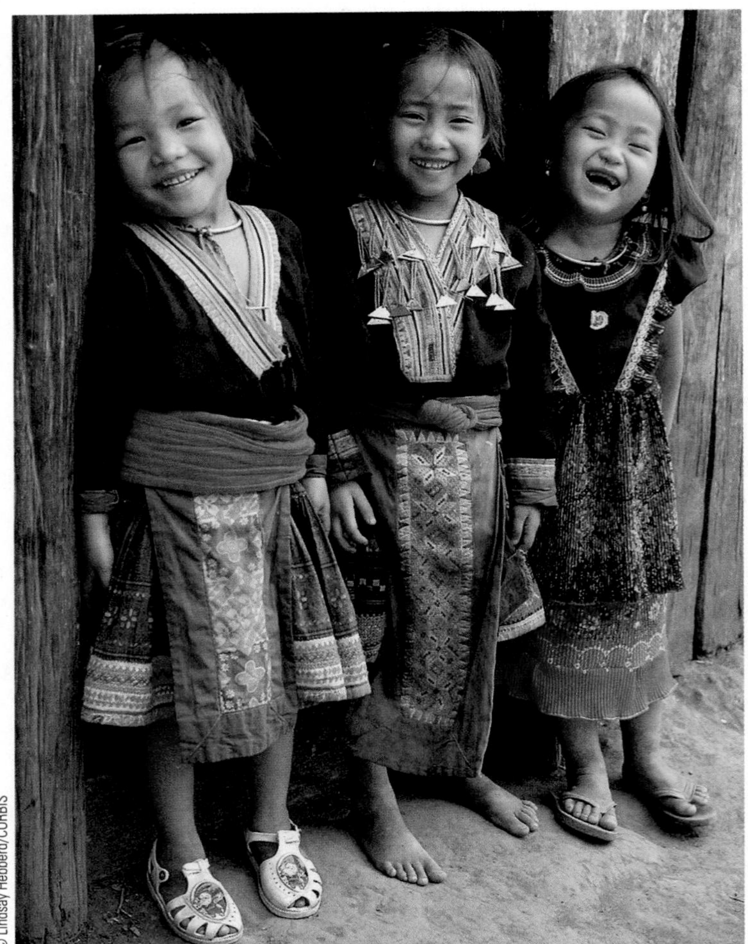
© Lindsay Hebberd/CORBIS

Cross-cultural studies allow researchers to explore the extent to which children's behaviors are universal or specific to a given culture. For example, are the emotions expressed by these Thai girls interpreted in common ways across cultures?

other hand, imply that the differences in the child's experiences weigh heavily in bringing about those behaviors. **Cross-cultural studies**, which compare children from different cultural groups on one or more behaviors or patterns of abilities, can be extremely useful in answering questions like these.

Take, for example, the development of play. One hypothesis put forward by Piaget is that there is a general progression in early childhood from *exploratory play*, in which the toddler throws, manipulates, and otherwise learns about the functions of objects, to *symbolic play*, in which he or she pretends with objects—for example, sipping from an empty cup or using a block as a telephone. Marc Bornstein and his colleagues (1999) recorded and coded the naturally occurring play behaviors of twenty-month-old children and their mothers in two countries, the United States and Argentina. Mother-child pairs were provided with the same set of eight toys and were told to play as they normally would for ten minutes. These researchers found that, despite being the same age, children in the United States engaged in more exploratory play with their mothers, whereas Argentine children engaged in more symbolic play. Moreover, mothers' play behaviors were strongly related to children's patterns of play. Thus, there were clear cultural differences, perhaps linked to the different social goals in the two groups. Exploratory play patterns, which involve manipulating and combining objects, are consistent with the emphasis on individual achievement, independence, and self-reliance in the United States. On the other hand, symbolic play patterns among Argentine mothers and their children often included social behaviors, such as feeding or putting a doll to sleep. These social behaviors are compatible with the orientation more frequent in Argentine society toward the larger, collective group. Thus, the transition from one form of play to another may be less influenced by universal processes, as suggested by Piaget, than by culture-specific experiences.

Cross-cultural studies can present unique challenges to the researcher. If children from two cultural backgrounds are being compared, the researcher must make sure the tasks are well understood and have equivalent forms despite differences in language or in the kinds of activities the children are used to doing (Peña, 2007). For example, children in some cultures may never have seen a photograph or a two-dimensional drawing. Asking these children to categorize objects in pictorial form may put them at an unfair disadvantage if they are to be compared with children who have extensive experience with two-dimensional representations. Moreover, if the researcher is an outsider to the cultural group being observed, he or she may provoke atypical reactions from the individuals under study. Parent-child interactions, peer play, and many other behaviors may not occur as they would in the natural course of events, because of the presence of an outside observer. Cross-cultural researchers must thus pay special attention to the possibility of *participant reactivity*.

For some researchers, cross-cultural studies play a different sort of role, in that they provide a way of understanding human development as it is shaped and formed by the unique contexts in which it occurs. From this perspective, a researcher may try to avoid imposing the values and concepts of his or her own culture on another, trying instead to discover the particular beliefs, values, and modes

cross-cultural study Study that compares individuals in different cultural contexts.

of thinking in the group under study. The goal is not to compare cultures in order to document similarities and differences; rather, it is to study cultures in an in-depth fashion in order to describe behaviors and underlying meaning systems *within* that culture (Miller, 1999; Saarni, 1998; Shweder et al., 2006; Super & Harkness, 1997). A research approach that is often used to achieve these goals is **ethnography**, a set of methods that includes observations of behaviors within the natural environment and interviews with individuals about values and practices within the culture. Ethnographers often live within a particular culture as *participant-observers*, immersing themselves over an extended period of time in the daily routines and practices of a culture (Weisner, 1996). Using these methods, researchers have obtained rich descriptions of what it means to be a child in cultures as diverse as the Gusii tribe of western Kenya (LeVine et al., 1994), Samoa (Ochs, 1988), and the poor neighborhoods of Brazil (Scheper-Hughes, 1992). Our understanding of important topics such as language acquisition, parenting styles, and children's social relationships has been enormously enhanced by this research tradition (LeVine, 2007).

The cross-cultural approach has benefits in terms of understanding human development as it occurs not only in other countries but also in our own society, in which cultural diversity is increasingly becoming a characteristic of the population. Consider some statistics. In Canada, approximately 21 percent of children age fourteen years and under come from non-Caucasian background cultures (Statistics Canada, 2009). In the United States, more than 40 percent of children under age eighteen are African American, Hispanic, Native American, or Asian (U.S. Census Bureau, 2008). Thus, to capture the elements of human development in the broadest and most meaningful sense, researchers will have to study concepts that are relevant and indigenous to these cultures. Individual autonomy and competition may be valued goals of socialization in middle-class Caucasian culture, for example, but they have less relevance in African American or Native American cultures (McLoyd, 1998). Cross-cultural studies can provide important insights into almost all aspects of child development. For this reason, we draw on available cross-cultural work as we discuss each aspect of the growth of children.

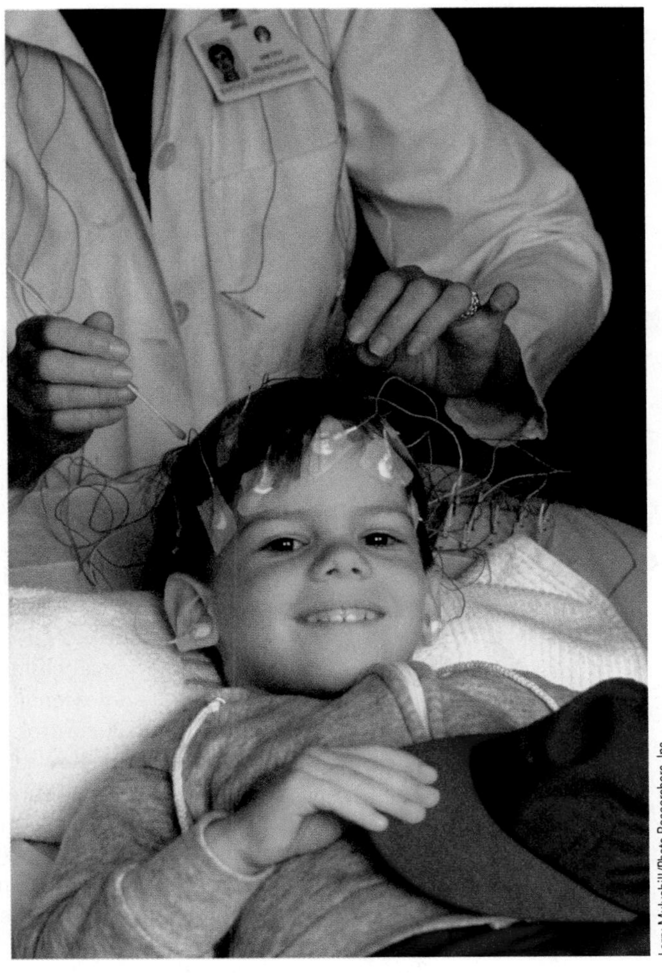
Larry Mulvehill/Photo Researchers, Inc.

Neuroscientists use a variety of techniques to record the activity of the brain while the individual engages in some sort of task. Here, a young child is participating in a study in which the electrical activity of the brain will be measured (ERP) as he responds to an event.

Neuroscience and Development

In no other time before now has the brain and its influence on the development of human behavior received more attention. Major advances in the field of *cognitive neuroscience*, the study of neural and other structures and systems of the brain associated with behavior, have produced insights and generated widespread interest among neuroscientists, child psychologists, parents, and the public about the relationship between the brain and behavior. Theoretical and practical questions about the importance of early experience and the possibility of critical periods for receiving certain kinds of stimulation have further fueled enthusiasm for studying the brain (Bruer, 1999). In large part, much of this movement has been spurred by the emergence of fascinating new technologies (Thompson & Nelson, 2001). Among these procedures are *positron emission tomography* (PET) scans, *functional magnetic resonance imaging* (fMRI), and the recording of

ethnography Set of methods, including observations and interviews, used by researchers to describe the behaviors and underlying meaning systems within a given culture.

event-related potentials (ERP). These techniques measure metabolic activity, blood flow, and electrical events, respectively, and provide clues about how the brain is functioning when an individual is engaged in motor, sensory, linguistic, emotional, and other information processing. At the present time, PET scans have limited utility for studying normal infants and children because they require injection of a radioactive substance. However, fMRI (which measures cerebral blood flow) and ERP (which is a measure of electrical activity generated by the synchronous firing of neurons) are among the more widely available noninvasive procedures that hold considerable promise for investigating normal and abnormal brain development (Casey, Thomas, & McCandless, 2001; Nelson & Monk, 2001).

There are some differences in the kinds of information yielded by these brain recording techniques. ERPs, typically used with infants and young children, tell researchers about the brain's almost immediate response to some event or stimulus, sometimes even if the child does not display an overt behavior. However, ERPs do not readily indicate which specific brain regions are responding. This latter type of information is best obtained with brain images from fMRI, which can show with some precision the areas that are activated when the child participates in a particular psychological task (Nelson, de Haan, & Thomas, 2006). Because fMRI scans require that children stay very still for somewhat prolonged periods of time, however, they are more difficult to obtain from infants and younger children.

Imaging can be especially useful in revealing differences in the brain functioning of normal and atypical children. Figure 2.10, for example, shows which regions of the brain "lit up" when adolescents who had experienced some form of earlier trauma or abuse were compared with a control group as they tried to inhibit a motor response. Participants in the control group showed greater activation in the left cortical regions. In contrast, participants who had experienced childhood trauma showed greater activation in an area called the *medial frontal gyrus*, a brain region associated with the inability to inhibit responses in other clinical populations (Carrion et al., 2008). Based on results such as these, researchers can start to uncover even more precisely the physiological events that occur when individuals experience severe stress.

Being able to see the brain as it functions "online" obviously holds great promise in complementing behavioral studies in illuminating both normal and atypical development. Because neuroscientific findings are now such an integral part of the field of developmental science, we will include them in several relevant portions of upcoming chapters.

Figure 2.10
Scanning the Human Brain
A technique called fMRI allows scientists to observe the functioning of the human brain as individuals perform some psychological task. Here, participants were instructed to press a button every time a letter popped up on a computer screen, except when the letter "X" appeared. The left image shows the regions of the brain that showed greater activation during the inhibition phase for a typical adolescent. The right image shows a different pattern of activation for an adolescent who had experienced trauma earlier in childhood.
Source: From Carrion et al., Depression and Anxiety 25:522. Copyright © 2008 by John Wiley & Sons, Inc. Reprinted by permission of John Wiley & Sons, Inc.

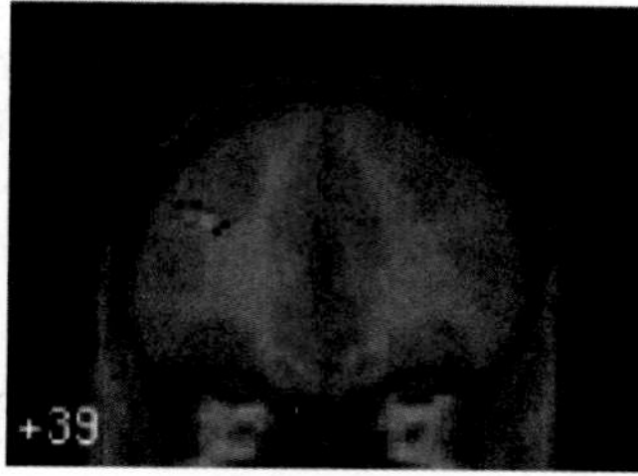

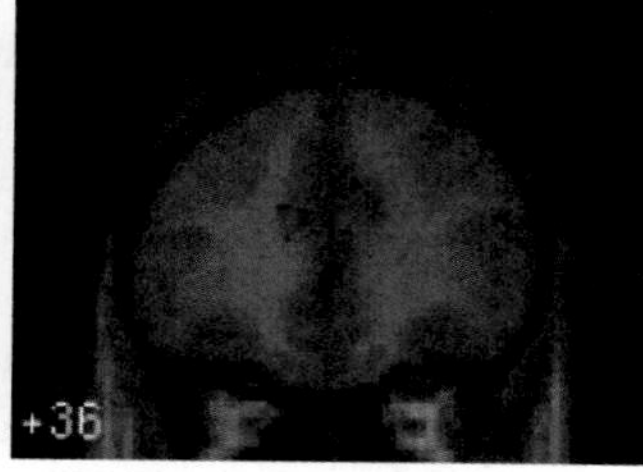

For Your Review and Reflection

- What four research tactics allow researchers to address questions about developmental change? What are the strengths and weaknesses of each tactic?
- What functions do different types of cross-cultural studies serve in developmental research?
- How do neuroscientific approaches enhance our understanding of development?

Ethical Issues in Developmental Research

All psychologists are bound by professional ethics to treat the participants under study humanely and fairly. In general, researchers try to minimize the risk of any physical or emotional harm that might come to participants from taking part in research and to maximize the benefits that will accrue from the findings of their work. In virtually all cases, the institutions in which researchers work require an Institutional Review Board (IRB) to review research projects to ensure that these general principles are met.

The American Psychological Association has drawn up the following specific guidelines for the use of human participants. First, participants must give **informed consent** before participating in a research project; that is, they must be told the purposes of the study and be informed of any potential risks to their well-being, and then they must formally agree to participate. Second, participants have the right to decline to participate or to stop participation, even in the middle of the experiment. Third, if participants cannot be told the true purpose of the experiment (sometimes knowing the experimenter's objective will influence how participants behave), they must be *debriefed* at the conclusion of the study. When participants are **debriefed**, they are told the true objective of the study and the reasons for any deception on the part of the experimenter. Finally, data collected from participants must be kept confidential. Names of participants must not be revealed, and care must be taken to protect their anonymity. To ensure that experimenters comply with these guidelines, virtually all research institutions in the United States are required to have review boards that evaluate any potential risks to participants and the researchers' compliance with ethical practice.

The same ethical guidelines apply to using children as participants in research, but frequently the implementation of these guidelines becomes a difficult matter. Who provides informed consent in the case of an infant or a young toddler, for example? (The parents do.) Is it proper to deceive children about the purposes of a study if they cannot understand the debriefing? (In general, it is a good idea to avoid any kind of deception with children, such as telling them you are interested in how quickly they learn a game when you are really interested in whether they will be altruistic with their play partner.) Are some subjects of study taboo, such as asking children about their concepts of death, suicide, or other frightening topics that might affect them emotionally? (Such studies, if conducted, must be planned very carefully and conducted only by trained professionals.) What about cases in which treatments are suspected to have beneficial outcomes for children? Can the control group properly have the treatment withheld? For example, if we suspect that children's participation in an early intervention preschool program will have real benefits for them, should children in the control group be kept out of it? (One solution to this thorny problem is to offer the control group the beneficial treatment as soon as possible after the conclusion of the study, although this is not always a satisfactory compromise. The control group still has to wait for a beneficial treatment or intervention.)

Many researchers assume that children's vulnerability to risk as they participate in psychological experiments decreases as they grow older. Because infants and young children have more limited cognitive skills and emotional coping strategies, they are viewed as less able to protect themselves and to understand their rights during participation in research. This assumption certainly has some logical

informed consent Participant's formal acknowledgment that he or she understands the purposes, procedures, and risks of a study, and agrees to participate in it.

debriefing Providing research participants with a statement of the true goals of a study after initially deceiving them or omitting information about its purposes.

TABLE 2.4 Ethical Guidelines in Conducting Research with Children

- *Nonharmful procedures:* The investigator may not use any procedures that could impose physical or psychological harm on the child. In addition, the investigator should use the least stressful research operation whenever possible. If the investigator is in doubt about the possible harmful effects of the research, he or she should consult with others. If the child will be unavoidably exposed to stress in research that might provide some diagnostic or therapeutic benefits to the child, the study should be reviewed by an institutional review board.
- *Informed consent:* The investigator should inform the child of all features of the research that might affect his or her willingness to participate and should answer all questions in a way the child can comprehend. The child has the right to discontinue participation at any time.
- *Parental consent:* Informed consent should be obtained in writing from the child's parents or from other adults who have responsibility for the child. The adult has the right to know all features of the research that might affect the child's willingness to participate and can refuse consent.
- *Deception:* If the research necessitates concealment or deception about the nature of the study, the investigator should make sure the child understands the reasons for the deception after the study is concluded.
- *Confidentiality:* All information about participants in research must be kept confidential.
- *Jeopardy:* If, during research, the investigator learns of information concerning a jeopardy to the child's well-being, the investigator must discuss the information with the parents or guardians and experts to arrange for assistance to the child.
- *Informing participants:* The investigator should clarify any misconceptions that may have arisen on the part of the child during the study. The investigator should also report general findings to participants in terms they can understand.

Source: Adapted from the ethical standards set by the Society for Research in Child Development, 2007.

basis and, in fact, is confirmed by research showing that second-graders have difficulty understanding the concept of confidentiality, as well as the contents of a debriefing statement (Hurley & Underwood, 2002). Some types of research, however, may actually pose a greater threat to older children. As Ross Thompson (1990) has pointed out, older children are developing a self-concept and a more elaborate understanding of the ways others evaluate them. Older children may thus be more susceptible to psychological harm than younger children when the researcher compares their performance with that of others or when they think teachers or parents may learn about their performance. In addition, older children may be more sensitive to research results that reflect negatively on their family or sociocultural group. These situations require awareness on the part of the researcher of the subtle ways children can be adversely affected by the research enterprise.

Table 2.4 sets forth the ethical guidelines on using children as participants in research established by the Society for Research in Child Development (2007). Probably the overriding guiding principle is that children should not be subjected to any physical or mental harm and should be treated with all possible respect. In fact, because children are frequently unable to voice their concerns and have less power than adults do, developmental researchers must be especially sensitive to their comfort and well-being.

what do you think? Should Researchers Reveal Information They Learn About Participants in Their Studies?

Researchers often study issues that are sensitive but that can have important consequences for the well-being of children. For example, a researcher might be interested in finding out the factors that predict the emergence of eating disorders in adolescents or the consequences of parental drug abuse for the child. However, research that can be very illuminating about the nature of childhood problems often raises difficult ethical dilemmas (Fisher, 1994).

Suppose the researcher discovers that a particular child has a serious eating disorder or that a young child has ingested harmful illegal drugs kept by the parents in the home. What are the ethical obligations of the researcher in such situations? Should the concerns about the welfare of individual children override any potential benefits of the research for children in general? Furthermore, should the identities of children with serious problems be revealed to parents, school personnel, or others responsible for their well-being, at the risk of violating children's trust that data will be kept confidential?

Ethical guidelines state that researchers who discover that a child is at risk must take steps to make sure that the child obtains appropriate assistance. Such action is based on the concept of "jeopardy" outlined by the Society for Research in Child Development and referred to in Table 2.4. The idea is that ethical concerns about the welfare of particular children should be a primary concern and override any potential benefits of the research for children in general. Also implicit in the concept of jeopardy is the notion that, in some circumstances, confidentiality must be broken to protect the best interests of the child. However, as a consequence of such actions, the child may drop out of the study in order to receive some form of treatment or intervention. If several children in the study drop out, the opportunity to complete the research project could be lost, along with the potential benefits of the results of the study for a larger group of children (Beauchamp et al., 1982). Some researchers believe that the benefits of a well-conducted study can override the obligation to help a particular child for whom a problem has been revealed.

In some cases, researchers may have a legal obligation to enforce the principle of jeopardy. A federal law, the Child Abuse Prevention and Treatment Act enacted in 1974, resulted in the creation of mandatory reporting procedures for suspected cases of child abuse and neglect in every state. In many states, researchers are included among individuals who are required to report. Thus, a researcher who discovers that a child has been abused or neglected, as in the preceding example of a child who has ingested parents' illegal drugs, may be required by law to report the case to the proper authorities. The fact that the child might drop out of the study or that confidentiality is broken is simply a necessary consequence.

In other cases, the issue may be more difficult to resolve. Research can be of help, though, in supplying information on how children themselves feel when such ethical dilemmas arise. Celia Fisher and her colleagues (1996) asked adolescents to judge what researchers should do if they discover that a child has a substance abuse problem, has been physically or sexually abused, displays a life-threatening behavior, or engages in delinquent behaviors. Most adolescents favored reporting instances of child abuse or threats of suicide to a responsible adult. For less severe problems, such as cigarette smoking and nonviolent delinquent acts, adolescents were more inclined to say that the researcher should do nothing. In cases like the latter, rather than reporting children to parents or authorities, researchers might decide to urge children to seek assistance on their own.

Other questions remain. Does the age of the child matter in such ethical decisions? Should these decisions be handled differently with adolescents than with younger children? How can research help us to address questions such as these?

For Your Review and Reflection

- What ethical guidelines apply to the participation of children in research?
- What ethical concepts should guide researchers who discover that children in their research projects may be experiencing some form of risk in their lives?

chapter recap

Chapter Review

Research Methods in Developmental Psychology

What issues must researchers pay attention to when they measure attributes and behaviors?

Like other scientists, developmental psychologists are concerned with using sound methodologies to glean information about children. The *scientific method* is used not only to test theories but also to gather information that can have applications in the lives of children. Researchers need to be concerned with *operationally defining* the *variables* in the study. That is, the variables must be specified in measurable terms. Variables must be *valid*; that is, they must actually measure the concept under consideration. Variables must also be *reliable*; that is, they must be obtained consistently from one time to another or from one observer to another.

What four information-gathering techniques do developmental researchers generally have available to them? What are the advantages and disadvantages of each technique?

Naturalistic observations involve the systematic recording of behaviors as they occur in children's everyday environments. Two special concerns in this approach are *participant reactivity,* the chance that children will react to the presence of an observer by behaving in atypical ways, and *observer bias,* the possibility that the researcher will interpret observations to be consistent with his or her hypotheses.

Structured observations, usually conducted in the laboratory, allow the experimenter more control over situations that accompany children's behaviors. Researchers can measure children's overt behaviors or obtain physiological measures, such as heart rate or brain wave activity. One limitation of this approach is that children may not act as they would in a natural context.

Researchers can employ *structured interviews* or *questionnaires* if they are interested in children's own reports of what they know or how they behave. Researchers need to be aware that children may not always answer questions truthfully and that systematic comparisons and unbiased interpretations by the researcher may be difficult to obtain.

Meta-analysis permits investigators to analyze the results of a large body of published research to draw general conclusions about behavior.

What are the different research designs that researchers might employ to study child development? What are the strengths and weaknesses of each design?

In *correlational studies,* the investigator attempts to see whether changes in one variable are accompanied by changes in another variable. Researchers may observe a *positive correlation,* in which increases in one variable are accompanied by increases in another, or a *negative correlation,* in which increases in one variable are accompanied by decreases in the other. The statistic used to assess the degree of relationship is the *correlation coefficient (r).* A related approach is *regression analysis,* in which researchers attempt to predict outcomes based on one or more predictor variables. One caution about these designs is that cause-and-effect conclusions cannot be drawn.

In the *experimental design,* the researcher manipulates one or more *independent variables* to see if they have an effect on the *dependent variable. Random assignment* of participants to different treatment groups helps ensure that only the independent variable varies from one group to the other. Therefore, cause and effect relationships among variables can be identified. Studies in which control procedures permit strong statements about cause and effect are said to have high *internal validity.* The concept of *external validity* refers to the ability to generalize a study's findings to other situations, contexts, or populations. Variations on the experimental technique are *field experiments,* in which the experimental manipulations are carried out in a natural setting, and *quasi-experiments,* in which the assignment of participants to experimental groups is determined by the participants' natural experiences. Because of this circumstance, researchers conducting quasi-experiments must be concerned with ruling out alternative explanations for their findings.

In *case studies* or the *single-case design,* the researcher intensively studies one or a few individuals over a period of time. The former usually involves a detailed narrative description, whereas the latter involves the systematic collection of data. The ability to generalize to a larger population may be limited with these approaches.

Special Issues in Developmental Research

What four research tactics allow researchers to address questions about developmental change? What are the strengths and weaknesses of each approach?

Longitudinal studies test the same participants repeatedly over an extended period of time. This approach requires a significant investment of time, may involve attrition of participants, and could be vulnerable to the *age-history confound.* It is the only method that allows researchers to examine the stability of traits.

Cross-sectional studies examine participants of different ages at the same time. Although this approach requires less time and fewer resources than the longitudinal approach, it is vulnerable to *cohort effects.*

Sequential studies examine children of two or more ages over a period of time, usually shorter than that used in longitudinal studies. This approach combines the advantages of the cross-sectional and longitudinal approaches but is also vulnerable to the problems associated with each.

Microgenetic studies require the close observation of children as they perform some task, in order to identify the specific processes that change with development. They require careful planning and the selection of tasks that will reveal developmental change, as well as intensive efforts at observation.

What functions do different types of cross-cultural studies serve in developmental research?

Cross-cultural studies, which compare individuals from different cultural groups, can be especially helpful in answering questions about universals in development. Researchers must make sure that tasks are comparable across cultural groups, however.

An important methodological tool, especially for those who wish to learn about the meaning systems within a culture, is *ethnography,* the use of observations and interviews by a researcher who acts as a participant-observer.

How do neuroscientific findings enhance our understanding of development?

New technologies in neuroscience allow researchers to observe the electrical activity of the brain (ERPs) or the rate of blood flow through different brain regions (fMRI). ERPs offer timed information about the brain's response to outside stimuli; fMRIs provide information about which brain regions are involved in processing particular kinds of events. These procedures allow us to observe changes in the structure and function of the brain with age and to identify brain processes and structures that distinguish typical and atypical development.

Ethical Issues in Developmental Research

What ethical guidelines apply to the participation of children in research?

Participants in research must be asked to provide *informed consent,* given the chance to decline participation, be *debriefed* if there has been any deception, and receive assurance that their data will be kept confidential.

What ethical concepts should guide researchers who discover that children in their research projects may be experiencing some form of risk in their lives?

Researchers should always be most concerned with the welfare of the child. In some cases, this concern may mean that confidentiality may have to be broken or that the child will have to drop out of the study to receive an intervention.

Key Terms and Concepts

age-history confound (p. 56)
case study (p. 53)
cohort effect (p. 58)
correlation coefficient (*r*) (p. 49)
correlational study (p. 48)
cross-cultural study (p. 62)
cross-sectional study (p. 57)
debriefing (p. 65)
dependent variable (p. 50)
ethnography (p. 63)
experimental design (p. 50)
external validity (p. 52)
field experiment (p. 52)
independent variable (p. 50)
informed consent (p. 65)
internal validity (p. 50)
longitudinal study (p. 56)
meta-analysis (p. 47)
microgenetic study (p. 60)
naturalistic observation (p. 43)
negative correlation (p. 48)
observer bias (p. 44)
operational definition (p. 43)
participant reactivity (p. 44)
positive correlation (p. 48)
quasi-experiment (p. 53)
questionnaire (p. 46)
random assignment (p. 50)
regression analysis (p. 49)
reliability (p. 43)
scientific method (p. 42)
sequential study (p. 59)
single-case design (p. 54)
structured interview (p. 46)
structured observation (p. 45)
validity (p. 43)
variable (p. 42)

Media Resources

Access an integrated eBook and chapter-specific interactive learning tools, including flashcards, quizzes, videos, and more, in your Developmental Psychology CourseMate, accessed through CengageBrain.com.

CHAPTER OUTLINE

PRINCIPLES OF HEREDITARY TRANSMISSION

The Building Blocks of Heredity

Cell Division and Chromosome Duplication

Gene Expression

Gene Functioning and Regulation of Development

GENE AND CHROMOSOMAL ABNORMALITIES

Gene Variations

Chromosome Variations

GENETIC COUNSELING

Prenatal Diagnosis

Ethical and Social Issues

WHAT DO YOU THINK? Should Sex Preselection Be Permitted?

DEVELOPMENTAL AND BEHAVIORAL GENETICS

The Methods of Behavioral Geneticists

Conceptualizing the Interaction Between Genotype and Environment

Conceptualizing the Correlation Between Genotype and Environment

Hereditary and Environmental Influences on Behavior

RESEARCH APPLIED TO PARENTING Treating Siblings Fairly

CHAPTER RECAP

[chapter 3]

Genetics and Heredity

KEY THEMES IN GENETICS AND HEREDITY

- **NATURE & NURTURE** How do nature and nurture interact in development?
- **RISK | RESILIENCE** What factors promote risk or resilience in development?

Michelle and Derek flopped down on the couch after a long evening of teacher conferences. They had coordinated the night so that Michelle visited all of Alison's fourth-grade teachers and Derek saw Keesha's sixth-grade teachers. Now they were ready to compare notes. "Keesha's doing just great," Derek reported. "Her teachers all say she's conscientious, responsible, and very meticulous about her work. No complaints whatsoever. In fact, she seems to be a real star in math and science. How's Alison doing?" Michelle looked at him and smiled, knowing that what she was about to say would not be a surprise to her husband. Since their daughters had been toddlers, both parents had noticed just how different their two little girls were. Keesha was so absorbed and focused on whatever she was doing and always cautious about trying new things. Alison, on the other hand, was a real free and creative spirit, willing to try anything and concerned less with the details of a task than with getting it done as quickly as possible. Michelle responded, "Well, Alison's going to have to get extra help in math, but her teacher says her poems and stories are very creative. In fact, she's putting one of her poems up in the showcase by the school office. She's just got to buckle down and make sure she gets all of her homework done, though, especially in math." Michelle and Derek prided themselves on being accepting of their girls' individual strengths and weaknesses—setting high expectations but respecting their individuality, too. But for both parents it was still a puzzle: how could two children growing up in the same house with the same family be so different? <<

Parents of more than one child are aware of similarities among them. However, they often take particular notice of the differences; for example, by pointing out how one child "takes after" his mother and another after her father. What are the mechanisms by which such resemblances and differences come about? Although we may grant the contribution of nature to eye color, gender, height, and many other physical traits, heredity's role in other characteristics, such as whether we are contented or quick-tempered, prone to alcoholism, likely to suffer depression, bright and quick-witted, active or more sedentary, is far less certain. Is Alison more impulsive and Keesha more cautious because these qualities developed as a result of their different genetic endowments or because their parents and others encouraged them to develop in these ways? Or did their individuality come about for more complex reasons—perhaps because Keesha and Alison actively pursued different paths of responding to their daily experiences as a result of their unique genetic makeup?

In this chapter, we examine hereditary contributions to development. Major advances in our understanding of the basic biological units of inheritance and their effects on behavior help us to appreciate better the mutual, interactive, and very complex relationship between nature and nurture. Experiences mold, modify, and enhance biological predispositions. In a similar manner, genetic endowment influences, perhaps even actively promotes, selection and preference for certain kinds of environments. Our goal is to understand just how such complex interactions evolve.

We begin with a brief overview of the principles of heredity. The blueprint for development is replicated in nearly every cell of our body. This blueprint includes genetic instructions that distinguish us from other species of plants and animals. Regardless of the language we speak, the work we do, the color of our skin, or how friendly we are, we share a genetic underpinning that makes each of us a human being. This biological inheritance also contributes to our individuality. With the exception of identical twins, each of us begins with a different set of genetic instructions. But even for identical twins, who have the same genetic makeup, the influence of distinctive experiences ensures that each of us is a unique individual, different from everyone else.

In this chapter, we also examine several examples of hereditary variations that pose problems for development. As researchers learn more about the ways in which genetic influences occur, we can design environments to help minimize the restrictions imposed by certain hereditary conditions. We consider, too, how genetic counseling assists parents in deciding whether to have children or how to prepare for a child who is likely to experience developmental problems.

Most psychological development, of course, cannot be linked to simple genetic instructions. Intelligence, temperament, and personality, along with susceptibility to various diseases and conditions, are the outcome of complex interactions between genetic and environmental events. In the final section of this chapter, we consider research involving identical and fraternal twins, siblings, adopted children, and other family relationships to help us understand the complex tapestry that genetic and environmental factors weave for cognitive, social-emotional, and personality development (Gottlieb, Wahlsten, & Lickliter, 2006; Rutter, 2006).

NATURE & NURTURE

Principles of Hereditary Transmission

Whether we have freckles, blond hair, or a certain type of personality can be influenced by genetic factors, but none of these characteristics is bestowed directly on us at conception. We must make a distinction between what our genetic makeup consists of and the kind of individual we eventually become. In other words, we must distinguish between the **genotype**, a person's constant, inherited genetic endowment, and the **phenotype**, his or her observable, measurable features, characteristics, and behaviors. A given phenotype is constructed from the complex interactions involving the genotype and the many events that are part of an individual's experience.

Modern theories of the genotype can be traced to a series of experiments reported in 1866 by Gregor Mendel, an Austrian monk. From his observations of the characteristics of successive generations of peas, Mendel theorized that hereditary characteristics are determined by pairs of particles called *factors* (later termed **genes**, the specialized sequences of molecules that form the genotype). He also proposed that the information provided by the two members of a pair of genes is not always identical. These different forms of a gene are today known as **alleles**. Sometimes many possible alternative versions exist for a particular gene.

Mendel also outlined the basic principle by which genes are transferred from one generation to another. He concluded that offspring randomly receive one member of every pair of genes from the mother and one from the father. This is possible because the parents' **gametes**, or sex cells (egg and sperm), normally carry only one member of each pair of genes. Thus, when egg and sperm combine during fertilization, a new pair of genes, one member of the pair inherited from each parent, is reestablished in the offspring. That individual, in turn, may transmit either member of this new pair to subsequent children. Thus, genetic information is passed on from one generation to the next.

At about the same time Mendel's research was published, biologists discovered **chromosomes**, long, threadlike structures in the nucleus of nearly every cell in the body. In the early 1900s, several researchers independently hypothesized that genes are located on chromosomes. Yet another major breakthrough occurred in 1953 when James Watson

genotype Total genetic endowment inherited by an individual.

phenotype Observable and measurable characteristics and traits of an individual; a product of the interaction of the genotype with the environment.

gene Large segment of nucleotides within a chromosome that codes for the production of proteins and enzymes. These proteins and enzymes underlie traits and characteristics inherited from one generation to the next.

allele Alternate form of a specific gene; provides a genetic basis for many individual differences.

gamete Sperm cell in males, egg cell in females, normally containing only twenty-three chromosomes.

chromosome Threadlike structure of DNA, located in the nucleus of cells, which forms a collection of genes. A human body cell normally contains forty-six chromosomes.

and Francis Crick deciphered the structure of chromosomes and, in so doing, proposed a powerfully elegant way by which genes are duplicated during cell division. By 1956, researchers had documented the existence of forty-six chromosomes in normal human body cells. Today, some fifty years after Watson and Crick's monumental discovery, the mapping of the sequence of the **human genome**—the nearly 3 billion chemical base pairs that make up every human's biological inheritance—is complete (Human Genome Management Information System (HGMIS), 2008).

The Building Blocks of Heredity

How could hereditary factors play a part in the differences displayed by Alison and Keesha or in a child's remarkable musical ability or in yet another's developmental delay? To understand the genotype and its effects on appearance, behavior, personality, or intellectual ability, we must consider genetic mechanisms at many different levels.

To begin with, every living organism is composed of cells—in the case of mature humans, perhaps as many as 100 trillion cells. As Figure 3.1 indicates, within the nucleus of nearly all cells are the chromosomes that carry genetic information critical to the cells' functioning. Genes, regions within the strands of chromosomes, determine the production of specific proteins in the cell. The genes, in turn, are made up of various arrangements of four different chemical building blocks called **nucleotides**, which contain one of four nitrogen-based molecules (*adenine, thymine, cytosine,* or *guanine*). The nucleotides pair together in one of only two ways to form the rungs of a remarkably long, spiral staircase-like structure called **DNA**, or **deoxyribonucleic acid** (see Figure 3.1).

Genes differ from one another in number and sequence of nucleotide pairings, and in their location on the chemical spiral staircases, or chains of DNA, that we call the chromosomes. Humans are believed to have between 20,000 and 25,000 *structural genes* coding for the production of proteins that govern the physiological functions of a cell (Genetics Home Reference, 2010c; Pennisi, 2007). Yet structural genes account for only about 2 percent of the nearly 3 billion base pairs estimated to make up the human genome (Plomin & Schalkwyk, 2007). Some of the remaining DNA consists of other types of genes that start and stop or modify the functioning of structural genes. But large stretches of DNA are made up of repeat sequences of base pairs or of other patterns that seem to have simply replicated themselves, and their functions, if any, remain unknown.

Just as Mendel theorized, hereditary attributes are, in many cases, influenced by pairs of genes or, more specifically, the two allelic forms of the pair. One member of the pair is located on a chromosome inherited from the mother; the other, on a similar, or *homologous*, chromosome acquired from the father. Figure 3.2 shows a **karyotype**, or photomicrograph of the forty-six chromosomes that humans (in this case, a male) normally possess.

As can be seen in Figure 3.2, the homologous sets of chromosomes that are not genetically involved in the determination of sex, called **autosomes**, can be arranged in pairs and numbered from 1 to 22 on the basis of their size. The remaining two chromosomes specify the genetic sex of an individual and differ for males and females. In females this pair consists of **X chromosomes**; both are relatively large and similar in size. The normal male has one X chromosome and a much smaller **Y chromosome**. The Y chromosome is believed to carry between 70 and 200 genes, in sharp contrast to the approximately 1,000 genes estimated to be on the X chromosome (Genetics Home Reference, 2010a).

human genome Entire inventory of nucleotide base pairs that compose the genes and chromosomes of humans.

nucleotide Repeating basic building block of DNA consisting of nitrogen-based molecules of adenine, thymine, cytosine, and guanine.

deoxyribonucleic acid (DNA) Long, spiral staircase-like sequence of molecules created by nucleotides identified with the blueprint for genetic inheritance.

karyotype Pictorial representation of an individual's chromosomes.

autosome One of twenty-two pairs of homologous chromosomes. The two members of each pair are similar in size, shape, and genetic function. The two sex chromosomes are excluded from this class.

X chromosome Larger of the two sex chromosomes associated with genetic determination of sex. Normally females have two X chromosomes and males, only one.

Y chromosome Smaller of the two sex chromosomes associated with genetic determination of sex. Normally males have one Y chromosome and females, none.

Figure 3.1
The Building Blocks of Heredity
Hereditary contributions to development can be observed at many levels. This figure depicts five major levels. Nearly every cell in the human body carries the genetic blueprint for development in the chromosomes. Specific regions on each chromosome, the genes, regulate protein production. Looked at in even more detail, the human genome consists of chemical molecules that are the building blocks for the genes. Each of these different levels of the individual's biological makeup can offer insights into the mechanisms by which the genotype affects the phenotype, the observable expression of traits and behaviors.
Source: Adapted from Isensee, W. (September 3, 1986). *The Chronicle of Higher Education.* Used with permission.

1. The **human body** has about 100 trillion cells. Proteins determine the structure and function of each cell.

2. Most **cells** contain a nucleus. Located within the nucleus are forty-six chromosomes that carry the instructions that signal the cell to manufacture various proteins.

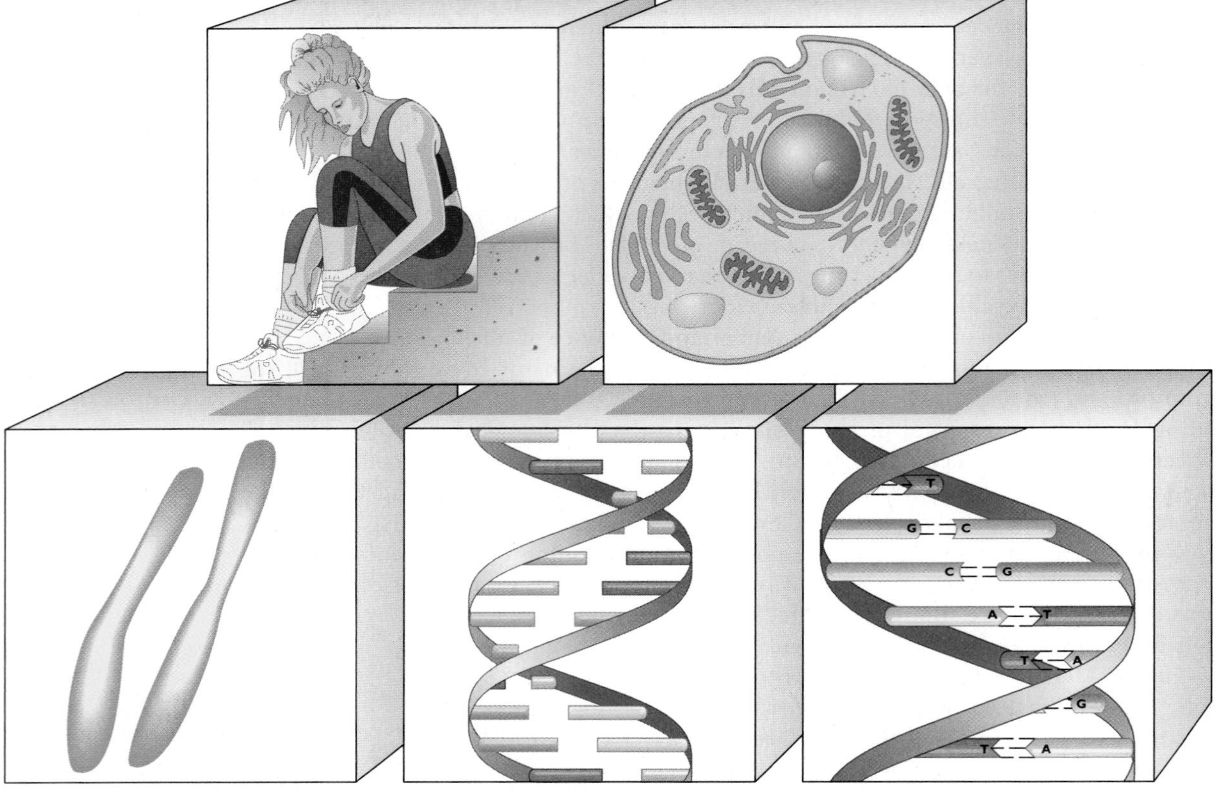

3. A **chromosome** is a long thin strand of DNA organized as a coiled double helix. A full set of forty-six chromosomes in humans is believed to contain somewhere between 20,000 and 25,000 genes.

4. A **gene** is made up of thousands of nucleotide pairs. Each gene typically has information designed to specify the production of one or more particular proteins.

5. **Nucleotides**, composed of four different kinds of chemical building blocks—adenine (A), thymine (T), cytosine (C), and guanine (G)—are the smallest genetic unit and are paired in specific combinations. Nearly 3 billion pairs of nucleotides make up the total complement of DNA in humans.

Cell Division and Chromosome Duplication

Each of us began life as a single cell created when a sperm cell, normally containing twenty-three chromosomes from the father, united with an ovum (egg), normally containing an additional twenty-three chromosomes from the mother. The developmental processes started by this fertilized egg cell, called a **zygote**, are more fully described in Chapter 4, "The Prenatal Period and Birth." Remarkably, however, nearly every one of the millions of different

zygote Fertilized egg cell.

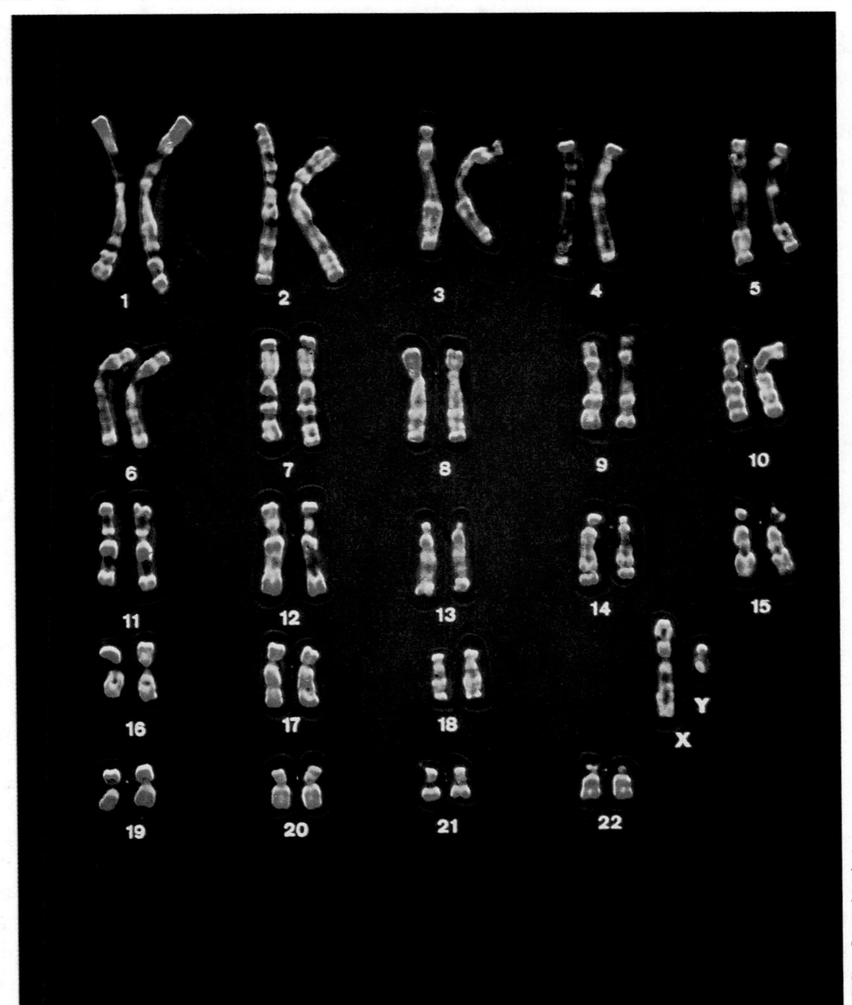

Figure 3.2
Chromosomes in the Normal Human Male
This karyotype depicts the twenty-two homologous pairs of autosomes and the two sex chromosomes in the normal human male. In females, the twenty-third pair of chromosomes consists of an XX pair instead of an XY pair.

cells in the newborn, whether specialized for bone or skin, heart or brain, or in some other way, contains the same genetic blueprint established in the initial zygote.

How does this extraordinary duplication of DNA from one cell to another and from one generation to the next take place? Most cells divide through the process called **mitosis**. During mitosis, genetic material in the nucleus of the cell is reproduced such that a full complement of DNA becomes available to each new cell. Even before cell division occurs, the chemical bonds linking the nucleotides that form the rungs of the DNA ladder weaken. The pairs of nucleotides separate as though they were being unzipped from each other. At the same time, additional nucleotides are manufactured in the cell and attach to the separated nucleotides. Because each nucleotide can combine with only one other type, the two newly formed strands of DNA are normally rebuilt in exactly their original sequence. The two newly formed copies of DNA eventually separate completely, so that one becomes a member of each of the two new daughter cells, as depicted in Figure 3.3.

The process of cell division associated with the gametes (the sex cells) is called **meiosis**. Meiosis, which results in twenty-three chromosomes in the egg and sperm cells, actually involves *two* successive generations of cell divisions. In the first stage, each of the forty-six chromosomes begins to replicate in much the same way as mitosis

mitosis Process of cell division that takes place in most cells of the human body and results in a full complement of identical material in the forty-six chromosomes in each cell.

meiosis Process of cell division that forms the gametes; normally results in twenty-three chromosomes in each human egg and sperm cell rather than the full complement of forty-six.

Figure 3.3

The Process of Mitosis

The process of mitotic cell division generates nearly all the cells of the body except the gametes. During mitosis, each chromosome replicates to form two chromosomes with identical genetic blueprints. As the cell divides, one member of each identical pair becomes a member of each daughter cell. In this manner, complete genetic endowment is replicated in nearly every cell of the body.

Cell nucleus (shown with a single pair of chromosomes).
Chromosomes split and replicate to produce two identical replicas of each chromosome.
The replicas separate, and the cell divides.
Each daughter cell now has a pair of chromosomes that is identical to the original pair.

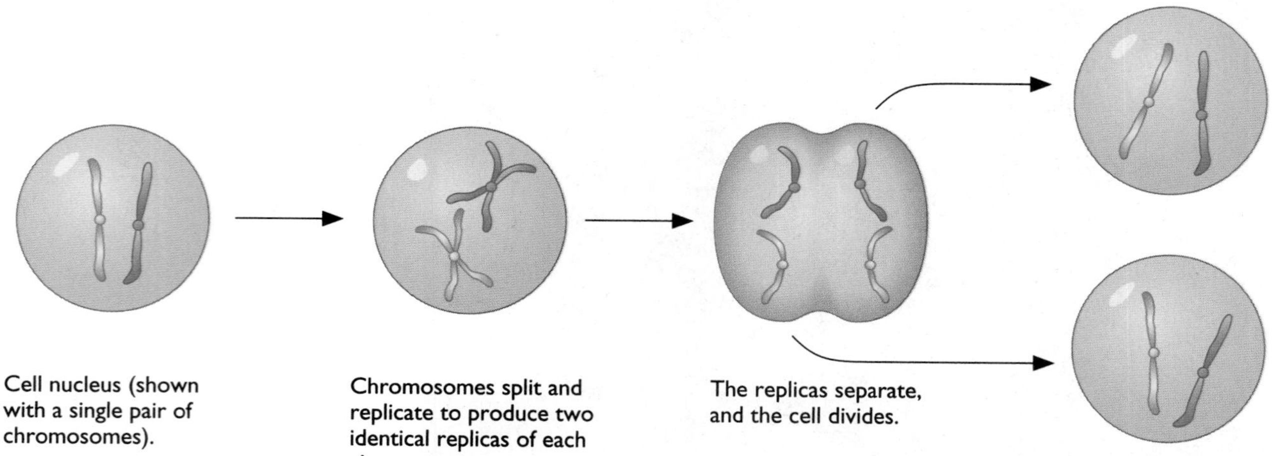

begins. However, before the identical replicas split apart, the cell divides, so that each daughter cell receives only one chromosome from each of the twenty-three pairs, as pictured in Figure 3.4. In the second stage, the replicas of the twenty-three chromosomes completely separate, and the cell divides once more, each cell again receiving one of the replicas. Thus, from these two successive divisions, four cells are produced, each with twenty-three chromosomes.

Random segregation of the twenty-three homologous chromosome pairs in the first stage of meiosis yields more than 8 million possible combinations of gametes with one or more different sets of chromosomes. Along with an equivalent number of possible unique arrangements from a mate, mother and father together have a gene pool of about 64 trillion different combinations from which their offspring may derive. But the potential for genetic variability is actually far greater because of another phenomenon known as **crossing over**, a key part of the first stage of meiosis. Before homologous chromosome pairs separate in the first cell division, they align, and segments of DNA may transfer, or cross over, from one member to the other member of the pair, as shown in Figure 3.5. This process of *genetic recombination* makes it virtually impossible for two individuals to have the same genetic makeup, even siblings, unless the two are identical twins.

Gene Expression

We have briefly described key structures of inheritance—nucleotides, genes, and chromosomes—and the way these are replicated in cells of the body, including gametes. But how does the genotype affect the phenotype? In other words, how does the underlying genetic blueprint promote the appearance of blue eyes, baldness, and dark skin or such complex traits as shyness, schizophrenia, and intelligent problem solving? The answer, according to classic genetics, begins with the alleles, the specific form a particular gene may take.

crossing over Process during the first stage of meiosis when genetic material is exchanged between autosomes.

Figure 3.4
The Process of Meiosis for Sperm Cells
As meiosis begins (A), DNA replicates as in mitotic cell division. However, before the replicated arms split apart, one member of each pair of homologous chromosomes moves to become part of each first-generation daughter cell (B). Once the first generation of daughter cells is established, DNA replicas split as part of the second meiotic division (C). Thus, one replica of one member pair of homologous chromosomes is contributed to each second-generation daughter cell (D). From these two successive divisions, four cells, each with twenty-three chromosomes, are produced.

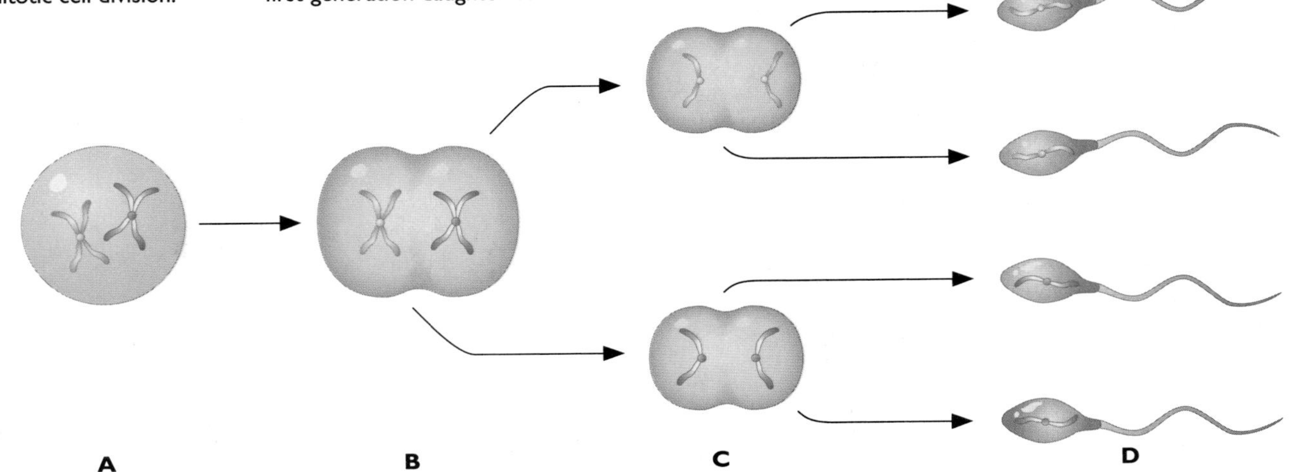

Cell with forty-six chromosomes (only one pair of homologous chromosomes is shown here). Each member of the pair has begun to replicate similar to mitotic cell division.
First meiotic cell division begins but does not proceed as in mitosis. Instead of the replicated chromosome splitting apart, one member of each homologous pair becomes a part of the first-generation daughter cell.
The second meiotic division proceeds after the first is completed; now the replicated chromosome acquired in the first-generation daughter cell splits apart.
Each of the four gametes produced by the two-step process now has acquired one member of the pair of homologous chromosomes.
A
B
C
D

The two genes that we inherit, one from our mother and the second from our father, which code for a particular protein in a cell, may be identical—that is, have the same allelic form—or they may differ. When both have the same allelic form, a person's genotype is said to be **homozygous** for whatever characteristic that gene affects. For example, three different alleles exist for the gene that governs blood type: A, B, and O. When both inherited alleles are A, both B, or both O, a person has a homozygous genotype for blood type. But, if an individual inherits two different alleles of the gene for blood type, let's say A and B, that person's genotype is **heterozygous**.

The consequences of a homozygous genotype are usually straightforward: the child's phenotype will be influenced by whatever characteristics are specified by that particular allelic form. But the effects of a heterozygous genotype depend on how the alleles influence each other. When a child's phenotype shows the effects of only one of the two allelic forms, the one whose characteristics are observed is **dominant**; the allelic form whose influence is not evident in the phenotype is **recessive**. For example, a person who inherits both an A and an O allele for blood type will be classified as having Type A; the allele for Type A is dominant, and the allele for Type O is recessive.

Cystic fibrosis, the most common autosomal recessive disorder in Western Europe (McGinniss & Kaback, 2002)

homozygous Genotype in which two alleles of a gene are identical, thus having the same effects on a trait.

heterozygous Genotype in which two alleles of a gene are different. The effects on a trait will depend on how the two alleles interact.

dominant allele Allele whose characteristics are reflected in the phenotype even when part of a heterozygous genotype. Its genetic characteristics tend to mask the characteristics of other alleles.

recessive allele Allele whose characteristics do not tend to be expressed when part of a heterozygous genotype. Its genetic characteristics tend to be masked by other alleles.

Figure 3.5
Crossing Over: The Exchange of Genetic Material Between Chromosomes
In the process known as crossing over, genetic material is exchanged between homologous pairs of chromosomes during the first stage of meiotic cell division. (A) Initially, autosomes that have begun DNA replication align with each other. (B) Genetic material between homologous chromosomes is exchanged. (C) One member of each homologous pair of chromosomes randomly segregates or relocates to two different regions of the parent cell, and the first generation of cell division in meiosis takes place.

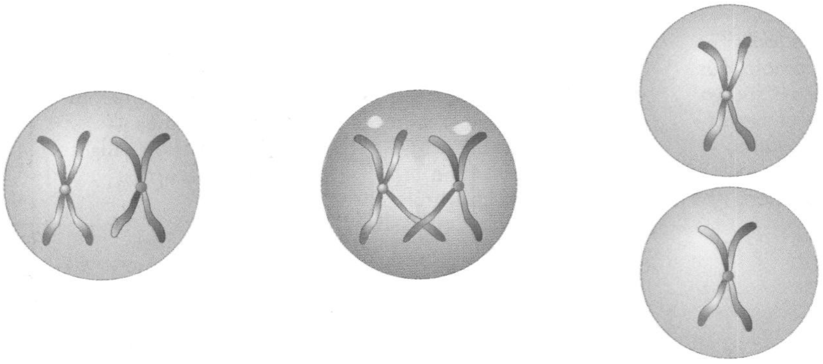

Alignment of homologous chromosomes, each a pair of sister chromatids
A

Crossover
B

First meiotic cell division
C

RISK | RESILIENCE

and a leading cause of childhood death among Caucasian children, provides another example of a dominant-recessive relationship between alleles. The shortened life span typically stems from a thickening of the mucus lining the respiratory tract, which interferes with breathing. Most Caucasian children inherit a gene pair that does not include the allelic form that codes for cystic fibrosis; they have a homozygous genotype that contributes to normal development. About one in twenty-five people of Caucasian ancestry, however, has a heterozygous genotype in which one gene is normal and the other carries the genetic information that can, if inherited, result in offspring with cystic fibrosis. The normal allele is *dominant*. Thus, someone who is heterozygous for this condition can lead an ordinary, productive life. But a child of a mother and father, each of whom has a heterozygous genotype, might inherit two alleles coding for cystic fibrosis (see Figure 3.6). In the latter condition, the two recessive alleles are no longer masked by a normal gene; this child (about 1 in every 3,000 Caucasian children) will suffer from cystic fibrosis. Medical researchers today are actively investigating the potential for *gene therapy*, the replacement of the gene that codes for a disorder, to reduce and even eliminate the devastating consequences of cystic fibrosis and other inherited diseases (Human Genome Project Information, 2009).

In some circumstances, the child's phenotype will reflect the influence of *both* allelic forms if they differ. When the characteristics of both alleles are observed, they exhibit **codominance**. For example, a child with Type AB blood has inherited a gene for Type A blood from one parent and a gene for Type B blood from the other parent.

Table 3.1 summarizes a number of traits and characteristics associated with dominant-recessive patterns. But we must be cautious when drawing inferences about these relationships. Many traits are **polygenic** in that they can be affected or determined by several genes, sometimes located on different sets of chromosomes. For example, the

codominance Condition in which individual, unblended characteristics of two alleles are reflected in the phenotype.

polygenic Phenotypic characteristic influenced by two or more genes.

Figure 3.6
The Pattern of Inheritance for Cystic Fibrosis
The inheritance of cystic fibrosis is one of many traits that are influenced by a single pair of genes. In this figure, F symbolizes a normal allele and f represents the allele for cystic fibrosis. When parents with heterozygous genotypes for this disease have children, their offspring may inherit a homozygous genotype with normal alleles (FF), a heterozygous genotype with one normal and one abnormal allele (Ff or fF), or a homozygous genotype with two abnormal alleles (ff). Because the normal allele dominates, children with a heterozygous genotype will not exhibit cystic fibrosis. When both alleles carry genetic information for the disease, however, cystic fibrosis will occur.

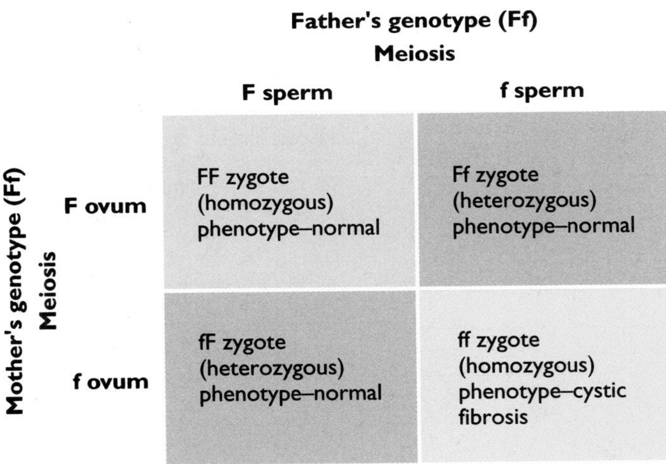

dominant-recessive relationship between the two inherited alleles that normally govern the inheritance of eye color, as indicated in Table 3.1, can be altered by other genes.

Gene Functioning and Regulation of Development

How do genes influence the development of a phenotype? A major field of study called *proteomics,* the investigation of the structures and functions of proteins, has emerged to attempt to answer precisely that question. We can give only a brief glimpse into this rapidly evolving area. Although exceptions exist, genetic information is typically conveyed from the DNA in the cell's nucleus to other parts of the cell. This process is performed by *messenger ribonucleic acid,* or *mRNA,* a molecule somewhat similar to DNA. Through this process, called *transcription,* mRNA replicates some segment of the DNA. The mRNA copy is transported to the cytoplasm, the region outside the nucleus of the cell where it then, through a process called *translation,* initiates a series of events that produce proteins to give the cell its unique ability to function.

New research on both the transcription of DNA to mRNA and the translation of mRNA into proteins is demonstrating that these processes are susceptible to environmental influences (Stiles, 2009). The field of **epigenetics** (derived from the combination of the word "genetics" along with the Greek word "epi" meaning "in addition to" or "on top of") is concerned with identifying modifications in gene expression that are not dependent on the genetic code itself (Masterpasqua, 2009). More specifically, genes can be silenced or turned on, not only by other genes, but also by certain environmental or experiential conditions. Radiation, foreign chemicals, nutrients available within the cell, and even influences as broad as early parenting are now known to have an impact on gene expression. But perhaps more remarkable is growing evidence that some of these alterations in gene expression can be passed on to succeeding generations of offspring. One of the best examples illustrating this

epigenetics The field of study concerned with how environmental factors interact with DNA and its transcription into mRNA to influence cell functioning and the phenotype.

TABLE 3.1 Alleles of Genes That Display a Dominant and Recessive Pattern of Phenotypic Expression

Dominant Traits	Recessive Traits
Brown eyes	Gray, green, blue, hazel eyes
Curly hair	Straight hair
Normal hair growth	Baldness
Dark hair	Light or blond hair
Nonred hair (blond, brunette)	Red hair
Normal skin coloring	Albinism (lack of pigment)
Immunity to poison ivy	Susceptibility to poison ivy
Normal skin	Xeroderma pigmentosum (heavy freckling and skin cancers)
Thick lips	Thin lips
Roman nose	Straight nose
Earlobe free	Earlobe attached
Cheek dimples	No dimples
Extra, fused, or short digits	Normal digits
Second toe longer than big toe	Big toe longer than second toe
Double-jointedness	Normal joints
Normal color vision	Red-green colorblindness
Farsightedness	Normal vision
Normal vision	Congenital eye cataracts
Retinoblastoma (cancer of the eye)	Normal eye development
Normal hearing	Congenital deafness
Type A blood	Type O blood
Type B blood	Type O blood
Rh-positive blood	Rh-negative blood
Normal blood clotting	Hemophilia
Normal metabolism	Phenylketonuria
Normal blood cells	Sickle cell anemia
Familial hypercholesterolemia (error of fat metabolism)	Normal cholesterol level at birth
Wilms tumor (cancer of the kidney)	Normal kidney
Huntington's disease	Normal brain and body maturation
Normal respiratory and gastrointestinal functioning	Cystic fibrosis
Normal neural and physical development	Tay-Sachs disease

NATURE & NURTURE

transgenerational effect has been demonstrated in rats. By feeding gestating rats with a particular diet, coat color in their offspring can be shifted from black to yellow. This change in coat color is then passed on to succeeding generations of offspring (Cropley et al., 2006). Differences in early caregiving also influence the responsiveness of some brain receptors to certain hormones that affect behavior in rodents. That responsiveness, in turn, can be transmitted to future generations of offspring (Champagne & Mashoodh, 2009). No changes in DNA have occurred but rather the switches affecting the functioning of the genes have been inherited. These modifications are hypothesized to have cascading and major consequences contributing to personality, cognition, and many other aspects of normal and abnormal development in humans as well. Thus, our appearance and behavior are the end result of an extensive chain of biochemical processes started by a template provided by the DNA. The instructions in that template are then implemented in particular ways depending on the cellular and biological environment as well as different kinds of experiences, that is, epigenetic events (Champagne & Mashoodh, 2009; Stiles, 2009).

Additional new discoveries are continuing to be made about genes and how they influence development. For example, sometimes it matters whether a particular gene has been inherited from the mother or the father. This phenomenon, called **genomic imprinting**, is best illustrated by the *Prader-Willi* and *Angelman syndromes*, each estimated to affect about 1 in 15,000 persons. Individuals with Prader-Willi syndrome display, among other physical and behavioral characteristics, short stature, feelings of hunger that often contribute to overeating and obesity, and mild to moderate intellectual impairment. In contrast, individuals with Angelman syndrome display marionettelike disturbances in gait, seizures, hyperactivity, and more severe learning difficulties, including minimal or no speech. Prader-Willi syndrome stems from the absence of a particular gene or set of genes on chromosome 15 inherited from the father and the inability of the mother's genetic material on the homologous chromosome to compensate for this loss. In contrast, Angelman syndrome arises from the absence of that same gene or set of genes inherited from the mother and the inability of the father's genetic material to compensate for the loss (Everman & Cassidy, 2000; Genetics Home Reference, 2010b). Susceptibility to certain cancers, growth disorders, and some types of diabetes are also known to occur as a result of genomic imprinting.

RISK | RESILIENCE

Substantial progress in understanding genetic influences has been made in recent years. However, important questions remain concerning the effects of the human genome on a wide range of complex human behaviors of interest to psychologists, an issue that will be discussed more fully later in this chapter. In the section that follows, we highlight additional examples of several specific gene mutations and chromosomal disturbances that can have profound repercussions for development. Keep in mind that serious consequences associated with gene and chromosomal deviations affect a relatively small number of individuals. Nevertheless, the consequences often reverberate and extend well beyond those individuals, to their families and others within the community.

For Your Review and Reflection

- What roles do genotype and the environment play in determining a phenotype?
- What is the human genome? How do the nucleus of the cell, chromosomes and DNA, genes, and nucleotides play a role in genetic influences on development?
- How many autosomes exist in the human karyotype? Of what importance are the X and Y chromosomes?
- What is the difference between mitosis and meiosis? What are the impacts of crossing over and the process of genetic recombination?
- In classic genetics, how do homozygous and heterozygous genes and the presence of dominant, recessive, and codominant allelic forms account for the inheritance patterns associated with various phenotypes? What are polygenic traits?

genomic imprinting Instances of genetic transmission in which the expression of a gene is determined by whether the particular allelic form has been inherited from the mother or the father.

- What are proteomics and mRNA? What roles do transcription and translation play in accounting for a gene's influence on development? How can environmental events affect genetic processes, and what are the implications of epigenetic processes for development?
- What is genomic imprinting?
- How might epigenetic processes increase risk or resilience in development?
- What behavioral and physical characteristics do you display that are likely a result of dominant and recessive genes or other gene/environment interactions?

Gene and Chromosomal Abnormalities

RISK | RESILIENCE

Changes in the structure of genes, or **mutations**, are able to introduce genetic diversity among individuals. Mutations occur surprisingly often; perhaps as many as half of all human conceptions occur with some kind of genetic or chromosomal change (Plomin et al., 2008). Most mutations are lethal, resulting in loss of the fertilized egg cell through spontaneous abortion very soon after conception, often before a woman even knows she is pregnant. A small number of other mutations will have little impact on development. However, some can have enduring, often negative, consequences for an individual and his or her quality of life, consequences that may be passed on from one generation to the next. In fact, more than 5 percent of all diseases observed in individuals before the age of twenty-five are at least in part the result of some type of genetic or chromosomal anomaly (Rimoin et al., 2002). Moreover, birth defects and genetically based diseases contribute to a disproportionately high number of hospitalizations and medical expenses in the United States (Yoon et al., 1997). Globally, almost 8 million children are born with genetically linked birth defects (Christianson, Howson, & Modell, 2006). We consider here the consequences of just a few of the more than 1,400 gene and chromosome anomalies that have been identified as influencing physical and behavioral development (Peltonen & McKusick, 2001).

Gene Variations

RISK | RESILIENCE

An estimated 120,000 infants are born each year in the United States with birth defects, many caused by the inheritance of a single dominant or pair of recessive genes (March of Dimes, 2010b). Table 3.2 lists a few of the more serious of the gene-based defects. In a good number of cases, the effects are evident at birth (*congenital*), but the consequences of some are not observed until childhood or even late adulthood. We will discuss several dominant and recessive disorders to illustrate their effects on development, the interventions and treatments available for them, and the insights they provide concerning the genotype's contribution to intellectual and behavioral capacities.

RISK | RESILIENCE

Williams Syndrome: Discordances in Language, Cognition, and Social Behavior About 1 in 20,000 children is born with **Williams syndrome**, caused by the deletion of a small number of genes on chromosome 7. The syndrome is autosomal dominant, although most occurrences are the result of a mutation. Children with Williams syndrome possess a distinctive set of facial features, including a short, upturned nose and full lips. They also display curvatures of the knee and hip that produce an unusual postural appearance and gait, and they often have heart and kidney abnormalities.

Individuals with Williams syndrome are typically mildly to moderately intellectually impaired. Perhaps most puzzling, however, is their strikingly uneven profile of cognitive and social strengths and weaknesses. For example, as young children they seem especially preoccupied with the faces of adults and show relatively few social inhibitions, even among strangers (Mervis, 2003).

mutation Sudden change in molecular structure of a gene; may occur spontaneously or be caused by an environmental event such as radiation.

Williams syndrome Dominant genetic disorder involving the deletion of a set of genes, which results in affected individuals' typically having a strong social orientation, good musical ability, and some unusual linguistic capabilities; accompanied by intellectual impairment and severe deficits in numerical and spatial ability.

Courtesy of Williams Syndrome Association

The smiling face of this girl with Williams syndrome epitomizes one of the behavioral characteristics common to such children, a strong orientation to initiating and maintaining social relationships. Their unusual pattern of strengths and weaknesses in various areas of cognition and language as well as their inquisitiveness about other people are of considerable interest to those who study child development. Such observations support the view that some aspects of development may be domain specific rather than more broadly determined by intelligence or personality.

TABLE 3.2 Some Inherited Gene Syndromes

Syndrome	Estimated Frequency (live births in U.S.)	Gene Located on Chromosome	Phenotype, Treatment, and Prognosis
Autosomal Dominant Syndromes			
Huntington Disease	1 in 15,000–30,000 among individuals with a western European heritage; less common in other populations.	4	Personality changes, depression, gradual loss of motor control and memory caused by massive neuronal cell death that often begins in mid-adulthood. Thus affected individuals may transmit the disease to another generation of offspring before becoming aware of the disease. In some individuals, symptoms may begin earlier and be more severe if the dominant gene is transmitted by the father, another example of genomic imprinting.
Marfan Syndrome	About 1 in 5,000	15	Tall, lean, long limbed, with gaunt face (some believe Abraham Lincoln had syndrome). Frequent eye and heart defects. Cardiac failure in young adulthood common. Suicide second most common cause of death. Associated with increased paternal age.
Neurofibromatosis Type I	1 in 3,500	17	Symptoms range from a few pale brown spots on skin to severe tumors affecting peripheral nervous system and distorting appearance. Minimal intellectual deficits in about 40% of cases. Other forms of neurofibromatosis are associated with genes located on other chromosomes.
Williams Syndrome	1 in 20,000	7	See text.

(continued)

TABLE 3.2 Some Inherited Gene Syndromes *(continued)*

Syndrome	Estimated Frequency (live births in U.S.)	Gene Located on Chromosome	Phenotype, Treatment, and Prognosis
Autosomal Dominant Syndromes			
Albinism	About 1 in 20,000 in overall population. Several forms. Most common occurs in about 1 in 15,000 African Americans, 1 in 40,000 Caucasians, but much more frequently among some Native American tribes (1 in 200 among Hopi and Navajo, 1 in 132 among San Blas Indians of Panama).	11 (other forms occur on Chromosomes 5, 9, 15, 16)	Affected individuals lack pigment *melanin*. Extreme sensitivity to sunlight and visual problems.
Cystic Fibrosis	About 1 in 3,000 Caucasians, 1 in 17,000 African-Americans, 1 in 31,000 Asian-Americans	7	Respiratory tract becomes clogged with mucus; lungs likely to become infected. Death often in young adulthood, but individuals may have children. Prognosis for females poorer than for males. Pulmonary therapy to remove mucus accumulation in lungs helps delay effects.
Galactosemia	1 in 60,000	9	Mental retardation, cataracts, cirrhosis of the liver caused by accumulation of galactose in body tissues because of absence of enzyme to convert this sugar to glucose. Heterozygous individuals have half the normal enzyme activity, enough for normal development. Galactose-free diet is only treatment, although many still display learning and behavioral problems.
Gaucher Disease	1 in 600 Ashkenazic Jews. Other, rarer forms found in all populations.	1	Enlarged spleen contributing to pain, cardiac failure, and failure to thrive. Frequent bone fractures, bruising, and bleeding. Limited treatment available.
Phenylketonuria	1 in 10,000–15,000 Causcasian and East Asian newborns; higher frequencies in some ethnic groups (Turks; Irish)	12	See text.
Sickle Cell Disease	About 1 in 500 African Americans; 1 in 1,000–1,400 Hispanic Americans.	11	See text.
Tay-Sachs Disease	1 in 3,600 Ashkenazic Jews.Very rare in other populations.	15	Signs of mental retardation, blindness, deafness, and paralysis begin 1 to 6 months after birth. No treatment available. Death normally occurs by 3 or 4 years of age.
ß–Thalassemia (Cooley's anemia)	1 in 800–3,600 in populations of Greek and Italian descent. Much less frequent in other populations.	11	Severe anemia beginning within 2 to 3 months of birth, stunted growth, increased susceptibility to infections. Death usually occurs in 20s or 30s.
Sex-Linked Syndromes			
Color vision deficiency (red-green)	About 1 in 100 males of Caucasian descent see no red or green. About 1 in 15 Caucasian males experience some decrease in sensitivity to red or green colors. Lower incidence of this deficiency in nearly all other populations.	X	If completely red-green colorblind, lack either green-sensitive or red-sensitive pigment for distinguishing these colors and see them as yellow. If decreased sensitivity to red or green, reds are perceived as reddish browns, bright greens as tan, and olive greens as brown.

(continued)

TABLE 3.2 Some Inherited Gene Syndromes (*continued*)

Syndrome	Estimated Frequency (live births in U.S.)	Gene Located on Chromosome	Phenotype, Treatment, and Prognosis
Sex-Linked Syndromes			
Duchenne Muscular Dystrophy	1 in 3,500–5,000 males. Most common of many different forms of muscular dystrophy. Several forms, including Duchenne, are X linked.	X	Progressive muscle weakness and muscle fiber loss. Mental retardation in about 1/3 of cases. No cure, and few live long enough to reproduce. Responsible gene located on short arm of X chromosome; appears to be massive in number of nucleotide pairs.
Fragile X Syndrome	1 in 4,000 males; 1 in 8,000 females.	X	See text.
Hemophilia A	1 in 4,000 males for hemophilia A; 1 in 20,000 males for another type, hemophilia B.	X	Failure of blood to clot. Several different forms; not all are sex linked. Queen Victoria of England was carrier for the most common form. Potential for bleeding to death, but administration of clot-inducing drugs and blood transfusions reduce hazard.

Sources: Amberger, Hamosh, & McKusick (2001); Genetics Home Reference (2009b). Additional information on these and many other inherited disorders may be found at Genetics Home Reference (2009b), a website provided by the U.S. National Library of Medicine; the Dolan DNA Learning Center (2002), and Medline Plus (2010c), a website provided by the U.S. National Library of Medicine and the National Institutes of Health.

When young, they are also extremely sensitive to certain sounds, such as those made by a drill or vacuum cleaner, or the loud noises produced by fireworks or the bursting of a balloon. Their ability to acquire language is initially slow and may never reach a high level (Marten, Wilson, & Reutens, 2008), and their visual-spatial skills may be especially limited (Mervis & Becerra, 2007). However, some with Williams syndrome display rather uncommon abilities with respect to creating and imitating music (Levitin & Bellugi, 1998). For example, some, after having heard a musical selection only once and regardless of the language in which it may have been sung, are able to reproduce the piece with extraordinary skill. Despite these strengths, children with Williams syndrome show poor planning and problem solving, and limited competence in acquiring numerical skills.

Individuals with Williams syndrome have become of special interest to developmental, cognitive, and social psychologists because of their unusual, and quite uneven, profile of intellectual and behavioral strengths and weaknesses. As is discussed later in this text, many cognitive abilities may be modular; that is, they may undergo relatively specific patterns of development that are distinct from other abilities. The observations of children with Williams syndrome are relevant in suggesting that some genes may have highly targeted consequences for intellectual, social, and other developmental capacities.

Sickle Cell Disease: A Problem Arising out of Adaptive Circumstance **Sickle cell disease** is a genetic disorder whose incidence is extremely high in many regions of West Africa and around the Mediterranean basin. Sickle cell disease is also found in nearly 1 of every 400 African Americans (Genetics Home Reference, 2010b) and in high numbers of Greek Americans and others whose ancestors came from regions in which malaria commonly occurs. The defect introduces a change in a single amino acid in hemoglobin, the molecule that permits the red blood cells to carry oxygen. As a result, red blood cells become crescent shaped rather than round.

Sickle-shaped cells are ineffective in transporting oxygen; they also survive for a much shorter duration than normal red blood cells, and the bone marrow has difficulty replacing them. The consequences are often

sickle cell disease Genetic blood disorder common in regions of Africa and other areas where malaria is found and among descendants of the people of these regions. Abnormal blood cells carry insufficient oxygen.

Individuals who suffer from sickle cell anemia, a genetically inherited disorder, have a large proportion of crescent-shaped red blood cells like the one shown at the bottom left. A normal red blood cell (upper right) is round and doughnut-shaped. Sickle-shaped cells are ineffective in transporting oxygen and may cause damage to various organs and pain by blocking small blood vessels.

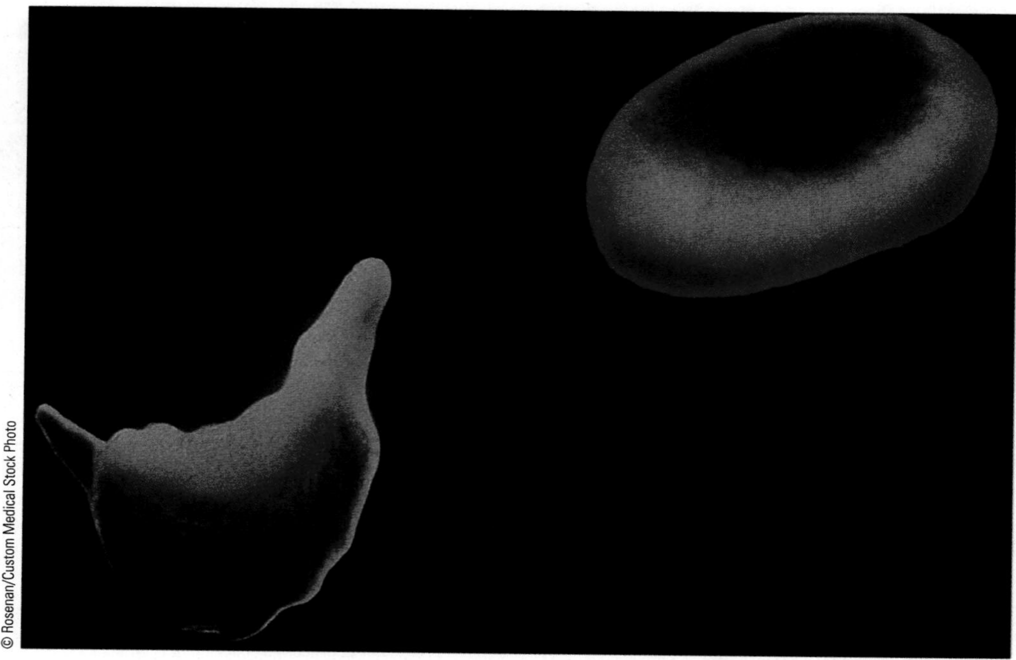

© Rosenan/Custom Medical Stock Photo

RISK | RESILIENCE

anemia, jaundice, low resistance to infection, and susceptibility to stroke, severe pain, and damage to various organs when the distorted cells block small blood vessels. Blood transfusions can help to alleviate the more serious problems. Despite their physical limitations, elementary school children with sickle cell disease appear quite similar to unaffected peers in terms of emotional well-being although they may be at somewhat increased risk for lowered intellectual development because of stroke and reduced oxygen distribution to the brain (Hogan et al., 2006).

About one in every twelve African Americans is a carrier of the sickle cell gene. These individuals, who possess a heterozygous genotype, have the **sickle cell trait**. They manufacture a relatively small proportion of cells with abnormal hemoglobin. Few of these individuals show symptoms of sickle cell disease; most live normal lives. But insufficient oxygen, which may occur in high-altitude regions, when flying in unpressurized airplane cabins, or after strenuous exercise, can trigger sickling of red blood cells in those who have the trait. Nevertheless, carriers of the sickle cell gene are more resistant to malaria than are individuals who have normal hemoglobin—an adaptive feature that accounts for the high incidence and persistence of the trait in regions where malaria is present.

Phenylketonuria: A Genetic Problem Modifiable by Diet **Phenylketonuria (PKU)**, a recessive metabolic disorder, provides a good illustration of how changing the child's cellular environment—in this case, through diet—can reduce a disorder's more harmful consequences. An infant with PKU appears normal at birth. However, intellectual impairment sets in soon thereafter and becomes severe by four years of age if the condition is untreated. The child may also have convulsions, hyperactivity, and other behavioral problems. In this condition, *phenylalanine*, an amino acid in milk and high-protein foods, such as meat, cannot be metabolized normally by the liver. As a result, phenylalanine and other metabolic products accumulate in the blood, and the nervous system becomes deprived of needed nutrients. Fortunately, screening blood samples collected a day or two after birth can detect elevated levels of phenylalanine. An infant identified as having PKU can then be placed on a diet low in phenylalanine to prevent its more serious effects. Experts agree that the diet must be started relatively early, within the first few weeks

sickle cell trait Symptoms shown by those possessing a heterozygous genotype for sickle cell anemia.

phenylketonuria (PKU) Recessive genetic disorder in which phenylalanine, an amino acid, fails to be metabolized. Unless dietary changes are made to reduce intake of phenylalanine, severe intellectual impairment occurs.

after birth, and continued at least through adolescence, to ensure nearly normal mental development (Phenylketonuria, 2000). Here, then, is an excellent example illustrating that genes by themselves do not necessarily cause particular developmental outcomes; environmental factors interact with the genotype to yield a specific phenotype.

NATURE & NURTURE

Even though quality of life and psychological adjustment for children with PKU can be nearly normal (Landolt et al., 2003), they may not be easy to achieve. The diet is difficult to maintain; it requires a careful balance between excessive phenylalanine to prevent damage to the nervous system and maintaining sufficient nutrients for normal development. Weekly blood tests may be necessary to keep metabolite concentrations within an acceptable range, a regimen for which child, parents, and testing centers may be ill prepared. The bland and unappetizing diet can be a source of conflict between child and caregiver as well, creating management problems within households attempting to lead relatively normal lives (Phenylketonuria, 2000).

NATURE & NURTURE

Even under optimal conditions, children with PKU may show some growth and intellectual deficiencies. For example, these children seem to have difficulty in planning and problem-solving tasks in which working memory or sustained attention is required to inhibit well-learned, simpler reactions in order to master new, more complex responses (Christ, Steiner, & Grange, 2006; Diamond et al., 1997). Moreover, individuals with PKU who successfully reach adulthood still need to be concerned about their diet. For example, children born to mothers who continue to display elevated levels of phenylalanine during pregnancy show increased risk for heart defects and intellectual impairment. If a mother returns to a low-phenylalanine diet before or early in her pregnancy, the risks can be reduced substantially (Koch et al., 2003; Widaman, 2009). Although dietary modifications are helpful, it remains unclear whether this intervention completely eliminates some negative consequences of PKU.

RISK | RESILIENCE

Sex-Linked Syndromes As already indicated, only a few dozen genes may be located on the Y chromosome, whereas the X chromosome carries many. This imbalance has substantial implications for a number of phenotypes said to be *sex linked* because the gene associated with them is carried only on the X chromosome. Hemophilia, some forms of red-green color vision deficiency, and Duchenne muscular dystrophy (see Table 3.2) are sex linked because they are inherited via specific genes on the X chromosome. Thus, they occur much more frequently in males than in females.

RISK | RESILIENCE

As with genes for autosomes, those that are sex linked often have a dominant-recessive relationship. Females, who inherit two genes for sex-linked traits, one on each X chromosome, are much less likely to display the deleterious effects associated with an abnormal recessive gene than are males, who, if they inherit the damaging allele, have no second, normal allele to mask its effects. Hemophilia, a condition in which blood does not clot normally, is a good example because it is nearly always associated with a defective gene on the X chromosome. Because the allele for hemophilia is recessive, daughters who inherit it typically do not exhibit this disorder; the condition is averted by an ordinary gene on the second X chromosome that promotes normal blood clotting. A female can, however, be a carrier. If she possesses a heterozygous genotype for hemophilia, the X chromosome with the abnormal allele has a fifty-fifty chance of being transmitted to either her son or her daughter, and, if inherited by a son, the Y chromosome does not contain genetic information to counter the allele's effects. If inherited by a daughter, she will be a carrier who may then transmit it to her sons and daughters, as has occurred in several interrelated royal families of Europe.

RISK | RESILIENCE

Fragile X Syndrome: A Sex-Linked Contributor to Intellectual Impairment Geneticists have identified a structural irregularity that consists of a pinched or constricted site near the end of the long arm of the X chromosome in some individuals (see Figure 3.7). This anomaly, termed **fragile X syndrome**, is now considered to be the most frequently inherited source of intellectual impairment associated with a specific gene for males (Medline Plus, 2010b). Males with fragile X syndrome commonly have a long, narrow face; large or prominent ears; and large testes. Cardiac defects and relaxed ligaments (permitting, for example, hyperextension of finger joints) are also

fragile X syndrome Disorder associated with a pinched region of the X chromosome; a leading genetic cause of intellectual impairment in males.

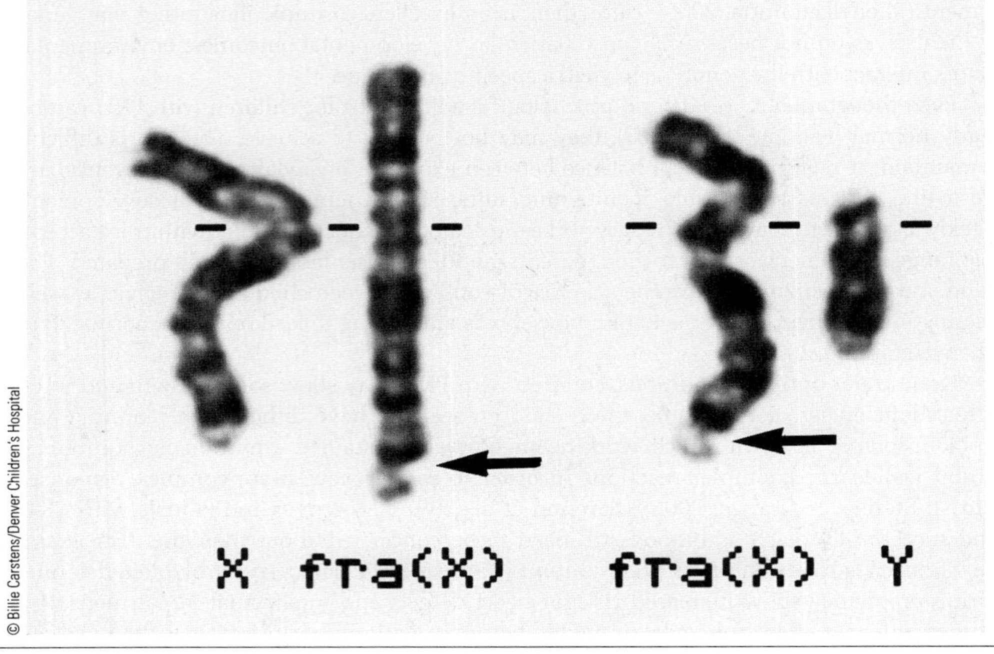

Figure 3.7
Chromosome Illustrating Fragile X Syndrome
Fragile X syndrome is one of the most frequently occurring genetic causes of intellectual impairment. This photomicrograph illustrates the pinched or constricted portion of one of the pair of X chromosomes in a heterozygous female and the X chromosomes in an affected male.

frequent components of the disorder. Behavioral attributes include poor eye contact and limited responsiveness to external stimulation, as well as hand flapping, hand biting, and other unusual mannerisms, such as mimicry. Females who possess a heterozygous genotype often show, to a much lesser extent, some of the physical characteristics of the disorder. Many of these women display a normal or nearly normal level of intelligence, although, as with other sex-linked gene disorders, they are carriers for the syndrome.

An unusual feature of fragile X syndrome is that its severity seems to increase as the abnormal gene is passed on from one generation to the next, a phenomenon termed *anticipation.* This progression begins when one set of three nucleotides, which repeats between 5 and 50 times in the normal gene, for some reason expands to 50 to 200 repetitions. Once this expansion begins, the gene seems to become unstable for subsequent offspring, so that more copies of the three nucleotides are spewed out, as though the replication process has difficulty turning off (Eliez & Reiss, 2000). Inheritance of this unchecked expansion beyond 200 repetitions is accompanied by a spectrum of learning difficulties ranging from mild to severe intellectual impairment. Thus, the size of the abnormal segment of the gene, along with the severity of the disorder, appears to increase as it is passed from a grandfather, in whom the initial amplification may occur (even if he shows no evidence of the disorder), to a daughter (who may be minimally affected because she has an additional X chromosome to compensate for the disorder), to a grandson (who now displays full-blown fragile X syndrome).

Chromosome Variations

Mutations in specific genes are only one of several sources of variation in the human genome. Occasionally, whole sections of a chromosome are deleted, duplicated, or relocated to another chromosome, or an extra chromosome is transmitted to daughter cells during cell division. When this happens, normal development is often disrupted. Perhaps as many as half of all conceptions that result in spontaneous abortion include such chromosomal abnormalities (Lebedev et al., 2004). If the child survives, structural aberrations of the chromosomes are often associated with mental impairment and severe physical deformations.

Human embryonic growth virtually never proceeds when a complete pair or even a member of one pair of autosomes is missing or when an extra pair of autosomes is inherited. **Trisomy**, the inheritance of one extra chromosome, also very often results in the loss of the

© Laura Dwight Photography

This 13-year-old boy with trisomy 21, or Down syndrome, has learned to read. He has made considerable progress in academic subjects as is evident from his contribution to this geography project. By being provided with an enriching environment, many with Down syndrome are able to accomplish levels of skill that permit them to engage in meaningful work and be active members of their community.

zygote or miscarriage in early pregnancy. However, three copies of chromosomes 13, 18, and 21 may be observed in surviving human newborns. Of these, trisomy 21, or Down syndrome, occurs most frequently. Even with this syndrome, however, fewer than 25 percent of conceptions survive to birth (Tolmie & MacFadyen, 2007).

Trisomy 21 (Down Syndrome) Trisomy 21, or **Down syndrome**, is one of the most common genetic causes of intellectual impairment, estimated at about 1 out of every 750 live births (Genetics Home Reference, 2010b). Physically observable features include an epicanthal fold that gives an almond shape to the eye, flattened facial features, poor muscle tone, short stature, and short, broad hands, including an unusual crease of the palm. About 40 percent of infants with Down syndrome have congenital heart defects. Cataracts or other visual impairments, as well as deficiencies in the immune system, are also common. Physical development is slowed compared with normal children. Language and memory abilities, in particular, are likely to be poor compared with children with similar levels of mental development (Vicari, 2006).

The vast majority of babies born with Down syndrome have an extra twenty-first chromosome, and most of these errors originate in egg cells, although some arise from errors during the production of sperm cells (Dolan DNA Learning Center, 2002). About 4 percent of infants with Down syndrome also have a segment of chromosome 21, perhaps as little as its bottom third, shifted to another chromosome. Still another small percentage have chromosomal deviations in only a portion of the body cells. The severity of Down syndrome in these latter individuals seems to be related to the proportion of cells exhibiting trisomy.

The probability of giving birth to an infant with trisomy 21 increases with the age of the mother, as is true for most other forms of trisomy (see Figure 3.8). Although mothers over thirty-five years of age give birth to only about 16 percent of all babies, they bear more than half of infants with Down syndrome. To explain these findings, experts have often proposed an "older egg" hypothesis. According to this view, the ova, which begin the first phases in meiosis even before the mother's own birth, change with age, either due to the passage of time or perhaps because of increased exposure to potentially hazardous biological and environmental conditions. These older egg cells, released during ovulation in the later childbearing years, are then more susceptible to chromosomal errors while undergoing the final steps of meiosis. Other researchers have proposed a "relaxed selection" hypothesis to account for the increased frequency of Down syndrome in

trisomy Inheritance of extra chromosome.

Down syndrome Disorder resulting from extra chromosomal material on pair number twenty-one; associated with intellectual impairment and distinct physical features.

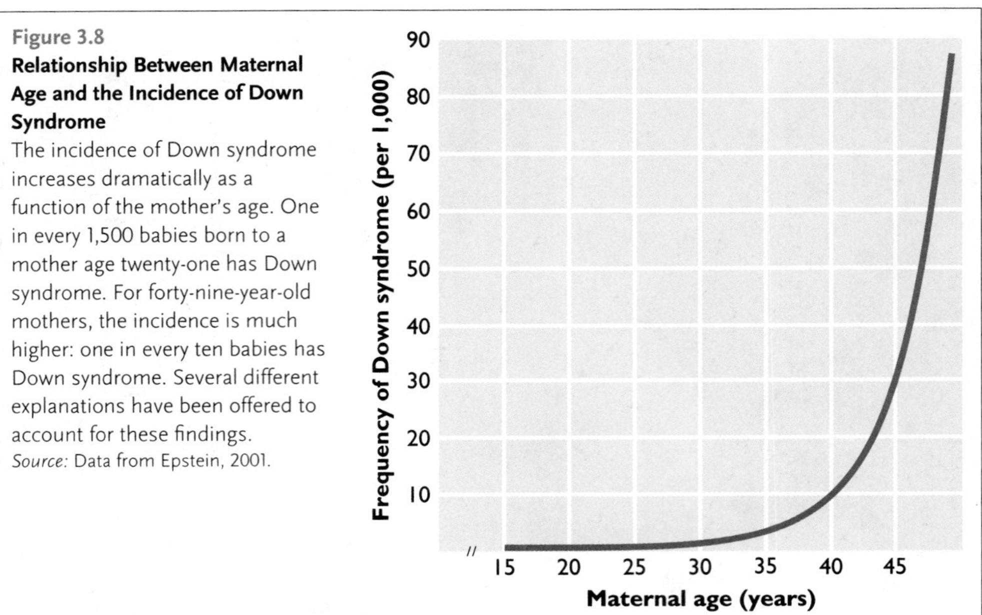

Figure 3.8
Relationship Between Maternal Age and the Incidence of Down Syndrome
The incidence of Down syndrome increases dramatically as a function of the mother's age. One in every 1,500 babies born to a mother age twenty-one has Down syndrome. For forty-nine-year-old mothers, the incidence is much higher: one in every ten babies has Down syndrome. Several different explanations have been offered to account for these findings.
Source: Data from Epstein, 2001.

older mothers. According to this view, older mothers are less likely than younger mothers to spontaneously abort a zygote with trisomy 21. Still another view is that egg cells containing the extra chromosome are unlikely to be selected during ovulation. However, as they become a proportionally larger pool of the available ova over time, the possibility that one is released during ovulation increases (Tolmie, 2002). New research suggests that the age of the father is also a factor in the incidence of Down syndrome. According to an analysis of data from 70,000 births in Denmark, fathers who were age 50 years or older were three times more likely to have a Down syndrome child than fathers age 29 years or younger (Zhu et al., 2005).

NATURE & NURTURE

RISK | RESILIENCE

Thanks to better medical and physical care, the majority of individuals born with Down syndrome may be expected to live more than fifty years (Tolmie, 2002). Many show considerable proficiency in reading and writing. But we still have much to discover about Down syndrome. For example, individuals with trisomy 21 who survive beyond age forty frequently develop the abnormal brain cells and show some of the same behavioral symptoms found in adults who acquire Alzheimer's disease (Miller, 2006). Alzheimer's disease is characterized by memory and speech disturbances, personality changes, and increasing loss of intellectual functioning, typically in individuals between fifty and seventy-five years of age. At least one form of Alzheimer's disease is thought to be inherited, and, not surprisingly, the responsible gene appears to be located on chromosome 21.

Sex Chromosome Syndromes As we have already noted, males normally have an X and a Y sex chromosome, and females have two X chromosomes. However, variations in the number of sex chromosomes as a result of errors during meiosis can occur in humans. For example, an individual may inherit only a single X, an extra chromosome (XXX, XXY, XYY), and, on rare occasions, even pairs of extra chromosomes (for example, XXXX, XXYY, XXXY). Table 3.3 describes several of these variations in more detail.

RISK | RESILIENCE

Although a number of aspects of development may be affected by chromosomal variations in those who do not possess the typical XX or XY complement, many, perhaps even the majority of these individuals, lead normal lives. They may, however, be more vulnerable to disruptive caregiving patterns than children with a normal complement of sex chromosomes. What matters most for individuals put at risk by sex chromosome variations, according to research, is the presence of a stable and supportive family environment that promotes positive development (Bender et al., 1995).

TABLE 3.3 Examples of Observed Sex Chromosome Syndromes

Disorder	Estimated Frequency (live births in U.S.)	Phenotype	Prognosis
45, X (Turner syndrome)	1 in 2,500 females (more than 90% are spontaneously aborted); 80% of cases involve the absence of the paternal X chromosome.	Short stature, usually normal psychomotor development but limited development of secondary sexual characteristics. Failure to menstruate and sterility due to underdeveloped ovaries. About 50% have webbed, short neck. Near-average range of intelligence but serious deficiencies in spatial ability and directional sense.	Increased stature and sexual development, including menstruation, but not fertility, can be induced through administration of estrogen and other hormones. In vitro fertilization permits carrying of child when adult.
47, XXX (Triple-X syndrome)	1 in 1,200 females; 90% have received two copies of maternal X chromosome.	Not generally distinguishable. Some evidence of delay in speech and language development, lack of coordination, poor academic performance, and immature behavior. Sexual development usually normal.Tendency for tall stature.	Many are essentially normal, but substantial proportion have language, cognitive, and social-emotional problems.
47, XXY (Klinefelter syndrome)	1 in 600 males (increased risk among older mothers); 56% received two maternal chromosomes, 44% two paternal sex chromosomes.	Tend to be tall, beardless, with feminine body contour, high-pitched voice. Some evidence for poor auditory short-term memory and difficulty with reading. Testes underdeveloped, individuals usually sterile.	Many with normal IQ, but about 20% may have occasional mild to moderate retardation.
47, XYY (XYY syndrome)	1 in 1,000 males	Above-average height; some have learning disabilities, but near-average range of intelligence.	Most lead normal lives and have offspring with a normal number of chromosomes. Higher proportion than normal incarcerated, but crimes no more violent than those of XY men.

Sources: Graham, Allanson, & Gerritson (2007); Amberger, Hamosh, & McKusick (2001); Genetics Home Reference, 2010b). Additional information on these and many other sex chromosome inherited disorders may be found at Genetics Home Reference (2010b), a website provided by the U.S. National Library of Medicine; the Dolan DNA Learning Center (2002), and Medline Plus (2010c), a website provided by the U.S. National Library of Medicine and the National Institutes of Health.

For Your Review and Reflection

- What is the basis for each of the following genetically influenced disorders?
  Williams syndrome — Sickle cell disease and sickle cell trait
  Phenylketonuria — Fragile X syndrome
- What phenotypes are associated with each? Why is each of interest to developmental scientists?
- What variations in the chromosomal makeup of an individual are possible? What is the most common example of chromosomal trisomy? What are examples of chromosomal variation associated with the sex chromosomes?
- What are factors that may or may not increase risk and resilience in individuals born with genetic disorders?
- If you have had the opportunity to become acquainted with others who possess a genetic disorder, what characteristics have you found to be most remarkable about them?

Genetic Counseling

Advances in detecting gene and chromosomal defects, as well as in understanding the biochemical and metabolic consequences of various inherited disorders, have led to a rapidly expanding medical and guidance specialty called **genetic counseling**. Obtaining a family history to

genetic counseling Medical and counseling specialty concerned with determining and communicating the likelihood that prospective parents will give birth to a baby with a genetic disorder.

summarize the occurrence of various diseases among ancestors and other relatives is usually the first step. If warranted, *parental* **genetic screening** may be carried out. For example, chromosomal abnormalities, as well as dominant and recessive genes associated with all of the disorders listed in Tables 3.2 and 3.3 (and many more not listed in these tables), can be detected through parental screening. Thus, genetic counselors can provide prospective parents with estimates of the likelihood of bearing a child with a specific problem, although parental screening, of course, does not identify new mutations that may arise in offspring. Prospective parents can then use this information to decide whether, for example, adoption or other new reproductive technologies, such as those discussed in Chapter 4, may be a better choice than bearing their own children.

Prenatal Diagnosis

There are many reasons for also carrying out **prenatal diagnostic tests**, tests carried out on the fetus. For example, such testing is often recommended for women who are older than thirty-five because of their increased risk for Down syndrome; when a genetic disorder has been reported in the family history; if parents are members of an ethnic group at risk for a specific genetic disease; or if delayed or unusual development of the fetus occurs during pregnancy (Cuniff & Committee on Genetics, 2004). The finding of a serious inherited disorder may lead to a decision to terminate the pregnancy if religious and ethical values allow such a choice. However, these tests can serve another important purpose: that of suggesting therapy and treatment designed to prevent or minimize the more devastating consequences of some metabolic disorders (Erbe & Levy, 2002).

Prenatal genetic screening procedures can now detect hundreds of genetically and environmentally induced defects in fetal development. Some of these, the prenatal diagnostic tests, provide unequivocal answers about the presence or absence of a problem. Others, often involving less invasive procedures, provide estimates of increased likelihood of the presence of some defect. If they are suggestive of a developmental disability, they may be followed by more conclusive diagnostic tests. One of the best-known definitive tests is **amniocentesis**, in which a small amount of amniotic fluid is withdrawn via a syringe inserted (under the guidance of an ultrasound image) in the woman's abdominal wall. Cells in the amniotic fluid are extracted and submitted to biochemical and chromosomal examination (see Figure 3.9). Amniocentesis is an especially effective procedure for detecting chromosomal variations, and it provides information about some metabolic problems as well. The test is usually performed between the thirteenth and eighteenth weeks of pregnancy and, although some risk to the fetus exists, recent research suggests that it is a relatively safe procedure (Eddleman et al., 2006; Shulman & Elias, 2007).

Another test that provides much the same information as amniocentesis but that can be carried out somewhat earlier in pregnancy (between ten and twelve weeks) is **chorionic villus sampling**. In this diagnostic procedure, a small sample of hairlike projections (*villi*) from the chorion, the outer wall of the membrane in which the fetus develops and that attaches to the woman's uterus, is removed by suction through a thin tube inserted through the vagina and cervix or, in some cases, through the abdominal wall. Information gained at this earlier time can reduce uncertainty and anxiety about the possibility of a developmental disability. However, chorionic villus sampling, in contrast to amniocentesis, does not provide information about possible neural tube defects; the procedure is somewhat more difficult to carry out; and, unless performed by skilled technicians or if performed before the tenth week of pregnancy, there may be a slightly increased risk for miscarriage and other consequences (March of Dimes, 2010a).

In **fetal blood sampling**, blood is withdrawn directly from the umbilical cord of the fetus for

genetic screening Systematic search using a variety of tests to detect the likelihood of increased developmental risk due to genetic or other anomalies.

prenatal diagnostic tests Procedures designed to provide unequivocal answers about the presence or absence of a prenatal problem.

amniocentesis Method of sampling the fluid surrounding the developing fetus through insertion of a needle; used to diagnose fetal genetic and developmental disorders.

chorionic villus sampling Method of sampling fetal chorionic cells; used to diagnose embryonic genetic and developmental disorders.

fetal blood sampling Method of withdrawing blood from the umbilical cord of the fetus; used to diagnose genetic disorders, especially those that affect the blood.

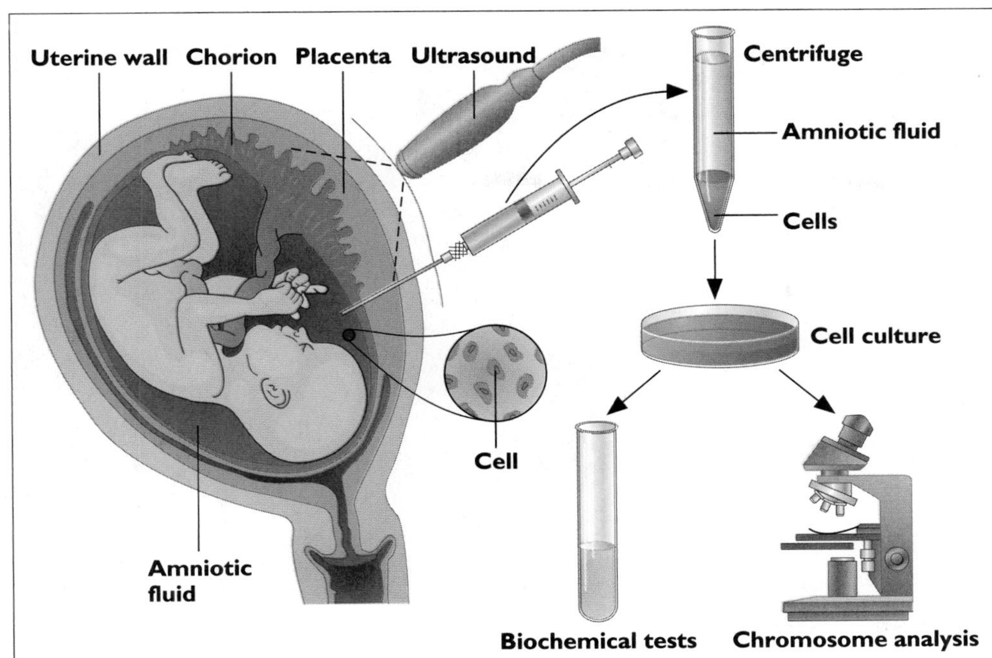

Figure 3.9
The Process of Amniocentesis
In this prenatal screening procedure, a needle is inserted into the amniotic fluid surrounding the fetus. A small amount is withdrawn, and cells shed by the fetus are separated from the fluid by centrifuge. The cells are cultured and submitted to various biochemical and other tests to determine whether chromosomal, genetic, or other developmental defects exist.
Source: Adapted from Knowles, R. V., 1985.

biochemical and chromosomal examination. This particular procedure, normally carried out from about the eighteenth week of pregnancy onward, permits the detection of various chromosomal and genetic errors and is especially useful in evaluating disorders associated with the blood. Although relatively safe, the procedure does need to be performed by specially trained physicians to reduce risk (University of Rochester Medical Center, 2010).

Because of the possible increase in risk and their relatively high cost, amniocentesis, chorionic villus sampling, and fetal blood sampling are normally performed only when there is some reason to believe that fetal abnormalities may occur. Other, less invasive procedures also exist. For example, several types of **maternal blood screening** tests, such as the *alpha fetoprotein test* and the more extensive and accurate *triple screen test,* can be carried out at around fifteen to twenty weeks of gestational age to provide evidence of increased risk for Down syndrome, neural tube defects, and certain kidney and other problems. Scientists have also begun to examine fragments of fetal DNA that circulate in the mother's bloodstream for indicators of genetic problems (South, Chen, & Brothman, 2008).

Certainly the most widespread of the noninvasive diagnostic procedures is **ultrasonography**, often called *ultrasound.* Ultrasound is now used routinely in many countries to help determine whether fetal growth is proceeding normally. Sound waves, reflecting at different rates from tissues of varying density, are represented on video monitors and often printed to form a picture of the fetus. The picture can reveal such problems as microcephaly (small head size), cardiac malformations, cleft lip and palate, and other physical disabilities (Gressens & Hüppe, 2007). In combination with a blood test, ultrasonography can be used to detect Down syndrome as early as eleven weeks prenatally (Malone et al., 2005).

Ultrasonography is also widely used to assist in carrying out other prenatal diagnostic tests, to verify the age of the fetus (interpretation of maternal and fetal blood tests is often highly dependent on an accurate assessment of age), and to monitor lifesaving operations that may on rare occasions be performed on the fetus within the womb (Harrison, 1996). Although limited in its use as a diagnostic tool, ultrasound has become a popular means of informing specialists and parents about the course of prenatal development.

maternal blood screening Tests performed on a woman's blood to determine whether the fetus she is carrying has an increased risk for some types of chromosomal and metabolic disorders.

ultrasonography Method of using sound wave reflections to obtain a representation of the developing fetus; used to estimate gestational age and detect fetal physical abnormalities.

The use of ultrasound to provide a visual image of the developing fetus has become a common practice in medical facilities around the world. Prospective parents are often thrilled by this opportunity to obtain a glimpse of the fetus. The use of ultrasound can also be important for obtaining a more accurate assessment of the age of the fetus. It provides assistance in carrying out other tests to determine if development is proceeding normally and, in some cases, permits surgical procedures designed to improve the likelihood of a healthy newborn.

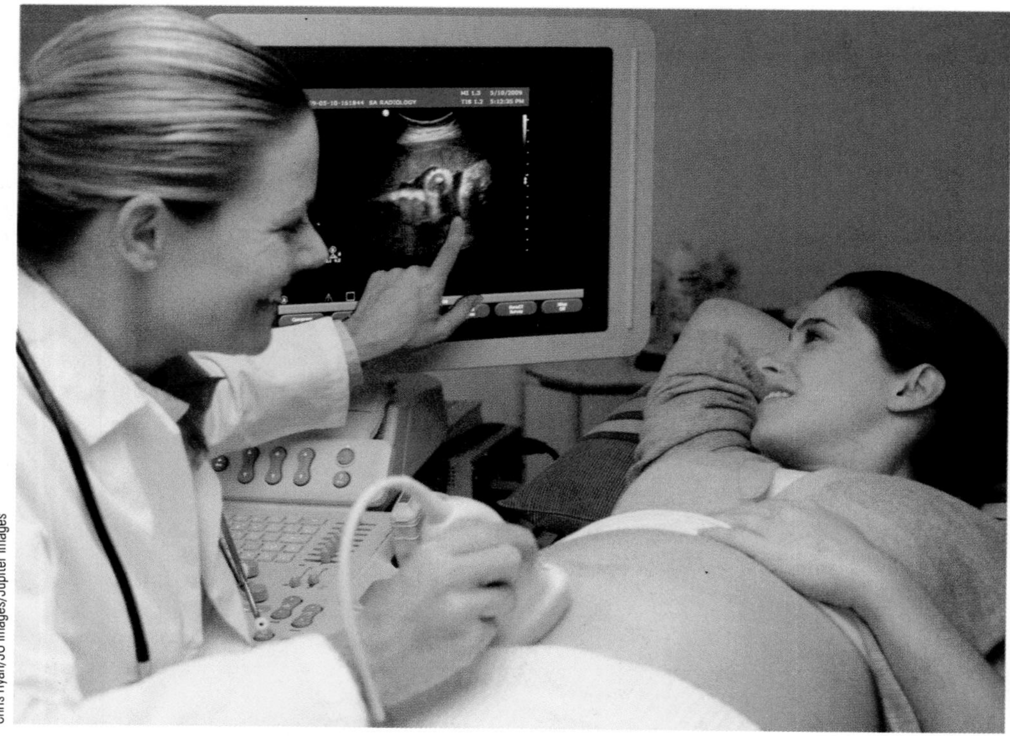

Chris Ryan/JO Images/Jupiter Images

Ethical and Social Issues

The major prenatal diagnostic tests are summarized in Table 3.4. Though they offer important information, their availability also raises a number of ethical and social issues. Note, for example, that many of these tests are carried out relatively late in pregnancy, and prospective parents may have to wait several weeks longer before they learn the results. This waiting period can create enormous apprehension, especially among those who have reason to believe that a problem may exist. Moreover, some expectant women feel almost coerced into using these technological advances to learn more about their pregnancies even when there is little to suggest a genetic problem (Henifin, 1993; Wertz & Fletcher, 1993).

TABLE 3.4 Prenatal Screening Tests

Prenatal Test	When Usually Administered (gestational age)	Typical Waiting Period for Results	Other Comments
Amniocentesis	13–18 weeks	About 2 weeks	Can be administered in weeks 11–14 but normally is not because the available supply of amniotic fluid is more limited.
Chorionic villus sampling	10–12 weeks	24–48 hours	Possibly a slightly greater risk than associated with amniocentesis, including limb deformities.
Fetal blood sampling	18 weeks or later	24–48 hours	Possibly somewhat greater risk than associated with amniocentesis.
Maternal blood screening	15–20 weeks	One week	Not definitive but provides information about increased risk for Down syndrome, and neural tube and some metabolic defects.
Ultrasonography	About 6 weeks and later	None	Provides picture of growing fetus. Not definitive for identifying many disorders. Little evidence of any risk. Often used to accompany other test procedures.

Some would say these tests are overused. Yet a physician who fails to at least offer prenatal diagnosis in circumstances in which it can be informative runs legal risks for incompetent obstetric practice (Wertz & Fletcher, 1998).

In many cases, those about to become parents would like to know about possible problems, if for no other reason than to effectively prepare for and address them even before birth. In fact, a substantial number of expectant women who learn that the fetus carries some abnormality still elect to continue the pregnancy, especially if the problem is less severe and possibilities exist for prenatal or postnatal therapy (Pride et al., 1993). Yet another issue concerns access to the results of these tests. For example, might insurance companies or other health organizations drop coverage if they become aware of results that indicate expensive medical treatment in the future? What about employers who might choose to hire on the basis of fewer health risks, as, for example, when genetic information hints at greater susceptibility to major diseases, such as cancer, diabetes, or heart disease, that could affect an individual's subsequent employment? And then there is the issue of sex preselection.

what do you think? Should Sex Preselection Be Permitted?

At one time in medieval Germany, couples placed a hammer under their bed if they wished to conceive a boy; in Denmark, they chose a pair of scissors for that location if they desired a girl (Golden, 1998). In China and India, where abortion is more widely practiced, evidence already exists that sex selection has been exercised; a disproportionate number of males have been born in these countries in recent years. As a consequence, China and India, as well as some other countries, have passed laws forbidding the use of prenatal tests solely to determine the sex of the fetus and to influence the course of pregnancy when the fetus is male or female (Wertz & Fletcher, 1998).

Although many adamantly oppose the use of a procedure that leads to the selective abortion of a healthy fetus on the basis of sex, what do you think about *preselection*, the effort to tilt the probability toward having either a male or a female conception? Previous preselection efforts focused on the timing or technique involved in procreation to increase conception of a male or female. These attempts have generally failed to provide a reliable method of conceiving a boy or a girl. However, in vitro fertilization (see Chapter 4) and other procedures could increase the likelihood of conception of a male or female (Fackelmann, 1998). For example, a difference exists in the amount of DNA found in the X and Y chromosomes. With the help of a dye that attaches to the DNA and glows when exposed to the light of a laser, sperm cells carrying an X chromosome shine more brightly because they contain about 2.8 percent more DNA than sperm cells carrying a Y chromosome. By introducing lopsided distributions of cells carrying the X chromosome into the uterus during periods when a woman might become pregnant, markedly higher numbers of successful pregnancies resulting in girls, or boys, might be expected. If you had a child, would you have a preference for a girl or a boy? To what extent do preferences for boys versus girls exist in your community? What social and cultural factors promote such a preference?

Parents in most Western countries do not show a strong preference for having a boy or a girl as their first child; but family balancing, having one boy and one girl, is frequently seen as the ideal family complement (Silver, 1998). Do you think that having children of both sexes is more desirable than having two boys or two girls? What about if you are a carrier for a sex-linked genetic disease? Might that change your views about sex preselection?

Do you think there is the possibility that sex preselection might be only a beginning step in the emergence of a "preference mentality"? Could this kind of mentality ultimately lead to an increased effort to develop procedures to preselect offspring on the basis of other desired traits and attributes intended to create "perfect" or "designer" children? Are we then treating children as a commodity, as some wrestling with this issue have proposed (Darnovsky, 2004)? Are we raising the possibility of potential discrimination against those who do not meet the ethnic, cultural, or community ideal? What kind of research might be carried out to begin to address these questions?

For Your Review and Reflection

- What are the major diagnostic tests for prenatal development? What are their limitations and their advantages?
- How do you think a photo of the fetus from an ultrasound might influence a prospective mother's perceptions about being pregnant? What about the prospective father's perceptions?
- What ethical and social issues emerge from the use of prenatal diagnostic tests?
- How might diagnostic tests increase risk or be used to enhance resilience?
- What is sex preselection, and what are arguments for and against its practice?

Developmental and Behavioral Genetics

NATURE & NURTURE

As our previous discussion indicates, chromosomal errors and particular genes can have drastic, often devastating, effects on physical, intellectual, and social development. Yet similarities observed among relatives—the wry sense of humor in a mother and daughter or the musical talent of a grandfather and his grandchildren—as well as many disorders are not likely to be linked to a single, isolated gene. Might these attributes and behaviors reflect a contribution from many genes? If so, how might genes have these effects and how important are the experiences shared by kin? Researchers engaged in **behavior genetics** attempt to learn to what extent the diversity of human traits, abilities, and behaviors is influenced by combinations of genes and by experience. Behavioral geneticists are helping to show that the entire realm of human behavior is influenced by nature and nurture and in complex, sometimes surprising, ways.

The Methods of Behavioral Geneticists

Behavior geneticists have available to them a number of different methods. One goal of many of these studies has been to provide an estimate of the heritability of various traits and behaviors. **Heritability** refers to the extent to which the variability in a sample of individuals on some characteristic, such as shyness or assertiveness, is a result of genetic differences among those individuals. Of course, the variability that is not accounted for by heritability may then be a result of the environmental circumstances those individuals have experienced. Thus, although research on heritability was initially designed to provide answers about the contribution of the genotype, it also helps to shed light on the role of experience in development (Plomin & Davis, 2009). It is important to keep in mind, however, that interpreting the degree of heritability of any particular phenotype is fraught with many problems, not only because of potential epigenetic influences, but also because of other difficulties that will become more apparent as we discuss the different methods used by behavior geneticists.

Selective Breeding Studies When studying the fruit fly or the mouse, behavior geneticists can use *selective breeding* experiments to learn whether certain phenotypic expressions can be increased or decreased in offspring. Members of a species that display a specific attribute are bred to each other, usually over many generations. If the attribute is inherited, subsequent generations of offspring can be expected to display it more and more frequently or strongly. For example, after thirty generations of selective breeding in which either highly active mice were bred only to each other or mice showing only a low level of activity were bred to each other, researchers observed no overlap in terms of the amount of activity displayed by members of the two groups (DeFries, Gervais, & Thomas, 1978). Those bred for high activity were thirty times more active; they would run the equivalent of 100 yards during

behavior genetics Study of how characteristics and behaviors of individuals, such as intelligence and personality, are influenced by the interaction between genotype and experience.

heritability Proportion of variability in the phenotype that is estimated to be accounted for by genetic influences within a known environmental range.

two three-minute test periods compared with the other mice, which would not even run one-tenth of that distance (Plomin et al., 2001). Selective breeding in various species of animals has revealed genetic contributions to many different attributes, including aggressiveness, emotionality, maze learning, and sex drive.

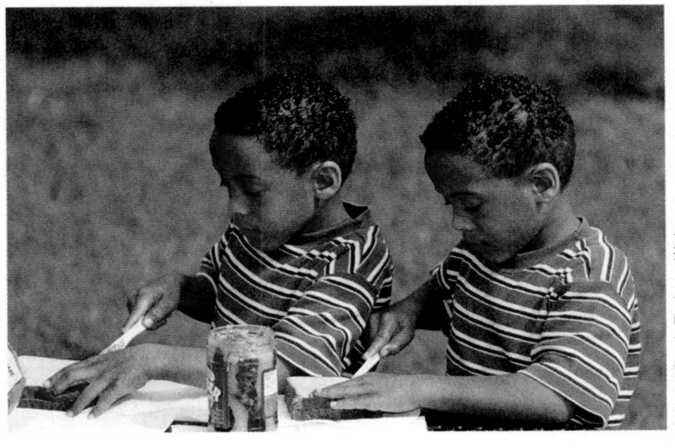

© Rachel Epstein/The Image Works

If you were given their names, would you be able to tell these twins apart once they moved and were no longer seated side by side? Virtually everyone would have a great deal of difficulty with such an assignment unless they could constantly keep an eye on at least one of them as he moved about. Because their genetic makeup is the same, identical or monozygotic twins typically look very much alike and display very similar traits and behaviors, as can be seen here. Twin studies provide important information about the contributions of heredity and environment to development.

Family Resemblance Studies Behavior geneticists gain information about hereditary and environmental influences on human behavior by examining resemblances among family members. These studies investigate similarities among *identical* and *fraternal twins*, siblings, and other members of families who are genetically different from one another to varying degrees. **Identical (monozygotic) twins** come from the same zygote: a single egg fertilized by a single sperm. A cell division early in development creates two separate embryos from this zygote, and the twins are genetically identical. **Fraternal (dizygotic) twins** come from two different zygotes, each created from a separate egg and a separate sperm. Fraternal twins are no more genetically similar than siblings born at different times, each averaging about half of their genes in common. However, they do share some of their prenatal environment and, by virtue of being the same age, may share other experiences to a greater extent than siblings born at different times.

If identical twins resemble each other more than fraternal twins in intelligence or shyness, one potential explanation for this similarity is their common genotype. The degree of resemblance is usually estimated from one of two statistical measures: concordance rate or correlation coefficient. The **concordance rate** is the percentage of pairs of twins in which both members display a specific attribute when one twin is identified as possessing it. Concordance rate is used when measuring characteristics that are either present or absent, such as schizophrenia or depression. If both members of every twin pair have a particular trait, the concordance rate will be 100 percent. If only one member of every pair of twins has some particular trait and the other does not, the concordance rate will be 0 percent. When attributes vary on a continuous scale, such that they can be measured in terms of amount or degree, resemblances are estimated from a *correlation coefficient*. This statistic helps to determine whether variables such as intelligence or shyness, which have some quantitative value, are more similar for identical than for fraternal twins or more similar among siblings than among unrelated children.

Adoption Studies Identical twins may resemble each other more than fraternal twins because identical twins share the same genotype. However, another explanation for any greater resemblance may be that identical twins share more similar experiences. One way to potentially reduce the effects of similarity in experience is to study biologically related family members who have been adopted or reared apart from each other. If an attribute is influenced by genetic factors, children should still resemble their biological siblings, parents, or other family members more than their adoptive relatives. On the other hand, if the environment is the primary determinant of an attribute, separated children can be expected to resemble their adoptive parents or other adopted siblings more closely than their biological parents or siblings.

Adoption studies, just as in the case of twin studies, pose many challenges for evaluating hereditary and environmental influences (Richardson & Norgate, 2006). For example, in the past, adopted children were often placed in a home similar to that of their biological parents. Under these circumstances, the relative contributions of family environment and heredity to an attribute are extremely difficult to distinguish. In addition, information on the biological family has not always been readily available in the case of adoption. Nevertheless, a number of large-scale and long-term investigations of genotype-environment effects involving

identical (monozygotic) twins Two individuals who originate from a single zygote (one egg fertilized by one sperm), which early in cell division separates to form two separate cell masses.

fraternal (dizygotic) twins Siblings who share the same womb at the same time but originate from two different eggs fertilized by two different sperm cells.

concordance rate Percentage of pairs of twins in which both members have a specific trait identified in one twin.

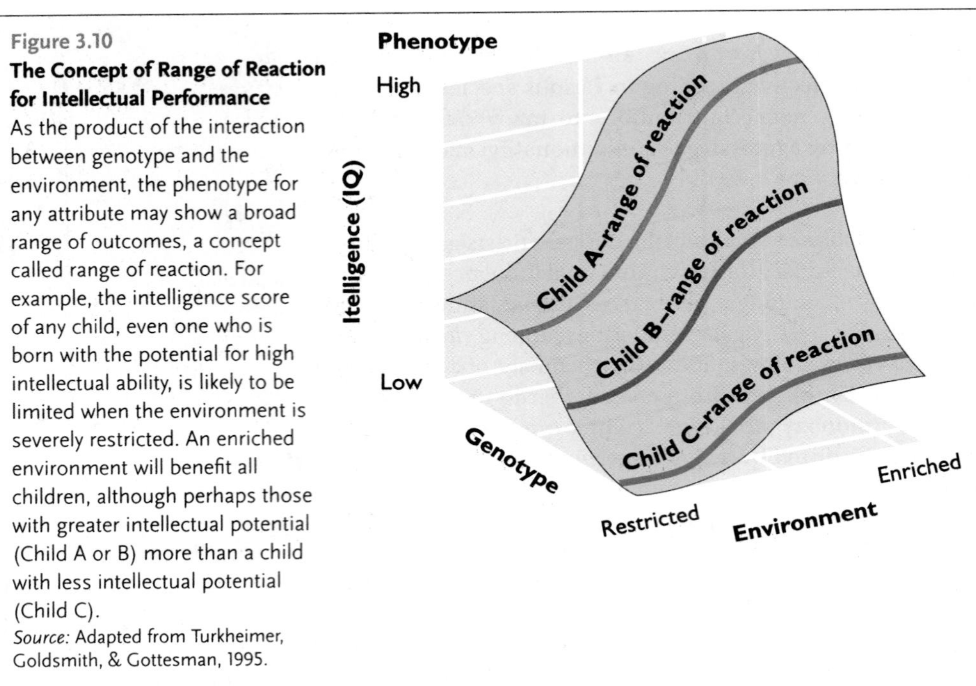

Figure 3.10
The Concept of Range of Reaction for Intellectual Performance
As the product of the interaction between genotype and the environment, the phenotype for any attribute may show a broad range of outcomes, a concept called range of reaction. For example, the intelligence score of any child, even one who is born with the potential for high intellectual ability, is likely to be limited when the environment is severely restricted. An enriched environment will benefit all children, although perhaps those with greater intellectual potential (Child A or B) more than a child with less intellectual potential (Child C).
Source: Adapted from Turkheimer, Goldsmith, & Gottesman, 1995.

twins, adopted children, siblings, half-siblings, and unrelated children in blended families have helped to shed light on the complex interactions and correlations that exist between heredity and experience (e.g., Boomsma, Busjahn, & Peltonen, 2002; Bouchard, 1997; Neiderhiser, Reiss, & Hetherington, 2007; Plomin, DeFries, & Fulker, 1988). For example, the Nonshared Environment in Adolescent Development (NEAD) project has been carrying out research involving hundreds of sets of adolescent twins and siblings as well as their parents to help understand genetic and family influences on adolescent adjustment (Neiderhiser et al., 2007). As an illustration of one of the many findings obtained from this longitudinal program, researchers found that, although depressive symptoms in adolescents showed a moderate genetic influence, environmental influences were the primary contributors to displays of extreme scores on depression (Rende et al., 1993).

Conceptualizing the Interaction Between Genotype and Environment

How a genotype influences development depends to a great extent on the environment. Likewise, how an environment affects behavior often depends on the genotype. These conditional relationships are the basis for complex *interactions* between heredity and experience; the influence of one on the other is not constant across individuals or environmental circumstances, or even during different periods of development (Balaban, 2006; Rutter & Silberg, 2002).

NATURE & NURTURE

Range of Reaction One component of the interactive relationship between genotype and environment can be conceptualized in terms of the concept of **range of reaction**, the idea that, depending on environmental conditions, a broad range of phenotypes may be expressed as a function of the genotype (Turkheimer, Goldsmith, & Gottesman, 1995). Figure 3.10 illustrates this concept for intellectual performance. Consider a child with Down syndrome (represented, for example, by Child C in Figure 3.10). Transferring this child from an unstimulating institutional setting (a restricted environment) and engaging him in supportive learning activities (more enriched environments) very likely will help him to achieve a much higher level of cognitive functioning (Feuerstein, Rand, & Rynders, 1988). The performances of

range of reaction Range of phenotypic differences possible as a result of different environments' interacting with a specific genotype.

children with other genotypes (as represented by Child A and Child B in Figure 3.10) can be affected, too, perhaps even more greatly, depending on whether they are reared in deprived or stimulating conditions. Yet we need to be cautious in considering the concept of range of reaction. The concept reflects only what we presently know about the way genotypes are expressed in environments familiar to us. For example, some day, when the ways in which trisomy 21 affects proteins essential to neural events are more fully understood, an environment may be fashioned to allow far higher levels of intelligent behavior in children with Down syndrome. Moreover, it is possible that some kinds of environments may prove to be relatively enriching for individuals with one level or form of a genotype but restrictive for individuals with another level or form of the genotype (Gottlieb, 2007).

Canalization The principle of **canalization**, a kind of "channeling" of development, suggests yet another way to think about genotype-environment relationships. A highly canalized attribute is one influenced primarily by the genotype; experiential factors can have an impact on the course of development, but only under extreme conditions (Waddington, 1971). For example, various aspects of early motor development such as the age at which infants begin to walk tend to emerge on a fairly regular basis during infancy. Presumably the genotype has carved a relatively deep course for their appearance. However, as you will soon learn, the emergence of early motor skills is not completely protected from disturbances in experience. Other aspects of early development, including some aspects of language acquisition and certain social behaviors, such as smiling, may also be highly canalized.

Gilbert Gottlieb (1991) has extended these ideas, proposing that the channeling process may come about not only through the genotype but also from early experiential influences. Exposure to certain types of stimulation during a critical period may steer development just as hereditary information can. As an example, Gottlieb looked at the early experiences of mallard ducklings. If prevented from hearing their own vocalizations and instead exposed to a chicken's call early in development, the ducklings later showed a preference for the chicken's call rather than for sounds produced by members of their own species.

As we have already learned, the genome itself is not isolated from the influences of the environment (Lickliter & Honeycutt, 2003). A classic example is evident in some reptiles—the temperature during incubation determines the sex of the offspring, a feature you might have thought was determined solely by genetics. As researchers learn more about the genotype, they have discovered many ways in which events taking place at cellular, neural, and broader physical and social levels can affect how the transcription and translation process takes place and may even change genetic mechanisms and gene expression themselves. In other words, we are beginning to more fully appreciate that development is epigenetic, that is, the outcome of bidirectional, multiple interactive genetic and environmental factors.

Conceptualizing the Correlation Between Genotype and Environment

NATURE & NURTURE

The task of determining how various traits derive from complex interactions between the genes and from the environment is laden with additional difficulties. Not only do genotype and environment interact, but they are also linked or *correlated* with each other in several ways (Moffitt, Caspi, & Rutter, 2005; Plomin et al., 2008; Reiss, 2005; Rutter, 2006; Scarr, 1992)

Passive Links One correlation between genotype and experience arises from the tendency for parents to establish a child-rearing environment in harmony with their own interests and preferences. Assume, for example, that sociability has some genetic basis. Sociable parents may transmit this orientation to their children through genes, via the social environment created in their home, or through both mechanisms. This kind of correlation between genotype and environment is labeled as *passive*, because it has been created for the child by the parents.

canalization Concept that the development of some attributes is governed primarily by the genotype and that only extreme environmental conditions will alter the phenotypic pattern for these attributes.

In most families, the correlation between the genetic and environmental components of child rearing is likely to be positive; that is, the environment will contain features that support and complement the child's genetic potential. But a negative correlation is also possible, as in cases in which parents elect to rear their children in ways that depart from their own backgrounds and genetic propensities. A parent who feels he or she was too shy during childhood and, as a consequence, missed out on many social opportunities may actively initiate play groups and other projects designed to promote sociability in a child.

Evocative Links Another type of correlation between genotype and environment, termed *evocative* or *reactive*, occurs when aspects of the environment, particularly other people, support or encourage behaviors that may have a genetic component; that is, other people's behavior occurs in response to or is evoked by the child's genotype. For example, an active preschooler is likely to prompt teachers to provide large-muscle toys to dissipate some of her energy. A ten-year-old's eagerness to read may encourage a teacher to offer additional opportunities for learning. A sociable child is more likely to attract the attention of peers than a shy or passive child. Thus, attributes that have a biological basis are likely to evoke patterns of behavior from others that complement the child's genetic tendencies. As an interesting demonstration of this effect, Thomas O'Connor and his colleagues (1998) examined whether children adopted shortly after birth, but whose biological parents had reported a history of antisocial behavior, would influence the way the adoptive parents treated their adopted children. In particular, would the adoptive parents engage in more negative interactions with these children than the adoptive parents of children whose biological parents did not report a history of antisocial behavior? Indeed, this was the finding, suggesting that something about the genotype inherited by the child was evoking more negative reactions from the adoptive parents. These children were, in fact, reported to engage in more antisocial behavior, thus perhaps drawing out the more negative reactions from their adoptive parents. However, we should also emphasize that other environmental factors, still unknown to these researchers, also seemed to play a role in increased negative parental reactions in some families.

Active, Niche-Picking Links In yet another type of correlation between genotype and environment, termed *active*, the child may be attracted by and eagerly seek out experiences more compatible with his or her genotype. Children who like music or science or art could prefer to engage in those activities with peers who have those same interests. The athletic

Jose Luis Pelaez Inc/Blend Images/Jupiter Images

Niche picking, the tendency for an individual to seek out and become attracted to activities that are compatible with his or her genotype, is an important aspect of the interaction between nature and nurture. Because of her interest in painting, this young person may be drawn to a future career or avocation involving art. She is also likely to pursue additional training and opportunities to become even more skilled as an artist.

child may find little pleasure in practicing the piano but spend countless hours skateboarding and playing basketball with others having the same preferences. Thus, any genetic basis for various traits and activities influences the kind of environment a child attempts to create and experience. Sandra Scarr and Kathleen McCartney (1983) described this kind of linkage as **niche picking**, to emphasize that children and adults selectively construct and engage environments responsive to their genetic orientations.

Scarr and McCartney (1983; Scarr, 1992) believe that the strength of passive, evocative, and active correlations between genotype and environment changes with development. The experiences infants receive are often determined for them by their caregivers. Thus, initial correlations between genotype and environment are more likely to be influenced by passive factors. As children gain greater independence and control of their environment, however, others around them are likely to notice and support their individual differences, and niche picking becomes an increasingly important possibility as children have the opportunity to choose their own interests and activities.

An important implication of these changing relationships is that children within the same family may become less similar to one another as they grow older and become freer of the common environment their parents provide. Older siblings can select niches befitting their individual genotypes more easily than can younger children. When Sandra Scarr and Richard Weinberg (1977) studied adopted children, they obtained support for this prediction. During early and middle childhood, adopted but biologically unrelated children in the same family showed similarities in intelligence, personality, and other traits. Perhaps these resemblances came about both as a result of adoption procedures that encouraged the placement of children in homes somewhat like their biological home and from the common family environment the adopted children now shared. As adopted siblings neared the end of adolescence, however, they no longer exhibited similarities in intelligence, personality, or other traits; the passive influence of the common environment established by the adoptive parents had become supplanted by active niche picking.

The notion of niche picking provides us with an even more startling prediction. When identical twins are reared apart, they may, with increasing age, actually come to resemble each other more, and perhaps as much as identical twins reared together! This greater correspondence could emerge as others react to their similar behaviors and as opportunities arise for the twins to make more choices. Some studies support this prediction. For example, pairs of identical twins, separated as infants and having no interactions with each other until well into adulthood, have sometimes shown remarkable similarities not only in gait, posture, gestures, and such habits as straightening eyeglasses, but also in storytelling skill, spontaneous giggling, phobic tendencies, hobbies, and interests, resemblances rarely observed between fraternal twins reared apart and usually not considered to have a strong genetic basis (Bouchard, 1984; Lykken et al., 1992). Furthermore, identical twins reared apart showed as high a correlation on many intellectual tasks and personality variables as those reared together. These results suggest that niche picking can be a powerful means of maintaining behaviors supported by the genotype.

Hereditary and Environmental Influences on Behavior

NATURE & NURTURE

Research findings involving studies of family resemblances, adopted children, and identical and fraternal twins can be, and often are, interpreted in many different ways precisely because of the complex interactions and relationships that genotype and environment share in shaping behavior. These interpretations sometimes have powerful implications for intervention and social policy (Baumrind, 1993; Jackson, 1993; Scarr, 1992, 1993). Should families or communities, for example, expend resources for educational and mental health efforts if a substantial biological basis for behavior exists? Or does this kind of question, concerned with *how much* heredity contributes to variations in the human phenotype, fail to recognize that educational and social opportunities are essential to maximize competencies, even where genetic contributions are considerable?

niche picking Tendency to actively select an environment compatible with a genotype.

Consider the following: About 90 percent of the variability in height among individuals is believed to be a consequence of genetic factors. However, the difference in the average height of North and South Koreans is a full 6 inches even though they essentially have the same hereditary background (Pak, 2004; Schwekendiek, 2008). Clearly, changes in the environment have had a profound impact on a characteristic that receives a significant contribution from genes. Environmental factors can surely be expected to have an impact on other inherited characteristics as well. In fact, environmental influences frequently account for *more* of the variability in human behavior than does the genotype (Plomin & Davis, 2009).

Intellectual Abilities Despite their many limitations, most studies have relied on IQ tests when attempting to measure the contributions of genotype and environment to intellectual abilities. Table 3.5 summarizes correlations on IQ test scores among individuals who share different genetic relationships with one another. Environmental influences are revealed by findings that individuals reared together show somewhat higher correlations for intelligence scores than those with the same genetic relationship reared apart. Nevertheless, the impact of the genotype on intelligence is also evident. The correlations for IQ increase as the similarity in genotypes rises.

We can make sense of several additional findings by considering correlations between genotype and environment. For example, IQ scores for younger adopted children reared together are positively correlated (about 0.20), as indicated in Table 3.5. However, they are much closer to 0.00 for adolescents. Moreover, intelligence has been found to be highly correlated in infancy and early childhood for *both* identical and fraternal twins and, with increasing age, to become *even greater* for identical twins but to decline to the level reported in Table 3.5 for fraternal (dizygotic) twins (Fischbein, 1981; Wilson, 1986). These findings probably reflect the impact of passive links (the similar rearing environment created by the parents) on intelligence early in childhood and more opportunity for niche picking later in development.

NATURE & NURTURE

Identical twins, however, do not always become more similar as they grow older. As twins who have been reared together become older, fraternal, and to some extent identical, twins become more dissimilar on many aspects of intelligence tests (McCartney, Harris, & Bernieri, 1990). Perhaps they, too, actively attempt to establish a *unique* niche in the family and community, efforts that may also be encouraged by parents of the twins (Schachter, 1982).

TABLE 3.5 Correlation in IQ as a Function of Genetically Related and Unrelated Individuals Living Together and Apart

Relationship	Raised	Observed
Monozygotic twins	Together	0.85
Monozygotic twins	Apart	0.74
Dizygotic twins	Together	0.59
Siblings	Together	0.46
Siblings	Apart	0.24
Midparent/child	Together	0.50
Single parent/child	Together	0.41
Single parent/child	Apart	0.24
Adopting parent/child	Together	0.20

Note: The data are based on a meta-analysis of 212 IQ correlations reported in various studies. In the case of twins and siblings, the heritability estimates are increased by an unspecified amount because of the common environmental contribution from the prenatal environment shared simultaneously by twins and sequentially by siblings. "Midparent" refers to the mean of the IQ scores of both parents.

Source: From Daniels, M., Devlin, B., & Roeder, K. (1997). Of genes and IQ. In B. Devlin, S. E. Feinberg, D. P. Resnick, & K. Roeder (Eds.), *Intelligence, genes, and success: Scientists respond to* The Bell Curve (pp. 45–70). New York: Springer–Verlag.

Despite the evidence that the heritability of intelligence is high, a classic investigation by Marie Skodak and Harold Skeels (1949) illustrates the substantial impact experience still has. One hundred children born to mentally retarded mothers, most of whom were from low socioeconomic backgrounds, were adopted before six months of age into homes that were economically and educationally well above average. These children displayed above-average intelligence throughout childhood and adolescence, and substantially higher IQs than their biological parents, an outcome reflecting the contribution of environmental factors. Nevertheless, the children's IQs were still correlated with those of their biological mothers, indicating hereditary influences on these scores as well.

More recent studies concerned with the genetic contributions to intellectual development focus on identifying locations of the many genes that affect brain development including, for example, the emerging neural networks underlying attention (Posner, Rothbart, & Sheese, 2007; Posthuma & de Gues, 2006). In addition, the effects of epigenetic influences on DNA clearly have implications for learning and memory. For example, silencing of some genes by certain types of chemical events triggered by fearful experiences has been shown to impair memory consolidation in rodents (Miller & Sweatt, 2007). These kinds of research efforts promise to yield new insights having important practical educational implications for learning, reading, and many other cognitive activities. However, the complexity of gene-environment interactions and their correlations make this research extremely challenging with respect to untangling the roles genotype and environment play in promoting intellectual development (Pennington et al., 2009).

Temperament and Personality Genetic influences are assumed to account for 20 to 50 percent of the variability in personality differences within a population (Bouchard, 2004; Plomin et al, 2008). **Temperament**, an early-appearing constellation of personality traits, has often been of interest in terms of possible genetic influences. A number of broad qualities characterize temperament. One of these is *sociability*, the tendency to be shy or inhibited and somewhat fearful of new experiences versus outgoing and uninhibited, characteristics that are likely precursors to introversion and extroversion, respectively, in older children and adults. Another trait is *emotionality*, the ease with which an individual becomes distressed, upset, or angry and the intensity with which these emotions are expressed. A third trait is *activity*, as evidenced by the tempo and vigor with which behaviors are performed. Identical twins consistently show higher correlations on these characteristics (typically between 0.40 and 0.60) than fraternal twins (typically between 0.10 and 0.30), suggesting an inherited component (Emde et al., 1992; Goldsmith, Buss, & Lemery, 1997; Robinson et al., 1992). Perhaps inherited differences in physiological reactivity underlie these differences. For example, with respect to sociability, young children who remain aloof and are reluctant to play with novel toys display increased heart rate and muscle tension in unfamiliar situations compared with children who are more outgoing and spontaneous (Kagan, 1994).

NATURE & NURTURE

Consistent racial and ethnic differences have been reported and attributed to genetic differences in temperament as well. When Daniel Freedman (1979) compared Caucasian and Chinese American newborns, he found that Caucasian babies were more irritable and harder to comfort than Chinese American infants. Similarly, research with four-month-olds from Boston, Dublin, and Beijing indicated that American infants were more active and fretful than those in Dublin, who in turn were more reactive than those in China (Kagan, 1994).

What aspects of the environment may also play an important role in temperament and other personality differences? Studies comparing the personalities of unrelated children in the same household report that the correlations are fairly low and often approach zero, especially in later childhood and adolescence (Plomin et al., 2008). *Shared environment*, the kinds of experiences children in a home or community have in common and that are assumed to foster similarity in children within the same family, simply does not have much effect for many aspects of personality. In contrast, *nonshared environment*, the experiences unique to individual children as they interact with parents, peers, and others, can play a powerful role in development, one that tends to make children in the family different rather than similar (Goldsmith, Buss, & Lemery, 1997; Plomin et al., 2008).

temperament Stable, early-appearing constellation of individual personality attributes believed to have a hereditary basis; includes sociability, emotionality, and activity level.

How can this be? One possibility is that peers, along with genes, play a pivotal role in determining the differences in personality and social adjustment displayed by children reared in the same family. Perhaps, too, parents actually do treat their children differently. Although mothers and fathers typically do not report much differential treatment, siblings frequently express another take on the matter. Observations of how parents interact with their sons and daughters seem to provide some ammunition in support of the children's perceptions. For example, the toys with which boys and girls are encouraged to play may differ considerably in some families (Lytton & Romney, 1991). And siblings do sometimes perceive that they are being treated unequally by their parents, a factor that can be related to a decline in the quality of their relationships with one another (Kowal & Kramer, 1997).

Treating Siblings Fairly | research applied to parenting

The girls woke up the next morning and started to prepare for school. As Keesha came down the stairs for breakfast, she asked, "Mom, can I have Stacy over after school? We want to practice gymnastics. Can she come over? Please?" Michelle answered without hesitating, "Of course, dear. Just be sure she has her parents' permission, OK?" Alison heard this exchange as she came out of her room and asked, "Can I have a friend over, too?" Michelle stiffened a little. She knew that Alison needed time for her homework after school, especially in light of what her math teacher had said the night before. "Alison, I'd love for you to have a friend over, but we really have to focus on your homework. After school today, let's lay out a plan so you can get your work done and then have some fun. But today is not a good day to have someone over." "That is so unfair!" Alison snapped back angrily. "How come she gets to have a friend over and I can't?" "Oh, boy!" thought Michelle to herself. "I'm going to have to figure out a way to handle this one!"

RISK | RESILIENCE

Should parents treat their children differently or in the same way? The answer is far from clear. For example, historically, identical twins were often dressed alike and treated almost as if they were one and the same individual. Today parents are advised to recognize their twins' individuality by encouraging them to gain unique experiences and to "pick out" their own niche in the family and community. As a consequence, they may be treated differently by parents and others. Other siblings, of course, share only about half of their genes and are quite distinct in physical appearance, personality, intellectual ability, and other characteristics. Parents may react to these differences in each child's characteristics. When is differential treatment a good thing? When is it a source of conflict? Research indicates that parents might consider some of these points when confronting this matter.

1. *Expect siblings to kindle different reactions from others.* Because all children, with the exception of identical twins, are born with different genotypes, they are likely to evoke distinctive kinds of responses from family members, teachers, peers, and others. These responses can, in turn, serve to magnify existing differences in the behaviors of siblings.
2. *Assume that siblings will actively search out ways to be different from one another.* Children very likely will engage in niche picking to set themselves apart from others within the family—a process called *sibling deidentification* (Feinberg & Hetherington, 2000). Such efforts may be observed even in identical twins. Whether it stems from biology or experience, the opportunity to find one's niche within the family, as well as the larger community, is an important aspect of development for all children.
3. *Anticipate that siblings will experience family events in different ways and will need to be treated differently in some circumstances.* Siblings within the same family—by virtue of their birth order, spacing, and unique events such as an illness, the death of a grandparent, or a move to a new neighborhood—will necessarily receive unique experiences because of their specific developmental status. In fact, distinct socialization practices for children of different ages is the norm, because treatment by caregivers could otherwise be developmentally inappropriate. Younger children typically need more nurturance and care; older children, increased independence and greater responsibility. Caregivers recognize that differential treatment is sometimes necessary. Children as young as five years of age notice these differences; younger children would prefer being the oldest in the family; that is, in their eyes, older siblings seem to have higher status (McHale et al., 1995). Furthermore, children and adolescents perceive greater differential

treatment of same-sex siblings than of brother-sister dyads by parents (McHale et al., 2000). Children do not always find differential treatment to be unfair. In fact, when children experience differential treatment on the part of their parents but feel it is justified—that is, equitable even though not equal—sibling relationships are generally positive (Kowal, Krull, & Kramer, 2004).

4. *Treat siblings impartially when possible and appropriate.* Impartial treatment of siblings by parents, to the extent that it is appropriate, is associated with less conflict among siblings and between children and their parents (Brody & Stoneman, 1994; McHale et al., 1995). In other words, parents who maintain a balance between socialization practices that are equitable within the limits of age-appropriate differences have children who interact effectively and in constructive ways with others, including their siblings. Differences in parenting arising from the individual needs of children can have positive consequences, but only as long as these differences do not reflect a form of parental "favoritism."

NATURE & NURTURE

Behavioral and Personality Disorders Table 3.6 summarizes the concordance rate for identical and fraternal twins for a variety of behavioral and personality disorders. None of these findings indicates 100 percent concordance even in identical twins, despite their matching genetic makeup. Thus, environmental factors play an important role in the manifestation of each of these problems. In fact, concordance measures for *conduct disorders* (fighting and aggressive behavior, failure to accept parental discipline) in both identical and fraternal twins are relatively high, suggesting that environmental factors contribute substantially to their appearance in both groups.

The genetic contribution to *bipolar disorder*, a disorder characterized by rapid and wide mood swings between feverish activity and withdrawn, depressed behaviors, appears to be substantial. Family studies reveal that children of a parent with bipolar disorder are at far greater risk for displaying the illness than children without such a parent. Research on adoptees provides further evidence that genotype plays a role; the risk for adopted children whose biological parents have the illness is about three times greater than for adopted children whose biological parents do not have it (Rutter et al., 1999). *Autism*, a disorder characterized by a lack of social communication (and more fully described later in this text), also reveals an ample hereditary contribution (Muhle, Trentacosa, & Rapin, 2004).

RISK | RESILIENCE

Alcoholism, although not linked to a single gene, shows a modest genetic component; other studies put the concordance rate at over 0.50 for identical twins and over 0.30 for fraternal twins who are male, somewhat higher than shown in Table 3.6 for the general population (Kendler et al., 1997; McGue, 1999). *Schizophrenia*, a form of psychopathology that includes

Parents with more than one child often want to treat each one of them equally but need to fine-tune their parenting efforts to the needs and age-appropriate activities of individual children. Fine motor skills demonstrated by the older sibling may permit her to engage in computer or other activities that are beyond the capacity of her younger sibling, who, as shown here, has found her own way to keep busy. By providing individual support and avoiding "favoritism," parents seem to help siblings learn to appreciate others' abilities.

TABLE 3.6 The Genetic Basis of Selected Behavioral and Personality Disorders: Twin Data

Evidence for the genetic basis of behavioral and personality disorders is often supported by studies of twins. For these disorders, the likelihood that both members of a pair will display the disorder, if exhibited by one, is greater when the pair are identical twins rather than fraternal twins. However, environmental factors may contribute to high concordance rates for both identical and fraternal twins, as is likely for conduct disorders.

Twin Concordances	Identical Twins	Fraternal Twins
Conduct disorder	.85	.70
Bipolar disorder	.65	.20
Autism	.65	.10
Unipolar depression	.45	.20
Alcoholism—males	.40	.20
Schizophrenia	.40	.10
Alcoholism—females	.30	.25

Source: Data from Plomin, 1994.

disturbances in thoughts and emotions, such as delusions and hallucinations, also exhibits some genetic contribution. Additional research raises the possibility that the *same* genes could have some role in different manifestations of psychopathology, including anxiety and depression or aggressive behavior and nonaggressive antisocial behavior (Eley, 1997; Plomin & Davis, 2009). These "general" genes, in other words, may contribute to wide variations in characteristics and behaviors that are often problematic for the individual. For example, anxiety and depression often co-occur in children and adolescents. One explanation for this relationship is that environmental factors are predisposing young people to the symptoms associated with both of these disorders. However, an alternative possibility is that although the same genes are contributing to the occurrence of both of these disorders, whether anxiety or depression is more likely to be displayed is dependent on the specific kind of environmental stress the individual experiences. Still other research indicates that some alleles of genes may be especially effective in moderating risk and increasing resilience in children exposed, for example, to maltreatment such as child abuse or neglect (Caspi & Moffitt, 2006; Kim-Cohen & Gold, 2009).

RISK | RESILIENCE

NATURE & NURTURE

Other Characteristics A host of other characteristics, including empathy, reading disabilities, sexual orientation, obesity, onset of pubertal development, susceptibility to various illnesses such as heart disease and cancer, and a propensity to be physically aggressive, to name just a few, have a genetic linkage (Brendgen et al., 2005; Fox et al., 2005; Harlaar, Dale, & Plomin, 2007; LeVay & Hamer, 1994; Mustanski et al., 2004; Plomin & Kovass, 2005). The influence of the genotype affects the entire breadth of human behavior, although the precise mechanisms by which it does often remain to be revealed. Perhaps more importantly, even when genetic influences are identified, social interventions can still make a difference. For example, while genes appear to predispose some youths to engage in risky problem behavior, initiating preventive programs designed to reduce that behavior can still be successful (Brody et al., 2009).

For Your Review and Reflection

- What are some of the methods behavior geneticists use to investigate the extent to which behavior is influenced by combinations of genes and experiences? Why are identical and fraternal twins—as well as adopted children—important in work designed to evaluate the heritability of behavior?
- How do concordance rate and correlation differ as measures in investigating genetic and environmental contributions to development?
- How are conceptualizations of the relationship between genotype and environment advanced by notions of range of reaction and canalization?

- In what ways do passive, evocative, and active niche-picking correlations between the genotype and experience differ from one another?
- To what extent are behavioral phenotypes, such as intelligence, personality and temperament, personality disorders, and other characteristics, influenced by heredity?
- Why are shared and nonshared environments important in accounting for similarities and differences in children's behavior?
- Why might parents treat siblings differently, and how do children interpret these differential treatments?
- If you have brothers and/or sisters, did your parents treat you the same or differently? Why do you think they may have done so?
- How might genetic factors play a role in the risk and resilience associated with personality disorders and behavioral problems?
- Consider some of the behavioral and personality differences between you and your siblings or, if an only child, siblings in other families that you know. How would you account for these differences and why?

chapter recap

Summary of Developmental Themes

Nature & Nurture

How do nature and nurture interact in development?

The phenotype, the observable behaviors and characteristics of an individual, is the product of complex, multiple factors interacting between genotype and environment. Environment includes biological contexts ranging from the composition of the cells to the foods we eat, but it also includes the experiences provided by caregivers and others. These environmental factors influence the functioning of genes immediately after conception and continue to have an impact throughout development. As a consequence, experiential factors are tightly interwoven with and may even modify the operation of genes to produce the range and variety of behaviors and characteristics an individual displays.

Determining the relationship between genotype and environment is further complicated by passive, reactive, and niche-picking correlations. For example, researchers recognize the child's active efforts to seek out environments that support and maintain behavioral orientations and preferences influenced by hereditary factors. As the child achieves greater control over the environment, he or she has increasing opportunities to find a niche. In other words, behaviors, activities, and skills that the child displays not only are a consequence of imposed social and physical experiences but also reflect the selective efforts of the child to discover interesting, challenging, and supportive environments.

Risk | Resilience

What factors promote risk or resilience in development?

Individual differences are pervasive in intellectual, temperamental, and a host of other cognitive, social, and emotional aspects of development. Hereditary and environmental factors work in combination to determine these differences. For example, inherited alleles of genes contribute to the wide range of physical, cognitive, emotional, and social adaptations displayed by individuals. Certain experiences also may turn the ability of genes on or off and therefore increase risk or resilience. A distinctive combination of genes and experiences underlies both the risk and the resilience we observe in human abilities and behavior.

Chapter Review

Principles of Hereditary Transmission

What roles do genotype and the environment play in determining a phenotype?

The genetic endowment inherited by an individual is the *genotype.* A *phenotype* refers to the traits and behaviors displayed by an individual. The phenotype is the result of complex, multiple factors interacting between the genotype and the experiences provided in the environment.

What is the human genome? How do the nucleus of the cell, chromosomes and DNA, genes, and nucleotides play a role in genetic influences on development?

The entire inventory of nucleotide base pairs that compose the genes and chromosomes in humans is called the *human genome.* The structures associated with the principles of heredity must be examined at several different levels. An individual's body is composed of trillions of cells. Twenty-three pairs of *chromosomes* (a total of forty-six), consisting of *deoxyribonucleic acid,* or *DNA,* are located in the nucleus of most cells in the human body. A central unit of hereditary information is the *gene,* a segment of a chromosome. *Nucleotides* are two different sets of pairs of repeating molecules that form the biochemical building blocks for the genes and the basic structure of the chromosomes.

How many autosomes exist in the human karyotype? Of what importance are the X and Y chromosomes?

The human *karyotype* consists of twenty-two pairs of *autosomes,* one member of each pair inherited from the mother, the second from the father. Males and females differ in the composition of the twenty-third pair of chromosomes. In females, both members of the pair normally are *X chromosomes*. In males, one is normally an X chromosome, and the other is a *Y chromosome*.

What is the difference between mitosis and meiosis? What are the impacts of crossing over and the process of genetic recombination?
Cell division in the human body takes place in two different ways. *Mitosis* is the process of cell division by which the forty-six chromosomes are duplicated in the body cells. The *gametes*, or sperm and egg cells, are formed by *meiosis*, a process of a cell division that results in twenty-three chromosomes in each of these cells. The random process by which a member of each of the twenty-three pairs of chromosomes is selected for the gametes, combined with *crossing over* during meiosis, ensures that every individual, with the exception of identical twins, has a unique hereditary blueprint. Once the gametes combine, the fertilized egg cell is called a *zygote*.

How do homozygous and heterozygous genes and the presence of dominant, recessive, and codominant allelic forms account for the inheritance patterns associated with various phenotypes? What are polygenic traits?
Variants of genes on the twenty-three pairs of chromosomes, or *alleles*, often interact with one another to establish probabilities of inheritance for particular traits or characteristics. A *dominant* allele will reflect its characteristics even when it is part of a *heterozygous* genotype, in which two alleles of a gene are different. A *recessive* allele is expressed only when it is part of a *homozygous* genotype, in which two alleles of a gene are the same. *Codominance* refers to the condition in which unblended characteristics of two alleles are reflected in the phenotype. Many human traits, however, are *polygenic*; that is, they are influenced by many different genes.

How do genes regulate the development of the phenotype? What is epigenetics? What is genomic imprinting?
Genetic information coded in DNA is recoded into mRNA (a process called transcription). The mRNA migrates to regions outside of the cell nucleus where the genetic information is translated into the production of proteins that result in different cell functions. The field of *epigenetics* is concerned with identifying how environmental conditions influence these processes of transcription and translation. *Genomic imprinting* refers to instances of genetic transmission in which the parental source of the gene, from mother or father, determines how the gene is expressed.

Gene and Chromosomal Abnormalities

What is the basis for and what phenotypes are associated with Williams syndrome, sickle cell disease and trait, phenylketonuria, and fragile X syndrome? Why is each of interest to developmental scientists?
Mutations, or spontaneous changes in the molecular structures of genes, can have wide-ranging influences on development, from almost no consequence to death. Some of these genetic or chromosomal problems can be passed from one generation to the next. *Williams syndrome* is caused by deletion of a small number of genes on chromosome 7. The phenotypic features include a short, upturned nose; full lips; and curvature of the knee and hips. Children with Williams syndrome display uneven developmental profiles; they often have unusual skill in music and show considerable attention to social stimuli but typically have poor spatial, numerical, and problem-solving skills.

Phenylketonuria (PKU) results from the presence of two recessive genes for the trait. Untreated children with PKU may exhibit convulsions, severe intellectual impairment, and hyperactivity. Early intervention with a modified diet can prevent many of these symptoms from manifesting themselves.

Sickle cell disease arises from the presence of two recessive genes that cause the red blood cells to become less efficient in transporting oxygen. The result can be anemia, jaundice, infection, and vulnerability to stroke, organ damage, and pain. An individual with *sickle cell trait* has only one of the recessive alleles but may still show symptoms under conditions of low oxygen. The presence of this allele provides protection against malaria.

Fragile X syndrome results from a constriction in one region of the X chromosome and is said to be sex linked. The phenotype will typically result in an individual having a long, narrow face, large ears, and large testes. Fragile X is the most frequently inherited source of intellectual impairment for males.

What variations in the chromosomal makeup of an individual are possible? What is the most common example of chromosomal trisomy? What are examples of chromosomal variation associated with the sex chromosomes?
The inheritance of only one chromosome on the autosomes does not permit survival in humans, but the presence of extra chromosomal material, or *trisomy*, can occur. A common disorder associated with inheritance of an extra chromosome and contributing to intellectual impairment is trisomy 21 (Down syndrome). Variations in number of sex chromosomes also occur but do not always contribute to behavioral or other developmental problems, especially if a supportive environment is available. Some of the patterns that can occur are X, XXX, and XYY.

Genetic Counseling

What are the major diagnostic tests for prenatal development? What are their limitations and their advantages?
Genetic counseling provides prospective parents with information on the probability of having children affected by birth defects. *Genetic screening* involves the use of systematic tests on parents or fetus to identify risks due to genetics. *Prenatal diagnostic tests* provide unequivocal answers about the presence or absence of a problem. *Amniocentesis* is effective for diagnosing many chromosomal and metabolic disorders. *Chorionic villus sampling* can be done earlier in pregnancy but cannot diagnose neural tube defects, requires more medical skill, and is associated with a slightly elevated risk of miscarriage. *Fetal blood sampling* can detect chromosomal and genetic errors and blood disorders but carries somewhat elevated risks. *Maternal blood screening* can assist in detecting neural tube defects and Down syndrome. *Ultrasonography* can show many physical abnormalities but does not indicate the presence of many other developmental disorders.

What ethical and social issues emerge from the use of prenatal diagnostic tests?
Controversial ethical and social issues include whether to have the tests in the first place, decisions made once the results of the tests are known, and the opportunity to carry out sex preselection.

What is sex preselection, and what are arguments for and against its practice?
Sex preselection refers to techniques that increase the likelihood that either a girl or a boy will be conceived. This technique allows for family balancing, may lead to a desirable parenting experience, and may prevent passing on sex-linked traits. Opponents argue that the practice may support sex bias and may lead to a "preference mentality" whereby children would be selected for other traits as well.

Developmental and Behavioral Genetics

What methods do behavior geneticists use to investigate the extent to which behavior is influenced by combinations of genes and experiences? Why are identical and fraternal twins—as well as adopted children—important in work designed to evaluate the heritability of behavior?
Behavior genetics is a method of attempting to determine the relative contribution of heredity and environment to traits and behaviors that are often the result of combinations of genes. To determine contributions from combinations of genes, behavioral geneticists frequently engage in selective breeding with lower organisms or compare findings among various family members, such as *identical twins, fraternal twins,* siblings, and adopted children, because these groups differ in the extent to which they share a common genotype. *Heritability* refers to the extent to which the variability on some characteristic in a sample of individuals is accounted for by genetic differences among those individuals.

How do concordance rate and correlation differ as measures in investigating genetic and environmental contributions to development?
The *concordance rate* refers to the percentage of pairs of twins who display the same characteristics. The correlation coefficient is a statistic that measures the degree of relationship between pairs of individuals of varying levels of biological relationship to one another.

How are conceptualizations of the interaction between genotype and environment advanced by notions of range of reaction and canalization?
The concept of *range of reaction* highlights the fact that a trait or behavior influenced by a person's genotype may be unique to a particular kind of environment. The principle of *canalization* emphasizes that some traits and characteristics are highly determined by the genotype or, conversely, that some environments may have a powerful influence on how these are displayed.

How do passive, evocative, and active niche-picking correlations between the genotype and experience differ from one another?
Correlations between genotype and environment may be *passive,* in that caregivers with specific genotypes are likely to provide environments supportive of their children's genotypes; *evocative,* in that parents, peers, and others are likely to react in ways that accommodate genetic inclinations; and *active,* in that children may attempt to find or create environments that support their individual genetic propensities (that is, engage in *niche picking*). These different correlations often make the task of determining how much the genotype accounts for the phenotypic expressions difficult to measure.

To what extent are behavioral phenotypes, such as intellectual abilities, personality and temperament, personality disorders, and other characteristics, influenced by heredity?
Intellectual abilities, *temperament* and other personality variables, social adjustment and behavioral disorders, and other traits and characteristics often display considerable heritability, suggesting that the genotype contributes substantially to variability among children for many aspects of development. More recent research examining genetic variations at the molecular level may help provide answers about how the interaction of genotype and environment influences the development of many of these behavioral phenotypes.

To what extent are shared and nonshared environments important in accounting for similarities and differences in children's behavior?
The shared environment provided by the family increases similarity among siblings, often to a limited extent. However, the nonshared environment that children within the same family experience contributes substantially to individual differences among children.

Why might parents treat siblings differently, and how do children interpret these differential treatments?
Different inherited characteristics among children may lead parents to treat them differently. Siblings perceive differential treatment from their parents, but when the differential treatment is interpreted as equitable, even if not equal, positive relationships between siblings are fostered.

Key Terms and Concepts

allele (p. 72)
amniocentesis (p. 92)
autosome (p. 73)
behavior genetics (p. 96)
canalization (p. 99)
chorionic villus sampling (p. 92)
chromosome (p. 72)
codominance (p. 78)
concordance rate (p. 97)
crossing over (p. 76)
deoxyribonucleic acid (DNA) (p. 73)
dominant allele (p. 77)
Down syndrome (p. 89)
epigenetics (p. 79)
fetal blood sampling (p. 92)
fragile X syndrome (p. 87)
fraternal (dizygotic) twins (p. 97)
gamete (p. 72)
gene (p. 72)
genetic counseling (p. 91)
genetic screening (p. 92)
genomic imprinting (p. 81)
genotype (p. 72)
heritability (p. 96)
heterozygous (p. 77)
homozygous (p. 77)
human genome (p. 73)
identical (monozygotic) twins (p. 97)
karyotype (p. 73)
maternal blood screening (p. 93)
meiosis (p. 75)
mitosis (p. 75)
mutation (p. 82)
niche picking (p. 101)
nucleotide (p. 73)
phenotype (p. 72)
phenylketonuria (PKU) (p. 86)
polygenic (p. 78)
prenatal diagnostic tests (p. 92)
range of reaction (p. 98)
recessive allele (p. 77)
sickle cell disease (p. 85)
sickle cell trait (p. 86)
temperament (p. 103)
trisomy (p. 89)
ultrasonography (p. 93)
Williams syndrome (p. 82)
X chromosome (p. 73)
Y chromosome (p. 73)
zygote (p. 74)

Media Resources

Access an integrated eBook and chapter-specific interactive learning tools, including flashcards, quizzes, videos, and more, in your Developmental Psychology CourseMate, accessed through CengageBrain.com.

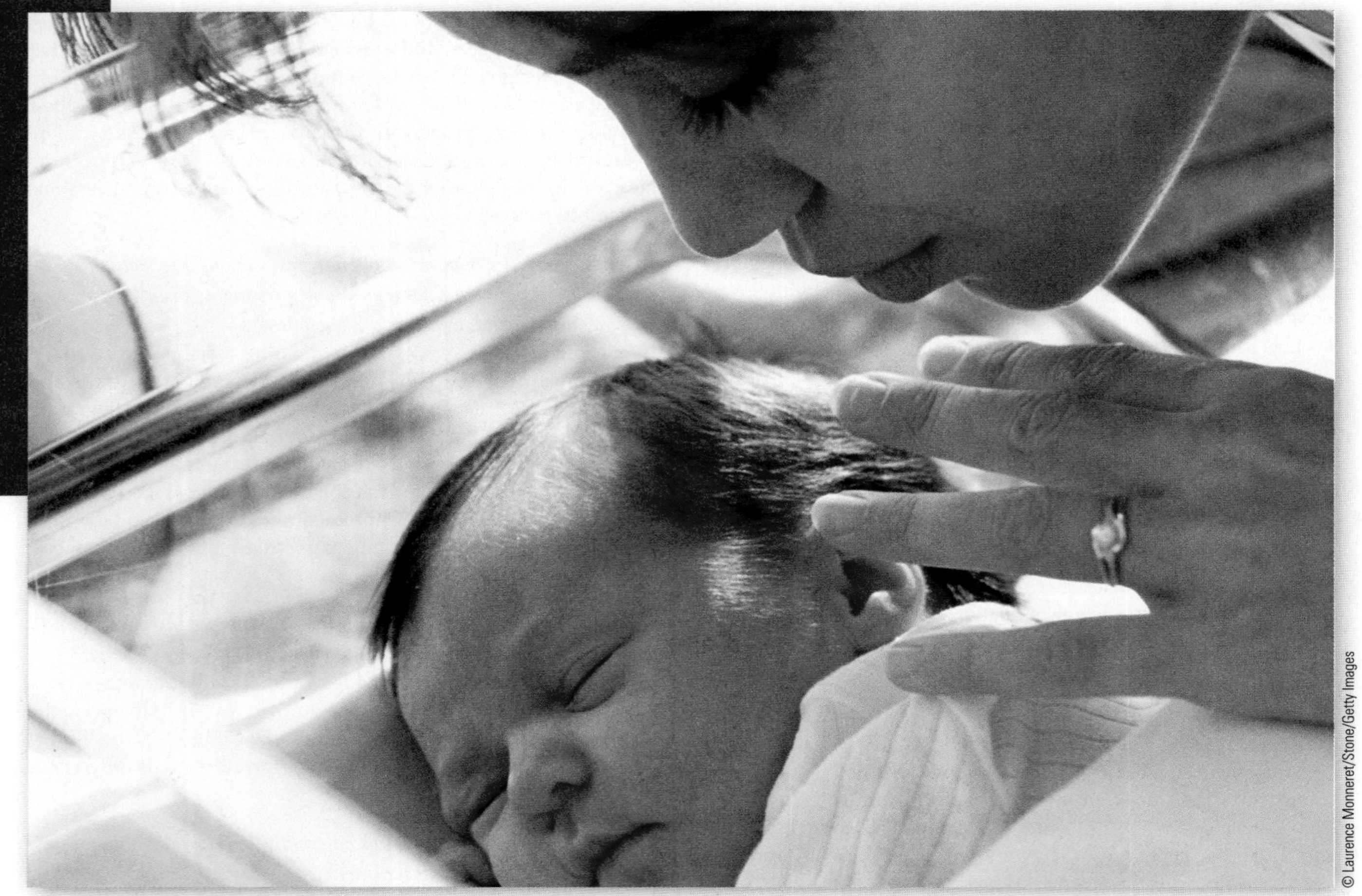

© Laurence Monneret/Stone/Getty Images

CHAPTER OUTLINE

[chapter 4]

The Prenatal Period and Birth

KEY THEMES IN THE PRENATAL PERIOD AND BIRTH

- **NATURE & NURTURE** How do nature and nurture interact during prenatal development and birth?
- **SOCIOCULTURAL INFLUENCE** How does the sociocultural context influence prenatal development and birth?
- **CONTINUITY | DISCONTINUITY** Is development before and after birth continuous or discontinuous?
- **RISK | RESILIENCE** What factors promote risk or resilience during prenatal development and birth?

It had been a long and tiring day. Elena had awoken at 4:00 a.m. and immediately realized it was time. Fortunately, the hospital was a short ride away. But as she now held her newborn daughter for the first time after 14 hours of labor, she no longer felt tired. She had wanted everything to go well, and it had. She avoided alcohol as soon as she learned of her pregnancy, made regular appointments to visit her obstetrician, and had taken additional folic acid and followed other recommendations made by her doctor about not including certain kinds of fish in her diet. She had been anxious about becoming a new mother, but she was feeling confident now as she watched every movement her daughter made in her arms.

As a high school counselor, Elena had worked with several students who had continued to smoke after becoming pregnant, who had delayed seeing an obstetrician because they had been reluctant to inform parents about their conditions, and, in some cases, whose families did not have the health insurance that would permit them to get the best possible care. Elena was well aware that these were among the many factors that could put newborns at risk; however, it had been difficult to persuade some of the teenagers to take these risks seriously. Several of their children, she knew, had been born with very low birth weight. Unfortunately, their mothers never returned to school, so she did not know how the babies were doing.

For now, Elena was grateful for all the support her husband had provided during her labor and throughout her pregnancy. "Sorry," she said as her husband fidgeted nearby. "I just have to hold my baby awhile longer; then you'll have your chance, OK?" <<

Most women experience both pride and apprehension when they learn they are pregnant. Those feelings are often influenced by a multitude of social and cultural views and ideas about pregnancy. Although societies differ enormously in their specific beliefs, anthropologists report that expectant women around the world are often urged to avoid certain activities and to carry out various rituals for the sake of their unborn. In Western cultures, admonitions about pregnancy exist as well; obstetricians may advise a pregnant woman to stop smoking, avoid alcohol, and let someone else clean the cat's litterbox.

Fortunately, the mysteries surrounding this remarkable time are beginning to become clearer. Our discussion of prenatal development opens with a brief description of the amazing sequence of events occurring between conception and birth. At no other time does growth take place so rapidly or do so many physical changes occur in a matter of weeks, days, and even hours. Some cultures, such as the Chinese, tacitly acknowledge these dramatic events by pronouncing the baby one year old at birth. In the typical nine months of confinement to the womb, the human organism indeed undergoes an epic journey.

Although fetal growth proceeds in a highly protected environment, we are also discovering the ways in which drugs, diseases, and other factors affect prenatal development. We summarize our current understanding of these influences and then consider the birth process, another point at which the influences on development can be significant.

The Stages of Prenatal Development

CONTINUITY | DISCONTINUITY

Three major overlapping periods define the life of a human organism. The **prenatal period** is launched from the moment of conception and continues until the beginning of labor. All but the first few days of this period are spent within the confines of the womb. The **perinatal period**, which can overlap with the prenatal period, dawns at about the seventh month of pregnancy and extends until twenty-eight days after birth. This phase is associated with the impending birth, the social and physical setting for delivery, and the baby's first adjustments to his or her new world. Among the events included in the perinatal period are the medical and obstetrical practices associated with delivery, and the preparations and care provided by parents and others to assist in the transition from the womb to life outside. The **postnatal** period, which can overlap with the perinatal period, begins after birth. The child's environment now includes the broader physical and social world afforded by caregivers and others responsible for the infant's continued growth.

The prenatal period is itself typically divided into three stages. The **germinal period**, also known as the *period of the zygote*, encompasses the first ten to fourteen days following conception. Cell division and migration of the newly fertilized egg, culminating with its implantation in the uterine wall, characterize the germinal period. The second stage, the **embryonic period**, continues from about two to eight weeks after conception. The formation of structures and organs associated with the nervous, circulatory, respiratory, and most other systems marks the embryonic period. The final stage, the **fetal period**, lasts from about eight weeks after conception until birth. This period is distinguished by substantial brain and physical growth; organs and systems are also further refined in preparation for functioning outside the womb.

Another way to describe the approximately thirty-eight weeks from conception to delivery that constitute a typical full-term human pregnancy is in terms of roughly equal three-month periods, or *trimesters*. You can see that partitioning the prenatal period in terms of trimesters does not neatly correspond to the germinal, embryonic, and fetal periods that we have just described. However, this system has a long-standing tradition of use within the healthcare community.

Fertilization

Even before her own birth, Elena, like most other human females, had formed approximately 2 million primitive egg cells in her ovaries. Their numbers, however, declined with development; by puberty, perhaps only 40,000 remained. Of this abundant supply, about 400 mature and are released for potential fertilization during the childbearing years (Moore & Persaud, 2008). In contrast, male sperm production begins only at puberty, when an incredible 100 million to 300 million sperm may be formed daily.

The opportunity for human conception begins about the fourteenth day after the start of the menstrual period. At this time, a capsule-like *follicle* housing a primitive egg cell in one of the ovaries begins to mature. As it matures and changes position, the follicle eventually ruptures and discharges its valuable contents from the ovary. After being expelled, the egg cell, or *ovum*, is normally carried into the Fallopian tube. This organ serves as a conduit for the egg, which moves toward the uterus at the leisurely rate of about one-sixteenth inch per hour. The Fallopian tube provides a receptive environment for fertilization if sperm are present. If unfertilized, the ovum survives only about twenty-four hours.

Sperm reach the Fallopian tube by maneuvering from the vagina through the cervix and uterus. Sperm can

prenatal period Period in development from conception to the onset of labor.

perinatal period Period beginning about the seventh month of pregnancy and continuing until about four weeks after birth.

postnatal period Period in development following birth.

germinal period Period lasting about ten to fourteen days following conception before the fertilized egg becomes implanted in the uterine wall. Also called *period of the zygote*.

embryonic period Period of prenatal development during which major biological organs and systems form; begins about the tenth to fourteenth day after conception and ends about the eighth week after conception.

fetal period Period of prenatal development, from about the eighth week after conception to birth, marked by rapid growth and preparation of body systems for functioning in the postnatal environment.

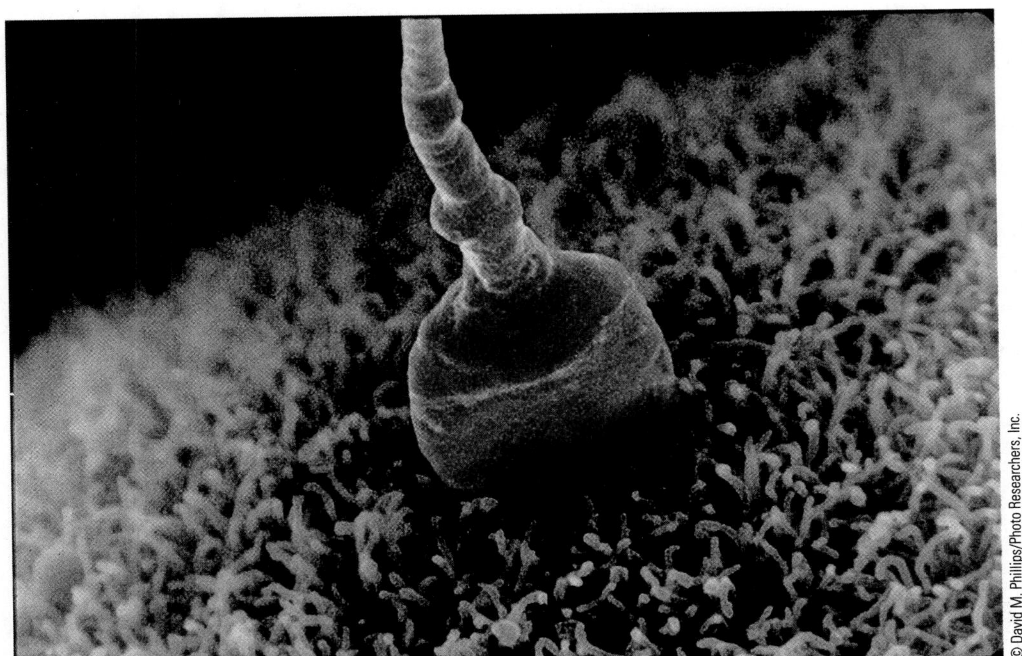

© David M. Phillips/Photo Researchers, Inc.

Human development begins with the penetration of the egg by a single sperm as shown here (egg and sperm are magnified greatly). Although the egg is the body's largest cell and the sperm the smallest, each contributes twenty-three chromosomes to form the hereditary basis for the development of a new living entity.

migrate several inches an hour with the assistance of their tail-like appendages. With each ejaculation, 300 to 500 sperm typically negotiate the approximately ten-hour trip into the Fallopian tube to reach the egg; these usually survive only about forty-eight hours.

If an ovum is present, sperm seem attracted to it, possibly because of scent-like chemical cues emitted by the egg (Spehr et al., 2003). The egg also prepares for fertilization in the presence of sperm. Cells initially surrounding the ovum loosen their protective grip, permitting the egg to be penetrated. As soon as one sperm cell breaks through the egg's protective linings, enzymes rapidly transform its outer membrane to prevent others from invading (Moore & Persaud, 2008). Genetic material from egg and sperm quickly mix to establish a normal complement of forty-six chromosomes. The egg, the body's largest cell, barely visible to the naked eye, weighs about 100,000 times more than the sperm, the body's smallest cell. Despite the enormous difference in size, both contribute equivalent amounts of genetic material to the zygote.

The Germinal Period

After fertilization, the zygote continues to migrate down the Fallopian tube (see Figure 4.1). Within twenty-four to thirty hours after conception, the single cell divides into two cells, the first of a series of mitotic divisions called *cleavages*. At roughly twelve- to twenty-hour intervals, these cells divide again to form four, then eight, then sixteen cells. During the cleavages, the zygote remains about the same size; thus, individual cells become smaller and smaller.

After three to four days, about the time the zygote is ready to enter the uterus, it has become a solid sphere of sixteen cells called a *morula*. Each cell is alike in its capacity to generate a separate, identical organism. About the fourth day after conception, however, the cells begin to segregate and carry out specific functions. One group forms a spherical outer cellular layer that eventually becomes various membranes providing nutritive support for the **embryo,** the label typically applied to the developing human organism from about two to eight weeks after conception. A second, inner group of cells organizes into a mass that will develop into the embryo. This differentiated group of cells is now called a *blastocyst* (Sadler, 2004).

About the sixth day after conception, the blastocyst begins the process of attaching to the uterine wall to tap a critical new supply of nutrients. By about the tenth to fourteenth day after conception, the implantation process is completed. In preparing for this event, the blastocyst began secreting

embryo Label typically applied to the developing organism from about two to eight weeks after conception.

Figure 4.1
Fertilization and the Germinal Period
During the early development of the human embryo, an egg cell is released from a maturing follicle within the ovary, and fertilization takes place in the Fallopian tube, transforming the egg cell or ovum into a zygote. Cleavage and multiplication of cells proceeds as the zygote migrates toward the uterus. Differentiation of the zygote begins within the uterus, becoming a solid sixteen-cell sphere known as the *morula*, then a differentiated set of cells know as the *blastocyst*, which prepares for implantation in the uterine wall. Once implanted, it taps a vital source of nutriments to sustain further development. (The numbers indicate days following fertilization.)
Source: Adapted from Moore, K. L., 1988.

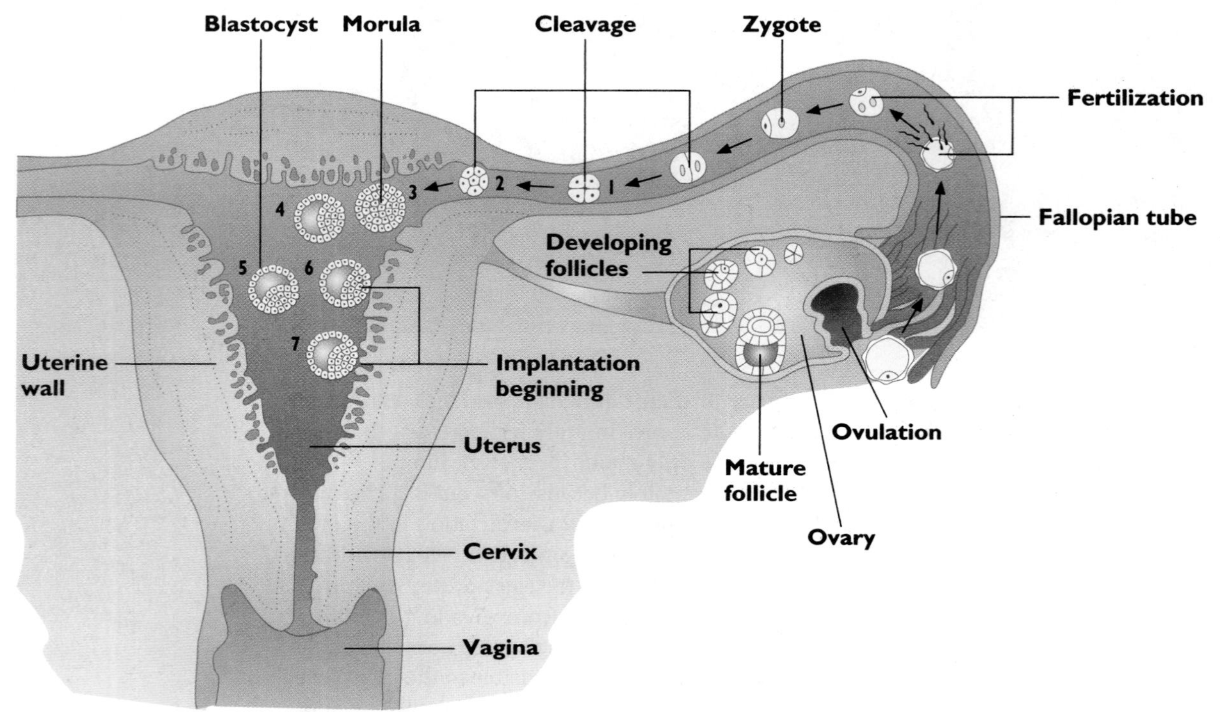

hormones and other substances to inhibit menstruation, or the shedding of the uterine lining, and to keep the woman's immune system from rejecting the foreign object. One of these hormones eventually becomes detectable in the woman's urine as a marker in pregnancy tests. If the zygote fails to attach to the uterine wall, it is expelled; the frequency of such events is unknown because a woman seldom realizes that a potential pregnancy has terminated.

The Embryonic Period

The embryonic period, which begins with the implantation of the blastocyst in the uterine wall and continues until about the eighth week after conception, is marked by the rapid differentiation of cells to form most of the organs and systems within the body. This differentiation, known as *organogenesis*, is achieved by the production and migration of specialized cells having distinctive functions.

Formation of Body Organs and Systems The first step in the formation of various body organs and systems involves the migration of unspecialized embryonic cells to establish a three-layered embryo. The three layers serve as the foundation for all tissues and organs in the body. The *endoderm*, or inner layer, will give rise to many of the linings of internal organs, such as lungs, the gastrointestinal tract, the liver, the pancreas, the bladder, and some glands. The *mesoderm*, or middle layer, eventually develops into skeleton and muscles, the urogenital system, the lymph and cardiovascular systems, and other connective tissues. The *ectoderm*, or outer layer, will form skin, hair, and nails, but its earliest derivatives will be the central nervous system and nerves.

How, by simply migrating to a layered configuration, do undifferentiated cells come to establish a highly distinctive set of organs and systems? Understanding this process remains one of the most important issues in prenatal development. The immediate environment surrounding a cell appears to play a major role. Although at first unspecialized, a cell's potential becomes constrained by its association with neighboring tissues, which secrete proteins called *paracrines*. The cells responding to paracrines may then activate or suppress genetic activity responsible for specialized functions (Gilbert, 2003). Thus, cells are induced by their surroundings to take on certain forms and functions. For example, if cells from the ectodermal layer are removed and placed in a culture so that they grow in isolation from other cell layers, they form epidermal, or skinlike, tissues. If placed with a layer of mesodermal cells, however, a nervous system will emerge (Abel, 1989). Cells also seem to be sensitive to the density of cells around them, releasing biochemical signals that slow down cell proliferation when an organ seems to have grown enough (Lien et al., 2006).

NATURE & NURTURE

Because the embryonic period is the major time for development of organs and systems, many possibilities for disruption exist. However, under normal conditions, the sequence of primary changes in prenatal development proceeds in a fairly regular pattern, as summarized in "Chronology: Prenatal Development."

Early Brain and Nervous System Development About the fifteenth day after conception, a small group of cells at one end of the ectoderm starts to grow rapidly. The growth creates a reference point for the cephalic (head) and caudal (tail) regions of the embryo, and helps to distinguish left from right side. The cells induce the development of the *neural tube*, which in turn initiates the formation of the spinal cord, nerves, and eventually the brain.

Rapid changes in the neural tube begin about the third week. At first, the neural tube is open at both ends. The tube begins closing in the brain region and, a few days later, in the caudal region. Its failure to knit shut at either end can have drastic consequences for development. In *anencephaly*, a condition in which the cephalic region of the neural tube does not close, the cerebral hemispheres fail to develop, and most of the cortex is missing at birth. Newborns with such a condition survive only a short time.

Spina bifida is a condition that arises when the caudal region of the neural tube fails to close. The resulting cleft in the vertebral column permits spinal nerves to grow outside the protective vertebrae. In more serious cases, the infant may be paralyzed and lack sensation in the legs. Surgery often must be performed. Sometimes it can be done even before birth to keep the condition from getting worse. But lost capacities cannot be restored, and malformations in brain development and impaired intellectual development may accompany spina bifida (Northrup & Volcik, 2000).

The frequency of both neural tube defects, now about 1 in every 1,000 births in the United States, has declined sharply over the last twenty years. One major contributor to this decrease, as illustrated in Figure 4.2, appears to be the consequence of taking nutritional supplements early in pregnancy, particularly folic acid and other components of the vitamin B complex. For example, in Canada, Chile, and Mexico, declines in spina bifida and anencephaly have been noted after efforts have been made to add supplements or fortify grain products with folic acid (de Villarreal, Arredondo, & Hernández 2006; De Wals et al., 2007; López-Camelo et al., 2005).

RISK | RESILIENCE

NATURE & NURTURE

The second month after conception is marked by continued rapid development of the head and brain. Nerve cells show an explosive increase in number; estimates are that as many as 250,000 neurons are generated every minute during this prenatal period (Dowling, 1998). Neurons also undergo extensive migration once the neural tube closes and they soon make contact with one another. The region of the head greatly enlarges relative to the rest of the embryo to account for about half of total body length. Although the embryo is still tiny, less than an inch long and half an ounce in weight, nearly all organs are established by this time, and the embryo is recognizably human.

One of the most striking milestones is reached about the sixth week after conception, when the nervous system begins to function. Now, irregular and faint brain wave activity can be recorded. Soon, if the head or upper body is touched, the embryo exhibits reflex movements. In a few more weeks, muscles may flex, but it will still be some time before the woman is able to feel any of these movements.

CHRONOLOGY Prenatal Development: Conception to 38 Weeks

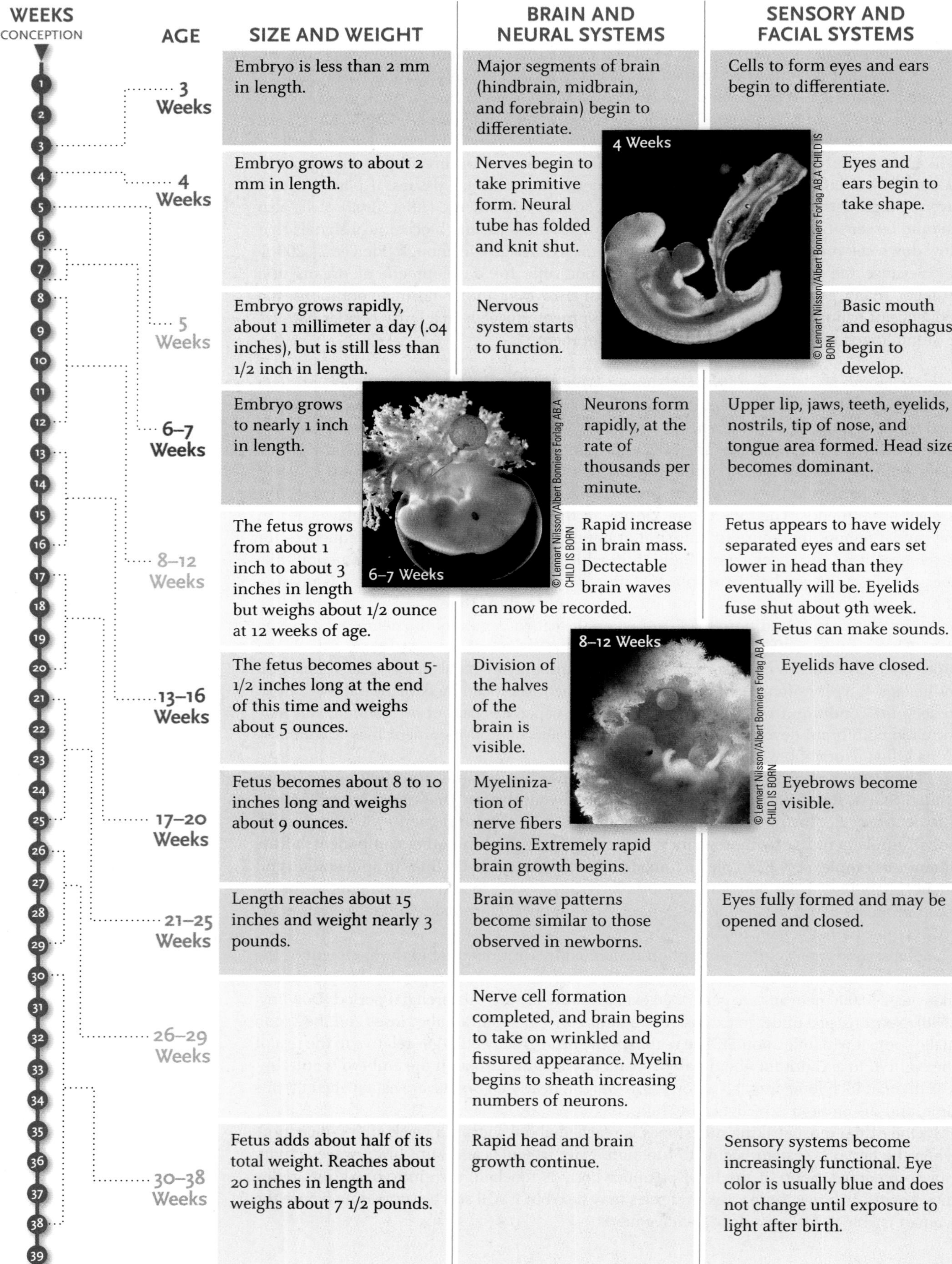

AGE (WEEKS FROM CONCEPTION)	SIZE AND WEIGHT	BRAIN AND NEURAL SYSTEMS	SENSORY AND FACIAL SYSTEMS
3 Weeks	Embryo is less than 2 mm in length.	Major segments of brain (hindbrain, midbrain, and forebrain) begin to differentiate.	Cells to form eyes and ears begin to differentiate.
4 Weeks	Embryo grows to about 2 mm in length.	Nerves begin to take primitive form. Neural tube has folded and knit shut.	Eyes and ears begin to take shape.
5 Weeks	Embryo grows rapidly, about 1 millimeter a day (.04 inches), but is still less than 1/2 inch in length.	Nervous system starts to function.	Basic mouth and esophagus begin to develop.
6–7 Weeks	Embryo grows to nearly 1 inch in length.	Neurons form rapidly, at the rate of thousands per minute.	Upper lip, jaws, teeth, eyelids, nostrils, tip of nose, and tongue area formed. Head size becomes dominant.
8–12 Weeks	The fetus grows from about 1 inch to about 3 inches in length but weighs about 1/2 ounce at 12 weeks of age.	Rapid increase in brain mass. Dectectable brain waves can now be recorded.	Fetus appears to have widely separated eyes and ears set lower in head than they eventually will be. Eyelids fuse shut about 9th week. Fetus can make sounds.
13–16 Weeks	The fetus becomes about 5-1/2 inches long at the end of this time and weighs about 5 ounces.	Division of the halves of the brain is visible.	Eyelids have closed.
17–20 Weeks	Fetus becomes about 8 to 10 inches long and weighs about 9 ounces.	Myelinization of nerve fibers begins. Extremely rapid brain growth begins.	Eyebrows become visible.
21–25 Weeks	Length reaches about 15 inches and weight nearly 3 pounds.	Brain wave patterns become similar to those observed in newborns.	Eyes fully formed and may be opened and closed.
26–29 Weeks		Nerve cell formation completed, and brain begins to take on wrinkled and fissured appearance. Myelin begins to sheath increasing numbers of neurons.	
30–38 Weeks	Fetus adds about half of its total weight. Reaches about 20 inches in length and weighs about 7 1/2 pounds.	Rapid head and brain growth continue.	Sensory systems become increasingly functional. Eye color is usually blue and does not change until exposure to light after birth.

4 Weeks © Lennart Nilsson/Albert Bonniers Forlag AB,A CHILD IS BORN

6–7 Weeks © Lennart Nilsson/Albert Bonniers Forlag AB,A CHILD IS BORN

8–12 Weeks © Lennart Nilsson/Albert Bonniers Forlag AB,A CHILD IS BORN

MUSCLE, SKIN, AND SKELETAL SYSTEMS	OTHER SYSTEMS	REFLEXIVE AND BEHAVIORAL RESPONSES
Precursors to vertebrae begin to organize.	Blood vessels form and connect to precursor of umbilical cord. Primitive one-chambered heart starts to beat by 21st day.	
Stripe of tissue forms on either side of trunk to begin chest and stomach muscle production. Arm buds appear by about 26 days. Similar swelling begins about 2 days later to form early buds for lower limbs. Tail-like cartilage appears to curve under rump.	Rudimentary liver, gall bladder, stomach, intestines, pancreas, thyroid, and lungs created. Red blood cells are formed by yolk sac.	
Elbow, wrist regions, and paddle-shaped plate with ridges for future fingers take shape.	Heart differentiates into upper and lower regions.	
Embryo possesses short webbed fingers, and foot plate has also begun to differentiate. Many muscles differentiate and take final shape. Tail-like cartilage regresses.	Heart divides into four chambers.	Embryo begins to show reflexive responses to touch, first around the facial region. Spontaneous movements of head, trunk, and limbs become possible.
Bones start to grow. Fingernails, toenails, and hair follicles form.	Fetus begins to show differentiation of external reproductive organs (if male, about 9th week; if female, several weeks later.)	Startle and sucking responses first appear. Fetus displays hiccups, flexes arms and legs, and also displays some facial expressions.
Spinal cord begins to form. Fingerprints and footprints established. Fetus sprouts soft, downlike hair at the end of this period.	If female, large numbers of primitive egg cells are created.	Other reflexes, including swallowing, emerge. Begins to display long periods of active movement. About 35 quarts of blood are pumped each day by the heart.
Fetus becomes covered by cheeselike, fatty material secreted by oil glands that probably protects the skin constantly bathed in amniotic fluid. Hair becomes visible. Fingerprints are formed.		Fetus often assumes a favorite position and displays sleep/wake cycles.
Skin appears wrinkled and has a pink to reddish cast caused by blood in capillaries, which are highly visible through translucent skin.	Lung functioning becomes possible but uncertain.	Fetus can see and hear and produces crying if born prematurely. Some indicators of stable states of sleep and wakefulness are exhibited.
Fat deposits accumulate beneath surface of skin to give fetus a much less wrinkled appearance. Hair may begin to grow on head. Lungs are sufficiently developed to permit breathing of air should birth occur.	Red blood cells now produced by bone marrow.	
Fat continues to accumulate, giving full-term newborn chubby appearance and helping to insulate baby from varying temperatures once born. Skin color turns from red to pink to white to bluish pink for all babies regardless of racial makeup.	About 300 quarts of blood pumped each day by the heart at birth.	Seeing, hearing, and learning are now possible.

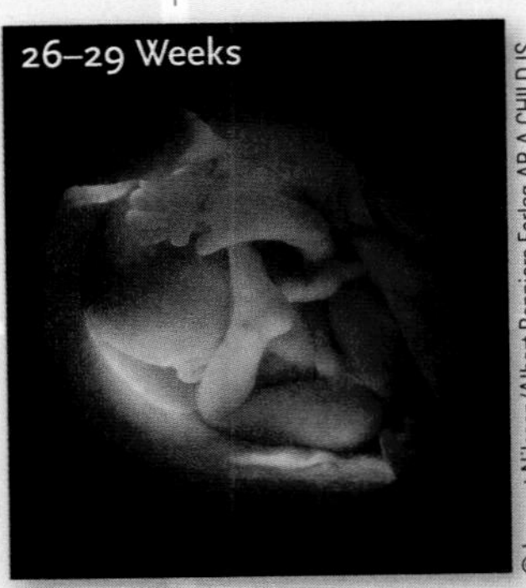

© Lennart Nilsson/Albert Bonniers Forlag AB,A CHILD IS BORN

For further information about fetal development see *http://www.visembryo.com/baby/index.html*

Figure 4.2

Decline in Neural Tube Defects Associated with the Increased Use of Folic Acid Supplements

Rates of neural tube defects (NTDs) have dropped substantially in the United States since 1991. During this same period, the use of folic acid supplements by women in their childbearing years increased, in part because of government recommendations, as well as regulations requiring that all enriched cereal grain products be fortified with folic acid. These factors very likely contributed to the substantial decline in NTDs.

Source: QuickStats: Spina Bifida and Anencephaly Rates* — United States, 1991, 1995, 2000, and 2005† (2008, January 11). http://www.cdc.gov/mmwr/preview/mmwrhtml/mm5701a7.htm.

*Based on birth certificates. However, birth certificates may underreport spina bifida and anencephaly so their numbers may be greater.

†Excludes data from Maryland, New Mexico, and New York, which did not require reporting for certain years.

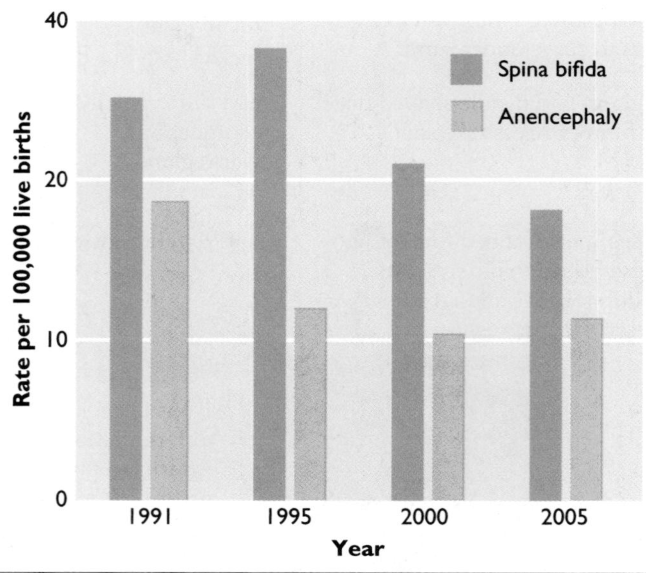

The Fetal Period

The change from embryo to **fetus,** the label typically applied to the developing human organism from about eight weeks after conception until birth, is signaled by the emergence of bone tissue at about the eighth week after conception. Organ differentiation continues, particularly in the reproductive system and the brain. However, the fetal period is best known for growth in size and the genesis of processes that help organs and systems to function. One positive consequence is that the fetus becomes much less susceptible to many potentially damaging environmental factors.

During the third month after conception, the fetus increases to about three and a half inches in length and about a half ounce in weight. Its movements become more pronounced. At nine weeks, the fetus opens and closes its lips, wrinkles its forehead, raises and lowers its eyebrows, and turns its head. By the end of twelve weeks, behaviors become more coordinated. The fetus can, for example, display sucking and the basic motions of breathing and swallowing. Fingers will bend if the arm is touched, and the thumb can be opposed to fingers, an indication that peripheral muscles and nerves are functioning in increasingly sophisticated ways.

The Second Trimester In the second of the three trimesters into which prenatal development is sometimes divided, the fetus's body grows more rapidly than at any other time. By the end of the fifth month, the fetus is about eight to ten inches long, although it still weighs only about nine ounces. During the sixth month, the fetus rapidly starts to gain weight, expanding to about one and a half pounds and reaching a length of about fourteen inches. Moreover, by the middle of the second trimester, fetal movements known as *quickening* become unmistakable to the woman. The fetus stretches and

fetus Label typically applied to the developing human organism from about eight weeks after conception until birth.

squirms as well. Near the end of this trimester, *myelin*, which helps to insulate and speed the transmission of neuronal impulses, begins to form and surround some nerve fibers. Brain wave patterns begin to look like those observed in the newborn, including patterns suggestive of different stages of sleep and wakefulness. Should birth occur at this time, there is some chance of survival if specialized medical facilities are available.

The Third Trimester The final months add finishing touches to the astonishing progression in prenatal development. The cerebral hemispheres, the regions of the brain most heavily involved in complex mental processing, grow rapidly, folding and developing fissures to give them a wrinkled appearance. The sense organs are developed sufficiently to enable the fetus to smell and taste, as well as to hear, see, and feel. The fetus continues to gain weight rapidly (nearly half a pound per week), although growth slows in the weeks just preceding birth. Control of body temperature and rhythmic respiratory activity remain problematic if birth occurs at the beginning of the third trimester. Nevertheless, **viability**, or the fetus's ability to survive outside the womb, dramatically improves over the course of these three months.

The onset of birth can be expected when the fetus reaches a gestational age of about 274 days. **Gestational age**, commonly employed in the medical profession to gauge prenatal growth, is derived from the date of onset of the woman's last menstrual period before conception. This method of calculation makes the embryo or fetus about fifteen days older than determining age from the date of conception. The average gestational period has declined in the last ten years in the United States and is now thirty-nine weeks (Davidoff et al., 2006). In addition, as any parent knows, variability in the timing of birth is the norm. Gestational age appears to be a few days shorter for Japanese and African American babies compared with Caucasian babies, for infants born to mothers younger than nineteen or older than thirty-four years, for second and later children compared with firstborns, and about a day shorter for girls than for boys (Divon et al., 2002; Mittendorf et al., 1993).

Assisted Reproduction

For many prospective parents, conceiving and having a baby proceeds as a normal part of the process of establishing a family. However, for some men and women, the opportunities to become a parent are limited or require special consideration. For many prospective parents, this may be due to difficulty in conceiving; others may be carriers of genetic diseases (see Chapter 3, "Genetics and Heredity") who wish to avoid the risk of passing these disorders to their offspring. For these prospective parents, advances in the field of reproductive technology have opened up many alternatives, in addition to adoption, in their efforts to become parents; these advances also are dramatically affecting traditional notions about what it means to be a mother or father.

Although not technically considered as a form of assisted reproductive technology, if a male is infertile or carries a genetic disorder or a single woman or lesbian couple would like to conceive, the prospective parent(s) may elect *artificial insemination by donor* (see Table 4.1). In this procedure, a donor, who is usually anonymous and is often selected because of similarity in physical and other characteristics to a prospective father, contributes sperm that are then artificially provided to the mother when ovulation occurs. If a female is infertile, a carrier of a genetic disease, or unable to complete a pregnancy for various reasons, assisted reproductive options may include *egg donation, gamete intrafallopian transfer (GIFT),* and *in vitro fertilization (IVF)* along with the administration of *fertility drugs*. In some of these practices, *surrogacy* or the use of another woman's womb during the gestational period may also be involved. In many cases, the surrogate mother may donate an egg for prenatal development, as well as her womb. The surrogate in that case is the biological mother as well as the bearer of the child who has been conceived by artificial insemination using the prospective father's sperm. Alternatively, with in vitro fertilization, eggs are removed from a woman's ovaries, fertilized in a laboratory dish with the prospective father's sperm, and transferred to another woman's uterus. In this situation, the biological and social mothers may be one and the same

viability Ability of the baby to survive outside the mother's womb.

gestational age Age of fetus derived from onset of mother's last menstrual period.

TABLE 4.1 Examples of Procedures Associated with Assisted Reproduction

Procedure	Description
Artificial Insemination by Donor	Sperm from a donor (often anonymous) are artificially provided to a woman during ovulation.
Egg Donation	An egg is harvested from a donor, fertilized, and inserted in another woman's uterus.
Fertility Drugs	Drugs are given to stimulate the development and release of egg cells from the ovary to increase the likelihood of conception by traditional means or to increase the harvest of eggs for other assisted reproduction technologies.
Gamete Intrafallopian Transfer (GIFT)	Surgical insertion of both sperm and eggs in the Fallopian tube, where fertilization normally occurs. Zygote intrafallopian transfer (ZIFT) is similar except that fertilization occurs in vitro and the zygote is inserted in the Fallopian tube.
In Vitro Fertilization (IVF)	Eggs are harvested from the ovaries and fertilized in a petri dish for subsequent implantation into a woman's uterus.
Surrogacy	A contractual arrangement in which a woman carries a pregnancy to term and in which the pregnancy involves either the surrogate's egg and sperm donated by the father or a couple's zygote established through in vitro fertilization.

except during the gestational period. Furthermore, a woman who cannot or chooses not to conceive in the traditional way might undergo in vitro fertilization and carry her own or another woman's fertilized egg during her pregnancy.

Legal, medical, and social controversies swirl around the technologies associated with assisted reproduction. For one thing, those who offer artificial insemination, apart from fertility clinics, are not always licensed, nor are they required to receive special training. Thus, the competence of the practitioners, the safety of their various activities, and the frequency of this practice may be unknown (Guinan, 1995). In addition, whereas adopted children are often informed of their status, children born as a result of, for example, artificial insemination by donor, may not know about their biological history. Even if told that their legal and biological fathers may be two different individuals, these offspring typically are unable to obtain further information, because doctors who draw on sperm banks are not required to keep records linking donors and recipients (Guinan, 1995). In some countries, such as Great Britain and Sweden, however, legislation has been enacted to permit individuals to obtain such information (Ethics Committee of the American Society for Reproductive Medicine, 2004). Legal debates can also erupt over who are the rightful parents when, for example, a surrogate mother resolves to keep the child she has carried to term.

The desire to have their own children is a powerful motive for many prospective parents. This is evident from the large number of fertility clinics—nearly 500 operating in the United States alone (Centers for Disease Control and Prevention, 2010a) and many more in other countries around the world. Nearly 60,000 births involving assisted reproduction occurred in the United States in 2007 (Centers for Disease Control and Prevention, 2010a). However, medical concerns are linked to the use of fertility drugs and assisted reproduction. For example, although about 1 percent of births in the United States (2 to 3 percent in some European countries) involve assisted reproduction, these account for about 18 percent of multiple births in the United States (Pauli et al., 2009; Wilkins-Haug, 2008). Multiple pregnancies, especially when they involve more than two fetuses, increase risks both to the woman and to her offspring. Evidence exists, too, that single children born to mothers who receive assisted reproduction, even with various factors such as maternal age controlled, tend to be of lower birth weight and are at increased risk for birth defects (Hansen et al., 2005; Reefhuis et al., 2009; Wilkins-Haug, 2008).

RISK | RESILIENCE

Despite the many concerns, studies conducted in Europe, the United States, and Taiwan reveal that children conceived by means of assisted reproduction show few emotional, behavioral, or other problems during their development (Hahn & DiPietro, 2001; Van Balen, 1998). For example, Susan Golombok and her colleagues (2002) have followed samples of children from the United Kingdom entering into adolescence who were conceived by in vitro fertilization or donor insemination. They found no differences between these children and children who were conceived without assistance on scales evaluating ability to function in school, peer relationships, and self-esteem. Parents, especially mothers, of children conceived as a result of assisted reproductive techniques are sometimes reported to display more positive parent-child relationships such as greater warmth and more concern than other parents, perhaps an indication of their commitment to and the value they place on their children (Golombok, MacCallum, & Murray, 2006; Hahn & DiPietro, 2001). The general conclusion from research is that the psychological risks to children born to parents who have been assisted in their reproductive efforts are low and that their social development is similar to that found in the larger population of children.

For Your Review and Reflection

- What constitutes the prenatal, perinatal, and postnatal periods of development?
- What are the major changes that take place following conception during the germinal, embryonic, and fetal periods of prenatal development?
- When are the major organs and systems of the body established? What is the course of brain and nervous system development in the embryo and fetus? What are some examples of how embryonic cellular differentiation and neural tube development are influenced by factors beyond genetic instructions?
- How can various kinds of assisted reproduction help prospective parents who have difficulty conceiving or are concerned about the inheritance of genetic disorders in their offspring? What are some of the medical and legal issues associated with various forms of assisted reproduction?
- What information do you think your parents had about prenatal development prior to your birth? How about your grandparents? What are some of the things you learned about this period of development that would be helpful should you ever have children?

Environmental Factors Influencing Prenatal Development

We can readily imagine that a host of events must occur, and at the right times, for prenatal development to proceed normally. What kinds of environmental support do embryo and fetus receive in their liquid, somewhat buoyant, surroundings, and how well protected are they from intrusions that can disrupt their development?

Support Within the Womb

The embryo and fetus are sustained by a number of major structures, including the placenta, the umbilical cord, and the amniotic sac. The **placenta**, formed by cells from both the blastocyst and the uterine lining, produces essential hormones for the fetus. Just as important, it serves as the exchange site at which oxygen and nutrients are absorbed from the woman's circulatory system, and at which carbon dioxide and waste products are excreted from the embryo's circulatory system. The transfer takes place through a network of intermingling, blood-rich capillaries originating in the woman's and the fetus's circulatory systems. Thus blood is not normally exchanged between a woman and her fetus. Although blood cells are too large to cross the membranes separating the two systems, smaller molecules of oxygen, carbon dioxide, nutrients, and hormones can traverse the barrier—so can some chemicals, drugs, and diseases that interfere with fetal development, as we will see shortly.

The **umbilical cord** is the conduit to and from the placenta for the blood of the fetus. The fetus lives in the womb

placenta Support organ formed by cells from both blastocyst and uterine lining; serves as exchange site for oxygen, nutrients, and waste products.

umbilical cord Conduit of blood vessels through which oxygen, nutrients, and waste products are transported between placenta and embryo.

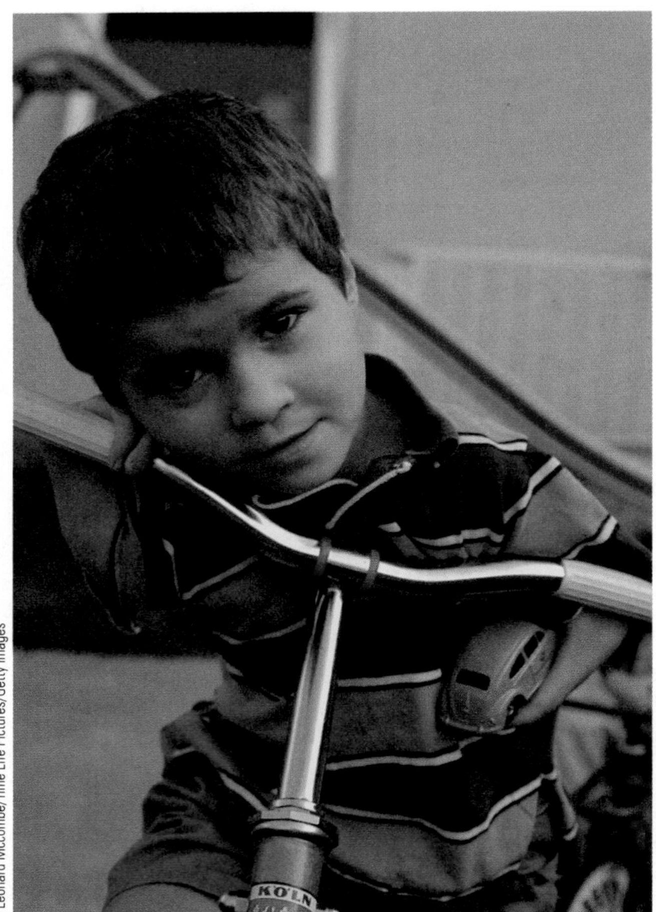

© Leonard Mccombe/Time Life Pictures/Getty Images

This young child with arm malformations illustrates the consequences of exposure to thalidomide during the embryonic stage of prenatal development.

surrounded by the fluid-filled **amniotic sac.** Amniotic fluid helps to stabilize temperature, insulates the fetus from bumps and shocks, and contains substances necessary for the development of the lungs. The fluid is constantly recirculated and renewed as the fetus ingests nutrients and urinates.

Principles of Teratology

Most fetuses negotiate the average thirty-seven- to thirty-eight-week period from conception to birth as healthy, vigorous newborns. Yet, as we discuss in Chapter 3, "Genetics and Heredity," genetic factors can modify normal progress. So, too, can environmental factors. The study of disabilities and problems that arise from environmental influences during the prenatal period is called *teratology*. Environmental agents that cause disruptions in normal development are known as **teratogens**.

The fact that external agents can upset the course of prenatal development in humans was first fully appreciated in 1941 when McAllister Gregg, an ophthalmologist, confirmed that rubella, commonly called German measles, causes visual anomalies in the fetus. During this same decade, many infants born to women exposed to the atomic bomb were reported to have birth defects. This finding, along with studies involving animals, implicated radiation as a teratogen (Warkany & Schraffenberger, 1947). The import of these early observations became even more greatly appreciated when researchers documented that women who had taken a presumably harmless antinausea drug called *thalidomide* frequently bore infants with severe arm and leg malformations (McBride, 1961).

The widely publicized thalidomide tragedy made it abundantly clear that environmental agents can seriously harm human embryos without adversely affecting the woman or others during postnatal development (Wilson, 1977). In fact, the embryo may be susceptible to virtually any substance if exposure to it is sufficiently concentrated. A number of broad generalizations have emerged from research on teratogens since the 1960s (Abel, 1989; Friedman & Hanson, 2007; Vorhees, 1986). These principles help to explain the sometimes bewildering array of adverse consequences that specific drugs, diseases, and other agents can have on development.

NATURE & NURTURE

RISK | RESILIENCE

CONTINUITY | DISCONTINUITY

- ***The Principle of Critical or Sensitive Periods: The extent to which a teratogen affects the fetus depends on the stage of development during which exposure occurs.*** Figure 4.3 shows that many human organs and systems are most sensitive to toxic agents during the third to eighth week after conception, when they are still being formed. However, vulnerability to teratogens exists throughout much of prenatal development. In fact, the brain continues to undergo substantial neural differentiation, migration, and growth during the second and third trimesters of pregnancy, as well as after birth. As a consequence, exposure to teratogens throughout prenatal development may have especially important behavioral consequences.
- ***The Principle of Susceptibility: Individuals within species, as well as species themselves, show major differences in susceptibility to different teratogens.*** Thalidomide provides a good example of this principle. Scientists knew that extremely large amounts of the drug caused abnormal fetal development in rats (Cohen, 1966). However, the doses given to pregnant women in Europe and Canada, where thalidomide was available as an over-the-counter preparation to reduce morning sickness and anxiety, were considerably smaller. For reasons

amniotic sac Fluid-filled, transparent protective membrane surrounding the fetus.

teratogen Any environmental agent that can cause deviations in prenatal development. Consequences may range from behavioral problems to death.

unknown, the embryos of humans between twenty and thirty-five days after conception are extremely sensitive to small amounts of thalidomide. More than 10,000 babies were born without limbs or with limb defects and intellectual disabilities. The genotype of an individual woman and her fetus may also affect susceptibility. Some fetuses were exposed to thalidomide during this sensitive period, yet at birth these babies showed no ill effects from the drug (Kajii, Kida, & Takahashi, 1973).

SOCIOCULTURAL INFLUENCE

- ***The Principle of Access: The accessibility of a given teratogen to a fetus or an embryo influences the extent of its damage.*** Many factors determine when and to what extent an embryo or a fetus is exposed to a teratogen. At one level, cultural and social practices may prevent a pregnant woman from using or encourage her to use drugs, prevent her from being inoculated or encourage her to be inoculated for certain diseases, or prevent her from being exposed to or allow her to be exposed to chemicals and other toxins. For example, use of alcohol may be socially approved in one segment of a culture and avoided in another. However, even when a teratogen is present, it must still gain access to the uterine environment—for example, through a woman's inhaling, ingesting, or injecting a drug intravenously. How a woman has been exposed to the agent, the way she metabolizes it, and how it is transported to the womb influence whether a teratogen reaches a sufficient threshold to have some effect on the fetus.
- ***The Principle of Dose-Response Relationships: The amount of exposure to or the dosage level of a given teratogen influences the extent of its damage.*** The severity of a teratogen often is related to level of dosage. The more a woman smokes, for example, the greater the likelihood that her baby will be of low birth weight. The concentration of a toxic agent reaching the fetus, however, cannot always be determined from the woman's exposure to it. The severity of an illness a woman experiences—for example, rubella—does not always predict the effect of the disease on the fetus.
- ***The Principle of Teratogenic Response: Teratogens do not show uniform effects on prenatal development.*** Teratogens may cause death or disrupt development of specific organs and systems. They may also have behavioral consequences, impairing sensorimotor, cognitive, social, and emotional development. The principles of species and individual differences, as well as the timing, duration, and intensity of exposure to the teratogen, govern the effect a specific teratogen will have on prenatal development. Alcohol, for example, can cause congenital defects during the embryonic period but may interfere with prenatal weight gain and contribute to postnatal behavioral problems if used during the second and third trimesters of pregnancy (Abel, 1989). One other important implication of this principle is that very different teratogenic agents can produce a similar pattern of disabilities. Thus, efforts to pinpoint why a baby was born with a given anomaly are not always successful.
- ***The Principle of Interference with Specific Mechanisms: Teratogens affect prenatal development by interfering with biochemical processes that regulate the differentiation, migration, or basic functions of cells.*** This principle helps to differentiate folk beliefs from scientific explanations of fetal anomalies. A woman's looking at a frightening visual stimulus, for example, has no direct consequence for the fetus. However, hormonal imbalances induced by chronic levels of stress may have an impact on development.
- ***The Principle of Developmental Delay and "Sleeper Effects": Some teratogens may delay development temporarily with no long-term negative consequences; others may cause developmental problems only late in development.*** Although some teratogenic effects can be observed at birth and are permanent and irreversible, others may be nullified, especially when a supportive caregiving environment is provided. However, the effects of teratogens on later development are probably substantially underestimated because some produce "sleeper effects." These are consequences that go unnoticed at birth but seed problems that become apparent in childhood and even later. For example, women treated with *diethylstilbestrol (DES)*, a hormone administered from the 1940s through the 1960s to prevent miscarriages, gave birth to daughters who showed a high rate of genital tract cancers and sons who displayed a high incidence of abnormalities of the testes when they reached adulthood.

Figure 4.3
Sensitive Periods in Prenatal Development
During prenatal development, organs and systems undergo periods in which they are more or less sensitive to teratogenic influences, environmental agents that can cause deviations in development. The potential for major structural defects (blue-colored sections) is usually greatest during the embryonic period, when many organs are forming. However, many regions of the body, including the central nervous system, continue to have some susceptibility to teratogens (yellow-colored sections) during the fetal period.
Source: From Moore, K. L., & Persaud, T. V. N. (2008). *The developing human: Clinically oriented embryology* (8th ed.). Philadelphia, PA: Saunders. p. 473. Reprinted by permission.

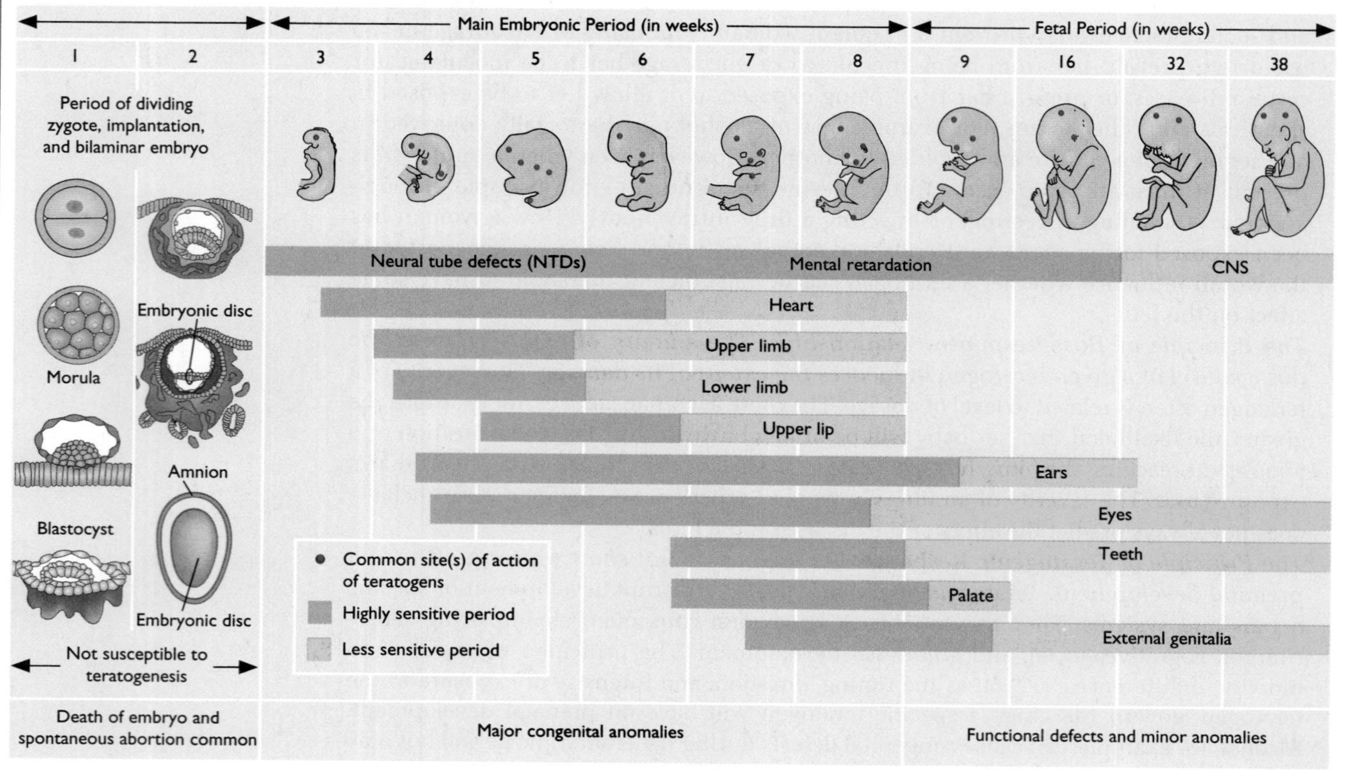

Drugs as Teratogens

Now that we have considered general principles involving teratogens, we can examine the effects that specific environmental agents have on the embryo or fetus. A number of substances that expectant women may use, either as medicine or as mood-altering devices, frequently become part of the intrauterine world. We focus on their consequences for both embryonic and fetal development.

RISK | RESILIENCE

Alcohol Because alcohol readily crosses the placenta, its concentration in the fetus is likely to be similar to that in the woman (Teratology Society, 2005). Moreover, because it lacks some enzymes to effectively degrade alcohol, the fetus may be exposed to it for a longer period of time (Reece et al., 1995). Among pregnant women in the Western world, alcohol is more widely used than any other teratogen and, according to some experts, is the single most frequent cause of reduced learning abilities in industrialized countries (Reece et al., 1995). Current data indicate that more than 10 percent of pregnant women have consumed alcohol and nearly 1 percent used it frequently (Substance Abuse and Mental Health Services Administration, 2009).

Widespread recognition of the dangers of alcohol emerged in the early 1970s, when three sets of characteristics were observed in a number of babies born to alcoholic women (Jones & Smith, 1973). These included prenatal and postnatal growth retardation including microcephaly (extremely small head size), abnormal facial features, and cognitive disabilities and other behavioral problems, such as hyperactivity and poor motor coordination, suggestive

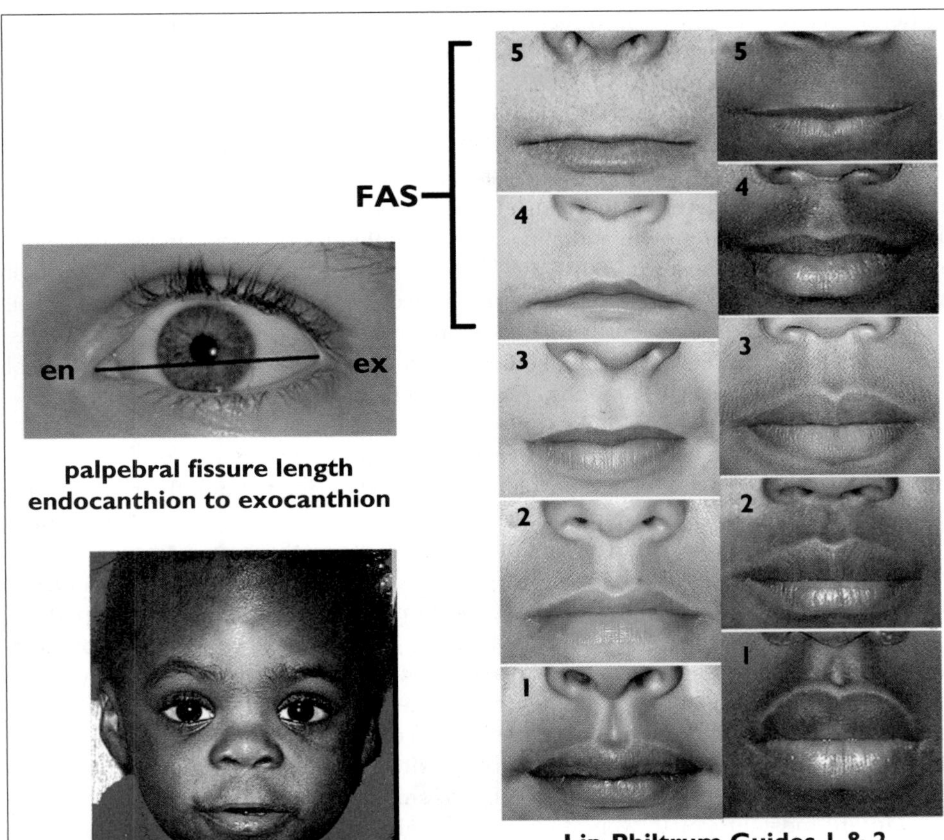

Facial features that are used to identify children with fetal alcohol syndrome are short palpebral fissures, a smooth philtrum, and a thin upper lip, as shown in this photo. Other physical characteristics, including microcephaly (small head size) and eyes widely set apart, are often accompanied by delayed physical growth and cognitive disabilities.
Source: Sokol, R. J., Delaney-Black, V., & Nordstrom, B. Fetal alcohol spectrum disorder. *Journals of the American Medical Association, 290,* 2996–2999. p. 2998.

of central nervous system dysfunction. This constellation of deficits, known as **fetal alcohol syndrome (FAS)**, appears in as many as 6 percent of infants born to alcoholic mothers (Day & Richardson, 1994). *Fetal alcohol spectrum disorders (FASD)* have been identified in many other children prenatally exposed to lesser amounts of alcohol. In addition to lower birth weight, these children may exhibit attentional, planning, problem solving, and other learning difficulties, along with social and behavioral problems (Bailey & Sokol, 2008; Kodituwakku, 2007). Perhaps as many as 1 in every 100 children born in the United States displays FAS or FASD.

Binge drinking, usually identified as five or more drinks within a short time, even if it takes place infrequently, can be especially hazardous because it exposes the fetus to highly concentrated levels of alcohol (Bailey et al., 2004; Streissguth et al., 1994). However, even limited alcohol consumption, some researchers report, is linked to an increase in spontaneous abortions and to reduced alertness, less vigorous body activity, more tremors, and slower learning in newborns compared with babies of women who do not drink (Jacobson & Jacobson, 1996; Streissguth et al., 1994). Work by Anne Streissguth and her colleagues shows that prenatal exposure to relatively moderate amounts of alcohol contributes to measurable deficits in attention and school performance, small declines in IQ, and more frequent behavioral problems in children and adolescents (Streissguth et al., 1994; Streissguth et al., 1999), problems that continue into adulthood (Spohr, Willms, & Steinhausen, 2007). For example, children and adolescents exposed to alcohol prenatally tended to be more impulsive and had difficulty organizing their work, especially under stress. Moreover, the tendency to display neurocognitive deficits was related to the amount of prenatal alcohol exposure, an example of the dose-related principle, and was especially evident when the woman engaged in occasional binge drinking.

fetal alcohol syndrome (FAS) Cluster of fetal abnormalities stemming from the mother's consumption of alcohol; includes growth retardation, defects in facial features, and intellectual retardation.

Nevertheless, there was no clear threshold at which negative consequences began to appear. As a result, Streissguth et al. (1999) and others (Sokol et al., 2003) conclude that even small amounts of alcohol can be harmful.

How does alcohol produce such effects? One way is by directly modifying cell functioning. Examination of infants with fetal alcohol syndrome who died shortly after birth reveals structural changes in the brain caused by delays and errors in the way neurons migrate to form the cortex, or outer layer, of the brain (Clarren et al., 1978). Alcohol consumption has also been linked to delayed growth and abnormalities of the frontal cortex and several other regions of the brain (Kodituwakku, 2007; Wass, Persutte, & Hobbins, 2001). The metabolism of alcohol requires substantial amounts of oxygen, so less oxygen may be available for normal cell functions. These findings provide further justification for the American Academy of Pediatrics' recommendation of complete abstinence, because "there is no known safe amount of alcohol consumption during pregnancy" (American Academy of Pediatrics, 2000).

Cigarette Smoking Among women 15 to 44 years of age in the United States, more than 16 percent of those who were pregnant report having smoked during the month prior to being interviewed in 2004 or 2005 (Substance Abuse and Mental Health Services Administration, 2009). That percentage is lower for pregnant women than for those who are not, at least for those over 18. Nevertheless, it is clear any risks to the fetus that might be found from smoking occur among a fairly substantial proportion of pregnant women, and particularly among those under age 25 (see Figure 4.4). The percentage is generally reported to be higher among Caucasian and African American women than among Hispanic women (Martin et al., 2008). It may also be far higher in other countries in which less effort has been directed toward publicizing the negative health consequences of smoking.

RISK | RESILIENCE

The risks to the fetus are, in fact, substantial. Nicotine and some other of the nearly 4,000 chemicals and compounds found in tobacco smoke have serious consequences for fetal and infant mortality, birth weight, and postnatal development (DiFranza, Aligne, & Weitzman, 2004; Lester, Andreozzi, & Appiah, 2004). Spontaneous abortions, stillbirths, and neonatal deaths increase in pregnant women who smoke (Streissguth et al., 1994).

Figure 4.4

Cigarette Use Among Women, Aged 15 to 44, by Age and Pregnancy Status

The potential negative effects of smoking on prenatal development have been widely publicized in recent years. The percentage of women smokers between 26 and 44 who smoked and were pregnant in 2004 and 2005 is much less than the percentage of women smokers of that same age who were not pregnant. A similar, but smaller, difference is found for women between 18 and 25 years of age. However, the message has not successfully led to reductions in the percentage of young women between 15 and 17 years who smoke and are pregnant.

Source: U.S. Department of Health and Human Services, 2006.

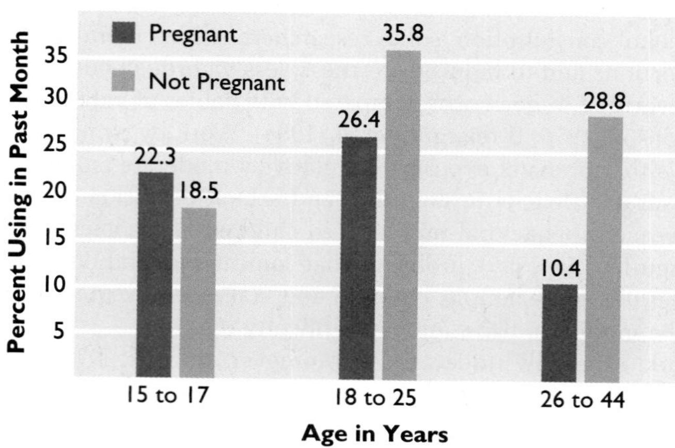

In fact, the U.S. Public Health Service estimates that the number of stillbirths and newborn deaths would decrease by 11 and 5 percent, respectively, if pregnant women in the United States stopped smoking (U.S. Department of Health and Human Services, 2004a). Another important finding from studies of babies born to smokers compared with nonsmokers is their smaller size (Aagaard-Tillery et al., 2008). The more and the longer a woman smokes during pregnancy, the lower her baby's average weight at birth, even when equated for length of gestation. Babies of women who smoke are also likely to be born a few days early (Shah & Bracken, 2000). Every cigarette smoked on a daily basis by a mother during the last trimester of pregnancy reduces the baby's weight by about one ounce (Bernstein et al., 2005).

As with alcohol consumption, a reduction in oxygen may account for these effects. Smoking increases carbon monoxide, which displaces oxygen, in the red blood cells of both woman and fetus. Nicotine also reduces blood flow to the placenta. Moreover, a fetus's heart rate goes up when a woman smokes, a reaction that may take place to maintain adequate oxygen. Babies of women who use tobacco have larger placentas and more frequent placental abnormalities than babies of the same weight born to nonsmoking women (Weinberger & Weiss, 1988). Nicotine may also interfere with metabolic activity important to cell regulation and differentiation.

Although some researchers have failed to find evidence of poorer performance on cognitive, academic, or other tasks for children exposed to smoke, most studies suggest negative behavioral and cognitive consequences (DiFranza, Aligne, & Weitzman, 2004; Huizink & Mulder, 2006; Monuteaux et al., 2006). For example, studies carried out in the United States, Finland, the Netherlands, and New Zealand reveal a small but significant increase in behavioral problems in children and adolescents whose mothers smoked during pregnancy (Kotimaa et al., 2003; Orlebeke, Knol, & Verhulst, 1999; Weitzman, Gortmaker, & Sobol, 1992). Moreover, infants born to smokers display greater irritability (Stroud et al., 2009), a higher-pitched cry (Nugent et al., 1996), and reduced visual and auditory alertness (Franco et al., 1999). Although efforts to control other factors potentially contributing to these observations have often been undertaken, genetic, family differences, and continued passive exposure to smoke from a caregiver or others in the family cannot be eliminated as possible causal contributors to these outcomes (American Academy of Pediatrics, 2000; Orlebeke et al., 1999). Once the child is born, passive exposure to environmental tobacco smoke created by others in the child's household also is associated with significantly increased health risks, such as sudden infant death and other respiratory problems (DiFranza, Aligne, & Weitzman, 2004).

Prescription and Over-the-Counter Drugs Legal drugs in addition to alcohol and tobacco can be hazardous for fetal development. Some are known teratogens (see Table 4.2), but knowledge of the effects of many remains perilously limited. Aspirin, for example, has been demonstrated to impair behavioral competence in the offspring of lower animals. One well-controlled study found that aspirin may also be associated with lower IQ in early childhood (Streissguth et al., 1984). Alternative pain relievers such as ibuprofen may also increase risk to the fetus (Dunlop et al., 2008).

Caffeine, too, has been implicated in birth defects in animals, although studies have failed to reveal any consistent link in humans. However, babies born to mothers who consume higher amounts of caffeine tend to have lower birth weight than babies of mothers who drink less coffee (Eskenazi et al., 1999). Caffeine also has a behavioral impact on the fetus. In biweekly two-hour ultrasound recordings of fetal activity during the final ten weeks of pregnancy in ten heavy-caffeine consumers (more than 500 milligrams, or five cups of coffee, daily) and ten low-caffeine consumers (less than 200 milligrams, or two cups of coffee, daily) fetuses were observed to have displayed considerably more arousal (defined by irregular heart rate and breathing activity, frequent body movements, and rapid eye movements) when exposed to the higher amounts of caffeine (Devoe et al., 1993). The more highly aroused infants may have consumed more energy, a factor that could contribute to their lower birth weight. However, the long-term implications of this difference in activity remain unknown.

RISK | RESILIENCE

TABLE 4.2 Prescription and Other Frequently Used Drugs and Their Effects on Prenatal Development

Drug	Description and Known or Suspected Effects
Alcohol	See text.
Amphetamines	Stimulants for the central nervous system, some types frequently used for weight control. Readily cross placental barrier. Fetal intrauterine growth retardation often reported but may be a result of accompanying malnutrition or multiple-drug use. Congenital anomalies and neural abnormalities reported (Aneja, Iqbal, & Ahmad, 2006).
Antibiotics (streptomycin, tetracycline)	Streptomycin associated with hearing loss.Tetracycline associated with staining of baby's teeth if exposure occurs during second or third trimester (Friedman & Polifka, 1996).
Antidepressants – Serotonin-Reuptake Inhibitors (SSRIs)	Evidence of slight increased risk for some types of birth defects but additional research is needed (Friedman & Hanson, 2007).
Antiepilectic drugs	Risk of congenital malformations. Little known about psychomotor development but some suggestive evidence of cognitive impairment in later development (Barrett & Richens, 2003).
Aspirin	Possibility of increased bleeding in both mother and infant (Hanson, 1997). See text for other complications that can arise.
Barbiturates (pentobarbital, phenobarbital, secobarbital)	Sedatives and anxiety reducers. Considerable evidence of neurobiological and behavioral complications in rats. Readily cross human placenta; concentrations in fetus may be greater than in woman. Newborns may show withdrawal symptoms (Friedman & Polifka, 1996). No consistent evidence of long-term effects in humans.
Benzodiazepines (chlordiazepoxide, diazepam)	Tranquilizers. Not shown to have teratogenic effects although newborns may display withdrawal symptoms with diazepam (Friedman & Polifka, 1996).
Caffeine	See text.
Lithium	Treatment for bipolar disorder. Crosses placenta freely. Known to be teratogenic in premammalian animals. Strong suggestive evidence of increased cardiovascular defects in human infants. Behavioral effects unknown. Administration at time of delivery markedly reduces infant responsivity (Friedman & Polifka, 1996).
Retinoids	An example is Accutane. See text.
Sex Hormones (androgens, estrogens, progestins)	Contained in birth control pills, fertility drugs, and other drugs to prevent miscarriages. Continued use of birth control pills during pregnancy associated with heart and circulatory disorders. Behavioral and personality implications suspected. Masculinization of female embryo from exposure to high doses of androgens or progestins.
Thalidomide	Reduces morning sickness and anxiety. Deformities of the limbs, depending on time of exposure, often accompanied by mental retardation (Friedman & Polifka, 1996).
Tobacco	See text.
Vitamins	Large amounts of vitamin A known to cause major birth defects. Excessive amounts of other vitamins may also cause prenatal malformations (Reece et al., 1995).

Note: This listing is not meant to be exhaustive, and other drugs may have teratogenic effects. No drug should be taken during pregnancy without consultation with a qualified physician.

Perhaps an even greater concern is the number of prescription and over-the-counter drugs consumed during pregnancy. Most expectant women use at least one medication (Werler et al., 2005), and the average may be as high as three (Dunlop et al., 2008). Little is known about the effects of many of these products, and even less is known about the interactive consequences when multiple drugs are used. In addition, as new drugs are developed, their impact as potential teratogens needs to be considered. The case of Accutane, a prescription medication used to treat acne, provides a vivid example. When first introduced as a treatment, Accutane taken by pregnant women resulted in a very high rate of physical deformities in the children who were born. Between 25 and 35 percent showed such irregularities as facial deformities, heart problems, and impairment of the nervous system

(Lammer et al., 1985). In general, expectant women are usually advised to take *no* drugs during pregnancy, including over-the-counter remedies, or to take them only under the close supervision of their physician.

Illicit Drugs Approximately 5 percent of women in the United States use illicit drugs during pregnancy (Substance Abuse and Mental Health Services Administration, 2009). However, the effects of illicit drugs, such as marijuana, heroin, and cocaine, on prenatal development are even more difficult to untangle than the effects of prescription and over-the-counter medications. Drug users are rarely certain of the contents or concentrations of the drugs they consume. Wide variation in frequency of use, the possibility of interactions from exposure to multiple drugs, poor nutritional status, inadequate or no prenatal care, and potential psychological and physiological differences both before and after taking such drugs compound the problem of isolating their teratogenic effects. The lifestyle of many illicit-drug users can be described as essentially chaotic (Chasnoff, 1992), so that conclusions about the impact of the drug itself are often difficult to make.

Efforts to determine the effects of marijuana on human fetal and postnatal development have revealed few consistent findings (Zuckerman & Bresnahan, 1991). As with tobacco, fetal weight and size appear to be reduced. Length of gestation may also be shorter for heavy marijuana users (Fried, 2002), a finding consistent with giving marijuana to speed labor, a practice carried out at one time in Europe.

Visual problems, lower scores on memory and verbal tasks, perhaps related to differences in neural activity even into adulthood, and more restless sleep patterns in early childhood are reported with prenatal exposure to marijuana (Dahl et al., 1995; Fried, 2002; Smith et al., 2006). In older children, some difficulties in executive functioning, the ability to organize and effectively regulate cognitive processes in goal-oriented activities, are also reported (Fried, 2002). However, social and economic differences in the backgrounds of the children could be contributing to many of these findings. In fact, in some cultures, such as Jamaica, marijuana use correlates positively with neonatal test performance (Dreher, Nugent, & Hudgins, 1994).

RISK | RESILIENCE

SOCIOCULTURAL INFLUENCE

The effects of heroin and morphine became a public concern as early as the late 1800s, when doctors reported withdrawal symptoms in newborns whose mothers used these substances (Zagon & McLaughlin, 1984). By the early 1900s, heroin and morphine were known to be transmitted through the placenta, as well as through the mother's milk. Although congenital defects have not been positively linked to heroin and methadone—a heroine substitute often given under regulated conditions—stillbirths and infant deaths are more frequent, and lower birth weight is common (American College of Obstetricians and Gynecologists, 1994). About 60 to 70 percent of infants born to heroin- and methadone-addicted women undergo withdrawal symptoms, such as diarrhea, sweating, a distinctively high-pitched cry, tremors, and irritability (Sprauve, 1996), and developmental difficulties continue to be observed in older children (Singer et al., 2008). High-quality caregiving, however, can play a powerful role in lessening the negative impact of prenatal exposure to heroin in children, at least for those who do not experience neurological damage (Ornoy et al., 1996).

Each year in the United States alone, well over 200,000 infants are estimated to be born to mothers who use illicit drugs (Lester, Andreozzi, & Appiah, 2004). However, few of these drugs have received more widespread attention than cocaine. Cocaine in its many forms—including crack, an especially potent and addictive variation—readily crosses the placenta. Once it reaches the fetus, it stays longer than in adults, because the immature organs of the fetus have difficulty breaking it down. Cocaine also can continue to influence the baby after birth through the mother's milk.

Dire effects for the fetus and subsequently for postnatal development as a result of exposure to cocaine have been widely publicized (Lester et al., 2004). Indeed, evidence exists that cocaine may be associated with prematurity and low birth weight (Bauer et al., 2005), as well as with attentional, cognitive, motor, and some early socio-emotional and neurobehavioral difficulties (Bennett, Bendersky, & Lewis, 2008; Lester et al., 2002; Singer et al., 2004; Stanwood & Levitt, 2001; Tronick et al., 2005). However, these observed relationships

what do you think? How Should We Respond to an Expectant Woman Who Abuses Drugs?

Consider the circumstances surrounding the prosecution of Cornelia Whitner of South Carolina. Her son was born with cocaine in his system. In 1992, Whitner pled guilty to a charge of child neglect after admitting to the use of cocaine in her third trimester of pregnancy. She was sentenced to eight years in prison. Since the mid-1980s, more than 200 American women in thirty states have been prosecuted on charges of child abuse and neglect, delivery of drugs to a minor, or assault with a deadly weapon for allegedly harming their offspring through prenatal exposure to cocaine or other illicit drugs (Armstrong, 2005; Lester et al., 2004). Do you think such approaches are an effective way to reduce the likelihood of drug use and any of its accompanying risks for the fetus? After all, anyone found to provide inappropriate drugs to a child would certainly expect to face criminal or other charges. Under such circumstances, should authorities also consider terminating the rights of the parents to rear the child? Alternatively, if known to be abusing drugs, could requiring an expectant mother to undergo some form of treatment to protect the fetus be another way to address the problem? What evidence is needed to support these kinds of efforts to reduce the likelihood that a fetus is exposed to drugs?

Others believe that criminal charges, imprisonment, or mandatory treatment may be counterproductive (Armstrong, 2005; Lester et al., 2004). Do you think, for example, that fear of being prosecuted might actually drive prospective mothers away from the care and treatment needed for both themselves and their fetuses? Moreover, could relying on criminal procedures limit the resources available for the implementation of innovative, well-funded public health efforts for treating addiction and its consequences for the fetus? Do you think sufficient knowledge and treatment facilities exist to assist expectant women in preventing drug abuse? Do women typically have the resources to gain access to such treatment when it is offered? What other social policies might be considered to help solve this very complex problem (cf. Lester et al., 2004)?

Consider another situation. Suppose one of your friends or a relative continues to smoke or to use alcohol during her pregnancy. What, if anything, would you say to this individual? What responsibility, if any, exists on your part to encourage an optimal start for every child at birth?

can often be explained by other factors known to interfere with development. As a result, some researchers suggest that exposure to cocaine for those undergoing a normal gestational period may not be the central factor contributing to poor physical growth or delayed acquisition of motor skills, lowered cognitive abilities, or behavioral, attentional, or affective disturbances in young children (Frank et al., 2001). A common thread of agreement emerging among researchers is that other risk factors regularly associated with the use of cocaine—such as increased exposure to tobacco and alcohol, poor nutrition, diminished parental responsiveness, abuse and neglect, social isolation of the family, and the increased stress typically accompanying poverty—may play just as important a role, perhaps even a *more important* role in negative outcomes for development during early and middle childhood than does cocaine itself (Frank et al., 2001; Jones, 2006). Thus, the prognosis for children subjected to cocaine and other illicit drugs in utero should and does improve substantially when interventions are undertaken to reduce or eliminate these other risk factors (Butz et al., 2001; Kilbride et al., 2000).

Diseases and Infections as Teratogens

RISK | RESILIENCE

Somewhere between 2 and 8 percent of babies born to American women are exposed to one or more diseases or other forms of illness during pregnancy (Landry, 2004). Fortunately, most babies are unaffected. Moreover, significant progress has been made in eliminating the potentially negative fetal consequences of several diseases, such as mumps and rubella (German measles), at least in some countries. Unfortunately, rubella, a highly preventable illness, continues to be a major cause of fetal malformations and death worldwide, because vaccination programs are limited in some regions of the world. Other diseases and infections, some of which are described in Table 4.3, pose risks for the fetus in even the most medically advanced countries. Their impact on the fetus can be serious, sometimes devastating, even when a woman is completely unaware of the illness.

Toxoplasmosis Toxoplasmosis is caused by a parasite found in many mammals and birds; perhaps as many as 60 million people in just the United States may be infected (Centers for Disease Control and Prevention, 2008). However, the disease is found with greater frequency in some European countries, including France and Austria, and in tropical regions. Humans occasionally contract the disease by touching cat feces containing the parasite or, even more frequently, by eating raw or partially infected cooked meat, especially pork and lamb. Children and adults are often unaware of their exposure, because the infection may have no symptoms or cause only a minor fever or rash.

Infections early in pregnancy can have devastating consequences; fortunately, risk of transmission to the fetus at this time is lowest (Foulon et al., 1999). Growth retardation, jaundice, accumulation of fluid in the brain, and visual and central nervous system damage are the most frequent teratogenic outcomes. Some infants show no symptoms at birth; only later may cognitive disabilities, neuromuscular abnormalities, impaired vision, and other eye problems become apparent. Treatment with antibiotics can be effective in reducing the likelihood of severe consequences if the fetus has been infected (Centers for Disease Control and Prevention, 2008). Clearly, the best course of action, however, is preventing infection from exposure to toxoplasmosis in the first place. Good sanitation procedures (e.g., washing counters, hands, and materials that may have been in contact with raw meats or fruits and vegetables), cooking meats thoroughly, and wearing gloves while gardening or working in soils that may contain cat feces and washing hands afterwards are among the steps that can be taken to reduce the likelihood of becoming infected.

Cytomegalovirus Cytomegalovirus (CMV), a member of the herpes family of viruses, causes swelling of the salivary glands and mononucleosis-like symptoms in adults. It is the single most frequent infection found in newborns today, affecting 1 to 2 of every 100 babies. As many as 10 percent of infected infants can be expected to sustain some congenital damage (Friedman & Hanson, 2002). No effective treatment exists.

CMV is most frequently reported in Asia, Africa, and lower socioeconomic groups, in which up to 85 percent of the population may be infected. Yet somewhere between 50 and 80 percent of adults in the United States are affected by age 40 (Centers for Disease Control and Prevention, 2010b). Transmission occurs through various body fluids. CMV can be passed easily between children playing together, for example, in daycare centers and in family daycare settings (Bale et al., 1999) and from child to adult through contact with body fluids. Most people show no signs of being infected nor is there any effective treatment for CMV. Although it may not be possible to avoid all risks of contracting CMV, thorough hand washing (especially after changing diapers), eliminating sharing of eating utensils, and kissing young children on the forehead or hugging them rather than kissing on the lips or cheek are recommended practices for reducing its transmission.

Fortunately, the aftermath of contracting the virus in early childhood is generally not serious. However, infection can occur within the womb, during birth, and through breast-feeding with more severe consequences (Adler, 1992; Hamprecht et al., 2004). The negative outcomes are typically greatest for the fetus if a woman contracts the disease for the first time during her pregnancy (Guerra et al., 2000). Growth retardation, jaundice, skin disorders, and small head size are common consequences. About one-third of infants showing these characteristics at birth will die in early infancy; a large percentage of those who survive will display cognitive disabilities. About half of infants sustaining congenital damage from CMV show no symptoms at birth, but many

TABLE 4.3 Diseases and Maternal Conditions That May Affect Prenatal Development

Disease	Physical and Behavioral Consequences for the Fetus
Sexually Transmitted Diseases	
Acquired Immunodeficiency Syndrome (AIDS)	See text.
Chlamydia	Nearly always transmitted to infant during delivery via infected birth canal. In the United States alone, more than 2 million individuals are estimated to be infected despite the fact that it can be treated (Datta et al., 2007). Often causes eye infection in infant and some increased risk of pneumonia. Other adverse effects suspected (Medline Plus, 2010a).
Gonorrhea	If acquired prenatally, may cause premature birth. Most frequently contracted during delivery through infected birth canal and may then attack eyes. In the United States and many other countries, antibiotic eye drops are administered to all newborns to prevent blindness.
Hepatitis B	Associated with premature birth, low birth weight, increased neonatal death, and liver disorders (Pass, 1987). Most frequently contracted during delivery through birth canal or postnatally. Can be prevented by vaccination.
Herpes Simplex	Of its two forms, only one is transmitted primarily through sexual activity. Both forms, however, can be transmitted to the fetus, causing severe damage to the central nervous system (Enright & Prober, 2004). Most infections occur during delivery through birth canal containing active herpes lesions.If untreated, the majority of infants will die or suffer central nervous system damage. Although current treatments may reduce these problems, significant difficulties remain for many infants (Enright & Prober, 2004). If known to carry the virus, women may need to be tested frequently during pregnancy to determine if the disease is in its active, contagious state because symptoms may not be present even when active. If the disease is active, cesarean delivery is used to avoid infecting the baby.
Syphilis	May cause death to fetus and low birth weight in newborns. Often results in learning disabilities and bone and other nervous system disorders (Chakraborty & Luck, 2008).
Other Diseases	
Cytomegalovirus	See text.
Influenza	Some forms linked to increased heart and central nervous system abnormalities, as well as spontaneous abortions (Reece et al., 1995).
Mumps	Increased risk of spontaneous abortion and stillbirth.
Rubella	Increased risk of spontaneous abortion and stillbirth. Growth retardation, cataracts, hearing impairment, heart defects, mental retardation also common and especially if exposure occurs in the first or second month of pregnancy and believed to increase the risk of schizophrenia in adulthood (Brown & Susser, 2002).
Toxoplasmosis	See text.
Varicella-zoster (chicken pox)	Increased risk of eye and ear defects, intrauterine growth retardation, limb defects, and learning disabilities (Enright & Prober, 2004).
Other Maternal Conditions	
Diabetes	Increased risk of stillbirths and fetal and infant mortality as well as excessive size of the baby at birth (Siddiqui & James, 2003). Effects are likely to be a consequence of metabolic disturbances rather than of insulin. Rapid advances in care have helped reduce risks substantially for diabetic women.
Hypertension (chronic)	Probability of miscarriage or infant death increased.
Obesity	Increased risk of diabetes and large-for-gestational-age babies (Lu et al., 2001).
Pregnancy-Induced Hypertension	5%–10% of expectant women experience significant increase in blood pressure, often accompanied by *edema* (swelling of face and extremities as a result of water retention), rapid weight gain, and protein in urine during later months of pregnancy. Condition is also known as *pre-eclampsia* (or *eclampsia*, if severe) and *toxemia*. Under severe conditions, woman may suffer seizures and coma.The fetus is at increased risk for death, brain damage, and lower birth weight. Adequate protein consumption helps minimize problems. Drugs used to treat high blood pressure may be just as hazardous to fetus as the condition itself.

(continued)

TABLE 4.3 Diseases and Maternal Conditions That May Affect Prenatal Development (continued)

Disease	Physical and Behavioral Consequences for the Fetus
Other Maternal Conditions	
Rh Incompatibility	Blood containing a certain protein is Rh positive, Rh negative if it lacks that protein. Hereditary factors determine which type the individual possesses. If fetus's blood is Rh positive, it can cause formation of antibodies in blood of woman who is Rh negative.These antibodies can cross the placental barrier to destroy red blood cells of fetus. May result in miscarriage or stillbirth, jaundice, anemia, heart defects, and mental retardation. Likelihood of birth defects increases with succeeding pregnancies because antibodies are usually not present until after birth of first Rh-positive child. A vaccine (Rhogam) can be administered to the mother within 3 days after childbirth, miscarriage, or abortion to prevent antibody formation.

Note: For more information on many of these diseases and maternal conditions see http://www.nlm.nih.gov/medlineplus/healthtopics.html.

will subsequently display progressive loss of hearing or other, subtler defects, including minimal brain dysfunction, visual or dental abnormalities, or motor and neural problems (Foulon et al., 2008; Landry, 2004).

Sexually Transmitted Infections and Sexually Transmitted Diseases Several infections and diseases identified as teratogenic are transmitted primarily through sexual contact, and the infection and its symptoms are usually concentrated in the genitourinary tract (see Table 4.3). Syphilis and certain strains of herpes simplex, for example, are virtually always contracted from infected sexual partners. On the other hand, some of these infections, such as acquired immunodeficiency syndrome (AIDS) and hepatitis B, can be acquired through exposure to infected blood as well.

Sexually transmitted infections (STIs), rather than sexually transmitted diseases (STDs), is the increasingly more preferred name for these viruses and bacteria because they may not show observable disease-like symptoms in some individuals. Nevertheless, STIs can interfere with reproduction in a number of ways. They may compromise the woman's health (AIDS, gonorrhea, hepatitis B, herpes simplex, syphilis), scar or disturb reproductive organs so that conception and normal pregnancy cannot proceed (chlamydia, gonorrhea), directly infect the fetus (AIDS, herpes simplex, syphilis), or interfere with healthy postnatal development (AIDS, hepatitis B, herpes simplex, syphilis) (Lee, 1988). In recent years, the frequency of STIs has risen rapidly in populations around the world. None, however, has had as dramatic an impact as AIDS.

Of the estimated 10,000 children under the age of fifteen having human immunodeficiency virus type 1 (HIV-1) in North America and the more than 3.2 million children currently living with the disease worldwide, most were infected prenatally, during birth, or shortly after birth through an infected mother's breast milk (Havens & Waters, 2004; National Institute of Allergy and Infectious Diseases, 2004). Prior to 1995, about 25 percent of infants born to HIV-positive women could be expected to eventually acquire AIDS. However, new anti-viral medical treatments have reduced the transmission rate to less than 2 percent, at least in countries in which such drugs are available (Fowler et al., 2007). An illustration of the effectiveness of these drugs in the United States can be seen in Figure 4.5.

RISK | RESILIENCE

Of those infants who do become infected with HIV, about 20 percent show rapid progression to AIDS and death in early childhood. However, with new advances in treatment, about two-thirds live more than five years; the average length of survival in Western countries is now greater than nine years; and about 25 percent of children do not show severe symptoms of AIDS until after ten years (Brown, Lourie, & Pao, 2000; European Collaborative Study, 2001; National Institute of Allergy and Infectious Diseases, 2004). Children receiving medication for HIV also show substantial benefits in terms of maintaining more normal levels of cognitive functioning throughout much of their childhood (Brown et al., 2000). Thus, the negative course of the disease can be slowed for cognitive and other aspects of development. Unfortunately, however, for many children around the world, limited medical services, poverty, and the absence of social support will adversely affect their development while living with the disease.

sexually transmitted infections (STIs) A group of infections such as chlamydia, syphilis, gonorrhea, herpes simplex, HIV, and hepatitis B often spread through sexual contact. Also frequently called sexually transmitted diseases (STDs).

Figure 4.5

Decline in HIV/AIDS Transmitted to Offspring via HIV-Infected Women

The transmission of HIV/AIDS infection to infants and children via HIV-infected women has declined dramatically in the United States from 1992 to 2004. This decline is primarily a result of treating infected women with zidovudine. Unfortunately, this and other drugs used to treat HIV/AIDS infection are often too expensive or unavailable in some regions of the world.

Source: From McKenna, M. T., & Hu, X. (2007). Recent trends in the incidence and morbidity that are associated with perinatal human immunodeficiency virus infection in the United States. *American Journal of Obstetrics and Gynecology, 197,* S10–S16. Reprinted by permission.

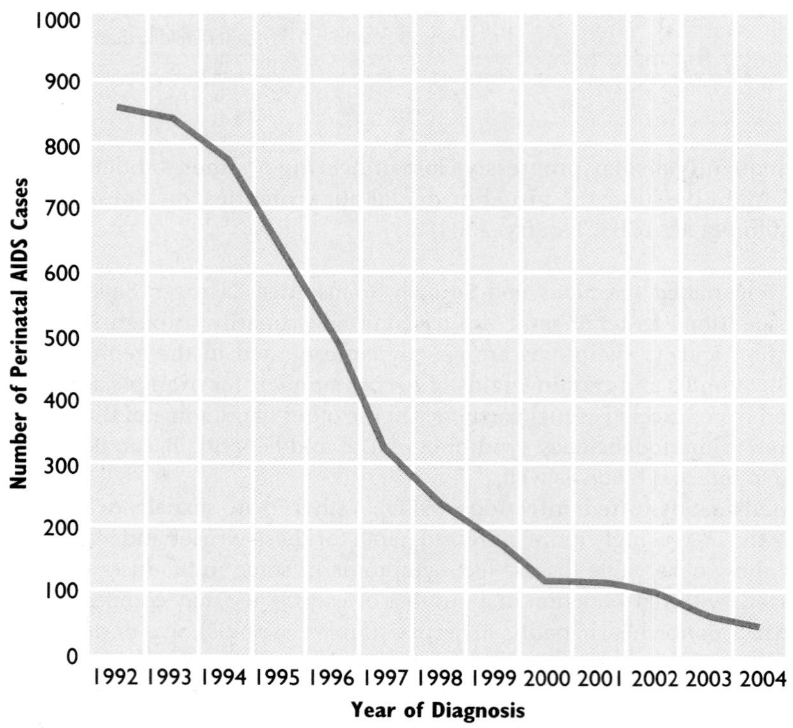

NATURE & NURTURE

Environmental Hazards as Teratogens

Radiation was one of the earliest confirmed teratogens, and it can cause genetic mutations as well. Radiation's effects include spontaneous abortion, small head size, and other defects associated with the skeleton, genitals, and sensory organs. Even low doses of radiation have been linked to increased risks of cancer and neural damage; pregnant women are urged to avoid unnecessary x-rays and other circumstances in which exposure might occur.

Chemicals and other elements in the environment pose another significant source of potential risks. Known teratogens include lead, mercury, and polychlorinated biphenyls, or PCBs (a synthetic hydrocarbon once used in transformers, hydraulic fluid, and other industrial equipment), as well as many elements found in paints, dyes and coloring agents, solvents, oven cleaners, pesticides, herbicides, food additives, artificial sweeteners, and cosmetic products (Hubbs-Tait et al., 2005; Needleman & Bellinger, 1994). Careless handling and disposal of such elements and their excessive production and use are one problem. They also pervade the foods we eat and the air we breathe. Mercury, for example, can occur in especially high concentrations in large predatory fish such as swordfish and tuna (Hubbs-Tait et al., 2005); the U.S. Food and Drug Administration recommends that pregnant and nursing mothers as well as young children avoid consuming these fish (U.S. Department of Health and Human Services, 2004b). In addition, many women of childbearing age are exposed in the workplace to hazardous substances such as lead, formaldehyde, and carbon monoxide.

Women's Conditions and Prenatal Development

In addition to teratogens, a number of health conditions are associated with increased risk during pregnancy. Several of these conditions (diabetes, pregnancy-induced and chronic hypertension, Rh incompatibility) and their consequences for the fetus are summarized in Table 4.3. Additional factors influencing the prenatal environment include the age of the woman, her nutritional status, and her emotional state.

Age The number of older mothers is on the rise in industrialized countries as women postpone pregnancy to establish careers or for other reasons. Is pregnancy riskier as women become older? As we show in Chapter 3, "Genetics and Heredity," the likelihood of having a child with Down syndrome increases dramatically during the later childbearing years, especially after age thirty-five. Some studies also report increased prematurity and mortality, as well as greater difficulty during labor, for women over thirty-five having their first child (Cleary-Goldman et al., 2005). The findings are likely due, in large part, to greater health problems (hypertension, diabetes, and others) that can accompany increased age. Despite these elevated risks, healthy women older than thirty-five routinely deliver healthy infants, just as do women between twenty and thirty-five years of age.

Teenagers, on the other hand, may be at considerably greater risk for delivering less healthy babies (Whitman et al., 2001). Lack of adequate prenatal care is one reason; pregnant teenagers in the United States, particularly those who are very young and unmarried, often do not seek medical services. Another reason pregnancy at these early ages poses more problems is the complicated nutritional needs of adolescents; many teenagers are still growing themselves. Although the rate of births to teenagers declined steadily in the United States between 1991 and 2006 (Martin et al., 2008), it is still substantially higher than in other industrialized nations and double or even triple the rate in most Western European countries. In any given year, about one in twenty-five fifteen- to nineteen-year-olds is likely to bear a child; this translates into more than 400,000 births per year to teens (Centers for Disease Control and Prevention, 2009b).

Nutrition What foods are needed for the health of the woman and her fetus? The seemingly obvious but important answer is a well-balanced diet. Extreme malnutrition during prenatal development can be especially detrimental. During World War II, famines occurred in parts of Holland and in Leningrad in the former Soviet Union. When the malnutrition occurred during the first few months of pregnancy, death, premature birth, and nervous system defects were especially frequent. When famine occurred later in prenatal

SOCIOCULTURAL INFLUENCE

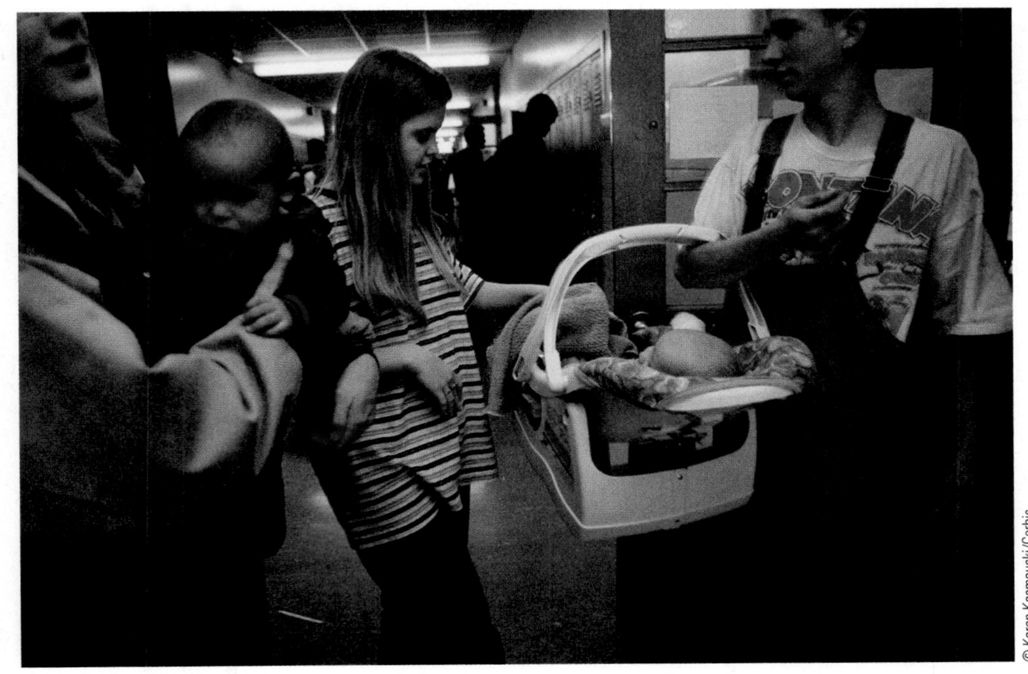

© Karen Kasmauski/Corbis

Teenage mothers give birth to more than 400,000 babies in the United States each year. Many of them will be unmarried teens who have received little or no prenatal care, factors that increase the risk for delivering less healthy babies.

development, retardation in fetal growth and low birth weights were more likely (Antonov, 1947). Although not everyone agrees about the guidelines, women of normal weight for their height are typically advised to gain about twenty-five to thirty-five pounds during pregnancy (Centers for Disease Control and Prevention, 2009a).

Diets must be not only sufficient in number of calories but also balanced with respect to adequate protein, vitamins, and other nutrients. In fact, intake of many nutrients should be increased during pregnancy, as Table 4.4 indicates. Fortunately, unless deficiencies are so severe that malformations and deficits in neuron formation cannot be overcome, many cognitive problems associated with prenatal undernutrition and the lowered birth weight that often accompanies it may still be reversed when adequate nourishment and stimulation are provided following birth (Pollitt, 1996).

SOCIALCULTURAL INFLUENCE

Stress Cultural beliefs about potentially harmful consequences of frightening or stressful events on fetal development are pervasive, and many societies encourage a calm atmosphere for pregnant women. In studies in which researchers have carefully measured anxiety, family conflict, positive and negative life events, and the availability of physical and social support for the woman, stress has been linked to greater complications during both pregnancy and birth. Anxiety appears to lengthen labor, increase the need for more anesthesia during delivery, and produce more birthing complications. High stress, particularly early in pregnancy, seems to contribute to a shorter length of gestation and therefore to more frequent preterm births and more infants with lower birth weight (Hobel, Goldstein, & Barrett, 2008). For example, women who had experienced an earthquake in the first trimester of pregnancy viewed the pregnancy as a more stressful period and also delivered their infants sooner than those who had experienced the earthquake in the second or third trimester (Glynn et al., 2001). In addition, fatigue associated with long hours at work, especially work that involves prolonged standing and physical strain, increases preterm birth and health problems for a pregnant woman (Schetter, 2009). Some stress is inevitable and limited levels for otherwise healthy mothers may even have beneficial consequences for the fetus (DiPietro et al, 2006). For example, sensory changes in the intrauterine environment introduced by moderate emotional variations experienced during pregnancy may enhance

TABLE 4.4 Nutritional Need Differences Between Nonpregnant and Pregnant Women 24 Years of Age

Nutrient	Nonpregnant	Pregnant	Percent Increase	Dietary Sources
Folic acid	180 mcg	400 mcg	+ 122	Leafy vegetables, liver
Vitamin D	5 μg	10 μg	+ 100	Fortified dairy products
Iron	15 mg	30 mg	+ 100	Meats, eggs, grains
Calcium	800 mg	1200 mg	+ 50	Dairy products
Phosphorus	800 mg	1200 mg	+ 50	Meats
Pyridoxine	1.6 mg	2.2 mg	+ 38	Meats, liver, enriched grains
Thiamin	1.1 mg	1.5 mg	+ 36	Enriched grains, pork
Zinc	12 mg	15 mg	+ 25	Meats, seafood, eggs
Riboflavin	1.3 mg	1.6 mg	+ 23	Meats, liver, enriched grains
Protein	50 g	60 g	+ 20	Meats, fish, poultry, dairy
Iodine	150 mcg	175 mcg	+ 17	Iodized salt, seafood
Vitamin C	60 mg	70 mg	+ 17	Citrus fruits, tomatoes
Energy	2200 kcal	2500 kcal	+ 14	Proteins, fats, carbohydrates
Magnesium	280 mg	320 mg	+ 14	Seafood, legumes, grains
Niacin	15 mg	17 mg	+ 13	Meats, nuts, legumes
Vitamin B-12	2.0 mcg	2.2 mcg	+ 10	Animal proteins
Vitamin A	800 μg	800 μg	0	Dark green, yellow, or orange fruits and vegetables, liver

Source: Reece et al., 1995.

neural development. Nevertheless, many studies have provided evidence that, when stress is very high, poorer developmental outcomes are more likely for infants and very young children (Huizink, Mulder, & Buitelaar, 2004; Laplante et al., 2004). The social support a pregnant woman receives from family and friends is an important factor that can mitigate potentially negative consequences of high levels of stress during pregnancy (Feldman et al., 2000). Among women who experience a variety of life changes before and during pregnancy, those with strong social and personal assistance—for example, those who can obtain a ride to work, get help when sick, or borrow needed money—have far fewer complications than women without such resources (Norbeck & Tilden, 1983).

RISK | RESILIENCE

After learning about the many teratogens and other factors that can affect prenatal development, we may be surprised that babies manage to be born healthy at all. But they do so every day. We should wonder, rather, at the rich complexity of prenatal development and appreciate more deeply that it proceeds normally so much of the time. Nearly 97 percent of babies born in the United States are healthy and fully prepared to adapt to their new environment. Knowledge of teratogens allows prospective parents as well as others in the community to maximize the chances that all infants will be equipped to enter the world with as many resources as possible.

For Your Review and Reflection

- What kinds of supportive functions do the placenta, umbilical cord, and amniotic sac provide for the embryo and the fetus?
- What are teratogens? What principles apply to how teratogens have their effects?
- How do alcohol, cigarette smoke, prescription or over-the-counter drugs, and illicit drugs affect prenatal development?
- What kinds of risks exist for the embryo and fetus exposed to rubella, toxoplasmosis, cytomegalovirus, and sexually transmitted infections?
- What maternal conditions affect the well-being of the fetus and embryo?
- What are some of the factors that increase resilience or risk to the fetus even if exposed to teratogens?
- What are steps that you personally could take to reduce the risk of fetal exposure to teratogens if you or someone you know becomes pregnant?

Birth and the Perinatal Environment

Societies vary enormously in the techniques and rituals that accompany the transition from fetus to newborn. Some interpret pregnancy and birth as natural and healthy; others, as an illness requiring medical care and attention (Newton, 1955). The !Kung, a hunting-and-gathering people living in the Kalahari Desert of Africa, build no huts or facilities for birthing. They view birth as part of the natural order of events, requiring no special intervention (Shostak, 1981). In contrast, pregnancy and childbirth in the United States and many other countries throughout much of the twentieth century were regarded more as illnesses to be managed by professionally trained medical personnel (Dye, 1986). In 1900 fewer than 5 percent of babies were born in hospitals in the United States. Today more than 99 percent of all babies in the United States are born in hospitals (Martin et al., 2009).

SOCIOCULTURAL INFLUENCE

Preparing for Childbirth

With the shift from childbirth at home to childbirth in the hospital came an increase in the use of medication during delivery. Concerns about the impact of these medications, along with reports of unmedicated but seemingly pain-free delivery by women in other cultures,

Societies differ enormously in their approach to the birth of a baby. In the United States, most births occur in hospitals. In contrast, more than four of every five births in the Trobriand Islands (part of Papua New Guinea) take place in villages where a midwife is in charge.

Peter Essick/Aurora Photos

prodded professionals and expectant parents alike to reconsider how best to prepare for the birth of a baby. After observing one woman who reported a pain-free delivery, Grantley Dick-Read, a medical practitioner in Great Britain, concluded that difficult childbirth was fostered largely by the tension and anxiety in which Western civilization cloaked the event. Dick-Read (1959) proposed that women be taught methods of physical relaxation, given information about the process of childbirth, and encouraged to cultivate a cooperative relationship with their doctors to foster a more natural childbirth experience. Others, including Fernand Lamaze (1970), adopted similar ideas, adding procedures to divert thoughts from pain and encouraging breathing activities to support the labor process.

In recent years, **prepared** (or **natural**) **childbirth**, which involves practicing procedures designed to minimize pain and reduce the need for medication during delivery, has become a popular birthing method. Women who attend classes and adhere to the recommendations of Lamaze and other childbirth education programs (such as the National Childbirth Trust in the United Kingdom) generally require fewer and lower amounts of drugs during delivery than women who have not participated in prepared childbirth. Women who attend childbirth classes may experience no less pain, but relaxation techniques and an additional element frequently promoted in these programs—the assistance of a coach or trainer, sometimes the partner—seem to help counter the discomfort and lead to a more positive evaluation of childbirth (Simkin & O'Hara, 2002).

prepared (natural) childbirth Type of childbirth that involves practicing procedures during pregnancy and childbirth that are designed to minimize pain and reduce the need for medication during delivery.

Nurturing and Caring During Labor | research applied to education

When Elena had awakened that early morning of her daughter's birth, she knew the signs of the onset of labor. Although taking longer than she would have liked, birthing had proceeded smoothly despite her anxieties about the whole process. Maybe it helped to have her husband participate with her in childbirth classes. During her pregnancy, she also had learned about other options, ranging from massage to hypnosis to traditional medication, even delivering the baby in water, an alternative the birthing center at the hospital offered for those who wished to do so. One other thing had been extremely helpful: the presence of a doula, another woman to accompany and support her throughout the entire period of labor. Elena was not certain about some of

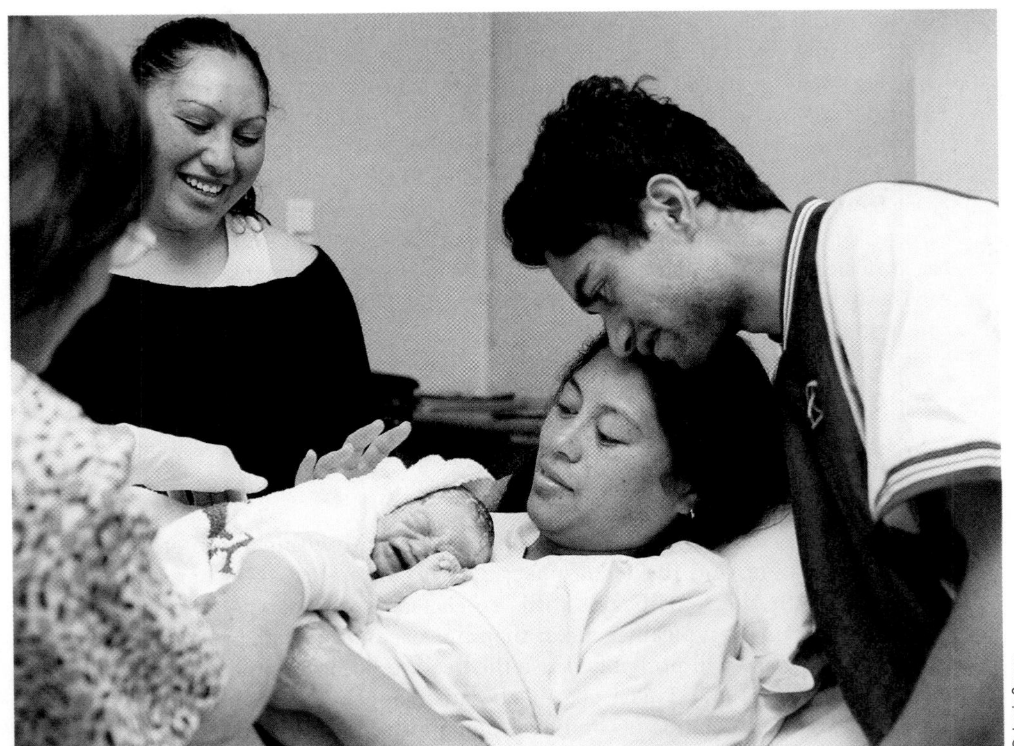

Today, partners, and sometimes other friends and family members, are encouraged to furnish social and emotional support to women who are about to deliver a baby. When such support is provided by a trusted companion, labor is shorter, fewer drugs are required, and babies are born exhibiting less distress. Nurse midwives, such as the one here who had been discussing the progress of labor with this mother as she was delivering her baby have demonstrated an excellent record in helping with the delivery of newborns.

the other alternatives for making the delivery easier and more comfortable. But of one thing she was very sure: in addition to her husband, she would have a doula with her throughout the birthing process.

Most women delivering a baby go through a lot of hard work and some, perhaps considerable, discomfort. It can be a very anxious time. Human birth differs from that of other species of mammals in that it typically requires some form of assistance (Rosenberg & Trevathen, 2001). In many cultures, the help comes from friends and relatives or from midwives, just as it did in the United States many decades ago. With the relocation of childbirth to hospitals, however, women became isolated from family and friends, and a more private and impersonal procedure emerged. Perhaps with that change something very important was lost. Research has helped to identify this loss and has led to alternatives in birthing practices that may benefit both men and women as they become new parents.

1. *Include a partner and/or some other trusted companion in preparing for and assisting during childbirth.* Studies carried out in numerous countries around the world as well as the United States reveal that having a continuously supportive companion during delivery can be helpful to women and their newborns (Simkin & O'Hara, 2002). For example, in one Guatemalan study, first-time mothers were assigned a doula, a woman experienced with delivery who stayed with the mother to provide emotional support, increase her physical comfort, inform her about what was happening during labor, and advocate for her needs (Klaus & Kennell, 1982). Women given these personal attendants spent a far shorter time in labor, required drugs or forceps less frequently, and delivered babies who showed less fetal distress and difficulty breathing than women who received only routine nursing care. Sometimes fathers or other partners are actively encouraged to take on some of these functions as well and can be very effective (Cunningham, 1993), although a doula may be able to provide a more balanced and informative perspective on the sequence of unfolding events (Ballen & Fulcher, 2006).
2. *Consider what type of practitioner might be most beneficial during childbirth.* Of course, fathers or other partners who assist in labor are not likely to be experts in the process. Midwives, nurses, or others far more experienced in childbirth, whose additional primary function is to provide personal assistance while managing labor, have received positive evaluations as well. Compared with physicians, having a midwife oversee birthing often results in, for example, lower rates of deliveries undergoing cesarean birth or other surgical procedures, less use of medication by

the mother, and greater maternal satisfaction with care (Butler et al., 1993; Oakley et al., 1996; Sakala, 1993). Whereas about 8 percent of births in the United States are now accompanied by midwives (Martin et al., 2009), the percent is far greater in a number of European countries.

3. *Explore the different alternatives available to assist in delivering a baby.* Some of the positive outcomes achieved by midwives may stem from an attitude that inspires women not just to deliver babies but also to draw on their own inner resources, as well as their support networks, for giving birth. Moreover, greater flexibility in positioning and moving about during labor, perhaps even soaking in a tub, standing, squatting, or sitting in special chairs, or even hanging from a bar, are increasingly being offered as alternatives to the traditional recumbent position for delivery. These choices can increase a woman's comfort and, in some cases, speed labor and thus reduce stress for both mother and baby (Simkin & O'Hara, 2002). In fact, in non-Western cultures, these alternative positions for childbirth may be the norm (Rosenberg & Trevathen, 2001).

Labor and Delivery

When labor begins, the wet, warm, and supportive world within the uterus undergoes a rapid transformation, and the fetus must adjust to an earthshaking series of changes. During normal birth, the fetus begins to be subjected to increasingly stronger pressure. Because the birth canal is typically smaller than the size of the head, pressure—as great as thirty pounds of force—will probably cause the head to become somewhat elongated and misshapen (Trevathen, 1987). This is possible because the cerebral plates are not yet knitted together, allowing them to slide up and over one another. At times the fetus may experience brief disruptions in oxygen as the flow of blood in the umbilical cord is temporarily obstructed. And then the infant emerges, normally head first, into a strange, new world, one drier, possibly colder, and often much brighter and noisier. Within minutes the new arrival must begin to take in oxygen. The baby must also soon learn to coordinate sucking, swallowing, and breathing to obtain sufficient nutrients.

Labor is a complicated, interactive process involving the fetus, the placenta, and the woman. What brings about its onset? The answer begins with the hypothalamus, pituitary, and adrenal glands of the fetus. When these become mature enough, they help to produce a cascading sequence of hormones and other events, including some in the placenta, that are especially important in initiating labor (Nathanielsz, 1996). In fact, measurement of one hormone in the placenta as early as the sixteenth to twentieth week of pregnancy can predict whether a delivery will occur somewhat before, somewhat after, or about the time of the anticipated due date (R. Smith, 1999).

The first of the three traditional stages of labor (see Figure 4.6) begins with brief, mild contractions perhaps ten to fifteen minutes apart. These contractions become increasingly frequent and serve to alter the shape of the cervix, preparing it for the fetus's descent and entry into the narrow birth canal. Near the end of the first stage, which on average lasts about eleven hours for firstborns and about seven hours for later-borns, dilation of the cervix proceeds rapidly to allow passage through the birth canal. The second stage consists of the continued descent and the birth of the baby. This stage usually requires a little less than an hour for firstborns and about twenty minutes for later-borns. It also normally includes several reorientations of both the head and shoulders to permit delivery through the tight-fitting passageway (Rosenberg & Trevathen, 2001). In the third stage, which lasts about fifteen minutes, the placenta is expelled. These durations are, however, averages; enormous variation exists from one woman to another.

Medication During Childbirth In Western societies, births are often accompanied by one of three different types of procedures to reduce pain. Systemic medications consisting of some type of narcotic and often accompanied by a tranquilizer affect the entire body and help to dull pain and reduce overall anxiety. An epidural—usually some type of anesthetic along with a narcotic and often given throughout much of labor—reduces pain to the lower part of the body. A spinal block—another type of anesthetic delivered directly into the spinal cord—quickly provides pain relief for a short period of time during labor. The drugs associated

© Jules Perrier/Corbis

This woman, who has just given birth, now has the opportunity to see and hold her infant for the first time. In contrast to earlier practices, parents in most hospital settings today are allowed ample time to become acquainted with their newborns immediately after birth.

with these procedures readily pass through the placenta and enter the fetus's circulatory system. As a consequence, babies whose mothers receive substantial amounts of some types of medication during labor may initially be less attentive and responsive to caregivers than babies of mothers who do not receive medication (Bricker & Lavender, 2002; Lieberman & O'Donoghue, 2002) and critics note that babies exposed to high doses of medication can be more irritable and gain weight more slowly than babies exposed to small amounts or no drugs at all (Brazelton, Nugent, & Lester, 1987; Emory, Schlackman, & Fiano, 1996).

Developmental differences between babies born to medicated and nonmedicated women, however, are not consistent. Some experts believe that reported negative effects of exposure to drugs at birth have been markedly overstated and occur only when medications are used excessively (Kraemer et al., 1985). Thus, women need not experience unreasonable pain or feel guilty if drugs are administered. Efforts to make the birth process gentler, such as by reducing illumination and noise or by delivering the baby underwater, have also been proposed (Daniels, 1989; LeBoyer, 1975), although the advantages of these practices for either women or infants have not been well documented (Simkin & O'Hara, 2002). The use of other complementary and alternative medical procedures, such as acupuncture and various relaxation techniques, also remains unproven with respect to benefits to mother or newborn (Allaire, 2001). However, as we have already discussed, providing a network of social support does help.

Cesarean Birth A *cesarean birth* is the delivery of a baby through a surgical incision in the woman's abdomen and uterus. Cesarean births are recommended, for example, when labor fails to progress normally, when the baby's head is very large, or when birth is *breech* (foot or rump first) rather than head first. Concerns about stress on the fetus that might lead to increased risk of brain damage, vaginal infections that might be transmitted to the baby, and expensive malpractice suits (should things go awry during vaginal delivery) have led to more than a fivefold increase in the frequency of cesarean sections in the past forty years in the United States. Today, more than 30 percent of deliveries in the United States are cesarean rather than vaginal (Martin et al., 2009).

RISK | RESILIENCE

Women who undergo cesarean section face an increased risk of infection and a longer hospital stay than women who give birth vaginally. Moreover, cesarean babies are likely to be exposed to greater maternal medication. Other concerns center on the different experiences

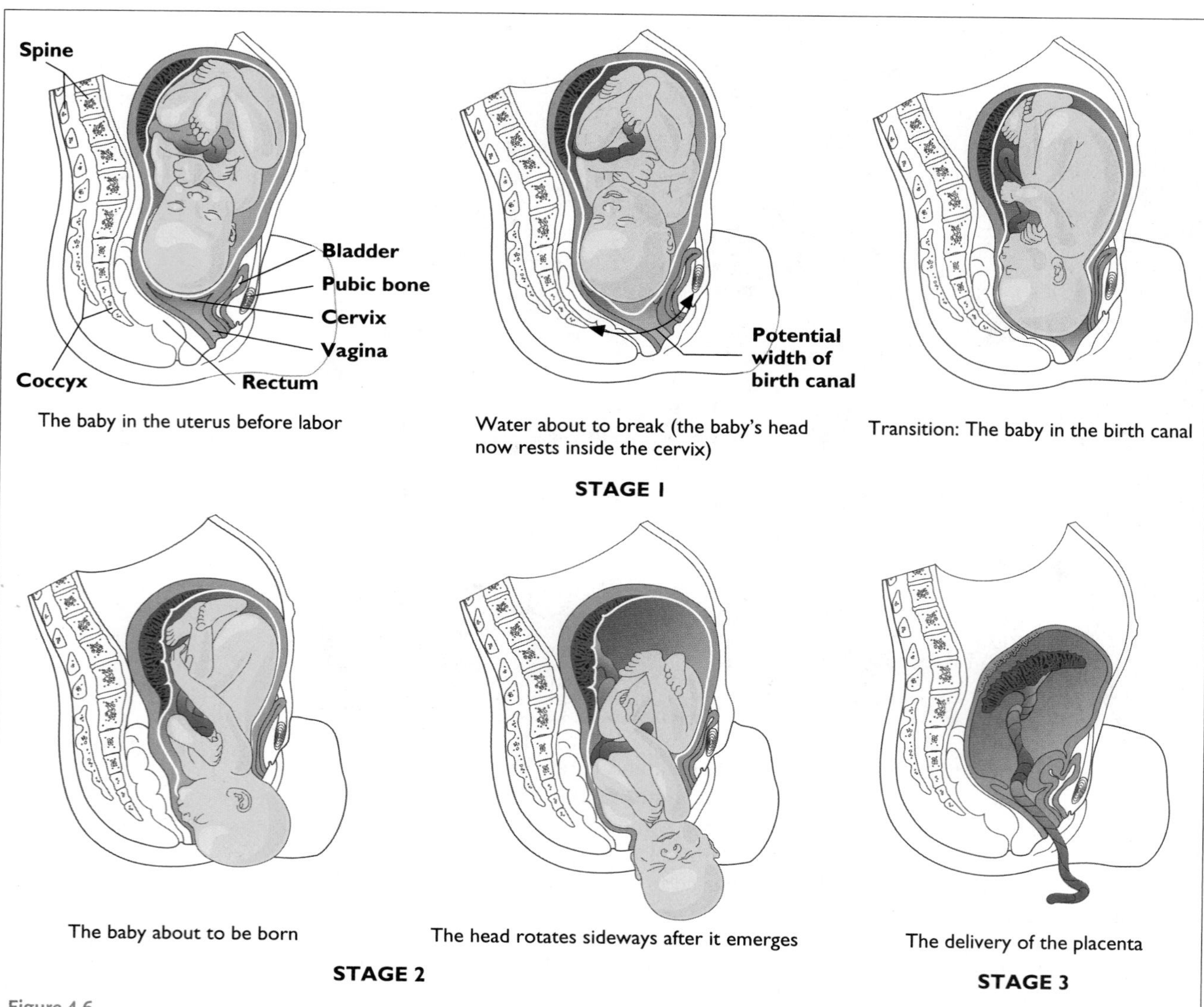

Figure 4.6

The Three Stages of Childbirth

In the first state of labor, the cervix, the neck of the uterus, dilates and thins to open a passage through the birth canal. The amniotic fluid, if not already lost, helps by exerting firm, even pressure on the cervix. When the pressure becomes too great, the sac containing the amniotic fluid will rupture, a process known as "breaking the water." The head of the fetus will soon enter the birth canal, and the second stage of labor begins. During the second stage of labor, each contraction continues to push the fetus farther along the approximately four inches of birth canal. During a normal delivery, the head emerges first (known as *crowning*), similar to pushing through the neck of a tight turtleneck sweater. The orientation of the head toward the mother's back is one of the reasons birthing for humans often needs the assistance of others (Rosenberg & Trevathen, 2001). Once the head has emerged, shoulders twist around in the birth canal, and the head turns sideways to permit delivery of the rest of the body. In the final stages of labor, the placenta is delivered.

that both mother and infant receive under such circumstances. For example, when cesarean babies are delivered before labor begins, they do not have a misshapen head and appear perfectly healthy. However, they have substantially lower levels of two stress hormones, adrenaline and noradrenaline, known to facilitate respiration by helping to keep the lungs open and clear. These hormones also enhance cell metabolism, circulation of the blood to the brain, and activity level, factors that help the infant make the transition to his or her new environment and become responsive to caregivers. Thus, cesarean babies generally tend to have more trouble breathing, are less active, sleep more, and cry less than other babies (Trevathen, 1987). Mothers, too, tend to evaluate their experience of a cesarean delivery less positively than those who deliver vaginally (Lobel & DeLuca, 2007). Nevertheless, the quality of mother-infant interactions and the psychosocial functioning of the infants a year after their birth appear quite similar regardless of type of delivery, suggesting that there are few long-term negative consequences of cesarean births (DiMatteo et al., 1996; Durik, Hyde, & Clark, 2000).

Birth Trauma The increase in the frequency of cesarean sections in the United States has come about partly because of concerns about birth trauma, or injuries sustained at birth. A potentially serious consequence is *anoxia*, or deprivation of oxygen. Anoxia can result from, for example, damage to or lengthy compression of the umbilical cord or head during birth, problems associated with the placenta, or failure of the baby to begin regular breathing after birth. If oxygen deprivation lasts more than a few minutes, severe damage to the central nervous system, including *cerebral palsy*, can result.

RISK | RESILIENCE

Fortunately, brief periods of anoxia have few long-lasting effects. Furthermore, an adequate postnatal caregiving environment can help to counter potentially negative outcomes for infants experiencing periods without oxygen (Sameroff & Chandler, 1975). Concerns about anoxia and other birth traumas have led to the widespread use of **fetal monitoring devices** during labor. Most of these devices record fetal heartbeat to determine whether the fetus is undergoing stress during delivery. However, some experts argue that overreliance on medically sophisticated equipment promotes interventions that only exacerbate the difficulty of delivery. In fact, by focusing on a supportive context to reduce anxiety, less birth trauma will occur compared with that which some medical interventions were designed to prevent (Hafner-Eaton & Pearce, 1994; Sakala, 1993).

Low Birth Weight

As infant and childhood diseases have come under greater control in recent decades, the treatment and prevention of **low-birth-weight (LBW)** infants (those weighing less than 2,500 grams, or five and a half pounds) has gained increased attention. In 2006, more than 8 percent of babies born in the United States fell into this category, the highest percent recorded in more than four decades (Martin et al., 2009). Survival improves rapidly as birth weight and gestational age increase to near-normal levels (Stephens & Vohr, 2009). For example, in the United States, nearly 2.5 percent of newborns weigh less than 1,500 grams (or three pounds and three ounces), yet these babies account for more than half of all neonatal deaths (Alexander et al., 2003). In fact, preterm births account for more neonatal deaths in the United States than do congenital malformations (Lang & Iams, 2009). Moreover, the United States has a higher proportion of infants born with low birth weight than many other developed countries, a major reason why its infant mortality rate is also higher than in many other industrialized countries (see Figure 4.7).

RISK | RESILIENCE

SOCIOCULTURAL INFLUENCE

Babies with low birth weight fall into two major groups: those born **preterm** (less than thirty-five weeks conceptual age), whose development has generally proceeded normally but has been cut short by early delivery, and those born **small for gestational age (SGA)**—that is, displaying intrauterine growth retardation, a much smaller weight than infants born at a comparable gestational age. Thus, low-birth-weight infants, often labeled premature infants, compose a heterogeneous group, perhaps needing separate types of medical treatment and intervention, and facing different developmental outcomes. Congenital anomalies are somewhat more frequent in SGA infants, for example, whereas respiratory distress is more likely among infants who are born preterm.

Caring for Infants with Low Birth Weight In general, infants born with low birth weight face numerous obstacles, not only in terms of survival but also throughout subsequent development (Lang & Iams, 2009). Cerebral palsy, seizure disorders, neurological difficulties that stem from hemorrhaging associated with regions of the brain, respiratory difficulties, and eye disorders are some examples of the physical problems observed. These difficulties are found especially frequently among infants born with *very low birth weight* (between 1,000 and 1,499 grams, or between two pounds, two ounces and three pounds, three ounces) and even more

fetal monitoring device Medical device used to monitor fetal heartbeat during delivery.

low birth weight (LBW) The label often given to any infant weighing less than 2,500 grams (or five and a half pounds) at birth.

preterm Any infant born prior to thirty-five weeks conceptual age (thirty-seven weeks gestational age).

small for gestational age (SGA) Any infant that displays intrauterine growth retardation, that is, weighs substantially less than infants born at a similar gestational age.

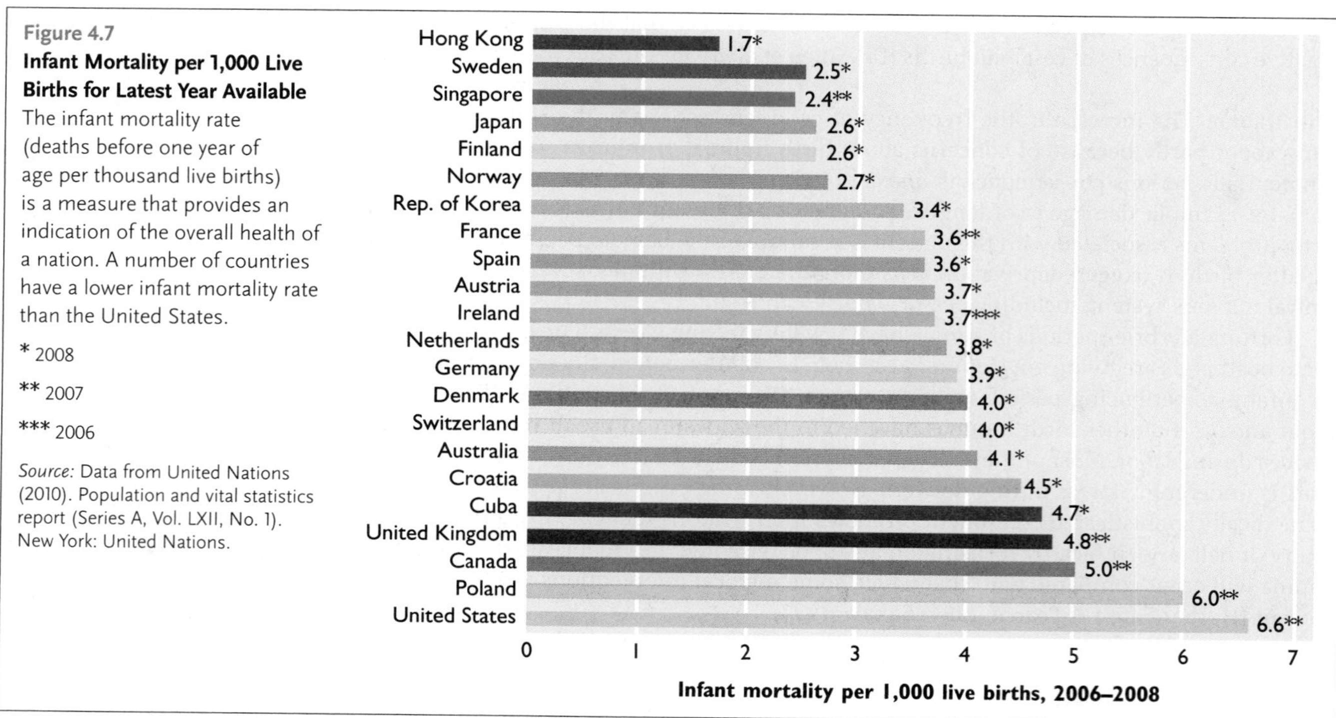

Figure 4.7
Infant Mortality per 1,000 Live Births for Latest Year Available
The infant mortality rate (deaths before one year of age per thousand live births) is a measure that provides an indication of the overall health of a nation. A number of countries have a lower infant mortality rate than the United States.

* 2008

** 2007

*** 2006

Source: Data from United Nations (2010). Population and vital statistics report (Series A, Vol. LXII, No. 1). New York: United Nations.

so among those with *extremely low birth weight* (less than 1,000 grams, or two pounds, two ounces) or who are born at less than twenty-seven weeks' gestational age. Brain scans of very early preterm infants reveal reduced brain volume and other neuroanatomic abnormalities lasting into early childhood, differences that continue to exist until twelve years of age and perhaps beyond, at least in preterm boys (Kesler et al., 2008). In addition to these problems, all low-birth-weight infants face the major task of maintaining physiological stability and achieving regular cycles of activity involving sleep and wakefulness. To deal with these problems, premature infants spend much of their time in an incubator, which carefully controls temperature and air flow with the aid of a respirator. They may be fed with a stomach tube and are often given painful heel pricks and other interventions to monitor the effects of medication and treatment.

The types of experiences that premature infants typically receive have been of considerable concern in terms of their consequences for social and psychological development. At one time parents were either excluded completely from neonatal intensive care units (NICUs), the specialized medical facilities designed to care for low-birth-weight infants (called *special care baby units* in Great Britain), or were given little opportunity to see or care for their newborns. However, that policy changed as evidence emerged showing the importance of appropriate stimulation for postnatal development. NICUs and parents now sometimes provide *compensatory stimulation*, experience to duplicate what the baby would have gained while still in the womb. For instance, the baby might be exposed to oscillating devices or waterbeds to simulate the movements the fetus experiences prenatally; muffled recordings of a human voice, a heartbeat, or other sounds to match those usually heard in the womb; reduced light and reduced exposure to noise; and opportunities for nonnutritive sucking, an activity in which the fetus occasionally engages (Field et al., 2006).

NATURE & NURTURE

Caregivers and others may also be encouraged to provide suitable *enriching stimulation:* visual and auditory experiences, prudent handling, and social and body contact more akin to the environment to which normal newborns are exposed, including body massage. Researchers have identified substantial benefits from both compensatory and enriching stimulation: more rapid weight gain, shorter hospital stays, fewer medical and eating problems, more regular breathing and heart rate, improvements in sensorimotor development, more stable and longer periods in quiet states, and smoother transitions from one state to another (Field, Diego, & Hernandez-Reif, 2007; Thoman 1993).

In recent years, *kangaroo care,* another kind of caregiving that combines both compensatory and enriching elements, has become widely adopted in NICUs (Field et al., 2006). First used in Bogotá, Colombia, several decades ago, kangaroo care involves resting the unclothed premature infant on the mother's body between her breasts for an hour or longer each day. This procedure helps the mother's own body temperature regulate the infant's body temperature, permits opportunity for nursing activity, and helps mother and child establish a social relationship with one another. Research has revealed that this experience, given to premature infants in the NICU for as little as an hour a day for fourteen days, facilitates infants' ability to regulate arousal, maintain a more consistent sleep-wake pattern, and engage in more mature attentional and exploratory behaviors as much as six months later, compared with premature infants not receiving kangaroo care (Feldman et al., 2002). Kangaroo care has also been found to enhance intellectual development (Tessier et al., 2003), and, in addition, the experience appears to positively affect how mothers view their infants and their role as a parent (Neu, 1999).

The opportunity to interact with each other shortly after birth has consequences for both mother and child. For children born with low birth weight, these occasions may be more difficult to arrange. Nevertheless, research reveals that encouraging parents to engage in these kinds of experiences is beneficial to children.

Promoting Psychological and Social Development in Low-Birth-Weight Children Fortunately, despite the hurdles they face, many low-birth-weight children do surprisingly well, as revealed by an analysis of data from more than eighty studies conducted in North America, Europe, Australia, and New Zealand (Aylward et al., 1989). However, in general, low-birth-weight infants, especially those with very or extremely low birth weight, lag behind other children throughout much of their development (Saigal et al., 2006). A higher proportion of very low- or extremely low-birth-weight children display visuomotor and language deficits; develop learning disabilities including deficits associated with attention, memory, and executive functioning; do more poorly on a variety of cognitive and intellectual tests; and show more behavior problems and fewer social skills than those born with normal birth weights (Anderson et al., 2004; Delobel-Ayoub et al., 2006; Shenkin, Starr, & Deary, 2004; Stephens & Vohr, 2009). Some of these problems likely are factors contributing to their poorer school achievement in mathematics, reading, and spelling (Aarnoudse-Moens et al., 2009) and the need for more special education intervention (Hollo et al., 2002).

NATURE & NURTURE

As we have begun to see in other examples of children with special needs, one very important factor contributing to positive developmental outcomes appears to be the support and encouragement of parents. Providing parents with opportunities to engage in suitable caregiving in the hospital setting, instructing them to recognize the specific needs of their infants and what behaviors to expect, and extending the emotional support of professional staff and other parents are types of assistance that have proven beneficial to low-birth-weight children (Achenbach et al., 1993; McCormick et al., 1993; Ramey et al., 1992). An example of such a program is the Newborn Individual Development Care and Assessment Program (NIDCAP), developed by Als (2009) and geared toward providing sensory stimulation appropriate to the level of the infant. Even very early preterm infants display observable behavioral changes in breathing patterns and color, motor activities such as finger movements and facial grimacing, and different states of arousal that signal stress or discomfort—messages that can be used by caregivers to help the infant regulate his or her behavior. In the NIDCAP program, the timing of various physical, medical, and social interventions is closely matched to recurring observations and assessments of the low-birth-weight infant's behavioral and physiological activities. Training involving the education and support of the parents as partners in the care of their infants is an essential ingredient within the program since NICU professionals often have many other obligations that draw them away from opportunities to respond to individual infants. This type of parent/professional cooperative effort appears to have some positive benefits, for example,

RISK | RESILIENCE

reduced lung disease, improved movement, reduced family stress, and a more positive perception by parents of their at-risk infants (Symington & Pinelli, 2006).

Additional support once the infant leaves the hospital is beneficial as well. When low-birth-weight children receive high-quality preschool interventions, they clearly benefit (Hill, Brooks-Gunn, & Waldfogel, 2003) and those benefits extend to early adulthood, at least for those not born with very or extremely low birth weights (McCormick et al., 2006). For example, Jeanne Brooks-Gunn and her colleagues (1993) found that low-birth-weight children who subsequently participated in educational daycare programs and whose families received regular home visits and joined in frequent parent group meetings were able to maintain higher levels of performance on cognitive tests than children in families for whom these resources were unavailable (see Figure 4.8). Family- and child-oriented services are especially important in helping to reduce stress, especially for those mothers who are less educated and may have fewer other resources available to cope with the considerable complexities associated with rearing a low-birth-weight child (Klebanov, Brooks-Gunn, & McCormick, 2001). Despite the continuing demands and increased burdens that are often a part of such childrearing, however, mothers of very low-birth-weight children report levels of satisfaction and positive feelings with respect to their parenting that are similar to those of mothers of normal-birth-weight children by the time their offspring reach three years of age (Singer et al., 1999).

Improved medical care in NICUs and supportive caregiving have permitted more low-birth-weight, especially extremely low-birth-weight, infants to survive and develop normally. These positive findings reflect more effective treatment (for instance, for respiratory distress) and management of the NICU (for example, reductions in bright light, loud noise, and sleep interruptions) designed to reduce stress in individuals who are among the least capable of responding to stress (Als et al., 1994; Bregman, 1998). However, perhaps because more extremely low-birth-weight infants are surviving as a result of these interventions, the proportion of children showing neurological or cognitive problems has remained stable over the past twenty years (Stephens & Vohr, 2009). Thus, a major assault on the problem has taken the form of prevention. Researchers have catalogued a long list of demographic, medical, and behavioral factors associated with low birth weight (Lang & Iams, 2009)—for example, inadequate prenatal care and nutrition, heavy smoking, and drug use as well as

Figure 4.8

Low-Birth-Weight Children's Cognitive Development as a Function of Intervention

In a large-scale study investigating the effects of providing home visits and educational child care for low-birth-weight infants and their families, Brooks-Gunn and her colleagues found that performance on measures of intellectual development was substantially better for those who received the intervention than for those who did not (the follow-up group). Although some decline in scores occurred even for the group receiving intervention, it was far less than for those who did not receive the intervention. Both groups performed similarly at the youngest age (twelve months), perhaps because tests measuring cognitive skills often are not very sensitive to differences at that age.

Source: Data from Brooks-Gunn et al., 1993.

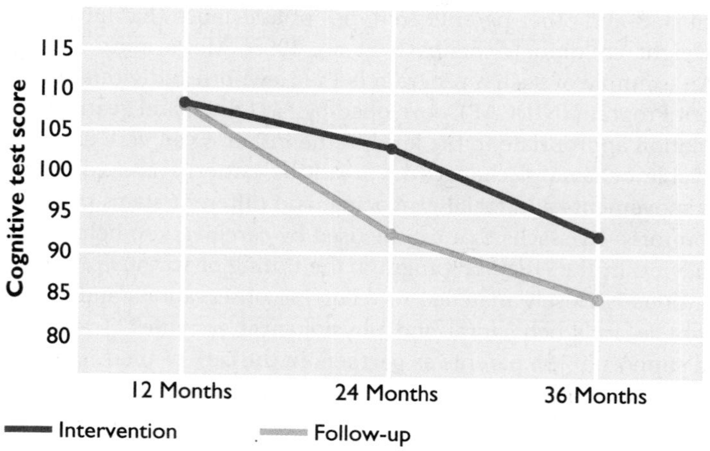

exposure to other teratogens, many of which we described in this chapter. Because so many of these factors are preventable, educational programs targeted toward pregnant women at high risk, including teenagers, have become increasingly important. These programs can reduce the incidence of low birth weight, especially when offered consistently and early in the course of pregnancy (Fangman et al., 1994; Seitz & Apfel, 1994). Indeed, future progress in addressing the problems that accompany low birth weight is likely to be as closely tied to improved and more widespread programs of prevention as to new medical advances.

For Your Review and Reflection

- What are the benefits of prepared childbirth and a supportive relationship with another individual for both parent and newborn child?
- What are the stages of delivery? How does medication during delivery affect the newborn?
- What are the benefits and disadvantages of cesarean births for mother and child? Why is this procedure often carried out?
- How do preterm and small-for-gestational-age infants differ? What are the factors that increase the likelihood of low birth weight? What is the difference between newborns identified as low birth weight, very low birth weight, and extremely low birth rate? What practices help children born with low birth weight?
- What are some of the factors that increase risk or improve resilience during the birth process and for preterm and low-birth-weight infants?
- Are you familiar with the circumstances surrounding your birth? What have been some of the most significant changes associated with birth practices since you were born?

Newborn Assessment

Even parents of a healthy infant may be in for a surprise when they see their baby for the first time. Unless delivered by cesarean section, the baby is likely to have a flattened nose and a large, distorted head from the skull bones' overriding one another during passage through the narrow birth canal. The skin of all babies, regardless of racial background,

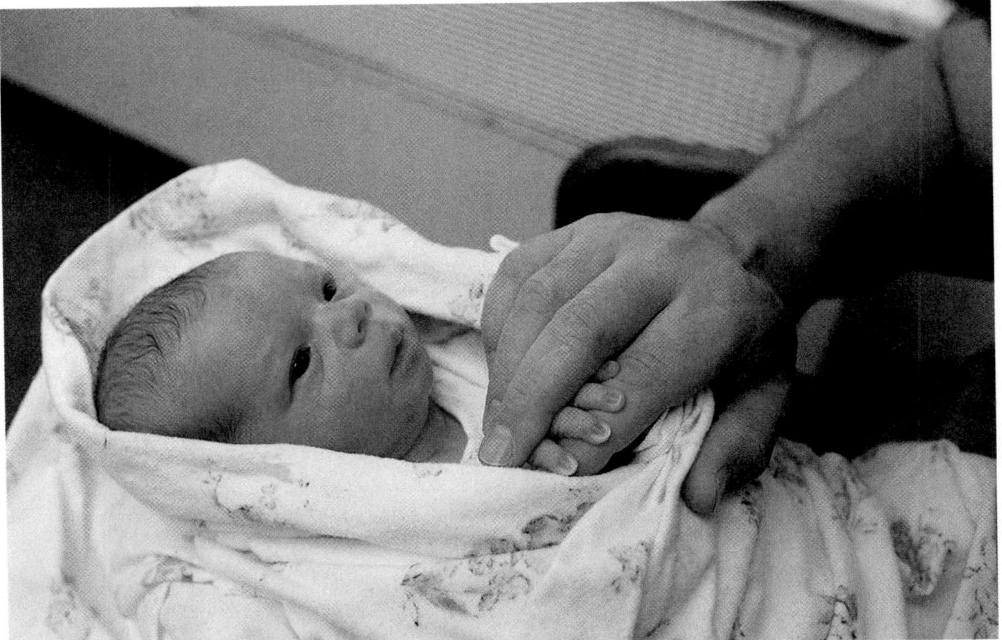

This two-day-old baby, holding her father's hand, has entered a world in which new forms of physical and social stimulation can be experienced. Although newborns and young infants spend much of their time sleeping, this infant is engaged in alert inactivity, a time in which she may be learning much about her environment.

is a pale pinkish color and often is covered with an oily, cheeselike substance (the *vernix caseosa*) that protects against infection. Sex organs are also swollen due to high levels of sex hormones from the mother.

An infant's most immediate need after emerging from the womb is breathing. Pressure on the chest during delivery probably helps to clear the baby's fluid-filled lungs, but the shock of cool air, perhaps accompanied by jiggling, a slap, or some other less-than-gentle activity by a birth attendant, makes the first breath more like a gasp, quickly followed by a reflexive cry. The umbilical cord may continue to pulse for several minutes after birth; in many societies, the cord is not cut until after it ceases to do so (Trevathen, 1987).

The second major task the baby must accomplish upon entering the world is regulating body temperature. Babies lose body heat about four times more rapidly than adults because of their lower fat reserve and relatively large body surface (Bruck, 1962). As a consequence, newborns, although they can effectively maintain their temperature when held close to a caregiver's body, are often quickly placed under heaters.

RISK | RESILIENCE

Newborns typically weigh five and a half to about nine pounds, and measure eighteen to twenty-two inches in length. Nearly all babies are screened for hearing loss before they leave the hospital. Many other procedures for evaluating their health have become available in recent years, but one that is routinely administered is the *Apgar Scale* (Apgar, 1953). Typically assessed at both one and five minutes after birth, the Apgar measures five vital signs: heart rate, respiratory effort, muscle tone, reflex responsivity, and color. Each vital sign is scored 0, 1, or 2 based on the criteria described in Table 4.5. In the United States, 90 percent of infants receive a total score of 7 or better; those who score lower than 4 are considered to be at risk.

A more extensive measure, developed by T. Berry Brazelton (1973) and given several days after birth to many infants, is the *Neonatal Behavioral Assessment Scale (NBAS)*. The NBAS evaluates, for example, the baby's ability to interact with the tester, responsiveness to objects in the environment, reflex motor capacities, and ability to control functions such as breathing and temperature. Newborn performance on the NBAS has been used to assess neurological condition and can indicate whether certain prenatal or perinatal conditions, as well as intervention programs, have had an effect (Korner, 1987; Tronick, 1987). An NBAS score can also predict later developmental outcomes. Babies who score poorly on the scale continue to be somewhat less responsive to caregivers in the first few months after birth (Vaughn et al., 1980). In general, however, the predictive validity of the NBAS (along with other infant tests) for long-term development is only modest at best (Brazelton, Nugent, & Lester, 1987). Nevertheless, parents who observe while examiners give the NBAS or who are trained to give it themselves seem to become more responsive to and effective in interactions with their infants (Worobey, 1985).

As this chapter has shown, there are numerous events in the period from conception to birth that lay important foundations for development. By the time the infant takes its first

TABLE 4.5 The Apgar Scoring System

Vital Sign	Ratings 0	1	2
Heart rate	Absent	Slow (below 100)	Over 100
Respiratory effort	Absent	Slow, irregular	Good, crying
Muscle tone	Flaccid	Some flexion of extremities	Active motion
Reflex responsivity	No response	Grimace	Vigorous cry
Color	Blue, pale	Body pink, extremities blue	Completely pink

Source: Adapted from Apgar, 1953. From V. Apgar, "A Proposal for a New Method of Evaluation of the Newborn Infant," *Anesthesia and Analgesia: Current Researches, 32*, 260–267. Copyright © 1953. Used by permission of Lippincott Williams & Wilkins. www.anesthesia-analgesia.org.

breath and utters its first cry, many of the first, and some very important, steps in his or her developmental story have already been taken.

For Your Review and Reflection

- What are the first tasks for the newborn following birth?
- Why are scores on the Apgar Scale and the Neonatal Behavioral Assessment Scale important?
- What are some of the individual differences that may exist among newborns that may increase their risk or resilience?
- How much did you weigh and what was your length when you were born? Was an Apgar score or any other type of assessment obtained for you at or shortly after your birth?

chapter recap

Summary of Developmental Themes

Nature & Nurture

How do nature and nurture interact during prenatal development and birth?

Prenatal development is the product of complex interactions involving genetic instructions inherited from parents and the expectant woman's physical and emotional conditions, as well as exposure to drugs, diseases, hazardous chemicals, and medications before and during pregnancy and during labor. We have seen, for example, that differentiation of organs and systems in the embryo typically obeys principles established by biochemical and physiological processes. Yet these processes do not operate in a vacuum. Teratogens and various intrauterine conditions can radically alter the normal developmental path. Thus, events in the life of the woman may change the immediate environment within her womb, with drastic consequences for the fetus.

Sociocultural Influence

How does the sociocultural context influence prenatal development and birth?

The immediate internal environment of the fetus and the perinatal environment provided for the newborn can be influenced dramatically by the larger social, economic, and cultural settings in which pregnancy and birth take place. The woman's actions during pregnancy are often modified or regulated by a network of expectations, advice, and resources within the culture in which she lives. An expectant woman in one community, for example, may have access to medical and other kinds of care that provide a more healthy environment for the fetus than a woman in another community. Industry or governmental units may legislate controls on chemical pollution in one country and ignore them in another. Scientific and technological advances in prenatal testing, birthing practices, and newborn care may be available in one region of the world but not in another; even when available, however, not all parents may have the economic resources or the desire to use them.

Continuous | Discontinuous

Is development before and immediately after birth continuous or discontinuous?

When the zygote attaches to the uterine wall and taps a new source of nourishment, its course of development changes dramatically. Once the various organs and systems are formed and become less susceptible to environmental disruptions, the fetus achieves a vastly different status. The process of birth itself is a major transition. Such spectacular changes fit with discontinuous or stagelike descriptions of development. So do the marked shifts in vulnerability to teratogens observed during prenatal development. Underlying the progressions, however, are biochemical and physiological processes governing cell proliferation, differentiation, and the emergence and functioning of biological systems that can be seen as continuous. Many dramatic changes are essentially the product of modest accumulative modifications in the multifaceted, complex environment that promotes development.

Risk | Resilience

What factors promote risk or resilience during prenatal development and birth?

Newborns everywhere undergo many common gestational experiences; however, differences in development arise because the fetus is not immune to the influences of the larger world. Because of exposure to teratogens and other maternal conditions, babies will differ in their physical and behavioral qualities, and their ability to cope with and adapt to their new environment. Low birth weight, for example, is an important element in increasing risk for a newborn. Greater knowledge of and sensitivity to those differences by caregivers, whether exhibited by a newborn with special needs, such as one with low birth weight, or by an infant who falls within the typical range for newborns, can help to ensure success for the continued development of every child.

Chapter Review

The Stages of Prenatal Development

What constitutes the prenatal, perinatal, and postnatal periods of development?
The *prenatal period* extends from conception to birth. The *perinatal period* extends from about the seventh month of pregnancy until twenty-eight days after birth. The *postnatal period* is the time that follows birth.

Where does fertilization of the egg cell by the sperm cell take place?
Fertilization normally takes place in the Fallopian tube when an ovum or egg cell is penetrated by a single sperm cell.

What are the major changes that take place following conception during the germinal, embryonic, and fetal periods of prenatal development?
During the *germinal period,* about the first ten to fourteen days after conception, the zygote migrates from the Fallopian tube to the uterus, becomes multicelled, and implants itself in the uterine wall to gain access to a new source of nutrients obtained from the mother. The *embryonic period* begins after implantation and continues until about the eighth week after conception. The embryonic period is marked by development of the placenta and other supportive structures within the uterine environment and by the differentiation of cells into tissues that form the major organs and systems of the embryo. The *fetal period,* beginning in about the eighth week after conception and lasting until birth, is marked by substantial growth and by refinement of organs and systems. By the last trimester, the ability of the fetus to survive on its own (*viability*) improves. For human infants, birth typically occurs around 274 days *gestational age.*

When are the major organs and systems of the body established? What is the course of brain and nervous system development in the embryo and fetus?
The major body organs and systems, including the brain and nervous system, differentiate during the embryonic phase. Neurons continue to form and migrate during the fetal period. Brain activity, sensory reactions, and movement are exhibited by the fetus.

How can various kinds of assisted reproduction and other procedures help prospective parents who have difficulty conceiving or are concerned about the inheritance of genetic disorders in their offspring? What are some of the medical and legal issues associated with various forms of assisted reproduction?
Among the assisted reproduction technologies and associated procedures used to facilitate the birth of offspring are artificial insemination by donor, egg donation, fertility drugs, gamete intrafallopian transfer, in vitro fertilization, and maternal surrogacy. Some of the issues raised by these technologies include the competence of the practitioners, the fact that children born with these methods may not know about their biological heritage, and the increased risk associated with multiple pregnancies that result from such procedures.

Environmental Factors Influencing Prenatal Development

What kinds of supportive functions do the placenta, umbilical cord, and amniotic sac provide for the embryo and the fetus?
The *placenta* serves as the major organ for transfer of nutrients from the mother's circulatory system and for expelling waste products from the fetus. The *umbilical cord* connects the fetus to the placenta. The *amniotic sac* provides a fluid-filled, protective surrounding in which development of the fetus occurs.

What are teratogens? What principles apply to how teratogens have their effects?
During both embryonic and fetal development, *teratogens,* or environmental agents harmful to the organism, can disrupt development and interfere with later behavior. The effects of teratogens differ depending on the genetic susceptibility of the embryo or fetus, how the teratogen reaches the prenatal environment, its level of dosage and manner of exposure, and where it interferes with cellular activity. A teratogen's effects also differ depending on the time at which exposure occurs during prenatal development. Not all the consequences are observed immediately; they may not even be evident until well into the postnatal years.

How do alcohol, cigarette smoke, prescription and over-the-counter drugs, and illicit drugs affect prenatal development?
Many different drugs are able to cross the placental barrier and can have teratogenic effects. Among those known to have the greatest impact on fetal development are alcohol, which can result in *fetal alcohol syndrome (FAS)* and other associated disorders, and cigarette smoke, which is linked to low birth weight. The effects of prescription and over-the-counter drugs on prenatal development are not always well known but can include low birth weight and lower IQ. Teratogenic effects, including lower birth weight and frequency of stillbirths as well as cognitive impairment, are linked to the use of many illicit drugs. However, their effects are often confounded with other events known to have significant negative consequences for the fetus. These factors include lack of proper nutrition, poor health of the mother, absence of medical care, lack of emotional and social support, and high levels of stress.

What kinds of risks exist for the embryo and fetus exposed to rubella, toxoplasmosis, cytomegalovirus, and sexually transmitted infections?
Diseases can have serious repercussions on both prenatal and postnatal development. Rubella is associated with visual, auditory, and heart defects, as well as cognitive disabilities. Toxoplasmosis can cause visual problems and intellectual impairment. Cytomegalovirus is also associated with cognitive disabilities, as well as sensory or motor problems. Sexually transmitted infections are associated with low birth weight, visual defects, cognitive disabilities, and in the most serious cases, death.

What environmental hazards can affect prenatal development?
Exposure to high levels of radiation is known to have serious physical consequences for fetal development. Exposure to lead, mercury, and many other chemical substances affects fetal development as well.

What maternal conditions affect the well-being of the fetus and embryo?
Less positive outcomes in prenatal development are possible if the mother is either very young or in the late childbearing years; has poor nutrition; has a high level of stress; lacks social support; or suffers from certain conditions, such as diabetes, obesity, and pregnancy-induced hypertension.

Birth and the Perinatal Environment

What are the benefits of prepared childbirth and a supportive relationship with another individual for both parent and newborn child?
Prepared (natural) childbirth may reduce the need for medication during delivery and often leads women to give more positive

evaluations of childbirth. The presence of someone familiar with the birth process but continuously present to provide emotional support and information to the mother, a doula, appears to have benefits for both mother and newborn.

What are the stages of delivery? How does medication during delivery affect the newborn?
Childbirth proceeds through three stages. In the first and longest stage, labor helps to initiate preparation of the birth canal. Passage of the fetus through the birth canal makes up the second stage. During the third stage, the placenta is delivered. Labor appears to be initiated by hormones produced by the fetus and the placenta. Concerns about too much reliance on medication during labor have led to efforts to initiate procedures that permit delivery with the use of fewer drugs. Newborns whose mothers receive extensive medication during delivery may show less responsiveness, greater irritability, and slower weight gain.

What are the benefits and disadvantages of cesarean birth for mother and child? Why is this procedure often carried out?
Cesarean deliveries are relatively common in the United States, despite their greater expense. They may lead to greater recovery time for the mother and the risk of exposure to medication for the newborn. Babies delivered via cesarean birth may also show greater initial breathing problems. The large number of cesarean births in the United States may stem, in part, from the extensive use of *fetal monitoring devices,* which signal fetal distress during delivery. Fetal distress is linked to concerns about the long-term negative consequences of birth trauma, such as exposure to oxygen deprivation.

How do preterm and small-for-gestational-age infants differ? What are the differences between low birth weight, very low birth weight, and extremely low birth weight? What are the factors that increase the likelihood of low birth weight? What practices help children born with low birth weight?
Preterm infants are born before thirty-five weeks conceptual age. Babies who are small for gestational age are born near their due date but show growth retardation. Low birth weight refers to infants born weighing between 1,500 and 2,500 grams, very low birth weight refers to infants weighing between 1,000 and 1,499 grams, and extremely low birth weight refers to infants weighing less than 1,000 grams. Risk factors for low birth weight include, for example, inadequate prenatal care, poor nutrition, smoking, and drug use. Infants born with very low birth weights or extremely low birth weights continue to show lower cognitive, social, and other competencies throughout development. However, compensatory and enrichment programs for low-birth-weight infants increase early weight gains and promote other positive developmental outcomes. Providing social and professional support to parents appears to be an especially important component to promoting development in low-birth-weight newborns.

Newborn Assessment

What are the first tasks for the newborn following birth?
Respiration and maintenance of body temperature are two immediate critical goals for the newborn.

Why are scores on the Apgar Scale and the Neonatal Behavioral Assessment Scale important?
Tests given to the newborn shortly after birth, such as the Apgar Scale and the Neonatal Behavioral Assessment Scale, provide some indication of the baby's physiological state and ability to interact with caregivers and respond to stimulation.

Key Terms and Concepts

amniotic sac (p. 122)
embryo (p. 113)
embryonic period (p. 112)
fetal alcohol syndrome (FAS) (p. 125)
fetal monitoring device (p. 143)
fetal period (p. 112)
fetus (p. 118)
germinal period (p. 112)
gestational age (p. 119)
low birth weight (p. 143)
perinatal period (p. 112)
placenta (p. 121)
postnatal period (p. 112)
prepared (natural) childbirth (p. 138)
prenatal period (p. 112)
preterm (p. 143)
sexually transmitted infections (STIs) (p. 133)
small for gestational age (SGA) (p. 143)
teratogen (p. 122)
umbilical cord (p. 121)
viability (p. 119)

Media Resources

Access an integrated eBook and chapter-specific interactive learning tools, including flashcards, quizzes, videos, and more, in your Developmental Psychology CourseMate, accessed through CengageBrain.com.

© Tripod/Siri Berting/Jupiter Images

CHAPTER OUTLINE

[chapter 5]

Brain, Motor Skill, and Physical Development

KEY THEMES

NATURE & NURTURE How do nature and nurture interact in brain, motor skill, and physical development?

SOCIOCULTURAL INFLUENCE How does the sociocultural context influence brain, motor skill, and physical development?

CONTINUITY | DISCONTINUITY Are brain, motor skill, and physical development continuous or discontinuous?

INTERACTION AMONG DOMAINS How do brain, motor skill, and physical development interact with other domains of development?

RISK | RESILIENCE What factors promote risk or resilience in brain, motor skill, and physical development during infancy?

She stared intently at the thirteen-year-old who had just finished her routine. Danielle couldn't believe what she had just seen. How could any girl her own age do that? Danielle's words expressed admiration and awe, but her voice was tinged with envy as she confided to her best friend, "We've been in gymnastics ever since we were five. If we tried that, we'd probably break our necks!"

Even as a toddler, Danielle had seemed captivated by leaping and tumbling. Her parents took great pride in their daughter's graceful athleticism and precocious motor skills. Danielle enrolled in ballet and gymnastics at an early age. Both activities had been fun. As Danielle became older and more skilled, she especially seemed to thrive on the competition that permeated gymnastics meets. She liked being good at what she did; she preferred being the best. Through the applause, her friend had no difficulty hearing Danielle mutter, "I'll bet I can do that. Watch me next time we're at practice." But she also knew that her body had changed. All of a sudden her legs seemed too long for the pommel horse, and her own program took more effort to carry out. She wondered silently if she really could complete a routine as challenging and remarkable as the one she had just observed. <<

Danielle, who is physically poised and skilled, displays a fair amount of confidence in the demands of learning a new and difficult gymnastic routine. Toward the end of childhood, many skills become highly specialized talents: young teens like Danielle are already accomplished athletes; others her age are concert musicians. But even before that, she, as well as other children, undergo substantial physical development and acquire a vast repertoire of motor skills and abilities, some simply taken for granted. Physical growth and advances in motor skills are among the most readily apparent signs of development. Parents are often astonished at just how quickly their infants, as well as their older children and adolescents, outgrow their newly purchased clothes. Few children become Olympic gymnasts, but beginning in infancy children rapidly acquire the ability to reach for objects, to walk, and then to run. These transformations are made possible and accompanied by less obvious, but no less revolutionary, changes in the brain.

The development of the brain, the acquisition of physical skills, and the growth of the body affect virtually every behavior displayed by the child and are, in turn, influenced by the social, emotional, and cognitive demands made on her as growth occurs. Consider how newfound motor coordinations may, for example, dramatically awaken cognition. The six-month-old who begins to reach for and grasp objects acquires a novel and powerful means of gaining information about the world and, at the same time, a new way to control and influence her environment. When children begin to crawl, they may confront new barriers and repeated choruses of "No, don't do that." How these freshly imposed limits, inspired by burgeoning physical and mental capacities, are faced and resolved can affect many other aspects of solving problems or building relationships with others. By the same token, the reactions of others to changing stature and physical accomplishments can arouse a child's pride and promote renewed efforts, or they can lead to discouragement and apprehension. Danielle's self-assurance from her prowess in gymnastics may

The infant's achievements in the domain of motor development often have profound consequences for other areas of development. Consider this infant's acquisition of the ability to reach for objects. He is now equipped to explore the textures and shapes of objects, and in some cases, their tastes. By reaching, he is also able to make requests for objects, thereby gaining a stronger sense of control over events in his life.

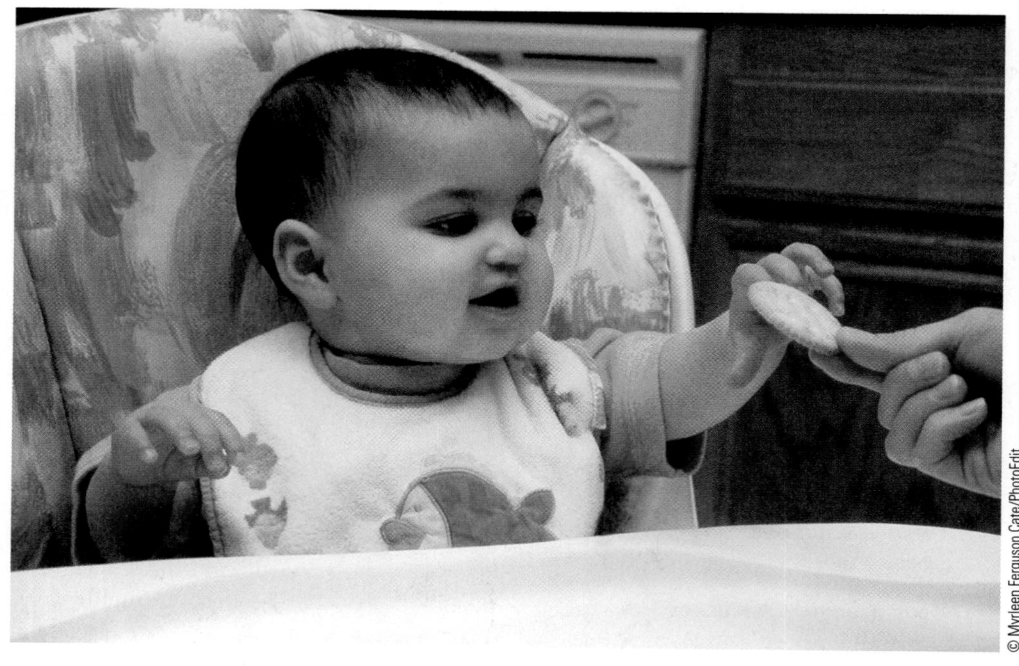

extend to her social interactions and her academic experiences. In contrast, the child who lacks various motor competencies or physical characteristics valued in a society—for example, is less coordinated, shorter, overweight, or otherwise physically distinctive—may receive strikingly different reactions from those around him and approach social and intellectual challenges with far less confidence.

How do brain, body, and motor skills develop? To what extent do parenting, culture, or other environmental events influence their course? Does the amount of sleep a child or adolescent receives have anything to do with these developments? How does physical prowess or appearance, early maturity, or height and weight, for example, affect other domains of development? In this chapter, we explore these questions and more. We first consider the developing brain, the structure that plays a central role in controlling and integrating the many changes observed in all aspects of behavior including motor skill and physical development.

The Brain and Nervous System

Imagine, for a moment, that you could observe a child's brain at work as it is engaged in solving a problem, responding to the reappearance of an absent mother's face, or processing the words of a foreign language. As we saw in Chapter 2, where methods of studying child development were introduced, new and highly sophisticated techniques have become available to provide glimpses into the operation and development of this remarkable organ. Our understanding of the neural structures and systems that contribute to the functioning of the brain remains at an early stage. However, we can outline some of the more important discoveries research in cognitive neuroscience has made about the developing human brain. Keep in mind that the architecture of the brain, although initially framed by genetic factors, is continually being modified by environmental factors critical to the eventual structure and function of this complex body part (Fox, Levitt, & Nelson, 2010).

The Developing Brain

Even before birth, brain growth is rapid. As Figure 5.1 shows, the size of the brain swiftly increases, from about 4 percent of its adult weight at five months after conception to about 25 percent at birth (Spreen, Risser, & Edgell, 1995). By age four years, the size of the brain is about 80 percent of its adult weight. The *brainstem* and *midbrain* (see Figure 5.2), which are

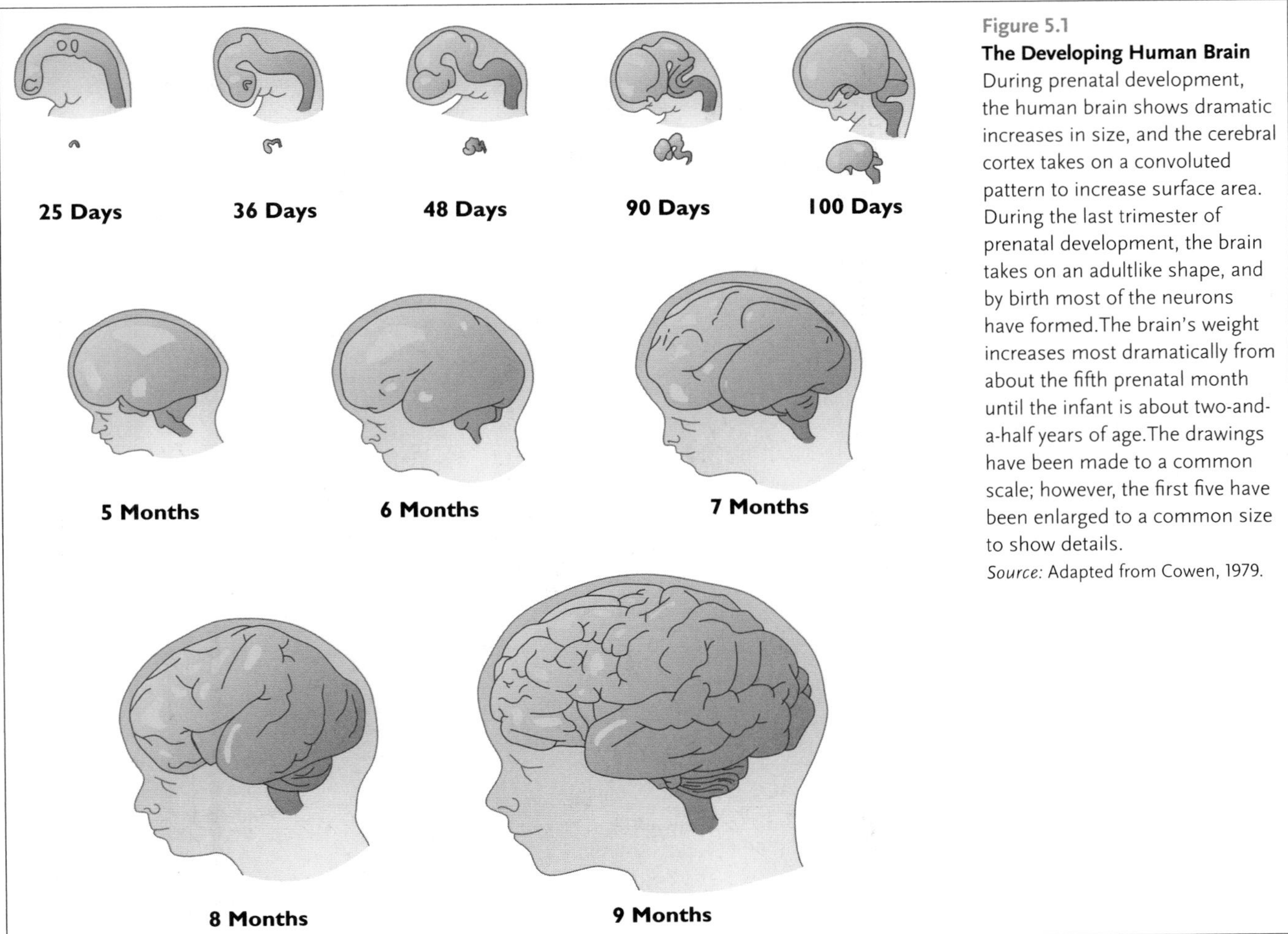

Figure 5.1
The Developing Human Brain During prenatal development, the human brain shows dramatic increases in size, and the cerebral cortex takes on a convoluted pattern to increase surface area. During the last trimester of prenatal development, the brain takes on an adultlike shape, and by birth most of the neurons have formed. The brain's weight increases most dramatically from about the fifth prenatal month until the infant is about two-and-a-half years of age. The drawings have been made to a common scale; however, the first five have been enlarged to a common size to show details.
Source: Adapted from Cowen, 1979.

involved in basic reflexes and sensory processing, as well as such essential biological functions as digestion, elimination, and respiration, are fairly well established at birth (Joseph, 2000). In contrast, neural changes in the *cortex,* the part of the brain most closely linked to sensation, motor responses, thinking, planning, and problem solving, continue to take place well after birth. Within the cortex, regions associated with sensory and motor functions tend to be among the earliest to mature. The frontal cortex, the region of the brain most directly involved in higher levels of cognition, tends to be among the latest.

At the cellular level, several important changes occur early in development in the **neurons**, the cells that carry electrochemical messages within various regions of the brain. These neuronal changes include *proliferation, migration,* and *differentiation.*

Neuron Proliferation The production of new nerve cells is known as *neuron proliferation.* Neuron production in humans begins near the end of the first month of prenatal development, shortly after the neural tube closes, and much of it, at least in the cerebral cortex, is completed by the sixth month of prenatal development. During the period of peak neuron proliferation, 20,000 neurons are generated every minute (Stiles, 2008). As a consequence, at a very early age, an extremely large number of young neurons—certainly well over 100 billion—have formed (Nelson, Thomas, & de Haan, 2006).

Neuron Migration Shortly after their formation, neurons move, or *migrate,* from the neural tube where they were produced to other locations. In some regions of the brain, this movement occurs passively, so that, as additional neurons are born, older ones are pushed farther to the outside of that portion of the brain. This type of growth

neuron Nerve cell within the central nervous system that is electrochemically designed to transmit messages between cells.

Figure 5.2

Cross-Section of the Human Brain

Certain regions of the brain are closely associated with specific functions. The overarching cortex is essential for most of behavior and includes regions associated with processing sensory and motor information, as well as areas heavily involved in thinking, planning, and problem solving. The anterior cingulate cortex (ACC) as well as the hypothalamus, amygdala, and brainstem may play pivotal roles in self-regulation. The early-developing midbrain and brainstem are important to basic biological functioning. The cerebellum is centrally involved in coordination and control of voluntary movements. Both the hypothalamus and pituitary glands are believed to play a major role in the regulation of physical growth. The amygdala additionally is highly involved in memory consolidation and the processing of emotions. The hippocampus is important for inhibiting behaviors, long-term memory, and spatial navigation.

Source: From Lewis, M. D, & Todd, R. M. (2007). The self-regulating brain: Cortical-subcortical feedback and the development of intelligent action. *Cognitive Development*, *22*, 406–430. Reprinted by permission of Elsevier.

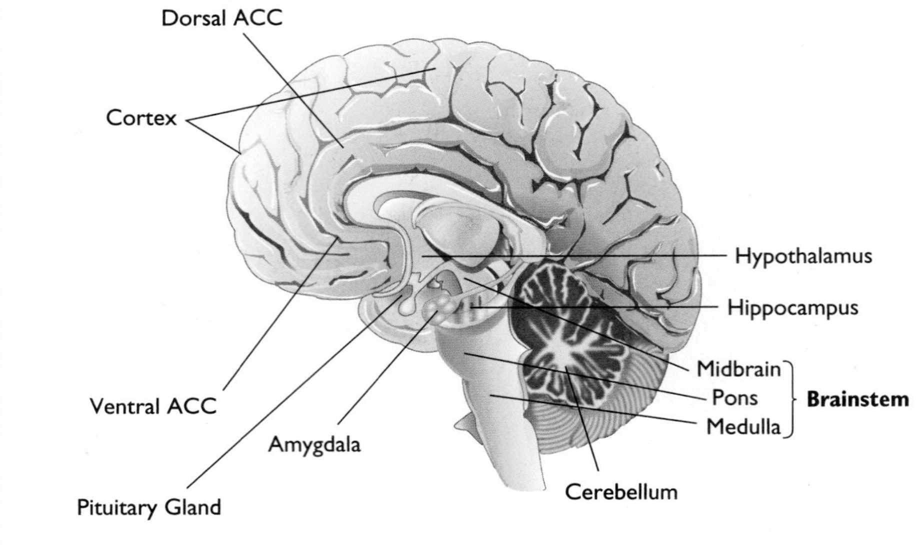

takes place, for example, in the hypothalamus, the brainstem, and the cerebellum. However, for many other regions of the brain, such as the cerebral cortex, the neurons may migrate a great distance, passing through levels of older neurons that already have reached their final destination. These regions of the brain are formed by an *inside-out* pattern of development in which layers of nerve cells nearer the outer surface are younger than layers deeper in the cortex (Nelson et al., 2006). Under these circumstances, how do neurons know where to migrate and when to stop migrating? Both neurochemical and mechanical information plays a role. Young neurons attach to and maneuver along the surfaces of fibers of *glial cells* radiating to the region of their destination, detaching from their guide, as shown in Figure 5.3, at programmed locations. Thus, one function of glial cells (from the Greek word for *glue*) is that of providing a scaffold or radial organization for neuron migration. Both the production and the migration of large numbers of neurons in the cortex occur in waves, especially during the seventh and eleventh weeks of gestational age (Spreen et al., 1995). However, some teratogens, including mercury and alcohol, are known to interfere with the onset and path of neuron migration. In fact, developmental defects ranging from intellectual disabilities to behavioral disorders have been linked to interference in the migratory patterns of nerve cells (Gressens, 2000).

RISK | RESILIENCE

Neuron Differentiation Whereas neuron proliferation and migration take place prenatally for the most part, neuron differentiation flourishes postnatally. *Neuron differentiation* is the process involved in the enlarging of the neurons, forming *dendrites* (the branching projections that establish synapses with other neurons), and the beginning functioning of many neurons. Neural differentiation contributes to the substantial increase in the size of the brain during the first four years after birth. A single neuron typically forms between 1,000 and 10,000 synaptic connections to establish a rich web of potential linkages to other neurons (Stiles, 2008).

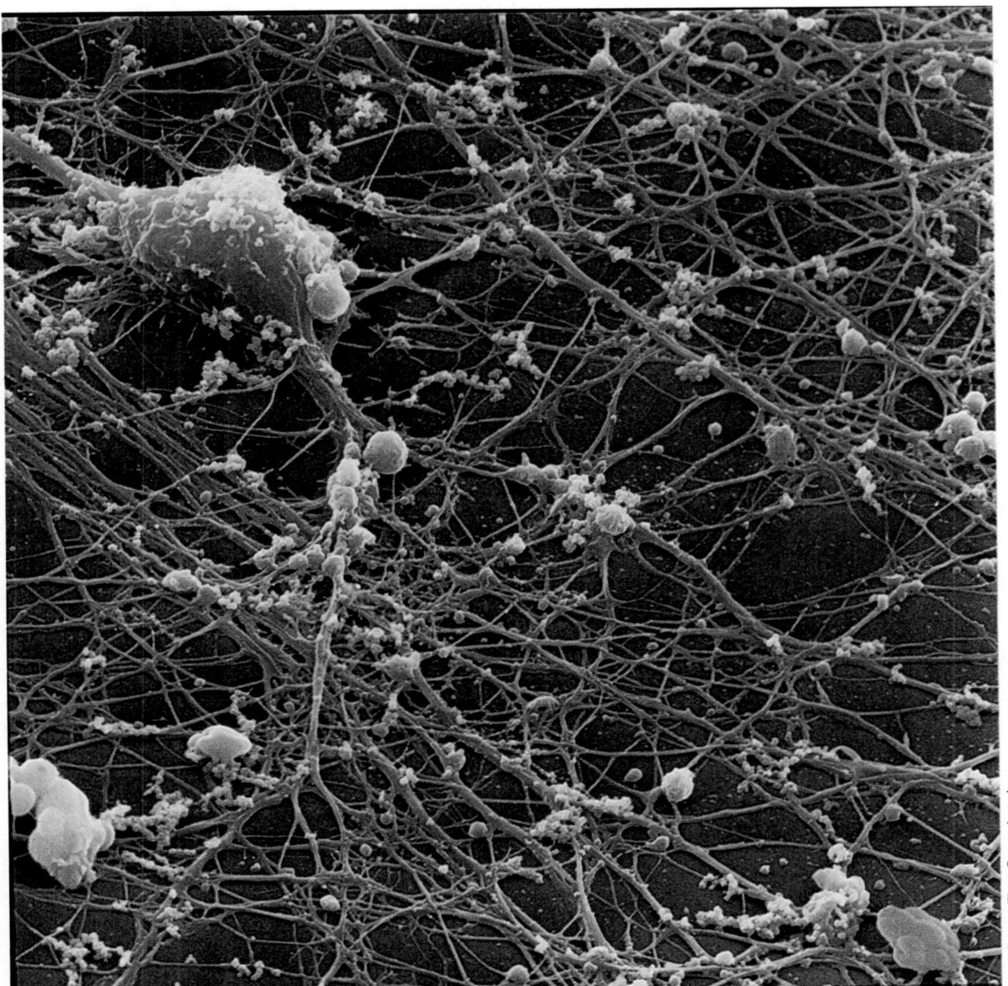

This color-enhanced photo, taken with a scanning electron microscope, shows a neuron. Neurons carry the electrochemical messages that are the basis for behavior. Even before birth, massive numbers of neurons are manufactured and migrate to various regions of the brain, where they begin to establish connections with other neurons.

Eye of Science/Photo Researchers, Inc.

NATURE & NURTURE

Some aspects of neuron differentiation proceed without external stimulation. Experience, however, plays a major role in the selection, maintenance, and strengthening of connections among many neurons (Nelson et al., 2006). Classic work investigating the effects of vision on brain development in cats illustrates this complex relationship (Hubel & Wiesel, 1979). By the time a kitten's eyes open, neurons in the visual receptor areas of the cerebral cortex have already established some connections and can respond, for example, to sensory information from either eye or to visual patterns with a broad range of characteristics. But the neurons become far more selective and tuned to particular kinds of sensory information as the kitten experiences specific forms of visual stimulation. If the kitten is exposed only to horizontal dark-light transitions in the visual field, for example, neurons begin to respond only to those patterns; likewise, exposure only to dark-light transitions that are vertical produces neurons sensitive only to that orientation.

Without stimulation and the opportunity to function, neurons are unlikely to establish or maintain many connections with other neurons; their synaptic density becomes substantially reduced. For example, in the visual cortex, the total number of synapses rises meteorically in the first few months after birth, but then these connective arms of the neuron show a substantial decline, a process called **synaptic pruning**, from about eight months of age to the late preschool years. Synaptic pruning continues at a slower rate between about four and ten years. In contrast, synaptic density in the auditory and prefrontal areas of the brain is greatest around five years of age, and pruning occurs somewhat later, especially in the prefrontal cortex. These age differences and the dramatic changes in synaptic density for these regions of the cortex can be seen

synaptic pruning The process by which weaker or less active dendrites of neurons are eliminated.

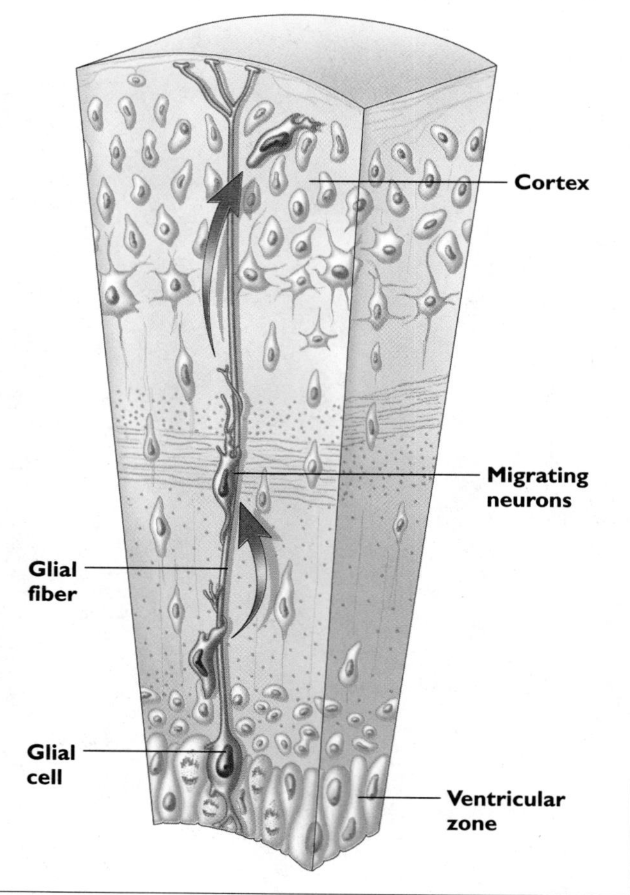

Figure 5.3
The Migration of Neurons via Glial Fiber
Wrapping themselves around glial fibers, neurons climb in spiral fashion to a particular layer in the cortex of the brain. Because the cortex of the brain develops in an inside-out pattern, earlier waves of neurons need to progress across shorter distances, and their migration may be completed within a day. However, later waves of neurons pass through earlier layers of the cortex and migrate across a greater distance, so that their journey may require several weeks. Some teratogens can interfere with this migratory pattern and, if the disruption is severe, result in a variety of developmental defects.
Source: Illustration by John W. Karapelou © 1998. Reprinted with permission of artist. www.karapelou.com.

in Figure 5.4. In addition, massive neuron cell death, a process called *apoptosis,* results in losses perhaps as high as 50 to 75 percent of neurons in some regions of the brain (Stiles, 2008). Thus, the typical infant is genetically equipped with many neurons that have the capacity to generate large numbers of synaptic connections, far more than a person will ever use. That surplus of neurons and dendrites, a major component of the gray matter located within the human brain, provides the opportunity for a rich variety of experiences to affect development; it also means that, if damage or destruction occurs to some synapses early in life, others may replace them.

Glial Cells and Myelination An estimated ten times more **glial cells** than neurons also form within the brain. These cells, which comprise about half the volume of the brain (Stiles, 2008), not only establish a scaffolding for neuron migration, as already mentioned, but also instruct the neurons to form synapses with other neurons (Ullian et al., 2001). One type of glial cell has another critical function: to provide the material from which **myelin**, the sheath of fatty substance (often described as white matter) that surrounds the axon of many neurons, is formed. Myelin serves to insulate and speed neural impulses up to 100 times faster than when it is absent (Fields, 2008).

glial cell Brain cell that provides a scaffolding for neuron migration and that nourishes neurons and assists in the production of myelin.

myelin Sheath of fatty cells that insulates and speeds neural impulses by about tenfold.

plasticity Capacity of immature systems, including regions of the brain and the individual neurons within those regions, to take on different functions as a result of experience.

Plasticity in Brain Development

Because of the unspecialized nature of young neurons, the immature brain displays substantial **plasticity**, or the ability, within limits, for alternate regions of the cerebral cortex to take on specialized sensory, linguistic, and other information-processing activity. Infants or children who suffer damage to regions of the cerebral cortex that process speech, for example,

Figure 5.4

Estimated Number of Synapses for Neurons in the Human Visual, Auditory, and Prefrontal Cortex as a Function of Age

Differentiation of the neurons in various regions of the human cortex proceeds rapidly shortly after birth, especially in the visual cortex. The rapid increment in neurons in the visual cortex occurs at a time when increased visual stimulation takes place and is correlated with significant improvements in visual abilities before a year of age. In comparison to the visual cortex, rapid neuron differentiation in the auditory and prefrontal cortex occurs somewhat later, as does synaptic pruning, especially in the prefrontal cortex. (Data from Huttenlocher & Dabholkar, 1997).

Source: From Thomas, M. S. C., & Johnson, M. H. (2008). New advances in understanding sensitive periods in brain development. *Current Directions in Psychological Science, 17,* 1–5. Reprinted by permission of the American Psychological Association.

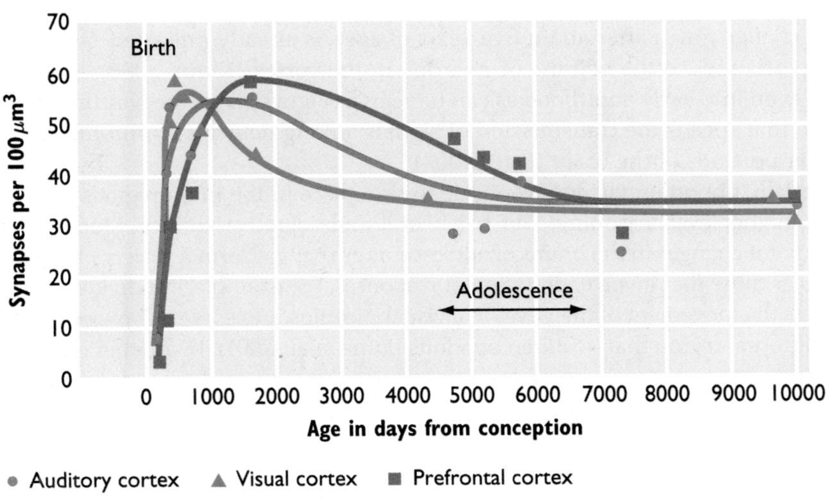

are often able to recover because neurons in other parts of the cortex take on this function. On the other hand, although considerable plasticity is retained by some regions of the mature adult brain (Thompson & Nelson, 2001), the prognosis for recovery of language in adults after an accident or a stroke is usually much poorer because the remaining neurons in the other regions now have already become dedicated to processing certain kinds of nonlinguistic experiences.

NATURE & NURTURE

William Greenough and his colleagues contend that neurons in human and other mammalian brains exhibit two different kinds of plasticity (Markham, Black, & Greenough, 2007). Some neurons are sensitive to *experience-expectant* information. As a result of a long evolutionary process, these neurons begin to grow and differentiate rapidly at about the time they can be expected to receive the kinds of stimulation important to their functioning. In many mammals, for example, parts of the visual cortex involved in depth or pattern perception develop quite rapidly shortly before and after the eyes open or, in the case of humans, shortly before and after birth. Research with lower animals indicates that visual deprivation during these periods—being reared in the dark or without patterned light, for example—results in the permanent loss of some kinds of depth and pattern vision, losses that do not occur when equivalent lengths of deprivation occur during other periods.

Other neurons are sensitive to *experience-dependent* information. Many opportunities for learning occur at unpredictable times during development. Each person learns different and unique things, even into old age. The distinctive perceptual features forming the image of a neighbor or the attributes defining the concept of democracy are unique representations registered within an individual's neural system. Here, then, is a form of plasticity that implicates neural differentiation as a critical aspect of brain functioning throughout a person's lifetime.

NATURE & NURTURE

How do neurons form connections with one another? A now-familiar mantra among contemporary neuroscientists is "Neurons that fire together wire together." As the organism encounters particular events in the world, whether they are sounds, visual stimuli, or other forms of stimulation, specific groups of neurons in the brain become activated. Each time neurons fire in synchrony, they are more likely to maintain connections with one another.

Implicated in this process is an amino acid called *glutamate*, which is one of several factors involved in communication among neurons. When neurons fire out of synchrony, however, they lose their connections, at least in part because the receptors for glutamate are altered or removed. Thus, the history of activity that neurons have with one another shapes the neuronal connections that remain versus those that are lost (Heynen et al., 2003; Penn & Shatz, 2002). Clearly, these findings from the laboratories of neuroscientists have important implications for the role of early experience in infancy and childhood.

Brain Development in Adolescence

For many years, scientists believed that by adolescence the growth of the brain is essentially complete. However, considerable evidence indicates that remodeling of the brain continues well into adulthood (Nelson et al., 2006) even though the total volume of the brain does not change much after about five years of age. As already indicated, synaptic pruning and apoptosis reduce the volume of neurons in the cortex (Kuhn, 2006). Offsetting these changes, even into early adulthood as can be seen in Figure 5.5, is the continued production of myelin that speeds the transmission of signals among neurons within the cortex as well as to other portions of the brain (Paus, 2004).

INTERACTION AMONG DOMAINS

Especially important changes continue to take place in the brain regions associated with planning, higher-level reasoning, and behavioral and cognitive control. Studies using fMRI scans pinpoint changes in the brains of adolescents as they perform a variety of cognitive tasks, in particular those that involve inhibition of responses. For example, if individuals are required to suppress the movement of their eyes to a visual stimulus, adolescents show greater activation of the prefrontal region than children or adults (Luna et al., 2001). In another experiment, adolescents were instructed to press a button in response to one visual target but avoid pressing it when they saw a different target. When fMRI scans of children at age nine were compared with their scans at age eleven, they showed an age-related decrease in activity in the prefrontal cortex. In addition, the areas that were activated were more localized rather than diffuse (Durston et al., 2006). All of this suggests that brain functioning becomes more effective and more specialized during adolescence. As brain researcher Linda Spear (2003) puts it, "The adolescent brain is a brain in the process of becoming leaner, more efficient, and less energy consuming" (p. 66).

Adolescents are often described as making risky choices in their behavior. The relatively late emergence of improved cognitive control compared with the relatively earlier development of subcortical regions of the brain known to be associated with risky choices and actions may be factors underlying that poor decision making. Thus, important additional changes continuing into adolescence and beyond are increased connectivity among various regions of the brain and a more effective balance between the earlier maturing and the later maturing regions (Casey, Getz, & Galvan, 2008).

Figure 5.5:

Myelination of Neurons Throughout Development

Although myelin covers relatively few neurons in very young children, it becomes an increasingly important component of brain development throughout childhood and is a process that continues even beyond adolescence. Myelin sheathes the axon of a neuron, helping to insulate it from other neurons and speeds neuronal transmission within the axon. Those neurons involved with vision (toward the back of the brain) are among the earliest to be myelinated, followed by those involved in language. Among the latest neurons to be myelinated are those in the prefrontal cortex, neurons which are typically involved with self-control and other more complex cognitive functions.

Source: Courtesy of Paul Thompson, Arthur Toga, Judith Rapoport/UCLA Lab of Neuro Imaging and NIMH.

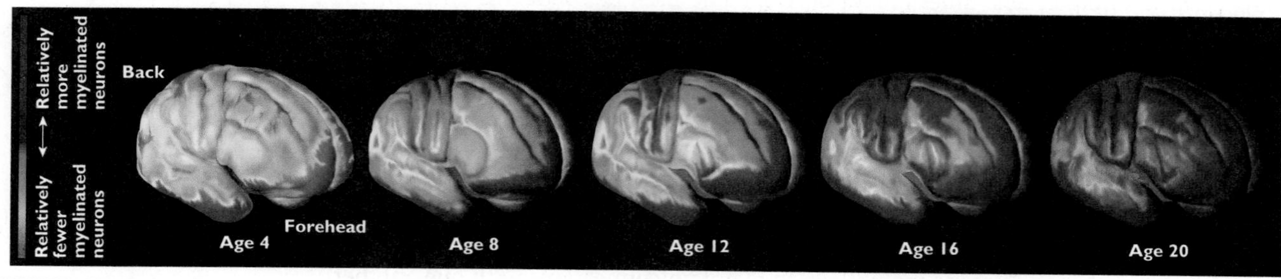

Brain Lateralization

One of the brain's most obvious physical characteristics is its two mirrorlike structures, a left and a right hemisphere. By and large, sensory information and motor responses on the left side of the body in humans are processed by the right hemisphere, and those on the right side of the body are processed by the left hemisphere. In addition, in most adults, the left hemisphere is especially involved in language functioning, whereas the right hemisphere is more typically engaged in processing certain types of spatial, emotional, or other nonverbal information. But these differences are by no means absolute. For example, speech is controlled primarily by the left hemisphere in about 98 percent of right-handed adults but in only about 70 percent of left-handed adults (Caplan & Gould, 2003). The reasons for brain lateralization in humans (and also when found in other species) remain unclear. One traditional perspective is that such specialization helps to minimize the need for duplication of the finite, and limited, neural circuitry within the brain.

Does hemispheric specialization already exist at birth, or does the brain show progressive **lateralization**, the process by which one hemisphere comes to dominate the other in terms of a particular function? Based on research on left-hemisphere damage in children, Eric Lenneberg (1967) proposed that, at least until age two, both hemispheres are capable of carrying out language functions equally well and that lateralization increases only gradually until adolescence. Other researchers, however, suggest that lateralization actually begins much earlier, perhaps as a consequence of exposure to fetal testosterone (Geschwind & Galaburda, 1987; Grimshaw, Bryden, & Finegan, 1995). For example, some physical differences in the two hemispheres already exist at birth (Kosslyn et al., 1999). Perhaps such brain asymmetries contribute to the observation that most infants lie with the head oriented to the right rather than to the left, an orientation that later predicts hand preference (Michel, 1988). Even before three months of age, most babies more actively use and hold objects longer in the right hand than in the left (Hawn & Harris, 1983). Most dramatic is evidence from ultrasound images of fifteen-week-old fetuses: 90 percent were observed to suck their right thumb, a preference that was linked consistently to handedness at ten to twelve years of age (Hepper, Wells, & Lynch, 2005).

For Your Review and Reflection

- Which regions of the brain develop earliest and latest? To what functions do those regions contribute?
- What developmental changes occur in neurons? How do myelin and glial cells contribute to neuronal development?
- When does the plasticity of the brain decline? What is the difference between experience-expectant and experience-dependent information? How do nature and nurture affect the development of the brain?
- What major changes occur in the brain during adolescence?
- What evidence exists for brain lateralization in infancy?
- Why might you claim that brain injuries, although serious at any age, are even more damaging as you become older?

Sleep

We often ignore consideration of sleep in discussions of development, perhaps because so little observable behavior is associated with this state. Yet sleep is an important behavioral state of increasing interest to researchers. Infants display a wide variety of behavioral states: crying, alert activity, alert inactivity, drowsiness, and regular and irregular sleep. Each of these states has distinctive features. For example, crying or distress usually begins

lateralization Process by which one hemisphere of the brain comes to dominate the other; for example, processing of language in the left hemisphere or of spatial information in the right hemisphere.

with whimpering but swiftly shifts to full-scale cries, often accompanied by thrashing of arms and legs. During alert activity, the infant also exhibits vigorous, diffuse motor activity, but such exertions are not accompanied by signs of distress. During alert inactivity, the baby is relatively quiet, at least in terms of motor activity, but actively engages in visual scanning of the environment. In this state, the baby appears to be most responsive to sensory stimulation and may be learning a great deal. But in early infancy sleep dominates in terms of amount of time spent among these various states. Perhaps not surprisingly, sleep plays a critical role in the development of both the brain and the body (Zee & Turek, 2006). And its regularity (or lack of it) is often of concern to parents, especially in the first few months when the adults in the household are awakened by the child's cries, sometimes several times in a night. Thus, it is important to consider some of the things we know about this topic, including changes in sleep patterns that bring the cycles of infants and caregivers into greater alignment with one another.

Patterns of Sleep in Infants

Although individual differences are great, newborns average sixteen to seventeen hours of sleep a day. Sleep and wake cycles are extremely short, and babies are easily disrupted by external stimulation. As the weeks pass, infants gradually sleep less but for longer periods; by about three to five weeks of age, a pattern begins to emerge in which the longest sleep periods take place at night (Thompson, 1982). But naps during the day continue to be a regular occurrence all the way through the preschool years. In fact, in some cultures, such naps are never eliminated.

SOCIOCULTURAL INFLUENCE

The development of sleep patterns differs substantially across various cultures. In most industrialized countries, parents eagerly look forward to having their infants adopt a routine that matches their own. A significant milestone is reached when the typical baby of three or four months finally sleeps through the night. In some cultures, such as the Kipsigi of rural Kenya, however, infants are permitted more flexibility and will not sleep through the night until much older (Super & Harkness, 1982).

Like adults, infants (even before they are born) display two distinct sleep states (Groome et al., 1997). During active or *REM (rapid eye movement)* sleep, eye movements and muscle jerks are frequent, and breathing and heart rate are irregular. During quiet sleep *(NREM)*, eye and muscle movements are few, and physiological activity is more regular. The proportion of time spent in the two states, however, shifts dramatically with development. About eight in sixteen hours of sleep are is spent in REM sleep as a newborn, but only about two in seven hours of sleep as an adult. Active or REM sleep has been linked to dreaming, but it is not clear whether young infants dream. However, REM sleep is believed to be important for normal brain activity (Roffwarg, Muzio, & Dement, 1966) including neuronal development and brain plasticity (Heraghty et al., 2008).

Sleeping Arrangements for Infants

SOCIOCULTURAL INFLUENCE

Where should infants sleep? The answer is very controversial. Historically, and in most cultures today (such as Japan), an infant and mother sleeping together—or *co-sleeping*—is the norm (Latz, Wolf, & Lozoff, 1999). In fact, Mayan mothers view putting very young children in a separate room at night as almost equivalent to child neglect (Morrelli et al., 1992). However, American mothers and others concerned about sleep issues typically suggest that having a separate space for sleeping, especially after the baby is a few months old, encourages self-reliance and independence. Decisions about sleeping arrangements are deeply ingrained in cultural beliefs concerning the values of closeness and interdependence, and of privacy and self-reliance. This being said, co-sleeping has become more common in American households. In one national study, 47 percent of mothers report sharing a bed with their infants either "sometimes" or "frequently" (Willinger et al., 2003).

What does research reveal about the risks or benefits of co-sleeping practices? One important consideration is how co-sleeping is defined. Sharing a bed is one form of co-sleeping, but sharing the same room (but a different bed) is often considered a co-sleeping arrangement as well. James McKenna and his colleagues contend that, when safe co-sleeping arrangements are initiated such as sharing the same room, mothers and infants engage in greater synchronized sleep, breathing, and arousal patterns that serve to protect infants from *apnea*, irregular patterns of temporary cessations in breathing. Those breathing cessations, in particular, can be related to tragic, unexplained deaths in infants (McKenna, Ball, & Gettler, 2007). Moreover, safe co-sleeping practices have the added advantage of promoting breast feeding. On the other hand, research suggests that under some circumstances bed sharing can actually put the infant at risk for death, especially if infants are younger than eleven weeks of age (Tappin, Ecob, & Brooke, 2005). Co-sleeping is especially hazardous on a couch or if the parent smokes, consumes alcohol, or uses other drugs (Hauck & Hunt, 2000). In response to this growing body of research, the American Academy of Pediatrics does not recommend bed sharing with infants (Task Force on Sudden Infant Death Syndrome, 2005). A far safer alternative to bed sharing for those who wish to be in close contact appears to be having the baby sleep within arm's length but in an infant crib.

RISK | RESILIENCE

research applied to parenting | Reducing Sudden Infant Death Syndrome

Danielle was proud of her gymnastics ability, but she also very much enjoyed helping to take care of her little brother born just three months ago. She delighted in playing with him and was eager to assist during bathing and in putting him to bed. Her mother, though, repeatedly commented about how different it was when Danielle's much older brother was a baby. Her mother insisted that Danielle's younger brother be placed on his back rather than on his stomach as she had done with her older brother. Her mother also now made sure that loose bedding and stuffed toys were removed from the crib, something that had not given her much concern during her firstborn's naps and bedtime. Her mother compulsively followed these practices and was very glad to have learned about these better ways to avoid having anything bad happen to this newest member of the family.

The abrupt, unexplained death of an infant less than one year of age who stops breathing during sleep is known as **sudden infant death syndrome (SIDS)**. These deaths, most frequently reported in babies about one to four months of age, are particularly tragic because they occur with no identifiable warnings. The highest incidence appears to occur at a time when basic automatic respiratory reflexes governed by the brainstem begin to be supplemented by voluntary, cortex-regulated breathing essential for vocalization and the emergence of speech (Lipsitt, 2003).

SIDS, once known as *crib death* or *cot death*, claimed the lives of between 1 and 2 of every 1,000 babies born in the United States in recent decades, and much higher rates have been reported in some other countries, such as New Zealand. Only congenital malformations and low birth weight or prematurity contribute to more deaths among infants (Xu, Kochanek, & Tejada-Vera, 2009). However, because of efforts to change sleeping arrangements for infants, the rate of SIDS has been cut by more than half in recent years (Hauck & Tanabe, 2008). Although researchers still do not know what causes SIDS, specific steps that parents can take are known to reduce its risk of occurring.

RISK | RESILIENCE

SOCIOCULTURAL INFLUENCE

1. *"Back to Sleep."* Up until the 1990s, parents were often advised to place their infants in a prone position (on their stomach) when ready for sleep. However, in 1994 pediatricians initiated a "Back to Sleep" campaign to encourage parents to place healthy infants on their backs to sleep. This change, designed to minimize the infant's breathing of expired carbon dioxide, has been estimated to reduce the incidence of SIDS as much as 80 percent in some nations and more than 50 percent in the United States (Hauck & Tanabe, 2008). Unfortunately, the proportion of parents placing their babies in a prone position when putting them to sleep has not changed significantly in

sudden infant death syndrome (SIDS) Sudden, unexplained death of an infant or toddler as a result of cessation of breathing during sleep.

Placing infants on their backs in preparation for sleep appears to have reduced the frequency of sudden infant death syndrome (SIDS). The decline in SIDS associated with this practice is reported in many countries, including the United States, where pediatricians in the 1990s launched a "Back to Sleep" campaign.

the United States over the last decade; more than 20 percent of parents continue to do so (Colson et al., 2009).

2. *Eliminate exposure to cigarette smoke and other drugs.* Numerous studies have confirmed that a mother's smoking or use of other drugs during pregnancy is associated with a greater likelihood of SIDS (Task Force on Sudden Infant Death Syndrome, 2005). Exposure even to passive smoke after birth (from mother, father, or other live-in adults) increases the risk as well.
3. *Provide firm bedding, and keep soft objects and loose bedding out of the crib.* The incidence of SIDS in Australia and New Zealand had been among the highest in the world. In these countries, less firm bedding (use of wool or of bark from the ti tree) appears to have contributed to the risk of SIDS for infants sleeping prone, perhaps again because of a tendency for this softer bedding to trap carbon dioxide. Soft objects and loose bedding pose a similar hazard.
4. *Avoid overheating.* High room temperature and high body temperature because of excessive bedding or clothing are also known to increase the incidence of SIDS (Task Force on Sudden Infant Death Syndrome, 2005). Adequate ventilation helps to prevent overheating of the infant, as well as to disperse carbon dioxide.
5. *Have the infant use a pacifier during sleep.* Although the mechanism is not yet understood, use of a pacifier is associated with a significant drop, sometimes as much as 90 percent, in the incidence of SIDS (Hauck, Omojokun, & Siadaty, 2005; Mitchell, Blair, & L'Hoir, 2006).

SIDS is associated with a number of other factors, including the colder months of the year, economically depressed neighborhoods, having a cold, being male, being a later-born or one of a multiple birth, and low birth weight. In addition to susceptibility to the buildup of carbon dioxide, other characteristics hypothesized to play a role in causing SIDS include abnormalities in neurons that project to areas influencing respiration in the brainstem and spinal cord and deficiencies associated with serotonin, an important neurotransmitter, in the brainstem (Duncan et al., 2010; Paterson et al., 2006).

Although the benefits far outweigh the drawbacks, one unintended outcome of having infants sleep on their back has been more frequent reports of flattening of the back of the head (Persing et al., 2003). The problem, not normally serious, can be substantially reduced by varying head position each time the baby is placed for sleep and giving the infant plenty of experience on his or her stomach during periods when awake and under the watchful eye of a parent (Graham, 2006).

Sleep in Adolescents

In recent years, concern often has been expressed about whether adolescents are typically receiving adequate amounts of sleep. Ask any parent of a teenager—adolescents tend to be night owls. Many go to bed late, often after 11:30 P.M. At the same time, because most high schools start earlier in the day than elementary schools, adolescents must wake up early, typically at 6 A.M. or even earlier, in order to make it to school on time. About 26 percent of adolescents get less than 6.5 hours of sleep per night (Wolfson & Carskadon, 1998). But teens may actually need more sleep, as much as 9 hours daily, compared with the typical 7 or 8 hours that we think of for adults (Carskadon, Harvey, & Duke, 1980). This means that many teenagers are not getting nearly enough rest to be alert during the day; by some estimates, as many as 85 percent can be categorized as sleep deprived (Dahl & Lewin, 2002; Wolfson & Carskadon, 1998).

RISK | RESILIENCE

Besides needing more sleep, adolescents also experience a phase shift in sleep cycle—a biological tendency to go to bed later and wake up later in the morning—which appears to be triggered by the onset of puberty (Carskadon, Acebo, & Jenni, 2004). Several other factors such as homework, computers and the Internet, and work schedules also contribute to the tendency for teens to stay up late. Sometimes teens try to catch up by sleeping more on weekends and holidays, but this further upsets the sleep-wake rhythm when they have to awaken early on the next school day (Dahl & Lewin, 2002).

INTERACTION AMONG DOMAINS

What are the consequences of insufficient sleep for adolescents? Lack of sleep is associated with lower grades in school, moodiness and depression, and lower self-esteem (Fredriksen et al., 2004; Millman et al., 2005; Wolfson & Carskadon, 1998). Excessive sleepiness is a special concern when teenagers drive; it is associated with the tendency to be involved in serious automobile accidents. The consequences of adolescent sleepiness are serious enough that several school districts across the United States have made changes toward later school start times for high school students. According to early reports from one of these districts, school attendance is up, and daytime sleepiness among students has declined (Wahlstrom, 2002).

For Your Review and Reflection

- What kinds of sleep patterns are found in newborns?
- Why does controversy exist concerning the sleeping arrangements for young infants?
- What factors increase risk associated with SIDS? What steps can caregivers follow to reduce the likelihood of SIDS?
- What kinds of sleeping arrangements did you experience as an infant? Were you placed on your back or on your stomach when put to sleep?
- How do patterns of sleep change in adolescence? What are the consequences of inadequate sleep? In what ways does sleep affect other domains of development? Did you feel that you received enough sleep during your adolescent years? How about now?

Motor Skill Development

During postnatal development, cartilage continues to be transformed into bone, and bones elongate and increase in number to become scaffolding to support the body in new physical orientations. As the brain and nervous system mature, neural commands begin to coordinate thickened and enlarged muscles, permitting more powerful and refined motor activities. For example, infants begin to roll from side to back, reach for objects, and eventually crawl, stand up, and walk. Two complementary patterns are evident in the emergence of motor activity: *differentiation*, the enrichment of global and relatively diffuse actions with more refined and skilled ones, and *integration*, the increasingly coordinated actions of muscles and sensory systems. Throughout infancy and childhood, motor skills become more efficient, coordinated, deliberate, or automatic as the task requires. Toward the end of childhood, many skills become highly specialized talents.

INTERACTION AMONG DOMAINS

For Jean Piaget, sensorimotor activity was essential to understand, for it served as the prototype and first stage in the construction of knowledge. Contemporary child development researchers, too, recognize that the acquisition, coordination, and integration of basic motor skills are not only interesting topics of study in their own right but also can give us important insights into early cognitive and perceptual development.

Among the reflexes that babies display is the swimming reflex. When young infants are placed in water, breathing is suspended, and they engage in swim-like movements with their arms and legs.

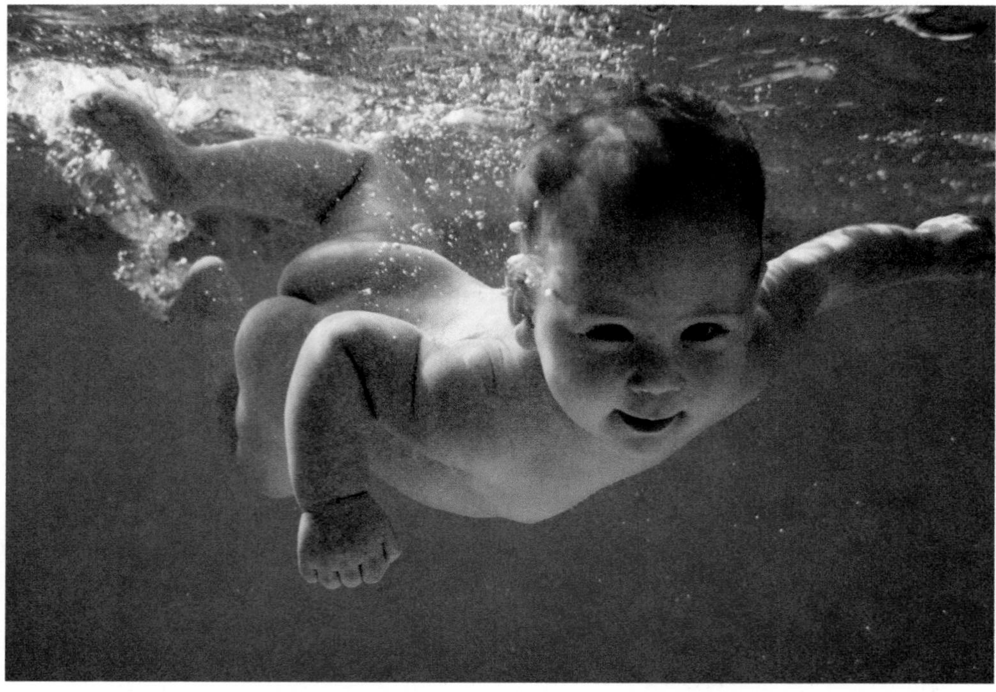

© Morgan McCauley/CORBIS

The First Actions: Reflexes

At first glance, newborns seem helpless and incompetent. Babies eat, sleep, and cry; their diapers always seem to need changing. Yet a more careful look reveals that infants enter their new world with surprisingly adept abilities, among them a set of **reflexes**, involuntary reactions to touch, light, sound, and other kinds of stimulation; some, such as sucking, are exhibited even prenatally.

Reflexes are among the building blocks that soon give rise to voluntary movements and the acquisition of *developmental milestones*—significant achievements in motor skills. Along with breathing and swallowing, *primitive reflexes,* such as rooting and sucking (see Table 5.1), provide nourishment for the infant's survival. Among our evolutionary ancestors, other reflexes, such as the Moro and palmar reflexes, helped to protect newborns from danger. *Postural reflexes,* including stepping, swimming, and body righting (which are surprisingly similar to later voluntary movements), appear to be designed to maintain a specific orientation to the environment. If primitive or postural reflexes are absent, are too strong or too weak, display unequal strength when normally elicited from either side of the body, or continue to be exhibited beyond certain ages, a pediatrician may begin to suspect cerebral palsy or some other neurological impairment and developmental difficulties for the baby.

Motor Milestones

Reflexes are often viewed as fixed responses to a stimulus. However, many early motor behaviors that young infants produce consist of coordinated actions. Repeated sequences of motions performed with no apparent goal such as rubbing one foot against the other, rocking back and forth, bouncing up and down, swaying side to side, striking or banging objects, mouthing and tonguing, and shaking and nodding the head may eventually be recruited and integrated into organized voluntary motor skills and activities such as grasping, crawling, and walking (Thelen, 1996). These latter motor milestones, once mastered, open up new worlds to the infant. Moreover, they lead caregivers to respond in different ways: childproofing the home to prevent accidents, allowing greater independence, expecting more mature behavior. Most gains in infant movement

reflex Involuntary reaction to touch, light, sound, and other kinds of stimulation.

TABLE 5.1 Typical Reflexes Observed in Newborns and Infants

Considerable variability exists among infants in their reflexes and the ages at which they can be elicited (Touwen, 1974). The presence or absence of any single reflex provides only one among many indicators of healthy or atypical development.

Name of Reflex	Testing Procedure	Response	Developmental Course	Significance
Primitive Reflexes				
Palmar or Hand Grasp	Place finger in hand.	Hand grasps object.	Birth to about 4 months.	Absence may signal neurological defects; persistence could interfere with voluntary grasping.
Rooting	Stroke corner of mouth lightly.	Head and tongue move toward stimulus.	Birth to about 5 months.	Mouth is brought to stimulus to permit sucking.
Sucking	Place finger in mouth or on lips.	Sucking begins.	Birth to about 6 months.	Ensures intake of potential nutrients.
Moro	(1) Sit child up, allow head to drop about 20 degrees backward, or (2) make a loud noise, or (3) lower baby rapidly.	Baby extends arms outward, hands open; then brings hands to midline, hands clenched, spine straightened.	Birth to about 5–7 months.	Absence may signal neurological defects; persistence could interfere with acquisition of sitting.
Babinski	Stroke bottom of foot.	Toes fan and then curl.	Birth to about 1 year.	Absence may signal neurological defects.
Asymmetric Tonic Neck Reflex	Place baby on back, arms and legs extended, and rotate head 90 degrees.	Arm on face side extends, arm on back side of head flexes.	About 1 month to 4 months.	Absence may signal neurological defects; persistence could prevent rolling over, coordination.
Postural Reflexes				
Stepping	Hold baby under arms, upright, leaning forward.	Makes walk-like stepping movements.	Birth to about 3 months.	Absence may signal neurological defects.
Labyrinthine	(1) Place baby on back. (2) Place baby on stomach.	Extends arms and legs. Flexes arms and legs.	Birth to about 4 months.	Absence may signal neurological defects.
Swimming	Place baby in water.	Holds breath involuntarily; arms and legs move as if trying to swim.	Birth to about 4–6 months.	Absence may signal neurological defects.
Placing	Hold baby under arms, upright, top of foot touching bottom edge of table.	Lifts foot and places on top of table.	Birth through 12 months.	Absence may signal neurological defects.
Landau Reaction	Place baby on stomach, hold under chest.	Lifts head, eventually other parts of body, above chest.	Head at 2 months, other parts of body later.	Absence may signal neurological defects; inadequate muscle tone for motor development.
Body Righting	Rotate hips or shoulder.	Rotates remainder of body.	4 months to more than 12 months.	Absence may signal neurological defects; difficulty in gaining postural control and walking.

illustrate progress in coordinating (1) *postural control,* the ability to maintain an upright orientation to the environment; (2) *locomotion,* the ability to maneuver through space; and (3) *manual control,* the ability to manipulate objects (Keogh & Sugden, 1985).

Postural Control Keeping the head upright and stable at about two to three months of age represents one of the first milestones in infant motor development. As the Motor Skill

CHRONOLOGY Development of Motor Skills: Birth to 7 Years

MONTHS BIRTH

YEARS BIRTH

2 Months
- Holds head steady when held upright.
- Lifts head up.

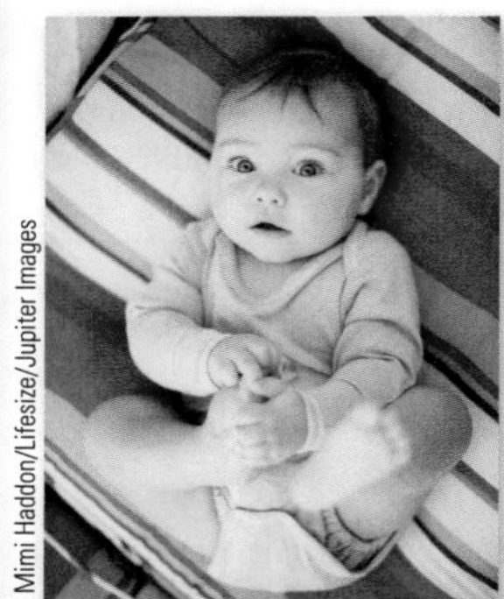
© Mimi Haddon/Lifesize/Jupiter Images

3 Months
- Holds head steady while being carried.
- Rolls over.
- Raises head and chest.

4 Months
- Grasps cube.

6 Months
- Sits without support.
- Stands holding on to something.

7 Months
- Rolls: back to stomach.
- Begins to attempt to crawl and/or creep.
- Displays true thumb opposition in holding cube.

8 Months
- Achieves sitting position without help.
- Pulls to standing.

9 Months
- Walks holding furniture (cruises).
- Demonstrates fine prehension (neat pincer grasp).
- Bangs two objects held in hands.

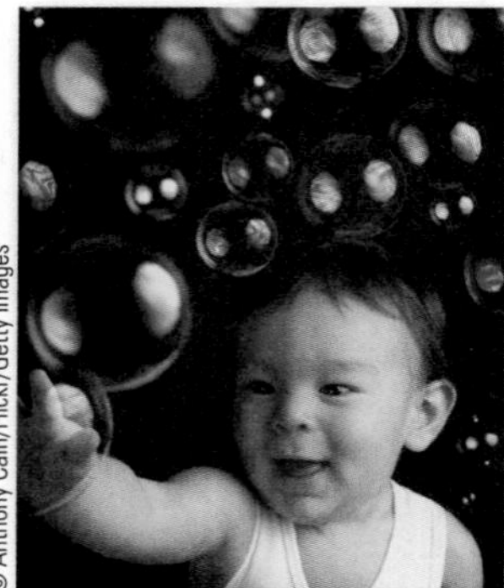
© Anthony Cain/Flickr/Getty Images

10 Months
- Walks with help.
- Plays pat-a-cake.

11 Months
- Stands alone.
- Turns pages of book.

12 Months
- Walks alone.
- Drinks from cup.

14 Months
- Builds tower using two cubes.
- Scribbles.

© JGI/Jamie Grill/Blend Images/Jupiter Images

15 Months
- Walks sideways and backward.
- Attempts to use spoon and fork.

17 Months
- Walks up steps.

18 Months
- Begins to run.

20 Months
- Kicks ball forward.
- Throws ball overhand.

2–3 Years
- Jumps up several inches using both feet.
- Begins to show true run rather than hurried walk.
- Balances on one foot for one second.
- Throws ball, but feet remain stationary.
- Outstretches arms to catch a ball.
- Draws primarily in the form of scribbles.
- Eats with a spoon.

© Steven Puetzer/Photographer's Choice RF/Getty Images

3–4 Years
- Walks upstairs, alternating feet.
- Able to produce standing long jump of about a foot.
- Flexes elbows to catch a ball and trap it against chest.
- Hops.
- Cuts paper with scissors.
- Uses lines to form boundaries of objects in drawing pictures.
- Brushes teeth without help.
- Puts on T-shirt.
- Buttons and unbuttons articles of clothing.

4–5 Years
- Walks downstairs, alternating feet.
- Gallops and skips by leading with one foot.
- Transfers weight forward to throw ball.
- Attempts to catch a ball with hands.
- Eats with a fork.
- Dresses without help.

© David Madison/Photographer's Choice RF/Getty Images

5–6 Years
- Walks on a balance beam.
- Jumps about one foot vertically, broad jumps about three feet.
- Displays adultlike skill in throwing and catching.

6–7 Years
- Ties shoes.
- Writes some numbers and words.

This chart describes the sequence of motor skill development based on the findings of research and indicates the age at which approximately half of the infants or children tested in the United States begin to demonstrate the skill. Children often show individual differences in the exact ages at which they display the various developmental achievements outlined here. Sources: Bayley, 1993: Cratty, 1986; Frankenburg et al., 1992; Gallahue, 1989; Newborg, Stock, & Wnek, 1984; Robertson, 1984; Winner, 1986.

Development chronology indicates, this achievement is followed by mastery of other significant postural skills, such as maintaining an upright sitting position, moving to a standing position, and standing without assistance. The milestones often follow the principle of **cephalocaudal development** (*cephalocaudal* combines the Greek words for "head" and "tail"). This principle describes the tendency for systems and parts of the body near the head to mature sooner than those more distant from the head. Head control, for example, precedes control of the trunk, and command of the legs is the last to develop. The integration of postural skills is also important. For example, the ability to keep the head upright while sitting or while standing on a stable surface is one thing; the ability to do this when being carried about or during self-movement requires integration of far more information.

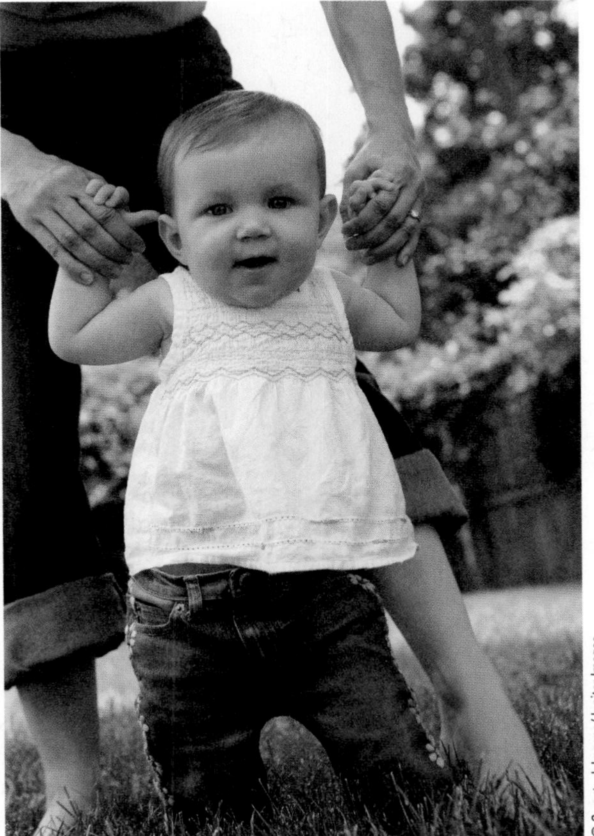

A major motor milestone that babies around a year of age typically reach is that of walking. Although this baby is not quite old enough to walk independently, infants show surprisingly coordinated leg movements well before this milestone is reached. Do you think this kind of practice might also help her to begin walking earlier? Although we typically think of the onset of walking as primarily the result of maturation, cross-cultural research suggests that, in communities in which a great deal of opportunity is provided to acquire this ability, children begin to walk at somewhat earlier ages.

Locomotion No one doubts that a monumental achievement in infancy is the ability to move about the environment. One early milestone in locomotion is the capacity to roll over. Then comes success at initiating forward motion, a skill marked by considerable variation. Some infants use arms to pull and legs to push, others use only arms or legs, and still others scoot forward while sitting.

Once babies are able to pull themselves upright, they often *cruise*; that is, move by holding onto furniture or other objects to help maintain their balance while stepping sideways. Forward walking holding onto someone's hand typically follows. By about twelve months of age, about half of American babies and infants in most cultures walk alone. Skill in walking continues to be refined throughout infancy and early childhood. The infant's steps become longer and show less side-to-side motion, while the toes point more forward, refinements that are linked with opportunities to practice walking. Walking up a flight of stairs begins much later, although children, much to the chagrin of many parents, first attempt to display success at crawling up stairs about a month before initially learning to walk (Berger, Theuring, & Adolph, 2007). Mothers often couple their negative emotional reactions, verbalizations, and gestures about risky locomotor responses with a rich array of positive responses designed to regulate, guide, and inform their infants about alternative courses of safe locomotor activity (Karasik et al., 2008).

Even before independent walking, many of the components of this ability are evident. For example, when babies six months of age are placed on a treadmill and held so they do not have to support their full weight, they display alternating stepping similar to that involved in walking (Thelen & Ulrich, 1991). The task constraints of maintaining upright posture, lifting the leg against gravity, moving forward, and other factors delay the onset of walking. And although crawling and walking appear to unfold in an orderly, well regulated fashion, the variety of terrains (for example, level or sloping, smooth or bumpy) over which infants are required to navigate reveal that considerable learning and problem solving is involved as well (Adolph, 2008).

Manual Control In the weeks that follow birth, infants make enormous progress in reaching, a major way of gaining access to and learning about objects. Moving the hand to the mouth appears to be among the earliest goal actions (Rochat, 1993). Systematic reaching for objects begins at about three months of age. By about five to six months, infants display mature, *ballistic* reaches to rapidly and accurately retrieve an object in the visual field, engaging in a series of submovements, not always perfectly executed but often quickly corrected, to meet the goal of obtaining the target (Berthier & Robin, 1998; Claxton, Keen, & McCarty, 2003). The ability to see their own hands is not necessary in early reaching; however, infants eventually make greater use of visual cues to help them accurately retrieve an object (Carrico & Berthier, 2008).

cephalocaudal development Pattern in which organs, systems, and motor movements near the head tend to develop earlier than those near the feet.

When first attempting to reach, very young infants typically keep their hands closed in fistlike fashion. By about four months of age, babies awkwardly pick up an object by grasping it with the palm of the hand. Over the next few months, they shift from using the inner palm to using opposing thumb and fingertips, a progression that culminates in a neat *pincer grasp* at about nine months of age.

Another important component of motor skill is increased coordination between the two hands. Very young infants often attempt to grasp objects with both hands, but once babies gain an ensemble of skills, including head control and postural balance while sitting by themselves and when leaning forward, one-handed reaches and more consistent, stable reaching become a part of their repertoire (Rochat & Goubet, 1995; Spencer et al., 2000). Nevertheless, two-handed reaches may re-emerge for a short period of time when first learning to walk (Corbetta & Bojczyk, 2002). Increased coordination is further reflected in the appearance of complementary hand orientations, such as holding a toy dump truck in one hand while using the other hand to fill it with sand. This *functional asymmetry* emerges at about five to six months of age but becomes especially refined as the child enters the second year and begins to display self-help and advanced motor tasks requiring sophisticated use of both arms and hands.

Motor Skills in the Preschool and Later-Childhood Years

Many fundamental motor skills that the child acquired in the first two years of life continue to be modified and refined in the preschool and elementary school years. For example, between two and six months after learning to walk, children typically begin to run. In the months and years that follow, they show increasingly effective body and eye-hand or eye-foot *coordination*, evident in their greater ability to hop and skip, or kick, dribble, and catch a ball. With increasing age, children also demonstrate better *balance*, reflected in the ability to walk greater distances on a beam or to stand on one foot for a longer period of time; increased *speed*, shown by running short distances more rapidly; improved *agility*, revealed, for example, in the ability to shift directions quickly while running; and greater *power*, shown by jumping higher or longer distances or throwing a ball farther and faster than at younger ages. Older preschoolers supplement their large-muscle and athletic exercises with coloring and drawing, cutting and sculpting, and other activities that demand greater neural control and small-muscle coordination, a longer attention span, and more sophisticated planning and organization. The Motor Skill Development chronology summarizes major accomplishments for some of these abilities during early childhood.

Motor skills during middle childhood become more efficient and better controlled, involve more complex and coordinated movements, and are exhibited more quickly and in a wider variety of contexts and circumstances (Keogh & Sugden, 1985). With the exception of balance, boys tend to slightly outperform girls on many gross-motor tasks by the time they enter elementary school (Gallahue, 1989). However, differences between boys and girls may become especially large for some activities as children approach the end of middle childhood and enter the adolescent years, as Figure 5.6 indicates for running speed and the distance a youngster can throw a ball.

As children grow older, differences in individual abilities often increase. Of course, to some degree, this may stem from practice—some children focus on acquiring particular competence relevant to their social and cultural milieus. The acquisition of expertise or specialized motor skills in sports, dance, crafts, hobbies, playing of musical instruments, and, in some cultures, trade- or work-related endeavors permits older children to become more effective members of their society and gain greater social status among peers and adults.

Determinants of Motor Development

NATURE & NURTURE

What roles do genetic or maturational factors play in motor development? What about practice, cultural, or other experiential factors? Many pioneers in developmental psychology advocated a strong maturational theory to explain the orderly acquisition of motor

Figure 5.6

Running Speed and Throwing Distance for Boys and Girls at Different Ages

Boys tend to outperform girls on many motor skill tasks during the elementary school years, as indicated by these data on speed of running and distance throwing a ball, summarized from a number of studies carried out since 1960. The differences between girls and boys often increase substantially as children enter adolescence.

Source: Data from Gallahue, 1989; adapted from Haubenstricker & Seefeldt, 1986.

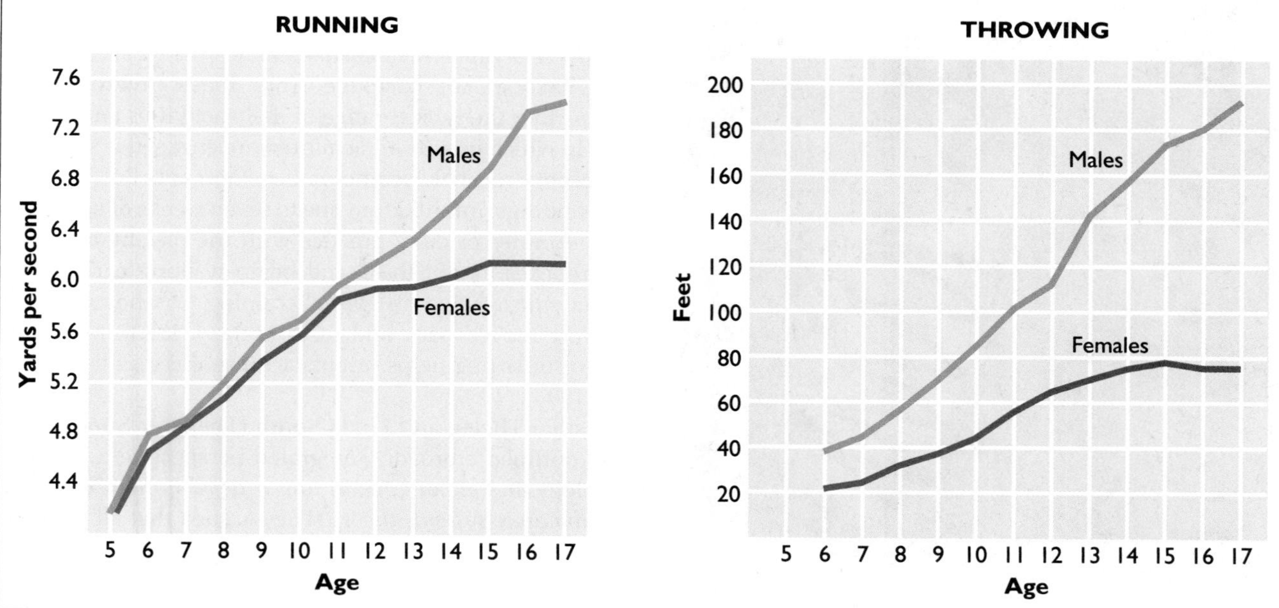

skills. But we now recognize that these changes are better understood in terms of the confluence of both biological and experiential factors.

Biological Contributions Supporting the role of genetics and maturation in the development of motor skills is their tendency to be displayed at predictable times and in similar ways in normal children. Moreover, the onsets of such skills as sitting and walking show greater concordance for identical than for fraternal twins. Greater similarity in gross motor activities, such as running, jumping, and throwing, is found in children who are more closely related biologically (Malina, 1980). Even intellectually and physically disabled babies attain major milestones in an orderly manner, although at a later age than other children. For example, blind children, who show substantial delays in acquiring postural, locomotion, and manual coordination skills, eventually acquire them (Tröster & Brambring, 1993).

Experiential Contributions With respect to the acquisition of expert motor skill, experience undoubtedly plays an important role. However, the same may be true for attaining basic developmental milestones. Lack of opportunity to engage in physical activity seriously interferes with reaching developmental milestones. For example, babies who spend most of their first year in an orphanage lying in cribs and receiving few other forms of stimulation typically do not walk before age three or four (Dennis, 1960). When special programs encourage blind infants to acquire self-initiated movement, they do so at ages more comparable to their sighted peers (Fraiberg, 1977).

RISK | RESILIENCE

Several investigators in the 1930s conducted studies with sets of twins to test the role of experience in motor skill development. Typically, one twin received extensive training in, say, handling blocks, climbing stairs, or roller skating; the other twin did not (Gesell & Thompson, 1934; Hilgard, 1932; McGraw, 1935). When given a chance to acquire the skills, the untrained twin often rapidly achieved the same level of skill displayed by the trained twin. In another early study, Wayne and Marsena Dennis investigated child-rearing practices among the Hopi Indians (Dennis & Dennis, 1940). Some Hopi Indian mothers followed the tribal tradition of tightly swaddling their babies in a cradleboard; the mother would strap the board to her back for all but about an hour a day during her waking hours for the first six to twelve months of her child's life. These Hopi babies had little opportunity to practice sitting up, crawling, and walking. Other Hopi mothers reared infants without swaddling. The researchers found that swaddling had little bearing on when infants initiated walking, an observation reconfirmed in a later study of the effects of Hopi rearing customs (Harriman & Lukosius, 1982).

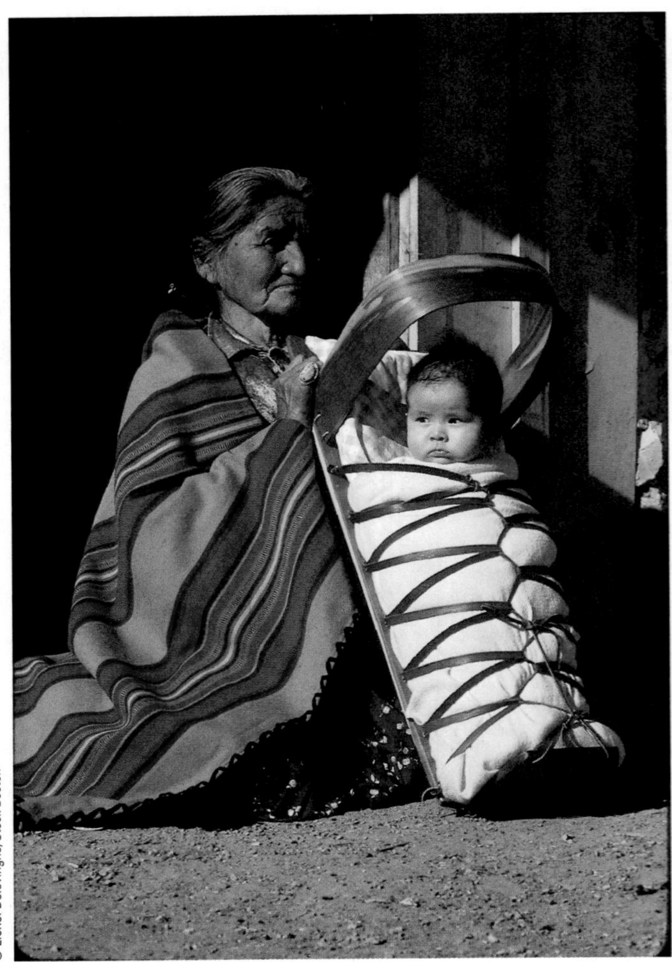

© Lionel Delevingne/Stock Boston

In the Navajo culture babies are often swaddled for most of the day. Wayne Dennis's research with Hopi infants who were also cared for in this way suggests that this baby, despite the lack of opportunity to practice sitting up, crawling, and standing alone, will begin to walk about the same time as an infant who has not been swaddled.

What can we conclude from these investigations? Perhaps that the typical range of daily activities and experiences in which infants and children are engaged is sufficient to promote normal locomotor development. But consider other findings. Infants from one to seven weeks of age, given a few minutes of daily practice with the placing and stepping reflexes, retain them and begin walking earlier than infants who receive no special training or whose legs are passively moved back and forth (Zelazo, 1983). Moreover, practice in sitting helps infants acquire these skills (Zelazo et al., 1993).

Esther Thelen and Linda Smith (Thelen & Smith, 1994, 2006) outlined a broadly integrated perspective to the role of biology and experience in motor development based on their *dynamic systems theory*. They argued that all complex motor skills require the assembling and reassembling of multiple processes involving, among other things, the following: motivation, elements of the nervous system that regulate posture and balance, increased bone and muscle strength, and changes in body proportions. These assemblages are further constrained by the biodynamics of the human body, as well as the situational context. However, when the right improvisation of components exists, infants display mastery of motor skills or advance to new levels of competence. Consider, for example, a six-month-old infant when first placed in a baby bouncer. She may initially show a few hesitant bounces up and down, but within a few weeks she very likely displays a highly coordinated bouncing pattern linked to the characteristics of the bouncer. No gene exists for such behavior, yet with the right physical resources, opportunities to practice, and a context that permits this activity, a sophisticated pattern of bouncing can be demonstrated. Biological and experiential factors comprise a dynamic, interactive system underlying motor development; its multiple components become "tuned" into sequences of more effective, self-organized actions over time.

NATURE & NURTURE

INTERACTION AMONG DOMAINS

SOCIOCULTURAL INFLUENCE

Cross-Cultural Differences

Given the multiple processes involved, it should not be surprising to learn that ethnic and cultural differences in motor development exist. At birth and throughout their first year, African American babies, as well as infants among the Wolof of Senegal, the Gusii of Kenya, the Yoruba of Nigeria, the Bantu of South Africa, and the Ganda of Uganda, typically outperform Caucasian infants on a variety of motor skills (Lester & Brazelton, 1982; Werner, 1972). Parents in a fairly prosperous rural community in Kenya made extensive efforts to teach their infants to sit or walk (Super, 1976). In fact, their language, as in some other regions of East Africa, contained distinctive words to denote the specialized training. The more caregivers promoted specific motor skills, the earlier their children tended to display them. For example, 93 percent of one group of caregivers said they taught their babies to crawl, and babies in this group began crawling at about five and a half months of age. In contrast, only 13 percent of the caregivers in a nearby group expressed support for such teaching, and their babies typically did not crawl until about eight months of age.

Many factors could contribute to the cultural differences, but one finding strongly implicates child-rearing efforts. Advanced motor development in this part of Kenya was limited to sitting, standing, and walking—skills considered culturally important. Other milestones not taught or valued, such as head control or the ability to roll over, were acquired later than they are by American infants. A similar observation comes from Jamaica. Some mothers in that country perform special stretching and massaging exercises to encourage their infants to sit and walk alone, and they do so earlier than other children (Hopkins & Westra, 1990).

We cannot be certain whether training focused on particular skills or more general experiences are responsible for cultural differences. Children in East Africa, for example, spend more time in an upright position, seated on a caregiver's lap or riding on her back, than children in the United States (Super, 1976). The activities may strengthen trunk and leg muscles to aid the earlier appearance of sitting, standing, and walking. However, gains achieved from training in one of two particular skills, such as stepping or sitting, do not appear to generalize to others (Zelazo, 1998; Zelazo et al., 1993). And infants who become increasingly proficient in crawling up and down a slope have to relearn how to go up and down the same slope when they start to walk (Adolph, 2008).

For Your Review and Reflection

- How do primitive and postural reflexes differ? What purpose do they serve for the infant?
- What are the major milestones associated with the development of postural control, locomotion, and manual control? How does the principle of cephalocaudal development apply to the emergence of the major motor milestones?
- What are the child's major achievements in motor skills during the preschool and later school years?
- What factors contribute to motor development? How do cultural practices influence their acquisition?
- Do you have records available for when you acquired various milestones in motor development? If they varied from the typical pattern, how would you explain these differences?

Body Growth and Development

Perhaps no more immediately apparent indicator of development exists than changes in a child's physical size. We often use the words *grow* and *develop* interchangeably in describing these physical transformations, but they do not refer to the same processes. Strictly speaking, *growth* is the increase in size of the body or its organs, whereas *development* refers not only to changes in size but also to the orderly patterns, such as growth spurts, and the more complicated levels of functioning that often accompany increases in height and weight.

Norms of Growth

By recording information about the height and weight of large numbers of children from diverse populations, we can determine whether a particular child's individual growth falls within the range expected for his or her chronological age and ethnic background. These **norms**, quantitative measures that provide typical values and variations in height and weight for children, have become an essential reference for attempting to answer questions about how biological and experiential factors influence growth.

norm Quantitative measure that provides typical values and variations in such characteristics as height and weight for children.

Length and Height The most rapid increase in body length occurs during the fourth month of prenatal development, when the fetus grows about 1.5 millimeters a day. The fetus continues to grow at a somewhat slower rate during the remaining prenatal weeks. The newborn maintains a high rate of growth for several months following birth. In fact, if growth rate during the first six months after birth were sustained, the average ten-year-old would be about 100 feet tall (McCall, 1979)! Girls can be expected to reach approximately half their adult height a little before two years of age and boys a little after two years of age (Fredriks et al., 2000).

Throughout much of early childhood, physical growth rate generally follows a slow and steady pace. The average preschooler grows from a little under three feet tall at age two to a little under four feet tall at age six. One of the more obvious differences you would notice between a six-year-old standing next to an eleven-year-old is that same disparity in their height—about a foot on average. Even more apparent is the growth spurt that takes place just prior to or during early adolescence. Although by this time parents may have dropped the typical childhood practice of penciling ever-higher marks on the bedroom wall, a long-absent aunt might still cry out, "My, how you've grown!" upon seeing her thirteen-year-old niece.

In the United States, the onset of rapid adolescent growth typically occurs between ages ten and fourteen for girls and between ages twelve and sixteen for boys (Sinclair, 1985). During this period, height increments occur at nearly double the rate in childhood. Because the growth spurt usually does not start in boys until about two years later, girls may tower head and shoulders over their male peers for a brief period in early adolescence. During the approximately three years over which the growth spurt occurs, girls add about twenty-eight centimeters (eleven inches) and boys about thirty centimeters (twelve inches), or about 17 percent of their total height (Abbassi, 1998). Figure 5.7 illustrates the growth typically observed in many populations of children during their first twenty years.

Figure 5.7

Growth in Height and Weight over the First Twenty Years

Height and, to a lesser extent, weight rapidly increase in the first two years following birth. Changes in height and weight continue at a fairly modest rate throughout childhood, followed by a brief, more rapid upturn sometime during the preadolescent or adolescent years. However, there is a wide range in height and weight among children, especially during the adolescent years. For example, this figure (based on children in the United States) shows height and weight growth charts for boys and girls between the 3rd and 97th percentiles.

Source: Data from Centers for Disease Control and Prevention, National Center for Health Statistics, 2000.

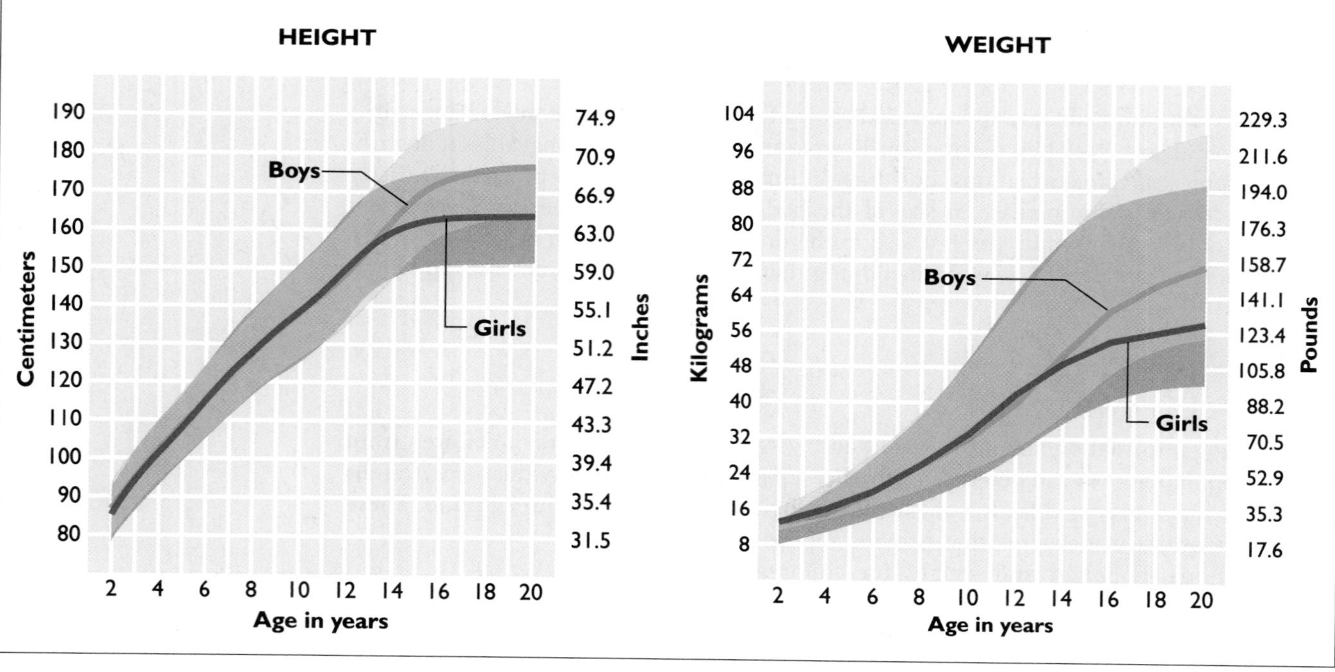

Figure 5.8

Changes in Body Proportions During Prenatal and Postnatal Growth

The size of the human head in proportion to the rest of the body shows striking changes over the course of prenatal to adult development. Two months after conception, the head takes up about half of the entire length of the body. By adulthood, the head makes up only about 12 to 13 percent of total body length. The head's tendency to grow more rapidly than regions of the body near the "tail" demonstrates the pattern of cephalocaudal development.

Source: Adapted from Robbins et al., 1928.

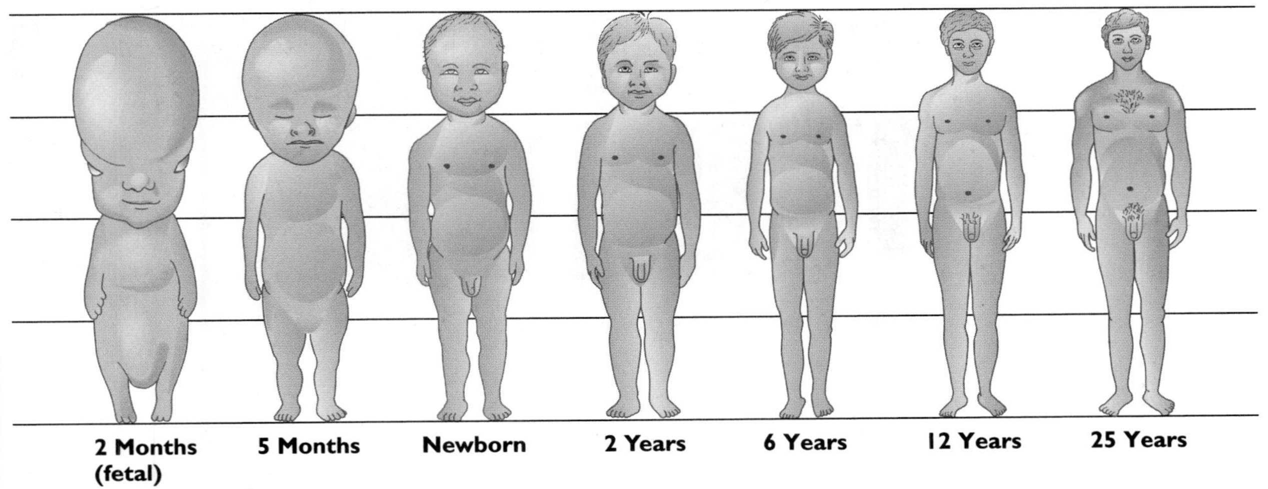

Weight In contrast to that of height, the maximum rate of increase in weight takes place shortly after birth. In their first few days, newborns typically lose excess body fluids and shed 5 to 10 percent of their birth weight. They then usually make rapid gains, normally doubling their birth weight in about five months and nearly tripling it by the end of the first year (Pinyerd, 1992).

Weight gains are smallest during childhood between ages two and three and gradually increase so that, by age six, most children weigh between thirty-five and sixty pounds. Slightly more rapid weight gain takes place during the middle school years and continues into adolescence (see Figure 5.7).

Patterns and Individual Differences in Body Growth

Specific organs and systems of the body often develop at rates different from that for the body as a whole. The most dramatic example is probably head size. Two months after conception, the head constitutes nearly 50 percent of total body length. By birth, however, head size represents only about 25 percent, and by adulthood only about 12 to 13 percent of total body length, as Figure 5.8 shows. The central nervous system, along with the head, undergoes an early and extremely rapid increase in weight. Other organs—for example, the muscles and the respiratory and digestive systems—follow a pattern similar to overall weight change: substantial gains during the first two years followed by a slower, more stable increase throughout childhood and perhaps a more rapid increase during adolescence. However, the reproductive system follows a strikingly different pattern: only during adolescence do organs associated with reproduction begin to mature and rapidly approach their adult size. These different patterns mirror the functional importance of various systems of the body at specific points in development.

Body growth generally follows the principle of cephalocaudal development. It also tends to reflect a pattern of **proximodistal development**. This principle asserts that

proximodistal development Pattern in which organs and systems of the body near the middle tend to develop earlier than those near the periphery.

Individuals differences in height and weight are already evident from birth and continue to be present in young children as can be seen here. However, such differences are likely to become even more apparent once these children approach the adolescent years.

regions nearer the trunk of the body tend to grow and become more differentiated earlier than those more peripheral to the body. For example, infants tend to gain control of their arms and legs sooner than areas more distant such as fingers and toes. However, physical growth does not necessarily conform to these principles during adolescence. During the adolescent growth spurt, for example, some parts of the body undergo rapid growth in a pattern almost the reverse of the proximodistal principle. We are all familiar with the teenager who seems to be all hands and feet. Hands and feet are in fact among the first body parts to show a dramatic change during this period; they are followed by arms and legs and, last of all, the trunk (Tanner, 1978). An adolescent, in other words, is likely to outgrow his shoes first, then his trousers, and finally his jacket.

Individual variations in size are already noticeable at birth. For example, boys tend to be slightly longer and heavier than girls at this time (Copper et al., 1993). Moreover, growth sometimes occurs in sudden spurts. One remarkable fact revealed by research is that growth of one-quarter to one-half inch can occasionally occur virtually overnight in infants and toddlers (Lampl, Veldhuis, & Johnson, 1992).

Individual differences in growth are especially evident during the adolescent years, when children are likely to show enormous variation in the timing, speed, and duration of the adolescent growth spurt. A girl who once was tallest among her childhood girlfriends may suddenly find at age thirteen that she is looking up to them, temporarily at least. A boy whose athletic skills were unremarkable may find himself the starting center for the middle school basketball team if he undergoes an early adolescent growth spurt.

Variability in growth occurs among ethnic and cultural groups as well. For example, although individual differences account for much of the variability in size, American infants of African heritage tend to weigh slightly less than American infants of European heritage at birth, even when social class, gestational age, and other factors known to affect birth weight are equated (Goldenberg et al., 1991). Variability in height among ethnically and culturally diverse populations is exhibited throughout childhood as well.

INTERACTION AMONG DOMAINS

Many societies share a mystique about tallness, the notion that height directly correlates with such traits as competence and leadership. Research has shown that height does affect impressions of a child's abilities. Mothers of young children of the same age, for example, perceive taller boys as more competent (able to get along better with others, less likely to cry when frustrated, and so forth). They treat smaller boys as younger and in a more overprotective manner (Sandberg, Brook, & Campos, 1994). The same is true of children judged on the basis of maturity of facial features (Zebrowitz, Kendall-Tackett, & Fafel, 1991). Despite these observations, lower self-esteem and other behavioral problems among children of short stature have not been consistently reported. And short adults typically function well within the norm socially and intellectually (Allen, 2006; Ulph et al., 2004).

Biological Determinants of Body Growth and Development

NATURE & NURTURE

What is the role of nature in human physical growth? The contributions of nature—that is, hereditary, neural, and hormonal factors—are suggested by research indicating significant biological influences on physical development as well as correlations among related family and cultural members in mature size and in the onset and pattern of physical changes.

Genetic Factors A person's height is likely to be closely related to that of his or her mother and father. What is true for the family in miniature is also true for larger human populations that are genetically related. The Lese of Zaire, for example, are much taller as a group than their nearby neighbors the Efe, tropical dwellers in the Ituri rain forest whose height is typically under five feet. Even body proportions differ among groups. For example, although much overlap occurs among people of different ethnic backgrounds, leg and arm lengths tend to be relatively greater in individuals of African descent, and even more so in Australian aborigines, than in other ethnic groups when length of the torso is equated (Eveleth & Tanner, 1990). Such similarities and differences implicate genetic factors in physical development. But genes do not control growth *directly*. Genes regulate physical development by means of neural and hormonal activity in different organs and body systems.

Neural Control Many researchers believe that the brain includes a growth center, a genetically established program or template that monitors and compares expected and actual rates and levels of growth for the individual. For example, **catch-up growth**, an increase in growth rate, often occurs after illness or malnutrition if duration and severity are limited and do not occur at some critical time. The acceleration continues until height "catches up" to the level expected, had no disruption occurred. The converse, **lagging-down growth**, also occurs (Prader, 1978). Some rare congenital and hormonal disorders produce unusually rapid growth. If the disorder is corrected, growth halts or slows until actual and projected height begin to match the trajectory established before the disruption. Where might this neural control center be located? Researchers theorize that the *hypothalamus*, a small region near the base of the brain, orchestrates the genetic instructions for growth.

Hormonal Influences **Hormones**, chemicals produced by various glands and secreted directly into the bloodstream, can circulate to influence cells in other locations of the body to furnish another key mechanism for converting genetic instructions into physical development. For example, hormones produced by cells in the hypothalamus trigger or inhibit production of still other hormones in the *pituitary gland*, including one known as *human growth hormone (HGH)*. Infants with insufficient HGH may be nearly normal in size at birth, but their growth slows dramatically over the ensuing months and years; they typically reach an adult height of only about four to four-and-a-half feet. HGH, however, only indirectly promotes growth. It spurs the production of *somatomedins*, specialized hormones manufactured by many other cells in the body that directly regulate cell division for growth (Underwood, 1991).

Until 1985, little could be done to alter the course of growth or eventual height for most children. Today, human growth hormone (HGH) can be produced synthetically and has been demonstrated to enhance stature for children whose bodies fail to produce sufficient amounts of this hormone or who have other biological conditions that typically result in limited height. However, increasing numbers of children with *idiopathic short stature,* that is, who are short but otherwise considered normal, are also being given HGH to speed up growth or increase their height, typically on the

catch-up growth Increase in growth rate after some factor, such as illness or poor nutrition, has disrupted the expected normal growth rate.

lagging-down growth Decrease in growth rate after some factor, such as a congenital or hormonal disorder, has accelerated the expected normal growth rate.

hormones Chemical secreted by various glands directly into the bloodstream and circulated to influence cells in other locations of the body.

order of 1 to 2.5 inches from what might have been anticipated without the treatment (Cuttler & Silvers, 2004). Should such efforts, which tend to be motivated by perceptions and expectations about the benefits of being tall, be encouraged? It is an expensive course of treatment, and benefits with respect to improved social abilities and personality have not been convincingly demonstrated (Theunissen et al., 2002; Wheeler et al., 2004).

For Your Review and Reflection

- What are norms for growth? How do they provide information about whether physical growth is proceeding normally?
- What patterns of growth are observed during infancy through adolescence? How do they differ for various parts of the body? How do they differ among individuals and ethnic groups?
- What evidence is there that nature influences physical growth? For example, how do genetic factors, neural control, and hormonal variations affect growth?
- What are catch-up and lagging-down growth?
- Did adults who were familiar with you throughout your development ever comment on how you have grown? What characteristics about body growth and development may have led them to make such a comment?

Nutrition and Psychological Factors Associated with Physical Development

INTERACTION AMONG DOMAINS

For a large proportion of the world's children, adequate nutrition and exposure to diseases may be the primary determinants of whether physical growth proceeds normally or even at all. Because the kinds and amounts of food we eat are factors that often immediately come to mind in influencing appearance and how we are perceived by others as well as our ability to learn and engage in various behaviors, we also consider here additional cognitive and social-emotional factors associated with nutrition and physical development.

SOCIOCULTURAL INFLUENCE

Nutrition and Health

Inadequate nutrition is estimated to be a contributing factor to more than one-third of deaths in children less than five years of age (UNICEF, 2009). Moreover, it results in stunted growth in an estimated one-third of children in underdeveloped countries (see Figure 5.9). The role of nutrition in growth can be documented in many ways. For example, during much of the first half of the twentieth century in Western Europe, the average height gain of children at various ages increased gradually over the years, except during World Wars I and II and other periods of agricultural and economic crisis, when food was far more limited. Moreover, after reunification in 1990, children in East Germany displayed increases in height and weight compared with children growing up earlier in the same region, presumably also because of better nutrition (Hesse et al., 2003). In 1984 a severe, three-month-long drought struck Kenya while researchers were engaged in a study of malnutrition in that region (McDonald et al., 1994). Food intake was cut sharply. The normal rate of weight gain among children was halved.

RISK | RESILIENCE

Severe protein-energy malnutrition can have a particularly devastating effect on development. Children with *marasmus* fail to grow because they lack sufficient calories. Consequences include eventual loss in weight; wrinkly, aged-looking skin; an often-shrunken abdomen; and a hollow body appearance, suggesting emaciation. Another prevalent form of protein-energy malnutrition is *kwashiorkor*, or failure to develop because the diet either contains an inadequate balance of protein or includes potentially harmful toxins. Kwashiorkor typically appears in one- to three-year-old children who have been

Figure 5.9

Undernutrition and Stunting of Growth in Children Under Age 5

Undernutrition contributes to large percentages of children who show stunted growth, that is, height substantially below what is expected for a child of that age. The percentages are especially high in underdeveloped countries. However, even in the United States, undernutrition may be a factor resulting in stunted growth for some children.

Source: Data from UNICEF (2009). Tracking progress on child and maternal nutrition. New York: United Nations Children's Fund.

Less than 5 percent
5–19 percent
20–29 percent
30–39 percent
40 percent or more
Data not available

weaned, usually because of the arrival of a newborn sibling, and whose subsequent sources of protein are inadequate or contaminated.

The symptoms of kwashiorkor include lethargic behavior and apathy, wrinkled skin, and thin, wispy, slightly reddish-orange hair, but most defining is edema, or swelling, especially of the stomach, giving the child a bloated appearance. Kwashiorkor not only disrupts physical growth but also brain development. However, when supplementary feeding has been provided to nutritionally deprived children, for example, in Colombia, Guatemala, Jamaica, Taiwan, and Indonesia, during the first few years of life, both motor and mental development are enhanced (Pollitt, 1994). Benefits to intellectual development extend into adolescence even when the supplementary diet is discontinued in the preschool years (Pollitt et al., 1993).

INTERACTION AMONG DOMAINS

As Figure 5.10 suggests, malnutrition operates at many levels to produce negative consequences for development. For example, cognitive deficits may stem from lessened motivation or curiosity and an inability to respond to or engage the environment. To illustrate, during the relatively brief drought in Kenya, schoolchildren became less attentive in class and less active on the playground (McDonald et al., 1994). To counter the disruption in motivation, attention, and activity level that can accompany malnutrition, some projects have been designed to encourage mothers to become more competent and effective teachers and caregivers for their young children. When nutritionally deprived children in Jamaica were given extra play opportunities and mothers were taught how to positively influence their children's development, children showed substantially higher performance on developmental and intelligence tests over a fourteen-year time period compared with children not receiving the intervention (Grantham-McGregor et al., 1994). However, the scores of malnourished children, even those given this kind of intervention, continue to fall below those of children who have been adequately nourished (Drewett et al., 2001). Even in the United States, lower academic performance and less positive interpersonal

Figure 5.10

The Many Routes by Which Malnutrition Affects Development

Nutritional deprivation can influence development at many different levels. More frequent and severe illness, delayed growth, and slower motor skill development are among the more visible consequences. Lower intellectual development is often an outcome as well. Malnutrition can damage the brain directly. However, limited capacity to engage the environment and other repercussions from the kinds of experiences a malnourished child receives may take a further toll on intellectual development. The context in which it often persists, such as poverty and the lack of essential resources, must also be factored into a consideration of how nutritional deprivation affects development.

Source: From Brown and Pollitt. Malnutrition, poverty and intellectual development. *Scientific American, 274* (Feb. 1996), pp. 38–43. Used by permission of Dimitry Schildlovsky.

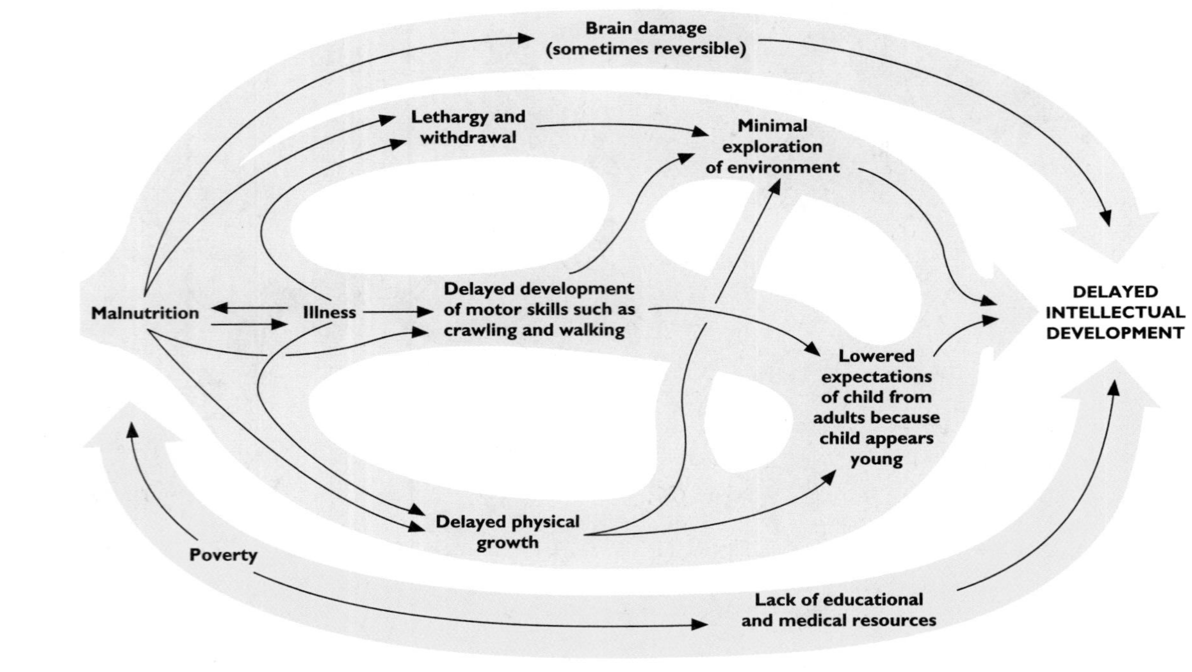

relationships are reported among large numbers of children living in families in which inadequate amounts of nutritional food are available (Alaimo, Olson, & Frongillo, 2001).

RISK | RESILIENCE

Deficiencies in specific nutritional elements—particularly iron and vitamin D, but also, for example, vitamins A, B complex, and K, as well as calcium—are also linked to growth disorders affecting countless numbers of children throughout the world (Suskind, 2009). Some of these disorders, especially iron-deficiency anemia, spawn lower performance on intelligence and other kinds of psychological tests. Although the problem is often assumed to be limited to low-income countries, iron-deficiency anemia is a major nutritional concern in the United States, affecting perhaps as much as 20 percent of some ethnic groups (Pollitt, 1994).

SOCIOCULTURAL INFLUENCE

Secular Trends Increased knowledge of nutrition and the ability to treat disease have yielded dramatic changes in patterns of growth in many societies in recent generations. These generational changes are termed **secular trends**. Children today grow faster and become taller as adults than did previous generations in most regions of the world. Between 1880 and 1950, the average height of Western European and American children increased by nearly four inches. A slower increase or even stability in size has been found since the 1960s. Similar findings have been reported for other cultures, although at different times. For example, in Japan the most substantial changes in height took place between 1950 and 1970 (Tanner, 1978). Improved nutrition, better medical care, and the abolition of child labor account not only for secular trends in greater height across generations but also for the larger size of children growing up in professional, highly educated, and urban families compared with children of poorer families and those in rural populations (Tanner, 1978).

secular trends Consistent pattern of change over generations.

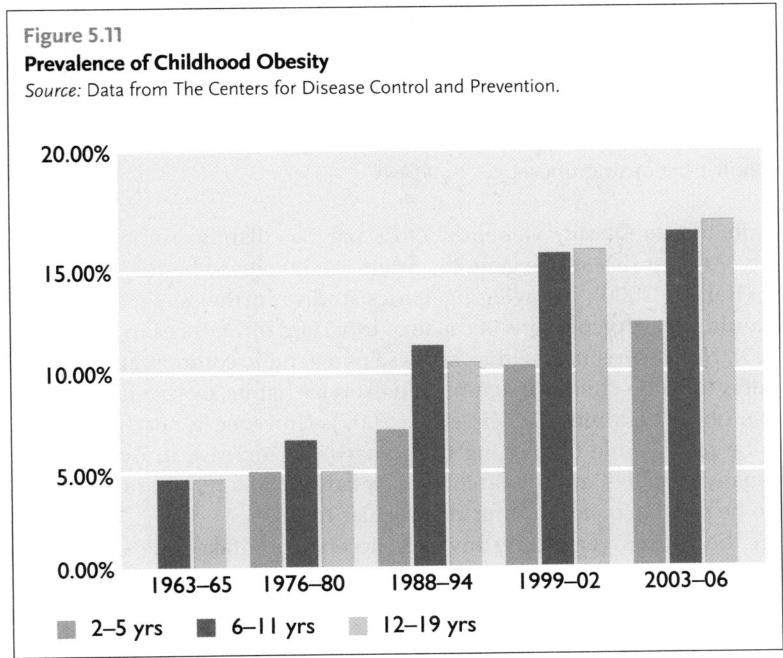

Figure 5.11
Prevalence of Childhood Obesity
Source: Data from The Centers for Disease Control and Prevention.

Failure to Thrive Some infants just don't seem to grow at the same pace as their agemates. Although no consistent criteria are used among researchers and pediatricians, if they remain below the third percentile for weight for a period of time, or if they show a notable deceleration in their rate of gaining weight from the time of birth, infants may be diagnosed as displaying **failure to thrive** (Olsen et al., 2007). Their small physical size may be accompanied by delays in acquiring developmental milestones—the ages at which they crawl, walk, or say their first words. Later in childhood, they may show lower intelligence test scores or other signs of problematic cognitive or social development (Corbett & Drewett, 2004).

RISK | RESILIENCE

The causes of failure-to-thrive syndrome are not entirely understood. For some infants, the origins may lie in a medical condition. But, for others, there is no clear organic basis. Researchers have come to realize that failure to thrive is often accompanied by a constellation of factors that may put the infant at risk: less responsive or more intrusive parenting, negative emotional experiences, but also greater familial exposure to poverty, violence, and other sources of stress.

Obesity

Few topics about physical development have received more attention in recent years than childhood obesity. And there is good reason for concern about this matter. For example, health surveys over the past three decades have revealed a worrisome increase in obesity among children and adolescents in the United States (see Figure 5.11). This increase has been especially pronounced among adolescents who grow up in poor families and among African American, Hispanic American, and Native American children (Barlow et al., 2007; Story, Sallis, & Orleans, 2009; Whitaker & Orzol, 2006). The problem, however, is not just limited to these groups nor even to this country (Anderson & Butcher, 2006). For example, if trends observed between 1980 and 2000 had continued, perhaps close to 50 percent of children living in North America would now be considered overweight or obese, and within the countries forming the European Union, it would be nearly 40 percent (Wang & Lobstein, 2006). As another example, between 1989 and 1997, obesity is estimated to have increased from 1.5 percent to 12.6 percent of two- to six-year-olds growing up in urban regions in China (Luo & Hu, 2002). Fortunately, at least within the United States, the percentage of children overweight or obese appears to have stopped increasing in the last decade although the numbers continue to remain perilously high (Ogden et al., 2010).

Most estimates of obesity are measured by *body mass index* (*BMI*). The BMI is determined by dividing the weight of a child or adult (in kilograms) by the square of his or her

failure to thrive Designation for a child whose growth in height or weight is below the third percentile for children of the same age.

height (in meters). Children and adults above the ninety-fifth percentile for their age on this measure compared with a reference population (which for the United States usually has been a large sample of children and adults who were tested in this country in the 1970s) or whose BMI is above 30 are considered obese. Children between the eighty-fifth and ninety-fifth percentile relative to other children their age are described as overweight and are considered at risk for becoming obese.

NATURE & NURTURE

Factors Contributing to Obesity Genetic factors may predispose some children to obesity in any society. At least five single gene disorders are known to be related to its early onset (Farooqi & O'Rahilly, 2000). Behavioral genetics studies further suggest a relationship as a function of multiple genes, perhaps because of inherited differences in metabolic processes (Strauss, 1999). Not surprisingly, either because of a genetic component or because parents serve as models for their children's eating and exercise habits, overweight parents are more likely to have obese children (Francis et al., 2007). However, a nearly "perfect storm" of factors may be responsible for fueling the remarkable increase in overweight and obese children in many societies, and researchers have advanced a number of hypotheses, many remaining to be proven, to account for this secular trend.

Some of the factors very likely involve the energy intake side of the equation. For example, ready access to fast foods and increased consumption of sugar-laden soft drinks and fruit juices are often considered culprits, and studies give some support for their role in accounting for weight gains (Anderson & Butcher, 2006; Barlow et al., 2007; Johnson et al., 2009). To counter these effects, consumption of more fresh fruits and vegetables is often recommended (Barlow et al., 2007).

INTERACTION AMONG DOMAINS

Perhaps of just as much concern are changes in energy output as a result of declines in physical activity (Anderson & Butcher, 2006). For example, compared with a generation ago, children today spend more time in sedentary activities. They are less likely to walk to and from school, and recess and physical education programs have been reduced in many schools in recent years. Evidence of substantial declines in unstructured outdoor activity also exists. For example, concern about neighborhood safety is related to increased obesity (Lumeng et al., 2006). Perhaps, then, it should come as no surprise that nearly two-thirds of high school students report not meeting recommended levels of daily physical activity (Centers for Disease Control and Prevention, 2008a). Even young children, whom we normally think of as being quite active, only spend about 3 percent of their time in preschool engaged in moderate to vigorous physical activity (Brown et al., 2009). In addition, research consistently shows that children, including preschool children, who watch more television per day have a higher BMI than

Parents can play an influential role in the development of childhood eating habits. When parents encourage children to finish everything on their plate or reward good behavior with sweets, children begin to rely more on external than internal cues for satiation, placing them at risk for obesity.

Figure 5.12

The Relationship Between Becoming Overweight, Amount of Physical Activity, and Hours of Television Viewing per Day

When children do not engage in sufficient physical activity (PA) and spend more than two hours per day watching media (MT), they are three to four times more likely to be overweight than children who are physically active and view lesser amounts of media. Both insufficient physical activity and excessive amounts of media viewing independently result in children being more likely to be overweight. However, when these two factors occur in combination, the likelihood of being overweight is greatest.

Source: Laurson, K. R., Eisenmann, J. C., Welk, G. J., Wickel, E. E., Gentile, D. A., & Walsh, D. A. (2008). Combined influence of physical activity and screen time recommendations on childhood overweight. *Journal of Pediatrics, 153*, 209–214. Reprinted by permission of Elsevier.

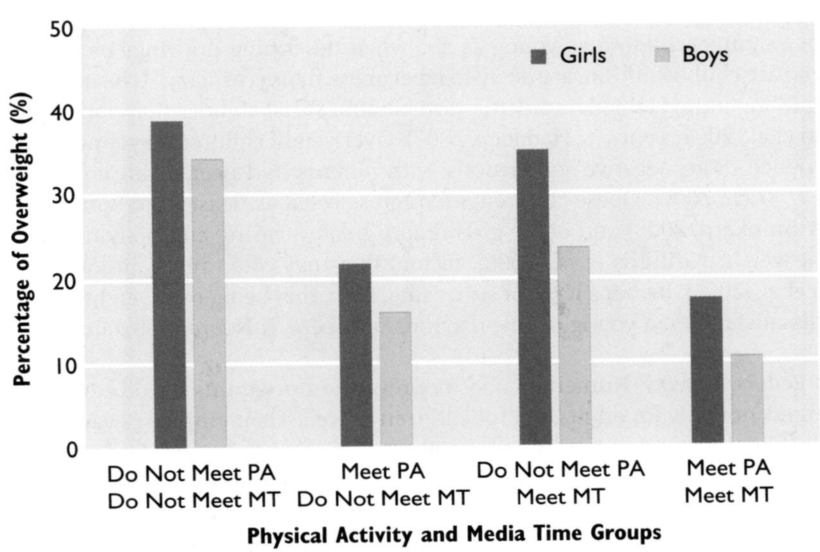

those who spend more time engaged in less sedentary activities (Barlow et al., 2007; Dennison, Erb, & Jenkins, 2002; Robinson, 2001). Children who fail to meet the American Academy of Pediatrics' recommended combination of physical activity (at least 13,000 pedometer steps per day for boys and 11,000 for girls) and media time (watching no more than two hours of media per day) have been found to be three to four times more likely to be overweight than children who meet these recommendations, as can be seen in Figure 5.12 (Laurson et al., 2008).

Parenting and social factors, as well as child characteristics, add yet another layer of potential factors contributing to obesity. For example, persistent tantrums over food and less sleep have been linked to increased weight in children (Agras et al., 2004; Snell, Adam, & Duncan, 2007; Taveras et al., 2008). So, too, has parenting style. Parents often described as *authoritarian*, that is, who place high demands on their children for self-control and tend to use strict disciplinary techniques, yet are relatively insensitive and offer low levels of emotional support, appear more likely to have children who are obese (Rhee et al., 2006). Furthermore, most parents of obese and overweight children tend to underestimate their child's weight, especially parents of boys (De La et al., 2009).

RISK | RESILIENCE

Controlling weight is complicated by the tendency for heavy children to be more responsive to external food-related cues and less responsive to internal hunger cues compared with their normal-weight peers (Ballard et al., 1980). Eleven-year-old obese children tend to eat faster than other children and fail to slow down their rate of food intake as they near the end of their meal, a pattern that is at odds with what is typically observed in children of normal weight (Barkeling, Ekman, & Rössner, 1992). Obese children are also somewhat less accurate in reporting how much they eat (Maffeis et al., 1994). In addition, eating with a larger group of peers (e.g., nine rather than three other preschoolers) seems to encourage intake of more food (Lumeng & Hillman, 2007). Leann Birch and her colleagues (cf. Birch & Davison, 2001) further believe that children can learn to become unresponsive to internal satiation cues through child-feeding practices imposed by parents. Parents may initiate meal-related efforts designed to encourage food consumption ("clean their plates") and use certain foods, such as sweets, to reward good behavior and to calm and quiet the child. These efforts, however, could have the unintended effect of shifting the child's reliance on internal signals for hunger to external signals based on how much has been eaten.

RISK | RESILIENCE

INTERACTION AMONG DOMAINS

SOCIOCULTURAL INFLUENCE

The Socioemotional Consequences of Obesity for Children and Adolescents Being overweight has strong social-emotional consequences in most cultures. In earlier times in industrialized societies, being heavier carried positive connotations of substance and prosperity—and still may in many developing countries (Sobal & Stunkard, 1989). For example, females in some regions of the world are encouraged to increase their body fat in preparation for marriage (Brown & Konner, 1987). However, in contemporary Western cultures, obesity is often viewed negatively, and children who are overweight face considerable social stigma (Puhl & Latner, 2007). For example, children as young as six, when describing drawings or photographs of people who are chubby or thin, are likely to label obese figures as "lazy," "cheater," or "liar" and as having more limited athletic, academic, artistic, and social abilities (Lawson, 1980; Musher-Eizenman et al., 2004; Penny & Haddock, 2007). Overweight children as young as seven years old experience more negative interactions with parents and peers than do other children (Davison & Birch, 2002). Obese children are often selected as "least liked" among their peers (Latner & Stunkard, 2003) and obese girls report greater teasing and bullying than children of normal weight (Griffiths et al., 2006), factors that may often result in lower self-esteem (Franklin et al., 2006). Perhaps it is not surprising, then, that being overweight is often related to body dissatisfaction in young people (Paxton, Eisenberg, & Neumark-Sztainer, 2006).

Efforts to Reduce Obesity Numerous obesity-prevention programs have been designed and implemented, not only for adults, but for children as well. Their emphases vary substantially. Some primarily focus on promoting physical activity among children and youth, others on eating more healthy foods, and still others work on combinations of practices oriented to improving health more generally. These programs may be carried out in schools, either by teachers or professionals, or in other venues, using a wide variety of approaches. Perhaps most noteworthy from the findings based on a meta-analysis of sixty-four intervention programs is that their benefits in promoting weight reduction have been quite small (Stice, Shaw, & Marti, 2006); compared with children in control groups, only thirteen programs reported a significant positive effect on participating children and youth. Those programs that were most likely to be effective were focused intensively on issues of weight (rather than more general health issues) and involved younger children or adolescents rather than preadolescents, but neither an emphasis on physical activity nor dietary intake seemed particularly effective, and long-term benefits from these programs have not always been reported.

Michelle Obama speaking about her campaign "Let's Move" designed to reduce obesity among children in the United States.

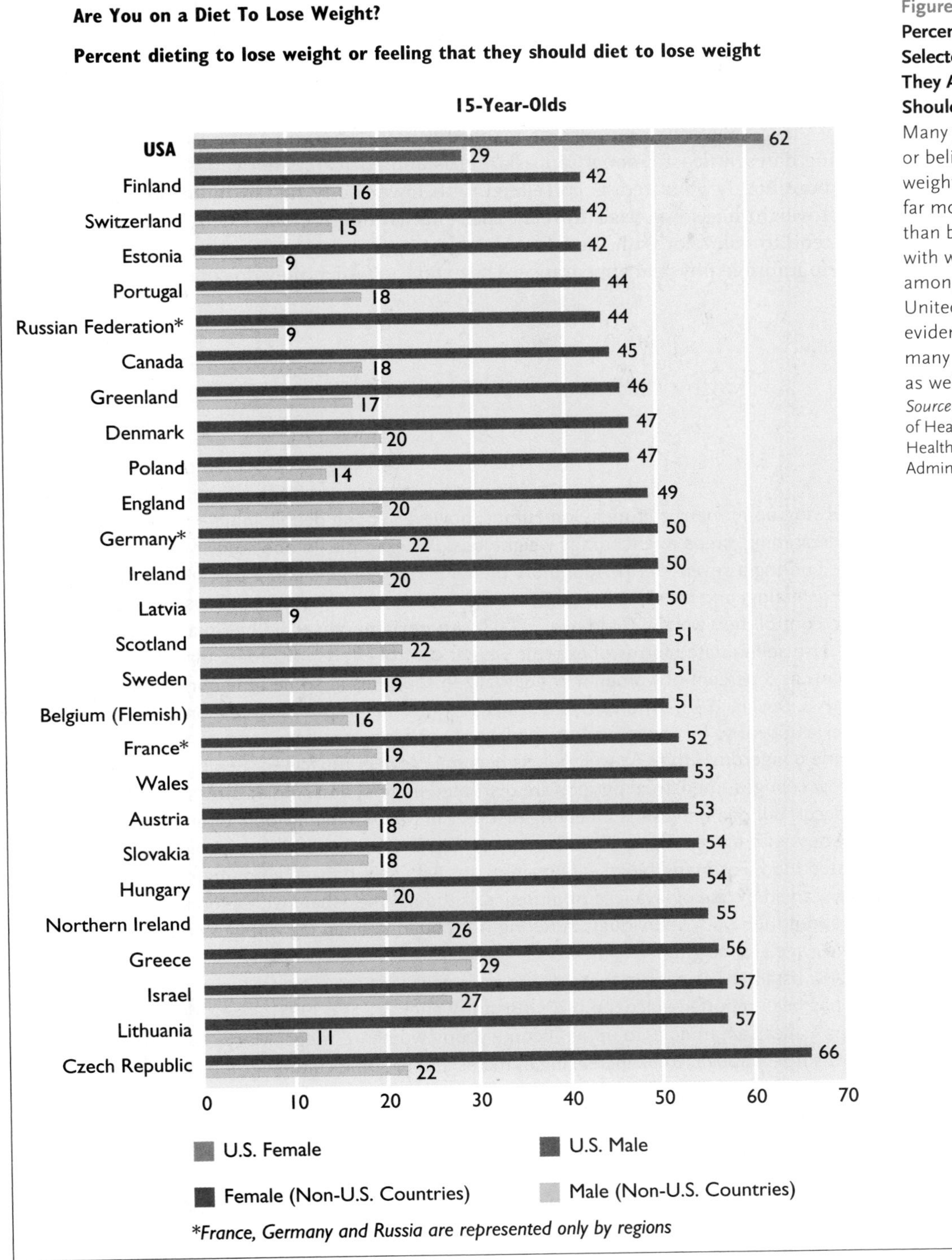

Figure 5.13

Percent of 15-Year-Olds in Selected Countries Who Report They Are Dieting or That They Should Lose Weight

Many youth are either on a diet or believe that they should lose weight. This concern is reported far more frequently by girls than by boys. Dissatisfaction with weight is especially strong among fifteen-year-olds in the United States but is clearly evident in Canada, Israel, and many European countries as well.

Source: Data from U.S. Department of Health and Human Services, Health Resources and Services Administration, 2003.

Being overweight seems to have contributed to another problem: efforts to initiate dieting, even by children who are within a normal weight range. In the United States, many young people, especially women, are dissatisfied with their weight. Girls as young as six express desires to be thin (Dohnt & Tiggeman, 2005). By five years of age, nearly half of all girls have some notion about what it means to diet (Abramovitz & Birch, 2000). Concerns about dieting can be seen among eight-year-olds from nearly all ethnic groups (Robinson et al., 2001), and various studies report that up to half of third-grade girls have attempted to diet (Strauss, 1999). By the time they get to high school, many youth, especially girls, and not just in the United States, are either dieting or feel that they should be (see Figure 5.13).

Yet this activity may actually backfire, resulting in greater weight gain than in children who do not attempt to diet (Field et al., 2003).

Repeated messages from fashion magazines, and sometimes from family and peers, stress the importance of slenderness for beauty and success and undoubtedly place enormous pressure on preteens and teens to control weight. During the adolescent years, many girls believe it is important to have a boyfriend and to be physically attractive. Having dates, at least among Caucasian girls and African American girls whose mothers are more highly educated, is correlated with lower body fat, an indication that concern about weight has some basis in real experience (Halpern et al., 1999). Many teenage girls also tend to talk a lot with their friends about appearance—about how to look good and how to improve physical appearance. The extent to which they do so, as well as the extent

Eating Disorders | atypical development

RISK | RESILIENCE

The large number of girls who attempt to diet has become an almost normative, although troubling, aspect of growing up in many cultures. Sometimes, however, young people initiate more drastic, even life-threatening, steps to encourage weight loss. For example, in one study of adolescents conducted during a seven-year period, more than 4 percent of girls and 2 percent of boys engaged in binge eating, and more than 5 percent of girls and nearly 1 percent of boys engaged in purging to control their weight (Field et al., 2008). **Anorexia nervosa** and **bulimia nervosa** are two long-term self-initiated forms of extreme weight control efforts, disorders that affect perhaps as many as 3 percent of women in industrialized countries at some time during their lifetimes (Walsh & Devlin, 1998). Anorexia nervosa is a kind of self-imposed starvation. Individuals with anorexia appear to be obsessed with the fear of appearing too heavy and, as a consequence, become dangerously thin. As weight loss becomes severe, muscle tissue degenerates, bone marrow changes, menstrual periods are disrupted in girls, and cardiac stress and arrhythmias can occur. Bulimia nervosa is an eating disorder in which the individual often engages in recurrent bouts of binge eating, sometimes consuming enormous quantities of high-calorie, easily digested food. For many, binge eating alternates with self-induced vomiting, actions sometimes accompanied by use of laxatives or diuretics. Although they share with anorexics an intense concern about their body, individuals suffering from bulimia often fall within a normal weight range for their age and height.

A substantial increase in these disorders, particularly the more frequent of the two, bulimia, has been reported since the 1970s (Bryant-Waugh & Lask, 1995). Its incidence is greatest among Caucasian, middle- to upper-income young women (Striegel-Moore & Bulik, 2007), but both disorders appear to be increasing in males and in some cultural groups that have begun to adopt Western values. Their frequency may also be greater in certain groups, such as athletes and dancers, who are especially concerned about weight gain. Perhaps eating disorders begin as part of the larger spectrum of anxieties that children, adolescents, and young adults experience about physical changes, especially as they approach and continue through puberty. For some individuals, an inherited, biological susceptibility may exist as well (Striegel-Moore & Bulik, 2007). Because sociocultural, psychological, and biological factors appear to interact, it should not be surprising that the treatments most effective for dealing with such disorders have been difficult to identify (Gowers & Bryant-Waugh, 2004). School intervention programs designed to promote good nutrition and physical activity can lead to substantial reductions in the number of adolescents reporting self-induced vomiting or use of laxatives to control weight (Austin et al., 2007). Moreover, about two-thirds of individuals who display anorexia nervosa show good recovery if treatment is begun early (Herpetz-Dahlmann et al., 2001). Because eating disorders can have serious long-term consequences, individuals experiencing one of them should be strongly encouraged to seek professional help.

anorexia nervosa An eating disorder involving self-imposed starvation.

bulimia nervosa A disorder involving recurrent bouts of binge eating and food purging.

to which they compare themselves with celebrities or other girls in school, or even see idealized thin bodies in commercials, predicts the degree of body dissatisfaction that they report (Hargreaves & Tiggemann, 2003; Jones, 2004).

For Your Review and Reflection

- What are the consequences of poor nutrition for growth? What are the differences between marasmus and kwashiorkor?
- What is a secular trend?
- What is failure to thrive and what are some of its consequences for development?
- How may sociocultural factors be contributing to the increase in obesity observed in many nations? How are interactions among domains evident in discussions of nutrition and obesity?
- Why are dieting and eating disorders of concern? What are anorexia nervosa and bulimia, and how do they affect development?
- Do you think that media, physical activity, and the perceptions of others have had an influence on your views about what to eat and the importance of exercise? In what ways?

© David Young-Wolff/PhotoEdit

Many children become sensitive to physical appearance, and weight, in particular, in the middle school years. Overweight individuals are viewed negatively in many contemporary Western cultures.

Physical Maturity

The growth spurt of early adolescence is only one of numerous indicators of approaching physical maturity. Accompanying the growth spurt are important progressions indicating sexual maturity. We briefly consider these and the psychological issues a young person may confront during the passage from late childhood to early adulthood.

Defining Maturity

One frequently used indicator of physical growth is **skeletal maturity**, the extent to which *ossification*, the chemical transformation of cartilage into bony tissue, has been completed. The change begins prenatally about the eighth week after conception, when cartilage in the ribs and in the center of the long bones of the arms and legs is transformed. The process continues into late adolescence or early adulthood, when bones in the wrist and ankle are finally completely formed. Other visible markers of approaching maturity appear just before and during the adolescent years. These important markers comprise a series of events associated with **puberty**, the developmental milestone reached when a young person gains the ability to reproduce.

CONTINUITY | DISCONTINUITY

During puberty, the *primary sexual organs*—testes and penis in males; vagina, uterus, and ovaries in females—enlarge and become capable of functioning. *Secondary sexual characteristics* that distinguish men and women, such as facial hair or breasts, also mature. Boys take on a more muscular and angular look as shoulders widen and the fat tissue of childhood is replaced with muscle. Girls' hips broaden, a change especially adaptive to bearing children. Like the growth spurt,

skeletal maturity Extent to which cartilage has ossified to form bone; provides estimate of how much additional growth will take place.

puberty Developmental period during which a sequence of physical changes takes place that transforms the person from an immature individual to one capable of reproduction.

CHRONOLOGY Adolescent Sexual Development: 9 Years to 16 Years

YEARS

GIRLS

© Fuse/Jupiter Images

Before 10 Years
- Adrenarche (see text).

10-11 Years
- Spurt in height begins.
- Breasts begin to show initial development.

11-12 Years
- First appearance of pubic hair.

12-13 Years
- Menarche (see text).
- Peak increase in height.

© Getty Images/Photos.com/Jupiterimages

13-14 Years
- Underarm hair begins to appear.

14-15 Years
- Growth of pubic hair completed.
- Growth of breasts completed.

BOYS

Before 10 Years
- Adrenarche (see text).

© Corbis Premium RF/Alamy

11-12 Years
- Testes begin to enlarge.

12-13 Years
- Spurt in height begins.
- First appearance of pubic hair.
- Growth of penis begins.

13-14 Years
- Spermarche (see text).

14 Years
- Peak increase in height.
- Voice begins to deepen.
- Underarm and facial hair begin to appear.

© Ableimages/Photodisc/Jupiter Images

15-16 Years
- Adult height reached.
- Growth of pubic hair completed.

These ages are typical for individuals reared in the United States and many other Western nations. However, considerable individual differences exist in the ages at which these various developmental changes occur. Sources: Malina & Bouchard, 1991; McClintock & Hardt, 1996; Tarner, 1990.

the timing of each of the many events associated with puberty differs enormously from one young person to another. As a rule, however, this cluster of characteristics tends to appear somewhat earlier in girls than in boys. The Adolescent Sexual Development chronology summarizes the approximate ages at which many of the developmental changes typically associated with the adolescent years take place for girls and boys growing up in North America and Europe.

Although there are numerous indicators of increasing sexual maturity, perhaps none is more significant than **menarche**, the first menstrual period in females, and **spermarche**, the occurrence of the first ejaculation of sperm in males. Menarche typically takes place between about twelve and thirteen years of age for females and spermarche between thirteen and fourteen years of age for males. However, as with other indicators of puberty, their initial appearance varies considerably from one individual to the next. For example, in

menarche First occurrence of menstruation.

spermarche The first ejaculation of sperm by males entering puberty.

the United States, the events accompanying sexual maturity begin somewhat earlier in African American girls than in Caucasian American girls (Biro et al., 2001; Mendle, Turkheimer, & Emery, 2007).

NATURE & NURTURE

What triggers these remarkable changes? The brain, including the hypothalamus and pituitary gland, and various hormones are centrally involved. *Adrenarche* initiates many of the changes taking place during early adolescence. Adrenarche refers to the maturation of the adrenal glands, small glands located above the kidneys. These glands release hormones important for the growth spurt and the emergence of underarm and pubic hair in girls. In addition, adrenarche may play an important role in the emergence of sexual attraction, which Martha McClintock and Gilbert Herdt (1996) argue typically occurs as early as ten years of age. In girls, the hypothalamus may monitor metabolic cues associated with body size or the ratio of fat to muscle; body mass index appears to be a good, although not the only, predictor of onset of menarche (Kaplowitz, 2008).

Still other *gonadotropic* (gonad-seeking) hormones released by the pituitary gland stimulate, in the case of females, the production of estrogen and progesterone by the ovaries and regulate the menstrual cycle. Estrogen promotes the development of the breasts, uterus, and vagina, as well as the broadening of the pelvis. Perhaps it is not surprising to find that exposure to certain environmental factors presumably affecting hormonal levels, for example, brominated flame retardants, DDT, and PCBs, may also influence pubertal timing (Buck Louis et al., 2008). Even family relationships, such as greater stress in the family, which can affect hormonal balances, may accelerate female development (Ellis, 2004; Ellis & Essex, 2007). In the case of males, hormones contribute to the production of sperm and elevate the production of testosterone by the testes. Testosterone, in turn, promotes further growth in height, an increase in size of the penis and testes, and the appearance of secondary sexual characteristics, such as pubic and facial hair.

Early Versus Late Maturity

Today adult height in most industrialized societies is typically reached by about age seventeen; a century ago, it often was not achieved until about age twenty-three (Rallison, 1986). Changes in the age of menarche reveal a similar trend in many countries toward increasingly early occurrences over recent generations (see Figure 5.14) and continue, although at a slower rate in the United States today (Anderson & Must, 2005).

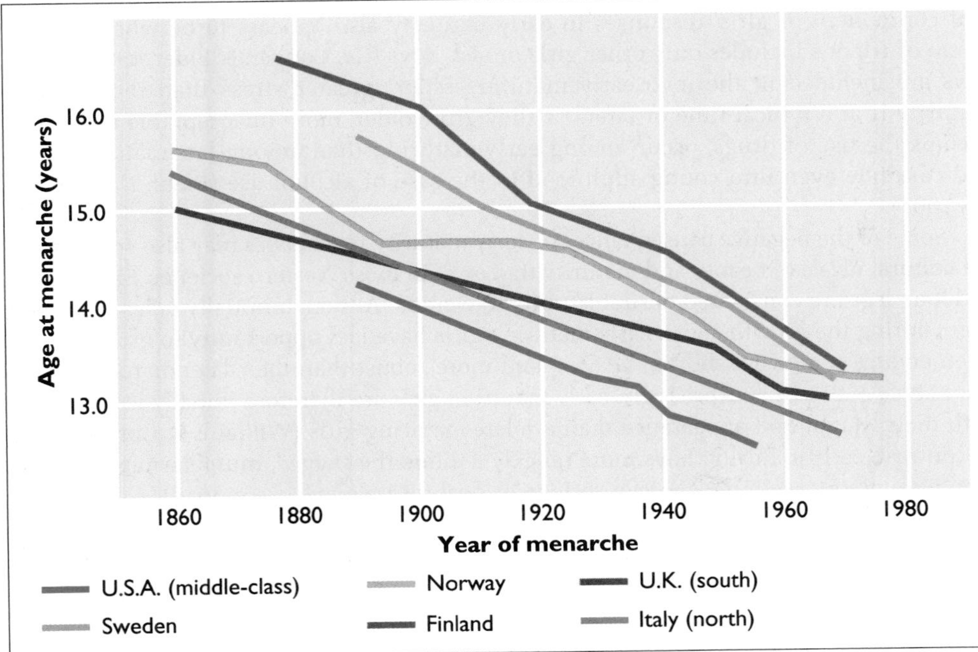

Figure 5.14
Secular Trends in the Age of Menarche
Evidence exists for a secular trend in the decrease in age of the onset of menarche from 1845 through 1960. Although most of the data were obtained by questioning adolescents and young adults, some, especially those from earlier generations, depended on the memories of older individuals.
Source: From Marshall, W. A., & Tanner, J. M. Puberty. In Falkner & J. M. Tanner (eds.), *Human Growth*, vol. 2, 2/e, p. 196. Copyright © 1986. Used by permission of Plenum Publishing Corporation.

SOCIOCULTURAL INFLUENCE

The secular changes stem from improved socioeconomic conditions, including more adequate nutrition. Girls who are unprepared for menarche, either due to lack of information or because of its early onset, perceive the event more negatively than other girls, whose reactions are often a mixture of positive and negative feelings (Koff & Rierdan, 1995; Ruble & Brooks-Gunn, 1982). However, thanks to greater communication within the family, including emotional support and assurance that menstruation is normal and healthy, girls' reactions to menarche today seem more positive than in previous times (Brooks-Gunn & Ruble, 1980; Koff & Rierdan, 1995).

INTERACTION AMONG DOMAINS

The limited research conducted with boys suggests that they are often uninformed, surprised, and confused about spermarche (Stein & Reiser, 1994). For many boys, sex education classes may either fail to explain what they need to know or are provided too late to prepare them. Their feelings about the event are mixed, and they seldom talk about it with others (Gaddis & Brooks-Gunn, 1985; Stein & Reiser, 1994). Nevertheless, early maturity seems to have a number of positive aspects for boys (Petersen, 1988; Taga et al., 2006). For example, compared with late maturers, early-maturing boys report more positive feelings about themselves, feel less rejected, express lower dependency and affiliative needs, and are less rebellious toward their parents (Mussen & Jones, 1957). Although late maturers want to be well liked and accepted, their efforts to obtain social approval often translate into attention-getting, compensatory, and childish behaviors disruptive to success with peers and adults (Mussen & Jones, 1958). Differences favoring early maturity in these areas, and also in career success and satisfaction with their marriages, continue to be observed even into adulthood (Jones, 1965; Taga et al., 2006).

What are girls' reactions to early and late maturity? Here the picture differs. Although early maturity may enhance status and prestige for girls just as for boys, it can also be embarrassing; decrease their popularity, at least among agemates; and lead to greater social pressure and expectations from older friends, parents, and other adults. Depression, eating disorders, and delinquent behaviors are reported more frequently among girls displaying early maturity (Ge et al., 2003; Mendle et al., 2007; Stice et al., 2001). For example, in research in Sweden, girls who reached menarche early were more likely than late-maturing girls to engage in a variety of norm-breaking activities, such as staying out late, cheating on exams, pilfering, or using alcohol (Magnusson, Stattin, & Allen, 1986). Early-maturing girls preferred older and more mature friends, who may have inspired their greater independence from socially approved conventions of behavior. Indeed, among those maturing early but reporting no older friends, the frequency of norm-breaking activities was about the same as for girls who matured later. An important component of girls' responses to early maturity also appears to be whether their group of friends includes only other girls or also boys (Ge, Conger, & Elder, 1996); when boys are included in the mix, early maturers report greater stress than those whose maturity is at a typical time or later. As they grow older, more unacceptable behaviors, such as the use of drugs, occur among early-maturing than among late-maturing girls and continue even into young adulthood in the case of alcohol use (Biehl, Natsuoki, & Ge, 2007).

SOCIOCULTURAL INFLUENCE

Some of the negative consequences of early maturity for females may also spring from the cultural ideals of beauty and maturity that exist in most Western societies. Slenderness and long legs are considered desirable traits in women. Although initially taller than their peers during the growth spurt, early-maturing girls have less opportunity to grow tall and often end up somewhat shorter, heavier, and more robust than their later-maturing peers (Biro et al., 2001). Not surprisingly, early-maturing girls are therefore initially less satisfied with their weight and appearance than are late-maturing girls (Williams & Currie, 2000). In contrast, early-maturing boys more quickly assume the rugged, muscular physique stereotypically portrayed in American society as ideal for men and are more pleased by their weight and appearance than late-maturing boys (Petersen, 1988). Even if they show depressive symptoms early in puberty, boys seem to bounce back two years later, a pattern that is not found for early-maturing girls (Ge et al., 2003).

Girls who mature early and boys who mature late are also out of step with most of their classmates. Young people usually prefer friends who share interests, and interests change with increasing maturity. Late-maturing boys may find that their peers move on to other pursuits, making it more difficult to maintain positive relationships with their friends. Early-maturing girls may redirect friendships to older peers and boys. In other words, biological, immediate social, and broader cultural factors combine to help define the consequences of early and late maturity.

Sexual Behavior

SOCIOCULTURAL INFLUENCE

Few changes accompanying puberty are as contentious in many families as the sexuality that attends physical maturity. Anthropological research indicates that the majority of cultures are likely to permit or at least tolerate some sexual activity during the teen years. But Western societies have generally been more restrictive in its expression (Schlegel & Barry, 1991). Many mothers in the United States tend to underestimate the extent of sexual activity among their offspring; their children, in turn, tend to underestimate the degree to which their mothers disapprove of this activity (Jaccard, Dittus, & Gordon, 1998). Nevertheless, large numbers of teenagers are sexually active, and at young ages. Forty-seven percent of ninth- through twelfth-graders state that they have engaged in sexual intercourse (Gavin et al., 2009).

RISK | RESILIENCE

What factors play a role in whether a teenager will engage in sexual activity? Several different family variables seem to be instrumental, according to a review by Brent Miller, Brad Benson, and Kevin Galbraith (2001). One especially important parameter is how the members of the family "connect" with one another. More specifically, when parents are warm and supportive of their children—that is, seem to be close and responsive to them—teenagers are more likely to remain sexually abstinent until they are somewhat older. Additionally, a similar outcome occurs when parents maintain relatively closer supervision and monitoring of their children's behavior, although evidence exists that there is a limit to this factor; when parents become intrusive and overcontrolling, sexual activity may be started somewhat earlier by their offspring. Not surprisingly, another important factor is the values parents hold concerning the appropriateness of sexual activity among teenagers. On the other hand, research on the extent to which parents communicate with their sons and daughters about sexual issues does not appear to be related to the timing with which sexual activity is initiated. However, few studies have examined when such communications begin; information about this subject may often be initiated by parents only after they are aware that their children are sexually active.

Other contextual variables associated with the family are also related to sexual activity. In general, children in families living in neighborhoods where there is greater poverty, higher crime rates, and less stability—factors that are generally correlated with lower education and income—tend to engage in earlier onset of sexual activity (Johnson & Tyler, 2007). Children of single parents are more likely to initiate sexual behavior earlier, and so are children who are growing up in abusive family environments or who have older teenage siblings who are already parents (East & Jacobson, 2001).

RISK | RESILIENCE

Aside from the moral and ethical issues that adolescent sexual behavior raises, there are important health and social consequences. Among the most frequent concerns are sexually transmitted diseases (STDs), teenage pregnancy, and the tendency of teenage parents to drop out of school. For example, nearly a quarter of female adolescents in the United States have a human papillomavirus (HPV) infection, and about 750,000 pregnancies occur in women under twenty years of age each year (Gavin et al., 2009). The rate of teen pregnancy has shown some decline throughout the 1990s and early 2000s but still remains far higher in the United States than in other technologically advanced countries (Hamilton, Martin, & Ventura, 2009). Moreover, 75 percent of all adolescents giving birth to a child each year will remain unmarried, a substantial increase from forty years ago, when only 15 percent who gave birth were unmarried (Allen et al., 1997; Coley & Chase-Lansdale, 1998). Only about half of these women can be expected to finish high school (Hotz, McElroy, & Sanders, 1997) and their children, in turn, are often likely to have difficulty when they begin school (Brooks-Gunn & Chase-Lansdale, 1995).

What Should Sex Education Programs Emphasize? what do you think?

Because of the risks associated with sexual activity, such as pregnancy and contracting STDs, many individuals working with elementary, middle, and high school students in the United States and other countries around the world have argued that young people need to be better educated about their sexuality.

Nearly everyone agrees that sex education should begin in the home at a young age, taught by parents. Moreover, most adults in the United States believe that sex education in the schools is appropriate, and when given the opportunity, only a small proportion of parents ask to have their children excused from sex education classes (Kaiser Family Foundation, 2004). In fact, sex education is either required or recommended in all states today and in most other countries in which formal education is offered. But beyond that, especially in the United States, much less accord exists about what the focus of the instructional content should be and the success of the various messages that are emphasized in such programs. What do you think contributes to an effective sex education program? Should the emphasis be on encouraging young people to abstain from sexual relationships until they are married? Or should sex education in the schools attempt to promote the acquisition of skills to handle maturely the complexities and consequences of relationships and provide clear information and access to resources that will help young people to think clearly about and be comfortable with their emerging sexuality? Do you think that promoting anything other than abstinence in sex education classes sends a mixed message that communicates a double standard: "Avoid sexual relationships, but in case you can't, here is what you should know"? How effective are abstinence-only sex education programs? Should the program be different for those adolescents who may already be engaging in sexual relationships? What types of programs do you think hold the most promise

© Laura Dwight Photography

Sex education is part of the school curriculum in most states and in many countries. However, many programs generate considerable controversy. What do you think should be the focus of such programs?

for delaying the onset of sexual activity or reducing the number of partners, unplanned pregnancies, or rate of sexually transmitted diseases? Should their focus be broader than sex education, for example, by involving high schoolers in voluntary community service and encouraging them to reflect on the normative tasks of adolescence, such as career goals and appropriate social relationships, so that only a small component of the curriculum is geared toward sex education? What role should the federal government play in providing funding for these various kinds of programs? Certainly more research is needed to help in arriving at informed decisions on these issues.

For Your Review and Reflection

- How is physical maturity defined?
- What are the developmental changes that accompany puberty?
- What are the social and behavioral consequences of early and late maturity for males and females?
- How do sociocultural factors influence adolescent views about their physical development?
- What factors are related to sexual behavior in adolescents? What are the health implications of such behavior?
- What were your reactions to becoming physically mature? What kind of sex education did you receive while growing up?

chapter recap

Summary of Developmental Themes

Nature & Nurture

How do nature and nurture interact in brain, motor skill, and physical development?

Brain development, the acquisition of motor skills, and physical development are the products of complex systems influenced by both biology and experience. For example, biological processes, both genetic and hormonal, augment the proliferation and migration of neurons. At the same time, environmental factors can have a potent effect on the way brain wiring proceeds. Although babies seem to be intrinsically motivated to exercise rudimentary motor skills, experiences such as practice and training can also encourage their acquisition. Once a child attains locomotion or other skills, she or he provokes new reactions from caregivers, which may include encouragement or restrictions of the types of behaviors the child displays. Genetic factors, brain centers that regulate growth, and hormones such as HGH, testosterone, and estrogen, among others, are biological factors that contribute to growth and physical maturity. However, adequate nutrition, stimulation, and the emotional and social support of caregivers are critical environmental factors as well. Moreover, the reactions of others to physical development (for example, early maturity or excessive weight gain) may result in differing behavioral consequences for children, including with whom they associate or whether they engage in practices involving dieting and eating that can influence health and physical well-being.

Sociocultural Influence

How does the sociocultural context influence brain, motor skill, and physical development?

Motor skill development and physical growth are embedded within settings, resources, and beliefs promoted by the society in which the child lives. For example, the extent to which a culture encourages specific skills, such as the acquisition of motor milestones and various physical skills, or provides positive evaluations for such things as being tall or slender, affects infants' and children's efforts to achieve various competencies and physical attributes. Knowledge about safe sleeping arrangements can reduce the occurrence of SIDS, and more access to nutritional resources has produced secular trends related to many changes in physical development such as greater height and the earlier appearance of menarche. Changes in eating habits, in physical activity, and in views about physical appearance are associated with social and cultural factors as well.

Continuity | Discontinuity

Are brain, motor skill, and physical development continuous or discontinuous?

Brain development, the acquisition of motor skills, and physical development show spurts at certain times in development. These patterns often give rise to conceptions of stagelike development. But even dramatic changes, such as those exhibited in attaining motor milestones in infancy or associated with puberty during the adolescence years, are grounded in processes undergoing continuous transformations. Small, incremental changes in the relative strength of muscles in infants, for example, or in the production of hormones during adolescence, may initiate substantive dynamic reorganizations of complex physical systems.

Interaction Among Domains

How do brain, motor skill, and physical development interact with other domains of development?

A child's physical size and weight, as well as improvements in the execution and coordination of motor skills, have dramatic influences on the responses and expectations of caregivers, peers, and others. Their reactions may well affect how the child feels about his or her body and abilities. For example, once capable of walking, the child has a greater ability to initiate independence and to explore the environment, enhancing cognitive development. At the same time, parents may become more restrictive, a dynamic that can have social and emotional repercussions. An adolescent's height or weight, even the degree to which he or she matures early or late, can have dramatic influences on the responses of caregivers and peers, and can influence the child's evaluation of self.

Risk | Resilience

What factors promote risk or resilience in brain, motor skill, and physical development during infancy?

Variations in brain development as well as motor skills and physical development come about for many reasons. For example, teratogens such as mercury and alcohol can interfere with the onset and path of neuron migration, leading to cognitive disabilities or behavioral disorders. Adequate hours of sleep during infancy can have consequences for weight and is important throughout childhood and adolescence for being alert. Parenting styles and practices may contribute to occurrences of SIDS and failure to thrive. Malnutrition poses a serious risk to children's physical and intellectual development. Excessive weight may lead to changes in self-esteem that encourage the child to initiate risky undertakings associated with attempts to initiate weight loss. These are factors that can be altered by parents or a society aware of and willing to make changes to reduce the risks.

Chapter Review

The Brain and Nervous System

Which regions of the brain develop earliest and latest? To what functions do those regions contribute?

Even before birth, brain growth is rapid. The brainstem and midbrain, which control essential biological functions, are fairly well established at birth. After birth, sensory and motor regions of the cortex develop earlier than the frontal portion of the brain that controls thinking, planning, and voluntary responses.

What developmental changes occur in neurons? How do glial cells and myelin contribute to neuronal development and functioning?

The three major changes that *neurons* undergo are proliferation (production of neurons), migration (movement of neurons to their final destination), and differentiation (formation of synapses with other neurons). The proliferation and migration of neurons take place largely during prenatal development. However, differentiation, the formation of dendrites and their synapses with other neurons, flourishes postnatally. Depending on various kinds of experience, neurons may undergo *synaptic pruning,* that is, a reduction in the density of the dendrites, and apoptosis, or cell death. *Glial cells* nourish and provide scaffolding for migrating neurons. They are also the source of *myelin,* the white matter that surrounds neurons and speeds neural impulses.

When does the plasticity of the brain decline? What is the difference between experience-expectant and experience-dependent information?

Plasticity of the brain is apparent in infancy and declines toward the end of childhood, although considerable plasticity is still evident in mature adult brains. Neuron differentiation may proceed at critical or sensitive times for experience-expectant information but occurs throughout development for experience-dependent information. An important principle underlying the development of neural connections is repeated episodes of firing in synchrony.

What major changes occur in the brain during adolescence?

Most brain changes during adolescence occur in the frontal regions. Neurons continue to become myelinated, and after a period of overabundance of synapses, the number of synapses declines. The prefrontal cortex is more active in adolescents than in other age groups when certain kinds of cognitive tasks are performed, leading some to conclude that the brain areas that control inhibition and other regulatory behaviors are still immature at this time.

What evidence exists for brain lateralization?

Infants display behaviors suggestive of hemispheric specialization, or *lateralization,* already prenatally and shortly after birth. Children and adults are more likely to process language in the left hemisphere, whereas emotional, spatial, and nonverbal information is more likely to be processed in the right hemisphere.

Sleep

What kinds of sleep patterns are found in newborns?

Newborns sleep for about two-thirds of the day but in short sleep-wake cycles. A relatively large proportion of the infant's time involves REM sleep, a state that may provide him or her with stimulation even while asleep.

Why does controversy exist concerning the sleeping arrangements for young infants?

Some cultures encourage the practice of co-sleeping. In addition, some researchers hypothesize that co-sleeping may help to prevent such problems as apnea in infants. These practices stand in contrast to the general belief in our culture that sleeping in one's own room promotes self-reliance and independence. The medical community currently advises against co-sleeping. One compromise is to have the infant sleep in a crib in the caregiver's room.

What steps can caretakers take to reduce the likelihood of SIDS? What factors are associated with SIDS?
The risk of *sudden infant death syndrome*, or *SIDS*, is highest at ages one to four months. To reduce the risk of SIDS, caregivers should place the infant to sleep on the back, provide a pacifier, eliminate exposure to cigarette smoke and co-sleeping in the same bed, remove soft bedding materials, and provide adequate ventilation in the child's room. SIDS is also associated with the colder months, poverty, low birth weight, having a cold, being a male, and being a later-born or multiple-birth child.

How do patterns of sleep change in adolescence?
Adolescents tend to need more sleep than younger children and show a shift toward a later sleep-wake cycle. Because these tendencies conflict with many of the daily demands placed on adolescents by school, work, and other forces, many adolescents are sleep-deprived.

Motor Skill Development

How do primitive and postural reflexes differ? What purpose do they serve for the infant?
Reflexes, involuntary responses to stimulation controlled by subcortical processes, are among the earliest motor actions displayed in newborns. Primitive reflexes (such as rooting and sucking) help to increase the likelihood of survival, whereas postural reflexes (such as stepping and swimming) help the infant to maintain a specific orientation in his or her environment.

What are the major milestones associated with the development of postural control, locomotion, and manual control? How does the principle of cephalocaudal development apply to the emergence of the major motor milestones?
Postural control includes keeping the head upright and balanced, maintaining an upright sitting position, and standing with, and later without, assistance. Locomotor skills include rolling over, crawling or creeping, cruising, and walking. Manual control includes prereaching, ballistic reaching, and a shift from reach with hands formed in a fist to use of a pincer grasp. The cephalocaudal principle highlights the fact that regions nearer the head tend to undergo more rapid development than regions farther away from the head.

What are the child's major achievements in motor skills?
During early childhood, children show advances in gross motor skills such as running, jumping, and skipping and fine motor skills, which enable children to use scissors, hold crayons, and perform other actions requiring small muscle movements. During the middle school years, children become more adept at fine-motor coordination and show more controlled, coordinated, and complex motor movements.

What factors contribute to motor development? How do cultural practices influence their acquisition?
Genetic preadaptation may contribute to the emergence of motor skills, but research indicates that experience can be important as well. Some societies promote the acquisition of basic motor skills, such as crawling and walking, and as a consequence, such skills often appear somewhat earlier among infants and very young children in those societies. The development of motor skills requires multiple elements becoming more and more integrated and organized over time.

Body Growth and Development

What are norms for growth? How do they provide information about whether physical growth is proceeding normally?
The term *grow* essentially applies to the increase in size of the body or its organs. The term *develop* refers not only to increases in size but also to any orderly pattern of change. *Norms* derived from measurements carried out on a large sample of individuals within a population provide an estimate of the range of what is considered typical in development. Growth norms reveal rapid height and weight just before and after birth, and much slower but regular increases in size beginning at about two years of age followed by the adolescent growth spurt.

How do patterns of growth differ for various parts of the body?
Some regions of the body—for example, the head—show faster rates of growth early in life than other regions in accord with the principle of *cephalocaudal development*. Regions nearer the center of the body also tend to develop somewhat sooner than regions more peripheral, a reflection of the principle of *proximodistal development*. Unlike the pattern observed earlier in childhood, physical growth during the adolescent growth spurt does not conform to the principles of cephalocaudal and proximodistal development. Boys tend to be larger than girls in early infancy, and ethnic groups also vary in height.

When are individual differences in growth most likely to be observed? What are the concerns about short stature in many cultures?
Individual differences in physical development are especially noticeable during the adolescent growth spurt. Children, especially boys, prefer being tall, but little evidence exists to indicate that those who develop normally but are constitutionally small are seriously disadvantaged.

How do genetic factors, neural control, and hormonal variations affect growth? What are catch-up and lagging-down growth?
Genetic factors predict a person's height and body proportions. Genetic factors work primarily through neural and hormonal activity. The hypothalamus contains cells that may determine whether growth is proceeding according to genetic instructions. These cells trigger human growth hormone, a substance that interacts in complex ways with other hormones to influence growth. *Catch-up growth* refers to the tendency for the rate of growth to increase for a period of time after disease or illness. *Lagging-down growth* is the tendency for it to decrease for a period of time after rapid gains.

Nutrition and Psychological Factors Associated with Physical Development

What are the consequences of poor nutrition for growth? What are marasmus and kwashiorkor?
Poor nutrition can result in decreased height and weight as well as loss of energy to sufficiently engage the environment. *Marasmus* is failure to grow because the infant lacks sufficient calories. *Kwashiorkor* is the result of inadequate protein in the diet or exposure to harmful toxins. Specific nutritional deficiencies, for example, of iron and vitamin D, affect large numbers of children and can result in lower intellectual development.

What is a secular trend?
A *secular trend* refers to a change in some aspect of development that occurs across generations. Height is an example of a secular trend, in that today's children grow faster and taller than in previous generations.

What is failure to thrive?
Failure to thrive is a label often applied to infants and very young children who are well below the norm for their age group in physical growth. Although some biological factor may underlie growth limitations, its occurrence is often accompanied by a constellation of parental and environment factors that put the child at increased risk.

What measure is typically used to determine obesity and being overweight? What factors may be contributing to the increase in obesity observed in many Western nations?
Body mass index is typically used to determine obesity and being overweight. The numbers of children who are obese or overweight have increased dramatically over the past several decades. Although genetic factors may play a role in obesity for some individuals, the dramatic change in its occurrence may be in part because of the increasing availability of calorie-laden convenience foods and drinks and in part because of a more sedentary lifestyle. Parenting practices may also influence weight gain, and children who are obese may be less responsive to cues associated with food ingestion.

What are the social-emotional consequences of being overweight? How effective are programs designed to reduce weight in obese children?
Obese and overweight children are often perceived as less capable and in a negative light by others. As a consequence, lower self-esteem and dissatisfaction with their bodies are frequently expressed by obese children. Many children and youth report attempts to diet or feel the desire to do so. Efforts to increase physical activity and to encourage better eating habits have had some, but limited, success in helping obese children to reduce their weight.

What factors may be contributing to eating disorders? What are anorexia nervosa and bulimia? Why are these eating disorders of concern?
Concerns about being attractive, especially by girls, and often promoted in the media and sometimes encouraged by peers and family members, may be among the factors leading to an increasing number of young people engaged in dieting and displaying eating disorders such as anorexia and bulimia. *Anorexia nervosa,* severe restriction on food intake over a long period of time, and *bulimia nervosa,* recurrent bouts of binge eating and self-induced vomiting, have negative and potentially life-threatening consequences for those who exhibit such disorders.

Physical Maturity

How is physical maturity defined?
Maturity is defined not by size but by ossification of bone material, or *skeletal maturity*. This process ends in late adolescence, when bones in the wrists and ankles complete their formation.

What are the developmental changes that accompany puberty? What factors are especially important in bringing about these changes?
Puberty is defined as the period during which the individual gains the ability to reproduce. *Menarche,* or the first occurrence of menstruation in females, and *spermarche,* the initial occurrence of ejaculation of sperm in males, signal this ability to reproduce. The primary sexual organs enlarge, and secondary sexual characteristics, such as facial hair and breasts, emerge. Hormones released by the pituitary gland and increased production of androgens such as testosterone and estrogen are largely responsible for these developmental changes.

What are the social and behavioral consequences of early and late maturity for males and females?
Boys seem to benefit from early maturity. They have more positive feelings about themselves and have better relationships with their parents and peers. For some girls, early maturity is associated with a decline in body satisfaction, depression, and increased norm-breaking activity.

What factors are related to sexual behavior in adolescents? What are the health implications of such behavior?
Among the factors that are related to whether youth engage in sexual behavior are the connectedness they feel with their families, the extent to which they are supervised, and the attitudes their parents hold with respect to sexual activity. Fewer resources in the family and the presence of a teenage sibling who is already a parent are among other factors. Health concerns include an increase in the incidence of sexually transmitted diseases and pregnancy. In addition, the likelihood of not completing a high school education is increased.

Key Terms and Concepts

anorexia nervosa (p. 186)
bulimia nervosa (p. 186)
catch-up growth (p. 177)
cephalocaudal development (p. 169)
failure to thrive (p. 181)
glial cell (p. 158)
hormones (p. 177)
lagging-down growth (p. 177)
lateralization (p. 161)
menarche (p. 188)
myelin (p. 158)
neuron (p. 155)
norm (p. 173)
plasticity (p. 158)
proximodistal development (p. 175)
puberty (p. 187)
reflex (p. 166)
secular trends (p. 180)
skeletal maturity (p. 187)
spermarche (p. 188)
sudden infant death syndrome (SIDS) (p. 163)
synaptic pruning (p. 157)

Media Resources

Access an integrated eBook and chapter-specific interactive learning tools, including flashcards, quizzes, videos, and more, in your Developmental Psychology CourseMate, accessed through CengageBrain.com.

© Elizabeth Crews/The Image Works

CHAPTER OUTLINE

[chapter 6]

Basic Learning and Perception

KEY THEMES

NATURE & NURTURE How do nature and nurture interact in learning and perceptual development?

SOCIOCULTURAL INFLUENCE How does the sociocultural context influence learning and perceptual development?

INTERACTION AMONG DOMAINS How do learning and perceptual development interact with other domains of development?

RISK | RESILIENCE What factors promote risk or resilience in learning and perceptual development?

The apartment had suddenly grown quiet. The three other babies and their mothers who had been helping to celebrate Chad's first birthday had departed. Only Tanya, Chad's mother, remained with him as the light faded at the end of the day. Picking up the torn gift wrappings, Tanya reflected on the events of the past year. She thought back to her first glimpse of Chad. She had counted his toes and fingers to make sure they were all there. She had wondered aloud, as she first held him, "What do you see? Do you recognize me? Can you hear me? Do you like my songs? What are you thinking?" Tanya had vowed to be a good mother, to help Chad learn. She couldn't afford the colorful playland that had beckoned to him at the toy store. But she had picked up some nice secondhand toys and books at a neighbor's yard sale and looked forward to showing them to Chad when the novelty of his new birthday gifts wore off. She wasn't sure if playing with him would make him smarter. She knew, though, that she loved those moments when he seemed to be captivated by her songs and stories about the world. <<

As you might have guessed from your reading so far, newborns are already engaging in the lifelong process of learning. Their vision, hearing, and other sensory capacities provide enormous amounts of information from which to learn. But exactly what are the developmental changes that take place with respect to these sensory systems? For example, do they see a mother's face as a whole or as a kaleidoscope of shadowy bits and pieces, perhaps with splashes of color to further attract their attention? Do they hear a father's lullaby as a rhythmical sequence of pleasant sounds and even discriminate a few of the sounds that differentiate the words that might be a part of the language they hear? And, as Tanya wondered, what part does the infant's early sensory stimulation play in later learning and perceptual development? Being reared in the angular world of city skyscrapers, might Chad, for example, see and learn in a far different way than a child growing up in a tropical rain forest?

These are precisely the kinds of questions psychologists have often asked. Why? Because learning and perception are fundamental processes by which children come to understand their world. *Perception*, the interpretation of sensory information from visual, auditory, and other receptors, is the vehicle by which we glean information about the world in the first place. *Learning*, a means of acquiring new skills and behaviors from experience, is an extremely important factor in helping children to avoid dangers, achieve satisfactions, and become contributing members of their families, communities, and culture. We begin this chapter by discussing basic processes in learning; then, we consider sensory and perceptual development in infants and children. These processes serve as the foundation for the more complex aspects of cognitive, intellectual, emotional, and social development examined in the chapters that follow.

NATURE & NURTURE

Basic Learning Processes in Infancy and Childhood

Infants come into the world remarkably well prepared to adapt to the environment. A fundamental ability evident right from birth is the capacity to learn. Learning helps children respond to the demands of their physical and social world, achieve goals, and solve problems. Infants and children learn, for example, that a stove can be hot, that hitting a sibling will provoke anger from their parents, and that the sound that makes the family dog arrive is the dog's name. What are the basic forms of learning? How early do these important capacities appear? We consider here four basic forms of learning: *habituation, classical conditioning, operant conditioning,* and *observational learning* as well as several other forms of learning that contribute to how we come to understand our world.

Habituation

The gradual decline in intensity, frequency, or duration of a response to the repeated occurrence of a stimulus is known as **habituation**. Even newborns display habituation. For example, they may show less arousal—that is, reductions in heart rate or fewer searching eye movements—as they are shown a colorful toy or hear the same bell ringing over and over. Habituation is thus a simple, adaptive form of learning to ignore things that offer little new information and that, in a sense, have become boring.

The finding that, once babies have habituated to an event, they often display a renewed response to a change in the stimulus indicates that habituation is a form of learning rather than merely fatigue or an inability to continue responding. For example, if touched on the leg instead of the arm or exposed to a sound other than the ringing of a bell, they may become aroused once again. The return of a response is an example of **recovery from habituation** (sometimes called **dishabituation**) and suggests that the baby perceives the new stimulus as different from the old one.

Low-birth-weight, brain-damaged, and younger babies tend to habituate less rapidly than older, more mature infants (Krafchuk, Tronick, & Clifton, 1983; Rovee-Collier, 1987). In fact, an infant's rapid habituation and recovery from habituation to new stimuli are associated with greater cognitive capacities in later childhood and adolescence (Bornstein et al., 2006; Dougherty & Haith, 1997; Rose et al., 2005). In addition, researchers have been able to capitalize on habituation responses in order to study a vast array of infants' perceptual, cognitive, and social abilities.

habituation Gradual decline in the intensity, frequency, or duration of a response over repeated or lengthy occurrences of the same stimulus.

recovery from habituation (dishabituation) Renewed response to a change in a stimulus, which indicates that the infant has detected that change.

unconditioned stimulus (UCS) Stimulus that, without prior training, elicits a reflexlike response (unconditioned response).

unconditioned response (UCR) Response that is automatically elicited by the unconditioned stimulus (UCS).

conditioned stimulus (CS) Neutral stimulus that begins to elicit a response similar to the unconditioned stimulus (UCS) with which it has been paired.

conditioned response (CR) Learned response that is exhibited to a previously neutral stimulus (CS) as a result of pairing the CS with an unconditioned stimulus (UCS).

Classical Conditioning

As we learned in Chapter 1, in *classical conditioning* a neutral event paired with a stimulus that triggers an inborn reaction can begin to elicit a response similar to the one initiated by the original stimulus. Consider a nipple placed in a newborn's mouth; it tends to elicit sucking. The nipple is an **unconditioned stimulus (UCS);** the sucking response is an **unconditioned response (UCR).** After a series of trials in which a neutral stimulus—say, a distinctive odor—is paired with the nipple (the UCS), the odor may also begin to elicit sucking even when the nipple is not present. The odor has become a **conditioned stimulus (CS),** and the sucking response it initiates, a **conditioned response (CR).** Figure 6.1 summarizes the sequence of steps in classical conditioning for this and other typical examples.

Figure 6.1
Examples of Classical Conditioning
Classical conditioning is learning in which a neutral event (conditioned stimulus), through its association with a cue (unconditioned stimulus) that naturally elicits a reflexlike response (unconditioned response), comes to elicit the same response (conditioned response).

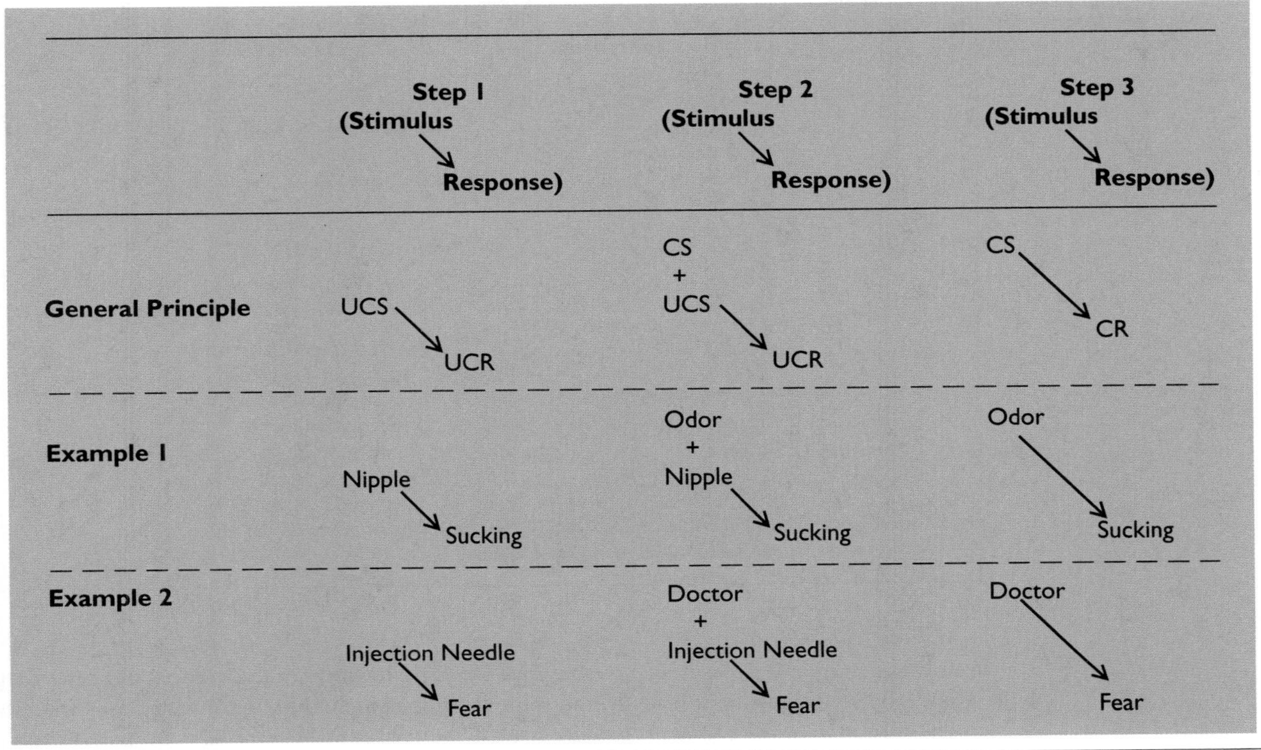

Infants display classical conditioning within hours of birth. For example, after pairing a tactile stimulus such as stroking their forehead (CS) with the delivery of a sugar solution to the mouth (UCS), an activity that normally elicits sucking (UCR), newborns learn to orient and initiate sucking (CR) in the presence of that tactile stimulus (CS) alone (Blass, Ganchrow, & Steiner, 1984). Thus, important associations, particularly those surrounding feeding activity, can be acquired through classical conditioning shortly after birth. On the other hand, infants do not display classical conditioning to aversive stimuli such as a loud noise or painful prick until they are about three or four weeks of age, perhaps because younger infants lack the motor and neural abilities needed to escape noxious events (Rovee-Collier, 1987). As infants become older, classical conditioning occurs more rapidly and involves a broader range of stimuli.

Operant Conditioning

In *operant* (or *instrumental*) *conditioning*, the frequency of spontaneous, sometimes novel behaviors changes as a result of positive and negative consequences. Put another way, behaviors tend to increase when followed by rewards **(positive reinforcement)** or the removal of aversive events **(negative reinforcement)** and to decrease when followed by the loss of rewards **(negative punishment)** or an aversive outcome **(positive punishment).** The term *positive* in this context indicates that, when a behavior occurs, it causes a stimulus event that either increases the rate of the response

positive reinforcement Occurrence of a stimulus that strengthens a preceding response. Also known as a *reward.*

negative reinforcement Removal of an aversive stimulus, which strengthens a preceding response.

negative punishment Removal or loss of a desired stimulus or reward, which weakens or decreases the frequency of a preceding response.

positive punishment Occurrence of an aversive stimulus that serves to weaken or decrease the frequency of a preceding response.

Figure 6.2

Positive and Negative Reinforcement and Punishment

Reinforcement leads to an increase in the rate of responding; punishment leads to a decrease in the rate of responding. *Positive* refers to the presentation of a stimulus following a response; *negative* refers to the removal of a stimulus following a response.

Rate of response

Response leads stimulus to be	**Increases**	**Decreases**
Delivered	**Positive reinforcement** (Increases behavior by delivering a desired stimulus) Example: Infant says, "cookie"→ Mother gives praise	**Positive punishment** (Decreases behavior by delivering an aversive stimulus) Example: Toddler throws toys → Father yells, "Stop it"
Removed	**Negative reinforcement** (Increases behavior by removing an aversive stimulus) Example: Child cleans messy room→ Parent stops "nagging"	**Negative punishment** (Decreases behavior by removing a desired stimulus) Example: Teenager out past curfew → Parent grounds teenager

(reinforcement) or decreases it (punishment). The term *negative* in this context indicates that, when a behavior occurs, it leads to the removal of a stimulus that either increases the rate of the response (reinforcement) or decreases it (punishment). Figure 6.2 summarizes these relationships and provides examples of positive and negative reinforcement and punishment.

Operant conditioning can be observed in infants within the first few hours of birth. For example, newborns will either increase or decrease pressure during sucking when the availability of milk, a positive reinforcer, is contingent on an increase or a decrease in pressure (Sameroff, 1972). And as with classical conditioning, operant conditioning seems to work best with behaviors important to infants, such as searching for (head turning, mouthing) and obtaining (sucking) food or other stimuli that are comforting. In other words, babies seem to be biologically prepared to learn about some things that are especially important for them.

Visual and auditory events can be especially powerful reinforcers for infants, too. Babies will work hard, modifying the frequency or rate of sucking, vocalizing, smiling, and other behaviors under their control, to see and hear things. These kinds of stimulation, of course, typically occur in the presence of parents, grandparents, neighbors, and siblings who, as major sources of reinforcers, encourage the baby to become responsive to them.

Classical and operant conditioning can explain the acquisition of many other behaviors throughout infancy and childhood. Through repeated associations of events and from positive (as well as negative) outcomes, including the reinforcing actions of caregivers or "instructors" (or their loss), children become more skilled and proficient in a rich variety of endeavors.

Observational Learning

Habituation, classical conditioning, and operant conditioning are the basis for mastering many vital tasks of infancy and childhood. However, one element that seems to be missing from this discussion so far is children's active role in observing and interpreting events that occur in their surroundings. As we saw in Chapter 1, social learning theorists have considered

Figure 6.3
Facial Imitation in Newborns
Within an hour after birth, babies in Nepal showed different responses when an experimenter used pursed versus widened lip movements. On the left, the baby broadens his lips in response to widened lips by the model. On the right, the baby exposes his tongue in response to pursed lips by the model. The findings support the highly controversial position that even newborns are capable of imitating facial gestures.
Source: © Nadja Reissland

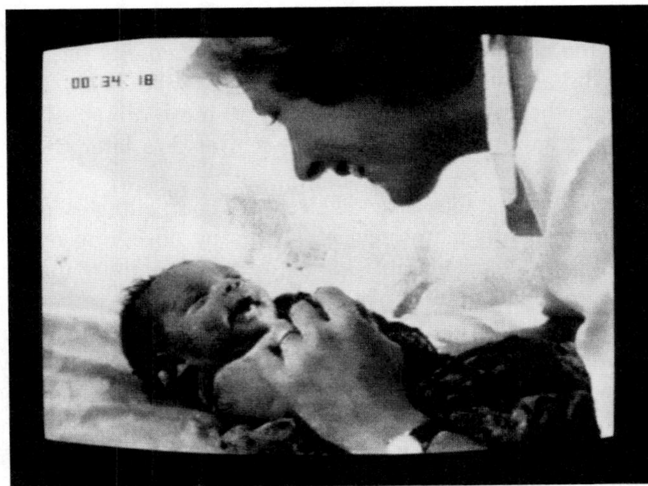

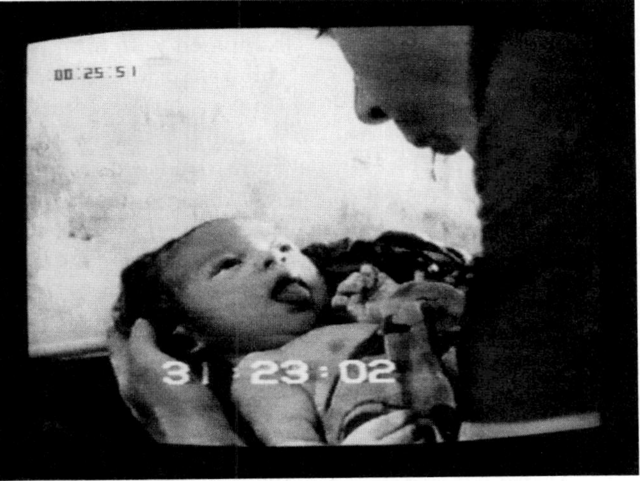

observational learning an important means by which children acquire many complex social and cognitive skills (Bandura, 1977b). Individuals often learn and reproduce behaviors important to the community by observing the activities of others, and others, in turn, may provide further behaviors and guidance that can be imitated. Imitation, then, becomes an increasingly important element in explaining learning throughout development.

When does imitation become possible? Some researchers argue that even newborns and very young infants imitate a variety of responses, including tongue protrusion, mouth opening, and possibly even facial expressions portraying such emotions as happiness, sadness, and surprise (Field et al., 1982; Meltzoff & Moore, 1999). For example, tongue protrusion, the most consistently reported behavior suggestive of imitation, has been observed in infants in rural Nepal only an hour after birth as can be seen in Figure 6.3 (Reissland, 1988).

More controversial, though, is what these imitative behaviors mean. Piaget (1962), for example, claimed that infants younger than eight to twelve months could imitate someone else's behavior but only when able to see themselves making these responses. Because babies cannot view their own faces, imitative facial gestures would be impossible, according to Piaget, until after about one year of age, when symbolic capacities emerge. From this perspective, then, imitative facial gestures such as tongue protrusion might be a stereotyped, rigid innate response triggered by or tethered, so to speak, to limited forms of stimulation. Perhaps tongue protrusion by a model, for example, also arouses the infant (Anisfeld, 2005), which in turn promotes a sucking response that naturally invokes this activity or it reflects an active effort to explore an interesting visual object (Jones, 1996; Karmiloff-Smith, 1995). However, Meltzoff and Moore (1999) have also proposed that infants imitate in order to continue interacting with others. For example, babies as young as six weeks will imitate some behaviors of a model up to twenty-four hours later. From this perspective, imitation is viewed as having an important social-communicative function and signals one of the earliest games babies play to learn about others in their surroundings.

INTERACTION AMONG DOMAINS

After six months of age, infants begin to display far more frequent and precise imitations, matching a wide range of modeled behaviors such as saying *ah*, tapping a table, and waving bye-bye (Jones, 2007). Moreover, they display **deferred imitation**, the ability to imitate a sequence of actions well after some activity has

deferred imitation Ability to imitate a model's behavior hours, days, and even weeks after observation.

been demonstrated. For example, six-month-olds may remove a mitten from a puppet's hand, shake it, and try to put it back on the puppet after observing this sequence of actions performed by a model twenty-four hours earlier (Barr, Dowden, & Hayne, 1996). Toddlers as young as fourteen months who see a peer pulling, pushing, poking, and inserting toys in the laboratory or at a daycare center will reproduce the behaviors in their own home two days later when given the same toys and imitate other novel behaviors as much as a week later (Meltzoff & Moore, 1999). These results accord well with research on memory (discussed in Chapter 8), showing that infants younger than one year can recognize stimuli hours and even days later. Enacting an observed activity, as compared with simply watching the actions performed by an adult, benefits recall for children at nine months of age who are observed a week later (Lukowski et al., 2005). However, after about a year of age, when memory abilities may be more robust, simply watching an event is often as effective for remembering the actions at a later time as immediately imitating the activity.

The findings of imitation at very young ages provide clear and compelling evidence that infants, as well as older children, learn many new behaviors by observing others. But very young children also demonstrate considerable flexibility and selectivity in their imitations. For example, fourteen- to eighteen-month-olds are more likely to imitate an adult's action that is accompanied by the verbal expression "There!"—indicating it was intentional—than an action accompanied by the verbal expression "Whoops!"—implying a mistake (Carpenter, Akhtar, & Tomasello, 1998). This and other findings suggest that, when the behaviors of another person appear to be intentional or geared toward reaching a goal, very young children are more likely to imitate their actions than when the purpose is unclear to them (Carpenter, Call, & Tomasello, 2005). As another illustration of selectivity in copying, year-old infants are more likely to move a toy directly to a goal when a barrier that required the model to initiate a more circuitous route has been removed (Schwier et al., 2006). Moreover, by three years of age, children are able to decide on whether their own solution to achieving a goal that requires a complex procedure, such as opening a drawer is better to use than an alternative method modeled by another person (Williamson, Meltzoff, & Markman, 2008). Clearly then, infants and young children are not merely copying behaviors, but instead are demonstrating selectivity about when imitating may be an efficient and adaptive means of acquiring important social and cultural skills engaged in by members of their community.

Talking on the telephone, often a favored activity of toddlers and young preschoolers, is a good example of behavior that is initiated as a result of the process of imitation.

Other Forms of Learning

Humans, including infants and young children, probably learn in many other ways. Various forms of **implicit learning,** learning about complex events without awareness, may be responsible for acquiring substantial knowledge about language, categories, and procedural routines that accompany many motor behaviors. Because much of the information in, for example, the visual-spatial environment and language is organized by patterns and rules, learning these systematic, co-occurring relationships is important for adaptation to both the physical and social worlds. Implicit learning may underlie much of *perceptual learning,* a topic that we cover more fully at the end of this chapter. For example, infants learn that banging certain toys results in the occurrence of specific sounds, that a particular person's voice is associated with that individual, and that after awakening in the morning they are likely to follow a routine involving dressing, eating, and getting ready to leave for the baby-sitter's house.

Another variant of implicit learning, *statistical learning,* emphasizes that associations are formed because some events, for example, the sounds expressed within a particular language, co-occur in a statistically predictable order (Saffran, Aslin, & Newport, 1996). In other words, infants and young children can learn from the many kinds of regularities that they experience in their world.

For Your Review and Reflection

- What are the basic principles of habituation, classical conditioning, and operant conditioning? What does recovery from habituation tell us about the habituation process?
- What are an unconditioned stimulus, an unconditioned response, a conditioned stimulus, and a conditioned response?
- How do positive reinforcement, negative reinforcement, negative punishment, and positive punishment affect behavior? Match the following examples with their corresponding types of reinforcement.

  (a) Not allowing a child to play with a toy after she has hit another child with it

  (b) Giving a child a dollar for cleaning his room

  (c) Showing anger at a child who spills her milk

  (d) Moving the family dog, who keeps taking the child's ball to another room

  Answers

  (a) negative punishment

  (b) positive reinforcement

  (c) positive punishment

  (d) negative reinforcement
- Why is observational learning an important component of learning theory? What evidence exists for imitation in early infancy? What is the significance of deferred imitation?
- In what other ways may infants and children be learning?
- Why might learning be a critical element in accounting for sociocultural differences in the many different kinds of behaviors infants and young children display?
- What are some examples of observational learning that you have seen infants display in their interactions with others? Why do you think infants and children often imitate the behavior of others?

implicit learning Learning abstract or correlated relationships among complex events without conscious awareness.

Sensory and Perceptual Capacities

Although various kinds of learning contribute to mastering new behaviors and enriching each individual's skills and competencies, these depend on other basic processes, including sensation and perception. Tanya's queries about whether Chad could see or hear as she first held her son are the kinds of questions many parents pose to their newborns even as they seem to provide their own answers by vocalizing, making funny facial expressions, touching, caressing, and rocking the baby. Still, the uncertainty remains: what exactly do infants *sense* and *perceive* when, for example, caregivers interact with them or when shiny new toys are given to them?

Sensation refers to the basic units of information recorded by a sensory receptor and the brain. **Perception** refers to the process of organizing and interpreting sensations. Sensations consist of, for example, registering different regions of brightness or of *contours*, the transitions in dark-light shading that signal borders and edges of elements in a visual array. With respect to auditory input, sensation refers to such abilities as discriminating a difference in the intensity or frequency of a sound. Perception, on the other hand, takes place when the infant recognizes his mother's face by sight or interprets a sequence of sounds as a familiar lullaby. Thus, sensations are typically thought to be the building blocks; perception, the order and meaning imposed on those basic elements.

NATURE & NURTURE

Is the world of the newborn a "great blooming, buzzing confusion" caused by a barrage of unorganized sensations, as proposed by William James (1890) more than a century ago? If so, the young infant would not apprehend objects or meaningful events at first. He or she would acquire the ability to do so only from learning, over a lengthy period of time, which pattern of basic sensory features is associated with a particular perceptual array. Perhaps, then, as a result of repeated experience with distinctive sensory input, the infant comes to recognize the human face or to perceive how far away an object is located or to hear a sequence of sounds as a lullaby. According to this viewpoint, perceptual development is a *constructive* process, that is, one of imposing sense and order on the multisensory external world.

James and Eleanor Gibson and many of their students offer a strikingly different opinion of the early perceptual capacities of infants (Pick, 1992). For them, babies come into the world well equipped to respond to the structure and organization of many stimuli and readily perceive the patterns afforded by objects and other sensory events. Some theorists go even further. According to some, the newborn from very early on has a set of *core principles* and mechanisms to process complex visual cues signifying objects and three-dimensional space, and to interpret other sensory input (Spelke & Kinzler, 2007). Of course, even within this framework, experience provides further opportunity to refine knowledge about which properties processed by the senses are stable and important, and which can be ignored as relatively uninformative.

Two broad observations about the research in this area are worth making at the outset. First, vision has been studied far more than any other sensory domain. To some extent, this bias reflects the widespread view that sight provides the major source of information for humans. Vision, however, has also been easier to study than hearing, smell, and other senses. Second, knowledge of sensory (and perceptual) development in newborns and young infants has expanded far more rapidly than knowledge of their development in older infants and children. The disparity reflects the efforts of researchers to uncover the earliest appearance of sensory and perceptual capacities, and the finding that many important changes in these domains occur in the first few months after birth.

Measuring Infant Sensory and Perceptual Capacities

How can we possibly know what babies see, hear, or smell when they are unable to tell us about it in words? Researchers have devised ingenious techniques, some quite simple, to help answer this question. Most of these procedures are based on measures of **attention**, that is, alertness or arousal focused on a specific aspect of the environment. For example, when

sensation Basic information in the external world that is processed by the sensory receptors.

perception Process of organizing and interpreting sensory information.

Figure 6.4
Visual Scanning
Using specialized techniques, researchers can often pinpoint the specific features in a visual stimulus at which infants are looking. Here the typical patterns of scanning these facelike stimuli by a one- and a two month-old have been recorded. Note how the younger infant's gaze tends to be directed to the outer or external regions of the facial stimulus, that is, hair and chin. The older infant's gaze is more frequently directed to inner features such as the eyes and mouth.
Source: Figure adapted with permission from "Pattern perception in early infancy" by P. Salapatek in *Infant Perception: From Sensation to Cognition*, Vol. 1 by L. B. Cohen and P. Salapatek (Eds.). Copyright © 1975 by Academic Press, reproduced by permission of the publisher.

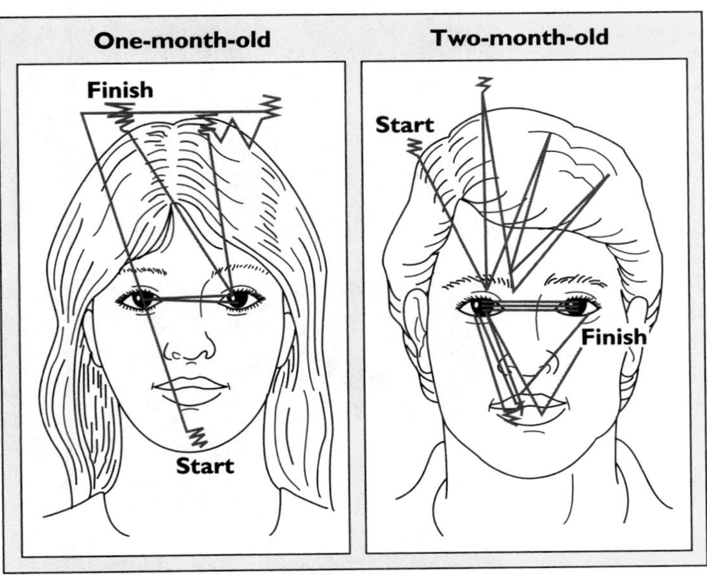

infants display attentional preferences by looking longer at one thing than at another, they are communicating that they perceive differences between visual arrays. Not only have the techniques for studying attentional preferences revealed much about infants' sensory and perceptual abilities, but they have also been enormously powerful in helping us to understand the cognitive capacities of infants that are discussed in later chapters.

Preferential Behaviors In 1958 Robert Fantz placed babies on their backs in an enclosed, criblike chamber. Through a peephole, he and his colleagues observed how long the babies gazed at different visual stimuli inserted in the top of the brightly illuminated chamber. Observers were able to determine where the infants were looking because the reflection of the stimulus could be seen on the cornea, the outer surface of the babies' eyes, as they looked at the perceptual arrays. Using this method, Fantz (1961) found that one- to six-month-olds attended to disks decorated with bull's-eyes, stripes, newsprint, or facelike figures far longer than to solid-colored circles.

This simple methodology encouraged many researchers to study the visual capacities of infants by recording their preferential looking. The procedure has some limitations, however. What can we conclude, for example, when the infant attends to both members of a pair of stimuli for the same length of time? Is the baby unable to discriminate the two, or does she prefer to look at one just as much as the other? Nor can we be certain about what features the infant is processing when gazing at a stimulus. Despite the limitations, babies often show preferences in what they attend to in their visual field. By using special photographic techniques involving infrared lights and appropriate film, or by using eye-tracking equipment, researchers can pinpoint specific regions and aspects of a figure at which the baby looks and how she or he inspects a stimulus. Such procedures have revealed, for example, which features of a human face infants are most likely to scan, as Figure 6.4 shows.

attention State of alertness or arousal that allows the individual to focus on a selected aspect of the environment.

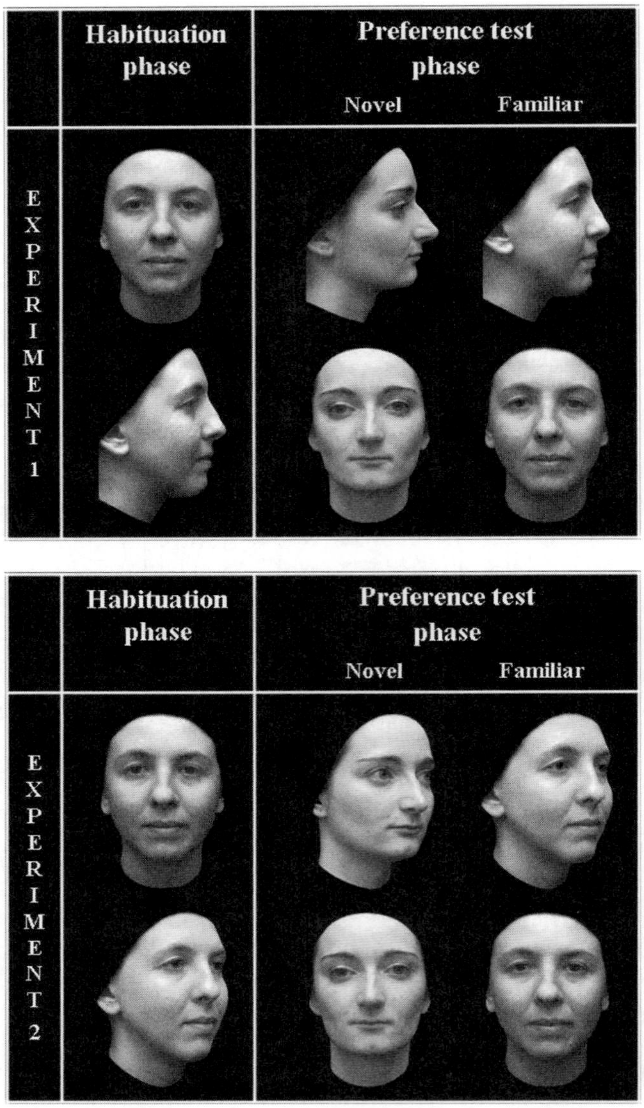

Figure 6.5
Infant Recognition of Different Facial Perspectives
After habituating to one of the faces in the left column, newborns were shown faces of the same individual in a different pose and a new individual with that same pose. When facial perspective changed 90 degrees (Experiment 1), infants did not show a preference for looking at either of the faces on test trials. However, when facial perspective changed 45 degrees (Experiment 2), they attended to the new face on test trials a greater proportion of the time than to the face of the individual they saw on habituation trials. What do you think findings such as these tell us about newborn infants' abilities?
Source: Reprinted from *Cognition*, vol. 106, 2008 pp. 1300–1321, Turati, C., Bulf, H., & Simion, F., "Newborns' face recognition over changes in viewpoint." with permission from Elsevier.

Habituation *Habituation* of attention, the simple form of learning described earlier, is another technique that capitalizes on the infant's tendency to prefer to look at some things more than others. Babies who see the same stimulus for relatively lengthy periods or over a series of trials pay less and less attention to it. A change in the stimulus, however, may elicit *recovery from habituation,* or, if the habituated stimulus is paired with one that is dissimilar, the infant may show a preference for the new one, both indicators that the child has perceived a difference.

To illustrate the use of a habituation procedure, consider the following study conducted with one- to three-day-old infants by Chiara Turati and colleagues (Turati, Bulf, & Simion, 2008). These researchers were interested in whether infants this young are able to recognize the same face even though there had been a change in facial orientation. Each infant was shown the face of a woman until he or she habituated to it. Then, the infant was shown that same face again, but now in a different orientation and paired with a novel face with that same orientation (see Figure 6.5). Would the infant recognize the original face by showing a preference for attending to the novel face even though the perspective of the familiar face had changed? The answer was yes, but only if the change in orientation of the face was 45 degrees and not 90 degrees. What could the researchers conclude since the infants showed no difference in responding when the face was rotated 90 degrees? Why do you think there was a difference in the findings for the two different orientations of the face? What would be interesting questions to ask in additional experiments concerned with very young infants' recognition of faces using habituation procedures? You can probably see why the habituation procedure, although simple in design, has yielded extraordinary insights into the capacities of even very young infants.

Operant Conditioning More complex forms of learning, such as operant conditioning, can also be used to further test an infant's ability to process sensory cues. To receive milk and other tangible rewards, such as interesting visual and auditory stimuli, babies will learn to suck faster or slower, turn their head, look, and perform other behaviors to indicate that they discriminate the arrays.

Operant conditioning procedures figure prominently in research on auditory perception. One procedure, established by Peter Eimas and his colleagues (1971), has proven especially informative. Babies are given a special nipple designed to record their rate of sucking. A baby who sucks energetically or at a rapid rate may be rewarded by hearing some pleasant sound—for example, the consonant-vowel pairing *pa*. After hearing *pa* repeatedly, the rate of sucking typically declines as the infant habituates to the stimulus. What will the baby do when a different sound, such as *ba*, is introduced? Infants as young as one month begin to suck at a high rate again in order to keep hearing *ba*. They can discriminate the new consonant-vowel pair from *pa*; they are already able to distinguish some important sounds that occur in language.

In addition to behavioral methods—preferential looking, habituation, and operant conditioning—physiological measures, such as heart rate or the neurological activity of the brain and even the firing of individual neurons, can be recorded to clarify the sensory and perceptual abilities of infants. Fortunately, the results of the various methods often complement one another in providing information about what infants are processing.

Vision and Visual Perception

The visual system of the newborn and young infant is not yet fully developed. The center of the retina (the *fovea*), the optic nerve, the visual cortex, and other parts of the visual apparatus all continue to mature in the weeks following birth (Hainline, 1998). Consequently, the very young baby does not see the world in the same way as an older child or adult. However, because newborns have limited motor skills, we are often tempted to assume that vision, along with other sensory systems, must be passive and that receptors merely await stimulation to develop. But Eleanor and James Gibson convincingly argue that perceiving is an active process (Gibson, 1966). For example, "We don't simply see, we look" (Gibson, 1988, p. 5). Even neonates actively mobilize sensory receptors to respond to stimulation flowing from their bustling environment, skills that become apparent when we examine their visual perceptual abilities.

Visuomotor Skills The eye includes a lens designed to refract, or bend, light. The lens focuses visual images onto the *retina*, the back of the eye that houses the *rods*, which are responsive to the intensity of light, and the *cones*, which are sensitive to different wavelengths of light. The lens of the human eye is variable; small, involuntary muscles change its shape so that images of objects viewed at different distances are brought into focus on the retina, a process called **visual accommodation.** When the lens works effectively, we can see things clearly.

Newborns display limited visual accommodation. However, the process improves rapidly to nearly adultlike levels by about three months of age (Aslin, 1987). Improvements in the physical characteristics of the eye and in paying attention to visual information may contribute to the developmental change (Hainline, 1998). In addition, the *pupillary reflex*, which controls the amount of light entering the eye, is sluggish during the first

visual accommodation Visuomotor process by which small involuntary muscles change the shape of the lens of the eye so that images of objects seen at different distances are brought into focus on the retina.

This young infant appears to be focusing on an important part of her environment. Visuomotor and other visual abilities rapidly improve during the first few months of life so that by the time she is ready to respond to solid foods, she very likely sees and anticipates what she is about to eat.

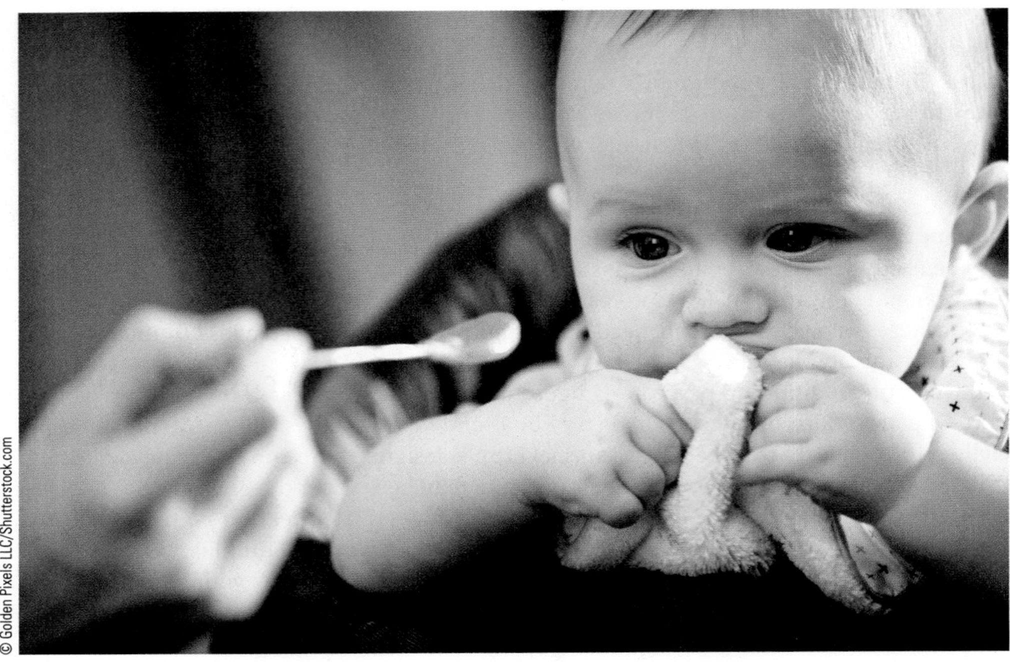

few months after birth, further reducing the ability to focus (Aslin, 1987). As a result, infants are unable to see details of stimuli. However, they discriminate best those patterns and objects about eight to twenty inches away, the typical distance of a caregiver's face when holding or feeding the baby.

Eye movements are another essential part of looking. **Saccades,** rapid movements of the eye to inspect an object or to look at something in the periphery of the visual field, are produced within hours of birth (Lewis, Maurer, & Kay, 1978). At first, the saccades are initiated slowly and cover only small distances; neonates must launch a sequence of them to "catch up" to a peripheral target (Aslin, 1993). Saccades typically become more accurate, especially during the first three to four months, and are more rapidly initiated over the years as children become older (Salman et al., 2006).

Humans exhibit another pattern of eye movements, **smooth visual pursuit,** which consists of maintaining fixation on a slowly moving target almost as though the eyes were locked onto it. Newborns display only brief periods of smooth pursuit, but its execution continues to improve through six to eight months of age (von Hofsten & Rosander, 1997), when it begins to appear adultlike. The development of both saccadic and smooth visual pursuit eye movements is closely linked to the improving capacity of infants to sustain attention to visual arrays (Richards & Holley, 1999).

In looking for an object, both eyes normally move together in the same direction. Sometimes, however, the eyes must rotate in opposite directions, turning toward each other as, for example, when a person tries to see a fly that has landed on his or her nose. This response, called **vergence,** occurs when fixations shift between far and near objects; otherwise, we would see double images. Vergence occurs irregularly in infants younger than two months, especially when objects are not static and move to different depths (Hainline & Riddell, 2002). For example, young babies' eyes may fail to rotate far enough toward each other to converge on a visual target.

saccades Rapid eye movement to inspect an object or view a stimulus in the periphery of the visual target.

smooth visual pursuit Consistent, unbroken tracking by the eyes, which serves to maintain focus on a moving visual target.

vergence Ability of the eyes to rotate in opposite directions to fixate on objects at different distances; improves rapidly during first few months after birth.

visual acuity Ability to make fine discriminations among elements in a visual array by detecting contours, transitions in light patterns that signal borders and edges.

Acuity How well are young infants able to see, despite their immature visuomotor skills? This question concerns **visual acuity.** One common test of visual acuity, the *Snellen test,*

Figure 6.6

What the Two-Month-Old Sees

Although adults with normal vision would see a clear image of this individual, as shown on the left, the two-month-old would perceive the same individual in far less detail as suggested by the photo on the right. Acuity in young infants, however, rapidly improves and typically approaches a normal level sometime between about six and twelve months of age.

Source: © Ray McVay/Photodisc/Getty Images

is based on identifying letters or other symbols on a chart twenty feet away. Babies, of course, cannot name letters, so other procedures are used to test their visual acuity. Several methods have been devised, but one that has proven reasonably good relies on *preferential looking*. As an array of, say, black and white stripes appears more frequently (the stripes become narrower), the pattern becomes more difficult to see, and the stimulus eventually appears gray. Infants unable to detect the stripes quickly lose interest, preferring to attend instead to a pattern they can still detect. By pairing stimuli with different frequencies of stripes and observing preferential looking, researchers can gauge the visual acuity of infants.

Two key findings emerge from the many investigations of visual acuity and *contrast sensitivity*, another more complex measure of visual capacity that takes into consideration ability to discriminate when illumination, orientation, and other aspects of contour also vary. First, even newborns detect contours, although their acuity and sensitivity to contrast is estimated to be about forty times poorer than in children or adults, as suggested in Figure 6.6 (Maurer et al., 1999), and as a result, they would be classified as legally blind. Second, acuity and contrast sensitivity improve rapidly during the first six months after birth and continue to improve at a slower rate for several years thereafter (Kellman & Arterberry, 2006). The gain, especially during early infancy, is owed to enhanced visuomotor skills and neural pathways for vision, changes in the shape and physical characteristics of the eye, and greater efficiency in the functioning of visual receptors in the retina.

Visual Problems in Infancy and Early Childhood | atypical development

NATURE & NURTURE

RISK | RESILIENCE

How important is visual sensory stimulation during infancy and early childhood for the development of the normal capacity to see? In Chapter 5, "Brain, Motor Skill, and Physical Development," we described research carried out on young kittens suggesting that early perceptual stimulation was essential for the growth of neurons in the visual receptor areas of the cortex. Several naturally occurring problems in infancy suggest similar consequences for the development of human visual abilities.

Approximately 1 in every 10,000 babies is born with *cataracts*, a clouding of part or all of the lens of the eye. Cataracts impair the capacity to see patterned stimulation (Sireteanu, 1999). If uncorrected, the baby's visual acuity, as well as other visual abilities, can be seriously impaired. Moreover, if the cataract is located in only one eye, the normal eye will actively suppress whatever responsiveness exists in the affected eye. The result is a lack of improvement in acuity in the affected eye, as well as impairment in depth perception because of the loss of binocular vision. Fortunately, cataracts are often relatively easy to detect. They can be surgically removed if medical resources are available, and substitute contact lenses can be implanted so that visual input will be focused on the retina. When such procedures are followed early in infancy, acuity in the affected eye or eyes improves rapidly, even after only an hour of patterned visual experience, and continues to improve rapidly with an outcome of normal visual development (Maurer et al., 1999).

Perhaps an even more frequent visual problem, affecting as many as 5 percent of infants and young children, is *amblyopia*, a condition sometimes called "lazy eye." Amblyopia refers to the failure of vision to develop in one eye, again because of suppression of visual input by the other eye. A common cause of amblyopia is *strabismus*, or the inability of the two eyes to display vergence. In many circumstances, strabismus is also relatively easy to detect; the eyes appear misaligned, or the child appears "cross-eyed" because muscles controlling the directionality of one of the eyes may be too strong or too weak. When strabismus is corrected early, normal depth perception and vision again become possible, as the two eyes begin to work together. However, for some infants and young children, the complementary functioning of the two eyes may go awry even without visible evidence of strabismus if, for example, the ability of one eye to focus is better than the other. A child with amblyopia displays the progressive loss of depth perception that vergence provides (Banks, Aslin, & Letson, 1975), and the weaker eye may become functionally blind. Fortunately, many procedures are available to correct such conditions, including patching the stronger eye for a period of time to strengthen the weaker one. If not performed early, preferably in toddlers and especially before the end of the preschool years, the loss of visual capacities can be permanent although more recent studies are suggesting that some recovery of vision in the weak eye is possible with special treatment programs even in older children and adults (National Eye Institute, 2008; Polat, Ma-Naim, & Spierer, 2009). Parents, and sometimes even pediatricians, may not always be aware of these visual problems. Thus, caregivers need to take the initiative in ensuring that their infants' and toddlers' vision is evaluated by experts who can conduct relatively simple tests for amblyopia; adequate perceptual stimulation early in development is an important ingredient to the emergence of normal visual capacities.

Color Perception Can babies see colors? The answer is yes, at least after a few months of age. Although very young infants may not see a complete range of colors because the cones are still limited in numbers and are not fully functioning together, perception of several hues is possible. For example, shortly after birth babies can detect red hues, especially if they are highly saturated; that is, contain relatively few wavelengths of other light (Adams & Courage, 1998). Detection of other hues, especially blue, comes later, but many color discriminations become adultlike by three to four months of age (Franklin & Davies, 2004; Kellman & Arterberry, 2006).

Perception of Patterns and Objects Few questions fascinate developmental scientists more than when and how infants recognize patterns and other configurations of visual arrays. We typically do not think about perception in terms of streams of light, but rather in ways

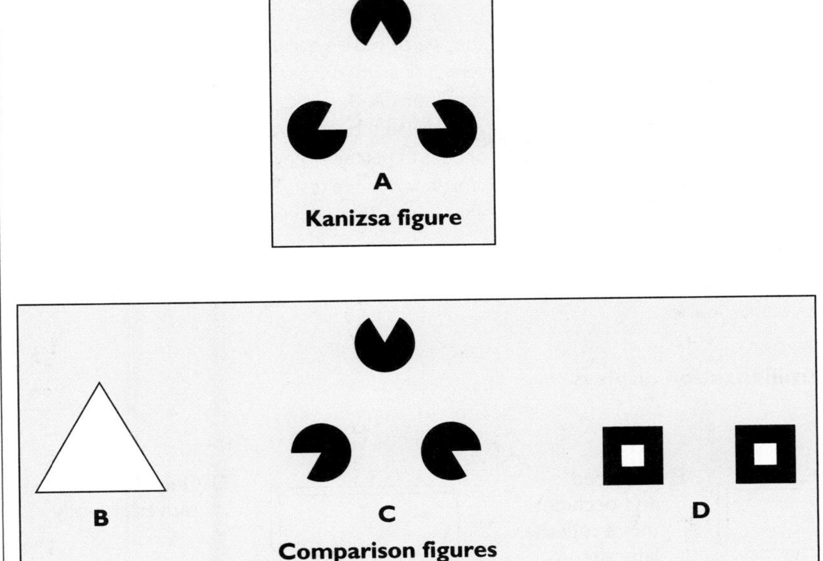

Figure 6.7
Infants' Subjective Perception of Form
Infants, as well as adults, perceive the subjective triangular figure (A) even though no contour is present to define it. After becoming habituated to the Kanizsa figure, babies are shown other figures, including a standard triangle formed by visible contours (B), the indented circular figures rotated to eliminate the subjective triangle (C), or a completely different array of stimuli (D). Infants show the least recovery from habituation to the traditional triangle (B), suggesting that they perceived the triangular shape produced by the Kanizsa figure.
Source: From Treiber et al., Perception of a 'subjective' contour by infants. *Child Development, 51*, 915–917. Used by permission of Society for Research in Child Development.

that lead us to interpret that light as depicting patterns or objects, and ultimately as sources of action and thought. Are babies then born with the ability to see objects rather than just variations in light? Some researchers think so. Others have argued the more traditional view: that this capacity is acquired only through extensive visual experience and that infants become aware of or construct perceptions of integrated, holistic, and meaningful visual figures through repeated opportunities to process contours, angles, shading, and other primary sensory features.

NATURE & NURTURE

As we have already learned, very young infants detect contours of visual stimuli. This information can help to differentiate the edges of objects (Kellman & Arterberry, 2006). They also respond to movement associated with contours. Does that necessarily mean that they see a unitary object or pattern? Perhaps not, but evidence suggests that, by two or three months of age, babies are likely to see the whole. Furthermore, by this age infants additionally inspect and analyze the components of complex stimuli, scanning a variety of their visual properties and carrying out a much more deliberate, organized search. A good example of this developmental change is demonstrated by the **externality effect:** infants younger than about two months of age are more likely to focus on the outer contours of a complex stimulus as if caught by this sensory feature, so that relatively less systematic exploration of its internal characteristics takes place. In contrast, older infants tend to scan more internal features (Maurer, 1983; Salapatek, 1975). We saw an illustration of the externality effect in the discussion of preferential looking. Babies younger than two months tend to fixate on the outer contours of the face, such as hair or the chin line; older infants much more frequently inspect internal features, such as the eyes or mouth (see Figure 6.4).

Other experiments provide further evidence that babies perceive entire forms and patterns at least within a few months after birth but continue to show improvement in form perception throughout infancy (Kellman & Arterberry, 2006). One especially convincing illustration involves subjective, or gradient-free, contours. Look at the Kanizsa figure shown in Figure 6.7. You should see a highly visible triangle appearing to stand "above" three black, disklike figures at each of its corners. But closer inspection will reveal that the brain subjectively assumes the triangular form; no contour is present to mark its edges. Infants, perhaps as young as one or two months, but very likely by three to four months, perceive subjective figures, too, a powerful demonstration that perception of form is not always based on

externality effect Tendency for infants younger than two months to focus on the external features of a complex stimulus and explore the internal features less systematically.

Figure 6.8
Inference of Unity and Coherence
Under some conditions, four-month-olds respond as if they perceived an occluded rod as a single complete figure. Infants are habituated to one of the seven familiarization displays shown here and are then presented with the test displays. After viewing conditions A, B, and C, infants respond to the complete rod in the test display as novel, indicating they perceived the rod in A, B, and C as being broken. When shown conditions D, E, F, or G, however, infants appear to perceive the rod as a connected whole, showing less attention to the complete rod than to the broken rod in the test display.The results indicate that young infants are able to infer unity and coherence for objects. Research suggests newborns do not make these perceptual inferences.
Source: Adapted from Spelke, E. S. Perception of unity, persistence and identity: Thoughts on infants' conceptions of objects. In J. Mehler and R. Fox (Eds.), *Neonate Cognition: Beyond the Blooming, Buzzing Confusion*. Copyright © 1985. Reprinted by permission of E. S. Spelke.

Familiarization displays
A Rod and occluder both remain stationary
B Both rod and occluder move together laterally
C Only the occluder moves laterally
D Only the rod moves laterally
E Only the rod moves vertically
F Rod moves to and away from occluder (change in distance)
G Only the rod moves laterally
Test displays
vs.

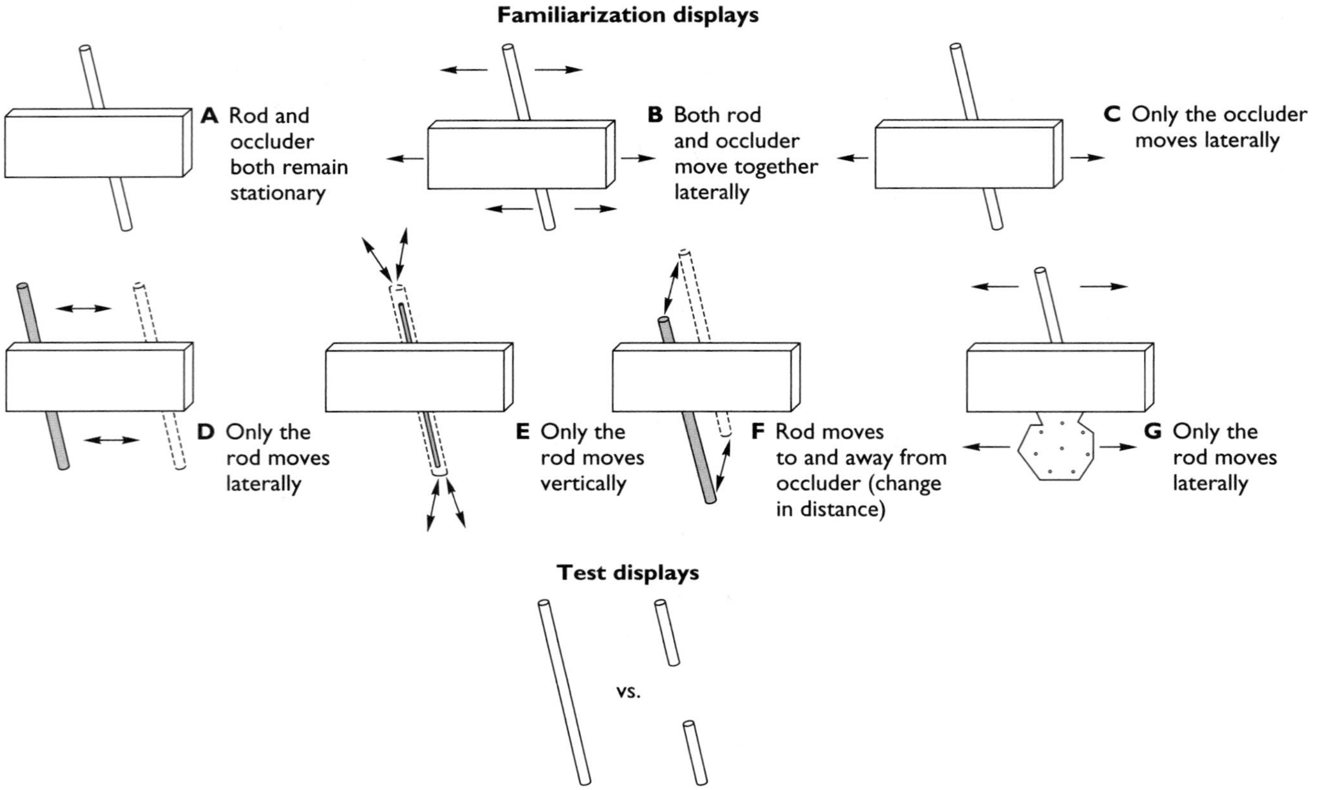

a detectable contour (Kavšek, 2009; Treiber & Wilcox, 1980). Moreover, by eight months of age, infants appear to treat such an illusory figure as if it has attributes much like a real object. For example, another object is perceived as if being occluded, that is, as if passing "under or behind" the triangle, if shown moving through its illusory boundaries (Csibra, 2001).

Research carried out by Philip Kellman, Elizabeth Spelke, and others suggests that an important aspect of perceiving an object is the relative motion of its associated features that help to segregate it from another object (Kellman, 1996; Kellman & Arterberry, 2006; Kellman & Spelke, 1983). A ball may be perceived as different from the floor, not only because of information associated with its contour and surface, but also from the continued association of the features of the ball as it rolls along the floor. Kellman, Spelke, and their colleagues initiated a number of studies investigating how a variety of movements involving an occluded rod influences an infant's inferences about the unity of that rod. Figure 6.8 illustrates some of the variations that infants were shown. Three- to four-month-olds interpreted the rod as complete and unbroken as long as its two protruding ends appeared to move together in the same direction and independently of the block during habituation trials, even if the two visible ends were of quite different shapes (Kellman & Banks, 1998).

If neither the rod nor the block moved, the rod and block shifted together in the same direction, or only the occluding block moved during habituation trials, the infants did not "fill in" the unseen portion of the rod; they treated the stimulus as two short pieces separated by an intervening space.

Still other researchers have argued that even newborns have some ability to detect object unity but have difficulty doing so because of limitations in processing the motion that is involved in testing with these kinds of relatively complicated displays (Valenza et al., 2006). What factors help infants detect object unity? Color, brightness, texture, and intersections of contour may help very young infants begin to segment their visual field and contribute to constructing their perception of objects (Johnson et al., 2008). Perhaps most importantly, according to Scott Johnson (2004; Johnson et al., 2008), infants must build their understanding of the unity of an obstructed object by integrating information about its motion and the position and orientation of its elements, as well as recognizing cues signaling depth perception; these processes take time to develop. This idea accords nicely with a suggestion by Amy Needham (2001) and her colleagues (Needham & Baillargeon, 1998; Needham & Modi, 2000) that yet another important factor is involved in object perception for infants, especially when perception takes place in a relatively cluttered environment in which many contours and surfaces are intermingled. Such a condition might exist, for example, when the infant is able to see a pacifier stuck among numerous toys in a box or among kitchen utensils in a drawer. Needham suggests that, in these circumstances, having viewed or manipulated the object as a separate entity at an earlier time is critical. Because the infant has memory for the segmented visual display on the basis of experience with it, he or she is able to perceive it in other contexts. Needham's work, then, points out the role that the infant's emerging motor and cognitive capacities might play in the very young infant's perception. In other words, perceiving an object may stem not only from processing features and characteristics of the external sensory environment but also from what the infant brings to the perceptual task in the form of motor skills and memory of having interacted with it before.

INTERACTION AMONG DOMAINS

Perception of Faces Some perceptual patterns are especially significant to the infant. One is the human face. Do even newborns recognize faces, perhaps even the faces of their caregivers? Based on the discussion so far, it should not be surprising to learn that, by about two months of age, infants do assign great importance to the face, attending to it more than to other, equally complex arrays. But an even earlier, perhaps innate preference also makes evolutionary sense, because faces are a vital source of information for social and emotional relationships.

INTERACTION AMONG DOMAINS

Some researchers have found evidence that newborns prefer, at least for moving configurations, a facelike image—two eyelike representations above a mouthlike feature—to other arrangements of the same components (Johnson et al., 1991). Mark Johnson suggests that this inborn preference arises from a fairly primitive subcortical visual system that functions in newborns (Johnson, 2005). Within about two months of age, this primitive system is supplanted by a more sophisticated cortical visual system that explores and discriminates faces from other, equally complex, stimuli (Mondloch et al., 1999; Pascalis & Kelly, 2009). The primitive system helps to ensure, however, that the infant gets off to the right start by preferring this extremely important perceptual array.

NATURE & NURTURE

On the other hand, infants' early preferences for faces simply may be a manifestation of their general tendency to prefer stimuli with certain kinds of configurations—in this case, stimuli with a top-heavy arrangement of features such as those shown in Figure 6.9. Research indicates that newborns show consistently greater interest in stimuli for which features cluster at the top; they show no specific preference for a correctly ordered human face when it is paired with another top-heavy, but rearranged, facelike stimulus (Macchi Cassia, Turati, & Simion, 2004; Turati, 2004). Additionally, the outline surrounding the configuration of elements within the stimulus may play a role; when, for example, both outline and elements are broader at the top or both are broader at the bottom, newborns prefer to look at such stimuli compared with when they do not match (Macchi Cassia et al., 2008). Thus, arrangements of arrays reflecting a more holistic agreement among various aspects

Figure 6.9
Preferences for Facelike and Non-Facelike Configurations
Newborns show a preference for looking at arrays of stimuli that tend to have more elements in the upper portion of the array than in the lower portion of the array (i.e., prefer attending to those shown in the left column more than those shown in the right column). These findings lend support to the view that general perceptual biases contribute to early preferences for faces in human infants.
Source: From Turati, C. (2004). Why faces are not special to newborns: An alternative account of the face preference. *Current Directions in Psychological Science, 13*, 5–8. Reprinted by permission of Sage.

of the stimulus seem to be preferred (Leo & Simion, 2009). Perhaps this factor also helps to explain why newborns display preferences for certain kinds of faces. For example, Alan Slater and his colleagues (Slater et al., 1998) showed babies between one and six days of age pairs of female faces that had been judged by adults as attractive and unattractive. These infants gazed at the attractive faces longer than the unattractive faces, a finding that has been obtained by other researchers testing older infants. By five months of age, they also prefer looking at pictures of faces with larger eyes, just as do adults (Geldart, Maurer, & Carney, 1999).

Although researchers offer different explanations for these early biases, recordings of brain wave activity reveal that, by three months of age, some regions of the cortex have become specialized for processing face stimuli; when babies at this age look at faces, brain wave patterns differ from those when looking at other equally complex visual arrays (Halit et al., 2004). And as is the case for adults, by seven months of age, brain wave patterns differ when looking at faces that depict a fearful expression compared with faces that display happy or neutral expressions (Leppänin et al., 2007). Nevertheless, faces in and of themselves do not automatically capture the attention of infants. For example, when five- to seven-month-olds view someone who is brushing her teeth or combing her hair, that dynamic activity is recognized just as well as the face of the person performing the activity (Bahrick & Newell, 2008).

When does a baby discriminate his or her mother's face from that of another person? As you might have guessed in reading about the habituation procedure, the answer is within days after birth (Bushnell, Sai, & Mullin, 1989; Slater & Quinn, 2001). By six months of age, differences in brain wave patterns are evident when a baby looks at her mother's face compared with a stranger's face (de Haan & Nelson, 1997). Moreover, a meta-analysis of studies examining looking behavior indicates that infants appear to have acquired information about female faces earlier and more quickly than male faces, perhaps because in most households, infants spend more time receiving care from women (Ramsey, Langlois, & Marti, 2005). From these various findings, we can conclude that infants are attracted to and identify significant aspects of the human face early in their development and make rapid strides in perceiving and recognizing this important social stimulus.

Biological Motion The important role of motion for early infant perceptual development was considered in our discussion of the perception of objects and is demonstrated in yet another phenomenon known as *biological motion.* Bennett Bertenthal (1993) and his colleagues (Proffitt & Bertenthal, 1990) carried out a series of studies in which infants were shown points of light moving as though attached to the head and major joints of a person walking. Adults who observe this pattern readily interpret the light movement as though it is someone walking. In other conditions, the pattern of lights was inverted, or an equivalent amount of motion was shown but with the lights scrambled so that the motion did not simulate the appearance of a person walking. Using attentional and habituation measures, these experiments demonstrated that, by the time infants have reached three to six months of age, the "walker" has taken on special meaning to them compared with other patterns of light motion.

Another recent study suggests that even newborns prefer attending to an upright display depicting biological motion over an inverted pattern of that same display or one showing random motion (Simion, Regolin, & Bulf, 2008). These findings support the argument that most human infants may be well prepared for acquiring social and cognitive information from motion cues (Yoon & Johnson, 2009). In fact, six- to ten-year olds with autism, children who typically have limited social cognitive skills, often have difficulty perceiving biological motion (Blake et al., 2003).

Depth Perception In addition to seeing to the left and right as well as above and below, babies see depth or distance. However, visual images are recorded on the retina in only two dimensions. When and how do we acquire depth perception? One source of information comes from *binocular vision.* Sensory information differs slightly for each eye. The ability to fuse the two distinct images to perceive a single object is called **stereopsis,** a capacity that improves markedly during the first four months after birth (Kellman & Arterberry, 2006). Stereopsis provides clues to depth as effectively for six-month-olds as for adults (Held, Birch, & Gwiazda, 1980).

Still other sources of information about depth and distance are available to infants. A classic series of studies involving the visual cliff suggests that **kinetic cues,** information provided by the movement of objects in the environment or resulting from changes in position of the eyes, head, or body, are among them. The **visual cliff** consists of a large sheet of glass bisected by a relatively narrow plank. A patterned surface is placed immediately under the glass on one side but much farther below it on the other side. Richard Walk (1968) found that an infant old enough to crawl could usually be coaxed to cross the shallow side but was much less likely to crawl over the deep side. The kinetic cues provided by moving his or her own head and body signaled depth; the babies showed the same response regardless of whether they could use one or both eyes.

Even babies too young to crawl react to the shallow and deep sides of the visual cliff differently. When placed face down on the glass surface, two- to three-month-olds become quieter, are less fussy, and show a greater decrease in heart rate on the deep side than on the shallow side (Campos, Langer, & Krowitz, 1970). Such reactions suggest that infants have not yet associated anxiety or fear with depth and find the visual information provided by the deep side more interesting than that on the shallow side. In fact, depth cues may already influence attention at birth, because newborns prefer looking at three-dimensional objects to looking at two-dimensional figures (Slater, Rose, & Morison, 1984).

Surprisingly, however, learning to avoid a drop-off occurs relatively independently when babies are acquiring the ability to sit, crawl, and walk. Karen Adolph has observed infants as they

stereopsis The ability to fuse the two distinct images from the eyes to perceive a single object.

kinetic cues Perceptual information provided by the movement of objects in the environment or changes in the positioning of the eyes, head, or body. Important source of information for depth perception.

visual cliff Experimental apparatus used to test depth perception, in which the surface on one side of a glass-covered table is made to appear far below the surface on the other side.

Figure 6.10

Avoiding a Risky Fall

Although infants at a very young age can perceive depth, their understanding of its consequences has to be relearned to fit the postural limitations associated with different motor skills. An infant may resist leaning too far to reach an attractive object located across a gap when sitting (A).However, that infant may readily try to crawl across a gap of a similar width and would fall if not caught by the experimenter (B). Similarly, in learning to locomote down an inclined plane, the child seems to have to relearn that he or she will fall down a steep slope that he or she can successfully negotiate when crawling. Coordinating perceptual information with permissible actions has to be relearned with each motor milestone in development.

Source: Adolph, K. E. (2000). Specificity of learning: Why infants fall over a veritable cliff. *Psychological Science, 11,* 290–295, Reprinted by permission of Sage.

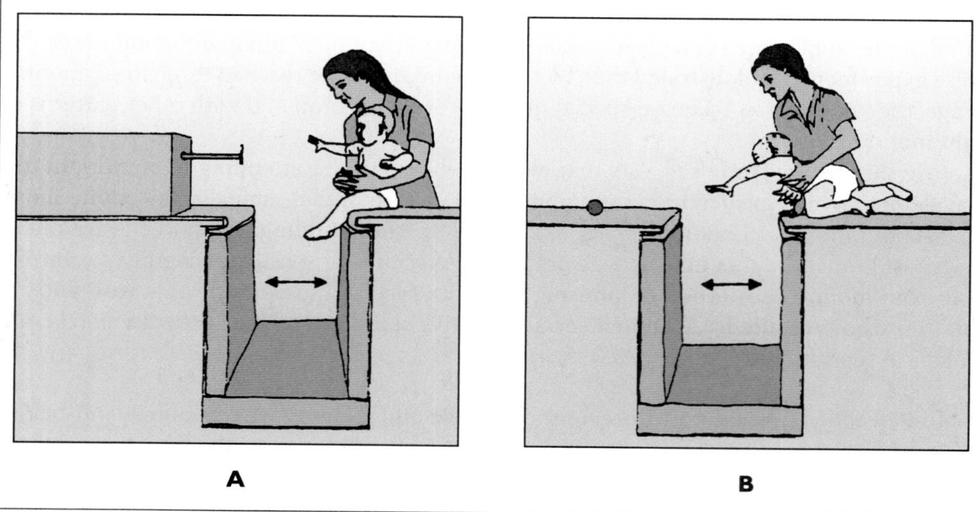

attempt to either reach across or crawl over a gap, and as they attempt to negotiate crawling or walking down a steeply inclined surface (Adolph, 1997, 2000). Whereas infants may avoid reaching across a gap that would cause them to lose their balance and fall from their seated position, they may readily attempt to crawl across a gap that is far too wide for them to avoid falling (see Figure 6.10). Similarly, even though they may have learned to safely crawl down an inclined plane, they seem to have to relearn the dangers of that same slope when beginning to walk. Thus infants need to learn to coordinate their perception of depth with safe actions for negotiating their surroundings as each new kind of postural and motor ability is acquired.

NATURE & NURTURE

Finally, other information, collectively described as *pictorial cues,* signals depth in photos or two-dimensional arrays. Pictorial cues include relative size (near objects appear larger), shadows, interposition of surfaces (one surface hides another), and linear perspective (lines converging toward a horizon). Infants begin to use many of these cues to identify nearer configurations beginning about five months of age (Kavšek, Granrud, & Yonas, 2009; Kellman & Arterberry, 2006; Yonas & Owsley, 1987). Thus, infants respond very early to abundant sources of information signaling depth and the three-dimensionality of objects. Many aspects of visual development during infancy are summarized in the Visual Development chronology.

For Your Review and Reflection

- What is the difference between sensation and perception?
- How are attention and other behavioral and physiological measures used to investigate infant sensory and perceptual capacities?

Visual Development: Birth to 8 Months

MONTHS

BIRTH

Newborn

- Shows minimal accommodation; limited, sluggish saccades; incomplete vergence.
- Detects contours, but acuity and contrast sensitivity remain relatively poor.
- Prefers attending to highly visible contour, angles, features in motion, and three-dimensional over two-dimensional stimuli.
- Exhibits externality effect.
- Demonstrates preference for facelike stimuli.

© Bill Gozansky/Alamy

1–3 Months

- Shows accommodation; near normal adultlike vergence.
- Smooth visual pursuit emerges.
- Discriminates cues to depth.

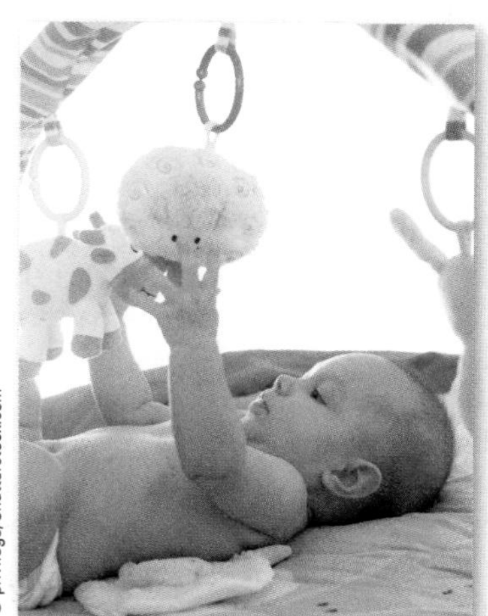

© privilege/Shutterstock.com

- Responds to rapidly expanding visual images.
- Explores internal as well as external features of stimuli.
- Recognizes shape of simple figures and more detailed patterns and objects.
- Prefers attending to increasingly complex patterns, including those with facelike organization.
- Detects basic colors.
- Infers "subjective" contour if defined by movement cues.
- Evidence for different brain wave patterns when processing faces than when processing other visual arrays.

4–8 Months

- Exhibits stereopsis.
- Saccadic eye movements become larger, more rapid, and accurate.
- Shows adultlike smooth visual pursuit.
- Acuity and contrast sensitivity approach normal.
- Displays fear of depth on visual cliff.
- Discriminates many pictorial (two-dimensional) cues to depth.
- Distinguishes symmetrical from asymmetrical patterns.
- Processses "subjective" contours even if arrays are static.
- Perceives occluded objects as wholes.
- Becomes responsive to "biological motion."

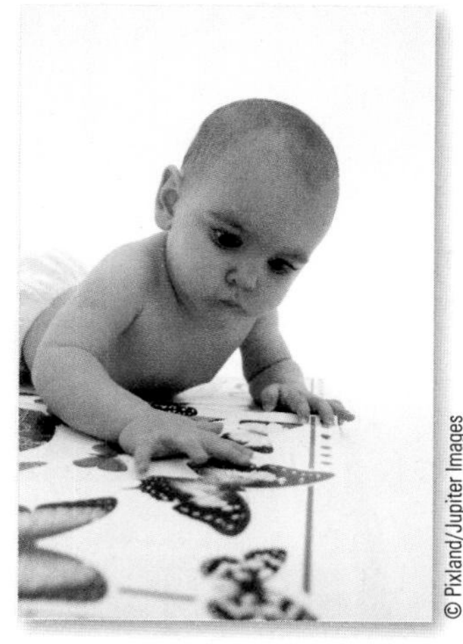

© Pixland/Jupiter Images

This chart describes the sequence of visual development in infancy based on the findings of research. Children often show individual differences in the exact ages at which they display the various developmental achievements outlined here.

- What limitations exist in infant visual accommodation, saccadic eye movements, smooth visual pursuit, vergence, and other visuomotor capacities? How quickly do these reach adultlike ability?
- What kinds of visual problems are found among infants? Why is the correction of these problems important in infancy or early childhood?
- What is the ability of infants to perceive color?
- How early do infants see patterns and forms in the visual world? What is the externality effect? How early and using what kinds of cues do infants perceive objects in their world?
- What is the developmental course of infant perception of faces? When can an infant distinguish the face of a caregiver from the face of another person?
- What is meant by the perception of biological motion?
- How early do infants perceive depth? What kinds of cues do infants use to perceive depth? What evidence exists to indicate that depth perception does not always produce appropriate responses to it?
- What arguments would you make to claim that nature plays an important role in infant visual development? What are examples of how experience affects visual development in infants and very young children?
- Why do developmental psychologists no longer believe the infant's visual world is simply a "blooming, buzzing confusion"?
- Why do you think that a mother nursing a very young infant might be providing optimal stimulation for early visual development?

Audition and Auditory Perception

Just as opinion once held that newborns are blind, so did it assert that newborns are deaf. However, the fetus is listening well before birth. Brain wave patterns, heart rate changes, and activity level observed on ultrasound scans reveal responses to vibroacoustic stimulation (Kisilevsky & Low, 1998). Low-frequency sounds, the kind that are produced in human speech, are detected by the fetus sometimes as early as twenty-three weeks of age (Kisilevsky & Low, 1998; Lecanuet, 1998). Sensitivity to a wide range of sounds at lower and lower intensities increases dramatically during the remainder of the prenatal period (Hepper & Shahidullah, 1994).

NATURE & NURTURE

Persuasive evidence that fetuses hear also comes from several studies indicating that newborns prefer to listen to the sounds they heard before birth. Anthony DeCasper and Melanie Spence (1986) asked expectant women to read aloud a passage from Dr. Seuss's *The Cat in the Hat* twice a day during the last six weeks of pregnancy. Their fetuses were exposed to the story for a total of about three and a half hours before birth. Two or three days after birth, the babies listened to either the same passage or a new story while outfitted with a special pacifier that recorded rate of sucking. Depending on the rate of sucking, the recording of the story would turn on or off. When newborns heard *The Cat in the Hat*, they changed their rate of sucking to listen to it but did not do so for the new story. Some kind of learning about the Dr. Seuss story apparently took place prenatally.

What precisely does the fetus hear, and what is it learning from these exposures? We are not really sure. As newborns, infants prefer to listen to their mother's voice rather than the voice of a stranger (DeCasper & Fifer, 1980), especially the lower-frequency sounds associated with their mother's voice (Spence & Freeman, 1996). Because the mother's body tissue and bones are very good conductors of sound, the newborn already has had considerable exposure to characteristics of the mother's speech (Lecanuet, 1998). Moreover, thirty-eight-week-old fetuses already show differential heart rate and behavioral

what do you think? Should the Fetus Be Exposed to Extra Auditory Stimulation?

An expectant mother, as we saw in Chapter 4, "The Prenatal Period and Birth," can initiate many practices that will foster healthy development during pregnancy. But with the advent of public awareness about the auditory and learning abilities of the fetus has come a new type of training that some parents have adopted to promote development in an effort to give their infant a psychological head start. This one involves the planned and regular exposure of the fetus to patterned sounds—simple, such as a heartbeat or drumbeat, or complex auditory and vibroacoustic events, such as classical or other kinds of music, and sometimes even words, numbers, and letters steadily relayed to the fetus via a belt or ear buds attached to an expectant woman's stomach. Others may expose the fetus to "daily lessons" in music or other forms of sensory stimulation via other means.

Research has demonstrated that, over the last trimester, the fetus displays increasing responsivity to music (Kisilevsky et al., 2004). Do you think the practice of regular exposure to music or other sounds might give the newborn a head start in life by stimulating intellectual processes? No evidence for this benefit for cognitive development currently exists. Alternatively, do you think that such exposure might promote a relaxing and comforting continuity to the newborn's world after birth? For example, could early exposure to (and any accompanying memory for) music or other kinds of auditory events promote emotional stability, serving as a kind of "security blanket" in the form of a soothing environmental context for the infant who is experiencing many additional stresses in negotiating her new world after birth? How could researchers design studies to answer these questions?

Can you think of any potential negative consequences of such early exposure? Could, for example, some level of intensity or too frequent exposure to sound be disruptive to prenatal development by damaging delicate sensory organs that are just beginning to function? For example, evidence exists that low-frequency sounds emanating from outside the womb are somewhat amplified for the fetus (Richards et al., 1992). Moreover, expectant women exposed to noisy workplaces or rock concerts sometimes report considerable activity in their fetus. Could such experiences, then, disrupt sleep patterns occurring prenatally, overstimulating and discomforting the fetus with the potential outcome of disrupting normal brain development?

Or is it possible that any benefits from this kind of activity occur as much for the prospective parents as for the newborn? For example, could gently talking to the fetus and reserving and organizing time for exposure to music or other sounds serve as a prelude to the type of attention and parenting schedule that the infant will very likely demand, and potentially benefit from, after birth? In other words, could these kinds of practices be good for adults as well as for infants? What do you think about exposing the fetus to extra auditory stimulation?

responses to the voice of the mother compared with that of a stranger (Kisilevsky et al., 2003). The fetus can learn something about the cadence of sound as well. After expectant women in France repeatedly recited a rhyme from the thirty-third to thirty-seventh week of their gestation period, changes in fetal heart rate in response to the rhyme revealed that the fetus differentiated it from another novel rhyme even when recited by someone else (DeCasper et al., 1994).

Hearing Physiological measures taken from the auditory brainstem suggest that responsivity to sounds is nearly adultlike for some frequencies in newborns, especially those in the middle range of sounds that humans can detect (Sininger, Doyle, & Moore, 1999). However, work using attentional and behavioral measures with older infants reveals marked improvement in most auditory skills throughout the first few months. Certainly by about six months of age, babies are able to detect and discriminate numerous features of sound, such as its frequency and intensity, almost as well as do adults (Saffran, Werker, & Werner, 2006; Trehub & Hannon, 2006).

Not all babies, however, are able to hear at birth. Moderate to profound deafness is estimated to affect approximately 5,000 newborns in the United States each year; additionally, between 1 and 2 out of every 1,000 infants born in the United States experience some kind of hearing difficulty (Kerschner, 2004). Lower rates are found in some Western European nations, such as France (Baille et al., 1996), but higher rates are reported in many other regions of the world. New screening techniques—for example, physiological measurements of neural activity in the auditory brainstem or recording the vibration of cells in the inner ear, brief procedures that are nonintrusive and painless—can be used with infants to detect the possibility of hearing loss. Although some nations now require universal screening for hearing in newborns, it is not yet required in all states in the United States. However, today most newborns in this country are tested (Biernath, Holstrum, & Eichwald, 2009). Such detection can lead to early interventions involving the use of hearing aids or sign language; activities that are especially important in normal language development.

RISK | RESILIENCE

Sound Localization Shortly after birth, babies display **sound localization,** the ability to locate a sound in space by turning their heads or eyes in the direction of the sound. This early ability, which may be reflexive, declines during the first two months and then reemerges at about four months of age in the form of a more deliberate search for sound (Muir & Hains, 2004). Ability to locate the precise position from which a sound originates improves markedly throughout infancy and into early childhood (Ashmead, Clifton, & Perris, 1987; Morrongiello, Fenwick, & Chance, 1990). By six to eight months of age, infants also begin to appreciate the distance from which a sound emanates. At this age, babies hearing a sound in the dark produced by an object beyond their reach are less likely to attempt to retrieve it than an object producing a sound that is within their reach (Clifton, Perris, & Bullinger, 1991).

Patterns of Sound In every culture that has been observed, caregivers sing or play music for their infants (Trehub & Trainor, 1998). Can babies distinguish music from noise? Might they even have a preference for some kinds of music? Two- and three-month-olds do recognize changes in tempo, the rate at which sounds occur (Baruch & Drake, 1997), and intervals between brief bursts of sound that denote simple rhythmic change (Demany, McKenzie, & Vurpillot, 1977). Between six months and one year of age, they also begin to distinguish between more complex rhythms and patterns of sounds (Clarkson, 1996; Morrongiello, 1984). For example, at eight months of age, babies recognize changes in short (six-note) melodies, including a transposition in key (e.g., from C to E flat) and the shift within the same octave to either a higher or a lower frequency (e.g., from B to D) (Trehub, Bull, & Thorpe, 1984; Trehub, Thorpe, & Morrongiello, 1985). Surprisingly, under some circumstances, eight-month-olds can keep track of absolute pitch better than adults can (Saffran, 2003).

In addition to detecting differences between sound patterns, infants show clear preferences for certain auditory events. Perhaps because of its voice quality or tempo, they prefer to listen to a song or lullaby directed by an adult to another infant over the same song or lullaby by the adult singing alone and a lower-pitched lullaby over a higher-pitched lullaby (Trainor, 1996; Volkova, Trehub, & Schellenberg, 2006). In fact, four-and-a-half-to six-month-olds can boast of some budding capacities as music critics. Carol Krumhansl and Peter Jusczyk (1990) chose short passages of Mozart minuets and introduced brief pauses at locations judged by adults to be either natural or awkward places for musical phrases to end. Babies preferred looking at a loudspeaker that played natural versions of the music to a speaker that played unnatural versions. Other research has shown that infants prefer the original passages of Mozart minuets over versions in which the intervals between sequences of notes have been altered to create a more dissonant, less pleasing sound, as heard by adults (Trainor & Heinmiller, 1998). In addition, after hearing two Mozart sonatas daily over

sound localization Ability to determine a sound's point of origin.

Auditory Development: Birth to 12 Months

CHRONOLOGY

MONTHS

BIRTH

Newborn

- Recognizes auditory events that were repeatedly produced by the woman when fetus was still in utero.
- Discriminates mother's and stranger's voices.
- Localizes sound reflexively.

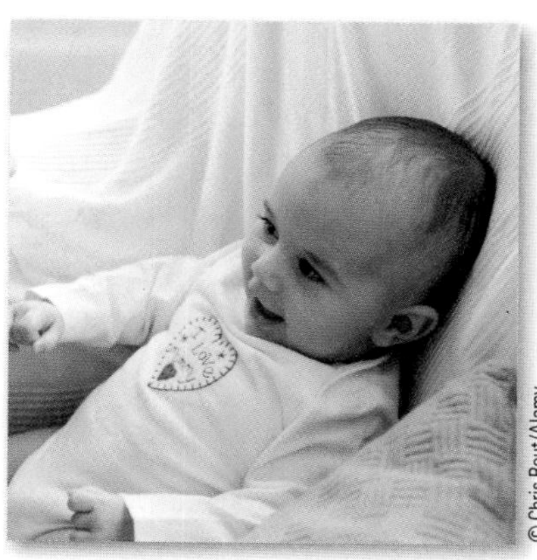

© Chris Rout/Alamy

1–3 Months

- Recognizes simple auditory patterns.
- Discriminates many, if not all, basic sounds used in language.
- Makes deliberate efforts to locate sound, an ability that continues to improve throughout early childhood.

4–8 Months

- Detects and discriminates high-frequency tones nearly as well as, sometimes better than, children or adults; ability to detect low-frequency tones continues to improve throughout childhood.
- Recognizes melodic rhythms, transposition in key, note changes, phrasing in music.

© moodboard/Alamy

9–12 Months

- Begins to lose some phoneme discriminations if not heard in native language.

This chart describes the sequence of auditory development in infancy based on the findings of research. Children often show individual differences in the exact ages at which they display the various developmental achievements outlined here.

several weeks' time, seven-month-olds can distinguish these from other Mozart sonatas, even when tested two weeks later (Saffran, Loman, & Robertson, 2000).

Another element in music is its meter—what is typically referred to as the pattern of strong and weak beats. In much of Western music, a simple and regular beat occurs. However, this degree of regularity in beat is not consistently found in the music of many other cultures in Eastern Europe, the Middle East, Africa, and South Asia. By four months of age, American infants typically prefer a simple and more regular beat over somewhat more complex patterns that are found, for example, in Balkan music (Soley & Hannon, 2010). In contrast, infants in Turkey, exposed to regular but also irregular metric patterns in the Balkan music with which they have experience, show no preference for the regular beat or the irregular structure and prefer both over a metric pattern with which they are not familiar. Thus, in the domain of music, even young infants display preferences for structural patterns common to their native culture.

SOCIOCULTURAL INFLUENCE

In conclusion, babies are indeed sensitive to rhythmic, melodic, and other aspects of music. Moreover, brain hemisphere asymmetries in responses to melodic changes

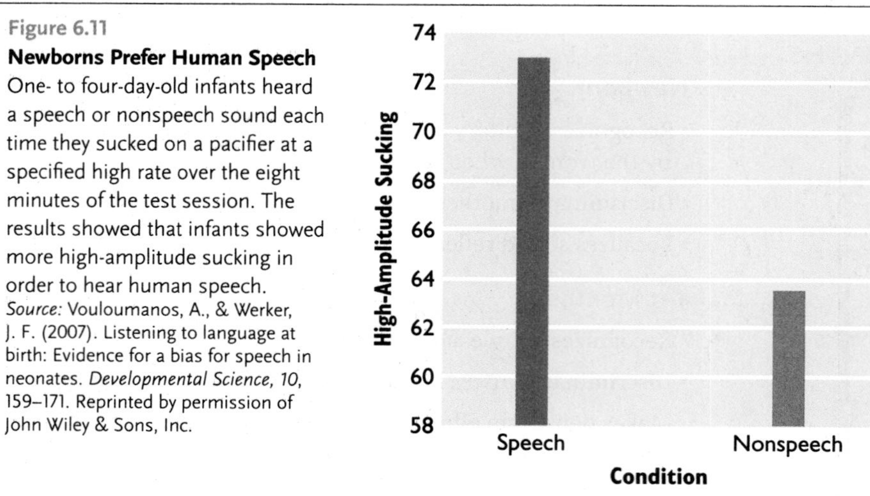

Figure 6.11
Newborns Prefer Human Speech
One- to four-day-old infants heard a speech or nonspeech sound each time they sucked on a pacifier at a specified high rate over the eight minutes of the test session. The results showed that infants showed more high-amplitude sucking in order to hear human speech.
Source: Vouloumanos, A., & Werker, J. F. (2007). Listening to language at birth: Evidence for a bias for speech in neonates. *Developmental Science, 10,* 159–171. Reprinted by permission of John Wiley & Sons, Inc.

(a left-ear/right-hemisphere advantage) are found in many young infants, just as they are observed in adults (Balaban, Anderson, & Wisniewski, 1998). A further implication of these many findings is that the ability to detect musical phrasings, even though it may not yet be fully adultlike by six months of age (Saffran et al., 2006), can also be important for detecting the phrasing and sound rhythms that commonly underlie speech. The Auditory Development chronology summarizes some of the early abilities infants display with respect to the perception of sound.

Speech Research on infants' hearing abilities has often been conducted to answer another question: How soon do babies perceive human speech? Practically right from birth, it seems. As Figure 6.11 shows, one- to four-day-old infants will suck more on a specially designed pacifier in order to produce a human voice saying speechlike sounds than to generate acoustically comparable nonspeech sounds (Vouloumanos & Werker, 2007). And the language areas of the brain show greater activation when infants only a few days old listen to speech as opposed to nonspeech sounds (Peña et al., 2003). Most important for our understanding of language development, however, infants respond in specific ways to small acoustic variations in human speech that distinguish one word or part of a word from another.

The smallest unit of sound that affects the meaning of a word is called a **phoneme.** Phonemes are surprisingly complicated bursts of acoustic energy. For example, a difference of less than one-fiftieth of a second in the onset or transition of a frequency of sound is enough for adults to discriminate the distinctive phonemes */p/, /b/,* and */t/* in the sounds *pa, ba,* and *ta.* (Linguists use slashes to identify the phonemes of a language.) Are infants able to hear the differences? Indeed they are. In fact, before six months of age, babies distinguish all the important sounds in any of the hundreds of languages spoken around the world (Werker & Desjardins, 1995).

From these findings, some who study language acquisition argue that babies are born with a "speech module," an innate capacity to detect and process the subtle and complicated sounds that make up human language (Fodor, 1983). The complexity of language acquisition, according to this view, requires a specialized ability because the cognitive skills of infants and young children are so limited. An alternative view is that phoneme discrimination hinges on broader, more general auditory capacities, capacities not limited to processing speech sounds or even necessarily unique to humans but that infants are able to exploit quite early in development.

NATURE & NURTURE

What evidence exists for either of these positions? Certain research findings contribute to the view that speech perception involves special language-oriented mechanisms. For example, an extremely complex relationship exists between the acoustic properties of sounds that are perceived to be the same phoneme. The */b/* phoneme in the words *beak* and *book* are quite different acoustically,

phoneme Smallest unit of sound that changes the meanings of words.

Figure 6.12

Categorical Perception in Adults and Infants

As can be seen in (A), an adult typically hears /ba/ when voice onset time falls on one side of a critical juncture, but /pa/ when it falls on the other side. Using habituation techniques, infants perceive these differences as well. Four-month-olds repeatedly heard a sound with the same voice onset time over a period of several minutes and then heard a change in that sound. As can be seen in (B), when the twenty-millisecond change crossed the critical juncture point, infants showed a significant increase in sucking rate. However, when the twenty-millisecond change occurred at a noncritical juncture point, the infants did not show a significant change in sucking rate. One-month-olds show a similar pattern of responding.

Sources: (A) From Aslin, R. N., & Pisoni, D. B. (1980). Some developmental processes in speech perception. In G. H. Yeni-Komshian, J. F. Kavanagh, & C. A. Ferguson (Eds.). *Child Phonology*, Vol. 2: Perception pp. 67–96. New York: Academic Press. Reprinted by permission. (B) Eimas, P. D., Siqueland, E. R., Jusczyk, P., & Vigorito, J. (1971). Speech perception in infants. *Science*, *171*, 303–306.

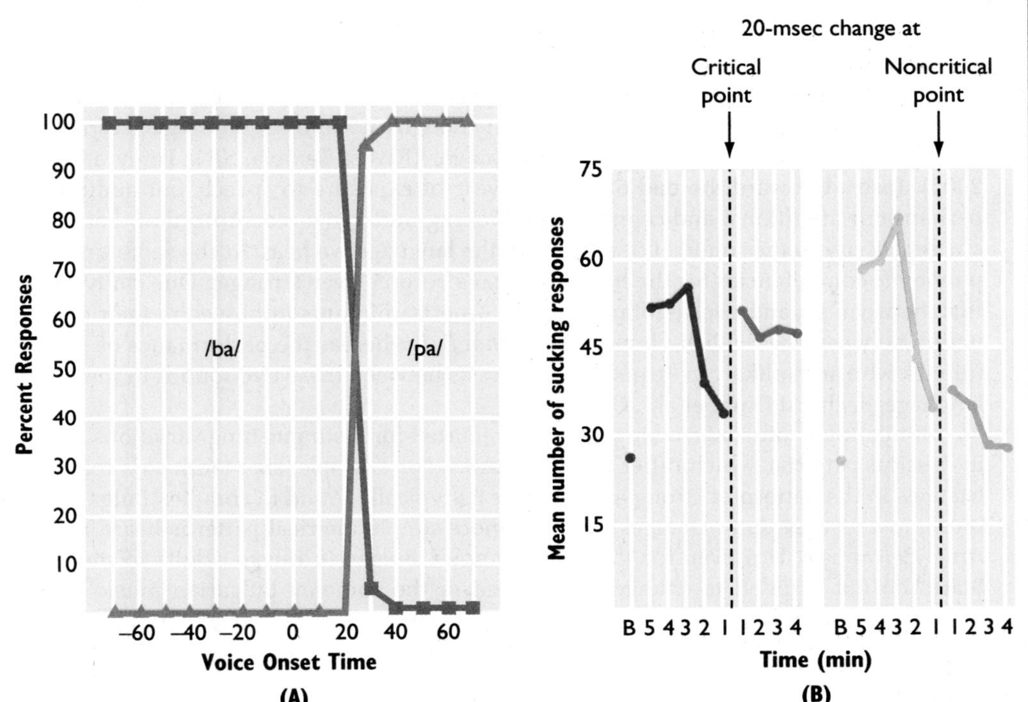

although we treat the sounds as equivalent. Researchers argue that the absence of a simple set of rules for signaling the phoneme */b/* in these two words makes the presence of a special mechanism for speech perception highly likely (Kuhl, 1987).

Categorical perception, the classification of sounds as the same even when they differ on some continuous physical dimension except when on opposite sides of a critical juncture, has also been used in support of a special mechanism for speech perception. For example, the English consonants */b/* and */p/* in the sounds *ba* and *pa* differ only in voice onset time (VOT), the period during which the vocal chords begin to vibrate relative to the release of air by the vocal apparatus. Small changes in VOT are typically not heard as more or less like *ba* or *pa*. Instead, English speakers hear only *ba* as long as VOT continues to fall on one side of the categorical boundary and only *pa* when it falls on the other side. But if the difference in VOT crosses a critical point, the phoneme boundary, the two sounds are readily distinguishable (see Figure 6.12). Infants as young as one month already demonstrate categorical perception for many different speech sounds (Saffran et al., 2006).

categorical perception Inability to distinguish among sounds that vary on some basic physical dimension except when those sounds lie at opposite sides of a critical juncture point on that dimension.

Many researchers, however, remain uncertain about whether babies are born with a special sensory mode for speech (Saffran et al., 2006). For one thing, categorical perception can be observed with some sounds other than those found in speech. For another, monkeys, and even chinchillas and other nonprimates, distinguish speech sounds categorically (Trehub & Hannon, 2006), a finding that further argues against a specialized innate human ability to process phonemes.

Auditory and Visual Perceptual Narrowing

Remarkably, young infants are able to detect phonemes and vowel sounds from a variety of languages. However, by six to twelve months of age, infants show a decline in the ability to distinguish basic sounds that are not heard within their native language (Saffran et al., 2006; Werker & Tees, 2005). For example, in one study, six- to eight-month-olds reared in an English-speaking environment could readily discriminate among phonemes used only in Hindi, whereas eleven- to thirteen-month-olds had more difficulty with this task (Werker & Lalonde, 1988). Adults can regain such lost discriminations only with considerable practice or under highly restricted listening conditions (Werker, 1989). Thus, it does not appear that we completely lose the capacity to make these distinctions; research with eleven-month-olds suggests that electrophysiological activity in the brain still reveals differentiation of non-native contrasts even though the infants no longer respond differently to the sounds in terms of their behavior (Rivera-Gaxiola, Silva-Pereyra, & Kuhl, 2005). Instead, toward the end of the first year of exposure to speech, our auditory and perhaps our attentional and cognitive functioning undergo a reorganization that reduces our sensitivity to the sounds not utilized in the language we hear. At the same time, early phonemic competencies for the native language become even stronger. One study showed that, between six and twelve months of age, American infants improved in their discrimination between the English phonemes /ra/ and /la/, whereas the performance of Japanese infants, who are unlikely to hear strong contrasts between these two sounds in their native language, declined (Kuhl et al., 2006).

SOCIOCULTURAL INFLUENCE

Similar perceptual narrowing has been reported for distinguishing variations in meter in musical patterns, which differ across cultures. For example, six-month-olds respond to changes in the pattern of strong and weak beats typically found in complex Bulgarian folk music just as they do to changes found in more simple metrical patterns heard in North American music. However, for the more complex Bulgarian music, adults in the United States do not respond to changes introduced in the complex Bulgarian music whereas adults in Bulgaria continue to do so (Hannon & Trehub, 2005). Moreover, this kind of developmental progression is found in visual processing as is evident from research on face perception (Pascalis & Kelly, 2009; Scott, Pascalis, & Nelson, 2007). For example, after seeing a single monkey face over a number of trials, infants at six months of age exhibit a preference for a novel monkey face when paired with the familiarized monkey face. However, by nine months of age, they no longer discriminate the familiar from the unfamiliar monkey faces. In contrast, after being familiarized to a human face, both six- and nine-month-olds discriminate the novel and familiar faces (Pascalis, de Haan, & Nelson, 2002; see Figure 6.13). These findings suggest that the visual perceptual processing of nine-month-olds has become more finely tuned to relevant (human faces) compared with irrelevant (monkey faces) stimuli. Nevertheless, if given the opportunity between six and nine months of age to repeatedly see faces of various monkeys in a picture book, babies, when tested at nine months of age, do display novelty preferences for monkey faces, suggesting that they have maintained the ability to discriminate these faces through experience (Pascalis et al., 2005).

NATURE & NURTURE

Similar findings have been reported for the perception of faces of different ethnic groups (Kelly et al., 2007). At three months of age, infants readily distinguish the faces of previously seen individuals from new faces, regardless of their racial or ethnic background. However, around six to nine months age, they begin to exhibit perceptual narrowing, showing novelty preferences for faces of individuals from only the ethnic group with which they are familiar. Combined, these results suggest that within the first year of life infants fine-tune both their auditory and visual systems to relevant information that most frequently occurs within their day-to-day experiences. As a result, they become better at discriminating sounds and faces that they hear or see often but may become poorer at discriminating sounds and faces that they hear or see less often.

SOCIOCULTURAL INFLUENCE

Figure 6.13
Discriminating Human and Monkey Faces
Infants six months of age readily discriminate and prefer looking at the face of a different human from the face of a human they have already seen; they also prefer looking at the face of a different monkey from the face of a monkey they have already seen. However, by about nine months of age, perceptual discrimination has apparently narrowed so that, unless they have had extended experience with monkey faces, infants do not typically respond as much to a change in a monkey face as to a change in a human face. The same appears to be true for adults; they show a clear preference for looking at a novel human face but do not look significantly more at a novel monkey face than at the face of a monkey that they have just seen.
Source: From "Discriminating Human and Monkey Faces" by Pascalis, O., de Haan, M., & Nelson, C. A. (2002). *Science 296*, 1321–1323. Reprinted with permission from AAAS.

Smell, Taste, Touch, and Sensitivity to Pain

Developmental researchers have given far less attention to smell, taste, and the cutaneous senses—the receptor systems of the skin responsible for perceiving touch, pressure, pain, and temperature—than to vision or hearing. Each of these senses also functions shortly after birth and furnishes crucial adaptive and survival cues for the baby. Smell, for example, may be critical for determining what is edible and may also be involved in early attachment to the caregiver.

Smell Facial expressions, changes in rate of respiration and blood flow in the brain, and approach-avoidance activities involving head turning are just a few of the responses indicating that newborns detect odors. Do babies turn up their noses at the unpleasant smell of rotten eggs? Can they detect the food-related smells of fish, butter, banana, or vanilla? They most certainly can (Steiner, 1979). In fact, at three to four days of age, infants show a preference for the smell of human breast milk as opposed to formula milk, even when they have been bottle-fed from birth (Marlier & Schaal, 2005). Moreover, newborns become increasingly sensitive to many smells during the first few days of life (Marlier, Schaal, & Soussignan, 1998).

NATURE & NURTURE

Parent-infant recognition occurs by odor among many species of animals. Can human infants identify their caregivers this way as well? Again, the answer is yes. By five days of age, infants turned their heads longer in the direction of a breast pad that had been worn by the mother than to an unused one. By six days of age, infants also preferred a pad obtained from their own mother to one from an unfamiliar mother (MacFarlane, 1975). By the same token, can family members identify their infants on the basis of odor? Indeed, within the

Figure 6.14
Discriminating Tastes
Babies produce different facial expressions depending on what they taste.The first column shows the resting faces of three newborns. Column 2 shows the same babies after they received distilled water—their expressions show very little change. After sweet stimulation, the babies' facial expressions are more positive and relaxed, resembling a smile or licking of the upper lip, as shown in column 3. However, their mouths become more pursed after sour stimulation (column 4) and more arch-shaped after bitter stimulation (column 5).
Source: Steiner, J. E. (1979). Human facial expressions in response to taste and smell stimulation. In H. W. Reese & L. P. Lipsitt (Eds.), *Advances in child development and behavior* (Vol. 13). New York: Academic Press.

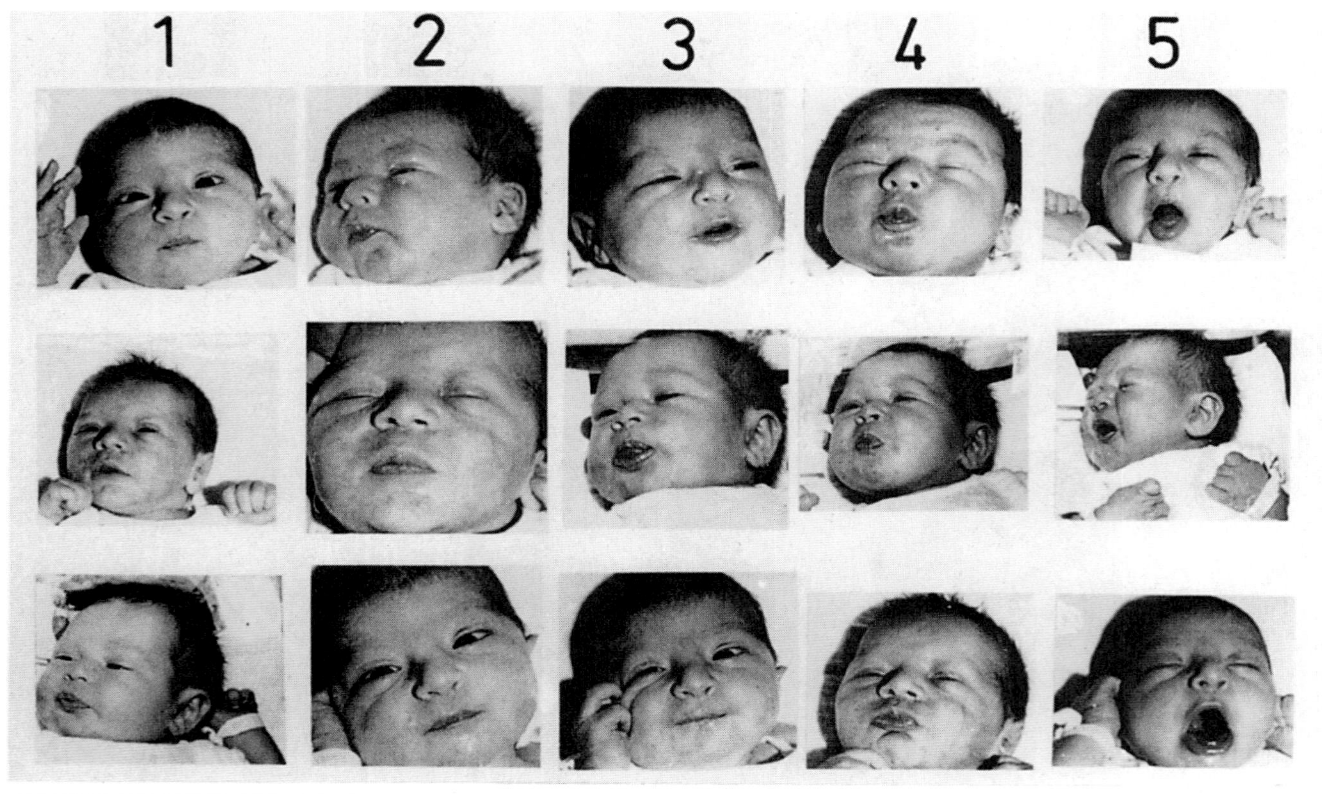

first few days of birth and after brief contact, not only mothers but also fathers, grandmothers, and aunts can recognize newborn kin by their smell alone. In other words, humans may inherit some family olfactory signature about which they are sensitive or learn very quickly (Porter, Balogh, & Makin, 1988).

Taste Receptors for the basic tastes of sweet, sour, salty, and bitter, located mostly on the tongue, develop well before birth; the fetus may already taste as it swallows amniotic fluid. Facial expressions and rate of sucking reveal more clearly that newborns can discriminate tastes (see Figure 6.14). Sweet stimuli, for example, elicit a relaxed facial expression resembling a smile; sour stimuli produce lip pursing or a puckered expression; and bitter stimuli elicit mouth opening as though expressing disgust (Steiner, 1979).

NATURE & NURTURE

Innate preferences for some tastes may help infants to meet nutritional needs and protect them from harmful or dangerous substances. And there may be a genetic basis for individual sensitivity to certain tastes, such as bitterness and sweetness (Mennella, Pepino, & Reed, 2005). Preferences can, however, be modified by early experience. For example, babies fed sweeter fluids in the first few months after birth ingest more sweet water at six months of age than babies not given this experience (Beauchamp & Moran, 1982). The desire for salt in a specific food may also be established early in infancy (Sullivan & Birch, 1990). Infants can detect flavors from their mother's milk as well—for example, garlic, alcohol, and vanilla—an ability that might familiarize them to the foods common to their family and culture (Mennella & Beauchamp, 1996). In fact, early exposure even to unpleasant tastes can make them more tolerable to infants. Julia Mennella and her colleagues exposed infants to Enfamil, a common milk-based formula, or Nutramigen, an unpleasant-tasting protein-based formula used to treat colic, starting at two weeks of age. Seven months later, all infants were given Enfamil, Nutramigen, and Alimentum, a novel unpleasant-tasting protein-based formula. Videotapes of each group of infants showed that those exposed early to the unpleasant-tasting formula were more accepting of both Nutramigen and Alimentum; they drank more and were more relaxed and happy as the formula was given to them (Mennella, Griffin, & Beauchamp, 2004).

Although learning appears to be important in the emergence of odor and taste preferences, we should emphasize one more thing. Until about two years of age, children will put just about anything into their mouths. Thus, among the most important things they must learn is what not to taste.

Touch and Temperature Infants are usually kissed, hugged, stroked, and maybe even sometimes poked or tickled. How much of this touching do they feel? And do they like to be touched? Skin contains more than 100 types of receptors sensitive to touch, pressure, temperature, and pain (Reisman, 1987). In fact, the skin is the body's largest organ, and its sensory receptors are the earliest to develop prenatally. As we saw in Chapter 4, even the fetus responds to touch. We have also already noted in Chapter 5 that tactile stimulation can elicit a variety of reflexes in the newborn. Clearly, then, even newborns can feel sensations on their skin.

Infants, for the most part, like to be touched. Touching, especially stroking as opposed to tickling or poking, often results in a smile or a coo and can settle crying (Peláez-Nogueras et al., 1997). And for infants born at risk because of low birth weight, massage therapy—the application of long strokes along the body and limbs—has been shown to accelerate weight gain (Field, 2001).

INTERACTION AMONG DOMAINS

As with smell, touch consists of an important sensory communication system that can facilitate social interactions between infant and caregiver (Hertenstein, 2002). Just as caregivers recognize their babies by odor shortly after birth, so can they recognize them by touch. After only sixty minutes of contact, mothers and fathers can identify their infants on the basis of stroking the backs of the babies' hands (Kaitz et al., 1994). This ability may be adaptive in encouraging caregivers to be responsive to their offspring.

A difficult problem for newborns, particularly premature infants, is regulation of body temperature. Cooling awakens babies, makes them more restless, and increases their oxygen consumption, responses that facilitate heat production. Because many newborns are unable to sweat or pant, exposure to high temperatures produces reddening of the skin, less activity, and more sleep, events that decrease heat production and assist heat loss (Harpin, Chellappah, & Rutter, 1983). When warm, babies also assume a sunbathing position, extending their extremities, perhaps a good clue for a caregiver who is trying to decide whether a baby is too warm (Reisman, 1987).

research applied to parenting | Reducing Sensitivity to Pain

Heel pricks, circumcision, immunizations, and other medical procedures involving newborns and young infants have come under increasing scrutiny in recent years because of concerns about the pain they may cause. Historically, newborns experiencing such invasive procedures were rarely given pain reduction medication and even major operations on very young infants were carried out with little or no effort to diminish pain. Why was this the case? The answer is that newborns were believed to have neither the neurological capacity to experience pain nor the ability to remember it (Kharasch, Saxe, & Zuckerman, 2003). An additional concern was the potential negative side effects of pain medication on an immature organism.

Today we know that brain centers involved in the detection of pain are well developed prenatally and that behavioral responses (such as crying and facial expressions) consistent with the discomfort associated with pain are readily displayed by preterm and full-term newborns as well as older infants. These facts should concern us given reports that preterm infants in neonatal intensive care units typically receive about sixteen painful events a day (Lago et al., 2009), and infants may even experience greater pain than older children and adults (Fitzgerald, 2005). Moreover, evidence has been gathered to suggest that exposure to painful circumstances early in infancy can lead to lasting changes in the endocrine and immune systems and to continued behavioral sensitivity to pain later in development (Kharasch et al., 2003; Porter, Grunau, & Anand, 1999). Medications may be an important part of efforts to manage pain, but what might parents and those professionals who work with infants additionally do to help manage pain?

NATURE & NURTURE

RISK | RESILIENCE

1. *Offer sucrose, some other sweetened liquid, or the opportunity to engage in nonnutritive sucking.* A number of research studies have demonstrated that offering sucrose, some other sweetened liquid, or even the opportunity to engage in nonnutritive sucking can be useful in reducing responses such as crying when carrying out some medical event that causes pain. Although the mechanisms by which sucrose, for example, works remain uncertain, some believe that it helps to release natural pain relievers in the brain that contribute to calming. Both premature and full-birth-weight infants benefit from this relatively simple procedure (Harrison, 2008; Lago et al., 2009).
2. *Holding, swaddling, or initiating kangaroo care before and during painful events can help* (Lago et al., 2009). These practices also may encourage calming and a more optimal state of quiet wakefulness. Not surprisingly, a mother's ability to sensitively read the infant's cues and to respond with appropriate affect can be important as well. Intrusive behaviors such as kissing repeatedly or attempting to dress the infant or other efforts to intervene while still distressed can increase the length or intensity of the infant's negative reactions (Din, Riddel, & Gordner, 2009).
3. *Nonintrusive visual and auditory stimulation—for example, exposure to some kinds of music—can be helpful, too.* This kind of experience probably promotes cognitive processing that serves as a distractor to attenuate the sense of pain (Anand et al., 2001; Lago et al., 2009).

Intermodal Perception

We have considered the development of seeing, hearing, and other senses in isolation from one another, but, of course, most objects and events bombard us with multiple sensory inputs. The sight of a cup provides information about how to shape the mouth to drink from it. The toddler who hears his mother's voice from another room expects to see her when he walks into that room. We often perceive these experiences as integrated and coordinated and draw perceptual inferences because of the typical relationships observed from multimodal stimulation. Sometimes, of course, we can be fooled by all these correlated experiences: a good ventriloquist really does make the dummy appear to be talking!

NATURE & NURTURE

How does the capacity to integrate several sensory inputs, referred to as **intermodal perception,** begin, and how important is it for development? One traditional view is that input received via the various senses is initially *unimodal*; that is, the senses function separately and independently. Only after repeated multimodal experiences, this argument runs, do babies come to recognize the correlations among various sensory inputs. Thus, intermodal perception involves, for example, learning that, when objects are shaken, some rattle and make a noise, but others do not; that material that feels soft can also look soft; and that a square-looking peg will not fit into a round-looking hole. According to this viewpoint, intermodal perception stems from *integration* or *enrichment* through the repeated association of sensations from two or more modalities. Alternatively, from a more Piagetian perspective, it is the outcome of constructing multisensory schemes from correlated sensory experiences (Lickliter & Bahrick, 2000).

But others have suggested that some intermodal perception is already possible at birth (Gibson, 1982; Gibson, 1979). According to this perspective, a primitive unity exists among the senses in early infancy, and with development and experience, **perceptual differentiation,** the ability to distinguish information coming through each particular sensory modality, occurs. A related aspect of this point of view is that

intermodal perception Coordination of sensory information to perceive or make inferences about the characteristics of an object.

perceptual differentiation Process postulated by Eleanor and James Gibson in which experience contributes to the ability to make increasingly finer perceptual discriminations and to distinguish stimulation arising from each sensory modality.

important sensory information is often *amodal*, that is, not tied to a particular sensory modality but shared across two or more of them. Examples of amodal characteristics of sensory input are *temporal synchrony*—that is, the correlated onset and offset of stimulation that can occur between two or more sensory modalities (such as hearing someone begin and stop speaking while simultaneously seeing their lips start and stop)—and tempo and rhythm, common components of both auditory and visual experience.

Some researchers believe that the ability to process amodal properties is especially important for early perceptual, cognitive, and social development. For example, Lorraine Bahrick, Robert Lickliter, and Ross Flom (2004) suggest that the intersensory redundancy associated with temporally synchronous perceptual cues attracts the infant's attention. As a consequence of this attentional bias, infants begin to learn about and remember correlated properties and qualities of objects and events, such as the voice that belongs to a particular parent, the bark that signifies the family's pet dog, or the verbal label for a particular color. Such learning likely begins at a very early age (Lewkowicz, 2010).

© Laura Dwight Photography

This toddler appears to be enjoying both the visual and tactual effects of playing with the water leaking from the flower pot. In fact, it would not be too surprising if she even began to taste it as well, although a caregiver might quickly discourage this behavior. Infants and young children experience events through multiple sensory modalities. At a very early age, they expect things to look, feel, taste, or sound in a particular way based on the information received from just one of these modalities.

Sight and Sound To determine whether infants link visual and auditory events, Elizabeth Spelke (1976) developed a simple procedure in which four-month-olds could look at either of two films shown side by side. At the same time, the infants could hear a soundtrack coming from a speaker located between the two viewing screens. The soundtrack matched events in one of the two films; for example, an unfamiliar woman engaged in a game of peekaboo or someone playing a percussion instrument. Would infants pay more attention to the film synchronized with the soundtrack? Spelke found this to be the case, at least when the percussion sounds could be heard.

Before four months of age, infants can also infer that a sound made by one object versus multiple objects hitting a surface should match up to visual arrays containing one object versus multiple objects (Bahrick, 2002). Five-month-olds even link sounds such as an auto or a train coming or going with concordant visual progressions of approaching and retreating movement (Pickens, 1994). Experience may have permitted learning about these relationships. However, other research suggests that newborns quickly master the association between a sound and a visible toy. After seeing a toy presented in several different locations and making a particular sound for brief periods of time, neonates displayed increased attention if the sound originated apart from the toy or if it accompanied a different toy (Morrongiello, Fenwick, & Chance, 1998). Thus, even newborns possess some kind of amodal process that guides and unifies sensory information from separate senses such as hearing and vision.

Intermodal perception in infants extends to social and linguistic information as well. For example, three-and-a-half-month-olds are likely to look at that parent, seated to one side, whose voice is coming from a speaker centered in front of the baby (Spelke & Owsley, 1979). By six months of age, babies hearing a strange male or female voice reciting a nursery rhyme look longer at a face of the same sex than at a face of the opposite sex (Walker-Andrews et al., 1991). In addition, babies are able to match the maturity of a face with its voice; they look more at the face of an adult or a child, depending on who is heard talking from a central speaker (Bahrick, Netto, & Hernandez-Reif, 1998). By two months of age, babies also recognize auditory-visual correspondence in people who are speaking, attending more to facial expressions articulating vowel sounds that match than to facial expressions that do not match what they hear (Patterson & Werker, 2003).

Intermodal cues can influence perception in some perhaps unexpected ways. Speech perception, for example, may be greatly affected by what a person sees. Harry McGurk and John MacDonald (1976) played videotapes of an adult uttering simple syllables such as *ba, ba.* Sometimes, however, the video picture was synchronized with another sound, such as *ga ga.* Three-year-olds through adults often reported hearing something quite different, for example, *da da* or another utterance. By two months of age, babies also recognize these kinds of auditory-visual correspondence, attending more to facial expressions articulating sounds that match than facial expressions that do not match what they hear (Patterson & Werker, 2003). Even newborns, although not yet producing the sounds, are more likely to show mouth movements that are similar to those they hear, for example, mouth opening to an *a* sound and, for an *m* sound, closing and then relaxing or moving lips back and forth together, another remarkable demonstration of just how effectively newborns may be tuned in to focus on important social and communicative resources in their environment (Chen, Striano, & Rakoczy, 2004).

Sight and Touch Even as newborns, babies who have just previously held an object by grasping it in their hand can recognize its shape by sight alone; they gaze at a different novel shape more than a shape that matches the one they had just been holding. However, they do not recognize that an object to which they have been habituated visually is the same as or different from the one they now are given the opportunity to hold. This finding suggests that there is not a global unity among these senses but rather that the information gathered for the property of shape by these two senses differs early in development (Sann & Streri, 2007). Coordination of some visual and tactile information provided by the mouth also exists by a month of age. In one experiment, one-month-olds showed greater visual attention to a hard, rigid object or a soft, deformable object, depending on which they had been given time to suck (Gibson & Walker, 1984). Moreover, infants soon begin to make cognitive inferences based on intermodal perception. For example, by five months of age, babies seem to recognize that a ball that can be squeezed, but not a hard ball, can go through a visible tube that is smaller than the ball's circumference (Schweinle & Wilcox, 2004).

For Your Review and Reflection

- What evidence exists to show that the fetus can detect vibroacoustic stimulation? What are potential benefits to the fetus if given extra external auditory stimulation? What are potential disadvantages from such extra stimulation?
- What are the basic auditory capacities of the infant? How does sound localization develop?
- What sound patterns do infants prefer to listen to?
- What arguments exist for or against the view that infants possess an innate capacity to detect phonemes? What is categorical perception?
- What is perceptual narrowing? When does it begin to play a role in auditory and visual perception? What are some of the sociocultural implications of perceptual narrowing?
- Can newborns and very young infants discriminate smells, tastes, touch, and temperature differences? Can they feel pain? What can parents do to help infants experiencing a painful event?
- How does intermodal perception develop? What evidence exists to show that infants recognize the correlation between visual and auditory information as well as visual and tactile cues?
- What are examples of how perceptual development interacts with other domains of development?
- Consider infants who might have been reared in an institutional setting. Given your knowledge of what infants can sense and perceive, why might such infants be at a serious disadvantage compared with those reared in a traditional family setting?

Perceptual Development Throughout Childhood

As we have already noted, research on sensory and perceptual development in preschoolers and older children has been carried out far less frequently than in neonates and infants. Nonetheless, researchers do find evidence of improved sensory processing, for example, auditory discriminations of different frequencies of sound and visual sensitivity to small changes in motion, during childhood (Armstrong, Maurer, & Lewis, 2009). Perceptual development also becomes more difficult to investigate without considering at the same time the child's improving attentional, linguistic, and cognitive skills. These latter factors may contribute to the observation that perceptual skills become more focused, organized, and confined to the meaningful and important features of the environment; in other words, perception becomes increasingly efficient with development.

INTERACTION AMONG DOMAINS

Perceptual Learning

Eleanor Gibson's influential theory of perceptual learning (1969, 1982, 1988) emphasizes three changes with age: increasing specificity in perception, improved attention, and more economical and efficient acquisition of perceptual information. Much of the child's first year is spent learning the sensory properties of objects, the spatial layout of her world, and the perceptual repercussions of her actions. But perceptual learning continues well after that. For example, children acquire new kinds of visual discriminations when they learn to read. They must begin to pay attention to consistencies and variations in letters and text.

To study perceptual learning, Eleanor Gibson and her colleagues (Gibson et al., 1962) created sets of letterlike figures, such as those shown in Figure 6.15. One member of each set was designated a standard, but each set included variations of that standard. A straight line, for example, might be redrawn as a curved line, the standard rotated or reversed, a break introduced in a continuous line, or the line's perspective changed by tipping or elongating some aspect of the figure. Children four through eight years of age were shown a stack of each set of figures and asked to pick out only those identical to the standard.

Children made many more errors for some kinds of variations than for others. Children of all ages seldom confused the standard with versions that contained breaks, perhaps because these features are important for identifying objects in the environment, as well as letters of the alphabet. However, older children did substantially better than younger children in discriminating rotations, reversals, and line-curve transformations, presumably because children who are learning to read must begin to distinguish such variations. Finally, children of all ages found it difficult to discriminate changes in perspective from the standard, a variation that can and normally should be ignored for identifying both physical objects and letters of the alphabet.

Eleanor Gibson believed the age-related improvements in performance on this activity did not come about by reinforcing children to make the discriminations. In fact, when asked to classify the letterlike forms over a series of trials, children showed steady improvement in sorting, without any feedback about their accuracy. Gibson argued that, through repeated exposure to and inspection of letters of the alphabet, children were afforded the opportunity to recognize certain critical features distinguishing such figures, an example of the powerful influence of implicit learning discussed earlier.

Experience and Perceptual Development

NATURE & NURTURE

How do experience and inborn sensory capacities interact to determine perception? Throughout the history of psychology, this has been an important question, and it continues to be so as medical and technical advances provide opportunities to compensate for some kinds of sensory disabilities. For example, blind children can perceive the existence of distant objects, presumably from changes in auditory cues they receive while moving about

Figure 6.15
Sensitivity to Perceptual Differences
Column 1 gives different letterlike forms used as standards in a sorting task. Columns 2 through 6 display various transformations of each standard. Four- to eight-year-olds, when shown a stack of the figures and asked to select only those identical to the standard, commit relatively few errors on variations that involve a break in the figure, presumably because the distinction is important for identifying many objects, as well as alphabetic symbols. With increasing age, errors involving rotation, reversal, and line/curve variations decrease substantially because, according to Eleanor Gibson, children who are beginning to learn to read must pay attention to these features of the stimuli. Errors involving perspective remain high at all ages, perhaps because the transformation is not important for identifying either objects or letters of the alphabet.
Source: Adapted from Pick, 1965.

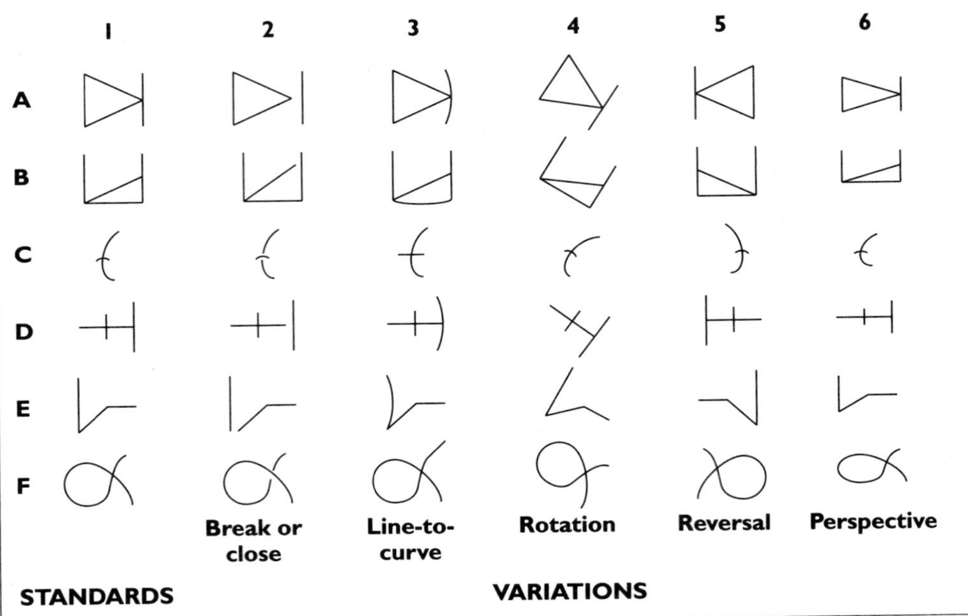

(Ashmead, Hill, & Talor, 1989). As a consequence, blind children may now be fitted with sonic devices to help them hear echoes to signal the direction, distance, and other qualities of objects.

The effects of these efforts with blind children are still to be demonstrated, but we can be sure of one thing from research discussed earlier in this chapter that showed evidence for sensitive periods in the development of vision: experience is extremely important for maintaining many perceptual capacities. Its important role in face perception has been demonstrated by research involving institutionalized children (Moulson et al., 2009). Such children are assumed to have relatively less opportunity to see adult faces because of the high ratio of children to caregivers compared with children reared in a traditional family setting. Perhaps just as importantly, their experiences are likely to be qualitatively different in that high turnover in caregivers provides less opportunity to have consistent exposure to familiar adults. Children from two-and-a-half to three-and-a-half years of age who continue to reside in an institutionalized setting show significantly reduced patterns of cortical ERP responses to pictures of faces compared with children who have never been institutionalized. On the other hand, foster care of previously institutionalized children can help to remediate this limitation.

RISK | RESILIENCE

Perceptual experience continues to be critical for modifying and enhancing the perceptual discrimination of faces throughout childhood and adolescence. For example, adults are able to recognize and distinguish countless numbers of faces that differ on various features such as the size of eyes and the spatial relationships between such features such as distance between the eyes. This ability continues to improve throughout childhood and early adolescence perhaps due to both improved visual skills and greater responsiveness in regions of the brain activated by seeing faces (Aylward et al., 2005; Johnson, Grossmann, & Kadosh, 2009). For example, the appearance of specific features such as the eyes or the mouth are recognized by children four years of age nearly as well as adults, but recognizing small differences in the spacing between these features continues to improve through early adolescence (Mondloch, Maurer, & Ahola, 2006; Mondloch & Thomson, 2008).

Experience also helps to explain cross-cultural differences in perception. Environments around the world differ in their degree of "carpenteredness" (Segall, Campbell, & Herskovits, 1966). In most urban societies, houses are constructed according to rectilinear principles, which involve perpendicular and right-angle dimensions. Even the layouts of roads and other artifacts of the environment often follow these principles. In other environments, such as in Oceanic and many African cultures, walls and roofs may be curved, and straight lines and angular intersections may be few.

INTERACTION AMONG DOMAINS

SOCIOCULTURAL INFLUENCE

In one study, field workers administered several optical illusions, such as the Müller-Lyer and horizontal-vertical illusions, whose effects depend on straight lines that intersect, to samples of children and adults in Africa, the Philippines, and the United States (Segall et al., 1966). The researchers theorized that individuals living in a carpentered environment, who often see intersecting rectangular contours, would be more susceptible to these illusions than people living in noncarpentered environments. In fact, the results conformed to their prediction. In a related set of findings, children and adults in cultures with minimal formal education, little experience with pictures, or artworks that incorporate few depth cues were unlikely to perceive pictures or photos in three dimensions (Pick, 1987). Thus, the ways in which children and adults interpret their sensory environment can be greatly affected by cultural opportunities, a finding that fits well with the conclusion that perception is influenced by experience.

For Your Review and Reflection

- What are the basic elements of Gibson's perceptual learning theory?
- How does experience influence perceptual development?
- What are some of the important developmental changes in face perception? Do you think research on the development of face perception should be an important topic to examine? If so, why?
- How might cross-cultural factors influence perceptual development?

© Betty Press

These children in the Sudan receive their education in front of a round schoolhouse. Does a child who grows up in a culture in which linear perspective is uncommon, as in many parts of Africa and island regions in the Pacific Ocean, perceive things differently than a child who grows up in an environment filled with straight lines, right angles, and many opportunities to see distances based on orderly linear cues?

chapter recap

Summary of Developmental Themes

Nature & Nurture

How do nature and nurture interact in learning and perceptual development?

We cannot help but be impressed by the remarkably adaptive resources immediately available to infants for gaining knowledge of their environment. The basic mechanisms of learning—habituation, classical and operant conditioning, and perhaps even observational learning—are ready to influence behavior at or shortly after birth. A newborn's sense organs are sufficiently developed to provide rudimentary capacities to see, hear, feel, taste, and smell, and they often function even before birth. We have also seen, however, that sensory and perceptual capacities change substantially as a result of experiential fine-tuning and perceptual narrowing. Thus, the environment plays an early and powerful role in determining which capacities are acquired and maintained.

Sociocultural Influence

How does the sociocultural context influence learning and perceptual development?

Experiences the culture provides—the behaviors that are reinforced and punished and opportunities to observe others engaged in work, play, and social interactions—have substantial effects on what a child learns. Although formal instruction and education are important in many kinds of learning, in all cultures the actions of caregivers and other models provide plentiful opportunities for children to gain knowledge of what is socially accepted and expected. Specific cultural demands, such as beginning to learn to discriminate letters; the opportunity to hear the sounds in a language and to view human faces, both members of one's own ethnic group as well as other ethnic groups; and even the physical layout of the environment, such as whether it is carpentered or not, can have considerable bearing on perceptual development.

Interaction Among Domains

How do learning and perceptual development interact with other domains of development?

Learning plays a substantial role in almost every aspect of development. The child acquires social skills, acceptable ways to express thoughts and feeling, techniques to achieve academic and occupational success, and numerous other behaviors through basic learning mechanisms. Such learning can provide the foundation for many aspects of cognitive development and the development of emotional relationships. Additionally, gains in perception are substantially influenced by physiological and neural advances. Because of perceptual narrowing, our responsiveness to others may be altered. Rapidly improving intellectual and motor skills introduce demands for making new perceptual discriminations (such as perceiving gaps or learning to read) that, when mastered, set the stage for further progress in cognitive, social, and other domains.

Risk | Resilience

What factors promote risk or resilience in learning and perceptual development?

Children need the opportunity to learn from others and to experience reinforcement from parents, teachers, and others who encourages and promotes the acquisition of effective social and cognitive skills. The extent to which the child is rewarded or punished for various behaviors as well as observes acceptable behaviors in others sets the stage for gaining resilience or for engaging in behaviors that potentially put him or her at risk. With respect to perceptual development, most children are born equipped to process the rich sensory experiences surrounding them. Of particular concern here is that the infant receive appropriate sensory and other environmental experiences during the time that neuronal differentiation is taking place in sensory regions of the cortex. For example, infants not treated for cataracts may experience permanent loss of vision later in development, and children being reared in institutional settings may not acquire important face perception skills.

Chapter Review

Basic Learning Processes in Infancy and Childhood

What are the basic principles of habituation, classical conditioning, and operant conditioning? What does recovery from habituation tell us about the habituation process?

Habituation refers to the gradual decline in responding as a result of repeated exposure to an event, a basic form of learning that helps in orienting to new information in the environment. Increased attention to new information following habituation indicates *recovery from habituation (dishabituation)*. This response suggests that infants are able to distinguish between familiar and new events. Classical conditioning involves the pairing of a neutral stimulus with one that naturally elicits a response. The neutral stimulus then begins to elicit the response as well. Operant conditioning involves the delivery or removal of a reinforcing or punishing stimulus so that behaviors preceding the stimulus increase or decrease.

What are an unconditioned stimulus, an unconditioned response, a conditioned stimulus, and a conditioned response?

The *unconditioned stimulus (UCS)* is the stimulus that elicits a reflexlike response. No training is required to obtain it. The *unconditioned response (UCR)* is the reaction that results from the presentation of the UCS. The *conditioned stimulus (CS)* is a neutral stimulus that begins to elicit a response similar to the UCS with which it has been paired. The *conditioned response (CR)* is the resulting learned response to the CS.

How do positive reinforcement, negative reinforcement, negative punishment, and positive punishment affect behavior?

Reinforcement increases the future likelihood of a behavior through the occurrence of a reward (*positive reinforcement*) or the removal of an aversive stimulus (*negative reinforcement*).

Punishment results in the decrease of a future behavior through the removal of a desired stimulus (*negative punishment*) or the application of an aversive stimulus (*positive punishment*).

Why is observational learning an important component of learning theory? What evidence exists for imitation in early infancy? What is the significance of deferred imitation?

Imitation is often the means by which infants and children learn the social and cultural behaviors that are important to their community. Research shows that newborns and young infants imitate behaviors such as tongue protrusion, mouth opening, and facial expressions of emotion. *Deferred imitation* refers to the infant's ability to reproduce a model's behavior at a later time. Its presence suggests a capacity for symbolic thinking.

What other forms of learning do children display?

Implicit learning refers to knowledge acquisition that takes place as a result of unintentionally abstracting patterns and rules that often underlie the structure of physical, linguistic, and social information. One form of implicit learning, statistical learning, arises from the repeated, regular, and predictable co-occurrences or ordering of experiences or events.

Sensory and Perceptual Capacities

What is the difference between sensation and perception?

Sensation refers to the receipt of information by the sensory receptors (for example, eyes and ears) and the brain. *Perception* refers to the organization and interpretation of that information.

How are attention and other behavioral and physiological measures used to investigate infant sensory and perceptual capacities?

Researchers rely on measures of *attention*, habituation and recovery from habituation, and learning, as well as measures of heart rate and neurological activity in the brain, to study infant sensory and perceptual capacities.

What limitations exist in infant visual accommodation, saccadic eye movements, smooth visual pursuit, vergence, acuity, and other visuomotor capacities? How quickly do these achieve adultlike ability?

The infant's *visual accommodation* response, the ability to focus at different distances, is initially limited but improves by three months of age. *Saccades*, rapid eye movements to inspect objects, are initially slow and cover small distances. Improvements are seen in the first three to four months and throughout childhood. *Smooth visual pursuit*, maintaining fixation on a moving target, is displayed for only brief periods by newborns but becomes adultlike by six to eight months. *Vergence*, the ability of the eyes to rotate in opposite directions, is irregular prior to two months. *Visual acuity*, a measure of how well infants can see, improves rapidly in the first six months.

What kinds of visual problems are found among infants? Why is the correction of these problems important in infancy or early childhood?

Among the problems infants may display are cataracts, the clouding of the lens, and amblyopia, the failure of vision to develop in one eye. Early treatment is important because visual input may influence the kinds of neural connections that are made. If treatment is delayed, visual capacities may be permanently lost.

What is the infant's ability to perceive color?

Color vision is limited prior to the age of three months. Initially infants detect primarily red hues but see the full range of colors in successive weeks.

How early do infants see patterns and forms in the visual world? What is the externality effect?

Newborns do not examine visual patterns systematically and are often attracted to external features that show high contrast (the *externality effect*) or movement. Within a few months, they engage in more systematic exploration of visual arrays.

How early do infants perceive objects in their world? What kinds of cues do they use?

Infants perceive objects as entities by at least three months of age but perhaps well before that. Their perception of the unity and coherence of objects is enhanced by motion cues and prior experience with the stimuli.

What is the developmental course of infant perception of faces? When can an infant distinguish the faces of caregivers from the faces of others?

Some research suggests that a preference for facelike forms shows up as early as the newborn period. Others propose that this preference reflects a more general bias to attend to visual arrays that are broader at the top than at the bottom. Nevertheless, infants show a clear preference for faces over other complex forms by two months of age. Infants may also be able to distinguish the caregiver's face a few days after birth, and this ability is likely associated with recognizing certain features in the face. Unique brain wave patterns associated with looking at faces are exhibited early in infancy.

What is meant by the perception of biological motion?

In some experiments, the only visual information provided is points of light attached to the joints of a moving organism. Infants seem to distinguish these stimuli as different and unique as compared with random motions of points of light.

How early do infants perceive depth? What kinds of cues do infants use to perceive depth? What evidence exists to indicate that depth perception does not always produce appropriate responses to the dangers associated with depth?

Depth information is provided to infants by *kinetic cues*, the differential flow of optic information that derives from self-induced movement or as a result of movement among arrays in the visual field. Depth perception is also provided by *stereopsis*, fusing the two images delivered by each eye into a single image. In addition, at about five to seven months of age, infants begin to process depth provided by pictorial cues. Infants also show recognition of depth cues when they are placed on an apparatus called the *visual cliff*. However, infants who are not yet crawling may not respond to the visual cliff as something to avoid. And although they may respond satisfactorily to depth when initiating one kind of movement (e.g., reaching for something), they may not do so when engaged in another kind of movement (e.g., crawling).

Why do developmental psychologists no longer believe the infant's visual world is simply a "blooming, buzzing confusion"?

Young infants do not respond to all visual stimuli with equal likelihood right from birth. The fact that they have preferences for some stimuli over others suggests that they are not bombarded with an array of visual information. In addition, perceptual development proceeds in an organized manner. For example, young infants primarily tend to scan only the exteriors of stimuli and begin to explore the interiors of stimuli more fully as they mature.

Is the fetus able to respond to sound?
The ability to process vibroacoustic stimulation begins prenatally during the third trimester of pregnancy, and very young infants can remember features of sounds that have been presented to them as fetuses. These observations have led some parents to stimulate the fetus with extra vibroacoustic experiences such as music. No research has demonstrated long-term benefits of such exposure to the developing child, and some believe that potentially negative consequences can occur under some circumstances.

What are the basic auditory capacities of the infant? How does sound localization develop?
Very young infants can detect different frequencies and intensities of sound and become increasingly responsive to variations in sound by six months of age. Their *sound localization* skills, the ability to determine where a sound is coming from, start out as reflexive but, by four months of age, become more deliberate and precise.

What sound patterns do infants prefer to listen to?
Infants show a preference for listening to human speech and to songs delivered in a child-oriented style. They also prefer musical patterns that conform to acceptable phrasing.

What arguments exist for or against the view that infants possess an innate capacity to detect speech and phonemes? What evidence is sometimes used to claim that infants use special auditory mechanisms to process human speech?
Young infants prefer listening to human speech more than other complex sounds, and greater neural activity in some regions of the brain can already be recorded when hearing speech. Young infants can also detect *phonemes*, the basic unit of sound used to differentiate the meaning of words in languages. Infants display *categorical perception;* they respond categorically to different phonemes. This finding is sometimes used to claim that infants process human speech with special auditory mechanisms. However, categorical perception for certain kinds of sounds can also be found in nonhumans as well.

What is perceptual narrowing? Why is it important?
Perceptual narrowing refers to the finding that, in contrast to younger infants, those about nine months of age become less responsive to phonemes they do not hear in their own language and to visual stimuli (such as faces of monkeys) with which they do not have much experience. Perceptual narrowing can also be seen in infants who have little opportunity to see faces of individuals from a different ethnic background. These findings, a kind of perceptual learning, suggest that infants fine-tune their auditory and visual systems to relevant information within their environment.

Can newborns and very young infants discriminate smells, tastes, touch, and temperature differences? Can they feel pain? What can parents do to help infants when experiencing a painful event?
Newborns and young infants are responsive to different smells, including the smell of their caregivers. They can discriminate tastes such as sweet, sour, and bitter. Newborns respond to tactile stimulation and changes in temperature, and show through their behavioral responses that they feel pain. By providing sweetened liquids or even the opportunity to suck; swaddling, holding, or kangaroo care; or mild auditory and visual stimulation that serves as a distracter, infants' negative responses to brief painful events can be reduced.

How does intermodal perception develop?
Intermodal perception is the ability to integrate information arising from more than one sensory modality. Some believe that this ability is acquired rapidly as a result of experiencing the correlations between sensory information arising from different modalities. Alternatively, another current position holds that intermodal perception is possible at birth and that *perceptual differentiation,* the ability to identify information coming from specific senses, arises with experience. Others propose that amodal properties of stimulation, such as temporal synchrony, may be highly salient to even very young infants and assist in their acquiring an understanding of the correlations that exist among the various sensory properties of objects and events.

What evidence exists to show that infants recognize the correlation between visual and auditory information as well as visual and tactile cues?
Infants will look at film sequences that correspond in tempo to sound tracks and at the face of the caregiver whose voice they hear on a speaker, indicating a recognition that certain sights go with particular sounds. Infants also show visual recognition of items they had previously put in their mouths, showing awareness of the correlation between visual and tactile cues.

Perceptual Development Throughout Childhood

What are the basic elements of Gibson's perceptual learning theory?
Gibson's theory emphasizes increasing specificity in perception, improved attention, and more efficient acquisition of perceptual information with experience. Reinforcement is not necessary for this form of learning to take place.

What role does experience play in the development of face perception? What aspects of face perception change during childhood?
Children reared in institutions have different patterns of brain responses than children who have been reared in traditional family settings when seeing faces. Although specific features of faces are well-recognized by children, recognizing changes in the spatial relations of those features continues to improve throughout childhood and early adolescence.

How might cross-cultural factors influence perceptual development?
Environments that are highly "carpentered" may be responsible for children's being more susceptible to visual illusions such as the Müller-Lyer and horizontal-vertical illusions. Also, children who live in cultures that do not emphasize formal education have difficulty perceiving depth cues in pictures and photographs.

Key Terms and Concepts

attention (p. 207)
categorical perception (p. 225)
conditioned response (CR) (p. 200)
conditioned stimulus (CS) (p. 200)
deferred imitation (p. 203)
externality effect (p. 213)
habituation (p. 200)
implicit learning (p. 205)
intermodal perception (p. 230)
kinetic cues (p. 217)
negative punishment (p. 201)
negative reinforcement (p. 201)
perception (p. 206)
perceptual differentiation (p. 230)
phoneme (p. 224)
positive punishment (p. 201)
positive reinforcement (p. 201)
recovery from habituation (dishabituation) (p. 200)
saccades (p. 210)
sensation (p. 206)
smooth visual pursuit (p. 210)
sound localization (p. 222)
stereopsis (p. 217)
unconditioned response (UCR) (p. 200)
unconditioned stimulus (UCS) (p. 200)
vergence (p. 210)
visual accommodation (p. 209)
visual acuity (p. 210)
visual cliff (p. 217)

Media Resources

Access an integrated eBook and chapter-specific interactive learning tools, including flashcards, quizzes, videos, and more, in your Developmental Psychology CourseMate, accessed through CengageBrain.com.

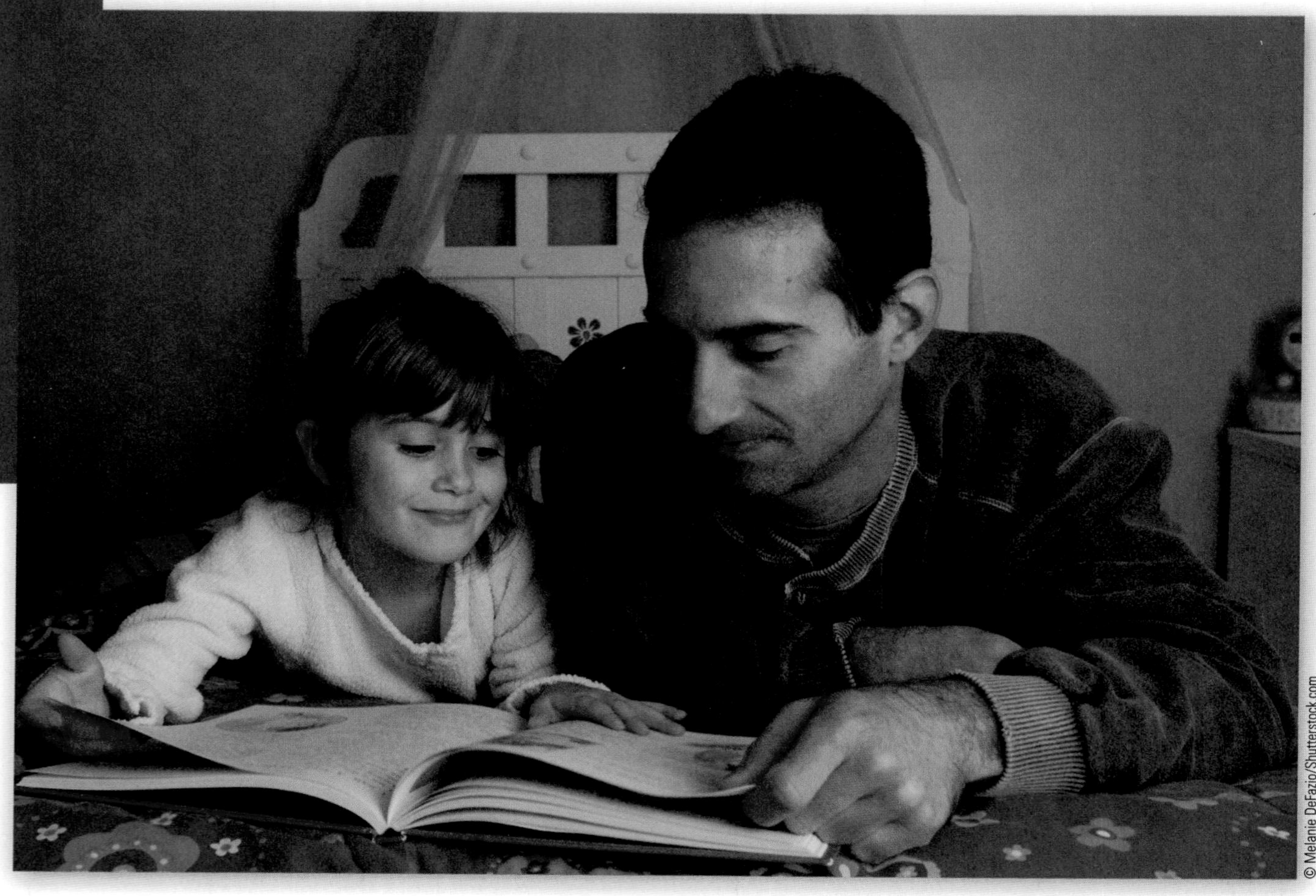
© Melanie DeFazio/Shutterstock.com

CHAPTER OUTLINE

[chapter 7]

Language

KEY THEMES IN LANGUAGE

- **NATURE & NURTURE** How do nature and nurture interact in the process of language development?
- **SOCIOCULTURAL INFLUENCE** How does the sociocultural context influence language development?
- **CONTINUITY | DISCONTINUITY** Is language development continuous or discontinuous?
- **INTERACTION AMONG DOMAINS** How does language development interact with development in other domains?
- **RISK | RESILIENCE** What factors promote risk or resilience in the process of language development?

The family reunion had been scheduled for months, and Tanya was looking forward to showing off one-year-old Chad. She was especially eager to compare notes with her cousin who also had a baby at just about the same time last year. As Tanya pulled into the driveway of her mother's home, she could see her cousin moving toward her, baby Lina in her arms. As mother and daughter got closer, Lina pointed at Chad seated in the back of the car and squealed, "Baby! Mama! Baby!" Tanya smiled and then, to her surprise, heard Chad for the first time make his own word, "Mama!" <<

Aside from walking, there are few accomplishments that parents focus on more than their baby's first use of language. The child's first words are typically recorded in the baby book with great excitement and are captured as quickly as possible with a camcorder. E-mails or text messages documenting the event fly to family and friends. Aside from denoting the infant's emerging and expected maturity, language means that the infant now has a way to participate in human interactions in a dramatically new way. He can express what he wants or needs with methods other than crying or making a facial expression. Language truly marks a significant turning point in the child's life.

There are several features of language development that are worth noting right from the outset. First, as mentioned in Chapter 6, "Basic Learning and Perception," children master the essential elements of language in a very short period of time and with seemingly little effort. Between infancy and age five, most children become highly proficient listeners and speakers, a marvel considering the overwhelming abundance of sounds, vocabulary words, grammatical rules, and social conventions that go into producing mature adult-sounding speech. How do infants and children accomplish all of this so quickly given these complexities?

Second, there is an order and regularity to how children around the world learn language. Even though young children may be exposed to sophisticated adult speech from many sources (for example, parents, siblings, baby-sitters, and television) and for extended periods of time, they do not start out by speaking in the same ways that adults do. There is *development*, and that development takes on a predictable pattern for children learning language under typical circumstances as well as those who are not. Consider two dramatic examples: One group of researchers studied several congenitally deaf preschool-age children who had not been taught sign language because parents were led to believe it would impede their ability to learn oral communication. None of them had learned to speak yet. Even so, the children had developed a unique gestural system of communication that followed the same sequence used by hearing children—that is, a one-symbol stage, followed by a two-symbol stage, and so forth (Feldman, Goldin-Meadow, & Gleitman, 1978). Similarly, studies of preschool children who were adopted and brought to the United States from China show that, despite their status as "older" learners of a second language, they progressed through the same sequence of language acquisition as young infants learning their first language (Snedeker, Geren, & Shafto, 2007). What factors are responsible for the striking regularities that we observe in children's language acquisition?

Also significant is the fact that children's use of language is *generative*. Children end up using language in creative and novel ways; most of what they say does not merely mimic the utterances they hear spoken around them. How do infants and children extract the regularities in the sounds, meanings, and word orders of the language they hear, and then use that information to say things they have never heard before?

In this chapter, we try to address these questions and more. First, we set the stage for our examination of language development by considering some foundational concepts and perspectives in language development. Next, we describe the major achievements in language and communication skills from infancy through childhood. Finally, we examine the functions of language as they interact with other aspects of the child's development.

Foundations for Language Development

What does it take to learn a language? If you have ever tried to communicate with someone who speaks a different language from you, you probably have a sense of just how remarkable children's mastery of communication is. When you first listen to a foreign language speaker, it may be difficult to discern even where individual words are located, let alone their meanings or the rules for putting words into meaningful orders. You can see how learning language requires the individual to master information at several different levels. Children seem to bring an array of predispositions and skills to the language acquisition process. For one thing, humans seem to be biologically prepared to engage in the process of language learning. Several regions of the brain appear to be specifically designed to process language and, perhaps, to assist in getting young children started on this remarkable journey. Children's general capacity to learn, think, and process social information also plays a role. Clearly, our ability to understand a sophisticated attainment like language requires us to draw on multiple perspectives.

The Elements of Language

A baby's contact with language is—initially, at least—noticeably one-sided. Although she may gurgle or coo, most of her experience is as a listener. Among her first tasks is to learn to identify the myriad sounds that make up her native language. In other words, she must distinguish specific sounds in the stream of spoken language, note the regularities in how they are combined, recognize which combinations constitute words, and eventually, when she makes the transition from listener to speaker, form the consonant-vowel combinations that are the building blocks of words and sentences. The fundamental sound units and the rules for combining them in a given language make up that language's **phonology**. If you have studied a foreign language, you will recognize that some sounds appear only in certain languages, such as the prolonged nasal *ñ* sound in Spanish and the French vowel that is spoken as though *e* and *u* are combined. Furthermore, each language has its own rules for combining sounds. In English, for example, the *sr* combination does not occur, whereas *sl* and *st* appear frequently. An important task for the child is to absorb the sounds and combinations of sounds that are acceptable in her native language and, eventually, to detect which of these sounds form words.

Another basic language skill that the child must master is linking the combinations of sounds he hears to the objects, people, events, or relationships they label. **Semantics** refers to the meanings of words (sometimes called the *lexicon*) or combinations of words. For example, *cookie* is an arbitrary grouping of sounds, but speakers of English use it to refer to a specific class of objects. The child thus attaches words to conceptual groups, learning when it is appropriate to use them and when it is not (for example, *cookie* does not refer to all objects or edible goods found in the bakery). The child also learns that some words describe actions (*eat*), whereas others describe relationships (*under* or *over*) or modify objects (*chocolate cookie*). Mapping combinations of sounds to their referents (that is, the things to which words refer) is a central element of language acquisition.

phonology Fundamental sound units and combinations of units in a given language.

semantics Meanings of words or combinations of words.

As the child begins to combine words, she learns the principles of **grammar**, the rules pertaining to the structure of language. Grammar includes two components, *syntax* and *morphology*. **Syntax** refers to the rules that dictate how words can be combined. The order in which words are spoken conveys meaning; for example, "Eat kitty" and "Kitty eat" do not mean the same thing, even in the simplified language of the young child. A word's position in a sentence can signify whether the word is an agent or the object of an action, for example. The rules of syntax vary widely from one language to another, but within a given language they operate with consistency and regularity. **Morphology** refers to the rules for combining the smallest meaningful units of language to form words. For example, the word *girl* has one morpheme (although it consists of several sounds, or *phonemes*). Adding *-s* to form *girls* makes the number of morphemes two and changes the meaning from singular to plural. Similarly, morphemes like *-ed* and *-ing* create a change in the tense of words. One of the most remarkable features of language acquisition is the child's ability to detect the rules of syntax and morphology and to use them to create meaningful utterances of his own with little direct instruction.

Just as important as semantic and syntactic rules are cultural requirements or customs pertaining to the proper use of speech in a social context. Is the child speaking with an elder or a peer? Is the context formal or informal? How does the speaker express politeness? Each situation suggests some unique characteristics of speech, a tone of voice, a formal or more casual syntactic structure, and the choice of specific words. In the context of playing with a best friend, saying, "Gimme that" might be perfectly appropriate; when speaking with the first-grade teacher, saying, "Could I please have that toy?" will probably produce a more favorable reaction. These examples demonstrate the child's grasp of **pragmatics**, the rules for using language effectively and appropriately according to the social context.

Clearly, using language is a multifaceted skill. Despite the complexities of learning all the elements that go into understanding and producing language, most children seem to master these challenges with relative ease.

The Brain and Language Acquisition

NATURE & NURTURE

The role of brain organization and functioning has occupied a very prominent place in the study of language acquisition for several decades. As new tools have become available to study human brain functioning, they have illuminated in even more detail the ways in which neuropsychological processes are associated with language development.

Brain Structures and Language The human brain contains several areas associated with the understanding and production of language. As you learned in Chapter 5, the right and left hemispheres of the brain have specialized functions, a phenomenon called *lateralization*. The primary regions that control language processing in most people are found in the left hemisphere. Neuropsychological studies reveal that several portions of the temporal, prefrontal, and visual areas of the brain are involved in language processing (Friederici & Wartenburger, 2010). However, studies of individuals who have suffered brain damage due to stroke, traumatic injury, or illness have pinpointed two specific regions in the left hemisphere that play a special role in the ability to use language (see Figure 7.1). The first is **Broca's area**, located in the left frontal region near the motor cortex. Patients who have damage in this region evidence **expressive aphasia**, or the inability to speak fluently, although their comprehension abilities remain intact. The second region, **Wernicke's area**, is in the temporal region of the left hemisphere, close to the areas of the brain responsible for auditory processing. Damage to Wernicke's area results in **receptive aphasia**, in which speech seems fluent—at least on the surface—but contains nonsense or incomprehensible words; the ability to understand the speech of others is also impaired.

grammar Rules pertaining to the structure of language.

syntax Grammatical rules that dictate how words can be combined.

morphology Rules of how to combine the smallest meaningful units of language to form words.

pragmatics Rules for using language effectively within a social context.

Broca's area Portion of the cerebral cortex that controls expressive language.

expressive aphasia Loss of the ability to speak fluently.

Wernicke's area Portion of the cerebral cortex that controls language comprehension.

receptive aphasia Loss of the ability to comprehend speech.

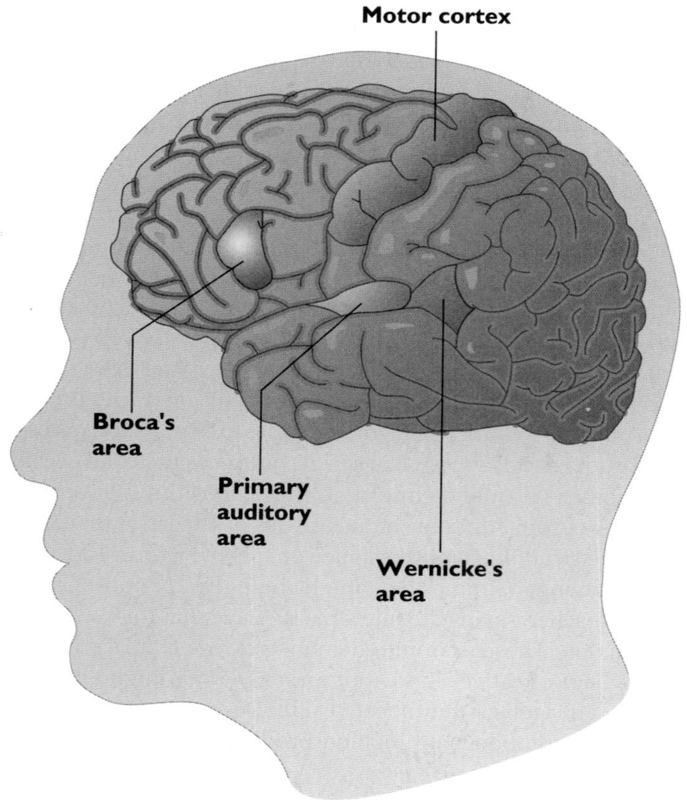

Figure 7.1
The Two Portions of the Left Cortex of the Brain Responsible for Language Processing
Broca's area governs the production of speech, and Wernicke's area is responsible for the comprehension of speech. Damage to the former produces expressive aphasia, whereas damage to the latter leads to receptive aphasia.

Does the presence of these specialized language regions in the brains of adults mean that language development is based on the unfolding of some biological or genetic program during childhood? Researchers' ability to record electrical activity and blood flow in the brain has yielded further information on the brain's involvement in language. Before young children begin speaking, brain wave activity as they listen to words they know and don't know is distributed across many regions of the brain. Once they start speaking, differences in brain waves become more focused in the left hemisphere for most children (Mills, Coffey-Corina, & Neville, 1997). Thus, some (but not all) language processing starts to become localized in the left hemisphere shortly after the first year. By the time children reach age seven years, patterns of brain activation indicate adult-like lateralization of language in the left hemisphere (Lee et al., 1999). Even deaf individuals learning sign language show brain activity in the left hemisphere similar to that of hearing individuals (Corina et al., 1999; McGuire et al., 1997). It is important to note, though, that the process of lateralization seems to be tied to the kinds of language experiences children have—the number of words they know, for example—rather than their age. That is, even though we might be tempted to conclude that brain development is driving the process of language development, the child's experiences with language, too, seem to play a role in how the brain becomes organized (Mills, Conboy, & Paton, 2005). One thing does seem clear—the brain organization we see in adults has its roots in some more primitive form in infants (Shafer & Garrido-Nag, 2007).

CONTINUITY | DISCONTINUITY

Critical Periods and Language Acquisition Is childhood an especially privileged time for learning language? Several decades ago, Eric Lenneberg (1967) claimed that, to speak and comprehend normally, children must acquire all language basics by adolescence, when physiological changes in the brain make language learning more difficult. He proposed a *critical period* for the acquisition of language. A few rare case studies of children who have been isolated from social contact or linguistic experience for protracted periods support his position. One girl, Genie, had minimal human contact from age twenty months until thirteen years, due to isolation imposed by her parents. She did not speak at all. After she was found and received extensive therapy, Genie made some progress in learning words but never learned to speak normally, showing special difficulty in completely mastering the rules of syntax (Curtiss, 1977). Another nineteen-year-old boy from rural Mexico, deaf since birth but given hearing aids at age fifteen years, spoke only in one- or two-word utterances and had difficulties with verb tenses, negation, and other elements of syntax, despite three years of exposure to language (Grimshaw et al., 1998). Studies of deaf people who learned American Sign Language (ASL) at different times in life provide additional support for the critical-period hypothesis. Elissa Newport (1990) found that individuals who learned ASL after age twelve showed consistent errors in the use of grammar, whereas those who were exposed to ASL from birth displayed a normal course in the development of the language.

Lenneberg's hypothesis also implies that children will find it difficult to learn a second language if they begin during or after adolescence. Here, too, there is evidence to support his ideas. Jacqueline Johnson and Elissa Newport (1989) assessed the ability of Chinese and Korean immigrants who learned English as a second language to judge the grammatical correctness of more than 200 English sentences. Some participants started to learn English as early as age three, others not until age seventeen or later. The older they were before learning English, the poorer were their scores on the grammar test (see Figure 7.2). Moreover, factors such as length of experience with English, amount of formal instruction in English, or identification with American culture could not account for the findings. Early exposure to a second language can also affect one's ability to pronounce it. One study found that, when individuals merely overheard Spanish before age six, they sounded more like native speakers when they went on to study Spanish as adults, as compared with individuals without that early experience (Au et al., 2002). Newport (1990) aptly summarizes findings like these by stating that "in language . . . the child, and not the adult, appears to be especially privileged as a learner" (p. 12).

Neuropsychological findings with bilingual speakers complement these findings. Participants in one study were Chinese adults who had acquired English as a second language at different points in their lifetimes. While participants read sentences that were either correct or violated semantic or syntactic rules, the researchers monitored their brain wave activity. Brain wave patterns suggested that the age of second-language acquisition made a special difference for syntactic tasks; if English had been acquired after age four, electrical activity in the left hemisphere showed a different pattern than if English had been acquired earlier in childhood (Weber-Fox & Neville, 1996). In another study, magnetic resonance imaging was used to study patterns of brain activation as bilingual individuals performed linguistic tasks in their native and second languages. When the second language was learned in adulthood,

Figure 7.2

Critical Periods for Language Acquisition

The performance of native Chinese or Korean speakers on a test of English grammar depends on the age at which they learned English. Evidence like this supports the idea that there is a critical period for the acquisition of language.

Source: From Johnson, J., & Newport, E. (1989). Critical period effects in second language acquisition: The influence of maturational state on the acquisition of English as a second language. *Cognitive Psychology, 21*, 60–99. Reprinted by permission of Elsevier.

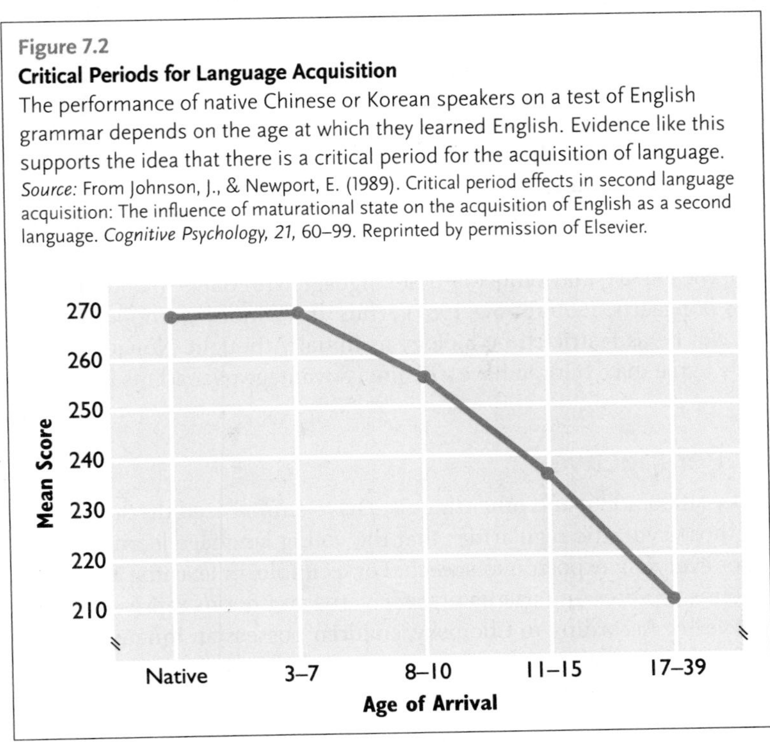

Figure 7.3

Brain Functioning in Bilingual Individuals

These two panels show activity patterns in the brains of two bilingual individuals as they engage in linguistic tasks in their native and second languages. The panel on the left shows brain activity for a native speaker of English who learned French in adulthood. Notice that two adjacent areas show activation. The panel on the right shows brain activity for a native speaker of Turkish who learned English in infancy. Here the areas activated for each language overlap. Neuropsychological findings such as these provide support for the critical-period hypothesis of language acquisition.

Source: Kim et al., 1997.

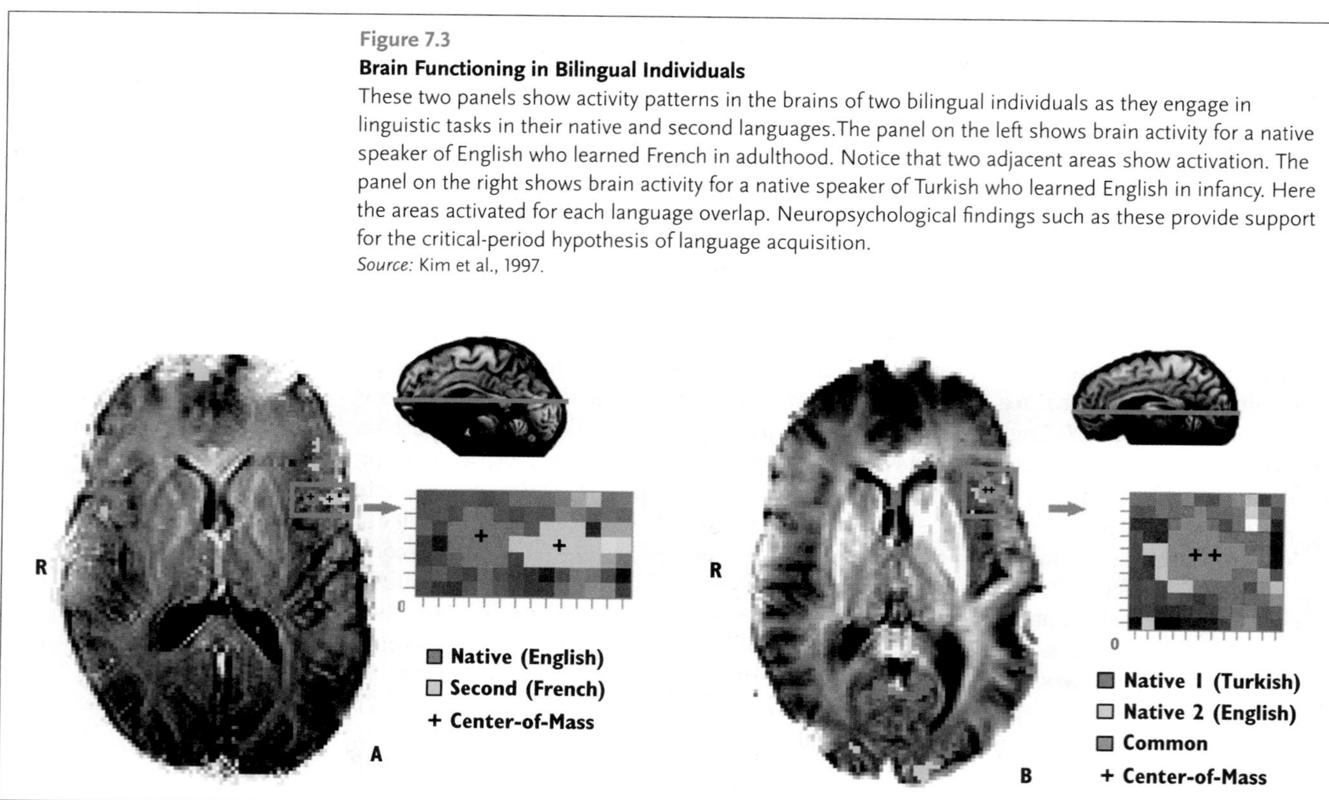

images of brain functioning showed that two adjoining but separate regions in Broca's area were activated (see the left panel of Figure 7.3). In contrast, when the second language was learned during infancy, overlapping regions in Broca's area showed activity (see the right panel of Figure 7.3) (Kim et al., 1997). Thus, the brain seems to respond, and perhaps become organized, differently depending on when the second language was learned.

Critics point to problems in interpreting some of the research cited in support of the critical-period hypothesis. Genie, for example, may have suffered serious cognitive, physiological, and emotional deficits because of her prolonged isolation from other humans, deficits that could well account for her lack of mature language. Furthermore, most studies of second-language learning, although controlling for many relevant variables, have not taken into account how much the later-learned second language is actually used (Bruer, 2001). One study showed that, even though they were learning English at age seventeen or later, the amount of English used by native Spanish speakers in talking to others predicted their facility with English (Birdsong & Molis, 2001). Finally, some individuals who learn a second language in adulthood acquire the phonology, vocabulary, and syntax of that language with native-like proficiency (Birdsong & Molis, 2001; Bongaerts, 1999; Snow, 1987). Thus, the window of opportunity for learning language may not be as restricted by biology as initially thought. Nonetheless, most experts would probably agree that children have a distinct advantage over adults in language learning.

Linguistic Perspectives

NATURE & NURTURE

Noam Chomsky (1980, 1986) and other linguists have emphasized the structures that all languages share, those syntactic regularities that the young language learner quickly identifies in the course of everyday exposure to speech. For example, in learning English, a child soon notices that nouns representing agents precede verbs and nouns representing the objects of actions follow verbs. According to Chomsky, children possess an innate system of language categories and principles, called *universal grammar,* which predisposes them to discover the general linguistic properties of any language. As children are exposed to a specific language, a process called *parameter setting* takes place; that is, the grammatical rules that distinguish

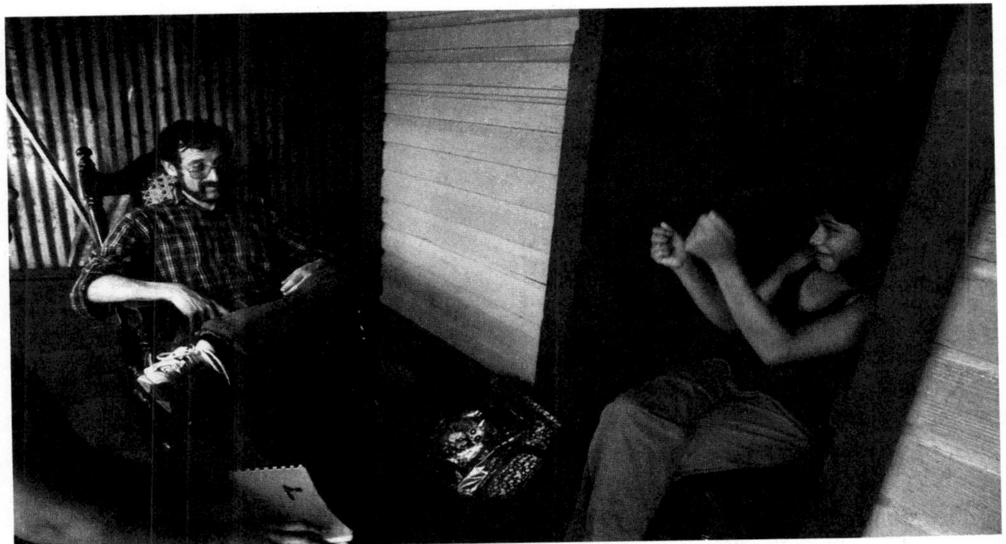

© Christina Gomez-Mira

A deaf community in Nicaragua has provided researchers with the unique opportunity to observe how a new language is created and then changes over time. The particular sign language developed in this community has become elaborated in ways that suggest a high degree of structure underlies the process.

English from Japanese or Arabic from French are set (Lidz & Gleitman, 2004). After abstracting the general rules of language, children apply them to form their own novel and creative utterances. Language learning, say many linguists, is different from other forms of learning; there are constraints on what the child will be predisposed to learn, and language learning is governed by its own set of principles. In other words, language learning is *modular*, separate and distinct from other kinds of processing. Furthermore, many linguists believe language is a uniquely human enterprise, one that is not part of the behavioral repertoire of other species.

Research evidence generally supports the idea that learning and applying rules is part of the process of learning language. Children rapidly learn syntactic rules for forming plurals, past tense, and other grammatical forms in their first five years and can even apply them to words they have never heard before. In a famous experiment, Jean Berko (1958) demonstrated this phenomenon by presenting children with several nonsense words, such as *wug*. Children were able to state correctly that the plural form of *wug* is *wugs*, although they had never heard made-up words like these. Even seven-month-old infants show evidence of being able to learn rules that can help them to learn language. In one study, infants heard several three-word sentences from an artificial language until they showed a decline in interest in them. For example, they heard constructions that had an ABA form such as "ga ti ga" and "li na li." During the test phase, though, they showed a distinct preference for sentences with an ABB construction, such as "wo fe fe." Likewise, infants who were habituated to the ABB structure preferred sentences with the ABA structure during the test phase (Marcus et al., 1998).

The drive to find structure in language is evident in another interesting way—in the development of *creole* languages, in which children in a particular cohort permanently embellish or expand the organization of the language they hear. Researchers have discovered a deaf community in Nicaragua in which individuals created their own version of sign language. With each new generation of children, the complexity of that language's structure increased (Senghas & Coppola, 2001). The implication is that children do not simply pattern their speech after what they hear; rather, they use language in creative but also highly organized ways.

Linguistic approaches help to explain just how children can master the complex, abstract rules that characterize all languages, given what some have called the "impoverished input"—the incomplete or ungrammatical utterances—that they typically hear (Lightfoot, 1982). They also help us understand how children learn language without explicit teaching of the rules of grammar or lists of vocabulary words.

Learning and Cognitive Perspectives

NATURE & NURTURE

Oftentimes, the child shows major advances in certain learning or cognitive (or thinking) skills right before he or she displays a major achievement in using language. For example, Elizabeth Bates and her colleagues found that abilities such as imitation, tool use, and the complex manipulation of objects predict language attainments (Bates et al., 1975). Alison Gopnik and Andrew Meltzoff (1986) have identified still other skills that seem to emerge just before certain language accomplishments. For example, children who can find a hidden object after it has been moved from one location to another begin within a few weeks to use words such as *gone* to signify disappearance. Similarly, they begin to use words representing success and failure (for example, *there* and *uh-oh*) after learning to solve a complex means-ends task, such as using a stick to obtain an object. Gopnik and Meltzoff (1987, 1992) also noted that children who are able to sort groups of toys into two distinct categories, such as dolls and cars or boxes and balls, have more words in their vocabulary. According to these researchers, children develop linguistic labels consistent with cognitive problems that interest them at a given stage of development. In addition, it may be no accident that children's first words tend to be nouns such as *dog* and not *animal* or *collie.* Learning to organize objects at this intermediate level seems to be easier for young children than using either broader or more specific categories (Rosch et al., 1976), and the child's language reflects this cognitive preference.

INTERACTION AMONG DOMAINS

Memory capabilities are involved in language acquisition, too. For example, at eight months of age, infants show a remarkable ability to remember particular words from stories they had heard two weeks earlier (Jusczyk & Hohne, 1997). This is precisely the age at which infants begin to show an increase in their comprehension of words spoken by others. Furthermore, the memory capacities of infants who are 12 months old are very good at predicting their language skills at 36 months of age (Rose, Feldman, & Jankowski, 2009). Among children who are four years old, short-term memory skills, especially the ability to reproduce the order in which stimulus words were heard, predict vocabulary acquisition one year later (Leclercq & Majerus, 2010).

Based on findings like these, some researchers argue that language acquisition is not so much based on modular and uniquely linguistic processes but rather on broader cognitive processing abilities that are responsible for development in all sorts of spheres. If we understand the general features of learning and cognitive processing, these theorists say, we will understand language acquisition.

CONTINUITY | DISCONTINUITY

One contemporary approach that emphasizes the role of general learning processes includes *connectionist models* of language acquisition. Connectionist models describe language development in terms of networks of associations that are organized in interconnected layers, much like the associations that form among neurons (see Figure 7.4

Figure 7.4

A Connectionist Model of Vocabulary Acquisition

Connectionist models emphasize the formation of elaborate networks of associations between incoming stimuli (images and labels, in this case) and internal representations, as well as associations of internal representations with outputs (e.g., saying a word). Connectionist models have been successful in simulating many aspects of language acquisition, including vocabulary development and syntax acquisition, suggesting that general cognitive processes may underlie the child's language achievements.

Source: From Nobre & Plunkett. The neural system of language: Structure and development. *Current Opinion in Neurobiology, 7,* pp. 262–268. Copyright © 1997. Reprinted with permission from Elsevier.

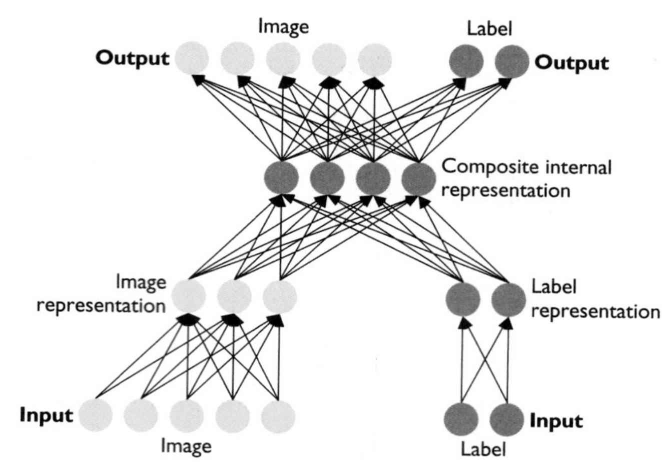

for one example). Repeated experiences with the linguistic environment are responsible for forming and strengthening associations between stimuli and the network of associations, among items within the network, and between the network and the individual's output or response (Klahr & MacWhinney, 1998; Plunkett, 1995). So far, connectionist models have done a good job of simulating several aspects of children's language acquisition, such as vocabulary and syntactic development (MacWhinney, 1998; Mayor & Plunkett, 2010; Plunkett & Marchman, 1996).

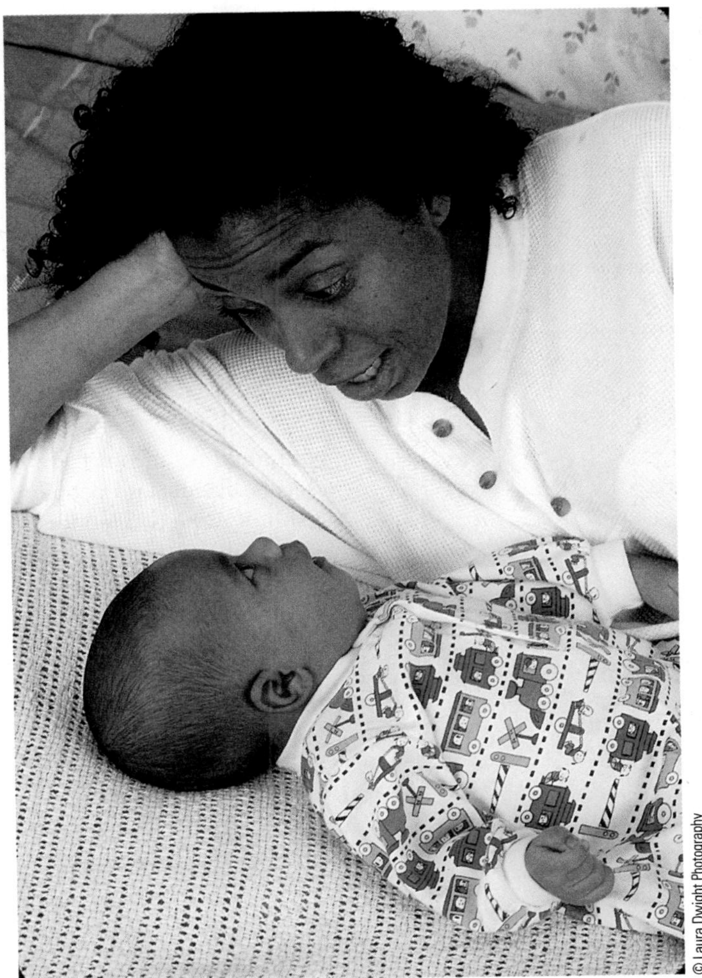

When caregivers talk to infants and young children, they employ simple sentences, exaggerate their intonation, and speak with a high pitch. Infants are especially responsive to these qualities of "motherese," which seem to provide a helpful framework for learning language.

Social Interaction Perspectives

Many researchers of child language hold as a central tenet that language is a social activity, one that arises from the desire to communicate with others and that is nurtured in social interactive contexts. They emphasize the role that experiences with more mature, expert speakers play in fostering linguistic skill. Social interaction researchers maintain that children need support and feedback as they make their first attempts at communication as well as models who, when speaking, do not produce utterances that exceed children's processing abilities. Many qualities of parental speech directed at children are well suited to the child's emerging receptive and productive skills, providing a *scaffolding*, or framework, from which the child can learn.

Parents have a unique way of talking to their young children. Most parents present a scaled-down version of spoken language as they interact with their young offspring, a version that contains simple, well-formed sentences and is punctuated by exaggerated intonation, high pitch, and clear pauses between segments of speech (Newport, 1977). Caregivers describe concrete events taking place in the present and often refer to objects with diminutives such as *kitty* or *doggie*. They also include repetitions of what the child has said, as well as many questions. Questions in particular serve to facilitate the occurrence of **turn taking**, the alternating vocalization by parent and child. Some questions are also used as **turnabouts**, elements of conversation that explicitly request a response from the child, as in "You like that, don't you?" or "What did you say?" Also, parents often follow the child's verbalization with a **recast**, repeating what the child has said but correcting any errors. **Expansions**—more elaborate verbal forms—may be added, too. Thus, when a child says, "Ball fall," his mother might reply, "Yes, the red ball [expansion] fell [recast]." Recasts and expansions provide children with cues about how their verbalizations need to change and can be improved. Children, in fact, often imitate and retain their parents' recasts (Farrar, 1992; Saxton, 1997).

NATURE & NURTURE

INTERACTION AMONG DOMAINS

The following exchange between one seven-month-old, Ann, and her mother illustrates several of these concepts (Snow, 1977):

Mother	Ann
Ghhhhh ghhhhh ghhhhh ghhhhh *Grrrrr grrrrr grrrrr grrrrr*	
	(protest cry)
Oh, you don't feel like it, do you?	
	aaaaa aaaaa aaaaa
No, I wasn't making that noise. I wasn't going *aaaaa aaaaa*.	
	aaaaa aaaaa
Yes, that's right.	

turn taking Alternating vocalization by parent and child.

turnabout Element of conversation that requests a response from the child.

recast Repetition of a child's utterance along with grammatical corrections.

expansion Repetition of a child's utterance along with a more complex form.

Mother	Ann
	(blowing noises)
That's a bit rude!	Mouth.
Mouth, that's right.	Face.
Face, yes, mouth is in your face. What else have you got in your face?	Face. (closing eyes)
You're making a face, aren't you?	

Notable in the exchange is the mother's pattern of waiting for her child's vocalization to end before she begins her response, an example of turn taking. If the child had spoken actual words, a real conversation would have taken place. The mother also repeated the child's vowel-like sound but embedded it in more elaborate speech. By the time the infant reaches eighteen months, the mother's tendency to expand or explain her utterances becomes even more pronounced, as in the brief episode on the left (Snow, 1977).

According to Snow (1984), two general principles operate during caregiver-child interactions. First, parents generally interpret their infants' behaviors as attempts to communicate, even when that interpretation may not seem warranted to an objective observer. Second, children actively seek relationships among objects, events, and people in their world and the vocal behaviors of their caregivers. The result of these two tendencies is that parents are motivated to converse with their children and children have a mechanism for learning language.

For Your Review and Reflection

- What are four kinds of skills that children master in the course of language development?
- What have studies shown about the involvement of the brain in language acquisition?
- What evidence supports a critical period hypothesis of language acquisition? What evidence is inconsistent with a critical period hypothesis?
- How does a linguistic perspective account for language acquisition? What research findings are consistent with a linguistic perspective?
- Which learning and cognitive skills are related to language acquisition?
- What are the unique features of a social interaction perspective on language acquisition?
- What research findings are consistent with the idea that social interactions play a role in language development?
- How does each of these perspectives concerning language address the five key themes?

Language Development in Infancy

Human infants display a striking preparedness to learn language. During the first two years of life, they show rapid advances in discerning and making the sounds of their native language, as well as understanding the meanings attached to those sounds.

Early Responses to Human Speech

NATURE & NURTURE

As we saw in Chapter 6, infants only a few weeks old prefer speech to nonspeech sounds (Vouloumanos & Werker, 2004). Young infants also show the ability to discriminate phonemes categorically. Although they can detect sounds from a variety of languages, their experiences with the language spoken around them quickly begin to constrain the small units of sound to which they are sensitive. That is, they show perceptual narrowing. Most

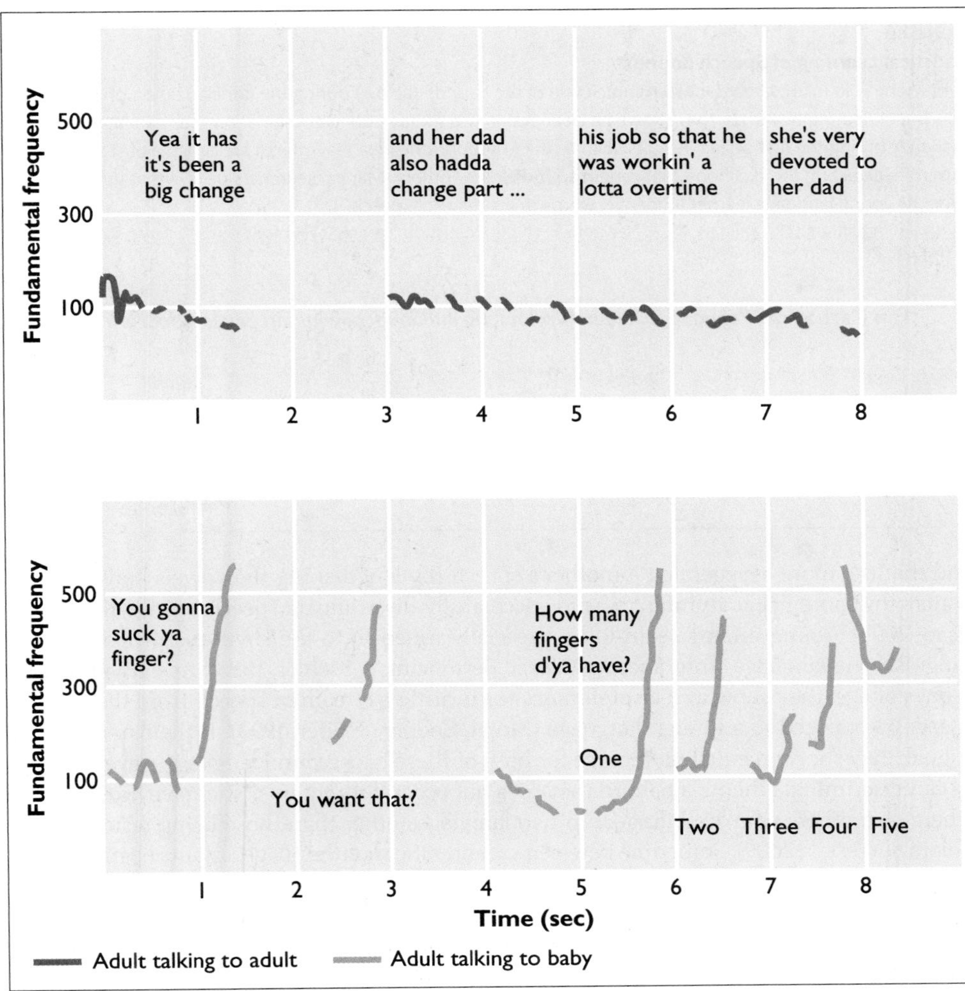

Figure 7.5
The Acoustical Properties of Maternal Speech to Infants
These two samples of maternal speech show the special acoustical qualities that make speech to infants (bottom) distinct from speech to adults (top). The vertical axis represents fundamental frequency, a measure of auditory pitch. Note the frequent use of modulation of pitch and the predominance of high pitch in maternal speech to infants. Babies seem to be especially responsive to the qualities of this type of speech.
Source: From Fernald, A. (1985). Four-month-olds prefer to listen to motherese. *Infant Behavior and Development, 8,* 181–195. Reprinted with permission of Ablex Publishing Corporation.

researchers concur: infants are born with auditory capabilities that allow them to start learning language (Gervain & Werker, 2008).

Sensitivity to Prosody Infants show an early sensitivity to **prosody**, the patterns of intonation, stress, and rhythm that communicate meaning. One example of a prosodic feature is the pattern of intonation that distinguishes questions from declarative statements. When you raise your voice at the end of a question, you are signaling a different communicative intent than when you let your voice fall at the end of a declarative sentence. Researchers have found that infants prefer the prosodic features associated with the high-pitched, exaggerated, musical speech, often called "baby talk," which mothers typically direct to their young children. Figure 7.5 illustrates some of the acoustical properties of **infant-directed speech** (or **parentese**) as this form of communication is called. In one study, Anne Fernald (1985) trained four-month-olds to turn their heads to activate a loudspeaker positioned on either side of them. The infants were more likely to make this response if their "reward" was a female stranger's voice speaking as the woman would speak to a baby than if she was using normal adult speech. Other research has shown that it is the positive affective tone of "baby talk" that infants are particularly attracted to (Singh, Morgan, & Best, 2002). In light of these preferences, it seems fitting that mothers from cultures as diverse as France, Italy, Germany, Britain, Japan, China, and the Xhosa tribe of southern Africa have been found to raise their pitch when they speak to their young infants (Fernald, 1991; Papousek, 1992).

Infants' sensitivity to the prosodic features of speech prepares them for the more complex aspects of language learning that lie before them. In one study, for example, researchers

prosody Patterns of intonation, stress, and rhythm that communicate meaning in speech.

infant-directed speech (parentese) Simple, repetitive, high-pitched speech of caregivers to young children; includes many questions.

Figure 7.6

Statistical Learning of Speech Sounds

Eight-month-old infants heard a two-minute cycle of the sounds (below) during the familiarization phase of an experiment. During test trials, they showed a clear preference for the sound combination they had heard less frequently during the first phase. Results such as these support the idea that infants are capable of statistical learning—detecting the likelihood that certain sounds follow others. Many researchers believe that this process helps the young language learner to identify words in a stream of speech.

Source: From Saffran, J. R., Aslin, R. N., & Newport, E. (1996). Statistical learning by 8-month-olds. *Science, 274,* 1926–1928. Reprinted by permission.

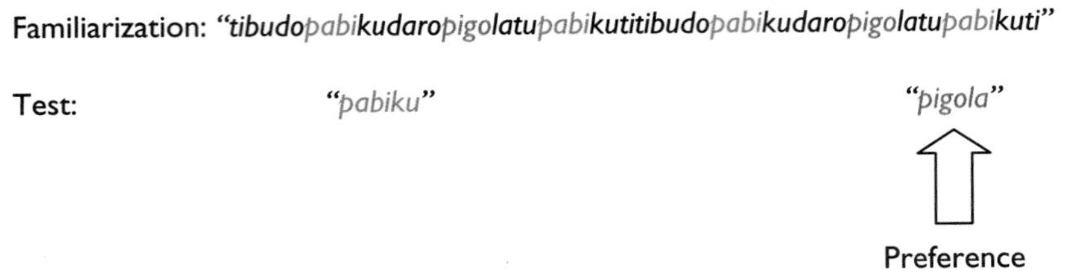

Familiarization: *"tibudopabikudaropigolatupabikutitibudopabikudaropigolatupabikuti"*

Test: *"pabiku"* *"pigola"*

Preference

found that the more exaggerated a mother's speech (by lengthening the vowels between consonants), the more likely an infant was to successfully discriminate speech sounds (Liu, Kuhl, & Tsao, 2003). Young infants seem to be especially tuned in to the rhythmic properties that distinguish one language from another (Nazzi, Bertoncini, & Mehler, 1998). As early as only a few days of age, they show a clear preference for hearing a stream of speech from their native language as opposed to a foreign language (Moon, Cooper, & Fifer, 1993). If their mothers are bilingual, they show an equal preference for both of these background languages (even though they can discriminate them), a pattern that does not occur with infants who have monolingual mothers or mothers who are bilingual in two languages other than those being tested (Byers-Heinlein & Werker, 2009). Sometime between six and nine months of age, infants begin to show a preference for listening to unfamiliar isolated words from their native language. For example, American infants prefer unfamiliar English words over Dutch words. At ten months of age, they also prefer words with a strong-weak stress pattern (for instance, *crossing* versus *across*), which are more common in English (Jusczyk, Cutler, & Redanz, 1993; Jusczyk et al., 1993).

Finding Words Perhaps most impressive is the finding that, between about six and eight months of age, infants show that they can detect the beginnings and endings of specific words in a stream of their native speech, a skill that should strike you as remarkable if you have ever tried to detect the presence of particular words when listening to someone speak an unfamiliar foreign language. To explore this ability, Sven Mattys and Peter Jusczyk (Mattys & Jusczyk, 2001) first familiarized infants with a single word, such as *dice*. Next, infants heard the target word within a passage, such as "Two dice can be rolled without difficulty," or they heard the same sound pattern but across two different words, as in "Wired ice no longer surprises anyone." Infants showed a clear preference for the first type of correctly segmented passage, probably using rhythmic cues, as well as detecting the different acoustic properties that phonemes have at the beginnings versus the ends of words (for instance, */d/* sounds slightly different at the beginning than at the end of a word). Words starting with vowels, though, are much harder for infants to locate in speech segments than words starting with consonants. Only sixteen-month-olds could locate words such as *ice* or *eel.*

The infant's capacity to extract information about the probability that one sound will follow another, a phenomenon called **statistical learning**, may be an important part of her ability to detect words in the speech stream (Saffran, 2001). In one experiment (see Figure 7.6), researchers exposed eight-month-olds to an unbroken stream of sounds, such as *tibudopabikudaropigolatupabikuti,* for two minutes. In this example, every instance of *pa* was followed by *bi.* On the other hand, *pi* was followed by *go* only one-third of the time. When later presented with *pabiku* versus *pigola,* infants showed a clear attentional preference for *pigola,* suggesting that they were sensitive to the chances that one sound would follow another (Saffran, Aslin, & Newport, 1996).

statistical learning The ability to discern the probability that one event follows another.

Studies show that several factors can help infants find words in a stream of speech. One is the use of infant-directed speech. Hearing new words spoken in the melodic rhythm of this form of language helps infants to distinguish those words from parts of words; hearing words spoken in regular adult tones makes the task more difficult (Thiessen, Hill, & Saffran, 2005). A second factor is the presence of the infant's name. In one study, when six-month-olds heard new words immediately after their own name (for example, "Emma's *cup* is here"), recognition for those words was greater than when they followed another novel word ("Autumn's *bike* is here"). Familiar words, such as one's own name, may thus help call out new words from the stream of speech and act as an important tool in language acquisition (Bortfeld et al., 2005).

Word recognition skills improve dramatically in the second year, especially as infants begin to use their knowledge of word meanings to decipher the sounds they hear. At eighteen months of age, for example, toddlers need to hear only the very first portion of a word, such as *daw* in *doggie*, in order to look at the picture the word represents (Fernald, Swingley, & Pinto, 2001). This relationship between meaning and sound is one example of how the various facets of language are, in fact, very much interrelated.

First Words

Once infants can locate words, the pathway is prepared for the next critical aspect of learning a language, namely, learning the meanings of those words and speaking them. The uttering of first words is a major accomplishment, marking the visible entry of the child into the world of spoken, shared communication.

Cooing and Babbling: Prelinguistic Speech Well before the child utters her first word, she produces sounds that increasingly resemble the language spoken in her environment. At birth, the infant's vocal capabilities are limited to crying and a few other brief sounds, such as grunts, sighs, or clicks. Between six and eight weeks, a new type of vocalization, **cooing**, emerges. These brief, vowel-like utterances are sometimes accompanied by consonants, usually those produced in the back of the mouth, such as */g/* or */k/*. Infants coo when they are in a comfortable state or when a parent has made some attempt to communicate, either with speech or with coos of his or her own. In the weeks that follow, the infant's vocalizations become longer and begin to include consonants formed at the front of the mouth, as in */m/* or */b/*.

The next significant accomplishment is the emergence of **babbling**, the production of consonant-vowel combinations such as *da* or *ba*. Most children begin to babble at about three to six months and refine their skills in the succeeding months. To many listeners, the infant's babbling sounds like active experimentation with the production of different sounds. These vocalizations are especially likely to occur in the context of mutually coordinated caregiver-child interactions (Hsu & Fogel, 2001), and they are often accompanied by such facial expressions as smiles or frowns (Yale et al., 1999), perhaps to emphasize the child's communicative intent. At about seven months, the infant will repeat well-formed syllables, such as *baba* or *dada*, a phenomenon called **canonical babbling**. It is almost as if the infant is trying to say words. At nine or ten months, the child's babbling includes more numerous and complex consonant-vowel combinations, as well as variations in intonation (Davis et al., 2000).

INTERACTION AMONG DOMAINS

The changes in children's productive capabilities are linked to physiological changes in their vocal apparatus and central nervous system that occur during the first year. In the months after birth, the infant's larynx descends farther into the neck, the oral cavity grows, and the baby can place her tongue in different positions in her mouth (not just forward and backward as at birth). At the same time, the cortex of the brain replaces the brainstem in controlling many of the child's behaviors. In general, early reflexlike vocalizations, such as cries, fade as more controlled voluntary utterances, such as coos and babbles, enter the child's repertoire.

Most infants, regardless of their culture, begin to coo and babble at similar ages. Even deaf children vocalize with coos and babbles in the first few months of life (Stoel-Gammon & Otomo, 1986), and both deaf and hearing

cooing Vowel-like utterances that characterize the infant's first attempts to vocalize.

babbling Consonant-vowel utterances that characterize the infant's first attempts to vocalize.

canonical babbling Repetition of simple consonant-vowel combinations in well-formed syllables.

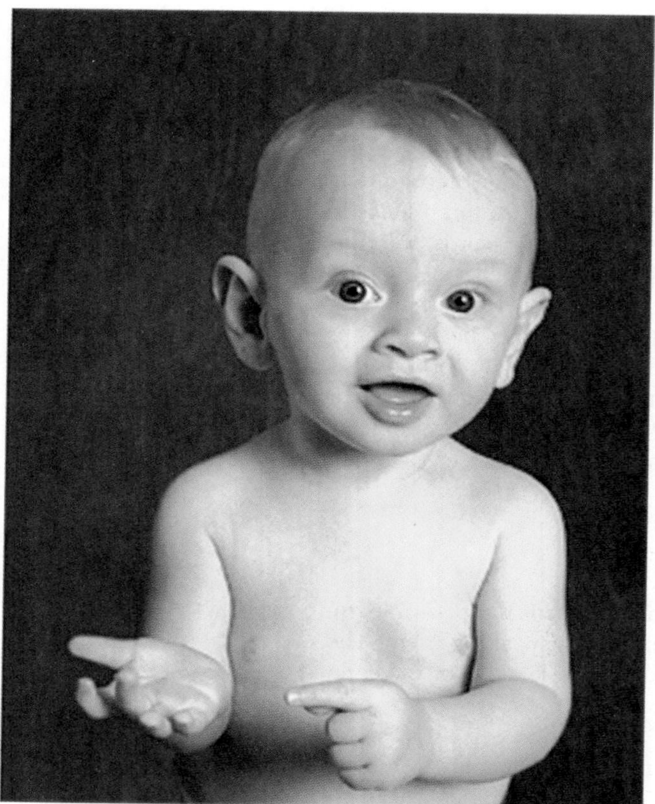

Research has shown that hearing children exposed to sign language by their deaf parents make hand gestures that correspond to the babbles made by most hearing children during the second half of the first year. Evidence like this supports the idea that human infants are prepared to respond to language input in highly specific ways.
Source: Adapted by permission from Macmillan Publishers, Ltd. Petitto, L. A., Holowka, S., Segio, L. E., & Ostry. (2001). Language rhythms in baby hand movements. *Nature, 413*, 35–36.

children exposed to sign language make repetitive, rhythmic hand gestures akin to babbling, prior to full-fledged signing (Petitto et al., 2001; Petitto & Marentette, 1991; Takei, 2001). The fact that the right side of the mouth opens wider than the left when children babble probably also signals the role of the left hemisphere in this process (Holowka & Petitto, 2002). Traditionally, evidence like this has been seen as support for the idea that nature plays a prominent role in the emergence of the child's utterances.

Even at this early stage of language development, however, the form the child's vocalizations take is influenced by the language spoken around her. Studies have shown identifiable differences in babbling among infants from varying cultures. One group of researchers conducted a spectral analysis of the vowel sounds made by ten-month-olds in Paris, London, Algiers, and Hong Kong. The procedure involved translating the acoustic properties of speech into a visual representation of the intensity, onset, and pattern of vocalization. Infants from different countries varied in the average frequencies of the sounds they produced; the differences paralleled those of adult speakers from the same countries (Boysson-Bardies et al., 1989). Thus, the child's linguistic environment has a distinct effect on his own speech before he can speak true words.

Gestures Late in the first year, before or as they speak their first words, many children begin to use such gestures as pointing, showing, or giving as a means to communicate with other people (Bates, Camaioni, & Volterra, 1975). Carlotta, a ten-month-old infant observed by Elizabeth Bates and her colleagues, provides some good examples of several kinds of nonverbal communication that seem to express meaning. In one observation, Carlotta held up her toy and extended her arm in a showing motion to an adult. Here her gesture functioned much as a declarative sentence does, calling the adult's attention to the object. Another time, Carlotta pointed to the kitchen sink and said, "Ha!" a communication intended to get the adult to do something (Bates, 1979). Often children's gestures are accompanied by direct eye contact with the communication's recipient. As children get older, they may add a vocalization to the gesture for added emphasis (Messinger & Fogel, 1998), much as Carlotta did when asking for water. Children may also repeat their communications if the messages are not understood. This constellation of behaviors and the context in which they occur suggest that children use gestures as a purposeful means to an end.

NATURE & NURTURE

Linda Acredolo and Susan Goodwyn (1988) found that a child between eleven and twenty-four months of age uses gestures not just to show or request but also to symbolize objects or events. The child may signify a flower, for example, by making a sniffing gesture or the desire to go outside with a knob-turning motion. A significant number of children's gestures re-create the functions of objects rather than their forms or shapes. For example, participants in the study would put their fist to one ear to signify a telephone or wave their hands to represent a butterfly.

INTERACTION AMONG DOMAINS

Acredolo and Goodwyn believe a strong relationship exists between the development of symbolic gestures and verbal abilities because both appear at approximately the same point in development, with gestures usually preceding words by a few weeks (Goodwyn & Acredolo, 1993). In fact, researchers have reported a tight correspondence between gestures for specific objects and the words that are produced for them several weeks later (Iverson & Goldin-Meadow, 2005). Recognizing that one thing can symbolize another represents a major cognitive advance, one that is essential for the use of both gestures and spoken language. Gestures, however, may simply be easier for the child to produce than the complex coordination required for a verbal utterance. Interestingly enough, when mothers observe their young children using gestures to point to an object, they often translate the gestures into words, thus providing a good model to the child for the next steps in attaining language (Goldin-Meadow et al., 2007). During their second year, infants begin to combine two distinct ideas with a gesture plus a word, for example, by pointing to a box and saying "open." These communications are the precursors of the more complex spoken speech the child will soon start to use at age two years (Goldin-Meadow, 2006).

By the middle of the second year, children are less likely to use gestures as their sole means of communication. Gestures unaccompanied by verbalization are less useful when the "listener" is out of view, and they are usually correctly understood by only a limited number of adults. Parents also probably tend to encourage the child's verbalizations more than they do the use of gestures (Acredolo & Goodwyn, 1990a). So oriented do hearing children become to words as a means of expression that, by two years of age, they are much more likely to learn new names for objects as opposed to new gestures to represent them (Namy & Waxman, 1998).

All of this is not meant to say that children stop using gestures entirely. In fact, quite the contrary is true. Both adults and children tend to use gestures as an accompaniment to their speech, giving emphasis to what they are saying or elaborating on a concept visually. Children begin to use gesture in these new ways as their speech gets more complex, at ages two and three (Mayberry & Nicoladis, 2000). Even blind children gesture while they speak to others, suggesting that this behavior is not merely an imitation of the communication styles of adults (Iverson & Goldin-Meadow, 2001). Rather, gesture seems to be very much intertwined with the communicative process.

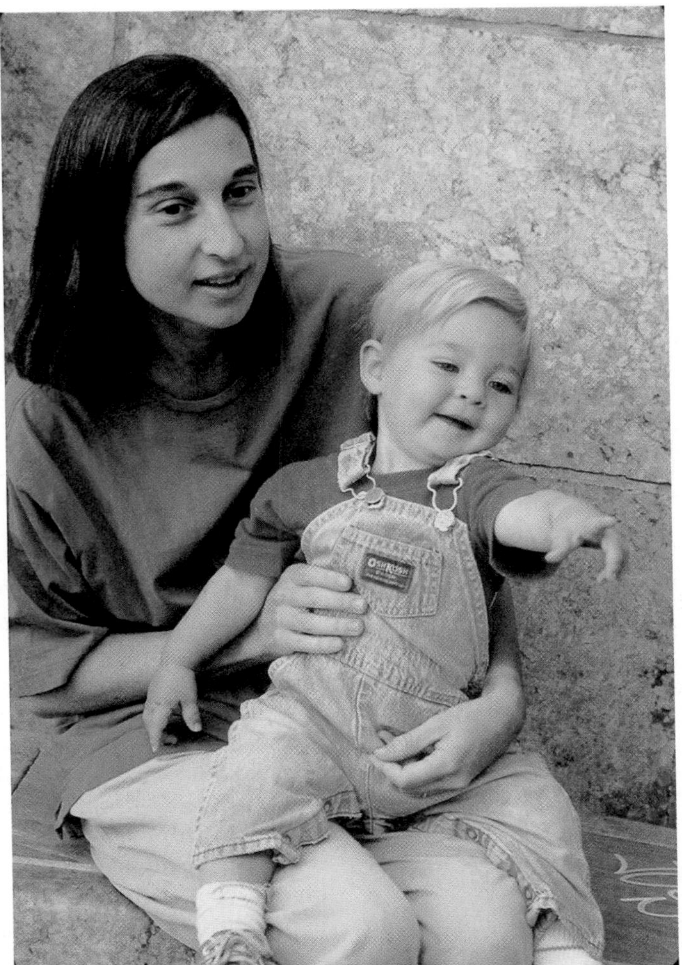

Late in the first year, many young children use gestures to communicate, either to call an adult's attention to an object or to get an adult to do something. Gestures typically drop out of the child's repertoire, though, as spoken language develops.

The One-Word Stage Typically at about one year of age, children say their first words, often *Mama, Dada,* or *bye*. From about twelve to twenty months of age, most children continue to speak only one word at a time. Children's first words are most frequently nouns, labels for objects, people, or events, although action words (*give*), modifiers (*dirty*), and personal-social words (*please*) also occur (Bates et al., 1994; Nelson, 1973). Children's early words usually refer to people or objects important in their lives, such as parents and other relatives, pets, and familiar objects. Children are also more likely to acquire labels for dynamic objects (*clock, car, ball*) or those they can use (*cup, cookie*) than for items that are stationary (*wall, window*). There is surprising regularity in the words that children from different background cultures first say. In research involving almost 1,000 one-year-olds from the United States, Beijing, and Hong Kong, Twila Tardif and her colleagues found that the following six words showed up most frequently in the children's first ten words regardless of culture: *Mommy, Daddy, bye, hi, uh-oh,* and *woof-woof* (Tardif et al., 2008).

Children acquire their first ten words slowly; the typical child adds about one to three words to his or her repertoire each month (Barrett, 1989). From about age eighteen months onward, however, many children show a virtual explosion in the acquisition of new words. This remarkable period in language development is called the **vocabulary spurt** (Barrett, 1985; Bloom, 1973). In one longitudinal study of vocabulary growth in one- to two-year-olds, some learned to say as many as twenty new words, mostly nouns, during each week of the vocabulary spurt (Goldfield & Reznick, 1990). Figure 7.7 shows the rapid rate of vocabulary growth for three children in the middle of their spurt. Within the same period, children also typically show a spurt in the number of words they understand (Reznick & Goldfield, 1992). When rapid vocabulary growth first begins, children also show a temporary increase in the number of errors they make in naming objects, forgetting words they recently learned. The influx of new words may temporarily interfere with knowledge that has been recently stored, a finding that is perhaps to be

vocabulary spurt Period of rapid word acquisition that typically occurs early in language development.

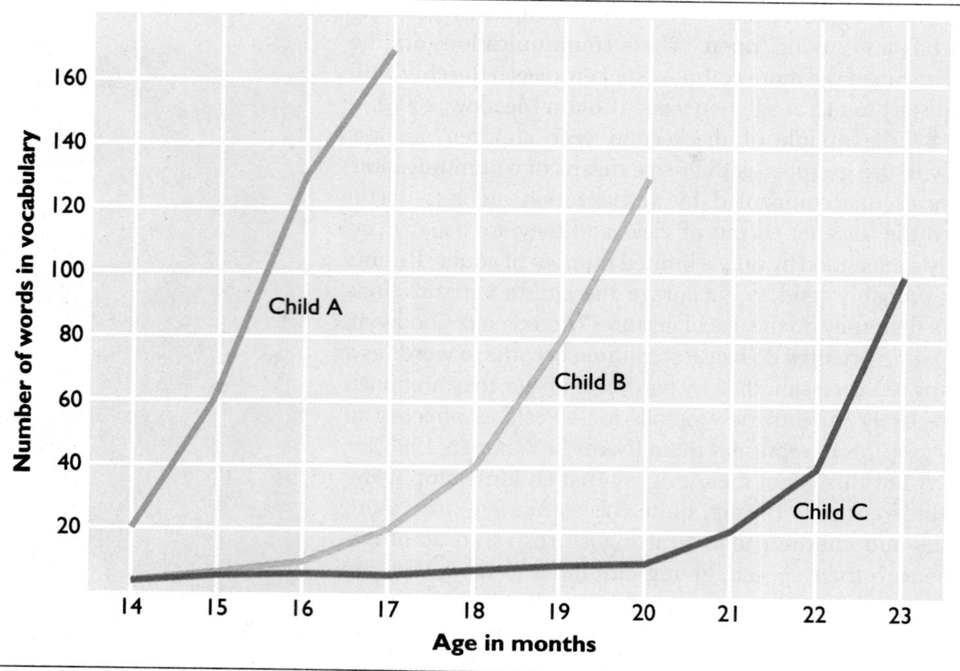

Figure 7.7
The Vocabulary Spurt in Three Young Children
Many children show a vocabulary spurt, a sharp rise in the number of new words they learn, as they approach two years of age. However, children may begin their spurts at different ages, as the graph clearly shows. Child A showed an early spurt, beginning at fifteen months. Child B's spurt began at the more typical age of eighteen months. Child C showed a late spurt at twenty-one months.
Source: Adapted from Goldfield & Reznick, 1990.

expected at this transitional time in language development (Dapretto & Bjork, 2000; Gershkoff-Stowe, 2001; Gershkoff-Stowe & Smith, 1997).

Once children enter a period of rapid vocabulary acquisition, between eighteen months and two years of age, the range of sounds they produce expands. Moreover, they link those sounds in the intonation patterns, or vocal melody, which characterize their native language (Snow, 2006). Certain kinds of errors are common, though, and may persist until children are in preschool or even elementary school. They might replace a *k* sound with a *t* to say *tootie* instead of *cookie* or substitute *w* for *r* in the word *rabbit.* Or children might delete a syllable that is unstressed, for example, saying *nana* for *banana*, or use reduplication, calling a bottle *baba* (Vihman, 1998). Children continue to develop the fine motor control that allows them to refine their speech articulation until age eight years and beyond (Singh & Singh, 2008).

INTERACTION AMONG DOMAINS

Most noticeable at this phase of language learning is the child's intense desire to communicate her thoughts, feelings, and desires. Even though her language skills are limited to one or, at most, two words at a time, the young child is enormously eager to find ways of talking about favorite people, toys, and objects (Bloom, 1998; Dromi, 1999).

Under- and Overextensions Some of the child's first words are bound to a specific context; that is, the child uses the word to label objects in limited situations. Lois Bloom (1973) observed that one nine-month-old used the word *car* only when she was looking out the living room window at cars moving on the street. She did not say "car" to refer to parked cars, pictures of cars, or cars she was sitting in. This type of utterance, used when the child applies a label to a narrower class of objects than the term signifies, is called an **underextension**. Over time, the child begins to use single words more flexibly in a wider variety of contexts (Barrett, 1986). Children may also show **overextension**, applying a label to a broader category than the term signifies. For example, a toddler may call a horse or a cow "doggie." The child often applies the same word to objects that look alike perceptually (Clark, 1973). At other times, the child may misuse a word when objects share functions, such as calling a rolling quarter a "ball" (Bowerman, 1978). As with underextensions, the child's use of overextensions declines after the second year.

underextension Application of a label to a narrower class of objects than the term signifies.

overextension Tendency to apply a label to a broader category than the term actually signifies.

Comprehension Versus Production If you have ever tried to learn a new language, you undoubtedly found it easier to understand what another speaker was saying than to produce a sentence in the new language yourself. An important point to remember about children's early language is that their **receptive language**, what they comprehend, far exceeds their **productive language**, their ability to say and use the words. In one study, parents reported an average of 5.7 words produced by their ten-month-olds but a comprehension average about three times greater, 17.9 words (Bates, Bretherton, & Snyder, 1988).

Infants show distinct signs of comprehending words as early as six months of age, well before they utter their first words. In one study, infants heard the word *mommy* or *daddy* produced by a synthetic voice in a gender-neutral frequency. As each word was repeated, they also saw side-by-side videos of their parents. Infants showed a clear preference for looking at the video of the parent who matched the spoken word. This preference was not evident in another group of infants who viewed strange men and women on videotape while listening to the words (Tincoff & Jusczyk, 1999). Thus, six-month-old infants show that they know the specific meanings of words, at least for people who are important in their lives. Over the course of the next year and a half, children show a dramatic increase in the speed and accuracy with which they understand spoken words (Fernald, Perfors, & Marchman, 2006; Hurtado, Marchman, & Fernald, 2008).

In general, infants comprehend the labels for nouns before they understand the labels for adjectives and verbs, no matter if they are learning English, Chinese, or Japanese (Booth & Waxman, 2009; Imai et al., 2008; Tomasello & Farrar, 1986). For example, although eighteen-month-olds show that they can learn what it means for a Lego car to *neem* ("push"), fourteen-month-olds have difficulty (Casasola & Cohen, 2000). One hypothesis for this delay in understanding verbs has to do with the notion that many verbs denote the actions or motions of objects. Thus, in order to understand a verb, the child has to first understand something about the object involved and the actions and motions it is capable of (Kersten, 1998). In fact, when young children are learning new verbs (such as "This one is *spogging*"), they often attend to how objects look as much as to what they do (Kersten & Smith, 2002).

That young children understand so much of what is said to them means they have acquired some important information about language before they actually speak. They know that people, objects, and events have names. They know that specific patterns of sounds represent objects and events in their environment. Most importantly, they begin to appreciate the usefulness of language as a means of expressing ideas, needs, and feelings.

Deriving the Meanings of Words: Constraints The number of new words that the child learns grows rapidly from age eighteen months through the preschool years. By the time they enter school, children know more than 14,000 words (Carey, 1978). How do children learn the meanings of so many new words in such a short period of time? The statistical learning that characterizes infants' abilities to detect words in the stream of speech similarly operates when young toddlers learn the labels for objects. A recent study showed that, if a word was applied to a given object 100 or 80 percent of the time, it was learned better than if the word referred to the object only 20 percent of the time (Vouloumanos & Werker, 2009). Thus, basic learning processes are part of the explanation.

Another way that the child acquires word meanings is by a process called **fast-mapping**, in which the context provides the key to the meanings of words that the child hears being spoken. Often the child's initial comprehension of a word is an incomplete guess, but a fuller understanding of its meaning follows from successive encounters with it in other contexts (Carey, 1978). Upon hearing the word *eggbeater* while watching someone unload various implements from the dishwasher, the child may think it is some kind of cooking tool; hearing the word again, as someone uses a specific object to mix a bowl of eggs, refines the meaning of the word in the child's mind. Children are often able to derive the meanings of words quickly, even when the exposure is brief, if the context in which they hear those words is meaningful (Rice & Woodsmall, 1988).

Many researchers believe that certain biases operate in the child's literal "search for meaning." Consider again the toddler who hears a new word, such as *eggbeater.* What does that word mean? Logically, it could refer to a host of objects

receptive language Ability to comprehend spoken speech.

productive language Meaningful language spoken or otherwise produced by an individual.

fast-mapping Process through which the context in which the child hears words spoken provides the key to their meanings.

Figure 7.8

The Taxonomic Constraint

Preschool children tend to extend novel words to other examples of the same taxonomic category. This is one type of constraint that guides young children's word learning.

Sources: (left) © Eric Isselée/Shutterstock.com, (right) © Fesus Robert/Shutterstock.com

"This is a dax!"

"Can you show me another dax?"

or perhaps an action instead of an object. Testing the numerous hypotheses could take an inordinate amount of time. Several researchers argue that children are biased to form more restricted hypotheses about the meanings of words; if they were not, they would not learn language so rapidly and with so few errors. **Constraints** on word learning give young children an edge in figuring out the meanings of words from the vast array of possibilities.

One of these constraints is that young children tend to assume that new words label unfamiliar objects, a phenomenon called the **mutual exclusivity bias** (Littschwager & Markman, 1994; Markman, 1987, 1990). Researchers have been able to demonstrate that children tend to treat new words as labels for new objects rather than as synonyms for words they already know. For example, Ellen Markman and Gwyn Wachtel (1988) showed three-year-olds pairs of objects; in each set, one object was familiar and the other was unfamiliar (for example, a banana and a pair of tongs). When children were told, "Show me the X" where X was a nonsense syllable, they tended to select the unfamiliar objects. That is, they assumed that the new word referred to the object for which they did not yet have a name. The mutual exclusivity bias emerges at about age three and is evident even in deaf children who use American Sign Language (Lederberg, Prezbindowski, & Spencer, 2000).

Researchers have examined other word learning constraints by examining how children *extend* new words. For example, if you look at Figure 7.8, children might be told that the picture at the top is a *dax*. Then they are asked "Can you find another *dax?*" To which other picture will they apply this new word? The choice they make is presumed to reveal something about the way in which they understand the word. Using this procedure, Ellen Markman and Jean Hutchinson (1984) found that four- and five-year-olds displayed the **taxonomic constraint**. Most children pointed to the cat, another member of the conceptual category *animals*, and not the bone, an item that is often associated with dogs in a functional way. In contrast, when children heard no label for the dog and were simply instructed to "find another one," they tended to associate the dog with the bone. Novel words, it seems, are extended to other items in similar conceptual categories.

Another bias in word learning, the **shape bias**, refers to the child's assumption that a new word labels an entire object, specifically its form. Young children learning that a

constraints The idea that children are biased to process information about language in limited ways.

mutual exclusivity bias Tendency for children to assume that unfamiliar words label new objects.

taxonomic constraint Tendency for children to assume that novel words label members of the same conceptual category.

shape bias The child's assumption that a new word labels an entire object, specifically its form.

new object is called a *zup,* for example, apply that word to other objects similar in shape, but not in color, rigidity, or other characteristics (Graham & Poulin-Dubois, 1999; Samuelson & Smith, 2000). Where do constraints on word learning come from? Some researchers believe they are innate and unique to word learning, that they are examples of highly specific linguistic processes (Waxman & Booth, 2000). Others suggest that they arise from growth in general knowledge about objects and their relationships to one another and, thus, that more general learning processes account for them (Smith, 1995; Smith, 1999). This is a debate that continues as researchers explore the bases of early word learning.

NATURE & NURTURE

Deriving the Meanings of Words: Social Processes The ways in which a parent speaks to the child—specifically, the use of infant-directed speech—may further assist the child's acquisition of word meaning. For example, mothers tend to say the names for objects more loudly than other words in their speech to infants, and often they place the object label in the last position in their sentence, as in "Do you see the *rattle*?" (Messer, 1981). Mothers also tend to highlight new words by raising their pitch as they say them (Fernald & Mazzie, 1991) or moving an object as they label it (Gogate, Bahrick, & Watson, 2000).

One of the most remarkable observations is that young language learners are able to use even more subtle social cues to figure out which objects new words are labeling. Suppose an adult says, "Let's find the *gazzer*" and looks at an object, rejects it, and excitedly picks up another object without naming it. The infant assumes the second object is the *gazzer* (Tomasello, Strosberg, & Akhtar, 1996). Or suppose an adult and an infant are playing with several unfamiliar, unnamed objects; then, the adult introduces a new object,

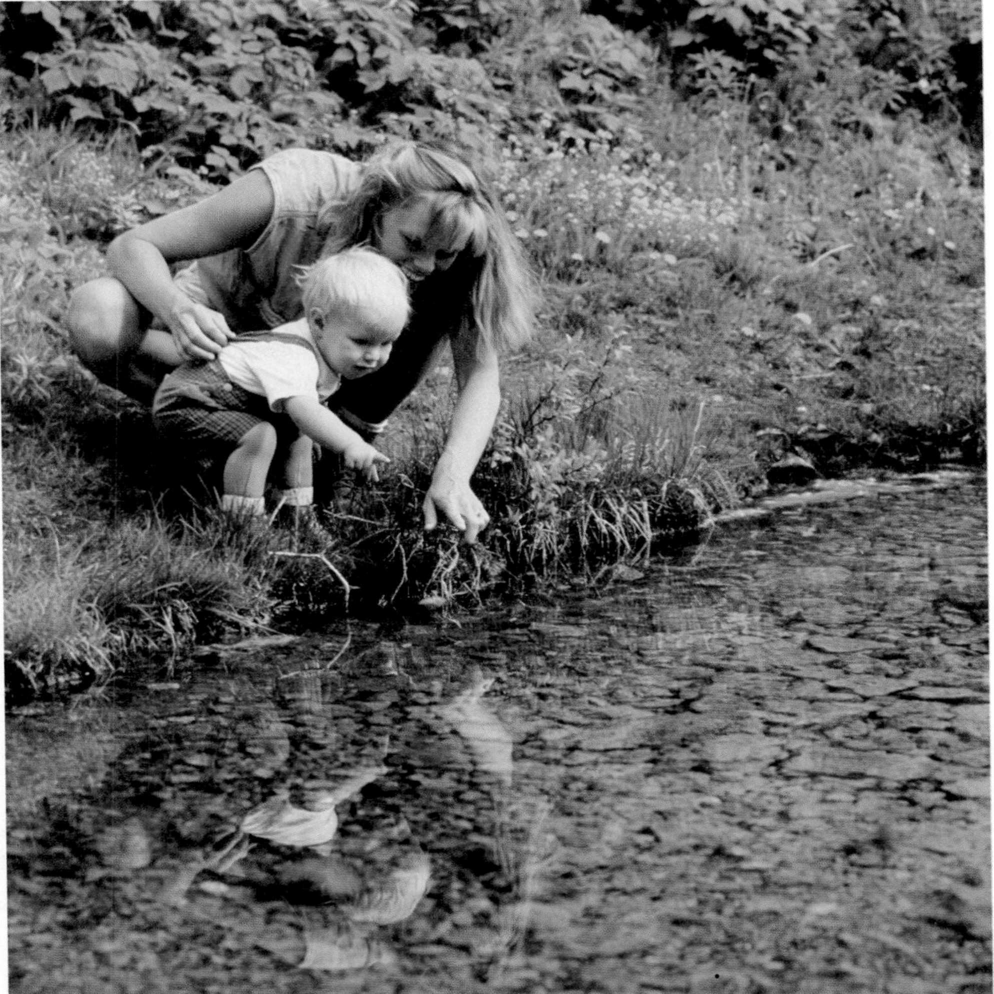

Episodes of joint attention between child and caregiver are important contexts for the acquisition of language and particularly for learning the meaning of words. Research shows that the amount of time infants spend in joint attention with their caregivers predicts their early language skills.

saying, "Look, I see a *modi*!" without pointing to any object. Again, the infant assumes the newest object is the *modi* (Akhtar, Carpenter, & Tomasello, 1996). These studies demonstrate that infants have an impressive ability to interpret social cues in deciding how labels and objects match up. They also show that episodes of **joint attention**, those times in which child and caregiver share the same "psychological space," are important contexts for language acquisition. Many parents and infants tend to spend substantial time in these moments of mutual engagement. For example, parents of infants tend to label many objects, often in the context of joint book reading or the child's manifest interest in a particular object or person in her surroundings (Ninio & Bruner, 1978). A typical scenario goes like this: The infant turns his head, points, and maybe even coos as the family dog enters the room. The mother also turns and looks, and says "doggie." These are precisely the conditions under which infants seem to remember the words that name objects (Masur, 1982).

Researchers have found that the amount of time infants spend in joint attention with their caregivers, whether in book reading or other contexts, is a strong predictor of their early language skills (Carpenter, Nagell, & Tomasello, 1998). According to Paul Bloom (2000), this evidence indicates that the child is actively seeking to find out what is on the minds of the adults with whom she is interacting—what their words refer to and what they are intending to communicate.

RISK | RESILIENCE

Researchers have observed that the more mothers talk with their children, the more words their children acquire (Huttenlocher et al., 1991; Olson, Bayles, & Bates, 1986). It is not just how much mothers talk to their children that makes a difference, however; *how* they talk also matters. When mothers use many directives to control their children's behaviors and are generally intrusive, language development is slowed. When mothers (or teachers) use questions, expansions, and conversational turn taking to elicit language from children or follow the children's vocalizations with a response, language development proceeds more rapidly (Hoff-Ginsberg, 1986; Nelson, 1973; Tamis-LeMonda, Bornstein, & Baumwell, 2001; Valdez-Menchaca & Whitehurst, 1992).

Linguistic exchanges with other interaction partners—fathers, siblings, peers, and others—may uniquely influence the child's eventual level of linguistic skill. For example, when fifteen-month-olds "converse" with their fathers, they experience more communication breakdowns than when they talk with their mothers. Fathers more often request clarification, change the topic, or do not acknowledge the child's utterance after they fail to understand what she or he said (Tomasello, Conti-Ramsden, & Ewert, 1990). Thus, in communicating with fathers, children are challenged to make adjustments to maintain the interaction. Children also learn language by overhearing it on educational television (Wright et al., 2001), in conversations between mothers and older siblings (Ashima-Takane, Goodz, & Derevensky, 1996), or even between two strangers (Akhtar, Jipson, & Callanan, 2001). Children are normally exposed to a rich and varied range of linguistic stimuli from different sources in the environment; many theorists believe this fact ensures that children will learn the details of linguistic structures that may not be present in the verbalizations of a single conversation partner, such as the mother (Gleitman, Newport, & Gleitman, 1984; Wexler, 1982).

Individual Differences in Language Development Although children show many common trends in the way they acquire language, they also show significant individual differences in rates and types of language production. You may have heard a family member or friend report that her child said virtually nothing for two or three years and then began speaking in complete sentences. Although such dramatic variations in language milestones are not frequent, children sometimes show unique patterns in their linguistic accomplishments, patterns that still lead to the attainment of normal language by later childhood.

One example of wide individual variation is the age at which children say their first word. Some children produce their first distinguishable word as early as nine months, whereas others may not do so until sixteen months (Barrett, 1989). Similarly, some children show good pronunciation, whereas others have difficulty making certain sounds, consistently substituting *t* for *k*, or *b* for *v*, for example (Smith, 1988). In addition, not all children

joint attention Episodes in which the child and another individual share the same psychological space as they encounter experiences in the world.

display the vocabulary spurt (Acredolo & Goodwyn, 1990b), or they may start their spurt at different ages, as Figure 7.7 indicates. The results of a study of more than 1,800 children underscore just how variable the size of children's vocabularies can be: at sixteen months of age, some children spoke 10 or fewer words, whereas others spoke as many as 180 words (Fenson et al., 1994).

Children may also differ in the content of their one-word speech. Most one-year-olds tend to use nominals predominantly, displaying what Katherine Nelson (1973) termed a

research applied to parenting | Reading to Children

It was only a couple of months later that Chad began to say a few different words. But after that, his vocabulary expanded rapidly, and he started stringing words together. Tanya marveled at the progress Chad was making as she prepared her son's bed. This was her favorite time of day. Every night, just before Chad was put to bed, Tanya would pull him up in her lap and take a picture book from the shelf. At first, she just pointed to and named things in the book, often encouraging Chad to participate by asking, "What's that?" As his vocabulary increased, Tanya elaborated on his answers and asked other questions: "What does the doggie say?" "Woof-woof!" squealed Chad, enjoying the ritual perhaps every bit as much, maybe even more, than his mother.

The research findings discussed earlier show that how and how often parents speak to children can influence language development. One context in which mothers' speech tends to be particularly lavish is during book reading. Erika Hoff-Ginsberg (1991) found that when mothers and two-year-olds were reading books, mothers showed the greatest diversity in the vocabulary they used, the greatest complexity of syntax, and the highest rate of replies to their children compared with other contexts, such as mealtime or toy play. Other research has shown that the amount of time parents spent reading stories to their twenty-four-month-olds predicted children's language ability up to two years later (Crain-Thoreson & Dale, 1992). As a result of such findings, many child development experts encourage parents to read to their young children.

Grover Whitehurst and his colleagues have developed a program called *dialogic reading* to stimulate language development in preschool children at risk for academic failure, but the general principles can be applied by any parent interested in promoting his or her child's language development. Here is some advice the researchers have developed for parents:

1. *Ask* what *questions (such as "What is this?") to stimulate the child to speak.* Avoid yes/no questions that require only brief answers.
2. *Follow the child's answer with a question.* Ask, for example, what shape or color an object has or what it is used for.
3. *Repeat the child's utterance in the form of an expansion.* For example, follow "Cow" with "Yes, that's right, it's a cow." This gives the child feedback that she is correct.
4. *If the child doesn't have an answer, provide a model and ask him to repeat.* For example, say "That's a bottle. Can you say bottle?"
5. *Be generous with praise and encouragement.* Make comments such as "Good talking" or "Nice job."
6. *Be responsive to the child's interests.* When the child expresses an interest in a picture or part of the story, follow her interest with encouragement to talk.
7. *Have fun.* Do not pressure the child; take turns with the child, and even make the activity a game.

Dialogic reading has been shown to increase language skills in children from different social classes when used by daycare teachers as well as parents (Arnold & Whitehurst, 1994) and in diverse cultures such as China (Chow et al., 2008) . Of course, children learn language skills in many other contexts, such as mealtime conversations (Snow, 1993). Thus, children whose parents do not read to them often are not necessarily fated to have poor language skills (Scarborough & Dobrich, 1993). Nonetheless, reading to children, even when they are as young as eight months old, leads to desirable outcomes in language development (DeBaryshe, 1993; Karrass & Braungart-Rieker, 2005).

Researchers have identified several techniques that parents can use to promote language development in the context of reading to their children. Among them are asking "what" questions, following the child's answer with a question, and using recasts. Making the experience positive and fun for the child is also important.

referential style. Other children show a different pattern: rather than naming objects, they frequently use words that have social functions, such as *hello* or *please,* thus displaying an **expressive style.** Expressive children use words to direct or comment on the behavior of other people. According to some research, referential children tend to have a larger vocabulary and show more rapid advances in language development, at least in the early stages (Bates et al., 1988; Nelson, 1973).

INTERACTION AMONG DOMAINS

How do we explain these individual differences in the rates and styles with which children acquire language? There are several hypotheses. Perhaps individual differences result from variations in the neurological structures that control language learning or from inborn differences in temperament. For example, referential children tend to have a long attention span, smile and laugh a lot, and are easily soothed (Dixon & Shore, 1997). Children who are more advanced in language comprehension and production show a similar profile (Dixon & Smith, 2000). This style might allow them to profit from incoming information about the names of objects. Some children also seem to be able to process information faster than others when asked to look at the correct picture as they hear "Where's the doggie?" Speed of reacting to these kinds of questions is a strong predictor of growth in vocabulary and grammar throughout early childhood (Fernald et al., 2006; Marchman & Fernald, 2008). Another possibility is that parents influence the rate and form of children's vocabulary development. Some parents, for example, may spend a great deal of time encouraging their infants to speak, focusing especially on labeling objects. Others may be more relaxed about letting the infant proceed at his or her own pace. Researchers have confirmed that the overall amount and variety of speech that parents produce for their infants is related to the acceleration of vocabulary growth (Hoff & Naigles, 2002; Huttenlocher et al., 1991).

NATURE & NURTURE

SOCIOCULTURAL INFLUENCE

Cultural Differences in Language Development There is substantial uniformity in the way children in different cultures learn to speak, but there are some notable differences, too. In Twila Tardif's study of infants from three cultures, the results (see Figure 7.9) show us that most first words label people, but there are cross-cultural variations in which other words appear in early vocabularies (Tardif et al., 2008). Cultural differences in how children speak in the one-word stage bolster the idea that what children hear others say influences what they themselves say. Unlike American children, Korean toddlers show a "verb spurt" before a "noun spurt" (Choi, 1998; Choi & Gopnik, 1995); similarly, Mandarin-speaking toddlers utter more verbs than nouns as they and their

referential style Type of early language production in which the child uses mostly nominals.

expressive style Type of early language production in which the child uses many social words.

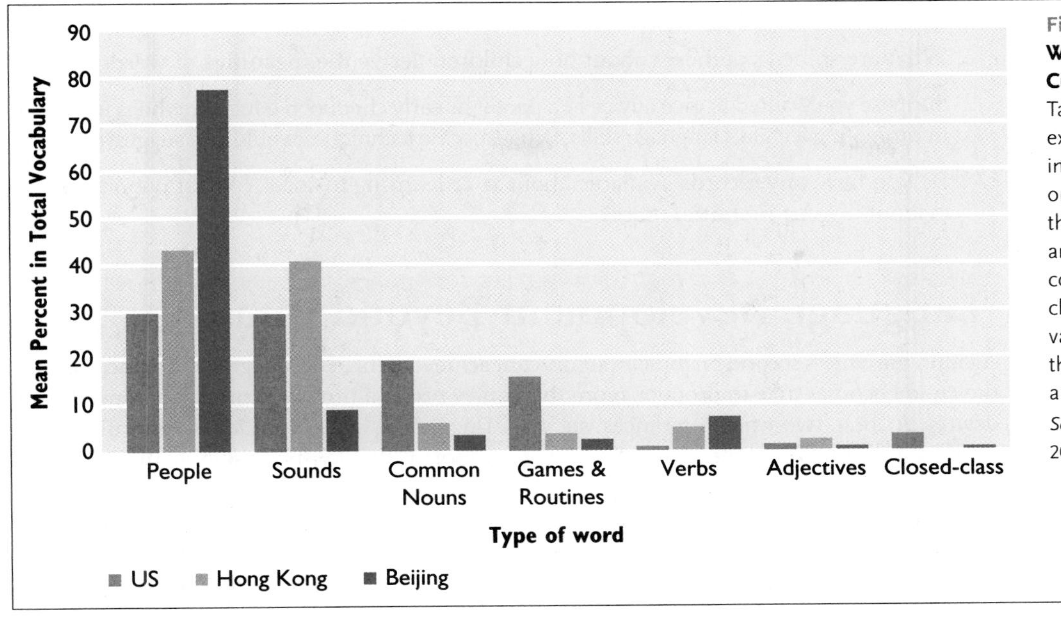

Figure 7.9
Word Learning in Three Cultures
Tardif and her colleagues examined the first ten words in the vocabularies of almost one thousand children from the United States, Hong Kong, and Beijing. The results show commonalities in the nature of children's first words, but also variations that may represent the influence of cultural values and practices.
Source: Data from Tardif, T. et al., 2008.

mothers play with toys (Tardif, 1996; Tardif, Gelman, & Xu, 1999). Mothers from both Asian groups pepper their speech with many more verbs and action sequences, saying things such as "What are you doing?" and "You put the car in the garage." American mothers, in contrast, use far more nouns (for instance, "That's a ball") and ask questions that require a nominal as an answer (such as "What is it?").

Consider the following two examples of maternal speech, one American and the other Japanese, as observed by Anne Fernald and Hiromi Morikawa (1993):

> *American mother*: That's a car. See the car? You like it? It's got nice wheels.
>
> *Japanese mother*: Here! It's a vroom vroom. I give it to you. Now you give it to me. Give me. Yes! Thank you.

Whereas American mothers tend to name objects and focus on the exchange of information, Japanese mothers rarely name objects, using them instead to engage their infants in social routines. Perhaps it is not surprising, then, that American infants use substantially more nouns in their speech at nineteen months of age. Thus, mothers may have different agendas as they speak with their children, and their style of speech may subtly shape the children's utterances.

Another example of variation in the use of infant-directed speech can be found in the Kaluli society of Papua New Guinea. In this culture, talking with others is a highly valued social skill, yet few adult verbalizations are directed to infants. Infants may be called by their names, but until they pass their first year, little else is said to them. When mothers do begin to talk to their babies, their speech contains few of the elements of parentese. Turn taking, repetitions, and elaborations are absent; usually mothers simply make directive statements that require no response from the child. Nevertheless, Kaluli children become proficient users of their language within developmental norms (Schieffelin & Ochs, 1983).

For Your Review and Reflection

- What kinds of phonological skills and preferences have researchers observed in infants?
- What are some of the features and patterns in infants' early vocalizations?
- How do young children use gestures in communication?
- What are the important features of children's language during the one-word stage?

- What are some of the individual and cultural variations in language acquisition?
- What are some hypotheses about how children derive the meanings of words?
- Suppose you wanted to give advice to a parent or early childhood educator who is interested in promoting a child's language skills. What specific techniques would you suggest?
- Do you have any records available about your learning to speak? What patterns are evident in your first utterances?

Language Development Beyond Infancy

Around the child's second birthday, a significant achievement in language production appears: the child becomes able to produce more than one word at a time to express ideas, needs, and desires. At first, two-word utterances, such as "Doggie go" and "More juice," prevail, but the child soon combines greater numbers of words in forms that loosely resemble the grammatical structure of his or her native language. When children combine words, they are stating more than just labels for familiar items; they are expressing relationships among objects and events in the world. Most impressive is that most of this process is conducted with relatively little deliberate instruction about grammar from adults. All of this represents no small feat for a two-year-old who is now mastering some of the more complex aspects of language.

Early Grammars: The Two-Word Stage

At first, children's two-word utterances consist of combinations of nouns, verbs, and adjectives, and omit the conjunctions, prepositions, and other modifiers that give speech its familiar flow. In addition, young talkers use very few morphemes to mark tense or plurals. Because speech at this stage usually contains only the elements essential to getting the message across, it has sometimes been described as **telegraphic speech**.

In his systematic observations of the language of three children, Martin Braine (1976) noted that speech at this stage contained a unique structure, which he dubbed *pivot grammar.* The speech of the children he observed contained noticeable regularities: one word often functioned in a fixed position, and other words filled in the empty slot. For example, one child said, "More car, more cookie, more juice, more read." Table 7.1 contains several other examples of a two-year-old's early word combinations.

More recent research has confirmed that children use nouns in particular in these pivot-type constructions, even when the noun is a nonsense word, such as *wug.* Thus, if a caregiver says, "Look! A wug!" children would say "More wug" or "Wug gone" (Tomasello et al., 1997). Children do not yet produce utterances according to a well-developed grammar, though; their constructions are probably based on the phrasings they hear as the adults around them speak (Tomasello & Brooks, 1999).

Many experts believe that no one syntactic system defines the structure of early language for all children (Maratsos, 1983; Tager-Flusberg & Zukowski, 2009). Some children speak with nouns, verbs, adjectives, and sometimes adverbs, whereas others infuse their speech with pronouns and other words such as *I, it,* and *here* (Bloom, Lightbown, & Hood, 1975). Most researchers agree, however, that individual children frequently use consistent word orders and that their understanding of at least a small set of semantic relationships is related to that word order. Moreover, numerous detailed observations of children's language indicate that they never construct "wild grammars"; some utterances, such as "Big he" or "Hot it," are simply never heard (Bloom, 1991). Such observations have distinct implications for explanations of syntactic development.

As we saw with learning the meanings of words, children just starting to use more complex speech are able to comprehend more information conveyed by different grammatical structures than they are able to produce. Two-year-olds, for example, demonstrate an understanding of singular versus plural words (Wood, Kouider, & Carey, 2009) and of the difference between past, present, and future tenses,

telegraphic speech Early two-word speech that contains few modifiers, prepositions, or other connective words.

TABLE 7.1 One Child's Early Grammar

This table shows several examples of one two-year-old's two-word speech. Frequently, one word—the pivot word—is repeated, while several other words fill the other slot. The pivot word can occupy either the first or second position in the child's utterances.

no bed	boot off	more car	airplane all gone
no down	light off	more cereal	Calico all gone
no fix	pants off	more cookie	Calico all done
no home	shirt off	more fish	all done milk
no mama	shoe off	more high	all done now
no more	water off	more hot	all gone juice
no pee	off bib	more juice	all gone outside
no plug		more read	all gone pacifier
no water		more sing	salt all shut
no wet		more toast	
		more walk	
		outside more	

Source: Adapted from Braine, 1976.

even though these distinctions do not typically appear in their own speech (Wagner, 2001). They also show that they understand the different meanings conveyed by transitive versus intransitive verbs (those with and without objects, respectively). In one study, twenty-five-month-old children saw a video of a duck bending a bunny over as both animals made arm circles. The experimenter said either, "The duck is blicking the bunny" or "The duck and the bunny are blicking," constructions that are more complex syntactically than the child's own spontaneous utterances. Then children saw two screens, one that portrayed bending and one that portrayed arm-circling. When asked to "Find blicking," children who had heard the term as a transitive verb looked at bending, and those who had heard the term as an intransitive verb looked at arm-circling (Naigles, 1990). Similarly, children just under two years of age are sensitive to the information provided by subjects versus targets of an action (see Figure 7.10) (Fisher et al., 2010).

Figure 7.10
Young Children Are Sensitive to Information Provided by Syntax
Twenty-one-month-old children who heard the top sentence looked longer at a video portraying the events on the right, but they looked at the video on the left when they heard the bottom sentence. These results suggest that young children already know where agents and targets of action belong in a sentence.
Source: From Fisher, C., Gertner, Y., Scott, R. M., & Yuan, S. WIRES Cognitive Science, 1st edition. Reprinted by permission of John Wiley & Sons, Inc.

The boy is gorping the girl!
The girl is gorping the boy!

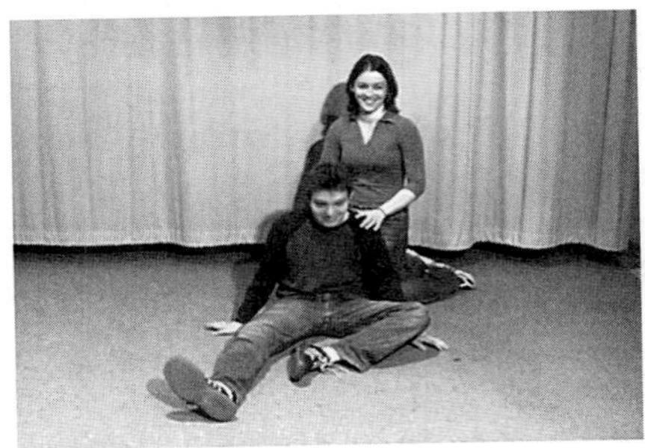

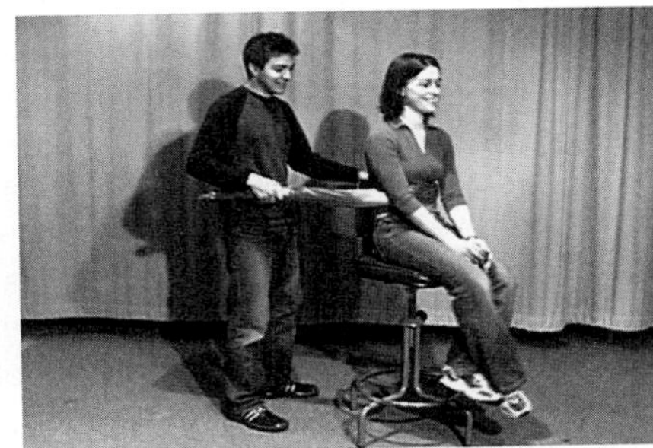

Figure 7.11

Two-Year-Olds Detect Incorrect Grammar

Portions of the left hemisphere of the brain show distinct responding when two-year-olds hear a speaker use incorrect grammar such as "then I take the eat" (left panel) as opposed to correctly stated "then I eat it" (right panel).

Source: From Bernal, S., Dehaene-Lambertz, G., Millotte, S., & Christophe, A. (2010). Two-year-olds compute syntactic structure online. *Developmental Science, 13*(1), 69–76. Reprinted by permission of John Wiley & Sons, Inc.

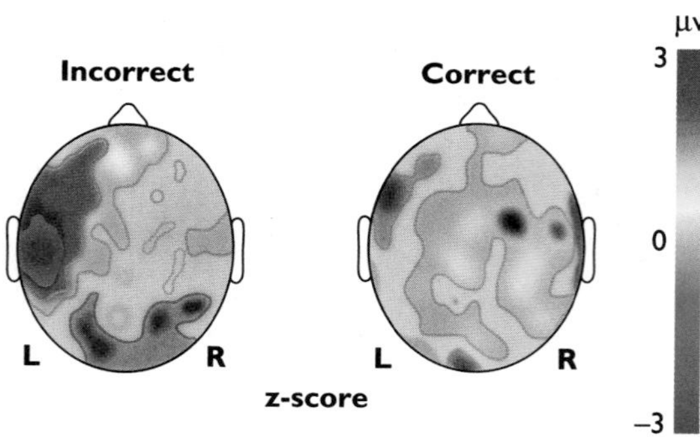

The child's ability to understand syntax shows up in measurements taken of electrical activity of the brain. Figure 7.11 shows how the brains of two-year-olds respond when they watch a video in which the speaker mixes up the positions of nouns and verbs, for example, instead of "then I *eat it*," saying "then I take *the eat*." Portions of the left hemisphere show activation in the presence of incorrect grammar, even among children who are not yet able to produce grammatically complex utterances (Bernal et al., 2010).

Later Syntactic Development

At age two and a half, children's speech often exceeds two words in length and includes many more of the modifiers and connective words that enrich the quality of speech. Adjectives, pronouns, and prepositions are added to the child's repertoire (Valian, 1986). Between ages two and five, the child's speech also includes increasingly sophisticated grammatical structures. *Morphemes*, such as *-s*, *-ed*, and *-ing*, are added to words to signal plurals or verb tense, and more articles and conjunctions are incorporated into routine utterances. The child also comes to use negatives, questions, and passives correctly.

Further information about children's syntactic development has been provided by a longitudinal study of sixty-five children conducted by Marina Vasilyeva and her colleagues (Vasilyeva, Waterfall, & Huttenlocher, 2008). Every four months, researchers obtained ninety-minute videotape samples of the speech of children as they matured from age twenty-two to forty-two months. These utterances were coded according to several linguistic categories including the types of sentences children used, as well as the presence of simple versus complex sentence constructions. Figure 7.12 shows some of the findings. You can see that children shifted from using a preponderance of imperatives to more well-formed declarative sentences over this time span. Early sentences tended to omit the subjects or objects, so children would say things like, "Want more cereal," or "I find." However, almost 70 percent of the twenty-two-month-olds used complete and well-formed simple sentences even at this young age. At twenty-six months, many children, but especially those with highly educated parents, started producing complex sentences like "You will be the prince and I will be the princess" or "There is a lot of stuff that has to come off." These are particularly striking examples of just how rapidly children become sophisticated users of grammatically correct speech.

Several other sophisticated forms of speaking emerge after age two, one of which is the use of negatives. In her examination of language acquisition in four children, Lois Bloom (1991) found a predictable sequence in the use of negatives. Initially, children use the negative to express the *nonexistence* of objects, as in "No pocket," said as the child searches for a pocket in her mother's skirt. In the second stage, children use the negative as they *reject* objects or events. For example, one of Bloom's participants said, "No sock" as

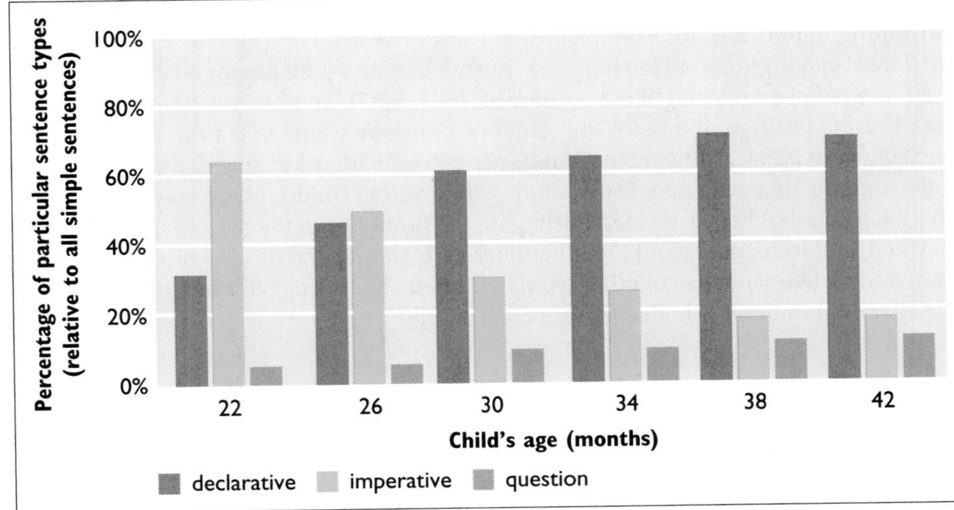

Figure 7.12
The Development of Syntax in Young Children
Researchers observed and coded the kinds of utterances made by children as they grew from 22 to 42 months of age. The results show distinct changes in the simple sentence types children produced over the year and a half.
Source: Vasilyeva, M., Waterfall, H., & Huttenlocher, J. (2008). Emergence of syntax: Commonalities and differences across children. *Developmental Science, 11*(1), 84–97. Reprinted by permission of John Wiley & Sons, Inc.

she pulled her sock off her foot. Finally, negatives are used to express *denial*, such as when the child states, "No dirty" in response to his mother's comment about his dirty sock. This sequence has also been observed cross-culturally, among Chinese children learning to speak Cantonese (Tam & Stokes, 2001). Young children form negatives not just by putting the negative marker at the beginning of an utterance but also by embedding it deep within a statement, as in "My sweetie's no gone" (de Villiers & de Villiers, 1979).

Questions, too, are formed in a fairly consistent developmental sequence, although not all children display the pattern we are about to describe (Maratsos, 1983). Children's earliest questions do not contain inverted word order but consist instead of an affirmative sentence or a declarative preceded by a *wh-* word (*who, what, why, when, where*), with a rising intonation at the end of the statement ("Mommy is tired?"). Subsequently, children form questions by inverting word order for affirmative questions ("Where will you go?") but not negative ones ("Why you can't do it?"). Finally, by age four, children form questions for both positive and negative instances as adults do (Klima & Bellugi, 1966).

One of the more difficult linguistic constructions for children to understand is the passive voice, as in "The car was hit by the truck." Children typically begin to comprehend the meaning of a passive construction by the later preschool years, but they may not use this grammatical form spontaneously and correctly until several years later. Prior to age four, children are also limited in their ability to generate sentences using subject-verb-object (the transitive) with novel verbs they have just learned, as in "He's meeking the ball" (Tomasello & Brooks, 1998). Michael Tomasello maintains that, when two- and three-year-olds do use more complex syntactic constructions, such as the passive and transitive voices, they are initially imitating what adults say. Only later in the preschool and early school years do they have a deeper appreciation for the forms that grammatical constructions can take (Brooks & Tomasello, 1999; Tomasello, 2000).

One particularly interesting phenomenon of the preschool and early school years is the child's tendency to use **overregularizations**, the application of grammatical rules to words that require exceptions to those rules. From time to time, for example, young children use words like *goed* or *runned* to express past tense, even if they previously used the correct forms, *went* and *ran*. Perhaps children make these mistakes because they forget the exception to the general rule for forming a tense (Marcus, 1996). Whatever the reason, these constructions suggest that the child is learning the general rules for forming past tense, plurals, and other grammatical forms (Marcus et al., 1992).

How exactly do children master the rules of syntax? Some clues may come from the phonology or sounds of language. Is the word *record* a noun or a verb, for example? The answer depends on which syllable is stressed. If the first, the word is a noun; if the second, it is a verb. Children may pick up cues from stress, the number of syllables in a word, or other tips from the sounds of language to help them classify words as nouns, verbs, or other grammatical categories (Kelly, 1992).

overregularization Inappropriate application of grammatical rules to words that require exceptions to those rules.

Other cues about syntax may come from the meanings of words. According to the **semantic bootstrapping hypothesis**, for example, when children learn that a certain animal is called a "cat," they also notice that it is a thing (noun) and, later in development, that it is an agent (subject) or a recipient (object) of action (Pinker, 1984, 1987). Thus, the word "cat" could not be placed in the position of a verb; the sentence "Mommy wants to cat me" would not be syntactically permissible. Noticing that adults use certain patterns of speech and understanding their contents may help, too. For example, when young children hear adults say, "Look! The dog's hurling the chair. See? He's hurling it," the pronouns in the pattern "He's [verb]ing it!" may help children understand the unfamiliar verb *hurling* and its use with a subject and object in a transitive sentence. In other words, children's knowledge of semantics influences their mastery of grammar (Childers & Tomasello, 2001).

Acquiring Social Conventions in Speech

When do children first understand that different situations call for different forms of speech? When Jean Gleason and Rivka Perlmann (1985) asked two- to five-year-olds and their parents to play "store," they observed that, at age three, some children modified their speech depending on the role they were playing. For example, one three-and-a-half-year-old boy who was the "customer" pointed to a fake milk bottle and said, "I want . . . I would like milk." His revision showed an understanding that an element of politeness is required of a customer. Preschoolers also have some limited understanding that different listeners are typically spoken to in different ways. In a study in which four- and five-year-olds were asked to speak to dolls portraying adults, peers, or younger children, the participants used more imperatives with dolls representing children and fewer with dolls representing adults and peers (James, 1978).

The child's facility with social forms of politeness increases with age. Researchers in one study instructed two- to six-year-olds to *ask* or *tell* another person to give them a puzzle piece. Older children were rated by adults as being more polite than the younger children, particularly when they were asking for the puzzle piece. Usually, older children included such words as *please* in their requests of another person (Bock & Hornsby, 1981).

NATURE & NURTURE

Parents undoubtedly play a significant role in at least some aspects of the acquisition of pragmatics, especially because they deliberately train their children to speak politely. Esther Greif and Jean Gleason (1980) observed the reactions of parents and children after children had received a gift from a laboratory assistant. If the child did not say "Thank you" spontaneously (and most of the preschoolers in the sample did not), the parent typically prompted the child with "What do you say?" or "Say thank you." Parents also serve as models for politeness routines; most parents in the study greeted the laboratory assistant upon entry and said good-bye when the assistant departed. In cultures such as Japan, in which politeness is a highly valued social behavior, children begin to show elements of polite language as early as age one year (Nakamura, 2001), probably because parents model and reinforce these verbal forms.

SOCIOCULTURAL INFLUENCE

Incorporating social conventions into language often involves learning subtle nuances in behaviors, the correct words, vocal intonations, gestures, or facial expressions that accompany speech in different contexts. Children may get direct instruction on the use of verbal forms of politeness, but it is not yet clear exactly how they acquire the other behaviors that accompany socially skilled communication.

Metalinguistic Awareness

Prior to age five, children may lack a full understanding of what it means for a sentence to be grammatical or how to gauge their linguistic competencies, even when their speech is syntactically correct and effective in delivering a communication. The ability to reflect abstractly on the properties of language and to conceptualize the self as a more or less proficient user of this communication tool is called **metalinguistic awareness**. By most accounts, children show thinking about language in this way during the early school years.

semantic bootstrapping hypothesis Idea that children derive information about syntax from the meaning of words.

metalinguistic awareness Ability to reflect on language as a communication tool and on the self as a user of language.

Reflecting on Properties of Language One of the first studies to explore children's thinking about language was conducted by Lila Gleitman and her colleagues (Gleitman, Gleitman, & Shipley, 1972); these researchers were interested in children's ideas about the function of grammar. The investigators had mothers read grammatically correct and incorrect passages to their two-, five-, and eight-year-old children. After each sentence, an experimenter said, "Good" at the end of an acceptable passage, such as "Bring me the ball," or "Silly" at the end of an unacceptable one, such as "Box the open." When the children were given the opportunity to judge sentences themselves, even the youngest children were generally able to discriminate between correct and incorrect versions. They were not able, however, to correct improper constructions or to explain the nature of a syntactic problem until age five.

In addition, it is not until age six or seven that most children appreciate that words are different from the concepts to which they are linked. For example, four-year-olds frequently believe *train* is a long word because its referent is long, in contrast to older children who understand the distinction (Berthoud-Papandropoulou, 1978). Such changes in metalinguistic understanding are undoubtedly linked to advances in cognition, particularly the development of more flexible and abstract thought.

Humor and Metaphor One visible way in which children demonstrate their metalinguistic awareness is through language play: intentionally mislabeling objects, creating funny words, telling jokes or riddles, or using words in a figurative sense. The earliest signs of humor have been documented shortly after the child begins speaking. Researcher Carolyn Mervis noted that her son Ari, at age fifteen months, called a hummingbird a "duck" (a word he had previously used correctly) and then looked at his mother and laughed (Johnson & Mervis, 1997). However, the ways in which children comprehend and produce humorous verbalizations undergo clear developmental changes from the preschool to later school years. Three- to five-year-olds experiment with the sounds of words, altering phonemes to create humorous facsimiles (for example, *watermelon* becomes *fatermelon*) (McGhee, 1979). By the early school years, the basis of children's humor expands to include riddles or jokes based on semantic ambiguities, as in the following:

QUESTION: *How can hunters in the woods find their lost dogs?*

ANSWER: *By putting their ears to a tree and listening to the bark.*

Still later—as every parent who has ever had to listen to a seemingly endless string of riddles and jokes from a school-age child can testify—children begin to understand and be fascinated by jokes and riddles that require them to discern syntactic ambiguities (Hirsch-Pasek, Gleitman, & Gleitman, 1978), as in the following:

QUESTION: *Where would you go to see a man-eating shark?*

ANSWER: *A seafood restaurant.*

Thus, children's appreciation of humor mirrors their increasingly sophisticated knowledge of the various features of language, beginning with its fundamental sounds and culminating with the complexities of syntactic and semantic rules.

Similarly, children's understanding of **metaphor**, figurative language in which a term that typically describes one object or event is applied to another context (for example, calling a shadow a "piece of the night" or skywriting a "scar in the sky"), undergoes developmental change. Preschoolers show a rudimentary ability to understand and produce figurative language, especially when it refers to perceptual similarities between two objects (Gottfried, 1997). A four-year-old understands expressions like "A string is like a snake," for example (Winner, 1979). But by middle childhood, children understand and even prefer metaphors grounded in conceptual relationships, like "The volcano is a very angry man" (Silberstein et al., 1982).

Throughout this chapter, we have described many developmental changes that take place in children's language skills. The attainments that take place from infancy through the early childhood years are summarized for you in the Language Chronology Chart on p. 270.

metaphor Figurative language in which a term is transferred from the object it customarily designates to describe a comparable object or event.

CHRONOLOGY Development of Language: Birth to 6+ Years

MONTHS BIRTH | YEARS BIRTH

Newborn
- Prefers human voices.
- Discriminates among phonemes.
- Discriminates own language from other languages.
- Cries.

© Purestock/Jupiter Images

1–5 Months
- Discriminates among vowels.
- Is sensitive to prosodic features of speech.
- Coos.

6–12 Months
- Babbles.
- Prefers unfamiliar words in own language to other languages.
- Detects words in a stream of speech.
- Produces gestures to communicate and to symbolize objects.
- Comprehends many words.

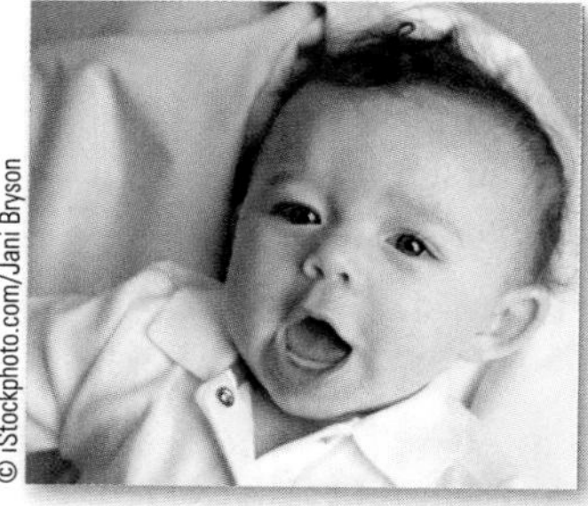
© iStockphoto.com/Jani Bryson

12–18 Months
- Produces single-word utterances.
- Comprehends fifty-plus words.

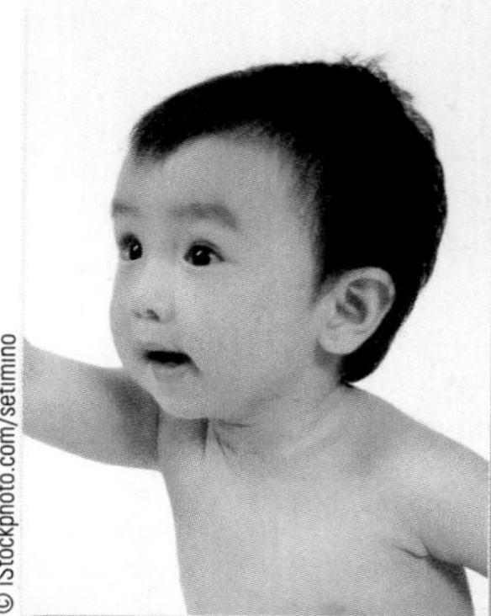
© iStockphoto.com/setimino

18-24 Months
- Displays vocabulary spurt.
- Begins to use two-word utterances.
- Comprehends tense and transitivity.

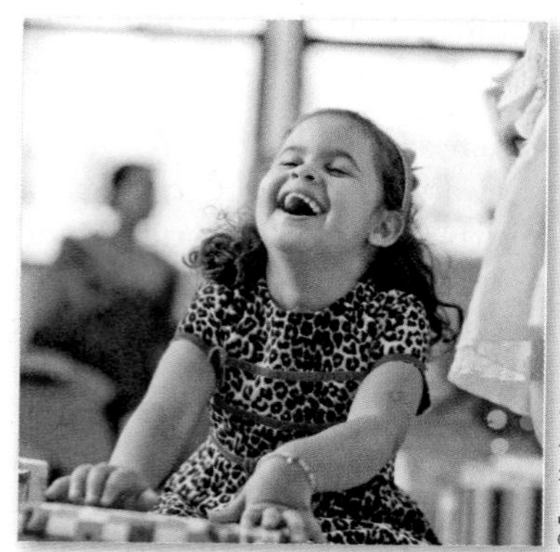
© Fuse/Jupiter Images

2½–5 Years
- Produces multiword utterances.
- Uses morphemes, negatives, questions, and passive voice.
- Shows growth in vocabulary and use of syntax.
- Displays overregularizations.
- Appreciates humor and metaphor.
- Shows growth pragmatics.

© Asia Images Group Pte Ltd/Alamy

6+ Years
- Shows metalinguistic awareness.

This chart describes the sequence of language development based on the findings of research. Children often show individual differences in the exact ages at which they display the various developmental achievements outlined here.

For Your Review and Reflection

- What are the major grammatical accomplishments of children in the two-word stage of language acquisition?
- What syntactic accomplishments follow the two-word stage?
- What aspects of pragmatics do children acquire in the preschool years?
- What are some examples of children's metalinguistic awareness?
- When you look at the Language Chronology Chart describing children's major achievements in this domain, are there one or two developments that are especially impressive or surprising to you? What is it that seems so noteworthy?

Functions of Language

Aside from its obvious usefulness as a social communication tool, what other functions does language serve? Does the human propensity to learn and employ language affect other aspects of functioning, specifically, mental processes, the regulation of behavior, and socialization? At the very least, language enriches the human experience by providing a useful vehicle for enhancing cognition and behavior; it also exerts powerful influences on other areas of human activity. In this section, we will examine briefly some broad effects of language on the domains of cognition, behavior, and socialization.

Language and Cognition

INTERACTION AMONG DOMAINS

The relationship between language and cognition has been an active area of exploration because most recognize the reciprocal relationship between these two domains. For now, let us consider how language might shape the child's thinking. How exactly might language have a powerful influence on the child's cognitive attainments?

Language, Memory, and Classification If you ask a child to perform a cognitive task, such as remembering a list of words or grouping a set of similar objects, you will notice that he will often spontaneously use language to aid his performance. Some of the best examples of this behavior come from research findings on developmental changes in children's memory. There are distinct differences in the way preschool and school-age children approach the task of remembering. Older children are far more likely than younger children to employ deliberate strategies for remembering, strategies that typically involve the use of verbal skills (Flavell, Beach, & Chinsky, 1966). The use of verbal labels seemed to bridge the gap between the time the items were first seen and the time they were to be recalled.

Language can also influence how children categorize related groups of objects. Stan Kuczaj and his colleagues showed children twelve unfamiliar objects that could be grouped into three sets (Kuczaj, Borys, & Jones, 1989). Children who were taught the names of one category member from each group were more successful in sorting the objects than children who were not given labels. Language provides children with cues that classes of stimuli differ from one another, and these cues can influence how children form conceptual groups. If some four-legged animals are called *dogs* and others are called *cats*, the different linguistic labels will highlight for the child that the features of these two groups differ.

Bilingualism and Cognition One of the more interesting ways in which the influence of language on thought has been studied has been to compare, on a variety of tasks, the performances of bilingual children equally fluent in two languages with monolinguals fluent in only one. Bilingual children have been characterized as more analytic and flexible in their approach to different types of thought problems. For example, bilingual children perform better than

Figure 7.13

Cognitive Achievements of Bilingual and Monolingual Children

Bilingual children outperform monolingual children on nonverbal tests such as the Raven Progressive Matrices, which requires participants to select the segment that correctly fits into the larger pattern. Bilingual children generally seem to be more analytical than monolingual children in their approach to various problem-solving tasks.

Source: From Raven's Standard Progressive Matrices. Used by permission of J.C. Raven Ltd.

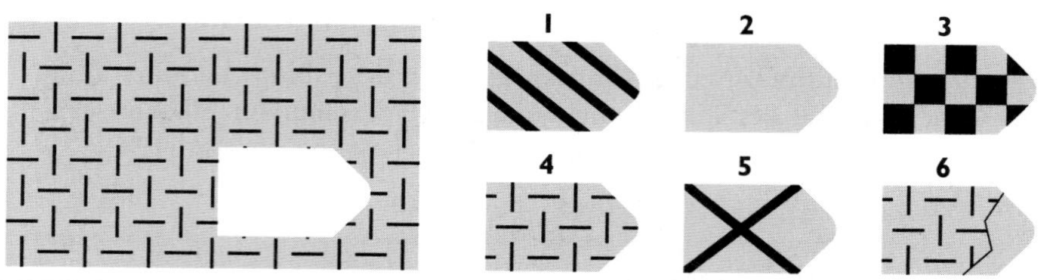

monolinguals on certain nonverbal problems, such as the Raven Progressive Matrices, which assess abstract reasoning (see Figure 7.13) (Hakuta & Diaz, 1985). Bilingual children have also been found to display greater metalinguistic awareness than monolingual children, even those who are chronologically older. When given sentences like "Why is the cat barking so loudly?" bilingual children were more likely than monolingual children to ignore conflicting semantic information and state that the sentences were grammatically correct (Bialystok, 1986). Finally, bilingual children perform better than monolingual children on tasks that require them to control and manage their cognitive processes. When signaled about the location of an interesting puppet to look at, infants reared in bilingual environments are better able to direct their looking to new or changed locations (Kovacs & Mehler, 2009). If instructed to sort a deck of cards based on one dimension—say, color—and then re-sort the deck on the basis of a different dimension—say, shape—bilingual children are better able to inhibit responses from the first task (Bialystok & Craik, 2010).

One hypothesis to explain their superior performance is that bilingual children are forced to think more abstractly and analytically because they have had experience with analyzing the structure and detail of not just one language but two. A second possibility is that they are generally more verbally oriented in their thinking and have a greater tendency to produce verbalizations that enhance their performance even in nonverbal tasks. Finally, they may have more control over cognitive processing because they are constantly having to inhibit one language when they speak (Bialystok, 1999, 2001; Diaz & Klingler, 1991). Whatever the mechanism, these studies demonstrate that speaking a second language affects cognitive processes, often in a favorable way.

How Should Bilingual Education Programs Be Structured? what do you think?

Estimates are that more than 5 million children (or 10 percent of children) attending public schools in the United States have limited English proficiency (National Clearinghouse for English Language Acquisition, 2010), a characteristic that could understandably hinder success in school. Many children who are learning English as a second language experience reading problems, for example (August et al., 2005). Given the ease with which young children learn language and the apparent connection between bilingualism and certain cognitive processes, are there any implications for how children learning English as a second language should be taught?

Philosophies of teaching language-minority children have varied. Some believe that children should receive most of their education in their primary language, whether it is Spanish, Cambodian, or French, and make the transition to English only when they are ready. At the other extreme are the advocates of immersion, the idea that children should be totally surrounded by the second language, learning it in the same way the young child learns the first language. Immersion has been in the public spotlight as states such as California and Massachusetts have mandated this approach to teaching children with limited English proficiency. Some bilingual programs fall between these two extremes, such that English is taught as an extra subject by a bilingual teacher while children take their core academic subjects in their native language.

Proponents of easing children into English by starting them in classes in their native language say that this approach promotes basic language development, which in turn creates the foundation for acquiring the second language. An underlying assumption is that learning two languages at once could interfere with the learning of English (Petitto et al., 2001). In addition, children will develop a sense of belonging in the school, and their self-esteem will be high (Fillmore & Meyer, 1992). Advocates of immersion generally say that children will have to learn English eventually and that it is better not to delay. This view is also consistent with a belief that language learning is generally easier for younger than for older children.

Some research findings suggest that allowing students to build their competence in their own native language assists in learning both core academic subjects and English (Bialystok, 2001; Meyer & Fienberg, 1992). On the other hand, immersion programs have been successful in Canada, Spain, and other countries (Artigal, 1991; Tucker & d'Anglejan, 1972). Unfortunately, evaluations of the effectiveness of bilingual education programs have been fraught with methodological difficulties (Willig & Ramirez, 1993). One issue is that many language-minority children come from a background of poverty, the effects of which may contribute to difficulties with school (Hakuta, 1999). Another problem is that the goal of most bilingual education programs for language-minority children is not, in reality, to make them bilingual but to emphasize speaking English (Petitto, 2009). In contrast, many successful immersion programs in Europe involve teaching both the native language and another highly valued language (Brisk, 1998). In Spain, for example, all children start learning a foreign language at age 3. Recent studies show that, when children learn two languages early in childhood, they can become proficient readers in ***both*** languages. Moreover, English-speaking monolingual children seem to profit from early bilingual education, too; they display better reading skills than children experiencing single language instruction (Kovelman, Baker, & Petitto, 2008). Finally, many children learning a second language are also learning about a second culture. Their degree of success in learning both the new language and the new culture may depend, at least in part, on how their culture of origin is viewed: is it valued or is there discrimination against it? In other words, learning a second language often takes place against a backdrop of complex social factors that are just as important to consider as the elements of linguistic development (Snow & Kang, 2006).

What does the research on the process of language development suggest about the best way to structure bilingual education programs? Aside from economic status, what other variables should future research evaluating bilingual education take into account? Do you know people who learned English as a second language while they were trying to learn academic subject matter in school? Which approach to bilingual education did they experience? Was their educational experience positive or negative? For what reasons?

How Language Influences Self-Regulation

INTERACTION AMONG DOMAINS

Language takes on an increasingly important role in regulating behavior as the child develops, according to two prominent Russian psychologists, Lev Vygotsky and Alexander Luria. Vygotsky (1962) believed the child's initial utterances serve an interpersonal function, signaling others about the child's emotional state. In the preschool years, however, speech takes on a different function. Specifically, the child's **private speech**, or overt, audible "speech-for-self," comes to guide his or her observable activities. If you have ever observed a toddler coloring and simultaneously saying something like "Now, I'll use the blue crayon. I'll make the sky blue," you have seen an example of private speech. Eventually, speech-for-self becomes interiorized; **inner speech** dictates the direction of the child's thoughts. Research has confirmed that audible private speech declines during middle childhood, but talking to one's self covertly increases (Winsler & Naglieri, 2003).

private speech Children's vocalized speech to themselves that directs behavior.

inner speech Interiorized form of private speech.

How important is private speech in directing behavior? You may have noticed that you tend to talk to yourself when

Young children often use private speech when they are engaged in tasks that require close attention. This overt "speech-for-self" guides children's actions and eventually becomes interiorized into a form called inner speech. Language thus helps children regulate their own behavior.

you are under stress or when you have a lot to do. Research has confirmed that children, like adults, use private speech when they find tasks difficult or when they make errors. In one study, researchers found that about 13 percent of three- and four-year-olds used private speech in some way during their spontaneous activities in preschool, but as Figure 7.14 shows, the older children were more likely to use private speech in the context of focused, goal-directed activities, such as doing a puzzle, rather than for nongoal-directed activities, such as wandering around the classroom (Winsler, Carlton, & Barry, 2000).

Similarly, Laura Berk (1986) noted that, when first-graders were solving math problems in school, they engaged in high levels of externalized private speech to guide their problem solving. Third-graders also showed evidence of private speech, but a more internalized form—through mutterings and lip movements—as they attempted to solve math problems. When children use task-relevant private speech, their performance on a variety of tasks improves (Berk, 1992). One longitudinal study demonstrated that, as children progress from overt to more internal private speech, they also show fewer distracting body movements

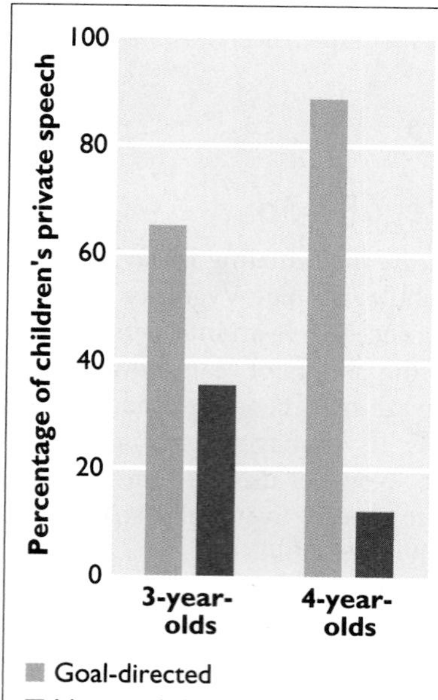

Figure 7.14
Private Speech in Preschoolers
Both three- and four-year-olds use private speech in the natural context of preschool, but four-year-olds are more likely to use private speech when they are engaged in focused, goal-directed activities. Private speech is one way in which language can regulate children's behaviors.
Source: Winsler, A., Carleton, M. P., & Barry, M. J. (2000). Age-related changes in preschool children's systematic use of private speech in a natural setting. *Journal of Child Language, 27,* 665–687. Reprinted with the permission of Cambridge University Press.

and greater sustained attention in school (Bivens & Berk, 1990). Such studies suggest that language becomes an increasingly powerful regulator of children's behavior as they develop.

How Language Influences Cultural Socialization

Still another way in which language can have a broad influence on development is by helping children discern the social roles, relationships, and values of their culture. Many languages have specific grammatical forms that are used to convey gender, age, or social power. In acquiring language, children are sensitized to the specific ways their own culture creates social order. For example, in Japanese, the word particle *zo* signifies affective intensity and a male speaker, and the particle *wa* conveys hesitancy and a female speaker. Children learning Japanese are therefore likely to associate hesitancy with females and forcefulness with males (Ochs, 1990). In many other languages, specific words have formal and informal versions, with the formal used when speaking with individuals who have more authority or power and the informal with individuals who share equal status or are related. Again, such linguistic distinctions highlight important social relationships within the cultural group.

SOCIOCULTURAL INFLUENCE

INTERACTION AMONG DOMAINS

A good example of how language can influence socialization comes from traditional Samoan culture, which emphasizes community and group accomplishments over the attainments of individuals. In Samoan speech, few verbalizations include praise or blame for individuals. Most statements concern the success or failure of the group and emphasize the life of the community. When Samoan children are exposed to verbalizations of this type, they are being socialized into the collective orientation of their culture (Ochs, 1990).

Researchers are just beginning to explore the ways in which the words and social conventions within a specific language are related to cultural values and beliefs. However, it is apparent that, through language, children learn far more than simply how to communicate; they also learn about the broader belief systems of their society.

For Your Review and Reflection

- In what ways does language influence cognitive processing?
- What are the specific effects of bilingualism on cognition?
- What are the functions of private speech for the developing child?
- In what ways does language provide clues about cultural values and socialization goals?
- Think about the structure of your native language. How might the elements of this language convey information about cultural values and norms?

chapter recap

Summary of Developmental Themes

Nature & Nurture

How do nature and nurture interact in the process of language development?

There are several indicators that, for humans, nature sets early predispositions to develop language in certain ways. For example, the fact that infants show an early sensitivity to phonemes and prosody in language, the child's tendency to progress through language milestones in a predictable sequence, and the devotion of certain portions of the brain to language are just some examples. However, we have also seen numerous examples of how interactions with more mature language users are also necessary for children to master the core elements and nuances of language in their culture.

Sociocultural Influence

How does the sociocultural context influence language development?

Cultures vary in the extent to which caregivers use parentese with their infants, a factor that may influence the rate of language acquisition. The specific elements of phonology, semantics, grammar, and pragmatics also vary across languages. Often the content and structure of a specific language provide cues about the culture's social order and values.

Continuous | Discontinuous

Is language development continuous or discontinuous?

Descriptions of early language development often seem stagelike because children appear to spend distinct periods of time in a babbling stage, a one-word stage, and so on. However, there are continuities among different events in language acquisition. For example, the sounds in infant babbling are related to the language the child will eventually speak. Contemporary theories, such as connectionism, emphasize continuous, non-stagelike processes in the emergence of language.

Interaction Among Domains

How does language development interact with development in other domains?
In early childhood, the ability to produce spoken language parallels physiological maturation of the vocal apparatus and the central nervous system. The emergence of language also coincides with the onset of certain cognitive skills, such as conceptual understanding. Language is nurtured largely within the context of social interactions with caregivers. Thus, physical, cognitive, and social factors affect the process of language development. By the same token, language affects other domains of development. Children's use of language enhances their ability to remember, form concepts, and as studies of bilingual individuals suggest, may even promote analytic and flexible thinking, as well as greater control over cognitive processes.

Risk | Resilience

What factors promote risk or resilience in the process of language development?
One domain in which children frequently show striking differences is in the rate at which they achieve language milestones. The type of speech they experience from caregivers has been shown to predict advances versus delays in the acquisition of language. Participation in joint activities with caregivers, especially in language-rich contexts such as reading books, has also been shown to promote children's language development.

Chapter Review

Foundations for Language Development

What are four kinds of skills that children master in the course of language development?
Children must master *phonology*, the basic sound units of language; *semantics*, or the meanings of words; *grammar*, the rules pertaining to the structure of language (including *syntax* and *morphology*); and *pragmatics*, the rules for using language in a social context.

What have studies shown about the involvement of the brain in language acquisition?
Specific brain structures are associated with *expressive aphasia* (*Broca's area*) and *receptive aphasia* (*Wernicke's area*). Children sustaining damage to these areas show a greater ability to recover language functions than adults do. Neuropsychological studies suggest that language functions begin to become lateralized shortly after the first year and look adult-like by age seven.

What evidence supports a critical period hypothesis of language acquisition? What evidence is inconsistent with a critical period hypothesis?
Children who have been deprived of language experience do not achieve fully developed language use. Children learning a second language in later childhood do not show a full mastery of syntax. At the same time, some late language learners achieve native-like mastery, probably because of the extent and depth of their experience with the second language.

How does a linguistic perspective account for language acquisition? What research findings are consistent with a linguistic perspective?
Linguistic theorists emphasize the child's abstraction of general grammatical principles from the stream of speech. They believe that language skills are modular. Data showing that children are able to learn and expand on rules in establishing creole languages are consistent with linguistic theory.

Which learning and cognitive skills are related to language acquisition?
Imitation, problem-solving, classification, and memory are related to language acquisition.

What are the unique features of a social interaction perspective on language acquisition? What research findings are consistent with the idea that social interactions play a role in language development?
Social interaction theorists state that several characteristics of caregiver-child speech, called *infant-directed speech* or *parentese*, facilitate development. Specific techniques include *turn taking*, *turnabouts*, *recasts*, and *expansions*. The amount and content of maternal speech to children, especially in episodes of joint attention, predict the rate and form of children's language acquisition.

Language Development in Infancy

What kinds of phonological skills and preferences have researchers observed in infants?
Newborns show a tendency to respond to language as a unique auditory stimulus. Young infants detect phonemes and vowel sounds from a variety of languages but show a decline in this ability by the second half of the first year. Infants show an early sensitivity to the *prosody*, patterns of intonation, stress, and rhythm that mothers around the world include in their speech to young children. Children's sensitivity to rhythmic properties of language helps them to differentiate their native language from others and possibly to detect the presence of specific words in a stream of speech.

What are some of the features and patterns in infants' early vocalizations?
Infants typically *coo* at six to eight weeks, *babble* at three to six months, and produce syllable-like *canonical babbling* at seven months.

How do young children use gestures in communication?
They might use a gesture to call attention to an object or to make a request. Sometimes children's gestures symbolize objects; later in development, gestures may accompany verbalization in order to elaborate a point.

What are the important features of children's language during the one-word stage?
By one year of age, most children are speaking one-word utterances, usually *nominals*, or nouns. At about eighteen months or so, children may show a particularly rapid phase of growth in word acquisition called the *vocabulary spurt*. At the earlier stages of word learning, children may restrict their use of some words to particular contexts (*underextension*) or apply them to too broad a category (*overextension*). Children comprehend word meanings much earlier than they are able to produce words. Their *receptive*

language exceeds their *productive language*. In most languages, labels for verbs are harder for children to understand than labels for nouns.

What are some of the individual and cultural variations in language acquisition?
Some children's early speech is *referential*; it includes mostly nominals. Other children are *expressive*; they use words with social functions. Fairly substantial individual differences also occur for the rate of language acquisition. Culture, too, can have an influence on the types of words children produce in the early stages of acquisition. For example, children from some Asian cultures learn verbs before they learn nouns.

What are some hypotheses about how children derive the meanings of words?
Children seem to learn the meanings of words by relying on constraints such as the *mutual exclusivity bias*, the *taxonomic bias*, and the *shape bias*. Episodes of *joint attention* also predict the rate and form of children's language acquisition.

Language Development Beyond Infancy

What are the major grammatical accomplishments of children in the two-word stage of language acquisition?
Two-year-olds begin to use two-word utterances, sometimes called *telegraphic speech* because it contains so few modifiers, prepositions, and connective words.

What syntactic accomplishments follow the two-word stage?
Children learn and apply the rules of grammar. These rules include both *syntax* and *morphology*. Children add morphemes, modifiers, prepositions, pronouns, and connective words to their speech. They begin to use negatives, questions, and eventually the passive voice. One interesting type of error they make is called *overregularization*, the application of grammatical rules to words that are exceptions. Children also evidence *semantic bootstrapping*, using the meanings of words to help them apply the rules of syntax.

What aspects of pragmatics do children acquire in the preschool years?
Children begin to show that different situations call for different forms of speech around age three. They adjust their speech, depending on the listener, and begin to use polite forms, probably because parents instruct them to.

What are some examples of children's metalinguistic awareness?
Examples of *metalinguistic awareness* include the ability to create humor and showing an understanding of *metaphor*.

Functions of Language

In what ways does language influence cognitive processing?
Language has been shown to influence specific cognitive processes such as memory and classification.

What are the specific effects of bilingualism on cognition?
Bilingual children are more flexible and analytic in certain cognitive tasks. They also perform better than monolingual children on tasks that require response inhibition.

What are the functions of private speech for the developing child?
Children often use *private speech*, and later *inner speech*, to direct their behavior. They tend to use private speech when tasks are difficult or goal directed.

In what ways does language provide clues about cultural values and socialization goals?
Language can be a vehicle to transmit to children the specific values and expectations of their native culture through formal and informal versions of words, gender categories of words, and even the specific words that are included or not included in the language.

Key Terms and Concepts

babbling (p. 253)
Broca's area (p. 243)
canonical babbling (p. 253)
constraints (p. 258)
cooing (p. 253)
expansion (p. 249)
expressive aphasia (p. 243)
expressive style (p. 262)
fast-mapping (p. 257)
grammar (p. 243)
infant-directed speech (parentese) (p. 251)
inner speech (p. 273)
joint attention (p. 260)
metalinguistic awareness (p. 268)
metaphor (p. 269)
morphology (p. 243)
mutual exclusivity bias (p. 258)
overextension (p. 256)
overregularization (p. 267)
phonology (p. 242)
pragmatics (p. 243)
private speech (p. 273)
productive language (p. 257)
prosody (p. 251)
recast (p. 249)
receptive aphasia (p. 243)
receptive language (p. 257)
referential style (p. 262)
semantic bootstrapping hypothesis (p. 268)
semantics (p. 242)
shape bias (p. 258)
statistical learning (p. 252)
syntax (p. 243)
taxonomic constraint (p. 258)
telegraphic speech (p. 264)
turn taking (p. 249)
turnabout (p. 249)
underextension (p. 256)
vocabulary spurt (p. 255)
Wernicke's area (p. 243)

Media Resources

Access an integrated eBook and chapter-specific interactive learning tools, including flashcards, quizzes, videos, and more, in your Developmental Psychology CourseMate, accessed through CengageBrain.com.

© Glow Images/Jupiter Images

CHAPTER OUTLINE

[chapter 8]

Cognition

KEY THEMES IN COGNITION

- **NATURE & NURTURE** How do nature and nurture interact in the process of cognitive development?
- **SOCIOCULTURAL INFLUENCE** How does the sociocultural context influence cognitive development?
- **CONTINUITY | DISCONTINUITY** Is cognitive development continuous or discontinuous?
- **INTERACTION AMONG DOMAINS** How does cognitive development interact with development in other domains?
- **RISK | RESILIENCE** What factors promote risk or resilience in cognitive development?

"Jeremy! Let's play a board game!" said Tommy to his three-year-old brother. "See. It's a memory game. I have two pictures of a truck, two pictures of a house, two pictures of everything. I flip them upside down, and we have to take turns trying to find two that match. It's fun, Jeremy. Let's try it." Tommy took pride in being a big brother; with seven years between them, he often baby-sat while his parents did chores around the house, and he especially enjoyed teaching Jeremy new things like this favorite childhood game of his.

"Okay," smiled Jeremy. But instead of flipping over only two tiles, he proceeded to turn over all of the tiles in the top row and then picked up and threw two of them over the couch. Tommy patiently retrieved the flying tiles, turned the visible pictures upside down again, and tried to show Jeremy how he should flip over only two. "See, Jeremy? Here is one truck. Now I have to try to remember where the other truck was. Do you remember?" But Jeremy had already scampered off into his bedroom, lured by the sound of the family cat meowing. <<

One of the most active research areas of child development focuses on **cognition**—those thought processes and mental activities, including attention, memory, concept formation, and problem solving, that are evident from early infancy onward. As the chapter opening scene suggests, younger children seem to think differently than older children. Jeremy did not seem to have the same kind of attention span as his older brother, and he seemed uninterested in playing a game that revolved around memory rather than throwing or jumping. In what other ways do children of different ages think differently? Do young children remember as well as older children do? Do older children solve problems the same way younger children do? When differences between younger and older children are found, what processes can account for these developmental changes? These are the types of questions that scientists interested in cognitive development ask.

Virtually every aspect of a child's development has some connection to emerging cognitive capabilities. For example, you will soon see that a child's use of language is linked to his or her growing conceptual development. Similarly, the child's increasing knowledge of the elements of effective social interaction or the way he interprets a social situation can influence the quality of relations with peers. In fact, you should find numerous examples throughout this text of how changes in thinking influence and interact with other areas of the child's development. Perhaps most important for those who are interested in applying research to children's lives, knowledge about the specific ways that children's thinking changes with development should have some clear implications for their education (see Chapter 10, "Achievement").

Theories of Cognitive Development

Several theoretical perspectives have guided research on cognitive development over the past several decades. During the early 1900s, Piaget and Vygotsky formulated rich and captivating ideas about the nature of children's thinking and the way it changed with development. Their ideas infiltrated mainstream thinking about cognitive development in the late 1960s and early 1970s. At just about the same time, information-processing models provided still a contrasting view of how children's thinking operated and changed with age. While many elements of each of these theories still inform some of our understanding of cognitive development, contemporary researchers now look to new theoretical ideas in their attempts to understand the nature of children's cognition. Core knowledge theory and dynamic systems theory are examples of these emerging perspectives.

Piaget's Theory

Jean Piaget (1896–1980) was a Swiss psychologist whose childhood interest in biology evolved into a general curiosity about how individuals acquire knowledge. Piaget saw himself as a *genetic epistomologist*, a scholar who was interested in the origins of knowledge from a developmental perspective. His desire to understand children's intellectual growth was probably sparked by his experiences working in the laboratories of Alfred Binet, in which the first intelligence test was developed. From the early 1920s, when his first books were published, to 1980, when he died, Piaget authored more than seventy books and scores of articles describing various aspects of children's thinking.

As we saw in Chapter 1, "Themes and Theories," Piaget promoted the idea that human thinking is characterized by *adaptation* and *organization*. One of the most important beliefs espoused by Piaget is that children actively construct their knowledge of the world, incorporating new information into existing knowledge structures, or *schemes*, through *assimilation*. As a result, schemes are modified or expanded through the process of *accommodation*. For example, the young infant may attempt to grasp a new, round squeeze toy, relying on a pre-existing scheme for grasping objects. As a consequence, that scheme becomes altered to include information about grasping round objects. The outcome is greater *equilibrium* or balance among the pieces of knowledge that make up the child's understanding. Thus, what a child can understand or mentally grasp at any given point in time is heavily influenced by what the child already knows or understands. At the same time, the child's schemes are constantly transformed, as equilibrium is continually disrupted by the never-ending flow of information from the surrounding world.

CONTINUITY | DISCONTINUITY

Piaget maintained that thought processes become reorganized into distinct stages at several points in development. Though the schemes in early stages lay the foundation for later knowledge structures, their reorganization is so thorough that schemes in one stage bear little resemblance to those in other stages. Piaget maintained that all children progress through the stages of cognitive development in an invariable sequence in which no stage is skipped. As described in Table 1.1 in Chapter 1, the child progresses through the *sensorimotor, preoperational, concrete operational,* and *formal operational* stages, reflecting major transitions in thought in which early, action-based schemes evolve into symbolic, then logical, and finally abstract mental structures. Piaget maintained that, for the most part, changes in mental structures—like the shift from sensorimotor to preoperational thought—are broad, sweeping reorganizations that influence thinking in multiple domains. Development, in this view, is said to be *domain-general*, that is, not tied to knowledge about any specific content (such as numbers versus spatial information).

cognition Thought processes and mental activities, including attention, memory, concept formation, and problem solving, that are evident from early infancy onward.

sensorimotor stage In Piagetian theory, the first stage of cognitive development, from birth to approximately two years of age, in which thought is based primarily on action.

The Sensorimotor Stage The most striking characteristic of human thinking during the **sensorimotor stage** is its solid basis in action. Each time the child reaches for an object, sucks on a nipple, or crawls along the floor, she is obtaining varied feedback about her body and its relationship to

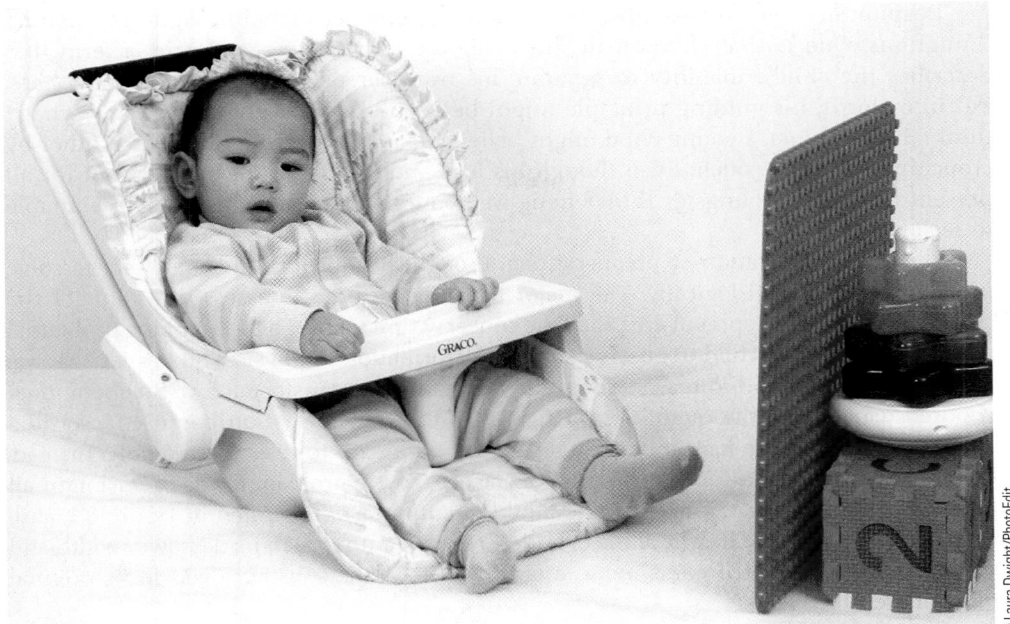

© Laura Dwight/PhotoEdit

A significant attainment in infancy is the child's understanding of object permanence. Children under three to four months of age act as if a hidden or obstructed object no longer exists. By age eight months, though, children will remove a barrier to look for a hidden object.

the environment that becomes part of her internal schemes. At first, the infant's movements are reflexive, not deliberate or planned. As the child passes through the sensorimotor period, her actions become increasingly goal directed and aimed at solving problems. Moreover, she is able to distinguish self from environment and learns about the properties of objects and how they are related to one another.

A particularly important accomplishment of this stage is the attainment of the **object permanence**, or *object concept*. Infants who possess object permanence realize that objects continue to exist even though they are not within immediate sight or within reach to be acted on. Up to three months of age, the saying "out of sight, out of mind" characterizes the child's understanding of objects. At about four months of age, he will lift a cloth from a partially covered object or show some reaction, such as surprise or puzzlement, when an object disappears. At about eight months of age, he will search for an object that has completely disappeared, for example, when it has been covered entirely by a cloth. In the last two phases of the attainment of object permanence, he will be able to follow visible and then invisible displacements of the object. In the first instance, the twelve-month-old will follow and find a toy that has been moved from under one cloth to another, as long as the movement is performed while he is watching. In the second instance, the eighteen-month-old can find an object moved from location A to location B, even if the displacement from A to B is done while he is not looking. The completion of the sensorimotor stage is signaled by the child's display of *deferred imitation*, the ability to imitate a model that is no longer present, as when the child mimics the temper tantrum displayed by another infant the day before. This ability requires the child to represent events and objects internally and marks the beginning of a major transition in thought.

The Preoperational Stage The key feature of the young child's thought in the **preoperational stage** is the *semiotic function*, the child's ability to use a symbol, an object, or a word to stand for something. The child can play with a cardboard tube as though it were a car or draw a picture to represent the balloons from her third birthday party. The semiotic function is a powerful cognitive ability because it permits the child to think about past and future events and to employ language. The semiotic function is also a prerequisite for imitation, imagery, fantasy play, and drawing, all of which the preschool child begins to manifest.

object permanence Realization that objects exist even when they are not within view. Also called *object concept*.

preoperational stage In Piagetian theory, the second stage of development, from approximately two to seven years of age, in which thought becomes symbolic in form.

Despite this tremendous advance in thinking, preoperational thought has distinct limitations. One is that children in this stage are said to be **egocentric**, a term that describes the child's inability to separate his own perspective from those of others. Put into words, his guiding principle might be "You see what I see, you think what I think." For example, a young child might believe he is hiding from his older brother by crouching behind a couch. Even though his legs and feet might be sticking out for all present to see, the youngster thinks he is well concealed because he himself is unable to see anyone.

The second limitation of preoperational thought lies in the child's inability to solve problems flexibly and logically. The major tasks Piaget used to assess the status of the child's cognitive development are called the **conservation tasks**. These "thinking problems" generally require the child to observe some transformation in physical quantities that are initially equivalent and to reason about the impact of the transformation. Preoperational children usually say the quantities change after the transformation because, according to Piaget, they lack the logical thought structures necessary to reason accurately. Instead, children display **centration**, focusing on one aspect of the problem to the exclusion of all other information. For example, in the liquid quantity task illustrated in Figure 8.1, children often focus on the height of the cylinder in Step 2 rather than its narrower width and mistakenly say it now contains more liquid than when the substance was in its original glass in Step 1.

The Concrete Operational Stage Children enter the **concrete operational stage** when they begin to be able to solve the conservation tasks correctly. The reason for this shift is that the child is now capable of performing **operations**, mental actions such as *reversibility*, that allow him to reason about the events that have transpired. For example, in the liquid quantity conservation task illustrated in Figure 8.1, he can pour the liquid back from the cylinder to the glass "in his head" to answer the question in Step 2 or think about the narrow width of the tall cylinder as compensating for its height. The concrete operational child is becoming a true "thinker," as long as there are specific objects to which he can apply his logic.

The Formal Operational Stage By the time the child reaches adolescence, she will most likely have moved to the final stage in Piaget's theory, the **formal operational stage**. Thinking in this stage is both logical and abstract. Problems such as "Bill is shorter than Sam but taller than Jim. Who is tallest?" can now be solved without seeing the individuals or conjuring up concrete images of them. The adolescent can also reason **hypothetically**; that is, she can generate potential solutions to problems in a thoroughly systematic fashion, much as a scientist approaches an experiment. In the social realm, achieving abstract thought means the adolescent can think about the nature of society and his own future role in it. Idealism is common at this developmental stage because he understands more fully concepts such as justice, love, and liberty and thinks about possibilities rather than just realities (Inhelder & Piaget, 1958). The development of formal operational thought represents the culmination of the reorganizations in thought that have taken place throughout each stage in childhood. For most adolescents, thought has become logical, flexible, and abstract, and its internal guiding structures are now highly organized.

Piaget is widely acknowledged as being one of the most influential of all thinkers in the history of psychology and a founder of the study of cognitive development as we know it (Brainerd, 1996; Flavell, 1996). By introducing questions about what develops as well as how development occurs, Piaget went well beyond the descriptions of norms of

egocentrism Preoperational child's inability to separate his or her own perspective from those of others.

conservation tasks Problems that require the child to make judgments about the equivalence of two displays; used to assess stage of cognitive development.

centration In Piagetian theory, tendency of the child to focus on only one aspect of a problem.

concrete operational stage In Piagetian theory, the third stage of development, from approximately seven to eleven years of age, in which thought is logical when stimuli are physically present.

operation In Piagetian theory, a mental action such as reversibility.

formal operational stage In Piagetian theory, the last stage of development, from approximately eleven to fifteen years of age, in which thought is abstract and hypothetical.

hypothetical reasoning Ability to systematically generate and evaluate potential solutions to a problem.

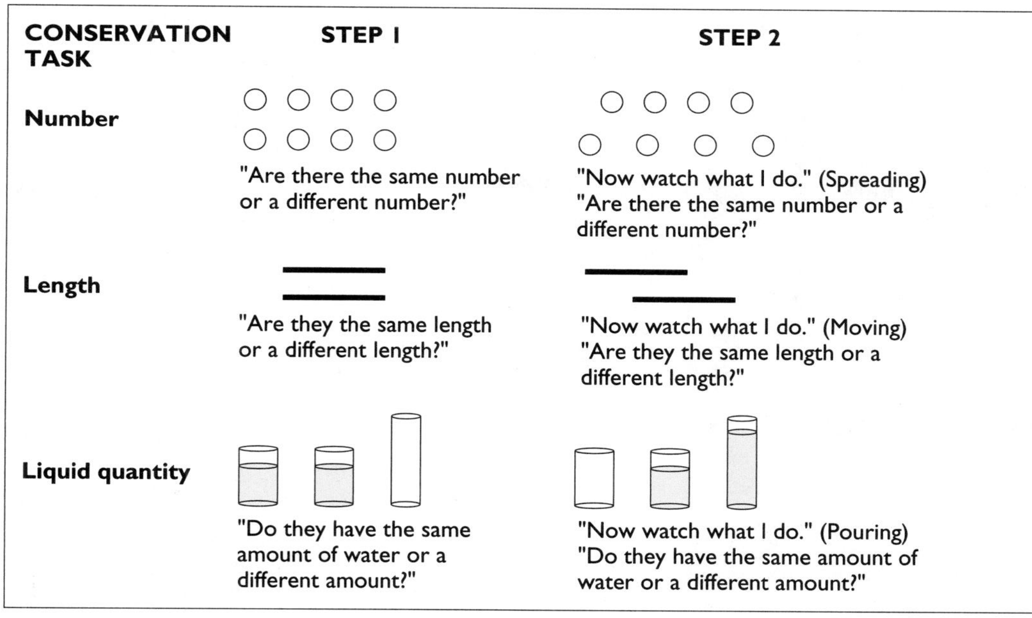

CONSERVATION TASK	STEP 1	STEP 2
Number	"Are there the same number or a different number?"	"Now watch what I do." (Spreading) "Are there the same number or a different number?"
Length	"Are they the same length or a different length?"	"Now watch what I do." (Moving) "Are they the same length or a different length?"
Liquid quantity	"Do they have the same amount of water or a different amount?"	"Now watch what I do." (Pouring) "Do they have the same amount of water or a different amount?"

Figure 8.1
Examples of Conservation Tasks
Depicted here are several Piagetian conservation tasks that children can solve once they reach the stage of concrete operations. Preoperational children usually say the quantities change after the transformation. Piaget believed they lack the logical thought structures necessary to reason correctly.

behavior that had been the staple of the early years of research in developmental psychology. Moreover, Piaget's method of closely watching the nuances of children's behaviors and listening as they explained their reasoning provided an important and inspiring lesson for developmental scientists: that "grand questions can actually be answered by paying attention to the small details of the daily lives of our children" (Gopnik, 1996, p. 225). At the same time, though, like all good theories, Piaget's ideas have spawned a host of debates about the nature of cognitive change as well as new perspectives on how to best characterize that change.

Vygotsky's Theory

Lev Vygotsky (1896–1934) lived in Russia at a time of great social and political upheaval—the Marxist revolution. No doubt influenced by the vigorous intellectual debates of the times, Vygotsky authored several landmark essays outlining his ideas on language, thought, and the sociocultural environment. His untimely death at the age of 38 cut short a rich and promising academic career.

SOCIOCULTURAL INFLUENCE

Standing in sharp contrast to Piaget's claims that cognitive processes function in similar ways across cultures, Vygotsky wrote that the child's cognitive growth must be understood in the context of the culture in which he or she lives. Vygotsky believed that, in formal and informal exchanges, caregivers, peers, and tutors cultivate in children the particular skills and abilities their cultural group values. Gradually, regulation and guidance of the child's behavior by others is replaced by internalized self-regulation. Lev Vygotsky made such social activity the cornerstone of his theory.

INTERACTION AMONG DOMAINS

The concept of **scaffolding** is a way of thinking about the social relationship involved in learning from another person. A scaffold is a temporary structure that gives the support necessary to accomplish a task. An effective caregiver or teacher provides such a structure in problem-solving situations, perhaps by defining the activity to be accomplished, demonstrating supporting skills and techniques in which the learner is still deficient, and motivating the beginner to complete the task. The collaboration advances the knowledge and abilities of the apprentice, as illustrated by the following study of a toddler learning to label objects. Anat Ninio and Jerome Bruner (1978) visited the child in his home every two weeks from age eight months to two years.

scaffolding Temporary aid provided by one person to encourage, support, and assist a lesser-skilled person in carrying out a task or completing a problem. The model provides knowledge and skills that are learned and gradually transferred to the learner.

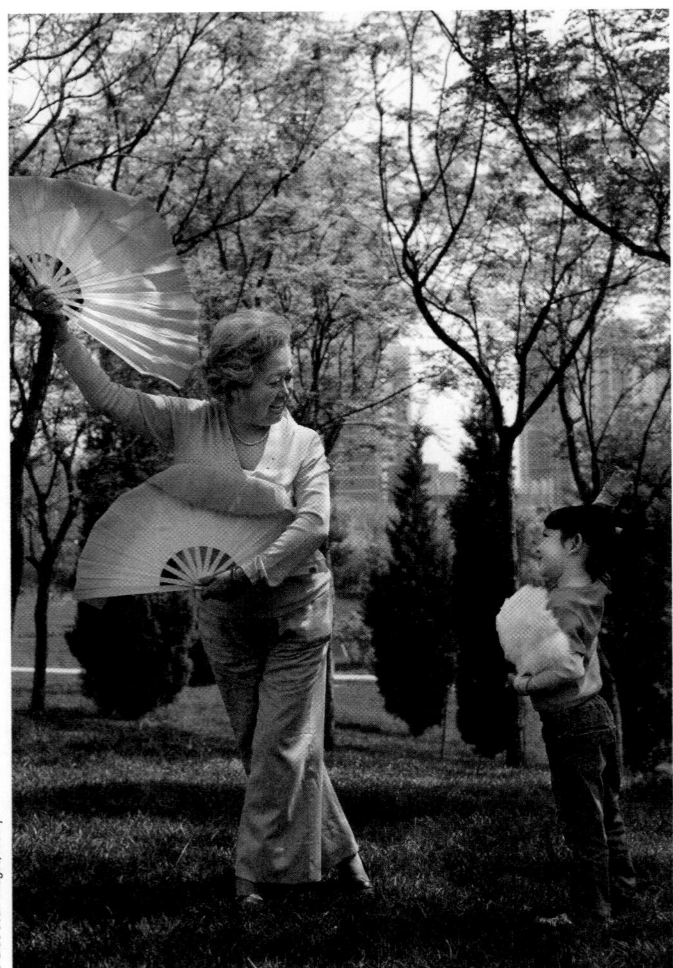

© Blue Jean Images/Alamy

By watching a skilled adult and participating in scaffolded learning, this young girl is learning a skill that is highly valued in her culture. Vygotsky emphasized the importance of sociocultural context in influencing which skills and abilities will be nurtured among children.

One commonly shared activity they observed was reading from a picture book, with the boy's mother providing the scaffold for the child to learn more about his language.

> *The mother's (often quite unconscious) approach is exquisitely tuned. When the child responds to her "Look!" by looking, she follows immediately with a query. When the child responds to the query with a gesture or a smile, she supplies a label. But as soon as the child shows the ability to vocalize in a way that might indicate a label, she raises the ante. She withholds the label and repeats the query until the child vocalizes, and then she gives the label if the child does not have it fully or correctly.*
>
> *Later, when the child has learned to respond with shorter vocalizations that correspond to words, she no longer accepts an indifferent vocalization. When the child begins producing a recognizable, constant label for an object, she holds out for it. Finally, the child produces appropriate words at the appropriate place in the dialogue. Even then the mother remains tuned to the developing pattern, helping her child recognize labels and make them increasingly accurate.* (Bruner, 1981, pp. 49–50)

This example illustrates what Vygotsky (1978) called the **zone of proximal development**, the span or disparity between what children are able to do without the assistance of others and what they are often able to accomplish by having someone more expert assist them at key points. Vygotsky claimed the most effective assistance from the expert is that just slightly beyond or ahead of the child's current capacities. Furthermore, a role model who is sensitive to the learner's level of knowledge contributes greatly to the effective transmission of skills.

Developmental scientists have shown widespread interest in Vygotsky's theory. Many have accepted his claims for the social basis of cognitive development and the importance of understanding the sociocultural context in which the child grows up.

Should Virtual Schools Be Promoted? what do you think?

Since the 1990s, virtual school experiences have been growing rapidly in the United States, Canada, Australia, and a number of other countries (Barbour & Reeves, 2009). In 2008–2009, forty-five states in the United States offered at least some online educational experiences to students in grades K to 12; in this same academic year, there were 320,000 course enrollments (one student in a semester-long course) in online learning (Watson et al., 2009). Virtual schooling is on the rise throughout the educational system.

What does the virtual school experience look like? Specific experiences can vary, but most courses share several characteristics. Teachers assign readings, which are usually delivered on the Internet. Students complete and submit assignments and projects and receive feedback from teachers electronically. Opportunities for discussion forums, instant messaging, and audio or videoconferencing with the teacher or other students are typically provided. Students can participate in their course on a flexible schedule, although they are usually required to complete a specified number of hours by the end of the term.

zone of proximal development Range of various kinds of support and assistance provided by an expert (usually an adult) who helps children to carry out activities they currently cannot complete but will later be able to accomplish independently.

Experts in online learning believe that this alternative vehicle for education is appealing to students who are bored or do not feel challenged by their courses in traditional schools. Virtual schools usually also provide more varied course selections than any individual school can offer, including advanced or honors courses. Moreover, students who have physical or medical conditions, who are high-school dropouts, or who have other challenges with traditional schools may be drawn to the options provided by a cyberschool (Barbour & Reeves, 2009). So far, research shows that students enrolled in virtual school courses learn as much or more than students in traditional classrooms (Barbour, 2009). However, dropout rates from virtual schools tend to be high, so that these comparisons may not provide the most accurate picture of the impact of online experiences. The students who remain in virtual schools may have unique traits, such as high levels of motivation, that account for their high levels of success (McLeod et al., 2005).

The theories of Piaget and Vygotksy offer clear implications for the ways in which children's educational experiences should be structured. What would each theorist say about the pros and cons of virtual schools? Would Piaget support the growth of virtual schools? Which parts of his theory lead you to your conclusion? Would Vygotsky have a different view about virtual schools? Why or why not? Would you be interested in more online learning opportunities in your own education? Which features of virtual schools do you find most appealing? What concerns do you have about virtual schools?

Information-Processing Theory

As we saw in Chapter 1, information-processing theorists believe that human cognition is best understood as the management of information through a system with limited space or resources. In the information-processing approach, mental processing is usually broken down into several components or levels of activity. For example, memory processes are often partitioned into *encoding, storage,* and *retrieval* phases. Information is assumed to move forward through the system, and each stage of processing takes some time.

Many traditional information-processing models are called **multistore models** because they posit several mental structures through which information flows, much as data pass through a computer. One example of this type of model is shown in Figure 8.2. Most multistore models distinguish between psychological structures and control processes. *Psychological structures* are analogous to the hardware of a computer. The *control processes* are mental activities that move information from one structure to another, much as software functions for the computer. Suppose someone asks you to repeat a list of words, such as *shoe, car, truck, hat, coat, bus.* If you have paid attention to all of the words and, like an efficient computer, "input" them into your cognitive system, processing will begin in the **sensory register**. Information is held here for a fraction of a second in a form very close to the original stimuli, in this case the audible sounds you experienced. Next, the words may move to the memory stores. **Working memory** (sometimes called *short-term memory*) holds information for no more than a couple of minutes. Many researchers consider working memory to be a kind of work space in which various kinds of cognitive tasks can be conducted. If you were to repeat the words over and over to yourself—that is, rehearse them—you would be employing a control process to retain information in working memory. You might also use the second memory store, **long-term memory**, the repository of more enduring information, and notice that the items belong to two categories, clothing and vehicles. The *executive control* oversees this communication among the structures of the

multistore model Information-processing model that describes a sequence of mental structures through which information flows.

sensory register Memory store that holds information for very brief periods of time in a form that closely resembles the initial input.

working (or short-term) memory Short-term memory store in which mental operations such as rehearsal and categorization take place.

long-term memory Memory that holds information for extended periods of time.

Figure 8.2

A Schematic Model of Human Information Processing

This highly simplified model includes several cognitive structures and processes that many information-processing theorists believe to be important in cognitive development. As the arrows indicate, information often flows in several directions between various structures. The goal of information-processing models is to identify those structures and processes that are at work when a child responds to his or her environment.

Source: Adapted from Atkinson & Shiffrin, 1968.

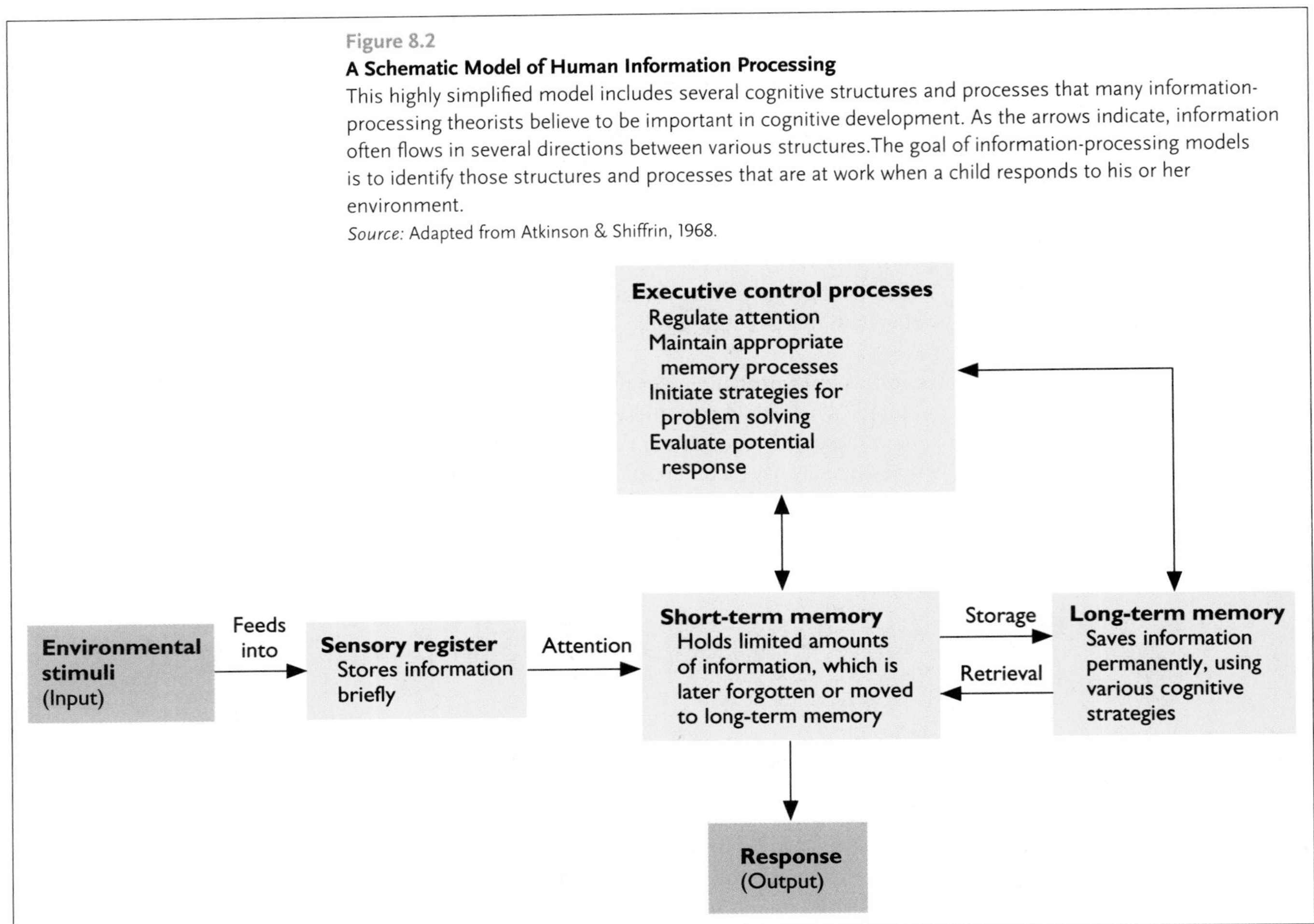

information-processing system. Finally, when you are asked to say the words aloud, your *response system* functions to help you reproduce the sounds you heard moments earlier.

Other theorists in this field have advanced a **limited-resource model** of the cognitive system that emphasizes a finite amount of available cognitive energy that can be deployed in numerous ways, but only with certain trade-offs. Limited-resource models emphasize the allocation of energy for various cognitive activities rather than the mental structures themselves. The basic assumption is that the pool of resources available for processing, retaining, and reporting information is finite (Bjorklund & Harnishfeger, 1990). In one such model, Robbie Case proposes an inverse relationship between the amount of space available for operating on information and that available for storage (Case, 1985; Case, Kurland, & Goldberg, 1982). *Operations* include processes such as identifying the stimuli and recognizing relationships among them; *storage* refers to the retention of information for use at a later time. If a substantial amount of mental effort is expended on operations, less space is available for storage or retention. In the simple memory experiment we just examined, the effort used to identify the words and notice the categorical relationships among them will determine the space left over for storing those words. If we are proficient at recognizing words and their relationships, storage space will be available. If these tasks cost us substantial effort, however, our resources will be taxed and little will be left for the task of remembering. As children grow older, they can mentally rotate images, name and compare objects,

limited-resource model Information-processing model that emphasizes the allocation of finite energy within the cognitive system.

and add numbers more rapidly (Kail, 1991; Kail & Ferrer, 2007), and as a consequence, more resources become available for other cognitive tasks.

How do these two general information-processing frameworks, the multistore model and the limited-resource model, account for cognitive development? Multistore models allow for two possibilities. Changes in cognition can stem from either an increase in the size of the structures—the "hardware"—or increasing proficiency in employing the "software," or control processes. For example, the capacity of the mental structure working memory may increase with age, or, as children grow older, they may increase their tendency to rehearse items to keep information in working memory or even push it into long-term memory. Limited-resource models suggest that what changes during development is processing efficiency. As children become more proficient in manipulating information, more internal space is freed up for storage.

CONTINUITY | DISCONTINUITY

Contemporary Theories of Cognitive Development

Today's theories of cognitive development have arisen from many decades of research that have provided a wealth of new information about how children think, results that have necessitated updated accounts of the developmental process. As an example, numerous studies have detailed surprising competencies in understanding properties of objects in three- and four-month-old infants. How can we explain this awareness when they have undergone only a limited degree of maturation or experienced very little learning at that point in their lives? Other research has revealed that, oftentimes, children's thinking is not influenced by just one or two factors or variables but rather by a multitude of forces that sometimes work simultaneously and oftentimes with great complexity. Simple, unidirectional explanations of development (for example, "heredity causes development" or "parenting styles cause development") do not seem to account for the differences we see in children, nor do they account for the reality that, at any one point in time, a number of factors are likely to influence exactly how children behave in a cognitive task.

Core Knowledge Theory **Core knowledge theory** proposes that young infants possess innate knowledge concerning many important aspects of the world, including the properties of objects, number, space, and perhaps even information about biological qualities or the social world (Baillargeon, 2001; Spelke & Hespos, 2001; Spelke & Kinzler, 2007). The idea is that even young infants exhibit a startling degree of competence as they encounter items and events in the world, a level of knowledge that probably stems from its adaptive value from an evolutionary perspective. Thus, it should not be surprising if many of the cognitive abilities displayed by young infants are also evident in other species. Core knowledge becomes elaborated with experience, according to these theorists, but essential understandings are present right from or shortly after birth. An important element of core knowledge theories is their claim that advances in thinking occur more rapidly in some domains than others (Hirschfeld & Gelman, 1994). In other words, core knowledge theories tend to be *domain-specific* and often posit specific *modules* that are responsible for a particular kind of knowledge.

NATURE & NURTURE

Dynamic Systems Theory Dynamic systems theories recognize that any account of cognitive development must consider many simultaneous forces that influence the child at one time. For cognitive development, these forces might include neuronal development, an array of environmental experiences that stretch the child's thinking abilities, past learning experiences, and motivations to learn new things. According to dynamic systems theories, each of these components is self-organizing, forming coherent patterns from repeated lower-level actions. However, each also can influence other systems and thus have an impact on the whole. Consider what happens as the infant begins to mature physically and be able to move about in the environment: new objects can be visually and manually

INTERACTION AMONG DOMAINS

core knowledge theory The idea that infants possess innate knowledge of certain properties of objects, as well as other basic concepts.

explored, parents may provide encouragement of that exploration (and perhaps even words to label the objects the infant handles), and the child derives emotional satisfaction from seeing the object roll or fall. Several systems (manual, linguistic, emotional, etc.) are developing and influencing the child all at once. Dynamic systems theories emphasize the coupling of several systems as a child encounters problems and tasks in the world; the overlapping integrations of these systems are what account for development (Smith & Breazeal, 2007).

For Your Review and Reflection

- What are the major characteristics of thinking in the sensorimotor, preoperational, concrete operational, and formal operational stages of cognitive development as described by Piaget?
- What are the essential elements of Vygotsky's sociocultural theory of cognitive development?
- Suppose you are a teacher creating a lesson plan for your students. How would Piaget's theoretical ideas influence the way you create this plan? How would a lesson plan created from Vygotsky's perspective be different?
- What are the general features of information-processing theories of cognitive development? How do multistore models differ from limited resource models?
- What are the major characteristics of core knowledge theory?
- What are the essential elements of dynamic systems accounts of cognitive development?
- How does each theory described in this section describe *development*?

Concept Development

When and how does the child begin to understand that horses, dogs, and cats all belong to a common category called "animals"? When does she realize that numbers such as 2 or 4 represent specific quantities, no matter what objects are being counted? And how does she mentally organize her spatial environment, such as the layout of her house or the path from home to school? In each case, we are concerned with the ways the child organizes a set of information about the world, using some general or abstract principle as the basis for that organization. In other words, we are describing the child's use of **concepts**.

As one psychologist put it, "Concepts and categories serve as the building blocks for human thought and behavior" (Medin, 1989). Concepts allow us to group isolated pieces of information on the basis of common themes or properties so that information is simplified and easier to make sense out of (Rakison & Oakes, 2003). The result is greater efficiency in cognitive processing. Suppose someone tells you, "A quarf is an animal." Without even seeing one, you already know many of the quarf's properties: it breathes, eats, locomotes, and so on. Because concepts are linked to one of the most powerful human capabilities—language—as well as other aspects of cognition, understanding how concepts develop is an important concern of developmental scientists.

Properties of Objects

The most fundamental early concepts, of course, have to do with the objects infants and young children encounter. What exactly do they understand about the properties of objects, most importantly, the fact of their continual existence?

concept Definition of a set of information on the basis of some general or abstract principle.

The Object Concept We already discussed how Piaget believed that significant accomplishments such as the object concept emerge late in the first year of life and do not become fully elaborated until the second year. However, experiments by researchers such as Renée Baillargeon suggest that, by three to four months of age, infants may actually understand far more about the properties of physical objects, including the object concept, than Piaget surmised (Baillargeon, 1987a; Baillargeon & DeVos, 1991). Baillargeon (1987a) conducted a unique experiment in which four-month-olds behaved as if they understood that an object continued to exist even when it was concealed by a screen. Figure 8.3 shows the phases of this experiment. At first, infants observed a screen that rotated back and forth 180 degrees over repeated trials. As you might expect, they eventually showed habituation of fixation to this display. Next, a box was placed behind the screen. Initially, when the screen was still flat against the table, the box was visible, but as the screen rotated away from the child, it hid the box from view. In the possible-event condition, the screen stopped moving at the point where it hit the box. In the impossible-event condition, the box was surreptitiously removed and the screen passed through the space the box would have occupied. As you already know, infants in a habituation experiment should look longer at the novel event, in this case, the screen that rotated only 112 degrees. However, infants looked significantly longer at the impossible event, apparently drawn in by the fact that the screen was moving through the space where the object should have been. Because infants are presumed to look longer at the stimulus display that goes against their internal knowledge, this procedure is often called the *violation-of-expectation* method.

Before the researcher could conclude that infants had the object concept, however, she had to rule out alternative explanations for the results. For example, what if infants simply prefer an arc of 180 degrees compared with an arc of 112 degrees, whether there is a box or not? Baillargeon included a control group of infants who saw the original habituation event followed by each of the test events (180 and 112 degrees) but without a box. In this condition, infants did not show preferences for the 180-degree rotation, indicating that the arc of the movement did not influence infants' responses.

Are there any other explanations for the results Baillargeon obtained? As noted, the possible test event was conceptualized by the experimenter as a novel occurrence. Some researchers point out, though, that the impossible test event (the screen rotating 180 degrees

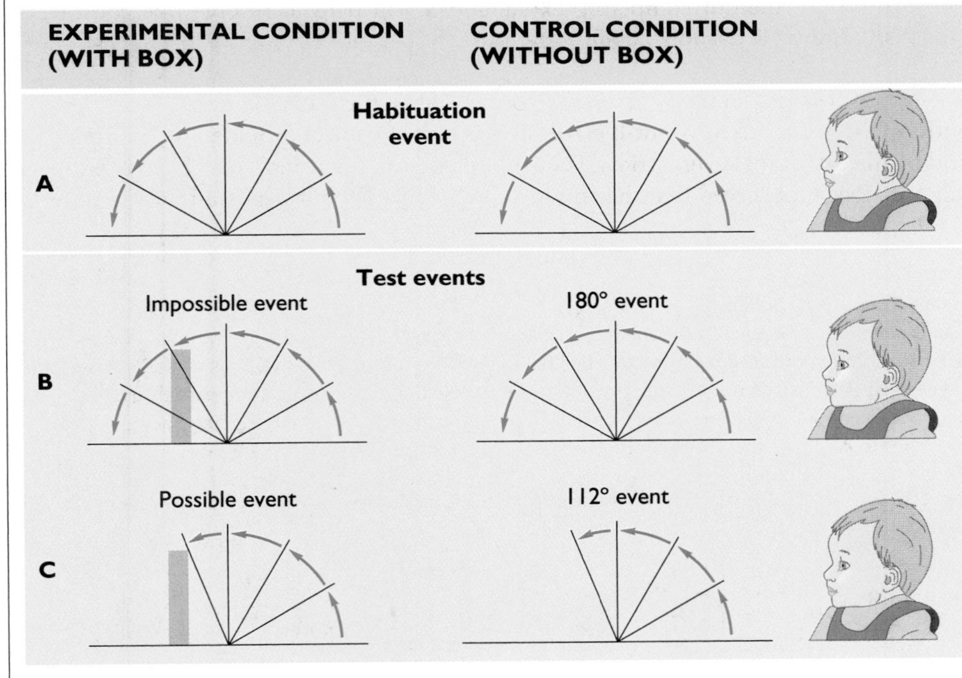

Figure 8.3
Do Infants Have an Object Concept?
In Baillargeon's experiment, infants were habituated to a screen rotating 180 degrees (A). Next, infants in the *impossible-event* condition saw the screen appearing to pass through the location of a box (B, on left), whereas infants in the possible-event condition saw the screen stop at the location of the box (C, on left). Infants in the *impossible-event* condition looked significantly longer at this event, suggesting that they were puzzled by what they saw and therefore had an object concept. The control conditions (shown at right) were included to make sure the infants were not responding to the arc of the screen's movement.
Source: Adapted with permission from Baillargeon, R. (1987). Do infants have an object concept?: Object permanence in 3 1/2–4 1/2 month-old infants. *Developmental Psychology, 23,* 655–664. Copyright © 1987 by the American Psychological Association.

apparently through the box) also contains novel elements; the presence of the box makes the event different from the original habituation event. Thus, novelty, and not knowledge about objects, could account for looking at the impossible event. In addition, there are some circumstances, particularly in the early stages of processing, in which infants may show a preference for familiar, rather than novel, stimuli. Preference for the impossible event could actually be based on a preference for familiarity, the 180-degree rotation, as opposed to knowledge about objects (Bogartz & Shinskey, 1998; Bogartz, Shinskey, & Speaker, 1997).

These controversies notwithstanding, Baillargeon claims that young infants not only understand that objects exist when out of sight but also understand that the objects' size matters in how far a screen can rotate (Baillargeon, 1987b). Apparently, young infants quickly move beyond simply understanding that an object exists under a cover or behind a barrier; they also develop ideas about physical properties of objects such as their height and rigidity and can calibrate the impact of these properties on a moving screen (Baillargeon, 1995).

Similarly, experiments by Elizabeth Spelke and her colleagues show that infants seem to appreciate the concept of *solidity*, the fact that one object cannot pass through the space occupied by another object. In one study, represented in Figure 8.4, two-and-a-half-month-old infants saw a ball roll across a ramp and behind a screen for several trials. Next they saw the ball roll as a partially visible box blocked its path. When the screen was removed, infants viewed the ball either resting in front of the box or at the end of the ramp. Infants looked significantly longer at the impossible result, the ball at the end of the ramp, suggesting to Spelke that infants recognize the concept of solidity. Some of Spelke's other experiments imply that young infants also understand the principle of *continuity*, the idea that objects move continuously in time and space (Spelke et al., 1992).

NATURE & NURTURE

The results of the violation-of-expectation experiments have led some researchers to see them as support for the core knowledge hypothesis. The contrasting point of view is that infants' performance in the violation-of-tasks is not due to innate core knowledge but rather to perceptual and memory processes that detect that "something is different" or "something is familiar" (Bogartz, Shinskey, & Schilling, 2000). It is wrong, say the critics, to imbue young infants with more advanced or specialized cognitive and representational skills than is warranted (Haith, 1998; Smith, 1999b). Rather, it is better to assume that basic, general cognitive processes are responsible for the behaviors we observe. Knowledge about objects is built, say many of these theorists, through rapid advances in attention and memory abilities, as well as the child's experiences in the world. Experts hope that well-designed experiments that rule out competing explanations will help to resolve this controversy (Aslin, 2000; Cohen & Cashon, 2006).

The A-Not-B Error A common error that occurs when the child is about seven to nine months of age is the $A\bar{B}$, or **A-not-B error**. In this task, an object is hidden in location A and found by the infant for several trials. Then, in full view of the infant, the object is hidden in location B. Piaget observed that the child would mistakenly but persistently search for the

Figure 8.4
Infants' Concepts of Solidity
In an experiment conducted by Elizabeth Spelke and her colleagues, two-and-a-half-month-old infants were habituated to the scene on the left, a ball rolling across a ramp. In the test phase, infants saw events that were either consistent or inconsistent with the principle that one object cannot pass through the space occupied by another. The infants looked longer at the inconsistent event, leading Spelke and her colleagues to postulate that this early knowledge about objects is innate.

Source: From Spelke, E., Breinlinger, K., Macomber, J., & Jacobson, K. (1992). Origins of knowledge. *Psychological Review, 99,* 605–632. Copyright © 1999 by the American Psychological Association. Adapted with permission.

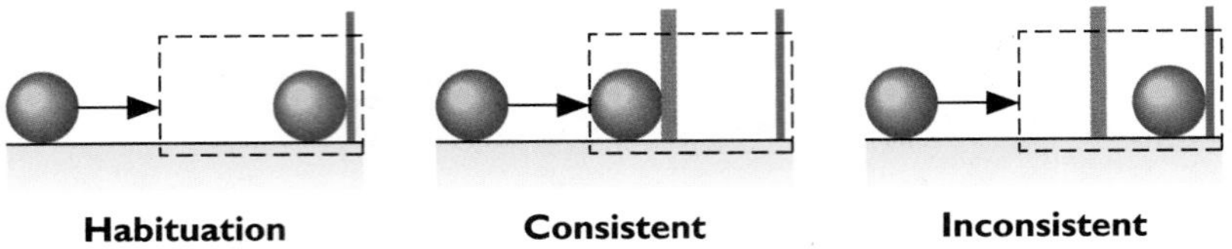

Figure 8.5

Alternative Explanations for the A$\bar{B}$ Error

A toy has been hidden first in the right well (location A), then is placed in the well on the left (location B) as shown in the first photograph.The next three photographs show that after the object is hidden, the infant reaches for location A even though he looks persistently at location B. The looking behavior suggests that he has the object concept when there are visible displacements of the object. Diamond (1991) believes that one reason infants reach for the incorrect location is because they fail to inhibit motor responses.

Source: © Adele Diamond

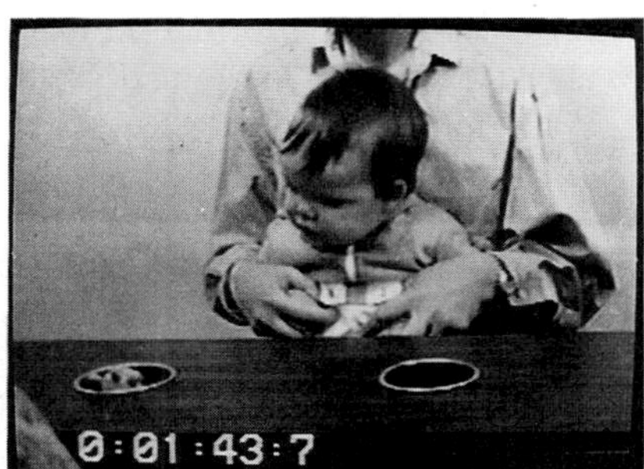

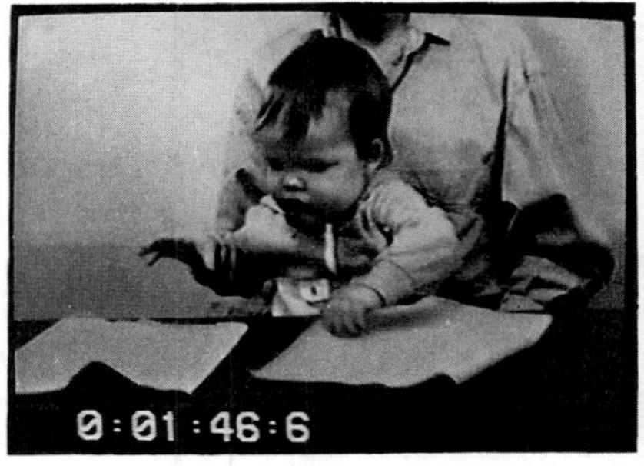

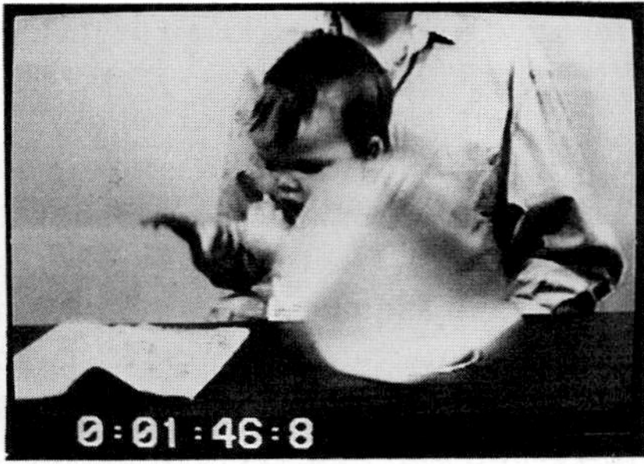

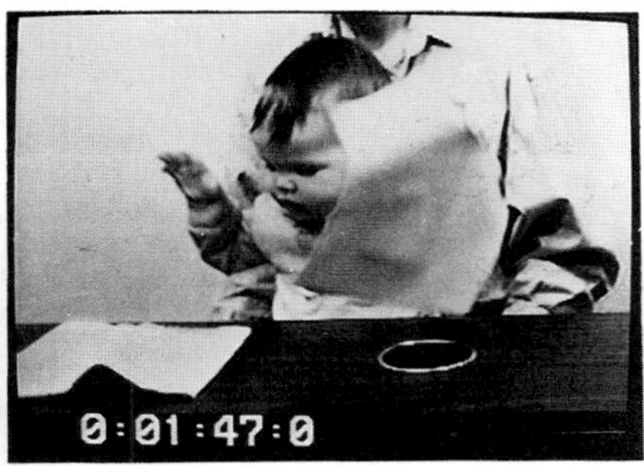

object in location A. He hypothesized that the infant's incomplete knowledge of the object concept leads to this error, in large part because the sensorimotor scheme for searching in location A still controls the child's thought. Researchers, however, have generated several alternative hypotheses about the reasons for the A-not-B error.

For one thing, memory difficulties may play a role. Eight- to twelve-month-old infants are less likely to make the A$\bar{B}$ error when they can search for the object at B immediately as opposed to after a delay. In addition, when watching infants make the A$\bar{B}$ error, Adele Diamond noticed that even though some infants mistakenly reached for A, they actually looked at B, the correct location of the hidden toy (see Figure 8.5) (Diamond, 1985). They behaved as though they knew the correct location of the toy but could not stop themselves from reaching to A. In other studies, adult monkeys, which normally perform successfully on the A$\bar{B}$ task, make mistakes identical to those of seven-to-nine-month-old human infants when lesions are made in very specific areas of their frontal cortex; these are the brain areas that control the inhibition of responses (Diamond & Goldman-Rakic, 1989). Diamond (1991) proposes that infants have the object concept well before age seven months but, due to the physical immaturity of this special cortical area, they cannot suppress their tendency to reach for location A. Lending support to this hypothesis are data showing that infants who are successful in the A$\bar{B}$ task display more powerful brain electrical activity from the same frontal region of the cortex (Bell & Fox, 1992). Moreover, when infants' responses to the A$\bar{B}$ situation are assessed using the habituation procedure rather than by the child's motor response, they look longer at an impossible event (a toy moves from A to B and is then found at A) than at a possible event (a toy moves from A to B and is found at B)

A-not-B error Error that an infant makes when an object is hidden in location A, found by the infant, and then, in full view of the infant, moved to location B.

(Ahmed & Ruffman, 1998). Thus, infants seem to know the correct location of the transposed object but do not show this knowledge when tasks require reaching.

Another account of the $A\bar{B}$ error states that infants may not be able to efficiently update their representation of the object's location after it is moved to B; in fact, they perform better when the A and B locations are covered with distinctive shapes and colors (Bremner & Bryant, 2001). Perhaps the most comprehensive description comes from a dynamic systems perspective. In this view, the infant's errors arise from competing tendencies of different strengths: the strong memory of the object at A and a deteriorating plan to look at location B in the face of few perceptual cues (Smith et al., 1999; Spencer, Smith, & Thelen, 2001). Any of several factors can improve performance: better memory for spatial locations, stronger perceptual cues about the object's location, or heightened attention to the events in the task.

Classification

Aside from learning about the properties of single objects, as in the object concept, children also quickly learn about relationships that can exist among sets of objects. Sometimes objects resemble one another perceptually and seem to "go together" because they are the same color or shape. At other times, the relationships among objects can be more complex; the perceptual similarities may be less obvious and, moreover, some sets can be embedded within others. Cocker spaniels and Great Danes, two different-looking dogs, can be classified together in the group "dogs," and both breeds fit into a larger category of "animals." Research has revealed a complex portrait of the emergence of this cognitive skill.

Early Classification One of the earliest signs of classification skills in young children occurs toward the end of the first year, when children begin to group perceptually similar objects together. Susan Sugarman (1982, 1983) carefully watched the behaviors of one- to three-year-olds as they played with successive sets of stimuli that could be grouped into two classes, such as plates and square blocks or dolls and boats. Even the youngest children displayed a spontaneous tendency to group similar-looking objects together by pointing consecutively to items that were alike. With the habituation paradigm, it has also been possible to show that three- and four-month-old infants respond to sets of items, such as dogs, cats, and horses, as if they belong to categories, using perceptual similarity as the basis for their behaviors (Oakes, Coppage, & Dingel, 1997; Quinn, Eimas, & Rosenkranz, 1993). Research with six-month-olds reveals that brain waves present distinct patterns of responses when infants are learning a category (that is, when they become familiarized with several different stimuli from the same category) and also when infants show behavioral preferences for items outside of the category (Quinn, Westerlund, & Nelson, 2006). Thus, the tendency to group objects together on the basis of shared perceptual characteristics emerges early in development and is accompanied by changes in physiological responding.

INTERACTION AMONG DOMAINS

Between ages one and three years, children experience a rapid growth in classification skills. One important way in which we see changes is in terms of the bases they use for grouping objects together. For example, at fourteen months of age, infants successively touch objects that appear in common contexts, such as "kitchen things" and "bathroom things" (Mandler, Fivush, & Reznick, 1987). Two-year-olds will match items on the basis of *thematic relations*, clustering items that function together or complement one another, such as a baby bottle and a baby (Markman & Hutchinson, 1984). They will also occasionally classify items *taxonomically*, grouping objects that may not look alike on the basis of some abstract principle, such as a banana with an apple (Ross, 1980). These broad distinctive categories seem to be more predominant in the thinking of twelve-month-olds who tend to point sequentially, for example, to all the animals in an array and then to all the vehicles (see Figure 8.6). It may be that the perceptual distinctiveness of the items in the two categories underlies these patterns of infant performance. Only later in development, beyond age 30 months, do children spontaneously point to "dogs" versus "horses," a more narrow conceptual grouping (Bornstein & Arterberry, 2010). As children develop, broad categories such as "animalness" become increasingly more fine-tuned and refined (Mandler, 2008).

Taxonomic classification is easier for young children when they hear that objects from the same category share the same label even though they may not look very much alike

Figure 8.6
Early Concepts
Infants and young children typically point in sequence to objects that belong to one category and then to objects in another category, displaying the basic elements of conceptual understanding. However, these behaviors are more obvious for objects from two broadly different groups, such as "animals" versus "vehicles" as opposed to "dogs" versus "horses."
Source: Bornstein, M. H., & Arterberry, M. E. (2010). The development of object categorization in young children: Hierarchical inclusiveness, age, perceptual attribute, and group versus individual analysis. *Developmental Psychology, 46*, 350–365.

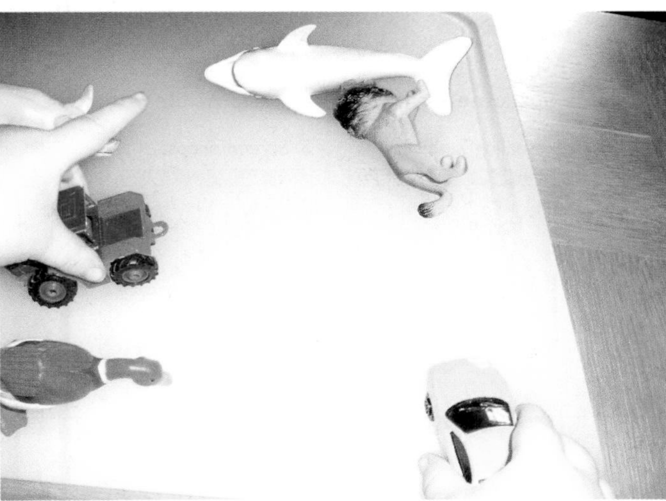

(e.g., a panther and a tabby house cat are both called "cats") or when their similarities are pointed out in some other way (Deák & Bauer, 1996; Nazzi & Gopnik, 2001). In fact, mothers often provide varied information of this sort to their young children about objects and their membership in categories, saying such things as, "That's a desk. That's a desk, too." Or they point sequentially to objects that come from the same conceptual group (Gelman et al., 1998). As children encounter new instances of a category, they incorporate information about those examples into their prior knowledge about the category (Carmichael & Hayes, 2001). And as children grow older, they become capable of understanding that objects (a *rubber duck*) can belong to more than one kind of classification system (*toys* and *bathroom things*) (Nguyen, 2007).

INTERACTION AMONG DOMAINS

Individual and Cultural Variations in Classification Implicit in many ideas about classification is the notion that there should be similarities in concept development among children, even those from different cultures. However, research suggests that this is not the case. For example, some three-year-olds show a clear propensity to use thematic classification, whereas others prefer taxonomic classification. Interestingly, these individual differences in classification preferences are linked to earlier unique profiles in play and language use. As one-year-olds, "thematic" children have been noted to play with objects in spatial, functional ways and, at age two, use words such as *in* and *down* more than "taxonomic" children do; that is, they have seemingly stable preferences to focus on how objects work in relation to one another (Dunham & Dunham, 1995).

SOCIOCULTURAL INFLUENCE

Cultural variations in classification occur, too. One group of researchers found that residents of rural Mexico with little formal schooling tended to group objects on the basis of their functional relations. "Chicken" and "egg" were frequently classified together because "the chicken lays eggs." On the other hand, individuals with more education relied on taxonomic classification, grouping "chicken" with "horse" because "they are animals" (Sharp, Cole, & Lave, 1979). It may be that taxonomic classification strategies are taught explicitly in schools or that education fosters the development of more abstract thought, a basic requirement for taxonomic grouping. Any full explanation of the development of classification skills will have to take into account the experiences of children within their specific sociocultural contexts.

Sequence of events I + I = I or 2

I. Object placed in case

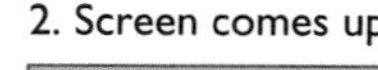

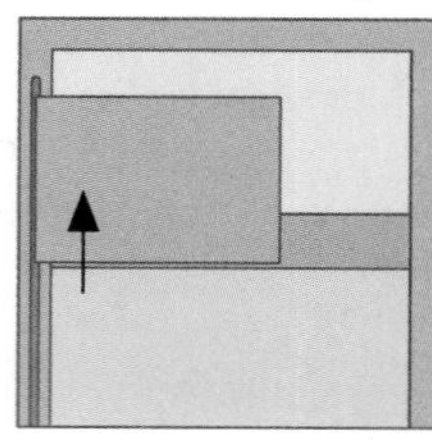

3. Second object added

4. Hand leaves empty

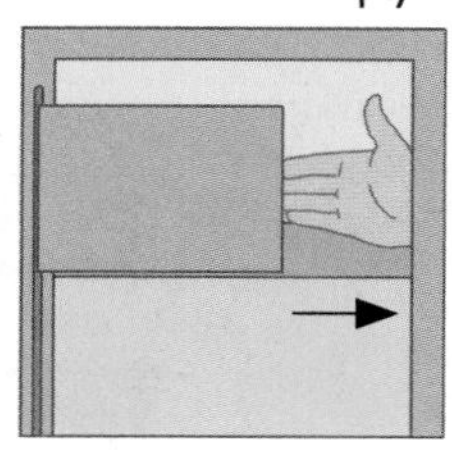

Then either: possible outcome

5. Screen drops....

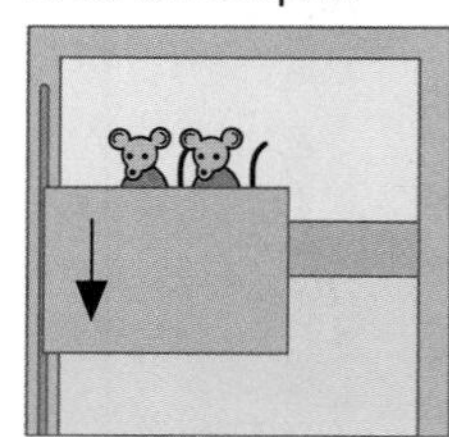

revealing 2 objects

or: impossible outcome

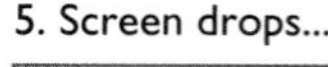

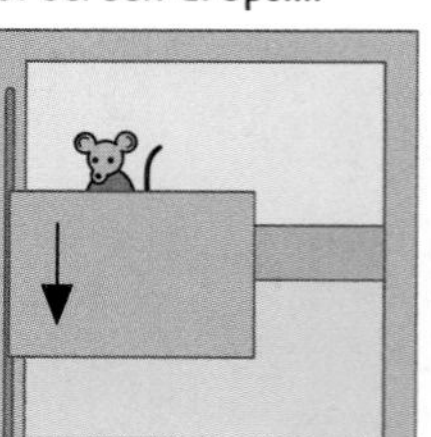

revealing I object

Figure 8.7
Can Infants Add?
This figure shows the sequence of events used in Wynn's (1992) experiments with five-month-olds. Infants first saw a hand place a mouse doll in the display. Next, a screen rotated up to hide the doll. A hand appeared with a second doll, placing it behind the screen and leaving the display empty-handed. During the test, the screen dropped down and revealed either two dolls (possible event) or one doll (impossible event). Infants looked longer at the impossible event, suggesting they knew something about the additive properties of numbers.
Source: Adapted from K. Wynn, Addition and subtraction by human infants. *Nature, 358,* pp. 749–750. Reprinted by permission from Nature, copyright 1992 Macmillan Magazines Ltd. Visit our website at www.nature.com.

Numerical Concepts

Another kind of conceptual understanding has to do with numbers. When and how do children begin to understand that some sets of objects have "more" than others? When do they appreciate that "2" is different from "4" and that the objects themselves do not matter when numerical entities are being compared? Thanks to a growing body of research, we now know that even infants and young children demonstrate sensitivity to basic aspects of numerical relationships.

Infants' Responses to Number Habituation studies show that newborns can detect differences in small numeric sets, such as two versus three dots (Antell & Keating, 1983). Infants even seem to understand something about additive properties of numbers. In one experiment, five-month-old infants watched as a toy was placed in a case and then was hidden by a screen. The infants watched as a second, identical toy was placed behind the screen (see Figure 8.7). When the screen was removed and only one toy remained—an impossible outcome if the infants appreciated that there should still be two toys—they showed surprise and looked longer than they did when two toys were visible (Wynn, 1992).

The preceding findings and the results of other studies suggest several interesting themes about the processes that underlie infants' behaviors. First, children's early numerical concepts do not rely on verbal skills. Infants are sensitive to changes in number well before they are able to talk. Second, early number concepts are inexact and rely on approximate judgments. For example, six-month-old infants respond to differences between eight versus sixteen dots, but not eight versus twelve dots (Lipton & Spelke, 2003; Xu & Spelke, 2000). At least early in infancy, children are best able to discriminate when one set of objects or events is at least double the size of the other (Wood & Spelke, 2005). Finally, many researchers believe that these early sensitivities to number provide another example of innate core knowledge (Feigenson, Dehaene, & Spelke, 2004; Wynn, 1998).

NATURE & NURTURE

Other researchers disagree and point out that the infants in these experiments might be responding on the basis of changes in the visual display other than number. For example, when stimulus items change in number, they also change in the amount of contour, or exterior boundary length, they contain; two mouse dolls have more total "outline" than one mouse doll. In a study in which the stimuli varied either in contour length or number, infants responded on the basis of contour length rather than number (Clearfield & Mix, 1999). Similarly, infants respond to changes in surface area of stimuli as opposed to their number (Clearfield & Mix, 2001). Recent studies, though, show that infants find changes in surface area to be more challenging than changes in number, suggesting that there is something about number concepts that is primary and fundamental in the way they think (Cordes & Brannon, 2008).

Early Number Concepts and Counting By the preschool years, many children start to count. Although a two- or three-year-old's rapid-fire pronouncement of "One, two, three, four, five" may seem to denote fairly impressive numerical thinking, their words do not necessarily indicate deep understanding of numbers. The count word "one," as it turns out, is quite well understood by most three-year-olds. They can give an adult "one" object when asked and can point to an array that has "one" object in it. But even though these young children may be able to count to ten, they make mistakes in labeling arrays of objects that have "five" versus "ten" items and cannot judge that ten objects are more than five. In these early years, the child's ability to understand that number words refer to highly specific and unique values develops slowly; their progression from understanding the meaning of "one" and "two" to "three" and "four" seems to require significant conceptual growth (Condry & Spelke, 2008; Huang, Spelke, & Snedeker, 2010).

By age four to five years, many children count to twenty—they say number words in sequence and, in so doing, appreciate at least some basic principles of numerical relationships (Lipton & Spelke, 2006). Rochel Gelman and her associates have argued that among the fundamental principles of counting that young children master are the following: (1) using the same sequence of counting words when counting different sets, (2) employing only one counting word per object, (3) using the last counting word in the set to represent the total number, (4) understanding that any set of objects can be counted, and (5) appreciating that objects can be counted in any order (Gelman & Gallistel, 1978; Gelman & Meck, 1983). Gelman and her colleagues believe that children's counting builds on their previous nonverbal understanding of number; it also serves as the basis for future numerical understanding (Gallistel & Gelman, 2005).

Many preschoolers are able to count, but recent research shows they may not fully understand the numerical concepts underlying the count words.

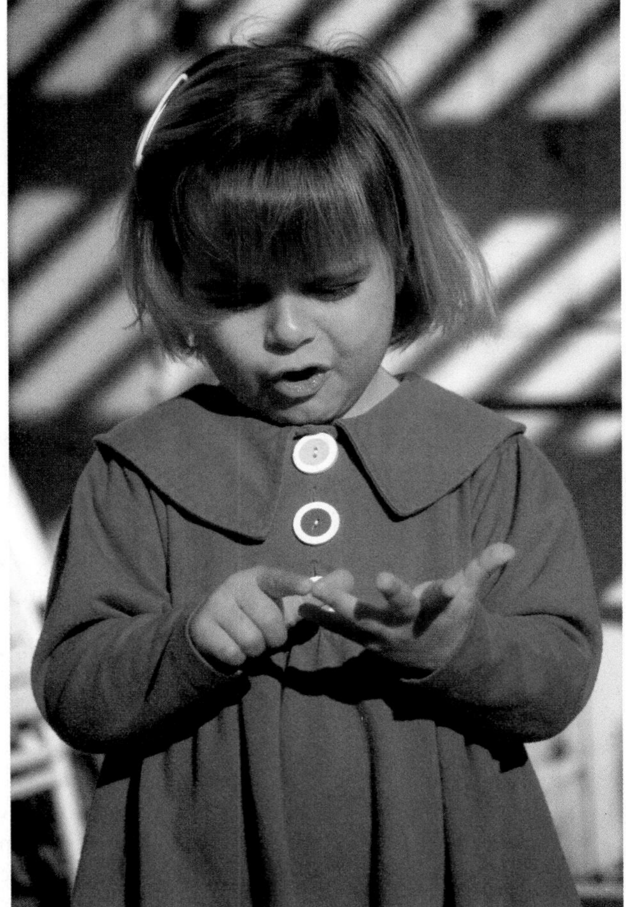

Four-year-olds show they are able to compare quantities, answering correctly such questions as "Which is bigger, five or two?" (Siegler & Robinson, 1982). Thus, their understanding of number terms includes relations such as "larger" and "smaller." One interesting pattern, though, is that young children have more difficulty in making such comparisons when the numbers themselves are large (ten versus fourteen) or when the difference between two numbers is small (eight versus nine). The same is true when children have to add, subtract, and perform other calculations with numbers (Levine, Jordan, & Huttenlocher, 1992). In contrast to the position that preschoolers' counting serves as the foundation for subsequent mastery of mathematical thinking, researchers such as Catherine Sophian believe that it is these early concepts of "greater than," "less than," and "equal to" that launch children into learning more advanced mathematical concepts (Sophian, 2007).

Children seem to have a good grasp of even more complex numerical concepts, such as fractions, by age four. Suppose a preschooler sees three-fourths of a circle hidden by a screen and then one-half of a circle come out from behind the screen. How much is still left behind the screen? A surprising number of four-year-olds can select a picture of one-fourth of a circle from a set of alternatives (Mix, Levine, & Huttenlocher, 1999). In addition, even a brief training session can help young children understand the basic concepts of fractions. When five-year-olds in one study had the opportunity to observe a whole pizza divided among different numbers of recipients, they began to understand that the size of each share of pizza depended on the number of individuals who were going to eat it (Sophian, Garyantes, & Chang, 1997).

Many people are surprised to learn about young children's abilities in mathematical reasoning. Researchers believe that the numerical competencies displayed by infants and young children likely serve as the foundation for more complex reasoning about quantities that emerges later in development (Canfield & Smith, 1996; Simon, Hespos, & Rochat, 1995). We will have more to say about children's mathematic thinking in Chapter 10, "Achievement."

Spatial Relationships

From early infancy onward, children organize the objects in their world in still another way: according to relationships in space. How does the child find his shoes, an enticing snack, or other objects? For the older child, spatial understanding extends to finding her way to school, grandparents' homes, or other, more remote locations.

Many researchers have found that infants, in the absence of any environmental cues, rely on the positions of their own bodies in space to locate objects. For example, in one study, nine-month-olds readily learned to locate an item hidden under one of two covers situated to either their left or their right. Shifted to the opposite side of the table, however, they looked in the wrong location because of their egocentric responding (Bremner & Bryant, 1977). When the investigator made the covers of the two hiding locations of distinctively different colors, infants were able to locate the hidden toy even when they were moved to a different position around the table (Bremner, 1978).

Toward the end of the first year, children quite literally reach out into the world for cues denoting spatial relationships. Infants slightly under nine months of age use landmarks denoting the physical locations of objects to find them in larger spatial environments. When playing peekaboo, infants in one study were assisted in locating a face by different-colored lanterns positioned by the correct window, even if their own positions were shifted (Lew, Bremner, & Lefkovitch, 2000). Likewise, preschoolers demonstrate that they can quickly learn that a distinctive color on a wall in a room can help them to locate a target object (Twyman, Friedman, & Spetch, 2007).

Young children also show a remarkable ability to use distance cues without the benefit of landmarks to search for objects. That is, they seem to have some way of representing how far apart objects are from each other, or how far an object is from a boundary in terms of metric length. Janellen Huttenlocher and her colleagues asked children ages sixteen to twenty-four months to find a toy buried in a five-foot-long sandbox that had no distinguishing landmarks (see Figure 8.8). The success rate for these young children was impressively high (Huttenlocher, Newcombe, & Sandberg, 1994). Using the habituation method, this same research team was able to show that five-month-olds reacted when hidden objects unexpectedly reappeared as little as eight inches from their original hiding location in a thirty-inch sandbox (Newcombe, Huttenlocher, & Learmonth, 2000).

Geometric cues—the shape of a room, for example—can also help young children to orient themselves in space. In one study, an experimenter showed three- and four-year-old children a green square in the corner of a rectangular room. The experimenter then flipped the square over so that it was blue, like the squares in all of the other corners. She also spun each child around approximately four times to disorient him or her. How did children locate the green square? Because there were no landmarks or distinguishing features in this particular condition of the experiment, successful performance depended on noticing the relationship of the short and long sections of the room in the corner in which the square was located. Children directed many more of their searches to the corners, which provided the correct spatial information, for example, "the short wall is on the left" than to corners that were not consistent with the original spatial information (Learmonth, Nadel, & Newcombe, 2002).

Taken together, these findings show that infants and toddlers have several ways to locate objects in space—referencing their own bodies, using landmarks, and employing distance and geometric cues. Marked improvements in locating objects in spatial environments seem to be especially noticeable at around age 18 months to two years, and may be linked to development of the hippocampus (Sluzenski, Newcombe, & Satlow, 2004). As with other forms of conceptual knowledge, researchers debate the degree to which this knowledge is innate and specialized versus acquired and due to more general processes (Huttenlocher & Lourenco, 2007; Spelke & Kinzler, 2007). Most agree, though, that infants

NATURE & NURTURE

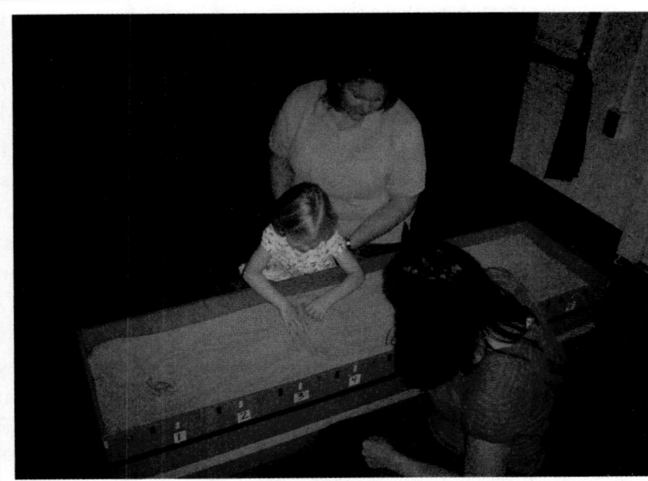

Figure 8.8
Spatial Reasoning in Young Children
Young children demonstrate the ability to use distance cues to locate objects hidden in a sandbox. This means that, in the absence of landmarks, children can rely on some understanding of metric distance to locate objects.
Source: Photo by Russell Richie, Courtesy of N. Newcombe, M. Hansen, and J. Sluzens

and young children improve these basic skills as they begin to move about—to crawl and walk around in their environments (Newcombe & Huttenlocher, 2006).

For Your Review and Reflection

- What kind of knowledge do infants display about the properties of objects?
- What developmental changes have researchers observed in children's classification skills?
- What developmental changes have researchers observed in children's numerical skills?
- What developmental changes have researchers observed in children's spatial concepts?
- Where do you stand in the debate between a core knowledge view and the idea that general learning principles explain children's concept development? What evidence leads you to this conclusion?

Attention

Have you ever noticed that sometimes a teenager can spend hours absorbed in a single activity, such as doing a jigsaw puzzle or playing a video game, whereas a toddler like Jeremy in this chapter's opening scene seems to bound from activity to activity? Most of us have a sense that older children are better able than younger ones to "pay attention" to a given task. Researchers have documented how children's attention processes undergo recognizable changes with development.

Attention has been conceptualized as a process that allows the individual to focus on a selected aspect of the environment, often in preparation for learning or problem solving (Kahneman, 1973). Attention represents the first step in cognitive processing and, as such, is a critical phase. Unless information enters the system in the first place, there will be few opportunities to develop memory, concepts, or other cognitive skills. Children with a poor capacity to attend will have difficulties in learning, the ramifications of which can be enormous, especially as they enter school. Research evidence corroborates that good attention skills at about age five or six years are among the strongest predictors of academic success in early elementary school (Duncan et al., 2007). Even at three months of age, infants who pay greater attention to stimuli have better recognition memory for them (Adler, Gerhardstein, & Rovee-Collier, 1998).

RISK | RESILIENCE

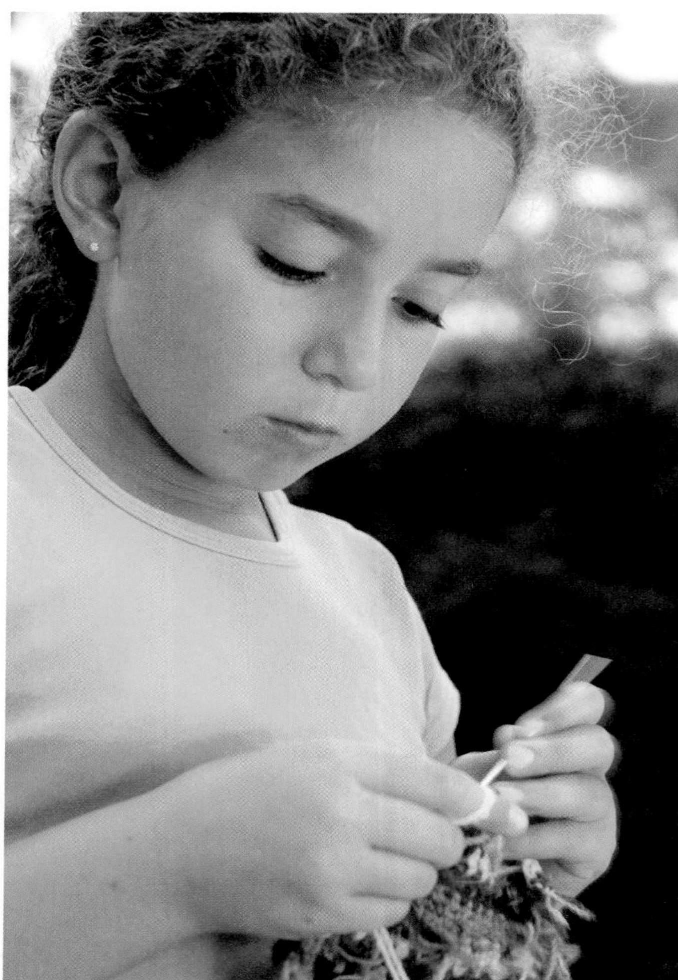

As children develop, their ability to focus and sustain their attention on a task grows noticeably, particularly around ten years of age.

Attention Span

One of the most obvious developmental trends is the dramatic increase in the child's ability to sustain attention on some activity or set of stimuli. Holly Ruff and Katharine Lawson (1990) observed one-, two-, and three-and-a-half-year-olds while the children played with an array of six toys. They observed a steady increase with age in the amount of attention directed to individual toys. On average, one-year-olds showed focused attention for 3.33 seconds, two-year-olds for 5.36 seconds, and three-and-a-half-year-olds for 8.17 seconds. Generally, at ages two and three, children show longer periods of attention to television and to toys they are playing with than to highly structured tasks. Between ages three and five years, though, children show growth in the ability to attend to tasks arranged by an adult (Ruff, Capozzoli, & Weissberg, 1998). The attention span continues to increase throughout the early school years and adolescence and shows a particularly marked improvement around age ten years (Milich, 1984; Yendovitskaya, 1971).

Why does sustained attention increase with age? Maturation of the central nervous system is partly responsible. The reticular activating system, the portion of the lower brainstem that regulates levels of arousal, is not fully mature until adolescence. Another factor may be the increasing complexity of the child's interests. Young children seem to be intrigued by the physical properties of objects, but because these are often not too complex, simply looking at or touching objects quickly leads to habituation. On the other hand, older children are more concerned with creative and varied ways of playing with objects (Ruff & Lawson, 1990). As children actively generate more possible uses for stimuli, their active engagement with stimuli captivates and feeds back to influence attention.

INTERACTION AMONG DOMAINS

Controlling Attention

A second developmental change in attentional processes involves the ability of children to control their attention in a systematic manner; that is, they increasingly deploy their attention effectively, such as when they are comparing two stimuli. At three-and-a-half months of age, shifts of attention from one stimulus to another appear to be reflexive in nature, but by five to six months of age, they are more deliberate and planned. During the period from about five to seven months, infants also exhibit a marked increase in the rate with which they shift attention from one stimulus to another. More rapid shifts probably reflect the infant's greater efficiency in processing information from the environment. Researchers hypothesize that the infant's ability to inhibit processing of one stimulus so that the next one can be attended to underlies more rapid shifts (Rose, Feldman, & Jankowski, 2001a). In addition, brain scans show that areas of the prefrontal cortex that are involved in arousal and attention show rapid improvements in organization and efficiency between four and seven months of age (Richards, Reynolds, & Courage, 2010).

INTERACTION AMONG DOMAINS

The classic studies of Eliane Vurpillot (Vurpillot, 1968; Vurpillot & Ball, 1979) illustrate developmental changes in how older children control their attention. Children were shown a picture of two houses, each having six windows, and were asked to judge whether the houses were identical (see Figure 8.9). As they inspected the houses, their eye movements were filmed. Preschoolers scanned the windows less thoroughly and systematically

Figure 8.9
Comparing Houses

Children were asked to explore houses to make judgments about whether they were the same or different while a camera photographed their eye movements. Preschoolers explored the windows less thoroughly, efficiently, and systematically than older children.

Source: From Vurpillot, E. (1968). The development of scanning strategies and their relation to visual differentiation. *Journal of Experimental Child Psychology*, 6, 632–650. Copyright © 1968 by Academic Press, reproduced by permission of the publisher.

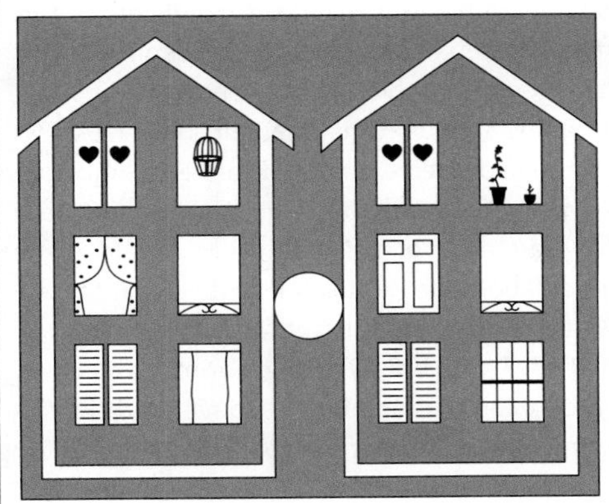

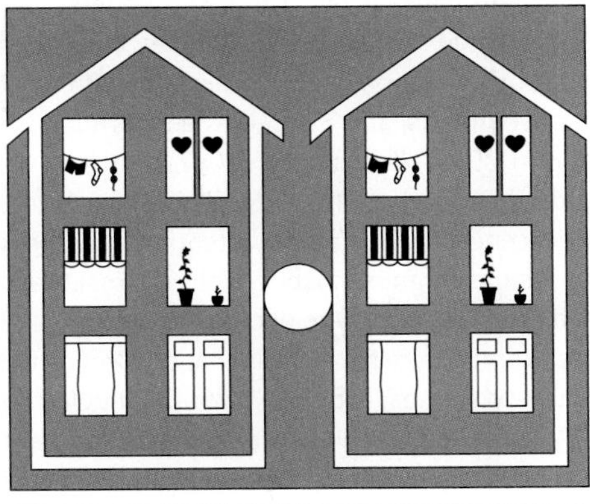

than older children. For example, when the houses were identical, four- and five-year-olds looked at only about half of the windows before making a decision, but older children looked at nearly all of them. When the windows differed, older children were more likely than younger children to stop scanning as soon as they detected a discrepancy. Finally, older children were more likely to look back and forth at windows in the same locations of the two houses; younger children displayed more haphazard fixations, looking at a window in one house, then a different window in the other house.

From middle childhood through about age sixteen years, children show improvements in the ability to control where their eyes look (Kramer, Gonzalez de Sather, & Cassavaugh, 2005) as well as in their ability to be *selective* (Goldberg, Maurer, & Lewis, 2001). In other words, older children are much more likely than younger children to ignore information that is irrelevant or distracts from some central activity or problem. This ability likely depends to some extent on the maturation of the prefrontal cortex, which we know is involved in selective attention in adults (Husain & Kennard, 1997). Also contributing to this change is the child's growing understanding that his attentional capacity is limited and that cognitive tasks are best accomplished with focused attention. Growth in this knowledge occurs during the preschool and early school years. Six-year-olds state that a person who is concentrating on one task will not pay much attention to other things, whereas four-year-olds do not exhibit this understanding (Flavell, Green, & Flavell, 1995).

INTERACTION AMONG DOMAINS

To some degree, the child's knowledge about attention may be gleaned from the kinds of behaviors that are emphasized in his or her culture. In our society, focusing on one thing at a time is probably considered by most parents and teachers to be a desirable goal (Ruff & Rothbart, 1996). However, this pattern is not universal. Children of Mexican heritage, when observed as they learned to make origami figures in a group context, engaged in much more simultaneous attention to multiple events than did European American children (Correa-Chávez, Rogoff, & Mejía Arauz, 2005). Cultural preferences and demands may thus guide the particular attentional style a child develops.

SOCIOCULTURAL INFLUENCE

Researchers find that individual differences in attention are evident by ages two to three years. Some children are able to resist distractors presented on a video screen while they are presented with toys to play with; at the same time, they show more sustained and focused attention while they are exploring those toys. Other children are less able to inhibit their responses to distractors in the environment and consequently may derive less benefit from full exploration of the objects (Kannass, Oakes, & Shaddy, 2006). These differences in attentional style may have cascading effects on cognitive development.

RISK | RESILIENCE

Approximately 5 percent of school-age children in the United States, usually boys, show a pattern of impulsivity, high levels of motor activity, and attention problems called *attention deficit hyperactivity disorder,* or *ADHD* (Bloom, Cohen, & Freeman, 2009). The disorder is puzzling because its cause is not completely understood, and an unambiguous diagnosis can be difficult to obtain. At the same time, for parents, teachers, and the children themselves, the consequences of the disorder—poor school achievement, behavior management problems, poor peer relationships, negative moods, and low self-esteem among them—can be serious (Erhardt & Hinshaw, 1994; Rapport, 1995; Whalen et al., 2002). Patterns of behavior associated with ADHD are evident before children start school (Loe et al., 2008), and whereas hyperactivity and impulsivity may decline in adolescence, problems with attention often persist for years (Hart et al., 1995).

As the diagnostic label implies, a major assumption about the nature of ADHD is that these children have some type of deficit in attention. But what precisely is the nature of that deficit? One prominent hypothesis is that children with ADHD have problems with higher-order executive control processes, especially those that help children to inhibit their tendencies to respond (Barkley, 1997; Pennington, 1998). In a type of experiment designed to assess this kind of skill, children sitting in front of a computer screen are instructed to hit one key if they see the letter "X" appear and to hit another key if the letter "O" pops up. However, if they first hear a tone, they must not hit a key at all. Children with ADHD have difficulty stopping themselves unless the tone is played much earlier than the letter appears (Schachar et al., 2000).

INTERACTION AMONG DOMAINS

Why do children with ADHD have these difficulties? Several studies implicate biological factors. Individuals with ADHD show abnormal brain wave activity, slower blood flow, and lower glucose metabolism in the prefrontal regions of the brain that are associated with regulating attention and motor activity (Rapport, 1995). Also, several brain regions, including the prefrontal cortex, are smaller in children with ADHD than in children without the diagnosis and develop more slowly (Giedd et al., 2001; Shaw et al., 2007). Accumulating evidence points to a strong genetic component to ADHD (Stevenson et al., 2005). In one investigation, 65 percent of the ADHD children in the sample had at least one relative with the disorder (Biederman et al., 1990). Other risk factors for attention problems include prenatal exposure to alcohol (Streissguth et al., 1995) and possibly nicotine, cocaine, or other drugs that may affect the developing brain of the fetus (National Institute of Mental Health, 1996). Low-level exposure to lead has also been implicated (Nigg, 2010).

NATURE & NURTURE

RISK | RESILIENCE

ADHD children are frequently treated with medications, such as Ritalin, that are classified as stimulants but that actually serve to "slow them down." This treatment helps many children, as does a combination of medication and behavior therapy, according to a major national study conducted in 1999 by the National Institute of Mental Health (MTA Cooperative Group, 1999). A more recent follow-up evaluating this group of children, however, found that the effects of medication waned after three years, perhaps because of less regulated administration of children's medicines or other factors that are not yet well understood (Jensen et al., 2007). Some experts worry that too many children are placed on medication simply because they exhibit behavior problems rather than genuine ADHD. Clearly, a better understanding of ADHD is needed to sharpen its clinical diagnosis and develop effective treatment strategies for these children.

For Your Review and Reflection

- What are two major ways in which attention changes with development?
- What factors seem to be responsible for developmental changes in attention?
- What is ADHD? What factors may be responsible for its occurrence?
- How would you characterize your own attentional style? Are you able to sustain your attention for long periods of time? Are you readily able to inhibit information that is distracting? Did you have this same style when you were a child?

- How does the research on attention illustrate the theme of risk and resilience? What kinds of developmental challenges do early attention problems seem to forecast? What do you think can be done to promote optimal development in children who show early attention problems?

Memory

Few cognitive skills are as basic as the ability to store information encountered at a given time for potential retrieval seconds, minutes, days, or even years later. It is hard to imagine how any other cognitive activity, such as problem solving, could take place without the ability to draw on previously experienced information. In one way or another, memory is a crucial element in most of our thinking.

Before we begin our discussion of memory, we need to consider some of the distinctions researchers have made concerning different types of memory. One contrast is the difference between recognition and recall memory. Tasks that measure **recognition memory** require participants to indicate somehow that they have experienced a picture, word, or other stimulus before. In other words, there has to be some behavioral response to the experimenter's question, "Have you encountered this item on previous trials of this experiment?" In **recall memory**, participants must reproduce previously presented stimuli. For example, they might be asked to generate a series of actions they had previously witnessed ("Can you show me how we fed the fish before?") or, among older children who can speak, to say a list of words or numbers they had previously heard.

Researchers sometimes also distinguish between episodic and semantic memory. **Episodic memory** is memory for events that occurred at a specific time and place in the past ("What did you do on your first day of school?"). **Semantic memory**, on the other hand, consists of general concepts or facts that are stored without reference to a specific previous event ("How many inches are in a foot?"). Finally, another contrast is sometimes made between explicit and implicit memory. **Explicit memory** refers to recollection of a past event or experience, such as hearing a story being read or viewing a picture of a female face in a laboratory experiment. Explicit memory is a conscious process and can be demonstrated via either recognition or recall. **Implicit memory** refers to nonconscious recollections of how to do something behaviorally, such as learning to use a spoon to eat cereal or, among older children, learning how to ride a bike. The child may have little awareness of all of the small improvements that have taken place in those skills over time. For the most part, the research described below concerns the development of explicit memory.

Studying Memory in Infants

Studying memory in infants presents some unique challenges because, of course, infants do not speak. How, then, can researchers determine anything about their memory capabilities? Two techniques used to study infant perception, *habituation* and *operant conditioning*, have been fruitful in studies of memory in young infants, especially recognition memory. In addition, researchers have developed several other ingenious procedures to shed light on young children's memory abilities.

Much of the earliest research on infant memory was conducted by Joseph Fagan, who used the habituation procedure to study recognition. First, a visual stimulus, such as a photograph of a human face or a geometric figure (some examples are shown in Figure 8.10) is presented to the infant for a predetermined period of time. On a subsequent trial, the same stimulus is paired with a completely new item, and the time the infant spends looking at each picture is recorded. In this *paired-comparison procedure*, infants typically look longer at the novel stimulus than at the familiar one, suggesting that

recognition memory Ability to identify whether a stimulus has previously been encountered.

recall memory Ability to reproduce stimuli that one has previously encountered.

episodic memory Memory for events that took place at a specific time and place.

semantic memory Memory for general concepts or facts.

explicit memory Conscious recollection of a past event or experience.

implicit memory Nonconscious recollections of how to do something behaviorally.

Figure 8.10
Infant Recognition Memory
Fagan tested infant recognition memory by using visual stimuli in a paired-comparison procedure. For each row, one of the stimuli was presented repeatedly until habituation occurred. Then one of the other stimuli in the row was paired with the familiar stimulus to see if infants preferred the novel item. Infants only a few months old looked longer at novel items up to fourteen days after the initial familiarization.

Source: Adapted from Fagan, J. F. (1974). Infant recognition memory: The effects of length. *Child Development, 45*, 351–356. Copyright © 1974. Used by permission of Society for Research in Child Development.

they remember the familiar item. Using this basic approach, Fagan (1974) demonstrated that five- to six-month-olds familiarized with black-and-white photos of human faces for only a few minutes retain information about them for surprisingly long periods of time. When the recognition test occurred three hours or up to fourteen days after the initial familiarization, infants showed consistently longer visual fixations to the novel stimulus. You will probably agree that this is an impressive level of performance for infants only a few months old!

Carolyn Rovee-Collier and her colleagues have used a different technique, relying on operant conditioning to demonstrate infants' early memory capabilities (Rovee-Collier & Hayne, 1987; Rovee-Collier & Shyi, 1992). As shown in Figure 8.11, an infant lies in a crib with a ribbon running from his ankle to an overhead mobile. Within a few minutes, the infant recognizes the contingency between his foot kicks and the movement of the mobile; his rate of kicking increases dramatically. Suppose, however, that the mobile is removed from the crib for two weeks. When the mobile is reintroduced, does the infant remember that this is the object that he can move with a foot kick? The answer is yes: three-month-olds vigorously kicked when the familiar mobile was replaced over the crib but did not kick as much when a brand-new mobile was put in the same position (Enright et al., 1983).

Studying infant recall requires different procedures. With one technique called *deferred imitation*, infants are shown a unique sequence of actions and then observed to see whether they imitate those behaviors at a later time. For example, in Andrew Meltzoff's studies, infants typically see the experimenter pull the square ends off a dumbbell or push a button on a box with a stick. When tested as long as four months later, a substantial number of fourteen-month-olds remembered the specific action sequences (Meltzoff, 1995). Similarly, Patricia Bauer and her colleagues have used a method they call **elicited imitation**, in which older infants and preschoolers must repeat a sequence of actions demonstrated by the experimenter. One sequence used in these studies is "making a gong." Children watch as the researcher shows three distinct steps to an event they have never seen before: (1) putting a bar across two posts, (2) hanging a plate from the bar, and (3) hitting the plate with a mallet (see Figure 8.12). Then, weeks or even months later, the children return to the laboratory and are asked to repeat the sequence of actions with the array of parts they see on the table. In other words, they must initially imitate and then later recall a correctly ordered set of behaviors. Bauer's studies show that, by the time most children start their second year, they need to see the sequence only once in order to remember it one month later. By twenty months of age, memories for the sequence can last for as long as twelve months (Bauer, 2002; Bauer, 2007). These studies provide dramatic evidence for the presence of recall memory well before children have fully developed their language skills.

elicited imitation Method in which older infants and preschoolers must repeat a sequence of actions demonstrated by the experimenter.

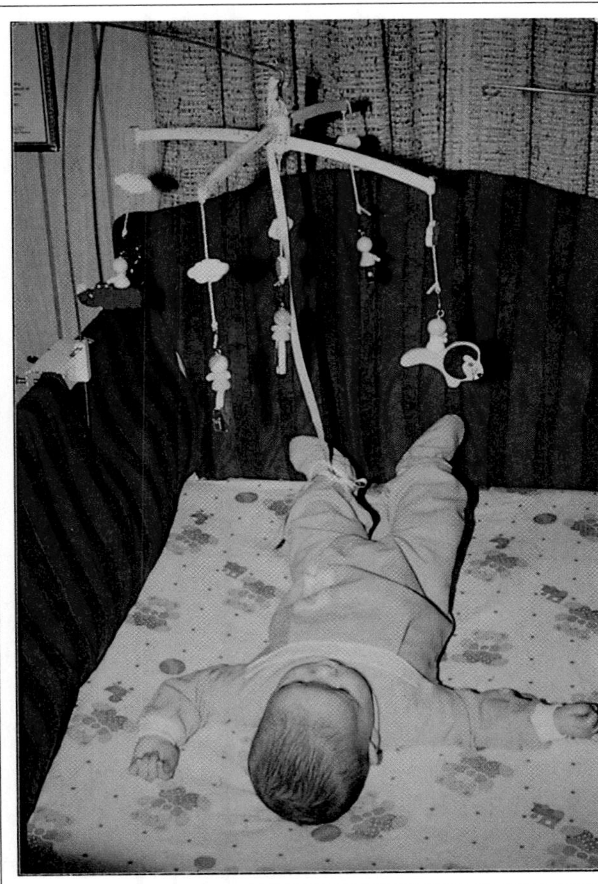

Figure 8.11
Using Operant Conditioning to Study Early Memory
Infants in Rovee-Collier's studies had a ribbon attached between their feet and an interesting mobile overhead. Infants quickly learned that kicking made the mobile move. When the mobile was removed and then reintroduced after a delay interval, infants showed that they "remembered" it by vigorously kicking again.
Source: Courtesy of Carolyn Rovee-Colliet.

Infant Memory Capabilities

Given what you have already learned about the evidence for some memory capacity for prenatal experiences, it should not be surprising to learn that newborns can also retain information and for at least a twenty-four-hour period (Swain, Zelazo, & Clifton, 1993). On the first day of one study, newborns heard a tape of a word, either *beagle* or *tinder*, that was repeated during the experimental session while an observer recorded the number of head turns the infants made toward the sound. As you would expect with the habituation procedure, the number of head turns declined over the session. One day later, one group of infants heard the same word again, whereas a second experimental group heard a new word. Infants in the first group made fewer head turns toward the stimulus word and more head turns away from it than infants in the second group. Evidently, they remembered some very specific properties of the auditory stimulus for a duration of many hours.

Early memories are easily disrupted, however, by changes in the context of the task. Suppose an infant in an operant-conditioning experiment learns the original contingency between a foot kick and the movement of the mobile when she is in a playpen lined with a yellow cloth with green squares. Twenty-four hours later, the mobile is reintroduced, but this time the cloth liner is blue with red stripes. Now the infant does not show a memory for the previous day's events; she does not kick nearly as much as she did at the end of training the previous day (Rovee-Collier et al., 1992). By the latter portion of the first year, however, infants are more likely to disregard differences in contextual cues when they are tested for memory, perhaps because their memories are more robust (Hartshorn et al., 1998). More broadly speaking, they can remember things that are learned in one place and tested in another (Rovee-Collier, 1999).

There are several other important developmental changes in both recognition and recall in the first two years. First, as infants mature, they store information more rapidly. Whether they are participating in a habituation, operant conditioning, deferred

Figure 8.12

An Example of Elicited Imitation

In this elicited imitation task, young children are shown the three steps involved in making a gong: (a) putting a bar between two posts, (b) hanging a plate, and (c) striking it with a mallet. After a delay of weeks, or even months, children return to the laboratory and are asked to make the gong. Memory for these kinds of sequences is generally very robust for two-year-olds.

Source: "Remembering the times of our lives: Memory in infancy and beyond." (2007) by Bauer, P. J. Reproduced by permission of Taylor & Francis Group, LLC., http://www.taylorandfrancis.com.

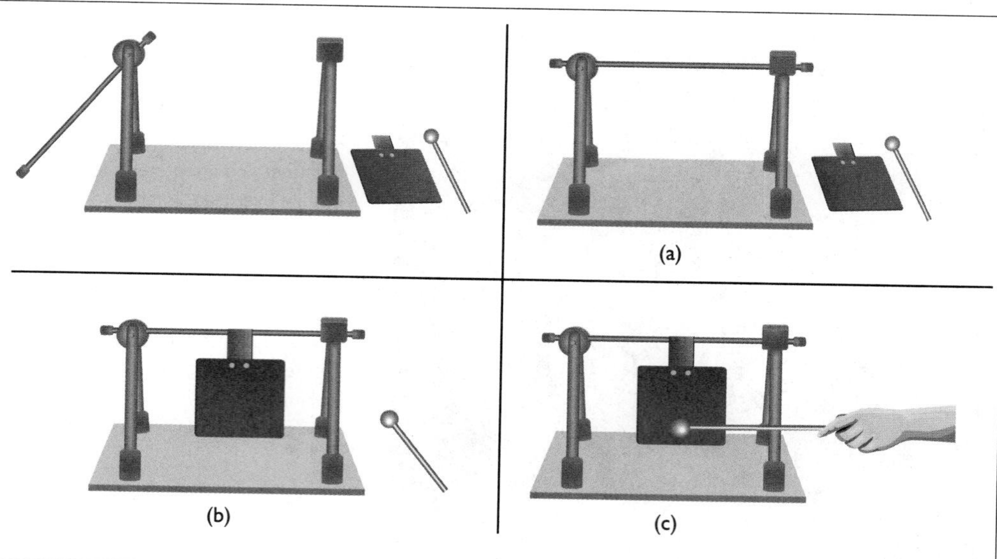

imitation, or elicited imitation experiments, they need fewer trials to "study" the items they are supposed to remember (Bauer, 2004; Courage & Howe, 2004; Hayne, 2004). In experiments using deferred imitation of a three-part sequence of actions, for example, six-month-olds typically need six exposures to the sequence in order to remember, while fourteen-month-olds need only one (Barr et al., 1996; Meltzoff, 1995). Second, infants can retain information for longer and longer periods of time. In deferred and elicited imitation tasks, the general finding is that six-month-olds can retain information over a twenty-four-hour period, nine-month-olds for up to five weeks, and twenty-month-olds for as long as twelve months (Bauer, 2004). Finally, as infants grow older, they remember a greater amount of information. While the majority of six-month-olds typically enact one segment of a three-part sequence in imitation tasks, nine-month-olds can reproduce more than one (Bauer, 2004). Using the habituation task, Susan Rose and her colleagues similarly found that, at five to seven months of age, infants had trouble recognizing a string of three or four different objects that were presented as part of one memory trial but that, by twelve months of age, almost half of infants were successful (Rose, Feldman, & Jankowski, 2001b).

Memory in Older Children

Researchers have used different types of tasks to assess the development of memory in children who are old enough to be able to talk, with most of them tapping recall memory. In studies using a *free-recall* task, children are asked to listen, for example, to a list of words, and then after a specified delay period, to repeat them in any order they wish. In other tasks, the order of the items must be preserved to measure what is called **memory span**, the number of stimulus items that can be recalled after the brief interval. As Figure 8.13 shows, two-year-olds typically remember only about two items in memory span tasks, four-year-olds about three or four, and seven-year-olds about five (Dempster, 1981). Most studies of recall memory, regardless of the specific procedure, show that older children remember more information than younger children.

Do these changes in memory occur because the storage capacity of memory increases? Probably not. Instead, children's tendency to employ **memory strategies**, activities to enhance the encoding and retrieval of information, increases with age. Children ages seven years and older are more likely than younger children to rehearse items, for example. At first they might repeat only the word they just heard, but after third grade, many children start to include that word plus at least one other item from the list to be remembered

memory span Number of stimulus items that can be recalled after a brief interval of time.

memory strategy Mental activity, such as rehearsal, that enhances memory performance.

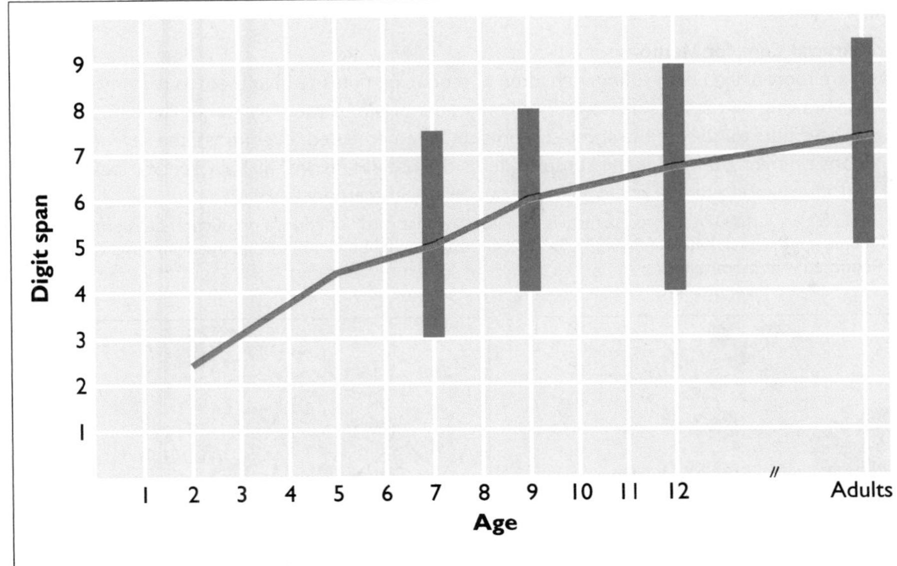

Figure 8.13
Developmental Changes in Memory Span
In the memory span task, participants are asked to repeat a string of digits after an interval of a few seconds. The points on the curve represent the average number of digits participants are able to recall. The bars represent the ranges of typical performance at each age. Memory span increases throughout childhood and approaches the adult level between ages ten and twelve years.
Source: From Dempster, F. N. (1981). Memory span: Sources of individual and developmental differences, *Psychological Bulletin, 89*, 1981, 63–100. Copyright © 1981 by the American Psychological Association. Reprinted with permission.

(Lehmann & Hasselhorn, 2007). Another strategy is to reorganize items into more meaningful, and hence more memorable, units. For instance, noting that the numbers 1, 3, 5, and 7 compose the sequence of odd numbers makes the list easier to recall. Or children can try to test themselves, covering items and saying their names to try to remember. As children grow older, they are likely to use several of these techniques to help themselves remember (Schwenck, Bjorklund, & Schneider, 2009).

Many memory strategies pertain mostly to encoding, or getting information into the memory stores, but older children are also better at retrieval, or getting it out. Figure 8.14 shows the sketches made by a first-grader and a seventh-grader who were asked in one study to "write or draw anything you want to help you win the game" as they played the memory game "Concentration." The first-grader's drawing had little to do with the game; it is simply a picture depicting an unrelated event. In contrast, the seventh-grader's notations contain important details about what the items are and their specific locations on the game board. Not surprisingly, the results of the study showed that the better the quality of children's notations, the fewer turns it took for them to win the game (Eskritt & Lee, 2002).

Changes in **processing speed**, the rapidity with which cognitive activities are carried out, also contribute to developmental gains in memory (Kail, 2007). Researchers have suggested that two types of processing speed are important. Among children ages seven to eight, the ability to speak digits or words rapidly—presumably indexing the *rate of verbal rehearsal*—is related to their memory span. Among children ages eleven and twelve, memory span is more closely linked to shorter silent pauses between the items as they are being recalled. This second measure is presumed to index the rate at which items are actually *retrieved* from memory. The data suggest that these different aspects of processing speed mature at different ages (Cowan, 1999; Cowan et al., 1998).

Developmental changes in memory can also be understood in terms of the child's increasing efficiency and control over cognitive processes. **Metamemory**, the child's understanding of memory, is one aspect of this process. It includes the ability to assess one's own memory characteristics and limitations, the demands made by different memory tasks, and the strategies likely to benefit memory (Flavell & Wellman, 1977; Guttentag, 1987). It also includes the ability to monitor the contents of one's own memory and to make decisions about how to allocate cognitive resources ("Have I memorized everything thoroughly? Do I still need to study some items?") (Kail, 1990). Advances in each of these aspects of metamemory are, to some degree, related to improvements in memory as children get older. For example, older children have a better understanding than younger children that longer lists are harder to remember than shorter ones and that events from the distant past are more difficult to

processing speed Rapidity with which cognitive activities are carried out.

metamemory The child's understanding of his or her own memory.

Figure 8.14

Generating Retrieval Cues for Memory

Older children are more skilled than younger children at producing notes to help them to remember information.The drawing on the left was made by a first-grader playing a memory game. The items in this child's drawing have little to do with the stimulus items to be remembered. In contrast, the seventh-grader's notations on the right include the stimulus items themselves, as well as their specific locations. Children who produce good external notes are more successful in memory tasks.

Source: Eskritt, M., & Lee, K. (2002). 'Remember where you last saw that card': Children's production of external symbols as a memory aid. *Developmental Psychology, 38*, 254–266. Copyright © 2002 by the American Psychological Association. Reprinted with permission.

remember than more recent events (Kreutzer, Leonard, & Flavell, 1975; Lyon & Flavell, 1993; Wellman, 1977). One consequence of this awareness is that children begin to see the need to use strategies (Schneider, 2000). Around age seven years, children improve in their efficiency in managing the complexities involved in many memory tasks: paying attention to new information while at the same time, maintaining in memory the information which has already been taken in (Barrouillet et al. 2009). By adolescence, children are able to judge whether they have studied enough, which memory strategies are the most effective for the material, and how much effort they need to allocate in order to improve recall (Schneider & Lockl, 2002).

Finally, growth in memory skills has been linked to the child's expanding base of general knowledge. In a unique experiment, Michelene Chi (1978) found that, in certain situations, children may actually remember more than adults. In this experiment, adults and children averaging ten years of age were asked to remember lists of ten digits presented by the experimenter. Typically, the adults' performance surpassed the children's. However, when the memory task consisted of reproducing chess positions previously seen for only ten seconds on a chessboard, children significantly outperformed adults. How did they accomplish this remarkable feat? Chi explains that the children who participated were experts in the game of chess, whereas the adults (who were college educated) had only casual knowledge of the game. By having greater knowledge, these children probably could encode the familiar patterns of chess pieces more efficiently, whereas adults were probably seeing random arrangements of rooks, knights, and pawns.

Brain Development and Memory

INTERACTION AMONG DOMAINS

Ultimately, any account of cognitive development will have to be connected to changes in the structures or processes that occur in the brain. Neuroscientists have been actively exploring brain functioning in both animals and humans to try to establish the underlying substrates of different cognitive processes, including memory. Fruitful approaches have included studying the memory performance of animals that have had different portions of the brain lesioned (or damaged), "scanning" the brain to measure metabolism and blood flow, and recording the electrical activity of the brain while individuals perform memory tasks.

We have already noted that even very young infants show a robust preference for novel stimuli, indicating their recognition memory for "old" items they have seen before. Infant monkeys show similar patterns of behavior; however, when their hippocampus is removed at fifteen days of age, preferences for novelty disappear (Bachevalier, Brickson, & Hagger, 1993). As Figure 8.15 shows, the hippocampus is a brain structure located below the cerebral cortex that has long been known to be involved in memory functioning. Apparently, the hippocampus, which is a part of the *limbic system*, is an early developing structure that is necessary for the display of fundamental memory processes such as recognition memory (Nelson, Thomas, & de Haan, 2006). The hippocampus continues to mature at least until two years of age (Seress & Abraham, 2008) and may thus be associated with growth in children's memory abilities beyond infancy.

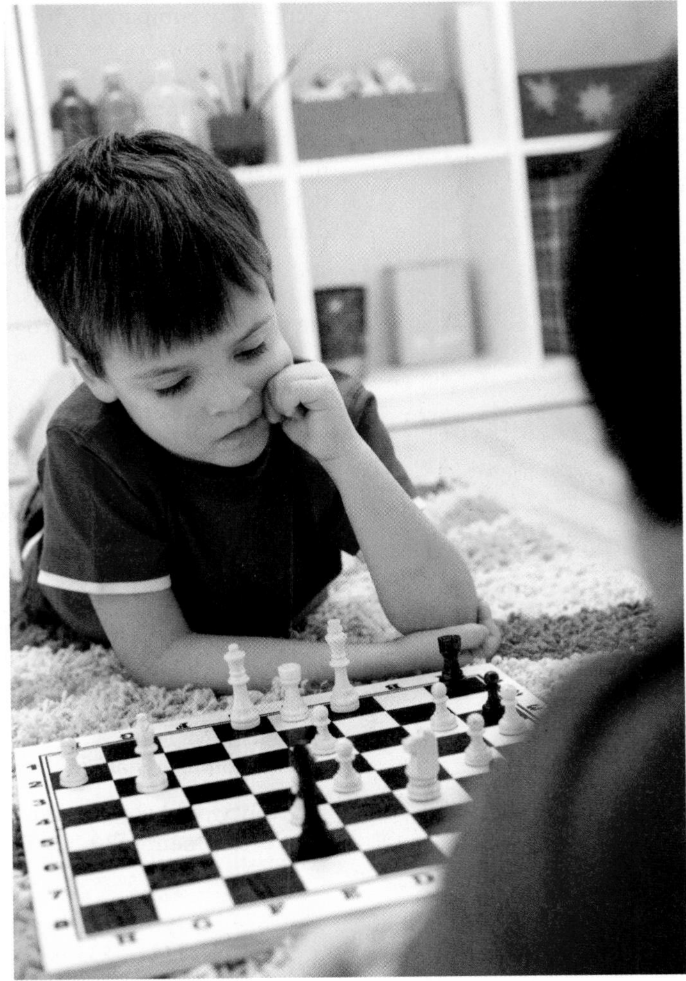

When children learn specific skills such as playing the game of chess, they may show greater memory for information related to the game than older individuals who do not have expertise in chess.

Toward the latter part of the first year, portions of the temporal and prefrontal lobes of the brain (see Figure 8.15) begin to mature, as is revealed by *positron emission tomography*, or PET, scans. PET scans allow neuroscientists to measure, among other things, the glucose activity in different portions of the brain. Interestingly, the levels of glucose metabolism in the temporal lobes of monkeys begin to look adultlike at four months of age, the age at which they begin to reach for a novel object after a short delay (Bachevalier, Hagger, & Mishkin, 1991). Similarly, glucose metabolism in the prefrontal lobes begins to appear mature in one-year-old human infants (Chugani, 1994). This is also the age at which infants correctly search for objects in the A-not-B task and at which they can locate objects after a delay (Nelson, 1995).

Researchers have also begun to record the electrical activity of the brain online while infants participate in memory tasks. In one study, five-month-old infants heard a succession of 100 identical stimuli, either a click or a tone. The next day, fifty of the "old" stimuli were presented with fifty "new" ones (e.g., a tone if a click had originally been heard). Electrical firing patterns of the brain were more pronounced for familiar than for unfamiliar stimuli. Brain waves also had less variable onset times for familiar stimuli on the

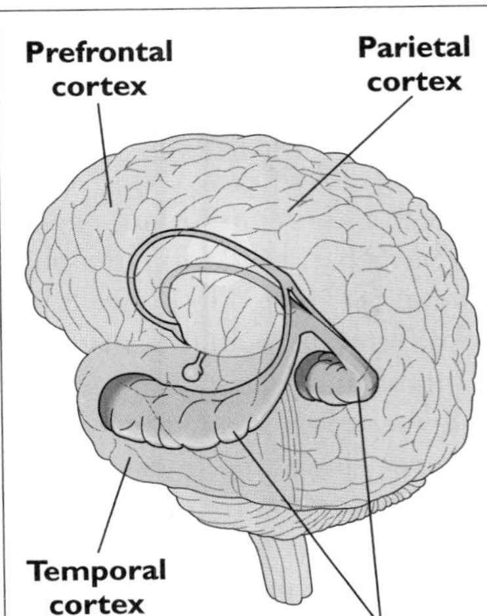

Figure 8.15

The Brain and Memory Development

Several regions of the brain are implicated in memory development. The hippocampus matures early, and part of its function may be to direct recognition memory. Portions of the temporal and prefrontal cortex mature later in the first year and apparently are involved in more demanding memory tasks.

second day compared with the first day (Thomas & Lykins, 1995). Put another way, physiological responses were more consistent and prominent for the stimuli that had been put into memory.

By the time children reach preadolescence, fMRI data show that their brains respond much as adults' brains do when they engage in a working memory task. Portions of the parietal and prefrontal areas of the cortex, in particular, show unique patterns of activation (Nelson et al., 2000). Thus, as the cortex develops, so does the ability to perform more demanding memory tasks.

Neuropsychological studies hold great promise in unlocking some of the mysteries of brain-behavior relationships. No doubt, they will also provide important information about the factors that influence cognitive development.

For Your Review and Reflection

- How do researchers study memory in infancy?
- What are the major features of memory during infancy?
- What factors are primarily responsible for developmental improvements in recall memory?
- Which memory strategies have you used to help yourself study or to remember other important information such as people's names, cell phone numbers, or street addresses? Do some strategies seem to work better for you than others? Why do you think this is so?
- What major changes in the brain accompany developmental improvements in memory?
- How would you answer this question: What is memory development the development of?

Problem Solving

One of the most powerful human cognitive skills is the ability to solve problems. Whether you are completing an analogy, computing an arithmetic solution, or testing a hypothesis, problem solving typically involves several steps or phases. Often you start with planning the steps to the solution of the problem, considering both the information you have at the start and the final goal. Clearly, you must attend to the portions of the problem that are relevant to its solution. You will probably select from a number of strategies to help you achieve your goal (for example, count on your fingers or use a calculator). In many cases, you must rely on your understanding of what different symbols in the problem (e.g., "+" or "=") represent. Frequently you must draw on a body of information from memory and examine relationships among several pieces of that information. Once you have the solution, you will often apply this new knowledge to similar contexts. Given the number of steps involved and the complex, intertwined relationships among them, you can see why problem solving is considered to be an example of what is called "higher-order thinking."

What are the earliest instances of problem-solving activity in humans? In an experiment conducted by Peter Willatts (1990), twelve-month-olds saw a barrier in front of a cloth on which was placed a string attached to a toy (similar to what is depicted in Figure 8.16). To get the toy, infants had to remove the barrier, pull the cloth, and then pull the string. In a control condition, the toy was not attached to the string. Infants in the first group tended to remove the barrier and then quickly pulled the cloth, and grasped the string to reach the toy. Their behavior suggested that reaching the attractive toy, which was of utmost interest to them, was possible by pulling the string. In contrast, infants in the control group played with the barrier, were slower to reach for the cloth, and frequently did not grasp the string, probably because they recognized that the barrier, cloth, and string could not help to bring the toy closer. Willatts (1990) concluded that infants are capable of putting together several subgoals with the deliberate intent of reaching a goal.

Figure 8.16
Transfer of Problem Solutions Among Infants
Even one-year-olds can transfer the solution of one problem to another when the goal sequences are similar. Each of these problems requires the child to bypass a barrier, pull the cloth, and grab the string to obtain the toy. Infants who were successful in solving one of these problems could typically solve the others, even though the problems were not perceptually identical.
Source: Adapted from Chen, Z., Sanchez, R. P., & Campbell, T. (1997). From beyond to within their grasp: The rudiments of analogical problem solving in 10- and 13-month-olds, *Developmental Psychology, 33*, 790–801. Copyright © 1997 by the American Psychological Association. Reprinted with permission.

Problem-solving skills become more elaborate and complex as children pass through the preschool and school years. Just think about the typical day of the average school-age child and you will undoubtedly discern many problem-solving situations the child encounters: a set of arithmetic problems to complete on a worksheet at school, a computer maze or jigsaw puzzle to solve for fun, or several bus routes to choose from to get to an after-school job. More mature and efficient problem solvers deploy several "executive" cognitive skills, much as the central processor directs the various functions of a computer. For instance, can I add these numbers in my head or should I get a calculator? What is the best strategy to use—should the puzzle be started with the edge pieces or the entire top left corner? Will learning how to do a simple computer maze provide any clues about how to do a more complex one? As researchers have explored children's problem solving, they have discovered a number of developmental changes in important components that characterize higher-order thinking.

Planning

One of the hallmarks of a mature problem solver is the ability to plan an approach to obtaining a goal. Planning, of course, depends on representational capacities, because symbols may be employed or manipulated as part of the plan. It also depends on having general knowledge about the events being planned for—what is involved in going grocery shopping versus taking a trip to the beach, for example (Hudson, Shapiro, & Sosa, 1995). Moreover, planning has at least two aspects: (1) deciding on the steps one needs to take ahead of time and (2) knowing when to be flexible and perhaps modify or discard advance plans if the situation calls for it (Baker-Sennett, Matusov, & Rogoff, 1993).

Planning can be observed as young children attempt to solve simple novel problems, such as in our earlier example of making a gong out of triangular supports, a metal plate, and a mallet. When two-year-olds in one study were shown the fully assembled gong first, they showed a high proportion of actions that would lead to successful problem solving. Showing the children the goal was much more effective than getting them started with the early steps in solving the problem. Thus, information about the end state of the problem was critical in prompting these young children to plan (Bauer et al., 1999). Similarly, in another experiment, ten-month-old infants were observed as they were encouraged either to throw a ball into a plastic tub or fit the ball into a tube. What happened when the experimenter offered them a ball in preparation for each action? Infants reached for the ball faster in the first instance, suggesting that they were planning their actions in accordance with their ultimate goal. When throwing (as opposed to fitting one object into another), their apparent intent was to initiate a faster, more forceful action (Claxton, Keen, & McCarty, 2003).

David Klahr's classic research using the Tower of Hanoi problem, illustrated in Figure 8.17, shows that there are clear developmental improvements in planning (Klahr, 1978; Klahr & Robinson, 1981). In this problem, one of three pegs has three cans of different sizes stacked on it. The goal is to move the cans to the third peg so they end up in the same order they were on the first peg. Two rules apply: only one item may be moved at a time, and a smaller can cannot be placed on a larger one. Klahr found that six-year-olds were better planners than three-year-olds in two respects: they were more likely to pursue long-term goals, and they could keep more subgoals in mind as they attempted to solve the problem. For example, three-year-olds single-mindedly moved the cans to the third peg without thinking of the intermediate steps that might be necessary; their plan encompassed only the short-term goal to get the cans to the final peg. They could think of only one or two steps to attain the goal and broke the rules of the game. In contrast, six-year-olds used five or six steps to solve the problem, looking ahead a step or more as they planned their moves and anticipating potential traps in or obstacles to their placement of the cans.

With development, children also show changes in the flexibility of their planning. This phenomenon is illustrated by another study in which children were asked to plan a route through a maze (Gardner & Rogoff, 1990). When the task involved no time pressure, seven- to ten-year-olds planned the entire route through the maze before they drew in the path. However, when the experimenter told children to work as fast as they could, these older children used a more efficient approach under the circumstances: they planned less. Younger children, ages four to seven years, were less likely to adapt their planning strategies to the particular demands of the task.

NATURE & NURTURE

Planning is likely to develop as children gain experiences with everyday routines in which specific events occur in a temporal order. Parental verbalizations about plans and the child's own emerging ability to verbalize probably also contribute (Benson, 1997). Another ingredient, according to Marshall Haith, is the child's "future orientation," his or her ability to think about events that are yet to come. Although early signs of future orientation are evident in infants—as they show anticipation about events in familiar routines, for example—a sense about the future probably undergoes more complex elaboration as the child matures (Haith, 1997).

Figure 8.17
The Tower of Hanoi
In the Tower of Hanoi problem, the child must move three cans stacked on the first peg to the third peg so that they end up in the same order. Only one can may be moved at a time, and a smaller can may not be placed on a larger one. This problem gives researchers the opportunity to study developmental changes in children's planning activities as they solve problems.

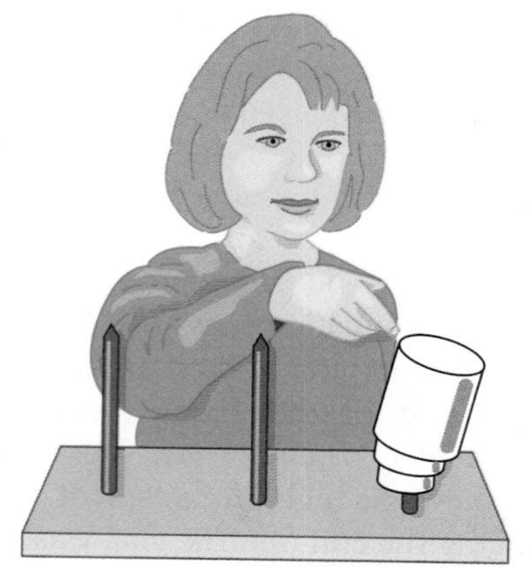

Strategy Choice

When a child encounters a problem—say, an addition problem—he will most likely choose from among several strategies. Robert Siegler has closely examined children's strategies as they solve simple addition problems and has found that children often rely on more than one approach (Siegler & Crowley, 1991; Siegler & Jenkins, 1989; Siegler & Shrager, 1984). Most children, he noted, first turned to one strategy but also usually had a backup strategy or two. Having multiple strategies affords the child useful flexibility as she encounters new situations and gains new knowledge (Siegler, 1989).

Suppose the child's assignment is to add the numbers 3 and 1. Several strategies are possible. The child can represent each number on his fingers and then count to the total. Alternatively, he can represent the larger number on his fingers and then count off the smaller number. Or he can simply retrieve the information from memory. Siegler found that, if the problem was simple, children drew on memory for the answer because that approach is the fastest. If the problem was more difficult, however, children used other strategies that ensured greater accuracy, such as counting on their fingers (Siegler & Shrager, 1984).

With development, as children have more successes with solving problems and become more confident about their approach, they are more likely to use memory as opposed to finger counting to solve addition problems. They also learn new strategies, often when they fail to solve a problem and need to search for alternative solutions. But children can learn from their successes, too. Siegler and Jenkins (1989) noticed that children often came up with new strategies for problems they had solved correctly earlier in the experiment. Children may also discover strategies simply by interacting with the materials for a problem (Thornton, 1999) or by hearing an expert explain a successful strategy (Crowley & Siegler, 1998).

Siegler's research shows that children do not merely substitute one strategy for another as they become more mature problem solvers. Rather, they incorporate new blends of strategies as they learn new ones and discard older ones. Children are constantly selecting from a pool of multiple strategies, depending on whether the task demands that they be fast or accurate and on what they remember about the success of the particular strategy in the past (Siegler, 1989). In their use of strategies, children frequently show variability from one problem-solving session to another, from one child to the next, and from one context to another, such as playing a board game versus doing math (Bjorklund & Rosenblum, 2002; Kuhn et al., 1995; Siegler, 1994). Variability, in fact, may enhance learning because it provides experiences with different problem-solving approaches and opportunities to discover those that work (Siegler, 1996).

Transferring Skills

One final essential element in higher-order thinking is the ability to use what you have learned in one situation and apply it to other, similar problems. How well do children extend their existing problem-solving skills to new circumstances? This has been a long-standing question in psychology, particularly among researchers who have studied the role of generalization in learning. It has also been a question of paramount importance to educators, who assume children will find some application in their everyday lives for what they have learned in the classroom. The ability to transfer knowledge requires that children learn the original problem well, note the resemblance between the old and new problems, and apply the appropriate activities to the new problem. This process is called **transfer** in that the child must notice the one-to-one correspondence that exists between the elements of one problem and those of another and then apply the familiar skills to the novel context.

An experiment by Ann Brown and her co-researchers illustrates how this process can occur (Brown, Kane, & Echols, 1986). Three- to five-year-olds were read a story in which a magical genie had to move his jewels from one bottle across a high wall to another bottle. Several items were available to help the genie: glue, paper clips, sheets of paper, and so on. The experimenter and each child enacted the solution,

transfer Ability to employ the solution to one problem in other, similar problems.

rolling up the paper into a tube and using it to transport the jewels from one bottle to the other. The children were then presented with a different problem having the same general solution (a rabbit that needs to get its Easter eggs across a river can roll paper into a tube to transport them). Whether the children were able to transfer the solution to a new problem depended on whether they recalled the goal structure of the previous problem. If they remembered the major actor, his goal, and the solution to his problem, even three-year-olds could solve the new problem.

NATURE & NURTURE

Brown hypothesized that, for transfer of problem solving to take place, the child must represent the problem in general mental terms, that is, abstract out the goal, problem, and solution dissociated from the specific fact that it was a genie who had to transfer jewels. Children can be encouraged to discern such common goal structures in consecutive problems. Zhe Chen and Marvin Daehler (1989) found that, when six-year-olds were explicitly prompted to formulate an answer to the question of how problems were alike, they performed significantly better on a transfer problem than control participants who did not receive this training. Even showing children a series of drawings that depict the goal structure of a problem can facilitate transfer to a new problem (Chen, 2003). The implication is that parents and teachers may play a crucial role in facilitating the transfer of learning by pointing out commonalities across several problems. In fact, there are some circumstances in which very young children can discern the similarities across problems themselves. For example, when problem-solving situations look perceptually different but share similar goal sequences (e.g., remove a barrier, pull the correct cloth, and pull the correct string to reach a toy, as shown in Figure 8.16), even infants who are one year of age show the ability to transfer the solution to other problems once they have been successful with the first (Chen, Sanchez, & Campbell, 1997).

Facilitating Transfer in the Classroom — research applied to education

As the teacher collected each student's paper, Tommy was thinking how glad he was to have the geography test over with. Science was next, and science was without doubt his favorite subject in school. The class was studying electricity and had learned about how to make a circuit, the properties of conductors and insulators, and the role of a battery. Now the teacher was asking pairs of students to make a series of three light bulbs work by putting together wires and batteries in the correct order. Tommy and his partner, Eliza, looked at the equipment before them and were stumped. How would they even begin? As they experimented, though, the principles they discussed in the previous day's lesson began to creep into their thinking. After only a few minutes, their bulbs were assembled and shining as brightly as their proud faces.

If you stop and think about it, probably the greatest overarching goal of education is to ensure that students transfer what they learn in one lesson, problem, or assignment to new situations both in and outside of the classroom. We expect students to go beyond the specific content of one particular mathematics problem, scientific experiment, or writing assignment and apply what they have learned in new situations. Is there anything teachers can do to promote this important process?

Robert Sternberg and Peter Frensch (1993) offer the following suggestions based on their review of numerous studies of both memory and transfer:

1. *"Teach for transfer" by providing multiple settings in which information is encoded.* This tactic, according to numerous studies of memory, should make retrieval of information more likely because there are more cues associated with it. Teachers should demonstrate to students how information they learn can be applied in different contexts and even ask students to think of applications themselves. That is, knowledge should not be "encapsulated" or taught as a "stand-alone" topic. As an example, principles of algebra could be taught in the context of a science class as well as a math class. The result should be that these principles are remembered better and their usefulness in different subject areas becomes more apparent to students.

2. *Organize information so that transfers are more likely to occur.* Classroom presentations should have an obvious organizational structure and should be connected to information students already have. Such an approach would provide students with a framework that would enhance understanding and learning. Sternberg and Frensch (1993) add that teachers rarely begin lessons with a discussion of why the information is important in students' lives (i.e., where it fits in their personal scheme of things), but to enhance learning, they should.
3. *Help students see the general features that are common across different content areas to be learned and that are specific to a given lesson.* Sternberg and Frensch (1993) describe a personal experience in learning Spanish in which the general features of the language were explicitly pointed out. At the same time, pronunciations and vocabulary that were unique to a given region or country were also highlighted for students. Learning should proceed more efficiently under circumstances in which common themes and exceptions to those themes are deliberately highlighted.
4. *Test students on their ability to apply what they have learned to new situations rather than on their ability to recall specific pieces of information.* This approach would establish in students a "mental set" for the idea that they will have to engage in transfer—that this is an important expectation of them.

All of these pointers have a common aim: to make students aware of transfer as an explicit goal of learning. In a sense, the preceding suggestions ask teachers and students to be more "metacognitive" about the learning process, to overtly and frequently discuss and reflect on how transfer might be promoted. The more teachers incorporate this goal into their daily classroom instruction, according to these researchers, the more likely students will learn in the truest sense of the word.

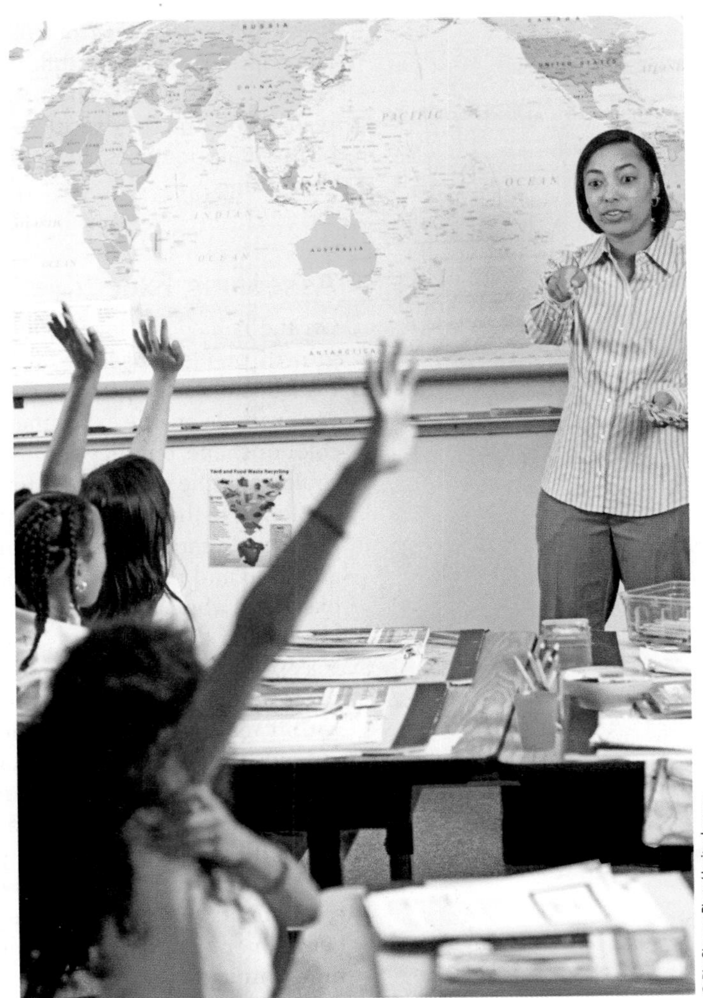

Teachers can use several techniques to facilitate transfer in the classroom. Transfer is one of the most important goals of formal instruction in school.

The Executive Function

Numerous times in this chapter, we have mentioned that, with development, children are better able to control their cognitive processing. As children develop, they become better able to analyze the tasks they face, size up their own capabilities, deploy and modify strategies, inhibit certain behaviors if they have to, and monitor the effectiveness of their approaches. The control of cognitive processing is also very important in problem solving, which, as we saw in this chapter, can involve complex tasks such as planning and transfer. Researchers have begun to turn their attention to understanding the role and development of this **executive function**, the portion of the information-processing system that coordinates various component processes in order to achieve some goal (Welsh, 2002). The development of executive function probably starts in the preschool years with the improvements in the attention system we described earlier in this chapter (Garon, Bryson, & Smith, 2008). In the school years and adolescence, children improve in their ability to inhibit their behavioral tendencies, regulate the information they hold in working memory, and finally, shift between the demands of one complex task to another (Best, Miller, & Jones, 2009).

executive function Portion of the information-processing system that coordinates various component processes in order to achieve some goal.

Neuropsychological studies of children who have experienced brain damage indicate that executive function skills seem to stand apart from other cognitive abilities; affected children may show normal language and sensory abilities but have difficulties with planning and inhibition (Espy & Kaufmann, 2002). The prefrontal cortex of the brain has been implicated as one area responsible for the executive function, although there may be others. Thus, as the cortex of the brain matures, we would expect children to show gains in their executive function capabilities.

INTERACTION AMONG DOMAINS

Assessing Executive Function

On the behavioral level, one manifestation of the child's executive function skills is the growth of *metacognition*, the child's awareness and knowledge of cognitive processes. Preschoolers often perform cognitive tasks without being fully reflective about their actions. For example, in one experiment, three-year-olds readily sorted objects on the basis of either color or shape, but they could not switch from one rule to the other. When questioned, they could state the second rule for sorting given to them by the experimenter, but they could not link it to their actions (Zelazo & Frye, 1998). As metacognitive awareness grows through the school years, so does the ability to act on that awareness, as you saw in our discussion of attention and memory. By adolescence, individuals decide what to think about in the first place and when (Kuhn, 2006). In essence, they become masters of their mental lives.

One of the laboratory tasks that researchers have used to examine executive function is a spatial working memory task in which an array of colored squares appears on a computer screen. The goal is to touch the squares one at a time in order to locate tokens hidden within and then "place" them in a special bin. How organized is the search process? And do individuals touch squares that have already been searched? Optimal performance requires participants to be systematic in their search—maybe by proceeding left to right or top to bottom—and once a token has been found and placed in the bin, to resume the search where it was left off. Touching squares in which tokens have already been found is considered an "error." This task is presumed to assess executive control because it has several components that have to be regulated; it requires participants to be organized, to remember, to monitor their performance, and to update information as progress is made. When nine- through twenty-year-olds were assessed on this task, individuals who were thirteen years of age and older did significantly better than younger children (Luciana et al., 2005).

Another situation that has been used to examine executive control is the Iowa Gambling Task. Here, four decks of cards are presented to individuals. Two decks have cards with high monetary rewards but also a few cards with high losses; the other two decks offer cards with smaller rewards but also many cards with small losses. The goal is to select cards from the decks to obtain the most money; in the long run, the decks with smaller rewards and losses are the best to choose. How do adolescents respond to this task in which the lure of big gains must be suppressed in order to "win" the most money? Monica Luciana and her colleagues (Hooper et al., 2004) found that preteens aged nine to ten years seemed to understand the task but were still tempted by the promise of big wins. Their choices tended to center on the decks with big wins and losses. In contrast, fourteen- to seventeen-year-olds were more likely to shift from the risky "big money" decks to the "safer" decks over the course of several trials. But even the older teenagers tended to make a greater number of riskier choices than those made by older adults. In other words, executive control shows signs of development throughout adolescence.

Judgment and Decision Making

Adolescents (or even adults) do not necessarily reach the most mature levels of metacognition (Kuhn, 2000a, 2000b). For example, adolescents and adults engaged in decision making are often influenced by their current belief systems, especially when confronted with real-life as opposed to laboratory problems. People of all ages, adolescents included, display **judgment biases**, tendencies to be influenced by inappropriate information at the expense of important and

judgment bias Tendency to be influenced by inappropriate information at the expense of important and perhaps more relevant facts.

Cognitive Development: Birth to 11 Years

MONTHS BIRTH | YEARS BIRTH

Newborn
- Shows recognition memory for simple stimuli.

4–9 Months
- Develops object concept.
- Shows sensitivity to changes in number.
- Notices changes in distance cues.
- Relies primarily on own body but also on simple landmark cues to locate objects in space.
- Shows more deliberate shifts of attention.

© thislife pictures/Alamy

12–18 Months
- Classifies objects according to physical similarities.
- Shows long-term recall in elicited imitation tasks.
- Performs simple problem solving by combining subgoals.
- Can transfer solutions across problems with similar goal sequences.

© Jose Luis Pelaez Inc/Blend Images/Jupiter Image

18–30 Months
- Classifies according to thematic and simple taxonomic relations.
- Understands the meaning of simple number terms.
- Uses distance cues to locate objects.
- Has memory span of about two items.
- Shows elementary planning capabilities.

3–4 Years
- Understands basic principles of counting.
- Displays intuitive concepts about numbers.
- Uses landmarks and geometric cues to negotiate spatial environments.

© fotovisage/Alamy

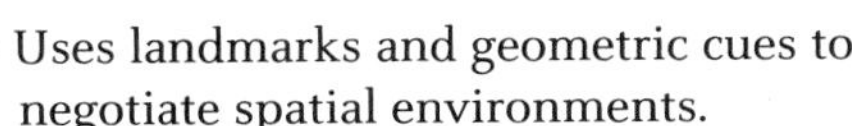

4–6 Years
- Uses systematic and efficient attention strategies.
- Has memory span of about four to five items.
- Can think of several steps in planning solutions to problems.
- Begins to show growth in executive function skills.

© 2008 Yellowdog Productions ALL RIGHTS RESERVED.

7–8 Years
- Produces rehearsal as a memory strategy.
- Has memory span of about five to six items.
- Shows flexibility in planning solutions to problems.
- Shows growth in metacognition.

9–11 Years
- Shows improvement in focused and selective attention.
- Produces organizational, elaboration, and retrieval strategies for memory.

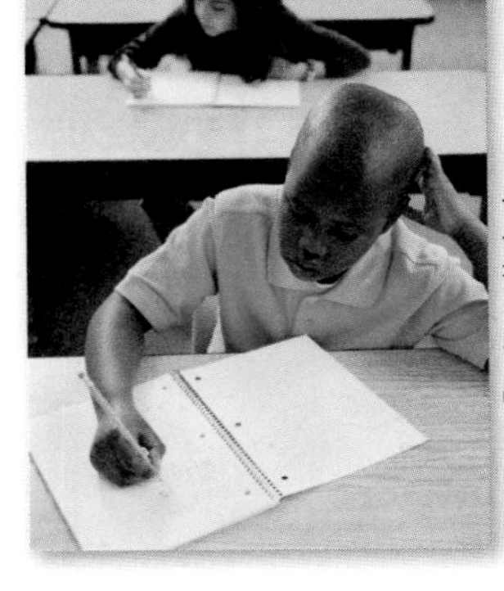
© Erik Isakson/Tetra Images/Jupiter Images

This chart describes the sequence of cognitive development based on the findings of research. Children often show individual differences in the exact ages at which they display the various developmental achievements outlined here.

perhaps more relevant facts. They also often operate according to their personal beliefs about social groups or how things look.

Most adolescents, for example, are vulnerable to the gambler's fallacy, saying that if a person has just won 75 percent of the time in video poker, she is destined to lose on the next turn. Rather than using information about statistics and probability, concepts that are within the grasp of children and adolescents, individuals make judgments on the basis of a small sample of events in which certain dramatic outcomes stand out (Klaczynski, 2001). Children and adolescents are also influenced by biases toward their own group, such as the social categories or religion to which they belong (Klaczynski, 2000). In the following scenario, for example, individuals can respond on the basis of statistical probability or a social stereotype:

INTERACTION AMONG DOMAINS

> In Juanita's class, ten girls are trying out to be cheerleaders, and twenty are trying out for the band. Juanita is very popular and very pretty. She is always telling jokes and loves to be around people. Do you think Juanita is trying out to be a cheerleader or for the band?

Children and preadolescents tend to say "cheerleader," responding to these types of questions on the basis of stereotypes even though, on a probabilistic basis, she is more likely to be one of the twenty trying out for the band than the ten trying out for cheerleading (Jacobs & Potenza, 1991).

Even though the story of cognitive development suggests that the eventual outcome is more efficient and rational thinking, the research on decision-making suggests that thought does not always stem purely from well-developed logic. Especially when situations involve self-interest or uncertainty, judgments are likely to be swayed by more informal, and sometimes emotional, beliefs (Jacobs & Klaczynski, 2002). What may develop, then, is the ability to inhibit quick, belief-based responding in favor of more reasoned, well-thought-out choices (Klaczynski, 2004).

The Cognitive Development Chronology on page 315 summarizes the child's major achievements in the domain of cognitive development. As the chart indicates, infants start this developmental journey with remarkable early capabilities. However, as you have also learned in this chapter, equally impressive is the number of sophisticated attainments children make in their thinking on so many different fronts.

For Your Review and Reflection

- When do children first evidence the ability to engage in problem solving? What types of studies have demonstrated this skill?
- What are the major ways in which children show changes in planning skills as they develop?
- How have the results of studies of problem solving challenged more traditional beliefs about children's strategy use?
- What factors encourage children to engage in the transfer of skills from one situation to another?
- What role does the executive function play in cognitive processing? In what ways does the executive function change with development?
- Recent research shows that the skills associated with executive function are strong predictors of children's academic success. Why would you not be surprised by this finding?
- Have you ever caught yourself making a decision on the basis of judgment biases? Do you think that knowing about the research on this subject will make you less vulnerable to making these kinds of errors in the future?

chapter recap

Summary of Developmental Themes

Nature & Nurture

How do nature and nurture interact in the process of cognitive development?

There are several indicators that nature sets early predispositions to think in certain ways. For example, young infants seem to understand the principle of solidity, the idea that one object cannot pass through the space occupied by another object. However, other evidence suggests that experiences, like formal schooling, can shape cognitive skills such as classification. Illuminating how nature and nurture work together to eventuate in cognitive growth remains an important goal for developmental researchers.

Sociocultural Influence

How does the sociocultural context influence cognitive development?

Ample evidence shows the influence of sociocultural factors on cognition. Children with formal schooling, for example, employ taxonomic classification more frequently than unschooled children. Cultural beliefs about other cognitive skills, such as attention, can be transmitted by the types of experiences provided by caregivers and, in particular, the scaffolding they supply.

Continuity | Discontinuity

Is cognitive development continuous or discontinuous?

Piaget stressed stagelike attainments in thinking. Others make claims for more continuous changes in cognition in their focus on the underlying basic processes that contribute to development. Unlike Piaget, Vygotsky, information-processing models, core knowledge approaches, and dynamic systems models do not emphasize discontinuities in development.

Interaction Among Domains

How does cognitive development interact with development in other domains?

Development in other domains can clearly influence cognitive growth. Perhaps the most obvious example is the fact that cognition is affected by maturation of the central nervous system, which is hypothesized to contribute to progress in the speed and efficiency of cognitive processing. The child's cognitive functioning is a contributor to development in many other domains, a fact that will become more obvious as you progress through this text.

Risk | Resilience

What factors promote risk or resilience in cognitive development?

Research indicates that children with poor attentional capacities can experience difficulties in other tasks requiring cognitive processing. Being able to attend to information is linked to better memory in infancy and higher intelligence test scores as well as better grades in school.

Chapter Review

Theories of Cognitive Development

What are the major characteristics of thinking in the sensorimotor, preoperational, concrete operational, and formal operational stages of cognitive development as described by Piaget?

The chief feature of the *sensorimotor stage* is that thought is based on action. Children develop means-ends behavior, separate the self from the external environment, and attain the *object concept.* The end of this stage is signaled by the child's ability to engage in deferred imitation, a form of representation. Children in the *preoperational stage* can think using symbols, but their thought is limited in that it is *egocentric.* Children fail *conservation tasks* because they do not yet have the logical thought structures that allow them to think about reversibility. The *concrete operational stage* is characterized by logical thought but only in the presence of real objects or images. By the time children reach the *formal operational stage,* they can think abstractly and hypothetically, generating multiple solutions to a problem. Thought is also systematic.

What are the essential elements of Vygotsky's sociocultural theory of cognitive development?

A principal feature of Vygotsky's theory is that the child's cognitive growth must be understood in terms of the sociocultural context in which he or she lives. *Scaffolding* is the temporary support provided by an expert to a learner who is trying to accomplish a task. Novice learners often get more support, but as their skills improve, that support is gradually withdrawn. Tutors often work within the child's *zone of proximal development,* the distance between what the child can do alone and what she can do with guidance.

What are the general features of information-processing theories of cognitive development? How do multistore models differ from limited resource models?

Information-processing theories emphasize the flow of information through the cognitive system. *Multistore models* include such structures as the *sensory register, working memory,* and *long-term memory,* as well as control processes such as rehearsal. *Limited-resource models* describe trade-offs between energy used to operate on stimuli and the capacity left over for storage.

What are the major characteristics of core knowledge theory?

Core knowledge theory proposes that infants possess innate knowledge of certain concepts such as the properties of objects, number, and space. This knowledge is thought to have arisen from evolutionary pressures and might be seen in other species, as well.

What are the essential elements of dynamic systems accounts of cognitive development?

Dynamic systems accounts of cognitive development emphasize the overlapping influence of different developmental forces, which when they become synchronized and coupled, can spur advances in thinking.

Concept Development

What kind of knowledge do infants display about the properties of objects?

Young infants seem to be sensitive to the permanence of objects, their height and rigidity, as well as to the concept of solidity, leading some researchers to formulate the core knowledge hypothesis, the idea that infants possess innate knowledge of certain properties of objects. Infants display the *A-not-B error* at about eight to twelve months of age. Explanations of this error include problems in memory, the failure to suppress an already made motor response, and an inability to update information about an object's changed location.

What developmental changes have researchers observed in children's classification skills?

One-year-olds group items together on the basis of perceptual similarities. Slightly older children rely on thematic and taxonomic relations. Children's early concepts are global and based on meanings, and they become more refined with development.

What developmental changes have researchers observed in children's numerical skills?

Newborns detect differences in small number sets, and five-month-olds respond to addition and subtraction of objects in a display. Some researchers believe that sensitivity to number is innate, but others say that infants may be responding on the basis of other attributes of the displays. By age four, children are able to count, and they display some knowledge of certain numerical principles. Preschoolers understand relations such as "bigger" and "smaller" but have more difficulty with large number sets and numbers that are close together. Preschoolers display good intuitions about how to add and form fractions. These understandings can form the basis for mathematical instruction.

What developmental changes have researchers observed in children's spatial concepts?

Infants first rely on the locations of objects relative to their own bodies, but they can soon use cues such as color and landmarks to locate objects in physical space. Infants and young children are also sensitive to distance and geometric cues in locating objects.

Attention

What are two major ways in which attention changes with development?

An important developmental change occurs in the ability to keep one's attention on some stimulus or activity. With development, children also gain in the ability to control their attention in a systematic and efficient manner. They are better able to be selective in what they attend to.

What factors seem to be responsible for developmental changes in attention?

Changes in attention span are due, in part, to maturation of the central nervous system, as well as the growing complexity of the child's interests. Changes in attentional control are linked to physiological maturation and the child's general increase in control over cognitive processes.

What is ADHD? What factors may be responsible for its occurrence?

ADHD is a developmental disorder linked to problems of attention. Problems with executive control are thought to underlie this disorder. Genetic factors, early exposure to teratogens, as well as slowed maturation of certain areas of the brain have been highlighted as causes of ADHD.

Memory

How do researchers study memory in infancy?

Habituation and operant-conditioning studies have been used to study recognition memory in infancy. Deferred imitation and *elicited imitation* have been useful techniques to study memory in older infants and preschoolers.

What are the major features of memory during infancy?

Infants show very good *recognition memory*. Stimuli seen for only brief periods can be remembered for days or weeks. Early memories are easily disrupted by changes in context, however. Developmental changes in recognition include an increase in the number of items that can be remembered, as well as an increase in the speed of remembering.

What factors are primarily responsible for developmental improvements in recall memory?

From preschool to preadolescence, children show an increase in *memory span*, the number of items that can be recalled after a brief period of time. Changes in processing speed, the rapidity with which cognitive activities can be carried out, contribute to this increase. Improvements in *recall memory* are also tied to children's increasing use of *memory strategies*, as well as increasing control over cognitive processing. One aspect of cognitive control is *metamemory*, the child's understanding of memory as a process.

What major changes in the brain accompany developmental improvements in memory?

Neuropsychological studies indicate that memory development is tied to maturation of several brain structures, including the hippocampus and temporal, prefrontal, and parietal lobes of the cortex.

Problem Solving

When do children first evidence the ability to engage in problem solving? What types of studies have demonstrated this skill?

Infants about one year of age show the ability to solve problems in that they will put together several steps to achieve a goal. For example, they will bypass a barrier, pull a cloth, and then reach for a string that is attached to a desirable toy.

What are the major ways in which children show changes in planning skills as they develop?

With development, children are better able to decide ahead of time which steps to take in solving a problem and keep more steps in mind. They also become more flexible in their strategy use.

How have the results of studies of problem solving challenged more traditional beliefs about children's strategy use?

Research using the microgenetic approach has found that children usually select from a pool of problem-solving strategies rather than simply switch from one strategy to another.

What factors encourage children to engage in the transfer of skills from one situation to another?

An important factor that can influence the likelihood of *transfer* is making the parallels between problems—their goal structures and solutions—more obvious, either through verbalizing them or showing images of them.

The Executive Function

What role does the executive function play in cognitive processing? In what ways does the executive function change with development? The *executive function* controls and coordinates one's cognitive processes. This ability increases with development, as is evidenced by advances in the child's metacognitive abilities. Metacognitive awareness grows through the school years and adolescence but, even then, may not reach full maturity. Adolescents and adults show *judgment biases* that reflect the influence of personal beliefs, dramatic outcomes, or social norms.

Key Terms and Concepts

A-not-B error (p. 291)
centration (p. 282)
cognition (p. 280)
concept (p. 288)
concrete operational stage (p. 282)
conservation tasks (p. 282)
core knowledge theory (p. 287)
egocentrism (p. 282)
elicited imitation (p. 302)
episodic memory (p. 301)
executive function (p. 313)
explicit memory (p. 301)
formal operational stage (p. 282)
hypothetical reasoning (p. 282)
implicit memory (p. 301)
judgment bias (p. 314)
limited-resource model (p. 286)
long-term memory (p. 285)
memory span (p. 304)
memory strategy (p. 304)
metamemory (p. 305)
multistore model (p. 285)
object permanence (p. 281)
operation (p. 282)
preoperational stage (p. 281)
processing speed (p. 305)
recall memory (p. 301)
recognition memory (p. 301)
scaffolding (p. 283)
semantic memory (p. 301)
sensorimotor stage (p. 280)
sensory register (p. 285)
transfer (p. 311)
working (or short-term) memory (p. 285)
zone of proximal development (p. 284)

Media Resources

Access an integrated eBook and chapter-specific interactive learning tools, including flashcards, quizzes, videos, and more, in your Developmental Psychology CourseMate, accessed through CengageBrain.com.

© Dmitriy Shironosov/Shutterstock.com

CHAPTER OUTLINE

[chapter 9]

Social Cognition

KEY THEMES IN SOCIAL COGNITION

- **NATURE & NURTURE** How do nature and nurture interact in the process of social cognitive development?
- **SOCIOCULTURAL INFLUENCE** How does the sociocultural context influence social cognitive development?
- **INTERACTION AMONG DOMAINS** How does social cognitive development interact with development in other domains?
- **RISK | RESILIENCE** What factors promote risk or resilience in social cognitive development?

"Jeremy! Let's play hide-and-seek!" shouted Tommy, trying once again to play with his three-year-old brother. Jeremy toddled into the family room as soon as he heard his big brother's voice. "See. You hide. I'll count to ten. Then I'll find you. It's fun, Jeremy. Let's try it." "Okay," smiled Jeremy. "I hide." The toddler stepped carefully over the family's Labrador retriever and plunked himself squarely behind the couch, or so he thought since he could not see his older brother. In the distance, he heard Tommy say, "Ten! Ready or not, here I come!" and held his breath. In barely a few seconds, though, Tommy was right in front of him, grinning widely. "Silly Jeremy," chuckled Tommy. "You can't let your legs stick out like that from behind the couch. I can see you!" <<

In this familiar scenario of a game of hide-and-seek, we see evidence of the varying ways in which children of two different ages understand the social world. Jeremy, a bright but still maturing three-year-old, thinks individuals around him see the world as he does. If he has his head completely hidden behind the couch so that he cannot see his older brother or anyone else in the room, he believes they cannot see him, even though other parts of his body are in plain view of those other observers. In contrast, Tommy understands that his perspective, visual and otherwise, may not be the same as that of other individuals. He comprehends that his own beliefs, desires, and intentions may, in fact, be quite different from those of his brother, parents, or friends. He even understands enough of the "mistakes" in the thinking of his younger brother to try to instruct him about how to hide more effectively. You might say that Tommy has greater "social intelligence."

In this chapter, we explore the development of children's thinking as it pertains to the social world, to children's understanding of the psychological qualities of other individuals as well as groups of individuals. We have already alluded several times in previous chapters to the idea that infants and children seem to be specially prepared to process social information. In Chapter 6, "Basic Learning and Perception," for example, we noted how infants more readily imitate actors' intentional actions over accidental ones, suggesting at least a primitive understanding of the goal-directedness of people's actions. In that chapter, too, we noted that infants are especially attuned to biological motion, indicating a special responsiveness to the perceptual cues offered by other living things. In Chapter 7, "Language," we discussed how episodes of mutual engagement—a sharing of psychological space—between child and caregiver present ideal conditions for the acquisition of language. In other words, much important learning depends on the child attending to, interpreting, and responding to social cues emitted by his or her partners in everyday interactions.

In past decades, many developmental researchers have operated as if there is a separation of sorts between the child's cognitive development and his or her social development. Increasingly, though, we recognize that there are strong connections between these broad domains of development. In this chapter, we focus on the

INTERACTION AMONG DOMAINS

emerging research on **social cognition**, those thinking processes and representations that are relevant to the social world (Olson & Dweck, 2008). This type of cognition, thinking about the self and its relationship to others, is a vital aspect of successful communication and social interaction, and also of the sophisticated and powerful attainments in thinking and reasoning that characterize human cognition.

Orienting to the Social World

The first signs of the infant's readiness to enter into the social arena appear at about two months of age, when she begins to have lengthier periods of alertness, displays a social smile, shows a distinct preference for scanning the human face, and exhibits a peak in crying (Rochat & Striano, 1999). The convergence of so many factors that just so happen to prepare the infant for social interactions has been dubbed the "two-month revolution" by Philippe Rochat (2004). The consequence of this newfound orientation is that caregivers and infants begin to participate in mutually rewarding playful exchanges, whether they are a game of peekaboo or a melodic exchange of smiles and vocalizations.

At nine months of age, the infant's social sophistication is even more obvious. Imagine a scene in which an adult shows an infant an interesting toy, and just as the infant is about to reach for it, the adult playfully pulls it away. Contrast this scenario with another one: the adult seems to accidentally drop the toy and is unable to reach for it. The infant is unable to touch the toy in both cases, but in the first, the adult apparently intends to tease the child. In the second case, the adult does not aim to frustrate the child. Nine-month-olds show signs of being able to tell the difference in adults' intentions; they reach for the toy more often in the "teasing" situation and also express more frustration (Behne et al., 2005). The infant's understanding of the motives of others can be thought of as a breakthrough acquisition. It signals the infant's more deliberate *contemplative* and *intentional* participation in the social world (Rochat, 2004, 2009). A number of research studies are beginning to reveal the remarkable sensitivities that infants show to the social cues displayed by the individuals who surround them.

Detecting Animacy

Before infants can *become* deliberately social, they have to understand what *is* social; that is, they must understand that some entities in the world are living things as opposed to inanimate objects and eventually that living things possess certain qualities like feelings, goals, and intentions. Children show a dramatically early ability to classify animate versus inanimate objects. For example, a twenty-four-month-old will show obvious surprise when a chair seems to move forward on its own (Golinkoff et al., 1984), and a twelve-month-old will fuss and cry more when a robot starts to move as opposed to a human stranger (Poulin-Dubois, Lepage, & Ferland, 1996). By the time they are three and four years old, children have a solid understanding of the categories of living versus nonliving things. They know that living things can eat and grow, but inanimate objects cannot; they say a person can feel sad, but a doll or a rock cannot (Gelman, Spelke, & Meck, 1983; Jipson & Gelman, 2007). They also ask different kinds of questions about objects versus living things: for the former, "What does it do?" is a common query; for the latter, "What does it eat?" is more frequently heard (Greif et al., 2006).

NATURE & NURTURE

Chapter 8, "Cognition," introduced you to the idea that some concepts may represent a form of *core knowledge* with which infants come into the world. Some developmental scientists have asserted that early responses to animacy represent still another case in which children seem to be programmed to learn about certain conceptual domains more quickly and effortlessly than others. In other words, some objects and events in the environment offer "privileged relationships" for the child to learn about (Gallistel et al., 1991). In this case, the so-called *natural domain* is knowledge about biological entities. Neuroscientific studies with adults suggest that once an individual has made the

social cognition Thinking processes and representations that are relevant to the social world.

Young infants seem to be particularly attracted to the eyes as features of the human face, a tendency which may help them to obtain important information from the environment.

decision that a particular thing in the environment is animate, the brain regions associated with processing social information such as biological motion and recognizing emotions are placed in a "ready state" (Wheatley, Milleville, & Martin, 2007). Recognizing animacy is thus an important first step in the emergence of social cognition.

Gaze Following

If "the eyes are the window to the soul," as an old saying goes, then even young infants somehow know that looking at another person's eyes provides valuable information, not just about their internal feelings and thoughts, but also about which information in the surrounding vicinity is worth attending to. Infants under six months of age prefer to look at eyes over other features of faces (Caron et al., 1973) and, a few months later, will follow the turn of an adult's head to see what she is looking at. But they follow the adult's head motion to look at a target only if the adult's eyes are open, not closed or covered by a blindfold. This suggests that infants are not led to look at an object by the sweep of motion created by the adult's physical head turn; rather, there is something significant about eyes themselves as infants interpret this event (Brooks & Meltzoff, 2002). By eighteen months of age, further progress is made: a shift in an adult's eye direction alone will lead the young child to follow the adult's gaze (Moore & Corkum, 1998). Infants react to these actions as if the adult "intends" to communicate something (Butler, Caron, & Brooks, 2000).

Being able to follow the eye gaze of another individual is an important milestone for the infant as she prepares to learn about objects in the world, what they are called, and how others react to them emotionally (Moore, 2008). In particular, following the gaze of an adult can lead to episodes of joint attention, those moments of shared mutual interaction that have been identified as so important to early learning (see Figure 9.1) (Mundy & Newell, 2007).

Social Referencing

In the latter half of the first year, a phenomenon called *social referencing* suggests another role for looking at the eyes and face of other individuals. **Social referencing**

social referencing Looking to another individual for emotional cues in interpreting a strange or ambiguous event.

Figure 9.1

Gaze-Following and Joint Attention

Infants often follow the gaze of an adult to locate objects, as shown in this scene from an experiment investigating the development of joint attention. These kinds of interactions are an important element of social cognition and provide a rich context for social and cultural learning.

Source: From Mundy, P. & Newell, L. (2007). Attention, joint attention, and social cognition. *Current Directions in Psychological Science, 16,* 269–274.

refers to infants' ability to modulate their own reactions to strange or new events depending on how they interpret the emotional expressions of others. If infants are placed in an unfamiliar situation or encounter a strange object and are uncertain how to respond, they often will look to their caregivers for cues. The facial expression the caregiver displays typically will influence the infant's own emotional response and subsequent actions. For example, in one study, twelve-month-olds were placed on the shallow side of the visual cliff apparatus, which is used to assess the perception of depth. They were coaxed to move toward the place on the cliff where the surface appears to drop off. At this point, half of the participants' mothers posed a happy expression, and the other half exhibited fear. Of the infants whose mothers smiled, 74 percent crossed the deep side of the cliff. In contrast, none of the infants whose mothers showed fear crossed the deep side. Moreover, these babies tended to produce fearful expressions on their own faces (Sorce et al., 1985). Thus, the infants not only "read" the expression they saw on their mothers' faces but also correctly interpreted its message.

Social referencing is a clear sign of the distinctly *interactive* nature of emotions. It is also a sign that infants begin to appreciate the referential nature of communication as well as the intentions of others. When infants in one study heard an experimenter say "Eew!" in a strong negative tone while looking at a toy, they were less likely to approach it than if she said "Nice!" However, if the experimenter made any of these comments while out of view, infants did not make use of the emotional tones in her messages (Moses et al., 2001). Infants seem to appreciate that, by expressing emotions—but specifically in a social context—individuals intend to communicate something about objects, people, or events. In that sense, social referencing is linked to advances in cognition. It is probably also an early indication of the child's internalization of the views and values of parents, a process that will continue throughout the early years of childhood (Desrochers et al., 1994; Kochanska, 1994).

INTERACTION AMONG DOMAINS

Understanding Others' Goals and Intentions

Suppose a six-month-old infant watches someone reach for a ball or teddy bear. How does she construe this event, as a series of perceptual moments devoid of any deeper social meaning or as a goal-directed act in which the person *intends* to reach for an object? Amanda Woodward (1998) attempted to answer just this question in a study that capitalized on the information provided by the visual habituation technique. Figure 9.2 shows the sequence of activities in this experiment. First, during habituation trials, infants repeatedly saw a hand reaching for one of two toys, in this case, the ball. Then, during the test trials, they were shown the same hand-reaching action, but aimed at a new toy—the teddy bear (the "new object")—or a hand reaching in a new location for the ball again (the "new side"). Infants showed greater looking times to the "new object" scenario, indicating that they found the change in target, as opposed to the change in location, to represent something new. Woodward and others interpret this result as indicating that, throughout the experiment, infants were paying attention to the "intent" of the person reaching: to obtain the ball. Bolstering this interpretation is the finding that this pattern of looking did not occur when the reaching was done by a mechanical claw; in this case, infants looked about the same amount of time at the two test situations. That is, looking based on the actor's intent was specific to conditions where the reaching was done by a human being.

Some researchers believe that the infant's ability to understand goals and intentions in others is yet another example of innately endowed knowledge that has an adaptive function for the growing infant (Biro & Leslie, 2007; Gergely & Csibra, 2003). On the other side of the debate are those who claim that infants' own experiences with goal-directed actions create the conditions for understanding intentional behaviors in others. Consider the "sticky mitten" experiment, for example. Here, three-month-old infants (who typically would not respond to intentions in others) had their hands covered with a Velcro mitten that could help them reach for and grab a teddy bear and a ball. After slightly

© Sabine Fritsch/STOCK4B/Getty Images

Infants and young children often rely on the emotional cues expressed by caregivers to interpret new or strange events. Is this animal an object to be approached or feared? The caregiver's positive emotional expression suggests that the former is the appropriate response.

NATURE & NURTURE

Figure 9.2
Understanding Actors' Goals
Six-month-old infants were habituated to a hand reaching for a particular object, in this case, the ball. During test trials, they showed greater looking toward the hand reaching for a new object, suggesting that that they were attending to the intent of the actor who was reaching ("get the ball") rather than the position of the reach.
Source: Adapted from Henderson, A. M. E., Gerson, S., & Woodward, A. L. (May, 2008). The birth of social intelligence. *Zero to Three*, 13–19.

Habituation

New Object

New Side

more than three minutes swiping and obtaining the toys, infants participated in the experiment described in Figure 9.2. Compared with a control group, these infants showed responses that were more typical of the six-month-olds described above (see Figure 9.3). They reacted on the basis of the actor's intentions rather than other dimensions of the experiment (Sommerville, Woodward, & Needham, 2005). Thus, it appears that the infant's own experience with being able to retrieve objects may be an important element in their beginning to understand intentionality in others.

What is the significance of the infant's rudimentary understanding of goal-directed behaviors? For one thing, infants may go on to imitate actions that have an intentional quality to them. After observing an adult reach for a toy in one experiment, seven-month-old infants imitated that action and reached for it themselves. This held true even if the adult did not complete the action of actually obtaining the toy. If the adult touched the object with the back of her hand, however, infants failed to imitate (Hamlin, Hallinan, & Woodward, 2008). Imitation is a powerful form of learning early in childhood, but children do not reproduce every single behavior they observe. By making judgments about which behaviors to emulate based on human intentions, infants are focusing their processing of information on behaviors that are relevant for their particular social and cultural environment.

SOCIOCULTURAL INFLUENCE

Speaking more broadly, understanding the goal-directed behaviors of other individuals paves the way for the collaborative kinds of learning that are responsible for the child's mastery of the social and cultural practices of society (Tomasello et al., 2005).

Representation

As infants progress in their understanding of the goals and intentions of others, the path is paved for acquiring one of the most powerful of human capabilities, the ability to understand and use symbols. Mastery of symbols—images, words, numbers, pictures,

Figure 9.3
The "Sticky Mittens" experiment
Three-month-old infants would not be expected to be sensitive to the goal-directed actions of an actor. However, once infants had brief experiences with "sticky mittens" that permitted them to have experiences with reaching for and obtaining toys, they were more likely than a control group to react to the goal-directed behaviors of an actor.
Source: From Woodward, A. L. (2009). Infants' grasp of others' intentions. *Current Directions in Psychological Science, 18,* 53–57.

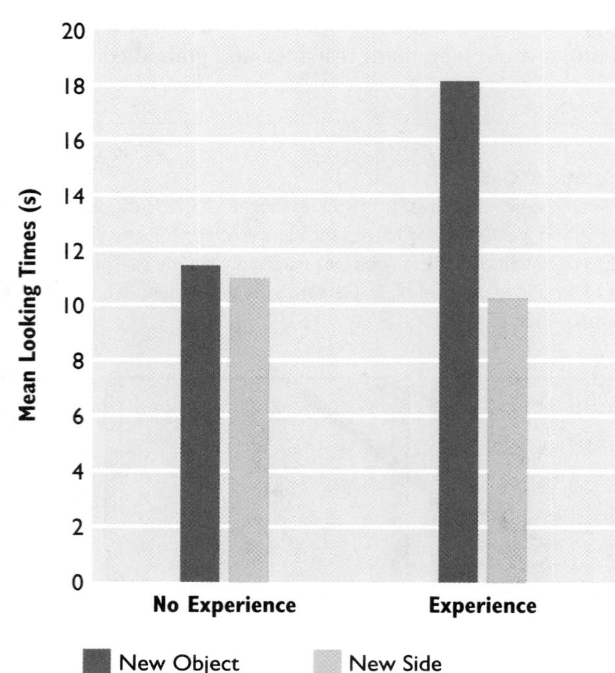

maps, or other configurations that represent real objects in the world—is considered to be a hallmark of human cognitive activity, setting humans apart from other species (Vygotsky, 1962). Children who understand symbols of various forms are catapulted into a whole new set of opportunities for learning, most notably through language, but also through the various other forms of representation that seem to be increasing in our contemporary society such as digital images, graphic symbols, and videos. An important component in the child's becoming "symbol-minded" is his or her appreciation for the fact that symbols were created by some other individual who *intended* them to stand for some real-world object, place, or concept (DeLoache, 2004). The child begins to understand, for example, that a drawing might be created by a person with the goal of reproducing a past experience or that a map is drawn to provide directions from home to a new location.

Piaget argued that children are unable to think with symbols, that is, use representations, until near the end of the sensorimotor stage of development at about eighteen months of age. Others, however, have challenged this position and argue that representational capacities are actually evident much earlier in infancy. Jean Mandler (1988, 1998) has pointed out a number of early abilities that infants display that support this thesis. For example, we noted in Chapter 7 that infants begin to use gestures to stand for objects or events prior to age one year. Similarly, young infants' apparent knowledge about the physical properties of objects, described in Chapter 8, suggests that they must hold some internal representation of them. Although infants may have basic representational capacities, toddlers and older children far more readily recognize that external symbols of real objects in the world can be used to further their problem-solving efforts.

Understanding Photographs and Drawings Nine-month-old infants show unique behaviors when they are shown highly realistic photos of common objects; they swipe at a photo of a toy car as if to pick it up or put their mouth on the picture of a baby bottle as if to drink from it (see Figure 9.4) (Pierroutsakos & DeLoache, 2003). To Judy DeLoache and her colleagues, these actions suggest that infants do not yet understand the symbolic nature of photographs; consequently, they perform the same actions on the images as they would on the real objects. By nineteen months of age, though, children's behavior changes; now children point to and talk about the pictures as if they are understood in a more abstract, representational way (DeLoache et al., 1998).

Even though the behavior of preschoolers suggests a basic understanding of the purpose of photos, they still show limitations in how they interpret them. Shown a pair

Figure 9.4

Infants Confuse Photos with Real Objects

Nine-month-olds physically explore photos of objects as if they were the real things, as this boy shows as he puts his mouth on the image of a bottle. Some researchers believe that behaviors like these indicate a failure to understand the representational nature of photographs and other symbols.

Source: From DeLoache, J. S. (2004). Becoming symbol-minded. *Trends in Cognitive Sciences, 8*, 66–70.

Figure 9.5

Developmental Changes in Responses to Photos

Preschool children were asked if a series of photographs were the same or different. Three-year-olds focused on the fact that identical objects were represented. Sensitivity to the photographer's techniques in creating images comes later in childhood.

Source: Reprinted from Liben, L. S. (2003). Beyond point and shoot: Children's developing understanding of photographs as spatial and expressive representations. In R. Kail (Ed.), *Advances in Child Development and Behavior.* Vol. 31. (pp. 1–42). San Diego, CA: Elsevier. With permission from Elsevier.

of images of the same item photographed from different perspectives (see Figure 9.5), preschoolers focus almost exclusively on the objects, no matter if they are depicted from the side or from above. Children ignore the different viewing angles used by the photographer and insist that the two photos are the same because the objects themselves are the same. Even when the experimenter stated, "Well, they're both of tulips, but is there anything different about the pictures?" a typical response from the young child was "Nope, this one [points] has the same stuff" (Liben, 2003, p. 15). Similarly, young children ignore darkness or lightness or other photographic elements in the images (Szechter & Liben, 2007). Front and center in the young child's mind are the objects shown in representations. Progress in understanding the ways in which images are created, the messages communicated by different design elements, and an appreciation for the fact that representations can help one's thinking and problem solving—all aspects of what is called *meta-representation*—emerges relatively slowly during the early and middle childhood years. A deep and full appreciation of these concepts may not occur until adolescence or even later (Liben, 2003).

Children's responses to drawings give us additional insights about the development of representational thinking. Two- and three-year-olds respond differently to pictures depending on if they are told someone painted them or created them by spilling paint on paper accidentally. They name the former as representing an object (e.g., "That's a man"), but describe the literal features of the latter (e.g., "That's paint") (Gelman & Ebeling, 1998). Likewise, consider the two pictures portrayed in Figure 9.6. Four-year-olds were asked to draw a balloon and a lollipop. Even though the two examples here look very much alike, this child insisted that each represented what he intended to draw, in this particular case, a lollipop on the left and a balloon on the right (Bloom & Markson, 1998). This finding leads us to the idea that children's understanding of the intentional nature of drawing might be linked to their own common experiences as budding artists, portraying their family members, flowers, the sun, and other common objects with crayons and markers, or even merely watching others draw. Indeed, Tara Callaghan has shown that, when two-year-olds are given multiple opportunities to watch an adult draw a series of common objects, they show greater understanding of the correspondence between objects and the pictures that portray them. Interestingly, they also show substantial growth in two other symbolic activities, language and symbolic play (Callaghan & Rankin, 2002).

NATURE & NURTURE

Figure 9.6
Children's Drawings Reveal an Understanding of Intent
What is represented in each of these drawings made by four-year-olds? The answer according to preschoolers is whatever the person drawing intended.
Source: From Bloom, P., & Markson, L. (1998). Intention and analogy in children's naming of pictorial representations. *Psychological Science, 9,* 200–204. Reprinted by permission of John Wiley & Sons, Inc.

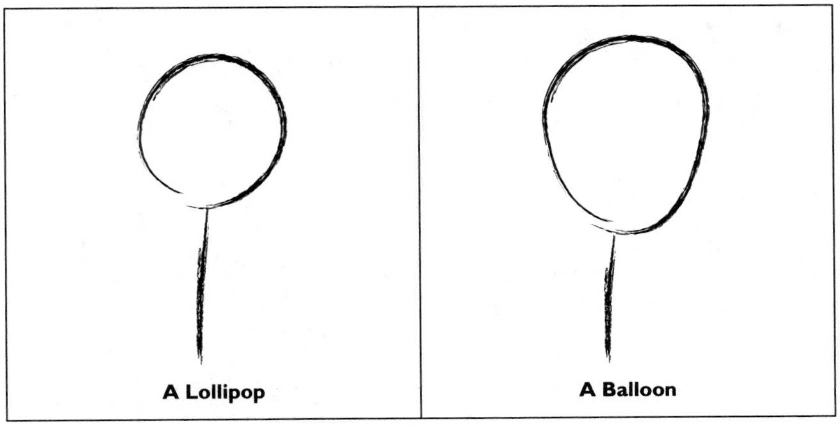

Representational Insight Very young children have some difficulty in recognizing that pictures are representations for real objects, and this difficulty extends to other kinds of situations as well, for example, when arrays of objects are used to represent things in the real world. In a well-known series of experiments, Judy DeLoache (1987) asked two- and three-year-olds to observe a small toy being hidden in a scale model of a room. Next, the children were brought into a life-size room that corresponded to the scale model they had just seen. Could they find the real-life toy that corresponded to the smaller replica in the previous segment of the experiment? If they saw a small Snoopy toy being hidden under a miniature couch, would they look for a large Snoopy under the couch in the life-size room? The three-year-olds could find the hidden object on more than 70 percent of the trials. But the two-year-olds could do so on only 20 percent of the trials. Later, when both age groups were asked to locate the toy back in the scale model, they did so with few errors. Thus, the search failures of two-year-olds in the life-size room were not due to memory problems. DeLoache believes that two-year-olds have difficulty with *dual representation*, that is, with understanding that a scale model can be both an object in its own right and a representation of a life-size room. By age three, however, children have the cognitive capacity, flexibility, and conceptual knowledge to appreciate that a symbol such as a model can "stand for" a real-life event. In other words, children gain **representational insight** (DeLoache, 2000; DeLoache & Smith, 1999).

NATURE & NURTURE

Some factors can accelerate the tendency of young children to develop representational insight. Repeated exposure to scale models, drawings, and live video photography helps children younger than three years to understand that these are symbols of real-world events (Callaghan & Rankin, 2002; DeLoache, 2004; Troseth, 2003). Also helpful can be explicit explanations that scale models have been created for the purpose of standing for corresponding large-scale objects and spaces. As young children generally become more aware of the intentions of others, they are better able to grasp that people create representations for this purpose (Sharon, 2005).

Reading Maps One of the practical ways in which representational skills (in combination with spatial skills) are exercised is in reading maps. From participating in a treasure hunt at a birthday party to traveling or learning geography in school, reading maps is part of many children's experiences, at least occasionally. Making use of a map involves several types of skills, including understanding that the symbols that the producer creates on the page are intended to refer to real objects or places,

representational insight The child's ability to understand that a symbol or model can stand for a real-life event.

An important cognitive skill that emerges at about age three is the understanding that a model may *represent* a real-life event. Representation is a powerful higher order cognitive skill.

© Michael Newman/PhotoEdit

appreciating the scale and alignment of the map in relation to the actual physical space, and, if one is actually navigating, planning an efficient route to get from one place to another.

Four-year-olds begin to show an ability to use simple maps to navigate a U-shaped route through a series of rooms (Uttal & Wellman, 1989). However, their skills are limited to maps for which there is a clear one-to-one correspondence between representations on the map (in this case, photographs of stuffed animals) and real objects in each of the rooms (actual stuffed animals). Also, the map must be aligned to match the actual physical space; rotating it to a different orientation presents problems. Map-reading skills improve in the next two years, though, so that by the time they are six, many children can use a map to plan an efficient route through a large-scale space (Sandberg & Huttenlocher, 2001). However, understanding maps that are not oriented in the same direction as the physical space remains challenging for children throughout the early school years (Liben & Downs, 1993). Also, children under age nine or ten years of age do not yet fully understand the role of maps in helping one navigate through space. After watching an adult placing stickers on a map to either mark the locations of objects or to make a map look pretty, young children could not correctly state that the former map would be more useful in locating hidden objects (Myers & Liben, 2008).

Why do children improve in map reading? One way to answer this question is to see which kinds of experiences improve children's ability to use maps. When experimenters highlight the connection between objects on the map and objects in the physical space by making explicit comparisons, young children's performance improves (Loewenstein & Gentner, 2001). Organizing the spatial relations among objects in the map—by making them into a drawing, for example—helps, too (Uttal et al., 2001). Asking children to explain why they place marks in certain places on maps is also beneficial (Kastens & Liben, 2007). Improvements in children's ability to use maps require an interesting intersection of two kinds of skills: understanding spatial relations and also appreciating the intentions of the creators of maps (Liben, 2009).

For Your Review and Reflection

- What is meant by the term social cognition? What kinds of information are included in this aspect of thinking and problem solving?
- What are four early signs that human infants are prepared to process social information?

- What evidence supports the idea that early social behaviors are a form of core knowledge? What evidence supports the idea that early social behaviors are learned?
- Aside from the specific skills mentioned in this section, what other capabilities do you think can be included as a part of "social intelligence"?
- What kinds of changes have researchers observed in young children's ability to demonstrate representational insight? How does the key theme of nature/nurture help us to understand this important aspect of cognitive development?

Understanding Psychological States

We have already seen that our general knowledge extends beyond understanding of physical objects, classes, number, and space even in the experiences of infants. It also includes an increasingly sophisticated awareness of our minds and how they and the minds of others work. As children get older, how do they understand and judge more complex qualities such as the motives, feelings, needs, interests, capacities, and thoughts of playmates, siblings, parents, and others? And how and when do children come to understand and reflect on the psychological states of the self?

In comparison to the world of physical objects and events, thinking about the social world presents unique challenges to the developing child. People may act unpredictably; their feelings and moods, and even their appearances, may shift unexpectedly. Just how children piece together their understanding of social experiences has been the focus of several lines of research. Contemporary researchers owe Piaget recognition for his initial efforts to study how children think about the perspectives and thinking of others.

Perspective Taking: Taking the Views of Others

Perspective taking is the ability to put oneself in another person's place, to consider that person's thoughts, feelings, or knowledge. One basic element of perspective taking is understanding what others see. For example, does the child realize that his sister, who is standing across the room, cannot see the brightly colored pictures in the book he is eagerly examining? In 1956, Jean Piaget and Barbel Inhelder published a classic experiment illustrating children's limited knowledge of the visual perspectives of others. Children seated in front of three different papier-mâché mountains (see Figure 9.7) were asked to indicate what a doll would see in viewing the array from various locations. Four- to six-year-olds showed considerable egocentrism in their responses; they typically indicated that the doll's view would be identical to their own. By six to nine years of age, children began to realize the doll's perspective would differ, although they still had difficulty figuring out what the doll would actually see. Nine- and ten-year-olds were able to determine the doll's perspective accurately. Subsequent research has shown that the difficulty of the doll and mountain task may have led Piaget and Inhelder to underestimate children's role-taking competence. When simpler visual arrays or familiar everyday scenes are used, or when the method of interviewing children is simplified, three- and four-year-olds can answer some of these kinds of questions reasonably well (Borke, 1975; Newcombe & Huttenlocher, 1992).

Visual perspective taking develops in two phases. At first, from late infancy until about age three years, children come to realize that their own and another's view are not identical. This is called *Level 1 perspective taking.* More advanced *Level 2 perspective taking* appears in three- and four-year-olds and continues to be refined for several years thereafter. Now children can determine the specific limitations of another's view, for example, whether an object or picture another person sees will look right side up or not (Flavell, 1978). These advances reflect cognitive gains in differentiating oneself from another and in knowledge of spatial relationships (Shantz, 1983).

Figure 9.7
Visual Perspective Taking
How well can children adopt another person's perspective? Piaget asked this question by seating a child at a table (location 1) containing three "mountains" of different size and color, then asking the child how the scene would look to a doll (or another person) seated at other locations (locations 2 and 3) around the table. Piaget found that preschoolers often chose a view similar to their own. More recent research indicates that preschoolers can more successfully accomplish this task when familiar and easily distinguishable scenes are used.

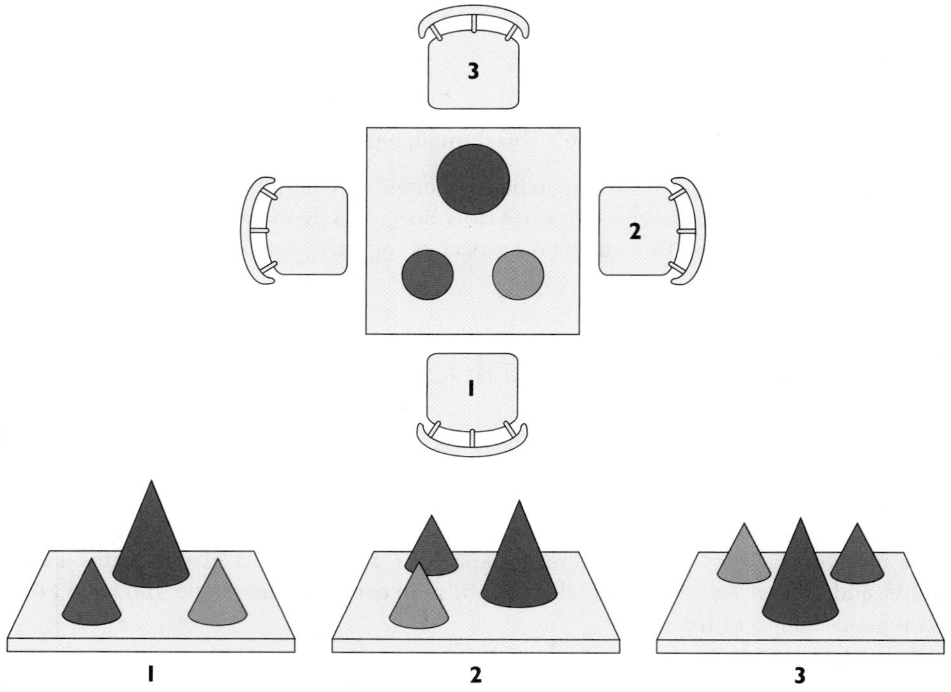

The Child's Theory of Mind

Children's understanding of their social world extends well beyond visual perspective-taking skills. Emerging among their competencies is an expanding and increasingly coherent appreciation of the kinds of mental qualities that contribute to the behavior of self and others. Did the playmate who broke a favorite toy *intend* to do the damage? Would a close friend *believe* that Mom will not let them go to the park alone? Many of our social behaviors are guided by the judgments and inferences we make about the desires, feeling states, beliefs, and thoughts of other people (Astington, Harris, & Olson, 1988; Wellman, 1990). In fact, it would be rare not to be concerned with the mental states of others in the normal course of interactions with them. For example, how would we be able to communicate effectively to someone if we did not have some appreciation of what that person already knows about the topic under discussion?

INTERACTION AMONG DOMAINS

When and how do children become aware of the concept of mental states, their own and those of others? That is, when and how do children develop a **theory of mind**? Once again, Piaget has provided much of the impetus for research on this topic. His position was quite clear. As Piaget put it, "The child knows nothing about the nature of thought . . ." (Piaget, 1929, p. 37). Dubbing this characteristic **realism**, Piaget maintained that children are not capable of distinguishing between mental and physical entities until the school years. To the child under age eight, dreams and mental images are as real as any event in waking, conscious life. To the same child, thinking is a behavior produced by the body, usually the mouth or the head; physical and mental acts are one and the same.

Understanding Mental States Despite Piaget's strong claims, developmental researchers have uncovered considerable evidence to the contrary. By age three, children readily distinguish between mental and physical entities and, after that age, show further developments in their understanding of their own mental states and those of others (Flavell, 1993).

In one classic experiment, three-year-olds were told stories such as the following: "Judy doesn't have a kitty, but right now she is thinking about a kitty." Children were then

theory of mind Awareness of the concept of mental states, both one's own and those of others.

realism Inability to distinguish between mental and physical entities.

asked: Could they see or touch the kitty? Could the kitty be seen by someone else or touched at some time in the future? Children had no problem identifying this as a mental event, one in which the kitty could not be seen or touched. In contrast, when they heard other stories, as in "Judy had a kitty," they correctly stated that these real events could be seen and touched (Wellman & Estes, 1986).

We have seen earlier in this chapter that some of the first signs of awareness of mental states are evident at eighteen months, when infants follow the gaze of an adult in episodes of joint attention. From there, preschoolers display an increasing repertoire of knowledge of mental states that starts with understanding the meaning of "desire," then "belief," and finally the concept of "false belief" (Wellman & Liu, 2004). Between ages six and ten, children begin to understand "the mind" as an active entity discrete from the self as they interpret metaphors such as "My mind was racing" or "My mind was hungry" (Wellman & Hickling, 1994). At age ten, children also understand that some mental states, such as "wanting" and "fearing," are more difficult to control than others, such as "paying attention" (Flavell & Green, 1999).

False Beliefs A particularly useful scenario to assess aspects of children's theory of mind has been the "false belief" task. The typical "false belief" task involves testing children's knowledge about what a naïve observer does or does not know about a visual scene that has been transformed. In one version (as illustrated in Figure 9.8), children are shown a doll named Maxi who puts some chocolate in a blue cupboard and leaves the scene. Maxi's mother moves the chocolate to a new location, a green cupboard. When Maxi returns, children are asked, "Where will he look for the chocolate?" Having seen the chocolate being moved, most three-year-olds say in the new location. Four-year-olds, though, recognize that Maxi holds a **false belief** and will look for the chocolate in the original cupboard (Wimmer & Perner, 1983).

NATURE & NURTURE

What factors account for the child's growing success on the false belief task and presumably his or her theory of mind? There is an ongoing debate. On the one hand, some researchers argue that the theory of mind is an innate, prepackaged, modular form of knowledge that becomes more elaborate with maturation (Baron-Cohen, 1995; Fodor, 1992; Leslie, 1994). In what might be viewed as support for this position, it is interesting to note that children from many cultures around the world, including China, Japan, and the preliterate Baka society of Cameroon, show similar timelines in improvements in their understanding of mental state terms such as "desire" and "belief" (Harris, 2006; Liu et al., 2008). Likewise, performance on the false belief task shows consistent developmental trends across many studies with North American populations (Callaghan et al., 2005; Wellman, Cross, & Watson, 2001). Recent evidence adds to the idea that some form of neurological maturity may be involved. Children who give accurate answers on the false belief task show corresponding changes in the electrical activity of the prefrontal cortex, patterns that are not evident in children who answer incorrectly (Liu et al., 2009).

In contrast, other researchers believe that a theory of mind arises from the child's socialization experiences, especially those that encourage an appreciation of others' mental states. Even simply sharing conversations with the caregiver or referring to other people in these conversations predicts the understanding of others' minds (Ensor & Hughes, 2008; Lu, Su, & Wang, 2008; Nelson, Adamson, & Bakeman, 2008). These are all the kinds of experiences that present opportunities for children to think about others' points of view. However, experiences with language may be especially crucial to the emergence of theory of mind. Mothers who use more language to describe mental states ("know" and "think") to their preschoolers, for example, have children who are more successful on the false belief task several months later (Adrián, Clemente, & Villanueva, 2007; Ruffman, Slade, & Crowe, 2002; Taumoepeau & Ruffman, 2008). Furthermore, recall our discussion in Chapter 7 of a community of deaf individuals in Nicaragua who formed their own version of an evolving sign language. Those adolescents and adults who had learned an earlier, more basic form of the language used fewer terms for mental states and made more errors on

false belief The child's mistaken understanding that a naïve or uninformed observer has the same information (and thus the same beliefs) as the child.

Figure 9.8
The False Belief Task
The false belief task is used to assess whether the child has mastered the concept of theory of mind. Children under age four typically respond that Maxi will look for the chocolate in the last place they themselves saw it hidden rather than in the location Maxi had witnessed.

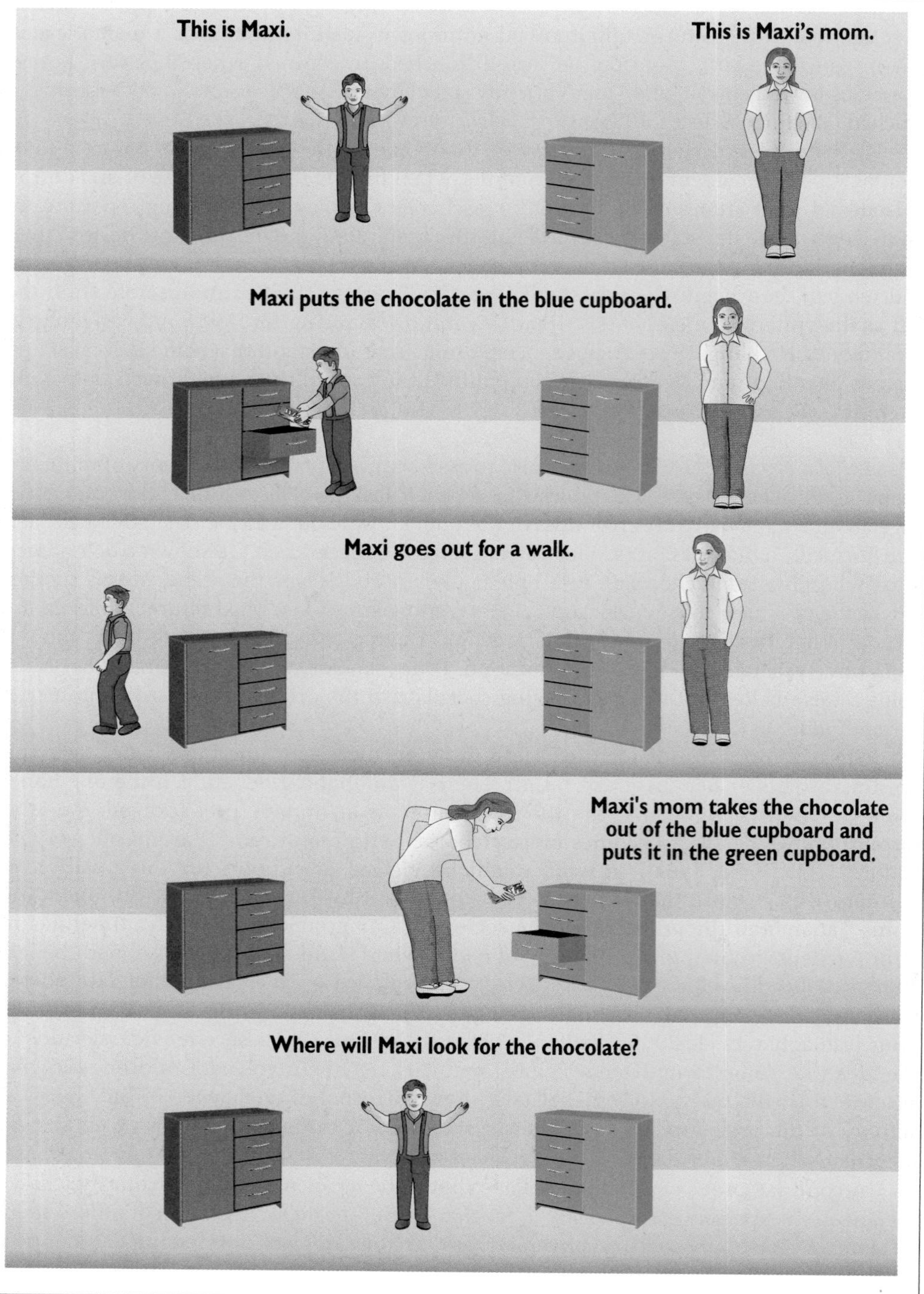

the false belief task. Among those who learned a more complex version of the language, mental state language (see Figure 9.9 for some examples) always developed before or simultaneously with competence on a false belief task. The reverse order—false belief performance before mental state language—never occurred (Pyers & Senghas, 2009).

This is Maxi.
This is Maxi's mom.
Maxi puts the chocolate in the blue cupboard.
Maxi goes out for a walk.
Maxi's mom takes the chocolate out of the blue cupboard and puts it in the green cupboard.
Where will Maxi look for the chocolate?

INTERACTION AMONG DOMAINS

The child's theory of mind is a key cognitive attainment bridging the self and social world. Researchers have noted, for example, that performance on the false belief task is related to the child's social skills with peers (Watson et al., 1999). You will encounter several other examples of the link between theory of mind and the child's social and emotional functioning in Chapter 15, "Peers."

Figure 9.9

Theory of Mind in Deaf Individuals

Members of a deaf community in Nicaragua developed their own sign language. As the language evolved and included more mental state words (such as "know" on the left and "doesn't know" on the right), individuals began to use more of these words and also showed greater success on a false belief test.

Source: From Pyers, J. E., & Senghas, A. (2009). Language promotes false-belief understanding: Evidence from learners of a new sign language. *Psychological Science, 20,* 805–811.

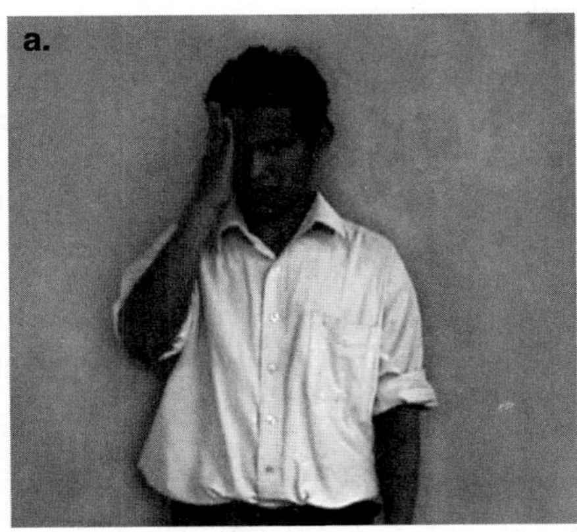

atypical development | Childhood Autism

Childhood autism is a puzzling disorder affecting about 1 in every 110 children born, according to government statistics collected in 2006 (Centers for Disease Control, 2010). The disorder, more common among boys than girls, is characterized by the child's preference to be alone, poor eye contact and general lack of social skills, often the absence of meaningful language, and a preference for sameness and elaborate routines. Some autistic children show unusual skills, such as being able to recite lengthy passages from memory, put together complex jigsaw puzzles, or create intricate drawings. Often these children show a fascination with spinning objects or repeating the speech patterns of someone else. The hallmark trait, though, is the lack of contact these children have with the social world, starting at an early age. Kanner's (1943) description of one autistic boy captures the syndrome well: "He seems almost to draw into his shell and live within himself" (p. 218).

Since Leo Kanner first identified this psychopathology, numerous causes of autism have been proposed, ranging from deprived early emotional relationships with parents to defective neurological wiring in the brain (Waterhouse, Fein, & Modahl, 1996). An intriguing more recent suggestion is that autistic children, for biological reasons, lack the ability to think about mental states; that is, they lack a "theory of mind" that most children begin to develop during the preschool years. Consider how autistic children behave in the "false belief" task described earlier. Whereas most normal four-year-olds are successful, most nine-year-old autistic children fail this problem (Baron-Cohen, Tager-Flusberg, & Cohen, 1993; Peterson, Wellman, & Liu, 2005). These results suggest that autistic children cannot conceptualize the mental state of another individual. Autistic children, the argument proceeds, have severe deficits in communication and social interaction precisely because they cannot appreciate what the contents of another person's mind might be (Frith & Happé, 1999).

Not all researchers believe that the absence of a "theory of mind" explains childhood autism. Some maintain that autistic children cannot disengage their attention from a stimulus on which they are focusing, such as the hiding location in the "false belief" task (Hughes & Russell, 1993). Others suggest that problems with memory, processing speech sounds, or executive control processes are responsible (Bennetto, Pennington, & Rogers, 1996; Carlson, Moses, & Hix, 1998; Whitehouse & Bishop, 2008). Moreover, even if autistic children lack a theory of mind, it may not be because of a neurological deficit.

Deaf children who are not exposed to sign language for several years, for example, perform similarly to autistic children on the false belief task. Thus, as discussed earlier, the opportunity to engage in conversations from which one might glean information about the mental states of others may be a crucial factor in the development of a theory of mind (Peterson & Siegal, 1999; Woolfe, Want, & Siegal, 2002).

Whatever the ultimate basis for autism, it seems likely that understanding basic cognitive processes will be helpful in deciphering the mechanisms underlying this perplexing childhood disorder. One outcome of this active area of research, for example, is awareness that autistic children show deficits in joint attention in the preschool years and as early as age one (Dawson et al., 2004; Osterling & Dawson, 1994), a finding that can be useful in early diagnosis and treatment of this disorder. For example, rewarding young autistic children for engaging in joint attention results in increases in this behavior, which may, in turn, have other beneficial consequences for social and cognitive development (Kasari, Freeman, & Paparella, 2006). A particularly promising line of research concerns how variations in the development of executive control—the ability to plan, inhibit, or choose responses flexibly—might explain some features of autism (Pellicano, 2010). Given the range in the seriousness of the symptoms of autism (hence the formal term *autism spectrum disorders*), as well as the number of different social behaviors for which these children show differences from the norm, it might be necessary to consider multiple cognitive deficits to explain this developmental disorder (Pellicano, 2010; Rajendran & Mitchell, 2007; Tager-Flusberg, 2007).

Deception Four- and five-year-old children perform successfully on the false belief task, but what about their ability to create false beliefs in others? In other words, when do children become capable of deception by intentionally making others believe something that is not true? When do children start to lie?

Probably by around age two years, according to one research study in which preschoolers were observed in their own homes over a period of many hours. In this set of observations, almost every single child participant—including the two-year-olds—lied at least once, but lying was more frequent among children aged four and six years (Wilson, Smith, & Ross, 2003). Another way to study the ability of children to deceive is to arrange a resistance-to-temptation situation. In one study, for example, three- to eight-year-old children were asked to turn away from the researcher and then identify the kind of toy the researcher was playing with based on only the sound it made. When there was one more toy still to go in the task, the experimenter abruptly left the room, reminding each child, "Don't peek!" Most children did peek, though, and 64 percent lied about it. The youngest children ended up being caught in their lies; when the experimenter asked what the toy was, they unwittingly answered correctly. In contrast, older children were more likely to continue the lie by giving fabricated explanations for how they had obtained the forbidden information (Talwar & Lee, 2008). The results of this study indicated that children's skills at deception were linked to their increasingly complex understanding in false belief tasks.

When and how do children detect when others are lying? Again, this seems to be a relatively early acquisition, starting at about six years of age, when children recognize that an important cue is the eye gaze of the perpetrator. Asked to judge whether video sequences of adults displayed lying or truthful responses, children were more likely to state that individuals who avert their gaze are lying (Einav & Hood, 2008). And when asked to lie themselves, preadolescent children realize that a way to maintain deceit is to *not* break eye gaze (McCarthy & Lee, 2009). These examples demonstrate that various facets of social cognition begin to extend to the domain of moral development, a topic that will be discussed later in this text.

INTERACTION AMONG DOMAINS

Referential Communication

A group of experiments that has been especially useful in providing information on children's awareness of themselves and others, now in the context of communication, centers on **referential communication**, situations that require the child to either talk about a topic specified by the experimenter or

referential communication Communication in situations that require the child to describe an object to a listener or evaluate the effectiveness of a message.

Figure 9.10

An Experiment in Referential Communication

In Krauss and Glucksberg's (1969) study of referential communication, four- and five-year-olds had to describe a series of unfamiliar geometric forms (pasted on blocks) to other children who could not see them. In this illustration, for example, the speaker on the left must explain to the listener on the right which forms to place on the stacking peg.The results showed that children this age are generally ineffective in transmitting this type of information. Research in more naturalistic settings, however, demonstrates that preschoolers can engage in effective referential communication.

Source: Adapted from Krauss & Glucksberg, 1969.

to evaluate the effectiveness of a message describing some sequence of events. Researchers note whether the child's message is sufficient to communicate his or her intent or, alternatively, whether the child is able to detect ambiguous or uninformative components in the messages heard.

In a classic study of referential communication, Robert Krauss and Sam Glucksberg (1969) asked four- and five-year-olds to describe a series of unfamiliar geometric forms to another child who could not see them (see Figure 9.10). The speaker had to provide the listener with enough information to duplicate an array the speaker was constructing. The results showed that children at this age often rely on personal descriptions of the stimuli (for instance, "It looks like Daddy's shirt"), messages that are not at all helpful to the listener. Thus, young children's ability to understand the requirements of the listener and to adjust their speech accordingly is limited when they are describing unfamiliar items and when the interaction is not face-to-face.

On the other hand, observations of children in more natural interactions with one another suggest that, well before they enter school, children appreciate at least some of the requirements of the listener and can modify their speech to make their communication effective. In a study of the communication skills of preschool-age children, Marilyn Shatz and Rochel Gelman (1973) asked four-year-olds to describe a toy to either an adult or a two-year-old listener. When the children spoke to the younger child, they shortened their utterances, used simple constructions, repeated utterances, and employed more attention-getting devices than when they spoke to the adult. Other researchers have also observed that even two-year-olds use techniques to make sure their messages get across during the normal interactions that occur in a nursery school. Children point, seek eye contact with listeners, and use verbal attention getters, such as "Hey," to ensure that listeners hear what they have to say (Wellman & Lempers, 1977). In addition, when a listener somehow indicates that he has misunderstood or says "What?", two- and three-year-olds attempt to make their communication more effective. They may repeat their statement or restate the utterance with a better choice of words, a change in verb form, or some other linguistic correction (Ferrier, Dunham, & Dunham, 2000; Levy, 1999; Shwe & Markman, 1997).

INTERACTION AMONG DOMAINS

RISK | RESILIENCE

Development of stronger referential communication skills is related to the child's achieving an understanding of theory of mind (Resches & Pérez Pereira, 2007). In addition, the mature use of language involves the ability to understand the demands of the situation, be sensitive to the needs of the listener, and employ subtle nuances in speech that are compatible with the situation. The child's failure to acquire the social skills that are part of effective communication can have broad consequences for the qualities of relationships that she or he establishes with parents, teachers, and peers, among others.

For Your Review and Reflection

- What developmental changes in visual perspective taking have been identified by researchers?
- What is meant by the child's "theory of mind"? What contrasting positions have been suggested as explanations for the development of theory of mind?
- What is childhood autism? What are some hypotheses about its causes?
- Research on the child's "theory of mind" has come to occupy a prominent place in developmental science. Why do you think scientists find this topic to be so important?
- How is the research on children's use of deception related to theory of mind?
- Explain the concept of referential communication. How might this behavior be related to the child's "theory of mind"?
- What kinds of statements would you expect to hear when your young niece, nephew, or family friend speaks to show that he or she has and uses a theory of mind?

Cognition in a Social Context

SOCIOCULTURAL INFLUENCE

So far in this chapter, we have focused on the child's social cognitive abilities. Here, we turn to a discussion of important cultural, educational, and social ways of tapping into and expanding upon these developments, i.e., the important ways sociocultural, parental, and peer processes can be and are implemented to take advantage of the child's growing social cognitive abilities. Cognitive development, as you can see, takes place in a distinctly social context, much as Vygotsky described in his sociohistorical theory of development (see Chapter 1, "Themes and Theories," and Chapter 8, "Cognition"). Of special importance is the child's collaboration with and internalization of social exchanges with parents, peers, and teachers (Rogoff, 1998). We have emphasized so far in this chapter that an important ingredient in this process is for young children and their caregivers or teachers to establish a psychologically meaningful social connection in the first place. In this section, we examine further the role that caregiver-child interactions, and more broadly speaking, societal expectations, play in some additional important cognitive attainments among children.

Skilled Collaborators and Guided Participation

Recall our earlier discussion in Chapter 8 of Vygotsky's theory in which we defined the concept of *scaffolding*. Scaffolding involves a teaching/learning relationship that uses the expert or tutor who intervenes as required and gradually withdraws as assistance becomes unnecessary. Patricia Greenfield (1984) observed this phenomenon among girls learning to weave in Zinacantan, Mexico. Beginners, in the presence of at least one expert weaver (usually the mother), started by weaving small items and performed only the simpler parts of the task. The more experienced the learner, the less likely the teacher was to intervene to complete the more technically difficult steps. Novices were more likely to receive direct commands from the teacher, whereas experienced weavers were more likely to receive statements or comments. Both verbal and nonverbal assistance declined as the girls became increasingly proficient weavers, although the expert continued to be a role model for both specific techniques and more general principles of weaving. Remarkably, the scaffolding that the tutor provided yielded a woven product from beginners indistinguishable from those completed by expert weavers.

As the phenomenon of scaffolding suggests, a role model who is sensitive to the learner's level of knowledge contributes greatly to the effective transmission of skills. The effect can be demonstrated in tasks as diverse as learning to distinguish the colors and shapes of pictures (Diaz, Neal, & Vachio, 1991) to finding out how to carry out long division in mathematics assignments (Pratt et al., 1992). Also important is the establishment of **intersubjectivity**, the mutual attention and shared communication that take place between expert and learner.

Of course, some tutors may be better at these activities than others. Barbara Radziszewska and Barbara Rogoff (1988) examined how nine- and ten-year-olds learned to plan errands. One group of children worked with their parents to organize a shopping trip through an imaginary town, while a second group of children worked with a peer to plan the expedition. Children who worked with adults were exposed to more sophisticated planning strategies; they explored a map of the town more frequently, planned longer sequences of activities, and verbalized more of their plans. Instead of using a step-by-step strategy ("Let's go from this store to the next closest store") as the peer pairs did, children working with adults formulated an integrated sequence of actions ("Let's mark all the stores we have to go to in blue and see what is the best way between them"). In the second part of the experiment, all of the children were observed as they planned a new errand in the same town, this time by themselves. Children who had initially worked with their parents employed more efficient planning strategies than children who had worked with peers.

Why does collaboration with adults work so well? In a follow-up study, Radziszewska and Rogoff (1991) observed that when children worked with adults, they participated in more discussion of the best planning strategy—more "thinking out loud"—than when they worked with peers who had expertise in planning. When working with adults, children were generally more actively involved in the cognitive task, whereas they tended to be more passive observers when their tutor was another child.

SOCIOCULTURAL INFLUENCE

Barbara Rogoff and her colleagues (Rogoff et al., 1993; Rogoff, 2003) have suggested that the extent to which children and adults take an active role in learning the skills, values, and knowledge of their community differs across cultures. In most communities adults provide scaffolding for children to begin engaging in mature activities, a process the researchers label **guided participation**. However, children take on a greater burden of responsibility for managing their attention, desire, and interest in mature activities in communities in which they are routinely in the company of adults. The guidance caregivers provide in this context is likely to be in the form of supporting children's observations and efforts rather than in the form of instruction. In contrast, when much of a child's day is spent separate from adults, the child will need more directed lessons and training to acquire mature skills. In this context, the caregivers assume comparatively greater responsibility in helping children to observe and understand the world.

Rogoff and her colleagues (Rogoff et al., 1993) found that in communities in India and Guatemala where young children could watch and enter into adult social and work activities, caregivers were likely to assist and support children in carrying out the more mature responsibilities, such as learning to dress themselves or play with a new toy. In other communities, children may be expected to learn merely by watching intently and quietly in order to master an adult's

intersubjectivity Mutual attention and shared communication that take place between two individuals.

guided participation Process by which a skilled collaborator transfers knowledge to a learner by providing support and gradually withdrawing it.

skillful activity. For example, in observing Mexican heritage children as they learned how to do origami, Rogoff and her colleagues found that these children asked fewer questions and paid closer attention than European American children while an adult folded paper to make various origami figures (Mejía-Arauz, Rogoff, & Paradise, 2005). On the other hand, in middle-income communities in Turkey and the United States, where children were more likely to be segregated (and parents could not be as consistently attentive and supportive), caregivers were likely to promote play and conversation or provide lessons or learning opportunities in interacting with children to teach them new skills. These interactions, in other words, looked more like the kind typically found with older children in formal school settings. Thus, although all caregivers provided guidance for more mature behavior in each community, its specific form differed, a confirmation of the diverse ways learning may be encouraged in various cultural contexts.

Reciprocal Teaching | research applied to education

Although Craig had always been impressed with his son Tommy's social skills, he and Marta, his wife, were more concerned with how Tommy was doing with reading in school. Tommy could read aloud fairly well, but he seemed to have consistent problems in understanding what he read. This was beginning to affect his performance in social studies, science, and other subjects in which students were expected to do quite a bit of independent fact-finding. Tommy seemed to stumble through these assignments and was beginning to feel embarrassed by the grades he was getting. At the last parent-teacher conference, though, Craig and Marta were reassured. The third-grade teacher was trying a new approach to reading called "reciprocal teaching," and she was very encouraged by the visible changes she saw in students' performance and attitudes toward their schoolwork.

Several facets of Vygotsky's theory can be seen in action in a special program developed to foster the emergence of reading comprehension strategies in junior high school students (Brown et al., 1991; Palincsar & Brown, 1984, 1986). The students received instruction in several important reading skills with an instructional method called *reciprocal teaching*. According to this method, teachers should do the following:

1. *Introduce students to four key reading comprehension strategies.* These strategies are summarizing, clarifying word meanings and confusing passages, generating questions about the passage, and predicting what might happen next.
2. *Provide the scaffolding for how to use comprehension strategies.* For one paragraph, the teacher models how to summarize the theme, isolate material that needs to be clarified, anticipate questions, and predict what will happen next.
3. *Ask students to engage in the same four activities for the next paragraph.* The teacher adjusts instructions according to the needs of the individual students, working within what Vygotsky would call each student's zone of proximal development. The teacher also provides feedback, praise, hints, and explanations. The teacher invites other students to react to a student's statements, adding other questions, making predictions, or requesting clarification. Teacher and students alternate paragraphs in the early stages of this process.
4. *Become less directive as the students become more skilled in each component of reading.* The students gradually take charge of the process, and the teacher becomes more of an observer, adding suggestions and support when necessary.

Table 9.1 gives an example of the teacher-student exchanges that typically occur with this method.

The results of training were impressive. Whereas during the pretests students averaged 20 percent correct in answering ten questions from reading a paragraph of material, after twenty sessions of reciprocal teaching they averaged 80 percent correct on similar tests. Six months later, students trained in this method moved up from the twentieth percentile in reading ability in their school to the fifty-sixth percentile. Several other studies have documented similar successes of

RISK | RESILIENCE

TABLE 9.1 An Example of Reciprocal Teaching

This conversation illustrates the types of exchanges that typify reciprocal teaching.The teacher and, eventually, the students model question asking, summarizing, clarifying, and predicting. In this particular excerpt, students have begun to assume control over their own learning. Students who participated in this program showed significant gains in reading comprehension.

Reciprocal Teaching	
Student 1:	(*Question*) My question is, what does the aquanaut need when he goes underwater?
Student 2:	A watch.
Student 3:	Flippers.
Student 4:	A belt.
Student 1:	Those are all good answers.
Teacher:	(*Question*) Nice job! I have a question too. Why does the aquanaut wear a belt? What is so special about it?
Student 3:	It's a heavy belt and keeps him from floating up to the top again.
Teacher:	Good for you.
Student 1:	(*Summary*) For my summary now: This paragraph was about what aquanauts need to take when they go under the water.
Student 5:	(*Summary*) And also about why they need those things.
Student 3:	(*Clarify*) I think we need to clarify gear.
Student 6:	That's the special things they need.
Teacher:	Another word for gear in this story might be equipment, the equipment that makes it easier for the aquanauts to do their job.
Student 1:	I don't think I have a prediction to make.
Teacher:	(*Prediction*) Well, in the story they tell us that there are "many strange and wonderful creatures" that the aquanauts see as they do their work. My prediction is that they'll describe some of these creatures. What are some of the strange creatures you already know about that live in the ocean?
Student 6:	Octopuses.
Student 3:	Whales?
Student 5:	Sharks!

Source: From Palincsar, A. S., & Brown, A. L. (1986, April). Interactive teaching to promote independent learning from text. *The Reading Teacher, 39*(8), 771–777. Reprinted with permission of Annemarie S. Palincsar and the International Reading Association.

reciprocal teaching from as early as first grade (Rosenshine & Meister, 1994; Spörer, Brunstein, & Kieschke, 2009).

The key to the success of reciprocal teaching, many experts believe, is the carefully modulated interaction between teacher and students, a point Vygotsky consistently emphasized and which resurfaces as an important theme as children acquire a range of cognitive skills.

Memory in a Social Context

It is tempting to think of memory as the ability to think of real events that occurred at some identifiable time and place in one's past, that memories are true to the actual details of the events that have transpired in an individual's life. That is, after all, how a camera memory card works; it records every visible detail that the open lens was pointed at.

However, cognitive and developmental scientists have learned that human memory does not operate in this way. Instead, our recollections of past events and experiences seem to be malleable and are influenced by our current state of knowledge and, in a more general way, by the kinds of emphases or values that are promoted by parents, teachers, and others in our social environments. Memory, as it turns out, is in many instances one's retelling of the past colored or guided by social conventions or other influences that have been absorbed over time.

Scripts One way to describe the effects of social experiences on memory is in terms of scripts. **Scripts** are the organized schemes of knowledge that individuals possess about commonly encountered events. For example, by the time they are three or four years old, most children have a general schematic representation for the events that occur at dinnertime—cooking the food, setting the table, sitting down to eat—as well as for other routine events, such as going to school or attending a birthday party. When asked to remember stories based on such familiar scripts, children typically recall script-based activities, such as "eating dinner," better than other details less closely related to scripts. Thus, scripts serve as general frameworks within which specific memories can be stored and may be one of the earliest building blocks for memory (Hudson & Mayhew, 2009).

Conversations with parents and others probably foster the formation of scripts. When parents reminisce using rich and detailed language about past events with their children, children have better recall about the past (Reese & Fivush, 1993; Reese, Haden, & Fivush, 1993). Within this framework, memory is better conceptualized as something children *use* than as something they *have* (Fivush, 1997). Moreover, as the following dialogue between a mother and child illustrates, conversations based on scripts can often shape still other cognitive skills, such as thinking about the concept of "future" as well as planning for those events that are going to occur:

Mother: Listen, we're gonna go to Nickelodeon Live on November 19th. Do you know what happens right after that? When do we eat lots of turkey: on what holiday?

Child: Thanksgiving.

Mother: That's right, when Thanksgiving comes.

Child: And what are we gonna do then?

Mother: What do we usually do?

Child: What?

Mother: Do we wake up early and go someplace? Where do we go? What do we see? Do we go to New York? And see what?

Child: What?

Mother: What do we do for Thanksgiving? Remember, when we went to New York City and we parked the car, then what did we do? We walked and walked and walked across the park. And then what did we see? Remember we sat on that hill and what goes by?

Child: The parade.

(Hudson, 2006, pp. 87–88)

Autobiographical Memory Think back to your childhood and try to identify your earliest memory. How old were you? It is unlikely that you will report that you were an infant or perhaps even a toddler. Most people are not able to recount memories for experiences prior to age three years (Pillemer & White, 1989; West & Bauer, 1999), a phenomenon called **infantile amnesia**. The question of why infantile amnesia occurs has intrigued psychologists for decades, especially in light of the ample evidence that infants and young children can display impressive memory capabilities. Many find that

script Organized scheme or framework for commonly experienced events.

infantile amnesia Failure to remember events from the first two to three years of one's life.

understanding the general nature of **autobiographical memories**, memories of events that have occurred in one's own life, can provide some important clues to this mystery. Between ages three and four, children begin to give fairly lengthy and cohesive descriptions of events in their past, often marking them with explicit references to time ("last Halloween" or "on my birthday") (Fivush, Haden, & Adam, 1995; Nelson & Fivush, 2004). What factors are responsible for this developmental turning point?

One explanation goes back to an idea raised by Piaget, namely, that children under age two years represent events in a qualitatively different form than older children. According to this line of thought, the verbal abilities that blossom in the two-year-old allow events to be coded in a form radically different from the action-based codes of the infant. The child's emerging verbal skills are, in fact, related to memory for personal experiences. Preverbal children who see unique events at age two do not describe them in verbal terms six months later when they are able to talk. Thus, early memories seem to be encoded in a format that cannot be translated into verbal terms later on (Simcock & Hayne, 2002).

INTERACTION AMONG DOMAINS

Another suggestion is that, before children can talk about past events in their lives, they need to have a reasonable understanding of the self as a psychological entity (Courage & Howe, 2004; Howe & Courage, 1997). As we will see in Chapter 12, "Self and Values," the development of the self becomes evident between the first and second years of life and shows rapid elaboration in subsequent years. The realization that the physical self has continuity in time, according to this hypothesis, lays the foundation for the emergence of autobiographical memory. Research has confirmed that the ability to recognize the self at nineteen months of age predicts the frequency with which children talk about past events when they are a few months older (Harley & Reese, 1999). And in cultures where there is more emphasis on individual notions of self (European American, for example), the individual's age in first memories is earlier than in cultures with a more collectivist orientation (Taiwanese, for example) (Wang, 2006a).

SOCIOCULTURAL INFLUENCE

A third possibility is that children will not be able to tell their own "life story" until they understand something about the general form stories take; that is, the structure of narratives (Nelson, 1993a). Knowledge about narratives arises from social interactions, particularly the storytelling children experience with parents and the attempts parents make to talk with children about past events in their lives (Reese et al., 1993). When parents talk with children about "what we did today" or "last week" or "last year," they guide the children's formation of a framework for talking about the past. They also provide children with reminders about the memory and relay the message that memories are valued as part of the cultural experience (Nelson, 1993b). It is interesting to note that European American children have earlier childhood memories than Korean children do (Mullen, 1994). American children also provide more extensive, detailed descriptions of events in their past than do Korean and Chinese children (Han, Leichtman, & Wang, 1998; Wang, 2004). By the same token, European American mother-child pairs talk about past events three times more often than do Korean mother-child pairs (Mullen & Yi, 1995). Moreover, European heritage mothers who ask their children many questions about past events, elaborating on their children's comments or asking for more details ("And what did Daddy do on the boat?"), tend to have children who talk more about the past (Harley & Reese, 1999). When mothers are trained to ask "what," "where," "when," and "who" questions as they reminisce about past events with their young children, children show more elaborate and detailed memories several months later (Reese & Newcombe, 2007). These kinds of studies demonstrate that the types of social experiences children have factor into the development of autobiographical memories.

NATURE & NURTURE

SOCIOCULTURAL INFLUENCE

A final suggestion is that children must begin to develop a "theory of mind" before they can talk about their own past memories. Once children begin to accurately answer questions like "What does it mean to *remember*?" and "What does it mean to *know* something?" improvements in memory also seem to occur (Perner & Ruffman, 1995). That is, understanding mental processes like "remember" and "know" may help the child actually use those activities to begin to tell a memory narrative about the self.

autobiographical memory Memory for specific events in one's own life.

The content of conversations between caregivers and children seems to influence the formation of scripts and autobiographical memory. When caregivers frequently prompt children to talk about past events, for example, children show more elaborate memories months later.

© Rob Marmion/Shutterstock.com

It may be that the developments just described are intertwined with and influence one another, that the ability to talk about one's past arises from the interplay of several factors, not just one (Pillemer, 1998). Increasingly, researchers are viewing autobiographical memory as arising from multiple factors that interact in the fashion of the dynamic systems model described in Chapter 1 (Reese, 2002).

How Reliable Is Children's Eyewitness Testimony?

what do you think?

The research on children's memory suggests that their ability to remember events from the past is very impressive. But as children are increasingly called on to testify in courts after they have witnessed or been victims of abuse, neglect, or other crimes, their capability to render an accurate account of past events has been called into question.

Just how reliable are children's memories when they are called on to give eyewitness testimony? Children's memory for events, even those that occurred months or years in the past, is remarkably good. On the other hand, children's memories are also susceptible to suggestive or leading questions by attorneys, clinicians, and other interrogators (Bruck & Ceci, 1999, 2004). The stakes are high regarding these issues. If children have been the victims of crime, the perpetrators should be punished; but if children's memories are inaccurate in these contexts, a criminal suspect might be falsely accused.

Some research indicates that children's recall of distinctive events such as a trip to Disney World or a medical emergency is surprisingly complete and accurate even four or five years after the event (Fivush & Schwarzmueller, 1998; Peterson & Whalen, 2001). For example, in one study of two- to thirteen-year-old children who had been treated in a hospital emergency room, even two-year-olds remembered a substantial amount about their injuries when they were interviewed five years later (Peterson & Whalen, 2001). Data such as this suggests that children's memories are reliable.

On the other hand, other studies have shown that children, especially preschoolers, are likely to misreport a past event if they are asked misleading questions. In some of the original studies of "false memories" in children, Stephen Ceci and his colleagues tested children ages three through twelve years on their ability to remember the details of a story (Ceci, Ross, & Toglia, 1987). A day later, children in one of the experimental conditions were asked leading questions that distorted the original information, such as "Do you remember the story about Loren, who had a headache because she ate her cereal too fast?" In the original story, Loren had a stomachache from eating her eggs too fast. Compared with children who did not hear misleading questions, children who heard biased questions made more errors on a subsequent test that required them to select pictures depicting the original story: they chose the pictures showing a girl eating cereal and having a headache. This tendency to err was especially pronounced in children ages four and under.

Many factors may influence just how suggestible children are. One is exactly who is doing the questioning. For example, in Ceci's study just described, misinformation provided by an adult tended to distort memory more than misinformation provided by another child; the perceived power of the questioner may make a difference. Second, some studies find that when children are asked questions repeatedly, particularly yes–no questions, they may change their answers or speculate inappropriately (Poole & White, 1991, 1993). Preschoolers especially may perceive the repeated question as a signal that their first answer was incorrect. Third, supplying dolls and props for children to reenact the event can lead to elevated false reports, especially among younger children (age three) and when this form of interview occurs after a delay of several weeks (Greenhoot et al., 1999). Finally, suggestibility may be reduced when children first are reminded to consider the basis of their information, a phenomenon called *source monitoring* (Poole & Lindsay, 2002; Thierry & Spence, 2002). In one laboratory study, for example, preschoolers were shown a video depicting a story about a boy feeding his dog accompanied by the experimenter's narrative. Some children were first asked to answer "Did you see it on the tape?" or "Did I tell you?" before they were asked leading questions about the story. This group was less likely to be influenced by leading questions compared with a group of children who were asked the leading questions first (Giles, Gopnik, & Heyman, 2002).

An important, and perhaps obvious, consideration in this discussion is that memories—those of both children and adults—generally decline with the passage of time. The results of one experiment showed that the amount and accuracy of information children spontaneously recalled about past events went down after two years, especially if they did not have an opportunity to be reminded of the original event. Under the latter conditions, up to 50 percent of the new information children added to their memories after being prompted by an experimenter was found to be inaccurate (Pipe et al., 1999). Research also shows that the effects of a biased interviewer are particularly strong after long delays (Quas et al., 2007). Because extended periods of time often elapse between a criminal event and the trial, these findings are especially relevant.

Given this information, what is the best way for professionals in the criminal justice system to encourage children to give reliable eyewitness accounts based on what we know from research? Who should do the interviewing? Someone such as a parent or someone who may be less well known to the child? What kind of training might interviewers benefit from before questioning children? What arrangements should be made to make children feel more comfortable when conveying their information? How often should children be asked to tell their stories? Should questions be open-ended or do young children need memory probes to help them remember events?

For Your Review and Reflection

- What do research findings tell us about the role of skilled collaborators in promoting children's cognitive advances? How do scaffolding and guided participation contribute to this process?
- What role do scripts play in children's memory?
- What four explanations have been offered for the emergence of autobiographical memory?
- What has research told us about the reliability of eyewitness testimony among children?
- What is the earliest memory that you have? How old were you?

Understanding Social Groups

In Chapter 8, we provided an overview of how children begin to form concepts pertaining to objects they encounter in the world. Here, we extend that discussion to how children conceptualize the social entities in their lives, with a particular eye toward how this form of "social intelligence" can ultimately either enhance or create risks in several spheres of development.

Forming Social Categories

Children form social categories early in infancy, even by six months of age. Researchers have uncovered this ability by using the habituation procedure introduced to you in Chapter 6, "Basic Learning and Perception." For example, suppose the infant is shown faces of several different females until the criterion for habituation is reached. Then the face of a male is displayed. Alternatively, the faces of several European Americans can be shown until the child has habituated to the stimuli, after which the face of an African-American is shown. In each case, infants show longer looking times to the face from a different gender or race compared with a new face from the original category (Katz & Kofkin, 1997). Results such as these indicate that, at the very least, infants are capable of perceptual discrimination of groups defined by gender or race.

Throughout the preschool and school years, children respond to social categories like race and ethnicity on the basis of concrete features: What foods does each group eat? What language do the people in the group speak? What is their skin color? Preadolescents are more likely to talk about abstract ideas, such as how social resources are allocated differently to various groups (Cooper et al., 2005). Adolescents also demonstrate another lesson that probably reflects the values of their social groups as well as their greater understanding of social norms: that it might be better not to even acknowledge sensitive issues such as race even when it is an obvious dimension of an experimental problem-solving task. When playing a game that involved guessing which photo of a person an experimenter had selected from an array, older children were less likely than younger children to mention the race of the person depicted (Apfelbaum et al., 2008).

In-Group Preferences

The formation of social concepts seems to parallel the formation of concepts for objects that we described in Chapter 8 in that children start out by using perceptual cues to cluster groups of individual items together, probably so that information about them can be processed more efficiently. In the social sphere, though, humans tend to go one step further—they assign a valence to some groups over others. Many different kinds of studies have documented the formation of **in-group preferences**, children's more positive reactions to groups to which they belong.

These preferences seem to show up early. Consider the experiment described in Figure 9.11. Ten-month-old infants in the United States and France saw and heard two strangers speaking on alternating trials: a native speaker of French and a native speaker of English. Then the two speakers appeared on a screen side-by-side, each offering the identical toy in synchrony and without speaking. Infants were more likely to reach for the toy from the speaker of their native language, indicating a preference for one's own group. This research also suggests the important role that language may play in marking social groups (Kinzler, Dupoux, & Spelke, 2007).

INTERACTION AMONG DOMAINS

A unique series of studies sheds further light on the factors that promote in-group preferences. Rebecca Bigler and her colleagues (Bigler, Jones, & Lobliner, 1997) divided children in each of several summer school classrooms into a "blue" group and a "yellow" group. For some children, their assignment to a group was based on a biological characteristic: whether their hair color was light or dark. For others, assignment to a group was random. Teachers in both groups were instructed to emphasize group membership with verbal comments and by other overt actions, such as seating children and having them line up for recess according to their group. Children in all the groups wore T-shirts bearing the color of their group (see Figure 9.12 depicting children from a similar study). The researchers also included a control group, in which children wore either yellow or blue T-shirts but did not experience emphasis on the groups from their teachers. At the end of four weeks, children were asked a series of questions evaluating their attitudes toward their own group (the in-group) and the other group (the out-group). Children in the experimental conditions showed a strong tendency to ascribe positive traits to *all* members of the in-group but to *none* of the members of the out-group. The control group, in contrast, did not show this pattern. Thus, when adults

in-group preferences Children's tendency to display more positive behaviors to members of their own social group or category.

Figure 9.11
Infants Display In-Group Preferences
Ten-month-old infants prefer to obtain toys from strangers who had previously spoken their own native language. The colors of the bars in the graph represent the language in which strangers had spoken to the infants before each offered a toy. Some researchers interpret this finding as showing a natural human tendency to prefer one's own social group, with language being an important marker of that group.
Source: From Kinzler, K. D., Dupoux, E., & Spelke, E. S. (2007). The native language of social cognition. *Proceedings of the National Academy of Sciences, 104,* 12577–12580.

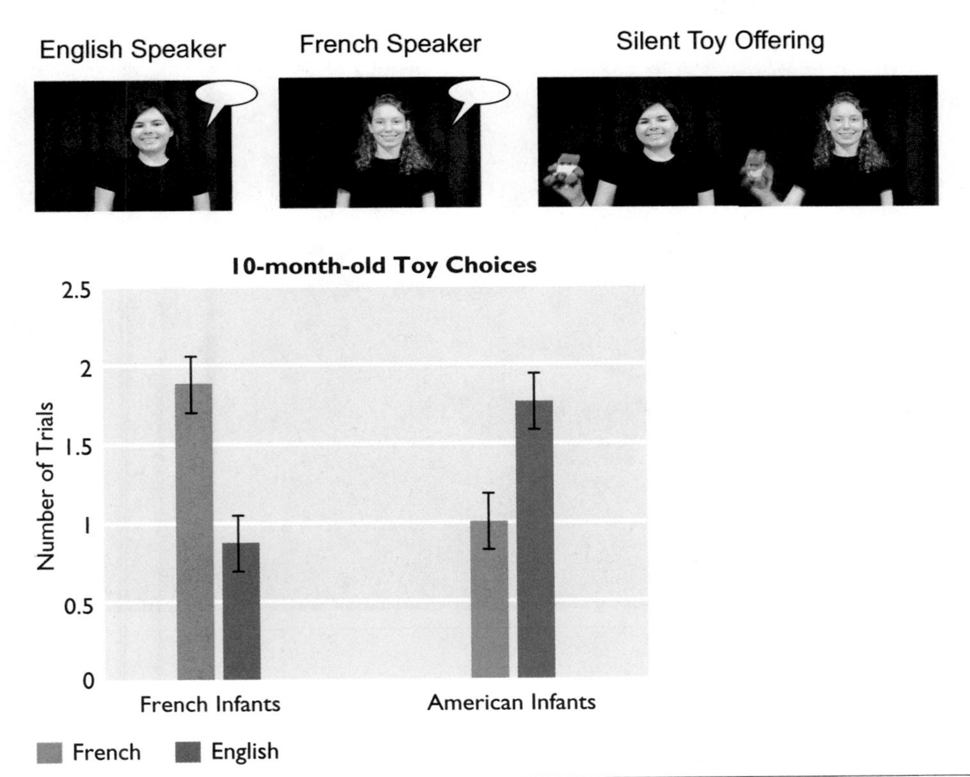

actively use obvious perceptual categories to describe children's groups, children exhibit strong favoritism toward their own group and bias against the out-group.

In-group favoritism does not operate in all circumstances, however. In a subsequent study, Bigler and her colleagues manipulated the status of the yellow and blue groups by displaying photographs of past winners of athletic and academic competitions on posters placed around the classrooms. They purposely showed more "winners" from the yellow group. Under these conditions, children in the low-status group, the blue group, did not show a bias toward their own group, whereas children in the high-status group did (Bigler, Brown, & Markell, 2001). These studies reveal important information about the factors that influence peer group dynamics, and especially biases toward certain groups. In particular, studies have shown that in-group biases are more likely to emerge when groups are made perceptually visible, when there are obvious differences in the size of groups, when social groups are clearly labeled by adults, and when adults display even subtle nonverbal cues about their feelings toward various groups (Bigler & Liben, 2006). In that sense, this body of research also provides clues about the strategies that can break down animosities among children's groups, findings that have implications for interventions aimed at reducing gender or racial and ethnic biases.

NATURE & NURTURE

Prejudice and Discrimination

When in-group preferences are accompanied by strong negative feelings about the out-group, children may develop feelings of prejudice. Research has shown that when children are the victims of prejudice—for example, when they experience racial discrimination—

Figure 9.12
Experimentally Creating In-groups and Out-groups
Rebecca Bigler's studies have demonstrated that when children are randomly assigned to one of two groups wearing either one color T-shirt or another, they quickly developed preferences for members of their own group and biases against children in the other group. This research shows that when adults mark children's groups in visible ways, significant outcomes in children's social attitudes typically follow.
Source: Copyright © James Shaffer/PhotoEdit

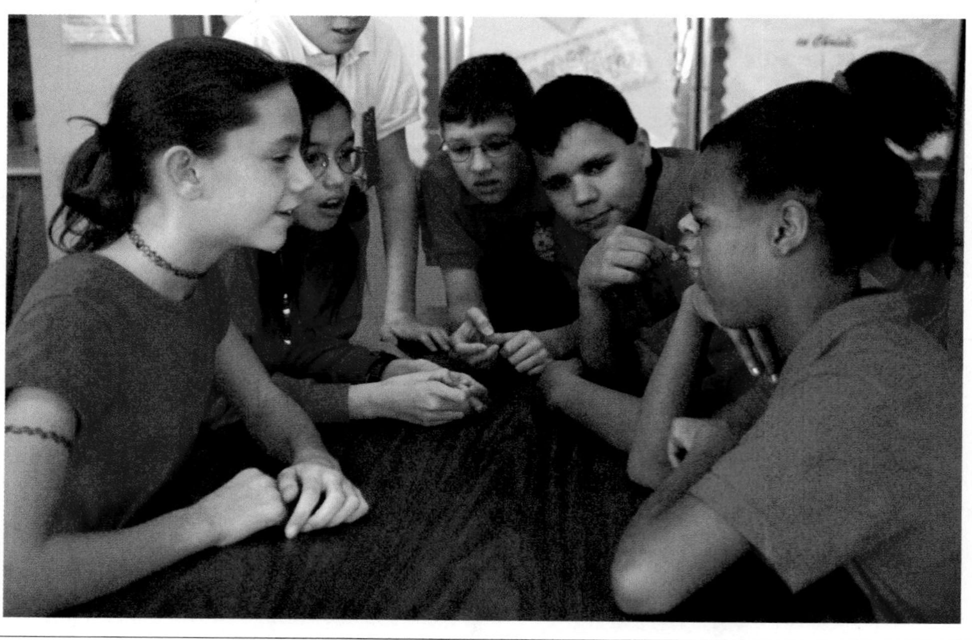

they are at risk for a number of serious problems such as depression, negative self-esteem, and lower satisfaction with life, as well as negative feelings about being a member of that race (Seaton, Yip, & Sellers, 2009; Spencer, 2006). Among a sample of Chinese American youth, discrimination experienced early in adolescence predicted feelings of depression, lower school engagement, and poorer academic grades in middle adolescence (Benner & Kim, 2009). These findings take on added significance when we consider the prevalence of discrimination on the basis of gender, race, and ethnicity. In one recent study, the majority of black youths perceived at least one incident of discrimination directed at them in the last year (Seaton et al., 2008).

RISK | RESILIENCE

Preschoolers seem to understand that it is unfair to exclude a person from an activity because of his or her gender or race (Killen & Stangor, 2001), and at age eight to ten years, children are able to recognize behavior that would typically be categorized as gender discrimination, such as giving more praise to a male student than an equally deserving female student (Brown & Bigler, 2004). Children's understanding of discrimination seems to depend on several factors: their ability to understand social comparisons, perspective taking, and people's intentions, as well as experiences children themselves have had with exclusion (Brown & Bigler, 2005; Killen, Sinno, & Margie, 2007). Direct teaching about what discrimination is by parents and others can influence children's understanding, as well (Hughes & Johnson, 2001). But if children understand discrimination as a process that is unfair, why does it still occur?

The answers provided by research are not so direct at this point, but several types of findings are instructive. Family influences matter in the attitudes children develop about different social groups such as race, but they matter less in the explicit messages that parents give to children than the implicit beliefs that they hold. Parents and children may not state directly that they prefer to associate with individuals who are white or black, but they may show differences in how they respond to positive and negative words when they are paired

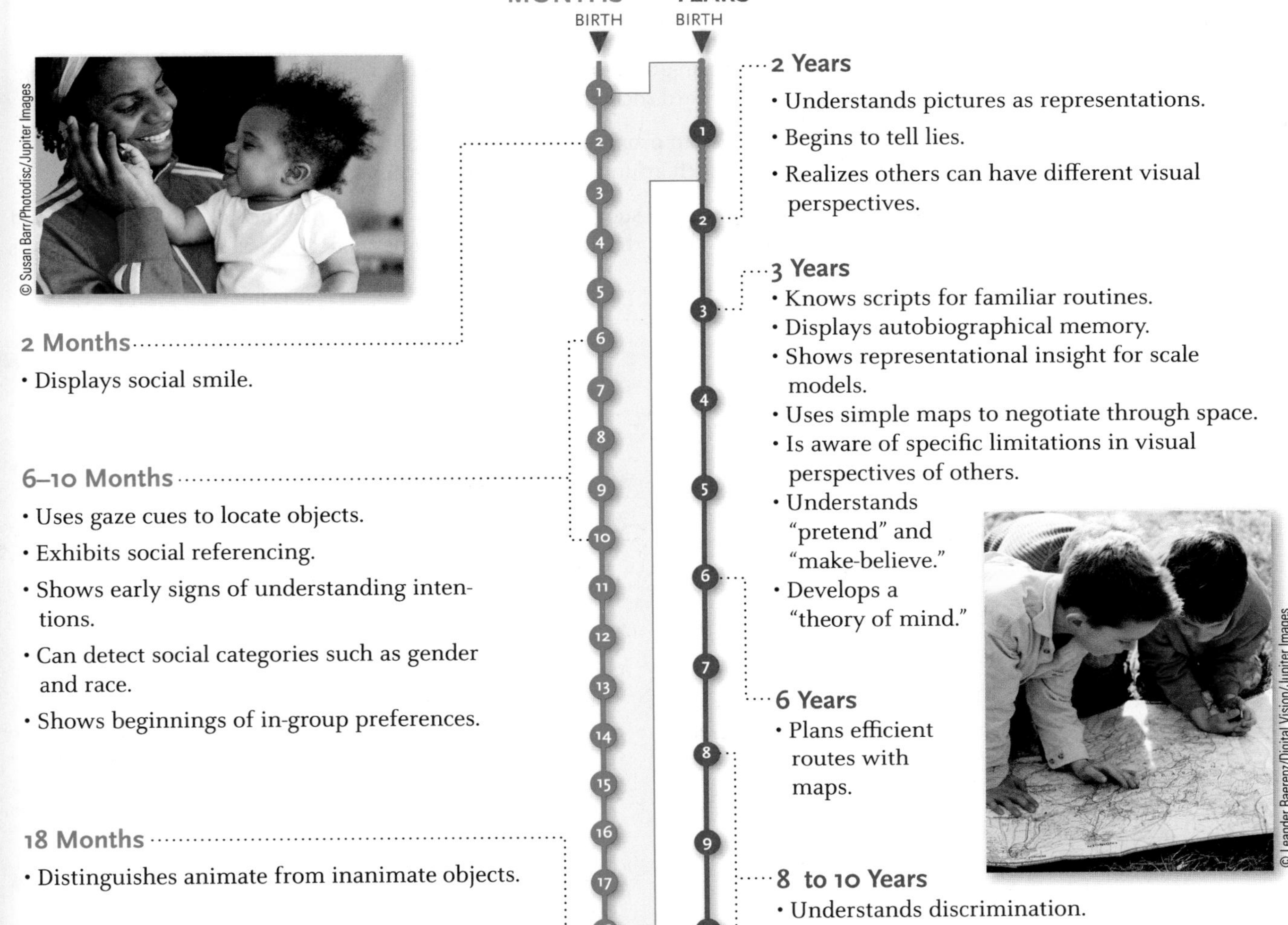

CHRONOLOGY
Development of Social Cognition: Birth to 10 Years
MONTHS
YEARS
BIRTH
BIRTH
© Susan Barr/Photodisc/Jupiter Images
2 Months
• Displays social smile.
6–10 Months
• Uses gaze cues to locate objects.
• Exhibits social referencing.
• Shows early signs of understanding intentions.
• Can detect social categories such as gender and race.
• Shows beginnings of in-group preferences.
18 Months
• Distinguishes animate from inanimate objects.
2 Years
• Understands pictures as representations.
• Begins to tell lies.
• Realizes others can have different visual perspectives.
3 Years
• Knows scripts for familiar routines.
• Displays autobiographical memory.
• Shows representational insight for scale models.
• Uses simple maps to negotiate through space.
• Is aware of specific limitations in visual perspectives of others.
• Understands "pretend" and "make-believe."
• Develops a "theory of mind."
6 Years
• Plans efficient routes with maps.
8 to 10 Years
• Understands discrimination.
© Leander Baerenz/Digital Vision/Jupiter Images

This chart describes the sequence of development of social cognition based on the findings of research. Children often show individual differences in the exact ages at which they display the various developmental achievements outlined here.

with pictures of white and black individuals, providing indirect information about their attitudes and feelings. It is not clear how implicit attitudes are transmitted from parent to child, but nonverbal messages are likely candidates (Castelli, Zogmaister, & Tomelleri, 2009).

It is also helpful to consider the factors that can break down feelings of prejudice and instances of discrimination. Some studies suggest that having a friendship with a peer from a different ethnic group can influence broader attitudes about that group, but so far, this effect seems to hold up only for higher status children who come from a majority group (Feddes, Noack, & Rutland, 2009). Finally, offering children lessons on the history of racism—as few as six classroom sessions—was found to influence attitudes toward different racial groups among elementary school children (Hughes, Bigler, & Levy, 2007).

Throughout this chapter, we have identified a number of ways in which social cognition undergoes development. The Social Cognition Chronology chart above summarizes the child's main achievements in this domain. You should find this information helpful as you reflect on the important changes that take place in children's thinking about social information and events.

For Your Review and Reflection

- When do children show the earliest signs of forming social categories?
- What is meant by in-group preferences? When do children show signs of displaying these attitudes toward social groups?
- What factors seem to promote the formation of in-group preferences? How might adults influence such attitudes toward social groups?
- What does the research suggest about ways to break down instances of prejudice and discrimination? Why is this topic considered one that carries risks during the process of development?

chapter recap

Summary of Developmental Themes

Nature & Nurture

How do nature and nurture interact in the process of social cognitive development?
Some researchers believe that the infant's tendency to attend in special ways to the behaviors of living things and human agents represents a form of core knowledge. At the same time, studies have demonstrated the role that learning and experience play in the emergence of phenomena such as sensitivity to goal-directed actions. Research in other domains of social cognition such as representation, theory of mind, and in-group bias shows the important influence of parents, teachers, and other adults in shaping children's understandings.

Sociocultural Influence

How does the sociocultural context influence social cognitive development?
The sociocultural context plays an essential role in social cognitive development. The goals and values of a social/cultural group are transmitted through the process of guided participation and can influence the development of cognitive processes such as autobiographical memory.

Interaction Among Domains

How does social cognitive development interact with development in other domains?
The child's emergent social cognitive skills interact with many other social capabilities. For example, children's understanding of theory of mind can have ramifications for their communications skills, for the emergence of autobiographical memory, and for their understanding of representations.

Risk | Resilience

What factors promote risk or resilience in social cognitive development?
Children's experiences of discrimination are related to depression, low self-esteem, and other poor developmental outcomes. Strategies to overcome prejudice and discrimination include encouraging friendships across social groups, as well as direct instruction on the historical events surrounding discrimination.

Chapter Review

Orienting to the Social World

What is meant by the term social cognition? *What kinds of information are included in this aspect of thinking and problem-solving?*
Social cognition refers to thinking and representations that are relevant to the social world. Included are the processes of understanding the psychological qualities of the self and others, engaging in joint attention with others, and understanding other social cues and concepts.

What are four early signs that human infants are prepared to process social information?
Infants distinguish animate from inanimate objects, detect and follow the gaze of others, engage in *social referencing,* and begin to appreciate the goal-directed intentions of human agents.

What evidence supports the idea that early social behaviors are a form of core knowledge? What evidence supports the idea that early social behaviors are learned?
Infants show a special sensitivity to living things as well as the goal-directed actions of human agents. Because these behaviors are displayed so early in life, some researchers argue that they represent a form of innate, core knowledge. At the same time, other studies have demonstrated the role that learning and experience play in infants' understanding of goal-directed actions.

What kinds of changes have researchers observed in young children's ability to demonstrate representational insight?
By age three, children attain *representational insight,* the ability to use a symbol such as a photograph or scale model to stand for a real-world event.

Understanding Psychological States

What developmental changes in visual perspective taking have been identified by researchers?
Children first recognize that their own view is not identical to that of another person (Level 1). Later in development, about age

three or four years, they can determine the specifics of the other's view (Level 2).

What is meant by the child's "theory of mind"? What contrasting positions have been suggested as explanations for the development of theory of mind?
Theory of mind refers to the child's awareness of his or her own mental states, as well as the mental states of others. The child's attainment of this understanding is often tested with *false belief* tasks. In contrast to Piaget's claims for early childhood *realism*, children can distinguish between mental and physical phenomena in the preschool years. Some researchers feel that theory of mind is an innate, modular form of knowledge, whereas others claim it arises from the child's experiences with language.

What is childhood autism? What are some hypotheses about its causes?
Childhood autism is a disorder in which children display a lack of contact with the social world, which is manifested by communication deficits. Some researchers believe autism arises from the lack of a theory of mind. Others suggest that information-processing deficits, such as attention, memory, or executive control processes, are responsible. Still others feel that multiple kinds of cognitive deficits underlie autism.

Explain the concept of referential communication. How might this behavior be related to the child's "theory of mind"?
Referential communication refers to the child's ability to take into account the needs of the listener in communicative settings. This process logically involves understanding the contents of the listener's mind.

Cognition in a Social Context

What do research findings tell us about the role of skilled collaborators in promoting children's cognitive advances? How do scaffolding and guided participation contribute to this process?
Research shows that adults play a critical role in the transmission of skills, probably because they encourage children to be active and to think aloud. Novice learners often get more support or scaffolding from experts, but as their skills improve, that support is gradually withdrawn. The latter phenomenon is called *guided participation.*

What role do scripts play in children's memory?
Preschoolers have clearly formed *scripts* for common events; these are organized schemes that include the repeated general elements of those events. Preschoolers show evidence of using scripts to recall the details of stories they have heard.

What explanations have been offered for the emergence of autobiographical memory?
Few people can remember events that occurred prior to age three, a phenomenon called *infantile amnesia*. Improvements in memory for specific events in one's life, or *autobiographical memory*, are tied to the child's emerging verbal skills, a growing awareness of the self, and increasing understanding of the form of a narrative.

What has research told us about the reliability of eyewitness testimony among children?
Young children's memories, like adults', are vulnerable to the influence of misleading questions. In fact, children under age four years may be especially susceptible. Factors such as a perceived powerful questioner, the use of repeated questions, and the use of props can exacerbate the distortion of memory. Encouraging source monitoring can reduce the influence of leading questions.

Understanding Social Groups

When do children show the earliest signs of forming social categories?
Infants as young as six months of age show they are able to form social categories such as gender and race based on perceptual features of the faces they see.

What is meant by in-group preferences? When do children show signs of displaying these attitudes toward social groups?
In-group preferences refer to children's more positive reactions to groups to which they belong. Such preferences show up as early as six months of age.

What factors seem to promote the formation of in-group preferences? How might adults influence such attitudes toward social groups?
In-group preferences are more likely to form when social groups are made perceptually discriminable, when social categories are overtly labeled, when one group is clearly larger in number than another, and when adults' implicit attitudes about groups become obvious to children.

What does the research suggest about ways to break down instances of prejudice and discrimination? Why is this topic considered one that carries risks during the process of development?
Adults' implicit attitudes can influence children's own beliefs and behaviors, so the subtle behaviors that convey them might need to be changed. Formal lessons on the history of discrimination, as well as friendships across group boundaries, can also make a difference.

Key Terms and Concepts

autobiographical memory (p. 343)
false belief (p. 333)
guided participation (p. 339)
infantile amnesia (p. 342)
in-group preferences (p. 346)
intersubjectivity (p. 339)
realism (p. 332)
referential communication (p. 336)
representational insight (p. 329)
script (p. 342)
social cognition (p. 322)
social referencing (p. 323)
theory of mind (p. 332)

Media Resources

Access an integrated eBook and chapter-specific interactive learning tools, including flashcards, quizzes, videos, and more, in your Developmental Psychology CourseMate, accessed through CengageBrain.com.

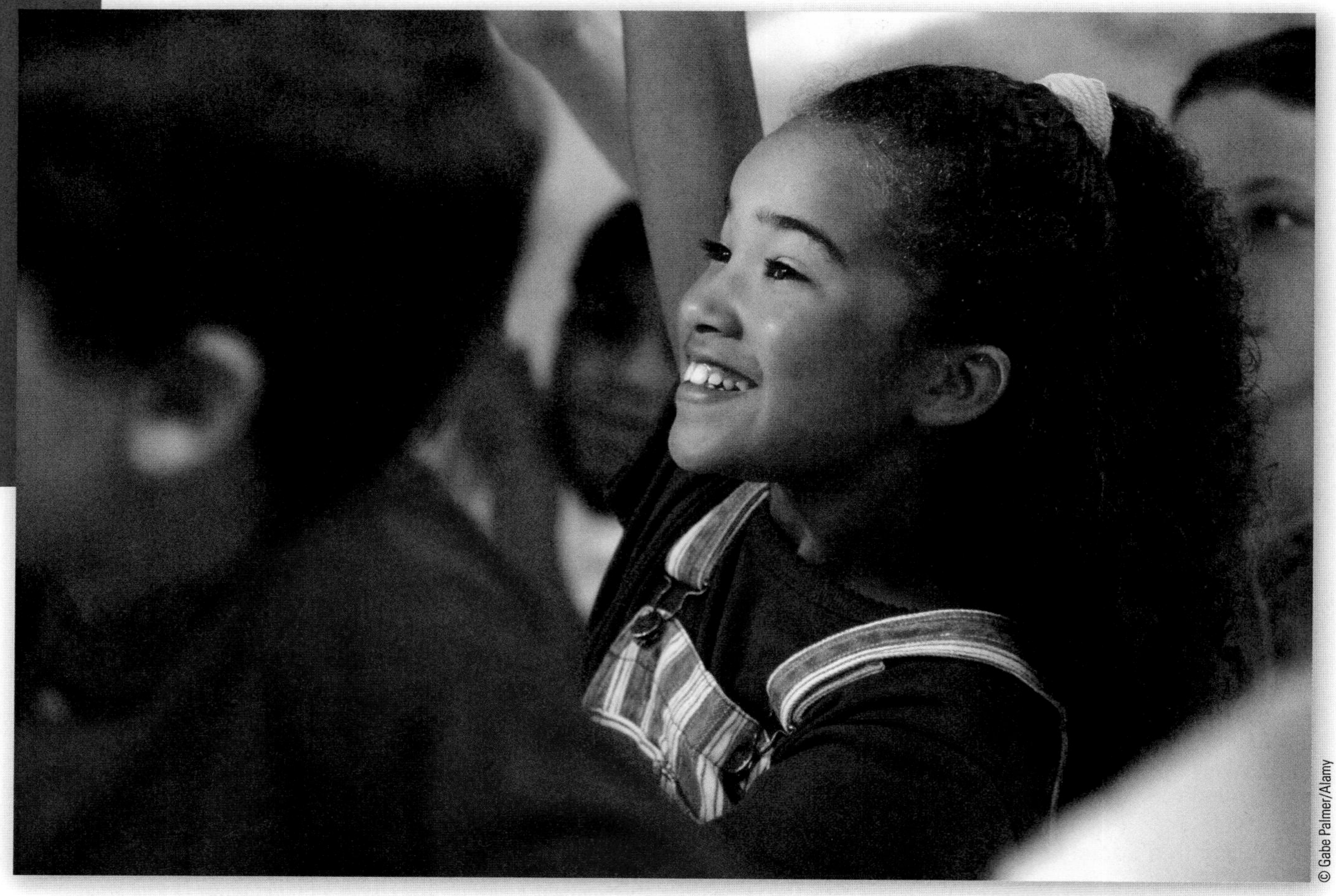
© Gabe Palmer/Alamy

CHAPTER OUTLINE

[chapter 10]

Achievement

KEY THEMES IN ACHIEVEMENT

- **NATURE & NURTURE** How do nature and nurture interact in children's achievement?
- **SOCIOCULTURAL INFLUENCE** How does the sociocultural context influence children's achievement?
- **INTERACTION AMONG DOMAINS** How does children's achievement interact with development in other domains?
- **RISK | RESILIENCE** What factors promote risk or resilience in children's achievement?

Lily stared intently at the school psychologist's desk. She was embarrassed to be stuck and especially embarrassed about the nature of the questions she was having trouble with. After three years in the United States, this ten-year-old was proud of the English she had learned. But she had been having serious problems with her reading and just couldn't stay focused on her work. The teacher had recommended to her parents that she be tested, but she really didn't understand what the test was for. She was relieved when the school psychologist announced that the test was done.

At lunchtime she approached Manuela, whom she considered to be an "expert" on American life because her family had lived in the States four years longer than Lily's family had. "What does *inscription* mean?" she asked Manuela.

"Oh, that's easy. It's words you write or carve on something, like a tombstone."

Lily was impressed but suspicious. "How did you know that?"

"It's the same as in Spanish: *inscripción*."

Manuela was acting so superior that Lily almost didn't want to confess her ignorance. When she asked her another question from the test, Manuela hooted with laughter. "Are you ever dumb! Don't you know anything? Everybody knows Christopher Columbus discovered America. We all knew that back in Chihuahua before we even moved here."

Lily's worst fears about herself had just been confirmed. Although the teacher and the school psychologist had tried to explain to her about the test she was to take, she had not really understood. Now she did. And at that moment the truth seemed all too plain to Lily: compared to Manuela, she was not intelligent and perhaps doomed to fail in school, a prospect she knew would be very upsetting to her parents. <<

Developmental scientists study the emergence of children's thinking for the purpose of learning how the human mind works. However, their findings also have relevance for understanding how we can optimize children's learning in school, a setting in which children are explicitly asked to remember, think conceptually and logically, and solve problems. The main aim of education is to provide children with the skills necessary to function as independent, responsible, and contributing members of society. Academic accomplishment and the development of cognitive skills are the chief points of emphasis. Societies vary in the extent to which they stress the experience of formal schooling; rural and agrarian subcultures in some countries, for example, do not have compulsory schooling. However, for most children growing up in the modern world, jobs in the professional and technical sectors will require that they have strong reading and writing skills as well as the ability to communicate, reason, and apply mathematical and scientific concepts. How can

Figure 10.1

High School Graduation Rates in the United States–2005

This figure shows the percent of students of different ethnic backgrounds estimated to graduate from public high schools in the United States in 2005. The percentage does not include students who eventually complete high school study through the General Education Development (GED) diploma or other routes.

Source: Data from Heckman, J. J., & LaFontaine, P. A. (2010). The American high school graduation rate: Trends and levels. *Review of Economics and Statistics, 92,* 244–262.

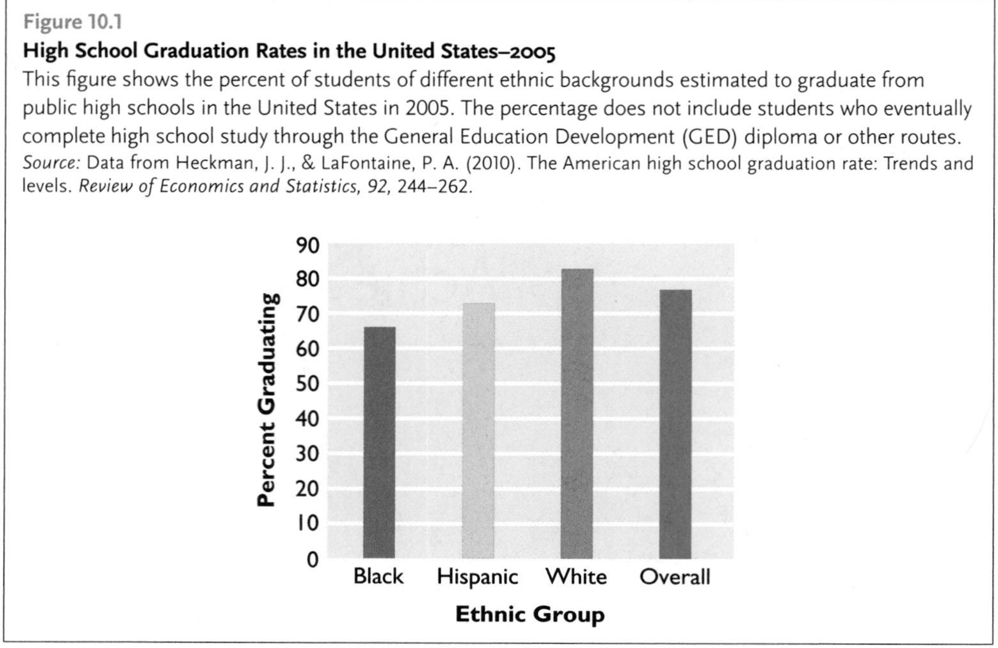

developmental science contribute to the effort to ensure that all children, including students like Lily who show signs of struggling in school, achieve at the highest levels?

In some measure, most children in the United States and many other countries attain the basic goals educators and parents have set for academic achievement in school. For example, in the United States, approximately 77 percent of young adults have completed high school. However, some would consider these completion rates to be unsatisfactory. Why do some students thrive in school and achieve at the highest levels while others find the challenges of school so difficult that they opt not to complete their education? How do individual differences in ability or learning styles contribute? What roles do factors outside of the cognitive domain, such as motivation and self-concepts, play? And how do children's experiences within the family and in school environments factor in? Moreover, high school completion rates are not the same for young adults of different ethnic backgrounds, as can be seen in Figure 10.1 (Heckman & LaFontaine, 2010). A major challenge for all of those concerned with the education of children is how to diminish this so-called *achievement gap.*

Adding to the concern are the results of major national and international surveys that often conclude that academic achievement among American students compares unfavorably with that of students from other industrialized countries. For example, by age seventeen, less than half of American students are judged as able to read and understand complicated information (Gonzales et al., 2000). The United States ranks below many countries in student performance on tests in science and mathematics, as indicated by the results of the Trends in International Mathematics and Science Study (TIMSS). This research project has included evaluations of academic performance by fourth-graders and eighth-graders in mathematics and science; the relative level of performance of the latter age group is shown in Figure 10.2. Because children in many East Asian and European nations perform better than those in the United States, the findings are among those that have created concern about children's learning in schools.

In this chapter, we consider the multiple factors that can contribute to children's achievement in educational settings. The research base on this topic is vast and spans a wide range of issues from characteristics of individuals to broader general concerns surrounding the behaviors of parents and teachers and the structures of schools (see Chapter 16), as well as the belief systems and values that characterize children's background cultures. We can only begin to scratch the surface in discussing a topic as broad as achievement. Nonetheless, it should quickly become apparent to you that developmental science has quite a bit to say about the factors that influence and can improve children's motivation and performance in schools.

Figure 10.2

International Comparisons of Mathematics and Science Achievement

This table presents the average scores of eighth-graders for the Trends in International Mathematics and Science Study conducted in 2007. The results have received considerable interest from educators and others concerned with the performance of students in the United States.

Source: Data from Gonzales, P., Williams, T., Jocelyn, L., Roey, S., Kastberg, D., and Brenwald, S. (2008). Highlights from TIMSS 2007: Mathematics and Science Achievement of U.S. Fourth- and Eighth-Grade Students in an International Context (NCES 2009–001 Revised). National Center for Education Statistics, Institute of Education Sciences, U.S. Department of Education. Washington, DC.

Average is higher than the U.S. average. Average is not measurably different from the U.S. average. Average is lower than the U.S. average.

Mathematics	Grade eight	Science	
Country	**Average score**	**Country**	**Average score**
TIMSS scale average	**500**	**TIMSS scale average**	**500**
Chinese Taipei	598	Singapore	567
Korea, Rep. of	597	Chinese Taipei	561
Singapore	593	Japan	554
Hong Kong SAR	572	Korea, Rep. of	553
Japan	570	England	542
Hungary	517	Hungary	539
England	513	Czech Republic	539
Russian Federation	512	Slovenia	538
United States	508	Russian Federation	530
Lithuania	508	Hong Kong SAR	530
Czech Republic	504	**United States**	520
Slovenia	501	Lithuania	519
Armenia	499	Australia	515
Australia	496	Sweden	511
Sweden	491	Scotland	496
Malta	488	Italy	495
Scotland	487	Armenia	488
Serbia	486	Norway	487
Italy	480	Ukraine	485
Malaysia	474	Jordan	482
Norway	469	Malaysia	471
Cyprus	465	Thailand	471
Bulgaria	464	Serbia	470
Israel	463	Bulgaria	470
Ukraine	462	Israel	468
Romania	461	Bahrain	467
Bosnia and Herzegovina	456	Bosnia and Herzegovina	466
Lebanon	449	Romania	462
Thailand	441	Iran, Islamic Rep. of	459
Turkey	432	Malta	457
Jordan	427	Turkey	454
Tunisia	420	Syrian Arab Republic	452
Georgia	410	Cyprus	452
Iran, Islamic Rep. of	403	Tunisia	445
Bahrain	398	Indonesia	427
Indonesia	397	Oman	423
Syrian Arab Republic	395	Georgia	421
Egypt	391	Kuwait	418
Algeria	387	Colombia	417
Colombia	380	Lebanon	414
Oman	372	Egypt	408
Palestinian Natl Auth.	367	Algeria	408
Botswana	364	Palestinian Natl Auth.	404
Kuwait	354	Saudi Arabia	403
El Salvador	340	El Salvador	387
Saudi Arabia	329	Botswana	355
Ghana	309	Qatar	319
Qatar	307	Ghana	303

Individual Differences in Ability

One factor that can influence academic achievement is the ability level children display when they engage in tasks that demand cognitive processing. Children and adults sometimes show noticeable differences in individual performance on tests of word meanings, general knowledge, and visual-spatial skill, a phenomenon that has been described by some psychologists in terms of the concept of intelligence. To the layperson, the term *intelligence* usually includes the abilities to reason logically, speak fluently, solve problems, learn efficiently, and display an interest in the world at large (Siegler & Richards, 1982; Sternberg et al., 1981). Most of us probably have a sense that the abilities to profit from experience and adapt to the environment are also part of intelligent human functioning. Yet despite the average person's ability to give what sounds like a reasonable description of intelligent behavior, in the field of psychology the formal definition of intelligence has proven surprisingly elusive. Although the concept has been the subject of research and theorizing for more than a century, no single definition has been commonly agreed on, and no one measurement tool assesses intelligence to everyone's satisfaction.

What Is Intelligence?

Among the many attempts to define intelligence, one prominent issue is whether intelligence is a unitary phenomenon or whether it consists of various separate skills and abilities. In the first view, an intelligent person has a global ability to reason and acquire knowledge that manifests itself in all sorts of ways, such as memorizing a long poem or solving a maze. Intelligence by this definition is a general characteristic that shows up in the multiple and varied observable behaviors and activities of any one person. In the second view, an intelligent person may possess specific talents in some areas but not in others and so, for instance, may be able to compose a sonata but be unable to solve a verbal reasoning problem. The various component skills of intelligence are seen as essentially independent, and each individual may have areas of strength and weakness.

A second major issue has been the best way to conceptualize intelligence. Should it be defined in terms of the *products* individuals generate, such as correct solutions to a series of mathematics problems or giving the precise definitions of words? Or should it be defined in terms of the *processes* people use to solve problems, such as the ability to integrate different pieces of information or to apply knowledge to new situations? The earliest theories about intelligence came from the *psychometric tradition*, which emphasized a product approach, quantifying individual differences in test scores to establish a rank order of capabilities among the participants tested. More recently, psychologists have put forth alternative ideas about the nature of intelligence based on theories about the cognitive processes people employ to acquire knowledge.

Psychometric Approaches The notion that human beings may differ from one another in certain skills originated in the late nineteenth century with the work of Sir Francis Galton. Galton (1883) believed people differ in their ability to discriminate among varying physical stimuli, such as auditory tones of different pitch, and in their speed of reaction to sensory stimuli. Such differences, according to Galton, are largely innate. Expanding on these ideas, James McKeen Cattell (1890) devised a series of psychophysical tests that assessed a person's ability to sense physical stimuli or perform different motor actions. It was Cattell who coined the term *mental test*. The first formal intelligence test was created in 1905 by Alfred Binet and Theodore Simon. Commissioned by the minister of public instruction in Paris to devise an instrument that would identify children who could not profit from the regular curriculum in the public schools due to lower mental abilities, Binet and Simon (1905) designed a test that assessed children's ability to reason verbally, solve simple problems, and think logically. With the Binet-Simon test, the mental testing movement was born, and psychometrics became firmly entrenched as a model for understanding intelligence.

Psychometric models of intelligence are based on the testing of large groups of individuals to quantify differences in abilities. The basic assumption is that some people will perform better than others and that those who perform below some average or normative level are less intelligent, whereas those who perform above that level are more intelligent. Within the general psychometric framework, however, theorists have taken contrasting positions on the exact nature of intelligence. Charles Spearman (1904) believed that intelligence consists of two parts: *g*, a general intelligence factor that he equated with "mental energy," and various *s*'s, specific knowledge and abilities such as verbal reasoning or spatial problem solving that are evident only in certain tasks. According to Spearman, *g* is a central aspect of any task requiring cognitive activity and accounts for commonalities in levels of performance that people typically demonstrate in various kinds of intellectual tasks. Thus, the influence of *g* might enable a person to obtain a high score on a verbal test, as well as on a test of visual-spatial skill.

In contrast, Louis Thurstone (1938) believed that intelligence is composed of several distinct fundamental capabilities that are completely independent of one another. He proposed that the following seven *primary mental abilities* are components of intelligence: *visual comprehension*, as measured by vocabulary and reading comprehension tests; *word fluency*, the ability to generate a number of words (for example, those beginning with *b*) in a short period of time; *number facility*, the ability to solve arithmetic problems; *spatial visualization*, the mental manipulation of geometric forms or symbols; *memory*, the ability to recall lists of words, sentences, or pictures; *reasoning*, the ability to solve analogies or other problems involving formal relations; and *perceptual speed*, the ability to recognize symbols rapidly.

Another way that intelligence has been conceptualized within the psychometric tradition has been put forth by Raymond Cattell and John Horn. According to their perspective, a distinction can be made between two types of intelligence, each with a unique developmental course (Cattell, 1971; Horn, 1968; Horn & Cattell, 1967). **Fluid intelligence** consists of biologically based mental abilities that are relatively free of cultural influence, such as the ability to remember a list of words or to group abstract figures together. **Crystallized intelligence** consists of skills one acquires as a result of living in a specific culture, such as knowledge of vocabulary, reading comprehension, or general information about the world. Cattell and Horn believed that fluid intelligence is tied to physiological maturation and that it increases until adolescence, when it levels off, and then declines in later adulthood. On the other hand, they hypothesized that crystallized intelligence increases over much of the life span because individuals continually acquire knowledge from the cultural groups in which they live. Researchers have found that fluid intelligence does eventually decline with age, especially after ages seventy to eighty. Crystallized intelligence increases through the middle adult years but also declines with aging, although on a somewhat slower trajectory than fluid intelligence (Kaufman, 2001; McArdle et al., 2002).

NATURE & NURTURE

SOCIOCULTURAL INFLUENCE

Intelligence as Speed of Processing Alternative theoretical ideas about intelligence are derived directly from the information-processing model of cognition. Rather than identifying the structures of mental ability, as the psychometricians did, information-processing theorists have focused on describing the mental processes necessary to accomplish different types of tasks.

Individuals vary in the speed with which they conduct certain cognitive activities. For example, consider a typical *choice reaction-time* task. A participant sits in front of an apparatus that contains eight lights, her finger resting on a "home" button. As soon as one of the eight lights comes on, the participant must move her finger to a button below that light to turn it off. People show notable differences in the speed with which they carry out this task. Several researchers have proposed that such individual differences in speed of processing information may be related to intelligence, particularly *g*, the general intelligence originally described by Spearman (Jensen, 1982; Vernon, 1983).

psychometric model Theoretical perspective that quantifies individual differences in test scores to establish a rank order of abilities.

fluid intelligence Biologically based mental abilities that are relatively uninfluenced by cultural experiences.

crystallized intelligence Mental skills derived from cultural experience.

According to Cattell and Horn, *crystallized intelligence* consists of skills that are acquired as the result of living in a specific culture. These Ugandan schoolgirls, for example, are learning to make baskets, a skill that is not likely to be acquired by children living in highly industrialized countries.

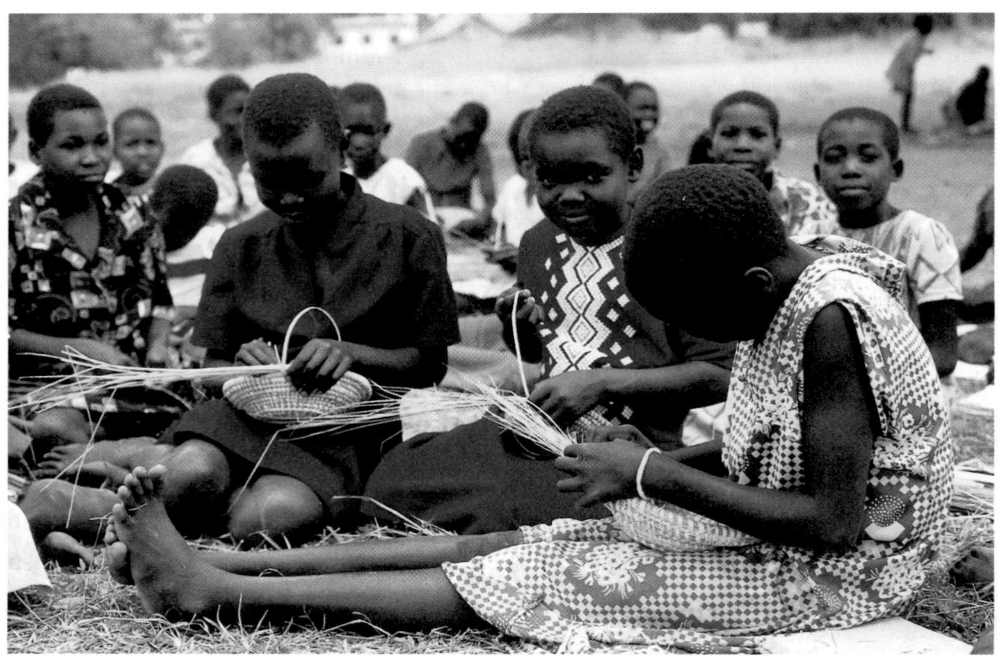

© Betty Press

Is there evidence that speed of information processing is a component of intelligence? Some relevant findings come from the results of the *Fagan Test of Infant Intelligence,* designed for infants between six and twelve months old and based on infants' recognition memory capabilities. During the test, the child sits on the parent's lap and views a picture for a predetermined period of time. The familiar picture is then presented alongside a novel one, and the infant's looking time to the novel stimulus is recorded. As you saw in Chapter 8, "Cognition," infants show their "memory" for the familiar stimulus by looking longer at the new item. In the test, several of these "novelty problems" are presented in succession. Infants show individual differences in the speed with which they acquire information about familiar items to the extent that their response to novelty is depressed. In one study, scores infants obtained on the Fagan Test of Infant Intelligence correlated in the range of +.44 to +.47 with their scores on several standard tests of intelligence at age eight years (Smith, Fagan, & Ulvund, 2002). Furthermore, a series of studies found that if infants directed less than 53 percent of their visual fixations to the novel stimuli, they were especially likely to fall into the category of "intellectually delayed" (Fagan & Montie, 1988). All of these findings suggest a role for the concept of speed of processing in understanding intelligence.

NATURE & NURTURE

RISK | RESILIENCE

Among older children and adults, researchers have observed at least moderate relationships between reaction-time measures and scores on standardized tests of intelligence (Jensen, 1982; Vernon, 1983); these relationships are weaker among young children (Miller & Vernon, 1996). It is important to keep in mind, though, that individuals may differ in their processing speed because of variations in motivation and attention to the task rather than differences in intellectual ability. Some participants in the choice reaction-time task may be distracted by the equipment in the experimental room or may become anxious, and hence slower, in their attempts to do their best. Because reaction times are measured in fractions of a second, they are particularly vulnerable to these types of disruptions. In addition, different cultures and ethnic groups place varying emphases on the value of speed in mental processes. In our own Western culture, we place high priority on getting things done quickly, but the same may not be true for cultures in which time is not a major factor in daily routines. A person who does not have a heightened consciousness of time and speed may not choose to perform mental tasks rapidly, even when he or she has the capability to do so (Marr & Sternberg, 1987). Finally, not all intelligent problem solving is done in a speedy way. Consider the problem of deciding on a career or whom to marry. Rushing to

SOCIOCULTURAL INFLUENCE

Figure 10.3
The Triarchic Theory of Intelligence
According to Robert Sternberg, intelligence has three major facets, or "subtheories," all based on the individual's ability to process information.

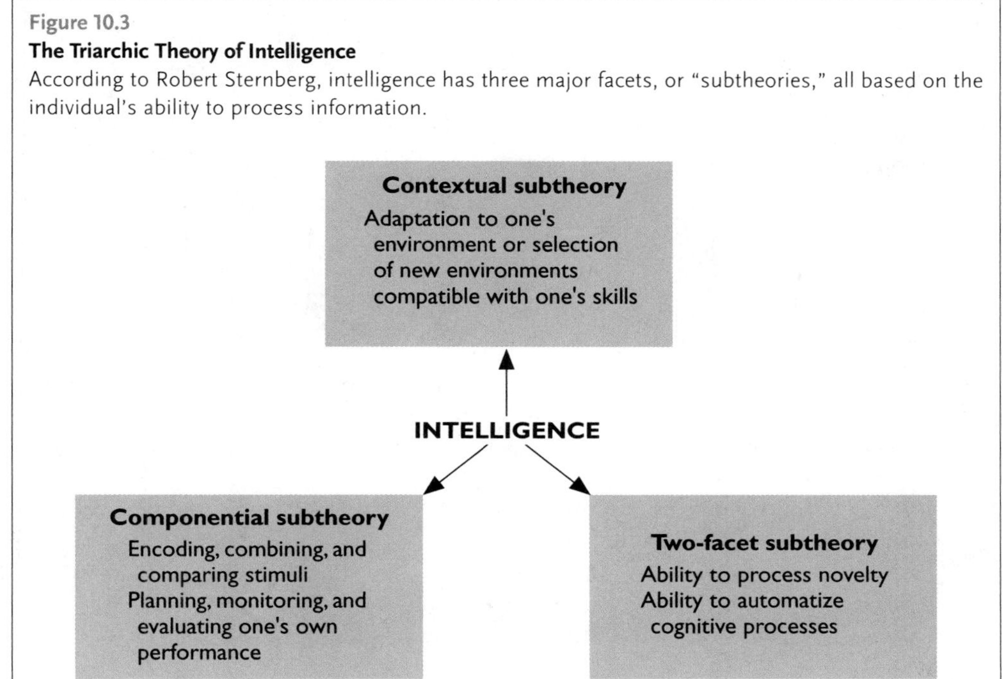

a solution can hardly be considered "smart" in these situations (Sternberg, 1982). Thus, we must be cautious in concluding that speed of processing is the only essential ingredient in intelligence.

Intelligence and Working Memory A promising approach to understanding intelligence examines individual differences in working memory. Recall from Chapter 8 that working memory involves a short-term psychological "work space" in which complex (and sometimes multiple) tasks are performed on incoming information. Individuals might be asked to read and confirm the truth value of a sentence and also to remember the last word in the sentence, for example. Researchers have reported that successful performance on working memory tasks is related to intelligence test scores and is also linked to specific patterns of brain activity in the parietal and occipital lobes (Van Rooy et al., 2001). Other research suggests that the capacity of working memory is an even better predictor of intelligence test scores than processing speed (Conway et al., 2002). Working memory probably involves some form of attentional control, the ability to regulate the amount of cognitive resources to perform the components of a complex task (Engle, 2002; Miyake et al., 2001). Some researchers postulate that individual differences in this ability represent an element of *g*, the concept of general intelligence identified by Spearman (Engle, Kane, & Tuholski, 1999).

Sternberg's Triarchic Theory of Intelligence Robert Sternberg (1985) has proposed a broad contemporary theory of intelligence based on the principles of information processing. The **triarchic theory** of intelligence (see Figure 10.3) consists of three major subtheories that describe mental functioning.

SOCIOCULTURAL INFLUENCE

The first of these subtheories, called the *contextual subtheory*, asserts that intelligence must be considered as an adaptation to the unique environment in which the individual lives. This means, for example, that we would not administer an intelligence test designed for children in the United States to children from a completely different culture, such as that of the Australian aborigines. In Sternberg's words, intelligence consists of "purposive adaptation to, and selection and shaping of, real-world environments relevant to one's life" (1985, p. 45).

triarchic theory Theory developed by Robert Sternberg that intelligence consists of three major components: (1) the ability to adapt to the environment, (2) the ability to employ fundamental information-processing skills, and (3) the ability to deal with novelty and automatize processing.

The contextual subtheory of Sternberg's triarchic theory of intelligence describes an individual's ability to adapt to the demands of the environment. Some cultures, for example, stress verbal abilities and literacy, but these skills may not be equally emphasized in other environments.

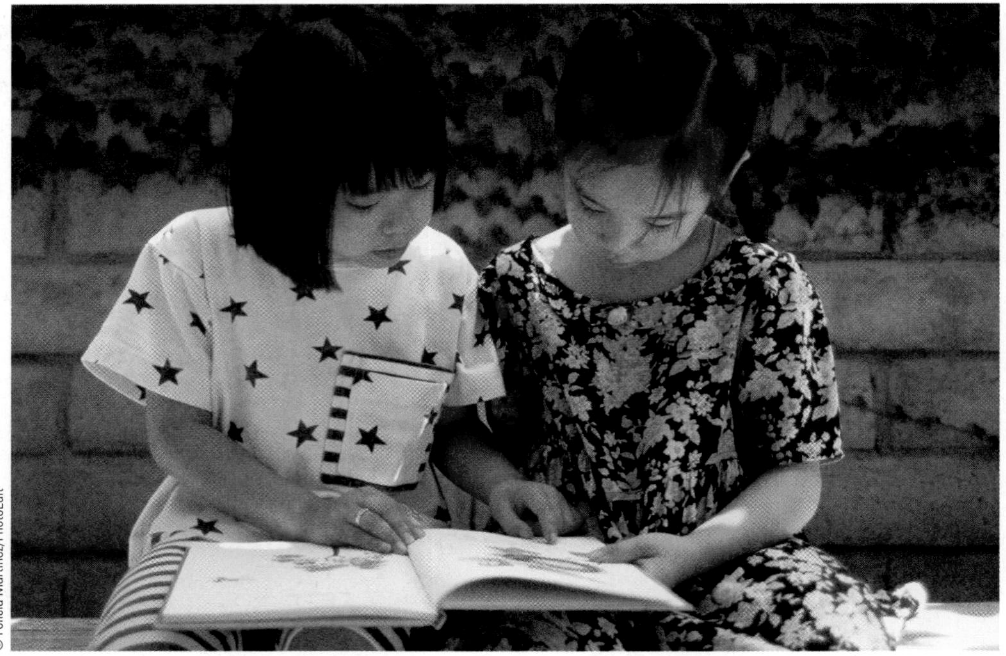

Intelligent people are thus able to meet the specific demands their environment places on them—by learning to hunt if their culture requires that skill or by perfecting reading or mathematical skills in societies that stress formal education. By the same token, intelligent people will change their environment to utilize their unique skills and abilities most effectively. For instance, changing jobs or moving to a different locale may demonstrate what Sternberg calls "successful intelligence," which may be equally as important as or more important than "academic intelligence" (Sternberg, 2001).

The *componential subtheory* focuses on the internal mental processes involved in intelligent functioning, including the ability to encode, combine, and compare stimuli—the basic aspects of the information-processing system. Other components of the componential subtheory are higher-order mental processes, such as relating new information to what one already knows. Finally, the ability to plan, monitor, and evaluate one's performance—the metacognitive activities we described in Chapter 8—is also part of intelligent functioning. Thus, Sternberg stresses how individuals acquire knowledge rather than what they know as indicators of intelligence.

The *two-facet subtheory* describes intelligent individuals in terms of (1) their ability to deal with novelty and (2) their tendency to automatize cognitive processes. Devising a creative solution to an unfamiliar problem or figuring out how to get around in a foreign country are examples of coping successfully with novelty. Automatization takes place when the individual has learned initially unfamiliar routines so well that executing them requires little conscious effort. Learning to read is a good example of this process. The beginning reader concentrates on the sounds symbolized by groups of letters and is very aware of the process of decoding a string of letters. The advanced reader scans groups of words effortlessly and may not even be aware of his mental activities while in the act of reading.

By including practical abilities, analytical abilities, and creative abilities, the triarchic theory captures the enormous breadth and complexity of what it means to be intelligent (Sternberg, 1998; Sternberg & Kaufman, 1998). Sternberg believes it is difficult to assess this human quality with one measure or test score because such a number would mask the extremely different patterns of abilities that individuals show. One child may have exceptional componential skills but behave maladaptively in her environment. Another may be highly creative in tackling novel problems but show poor componential skills.

Gardner's Theory of Multiple Intelligences Howard Gardner defines intelligence as "an ability (or skill) to solve problems or to fashion products which are valued within one or more cultural settings" (1986, p. 74). Like Sternberg, Gardner believes that information-processing abilities are at the core of intelligence. Gardner's (1983, 1998) emphasis, though, is on the idea that people often show marked individual differences in their ability to process specific kinds of information. Accordingly, he identified the following eight distinct intelligences:

- *Linguistic:* Sensitivity to the meanings and order of words, as well as the functions of language
- *Musical:* Sensitivity to pitch, tone, and timbre, as well as musical patterns
- *Logico-mathematical:* The ability to handle chains of reasoning, numerical relations, and hierarchical relations
- *Spatial:* The capacity to perceive the world accurately and to transform and re-create perceptions
- *Bodily-kinesthetic:* The ability to use one's body or to work with objects in highly differentiated and skillful ways
- *Intrapersonal:* The capacity to understand one's own feelings and use them to guide behavior
- *Interpersonal:* The ability to notice and make distinctions among the moods, temperaments, motivations, and intentions of others
- *Naturalistic:* The ability to distinguish among, classify, and see patterns in aspects of the natural environment.

According to Gardner's theory of multiple intelligences, children may show exceptional abilities in some domains but not others. Among the eight types of intelligence he hypothesizes is musical intelligence, a sensitivity to pitch, tone, timbre, and musical patterns.

Gardner claims support for the existence of these discrete areas of intelligence on several fronts. For each skill, he says, it is possible to find people who excel or show genius, such as Mozart, T. S. Eliot, and Einstein. It is also possible, in many instances, to show a loss of or a deficit in a specific ability due to damage to particular areas of the brain. Lesions to the parts of the left cortex specifically dedicated to language function, for example, produce a loss of linguistic intelligence. Yet the other intelligences usually remain intact. Finally, it is possible to identify a core of information-processing operations uniquely relevant to each area. For musical intelligence, one core process is sensitivity to pitch. For bodily-kinesthetic intelligence, it is the ability to imitate the movement made by another person.

How does each of the intelligences develop? Gardner believes propensities or talents in certain areas may be inborn, but the child's experiences are also of paramount importance. Some children, for example, may show a unique ability to remember melodies, but all children would profit from exposure to musical sequences. Moreover, Gardner reminds us that it is important to remember the cultural values to which the child is exposed. In our culture, linguistic and logico-mathematical skills are highly valued and are emphasized as measures of school success. Among the Puluwat islanders of the South Pacific, the navigational skills required for successful sailing are critical, and hence spatial intelligence receives great recognition in that culture.

Gardner's theory has appealed to many educators and parents in its positive emphasis on each child's unique talents. Some researchers caution, though, that more independent empirical evidence is necessary before we can accept its key tenets and assumptions (Klein, 1997).

Figure 10.4
How Intelligence Is Distributed in the General Population
Intelligence scores are assumed to be normally distributed in the population, with a mean score of 100. Most people's scores fall within 15 points (or one standard deviation) above or below the mean, and almost the entire population falls within three standard deviation units of the mean. In reality, a slightly greater number of individuals than we would theoretically expect fall at the lower end of the distribution, probably due to genetic, prenatal, or early postnatal risks that can affect intelligence.

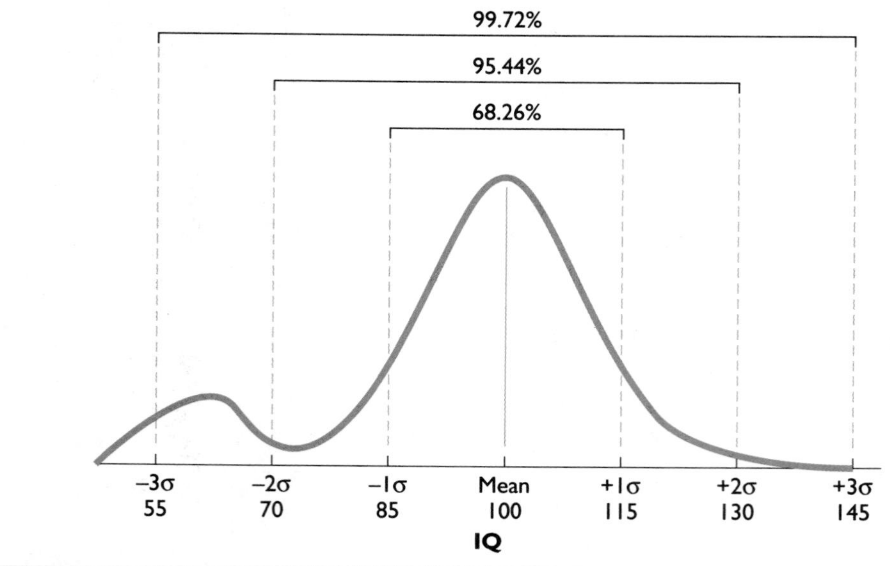

Measuring Intelligence

Over the years, we have come to use the term *IQ* as a synonym for intelligence. In fact, the abbreviation IQ means **intelligence quotient** and refers only to the score a person obtains on the standardized intelligence tests now fairly widely used in Western societies. The results of these tests have become so closely associated with intelligence as an attribute of human functioning that we have virtually ceased to make a distinction between them. Yet, as we may suspect from the opening scene describing Lily, the IQ score may or may not be a good indicator of intelligent functioning.

The Distribution of IQ Scores Standardized tests of intelligence are based on many shared assumptions about how this characteristic is distributed among individuals. As Figure 10.4 shows, IQ scores are assumed to be normally distributed in the population, with the majority falling in the middle of the distribution and fewer at the upper and lower extremes. The average or *mean* IQ score on most tests is 100. Usually a statistical measure of the average variability of scores around the mean, or *standard deviation*, is also calculated. The standard deviation gives a picture of how clustered or spread out the scores are around the mean. On many tests, the standard deviation has a value of 15.

The normal distribution of scores can also be partitioned into "standard deviation units." As Figure 10.4 shows, the majority of IQ scores (about 68 percent) fall within one standard deviation on either side of the mean, and almost all scores in the population (about 99 percent) fall within three standard deviations above or below the mean. In reality, the percentage of scores below the mean is slightly greater than the theoretical normal distribution would predict. This fact is probably

intelligence quotient (IQ) Numerical score received on an intelligence test.

the result of genetic, prenatal, or early postnatal factors that can put young infants at risk for lower intellectual development (Vandenberg & Vogler, 1985; Zigler, 1967).

RISK | RESILIENCE

IQ Tests Educators, clinicians, and others who must assess and diagnose children have a number of standardized tests to choose from. Usually intelligence tests are administered in special situations, such as when parents or teachers suspect that a child is unusually gifted. Alternatively, there may be a need to assess a child whose schoolwork falls below the level of other children in the class, as in the case of Lily described at the beginning of this chapter. Does the child have a learning disability (which is usually accompanied by normal intellectual functioning), or is the child's general ability to learn impaired? Are there other reasons (for example, emotional factors) why the child is not performing well? A special educational plan designed to meet the needs of the student may then be implemented. Intelligence tests may also be employed to assess the developmental progress of children who are at risk for any number of reasons; perhaps they were premature at birth or suffered some trauma that could affect their ability to learn. Although many children will not have the experience of taking an IQ test, a variety of special circumstances may dictate administering such a test.

How are IQ tests designed? *Psychometricians*, psychologists who specialize in the construction and interpretation of tests, typically administer a new test to a large sample of individuals during the test construction phase, both to assess the test's *reliability* and *validity* (see Chapter 2, "Studying Child Development") and to establish the norms of performance against which to compare other individuals. A central concern is to ensure that each item included in the test is related to the overall concept being measured, in this case, intelligence. Moreover, if the test is valid, the scores obtained should be related to scores on other, similar tests. Needless to say, the business of designing intelligence tests requires careful thought and skill. Some intelligence tests are designed to be administered to individual children; others can be given to large groups. Ethical standards dictate that psychologists be carefully trained in both the administration and scoring of IQ tests before being permitted to administer them.

Most tests of infant intelligence are based on norms for behaviors that are expected to occur in the first year or two of life. Because most of the infant's accomplishments are in the domains of motor, language, and socioemotional development, these areas appear most frequently on the various tests. Almost without exception, the tests are administered individually to infants. Perhaps the most widely used infant test is the *Bayley Scales of Infant and Toddler Development*, originally designed by Nancy Bayley (2005) to predict later childhood competence. The test consists of several scales. The Cognitive and Language scales assess the young child's sensory and perceptual skills, memory, learning, acquisition of the object concept, and linguistic skill. The Motor Scale measures the child's ability to control and coordinate the body, from large motor skills to finer manipulation of the hands and fingers. Table 10.1 shows some sample items from each scale. Designed for infants from one through forty-two months of age, the test yields a *developmental index* for both the mental and the motor scale. That is, the infant's scores are compared with the scores for the standardization sample (the large sample of normal infants whose performance was assessed at the time the test was developed) and are expressed in terms of how much they deviate from the average scores of that sample. The Bayley scales also contain a Behavior Rating Scale to assess the infant's interests, emotions, and general level of activity compared with the standardization sample.

One of the more widely used individually administered intelligence tests for school-age children is the *Wechsler Intelligence Scale for Children*, scaled for use with children ages six through sixteen years. The original version was constructed in 1949 by David Wechsler and most recently revised in 2003. The revised version, called the WISC-IV, contains five scales: (1) the Verbal Comprehension Scale, which assesses the child's ability to understand and use words to express thinking; (2) the Perceptual Reasoning Scale, which includes tests of nonverbal reasoning skills; (3) the Working Memory Scale, which appraises attention and retention skills; (4) the Processing Speed Scale, which requires children to scan symbols and make decisions about them; and (5) the Full Scale IQ, which represents a composite

TABLE 10.1 Sample Items from the Bayley Scales of Infant and Toddler Development

Age	Cognitive/Language Scales	Motor Scale
2 months	Turns head to sound Plays with rattle Reacts to disappearance of face	Holds head erect and steady for 15 seconds Turns from side to back Sits with support
6 months	Lifts cup by handle Looks for fallen spoon Looks at pictures in book	Sits alone for 30 seconds Turns from back to stomach Grasps foot with hands
12 months	Builds tower of 2 cubes Turns pages of book	Walks with help Throws ball Grasps pencil in middle
17–19 months	Imitates crayon stroke Identifies objects in photograph	Stands alone on right foot Walks up stairs with help
23–25 months	Matches pictures Uses pronoun(s) Imitates a 2-word sentence	Laces 3 beads Jumps distance of 4 inches Walks on tiptoe for 4 steps
38–42 months	Names 4 colors Uses past tense Identifies gender	Copies circle Hops twice on 1 foot Walks down stairs, alternating feet

Source: Bayley Scales of Infant and Toddler Development. "Bayley Scales of Infant Development" is a registered trademark of The Psychological Corporation.

Figure 10.5

Sample Items from the Wechsler Intelligence Scale for Children-IV

Shown here are two items similar to those that appear on the Perceptual Reasoning Scale of the WISC-IV. This particular scale measures children's ability to think and solve problems without using words. In the first example, children are to complete the sequence based on the other items in the array. In the second example, children must select the two items that belong to the same category.

Source: http://psychcorp.pearsonassessments.com/HAIWEB/Cultures/en-us/Productdetail.htm?Pid=015-8979-044.

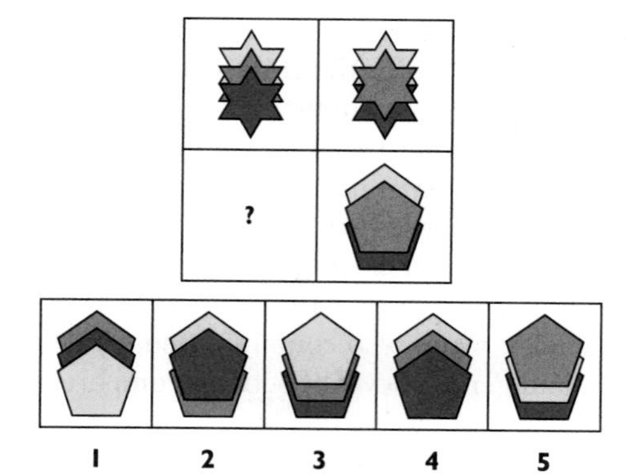

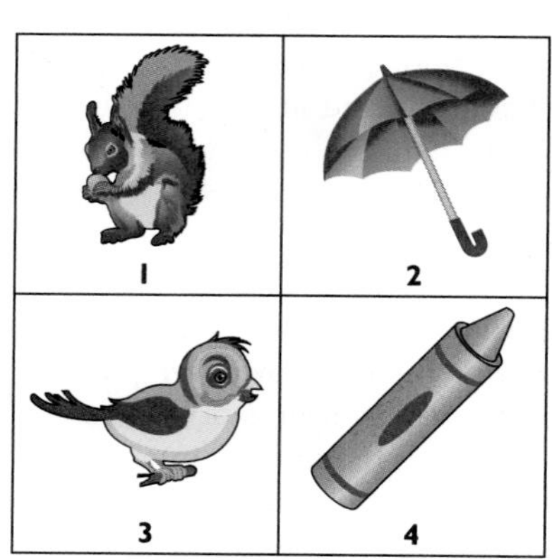

of all of the scales. Thus, this test allows the examiner to assess patterns of strength and weakness in the child's mental abilities. The child's score on the WISC-IV is computed on the basis of the **deviation IQ**, a measure that is computed by comparing the child's score with a standardization sample of similar-age children. Figure 10.5 shows some items resembling those from the WISC-IV.

deviation IQ IQ score computed by comparing the child's performance with that of a standardization sample.

atypical development | Giftedness

A small number of children measure well above the scores that most children obtain on intelligence tests—in some cases, two standard deviations or more above the mean. According to the U.S. Department of Education (1993), these gifted children show "high performance capability in intellectual, creative, and/or artistic areas, possess an unusual leadership capacity, or excel in specific academic fields." Gifted children may already display remarkably high levels of performance compared with other children of similar age or background experiences, or they may show the potential to perform at those high levels. Although unusual talent has been measured traditionally by IQ scores, more contemporary views provide alternative ways of understanding giftedness.

For example, drawing on his triarchic theory of intelligence, Robert Sternberg (1981, 1986) has demonstrated that gifted children show several unique information-processing skills. First, when solving problems, they tend to spend much of their time in planning—selecting and organizing strategies and information, for example—and less time in encoding the details stated in the problem. That is, their approach tends to be more "global" than "local," reflecting greater metacognitive skills, an idea that has received support in several studies of gifted children (Alexander, Carr, & Schwanenflugel, 1995). Second, Sternberg hypothesizes that gifted children are better able to deal with novelty and to automatize their information processing. Given novel, unusual insight problems, for example, gifted children are better able than children of average ability to recognize useful strategies for solutions (Sternberg, 1986).

Gifted children are also apparently more efficient and speedier in processing stimuli that match their particular talents. Veronica Dark and Camilla Benbow (1993) asked extremely gifted seventh- and eighth-graders to judge, as quickly as they could, whether two stimuli were the same or different. When the stimuli were digits, the response patterns of students most gifted in mathematics showed faster access to numerical representations than those of other children. The response patterns of students most gifted in verbal skills showed faster access to verbal representations when the stimuli were words. Based on their analyses of many studies of giftedness, Dark and Benbow concluded that the difference between gifted and other children is not qualitative; rather, it is simply a matter of degree, in this case, the degree to which basic cognitive skills are used quickly and efficiently.

What else do we know about the characteristics of gifted children? One of the most extensive studies was conducted by Lewis Terman beginning in 1921 (Terman, 1954; Terman & Oden, 1959). More than 1,000 children with IQ scores of 140 or greater were studied longitudinally from early adolescence into their adult years. Contrary to popular stereotypes, they were not frail, sickly, antisocial, "bookish" types. They tended to be taller than average, were physically healthy, and often assumed positions of leadership among their peers. By the time they were young adults, about 70 percent of those in the sample had completed college (a very high proportion for that generation), and many had obtained advanced degrees. The majority entered professional occupations in which they became very productive as adults—authoring books, plays, and scientific articles, for example. Unfortunately, however, because the children in Terman's sample were nominated by their teachers, gifted children who were quieter or did not fit a teacher's conception of a "good student" were probably overlooked. Thus, Terman's results must be viewed with caution.

Other more recent research has found that gifted children take advantage of accelerated educational opportunities and are far more likely to pursue postgraduate degrees than is the norm. They generally show healthy peer relationships, have good self-concepts, are well adjusted, and express high career and life satisfaction in their adult lives (Lubinski et al., 2001, 2006). Those at the extreme end of the continuum, though, are more likely to be socially isolated and feel unhappy, probably because they are so different from their peers and have trouble "fitting in" (Robinson & Clinkenbeard, 1998; Winner, 1996, 1997).

NATURE & NURTURE

Does giftedness simply reveal itself naturally during the childhood years? Not according to other researchers examining the underpinnings of exceptional talent. In one study, two children who were expert chess players and one who was an accomplished musician were found to spend many hours practicing their skills under the tutelage of special teachers (Feldman, 1979). In another study, world-class musicians, mathematicians, and athletes reported that their childhood years were marked by strong encouragement of their early natural abilities. Parents, coaches, and teachers were important sources of motivation, and typically these talented individuals spent years in intensive training of their skills (Bloom, 1982). Because of the exceptional drive and hard work that are involved in achieving high levels of success, most gifted children do not become unusually accomplished or eminent adults (Winner, 1997). A special concern for many researchers and educators is that the talents of gifted children be nurtured so that their potential can be realized (Winner, 2000).

What Does IQ Predict?

IQ tests do a good job of telling us which children will be successful in school and which will have difficulties. Most studies have found that the correlations between intelligence tests and measures of educational achievement average about .50, with the correlations slightly higher for elementary school children than for high school or college students (Brody & Brody, 1976; Jensen, 1980). In addition, the correlations are strongest with academic subjects that emphasize verbal skills, such as reading (Horn & Packard, 1985). One reason IQ scores predict school achievement so successfully is that many of the skills assessed in intelligence tests overlap with the skills essential to educational success. Verbal fluency, the ability to solve arithmetic problems, and rote memory—some of the abilities IQ tests measure—are part of most children's school routines. Thus, IQ tests predict best exactly what Binet originally designed them to foretell.

Do IQ tests predict any developmental outcomes other than school success? As we saw above in our discussion of giftedness, IQ scores are related to job status during adulthood. Terman's longitudinal study of children with IQs of 140 or higher (Terman, 1925; Terman & Oden, 1959) found that many of these exceptionally bright individuals eventually became scientists, executives, and college faculty members. As usual, however, we must be cautious about how we interpret correlational data. As we saw earlier, IQ scores are strongly related to educational achievement. They are also related to how many years an individual will actually spend in school (Neisser et al., 1996). It may be that occupational success is the result of education and not a direct outcome of IQ (Ceci & Williams, 1997; Fulker & Eysenck, 1979; Jencks, 1972).

Aside from these relationships, do IQ scores predict other measures of success in life? Social scientists disagree. According to some, IQ scores predict economic status in adulthood (Herrnstein & Murray, 1994); others claim that IQ scores do not necessarily forecast the amount of money an individual earns, physical or mental health, job satisfaction, or general life satisfaction (Lewis, 1983; McClelland, 1973; Sternberg, 1995). The debate abounds with disagreements about the proper use of statistical techniques as well as whether various measures of IQ are valid (Fraser, 1995). Suffice it to say that this topic has strong roots in the nature–nurture controversy. Generally, advocates of a nature position believe intelligence is a stable trait that affects later developmental outcomes, whereas those who favor a nurture position believe intelligence is malleable, depending on the quality of a child's experiences, and thus may not reliably forecast long-term future outcomes.

NATURE & NURTURE

Group Differences in IQ Scores

Children from different socioeconomic and ethnic backgrounds do not perform equally well on traditional IQ tests. One finding has been that African American children in the United States typically score fifteen points lower than Caucasian children on tests such as the WISC (Jensen, 1980; Loehlin, Lindzey, & Spuhler, 1975). This difference in scores has diminished over the past thirty years, however, by up to seven points according to some estimates (Dickens & Flynn, 2006). Another finding is that children from lower socioeconomic classes obtain lower IQ scores than those from middle and upper classes (Deutsch,

Katz, & Jensen, 1968; Lesser, Fifer, & Clark, 1965). Of the many hypotheses put forward about the sources of these differences, some have rekindled the nature–nurture debate, and others have focused on the validity of IQ tests for children who come from diverse backgrounds.

NATURE & NURTURE

Race, IQ, and Nature Versus Nurture In 1969, Arthur Jensen published a paper suggesting that racial differences in IQ scores could, in large part, be accounted for by heredity. According to Jensen, there is a high degree of *heritability* in IQ; that is, about 80 percent of the variation in IQ scores in the population could be explained by genetic variation. He argued that, because racial and ethnic subgroups within the population tend not to marry outside their groups, African American–Caucasian differences in IQ scores have a strong genetic component.

Jensen's propositions created a storm of controversy, one that reemerged as a result of similar claims made a few decades later by Richard Herrnstein and Charles Murray (1994). One of the most immediate criticisms of these researchers' arguments was that within-group estimates of heritability cannot be used to explain between-group differences in performance. Even if the heritability of IQ were .80 for both Caucasian and African American populations (actually, the heritability estimates for IQ were derived solely from samples of Caucasian children and their families), other factors, such as differences in the environmental experiences of each group, could not be ruled out in explaining racial differences in IQ scores (Loehlin et al., 1975). For example, a fifteen-point difference in IQ could still arise if most Caucasian children grew up in enriched environments and most African American children experienced environments that did not promote optimal intellectual development.

NATURE & NURTURE

A *cross-fostering study* by Sandra Scarr and Richard Weinberg (1976, 1978, 1983) that examined children who were raised in environments markedly different from those of their biological families demonstrated just how this effect might take place. In their transracial adoption study, Scarr and Weinberg selected 101 Caucasian middle-class families that had adopted African American children, most of whom were under one year of age at the time of adoption. Many of these families also had biological children of their own. The adoptive families were highly educated, were above average in occupational status and income, and had high IQ scores. The biological families of the adopted children had lower educational levels and lower-status occupations. Scarr and Weinberg found that the average IQ among the African American adopted children was 106, higher than the average score of both African American children and those in the general population. The researchers argued that, because the adopted children were raised in environments that exposed them to Caucasian culture and the verbal and cognitive skills customarily assessed in IQ tests, they performed better than African American children with similar genetic backgrounds who did not have that experience. At the same time, however, the IQs of the adopted children were more strongly correlated with the educational levels of their biological parents ($r = 0.36$) than with the IQs of their adoptive parents ($r = 0.19$). Thus, some role involving heredity cannot be ruled out either.

Many researchers reject a genetic explanation of racial differences in IQ as too simplistic. We saw in Chapter 3, "Genetics and Heredity," that heredity and environment interact in complex ways to produce varied developmental outcomes; neither by itself is sufficient to explain human behaviors. In fact, because an individual's genotype influences the type of environment he or she will experience, heritability estimates may actually include environmental effects (Dickens & Flynn, 2001). Furthermore, in the United States, race is a variable confounded by the other variables of social class, educational achievement, educational opportunities, and income. All of these factors can contribute to the types of learning experiences young children undergo. Parents with greater financial resources can provide the books, toys, and other materials that stimulate intellectual growth. Moreover, families with economic stability are likely to experience less stress than economically unstable families, a factor that can be related to intellectual performance. Finally, research shows that heritability estimates can vary depending on family background variables. For families in which parents were well educated, heritability of verbal IQ for children was estimated to be .74, whereas when parents were poorly educated, the heritability estimate was .26 (Rowe, Jacobson, & Van den Oord, 1999). Rather than settling the nature–nurture question, then, racial differences in IQ have served to highlight the complexity of interactions among variables associated with intelligence.

Test Bias A major hypothesis put forth to account for group differences in IQ scores is based on the notion of **test bias**. According to this view, the content of traditional tests is unfamiliar to children from some social or cultural backgrounds. In other words, traditional psychometric tests are not culturally fair. Recall the dilemma Lily faced at the beginning of this chapter and the erroneous conclusion she drew about her own intelligence based on her failure to define *inscription* and to answer the question "Who discovered America?" Unfortunately, her IQ test score may reflect the same conclusion. Individuals who have not encountered such specific information in their own cultural experiences will fail those items and score lower on many intelligence tests (Fagan & Holland, 2002).

SOCIOCULTURAL INFLUENCE

What happens when tests that are more culturally fair are administered to children from varied sociocultural backgrounds? The research findings are mixed. In Chapter 7, "Language," you were introduced to the Raven Progressive Matrices, a nonverbal test of reasoning ability that is assumed to contain minimal cultural bias. Caucasian children still score significantly higher on this test than African American children do (Jensen, 1980). Yet when another culturally fair test, the Kaufman Assessment Battery, was administered to children of different cultural backgrounds, the difference in test scores between Caucasian and African American children was smaller than when tests such as the WISC were given (Kaufman, Kamphaus, & Kaufman, 1985).

what do you think?

Are IQ Tests Helpful in Assessing Individual Differences in Ability?

Because of the controversy surrounding IQ tests and because scores on IQ tests can fluctuate markedly for any individual child (in some cases as much as forty points from one test time to another), many psychologists advocate that educators and parents use caution when interpreting them. When IQ scores form the basis for children to be labeled by parents and teachers as "underachievers" or "slow learners," the result can be a self-fulfilling prophecy. Children may show lower achievement simply because of the lower expectations of others. In addition, unless the test is based on specific kinds of cognitive processing abilities, IQ scores may not have direct implications for specific educational strategies or instructional interventions. Finally, it is important to consider that, while IQ scores have been shown to have moderate success in forecasting school achievement, an even stronger factor in predicting school performance is the degree to which children show self-discipline. Compared with children who are unable to regulate their behaviors, children who can inhibit impulsive behaviors and who can delay their access to rewards tend to receive higher grades in school, gain admission to more selective high schools, and perform better on several other measures of academic achievement. Measures of self-discipline have more than twice the statistical power of IQ scores in predicting these achievement-related outcomes (Duckworth & Seligman, 2005).

RISK | RESILIENCE

At the same time, many psychologists who work with children in clinical settings find that the results of IQ tests can offer a good sense of a child's pattern of strengths and weaknesses. The tests can assist in diagnosis of learning problems (e.g., Does the child show more aptitude than his or her school grades suggest?) and offer other important clinical insights (e.g., What is the child's behavioral style in approaching a cognitive task? Is she impulsive and careless, or methodical and less error-prone, for example?).

test bias Idea that the content of traditional standardized tests does not adequately measure the competencies of children from diverse cultural backgrounds.

What do you think are the best ways to assess a child's skills and abilities as they pertain to academic achievement? If IQ tests are used, what advice would you offer to parents and teachers about how to interpret and use them wisely? Are there any implications of this discussion for how IQ tests should be constructed?

For Your Review and Reflection

- What major questions have surrounded attempts to define intelligence?
- What are the main features of psychometric approaches to intelligence?
- What are the principal ideas underlying the theories of Spearman, Thurstone, and Cattell and Horn?
- What are the main features of information-processing approaches to intelligence?
- What assumptions do psychologists make about the distribution of IQ scores in the population?
- What are some major tests that have been used to assess intelligence in infants and children? What are the primary features of each in terms of how they measure intelligence?
- How is giftedness defined? What are the unique ways in which gifted individuals process information? What are the behavioral characteristics of gifted children?
- What kinds of outcomes do IQ scores predict?
- What are the complexities involved in trying to assess the contributions of heredity to group differences in IQ?

Self-Concepts and Achievement

A growing body of research points to the idea that how children *think* about their abilities may be just as important in understanding their achievement as their *actual level of ability*. The ideas that children hold about their own competence, as well as the cognitions they hold about the abilities of the gender or ethnic group to which they belong, can have startling effects on performance on cognitive and school-related tasks.

Motivational Belief Systems

INTERACTION AMONG DOMAINS

The development of the child's understanding of self as someone who is an agent of change and who can successfully solve problems and achieve goals can be a substantial factor in explaining achievement. Just as we can ask a child what she knows about her physical features or personal characteristics, so too can we ask whether she realizes that she influences and controls her surroundings. Such questions inquire about a child's understanding of her sense of agency or autonomy. What do children know about such matters?

The Sense of Agency The belief that a person can determine and influence his or her surroundings probably has its roots in infancy. Robert White (1959) suggested that babies are born with a desire to master their environment, an ambition he termed **effectance motivation**. The active

effectance motivation Inborn desire theorized to be the basis for the infant's and child's efforts to master and gain control of the environment.

infant repeatedly stacks blocks, bangs pots, smiles at caregivers, and plays peek-a-boo, activities that often lead to consequences that he anticipates. If he cries, he typically is picked up, rocked, and comforted. The one-year-old who says "Mama" or another new word often becomes the center of attention. From the feedback associated with these actions, infants may learn to expect outcomes and how to make them happen again. Eventually, they see themselves as being in control, capable of reaching desired goals, and having the means to do so as they interact with both their physical and social environments (Wachs & Combs, 1995). For example, when babies can make a mobile rotate rapidly by moving their heads on a pressure-sensitive pillow, they quickly learn to do so. But if their head movements on the pillow initially fail to have any consequences, they are far less likely to learn a contingency-related outcome when it is established (Watson, 1971; Watson & Ramey, 1972).

Self-Determination Toward the end of the first year and continuing into the second, children start to initiate efforts to share interesting sights and activities with caregivers and playmates, an important step in becoming aware of their ability to influence what others see and do. After about two years of age, many will protest the attempts of caregivers to help them in an activity such as dressing or eating. Some researchers believe such protests further reveal an early desire to be an agent or to master an activity (Kagan, 1981; Lutkenhaus, Bullock, & Geppert, 1987). At about this same time, children also look to adults after completing a task as though to share their success or turn away and hunch their shoulders after failure (Stipek, Recchia, & McClintic, 1992). The feedback mothers provide to two-year-olds following their efforts to solve a problem plays an important role in the way they subsequently respond to a challenging task. When mothers are more negative and critical, their children are increasingly likely to display shame in confronting a difficult problem as three-year-olds. Mothers who are more supportive and provide a scaffold to assist in solving a problem have children who, when they are older, display greater persistence if confronted with an achievement-oriented task (Kelley, Brownell, & Campbell, 2000).

NATURE & NURTURE

Children become increasingly sophisticated about how the world responds to their actions. For example, if asked, "How did you get to be the way you are?" a preschooler is likely to refer to uncontrollable factors ("I just grew . . . . My body just got bigger"), whereas a ten-year-old mentions her own efforts ("From getting good grades in school from studying"). By age thirteen, children also acknowledge the contributions of others to their sense of agency ("I learned from my parents, I even learned from friends, just listening to them and talking to them"). Most children believe that individual effort is an important aspect of achieving success and avoiding failure, even in societies that have emphasized a more collective orientation, such as Russia (Stetsenko al., 1995). For example, elementary school children in Los Angeles, Tokyo, Berlin, Moscow, and Prague are in close agreement in their views that effort, in particular, rather than other factors, such as the teacher or luck or even ability, is the most important determinant of school performance (Little & Lopez, 1997).

Mastery Beliefs Within every community, individuals can differ substantially in their sense of self-determination and control. Some children are convinced that what happens to them depends on their actions, that their choices, decisions, and abilities govern whether outcomes are good or bad, successful or unsuccessful. When asked how to find a friend, such a child might say, "Go up to someone you like and ask them to play with you." When asked how to do well on a test, the child might answer, "Study for it, and you'll get smarter!" Such children have a strong **mastery orientation,** a belief that success stems from trying hard; failures, these children presume, are conditions to be overcome by working more or by investing greater effort (Dweck & Elliott, 1983).

mastery orientation Belief that achievements are based on one's own efforts rather than luck or other factors beyond one's control.

Other children, in contrast, believe luck, fate, or other people have an inordinate influence on what happens to them. When asked why he cannot catch a ball, such a child might say, "The others throw it too fast." When asked why he got a poor grade, he might say, "The teacher doesn't like me." His explanation for a good grade might be, "I was lucky." Such children often express little confidence in their ability and feel powerless to influence the future. They perceive themselves as being unable to achieve, perhaps because their efforts have not led to regular success. In place of a sense of mastery, they have a sense of **learned helplessness** (Dweck & Elliott, 1983).

These differing interpretations about success and failure are linked to another property of the belief system. To the extent that children think the characteristics they and others display are stable *entities*, that is, fixed or unchangeable qualities or traits such as being smart, friendly, or popular, the more vulnerable they are to a helpless orientation. As a consequence, when faced with a challenging situation, the focus tends to be on evaluating how well they perform or "measure up" rather than on what steps might be taken to improve their performance or activity. In contrast, when children hold beliefs that characteristics or traits of individuals are *incremental* or malleable and can therefore be changed, their focus in challenging situations is more likely to be directed toward learning procedures and strategies reflecting resilience and increased effort (Erdley et al., 1997; Heyman & Dweck, 1998). Why might this be so? If traits are seen as enduring characteristics, little can be done to change them; thus, the child places greater emphasis on determining the degree to which he or she (and others) possesses them as indicated by *performance* on the problem or task. On the other hand, if traits are seen as temporary characteristics, then the child can focus on the processes required to improve on or modify them, that is, on better ways of *learning* the task or how to solve the problem (Dweck, 1999).

RISK | RESILIENCE

Differing beliefs about the degree to which traits are fixed or modifiable and the causes of success or failure have a powerful bearing on academic achievement, participation in athletics and other physical activities, efforts to establish social relationships, self-esteem, and career aspirations (Bandura et al., 2001; Chapman, Skinner, & Baltes, 1990; Heyman & Dweck, 1998). Children who display evidence of learned helplessness in school, for example, may be caught in a vicious cycle involving self-fulfilling anticipation of failure accompanied by excuses that they have little control over what happens to them (Bandura et al., 1996). They are especially likely to expect failure on tasks found difficult in the past and may avoid them when given further opportunity to work on them (Dweck, 1991; Erdley et al., 1997). Note that high ability is not the factor that determines a mastery orientation (Dweck, 1999).

A mastery-versus-helplessness orientation can be observed in kindergartners and remains stable for up to five years (Ziegert et al., 2001). However, teachers can have an important influence on children's beliefs about their academic competence. When teachers provide a supportive, responsive learning environment, children come to believe that they have greater control over their understanding of academic materials and, as a consequence, become more actively engaged, as well as more successful in their efforts. Where learning environments are unsupportive, children are more likely to conclude that external factors are responsible for what happens, which, in turn, leads to less satisfaction and lower achievement in the classroom. Longitudinal data reveals that these differences in perceived control form a cyclic pattern of confidence and success that feeds into and magnifies individual differences in children's views of beliefs about their achievements and failures in the classroom (Skinner, Zimmer-Gembeck, & Connell, 1998). What specific teacher behaviors might make a difference? In one recent study, when seventh-graders were provided with the opportunity to gain knowledge about how learning can change the brain, how self-cognitions can influence performance, and were also supplied with information about specific study skills that can improve performance, they showed notable increases in mastery orientation as well as a rising trajectory in their grades in school (Blackwell, Trzesniewski, & Dweck, 2007).

learned helplessness Belief that one has little control over situations, perhaps because of lack of ability or inconsistent outcomes.

The rule in Lily's house was that, once homework was finished, the remaining time before bedtime was hers to do with as she wished. She often played chess or worked on a jigsaw puzzle with her grandfather. This evening, however, her grandfather had become busy on another project. "Perhaps just as well," thought Lily. She texted her friend Manuela. "Do you want to come over and hang out?" she queried. "You must have finished your math already," Manuela replied. "I hate math, still have a lot more problems to do," she continued. Lily quickly replied, "You did really well on that last test." But Lily already knew what Manuela's reply would be: "I was lucky. The teacher asked the right questions. I wish I was good at math."

Children who gain little mastery over their environment or face conflicting and inconsistent reactions, such as those they might receive from parents who are abusive, are among the most likely to display learned helplessness. But even well-intentioned parents and teachers may unwittingly help to foster a sense of helplessness. For example, when parents generally believe they can promote their children's intellectual development, their children seem to benefit (Bandura et al., 1996). The seeds of a sense of helplessness, Carol Dweck (1999) believes, are sown in preschoolers who tend to judge their performance on tasks as "good" or "bad." When the value of self becomes contingent on feeling worthy or unworthy, young children become especially vulnerable to learned helplessness.

A study conducted by Melissa Kamins and Carol Dweck (1999) provides some experimental evidence to indicate that certain types of feedback with respect to either criticism or praise can lead to a more helpless orientation when children are subsequently confronted with similar situations involving a setback. In this study, five- and six-year-olds engaged in role-playing a series of four different stories that involved various tasks. In each of these tasks, children acted in the role of a doll, either making an error or completing the task successfully. At the end of each story, the experimenter (who was engaged in role-playing as the teacher) provided one of three different types of feedback. When the task involved an error, the feedback from the "teacher" was directed either at the person (e.g., "I'm very disappointed in you"), at the outcome of the task ("That's not the right way to do it"), or at the process that contributed to the error in the task ("Maybe you can think of another way to do it"). (Special effort was made to ensure that the children understood they were role-playing and that the scenarios were pretend situations.) When praise for success was administered, the child heard something like, "I'm very proud of you," or "That's the right way to do it," or "You must have tried really hard" for the person, outcome, and process feedback conditions, respectively.

How would children respond after role-playing in a similar but new task when a setback occurred? To answer this question, the researchers asked children to evaluate how well the new problem had been completed (product rating); how performance in the task reflected abilities such as being good, bad, smart, not so smart, and so forth (self-assessment); whether they felt happy or sad (affect); and their willingness to continue in the role-playing activity or to attempt to correct the error (persistence). The results are shown in Figure 10.6. Higher scores indicate a more positive rating.

The results revealed a consistent pattern of reactions typical of helplessness when the emphasis in the feedback had been on the person (and to a lesser extent, on the outcome) than when the feedback focused on the process of completing the task effectively. Somewhat surprisingly, this relationship held up whether the children had been exposed earlier to criticism or to praise in the role-playing activity, an outcome reported by other researchers, as well (Henderlong & Lepper, 2002). These findings and the research of many others suggest that parents (and teachers) can take several steps to reduce the likelihood that children will acquire a sense of learned helplessness:

1. *Avoid frequent criticism and punishment, especially of younger children.* The younger child who is often criticized or punished for, say, being messy or failing to finish a task may be particularly susceptible to the belief that he is "bad." In arriving at this stable view of his personality, he may have little reason to try to do better or may shun similar challenges to

Figure 10.6

The Consequences of Different Types of Feedback for Learned Helplessness

Children who hear *person-oriented feedback* evaluate the outcome of new work less positively (product rating), view themselves as having fewer positive abilities (self-assessment), feel less happy with themselves (affect), and are less willing to continue the activity (persistence) than children who receive *process-oriented feedback*. Outcome-oriented feedback also produces less desirable outcomes.
Source: Adapted from Kamins & Dweck, 1999.

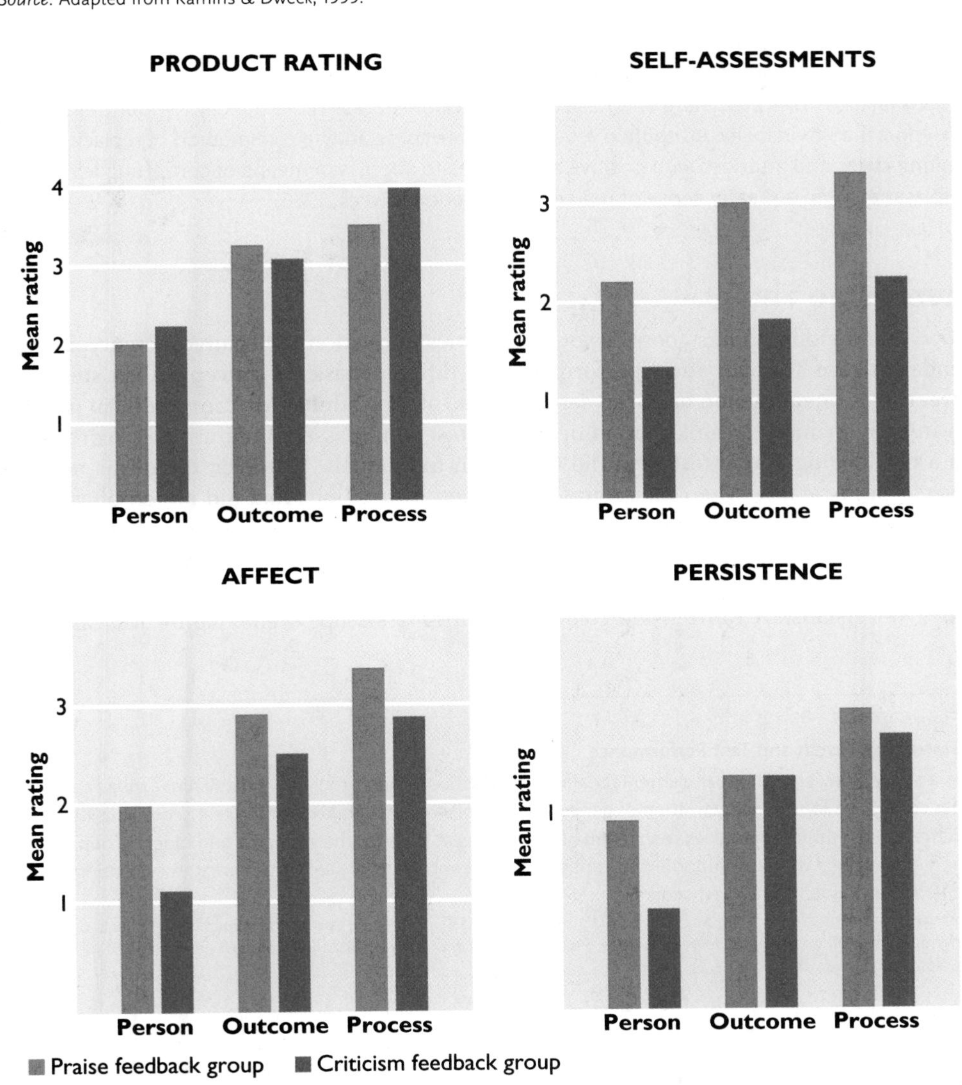

avoid receiving further negative evaluations. Thus, it is important that parents and teachers help the younger child to avoid feelings of shame or limited self-worth when evaluating behavior (Kelley et al., 2000).

2. *Motivate effort by identifying positive process approaches to problem solving.* As children become older and more knowledgeable, parents and teachers can promote a mastery orientation by emphasizing the various skills and procedures important to success, that is, what children can do to more effectively achieve a goal. Such feedback should help children to appreciate the malleability of traits and capacities (Blackwell et al., 2007).
3. *Attribute poor performance to factors other than ability.* When a child does perform poorly, a parent's or teacher's evaluation should focus on nonintellectual and temporary factors that may have reduced the child's performance rather than on her intrinsic ability, thereby inspiring effort when the next opportunity arises.

4. *View activities as opportunities to learn rather than as tests of ability.* Parents and teachers can encourage children to approach academic tasks as opportunities to learn rather than as situations in which their performance will be evaluated in terms of competence (or lack of competence) (Dweck, 1999; Erdley et al., 1997).

Younger children must be convinced that their failures and successes are not the outcome of being "bad" or "good." Older children should be assured that shortcomings in performance on, say, academic tasks stem less from lack of ability than from insufficient effort or some other factor that can be modified. Children who already have acquired an orientation to learned helplessness can benefit from *attribution retraining,* a procedure designed to change their beliefs about the cause of their failures. This procedure emphasizes tying lack of success more directly to poor or ineffective effort than to inability. Attribution retraining has become an effective method of replacing self-limiting styles and attitudes with positive approaches to success, a means of converting learned helplessness into a greater sense of mastery and agency (Dweck, 1986).

Stereotype Threat

How an individual thinks about his or her abilities in relation to negative stereotypes about gender or race also can affect performance on different tasks, a concept called **stereotype threat**. This phenomenon has been demonstrated among adults: African American individuals initially primed to think that an upcoming test would assess their abilities scored lower on a challenging verbal test than did Caucasian individuals. However, there was no difference in performance when the groups were given instructions that did not emphasize ability testing (Steele & Aronson, 1995). Similar findings have been reported with upper and lower elementary and middle school Asian American girls given a standardized math test. Right before taking the test, each girl colored a picture that activated stereotypes about either "girls" or "Asians." A third group colored a neutral landscape scene. Figure 10.7 shows the

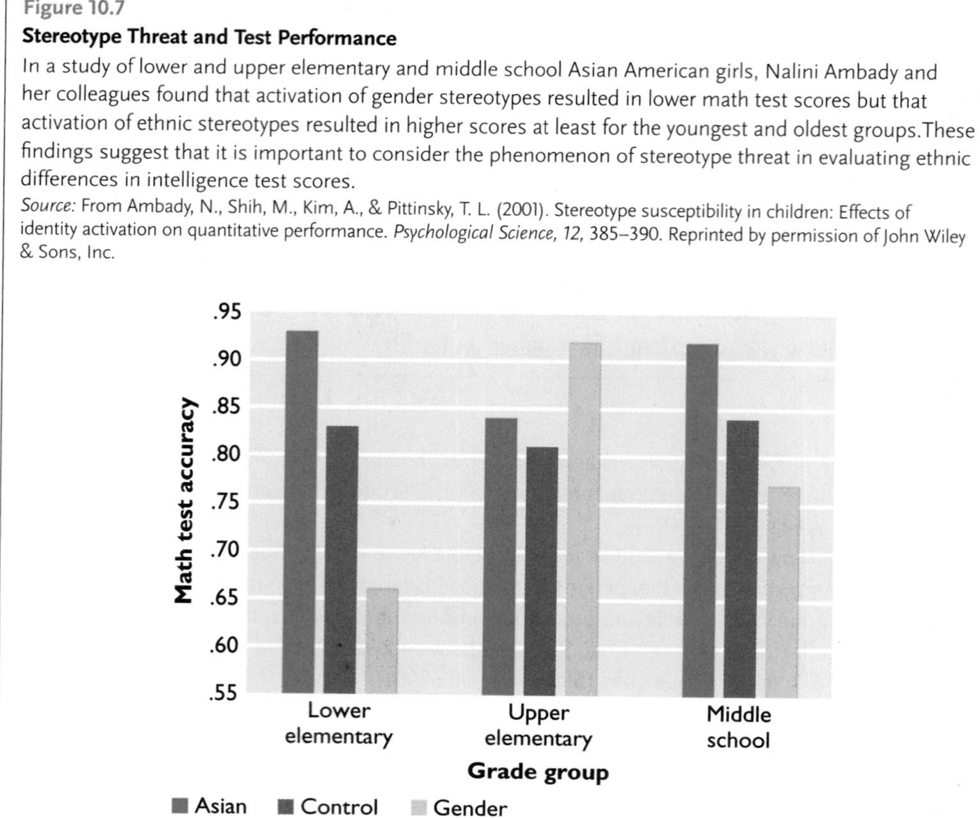

Figure 10.7

Stereotype Threat and Test Performance

In a study of lower and upper elementary and middle school Asian American girls, Nalini Ambady and her colleagues found that activation of gender stereotypes resulted in lower math test scores but that activation of ethnic stereotypes resulted in higher scores at least for the youngest and oldest groups.These findings suggest that it is important to consider the phenomenon of stereotype threat in evaluating ethnic differences in intelligence test scores.

Source: From Ambady, N., Shih, M., Kim, A., & Pittinsky, T. L. (2001). Stereotype susceptibility in children: Effects of identity activation on quantitative performance. *Psychological Science, 12,* 385–390. Reprinted by permission of John Wiley & Sons, Inc.

performance of each of the groups on the math component of the Iowa Test of Basic Skills. For the youngest and oldest age groups, activating stereotypes about girls resulted in lower math test scores, whereas activating stereotypes about ethnicity resulted in higher scores (Ambady et al., 2001). (It is unclear why upper elementary students did not fit this pattern of performance.)

If thinking about negative connotations of stereotypes can lead to decrements in performance, can the reverse happen? Can thinking about positive attributes of one's group or the self result in enhanced achievement? Some provocative studies suggest that this may be the case. In one study, African American seventh-graders were randomly assigned to one of two groups. At the start of the school year, children in the experimental group were asked to write about an important personal value—their friendships or their religion, for example. Children in the control condition wrote an essay on a neutral topic. Remarkably, children who received the brief intervention in the experimental group earned higher grades in the course at the end of the term than those in the control group. The experience of *self-affirmation*, these results suggest, can have powerful and long-lasting effects on achievement (Cohen & Garcia, 2008; Cohen et al., 2006).

RISK | RESILIENCE

For Your Review and Reflection

- How does effectance motivation begin and develop?
- What factors contribute to mastery orientation and learned helplessness? What steps can parents and teachers take to reduce learned helplessness in children?
- What examples of mastery orientation and learned helplessness have you observed among your friends or among children with whom you have worked?
- How does the concept of stereotype threat help us to understand group differences in achievement?

Contextual Influences on Achievement

There is no question that another critical factor in any child's successful achievement is the school that he or she attends. In Chapter 16, we discuss how the organization and structure of schools can enhance or detract from learning. Here, we focus on how the people involved in the child's schooling experiences—parents, peers, and teachers—contribute to the child's experiences of success or failure.

Parents, Peers, and School Achievement

NATURE & NURTURE

RISK | RESILIENCE

Not surprisingly, parents are of paramount importance in understanding children's achievement in school. A model proposed by Wendy Grolnick and her colleagues (Grolnick, Ryan, & Deci, 1991) and illustrated in Figure 10.8 shows one conceptualization of how parents play a role. According to these researchers, parental support for their children's autonomy (e.g., encouraging independent decision making) and involvement with their children (such as spending time talking with them about the children's problems) are related to the strength of children's "inner resources." That is, children develop feelings of competence, autonomy, and control, which in turn influence academic performance. To test these ideas, the researchers measured both parental and child qualities that were components of the model, as well as children's academic success. Using sophisticated statistical techniques, they were able to show the relationships they had predicted. Other researchers have confirmed the importance of mothers' and fathers' autonomy support for predicting children's success in key academic subjects such as reading and mathematics (National Institute of Child Health and Human Development Early Child Care Research Network, 2008).

stereotype threat The psychological impact of negative social stereotype in an individual.

Figure 10.8

A Model of Parental Influences on Children's Academic Achievement

One model of children's academic achievement suggests that parental involvement and support of children's autonomy predict children's "inner resources." These resources include children's feelings of control, competence, and autonomy. These characteristics, in turn, predict academic achievement. Research has found support for the major elements of this model.

Source: Adapted from Grolnick, Ryan, & Deci, 1991.

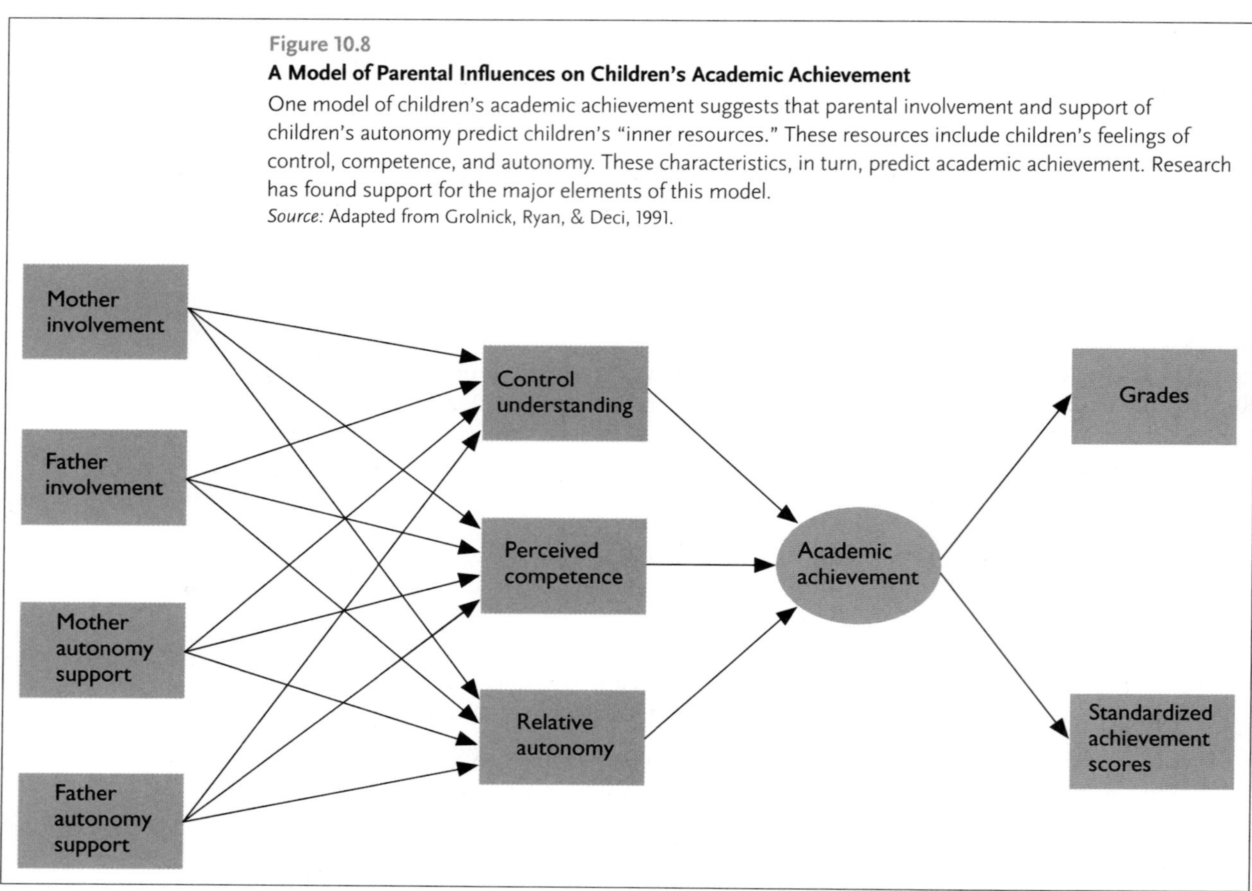

Researchers have also found that *authoritative parenting* (characterized by warmth and extensive verbal explanation) and the *social support* parents provide predict, at least indirectly, how well children will do in school during middle childhood and adolescence (DeBaryshe, Patterson, & Capaldi, 1993; Dubow et al., 1991; Steinberg et al., 1992). Frequent transitions in parenting (e.g., divorce and remarriage followed by another divorce) and a more discordant family climate, on the other hand, are related to less positive outcomes in school (Kurdek, Fine, & Sinclair, 1995).

An especially important way that parents can bolster their children's school-related motivations is to be involved in schooling. When parents attend open houses, parent-teacher conferences, and other school functions, and when they keep track of how their children are doing in school, children from diverse ethnic and social class backgrounds show higher academic motivation and better performance in school (Benner, Graham, & Mistry, 2008; Eamon, 2005; Woolley & Grogan-Kaylor, 2006). By being involved and communicating with teachers, parents learn about how to handle the challenges their children face in school, and children receive an important message—that parents and teachers agree on objectives and standards for behavior (Hill & Taylor, 2004). Moreover, when parents express values that education and academic achievement are important—by taking trips to museums and libraries or purchasing educational materials, for example—children's academic achievement grows in a positive direction (Hill & Tyson, 2009).

Peers make a difference, too. As early as fourth grade, children tend to sort themselves into groups that have different levels of school motivation, and children who are members of a particular group at the start of the school year become even more aligned with the group's motivation level by the end of this period (Kindermann, 1993, 2007). Moreover, the information children get from peers about their academic competence has an influence on their subsequent behaviors. Children who develop reputations among their peers for academic success show discernable gains in their academic self-concept, the effort they put into school-related tasks, and their academic performance over time (Gest et al., 2008).

Peers may also enhance or offset the effects of different parenting styles on children's academic achievement. Laurence Steinberg and his associates found that among Asian American adolescents, for example, peer support for academic excellence lessened the negative effects of *authoritarian parenting* on academic achievement. For Caucasian adolescents, peer support for achievement complemented parents' tendency to be *authoritative* (Steinberg, Dornbusch, & Brown, 1992). (See Chapter 14, "The Family," for further discussion of the difference between authoritarian and authoritative parenting.) A supportive family context may be an important factor in encouraging children to gain the interpersonal and cognitive skills that will lead to interactions with peers who promote academic success in the first place (Kurdek et al., 1995; Steinberg, 1996).

Finally, the availability of a mentor can be an important contributor to success in the schools for adolescents. For example, research on Big Brother and Big Sister programs has revealed a positive influence on grades, attendance, and perceived competence with respect to academic subjects (Grossman & Tierney, 1998). Perhaps a bit surprising, however, is that many of these benefits seemed to be mediated by adolescents establishing better parental relationships rather than as a direct consequence of the mentor's activities with the student (Rhodes, Grossman, & Resch, 2000).

Teachers: Key Agents of Influence

No single factor in the school experience plays a more critical role in student achievement and self-esteem than teachers. The expectations teachers have of students, their classroom management strategies, and the climate they create in the classroom are all major elements in student success or failure.

NATURE & NURTURE

Teacher Expectations A highly publicized study conducted by Robert Rosenthal and Lenore Jacobson several decades ago (1968) documented how teachers' expectations of students' performance can affect students' actual attainments. The researchers told teachers that certain elementary school children could be expected to show sudden gains in intellectual skills during the course of the school year based on their scores on an IQ test administered at the beginning of the term. In reality, the students they designated as "rapid bloomers" were chosen randomly. An IQ test administered at the end of the school year revealed that the targeted children indeed showed significantly greater improvement than other students in the class, an outcome called the *Pygmalion effect.* The investigators explained the findings by suggesting that teachers somehow treated the targeted children differently based on their beliefs about the children's intellectual potential, thereby creating a self-fulfilling prophecy.

Differing expectations, especially when they are clearly evident to students, have consequences for achievement, as well. Margaret Kuklinski and Rhona Weinstein (2001) looked at children in grades one through five to determine whether teacher expectations affected performance on reading achievement. As Figure 10.9 suggests, the researchers anticipated

Figure 10.9
Teacher Expectancy Effects on Children's Reading Achievement
Teacher expectancies may not only have a direct effect on reading achievement but can also influence behavior by modifying children's own expectations for themselves, as this model suggests. Margaret Kuklinsky and Rhona Weinstein(2001) obtained support for this model, especially in classrooms in which teacher expectancies could be recognized easily by children.The impact of the children's own self-perceptions pertaining to reading, as influenced by teacher expectations, was especially evident when children were in fifth grade but far less evident in earlier grades.
Source: Adapted from Kuklinski & Weinstein, 2001, p. 1557.

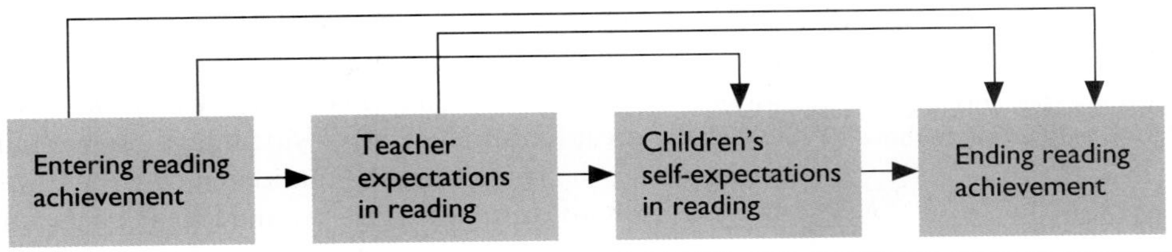

Entering reading achievement → Teacher expectations in reading → Children's self-expectations in reading → Ending reading achievement

that teacher expectations about reading ability would influence not only achievement in reading at the end of the school year but also the children's own self-perceptions of their reading ability. These self-perceptions would, in turn, also influence their reading achievement. The results of the study generally supported these hypotheses, especially in classrooms in which teacher expectations were more readily apparent to children, although children's self-perceptions tended not to become a factor until they reached the fifth grade.

Other studies have confirmed that high achievers *are* treated differently in the classroom by many teachers; they are given more opportunities to participate, are given more time to answer questions, receive more praise for being correct, and receive less criticism than lower achievers (Minuchin & Shapiro, 1983). In other words, the classroom climate is most supportive for those who have already demonstrated success, whereas those who most need the teacher's attention and encouragement may actually get them least.

Classroom Management Strategies Students achieve most in school when their teachers maximize the time spent in actual learning. This statement may seem obvious, but not all school time is spent in direct instruction. Effective teachers plan their lessons well, monitor the entire classroom continuously, minimize the time spent in disciplining children who misbehave, and keep transitions between activities brief and smooth (Brophy, 1986). They make sure there is little "dead time" in the classroom when students are unoccupied, and they keep the focus on instruction.

Another key ingredient in a teacher's success is active involvement in the learning process. This means teachers remain personally involved in every phase of instruction, from the initial presentation of a new lesson to supervising the individual work of students. Involvement also refers to the teacher's enjoyment and knowledge of students. Even when students are working in groups, teachers who guide the discussion or progress of the group will foster higher levels of mastery and greater feelings of competence than those who leave students completely on their own (Brophy, 1986; Skinner & Belmont, 1993). Effective teachers also provide students with clear feedback on the quality of their performance and on what is expected of them (Rutter, 1983).

Creating peer-centered learning experiences can be an effective means of involving students in the educational enterprise of the school. In studies of **cooperative learning**, students work in groups rather than individually to solve academic problems. These groups, for example, may consist of four or five students, some boys and some girls, with a range of abilities and from diverse backgrounds. The teacher is usually instrumental in introducing a topic or set of materials, but then the team members work and study together on the problems, quizzing one another until they decide collectively that they understand the unit. Cooperative learning is associated with increases in affiliations among students from diverse backgrounds (e.g., cross-racial friendships), improvements in self-esteem, more favorable attitudes toward academic achievement, and better academic performance. (Roseth, Johnson, & Johnson, 2008; Slavin, 1990).

As an illustration of the effectiveness of cooperative learning, Hanna Shachar and Shlomo Sharan (1994) compared the communication and achievement skills of 197 eighth-graders assigned to cooperative learning classrooms in history and geography with those of 154 students in classrooms taught by traditional teacher-led methods. The study, carried out in Israel, included Jewish students from Western and Middle Eastern backgrounds. The classes were taught for six months. The cooperative learning groups were reconstituted several times throughout the year to give students the opportunity to work with a number of different peers. At the end of the year, a videotaped discussion of a topic in history and geography involving six-person groups revealed that those who participated in cooperative learning expressed themselves more frequently, were more likely to take a personal position and expand on the ideas brought up by another student, and were less likely to interrupt their peers than students who participated in traditional classrooms. The gains in communication skills were especially great for Middle Eastern students; those with this background who came from the traditional classroom were far less likely to express themselves than their peers from

cooperative learning Peer-centered learning experience in which students work together in small groups to promote the learning of each group member.

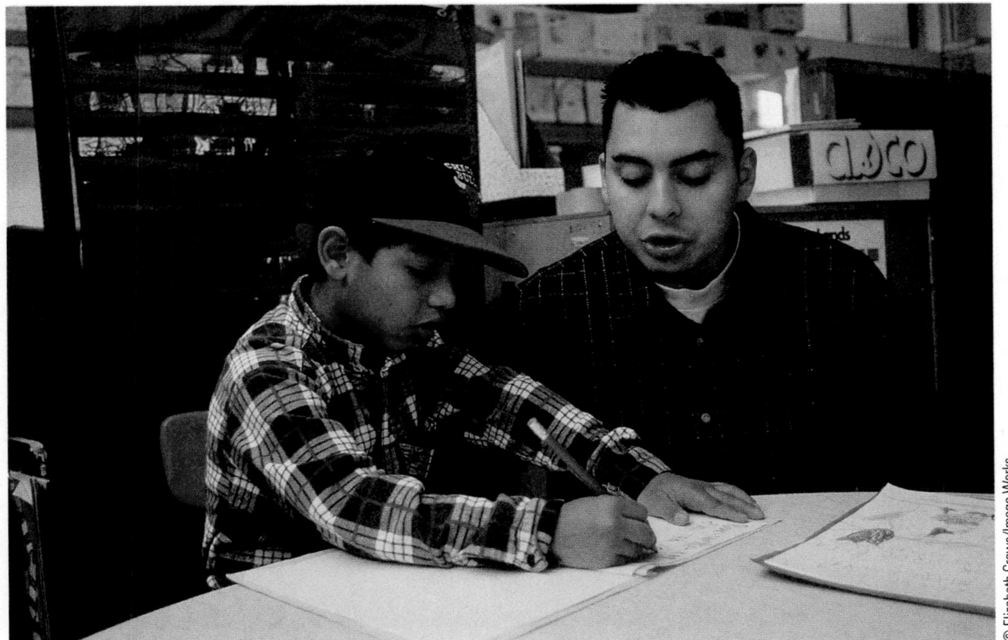

© Elizabeth Crews/Image Works

One of the most important factors in a child's school experience is teacher encouragement. This boy is receiving the kind of assistance with writing that will promote learning. Effective teachers are involved in all phases of instruction, provide clear feedback, and create a positive emotional climate in the classroom.

Western backgrounds. Gains in scores on achievement tests in history were also much higher among students who participated in the cooperative groups than among students in the traditional classroom.

Another form of peer-centered education is called **collaborative learning**. Here students work jointly on the same problems, often without competing with other groups but with the goal of arriving at solutions jointly, solutions that would be unlikely to arise from students working by themselves (Littleton & Häkkinen, 1999). For example, in one study, fourth-graders worked in pairs on mathematics and spatial reasoning problems, some that required rote learning and copying and some that required formal reasoning (Phelps & Damon, 1989). After six sessions of collaboration, children showed significant gains in performance on math and spatial problems compared with a control group of children who did not participate in collaborative efforts. This effect occurred for tasks that required formal reasoning but not for those that required rote learning or copying. Another interesting outcome was that the superiority of boys over girls on spatial problems at the start of the study significantly diminished. In fact, other research indicates that cooperative and collaborative learning may be especially beneficial in certain areas for students, such as, for example, girls learning math or science. These gains could come about because girls now have a chance to take on leadership roles or because cooperative or collaborative learning more closely fits their preferred style of learning and helps to maintain interest in these subjects (Eccles & Roeser, 1999; Peterson, Johnson, & Johnson, 1991).

The Classroom Climate When students participate in cooperative and collaborative learning efforts, they may get the idea that the teacher and the school are promoting *autonomy* or increased student initiative within the classroom, a perception that appears to be beneficial to student progress (Boggiano et al., 1992; Valeski & Stipek, 2001). Children who view their teachers as giving them greater responsibility within the classroom have higher self-esteem scores than those who perceive teachers as controlling and directive (Ryan & Grolnick, 1986). Moreover, teachers who display the kinds of qualities associated with good parenting—that is, who have high expectations for their students and who show caring, supportive, and nurturant qualities in contrast to an emphasis on negative feedback in their educational approach—are more effective in promoting student adjustment to the

collaborative learning Peer-centered learning in which students work together on academic problems with the goal of arriving at solutions that are more effective than solutions that could have been derived from individual effort alone.

An important form of learning is *cooperative learning*, in which small groups of students work together. The four students participating in this project can learn a great deal from each other. Students engaged in cooperative learning, compared with those who receive more traditional methods of instruction, often display significantly higher performance in subjects on which they work as a group.

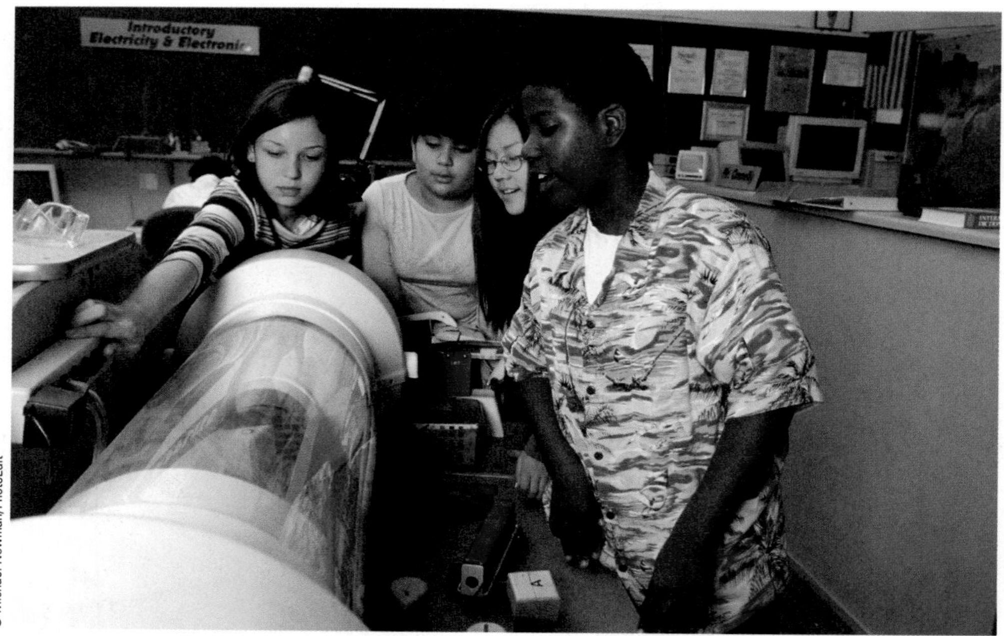

© Michael Newman/PhotoEdit

classroom and high academic performance in early adolescence (Linney & Seidman, 1989; Rutter, 1983; Rutter et al., 1979; Wentzel, 2002).

Children are able to recognize the strength of their interpersonal relationship with a teacher as early as first grade. When they perceive that teachers care about them, children have more favorable attitudes toward school (Valeski & Stipek, 2001). Moreover, teacher–child relationships that begin early in the schooling process have long-term outcomes. Bridget Hamre and Robert Pianta (2001) asked kindergarten teachers in a small community to assess their personal relationships with each of their students. Nearly 200 of these students were followed through eighth grade. Those reported to have had a negative relationship with the teacher as kindergartners, for example, showing conflict and overdependency, continued to have difficulties with school over the next eight years. However, if children who displayed behavior problems in kindergarten were able to develop positive relationships with their kindergarten teachers, it helped to counter behavioral difficulties in the later school years, a finding that has considerable implications for the importance of a young student's relationship with his or her teacher and academic success.

RISK | RESILIENCE

Cultural Differences in School Achievement

SOCIOCULTURAL INFLUENCE

The school experience is not necessarily the same for children of different racial and ethnic backgrounds. Children who attend school bring with them attitudes about school that are first nurtured within their families, as well as cultural beliefs that may be in synchrony or in conflict with the predominant belief system of the school (Gibson & Ogbu, 1991). For example, are schools a vehicle for economic and personal advancement? Cultural and ethnic groups may vary in their responses to this question. Is verbal, rational expression (which schools emphasize) the optimal means of human communication as opposed to emotional or spiritual sharing? Again, cultures sometimes differ in the extent to which they value these various skills. One of the major challenges facing educators is how to ensure the academic success of children who come from a range of cultural-ethnic backgrounds.

RISK | RESILIENCE

The Achievement Gap A concern arising from research on school achievement in the United States is that a significant number of children from some groups—for example, African American and Hispanic children—score lower than Caucasian children on measures of academic performance. In the 1960s, the prevailing explanation for these school difficulties centered on the *cultural deficit hypothesis*, the notion that some deficiency in the backgrounds of diverse children hindered their preparation for the academic demands of school. However, researchers like Herbert Ginsberg (1972) pointed out that a more useful way to think about these issues is that minority children are *culturally different*; that is, the behaviors minority children display help them to adapt to their specific life circumstances. For example, rather than concluding that they have poor language skills, it is important to notice that African American children display rich images and poetic forms when speaking to one another. According to the *cultural compatibility hypothesis*, school instruction produces greater improvements in learning if it is consistent with the practices of the child's own culture (Tharp, 1989).

Some provocative questions arise when we examine the developmental pattern related to the achievement gap between students from different cultural and ethnic backgrounds. In a study of children in the first two years of school, Karl Alexander and Doris Entwisle (1988) found that African American and Caucasian first-graders did not differ significantly on a standardized test of verbal and quantitative achievement when they were assessed at the beginning of the school year. But by the end of the year and during the second year, the scores of African American and Caucasian students began to diverge noticeably. Why did measurable differences in achievement show up, but only after one year of school?

In keeping with the cultural compatibility hypothesis, some have argued that for many African American students, a conflict exists between their background culture and the social and cognitive structure of traditional schools. For example, the spiritualism, expressiveness, and rich oral tradition characteristic of the African American heritage frequently clash with the materialism, emotional control, and emphasis on printed materials characteristic of European Americans and their schools (Boykin, 1986; Heath, 1989; Slaughter-Defoe et al., 1990). Some African American children may also perceive that academic success does not necessarily lead to occupational or economic success and therefore do not take academic performance seriously (Ogbu, 1974). Furthermore, many African American children believe they will do well in school even though past performance indicates they are likely to do otherwise. These children may need not only to overcome the hurdles imposed by racism and economic hardship but also to more fully understand what behaviors will be necessary to achieve their expectations, that is, to become motivated to master the academic materials and skills necessary to achieve their goals (Alexander, Entwisle, & Bedinger, 1994; Steinberg, 1996).

In focusing on cultural differences, however, researchers need to recognize that they may be unwittingly contributing to stereotypes. After all, many children in all cultural and ethnic groups in the United States are doing well in school. What factors are contributing to their success? Tom Luster and Harriette McAdoo (1994, 1996) have provided some answers for African American children, and the answers should not be too surprising. African American children who are high achieving, just as other children who are high achieving, experience relatively supportive home environments in which mothers display self-esteem and are members of smaller families whose incomes are above the poverty line. Luster and McAdoo (1996) followed African American children from preschool age until young adulthood. All the children lived in families with low socioeconomic status during the preschool period. Consistent with our earlier discussion emphasizing the importance of parents in promoting school success, the cognitive competence and academic motivation these children brought to the public school setting, as well as their degree of social adjustment, predicted performance on achievement tests during the elementary school years. Children of mothers who were more involved with their children's schooling also tended to do better in the lower grades, although this relationship did not hold up during adolescence. However, parents' expectations for success in the classroom were correlated with achievement throughout the school years. These findings further confirm the important role families play in the education of all children (Fuligni, 1997; Steinberg, 1996).

RISK | RESILIENCE

The most recent findings also now indicate that strong racial identity among African American adolescents may actually be a protective factor in explaining school success, rather than being the risk that some earlier researchers had suggested. Young people who show strong positive affiliations with their race may have in place sources of cultural and psychological support that can promote feelings of self-efficacy, high motivation to succeed in academics, and high levels of attainment in school (Chavous et al., 2008; Wong, Eccles, & Sameroff, 2003). In the end, it seems that no matter what their race or ethnic background, children respond to strong encouragement from parents and teachers, as well as the high expectations the adults in their lives set for success in school (Honora, 2003).

Achievement Among Asian Children Beginning in the mid-1980s, Harold Stevenson and his associates conducted comparative research on the academic abilities of Taiwan Chinese, Japanese, and American students. This research was guided by an effort to understand why Asian students seem to do particularly well in the areas of mathematics and science. First- and fifth-grade students from middle- to upper-class backgrounds in all three countries were tested on a battery of specially designed cognitive tasks that assessed, among other things, spatial relations, perceptual speed, auditory and verbal memory, and vocabulary, along with reading and mathematics achievement (Stevenson, Lee, & Stigler, 1986).

Most noteworthy about the findings was that American children scored far lower in mathematics than the other two groups (see Figure 10.10). The distinctive patterns of achievement could not be explained by superior cognitive skills in any one group. The researchers found no predictive relationships between scores on the various cognitive assessments and scores on achievement tests. In fact, the children's cognitive profiles were quite similar across cultural groups by the time they reached fifth grade (Stevenson et al., 1985). When again tested in eleventh grade, American children continued to lag well behind the Chinese and Japanese in mathematics achievement, although, as Figure 10.10 shows, on age-appropriate tests of general information (e.g., "What are two things a plant needs in order to grow?" or "Why has it been possible to make smaller computers in recent years?"), the Asian children were not superior to the American children (Stevenson, Chen, & Lee, 1993).

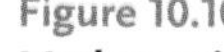
SOCIOCULTURAL INFLUENCE

What accounts for this pattern of findings? Stevenson's research group reported significant differences in children's school routines and parents' attitudes and beliefs among the Taiwan Chinese, Japanese, and American groups, as well as differences between Asian American and Caucasian American families. For example, during the year, Taiwan Chinese and Japanese children attend school about fifty more days than American children do. Furthermore, Asian high school students spend close to fifty hours a week in school while

Figure 10.10

Mathematics Achievement and General Information Scores as a Function of Sociocultural Context

Chinese and Japanese students score higher than American students on tests of mathematics achievement beginning in first grade, and their superiority in this area continues throughout high school.However, on tests of general information, children from all three cultures perform at similar levels, especially in the higher grades. The better performance on mathematics tests by East Asian children may reflect both school- and family-related cultural influences.

Source: Reprinted with permission from H. W. Stevenson, C. Chen, and S. Y. Lee,"Mathematics Achievement of Chinese, Japanese, and American Children: Ten Years Later," *Science, 259*, 53–58. Copyright © 1993 American Association for the Advancement of Science.

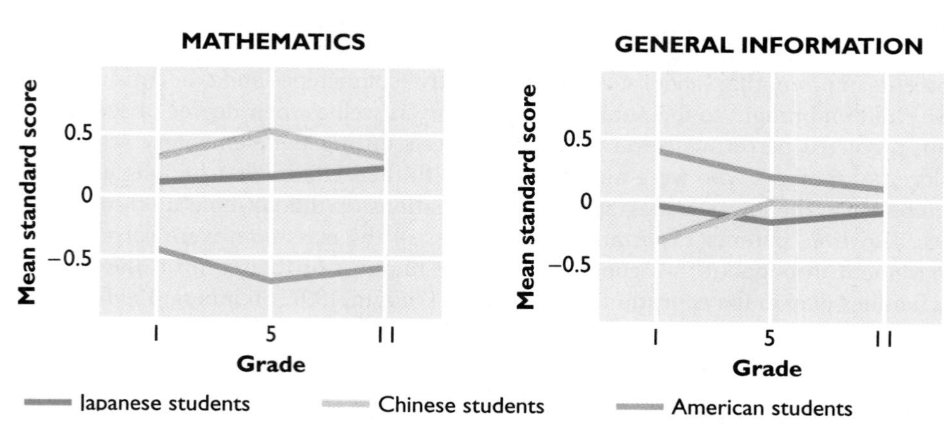

students in the United States spend about thirty-six (Fuligni & Stevenson, 1995). The percentage of classroom time actually spent in academic activities also differs. For fifth-grade students, the figures were 64.5 percent of the time for American children, 91.5 percent for Taiwan Chinese children, and 87.4 for Japanese children. Furthermore, American children studied language arts more than twice as long as they did mathematics, whereas the Asian children spent equal amounts of time on each subject. Thus, the American children received far less instruction in mathematics than their Taiwanese and Japanese counterparts did (Stevenson et al., 1986). In addition, the Asian teachers were far more likely to use their time in mathematics classes directly teaching the entire class, whereas American children spent more than half their time in mathematics classes working alone (Stigler, Lee, & Stevenson, 1987).

Stevenson's research group also examined attitudes and behaviors related to homework. American children devoted substantially less time to doing homework—an average of 46 minutes per day among fifth-graders, according to mothers' estimates—compared with 114 and 57 minutes for Taiwanese and Japanese children, respectively. American mothers were not dissatisfied with the small amount of homework their children received, nor were Taiwan Chinese and Japanese mothers dissatisfied with the large amounts their children were assigned (Stevenson et al., 1986). In addition, compared with American students, high school students, their peers, and their parents in the two Asian cultures seemed to expect higher standards and voiced greater concern about education (Chen & Stevenson, 1995). American high school students were also far more likely to work, date, and engage in other leisure time activities than Asian students. Finally, Asian students were more likely than American students to believe their own effort was the best route to accomplishments (Chen & Stevenson, 1995). Indeed, effort is a central component of the socialization process in many Asian cultures; that is, the procedures by which one achieves a goal are considered extremely important (Bempechat & Drago-Severson, 1999). Effort and persistence are seen as elements that help the individual to develop a strong and virtuous character, a value that is held in high regard in Chinese culture, for example (Li, 2005).

These data confirm that a number of factors other than pure cognitive ability determine the child's level of achievement in school. As we have seen throughout this section, the events that transpire in the classroom, parental attitudes, and larger cultural influences are all related to patterns of academic success or failure. If we are concerned about the educational attainments of students and their overall psychological development, research on the influence of schools reveals that there are many ways to more fully engage children of all ability levels and diverse sociocultural backgrounds (Steinberg, 1996).

For Your Review and Reflection

- How do parents and peers influence school achievement?
- How do teacher behaviors influence school achievement?
- What factors seem to be related to the achievement behaviors of children from different cultural groups?
- What factors seem to contribute to risks to children's academic achievement?
- How important have these various contextual influences been for you and your achievements in school and in other activities?

Applied Developmental Science and Academic Learning

It is increasingly apparent that research findings on early children's learning experiences and the qualities of children's thinking can inform the world of practice and social policy in important ways. Here we highlight a few of the domains in which several decades of research have uncovered information that can guide the construction of children's learning environments so that they are maximally effective and help us achieve the goal of optimizing the development of all children, regardless of whether their early environments presented them with risks and challenges.

Early Intervention

NATURE & NURTURE

RISK | RESILIENCE

During the 1960s, the idea of compensatory education became popular in the United States. Researchers wanted to see if children who were at risk for lower academic achievement could improve if they received the kinds of cognitive stimulation presumably available to middle-class children. More recently, our understanding of the role of early experience during the first three or four years of life has prompted renewed attention to the idea of early intervention. Because we now understand that neurotransmitter functioning, synaptic formation, and gene activation are influenced by environmental conditions, some researchers argue that there is more urgency in providing optimal learning environments for young children (Shore, 1997). Indeed, more and more research is accumulating on the importance of building strong foundations for academic success in children's preschool experiences (Pianta et al., 2010). The skills that three- and four-year-olds build in their mathematical reasoning, self-regulation behaviors, and beginning literacy concepts are strong predictors of academic success several years later in elementary school (Duncan et al., 2007). Are there certain things that parents and teachers can do that are linked to the child's greater success in school? Some of the answers come from studies of how parents and children interact in their homes.

The HOME Inventory In 1970, an ambitious project got under way in Little Rock, Arkansas. Initiated by Bettye Caldwell and her associates (Caldwell & Bradley, 1978), the goal of the project was to identify characteristics of the young child's environment that might be related to later competence, including intellectual achievement. A sample of infants and their parents was recruited for a longitudinal study that would last eleven years.

The *Home Observation for Measurement of the Environment* (*HOME*) inventory was designed to measure a number of characteristics of the child's home surroundings, including the quality of caregiver–child interactions, the availability of objects and activities to stimulate the child, and the types of experiences family members provide to nurture the child's development (see Table 10.2 for the subscales and some sample items). Researchers collected data for the inventory through interviews and direct observations in the children's homes and gave children in the sample standard intelligence and school achievement tests.

TABLE 10.2 Subscales of the Home Observation for Measurement of the Environment (HOME)

The HOME inventory assesses several features of the home environment. Subscales 1, 4, and 5 were found to be significantly correlated with the child's later IQ and language competence.

1. **Emotional and verbal responsivity of mother**
   Sample item: Mother caresses or kisses child at least once during visit.
2. **Avoidance of restriction and punishment**
   Sample item: Mother does not interfere with child's actions or restrict child's movements more than three times during visit.
3. **Organization of physical and temporal environment**
   Sample item: Child's play environment appears safe and free of hazards.
4. **Provision of appropriate play materials**
   Sample item: Mother provides toys or interesting activities for child during interview.
5. **Maternal involvement with child**
   Sample item: Mother tends to keep child within visual range and to look at the child often.
6. **Opportunities for variety in daily stimulation**
   Sample item: Child eats at least one meal per day with mother and father.

Source: From R. Elardo & R. H. Bradley, The Home Observation of the Environment (HOME) Scale: A review of research, *Developmental Review, 1,* 113–145. Copyright © 1981 by Academic Press, reproduced by permission of the publisher.

The results identified several key features of the home environment as being related to subsequent IQ (Bradley, 1989). Significant correlations were found among measures of the home environment taken at age twelve months and children's IQ scores at ages three and four-and-a-half years. Particularly important were scales that measured parental emotional and verbal responsivity to the child, the availability of appropriate play materials, and parental involvement with the child (Bradley & Caldwell, 1976; Elardo, Bradley, & Caldwell, 1975). In addition, HOME scores at age two years, and especially these same three scales, were significantly related to language competencies at age three years (Elardo, Bradley, & Caldwell, 1977). A follow-up of these children showed that parental involvement and availability of toys at age two years were significantly related to school achievement at age eleven years (Bradley, 1989).

This series of studies shows that important processes occur between children and their parents early in life that can have long-lasting implications for future intellectual achievement. For one thing, children who have responsive parents may develop a sense of control over their environments, and their resulting general socioemotional health may facilitate intellectual growth. In addition, the opportunity to play with toys may provide contexts for children to learn problem-solving skills from their parents, as well as the chance to develop knowledge from direct manipulation of the play materials. Language development is also enhanced because verbal interactions with parents during play and at other times teach children the properties of spoken speech (Bradley & Caldwell, 1984). One project demonstrated that, when mothers provided an environment rich in learning experiences such as those described in the HOME studies, the difference in IQ scores between African American and Caucasian children dropped by 28 percent (Brooks-Gunn, Klebanov, & Duncan, 1996).

Project Head Start The first federally funded program for compensatory education was Project Head Start, begun in the 1960s as a preschool enrichment program for "underprivileged children." Currently enrolling more than 900,000 children (Levinson, 2007), the program includes nutritional and medical assistance, as well as a structured educational program designed to provide cognitive stimulation. The first evaluations of Head Start were disappointing. In 1969, the Westinghouse Learning Corporation/Ohio University report compared the intellectual development of about 4,000 children from similar backgrounds, half of whom had participated in the first Head Start programs around the country and half of whom did not participate. Essentially no differences were found in the intellectual performance of the two groups; both remained below the norms for their age groups. This evaluation, however, was criticized on a number of grounds, including the fact that the evaluation was done prematurely, just barely after the program got off the ground.

Subsequent evaluations of Head Start have yielded more optimistic results. The Head Start Evaluation, Synthesis, and Utilization Project was an attempt to summarize all research on the impact of Head Start (McKey et al., 1985). This review concluded that Head Start produced significant effects on the intellectual performance of program participants, at least for the short term. Head Start children performed well in the first year or two after they started elementary school, showing average gains of ten points in IQ score, but the effects of the program faded in subsequent years.

One of the issues facing Head Start has been the great variability in the instructional practices used by teachers in programs across the country. What happens, though, when some of the most robust findings in developmental science are applied to Head Start classrooms in a deliberate and systematic way? In a study that randomly assigned Head Start children to either a control group or a group that received a research-based curriculum focused on social-emotional skills (such as conflict resolution, emotion expression, and emotion understanding) and vocabulary and literacy skills (such as awareness of the sounds made by different letters in words), children in the latter group showed substantial gains in multiple skills in both literacy and social problem solving over the course of a school year (Bierman et al., 2008). Results like these suggest that targeted interventions based on scientific findings may be an important strategy in getting children off to a good start in school achievement, and perhaps also in reducing the achievement gap.

One example of an early intervention program is Project Head Start, a federal program designed to provide nutritional and medical assistance, as well as school readiness skills, to children growing up in poverty. Children who attend Head Start show gains in some measures of educational achievement and at least short-term increases in IQ scores.

The Carolina Abecedarian Project Another important early intervention project, the Carolina Abecedarian Project, begun in 1972, aimed to prevent the lower intellectual functioning of children at risk (Ramey & Campbell, 1981; Ramey, Lee, & Burchinal, 1989). A sample of 121 low-income pregnant women with low educational achievement and IQ scores (an average of 84) was selected. Once the infants were born, roughly half were assigned to the experimental group and half to the control group. Infants in the experimental group received medical care, nutritional supplements, and a structured program of day care that emphasized the development of cognitive, language, social, and motor skills. In addition, the researchers provided a toy-lending library and a home visiting program, as well as parent support groups. During the first year, few differences on Bayley scores were found between infants in the experimental and control groups. From age eighteen months onward, however, the IQs of the experimental group consistently exceeded those of the control group, even when the children reached young adulthood (see Figure 10.11) (Campbell & Ramey, 1994; Campbell et al., 2001). Some researchers have voiced pessimism about the significance of these findings. For example, Herman Spitz (1986) pointed out that, by age five years, the differences between the experimental and control groups diminished to an average of only seven points. Also, scores for the experimental group never really increased (Spitz, 1999). Therefore, say the critics, the effects of this intensive intervention were not substantial.

An important issue concerns why the initial gains of Head Start and Abecedarian children "washed out" to some extent in successive years. Perhaps early intervention is not enough to inoculate children from the pervasive and continuing effects of poverty and understimulating environments as they advance into the school years. Perhaps, too, IQ scores are not the best indicators of the impact of Head Start and other early intervention programs. One collaborative study of the effects of eleven early intervention programs showed that children who had participated were less likely than nonparticipants to be assigned to special education classes, less likely to be "held back" a grade, and more likely to cite their school achievements as a source of pride (Lazar & Darlington, 1982). Data from the Chicago Longitudinal Study, assessing the impact of intensive center-based preschool programs for children living in poverty, show that by the time children were teenagers, they finished more years of school and had lower rates of juvenile delinquency than nonparticipants (Reynolds et al., 2001). Statistical analyses suggest that these effects are connected to growth in children's scholastic skills, good-quality educational experiences following the preschool program, and a high level of parental involvement (Reynolds, Ou, & Topitzes, 2004).

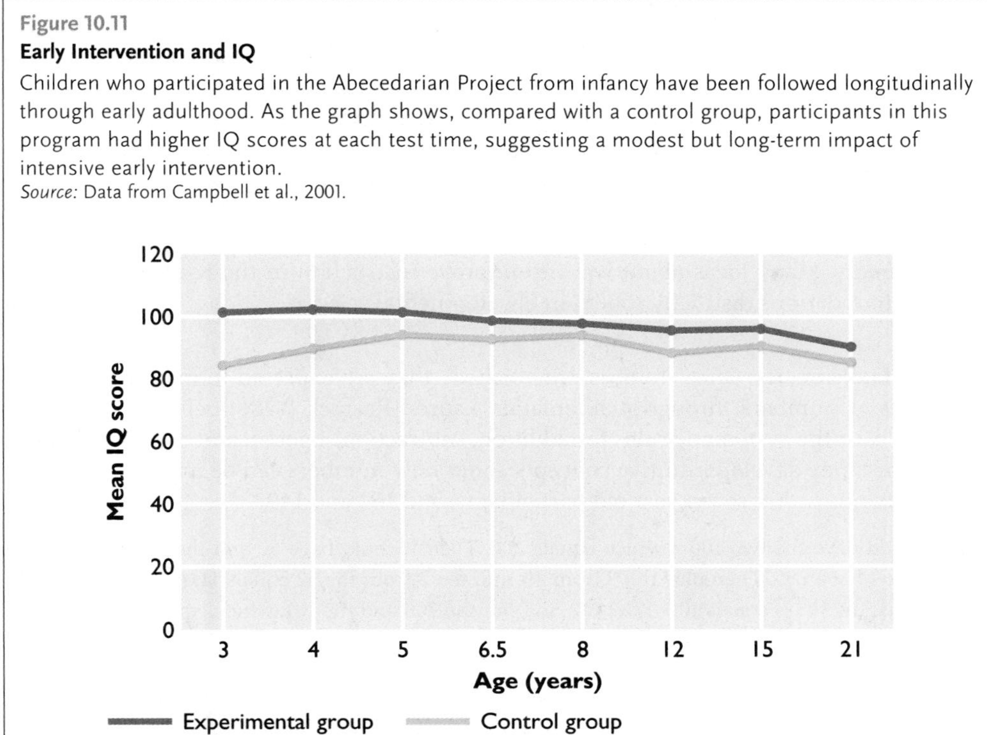

Figure 10.11
Early Intervention and IQ
Children who participated in the Abecedarian Project from infancy have been followed longitudinally through early adulthood. As the graph shows, compared with a control group, participants in this program had higher IQ scores at each test time, suggesting a modest but long-term impact of intensive early intervention.
Source: Data from Campbell et al., 2001.

Craig and Sharon Ramey (1998), pioneers in the Abecedarian Project, suggest that, to be effective, early intervention programs need to target children early in development, include substantial contact with children and families who participate, and provide direct learning experiences for children. Programs should also provide a broad array of services, including health and social services, as well as transportation. Finally, to have long-lasting impact, continuous intervention and support should take place beyond the preschool years.

Early Head Start In 1994 the federal government launched Early Head Start, a comprehensive national early intervention program targeted toward low-income children from birth to three years of age. Providing center-based services, home-based services, or both, the program focuses on health care, nutrition, early education of children, and parent education and support. Currently, slightly more than 60,000 children participate in Early Head Start (Hamm & Ewen, 2006). To evaluate the impact of the program, 3,000 families from seventeen programs in diverse regions of the country were recruited; half were randomly assigned to receive Early Head Start services, and half served as the control group. Children were assessed on a number of measures of cognitive and social development at ages fourteen, twenty-four, and thirty-six months. Several measures of parenting effectiveness were also obtained. The results showed that, by age three years, Early Head Start children outscored the control group in several important domains, including levels of cognitive functioning, language development, engagement with parents, and self-control. Parents showed differences, too; Early Head Start parents were more likely to read to their children and less likely to spank them. Overall, these parents were judged to provide a more supportive learning environment for children in their homes. Most effective were those programs that combined center-based care with home visits (Love et al., 2005).

Researchers acknowledge that, although the gains Early Head Start children showed were modest, they still presented a better profile than did the control children (Love et al., 2005), no small accomplishment considering that their annual family income was at the federal poverty level (for example, $19,350 for a family of four in 2005). The data echo an important theme: that intensive intervention, started early and involving parents, can indeed have an impact on children who are at risk.

Learning Academic Subjects

Although much of the research on children's cognitive development has traditionally focused on growth of general skills such as memory and problem-solving (see Chapter 8, "Cognition"), developmental scientists have also focused more and more on how children learn specific academic subjects. The science of understanding how children learn to read, for example, has grown tremendously and has greatly influenced programmatic approaches to reading instruction (Paris & Paris, 2006). Likewise, information on how children learn mathematics and science, two topics of high interest to educators and policymakers, has grown rapidly. Many ideas about ways to improve instruction in the K-12 school system build on foundations distinctly rooted in developmental science.

Learning Mathematics Once children enter school, they are expected to master the formal properties of numbers through mathematics. Lauren Resnick (1986) believes that before children learn the systematic rules for addition, subtraction, algebra, and other mathematical systems, they develop intuitive concepts about how numbers can be manipulated. How would Pitt, one of her seven-year-old participants, add 152 and 149?

> I would have the two 100's, which equals 200. Then I would have 50 and the 40, which equals 90. So I have 290. Then plus the 9 from 49, and the 2 from the 52 equals 11. And then I add the 90 plus the 11 . . . equals 102. 102? 101. So I put the 200 and the 101, which equals 301. (p. 164)

All of this came from a young boy who had mastered only first-grade arithmetic!

In fact, children seem to have a good basic grasp of even more complex numerical concepts, such as fractions, by age four. Suppose a preschooler sees three-fourths of a circle hidden by a screen and then one-half of a circle come out from the screen. How much is left behind the screen? A surprising number of four-year-olds can select a picture of one-fourth of a circle from a set of alternatives (Mix, Levine, & Huttenlocher, 1999). In addition, even a brief training session can help young children understand the basic concepts of fractions. When five-year-olds in one study had the opportunity to observe a whole pizza divided among different numbers of recipients, they began to understand that the size of each share of pizza depended on the number of individuals who were going to eat it (Sophian, Garyantes, & Chang, 1997). Given such findings, it is puzzling that many children experience difficulties with mathematics in school. Perhaps, as Resnick suggests, teachers should frame more complex mathematical operations, such as ratios and algebraic expressions, in terms of simple additive properties or other intuitions children have about numbers, at least when they are first being learned (Resnick, 1995; Resnick & Singer, 1993).

SOCIOCULTURAL INFLUENCE

Because Asian students score significantly higher than students from the United States on tests of mathematics (Fuligni & Stevenson, 1995; Geary et al., 1993; Stevenson et al., 1993), examining the source of their mathematical proficiency can be especially instructive. Asian children use different strategies to solve mathematics problems than American children usually do. Korean and Japanese children, for example, add the numbers 8 + 6 by first trying to reach 10; that is, they add 8 + 2 to make 10 and then add the difference between 6 and 2 to reach the answer, 14. It is interesting to note that, in these Asian languages, names for numbers in the teens are "ten one" (eleven), "ten two" (twelve), and so on. Thus, children may be used to thinking in terms of tens. Addition and subtraction strategies based on a system of tens are also taught explicitly in Korea and Japan (Fuson & Kwon, 1992; Naito & Miura, 2001); as amount of schooling increases, so does children's use of the base ten approach (Naito & Miura, 2001). Findings such as these offer interesting potential ways of enhancing children's already sound mathematical understanding.

Researchers have identified several mathematical skills that seem to be especially important in predicting successful achievement in this subject several years later. Among them are familiarity with the symbolic representations of numbers, being able to place numbers correctly on a line representing magnitude, and understanding the meanings of the various symbols used in mathematics (e.g., +, =) (Berteletti et al., 2010; Booth & Siegler, 2008; Siegler, 2003). Along with the knowledge of the concepts that build strong foundations in children's mathematical understanding, research has also uncovered some relatively simple interventions that can enhance children's mastery of numbers. For example,

NATURE & NURTURE

just four 15-minute sessions of playing a board game that involves counting spaces from start to finish—in a straight line—can improve children's performance on tests of number identification, number comparisons, addition, and other key measures of numerical competency (Siegler, 2009).

Development of Scientific Thinking Most of us have received at least some formal training in the complex type of reasoning called *scientific thinking.* Scientific reasoning involves formulating a hypothesis, designing experiments in which one factor varies while others are held constant, and deciding on the validity of the hypothesis based on the observable evidence. According to Piaget, you will recall, this form of logical thought is not observed prior to the start of the formal operational stage, usually at preadolescence. Contemporary research confirms that there are indeed observable developmental accomplishments in scientific reasoning; however, even children who are just starting school show impressive knowledge about some of the basic tenets of scientific thinking.

One element of scientific thinking is the ability to distinguish between theory and evidence. Preschoolers often behave as if there is no distinction between the two. Shown a series of pictures depicting two runners in a race, younger children typically answer the questions, "Who won?" and "How do you know?" with theory (e.g., "He has fast sneakers") rather than evidence (e.g., "He's holding the trophy"). By age six, though, children are likely to cite objective evidence (Kuhn & Pearsall, 2000).

A related skill is the capacity to see which conclusions are warranted by the evidence. Let us consider one example in which the child is presented with a series of pictures depicting the phases of the moon along with two theories about why they occur: (1) clouds cover different portions of the moon at different times, or (2) the moon has a dark and a light side. Then the child hears the evidence: an astronaut reports that the moon is dry and has no water, that he landed on some white rock, and that he later walked on black gravel. Which theory about the moon could possibly be correct? Most first-, third-, and fifth-graders in this study chose the second theory, the one that was consistent with the evidence (Samarapungavan, 1992). Other researchers have confirmed that first-graders can correctly identify whether a specific piece of empirical evidence provides conclusive or inconclusive support for a hypothesis (Sodian, Zaitchik, & Carey, 1991).

Yet scientific thinking involves greater complexities. For example, hypotheses must be formed in the first place, and usually several hypotheses are concurrently in the mind of the scientist. Often several variables operate at the same time. Experiments must be designed and conducted and their outcomes coordinated with the hypotheses to determine which variable causes the observed outcomes (Klahr & Dunbar, 1988). It is here that developmental changes are most apparent. When third-graders are asked to generate and evaluate hypotheses by running a series of experiments, they usually are not systematic in designing experiments that isolate the key variable and do not write down the outcomes of their experiments. Sixth-graders show improvements but still design a limited number of experiments, and their experiments are often difficult to interpret. In one study in which sixth-graders were asked to use a software package to test which variables played a role in the risk of earthquakes, 83 percent of the students investigated three or more variables at once (Kuhn & Dean, 2005). Adults do the best but not because their reasoning about the relationship between theory and evidence is stronger. Rather, adults can coordinate the generation of hypotheses with the design of the set of experiments necessary to test them (Klahr, Fay, & Dunbar, 1993).

NATURE & NURTURE

When children are encouraged to engage repeatedly in scientific problem solving, their skills improve noticeably. Deanna Kuhn and her colleagues (Kuhn, Schauble, & Garcia-Mila, 1992) asked preadolescents to identify which variables affected the speed of a model boat being towed in a tank of water: the water depth, boat size, boat weight, sail color, or sail size. The instructor gave minimal feedback to the students, but they were encouraged to make a plan about what they wished to find out, state what they found out after each experiment, and record their findings in a notebook. The results showed that over only a few weeks of repeated exposure to these problems, students became markedly more proficient at designing valid and focused experiments and at drawing valid inferences from the data they collected. Follow-up studies show that this knowledge is subsequently applied to new

Children's scientific reasoning can be encouraged by providing opportunities for students to record their plans and their findings at each stage of solving a scientific problem.

Michael Newman/PhotoEdit Inc.

problems (Kuhn et al., 1995; Schauble, 1996). Even hinting to students that they should limit their investigations to a single variable helps. Sixth-graders who received this tip during science instruction were more likely than those in a control group to conduct valid experiments and to draw appropriate conclusions (Kuhn & Dean, 2005).

Direct instruction helps children master principles of scientific reasoning, too. In one study, seven- to ten-year-olds received explicit training on the concept "controlling variables in an experiment." They were provided with examples of confounded and unconfounded experiments and were then asked to apply their knowledge to a sample experiment. Children who had received this training were able to apply the principle of "controlling variables" to several different experiments and were more likely to do so than children who had not received instruction. Thus, the ability to reason like a scientist is clearly within the grasp of elementary school students (Chen & Klahr, 1999; Klahr, Chen, & Toth, 2001).

A good way to capture the development of scientific thinking is provided by Deanna Kuhn and her colleagues, who say that children acquire increasing control over their own thought processes. By becoming aware of the differences between theory and evidence, fact and opinion, and by coordinating theories with evidence, children begin to be able to "know how they know" (Kuhn & Pearsall, 2000). In that sense, the steps in the development of scientific reasoning may reflect broader accomplishments in the cognitive domain.

These studies give you a glimpse of how the science of learning and cognition can serve as the springboard for educational practices that capitalize on our knowledge about the child—his or her capabilities, qualities as a thinker, and potential as a learner. In recognition of the potential contributions that developmental science and educational psychology can make to children's academic achievement, more and more policymakers are asking that educational innovations be firmly grounded in this type of "evidenced-based practice."

For Your Review and Reflection

- Which specific aspects of the home environment are related to subsequent IQ scores in children?
- What has research revealed about the effects of early intervention programs for children? What factors are most important in promoting successful outcomes?

- What forms of mathematical reasoning do young children display? How can educators capitalize on these basic skills?
- What basic scientific reasoning skills do children bring to their early experiences in school? What kinds of changes occur in these skills with development?
- What additional research do you think developmental scientists should carry out to illustrate the role of early experience on academic and other kinds of learning?

chapter recap

Summary of Developmental Themes

Nature & Nurture

How do nature and nurture interact in children's achievement?
The nature–nurture debate becomes an especially thorny issue in the matter of intelligence and academic achievement. Few psychologists would dispute that heredity plays a role in the child's intellectual development. For example, early individual differences in the speed of infant habituation and recognition memory may signal differences in some aspects of later intellectual functioning. In addition, genetic effects such as Down syndrome and the high correlations between IQ scores of identical twins reared apart suggest a role for "nature." Yet research also shows that children's early experiences within the home, together with the intellectual skills touted by the larger culture, modulate how their genetic blueprints unfold.

Sociocultural Influence

How does the sociocultural context influence children's achievement?
Culture broadly influences the kinds of skills that its members value and nurture and that are believed to constitute intelligence as well as achievement. Is speed of executing tasks important? Are good visual-spatial or verbal skills essential for successful adaptation to the environment? A culture's demands and expectations frame the way intelligent behavior will be defined in the first place. From the narrower perspective of performance on standardized IQ tests, children who have experiences consistent with the knowledge tapped by test items will perform well, whereas those with more impoverished backgrounds will be at a disadvantage. Other sociocultural factors often associated with social class, such as parental emphasis on intellectual efforts or the amount of emotional stress within the family system, can also impinge on academic achievement.

Interaction Among Domains

How does children's achievement interact with development in other domains?
Children who obtain high scores on intelligence tests are more likely to be successful in school and, as adults, to hold high-status jobs and be productive in those jobs. Thus, to some extent, IQ scores can predict certain aspects of accomplishment in life. Achievement can be influenced in significant ways by the child's beliefs about the self. A sense of agency, mastery beliefs, and views of intelligence as malleable are all associated with higher levels of performance in the academic sphere.

Risk | Resilience

What factors promote risk or resilience in children's achievement?
Studies of environmental influences suggest that an individual's score on an IQ test or on measures of academic achievement can be a function of the specific parenting practices she or he has experienced or other elements of the childhood environment. For example, children who are successful in school tend to have parents and teachers who foster agency and peers who support academic attainment. Early intervention programs can result in long-term gains in achievement for children who start their lives at risk for intellectual and academic delays.

Chapter Review

Individual Differences in Ability

What major questions have surrounded attempts to define intelligence?
Definitions of intelligence vary in two major ways: whether intelligence is seen as a global characteristic or as a set of separate abilities, and whether the emphasis is on the products or the processes of intelligent behavior.

What are the main features of psychometric approaches to intelligence?
The *psychometric model* of intelligence emphasizes individual differences in test scores. The idea is to compare an individual's score with the performance of the many children or adults who constitute the standardization sample.

What are the principal ideas underlying the theories of Spearman, Thurstone, and Cattell and Horn?
Spearman conceptualized a general intelligence factor called *g*, and Thurstone believed in seven primary mental abilities. In Cattell and Horn's view, intelligence could be seen as having two components: *fluid intelligence*, which is free of cultural influence, and *crystallized intelligence*, which refers to culturally derived skills. Fluid intelligence shows an earlier developmental decline than crystallized intelligence.

What are the main features of information-processing approaches to intelligence?
Information-processing models focus on the mental activities of individuals as they engage in problem solving. Speed of processing

and working memory capacity are two information-processing activities thought to be involved in intelligence.

What assumptions do psychologists make about the distribution of IQ scores in the population?
IQ scores are normally distributed in the population. The mean IQ is 100, and the standard deviation is 15. Individuals who fall beyond two standard deviations from the mean are considered to be exceptional.

What are some major tests that have been used to assess intelligence in infants and children? What are the primary features of each in terms of how they measure intelligence?
The Bayley Scales of Infant and Toddler Development are used to assess the intellectual capabilities of infants. Scores on tests of cognition, language, motor control, and behavior can indicate if an infant is at risk for developmental delay. The WISC-IV contains scales that assess verbal comprehension, perceptual reasoning, working memory, and processing speed. The child's score is expressed as a *deviation IQ*, a measure that compares his or her performance to that of the standardization sample.

How is giftedness defined? What are the unique ways in which gifted individuals process information? What are the behavioral characteristics of gifted children?
A child who scores more than two standard deviations above the mean for IQ is generally regarded as gifted. Gifted children are good planners and show skill in dealing with novelty. They are also fast and efficient in processing information. Gifted children tend to take advantage of educational opportunities, have good relationships with peers, and are generally well adjusted.

What kinds of outcomes do IQ scores predict?
IQ scores generally predict academic success but are not necessarily related to other measures of life satisfaction.

What are the complexities involved in trying to assess the contributions of heredity to group differences in IQ?
Social class and racial differences in IQ scores illustrate the difficulty of drawing simple conclusions about the sources of intelligence. One problem is that estimates of heritability derived from only one group do not necessarily explain between-group differences in scores. Cross-fostering studies of children who were raised in environments that differ from those of their biological parents indicate that IQ scores rise in enriched environments but that scores are still more strongly related to educational levels of biological parents than to IQ levels of adoptive parents. *Test bias* may also contribute to between-group differences.

Self-Concepts and Achievement

How does effectance motivation begin and develop?
Infants seem to be born with an intrinsic desire (*effectance motivation*) to gain control of their world. To the extent that the environment provides consistent feedback in response to children's actions, children acquire an increasing sense of agency.

What factors contribute to mastery orientation and learned helplessness? What steps can parents and teachers take to reduce learned helplessness in children?
Children with a *mastery orientation* believe they have considerable influence over what happens to them. Those who experience *learned helplessness* believe they have little influence over what happens to them. Mastery orientation and learned helplessness are determined in part by the extent to which children perceive their abilities as entity-based or as a result of their own effort. Learned helplessness can be reduced by helping children focus on their effort and by avoiding praise or criticism of stable traits.

How does the concept of stereotype threat help us to understand group differences in achievement?
Stereotype threat, the negative psychological impact of being sensitized to a stereotype about gender or ethnicity, has been linked to diminished performance on standardized tests.

Contextual Influences on Achievement

How do parents and peers influence school achievement?
Parents who are involved with their children and who encourage their autonomy tend to have children with higher academic achievement. The peers with whom a child aligns himself or herself can affect school motivation.

How do teacher behaviors influence school achievement?
Teacher expectations about students' abilities can have important consequences for their school achievement. Certain classroom management styles can be influential; studies of *cooperative* and *collaborative learning* reveal more favorable outcomes for students. In addition, teachers have a positive impact on students when they encourage autonomy and initiative, and when they form close interpersonal relationships with their students.

What factors seem to be related to the achievement behaviors of children from different cultural groups?
According to the cultural compatibility hypothesis, children's academic performance rises when educational practices incorporate elements of the child's background culture. Children in Asian societies experience more learning time, greater demands for homework, and a greater press for achievement from parents than children in the United States. They also believe in the importance of effort for academic success. This constellation of factors may contribute to higher levels of achievement.

Applied Developmental Science and Academic Learning

Which specific aspects of the home environment are related to subsequent IQ scores in children?
Studies using the HOME Inventory show that several factors in the child's home environment are related to higher IQ scores. Particularly important are parental responsiveness to the child, provision of appropriate play materials, and parental involvement with the child.

What has research revealed about the effects of early intervention programs for children? What factors are most important in promoting successful outcomes?
Evaluations of the effectiveness of early intervention programs such as Head Start and the Abecedarian Project show intellectual and academic gains by children who have participated. However, some earlier research showed that the increases shown by Head Start children often fade after a few years. Critics of the Abecedarian Project say that increases in IQ scores are modest at best. Some

researchers argue that more intensive and continuous intervention is necessary to produce more dramatic outcomes. Research on Early Head Start confirms the importance of these factors.

What forms of mathematical reasoning do young children display? How can educators capitalize on these basic skills?
Preschoolers display good intuitions about how to add and how to form fractions. Educators can try to frame more complex mathematical concepts in terms of their additive properties to take advantage of the mathematical understanding children have already.

What basic scientific reasoning skills do children bring to their early experiences in school? What kinds of changes occur in these skills with development?
Before adolescence, children display the ability to distinguish between theory and evidence and can identify which evidence supports a given hypothesis. Developmental changes are most apparent in the ability to design systematic experiments to test hypotheses. This ability can be enhanced with increased experiences in scientific problem solving as well as with direct instruction on how to design an experiment without confounds.

Key Terms and Concepts

collaborative learning (p. 378)
cooperative learning (p. 379)
crystallized intelligence (p. 357)
deviation IQ (p. 364)
effectance motivation (p. 369)
fluid intelligence (p. 357)
intelligence quotient (IQ) (p. 362)
learned helplessness (p. 371)
mastery orientation (p. 370)
psychometric model (p. 357)
stereotype threat (p. 375)
test bias (p. 368)
triarchic theory (p. 359)

Media Resources

Access an integrated eBook and chapter-specific interactive learning tools, including flashcards, quizzes, videos, and more, in your Developmental Psychology CourseMate, accessed through CengageBrain.com.

© Hideki Nawate/amanaimagesRF/Jupiter Images

CHAPTER OUTLINE

[chapter 11]

Emotion

KEY THEMES IN EMOTIONAL DEVELOPMENT

- **NATURE & NURTURE** How do nature and nurture interact in emotional development?
- **SOCIOCULTURAL INFLUENCE** How does the sociocultural context influence emotional development?
- **INTERACTION AMONG DOMAINS** How does emotional development interact with other domains of development?
- **RISK | RESILIENCE** What factors promote risk or resilience in emotional development?

It's a quiet time on Sunday morning, just after a big breakfast, and Cindy admires her eight-month-old son, Michael, as he sits in his infant seat. He is looking at her so intently, raising his eyebrows a bit and scanning her face, gurgling contentedly. Suddenly the phone rings. Michael falls silent and opens his eyes wide. Cindy raises her eyebrows into two big arches and opens her mouth, making an exaggerated "Oohh" sound, suggesting surprise. Her baby eyes her with fascination, chortles, then smiles broadly. Cindy smiles back, chuckles, and says, "Must be Grandma calling to see how you are. Let me answer the phone, okay, honey?" She touches Michael affectionately under the chin as she gets up to reach for the phone. The baby lets out a shriek of delight and smiles again. Cindy can't help but laugh at the antics of her young son.

This scene, in all its simplicity, is a typical one in many families. Babies and caregivers revel in each other's company, and although the infant cannot yet speak, he participates fully in the interaction in nonverbal ways. The communication relies less on language than on both overt and subtle nuances in facial expressions and sounds that communicate emotional states. Some have characterized the back-and-forth nature of this exchange as a well-choreographed "waltz" wherein each partner looks to the other for cues about what to do next so the interaction proceeds smoothly and enjoyably. The episode also suggests some fundamental questions about the nature of human emotions and the forces that guide emotional development. In what ways, if any, are our emotions innately influenced, the result of a biological "prewiring"? And how are our displays and conceptions of emotions derived from learning the rules and conventions of our culture?

The interaction between Cindy and her infant suggests that emotions play a key role in social exchanges between infants and adults. This may not always be the case, as illustrated most dramatically by the Gusii of Kenya. The Gusii culture places great emphasis on suppressing intense emotions, probably to maintain harmony in the small, tribal living units characteristic of that group. Consequently, mothers maintain a bland, neutral expression when interacting with their infants and try to inhibit strong shows of emotion from their children (Dixon et al., 1981). Differing cultural norms are reflected in the parenting styles we see in various cultures and the specific emotional behaviors children eventually display. At the same time, however, research with young infants in many other cultures confirms the general principle that emotions are an integral part of the social lives of infants and their caregivers.

In this chapter, we see how children's expression and understanding of emotions change with age. Many of these accomplishments are tied to advances in cognition that permit children to think about complex feeling states within themselves as well as in others. An important part of the process of emotional growth also involves the child's ability to regulate his emotions—to cool down, for example, if he is feeling angry and frustrated. In addition, even though emotions are the personal expressions of the individual's moods or feeling states, they also function as a mode of communicating with others. Given the social dimension of emotions, we will investigate the role they play in the child's relationships with others, specifically in the special "attachments" that emerge between child and caregivers. What is the psychological significance of these early emotional bonds, and how do they influence the child's later development?

What Are Emotions?

INTERACTION AMONG DOMAINS

Emotions are a complex set of behaviors produced in response to some external or internal event, or elicitor, which serve to motivate and direct thoughts and actions. Emotions include several components. First, they have a *physiological* component, involving changes in autonomic nervous system activities such as respiration and heart rate. Fear or anxiety, for example, may be accompanied by more rapid breathing, increased heart rate and blood pressure, and perspiration. Second, emotions include an *expressive* component, usually a facial display that signals the emotion. Smiles, grimaces, cries, and laughter overtly express a person's emotional state. Third, emotions have an *experiential* component, the subjective feeling or cognitive judgment of having an emotion. Just how a person interprets and evaluates an emotional state depends on his level of cognitive development and the past experiences he has had. For a child to be able to state, "I feel happy," he must recognize the internal cues and external contexts associated with "happiness," which are derived from experience. In addition, he must have a relatively mature concept of the self as a feeling, responding being—a sign of cognitive maturity.

The Functions of Emotions

What role do emotions play in the psychological development of the child? On one level, they serve to organize and regulate the child's own behavior. If a child is learning to ride a two-wheeled bicycle and succeeds in tottering down the sidewalk without keeling over, she undoubtedly will feel elated and probably more motivated to practice this new skill for a few more minutes or even hours. If, on the other hand, she falls repeatedly or even injures herself, she may feel angry and discouraged and quit riding for a few days. Thus, the child's emotional states influence what she will decide to do (Saarni et al., 2006).

INTERACTION AMONG DOMAINS

A child's emotional state can also influence cognitive processes. One example concerns the relationship between emotion and learning. Research indicates that children who show an interest in certain objects or topics—a strong feeling of attraction or pleasure—pay more attention to those stimuli and remember them better in a subsequent memory test compared with objects that do not interest them (Renninger, 1992).

Of special importance is the fact that emotions serve to initiate, maintain, or terminate interactions with others. The baby's cry or smile almost invariably prompts contact with the caregiver. A toddler's frustration and anger over an unshared toy may lead him to abandon a playmate temporarily. In fact, a social dialogue completely devoid of emotional content is unusual. "Moods," more enduring emotional states, may help us understand the child's personality attributes, such as the tendency to be shy, dependent, or aggressive. These traits, in turn, can influence the frequency and form of the child's social contacts. Thus, understanding emotional development can increase our appreciation of a broad range of children's accomplishments in other domains.

Measuring Emotions

Given the complex nature of emotions, measuring them becomes an important issue for researchers because all three dimensions—physiological, expressive, and cognitive—must be considered. One approach is to record changes in physiological functions such as heart rate (acceleration or deceleration), heart rate variability (the individual's basic heart rate pattern), or electroencephalogram (EEG) patterns showing brain activity as affective stimuli are presented (Marshall & Fox, 2008; Fox & Davidson, 1986). Newer technologies, such as *positron*

emotions Complex behaviors involving physiological, expressive, and experiential components produced in response to some external or internal event.

emission tomography (PET) and *functional magnetic resonance imaging* (fMRI) (see Chapter 2, "Studying Child Development"), are also being used to track the activities of the brain as emotions are being experienced (Wager et al., 2008). Another strategy is to conduct fine-grained analyses of the child's facial expressions or vocalizations. Tiny movements of the muscles in the brow, eye, and mouth regions produce the facial configurations associated with joy, sadness, anger, and other emotions. An example of a coding scheme developed to score ten facial expressions is the AFFEX developed by Carroll Izard and his associates (Izard & Dougherty, 1982). Each emotional expression is associated with discrete movements that are carefully described in the coding scheme. Figure 11.1 shows several components of the expression for anger, for example, including brows lowered and drawn together, eyes narrowed or squinted, and the mouth squarish and angular. When all three components are present, the appearance of anger is said to be observed. Similarly, combinations of facial movements for other emotions are detailed in the coding scheme.

Figure 11.1

Identifying Facial Expressions of Anger in Infants

This series of drawings shows the elements of anger that are part of the AFFEX system for scoring facial expressions. Panel A shows the brows lowered and drawn together. Panel B shows the eyes narrowed. Panel C shows the angular or square-shaped mouth. When all of these elements appear together (as in Panel D), the emotion expressed is scored as anger.

Source: Adapted from Izard & Dougherty, 1982.

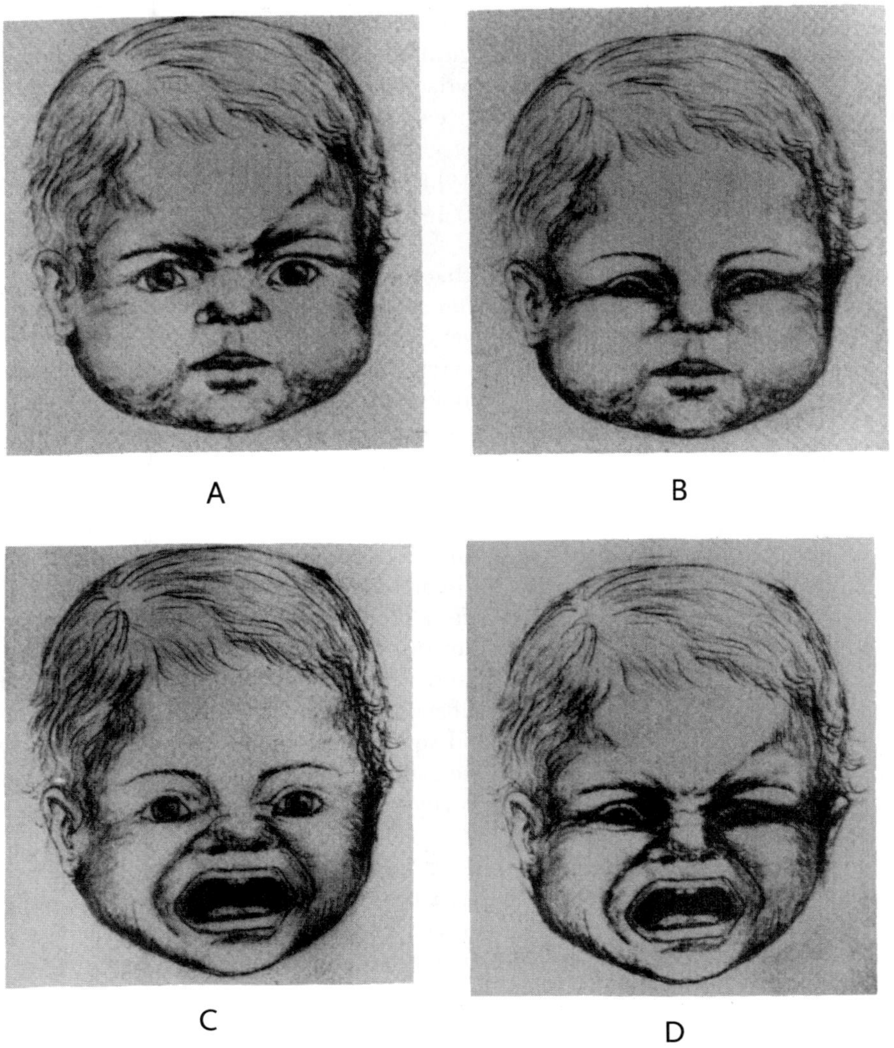

A

B

C

D

The frequency, loudness, duration, and sound patterns of the child's vocalizations can also indicate emotion (Papousêk, Papousêk, & Koester, 1986). Often facial expressions, body movements, and vocalizations function as an ensemble of emotion indicators; for example, a facial expression of anger, raising arms upward, and crying combine to signal "pick me up" (Weinberg & Tronick, 1994). Finally, the child's interpretations of her own and others' emotions can be assessed through the use of self-report measures (e.g., "Tell me how often you felt cheerful in the last week") and tasks requiring the child to label, match, or produce emotional expressions ("Tell me how the person in this picture feels" or "Show me the person who feels sad").

Although each methodological approach has helped to illuminate aspects of the child's emotional life, researchers must be cautious when interpreting their data. When physiological changes such as decelerated heart rate occur as the infant watches a lively segment of "Sesame Street," is he experiencing interest or surprise? The emotion that corresponds to a specific reaction of the nervous system is not always clear. Likewise, an overt emotional expression such as crying might represent a number of possible internal emotional states, such as sadness, joy, or fear. Self-reports of the child's emotional states present their own difficulties. As we saw in Chapter 2, some children may answer researchers' questions based on the way they think they should reply rather than on how they feel. Others may be reluctant to discuss their inner feelings at all. Despite these methodological difficulties, researchers have learned a good deal about emotional development in the past three decades.

Theoretical Perspectives on Emotional Development

To what degree are human emotions biologically based, preprogrammed responses to specific environmental stimuli? How do the myriad learning experiences that accumulate over the course of infancy and childhood influence emotional development? Do emotions function in neat, discrete packages—anger being separate from sadness and fear? Or are different emotions simply points on a continuum of positive or negative arousal? These are some of the questions addressed by contemporary perspectives on emotion.

NATURE & NURTURE

Biologically Based Explanations The main champions of a strong biological view of emotions are Paul Ekman and Carroll Izard. After studying people in various cultures, Ekman (1972, 1973) concluded that there are universal facial expressions for certain basic emotions that are interpreted in similar ways across cultures. Ekman showed photographs of six faces, each depicting a particular emotion—happiness, sadness, anger, fear, surprise, or disgust—to participants in the United States, Japan, Chile, Brazil, and Argentina. As they looked at each photograph, participants were asked to identify the emotion displayed. Ekman found a high degree of accuracy across cultures as to which emotions were represented. A meta-analysis of ninety-seven studies confirms what Ekman first reported—that individuals from a wide variety of cultures correctly recognize fundamental emotions, showing the highest degree of accuracy for happiness (Elfenbein & Ambady, 2002).

Similarly, Izard believes that because certain emotional expressions are displayed by very young infants and there is little variation across individuals and cultures in how they are expressed, they are necessarily innate and have distinct adaptive value (Izard, 2007). When the newborn infant tastes a bitter substance such as quinine, for example, she will pull up her upper lip, wrinkle her nose, and squint her eyes, indicating she has detected the unpleasant stimulus. No learning is necessary to produce this reaction of disgust. The caregiver observing this signal might respond by removing a potentially harmful substance from the baby's mouth, thereby ensuring her well-being.

The experience of emotion, Izard states, is the automatic product of the internal sensory feedback the individual receives from making the facial expression; wrinkling the face produces the feeling of disgust. Izard also maintains that once an emotion is activated, it in turn motivates the individual to act. The experience of disgust, in other words, may lead the baby to spit out the distasteful substance. According to Izard, infants show a small set of discrete emotions, such as joy, anger, fear, sadness, interest, and disgust, which function independently of one another. With development, these emotions become more interrelated and

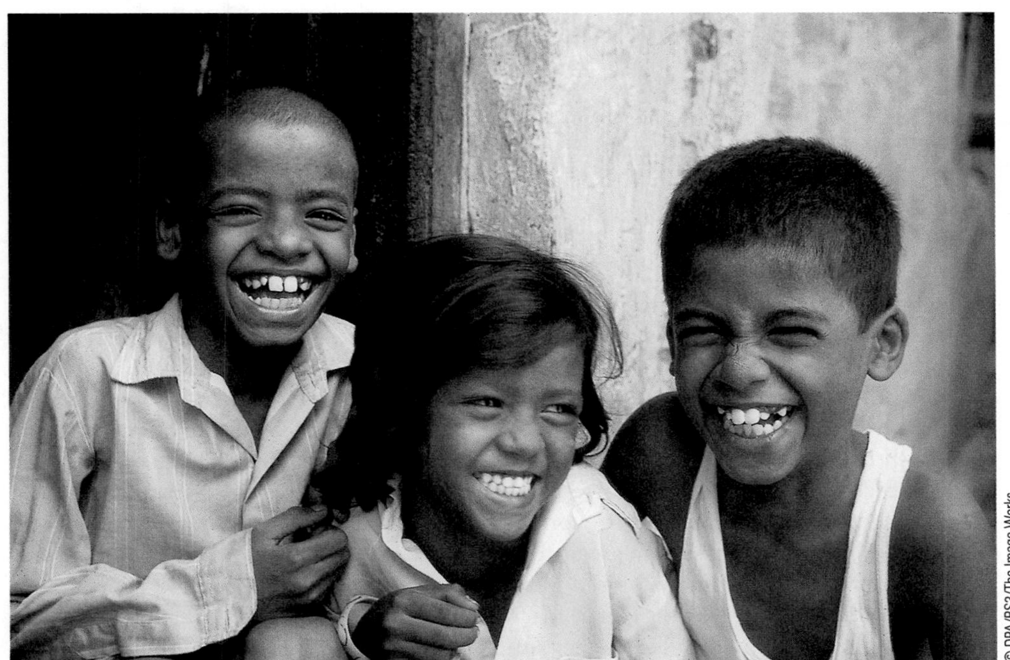

© DPA/RS3/The Image Works

There are many cross-cultural similarities in the expression and interpretation of emotions. Most of us, for example, would recognize these Indian children's expressions as indicating happiness.

connected to cognition (Ackerman, Abe, & Izard, 1998). Furthermore, different patterns of expressing emotions eventually become organized as personality traits that can vary across individuals (Izard & Ackerman, 2000).

INTERACTION AMONG DOMAINS

Both Ekman and Izard acknowledge that learning may play a role in emotional development, especially as children learn to control and regulate their emotions. They maintain, however, that the role of biological factors is paramount and that emotions originate in the genetic blueprints with which the child begins life.

A Cognitive-Socialization Explanation Michael Lewis and Linda Michalson (1983) have provided an account of the emotional life of the child that emphasizes the cognitive activities involved in emotional experiences. According to these theorists, an environmental event does not directly produce an emotional expression. Instead, the child relies on cognitive processes to assess the event, how it compares with past events, and the social rules surrounding the event. Suppose, for example, the child encounters a barking dog. Whether he cries with fear or smiles at the noisy animal depends on his past experiences with dogs (has he ever been bitten?) and on what parents and others have instructed him to believe about animals ("Barking dogs will bite—stay away!" or "Some dogs get excited when they want to play—it's okay"). Cognitive processes thus act as *mediators,* or mental events that bridge the gap between environmental stimuli and the response the individual ultimately expresses. This conceptualization accounts for individual differences in emotional reactions when the same event produces different responses from two people.

INTERACTION AMONG DOMAINS

According to Lewis and Michalson, socialization plays an important role in shaping the time and the manner in which emotions are displayed. Children in our culture learn that it is appropriate to feel happy at birthday parties and sad when a friend's grandmother dies and that a smiling face and a sad face should be made under these respective circumstances. Socialization also guides the way emotions are managed. Young children in many cultures, for example, learn to inhibit expressions of fear and anger. Finally, socialization directs the way children label and interpret emotions. When the young child cries due to a physical injury and the parent says, "That hurts, doesn't it?" the interpretation provides pain as the reason for the tears. When crying is the response to the collapse of a tower of toy blocks, the parent may provide a different interpretation for the child, such as "That's frustrating." These kinds of communications serve as an important vehicle by which children learn how to interpret their own emotional states.

NATURE & NURTURE

NATURE & NURTURE

INTERACTION AMONG DOMAINS

Emotion as Part of a Social Context For some theorists, such as Joseph Campos and Carol Saarni (Campos et al., 1994; Saarni, 1999; Saarni et al., 2006), emotions are deeply and inextricably intertwined with the social environment. Children's understanding of their own and others' emotions and how they regulate their emotional states arise from the crossroads of personal goals and social interactions with others. What the child wants and desires, as well as the reactions of those in the social environment, create the "mix" for experiences of emotions. Emotions serve to motivate the individual toward particular social actions. For example, the emotion of "pride" can be the outcome of glowing comments from the parents after a child produces a colorful drawing. For that same child, the experience of pride will likely motivate her to share a newly written poem with a visiting grandmother. Emotions also surface when the emotions of others are observed (e.g., a mother shows great fear at the sound of thunder) or when one remembers emotional experiences from the past.

Rather than describe discrete emotions such as joy or fear, contextual theorists emphasize the intensity and positive or negative tone of emotions. Emotions are not conceptualized as *entities* but instead are viewed as *processes* embedded in social interactions and undergirded by neural functions (Barrett & Wager, 2006). In other words, it is of paramount importance to understand how they work or function. According to this perspective, considerable attention is necessarily given to the process of socialization and to the role of culture. How do families help children to regulate their emotions, to control, for example, angry outbursts or overt expressions of fear? How do different cultures conceptualize emotions, and what emotional styles do they emphasize, being expressive or more restrained, for example? These are the types of research questions that are motivated by this important perspective on emotional development.

For Your Review and Reflection

- What are the three components of emotions? How are these related to the ways in which researchers measure emotions?
- What functions do emotions serve in the various aspects of the child's psychological life?
- What are the main ways in which biological, cognitive-socialization, and social-contextual theories of emotion differ from one another?
- How does each of these theories address the issue of the interaction of nature and nurture?
- How closely do you think physiological, expressive, and cognitive interpretations of emotions are tied together during infancy? During childhood? During adolescence?

Expressing and Understanding Emotions

Researchers focus on emotional development from various angles. First, they examine whether children change in the way they express their own emotions. Do infants exhibit the full range of emotions that we see in adults, or does a developmental progression occur in the types of emotions children display? Second, how do children change in their ability to understand emotions in themselves and others, to read facial expressions and interpret them, to know the circumstances that lead positive and negative emotions to arise, and to appreciate the consequences of different emotions?

Early Emotional Development

Much of the groundwork for emotional development occurs during the first year or so of life. Parents and young infants frequently rely on nonverbal signals laden with emotional overtones to communicate with one another, as we saw with Cindy and Michael at the start of this chapter. Just what behaviors are infants capable of showing and "reading"?

Emotional Expression in Infancy Even infants only a few days or weeks old are capable of producing the facial expressions associated with several emotions, including interest, distress, disgust, joy, sadness, anger, and surprise (Field et al., 1982; Izard, 1978; Izard et al., 1995). By seven months of age, the infant has added expressions of fear to his repertoire (Izard et al., 1980). The fact that these discrete facial expressions appear so early in infancy, before much learning can have taken place, provides strong support for the idea that emotional expressions are to some extent biologically determined. These emotions are often called **basic** (or *primary*) **emotions.**

NATURE & NURTURE

Although even the earliest displays of basic emotions usually are recognized readily by adults, their form and the conditions that elicit them may change over the first few months. Two important emotional expressions in infancy, smiling and crying, demonstrate these changes. The smile is one of the most captivating and irresistible infant behaviors. In the newborn, this behavior occurs primarily during the state of REM sleep, when dreaming is thought to occur, in bursts of several smiles in succession (Emde & Koenig, 1969). The mouth stretches sideways and up, producing a simple version of the smile. Although many hypotheses attempt to explain why very young infants produce this facial gesture (including the popular but mistaken notion that "gas" is responsible), the most consistent finding is that neonates smile when they experience a shift in physiological arousal state, such as when they fall asleep or become drowsy (Wolff, 1987).

At approximately two weeks of age, the form of the smile changes. After the initial broadening of the lips, the corners of the lips retract even farther (with the mouth often opening), the cheek muscles contract, and the skin around the eyes wrinkles (Messinger, Fogel, & Dickson, 1999). Now the infant smiles during states of wakefulness, sometimes in response to familiar voices and sounds, sweet tastes, and pleasant food odors (Fogel, 1982; Steiner, 1979). By three months of age, smiles increase in frequency, and full-blown smiles—with open mouth and cheeks raised—become increasingly reserved for interactions in which the infant looks at a smiling mother (Messinger, Fogel, & Dickson, 2001). Because the "social smile" plays a substantial role in initiating and maintaining interactions between the infant and significant adults in her life, it is considered an important milestone in infant development. The shift from smiling as a reflex-like behavior to a controlled, voluntary response parallels the increasing maturation of the cerebral cortex, which is responsible for higher-order mental processes and deliberate, goal-directed behaviors.

INTERACTION AMONG DOMAINS

Crying is another common way in which infants express emotion. Newborn babies cry for a variety of reasons but primarily because they are hungry, cold, wet, in pain, or disturbed out of their sleep. The nature of the baby's distress is often reflected in the type of cry she emits. In an extensive study of eighteen infants observed in their homes, Peter Wolff (1969) identified three patterns of crying. The first is the *basic* (or hungry) *cry,* a rhythmical sequence consisting of a vocalization, a pause, an intake of air, and another pause. The second is the *angry cry,* in which extra air is forced through the vocal cords during the vocalization segment of the basic cry. Finally, in the *pain cry,* the infant produces a long vocalization followed by an even longer silence as he holds his breath and then gasps.

Like smiling, crying is a response that promotes contact between the infant and the caregiver. Mothers usually react to their young infants' cries promptly, especially an angry or a pain cry, and when they do, infants actually cry less in succeeding weeks and months (Bell & Ainsworth, 1972; Wolff, 1969). Usually the first order of business is to make sure the infant's physical needs are met. Other effective techniques for soothing the crying infant include providing a pacifier, swaddling with a blanket, and tapping some part of his body, that is, providing some form of rhythmic or continuous stimulation (Brackbill, 1975). Picking up the baby and holding her on one's shoulder also is soothing, probably because this act provides the infant with a broad range of stimulation that distracts her from crying (Korner, 1972).

By the time the infant is about two months of age, the causes of crying are no longer purely physiological. An infant might cry when the caregiver puts him down in his crib or when a favorite toy is removed from his grasp. At about this time, a new type of cry emerges: the *fussy* or *irregular cry,* which varies in intensity, is less rhythmical,

basic emotion Emotion such as joy, sadness, or surprise that appears early in infancy and seems to have a biological foundation. Also called *primary emotion.*

and seems to function as a demand for particular objects or actions. At eight months of age, the infant will pause in crying to see if the mother or other adults are receiving the message (Bruner, 1983). As the infant gains more voluntary control over his vocalizations, crying patterns become even more varied and controlled and are displayed in a wider range of situations to signal an assortment of messages. Individual differences in the crying patterns of some infants are useful in diagnosing developmental abnormalities. Malnourished infants, those exposed prenatally to certain drugs, and infants who have suffered oxygen deprivation show unique profiles in the pitch and length of their cries (Michelsson, Sirvio, & Wasz-Hockert, 1977; Quick, Robb, & Woodward, 2009; Zeskind, 1981).

Recognizing Others' Emotions Besides producing expressions themselves, infants are capable of discriminating and responding to emotional displays in others. Several remarkable studies conducted by Tiffany Field and her colleagues suggest that three-day-old infants are capable of imitating the facial expressions for happiness, surprise, and sadness when an adult models these expressions (Field et al., 1982, 1983). Infants widened their eyes and opened their mouths on "surprise" trials, drew back their lips on "happiness" trials, and tightened their mouths and furrowed their brows on "sadness" trials (see Figure 11.2). Although some researchers offer alternative explanations for these findings (see Chapter 6, "Basic Learning and Perception"), many believe they show that infants have an early sensitivity to emotional expressions in others.

Two emotions seem to generate especially strong responses in infants: anger and fear. Infants look more at angry faces than at other emotions expressed facially and show a distinct neural response when viewing an angry face with eyes looking directly at them (Hoehl & Striano, 2008; Montague & Walker-Andrews, 2001). Similarly, as Figure 11.3 reveals, they show greater attention to faces displaying fear than other expressions (Peltola et al., 2008). Why this distinct pattern of responses to anger and fear? One obvious suggestion comes from an evolutionary perspective: that there is adaptive value for organisms to be able to detect faces posing a threat. To examine this hypothesis, researchers are actively studying the responses of other species to facial displays of emotion, as well as the neural mechanisms that underlie what might be built-in responses (Vuilleumier, 2005).

Do infants derive meaning from the facial expressions they observe in others, or do they simply respond to changes in isolated facial features that contribute to these expressions (e.g., the upward curve of the mouth in the smile)? Our discussion of *social referencing* in Chapter 9, "Social Cognition," suggests an infant's ability to interpret facial expressions. When infants "read" the expression they see on their mothers' faces before they cross the visual cliff apparatus, for example, and then decide not to cross in the presence of her negative emotion, they are interpreting the emotional message. Interestingly enough, a mother's negative emotion (for example, fear) seems to have more influence on the child's behavior than a positive emotion (for example, happiness) (Vaish, Grossmann, & Woodward, 2008).

Emotions as Regulators of Social Interactions Given infants' ability to express and identify emotions in the context of interactions with others, developmental psychologists now recognize that emotions serve an important function in regulating and modulating early social exchanges. This dynamic process begins at about two or three months of age, when the infant looks into the adult's eyes and produces a "social smile" or a cry, to which the adult responds. The adult vocalization or facial expression, in turn, often precipitates another emotional response from the infant. Such episodes of reciprocal, mutually engaging cycles of caregiver–child behaviors are called **interactive synchrony.** These symmetrical interactions increase noticeably over the first six months of life (Hsu & Fogel, 2003). During the child's first year, interactive synchrony characterizes about 30 percent of face-to-face interactions between infant and caregiver (Tronick & Cohn, 1989).

At about three months, primary caregivers typically assume the major responsibility for guiding interactions, producing repetitions of exaggerated faces and vocalizations to which the infant pays rapt attention (Stern, 1974). Infants, without doubt, notice and react to their mothers' expressive displays. They especially attend when the mother's actions are contingent on their own behaviors; that is, the mother's smile or vocalization

interactive synchrony Reciprocal, mutually engaging cycles of caregiver–child behaviors.

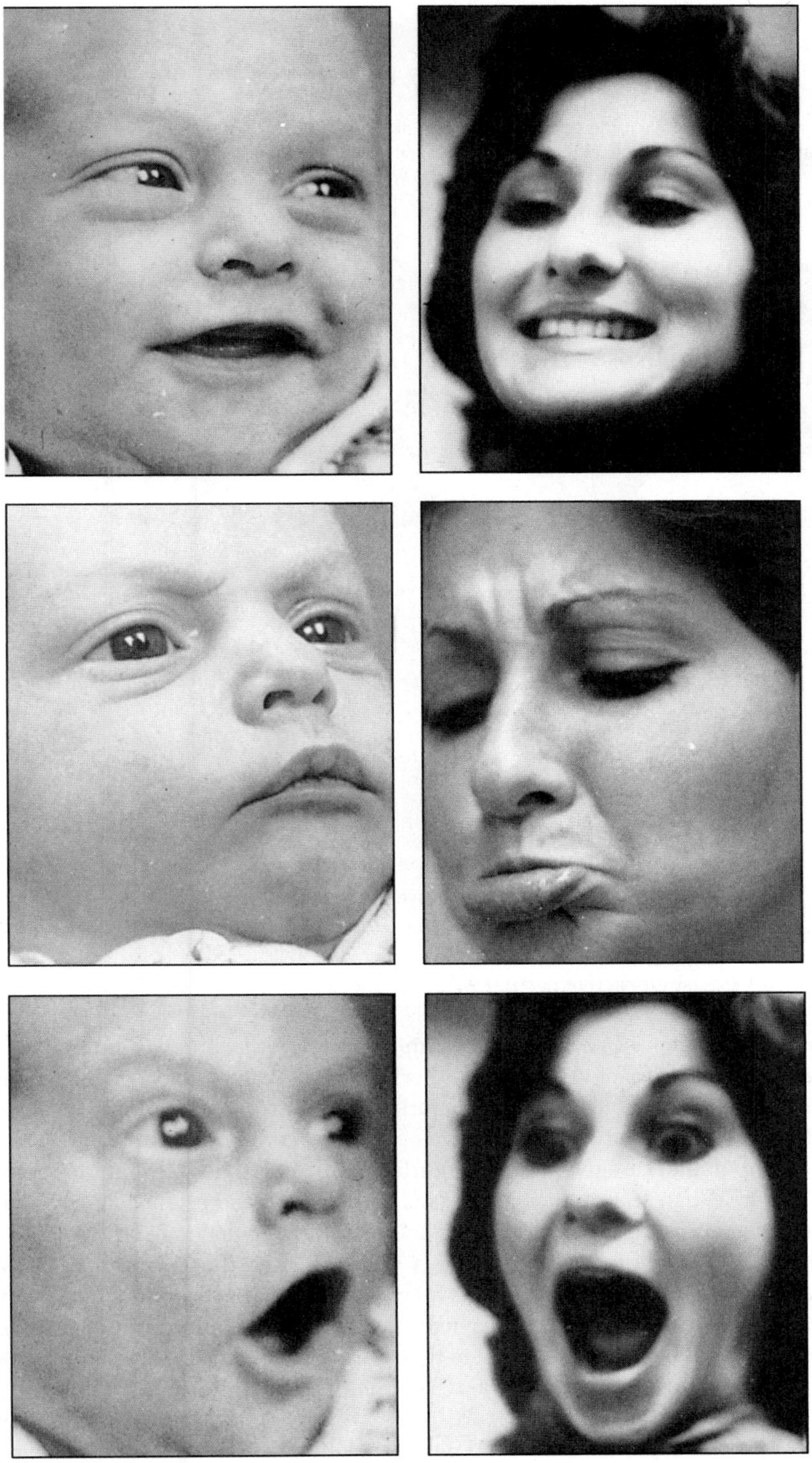

Figure 11.2
Infants' Imitation of Facial Expressions
According to some research, three-day-old infants are capable of imitating expressions for happiness (top), sadness (middle), and surprise (bottom) when they are modeled by an adult. These emotions are categorized as *basic emotions*.
Source: From Field, T. M., Woodson, R., Greenberg, R., & Cohen, D. (1982). Discrimination and imitation of facial expressions by neonates. *Science, 218*, 179–181. Reprinted with permission from AAAS.

directly follows the infant's behavior (Bigelow & DeCoste, 2003). When mothers do not return a smile but show a *still face* or a neutral pose, infants respond with a quizzical or sober look, avert their gaze, and touch themselves or some nearby object. When mothers show a positive expression, infants follow suit. If mothers look depressed, infants react by averting their gaze and sometimes crying (Cohn & Tronick, 1983; Toda & Fogel, 1993; Tronick et al., 1978). By about six to nine months of age, infants more clearly take the initiative; their displays of positive affect now more often precede their mothers' (Cohn & Tronick, 1987). Thus, throughout early infancy,

Figure 11.3

Infants' Responses to Fearful Faces

Seven-month-old infants showed longer looking times and longest single looks to a face displaying fear as opposed to happiness. This response was not likely due to the novel nature of the fearful face, as another unique facial expression did not elicit the same amount of looking.

Source: From Peltola et al., (2008). Fearful faces modulate looking duration and attention disengagement in 7-month-old infants. *Developmental Science, 11,* 60–68. Copyright © 2008 by John Wiley & Sons, Inc. Reprinted by permission of John Wiley & Sons, Inc.

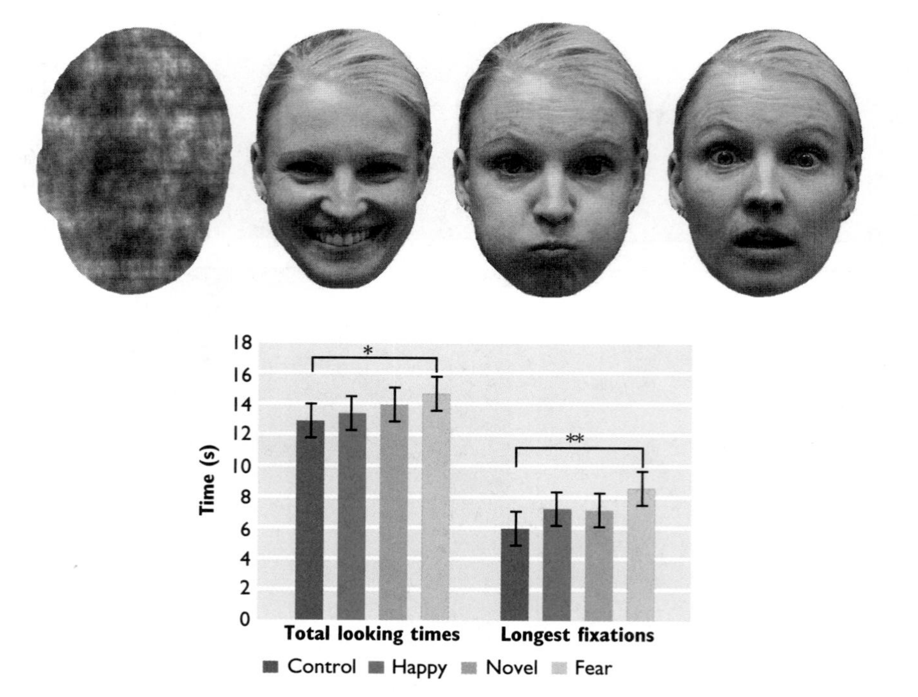

the child becomes an increasingly active partner in an emotionally toned, interactive "duet" with the caregiver.

But what about the other 70 percent of the time, when infant–caregiver interactions are *asynchronous,* or uncoordinated with each other? Edward Tronick and his colleagues believe these episodes, which constitute the majority of infant–caregiver relations, also play an important part in normal emotional development. A common occurrence after a sequence in which infant and caregiver are not coordinated is the infant's attempt to repair the "interactive error." When the mother looks sad, for example, the infant's subsequent gaze aversion or crying encourages the mother to modify her own behavior, and frequently she does (Tronick, 2003). If the mother has made a "still-face" and then reverts back to a responsive social interaction style, the infant shows greater ability to rebound emotionally (Haley & Stansbury, 2003). Thus, episodes of asynchrony give infants opportunities to learn about the rules of interaction and, in cases where they are able to repair an interaction, give them a sense of mastery or control over their environment (Tronick, 2003).

RISK | RESILIENCE

The kinds of affective exchanges that take place between infant and caregiver lay the groundwork for social behavior and emotional dispositions at later ages. Researchers are increasingly pointing to the risks created for infants when mothers are depressed. Depressed mothers tend to be less positive in face-to-face interactions with their infants (Campbell, Cohn, & Meyers, 1995). Perhaps as a consequence, infants of clinically depressed mothers express a good deal of negative affect in face-to-face interactions. They tend to express more sadness and anger, and their negative affect extends to other adults who are not depressed (Field, 1995; Field et al., 1988; Pickens & Field, 1993). These infants also show brain wave patterns similar to those of depressed adults (Dawson, 1994; Field et al., 1995). Thus, the dominance of negative emotions during early mother–child interactions culminates in a general mood or background emotional state that apparently pervades the child's own behaviors (Tronick, Ricks, & Cohn, 1982). The child may bring this general affective tone to new situations; for example, an anxious child is likely to interpret a new event as frightening, whereas a happy child may react with curiosity.

The nature of the affective exchanges between mother and child also influences the strength of the emotional bond, or *attachment,* between them. Infants who attempt to elicit responses from their mothers by smiling, vocalizing, or crying at six months of age are more likely to have healthy attachments at age one year than children who withdraw from such interactions (Tronick et al., 1982). Depressed mothers tend to have children with poorer quality attachments (Campbell et al., 2004; Teti et al., 1995). As is discussed later in this chapter, healthy attachments, in turn, are correlated with many other positive developmental outcomes in social and cognitive functioning. Also of concern is the finding that maternal depression when the child is eighteen months old is correlated with his or her own depression as far down the road as twelve to thirteen years of age, even when other risk factors are taken into account (Karevold et al., 2009). Hence, the tone of early infant–caregiver interactions appears to be a crucial facet of child development.

Emotions During Early and Middle Childhood

By their second year, many children begin to show emotions that reflect a more complex understanding of the self and social relationships such as *shame, guilt,* and *envy,* for example. Each of these emotions requires the child to understand the perspective of another person—that the person may be disappointed with the child, may be hurt, or may feel affection for a third party. Such emotions also require a consciousness about the self and one's relations to others (Saarni et al., 2006), a facet of development described in Chapter 12, "Self and Values". Accordingly, emotions such as envy and guilt are known as **self-conscious emotions.**

INTERACTION AMONG DOMAINS

The visible signs of self-conscious emotions can be multifaceted: a child displaying shame lowers her head and eyes, collapses her body, and often has an odd smile on her face (Lewis, Alessandri, & Sullivan, 1992). Asked to dance in front of people or told that he or she has failed a task, a preschooler might show embarrassment with a smiling face, a look away, and nervous body movements (Lewis & Ramsay, 2002). Feelings of shame are of particular concern because they are linked with the physical manifestations of psychological stress. Cortisol levels—indicators of stress—obtained after preschoolers failed a task such as stacking a graduated series of cups or completing a puzzle rose significantly compared with baseline levels (Mills et al., 2008).

The expression of self-conscious emotions can change with age. At age two years, children show discernible signs of jealousy. The child may wedge himself between his mother and father as they are hugging or hit a sibling whom his parent has just kissed (Cummings, Zahn-Waxler, & Radke-Yarrow, 1981). As children get older, they are better able to manage their jealousy, especially in front of their parents (Miller, Volling, & McElwain, 2000). Basic emotions, such as fear, also undergo developmental changes, particularly in the types of stimuli that elicit them. Whereas early expressions of fear result from loud noises or strange people, later in childhood, fear occurs as a response to more complex events such as the possibility of failing in school or being rejected by peers (Morris & Kratchowill, 1983; Rutter & Garmezy, 1983). Thus, as the child's cognitive skills and social awareness grow, he expresses more complex emotions or more elaborate and controlled forms of the basic emotions.

Talking About and Understanding Emotions With the advent of language, children begin communicating feelings by verbalizing instead of just furrowing their brows and crying or making some other facial display. Children begin to use language to describe feeling states between eighteen and thirty-six months of age, shortly after they begin to talk. Inge Bretherton and Marjorie Beeghly (1982) asked mothers of twenty-eight-month-olds to keep a diary of their children's verbalizations that referred to psychological states. Besides being able to apply a wide range of terms to express both positive and negative feelings, these children were able to

INTERACTION AMONG DOMAINS

self-conscious emotion Emotion such as guilt and envy that appears later in childhood and requires knowledge about the self as related to others.

By age three or four, children's understanding of emotions includes knowledge about how to soothe others' negative emotions. Preschoolers might suggest hugging or sharing a toy with a distressed child, for example.

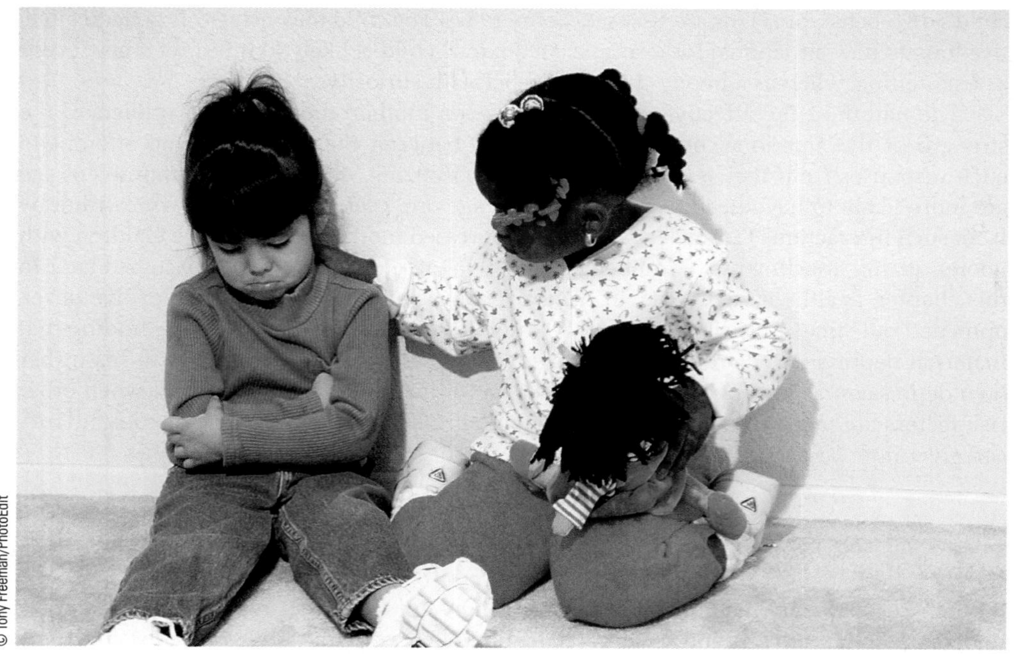

discuss the conditions that led to a specific emotion and the actions that followed as a consequence. Several children, for example, made statements similar to "Grandma mad. I wrote on wall," suggesting an understanding of the reasons for another's emotion. Another type of utterance made by several children—"I cry. Lady pick me up and hold me"—signifies an understanding that emotions may be related to subsequent actions.

From age three to four years and older, children use more varied and complex emotion words (Fabes, Eisenberg et al., 2001). At this age, children also become more proficient in verbally describing the causes and consequences of emotions (Barden et al., 1980). They tend to agree that certain events, such as receiving a compliment, lead to happy emotions, whereas others, such as being shoved, lead to negative feelings. Furthermore, they are able to suggest ways to ameliorate another's negative emotions, such as hugging a crying sibling or sharing toys to placate an angered playmate (Fabes et al., 1988).

Between roughly ages eight and ten, many children understand the emotional behaviors prescribed by cultural rules (e.g., you are supposed to look happy when you receive a gift even if you don't like it) or behaviors necessary to obtain certain goals (you should smile even if you don't feel well if you want your mother to allow you to go to a friend's party). In such cases, the individual masks or "fakes" an emotional state. Paul Harris and his associates (Harris et al., 1986) examined this skill in using emotional **display rules**—the cultural guidelines governing when and how to express emotions—by asking six- and ten-year-olds to listen to stories in which the central character felt either a positive or a negative emotion but had to hide it. After hearing the story, children were to describe verbally the facial expression of the protagonist, along with how this person really felt. Even six-year-olds could state that the emotion displayed would not match the emotion felt, although ten-year-olds provided a fuller explanation. These results suggest that, by the middle school years, children have developed a broad understanding of the social norms and expectations that surround the display of feelings.

INTERACTION AMONG DOMAINS

Knowledge about emotions can have significant ramifications for the child's social development. For example, five-year-old-children who are able to label correctly facial expressions of emotions are more likely to display positive social behaviors at age nine (Izard et al., 2001). Moreover, children who have substantial knowledge about the emotions that usually accompany given situations have higher scores on tests of moral development, are less likely to evidence behavior problems, and

display rules The cultural guidelines governing when, how, and to what degree to display emotions.

are better liked by their peers (Cook, Greenberg, & Kusche, 1994; Denham et al., 1990; Dunn, Brown, & Maguire, 1995). The reason may be that children who have greater knowledge about emotions are more likely to respond appropriately to the emotional expressions of their agemates—they have greater social skills (Mostow et al., 2002).

INTERACTION AMONG DOMAINS

Knowledge about emotions is probably gleaned, at least in part, from parents. Children who have greater knowledge about emotions—who can label emotional expressions on faces, describe the feelings of another person in an emotion-related situation, and talk about the causes of emotions—typically have mothers who discuss and explain emotions, often in the context of the child expressing a negative emotion himself. In other words, these mothers are good "coaches." On the other hand, when parents display more negative affect themselves or dismiss children's experiences of emotions (e.g., "You're overreacting!"), children's understanding of emotions is poorer and they are less socially competent (Denham et al., 1997; Dunn & Brown, 1994; Laible & Thompson, 2002). Parents who engage in such behaviors are probably missing opportunities to explain to their children the important elements of emotional responding. The extreme case is represented by children who are physically abused or neglected by their parents. These children have noticeable deficits in their ability to identify the emotional expressions that correspond to particular situations, such as going to the zoo and getting a balloon or losing a pet dog to disease. Physically abused children, perhaps not surprisingly, have a bias toward selecting angry expressions (Pollak et al., 2000).

NATURE & NURTURE

Emotional development in older children is closely affiliated with advances in cognition that allow them to think in more complex, abstract terms. By the time they enter school, children begin to understand that changes in thoughts may lead to changes in feelings—that thinking happier thoughts, for example, might make a sad mood go away (Weiner & Handel, 1985). In addition, they comprehend the possibility of experiencing two contrasting emotions at the same time, such as feeling happy at receiving a gift but disappointed that it cannot yet be opened (Brown & Dunn, 1996). As children approach adolescence, their concepts of emotions center increasingly on internal psychological states. That is, whereas younger children identify their own emotional states based on the situations they are in ("I'm happy when it's my birthday"), preadolescents and adolescents refer more frequently to their mental states ("I'm happy when I feel good inside") (Harris, Olthof, & Meerum Terwogt, 1981).

INTERACTION AMONG DOMAINS

Emotions During Adolescence

By many popular accounts, adolescence is a unique phase in emotional development. Many laypeople, as well as professionals, believe adolescence is a time of "storm and stress," of emotional turmoil and extreme moodiness. Does research substantiate this belief? And what other changes do we see in the emotional lives of teens?

Although the evidence is somewhat mixed, several studies suggest that adolescents do experience more negative emotions than children of other ages. In one study, for example, fifth- through ninth-graders wore electronic pagers for one week as they went through their normal daily routines. At random times over the week, the researchers "beeped" the participants to indicate they should rate their mood just before the signal. In addition, the children and their parents filled out questionnaires assessing the number of positive and negative life events they experienced in the past six months. Figure 11.4 shows the results. Ninth-graders reported more negative affect than fifth-graders; moreover, for these young adolescents, negative emotions were associated with a greater number of negative life events, such as changing schools, breaking up with a boyfriend or girlfriend, or getting along poorly with parents (Larson & Ham, 1993). By grade ten, though, adolescents' emotional states become more stable and stop moving in a negative direction (Larson et al., 2002).

In addition, adolescents and their parents express increased negative emotions to each other from age twelve to about age fifteen, after which negativity declines. These parent–child interactions involve mutual reciprocal influences. Parents who receive a large amount of expressed negative affect from their adolescent children escalate in their own negative emotions over time; likewise, adolescents whose parents express negative emotions toward them increase in their negative affect (Kim et al., 2001). These results illustrate an important

Figure 11.4

Frequency of Negative Affect Among Adolescents

To assess the types of emotions experienced by older children and adolescents, researchers "beeped" participants during their daily routines and asked them to report how they felt. The mean percentage of negative affect is shown along the vertical axis. The percentages indicated within the graph show the proportion of students in each grade reporting low, medium, or high stress associated with negative life events. Ninth-graders reported more negative affect than fifth-graders, and those who reported more stress in their lives were especially likely to experience negative emotions.

Source: From R. Larson & M. Ham, Stress and 'storm and stress' in early adolescence: The relationship of negative effects with dysphoric affect. *Developmental Psychology, 29,* 136. Copyright © 1993 by the American Psychological Association. Reprinted with permission.

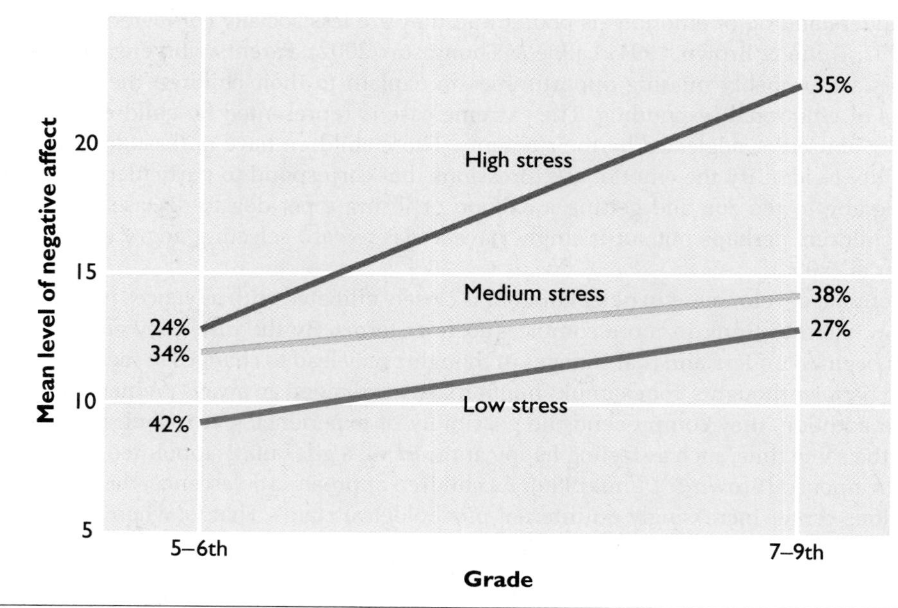

principle that we have introduced in this chapter and will discuss again in Chapter 14, "The Family": that parents and their children are often involved in a mutually influencing spiral of interactions, sometimes affecting each other in important and enduring ways.

INTERACTION AMONG DOMAINS

By adolescence, the brain and cognitive processes that are presumed to support the regulation of emotions are maturing (Spear, 2000). In addition, cognitive advances make it possible for adolescents to consider the complexities of many situations, including the possibility that events and experiences can lead to feelings that are equally complex and even sometimes in opposition to one another. Children are now more likely to express conflicting emotions, making statements such as "I love my dad even though I am mad at him right now" or "Watching the end of that movie makes me feel both sad and happy at the same time" (Harter & Whitesell, 1989; Larsen, To, & Fireman, 2007). The abilities to consider multiple sides of a problem and to think abstractly no doubt play a part in the emergence of such many-sided feelings.

For many children, the various facets of emotional development that we have discussed throughout this chapter now culminate in a more mature state of *emotional self-efficacy,* the ability to accept and feel in control of one's emotions. By the time they pass through adolescence, well-adjusted individuals are able to handle challenging emotional encounters with an appropriate emotional tone. They accept their emotional experiences, both good and bad, and feel they are able to manage them. Emotional challenges are met with a sense of wanting to move forward in a positive way. All of these qualities are part and parcel of an evolving general sense of positive self-regard (Saarni et al., 2006). You can probably see, too, that developing emotional self-efficacy has enormous implications for the success of the adolescent's social interactions, not only with casual acquaintances, but also with those who form his or her network of close relationships.

For Your Review and Reflection

- What are the differences between basic and self-conscious emotions? Give some examples of basic emotions that researchers have observed in young infants. Give some examples of self-conscious emotions that emerge later in childhood.
- What are the dynamics of synchronous and asynchronous interactions between infant and caregiver? What is the significance of these types of interactions for later emotional development?
- What types of knowledge about emotions do children acquire in the years from preschool to adolescence? How can parents and caregivers promote emotion knowledge among children?
- What are the distinctive features of emotional development in adolescence?

Regulating Emotions

Researchers are increasingly pointing to an achievement considered to be pivotal in socio-emotional development: the ability to regulate one's own emotions. During the early and middle school years, children generally become better able to control their own emotional states. Part of the process of enacting display rules—to smile even when a gift is not exactly what one wanted—depends on the capacity to control one's actions (Kieras et al., 2005). Behaviors such as calming down after getting angry or actively managing sad or depressed feelings have important repercussions for the child's social relationships and, significantly, for mental health (Cicchetti, Ackerman, & Izard, 1995; Cole, Luby, & Sullivan, 2008; Kovacs, Joormann, & Gotlib, 2008; Zhou et al., 2004). Much of the development of emotion that we have described previously—expressing, recognizing, and understanding emotions, as well as socialization experiences regarding emotions—culminates in the ability to regulate one's affective state (Denham, 1998).

RISK | RESILIENCE

Emotion Regulation in Infancy and Early Childhood

Emotion regulation has its earliest roots in infancy. In general, infants rely on caregivers to help them regulate their emotions with carrying, rocking, or soft vocalizations. Distraction also helps, at least in the short run (Harman, Rothbart, & Posner, 1997). Even young babies, however, make some attempts to regulate their own affective states, whether it be by sucking on a pacifier, by looking away if they become too aroused (as noted earlier in this chapter), or even by falling asleep (Kopp, 1989; Walden & Smith, 1997). Specific emotions may cause specific regulatory behaviors. For example, infants who experience fear when seeing an unpredictable mechanical toy withdraw from the stimulus or look at the mother. When frustrated and angered by the removal of an attractive toy, infants distract themselves or try to approach the toy (Buss & Goldsmith, 1998).

Two-year-olds continue to use strategies such as distraction; when they are presented with a snack or a gift but must wait to obtain it, they typically shift their attention to other objects. Normally, this strategy alleviates their distress (Grolnick, Bridges, & Connell, 1996). But when young children focus on the source of their frustration, their anger tends to increase (Gilliom et al., 2002). By age three, many children show fewer tantrums and intense negative outbursts as they increasingly rely on language to communicate their intents and desires (Kopp, 1992). Physiological maturation probably contributes, too. Researchers suspect that early childhood is a time when the frontal portions of the brain, which control excitation and inhibition of emotion-linked behavior, are maturing (Fox, 1994; Schore, 1996).

INTERACTION AMONG DOMAINS

One of the most important aspects of emotion regulation is what it predicts later in development. Infants who have difficulty regulating their emotions at six months of age, for example, are more likely to be noncompliant with their parents at age three (Stifter, Spinrad, & Braungart-Rieker, 1999). Similarly, preschoolers and elementary-age children

RISK | RESILIENCE

who express a lot of anger, hostility, and other negative emotions show poorer social competence in school and are isolated from or rejected by peers (Eisenberg et al., 1997; Fabes et al., 2002; Hubbard, 2001).

Perhaps of most concern, researchers have found that the inability to regulate negative emotions is part of the behavioral profile of children with conduct problems. In one study, preschool-age children, some of whom were identified as being at risk for behavior problems, were invited to a laboratory to participate in several cognitive tasks. After each child finished the session, he or she was offered a prize that was undesirable and disappointing. The children's emotional expressions were observed in both the presence and absence of the experimenter. As Figure 11.5 indicates, boys who were at risk for conduct problems expressed more anger, speaking rudely and with obvious negative emotion, compared with low-risk boys. High-risk boys also maintained that anger for longer periods of time while in the presence of the experimenter. Low-risk boys showed anger, too, but only when they were alone. The pattern for girls differed: girls from almost all risk categories expressed fewer negative emotions. These results suggest that boys who are reported by parents and teachers to have fewer behavior problems are better able to manage their emotions when in a social setting. Boys with conduct problems, on the other hand, seem to have difficulty regulating their anger, a fact that could be a source of their generally disruptive behavior (Cole et al., 1994). The evidence linking emotion regulation and later social development continues to mount, not only for children in the United States but also for those in other cultures, such as Indonesia (Eisenberg, Pidada, & Liew, 2001).

NATURE & NURTURE

The way children learn to manage their emotions depends, at least in part, on the kinds of experiences their parents provide (e.g., do parents provide opportunities for children to

Figure 11.5

Emotion Regulation in Children at Risk for Conduct Problems

What happens when children who are at risk for behavior problems experience disappointment? In a study assessing this question, children who had been identified as being at high, medium, or low risk for conduct problems were given a prize that was disappointing to them. The graph shows that boys who were at risk showed a high percentage of negative emotions whether or not the experimenter was in the room with them. Low-risk boys were better able to regulate their negative feelings when someone was present in the room with them. Girls, in general, expressed fewer negative emotions regardless of whether or not they were with someone. The exception was low-risk girls, who expressed more negative emotions when alone.

Source: From Cole, P. M., Zahn-Waxler, C., & Smith, K. D. (1994). Expressive control during a disappointment: Variations related to preschoolers' behavior problems. *Developmental Psychology, 30,* pp. 835–846. Copyright © 1994 by the American Psychological Association. Reprinted with permission.

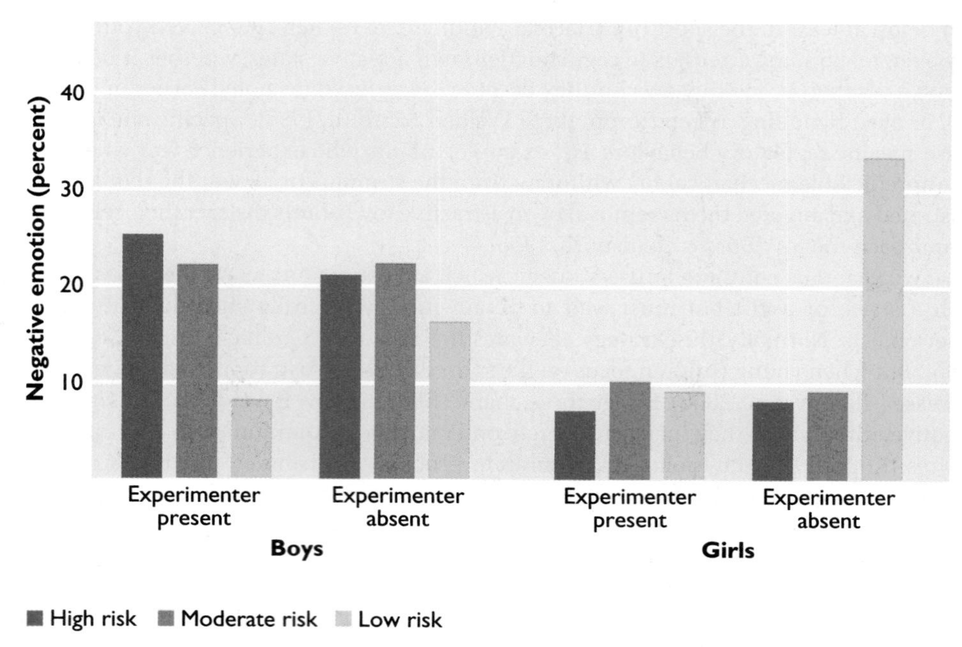

become aroused or to calm down?), as well as what children learn are the consequences of their own emotional displays (e.g., what happened when I had an angry tantrum versus when I "used my words"?). When parents become distressed at their children's display of negative emotions and punish them, children later tend to express more anger and hostility and have more behavior problems and poorer social functioning in school (Eisenberg, Fabes et al., 1999; Fabes, Leonard et al., 2001). On the other hand, when parents provide supportive coaching and guidance for children's expression of emotion—by helping children talk about how they feel and suggesting ways of dealing with their emotions—children are better able to soothe themselves and moderate their negative emotions (Gottman, Katz, & Hooven, 1997). The general emotional tone of interactions with parents may play a role, too. Nancy Eisenberg and her colleagues found that mothers who were more positive in their emotional expressivity, in contrast to mothers who generally expressed negative emotions, had children who were better able to regulate their own emotions. The children of more negative mothers also behaved more aggressively and were rated as less socially competent by parents and teachers (Eisenberg, Gershoff et al., 2001; Eisenberg, Valiente et al., 2003).

It is important to remember that all of these findings need to be considered within the context of the child's temperament style. Some children tend to be more impulsive and quick to react than others, qualities that are related to their greater emotional expressiveness. Other children are cautious and deliberate, and more likely to hide their feelings. Parental behaviors can both shape and be a reaction to their children's tendencies (Eisenberg, Zhou et al., 2003), yet another manifestation of the complex ways in which developmental outcomes are influenced by dynamic, mutually influential interactions. Longitudinal evidence suggests, though, that the chain of events that seems to make the most sense given the data is that parental warmth helps children's emotion regulation which, in turn, results in fewer behavior problems as rated by parents and teachers (Eisenberg et al., 2005). In terms of emotion regulation, with development, children too probably become more aware of their own emotional styles and seek out experiences that are compatible with their needs; some children may learn that sitting alone and playing is soothing, for example, whereas others may seek the emotional release of a fast-paced basketball game (Thompson, 1994).

INTERACTION AMONG DOMAINS

Neuroscientific research indicates that children's increasing ability to regulate behaviors, and emotions in particular, is accompanied by distinct changes in how the brain functions. In one study, children played a computer game in which they were required to press a button when certain target stimuli appeared on the screen but not to press when a nontarget showed up. In this case, children were told, "Catch all the Pokemon except for Meowth." Brain scans (fMRI) obtained while children played this game revealed that there was pronounced activation of the prefrontal and parietal regions of the brain when responses had to be inhibited (see Figure 11.6), much more so than was observed when adults played the same game (Durston et al., 2002). Other researchers have focused on changes in electrophysiological responding of regions of the brain involved in the inhibition and control of behaviors. When children played a computer game in which they suddenly and briefly lost all of the "points" they had earned (and thus experienced a negative emotion), areas of the prefrontal cortex showed particular patterns of electrophysiological activity. For older children, those physiological responses were quicker, less dramatic, and more localized in the prefrontal regions, a pattern suggesting that development of emotion regulation corresponds to greater neural efficiency in specific regions of the brain (Lewis et al., 2006).

Emotion Regulation in Adolescence

RISK | RESILIENCE

A new school, perhaps a new circle of friends, budding romantic relationships, greater challenges and pressures in academics, shifting relationships with parents—adolescents have reasons to experience more numerous and powerful bouts of emotion. Just how adolescents manage these emotions, as it turns out, can be a significant predictor of their mental health. Psychologists typically describe two broad categories of adjustment problems that sometimes face older children and adults: internalizing and externalizing. **Internalizing** refers to disturbances of mood, such as experiences of

internalizing An emotional style that is inner-directed and results in emotions such as guilt or sadness.

Figure 11.6
Brain Areas Associated with Inhibition
Recent fMRI studies have shown that children display elevated activation in the prefrontal cortex and the parietal lobes when they are involved in tasks that require them to inhibit a response. Adults show less dramatic levels of activation in these brain areas.

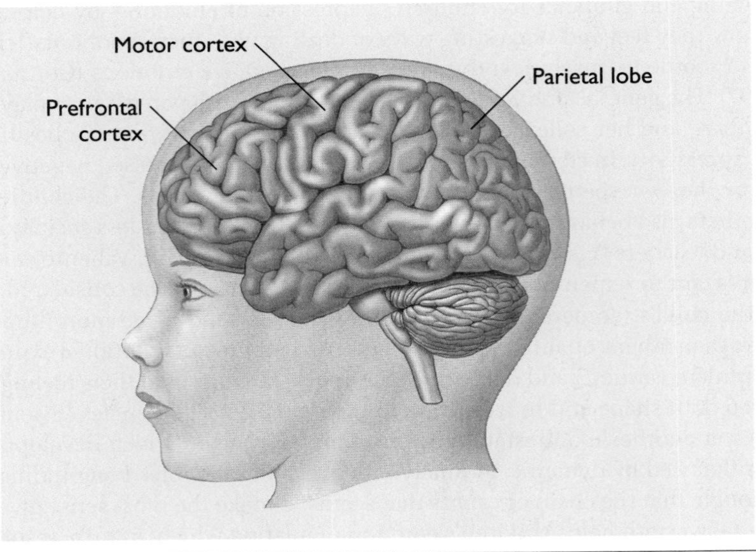

guilt and sadness, and in more severe cases, anxiety and depression. As the name implies, this emotional style of the individual is inner-directed but exacts a psychological cost. **Externalizing** pertains to outward-directed behavioral manifestations, usually aggression or temper tantrums, which are typically driven by anger. Research is beginning to suggest that adolescents who develop and use ineffective emotion-regulation strategies are more prone to both of these types of problematic styles.

In one study, seventh- and tenth-graders were cued at various times of the day to report on their feelings over the past hour. Then, thinking about their most negative emotions, participants were asked to indicate which strategies they used in order to cope with their stress. Adolescents reported feeling a wide range of emotions, some connected to embarrassing situations, others to romantic relationships, sexual activity, or substance use. The most frequent ways adolescents dealt with their negative emotions included expressing their feelings, trying to solve the problem, acceptance of the problem, distraction, or thinking more positively. These strategies did not always work to make participants feel better, but they did signal active attempts to try to resolve their feelings. A smaller proportion of participants reported using less effective strategies such as denial or rumination (persistent worrying). These adolescents were more likely to continue to feel anger or sadness. Most importantly, frequent use of strategies such as denial or rumination was correlated with a greater incidence of internalizing and externalizing problems (Silk, Steinberg, & Morris, 2003).

In studying how adolescents cope with stress in their lives, Bruce Compas has proposed that it is first important to establish the context within which negative pressures are occurring. Is the factor causing stress perceived as controllable or not? For example, adolescents are less likely to perceive control when their distress is associated with parental divorce or economic strain within the family. Under such conditions, coping strategies such as distraction seem to be most helpful. On the other hand, adolescents may perceive more control over other sources of stress such as getting a poor grade on an exam or having an argument with a friend. In this latter case, the use of active problem-solving strategies is most beneficial. In most cases, though, denial and avoidance are ineffective coping strategies regardless of the degree of perceived

externalizing An emotional style that is outward-directed and results in behavioral manifestations such as aggression or temper tantrums.

control (Compas, 2004). The links between emotion regulation and psychopathology suggest that this is a very important area for future research and intervention. Promoting healthy coping skills may be one of the best ways to promote resilience among adolescents, not only those who experience normal developmental challenges, but also those who are exposed to aversive conditions, such as parental depression, poverty, abuse, and violence (Compas, 2004; Compas et al., 2002).

RISK | RESILIENCE

atypical development | Adolescent Depression and Suicide

For some adolescents, negative emotional states become extreme and manifest themselves as *depression,* a psychological disorder characterized by dejected mood for lengthy periods of time, eating and sleeping problems, low self-esteem, loss of energy, and other symptoms. According to research estimates, roughly 35 percent of adolescents experience depressed mood and about 9 percent meet the criteria for clinical depression, with girls experiencing higher rates of depression than boys (Office of Applied Studies, 2005; Petersen et al., 1993; Wichstrøm, 1999).

The causes of depression in adolescents are complex and not completely understood by developmental scientists, but researchers have noticed that depressed children often have depressed parents. Studies of family relationships suggest that there is a genetic component to depression (Pike et al., 1996) but also that certain family climates are typical among children who are depressed. Parents who express less warmth and supportiveness and who participate in more conflicts with their children are more likely to have adolescents who are depressed (Ge, Best et al., 1996; Greenberger & Chen, 1996; Messer & Gross, 1995). Children who witness or are victims of domestic violence are also at risk for depression (Downey et al., 1994; Sternberg et al., 1993). Perhaps these parents, whose poor parenting skills may be due to their own depression, weaken their children's ability to regulate their own emotions or influence their children to form negative ideas about social relationships (Cummings, 1995). The result is that the child, too, may become depressed.

NATURE & NURTURE

Why are adolescents especially vulnerable? Several explanations are possible. Cognitive growth may mean the adolescent thinks more about the self and the future. A switch from elementary to secondary school may mean adjustments in peer group relationships. Family relationships may be changing; for example, parents may have reached a stage in their relationship at which they are considering divorce (Petersen et al., 1993; Rutter, 1991). Changes in self-image may accompany the many biological changes in the body associated with puberty. For girls, depression is often linked to issues of self-concept and interpersonal stress (Donnelly & Wilson, 1994; Rudolph & Hammen, 1999). According to Susan Nolen-Hoeksma, these findings can be understood as the result of several factors that girls experience to a greater degree than boys: greater exposure to stressful life events (e.g., sexual abuse), greater biological responses to stress, and coping styles that involve focusing inward on feelings of distress (Nolen-Hoeksma, 2001). Finally, some researchers believe that changes in hormone levels that occur during puberty may activate genes that put individuals at risk for psychological problems (Walker, 2002). Clearly, understanding and preventing depression in adolescents requires a consideration of several domains of development.

INTERACTION AMONG DOMAINS

The most serious concern about adolescents who are depressed is their risk for committing suicide. Surveys show that, in 2005, one in five high school students seriously considered or attempted suicide and that suicide is the third leading cause of death among thirteen- to nineteen-year-olds (MacKay & Duran, 2008). Although the number of attempted suicides is greater in females than in males, completed suicides are more frequent among males than females. This difference is the consequence of the fact that males typically choose more lethal means of attempting suicide than females do. Homosexual male adolescents are at particular risk for suicide (Remafedi et al., 1998).

Some of the warning signs that a young person may be thinking about suicide include falling grades in school, drug or alcohol use, withdrawal from family or friends, or avoidance of social and sporting events. When these behaviors are combined with becoming especially quiet, changes in eating or sleeping patterns, giving away valued possessions, or talking or writing about suicide, the adolescent may be signaling a need for help. Experts recognize that an array of genetic, social, and cultural factors can contribute to depression, but also that fostering strong relationships for adolescents at risk for depression is an important organizing theme for intervention. The Centers for Disease Control (2008) suggest that front-line strategies should aim to promote strong, positive relationships between individuals and their families, as well as with social institutions such as schools and community organizations. Such relationships provide the kind of close, strong support that nurtures healthy development, as well as information about how to prevent and treat suicide.

RISK | RESILIENCE

For Your Review and Reflection

- What strategies do infants and children typically use to regulate their emotions? What is the significance of the child's ability to regulate his or her own emotions?
- How can parents and caregivers promote emotion regulation among children?
- Much of the discussion in this section identifies risks to infants and children. What are the implications for promoting emotional resilience in individuals?
- What factors are related to depression during adolescence?
- If you know of a teenager who appears to be depressed, what steps might you take to address this problem?

Variations in Emotional Development

So far, our account of emotional development has emphasized commonalities across children in the expression and interpretation of emotions. Despite the generalities we have observed, however, there are noteworthy variations in emotional development among individuals and cultural groups.

Temperament

Emotions are not just transitory states of feeling and expression; often we discern a child's more enduring emotional mood and describe her personality as "cheerful" or "hostile," "easygoing" or "irritable." As we saw in Chapter 3, "Genetics and Heredity," researchers have found that infants and children vary in *temperament,* a style of behavioral functioning that encompasses the intensity of expression of moods, distractibility, adaptability, and persistence. Individual differences among infants in these qualities often remain relatively stable over time and across different situations (Rothbart & Bates, 2006).

Patterns of Temperament In a classic body of research, Stella Chess and Alexander Thomas (1982, 1990, 1991) have offered one conceptualization of temperament, identifying three basic patterns that many children display:

- The *easy* child generally has positive moods, regular body functions, a low to moderate energy level in responses, and a positive approach to new situations. This child establishes regular feeding and sleeping schedules right from early infancy and adapts quickly to new routines, people, and places.
- The *difficult* child is often in a negative mood, has irregular body functions, shows high-intensity reactions, withdraws from new stimuli, and is slow to adapt to new situations. The difficult child sleeps and eats on an unpredictable schedule, cries a good deal (and loudly), and has trouble adjusting to new routines.
- The *slow-to-warm-up* child is somewhat negative in mood, has a low level of activity and intensity of reaction, and withdraws from new stimuli. However, with repeated exposure to new experiences, she or he begins to show interest and involvement.

Chess and Thomas (1991) note that children with different temperaments will evoke different patterns of reactions from their parents, teachers, and peers. "Easy" children usually elicit the most positive reactions from others, whereas children from the other two temperament categories typically draw more negative reactions. Later in life, children with "easy" temperaments may adjust more readily to important transitions, such as the start of school or making new friends. An important dimension of development, say Chess and Thomas, is the "goodness of fit" between the child's temperament and the demands placed on the child by the environment, specifically parents, teachers, peers, and others.

Other researchers have proposed alternative descriptions of temperament types. For example, Jerome Kagan and his colleagues (Kagan, Reznick, & Snidman, 1988) noted that some infants tend to show wariness and fearfulness when they encounter unfamiliar people, objects, or events, and others react with interest, spontaneity, and sociability. Longitudinal studies show that both the first group, called *inhibited,* and the second, called *uninhibited,* tend to maintain their distinctive styles from infancy through early childhood.

Mary Rothbart and her colleagues (Rothbart, Derryberry, & Posner, 1994; Rothbart & Hwang, 2005) have offered another increasingly influential description of temperament. Infants are thought to differ in terms of *reactivity,* or how easily the child becomes aroused in response to events in the environment. Some children react quickly and intensely, whereas others are slower to react and are generally calmer. A second dimension of temperament in this model is the ability to *regulate the self,* to adjust one's level of arousal and to soothe oneself. Some children are better able than others to shift their attention or to inhibit behaviors in order to bring themselves back to a calm state.

One caution about categorizing infant styles concerns the cross-cultural dimensions of temperament. Although the preceding categories may capture individual differences in the emotional styles of Western infants, they may not apply to children from other cultures. For example, when Japanese mothers were asked to describe the behavioral styles of their infants, the "easy/difficult" dimension appeared in their responses, but so did unique qualities such as "self-assertiveness" (e.g., a tendency to like pleasant sounds, enjoy exercising the body, and feed quickly) (Shwalb, Shwalb, & Shoji, 1994). Cultural differences in parental expectations regarding children's temperament may, in turn, lead to differences in parenting styles that circle back to influence the child's style of responding to people and objects.

SOCIOCULTURAL INFLUENCE

Biological Bases of Temperament There are good reasons to believe that individual differences in temperament are rooted in biology. For example, children in Kagan's two temperament categories show different profiles of physiological responsiveness. Inhibited children show more pronounced cardiac reactions, a greater rise in blood pressure when changing from a sitting to a standing position, and more tension in skeletal muscles compared with uninhibited children. As adolescents, inhibited children exhibit a greater response of the brainstem to auditory stimulation (Woodward et al., 2001). Kagan and his colleagues postulate that differential responsiveness in the limbic system, the portion of the brain below the cortex that controls emotions, may lie at the root of temperament differences (Kagan, Snidman, & Arcus, 1993).

NATURE & NURTURE

Infants who are prone to be irritable also show distinct patterns of brain wave functioning. In one study, infants were observed as they saw and heard novel stimuli; their level of motor activity and emotional responses were of particular interest. Then, when the infants were nine months of age, patterns of EEG activity were measured. Compared with other infants in the study, active, irritable children who were hard to soothe at four months of age showed greater brain wave activity in the right frontal lobe, the portion of the brain thought to be involved in the expression and processing of emotions (Tucker, 1981). These same infants, at twenty-four months of age, tended to be fearful and inhibited (Calkins, Fox, & Marshall, 1995).

Stephen Porges and his associates (Porges, Doussard-Roosevelt, & Maiti, 1994) have focused on *cardiac vagal tone* as a physiological component of temperament. This measure assesses the degree to which the heart is influenced by the vagus nerve, one of the principal nerves in the autonomic nervous system originating in the brainstem. Infants who show high baseline cardiac vagal tone tend to be reactive; they respond both positively and negatively in stressful situations compared with infants with low cardiac vagal tone (Gunnar et al., 1995; Huffman et al., 1998; Stifter, Fox, & Porges, 1989). In addition, infants who show declines in vagal tone while a series of novel stimuli are presented are more attentive and easier to soothe (Huffman et al., 1998). Perhaps these infants are better able to regulate their emotional states. It is worth noting that these two patterns of physiological responding—reactivity and self-regulation—correspond to the two major dimensions of temperament proposed by Rothbart.

If individuals differ in the ways their bodies tend to react emotionally, then it is logical to presume that genetics plays a role in temperament. As we noted in Chapter 3, studies comparing identical and fraternal twins and parents and children on dimensions of temperament suggest that they have a genetic component. Even so, most researchers of temperament agree that biology only sets in place certain predispositions. Any explanation of a child's personality development most certainly needs to include the complex interplay between initial behavior patterns and environmental experiences (Kagan & Fox, 2006; Rothbart & Bates, 2006).

Temperament and Later Development Does early temperament forecast any of the child's characteristics later in life? It appears so. For example, the extent to which an infant tends to show negative emotions at three months of age predicts poorer cognitive abilities for that child at age four years, even when factors such as the mother's responsiveness are ruled out as influences on the child (Lewis, 1993). In the domain of social relationships, preschool boys who tend to exhibit negative affect often have poorer social skills and lower status among their peers (Eisenberg et al., 1993). Similarly, infants who tend to express anger and frustration score higher on measures of aggression at age six to seven years than children who express less anger as infants (Rothbart, Ahadi, & Hershey, 1994). Likewise, a relationship exists between a child's negativity, short attention span, and swings in emotions at age three and hyperactivity, attention problems, and antisocial behavior in adolescence (Caspi et al., 1995). It seems that the relatively stable emotional style a particular child displays early in life may have a far-reaching impact on both cognitive and social functioning later on and these relationships hold up regardless of the culture in which a child grows up (Zhou, Lengua, & Wang, 2009). According to some researchers, early temperament styles are likely to have a strong relationship to adult personality types (Rothbart, Ahadi, & Evans, 2000).

RISK | RESILIENCE

Sex Differences in Emotions

According to the familiar stereotype, females are more emotionally expressive and more sensitive to the emotional states of others than are males. Do boys and girls actually differ in any facet of emotional development? It seems that for the most part the answer is yes—that girls are more emotionally expressive and more attuned to emotions than are boys.

During infancy and the preschool years, there do not appear to be strong, clear-cut sex differences. Some studies find that girls tend to show more positive emotions than do boys (e.g., Matias & Cohn, 1993), but others show that boys are more expressive in general (Weinberg et al., 1999). By elementary school, though, girls show a greater range of emotions than boys. In one study, when seven- and twelve-year-olds played a game with a peer, girls were more likely than boys to show a positive or negative emotion when the peer made a comment such as "she looks friendly" or "she doesn't look nice" (Casey, 1993). Later in adolescence, girls smile more than boys both on their own initiative and in response to the smile of another (Hall & Halberstadt, 1986). Girls also begin to show more anxieties than boys during the school years—fears about tests, family issues, health, and other concerns (Orton, 1982; Scarr et al., 1981). Finally, some researchers report that girls are better than boys at decoding the emotional expressions of others (Brown & Dunn, 1996; Hall, 1978, 1984).

NATURE & NURTURE

Observations of parents' behaviors suggest that many of these sex differences may be taught or modeled directly. For example, mothers and fathers spend more time trying to get their infant daughters to smile than they do their infant sons (Moss, 1974). Mothers of preschoolers also mention feeling states more often and discuss a wider variety of emotions when they talk with their daughters than when conversing with their sons (Dunn, Bretherton, &

© Michael Newman/PhotoEdit

Girls may be more emotionally expressive than boys as a consequence of the kinds of experiences they have had with their caregivers. For example, mothers tend to be more facially expressive when they play with their preschool-aged daughters than with their sons.

Munn, 1987; Kuebli, Butler, & Fivush, 1995). Mothers are also more facially expressive when they play with their two-year-old girls than with boys, thus exposing girls to a greater range of emotions and displaying more social smiles to them (Malatesta et al., 1989). In general, parents encourage girls to maintain close emotional relationships and to show affection, whereas they instruct boys to control their emotions (Block, 1973). Thus, although biological explanations of sex differences cannot be ruled out completely, many of the emotional behaviors we see in males and females appear to be influenced by their learning histories.

Differences in how boys and girls regulate their emotions are of special interest to researchers trying to identify the precursors of adjustment difficulties in childhood. When girls experience challenges or problems, they tend to employ internalizing strategies for coping, such as worrying or becoming anxious or depressed. In contrast, when boys experience difficulties, they tend to engage in externalizing behaviors, such as aggression (Rossman, 1992; Zahn-Waxler, Cole, & Barrett, 1991). Understanding the sources of emotion regulation in boys and girls thus has implications for the treatment and prevention of psychological problems that are associated with each sex.

Cultural Differences in Emotions

SOCIOCULTURAL INFLUENCE

The tendency of children to express and detect emotions varies as a function of the culture in which they are raised. American children, for example, tend to smile more than Chinese infants (Camras et al., 1998). On the other end of the emotional spectrum, Chinese children are better able to identify fearful and sad situations than are American children, and they cry less (Borke, 1973; Camras et al., 1998). These differences may reflect the child's incorporation of particular cultural beliefs about emotions.

An examination of two different cultural groups in rural Nepal further illustrates this concept. Pamela Cole and her colleagues (Cole, Bruschi, & Tamang, 2002) studied children in two small villages, each comprising a different ethnic group—one Brahmin and the other Tamang. The Brahmins subscribe to a caste system in which strict rules dictate which social groups may interact. They are very oriented to status differences and the power of authority, and they have a great deal of pride in their own ethnic group. The Tamang, on the other hand, place great value on community rather than on the individuals within the group. Resources are shared, and important decisions are made by consulting all group members, in accordance with their Buddhist values of selflessness. How do school-age children in these two very different cultures express emotions? All children were asked to react to scenarios likely to lead to an emotional reaction, such as having a friend snatch away a piece of candy or watching as a parent spills tea all over homework papers. Brahmin children, although they expected to feel anger in such situations, clearly stated that anger should not be expressed, primarily because authority needed to be respected and group orderliness preserved. Tamang children, in contrast, did not express anger; rather, they reported a feeling of *thiken,* or making the mind calm, in accordance with their Buddhist beliefs. American children, also participants in this study, endorsed anger as an appropriate response. This belief is consistent with the value we place on self-assertion and independence in our culture (Cole et al., 2002).

Cultural belief systems extend to the kinds of temperamental styles that are valued. A good example is the dimension of shyness and inhibition. In European families, this personality profile is often seen as a liability; we expect our children to be outgoing, sociable, and eager to interact with the environment. In Chinese society, though, shyness is a valued trait. Parents and teachers believe that shy children are well behaved, and shy children have positive views of themselves (Chen, Rubin, & Li, 1997; Chen et al., 1999). These cultural beliefs are likely to be expressed in the socialization practices of parents and others.

Finally, cultures differ in the extent to which children are exposed to emotional events. Infants in northern Germany experience frequent separations from their mothers, whereas Japanese infants do not (Saarni et al., 2006). It should not be surprising, then, if children show varying patterns of emotional reactions to the same event—in this case, the mother's departure.

For Your Review and Reflection

- What are the different ways in which child temperament has been conceptualized? How would you characterize your temperament?
- What is the evidence for a biological basis for temperament?
- How is temperament related to later development?
- How do boys and girls differ in the expression of emotions? What factors might be responsible for these differences?
- In what ways does the development of emotion vary across cultures? What values does your own background culture have about emotions?
- When interacting with children, what differences in temperament have you noticed? How would you account for why those differences exist?

Attachment: Emotional Relationships with Others

One of the most widely discussed and actively researched aspects of emotional and social development is **attachment,** the strong emotional bond that emerges between infant and caregiver. The concept of attachment occupies a prominent place in developmental psychology because of its link with successful cognitive, social, and emotional development throughout childhood.

How does attachment emerge between infant and caregiver? In what ways is this emotional bond expressed? What roles do the caregiver and infant play in its formation? What is the significance of attachment in the later development of the child? Do we observe the same patterns of attachment among children across cultures? In this portion of the chapter, we will examine the course of attachment in infancy and early childhood and explore the answers to these questions.

attachment Strong emotional bond that emerges between infant and caregiver.

The Origins of Attachment: Theoretical Perspectives

What forces govern the emergence of attachment? Historically, there have been two important perspectives on this question, learning theory and ethological theory.

Learning Theory Learning theorists believe that certain basic drives, such as hunger, are satisfied by **primary reinforcers,** rewards that gratify biological needs. In the case of the young infant, an important primary reinforcer is food. Other rewards, called **secondary reinforcers,** acquire their reinforcing qualities from their association with primary reinforcers. Because they are connected repeatedly with the reduction of the hunger drive, mothers acquire secondary reinforcing properties. Eventually the mother's presence in contexts outside feeding is rewarding to the infant.

NATURE & NURTURE

Is the activity of feeding related to the emergence of infant-mother attachments, as learning theorists predict? Evidently not, according to a series of classic experiments conducted by Harry Harlow and his associates (Harlow & Zimmerman, 1959). These investigators separated infant monkeys from their mothers and provided them instead with extended contact with two surrogate mothers, one a figure made of wire mesh and the other a figure covered with terry cloth. The wire surrogate was equipped for feeding half of the monkeys; the terry-cloth surrogate fed the other half. The infant monkeys lived with both their surrogates for at least 165 days, during which time several observations were made of the monkeys' behaviors. One measure was the number of hours per day spent with each surrogate. As Figure 11.7 shows, infant monkeys preferred the cloth "mother" regardless of which surrogate was providing nourishment. In a subsequent test of attachment, when a frightening stimulus such as a mechanical spider was introduced into the monkeys' cage, the monkeys chose the cloth mother to run and cling to, even if they had been fed by the wire mother.

Harlow Primate Laboratory, University of Wisconsin

Harlow's experiments showed that infant monkeys reared with surrogate mothers preferred the cloth mother even when the wire mother provided nourishment. Here, the infant monkey is actually nursing from the wire mother but still maintains contact with the cloth mother. These findings challenge the hypothesis that attachment arises from the caregiver's association with feeding the child.

Harlow's findings challenged the view that attachments are based on the mother's acquisition of secondary-drive characteristics. The fact that the infant monkeys did not seek out the surrogate that fed them under either normal or stressful conditions led Harlow to conclude that "contact comfort," the security provided by a physically soothing object, played a greater role in attachment than the simple act of feeding.

The Ethological View Proponents of the ethological position state that attachments occur as the result of the infant's innate tendency to signal the caregiver and the caregiver's corresponding predisposition to react to these signals. As a result, infant and caregiver are brought together, a bond is forged between them, and the survival of the infant is ensured. In other words, attachment is an adaptive, biologically programmed response system that is activated early in the infant's development and follows many of the principles of *imprinting* described in Chapter 1, "Themes and Theories." The principal spokesperson for this perspective, John Bowlby (1958, 1969), initially was concerned with the detrimental effects of institutionalization on infants and young children. Scientists in the late 1940s had reported that children who spent extended periods of time in hospitals and orphanages during their early years often showed serious developmental problems, including profound withdrawal from social interactions, intellectual impairments, and, in

NATURE & NURTURE

primary reinforcer Reward that gratifies biological needs or drives.

secondary reinforcer Object or person that attains rewarding value because of its association with a primary reinforcer.

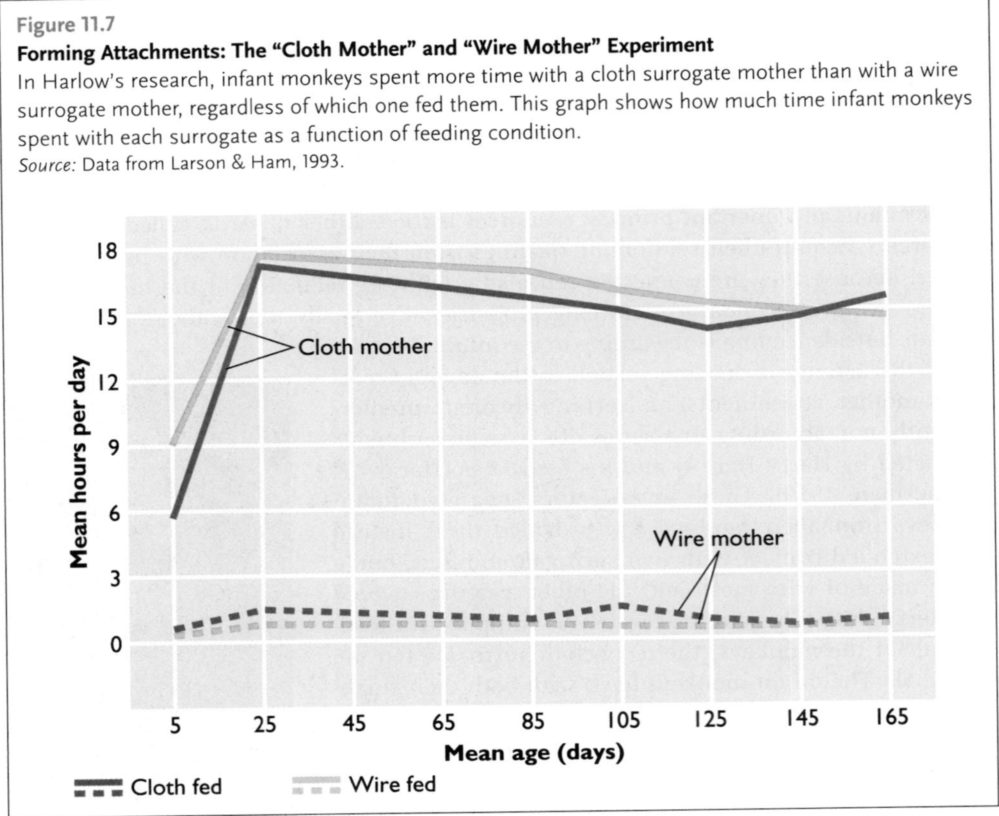

Figure 11.7
Forming Attachments: The "Cloth Mother" and "Wire Mother" Experiment
In Harlow's research, infant monkeys spent more time with a cloth surrogate mother than with a wire surrogate mother, regardless of which one fed them. This graph shows how much time infant monkeys spent with each surrogate as a function of feeding condition.
Source: Data from Larson & Ham, 1993.

some cases, physical delays (Skodak & Skeels, 1949; Spitz, 1946a). Bowlby proposed that the cause lay in the lack of a close emotional bond between child and primary caregiver.

Bowlby (1969) maintained that attachments develop in a fixed sequence:

- In the first two months, infants emit *signaling behaviors,* such as crying and smiling, which bring the caregiver physically close to the infant. Infants emit these signals indiscriminately, but as caregivers respond, stable patterns of interaction emerge.
- Between two and six months of age, smiles and cries become increasingly restricted to the presence of the caregiver, usually the mother.
- From six to twelve months of age, clearer signs of the infant's strong attachment to the caregiver develop. At this point, most infants become visibly upset at the mother's departure, a phenomenon called **separation anxiety,** and also show signs of **reunion behavior,** happily greeting the mother on her return. Once they are able to move about, infants will ensure their nearness to their mothers by approaching and clinging to them. About the same time, they also display **stranger anxiety,** a wariness or fear at the approach of someone unfamiliar.
- The final phase of attachment occurs at about three years of age, when the relationship between mother and child becomes more of a partnership and the child comes to appreciate the mother's feelings, motives, and goals.

The regularity with which infants show this sequence of behaviors and the adaptive function they serve, says Bowlby, suggests its biological and evolutionary basis.

According to Bowlby, infants become attached to those who respond consistently and appropriately to their signaling behaviors. Thus, Bowlby saw the maladaptive development of institutionalized infants as a consequence of the absence of the dynamic, contingent interaction between

separation anxiety Distress the infant shows when the caregiver leaves the immediate environment.

reunion behavior The child's style of greeting the caregiver after a separation.

stranger anxiety Fear or distress an infant shows at the approach of an unfamiliar person.

child and caregiver. Although institutional settings met children's basic physical needs, they often did so at the convenience of the caregiver's schedule rather than in response to the child's behaviors. Modern-day studies of infants growing up in orphanages in Romania echo these important themes. In one recent report, for example, less than 20 percent of 95 infants raised in an institutional setting showed signs of healthy attachments. An important predictor of those healthy emotional relationships was the quality of caregiving in the institution—that is, the emotional involvement, sensitivity, and responsiveness of the adults who worked in the orphanage (Zeanah et al., 2005). Bowlby's general scheme concerning the origins and course of attachment has framed literally hundreds of investigations of the development of attachment.

The Developmental Course of Attachment

For the most part, research has confirmed the sequence of behaviors outlined by Bowlby in the emergence of attachment. Infants can discriminate their mothers' faces from those of strangers at two days of age and their mothers' voices and odors a few days after that (DeCasper & Fifer, 1980; Field et al., 1984; MacFarlane, 1975). However, they emit their signals to anyone who is available. By about seven months of age, these indiscriminate behaviors give way to attachments to specific people, most notably the mother or primary caregiver. Stranger anxiety becomes full blown, and separation anxiety is usually manifested as well. In the months that follow, children show evidence of multiple attachments to fathers, substitute caregivers, and grandparents (Schaffer & Emerson, 1964).

At age two years most children continue to show strong attachments, but by three years some of the manifestations of this bond begin to change. Separation distress diminishes for most children, probably due to advances in cognition. For example, children begin to appreciate the fact that even though the caregiver may depart for several hours, she always returns (Marvin, 1977). The impact of repeated experience with separation and reunion episodes may extend to a more general understanding that negative emotional experiences often yield to strong positive affect, that distress can be followed by stability (Schore, 1994). As children develop insights into the perspectives of others and as their communication skills improve, they can better understand the reasons for temporary separations and can express their emotions in ways other than crying or clinging. The Emotional Development Chronology summarizes the sequence of many of the changes in both emotional development and attachment.

INTERACTION AMONG DOMAINS

Measuring Attachment The **Strange Situation,** developed by Mary Ainsworth and her associates, is a standardized test frequently employed to measure the quality of the child's emotional ties to her primary caregiver, usually her mother (Ainsworth et al., 1978). Table 11.1 shows the eight episodes that compose this measure, which is administered in a laboratory setting.

On the basis of her extensive observations of the patterns of behaviors shown by infants, Ainsworth (Ainsworth et al., 1978) distinguished three patterns of attachment: *secure attachment* and two categories of *insecure attachment, avoidant* and *ambivalent attachment.* More recently, other researchers have identified still a third type of insecure attachment called *disorganized/disoriented attachment.* These attachment categories are described as follows.

Secure attachment Children in the **secure attachment** group show many clear signs of attachment by displaying stranger anxiety and separation protest and greeting the mother enthusiastically upon her return. They also use the mother as a **secure base** for exploration, exploring their new surroundings but looking or moving back to the mother as though to "check in" with her. They obviously feel comfortable in the presence of the mother and distressed and apprehensive in her absence.

Strange Situation Standardized test that assesses the quality of infant-caregiver attachment.

secure attachment Attachment category defined by the infant's distress at separation from the caregiver and enthusiastic greeting upon his or her return. The infant also displays stranger anxiety and uses the caregiver as a secure base for exploration.

secure base An attachment behavior in which the infant explores the environment but periodically checks back with the caregiver.

CHRONOLOGY Emotional Development: Birth to 12 Years

MONTHS BIRTH | YEARS BIRTH

Newborn
- Discriminates mother's face, voice, and smell from others'.
- Expresses interest, distress, disgust, joy, sadness, anger, and surprise.
- Imitates facial expressions for happiness, surprise, and sadness.
- Smiles during REM sleep.
- Cries to express physical needs.

2 Months
- Displays "fussy cry."

© JGI/Blend Images/Jupiter Images

3 Months
- Smiles at caregiver.
- Distinguishes happiness from anger, surprise, and sadness.
- Participates in interactive synchrony.

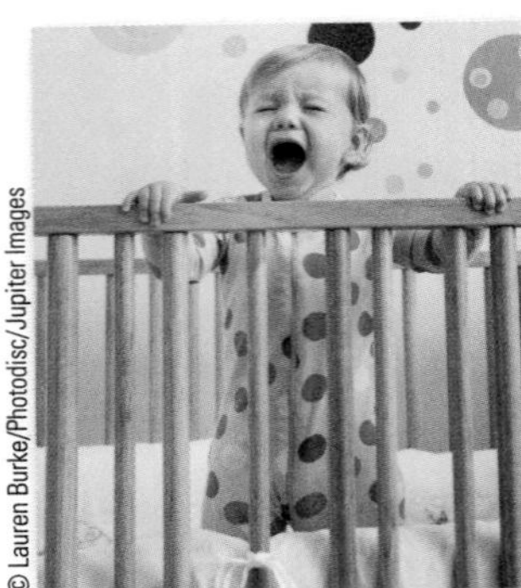
© Lauren Burke/Photodisc/Jupiter Images

7 Months
- Expresses fear.
- Shows specific attachments, stranger anxiety, and separation anxiety.

12 Months
- Shows social referencing.

18–24 Months
- Displays guilt, shame, and envy.
- Uses words to describe feeling states.
- Regulates emotions by shifting attention to objects that do not cause distress.

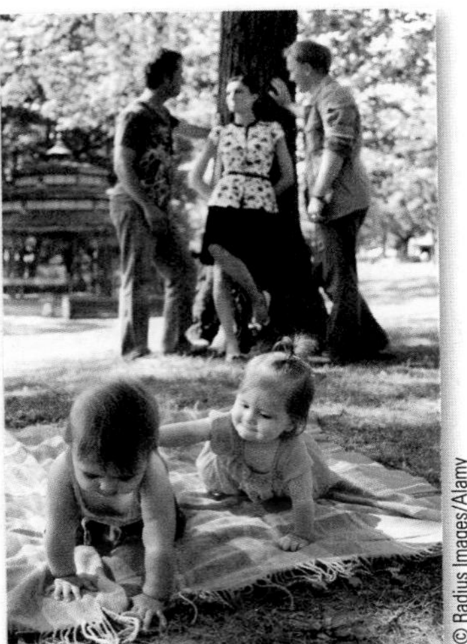
© Radius Images/Alamy

3–4 Years
- Describes the causes and consequences of emotions.
- Shows decline in tantrums and negative outbursts.
- Shows decline in separation distress and other attachment behaviors typical of infancy.

6–7 Years
- Understands that emotions fade with time and that thoughts can control emotions.
- Understands the possibility of feeling two emotions at once.

© JGI/Blend Images/Jupiter Images

10–12 Years
- Can mask or "fake" emotions.
- Has concepts of emotions based on internal feeling states.

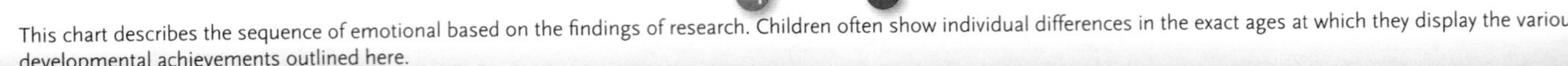
This chart describes the sequence of emotional based on the findings of research. Children often show individual differences in the exact ages at which they display the various developmental achievements outlined here.

TABLE 11.1 The Episodes of the Strange Situation

Episode*	Persons Present	Action	Attachment Behaviors Assessed
1	Caregiver, baby, observer	Observer introduces mother and baby to experimental room and leaves.	
2	Caregiver, baby	Baby explores and plays while caregiver is passive.	Secure base
3	Stranger, caregiver, baby	Stranger enters room, converses with caregiver, and approaches baby.	Stranger anxiety
4	Stranger, baby	Caregiver leaves room unobtrusively.	Separation anxiety
5	Caregiver, baby	Caregiver returns and greets baby.	Reunion behavior
6	Baby	Caregiver leaves room, saying "bye-bye."	Separation anxiety
7	Stranger, baby	Stranger enters and orients to baby.	Stranger anxiety
8	Caregiver, baby	Caregiver returns and greets baby.	Reunion behavior

*Each episode except the first lasts for about three minutes.

Source: Adapted from Ainsworth et al., 1978.

Avoidant Attachment Infants in the **avoidant attachment** category are less distressed when the mother leaves and less enthusiastic in greeting her when she returns. They tend to avoid or ignore her, playing in isolation even when she is present in the room. All of these behaviors, according to Ainsworth, constitute a form of insecure attachment.

Ambivalent (or Resistant) Attachment Tension characterizes the behaviors **ambivalent (resistant) attachment** children show toward their mothers. Although they display noticeable proximity-seeking behaviors when the mother is in the room, sometimes clinging excessively to her, they also show angry, rejecting behavior when she returns, even hitting or pushing her away. Some children in this category are extremely passive, showing limited exploratory play except for bouts of crying that are used as signals to be picked up and held. These children, too, are considered insecurely attached.

Disorganized/Disoriented Attachment Children in the **disorganized/disoriented attachment** category show fear of their caregivers, confused facial expressions, and an assortment of avoidant and ambivalent attachment behaviors in the Strange Situation (Main & Solomon, 1986). These behaviors are accompanied by physiological signs of stress (Hertsgaard et al., 1996).

In the United States, about 65 percent of infants are typically categorized as securely attached, about 20 percent as avoidantly attached, and about 10 percent as ambivalently attached

avoidant attachment Insecure attachment in which the infant shows little separation anxiety and does not pay much attention to the caregiver's return.

ambivalent (resistant) attachment Insecure attachment in which the infant shows separation protest but also distress upon the caregiver's return.

disorganized/disoriented attachment Infant-caregiver relations characterized by the infant's fear of the caregiver, confused facial expressions, and a combination of avoidant and ambivalent attachment behaviors.

(van IJzendoorn & Sagi, 1999). Other data suggest that perhaps as many as 15 percent of infants show signs of disorganized attachments (Lyons-Ruth & Jacobvitz, 1999).

Another way to measure attachment is the *Q-sort*. In this method, mother and infant are observed for a specified period of time, after which the observer sorts through a series of 90 cards containing descriptions of the mother-infant relationship. Several piles are created, from "least characteristic" to "most characteristic" of the child. The child's attachment score is based on the extent to which these ratings correlate with the characteristics of a securely attached child that have been defined by a panel of experts on childhood attachment (Waters & Deane, 1985). The use of the Q-sort has permitted researchers to study attachment in a broader range of contexts and in a wider age range of children than has the Strange Situation (Thompson, 2006).

The Antecedents of Secure Attachment How do secure, high-quality attachments develop? Research by Mary Ainsworth and her colleagues (Ainsworth, Bell, & Stayton, 1971, 1972, 1974) suggests that the caregiver's style of interacting with the infant and his or her responsiveness to the baby's signals are key factors.

NATURE & NURTURE

Ainsworth and her associates visited the homes of twenty-six infants and their mothers for about four hours every three weeks during the entire first year of the infants' lives. When they were about one year old, the infants were brought to the laboratory to be tested in the Strange Situation and were classified according to the quality of attachment to their mothers. An attempt then was made to find relationships between the attachment classification and specific maternal behaviors observed earlier. The results of this study indicated that mothers of securely attached infants were *sensitive* to their children's signals, noticing their cues and interpreting them correctly. These mothers were *accepting* of their role as caregiver. They displayed *cooperation;* mothers of securely attached infants would wait until the child finished her activity or was in a good mood before imposing a request. They used gentle persuasion rather than assertive control. Mothers in this group were also *accessible,* providing quick responses to the child's signals, particularly crying. They were not distracted by their own thoughts and activities. In contrast, mothers of the insecurely attached group were often rigid, unresponsive, and demanding in their parenting style and did not feel positively about their role as caregiver.

A meta-analysis of sixty-six studies showed that maternal sensitivity is indeed strongly related to attachment (De Wolff & van IJzendoorn, 1997). However, the emotional tone of early mother-child interactions is also important to consider. Mothers of securely attached children have been found to be more affectionate, more positive, and less intrusive in their vocalizations than mothers of insecurely attached infants, toddlers, and young school-age children (Bates, Maslin, & Frankel, 1985; Isabella, 1993; Izard et al., 1991; Stevenson-Hinde & Shouldice, 1995). In a study of children who were about to enter school, those who were insecurely attached and who showed the most behavior problems two years later had mothers who displayed the highest levels of negativity and tension of all the participants (Moss et al., 1998). Even when mothers and their children have conflicts, mothers of securely attached children use explanations of their positions and show a willingness to compromise. In other words, they are excellent communication partners (Laible, Panfile, & Makariev, 2008).

RISK | RESILIENCE

Interactive synchrony also influences the emergence of attachments. One group of researchers observed the interactions of mothers and their infants at one, three, and nine months of age, recording each instance in which the infants' and mothers' behaviors co-occurred and produced a mutually satisfying outcome. For example, if the infant gazed at the mother, the mother verbalized, or if the infant fussed and cried, the mother soothed him. The infants' attachments were then assessed at one year of age. According to the results, securely attached infants had experienced a greater number of synchronous interactions in the prior months, a finding other researchers have replicated (Isabella, Belsky, & von Eye, 1989; Schölmerich et al., 1995). Therefore, in accounting for the emergence of secure attachment, it is important to consider maternal behavior as it is related to the child's behavior.

It is worth noting that siblings reared in the same family are at least moderately similar to each other in their attachment classifications and that identical twins are no more similar than fraternal twins in their attachment styles (O'Connor & Croft, 2001; van IJzendoorn et al., 2000). This pattern of results is consistent with the notion that the events that transpire within the family are a key ingredient in shaping attachments.

Attachments to Fathers Because mothers traditionally have fulfilled the role of primary caregiver, most of the emphasis in research has been on the emotional bond that develops between child and mother. With large numbers of women participating in the labor force, however, and challenges to the assumption that females have the exclusive role in child care, many caregiving responsibilities have been assumed by others either within or outside the family. Moreover, researchers in developmental science have recognized the glaring absence of information on how another important family member, the father, interacts with his children. The result has been a growing literature on father–child interaction.

In this chapter, we have underscored maternal sensitivity and responsiveness as key factors in fostering optimal child development. Studies have shown that fathers are just as responsive as mothers to the signals of their infants, and when given the opportunity, they interact with their babies in ways similar to mothers. One team of researchers measured the physiological responsiveness of mothers and fathers as they observed quiet, smiling, or crying babies on a video monitor (Frodi et al., 1978). Mothers and fathers showed similar changes in heart rate, blood pressure, and skin conductance when the babies smiled or cried. In another study of maternal and paternal behaviors toward infants in the newborn nursery, Ross Parke and Sandra O'Leary (1976) found that fathers were just as likely as mothers to hold, touch, and vocalize to their babies.

After the newborn period, fathers and mothers begin to manifest somewhat different styles of interacting with their infants. When they play face to face with their babies, fathers tend to provide physical and social stimulation in staccato bursts, whereas mothers tend to be more rhythmic, positive in emotional tone, and soothing (Forbes et al., 2004). Fathers typically engage in physical and unpredictable "idiosyncratic" play with their infants—throwing them up in the air, moving their limbs, and tickling them—whereas mothers spend more time in caregiving activities or calm games like "pat-a-cake" (Lamb, 1997; Yogman, 1982). As a consequence, infants prefer fathers when they wish to play and seek out mothers when they desire care and comfort. At the same time, fathers from diverse backgrounds have also been observed to engage in at least moderate amounts of responsive, positively toned interaction with their young infants (Shannon, Tamis-LeMonda, & Margolin, 2005). Physical play is not the exclusive style that fathers display.

In general, fathers spend less time interacting with and caring for their children than mothers do. Nevertheless, infants clearly do form attachments to their fathers. In the Strange Situation, infants show signs of separation anxiety when the father leaves the room and greet him on his return. They also use him as a secure base for exploration (Kotelchuk, 1976). In most cases, when infants are attached to their mother, they are also attached to their father (Rosen & Burke, 1999). As is the case with mothers, when fathers spend time in face-to-face interactions with their infants, but particularly when they show sensitivity in their play, their infants show clear signs of attachment to them (Cox et al., 1992; Grossmann et al., 2002). Securely attached infants also tend to have fathers who are sociable, are agreeable, and express positive emotions (Belsky, 1996). Given the opportunity to be nurturant and responsive, fathers, like mothers, can become partners in strong, secure attachments.

The opportunity for infants to develop attachments to fathers matters. Children who have secure attachments to *both* mothers and

Infants show clear signs of attachment to fathers, especially when fathers spend time in rewarding, mutually engaging interactions with them. Research shows that children who have healthy attachments to mothers *and* fathers show higher self-esteem and greater social competence than children who are securely attached to only one or neither parent.

RISK | RESILIENCE

fathers show higher self-esteem and greater social competence than children who have secure attachments to only one or to neither parent (Verschueren & Marcoen, 1999). Moreover, healthy relationships with fathers can buffer children who are at risk due to impaired interactions with their mother. Recall how infants with a depressed mother often have poor-quality interactions with them. One group of researchers found that infants with a depressed mother often developed more positive interactions with their father (Hossain et al., 1994). Studies like these suggest that fathers fulfill a very important role in the family—one that simply cannot be ignored.

Temperament and Attachment Caregivers are not solely responsible for the emergence of attachment. Because attachments form in the context of interactions between caregiver and infant, it seems reasonable to postulate that the infant's own style as a communication partner contributes significantly to the growth of an affectional bond.

Several researchers have reported a link between infant characteristics such as irritability and proneness to distress and subsequent attachment behaviors in the Strange Situation (Bates et al., 1985; Goldsmith & Alansky, 1987; Miyake, Chen, & Campos, 1985). For example, two-day-old infants' proneness to distress when a pacifier is removed from their mouths is related to insecure attachment at fourteen months of age (Calkins & Fox, 1992). Similarly, in a study of Dutch infants who were identified as very irritable newborns, 74 percent were classified as insecurely attached at eighteen months of age (van den Boom, 1994, 1995). Yet early irritability does not necessarily predispose children to become insecurely attached. In the same study of Dutch infants, a second group of irritable newborns and their mothers participated in an intervention program that resulted in only 28 percent being scored as insecurely attached later in infancy.

Promoting Secure Attachment in Irritable Infants | research applied to parenting

The phone call turned out to be from Gwen, Cindy's close friend. The two of them had shared many life experiences since their childhood days, but Cindy still found it remarkable that they had had their babies within three months of each other. Cindy knew, though, that motherhood was a challenge for Gwen. Gwen's son, unlike Michael, was hard to figure out and to keep happy. He didn't seem to like being held very much and was often cranky both before and after feeding. Gwen was a loving mother, but at times she was at her wits' end trying to think of ways to soothe her baby. When Cindy picked up the phone, she could tell from Gwen's voice that she was looking for advice on how to handle her difficult child.

What can parents do if their infant is born with a "difficult" temperamental style, showing more negative than positive emotions, fussing and crying, and smiling infrequently? Research carried out in the Netherlands—in which mother–child interaction was observed in the home monthly up until the infants were six months of age—shows that mothers of irritable infants displayed distinct patterns of reactions. They exhibited less visual and physical contact with their babies, were less involved with them, and responded less when their babies smiled or showed other positive social behaviors (van den Boom & Hoeksma, 1994). Although many of the differences between mothers of irritable and nonirritable infants disappeared by the time their children were six months old, such negative parent–child interactions may predispose children to develop insecure attachments.

In a second study (van den Boom, 1994, 1995), mothers of irritable newborns were randomly assigned to either an intervention group or a control group when their infants were six months of age. During three in-home training sessions conducted every three weeks, mothers in the intervention group were taught to be more responsive to the cues their infants provided. The infants and mothers were observed again when the children were twelve, eighteen, twenty-four, and forty-two months of age. The benefits of the intervention were clear: Children in the experimental group were far more likely to be securely attached than children in the control group, even into toddlerhood. These children were also more cooperative, displayed fewer behavior problems, and engaged in more activities and verbal interactions with their mothers than the control group children. Even though mothers had received training up to several years earlier, they continued to show responsive, sensitive parenting.

What exactly were mothers in the intervention group taught? Following are the essential ingredients of the training package:

1. *Attend to the infant's signals, especially by imitating the baby's behaviors and repeating one's own verbalizations.* If the infant coos, respond by making a similar sound. When speaking to the infant, say words slowly and repeat them. If the infant averts his gaze, remain silent, because gaze aversion often means the caregiver has not interpreted the child's signals correctly. These techniques aim to slow down the tempo of mother–infant interactions and to simplify them. The overall goal of these procedures is to help the mothers perceive and interpret infant signals accurately.
2. *Try to soothe the fussing or crying infant.* Because some infants seem to respond negatively to being cuddled or held in close physical contact, try to find a technique suitable for the particular child and her preferences, for example, feeding or vocalizing to her. Once an effective technique is identified, stick with it. Again, the idea is to avoid rapid changes in maternal behavior that might create further frustration and distress in the infant.
3. *Pay attention to the infant's positive signals instead of focusing on his negative behaviors.* Mothers of irritable infants are often so focused on their negative behaviors that they ignore the infant's positive signals. Create opportunities for positive interactions. Play with the infant using games and toys, paying attention to how he responds, especially if the response is a smile or a laugh.

In general, the goal of the program was to help mothers correctly read and respond to their own infants' signals, characteristics of mothering that Ainsworth's early studies identified as precursors of secure attachment. Infants who participated in this and other similar interventions show many desirable outcomes even years after the intervention itself was terminated (van Doesum et al., 2008).

Attachment and Later Development The importance of attachment has been underscored by research findings showing that secure attachments are related to positive developmental outcomes in both social and cognitive spheres when children become older. Leah Matas and her associates assessed the quality of attachments of forty-eight infants when they were eighteen months of age (Matas, Arend, & Sroufe, 1978). Six months later, these same children were observed for the quality of their play and their problem-solving styles. Children who had earlier been categorized as securely attached were more enthusiastic and compliant with their mothers' suggestions in the problem-solving tasks and showed more positive affect and persistence than their insecurely attached counterparts. They also engaged in more symbolic play and displayed less crying and whining. Other researchers have noted that securely attached children show advantages in language acquisition and cognitive reasoning from toddlerhood well into the middle school years and adolescence. Perhaps the secure child's readiness to explore the environment provides the kind of intellectual stimulation that leads to better cognitive performance (Jacobsen, Edelstein, & Hofman, 1994; Meins, 1998). Perhaps, too, the style of maternal interaction that leads to secure attachment also promotes language and cognitive development.

INTERACTION AMONG DOMAINS

Securely attached children have also been found to be more socially competent with their peers as preschoolers, showing more leadership, greater sympathy, less aggression, and less withdrawal from social interactions (DeMulder et al., 2000; Booth-LaForce & Kerns, 2009; Waters, Wippman, & Sroufe, 1979). They evidence stronger signs of "ego resiliency" at age five years, meaning they respond to problems in a flexible, persistent, and resourceful manner (Arend, Gove, & Sroufe, 1979). In contrast, insecurely attached infants, particularly those who show avoidant patterns, do not fare so well in the preschool years, according to other research. Children with this attachment classification are found to display many maladaptive and undesirable behaviors, such as high dependency, noncompliance, and poor social skills in peer interactions. They are described by teachers as hostile, impulsive, and withdrawn (Erickson, Sroufe, & Egeland, 1985; Laible & Thompson, 2000). Moreover, avoidant children tend to have negative representations of peers, interpret peers' behaviors as hostile, and become more fearful with age (Cassidy et al., 1996; Kochanska, 2001). A recent meta-analysis of research studies that represented the data of nearly 6,000 children demonstrated that insecure attachments are very strong predictors of externalizing behaviors later in childhood (Fearon et al., 2010).

RISK | RESILIENCE

The effects of early attachments may carry over well into adolescence and the adult years. Adolescents who evidence secure attachments to their parents, in the sense of expressing affection for and trust in them, generally have high self-esteem, have a strong sense of personal identity, have fewer depressive symptoms, and display social competence (Cooper, Shaver, & Collins, 1998; Rice, 1990). They also engage in more constructive problem solving when discussing controversial topics, such as dating and household rules, with their parents (Kobak et al., 1993) and generally show successful psychological adjustment in the sense of displaying fewer internalizing and externalizing behaviors (Allen et al., 2007). Longitudinal data also suggest that children who showed the ambivalent attachment pattern as infants are more prone than secure infants to develop anxiety disorders and have poorer social competence in adolescence (Warren et al., 1997; Weinfield, Ogawa, & Sroufe, 1997).

Internal Working Models and Later Relationships One of the most provocative and interesting findings emerging in attachment research is that the quality of an individual's attachment during childhood may influence his interpersonal relationships as an adolescent or adult. In Bowlby's (1973) theory, as children experience ongoing interactions with parents, they develop mental frameworks of those relationships called **internal working models of relationships.** These internal working models can, in turn, influence representations of other close relationships that emerge later in life, such as those with friends and romantic partners. Secure attachments, according to the theory, help foster healthy close relationships later in life; insecure attachments, however, can forecast problems in subsequent close relationships. Consistent with this theory are the results of a meta-analysis of sixty-three studies of attachment that found that secure attachment was more strongly associated with friendship quality than with peer relations in general (Schneider, Atkinson, & Tardif, 2001). In a more direct exploration of how early representations of relationships are related to later representations, Wyndol Furman and his colleagues (Furman et al., 2002) administered the Adult Attachment Interview to a group of high school seniors. This attachment measure requires participants to describe and evaluate their own childhood attachment relations; participants are then placed in the appropriate attachment category based on their responses. Working models of friendships and romantic partners were also assessed, using questions about support, caregiving, and cooperation in these relationships. The results showed a strong relationship between working models of relationships with parents and those with friends, but those with romantic relationships were less strong.

Internal working models of relationships may even extend to how a parent conceptualizes his or her relationship and interacts with the child (Bowlby, 1973; Main, Kaplan, & Cassidy, 1985). Researchers have noted significant relationships between the attachment classifications given to parents through the Adult Attachment Interview and the attachment styles of their infants (Benoit & Parker, 1994; Steele, Steele, & Fonagy, 1996; van IJzendoorn, 1995). Mothers who have positive concepts of their own attachments express more joy and pleasure in the relationship with their own child; they also display more emotional availability and use more positive and sensitive parenting behaviors (Aviezer et al., 1999; Pederson et al., 1998; Slade et al., 1999).

Cross-Cultural Variations in Patterns of Attachment Overall, children in most countries around the world show behaviors indicating secure attachment even if they have been reared in very different circumstances (Posada et al., 1995; van IJzendoorn, 1995). Studies of children in Israel are good examples. Many Israeli infants are raised in the group setting of the kibbutz. While parents go to work, children are cared for by the *metapelet,* or caregiver, beginning sometime between six and twelve weeks of age and continuing after the first year. Children go to the group caregiving center (called the "children's house") in the morning and return home in the late afternoon, but most of their time is spent with the nonparental caregiver and peers. Do such arrangements interfere with the formation of attachments to mothers? One study showed that 80 percent of infants were securely attached to their mothers; interestingly, however, this finding held true only for infants who came home to sleep for the evening. Some infants sleep overnight at the "children's house," in

internal working models of relationships Mental frameworks of the quality of relationships with others, developed as a result of early ongoing interactions with caregivers.

keeping with more traditional practices of the kibbutz; among this group, only 48 percent were securely attached to their mothers (Sagi et al., 1994). Children raised on the kibbutz also showed notable attachments to their metapelet; 53 percent of infants were classified as securely attached to the caregiver (Sagi et al., 1985).

Observations of infants in Germany show a different pattern of results. In one study, about 49 percent of infants were scored as avoidantly attached (Grossmann et al., 1985). As in the Ainsworth studies, these researchers noted a relationship between maternal sensitivity and infant attachment: securely attached infants had mothers who interacted with them in a warm, responsive manner. However, although mothers varied in the sensitivity of responding when infants were two months of age, they did not vary by the time the infants were ten months old; most mothers had *low* sensitivity ratings by this time. Grossmann and her colleagues interpreted their findings in the context of the different attitudes toward child rearing held by parents in Germany and the United States. The emphasis in German culture is on fostering independence in one's offspring, encouraging the development of an obedient child who does not make demands on the parents. Responding to the infant's every cry is considered inappropriate. Thus, German mothers' tendency to pick up their children less frequently and for shorter periods of time and to display less affection reflects the goals of socialization in that culture.

SOCIOCULTURAL INFLUENCE

Finally, a study of Dogon mothers and infants in northwestern Africa found that, although infants assessed in the Strange Situation fell into the secure category at the same rate as Western samples, no infants were classified as avoidant. Recall that in North America about 20 percent of infants are avoidant. The researchers attribute the results to the fact that Dogon mothers feed their infants on demand, responding immediately to their infants' cries of hunger and distress. The high degree of responsiveness of mothers, say the researchers, makes avoidant behavior highly unlikely (True, Pisani, & Oumar, 2001).

Taken together, these studies suggest that the central ideas of attachment theory hold up under a wide variety of cultural circumstances. They show, in particular, that the mother's sensitivity and responsiveness are indeed related to the type of attachment style the infant displays. Yet some researchers caution that the Strange Situation may not take into account specific cultural practices as they relate to separation of the mother and infant. In Japan, for example, mothers and infants are rarely apart from one another, and infants respond with distress when the mother departs and then returns as part of the Strange Situation. Infants may be classified as insecure when they are really just responding to a breach of cultural practice (Takahashi, 1990). More broadly, say the critics, theorists need to consider the goals of socialization in a particular culture; not all cultures equally value the emergence of independence and exploration. Nor do all cultures define maternal sensitivity and responsiveness in the same way. Thus, attachment should be studied within the context of a particular culture's belief systems and practices (Rothbaum et al., 2000).

Child Care and Attachment One of the most difficult decisions many parents face concerns alternative child care arrangements when they work. As Table 11.2 shows, more than 60 percent of mothers with preschool-age children work, and almost 60 percent of women with infants under one year of age are employed (U.S. Census Bureau, 2010c). A substantial number of children are therefore receiving nonparental care, many beginning very early in life. Does this form of early experience influence the formation of attachments?

One problem in answering this question is that many variables operate when the child receives nonparental care. Is it the mother's absence or the quality of substitute care that produces any observable effects on child behavior? These two factors are difficult to separate. Does it matter whether the child receives full-time or part-time care? Perhaps, but the tremendous variation in caregiving schedules has made this factor difficult to control in research studies. In addition, the kinds of alternative care children receive vary a great deal, ranging from a single caregiver coming to the home to out-of-home family daycare in which another parent provides care for several children to center-based care.

The most recent information shows that early daycare does not put children at risk for insecure attachments. In a major study of more than 1,000 infants attending ten centers, researchers found that children who attended daycare did not differ from home-reared children in their reactions during reunions with their mothers and in overall attachment security. In addition, age at which daycare began, the amount of weekly time spent in

TABLE 11.2 Labor Force Participation Rates for Women with Children Under Age 18

This table shows the percentage of women with children under age eighteen who were employed outside the home in 2007 (the table shows only the data for married women whose husbands are present in the home).

Age of Child	Percentage of Women in the Labor Force
Under 18	69.4
Under 6, total	61.6
Under 3	58.8
1 year or under	57.8
2 years	61.4
3–5 years	65.6
6–13 years	74.5
14–17 years	79.8

Source: Data from U.S. Census Bureau, 2010c.

daycare, the quality of care, and the type of care (e.g., home with a relative, home with a nonrelative, center-based care) did not influence children's attachments in infancy or during the preschool years. There were some conditions under which insecure attachments were more likely, however: when maternal insensitivity co-occurred with extensive or poor-quality child care. In these cases, children were particularly at risk for ambivalent attachments (NICHD Early Child Care Research Network, 1997, 2001b).

RISK | RESILIENCE

A study conducted in Australia reiterates that what is important are the attitude and behaviors of the mother. The researchers found that mothers who returned to work by the time an infant was five months of age and who were committed to combining their roles as mothers with their work roles were more likely to have secure infants. These mothers, as it turned out, were also less anxious about child care and were more sensitive in their parenting styles (Harrison & Ungerer, 2002). Taken together, the studies on child care and attachment indicate that what matters most is the context in which child care is taking place—the emotional climate that parents create in the home and the quality of the interactions infants have with their parents.

Disruptions in Attachment

In some contexts, the ideal pattern of caregiver–child interaction may be disrupted, for example, when mother and infant are physically separated during the early days of their partnership due to the infant's premature birth or when the child is placed for adoption and nonbiological parents assume the caregiving role. Other children are the victims of physical abuse or neglect. What might be the impact of such disruptions on attachment? A consideration of these issues will further illuminate the ways in which early caregiver–child relationships influence subsequent child development.

RISK | RESILIENCE

Prematurity The preterm infant looks and behaves differently from the infant with the benefit of a full thirty-eight weeks in utero. In all likelihood, the premature infant will be very small and fragile looking, less alert and responsive to stimulation, and more difficult to comfort. Cries, but not smiles, are very frequent (Goldberg, 1979). In addition, mothers and their premature infants usually are separated physically, sometimes for several weeks, while the babies receive the medical care necessary to ensure their well-being or even their survival. If attachments were based largely on mutually rewarding infant–caregiver interactions, we might expect premature infants to develop insecure attachments with their mothers.

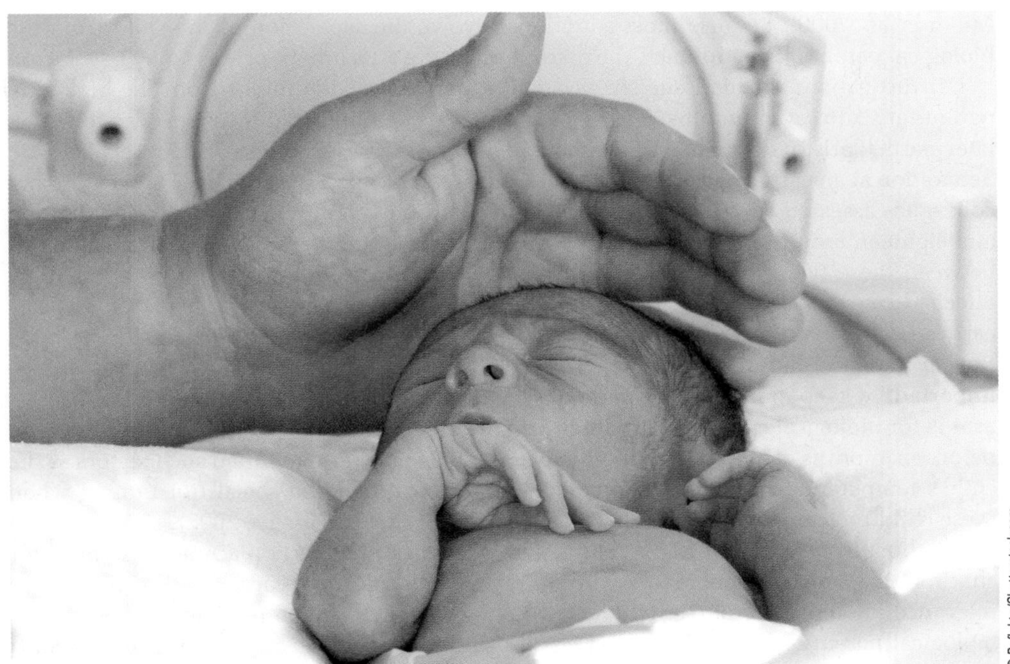

Because of their physical appearance, behavioral unresponsiveness, and separation from caregivers, premature infants can be at risk for insecure attachments. However, the presence of a sensitive, supportive caregiver can mitigate that risk.

In the hospital nursery, mothers of premature infants indeed behave in a markedly different manner than mothers of full-term infants do. Mothers of premature babies touch, hold, and smile at their babies less often than do mothers of full-term infants (DiVitto & Goldberg, 1979). As their babies get older, however, mothers of premature infants actually become more active than mothers of full-term babies in stimulating them: they initiate and maintain more interactions, even to the point of being excessive. These behaviors may stem from the mother's desire to alter the premature's unresponsive pattern or to stimulate the child in an effort to spur slowed development. Infants often react to these maternal behaviors by averting their gaze, as though to shut out the added stimulation (Field, 1977, 1982).

Given the differences in maternal styles with premature babies, is there a corresponding impact on the attachments of these infants? In a comparison of twenty full-term and twenty premature infants at eleven months of age, Ann Frodi and Ross Thompson (1985) observed no significant differences in the patterns of attachments. Most of the children in both groups were observed to be securely attached. By one year of age, many premature infants "rebound" from the negative effects of early birth, especially if they encounter a responsive, supportive environment. Mothers may also adapt their styles in later months to conform more closely to the rhythms and needs of the child. Thus, the early developmental risk posed by prematurity does not automatically lead to persistent problems in mother–child relations or other developmental patterns. On the other hand, very-low-birthweight infants—those under 1,250 grams—have been found to be at risk for insecure attachments at nineteen months of age (Mangelsdorf et al., 1996). These infants in particular may present greater stresses and challenges for their caregivers. It may be that many of the hospital practices designed to promote responsive parenting of prematures described in Chapter 4, "The Prenatal Period and Birth," can benefit the formation of attachments in these at-risk infants. We will have to wait for the results of future research to know more about these specific kinds of impacts.

Adoption and Foster Care By the time they reach middle childhood and adolescence, adopted children show a noticeably higher incidence of psychological and academic problems compared with nonadopted children (Brodzinsky et al., 1984; Fergusson, Lynskey, & Horwood, 1995; Sharma, McGue, & Benson, 1998). They are at greater risk for substance abuse, health problems, emotional distress, and fighting (Juffer & van IJzendoorn, 2005;

RISK | RESILIENCE

Miller et al., 2000). Because most adoptions involve the separation of the child from the biological parent during infancy, the disruption of the attachment process may be a factor.

Investigations of this issue showed that separation of the infant from the biological parents at six to seven months of age can produce socioemotional difficulties even ten years later, particularly in the child's ability to form relationships with others (Yarrow et al., 1973). Separation at an earlier age, however, may have a lesser impact. When Leslie Singer and her colleagues assessed the attachments of adopted and nonadopted infants between thirteen and eighteen months of age, they found no difference in the classifications of attachments between these two groups (Singer et al., 1985). Most of the infants fell into the securely attached category. In this group, most of the adoptive placements had occurred at fairly early ages, the majority by three months of age. At this age children have not yet developed the early manifestations of attachment, such as stranger and separation anxiety. It is also important to keep in mind that maternal sensitivity is important for adopted children, just as it is for biological caregivers and their infants. In a Dutch study of 146 children adopted before six months of age, maternal sensitive responsiveness—more than such factors as the child's temperament or gender—predicted better cognitive and social functioning when these children were seven years old (Stams, Juffer, & van IJzendoorn, 2002).

Although the studies of adoption generally suggest that early placement is better for children than later placement, the findings on the importance of caregiver sensitivity have relevance for another group of children who experience disrupted relationships with their biological parents—foster children. Mary Dozier and her colleagues (Dozier et al., 2001) found that infants placed in foster homes at age eighteen months can still develop secure attachments provided that their caregivers both value relationships and had strong attachments to their own parents. This pattern occurred even if the infants had experienced neglect, physical abuse, and frequent turnover in caregivers. These data speak to the remarkable resilience of young children when they are provided with loving, nurturant homes.

what do you think?

Should International Adoptions Be Encouraged?

Between 1988 and 2001, international adoptions of children increased by 79 percent to include more than 34,000 children from more than fifty countries, with families in the United States adopting more than any other country (UNICEF, 2003). Parents adopt children for many reasons: They may want to help children who are in need, they may be seeking a way to raise children if they are unable to have offspring of their own, or both. However, as we saw above, children who are adopted face a number of developmental risks including attachment problems, especially if their transition to a new family occurs after age two years. Children who are adopted from another country show many of these same patterns; they are generally at more risk for behavior problems that persist over time if they are placed in their new homes after age twenty-four months (Gunnar & van Dulmen, 2007; Lee et al., 2010; Rutter et al., 2009).

However, international adoptions raise a whole set of other questions that are unique to this particular situation. For example, what happens if parents are unprepared to raise a child who has experienced severe early deprivation in a foreign orphanage or serious maltreatment during early care (O'Connor, 2005)? How do children fare when their ethnic heritage is different from that of their adoptive parents? One recent study, for example, showed that Asian children who are adopted by Euro Americans were not seen as part of the Asian American immigrant community in the same way that children from Asian families were (Lee & Miller, 2009). Other critics point to serious ethical issues that are often connected to international adoption, claiming that such practices disproportionately affect biological parents who are poor and do not have the power or resources to keep their own children. This social context can promote child trafficking, kidnapping, and other serious problems that affect children who are already vulnerable (Hollingsworth, 2003).

What do you think about the appropriateness of international adoptions? Do the benefits to children outweigh the risks outlined above? How can the research in developmental science help to resolve some of these complex and troubling issues?

Abuse Physically or psychologically abused children are at risk for an assortment of cognitive and socioemotional difficulties. Because the trauma that accompanies within-family violence can be enduring, especially with repeated episodes of abuse, it is not surprising that attachments between abused children and their parents take on an aberrant character.

RISK | RESILIENCE

Infants and toddlers who have been maltreated by their caregivers are likely to fall into the category of insecure attachment, called *disorganized/disoriented attachment.* Approximately 80 percent of maltreated infants fit this attachment profile (Carlson et al., 1989; Cicchetti, Toth, & Lynch, 1995). Like other attachment categories, the disorganized/disoriented pattern may predict later developmental outcomes. In one study, 71 percent of preschoolers who showed high levels of hostile behavior toward peers had been categorized as having disorganized attachments during infancy (Lyons-Ruth, Alpern, & Repacholi, 1993). In another, researchers found that when children with disorganized/disoriented attachments were six years old, they tended to be depressed, disorganized in behavior, and even self-destructive in response to questions about their parents or family life (Main et al., 1985). Disorganized children also tend to express more anger over time (Kochanska, 2001).

Why do these maladaptive attachments form? Abusive parents tend to react negatively to many of their children's social signals, even positive ones. When Ann Frodi and Michael Lamb (1980) observed the reactions of abusive and nonabusive mothers to videotapes of smiling and crying infants, abusive mothers were more aroused physiologically by both cries and smiles than were nonabusive mothers and were less willing to interact with an infant, even a smiling one. These findings suggest, at the very least, that the abused infant has an unwilling and psychologically distant interaction partner. In addition, mothers of disorganized/disoriented children tend to be intrusive and insensitive in their parenting styles independent of the temperamental characteristics of their children (Carlson, 1998).

Studies of premature, adopted, and abused children reveal that secure attachment relationships can develop in circumstances that are less than optimal during the early part of infancy. At the same time, however, when interactions between caregivers and infants deviate too widely from the ideal, especially in terms of the emotional tone of interactions, the consequences for the child can be serious and enduring.

Early Emotional Experiences and the Brain One of the most valuable outcomes of the studies conducted on disrupted infant–caregiver attachments has been an accumulating appreciation for the role of early experiences in children's emotional lives. Recent physiological evidence suggests that changes in the functioning of the nervous system may accompany early social-emotional interactions and, furthermore, that the first two to three years of life may represent a critical period in laying down the "hardwiring" of emotional responding. For example, research with children who have suffered deprivation due to being reared in orphanages shows that their brains emit less electrical activity when they are shown pictures of faces (Nelson, 2007). These kinds of findings lead us to ask about the details of how these changes in brain functioning happen.

INTERACTION AMONG DOMAINS

One physiological system that has been examined is the action of the stress hormone *cortisol.* Researchers have observed that infants with a tendency to be fearful, inhibited, or angry sometimes show elevation of the amount of cortisol in their saliva, reflecting their experience of stress (Stansbury & Gunnar, 1994). In one study, though, inhibited infants with secure attachments did not show these typical elevations when confronted with fear-provoking stimuli, as indicated in Figure 11.8 (Nachmias et al., 1996). In contrast, inhibited infants who were insecurely attached did show a rise in levels of cortisol. Because these data are correlational, the usual precautions about interpreting the results apply. Nonetheless, there are some interesting potential implications of studies such as this one. Cortisol is released by the adrenal glands and can influence the hippocampus (which is involved in learning and memory), the frontal areas of the brain, and portions of the limbic system (connected with emotional responding). In animals, excessive exposure to cortisol results in the death of neurons and the atrophy of dendrites. Although the impact of too much exposure to cortisol on the human brain has not yet been studied directly, one implication is that early and prolonged exposure to stress can have negative consequences on the structure of important brain systems. Healthy attachments, however, might buffer those effects (Gunnar, 1998; Gunnar & White, 2001).

Figure 11.8

Physiological Stress Responses in Young Infants

In a study in which inhibited and uninhibited eighteen-month-olds were exposed to stressful situations (e.g., a noisy mechanical robot), inhibited children showed elevated levels of the stress hormone cortisol, but only if they were insecurely attached. The green bars represent baseline levels of cortisol in the saliva prior to the fearful situation, and the purple bars represent levels of cortisol after the fearful event. These findings suggest that secure attachments might buffer the physiological stress responses of inhibited children.

Source: Adapted from Nachmias, M., Gunnar, M., Mangelsdorf, S., Parritz, R., & Buss, K. (1996). Behavioral inhibition and stress reactivity: Moderating role of attachment security. *Child Development*, *67*, pp. 508–522. Copyright © 1996. Used by permission of Society for Research in Child Development.

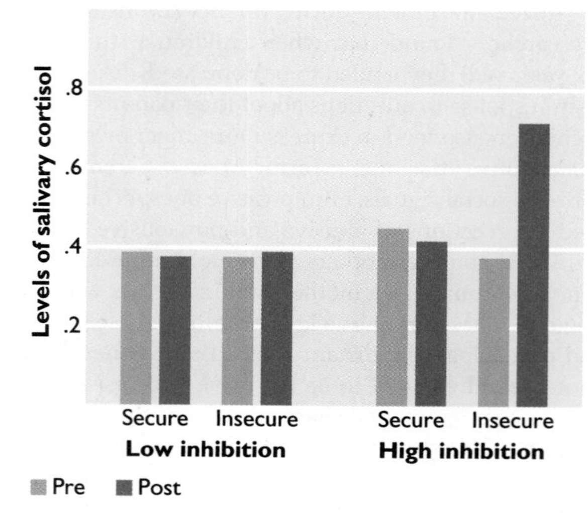

Another biochemical substance, the neurotransmitter norepinephrine, has also been implicated in early emotional development. Infant monkeys deprived of contact with their mothers show depressed levels of norepinephrine. Similarly, emotionally disturbed children who have suffered neglect show lower levels of norepinephrine, as well as oxytocin—a hormone that acts as a neurotransmitter, than children who are not neglected (Pollak et al., 2010; Rogeness & McClure, 1996). Researchers are further exploring the relationship of attachment with these biochemical systems as well.

We now know that many of the brain systems involved in emotional responding—the hippocampus, the amygdala, and the prefrontal cortex—are malleable and plastic in early infancy. Because of their malleability, they may be especially vulnerable to the differing types of emotional experiences, positive and negative, to which children are exposed (Post & Weiss, 1997). Given these findings, it is vital that researchers continue to explore the role that early emotional experiences play in development.

For Your Review and Reflection

- What theoretical perspectives have influenced our understanding of attachment?
- What changes in attachment behaviors are typically seen over the course of development? Which behaviors are special hallmarks of attachment?
- How is attachment accessed in young children? What categories are used to classify children?
- What factors have been shown to promote secure attachments?
- What are the consequences of attachment styles for later development?
- How are attachment behaviors similar or different across cultures? What is the significance of these findings?

- What is the impact of child care on attachment? How are your own feelings about child care influenced by these research findings?
- What do the cases of prematurity, adoption, and abuse tell us about the concept of attachment?
- What is the relationship between early emotional experiences and the development of the brain?
- What are the implications of attachment styles for risk and resilience in development?
- Why do you think attachment is such an important factor in development? How have the early relationships established with your caregivers played an influential role in your development?

chapter recap

Summary of Developmental Themes

Nature & Nurture

How do nature and nurture interact in emotional development?
As has been stressed throughout this chapter, both nature and nurture contribute to the child's emotional development. Biology assumes a larger role in the child's early emotional capacities, for example, in the infant's ability to express and detect basic emotions such as joy and sadness. However, socialization and cognitive development become more prominent explanations for later emotional expression, particularly for self-conscious emotions such as guilt and envy and for emotion regulation. Ethologists and child temperament researchers maintain that nature guides the formation of attachments between children and caregivers, but other researchers show how qualities of parenting style are equally important. Many aspects of emotional development in adolescence highlight the interaction between heredity and environment. Depression, for example, can be best understood as emerging from biological risks that meet with socialization or contextual risks.

Sociocultural Influence

How does the sociocultural context influence emotional development?
Different cultures place varying emphasis on emotionality itself and on the specific emotions considered appropriate to display. For example, Chinese infants smile and cry less than American infants. A culture's beliefs and values also can influence the child's responses in the Strange Situation. For example, Japanese children are more frequently classified as insecurely attached, but their behavior may simply reflect a response to changes in normative cultural practice.

Interaction Among Domains

How does emotional development interact with other domains of development?
Emotions are closely intertwined with both cognition and social behavior. On the one hand, cognitive achievements, such as the ability to interpret social and personal experiences, lay the groundwork for advances in attachment and emotional expression. Similarly, children often learn about emotions through social experiences, such as interactions with their caregivers. On the other side of the equation, successful emotional development in the form of attachment is associated with positive social and cognitive achievements later in childhood. Children who are skilled at understanding, expressing, and regulating emotions also have better relations with their peers.

Risk | Resilience

What factors promote risk or resilience in emotional development?
Some children may be "easy," "difficult," or "slow to warm up" in temperament, or they may display inhibited or uninhibited styles. These relatively stable individual differences may affect how parents and others react to the child and, in turn, influence other developmental outcomes such as attachment. The child's ability to regulate his or her emotions is another predictor of successful development later on. Among adolescents, the failure to regulate emotions and propensities for depression can create risks. In general, responsive and supportive caregiving practices can promote resilience in these kinds of circumstances.

Chapter Review

What Are Emotions?

What are the three components of emotions? How are these related to the ways in which researchers measure emotions?
Emotions are a complex set of behaviors produced in response to some event. Emotions have physiological, expressive, and experiential components.

What functions do emotions serve in the various aspects of the child's psychological life?
Emotions can regulate overt actions; influence cognitive processing; and, most important, initiate, maintain, or terminate social interactions.

What are the main ways in which biological, cognitive-socialization, and social-contextual theories of emotion differ from one another?
Biological theories state that infants are born with the ability to express certain basic emotions. Making the facial expressions for these emotions leads to the experience of the emotion. Cognitive-

socialization theories emphasize the child's knowledge about the appropriate times and ways of expressing emotions, knowledge that is gleaned from socialization experiences. Social-contextual theories state that emotions must be understood as processes embedded in social interactions. The positive or negative tone and their intensity are especially important.

How does each of these theories address the issue of the interaction of nature and nurture?
By their very nature, biological theories stress how nature sets the foundations for emotional development. Cognitive-socialization theories emphasize the role of environmental experiences in shaping how children understand their emotional experiences. Social-contextual theories, too, ascribe a large role to nurture.

Expressing and Understanding Emotions

What are the differences between basic and self-conscious emotions? Give some examples of basic emotions that researchers have observed in young infants. Give some examples of self-conscious emotions that emerge later in childhood.
Basic emotions appear early in infancy and, for the most part, appear similar across cultures. Examples include joy, sadness, and surprise. *Self-conscious emotions* require more sophisticated cognitive and social understanding on the part of the child. They require knowledge about the self as related to others. Examples include shame, guilt, and jealousy.

What are the dynamics of synchronous and asynchronous interactions between infant and caregiver? What is the significance of these types of interactions for later emotional development?
During *interactive synchrony,* infants' emotional expressions occur in contingent exchanges with the caregiver. The reactions of one individual follow the expressions of the other. Infants learn important lessons about the rules of interaction and the ability to regulate interactions in the context of these, as well as asynchronous, interactions.

What types of knowledge about emotions do children acquire in the years from preschool to adolescence? How can parents and caregivers promote emotion knowledge among children?
Preschoolers begin to understand many of the situations that give rise to specific emotions and the consequences of displaying them. They also begin to understand how to manage negative emotions. School-age children begin to appreciate cultural *display rules* that dictate when and how emotions should be displayed. They also understand that they can control emotions with their own thoughts and that sometimes two emotions can be experienced simultaneously.

What are the distinctive features of emotional development in adolescence?
Adolescents experience more negative emotions and have more negative interactions with their parents than children of other ages.

Regulating Emotions

What strategies do infants and children typically use to regulate their emotions? What is the significance of the child's ability to regulate his or her own emotions?
Infants may distract themselves, look away, or look at the caregiver in order to regulate their emotional states. Older children typically use distraction to regulate their emotions. The ability to regulate emotions is important because it predicts behavioral conduct and the quality of social relationships later in childhood. Adolescents who use active emotion regulation strategies, such as problem solving rather than denial or rumination, are less likely to develop adjustment problems such as *internalizing* or *externalizing.*

How can parents and caregivers promote emotion regulation among children?
Parents who provide supportive guidance, who offer positively toned interactions, and who at least attempt to help children manage their emotions have children who are better at emotion regulation.

Much of the discussion in this section identifies risks to infants and children. What are the implications for promoting emotional resilience in individuals?
Resilience can be promoted by being responsive to the social bids and emotions expressed by infants and by encouraging older children to learn how to appropriately express and manage their emotions. There are many positive consequences of these tactics, especially for the child's social development.

What factors are related to depression during adolescence?
Depression may have a genetic component but is also linked to family conflict. Adolescents may be especially prone to depression because of the large number of cognitive, physical, emotional, and social changes that take place at this time.

Variations in Emotional Development

What are the different ways in which child temperament has been conceptualized?
Different temperament categories include the easy, difficult, and slow-to-warm-up styles identified by Chess and Thomas, the inhibited versus uninhibited styles researched by Kagan and his colleagues, and the dimensions of reactivity and self-regulation focused on by Rothbart and her colleagues.

What is the evidence for a biological basis for temperament?
Children with different temperament styles show differences in such physiological responses as heart rate, EEG patterns, and cardiac vagal tone.

How is temperament related to later development?
Early temperament styles predict social behaviors, peer relations, and cognitive functioning later in development.

How do boys and girls differ in the expression of emotions? What factors might be responsible for these differences?
Sex differences in emotions are more likely to show up later in childhood. Girls tend to express a wider range of emotions and are better at identifying emotional expressions in others than boys. These sex differences may arise from socialization experiences that take place early in childhood. Mothers are more expressive with and tend to engage in more "emotion talk" with their daughters than their sons. Parents also encourage girls to maintain emotional closeness and boys to control their emotions.

In what ways does the development of emotion vary across cultures?
Different cultures encourage the expression of some emotions over others, depending on the broader values and belief systems they hold. They may also value some temperament styles over others.

Attachment: Emotional Relationships with Others

What theoretical perspectives have influenced our understanding of attachment?
Learning theory has emphasized the mother's association with feeding (a *primary reinforcer*) and other activities that the infant finds pleasurable. As a result of this association, she is said to acquire *secondary reinforcing* attributes. Harlow's classic experiments with surrogate monkeys showed that contact comfort played a more important role in *attachment* than feeding. Ethological theorists view attachment as an innate, adaptive phenomenon that promotes proximity between the infant and caregiver and thus ensures the infant's survival.

What changes in attachment behaviors are typically seen over the course of development? Which behaviors are special hallmarks of attachment?
Several behaviors mark the child's emerging attachment to the caregiver at about six months of age. These include using the caregiver as a *secure base, separation anxiety, reunion behavior,* and *stranger anxiety.*

How is attachment accessed in young children? What categories are used to classify children?
Attachment is measured by observing the infant's responses to the *Strange Situation,* a standardized laboratory task that assesses the infant's use of the caregiver as a secure base for exploration, stranger anxiety, separation anxiety, and reunion behavior. The different categories include *secure attachment* and three categories of *insecure attachment—avoidant, ambivalent* (or *resistant*), and *disorganized/disoriented attachment.*

What factors have been shown to promote secure attachments?
Several variables predict the formation of secure attachments, including the sensitivity and responsiveness of the caregiver, the synchrony of child–caregiver interactions, and the temperament of the child.

What are the consequences of attachment styles for later development?
Security of attachment predicts a number of important developmental outcomes, including cognitive performance, social competence, and high self-esteem. The *internal working models of relationships* that children develop as a part of the attachment process are related to qualities of other close relationships later in life.

How are attachment behaviors similar or different across cultures? What is the significance of these findings?
The proportion of infants placed in various attachment categories can vary cross-culturally, but these studies still confirm that caregiver sensitivity is an important factor in the emergence of secure attachment. At the same time, it is important to consider the goals of socialization in a particular culture as attachment concepts are applied in different cultural contexts.

What is the impact of child care on attachment?
The most recent data show that, in general, early experiences in child care do not lead to disruptions in attachment. Rather, it is important to consider the emotional climate of the home and the quality of interactions that parents and infants have when both parents work.

What do the cases of prematurity, adoption, and abuse tell us about the concept of attachment?
Studies of premature infants, adoptees, foster children, and abused children indicate that attachments can form under less than optimal circumstances but that extreme deviations in caregiver–child interaction patterns can have serious negative consequences for the child.

What is the relationship between early emotional experiences and the development of the brain?
There is growing evidence to suggest that early emotional experiences are linked to changes in the underlying physiology of the central nervous system. Changes in the action of cortisol and neurotransmitters have been observed in young organisms that experience prolonged early stress.

Key Terms and Concepts

ambivalent (resistant) attachment (p. 423)
attachment (p. 418)
avoidant attachment (p. 423)
basic emotion (p. 401)
disorganized/disoriented attachment (p. 423)
display rules (p. 406)
emotions (p. 396)
externalizing (p. 412)
interactive synchrony (p. 402)
internalizing (p. 411)
internal working models of relationships (p. 428)
primary reinforcer (p. 419)
reunion behavior (p. 420)
secondary reinforcer (p. 419)
secure attachment (p. 421)
secure base (p. 421)
self-conscious emotion (p. 405)
separation anxiety (p. 420)
stranger anxiety (p. 420)
Strange Situation (p. 421)

Media Resources

Access an integrated eBook and chapter-specific interactive learning tools, including flashcards, quizzes, videos, and more, in your Developmental Psychology CourseMate, accessed through CengageBrain.com.

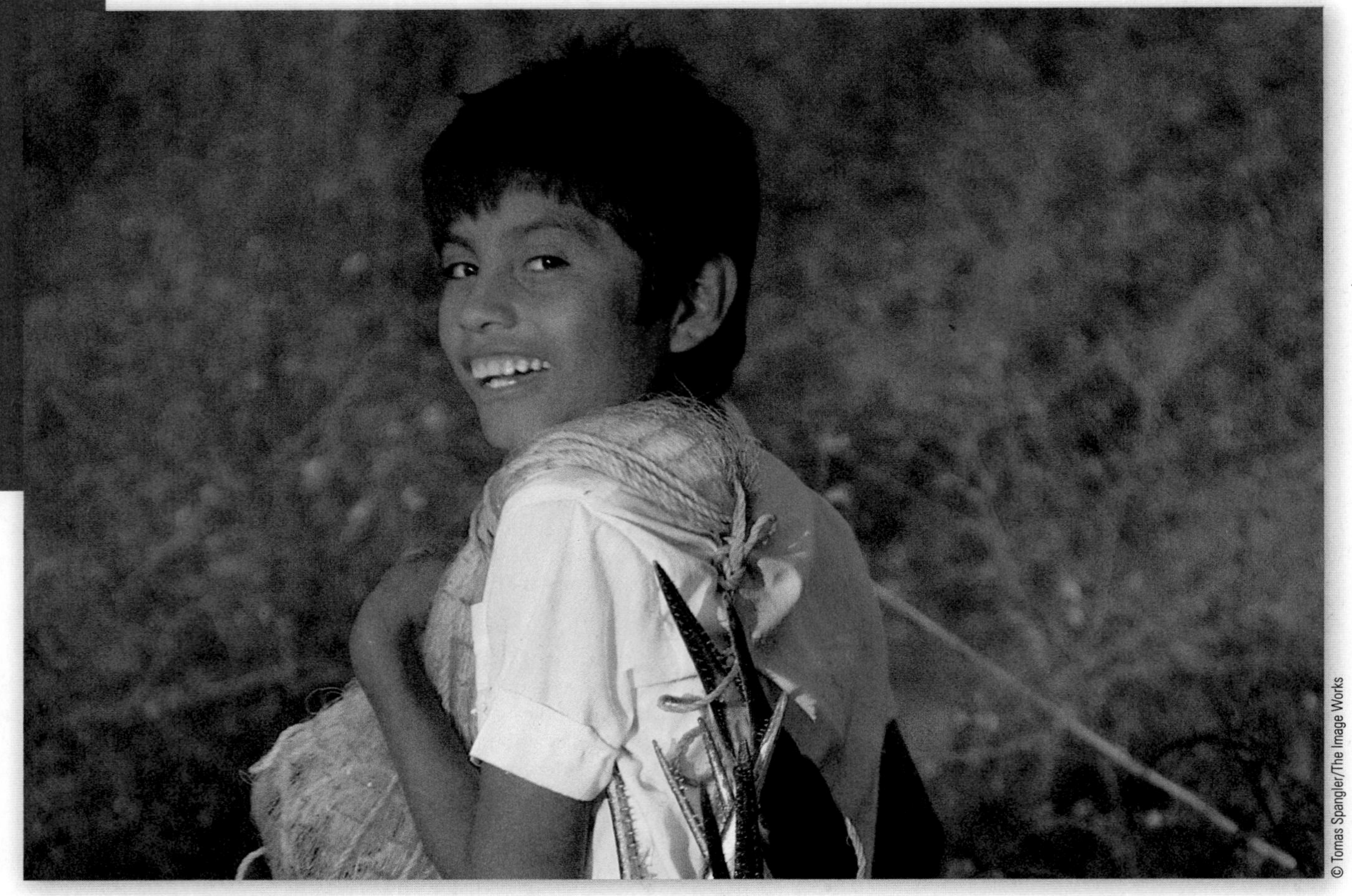

© Tomas Spangler/The Image Works

CHAPTER OUTLINE

[chapter 12]

Self and Values

KEY THEMES IN SELF AND VALUES

- **NATURE & NURTURE** How do nature and nurture interact in the development of self and of values?
- **SOCIOCULTURAL INFLUENCE** How does the sociocultural context influence the development of self and values?
- **CONTINUITY | DISCONTINUITY** Is the development of self and values continuous or discontinuous?
- **INTERACTION AMONG DOMAINS** How do self and values interact with other domains of development?
- **RISK | RESILIENCE** What factors promote risk or resilience in the development of self and values?

Michael had just finished his math assignment when he heard the door slam. Then he heard the loud, angry voice. "Kids today!" his grandfather fumed to no one in particular. "A couple of 'em almost ran me down on the sidewalk. Didn't bother to apologize. One even yelled, 'Get out of my way!' as she chased after her friends. Kids don't respect anybody, not even themselves—wearing those weird clothes, dyeing their hair every color you can think of, poking holes in their ears, even their noses! I suppose if I had stopped 'em, they'd have taken a swing at me or even worse. . . ." His voice trailed off to a mutter.

Michael had heard such tirades before: how the world has changed, how children today don't know right from wrong. Michael also worried about reports on the news: the first-grader who punched his teacher, the large number of sixth-graders who felt cheating was okay. Did his grandfather have a valid point? But he also thought about the fund raiser he and his friends had held to help earthquake victims whose homes and neighborhoods had been destroyed in other parts of the world. Collecting bottles and cans from the school cafeteria, as well as those brought by community members to a drop-off spot at school, they had managed to raise more than $500 to send to a relief agency. It made him feel good to be able to do even such a small thing to help people in those devastated regions. "Grandpa," he now said, hoping to placate his grandfather, "don't worry. Next time you go out for a walk, I'll go with you. Now would you like me to make you a cup of hot tea?" <<

To instill in children a sense of satisfaction with who they are and recognition of the standards of conduct considered acceptable and ethical within their community are among the most important goals of society. We expect children and adults to take pride in their accomplishments, learn to judge right from wrong, and refrain from actions that harm family, friends, or neighbors. Broadly speaking, survival in a social community depends on helping, cooperation, and sharing—behaviors that benefit others. Children display an awareness of self and the consequences of their conduct, both good and bad, early on, but these understandings undergo noticeable changes with development.

Michael's grandfather believes his generation has witnessed a decline in a positive sense of self and in courtesy and concern for others. Although one might debate whether such a change has actually taken place, the concerns voiced by Michael's grandfather are not new. Philosophers, theologians, and scientists have argued for decades about whether human nature is good or evil and how experience serves to channel children's inborn tendencies in either direction. In this chapter, we look first at the nature of "self" and how it relates to self-esteem and identity. We consider too how self-regulation contributes to our development. We then examine what theories and research tell us about moral development. Finally, we look at the course of development of altruistic and prosocial values as well as the factors that contribute to their counterpart: antisocial behavior.

The Concept of Self

"I know how."
"Look! See what I did!"
"I'm smart."
"I'm stronger than you!"
"I'm really good at this!"

These declarations express in no uncertain terms what children believe they can do, what they think they are like, and how they feel about their abilities. The statements reveal the child's awareness of self. How does this understanding of *self*—as someone who is an independent, unique person, able to reflect on his or her own beliefs and characteristics—develop?

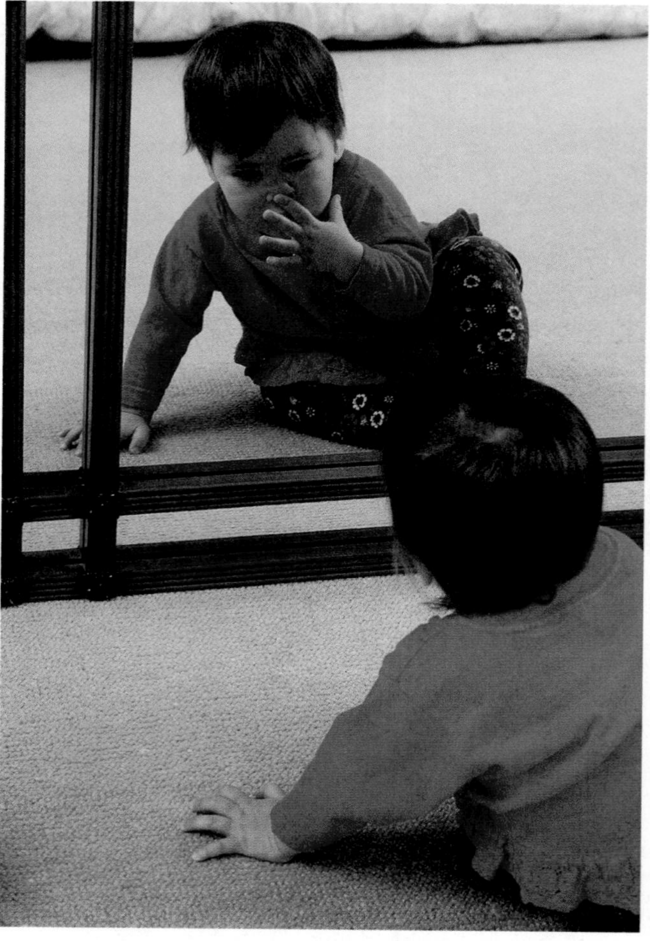

© Laura Dwight/PhotoEdit

In touching her nose while looking in the mirror, this eighteen-month-old illustrates one way a toddler tells us something about the knowledge she has about herself. After having a small spot of rouge surreptitiously placed on the tip of her nose, she seems to be indicating by touching her nose that the reflection is of "me." Before about fifteen to eighteen months of age, children typically do not respond to their reflections in the mirror because they still have a very limited understanding of self.

More than a century ago, William James (1892) suggested that there were two major components associated with the concept of self: the "me," or *objective self*, and the "I," or *subjective self*. James's objective, or the "me" aspect of self, is often called **self-concept**. An individual's self-concept includes an understanding of his or her physical qualities, possessions and status, skills, and psychological characteristics, including personality, beliefs, and value systems. The "I," or the subjective component, is made up of several additional key realizations, perhaps the most important of which is that "I" can be an agent of change and can control events in my life (sense of autonomy). We already considered some major developmental changes associated with the child's understanding of his or her sense of autonomy in Chapter 10, "Achievement," when discussing mastery orientation. But what about self as object?

Self as Object

When do children become aware of themselves as entities distinct from others? It is fairly obvious that they possess *self-awareness* when they say "That's me!" while looking at a family photo or vacation video or stake a claim to a particular toy with a boisterous self-reference of "That's mine!" But do infants, even before they talk, show any signs of self-recognition or this "idea of me"?

Self-Recognition in Infants and Toddlers The seeds of self-awareness already may be sown in infants' recognition of how their own body movements take place. For example, the attentional preferences of babies as young as three months suggest that they recognize when the left and right position and movements of their legs, viewed on videotape, are inverted (Rochat & Morgan, 1995). Other research reveals that infants recognize their own voice, face, and body movements as different from those of others, suggesting the origins of a rudimentary understanding of self as separate and distinct from other people and objects well before the end of the first year (Legerstee, Anderson, & Schaffer, 1998; Rochat & Striano, 2002). These capacities very likely serve as precursors to the fuller representation of self.

self-concept Perception, conceptions, and values one holds about oneself.

The household mirror has become an especially helpful research tool in answering the question of when self-recognition emerges. A toddler younger than fifteen to eighteen months shows little evidence of recognizing herself in a mirror. How do

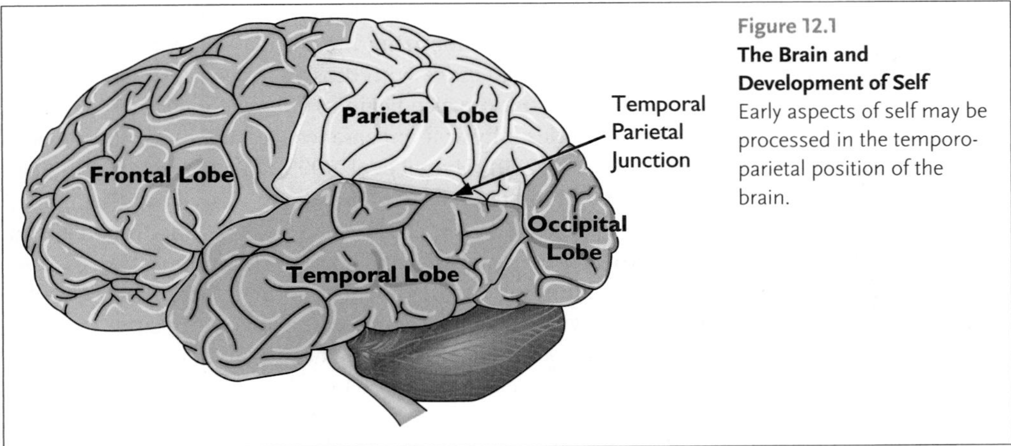

Figure 12.1
The Brain and Development of Self
Early aspects of self may be processed in the temporo-parietal position of the brain.

we know? If a spot of rouge is placed surreptitiously on her nose, it is not until she is older than this age that she will touch or rub her nose while looking in the mirror. Such behavior suggests that she has formed a concept of the details that ordinarily make up her appearance. Children who display self-recognition in the mirror, compared with those who do not, also include more personal pronouns such as "me," "my," and "mine" in their communications and engage in more pretend play (Lewis & Ramsay, 2004); the extent to which the left temporo-parietal junction of the brain has matured appears to be correlated with these measures (Lewis & Carmody, 2008—see Figure 12.1).

At a very young age, then, children have begun to unwrap a major piece of the total package of their self-concept. Furthermore, the implications of becoming aware of one's appearance can be enormous. For one thing, it may provide the basis for the onset of self-conscious emotions such as embarrassment, shame, and pride, which emerge in toddlers (see Chapter 11, "Emotions"). For another, self-recognition seems to develop hand in hand with a growing awareness of others as distinct individuals. For example, a child who displays self-recognition on the mirror task is also likely to attend to a partner of a similar age and to encourage him or her to play with matching toys, an indication of increased interest in sharing and enjoyment of the other child's activities (Asendorpf & Baudonnière, 1993).

Self-Definition in Childhood The early childhood years herald several important changes in concepts of self. If asked to answer the question "Who are you?" a preschooler might say, "I'm a boy. I'm strong. I know the letters of the alphabet. I like pizza. I live with my mother and father. I go to nursery school." Thus, during the preschool years, knowledge of self includes one's own physical features but also begins to include activities the child likes and is good at, his possessions, and his relationships with others. In defining themselves, children at this age commonly establish a **categorical self**; that is, they classify themselves in terms of membership in certain groups based on their sex, age, skills, what they own, where they live, and who their friends are.

INTERACTION AMONG DOMAINS

Are very young children also aware of having psychological and social attributes? As we pointed out in Chapter 9, "Social Cognition," preschoolers know quite a bit about their own mental activities. They possess knowledge of themselves that goes beyond physical appearance and actions. Thus, responses like "I have a friend" or "I'm a happy person" are among their self-descriptions, as are other comments about moods, feelings, achievements, and other psychological and social orientations. Self as object, as *me*, even for a young child, includes a sense of a psychological and social being (Damon & Hart, 1988; Harter, 1999).

When children reach about seven years of age, a new element enters their self-descriptions. Whereas younger children describe themselves in terms of typical physical characteristics and activities ("I run fast"), older children begin to make relational statements. For example, in response to the question "Who are you?" an older child might say, "I can run faster than anyone

categorical self Self-classification in terms of membership in certain groups based on sex, age, skills, what one owns, where one lives, and who one's friends are.

else in my class," "I'm not as pretty as my big sister," or "Other kids in my class are better than I am at math." In other words, instead of itemizing their skills, actions, or social and psychological qualities, they compare their qualities with those of others (Harter, 1999).

During the elementary school years, children also begin to effectively distinguish self in terms of separate skills: academic abilities, physical appearance, behavioral conduct, social skills, and athletic competence (Cole et al., 2001; Hymel et al., 1999). In addition, they increasingly indicate that they, not a parent or another adult, are a better authority in assessing their abilities, thoughts, and feelings (Burton & Mitchell, 2003). Such recognition strengthens an increasing awareness of their own uniqueness as individuals. As children acquire a better understanding of their strengths and limitations, their evaluation of self may be somewhat less positive than during the preschool years. Their self-concept shows some positive increases in most domains in the later elementary school years but then once again tends to dip as they begin to enter the adolescent years. Moreover, gender differences exist in how favorable these different domains of self are perceived; boys tend to view themselves more positively with respect to appearance and athletic ability, girls with respect to their conduct (Harter, 1999).

Self-Definition During Adolescence During adolescence, "self" as a concept not only begins to be viewed from multiple perspectives but sometimes even in conflicting ways. Susan Harter (1986a) asked children whether someone can have both positive and negative qualities. Can a person be both "smart" and "dumb," or "nice" and "nasty"? She found a substantial increase in the belief in this possibility between the seventh and ninth grades. The number of opposite perspectives, as well as concerns about feeling confused or bothered by qualities of self that conflict when, for example, interacting with parents, with friends, in a romantic relationship, or as a member of the classroom, become greatest during middle adolescence, as Figure 12.2 indicates (Harter & Monsour, 1992).

The impetus for conflicting selves may arise from a desire to impress or gain increased acceptance or simply as part of experimentation during the teenage years. Teens are certainly sensitive to the social implications of their self-portrayals. This awareness is evident in such responses from young adolescents as "I play sports . . . because all the kids like athletes" and "I'm an honest person . . . people trust me because of it" (Damon & Hart, 1988).

Figure 12.2
Concerns About Opposing Attributes
From early to middle adolescence, students increasingly report conflicting descriptions of self that depend on whether their evaluations are framed within the perspective of classroom, friends, close relationships, or parents. Concerns about these conflicting views increase at the same time. However, both the number of opposite attributes assigned to self and concerns about their effects on defining self begin to decline in later adolescence, as young people establish a more integrated identity and recognize that contradictions may be normal and even of some value.
Source: Data from Harter & Monsour, 1992.

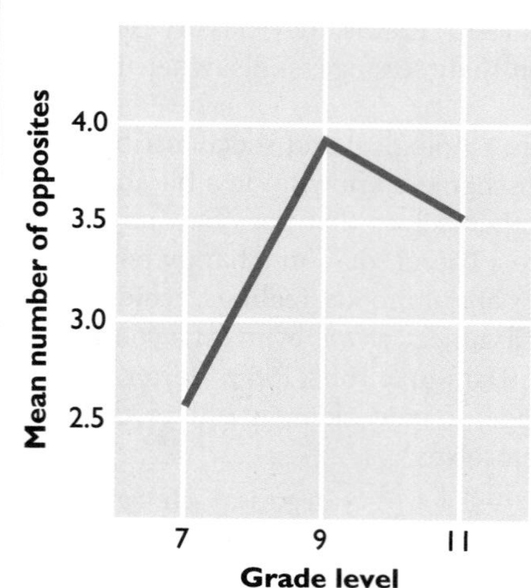

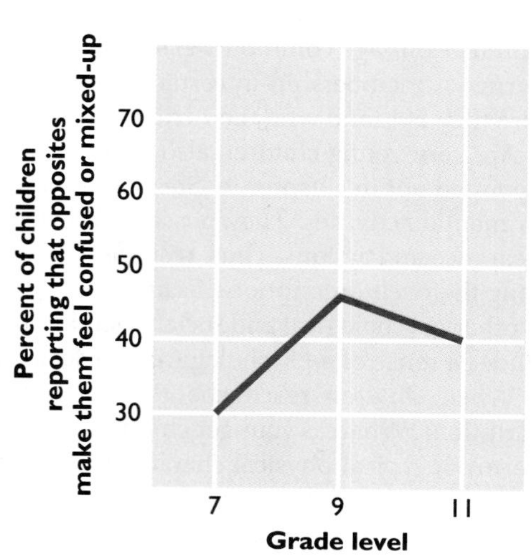

Under these circumstances, "false" selves appear to be a normal and even healthy aspect of development. However, if the inconsistencies arise from a belief that approval is contingent on "showing different faces" at the expense of one's "true self," these conflicts may lead to more serious consequences, such as feeling depressed and confused about self (Harter et al., 1996). Fortunately, concerns about conflicting selves typically lessen for most adolescents as they become older. With increasing maturity, they come to establish a higher-order, coherent picture of self based on principled ideas and comprehensive plans, which include a more extended future and greater understanding of their strengths and limitations (Harter, 2006).

RISK | RESILIENCE

SOCIOCULTURAL INFLUENCE

Sociocultural Influences on Definitions of Self Can cultural, religious, and social class differences, which are highly laden with values in their own right, influence the development of self-concepts? Children in Western societies tend to use many personal references in responding to questions about things that "tell about you." They might say, "I am a very smart person" or "I like hockey." However, in other societies, membership in the family or a social group may be far more important in determining perceptions of self than individual qualities or abilities unrelated to other people.

As an illustration of these sociocultural differences, compared with middle-income youngsters in the United States, poor children who were living in a fishing village in Puerto Rico were far more likely to voice expressions about themselves in terms of whether their behavior was good or bad rather than competent or talented (Damon & Hart, 1988). For example, a twelve-year-old might describe himself as someone who is nice or respects others because, if not, "everybody will hit me and hate me or not help me." These children consistently expressed greater concern about whether others approved of their actions than about their relative competence with respect to some skill or capacity.

In still other cultures that place greater emphasis on contributions to the collective community than on individual accomplishments—for example, the Samoan society and in many Asian countries—evaluations of self in terms of particular competencies may not be seen as desirable. As a consequence, greater modesty is demanded in describing one's personal qualities. To illustrate this difference, children from China tend to comment on their social networks or social interactions. They are more likely to say, for example, "I like to help my mom wash dishes" or offer other self-descriptions involving some quality consistent with their culture's emphasis on the connections among individuals in the social group (Wang, 2004).

At the same time, social philosophies, such as the Confucian belief in striving for self-perfection, can result in notions of self that reference the individual, even in collective societies. When asked to describe themselves as learners, for example, Chinese adolescents often talk about enhancing their own skills, personal achievements, and self-fulfillment (Li, 2006). Because children's views of themselves are heavily influenced by social structure and the expectations of the community, as well as styles of parenting and formal education, the picture of an emerging self in many societies is remarkably complex and may differ substantially from that typically observed in many Western nations.

Social Comparison

During the early and middle school years, as we already indicated, children begin to reference others in describing themselves. Whether Jim feels he is nice or can run fast, or Ellen believes she is smart or throws a ball well, depends on how Jim or Ellen thinks he or she stacks up against agemates and friends. How important is the process of **social comparison**—the tendency of people to use others as mirrors to evaluate their own abilities, interests, and values? The answer appears to be that it becomes increasingly important as children move through the elementary school years. For example, nine-year-olds who could not actually determine their success but were told that they did better than, or not as well as, peers in a ball-throwing contest predicted future performance based on the feedback they received. If told they were successful, they expected to show continued superior ability; if told they were less successful, they expected to continue to perform more poorly than children who received no feedback. Five- and seven-year-olds,

social comparison Process of defining oneself in relation to the skills, attributes, and qualities of others.

Social comparison, the tendency to evaluate one's own competencies on the basis of observing the competencies displayed by others, becomes an increasingly important component in defining self as children become older.

© China Photos/Getty Images

however, were unaffected by the information; they predicted that they would do equally well, regardless of how they compared with others (Ruble et al., 1980).

In fact, young children frequently are unrealistic about their skills; they claim they will do far better than they actually can (Harter, 1999). Kindergartners rate themselves more positively than older children do and tend to ignore feedback to adjust their evaluations, particularly when information about failure is given to them (Ruble, Eisenberg, & Higgins, 1994). By attending to the attributes and qualities of others, older children may begin to gain a more realistic means of predicting how well they can do. For example, Diane Ruble (1987) found that children in kindergarten and first grade who more frequently made social comparisons involving achievement tended to have greater knowledge of their relative standing in the classroom. Comments from classmates make a difference, too. When other children say things like "You're good at math," children acquire a sense about the academic areas in which they do or do not excel (Altermatt et al., 2002).

Older school-age children engage in increasingly subtle, indirect social comparisons to determine how well they are doing, perhaps because more conspicuous forms of information gathering are perceived as inappropriate behaviors. For example, nine- or ten-year-olds are more likely than younger children to ask classmates, "What question are you on?" to assess their progress among peers (Pomerantz et al., 1995). On the other hand, the kind of educational environment in which children participate also influences this behavior. In Israel, for example, children in kibbutz schools, which place greater emphasis on cooperative activity than more traditional urban schools in that country, continue to be more likely to interpret glances among one another as efforts to increase mastery rather than as social comparisons (Butler & Ruzany, 1993).

SOCIOCULTURAL INFLUENCE

As children approach the adolescent years and become more competent, they become less likely to look to others to evaluate themselves and increasingly rely on their own measures of performance on a task to judge success (Ruble & Flett, 1988). This change indicates a shift from social comparison to a more self-reliant and principled standard for evaluating self.

self-esteem One's feelings of worth; extent to which an individual senses his or her attributes and actions as good, desired, and valued.

Self-Esteem: Evaluating Self

A child's description of self often includes an evaluative component. **Self-esteem** or self-worth is specifically concerned with the positive feelings of merit and the extent to which the child believes his or her attributes and actions are good, desired, and valued. This aspect of self appears to be related to social affiliations, success in school, happiness, and some aspects of mental and physical health including reduced likelihood of eating disorders (Baumeister et al., 2003; Harter, 1999). Depression, anxiety, and poor adjustment in school and social relationships, including antisocial behaviors, aggression, and delinquency, also have been associated with low self-esteem (Damon, 1983; Donnellan et al., 2005; Rubin, Coplan, & Bowker, 2009).

INTERACTION AMONG DOMAINS

RISK | RESILIENCE

As already pointed out, children often give different evaluations of self; when asked about academic competence, athletic skill, social acceptance, or physical appearance, they may evaluate themselves highly in some areas, but less so with respect to other qualities. Still, by about eight years of age, children can give answers to such global questions as "Do you like yourself?" and "Are you happy the way you are?" The responses to these broad inquiries, however, are not simply the sum of all the different evaluations made of one's attributes and abilities, and they can vary across situations and time (Harter, Waters, & Whitesell, 1998). What, then, are some of the factors that influence how a child arrives at a global sense of worth?

Origins of Self-Esteem William James (1892) theorized that self-esteem depends on the success a person feels in areas in which she wants to succeed. Other theories emphasize that self-esteem originates in how a person thinks others see him; the *generalized other*—the combined perceived evaluations of parents, peers, and teachers influential in a person's life—helps to determine sense of worth (Cooley, 1902; Felson, 1993; Mead, 1934).

Both success in a highly regarded domain and the perceived evaluations of others do appear to affect self-esteem. Susan Harter (1987) obtained ratings of how children viewed themselves in scholastic competence, athletic competence, social acceptance, physical appearance, and behavioral conduct, as well as in terms of global success. Children were also asked how critical it was for them to do well in each of these domains. Harter reasoned that greater discrepancies between perceived competence and the importance of a domain, especially one highly valued, would be linked to lower self-esteem. Children also rated how others (parents, peers) viewed them, ranked their importance, liked them, and so on.

For children in the third to eighth grades, the more an area rated as important to themselves outstripped perception of their competence in that area, the lower was their sense of overall worth. In fact, children with low self-esteem seemed to have trouble disregarding the significance of domains in which they were not skilled (Harter, 1986b). In contrast, children with high self-esteem minimized the value of those fields in which they were not especially competent and gained considerable satisfaction from areas in which they were relatively successful.

Are some domains more important than others for a child's overall sense of worth? The answer appears to be yes. Boys and girls of elementary and middle school age who are dissatisfied with and keenly concerned about their physical appearance tend to have lower self-esteem. In fact, if already concerned about their thinness as young as five years of age, girls can soon begin to have lowered self-esteem (Dohnt & Tiggeman, 2006). In American culture, this relationship probably stems in part from the enormous emphasis in movies, television, and magazines on physical appearance as the key to success and acceptance. Although discrepancies are also important in other domains, they correlate less highly with judgments of overall self-worth. Positive assessments of physical appearance continue to be an important predictor of higher self-esteem for boys and girls as they enter the adolescent years (DuBois et al., 2000).

Harter also found that the perceived social support of others was correlated with the child's sense of self-worth. Elementary school children with low discrepancy *and* high social support scores showed superior levels of self-worth. Children with high discrepancy and low social support displayed the lowest levels of self-esteem. The opinions of others do matter in children's feelings of self-worth (Thomaes et al., 2010). Moreover, some children seem to respond more to the degree of approval they get from others, some to how much disapproval they receive, and still others to both (Rudolph, Caldwell, & Conley, 2005). Thus, efforts to improve self-esteem in children may require the formation and acceptance of realistic personal goals, as well as an understanding of how the need for approval works for each individual child.

Although self-esteem is influenced by many different factors, one that appears to be especially influential for older children and adolescents is their physical appearance. Perhaps, then, it is no wonder that interest in magazines and other media that focus on physical appearance is so high for these youths.

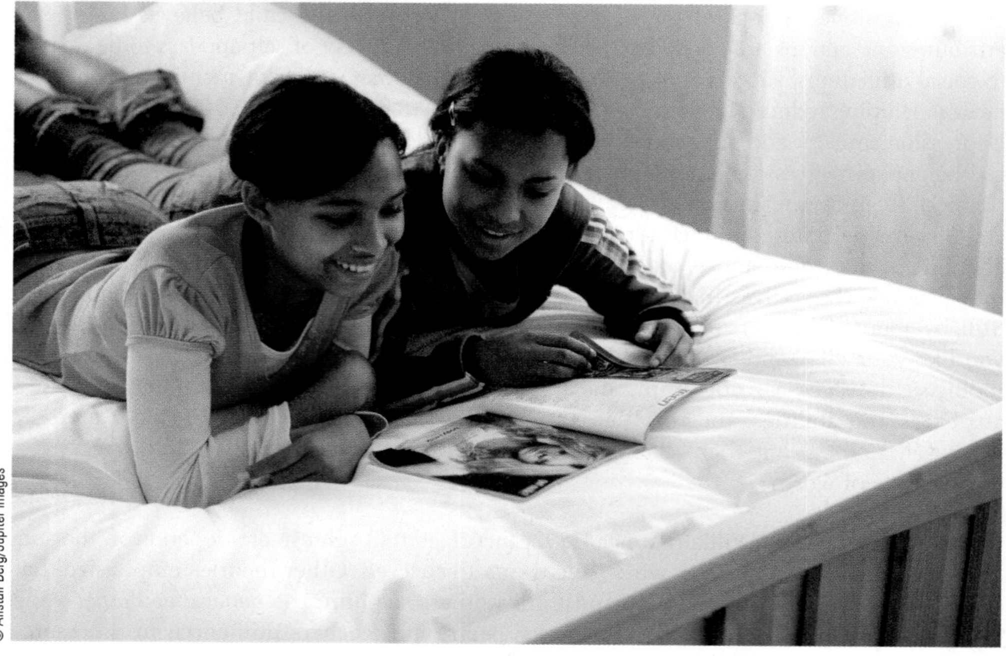

Developmental Changes in Self-Esteem In general, the self-esteem of children in early elementary school is high. Yet as they enter adolescence, a meta-analysis based on findings from numerous studies has revealed that self-esteem for many young people dips substantially, and this change is greater for girls (Robins & Trzesniewski, 2005). An example of such a developmental change from just one study can be seen in Figure 12.3 (Baldwin & Hoffman, 2002). The change accompanies major transitions, such as the onset of puberty,

Figure 12.3
Self-Esteem During Adolescence
Research has consistently shown a decline in self-esteem during the adolescent years. This decline tends to begin at an earlier age in girls than in boys and is more substantial for girls.
Source: From Baldwin, S. A., & Hoffman, J. P. (2002). The dynamics of self-esteem: A growth curve analysis. *Journal of Youth and Adolescence, 31,* 101–113. Reprinted by permission.

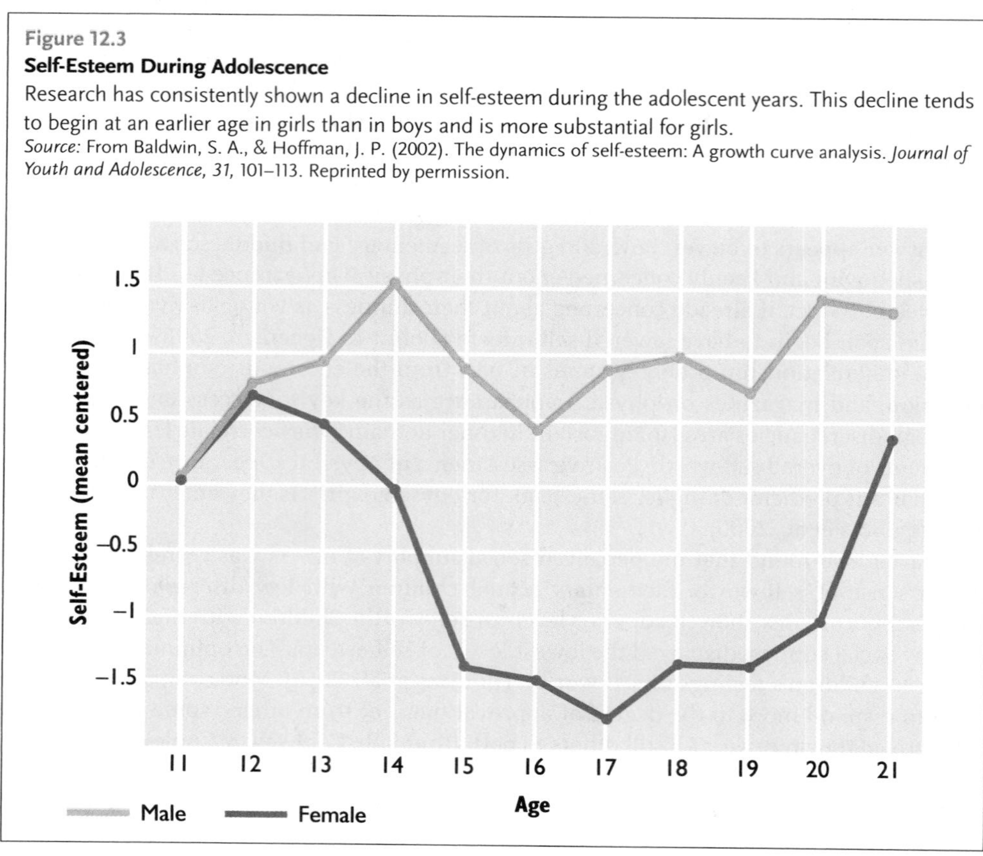

entry into junior high school, and substantial realignments in friendship patterns. During the change to junior high, daily hassles tend to increase, whereas teacher support and extracurricular activities decline, all factors correlated with a decrease in self-esteem, especially among low-income children regardless of ethnic or racial background (Seidman et al., 1994). Often the decline accompanies a lowering of perceived competence in academic subjects, such as mathematics.

RISK | RESILIENCE

However, when adolescents retain a warm, strong orientation toward others and perceive their parents as being affectionate, attuned to, and supportive of their efforts in decision making, they are more likely to maintain high self-esteem throughout these transitions (Laible & Carlo, 2004; Ojanen & Perry, 2007). Coping strategies that lead young people to attribute success to their competence and mastery are another critical element in maintaining high self-esteem (Brooks, 1992).

High self-esteem continues to be associated with positive developmental outcomes for adolescents, just as it is for younger children. High self-esteem is associated with low levels of emotional and behavioral problems in the teenage years; externalizing problems are especially less likely when parents (as opposed to peers) are the source of children's self-esteem (DuBois et al., 2002). A major longitudinal study conducted in New Zealand adds further weight to the importance of self-esteem. The data indicate that low self-esteem in adolescence is correlated with several negative outcomes in adulthood (age twenty-six years), among them poorer physical and mental health, money and work problems, and more criminal convictions (Trzesniewski et al., 2006).

SOCIOCULTURAL INFLUENCE

Research involving several studies comparing children from the United States and Taiwan has revealed a consistent cross-cultural pattern: Taiwanese children report lower self-esteem than their counterparts in the United States (Chiu, 1992–1993; Stigler, Smith, & Mao, 1985). The reasons may stem from socialization patterns in Taiwan that emphasize humility rather than pride in one's accomplishments or qualities and provide less opportunity to receive social or public displays of success in academic and other settings. Also, Taiwanese family-rearing patterns emphasize obedience rather than individual achievement, and although children in Taiwan often do excel academically, other ways of gaining high self-esteem may be less available to them. Even Asian American adolescents growing up in the United States continue to display lower self-esteem than their Caucasian American counterparts (Rhee, Chang, & Rhee, 2003).

Identity

The burgeoning sense of self, along with the capacity to reflect on individual qualities that include the evaluative elements associated with self-esteem, serves as the nucleus for the construction of an **identity**, a broad, coherent, internalized view of who a person is and wants to be, and what a person believes and values. A sense of identity solidifies and gives meaning to such fundamental questions about self as: Who am I? Why do I exist? What am I to become? The development of a healthy identity, as Erik Erikson pointed out (see Chapter 1, "Themes and Theories"), is a lifelong process that builds on earlier gains in accepting and trusting others, in being encouraged to explore interests and desires, and in acquiring feelings of competence and skill. However, it undergoes further important changes during adolescence and early adulthood. By formulating a unified sense of self as an agent separate from others and as someone capable of reflecting on one's own agency, the adolescent creates a more fully integrated identity and sets the stage for developing a healthy personality to accompany the transition to mature adulthood.

Based on their responses to questions involving, for example, occupational concerns, political and religious ideas, and views about sexual activity, James E. Marcia (1980, 1993) found that adolescents often report different views of their identity at different times during this part of their lives. Some have little interest in these topics or a desire to become

identity (personal) Broad, coherent, internalized view of who a person is and wants to be, and what a person believes and values, that emerges during adolescence.

© Condor 36/Shutterstock.com

Parents are not always enthusiastic about some of the things their children do. During the adolescent years, decisions about dress and appearance are especially common sources of tension within families. However, these efforts to distinguish themselves are typically part of an ordinary developmental process accompanying the transition to mature adulthood. They probably reflect the increasing independence that young people desire, and may need, in their efforts to construct their own identity.

involved with them, a status Marcia labeled *identity-diffusion.* For example, in responding to questions bearing on political issues, the adolescent may say "I don't really care about politics; I wouldn't say I'm a Democrat or a Republican." Others have avoided wrestling with these topics by accepting an identity largely influenced by what others value and believe, a status labeled *foreclosure* (e.g., "My parents are both Democrats, and so am I"). Others, although actively exploring these issues, have still to make any clear commitment about them, a status labeled *moratorium* (e.g., "I think I support the social platform of Democrats but in the past have labeled myself a Republican, so I'm not sure yet"). And, finally, others have clear views about these issues based on their own decision making, a status labeled *identity achievement* (e.g., "My parents raised me as a Republican, but in the last election, I helped the Democratic senator in my state with her campaign, as I fully endorsed her platform"). These four identity statuses appear to reflect different approaches adopted by adolescents in their identity formation and are correlated with different personality characteristics. For example, those with foreclosure status tend to be more conforming and less open to new experiences whereas those with achievement status tend to be more outgoing and open to new experiences (Crocetti et al., 2008). Adolescents with identity-diffusion and moratorium statuses tend to move to identity achievement later in adolescence or early adulthood (Berzonsky & Adams, 1999; Meeus et al., 1999).

The Adolescent Identity Crisis Despite the many differences that may exist in identity statuses, the period of adolescence has sometimes been viewed as filled with stress and uncertainty about self, riddled with sudden and frequent mood shifts, a time dubbed the **identity crisis**. Increased conflict with parents and the initiation of more risky and socially disruptive behavior are said to be a part of this developmental period as well (Arnett, 1999).

As they approach the teen years, children frequently engage in new ways of behaving and thinking that involve greater autonomy, independence, and expressions of intimacy with others (Collins & Steinberg, 2006). For example, teenagers increasingly view their actions and conduct as personal—their own business, so to speak—and believe that such matters as family chores, eating habits, curfews, and personal appearance are up to them, not their parents. Needless to say, this view can introduce conflict within the family, especially for parents who wish to maintain control. Meta-analyses of the findings of numerous studies reveal that the frequency of conflict within the family is greatest early in adolescence and declines over the teenage years (Laursen, Coy, & Collins, 1998). For many adolescents, however, conflict is far less frequent than the idea of a crisis would suggest (Hill, 1987; Powers, Hauser, & Kilner, 1989).

RISK | RESILIENCE

One key to successfully negotiating this period appears to be having a family, an educational environment, and a social milieu that support the needs and interests of adolescents (Eccles et al., 1993; Schwartz, 2008). For example, as young teens progress from elementary to junior high school, they find greater emphasis on control and discipline, less positive personal support from teachers, and more competitiveness and public evaluation of their work. Such changes may conflict with the adolescents' need for fewer intellectual pressures and more opportunity to take charge in exploring and resolving uncertainties about their identity (Eccles et al., 1993). Yet by bargaining over everything from their choices of friends and activities to their use of cell phones and computers or the family car, adolescents test new ways of communicating with and relating to parents and others

identity crisis Period, usually during adolescence, characterized by considerable uncertainty about the self and the role the individual is to fulfill in society.

in authority, which helps to promote a sense of self in relation to the other (Powers et al., 1989). Being able to establish a point of view thus seems to promote a strong sense of personal identity (Grotevant & Cooper, 1986; Hauser et al., 1987). Parental support and the ability to communicate with their teenagers appear to reduce the likelihood of behavior problems in many different families including, as just one example, Hispanic immigrant adolescents (Schwartz et al., 2005). Parents, teachers, and others play an important role in providing reassurance and support while permitting teenagers to weigh their ideas and explore their identities.

Cultural differences exist in the extent to which "storm and stress" during adolescence are reported as well (Arnett, 1999). Whereas children in the United States report a declining quality in their relationships with parents as they move through early adolescence, this decline is not reported by Chinese teenagers (Pomerantz et al., 2009). Within the United States, less conflict is also reported between adolescents and adults in Mexican American families than in Caucasian American middle-class families (Suarez-Orozco & Suarez-Orozco, 1996). Nevertheless, as families assimilate Western culture over generations, the conflict seems to increase. For example, adolescents in those generations of Asian American families that have been in the United States longer are likely to display greater evidence of characteristics suggestive of an identity crisis (Steinberg, 1996).

SOCIOCULTURAL INFLUENCE

Ethnic Identity Among the factors affecting a young person's identity is ethnic and racial background. **Ethnic identity** refers to the sense of belonging to a specific cultural group as opposed to simply adopting its social practices, known more generally as *acculturation* (Phinney, 1990). Thinking about one's ethnic roots is not particularly common among European American adolescents, who generally describe themselves as "white" or "American," rather than referring to their ancestors' countries of origin. On the other hand, Mexican and Chinese youth in the United States, particularly those who are immigrants, frequently identify themselves solely in terms of their country of origin. Second- and third-generation youth are more likely to add hyphenated terms, saying that they are "Mexican-American" or "Asian-American" (Fuligni, Witkow, & Garcia, 2005).

SOCIOCULTURAL INFLUENCE

Because the majority culture often views minority groups in a stereotypical and negative light, identifying with a minority ethnic or racial group was once thought to set the stage for personal conflict and confusion. Early studies with preschool and younger children reported a bias for choosing dolls or pictures that depict the majority group—in this case, Caucasian children—even by members of a minority group (Gray-Little & Hafdahl, 2000). But this measure may be methodologically biased, or other factors may be influencing children's choices; the preference has been observed even in the West Indies, where Caucasians are the minority. Other measures used to assess the value given to one's own racial group have not shown any disadvantage to children with a strong ethnic identity. In fact, two large-scale meta-analyses of self-esteem in majority and minority groups in the United States have revealed that self-esteem among African American children and adolescents, especially for girls, is higher than among Caucasians. It does, however, tend to be lower for Hispanic, Asian, and Native Americans than for Caucasians among both boys and girls (Gray-Little & Hafdahl, 2000; Twenge & Crocker, 2002).

Ethnic identity formation is thought to involve at least two components: *group esteem*, or feeling pride in belonging to an ethnic group, and *exploration*, attempting to learn more about the meaning of being part of an ethnic group. Longitudinal research including African American, Latino American, and European American youth shows that each component takes a slightly different developmental course. As Figure 12.4 shows, group-esteem rises in early and middle adolescence, and growth is especially pronounced for non-European children. Exploration of ethnic identity seems to be a later-occurring process and may be facilitated when adolescents find themselves in more diverse environments, such as racially mixed schools (French et al., 2000, 2006).

ethnic identity The sense of belonging to a particular cultural group.

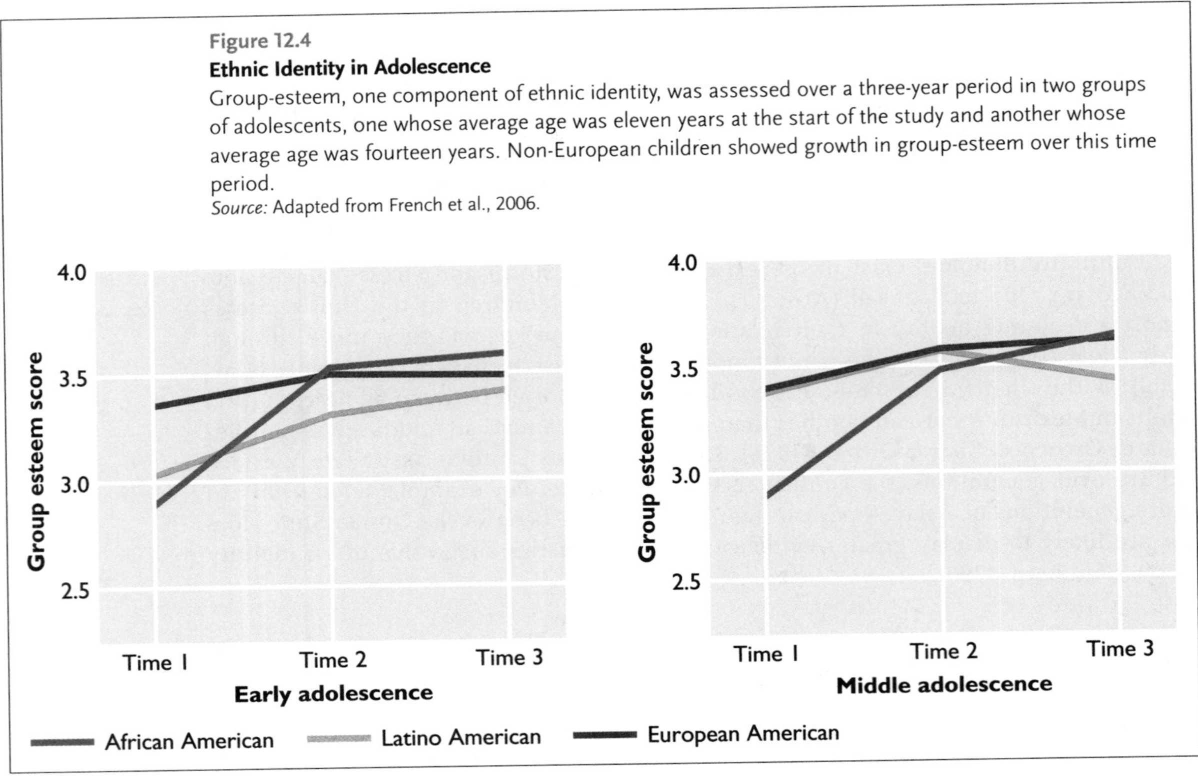

Figure 12.4
Ethnic Identity in Adolescence
Group-esteem, one component of ethnic identity, was assessed over a three-year period in two groups of adolescents, one whose average age was eleven years at the start of the study and another whose average age was fourteen years. Non-European children showed growth in group-esteem over this time period.
Source: Adapted from French et al., 2006.

RISK | RESILIENCE

Becoming comfortable with one's own ethnic identity is associated with several positive outcomes. For one thing, it can lead to greater acceptance of and a more favorable attitude toward other ethnic groups (Phinney, Ferguson, & Tate, 1997; Valk, 2000). A strong ethnic identity, especially in the sense of feeling pride and emotional attachment to one's ethnic group, can also serve as a buffer against the negative consequences of perceived discrimination from peers (Greene, Way, & Pahl, 2006). Moreover, an increase in ethnic identity during early adolescence in African Americans has been found to decrease the likelihood of their reporting depressive symptoms (Mandara et al., 2009). Valuing one's ethnicity seems to be fostered by responsive parents who are sensitive to ethnic issues (Phinney & Rosenthal, 1992). However, ethnic socialization by minority parents is usually carried out within, not at the expense of, broader child-rearing goals emphasized in most families: getting a good education, being a good human being, feeling satisfied about oneself, and working hard.

For Your Review and Reflection

- When do various aspects of self-concept appear? What do we mean by self-recognition and self-definition?
- What is the role of social comparison in developing a self-concept?
- What aspects of self do you feel are most important to you? How have sociocultural factors influenced the development of your self-concept?
- What contributes to high self-esteem? How does self-esteem change over development? How do sociocultural factors influence self-esteem?
- Did your self-esteem change during the adolescent years? What factors do you think either helped maintain your self-esteem or resulted in its changing during those years?

- What is an identity crisis?
- Does an ethnic identity play an important role for your self-concept? If so, has it affected your self-esteem? In what ways?

Self-Regulation

Impulsive and easily upset, young children typically have difficulty behaving in a patient or deliberate manner. Eventually, however, parents and others demand that children acquire **effortful control**, the ability to suppress undesirable responses for less dominant ones that are considered socially or morally more acceptable. A three-year-old needs to stay away from an attractive fireplace, use the toilet, say thank you, and share and put away toys. Older children and teenagers must assume ever greater responsibility for their actions and are expected to conform to socially accepted rules and standards. But becoming responsible and self-reliant can be a long and difficult transition. **Self-regulation** refers to the capacity to monitor, direct, and flexibly adapt one's behaviors and activities to achieve certain goals or meet the demands imposed by others.

Developmental Changes

For very young children, regulation of behavior might best be labeled *co-regulation* (Kopp, 1987), because children and their caregivers jointly manage behavior. In many families, efforts to limit activities begin when babies are about eight or nine months old. At this time, newly acquired motor skills increase risk of injury, heralding the need for restraining devices, such as playpens and gates. Infants about one year of age may be warned to avoid dangerous or health-threatening objects and situations ("Don't touch the knife," "Don't play with the cat litter," "Hold onto my hand"). Efforts to preserve possessions ("Stay away from the VCR") and avoid harm to others ("Don't pinch") are also common concerns at about this time (Gralinski & Kopp, 1993).

As toddlers move beyond eighteen months of age, adults often supplement these *caregiving demands* with additional *demands for appropriate behavior*, such as keeping quiet and sitting up straight, and *demands for competent action*, such as helping to set the table or participating in social and family activities (Kuczynski & Kochanska, 1995). These efforts focus on encouraging acceptable social interactions, taking part in family routines and chores, and cultivating self-care and greater independence, such as walking rather than being carried (Gralinski & Kopp, 1993). By the time children reach twenty-four to thirty months of age, parental demands may decline in frequency as children become familiar with and respond to requests more routinely (Kopp, 1987). In general, girls tend to be more compliant than boys (Kochanska, Murray, & Harlan, 2000).

Children's self-initiated attempts to obey appear during the second year. A thirteen-month-old, for example, may look at, and perhaps even approach and touch, an electrical outlet while saying, "No, no!" But over the next few years, self-restraint improves rapidly. For example, in a **delay-of-gratification** task, in which the child is asked to wait some period of time before performing an activity or attaining some highly desired outcome (such as playing with an attractive toy or eating a piece of candy), eighteen-month-olds have great difficulty complying. Between two and three years of age, children become increasingly more effective in delaying their behavior (Vaughn, Kopp, & Krakow, 1984). Thus, although self-control begins with attempts by others to govern the young child's actions, their efforts are transferred and gradually relinquished as warnings and guidance become less direct and as the child takes on more responsibility for regulating his behavior.

The Development of Self and Self-Regulation Chronology summarizes major transitions in this ability to regulate one's own behavior, along with the development of self.

effortful control Ability to suppress undesirable responses for less dominant ones that are considered socially or morally more acceptable.

self-regulation Capacity to monitor, direct, and flexibly adapt one's behaviors and activities to achieve certain goals or meet the demands imposed by others.

delay of gratification Capacity to wait before performing a tempting activity or attaining some highly desired outcome; a measure of ability to regulate one's own behavior.

CHRONOLOGY Development of Self and Self-Regulation: Birth to 13+ Years

© Jamie Grill/Tetra Images/Jupiter Images

© Radius Images/Jupiter Images

8–9 Months
- Parent initiates attempts to regulate infant's behavior.

12–15 Months
- Parent's efforts to control behavior emphasize toddler's safety, preservation of property, and avoidance of harm to others.
- Toddler shows the first signs of self-regulation.

© Marcin Balcerzak/Shutterstock.com

15–18 Months
- Recognizes self in mirror and photos.
- Parent's increased efforts at co-regulation emphasize family routines, self-care, and increased independence.

18–30 Months
- Begins to be capable of delaying gratification.

2 ½–6 Years
- Defines self by categorical judgments.
- Recognizes agency for physical and cognitive achievements.
- Exercises overt self-regulation using language.
- Recognizes increasingly effective ways to delay gratification.

6–9 Years
- Defines self by social comparisons.
- Displays global self-esteem.
- Recognizes agency for social achievements.
- Exercises self-regulation through internalized language.

10–13 Years
- Defines self in terms of social roles.
- Begins to use autonomous criteria for evaluating of self.
- Recognizes contradictory views of self.
- Shows metacognitive understanding of self-regulation.

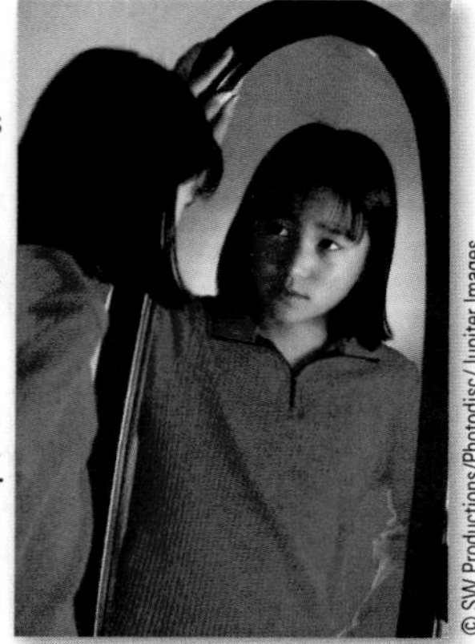
© SW Productions/Photodisc/Jupiter Images

13+ Years
- Defines self in terms of principled values.
- Begins to accept and resolve contradictory views of self.
- Begins to address issues of identity.
- Recognizes self within the broader society.

This chart describes the sequence in the development of understanding the self and self-regulation based on the findings of research. Children often show individual differences in the exact ages at which they display the various developmental achievements outlined here.

research applied to parenting | Encouraging Young Children's Compliance

Even though preschoolers are beginning to exert signs of self-control, most parents still provide their young children with a hefty dose of supervision. And with their rising independence, children are not always ready to accept it. The frequency with which conflict occurs between parents and children in American families—for example, asking the child to delay a response, slow down an activity, stop an unacceptable behavior, pay attention, or help out with an uninteresting task—is typically high, perhaps on the order of fifteen to twenty times per hour (Laible & Thompson, 2002). The commitment to complying with a "don't" uttered by caregivers appears to be acquired somewhat earlier and more rapidly by children in American families than consistency in responding to a "do." This difference may be because parents are more likely to enforce the former than the latter or because they persist more in prohibiting negative behaviors (Kochanska, 2002; Kochanska, Coy, & Murray, 2001). Can caregivers do anything to encourage the emergence of socially acceptable and compliant behaviors during early childhood? Research findings suggest that there is a link between child compliance and several characteristics of caregivers.

1. *Be supportive, responsive, accepting, sensitive, and emotionally available to children.* Researchers have found that, when mothers showed eager responsiveness to their toddlers and were generally positive in the emotions they expressed, their children often responded in kind, with cooperation and enthusiasm. When mother–child pairs displayed this *mutually responsive orientation*, the children were likely to continue to comply with mothers' requests even several years later (Kochanska & Murray, 2000).
2. *Justify the need for children to act in certain ways.* Researchers have noted that mothers who used a high level of justification when their children were thirty months old also had children who were more compliant with adult requests six months later. When caregivers make statements like "You need to eat your dinner, so that you will not be hungry later," they are helping their children to understand multiple perspectives on social conflicts, offering an opportunity for growth (Laible & Thompson, 2002).
3. *Offer a compromise or provide a benefit for alternative responses.* When caregivers show an interest in putting an end to a conflict ("I'll let you have a cookie if you eat your dinner"), children are learning an important lesson: that relationships are important and that conflict resolution skills are useful in preserving those relationships (Laible & Thompson, 2002).
4. *Emphasize behaving competently over inhibiting activities.* When mothers emphasize "do" over "don't" in their toddlers and preschoolers, fewer compliance and behavior problems arise at age five. Perhaps by encouraging children to perform various activities, such as household tasks ("Clean up") or self-care behaviors ("Tie your shoe"), parents are fostering feelings of competence that have repercussions for the child's future willingness to comply with parental requests (Kuczynski & Kochanska, 1995).

Factors Contributing to Self-Regulation

The degree to which preschool children achieve the ability to regulate their own behaviors has been linked not only to better literacy, vocabulary, and mathematics skills (Duncan et al., 2007; McClelland et al., 2007) but also to important positive outcomes even many years later. For example, adolescents who had greater self-regulatory capacities as preschoolers are described by their parents as more academically and socially competent and better able to handle frustration and temptation. They are also reported to be more attentive, deliberate, and intelligent, and they seem better able to tolerate stress and cope with social and personal problems, even when their intellectual performance is similar to that of peers less able to delay gratification when they were younger (Mischel, Shoda, & Rodriguez, 1989; Shoda, Mischel, & Peake, 1990). Not surprisingly, they also are better at being able to inhibit responses that are not relevant to a task (Eigsti et al., 2006).

INTERACTION AMONG DOMAINS

What are some of the processes involved in both the development of self-regulation and these individual differences? Figure 12.5 illustrates a few of these essential

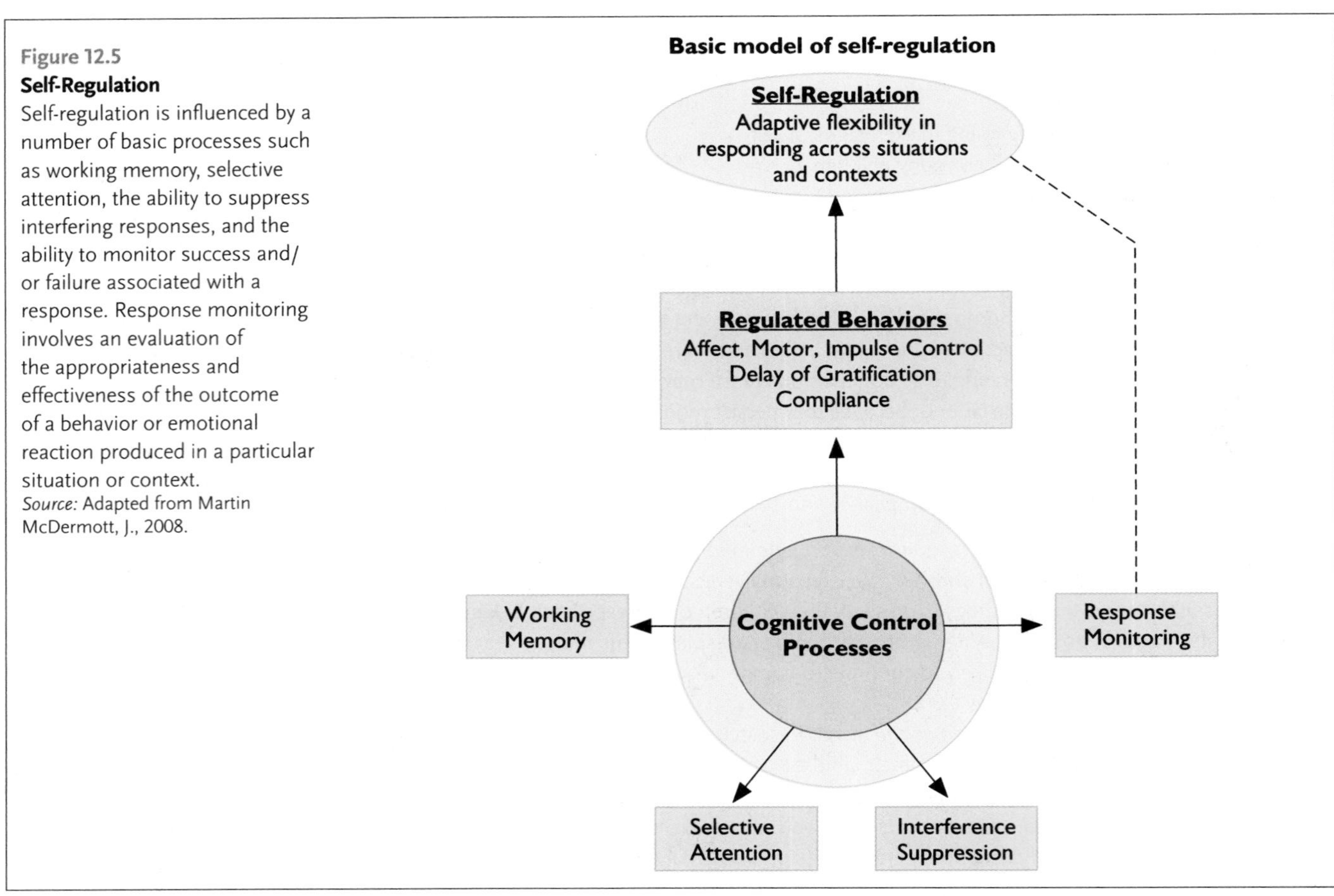

Figure 12.5
Self-Regulation
Self-regulation is influenced by a number of basic processes such as working memory, selective attention, the ability to suppress interfering responses, and the ability to monitor success and/or failure associated with a response. Response monitoring involves an evaluation of the appropriateness and effectiveness of the outcome of a behavior or emotional reaction produced in a particular situation or context.
Source: Adapted from Martin McDermott, J., 2008.

components. Working memory, selective attention, and the ability to suppress interfering responses and monitor the appropriateness of initiated responses are likely to be important elements in the cognitive control processes that contribute to various aspects of self-regulation. Consider, for example, attentional factors. The child directed not to eat a marshmallow who says, "The marshmallow is yummy"—words that focus attention on the forbidden treat—or who talks about sad things, such as falling and hurting himself—ideas that provide little diversion—shows less ability to inhibit his behavior than a child who sings a pleasant but distracting nursery rhyme, such as "Three Blind Mice" (Mischel, Ebbesen, & Zeiss, 1972).

For very young children, caregivers are likely to assist with these attentional mechanisms. Think about parents and two-and-a-half-year-olds shopping at a grocery store, an activity that can test the limits of most caregivers because grocery displays are enticing. In this setting, parents are frequently forced to respond to their children's requests, and they use a variety of tactics to do so: reasoning, not responding, physically or verbally intervening, acknowledging children's desires, and attempting to distract children. However, parents who try to anticipate conflicts, either by diverting children's attention in advance or by engaging them in an interesting conversation, are most effective in preventing conflict while grocery shopping (Holden, 1983).

During the later preschool and early school years, children display their own attentional strategies to keep on track and support their goals. For example, in a delay-of-gratification task, preschoolers often place a tempting reward in front of themselves rather than a picture of it or some other, irrelevant item. In doing so, they increase their exposure to the forbidden object, look at it more, and have greater difficulty delaying their response to it. By age five, children are less likely to create such self-defeating arrangements. They prefer to wait with the tempting reward covered rather than uncovered

(Mischel & Mischel, 1983). Some will even shield their eyes, play games with their hands and feet, or try to go to sleep to help manage the delay (Cournoyer & Trudel, 1991; Mischel, Shoda, & Rodriguez, 1989). Older children can even articulate these notions. For example, an eleven-year-old might offer the following in a tempting situation: "Take your mind off of it; think of something else!"

Language may also play a critical role in the child's ability to regulate his or her own behavior (Luria, 1961, 1969; Vygotsky 1962). As noted in Chapter 7, "Language," a preschool child, for example, may engage in *private speech* intended for no one else but that helps to direct attention to key dimensions and features of a task. Private speech assists in establishing and organizing ways to carry out an activity and in preserving important task-related information in memory—or in the example above, avoiding a forbidden object (Meichenbaum, 1977). Yet children's observable private speech is not always correlated with effective problem solving. Perhaps this finding should be expected, as the production of private speech is more likely in especially challenging circumstances where successes are harder to come by (Frauenglass & Diaz, 1985).

What aspects of brain development may be especially important for self-regulation? As noted in Chapter 5, "Brain, Motor Skills, and Physical Development" (see Figure 5.2), the anterior cingulate cortex, part of the prefrontal cortex, very likely plays a significant role (Lewis & Todd, 2007). The hypothalamus, amygdala, and brainstem are instrumental in various aspects of self-regulation as well. Many of the developmental changes in this capacity also probably arise from the increasing coordination among these different component systems as well as other regions of the brain, as noted in Chapter 5.

For Your Review and Reflection

- What is meant by effortful control and self-regulation?
- How does self-regulation change during childhood?
- What factors seem to promote young children's compliance? If you were working with young children, what practices would you follow to encourage them to help regulate their own behavior?
- How do other domains of development interact with increasingly effective self-regulation?

Moral Development

As children gain greater knowledge of the self and more skill in regulating their own behavior, they are expected to increasingly conform to the socially acceptable rules and regulations of their community. We are talking here about *moral development*, the process by which an individual comes to understand what society accepts as right and wrong. Researchers have focused on several key components of moral development: the development of *conscience*, a powerful cognitive-emotional influence on morality; *moral behavior*, the performance of actions consistent with principles of right and wrong; and *moral reasoning*, or the decision processes involved in arriving at a course of action about what is right or wrong.

The Development of Conscience

Freud theorized that the development of **conscience**, a mechanism that governs what a child should not do, and an *ego ideal*, a mechanism that promotes appropriate and desirable behaviors, arises during the preschool years from the process of strongly identifying with a

conscience A regulatory mechanism involving the ability to feel moral emotions, such as guilt and empathy, and the tendency to follow rules set forth by adults.

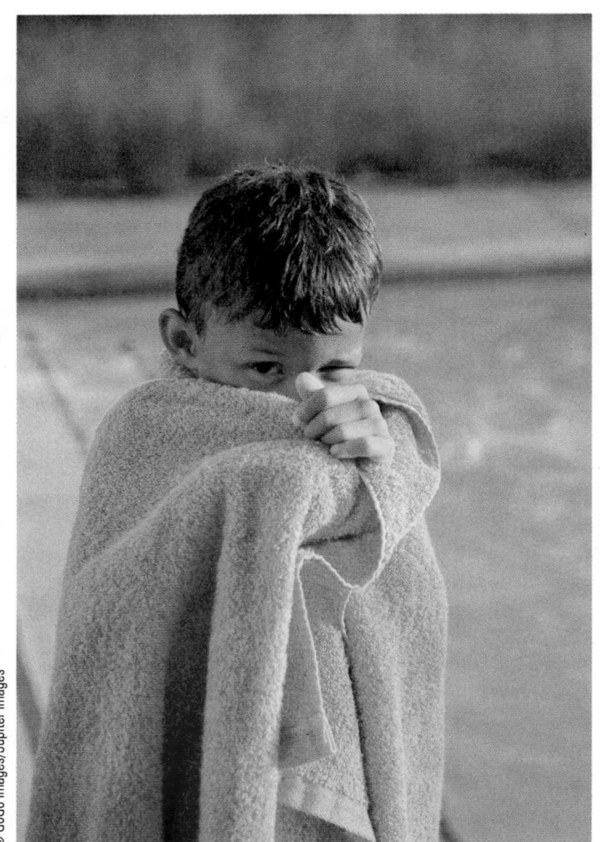
© GoGo Images/Jupiter Images

This child displays a typical response of hiding his face, after committing a transgression at the swimming pool. Research on moral development and the development of values has examined the roles of affect, reinforcement and punishment, and cognition in efforts to fully understand the socialization of culturally permissible behavior.

parent or caregiver of the same sex. Combined, conscience and ego ideal constituted what Freud described as the *superego*. However, in theories of moral development today, the term *conscience* is more broadly used to capture the notion of an internalized self-regulatory executive system consisting of two components: the ability to feel moral emotions, such as guilt and empathy, and the tendency to follow rules set forth by adults, even when children are not being watched (Kochanska & Aksan, 2006).

We see evidence of both of these elements in early childhood. By age three years, some children willingly comply with the requests of their parents to complete certain activities (such as putting away toys) and to avoid others (such as touching prohibited objects), even when the parents are no longer present (Kochanska, Aksan, & Koenig, 1995). Three-year-olds also notice flawed objects (such as a teddy bear with stuffing coming out or a broken cup), and if led to believe the flaws are the consequence of their own behavior, may voice apologies ("Sorry," "Didn't mean to"), offer reparations ("Put back in," "Clean up"), and exhibit distress ("Take this away," "I wanna go")—expressions of guilt and shame that are frequently manifestations of conscience (Kochanska, Casey, & Fukumoto, 1995). Girls tend to display more guilt than boys (Kochanska et al., 2002). This combination of moral feelings and moral actions typically melds into a more cohesive form of conscience by the time the child approaches age four years (Aksan & Kochanska, 2005).

What forces are responsible for the emergence of conscience? One factor may be the child's ability to recognize positive emotional reactions as well as anger or displeasure in the communications of caregivers. These emotions give children clear messages about what adults deem to be appropriate behavior. Another factor is the increasing ability to regulate and inhibit behavior (Kochanska, 2002; Kochanska, Murray, & Coy, 1997; Kochanska, Tjebkes, & Forman, 1998).

INTERACTION AMONG DOMAINS

Other parental behaviors are involved as well. Positive emotional relationships and mutual responsiveness between mother and child are closely aligned with a healthy conscience for both boys and girls (Kochanska & Aksan, 2006). But the relationship between parenting style and the child's conscience is especially strong when children show a secure attachment to their parents (Kochanska et al., 2004). At the same time, some young children seem to be more willing and eager than others to learn what parents teach. For example, the degree to which fourteen-month-olds imitate their mothers in a chore like "Clean the table" predicts their levels of conscience and guilt at three and four years of age (Forman, Aksan, & Kochanska, 2004). One major source of these individual differences may be the child's temperament; for example, young children who tend to be more fearful are more likely to display indicators of guilt such as gaze aversion, confession, apology, and self-blame in response to a transgression (Kochanska & Aksan, 2006).

Social Learning Theory and Moral Behavior

NATURE & NURTURE

CONTINUITY | DISCONTINUITY

Social learning theories emphasize the child's acquisition of *moral behaviors*, such as behaving acceptably and resisting temptation. According to social learning theory, the rewards and punishments dispensed by parents and others shape the child's conduct, as do the actions and verbalizations that a child sees or hears. Social learning theorists view morality as a process of incremental growth in appropriate actions and increasing conformity with the rules of society.

How convincingly does the social learning model explain moral development? Studies investigating the child's ability to resist temptation have often used the "forbidden toy" situation; the child must learn not to play with an attractive and enticing toy placed in the room with the child. The results suggest that reinforcement history is indeed a factor in moral behavior. Children often quickly learn not to touch an attractive toy if an adult mildly reprimands them for initiating activities with it. In other words, they respond to the punishments the adult doles out.

Several factors influence children's tendency to transgress when left alone in a room with a forbidden toy after they have been punished. First, as social learning theory predicts, the timing of the punishment plays a role. Punishments are most effective if they closely follow the undesired behavior—for example, when the child first reaches for a forbidden toy rather than after he has picked it up. Second, providing a verbal explanation of why the toy is prohibited also has an effect. When children are told, for example, that the attractive toy might break if it is handled, they are much less likely to violate the adult's prohibition. According to social learning theorists, verbalizations facilitate the internalization of morally acceptable and unacceptable behaviors (Aronfreed, 1976).

INTERACTION AMONG DOMAINS

Parents and others also serve as models for moral behavior. Children who observe a model commit a prohibited act, such as touching a forbidden toy, are more likely to perform the act themselves, whereas children observing a model who resists temptation will commit fewer transgressions (Rosenkoetter, 1973). However, models appear to be more powerful in *disinhibiting* than in inhibiting behavior that violates a rule or an expectation. Children are more likely to follow someone's deviant behaviors than his or her compliant ones (Hoffman, 1970).

Albert Bandura's social cognitive theory (1986) assigns a larger role to cognitive processes in the emergence of moral values. According to this view, children develop internalized standards of conduct, cognitive representations derived from observing others and used in processing their explanations for moral behavior. Children, especially to the extent to which they accept and accurately perceive communications, attempt to behave in ways consistent with those representations (Grusec & Goodnow, 1994).

Cognitive-Developmental Theories

Like Michael, the child in this chapter's opening vignette, school-aged children typically have daily opportunities to make decisions that have a moral dimension to them. From choosing how to respond to a sibling who absconds with a favorite toy ("Should I hit him, or should I share?") to deciding whether to tell parents about a misbehavior at school ("Should I confess, or should I hide the truth for as long as I can?") to selecting a way to handle an irritated grandfather ("Should I talk back, or should I find a way to make him feel better?"), children's behaviors often reflect the value systems that their parents, teachers, and others have tried to pass on to them. But when parents and teachers engage in "moral education," what can they expect the child to understand about these all-important lessons? And even if children understand what is right and what is wrong, how can they be encouraged to behave in ways that reflect those judgments? Some of the answers arise from a long line of theory and research on children's moral development.

INTERACTION AMONG DOMAINS

Cognitive-developmental explanations of moral development highlight the ways children *reason* about moral problems. Should a person ever steal, even if the transgression would help another person? Are there circumstances under which lying is acceptable? The child's capacity to think through the answers to such questions depends on his ability to consider the perspectives, needs, and feelings of others. In other words, moral development is intimately connected with advances in general thinking abilities. The two earliest and most prominent cognitive-developmental theorists concerned with moral development, Jean Piaget and Lawrence Kohlberg, have suggested stage theories in which children's reasoning about moral issues is qualitatively different depending on their level of development.

CONTINUITY | DISCONTINUITY

Piaget's Theory Piaget (1932/1965) derived many of his ideas about moral development from two contexts: as children played a formal game with a shared set of rules and as they encountered moral dilemmas created to assess thinking about ethical problems.

Preschoolers, Piaget stated, are not guided by rules. They engage in an activity for the pure pleasure it provides. Thus, young children playing a game of marbles, for example, may hide them or move them randomly, ignoring the formal rules of the game. By about age six, however, rules become sacred and inviolable. The rules must be respected and have always existed in the same form; people played marbles in exactly the same way over the years. By about ten years of age, children begin to understand rules to be the result of cooperation and mutual consent among all the participants in the game; thus, rules may be modified to suit the needs of the situation if all the players agree. Recent research, however, suggests that Piaget underestimated the very young child's understanding of rules associated with simple games. For example, in one study, three-year-olds watched a puppet perform a game-like activity with an object in a way that did not match what an adult had modeled as an appropriate way to use the object. Children often responded to the puppet's misguided actions with comments such as "No, it does not go like this!" or "No, not in this hole!" (Rakoczy, Warneken, & Tomasello, 2008).

The second method Piaget used to study moral development consisted of noting children's responses to moral dilemmas, stories in which a central character committed a transgression. The intentions of that character and the consequences of his or her act varied, as the following stories illustrate:

> A. A little boy who is called John is in his room. He is called to dinner. He goes into the dining room. But behind the door there was a chair, and on the chair there was a tray with fifteen cups on it. John couldn't have known that there was all this behind the door. He goes in, the door knocks against the tray, bang go the fifteen cups, and they all get broken!
>
> B. Once there was a little boy whose name was Henry. One day when his mother was out he tried to get some jam out of the cupboard. He climbed up onto a chair and stretched out his arm. But the jam was too high up and he couldn't reach it and have any. But while he was trying to get it he knocked over a cup. The cup fell down and broke. (Piaget, 1932/1965, p. 122)

Which boy is naughtier? Younger children typically choose John, the child who broke more cups. According to Piaget, children younger than about ten are in the stage of moral development called **moral realism**, or *heteronomy*. They judge the rightness or wrongness of an act by the objective visible consequences—in this case, how many cups were broken. They do not consider the boys' intentions to behave well or improperly. In this stage, rules are viewed as unbreakable; if the rules are violated, the child sees punishment as the inevitable consequence. A belief in **immanent justice** is also reflected in such statements as "That's God punishing me," made when the child accidentally falls off a bike after lying to her mother, for example. Although the fall is unrelated to the child's transgression, she believes the causal link exists. Children in this stage also believe that a punishment need not be related to the wrongful act if it is severe enough to teach a lesson. Thus, stealing a friend's toy can be punished by any means, not necessarily by returning the toy or making reparations.

From a limited ability to reason about moral issues, children progress to **moral relativism**, or *autonomy*. Now the transgressor's motives are taken into account. Thus, Henry is named as the naughtier boy. In addition, the child no longer believes every violation will be punished. Punishments, however, should relate to the misdemeanor so that the individual appreciates the consequences of his act.

What precipitates the shift from moral realism to moral relativism? Piaget points to changes in the child's cognitive capabilities, especially decreasing egocentrism, as one

moral realism In Piaget's theory of moral development, the first stage of moral reasoning, in which moral judgments are made on the basis of the consequences of an act. Also called *heteronomy*.

immanent justice Young child's belief that punishment will inevitably follow a transgression.

moral relativism In Piaget's theory of moral development, the second stage of moral reasoning, in which moral judgments are made on the basis of the actor's intentions. Also called *autonomy*.

important element. To understand another's intentions, for example, the child must be able to appreciate the point of view of that person as distinct from her own. Another important factor is the opportunity to interact with peers. Peer interactions force the child to consider the thoughts and feelings of others and eventually lead to an understanding of their intentions and motives. Parents can further promote the shift from realism to relativism, notes Piaget, by encouraging mutual respect and understanding, pointing out the consequences of the child's actions for others, and articulating their needs and feelings as parents.

INTERACTION AMONG DOMAINS

Research confirms that reasoning about moral problems shifts as children grow older. With development, children from diverse cultures, from different social classes, and of varying intellectual abilities more fully consider intentions in judging the actions of another person. However, researchers have also found that younger children can be sensitive to the motives behind a given act—that intentional hitting is worse than accidental hitting or that actions that produce psychological consequences (such as causing embarrassment or being frightening or upsetting to another person) are also possible and inappropriate (Helwig, Zelazo, & Wilson, 2001; Leslie, Knobe, & Cohen, 2006; Zelazo, Helwig, & Lau, 1996).

Kohlberg's Theory Like Piaget, Kohlberg (1976, 2008) proposed a stage theory of moral development in which progress through each stage proceeds in a universal order and regression to earlier modes of thinking is rare. Kohlberg based his theory on children's responses to a set of dilemmas that put obedience to authority or the law in direct conflict with helping a person in need ("Should a man steal an overpriced drug that he cannot obtain legally in order to save his wife?").

CONTINUITY | DISCONTINUITY

Kohlberg identified three general levels of moral orientation, each with two substages, used to explain the varying responses of his participants, boys from ten to sixteen years of age (see Table 12.1). At the **preconventional level**, the child's behavior is motivated by external pressures: avoidance of punishment, attainment of rewards, and preservation of self-interests. At this level, norms of behavior are primarily derived from the child's needs and desires. At the **conventional level**, conforming to the norms of the majority and maintaining the social order have become central to the child's reasoning. The child now considers the points of view of others, along with their intentions and motives. The child also feels a sense of responsibility to contribute to society and to uphold the laws and institutions that serve its members. Finally, at the **postconventional level**, the individual has developed a fuller understanding of the basis for laws and rules. They are now seen as a social contract that all individuals must uphold because of shared responsibilities and duties. The individual recognizes the relative, and sometimes arbitrary, nature of rules. Certain principles and values—in particular, justice and human dignity—must be preserved at all costs. Kohlberg also emphasized that changes in the child's perspective-taking ability are the basis for shifts in moral reasoning. Changes in perspective-taking ability are promoted by opportunities for children to discuss others' points of view, a position for which research provides some support (Walker, Hennig, & Krettenauer., 2000).

Numerous investigations of Kohlberg's theory have confirmed stagelike transitions in moral reasoning. For example, in one longitudinal study following children and adults over a twenty-year period, changes in responses to moral dilemmas, as can be seen in Figure 12.6, typically fit the stagelike progression delineated by Kohlberg (Colby et al., 1983). In another study, six- through fifteen-year-olds tested during a two-year period gained in moral reasoning, and few children skipped stages or regressed to earlier forms of reasoning (Walker, 1989). Children also judge the sophistication of alternative responses to moral dilemmas in accordance with stage theory, as long as the alternatives are below their current level of reasoning about moral development (Boom, Brugman, & van der Heijden, 2001).

Cross-cultural studies in more than twenty different countries as diverse as India, Turkey, Japan, Nigeria, and

preconventional level In Kohlberg's theory, the first level of moral reasoning, in which morality is motivated by the avoidance of punishments and attainment of rewards.

conventional level In Kohlberg's theory, the second level of moral reasoning, in which the child conforms to the norms of the majority and wishes to preserve the social order.

postconventional level In Kohlberg's theory, the third level of moral reasoning, in which laws are seen as the result of a social contract and individual principles of conscience may emerge.

TABLE 12.1 Kohlberg's Six Substages of Moral Development

Stage	Motivation	Typical Moral Reasoning
Preconventional Level		
1 **Punishment and obedience orientation**	The primary motive for action is the avoidance of punishment:	*Pro:* If you let your wife die, you will get in trouble. You'll be blamed for not spending the money to save her and there'll be an investigation of you and the druggist for your wife's death. *Con:* You shouldn't steal the drug because you'll be caught and sent to jail if you do. If you do get away, your conscience would bother you thinking how the police would catch up to you any minute. (Kohlberg, 1984, p. 52)
2 **Naive instrumental hedonism**	Actions are motivated by the desire for rewards:	*Pro:* If you do happen to get caught you could give the drug back and you wouldn't get much of a sentence. It wouldn't bother you much to serve a little jail term, if you have your wife when you get out. *Con:* He may not get much of a jail term if he steals the drug, but his wife will probably die before he gets out, so it wouldn't do him much good. If his wife dies, he shouldn't blame himself; it isn't his fault she has cancer. (Kohlberg, 1984, p. 52)
Conventional Level		
3 **Good-boy morality**	The child strives to avoid the disapproval of others (as distinct from avoidance of punishment):	*Pro:* No one will think you're bad if you steal the drug but your family will think you're an inhuman husband if you don't. If you let your wife die, you'll never be able to look anyone in the face again. *Con:* It isn't just the druggist who will think you're a criminal, everyone else will, too. After you steal it, you'll feel bad thinking how you've brought dishonor on your family and yourself; you won't be able to face anyone again. (Kohlberg, 1984, p. 52)
4 **Authority-maintaining morality**	An act is always wrong if it violates a rule or does harm to others:	*Pro:* You should steal it. If you did nothing you'd be letting your wife die; it's your responsibility if she dies.You have to take it with the idea of paying the druggist. *Con:* It is a natural thing . . . to want to save his wife but it's always wrong to steal. He still knows he's stealing and taking a valuable drug from the man who made it. (Kohlberg, 1984, p. 50)
Postconventional Level		
5 **Morality of contract and democracy**	The individual is concerned with self-respect and maintaining the respect of others. Laws must be obeyed, because they represent a social contract, but they may sometimes conflict with moral values:	*Pro:* The law wasn't set up for these circumstances.Taking the drug in this situation isn't really right, but it's justified to do it. *Con:* You can't completely blame someone for stealing, but extreme circumstances don't really justify taking the law in your own hands. You can't have everyone stealing when they get desperate.The end may be good, but the ends don't justify the means. (Kohlberg, 1984, p. 50)
6 **Morality of individual principles of conscience**	Individuals are concerned with upholding their personal principles and may sometimes feel it necessary to deviate from rules when the rules conflict with moral principles:	*Pro:* This is a situation that forces him to choose between stealing and letting his wife die. In a situation in which the choice must be made, it is morally right to steal. He has to act in terms of the principle of preserving and respecting life. *Con:* [The man] is faced with the decision of whether to consider other people who need the drug just as badly as his wife. [He] ought to act not according to his particular feelings toward his wife but considering the value of all the lives involved. (Kohlberg, 1984, p. 51)

Finland have also found that children generally show development of moral reasoning, at least from preconventional to the first of the conventional levels (Gibbs et al., 2007; Jensen, 2008). Note, though, that most individuals as adults still reason at the conventional level (see Figure 12.6). Moral development has been found to correlate positively with IQ, educational level, and the opportunity to engage in diverse social interactions consistent with Kohlberg's emphasis on the cognitive and perspective-taking basis for moral judgment (Gibbs et al., 2007). However, researchers have been unable to confirm some specific propositions in Kohlberg's outline of moral development. For example, do individuals within a stage respond consistently to different moral dilemmas? In one study of seventy-five college students who responded to five moral dilemmas, not one person received the same stage score for all stories (Fishkin, Keniston, & MacKinnon, 1973). Thus, individuals may display considerable variation in their reasoning about moral issues.

SOCIOCULTURAL DIFFERENCES

Kohlberg's theory also may not capture the many modes of moral reasoning evident in individuals in some cultural groups. For example, in responding to moral dilemmas, people growing up on the Israeli kibbutz often address the importance of the principle of happiness for everyone (Snarey, 1985). Asian cultures are more likely to emphasize the idea of the collective good and a harmonious social order than are Western cultures. From this perspective, the desirable way to resolve disputes is to reconcile people who are in conflict rather than rely on laws to control their behavior. Kohlberg's moral dilemmas, which require a choice between rules and the needs of individuals to bring about justice, do not permit the expression of this cultural principle (Dien, 1982; Ma & Cheung, 1996). Evaluations of the appropriateness of telling the truth or lying also differ between Chinese and Canadian children, as might be predicted from the differing emphasis on modesty and humility reported for these two cultures (Lee et al., 1997). Likewise, Indian cultures emphasize the value of all life, not just human life; thus, a most serious transgression, as expressed by Hindu children

Figure 12.6

The Development of Moral Reasoning

In a longitudinal follow-up study of Kohlberg's original sample, Anne Colby and her colleagues confirmed that participants showed consistent upward advances in moral reasoning with age.The graph shows the extent to which participants gave responses characteristic of each of Kohlberg's six stages from age ten through adulthood. With development, responses associated with the preconventional level (stages 1 and 2) declined, and responses associated with the conventional level (stages 3 and 4) increased. Few young adults moved to the postconventional level of moral reasoning.

Source: From Colby, A., Kohlberg, L., Gibbs, J., & Lieberman, M. (1983). A longitudinal study of moral judgment. *Monographs of the Society for Research in Child Development, 48* (No. 1–2, Serial No. 200). Reprinted by permission of The Society for Research in Child Development.

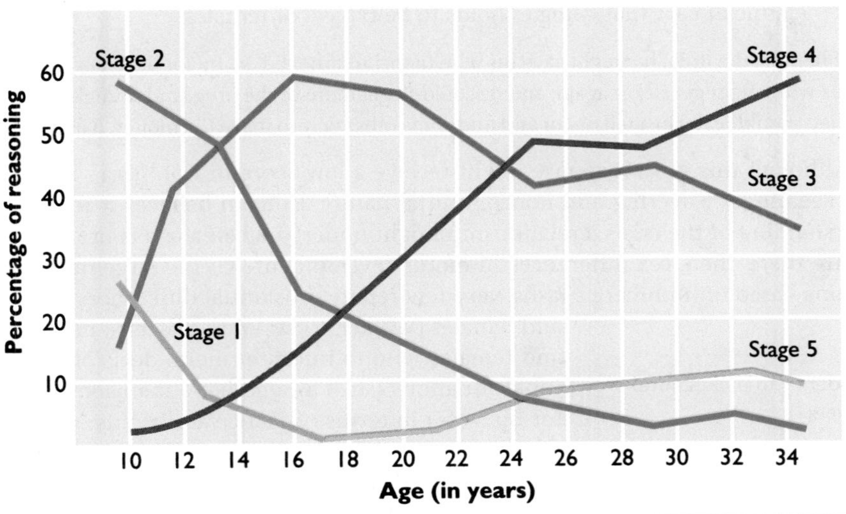

Kohlberg's theory of moral development has been criticized for failing to measure the values found in other cultures. Here young boys are learning appropriate behaviors to display during prayer time in a mosque in Malaysia. Our understanding of the development of moral reasoning will remain incomplete until we explore how these and other religious experiences and cultural traditions influence development.

© Ron Yue/Alamy

and adults, is eating beef, chicken, or fish (Shweder, Mahapatra, & Miller, 1987). Buddhist beliefs about limits to self and to the value of intervention in preventing suffering are also difficult to reconcile within Kohlberg's framework (Huebner & Garrod, 1991). Thus, the movement of the individual toward the fullest understanding of morality as conceptualized by Kohlberg may be primarily a Western phenomenon.

Gilligan's Theory The failure to consider alternative modes of moral reasoning has been an especially sensitive issue with respect to possible sex differences in moral development. In one early study, Kohlberg reported that most males function at the higher stage, whereas most females reason at the lower stage, within the conventional level of moral reasoning (Kohlberg & Kramer, 1969). The report provoked a strong reaction from some members of the psychological community and led Carol Gilligan to propose that moral development takes a different, not an inferior, course in females (Gilligan, 1982). Because females tend to be concerned with relationships, caregiving, and intimacy, they typically develop a **morality of care and responsibility** in contrast to the **morality of justice** described by Kohlberg. The morality of care and responsibility concerns self-sacrifice and relationships with others, rather than the tension between rules and the needs and rights of the individual.

An eleven-year-old girl's response to the story about whether or not to steal a drug illustrates the ethic of care that Gilligan holds to be typical of females:

> If he stole the drug, he might save his wife then, but if he did, he might have to go to jail, and then his wife might get sicker again, and he couldn't get more of the drug, and it might not be good. So, they should really just talk it out and find some other way to make the money. (Gilligan, 1982, p. 28)

Although this girl's response might receive a low score in Kohlberg's system because of its seemingly wavering and noncommittal nature, Gilligan believes it reflects a mature understanding of the crisis a relationship might undergo when a law is broken.

Are there, then, sex differences in moral development? Of the large number of investigations based on Kohlberg's tasks, very few report substantial differences between males and females (Walker, 1984; Wark & Krebs, 1996). Both males and females tend to interpret moral decisions about impersonal situations (such as whether a man should steal a drug for his wife) in terms of justice and rights; decisions about dilemmas that they have personally confronted are more frequently made in terms of the ethic of care (Walker, 1996). Regardless of whether sex differences in moral development

morality of care and responsibility Tendency to make moral judgments on the basis of concern for others.

morality of justice Tendency to make moral judgments on the basis of reason and abstract principles of equity.

exist, Gilligan's work has shown that researchers need to expand their understanding of what constitutes moral values.

Morality as Domain-Specific Knowledge Definitions of morality can vary enormously and are often embedded within the broad fabric of social knowledge and values represented in culture (Turiel & Wainryb, 1994; Turiel, 2006). Perhaps, then, a distinction needs to be made between moral and societal beliefs. The moral domain consists of rules that regulate a person's own or another's rights or welfare; examples are the concepts of justice and responsibility toward others. The societal domain pertains to knowledge of **social conventions**, the rules that regulate such social interactions as how to dress appropriately for a given occasion and what degree of formality to use in speaking to someone—factors that can vary dramatically from one culture to another. A third domain, personal views, for example, about whom to become friends with and how to spend time in various leisure activities, may also be a component of moral development.

Moral and societal domains of knowledge, along with personal views, may develop along separate paths (Turiel, 2006); most theories of moral development have confused the different domains. Children begin distinguishing moral and social-conventional rules by age three (Smetana & Braeges, 1990). To illustrate, young children will respond differently to their playmates' transgressions depending on whether the actions violate a social or a moral rule. When a child violates a moral rule, for example, by intentionally inflicting harm or taking another's possessions, other children typically react by physically intervening or making statements about the pain the victim experienced. On the other hand, when children observe another person violating a social convention, such as eating while standing instead of sitting, they either do not react or simply comment on the rules that surround proper social behavior (Nucci & Turiel, 1978). When questioned about social-conventional transgressions, most children say such an act would be acceptable if no rule existed about it in school, whereas moral transgressions are wrong, are more serious, and should receive greater punishment, even if the school has no rule pertaining to them (Smetana, Schlagman, & Adams, 1993). Children and adolescents are likely to be relatively intolerant about others' holding moral beliefs with which they disagree, but they also readily recognize that others need not share beliefs about social conventions (Wainryb et al., 2001). Moreover, disagreements with parents are far more likely to emerge with respect to social conventions than moral values as children move into and through adolescence in many different cultures (Smetana, 2002).

INTERACTION AMONG DOMAINS

How do children come to appreciate the distinction between moral and social conventions? Perhaps it is through the greater emotional affect associated with moral transgressions than with social infractions. For example, when first- and third-graders are asked to rate how they would feel if they were hit without provocation or if another child stole their toys, they are more likely to indicate a negative emotion than if the scenario described lining up outside the wrong classroom. Children frequently justify intervening in a moral transgression by referring to either their own or the victim's emotional state (Arsenio & Ford, 1985). Adults also may react differently to transgressions associated with moral issues compared with social conventions; as a result, the child learns to discriminate between these two domains (Glassman & Zan, 1995).

Moral Reasoning Versus Moral Behavior Cognitive-developmental approaches fill a void left by social learning theories by acknowledging that how the child thinks about moral situations and social conflict may be as important as how she behaves. However, is moral reasoning related to moral behavior? As one researcher put it, "Knowing the good is not always sufficient to motivate someone to do the good" (Nucci, 2001, p. 196). Scores on moral reasoning tests do not always correlate with tendencies to avoid cheating, to help others, or to abide by rules (Richards et al., 1992). The closest relationships are found between moral reasoning and specific negative social behaviors, such as aggression and delinquency (Blasi, 1980; Gregg, Gibbs, & Basinger, 1994). These issues aside, it remains important to understand how children make judgments about what is right and wrong and, in addition, to know more about how the motivations to act on those judgments arise (Arsenio & Lemerise, 2004).

social conventions Behavioral rules that regulate social interactions, such as dress codes and degrees of formality in speech.

Who Is Responsible for Moral Development?

what do you think?

At the beginning of this chapter, Michael's grandfather complained about young people's lack of respect for and treatment of others today. It may be a view commonly expressed by others as well. We often hear about adolescents, even children, breaking the law or engaging in behaviors that are not morally or socially acceptable. But do you think children and adolescents are less moral today than in previous generations? No study is likely to be able to provide a clear answer to this question, but it raises an interesting further question. Who is responsible for a child's moral development?

Few would argue against parents and children themselves having a major role in this process. But might it "take a village" to raise a child? In other words, do you think the school and the broader community should be involved in promoting moral development as well? If so, in what ways? Should there, for example, be a moral or "character" education component in school curriculums? If so, what should be included in it? For example, should it encourage developing a sensitivity to others by emphasizing the emotional consequences of unacceptable behaviors such as lying, cheating, hitting, or being disrespectful to others? Should such programs include training in ethics or serving in volunteer activities? Could members of the community establish more coherent programs for communicating standards and expectations about acceptable behavior for children and adolescents (Damon, 1997)? For example, what role might organized athletic programs, religious activities, boys' and girls' clubs, and other efforts undertaken by the community play in this process? What has been your experience with these kinds of programs? How have they played a role in your views about what is morally right or acceptable behavior?

For Your Review and Reflection

- What are the signs of the development of conscience in the early childhood years? What factors are related to the development of conscience?
- How does social learning theory account for the development of moral behaviors?
- What are the basic elements of Piaget's theory of moral development? What elements of his theory are supported or refuted by research evidence?
- What are the primary stages of moral development according to Kohlberg?
- What kinds of data support Kohlberg's theory? What are some of the major criticisms of his perspective?
- What is the distinction between a morality of justice and a morality of care and responsibility?
- What evidence suggests that the development of knowledge in the moral domain should be distinguished from the development of knowledge about social conventions?
- How are interactions among domains reflected in moral development? What are some sociocultural influences on moral development?
- How well do you think conscience, behavior, and reasoning are coordinated in accounting for a child's moral development?

Prosocial Behavior and Altruism

prosocial behavior Positive social action performed to benefit others.

A young child consoles a friend in distress, helps her pick up the pieces of a broken toy, or shares a snack. These **prosocial behaviors**, social actions performed to benefit others and perhaps the self, have come under increasing investigation as another way to understand the development of values and moral behavior in children. Among prosocial behaviors is **altruism**, behavior carried out to help others without expectation of rewards for oneself. In contrast to research that focuses on justice and rights, prosocial and altruistic responses have a less obligatory, legalistic quality about them (Kahn, 1992).

The Development of Prosocial Behavior and Altruism

Several contemporary theorists believe an essential element underlying prosocial or altruistic behavior is **empathy**, a vicarious, shared emotional response involving an understanding and appreciation of the feelings of others, which includes sympathetic concern for the person in need of assistance (Eisenberg, Fabes, & Spinrad, 2006). Perhaps humans are biologically predisposed to exhibit such a trait. Even infants show signs of sensitivity to the distress of others. Two- and three-day-olds may cry when other infants cry, but not in response to other, equally loud noises (Simner, 1971). In addition to crying, ten- to fourteen-month-olds may whimper or silently attend to expressions of distress from another person. Often they respond by soothing themselves, sucking their thumbs, or seeking a parent for comfort (Radke-Yarrow & Zahn-Waxler, 1984).

NATURE & NURTURE

Between one and two years of age, empathy promotes new behaviors, typically called *sympathy*: touching or patting the distressed person as though to provide solace, seeking assistance for the person, or even giving the person something to provide comfort, such as a cookie, blanket, or teddy bear. The person's emotional state may also be labeled with such expressions as "Cry," "Oh-oh!" or "Hurting." Slightly older children display more varied and complex responses, including comforting and helping the troubled child, asking questions of her, punishing the agent of the child's distress, protecting the child, and asking an adult for help (Radke-Yarrow & Zahn-Waxler, 1984; Zahn-Waxler et al., 1992). Such expressions and actions are not uncommon. In one study of toddlers playing at home with familiar peers, almost half of the children who observed distress in their peers responded with an attempt to comfort or assist them. They were especially likely to do so if they themselves had caused the distress (Demetriou & Hay, 2004). Toddlers will even display sympathetic responses if someone shows no signs of emotion after being harmed (Vaish, Carpenter, & Tomasello, 2009). Research indicates that several areas of the prefrontal cortex are involved in activities eliciting empathetic responses (Light et al., 2009).

Many researchers report that helping and sharing increase with age (Eisenberg et al., 2006), but others note that older children may actually help or share less (Nantel-Vivier et al., 2009). Beyond age six, increasing concerns about self-interest, the expectations of others, and greater consideration of the consequences of their actions can enter into children's decisions about assisting a person in need or performing a prosocial activity (Eisenberg et al., 1995; Krebs & Van Hesteren, 1994).

Are girls, often believed to be more nurturing, caring, and empathic than boys, also more altruistic? On the whole, children display few gender differences in the amount of helping and sharing they exhibit. For example, when in the presence of a crying baby, girls are no more likely to assist than boys (Zahn-Waxler, Friedman, & Cummings, 1983). But some gender differences are observed favoring girls, and the differences tend to increase with age. These differences are more evident when measures of prosocial behavior involve being kind or considerate, rather than when the activity demands helping, comforting, or sharing. In addition, they are more likely to be found when self-reports rather than observational methods are used to measure prosocial activity (Eisenberg et al., 2006).

What factors lead to increases in prosocial behavior? Some researchers believe there is a link between prosocial behavior and empathy. Behaving prosocially, such as attempting to alleviate distress in others, may be a way to relieve a child's own empathic distress (Hoffman, 1976, 1982). Thus, if a boy sees that a friend who has just fallen down on the playground is crying, he feels uncomfortable. He knows how painful a skinned knee feels and shares his friend's anguish. To feel better himself, the boy rushes to help his playmate to the school nurse's office. When children are asked to report their feelings, a consistent link between empathy and assisting others has not always been

altruism Behavior carried out to help another without expectation of reward.

empathy Understanding and sharing of the feelings of others.

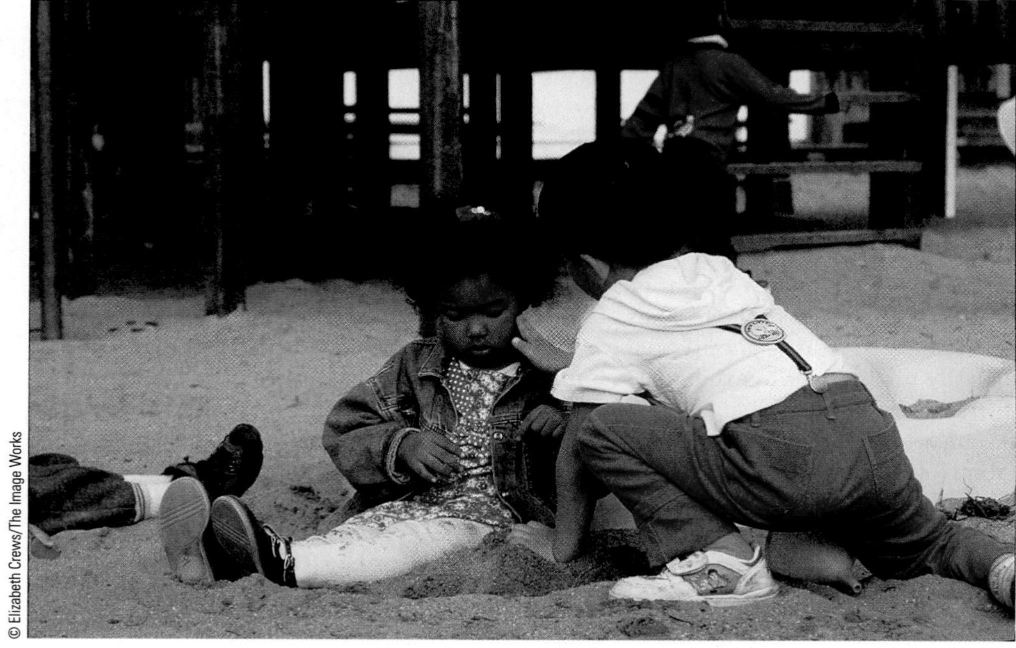

© Elizabeth Crews/The Image Works

Even preschoolers display care and concern about others. Here a boy brushes sand from the face of his younger sister in an effort to keep her from becoming upset. These kinds of actions suggest that prosocial behavior is an early aspect of human development. Moreover, its expression is very likely influenced by the socialization practices of parents and other caregivers.

shown. However, when empathy is assessed by using nonverbal measures, for example, facial expressions such as sadness or behavioral gestures such as looking toward the distressed person, there is a relationship with helping and sharing. Older children who report feeling, or who are reported by others to show, greater sympathy are also described by others as being more prosocial in their behavior (Malti et al., 2009). As children grow older, that relationship grows distinctly stronger (Eisenberg & Miller, 1987; Roberts & Strayer, 1996).

A younger child may show signs of empathic distress but not know exactly how to help (Hoffman, 1976). If a playmate is crying as the result of a fall, should she be helped to stand up or be left alone? Should the child say something comforting or reassuring, or simply keep silent? As children mature, they are learning about the social and emotional worlds on a number of fronts. They are better able to interpret the emotions they are feeling (including empathy), may experience them more strongly, and learn about the range of prosocial behaviors they can express. Unfortunately, if the emotional arousal is either too limited or becomes too great, children may either ignore the other person or focus on their own uncomfortable feelings at the expense of helping (Fabes et al., 1994; Miller et al., 1996; Young, Fox, & Zahn-Waxler, 1999). The distinction between self and other also matures and, with it, the realization that the other person's distress can be relieved by taking some action. In this regard, individual differences in helpfulness do exist (Hay et al., 1999). Children who show more prosocial behaviors are better able to take the perspective of another and therefore to feel sympathy for that individual (Eisenberg et al., 1999).

INTERACTION AMONG DOMAINS

Prosocial Reasoning

Just as moral reasoning associated with justice changes with development, so does reasoning associated with prosocial behavior. Nancy Eisenberg (1986) formulated prosocial dilemmas in which the interests of one person are in conflict with those of another individual or group. For example, a child on the way to a birthday party sees another child who has hurt her leg. Should she go find that child's parent in order to get her to a doctor? Or should she continue on to the birthday party so as not to miss the fun? In justifying their answers to such a dilemma, many preschool and some young school-age children in the United States say they would help in order to gain affection or material rewards, such as candy or cake. Early elementary school children are more likely to express a concern for the physical or psychological needs of others ("He needs help"; "She's hurt"). In the middle childhood years, the child's responses increasingly take into consideration the reactions of others ("The child

© Sean Sprague/The Image Works

Some children grow up in cultures in which they contribute to the needs of the entire community. Here children in India assist by carrying firewood to their local rural village. Children reared in group-oriented societies tend to engage in more prosocial behavior than children reared in settings that emphasize individualism.

should help because the other person would like her"). During the later elementary years and into high school, more reflective and empathic responses emerge ("I'm trying to put myself in that person's shoes"). Older adolescents tend to focus on behavior concerned with fulfilling societal obligations, avoiding guilt, and maintaining self-respect. As with moral development, prosocial reasoning progresses from concern for external consequences to a more internalized, principled basis on which to act.

Culture and Prosocial Reasoning and Behavior When asked to reason about prosocial dilemmas, children in other Western industrialized societies display similar patterns of development. German, Italian, and Polish children, for example, show the same progression as children in the United States (Boehnke et al., 1989; Eisenberg et al., 1985). In other cultures, however, variations have been found. For example, elementary school children reared on the Israeli kibbutz reflect a more mature level of prosocial reasoning, voicing concern about the humaneness of the central character and the importance of internalized norms ("She has a duty to help others") (Eisenberg, Hertz-Lazarowitz, & Fuchs, 1990). A somewhat different picture emerges for children from the Maisin tribe, a coastal village society of Papua New Guinea. Here children maintain a concern about the needs of others well into adolescence and even adulthood (Tietjen, 1986). These developmental patterns mirror the values emphasized by each culture. On the Israeli kibbutz, the goal of contributing to the good of the entire community is stressed, whereas, among the Maisin, children are taught explicitly to be aware of and respond to the needs of specific others rather than to those of the larger social group.

SOCIOCULTURAL INFLUENCE

Might children also show cross-cultural differences in behaving prosocially? Nancy Graves and Theodore Graves (1983) studied the inhabitants of Aitutaki Island, one of the Cook Islands in the South Pacific. A tremendous economic shift, from a subsistence to an industrialized market economy, took place on parts of this island and produced corresponding changes in family structure and the roles of family members. Children living in the unaffected rural villages grow up in extended families in which they make substantial contributions to family and community goals. They participate in most community affairs, are sent by elders to share food and goods with other village members, and bring the family contribution to church each week. In contrast, children growing up in urban, more modernized settings are reared in nuclear families and participate less in both family and community functions.

Graves and Graves (1983) observed that children five and six years of age in the urban communities were less likely to assist others in their home and surrounding environs than were children in rural settings. The researchers concluded that prosocial behavior is more likely in societies in which the predominant ethic is one of interdependence and group

CHRONOLOGY Moral and Prosocial Development: Birth to 16+ Years

MONTHS — BIRTH | YEARS — BIRTH

Newborn–9 Months

- Reacts to cries of other infants in primitive empathic way.

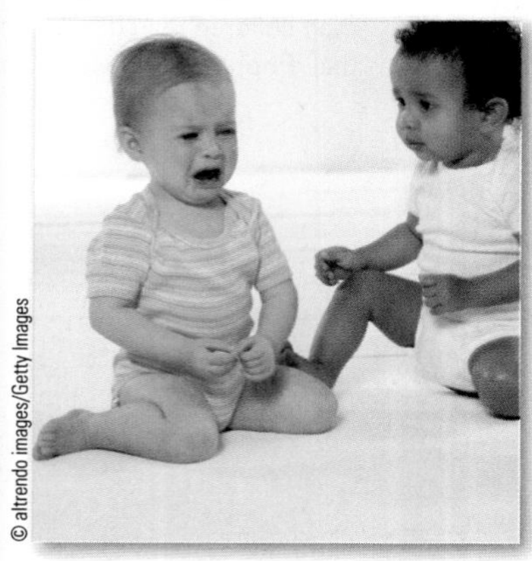
© altrendo images/Getty Images

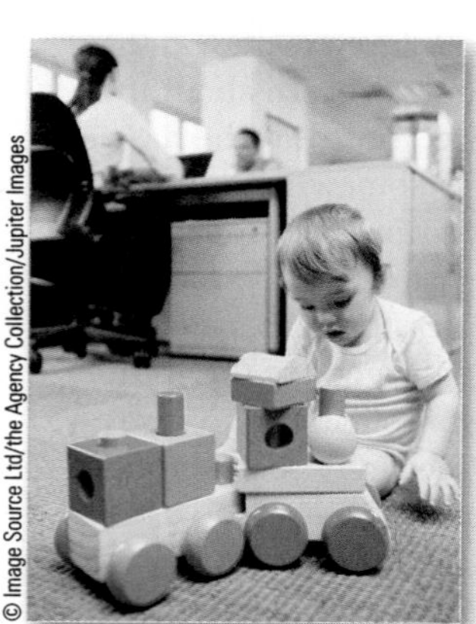
© Image Source Ltd/the Agency Collection/Jupiter Images

10–14 Months

- Shows various signs of empathy to distress of another but often soothes the self.

1–2 Years

- Assists another in distress by patting, touching, or offering material objects.

2–3 Years

- Begins to show signs of guilt and remorse for misdeeds.

3–6 Years

- Discriminates moral and social-conventional rules.
- Judges moral dilemmas according to objective consequences and believes in immanent justice.
- Hedonistic and needs-oriented judgments dominate prosocial decisions.

© iStockphoto.com/Franky De Meyer

7–10 Years

- Reasons according to rewards and punishments expected from authority figures.
- Approval and concerns about the reactions of others guide judgments about assisting others.

10–16 Years

- Judges moral dilemmas according to intentions of actor.
- Reasons on the basis of rules and laws with a belief in maintaining social order.
- Empathic reasoning appears in prosocial judgments.

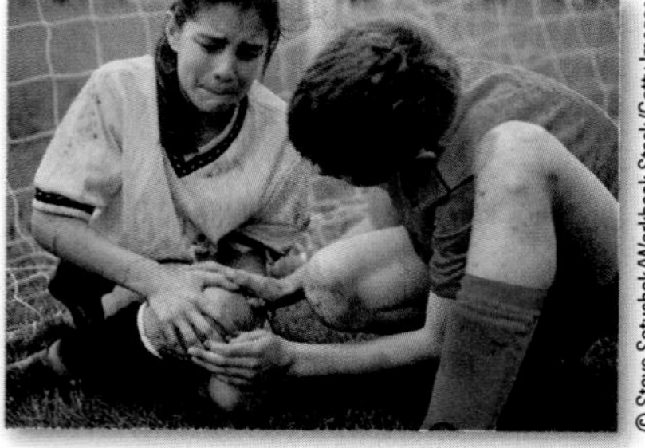
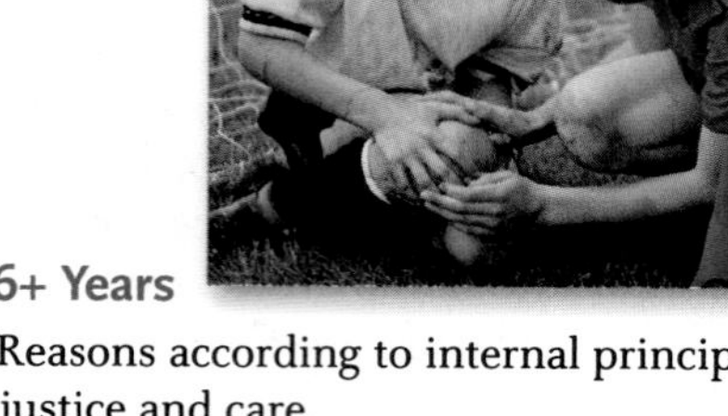
© Steve Satushek/Workbook Stock/Getty Images

16+ Years

- Reasons according to internal principles of justice and care.
- Internalized principles guide prosocial behavior.

This chart describes the sequence in the development of moral and prosocial behavior based on the findings of research. Children often show individual differences in the exact ages at which they display the various developmental achievements outlined here.

orientation, and in which the child participates in cooperative work experiences, than it is in cultures that emphasize individualism and self-reliance. In general, children from traditional rural communities tend to be more cooperative than children from urban cultures (Eisenberg & Mussen, 1989). Also, children from more communal cultures (typical of Asian countries) tend to share more than children from cultures emphasizing individualism (typical of Western countries) (Rao & Stewart, 1999).

Factors Influencing Prosocial Behavior

What role do child-rearing techniques play in the emergence of prosocial behavior? As social learning theory would predict, reinforcement can be influential. But material rewards (money, candy, tokens) do not appear as effective as social rewards ("You're a good boy!" or "That's really nice") in increasing the likelihood that children will share, help, or show concern for others (Grusec, 1991; Warneken & Tomasello, 2008). Opportunities for observational learning are another potent factor. When a child sees someone make a donation to a needy person or group, he is likely to be charitable as well (Grusec & Skubiski, 1970).

NATURE & NURTURE

What models do appears to be more important than what they say (Rushton, 1975), yet the nature of caregivers' verbal communications also has a bearing on prosocial behavior. When parents use **induction**—that is, explain why transgressions are wrong, provide a rationale for rules and regulations, present a reason for prosocial activity, and express disappointment at specific behaviors when exhibited inappropriately—their children are more likely to practice prosocial behaviors (Hastings et al., 2000; Hoffman, 1975; Krevans & Gibbs, 1996). For example, a parent might say, "Don't pull Sam's hair! That hurts him. You don't like to have your hair pulled, do you?" Such messages emphasize clear communication about standards for behavior, arouse empathic feelings, and stimulate perspective taking (Eisenberg & Mussen, 1989). In contrast, a far less effective means of fostering prosocial behavior involves **power assertion**, using forceful commands, physical punishment, or removal of material objects or privileges to influence behavior. For example, the parent might yell, "Stop that! You're not watching TV tonight!" as her son pulls his brother's hair.

Assigning responsibility to children, particularly for tasks that benefit others rather than to themselves, also has an impact. For example, having children contribute to household chores, such as gardening, helping to prepare meals, keeping the family room clean, or other activities beneficial to the family as a whole, is related to more prosocial activities than is taking responsibility for tasks that directly profit only oneself, such as taking care of one's own room or cleaning up one's own space (Grusec, Goodnow, & Cohen, 1996). Moreover, prosocial actions are increased when children are "expected" to initiate and routinely complete these helping activities—that is, when children must self-regulate their actions in these realms rather than when they are requested to carry out the chores only on particular occasions.

Another socialization technique that may be as effective as induction is to emphasize the child's prosocial characteristics. When a child is told, "I guess you're the kind of person who helps others whenever you can," her tendency to behave prosocially increases greatly (Mills & Grusec, 1989). Perhaps attributing to the child a sense of concern for others changes her self-concept, and she strives to behave in a manner consistent with that image (Grusec, 1982). Parents do not make prosocial attributions about their children often, but it is precisely the rarity of these comments that may make them so powerful in the eyes of the child (Grusec, 1991).

NATURE & NURTURE

Additional Correlates of Prosocial Behavior Grade school children who tend to help others have better social skills (Eisenberg & Mussen, 1989), are more popular with peers (Gottman, Gonso, & Rasmussen, 1975; McGuire & Weisz, 1982), and are more self-confident, self-assured, and better adjusted than those who do not. Children who think prosocially—who tend to think in terms of helping others in distress—have more friends and higher-quality relationships with their friends (Rose & Asher, 2004).

induction Parental technique that relies on the extensive use of reasoning and explanation, as well as the arousal of empathic feelings, to influence behavior.

power assertion Parental technique that relies on the use of forceful commands, physical punishment, and removal of material objects or privileges to influence behavior.

Perhaps it is not surprising that prosocial behaviors are associated with many desirable outcomes, particularly in children's social relationships.

Research has revealed other intriguing links, as well. For example, relationships have been reported between prosocial behavior and academic achievement. In one study, eight- to nine-year-olds in a community near Rome, Italy, were revisited five years later as adolescents. Teachers, peers, and the children themselves rated their willingness to help, share, be cooperative, and be kind. Even after controlling for level of early academic achievement as third-graders, the researchers found that higher levels of prosocial behavior displayed at this younger age subsequently predicted greater achievement in school as adolescents (Caprara et al., 2000). In another study carried out in Shanghai, China, a greater prosocial orientation among sixth-graders also was correlated with greater academic achievement two years later (Chen et al., 2000). These results suggest that educational environments might benefit from emphasizing prosocial behaviors.

INTERACTION AMONG DOMAINS

Surprisingly, developmental researchers have seldom investigated the many potential influences that exposure to religious education and other social organizations, such as scouting, boys' and girls' clubs, and other community programs, may have on the development of prosocial responses and values. Yet many parents would claim that such activities also play a vital role in the development of socially acceptable behaviors. You may have thought so as well when thinking about the questions posed earlier concerning who is responsible for moral development. In one study of children given training in their Jewish or Christian faith, participants as young as ten years were found to distinguish between moral issues that they considered to be unalterable (stealing, hitting, damaging another's property) and conventional religious practices that might change in certain circumstances or not apply to other individuals (dress customs, dietary laws, worship activities). Thus, they could distinguish moral issues involving justice and human welfare from social conventions that arise from exposure to their particular faith (Nucci & Turiel, 1993). In other words, recognizing what is moral and what is socially determined very likely is influenced not only by parental teachings and school practices but also by the myriad other activities and examples to which children are exposed in their particular social contexts, including religious training. Moreover, those who identify themselves as religious report that they engage in or are rated by others as displaying more prosocial and civic behavior, a finding observed not only from research involving middle-class children in the United States but also among Muslim adolescents in Indonesia (French et al., 2008; Furrow, King, & White, 2004; Kerestes, Youniss, & Metz, 2004). Issues of fairness and rights, caring and cooperation, and duties and personal responsibility are among those that individuals in most cultures believe are too important to be left to just one component of the child's experiences.

For Your Review and Reflection

- What evidence shows that children are capable of prosocial behaviors in early childhood? What is the relationship between empathy and prosocial behavior?
- What are some of the developmental changes in how children reason about prosocial behavior?
- How do socialization practices, cross-cultural differences, and other activities influence prosocial behavior?
- In situations where someone needs help, how do you think the ways you would respond have changed as you have become older? Why do you think those changes occurred?

Antisocial Behavior

Antisocial behavior is used to label a number of different activities in children and adolescents. For example, frequent temper tantrums in the very young child, a tendency to lie in the preschooler, being argumentative, belligerent, or stealing in the older child, and engaging in acts of vandalism or the destruction of property by an adolescent are often considered instances of antisocial behavior. However, it is **aggression**, the effort to intentionally harm another person, either physically or psychologically, or to destroy property that probably first comes to mind when we think about antisocial behavior.

Aggression

If you have watched a group of children on the playground, helped in babysitting for a family with several young children, or overheard a group of adolescents describing an unpopular peer, you have undoubtedly witnessed instances of aggressive behavior. Such behavior seems to be a staple of many social interactions; perhaps you have been a victim as well as an instigator of such activity. Aggressive behavior has many dimensions and forms. For example, **instrumental aggression** (sometimes called *proactive aggression*) is carried out for self-serving purposes, that is, to achieve a goal such as a desired toy or someone else's valued possession. Not surprisingly, under some circumstances, that kind of behavior can elicit *reactive aggression,* a retaliation in response to that other person's efforts to obtain the toy or possession or, in other cases, in response to an unflattering or negative comment made by another person. **Relational aggression**, such as taunting, name-calling, and malicious gossip, on the other hand, is a form of antisocial behavior designed to harm someone psychologically rather than physically, for example, to hurt their feelings, threatening to end their friendship, or to "put them down" in some other way. This form of aggression goes by many other names, such as *indirect, covert,* and *social aggression* (Card et al., 2008).

The Development of Aggression When do we first see evidence of aggressive behavior in children? What form does it take? In what way does aggressive behavior change with development? Whereas very young infants may show emotional responses such as anger in frustrating situations, intent to harm, a key ingredient for defining aggressive behavior, probably does not enter into a child's repertoire until near the end of the first year of life (Dodge, Coie, & Lynam, 2006). At this time children are beginning to take interest in specific toys and possessions and start to display more control and independence. Not surprisingly, their protests to someone taking away a valued possession or the limitations a caregiver might impose for their safety can often lead to physical outbursts such as hitting, slapping, or having a temper tantrum. However, as toddlers and preschoolers gain more linguistic skills, responses involving verbal aggression take on increasing frequency.

During the elementary school years, physical aggression typically declines as children gain greater ability to regulate emotions, delay gratification, and draw on more effective cognitive skills for interacting with others (Dodge et al., 2006). Nevertheless, relational aggression begins to increase at this time. Moreover, a small proportion of children, especially boys, now become of special concern to others because of frequent displays of antisocial behavior. Such children, who may be highly aggressive even as young as four to six years of age, are likely to continue to be so even into adulthood (Asendorpf, Denissen, & van Aken, 2008).

INTERACTION AMONG DOMAINS

Aggressive behavior generally continues to decline during adolescence, but when it does occur, far more serious acts of violence often may be displayed; if an individual is going to be involved in serious violence, adolescence is when it typically begins (Dodge et al., 2006). For example, in the United States, youths under eighteen years of age account for about 16 percent of all arrests for violent crimes and 26 percent of all arrests for property crimes (Puzzanchera, 2009); fifteen- to seventeen-year-olds in the United States have the highest homicide rate of any age group although this rate has declined substantially in the past twenty years (Baum, 2005).

Gender differences are apparent in some forms of aggressive behavior. Boys are far more likely to display physical aggression than are girls beginning already in the preschool years. However, the frequency of relational aggression, contrary to the views of many, does not differ between boys and girls. Moreover, children and adolescents, especially boys, who display high levels of physical aggression are likely also to show greater amounts of relational aggression (Card et al., 2008).

aggression Behavior that is intentionally carried out to harm another person.

instrumental aggression Behavior motivated to obtain some concrete object or goal and that causes potential or real physical harm to another. Sometimes called *proactive aggression.*

relational aggression Behavior motivated to hurt another's feelings. Sometimes called *indirect, covert,* or *social aggression.*

Factors Associated with Aggressive Behavior in Children and Adolescents What are the variables that researchers have found to be associated with the development of aggressive behavior? The list is quite long, as can be seen in Table 12.2 (Dodge et al., 2006).

RISK | RESILIENCE

We need to be cautious, however, in interpreting how these factors are related to aggression. In some cases, they may not be causal. For example, being rejected by peers may not increase aggression in children but is instead the response by peers to the child's own display of antisocial behavior. Being friends with an antisocial adolescent may not contribute to increased aggression but may be the result of seeking out others with similar behavioral tendencies. Likewise, does increased use of physical punishment cause aggressive behavior, or could it be the response of parents to a child who is difficult to manage?

A second problem is that accounting for aggressive or antisocial behavior in terms of any one or a small set of individual causes may be quite limiting in trying to understand its development. Many contemporary researchers have found it useful to understand aggression in terms of how multiple forces, some positive and some negative, interact with each other. Which factors put children at risk, which are protective, and how do they interrelate? One good example of these multiple forces comes from research showing that, when males are victims of maltreatment, they tend to become aggressive, but only when they have a particular genotype, the one that depresses levels of MAO-A (Caspi et al., 2002). MAO-A is an enzyme that metabolizes certain neurotransmitters and is found on the X chromosome. A second set of research findings demonstrated a similar relationship between MAO-A genotype and, for example, parental neglect and inconsistent discipline in contributing to increased aggression (Foley et al., 2004). Thus, genetic risk alone is not sufficient to predict aggressive behavior. Rather, it is its co-occurrence with maltreatment, parental neglect, or inconsistent parenting that links it to elevated aggression.

INTERACTION AMONG DOMAINS

As another example, consider parental disciplining techniques such as frequent use of corporal punishment and yelling. These factors are associated with increased aggressive behavior in children and fairly convincing data exist to suggest that there is a causal relationship. However, their negative consequences may be moderated by the perceptions within families of whether these disciplining techniques are normative or typical practices of parents. In a recent study, disciplining techniques and aggressive behavior were evaluated in families from six different countries (China, India, Italy, Kenya, Philippines, and Thailand). Although corporal punishment and yelling were correlated with increased aggressive behavior in the children interviewed in all of these countries, the relationship was not as strong where cultural practices may lead children to perceive that it is a fair and reasonable disciplinary technique (Gershoff et al., 2010).

SOCIOCULTURAL INFLUENCE

TABLE 12.2 Some Factors Often Found to Be Associated with Incidences of Aggressive and Antisocial Behavior in Children and Adolescents

- Behavioral genetics studies involving twins, siblings, and others with varying degrees of genetic linkage between family members suggest a genetic relationship, as do some variations in specific genes (for example, the MAO-A gene involved in metabolizing neurotransmitters such as norepinephrine, dopamine, and serotonin)
- Dispositional factors such as a difficult temperament and low scores on personality measures such as agreeableness and constraint
- Neuropsychological factors such as relatively low verbal ability and deficiencies in executive control
- Biological factors such as experiencing complications prenatally or perinatally, prenatal exposure to nicotine, and low resting heart rate
- Community factors such as residing in neighborhoods with low economic status and high unemployment
- Parenting factors including marital conflict, low parental warmth, abusive parenting
- Contextual factors such as out-of-family day care of low quality
- Sociocultural factors such as inconsistent disciplinary practices and reliance on physical punishment where it is not routinely accepted in the child's culture
- Social factors such as peer rejection, friendship with a deviant peer
- Family factors such as lack of parental monitoring (adolescents)

Note: See Dodge, Coie, & Lynam (2006) for more information on these factors and references to research studies demonstrating these findings.

Still another example comes from a study of twelve- and thirteen-year-olds whose risk for aggressive behaviors was related to poverty within the family and neighborhood. The likelihood of aggression for this vulnerable group was reduced when parents monitored their child's location and peer contacts (Pettit et al., 1999). Studies like these underscore that understanding children's and adolescent's antisocial behavior requires casting a wide net—considering characteristics of the person, his social environment, and the larger community in combination—rather than targeting one or two causal variables.

atypical development | Conduct Disorder

Conduct disorder is a psychiatric designation applied to children and adolescents who, for an extended period of time (typically six months or longer), violate or seriously disregard the social norms and rules of the family, school, or society (American Psychiatric Association, 2000). The range of problem behaviors may include bullying, threatening, fighting, physical cruelty to animals, destroying property, lying, and stealing. Depending on how it is defined, as many as 5 percent of children around the world and up to 4 percent of nine- to seventeen-year-olds in the United States are estimated to display conduct disorders (Scott, 2007; Shaffer et al., 1996). As might be expected, it is more likely to occur in boys than in girls.

The factors hypothesized to contribute to the development of conduct disorders in children and adolescents are as varied as the types of problem behaviors that are identified as antisocial. For example, genetic and temperamental predispositions, along with inconsistent and coercive parenting practices—especially when discipline is based on physical punishment or includes abuse and maltreatment, frequent parental discord and conflict, or limited cognitive skills associated with perspective taking—are just a few of the factors theorized to play some part in contributing to conduct disorders (McMahon, Wells, & Kotler, 2006).

NATURE & NURTURE

Is it possible that a child or adolescent who exhibits conduct disorders also might be deficient in empathy? In other words, are some children unable to emotionally share others' feelings and to understand the negative impact of their actions on others? To examine this question, Douglas Cohen and Janet Strayer (1996) asked young people (ages fourteen to seventeen) who had been diagnosed as conduct disordered and were residing in a residential treatment center, and a comparison group of normal young people from the same community, to observe and respond to a videotaped set of vignettes depicting individuals in emotionally laden situations. They also completed a set of questionnaires about how certain types of situations made them feel ("Seeing [a child] who is crying makes me feel like crying" or "I am often very touched by the things that I see happen"). These various measures revealed that young people who display conduct disorders exhibit substantially less empathy than a comparison group; they are less likely to identify the emotions of others and to show responses concordant with and responsive to the emotional states of others.

Cohen and Strayer's research did not reveal why the differences in empathy between conduct-disordered and normal adolescents might exist. Perhaps family socialization practices that differ in the extent to which the youths' emotional needs are met or experienced are part of the answer. For example, concern for others is found more frequently in families in which warmth is high, in which parents point out the consequences of harmful behavior, and in which altruistic activities are modeled (Robinson, Zahn-Waxler, & Emde, 1994). Perhaps, too, children who begin to engage in antisocial conduct become less sensitive to and less willing to interpret empathic cues in others, growing increasingly callous to such information. Children who, as preschoolers, show signs of behavioral problems display levels of concern for others that are similar to those of children who display normative behavior. But by six to seven years of age, they no longer exhibit as much concern for others (Hastings et al., 2000). These results raise the question of how important empathic training might be for effective treatment of children who display conduct disorders.

Recent research also suggests that responses in certain regions of the brain that are involved in sensitivity to pain and emotion regulation such as the amygdala differ for adolescents with conduct disorders compared with other adolescents (Decety, Michalska, & Akitsuki, 2008; Decety et al., 2009). Relatively more activation in some of these areas occurs when intentional or accidental pain is observed in those diagnosed with conduct disorders as suggested in Figure 12.7. This finding

INTERACTION AMONG DOMAINS

Figure 12.7

Conduct Disorders and Responses in the Brain

When adolescents with a conduct disorder (CD) observed a scene involving intentional or accidental pain, regions of the brain sensitive to processing of pain showed increased responsivity compared with adolescents who were not diagnosed with this disorder.

Sources: Copyright 2009 "Atypical empathic responses in adolescents with aggressive conduct disorder: a functional MRI Investigation" Decety, J., Michalska, K. J., Akitsuki, Y., & Lahey, B. Reproduced by permission of Taylor & Francis Group, LLC., http://www.taylorandfrancis.com.

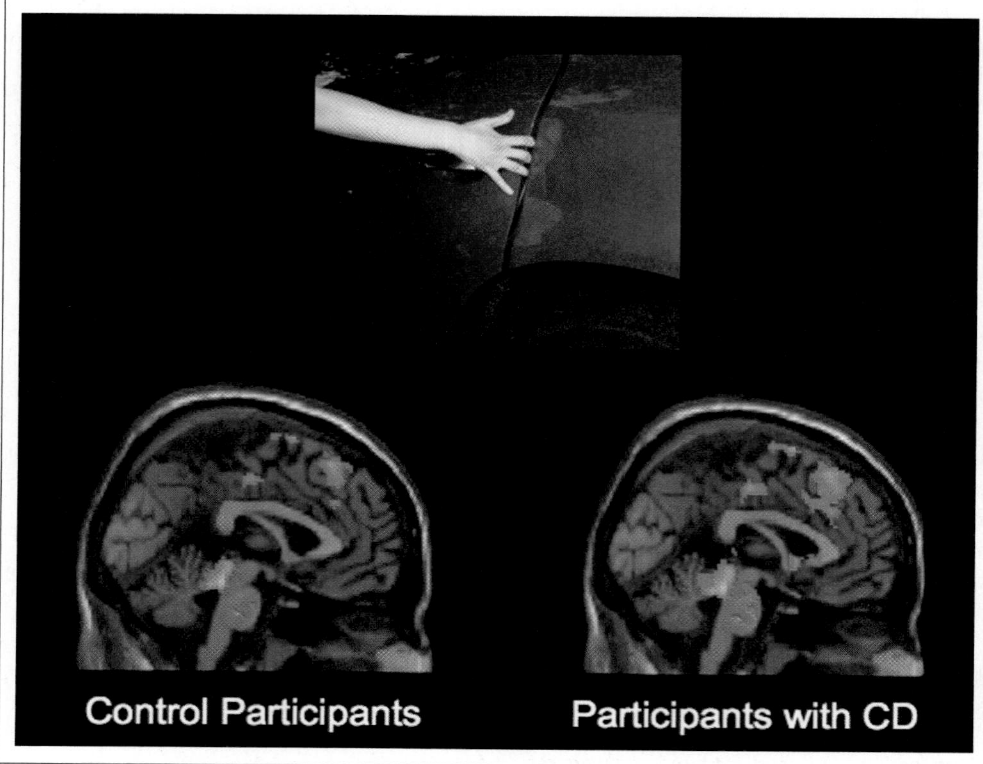

with this disorder may find observing a painful event to be more rewarding. For example, the amygdala is sometimes linked to responses involving positive affect. Alternatively, because youth with conduct disorders may be responding more strongly, they may have greater difficulty regulating their emotions under such circumstances and, as a consequence, display increased aggressive and violent behavior. Moreover, other regions of the brain associated with social relationships and moral reasoning (for example, the temporal parietal junction), show less activation, again suggesting the possibility that empathic responding is more limited for children and youth with conduct disorders. What is also clear from the extensive research carried out on children with conduct disorder is that we have much to learn about what leads to it as well as what kinds of programs may be established to minimize its occurrence (Scott, 2007).

For Your Review and Reflection

- What is aggression? What is the difference between instrumental and relational aggression? What other labels are sometimes used to refer to these different forms of aggression?
- What developmental changes occur in the display of aggressive behaviors?
- What factors increase risk for antisocial behavior? What recommendations would you suggest for parents and policy advocates in their efforts to reduce aggression and violence in children and youth?
- What is a conduct disorder? What factors may influence the development of a conduct disorder?

chapter recap

Summary of Developmental Themes

Nature & Nurture

How do nature and nurture interact in the development of self and of values?

Although early, biologically-based tendencies for children to display empathy may exist, most researchers have described how the child's cognitions and social experiences shape self and values. For example, feedback from others certainly plays an enormous role in the child's characterization of self and prosocial behavior. Theorists such as Piaget and Kohlberg suggest that maturation contributes in part to changes in moral reasoning. But even they believe children's experiences with peers and other socializing agents play a large role in spurring moral reasoning.

Sociocultural Influence

How does the sociocultural context influence the development of self and values?

Children's evaluations of self are greatly determined by the extent to which they display autonomy, loyalty, cooperation, perseverance, and other qualities stressed by the culture. Self-esteem is affected by how well children live up to the society's expectations concerning beauty, athletic skill, academic ability, and other attributes the culture values. Moral reasoning and behavior further reflect the values of a culture. When responsibilities to the larger social group are emphasized, children tend to be more caring and display more prosocial reasoning than when the culture emphasizes the role of the individual. In addition, groups place different weights on law and justice versus other values, such as harmonious interactions with others. Children's responses to moral dilemmas often reflect their culture's unique beliefs.

Continuity | Discontinuity

Is the development of self and values continuous or discontinuous?

Although the child's understanding of self undergoes many developmental changes, evidence that these changes are stagelike remains limited. Even the identity crisis, often considered a hallmark of adolescence, may not be experienced by all young people and reflects a culmination of many earlier, gradual changes. Several influential theories of moral development are stage theories, specifically those of Piaget and Kohlberg. The empirical evidence, however, suggests that reasoning about moral, prosocial, and other values may occur at several levels within the same individual. Although stage theories are popular, domain-specific approaches emphasizing continuous growth are prominent as well.

Interaction Among Domains

How do self and values interact with other domains of development?

Cognitive skills, such as the ability to reason abstractly about the feelings and intentions of others, play a role in evaluations of self and moral judgments. Physical changes and capacities, as well as the social environment, can dramatically affect self-esteem and the emergence of identity. Emotions such as empathy contribute to prosocial behaviors and altruism. At the same time, development of the self and of values has an effect on other domains. For example, high self-esteem and prosocial activity are associated with healthy peer interactions. Development of the self and of values represents an important interaction among affect, cognition, and social experience.

Risk | Resilience

What factors promote risk or resilience in the development of self and values?

The development of self plays an important role in how children view themselves. Low self-esteem and a lower prosocial orientation are linked to poorer outcomes later in development. So, too, are a number of factors such as genetic, dispositional, biological, community, and parenting practices that are correlated with tendencies for increased aggression. On the other hand, research has also identified several factors that are protective and promote resilience, for example, high self-esteem, a strong ethnic identity, and good self-regulatory abilities.

Chapter Review

The Concept of Self

What are the early indications of the concept of self during infancy? How do researchers measure self-recognition?

Infants recognize the movement of their own legs at three months and their own face especially between fifteen and eighteen months of age. To measure self-recognition, researchers often observe infants' reactions to a spot of rouge placed on the nose as infants look in the mirror. Such behavior reflects early evidence for the child's emerging *self-concept*, perceptions, and, in older children, conceptions and values one holds about oneself.

What are the features of the self-concept during early childhood? During middle childhood? During adolescence?

Preschool-aged children typically define themselves in terms of a *categorical self*; that is, by referring to various categories that provide membership in one group or another. *Social comparison* becomes an increasingly important aspect influencing self-concept during middle childhood.

During adolescence, definitions of self may include conflicting dimensions, probably in response to demands from different social groups (for instance, friends versus parents). A reliance on social comparison diminishes in concepts of self as adolescents develop a firm sense of personal identity. They are more likely than younger children to acknowledge the influence of others and to draw on psychological, internal qualities as opposed to physical traits.

How does social comparison contribute to the concept of self?

By engaging in *social comparison*, children gain knowledge of their relative standing among their peers, an important component in their understanding of self. Most five- to seven-year-olds do not respond to this form of feedback about their successes or failures in assessing themselves, but older school-age children do.

What factors contribute to high self-esteem? What developmental changes are reported for self-esteem?

Self-esteem arises from the evaluations of others, as well as the extent to which the child feels successful in those areas thought to be important. Many researchers have reported a drop in self-esteem as children enter adolescence, and somewhat more for girls. The most important aspect of self-esteem is that it is associated with a number of positive developmental outcomes, including those that are long term.

What is an identity crisis? Is there evidence that this is a significant part of adolescent development?
Adolescents normally acquire a broad, coherent, and internalized view of themselves that comprises their *identity (personal)*. The *identity crisis* refers to the idea that, during this time, adolescents may experience a period of uncertainty about who they are and what roles they will fill in society. Although research indicates that this is a time of heightened conflicts with parents as they explore new ways of behaving, most teenagers negotiate this time without undergoing a "crisis."

How important is ethnic group identity for young people?
Ethnic identity, a sense of belonging to one's own cultural group, seems to benefit children and improve their understanding of others. It can also serve as a buffer against perceived discrimination and a source of increased self-esteem.

Self-Regulation

When are children expected to demonstrate effortful control? What do we mean by self-regulation?
Parents expect children to begin to respond to their requests for *effortful control,* the ability to suppress undesirable responses, typically beginning about a year of age. *Self-regulation* refers to the child's ability to control his or her own behaviors in accordance with the expectations of caregivers and other adults.

How does self-regulation change during early childhood?
Regulation of the child's behaviors typically shifts from parents to children in the second year. On *delay-of-gratification* tasks, in which children are asked to wait for some period of time before attaining a highly desirable object, children become increasingly able to delay their behavior. Progress in language development and cognitve control capacities seem to be related to this ability.

What factors seem to promote children's compliance?
Children's compliance is facilitated when parents are responsive and supportive, justify their demands, offer compromises, and focus on "do" rather than "don't."

Moral Development

What are the signs of the development of conscience in children?
Signs of the development of *conscience*, a sense of what is acceptable and unacceptable behavior, include the display of moral emotions, such as guilt or shame, as well as an increasing willingness to comply with adult rules, even when adults are not present.

What factors are related to the development of conscience?
Children are increasingly able to recognize the adult emotions that give them feedback about appropriateness of their own actions. They are also better able to regulate their own behaviors. Positive and mutually responsive interactions with caregivers are also important in conscience development.

How does social learning theory account for the development of moral behavior?
Social learning theory emphasizes the reinforcements that children receive from parents and other agents of socialization, as well as their observations of the behaviors of others, in explaining moral development.

What are the basic elements of Piaget's theory of moral development? What elements of his theory are supported or refuted by research evidence?
In Piaget's theory, children progress from *moral realism* to *moral relativism* as their cognitive capabilities mature. In moral realism, children focus on the visible consequences of an act, believe in *immanent justice,* and do not see a need for punishments to fit the transgression. In moral relativism, children focus on the intentions behind an act, shed their belief in immanent justice, and believe that punishments should relate to misdemeanors. The child's increasing perspective-taking skills, as well as opportunities to interact with peers, are major factors in promoting this shift.

Research confirms that children more fully consider intentions and show fewer beliefs in immanent justice and arbitrary punishment as they grow older. But even preschoolers have been shown to recognize actors' intentions, and the contributions of parents (not just peers) have also been demonstrated in children's moral reasoning.

What are the primary stages of moral development according to Kohlberg? What kinds of data support his theory? What are some of the major criticisms of his perspective?
In Kohlberg's view, most children advance through *preconventional, conventional,* and *postconventional* levels of moral reasoning. During the preconventional stage, morality is motivated by the avoidance of punishments and attainment of rewards; during the conventional stage, morality is governed by conforming to the norms of the majority and wishes to preserve the social order; and during the postconventional stage, morality is increasingly viewed as a social contract and individual principles of conscience dominate. Kohlberg maintains that the child's increasing perspective-taking skills, amplified by opportunities to discuss the points of view of others, are responsible for progress through the stages.

Research supports the idea that there are stagelike progressions in moral thinking and that moral reasoning is related to advances in cognition. But critics point out that most people do not reason above the conventional level and that values drawn from various cultures are not well represented in the theory.

What is the distinction between a morality of justice and a morality of care and responsibility?
Kohlberg's theory focuses on a *morality of justice,* the tendency to make moral judgments based on considerations of rules versus the rights of the individual. A *morality of care and responsibility* refers to moral judgments based on concerns of self-sacrifice and relationships with others.

What evidence suggests that the development of knowledge in the moral domain should be distinguished from the development of knowledge about social conventions?
Children tend to take action when moral rules, as opposed to *social conventions,* rules that relate to culturally emphasized practices, are violated. They also believe that moral transgressions are wrong, even if there are no explicit rules about them. Social conventions, they say, are dependent on rules.

Prosocial Behavior and Altruism

What is the evidence that children are capable of prosocial behaviors in early childhood? What is the relationship between empathy and prosocial behavior?
Prosocial behaviors, social actions performed to benefit others, include *altruism,* behavior carried out to help others without

expecting a reward for one's self. Some signs of concern about others in early childhood include the following: displays of *empathy* (a vicarious, shared emotional response) for the distress of others, soothing a person in distress, and seeking assistance for that person.

When empathy is assessed via facial expressions or other observable behaviors, it has been shown to be related to prosocial behavior. This relationship is assumed to grow stronger with development.

What are the stages of prosocial reasoning according to recent theory and research?
Children typically progress through the following steps in prosocial reasoning: believing that prosocial behaviors should be displayed because they are rewarded, a concern for the needs of others, a concern for the approval of others, an empathy orientation, and finally, a focus on self-respect and fulfillment of societal obligations.

How do cross-cultural differences in child rearing, socialization factors, and other activities influence displays of prosocial behavior?
Children are more likely to engage in mature prosocial reasoning and display a greater number of prosocial behaviors in cultures that promote a community orientation and group values. Children who are rewarded for prosocial behaviors and who observe parents and others acting prosocially tend to be more helpful than other children. Children whose parents use *induction* rather than *power assertion* as a disciplinary technique are also more likely to demonstrate care and concern for others. Religious education and participation in other social organizations is likely to encourage children to engage in more prosocial behavior.

What is the relationship between prosocial behavior and other aspects of development?
Children who display prosocial behaviors are more popular with peers and have stronger friendships. They are also more likely to have higher academic achievement.

Antisocial Behavior

What is aggression, and how do instrumental and relational aggression differ?
Aggression is behavior that is intentionally carried out to harm another person or another's possessions. *Instrumental aggression,* sometimes called proactive aggression, is a form of aggression designed to obtain some concrete object or goal and that causes potential or real physical harm to another. *Relational aggression,* sometimes called indirect, covert, or social aggression, is behavior designed to hurt another's feelings.

How does aggressive responding change with development?
The earliest forms of aggressive behavior are often in response to frustrating situations, but as preschoolers acquire desires for certain things and begin to express increasing independence, physical aggression dominates. Relational aggression also begins early in development and typically becomes more influential in later childhood and adolescence. For some adolescents, violent aggressive acts are also exhibited.

What factors are related to increased aggressive and antisocial behaviors in children and adolescents?
Researchers have identified genetic, dispositional, biological, contextual, and parenting and socialization factors that contribute to the occurrence of aggressive and antisocial behaviors. Multiple forces, some positive and some negative, often interact with each other to increase or reduce the likelihood of aggression.

What is a conduct disorder? What factors may contribute to its occurrence?
Some children and adolescents display frequent bullying, threatening, fighting, cruelty to animals, destruction of property, and lying and stealing for an extended period of time. These individuals are said to possess a conduct disorder. A decline in feelings of empathy may play a special role in the development of highly aggressive youth.

Key Terms and Concepts

aggression (p. 471)
altruism (p. 465)
categorical self (p. 441)
conscience (p. 455)
conventional level (p. 459)
delay of gratification (p. 451)
effortful control (p. 451)
empathy (p. 465)
ethnic identity (p. 449)
identity crisis (p. 448)
identity (personal) (p. 447)
immanent justice (p. 458)
induction (p. 469)
instrumental aggression (p. 471)
morality of care and responsibility (p. 462)
morality of justice (p. 462)
moral realism (p. 458)
moral relativism (p. 458)
postconventional level (p. 459)
power assertion (p. 469)
preconventional level (p. 459)
prosocial behavior (p. 464)
relational aggression (p. 471)
self-concept (p. 440)
self-esteem (p. 444)
self-regulation (p. 451)
social comparison (p. 443)
social conventions (p. 463)

Media Resources

Access an integrated eBook and chapter-specific interactive learning tools, including flashcards, quizzes, videos, and more, in your Developmental Psychology CourseMate, accessed through CengageBrain.com.

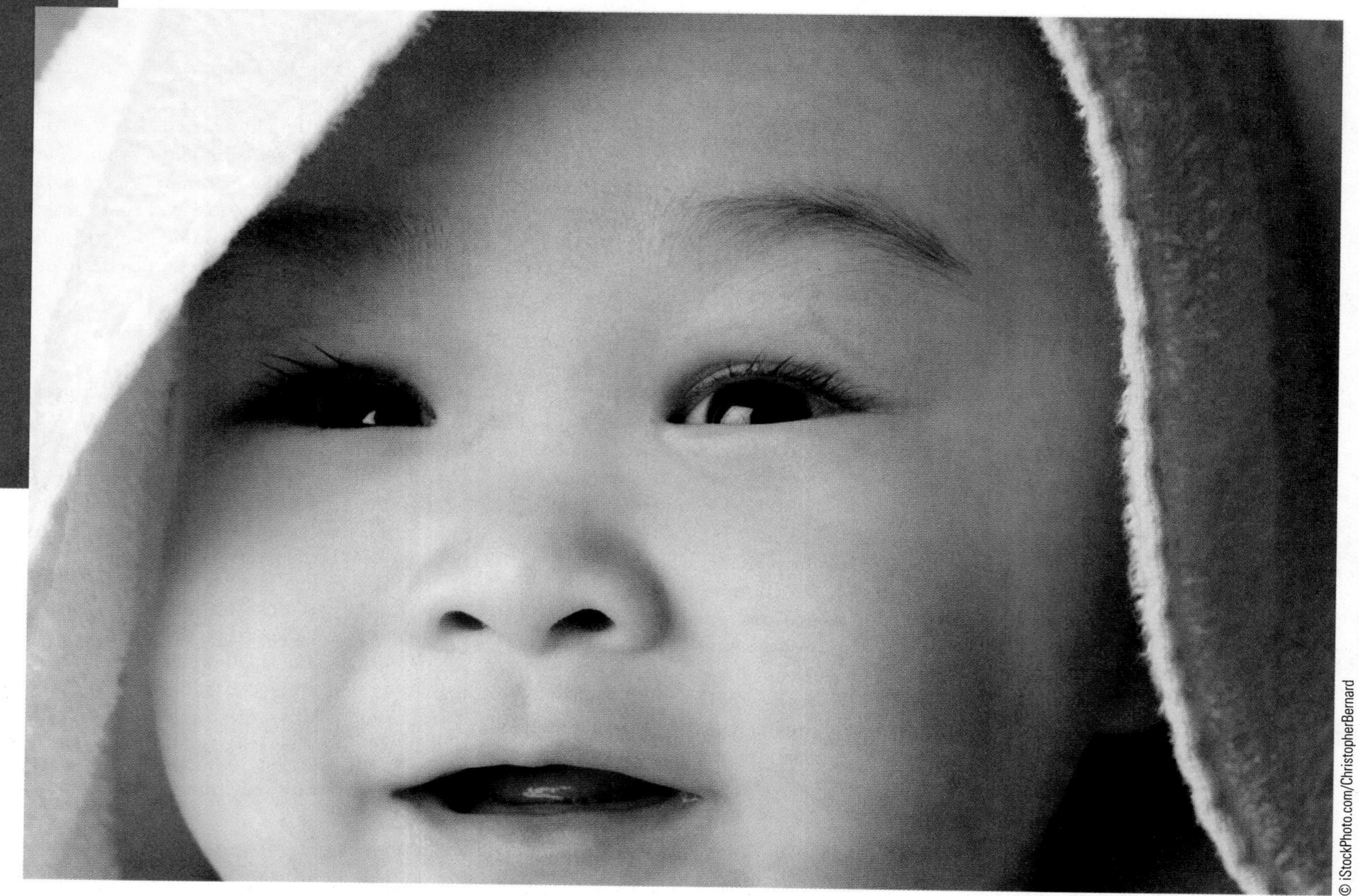

© iStockPhoto.com/ChristopherBernard

CHAPTER OUTLINE

[chapter 13]

Gender

KEY THEMES IN GENDER DEVELOPMENT

- **NATURE & NURTURE** How do nature and nurture interact in gender development?
- **SOCIOCULTURAL INFLUENCE** How does the sociocultural context influence gender development?
- **CONTINUITY | DISCONTINUITY** Is gender development continuous or discontinuous?
- **INTERACTION AMONG DOMAINS** How does gender development interact with development in other domains?
- **RISK | RESILIENCE** What factors promote risk or resilience in gender development?

"Nicky," one of the authors said to her then five-year-old son, "what do you think should be on the cover of this book? It's about children, you know."

"Well," he thought for a moment, "how about a picture of a child?"

"A boy or a girl?" asked the mother.

"How about one of each?" he suggested. The mother was pleased that her son chose a girl as well as a boy. She had tried hard to teach him to think about gender in nonstereotypical ways, and his willingness to include girls seemed to indicate that her efforts were successful.

"What should they be doing?" the mother continued.

"Well, how about having the boy play with a computer?" he quickly responded.

"And the girl?" she asked.

"I think she should have a tea party or something." <<

This five-year-old's response is consistent with many **gender stereotypes** that exist in our society, that is, our beliefs and expectations about the characteristics of females and males. Boys, according to these stereotypes, are active, aggressive, independent, and interested in science. Girls, on the other hand, are passive, nonaggressive, and socially oriented. At what ages and to what extent do children have knowledge of these stereotypes? Furthermore, are such common beliefs actually manifested in the everyday behaviors of children? Are any differences we might observe due to the biological makeup of males and females? What part does socialization play in this process? We will address these central questions in this chapter as we discuss **gender-role development**, the process by which children acquire the characteristics and behaviors prescribed for males and females in their culture.

Before the mid-1960s, most psychologists regarded the socialization of children into traditional masculine and feminine roles as both a natural and a desirable outcome of development. Behavioral sex differences were viewed as inevitable and were linked to comparable sex differences among nonhumans (Kohlberg, 1966; Mischel, 1966; Shaw & Darling, 1985). But changes in social values in the mid-1960s, especially those accompanying the women's movement, shifted the ways in which psychologists approached sex differences and gender-role socialization. Many of the questions that interest developmental psychologists today represent both a challenge to traditional assumptions about the nature and origins of gender roles and sex differences and a concerted effort to determine the developmental processes that underlie children's acquisition and enactment of gender roles.

Gender Stereotypes Versus Actual Sex Differences

Throughout the recorded history of Western civilization, females and males have been assumed to differ in temperament and interests, among other characteristics. Many of these beliefs persist unchanged in contemporary gender stereotypes.

The Stereotypes: What Are They?

Suppose a group of college students is asked to rate the "typical" boy or girl on a number of psychological attributes. Will the students rate certain traits as more typical of males than of females, and vice versa? College students respond that characteristics such as independence, aggression, and self-confidence are associated with masculinity. In general, attributes such as these, which are associated with acting on the world, are classified as **instrumental**. In contrast, emotional expressiveness, kindness, and gentleness are linked with femininity. These perceived feminine characteristics are often classified as **expressive**, or associated with emotions and interactions with other people. Table 13.1 shows other traits often associated with masculinity and femininity (Martin, 1995).

These gender stereotypes are not limited to our own society. Researchers asked children and adults from thirty nations in North and South America, Europe, Africa, and Asia to indicate whether certain traits are more frequently associated with men or women in their culture. The results showed many cross-cultural similarities in the stereotypes adults attributed to males and females (Williams & Best, 1982).

SOCIOCULTURAL INFLUENCE

Despite the many similarities in gender stereotypes across cultures, some differences occurred among nations in the specific characteristics attributed to males and females. For example, Italian adults stereotypically associated "endurance" with women, although most adults in other countries believed this to be a masculine trait. Nigerian adults believed "affiliation" to be neutral, whereas adults in other countries said it was a feminine characteristic. Thus, we cannot say that specific characteristics are always attributed to males or to females. We can say, however, that the tendency to stereotype on the basis of sex is found in a variety of cultural settings.

Children's Knowledge of Gender Stereotypes

Children begin to acquire gender-role stereotypes and employ them as guides for their behavior at a surprisingly early age—from two years onward. At eighteen months of age, infants prefer to look at toys stereotypically associated with their own sex (Serbin et al., 2001). By age two, children look longer at images of males (as opposed to females) putting on lipstick and females (as opposed to males) tying a necktie, indicating through their behavior that they notice when males and females violate stereotypes (Hill & Flom, 2007). Now, too, boys prefer to play with cars, balls, and trains, whereas girls prefer dolls, cooking utensils, and brush and comb sets (Campbell, Shirley, & Caygill, 2002). Preschoolers' knowledge about gender stereotypes is extensive; it includes personality traits, occupations, appearance qualities, and household activities that are associated with males and females (Bauer, Liebl, & Stennes, 1998; Poulin-Dubois et al., 2002). Their thinking about gender stereotypes even extends beyond these qualities to items that may serve as metaphors for masculinity and

gender stereotypes Expectations or beliefs that individuals within a given culture hold about the behaviors characteristic of males and females.

gender-role development Process by which individuals acquire the characteristics and behaviors prescribed by their culture for their sex. Also called *sex typing*.

instrumental characteristics Characteristics associated with acting on the world; usually considered masculine.

expressive characteristics Characteristics associated with emotions or relationships with people; usually considered feminine.

TABLE 13.1 Stereotypic Characteristics Attributed to Males and Females

When college students were asked to rate a typical boy or girl on a number of personality traits, strong patterns emerged among traits that were seen as being associated with each sex. Male traits generally fall into a cluster called *instrumentality* and female traits into a cluster labeled *expressiveness.*

Mean Typicality Ratings by Sex of Child Target[a]		
Item Type	**Boys**	**Girls**
Sex-typed Masculine[b]		
Self-reliant	5.05	3.69
Does dangerous things	4.96	2.57
Enjoys mechanical objects	5.57	2.68
Dominant	5.36	3.54
Enjoys rough play	6.09	3.07
Independent	4.95	3.59
Competitive	5.70	4.16
Noisy	5.78	3.93
Physically active	6.23	4.80
Aggressive	5.60	3.41
Conceited	4.38	3.46
Sex-typed Feminine[c]		
Gentle	3.21	5.36
Neat and clean	3.05	5.42
Sympathetic	3.42	5.33
Eager to soothe hurt feelings	3.35	5.33
Well-mannered	4.01	5.44
Cries and gets upset easily	3.20	4.95
Easily frightened	3.27	4.89
Soft-spoken	3.00	4.64
Helpful around the house	3.27	5.31
Gullible	3.74	4.33
Reliable	4.33	4.74
Truthful	4.31	4.91
Likeable	4.99	5.68
Non-sex-typed		
Adaptable	4.90	4.72

[a]Maximum scores = 7.0.
[b]Indicates that ratings for boys were significantly higher than for girls.
[c]Indicates that ratings for girls were significantly higher than for boys.

Source: From Martin, C. L. (1995). Stereotypes about children with traditional and nontraditional gender roles. *Sex Roles, 33*, pp. 727–751.

femininity; they believe, for example, that fir trees and bears are "for boys" and that maple trees and butterflies are "for girls" (Leinbach, Hort, & Fagot, 1997).

By age six or seven, children's knowledge of gender stereotypes is well established. Lisa Serbin and her colleagues (Serbin, Powlishta, & Gulko, 1993) asked five- through twelve-year-olds to state whether twenty stereotyped objects (for example, *hammer, rifle, stove, broom*) belonged to male or female categories. As Figure 13.1 indicates, all

© Jacek Chabraszewski/Shutterstock.com

Children's knowledge of gender stereotypes includes personality traits, appearance qualities, household activities, and occupations. Knowledge of stereotypes begins as early as age two and is well established by age six or seven.

children, regardless of age, showed wide-ranging knowledge of the stereotypes. The figure also shows that children's knowledge of stereotyped personality traits (for example, *gentle, emotional, adventurous, messy*) expands through the middle school years. Throughout childhood, a substantial number of children's stereotypes about girls center on their appearance (e.g., they are pretty, have long hair, and wear dresses) while stereotypes about boys focus largely on their traits and activities (e.g., they like sports, fight, and play rough) (Miller et al., 2009).

As children grow older, their knowledge of stereotypes becomes more flexible in that they are more likely to say that both males and females can possess certain traits. For example, many teens say that "independence" can be a male or a female trait, or that both boys and girls can be "gentle" (Liben & Bigler, 2002). Flexibility concerning gender stereotypes is especially high right when young adolescents experience a life transition that may involve reevaluation of past beliefs, such as entering junior high school (Alfieri, Ruble, & Higgins, 1996).

Some evidence suggests that, later in adolescence, when individuals are more likely to be thinking about their future roles and responsibilities, flexibility regarding gender stereotypes declines (Alfieri et al., 1996). Researchers have described this return to traditional beliefs about gender during adolescence as *gender intensification* (Hill & Lynch, 1983). Societal expectations that teens will begin dating may create pressures to conform to more rigid masculine and feminine roles. Those who socialize them—their parents, teachers, and others—may

Figure 13.1

Developmental Trends in Gender-Role Knowledge

When kindergartners through sixth-graders were asked to identify which of twenty stereotyped objects were masculine and which were feminine, all children gave at least 90 percent correct answers (see the line for "activity knowledge"). If they were asked to indicate whether objects could be used by both sexes, a developmental increase in flexibility was also observed (see the line for "activity flexibility"). In addition, knowledge of stereotyped traits and flexibility with regard to those traits both increased over the age span studied.

Source: From Serbin, L. A., Powlishta, K. K., & Gulko, J. The development of sex typing in middle childhood. *Monographs of the Society for Research in Child Development*. Reprinted by permission of The Society for Research in Child Development.

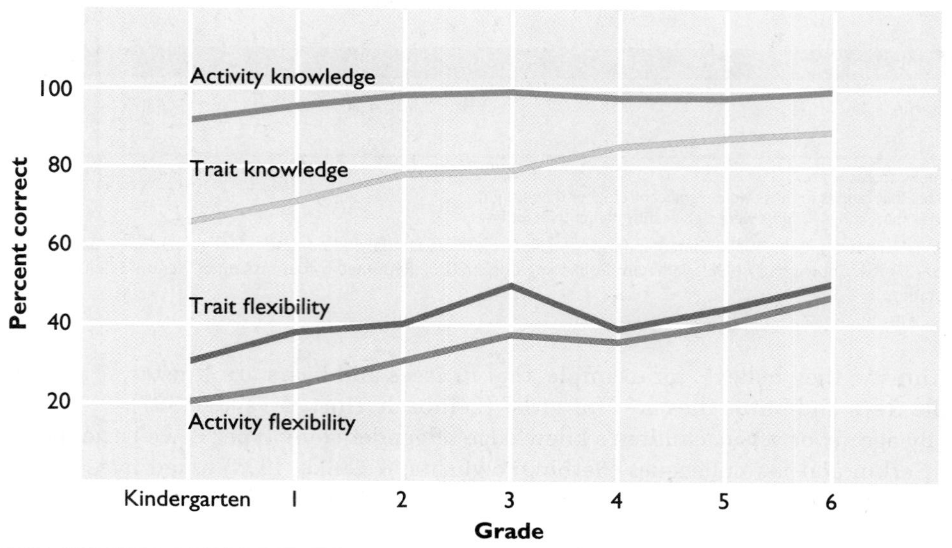

feel they have to encourage that conformity as well. Do adolescent boys, then, become increasingly masculine and girls more feminine?

To some extent, yes, they do, particularly in the context of conventional parental influences. When parents assume traditional roles in household tasks, or when they openly encourage stereotyped chores, girls and boys do indeed assume more gender-typed roles around the house over time. Teenage girls do more of the cleaning, food preparation, and laundry, whereas boys take out the garbage, do yard work, and repair household items (Antill et al., 1996; Crouter, Manke, & McHale, 1995). Furthermore, when high school students were asked in one study to consider their "possible selves"—that is, the future roles they envisioned for themselves—girls favored the arts and communication, whereas boys favored math and science (Lips, 2004). However, other longitudinal research indicates that gender differences in some areas might actually decrease over adolescence. For example, boys and girls express differences in their feelings of math competence in elementary school, but those differences practically vanish by the senior year of high school. Similarly, sex differences in ratings of language competence diminish over the middle and high school years (Jacobs et al., 2002). Given the ambiguities in the data, perhaps the safest conclusion is that gender intensification is not a robust phenomenon (Galambos, 2004; Ruble, Martin, & Berenbaum, 2006).

Enacting Stereotypes

Given their far-reaching knowledge, to what degree do children actually enact gender stereotypes? Quite a bit, according to studies that have asked children to report how they spend their leisure time. Eight-year-old girls in one study said that they spent much more time in feminine activities, such as dance, crafts, gymnastics, and art, than in masculine activities, such as competitive sports, building, and fishing. As they grew older, however, the difference between time spent in feminine and masculine activities diminished (McHale, Shanahan et al., 2004). Boys tend to be even more stereotyped in their activities, especially when they are with other boys. In this context, they spend seven times the amount of time in masculine activities as compared with feminine ones (McHale, Kim et al., 2004). In addition, children who start out showing strong sex-typed behaviors as preschoolers continue to show these stereotyped patterns of behaviors as eight-year-olds (Golombok et al., 2008).

The strong pattern of preferring sex-typed activities breaks down under certain circumstances. Playing with a sibling of the opposite sex makes a difference (McHale, Kim et al., 2004). Culture matters, too. Perhaps the most comprehensive cross-cultural comparison of children and the factors that influence their development was conducted by Beatrice Whiting and Carolyn Pope Edwards. In their Six-Culture study, these researchers examined aggression, nurturance, help seeking, sociability, and other social behaviors in children ages three to eleven living in Kenya, Okinawa, India, the Philippines, Mexico, and the United States (Whiting & Edwards, 1988; Whiting & Whiting, 1975). The results showed that differences between boys and girls were more exaggerated in some cultures than in others; in fact, they were least pronounced for the American children in the sample. Furthermore, sex differences between males and females diminished when both boys and girls were involved in household tasks, particularly the care of younger siblings. For example, Nyansango boys in East Africa scored higher than girls on their tendency to offer help and support to others; they were also as likely as girls to retreat from aggression. Interestingly, many boys in this culture tend to babies and perform other domestic chores, tasks that encourage nurturance and collaboration.

SOCIOCULTURAL INFLUENCE

What Sex Differences Actually Exist?

In light of such durable and pervasive stereotypes about "femaleness" and "maleness," it is logical to ask whether researchers have documented actual differences in the characteristics or behaviors of females and males. For many human traits, the data show that average differences *between* the sexes are smaller than the variability in performance *within* each

Similar gender-typed behaviors have been observed in several different cultures, including Mexico, this girl's home. Women and girls are expected to participate in household tasks and the care of children. Variations in gender roles across cultures have also been observed, however, suggesting that biology alone cannot account for their occurrence.

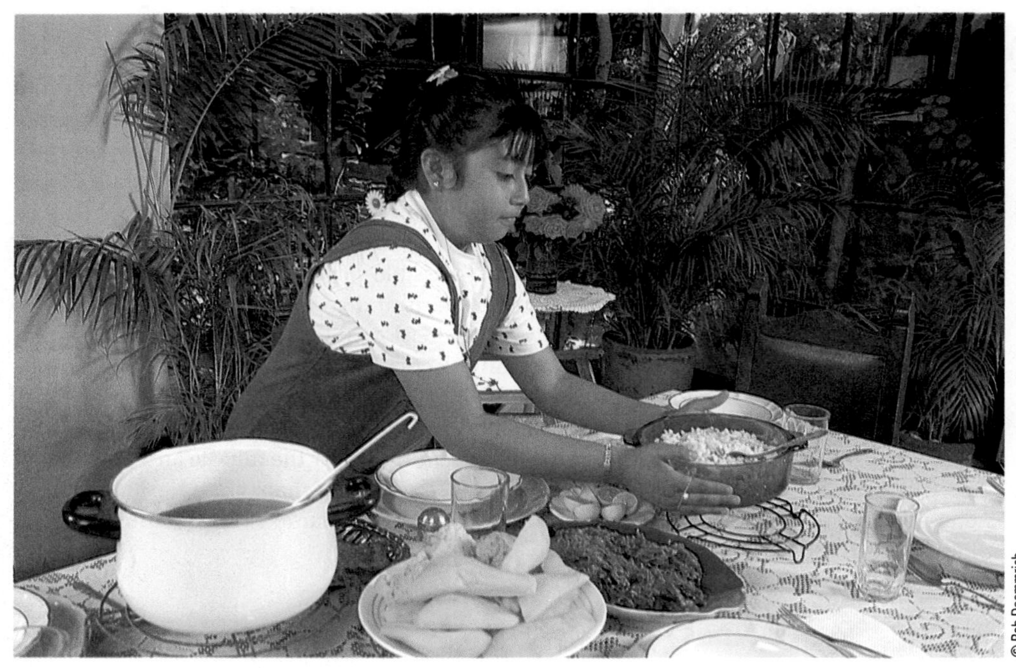

© Bob Daemmrich

sex. Nonetheless, in some domains the characteristics of females and males have been found to differ.

Physical Attributes Females and males physically differ in a number of ways, including the makeup of their chromosomes, their genitalia, and levels of certain hormones. Females are physically more mature at birth, whereas males show a special physical vulnerability during infancy. Compared with females, males are more likely to be miscarried, die in infancy, or develop hereditary diseases (Jacklin, 1989). Later in infancy and childhood, females walk, talk, and reach other developmental milestones earlier than males. Males, on the other hand, are more physically active and are more likely to engage in vigorous rough-and-tumble play (Pellegrini & Smith, 1998; Ruble et al., 2006). By later childhood and adolescence, females reach puberty earlier, and males develop greater height, weight, and muscle mass than females (Maccoby & Jacklin, 1974).

Cognition One aspect of cognition for which males and females have been thought to differ is in verbal abilities. The popular belief has been that girls are more skilled than boys at verbal tasks, a belief that was modestly substantiated by an early review of the relevant research (Maccoby & Jacklin, 1974). Meta-analyses of cognitive sex differences, however, indicate only small sex differences in verbal skills favoring females (Feingold, 1988; Hyde & Linn, 1988). Females have a slight advantage on tests that measure reading comprehension, spelling, word meaning, or grammar (Feingold, 1993; Halpern, 1997), but most researchers agree that the differences are not large enough to warrant much notice.

Similarly, researchers examining data available in two major studies involving sixty-nine countries and almost half a million children have found that in most countries there are negligible differences in the mathematics performance of boys versus girls (Else-Quest, Hyde, & Linn, 2010). Figure 13.2 illustrates the average magnitude of this sex difference. These researchers did find, however, that even though performance differences did not show up, boys reported more confidence, less anxiety, and more motivation in doing mathematics than girls. Results such as these point to the need to understand the social and cultural factors that sway children's thinking about mathematics.

In fact, the only notable sex difference in cognitive skills currently supported by empirical evidence involves visual-spatial abilities. Visual-spatial skills include a number

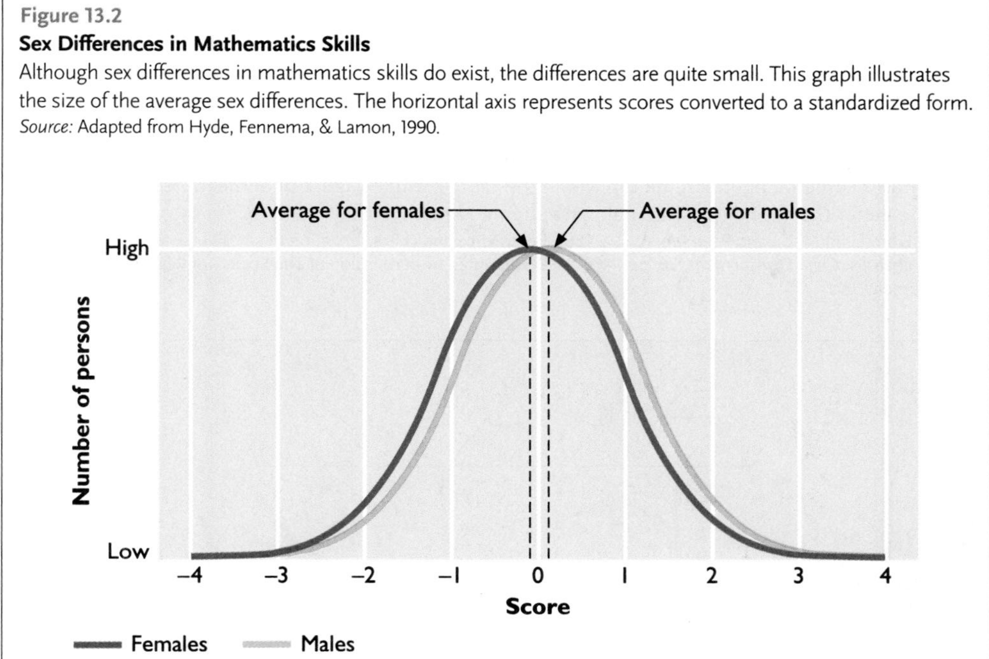

Figure 13.2
Sex Differences in Mathematics Skills
Although sex differences in mathematics skills do exist, the differences are quite small. This graph illustrates the size of the average sex differences. The horizontal axis represents scores converted to a standardized form.
Source: Adapted from Hyde, Fennema, & Lamon, 1990.

of processes, all of which require the ability to visualize and transform figures or objects in the mind. Figure 13.3 illustrates three tests of visual-spatial skills: spatial perception, mental rotation, and spatial visualization. As you can see, spatial perception tasks require participants to ignore distracting information to locate horizontal and vertical orientation. Mental rotation tasks demand that participants transform two- and three-dimensional figures "in their heads." Spatial visualization tasks require them to analyze relationships among different spatial representations.

In general, results indicate no sex differences on spatial visualization tasks. Males do, however, show superior performance on mental rotation and, to a lesser extent, spatial perception (the tasks depicted in the middle and top portions of Figure 13.3, respectively) (Linn & Peterson, 1985, 1986; Voyer, Voyer, & Bryden, 1995). Habituation experiments show that sex differences in mental rotation skills are evident in infants as young as three to five months of age (Moore & Johnson, 2008; Quinn & Liben, 2008). For example, males are more likely to show shorter looks to a novel rotation of a familiar stimulus than to a novel mirror image of that stimulus whereas girls are likely to look about equally at both of these stimuli. However, the magnitude of sex differences in this domain increases with age (Voyer et al., 1995).

Social Behaviors Researchers who have examined the results of hundreds of studies of social behaviors and personality characteristics have concluded that few actual sex differences exist in the area of social behaviors (Feingold, 1994a; Maccoby & Jacklin, 1974). Although average scores of boys and girls consistently differ in some areas, it is also true that the performance of children within each sex shows considerable variability.

One of the most consistent findings in the research on sex differences is that, beginning in the preschool years, males are more aggressive than females. They engage in more rough-and-tumble play, display more physical aggression, try to dominate peers, and subsequently display more antisocial behaviors than girls (Archer, 2004; Card et al., 2008; Loeber & Hay, 1997). Meta-analyses substantiate that sex differences in aggression are greatest among preschoolers and decrease through the college years (Eagly & Steffen, 1986; Hyde, 1984, 1986). Even though males generally are more aggressive than females, however, the magnitude of the sex difference varies as a function of where the aggression occurs and the type of aggression being measured. The largest sex differences are found in naturalistic settings, such as playgrounds, and when physical aggression is being mea-

Figure 13.3

Sex Differences in Visual-Spatial Skills

Tests of visual-spatial skills typically assess spatial perception (top), mental rotation ability (middle), or spatial visualization (bottom). In the top panel, participants are asked to indicate which bottle has a horizontal water line. In the middle panel, participants must identify the two responses that depict rotated versions of the standard. In the bottom panel, participants are asked to identify the simple geometric figure on the top within the more complex figure underneath. Generally, males perform better than females on spatial perception and mental rotation tasks.

Source: From Linn, M. C., and Peterson, A. C. (1988). Emergence and characterization of sex difference in spatial ability: A meta-analysis. *Child Development, 56,* pp. 1479–1498. Reprinted by permission of The Society of Research for Child Development, Inc.

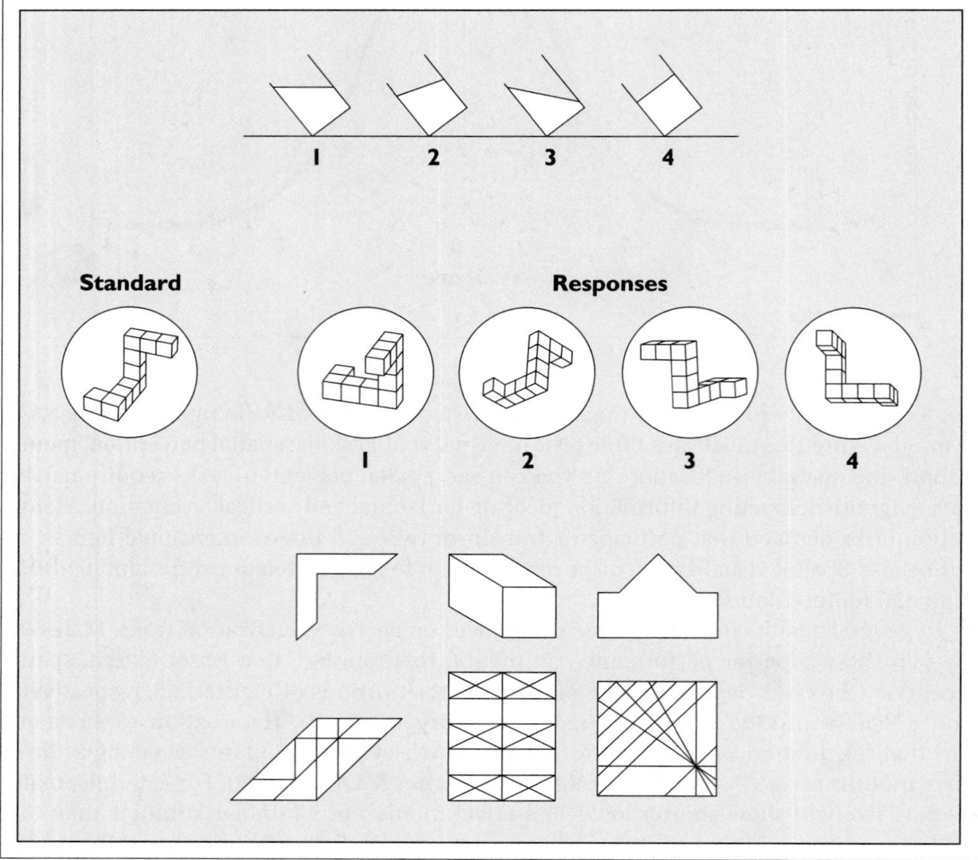

sured. Conclusions about sex differences in aggression must be tempered by how this construct is defined, however. When aggression is described as an attempt to harm another person through manipulation, gossip, or excluding peers from a social group (called *indirect* or *relational aggression,* as we saw in Chapter 12), boys and girls are found to be equally aggressive (Card et al., 2008).

Other sex differences occur in the verbal and nonverbal behaviors that boys and girls use as they participate in social communication. Boys generally issue more directive statements (e.g., "Put that block over here!"), attempt to gain the floor, and engage in one-upmanship as they speak. Girls, on the other hand, tend to verbally reinforce their conversation partners and follow the ongoing themes of conversations (Carli & Bukatko, 2000). Girls are especially likely to display these affiliative behaviors when they are interacting with other girls (Strough & Berg, 2000). Girls also display more social smiles and gazing than boys do, especially in late adolescence (Eisenberg & Lennon, 1983; Hall & Halberstadt, 1986).

Emotions To some degree, girls show a heightened sensitivity to emotions compared with boys. For example, female children and adults from widely varying cultures

© iStockphoto.com/yellowsarah

One of the most consistent sex differences is the tendency for boys to display more rough-and-tumble play and physical aggression than girls, especially during the preschool years. In the domain of relational aggression, however, boys and girls are equally aggressive.

are better than males at identifying the positive and negative emotions displayed on faces (Hall, 1984). Moreover, girls tend to display more positive and negative emotions themselves (Casey, 1993). Females also show more anxieties and worrying about social and problem-solving situations than do males (Block, 1983; LaGreca & Lopez, 1998; Silverman, LaGreca, & Wasserstein, 1995). Such findings must be interpreted with caution, however, because females may simply be more likely than males to report their feelings and emotional states. The case of empathy provides a good example of this problem. Females report that they are more empathic and cry more than males do, but no sex differences emerge when physiological or unobtrusive measures are used to assess empathy (Eisenberg & Lennon, 1983).

In addition, some researchers have found sex differences in self-esteem. Surveys of middle-class girls indicate that, when they reach adolescence, girls report a decline in their feelings about their self-worth (American Association of University Women, 1992). Other research, however, indicates that the size of the difference in self-esteem between boys and girls is generally small (Kling et al., 1999) and that there is more variability in self-esteem within groups of boys and girls than there is between them (Eccles et al., 1999).

RISK | RESILIENCE

Perhaps of greatest concern is the fact that, beginning in adolescence, girls show a sharp rise in the rates of depression they experience compared with boys (see Chapter 11, "Emotion"); by late adolescence, they are twice as likely as boys to be depressed. According to Susan Nolen-Hoeksma, these findings can be understood as the result of several factors that girls experience to a greater degree than boys: greater exposure to stressful life events (e.g., sexual abuse), greater biological responses to stress, and coping styles that involve focusing inward on feelings of distress (Nolen-Hoeksma, 2001). Because adolescence is the time during which we usually begin to see this gender difference, researchers are trying to understand how the complex changes that occur at this developmental stage might be responsible.

Sex Differences in Perspective

Perhaps because of our tendency to think in terms of gender stereotypes, we might assume sex differences will be numerous. In fact, research on actual sex differences indicates that the behavior of people in general shows great variability and that males and females often are more alike than different. If the research indicates more similarities than differences between males and females, why do stereotypical beliefs persist? One explanation may be that we notice, and therefore retain, our beliefs when boys and girls display behaviors consistent with stereotypes. In contrast, when a girl or a boy behaves in a manner inconsistent with a stereotype, we ascribe this pattern to an individual difference. Thus, when a boy fights (a stereotypically masculine activity), we say that "boys will be boys." But when he cooks and helps around the house in stereotypically feminine tasks, we comment on how "helpful" (not how "feminine") he is compared with other boys his age. Perhaps, too, stereotypes result from the tendency of children (and adults) to form cognitive categories of social groups (Martin, 1991). On seeing one similarity among people in a group (for example, in terms of physical characteristics), we may be tempted to conclude that they resemble one another in other ways, too.

For Your Review and Reflection

- What are the characteristics associated with masculine and feminine stereotypes?
- What do cross-cultural studies reveal about the nature of gender stereotypes?
- How do children's concepts of gender stereotypes change with age?
- What actual sex differences exist in the physical, cognitive, and social domains?
- Why do you think gender is such a salient social category in many cultures?

Theories of Gender-Role Development

What are the origins of sex differences in behavior? Even though contemporary research shows that actual sex differences in behavior are relatively few, boys and girls can still show different profiles in some domains of behavior. Most researchers acknowledge that a complex interplay of biology, socialization, and the child's understanding underlies this process, leading some to argue that the best overarching theoretical approach to apply might be a dynamic systems model (Martin & Ruble, 2010). That is, different influences on the emergence of gender roles may have their most pronounced impact at different times in development, and factors both internal and external to the individual interact in mutually influential ways to produce the behaviors and cognitions we see in boys and girls. Here we explore the contributions of some of these factors to gender-role development.

NATURE & NURTURE

Contributions of Biology

The role of biology in accounting for sex differences focuses largely on the influence of chromosomes, hormones, and the structure of the brain on behavior. These factors often work in ways that illustrate the complex interactions of biological systems to produce sex-differentiated behaviors.

As we saw in Chapter 3, the presence of an X or a Y sex chromosome begins a complex process that leads to sexual differentiation. Between six and twelve weeks after conception, the XY chromosomal configuration leads to the development of testes and the secretion of a class of male hormones called **androgens**, a process that results in further sexual differentiation. The penis and scrotum develop in response to the metabolism of *testosterone,* an androgen that is actually present in both sexes but in greater amounts in males (Whalen, 1984). Similarly, new research is suggesting that messages initiated by a gene located on chromosome X may set in motion the development of female structures including the ovaries (Ottolenghi et al., 2007). These differences in biological structures form the bases by which a child is labeled "boy" or "girl," the categorization of biological sex.

androgen Class of male or masculinizing hormones.

Hormones and Behavior Prenatal exposure to hormones, particularly androgens, influences the developing fetus in ways that may have an impact on biology and, perhaps, postnatal behavior. Most important for our discussion, androgens influence the developing organization of the central nervous system and the brain (Gorski, 1980; MacLusky & Naftolin, 1981; Overman et al., 1997). Hormone-related sex differences in the central nervous system may, in turn, have important influences on behavior and abilities.

Take the example of aggression. Explanations of sex differences in aggression from a biological perspective have relied largely on experiments in which androgens were administered systematically to female animals during prenatal development. The animal studies show that these hormonally treated females subsequently display increased aggressive behaviors, such as threats and rough-and-tumble play, compared with normally developing females. These findings have been replicated in rats, monkeys, and a number of other species (Goy, 1970; Parsons, 1980).

Although this type of evidence implies a causal link between male hormones and aggression, some controversy concerning the relationship exists (Tieger, 1980). First, although hormones have been shown to precede and presumably influence certain behaviors, such as aggression, those behaviors may themselves have an impact on hormone levels. That is, levels of hormones, including testosterone, can also change *in response to* changes in the environment. Among nonhuman males, for example, increases in androgen levels frequently follow, rather than precede, an aggressive encounter (Hood et al., 1987). Thus, the link between aggression and levels of androgens is not unidirectional, and it is difficult to make causal statements. Second, because human beings have a nervous system that differs in important ways from those of other species—particularly in the size of the cortex, which directs voluntary behavior—it is not clear that findings from animal studies can be generalized to humans (Fausto-Sterling, 1992). Nevertheless (and still keeping the aforementioned cautions in mind), the data from recent studies with humans show that the more testosterone women had in their bloodstream during pregnancy, the more likely their daughters and sons were to show preferences for masculine activities when they were preschoolers. In contrast, social factors such as parental sex-role beliefs did not predict these girls' behaviors (Auyeung et al., 2009; Hines et al., 2002).

INTERACTION AMONG DOMAINS

atypical development | Hormonal Disorders in Children

Among humans, there are several conditions in which genetic males or females may be exposed to a hormonal environment that is not typical for their sex. One such disorder is *congenital adrenal hyperplasia (CAH)*, a condition that occurs in about 1 in 15,000 births (Nimkarn & New, 2010). This genetic disorder causes a deficiency in the production of adrenal steroids, with the result that high levels of androgens begin to be produced during the prenatal period. If the child is a genetic female, for example, she will be born with masculinized genitalia. Usually her physical appearance is surgically corrected, hormone therapy is begun to regulate the levels of androgens circulating in her body, and the child is raised as a girl. Even following treatment, however, CAH girls have been found to show many behavioral patterns that are "typical" of boys. They prefer toys geared for boys, like rough-and-tumble play, and show enhanced visual-spatial skills (Collaer & Hines, 1995; Hampson, Rovet, & Altmann, 1998).

Among boys, a failure of androgen to bind with its receptors can result in *androgen insensitivity (AI) syndrome*. Because the boy is born with female-looking genitalia, he is usually raised as a girl; the disorder is typically discovered at puberty, when menstruation fails to begin (Breedlove, 1994). These children commonly show "female" play interests and visual-spatial skills that are poorer than those of normal females who served as controls (Collaer & Hines, 1995).

It is tempting to conclude from these hormonal disorders that biological factors are responsible for sex differences in patterns of social behaviors and cognitive skills. CAH girls do, in fact, have masculine-typed behaviors and were exposed to unusually high levels of androgens even though they were later socialized as girls. AI boys have lower levels of androgens and, even though they are socialized as girls, their performance on some cognitive tasks is actually lower than that of the average female. Thus, it is difficult to argue simply for the effect of socialization on their behavior. At the same time, studies of androgenized girls can be difficult to interpret because parents were aware of their daughters' masculinized appearance at birth and may have tolerated or even encouraged more "boylike" behaviors. Moreover, their enhanced visual-spatial skills may be the result of their masculine play styles rather than hormone levels per se (Liben & Bigler, 2002).

Cases of ambiguous biological sex demonstrate very clearly the complexities involved in discussing concepts of gender. That is, even though an XX or XY genotype may lay out a blueprint for individuals to become either males or females, the phenotype may not always express that "either-or" pattern. What other complexities arise as you think about the consequences of ambiguous sex for gender-typed behaviors or even for sexual orientation?

Brain Lateralization A second way in which biology can influence sex differences in behavior is through the organization and functions of the brain. A prominent biological explanation for sex differences in visual-spatial skills involves the process known as *lateralization of the brain.* During the course of development, as we saw in Chapter 5, "Brain, Motor Skill, and Physical Development," the two halves of the brain become increasingly specialized to handle different types of information, such as speech perception and speech production. According to one version of the lateralization hypothesis, girls' brains mature more quickly and lateralize earlier than boys'. Because verbal skills are thought to develop sooner than visual-spatial skills, and because rapid maturation of the brain is assumed to produce less eventual lateralization, the verbal skills of girls are presumed to be more evenly distributed across the hemispheres. Verbal processing in the right and left hemispheres, in turn, interferes with the visual-spatial processing that usually takes place predominantly in the right hemisphere. Because lateralization takes longer in boys, their cerebral hemispheres are thought to become more specialized than girls'. The net result is that their visual-spatial skills are stronger. Some research evidence confirms that children (regardless of sex) who mature early score better on verbal tasks than on spatial tasks, whereas the reverse pattern holds for late maturers (Waber, 1976).

Before we accept the lateralization hypothesis, however, we should note that there are also nonbiological explanations of sex differences in visual-spatial skills. One such explanation relies on the contrasting play experiences of boys and girls. According to this formulation, stereotypically masculine play activities, such as using building blocks or video games, facilitate the development of visual-spatial skills in boys (Block, 1983; Greenfield, 1994). Evidence for this explanation was found in a study in which ten- to eleven-year-old boys and girls were given practice in playing either a visual-spatial or verbal video game. The results showed that both boys and girls who played the visual-spatial game improved in their visual-spatial skills, whereas those who played the word game did not improve (Subrahmanyam & Greenfield, 1994). Thus, sex-typed play activities may account, at least in part, for sex differences in visual-spatial skills.

Social Cognitive Theory

One of the primary mechanisms accounting for sex differences in behavior, social cognitive (and before them, social learning) theorists maintain, is sex-differentiated treatment of boys and girls. According to this position, boys and girls are reinforced and punished differentially for specific behaviors, which leads them to behave in sex-typed ways. Girls, for example, may be rewarded for playing with dolls and punished for climbing trees, whereas boys may receive the opposite treatment. Thus, because children are motivated to seek reinforcement and avoid punishment, they will behave in a sex-typed fashion.

Children attend both to the consequences of their own behavior and to the consequences others face for their behavior. In fact, imitation, or modeling, may be an even more powerful means by which children learn gender roles. By observing the experiences of other people, children develop expectations for reinforcement and punishment of their own behavior. These expectations may influence their behavior as strongly as the actual experiences of reward or punishment do (Bandura, 1969, 1977a). Children have numerous opportunities to observe models behaving in gender-stereotypic ways in the home, in the outside world, and in the media. Studies show that gender stereotypes are frequently evident in television, video games, the Internet, and children's literature (Ruble et al., 2006; Signorielli, 2001). They also show that, within families, women still do the bulk of such household tasks as cooking and cleaning (Coltrane, 2000). Each time a child sees that Dad fixes things around the house and Mom does most of the cooking and cleaning, or that most little boys play baseball and little girls play house, she is adding to her storehouse of sex-typed behaviors.

© Michael Newman/PhotoEdit

According to social learning theory, a powerful vehicle for the transmission of gender roles is imitation. Parents can be especially potent models for gender-typed behaviors.Thus the roles they take on in the household, as well as their attitudes and beliefs, can have an impact on the gender-role development of their children.

Several factors influence whether children will imitate the sex-typed behaviors of others. Albert Bandura and other researchers who take a social cognitive view have proposed that children's *attention* to models in the first place is influenced by both the sex of the model and the **sex typicality** of the model's behavior, that is, how characteristic it is of the model's own sex (Bandura, 1977a; Bandura & Bussey, 2004; Perry & Bussey, 1979). According to this hypothesis, boys would, in general, be more likely than girls to attend to the behavior of male models, although they would be less likely to attend to a male model who was exhibiting "feminine" behavior. The prediction that individuals will pay greater attention to same-sex models is based on the notion that observation of same-sex models should provide children with greater information about potential consequences for their own behavior. In addition, Bandura suggests, children *recognize* that certain behaviors are sex-typed, especially as they observe the frequency with which males and females, as a group, perform certain behaviors. Finally, Bandura (1977a) proposes that *motivational* factors, such as reward seeking and attempts to retain a sense of mastery, will influence behavior in a variety of realms. As children grow older, they rely less on others to regulate their behavior and more on *self-regulation,* based on personal standards of gender-appropriate behavior (Bandura, 1986).

INTERACTION AMONG DOMAINS

Research has supported several of the predictions of social cognitive theory. Children are indeed more likely to imitate same-sex than other-sex models (Bussey & Bandura, 1984; Bussey & Perry, 1982). Thus, same-sex parents, peers, and characters in the media can be powerful influences on the child. In addition, other studies have found that children are more likely to imitate models who behave in sex-typical ways than models who behave in sex-atypical ways (Perry & Bussey, 1979). Moreover, the amount of time children spend in gendered environments does predict their tendency to act in gender-stereotyped ways (McHale et al., 2009). Finally, self-regulation of sex-typed behavior does seem to increase with development, as a study by Kay Bussey and Albert Bandura (1992) shows. Two- to four-year-olds privately rated how they would feel if they played with a series of toys, some of which were masculine (for example, a dump truck), some feminine (for example, a baby doll), and some neutral (for example, a xylophone). As Figure 13.4 shows, younger children expressed relatively neutral self-evaluations regarding playing with masculine and feminine toys. Older children, in contrast, indicated more positive self-evaluations when visualizing themselves playing with toys geared for their own sex.

sex typicality Extent to which a behavior is usually associated with one sex as opposed to the other.

Figure 13.4

Self-Evaluations During Same-Sex Activities

Two- and four-year-olds rated how they would feel while playing with masculine, feminine, or neutral toys. The higher the score, the more favorable the self-evaluation. As the graph indicates, younger children, especially girls, gave relatively neutral self-evaluations for playing with masculine and feminine toys. In contrast, older children said they would feel better about themselves when they played with same-sex toys.

Source: Adapted from Bussy, K. and Bandura, A. (1992). Self-regulatory mechanisms governing gender development. *Child Development, 63,* p. 1243. Copyright © 1992 The Society for Research in Child Development, Inc. Used with permission.

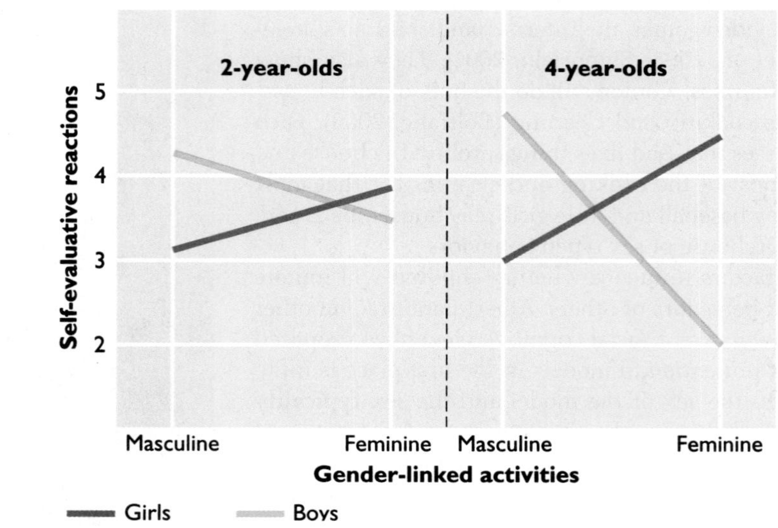

Social cognitive theory makes an important contribution to our understanding of gender-role development in that it provides a way for us to understand how broader societal beliefs and values are transmitted to individual children. As Bussey and Bandura (1999) state, labeling boys as boys and girls as girls would have very little consequence if there were no social repercussions to acting in masculine and feminine ways.

Cognitive-Developmental Theories

INTERACTION AMONG DOMAINS

Cognitive-developmental theories focus on the ways children understand gender roles, in general, and themselves as males or females, in particular. In cognitive-developmental theories, *gender* is emphasized as a conceptual category, a way of classifying people on the basis of their overt appearance or behaviors.

CONTINUITY | DISCONTINUITY

Kohlberg's Cognitive-Developmental Theory Lawrence Kohlberg (1966) proposed that gender roles emerge as a consequence of stagelike developments in cognition. The most basic of these cognitive milestones is acquisition of **gender identity**, the knowledge that self and others are female or male. This concept, which is acquired between ages two and three years, is crucial to later gender-role development because it provides a basic categorizing principle with which children begin to divide the world. After acquiring gender identity, around their fourth birthday, children develop **gender stability**, a sense that gender does not change over time. Children who have acquired gender stability recognize that they were born one sex and will grow up to be a member of that same sex. Despite this knowledge, however, they may not yet be aware of the fact that genitalia determine biological sex. Rather, children assume external factors (such as clothing or hair length) are the determinants of sex. Thus, a young boy may believe he was a baby boy and will grow up to be a "daddy" (gender stability) but only if his behavior and physical characteristics (such as hair length)

gender identity Knowledge, usually gained by age three years, that one is male or female.

gender stability Knowledge, usually gained by age four years, that one's gender does not change over time.

remain masculine. By age six, most children acquire **gender constancy**, the awareness that changes in external characteristics, behaviors, or desires do not lead to a change in biological sex. Thus, a boy may wear a dress and a girl may play with toy soldiers without altering their respective biological sexes. For Kohlberg, the acquisition of gender constancy marks the child's mature awareness of the concept of gender differentiation.

Because children value both their own sex and themselves, they are motivated to behave in a gender-typical fashion. From Kohlberg's perspective, cognitive development facilitates **self-socialization** among children. Kohlberg believed that, once children attain gender constancy, they are internally motivated by their positive self- and same-sex evaluations to behave in a manner consonant with their conceptions of what is sex appropriate. External motivators (such as reinforcements and punishments) are of minimal importance in the process of self-socialization.

Research has confirmed that children progress from attaining gender identity to gender stability and, finally, gender constancy from about two to nine years of age (Fagot, 1985; Slaby & Frey, 1975; Ruble et al., 2007). This trend appears among children from several cultures, including Argentina, Belize, Kenya, Nepal, and American Samoa (DeLisi & Gallagher, 1991; Munroe, Shimmin, & Munroe, 1984). At about eighteen months of age, children indicate some knowledge of gender categories by matching up the faces and voices of adult males and females (Poulin-Dubois, Serbin, & Derbyshire, 1998). Between ages two and three, most children are able to label themselves as male or female (Huston, 1985). Once children apply gender labels correctly to themselves and others—in some children as early as the months preceding age two years—they typically also start to engage in more gender-stereotyped play (Zosuls et al., 2009).

How does gender identity develop? Perhaps parents and others provide this information directly by saying things to their young children such as "There's another little boy just like you" or "Be a good girl now, won't you?" Beverly Fagot's research also shows that children who are adept at using gender labels tend to have mothers who engage in sex-typed play with their children and espouse traditional beliefs about gender roles themselves (Fagot, Leinbach, & O'Boyle, 1992). Many researchers contend, however, that the messages about gender roles are so clear and pervasive in our society that, even aside from the role parents may play, children cannot help but notice them and categorize themselves as males or females.

Perhaps the biggest contribution of Kohlberg's theory is in the claim that attaining gender constancy has organizing effects on the child's subsequent gendered behaviors. Does this hypothesis stand up to research? A study conducted by Diane Ruble and her colleagues shows that as children are building concepts of gender stability, from ages three through five years, their belief in rigid sex roles also increases. However, once children attain a mature understanding of the constancy of gender, their sex-role beliefs actually become more flexible. That is to say, once children comprehend that gender is not defined merely by superficial factors such as how one dresses or acts, they are more willing to tolerate violations of gender-role norms. Children now understand that the "essence" of the boy who behaves in gender-atypical ways is still male and likewise for girls (Ruble et al., 2007).

The concept of gender identity is actually more complicated than the above description suggests. In the middle childhood years, children begin to think about *gender typicality,* the degree to which they conform to society's expectations about boys and girls. They also make evaluative judgments about the extent to which they feel content about their assigned gender. Research has shown that the degree to which children view themselves as compatible with their gender is related to psychological adjustment. Preadolescents who express contentment with their own gender and see themselves as typical for their sex have higher self-esteem, for example (Egan & Perry, 2001). When preteens score low on measures of gender typicality, however, they are at risk for low self-esteem in later years. These children are also more likely to experience internalizing problems, such as depression and anxiety, if they feel pressured to conform to gender expectations for boys and girls (Yunger, Carver, & Perry, 2004).

RISK | RESILIENCE

gender constancy Knowledge, usually gained around age six or seven years, that one's gender does not change as a result of alterations in appearance, behaviors, or desires.

self-socialization Children's tendency to seek out information about gender and comply with norms for gendered behavior once they have achieved an understanding of the concept of gender.

Some preadolescents also begin to question their identities as heterosexual individuals. They may be unsure of whether they will get married, have a family, take on traditional parental roles, or fall in love with a member of the opposite sex. Children who express these ideas tend to feel subsequent distress about their relationships with peers, although these effects are not necessarily very large. Perhaps the most important point is that, for some children, ideas about the nature of the "sexual self" begin to take shape prior to adolescence, contrary to what many researchers had previously thought (Carver, Egan, & Perry, 2004). For thirteen- to fifteen-year-olds who report attraction to members of the same sex, though, risks for depression, low self-esteem, and poor school performance start to become apparent (Bos et al., 2008).

RISK | RESILIENCE

Gender Schema Theory Another influential cognitive-developmental view is *gender schema theory* (Bem, 1981; Martin & Halverson, 1981, 1987). Like Kohlberg's theory, gender schema theory stresses the importance of the acquisition of gender identity and children's intrinsic motivations to behave in a gender-typical manner. Unlike Kohlberg's theory, however, gender schema theory places little stress on the attainment of gender constancy; rather, it focuses on how children's active construction of gender knowledge influences their behavior (Bem, 1981; Martin & Halverson, 1987; Signorella, 1987).

Carol Martin and Charles Halverson (1981) proposed that children first acquire gender identity and then, in their attempts to create order in their social worlds, begin to construct two **gender schemas**, or cognitive organizing structures for information relevant to gender. The first one, the *same-sex/opposite-sex schema,* refers to the child's knowledge of one sex or the other. This is a fairly primitive cognitive structure composed largely of gender stereotypes, such as "boys fix cars" and "girls sew." Children also begin to develop a second, more elaborate gender schema about behaviors relevant to their own sex. This *own-sex schema* provides a basis for guiding children's behavior. Thus, even though both boys and girls know that girls sew, girls are more likely to be motivated to learn to sew, whereas they may not want to learn how to fix a car. Researchers have confirmed that children explore and prefer neutral objects labeled as intended for their own sex more than they do objects labeled for the other sex. Moreover, up to one week later, children remember more details about the "same-sex" objects than they do about the "other-sex" objects, even when they are offered a reward for remembering details (Bradbard et al., 1986; Martin, Eisenbud, & Rose, 1995).

According to Martin and Halverson (1981), children's gender schemas serve as a potent means of organizing information about their social worlds. Some children tend to be *gender schematic*; that is, they possess a strong gender schema, exhibit more consistent sex typing in their behavior, and process information along gender lines. In contrast, children who are *gender aschematic* possess a weaker gender schema, are less sex typed behaviorally, and focus their attention on aspects of information that are not related to gender. Gender-schematic children often distort information according to their beliefs about gender and are unlikely to remember events that are inconsistent with those beliefs. For example, gender-schematic children find it difficult to remember information about pictures of people engaged in sex-atypical activities, such as a boy playing with a doll, whereas they can easily remember information about people engaged in sex-typical activities, such as a girl playing with a tea set (Signorella, 1987; Welch-Ross & Schmidt, 1996). These effects are apparent as early as age twenty-five months, at least among boys (Bauer, 1993). Even more dramatic is the finding that children distort stereotype-inconsistent information by actually changing the sex of the person engaged in the sex-atypical behavior. Gender-schematic children who see a picture of a boy playing with a doll are more likely to remember seeing a picture of a girl playing with a doll than a picture of a boy playing with a gender-typical toy (Carter & Levy, 1988).

NATURE & NURTURE

Why do many children become gender schematic? According to Bem (1983), it depends on the extent to which they experience gender as a relevant social category. Thus, for example, when differences between males and females are frequently pointed out to them by parents, teachers, or peers, children themselves will use gender as a way to classify social information. Furthermore, both peers and adults stress conformity to gender-typical roles, a fact that makes it difficult for most children in our society to become truly gender aschematic.

gender schema Cognitive organizing structure for information relevant to sex typing.

Gender-Role Development: Birth to 18 Years

MONTHS | YEARS

PRENATAL | BIRTH

BIRTH

Prenatal Period

- Sex chromosomes and genitalia develop.
- Sex hormones influence brain and physical development.

Birth

- Infant receives label as boy or girl.

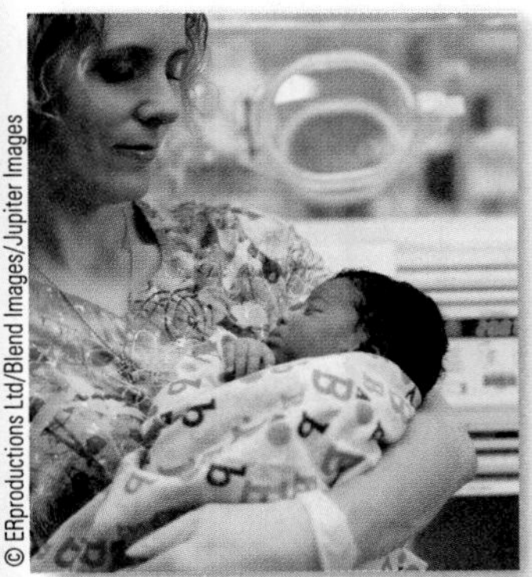

© ERproductions Ltd/Blend Images/Jupiter Images

© Indeed/Stockbyte/Jupiter Images

18 Months

- Can categorize males versus females by matching up faces and voices.

2–3 Years

- Child labels own gender.
- Identifies pictures labeled as "boy" or "girl."
- Shows knowledge of gender-role stereotypes.
- Prefers same-sex playmates and toys.

© Picture Partners/Alamy

4–5 Years

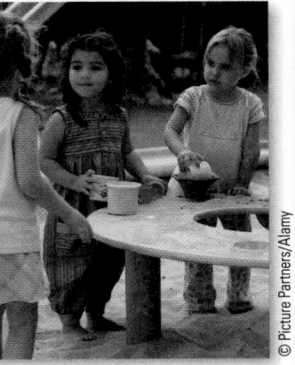

- Attains gender stability.
- Shows even stronger preferences for same-sex playmates and toys.
- Displays decline in cross-gender behavior.
- Enforces gender-role norms in peers.
- If boy, shows greater visual-spatial skills.
- If boy, shows more physical aggression.
- If girl, shows more relational aggression.

6–12 Years

- Attains gender constancy.
- Responds increasingly negatively to cross-gender play in peers.
- Shows more knowledge of and flexibility in gender-role stereotypes.
- Shows awareness of gender typicality.

13–18 Years

© PhotoAlto Agency/Jupiter Images

- Shows less interest in sex-segregated interactions.
- If girl, shows more social smiles and gazing.
- If girl, may be vulnerable to depression.
- Shows greater tolerance for sex-atypical behaviors.
- Sex differences in aggression diminish.
- May show gender intensification.

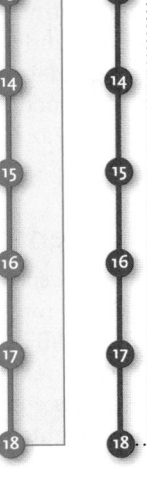

This chart describes the sequence of gender-role development based on the findings of research. Children often show individual differences in the exact ages at which they display the various developmental achievements outlined here.

To sum up, each of the preceding theories has some value for explaining the source of sex differences, many of which are outlined in the Gender Development Chronology. Biologically oriented research helps us to understand the physiological underpinnings of male and female behavior. Social cognitive theory provides a mechanism for explaining how children learn discrete aspects of sex-typical behavior. Cognitive-developmental approaches explain how children's concepts of gender become integrated in their minds. Although each theory explains a specific feature of gender-role development better than the other theories do, none of them taken alone is adequate to explain the multifaceted nature of this aspect of development.

For Your Review and Reflection

- What are the major ways in which biology is thought to influence gender-role development? What specific research findings support a biological perspective? What research findings challenge the idea that biology alone is responsible for gender-role development?
- How does social cognitive theory account for gender-role development? What research findings support the social cognitive perspective?
- What are the essential features of Kohlberg's cognitive-developmental theory of role development? What specific research findings support Kohlberg's theory?
- What are the elements of gender schema theory? What specific research findings support gender schema theory?
- Why do you think that each of these different theories of gender-role development is important to consider for our understanding of this process?
- How do these theories reflect interactions among various domains of development?

The Socialization of Gender Roles

NATURE & NURTURE

Whatever biological tendencies are associated with being a male and a female, it is worth exploring further the influences of the social environment on gender-role development and how they intersect with the child's developing cognitions about gender. Particularly if we are concerned about the gender-associated problems children face, whether it be aggression among boys or the anxieties experienced by girls, we need to understand how social experiences can promote optimal development for both sexes.

The earliest messages about the social world, of course, come from the child's parents. From the moment of birth, when parents in our culture ask, "Is it a boy or a girl?" the sex of their child is a very prominent characteristic, one that elicits specific behaviors and reactions from mother and father. As children branch out to social relationships with peers, gender-role socialization continues in very powerful ways—in the games children play, in the relationships they form, and how they react to one another's behaviors. Finally, another significant influence on gender-role development is the child's experiences in schools, in which teachers and the instructional materials they use can confirm (or disconfirm) early gender-role beliefs and behaviors.

The Influence of Parents

Traditionally, developmental scientists have believed one of the most important sources of information about gender for children is the behavior of their parents and the environment parents create (Katz, 1987). Sometimes the messages are subtle. Parents commonly provide their children with sex-differentiated toys and room furnishings (Rheingold & Cook, 1975). They buy sports equipment, tools, and vehicles for their sons, and dolls and doll furniture for their daughters. Boys' rooms typically are decorated in blue, girls' in yellow (Pomerleau et al., 1990). When parents provide boys and girls with different physical environments, they send messages that boys are indeed different from girls and set sex-related limits on the types of behavior that are acceptable and appropriate.

Another way in which parents influence their children's gender-role development is through their own general beliefs about masculine and feminine roles. Many parents believe children as young as two years differ along gender-stereotypic lines (McGuire, 1988). They report, for example, that their own sons like sports, enjoy tools, and are energetic. On the other hand, parents of girls say their daughters like to be admired, enjoy playing with dolls, and like clothes. Parents' gender beliefs are related to their children's gender beliefs (Tenenbaum & Leaper, 2002). Those beliefs are frequently translated into sex-differentiated patterns in the types of chores boys and girls are assigned to do around the house: boys take out the garbage and mow the lawn; girls do more chores within the house, such as cleaning and cooking (Goodnow, 1988; Lackey, 1989). The tendency of children to participate in household tasks associated with their gender increases in early adolescence, especially if their own parents assume traditional roles in household tasks or parents openly encourage traditional chores (Antill et al., 1996; Crouter, Manke, & McHale, 1995).

Parental Behavior Sometimes parents' messages about gender are more direct. Research shows that parents treat children differently on the basis of sex in early infancy, beginning at ages younger than those at which actual behavioral sex differences emerge (Fagot & Leinbach, 1987). Right in the first week following the birth of their child, parents of daughters describe their infants as more delicate and less strong and as having finer features than do parents of boys (Karraker, Vogel, & Lake, 1995). Adults play more roughly with a male infant, tossing him in the air and tickling him vigorously, than they do with a female infant (Huston, 1983). During infancy and childhood, girls are more likely than boys to be protected and sheltered by adults, whereas boys are given greater opportunities than girls to explore their environments (Block, 1983; Burns, Mitchell, & Obradovich, 1989). When their children are preschoolers, parents react more negatively when their daughters assert themselves than when their sons do. Fathers in particular tend to react positively when their daughters display compliant behavior and reward their sons for assertiveness (Kerig, Cowan, & Cowan, 1993). In addition, parents give boys more positive evaluations and girls more negative evaluations when children are working on solving problems (Alessandri & Lewis, 1993).

Both mothers and fathers use more emotion words when speaking with their preschool-age daughters than with their sons (Adams et al., 1995; Kuebli, Butler, & Fivush, 1995). Parents also respond positively to boys who play with blocks, manipulate objects, and engage in physical play. With girls, parents tend to encourage play that involves dolls, domestic themes, and "pretending" (Fagot & Leinbach, 1987; Farver & Wimbarti, 1995; Lindsay, Mize, & Pettit, 1997). Fathers appear to be especially concerned about what they perceive as masculinity in their sons, at least during the preschool years (Jacklin, DiPietro, & Maccoby, 1984). Such concern is often expressed in parental interviews as well as in the consistently negative manner in which many fathers respond to sex-atypical behavior in their sons.

However, a meta-analysis of 172 studies of parents' differential socialization of girls and boys suggests that we must be cautious about how much weight we give to the role of direct parental reinforcement in accounting for the various facets of gender-role development. In general, the overall impact of parental behaviors was judged to be small in most areas of socialization, including achievement expectations, dependency, and aggression. The only socialization area that showed a significant effect was parental encouragement of sex-typed activities, such as doll play for girls and tool play for boys (Lytton & Romney, 1991).

There are several ways to interpret these somewhat surprising findings. It may be that children's participation in sex-typed play is a particularly important context for acquiring well-defined ideas about masculinity and femininity. Studies show that children's activity interests and how they spend their leisure time are indeed gender-stereotyped—even more so than their beliefs about gender or their personality characteristics. Boys tend to prefer and engage in activities such as competitive sports and building, whereas girls prefer and participate in activities such as dance and writing (McHale, Crouter, & Tucker, 1999, 2001). Even at age three, girls spend more of their weekend time in socializing, personal care activities and educational activities, whereas boys engage in more video game playing

When fathers assume a greater role in parenting, children show less knowledge of stereotypes and are slower to acquire gender labels.

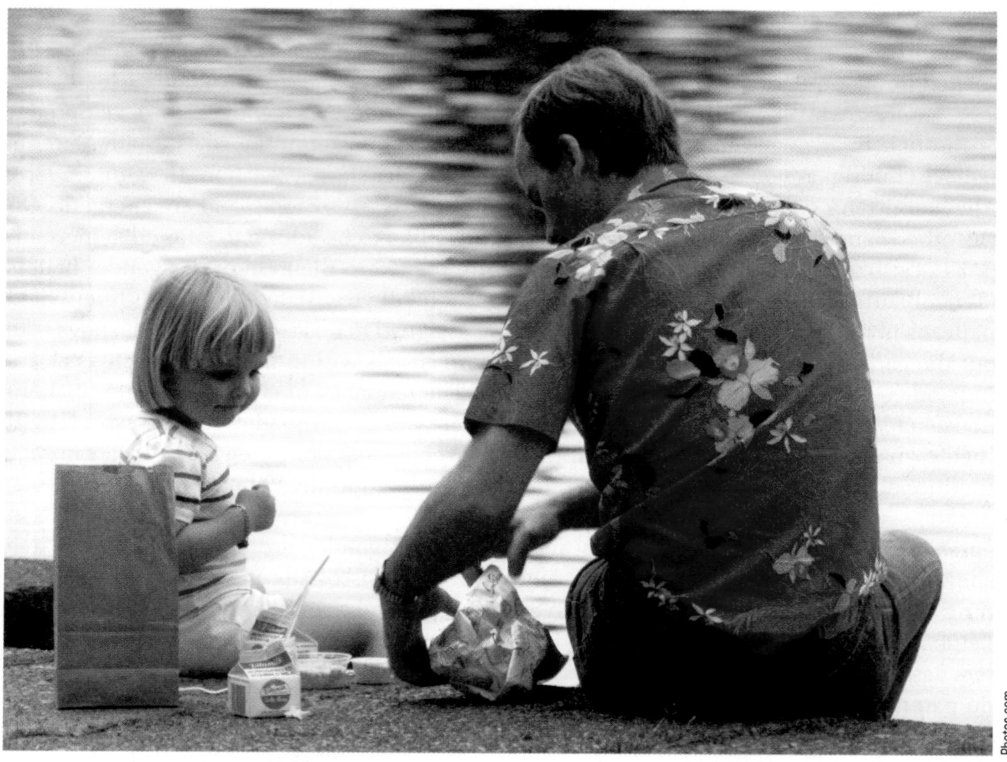

Photos.com

(Huston et al., 1999). Some of these contexts are more conducive to fostering collaboration, whereas others tend to promote competition and assertiveness (Leaper, 2000). Also important to consider is the possibility that children's gender-role socialization may be more heavily influenced by broader social forces than by parental behaviors (Harris, 1995; Martin & Ruble, 1997). For example, peer experiences and exposure to gender-typed media messages may be far more important in gender socialization.

Parents' roles in gender-role socialization may generally be more indirect but still powerful. For example, mothers in one study were observed as they spoke to their preschoolers about a picture book they were reading together. A substantial proportion of mothers were observed to make implicit references to gender by making statements like "That's a lady sewing a dress, right?" and "Can girls play football?" By highlighting gender as a social category and by contrasting male versus female roles, parents may be inadvertently sending signals about gender stereotypes to children whose minds are actively processing social information (Gelman, Taylor, & Nguyen, 2004).

Gender Roles in Nontraditional Families A series of profound changes in the traditional American family over the last several decades has had an impact on gender-role development. As we described in Chapter 11, "Emotion," mothers increasingly are employed outside the home while their children are still young. These women may be providing their children with alternative models for feminine behavior.

In general, maternal employment facilitates the development of flexibility in children's conceptions of gender roles. Children with employed mothers are more likely to believe both males and females can exhibit a wide variety of behaviors and personality characteristics than are children whose mothers are not employed outside the home. The effects on daughters of employed mothers are particularly dramatic. Daughters of mothers who work outside the home show higher levels of achievement motivation and are more likely to have personality styles that blend male-typed and female-typed traits than are the daughters of nonworking mothers (Hoffman, 1979; Ruble et al., 2006).

RISK | RESILIENCE

Psychologists are also interested in the effects of nontraditional fathers—those who take on at least equal responsibility for child care—on children's gender-role development. Children whose mothers and fathers make a deliberate effort to share parenting are slower to adopt gender labels and show less knowledge of gender stereotypes during the children's preschool years (Fagot & Leinbach, 1995). Research shows that girls in particular profit from the involvement of fathers in child-oriented activities. Elementary school–age girls whose parents were less stereotyped in their marital and child-rearing roles also showed more independence and feelings of being in control over events in their lives (Hoffman & Kloska, 1995). In another research project that included traditional parents as well as parents who shared equally in child-related responsibilities, adolescent girls from egalitarian families maintained high levels of school achievement, whereas girls from traditional families showed declines in science and mathematics achievement as they made the transition to seventh grade. Boys showed no differences in achievement associated with parenting styles (Updegraff, McHale, & Crouter, 1996).

The Influence of Peers

An extremely powerful influence on children's gender-role development is the peer group. Peer groups not only provide children with opportunities for particular kinds of play but also offer a forum in which children can learn about social behavior and social interactions by watching models and obtaining feedback about their own behaviors. Although peers influence children on a variety of social dimensions, nowhere is their influence more marked than in the area of gender-role socialization (Carter, 1987).

Early Play Patterns The influence of peers on gender-role development can be observed even among very young children. Carol Jacklin and Eleanor Maccoby (1978) observed same-sex and mixed-sex pairs of unacquainted two-year-olds to determine the influence of peers on toddlers' behavior. Children were dressed in a sex-neutral fashion (in yellow jumpsuits) and allowed to play in a room with their mothers present but nondirective. As Figure 13.5 shows, the toddlers' behavior varied as a function of the sex of their play partner even though the children were unaware of the true sex of the other child. In other words, the behaviors of the neutrally dressed children seemed to precipitate different reactions in their play partners. In general, children displayed more social behaviors, both positive overtures and negative acts, when they played with a peer of the same sex. Girls were more likely to be passive when they played with a boy peer than when they played with a girl peer. In addition, girls in girl-girl pairs exhibited greater sharing of toys and were less likely to become upset and cry than when they were in mixed-sex pairs. Finally, boys were less likely to obey a verbal prohibition from a girl than from a boy. Already at this young age, the dynamics of peer interactions were markedly influenced by the sex of the partners.

Figure 13.5

Social Behavior as a Function of the Child's Play Partner

In a study by Jacklin and Maccoby, unacquainted two-year-olds were observed as they interacted with either a same-sex or an opposite-sex partner. The amount of social behavior (both positive overtures and negative acts such as aggression) was greater when children played with a peer of the same sex.

Source: Adapted with permission from Jacklin, C. N., et al. Social behavior as a function of the child's play partner: Social behavior at 33 months. *Child Development, 49,* pp. 557–559. Copyright The Society of Research for Child Development, Inc.

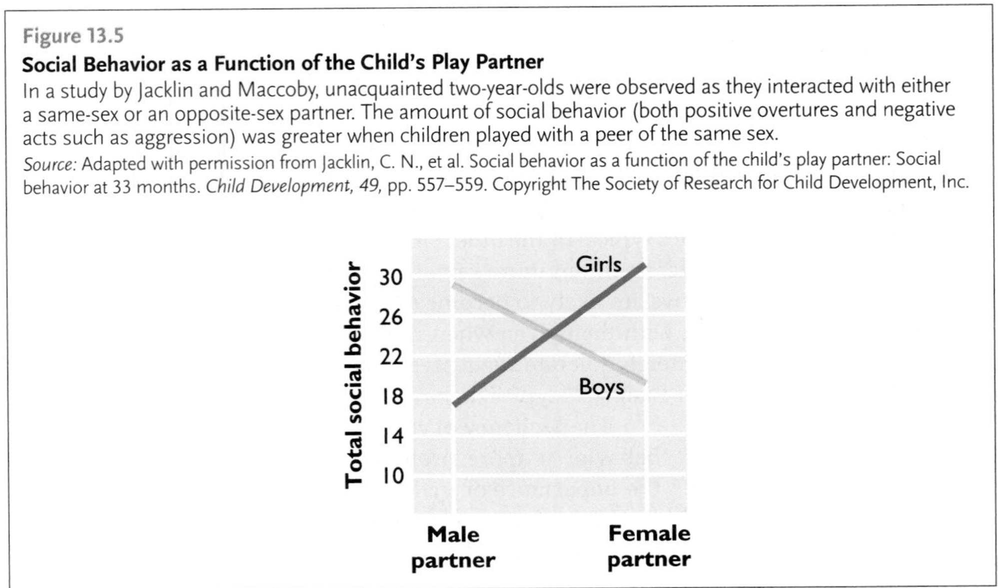

Both boys and girls may engage in cross-gender activities. However, it is usually easier for girls to cross gender boundaries than for boys; peers usually react more negatively in the latter case.

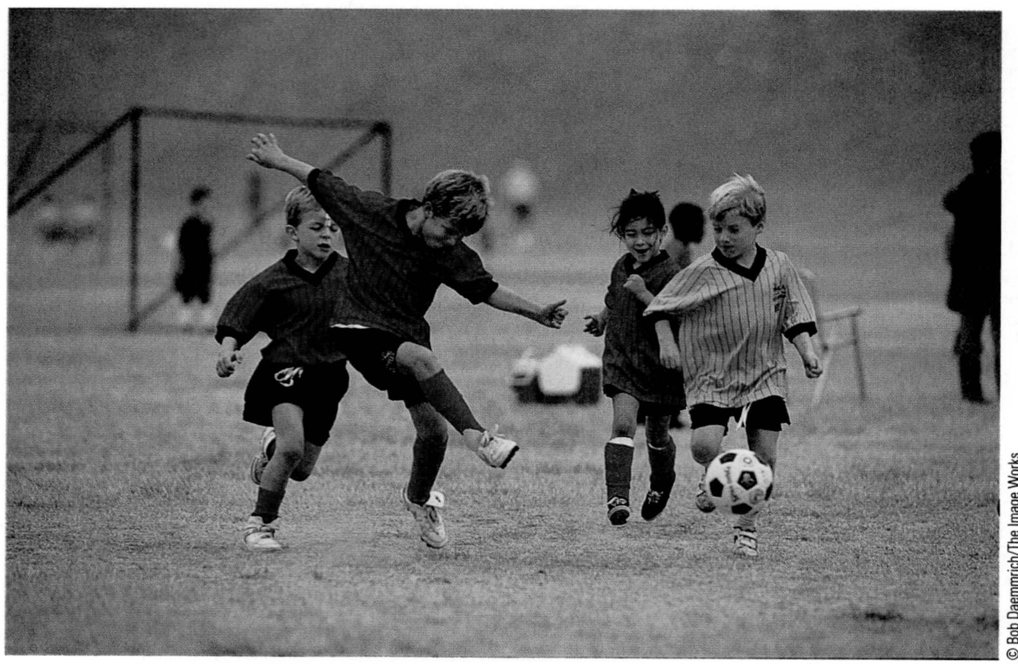

© Bob Daemmrich/The Image Works

Peer Enforcement of Gender Roles Peers continue to exert a strong influence on children's adoption of sex-typical behaviors as they begin preschool. A number of studies have shown, for example, that children respond differentially to sex-typical and sex-atypical behavior in their peers. Children may reward behavior they like by complimenting a child or by engaging in mutual play, and they may punish a behavior they do not approve of by name calling. Preschoolers and kindergartners reliably punish boys who engage in sex-atypical behavior, such as playing with dolls, while rewarding them for engaging in sex-typical behavior, such as playing with trucks (Fagot, 1977; Lamb, Easterbrooks, & Holden, 1980; Lamb & Roopnarine, 1979). In contrast, girls are rewarded for engaging in sex-typical behavior, such as playing house, but apparently they experience no consequences when they engage in sex-atypical behavior (Fagot, 1977).

The pressures the peer group exerts apparently work. Children are responsive to the positive and negative feedback they receive from their peers. They are likely to continue to engage in a sex-typical behavior in response to reinforcement and to terminate behaviors their peers punish (Lamb, Easterbrooks, & Holden, 1980). Furthermore, feedback from same-sex peers may be especially important. Beverly Fagot (1978a) found that both girls and boys age two years were more likely to continue a behavior if a same-sex peer responded positively and to discontinue a behavior if a same-sex peer reacted negatively. If the peer was of the other sex, however, the peer's feedback was largely ineffective.

Cross-Gender Behavior Some children (between 20 and 40 percent), more often girls than boys, do not respond to their peers' disapproval of sex-atypical behavior (Sandberg et al., 1993). These children exhibit **cross-gender behavior**; that is, they adopt, in whole or in part, a variety of characteristics typical of the other sex (Fagot, 1977). Cross-gender boys, for example, exhibit a strong interest in feminine games and activities and play "dress-up" in girls' clothes. Cross-gender boys are likely to become social isolates over time because their male peers refuse to interact with them even when they play in a masculine fashion, and their female peers seem to merely tolerate their presence. Cross-gender girls, in contrast, appear to suffer very little for their sex-atypical behavior, at least in the preschool years.

RISK | RESILIENCE

SOCIOCULTURAL INFLUENCE

The tendency of children to disapprove of cross-gender behavior is more pronounced in cultures that emphasize the importance of traditions and adherence to social norms (for example, Taiwan) as opposed to freedom to break from traditions and individualism, as in Israel (Lobel et al., 2001). This tendency also increases with age. When researchers

cross-gender behavior Behavior usually seen in a member of the opposite sex. Term generally is reserved for behavior that is persistently sex atypical.

interviewed kindergartners through sixth-graders to determine how these children would respond to hypothetical cases of cross-gender behavior in their peers, older children reported they would respond more negatively to cross-gender behavior than did younger children. Moreover, children stated they would respond more negatively to cross-gender behavior in their male peers than in their female peers. The degree of negativity children exhibited was particularly surprising. Only one child reported she would respond positively toward a cross-gender child, and children were virtually unanimous in their assertion that they would not want to play with a cross-gender child. Children's reports of how they would respond ranged from fairly innocuous comments (such as "I'd stay away") to statements indicating they would physically abuse cross-gender children (Carter & McCloskey, 1984).

Similar results were obtained when researchers asked preadolescents to describe the personal qualities of an actor who played a gender-inappropriate game with children of the opposite sex. If a boy actor played jump rope with a group of girls, he was viewed as significantly less popular than a female actor or a male actor playing a masculine game (Lobel et al., 1993). As we will see in Chapter 15, "Peers," popularity with peers is, in turn, associated with other significant developmental outcomes. Children who are unpopular often have low self-esteem and poor academic achievement, and they may be prone to aggression. Thus, cross-gender behavior can be stigmatizing and potentially far-reaching in its effects.

what do you think? Is Gender Identity Disorder Really a Disorder?

According to the *Diagnostic and Statistical Manual of Mental Disorders* (DSM-IV) of the American Psychiatric Association, cross-gender children may qualify for a diagnosis of *gender identity disorder* if they express a strong desire to be a member of the opposite sex or claim to be unhappy as a boy or a girl (American Psychiatric Association, 1994). Children may insist on wearing clothing or hairstyles stereotypical of the opposite sex or may display significant problems at home or school, sometimes to the extent that parents seek out professional help (Zucker & Bradley, 2000).

The main point of contention is whether gender identity disorder is a genuine problem residing within an individual or whether the problem lies in our broader society's intolerance for behaviors that violate gender boundaries. When these children experience distress, for example, is it because of some inner turmoil associated with personal adjustment issues or is it due to the highly negative reactions of peers and parents to cross-gender behaviors?

The criteria for mental disorder in the DSM-IV include an individual's experience of severe distress or increased risk of harm. Mental health professionals note that children with gender identity disorder are prone to depression and behavior problems similar to those of children with other clinical diagnoses (Zucker & Bradley, 2000). Therefore, some say that gender identity disorder is a legitimate psychiatric problem. Critics point out that gender identity disorder does not necessarily lead to adjustment problems later in adolescence and adulthood. Many of these children, for example, eventually identify themselves as homosexual, which is not a psychiatric condition in DSM-IV. Moreover, the distress children experience is not due to cross-gender behaviors—these children are perfectly happy when they perform such behaviors. It is the reactions of peers and others that cause them such great difficulty. Critics believe that gender identity disorder should be removed from the DSM-IV (Bartlett, Vasey, & Bukowski, 2000).

Research has shown that the degree to which children view themselves as compatible with their gender is indeed related to psychological adjustment. Preadolescents who express contentment with their own gender and see themselves as typical for their sex have higher self-esteem, for example (Egan & Perry, 2001). Thus, "fitting in" with one's gender is associated with indicators of mental health. However, when children with gender identity disorder report distress, the cause is usually problems with peers or unhappiness at having to stop their cross-gender behaviors, not a disturbance of gender. Also important to consider is the fact that definitions of masculinity and femininity can vary across cultures and historical times. Nancy Bartlett and her colleagues point out that, in other eras, for example, men who stayed at home with their children might have been seen as mentally ill for violating a gender norm (Bartlett et al., 2000).

Perhaps it would be helpful to conduct more longitudinal studies of cross-gender children to observe developmental changes in their adjustment, as well as the specific antecedents and consequences of their cross-gender behaviors. One recent study of girls with gender identity disorder found, for example, that very few of these individuals experienced distress as young adults (Drummond et al., 2008). What do findings such as these suggest about this controversy? What other kinds of studies might be useful in sorting out the issues relevant to considering whether gender identity disorder is really a disorder? If the problem resides in the ways that peers react to the nontraditional behaviors of some children, can those peer reactions be altered or changed in any way? Should they be?

Sex Segregation One of the things even a casual observer would notice on the typical school playground is that boys and girls tend to interact in separate groups: boys play with boys, and girls play with girls (Maccoby, 1988, 1990). This phenomenon is called **sex segregation**. In one observation of 100 children on their preschool playgrounds, four-year-olds spent three times as much of their play activity with same-sex partners as with opposite-sex partners. By age six, they spent eleven times more time with peers of the same sex (Maccoby & Jacklin, 1987). In fact, only about 10 percent of young children's peer interactions are with members of the opposite sex (Martin & Fabes, 2001). This tendency to prefer same-sex peers persists at least until early adolescence (Maccoby, 1990). Interestingly enough, when young children are asked if a boy can join a group of girls playing with dolls (or if a girl can join a group of boys playing with trucks), almost 90 percent say, "Yes" and justify their responses on moral grounds. It wouldn't be right or fair, they say, to exclude the member of the opposite sex (Killen et al., 2001). Yet, when confronted with social interactions with an opposite-sex peer, elementary school–age children express more negative emotion toward and less liking of that child (Underwood, Schockner, & Hurley, 2001). Sex segregation is a potent phenomenon in the social lives of young children.

Eleanor Maccoby (1990, 2002) believes children's experiences in same-sex groups constitute an extremely powerful socialization environment. As boys play in their characteristic rough-and-tumble fashion or in team sports and games, they develop assertive, dominance-seeking styles of interaction. In contrast, girls' groups, which are oriented toward relationships and shared intimacy, promote cooperation and mutual support as well as a tendency to preserve the cohesiveness of the group. A study of preschool and kindergarten children over a six-month period confirmed that, as children spent more time in same-sex groups, their conformity with gender-stereotyped behaviors increased. Boys who spent more time with boys became more active and rough in their play. Similarly, girls who spent more time with girls played more calmly over time and engaged in more gender-stereotyped play, such as dressing up and interacting with dolls (Martin & Fabes, 2001).

Sex segregation begins to break down as children enter adolescence and begin to think about dating (Richards et al., 1998). The pressures of heterosexual interactions, however, may enhance rather than diminish the push toward conformity with gender-role norms (Eccles, 1987; Petersen, 1980). This pattern is particularly obvious among teenage girls, many of whom abandon "tomboyish" behaviors that were acceptable during an earlier period of development (Huston & Alvarez, 1990).

Adolescent Peer Influences Peer acceptance and rejection become increasingly important during adolescence. Although sex-typing pressures remain high, popularity among adolescents of both sexes relies more on positive personality characteristics, such as leadership abilities and politeness, rather than merely the presence of sex-typed behavior (Sigelman, Carr, & Begley, 1986). Thus, the presence of cross-gender personality characteristics or behaviors may not lead to isolation from peers among older adolescents to the extent that it does for younger children (Huston & Alvarez, 1990; Katz & Ksansnak, 1994). Adolescents' greater tolerance for sex-atypical personality characteristics may reflect their increasing cognitive abilities,

INTERACTION AMONG DOMAINS

sex segregation Clustering of individuals into same-sex groups.

© iStockphoto.com/RonTech2000

Research has shown that boys typically receive more attention from teachers than girls. Teachers can promote gender equity in the classroom by calling on girls to answer questions and waiting a few moments to give girls a chance to participate.

specifically their ability to consider multiple dimensions as they make judgments about individuals, including abstract qualities such as trustworthiness or loyalty (Eccles, 1987).

The Influence of Teachers and Schools

Teachers, like peers and parents, sometimes treat children differentially according to sex, reinforce and punish sex-typed behaviors, and model sex-typical behavior for their students. Moreover, schools may foster sex typing through the teaching materials and curriculum to which children are exposed. For example, one survey of children's readers found that, although boys and girls were portrayed with almost equal frequency, girls were more often the characters in stories in need of rescue, and boys were rarely shown doing housework or displaying emotions (Purcell & Stewart, 1990).

Teacher Attitudes and Behaviors Teachers, like other adults, may express stereotypical, gender-based views about the capacities of their students. They believe female students are feminine and male students are masculine, although more experienced teachers are less likely to hold stereotyped beliefs and more likely to treat students in an egalitarian fashion than are less experienced teachers (Fagot, 1978a; Huston, 1983). When teachers are asked to nominate their best students or those with the most potential, they are more likely to nominate boys than girls. They are especially likely to name boys as most skilled in mathematics. When asked to think of students who excel in language or social skill, teachers are more likely to name girls (BenTsvi-Mayer, Hertz-Lazarowitz, & Safir, 1989). These patterns in teacher responses occur despite the fact that actual sex differences in many of these domains are minimal.

In addition, teachers respond differently to students on the basis of sex as opposed to behavior. Boys, for example, receive more disapproval from teachers than girls do during preschool and elementary school, even when boys and girls engage in similar amounts of disruptive behavior (Huston, 1983; Serbin et al., 1973). Teachers' behavior may reflect a belief that boys are more likely than girls to cause trouble in the classroom unless rules are strictly enforced (Huston, 1983). On the other hand, teachers pay more attention to a girl when she sits quietly in the front of the classroom, whereas the amount of attention paid to a boy is high regardless of where he sits (Serbin et al., 1973). Within elementary school classrooms, teachers tend to call on boys more often than girls and give them more explicit feedback regarding their answers. When girls answer, they are more likely to receive a simple acceptance from the teacher ("okay"), whereas boys tend to receive more praise, constructive criticism, or encouragement to discover the correct answer (Sadker & Sadker, 1994). Thus, boys receive more explicit academic instruction and tend to dominate classroom interactions.

As we saw in Chapter 9, "Social Cognition," teachers can influence the degree to which children pay attention to stereotypes when they highlight gender as a relevant social grouping. In one study, teachers in one set of classrooms were told to behave in ways that emphasized gender groups. For example, they used separate bulletin boards to display girls' and boys' artwork and made frequent comments such as, "All the boys should be sitting down" or "Amber, you can come up for the girls." Teachers in this group made an average of 7.2 references to gender per twenty-minute time period. Compared with a control group in which teachers were instructed to refer to children as individuals rather than according to gender, children in the "gendered" classrooms showed significant increases in stereotyping over the course of four weeks (Bigler, 1995).

Promoting Gender Equity in the Classroom

research applied to education

Now eight years old, Nicky is sitting in a circle with the other third-graders in his class, listening to Brittany read the story she wrote during Writing Workshop. The children seem captivated by her story; even the most restless among them sits quietly, eyes glued on the storyteller. When Brittany is done, Ms. Klein says, "Okay, does anyone have any questions or comments about Brittany's story? Go ahead, Brittany. You can call on someone." Hands fly up eagerly.

"Stephen," says Brittany.

"Why did you make the character live by a pond?" asks Stephen.

"Because he has a lot of animal friends that live there," she responds.

More hands churn in the air. "Nicky," she calls out next.

"Wait a minute," says Ms. Klein. "Remember our rule. You have to call on a girl next."

"Reesha," Brittany calls out.

"I like how the words you picked make me think of beautiful pictures in my head," comments Reesha.

"Thank you," responds Brittany, a little shyly.

Nicky's mother, observing all of this, thinks maybe her son feels slighted for being passed over. Later, when she asks him about this, he firmly proclaims, "All Ms. Klein is trying to do is to be fair to the boys and girls in the class. I didn't feel bad at all. I think it's the right thing to do."

Just as teacher behavior can perpetuate stereotypes, it can change sex-typing patterns among children in classroom settings. A collection of studies suggests some specific techniques teachers can use to reduce sex segregation, modify children's beliefs about gender, and promote the participation of girls in the classroom.

1. *Use reinforcement to facilitate cooperative cross-sex play.* In one study involving preschoolers and kindergartners, teachers praised children who played in mixed-sex groups by pointing out their cooperative play to the class and complimenting the children. Cross-sex play subsequently increased (Serbin, Connor, & Iler, 1979; Serbin, Tonick, & Sternglanz, 1977).
2. *Prepare lessons that explicitly allow children to question gender stereotypes about personal qualities, occupations, and activities.* Researchers in Dublin, Ireland, had student teachers present a series of lessons to children in the first through sixth grades. The lessons encouraged children to think of counterexamples to common stereotypes, for example, instances in which women show an interest in football or in which men have been observed to be warm and gentle. Discussions were supplemented by opportunities to meet people who worked in nontraditional roles, such as a male nurse and a female veterinary surgeon. In addition, children read poetry, read fairy tales, and had worksheets that brought up themes counter to traditional stereotypes. At the end of four months, children who had experienced the lessons had significantly lower stereotype scores than those in a control group (Gash & Morgan, 1993).

3. *Be conscious of the need to give girls a chance to participate.* One way to do this is to wait three to five seconds before calling on a student to answer a question. Girls, especially those who are shy or less confident, may need time to formulate their answers and decide they are willing to share them with the class. Also, do not just call on students who volunteer, because these are more likely to be boys. Teachers can even have an observer record the number of times they call on boys versus girls. Myra and David Sadker (1994) found that, when teachers saw the results of such observations, and, further, when they received training on how to be more gender equitable, girls in their elementary and secondary school classrooms became more equal partners with boys in class participation.

Student Attitudes Toward Coursework Research indicates that students, teachers, and parents alike view some academic subjects as masculine and others as feminine (Huston, 1983). As we noted earlier, mathematics is generally seen as a masculine activity, and reading is viewed as feminine (Eccles et al., 1983; Eccles, Wigfield et al., 1993; Huston, 1983; Yee & Eccles, 1988). Such sex typing is not limited to American schoolchildren. In a study of first- through fifth-grade Chinese, Japanese, and American boys and girls, the investigators found that most children believed boys are better in mathematics and girls are better at reading (Lummis & Stevenson, 1990). Moreover, boys in these three societies predicted they would do better in mathematics in high school than girls predicted they would do, although no sex differences were found in children's predictions of their future reading skills.

Society's messages about girls' mathematical abilities may be changing, however. In a study including data from children in first through twelfth grades, researchers asked children to report how competent they felt in math. Although in the early grades boys clearly felt more capable in math than girls, the gender gap in beliefs declined with age such that by twelfth grade there was virtually no difference between boys and girls. The researchers suggest that one reason for this shift may be a general societal push for girls to participate in math courses and activities (Fredricks & Eccles, 2002). Researchers have also begun to identify other factors that encourage and support girls' participation in and attitudes about math. For example, one important influence on boys, but especially on girls, is having a group of high-achieving peers who also enroll in advanced mathematics courses in high school (Crosnoe et al., 2008).

Sex Differences in Academic Self-Evaluations Girls generally show greater self-criticism of their academic work than boys do. Karin Frey and Diane Ruble (1987) have studied instances of self- and peer criticism for academic work in classroom settings. Children between ages five and ten years were observed at work in academic tasks in their classrooms, and their spontaneous critical and complimentary comments about themselves and their peers were tallied. Several sex differences emerged in the nature of comments children made. Overall, both girls and boys made more self-compliments than self-criticisms, but boys made a greater number of self-congratulatory statements relative to self-criticisms than girls did. Boys complimented themselves and criticized their peers more than girls did, whereas girls criticized themselves and complimented their peers more than boys did. Girls also were more likely to attribute their failures to a lack of ability ("I'm so stupid") than boys were. If girls tend to take greater responsibility for their own failures than boys do, it is possible that there may be emotional consequences for them, for example, greater anxiety and depression.

RISK | RESILIENCE

The link between emotions and academic self-evaluations was demonstrated in a longitudinal study in which third- and sixth-graders were asked to evaluate their scholastic competence each year for a period of three years. Teachers also evaluated children's academic abilities. Boys and girls were similar in their estimates of their academic ability in grade three, but in successive years, their profiles diverged. As Figure 13.6 illustrates, starting at about fourth grade and continuing through eighth grade, boys tended to overestimate their academic abilities, and girls tended to underestimate theirs. In addition, symptoms of anxiety and depression were negatively correlated with the tendency to overestimate one's abilities (Cole et al., 1999). Thus, gender differences in self-evaluations can have important connections to children's emotional well-being.

INTERACTION AMONG DOMAINS

Figure 13.6
Gender Differences in Academic Self-Evaluations
In a study by Cole et al. (1999), third- and sixth-graders were asked to evaluate their scholastic competence each year for a period of three years. Teachers also evaluated children's academic abilities. The graph shows that there are sex differences in children's tendency to overestimate their academic abilities starting at about fourth grade and continuing through eighth grade. (The y-axis shows a statistical estimate of the tendency to overestimate such that a higher positive number indicates greater overestimation.)
Source: From Cole, D. A., Martin, J. M., Peeke, L., Seroczynski, A. D., & Fier, J. (1999). Children's over-and-underestimation of academic competence: A longitudinal study of gender differences, depression, and anxiety. *Child Development, 70,* pp. 459–473. Copyright © 1999. Reprinted with permission of the Society for Research in Child Development.

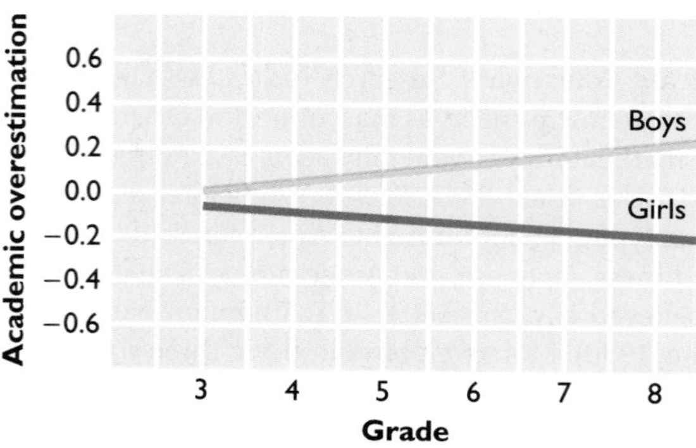

Sexual Harassment A national survey of more than 2,000 middle and high school students reveals that a surprising number, 83 percent of girls and 79 percent of boys, report that they have experienced sexual harassment from either a peer or an adult (American Association of University Women Educational Foundation, 2001). Another survey of 600 teenage girls indicates that 90 percent report being the victims of sexual harassment (Leaper & Brown, 2008). Sexual harassment in one form or another is part of the routine, everyday experiences of many teens, often in the hallways and classrooms of schools. Forms of harassment can vary from spreading rumors about sexual activity, to telling sexual jokes, to forcing participation in kissing or a sexual act. Of most concern, of course, is the impact on the victims; the consequences can range from feeling embarrassed to extremely upset. For girls, who are more likely than boys to experience physical forms of harassment, fear of the perpetrator is often the outcome (Hand & Sanchez, 2000).

RISK | RESILIENCE

Sexual harassment is in violation of Title IX, the federal law protecting the civil rights of students. Most schools have formal policies against sexual harassment, in part to protect against litigation. Then why is sexual harassment so common? First, even though schools may have policies, it is not always clear how students are made aware of them. Researcher Nan Stein (1995, 2007) also notes that there tends to be tacit approval by teachers and parents when they witness sexual harassment. Adults are not always prepared to challenge this behavior when they witness adolescents displaying it in school hallways, classrooms, and sports playing fields. Finally, students themselves may not be fully aware of the behaviors that fall within the scope of sexual harassment. High schoolers are usually able to identify physical acts as harassment but often do not label sexist jokes or sexual remarks in the same way. Perhaps, because of this, these latter behaviors have simply become normative in the high school environment (Terrance, Logan, & Peters, 2004).

For Your Review and Reflection

- What are some of the ways in which parents influence children's gender-role development?
- What effects do nontraditional parents have on gender-role development?

- What do early play patterns reveal about the role of peers in gender-role development?
- What role do peers play in the enforcement of sex-typed behaviors?
- What are the consequences of cross-gender behaviors for boys and for girls?
- How does sex segregation contribute to the development of gender roles?
- In what ways do teachers sometimes contribute to sex-typed behaviors in children?
- What attitudes do boys and girls hold about academic subjects and academic evaluations?
- What forms of intervention would you suggest to reduce the levels of sexual harassment experienced by children in schools?

chapter recap

Summary of Developmental Themes

Nature & Nurture

How do nature and nurture interact in gender development?
Biological influences on gender-role development include hormones and brain structures that may underlie sex differences in aggression and visual-spatial skill. According to social cognitive theorists, the child's socialization experiences with parents and peers and in school contribute substantially to observed sex differences, as does the child's knowledge of gender-role stereotypes. Children learn about gender roles very early in life, well before actual sex differences in most behaviors are observed. Research shows that parents, peers, and teachers treat boys and girls differently, providing support for the role of nurture in gender-role development.

Sociocultural Influence

How does the sociocultural context influence gender development?
Most cultures hold stereotypical beliefs about gender roles, although the specific characteristics associated with each sex can vary. The particular behaviors exhibited by males and females can also vary according to culture. Such findings demonstrate that, although the tendency to stereotype is widespread, the characteristics associated with each sex are not necessarily fixed. Changes within American society, such as the increased proportion of women employed outside the home, underscore the idea that children's gender-role development can be affected by shifting sociocultural trends.

Continuity | Discontinuity

Is gender development continuous or discontinuous?
Theorists such as Lawrence Kohlberg describe gender development as a stagelike process. Kohlberg hypothesized that children progress through a sequence of attaining gender identity, gender stability, and gender constancy. Research evaluating stage theories has confirmed that children pass through the general sequence of gender awareness outlined by Kohlberg. In contrast, social cognitive theorists describe the cumulative and incremental effects of reinforcement and modeling on gender-role development.

Interaction Among Domains

How does gender development interact with development in other domains?
Attainments in cognition are thought to be related to many aspects of gender-role development. Bandura describes cognitive processes, such as attention, that influence which models, male or female, children will imitate. Kohlberg suggests that general cognitive advances pave the way for gender knowledge, such as gender constancy. By the same token, the child's state of gender-role development can influence cognitive processing. Gender-schematic children, for example, may show memory distortions consistent with their gender-role beliefs.

Risk | Resilience

What factors promote risk or resilience in gender development?
Some children exhibit patterns of cross-gender behavior. These tendencies are usually met with negative feedback from peers, especially if the cross-gender child is a boy. Risks can also be associated with parental and teacher practices that limit children's activities on the basis of gender. At the same time, the greater confidence and participation of girls in mathematics activities are a sign that risks (in this case, the restriction of potential career paths) can be minimized through societal changes.

Chapter Review

Gender Stereotypes Versus Actual Sex Differences

What are the characteristics associated with masculine and feminine stereotypes?
Gender stereotypes are the expectations or beliefs that individuals within a given culture hold about the characteristics of females and males. Children learn about these stereotypes as part of the process of *gender-role development.* Stereotypes of masculinity center on *instrumentality,* qualities associated with acting on the world. Stereotypes of femininity center on *expressiveness,* qualities associated with emotions and relationships.

What do cross-cultural studies reveal about the nature of gender stereotypes?
Although there are many cross-cultural similarities in the content of gender stereotypes, there are also notable variations. For example, in Italy, the trait of "endurance" is associated with females, and, in Nigeria, "affiliation" is seen as gender neutral. Thus, specific characteristics are not always associated with males or females.

How do children's concepts of gender stereotypes change with age?
Children demonstrate knowledge of gender stereotypes as early as age two. They are familiar with the personality traits, occupations, appearance qualities, and household activities associated with males and females. With development, knowledge about stereotypes becomes more extensive but also more flexible.

What actual sex differences exist in the physical, cognitive, and social domains?
Males and females differ in several physical qualities, including activity level, rate of maturity, and physical size. The most notable sex differences in cognition are in visual-spatial tasks. Males tend to perform better than females on tasks on mental rotation and spatial perception tasks. In the social domain, males tend to be more physically aggressive than females, although definitions of aggression, context, and age all make a difference in how this quality is expressed. Girls show a heightened sensitivity to emotions and are more vulnerable than boys to depression.

Theories of Gender-Role Development

What are the major ways in which biology is thought to influence gender-role development? What specific research findings support a biological perspective? What research findings challenge the idea that biology alone is responsible for role development?
Biological theories emphasize the role of hormones such as androgens and differences in the structures of male and female brains in explaining sex differences in behaviors such as aggression and visual-spatial skills. Animal and human studies show that prenatal exposure to androgens is related to aggressive, rough-and-tumble behavior, and male-type play. However, hormone levels can change in response to environmental events, indicating that caution is in order when interpreting findings about biology and gender.

How does social cognitive theory account for gender-role development? What research findings support the social cognitive perspective?
Social cognitive theory emphasizes the roles of reinforcement, imitation, and, eventually, self-regulation in producing sex-typed behaviors. An important factor influencing the likelihood of imitation is the *sex typicality* of the model's behavior. Research shows that children are more likely to imitate same-sex than other-sex models and that self-regulation of sex-typed behaviors increases with development.

What are the essential features of Kohlberg's cognitive-developmental theory of gender-role development? What specific research findings support Kohlberg's theory?
Kohlberg's theory hypothesizes that children's awareness of gender grows through successive mastery of *gender identity, gender stability,* and *gender constancy.* Cross-cultural research has confirmed this developmental sequence. In addition, recent research has supported the claim that gender constancy predicts the child's subsequent gender-type behavior.

What are the elements of gender schema theory? What specific research findings support gender schema theory?
Gender schema theory states that children first form cognitive representations of same-sex/opposite-sex schema and then form more elaborate schemas for their own sex. Research has shown that children prefer neutral objects labeled for their own sex and that gender schemas can have an impact on social information processing. For example, gender-schematic children distort information about sex-atypical behaviors.

The Socialization of Gender Roles

What are some of the ways in which parents influence children's gender-role development?
Many parents express stereotypical attitudes and beliefs about their male and female children. They also treat children differently based on their biological sex, from the way they furnish their rooms to the kinds of activities and play they encourage.

What effects do nontraditional parents have on gender-role development?
Children who have nontraditional parents show less knowledge of gender stereotypes, and girls show more independence and achievement.

What do early play patterns reveal about the role of peers in gender-role development?
Children show more positive and negative social behaviors when they play with a peer of the same sex. Girls in mixed-sex pairs are more likely to be passive and to become upset. These gender-role dynamics are already apparent at age two years.

What role do peers play in the enforcement of sex-typed behaviors?
Peers reward sex-typical play and reliably punish sex-atypical behaviors in children, especially boys.

What are the consequences of cross-gender behaviors for boys and for girls?
Children, especiallly boys, who consistently display cross-gender behaviors are likely to be isolated from their peer groups.

How does sex segregation contribute to the development of gender roles?
Sex segregation is a robust phenomenon through the early school years and provides differential socialization experiences for boys and girls. Boys' groups promote dominance and assertiveness, whereas girls' groups promote a relationship orientation and shared intimacy.

In what ways do teachers sometimes contribute to sex-typed behaviors in children?
Teachers may contribute to gender-role socialization through their attitudes and behaviors. Teachers may have different expectations about the academic skills of boys and girls and often focus more attention on boys than on girls.

What attitudes do boys and girls hold about academic subjects and academic evaluations?
Students' own beliefs about their academic skills may be stereotyped, but at least in the domain of mathematics, girls' beliefs in their competence seem to be increasing. Girls often underestimate their academic abilities and attribute failures to lack of ability.

Key Terms and Concepts

androgen (p. 488)
cross-gender behavior (p. 500)
expressive characteristics (p. 480)
gender constancy (p. 493)
gender identity (p. 492)
gender-role development (p. 480)
gender schema (p. 494)
gender stability (p. 492)
gender stereotypes (p. 480)
instrumental characteristics (p. 480)
self-socialization (p. 493)
sex segregation (p. 502)
sex typicality (p. 491)

Media Resources

Access an integrated eBook and chapter-specific interactive learning tools, including flashcards, quizzes, videos, and more, in your Developmental Psychology CourseMate, accessed through CengageBrain.com.

CHAPTER OUTLINE

[chapter 14]

The Family

KEY THEMES IN THE FAMILY

SOCIOCULTURAL INFLUENCE How does the sociocultural context influence family processes?

INTERACTION AMONG DOMAINS How do family processes interact with other domains of development?

RISK | RESILIENCE What factors promote risk or resilience in family processes?

Seven-year-old Joey looked at his loaded dinner plate and announced, "I'm not hungry. Can I just have dessert?" "No, you may not!" his embarrassed mother replied as she turned toward her houseguest. "I can't think why he gets like this. He's stubborn as a mule." The guest wondered why no one mentioned that Joey, in full view of his mother, had eaten most of a gift box of cookies before dinner.

"I don't want this! It stinks! You stink!" Joey shouted. He pushed away his plate, got up from the table, and ran to the television, which he turned up to full volume.

"Turn that down this minute, or go to your room!" his mother ordered. Joey ignored her. "He's been like this since his father and I split up," she told her guest in a lowered voice. "Everything's so different now. I feel like I have to be two parents instead of one. He used to be such a good boy." Spying Joey reaching for the cookie box, she warned, "Don't take that cookie!" Joey removed his hand from the box and gave his mother a mournful, pleading look. "All right, but just one!" she conceded. Joey took two and returned to the TV. <<

This episode represents only one brief experience in Joey's life, but the accumulation of experiences such as this within the context of the family can have a distinct effect on the developing child. Families are central to the process of **socialization**, the process by which children acquire the social knowledge, behaviors, and attitudes valued by the larger society. Parents, siblings, and others within the family unit are the people with whom the child usually spends the most time and forms the strongest emotional bonds, and they thus exert an undeniable influence in the child's life.

The study of the impact of the family is no simple matter. For one thing, the child's experiences within the family can be affected by many factors such as divorce or parental employment status, elements that can change the nature of interpersonal dynamics within the family. Joey's family experiences both before and after his parents' separation, for example, can have potentially long-lasting effects on his development. Moreover, the direction of influence within families runs along several paths. Just as parents and siblings affect the child's behavior, the child affects the reactions of other family members. Because the family experience includes fluid, constantly changing effects and outcomes for its various members, studying the impact of the family presents a special research challenge to developmental scientists.

In a sense, virtually every domain of development is deeply influenced by the family environment. Cognition, moral awareness, gender identity, and emotional growth are all nurtured largely within the family. In this chapter, we focus on the roles specific family members play in the child's social development, with special attention to adaptive and maladaptive patterns of interaction. We will also see how the family is a structure in flux, shaped by cultural values and shifting demographic trends such as divorce and single parenthood. The effects of these changes in family structure—and whatever consequences they might have on interactions among individuals within the family—are a major concern for developmental scientists.

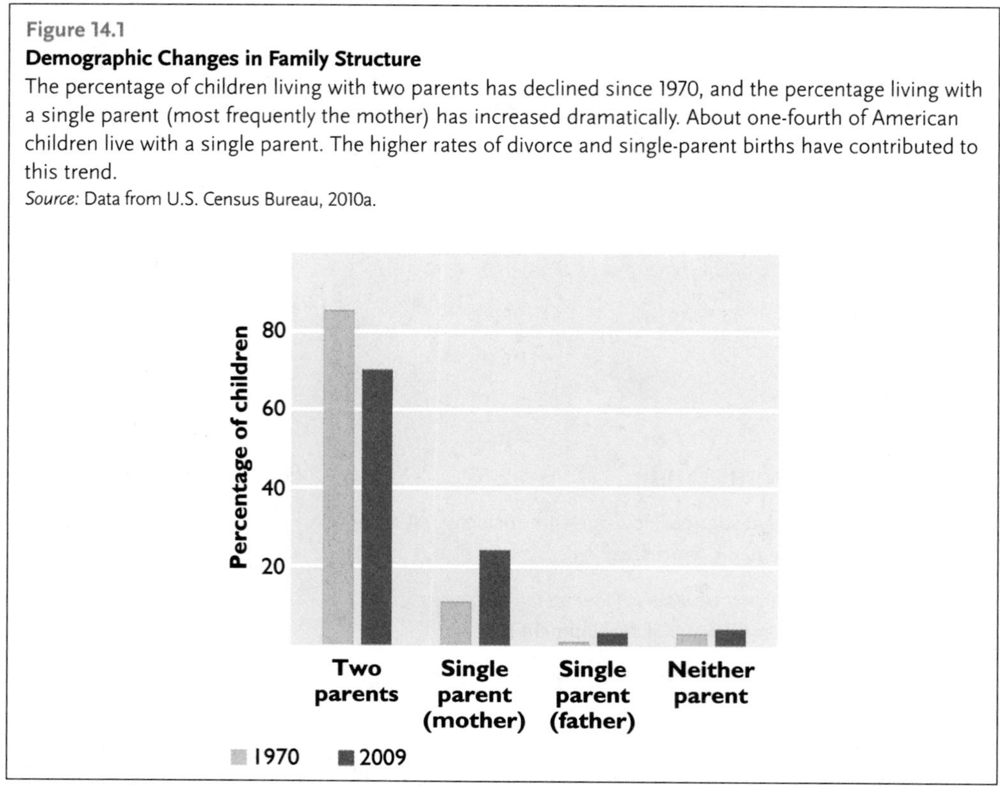

Figure 14.1
Demographic Changes in Family Structure
The percentage of children living with two parents has declined since 1970, and the percentage living with a single parent (most frequently the mother) has increased dramatically. About one-fourth of American children live with a single parent. The higher rates of divorce and single-parent births have contributed to this trend.
Source: Data from U.S. Census Bureau, 2010a.

Understanding the Family

Historians, sociologists, and anthropologists who study the family as a social unit point to the changes in its structure and functions over the past two centuries. With the industrialization of nineteenth-century America, for example, the extended family, in which secondary relatives such as grandparents, aunts and uncles, or cousins live in the same household as the primary family, gave way to the nuclear family, consisting solely of parents and their offspring living in a single household. Similarly, as we saw in Chapter 1, "Themes and Theories," the modern notion that families are havens for nurturing the child's growth and development was not always prevalent. As we look back in history, we see that the family has been a changing social structure, and all signs indicate it will continue to take different shapes in the future to reflect larger social, economic, and historical trends.

The Demographics of the American Family

SOCIOCULTURAL INFLUENCE

No one family structure typifies contemporary American society. The 1950s model of a two-parent family with two children and a nonworking mother no longer applies. For example, as Figure 14.1 shows, only 70 percent of children younger than eighteen years lived with two parents in 2009, compared with 82 percent in 1970. Twenty-six percent of American children live with only one parent (U.S. Census Bureau, 2010a). High rates of divorce and single-parent births have contributed to this trend. Projections are that about 50 percent of current marriages will end in divorce (compared with about 15 percent in 1960), and about 28 percent of all births are to single women (U.S. Census Bureau, 2010b). Moreover, about 2 percent of children live solely with their grandparents (U.S. Census Bureau, 2010a), and a growing number live with gay or lesbian parents. Finally, more than 70 percent of married

socialization Process by which children acquire the social knowledge, skills, and attitudes valued by the larger society.

Figure 14.2
The Systems Model of the Family
According to systems theorists, reciprocal influences among family members occur at three levels: the individual or microlevel, the family environment, and the larger social context. At the microlevel, parent and child influence each other directly. Within the family, relationships among particular individuals, such as husband and wife, can affect interactions with children. Finally, larger social factors, such as the presence of economic stress, can affect parent-child relations. The individual child's development is thus embedded in this network of multidirectional interactions.
Source: From Peterson, G. W., and Rollins, B. C. (1987). Parent-child socialization in M. B. Sussman and S. K. Steinmetz (Eds.), *Handbook of Marriage and the Family*. Reprinted by permission of Plenum Publishing Corporation.

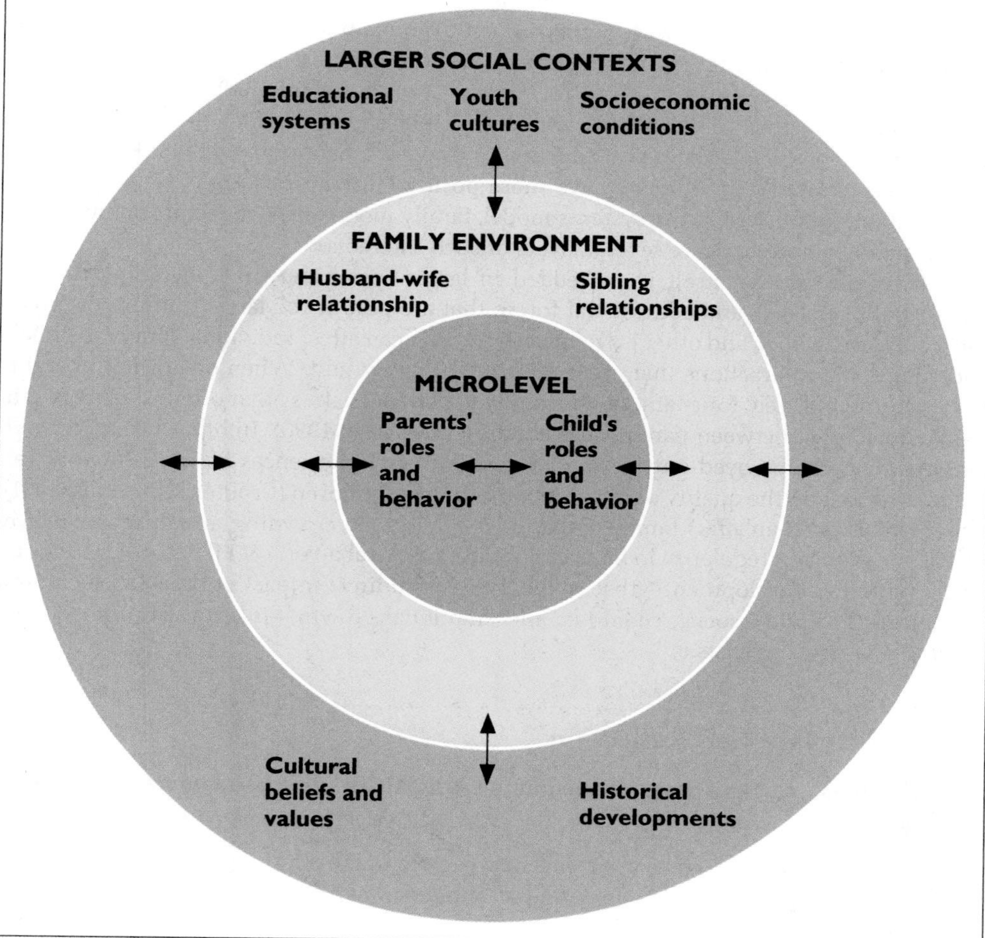

women with children younger than eighteen years work outside the home, compared with about 45 percent in 1975. All of these changes in family structure have distinct implications for the child's experiences within the family.

A Systems Approach

Many child development researchers have found it fruitful to focus on family dynamics, the interactions among all members of the group, rather than on the structure of the family per se as they study the impact of the family. An important influence on contemporary thinking about the family is **systems theory**. The premise is that all members influence one another simultaneously, and the interactions flow in a circular, reciprocal manner. In systems theory (see Figure 14.2), the individual child's development is understood as being embedded in the complex network of multidirectional interactions among all family members (Bronfenbrenner, 1986; Cox & Paley, 2003).

systems theory Model for understanding the family that emphasizes the reciprocal interactions among various members.

Systems theory assumes that families undergo periods of stability and change. The family tends to adapt to maintain a state of *homeostasis*, or equilibrium. Thus, as children attain milestones such as going to school or entering adolescence, the family system must readjust to absorb the child's new routines or demands for independence. At other times, families may experience crises, such as financial hardship, moving, or divorce. In these instances, changing external circumstances require the child and all other family members to adapt to the new situation. Systems theory, then, regards families as dynamic, self-regulating social groups (Minuchin, 1988).

Families usually contain several subsystems, such as the relations maintained between spouses, among siblings, and between parent and child. A single family member is usually a member of more than one subsystem at the same time. The child has a relationship with each parent, as well as with perhaps one or more siblings; mothers and fathers are spouses as well as parents. The quality of each of these separate relationships can have an impact on other relationships. Thus, for example, when parents have high-quality marital relationships, their relationships with their children are warmer, and their children show more favorable psychological adjustment (Davies & Scummings, 1998; Harold et al., 1997; Miller et al., 1993). Siblings have more positive interactions with one another, too (MacKinnon, 1988). Within the systems model, family members have reciprocal influences on one another, and there are several layers of such interactions.

SOCIOCULTURAL INFLUENCE

The family system itself is embedded in larger social networks, including the economic, political, legal, and educational forces that are part of the larger culture. Events in the workplace, school, and other extrafamilial settings can affect individual family members and, hence, the interactions that occur within the family unit. When one or both parents becomes unemployed, for example, the family experiences stress that often is expressed in increased conflict between parents and children (Flanagan, 1990). In other instances, both parents may be employed outside the home, and their experiences of stress at work can have an impact on the quality of interactions with their children (Crouter & Bumpus, 2001). Other factors that can affect family dynamics include noise, crowding, and the general level of organization and regularity in household routines (Atzaba-Poria & Pike, 2008). The *social ecology* of child development—that is, the direct or indirect impact of broad sociocultural factors on the child's social, cognitive, and emotional growth—is critical to understand, according to psychologists.

For Your Review and Reflection

- What major changes have occurred in the structure of American families in the past thirty years?
- What does it mean to take a systems approach to understanding the family? Give examples of how influences on one subsystem within the family can have consequences for another subsystem.
- What are examples of major changes that took place within your family during your childhood and adolescence?

Parents and Socialization

In most cultures, the primary agents of the child's socialization are parents. As we will see in the next two chapters, peers, teachers, and broader social factors also play a significant role. But perhaps no other individuals in the child's life have the powerful influence on future behaviors, attitudes, and personality that parents do.

Parents affect children's socialization in three primary ways. First, they socialize their children through direct training, providing information or reinforcement for the behaviors they find acceptable or desirable. Parents may, for example, encourage their children to share with playmates or instruct them on how to become acquainted with an unfamiliar peer. Second, as they interact with their children, parents serve as models for the children's attitudes, beliefs, and actions. For example, parents who are warm, engaging, and verbally stimulating tend to have children who are popular in school. Finally, parents manage other aspects of their children's lives that in turn can influence children's social development. Parents choose the neighborhood in which the family lives; they also may enroll children in sports programs, arrange birthday parties, and invite children's friends to spend the night, all of which influence children's peer networks (Parke & Buriel, 2006).

Parents' major concerns and activities shift as the child develops. Whereas parents of infants focus on caregiving activities and helping the child to learn such skills as self-feeding, dressing, and toileting, parents of preschoolers begin more deliberate attempts at socialization. They help their children to regulate their emotions—to control angry outbursts, for example—and start to instill social skills, such as polite forms of speech and sharing during play with peers. Parents of elementary school children are likely to be concerned with their children's academic achievement. When their children approach adolescence, most parents encourage independent, rational, and value-based decision making as their youngsters prepare to enter their own adult lives.

Parental roles shift with development. Throughout early childhood, parents closely monitor much of their children's activity. Once children enter school, parents play less of a supervisory role. They begin to expect their children to be cooperative members of the family by avoiding conflicts and sharing in household tasks. Parents and children begin to negotiate as they make decisions and solve family problems. Finally, during adolescence, parents observe children's participation in the larger world, in school and community activities and close personal relationships with peers. While parents are encouraging independence in some domains, such as school achievement, they may also be exerting more control in other domains, such as their children's social activities (Maccoby, 1984; Maccoby & Martin, 1983; McNally, Eisenberg, & Harris, 1991).

INTERACTION AMONG DOMAINS

As this quick sketch suggests, the child's own development often precipitates shifts in parental roles. As the child's language and cognitive skills mature, parents place greater expectations on her social communication behaviors. As she enters school, parents nurture greater independence. The physical changes associated with puberty often signal to parents that more mature child–adult interactions, such as deferring at times to the child's wishes rather than rigidly restricting his activities, are warranted (Steinberg, 1981). As systems theory suggests, the individual child's development within the family represents an ongoing give-and-take between child and parent, necessitating continual readjustment by all members to reinstate family equilibrium.

Styles of Parenting

Even the casual observer of parents interacting with their children in public places such as parks, shopping malls, and supermarkets will notice markedly different styles of parental behavior. Some parents are extremely controlling, using crisp, firm commands devoid of explanations to restrict their children's behavior. Others seem not to notice as their charges create chaos and pandemonium. Researchers have established that the pattern of interactions a parent adopts is an important variable in influencing the child's later development.

In a landmark series of observational studies, Diana Baumrind (1971, 1973) recorded the interpersonal and behavioral styles of nursery school children as they engaged in normal school activities. She also watched as they worked on a series of standardized problem-solving tasks, such as completing a set of puzzles. In addition, Baumrind gathered information on parenting styles by observing how mothers interacted with their children in both play and structured teaching settings, watching parents and their children in the home, and interviewing parents about their child-rearing practices. The children and parents were observed again when children were eight or nine years old. Based on these extensive observations, Baumrind identified several distinct patterns of parenting.

Some parents, Baumrind found, were extremely restrictive and controlling. They valued respect for authority and strict obedience to their commands and relied on coercive techniques, such as threats or physical punishment, rather than on reasoning or explanation, to regulate their children's actions. They were also less nurturant toward their children

Research has shown that parents who expect mature behavior from their children, provide explanations for their requests, and are supportive and warm in their interactions have children who display instrumental competence. These parents display what is called an *authoritative style.*

© Golden Pixels LLC/Shutterstock.com

than other parents in the study. Baumrind identified this group as **authoritarian parents.** The second parenting style belonged to the group she called **permissive parents**. These parents set few limits and made few demands for mature behavior from their children. Children were permitted to make their own decisions about many routine activities such as TV viewing, bedtime, and mealtimes, for example. Permissive parents tended to be either moderately nurturant or cool and uninvolved. The third group of parents was high on both control and nurturance. These **authoritative parents** expected their children to behave in a mature fashion but tended to use rewards more than punishments to achieve their ends. They communicated their expectations clearly and provided explanations to help their children understand the reasons for their requests. They also listened to what their children had to say and encouraged a dialogue with them. Authoritative parents were distinctly supportive and warm in their interactions with their children. Figure 14.3 summarizes the characteristics of these three parental styles, as well as a fourth style, *uninvolved parents,* which has been described in later research and will be discussed shortly.

RISK | RESILIENCE

Baumrind found a cluster of behavioral characteristics in children linked with each parental style. The offspring of authoritative parents were friendly with peers, cooperative with adults, independent, energetic, and achievement oriented. They also displayed a high degree of self-control. This set of characteristics often is termed **instrumental competence.** In marked contrast, children of authoritarian and permissive parents did not exhibit the social responsibility and independence associated with instrumental competence. Children who had authoritarian parents appeared unhappy; also, boys tended to be aggressive, whereas girls were likely to be dependent. Children of permissive parents, on the other hand, were low on self-control and self-reliance.

INTERACTION AMONG DOMAINS

authoritarian parent Parent who relies on coercive techniques to discipline the child and displays a low level of nurturance.

permissive parent Parent who sets few limits on the child's behavior.

authoritative parent Parent who sets limits on a child's behavior using reasoning and explanation and displays a high degree of nurturance.

instrumental competence Child's display of independence, self-control, achievement orientation, and cooperation.

The effects of parenting style extend to other dimensions of child development and reach into the adolescent years. Authoritarian parenting, especially with its use of coercive techniques for controlling behavior, is associated with less advanced moral reasoning and less prosocial behavior (Boyes & Allen, 1993; Krevans & Gibbs, 1996), as well as lower self-esteem (Loeb, Horst, & Horton, 1980), and poorer adjustment starting school (Barth & Parke, 1993). Extremely controlling parenting and the use of coercive techniques are also associated with higher levels of aggression in children (Dodge, Coy, & Lynam, 2006; Xu, Farver, & Zhang, 2009), poor peer relations (Pettit et al., 1996; Putallaz, 1987), and lower

Figure 14.3

Patterns of Parenting as a Function of Control and Nurturance

Four parenting styles can be identified in terms of the extent to which parents set limits on the child's behavior (control) and the level of nurturance and responsiveness they provide.

Source: Adapted from Maccoby, E. E., & Martin, J. A. (1983). Socialization in the context of the family: Parent-child interaction in E. M. Hetherington (Ed.), *Handbook of Child Psychology*, Vol. 4. Socialization, Personality, and Social Development. Copyright © 1983. Used by permission of John Wiley & Sons, Inc.

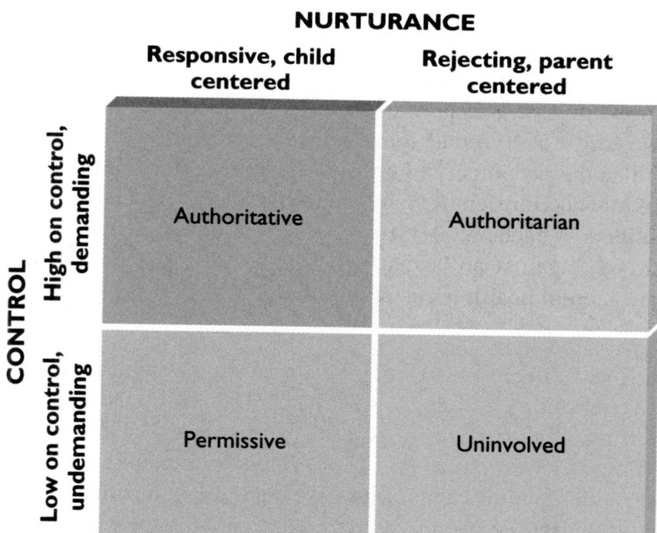

school achievement in adolescence (Dornbusch et al., 1987). In contrast, by the time children reach adolescence, those with authoritative parents demonstrate all sorts of positive developmental outcomes. They show higher school achievement, have higher self-esteem, display lower depression and anxiety, and perform fewer risky and antisocial behaviors (Collins & Steinberg, 2006; Steinberg, 2001).

Researchers have also identified a fourth parenting style: the **uninvolved**, or *neglectful*, **parent** (Maccoby & Martin, 1983). These parents seem to be uncommitted to their parental role and emotionally detached from their children, often giving greater priority to their own needs and preferences than to the child's. These parents may be uninterested in events at the child's school, be unfamiliar with his playmates, and have only infrequent conversations with him. Uninvolved parenting is related to children's lower self-esteem (Loeb et al., 1980), heightened aggression (Hatfield, Ferguson, & Alpert, 1967), and lower control over impulsive behavior (Block, 1971). As older adolescents, children with uninvolved parents show more maladjustment, lack of creativity, and greater alcohol consumption than adolescents who experienced other parenting styles (Weiss & Schwarz, 1996). Some believe that uninvolved parenting may present the greatest risks of all to healthy long-term development (Steinberg et al., 1994).

RISK | RESILIENCE

Why does authoritative parenting work so well? Several explanations are possible. First, when parents make demands for mature behavior from their children, they make explicit the responsibilities individuals have toward one another when they live in social groups. When parents set forth clear, consistent guidelines for behavior, they make the child's job of sorting out the social world much easier. Second, when parental demands are accompanied by reasonable explanations, the child is more likely to accept the limitations on her actions. Third, when parents take into account the child's responses and show affection, he is likely to acquire a sense of control over his actions and derive the sense that he has worth. Studies confirm that adolescents who have authoritative parents have a healthy sense of autonomy and personal responsibility, and feel a sense of control over their lives (Glasgow et al., 1997; Steinberg, Elmen, & Mounts, 1989). Thus, the net outcome of authoritative parenting is a competent child who shows successful psychological adjustment.

uninvolved parent Parent who is emotionally detached from the child and focuses on his or her own needs as opposed to the child's.

Effective Parenting

Baumrind's research showed that the most desirable developmental outcomes are with parenting that has two key characteristics: responding to the child's needs and actions with warmth and nurturance and setting limits on the child's behavior. These themes echo the discussion of sensitive parenting and attachment presented in Chapter 11, "Emotion."

No matter what the age of the child, whether he is a toddler exhibiting a fierce temper tantrum or an adolescent testing a curfew, research shows that parenting based on strong expressions of warmth, involvement with children's lives, and clear limit setting results in successful developmental outcomes. Even when families are faced with stresses and challenges, these techniques can mitigate potentially negative long-term outcomes for children. Parents who express warmth and support, who are good communicators with their children, and who continue to retain some control over them seem to buffer their children against risks such as the propensity to engage in violence and to use alcohol, tobacco, and marijuana (Brookmeyer, Henrich, & Schwab-Stone, 2005; Cleveland et al., 2005; Fletcher, Steinberg, & Williams-Wheeler, 2004). In general, research shows that the role of parental firmness is to protect against antisocial behavior, while parental warmth contributes in important ways to mental health (Gray & Steinberg, 1999).

RISK | RESILIENCE

Parental Warmth A series of studies has singled out parental warmth, the tendency of parents to express positive emotions and approval toward their children, as an important feature of effective parenting. Children whose parents express warmth and support tend to have higher self-esteem, greater empathy, and fewer behavioral problems (Cox & Harter, 2003; Zhou et al., 2002). Among adolescents, who may begin to experiment with risky behaviors, parental support and warmth are related to a decreased likelihood of teen pregnancy, less aggression, and less association with deviant peers (Scaramella et al., 2002; Young et al., 1995). Several messages are communicated to adolescents when parents express warmth and affection: "You are secure, you are valued, and you are worthwhile." These messages may be especially critical for children to hear at a time when they are at risk for experiencing a drop in self-esteem or feelings of anxiety or depression. In contrast to parents who express hostility to their adolescent children, parents who are high on warmth tend to have children with fewer internalizing and externalizing problems overall. Furthermore, warm parenting seems to slow many teens' tendency to increase in acting-out behaviors, depression, and anxiety over time (Scaramella, Conger, & Simons, 1999).

On the other hand, parental negativity is related to less compliance on the part of the child, poor peer relationships, and delinquency (Deater-Deckard et al., 2001; Isley et al., 1999; Simons et al., 2001). Parental warmth may even serve as a protection of sorts for children who are highly aggressive as youngsters and who are at risk for later developmental problems. When these children experience warm and affectionate parenting, they are less likely to show a decline in empathy, school problems, and adulthood unemployment that many other children in this category display (Hastings et al., 2000; Kokko & Pulkkinen, 2000).

Parental warmth probably works in a number of ways. One outcome of parental warmth and supportiveness is the child's perception of his or her own competence. As we saw in Chapter 12, "Self and Values," parental support is an important contributor to the growth of children's self-esteem, which in turn has consequences for many other aspects of the child's social and cognitive development. Some researchers believe the real underlying value of parental warmth is that it sets a positive emotional tone in parent–child interactions, one that fosters harmony and connection among family members (Collins & Steinberg, 2006). Moreover, warm parents, in their expression of positive emotions, may encourage a process of "emotion matching" in their children. Positive parental emotions are associated with positive emotions in children (Kochanska, 1997). On the other hand, Kee Kim and associates found that a high level of negative affect expressed by parents of adolescents predicted the rate at which adolescents increased their own expressions of negative affect (Kim et al., 2001). Considering that negative emotions are generally associated with unsuccessful social interactions, not just with parents but also with peers and others, learning how to maintain a positive emotional tone may be an important social skill for children to acquire.

INTERACTION AMONG DOMAINS

Parental Control Effective parenting also includes the ability of parents to control their children's behavior, setting limits when appropriate. However, researchers are finding that a distinction needs to be made between *behavioral control*, monitoring and regulating the child's actions, and *psychological control*, intrusive and domineering parenting that can interfere with the child's growing needs for autonomy (Barber, 2002). Gregory Pettit and his colleagues found that adolescents whose parents were high on monitoring (that is, they were aware of their activities, friends, and how they spent their time) were less likely to become involved in delinquent behaviors. In contrast, those with parents who exerted a high degree of psychological control were more likely to display delinquent behaviors and also expressed higher levels of anxiety and depression (Pettit et al., 2001). Similar outcomes have been reported in a study of American and Chinese young adolescents. When parents were involved in regulating activities such as going out after school, children showed higher academic achievement. When parents used guilt and withdrawal of affection in response to behaviors they did not approve of, children showed signs of poorer emotional functioning, expressing greater shame, worry, and anger (Wang, Pomerantz, & Chen, 2007).

Effective parents do not engage in close surveillance or spying. Rather, they create an atmosphere in which adolescents feel comfortable talking with parents and disclosing information about how things are going in school or where they are spending their free time. According to some experts, it is parental knowledge gained through open communication, rather than monitoring per se, that predicts less risky and delinquent behavior in teens (Soenens et al., 2006; Smetana, 2008). Fewer risky behaviors occur when parents have developed a close relationship with their children—which allows for disclosure—than when parents gain knowledge about their children from other sources, such as teachers, neighbors, and the child's friends (Crouter et al., 2005).

As you can see, parenting—especially parenting of adolescents—can require a delicate balancing act between controlling children's behavior and respecting children's need to develop a sense of identity and independent decision making. When parents allow autonomy in decisions about how to spend allowance or free time, self-esteem rises and depression declines (Hasebe, Nucci, & Nucci, 2004; Smetana, Campione-Barr, & Daddis, 2004). But when they are overbearing and controlling, parents are simply exerting their power in a style reminiscent of authoritarian parenting. It should not be surprising, then, that the consequences of this approach to parental control are often negative (Barber & Harmon, 2002). Research shows that, if teens experienced a high level of parental intrusiveness in seventh grade, they had more unsupervised peer contact in eighth grade and more problem behaviors in eleventh grade. By the same token, a similar pattern unfolded if seventh-graders had high levels of freedom in deciding how late to stay out or whether they could date (Goldstein, Davis-Kean, & Eccles, 2005). Balance is indeed the key, and finding the right balancing point between control and autonomy promotion often offers a distinct challenge to parents.

RISK | RESILIENCE

Punishment In recent decades, the most widely discussed parental control technique has been *punishment*, the administration of an aversive stimulus or withdrawal of rewards to decrease the frequency of undesirable behaviors (see Chapter 6, "Basic Learning and Perception"). A form of power assertion, punishment can include spanking, sharp verbal rebukes, or the loss of such privileges as TV viewing time or playtime with friends.

Laboratory studies carried out in the tradition of learning theory show that certain ways of administering punishment are more effective than others. One important factor is making sure the punishment closely follows the child's transgression so that the child makes the connection between her behavior and the consequences. Another powerful factor is providing an explanation for why the behavior is not desirable (Parke, 1969). The effectiveness of punishment also depends on the consistency with which it is applied. As we saw in the case of Joey and the cookies at the beginning of the chapter, children can become particularly disobedient and aggressive when parents prohibit a behavior on one occasion and permit it on another. Consistency among caregivers (**interagent consistency**) and consistency of one caregiver from one occasion to the next (**intra-agent consistency**) are both important in giving children clear, unambiguous messages about acceptable and unacceptable behaviors (Deur & Parke, 1970; Sawin & Parke, 1979).

interagent consistency Consistency in application of disciplinary strategies among various caregivers.

intra-agent consistency Consistency in a single caregiver's application of discipline from one situation to the next.

Should Parents Spank Their Children? what do you think?

Most often, when parents think of punishment, they think of spanking the child. In a survey of almost 1,000 parents, Murray Straus and Julie Stewart found that 94 percent of parents of three- and four-year-olds reported striking their children in the previous year. Infants and adolescents were spanked less often (Straus & Stewart, 1999). However, even half of adolescents report being hit by their parents, with an average of six to eight times in a year (Straus & Donnelly, 1993). Thus, in the United States, many parents resort to physical punishment, at least on occasion, to control their child's behavior.

Many psychologists believe that physical tactics such as hitting and spanking should not be used at all. They argue that by using physical punishment, parents are serving as models for aggression. Following the tenets of social learning theory, we should not be surprised if the chief lesson children learn from parents who spank is that physical aggression is a way to resolve conflicts (Parke & Slaby, 1983). Also, an overreliance on physical punishment may set the stage for child abuse (Parke & Collmer, 1975). Caught up in the escalating emotions of a confrontation with their children, parents who are already willing to spank, hit, or pinch do not have far to go before they cause more serious physical injury.

A contrasting position is that occasional spanking has no long-lasting negative effects. In fact, spanking, judiciously used, may be a necessary tactic when children are unrelentingly noncompliant. In this line of thinking, parents should consider spanking only when other nonphysical disciplinary tactics have failed. When parents are warm and supportive, however, an occasional spanking is not harmful; rather, it may be necessary to help children learn to be compliant and to regulate their own behavior (Baumrind, 1996).

Some research suggests that the children of parents who use occasional spanking do not have different profiles from children whose parents never spank. In one study of twenty-one-month-olds, for example, children whose mothers used frequent physical punishment scored lower on their ability to regulate their behaviors. However, children whose mothers used occasional physical punishment did not differ from children whose mothers never spanked them—both fared better than the high-physical-punishment group (Power & Chapieski, 1986). Additional evidence suggests that the link between spanking and aggression in children, and spanking and child abuse, is not necessarily clear. For example, since 1995, when Sweden passed a law to ban physical punishment, aggression in teenagers has increased (and not decreased), as has the number of cases of child abuse (Baumrind, 1996).

Supporting the other side of the debate are the results of a meta-analysis of eighty-eight studies evaluating the impact of physical punishment on children. The findings indicated that physical punishment had a strong relationship to the child's immediate compliance. However, there was also a strong association between the use of physical punishment and child abuse. Lesser, but still significant, associations were found between increased use of physical punishment and heightened aggression, risk for mental health problems, and lower moral internalization in children (Gershoff, 2002). A study of children from six countries in Africa, Asia, and Europe provides support for this theme: when parents use physical punishment, their children tend to exhibit more aggressive behaviors (Gershoff, Grogan-Kaylor et al., 2010).

Where do you stand on the use of even occasional spanking to regulate children's behavior? Are there any circumstances where you think spanking might be warranted? What is the basis for your decision? If you observed a parent physically punishing a child, at what point might you intervene or express concerns about such activity?

Managing Noncompliant Children research applied to parenting

After her dinner guest left and Joey was put to bed (with yet another struggle), his mother sat exhausted on the couch and thought about the difficulties she was having in controlling her child's behavior. Her embarrassment in front of her guest was just a small problem compared with the negative cycle in which she and Joey always seemed to end up. She loved her child beyond words, but things were just too far out of control,

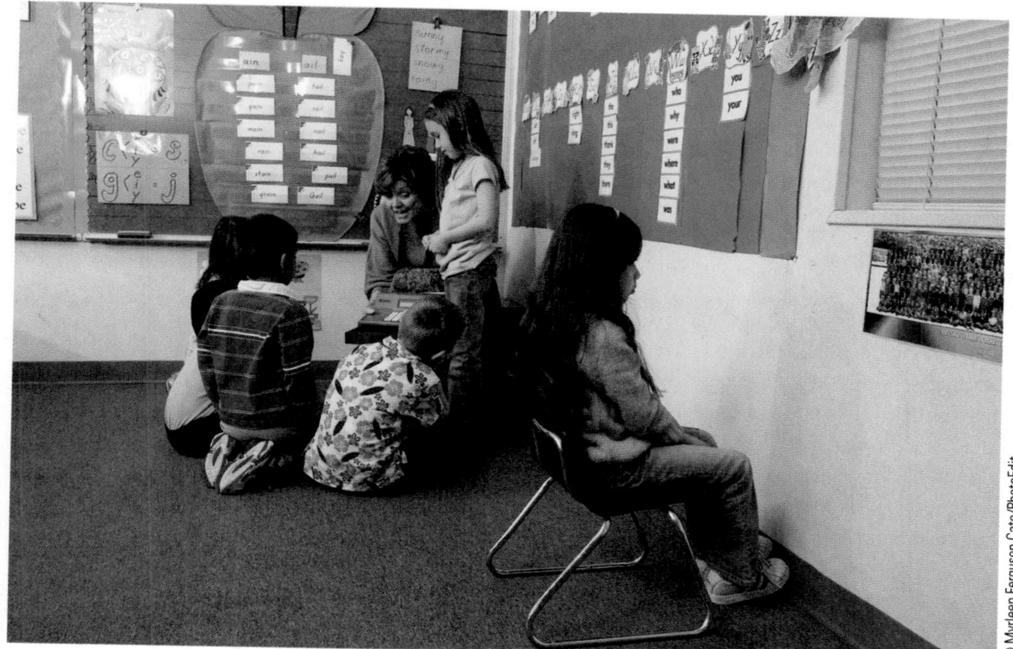

© Myrleen Ferguson Cate/PhotoEdit

One effective technique for managing a child's behavior is the use of "time-out"—sending the child to a neutral area for a specific amount of time after she or he misbehaves. Time-out has been found to reduce or eliminate a variety of behavior problems among children.

and she needed help. A friend had suggested that she see a clinical psychologist for advice. She went to her dresser drawer and pulled out the psychologist's card; she would call Dr. Nagle in the morning.

At the visit with Dr. Nagle two weeks later, Joey's mother described some examples of her son's noncompliant behavior. Dr. Nagle nodded knowingly and then spoke of the need for parents to maintain reasonable control over their child's behavior. "Just how can I do that?" asked Joey's mother. "I don't believe in spanking. What else can I do to get him to listen to me?" Dr. Nagle then proceeded to outline the elements of a parent behavior management program.

One of the most common problems parents face is the oppositional behavior their children show, often beginning at age two or three. A parent makes a request (e.g., "Time to go to bed"), and the child simply refuses to comply, adding a loud "No!" for emphasis. The child's response may reflect a healthy, growing desire for independence and self-assertion. But this pattern, if repeated for a length of time, can quickly lead to conflicts with parents and frustration on their part. For the child, persistent noncompliance has the potential to lead to major behavior problems, including aggression.

Rex Forehand and his colleagues (McMahon, Forehand, & Foster, 2003) have described some basic behavior management techniques that can help parents control children's negative behaviors without resorting to spanking or physical punishment. They are based on having parents avoid two kinds of traps: a negative reinforcement trap and a positive reinforcement trap. In the first case, a parent issues a command, but the child whines, protests, and does not listen. If the parent gives in, the child has received a negative reinforcement, learning that whining will remove an aversive stimulus (the parent's commands). In the second case, the child's noncompliance receives a positive consequence—that is, extra attention—if parents spend a lot of time and effort talking with her about why she should obey. Therefore, parents should try to adhere to the following principles:

1. *Attend to the child's appropriate behavior each day.* Notice what children do and label their appropriate behaviors (e.g., "You are speaking in your normal voice"). Children will learn that attention and rewards follow when they behave as parents expect them to. When attending to the child's desirable behavior, avoid using commands, questions, and criticisms, all of which are associated with the child's noncompliance.
2. *Reward the child's compliance.* Parents should respond quickly with positive attention when children display appropriate behaviors. Saying "Wonderful job" or "Thanks for helping me" can go a long way in shaping children's positive behaviors.
3. *Ignore inappropriate behaviors that are minor, such as crankiness and whining.* The lack of attention should cause the behavior to decrease.

4. *Give clear, succinct commands, and reward the child with verbal praise for following them.* Do not engage in a long discussion with the child (which amounts to too much attention), but make sure the child understands what is expected.
5. *Use a technique called "time-out" if the child does not comply with a command.* Remove the child from all possible sources of reward, even subtle or accidental ones. Take him immediately to a quiet, neutral place and leave him alone there until a short period of time, usually two to five minutes, has elapsed. Time-out has been found to be effective in reducing or eliminating a variety of troublesome behaviors in children, including temper tantrums, fighting, and self-injurious behaviors (Varni, 1983). Time-out also gives both children and parents the opportunity to "cool down" after all parties have become aroused.

The techniques just described have been found to significantly reduce noncompliance in children who were referred to a clinic for their behavior problems. Not only did their behavior improve relative to their pre-treatment baseline, but it also compared favorably with that of a group of control children who had not been referred to the clinic (Forehand & Long, 1988). These techniques have also been shown to reduce children's problem behaviors when parents learned about them through reading a "parenting book." Even a brief five-week intervention was successful in reducing many of the child behaviors that parents found to be challenging to manage (Forehand et al., 2010).

Factors That Influence Parenting Strategies

As they engage in interactions with each other, parents and children interpret each other's behaviors; these judgments, in turn, influence the specific behaviors they display toward each other. In addition, parents hold beliefs about their own competence and effectiveness as parents; these beliefs are also related to the quality of parenting (Coleman & Karraker, 1998). Finally, children's behaviors, specifically the extent to which they escalate the intensity of interactions, can determine parental styles. In short, parenting strategies arise from a complex interplay of cognitions and reactions to the dynamics of the situation.

INTERACTION AMONG DOMAINS

Parental Cognitions One way to understand parents' cognitions is in terms of their *attributions* about children's behaviors: Why are their children acting the way they do? Theodore Dix and Joan Grusec (1985; Dix, 1993) hypothesize that the kinds of attributions parents make about the causes of their children's behaviors will influence the parenting strategies they adopt. If, for example, a parent believes his three-year-old is throwing a tantrum at the dinner table because she wants her dessert immediately, he will probably insist that she first eat all her vegetables. If, on the other hand, the parent suspects the child is ill, he will probably remove the child from the dinner table and nurture and console her.

Figure 14.4 presents a schematic diagram of Dix and Grusec's (1985) attribution model of socialization. The flow of events proceeds as follows. First, the parent observes the child's behavior and judges whether it is typical for the child or normative for her age group. The parent assesses whether the child has the skills, knowledge, and motive to behave intentionally in a certain way. Do most three-year-olds throw tantrums to get dessert? Is throwing a tantrum a typical behavior for that child? Parents make a causal attribution about the child's intentions. Next, parents' attributions affect their emotional and behavioral responses to the child. Parents become more upset and act more forcefully if they believe the child intends to misbehave—in this case, screaming for the explicit purpose of getting dessert. Finally, if parents have made the correct attribution, they will be effective in controlling the child. But if they are wrong, the child may continue to misbehave, and both parents and child may feel negative emotions rising.

Research confirms that parents make more attributions about children's intentions as the children get older. Furthermore, when parents believe that a child intends to misbehave, they feel more upset and think it is important to respond forcefully (Dix et al., 1986; Dix, Ruble, & Zambarano, 1989). Mothers who tend to attribute hostile intentions to children's actions are likely, in fact, to use harsh discipline practices; their children, in turn, tend to have problems with aggression in school (Nix et al., 1999; Rudy & Grusec, 2006).

Figure 14.4
The Attribution Model of Socialization
Dix and Grusec (1985) hypothesize that parents' judgments about the child's intentionality in misbehaving are critical in determining their response. Parents become more upset if they believe the child intended to transgress and select more forceful control strategies than they do if they believe the transgression was unintentional. If their attributions are correct, they will effectively control behavior. If they make an incorrect attribution, however, they will be less effective, may escalate the level of punishment, and may produce negative emotions in themselves and the child.
Source: Adapted from Dix, T. H., & Grusec, J. E. (1985). Parent attribution in the socialization of children in I. E. Sigel (Ed.), *Parental Belief Systems: The Psychological Consequences For Children*. Copyright © 1985 by Lawrence Erlbaum Associates, Inc. Reprinted by permission of Lawrence Erlbaum Associates, Inc.

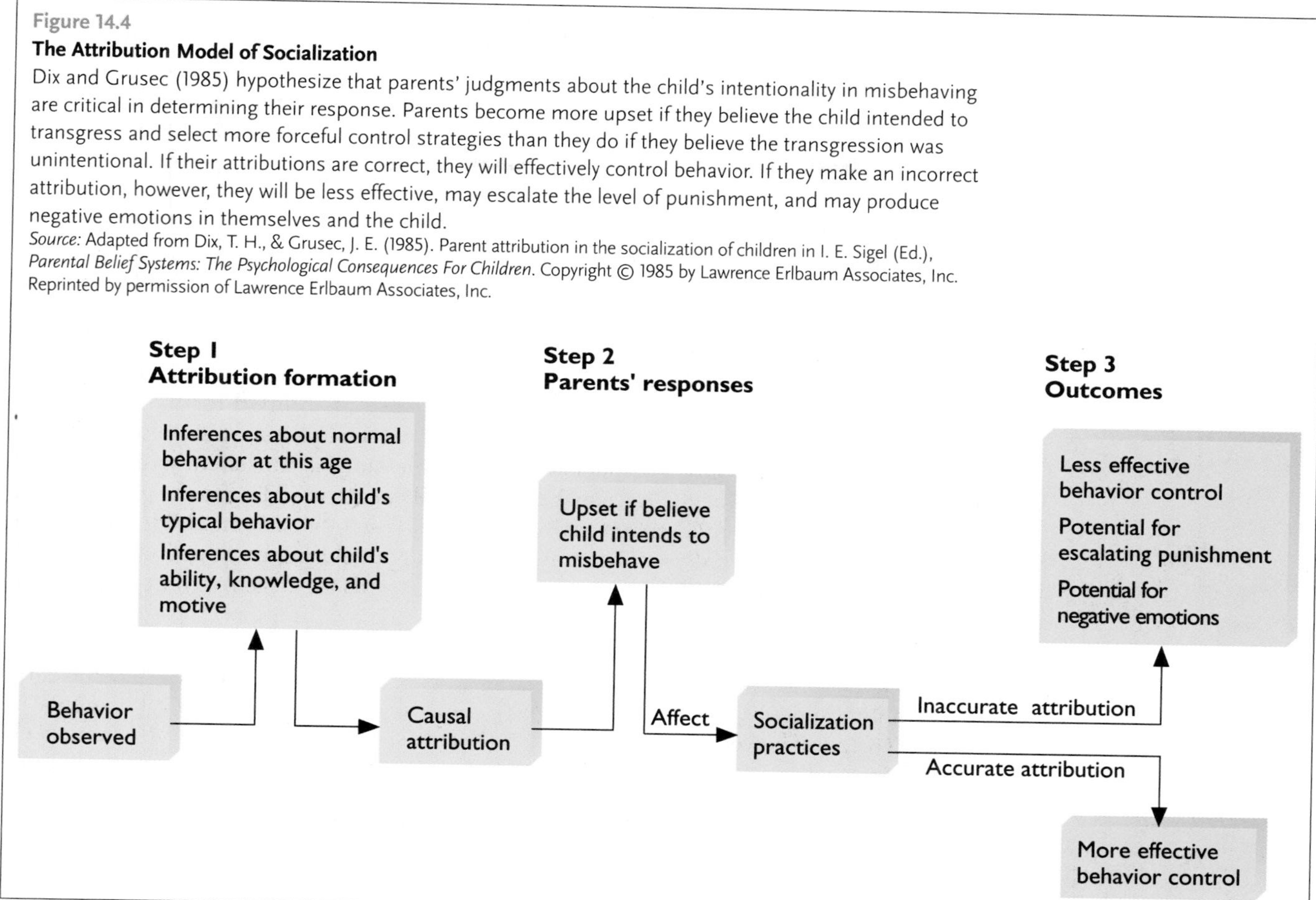

Another dimension of parental cognitions is their beliefs about their own *efficacy*: Do parents see themselves as competent and able to control their children's behaviors? For example, some parents see themselves as powerless relative to their children. Oftentimes, in an attempt to regain their power and control, these parents engage in conflict and harsh discipline with their children (Bugental & Lewis, 1998; Bugental et al., 1997). However, their inconsistent style may send mixed messages to the child. For example, a harsh command might be followed by "just kidding" or some other form of appeasement (Bugental, Blue, & Cruzcosa, 1989). Children tend to become inattentive when they experience this type of ambiguous communication style from adults and may thus become unresponsive to their requests (Bugental et al., 1999). Parental beliefs about their own efficacy can be influenced by diverse factors, including financial stress (Brody, Flor, & Gibson, 1999), the degree to which the child's temperament challenges the parent (Teti & Gelfand, 1991), and the parent's "working models" of interpersonal relationships (Grusec, Hastings, & Mammone, 1994).

Finally, it is important to consider the different goals that parents have as they raise their children. These goals typically extend beyond simply controlling their children's behavior—parents want their children to be happy, have strong values, and have a trusting and loving relationship with them. Parents rely on different strategies depending on the goals they have in mind. When parents want to resolve quickly a disagreement with the child, for example, they most often use power assertion. When they wish to teach a child specific values, on the other hand, they tend to use explanation and open communication (Hastings & Grusec, 1998).

The Child's Characteristics and Behaviors In his **control theory**, Richard Bell (1968; Bell & Harper, 1977) suggests that children play a distinct role in the types of behaviors that parents display toward them. Parents and children have upper and lower limits of tolerance for the types of behavior

control theory Hypothesis about parent–child interactions suggesting that the intensity of one partner's behavior affects the intensity of the other's response.

each shows the other. When the behavior of one approaches the other's upper limit, the recipient tries to reduce the excessive behavior with increasing levels of intensity. Thus, for example, a parent whose son is having a temper tantrum might first try to talk to him, next remove him to his room, and finally resort to physical punishment. Likewise, if the child's behavior approaches the parent's lower limits—in the child's shyness or withdrawal at the doctor's office, for example—the parent may try to stimulate the child by coaching her to speak and then promising her a reward if she vocalizes.

Control theory implies that, when children's behavior pushes parents to their limits, parents will respond with more forceful and firmer control techniques. Furthermore, some children may transgress to this extent more frequently than others. Support for this idea comes from research that shows that aggressive, difficult children elicit more negative reactions from adults than more compliant, nonaggressive children (Anderson, Lytton, & Romney, 1986). In addition, in a study of identical and fraternal twins and biologically related and unrelated siblings, genetic factors accounted for the relationship between parents' negativity and problem behaviors (Neiderhiser et al., 1999). The idea that the child's temperament influences parental reactions is consistent with these data.

The research of Grazyna Kochanska and her colleagues is adding to the growing body of evidence that some children are easier to socialize than others. Some children, she finds, display *committed compliance.* Even as fourteen-month-old infants, these children seem eager to respond to their mothers, imitating them eagerly as they teach or complying quickly and enthusiastically with their requests. Other children may comply with parental requests only as particular situations demand, and still others seem to be generally unresponsive to their parents (Forman & Kochanska, 2001). These qualities of the child are, in turn, related to parenting styles. When children display committed compliance, for example, parents are less likely to use power-assertive techniques (Kochanska, 1997). Parents are also more likely to provide higher levels of guidance in cognitive tasks, behaviors that provide more opportunities for learning, as opposed to trying to continue to regulate the child's noncompliant behavior with directive commands (Gauvain & Perez, 2008).

INTERACTION AMONG DOMAINS

Children's cognitions about their parents' demands probably also make a difference in how they react. Do children see their parents' requests as fair and appropriate? Are children motivated to comply? Do they feel internally motivated rather than pressured by others to respond? These are some of the factors that likely play a part in the tone and outcomes of parent–child interactions (Grusec & Goodnow, 1994). For example, in countries where children perceive parental scolding and corporal punishment to be normative, there is less of a relationship between these parental behaviors and children's aggression (Gershoff, Grogan-Kaylor et al., 2010). When adolescents believe parents have the right to control their behaviors, they are more willing to obey them (Cumsille et al., 2009). Researchers are just beginning to explore the role of children's cognitions in parent–child interactions.

Problems in Parenting

There is no doubt that being a parent presents special rewards but also distinct challenges. In some instances, such extreme maladaptive styles of interaction develop between parent and child that physical and psychological harm can occur to both. Understanding the dynamics of these families is essential to any attempt at intervention and also provides an even greater understanding of how all families, both healthy and dysfunctional, work as systems.

RISK | RESILIENCE

Coercive Cycles Sometimes problems in parenting result from a pattern of negative reciprocal interactions between parent and child called **coercive cycles** (depicted in Figure 14.5). Gerald Patterson and his colleagues (Patterson, 1982, 1986; Patterson, Reid, & Dishion, 1992) conducted extensive longitudinal studies of boys who exhibited pathological aggression and concluded that they acquired their behavior from routine family interactions in which both parents and children engaged in coercive behavior.

coercive cycle Pattern of escalating negative reciprocal interactions.

In Patterson's studies, preadolescent boys labeled as highly aggressive by schools, courts, or the families

Figure 14.5

A Coercive Cycle of Parent-Child Interaction

In a coercive cycle, the parent makes a request of a child, which is met with resistance and hostility. The child's behavior escalates the parent's anger, which results in harsher commands and more negative emotions. This parent behavior results in even greater resistance and hostility in the child. If the parent backs down from the request, the child's unacceptable behavior has been negatively reinforced. (Do you see why?)

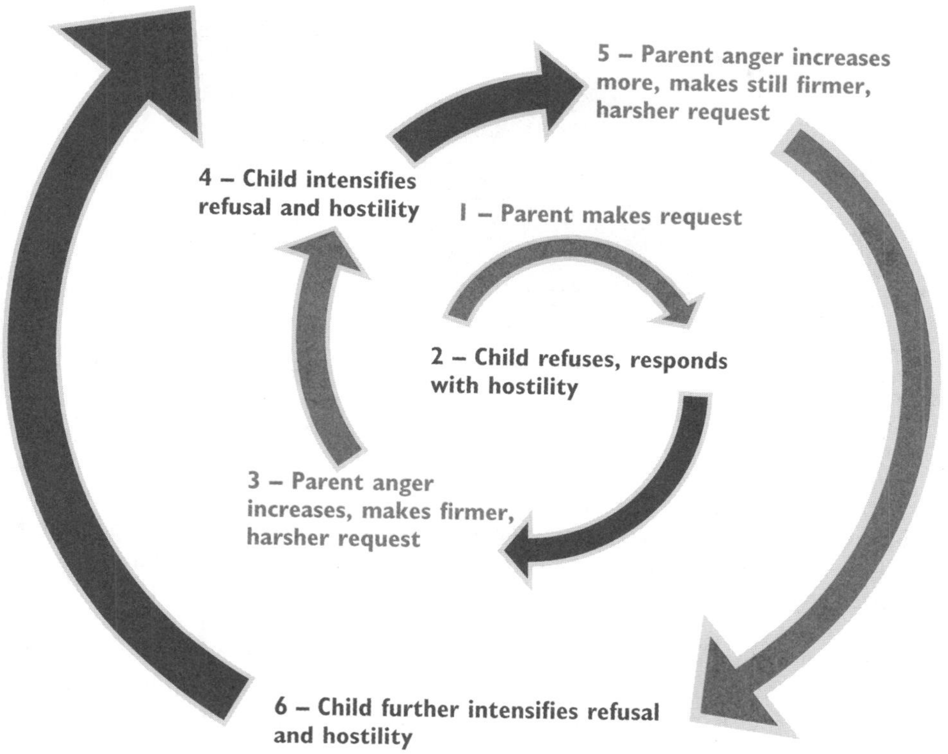

5 – Parent anger increases more, makes still firmer, harsher request

4 – Child intensifies refusal and hostility

1 – Parent makes request

2 – Child refuses, responds with hostility

3 – Parent anger increases, makes firmer, harsher request

6 – Child further intensifies refusal and hostility

themselves were compared with nonaggressive boys from "normal" families over a period of several months. Detailed observations were made of family interactions in the home, including the sequences of behaviors displayed by parents, the target children, and their siblings. Patterson learned that the families of antisocial boys were characterized by high levels of aggressive interaction that rewarded coercive behaviors. When younger, the antisocial boys exhibited minor negative behaviors, such as whining, teasing, or yelling, in response to the aggression of another family member. About 70 percent of these behaviors were reinforced by the acquiescence of the child's interaction partner; in other words, the parent or sibling backed down, and the submission negatively reinforced the child's aggression. In addition, although parents were observed to nag, scold, or threaten their children, they seldom followed through on their threats. Such sequences between the target child and other family members occurred as often as hundreds of times each day in the aggressive families. Over time, the target boys' aggression escalated in frequency and progressed to physical assaults.

At this point, many parents attempted to control their sons' aggressive behaviors, but in doing so they too became highly aggressive. The chains of coercion increased in duration to form long bursts of negative interactions and often resulted in hitting between parent and child. After extended experience in these maladaptive familial exchanges, boys became out of control and acted violently in settings outside the home, such as the school. Aggression in school was related, in turn, to poor peer relations and academic failure, adding to the chain of negative events in the boys' lives.

Can such extreme patterns of aggression be controlled? Patterson and his colleagues have intervened in the maladaptive interactions of aggressive families by training parents in basic child management skills (Patterson et al., 1975; Snyder, Reid, & Patterson, 2003).

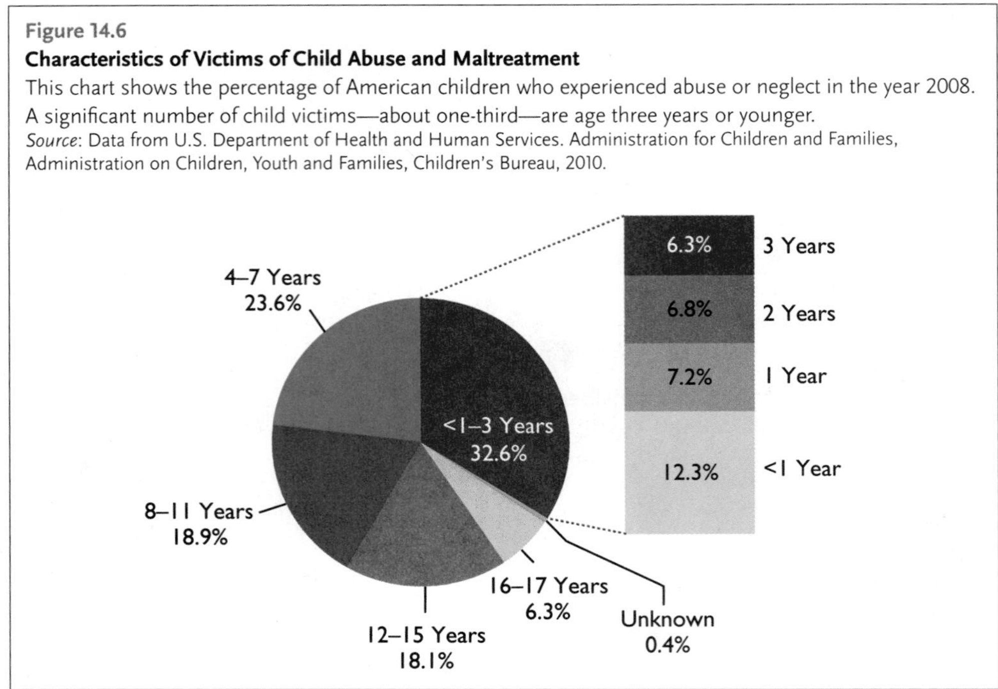

Figure 14.6
Characteristics of Victims of Child Abuse and Maltreatment
This chart shows the percentage of American children who experienced abuse or neglect in the year 2008. A significant number of child victims—about one-third—are age three years or younger.
Source: Data from U.S. Department of Health and Human Services. Administration for Children and Families, Administration on Children, Youth and Families, Children's Bureau, 2010.

They focused on teaching parents to use discipline more effectively by dispensing more positive reinforcements for prosocial behaviors, using reasoning, disciplining consistently, and setting clear limits on even minor acts of aggression. Children significantly decreased their rates of deviant behavior after only a few weeks, and the results were maintained for as long as twelve months after the initial training period (Patterson & Fleischman, 1979). As an added benefit, parents' perceptions of their children became more positive (Patterson & Reid, 1973). More recent studies have shown that even brief prevention-focused interventions that help parents to attend to their young children's positive behaviors, anticipate conflicts, and become more engaged and involved with their children can have long-lasting effects on reducing problem behaviors in children (Dishion et al., 2008).

Child Abuse In 2008, almost 700,000 children in the United States were confirmed victims of abuse or neglect (U.S. Department of Health and Human Services, 2010). Figure 14.6 shows the ages at which children are the victims of maltreatment. Aside from the immediate physical and psychological consequences of abuse, children who are the victims of family violence are predisposed to a number of developmental problems. Maltreated infants and toddlers are more likely to be anxiously attached to their mothers than are children who are not maltreated (Egeland & Sroufe, 1981; Schneider-Rosen et al., 1985). These children are thus vulnerable to the social, emotional, and cognitive impairments associated with insecure attachment. Preschool and school-age children with a history of abuse score lower on tests of cognitive maturity and academic engagement and manifest low self-esteem and school learning problems (Eckenrode, Laird, & Doris, 1993; Hoffman-Plotkin & Twentyman, 1984; Shonk & Cicchetti, 2001). Emotionally, they may display withdrawal and passivity or, on the other hand, aggressive, oppositional patterns of behavior, patterns that are linked to their generally poor relationships with peers (Salzinger et al., 1993; Shonk & Cicchetti, 2001). They also frequently display symptoms of clinical depression (Sternberg et al., 1993). Finally, abused and neglected children are at risk for delinquency and violent criminal behavior in adulthood (Widom, 1989) and may be prone to become abusive parents themselves (Egeland, Jacobvitz, & Papatola, 1987).

INTERACTION AMONG DOMAINS

The causes of abuse are neither simple nor easily ameliorated. Research on the interaction patterns in abusive families suggests that they differ in several respects from those in nonabusive families. Perhaps most significantly, parents in abusive families tend to rely on coercive or negative strategies to modify their children's behavior, even for routine or mild discipline problems. In one study, abusive and nonabusive mothers were observed as they engaged in a sequence of preparing a meal, playing, and cleaning up with their preschool-age children. Abusive mothers relied heavily on power-assertive techniques, such as threats, humiliation, or physical contact, to alter their children's behavior, whereas nonabusive mothers used predominantly positive strategies, including reasoning, bargaining, or modeling. Abusive mothers issued more than twice as many commands to their children as nonabusive mothers and also were inconsistent in reinforcing their children's compliance (Oldershaw, Walters, & Hall, 1986). As we saw earlier, inconsistent punishment usually leads to the persistence of undesirable behaviors in children.

Certain characteristics of children are also more commonly observed in abusive families. Parents often describe the abused child as irritable, difficult to put to sleep, and prone to excessive crying (Ounsted, Oppenheimer, & Lindsay, 1974). A group at special risk for abuse is premature infants, who tend to have high-pitched, aversive cries and a less attractive appearance (Parke & Collmer, 1975). Abusive parents become especially sensitized to some of the child's objectionable behaviors and show heightened emotional reactivity to the child's cries or noncompliance (Frodi & Lamb, 1980; Wolfe et al., 1983). Abuse is especially likely to occur when mothers of premature and at-risk children feel unable to control their children's behavior and experience depression (Bugental & Happaney, 2004).

Finally, abusive families tend to be isolated from the outside world and have fewer sources of social support than nonabusive families. In one study, abusive parents reported they were less involved with the community than nonabusive parents were; they tended not to join sports teams, go to the library, or take classes (Trickett & Susman, 1988). In another study, some mothers who were at risk for becoming abusive because of their own family history had normal, positive relationships with their children. These mothers had extensive emotional support from other adults, a therapist, or a mate. In contrast, high-risk mothers who subsequently became abusive experienced greater life stress and had fewer sources of psychological support (Egeland, Jacobvitz, & Sroufe, 1988).

How can the spiral of abuse be broken? Researchers suggest that interventions should teach basic parenting skills, provide parents with mechanisms to cope with their emotional tension, and offer social support such as child care or counseling services (Belsky, 1993; Wolfe, 1985). Especially promising are programs in which home visitors provide parent education and support. Daphne Bugental and her colleagues demonstrated remarkable success in reducing the prevalence of abuse in at-risk families—from 26 percent in a control condition to 4 percent in a specially designed intervention program. What were the key ingredients in the successful program? First, mothers were taught by home visitors how to read and interpret their infants' distress signals. For example, they were informed that infants were not intending to behave negatively or challenge parental power. Second, mothers were equipped with a problem-solving approach to dealing with their children's difficult behaviors. They were encouraged to think about reasons for their infants' behaviors, generate potential solutions to the problem, and assess how effective their strategies were (Bugental et al., 2002; Bugental & Schwartz, 2009). Programs that offer parent education and support not only reduce the incidence of child abuse and neglect but also result in increases in the psychological well-being of young children who had previously been maltreated; these children evidence fewer negative representations of the self as a consequence of such targeted interventions (Cicchetti & Toth, 2006).

SOCIOCULTURAL INFLUENCE

Observers have noted our society's general acceptance of violence as a means of solving problems. This tendency is evident in the widespread endorsement of physical punishment as a technique for disciplining children, as well as in the pervasive displays of violence in the media (Belsky, 1980, 1993; Hart & Brassard, 1987). Altering broader societal attitudes about violence may thus be an additional and necessary step in breaking the cycle of child abuse. Finally, a national study of more than 6,000 households showed that violence toward children was more prevalent in families experiencing unemployment, substance abuse, and financial difficulties (Wolfner & Gelles, 1993). As daunting as the task may seem, a broad attack on more general social problems may help to ameliorate the problem of child abuse.

Posttraumatic Stress Disorder atypical development

Children who are the victims of physical or sexual abuse or who have witnessed wars, disasters, acts of terrorism, or other traumatic events may experience the symptoms of **posttraumatic stress disorder**, or **PTSD** (Dubner & Motta, 1999; Famularo et al., 1994; Klingman, 2006). This diagnosis was originally formulated in studies of adults' responses to extremely stressful events such as wars and natural disasters, but many of the symptoms have also been observed in children who have experienced psychological traumas. Chief among them are sleep disturbances and nightmares, angry outbursts, stomachaches and headaches, depression, and difficulties in school. Some may also show the repetitive, intrusive thoughts and vivid flashbacks of the episode that adults often display (Milgram, 1998; Yule, 1998). According to one representative national sample, as many as 14 percent of children in the United States have been exposed to violence or disaster and, thus, may be at risk for PTSD (Becker-Blease, Turner, & Finkelhor, 2010).

Physiological changes in the central nervous system may accompany PTSD. Studies with animals and adult humans have shown that extreme stress is associated with decreases in the size of the hippocampus and declines in short-term memory performance (Bremner, 1999; Bremner & Narayan, 1998). More volatile functioning of the neurochemical system that responds to stress has also been observed in adults and adolescents who have experienced trauma (Golier & Yehuda, 1998; Southwick, Yehuda, & Charney, 1997). The possibility that stress can cause permanent changes to the structure of the brain and affect children's learning abilities is particularly disturbing.

Many children who have been exposed to extreme stress or trauma rebound to their previous level of functioning within a relatively short period of time. In recent studies of children who were directly affected by 9/11 and Hurricane Katrina, most children showed no significant signs of poor mental health one year later (Gershoff, Aber et al., 2010; Kronenberg et al., 2010). However, re-exposure to trauma or the added impact of ongoing stressors can prolong children's recovery. So can the experience of PTSD in children's caregivers (American Psychological Association, 2008; Catani et al., 2010; Chemtob et al., 2010).

RISK | RESILIENCE

The most successful treatments of PTSD in children and adults have used a cognitive-behavioral approach (Foa & Meadows, 1997). Typically, the child is given relaxation training along with suggestions for how to control thoughts about the traumatic event. As pointed out in Chapter 16, "Beyond Family and Peers," research also shows that providing children with ongoing support—not just from family members but from various segments of the community including schools—can be critical (Kronenberg et al., 2010). In general, when children return to stable routines, when multiple sources of stress are reduced, and when caregivers and other adults offer them emotional support, children seem to recover more quickly from initial episodes of PTSD.

Cultural and Social Class Variations in Parenting

SOCIOCULTURAL INFLUENCE

Do broader sociocultural beliefs and values play a role in parental socialization practices? If so, do children show specific patterns of behavior as a result of their different cultural experiences? Recent research suggests that the answer to both questions is yes.

Cross-Cultural Differences Beatrice Whiting and Carolyn Pope Edwards (1988) have provided an extended analysis of variations in parenting by comparing societies as diverse as rural Kenya, Liberia, and the Philippines with urban America. Despite vast differences in economic, social, and political conditions, many similar, overarching patterns are apparent in the ways parents socialize their children. With infants and toddlers, the universal emphasis is on nurturance, that is, providing routine care along with attention and support. By the time the child reaches age four or five years, most parents shift their focus to control, correcting or reprimanding misbehavior. Finally, when children reach school age, parents become concerned with training their children in the skills and social behavior their cultural group values.

posttraumatic stress disorder (PTSD) A response to extreme stress characterized by sleep disturbances, bodily complaints, and depression.

At the same time, though, Whiting and Edwards (1988) observed notable differences in parenting behaviors. For example, mothers from rural villages in Kenya and Liberia emphasized training children to do chores responsibly and placed a high premium on obedience. From an early age, children were taught how to care for the family's fields and animals, and they assumed a major role in caring for younger siblings. Children were punished for performing tasks irresponsibly and were rarely praised. Consistent with this orientation to child rearing was the family's dependence on women and children for producing food. Because women in these cultures typically had an enormous workload, they delegated some tasks to children as soon as children were physically capable of managing them; because accidents and injury to infants and the family's resources must be prevented, deviant behaviors were not tolerated in children. Children growing up in these communities were highly compliant to mothers' commands and suggestions.

An even more controlling style characterized the Tarong community in the Philippines, in which subsistence farming was the mainstay but responsibilities for producing food were more evenly distributed among the group's members. When the mother did not rely so heavily on her children to work for the family's survival and when the goals of training were thus less clear, arbitrary commands and even punishing became more common. Children were scolded frequently for being in the way of adults or playing in inappropriate places. By middle childhood, Tarong children showed a marked decline in their tendency to seek attention from or be close to their parents.

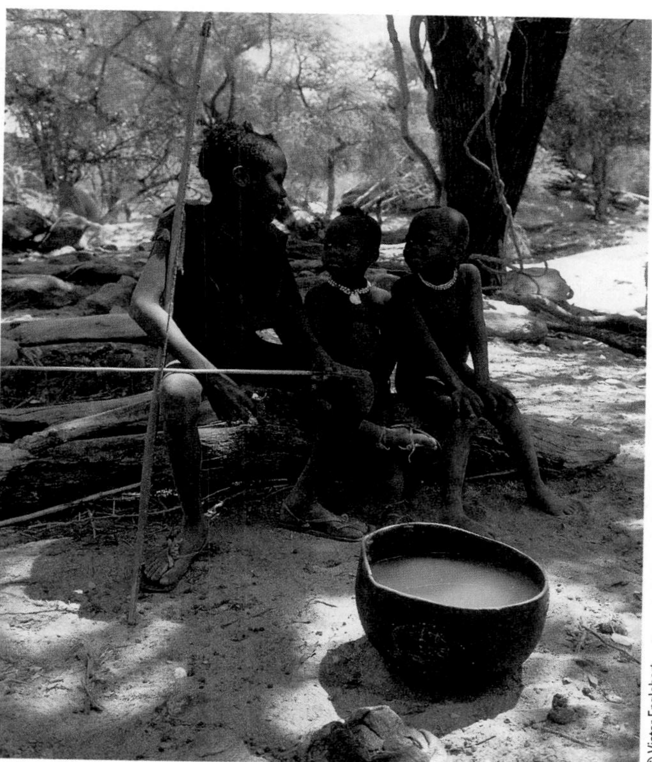

© Victor Englebert

Children's socialization experiences are influenced by cultural values and beliefs. For example, in rural Kenya, children care for the family's fields and animals and have responsibility for younger siblings. Children growing up in such communities were found to display a high degree of compliance to mothers' requests.

These patterns provided a striking contrast to the "sociability" that characterized the middle-income American mothers in the sample. Interactions between mothers and children consisted of significant information exchange and warm, friendly dialogues. Mothers emphasized verbalization, educational tasks, and play, and they were liberal in their use of praise and encouragement. Because children in American society normally do not work to ensure the economic survival of the family unit, firm training and punishing were not part of these parents' styles. The emphasis on verbalization and educational activities was consistent with the high value Americans place on social interactions and schooling.

Other researchers examining parent–child relationships in Asian cultures have reaffirmed the idea that culture affects parenting styles. Japanese mothers use less physical punishment and more verbal reasoning to control their children than American mothers (Kobayashi-Winata & Power, 1989). Japanese culture emphasizes responsibilities and commitments to others, a socialization goal that is achieved more effectively through reasoning than through power-assertive techniques. Japanese children, in fact, comply with rules at home and in school more than their American counterparts do. Similarly, both Chinese parents and children report a greater emphasis on parental behavioral control and press for achievement in their culture than do Americans (Chao, 1994; Chao & Kanatsu, 2008). In Chinese society, character development and educational attainment are highly valued, and parental practices follow directly from these larger societal goals.

As Whiting and Edwards (1988) point out, parents around the world resemble one another in numerous ways because of the universal needs children have as they grow and develop. But it is also true that the specific ecology of each culture, its socialization goals, and the demands it places on the family unit can dramatically shape parenting practices and the course of the individual child's socialization.

Social Class and Ethnic Differences Reliable social class differences exist in parenting practices. Middle-class mothers use induction, or reasoning, as they discipline their children more frequently than do lower-class mothers, who tend to use power-assertive techniques.

Figure 14.7
Effective Parenting and Peer Influences
The style of parenting that best predicts successful developmental outcomes may depend on other influences in the child's life. For example, researchers have found that for lower- and working-class adolescents, a more controlling style of parenting may lead to fewer problem behaviors if peers exert a negative influence. In this study, adolescents were divided into two groups: those who were above and below average in their exposure to negative peer influences. The amount of control parents exhibited was divided into four categories, from least to most control (where 1 was equal to least control). As the graph shows, for adolescents exposed to higher-than-average negative peer influences, greater parental control was associated with fewer behavior problems. Levels of parental control mattered less for adolescents exposed to lower-than-average negative peer influences.
Source: From Mason, C. A., Cauce, A. M., Gonzales, N., & Hiraga, Y. (1996). Neither too sweet nor too sour: Problem peers, maternal control, and problem behavior in African American adolescents. *Child Development, 67,* pp. 2115–2130. Reprinted by permission of The Society for Research in Child Development, Inc.

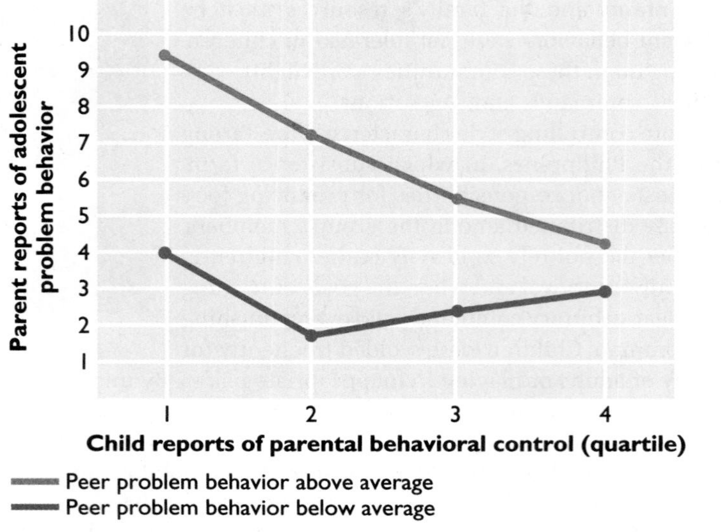

Middle-class mothers also praise their children liberally and generally verbalize more than lower-class mothers, who in turn more frequently utter such commands as "Do it because I say so!" and dispense less positive reinforcement (Hoffman, 1984).

Social class by itself, however, is not a variable that provides neat or meaningful explanations, because it is usually associated with other variables, such as access to health care, nutrition, physical environment, and educational experiences. Moreover, even within low-income families, significant variations in parenting styles can occur; a single characteristic style may not exist. For example, among low-income families, older mothers and mothers who are more religious tend to rely less on power-assertive parenting styles than younger mothers or those who are less religious (Kelley, Power, & Wimbush, 1992). Another factor to consider is how parenting practices might be related to the type of peer influence to which children are exposed. In one study, African American adolescents from lower- and working-class families were divided into two groups, those who were above and below average in their exposure to peer problem behaviors. As Figure 14.7 shows, for adolescents exposed to negative peer influences, fewer behavior problems occurred when parents exerted more control over their children. When exposure to negative peer influences was lower, the type of parental control made less of a difference (Mason et al., 1996). Although we have seen in much of this chapter that high parental control is associated with negative child outcomes, under some circumstances this type of parenting may actually be advantageous.

Vonnie McLoyd (McLoyd, 1990; McLoyd et al., 1994) has provided an extended analysis of the growing literature on families under economic stress that illuminates the effects of social class. Because African American children experience a disproportionate share of the problems of poverty (a rate of 41 percent for African American children at the time of her analysis compared with 13 percent for Caucasian children), McLoyd focused on the social and family dynamics that can affect this racial minority. In McLoyd's analysis, economic hardship has a serious negative impact on children's socioemotional development because of the psychological distress it causes parents. Parents under stress have a diminished ability to provide nurturant, consistent, involved care for their children. Children growing up with poverty are thus at risk for depression, poor peer relations, lower self-esteem, and conduct disorders. In one study of African American mothers, mothers' job loss was related to the tendency to report symptoms of depression. This fact was, in turn, related to their use of punishment and less parental nurturance (McLoyd et al., 1994).

Similar findings have been reported for Caucasian middle-class families from the Midwestern United States during a time of economic downturn. Rand Conger and his colleagues (Conger et al., 1992) found that parents who experienced economic hardship reported greater emotional distress, which was related to less skillful parenting. The disruptions in parenting were associated with adjustment problems among the adolescent boys in the sample. These seventh-graders reported more feelings of hostility and depression than those whose families were not experiencing economic hardship. The effects of financial stress have been observed in many types of families. Both one- and two-parent families of African American, Latino, and European American backgrounds show more negative parent–child relationships in the context of financial strain (Conger et al., 2002; Gutman & Eccles, 1999; Parke et al., 2004).

The demands poverty makes on many African American families may be related to unique family structures that are adaptive for their situation and help them to cope. For example, a significant number of African American children grow up in an extended family. About 8 percent of African American children younger than eighteen years—almost three times as many as Caucasian children—grow up with a live-in grandparent (Livingston & Parker, 2010). Extended family members often bring additional income, child care assistance, and emotional support and counseling to families under stress, especially when the parent is single (Wilson, 1986). Extensive networks of social support have, in turn, been associated with responsive and involved parenting styles among low-income African American mothers (Burchinal, Follmer, & Bryant, 1996). Among African American adolescents, those who perceived their families as having extensive social support from relatives also perceived their homes as being organized and their parents as being involved in their schooling; these beliefs were linked to fewer problem behaviors, greater self-reliance, and higher grades in school than for adolescents whose perceptions differed (Taylor, 1996). The higher levels of involvement of African American families in religion also have a positive impact on children. Children of religious parents show less aggression and depression than those whose parents are less involved in religion (Brody, Stoneman, & Flor, 1996). Thus, although economic stress can have a negative effect on family dynamics, it can also foster alternative family structures and socialization goals that help to meet the needs of children.

For Your Review and Reflection

- What are the characteristics of the four major styles of parenting? What child behaviors are associated with each parental style? Which parenting style did you experience when you were growing up?
- What are some of the specific effects of parental warmth on the developing child?
- Which principles of learning theory help to explain effective punishment?
- In what ways do parental cognitions play a role in parenting strategies?
- What are some ways in which the characteristics of the child can influence parenting strategies?
- How do coercive cycles of maladaptive parent–child interactions arise? What can be done to intervene in these maladaptive interactions?
- What are some of the factors associated with the incidence of child abuse?

- In what ways do parenting strategies vary across different cultural and socioeconomic groups?
- When you consider all of the research described in this section, which parenting behaviors emerge as most critical in promoting healthy development and resilience to risks in children?

Relationships with Mothers, Fathers, and Siblings

Because women traditionally have been seen as the primary caregivers for children, most studies of parenting practices in the psychological literature have focused on mothering. More than two decades of research on fathers, however, as well as even more recent studies of sibling relationships, have provided a much broader understanding of how each distinct relationship within the family influences the individual child's development.

Mothering Versus Fathering: Are There Differences?

Historically, mothers have borne most of the responsibility for child rearing in American society, whether or not they have been employed outside the home. However, the number of fathers participating in child care is increasing. For example, about 19 percent of single parents are now fathers. In addition, fathers assume primary child care responsibilities in about 25 percent of families while mothers of preschoolers are working (U.S. Census Bureau, 2010a). Research resoundingly reveals that fathers are significant figures in their children's lives and are clearly competent in their parental role.

In this chapter, as well as in Chapter 11, "Emotion," we have underscored maternal sensitivity and responsiveness as key factors in fostering optimal child development. Studies have shown that fathers are just as responsive as mothers to the signals of their infants, and, when given the opportunity, they interact with their babies in ways similar to mothers. Several decades ago, a team of researchers measured the physiological responsiveness of mothers and fathers as they observed quiet, smiling, or crying babies on a video monitor (Frodi et al., 1978). Mothers and fathers showed similar changes in heart rate, blood pressure, and skin conductance when the babies smiled or cried. In another study of maternal and paternal behaviors toward infants in the newborn nursery, Ross Parke and Sandra O'Leary (1976) found that fathers were just as likely as mothers to hold, touch, and vocalize to their babies.

After the newborn period, fathers and mothers begin to manifest somewhat different styles of interacting with their infants. When they play face to face with their babies, fathers tend to provide physical and social stimulation in staccato bursts, whereas mothers tend to be more rhythmic and soothing. Fathers engage in physical and unpredictable "idiosyncratic" play with their infants—throwing them up in the air, moving their limbs, and tickling them—whereas mothers spend more time in caregiving activities or calm games such as "pat-a-cake" (Lamb, 1997; Yogman, 1982). As a consequence, infants prefer fathers when they wish to play and seek out mothers when they desire care and comfort. This dichotomy in parental styles of interaction continues at least until middle childhood (Russell & Russell, 1987).

Despite their responsiveness and competence as parents, many fathers spend less time with their children than mothers do. In general, fathers spend about one-half to two-thirds the time mothers do in direct contact with their children, even when the mother works outside the home (National Research Council and Institute of Medicine, 2003). This pattern has been found in diverse ethnic groups and cultures, including African American, Chinese, and Japanese families (Hossain & Roopnarine, 1994; Ishii-Kuntz, 1994; Sun & Roopnarine, 1996).

Why are fathers less involved? Some may hold traditional beliefs about which family member should be responsible for child care. Another reason may be that fathers are not confident in their caregiving skills. Because males typically are not exposed to child care

© AresT/Shutterstock.com

When given the opportunity, fathers respond to their children by touching, holding, and vocalizing to them in much the same way that mothers do. They do, however, engage in more physical play with their children than mothers. When fathers participate in child care, their children show favorable developmental outcomes.

through such experiences as baby-sitting or courses on parenting and child development, they may feel insecure about feeding, bathing, or diapering a child (Lamb et al., 1987). On the other hand, some circumstances predict greater father involvement in child care: fewer hours at work, the fact that the mother works, and the father's memories of his own relationship with his father (Gottfried, Bathurst, & Gottfried, 1994; NICHD Early Child Care Research Network, 2000a; Radin, 1994). In some cases, the father may have learned to extend his caregiving role from observing the participation of his father; in other cases, he may be trying to have a better relationship with his own children than he had with his uninvolved father.

Demographers project that more and more children will be cared for by fathers for longer periods of time (Casper & O'Connell, 1998). It seems, then, that the concept of the father as an equal partner in parenthood is gaining hold (Pleck, 2010).

The Father's Influence on Child Development Do fathers have a different influence than mothers on the process of child development? During the 1960s and 1970s, psychologists believed they did, based on studies of the effects of father absence, especially on boys. Boys growing up without fathers were more likely to have problems in academic achievement, gender-role development, and control of aggression (Biller, 1974; Lamb, 1981). An important theoretical construct driving much of the older research was *identification*: the idea that boys assimilate the characteristics, attitudes, and behaviors of their fathers as they form an intense emotional bond with them. Presumably, boys without fathers did not have an identity figure or model for appropriate masculine, instrumentally competent behavior and thus suffered deficits in cognitive, social, and emotional domains.

Identification with the father may be less important than other variables, however. Michael Lamb (2010) points out that the effects of father absence may result not from the loss of a masculine identity figure for the son but from the loss of a source of emotional and financial support for the entire family. The tension and stress that result may produce maladaptive patterns of parenting, which in turn generate undesirable developmental outcomes for boys. Boys may be particularly vulnerable because they seem to be more generally susceptible than girls to the effects of deviant environments (Rutter, 1986).

Risk | Resilience

A more contemporary view is that fathers make recognizable contributions to family life in general, and child development in particular, but that those contributions simply reflect aspects of good parenting. In other words, good fathering resembles good mothering, and the child will thrive by having two parents who fill those roles instead of just one. Research confirms that the mere presence of a father is not associated with benefits to children's development. Instead, it is when fathers are nurturant, responsive, and involved with their children that children show higher cognitive, language, and social functioning (Black, Dubowitz, & Starr, Jr., 1999; Cabrera, Shannon, & Tamis-LeMonda, 2007; Jaffee et al., 2003).

INTERACTION AMONG DOMAINS

Siblings

Like parents, siblings serve as important sources of the child's social attitudes, beliefs, and behaviors. Although they may not wield as much power as parents, siblings certainly do attempt to control one another's behaviors (ask anyone who is not an only child!) and may be models for both desirable and undesirable actions. An emerging body of research on sibling relationships has provided yet another perspective on how families influence development.

The Only Child One way to assess the impact of siblings on development is to examine children who have none. Are there notable differences between only children and children with one or more sisters or brothers? Popular opinion depicts the only child as spoiled, demanding, self-centered, and dependent. But research evidence suggests the contrary, that only children may enjoy the benefits of having their parents' exclusive attention. Toni Falbo and Denise Polit (1986) summarized the results of 115 studies of only children and concluded that, overall, only children showed higher achievement and intelligence scores than children with siblings. In addition, only-borns ranked higher on measures of character—that is, tendencies toward leadership, personal control, and maturity—than children with siblings. No overall differences emerged between only children and children with siblings on assessments of sociability and personal adjustment.

INTERACTION AMONG DOMAINS

In explaining these findings, Falbo and Polit (1986) found support for the hypothesis that features of the parent–child relationship account for the advantages only children enjoy in certain domains. Only children were found to have more positive relationships with their parents than children having siblings. This effect probably occurs because parents of one child have more time to spend with their son or daughter and generally have high-quality interactions with their child (Falbo & Cooper, 1980). Parents and children in one study, for example, exchanged more in mealtime conversations in one-child families than in families having two or three children (Lewis & Feiring, 1982). First-time parents are also more anxious about their child-rearing techniques and may thus be more vigilant and responsive to their child's behaviors (Falbo & Polit, 1986).

Falbo and Polit's (1986) meta-analysis showed that parent–child relations in one- and two-child families are actually more similar than different. Only when a third child is born does the quality of parent–child relations diminish significantly. Parents of more than two children probably become more relaxed about their child-rearing strategies and also have significantly more demands placed on their time. The result is less responsiveness and fewer deliberate attempts to instruct their children, aspects of parenting found to be related to cognitive achievements.

Family Size and Birth Order Children growing up in contemporary American society have fewer siblings than children in earlier eras. In 2009, the typical American family with children had one or two children (U.S. Census Bureau, 2010a). Many children thus grow up with only one other sibling. Does the size of the family make any difference in child development?

INTERACTION AMONG DOMAINS

In general, children from smaller families have higher intelligence test scores, achieve higher levels of education, and display greater self-esteem (Blake, 1989; Wagner, Schubert, & Schubert, 1985). As we have just seen, one reason for these effects may be that parents in larger families have less time to spend with their children and may not provide the kind of cognitive stimulation children in smaller families receive. Another important factor is financial circumstances: parents with a larger number of children often experience greater economic stress, which in turn may diminish the quality of their parenting (Rutter & Madge, 1976).

Regardless of family size, the child's birth order, whether firstborn or later born, can also be a factor in development. Like only children, firstborns tend to score higher on IQ tests and have higher achievement motivation than other children (Glass, Neulinger, & Brim, 1974; Zajonc, Markus, & Markus, 1979). They also tend to be more obedient and socially responsible (Sutton-Smith & Rosenberg, 1970). These effects probably stem from the greater attention and autonomy parents give to their first children (Bumpus, Crouter, & McHale, 2001). Later-borns seem to have an advantage in the social sphere, however. Youngest siblings tend to have better peer relationships than first-borns and are more confident in social situations (Lahey et al., 1980; Miller & Maruyama, 1976).

The Impact of a Sibling's Arrival The birth of a sibling can have a dramatic effect on the life of a firstborn child. Research on the consequences of a second child's arrival generally confirms that "sibling rivalry" is no myth. Judy Dunn and Carol Kendrick (1982) followed the progress of family relationships among forty firstborn children who experienced the arrival of a sibling sometime between their first and fourth birthdays. Dunn and Kendrick observed normal home routines during the mother's last month of pregnancy and again when the baby sibling was one, eight, and fourteen months old. They also interviewed the mother at each stage about the older child's eating and sleeping habits, moods, and other routine behaviors.

For the majority of children, the arrival of a sister or brother led to marked changes in behavior; they became more demanding, clingy, unhappy, or withdrawn. Accompanying these changes in their behavior were significant decreases in maternal attention toward them; mothers engaged in less joint play, cuddling, and verbalization with their first-borns and in general initiated fewer interactions with them. At the same time, restrictive and punitive maternal behaviors increased. Over time, Dunn and Kendrick (1982) noted, two distinct patterns of sibling relationships emerged. Among some sibling pairs, almost all interactions eventually became friendly and positive; for others, a persistent pattern of hostility and aggression became the norm. The first pattern was more likely if mothers had previously prepared the older child for the newborn's arrival by referring to the infant as a person with needs and desires. Engaging the older child in caring for the infant also seemed to have positive consequences. In contrast, negative relationships between siblings resulted if the older child experienced a sharp drop in maternal contact. The discrepancy in pre- and post-sibling maternal contact made the most difference: children who had less contact with their mothers before the sibling's birth were less profoundly affected by her attention to the new infant.

The timing of a sibling's arrival may also be important. Researchers have noted a drop in the security of a child's attachment to the mother following the birth of a second child. However, the decrease in attachment security was less noticeable if the older child was twenty-four months of age or younger (Teti et al., 1996). Younger children may not yet have the social cognitive capacities to see the new arrival as a threat or cause of change in family routines.

The arrival of a sibling demands a big adjustment for the older child, especially because another individual begins to compete for the parents' attention and affection. As already noted in Chapter 3, "Genetics and Heredity," siblings are aware of the differential treatment parents may knowingly or unwittingly bestow on them (Kowal & Kramer, 1997; McHale et al., 1995). The greater the perceived discrepancy is, the greater the sibling conflict will be (Dunn, 1988). But certainly not all aspects of sibling relationships are negative. Dunn and Kendrick (1982) noted that, in certain circumstances, siblings fill a void in parent–child relationships. When the mother and her older child have difficulties in their interactions, siblings may provide the attention and affection missing from the maternal relationship, thus helping to keep the family system in equilibrium. When parents display a high degree of marital conflict or even undergo divorce, siblings show an increase in emotional closeness and positive, friendly behavior toward one another (Dunn, 1996).

Sibling Interactions Among Older Children How do older children interact as siblings? For one thing, children tend to fight more with their siblings than with their friends. When fifth- through eighth-graders were asked to describe conflicts with their siblings,

This young boy's reaction to a new sibling is typical. Although many children become clingy, withdrawn, or demanding when a new sibling first arrives, these reactions can be diminished if parents prepare the older child for the infant's arrival and involve him in the infant's care. Adjustment is also more difficult if the older child perceives that he must compete for the parents' affection and attention.

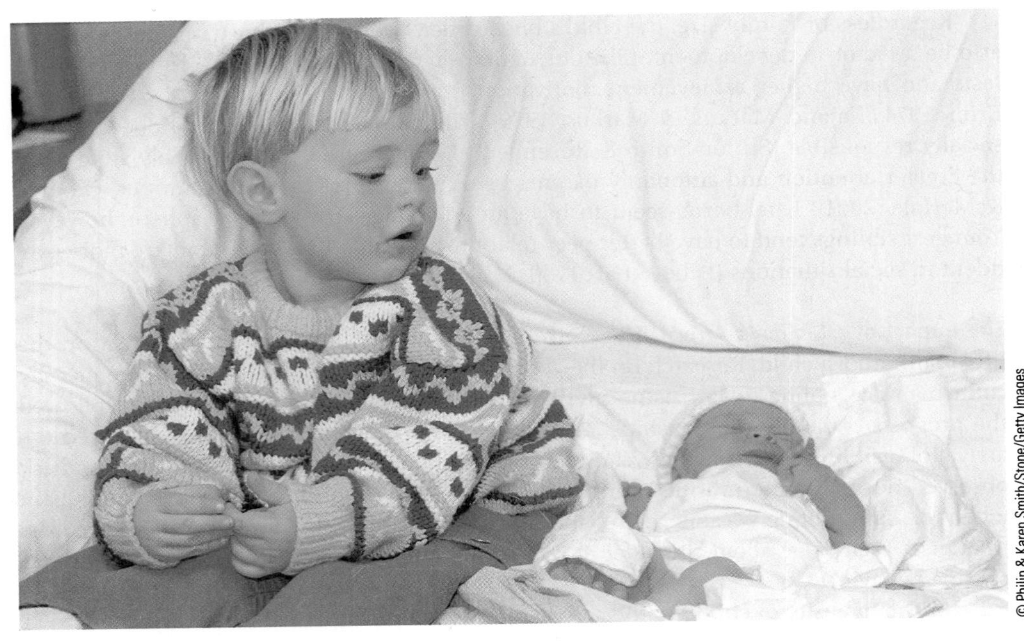

© Philip & Karen Smith/Stone/Getty Images

they reported that they allowed quarrels with siblings to escalate, whereas they tried to resolve conflicts with friends. Most of the time, siblings fight about privacy and interpersonal boundaries, such as one sibling borrowing an item from another without permission or entering a sibling's room (Campione-Barr & Smetana, 2010; Raffaelli, 1997). Typically, parents do not intervene in sibling conflicts, and when they do not, those conflicts continue (Perozynski & Kramer, 1999). On the other hand, when parents discuss each child's needs (as opposed to using controlling tactics), subsequent conflicts between siblings are less likely (Kramer, Perozynski, & Chung, 1999). Researchers have noted that the degree of conflict in sibling relationships is related to the amount of aggression a child shows in school, whereas the amount of warmth in sibling relationships is linked to emotional control and social competence in school (Garcia et al., 2000; Stormshak et al., 1996).

INTERACTION AMONG DOMAINS

Whether positive or negative, sibling relationships in early childhood tend to remain stable through middle childhood (Dunn, Slombowski, & Beardsall, 1994) and then typically change from middle childhood through adolescence. Duane Buhrmester and Wyndol Furman (1990) administered the Sibling Relationship Questionnaire to third-, sixth-, ninth-, and twelfth-graders to assess several dimensions of sibling interactions. Older siblings reported being more dominant and nurturant toward their younger siblings, and younger siblings confirmed that they received, more often than dispensed, dominance and nurturance. These differences between older and younger siblings apparently disappear over time, however. The older children in the sample reported having more egalitarian relationships with their siblings, as well as less intense feelings of both warmth and conflict. Initial differences in power and nurturance usually disappeared when the younger sibling was twelve years old, by which time she or he had become more competent and needed less guidance and emotional support. Thus, generally speaking, the emotional intensity—both positive and negative—that typically surrounds sibling interactions declines from middle childhood to early adolescence (Slomkowski & Manke, 2004).

Although the presence of siblings may mean the child has fewer opportunities to interact with parents, it also provides the context for developing other unique skills. Older siblings have opportunities to become nurturant and assertive, and younger siblings have more models for a range of behaviors than only children. Older siblings may also regulate their younger brother's or sister's opportunities to interact with other children in their school or neighborhood (Zukow-Goldring, 2002). Although many children grow up with siblings, we are just beginning to understand the role brothers and sisters play in child development.

For Your Review and Reflection

- What are the major differences between mothers and fathers in parenting styles?
- In what ways do fathers make important contributions to child development?
- How do family size and birth order have an impact on child development?
- In what ways can parents facilitate a child's transition to having a new sibling?
- What role do siblings play in the development of younger children in the family?
- Which of the five key themes in development stands out for you in this section of the chapter? Why?

Families in Transition

As we saw at the start of this chapter, the traditional nuclear family has been slowly disappearing from mainstream American society. Single-parent families, dual-wage-earner families, and reconstituted families (in which adults who remarry bring their respective children into new families) are becoming more and more prevalent and offer new circumstances to which children must adapt. What are the effects of these emerging family structures on child development? Research shows that child development is influenced not so much by changes in family structure per se as by the ways in which structural changes affect interpersonal relations within the family.

Maternal Employment

In the past four decades, the percentage of married women with children in the labor force has increased dramatically. The working mother is now the norm. What is the effect of maternal employment on child development?

When psychologists compare children of employed mothers with children of women who remain at home, few differences emerge on measures of cognitive achievement and socioemotional development, at least among middle-class participants. If anything, daughters of employed mothers derive some benefit; they are likely to show greater independence, greater achievement, and higher self-esteem than daughters of nonworking mothers (Gottfried, Gottfried, & Bathurst, 2002; Hoffman & Youngblade, 1999). Apparently these girls profit from having a successful, competent role model, at least as the larger society recognizes these qualities. (Women who remain at home "work" too, but traditionally they have not been afforded recognition or status for that role.)

When a mother returns to work seems not to be an important factor. In an analysis of data collected from several thousand participants in the National Longitudinal Survey of Youth, Elizabeth Harvey (1999) found that the timing of mother's entry or return to the work force was not associated with children's development. The number of hours mothers work can make a difference, however. Two studies of mostly Caucasian middle-class women found that the more hours mothers worked, the lower was the academic achievement of their preschool and early school-age children (Brooks-Gunn, Han, & Waldfogel, 2002; Goldberg, Greenberger, & Nagel, 1996). On the other hand, comprehensive longitudinal studies of children from infancy through age twelve have found that although academic achievement was negatively related to the number of hours the mothers worked when children were ages five and six, this relationship was modest and was not apparent as children grew older (Gottfried et al., 1994; Harvey, 1999).

For low-income families, maternal employment is related to some clear benefits for children. One longitudinal study examined 189 second-graders; most were born to adolescent mothers, and 41 percent lived in households with incomes below the poverty level. For this sample, maternal employment during the child's first three years was associated with greater household income, a higher-quality home environment as assessed by the HOME inventory

© Manchan/Digital Vision/Jupiter Images

When mothers work, their children are less likely to hold stereotyped beliefs about gender, probably because they see both parents in multiple roles.

(see Chapter 10, "Achievement"), and higher mathematics achievement in school for the child compared with the effects when mothers did not work (Vandell & Ramanan, 1992).

In general, the clearest effect of maternal employment involves the gender-role attitudes of both sons and daughters. As we saw in Chapter 13, "Gender," when mothers work outside the home, their children are less likely than children of at-home mothers to hold stereotypical beliefs about males and females and more likely to see both sexes as competent (Hoffman & Youngblade, 1999). When both mother and father work, sons and daughters have the opportunity to see both parents in multiple roles—as powerful, competent wage earners and nurturant, warm caregivers—a factor that probably contributes to more egalitarian beliefs.

Overall, maternal employment is not a simple, "neat" variable in studying child development. Some mothers work out of sheer economic necessity, whereas others are more concerned with realizing personal or career goals, for example. As researchers point out, the impact of maternal employment is better understood through its effects on family dynamics, parental attitudes, and the alternative child care arrangements the family chooses. It is to these factors that we now turn our attention.

Maternal Employment and Parent–Child Interaction In terms of direct, one-to-one mother–child interaction, no significant differences have been found between employed and nonemployed mothers (Gottfried et al., 2002). Employed mothers often compensate for the time they miss with their children during the workweek by allocating more time for them during mornings and evenings (Ahnert, Rickert, & Lamb, 2000). In many instances, fathers assume more responsibilities for child care when the mother works, especially when parents have nonstandard work schedules and when they hold nontraditional beliefs about child care (Han, 2004; NICHD Early Child Care Research Network, 2000b). As we saw in our earlier discussion, responsive and sensitive "fathering" provides the same benefits to children as effective "mothering."

Overall, what matters more than whether the mother works is her attitude toward mothering and work and why she is working or staying home. In one study of mothers of infants, women who remained at home contrary to their preference had higher scores on tests of depression and stress than mothers who preferred to be at home and were not in the labor force and employed mothers who valued their positions in the work world (Hock & DeMeis, 1990). We saw earlier in this chapter that parental stress has been implicated as a factor in less consistent and less nurturant parenting. On the other hand, when maternal employment is the factor that produces tension, parenting practices also may suffer. Researchers have found that mothers who worked more than forty hours per week, for example, were more anxious and unhappy and had less sensitive and less animated interactions with their infants than mothers who worked less than forty hours per week (Owen & Cox, 1988). In general, family factors continue to predict child outcomes, even though, when mothers work, their children are likely to be enrolled in full-time child care. Variables such as parental child-rearing style, psychological well-being, and sensitivity are associated with children's cognitive and social development irrespective of the child's caregiving context (NICHD Early Child Care Research Group, 1998b). First and foremost, it is parents who play a primary role.

The Effects of Daycare About one-fourth of children enter child care during the first five months after birth, according to one national survey. About half begin regular child care before they turn three (Singer et al., 1998). Child care arrangements take various forms, from in-home care provided by a relative or paid caregiver to group care in a formal, organized

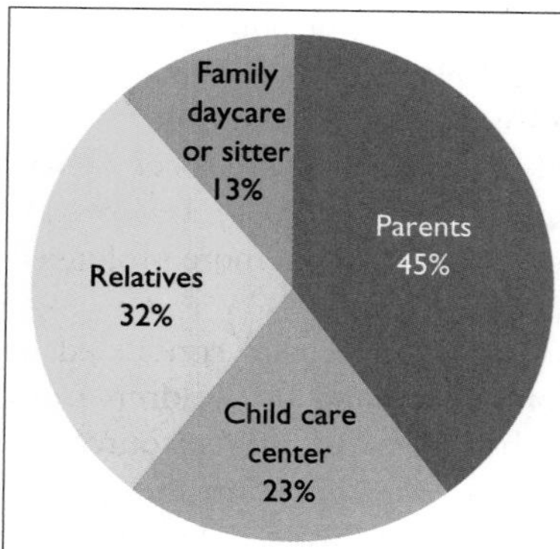

Figure 14.8
Child Care Arrangements for Children Under Age 5, 2005/2006
This chart shows the percentage of American children who receive different forms of child care. Forty-five percent of infants, toddlers, and preschoolers are cared for by parents. Of the remainder, most are cared for by relatives or attend a formal child care center. (Note that the percents do not add up to 100 percent because some children receive more than one form of care.)
Source: Data from National Center for Educational Statistics, 2001.

center. As Figure 14.8 shows, about 45 percent of children under age five are cared for by their parents. Of those who receive full-time nonparental care, a significant percentage attends organized child care centers.

One area in which some (but not all) researchers have noted an effect of daycare is in intellectual performance. Daycare children tend to outperform children reared at home by parents on standardized tests of IQ, as well as measures of problem-solving ability, creativity, language development, and arithmetic skills (Lamb & Ahnert, 2006). Daycare programs that stress cognitive activities have a greater effect on IQ scores than those that simply provide caregiving (NICHD Early Child Care Research Network, 2003b). Moreover, the effect of high-quality care on intellectual and academic achievement shows up many years later, when children are fifteen years of age (see Figure 14.9). The experience of high-quality care from birth to age four-and-a-half years predicts higher scores on measures of vocabulary, reading comprehension, verbal reasoning, and mathematical problem solving (Vandell et al., 2010).

Daycare is also associated with effects in the realm of social development. Specifically, children with experience in daycare are more socially competent with peers. They show more frequent nonnegative interactions, more complex and reciprocal play, and more positive engagement with peers compared with children not in child care. Important to note is the finding that responsiveness of caregivers in daycare centers was associated with these positive peer interactions (NICHD Early Child Care Research Network, 2001a). In addition to showing

Figure 14.9
High Quality Child Care and Cognitive Development
Children show long-term gains in cognitive development when they attend high-quality child care programs. As can be seen in this figure, gains show up once the measured quality reaches a certain level and accelerate as the quality of the program is rated increasingly higher.
Source: From Vandell, D. L., Belsky, J., Burchinal, M., Steinberg, L., Vandergraft, N., & NICHD Early Child Care Research Network. (2010). Do effects of early child care extend to age 15 years? Results from the NICHD study of early child care and youth development. *Child Development, 81*, pp. 737–756. Reprinted by permission of The Society for Research in Child Development, Inc.

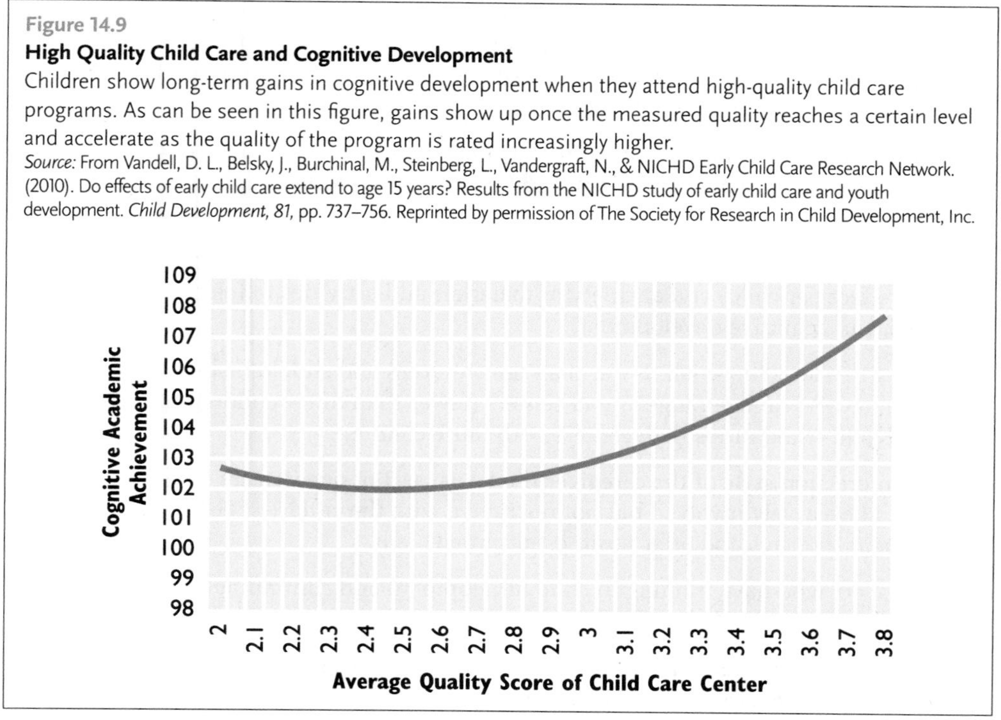

more positive behaviors, some studies suggest that daycare children may display more aggression with peers and noncompliance with adults (Bates et al., 1994; Baydar & Brooks-Gunn, 1991). A national study of more than 1,000 children in daycare centers across the United States found that the amount of time spent in child care predicted children's problem social behaviors at age four and a half (NICHD Early Child Care Research Network, 2003a). However, if there are negative effects, some researchers caution that they may arise from more prolonged experiences in low-quality centers (Lamb & Ahnert, 2006; Love et al., 2003).

RISK | RESILIENCE

It is important to remember that many studies of daycare have been conducted in high-quality centers, often associated with universities and populated by children from middle- to upper-class families. But not all parents have the opportunity or resources to send their children to such high-caliber programs. In a disturbing report on the quality of child care centers in the United States, only 14 percent of centers were judged to offer care that promotes children's development; most provided only custodial-level care, and 12 percent were found to jeopardize children's development (Children's Defense Fund, 1996). Another national report characterizes the average level of child care in the United States as "mediocre" (National Research Council and Institute of Medicine, 2003). What are the effects of less-than-excellent programs on children? Research suggests that when children are enrolled in low-quality centers before age one, they have more difficulty with peers and are distractible and less task oriented in kindergarten than children who are enrolled at later ages and those who attend high-quality centers (Howes, 1990). Children in low-quality child care also tend to score lower on tests of cognitive and language skills than children in high-quality care (Burchinal et al., 2000; NICHD Early Child Care Research Network, 2000b; Peisner-Feinberg et al., 2001). Evidence is accumulating that quality of child care makes a difference. Thus, it is essential that parents be aware of the elements of high-quality daycare.

Choosing a Daycare Center Both the federal government and many states have set minimum requirements for daycare services that regulate the qualifications of teachers, staff–child ratios, the size and safety of the facility, and the provision of nourishing meals. Although the guidelines and laws provide for minimum standards, most parents are concerned with providing their children with the best possible care during the hours they are at work. Alison Clarke-Stewart and Virginia Allhusen (2005) have drawn on the expanding body of research findings on daycare to compile the following suggestions for parents:

- Center-based care is more likely to include educational opportunities for children than home-based care, such as that provided by baby-sitters and family daycare. On the other hand, children are more likely to receive one-to-one supervision and authoritative discipline in home-based care.
- Children are most likely to thrive intellectually and emotionally in programs that offer a balance between structured educational activities and an open, free environment.
- The caregiving environment should provide ample physical space (at least twenty-five square feet per child) and a variety of materials and activities to foster sensorimotor, social, and cognitive development.
- Class size should be small (fewer than ten children) and should include children within a two-year age range. Small centers (fewer than thirty children) usually have better staff–child ratios than centers with more children.
- The interaction style of the caregiver is a key aspect of quality care. The caregiver should be actively involved but not restrictive with the children. The caregiver should also be responsive and offer positive encouragement.
- Caregivers who have training in child development and continuing opportunities for education are most likely to provide high-quality care.
- The individual characteristics of the child should be taken into account. Some children will probably do well in a program that balances structure and openness; others may profit from either more structure or a more flexible and relaxed program.

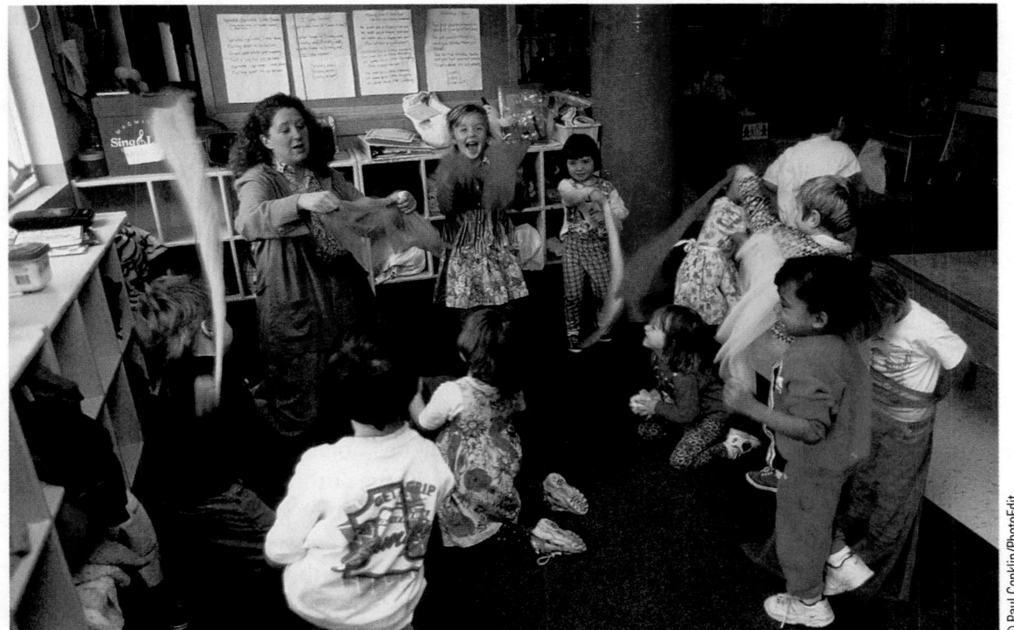

© Paul Conklin/PhotoEdit

Research shows that daycare has few negative effects on young children and may even facilitate cognitive and social development. High-quality centers generally have small group size, favorable staff-to-child ratios, and responsive, warm caregivers.

Other important factors include a high staff–child ratio and low staff turnover. Research shows, for example, that when the staff–child ratio is at least one to three for infants, one to four for toddlers, and one to nine for preschoolers, the quality of caregiving and of children's activities within the center are both good. Likewise, when the overall class size is six or fewer for infants, twelve or fewer for toddlers, and eighteen or fewer for preschoolers, children have better-quality experiences than those in larger groups (Howes, Phillips, & Whitebook, 1992).

In essence, the qualities of good daycare mirror the qualities of good parenting. In fact, the reason that factors such as good staff–child ratios and education of caregivers are important is because they are related to the quality of caregiving (NICHD Early Child Care Research Network, 2002). In choosing a daycare center, parents should seek a warm, responsive environment that provides the child, at least some of the time, with opportunities for structured play and prosocial learning.

Divorce

As we pointed out at the start of this chapter, the statistics are dramatic: the divorce rate among couples in the United States is a little under 50 percent, and estimates suggest that 40 percent of children will live through the divorce of their parents (Bramlett & Mosher, 2001; Cherlin, 1992; Furstenberg, 1994). Far from being an atypical event, divorce affects a significant proportion of American children. Unfortunately, the effects of divorce on children are rarely positive; the absence of one parent, the emotional and financial tension, and sometimes continuing conflicts between parents that accompany divorce frequently lead to a range of psychological problems for both boys and girls, at least in the period immediately following the breakup of the family. The ability of children to cope with the stresses of divorce, particularly in the long run, depends on a number of variables. Most important is the way parents manage the transition in family structure.

RISK | RESILIENCE

A major longitudinal study of the effects of divorce on parents and children conducted by E. Mavis Hetherington and her associates illuminated how parental separation affects children and how the nature of parent–child interactions changes (Hetherington, Cox, & Cox, 1982). The researchers compared two groups over a period of two years, a sample of forty-eight preschool-age, middle-class children whose parents divorced and another group of forty-eight middle-class children matched on several variables, such as age and sex, whose families were intact. In all the divorced families, mothers had custody of their children. During the course of the study, the researchers made several assessments of both parents and children, including parental interviews, observations of parent–child interactions in the laboratory and at home, observations and ratings of children's behavior in the home and at school, and personality tests.

The results of the study indicated that the worst period for most children was the first year after the divorce, when they exhibited many negative characteristics such as aggression, distractibility, and noncompliance. The extent of their undesirable behaviors surpassed those of children from intact families with a high level of conflict; it was particularly noticeable in boys. Two years after the divorce, many of the effects on children had diminished, especially for girls. In a six-year follow-up, however, many boys continued to show patterns of aggression and noncompliance, academic difficulties, poor relations with peers, and extremely low self-esteem (Hetherington, 1989).

INTERACTION AMONG DOMAINS

A look at family interaction styles after divorce helps to account for the poor initial adjustment of children. Hetherington and her colleagues noted that, soon after they separated from their husbands, mothers tended to adopt a more authoritarian style of parenting (Hetherington et al., 1982; Hetherington & Kelly, 2002). They gave out numerous commands and prohibitions and displayed little affection or responsiveness to their children. These mothers were undoubtedly having problems coping with their new status as single parents in both emotional and practical terms. At the same time, the fathers withdrew, participating little in the management of their children's behavior. Children, particularly boys, became less compliant, and mothers in turn responded with increased restrictiveness and punitiveness. Caught up in a spiral of frustration, helplessness, and feelings of incompetence, these mothers responded negatively to many of their children's behaviors, even those that were neutral or positive, and, despite their harsh threats, followed up on few of the directives they gave. The result was a coercive cycle of parent–child interaction such as that described earlier in this chapter and typified by this chapter's opening scene between Joey and his mother.

Other researchers have confirmed that many children show more heightened aggression, lower academic achievement, disruptions in peer relationships, and depression after their parents' divorce than they had previously (Amato, 2001; Emery, 1999b; Stolberg & Anker, 1984; Wallerstein, Corbin, & Lewis, 1988). Research on how children respond to parental conflict suggests that children either blame themselves or perceive a personal threat when their parents fight, judgments that are linked to their own psychological adjustment (Grych, Harold, & Miles, 2003). Sibling interactions also suffer. Carol MacKinnon (1989) observed elementary school-age children as they played games with their siblings in the laboratory. Siblings whose parents had been divorced for one year or longer showed more teasing, quarreling, physical attacks, and other negative behaviors toward one another than children from intact families. Children ages six to eight years seem to have the most difficulty adjusting to divorce; they are old enough to recognize the seriousness of the family's situation but do not yet have the coping skills to deal with feelings of sadness and guilt that often accompany the change in family structure (Wallerstein & Kelly, 1980). Older children often have a better understanding of divorce and the notion that conflicts between parents must somehow be resolved (Kurdek, 1989). However, even adolescents often suffer negative psychological consequences after their parents divorce. Adolescent boys in particular were found to be more likely to use alcohol or illicit drugs after their parents separated than boys in a control group whose parents remained married (Doherty & Needle, 1991).

INTERACTION AMONG DOMAINS

For some individuals, the aftermath of divorce may last well into young adulthood. According to data collected as part of a major longitudinal study in Great Britain, young adults whose parents had previously divorced reported more depression, anxiety, and other emotional problems than adults from intact families (Chase-Lansdale, Cherlin, & Kiernan, 1995). In addition, in a twenty-year follow-up of her original sample, Hetherington (1999) found that young adults whose parents had divorced were less likely to finish high school, had smaller social networks, experienced more conflicts with siblings and friends, and had more conflicts in their own marriages. The results of another longitudinal study show that adults whose parents had divorced were more likely to experience a breakup of their own marriages (Amato, 1999).

Adjusting to Divorce The consequences of divorce are not always so grim for all children. In fact, most children whose parents have divorced do not look different from children in intact families when they are followed over time (Emery, 1999a). We need to remember that the psychological distress experienced by children at the time of divorce is different from a long-term psychological disorder (Emery, Otto, & O'Donohue, 2005). E. Mavis Hetherington (1989) observed that, after six years, some of the children in her original study recovered from the family crisis and showed a healthy adaptation to their new family lifestyle whether or not their mothers remarried. These children displayed few behavior problems, high self-esteem, successful academic performance, and positive relations with peers.

RISK | RESILIENCE

What factors were associated with this favorable pattern of adjustment? For one thing, mothers of children in this group had become less authoritarian and more authoritative in their parental style, encouraging independence but also providing a warm, supportive climate for their sons and daughters. If the mother was not available, many of these children had contact with some other caring adult, such as a relative, teacher, or neighbor. In addition, several children in this category had responsibility for the care of another individual: a younger sibling, an aging grandparent, or someone with a physical or emotional problem. These relationships may have offered children an opportunity to feel needed and provided an alternative source of emotional gratification and support. In contrast, mothers of children with long-lasting adjustment problems continued to manifest coercive styles of interaction. Mothers and sons were especially likely to fall into this pattern. Children are also more likely to show successful adjustment to divorce when conflict between divorced parents is low, when the child does not feel "caught" between the two parents, and when the child does not feel that he or she will be abandoned (Amato & Rezac, 1994; Buchanan, Maccoby, & Dornbusch, 1991; Wolchik et al., 2002). Maintaining a close relationship with grandparents can also help (Lussier et al., 2002).

Divorce represents a difficult transition for all members of the family. Some of the effects of divorce on children may actually be due to personal attributes in parents that are passed on genetically to children. Parents and children may share biological predispositions for low social and academic skills, and these may be the very characteristics that lead to marital problems for parents, as well as problematic post-divorce behaviors in children (O'Connor et al., 2000). However, research also suggests that a key variable to understanding the effects of divorce is the quality of relationships among all family members: the more conflict and negative emotion associated with the process and the more prolonged the maladaptive patterns of interaction, the worse the outcomes for the child. In addition, the child's overall adjustment needs to be considered in the broader context of factors such as socioeconomic status, neighborhood, and parental emotional state. These risk factors operate in a similar fashion whether the parents are divorced or not (Deater-Deckard & Dunn, 1999).

Custody Arrangements After divorce, most children reside with their mothers, in large part because of long-standing societal beliefs about the privileged nature of mother–child relationships. Yet when children live with their mothers after a divorce, they are more likely to experience economic hardship than if they live with their fathers. Studies have found that income for divorced women with children declines an average of 30 percent, whereas income for fathers declines much less or even increases (Burkhauser et al., 1991; Weitzman, 1985). Children living with their mothers also typically show a dramatic impairment in relationships with their fathers. For example, according to one national study, more than a third of the children in the sample did not see their fathers *at all* or saw them only a few times a year (Selzer, 1991).

Many states now have laws that favor joint custody of children following divorce. In most cases, this means both parents have equal responsibility for making decisions about the child's medical care and education; that is, they have *joint legal custody*. In other cases, children reside for substantial periods of time with each parent; this arrangement refers to *joint physical custody*. A meta-analysis of studies comparing the effects of joint custody versus sole custody shows that joint custody—whether it is legal or physical—generally has greater benefits for children. Children in joint custody display higher self-esteem and

Children often have a difficult time adjusting to the presence of stepparents, generally because stepparents do not take an active role in disciplining and showing affection to their "new" children. Problems are more likely to occur when children from each parent's prior marriage become part of the new "blended" family.

© Michael Newman/PhotoEdit

fewer behavioral and emotional problems than children in sole custody. An important factor related to these benefits is the ability of children to spend time with each parent; also, parents of children in joint custody tend to have fewer conflicts than parents in a sole-custody situation (Bauserman, 2002). However, it may not be the custody situation per se that influences children's well-being. Rather, it may be that parents who select this custody arrangement tend to have a low conflict style to begin with (Emery et al., 2005). Researchers have also reported that parental participation in a wide range of activities, even everyday ones such as shopping and watching TV together, predicted children's successful adjustment better than the frequency of special trips or activities (Clarke-Stewart & Hayward, 1996).

Relationships with Stepparents Approximately 75 to 80 percent of divorced individuals remarry, the majority within five years after their divorce (Cherlin, 1992). As a consequence, a significant number of children, often teenagers by virtue of the timing of these events, live with a stepparent. For children who have just experienced the separation of their parents, the introduction of a new "parent" can represent yet another difficult transition even though parental remarriage holds the promise of greater financial security and emotional support for both parents and children (Zill, Morrison, & Coiro, 1993).

Like divorce, a parent's remarriage often leads to aggression, noncompliance, poor peer relations, and academic difficulties among children (Bray, 1988; Zill, 1988). In fact, children with stepparents often resemble children with single parents on measures of problem behavior, academic success, and psychological adjustment (Hetherington & Henderson, 1997). As Figure 14.10 shows, a survey of more than 10,000 children in grades six through twelve showed that children in stepfamilies look similar to children from single-parent families in the number of school-related problems experienced; both groups have more problems than children from two-parent families (Zill, 1994). The child usually has more difficulty adjusting when stepparents have larger numbers of their own children, when children from two previous marriages are assimilated into one family, and when the custodial parent and stepparent have a new biological child of their own (Hetherington, 1999; Hetherington, Henderson, & Reiss, 1999; Santrock & Sitterle, 1987; Zill, 1988). Adolescents have more problems adjusting to their new families than younger children, perhaps because their growing autonomy leads them to be more confrontational with parents (Brand, Clingempeel, & Bowen-Woodward, 1988; Hetherington & Jodl, 1994). Even if children had shown previous adjustment to the remarriage of their parents, problems can resurface in

Figure 14.10

Family Type and Percentage of Children Experiencing Problems in School

According to a national study involving more than ten thousand children in grades six through twelve, children living in stepfamilies resemble those living in single-parent homes (with their mothers) in the patterns of difficulties they show in school. Both groups have more problems than children living in two-parent families, probably due to differences in parenting styles among the groups.

Source: Adapted from Zill, N. (1994). Understanding why children in stepfamilies have more learning and behavior problems than children in nuclear families in A. Booth & J. Dunn (Eds.), *Stepfamilies: Who Benefits? Who Does Not?* Copyright © 1994 by Lawrence Erlbaum Associates, Inc. Reprinted by permission of Lawrence Erlbaum Associates, Inc.

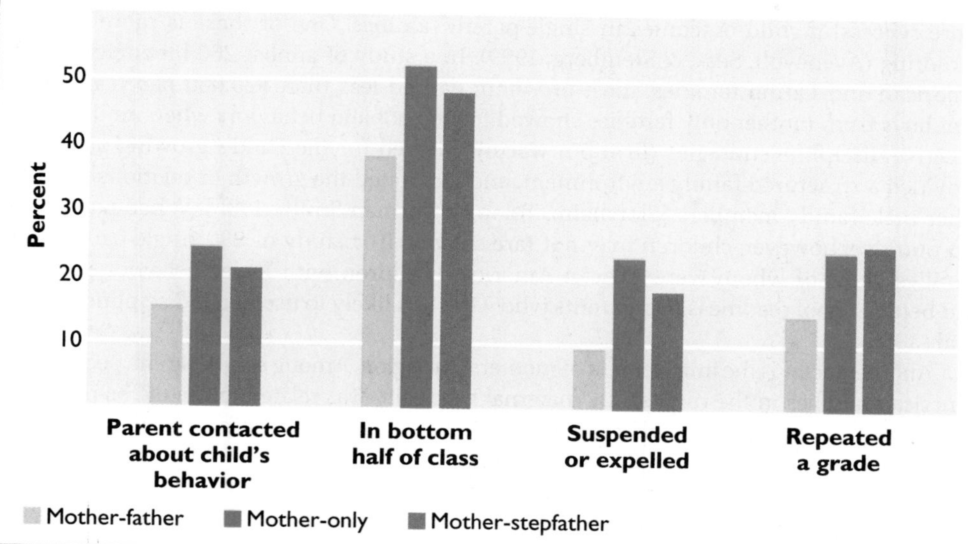

adolescence (Bray, 1999). In addition, girls in the middle school and adolescent years do not adjust as well as boys to parental remarriage; girls especially withdraw from their stepfathers (Brand et al., 1988; Vuchinich et al., 1991).

Drawing from data collected in a national survey of parent–adolescent relations, Frank Furstenberg (1987) found that stepparents had reservations about their ability to discipline and provide affection to stepchildren. At the same time, stepchildren corroborated that stepparents were less involved than their biological parents in care and supervision. Other researchers examining stepparent–stepchild relationships over time confirm that stepparents typically do not fit the profile of authoritative parenting described earlier in this chapter (Hetherington & Jodl, 1994), and thus the benefits of that parenting style for children are not realized. If anything, stepparents often look like the disengaged parents described at the beginning of this chapter; they provide less support for and control over the behavior of their stepchildren compared with their biological children (Mekos, Hetherington, & Reiss, 1996). Moreover, when stepparents do exert control, adolescents tend to show greater aggression, noncompliance, and other problem behaviors (Kim, Hetherington, & Reiss, 1999).

Some difficulties in stepfamilies may stem from the uncertain social roles of stepparents. Stepparents believe that they should play an active role in parenting but are also reluctant to become too involved with their stepchildren (Fine, Coleman, & Ganong, 1999). The advice given by one sixteen-year-old stepson reveals just how delicate a balance stepparents must strike:

> *The stepparent first would be to give room to the children, but still on the same spectrum, keep control basically, keep disciplining but I wouldn't say that you should make them, kinda let them ease into it. You shouldn't jump into something right away which is completely new.* (Fine et al., 1999, p. 283)

Parental remarriage presents special challenges to all family members that researchers are just beginning to explore.

Single-Parent Families

RISK | RESILIENCE

About one-third of American children are born to single mothers (Hamilton et al., 2005). Children growing up in single-parent families are at greater risk for a broad array of developmental problems, including poor academic achievement, behavior problems, and high-risk behaviors such as substance abuse (Barber & Eccles, 1992; Demo & Acock, 1996; Turner, Irwin, & Millstein, 1991). It is also important to note that the poverty rate for families headed by single mothers is almost 30 percent higher than for any other family type (DeNavas-Walt, Proctor, & Lee, 2005).

In light of these risks, it is important for research to identify the factors associated with more successful child outcomes in single-parent families. One of these is more involved parenting (Avenevoli, Sess, & Steinberg, 1999). In a study of almost 200 inner-city African American and Latino families, most of whom earned less than $20,000 per year, adolescent boys from mother-only families showed fewer problem behaviors when mothers used effective discipline strategies (firm but warm), allowed for the child's growing autonomy, provided a structured family environment, and facilitated the growth of relationships with other male family members (Florsheim, Tolan, & Gorman-Smith, 1998). When parents are too punitive, however, children may not fare so well. In a study of 290 single-parent, poor families, most of whom were African American, children with fewer behavior problems and better school readiness had parents who were less likely to use harsh discipline (Zaslow et al., 1999).

Another factor is the involvement of mothers in religion. Among single-parent, poor African American families in the rural south, maternal religiosity was related to use of "no-nonsense" parenting (firm but warm), higher quality of mother–child relationships, and more maternal involvement in school. These latter variables, in turn, were linked to the child's overall successful development in cognitive, social, and behavioral domains (Brody & Flor, 1998).

Studies of single-parent families, as well as families who are undergoing other types of transitions, emphasize that it is important to find ways to promote healthy, positive interactions between parents and children. Effective parents are involved and nurturant and provide firm, steady guidance to their children. When parents are stressed or distracted, or when they are unaware of the importance of parenting style, they are less likely to engage in successful interactions with their children. Assistance with child care, parent training programs, and counseling support for families experiencing stress are some of the societal programs that can be helpful.

Gay and Lesbian Parents

Because of the legal and social controversies surrounding gay and lesbian parenting, it is difficult to obtain accurate estimates of how many children grow up in families with same-sex parents. But most experts agree that the numbers are rising and might be in the millions. Research on the impact of growing up in families in which parents are gay or lesbian is clearer, however. When children whose parents are homosexual are compared with children whose parents are heterosexual, there are virtually no identifiable differences in their academic performance, social development, peer relationships, mental health, or sexual orientation (Patterson, 2000; Wainright, Russell, & Patterson, 2004; Wainright & Patterson, 2008). As with most studies of the impact of the family on child development, what matters most, say the results, is the quality of the day-to-day interactions that family members have with one another.

A study by Susan Golombok and her colleagues (Golombok et al., 2003) is representative of this body of research. Samples of seven-year-old children with two lesbian parents, two heterosexual parents, or single heterosexual mothers were compared on a number of measures of social and emotional well-being, including self-esteem, peer relations, gender-role activities, and mental health. Parental warmth, emotional involvement, and conflict resolution styles were also assessed. The findings showed that, in general, lesbian mothers were not significantly different from heterosexual mothers on most dimensions of parenting. In fact, lesbian mothers spanked their children less and engaged in more imaginative play. No differences were found in the adjustment scores of children from the various groups. Most revealing was the finding that the strongest predictor of children's adjustment was not mothers' sexual orientation or the structure of the family but rather the amount of stress parents reported. For children in all families, the greater the difficulty mothers reported in their parental roles, the more likely were children to experience adjustment problems.

For Your Review and Reflection

- What are some of the effects of maternal employment on child development? How are mother–child interactions affected?
- What has research shown about the effects of child care on the cognitive and social development of children?
- What are the effects of divorce on child development? What factors can help children adjust to the divorce of their parents?
- What are some typical characteristics of stepparent–child relationships?
- What factors are associated with successful outcomes in single-parent families?
- What does research indicate about the impact of having gay or lesbian parents?

chapter recap

Summary of Developmental Themes

Sociocultural Influence

How does the sociocultural context influence family processes?
Many goals parents have for their children's socialization are governed by attitudes the larger society holds, values and beliefs that change over time. Parents will emphasize cooperation, achievement, and sociability, for example, to the extent that the larger group values these characteristics. Culture also influences who participates in child care and to what extent; in some cultures, for example, fathers and siblings take part in many routine child care tasks. Finally, economic and social trends, such as family size, single parenthood, maternal employment, alternative child care, divorce, and remarriage, can alter family structures. The changes in family dynamics these factors introduce can have far-reaching consequences for child development.

Interaction Among Domains

How do family processes interact with other domains of development?
The child's experiences within the family, particularly the type of parenting style to which the child is exposed, can have broad consequences for development. For example, children who experience authoritarian parenting show less advanced moral reasoning, lower self-esteem, poorer relations with peers, poorer school adjustment, and higher levels of aggression than children who experience authoritative parenting. Similarly, interactions with siblings often provide children with opportunities to develop such social skills as nurturance and assertiveness. Finally, transitions in families can introduce both new opportunities and new stresses that can affect children's emotional, social, and cognitive development.

Risk | Resilience

What factors promote risk or resilience in family processes?
Certain styles of parenting or parenting behaviors may put children at risk. In general, authoritative parents who display warmth and responsiveness are most effective. Divorce and single parenthood can put children at risk, but the practice of effective parenting can override the effects that these variations in family structure might have. Ultimately, the style of parenting is the more important element in leading to risk or providing resilience for a child than is the structure of the family in which the child lives.

Chapter Review

Understanding the Family

What major changes have occurred in the structure of American families in the past thirty years?
The demographics of the family have changed in the past thirty years such that more children live in single-parent families, with grandparents, with gay or lesbian parents, or in families in which both parents work outside the home.

What does it mean to take a systems approach to understanding the family? Give examples of how influences on one subsystem within the family can have consequences for another subsystem.
In *systems theory*, the reciprocal interactions among various members are recognized. As just one example, problems in marital relationships can have an impact on parent–child interactions.

Parents and Socialization

What are the characteristics of the four major styles of parenting? What child behaviors are associated with each parental style?
Authoritarian parents display a low degree of warmth and tend to use coercive techniques. Their children tend to be less happy; boys are more aggressive, and girls are more dependent. *Permissive parents* set few limits on children's behaviors. Their children tend to be low on self-control and self-reliance. *Uninvolved parents* are emotionally detached from their children and uncommitted to the parental role. Their children tend to be more aggressive, display low self-esteem, and engage in risky behaviors. *Authoritative parents* are high on warmth and use reasoning and explanation to control their children. Their children tend to display a high degree of *instrumental competence*, showing independence, self-control, achievement orientation, and cooperation.

What are some of the specific effects of parental warmth on the developing child?
Parental warmth is associated with higher self-esteem, greater empathy, and fewer behavioral problems such as aggression in children.

Which principles of learning theory help to explain effective punishment?
To be effective, punishment should closely follow the child's transgression and should be consistently applied. Both *interagent* and *intra-agent consistency* are important. Punishment should also be accompanied by an explanation for why the behavior is undesirable. An effective alternative to physical punishment is a technique called time-out.

In what ways do parental cognitions play a role in parenting strategies?
Parents' attributions about their children's behaviors, their beliefs in their own efficacy, and their socialization goals affect their parenting strategies.

What are some ways in which the characteristics of the child can influence parenting strategies?
Control theory holds that children's behavior can influence the intensity of a parent's response. The child's temperament and the degree to which he or she exhibits committed compliance are often related to parenting strategies.

How do coercive cycles of maladaptive parent–child interactions arise? What can be done to intervene in these maladaptive interactions?
Coercive cycles develop when parents do not deliver consequences to the aggressive behaviors of their children, thus tacitly reinforcing them. Children's aggression increases, and a cycle of escalating negative interactions ensues. To break this cycle, parents should focus on their children's positive behaviors, apply discipline consistently, and set clear limits on negative behaviors.

What are some of the factors associated with the incidence of child abuse?
Child abuse is more likely to occur when parents rely on harsh, coercive control techniques, are isolated from the outside world, and have few sources of social support. Certain children, such as those born prematurely, are at risk for abuse. One of the possible consequences of the child's repeated exposure to abuse or trauma is *posttraumatic stress disorder (PTSD)*.

In what ways do parenting strategies vary across different cultural and socioeconomic groups?
Cultures vary in the degree to which children must contribute to the family's subsistence, do chores, and obey their parents. In some cultures, parents demand a very high degree of compliance whereas, in others, the emphasis in parent–child interactions is sociability. With regard to social class, lower-class mothers tend to use more power-assertive parenting techniques than do middle-class mothers. Economic stress is associated with a diminished ability to offer warm, supportive care. At the same time, families undergoing stress can develop positive coping strategies such as the support of extended families and involvement in religion.

Relationships with Mothers, Fathers, and Siblings

What are the major differences between mothers and fathers in parenting styles?
Even though fathers typically spend less time with their children than do mothers, they behave similarly when they are given the opportunity. One difference is that fathers engage in more physical interactions with their infants and young children than mothers.

In what ways do fathers make important contributions to child development?
Sensitive, responsive fathering is associated with children's higher academic achievement, better social functioning, and less rigid gender-role stereotypes.

How do family size and birth order have an impact on child development?
In general, children raised in smaller families tend to display higher levels of achievement, probably because they experience higher-quality interactions with their parents. Firstborns tend to excel in academic and intellectual achievements, whereas laterborns tend to be more socially oriented.

In what ways can parents facilitate a child's transition to having a new sibling?
The child's adjustment to the arrival of a new sibling is smoother when parents prepare him or her for the arrival of the new child and when the older child is involved in the new sibling's care.

What role do siblings play in the development of younger children in the family?
Older siblings act as teachers, models, and sources of social support for younger children in the family. Older siblings are usually more dominant and nurturant than younger siblings, but these differences diminish as children get older.

Families in Transition

What are some of the effects of maternal employment on child development? How are mother–child interactions affected?
Maternal employment is associated with higher levels of achievement, independence, and self-esteem in girls and less stereotyped gender-role attitudes in both boys and girls. More important than the fact of maternal employment is the mother's interaction style and the quality of substitute care the child receives. Mothers who are satisfied with their life circumstances and who display adaptive parenting techniques tend to have well-adjusted children regardless of their employment status.

What has research shown about the effects of child care on the cognitive and social development of children?
Studies of child care generally show that children who attend high-quality daycare are more cognitively and socially competent than children who are reared solely at home by their parents. High-quality child care provides the same sensitive, responsive caregiving that good parenting provides.

What are the effects of divorce on child development? What factors can help children adjust to the divorce of their parents?
Children whose parents divorce evidence socioemotional and academic difficulties, especially boys. Many effects disappear after the first year following divorce, however. More positive adjustment to divorce is associated with a shift from power-assertive to authoritative parenting, low parental conflict after separation, and the presence of social support for children outside the immediate family.

What are some typical characteristics of stepparent–child relationships?
Children and stepparents often experience conflicts in their relationships with each other. Part of the problem may be the reluctance of stepparents to exhibit the qualities of authoritative parenting that are associated with positive child outcomes—in particular, support for and control over their stepchildren's behaviors.

What factors are associated with successful outcomes in single-parent families?
Children do best when their single parents are involved, use effective discipline strategies, and display warmth. Assistance with sources of stress, such as help with child care and counseling, can be helpful in alleviating some of the stresses single parents face.

What does research indicate about the impact of having gay or lesbian parents?
Research shows that children growing up with same-sex parents do not differ from children with heterosexual parents on academic, social, or emotional traits. What matters most for all children is the quality of caregiver interactions they experience.

Key Terms and Concepts

authoritarian parent (p. 516)
authoritative parent (p. 516)
coercive cycle (p. 524)
control theory (p. 523)
instrumental competence (p. 516)
interagent consistency (p. 519)
intra-agent consistency (p. 519)
permissive parent (p. 516)
posttraumatic stress disorder (PTSD) (p. 528)
socialization (p. 512)
systems theory (p. 513)
uninvolved parent (p. 517)

Media Resources

Access an integrated eBook and chapter-specific interactive learning tools, including flashcards, quizzes, videos, and more, in your Developmental Psychology CourseMate, accessed through CengageBrain.com.

© Monkey Business Images/Shutterstock.com

CHAPTER OUTLINE

[chapter 15]

Peers

KEY THEMES IN PEER RELATIONS

- **SOCIOCULTURAL INFLUENCE** How does the sociocultural context influence peer relations?
- **INTERACTION AMONG DOMAINS** How do peer relations interact with other domains of development?
- **RISK | RESILIENCE** What factors promote risk or resilience in peer relations?

It was the start of the first day of school. Ms. Nakamura, the sixth-grade teacher, surveyed her new charges as they played in the schoolyard before the bell rang. It was a familiar scene: The boys played a raucous game of soccer, cheering their teammates and urging victory. The girls gathered in smaller groups, talking with great animation about their summer experiences and their excitement about school. As always, certain children in both groups were the center of activity; they seemed to attract their agemates as a pot of honey draws bees. Other children stayed on the fringes of the playground; few of their peers approached or spoke to them. Already Ms. Nakamura had a sense that sixth grade would be easier on some of these fresh new faces than others. <<

In many ways, Ms. Nakamura's intuitions were correct. She would find, as she learned to match names to faces in this year's class, that many of the children she was observing would make the transition to this new grade more easily than some of the less popular children. Research evidence suggests that the ability to have successful and rewarding interactions with peers during childhood can be the harbinger of successful later adjustment and that poor peer relations are often associated with a range of developmental problems. Boys and girls who have good peer relationships are less likely to experience academic difficulties, drop out of school, or commit delinquent acts in later years than classmates who relate poorly with their peers (Morison & Masten, 1991; Parker & Asher, 1987; Rubin, Bukowski, & Parker, 2006; Wentzel, 2009). Children who are accepted by their peers are also less likely to report feeling lonely, depressed, and socially anxious than children who are rejected (Barker et al., 2008; Cassidy & Asher, 1992; Gazelle & Ladd, 2003; Rubin, Coplan, & Bowker, 2009). Of course, the quality of peer relations is not the only factor that predicts later developmental outcomes. But it is hard to deny that experiences with peers play a substantial role in the lives of most children. Thus, peer relationships have become an important focus of developmental research.

What do child development experts say about the role of peers? Social learning theorists believe peers exert a powerful influence on the child's socialization by means of modeling and reinforcement. According to social learning theory, the greater the similarity between a model and an observer, the more likely it is that the observer will imitate the model's behavior (Bandura, 1969). Peers therefore are prime candidates for prompting imitation in children. Although peer imitation declines by middle childhood, it occurs quite frequently in the early years. In one study, the number of imitative acts occurring in the free play of preschoolers averaged 14.82 per hour (Abramovitch & Grusec, 1978). Needless to say, these imitations may be positive, such as promoting sharing and altruistic acts, or negative, such as encouraging aggressive or other antisocial behavior. Peer models can also influence gender-role behaviors. Most children are reluctant to play with toys meant for the opposite sex. Yet if a peer model displays cross-sex play, children's tendency to follow suit increases (Kobasigawa, 1968; Wolf, 1973). Especially in the realm of social behaviors, children may imitate competent peer models over adult models because they see the behaviors selected by peers as more appropriate for themselves.

Peers not only model certain behaviors but also actively reinforce their friends' behaviors. Peers communicate clear signals about the social behaviors they prefer and those they won't tolerate, messages that may either maintain or inhibit the child's behaviors. In addition, peer reactions can influence the frequency of behaviors such as aggression. For example, in their observations of preschoolers, Gerald Patterson and his colleagues noted that about three-fourths of the aggressive behaviors that took place were reinforced by victims' compliance or submission (Patterson, Littman, & Bricker, 1967). The consequence was that aggressors maintained their combative styles of interaction. If a peer responded with counteraggression, however, the perpetrator was less likely to repeat the action with that child, choosing either another victim or another behavior. Thus, peers powerfully affect one another by means of their positive and negative reactions.

Piaget (1932/1965) and Vygotsky (1978) have emphasized the ways in which peer contacts alter the child's cognitions, which can, in turn, direct social behavior. Piaget contended that peer interactions prompt, or even coerce the child to consider the viewpoints of others, thus broadening her social perspective-taking ability and diminishing her egocentrism. The result is a greater capacity for social exchange. Vygotsky maintained that contact with peers, especially those who are more skilled in a given domain, stretches the child's intellectual and social capacities. As a result of experiences with peers, the child internalizes new modes of thinking and social interaction and then produces them independently.

The number of studies examining peer relations in childhood and adolescence has skyrocketed in the past two decades, due in part to recognition of the prevalence of peer experiences in children's lives and the power of peers as socializing agents (Rubin et al., 2006). Because we humans are "social" beings, it is not surprising that our childhood experiences in social groups play such a large part in making us who we are.

Developmental Changes in Peer Relations

Compared with any other human relationship, the special feature of peer relations is their egalitarian nature. In fact, strictly speaking, the term **peer** refers to a companion who is of approximately the same age and developmental level. Parent–child interactions are characterized by a distinct dominant–subordinate hierarchy; parents use their authority to transmit information about social rules and behaviors. Peers, however, often function far more equally, and it is primarily among equals that children can forge such social skills as compromising, competing, and cooperating. Thus, experiences with peers afford the child unique opportunities to construct social understanding and to develop appropriate social responses.

INTERACTION AMONG DOMAINS

Relationships with peers also contribute to the child's developing sense of self. Peers provide the child with direct feedback (verbal and sometimes nonverbal) about how well he is doing in the academic, social, and emotional realms, information that can significantly influence his self-esteem. Peers provide a natural comparison against which the child can gauge his own accomplishments: "Am I really a good athlete?" "How am I doing as a student?" A child can answer questions such as these by comparing his own abilities with those of his peers as already discussed in Chapter 12, "Self and Values."

The way in which children relate to their peers undergoes significant developmental changes. At first, peers are simply interesting (or, at times, annoying) companions in play, but eventually they assume a larger and more crucial part in the child's social and emotional life. Children's peer networks start out small. But as children enter daycare and school—and as their cognitive, language, and social skills develop—their peer networks expand, and their relationships with a subset of those peers grow in intensity.

Early Peer Exchanges and Play

Infants show distinct reactions to peers even in the first few months of life. The sight of another baby often prompts a three-month-old to become generally aroused and active, a reaction that is very different from the ritualized greeting she usually reserves for her mother (Fogel, 1979) or the rapt and quiet attention she displays to her reflected image (Field, 1979). At six months, diffuse responses to peers give

peer Companion of approximately the same age and developmental level.

way to more specific signals, such as smiles, squeals, touching, and leaning in their direction (Hay, Nash, & Pedersen, 1983; Vandell, Wilson, & Buchanan, 1980). Older babies crawl toward one another and explore one another's facial features (Vandell & Mueller, 1980). Thus, from early on, infants recognize something special and interesting about strangers who resemble them in size and features. At the same time, most peer interactions during infancy are brief, lasting only a few seconds, and usually do not involve mutual exchanges of behaviors.

In the second year, social exchanges with peers become longer and more coordinated. Two children will jointly manipulate toys and other objects, each child taking a turn playing and then offering the object to the playmate; the latter behavior serves as an especially effective means of maintaining interactions with a peer (Williams, Ontai, & Mastergeorge, 2010). Children also begin to play simple games together, such as hide-and-seek or tag, activities that require taking turns and switching roles (Hay, Kaplan, & Nash, 2009; Howes, 1987). Later in toddlerhood, between ages two and three years, children engage in peer interactions more frequently. Instead of primarily revolving around objects such as toys, these interactions contain many positive social and affiliative behaviors, such as giving attention, smiling, sharing, and cooperating (Bronson, 1981).

In her classic studies of children's play, Mildred Parten (1932) found that the peer relations of young children are characterized by three forms. In *solitary* play, children play alone with toys, apart from other children and without regard for what they are doing. One child might be stacking rings while another does a puzzle; neither notices or cares about the other's activities. In *parallel* play, children play independently while alongside or close to other children. Several children might be gathered at a sandbox, one digging with a shovel, another making "pies," and still another dragging a truck through the sand. Even though they are in close proximity, one child's activities do not influence the play of the others. Yet such behavior initially may provide an important means for encouraging a child to move into more sophisticated *cooperative* play (Robinson et al., 2003). In cooperative play, children interact. They share toys, follow one another, and make mutual suggestions about what to do next. Although Parten believed that a stagelike developmental progression takes place from solitary to parallel and then cooperative play, research suggests that all three types of play occur among preschoolers (Barnes, 1971; Rubin, Maioni, & Hornung, 1976).

The type of play exhibited by preschoolers may depend on the socialization goals of parents and teachers. For example, in Korean American preschools, teachers encourage individual academic achievement and task persistence rather than social interaction with other children. Korean American preschoolers engage in significantly less cooperative play and more parallel play than Anglo American preschoolers do (Farver, Kim, & Lee, 1995). A child's preferred form of play might also be an early indicator of possible problems in peer relationships. For example, preschoolers who engage in higher levels of solitary play in earlier months have been found to exhibit less ability to regulate their behaviors. They are also more likely to be excluded by peers than children with lower levels of solitary play (Spinrad et al., 2004).

SOCIOCULTURAL INFLUENCE

RISK | RESILIENCE

One of the most interesting, and increasingly common, forms of play seen in preschoolers is **social pretend play** (also called *sociodramatic play* and *symbolic play*), in which they invoke "make believe" to change the functions of objects, create imaginary situations, and enact pretend roles, often with the cooperation of one or two peers (Smith, 2005). Simple forms of pretense begin already by sixteen to eighteen months of age; for example, pretending to drink from an empty glass of water (Bosco, Friedman, & Leslie, 2006). Older children use sticks and pots as band instruments, ride "magic carpets" together, and play "Mommy and Daddy." Furthermore, by three years of age, children are able to pretend that a single object can have alternative identities as they move back and forth between different play activities (Wyman, Rakoczy, & Tomasello, 2009). Growth in the child's cognitive, perspective-taking, and communication skills helps to explain these changes. To conceive of a stick as representing a flute, for example, the child must develop symbolic capabilities that allow him to let one object represent another. To play "Mommy," a young girl must relinquish her own perspective and appreciate another person's social role: what

INTERACTION AMONG DOMAINS

social pretend play Play that makes use of imaginary and symbolic objects and social roles, often enacted among several children. Also called *sociodramatic play* and *symbolic play*.

Preschoolers often show social pretend play in which they invoke "make believe" to create imaginary situations, change the functions of objects, or enact pretend roles. Social pretend play has been observed in children from diverse cultures.

© Monkey Business Images/Shutterstock.com

"mommies" do and how they speak to children. For complex and coordinated exchanges of pretend play to occur, such as when one child sets the table and prepares the food while the other cries like a baby, children must understand the rules of social dialogue and communication. When we watch three-year-olds engage in pretend play with one another, we are witnessing an intersection of their growing competence in several arenas: social, language, and cognitive skills.

The tendency for three- and four-year-olds to engage in social pretend play has been observed among children from diverse cultural backgrounds, including Chinese, Korean American, and Irish American groups, suggesting that this form of play may be a universal developmental acquisition. It is interesting to note that this is the age at which children from different cultures acquire a "theory of mind" (see Chapter 9, "Social Cognition") and that children who engage in pretend play are advanced in theory-of-mind tasks (Harris, 2005). At the same time, the child's culture influences the specific content of pretend play. Korean American children, for example, typically enact family and everyday themes (e.g., eating, sleeping, going places) in their play, whereas American children display themes of danger (e.g., crashes, injuries) and fantasy characters (Farver & Shin, 1997). Irish American children spend substantial time pretending with toys purchased by their families, whereas Chinese children rely more on social routines than on props (Haight et al., 1999). Thus, cultural values and resources are often vividly reflected in children's play.

SOCIOCULTURAL INFLUENCE

The Middle Childhood Years

Elementary school-age children begin to participate more in group activities than in the dyads (two-person groups) that are more likely to characterize earlier peer interactions. As noted in Chapter 13, "Gender," they show a clear preference for same-sex peers and, to a lesser extent, for children who are racially similar. In fact, as Figure 15.1 shows, the tendency to play with other children of the same sex begins in the preschool years and grows stronger throughout the elementary school years (Maccoby & Jacklin, 1987). As with younger children, they prefer to associate with peers who have similar behavior styles; for example, aggressive children tend to "hang out" with other aggressive children, and children motivated to perform well academically tend to interact with those who do well in school (Rubin et al., 2006). In general, quarrels and physical aggression with peers eventually wane, and prosocial behaviors such as sharing and helping others increase.

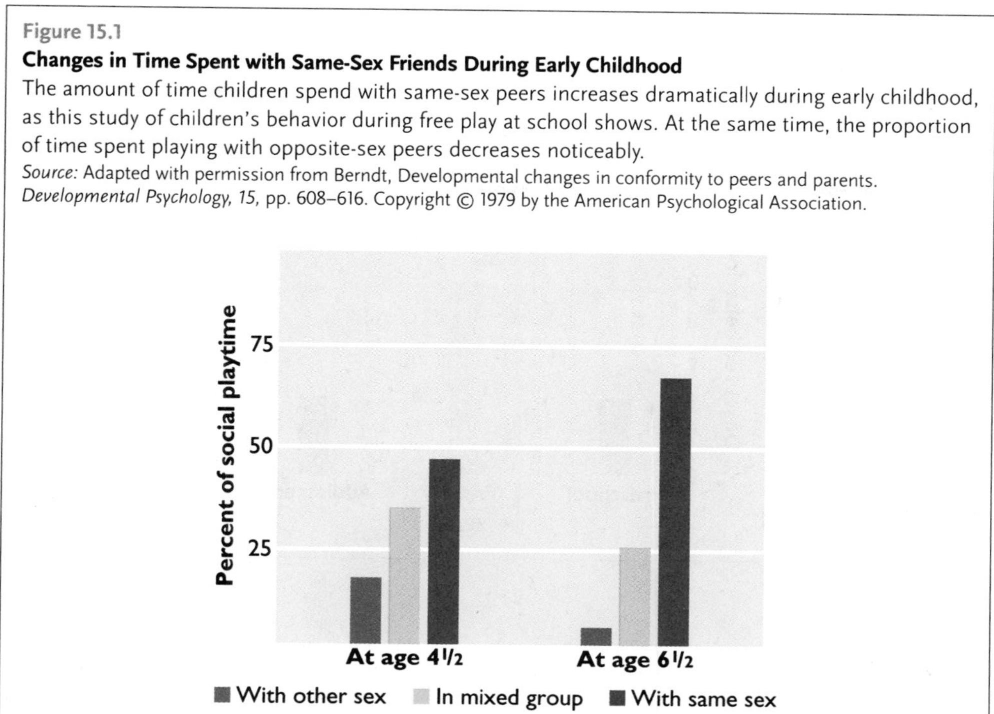

Figure 15.1
Changes in Time Spent with Same-Sex Friends During Early Childhood
The amount of time children spend with same-sex peers increases dramatically during early childhood, as this study of children's behavior during free play at school shows. At the same time, the proportion of time spent playing with opposite-sex peers decreases noticeably.
Source: Adapted with permission from Berndt, Developmental changes in conformity to peers and parents. *Developmental Psychology, 15,* pp. 608–616. Copyright © 1979 by the American Psychological Association.

A special form of play, called **rough-and-tumble play,** emerges around age two years but becomes more visible during the elementary school years, especially among boys, declining once again during adolescence (see Figure 15.2). Children chase one another, pretend to fight, or sneak up and pounce on one another. Rough-and-tumble play differs from aggression in that children do not intend to hurt other players and it often occurs among children who like one another. Smiling and laughing typically accompany the exaggerated movements and soft hits and kicks that comprise rough-and-tumble play, signs that these interactions are friendly rather than aggressive (Pellegrini, 2007). For example, episodes of rough-and-tumble play may be routinely followed by organized games with rules or a playful chase in a game of tag. Thus, rough-and-tumble play can provide a context for learning role exchange (e.g., "Now you chase me") and prosocial behaviors such as cooperation. On the other hand, especially among unpopular children, rough play can end up in a real physical fight. In one study, the rough-and-tumble play of unpopular children escalated into aggression 28 percent of the time and was positively correlated with a measure of antisocial behavior (Pellegrini, 1988). In general, rough-and-tumble play seems to be a way for boys, especially as they approach adolescence, to establish their dominance and status among peers (Pellegrini, 2007).

Adolescence

By the time they reach adolescence, children spend considerable free time with their peers, at least in the United States. In a review of forty-five studies of how adolescents in different countries spend their daily time (see Table 15.1), Reed Larson found that American youth have more unrestricted time than children in Europe or Asia and that much of this time is spent with friends (Larson, 2001). Although time spent with peers might provide important opportunities to develop social skills and supportive relationships, some research is beginning to indicate that the amount of unstructured time spent with peers without adult supervision is related to depression, conduct problems, and lower grades in school. On the other hand, free time spent with parents and other adults or participating

SOCIOCULTURAL INFLUENCE

rough-and-tumble play Active, physical play that carries no intent of imposing harm on another child.

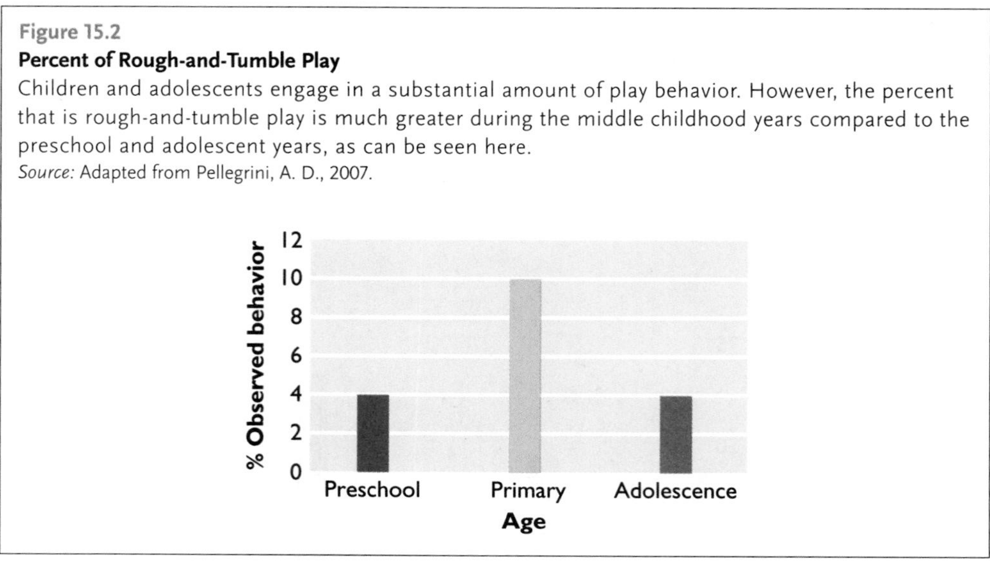

Figure 15.2
Percent of Rough-and-Tumble Play
Children and adolescents engage in a substantial amount of play behavior. However, the percent that is rough-and-tumble play is much greater during the middle childhood years compared to the preschool and adolescent years, as can be seen here.
Source: Adapted from Pellegrini, A. D., 2007.

RISK | RESILIENCE

in structured activities such as hobbies, sports, and extracurricular activities at school predicts better school success and fewer conduct problems (Mahoney, 2000; McHale, Crouter, & Tucker, 2001).

Peer relations during adolescence become more intense on one level and involve larger networks on another level. Adolescents form close, intimate friendships with a subset of their peers, often those who resemble themselves in certain traits, such as an orientation to academics or aggressive activity. Many children also form **cliques**, groups of three to nine children who often interact together (Rubin et al., 2006). Clique membership is frequently supplemented by identification with a **crowd**, a larger group of peers with a specific reputation, such as "jocks" or "brains." Members of crowds do not necessarily spend time together but share a label based on a stereotype. Interestingly, even though youngsters may see themselves as members of particular cliques, their membership in crowds is often identified or labeled by others (Brown, 1989). That is, a girl may not see herself as a "brain" but receive that label from peers who observe her academic achievements and studious behaviors. Membership in cliques and crowds in the middle and later school years reflects the child's growing need for group belonging at a time when he is orienting away from parents and other adults. At the same time, the values parents encourage can influence the crowds with which their adolescent children affiliate. If a parent encourages achievement, for example, the child's academic success may place her in the group of "brains" (Brown et al., 1993). The norms of cliques and crowds can be powerful shapers of behavior; they often provide the adolescent with prescriptions on how to dress, act, and even what ambitions to have for the future. However, the degree to which the group has influence depends on how strongly the adolescent identifies with that group (Kiesner et al., 2002).

As adolescents approach young adulthood and feel more secure about their self-identities, they are less interested in cliques and crowds and increasingly become oriented once again toward relationships with individuals (Rubin et al., 2006). One other significant change in adolescence is that some peer relations begin to reflect interest in the opposite sex. The time spent with same-sex peers does not decline in adolescence, but time spent with an opposite-sex peer increases substantially during high school (Richards et al., 1998). As they grow older, and as they begin to spend increasing time with their romantic partners, adolescents spend less time with family members. Nonetheless, they still maintain close emotional ties with families, rating parents and romantic partners as their most influential relationships (Laursen & Williams, 1997).

clique Peer group of three to nine same-sex children who frequently interact together.

crowd Large group of peers characterized by specific traits or reputation.

TABLE 15.1 How Do Adolescents Spend Their Free Time?

Reed Larson has compiled the results of forty-five studies of how adolescents in various cultures spend their work and free time hours per day. A portion of the results is shown here. You should note that several of the activities in "free time" include opportunities to interact with peers. What do the data suggest about cross-cultural differences in how adolescents spend their time?

Activity	United States	Europe	East Asia
Household labor	20–40 min	20–40 min	10–20 min
Paid labor	40–60 min	10–20 min	1–10 min
Schoolwork	3.0–4.5 hr	4.0–5.5 hr	5.5–7.5 hr
Total work time	**4–6 hr**	**4.5–6.5 hr**	**6–8 hr**
TV viewing	1.5–2.5 hr	1.5–2.5 hr	1.5–2.5 hr
Talking	2–3 hr	Insufficient data	45–60 min
Sports	30–60 min	20–80 min	1–20 min
Structured voluntary activities	10–20 min	1.0–20 min	0–10 min
Total free time	**6.5–8.0 hr**	**5.5–7.5 hr**	**4.0–5.5 hr**

Source: Larson, 2001.

For Your Review and Reflection

- What developmental outcomes usually accompany good peer relationships during childhood?
- What are the different forms of play exhibited by toddlers, preschoolers, and elementary school children? What factors are related to the emergence of these different types of play?
- What are the characteristics of peer relationships during the preschool and elementary school years? How do these characteristics change in later childhood and during adolescence?
- What are some of the factors that influenced which peers you interacted with during your childhood and adolescence? Were you a member of a clique or crowd? How important were these experiences for your own development?
- What do you think may be factors in peer interactions that promote risk or resilience?

Children's Friendships

And Pooh said to Piglet, 'Life is so much friendlier with two.' (A.A. Milne, author)

Certain peer relations are special. They are marked by shared thoughts and experiences, trust, intimacy, and joy in the other's company. Children's relationships with friends differ from those with other peers. They are a dyadic relationship; both members of a pair voluntarily identify each other as friends. Friends express more emotion and loyalty toward each other, see each other more frequently, and both cooperate and disagree more than mere acquaintances do (Newcomb & Bagwell, 1995; Rubin et al., 2006; Rubin, Fredstrom, & Bowker, 2008). Even though childhood friendships may not endure, their impact on social and emotional development can rival that of the family and may provide a needed buffer when children feel psychological strains. Friendships are also an important source of cognitive and social support (Hartup, 1996).

Children's Patterns and Conceptions of Friendship

Even infants and toddlers may display friendships. They may prefer to interact socially with a particular child, more frequently repeat activities that have been carried out together in the past, imitate each other and jointly participate in pretend activities, and separate and even exclude others from the larger group of which they may be a part (Hay, Caplan, & Nash, 2009). However, it is slightly later during early childhood that friendships typically begin to be obvious.

Early Childhood About 80 percent of three- to four-year-olds spend a substantial amount of time with at least one peer who is a "strong associate" or friend. Most preschoolers observed in their nursery school classrooms spend at least 30 percent of their time with one other peer, usually someone of the same sex (Hinde et al., 1985). For the three-year-old, however, the concept of friend does not encompass the full range of psychological complexities that it does for the older child. At this age, the term is virtually synonymous with playmate.

Preschoolers' activities with friends usually consist of games, object sharing, and pretend sequences (e.g., "You be the baby, and I'll be the mommy"). Conversations between friends often contain a good deal of social comparison, a search for differences as well as similarities. Preschool children are fascinated not so much by the specific things they have in common as by the fact that they have things in common. Hence the following typical conversation recorded by Jeffrey Parker and John Gottman (1989):

Child A: We both have chalk in our hands.

Child B: Right!

Preschoolers especially value friends who give them positive feedback, prefer to play with them over other children, and engage in low levels of conflict with them (Ladd, Kochenderfer, & Coleman, 1996). The qualities of preschoolers' friendships are associated with other dimensions of their social functioning. When children offer support to their friends, they tend to be more prosocial in general. When they have a high degree of conflict in their friendships, they tend to be more aggressive compared to other dyads. Perhaps somewhat surprising is the finding that preschoolers who tend to have close, intimate friendships with only a few peers tend to show greater relational aggression. These children may already be learning how to manipulate their peers through gossip, threats, or exclusion to achieve their personal and social goals (Sebanc, 2003).

INTERACTION AMONG DOMAINS

Middle Childhood In the middle-school years (roughly ages eight through twelve), children are very concerned with being accepted by their peers and avoiding the insecurity peer rejection brings; both factors motivate friendship formation. Most friends are of the same age and sex, although relationships with younger and older children occasionally occur as well. Cross-sex friendships are rare, however, constituting only about 5 percent of the mutual friendships reported in one study of more than 700 third- and fourth-graders (Kovacs, Parker, & Hoffman, 1996). Researchers in another study even found their fifth-grade participants to be openly resistant to the idea that they might have a friend of the opposite sex (Buhrmester & Furman, 1987). By the time children approach preadolescence, the time they spend with same-sex friends surpasses the time they spend with either parent.

Friendship partners may change, though, sometimes rather frequently, over the childhood years. As part of a comprehensive longitudinal study of the social development of children beginning in fourth grade, Robert and Beverly Cairns (1994) asked children to name their best friends each year through eleventh grade. Figure 15.3 shows that the friend named in fourth grade was unlikely to be named again in successive years. Friendships can even shift within a time span of a few weeks. When Robert Cairns and his colleagues observed the nature of fourth- and seventh-graders' friendships, they found that children who mutually nominated each other as friends the first time they were interviewed usually did not name each other as close friends three weeks later (Cairns et al., 1995). However, the tendency for children to have new mutual friends at different points in time may depend on the characteristics of the child. In another project, children who switched friends more frequently over the four weeks of a summer camp session tended to be perceived by other

Figure 15.3
Changes in Best Friends
In a longitudinal study of best friends, Cairns and Cairns (1994) found that children named as best friends in fourth grade were seldom renamed as best friends in successive years. Friendships may therefore be less stable than generally thought. On the other hand, other research suggests that the stability of friendships over time may depend on the specific personality characteristics of individual children.
Source: From Cairns, R. B., & Cairns, B. D. (1994). Lifelines and risks: Pathways of youth in our time. Copyright © 1994. Reprinted with the permission of Cambridge University Press.

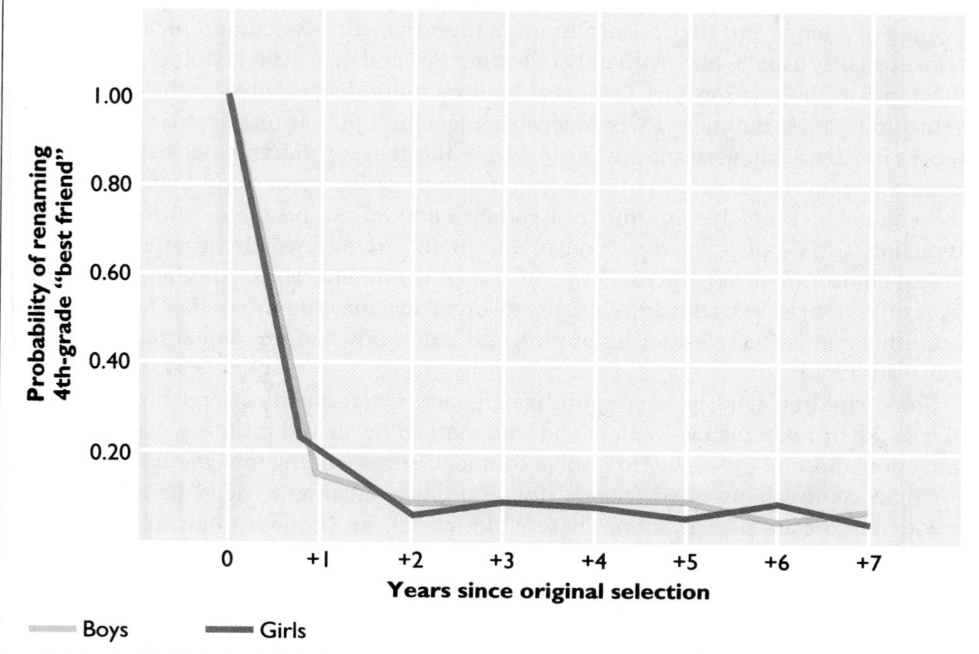

children as playful, humorous, and "gossipy," but also as aggressive, unreliable, and untrustworthy; that is, they had qualities that probably both attracted and disappointed friends (Parker & Seal, 1996).

In middle childhood, friendship interactions typically include conflicts as well as cooperation (Hartup et al., 1993), and gossip becomes a predominant format for communication, as the following episode between two girls illustrates:

E: Oh, see, um, you know that tub she gave us for the spider?

M: Yeah.

E: She acts like she owns the whole thing.

M: The whole spider.

E: I know. (Parker & Gottman, 1989, p. 114)

Parker and Gottman (1989) believe that gossip allows children to sample the attitudes and beliefs of their agemates without taking the risk of revealing their own views. Because gossip involves the sharing of "privileged" information, it also solidifies the child's membership in the friendship circle.

During this age period, the internal psychological aspects of friendship grow in importance. When sixth-graders are asked, "How do you know that someone is your best friend?" they respond with statements such as "I can talk to her about problems" or "He'll keep a secret if you tell him." In other words, intimacy and trust as well as loyalty, generosity, and helpfulness become integrated into the child's understanding of friendship (Berndt, 1981). Girls in particular speak about the value they place on intimacy in friendship relations. Girls cite the importance of sharing confidences and private feelings with friends far more frequently than boys do and find that their same-sex friendships provide more support than boys find in their friendships (Buhrmester & Furman, 1987; Furman & Buhrmester, 1992; Jones & Dembo, 1989). This tendency, however, may stem in part from their stereotyped knowledge that female relationships are supposed to be close (Bukowski & Kramer, 1986).

Sex differences in concepts of friendship are accompanied by heightened differences in the structure of boys' and girls' friendship networks during the middle-school years. Boys' friendships are usually *extensive*; their circle of friends is larger, and play is frequently enacted in groups. For boys, friendship is oriented around shared activities, especially sports. In contrast, girls' friendships tend to be *intensive*. Girls have smaller networks of friends, but they engage in more intensive affective communication and self-disclosure. Girls usually play with only one other girl and may even be reluctant to include a third girl in the relationship. Girls also become more distressed over the breakup of a friendship (Eder & Hallinan, 1978; Maccoby & Jacklin, 1987). It may be that these sex differences in friendship patterns are derived from the games children have historically been expected to play. Boys are often encouraged to play group games and team sports, such as baseball, which involve a number of children and do not promote intimacy and close interaction. Girls' games, such as "house" and "dolls," involve smaller groups and provide an ideal environment for the exchange of thoughts and emotions. Another possibility is that sex differences in friendships are due to larger socialization forces that foster sensitivity to others and affective sharing in girls and autonomy and emotional reserve in boys (Winstead, 1986).

INTERACTION AMONG DOMAINS

Some children tend to have more friends and better-quality friendships than other children. Their relationships with friends are marked by shared intimacy, caring, support, companionship, and the ability to resolve conflicts. In responding to vignettes about potential situations involving good friends (for example, watching a friend being laughed at for botching a class presentation), these children did not propose to avoid or blame the friend ("I'd stay away from my friend"; "It was his own fault") (Rose & Asher, 2004). In other vignettes in which there was a conflict with a friend (for example, the friend changes the television channel), these children refrained from using revenge as a motive for their actions (Rose & Asher, 1999). Such information about the specific goals and behaviors used by children who are good friendship partners may be useful in designing interventions for children who have few friends.

Adolescence By adolescence, the importance of close friendship is firmly solidified. Adolescents from diverse cultures such as China and Iceland claim strong loyalty to their close friends (Keller et al., 1998). Why are friends important? In the United States, adolescents say they value the ability to share thoughts and feelings with friends and expect mutual understanding and self-disclosure in friendships (Bigelow & LaGaipa, 1975; Furman & Bierman, 1984). During this time, friends also become increasingly more positive and reciprocally supportive of one another (De Goede, Branje, & Meeus, 2009). They share

© iStockphoto.com/Andrea Gingerich

© Image Source/Jupiter Images

Boys and girls differ in the patterns of their friendships and the types of activities they engage in with friends. Boys tend to have larger networks of friends, and they tend to participate in shared activities with them. Girls' networks, on the other hand, are smaller and center on affective communication and self-disclosure.

problems, solutions to those problems, and private feelings. These qualities fit the needs of individuals who may be struggling to define who they are and who they will become. A sample exchange between two adolescent friends drawn from Parker and Gottman's (1989) research illustrates these themes:

A: I don't know. Gosh, I have no idea what I want to do. And it really doesn't bother me that much that I don't have my future planned. [laughs]

B: [laughs]

A: [laughs] Like it bothers my dad a lot, but it doesn't bother me.

B: Just tell your dad what I always tell my dad: "Dad, I am."

A: [laughs] Exactly!

B: "And whatever happens tomorrow, I still will be!"

Adolescents continue to prefer same-sex friends, although the frequency of boy–girl interactions increases. At this age, similarities in attitudes about academics, dating, drinking, smoking, and drug use influence whether children become friends (Dishion, Andrews, & Crosby, 1995; Epstein, 1983; Tolson & Urberg, 1993). Adolescent friendships become more selective with age; teenagers have fewer mutual friends than younger children do, but mutual friends comprise a greater proportion of their total network of friends. The tendency for girls to have smaller friendship networks than boys, observed earlier in childhood, disappears to some degree, but girls' friendships remain marked by emotional intensity and, perhaps because of this, even fragility (Benenson & Christakos, 2003; Urberg et al., 1995). Adolescents also say that the time they spend with their friends is the most enjoyable part of their day (Csikszentmihalyi & Larson, 1984). Friendship is thus a key element in the social and emotional life of the older child.

INTERACTION AMONG DOMAINS

The Development of Peer Relations Chronology summarizes many of the changes in peer relations and friendships that occur during childhood and adolescence.

How Children Become Friends

How do two previously unacquainted children form a friendship? What behaviors must occur to produce an affiliative bond between these two peers? A time-intensive investigation by John Gottman (1983) provides a fascinating glimpse into the process of friendship formation among children who initially met as strangers. Gottman's method involved tape-recording the conversations of eighteen unfamiliar dyads ages three to nine years as they played in their homes for three sessions. Even in this short time, friendships among some of the pairs began to emerge. In all cases, each member of the pair was within one year of the age of the other. Some were same-sex pairs, others opposite-sex. The behaviors of the child whose home it was (the host child) and the visiting child (the guest) were coded separately; the sequences of behaviors these children displayed—that is, how one child's behavior influenced the other's—were also analyzed.

Children who "hit it off" in the first play session showed several distinct patterns of interaction. First, they were successful in exchanging information, as in the following conversation one pair had:

A: Hey, you know what?

B: No, what?

A: Sometime you can come to my house.

Children who became friends made efforts to establish a common ground by finding activities they could share or by identifying similarities and differences between them.

In addition, any conflicts that occurred as they played were successfully resolved, either by one member of the dyad explaining the reason for the disagreement or by one child complying with the other child's demands, as long as they were not excessive or unreasonable. Alternatively, as activities escalated from simply coloring side by side ("I'm

CHRONOLOGY Development of Peer Relations: Birth to 18 Years

MONTHS BIRTH

YEARS BIRTH

© Ryan McVay/Photodisc/Jupiter Images

3 Months

- Reacts with arousal or attention to presence of a peer.

6–9 Months

- Directs smiles, touches, and other signals toward peers.
- Approaches peers.

2–4 Years

- Jointly manipulates objects with one or two other peers.
- Engages in simple turn-taking games with peers.
- Shares, smiles, and cooperates with peers.
- Shows bouts of physical aggression with peers.
- Displays solitary, parallel, cooperative, and social pretend play.
- Increasingly prefers certain playmates.

5–9 Years

- Participates in group activities.
- Displays less physical aggression and more prosocial behaviors toward peers.
- Displays rough-and-tumble play.
- Shows increasing concern about being accepted by friends.
- Cross-sex friendships become rare.

10–14 Years

- Forms intimate friendships.
- Joins cliques.
- Becomes affiliated with a crowd.
- Feels greater peer pressure to conform.
- Psychological aspects underlying friendship become more important.
- Incidences of bullying peak.

© Photos.com/Jupiterimages

15–18 Years

- Participates less frequently in cliques and crowds.
- Becomes more interested in peers of the opposite sex.
- Frequency of romantic relationships increases.

This chart describes the sequence of peer relations based on the findings of research. Children often show individual differences in the exact ages at which they display the various developmental achievements outlined here.

coloring mine green") to one child issuing a command ("Use blue. That'd be nice"), children who became friends tempered potential conflict by de-escalating the intensity of play (in this case, going back to side-by-side coloring) or using another element of play that was "safe"—namely, information exchange (e.g., "I don't have a blue crayon. Do you?"). In contrast, children who did not become friends often persisted in escalating their play until the situation was no longer amicable. Children who became friends thus modulated their interactions to preserve a positive atmosphere. Over time, other social processes also came into play; clear communication and self-disclosure (the revelation of one's feelings) were among these.

Generally speaking, children become friends with agemates who resemble themselves on a number of dimensions. Young children and their friends often share similar play styles and language skills (Dunn & Cutting, 1999; Rubin et al., 1994). Among older children, friends are similar in temperament, popularity, and the tendency to behave prosocially or aggressively (Haselager et al., 1998). By becoming friends with like-minded agemates, children select contexts in which some of their own initial tendencies—their aggression or prosocial behavior, for example—may become even more accentuated. In fact, friends become more similar to one another as their relationship continues (Newcomb, Bukowski, & Bagwell, 1999).

INTERACTION AMONG DOMAINS

The Functions of Friendship

By virtue of their special qualities, friendships contribute to the child's development in ways that differ from other, more transient peer interactions. Friendships involve a distinct sense of mutual reciprocity between peers and a significant affective investment from each child (Hartup & Stevens, 1999). Thus, they provide a fertile ground for the child's social and emotional development.

INTERACTION AMONG DOMAINS

Interactions with friends provide a context for the development of social skills such as cooperation, competition, and conflict resolution. In one study, researchers observed teams of four- and five-year-olds playing a game in which cooperation led to both partners winning, whereas competition led to losses for both (Matsumoto et al., 1986). Teachers independently rated the degree of friendship for each pair of children. The results showed that the greater the degree of friendship, the more the children cooperated to win the game. Because of their investment in friendships, when children have conflicts with friends, they frequently seek to negotiate and resolve those conflicts by, for example, turning away from the situation, rather than letting the argument escalate or terminating the friendship (Fonzi et al., 1997; Hartup et al., 1988). Friends can also encourage many positive qualities, such as the tendency to engage in prosocial behavior. When their friends are prosocial, adolescents express more altruistic goals (for instance, they say that they try to share or cheer someone up if something has gone wrong) and are described by peers as behaving prosocially a year later (Barry & Wentzel, 2006).

Because friendships include the sharing of affection and emotional support, especially among older children, they may play a vital role in protecting children from anxiety and stress, particularly when there are problems in the family. For example, boys seem to adjust better to the practical and psychological consequences of divorce when they have friends (Wallerstein & Kelly, 1980). When children come from harsh, punitive home environments, they are at risk for becoming the victims of peer aggression and for behaving aggressively and defiantly; however, this risk is diminished for children who have friends (Criss et al., 2002; Schwartz et al., 2000).

RISK | RESILIENCE

Children who have close and intimate friendships experience less anxiety and depression, and are more sociable in general than those with few close friends (Buhrmester, 1990; Sund, Larsson, & Wichstrøm 2003). Friendships also appear to help dampen potential negative outcomes for children who experience loneliness (Laursen et al., 2007). However, simply having friends may not insulate children from, for example, increases in depression that are sometimes observed during the adolescent years. Mara Brendgen and colleagues assessed levels of depressed mood in a longitudinal study of adolescents between eleven

Figure 15.4
Friendship as a Buffer Against Loneliness
Having even one "best friend" can significantly lower children's reports of loneliness. In this study, third- through sixth-graders filled out a questionnaire assessing their feelings of loneliness and social dissatisfaction partway through the school year. A high score indicated greater feelings of loneliness. Children who had a reciprocal relationship with at least one friend had significantly lower loneliness scores than children who had no such relationship.
Source: From Renshaw, P. D., & Brown, P. J. (1993). Loneliness in middle childhood: Concurrent and longitudinal predictors. *Child Development, 64,* pp. 1271–1284. Copyright © 1993. Reprinted with permission of the Society for Research in Child Development.

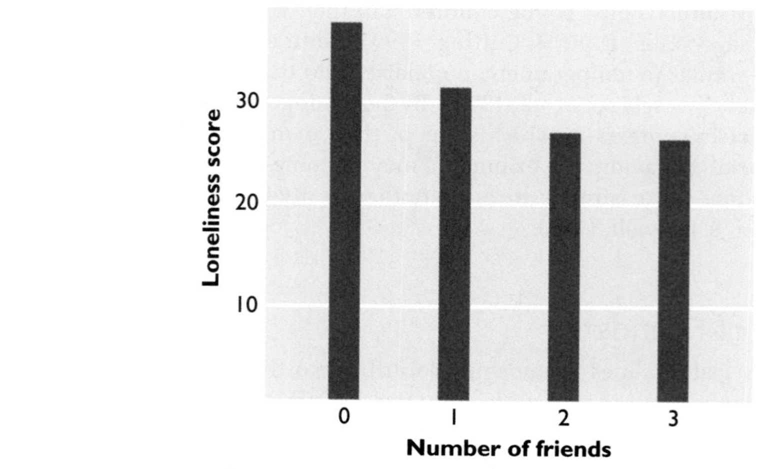

and thirteen years of age (Brendgen et al., 2010). Most youths showed low levels and little change in depressed mood over this time frame. However, 15 percent of children showed a substantial increase on this measure, and another 10 percent scored high in depressed mood at both ages. Those who had no friends were more likely to show an increase in depressed mood than those who had nondepressed friends. But the increase in depressed mood was even greater when a friend scored high on this same measure. Thus, lack of friends had some impact on changes in depressed mood, but an even more substantial impact in depressed mood was found in children when their friends displayed elevated levels of depression. Thus, having a friend may protect against depression but not if that friend is himself depressed.

Because many studies of friendship are correlational, the direction of influence is not always clear. For example, less anxious or more depressed children may be more capable of forming intimate friendships, or the reverse may be true: friendships may make them less anxious or depressed. Nonetheless, it is reasonable to hypothesize that friends provide an important source of social support for and feedback about one's competence and self-worth. In fact, as Figure 15.4 shows, having even just one "best friend" can mean less loneliness for the child (Parker & Asher, 1993; Renshaw & Brown, 1993).

Although friends can have exceedingly positive benefits for development, in some cases friendships may not be emotionally supportive. For children who are not liked by other children, for example, interactions with their friends tend to be more negative than among other children (Rubin et al., 2006). Friends can also be a factor in deviant behavior, especially among children who are predisposed to have conduct problems themselves. Thomas Dishion and his colleagues (Dishion, Patterson, & Griesler, 1994) observed that ten-year-old aggressive boys who had been rejected by most of their peers often became friends with other aggressive boys. Over time, they conversed more about deviant behavior such as substance abuse and delinquency (Dishion et al., 1996). By age fourteen, association with antisocial friends was found to contribute statistically to the tendency to engage in deviant behaviors. In addition, having a close friend who engages in other risky activities such as binge drinking or who is sexually active also increases the likelihood of these behaviors. Nevertheless, these effects are quite small, suggesting that a close friendship is just one of many factors that influence such risk behaviors (Jaccard, Blanton, & Dodge, 2005). Although monitoring friendship networks may be important, breaking the cycle of various antisocial behaviors requires more than intervening in those friendships. For example, association with deviant friends is more likely when parents fail to be nurturant and involved, are unsupportive and do not monitor their adolescents' behaviors, or when a larger network of friends engages in such behaviors (Jaccard et al., 2005; Scaramella et al., 2002).

what do you think? What Are the Consequences of Friending and Defriending?

No one doubts that technology has dramatically changed our lives over the past several decades. And those changes may also be affecting how peers relate to one another and what is meant by being a friend. Social networking and texting have become a major part of many teenagers' Internet-savvy activities. For example, 93 percent of teenagers in the United States use the Internet and 73 percent of them access social network sites (Lenhart et al., 2010).

Although considerable interest has been focused on the intellectual impact of Internet use and the potentially negative influences associated with cyberbullying and sexual communications via such media, might this activity also be changing how we develop and interact with friends? Do you think, for example, that as a result of greater use of electronic communications, children and teenagers may have fewer face-to-face interactions with their friends, a trend that has been suggested by some researchers (Subrahmanyam & Greenfield, 2008)? Does this means of maintaining contact with others provide as much emotional support and trust, a hallmark of strong friendships, as that which occurs when individuals interact with one another in person? What might be the consequences of missing the visible social cues and subtle emotional variations that are difficult to convey outside of the immediate one-to-one context that has historically served to support friendships? As a result, are children and teenagers becoming less adept at reading these cues when the opportunities arise? And what might be the impact of such communications because they are often more public, that is, possibly viewed by many others? Could texting and communicating via social networks to establish and maintain friendships then lead to more superficial interactions? Or could such activities actually make friends more available and thus permit the establishment of tighter and closer bonds with each other? Might these various means of communication, for example, help shy children and adolescents reach out to and stay in touch with others?

There are additional issues regarding the dynamics of children's friendships. Have you ever been defriended or invited someone to be a friend who failed to answer your request to become one? What do you think the reactions of children and teenagers are to this kind of "social" exchange? Is it likely to be the same as when friends have unsuccessful social interactions in person? Is it a "convenient," less emotionally difficult way of letting someone know your feelings about them or, in the case of defriending, is it likely to be communicated and then perceived as a less polite, harsher, and, as a consequence, more negative interaction than a face-to-face rejection? How do you think these newer ways of establishing, maintaining, and changing friends assist or complicate social relationships for children and teenagers?

Romantic Relationships

The relationship styles cultivated in friendships may extend to relations with others later in life. Harry Stack Sullivan (1953) believed that the capacity for intimacy nurtured by same-sex friendships in childhood provides the foundation for intimacy in more mature adult relationships. As well, the quality of adolescent romantic relations has been found to be associated with the quality of relations the teenagers experienced within their own family, beginning at birth (Furman & Collins, 2009).

The emergence of romantic relationships is typically reported among adolescents in most Western societies. However, in other cultures such interactions are not encouraged and are less likely to be observed during this time.

For many adolescents, romantic relationships seem to follow a specific pattern. They usually begin with mixed-sex interactions that involve casual and informal boy–girl groups in early adolescence. This type of interaction is then replaced by group dating and, finally, romantic relationships with a single partner (Connolly et al., 2004). Most teens in the United States report that they have "fallen in love" and that they have engaged in a serious romantic affair in high school (Regan et al., 2004). In one study, the percentage of seventh-, ninth-, and eleventh-grade adolescents indicating that they have been romantically involved during the preceding year was reported to be 32, 41, and 59 percent, respectively (Giordano, Manning, & Longmore, 2006).

SOCIOCULTURAL INFLUENCE

Although romantic experiences are typical during the adolescent years in Western societies, such may not be the case in many regions of the world. For example, in China adolescent romantic involvement is neither encouraged nor as readily accepted by parents and other family members despite recent changes in that country. Thus, tenth- and eleventh-graders living in Canada say they have experienced a romantic relationship far more often than those living in China (Li et al., 2010). Furthermore, in the United States, Asian American adolescents are less likely to have had a romantic relationship than adolescents belonging to other ethnic and racial groups (Carver, Joyner, & Udry, 2003). In general, however, adolescent romantic relationships tend to be short lived, typically lasting less than a year (Connolly & McIssac, 2009).

Adolescents who become romantically involved with each other are not only likely to be similar in racial, ethnic, and other demographic characteristics such as social class, but also with respect to social and psychological qualities including popularity, physical attractiveness, and tendency to display aggression or delinquent behavior and depression (Furman & Simon, 2008; Simon, Aikins, & Prinstein, 2008). Perhaps somewhat more surprising is that both physical and/or relational aggression are reported to occur in many of these relationships, perhaps as high as 40 percent according to some studies (Collins, Welsh, & Furman, 2009). For males, such aggression appears to be correlated with exposure to conflict between parents, but parental conflict seems unrelated to aggression instigated by females involved in a romantic relationship (Kinsfogel & Grych, 2004).

INTERACTION AMONG DOMAINS

Unlike more mature romantic relationships, which offer mutual support and caregiving, early romantic interactions take on significance because adolescents feel it is important to be involved with someone and because of the status it often affords them (Collins et al., 2009). Early romantic relationships function as opportunities to explore sexuality and are a source of companionship; later romantic relations increasingly become a strong source of emotional support (Furman & Simon, 2008).

For Your Review and Reflection

- What are the qualities of children's friendships during the preschool, middle-childhood, and adolescent years?
- What factors influence the formation of children's friendships?
- How do friendships contribute to the child's social and emotional development?
- What are the qualities of romantic relationships in adolescence?
- Why might romantic relationships differ across various cultures?
- Think about the friendships that you established in childhood and during your adolescent years. Why were they important to you? How did they change as you became older?

Peer Group Dynamics

Preschoolers and elementary-school children often associate in groups. Groups of peers interacting together, however, begin to become especially visible and significant during the middle-school and early secondary-school years. Adolescents frequently "hang out" in groups, desire to be members of the most popular groups, and look to the peer group for standards of appearance, conduct, and attitudes. Parents may find that their son or daughter must have a certain haircut or must buy a particular video game, only to discover that everyone else in the child's circle of friends has the same "look" or library of games. The social dynamics of large groups often differ from the dynamics of dyads; the power exerted by the group in shaping how the child acts and thinks can be enormous.

Peer Group Formation

How do peer groups form in the first place? Undoubtedly, they coalesce on the basis of shared interests, backgrounds, or activities. Children associate with other members of their classroom, soccer team, or school band, for example. Other variables, such as socioeconomic status or ethnic and racial group membership, can also contribute. For example, young

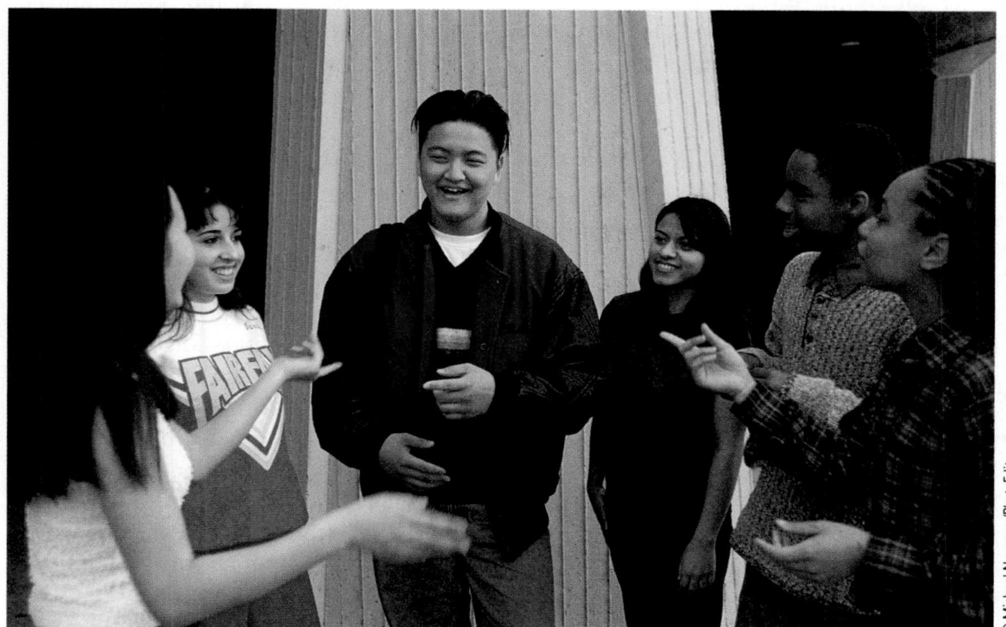

© Michael Newman/PhotoEdit

During adolescence, peer groups form on the basis of shared interests or common activities. Mixed-sex interactions are more likely to occur than in the earlier years of childhood.

children often choose playmates with a similar racial background, and adolescents whose friends have a similar ethnic background are more likely to affiliate with a larger crowd whose members have that same background (Brown et al., 2008; Leman & Lam, 2008). As we have seen in Chapter 13, "Gender," and in this chapter, gender is another powerful variable; groups, for the most part, tend to be of the same sex throughout childhood and early adolescence.

A particularly enlightening description of how peer groups form and operate can be found in a classic experiment called the Robber's Cave Study, named after the state park in Oklahoma where it took place. Muzafer Sherif and his colleagues invited twenty-two fifth-grade boys who did not know one another to participate in a summer camp program (Sherif et al., 1961). The boys were divided into two groups housed in separate parts of the state park. Initially, each group participated in its own program of typical camp activities—hiking, crafts, structured games—and was unaware of the existence of the other group. In this initial period of the experiment, each group began to develop a unique identity, and individual members performed distinct roles in relation to this group identity. One group became "tough"; the boys swore, acted rough, and ridiculed those who were "sissies." Members of the other group were polite and considerate. As group solidarity grew, members decided to name themselves, the former calling themselves the Rattlers and the latter the Eagles.

The experimenters found that when they deliberately structured certain situations to encourage cooperation, group identities could be further strengthened. One day, for example, each group returned to the campsite to find that the staff had not prepared dinner; only the uncooked ingredients were available. The boys quickly took over, dividing up the tasks so that some cooked, others prepared drinks, and so forth. Some boys assumed a leadership role, directing the suppertime activities, and others followed their directives. It was quite apparent that the boys had a strong sense of identity with the group and that the group had a clear structure. In other words, for both the Rattlers and the Eagles, there was strong intragroup cooperation and identity.

Another change in circumstances made the group identities even more pronounced. The camp counselors arranged for the Rattlers and Eagles to meet and organized a series of competitions for them, including games such as baseball and tug-of-war. The effects of losing in these competitions were dramatic. The losing group became very disharmonious and conflict ridden. Members accused one another of causing the loss, and some boys who had previously enjoyed status and prestige were demoted in standing if they had contributed to the group's humiliation.

After these initial conflicts, however, group identity became stronger than ever. The effects of competition on behavior between the groups were even more pronounced. The Rattlers and Eagles verbally antagonized each other and retaliated for a loss in competition by raiding each other's campsites and stealing possessions such as comic books and clothing. Each episode forged intragroup identity but also increased intergroup hostility.

In the last phase of this social experiment, the counselors attempted to lessen the bad feelings between the Rattlers and the Eagles by having them share meals or watch movies together. Instead of promoting harmony between the groups, however, this tactic produced continuing hostilities, punctuated with fights and verbal assaults. In contrast, when the experimenters created situations in which the two groups had to work together to achieve some common goal, antagonisms between them began to crumble. One hot day, for example, when the counselors "discovered" that the water pipeline for the campsites was broken, both Rattlers and Eagles began to search together for the broken pipes. On another occasion, the food delivery truck broke down; again, the boys all worked together to restart the engine. The acrimonious behavior between the two groups diminished, and boys from the two groups actually began to form friendships with one another. Thus, the Robbers Cave study reveals important information about the factors that influence peer group dynamics. It provides clues about the strategies that either promote or break down animosities among children's groups, findings that have implications for interventions aimed at reducing gender or racial and ethnic biases, as already discussed in Chapter 9, "Social Cognition."

Dominance Hierarchies

The scene: a standard laboratory playroom on a university campus. Six elementary school boys, strangers to one another, are brought together to play for forty-five minutes, five days in a row. Beginning the first day, researchers discover, the boys establish dominance hierarchies, distinct levels of social power in the relationships among group members. Some boys initiate more activity, verbally persuade the other group members to act a certain way, or use aggression to get their way. Others play a more submissive role, giving in to the actions of the dominant boys. Based on the frequencies with which they display these behaviors, each boy can be rated as most or least dominant or somewhere in between (Pettit et al., 1990).

As laboratory studies and field experiments such as the Robber's Cave Study show, the dominance relations among members of the peer group form quickly and remain stable over a period of months or even longer. Especially among younger children, dominance is established through, for example, success in competition, which may be accompanied by physically coercing or threatening the other members of the group. As children approach adolescence, the basis for dominance within some groups may also include social and other resources: in a classroom setting, for example, attention and factors associated with intelligence, creativity, and interpersonal skill (Jonkmann, Trautwein, & Lüdtke, 2009; Pettit et al., 1990; Savin-Williams, 1980).

What function do dominance hierarchies serve in the social behavior of children? First, groups can more easily meet their objectives when certain individuals within the group assume a leadership role. Ethologists have long observed that many species of animals, especially primates, have clear lines of power that probably enhance the obtaining of food, protection against natural enemies, and control of reproduction. Among children, dominance hierarchies can serve to get games going on the playground or accomplish school projects that require group efforts. Second, dominance hierarchies make social relationships more predictable for members of the group. Each individual has a specific role, whether as leader or follower, and the behaviors associated with those roles are often clearly defined. Finally, dominance hierarchies are thought to control aggression among members of the group. Usually, once the most dominant members of the group have emerged, few other members resort to aggression.

INTERACTION AMONG DOMAINS

Peer Pressure and Conformity

One of the most widely accepted beliefs about peer groups is that they control the behavior of children, sometimes more than parents and other adults would like. How willing are children to conform to peer pressures? Relative to other ages, vulnerability to peer pressure peaks in early adolescence, usually between the sixth and ninth grades. Around this age, too, when asked to rate two alternative vignettes—one that enhances or maintains their status with peers versus one that emphasizes achieving an academic or athletic goal, maintaining a friendship, pursuing a romantic relationship, showing compassion for a rejected peer, or obeying a rule—adolescents are particularly likely to rate scenarios that enhance their status with peers higher. For example, after hearing or reading a pair of vignettes, children might be asked "How likely are you to choose the person who is popular but not a good player?" Even elementary school children show some preference for increasing their status among peers. However, this preference becomes dramatically stronger for adolescents and especially when that choice is pitted against adhering to rules, as can be seen in Figure 15.5 (LaFontana & Cillessen, 2010).

For some children, the peer group may play an especially important part in influencing behaviors and choices. For example, when parents of adolescents are unresponsive to their children and maintain their power and restrictiveness, their children tend to be more noticeably oriented to their peer group (Bogenschneider et al., 1998; Fuligni & Eccles, 1993). Adolescents who develop an extreme orientation to their peer group, to the extent that they will ignore parents and schoolwork in order to remain popular, are more likely to become involved with alcohol and drug use, to skip classes, and to demonstrate other problem behaviors (Fuligni et al., 2001). The roles that specific peers play in the child's development may be especially revealing. For example, some friends may be more influential than others, and their influence may be greater in some domains than in others, such as

RISK | RESILIENCE

Figure 15.5

Importance of Perceived Status Compared to Other Domains

When asked to rate their choice of two vignettes, one enhancing or maintaining their status with peers versus the other emphasizing achieving an academic or athletic goal, maintaining a friendship, pursuing a romantic relationship, showing compassion for a rejected peer, or obeying a rule, adolescents are particularly likely to rate scenarios that enhance their status with peers higher.

Source: From LaFontana, K. M., & Cillessen, A. H. N. (2010). Developmental changes in the priority of perceived status in childhood and adolescence. *Social Development, 19*, pp. 130–147. Reprinted by permission of John Wiley & Sons, Inc.

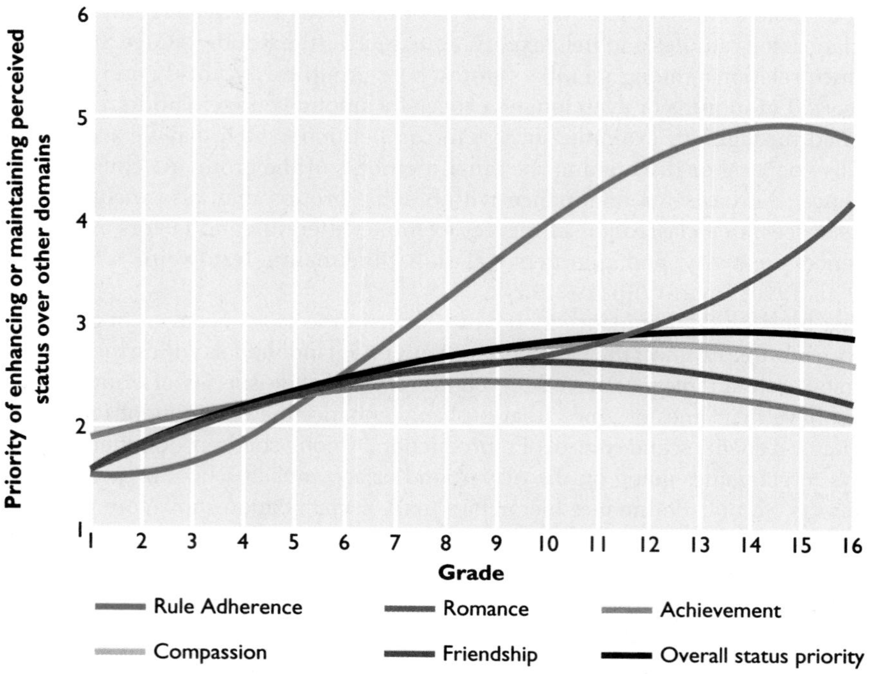

Priority of enhancing or maintaining perceived status over other domains

6
5
4
3
2
1

1 2 3 4 5 6 7 8 9 10 11 12 13 14 15 16

Grade

Rule Adherence
Romance
Achievement
Compassion
Friendship
Overall status priority

aggression as opposed to school achievement. Thus, a full understanding of peer influences will have to take these complexities into account.

For Your Review and Reflection

- What factors promote the formation of peer group identities? What factors can lessen hostilities between groups of peers?
- How do dominance hierarchies form in children's peer groups? What functions do they serve?
- When does conformity to peer pressure reach its peak? What are some factors related to a stronger orientation to the peer group?
- How did peers influence your behavior during middle childhood and adolescence? When were you most susceptible to their influence? Why?
- How might different abilities in various domains affect peer group formation, dominance, and conformity?

Peer Popularity and Social Competence

Parents, teachers, and others who have the opportunity to observe children over time usually notice the two extreme ends of the sociability spectrum: some children seem to be at the center of many activities, from school projects to playground games, whereas others are ridiculed or ignored. Frequently the patterns of peer acceptance that become established in

Figure 15.6

Classifications of Peer Status

The number of positive and negative peer nominations received determines whether a child's peer status is classified as controversial, rejected, neglected, or popular. Average children receive less extreme scores on peer nomination measures.

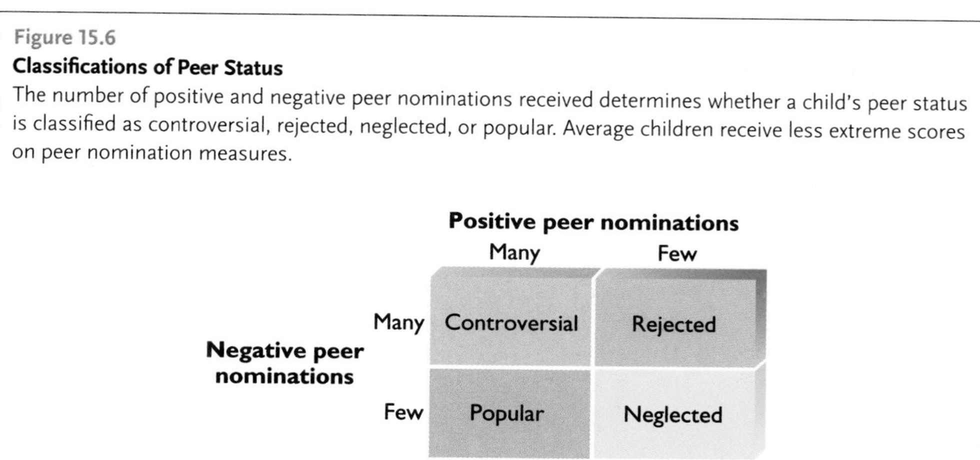

the early school years persist for years afterward, along with the psychological rewards or disappointments that accompany them.

Various systems for observing and coding peer interactions exist (Bierman, 2004), but because they may require substantial time and expenditures, psychologists often assess the quality of peer relations by administering questionnaires to children, asking about the social standing of their agemates. Peer assessments frequently consist of a **sociometric nomination** measure in which children are asked to name a specified number of peers (usually between three and five) who fit a certain criterion. For example, children might be asked to "name three classmates you especially like (or dislike)" or "list three peers you would like to walk home from school with." The number of positive or negative nominations the child receives from other children serves as a measure of his popularity. Alternatively, children are sometimes asked to rate each peer in the class or group, or are rated by some other person such as a teacher who is familiar with the children, on a **sociometric rating scale**. A series of items, such as "How much do you like to be with this person at school?" is asked when peers are engaged in this evaluation process. The target child's average rating by the other children is the index of peer acceptance.

Peer nomination measures are often used to classify children's peer status (Rubin et al., 2006). *Popular* children receive many more positive ("like") than negative ("dislike") nominations. *Rejected* children, in contrast, receive few positive but many negative nominations. *Neglected* children receive low numbers of nominations in either category; although they lack friends, they are not actively disliked. *Controversial* children receive high numbers of both positive and negative nominations. They have a high degree of "social impact" because they are active and visible, but they are generally not preferred as social partners. Finally, average children do not receive extreme scores on peer nomination measures. Figure 15.6 summarizes these categories of peer status.

The use of sociometric questionnaires, although important to research on peer relations, raises some interesting questions. First, do researchers and children agree on the connotations of popularity? In one study, fourth- and fifth-graders were shown photographs of three children; one was described as popular, one was described as unpopular, and one was presented as neutral. Children were asked to imagine several different social encounters with each of the children (e.g., meeting in the lunch room) and to rate how positive and negative these interactions would be. Children were also asked to rate how much they liked each target child. The results showed that, although unpopular targets were liked less than the other two targets, popular children were not liked any more than neutral targets (LaFontana & Cillessen, 1998). Popular peers, as defined by children, also may be viewed as more aggressive, dominant, and "stuck up" than popular children as defined by other sociometric measures (LaFontana & Cillessen, 2002). Thus, researchers' and children's notions of popularity may not have exactly the same meaning.

sociometric nomination Peer assessment measure in which children are asked to name a specific number of peers who fit a certain criterion, such as "peers you would like to walk home with."

sociometric rating scale Peer assessment measure in which children rate peers on a number of social dimensions.

Figure 15.7
A Composite Social Map
Illustrated here is a composite social map for girls in a fourth-grade classroom. Children are asked to report on the social affiliations of others in their classroom, and their responses are tallied and diagrammed. The map shows four peer groups of various sizes in this particular classroom, some of them with overlapping members.
Source: Adapted from Kindermann, 1998.

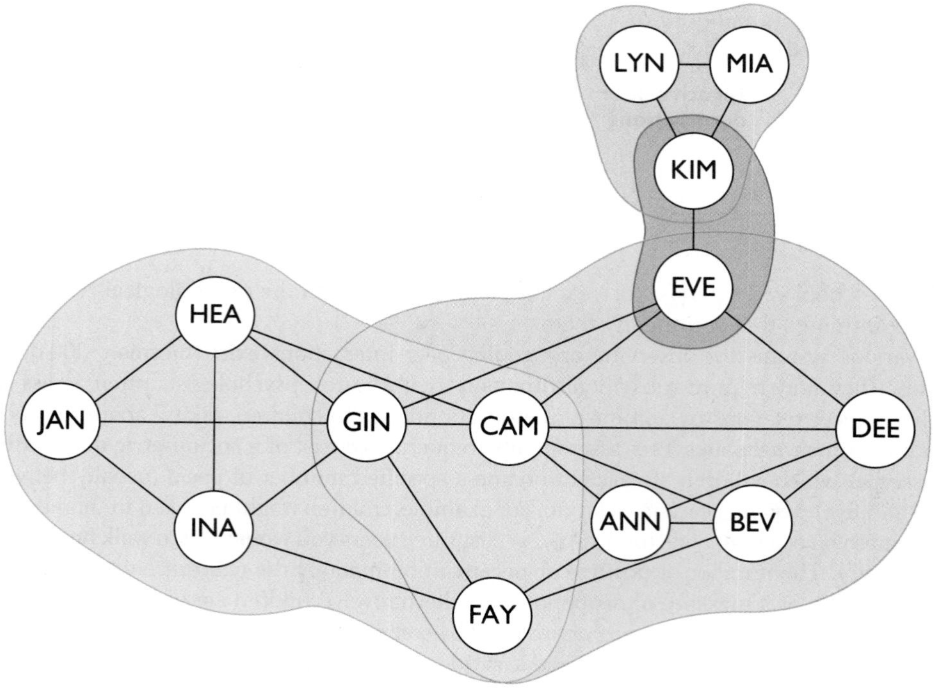

Second, most sociometric measures assess an individual child's one-on-one relationships with a few children. However, as the Robbers Cave study so vividly demonstrated, much of children's experience with peers is in the context of larger groups. Because understanding children's leadership, dominance, and status requires an examination of their functioning in a broader social network, approaches that capture the complexities of children's peer networks are needed. One such approach involves creating composite social maps of children's peer group relations. To create one, several children are asked to report with whom various other children associate; these reports are tallied up and diagrammed (see Figure 15.7 for an example).

RISK | RESILIENCE

Characteristics of Popular and Unpopular Children

What exactly is it about unpopular children that makes them so unappealing to their agemates and places them so consistently in an undesirable status? This is a particularly important question for those attempting to intervene in these children's "at-risk" circumstances. Peer popularity, as defined by sociometric measures, is related to a number of variables, some of which lie within the child's control, and some of which, unfortunately, do not.

INTERACTION AMONG DOMAINS

Physical Attractiveness and Motor Skills When asked to rate other children, sometimes based on photographs of those whom they do not know and sometimes based on ratings of those whom they do know, children from preschool through high school identify others who are considered physically attractive as more friendly, intelligent, and socially competent than unattractive agemates (Dion & Berscheid, 1974; Langlois & Stephan, 1981; Vannatta et al., 2009). These stereotypic beliefs can lead to self-fulfilling behaviors in children who have been labeled. For example, a child who receives peer attention because of attractiveness may have numerous opportunities to develop the social skills that lead to even greater peer acceptance.

Another factor related to peer acceptance is the child's proficiency in motor activities. Both boys and girls who are coordinated, strong, and skilled in athletic activities are rated as more popular by peers (Vannatta et al., 2009) and as more socially competent by their teachers and parents (Hops & Finch, 1985). Perhaps the value our society places on athletic prowess is reflected in children's preferences in playmates. Alternatively, motor skill may help to establish leadership in the manipulation of objects and game playing, which constitutes a large part of children's shared activities. Those who are talented in this arena will naturally have more peer contacts and eventually be better liked.

Social Skills One of the most important factors in peer acceptance is the constellation of social behaviors displayed by popular and unpopular children. Researchers who have observed the overt activities of accepted and unaccepted peers have learned that each presents a distinct behavioral profile. In general, popular children engage in prosocial, cooperative, and normative behaviors and show a high degree of social skill. For example, when Gary Ladd (1983) observed third- and fourth-grade students during recess, he noted several differences in the behavioral styles of popular and rejected children. Popular children spent more time in cooperative play, social conversation, and other positive social interactions with peers than their rejected counterparts. Rejected children, on the other hand, spent more time engaging in antagonistic behaviors such as arguing and playing in a rough-and-tumble fashion, or playing or standing alone at a distance from peers; about 50 percent of rejected children are aggressive (Bierman, Smoot, & Aumiller, 1993), and about 20 percent are highly socially withdrawn (Volling et al., 1993). Both of these types of rejected children, as well as neglected children, display socially inappropriate behaviors for which they receive little social reinforcement (Parkhurst & Asher, 1992; Pettit et al., 1996).

INTERACTION AMONG DOMAINS

RISK | RESILIENCE

In another study that examined the peer-directed behaviors of first- and third-grade boys, neglected boys were found to be the least aggressive of any group observed (Coie & Dodge, 1988). They tended to engage in isolated activities and had low visibility with peers. Controversial boys were intellectually, athletically, or socially talented and very active, but they were sometimes prone to anger and rule violations. The mixture of their positive and negative social behaviors thus elicited a similarly mixed reaction from their classmates. Thus, children may be unpopular with their peers for a number of reasons, ranging from social withdrawal to outright aggression.

The social competence of popular children becomes markedly apparent when they are asked to enter a group of unfamiliar children who are already at play (Dodge et al., 1983). Popular children seem to know exactly what to do. Rather than calling attention to themselves or disrupting the group's activities, they make statements about their peers or what they are doing, such as "That looks like a fun game you are playing." These diplomatic verbalizations pave the way for their smooth integration into the group. Rejected children tend to disrupt the group's ongoing activity by pushing the blocks off the table or making intrusive or unrelated statements about the activity, usually about themselves (e.g., "I have a baby brother"). In return, their peer hosts respond negatively to them. Neglected children are not disruptive but employ another ineffective strategy. Instead of making some verbal or nonverbal attempt to join the group, these children passively watch as their peers play—and they are ignored.

Emotion Regulation Research increasingly points to a link between children's ability to regulate their own emotions and the reactions they receive from peers. For example, in one study, peers reported that children they had categorized as rejected were irritable and inattentive in their behaviors. Peers saw them as complaining and getting upset when things went wrong and as being easily distracted (Pope & Bierman, 1999). In fact, rejected children do tend to express more anger, both in their facial expressions and their verbalizations, in contexts such as losing a game (Hubbard, 2001). Or they may show inappropriate happiness as they behave aggressively with their peers (Arsenio, Cooperman, & Lover, 2000). Observations of preschool- and kindergarten-age children show that there is a relationship

INTERACTION AMONG DOMAINS

Children who lack social skills may be rejected or neglected by their peers. In contrast, popular children display prosocial behaviors and a wide range of social knowledge.

© Bob Daemmrich/Stock Boston

between the ability to inhibit undesirable behaviors and social competence with peers, a pattern of findings that also has been observed in varying cultures, such as Indonesia, for example (Eisenberg, Pidada, & Liew, 2001).

Do children's socioemotional skills actually increase their popularity? Gary Ladd and his associates examined this question more closely by observing preschool children in the playground during three six-week intervals at the beginning, middle, and end of the academic year (Ladd, Price, & Hart, 1988). Episodes of cooperative play, arguments, and other positive and negative forms of interaction were recorded. In addition, children's sociometric status was assessed at each of these three points in time. The results showed that children who engaged in more cooperative play at the beginning of the school year made gains in peer acceptance by the end of the school year, whereas children who frequently argued showed a decline in acceptance by the middle of the school year. These results are consistent with the idea that children's behaviors precede their social status.

RISK | RESILIENCE

Perhaps of more concern is the finding that once children are rejected by peers, they are on a trajectory that oftentimes leads to lower school achievement and emotional problems. In another study, Ladd observed children both in the fall and spring of their kindergarten year, noting their peer status, peer interactions, classroom participation, and emotional adjustment at these times. The data fit the model depicted in Figure 15.8. Rejected children were subjected to more negative treatment from peers (e.g., exclusion from peer activities, victimization) and participated less in classroom activities later in the school year, which in turn predicted lower achievement and emotional difficulties (Buhs & Ladd, 2001). This pattern of decline continues to be evident for many rejected children as they move through the later school years (Ladd, Herald-Brown, & Reiser, 2008). Another more recent study involving Italian young school children revealed a similar finding: rejected children were more likely to show a decline in academic achievement, and popular children an increase in school performance (Greenman, Schneider, & Tomada, 2009). Given the developmental pathway that many rejected children follow, finding ways to help them negotiate their social world in the school seems all the more important. For example, children rejected by peers during their early school years but who begin to become more accepted by the fourth through sixth grades often display improved independent and cooperative classroom participation (Ladd et al., 2008).

INTERACTION AMONG DOMAINS

Peer popularity may have both positive and negative consequences associated with it. In one study, popular teens tended to show good self-control, sensitivity to the views of

Figure 15.8

The Impact of Peer Rejection

Peer rejection is associated with negative consequences among children, including emotional and academic problems. To study more closely the dynamics of this process, Eric Buhs and Gary Ladd (2001) monitored kindergarten children's peer status, peer interactions, classroom participation, and eventual adjustment over the school year.They found that the results of the study generally supported a model like that depicted here.

Source: Adapted from Buhs & Ladd, 2001.

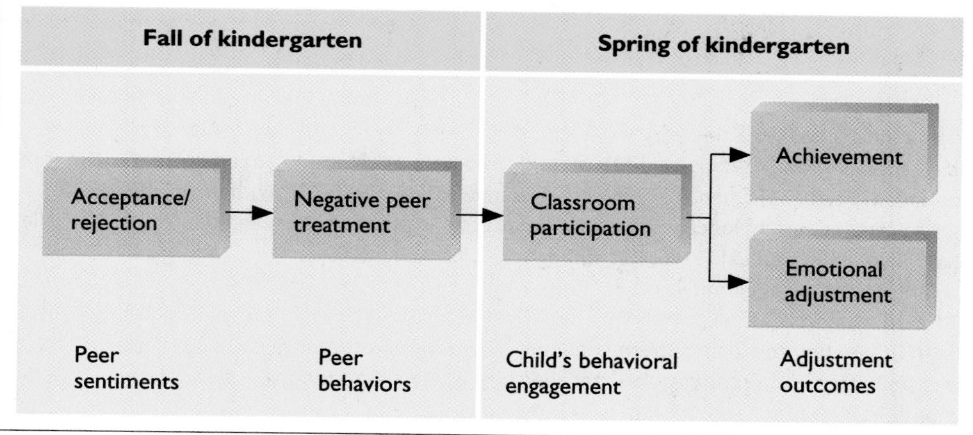

others, and healthy emotional relationships with parents and friends. At the same time, those who were popular at age thirteen were more likely to show increases in alcohol and marijuana use and minor delinquent behavior a year later. According to the *popularity-socialization hypothesis,* popular teens experience more opportunities to be socialized by their agemates than those who are less popular, subjecting them to both the positive and the negative influences of peers (Allen et al., 2005).

What personal qualities are associated with developmental changes in peer popularity? Social skills, no doubt, continue to play an important role throughout childhood and adolescence, but the impact of certain dimensions of personal behavior such as aggression, already noted to be associated with unpopularity in middle childhood, may change in adolescence. According to Terrie Moffitt (1993), the adolescent years are a time when some teens see antisocial behavior as more desirable because it is a clear sign of breaking away from the control of parents. Consistent with this idea, some studies indicate that, in early adolescence, antisocial behavior may actually be associated with peer popularity, especially if it is conceived of as *perceived popularity,* or high visibility (as opposed to being well liked). Thus, for example, eighth-grade children described by peers and teachers as antisocial were named as individuals children would want to spend time with after school (Kiesner & Pastore, 2005).

INTERACTION AMONG DOMAINS

Various studies provide some additional clues about the social dynamics of aggression and popularity. Thomas Farmer and his colleagues (Farmer et al., 2003) surveyed seventh- and eighth-graders, as well as their peers and teachers, and found two types of aggressive children: "tough" boys who were aggressive but also popular and socially skilled, and "troubled boys" who were aggressive, unpopular, and unskilled socially. The first group, more than the second, tended to be leaders who were involved in extracurricular activities and were very influential in peer groups.

RISK | RESILIENCE

Other researchers have also shown that overt, but especially *relational,* aggression is associated with perceived popularity (Cillessen & Mayeux, 2004; Hoff et al., 2009; Rose, Swenson, & Waller, 2004). Recall that relational aggression refers to tactics such as ignoring others, leaving them out of social activities, or gossiping about them. Together, these research findings seem to tell a more complicated story: that, in the transition from elementary school to middle school, when many peer groups become shifted or realigned, some children find forceful ways to exert social power. They manipulate others, assert themselves, and generally "call the shots" with their peers. In many cases, their efforts at using aggression to attain social status are successful, at least in the short run. However, the long-term outcomes of behaving in this way are still not known (Cillessen & Rose, 2005).

Social Withdrawal — atypical development

Some children are "loners." They have few or no friends, and they end up playing or doing their schoolwork on their own, even if surrounded by other children. Along with aggression, social withdrawal is considered by many child development experts to be one of the two most important indicators of a behavior problem (Rubin & Asendorpf, 1993). Withdrawn children are prone to express anxiety, loneliness, negative conceptions of themselves, and depression (Gazelle & Ladd, 2003; Kingery et al., 2010; Rubin, Bowker, & Kennedy, 2009).

Children may have limited interactions with their peers for a number of reasons. Some children may simply prefer to play by themselves, curling up with a book or becoming involved with an interesting toy. This pattern is usually noted in the preschool and early school years and is not necessarily an indication that the child is at risk for abnormal development. A second pattern is that of the shy child, who is nervous about being in new environments or with strangers but generally desires social interactions. This characteristic may stem from a biologically based temperament that results in the child's wariness and inhibition (Kagan, Snidman, & Arcus, 1993). Early negative experiences due to a shy temperament can escalate into more severe social withdrawal as the childhood years progress. A third category is children who desire social interactions but, because of their inept social skills or other factors, are avoided by their peers. These children may react with aggression, which further contributes to their isolation (Rubin & Asendorpf, 1993).

RISK | RESILIENCE

Researchers are beginning to understand some of the processes that complement biological temperament in contributing to social withdrawal in children. To illustrate, children who follow a trajectory of increasing social withdrawal over the elementary school years display poor inhibitory control; for example, they have difficulty waiting or stopping an activity when asked to do so (Booth-LaForce & Oxford, 2008). Parenting style can play a key role as well. When their children are attempting to initiate social interactions, mothers who tend to be overprotective, overcontrolling, or intrusive may promote a cycle of inadequacy and feelings of incompetence in their offspring, fostering anxiety about initiating social contact with others (Rubin et al., 2009). The reactions of peers may make a difference too. First-grade children do not seem to think about social withdrawal as a liability when asked to rate the likability of children described in vignettes. By age ten, though, social withdrawal is viewed as an abnormal behavior (Younger, Gentile, & Burgess, 1993). Interestingly, even in China, where adults value shyness as a personality trait, children shift from positive to negative evaluations of shy children at around age twelve (Chen, Rubin, & Li, 1995). Unfortunately, children who display anxiety in social situations are often hesitant about making social contact with other children and are unlikely to persist if initially rejected by peers. That course of action may then further heighten the likelihood of their socially withdrawing (Gazelle & Druhan, 2009). Thus child characteristics, socialization practices of parents, and the reactions of peers are among the many factors that can lead to social withdrawal.

Despite these complexities, it is important that researchers continue to examine the nature of social withdrawal in childhood because of its potential lingering impact even well into adulthood. Kenneth Rubin gives one example in a letter he received from a fifty-one-year-old individual who had read about his research:

> I recall one instance in my third year of grade school and my teacher approached me after recess with the enquiry "have you no one to play with—I have noticed you standing by yourself at recess for several days now." I recalled replying and LYING—"yes I've friends." The teacher was observant and I give her credit for this, however, I wish, oh how I wish, something had been done about my isolation at the tender age of 7 or 8. It has been a long, lonely road. (Rubin & Asendorpf, 1993, p. 4)

© altrendo images/Stockbyte/Jupiter Images

Researchers are actively exploring the ways young children develop social skills. Parenting influences are important as are the child's cognitive skills such as correctly encoding and interpreting the cues other children in the group display in deciding how to interact with them.

The Origins of Social Competence

What factors are responsible for **social competence**, the ability to function well with others while still achieving one's own personal goals, achievements that stand in stark contrast to the social ineptness displayed by some? You will already be able to identify some of these factors from our earlier discussion of popular and unpopular peers. Researchers draw their answers from a number of perspectives, from the early attachment relationships children form with their caregivers to capabilities in processing the subtle cues that form such an integral part of social interactions.

INTERACTION AMONG DOMAINS

Attachment Relationships Attachment teaches children about emotional ties: how to recognize affection and how to show it. This knowledge and the "internal working models" that children construct regarding relationships in forming attachments may assist them as they expand their social world to include others (Booth-LaForce & Kerns, 2009). Longitudinal studies confirm that children and adolescents who have more positive relationships with peers tended to have secure attachments with their parents during infancy and toddlerhood (Booth-LaForce & Oxford, 2008; NICHD Early Child Care Research Network, 2006; Sroufe et al., 2005). But early attachment relationships are only part of the many conditions involved in contributing to social competence. When the quality of parenting improves as children become older, for example, if mothers become more supportive, permit greater autonomy, and show less hostility toward their children, social competence improves, and the initial influence of type of attachment decreases (NICHD Early Child Care Research Network, 2006). Not surprisingly, then, parenting styles are clearly important throughout the child's development, not just during infancy.

RISK | RESILIENCE

Parental Influences In their relationships with caregivers, children have the opportunity to learn and practice a variety of social skills, such as turn taking, compromise, and effective communication. Once honed and refined, these abilities can later be employed with peers and other individuals in the child's life. Thus, parenting practices play an influential role in the relationships their children form with peers. Broadly speaking, parents who exhibit an authoritative style (see Chapter 14, "The Family")—that is, are responsive, are nurturant, and provide verbal explanations—tend to have children who are popular and who display prosocial behaviors with peers. In contrast, children of authoritarian, power-assertive parents are more likely to be classified as rejected (Ross & Howe, 2009; Pettit, Bates, & Dodge, 1997).

social competence The ability to function well with others while still achieving one's own personal goals.

Parents serve as important models of social competence for their children, create opportunities for their children to interact with peers, and provide explicit instruction on appropriate ways to behave in social situations (McDowell & Parke, 2009). In one study, mothers of popular and unpopular preschoolers were observed as they introduced their children to a pair of peers busily playing with blocks. Mothers of unpopular children tended to disrupt the ongoing play and use their authority to incorporate their own child into the group. In many ways, their behaviors resembled those of the unpopular children we discussed earlier. In contrast, mothers of popular children encouraged their offspring to become involved in play without intervening in the activity of the host peers. Moreover, in a subsequent interview, these mothers displayed greater knowledge of how to encourage their children to make friends, resolve conflicts, and display other positive social behaviors (Finnie & Russell, 1988). Others have noted that, compared with parents of less popular children, parents of popular and socially competent children are generally less disagreeable and demanding and express less negative affect when they play with their children (Isley et al., 1999; Putallaz, 1987). In addition, both mothers and fathers of unpopular children have been found to shift conversations to irrelevant topics, speak while someone else is talking, and ignore their children's requests. Perhaps not surprisingly, their children showed similar ineffective communication styles (Black & Logan, 1995).

Parents can influence children's social competence on another level: by managing their children's social activities and experiences that provide the context for the emergence of social skills. Some parents seek out play groups for their preschoolers or periodically get together with friends who have children. When parents deliberately arrange peer contacts for their preschoolers, their children have a greater variety of playmates and a larger number of consistent play partners, display more prosocial behaviors at preschool, and have higher sociometric status (at least among boys) than when parents do not make such efforts (Ladd & Golter, 1988; Ladd & Hart, 1992). Opportunities to interact with peers provide the child with a natural arena to discover those behaviors that generate positive responses from peers and those that do not.

INTERACTION AMONG DOMAINS

Social-Cognitive Development Children's social competence includes an array of intertwined cognitive and behavioral skills. An information-processing model of social competence formulated by Nicki Crick and Kenneth Dodge (see Figure 15.9) suggests more precisely how cognitions and behaviors are related and where problems in social functioning might occur (Crick & Dodge, 1994).

According to the model, the first step in processing social information is to focus on the correct cues. For example, suppose a boy initiates a conversation with a peer. It is more important for the child to encode the peer's facial expression ("Is that a smile or a sneer?") than the color of her clothing. Second, the child must meaningfully interpret the social cues based on his past experiences. Most children would interpret a scowl on a peer's face as a sign of hostility and a smile as a mark of friendliness. In the third step of processing, the child selects a goal for the situation, such as retaliating against an aggressor or making a friend. Fourth, the child generates one or more potential behavioral responses. If he perceives the peer as hostile, he may contemplate avoiding her or matching her hostility. If he reads her signals as friendly, he may consider smiling back or beginning to talk. Fifth, the child evaluates the potential consequences of each possible behavior. Hostility and aggression could lead to physical harm whereas avoidance might not, and hence avoidance might be preferable. Finally, the child enacts the chosen response verbally or physically, monitors the outcome of his behavior, and, if necessary, modifies it, engaging in the six-step cycle over again. This model thus includes a number of steps at which things can go wrong to disrupt a smooth, mutually rewarding social interaction.

RISK | RESILIENCE

Studies of peer relations suggest that popular children are more skillful than unpopular (and, in particular, rejected) children at several steps in the model. First, they are better able to encode and decipher social information correctly. In one study, elementary school children were asked to label the emotions depicted in sets of pictures. For example, one was a series of faces depicting anger, happiness, sadness, disgust, surprise, and fear. Rejected children were less able than popular children to correctly identify the emotions represented in these stimuli (Monfries & Kafer, 1987). As another illustration of how selective processes

Figure 15.9

Social Competence: An Information-Processing Model

Crick and Dodge (1994) have proposed a six-step model of social competence based on the child's growing social information-processing skills. The process begins when the child is able to correctly encode and then interpret a social cue. Next, the child generates a set of social goals and possible responses to achieve them. Finally, the child evaluates those responses and enacts the behavior he or she internally selected. Children low in social competence may have difficulties at any step in this model.

Source: From Crick, N. R., & Dodge, K. A. (1994). A review and reformulation of social information-processing mechanisms in children's social adjustment. *Psychological Bulletin, 115,* pp. 74–101.

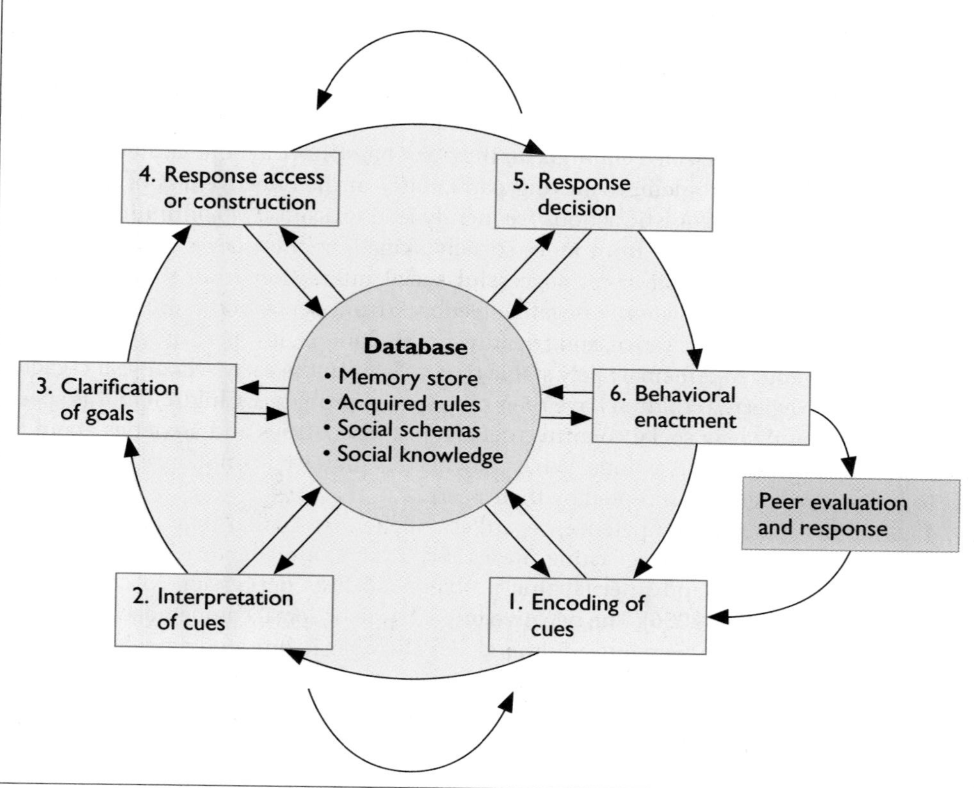

in social information processing might work, children who have been physically abused tend to focus on angry rather than happy faces and have difficulty avoiding attention to angry faces (Pollak & Tolley-Schell, 2003).

Second, some rejected children tend to make incorrect attributions about the behaviors of peers. In one experiment, researchers asked children to view videotaped episodes of an actor destroying a second actor's toy with hostile, prosocial, accidental, or ambiguous intent. Both rejected and neglected children tended to attribute hostile intentions to the actor's actions, even when the acts were accidental or prosocial. Popular children were more often correct in their judgments (Dodge, Murphy, & Buchsbaum, 1984). Numerous studies have confirmed that aggressive children in particular tend to make more hostile attributions about the intentions of others than nonaggressive children (Dodge, Coie, & Lynam, 2006). The tendency to hold negative beliefs about peers is linked to two factors: prior negative experiences with parents and past low social acceptance from peers (MacKinnon-Lewis, Rabiner, & Starnes, 1999). As a result of these mistaken attributions, aggressive children often retaliate with further negative behavior.

Third, some rejected children tend to suggest inappropriate strategies to resolve social problems and have difficulty devising alternative paths to attain their social goals (Rubin & Krasnor, 1986). Researchers typically assess social problem-solving skills by presenting children with hypothetical social dilemmas and examining their proposed solutions. Researchers in one study asked kindergartners to react to a series of dilemmas in which, for example, one child takes away another's toy. Unpopular children were much more likely than popular children to recommend an aggressive solution, such as "Punch him" or "She could beat her up" (Dodge et al., 2003). In addition, when Kenneth Rubin and Linda Krasnor observed children's strategies for handling social problems in naturalistic settings, they noted that rejected children were rigid in their attempts (Rubin & Krasnor, 1986). If, for example, a rejected child failed to convince another child to give him an object, he simply repeated the same unsuccessful behavior. Popular children often tried a different approach to attaining their goal, indicating a broader and more flexible repertoire of social problem-solving skills.

Popular children thus possess social knowledge that leads to successful interactions with their peers and also behave in ways that manifest this expertise. They know what strategies are needed to make friends (e.g., ask others their names, invite them to do things) and can describe prosocial behaviors that tend to foster peer relationships (e.g., be generous, keep promises). They also recognize that the achievement of their social goals may require time and work and adjust their behaviors according to the sometimes subtle demands of the situation (Asher, 1983). Rejected children, on the other hand, have a more limited awareness of how to solve social problems, believing particularly in the effectiveness of aggression. Unfortunately, their antagonistic actions frequently lead to a spiral of continuing rejection. As they become disassociated from more socially skilled, popular peers, they have fewer opportunities to learn the basics of successful social interaction from them. Moreover, the child who receives consistently negative feedback from peers would probably be hard pressed to be positive, cooperative, and friendly. In this context, it is perhaps not surprising that aggression tends to remain a fairly stable trait, at least in the early school years (Ladd & Burgess, 1999). Neglected children have their own special problems. Children in this special category may not display social cognitive deficits but insecurities and anxieties about the consequences of their social actions. What they need is more self-confidence in their abilities to interact with and be accepted by their peers.

Limitations in social competence, regardless of the factors that may be contributing to this assessment, can be long-lasting. Researchers have often reported a link between poor social competence and internalizing problems such as depression in children and adolescents (Rubin et al., 2006). The negative impact of poor social competence on internalizing problems continues even into adulthood. For example, in one study in which children eight to twelve years of age were tested again seven, ten, and twenty years later, findings suggested that internalizing problems continued to increase above and beyond the symptoms displayed at earlier ages for those who initially displayed poor social competence

RISK | RESILIENCE

© MANDY GODBEHEAR/Shutterstock.com

Bullying has become a major concern in many communities. Although it is often thought of in terms of physical aggression directed toward another person, teasing, taunting, and making derogatory comments about another person can have devastating effects on the target of this behavior as well.

(Burt et al., 2008). In other words, peer rejection and the inability to maintain close friendships, indicators of poor social competence, can have negative implications that extend and increase well beyond the childhood and adolescent years.

research applied to parenting | Preventing Bullying

Ms. Nakamura's attention was drawn to the loud shouts of a circle of boys at the back of the playground. As she approached, she saw two boys in the middle of the circle, one waving clenched fists and yelling at the other. Quickly she stepped in and broke up the fight, fortunately before anyone got hurt. She recognized the older of the two boys; he was a fourth-grader who had a reputation for being a "bully." The other child was a small, frightened-looking second-grader who was on the verge of tears. Ms. Nakamura knew that this was a serious situation because it had been going on a while. What should she do about it?

Bullying has become a major concern for parents, teachers, and those responsible for the safety of children and adolescents. A cross-national survey conducted in the 2005–2006 academic years indicated that bullying is a problem for eleven- to fifteen-year-olds in many countries, as can be seen in Figure 15.10 (Craig et al., 2009). The number of children reporting being bullied declined over the decade preceding this latest survey in most countries, but not in the United States, Canada, Ireland, England, Scotland, and Wales (Molcho et al., 2009). Some might argue that it has become an even more serious problem with the rise of the Internet, texting, and social networks in part because such activity can be carried out with some anonymity and with great frequency. Especially disturbing, however, is that bullying can have a deadly dimension; suicides associated with being a victim of bullying have received enormous attention in the media in recent years.

SOCIOCULTURAL DIFFERENCES

Bullying exists in many different forms: *physical*, for example, hitting, kicking, or beating another; *verbal*, for example, making derogatory remarks, taunting, or teasing; *relational*, for example, ignoring or gossiping about another; and *cyberbullying*, the electronic form of bullying, which has become increasingly publicized. It may begin as early as kindergarten but seems to reach its zenith between about eleven and fourteen years of age. It occurs somewhat more frequently among boys than girls, as Figure 15.10 indicates, and most of it is directed at same-sex peers (Ladd, 2005).

Researchers have documented many of the characteristics of children who are bullies and also the characteristics of the victims of this form of aggression. One common observation among those who bully is that it is carried out to gain status among peers (Salmivalli & Peets, 2009). Bullies tend to be more aggressive than their victims, and their actions are more likely to be implemented when their targets are of relatively low status, thus not threatening disapproval from peers and particularly from peers with whom the bully wishes to be more popular (Olthof & Goossens, 2008; Veenstra et al., 2007). Bullies are also more likely to be insecurely attached to their parents, and their parents, in turn, are more likely to be neglecting or rejecting (Duncan, 2004; Holmes & Holmes-Lonergan, 2004).

Most targets of perpetrators are peers for whom bullying provides an easy victory because they are not assertive; thus, the recipients are identified frequently as passive victims (Salmivalli & Peets, 2009). A smaller number of targets, identified as provocative victims, seem to provoke attacks from bullies. In general, children who are targeted tend to have low self-esteem and are more likely to experience loneliness and depression (Hawker & Boulton, 2000). Given these characteristics, is there anything parents (and perhaps teachers) can do to stop this negative cycle?

Dan Olweus (1993) initiated a major intervention program to deal with the problems of bullying in Norway. The program involved about 2500 students from forty-two elementary and junior high schools, as well as their parents and teachers. The power asymmetry that research has demonstrated to occur between bullies and victims contributed to the following advice to the parents of chronic victims:

1. *Help the child to develop self-confidence by encouraging special talents or abilities he displays.* Children who gain confidence are more likely to be assertive and refuse to tolerate the behaviors of bullies.
2. *Encourage the child to undertake some form of physical training or participate in sports.* By doing so, he will feel less anxiety about his body and send out "signals" of strength rather than weakness to potential aggressors.

Figure 15.10

Bullying: an International Problem

A representative sample of over 200,000 11- to 15-year-olds in 40 different countries responded to survey questions asking whether they had bullied or were the victim of bullying. The percentage of those reporting they had bullied, were a victim, or both two or more times in the previous two months are shown for each of these countries. As can be seen here, countries differed considerably in the percent of children reporting bullying or victimization; the problem appears to be especially severe in Baltic countries. Boys reported being a bully more frequently than girls in all countries; girls reported being the victim more often than boys in most countries.

Source: Data from Craig, W., Harel-Fisch, Y., Fogel-Grinvald, H., Dostaler, S., Hetland, J., Simons-Morton, B., ... HBSC Violence & Injuries Prevention Focus Group, & HBSC Bullying Writing Group. (2009). A cross-national profile of bullying and victimization among adolescents in 40 countries. *International Journal of Public Health, 54* (Supplement 2), 216–224.

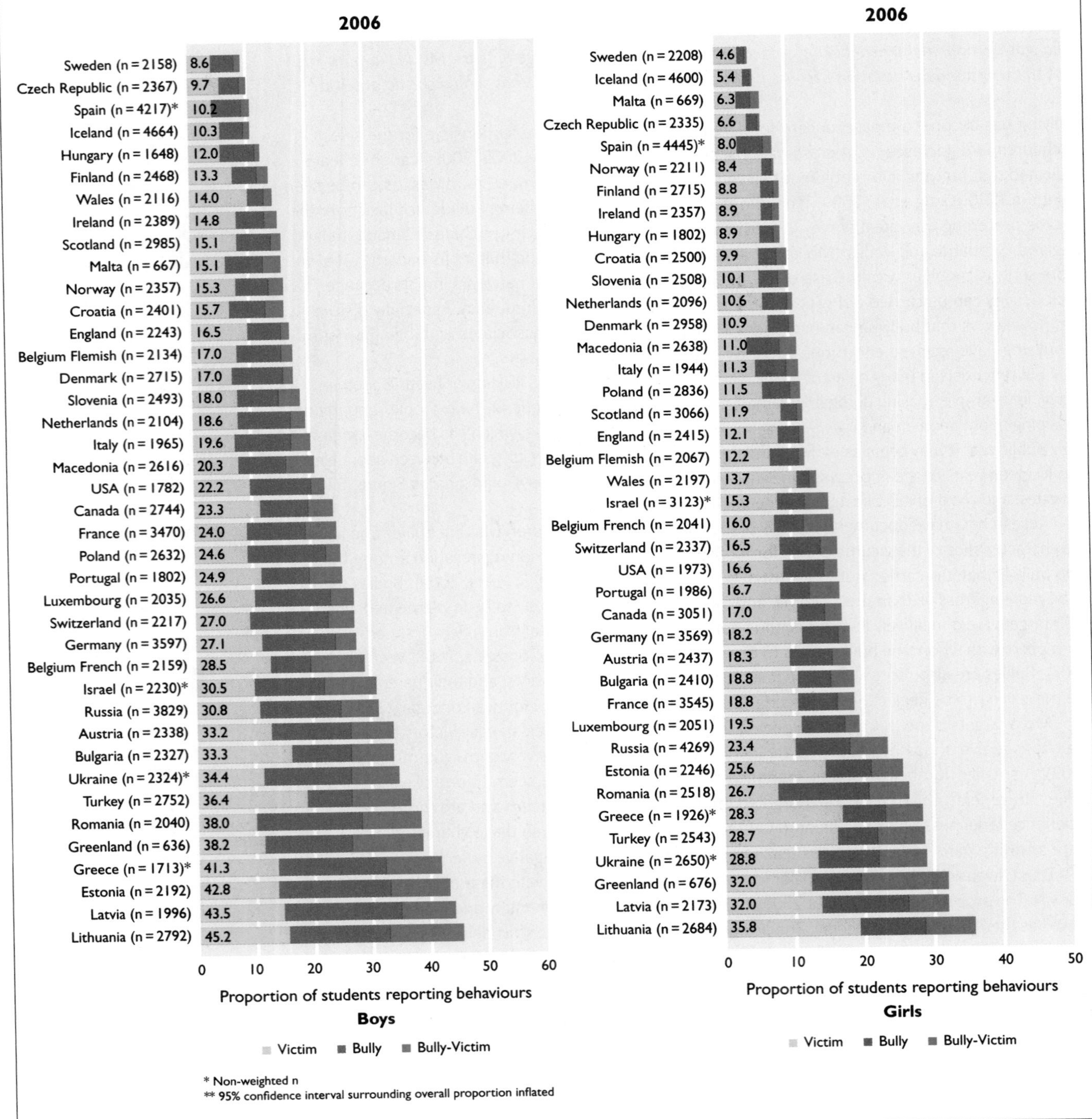

3. *Help the child get to know a friendly student in the class who has similar interests or is also looking for a friend.* A relationship with another peer can help with feelings of loneliness and depression.
4. *Encourage the child's attempts to become involved with people or activities outside the family.* This suggestion is especially helpful if the family tends to attempt to protect the child every time he is attacked.

This advice was combined with several other programmatic changes involving the school, including institution of class rules against bullying, better supervision of lunch and recess, talks with the parents of bullies and victims, and promotion of more cooperative learning and positive classroom experiences (Olweus, 1993). The results showed a 50 percent reduction in the number of children being bullied (and in those acting as bullies as well). In addition, the incidence of other antisocial behavior such as thefts and vandalism was reduced, and the social climate of the classroom became more positive. A key to the program's success was the involvement of all children in the program (not just bullies and victims), greater supervision of children during the school day, and good communication between teachers and parents (Olweus, 1997).

An important strategy that may further stem bullying involves encouraging bystanders to help in defending victims. Even when just one individual stands up for the target of bullying and expresses disapproval of a bully's actions, the likelihood of the perpetrator gaining status from such behavior is reduced (Salmivalli, 2010). What is most apparent, though, from the research conducted on attempts to reduce bullying is that dealing with the problem requires a concerted effort at many different levels. School administrators need to establish rules, implement clear consequences for bullying, and promote a climate in which it is no longer "cool" to engage in such activity. Parents, teachers, and other adults working with children need to encourage children to feel comfortable about reporting bullying, take those reports seriously, and communicate their concerns, not only to the child committing the bullying and the victim of such actions, but to others who are responsible for children as well. In addition, peers need to carry out discussions in the classroom and other settings that emphasize the unacceptability of bullying, defend and provide support to victims, and recognize the potentially very harmful consequences of çmessages, images, and videos that may be seen by countless numbers of others when cyberbullying. In other words, approaches for dealing with bullying must consider characteristics of not only the bullying–victim dyad but also the peer group and the institutional context and social environment in which it takes place if programs to reduce this form of aggression are to be successful (Berger, Karimpour, & Rodkin, 2008).

Training Social Skills

Can children be taught the elements of socially skilled behavior and thereby gain greater acceptance from their peers? Answering this question is important in light of findings that children who experience rejection from peers are more likely to have academic, social, and psychological problems (Rubin et al., 2006). Several forms of intervention, usually employed in schools and clinical settings, have produced improvements in children's interpersonal strategies.

Modeling One effective training technique is modeling, that is, exposing children to live or recorded models displaying desirable behaviors. For example, one research team presented a group of socially withdrawn preschoolers with short videotapes depicting young children engaging in social behaviors accompanied by a narration of their thoughts (Jakibchuk & Smeriglio, 1976). The soundtrack included the following self-directed statements as the model approached a group of peers: "Those children over there are playing together. . . . I would like to play with them. But I'm afraid. I don't know what to do or say. . . . This is hard. But I'll try. . . . I'm close to them. I did it. Good for me. . . ." Compared with their baseline behaviors, withdrawn children who watched these videotapes for four days increased the number of their social interactions and in turn were the objects of more positive social

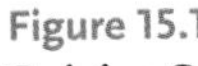

Figure 15.11
Training Social Skills
In an experiment that evaluated the effects of several treatment strategies with socially withdrawn preschoolers, researchers found that children who observed a model approach a group of peers while verbalizing his thoughts later increased their number of social interactions compared with the pretreatment (or baseline) period.These children also experienced more positive social behaviors from others.The graphs show both measures for this treatment group compared with a group that saw a neutral film and with a no-treatment control group.These last two groups were included to ensure that any gains in social behavior were not the result of simple contact with the experimenters or exposure to a film per se.
Source: Adapted from Jakibchuk & Smeriglio, 1976.

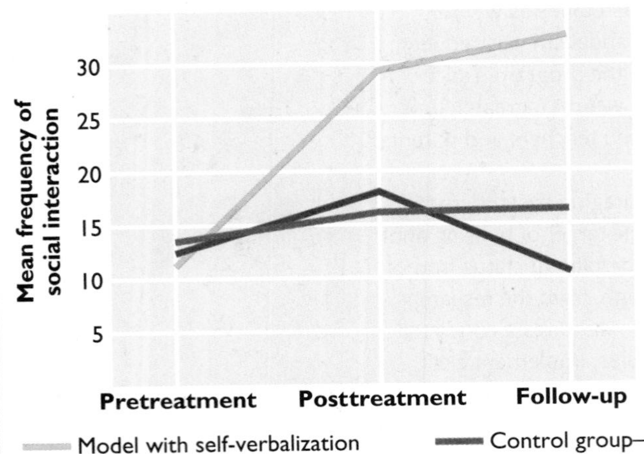

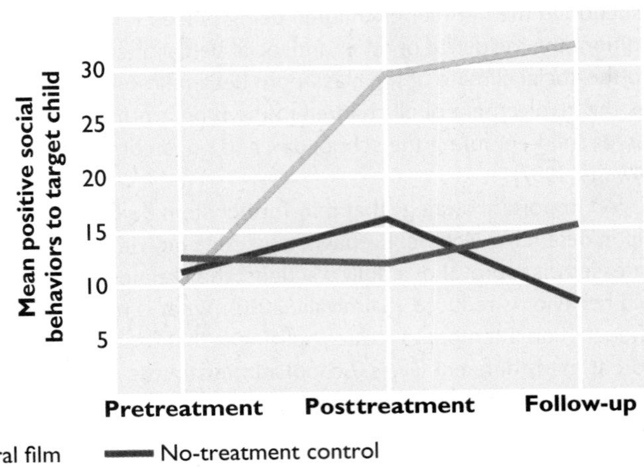

Model with self-verbalization — Control group—neutral film — No-treatment control

behaviors from others. Figure 15.11 shows dramatic results when children who received this treatment were compared with children who received no intervention at all or who saw a film on another subject. From the perspective of social learning theory, by identifying with the model, observing how the model acted, and noting the positive consequences of the model's behavior, children were able to expand their repertoire of social behaviors and increase their likelihood of performing them successfully.

INTERACTION AMONG DOMAINS

Reinforcement A second type of intervention uses social or material reinforcement to shape socially skilled behaviors and increase their frequency, a technique of operant conditioning (see Chapter 6, "Basic Learning and Perception"). Suppose a withdrawn child merely looks at a group of peers playing on the opposite side of the room. The teacher or parent immediately reacts with a "Good!" or a pat on the head. Next, the young child might take a few steps in the direction of the group. Again, the adult promptly delivers a reinforcer. The teacher or parent rewards each successive approximation to the target behavior—in this case, joining the group—until the child has actually entered the group. In general, direct reinforcement of social behaviors is a very effective technique, especially for increasing their frequency (Schneider & Byrne, 1985).

Sometimes the operant approach is combined with other techniques, such as modeling. In one investigation, withdrawn nursery school children received social reinforcement whenever they interacted with their peers. Those who also saw a model demonstrating social interactions showed the greatest gains in the amount of time spent with peers (O'Connor, 1972).

Coaching Perhaps the most popular training technique has been coaching, or direct instruction in displaying an assortment of social behaviors. In this approach, a verbal presentation of the "right" and "wrong" ways to act is frequently accompanied by discussion about why certain techniques, both positive and negative, work or do not work and by opportunities for children to role-play, or act out the desirable behaviors (Bierman & Powers, 2009). The goal is to expand children's knowledge of socially desirable behaviors and develop social problem-solving skills. For example, in one social skills training program, elementary school children learn how to join a conversation:

> Teacher: Chances are that if you don't know how to start talking with another person or join in when others are talking, you won't be a part of many conversations. . . . For example, pretend that some of your classmates are talking about a TV show that you happened to see last night and you want to get in on the conversation. . . . What you might do is walk over to the group and, when there is a slight pause in the talking, say something like, "Are you talking about 'Star Trek'? I saw that and really liked it a lot too." At this point you have joined the conversation.
>
> Next, you want to make sure that you participate in what's going on. You should listen and add comments to what is being said. . . . Can you give me different examples of how you can now add to or take part in a conversation or what else you would say? (Michelson et al., 1983, pp. 116–117)

Karen Bierman (1986) has added still another component to a social skills training program based on coaching: conducting the intervention as a cooperative activity among both popular and unpopular peers. Each target child in her group of preadolescents met with two socially accepted classmates for ten half-hour sessions to produce a film together but also to receive coaching on expressing feelings, asking questions, and displaying leadership. This two-pronged approach led to greater improvements in conversational skills than social skills training alone, possibly because peers could observe firsthand the positive changes occurring in initially unskilled children and could reinforce them immediately. Perhaps this finding should not be surprising; as we saw in Chapter 10, "Achievement," cooperative efforts within the classroom, in general, have been found to be more effective in promoting higher academic achievement and more positive peer relationships than efforts encouraging competitive or individual goals (Roseth, Johnson, & Johnson, 2008).

Over the years, many refinements have been incorporated into programs designed to train social skills in children, and there is good evidence for their effectiveness in promoting social abilities along with positive peer interactions for many children and youth. Gains, however, have been less clearly established for those with serious disorders and who are at higher levels of developmental risk (Bierman & Powers, 2009). However, integrated training efforts incorporating social skill training with a focus on the early development of, for example, emotional and executive functioning, hold promise for additional success for these children as well (Domitrovich, Cortes, & Greenberg, 2007; Greenberg, 2006; Mostow et al., 2002).

For Your Review and Reflection

- What methods do researchers use to assess children's peer status?
- What are some of the characteristics displayed by popular children? What are some of the specific elements of their socioemotional behaviors?
- How do popular and rejected children differ in the ways they process social information?
- What factors increase risk, and what factors increase resilience, for children as they engage in social interactions with each other?
- How extensive is bullying in children and adolescents? Why might bullies engage in such behavior? What are some of the recommendations for dealing with bullies and for helping victims of bullying?
- Were you ever a victim of bullying, or did you engage in bullying activity? Why do you think you were a victim or perpetrator? Did these events have an effect on you, and, if so, how have you addressed them?
- What are some of the influences on the development of children's social competence?
- What are some techniques for promoting children's social skills?

chapter recap

Summary of Developmental Themes

Sociocultural Influence

How does the sociocultural context influence peer relations?

In general, children who spend more time with peers show advances in social development and often tend to prefer cooperation to competition. Culture can also influence children's play styles, the likelihood of observing romantic relationships among teenagers, and the standards that shape peer acceptance. For example, our society highly values athletic capabilities and social skill, and consequently children who are proficient in these domains typically enjoy more peer popularity. In addition, bullying and victimization appear to be far more prevalent in some societies than in others.

Interactions Among Domains

How do peer relations interact with other domains of development?

On one level, many of the physical qualities the child possesses influence the reactions of peers. Physical attractiveness, body build, motor skill, and rate of maturation all engender different responses from other children. On another level, the child's social and emotional skills clearly affect how peers react. Children who can accurately read the emotions of others, gauge the consequences of their own behaviors on others, and employ the strategies that facilitate effective social interactions are more popular with their peers. Similarly, children who are aggressive and display physical power often rise to the top of peer group dominance hierarchies but may become unpopular with peers, as evidenced when those peers are asked to name children they like or prefer to associate with. The formation of early emotional attachments and growth in social knowledge may also play a role in popularity.

Risk | Resilience

What factors promote risk or resilience in peer relations?

Children vary in the extent to which they are accepted by their peers. Some children are popular, whereas others are rejected, neglected, or controversial. Healthy relations with peers are associated with a number of successful developmental outcomes in other arenas. Popular children do well in school, have high levels of self-esteem, and suffer fewer emotional difficulties, such as depression, than unpopular children. Unpopular children are at greater risk for social withdrawal, which can contribute to a variety of internalizing problems such as anxiety and feelings of loneliness in addition to depression. The child's emerging cognitive capabilities, especially perspective-taking skills, allow the child to think about the reactions and expectations of others and to anticipate the consequences of his or her own behaviors. The desire to gain status may be a major impetus to engaging in bullying and the victims of such attacks may be at risk for loss of confidence. However, having a friend to counter a bully's behavior enhances the resilience of those who are bullied. Successful peer interaction is thus both a product of and a contributor to the child's emotional, cognitive, and social achievements.

Chapter Review

Developmental Changes in Peer Relations

What are some of the major changes in peer relations from infancy through adolescence?

Infants show a direct interest in *peers,* other children about the same age, through visual attention, smiles, and touches. By age two, children show coordinated social interactions with agemates in their play behavior. Elementary school children engage in group activities that involve larger numbers of children and often primarily include only members of their own sex. Children increasingly spend more time with peers as they approach the adolescent years and form more intense relationships with certain peers as well as romantic relationships.

What are the different forms of play exhibited by preschoolers and during middle childhood? What factors are related to the emergence of these different types of play?

Preschoolers typically engage in three forms of play: solitary play; parallel play, where one child often matches the activity of a peer; and cooperative play, where children share, engage in turn-taking activities, and mutually influence what they do together. Preschoolers also engage in considerable *social pretend play,* sometimes called sociodramatic or symbolic play, a form of activity that is linked to advances in cognition, language, and social understanding. *Rough-and-tumble play,* physical interactions that are not intended to harm a playmate, also emerges during the preschool years and increases during the early elementary school years, especially among boys. This form of play may function as a way to establish dominance relationships among peers.

What are the characteristics of peer relationships during adolescence?

Adolescents form larger groups called *cliques* and *crowds.* They also form more intense relationships with friends and start to spend more time with peers of the opposite sex.

Children's Friendships

What are the qualities of children's friendships during the preschool years, during middle childhood, and during adolescence?

Preschoolers view friends as peers to play with rather than as individuals valued for their psychological qualities. However, they are already beginning to establish friendships with peers who show similar characteristics such as prosocial behavior or aggression. During middle childhood, children begin to increasingly value friends for their psychological qualities, rather than the fact that friends share activities with them. Friendships may be of short duration, and cross-sex friendships are relatively rare. Adolescents see friends as providing trust and intimacy. Opposite-sex as well as same-sex friendships are increasingly observed. Friends increasingly influence prosocial as well as antisocial behaviors.

What factors influence the formation of children's friendships?

Children become friends with peers who share interests, personality qualities, or other behaviors and characteristics with them. Children form friendships by keeping social interactions positive in tone and de-escalating conflicts, exchanging information, and, at later ages, engaging in self-disclosure.

How do friendships influence a child's development?
Friendships provide a context for developing social skills such as cooperation and conflict resolution and may help the child learn the benefits of intimacy in relationships. Friendships may often protect children from anxiety and stress and are associated with higher levels of self-esteem. However, the benefits of friends may not always be positive. Having friends who are depressed may promote similar feelings; having friends who are antisocial or show other deviant forms of behavior may encourage the display of similar problem behavior.

What are the qualities of romantic relationships in adolescence?
Romantic relationships among teens evolve from more casual mixed-sex groups and provide opportunities for companionship and exploration of sexuality. Their occurrences are influenced by cultural values. Most involved couples have similar interests; however, adolescents' romantic relationships usually do not show the same mutually supportive, caregiving qualities as more mature adult relationships.

Peer Group Dynamics

What factors promote the formation of peer group identities? What factors can lessen hostilities among groups of peers?
Peer groups often form because of shared interests and activities among their members. Children may form especially strong identities with the group to which they belong when groups compete against one another. Peer groups show in-group favoritism when their group is highly defined and when their group has high status. Intergroup hostilities can be reduced by having groups work together on some common goal.

What functions do dominance hierarchies serve in peer groups?
Peer groups quickly form dominance hierarchies, organized structures in which some children become leaders and some become followers. Dominance hierarchies may help facilitate completion of activities by the peer group and seem to serve adaptive social functions, such as controlling aggression.

When does peer pressure reach its peak? What factors are related to vulnerability to peer pressure?
Susceptibility to peer pressure heightens during early adolescence but declines in young adulthood. For some children, extreme orientation to the peer group is associated with deviant behaviors. Children who have parents that are unresponsive and uninvolved may be more vulnerable to peer pressure.

Peer Popularity and Social Competence

How do researchers assess children's peer status?
Peer status is typically measured through assessment devices such as *sociometric nominations,* where children identify peers on the basis of some criteria; *sociometric rating scales,* where children are rated on some criteria, often by peers; and sometimes by the evaluations of others such as teachers who are familiar with the children. Newer approaches might create composite social maps that help to identify more complex relationships among peers.

What are some of the characteristics displayed by popular children?
Popular children tend to engage in prosocial behaviors, but popularity is also influenced by attractiveness, motor skills, and the ability to regulate emotions. Popular children know how to enter peer groups and effectively maintain cohesive social interactions. They engage in fewer antagonistic behaviors than neglected or rejected children. However, during adolescence, popularity is sometimes linked to aggression. Adolescents who are socially skilled and involved in school activities may use aggression as a means of establishing social status and power.

What are factors contributing to social withdrawal?
Some children simply prefer to interact with a limited number of peers; others may do so because of anxiety associated with social interactions or limited skills to do so effectively. Temperament or lack of opportunity to acquire effective techniques for socializing may underlie children's social withdrawal.

What are some of the factors that influence the development of children's social competence?
Social competence has its roots in the child's earliest attachment relationships but is also influenced by parental styles of social interaction. Parents serve as models for and often directly teach, as well as create opportunities for, their children to interact with others. Cognitive skills such as the ability to perceive and interpret social cues accurately, select an appropriate goal, generate and choose an appropriate response, and learn from the outcome of one's actions are important.

What are some of the ways social skills may be facilitated in children? How effective are they?
Modeling, reinforcement, and coaching are some of the techniques used to enhance social skills in children who display problem behaviors such as aggression and social withdrawal. They have been shown to be effective for many children. Newer approaches incorporating an added emphasis on social and executive functioning may be especially important for children who show serious disorders and who are at higher developmental risk.

Key Terms and Concepts

Media Resources

Access an integrated eBook and chapter-specific interactive learning tools, including flashcards, quizzes, videos, and more, in your Developmental Psychology CourseMate, accessed through CengageBrain.com.

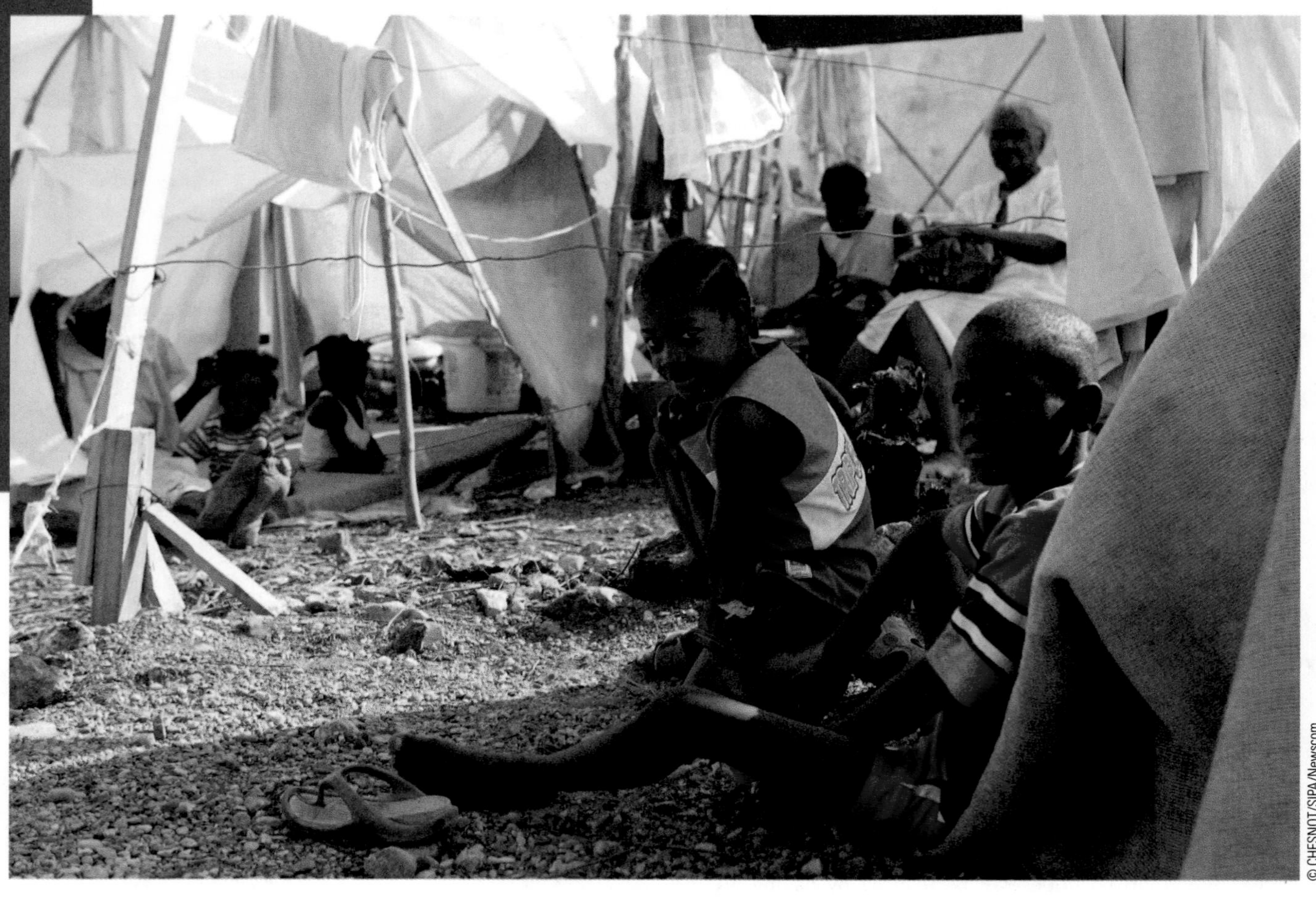
© CHESNOT/SIPA/Newscom

CHAPTER OUTLINE

[chapter 16]

Beyond Family and Peers

KEY THEMES BEYOND FAMILY AND PEERS

SOCIOCULTURAL INFLUENCE How does the sociocultural context influence the child's experiences with media, computers, schools, and the broader world in which children live?

INTERACTION AMONG DOMAINS How do the child's experiences with media, computers, schools, and the broader world in which children live interact with development in various domains?

RISK | RESILIENCE How are risk or resilience influenced by the child's experiences with media, computers, schools, and the broader world in which children live?

Jeremy slammed the door behind him, flicked the lock, and headed to the refrigerator. It was his regular routine after school. Come home, get a snack, and turn on the television to watch cartoons. He wasn't allowed to go out to play—too dangerous, his mother claimed. If he had already seen the cartoons, he might play a video game for a while. But because he couldn't have anyone over until his mother returned from work, that wasn't much fun, either. He dreamed of living in a house with a big yard, maybe even a swimming pool in the back and a park nearby. But that wasn't the neighborhood he was living in. <<

Children grow up in many different contexts. In contrast to Jeremy, some go to soccer practice or music lessons after school or stay at school until a parent picks them up an hour or two later. Some spend their time chatting on the computer with their friends. Some, like Jeremy, watch a lot of television.

Historically, of course, parents, peers, and other familiar adults such as teachers and grandparents have played a major role in socializing children as well as helping them build their cognitive skills. They continue to serve this function for many children in contemporary society. However, the second half of the twentieth century began what some have called a "media revolution" affecting the lives of children (Comstock & Scharrer, 2006; Roberts & Foehr, 2004). Television, DVDs, video games, computers, cell phones, and other electronic devices have become a staple in the everyday experiences of many children and adolescents. For example, Table 16.1 provides an indication of just how much time children are exposed to five different kinds of media. Some wonder if the influence of media has encroached on the ability of parents to control the events to which their offspring are exposed. Does the violence in much of contemporary media, for example, have a detrimental impact on children and adolescents? Is there any consequence of this extensive media exposure for cognitive development? In this chapter, we begin to examine some of these issues.

We also explore potential influences of the broader context in which children live and how it affects their development. Neighborhoods for many today are less likely to include nearby family members or opportunities to establish close-knit relationships with others. What might some of the implications of this change be for children? Furthermore, children are sometimes affected by war or natural disasters. How might these kinds of cataclysmic circumstances affect their social, emotional, and cognitive development? And, of course, socioeconomic conditions can differ tremendously for families. Poverty or homelessness may provide serious challenges to children in their efforts to adapt to the world around them. As Urie Bronfenbrenner emphasized in his bioecological model (Bronfenbrenner & Morris, 2006), these various contexts cannot be ignored in attempting to understand children's development.

TABLE 16.1 Average Amount of Time (in Hours and Minutes) Children Are Exposed to Five Different Kinds of Electronic Media

Even young children in the United States are exposed to various kinds of media for extensive periods of time each day. The amount of exposure increases substantially for older children.

Research Sample	Television	Video and Movies	Audio	Video Games	Computer
Children 0–6 Years of Age	0:59	0:24	0:48	0:06	0:07
Children 8–18 Years of Age	3:04	1:11	1:44	0:49	1:02

Source: Data on sample of children 0–6 years (2005) from Rideout and Hamel (2006, see table 1); on sample 8–18 years (2004) from Roberts, Foehr, and Rideout (2005, see table 1).
Table adapted from Roberts & Foehr, 2008, p. 18.

Television and Related Visual Media

American children watch a great deal of television. In fact, children between birth and six years of age will have spent about as much time watching television programs, videos, or DVDs, and playing video games as playing outside, and only about one-third as much time reading or being read to (see Figure 16.1). On average children less than a year of age are exposed to television and videos or DVDs nearly about an hour a day (Anand & Krosnick, 2005; Hollenbeck & Slaby, 1979). The amount of time children are exposed to visual media increases substantially during the preschool years (to between two and a half and three hours a day), shows a small decline once children enter elementary school, and then increases again to about four hours a day by twelve years of age. Television viewing once again declines a bit during adolescence when involvement in athletic programs, listening to music, dating, and other activities increase (Comstock & Scharrer, 2006; Huston et al., 1990; Roberts, Foehr, & Rideout 2005). Children, at least in the United States, spend more time watching television

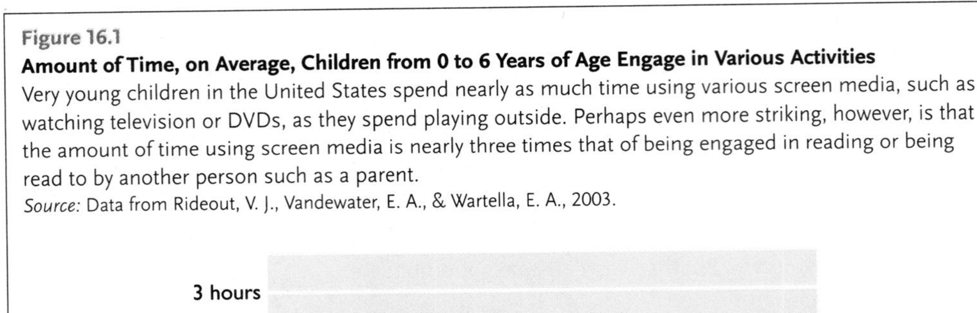

Figure 16.1
Amount of Time, on Average, Children from 0 to 6 Years of Age Engage in Various Activities
Very young children in the United States spend nearly as much time using various screen media, such as watching television or DVDs, as they spend playing outside. Perhaps even more striking, however, is that the amount of time using screen media is nearly three times that of being engaged in reading or being read to by another person such as a parent.
Source: Data from Rideout, V. J., Vandewater, E. A., & Wartella, E. A., 2003.

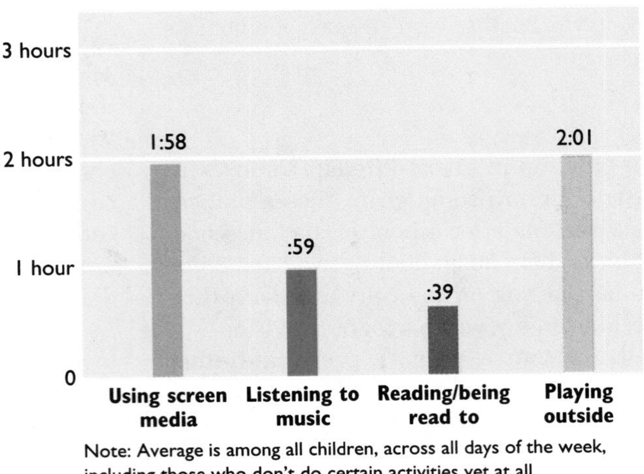

© Wu Wei/Xinhua/Photoshot/Newscom

Young children in most families spend many hours watching television. As a consequence, television can have a powerful influence on their development. According to some estimates, as much as one-third of a child's waking life will have been spent watching television, and a good portion of the programming young children see will be cartoons.

than at any other activity except sleep (Roberts et al., 1999). By high school graduation, three years will, on average, have been given to watching television (Strasburger, 1993).

Television viewing among children shows large individual differences. Some three- to five-year-olds watch very little television; others watch as much as seventy-five hours per week. In households where books are less available and the TV is more likely to be on constantly, the amount of viewing by children is typically greater (Comstock & Scharrer, 2006; Roberts & Foehr, 2004). Individual patterns of TV viewing remain stable over the years. Thus, the television-viewing habits children acquire in early childhood can be relatively long lasting (Huston & Wright, 1998).

As they grow older, children typically show changes in the types of programs they prefer to watch. Preschoolers are more likely to view educational programs designed for children, such as *Sesame Street*, as well as cartoons. Interest in child-centered educational programs is relatively greater among younger preschoolers than older children (Wright et al., 2001). By ages five to seven, children begin to watch comedies and entertainment shows aimed at general audiences, shows that make increasing demands on their ability to comprehend plots and themes (Huston et al., 1990). Boys tend to watch more television than girls (Huston & Wright, 1998) and African American children more than European American children (Comstock, 1991). Children from lower socioeconomic levels are more frequent viewers than children from higher-income backgrounds (Greenberg, 1986).

Children's Comprehension of Television Programs

Contrary to popular belief, television viewing is usually not a passive process in which a mesmerized child sits gazing at the screen. The fact that preferences for shows change with age is just one example of the ways children actively control their TV viewing. Daniel Anderson and his colleagues have conducted numerous studies demonstrating that children's selection of television programs is influenced by their ability to comprehend content (Anderson & Burns, 1991). Certain formal, or structural, features of television serve to draw the viewer in, particularly such sound effects as laughter, music, and children's and women's voices. Other features, such as visual cuts, motion, and special sound effects, hold the child's attention (Schmitt, Anderson, & Collins, 1999).

The formal features of television and visual media programs may have some influence on very young children's attention to the television, but when do children comprehend the messages being conveyed by such material? The answer, of course, depends in part on the kind and complexity of the material being shown. For example, when preschoolers

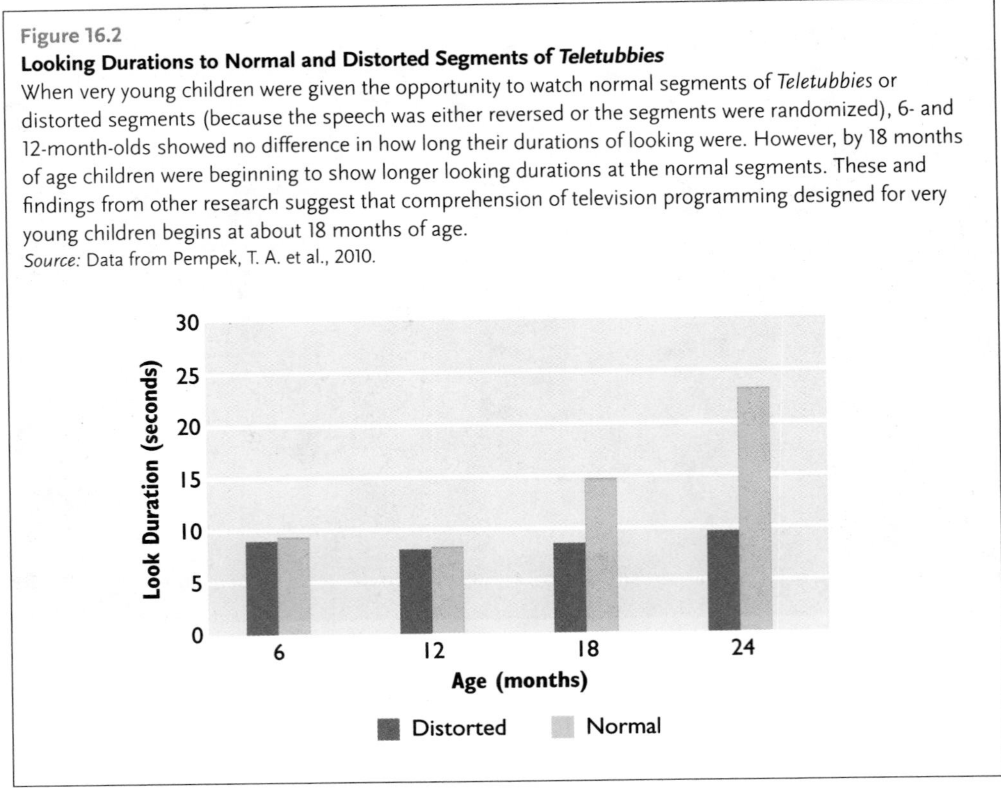

Figure 16.2
Looking Durations to Normal and Distorted Segments of *Teletubbies*
When very young children were given the opportunity to watch normal segments of *Teletubbies* or distorted segments (because the speech was either reversed or the segments were randomized), 6- and 12-month-olds showed no difference in how long their durations of looking were. However, by 18 months of age children were beginning to show longer looking durations at the normal segments. These and findings from other research suggest that comprehension of television programming designed for very young children begins at about 18 months of age.
Source: Data from Pempek, T. A. et al., 2010.

watch segments of *Sesame Street* in which the comprehensibility of the program has been altered, that is, presented in a foreign language or played backward, attention declines even though the formal features remain constant (Anderson et al., 1981). In other words, children actively direct their attention to those portions of the show that they most readily understand; they are not influenced by sound effects or visual cuts alone.

Is viewing by even younger children influenced by the content of the program? The answer, in fact, appears to depend on the age of the child. In a recent study, looking behavior of children six, twelve, eighteen, and twenty-four months of age was recorded while they were watching *Teletubbies,* a program designed to be of special interest to infants and toddlers (Pempek et al., 2010). Children watched both a normal clip from the program and a segment containing the same material but in which the dialogue was either reversed to create backward speech or the scenes were randomly ordered. As can be seen in Figure 16.2, not until eighteen months of age did children show an increase in the duration of their looks at the normal segment compared with the distorted segment. Processing of comprehensible sequences of a televised program may be beyond the ability of children less than about eighteen months of age because of limits associated with development in a number of cortical areas known to be activated in adults when processing comprehensible sequences rather than random sequences of televised content (Anderson et al., 2006).

INTERACTION AMONG DOMAINS

Many television shows have complex plots and use subtle cues that require inferences about characters' motives, intentions, and feelings. In addition, most programs contain changes of scene that require viewers to integrate information across several scenes. Research indicates that clear developmental differences exist in children's ability to understand information from television shows, differences that accompany changes in cognitive processing. Preschoolers can understand short story segments and remember the most central elements of each story (Lorch, Bellack, & Augsbach, 1987). When the plots and themes of television shows thicken, however, young children have difficulties. More specifically, when they watch programs designed for general audiences, younger children are less likely than older children to remember the explicit content, that is, the discrete scenes that are essential to understanding the plot. Even when they do remember explicit information, younger children frequently fail to grasp the implicit content communicated by relationships among scenes (Collins et al., 1978). For example, young children may fail to understand a character's motive for aggression if the message is communicated in two scenes separated by several other sequences (Collins, 1983).

In addition, children's general knowledge and previous experiences can affect their comprehension of the programs they watch. Suppose, for example, that children are asked to retell the content of a show about a murder and the suspect's eventual capture. Children frequently mention script-based knowledge (see Chapter 9, "Social Cognition"), drawing from their general storehouse of information on the events that surround the relationships between police and criminals. Older children are more likely than younger children, however, to describe content specific to the program they watched, such as the fact that some police officers in the show did not wear uniforms (Collins, 1983). As children's general knowledge about the world grows, their comprehension of more detailed information in television programs expands as well. For example, the ability to comprehend dramatic narratives continues to improve until at least thirteen years of age (Collins & Wellman, 1982).

Other research has shown that children's growing verbal competency underlies their ability to understand TV programs. When five-year-olds were given standardized IQ tests and tested on their memory of the central and incidental events in a thirty-five-minute television program, their scores on the verbal subscales of the tests correlated significantly with their ability to comprehend the show's central events (Jacobvitz, Wood, & Albin, 1991).

One other important developmental change is in children's ability to recognize that most television programming is fictional. Preschoolers often have difficulty distinguishing the boundaries between events that occur on television and those that take place in the real world (Flavell et al., 1990; Jaglom & Gardner, 1981). For example, preschoolers may think that Sesame Street is a place where others live, that individuals portrayed on television can see and hear their viewers, and that the things seen on TV exist inside it (Nikken & Peeters, 1988).

Many five- and six-year-olds do not fully understand that television characters are actually actors playing roles; not until age eight and older do the majority of children grasp this concept. However, even kindergartners realize that cartoons are fantasy. They are also quite accurate about deciding whether their favorite programs occur as part of real life or just on television. In fact, by this time they tend to be biased in assuming that most television programming does not occur in real life (Wright et al., 1994). Thus, the developmental course seems to progress from failing to make a distinction between events on television and events in the real world to a belief that few events depicted on television occur in the real world to, finally, a more complete understanding of which events occurring on television are fictional and which are not (Wright et al., 1994).

Television's Influence on Cognitive and Language Development

INTERACTION AMONG DOMAINS

Today many children in the United States and most Western countries have ready access to programs specifically designed to teach cognitive skills. What, if anything, are they learning from such programs? This question has become especially controversial with respect to infants and toddlers (Anderson & Pempek, 2005; Courage & Howe, 2010; Courage & Setliff, 2009). For example, the American Academy of Pediatrics (1999) continues to recommend that children less than twenty-four months of age not view televised material. Yet numerous videos, some making substantial claims for enhancing cognitive development, and several television series designed to attract the attention of infants and toddlers, have been produced over the past two decades. Is there any evidence to indicate that there are benefits from watching these programs at this early age?

Influences on Infants and Toddlers At the present time, little data exists to demonstrate that the cognitive and language development of infants and toddlers is fostered by televised programming despite the belief by many parents that it does have significant consequences for their children (Calvert et al., 2005; Courage & Howe, 2010). In Chapter 9, "Social Cognition," the difficulty very young children have with processing pictures was noted. Thus it should not be surprising to find that learning from television is not simple either. Watching material on television is not the same as observing events in the real world (Anderson & Hanson, 2010). For example, visual scenes presented on television are more impoverished because the picture lacks depth and the scenes are spatially constrained by limits imposed by the available image. Segments include transitions such as cuts and changes in perspective that require integration not typically experienced in the real world. In addition, the viewer cannot engage in or alter the events taking place on the screen. These and other conventions associated with televised material are readily interpreted by the experienced viewer, but they may provide substantial challenges for the infant and toddler. For example, one-year-olds are much less likely to look at an object that is labeled in the audio track while watching *Sesame Street* than is a more mature viewer (Kirkorian, Anderson, & Keen, 2008), and, as we have already learned, viewing at this early age seems unaffected by disruptions in the comprehensibility of the material being presented.

Other research has demonstrated that children less than about thirty to thirty-six months of age seem to display a *video deficit,* that is, learn less from even simple videotaped presentations than when information is provided by a live person (Anderson & Hanson, 2010; Anderson & Pempek, 2005; Barr, 2010). For example, when asked to imitate a simple sequence of removing a mitten, shaking it to hear the sound of a bell inside the mitten, and then removing the bell, one- and two-year-olds are much less likely to be successful if they observe these events on video than if watching a live person perform them (Barr & Hayne, 1999). Furthermore, not until they are older than two years of age do children seem to realize that seeing a toy being hidden in a room on television can help them solve the problem of finding that toy in that room (Schmitt & Anderson, 2002; Troseth & DeLoache, 1998). On the other hand, if while behind a window, they observe a live person hiding the toy, children are more likely to be able to retrieve the toy when given the opportunity to do so. The greater perceptual and cognitive demands required in processing video material may be contributing to these findings (Barr, 2010; Troseth, 2010). Very young children also may not yet be fully aware that television can provide useful information to them since it is different from the real world and the events occurring on it are typically not affected by the child's behavior (Cleveland & Striano, 2008; Troseth, 2010).

Studies examining the effects of television on language acquisition and verbal expression and comprehension in infants and toddlers have yielded mixed findings. For example, very young children are about as likely to learn labels for objects when taught by a live model as when observing a similar model on a television screen. However, when a voice simply labels a novel object as it appears on the screen, they do not do as well (Krcmar, Grela, & Lin, 2007). If infants beginning at twelve to fifteen months of age are given multiple opportunities over a six-week period to watch a DVD (*Baby Wordsmith*) specifically designed to encourage learning by pairing pictures of common objects with their appropriate labels, they show no greater expressive or receptive language development than a control group not shown the video (Robb, Richert, & Wartella, 2009).

A longitudinal project carried out by Deborah Linebarger and Dale Walker (2005), however, found a positive relationship between vocabulary size and complexity of speech when infants and toddlers watched some kinds of child-oriented programs more frequently. Beginning at six months of age and for every three months until they reached age three, parents recorded the length of time their children watched certain televised programs. Those who spent more time watching *Dora the Explorer* and *Blues Clues*—shows where characters often label objects, direct much of their speech to the child, and ask the viewer to respond to their verbal queries—acquired larger vocabularies and expressed more complex speech by three years of age. The same was found for children who watched *Arthur, Clifford,* and *Dragon Tales* more—shows that have a storybook-like quality to them. However, children who watched *Teletubbies* and *Barney and Friends* more did not exhibit as much progress in language development as those who watched less of these programs. This study was correlational in nature, so it is not possible to conclude that the observed language differences were caused by the differential exposure to these programs; other factors may have contributed to why children preferred watching some programs more than others as well as differences in language development. Nevertheless, the findings suggest interesting possibilities about the kinds of viewing content that might be more likely to help very young children begin to learn from television.

Influences on Cognitive Development for Preschoolers and Older Children Although the benefits of television viewing for infants and toddlers remain unclear, preschoolers clearly can learn a lot from visual media, according to research on educational television. Evaluations

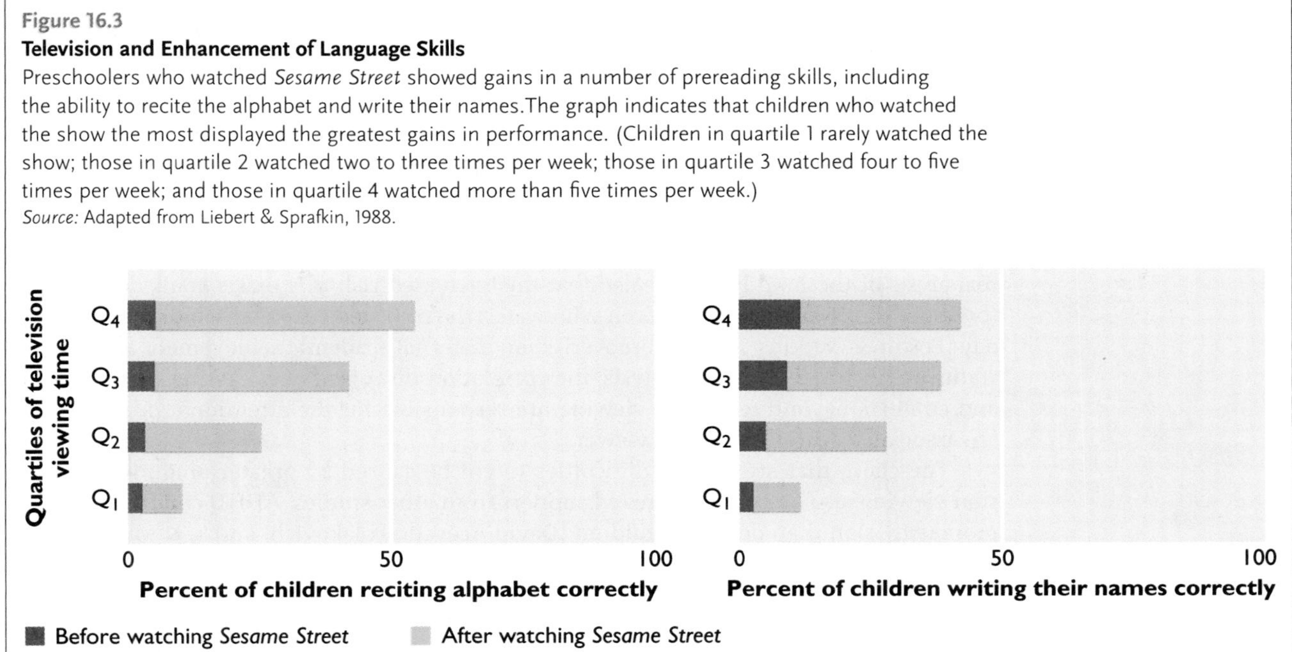

Figure 16.3
Television and Enhancement of Language Skills
Preschoolers who watched *Sesame Street* showed gains in a number of prereading skills, including the ability to recite the alphabet and write their names.The graph indicates that children who watched the show the most displayed the greatest gains in performance. (Children in quartile 1 rarely watched the show; those in quartile 2 watched two to three times per week; those in quartile 3 watched four to five times per week; and those in quartile 4 watched more than five times per week.)
Source: Adapted from Liebert & Sprafkin, 1988.

of the effects of such programs as *Sesame Street* demonstrate that television can teach children a range of problem-solving, mathematical, reading, and language skills (Huston & Wright, 1998).

Sesame Street was specifically designed to provide entertaining ways to teach children, especially those who might be underprepared for school, the letters of the alphabet, counting, vocabulary, and similar school-readiness skills. The programs also deliberately include both male and female characters from many racial and ethnic backgrounds. Preschoolers, many from disadvantaged backgrounds, who watched *Sesame Street* most frequently were found to show the greatest gains on several skills, including writing their names and knowing letters, numbers, and forms (see Figure 16.3). Frequent viewers also obtained higher scores on a standardized vocabulary test, adapted better to school, and had more positive attitudes toward school and people of other races than nonwatchers (Bogatz & Ball, 1972; Rice et al., 1990). Thus the program had effects not only on children's cognitive skills but also on their prosocial attitudes.

Not only does educational programming have immediate effects on children's cognitive abilities, but these effects can be long lasting. For example, children in low-income families who spent relatively greater amounts of time watching *Sesame Street* and other television shows geared to educational goals at two and three years of age did well on measures of reading, math, language abilities, and other indicators of school readiness three years later (Wright et al., 2001). This effect may, in part, stem from their increased interest in continuing to watch informative television as they became older.

A longitudinal study carried out on high schoolers in working- and middle-class families for whom television viewing habits had been recorded as preschoolers suggests a positive impact of having watched informative educational programming more than a decade earlier. Compared with those who watched more violent or entertainment-oriented shows as preschoolers, those who watched more educational programming had higher grades in English, math, and science; read more books; and were more achievement oriented as teenagers (D. R. Anderson et al., 2001). This relationship was somewhat greater for males than females, although a similar pattern was found for both sexes. Because the data on long-term effects of television viewing are correlational in nature, it is not possible to completely rule out other factors that could account for the positive relationships that were observed in the longitudinal study. For example, either individual differences or parental encouragement of educational and achievement goals throughout childhood may help to explain some of these findings. Nevertheless, the results considerably blunted many of the strong objections that have been raised about television's negative influence on development, especially if children are observing programming designed to be educationally informative.

RISK | RESILIENCE

One substantive concern about infants, toddlers, and preschoolers who watch large amounts of television involves the potential for developing attentional problems (Courage & Setliff, 2009; Schmidt & Vandewater, 2008). For example, one study raising considerable public interest reported a significant correlation between the amount of television children had watched as one- and three-year-olds and attentional difficulties, similar to those exhibited by children with ADHD, at seven years of age (Christakis et al., 2004). However, a recent reanalysis of these findings revealed that this increased risk, if it exists at all, does so only for about the 10 percent of children who watch the most television, seven or more hours a day (Foster & Watkins, 2010). Moreover, when maternal academic achievement and poverty status are factored into the analysis, the correlation disappears, suggesting that processes and contexts beyond television viewing are responsible for the attentional problems that are associated with these heavy viewers.

The claim that attentional difficulties might be caused by greater amounts of television viewing also has received mixed support from other studies. ADHD children do watch more television than do other children (David Acevedo-Polakovich, Lorch, & Milich, 2007). However, when factors such as the mother's education and whether a television is present in the child's bedroom are taken into account, this linkage disappears. For example, ADHD children are twice as likely to have a television in their bedroom than are other children. On the other hand, other studies have reported some increase in attentional problems among adolescents who watched greater amounts of television at earlier ages even when attentional difficulties at earlier ages were taken into account (Johnson et al., 2007; Landhuis et al., 2007). Clearly more research is needed to untangle the extent to which television viewing or other factors may account for attentional differences.

Researchers have also found that the amount of time children watch television sometimes shows a modest negative link with school achievement (Schmidt & Vandewater, 2008). However, the general consensus is that such a conclusion also masks the complexity of factors contributing to this finding. Those who watch television a great deal of time generally do poorly on academic achievement tests. But moderate amounts of television viewing, for example, between about one and ten hours a week, seem to be beneficial to academic achievement. Thus there may be a curvilinear relationship between television viewing and academic achievement; some television viewing, especially if it consists primarily of educational programming, may be beneficial. In contrast, a great deal of TV viewing, especially when it involves a lot of programming that contains violence, may be harmful. In addition, the amount of viewing time that is optimal may decrease with age, for example, from about two hours a day for nine-year-olds to less than an hour a day for seventeen-year-olds (Razel, 2001). Greater amounts of television viewing also appear to have negative consequences for children whose families are better off, but little or even small positive benefits for children who are disadvantaged (Schmidt & Vandewater, 2008).

INTERACTION AMONG DOMAINS

Influences on Language Development for Preschoolers and Older Children Mabel Rice and her colleagues (1990) suggest that television promotes preschoolers' language development. Many programs targeted for children include simplified speech, repetitions, recasts, and elaboration on the meanings of words. As we saw in Chapter 7, "Language," these devices can enhance the child's acquisition of vocabulary and syntax (Rice, 1983). Parents also sometimes use television as a "video picture book" in which events portrayed on the show stimulate verbal exchanges and language learning. For example, when mothers watch television with their preschoolers, they frequently identify objects, repeat new words, ask questions, or relate the content of the show to the child's own experiences (Lemish & Rice, 1986).

Is there direct evidence that television can function as a vehicle for vocabulary acquisition? Investigators exposed three- and five-year-olds to twenty new words in a fifteen-minute animated television story and found that both age groups showed gains in comprehension after only two viewings. Three-year-olds learned an average of one to two new words, and five-year-olds learned four to five words (Rice & Woodsmall, 1988). These findings are all the more impressive considering the brevity of the children's exposure to new vocabulary items and the limited efforts of the experimenters to highlight or exaggerate the new words.

Television's Influence on Social Development

INTERACTION AMONG DOMAINS

Whipping a towel over his shoulders, a seven-year-old jumps off the couch after watching the movie *Superman* on television. A brother and sister brandish toy swords, the brother mimicking the action of a favorite cartoon character. These common scenes in American households illustrate the power of television to influence children's behavior by providing models for direct imitation. Sometimes the messages are more subtle: a male announcer's authoritative voice decrees that this toy is the one all your friends want or that a sugary cereal is fortified with vitamins. When mostly men's voices appear in television commercials, the indirect message is that males more than females have the knowledge and authority to make such definitive statements. Whether by directly providing models for children to imitate or by indirectly offering messages about social categories, television has the possibility of promoting behaviors as diverse as aggression and sex typing. Psychologists and social policymakers have been particularly concerned about how television affects the child's social behavior and understanding, for better or worse.

Aggression Any child who turns on the television in the United States and many other countries around the world has an extraordinarily good chance of encountering a portrayal of violence. Approximately 60 percent of the programming shown between 6 a.m. and 11 p.m. in the United States contains violent scenes (and sometimes many of them). Moreover, that rate is even higher in children's programming, especially cartoons (Center for Communication and Social Policy, 1998). As a consequence, children will see an average of 10,000 acts of violence every year (Federman, 1998). Does this heavy dose of televised violence viewing produce aggression in children? Hundreds of research studies have examined this issue, and the consensus is clearly yes (Murray, 2008; Wilson, 2008). Meta-analyses of the large number of studies investigating this question find that a small but consistent causal relationship exists between viewing aggression on TV and aggressive behavior in children (Comstock & Scharrer, 2006; Anderson et al., 2003). The first column of Figure 16.4 provides an indication of the modest effect sizes associated with TV violence and aggressive behavior.

RISK | RESILIENCE

In keeping with the principles of social learning theory, a regular diet of viewing aggressive models may suggest to the child that physical attacks are acceptable in a person's repertoire of behaviors. Two processes could be operating. First, children can learn new acts of aggression from the models they observe. Second, aggressive behaviors already in the

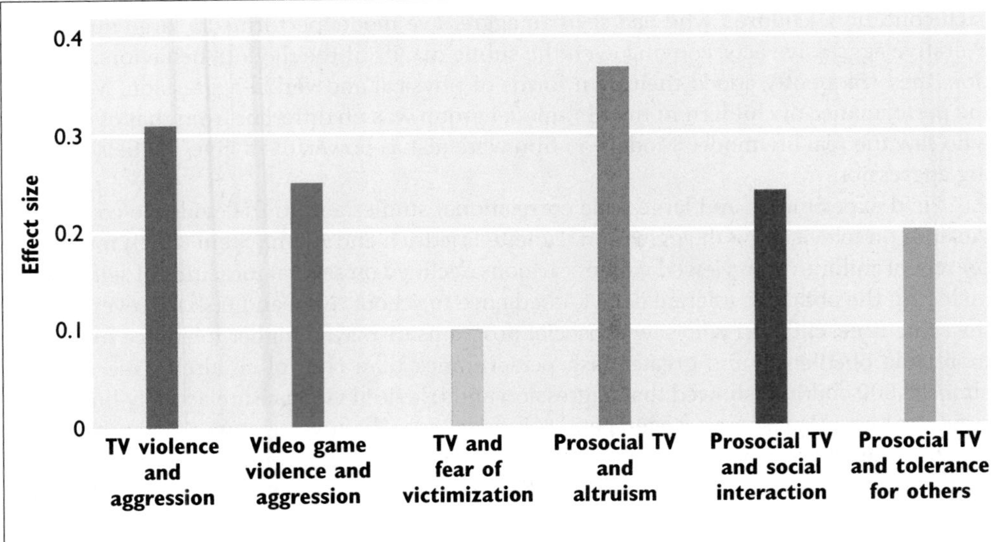

Figure 16.4
Social Outcome Effect Sizes for the Content of Various Types of Media Based on Meta-analytic Studies
Numerous meta-analytic studies have been carried out examining the impact of different types of media content on social behavior. These effect sizes are modest but illustrate that video content may have an impact on children's behavior and attitudes.
Source: Data from Wilson, B. J., 2008.

These photos, taken from Bandura's classic experiments, illustrate with stark clarity the power of imitation in influencing children's aggression. In the top row, an adult model displays various aggressive actions against a "Bobo doll." The middle and bottom rows depict the sequence of imitative aggression shown by a male and female participant in the experiment.Their behaviors closely mimic the specific actions they had previously seen the adult perform.

child's repertoire may be disinhibited (Bandura, 1969). In a classic set of laboratory studies, Albert Bandura and his colleagues (Bandura, Ross, & Ross, 1963a, 1963b) explored the effects of viewing aggression. Nursery school children in one experiment were randomly assigned to one of five experimental conditions. The first group watched from behind a one-way mirror as a model in the next room performed a series of unusual acts of physical and verbal aggression on a plastic, inflated Bobo doll. For example, the model hit the doll with a hammer, kicked it, and said, "Hit the Bobo doll!" and "Kick the Bobo doll!" A second group of children watched a model perform the same actions, but the presentation was on film. A third group watched an adult disguised as a cartoon figure behave like the models in the previous two conditions. A fourth group observed an adult model behaving in a non-aggressive manner, sitting quietly and ignoring the Bobo doll and the toys associated with aggressive behavior. The last group of children saw no model at all.

Figure 16.5 shows the mean number of aggressive responses displayed by children in each condition. Children who had seen an aggressive model performed a large number of imitative aggressive acts, copying even the subtle details of the model's behaviors. In addition, they frequently added their own forms of physical and verbal aggression. Moreover, the performance of children in the film-model group was no different from that of children who saw the real-life model. Models on film were just as powerful as "live" models in eliciting aggression.

Field experiments and large-scale correlational studies add to the evidence connecting violence on television with aggression. Lynette Friedrich and Aletha Stein (1973) found that preschool children who viewed violent cartoons declined on several measures of self-control, including the ability to tolerate delays, obedience to school rules, and task perseverance. At the same time, children who saw prosocial programs displayed higher tolerance for delays, more rule obedience, and greater task perseverance than control children. One study of almost 1,000 children showed that aggression and televised violence are actually linked in a reciprocal way (Huesmann, Lagerspetz, & Eron, 1984). The investigators asked each child's peers to rate how aggressive the child was, and they also noted how much television violence each child watched. The number of violent TV shows children saw at the start of the study predicted how aggressive they were three years later. In turn, aggression also influenced TV

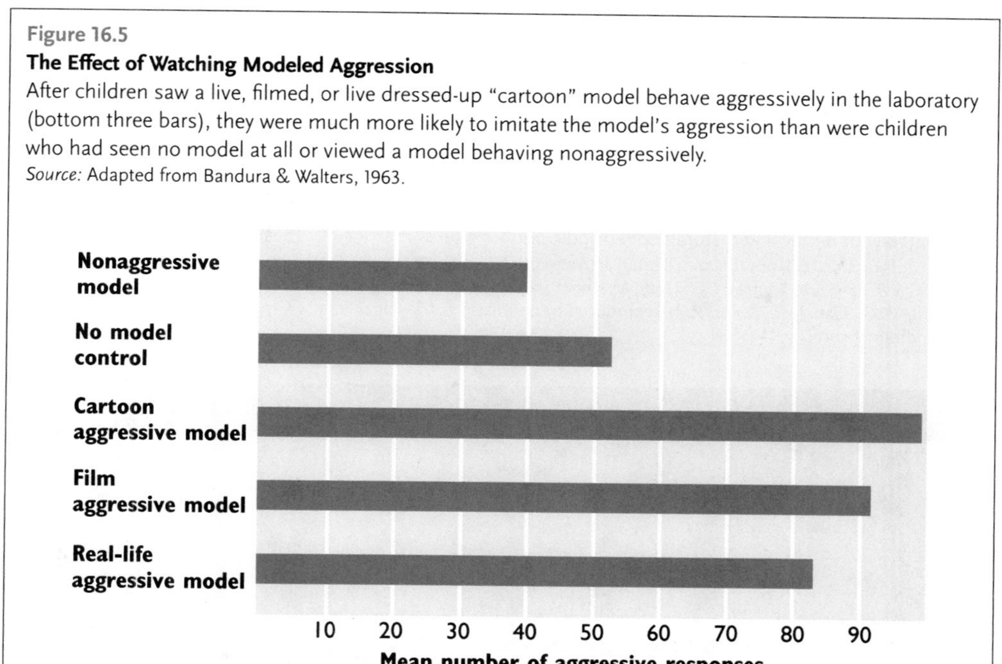

Figure 16.5

The Effect of Watching Modeled Aggression

After children saw a live, filmed, or live dressed-up "cartoon" model behave aggressively in the laboratory (bottom three bars), they were much more likely to imitate the model's aggression than were children who had seen no model at all or viewed a model behaving nonaggressively.

Source: Adapted from Bandura & Walters, 1963.

viewing. Children who were aggressive at the start of the study watched more violent shows three years later than they did initially. The findings are consistent with a bidirectional model of influence: children become more aggressive after a diet of violent television, and their aggression seems to stimulate even more viewing of violent shows. The tendency to view high amounts of violence as preschoolers correlates not only with more aggression in adolescence but also with poorer academic success (D. R. Anderson et al., 2001). In fact, the impact of viewing televised violence may be greatest for younger children (Wilson, 2008).

INTERACTION AMONG DOMAINS

Recent studies have begun to explore what may be happening in the brain when children watch violent versus nonviolent television programs. For example, John Murray and his colleagues (Murray et al., 2006) used fMRI to investigate whether certain regions of the brain were more responsive to violent video content than to nonviolent content. Eight children between nine and thirteen years of age were shown two three-minute videos depicting violence (two boxing scenes from *Rocky IV*) and two three-minute videos showing nonviolent activity (one scene from *Ghostwriter*, a PBS children's program, and the other a National Geographic animal program designed for children). The researchers found greater activation in a number of areas of the brain, especially in the right hemisphere, for the violent sequences. These regions included the right posterior cingulate, motor cortex, and amygdala, as well as specific areas of the hippocampus, parietal, and prefrontal cortex (see Figure 16.6). Several of these areas appear to be linked to increased arousal and attention, detection of threat, and encoding and retrieval of episodic memories and long-term memory. These findings suggest that considerable emotional processing may be taking place when children watch violent videos, as might be expected, but also that the content is likely to be remembered.

Can parents do anything to mitigate the potentially harmful consequences of television shows on their children's behavior? One obvious tactic is to limit the amount of time children are permitted to watch violent programs. Another is to suggest prosocial methods of conflict resolution when violence is displayed. In a school-based intervention program, 170 children who frequently watched violent programs were divided into an experimental and a control group. During a period of six to eight weeks, children in the experimental group participated in regular training sessions in which they were taught, after watching high-action, "superhero" shows, that (1) the behaviors of aggressive TV characters are not representative of the way most people act, (2) aggressive scenes on TV are not real but are staged by means of special effects and camera techniques, and (3) the average person uses more positive strategies to resolve interpersonal problems than those shown on violent TV programs. During the same

Figure 16.6

Activation Patterns in Children Viewing a Violent Video

Eight children 9 to 13 years of age who viewed a violent video compared to a nonviolent video showed more activation in several regions of the brain including the posterior cingulate and amygdala, especially in the right hemisphere, as well as the precuneous and hippocampus. The pattern of activation within these and other regions of the brain suggests that the observation of violent scenes is emotionally arousing, involves activation of systems for detecting fear or threat, and activates regions of the brain associated with retrieval and storage of episodic and long-term memory for these events.

Source: Copyright 2006 From Children's brain activations while viewing televised violence revealed by fMRI. *Media Psychology, 8,* 25–37, by Murray, J. P., Liotti, M., Ingmundson, P. T., Mayberg, H. S., Pu, Y., Zamarripa, F., Liu, Y., Woldorff, M. G., Gao, J.-H., & Fox, P. T. Reproduced by permission of Taylor & Francis Group, LLC., http://www.taylorandfrancis.com.

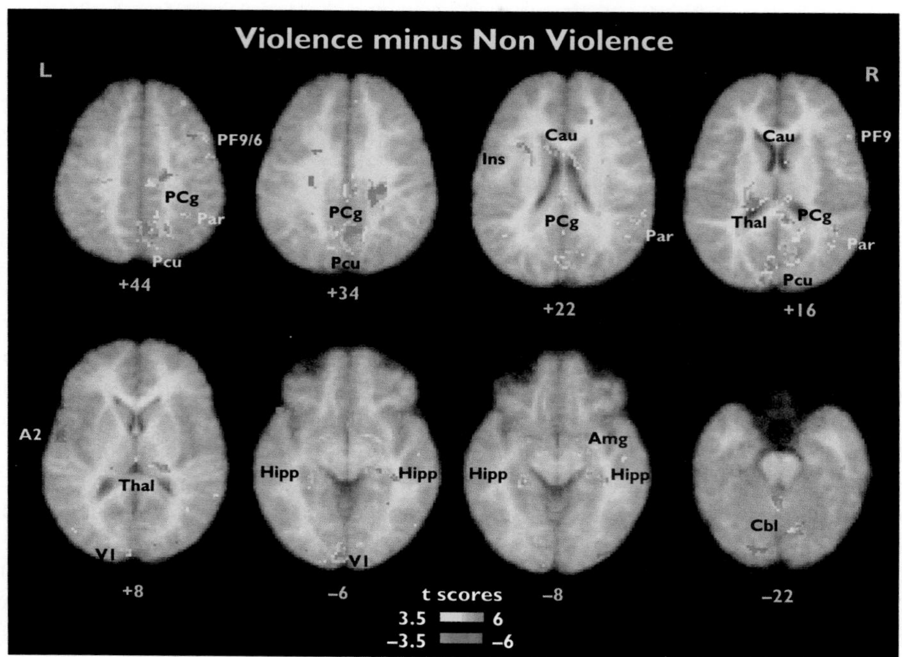

Note: Brain regions identified in the figure are : PF9/6 and PF9 (prefrontal cortex-Brodmann's area); PCg (posterior cingulate gyrus); Par (parietal lobe); Pcu (precuneous); Ins (insula); Cau (caudate nucleus); Thal (thalamus); A2 (secondary auditory area); V1 (visual area); Hipp (hippocampus); Amg (Amygdala); Cbl (cerebellum). Numbered images depicted are from the upper (superior) to lower (inferior) regions of the brain. L = left hemisphere; R = right hemisphere.

time period, control participants saw nonviolent shows and engaged in neutral discussions. By the end of the study, children in the experimental group were significantly less aggressive than the control children, demonstrating that the real-life behaviors of children can be modified by effecting changes in their attitudes about television (Huesmann et al., 1983).

Prosocial Behavior Just as television can encourage negative social behaviors, it can foster prosocial development. Friedrich and Stein (1973) found that children who watched *Mister Rogers' Neighborhood* for a four-week period showed increases in prosocial interpersonal behaviors. Many other researchers have also found that programs that contain messages about cooperation, altruism, and sharing promote these behaviors in children. Meta-analyses of studies of prosocial television indicate that such programs can have powerful effects. In fact, as can be seen in Figure 16.4, the effects of prosocial programming can be even greater than the effects of antisocial programming on some aspects of children's behavior (Hearold, 1986; Mares & Woodard, 2005).

Gender Stereotypes Television does occasionally portray males and females in nontraditional roles: fathers cook and care for their children, and women are employed outside the home. These programs, however, are not standard fare on commercial television. Working women, when they are shown, are likely to be employed in gender-typical roles (e.g., as secretaries and nurses); if they occupy positions of authority, they are often cast as villains

(Huston & Wright, 1998). Consistent with stereotypes of female behavior, girls and women on television act nurturantly, passively, or emotionally. In contrast, males are more frequently the central characters of television shows, and they act forcefully, have more power and authority than women, and display reason rather than emotion. Portrayal of these gender stereotypes may be declining, but they continue to exist in much of television programming (Signorelli & Bacue, 1999). Moreover, the greatest stereotyping tends to be found in programs aimed at children (Signorielli, 2001).

Children's attention to these stereotypes very likely depends on other developmental changes children undergo. For example, five-year-old boys who demonstrate gender constancy (see Chapter 13, "Gender") are more likely to watch male characters on television and prefer programs that contain a greater proportion of males than five-year-old boys who do not display gender constancy (Luecke-Aleksa et al., 1995). In addition, gender-constant boys are more likely to watch shows created for adult entertainment, particularly sports and action shows, than do their counterparts who still do not exhibit gender constancy. This difference in viewing preferences does not seem to be linked to earlier maturity in other cognitive abilities.

INTERACTION AMONG DOMAINS

In contrast, gender constancy in five-year-old girls has relatively little effect on their television preferences or viewing habits. Perhaps this sex difference reflects the greater attractiveness of male roles on much of television and, therefore, accounts for such programs' increased interest value for boys who have gained gender constancy. Alternatively, perhaps this sex difference reflects a lessened need on the part of girls to exploit television as a basis for gender-role differentiation.

Ethnic Considerations The characters on American television are predominantly white. African Americans are occasionally shown, but Hispanic, Asian, and Native American individuals are much less likely to be seen (Greenberg & Brand, 1994). This portrait applies to commercial entertainment programs for children as well, although in both commercial and public educational programming for children about one-fourth to more than one-third of the characters are minorities, and minorities are becoming represented in increasing numbers on American television (Calvert, 1999). Relatively little research has been carried out to determine how important the representation of ethnic minorities may be to young children. However, African American young people tend to prefer to watch and identify with African American characters (Greenberg & Brand, 1994). The extent to which they do so has been found to be positively related to self-esteem (McDermott & Greenberg, 1984) and, in some cases, although not consistently, to positive attitudes about their own race (Graves, 1993).

Exposure to Sexual Content What other things might young people be learning from television and other media? In one study, twelve- to fourteen-year-old children were interviewed about the television shows, music, movies, and magazines they used. The researchers were able to compute an index of these teens' "sexual media diet" by noting the extent of sexual content in the shows, music, movies, and magazines. When the participants were interviewed again two years later, those who had experienced heavy exposure to sexual content in the media were more than twice as likely to report engaging in sexual intercourse (Brown et al., 2006). Among African American teenagers, heavy exposure to music videos and sports programming on television was found to be linked to lower self-esteem. However, adolescents who expressed strong identification with popular black (and not white) television characters had high self-esteem (Ward, 2004). Thus, the way in which media influences children—either positively or negatively—depends not only on the content of what they watch but also on the characteristics of the viewer.

The potential consequences of extensive exposure to sexual content through media, however, are important to consider. For example, a large sample of twelve- to seventeen-year-olds who were included in a national longitudinal survey in the United States were asked how frequently they viewed a variety of programs that were considered to contain a high degree of sexual content. Three years later, girls were asked if they had become pregnant, and boys were asked if they had ever gotten a girl pregnant (Chandra et al., 2008). Those who were in the top 10 percent of viewers of sexual content were twice as likely to have been linked to a pregnancy as were other teenagers. Although the claim for a definitive causal link between television exposure to sexual content and teenage pregnancy

© Mary Kate Denny/PhotoEdit

In addition to concerns about exposure to aggressive behaviors and sexual content on television, young children also see many commercials. The products promoted in these commercials may include candy, snacks, and fast food meals that may not be particularly healthy for them, as well as toys and other items that are expensive and of relatively little educational value.

cannot be made from this study, these findings raise further questions and concerns about what television programming is offering to children and youths.

Consumer Behavior Because of their tremendous spending power, either directly or through their parents, children are the targets of a significant number of television commercials; on average, children see approximately 40,000 commercials a year (Kunkel, 2001; Strasburger, 2001). Of concern to many child advocates are the kinds of products that are heavily marketed on television (e.g., sugar-coated cereals, candy and snacks, toys, and meals at fast-food restaurants), the proliferation of shows linked to specific toys (e.g., cartoon shows that portray the same characters as toys), and product endorsements for expensive items, such as athletic shoes by popular sports figures and other celebrities—all of which put pressure on children and adolescents (and their parents) to spend money.

Children do respond to the messages of commercials. For one thing, they frequently request the cereals and other foods they see advertised (Taras et al., 1989). By age three, children distinguish commercials from other programming, but they do not always recognize commercials as messages specifically intended to influence their behavior; four- and five-year-olds, for example, believe "commercials are to help and entertain you" (Ward, Reale, & Levinson, 1972). Young children are especially likely to confuse programs with commercials if toys or cartoon characters appear in both (Wilson & Weiss, 1992). By about seven to eight years of age, most children begin to recognize that commercials are intended to influence viewers' buying habits (Andronikidis & Lambrianidou, 2010; Owen et al., 2007). Because young children are not able to evaluate critically the information presented to them in commercials, they may pressure their parents to purchase expensive toys and clothes, heavily sugared foods, and other products (Calvert, 2008).

In more recent years, controversy has swirled around the introduction of Channel One and similar programs in public schools. Channel One programming consists of ten minutes of news and two minutes of commercials for products of interest to young people. If a school agrees to air these broadcasts to students, free televisions are provided. It has become a popular idea in the American school systems; nearly 6 million middle and high school students are able to see the program in approximately 8,000 schools (Channel One News, 2009). In general, students seem to learn about current events from such programming, and teachers and principals like it (Johnston, Brzezinski, & Anderman, 1994). But the commercials also are reported to be effective as well; students more positively evaluate and express greater interest in buying the products that are advertised (Brand & Greenberg, 1994). Other companies are furnishing school computer labs with free equipment in which the advertising is available continuously on a small part of the screen (Calvert, 2008). In addition, based on information provided when the student logs on, these companies are collecting information about the age and gender of children working with the computer, as well as the kinds of websites they visit. Although schools are being provided with state-of-the-art computer facilities, critics worry about the potential invasion of privacy and the consequences of what could be interpreted as school-sanctioned commercialism from these kinds of arrangements.

research applied to parenting | Encouraging Critical Skills in Television Viewing

Jeremy finished his homework just before his mother came home. Fortunately, there still was enough daylight for his best friend, Aaron, to come over for a visit. As soon as he arrived, the conversation turned to the afternoon's television fare and some of the toys that were advertised on their favorite shows. "Hey, did you see that car that spins off the race track? That is really awesome." "Yeah," Aaron replied. "I really want to get one." "Me, too. And I want that robot they showed after that," Jeremy proclaimed. Jeremy's mother worried when she overheard this conversation. Was this generation of kids being steered to buy more consumer goods than children in prior years had been? These fears were added to her growing concerns about the effects of watching all of that violence on television. Was there anything she could do to control the large impact of television on the thinking and behavior of her young son?

As we have seen, television holds enormous promise to enhance children's intellectual and social functioning. However, there is also clear evidence of potential dangers, especially when television viewing takes up much of a child's time or is directed at programs that are age inappropriate. Apart from the option not to have a television set available in the home (an alternative that relatively few parents defend), what steps might parents take to promote positive benefits from this medium? Any recommendations will, of course, depend on the maturity of the child, as well as the values caregivers wish to promote. However, developmental scientists and others concerned about the influence of television on children generally agree with the following guidelines:

1. *Be aware of how much time is being spent watching television and what is being watched.* Parents may not always realize how much of the day their children spend in front of the television set, what they are watching, or how the program is affecting them. Continuous supervision may not be possible when parents are busy with other household duties or away at work. However, knowing what children are watching, and for how long, is the first step in understanding what they might be learning from television.
2. *Decide what is acceptable to watch.* Even very young children may be attracted to programming that is frightening or inappropriate, not because they necessarily enjoy it, but because the rapid pace of events or some other convention of the programming is attracting their attention. Parents have the responsibility to determine which programs are permissible and ensure that children limit their television viewing to those they consider acceptable. Recognize, however, that as children become older and more independent, parental monitoring will be more difficult. Older children must learn to take increasing responsibility for their own television viewing.
3. *Establish acceptable times for watching television.* Family members need to know when they can watch television. For example, can the television be on during the dinner hour? Is watching television permitted if homework, chores, or other obligations are not yet finished? How late in the evening is television viewing allowed?
4. *Watch television with children whenever possible.* When jointly watching programs with their children, parents have the opportunity to discuss such things as what is real and what is fantasy, how conflict might be resolved other than through violence, the stereotypes being portrayed, the goals of advertising, and many other issues presented through this medium that

The effects of television viewing on children's development probably depend on the types of programs watched, as well as how much time is spent in front of the television set. When parents view television programs along with their children, opportunities become available for parents to promote a variety of critical skills in their children's thinking.

© Mat Hayward/Fotolia

are valued or not approved within the household. In addition, by commenting on the material, parents can stimulate vocabulary development and provide different perspectives that may promote cognitive and social skills. Unfortunately, coviewing involving active discussion of television content appears to be infrequent in most families (Huston & Wright, 1998).

5. *If not interested in watching a program, turn the television off.* In many American homes, the television is on "most of the time" or "always" for more than one-third of children under three years of age (Rideout & Hamel, 2006). Children's play, either alone or with a parent, often occurs while programming designed for adult viewing is playing in the background (Masur & Flynn, 2008). However, children's play episodes are shorter and less focused under these conditions, and both the quantity and quality of parent–child interactions are lower (Schmidt et al., 2008; Kirkorian et al., 2009). Thus, the presence of background television seems to offer little for promoting positive cognitive and social opportunities for young children.

For Your Review and Reflection

- How much time do children of different ages spend viewing television? What kinds of programs are they attending to, and how are they watching them?
- When do children begin to comprehend television programming? How does this comprehension change with development? What factors may be contributing to their increasing comprehension of video?
- What evidence exists to suggest that infants' and toddlers' cognitive development and language are influenced by televised material? Why have some researchers suggested that very young children have a video deficit?
- Summarize the evidence suggesting that attentional processes and cognitive and language development of preschoolers and older children are influenced by viewing television.
- What influence does television viewing have on aggression and other aspects of social development?
- How might caregivers influence television viewing for their children?

- What potential risks are associated with extensive television viewing during childhood?
- When did you begin to watch television as a child? What programs did you prefer, and why do you think these were of interest to you? How did your parents or other adults influence your television viewing?

Computers, Social Media, and Video Games

Just as most adults in many countries are now likely to encounter computers in their daily experiences, so are children—even very young children. For example, in one study, parents reported that 21, 58, and 77 percent of children two years of age and younger, three to four years of age, and five to six years of age, respectively, had used a computer. Among those children, about 14 percent used it every day (Calvert et al., 2005). Figure 16.7a illustrates the kinds of activities children beginning to become computer-savvy carry out. As can be seen in Figure 16.7b, on any typical day, the percentage of children engaged in some kind of computer activity increased as they became older. Among those children who use a computer, 42 percent have asked to view one or more websites designed for children and, with the help of a parent, have sent an e-mail. On any particular day, about 15 percent played a video game on the computer; in fact, most of the time children used the computer was spent playing a video game (Calvert et al, 2005). More than 90 percent of adolescents, both males and females, typically use the Internet about one to two hours a day. About 80 percent of adolescent boys report using the computer for playing games, typically about one to two hours a day, but less than 30 percent of girls indicate that they use the computer for this activity, and typically for less than one hour a day (Willoughby, 2008). These kind of data begin to illustrate the pervasive role that computers play in the lives of many children.

What are the effects of computers and video games on children's development? Does experience with computers and video games influence the ways in which children tackle problem solving and other cognitive tasks? Are young "keyboard junkies" who spend long hours glued to the computer screen missing other critical experiences, particularly the social interactions crucial to their socioemotional development? The pervasive presence of computers in today's world makes these questions well worth exploring. The emerging answer is clear: there is little, if any, such thing as an "effect of computers" or video games per se on child development. What matters, rather, is the way children use them (Behrman, 2000).

Academic Mastery and Cognition

INTERACTION AMONG DOMAINS

The first relatively widespread use of computers in education began in the 1960s, when **computer-assisted instruction (CAI)** was touted as a valuable, efficient educational tool. CAI programs serve primarily to supplement classroom instruction, providing highly structured tutorial information along with drill-and-practice exercises in content areas such as mathematics and reading. Several principles are presumed to make CAI programs effective teaching tools. First, the child can work through a lesson at her own pace, reviewing topics if necessary. CAI thus provides an individually paced learning experience in which the content can be tailored to the specific needs of the student. Second, the child receives immediate feedback about the correctness of his responses to questions and exercises and may even receive periodic summaries of performance. Finally, CAI programs often employ sound effects and graphics designed to promote the child's attention to and interest in the material being presented.

computer-assisted instruction (CAI) Use of computers to provide tutorial information and drill-and-practice routines.

How effective are CAI approaches to instruction? Meta-analyses of hundreds of studies have shown that, on average, students with CAI experience improve in achievement test scores

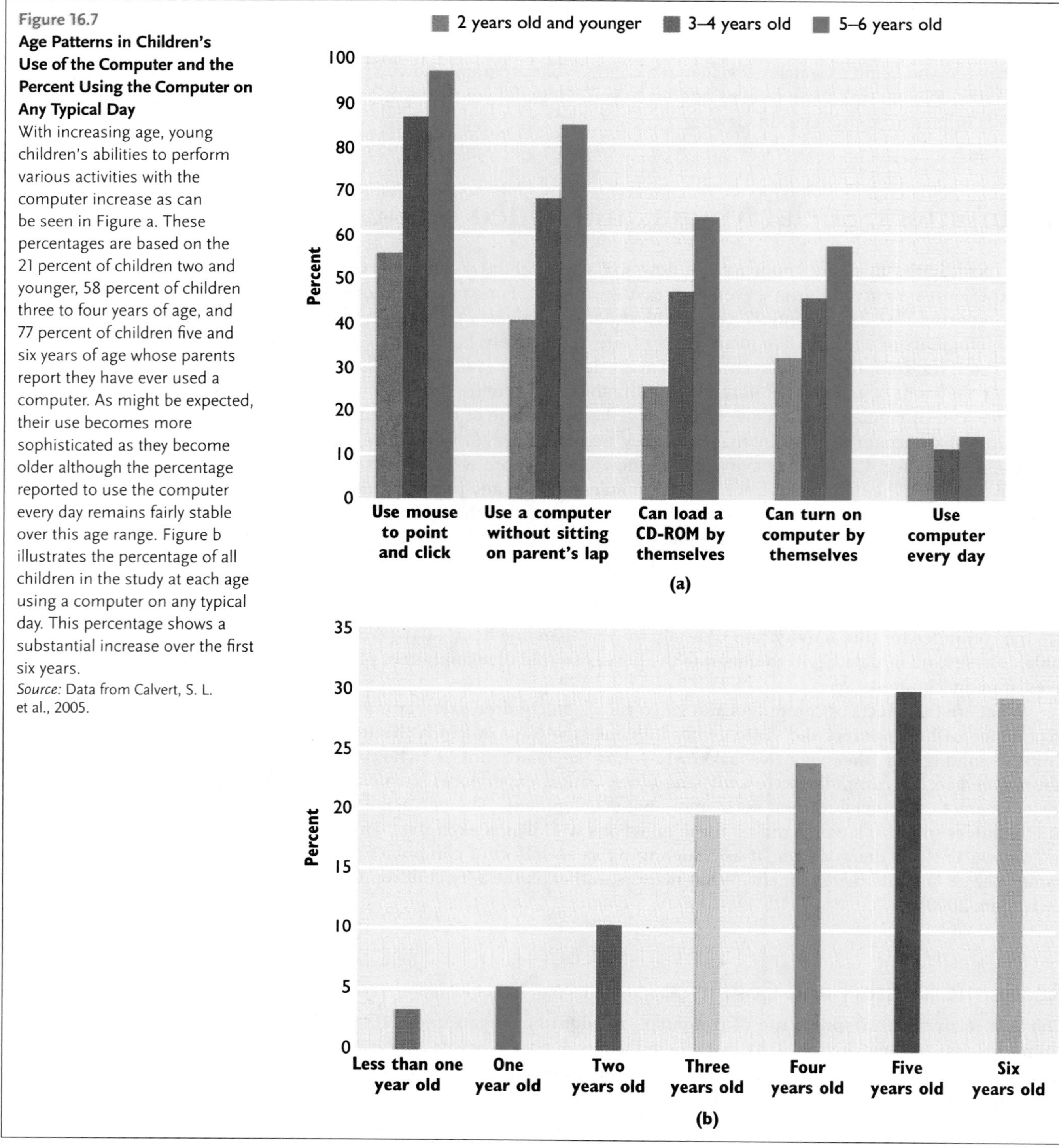

Figure 16.7
Age Patterns in Children's Use of the Computer and the Percent Using the Computer on Any Typical Day
With increasing age, young children's abilities to perform various activities with the computer increase as can be seen in Figure a. These percentages are based on the 21 percent of children two and younger, 58 percent of children three to four years of age, and 77 percent of children five and six years of age whose parents report they have ever used a computer. As might be expected, their use becomes more sophisticated as they become older although the percentage reported to use the computer every day remains fairly stable over this age range. Figure b illustrates the percentage of all children in the study at each age using a computer on any typical day. This percentage shows a substantial increase over the first six years.
Source: Data from Calvert, S. L. et al., 2005.

and that this effect is moderately strong (Lepper & Gurtner, 1989). CAI is especially effective with elementary school and special-needs children, who seem to profit most from individualized approaches to learning (Kulik, Kulik, & Bangert-Drowns, 1985; Niemiec & Walberg, 1987).

Newer educational software places less emphasis on rote memorization and more on providing children with opportunities to use higher-order thinking skills as they master academic subjects. To date, the effects of these efforts have been mixed (Roschelle et al., 2000). For example, math education programs designed to encourage children to think more fully seem to have positive effects, whereas those that are oriented toward making repetitive math learning more fun seem to have no, and perhaps even detrimental, effects on learning (Wenglinsky, 1998). In general, however, the areas in which computer learning seems to have the greatest benefits are in science and mathematics (Roschelle et al., 2000). Being able to visualize and observe simulations of scientific concepts appears to encourage children to engage in more advanced levels of thinking than had been thought possible. Another factor associated with computers that may have powerful benefits is the opportunity to work on real-world problems that are available through the Internet. More specifically, with increased access to recently collected data from scientific research, children and adolescents can engage in the very same types of activities of experimentation, design, and reflection that scientists and researchers carry out in their efforts to make contributions to understanding the environment, society, and the physical and biological world.

Other major advantages of the computer, especially with Internet access, stem from the opportunity to learn about issues and topics that simply would not be available to most children any other way. For example, with very little investment, children can explore and even design art and music, choreograph dramatic scenes, acquire information about other cultures (both existing and extinct), and communicate with other peoples. Among cognitive skills that may be enhanced are spatial representation, iconic skills, and increased ability to attend to multiple events, as is often required for playing action video games (Subrahmanyam et al., 2001). In general, moderate use of the computer tends to be correlated with a positive academic orientation such as higher educational aspirations, a sense of the importance of doing well in school, and, in particular, higher school grades (Willoughby, 2008). Among children in low-income families, the amount of time spent on the Internet is positively associated with grade point average as well as reading achievement (Jackson et al., 2006).

Social Development

INTERACTION AMONG DOMAINS

RISK | RESILIENCE

With the advent of e-mail, chat rooms, and other early online communication technologies in the lives of children and youths, researchers initially theorized that traditional social connections with friends and family would be disrupted. Early research studies conducted in the 1990s with adolescents gave some support to this assumption (Valkenburg & Peter, 2009). Older children and adolescents do spend much of their time at the computer alone. Adolescents who, for example, put in more than two hours a day on the computer have sometimes reported fewer and poorer social interactions with parents and friends (Sanders et al., 2000). However, as Patti Valkenburg and Jochen Peter (2009) have recently pointed out, two changes in the past decade emerged to challenge concerns about the influence of the computer on social relationships. First, computer and Internet use has become so common that adolescents can now more readily maintain their social interactions with many others via this technology (Lenhart & Madden, 2007). Second, new communication technologies (e.g., instant messaging and social networking sites such as Facebook) have become an increasingly popular means of encouraging social interactions with others. For example, about 85 percent of adolescents in Europe and the United States use instant messaging to talk to their friends (Gross, 2004; Valkenburg & Peter, 2007).

Researchers often now report findings of greater social connectedness and a sense of well-being (e.g., fewer instances of feelings of loneliness, low self-esteem, and depressive moods) among adolescents who engage in these kinds of online communication (Valkenburg & Peter, 2009). However, there are several caveats to this broad conclusion. For example, among adolescents who report feelings of loneliness, instant messenger use tends to decline rather than becoming an increasingly frequent means of communication with others (van den Eijnden et al., 2008). Thus, using electronic social technologies is not always a practice implemented to enhance a sense of well-being. Moreover, when online communications focus more on establishing contacts or talking with new people rather than friends, these positive benefits are no longer found. Not surprisingly, then, one major concern is what kinds of social interactions may be occurring during some of these online activities, especially when they involve individuals with whom the young person is not acquainted.

What Regulations Should Exist for Children's Access to the Internet and Other New Technologies?

what do you think?

With the emergence of new technologies often come new challenges and dilemmas for parents and society. Because computers, the Internet, and other social technologies have become such prevalent parts of the environment for many children, these new resources have generated their own set of controversies. As we have just seen, many positive advantages can exist for children using these new technologies. For example, learning benefits may come from being able to readily obtain in-depth information about a topic. But easily accessible Internet sites and social network information may also make available some material not considered appropriate for children. Among these are ways to engage in violent activity, viewing information from groups that promote hatred and bigotry (both to groups and to individuals), and sexually explicit imagery and explicit verbal exchanges encouraging risky behavior.

Little research exists on what children and youth are actually viewing or saying on the Internet or via other technologies. However, one study of the chat-room conversations of more than 500 teenagers found that almost 30 percent of participants talked about sexual themes, and, within communications, there was one sexual comment per minute (Subrahmanyam, Smahel, & Greenfield, 2006). Another analysis found that more than 400 message boards on the Internet were devoted to the topic of self-injurious behaviors in teens. Although many of these provided a way for adolescents with a particular problem to engage in mutual support for each other, a fair number were judged to encourage even more of these damaging and harmful behaviors (Whitlock, Powers, & Eckenrode, 2006). Still another project, a national survey of adolescents and young adults fourteen to twenty-two years of age who indicated using MySpace or similar social networking sites, revealed that 40 percent of them had been contacted by someone whom they did not know (Annenberg Public Policy Center, 2006). Children also may be constantly bombarded with advertising and other images that can promote certain points of view that children have difficulty understanding and that parents may find objectionable. What do you think about regulating such activities when, in some cases, there may be serious consequences for those who are exposed to such messages? What steps do you think parents and others should take to limit unacceptable Internet and other information from being received in the home? What steps should teachers or librarians take in the more public settings of schools and libraries? For example, should filters and blocking devices be installed on computers in the home and in publicly accessible locations as well? Do you think such restrictions are appropriate in public facilities given that they interfere with the rights of adults? Might such restrictions also limit some helpful resources, especially for older children and adolescents—for example, in cases where a young person (and his or her parents) may feel uncomfortable or unwilling to discuss sexuality?

Do you think parents are fully aware of how their children are using the computer? Is there a need to develop programs to teach children and adolescents about appropriate online computer usage? To what extent do you think *mentoring*, or *monitoring*, is needed when it comes to children and adolescents using the Internet and the increasingly greater number of other new technologies, which they often embrace so readily?

Video Games

Many parents express concerns about the content of and how much time their children spend playing video games (Gentile, 2009). A nationally representative sample of nearly 1,200 children and youths between eight and eighteen years of age from the United States surveyed in 2007 revealed that many children and adolescents, especially boys, play video games at least once a day (see Table 16.2). Moreover, a substantial portion of respondents indicated that they sometimes skipped chores and schoolwork to play video games (33 percent and 25 percent, respectively), and 20 percent indicated that they had done poorly on schoolwork or a test because of their game playing. The nearly 10 percent of respondents who showed the greatest tendencies to engage in behaviors suggestive of an addiction to game playing (e.g., playing for twenty-four hours per week, using game playing

INTERACTION AMONG DOMAINS

TABLE 16.2 Frequency Children and Adolescents Report Playing Video Games and How Mature-Rated Video Games Were Obtained

Substantial numbers of children and adolescents report that they play video games, and many are doing so at least once a day. The frequency of playing video games declines during older adolescence. Boys are far more likely to engage in this activity than girls, and many boys, even as young as eight to eleven years, own a mature-rated game. Children and adolescents obtain mature-related games largely as gifts from others.

		Sex		Age range		
Measure	**Overall**	**Boys**	**Girls**	**8–11**	**12–14**	**15-18**
Frequency of video-game play						
At least once a day	23	33	12	26	26	17
5 or 6 times a week	13	20	6	16	14	11
3 or 4 times a week	16	17	14	17	19	12
Once or twice a week	16	15	18	16	16	16
A couple of times a month	9	6	11	10	7	8
About once a month	4	3	6	4	5	4
Less than once a month	7	3	12	5	4	13
Never	12	3	21	6	9	19
Obtained a mature-rated video game...						
As a gift	26	35	16	16	31	34
With own money, and parents knew about it	22	33	9	7	23	37
With parents' money, and parents knew about it	13	18	6	7	16	17
With own money, and parents did not know about it	4	7	1	2	2	9
With parents' money, and parents did not know about it	1	2	0	1	0	2
Percentage who own a mature-rated game	39	54	20	22	41	56

Note. All numbers in the table are percentages.
Source: Gentile, D., 2009.

to escape problems, skipping chores and schoolwork to play, etc.) were less likely to do well in school, had trouble paying attention in school, and experienced more health problems (e.g., hand and wrist pain) very likely related to game playing (Gentile, 2009).

RISK | RESILIENCE

Because the data are correlational, much remains to be learned about whether excessive game playing caused some of these difficulties, but the findings suggest that extensive video game playing could be a contributing factor to problems in school. Moreover, the findings complement results from other studies. For example, those who are engaged in game playing spend 34 percent less time on homework and 30 percent less time reading (Cummings & Vandewater, 2007). In addition, six- to nine-year-olds who were randomly given a video game system spent less time involved in academic activities after school and showed lower academic achievement in reading and writing four months later compared with children who were not given the system (Weis & Cerankosky, 2010). Perhaps discouraging to those concerned about video game activity is that games labeled as designed for older audiences (e.g., eighteen or older) and games that contain violent actions appear to increase their attractiveness, even to children as young as seven or eight years of age (Bijvank et al., 2009).

Are there potential benefits from playing video games? When asked why they play, twelve- to fourteen-year-olds often indicate that it is, in some sense, a social activity. Many adolescents talk to each other about games, and they also report positive experiences associated with teaching others how to play them (Olson, 2010). In addition, young people frequently say that game playing is relaxing as well as provides intellectual challenges. It may be possible that such games can also enhance attentional and spatial skills, at least among adults and older people (Spence & Feng, 2010), but evidence for such benefits for children or adolescents has not been reported.

Do children and youths spend too much time playing video games? Girls tend to spend less time in this activity than boys. Why might this be so? Nevertheless, one potential benefit for both girls and boys may be the social engagement that is often a part of this activity.

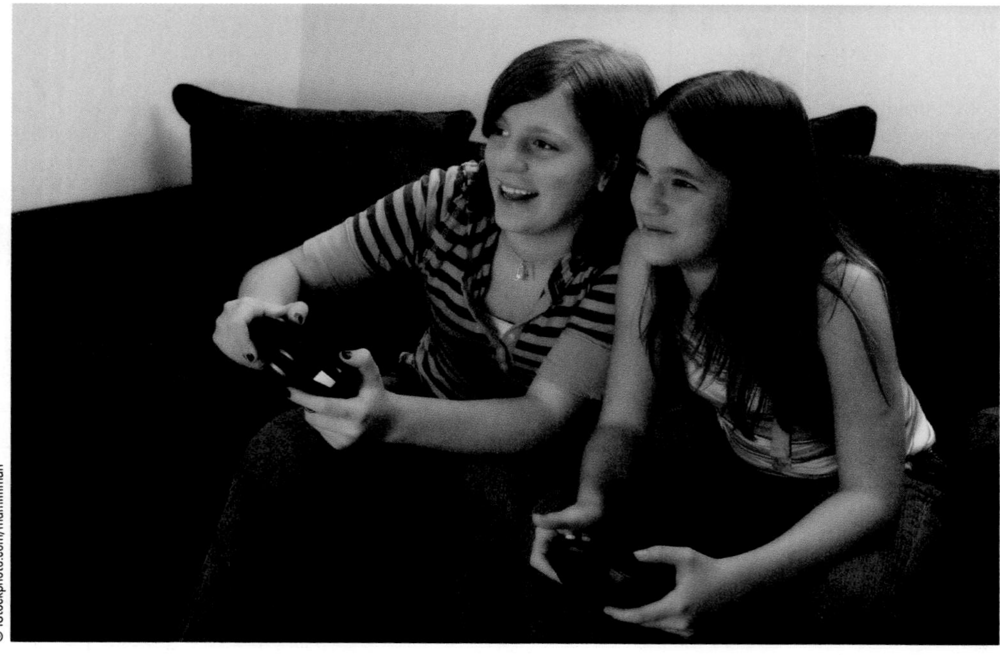

For Your Review and Reflection

- How has computer use changed over the past several decades?
- What benefits do computers provide in the mastery of academic material? How have new technologies influenced the use of computers for social interactions? What has been the impact of these new technologies on social development?
- How do boys and girls differ in their use of and attitudes toward computers and video games?
- What controversies exist concerning children's access to computers?
- How much time do children and adolescents spend playing video games? What aspects of children's behavior are correlated with playing video games? What are the potential benefits and risks of extensive video game playing?
- How might the availability of Internet and social networks increase risk for children and adolescents? How might their availability enhance resilience?
- Were you actively involved with social network sites as a child or adolescent? In what ways did you find them beneficial for your development? In what ways did you find that they posed challenges for your development?

Schools

In Chapter 10, "Achievement," we examined many aspects of schooling and how it affects academic success for children. Here we take a closer look at the environment associated with schooling such as size of the school, important transitions taking place as children progress through school, and school violence. The emphasis is on the influence of these factors not only on academic success but also on their social and emotional consequences for children and youths.

School and Classroom Size

Schools can vary substantially in their organization and structure. Although the one-room classroom is rarely found today in the United States, schools can be large or small, depending

© iStockphoto/monkeybusinessimages

Many factors can influence children's success in school. Perhaps because teachers can retain their attention more effectively, students in classrooms with fewer numbers of children seem to do better academically than students with higher numbers of classmates.

on the community, and they are likely to increase in size in the upper grades. Some children may also attend crowded classrooms, thus limiting the amount of time teachers spend with each child. What are some of the effects of these factors?

School Size Although some controversy surrounds the importance of school size, any significant effects researchers have found usually favor students from smaller schools (Moore & Lackney, 1993; Rutter, 1983). In a major study of thirteen high schools ranging in size from 13 to more than 2,000 students, researchers noted that students from smaller schools were less alienated, participated more in school activities, felt more competent, and found themselves more challenged (Barker & Gump, 1964). Students in smaller schools may need to fill more roles, particularly leadership roles such as editing the school newspaper or being captain of the band, for which positive feedback from parents, teachers, and peers is received. They are also likely to identify strongly with the school and develop a greater sense of personal control and responsibility. Furthermore, participating in school-based extracurricular programs seems to reduce the likelihood that young people will drop out of school, especially among those who are less academically competitive (Mahoney & Cairns, 1997). These kinds of findings have been among the factors influencing substantial efforts to create smaller schools. For example, in the past decade, the Bill and Melinda Gates Foundation invested more than $800 million to establish 2,000 small high schools designed, in particular, to help underserved minority children (SRI/AIR, 2002).

INTERACTION AMONG DOMAINS

Class Size Class size is another important aspect of school structure. Many countries around the world, as well as numerous states within the United States, have invested huge amounts of money to reduce class size (Ehrenberg et al., 2001b; NICHD Early Child Care Research Network, 2004). For example, the number of students per teacher in elementary school classrooms in the United States fell from 25.1 to 18.3 over the three decades from about 1970 to 2000; a similar decrease, from 19.7 to 14.0, occurred in secondary schools (Ehrenberg et al., 2001b). Although research has not always revealed a consistent benefit from such efforts, the general consensus is that children in small classes, especially in the earlier grades, show some academic advances over children in large classes and receive higher-quality instruction and emotional support (Ehrenberg et al., 2001a; NICHD Early Child Care Research Network, 2004). One of the most influential of these studies was carried out in Tennessee and involved seventy-six schools. Kindergarten children and teachers were randomly assigned to classes of different sizes (thirteen to seventeen versus twenty-two to twenty-five pupils per class). By the end of first grade, children in the small classes showed marked improvement in performance on standardized tests of reading and mathematics compared with children from regular-size classes. The benefits of small classes were especially pronounced for minority children (Finn & Achilles, 1990).

The long-term consequences of smaller class size were also favorable. Children in small classes in kindergarten through third grade in the Tennessee study continued to do better than their classmates assigned to larger classes, even after entering regular-size classrooms beginning in fourth grade (Mosteller, 1995). These benefits from the smaller-class experience were exhibited by children in later grades as well. Moreover, when small class sizes were introduced to the poorest districts in the state, children in these districts moved from displaying reading and mathematics scores that were well below average to scores above average for the state.

Why do smaller classes work? For one thing, teachers probably have greater enthusiasm and higher morale when they are not burdened with large numbers of students. Teachers also have more time to spend with individual children, and students are more likely to be attentive and engaged in classroom activities and show fewer behavioral problems in small classes (Finn & Achilles, 1990; Mosteller, 1995). But it is likely that benefits of reduced class size emerge only when teachers are trained to take advantage of the opportunities of working with smaller numbers of students (Bennett, 1998; Ehrenberg et al., 2001a, 2001b).

School Transitions

In addition to the size of the school and the classroom, the school transitions children are expected to make at specific ages may influence development. Most children begin kindergarten at age five or six, and the way in which they adjust to this first experience of school frequently determines how much they will like later grades. A second important transition occurs in adolescence, when entering junior or senior high school makes new academic and social demands on students.

Starting School Few occasions in a child's life are as momentous as the first day of school. Parents typically find this a time of mixed emotions, of eager anticipation about the child's future accomplishments coupled with anxieties about whether school will provide positive and rewarding experiences for their child. Children have many major adjustments to handle, including acclimating to a teacher and a new physical environment, making new

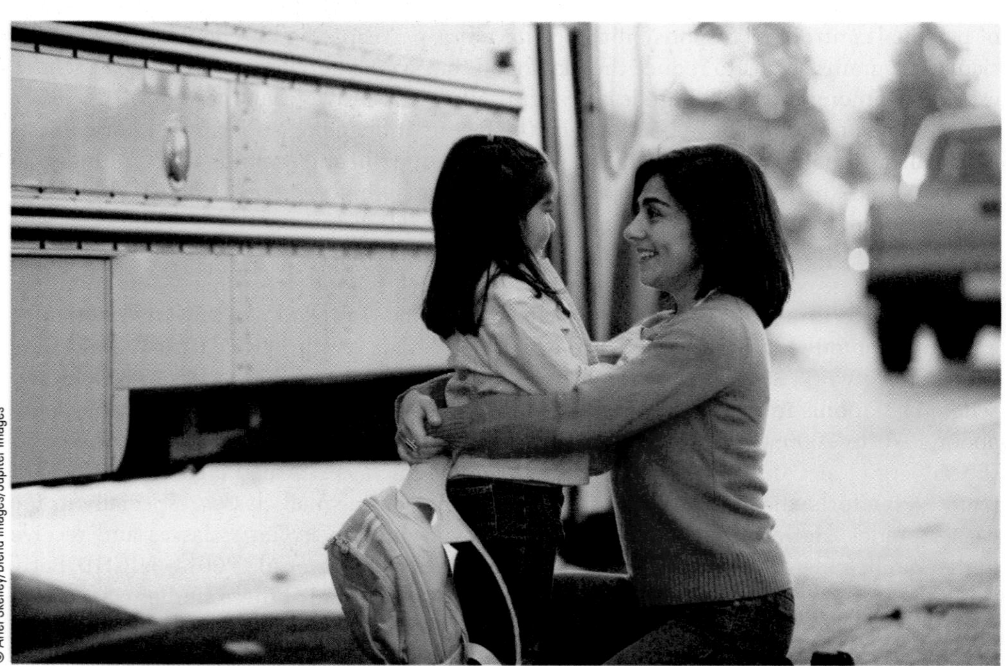

© Ariel Skelley/Blend Images/Jupiter Images

A major adjustment for children and their relationships with others often begins on the first day of school. Those who already display positive social behaviors and strong cognitive and linguistic skills promoted by supportive parents are more likely to thrive in this new environment.

friends, and mastering new academic challenges. Success in making the initial transition to school can set the tone for later academic and socioemotional development.

Not surprisingly, children who bring to school certain entry-level skills, such as a battery of positive social behaviors (e.g., cooperativeness in their preschool play or friendliness in their interactions with peers), and who exhibit cognitive and linguistic maturity (e.g., ability to engage in or be ready for school-related activities as a result of preschool and family experiences) do better in kindergarten (Entwisle, 1995; Ladd, Birch, & Buhs, 1999; Ladd & Price, 1987). Gary Ladd and his colleagues (Ladd et al., 1999), testing several hundred kindergartners throughout the school year, found that positive behavioral orientations exhibited by children in the first weeks of kindergarten fostered the formation of friendships and peer acceptance, whereas antisocial behaviors resulted in children being less liked by peers over the year and having greater conflict with teachers. The negative qualities displayed by some children (lack of friends, peer rejection, poor teacher–child relationship) seemed to be increasingly detrimental for adjustment to this new environment. These findings confirm that many factors working within the school, as well as the qualities children bring to the school environment, affect their early academic success.

INTERACTION AMONG DOMAINS

RISK | RESILIENCE

The presence of familiar peers in the kindergarten classroom also facilitates peer acceptance and is related to more positive attitudes toward school and fewer anxieties at the start of the school year (Ladd & Price, 1987). In general, factors promoting continuity between the preschool and kindergarten experiences seem beneficial to the child's adjustment, suggesting that parents should consider ways to foster their children's friendships with peers who will be future classmates. These results underscore the fact that the transition to school can be a particularly crucial time and that successes in one domain (peer relations) are related to successes in another (competence in school).

Another controversy that surrounds this first school transition is the age of the child upon school entry. Some researchers claim the younger members of the classroom do not perform as well academically as the older members and continue to have difficulty in the later school years (Breznitz & Teltsch, 1989; May, Kundert, & Brent, 1995). Others, however, have pointed out methodological and other problems in this research and have failed to find evidence that younger and older children in the classroom differ in any meaningful way (Alexander & Entwisle, 1988; Shepard & Smith, 1986). Frederick Morrison and his colleagues have carried out further work on this issue with Canadian schoolchildren (Morrison, Griffith, & Alberts, 1997). They found that younger children do tend to score below older children on reading and mathematics achievement tests at the end of the school year. However, the same is true even at the beginning of the school year. In fact, when measures of progress in reading and mathematics were used as the criteria, younger first-graders gained just as much as older first-graders. Furthermore, the first-graders, whether younger or older, gained more than children who remained in kindergarten but could have been enrolled in first grade. Although additional research needs to be carried out, these findings suggest that entrance age by itself may not be an important factor in academic progress and that children should not be delayed in entering school on that basis alone.

A Second Transition: Junior High Another important transition occurs later in many children's schooling careers, when they move from elementary school to a middle or junior high school. In the United States, this transition is usually the visible signal of childhood's end and the beginning of adolescence. Once again, children must adapt to a new physical environment, new teachers, and, often, new peers. Now, rather than staying with the same classmates in the same room for most of the school day, they move from class to class, each usually with its own set of students. Frequently, the difference in student body size is dramatic. In one study, the mean school size from grade six to grade seven increased from 466 to 1,307, and the mean number of children in each grade went from 59 to 403 (Simmons et al., 1987). It is no wonder that many researchers report a decline in school satisfaction and academic motivation in pre- and early adolescence, as well as a drop in grades and participation in extracurricular activities (Eccles, Midgley et al., 1993; Hirsch & Rapkin, 1987; Simmons & Blyth, 1987).

We noted in Chapter 12, "Self and Values," that some researchers have observed a decline in self-esteem at this time, particularly among preadolescent girls (Hirsch & Rapkin,

Entry into junior high or middle school is a source of new opportunities for learning, as well as new challenges and difficulties. In making the change, students such as these in the school cafeteria often find themselves in a much larger school and as a result may need to build new friendships.

© David R. Frazier

1987; Simmons et al., 1979). Early-maturing sixth-grade girls display better images of themselves when they attend schools with kindergarten through eighth-grade classes, presumably because they feel less pressured to adopt dating and other activities that become prevalent among seventh- and eighth-graders. Girls entering puberty at more typical ages and at about the same time at which they enter a new school program or undergo other significant transitions tend to have lower self-images and more difficulties in school, possibly because multiple changes in life are difficult to handle (Simmons et al., 1987). Boys and girls who feel they have little control over their academic progress and are less personally invested in succeeding in school also benefit by not having to undergo a school transition between fifth and sixth grades (Rudolph et al., 2001).

RISK | RESILIENCE

For some adolescents, the difficulties encountered during school transitions continue to be reflected in lower self-esteem and continuing emotional distress such as high levels of depression and greater drug and alcohol use through the later school years (Aikins, Bierman, & Parker, 2005; Rudolph et al., 2001). These difficulties may even set in motion a pattern of academic decline that leads them to drop out of school (Eccles et al., 1997; Eccles & Midgley, 1989). Perhaps school transitions do not fit the specific developmental needs of many preadolescents. At a time during which youngsters seek stronger peer associations and a supportive climate for resolving identity issues, they confront an educational environment that is more impersonal than the one they had experienced in elementary school and which fragments peer relationships. In fact, children who enter the junior high years with good social skills continue to do well perhaps because of their ability to maintain and establish new friendships (Aikins et al., 2005). Compared with elementary school, junior high school classrooms also tend to emphasize greater teacher control and discipline, offer fewer personal and positive teacher–student interactions, use a higher standard of evaluating student competence while focusing on more public evaluation of the quality of work, and can often be less cognitively challenging as classrooms become more teacher directed and provide fewer opportunities for student-initiated learning (Eccles, Midgley et al. 1993; Eccles & Roeser, 1999).

What happens when alternatives to the traditional junior high school and high school structures are instituted? When teachers offer greater academic and personal counseling, contact parents when students are absent, and encourage communication with parents and when students are assigned to classes with many of the same classmates, students show higher levels of academic success, less psychological dysfunction, and a substantially lower school dropout rate than students who experience more traditional school changes (Felner & Adan, 1988).

atypical development | Educating Youths with Serious Emotional Disturbances

The goal of public education in the United States is to help all children achieve at the highest level they can. As a consequence, schools are responsible for educating every child regardless of his or her background or ability. Children enter the public schools with various strengths and sometimes with disabilities. In fact, approximately 11 percent of students in the United States have one or more disabilities (Wagner, 1995). How well do such students do? There is no simple story to tell because enormous variability occurs among this population of children. Some children—for example, those with sensory impairments—are just as likely to further their educations beyond high school as youngsters in the general population, but they may not do as well in the labor market. Others, such as those with learning disabilities, often obtain jobs quickly after high school, although they are less likely to pursue further education.

One group of youths seems to have an especially difficult time both in school and afterward. This group includes those with serious emotional disturbances who display problems over a long period of time—such as unexplained difficulty in learning, inability to establish satisfying interpersonal relationships with peers or adults, pervasive depression or fears, or other inappropriate behaviors or emotions in normal circumstances. These children typically become disengaged from school, as evidenced by frequent absenteeism and failure to make friends among schoolmates. The consequence is often poor school performance and dropping out. Only a relatively small proportion continue their education (Wagner, 1995).

Are there ways the schools can improve on these outcomes? One concern is that these students be provided the kind of support they need to achieve their goals. For example, the few special services they are likely to receive are academic (tutoring, slower-paced instructions, and so forth) rather than assistance with emotional or behavioral problems. Moreover, the vast majority of youths with serious emotional disturbances are expected to compete just as other students do, despite their additional needs and different career goals. Under these sink-or-swim conditions, perhaps it is little wonder that youngsters with serious emotional disorders often find school frustrating and difficult; even those who do graduate still have difficulty obtaining jobs.

What interventions might help these children? The involvement of parents in promoting learning, holding high expectations for their children's efforts, and becoming involved in the school all seem to contribute to success for youngsters with serious emotional disorders (Henderson, 1994). However, schools may need to offer these students more, and perhaps earlier, vocational and technical courses that maintain their interest in education and provide the job skills needed for success (Wagner, Blackorby, & Hebbeler, 1993). When student interest is maintained, participation in regular courses in the later school years is likely to be more positive. Finally, fostering integration with other students, through sports, hobbies, or other social activities, along with greater collaboration with mental health and social service agencies to address the specific needs of individual children, can also yield positive outcomes for youngsters with serious emotional disturbances (Wagner, 1995).

School Violence

Violence in the schools has become a growing concern. Violent behavior may range from attacks on children or teachers that result in physical and psychological damage, to even death. Youth violence resulting in deaths in the schools in the United States increased substantially in the late 1980s in disadvantaged urban schools among African American and Hispanic youths. However, in the latter half of the 1990s, violence was reported with increased frequency in suburban and rural communities and at the hands of middle-class Caucasian American youths (National Research Council and Institute of Medicine, 2002b). Shootings in schools have resulted in deaths not only in the United States but also in Western Europe and other nations. Fortunately, such incidents remain quite rare. Nevertheless, they have received enormous attention in the media and have contributed to considerable public alarm (M. Anderson et al., 2001).

The violence associated with inner-city schools often appears to be an extension of the violence found in urban neighborhoods (National Research Council and Institute of Medicine, 2002b). Problems involving poverty, racial segregation, and illegal drug activity very likely spill over from the neighborhood and into the school in urban communities and typically involve specific grievances held by the perpetrators against particular individuals. However, in suburban and rural schools, the violence seems more like the kind of "rampage" shootings by adults that occur in workplaces or in other public locations (National Research Council and Institute of Medicine, 2002b).

RISK | RESILIENCE

Case studies of a number of these rampage-type events reveal few similarities among the students committing these acts of violence other than that the perpetrators are virtually always male. They tend to come from regions of the country where a somewhat higher sense of honor about self, reputation, and property exists within the broader culture. When this sense is violated in some way and combined with tendencies toward aggressive responding, the likelihood of bringing a gun to school or of committing some violent act is increased (Brown, Osterman, & Barnes, 2009). But among other factors shared by some of the perpetrators are a recent drop in grades, the tendency to be associated with or engage in delinquent behavior, serious mental health problems (not typically recognized by either parents or the school), and easy access to guns. A stereotyped picture of a child who is a member of a dysfunctional family, who is a loner, and whom adults believe to be at high risk for committing violence is not usually found in the cases that have been studied. Although the youths who committed lethal violence were often members of some student groups and informal cliques—that is, they were not completely outside the configuration of social participation with other peers—they often were likely to be only marginally associated with the group. At least some adults had hints that these boys might commit violent acts; however, the gap between the young persons who displayed such clues and their parents or others who might have been able to obtain help was never bridged. Some of the youths' friends had an even greater sense of the potential danger of violence. However, they, too, failed to communicate this information to appropriate authorities who might have been able to intervene.

SOCIOCULTURAL INFLUENCE

Several steps can be taken to reduce or eliminate such rampages in the future and to make schools safer. For example, more extensive mental health services should be provided in the schools for children in need of them. Additionally, greater efforts may be required to limit young people's access to weapons, such as guns, because their use has been the primary means by which violent acts resulting in death have occurred. However, the most important step in reducing violent lethal behavior may be to establish a climate, not just in the schools but in other locations within the community as well, in which adults and young people can communicate with each other and work together to provide a supportive network committed to the safety and well-being of all youth (National Research Council and Institute of Medicine, 2002b).

For Your Review and Reflection

- How do school and class size influence performance in the classroom?
- Why are school transitions difficult, and what practices can be implemented to make them easier for children?
- How might cognitive and emotional domains of development interact to promote resilience or to increase risk in completing school?
- What responsibility does public education have toward children who are emotionally disturbed? How successful are such children in the classroom?
- What explanations exist for violent behavior in schools?
- What were your experiences when you started school? What kind of climate existed in the school you attended during adolescence? What resources were available in your school to help those who might have special needs?

Neighborhoods

In many cultures and societies, rearing children is considered a communal effort. Even in the United States, with its emphasis on the family as the bedrock for the transmission of cultural values and beliefs, neighbors and other community members often provide resources to families in their efforts to create a supportive rearing environment (National Research Council and Institute of Medicine, 2002a). Of course, at one time, neighbors might often have included distant family members. But today, increased family mobility; less visibility in the community because of long absences for work; more heterogeneous interests among the residents; and the deterioration of some areas as a result of crime, drugs, and poverty have made questions about the neighborhood's role in development—that is, the broader ecological context in which children live—even more important.

Do Neighborhoods Matter?

A review of the literature on neighborhoods' effects on developmental outcomes by Tama Leventhal and Jeanne Brooks-Gunn (2000) indicates that they do matter. Neighborhoods matter, for example, with respect to school readiness and achievement; children who grow up in neighborhoods in which the residents have higher socioeconomic status do better in school and are more likely to graduate from high school and to attend college. Adolescents living in poor families, but who reside in communities where a high proportion of neighbors are considered middle class, perceive education as more important and useful, and they put more effort into academic work (Ceballo, McLoyd, & Toyokawa, 2004). Neighborhoods matter, too, with respect to behavioral and emotional problems; both are more likely to be present among children residing in neighborhoods with lower socioeconomic status. And youths living in neighborhoods with higher socioeconomic status tend to delay engaging in sexual activity and are less likely to bear children as teenagers (Leventhal & Brooks-Gunn, 2000). For example, in a nationally representative study recently carried out in Canada, girls with conduct problems in less affluent neighborhoods were found to initiate sexual activity earlier than girls with conduct problems in more affluent neighborhoods (Dupéré et al., 2008).

SOCIOCULTURAL INFLUENCE

RISK | RESILIENCE

These findings are probably not too surprising. However, a more important question is how neighborhoods might influence these kinds of outcomes. Leventhal and Brooks-Gunn (2000) propose three different pathways by which neighborhoods can have an impact. One

© David Young-Wolff/PhotoEdit

The neighborhood in which they live can have a major influence on children's development. Those neighborhoods that are viewed as safe, include many educational and leisure resources, and offer programs to support the values of the community in which they reside are likely to benefit children the most.

pathway is via the availability of institutional resources such as libraries, educational programs, and museums designed to promote achievement. Such resources also extend to the availability of quality child care and the presence of good schools and medical services and, in the case of adolescents, employment opportunities that encompass visible opportunities for "getting ahead" through the acquisition of job-relevant skills. The benefits of high-quality child care and good schools are well documented, although evidence that other institutional resources make a difference needs more thorough research.

A second pathway by which neighborhoods may have an effect on development is through the parenting styles caregivers engage in and the interpersonal support networks that are available to parents. Indeed, parenting is affected by a mother's perception of the neighborhood, such as how safe it is. As an illustration, mothers who have a negative view of their neighborhoods are more likely to show greater supervision of their children's activities than mothers who view their neighbors as a source of help (O'Neil, Parke, & McDowell, 2001). Nevertheless, more restrictive parental practices in poorer, high-crime neighborhoods may be beneficial to children, as the findings of a study carried out by Rosario Ceballo and Vonnie McLoyd (2002) indicate. Perhaps such parental practices reduce opportunities for children to be influenced by peers who may encourage them to engage in less desirable activities (Jarrett, 1997). Even so, an important beneficial component to children of concerned and involved parents in poor neighborhoods continues to be nurturance rather than harsh and inconsistent socialization practices (Brody et al., 2001). When parents have greater social support from family and friends within the community, the negative effects that often accompany increased parental stress in poor neighborhoods may also be reduced.

Yet a third pathway for influences on development occurs through the individual and community-level offerings provided within neighborhoods to supervise young people and to reduce the risks that they may experience. This pathway is sometimes referred to in terms of the norms or collective efforts of neighbors (Leventhal & Brooks-Gunn, 2000). The social cohesion—that is, the willingness of residents to intervene or establish alternatives such as athletic activities, after-school programs, and social clubs designed to promote the values and goals of the community—may differ substantially from one neighborhood to another. Yet when residents are willing to take the initiative in monitoring or overseeing the doings of children and youths, neighborhoods tend to experience less violence and fewer deviant behaviors among the young (Brody et al., 2001; Sampson, Raudenbush, & Earls, 1997).

These various neighborhood effects on development are not large (Caspi et al., 2000; Leventhal & Brooks-Gunn, 2000). For example, research involving identical twins growing up in a range of communities suggests that neighborhood differences account for about 5 percent of the variability associated with their mental health. Although this impact may seem small, when the interventions designed to improve institutional resources, interpersonal support, and the norms and collective efforts of a community are extended to a large number of children within a neighborhood, the costs are small and the benefits quite high. Thus social policies designed to enhance the institutional resources within the community, parental perceptions of support and other features that uphold desirable parenting practices, and the individual and collective efforts of the community members to monitor and assist in the supervision of children and adults may be important avenues for promoting child and youth development.

SOCIOCULTURAL INFLUENCE

Neighborhoods, Low Income, and Children in Poverty

We have already seen some of the findings associated with low-income neighborhoods and identified three pathways for how these outcomes might occur. Here we take a closer look at some research that has examined the relationship among neighborhoods, low income, and children in poverty. As a result of a court order implemented to desegregate public housing in Chicago several decades ago, parents with children were provided vouchers that allowed them to relocate to other neighborhoods. The assignment of families to various neighborhoods, based on the availability of housing, was random. When these families were studied ten years later, youths who had the opportunity to reside in more affluent suburban neighborhoods did much better academically than youths who were relocated and continued to reside in poorer urban neighborhoods (Rubinowitz & Rosenbaum, 2000; Leventhal & Brooks-Gunn, 2003).

In another demonstration of the impact of neighborhoods on children's academic success, Leventhal and Brooks-Gunn (2004) initiated a study of children of low-income families, predominantly minority families in New York City, who had been assigned randomly by the U.S. Department of Housing and Urban Development (HUD) to live in communities that differed in their economic resources. Some of the families received vouchers that permitted them to move into private housing in residential areas where poverty was low (fewer than 10 percent of the residents were poor), others to a neighborhood of their choice, and still others continued to live in public housing where family incomes were low. How did children in these three groups of families fare three years later? The benefits of moving from a high- to low-poverty neighborhood were especially great for boys eleven to eighteen years of age. For example, their performance on verbal tasks such as naming letters and reading words as well as solving mathematical word problems was significantly better than the performance by boys of the same ages in the other two groups. Although low-income pre-adolescent and adolescent boys typically fare much more poorly than girls on these two kinds of tasks, boys who had moved out of the high-poverty neighborhoods now demonstrated academic competencies similar to those displayed by girls. These findings were accompanied by reports from the boys indicating that they were spending more time on homework than boys in the other two groups. Parents also believed their children's academic improvement stemmed from improved school safety in the low-poverty neighborhoods.

For younger children (ages six to ten), such differences were not found. Moreover, there was a tendency for these children, now living in more affluent neighborhoods, to be retained in a grade more frequently, a result that may stem from the higher standards that schools in these neighborhoods held for students. However, the most important message from this research is that, where older children and adolescent boys reside can have a major impact on eliminating gender differences, differences typically found among low-income families when boys grow up in economically and socially disadvantaged neighborhoods (Leventhal & Brooks-Gunn, 2004).

RISK | RESILIENCE

Other research demonstrates the extent to which children in low-income families miss opportunities to participate in organized activities. For example, only one in ten children from poor families enrolls in sporting programs and clubs outside of school whereas more than nine out of ten children from higher-income families do so—and often in multiple programs (Theokas & Bloch, 2006). Although many efforts to increase the availability and affordability of activities within low-income communities in the United States have been initiated, differences still exist. For example, in one recent study, children from low-income families were found to participate less in athletic or community groups and programs (e.g., scouting), lessons (e.g., music), and summer camp activities as well as activities outside of church than children from families that were better off economically (Dearing et al., 2009). The one exception was with respect to participation in church-related activities; children in low-income families were more likely to participate in this kind of activity than children from more affluent families. Income was a major factor in accounting for these findings; however, the extent to which parents emphasized cognitive stimulation in the home contributed as well. Thus, having affordable activities available is important but so too may be the need for interventions that provide parents with training and education about the value of engaging their children in reading, problem solving, and other cognitively challenging undertakings. These kinds of learning opportunities may, in turn, foster increased interest in pursuing opportunities to participate in programs available outside the home.

INTERACTION AMONG DOMAINS

RISK | RESILIENCE

Living in communities where poverty is high includes many different risk factors for children (Evans, 2004). These risk factors extend beyond just the family—where there is an increased likelihood of more punitive parenting, where children often live with a single parent or one who is out of work, and where there are fewer supportive social networks for family members. For example, exposure to factory pollutants is much greater for the 10 percent of families most deprived living in England, as can be seen in Figure 16.8. Noise levels are likely to be higher and adequate water and sanitation facilities less available in poor communities as well. Children in these neighborhoods are also exposed to more street traffic, and play spaces tend to be more hazardous.

Gary Evans and Kimberly English (2002) examined a number of risk factors to see if their combination was greater for eight- to ten-year-olds living in poverty compared with

Figure 16.8

Factory Pollution and Deprivation

One of many potentially negative influences on optimal development in children is their greater exposure to pollutants. As this study carried out in England indicates, those who live in the most deprived neighborhoods are exposed to far more factory pollution than those who live in more affluent neighborhoods.

Source: Data from Friends of the Earth, United Kingdom, 2001. *Pollution and poverty: Breaking the link.* London: Author.

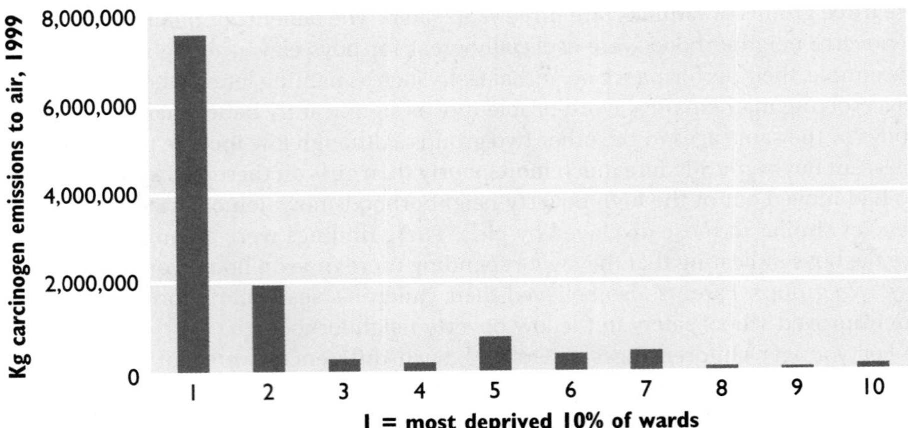

Note: Wards are subdivisions of local authorities in England, averaging approximately 8,000 persons per ward. Deprivation (corrected for ward population size) is a weighted estimate based on income (25%), employment (25%), health status and benefits (15%), educational levels (15%) house quality (10%), and access to basic services (10%). The 8,414 wards were broken into 10 parts (on the graph, 1 = the most deprived 10% of wards [Wards 1–842]; 2 is the next most deprived 10% [Wards 842–1682], etc). The pollution data covered all factories in England emitting more than 1,000 kilograms of carcinogens into the air in 1999. There are 156 of these factories.

children in middle-income homes and whether this cumulative risk exposure could partially account for differences in socioemotional adjustment for children. They identified three physical risk factors: crowding as measured by the number of individuals per room; housing quality as measured by structural quality, cleanliness, clutter, resources, and safety within the home; and noise level in the living room. They also identified three psychosocial risk factors as measured by the responses of the mother to questions about her child's exposure to violence, exposure to family arguments, and occurrences of separation from the family. Children living in poverty were likely to be exposed to a greater number of these risk factors. Moreover, exposure to the accumulated number of stressors helped to further account for the poorer socioemotional adjustment displayed by children living in poverty. In other words, within the constraints known to exist with correlational findings, the results raise the possibility that exposure to multiple stressors elevates poorer adjustment above and beyond that which might be explained by the simple increase in individual stressors. Other factors, of course, may contribute to the effects of poverty. As just one example, the longer families live in poverty, the more serious consequences this may have for their children (Evans, 2004). The design and implementation of programs helpful for such children remains an enormously important, but difficult, problem for researchers and those concerned with the implications for public policy to address.

Affluent Communities

RISK | RESILIENCE

We often think that children growing up in affluent communities are protected from risks in development, but this is not necessarily the case. Suniya Luthar and her colleagues have conducted several studies that show that, for some children from wealthy families, the pressures placed on them by families with hard-driving schedules and high expectations may exact psychological costs. In one study, one in five tenth-grade girls reported that they were depressed, a rate that was three times higher than average among girls this age. In addition, 72 percent of adolescents reported that they had used alcohol at least once in the past, compared with 61 percent for teens of this age on average (Luthar & D'Avanzo, 1999). In another study, a sample of 300 sixth- and seventh-graders from a high-income neighborhood (the median income was about $100,000 per year) showed high rates of depression among girls and high levels of substance use among boys and girls, a phenomenon that was linked to their anxiety and depression. Related to these behaviors was the feeling of being pressured toward academic achievement, a sentiment that caused them to set very high standards for themselves.

Researchers do not yet fully understand why children from privileged backgrounds might experience such serious social and emotional problems, but they have some suspicions. For one thing, apparently many of the parents of these children focused more on their children's accomplishments than on their personal qualities and character. Many of these children also experienced a lack of emotional connection to their parents. Involved in a pattern of extensive after-school activities, or spending significant time alone while their professional parents worked, these children did not feel much emotional closeness to their parents (Luthar & Becker, 2002; Luthar & Latendresse, 2005). Students and parents were both apparently caught up in highly overscheduled days, with little "down time" in which emotional support could be provided. In conclusion, even some children in families with high levels of material wealth may not always be happy (Luthar & Sexton, 2004).

INTERACTION AMONG DOMAINS

Exposure to Violence

A nationally representative sample of children and adolescents under eighteen years of age in the United States responding to a telephone interview (or a parent in the case of children under ten years of age) revealed that many are exposed to some form of violence, as is evident from Figure 16.9 (Finkelhor et al., 2009). Among youths living in urban neighborhoods, those percentages are higher, and they are more likely to consist of witnessing such events directly (Kracke & Hahn, 2008). For some in urban communities, this experience is the result of gang activity. Gangs in the United States are estimated to number nearly 28,000 with approximately 774,000 members (Egley, Howell, & Moore, 2010). Regardless of the source of exposure to violence, it puts youth at risk for posttraumatic stress disorder, depression, anxiety, and substance abuse; children who witness violence are also more likely to enact violent behaviors themselves (Cooley-Strickland et al., 2009; Farver et al., 2005; Kelly, 2010).

Parents play an influential role in how adolescents cope with exposure to violence. In one study, young adolescents and their female caregivers living in a violent section of an urban area were interviewed about how they coped with this problem. Caregivers were also asked to describe the types of discussions they had with children about violence in their neighborhood. Children whose parents encouraged them to take an active, problem-focused, or preventive approach showed gains in self-esteem, grades in school, and mental health. These gains were not observed when children were encouraged to ignore the problem or to respond with aggression. Talking to children about violence, as opposed to ignoring it, and serving as a good role model for how to cope can provide children with a means to achieve successful outcomes (Kliewer et al., 2006). In addition, adolescents who report that they are religious, in the sense of being spiritual and engaging in personal religious experiences, seem to be protected to some degree from the negative impact of exposure to violence (Pearce et al., 2003).

War, Natural Disasters, and Children

Perhaps no other tragedy aside from natural calamities such as earthquakes, floods, or famine is more disruptive to neighborhoods than war. But wars often have an impact on large numbers of communities and are the result of human motivation; they are therefore subject to a form of intervention that is not available for many other kinds of disasters. The consequences of war for young people can be devastating. For example, as a result of

RISK | RESILIENCE

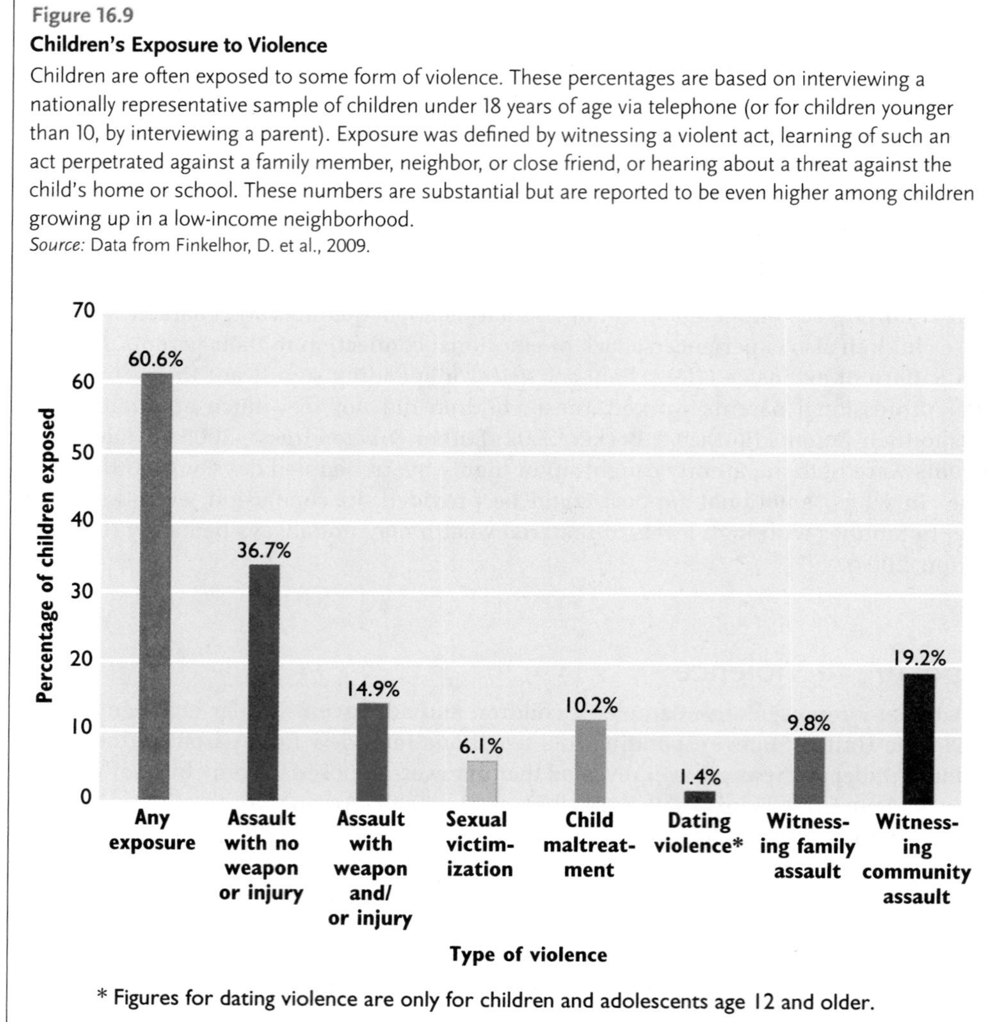

Figure 16.9
Children's Exposure to Violence
Children are often exposed to some form of violence. These percentages are based on interviewing a nationally representative sample of children under 18 years of age via telephone (or for children younger than 10, by interviewing a parent). Exposure was defined by witnessing a violent act, learning of such an act perpetrated against a family member, neighbor, or close friend, or hearing about a threat against the child's home or school. These numbers are substantial but are reported to be even higher among children growing up in a low-income neighborhood.
Source: Data from Finkelhor, D. et al., 2009.

conflicts between 1990 and 2000, perhaps as many as 2 million children around the world lost their lives, 6 million were injured or disabled, 12 million were left homeless, and 1 million were orphaned (UNICEF, 2002).

Of children who experience and survive war in their neighborhoods, substantial numbers have been reported to display posttraumatic stress disorder (PTSD), a disorder that was described with respect to physical and sexual abuse in Chapter 14, "The Family." In the case of war, multiple factors may contribute to the appearance of PTSD. Children may witness violent acts such as killing, rape, and torture (or even experience some of these) or see the physical manifestations of war, including dead bodies or destroyed buildings. They may also be subjected to homelessness, starvation, relocation to refugee camps, and separation from family and friends, additional factors that can contribute to the occurrence of PTSD (Allwood, Bell-Dolan, & Husain, 2002). The extent of stress reported by children is influenced by the degree to which they report experiencing the more traumatizing aspects of war (Smith et al., 2001). Not surprisingly, studies vary widely with sometimes as many as 25 to 90 percent of children reported to be experiencing some aspects of posttraumatic stress reaction as the result of war-related events (Barenbaum, Ruchkin, & Schwab-Stone, 2004).

In general, the symptoms of PTSD are most evident within the first year of exposure to war events; after one year, they decline. However, some stressors, such as relocation and separation from family, may be ongoing for years, and, as a consequence, children may remain vulnerable to PTSD for long periods of time (Thabet & Vostanis, 2000). Nevertheless, some children show exceptional resilience in the face of such tragedy. At the present time, researchers know little about the factors that might promote this resilience; however, the availability of some kind of social support is often theorized to be one important element. That support usually comes from a mother. Her reactions to the war experience do have an impact on the child's level of distress (Barenbaum et al., 2004; Smith et al., 2001).

RISK | RESILIENCE

Other effective ways to treat children experiencing the stresses of war may be needed. Perhaps a first step is to establish a secure environment for children, often an extremely difficult task given the possibilities of continued conflict, the uncertainties associated with living under refugee conditions, and the suspicions that can pervade attitudes toward others who may not be well known by the children. Psychosocial intervention efforts designed to assist the mothers of children exposed to war so that they, in turn, can be more helpful to their children show promise of positive benefits (Dybdahl, 2001). However, the availability of a well-functioning parent may not be a panacea by itself (Barenbaum et al, 2004). Reestablishing educational facilities with supportive teachers as well as other community resources can be helpful, as may other more intensive therapeutic procedures (Barenbaum et al., 2004; Klingman, 2006). Vast amounts of support are typically needed for children who have experienced this kind of disruption in their lives. In addition, well-designed research to evaluate the procedures that can help the most should be a priority until such time as neighborhoods are safe from the ravages of war, no matter where children reside.

In the same nationally representative sampling of children and adolescents under eighteen years of age in the United States that were asked about exposure to violence, another question asked about having experienced a calamitous event such as a "very bad fire, explosion, flood, tornado, hurricane, earthquake or other disasters" (Becker-Blease, Turner, & Finkelhor, 2010). Approximately 14 percent had been involved in one or more of these kinds of disasters during their lifetime, and 4 percent had experienced such an event within the past year. By the end of this past century, an estimated 67 million children worldwide were being affected by natural disasters every year (Penrose & Takaki, 2006). Although typically of shorter duration, natural disasters and terrorist attacks are often described as having similar consequences as war on children and adolescents. Such events disrupt families, the neighborhood (if neighborhoods still remain), and community resources. For example, thirty-three months after Hurricane Katrina devastated the New Orleans area, nearly 50 percent of fourth- through sixth-graders in six different schools (some severely damaged, others less so) still reported moderate to severe symptoms of PTSD (Moore & Varela, 2009). Depression and anxiety have also been found to be substantially higher one and two years after Hurricane Katrina struck than before among eleven- to eighteen-year-olds (Roberts et al., 2010). In addition, relational aggression and bullying levels post-hurricane, relative to pre-hurricane, have been found to increase (Terranova, Boxer, & Morris, 2009), further illustrating the myriad of problems in addition to PTSD that youth experience following a natural disaster (Roberts et al, 2010).

The extent to which these symptoms remained seemed to be closely linked to the severity of disruptions (for example, a damaged home still not fixed, having to move to a different home several times) in the lives of these children after the hurricane. On the other hand, being able to make new friends among classmates or the continued support of their friends in the aftermath of this disaster had a substantial positive effect in reducing the effects of PTSD (Roberts et al., 2010). Other recent research also reveals that having supportive relationships as well as reconstruction of schools can enhance resilience in children who experienced Hurricane Katrina (Kronenberg et al., 2010). These findings suggest that the events following the hurricane may be more important in lowering levels of PTSD symptoms than the degree of traumatic exposure to the initial occurrence of the hurricane.

INTERACTION AMONG DOMAINS

As might be anticipated from the findings of the importance of a supportive parent for children affected by war, the loss of a parent from a natural disaster can be especially devastating. In 2003, an earthquake measuring 6.7 on the Richter Scale destroyed the city of Bam in Southeast Iran, killing an estimated 26,000 inhabitants. Four years later, eighty-six children averaging nine years of age who had lost one or both parents during the earthquake were matched with eighty-six children who had not suffered this particular loss. In

The children shown here outside the Superdome in New Orleans are guarding the small number of possessions that their mother could take with her after flooding caused by Hurricane Katrina destroyed their home. Many children exposed to this disaster experienced depression and symptoms suggestive of posttraumatic stress disorder (PTSD). Having a supportive relationship with others and returning to classrooms with friends in reconstructed schools are among the factors that can help to reduce the risks associated with natural disasters and other severe disruptions in children's lives.

RISK | RESILIENCE

accord with predictions, those without one or both parents continued to experience more severe emotional and behavioral problems at this later time (Kalantari & Vostanis, 2010). The severity of their problems was greater when a surviving parent also demonstrated more mental health problems, a finding that has been reported in other research involving the impact of earthquakes on children and their families (Margolin, Ramos, & Guran, 2010). Thus, we see again how the parental support system available to children following a natural disaster plays an important role in the mental health of these children.

Terrorist attacks do not leave children unscathed either. Six months following the destruction of the World Trade Center in New York City on September 11, 2001, samples of children attending schools in that city were surveyed. Some of the children were enrolled in schools near "ground zero," others from schools more distant from the disaster. Information also was obtained about whether the child was directly exposed to the attack (e.g., harmed, witnessed the event, near the cloud of smoke, evacuated to safety) and whether any family members (including grandparents and aunts and uncles) were affected by it. Nearly 30 percent of the children reported one or more probable anxiety or depressive disorders, and this rate was highest among children who were themselves or who had a member of their family directly exposed to the event (Hoven et al., 2005). In fact, degree of exposure to the attack for a family member increased the likelihood of a mental disorder even more than degree of exposure for the child, suggesting that professionals dealing with the aftermath of this kind of disaster need to address the impact on the family as well as on the child. Surprisingly, proximity of the school the child attended did not have a bearing on increased mental disorders. One additional finding was that children's earlier exposures to some kind of traumatic event seemed to make them more vulnerable to experiencing symptoms after the terrorist attack. This finding of amplification of the effects due to other traumas has also been reported in studies involving preschoolers (Chemtob, Nomura, & Abramovitz, 2008). Children this age who directly saw the consequences of the attack (for example, an injured person or the towers collapsing) but had not experienced prior traumas such as an interpersonal loss, serious accident or illness, or natural disaster subsequently showed no greater likelihood of behavioral problems than those who did not directly witness the attack. However, if they had experienced some other traumatic event, behavioral problems were more likely to be exhibited. One important conclusion that these kinds of findings suggest is that children can be resilient in dealing with some level of trauma. However, the stresses associated with multiple traumas may substantially increase the risks for normal development in children.

For Your Review and Reflection

- What aspects of development are known to be influenced by the neighborhood?
- What are some of the consequences of living in low-income neighborhoods and poverty?
- What adverse developmental outcomes do some children from affluent families manifest?
- What is the impact of exposure to violence on adolescents? What factors promote successful adaptation to this exposure?
- What factors increase the risk and resilience of children living in low-income and middle-income neighborhoods?
- What are the most serious outcomes for children experiencing war, and what factors may be most important in dealing with these consequences?
- What are some of the consequences of children's exposure to natural disasters and to terrorist activities?
- What kind of neighborhood did you reside in when you were growing up? How did your experiences in that neighborhood benefit by the resources already available in it? How might your experiences have been different if additional resources had been available?
- As a child or adolescent, you may have been part of, or at least heard about, natural disasters and terrorist events on television or from friends. What was your reaction to this kind of experience?

chapter recap

Summary of Developmental Themes

Sociocultural Influence

How does the sociocultural context influence the child's experiences with media, computers, schools, and the broader world in which children live?

The society in which the child grows up determines what kind of exposure she will have to television, computers, schools, and the availability of various neighborhood resources. Not all cultures emphasize formal schooling, and not all children have access to television or computers. In addition, exposure to war varies considerably, depending on the society in which a child is living.

Interaction Among Domains

How do the child's experiences with media, computers, schools, and the broader world in which children live interact with development in various domains?

As children's cognitive skills grow, so does their ability to comprehend information portrayed on television and their ability to learn even more from the programming that is broadcast. Television can also influence social behavior through the strong messages it portrays about violence, prosocial acts, and gender-role stereotypes. Experiences with computers can facilitate cognitive and social development as well. Children who have good peer relations are more likely to adjust well to school and, therefore, benefit academically. Once in school, children typically have experiences that can promote their intellectual advancement, peer relations, and self-concept.

Risk | Resilience

How are risk or resilience influenced by the child's experiences with media, computers, schools, and the broader world in which children live?

Exposure to a heavy diet of media violence early in childhood may put a child at risk for aggression later in childhood. The ready availability of the Internet and use of social networks can put children at risk for exposure to early and predatory sexual activity. Extensive video game activity may disrupt academic activity. Children seem to benefit from small classes and schools and thrive if they experience smooth transitions when beginning school and moving to junior high and high school. The kind of neighborhood in which a child lives may be relatively safe or dangerous. For example, exposing the child to violent behavior and limited resources for healthy and supportive organizations available within the community increases risks. War, natural disasters, and terrorist activities affecting a community can increase risks to safety and mental health, and they may have especially negative consequences when supportive parenting is no longer available or when several kinds of trauma are experienced.

Chapter Review

Television and Related Visual Media

How much time do children and adolescents spend watching television?
On average, children about a year of age are exposed to television about one hour a day, preschoolers watch between two and three hours each day, younger elementary school students somewhat less, and early adolescents as much as four hours a day, after which viewing time declines somewhat.

What do very young children comprehend about television programming?
Although the formal features of television often guide their attention, children less than about eighteen months of age typically watch randomized scenes or scenes accompanied by incomprehensible language about as much as comprehensible programming. As children's cognitive and verbal skills expand, so does their ability to comprehend both more complex plots and the conventions associated with television programs. Young children progress from failing to make a distinction between events on television and events in the real world, to a belief that events depicted on television do not occur in the real world, to a more complete understanding of which events occurring on television are fictional and which are not.

How are cognitive and language development influenced by viewing television?
Despite the belief by many parents (and claims by producers of television programs and DVDs), little evidence exists to show that infants and children less than about eighteen months of age learn much from television. Furthermore, children less than thirty to thirty-six months of age often display a video deficit; that is, they imitate and learn less from televised tasks than from tasks carried out by a live person. Although there may be limited benefits to infants and young toddlers for language acquisition, much clearer benefits for cognitive and language development are evident among preschoolers. Television can promote certain pre-reading skills, such as knowledge of the alphabet and numbers, and television can increase preschoolers' language development and vocabulary. Children who watch relatively greater amounts of educational television as preschoolers continue to demonstrate greater academic achievement during the high school years. However, concerns continue to exist about the relationship between television viewing and attentional difficulties.

What is the relationship between watching television and aggression?
Children who observe aggressive events on television learn such behaviors and can demonstrate them in similar situations. Viewing high levels of violence on television is associated with greater aggression in children and youths.

What other consequences are associated with watching television?
Prosocial behaviors can be learned via television and may even be more influential than violent content. Gender stereotypes are commonly exhibited in television programming. Children's attention to these stereotypes appears to be dependent on an understanding of their own gender. Children watch and identify with television characters that belong to their own ethnic group, and the extent to which they do so is linked to positive self-esteem. Adolescents who consume a heavy diet of sexual content via various forms of media tend to have sexual relations earlier, and the risk of teenage pregnancy is increased.

How is television viewing related to children's consumer behavior?
Children do not understand that commercials are intended to influence consumer behavior until about age eight. Children tend to request the products they have seen on television commercials. Commercials are now seen on some television programming designed to be shown in public schools, a practice that has generated considerable controversy.

What can parents do to encourage positive benefits from television?
Parents should be aware of their children's viewing habits, select acceptable programs for viewing at appropriate times, comment on the programming to assist children in their understanding of it, and turn the television off when engaged in other activities.

Computers, Social Media, and Video Games

How extensive is computer use by children?
Most children, even preschoolers, now have access to computers in the home, at school, or in both locations. Even preschoolers are able to use at least some of the computer's features. Older children use the Internet for a variety of purposes, including for various social functions.

What benefits do computers provide in the mastery of academic material?
Computer-assisted instruction may result in gains in achievement in various subjects. The largest gains in achievement occur when children are required to think more fully about a topic and are frequently reported in the areas of mathematics and science. Children can access real-world data online and learn about a wide array of topics and issues that might not normally be available to them. Among the cognitive skills that appear to benefit from children's use of computers and other electronic technologies are spatial representation, iconic skills, and the ability to attend to multiple events.

What has been the impact of computers on children's social development?
Computers can promote social involvement, especially when they are used for group projects. Even when children and adolescents are on the computer alone, they are often engaged in social networking through e-mail, social networks, and instant messaging.

What controversies exist concerning children's access to computers?
Controversies exist over how to regulate access to the Internet, as some material available on it may not be suitable for children. A major unresolved issue is the extent to which children should be either educated about or monitored in the use of the Internet.

What are some of the findings associated with video game playing?
Children and adolescents, especially boys, spend considerable time playing various video games. Many, even younger children, have access to games designed for mature audiences. Excessive time spent in game playing has been associated with poorer academic achievement and with attentional problems.

Schools

What are some of the effects of classroom and school size on various aspects of development?
Some evidence exists to suggest that children enrolled in small classes and who attend smaller schools benefit socially, emotionally, and academically. For some children, these benefits may continue to be observed as they progress through school.

What factors help to promote a smooth transition to the start of school?

Children who initially demonstrate competence with respect to social behaviors and cognitive and linguistic skills tend to make smoother transitions to the start of school. Entering school with familiar peers has advantages as well.

What are the effects of the transition from elementary school to middle school or junior high school?

The transition from elementary to junior high school can be difficult for many children, especially if they experience other developmental transitions at the same time. Children may exhibit a drop in self-esteem, depression, anxiety, and greater participation in risky behaviors. The kinds of interactions that occur in the more advanced grades may be difficult for children if they feel they have little control over their academic progress or are not personally invested in succeeding in the classroom.

How well do children with emotional disturbances do in school? What factors may help them to succeed?

Children with emotional disturbances often have a difficult time in school and after leaving school. Greater absenteeism and dropping out before completing high school often accompany children with emotional disturbances. Academic and social counseling are important, but additional mental health resources and schooling experiences designed to complement their interest and skills are needed as well.

What explanations exist for violent behavior in schools?

In urban communities, school violence tends to reflect an extension of violence found in the neighborhood. In suburban and rural communities, the violence is more likely the result of a youth engaging in a "rampage." Few commonalities are shared by perpetrators, and although both adults and peers may show some signals that anticipate these actions, the signs are often not sufficiently visible to encourage others to carry out some type of intervention.

Neighborhoods

What aspects of development are known to be influenced by neighborhoods?

The neighborhoods in which children grow up have an effect on academic success, mental health, and sexual behavior. Neighborhoods influence development through the institutional resources they provide, the parenting style practiced in response to safety, the support network perceived to exist in the neighborhood, and the individual and collective efforts of community residents to supervise and monitor the development of youth.

How are low-income families and children in poverty affected by the neighborhood?

Adolescents, at least boys, benefit academically when they have the opportunity to move into neighborhoods that have fewer families in poverty. As a result of living in poverty, children have fewer opportunities to engage in a variety of extracurricular activities. They are also likely to be exposed to more polluted air and a number of other risk factors that may magnify developmental problems.

What adverse developmental outcomes do some children from affluent families display?

For some children from affluent families, high pressures to achieve, combined with lack of emotional connection to parents, are associated with depression, anxiety, and substance use.

What are some of the consequences for children and youth exposed to violence?

Posttraumatic stress disorder, depression, anxiety, and substance abuse as well as a greater tendency to enact violent behaviors are more frequently reported among children exposed to substantial amounts of violence in their neighborhood.

What are the most serious consequences for children experiencing war, and what procedures may be most effective in dealing with those consequences?

Children who witness war evidence many of the symptoms associated with PTSD, especially within the first year of their exposure. Successful interventions have involved placing children in a secure environment as well as providing support to caregivers, who have the potential to, in turn, be helpful to their children. In addition, reestablishing educational opportunities and supportive community resources benefits children from war-torn neighborhoods.

What are some consequences of natural disasters and terrorist activity for children?

Similar outcomes are associated with natural disasters as those stemming from war. PTSD and other disorders remain higher several years after the event and are reduced, in part, as a result of acquiring or retaining close friends and families who are able to provide a supportive environment. The degree of long-term problems appears to be related to the extent to which children have been exposed to previous traumatic events.

Key Terms and Concepts

computer-assisted instruction (CAI) (p. 605)

Media Resources

Access an integrated eBook and chapter-specific interactive learning tools, including flashcards, quizzes, videos, and more, in your Developmental Psychology CourseMate, accessed through CengageBrain.com.

Glossary

Accommodation In Piagetian theory, a component of adaptation; process of modification in thinking (schemes) that takes place when old ways of understanding something no longer fit.

Adaptation In Piagetian theory, the inborn tendency to adjust or become more attuned to conditions imposed by the environment; takes place through assimilation and accommodation.

Age-history confound In longitudinal studies, the co-occurrence of historical factors with changes in age; affects the ability to interpret results.

Aggression Behavior that is intentionally carried out to harm another person.

Allele Alternate form of a specific gene; provides a genetic basis for many individual differences.

Altruism Behavior carried out to help another without expectation of reward.

Ambivalent (resistant) attachment Insecure attachment in which the infant shows separation protest but also distress upon the caregiver's return.

Amniocentesis Method of sampling the fluid surrounding the developing fetus through insertion of a needle; used to diagnose fetal genetic and developmental disorders.

Amniotic sac Fluid-filled, transparent protective membrane surrounding the fetus.

Androgen Class of male or masculinizing hormones.

Anorexia nervosa An eating disorder involving self-imposed starvation.

A-not-B error Error that an infant makes when an object is hidden in location A, found by the infant, and then, in full view of the infant, moved to location B.

Assimilation In Piagetian theory, a component of adaptation; process of interpreting an experience in terms of current ways (schemes) of understanding things.

Attachment Strong emotional bond that emerges between infant and caregiver.

Attention State of alertness or arousal that allows the individual to focus on a selected aspect of the environment.

Authoritarian parent Parent who relies on coercive techniques to discipline the child and displays a low level of nurturance.

Authoritative parent Parent who sets limits on a child's behavior using reasoning and explanation and displays a high degree of nurturance.

Autobiographical memory Memory for specific events in one's own life.

Autosome One of twenty-two pairs of homologous chromosomes. The two members of each pair are similar in size, shape, and genetic function. The two sex chromosomes are excluded from this class.

Avoidant attachment Insecure attachment in which the infant shows little separation anxiety and does not pay much attention to the caregiver's return.

Babbling Consonant-vowel utterances that characterize the infant's first attempts to vocalize.

Basic emotion Emotion such as joy, sadness, or surprise that appears early in infancy and seems to have a biological foundation. Also called primary emotion.

Behavior genetics Study of how characteristics and behaviors of individuals, such as intelligence and personality, are influenced by the interaction between genotype and experience.

Behaviorism Learning theory perspective that explains the development of behavior according to the principles of classical and operant conditioning.

Bioecological model Bronfenbrenner's theory that development is influenced by experiences arising from broader biological, social, and cultural systems as well as a child's immediate surroundings.

Broca's area Portion of the cerebral cortex that controls expressive language.

Bulimia nervosa A disorder involving recurrent bouts of binge eating and food purging.

Canalization Concept that the development of some attributes is governed primarily by the genotype and that only extreme environmental conditions will alter the phenotypic pattern for these attributes.

Canonical babbling Repetition of simple consonant-vowel combinations in well-formed syllables.

Case study In-depth description of psychological characteristics and behaviors of an individual, often in the form of a narrative.

Catch-up growth Increase in growth rate after some factor, such as illness or poor nutrition, has disrupted the expected normal growth rate.

Categorical perception Inability to distinguish among sounds that vary on some basic physical dimension except when those sounds lie at opposite sides of a critical juncture point on that dimension.

Categorical self Self-classification in terms of membership in certain groups based on sex, age, skills, what one owns, where one lives, and who one's friends are.

Centration In Piagetian theory, tendency of the child to focus on only one aspect of a problem.

Cephalocaudal development Pattern in which organs, systems, and motor movements near the head tend to develop earlier than those near the feet.

Chorionic villus sampling Method of sampling fetal chorionic cells; used to diagnose embryonic genetic and developmental disorders.

Chromosome Threadlike structure of DNA, located in the nucleus of cells, which forms a collection of genes. A human body cell normally contains forty-six chromosomes.

Chronosystem In Bronfenbrenner's ecological systems theory, the constantly changing temporal component of the environment that can influence development.

Clique Peer group of three to nine same-sex children who frequently interact together.

Codominance Condition in which individual, unblended characteristics of two alleles are reflected in the phenotype.

Coercive cycle Pattern of escalating negative reciprocal interactions.

Cognition Thought processes and mental activities, including attention, memory, concept formation, and problem solving, that are evident from early infancy onward.

Cognitive-developmental theory Theoretical orientation, most frequently associated with Piaget, emphasizing the active construction of psychological structures to interpret experience.

Cohort effect All the characteristics shared by individuals growing up in a specific social and historical context.

Collaborative learning Peer-centered learning in which students work together on academic problems with the goal of arriving at solutions that are more effective than solutions that could have been derived from individual effort alone.

Computer-assisted instruction (CAI) Use of computers to provide tutorial information and drill-and-practice routines.

Concept Definition of a set of information on the basis of some general or abstract principle.

Concordance rate Percentage of pairs of twins in which both members have a specific trait identified in one twin.

Concrete operational stage In Piagetian theory, the third stage of development, from approximately seven to eleven years of age, in which thought is logical when stimuli are physically present.

Conditioned response (CR) Learned response that is exhibited to a previously neutral stimulus (CS) as a result of pairing the CS with an unconditioned stimulus (UCS).

Conditioned stimulus (CS) Neutral stimulus that begins to elicit a response similar to the unconditioned stimulus (UCS) with which it has been paired.

Conscience A regulatory mechanism involving the ability to feel moral emotions, such as guilt and empathy, and the tendency to follow rules set forth by adults.

Conservation tasks Problems that require the child to make judgments about the equivalence of two displays; used to assess stage of cognitive development.

Constraints The idea that children are biased to process information about language in limited ways.

Control theory Hypothesis about parent–child interactions suggesting that the intensity of one partner's behavior affects the intensity of the other's response.

Conventional level In Kohlberg's theory, the second level of moral reasoning, in which the child conforms to the norms of the majority and wishes to preserve the social order.

Cooing Vowel-like utterances that characterize the infant's first attempts to vocalize.

Cooperative learning Peer-centered learning experience in which students work together in small groups to promote the learning of each group member.

Core knowledge theory The idea that infants possess innate knowledge of certain properties of objects, as well as other basic concepts.

Correlation coefficient (*r*) Statistical measure, ranging from +1.00 to −1.00, that summarizes the strength and direction of the relationship between two variables; does not provide information about causation.

Correlational study Study that assesses whether changes in one variable are accompanied by systematic changes in another variable.

Cross-cultural study Study that compares individuals in different cultural contexts.

Cross-gender behavior Behavior usually seen in a member of the opposite sex. Term generally is reserved for behavior that is persistently sex atypical.

Crossing over Process during the first stage of meiosis when genetic material is exchanged between autosomes.

Cross-sectional study Study in which individuals of different ages are examined at the same point in time.

Crowd Large group of peers characterized by specific traits or reputation.

Crystallized intelligence Mental skills derived from cultural experience.

Debriefing Providing research participants with a statement of the true goals of a study after initially deceiving them or omitting information about its purposes.

Deferred imitation Ability to imitate a model's behavior hours, days, and even weeks after observation.

Delay of gratification Capacity to wait before performing a tempting activity or attaining some highly desired outcome; a measure of ability to regulate one's own behavior.

Deoxyribonucleic acid (DNA) Long, spiral staircase-like sequence of molecules created by nucleotides identified with the blueprint for genetic inheritance.

Dependent variable Behavior that is measured; suspected effect of an experimental manipulation.

Development Physical and psychological changes in the individual over a lifetime.

Developmental psychology Systematic and scientific study of changes in human behaviors and mental activities over time.

Developmental science The interdisciplinary field of research and theories concerned with studies and explanations of human development.

Deviation IQ IQ score computed by comparing the child's performance with that of a standardization sample.

Disorganized/disoriented attachment Infant-caregiver relations characterized by the infant's fear of the caregiver, confused facial expressions, and a combination of avoidant and ambivalent attachment behaviors.

Display rules The cultural guidelines governing when, how, and to what degree to display emotions.

Dominant allele Allele whose characteristics are reflected in the phenotype even when part of a heterozygous genotype. Its genetic characteristics tend to mask the characteristics of other alleles.

Down syndrome Disorder resulting from extra chromosomal material on pair number twenty-one; associated with intellectual impairment and distinct physical features.

Dynamic systems theory Theoretical orientation that explains development as the emerging organization arising from the interaction of many different processes.

Effectance motivation Inborn desire theorized to be the basis for the infant's and child's efforts to master and gain control of the environment.

Effortful control Ability to suppress undesirable responses for less dominant ones that are considered socially or morally more acceptable.

Egocentrism Preoperational child's inability to separate his or her own perspective from those of others.

Elicited imitation Method in which older infants and preschoolers must repeat a sequence of actions demonstrated by the experimenter.

Embryo Label typically applied to the developing organism from about two to eight weeks after conception.

Embryonic period Period of prenatal development during which major biological organs and systems form; begins about the tenth to fourteenth day after conception and ends about the eighth week after conception.

Emotions Complex behaviors involving physiological, expressive, and experiential components produced in response to some external or internal event.

Empathy Understanding and sharing of the feelings of others.

Empiricism Theory that environmental experiences shape the individual; more specifically, that all knowledge is derived from sensory experiences.

Epigenetics The field of study concerned with how environmental factors interact with DNA and its transcription into mRNA to influence cell functioning and the phenotype.

Episodic memory Memory for events that took place at a specific time and place.

Equilibration In Piagetian theory, an innate self-regulatory process that, through accommodation and assimilation, results in more organized and powerful schemes for adapting to the environment.

Ethnic identity The sense of belonging to a particular cultural group.

Ethnography Set of methods, including observations and interviews, used by researchers to describe the behaviors and underlying meaning systems within a given culture.

Ethology Theoretical orientation and discipline concerned with the evolutionary origins of behavior and its adaptive and survival value in animals, including humans.

Executive function Portion of the information-processing system that coordinates various component processes in order to achieve some goal.

Exosystem In Bronfenbrenner's ecological systems theory, environmental settings that indirectly affect the child by influencing the various microsystems forming the child's immediate environment.

Expansion Repetition of a child's utterance along with a more complex form.

Experimental design Research method in which one or more independent variables are manipulated to determine the effect on other, dependent variables.

Explicit memory Conscious recollection of a past event or experience.

Expressive aphasia Loss of the ability to speak fluently.

Expressive characteristics Characteristics associated with emotions or relationships with people; usually considered feminine.

Expressive style Type of early language production in which the child uses many social words.

External validity The ability to generalize the findings of a study to other situations, contexts, or individuals.

Externality effect Tendency for infants younger than two months to focus on the external features of a complex stimulus and explore the internal features less systematically.

Externalizing An emotional style that is outward-directed and results in behavioral manifestations such as aggression or temper tantrums.

Failure to thrive Designation for a child whose growth in height or weight is below the third percentile for children of the same age.

False belief The child's mistaken understanding that a naïve or uninformed observer has the same information (and thus the same beliefs) as the child.

Fast-mapping Process through which the context in which the child hears words spoken provides the key to their meanings.

Fetal alcohol syndrome (FAS) Cluster of fetal abnormalities stemming from the mother's consumption of alcohol; includes growth retardation, defects in facial features, and intellectual retardation.

Fetal blood sampling Method of withdrawing blood from the umbilical cord of the fetus; used to diagnose genetic disorders, especially those that affect the blood.

Fetal monitoring device Medical device used to monitor fetal heartbeat during delivery.

Fetal period Period of prenatal development, from about the eighth week after conception to birth, marked by rapid growth and preparation of body systems for functioning in the postnatal environment.

Fetus Label typically applied to the developing human organism from about eight weeks after conception until birth.

Field experiment Study in which the experimental manipulations are carried out in a natural setting.

Fluid intelligence Biologically based mental abilities that are relatively uninfluenced by cultural experiences.

Formal operational stage In Piagetian theory, the last stage of development, from approximately eleven to fifteen years of age, in which thought is abstract and hypothetical.

Fragile X syndrome Disorder associated with a pinched region of the X chromosome; a leading genetic cause of intellectual impairment in males.

Fraternal (dizygotic) twins Siblings who share the same womb at the same time but originate from two different eggs fertilized by two different sperm cells.

Gamete Sperm cell in males, egg cell in females, normally containing only twenty-three chromosomes.

Gender constancy Knowledge, usually gained around age six or seven years, that one's gender does not change as a result of alterations in appearance, behaviors, or desires.

Gender identity Knowledge, usually gained by age three years, that one is male or female.

Gender schema Cognitive organizing structure for information relevant to sex typing.

Gender stability Knowledge, usually gained by age four years, that one's gender does not change over time.

Gender stereotypes Expectations or beliefs that individuals within a given culture hold about the behaviors characteristic of males and females.

Gender-role development Process by which individuals acquire the characteristics and behaviors prescribed by their culture for their sex. Also called *sex typing.*

Gene Large segment of nucleotides within a chromosome that codes for the production of proteins and enzymes. These proteins and enzymes underlie traits and characteristics inherited from one generation to the next.

Genetic counseling Medical and counseling specialty concerned with determining and communicating the likelihood that prospective parents will give birth to a baby with a genetic disorder.

Genetic screening Systematic search using a variety of tests to detect the likelihood of increased developmental risk due to genetic or other anomalies.

Genomic imprinting Instances of genetic transmission in which the expression of a gene is determined by whether the particular allelic form has been inherited from the mother or the father.

Genotype Total genetic endowment inherited by an individual.

Germinal period Period lasting about ten to fourteen days following conception before the fertilized egg becomes implanted in the uterine wall. Also called *period of the zygote.*

Gestational age Age of fetus derived from onset of mother's last menstrual period.

Glial cell Brain cell that provides a scaffolding for neuron migration and that nourishes neurons and assists in the production of myelin.

Grammar Rules pertaining to the structure of language.

Guided participation Process by which a skilled collaborator transfers knowledge to a learner by providing support and gradually withdrawing it.

Habituation Gradual decline in the intensity, frequency, or duration of a response over repeated or lengthy occurrences of the same stimulus.

Heritability Proportion of variability in the phenotype that is estimated to be accounted for by genetic influences within a known environmental range.

Heterozygous Genotype in which two alleles of a gene are different. The effects on a trait will depend on how the two alleles interact.

Homozygous Genotype in which two alleles of a gene are identical, thus having the same effects on a trait.

Hormones Chemical secreted by various glands directly into the bloodstream and circulated to influence cells in other locations of the body.

Human genome Entire inventory of nucleotide base pairs that compose the genes and chromosomes of humans.

Hypothetical reasoning Ability to systematically generate and evaluate potential solutions to a problem.

Identical (monozygotic) twins Two individuals who originate from a single zygote (one egg fertilized by one sperm), which early in cell division separates to form two separate cell masses.

Identity (personal) Broad, coherent, internalized view of who a person is and wants to be, and what a person believes and values, that emerges during adolescence.

Identity crisis Period, usually during adolescence, characterized by considerable uncertainty about the self and the role the individual is to fulfill in society.

Identity In Eriksonian psychosocial theory, the acceptance of both self and society, a concept that must be achieved at every stage but is especially important during adolescence.

Immanent justice Young child's belief that punishment will inevitably follow a transgression.

Implicit learning Learning abstract or correlated relationships among complex events without conscious awareness.

Implicit memory Nonconscious recollections of how to do something behaviorally.

Imprinting Form of learning, difficult to reverse, during a sensitive period in development in which an organism tends to stay near a particular stimulus.

Independent variable Variable manipulated by the experimenter; the suspected cause.

Individual differences Unique characteristics that distinguish a person from other members of a larger group.

Induction Parental technique that relies on the extensive use of reasoning and explanation, as well as the arousal of empathic feelings to influence behavior.

Infant-directed speech (parentese) Simple, repetitive, high-pitched speech of caregivers to young children; includes many questions.

Infantile amnesia Failure to remember events from the first two to three years of one's life.

Information processing Theoretical approach that views humans as having a limited ability to process information, much like computers.

Informed consent Participant's formal acknowledgment that he or she understands the purposes, procedures, and risks of a study, and agrees to participate in it.

In-group preferences Children's tendency to display more positive behaviors to members of their own social group or category.

Inner speech Interiorized form of private speech.

Instrumental aggression Behavior motivated to obtain some concrete object or goal and that causes potential or real physical harm to another. Sometimes called proactive aggression.

Instrumental characteristics Characteristics associated with acting on the world; usually considered masculine.

Instrumental competence Child's display of independence, self-control, achievement orientation, and cooperation.

Intelligence quotient (IQ) Numerical score received on an intelligence test.

Interactive synchrony Reciprocal, mutually engaging cycles of caregiver–child behaviors.

Interagent consistency Consistency in application of disciplinary strategies among various caregivers.

Intermodal perception Coordination of sensory information to perceive or make inferences about the characteristics of an object.

Internal validity The ability to draw cause-and-effect conclusions by controlling for extraneous variables in an experimental study.

Internal working models of relationships Mental frameworks of the quality of relationships with others, developed as a result of early ongoing interactions with caregivers.

Internalizing An emotional style that is inner-directed and results in emotions such as guilt or sadness.

Intersubjectivity Mutual attention and shared communication that take place between two individuals.

Intra-agent consistency Consistency in a single caregiver's application of discipline from one situation to the next.

Joint attention Episodes in which the child and another individual share the same psychological space as they encounter experiences in the world.

Judgment bias Tendency to be influenced by inappropriate information at the expense of important and perhaps more relevant facts.

Karyotype Pictorial representation of an individual's chromosomes.

Kinetic cues Perceptual information provided by the movement of objects in the environment or changes in the positioning of the eyes, head, or body. Important source of information for depth perception.

Lagging-down growth Decrease in growth rate after some factor, such as a congenital or hormonal disorder, has accelerated the expected normal growth rate.

Lateralization Process by which one hemisphere of the brain comes to dominate the other; for example, processing of language in the left hemisphere or of spatial information in the right hemisphere.

Learned helplessness Belief that one has little control over situations, perhaps because of lack of ability or inconsistent outcomes.

Learning Relatively permanent change in behavior as a result of such experiences as exploration, observation, and practice.

Limited-resource model Information-processing model that emphasizes the allocation of finite energy within the cognitive system.

Longitudinal study Research in which the same participants are repeatedly tested over a period of time, usually years.

Long-term memory Memory that holds information for extended periods of time.

Low birth weight (LBW) The label often given to any infant weighing less than 2,500 grams (or five and a half pounds) at birth.

Macrosystem In Bronfenbrenner's ecological systems theory, major historical events and the broad values, practices, and customs shared by a culture.

Mastery orientation Belief that achievements are based on one's own efforts rather than luck or other factors beyond one's control.

Maternal blood screening Tests performed on a woman's blood to determine whether the fetus she is carrying has an increased risk for some types of chromosomal and metabolic disorders.

Meiosis Process of cell division that forms the gametes; normally results in twenty-three chromosomes in each human egg and sperm cell rather than the full complement of forty-six.

Memory span Number of stimulus items that can be recalled after a brief interval of time.

Memory strategy Mental activity, such as rehearsal, that enhances memory performance.

Menarche First occurrence of menstruation.

Mesosystem In Bronfenbrenner's ecological systems theory, the environment provided by the interrelationships among the various settings of the microsystem.

Meta-analysis Statistical examination of a body of research studies to assess the effect of the common central variable.

Metalinguistic awareness Ability to reflect on language as a communication tool and on the self as a user of language.

Metamemory The child's understanding of his or her own memory.

Metaphor Figurative language in which a term is transferred from the object it customarily designates to describe a comparable object or event.

Microgenetic study A research approach in which close observations are made of the individual child's behavior from one trial to the next.

Microsystem In Bronfenbrenner's ecological systems theory, the immediate environment provided in such settings as the home, school, workplace, and neighborhood.

Mitosis Process of cell division that takes place in most cells of the human body and results in a full complement of identical material in the forty-six chromosomes in each cell.

Moral realism In Piaget's theory of moral development, the first stage of moral reasoning, in which moral judgments are made on the basis of the consequences of an act. Also called *heteronomy.*

Moral relativism In Piaget's theory of moral development, the second stage of moral reasoning, in which moral judgments are made on the basis of the actor's intentions. Also called *autonomy.*

Morality of care and responsibility Tendency to make moral judgments on the basis of concern for others.

Morality of justice Tendency to make moral judgments on the basis of reason and abstract principles of equity.

Morphology Rules of how to combine the smallest meaningful units of language to form words.

Multistore model Information-processing model that describes a sequence of mental structures through which information flows.

Mutation Sudden change in molecular structure of a gene; may occur spontaneously or be caused by an environmental event such as radiation.

Mutual exclusivity bias Tendency for children to assume that unfamiliar words label new objects.

Myelin Sheath of fatty cells that insulates and speeds neural impulses by about tenfold.

Naturalistic observation Study in which observations of naturally occurring behavior are made in real-life settings.

Nature-nurture debate Historically, the theoretical controversy over whether development is the result of the child's genetic endowment or environmental influences.

Negative correlation Relationship in which changes in one variable are accompanied by systematic changes in another variable in the opposite direction.

Negative punishment Removal or loss of a desired stimulus or reward, which weakens or decreases the frequency of a preceding response.

Negative reinforcement Removal of an aversive stimulus, which strengthens a preceding response.

Neuron Nerve cell within the central nervous system that is electrochemically designed to transmit messages between cells.

Niche picking Tendency to actively select an environment compatible with a genotype.

Norm Quantitative measure that provides typical values and variations in such characteristics as height and weight for children.

Nucleotide Repeating basic building block of DNA consisting of nitrogen-based molecules of adenine, thymine, cytosine, and guanine.

Object permanence Realization that objects exist even when they are not within view. Also called *object concept.*

Observational learning Learning that takes place by simply observing another person's behavior.

Observer bias Tendency of researchers to interpret ongoing events as being consistent with their research hypotheses.

Operation In Piagetian theory, a mental action such as reversibility.

Operational definition Specification of variables in terms of measurable properties.

Organization In Piagetian theory, the inborn tendency for structures and processes to become more systematic and coherent.

Overextension Tendency to apply a label to a broader category than the term actually signifies.

Overregularization Inappropriate application of grammatical rules to words that require exceptions to those rules.

Participant reactivity Tendency of individuals who know they are under observation to alter natural behavior.

Peer Companion of approximately the same age and developmental level.

Perception Process of organizing and interpreting sensory information.

Perceptual differentiation Process postulated by Eleanor and James Gibson in which experience contributes to the ability to make increasingly finer perceptual discriminations and to distinguish stimulation arising from each sensory modality.

Perinatal period Period beginning about the seventh month of pregnancy and continuing until about four weeks after birth.

Permissive parent Parent who sets few limits on the child's behavior.

Phenotype Observable and measurable characteristics and traits of an individual; a product of the interaction of the genotype with the environment.

Phenylketonuria (PKU) Recessive genetic disorder in which phenylalanine, an amino acid, fails to be metabolized. Unless dietary changes are made to reduce intake of phenylalanine, severe intellectual impairment occurs.

Phoneme Smallest unit of sound that changes the meanings of words.

Phonology Fundamental sound units and combinations of units in a given language.

Placenta Support organ formed by cells from both blastocyst and uterine lining; serves as exchange site for oxygen, nutrients, and waste products.

Plasticity Capacity of immature systems, including regions of the brain and the individual neurons within those regions, to take on different functions as a result of experience.

Polygenic Phenotypic characteristic influenced by two or more genes.

Positive correlation Relationship in which changes in one variable are accompanied by systematic changes in another variable in the same direction.

Positive punishment Occurrence of an aversive stimulus that serves to weaken or decrease the frequency of a preceding response.

Positive reinforcement Occurrence of a stimulus that strengthens a preceding response. Also known as a *reward.*

Postconventional level In Kohlberg's theory, the third level of moral reasoning, in which laws are seen as the result of a social contract and individual principles of conscience may emerge.

Postnatal period Period in development following birth.

Posttraumatic stress disorder (PTSD) A response to extreme stress characterized by sleep disturbances, bodily complaints, and depression.

Power assertion Parental technique that relies on the use of forceful commands, physical punishment, and removal of material objects or privileges to influence behavior.

Pragmatics Rules for using language effectively within a social context.

Preconventional level In Kohlberg's theory, the first level of moral reasoning, in which morality is motivated by the avoidance of punishments and attainment of rewards.

Prenatal diagnostic tests Procedures designed to provide unequivocal answers about the presence or absence of a prenatal problem.

Prenatal period Period in development from conception to the onset of labor.

Preoperational stage In Piagetian theory, the second stage of development, from approximately two to seven years of age, in which thought becomes symbolic in form.

Prepared (natural) childbirth Type of childbirth that involves practicing procedures during pregnancy and childbirth that are designed to minimize pain and reduce the need for medication during delivery.

Preterm Any infant born prior to thirty-five weeks conceptual age (thirty-seven weeks gestational age).

Primary reinforcer Reward that gratifies biological needs or drives.

Private speech Children's vocalized speech to themselves that directs behavior.

Processing speed Rapidity with which cognitive activities are carried out.

Productive language Meaningful language spoken or otherwise produced by an individual.

Prosocial behavior Positive social action performed to benefit others.

Prosody Patterns of intonation, stress, and rhythm that communicate meaning in speech.

Proximodistal development Pattern in which organs and systems of the body near the middle tend to develop earlier than those near the periphery.

Psychometric model Theoretical perspective that quantifies individual differences in test scores to establish a rank order of abilities.

Psychosocial theory of development Erikson's theory that personality develops through eight stages of adaptive functioning to meet the demands framed by society.

Puberty Developmental period during which a sequence of physical changes takes place that transforms the person from an immature individual to one capable of reproduction.

Quasi-experiment Study in which researchers investigate the effects of independent variables that they do not manipulate themselves but that occur as a result of participants' natural experiences.

Questionnaire Set of standardized questions administered to participants in written form.

Random assignment Use of principles of chance to assign participants to treatment and control groups; avoids systematic bias.

Range of reaction Range of phenotypic differences possible as a result of different environments interacting with a specific genotype.

Realism Inability to distinguish between mental and physical entities.

Recall memory Ability to reproduce stimuli that one has previously encountered.

Recast Repetition of a child's utterance along with grammatical corrections.

Receptive aphasia Loss of the ability to comprehend speech.

Receptive language Ability to comprehend spoken speech.

Recessive allele Allele whose characteristics do not tend to be expressed when part of a heterozygous genotype. Its genetic characteristics tend to be masked by other alleles.

Recognition memory Ability to identify whether a stimulus has previously been encountered.

Recovery from habituation (dishabituation) Renewed response to a change in a stimulus, which indicates that the infant has detected that change.

Referential communication Communication in situations that require the child to describe an object to a listener or evaluate the effectiveness of a message.

Referential style Type of early language production in which the child uses mostly nominals.

Reflex Involuntary reaction to touch, light, sound, and other kinds of stimulation.

Regression analysis A correlation-based statistical technique that allows researchers to make predictions about outcome variables based on one or more predictor variables.

Relational aggression Behavior motivated to hurt another's feelings. Sometimes called indirect, covert, or social aggression.

Reliability Degree to which a measure will yield the same results if administered repeatedly.

Representational insight The child's ability to understand that a symbol or model can stand for a real-life event.

Reunion behavior The child's style of greeting the caregiver after a separation.

Rough-and-tumble play Active, physical play that carries no intent of imposing harm on another child.

Saccades Rapid eye movement to inspect an object or view a stimulus in the periphery of the visual target.

Scaffolding Temporary aid provided by one person to encourage, support, and assist a lesser-skilled person in carrying out a task or completing a problem. The model provides knowledge and skills that are learned and gradually transferred to the learner.

Scheme In Piagetian theory, the mental structure underlying a coordinated and systematic pattern of behaviors or thinking applied across similar objects or situations.

Scientific method Use of objective, measurable, and repeatable techniques to gather information.

Script Organized scheme or framework for commonly experienced events.

Secondary reinforcer Object or person that attains rewarding value because of its association with a primary reinforcer.

Secular trends Consistent pattern of change over generations.

Secure attachment Attachment category defined by the infant's distress at separation from the caregiver and enthusiastic greeting upon his or her return. The infant also displays stranger anxiety and uses the caregiver as a secure base for exploration.

Secure base An attachment behavior in which the infant explores the environment but periodically checks back with the caregiver.

Self esteem One's feelings of worth; extent to which and individual senses one's attributes and actions as good, desired, and valued.

Self-concept Perception, conceptions, and values one holds about oneself.

Self-conscious emotion Emotion such as guilt and envy that appears later in childhood and requires knowledge about the self as related to others.

Self-regulation Capacity to monitor, direct, and flexibly adapt one's behaviors and activities to achieve certain goals or meet the demands imposed by others.

Self-socialization Children's tendency to seek out information about gender and comply with norms for gendered behavior once they have achieved an understanding of the concept of gender.

Semantic bootstrapping hypothesis Idea that children derive information about syntax from the meaning of words.

Semantic memory Memory for general concepts or facts.

Semantics Meanings of words or combinations of words.

Sensation Basic information in the external world that is processed by the sensory receptors.

Sensitive period Brief period during which specific kinds of experiences have significant positive or negative consequences for development and behavior; also called *critical period.*

Sensorimotor stage In Piagetian theory, the first stage of cognitive development, from birth to approximately two years of age, in which thought is based primarily on action.

Sensory register Memory store that holds information for very brief periods of time in a form that closely resembles the initial input.

Separation anxiety Distress the infant shows when the caregiver leaves the immediate environment.

Sequential study Study that examines groups of individuals of different ages over a period of time; usually shorter than a longitudinal study.

Sex segregation Clustering of individuals into same-sex groups.

Sex typicality Extent to which a behavior is usually associated with one sex as opposed to the other.

Sexually transmitted infections (STIs) A group of infections such as chlamydia, syphilis, gonorrhea, herpes simplex, HIV, and hepatitis B often spread through sexual contact. Also frequently called sexually transmitted diseases (STDs).

Shape bias The child's assumption that a new word labels an entire object, specifically its form.

Sickle cell disease Genetic blood disorder common in regions of Africa and other areas where malaria is found and among descendants of the people of these regions. Abnormal blood cells carry insufficient oxygen.

Sickle cell trait Symptoms shown by those possessing a heterozygous genotype for sickle cell anemia.

Single-case design Study that follows only one or a few participants over a period of time, with an emphasis on systematic collection of data.

Skeletal maturity Extent to which cartilage has ossified to form bone; provides estimate of how much additional growth will take place.

Small for gestational age (SGA) Any infant that displays intrauterine growth retardation, that is, weighs substantially less than infants born at a similar gestational age.

Smooth visual pursuit Consistent, unbroken tracking by the eyes, which serves to maintain focus on a moving visual target.

Social cognition Thinking processes and representations that are relevant to the social world.

Social comparison Process of defining oneself in relation to the skills, attributes, and qualities of others.

Social competence The ability to function well with others while still achieving one's own personal goals.

Social conventions Behavioral rules that regulate social interactions, such as dress codes and degrees of formality in speech.

Social learning theory Theoretical approach emphasizing the importance of learning through observation and imitation of behaviors modeled by others.

Social policy Programs and plans established by local, regional, or national public and private organizations and agencies designed to achieve a particular social purpose or goal.

Social pretend play Play that makes use of imaginary and symbolic objects and social roles, often enacted among several children. Also called *sociodramatic play* and *symbolic play.*

Social referencing Looking to another individual for emotional cues in interpreting a strange or ambiguous event.

Socialization Process by which children acquire the social knowledge, skills, and attitudes valued by the larger society.

Sociocultural theory Vygotsky's developmental theory emphasizing the importance of cultural tools, symbols, and ways of thinking that the child acquires from more knowledgeable members of the community.

Sociometric nomination Peer assessment measure in which children are asked to name a specific number of peers who fit a certain criterion, such as "peers you would like to walk home with."

Sociometric rating scale Peer assessment measure in which children rate peers on a number of social dimensions.

Sound localization Ability to determine a sound's point of origin.

Spermarche The first ejaculation of sperm by males entering puberty.

Stage Developmental period during which the organization of thought and behavior is qualitatively different from that of an earlier or later period.

Statistical learning The ability to discern the probability that one event follows another.

Stereopsis The ability to fuse the two distinct images from the eyes to perceive a single object.

Stereotype threat The psychological impact of negative social stereotypes in an individual.

Strange Situation Standardized test that assesses the quality of infant-caregiver attachment.

Stranger anxiety Fear or distress an infant shows at the approach of an unfamiliar person.

Structured interview Standardized set of questions administered orally to participants.

Structured observation Study in which behaviors are recorded as they occur within a situation constructed by the experimenter, usually in the laboratory.

Sudden infant death syndrome (SIDS) Sudden, unexplained death of an infant or toddler as a result of cessation of breathing during sleep.

Synaptic pruning The process by which weaker or less active dendrites of neurons are eliminated.

Syntax Grammatical rules that dictate how words can be combined.

Systems theory Model for understanding the family that emphasizes the reciprocal interactions among various members.

Systems views Theories of development that are concerned with the effects of a broad range of biological, physical, and sociocultural settings on the process of development.

Taxonomic constraint Tendency for children to assume that novel words label members of the same conceptual category.

Telegraphic speech Early two-word speech that contains few modifiers, prepositions, or other connective words.

Temperament Stable, early-appearing constellation of individual personality attributes believed to have a hereditary basis; includes sociability, emotionality, and activity level.

Teratogen Any environmental agent that can cause deviations in prenatal development. Consequences may range from behavioral problems to death.

Test bias Idea that the content of traditional standardized tests does not adequately measure the competencies of children from diverse cultural backgrounds.

Theories Sets of ideas or propositions that help to organize or explain observable phenomena.

Theory of mind Awareness of the concept of mental states, both one's own and those of others.

Transfer Ability to employ the solution to one problem in other, similar problems.

Triarchic theory Theory developed by Robert Sternberg that intelligence consists of three major components: (1) the ability to adapt to the environment, (2) the ability to employ fundamental information-processing skills, and (3) the ability to deal with novelty and automatize processing.

Tiresome Inheritance of extra chromosome.

Turn taking Alternating vocalization by parent and child.

Turnabout Element of conversation that requests a response from the child.

Ultrasonography Method of using sound wave reflections to obtain a representation of the developing fetus; used to estimate gestational age and detect fetal physical abnormalities.

Umbilical cord Conduit of blood vessels through which oxygen, nutrients, and waste products are transported between placenta and embryo.

Unconditioned response (UCR) Response that is automatically elicited by the unconditioned stimulus (UCS).

Unconditioned stimulus (UCS) Stimulus that, without prior training, elicits a reflexlike response (unconditioned response).

Underextension Application of a label to a narrower class of objects than the term signifies.

Uninvolved parent Parent who is emotionally detached from the child and focuses on his or her own needs as opposed to the child's.

Validity Degree to which an assessment procedure actually measures the variable under consideration.

Variable Factor having no fixed or constant value in a given situation.

Vergence Ability of the eyes to rotate in opposite directions to fixate on objects at different distances; improves rapidly during first few months after birth.

Viability Ability of the baby to survive outside the mother's womb.

Visual accommodation Visuomotor process by which small involuntary muscles change the shape of the lens of the eye so that images of objects seen at different distances are brought into focus on the retina.

Visual acuity Ability to make fine discriminations among elements in a visual array by detecting contours, transitions in light patterns that signal borders and edges.

Visual cliff Experimental apparatus used to test depth perception, in which the surface on one side of a glass-covered table is made to appear far below the surface on the other side.

Vocabulary spurt Period of rapid word acquisition that typically occurs early in language development.

Wernicke's area Portion of the cerebral cortex that controls language comprehension.

Williams syndrome Dominant genetic disorder involving the deletion of a set of genes, which results in affected individuals' typically having a strong social orientation, good musical ability, and some unusual linguistic capabilities; accompanied by intellectual impairment and severe deficits in numerical and spatial ability.

Working (or short-term) memory Short-term memory store in which mental operations such as rehearsal and categorization take place.

X chromosome Larger of the two sex chromosomes associated with genetic determination of sex. Normally females have two X chromosomes and males, only one.

Y chromosome Smaller of the two sex chromosomes associated with genetic determination of sex. Normally males have one Y chromosome and females, none.

Zone of proximal development Range of various kinds of support and assistance provided by an expert (usually an adult) who helps children to carry out activities they currently cannot complete but will later be able to accomplish independently.

Zygote Fertilized egg cell.

References

Aagaard-Tillery, K. M., Porter, T. F., Lane, R. H., Varner, M. W., & Lacoursiere, D. W. (2008). In utero tobacco exposure is associated with modified effects of maternal factors on fetal growth. *American Journal of Obstetrics and Gynecology, 198,* 66.e1–66.e6.

Aarnoudse-Moens, C. S. H., Wiesglas-Kuperus, N., van Goudoever, J. B., & Oosterlaan, J. (2009). Meta-analysis of neurobehavioral outcomes in very preterm and/or very low birth weight children. *Pediatrics, 124,* 717–728.

Abbassi, V. (1998). Growth and normal puberty. *Pediatrics, 102,* 507–511.

Abel, E. L. (1989). *Behavioral teratogenesis and behavioral mutagenesis: A primer in abnormal development.* New York, NY: Plenum Press.

Abramovitch, R., & Grusec, J. E. (1978). Peer imitation in a natural setting. *Child Development, 49,* 60–65.

Abramovitz, B. A., & Birch, L. L. (2000). Five-year-old girls' ideas about dieting are predicted by their mothers' dieting. *Journal of the American Dietetic Association, 100,* 1157–1163

Acevedo-Polakovich, I., Lorch, E. P., & Milich, R. (2007). Comparing television use and reading in children with ADHD and non-referred children across two age groups. *Media Psychology, 9,* 447–472.

Achenbach, T. M., Howell, C. T., Aoki, M. F., & Rauh, V. A. (1993). Nine-year outcome of the Vermont Intervention Program for Low Birth Weight Infants. *Pediatrics, 91,* 45–55.

Ackerman, B. P., Abe, J. A., & Izard, C. E. (1998). Differential emotions theory and emotional development. In M. F. Mascolo & S. Griffin (Eds.), *What develops in emotional development?* (pp. 85–106). New York, NY: Plenum.

Acredolo, L. P., & Goodwyn, S. W. (1988). Symbolic gesturing in normal infants. *Child Development, 59,* 450–466.

Acredolo, L. P., & Goodwyn, S.W. (1990a). Sign language among hearing infants: The spontaneous development of symbolic gestures. In V. Volterra & C. J. Erting (Eds.), *From gesture to language in hearing and deaf children* (pp. 68–78). New York, NY: Springer-Verlag.

Acredolo, L. P., & Goodwyn, S.W. (1990b). Sign language in babies: The significance of symbolic gesturing for understanding language development. In R. Vasta (Ed.), *Annals of child development* (Vol. 7, pp. 1–42). Greenwich, CT: JAI Press.

Adams, R. J., & Courage, M. L. (1998). Human newborn color vision: Measurement with chromatic stimuli varying in excitation purity. *Journal of Experimental Child Psychology, 68,* 22–34.

Adams, S., Kuebli, J., Boyle, P. A., & Fivush, R. (1995). Gender differences in parent-child conversations about past emotions: A longitudinal investigation. *Sex Roles, 33,* 309–323.

Adler, S. A., Gerhardstein, P., & Rovee-Collier, C. (1998). Levels-of-processing effects in infant memory? *Child Development, 69,* 280–294.

Adler, S. P. (1992). Cytomegalovirus and pregnancy. *Current Opinions in Obstetrics and Gynecology, 4,* 670–675.

Adolph, K. E. (1997). Learning in the development of infant locomotion. *Monographs of the Society for Research in Child Development, 62* (3, Serial No. 251).

Adolph, K. E. (2000). Specificity of learning: Why infants fall over a veritable cliff. *Psychological Science, 11,* 290–295.

Adolph, K. E. (2008). Learning to move. *Current Directions in Psychological Science, 17,* 213–218.

Adrián, J. E., Clemente, R. A., & Villanueva, L. (2007). Mothers' use of cognitive state verbs in picture-book reading and the development of children's understanding of mind: A longitudinal study. *Child Development, 78,* 1052–1067.

Agras, W. S., Hammer, L. D., McNicholas, F., & Kraemer, H. C. (2004). Risk factors for childhood overweight: A prospective study from birth to 9.5 years. *Journal of Pediatrics, 145,* 20–25.

Ahmed, A., & Ruffman, T. (1998). Why do infants make A not B errors in a search task, yet show memory for location of hidden objects in a nonsearch task? *Developmental Psychology, 34,* 441–453.

Ahnert, L., Rickert, H., & Lamb, M. E. (2000). Shared caregiving: Comparisons between home and child-care settings. *Developmental Psychology, 36,* 339–351.

Aikins, J. W., Bierman, K. L., & Parker, J. G. (2005). Navigating the transition to junior high school: The influence of pre-transition friendship and self-system characteristics. *Social Development, 14,* 42–60.

Ainsworth, M. D. S., Bell, S. M., & Stayton, D. J. (1971). Individual differences in Strange Situation behavior of one-year-olds. In H. R. Schaffer (Ed.), *The origins of human social relations* (pp. 17–57). London, UK: Academic Press.

Ainsworth, M. D. S., Bell, S. M., & Stayton, D. J. (1972). Individual differences in the development of some attachment behaviors. *Merrill-Palmer Quarterly, 18,* 123–143.

Ainsworth, M. D. S., Bell, S. M., & Stayton, D. J. (1974). Infant-mother attachment and social development: "Socialization" as a product of reciprocal responsiveness to signals. In M. R. Richards (Ed.), *The integration of the child into a social world* (pp. 99–135). London, UK: Cambridge University Press.

Ainsworth, M. D. S., Blehar, M. C., Waters, E., & Wall, S. (1978). *Patterns of attachment: A psychological study of the strange situation.* Hillsdale, NJ: Erlbaum.

Akhtar, N., Carpenter, M., & Tomasello, M. (1996). The role of discourse novelty in early word learning. *Child Development, 67,* 635–645.

Akhtar, N., Jipson, J., & Callanan, M. A. (2001). Learning words through overhearing. *Child Development, 72,* 416–430.

Aksan, N., & Kochanska, G. (2005). Conscience in childhood: Old questions, new answers. *Developmental Psychology, 41,* 506–516.

Alaimo, K., Olson, C. M., & Frongillo, E. A., Jr. (2001). Food insufficiency and American school-aged children's cognitive, academic, and psychosocial development. *Pediatrics, 108,* 44–53.

Alessandri, S. M., & Lewis, M. (1993). Parental evaluation and its relation to shame and pride in young children. *Sex Roles, 29,* 335–343.

Alexander, G. R., Kogan, M., Bader, D., Carlo, W., Allen, M., & Mor, J. (2003). U.S. birth weight/gestational age-specific neonatal mortality: 1995–1997 rates for whites, Hispanics, and blacks. *Pediatrics, 111,* e61–e66.

Alexander, J. M., Carr, M., & Schwanenflugel, P. J. (1995). Development of metacognition in gifted children: Directions for future research. *Developmental Review, 15,* 1–37.

Alexander, K. L., & Entwisle, D. R. (1988). Achievement in the first 2 years of school: Patterns and processes. *Monographs of the Society for Research in Child Development, 53* (2, Serial No. 218).

Alexander, K. L., Entwisle, D. R., & Bedinger, S. D. (1994). When expectations work: Race and socioeconomic differences in school performance. *Social Psychology Quarterly, 57,* 283–299.

Alfieri, T., Ruble, D. N., & Higgins, E. T. (1996). Gender stereotypes during adolescence: Developmental changes and the transition to junior high school. *Developmental Psychology, 32,* 1129–1137.

Allaire, A. D. (2001). Complementary and alternative medicine in the labor and delivery suite. *Clinical Obstetrics and Gynecology, 44,* 681–691.

Allen, D. B. (2006). Growth hormone therapy for short stature: Is the benefit worth the burden? *Pediatrics, 118,* 343–348.

Allen, J. P., Philliber, S., Herrling, S., & Kuperminc, G. P. (1997). Preventing teen pregnancy and academic failure: Experimental evaluation of a developmentally based approach. *Child Development, 64,* 729–742.

Allen, J. P., Porter, M., McFarland, C., McElhaney, K. B., & Marsh, P. (2007). The relation of attachment security to adolescents' paternal and peer relationships, depression, and externalizing behavior. *Child Development, 78,* 1222–1239.

Allen, J. P., Porter, M. R., McFarland, F. C., Marsh, P., & McElhaney, K. B. (2005). The two faces of adolescents' success with peers: Adolescent popularity, social adaptation, and deviant behavior. *Child Development, 76,* 747–760.

Allwood, M. A., Bell-Dolan, D., & Husain, S. A. (2002). Children's trauma and adjustment reactions to violent and nonviolent war experiences. *Journal of the American Academy of Child and Adolescent Psychiatry, 41,* 450–457.

Als, H. (2009). Newborn Individualized Developmental Care and Assessment Program (NIDCAP): New frontier for neonatal and perinatal medicine. *Journal of Neonatal-Perinatal Medicine, 2,* 135–147.

Als, H., Lawhon, G., Duffy, F. H., McAnulty, G. B., Gibes-Grossman, R., & Blickman, J. G. (1994). Individualized developmental care for the very low-birth-weight preterm infants: Medical and neurofunctional effects. *Journal of the American Medical Association, 272,* 853–858.

Altermatt, E. R., Pomerantz, E. M., Ruble, D. N., Frey, K., & Greulich, F. K. (2002). Predicting changes in children's self-perceptions of academic competence: A naturalistic examination of evaluative discourse among classmates. *Developmental Psychology, 38,* 903–917.

Amato, P. R. (1999). Children of divorced parents as young adults. In E. M. Hetherington (Ed.), *Coping with divorce, single parenting, and remarriage* (pp. 147–163). Mahwah, NJ: Erlbaum.

Amato, P. R., & Rezac, S. J. (1994). Contact with nonresident parents, interparental conflict, and children's behavior. *Journal of Family Issues, 15,* 191–207.

Ambady, N., Shih, M., Kim, A., & Pittinsky, T. L. (2001). Stereotype susceptibility in children: Effects of identity activation on quantitative performance. *Psychological Science, 12,* 385–390.

Amberger, J. S., Hamosh, A., & McKusick, V. A. (2001). Morbid anatomy of the human genome. In C. R. Scriver, A. L. Beaudet, W. S. Sly, & D. Valle (Eds.), *The metabolic & molecular bases of inherited disease* (8th ed., Vol. 1, pp. 47–111). New York, NY: McGraw-Hill.

American Academy of Pediatrics. (1999). Media education. *Pediatrics, 104,* 341–342.

American Academy of Pediatrics. (2000). Committee on Substance Abuse and Committee on Children with Disabilities. Fetal alcohol syndrome and alcohol-related neurodevelopmental disorders. *Pediatrics, 106,* 358–361.

American Association of University Women. (1992). *How schools shortchange girls.* Washington, DC: AAUW Educational Foundation.

American Association of University Women Educational Foundation. (2001). *Hostile hallways: Bullying, teasing, and sexual harassment in school.* Washington, DC: AAUW Educational Foundation.

American College of Obstetricians and Gynecologists. (1994). Substance abuse in pregnancy. *ACOG Technical Bulletin No. 195.*

American Psychiatric Association. (1994). *Diagnostic and statistical manual of mental disorders* (4th ed.). Washington, DC.

American Psychiatric Association. (2000). *Diagnostic and statistical manual of mental disorders* (Revised 4th ed.). Washington, DC: Author.

American Psychological Association (2008). *Presidential Task Force on posttraumatic stress disorder and trauma in children and adolescents.* Retrieved September 23, 2010, from http://www.apa.org/pi/families/resources/children-trauma-update.aspx

Anand, K. J. S., and the International Evidence-Based Group for Neonatal Pain. (2001). Consensus statement for the prevention and management of pain in the newborn. *Archives of Pediatric and Adolescent Medicine, 155,* 173–180.

Anand, S., & Krosnick, J. A. (2005). Demographic predictors of media use among infants, toddlers, and preschoolers. *American Behavioral Scientist, 48,* 539–561.

Anderson, C. A., Berkowitz, L., Donnerstein, E., Huesmann, L. R., Johnson, J. D., Linz, D., et al. (2003). The influence of media violence on youth. *Psychological Science in the Public Interest, 4,* 81–110.

Anderson, D. R., Fite, K. V., Petrovich, N., & Hirsch, J. (2006). Cortical activation while watching video montage: An fMRI study. *Media Psychology, 8,* 7–24.

Anderson, D. R., & Hanson, K. G. (2010). From blooming, buzzing confusion to media literacy: The early development of television viewing. *Developmental Review, 30,* 239–255.

Anderson, D. R., Huston, A. C., Schmitt, K. L., Lineberger, D. L., & Wright, J. C. (2001). Early childhood television viewing and adolescent behavior: The recontact study. *Monographs of the Society for Research in Child Development, 66* (Serial No. 264).

Anderson, D. R., Lorch, E. P., Field, D. E., & Sanders, J. (1981). The effects of TV program comprehensibility on preschool children's television viewing behavior. *Child Development, 52,* 151–157.

Anderson, D. R., & Pempek, T. A. (2005). Television and very young children. *American Behavioral Scientist, 48,* 505–522.

Anderson, K. E., Lytton, H., & Romney, D. M. (1986). Mothers' interactions with normal and conduct-disordered boys: Who affects whom? *Developmental Psychology, 22,* 604–609.

Anderson, M., Kaufman, J., Simon, T. R., Barrios, L., Paulozzi, L., Ryan, G., et al. (2001). School-associated violent deaths in the United States, 1994–1999. *Journal of the American Medical Association, 286,* 2695–2702.

Anderson, P. J., Doyle, L. W., & the Victorian Infant Collaborative Study Group. (2004). Executive functioning in school-aged children who were born very preterm or with extremely low birth weight in the 1990s. *Pediatrics, 114,* 50–57.

Anderson, P. M., & Butcher, K. F. (2006, Spring). Childhood obesity: Trends and potential causes. *Future of Children: Childhood Obesity, 16,* 19–45.

Anderson, S. E., & Must, A. (2005). Interpreting the continued declines in the average age at menarche: Results from two nationally representative surveys of U.S. girls studied 10 years apart. *The Journal of Pediatrics, 147,* 753–760.

Andronikidis, A. I., & Lambrianidou, M. (2010). Children's understanding of television advertising: A grounded theory approach. *Psychology & Marketing, 27,* 299–322.

Aneja, A., Iqbal, M. M., & Ahmed, K. (2006). The effects of amphetamine use during pregnancy and lactation. *Directions in Psychiatry, 26,* 237–251.

Anisfeld, M. (2005). No compelling evidence to dispute Piaget's timetable of the development of representational imitation in infancy. In S. Hurley & N. Chater (Eds.), *Perspectives on imitation: From neuroscience to social science* (Vol. 2, pp. 55–77). Cambridge, MA: MIT Press.

Annenberg Public Policy Center (2006). *Stranger contact in adolescent online social networks.* Philadelphia, PA: Annenberg Public Policy Center, University of Pennsylvania. Retrieved July 20, 2010, from http://www.annenbergpublicpolicycenter.org/Downloads/Releases/Release_HC20060920/Report_HC20060920.pdf

Antell, S. E., & Keating, D. P. (1983). Perception of numerical invariance in neonates. *Child Development, 54,* 695–701.

Antill, J. K., Goodnow, J. J., Russell, G., & Cotton, S. (1996). The influence of parents and family context on children's involvement in household tasks. *Sex Roles, 34,* 215–236.

Antonov, A. N. (1947). Children born during the siege of Leningrad in 1942. *Journal of Pediatrics, 30,* 250–259.

Apfelbaum, E. P., Pauker, K., Ambady, N., Summers, S. R., & Norton, M. I. (2008). Learning (not) to talk about race: When older children underperform in social categorization. *Developmental Psychology, 44,* 1513–1518.

Apgar, V. (1953). A proposal for a new method of evaluation of the newborn infant. *Anesthesia and Analgesia: Current Researches, 32,* 260–267.

Archer, J. (2004). Sex differences in aggression in real-world settings: A meta-analytic review. *Review of General Psychology, 8,* 291–322.

Arend, R., Gove, F. L., & Sroufe, L. A. (1979). Continuity of individual adaptation from infancy to kindergarten: A predictive study of ego-resiliency and curiosity in preschoolers. *Child Development, 50,* 950–959.

Ariès, P. (1962). *Centuries of childhood: A social history of family life* (R. Baldick, Trans.). New York, NY: Vintage.

Armstrong, E. M. (2005). Drug and alcohol use during pregnancy: We need to protect, not punish, women. *Women's Health Issues, 15,* 45–47.

Armstrong, V., Maurer, D., & Lewis, T. L. (2009). Sensitivity to first- and second-order motion and form in children and adults. *Vision Research, 49,* 2774–2781.

Arnett, J. J. (1999). Adolescent storm and stress, reconsidered. *American Psychologist, 54,* 317–326.

Arnold, D. S., & Whitehurst, G. J. (1994). Accelerating language development through picture book reading: A summary of dialogic reading and its effects. In D. K. Dickinson (Ed.), *Bridges to literacy: Children, families, and schools* (pp. 103–128). Cambridge, MA: Blackwell.

Aronfreed, J. (1976). Moral development from the standpoint of a general psychological theory. In T. Lickona (Ed.), *Moral development and moral behavior* (pp. 54–69). New York, NY: Holt, Rinehart & Winston.

Arsenio, W. F., & Ford, M. E. (1985). The role of affective information in social-cognitive development: Children's differentiation of moral and conventional events. *Merrill-Palmer Quarterly, 31,* 1–17.

Arsenio, W. F., & Lemerise, E. A. (2004). Aggression and moral development: Integrating social information processing and moral domain models. *Child Development, 75,* 987–1002.

Arsenio, W. F., Cooperman, S., & Lover, A. (2000). Affective predictors of preschoolers' aggression and peer acceptance: Direct and indirect effects. *Developmental Psychology, 36,* 438–448.

Artigal, J. M. (1991). *The Catalan immersion program: A European point of view.* Norwood, NJ: Ablex.

Asendorpf, J. B., & Baudonnière, P-M. (1993). Self-awareness and other-awareness: Mirror self-recognition and synchronic imitation among unfamiliar peers. *Developmental Psychology, 29,* 88–95.

Asendorpf, J. B., Denissen, J. J. A., & van Aken, M. A. G. (2008). Inhibited and aggressive preschool children at 23 years of age: Personality and social transitions into adulthood. *Developmental Psychology, 44,* 997–1011.

Asher, S. R. (1983). Social competence and peer status: Recent advances and future directions. *Child Development, 54,* 1427–1434.

Ashima-Takane, Y., Goodz, E., & Derevensky, J. L. (1996). Birth order effects on early language development: Do secondborn children learn from overheard speech? *Child Development, 67,* 621–634.

Ashmead, D. H., Clifton, R. K., & Perris, E. E. (1987). Precision of auditory localization in human infants. *Developmental Psychology, 23,* 641–647.

Ashmead, D. H., Hill, E. W., & Talor, C. R. (1989). Obstacle perception by congenitally blind children. *Perception & Psychophysics, 46,* 425–433.

Aslin, R. N. (1987). Motor aspects of visual development in infancy. In P. Salapatek & L. Cohen (Eds.), *Handbook of infant perception: From sensation to perception* (Vol. 1, pp. 43–113). Orlando, FL: Academic Press.

Aslin, R. N. (1993). Perception of visual direction in human infants. In C. Granrud (Ed.), *Visual perception and cognition in infancy* (pp. 91–119). Hillsdale, NJ: Erlbaum.

Aslin, R. N. (2000). Why take the cog out of infant cognition? *Infancy, 1,* 463–470.

Aslin, R. N., & Pisoni, D. B. (1980). Some developmental processes in speech perception. In G. H. Yeni-Komshian, J. F. Kavanagh, & C. A. Ferguson (Eds.), *Child phonology, Vol. 2: Perception* (pp. 67–96). New York, NY: Academic Press.

Astington, J. W., Harris, P. L., & Olson, D. R. (1988). *Developing theories of mind.* New York, NY: Cambridge University Press.

Atzaba-Poria, N., & Pike, A. (2008). Correlates of parental differential treatment: Parental and contextual factors during middle childhood. *Child Development, 79,* 217–232.

Au, T. K.-F., Knightly, L. M., Jun, S.-A., & Oh, J. S. (2002). Overhearing a language during childhood. *Psychological Science, 13,* 238–243.

August, D., Carlo, M., Dressler, C., & Snow, C. (2005). The critical role of vocabulary development for English language learners. *Learning Disabilities Research & Practice, 20,* 50–57.

Austin, S. B., Kim, J., Wiecha, J., Troped, P. J., Feldman, H. A., & Peterson, K. E. (2007). School-based overweight preventive intervention lowers incidence of disordered weight-control behaviors in early adolescent girls. *Archives of Pediatric & Adolescent Medicine, 161,* 865–869.

Auyeung, B., Baron-Cohen, S., Ashwin, E., Knickmeyer, R., Taylor, K., Hackett, G., & Hines, M. (2009). Fetal testosterone predicts sexually differentiated childhood behavior in girls and in boys. *Psychological Science, 20,* 144–148.

Avenevoli, S., Sess, F. M., & Steinberg, L. (1999). Family structure, parenting practices, and adolescent adjustment: An ecological examination. In E. M. Hetherington (Ed.), *Coping with divorce, single parenting, and remarriage* (pp. 65–90). Mahwah, NJ: Erlbaum.

Aviezer, O., Sagi, A., Joels, T., & Ziv, Y. (1999). Emotional availability and attachment representations in kibbutz infants and their mothers. *Developmental Psychology, 35,* 811–821.

Aylward, E. H., Park, J. E., Field, K. M., Parsons, A. C., Richards, T. L., Cramer, S. C., & Meltzoff, A. N. (2005). Brain activation during face perception: Evidence of a developmental change. *Journal of Cognitive Neuroscience, 17,* 308–319.

Aylward, G. P., Pfeiffer, S. I., Wright, A., & Verhulst, S. J. (1989). Outcome studies of low birth weight infants published in the last decade: A metaanalysis. *Journal of Pediatrics, 115,* 515–520.

Bachevalier, J., Brickson, M., & Hagger, C. (1993). Limbic-dependent recognition memory in monkeys develops early in infancy. *Neuro Report, 4,* 77–80.

Bachevalier, J., Hagger, C., & Mishkin, M. (1991). Functional maturation of the occipitotemporal pathway in infant rhesus monkeys. In N. A. Lassen, D. H. Ingvar, M. E. Raichle, & L. Friberg (Eds.), *Brain work and mental activity* (pp. 231–240). Copenhagen: Munksgaard.

Bahrick, L. E. (2002). Generalization of learning in three-and-a-half-month-old infants on the basis of amodal relations. *Child Development, 73,* 667–681.

Bahrick, L. E., Lickliter, R., & Flom, R. (2004). Intersensory redundancy guides the development of selective attention, perception, and cognition in infancy. *Current Directions in Psychological Science, 13,* 99–102.

Bahrick, L. E., Netto, D., & Hernandez-Reif, M. (1998). Intermodal perception of adult and child faces and voices by infants. *Child Development, 69,* 1263–1275.

Bahrick, L. E., & Newell, L. C. (2008). Infant discrimination of faces in naturalistic events: Actions are more salient than faces. *Developmental Psychology, 44,* 983–996.

Bailey, B. A., & Sokol, R. J. (2008). Pregnancy and alcohol use: Evidence and recommendations for prenatal care. *Clinical Obstetrics & Gynecology, 51,* 436–444.

Bailey, B. N., Delaney-Black, V., Covington, C. Y., Ager, J., Janisse, J., Hannigan, J. H., & Sokol., R. J. (2004). Prenatal exposure to binge drinking and cognitive and behavioral outcomes at age 7 years. *American Journal of Obstetrics and Gynecology, 191,* 1037–1043.

Baillargeon, R. (1987a). Object permanence in 3 1/2- and 4 1/2-month-old infants. *Developmental Psychology, 23,* 655–664.

Baillargeon, R. (1987b). Young children's reasoning about the physical and spatial characteristics of a hidden object. *Cognitive Development, 2,* 179–200.

Baillargeon, R. (1995). Physical reasoning in infancy. In M. S. Gazzaniga (Ed.), *The cognitive neurosciences* (pp. 181–204). Cambridge, MA: MIT Press.

Baillargeon, R. (2001). Infants' physical knowledge: Of acquired expectations and core principles. In E. Dupoux (Ed.), *Language, brain, and cognitive development: Essays in honor of Jacques Mehler* (pp. 341–361). Cambridge, MA: MIT Press.

Baillargeon, R., & DeVos, J. (1991). Object permanence in young infants: Further evidence. *Child Development, 62,* 1227–1246.

Baille, M.-F., Arnaud, C., Cans, C., Grandjean, H., du Mazaubrun, C., & Rumeau-Rouquette, C. (1996). Prevalence, aetiology, and care of severe and profound hearing loss. *Archives of Disease in Childhood, 75,* 129–132.

Baker-Sennett, J., Matusov, E., & Rogoff, B. (1993). Planning as a developmental process. In H. W. Reese (Ed.), *Advances in child development and behavior* (Vol. 24 , pp. 253–281). San Diego, CA: Academic Press.

Balaban, E. (2006). Cognitive developmental biology: History, process and fortune's wheel. *Cognition, 101,* 298–332.

Balaban, M. T., Anderson, L. M., & Wisniewski, A. B. (1998). Lateral asymmetries in infant melody perception. *Developmental Psychology, 34,* 39–48.

Baldwin, J. M. (1930). Autobiography of James Mark Baldwin. In C. Murchison (Ed.), *A history of psychology in autobiography* (Vol. 1, pp. 1–30). Worcester, MA: Clark University Press.

Baldwin, S. A., & Hoffman, J. P. (2002). The dynamics of self-esteem: A growth curve analysis. *Journal of Youth and Adolescence, 31,* 101–113.

Bale, J. F., Jr., Zimmerman, B., Dawson, J. D., Souza, I. E., Petheram, S. J., & Murph, J. R. (1999). Cytomegalovirus transmission in child care homes. *Archives of Pediatrics and Adolescent Medicine, 153,* 75–79.

Ballard, B. D., Gipson, M. T., Guttenberg, W., & Ramsey, K. (1980). Palatability of food as a factor influencing obese and normal-weight children's eating habits. *Behavior Research and Therapy, 18,* 598–600.

Ballen, L. E., & Fulcher, A. (2006). Nurses and doulas: Complementary roles to provide optimal maternity care. *Journal of Obstetric, Gynecologic, & Neonatal Nursing, 35,* 304–311.

Bandura, A. (1965). Vicarious processes: A case of no-trial learning. In L. Berkowitz (Ed.), *Advances in experimental social psychology* (Vol. 2, pp. 1–55). New York, NY: Academic Press.

Bandura, A. (1969). *Principles of behavior modification.* New York, NY: Holt, Rinehart & Winston.

Bandura, A. (1977a). Self-efficacy: Toward a unifying theory of behavioral change. *Psychological Review, 84,* 191–215.

Bandura, A. (1977b). *Social learning theory.* Englewood Cliffs, NJ: Prentice-Hall.

Bandura, A. (1986). *Social foundations of thought and action: A social cognitive theory.* Englewood Cliffs, NJ: Prentice-Hall.

Bandura, A. (1989). Social cognitive theory. In R. Vasta (Ed.), *Annals of child development: Vol. 6. Six theories of child development: Revised formulations and current issues* (pp. 1–60). Greenwich, CT: JAI Press.

Bandura, A., Barbaranelli, C., Caprara, G. V., & Pastorelli, C. (1996). Multifaceted impact of self-efficacy beliefs on academic functioning. *Child Development, 67,* 1206–1222.

Bandura, A., Barbaranelli, C., Caprara, G. V., & Pastorelli, C. (2001). Self-efficacy beliefs as shapers of children's aspirations and career trajectories. *Child Development, 72,* 187–206.

Bandura, A., Ross, D., & Ross, S. A. (1963a). Imitation of film-mediated aggressive models. *Journal of Abnormal and Social Psychology, 66,* 3–11.

Bandura, A., Ross, D., & Ross, S. A. (1963b). Vicarious reinforcement and imitative learning. *Journal of Abnormal and Social Psychology, 67,* 601–607.

Bandura, A., & Bussey, K. (2004). On broadening the cognitive, motivational, and sociostructural scope of theorizing about gender development and functioning: Comment on Martin, Ruble, and Szkrybalo (2002). *Psychological Bulletin, 130,* 691–701.

Bandura, A., & Walters, R. H. (1959). *Adolescent aggression.* New York, NY: Ronald Press.

Bandura, A., & Walters, R. H. (1963). *Social learning and personality development.* New York, NY: Holt, Rinehart & Winston.

Banks, M. S., Aslin, R. N., & Letson, R. D. (1975). Sensitive period for the development of human binocular vision. *Science, 190,* 675–677.

Barber, B. K. (2002). *Intrusive parenting: How psychological control affects children and adolescents.* Washington, DC: American Psychological Association.

Barber, B. L., & Eccles, J. S. (1992). Long-term influence of divorce and single-parenting on adolescent family- and work-related values, behaviors, and aspirations. *Psychological Bulletin, 111,* 108–126.

Barber, B. K., & Harmon, E. L. (2002). Violating the self: Parental psychological control of children and adolescents. In B. K. Barber (Ed.), *Parental psychological control of children and adolescents* (pp. 15–52). Washington, DC: American Psychological Association.

Barbour, M. (2009). Today's student and virtual schooling: The reality, the challenges, the promise. *Journal of Distance Learning, 13,* 5–25.

Barbour, M. K., & Reeves, T. C. (2009). The reality of virtual schools: A review of the literature. *Computers & Education, 52,* 402–416.

Barden, R. C., Zelko, F., Duncan, S. W., & Masters, J. C. (1980). Children's consensual knowledge about the experiential components of emotion. *Journal of Personality and Social Psychology, 39,* 968–976.

Barenbaum, J., Ruchkin, V., & Schwab-Stone, M. (2004). The psychosocial aspects of children exposed to war: Practice and policy initiatives. *Journal of Child Psychology and Psychiatry and Allied Disciplines, 45,* 41–62.

Barkeling, B., Ekman, S., & Rössner, S. (1992). Eating behaviour in obese and normal weight 11-year-old children. *International Journal of Obesity, 16,* 355–360.

Barker, E. D., Boivin, M., Brendgen, M., Fontaine, N., Arseneault, L., Vitaro, F., et al. (2008). Predictive validity and early predictors of peer victimization trajectories in preschool. *Archives of General Psychiatry, 65,* 1185–1192.

Barker, R., & Gump, P. (1964). *Big school, small school: High school size and student behavior.* Stanford, CA: Stanford University Press.

Barkley, R. A. (1997). *ADHD and the nature of self-control.* New York, NY: Guilford Press.

Barlow, S. E., and the Expert Committee. (2007). Expert Committee recommendations regarding the prevention, assessment, and treatment of child and adolescent overweight and obesity: Summary report. *Pediatrics, 120,* S164–S192.

Barnes, K. (1971). Preschool play norms: A replication. *Developmental Psychology, 5,* 99–103.

Baron-Cohen, S. (1995). *Mindblindness: An essay on autism and theory of mind.* Cambridge, MA: MIT Press.

Baron-Cohen, S., Tager-Flusberg, H., & Cohen, D. J. (1993). *Understanding other minds: Perspectives from autism.* New York, NY: Oxford University Press.

Barr, R. (2010). Transfer of learning between 2D and 3D sources during infancy: Informing theory and practice. *Developmental Review, 30,* 128–154.

Barr, R., Dowden, A., & Hayne, H. (1996). Developmental change in deferred imitation by 6- to 24-month-old infants. *Infant Behavior and Development, 19,* 159–170.

Barr, R., & Hayne, H. (1999). Developmental changes in imitation from television during infancy. *Child Development, 70,* 1067–1081.

Barrett, C., & Richens, A. (2003). Epilepsy and pregnancy: Report of an Epilepsy Research Foundation Workshop. *Epilepsy Research, 52,* 147–187.

Barrett, L. F., & Wager, T. D. (2006). The structure of emotion: Evidence from neuroimaging studies. *Current Directions in Psychological Science, 15,* 79–83.

Barrett, M. D. (1985). Issues in the study of children's single-word speech. In M. D. Barrett (Ed.), *Children's single-word speech* (pp. 1–19). Chichester, UK: Wiley.

Barrett, M. D. (1986). Early semantic representations and early word usage. In S. A. Kuczaj & M. D. Barrett (Eds.), *The development of word meaning* (pp. 39–67). New York, NY: Springer-Verlag.

Barrett, M. D. (1989). Early language development. In A. Slater & G. Bremner (Eds.), *Infant development* (pp. 211–241). London, UK: Erlbaum.

Barrouillet, P., Gavens, N., Vergauwe, E., Gaillard, V., & Camos, V. (2009). Working memory span development: A time-based resource-sharing model account. *Developmental Psychology, 45,* 477–490.

Barry, C. M., & Wentzel, K. R. (2006). Friend influence on prosocial behavior: The role of motivational factors and friendship characteristics. *Developmental Psychology, 42,* 153–163.

Barth, J. M., & Parke, R. D. (1993). Parent-child relationship influences on children's transition to school. *Merrill-Palmer Quarterly, 9,* 173–195.

Bartlett, N. H., Vasey, P. L., & Bukowski, W. M. (2000). Is gender identity disorder in children a mental disorder? *Sex Roles, 43,* 753–785.

Baruch, C., & Drake, C. (1997). Tempo discrimination in infants. *Infant Behavior and Development, 20,* 573–577.

Bates, E., Bretherton, I., & Snyder, L. (1988). *From first words to grammar.* Cambridge, UK: Cambridge University Press.

Bates, E., Camaioni, L., & Volterra, V. (1975). The acquisition of performatives prior to speech. *Merrill-Palmer Quarterly, 21,* 205–226.

Bates, E., Marchman, V., Thal, D., Fenson, L., Dale, P., Reznick, J. S., et al. (1994). Developmental and stylistic variation in the composition of early vocabulary. *Journal of Child Language, 21,* 85–123.

Bates, J. E., Maslin, C. A., & Frankel, K. A. (1985). Attachment security, mother-child interaction, and temperament as predictors of behavior-problem ratings at age three years. In I. Bretherton & E. Waters (Eds.), *Growing points of attachment theory and research. Monographs of the Society for Research in Child Development, 50 (1–2, Serial No. 209).*

Bates, J., Marvinney, D., Kelly, T., Dodge, K., Bennett, T., & Pettit, G. (1994). Child-care history and kindergarten adjustment. *Developmental Psychology, 30,* 690–700.

Bauer, C. R., Langer, J. C., Shankaran, S., Bada, H. S., Lester, B., Wright, L. L., . . . & Verter, J. (2005). Acute neonatal effects of cocaine exposure during pregnancy. *Archives of Pediatric and Adolescent Medicine, 159,* 824–834.

Bauer, P. J. (1993). Memory for gender-consistent and gender-inconsistent event sequences by twenty-five-month-old children. *Child Development, 64,* 285–297.

Bauer, P. J. (2002). Long-term recall memory: Behavioral and neurodevelopmental changes in the first 2 years of life. *Current Directions in Psychological Science, 11,* 137–141.

Bauer, P. J. (2004). Getting explicit memory off the ground: Steps toward construction of a neuro-developmental account of changes in the first two years of life. *Developmental Review, 24,* 347–373.

Bauer, P. J. (2007). *Remembering the times of our lives: Memory in infancy and beyond.* Mahwah, NJ: Erlbaum.

Bauer, P. J., Liebl, M., & Stennes, L. (1998). PRETTY is to DRESS as BRAVE is to SUITCOAT: Gender-based property-to-property inferences by 4-1/2-year-old children. *Merrill-Palmer Quarterly, 44,* 355–377.

Bauer, P. J., Schwade, J. A., Wewerka, S. S., & Delaney, K. (1999). Planning ahead: Goal-directed problem solving by 2-year-olds. *Developmental Psychology, 35,* 1321–1337.

Baum, K. (2005, April). *Juvenile victimization and offending, 1993–2003.* Bureau of Justice Special Report, Department of Justice, NCJ 209468.

Baumeister, R. F., Campbell, J. D., Krueger, J. I., & Vohs, K. D. (2003). Does high self-esteem cause better performance, interpersonal success, happiness, or healthier lifestyles? *Psychological Science in the Public Interest, 4,* 1–44.

Baumrind, D. (1971). Current patterns of parental authority. *Developmental Psychology Monographs, 4* (1, Pt. 2).

Baumrind, D. (1973). The development of instrumental competence through socialization. In A. Pick (Ed.), *Minnesota symposium on child psychology* (Vol. 7, pp. 3–46). Minneapolis, MN: University of Minnesota Press.

Baumrind, D. (1993). The average expectable environment is not good enough: A response to Scarr. *Child Development, 64,* 1299–1317.

Baumrind, D. (1996). Parenting: The discipline controversy revisited. *Family Relations, 45,* 405–414.

Bauserman, R. (2002). Child adjustment in joint-custody versus sole custody arrangements: A meta-analytic review. *Journal of Family Psychology, 16,* 91–102.

Baydar, N., & Brooks-Gunn, J. (1991). Effects of maternal employment and child care arrangements on preschoolers' cognitive and behavioral outcomes: Evidence from the children of the National Longitudinal Survey of Youth. *Developmental Psychology, 27,* 932–945.

Bayley, N. (2005). *Bayley Scales of Infant and Toddler Development* (3rd ed., Bayley-III). San Antonio, TX: Pearson.

Beauchamp, G. K., & Moran, M. (1982). Dietary experience and sweet taste preferences in human infants. *Appetite, 3,* 139–152.

Beck, R. W., & Beck, S. H. (1989). The incidence of extended households among middle-aged black and white women. *Journal of Family Issues, 10,* 147–168.

Becker-Blease, K. A., Turner, H. A., & Finkelhor, D. (2010). Disasters, victimization, and children's mental health. *Child Development, 81,* 1040–1052.

Behne, T., Carpenter, M., Call, J., & Tomasello, M. (2005). Unwilling versus unable: Infants' understanding of intentional action. *Developmental Psychology, 41,* 328–337.

Behrman, R. E. (Ed.) (2000). Children and computer technology [Special issue]. *The Future of Children, 10*(2).

Beilin, H. (1989). Piagetian theory. In R. Vasta (Ed.), *Annals of child development: Vol. 6. Six theories of child development: Revised formulations and current issues* (pp. 85–131). Greenwich, CT: JAI Press.

Beilin, H., & Fireman, G. (1999). The foundation of Piaget's theories: Mental and physical action. *Advances in child development and behavior* (Vol. 27, pp. 221–246). San Diego, CA: Academic Press.

Bell, M. A., & Fox, N. A. (1992). The relations between frontal brain electrical activity and cognitive development during infancy. *Child Development, 63,* 1142–1163.

Bell, R. Q. (1968). A reinterpretation of the direction of effects in studies of socialization. *Psychological Review, 75,* 81–95.

Bell, R. Q., & Harper, L. V. (1977). *Child effects on adults.* Hillsdale, NJ: Erlbaum.

Bell, S. M., & Ainsworth, M. D. S. (1972). Infant crying and maternal responsiveness. *Child Development, 43,* 1171–1190.

Belsky, J. (1993). Etiology of child maltreatment: A developmental-ecological analysis. *Psychological Bulletin, 114,* 413–434.

Belsky, J. (1996). Parent, infant, and social-contextual antecedents of father-son attachment security. *Developmental Psychology, 32,* 905–913.

Bem, S. L. (1981). Gender schema theory: A cognitive account of sex-typing. *Psychological Review, 88,* 354–364.

Bem, S. L. (1983). Gender schema theory and its implications for child development: Raising gender aschematic children in a gender schematic society. *Signs, 8,* 598–616.

Bempechat, J., & Drago-Severson, E. (1999). Cross-national differences in academic achievement: Beyond etic conceptions of children's understanding. *Review of Educational Research, 69,* 287–314.

Bender, B. G., Harmon, R. J., Linden, M. G., & Robinson, A. (1995). Psychosocial adaptation of 39 adolescents with sex chromosome abnormalities. *Pediatrics, 96,* 302–308.

Benenson, J. F., & Christakos, A. (2003). The greater fragility of females' versus males' closest same-sex friendships. *Child Development, 74,* 1123–1129.

Benner, A. D., Graham, S., & Mistry, R. S. (2008). Discerning direct and mediated effects of ecological structures and process on adolescents' educational outcomes. *Developmental Psychology, 44,* 840–854.

Benner, A. D., & Kim, S. Y. (2009). Experiences of discrimination among Chinese American adolescents and the consequences for socioemotional and academic development. *Developmental Psychology, 45,* 1682–1694.

Bennett, D. S., Bendersky, M., & Lewis, M. (2008). Children's cognitive ability from 4 to 9 years old as a function of prenatal cocaine exposure, environmental risk, and maternal verbal intelligence. *Developmental Psychology, 44,* 919–928.

Bennett, N. (1998). Annotation: Class size and the quality of educational outcomes. *Journal of Child Psychology and Psychiatry, 39,* 797–804.

Bennetto, L., Pennington, B. F., & Rogers, S. J. (1996). Intact and impaired memory functions in autism. *Child Development, 67,* 1816–1835.

Benoit, D., & Parker, K. (1994). Stability and transmission of attachment across three generations. *Child Development, 65,* 1444–1456.

Benson, J. B. (1997). The development of planning: It's about time. In S. L. Friedman & E. K. Scholnick (Eds.), *The developmental psychology of planning: Why, how, and when do we plan?* (pp. 43–75). Mahwah, NJ: Erlbaum.

BenTsvi-Mayer, S., Hertz-Lazarowitz, R., & Safir, M. P. (1989). Teachers' selections of boys and girls as prominent pupils. *Sex Roles, 21,* 231–245.

Berger, C., Karimpour, R., & Rodkin, P. C. (2008). Bullies and victims at school: Perspectives and strategies for primary prevention. In T. W. Miller (Ed.), *School violence and primary prevention* (pp. 295–322). New York, NY: Springer Science + Business Media.

Berger, S. E., Theuring, C., & Adolph, K. E. (2007). How and when infants learn to climb stairs. *Infant Behavior and Development, 30,* 36–49.

Berk, L. E. (1986). Relationship of elementary school children's private speech to behavioral accompaniment to task, attention, and task performance. *Developmental Psychology, 22,* 671–680.

Berk, L. E. (1992). Children's private speech: An overview of theory and the status of research. In R. M. Diaz & L. E. Berk (Eds.), *Private speech: From social interaction to self-regulations* (pp. 17–53). Hillsdale, NJ: Erlbaum.

Berko, J. (1958). The child's learning of English morphology. *Word, 14,* 150–177.

Bernal, S., Dehaene-Lambertz, G., Millotte, S., & Christophe, A. (2010). Two-year-olds compute syntactic structure on-line. *Developmental Science, 13,* 69–76.

Berndt, T. J. (1981). Relations between social cognition, nonsocial cognition, and social behavior: The case of friendship. In J. H. Flavell & L. D. Ross (Eds.), *Social cognitive development: Frontiers and possible futures* (pp. 176–199). Cambridge, UK: Cambridge University Press.

Bernstein, I. M., Mongeon, J. A., Badger, G. J., Solomon, L., Heil, S. H., & Higgins, S. T. (2005). Maternal smoking and its association with birth weight. *Obstetrics & Gynecology, 106,* 986–991.

Berteletti, I., Lucangeli, D., Piazza, M., Dehaine, S., & Zorzi, M. (2010). Numerical estimation in preschoolers. *Developmental Psychology, 46,* 545–551.

Bertenthal, B. I. (1993). Infants' perception of biomechanical motions: Intrinsic image and knowledge-based constraints. In C. Granrud (Ed.), *Visual perception and cognition in infancy* (pp. 175–214). Hillsdale, NJ: Erlbaum.

Berthier, N. E., & Robin, D. J. (1998). Midreach correction in 7-month-olds. *Journal of Motor Behavior, 30,* 290–300.

Berthoud-Papandropoulou, I. (1978). An experimental study of children's ideas about language. In A. Sinclair, R. J. Jarvella, & W. J. M. Levelt (Eds.), *The child's conception of language* (pp. 55–64). Heidelberg: Springer-Verlag.

Berzonsky, M. D., & Adams, G. R. (1999). Reevaluating the identity status paradigm: Still useful after 35 years. *Developmental Review, 19,* 557–590.

Best, J. R., Miller, P. H., & Jones, L. L. (2009). Executive functions after age 5: Changes and correlates. *Developmental Review, 29,* 180–200.

Bialystok, E. (1986). Factors in the growth of linguistic awareness. *Child Development, 57,* 498–510.

Bialystok, E. (1999). Cognitive complexity and attentional control in the bilingual mind. *Child Development, 70,* 636–644.

Bialystok, E. (2001). *Bilingualism in development: Language, literacy, and cognition.* Cambridge, UK: Cambridge University Press.

Bialystok, E., & Craik, F. I. M. (2010). Cognitive and linguistic processing in the bilingual mind. *Current Directions in Psychological Science, 19,* 19–23.

Biederman, J., Faraone, S. V., Keenan, K., Knee, D., & Tsuang, M. T. (1990). Family-genetic and psychosocial risk factors in DSM-III attention deficit disorder. *Journal of the American Academy of Child and Adolescent Psychiatry, 29,* 526–533.

Biehl, M. C., Natusaki, M. N., & Ge, X. (2007). The influence of pubertal timing on alcohol use and heavy drinking trajectories. *Journal of Youth and Adolescence, 36,* 153–168.

Bierman, K. L. (1986). Process of change during social skills training with preadolescents and its relation to treatment outcome. *Child Development, 57,* 230–240.

Bierman, K. L. (2004). *Peer rejection: Developmental processes and intervention.* New York, NY: Guilford.

Bierman, K. L., Domitrovich, C. E., Nix, R. L., Gest, S. D., Welsh, J. A., Greenberg, M. T., Blair, C., Nelson, K. E., & Gill, S. (2008). Promoting academic and social-emotional school readiness: The Head Start REDI Program. *Child Development, 79,* 1802–1817.

Bierman, K. L., & Powers, C. J. (2009). Social skills training to improve peer relations. In K. H. Rubin, W. M. Bukowski, & B. Laursen (Eds.) *Handbook of peer interactions, relationships, and groups* (pp. 603–621). New York, NY: Guilford Press.

Bierman, K. L., Smoot, D. L., & Aumiller, K. (1993). Characteristics of aggressive-rejected, aggressive (nonrejected), and rejected (nonaggressive) boys. *Child Development, 64,* 139–151.

Biernath, K., Holstrum, W. J., & Eichwald, J. (2009). Hearing screening for newborns: The midwife's role in early hearing detection and intervention. *Journal of Midwifery & Women's Health, 54,* 18–26.

Bigelow, A. E., & DeCoste, C. (2003). Sensitivity to social contingency from mothers and strangers in 2-, 4-, and 6-month-old infants. *Infancy, 4,* 111–140.

Bigelow, B. J., & LaGaipa, J. J. (1975). Children's written descriptions of friendship: A multidimensional analysis. *Developmental Psychology, 11,* 857–858.

Bigler, R. S. (1995). The role of classification skill in moderating environmental effects on children's gender stereotyping: A study of the functional use of gender in the classroom. *Child Development, 66,* 1072–1087.

Bigler, R. S., Brown, C. S., & Markell, M. (2001). When groups are not created equal: Effects of group status on the formation of intergroup attitudes in children. *Child Development, 72,* 1151–1162.

Bigler, R. S., Jones, L. C., & Lobliner, D. B. (1997). Social categorization and the formation of intergroup attitudes in children. *Child Development, 68,* 530–543.

Bigler, R. S., & Liben, L. S. (2006). A developmental intergroup theory of social stereotypes and prejudice. In R. V. Kail (Ed.), *Advances in child development and behavior,* Vol. 34 (pp. 39–89). London, UK: Elsevier.

Bijvank, M. N., Konijn, E. A., Bushman, B. J., & Roelofsma, P. H. M. P. (2009). Age and violent-content labels make video games forbidden fruits for youth. *Pediatrics, 123,* 870–876.

Biller, H. B. (1974). *Paternal deprivation: Family, school, sexuality and society.* Lexington, MA: Heath.

Billing, L., Eriksson, M., Jonsson, B., Steneroth, G., & Zetterström, R. (1994). The influence of environmental factors on behavioral problems in 8-year-old children exposed to amphetamine during fetal life. *Child Abuse & Neglect, 18,* 3–9.

Binet, A., & Simon, T. (1905). Méthodes nouvelles pour le diagnostic du niveau intellectuel des anormaux. *L'Anée Psychologique, 11,* 191–244.

Birch, L. L., & Davison, K. K. (2001). Family environmental factors influencing the developing behavioral controls of food intake and childhood overweight. *Pediatric Clinics of North America, 48,* 893–907.

Birdsong, D., & Molis, M. (2001). On evidence for maturational constraints in second-language acquisition. *Journal of Memory and Language, 44,* 235–249.

Biro, F. M., McMahon, R. P., Striegel-Moore, R., Crawford, P. B., Obarzanek, E., Morrison, J. A., et al. (2001). Impact of timing of pubertal maturation on growth in black and white female adolescents: The National Heart, Lung, and Blood Institute Growth and Health Study. *Journal of Pediatrics, 138,* 636–643.

Biro, S., & Leslie, A. M. (2007). Infants' perception of goal-directed actions: Development through cue-based bootstrapping. *Developmental Science, 10,* 379–398.

Bivens, J. A., & Berk, L. E. (1990). A longitudinal study of the development of elementary school children's private speech. *Merrill-Palmer Quarterly, 36,* 443–463.

Bjorklund, D. F., & Harnishfeger, K. K. (1990). The resources construct in cognitive development: Diverse sources of evidence and a theory of inefficient inhibition. *Developmental Review, 10,* 48–71.

Bjorklund, D. F., & Rosenblum, K. E. (2002). Context effects in children's selection and use of simple arithmetic strategies. *Journal of Cognition and Development, 3,* 225–242.

Black, B., & Logan, A. (1995). Links between communication patterns in mother-child, father-child, and child-peer interactions and children's social status. *Child Development, 66,* 255–271.

Black, M. M., Dubowitz, H., & Starr, R. H., Jr. (1999). African American fathers in low income, urban families: Development, behavior, and home environment of their three-year-old children. *Child Development, 70,* 967–978.

Blackwell, L. S., Trzesniewski, K. H., & Dweck, C. S. (2007). Implicit theories of intelligence predict achievement across an adolescent transition: A longitudinal study and an intervention. *Child Development, 78,* 246–263.

Blake, J. (1989). Number of siblings and educational attainment. *Science, 245,* 32–36.

Blake, R., Turner, L. M., Smoski, M. J., Pozdol, S. L., & Stone, W. L. (2003). Visual recognition of biological motion is impaired in children with autism. *Psychological Science, 14,* 151–157.

Blasi, A. (1980). Bridging moral cognition and moral action: A critical review of the literature. *Psychological Bulletin, 88,* 1–45.

Blass, E. M., Ganchrow, J. R., & Steiner, J. E. (1984). Classical conditioning in newborn humans 2–48 hours of age. *Infant Behavior and Development, 7,* 223–235.

Block, J. H. (1971). *Lives through time.* Berkeley, CA: Bancroft Books.

Block, J. H. (1973). Conceptions of sex role: Some cross-cultural and longitudinal perspectives. *American Psychologist, 28,* 512–526.

Block, J. H. (1983). Differential premises arising from differential socialization of the sexes: Some conjectures. *Child Development, 54,* 1335–1354.

Bloom, B., Cohen, R. A., & Freeman, G. (2009). *Summary health statistics for U. S. children: National Health Interview Survey, 2008.* National Center for Health Statistics: Vital Health Statistics 10(244).

Bloom, B. S. (1982). The role of gifts and markers in the development of talent. *Exceptional Children, 48,* 510–522.

Bloom, L. (1973). *One word at a time.* The Hague: Mouton.

Bloom, L. (1991). *Language development from two to three.* Cambridge, UK: Cambridge University Press.

Bloom, L. (1998). Language acquisition in its developmental context. In W. Damon (Series Ed.) & D. Kuhn & R. S. Siegler (Vol. Eds.), *Handbook of child psychology: Vol. 2: Cognition, perception, and language.* (5th ed., pp. 309–370). New York, NY: Wiley.

Bloom, L., Lightbown, P., & Hood, L. (1975). Structure and variation in child language and the acquisition of grammatical morphemes. *Monographs of the Society for Research in Child Development, 40* (2, Serial No. 160).

Bloom, P. (2000). *How children learn the meanings of words.* Cambridge, MA: MIT Press.

Bloom, P., & Markson, L. (1998). Intention and analogy in children's naming of pictorial representations. *Psychological Science, 9,* 200–204.

Bock, J. K., & Hornsby, M. E. (1981). The development of directives: How children ask and tell. *Journal of Child Language, 8,* 151–163.

Boehnke, K., Silbereisen, R. K., Eisenberg, N., Reykowski, J., & Palmonari, A. (1989). Developmental pattern of prosocial motivation: A cross-national study. *Journal of Cross-Cultural Psychology, 20,* 219–243.

Bogartz, R. S., & Shinskey, J. L. (1998). On perception of a partially occluded object in 6-month-olds. *Cognitive Development, 13,* 141–163.

Bogartz, R. S., Shinskey, J. L., & Schilling, T., H. (2000). Object permanence in five-and-a-half-month-olds? *Infancy, 1,* 403–428.

Bogartz, R. S., Shinskey, J. L., & Speaker, C. J. (1997). Interpreting infant looking: The event set X event set design. *Developmental Psychology, 33,* 408–422.

Bogatz, G., & Ball, S. (1972). *The second year of Sesame Street: A continuing evaluation.* Princeton, NJ: Educational Testing Service.

Bogenschneider, K., Wu, M., Raffaeilli, M., & Tsay, J. C. (1998). Parent influences on adolescent peer orientation and substance abuse: The interface of parenting practices and values. *Child Development, 69,* 1672–1688.

Boggiano, A. K., Shields, A., Barrett, M., Kellam, T., Thompson, E., Simons, J., & Katz, P. (1992). Helplessness deficits in students: The role of motivation orientation. *Motivation and Emotion, 16,* 271–296.

Bongaerts, T. (1999). Ultimate attainment in foreign language pronunciation: The case of very advanced foreign language learners. In D. Birdsong (Ed.), *Second language acquisition and the critical period hypothesis* (pp. 133–159). Mahwah, NJ: Erlbaum.

Boom, J., Brugman, D., & van der Heijden, P. G. M. (2001). Hierarchical structure of moral stages assessed by a sorting task. *Child Development, 72,* 535–548.

Boomsma, D. I., Busjahn, A., & Peltonen, L. (2002). Classical twin studies and beyond. *Nature Reviews: Genetics, 3,* 872–882.

Booth, A. E., & Waxman, S. R. (2009). A horse of a different color: Specifying with precision infants' mappings of novel nouns and adjectives. *Child Development, 80,* 15–22.

Booth, J. L., & Siegler, R. S. (2008). Numerical magnitude representations influence arithmetic learning. *Child Development, 79,* 1016–1031.

Booth-LaForce, C., & Kerns, K. A. (2009). Child-parent attachment relationships, peer relationships, and peer-group functioning. In K. H. Rubin, W. M. Bukowski, & B. Laursen (Eds.), *Handbook of peer interactions, relationships, and groups* (pp. 490– 507). New York, NY: Guilford.

Booth-LaForce, C., & Oxford, M. L. (2008). Trajectories of social withdrawal from grades 1 to 6: Prediction from early parenting, attachment, and temperament. *Developmental Psychology, 44,* 1298–1313.

Borke, H. (1973). The development of empathy in Chinese and American children between three and six years of age: A cross-culture study. *Developmental Psychology, 9,* 102–108.

Borke, H. (1975). Piaget's mountains revisited: Changes in the egocentric landscape. *Developmental Psychology, 11,* 240–243.

Bornstein, M. H., & Arterberry, M. E. (2010). The development of object categorization in young children: Hierarchical inclusiveness, age, perceptual attribute, and group versus individual analyses. *Developmental Psychology, 46,* 350–365.

Bornstein, M. H., Hahn, C.-S., Bell, C., Haynes, O. M., Slater, A., Golding, J., Woke, D., & the ALSPAC Study Team (2006). Stability in cognition across early childhood: A developmental cascade. *Psychological Science, 17,* 151–158.

Bornstein, M. H., Haynes, O. M., Pascual, L., Painter, K. M., & Galperín, C. (1999). Play in two societies: Pervasiveness of process, specificity of structure. *Child Development, 70,* 317–331.

Bortfeld, H., Morgan, J. L., Golinkoff, R. M., & Rathbun, K. (2005). Mommy and me: Familiar names help launch babies into speech-stream segmentation. *Psychological Science, 16,* 298–304.

Bos, H. M. W., Sandfort, T. G. M., de Bruyn, E. H., & Hakvoort, E. M. (2008). Same-sex attraction, social relationships, psychosocial functioning, and school performance in early adolescence. *Developmental Psychology, 44,* 59–68.

Bosco, F. M., Friedman, O., & Leslie, A. M. (2006). Recognition of pretend and real actions in play by 1- and 2-year-olds: Early success and why they fail. *Cognitive Development, 21,* 3–10.

Bouchard, T. J., Jr. (1984). Twins reared together and apart: What they tell us about human diversity. In S.W. Fox (Ed.), *Individuality and determinism: Chemical and biological bases* (pp. 147–184). New York, NY: Plenum Press.

Bouchard, T. J., Jr. (1997). IQ similarity in twins reared apart: Findings and responses to critics. In R. J. Sternberg & E. Grigorenko (Eds.), *Intelligence, heredity, and environment* (pp. 126–160). New York, NY: Cambridge University Press.

Bouchard, T. J., Jr. (2004). Genetic influences on human psychological traits. *Current Directions in Psychological Science, 13,* 149–151.

Bowerman, M. (1978). The acquisition of word meaning: An investigation of some current conflicts. In N. Waterson & C. Snow (Eds.), *The development of communication* (pp. 263–287). New York, NY: Wiley.

Bowlby, J. (1958). The nature of the child's tie to his mother. *International Journal of Psychoanalysis, 39,* 350–373.

Bowlby, J. (1969). *Attachment and loss: Vol. 1. Attachment.* New York, NY: Basic Books.

Bowlby, J. (1973). *Attachment and loss. Vol. 2. Separation: Anxiety and anger.* New York, NY: Basic Books.

Boyes, M. C., & Allen, S. G. (1993). Styles of parent-child interaction and moral reasoning in adolescence. *Merrill-Palmer Quarterly, 39,* 551–570.

Boykin, A. W. (1986). The triple quandary and the schooling of Afro-American children. In U. Neisser (Ed.), *The school achievement of minority children: New perspectives* (pp. 57–92). Hillsdale, NJ: Erlbaum.

Boysson-Bardies, B. de, Halle, P., Sagart, L., & Durand, C. (1989). A crosslinguistic investigation of vowel formants in babbling. *Journal of Child Language, 16,* 1–17.

Brackbill, Y. (1975). Continuous stimulation and arousal level in infancy: Effects of stimulus intensity and stress. *Child Development, 46,* 364–369.

Bradbard, M. R., Martin, C. L., Endsley, R. C., & Halverson, C. F. (1986). Influence of sex stereotypes on children's exploration and memory: A competence versus performance distinction. *Developmental Psychology, 22,* 481–486.

Bradley, R. H. (1989). The use of the HOME inventory in longitudinal studies of child development. In M. H. Bornstein & N. A. Krasnegor (Eds.), *Stability and continuity in mental development: Behavioral and biological perspectives* (pp. 191–215). Hillsdale, NJ: Erlbaum.

Bradley, R. H., & Caldwell, B. M. (1976). The relation of infants' home environments to mental test performance at fifty-four months: A follow-up study. *Child Development, 47,* 1172–1174.

Bradley, R. H., & Caldwell, B. M. (1984). The relation of infants' home environments to achievement test performance in first grade: A follow-up study. *Child Development, 55,* 803–809.

The Brain Matures (2008, March). *Scientific American, 298,* 60–61.

Braine, M. D. S. (1976). Children's first word combinations. *Monographs of the Society for Research in Child Development, 41* (1, Serial No. 164).

Brainerd, C. J. (1996). Piaget: A centennial celebration. *Psychological Science, 7,* 191–195.

Bramlett, M. D., & Mosher, W. D. (2001). *First marriage dissolution, divorce, and remarriage: United States* (Advance Data from Vital and Health Statistics No. 323). Hyattsville, MD: National Center for Health Statistics.

Brand, E., Clingempeel, W. E., & Bowen-Woodward, K. (1988). Family relationships and children's psychological adjustment in stepmother and stepfather families: Findings and conclusions from the Philadelphia Stepfamily Research Project. In E. M. Hetherington & J. D. Arasteh (Eds.), *Impact of divorce, single-parenting, and stepparenting on children* (pp. 299–324). Hillsdale, NJ: Erlbaum.

Brand, J. E., & Greenberg, B. S. (1994). Commercials in the classroom: The impact of Channel One advertising. *Journal of Advertising Research, 34,* 18–27.

Bray, J. H. (1988). Children's development during early remarriage. In E. M. Hetherington & J. D. Arasteh (Eds.), *Impact of divorce, single parenting, and stepparenting on children* (pp. 279–298). Hillsdale, NJ: Erlbaum.

Bray, J. H. (1999). From marriage to remarriage and beyond: Findings from the Developmental Issues in Stepfamilies Research Project. In E. M. Hetherington (Ed.), *Coping with divorce, single parenting, and remarriage* (pp. 253–271). Mahwah, NJ: Erlbaum.

Brazelton, T. B. (1973). *Neonatal Behavioral Assessment Scale.* Philadelphia: J. B. Lippincott.

Brazelton, T. B., Nugent, J. K., & Lester, B.M. (1987). Neonatal Behavioral Assessment Scale. In J. D. Osofsky (Ed.), *Handbook of infant development* (2nd ed., pp. 780–817). New York, NY: Wiley.

Breedlove, S. M. (1994). Sexual differentiation of the human nervous system. *Annual Review of Psychology, 45,* 389–418.

Bregman, J. (1998). Developmental outcome in very low birthweight infants: Current status and future trends. *Pediatric Clinics of North America, 45,* 673–690.

Bremner, A., & Bryant, P. (2001). The effect of spatial cues on infants' responses in the AB task, with and without a hidden object. *Developmental Science, 4,* 408–415.

Bremner, J. D. (1999). Does stress damage the brain? *Biological Psychiatry, 45,* 797–805.

Bremner, J. D., & Narayan, M. (1998). The effects of stress on memory and the hippocampus throughout the life cycle: Implications for childhood development and aging. *Development and Psychopathology, 10,* 871–885.

Bremner, J. G. (1978). Egocentric versus allocentric spatial coding in nine-month-old infants: Factors influencing the choice of code. *Developmental Psychology, 14,* 346–355.

Bremner, J. G., & Bryant, P. E. (1977). Place versus response as the basis for spatial errors made by young infants. *Journal of Experimental Child Psychology, 23,* 162–171.

Brendgen, M., Dionne, G., Girard, A., Boivin, M., Vitaro, F., & Pérusse, D. (2005). Examining genetic and environmental effects on social aggression: A study of 6-year-old twins. *Child Development, 76,* 930–946.

Brendgen, M., Lamarche, V., Wanner, B., & Vitaro, F. (2010). Links between friendship relations and early adolescents' trajectories of depressed mood. *Developmental Psychology, 46,* 491–501.

Bretherton, I., & Beeghly, M. (1982). Talking about internal states: The acquisition of an explicit theory of mind. *Developmental Psychology, 18,* 906–921.

Breznitz, Z., & Teltsch, T. (1989). The effect of school entrance age on academic achievement and social-emotional adjustment of children: Follow-up study of fourth graders. *Psychology in the Schools, 26,* 62–68.

Bricker, L., & Lavender, T. (2002). Parenteral opioids for labor pain relief: A systematic review. *American Journal of Obstetrics and Gynecology, 186,* S94–S109.

Brisk, M. (1998). *Bilingual education: From compensatory to quality schooling.* Mahwah, NJ: Erlbaum.

Brody, E. B., & Brody, N. (1976). *Intelligence: Nature, determinants, and consequences.* New York, NY: Academic Press.

Brody, G. H., Beach, S. R., Philibert, R. A., Chen, Y.-F., & Murry, V. M. (2009). Prevention effects moderate the association of 5-HTTLPR and youth risk behavior initiation: Gene X environment hypothesis tested via a randomized prevention design. *Child Development, 80,* 645–661.

Brody, G. H., & Flor, D. L. (1998). Maternal resources, parenting practices, and child competence in rural, single-parent African American families. *Child Development, 69,* 803–816.

Brody, G. H., Flor, D. L., & Gibson, N. M. (1999). Linking maternal efficacy beliefs, developmental goals, parenting practices, and child competence in rural single-parent African American families. *Child Development, 70,* 1197–1208.

Brody, G. H., Ge, X., Conger, R., Gibbons, F. X., Murry, V. M., Gerrard, M., & Simons, R. L. (2001). The influence of neighborhood disadvantage, collective socialization, and parenting on African American children's affiliation with deviant peers. *Child Development, 72,* 1231–1246.

Brody, G. H., & Stoneman, Z. (1994). Sibling relationships and their association with parental differential treatment. In E. M. Hetherington, D. Reiss, & R. Plomin (Eds.), *Separate social worlds of siblings* (pp. 129–142). Hillsdale, NJ: Erlbaum.

Brody, G. H., Stoneman, Z., & Flor, D. (1996). Parental religiosity, family processes, and youth competence in rural, two-parent African American families. *Developmental Psychology, 32,* 696–706.

Brodzinsky, D. M., Schecter, D. E., Braff, A. M., & Singer, L.M. (1984). Psychological and academic adjustment in adopted children. *Journal of Consulting and Clinical Psychology, 52,* 582–590.

Bronfenbrenner, U. (1977). Toward an experimental ecology of human development. *American Psychologist, 32,* 513–531.

Bronfenbrenner, U. (1986). Ecology of the family as a context for human development: Research perspectives. *Developmental Psychology, 22,* 723–742.

Bronfenbrenner, U. (1989). Ecological systems theory. In R. Vasta (Ed.), *Annals of child development: Vol 6. Six theories of child development: Revised formulations and current issues* (pp. 187–251). Greenwich, CT: JAI Press.

Bronfenbrenner, U. (1995). Developmental ecology through space and time: A future perspective. In P. Moen, G. H. Elder, & K. Luescher (Eds.), *Examining lives in context: Perspectives on the ecology of human development* (pp. 619–647). Washington, DC: American Psychological Association.

Bronfenbrenner, U., & Morris, P. A. (2006). In W. Damon & R. M. Lerner (Series Ed.) & R. M. Lerner (Vol. Ed.) *Handbook of child psychology: Vol. 1. Theoretical models of human development.* (6th ed., pp. 793–828). Hoboken, NJ: John Wiley & Sons.

Bronson, W. (1981). Toddlers' behavior with age-mates: Issues of interaction, cognition, and affect. In L. Lipsitt (Ed.), *Monographs on infancy* (Vol. 1, pp. 1–127). Norwood, NJ: Ablex.

Brookmeyer, K. A., Henrich, C. C., & Schwab-Stone, M. (2005). Adolescents who witness community violence: Can parent support and prosocial cognitions protect them from committing violence? *Child Development, 76,* 917–929.

Brooks-Gunn, J., & Chase-Lansdale, P. L. (1995). Adolescent parenthood. In M. H. Bornstein (Ed.), *Handbook of parenting: Vol. 3. Status and social conditions of parenting* (pp. 113–149). Mahwah, NJ: Erlbaum.

Brooks-Gunn, J., Han, W. J., & Waldfogel, J. (2002). Maternal employment and child cognitive outcomes in the first three years of life: The NICHD study of early child care. *Child Development, 73,* 1052–1072.

Brooks-Gunn, J., Klebanov, P. K., & Duncan, G. J. (1996). Ethnic differences in children's intelligence test scores: Role of economic deprivation, home environment, and maternal characteristics. *Child Development, 67,* 396–408.

Brooks-Gunn, J., Klebanov, P. K., Liaw, F., & Spiker, D. (1993). Enhancing the development of low-birthweight, premature infants: Changes in cognition and behavior over the first three years. *Child Development, 64,* 736–754.

Brooks-Gunn, J., & Ruble, D. (1980). Menarche: The interaction of physiology, cultural, and social factors. In A. J. Dan, E. A. Graham, & C. P. Beecher (Eds.), *The menstrual cycle: A synthesis of interdisciplinary research* (pp. 141–159). New York, NY: Springer-Verlag.

Brooks, P. J., & Tomasello, M. (1999). Young children learn to produce passives with nonce verbs. *Developmental Psychology, 35,* 29–44.

Brooks, R. B. (1992). Self-esteem during the school years: Its normal development and hazardous decline. *Pediatric Clinics of North America, 39,* 537–550.

Brooks, R., & Meltzoff, A. N. (2002). The importance of eyes: How infants interpret adult looking behavior. *Developmental Psychology, 38,* 958–966.

Brophy, J. (1986). Teacher influences on student achievement. *American Psychologist, 41,* 1069–1077.

Brown, A. L., Campione, J. C., Ferrara, R. A., Reeve, R. A., & Palincsar, A. S. (1991). Interactive learning and individual understanding: The case of reading and mathematics. In L. T. Landsmann (Ed.), *Culture, schooling, and psychological development* (pp. 136–170). Norwood, NJ: Ablex.

Brown, A. L., Kane, M. J., & Echols, C. H. (1986). Young children's mental models determine analogical transfer across problems with a common goal structure. *Cognitive Development, 1,* 103–121.

Brown, A. S., & Susser, E. S. (2002). In utero infection and adult schizophrenia. *Mental Retardation and Developmental Disabilities Research Reviews, 8,* 51–57.

Brown, B. B. (1989). The role of peer groups in adolescents' adjustment to secondary school. In T. J. Berndt & G. W. Ladd (Eds.), *Peer relationships in child development* (pp. 188–215). New York, NY: Wiley.

Brown, B. B., Herman, M., Hamm, J. V., & Heck, D. J. (2008). Ethnicity and image: Correlates of crowd affiliation among ethnic minority youth. *Child Development, 79,* 529–546.

Brown, B. B., Mounts, N., Lamborn, S. D., & Steinberg, L. (1993). Parenting practices and peer group affiliation in adolescence. *Child Development, 64,* 467–482.

Brown, C. S., & Bigler, R. S. (2004). Children's perceptions of gender discrimination. *Developmental Psychology, 40,* 714–726.

Brown, C. S., & Bigler, R. S. (2005). Children's perceptions of discrimination: A developmental model. *Child Development, 76,* 533–553.

Brown, J. D., L'Engle, K. L., Pardun, C., Guo, G., Kenneavy, K., & Jackson, C. (2006). Sexy media matter: Exposure to sexual content in music, movies, television, and magazines predicts black and white adolescents' sexual behavior. *Pediatrics, 117,* 1018–1027.

Brown, J. R., & Dunn, J. (1996). Continuities in emotion understanding from three to six years. *Child Development, 67,* 789–802.

Brown, L. K., Lourie, K. J., & Pao, M. (2000). Children and adolescents living with HIV and AIDS: A review. *Journal of Child Psychology and Psychiatry, 41,* 81–96.

Brown, P. J., & Konner, M. (1987). An anthropological perspective on obesity. *Annals of the New York Academy of Sciences, 499,* 29–46.

Brown, R. P., Osterman, L. L., & Barnes, C. D. (2009). School violence and the culture of honor. *Psychological Science, 20,* 1400–1405.

Brown, W. H., Pfeiffer, K. A., McIver, K. L., Dowda, M., Addy, C. L., & Pate, R. R. (2009). Social and environmental factors associated with preschoolers' nonsedentary physical activity. *Child Development, 80,* 45–58.

Bruck, K. (1962). Temperature regulation in the newborn infant. *Biological Neonatorum, 3,* 65–119.

Bruck, M., & Ceci, S. (2004). Forensic developmental psychology. *Current Directions in Psychological Science, 13,* 229–232.

Bruck, M., & Ceci, S. J. (1999). The suggestibility of children's memory. *Annual Review of Psychology, 50,* 419–439.

Bruer, J. T. (1999). *The myth of the first three years.* New York, NY: Free Press.

Bruer, J. T. (2001). A critical and sensitive period primer. In D. B. Bailey, J. T. Bruer, F. J. Symons, & J.W. Lichtman (Eds.), *Critical thinking about critical periods* (pp. 3–26). Baltimore, MD: Brookes.

Bruner, J. S. (1983). *Child's talk: Learning to use language.* New York, NY: W. W. Norton.

Bryant-Waugh, R., & Lask, B. (1995). Annotation: Eating disorders in children. *Journal of Child Psychology and Psychiatry, 36,* 191–202.

Buchanan, C. M., Maccoby, E. E., & Dornbusch, S. M. (1991). Caught between parents: Adolescents' experience in divorced homes. *Child Development, 62,* 1008–1029.

Buck Louis, G. M., Gray, L. E., Jr., Marcus, M., Ojeda, S. R., Pescovitz, O. H., Witchel, S. F., & Euling, S. Y. (2008). Environmental factors and puberty timing: Expert panel research needs. *Pediatrics 2008, 121,* S192–S207.

Bugental, D. B., Blue, J. B., & Cruzcosa, M. (1989). Perceived control over caregiving outcomes: Implications for child abuse. *Developmental Psychology, 25,* 532–539.

Bugental, D. B., Ellerson, P. C., Lin, E. K., Rainey, B., Kokotovic, A., & O'Hara, N. (2002). A cognitive approach to child abuse prevention. *Journal of Family Psychology, 16,* 243–258.

Bugental, D., & Happaney, K. (2004). Predicting infant maltreatment in low-income families: The interactive effects of maternal attributions and child status at birth. *Developmental Psychology, 40,* 234–243.

Bugental, D. B., & Lewis, J. (1998). Interpersonal power repair in response to threats to control from dependent others. In M. Kofta, G. Weary, & G. Sedek (Eds.), *Personal control in action: Cognitive and motivational mechanisms* (pp. 341–362). New York, NY: Plenum.

Bugental, D. B., Lyon, J. E., Krantz, J., & Cortez, V. (1997). Who's the boss? Accessibility of dominance ideation among individuals with low perceptions of interpersonal power. *Journal of Personality and Social Psychology, 72,* 1297–1309.

Bugental, D. B., Lyon, J. E., Lin, E. K., McGrath, E. P., & Bimbela, A. (1999). Children "tune out" in response to the ambiguous communication styles of powerless adults. *Child Development, 70,* 214–230.

Bugental, D. B., & Schwartz, A. (2009). A cognitive approach to child mistreatment prevention among medically at-risk infants. *Developmental Psychology, 45,* 284–288.

Buhrmester, D. (1990). Intimacy of friendship, interpersonal competence, and adjustment during preadolescence and adolescence. *Child Development, 61,* 1101–1111.

Buhrmester, D., & Furman, W. (1987). The development of companionship and intimacy. *Child Development, 58,* 1101–1113.

Buhrmester, D., & Furman, W. (1990). Perceptions of sibling relationships during middle childhood and adolescence. *Child Development, 61,* 1387–1398.

Buhs, E. S., & Ladd, G. W. (2001). Peer rejection as an antecedent of young children's school adjustment: An examination of mediating processes. *Developmental Psychology, 37,* 550–560.

Bukowski, W. M., & Kramer, T. L. (1986). Judgments of the features of friendship among early adolescent boys and girls. *Journal of Early Adolescence, 6,* 331–338.

Bumpus, M. F., Crouter, A. C., & McHale, S. M. (2001). Parental autonomy granting during adolescence: Exploring gender differences in context. *Developmental Psychology, 37,* 163–173.

Burchinal, M. R., Follmer, A., & Bryant, D. M. (1996). The relations of maternal social support and family structure with maternal responsiveness and child outcomes among African American families. *Developmental Psychology, 32,* 1073–1083.

Burchinal, M. R., Roberts, J. E., Riggins, R., Jr., Zeisel, S. A., Neebe, E., & Bryant, D. (2000). Relating quality of center-based child care to early cognitive and language development longitudinally. *Child Development, 71,* 338–357.

Burkhauser, R. V., Duncan, G. J., Hauser, R., & Bernsten, R. (1991). Wife or frau, women do worse: A comparison of men and women in the United States and Germany after marital dissolution. *Demography, 28,* 353–360.

Burns, A. L., Mitchell, G., & Obradovich, S. (1989). Of sex role and strollers: Attention to toddlers at the zoo. *Sex Roles, 20,* 309–315.

Burt, K. B., Obradović, J., Long, J. D., & Masten, A. S. (2008). The interplay of social competence and psychopathology over 20 years: Testing transactional and cascade models. *Child Development, 79,* 359–374.

Burton, S., & Mitchell, P. (2003). Judging who knows best about yourself: Developmental change in citing the self across middle childhood. *Child Development, 74,* 426–443.

Bushnell, I. W. R., Sai, F., & Mullin, J. T. (1989). Neonatal recognition of the mother's face. *British Journal of Developmental Psychology, 7,* 3–15.

Buss, K. A., & Goldsmith, H. H. (1998). Fear and anger regulation in infancy: Effects on the temporal dynamics of affective expression. *Child Development, 69,* 359–374.

Bussey, K., & Bandura, A. (1984). Influence of gender constancy and social power on sex-linked modeling. *Journal of Personality and Social Psychology, 47,* 1292–1302.

Bussey, K., & Bandura, A. (1992). Self-regulatory mechanisms governing gender development. *Child Development, 63,* 1236–1250.

Bussey, K., & Bandura, A. (1999). Social cognitive theory of gender development and differentiation. *Psychological Bulletin, 106,* 676–713.

Bussey, K., & Perry, D. G. (1982). Same-sex imitation: The avoidance of cross-sex models or the acceptance of same-sex models. *Sex Roles, 8,* 773–784.

Butler, J., Abrams, B., Parker, J., Roberts, J. M., & Laros, R. K., Jr. (1993). Supportive nurse-midwife care is associated with a reduced incidence of cesarean section. *American Journal of Obstetrics and Gynecology, 168,* 1407–1413.

Butler, R., & Ruzany, N. (1993). Age and socialization effects on the development of social comparison motives and normative ability assessment in kibbutz and urban children. *Child Development, 64,* 532–543.

Butler, S. C., Caron, A. J., & Brooks, R. (2000). Infant undestanding of the referential nature of looking. *Journal of Cognition and Development, 1,* 359–377.

Butz, A. M., Pulsifer, M., Marano, N., Belcher, H., Lears, M. K., & Royall, R. (2001). Effectiveness of a home intervention for perceived child behavioral problems and parenting stress in children with in utero drug exposure. *Archives of Pediatric and Adolescent Medicine, 155,* 1029–1037.

Byers-Heinlein, K., & Werker, J. F. (2009). Monolingual, bilingual, trilingual: Infants' language experience influences the development of a word-learning heuristic. *Developmental Science, 12,* 815–823.

Cabrera, N. J., Shannon, J. D., & Tamis-LeMonda, C. (2007). Fathers' influence on their children's cognitive and emotional development: From toddlers to pre-K. *Applied Developmental Science, 11,* 208–213.

Cairns, R. B. (1992). The making of developmental science: The contributions and intellectual heritage of James Mark Baldwin. *Developmental Psychology, 28,* 17–24.

Cairns, R. B., & Cairns, B. D. (1994). *Lifelines and risks: Pathways of youth in our time.* Cambridge, UK: Cambridge University Press.

Cairns, R. B., & Cairns, B. D. (2006). The making of developmental psychology. In W. Damon & R. M. Lerner (Editors-in-Chief) & R. M. Lerner (Vol. Ed.), *Handbook of child psychology: Vol. 1. Theoretical models of human development* (6th ed., pp. 89–165). Hoboken, NJ: Wiley.

Cairns, R. B., Leung, M., Buchanan, L., & Cairns, B. D. (1995). Friendships and social networks in childhood and adolescence: Fluidity, reliability, and interrelations. *Child Development, 66,* 1330–1345.

Cairns, R. B., & Ornstein, P. A. (1979). Developmental psychology. In E. Hearst (Ed.), *The first century of experimental psychology* (pp. 459–510). Hillsdale, NJ: Erlbaum.

Caldwell, B. M., & Bradley, R. H. (1978). *Home Observation for Measurement of the Environment.* Little Rock, AR: University of Arkansas.

Calkins, S. D., & Fox, N. A. (1992). The relations among infant temperament, security of attachment, and behavioral inhibition at twenty-four months. *Child Development, 63,* 1456–1472.

Calkins, S. D., Fox, N. A., & Marshall, T. R. (1995). Behavioral and physiological antecedents of inhibition in infancy. *Child Development, 67,* 523–540.

Callaghan, T. C., & Rankin, M. P. (2002). Early understanding and production of graphic symbols. *Child Development, 70,* 1314–1324.

Callaghan, T., Rochat, P., Lillard, A., Claux, M. L., Odden, H., Itakura, S., Tapanya, S., et al. (2005). Synchrony in the onset of mental-state reasoning. *Psychological Science, 16,* 378–384.

Calvert, S. (1999). *Children's journeys through the information age.* New York, NY: McGraw-Hill.

Calvert, S. L. (2008). Children as consumers: Advertising and marketing: Special issue: Children and electronic media. *The Future of Children, 18,* 205–234.

Calvert, S. L., Rideout, V., Woolard, J., Barr, R., & Strouse, G. (2005). Age, ethnicity, and socioeconomic patterns in early computer use: A national survey. *American Behavioral Scientist, 48,* 590–607.

Cammilleri, A. P., & Hanley, G. P. (2005). Use of a lag differential reinforcement contingency to increase varied selections of classroom activities. *Journal of Applied Behavior Analysis, 38,* 111–115.

Campbell, A., Shirley, L., & Caygill, L. (2002). Sex-typed preferences in three domains: Do two-year-olds need cognitive variables? *British Journal of Psychology, 93,* 203–317.

Campbell, F. A., Pungello, E., Miller-Johnson, S., Burchinal, M., & Ramey, C. T. (2001). The development of cognitive and academic abilities: Growth curves from an early childhood educational experiment. *Developmental Psychology, 37,* 231–242.

Campbell, F. A., & Ramey, C. T. (1994). Effects of early intervention on intellectual and academic achievement: A follow-up study of children from low-income families. *Child Development, 65,* 684–698.

Campbell, S. B., Brownell, C. A., Hungerford, A., Spieker, S. J., Mohan, R., & Blessing, J. S. (2004). The course of maternal depressive symptoms and maternal sensitivity as predictors of attachment security at 36 months. *Development and Psychopathology, 16,* 231–252.

Campbell, S. B., Cohn, J. F., & Meyers, T. (1995). Depression in first-time mothers: Mother-infant interaction and depression chronicity. *Developmental Psychology, 31,* 349–357.

Campione-Barr, N., & Smetana, J. G. (2010). "Who said you could wear my sweater?" Adolescent siblings' conflicts and associations with relationship quality. *Child Development, 81,* 464–471.

Campos, J. J., Langer, A., & Krowitz, A. (1970). Cardiac responses on the visual cliff in prelocomotor human infants. *Science, 170,* 196–197.

Campos, J., Mumme, D., Kermoian, R., & Campos, R. G. (1994). A functionalist perspective on the nature of emotion. In N. Fox (Ed.), The development of emotion regulation: Behavioral and biological considerations. *Monographs of the Society for Research in Child Development, 59* (2–3, Serial No. 240).

Camras, L. A., Oster, H., Campos, J., Campos, R., Ujie, T., Miyake, K., et al. (1998). Production of emotional facial expressions in European, American, Japanese, and Chinese infants. *Developmental Psychology, 34,* 616–628.

Canfield, R. L., & Smith, E. G. (1996). Number-based expectations and sequential enumeration by 5-month-olds. *Developmental Psychology, 32,* 269–279.

Caplan, D. N., & Gould, J. L. (2003). Language and communication. In L. Squire, F. Bloom, S. McConnell, J. Roberts, N. Spitzer, & M. Zigmond (Eds.), *Fundamental neuroscience* (2nd ed., pp. 1329–1352). San Diego, CA: Academic Press.

Caprara, G. V., Barbaranelli, C., Pastorelli, C., Bandura, A., & Zimbardo, P. G. (2000). Prosocial foundations of children's academic achievement. *Psychological Science, 11,* 302–306.

Card, N. A., Stuckey, B. D., Sawalani, G. M., & Little, T. D. (2008). Direct and indirect aggression during childhood and adolescence: A meta-analytic review of gender differences, intercorrelations, and relations to maladjustment. *Child Development, 79,* 1185–1229.

Carey, S. (1978). The child as word learner. In M. Halle, J. Bresnan, & G. A. Miller (Eds.), *Linguistic theory and psychological reality* (pp. 264–293). Cambridge, MA: MIT Press.

Carli, L. L., & Bukatko, D. (2000). Gender, communication, and social influence: A developmental perspective. In T. Eckes & H. M. Trautner (Eds.), *The developmental social psychology of gender* (pp. 295–331). Mahwah, NJ: Erlbaum.

Carlson, S. M., Moses, L. J., & Hix, H. R. (1998). The role of inhibitory processes in young children's difficulties with deception and false belief. *Child Development, 69,* 672–691.

Carlson, V., Cicchetti, D., Barnett, D., & Braunwald, K. (1989). Contributions of the study of maltreated infants to the development of the disorganized ("D") type of attachment relationship. In D. Cicchetti & V. Carlson (Eds.), *Child maltreatment: Theory and research on the causes and consequences of child abuse and neglect* (pp. 495–528). Cambridge, UK: Cambridge University Press.

Carmichael, C. A., & Hayes, B. K. (2001). Prior knowledge and exemplar encoding in children's concept acquisition. *Child Development, 72,* 1071–1090.

Caron, A. J., Caron, R. F., Caldwell, R. C., & Weiss, S. J. (1973). Infant perception of the structural properties of the face. *Developmental Psychology,* 385–399.

Carpenter, M., Akhtar, N., & Tomasello, M. (1998). Fourteen- through 18-month-old infants differentially imitate intentional and accidental actions. *Infant Behavior and Development, 21,* 315–330.

Carpenter, M., Call, J., & Tomasello, M. (2005). Twelve- and 18-month-olds copy actions in terms of goals. *Developmental Science, 8,* F13–F20.

Carpenter, M., Nagell, K., & Tomasello, M. (1998). Social cognition, joint attention, and communicative competence from 9 to 15 months of age. *Monographs of the Society for Research in Child Development, 63* (4, Serial No. 176).

Carrick, N., & Quas, J. A. (2006). Effects of discrete emotions on young children's ability to discern fantasy and reality. *Developmental Psychology, 42,* 1278–1288.

Carrico, R. L., & Berthier, N. E. (2008). Vision and precision reaching in 15-month-old infants. *Infant Behavior and Development, 31,* 62–70.

Carrion, V. G., Garrett, A., Menon, V., Weems, C. F., & Reiss, A. L. (2008). Posttraumatic stress symptoms and brain function during a response-inhibition task: An fMRI study in youth. *Depression and Anxiety, 25,* 514–526.

Carskadon, M. A., Acebo, C., & Jenni, O. G. (2004). Regulation of adolescent sleep: Implications for behavior. *Annals of the New York Academy of Sciences, 1021,* 276–291.

Carskadon, M. A., Harvey, K., & Duke, P. (1980). Pubertal changes in daytime sleepiness. *Sleep, 2,* 453–460.

Carter, D. B. (1987). The roles of peers in sex role socialization. In D. B. Carter (Ed.), *Current conceptions of sex roles and sex-typing: Theory and research* (pp. 101–121). New York, NY: Praeger.

Carter, D. B., & Levy, G. D. (1988). Cognitive aspects of early sex-role development: The influence of gender schemas on preschoolers' memories and preferences for sex-typed toys and activities. *Child Development, 59,* 782–792.

Carter, D. B., & McCloskey, L. A. (1984). Peers and the maintenance of sex-typed behavior: The development of children's understanding of cross-gender behavior in their peers. *Social Cognition, 2,* 294–314.

Carver, K., Joyner, K., & Udry, J. R. (2003). National estimates of adolescent romantic relationships. In P. Florsheim (Ed.), *Adolescent romantic relationships and sexual behavior: Theory, research, and practical implications* (pp. 291–329). New York, NY: Cambridge University Press.

Carver, P. R., Egan, S. K., & Perry, D. G. (2004). Children who question their heterosexuality. *Developmental Psychology, 40,* 43–53.

Casasola, M., & Cohen, L. B. (2000). Infants' association of linguistic labels with causal actions. *Developmental Psychology, 36,* 155–168.

Case, R. (1985). *Intellectual development: A systematic reinterpretation.* New York, NY: Academic Press.

Case, R., Kurland, D. M., & Goldberg, J. (1982). Operational efficiency and the growth of short term memory span. *Journal of Experimental Child Psychology, 33,* 386–404.

Casey, B. J., Getz, S., & Galvan, A. (2008). The adolescent brain. *Developmental Review, 28,* 62–77.

Casey, B. J., Thomas, K. M., & McCandless, B. (2001). Applications of magnetic resonance imaging to the study of development. In C. A. Nelson & M. Luciana (Eds.), *Handbook of developmental cognitive neuroscience* (pp. 137–148). Cambridge, MA: MIT Press.

Casey, R. J. (1993). Children's emotional experience: Relations among expression, self-report, and understanding. *Developmental Psychology, 29,* 119–129.

Casper, L. M., & O'Connell, M. (1998). Work, income, the economy, and married fathers as child care providers. *Demography, 35,* 243–250.

Caspi, A., Henry, B., McGee, R. O., Moffitt, T. E., & Silva, P. A. (1995). Temperamental origins of child and adolescent behavior problems: From age three to age fifteen. *Child Development, 66,* 55–68.

Caspi, A., & Moffitt, T. E. (2006). Gene-environment interactions in psychiatry: Joining forces with neuroscience. *Nature Reviews. Neuroscience, 7,* 583–590.

Caspi, A., McClay, J., Moffitt, T., Mill, J., Martin, J., Craig, I., Taylor, A., & Poulton, R. (2002). Evidence that the cycle of violence in maltreated children depends on genotype. *Science, 297,* 851–854.

Caspi, A., Taylor, A., Moffitt, T. E., & Plomin, R. (2000). Neighborhood deprivation affects children's mental health: Environmental risks identified in a genetic design. *Psychological Science, 11,* 338–342.

Cassidy, J., & Asher, S. R. (1992). Loneliness and peer relations in young children. *Child Development, 63,* 350–365.

Cassidy, J., Kirsh, S. J., Scolton, K. L., & Parke, R. D. (1996). Attachment and representations of peer relationships. *Developmental Psychology, 32,* 892–904.

Castelli, L., Zogmaister, C., & Tomelleri, S. (2009). The transmission of racial attitudes within the family. *Developmental Psychology, 45,* 586–591.

Catani, C., Gewirtz, A. H., Wieling, E., Schauer, E., Elbert, T., & Neuner, F. (2010). Tsunami, war, and cumulative risk in the lives of Sri Lankan schoolchildren. *Child Development, 81,* 1176–1191.

Cattell, R. B. (1971). *Abilities: Their structure, growth, and action.* Boston, MA: Houghton Mifflin.

Ceballo, R., & McLoyd, V. C. (2002). Social support and parenting in poor, dangerous neighborhoods. *Child Development, 73,* 1310–1321.

Ceballo, R., McLoyd, V. C., & Toyokawa, T. (2004). The influence of neighborhood quality on adolescents' educational values and school effort. *Journal of Adolescent Research, 19,* 716–739.

Ceci, S. J., Ross, D. F., & Toglia, M. P. (1987). Suggestibility of children's memory: Psychological implications. *Journal of Experimental Psychology: General, 116,* 38–49.

Ceci, S. J., & Williams, W. M. (1997). Schooling, intelligence, and income. *American Psychologist, 52,* 1051–1058.

Center for Communication and Social Policy (1998). *National Television Violence Study* (Vol. 3). Newbury Park, CA: Sage.

Centers for Disease Control (2008). *Strategic direction for the prevention of suicidal behavior: Promoting individual, family, and community connectedness to prevent suicidal behavior.* Retrieved June 13, 2010, from http://www.cdc.gov/violenceprevention/pdf/Suicide_Strategic_Direction_Full_Version-a.pdf

Centers for Disease Control (2010). *Autism and Developmental Disabilities Monitoring (ADDM) Network.* Retrieved October 3, 2010, from http://www.cdc.gov/ncbddd/autism/addm.html

Centers for Disease Control and Prevention, National Center for Health and Statistics, Individual growth charts, summary files (2000). *CDC growth charts: United States.* Retrieved August 27, 2010, from http://www.cdc.gov/growthcharts/charts.htm#Set1

Centers for Disease Control and Prevention (2008a). 2007 National Youth Risk Behavior Survey overview. *MMWR, 57(SS04), 1–13.* Retrieved August 27, 2010, from http://www.cdc.gov/mmwr/preview/mmwrhtml/ss5704a1.htm?s_cid=ss5704a1_e#tab74

Centers for Disease Control and Prevention (2008b). *Fact sheet: Toxoplasmosis.* Retrieved August 23, 2010, from http://www.cdc.gov/toxoplasmosis/factsheet.html

Centers for Disease Control and Prevention (2009a). *Birth outcome and risk factor analysis.* Retrieved August 23, 2010, from http://www.cdc.gov/PEDNSS/how_to/read_a_data_table/prevalence_tables/birth_outcome.htm

Centers for Disease Control and Prevention (2009b). *NHANES Surveys (1976–1980 and 2003–2006).* Retrieved February 9, 2010, from http://www.cdc.gov/nccdphp/dnpa/obesity/childhood/prevalence.htm

Centers for Disease Control and Prevention (2009c). *Teen births.* Retrieved August 23, 2010, from http://www.cdc.gov/nchs/fastats/teenbrth.htm

Centers for Disease Control and Prevention (2010a). *2007 assistive technology report.* Retrieved August 20, 2010, from http://www.cdc.gov/art/ART2007/index.htm

Centers for Disease Control and Prevention (2010b). *Cytomegalovirus (CMV) and congenital CMV infection.* Retrieved August 23, 2010, from http://www.cdc.gov/cmv/overview.html

Chakraborty, R., & Luck, S. (2008). Syphilis is on the increase: The implications for child health. *Archives of Disease in Childhood, 93,* 105–109.

Champagne, F. A., & Mashoodh, R. (2009). Genes in context: Gene–environment interplay and the origins of individual differences in behavior. *Current Directions in Psychological Science, 18,* 127–131.

Chandra, A., Martino, S. C., Collins, R. L., Elliott, M. N., Berry, S. H., Kanouse, D. E., & Miu, A. (2008). Does watching sex on television predict teen pregnancy? Findings from a national longitudinal survey of youth. *Pediatrics, 122,* 1047–1054.

Channel One News (2009). *Who are we?* Retrieved July 8, 2010, from http://www.channelone.com/about/

Chao, R. K. (1994). Beyond parental control and authoritarian parenting style: Understanding Chinese parenting through the cultural notion of training. *Child Development, 65,* 1111–1119.

Chao, R., & Kanatsu, A. (2008). Beyond socioeconomics: Explaining ethnic group differences in parenting through cultural and immigration processes. *Applied Developmental Science, 12,* 181–187.

Chapman, M., Skinner, E. A., & Baltes, P. B. (1990). Interpreting correlations between children's perceived control and cognitive performance: Control, agency, or means-ends beliefs? *Developmental Psychology, 26,* 246–253.

Chase-Lansdale, P. L., Cherlin, A. J., & Kiernan, K. E. (1995). The long-term effects of parental divorce on the mental health of young adults: A developmental perspective. *Child Development, 66,* 1614–1634.

Chasnoff, I. J. (1992). Cocaine, pregnancy, and the growing child. *Current Problems in Pediatrics, 22,* 302–321.

Chavous, T. M., Smalls, C., Rivaz-Drake, D., Griffin, T., & Cogburn, C. (2008). Gender matters, too: The influences of school racial discrimination and racial identity on academic engagement outcomes among African American adolescents. *Developmental Psychology, 44,* 637–654.

Chemtob, C. M., Nomura, Y., & Abramovitz, R. A. (2008). Impact of conjoined exposure to the World Trade Center attacks and to other traumatic events on the behavioral problems of preschool children. *Archives of Pediatric & Adolescent Medicine, 162,* 126–133.

Chemtob, C. M., Nomura, Y., Rajendran, K., Yehuda, R., Schwartz, D., & Abramovitz, R. (2010). Impact of maternal posttraumatic stress disorder and depression following exposure to the September 11 attacks on preschool children's behavior. *Child Development, 81,* 1129–1141.

Chen, C., & Stevenson, H. W. (1995). Motivation and mathematics achievement: A comparative study of Asian-American, Caucasian-American, and East Asian high school students. *Child Development, 66,* 1215–1234.

Chen, X., Li, D., Li, Z., Li, B., & Liu, M. (2000). Sociable and prosocial dimensions of social competence in Chinese children: Common and unique contributions to social, academic, and psychological adjustment. *Developmental Psychology, 36,* 302–314.

Chen, X., Rubin, K. H., & Li, B. (1997). Maternal acceptance and social and school adjustment: A four-year longitudinal study. *Merrill-Palmer Quarterly, 43,* 663–681.

Chen, X., Rubin, K. H., Li, B., & Li, D. (1999). Adolescent outcomes of social functioning in Chinese children. *International Journal of Behavioral development,* 23, 199–223.

Chen, X., Rubin, K. H., & Li, Z. (1995). Social functioning and adjustment in Chinese children: A longitudinal study. *Developmental Psychology, 31,* 531–539.

Chen, X., Striano, T., & Rakoczy, H. (2004). Auditory–oral matching behavior in newborns. *Developmental Science, 7,* 42–47.

Chen, Z. (2003). Worth one thousand words: Children's use of pictures in analogical problem-solving. *Journal of Cognition and Development, 4,* 415–434.

Chen, Z., & Daehler, M. W. (1989). Positive and negative transfer in analogical problem-solving by 6-year-olds. *Cognitive Development, 4,* 327–344.

Chen, Z., & Klahr, D. (1999). All other things being equal: Acquisition and transfer of the control of variables strategy. *Child Development, 70,* 1098–1120.

Chen, Z., Sanchez, R. P., & Campbell, T. (1997). From beyond to within their grasp: The rudiments of analogical problem solving in 10- and 13-month-olds. *Developmental Psychology, 33,* 790–801.

Cherlin, A. J. (1992). *Marriage, divorce, remarriage* (Rev. ed.). Cambridge, MA: Harvard University Press.

Chess, S., & Thomas, A. (1982). Infant bonding: Mystique and reality. *American Journal of Orthopsychiatry, 52,* 213–222.

Chess, S., & Thomas, A. (1990). Continuities and discontinuities in temperament. In L. N. Robins & M. Rutter (Eds.). *Straight and devious pathways from childhood to adolescence* (pp. 205–220). Cambridge, UK: Cambridge University Press.

Chess, S., & Thomas, A. (1991). Temperament and the concept of goodness of fit. In J. Strelau & A. Angleitner (Eds.), *Explorations in temperament: International perspectives on theory and measurement* (pp. 15–28). New York, NY: Plenum.

Chi, M. T. H. (1978). Knowledge structure and memory development. In R. Siegler (Ed.), *Children's thinking: What develops?* (pp. 73–96). Hillsdale, NJ: Erlbaum.

Childers, J. B., & Tomasello, M. (2001). The role of pronouns in young children's acquisition of the English transitive construction. *Developmental Psychology, 37,* 739–748.

Children's Defense Fund. (1996). *The state of America's children: Yearbook.* Washington, DC: Author.

Chiu, L. H. (1992–93). Self-esteem in American and Chinese (Taiwanese) children. *Current Psychology: Research & Reviews, 11,* 309–313.

Choi, S. (1998). Verbs in early lexical and syntactic development in Korean. *Linguistics, 36,* 755–780.

Choi, S., & Gopnik, A. (1995). Early acquisition of verbs in Korean: A cross-linguistic study. *Journal of Child Language, 22,* 497–529.

Chomsky, N. (1980). *Rules and representations.* New York, NY: Columbia University Press.

Chomsky, N. (1986). *Knowledge of language: Its nature, origin, and use.* New York, NY: Praeger.

Chow, B. W., McBride-Chang, C., Cheung, H., & Chow, C. S. (2008). Dialogic reading and morphology training in Chinese children: Effects on language and literacy. *Developmental Psychology, 44,* 233–244.

Christ, S. E., Steiner, R. D., & Grange, D. K. (2006). Inhibitory control in children with phenylketonuria. *Developmental Neuropsychology, 30,* 845–864.

Christakis, D. A., Zimmerman, F. J., DiGiuseppe, D. L., & McCarty, C. A. (2004). Early television exposure and subsequent attentional problems in children. *Pediatrics, 113,* 708–713.

Christianson, A., Howson, C. P., & Modell, B. (2006). *March of Dimes global report on birth defects: The hidden toll of dying and disabled children.* White Plains, NY: March of Dimes Defects Foundation.

Chugani, H. T. (1994). Development of regional brain glucose metabolism in relation to behavior and plasticity. In G. Dawson & K. Fischer (Eds.), *Human behavior and the developing brain* (pp. 153–175). NewYork: Guilford.

Cicchetti, D., Ackerman, B., & Izard, C. (1995). Emotions and emotion regulation in developmental psychopathology. *Development and Psychopathology, 7,* 1–10.

Cicchetti, D., & Toth, S. L. (2006). Developmental psychopathology and preventive intervention. In W. Damon & R. M. Lerner (Editors-in-Chief) & K. A. Renninger & I. E. Sigel (Vol. Eds.), *Handbook of child psychology, Vol. 4. Child psychology in practice* (6th ed., pp. 497–547). Hoboken, NJ: Wiley.

Cicchetti, D., Toth, S. L., & Lynch, M. (1995). Bowlby's dream comes full circle: The application of attachment theory to risk and psychopathology. *Advances in Clinical Child Psychology, 17,* 1–75.

Cillessen, A. H. N., & Mayeux, L. (2004). From censure to reinforcement: Developmental changes in the association between aggression and social status. *Child Development, 75,* 147–163.

Cillessen, A. H. N., & Rose, A. J. (2005). Understanding popularity in the peer system. *Current Directions in Psychological Science, 14,* 102–105.

Clark, E. V. (1973). What's in a word? On the child's acquisition of semantics in his first language. In T. E. Moore (Ed.), *Cognitive development and the acquisition of language* (pp. 27–63). New York, NY: Academic Press.

Clarke-Stewart, A., & Allhusen, V. (2005). *What we know about childcare.* Cambridge, MA: Harvard University Press.

Clarke-Stewart, K. A., & Hayward, C. (1996). Advantages of father custody and contact for the psychological well-being of school-age children. *Journal of Applied Developmental Psychology, 17,* 239–270.

Clarkson, M. G. (1996). Infants' intensity discrimination: Spectral profiles. *Infant Behavior and Development, 19,* 181–190.

Clarren, S. K., Alvord, E. C., Suni, S. M., & Streissguth, A. P. (1978). Brain malformations related to prenatal exposure to ethanol. *Journal of Pediatrics, 92,* 64–67.

Claxton, L. J., Keen, R., & McCarty, M. E. (2003). Evidence of motor planning in infant reaching behavior. *Psychological Science, 14,* 354–356.

Clearfield, M. W., & Mix, K. S. (1999). Number versus contour length in infants' discrimination of small visual sets. *Psychological Science, 10,* 408–411.

Clearfield, M. W., & Mix, K. S. (2001). Amount versus number: Infants' use of area and contour length to discriminate small sets. *Journal of Cognition and Development, 2,* 243–260.

Cleary-Goldman, J., Malone, F. D., Vidaver, J., Ball, R. H., Nyberg, D. A., & Comstock, C. H. (2005). Impact of maternal age on obstetric outcome: Increasing maternal age is a risk factor for miscarriage, chromosomal abnormalities, gestational diabetes, placenta previa, placental abruption, cesarean delivery, and perinatal loss, but not for hypertensive complications. *Obstetrics & Gynecology, 105,* 983–990.

Cleveland, A., & Striano, T. (2008). Televised social interaction and object learning in 14- and 18-month-olds. *Infant Behavior and Development, 31,* 326–331.

Cleveland, M. J., Gibbons, F. X., Gerrard, M., Pomery, E. A., & Brody, G. H. (2005). The impact of parenting on risk cognitions and risk behavior: A study of mediation and moderation in a panel of African American adolescents. *Child Development, 76,* 900–916.

Clifton, R., Perris, E., & Bullinger, A. (1991). Infants' perception of auditory space. *Developmental Psychology, 27,* 187–197.

Cohen, D., & Strayer, J. (1996). Empathy in conduct-disordered and comparison youth. *Developmental Psychology, 32,* 988–998.

Cohen, G. L., & Garcia, J. (2008). Identity, belonging, and achievement: A model, interventions, implications. *Current Directions in Psychological Science, 17,* 365–369.

Cohen, G. L., Garcia, J., Apfel, N., & Master, A. (2006). Reducing the racial achievement gap: A social-psychological intervention. *Science, 313,* 1307–1310.

Cohen, L. B., & Cashon, C. H. (2006). Infant cognition. In W. Damon & R. M. Lerner (Editors-in-Chief) & D. M. Kuhn & R. S. Siegler (Vol. Eds.), *Handbook of child psychology: Vol. 2, Cognition, perception, and language* (6th ed., pp. 214–251). Hoboken, NJ: Wiley.

Cohen, R. L. (1966). Experimental and clinical chemateratogenesis. *Advances in Pharmacology, 4,* 263–349.

Cohn, J. F., & Tronick, E. Z. (1983). Three-month-old infants' reaction to simulated maternal depression. *Child Development, 54,* 185–193.

Cohn, J. F., & Tronick, E. Z. (1987). Mother-infant face-to-face interaction: The sequence of dyadic states at 3, 6, and 9 months. *Developmental Psychology, 23,* 68–77.

Coie, J. D., & Dodge, K. A. (1988). Multiple sources of data on social behavior and social status in the school: A cross-age comparison. *Child Development, 59,* 815–829.

Colby, A., Kohlberg, L., Gibbs, J., & Lieberman, M. (1983). A longitudinal study of moral judgment. *Monographs of the Society for Research in Child Development, 48* (1–2, Serial No. 200).

Cole, D. A., Martin, J. M., Peeke, L. A., Seroczynski, A. D., & Fier, J. (1999). Children's over- and underestimation of academic competence: A longitudinal study of gender differences, depression, and anxiety. *Child Development, 70,* 459–473.

Cole, D. A., Maxwell, S. E., Martin, J. M., Peeke, L. G., Seroczynski, A. D., Tram, J. M., et al. (2001). The development of multiple domains of child and adolescent self-concept: A cohort sequential longitudinal design. *Child Development, 72,* 1723–1746.

Cole, P. M., Luby, J., & Sullivan, M. W. (2008). Emotions and the development of childhood depression: Bridging the gap. *Child Development Perspectives, 2,* 141–148.

Coleman, P. K., & Karraker, K. H. (1998). Self-efficacy and parenting quality: Findings and future applications. *Developmental Review, 18,* 47–85.

Coley, R. L., & Chase-Lansdale, P. L. (1998). Adolescent pregnancy and parenthood: Recent evidence and future directions. *American Psychologist, 53,* 152–166.

Collaer, M. L., & Hines, M. (1995). Human behavioral sex differences: A role for gonadal hormones during early development? *Psychological Bulletin, 118,* 55–107.

Collins, W. A. (1983). Social antecedents, cognitive processing, and comprehension of social portrayals on television. In E. T. Higgins, D. N. Ruble, & W. W. Hartup (Eds.), *Social cognition and social development* (pp. 110–133). Cambridge, UK: Cambridge University Press.

Collins, W. A., & Steinberg, L. (2006). Adolescent development in interpersonal context. In W. Damon & R. M. Lerner (Editors-in-Chief) & N. Eisenberg (Vol. Ed.), *Handbook of child psychology: Vol. 3. Social, emotional, and personality development* (6th ed., pp. 1003–1067). Hoboken, NJ: Wiley.

Collins, W. A., & Wellman, H. M. (1982). Social scripts and developmental patterns in comprehension of televised narratives. *Communication Research, 9,* 380–398.

Collins, W. A., Wellman, H., Keniston, A. H., & Westby, S. D. (1978). Age-related aspects of comprehension and inference from a televised dramatic narrative. *Child Development, 49,* 389–399.

Collins, W. A., Welsh, D. P., & Furman, W. (2009). Adolescent romantic relationships. *Annual Review of Psychology, 60,* 631–652.

Colson, E. R., Rybin, D., Smith, L. A., Colton, R., Lister, G., & Corwin, M. J. (2009). Trends and factors associated with infant sleeping position: The National Infant Sleep Position Study, 1993–2007. *Archives of Pediatric & Adolescent Medicine, 163,* 1122–1128.

Coltrane, S. (2000). Research on household labor: Modeling and measuring the social embeddedness of routine family work. *Journal of Marriage and the Family, 62,* 1208–1233.

Compas, B. E. (2004). Processes of risk and resilience during adolescence: Linking contexts and individuals. In R. M. Lerner & L. Steinberg (Eds.), *Handbook of adolescent psychology* (2nd ed., pp. 263–296). Hoboken, NJ: Wiley.

Compas, B. E., Langrock, A. M., Keller, G., Merchant, M. J., & Copeland, M. E. (2002). Coping with parental depression: Processes of adaptation to chronic stress. In S. H. Goodman & I. H. Gotlib (Eds.), *Children of depressed parents: Mechanisms of risk and implications for treatment* (pp. 227–252). Washington, DC: American Psychological Association.

Comstock, G. (1991). *Television and the American child.* Orlando, FL: Academic Press.

Comstock, G., & Scharrer, E. A. (2006). Media and popular culture. In W. Damon & R. M. Lerner (Editors-in-Chief) & K. A. Renninger & I. E. Sigel (Vol. Eds.), *Handbook of child psychology: Vol. 4. Child psychology in practice* (6th ed., pp. 817–863). Hoboken, NJ: Wiley.

Condry, K. F., & Spelke, E. S. (2008). The development of language and abstract concepts: The case of natural number. *Journal of Experimental Psychology: General, 137,* 22–38.

Conger, R. D., Conger, K. J., Elder, G. H., Jr., Lorenz, F. O., Simons, R. L., & Whitbeck, L. B. (1992). A family process model of economic hardship and adjustment of early adolescent boys. *Child Development, 63,* 526–541.

Conger, R. D., Wallace, L. E., Sun, Y., Simons, R. L., McLoyd, V. C., & Brody, G. H. (2002). Economic pressure in African American families: A replication and extension of the family stress model. *Developmental Psychology, 38,* 179–193.

Connolly, J. A., Craig, W. Goldberg, A., & Pepler, D. (2004). Mixed gender groups, dating, and romantic relationships in early adolescence. *Journal of Research on Adolescence, 14,* 185–207.

Connolly, J., & McIsaac, C. (2009). Adolescents' explanations for romantic dissolutions: A developmental perspective. *Journal of Adolescence, 32,* 1209–1223.

Conway, A. R. A., Cowan, N., Bunting, M. F., Therriault, D. J., & Minkoff, S. R. B. (2002). A latent variable analysis of working memory capacity, short-term memory capacity, processing speed, and general fluid intelligence. *Intelligence, 30,* 163–184.

Cook, E. T., Greenberg, M. T., & Kusche, C. (1994). The relations between emotional understanding, intellectual functioning, and disruptive behavior problems in elementary-school-aged children. *Journal of Abnormal Child Psychology, 22,* 205–219.

Cooley, C. H. (1902). *Human nature and the social order.* New York, NY: Scribner's.

Cooley-Strickland, M., Quille, T. J., Griffin, R. S., Stuart, E. A., Bradshaw, C. P., & Furr-Holden, D. (2009). Community violence and youth: Affect, behavior, substance use, and academics. *Clinical Child and Family Psychology Review, 12,* 127–156.

Cooper, C. R., García Coll, C., Thorne, B., & Orellana, M. F. (2005). Beyond demographic categories: How immigration, ethnicity, and "race" matter for children's identities and pathways through school. In C. R. Cooper, C. Garcia Coll, T. Bartko, H. Davis, & C. Chatman (Eds.). *Developmental pathways through middle childhood: Rethinking context and diversity as resources* (pp. 181–205). Mahwah, NJ: Erlbaum.

Cooper, M. L., Shaver, P. R., & Collins, N. L. (1998). Attachment styles, emotion regulation, and adjustment in adolescence. *Journal of Personality and Social Psychology, 74,* 1380–1397.

Copper, R. L., Goldenberg, R. L., Cliver, S. P., DuBard, M. B., Hoffman, H. J., & Davis, R. O. (1993). Anthropometric assessment of body size differences of full-term male and female infants. *Obstetrics and Gynecology, 81,* 161–164.

Corbett, S. S., & Drewett, R. F. (2004). To what extent is failure to thrive in infancy associated with poorer cognitive development? A review and meta-analysis. *Journal of Child Psychology and Psychiatry and Allied Disciplines, 45,* 641–654.

Corbetta, D., & Bojczyk, K. E. (2002). Infants return to two-handed reaching when they are learning to walk. *Journal of Motor Behavior, 34,* 83–95.

Cordes, S., & Brannon, E. M. (2008). The difficulties of representing continuous extent in infancy: Using number is just easier. *Child Development, 79,* 476–489.

Corina, D. P., McBurney, S. L., Dodrill, C., Hinshaw, K., Brinkley, J., & Ojemann, G. (1999). Functional roles of Broca's area and supramarginal gyrus: Evidence from cortical stimulation mapping of a deaf signer. *NeuroImage, 10,* 570–581.

Correa-Chávez, M., Rogoff, B., & Mejía Arauz, R. (2005). Cultural patterns in attending to two events at once. *Child Development, 76,* 664–678.

Courage, M. L., & Howe, M. L. (2004). Advances in early memory development research: Insights about the dark side of the moon. *Developmental Review, 24,* 6–32.

Courage, M. L., & Howe, M. L. (2010). To watch or not to watch: Infants and toddlers in a brave new electronic world. *Developmental Review, 30,* 101–115.

Courage, M. L., & Setliff, A. E. (2009). Debating the impact of television and video material on very young children: Attention, learning, and the developing brain. *Child Development Perspectives, 3,* 72–78.

Cournoyer, M., & Trudel, M. (1991). Behavioral correlates of self-control at 33 months. *Infant Behavior and Development, 14,* 497–503.

Coustan, D. R., & Felig, P. (1988). Diabetes mellitus. In G. N. Burrow & T. F. Ferris (Eds.), *Medical complications during pregnancy* (3rd ed., pp. 34–64). Philadelphia: W. B. Saunders.

Cowan, N. (1999). The differential maturation of two processing rates related to digit span. *Journal of Experimental Child Psychology, 72,* 193–209.

Cowan, N., Wood, N. L., Wood, P. K., Keller, T. A., Nugent, L. D., & Keller, C. V. (1998). Two separate verbal processing rates contribute to short-term memory span. *Journal of Experimental Psychology: General, 127,* 141–160.

Cowan, W. M. (1979, September). The development of the brain. *Scientific American, 241,* 113–133.

Cox, M. J., & Harter, K. S. M. (2003). Parent-child relationships. In M. H. Bornstein, L. Davidson, C. Keyes, & K. Moore (Eds.), *Well-being: Positive development across the lifespan* (pp. 191–203). Mahwah, NJ: Erlbaum.

Cox, M. J., Owen, T. J., Henderson, V. K., & Margand, N. A. (1992). Prediction of infant-father and infant-mother interaction. *Developmental Psychology, 28,* 474–483.

Cox, M. J., & Paley, B. (1997). Families as systems. *Annual Review of Psychology, 48,* 243–267.

Craig, W., Harel-Fisch, Y., Fogel-Grinvald, H., Dostaler, S., Hetland, J., Simons-Morton, B., . . . HBSC Violence & Injuries Prevention Focus Group, & HBSC Bullying Writing Group (2009). A cross-national profile of bullying and victimization among adolescents in 40 countries. *International Journal of Public Health, 54 (Supplement 2),* 216–224.

Crain-Thoreson, C., & Dale, P. S. (1992). Do early talkers become early readers? Linguistic precocity, preschool language, and emergent literacy. *Developmental Psychology, 28,* 421–429.

Crick, N. R., & Dodge, K. A. (1994). A review and reformulation of social information-processing mechanisms in children's social adjustment. *Psychological Bulletin, 115,* 74–101.

Criss, M. M., Pettit, G. S., Bates, J. E., Dodge, K. A., & Lapp, A. L. (2002). Family adversity, positive peer relationships, and children's externalizing behavior: A longitudinal perspective on risk and resilience. *Child Development, 73,* 1220–1237.

Crocetti, E., Rubini, M., Luyckx, K., & Meeus, W. (2008). Identity formation in early and middle adolescents from various ethnic groups: From three dimensions to five statuses. *Journal of Youth and Adolescence, 37,* 983–996.

Cropley, J. E., Suter, C. M., Beckman, K. B., & Martin, D. I. K. (2006). Germ-line epigenetic modification of the murine Avy allele by nutritional supplementation. *Proceedings of the National Academy of Science USA, 103,* 17308–17312.

Crosnoe, R., Riegle-Crumb, C., Field, S., Frank, K., & Muller, C. (2008). Peer group contexts of girls' and boys' academic experiences. *Child Development, 79,* 139–155.

Crouter, A. C., & Bumpus, M. F. (2001). Linking parents' work stress to children's and adolescents' psychological adjustment. *Current Directions in Psychological Science, 10,* 156–159.

Crouter, A. C., Bumpus, M. F., Davis, K. D., & McHale, S. M. (2005). How do parents learn about adolescents' experiences? Implications for parental knowledge and adolescent risky behavior. *Child Development, 76,* 869–882.

Crouter, A. C., Manke, B. A., & McHale, S. M. (1995). The family context of gender intensification in early adolescence. *Child Development, 66,* 317–329.

Crowley, K., & Siegler, R. S. (1998). Explanation and generalization in young children's strategy learning. *Child Development, 70,* 304–316.

Csibra, G. (2001). Illusory contour figures are perceived as occluding surfaces by 8-month-old infants. *Developmental Science, 4,* F7–F11.

Csikszentmihalyi, M., & Larson, R. (1984). *Being adolescent.* New York, NY: Basic Books.

Cummings, E. M. (1995). Security, emotionality, and parental depression: A commentary. *Developmental Psychology, 31,* 425–427.

Cummings, E. M., Zahn-Waxler, C., & Radke-Yarrow, M. (1981). Young children's responses to expressions of anger and affection by others in the family. *Child Development, 52,* 1274–1282.

Cummings, H. M., & Vandewater, E. A. (2007). Relation of adolescent video game play to time spent in other activities. *Archives of Pediatric & Adolescent Medicine, 161,* 684–689.

Cumsille, P., Darling, N., Flaherty, B., & Loreto Martínez, M. (2009). Heterogeneity and change in the patterning of adolescents' perceptions of the legitimacy of parental authority: A latent transition model. *Child Development, 80,* 418–432.

Cuniff, C., & Committee on Genetics. (2004). Prenatal screening and diagnosis for pediatricians. *Pediatrics, 114,* 889–894.

Cunningham, J. D. (1993). Experiences of Australian mothers who gave birth either at home, at a birth centre, or in hospital labour wards. *Social Science and Medicine, 36,* 475–483.

Curtiss, S. (1977). *Genie: A psycholinguistic study of a modern-day "wild child."* New York, NY: Academic Press.

Cuttler, L., & Silvers, J. B. (2004). Growth hormone treatment for idiopathic short stature: Implications for practice and policy. *Archives of Pediatrics and Adolescent Medicine, 158,* 108–110.

Dahl, R. E., & Lewin, D. S. (2002). Pathways to adolescent health: Sleep regulation and behavior. *Journal of Adolescent Health, 31,* 175–184.

Dahl, R. E., Scher, M. S., Williamson, D. E., Robles, N., & Day, N. (1995). A longitudinal study of prenatal marijuana use: Effects on sleep and arousal at age 3 years. *Archives of Pediatric and Adolescent Medicine, 149,* 145–150.

Damon, W. (1983). *Social and personality development: Infancy through adolescence.* New York, NY: W. W. Norton.

Damon, W. (1997). Learning and resistance: When developmental theory meets educational practice. In E. Amsel & K. A. Renninger (Eds), *Change and development: Issues of theory, method, and application* (pp. 287–310). Mahwah, NJ: Lawrence Erlbaum.

Damon, W., & Hart, D. (1988). *Self-understanding in childhood and adolescence.* New York, NY: Cambridge University Press.

Daniels, K. (1989). Waterbirth: The newest form of safe, gentle and joyous birth. *Journal of Nurse-Midwifery, 34,* 198–205.

Daniels, M., Devlin, B., & Roeder, K. (1997). Of genes and IQ. In B. Devlin, S. E. Feinberg, D. P. Resnick, & K. Roeder (Eds.), *Intelligence, genes, and success: Scientists respond to* The Bell Curve (pp. 45–70). New York, NY: Springer–Verlag.

Dapretto, M., & Bjork, E. L. (2000). The development of word retrieval abilities in the second year and its relation to early vocabulary growth. *Child Development, 71,* 635–648.

Dark, V. J., & Benbow, C. P. (1993). Cognitive differences among the gifted: A review and new data. In D. K. Detterman (Ed.), *Current topics in human intelligence. Vol. 3. Individual differences and cognition* (pp. 85–120). Norwood, NJ: Ablex.

Darnovsky, D. M. (2004). Revisiting sex selection: The growing popularity of new sex selection methods revives an old debate. *Gene Watch, 17,* 3–6.

Darwin, C. (1877). A biographical sketch of an infant. *Mind, 2,* 285–294.

Datta, S. D., Sternberg, M., Johnson, R. E., Berman, S., Papp, J. R., McQuillan, G., & Weinstock, H. (2007). Gonorrhea and chlamydia in the United States among persons 14 to 39 years of age, 1999 to 2002. *Annals of Internal Medicine, 147,* 89–96.

Davidoff, M. J., Dias, T., Damus, K., Russell, R., Bettegowda, V. R., Dolan, S., . . . & Petrini, J. (2006). Changes in gestational age distribution among U.S. singleton births: Impact on rates of late preterm birth, 1992–2002. *Seminars in Perinatology, 30,* 8–15.

Davies, P. T., & Scummings, E. M. (1998). Exploring children's emotional security as a mediator of the link between marital relations and child adjustment. *Child Development, 69,* 124–139.

Davis, B. L., MacNeilage, P. F., Matyear, C. L., & Powell, J. K. (2000). Prosodic correlates of stress in babbling: An acoustical study. *Child Development, 71,* 1258–1270.

Davison, K. K., & Birch, L. L. (2002). Processes linking weight status and self-concept among girls from ages 5 to 7. *Developmental Psychology, 38,* 735–748.

Dawson, G. (1994). Development of emotion expression and emotion regulation in infancy. In G. Dawson & K. W. Fischer (Eds.), *Human behavior and the developing brain* (pp. 346–379). New York, NY: Guilford.

Dawson, G., Toth, K., Abbott, R., Osterling, J., Munson, J., Estes, A., & Liaw, J. (2004). Early social attention impairments in autism: Social orienting, joint attention, and attention to distress. *Developmental Psychology, 40,* 271–283.

Day, N. L., & Richardson, G. A. (1994). Comparative teratogenicity of alcohol and other drugs. *Alcohol Health and Research World, 18,* 42–48.

Deák, G. O., & Bauer, P. J. (1996). The dynamics of preschoolers' categorization choices. *Child Development, 67,* 740–767.

Dearing, E., Wimer, C., Simpkins, S. D., Lund, T., Bouffard, S. M., Caronongan, P., Kreider, H., & Weiss, H. (2009). Do neighborhood and home contexts help explain why low-income children miss opportunities to participate in activities outside of school? *Developmental Psychology, 45,* 1545–1562.

Deater-Deckard, K., & Dunn, J. (1999). Multiple risks and adjustment in young children growing up in different family settings: A British community study of stepparent, single mother, and nondivorced families. In E. M. Hetherington (Ed.), *Coping with divorce, single parenting, and remarriage* (pp. 65–90). Mahwah, NJ: Erlbaum.

Deater-Deckard, K., Pike, A., Petrill, S. A., Cutting, A. L., Hughes, C., & O'Connor, T. G. (2001). Nonshared environmental processes in social-emotional development: An observational study of identical twin differences in the preschool period. *Developmental Science, 4,* F1–F6.

DeBaryshe, B. D. (1993). Joint picture-book reading correlates of early oral language skill. *Journal of Child Language, 20,* 455–461.

DeBaryshe, B. D., Patterson, G. R., & Capaldi, D. M. (1993). A performance model for academic achievement in early adolescent boys. *Developmental Psychology, 29, 795–804.*

DeCasper, A. J., & Fifer, W. P. (1980). Of human bonding: Newborns prefer their mothers' voices. *Science, 208,* 1174–1176.

DeCasper, A. J., Lecanuet, J.-P., Busnel, M.-C., Granier-Deferre, C., & Maugeais, R. (1994). Fetal reactions to recurrent maternal speech. *Infant Behavior and Development, 17,* 159–164.

DeCasper, A. J., & Spence, M. J. (1986). Prenatal maternal speech influences newborns' perception of speech sounds. *Infant Behavior and Development, 9,* 133–150.

Decety, J., Michalska, K. J., & Akitsuki, Y. (2008). Who caused the pain? A functional MRI investigation of empathy and intentionality in children. *Neuropsychologia, 46,* 2607–2614.

Decety, J., Michalska, K. J., Akitsuki, Y., & Lahey, B. (2009). Atypical empathic responses in adolescents with aggressive conduct disorder: A functional MRI investigation. *Biological Psychology,* 80, 203–211.

DeFries, J. C., Gervais, M. C., & Thomas, E. A. (1978). Response to 30 generations of selection for open-field activity in laboratory mice. *Behavior Genetics, 8,* 3–13.

De Goede, I. H.A., Branje, S. J. T. & Meeus, W. H. J. (2009). Developmental changes and gender differences in adolescents' perceptions of friendships. *Journal of Adolescence, 32,* 1105–1123.

de Haan, M., & Nelson, C. A. (1997). Brain activity differentiates face and object processing in 6-month-olds. *Developmental Psychology, 35,* 1113–1121.

De La O., A., Jordan, K. C., Ortiz, K., Moyer-Mileur, L. J., Stoddard, G., Friederichs, M., . . . & Mihalopoulos, N. L. (2009). Do parents accurately perceive their child's weight status? *Journal of Pediatric Health Care, 23,* 216–221.

DeLisi, R., & Gallagher, A. M. (1991). Understanding of gender stability and constancy in Argentinian children. *Merrill-Palmer Quarterly, 37,* 483–502.

DeLoache, J. (1987). Rapid change in the symbolic functioning of young children. *Science, 238,* 1556–1557.

DeLoache, J. S. (2000). Dual representation and young children's use of scale models. *Child Development, 71,* 329–338.

DeLoache, J. S. (2004). Becoming symbol-minded. *Trends in Cognitive Sciences, 8,* 66–70.

DeLoache, J. S., Pierroutsakos, S. L., Uttal, D. H., Rosengren, K. S., & Gottlieb, A. (1998). Grasping the nature of pictures. *Psychological Science, 9,* 205–210.

DeLoache, J. S., & Smith, C. M. (1999). Early symbolic representation. In I. E. Sigel (Ed.), *Development of mental representation: Theories and applications* (pp. 61–86). Mahwah, NJ: Erlbaum.

Delobel-Ayoub, M., Kaminski, M., Marret, S., Burguet, A., Marchand, L., N'Guyen, S., . . . , & Larroque, B. (2006). Behavioral outcome at 3 years of age in very preterm infants: The EPIPAGE Study. *Pediatrics, 117,* 1996–2005.

Demany, L., McKenzie, B., & Vurpillot, E. (1977). Rhythm perception in early infancy. *Nature, 266,* 718–719.

Demetriou, H., & Hay, D. F. (2004). Toddlers' reactions to the distress of familiar peers: The importance of context. *Infancy, 6,* 299–318.

Demo, D. H., & Acock, A. C. (1996). Family structure, family process, and adolescent well-being. *Journal of Research on Adolescence, 6,* 457–488.

Dempster, F. N. (1981). Memory span: Sources of individual and developmental differences. *Psychological Bulletin, 89,* 63–100.

DeMulder, E. K., Denham, S., Schmidt, M., & Mitchell, J. (2000). Q-sort assessment of attachment security during the preschool years: Links from home to school. *Developmental Psychology, 36,* 274–282.

DeNavas-Walt, C., Proctor, B. D., & Lee, C. H. (2005). Income, poverty, and health insurance coverage in the United States: 2004. *Current Population Reports* (P60–229). Washington, DC: U.S. Government Printing Office.

Denham, S. A. (1998). *Emotional development in young children.* New York, NY: Guilford.

Denham, S. A., McKinley, M., Couchoud, E. A., & Holt, R. (1990). Emotional and behavioral predictors of preschool ratings. *Child Development, 61,* 1145–1152.

Denham, S. A., Mitchell-Copeland, J., Strandberg, K., Auerbach, S., & Blair, K. (1997). Parental contributions to preschoolers' emotional competence: Direct and indirect effects. *Motivation and Emotion, 21,* 65–86.

Dennis, W. (1960). Causes of retardation among institutional children: Iran. *Journal of Genetic Psychology, 96,* 47–59.

Dennis, W., & Dennis, M. G. (1940). The effect of cradling practices upon the onset of walking in Hopi children. *Journal of Genetic Psychology, 56,* 77–86.

Dennison, B. A., Erb, T. A., & Jenkins, P. L. (2002). Television viewing and television in bedroom associated with overweight risk among low-income preschool children. *Pediatrics, 190,* 1028–1035.

Desrochers, S., Ricard, M., Decarie, T. G., & Allard, L. (1994). Developmental synchrony between social referencing and Piagetian sensorimotor causality. *Infant Behavior and Development, 17,* 303–309.

Deur, J. L., & Parke, R. D. (1970). Effects of inconsistent punishment on aggression in children. *Developmental Psychology, 2,* 403–411.

Deutsch, M., Katz, I., & Jensen, A. R. (1968). *Social class, race, and psychological development.* New York, NY: Holt, Rinehart & Winston.

de Villarreal, L. E. M., Arredondo, P., & Hernández, R. (2006). Weekly administration of folic acid and epidemiology of neural tube defects. *Maternal & Child Health Journal, 10,* 397–401.

de Villiers, P. A., & de Villiers, J. G. (1979). Form and function in the development of sentence negation. *Papers and Reports in Child Language, 17,* 57–64.

De Wals, P., Tairou, F., Van Allen, M. I., Uh, S. H., Lowry, R. B., Sibbald, B., . . . & Niyonsenga, T. (2007). Reduction in neural-tube defects after folic acid fortification in Canada. *New England Journal of Medicine, 12,* 135–142.

De Wolff, M. S., & van IJzendoorn, M. H. (1997). Sensitivity and attachment: A meta-analysis on parental antecedents of attachment. *Child Development, 68,* 571–591.

Devoe, L. D., Murray, C., Youssif, A., & Arnaud, M. (1993). Maternal caffeine consumption and fetal behavior in normal third-trimester pregnancy. *American Journal of Obstetrics and Gynecology, 168,* 1105–1112.

Diamond, A. (1985). The development of the ability to use recall to guide action as indicated by infants' performance on A$\bar{B}$. *Child Development, 56,* 868–883.

Diamond, A. (1991). Neuropsychological insights into the meaning of object concept development. In S. Carey & R. Gelman (Eds.), *The epigenesis of mind: Essays on biology and cognition* (pp. 67–110). Hillsdale, NJ: Erlbaum.

Diamond, A., & Goldman-Rakic, P. S. (1989). Comparison of human infants and rhesus monkeys on Piaget's AB task: Evidence for dependence on dorsolateral prefrontal cortex. *Experimental Brain Research, 74,* 24–40.

Diamond, A., Prevor, M. B., Callender, G., & Druin, D. P. (1997). Prefrontal cortex cognitive deficits in children treated early and continuously for PKU. *Monographs of the Society for Research in Child Development, 62* (4, Serial No. 252).

Diaz, R. M., & Klingler, C. (1991). Towards an explanatory model of the interaction between bilingualism and cognitive development. In E. Bialystok (Ed.), *Language processing in bilingual children* (pp. 167–192). Cambridge, UK: Cambridge University Press.

Diaz, R. M., Neal, C. J., & Vachio, A. (1991). Maternal teaching in the zone of proximal development: A comparison of low- and high-risk dyads. *Merrill-Palmer Quarterly, 37,* 83–108.

Dickens, W. T., & Flynn, J. R. (2001). Heritability estimates versus large environmental effects: The IQ paradox resolved. *Psychological Review, 108,* 346–369.

Dickens, W. T., & Flynn, J. R. (2006). Black Americans reduce the racial IQ gap. *Psychological Science, 17,* 913–920.

Dick-Read, G. (1959). *Childbirth without fear.* New York, NY: Harper & Row.

Dien, D. S. (1982). A Chinese perspective on Kohlberg's theory of moral development. *Developmental Review, 2,* 331–341.

DiFranza, J. R., Aligne, A., & Weitzman, M. (2004). Prenatal and postnatal environmental tobacco smoke exposure and children's health. *Pediatrics, 113,* 1007–1015.

DiMatteo, M. R., Lepper, H. S., Damush, T. M., Morton, S. C., Carney, M. F., Pearson, M., & Kahn, K. L. (1996). Cesarean childbirth and psychosocial outcomes: A meta-analysis. *Health Psychology, 15,* 303–314.

Din, L., Riddell, R., & Gordner, S., (2009). Brief report: Maternal emotional availability and infant pain-related distress. *Journal of Pediatric Psychology, 34,* 722–726.

Dion, K. K., & Berscheid, E. (1974). Physical attractiveness and peer perception among children. *Sociometry, 37,* 1–12.

DiPietro, J. A., Novak, M. F. S. X., Costigan, K. A., Atella, L. D., & Reusing, S. P. (2006). Maternal psychological distress during pregnancy in relation to child development at age two. *Child Development, 77,* 573–587.

Dishion, T. J., Andrews, D. W., & Crosby, L. (1995). Anti-social boys and their friends in early adolescence: Relationship characteristics, quality, and interactional process. *Child Development, 66,* 139–151.

Dishion, T. J., Patterson, G. R., & Griesler, P. C. (1994). Peer adaptations in the development of antisocial behavior: A confluence model. In L. R. Huesmann (Ed.), *Aggressive behavior: Current perspectives* (pp. 61–95). New York, NY: Plenum.

Dishion, T. J., Shaw, D., Connell, A., Gardner, F., Weaver, C., & Wilson, M. (2008). The Family Check-up with high-risk indigent families: Preventing problem behavior by increasing parents' positive behavior support in early childhood. *Child Development, 79,* 1395–1414.

Dishion, T. J., Spracklen, K. M., Andrews, D. W., & Patterson, G. R. (1996). Deviancy training in male adolescent friendships. *Behavior Therapy, 27,* 373–390.

DiVitto, B., & Goldberg, S. (1979). The effect of newborn medical status on early parent-infant interactions. In T. M. Field, A. M. Sostek, S. Goldberg, & H. H. Shuman (Eds.), *Infants born at risk* (pp. 311–332). New York, NY: S. P. Medical & Scientific Books.

Divon, M. Y., Ferber, A., Nisell, H., & Westgren, M. (2002). Male gender predisposes to prolongation of pregnancy. *American Journal of Obstetrics and Gynecology, 187,* 1081–1083.

Dix, T. (1993). Attributing dispositions to children: An interactional analysis of attribution in socialization. *Personality and Social Psychology Bulletin, 19,* 633–643.

Dix, T. H., & Grusec, J. E. (1985). Parent attribution processes in the socialization of children. In I. E. Sigel (Ed.), *Parental belief systems: The psychological consequences for children* (pp. 201–234). Hillsdale, NJ: Erlbaum.

Dix, T. H., Ruble, D. N., Grusec, J. E., & Nixon, S. (1986). Social cognition in parents: Inferential and affective reactions to children of three age levels. *Child Development, 57,* 879–894.

Dix, T. H., Ruble, D. N., & Zambarano, R. J. (1989). Mother's implicit theories of discipline: Child effects, parent effects, and the attribution process. *Child Development, 60,* 1373–1391.

Dixon, S., Tronick, E., Keeler, C., & Brazelton, T. B. (1981). Mother-infant interaction among the Gusii of Kenya. In T. M. Field, A. M. Sosteck, P. Vietze, & P. H. Leiderman (Eds.), *Culture and early interactions* (pp. 149–168). Hillsdale, NJ: Erlbaum.

Dixon, W. E., Jr., & Shore, C. (1997). Temperamental predictors of linguistic style during multiword acquisition. *Infant Behavior and Development, 20,* 99–103.

Dixon, W. E., Jr., & Smith, P. H. (2000). Links between early temperament and language acquisition. *Merrill-Palmer Quarterly, 46,* 417–440.

Dodge, K. A., Coie, J. D., & Lynam, D. (2006). Aggression and antisocial behavior in youth. In W. Damon & R. M. Lerner (Editors-in-Chief) & N. Eisenberg (Vol. Ed.), *Handbook of child psychology: Vol. 3. Social, emotional, and personality development* (6th ed., pp. 719–788). Hoboken, NJ: Wiley.

Dodge, K. A., Lansford, J. E., Burks, V. S., Bates, J. E., Pettit, G. S., Fontaine, R., & Price, J. M. (2003). Peer rejection and social information-processing factors in the development of aggressive behavior problems in children. *Child Development, 74,* 374–393.

Dodge, K. A., Murphy, R. R., & Buchsbaum, K. (1984). The assessment of intention-cue detection skills in children: Implications for developmental psychopathology. *Child Development, 55,* 163–173.

Dodge, K. A., Pettit, G. S., & Bates, J. E. (1994). Socialization mediators of the relation between socioeconomic status and child conduct problems. *Child Development, 65,* 649–665.

Dodge, K. A., Schlundt, D. C., Schocken, I., & Delugach, J. D. (1983). Social competence and children's sociometric status: The role of peer group entry strategies. *Merrill-Palmer Quarterly, 29,* 309–336.

Doherty, W. J., & Needle, R. H. (1991). Psychological adjustment and substance use among adolescents before and after parental divorce. *Child Development, 62,* 328–337.

Dohnt, H. K., & Tiggemann, M. (2005). Peer influences on body image and dieting awareness in young girls. *British Journal of Developmental Psychology, 23,* 103–116.

Dohnt, H., & Tiggemann, M. (2006). The contribution of peer and media influences to the development of body satisfaction and self-esteem in young girls: A prospective study. *Developmental Psychology, 42,* 929–936.

Dolan DNA Learning Center. (2002). Your genes, your health. Retrieved August 19, 2010, from www.ygyh.org

Domitrovich, C. E., Cortes, R., & Greenberg, M. T. (2007). Improving young children's social and emotional competence: A randomized trial of the preschool PATHS curriculum. *Journal of Primary Prevention, 28,* 67–91.

Donnellan, M. B., Trzesniewski, K. H., Robins, R. W., Moffitt, T. E., & Caspi, A. (2005). Low self-esteem is related to aggression, antisocial behavior, and delinquency. *Psychological Science, 16,* 328–335.

Donnelly, M., & Wilson, R. (1994). The dimensions of depression in early adolescence. *Personality and Individual Differences, 17,* 425–430.

Dornbusch, S. M., Ritter, P. L., Leiderman, P. H., Roberts, D. F., & Fraleigh, M. J. (1987). The relation of parenting style to adolescent school performance. *Child Development, 58,* 1244–1257.

Dougherty, T. M., & Haith, M. M. (1997). Infant expectations and reaction time as predictors of childhood speed of processing and IQ. *Developmental Psychology, 33,* 146–155.

Dowling, J. E. (1998), *Creating mind: How the brain works.* New York, NY: Norton.

Downey, G., Feldman, S., Khuri, J., & Friedman, S. (1994). Maltreatment and childhood depression. In W. M. Reynolds & H. F. Johnston (Eds.), *Handbook of depression in children and adolescents: Issues in clinical child psychology* (pp. 481–508). New York, NY: Plenum.

Dozier, M., Stovall, K. C., Albus, K. E., & Bates, B. (2001). Attachment for infants in foster care: The role of caregiver state of mind. *Child Development, 72,* 1467–1477.

Dreher, M. C., Nugent, J. K., & Hudgins, R. (1994). Prenatal marijuana exposure and neonatal outcomes in Jamaica: An ethnographic study. *Pediatrics, 93,* 254–260.

Drewett, R., Wolke, D., Asefa, M., Kaba, M., & Tessema, F. (2001). Malnutrition and mental development: Is there a sensitive period? A nested case-control study. *Journal of Child Psychology and Psychiatry, 42,* 181–187.

Dromi, E. (1999). Early lexical development. In M. Barrett (Ed.), *The development of language* (pp. 99–131). East Sussex, UK: Psychology Press.

Drotar, D., & Robinson, J. (2000). Developmental psychopathology of failure to thrive. In A. J. Sameroff & M. L. Lewis (Eds.), *Handbook of developmental psychopathology* (2nd ed., pp. 351–364). Dordrecht, Netherlands: Kluwer.

Drummond, K. D., Bradley, S. J., Peterson-Badali, M., & Zucker, K. J. (2008). A follow-up study of girls with gender identity disorder. *Developmental Psychology, 44,* 34–45.

Dubner, A. E., & Motta, R. W. (1999). Sexually and physically abused foster care children and posttraumatic stress disorder. *Journal of Consulting and Clinical Psychology, 67,* 367–373.

DuBois, D. L., Burk-Braxton, C., Swenson, L. P., Tevendale, H. D., Lockerd, E. M., & Moran, B. L. (2002). Getting by with a little help from self and others: Self-esteem and social support as resources in early adolescence. *Developmental Psychology, 38,* 822–839.

DuBois, D. L., Tevendale, H. D., Burk-Braxton, C., Swenson, L. P., & Hardesty, J. L. (2000). Self-system influences during early adolescence: Investigation of an integrative model. *Journal of Early Adolescence, 20,* 12–43.

Dubow, E. F., Tisak, J., Causey, D., Hryshko, A., & Reid, G. (1991). A two-year longitudinal study of stressful life events, social support, and social problem-solving skills: Contributions to children's behavioral and academic adjustment. *Child Development, 62,* 583–599.

Duckworth, A. L., & Seligman, M.E. P. (2005). Self-discipline outdoes IQ in predicting academic performance of adolescents. *Psychological Science, 16,* 939–944.

Duncan, G. J., Dowsett, C. J., Claessens, A., Magnuson, K., Huston, A. C., Klebanov, P., . . . & Japel, C. (2007). School readiness and achievement. *Developmental Psychology, 43,* 1428–1446.

Duncan, J. R., Paterson, D. S., Hoffman, J. M., Mokler, D. J., Borenstein, N. A., Belliveau, R. A., . . . & Kinney, H. C. (2010). Brainstem serotonergic deficiency in sudden infant death syndrome. *JAMA, 303,* 430–437.

Duncan, R. D. (2004). The impact of family relationships on school bullies and their victims. In D. L. Espelage & S. M. Swearer (Eds.), *Bullying in American schools* (pp. 227–244). Mahwah, NJ: Erlbaum.

Dunham, P., & Dunham, F. (1995). Developmental antecedents of taxonomic and thematic strategies at 3 years of age. *Developmental Psychology, 31,* 483–493.

Dunlop, A. L., Gardiner, P. M., Shellhaas, C. S., Menard, M. K., & Diarmid, M. A. (2008). The clinical content of preconception care: The use of medications and supplements among women of reproductive age. *American Journal of Obstetrics and Gynecology, 199,* S367–S372.

Dunn, J. (1988). Connections between relationships: Implications of research on mothers and siblings. In R. A. Hinde & J. Stevenson-Hinde (Eds.), *Relationships within families: Mutual influences* (pp. 168–180). Oxford: Clarendon Press.

Dunn, J. (1996). Brothers and sisters in middle childhood and early adolescence: Continuity and change in individual differences. In G. H. Brody (Ed.), *Sibling relationships: Their causes and consequences* (pp. 31–46). Norwood, NJ: Ablex.

Dunn, J., Bretherton, I., & Munn, P. (1987). Conversations about feeling states between mothers and their young children. *Developmental Psychology, 23,* 132–139.

Dunn, J., & Brown, J. R. (1994). Affect expression in the family, children's understanding of emotions, and their interactions with others. *Merrill Palmer Quarterly, 40,* 120–137.

Dunn, J., Brown, J. R., & Maguire, M. (1995). The development of children's moral sensibility: Individual differences and emotion understanding. *Developmental Psychology, 31,* 649–659.

Dunn, J., & Cutting, A. L. (1999). Understanding others, and individual differences in friendship interactions in young children. *Social Development, 8,* 201–219.

Dunn, J., & Kendrick, C. (1982). *Siblings: Love, envy, and understanding.* Cambridge, MA: Harvard University Press.

Dupéré, V., Lacourse, E., Willms, J. D., Leventhal, T., & Tremblay, R. E. (2008). Neighborhood poverty and early transition to sexual activity in young adolescents: A developmental ecological approach. *Child Development, 79,* 1453–1476.

Durik, A. M., Hyde, J. S., & Clark, R. (2000). Sequelae of Cesarean and vaginal deliveries: Psychosocial outcomes for mothers and infants. *Developmental Psychology, 36,* 251–260.

Durston, S., Davidson, M. C., Tottenham, N., Galvan, A., Spicer, J. et al. (2006). A shift from diffuse to focal cortical activity with development. *Developmental Science, 9,* 1–8.

Durston, S., Thomas, K. M., Yang, Y., Ulug, A. M., Zimmerman, R. D., & Casey, B. J. (2002). A neural basis for the development of inhibitory control. *Developmental Science, 5,* F9–F16.

Dweck, C. S. (1986). Motivational processes affecting learning. *American Psychologist, 41,* 1040–1048.

Dweck, C. S. (1991). Self-theories and goals: Their role in motivation, personality, and development. In R. Diestbier (Ed.), *Nebraska Symposium on Motivation, 1990* (Vol. 36, pp. 199–235). Lincoln, NE: University of Nebraska Press.

Dweck, C. S. (1999). *Self-theories: Their role in motivation, personality, and development.* Philadelphia, PA: Psychology Press.

Dweck, C. S., & Elliott, E. S. (1983). Achievement motivation. In E. M. Hetherington (Ed.), *Handbook of child psychology: Vol. IV. Socialization, personality, and social development* (4th ed., pp. 643–691). New York, NY: Wiley.

Dybdahl, R. (2001). Children and mothers in war: An outcome study of a psychosocial intervention program. *Child Development, 72,* 1214–1230.

Dye, N. S. (1986). The medicalization of birth. In P. S. Eakins (Ed.), *The American way of birth* (pp. 21–46). Philadelphia: Temple University Press.

Eagly, A. H., & Steffen, V. J. (1986). Gender and aggressive behavior: A meta-analytic review of the social psychological literature. *Psychological Bulletin, 100,* 309–330.

Eamon, M. K. (2005). Social-demographic, school, neighborhood, and parenting influences on the academic achievement of Latino young adolescents. *Journal of Youth and Adolescence, 34,* 163–174.

East, P. L., & Jacobson, L. J. (2001). The younger siblings of teenage mothers: A follow-up of their pregnancy risk. *Developmental Psychology, 37,* 254–264.

Eccles, J., Adler, T. F., Futterman, R., Goff, S. B., Kaczala, C. M., Meece, J. L., & Midgley, C. (1983). Expectancies, values, and academic behaviors. In J. T. Spence (Ed.), *Achievement and achievement motives: Psychological and sociological approaches* (pp. 75–146). San Francisco, CA: W. H. Freeman.

Eccles, J., Barber, B., Jozefowicz, D., Malenchuk, O., & Vida, M. (1999). Self-evaluations of competence, task values, and self-esteem. In N. G. Johnson, M. C. Roberts, & J. Worell (Eds.), *Beyond appearance: A new look at adolescent girls* (pp. 53–83). Washington, DC: American Psychological Association.

Eccles, J. S. (1987). Adolescence: Gateway to androgyny? In D. B. Carter (Ed.), *Current conceptions of sex roles and sex typing: Theory and research* (pp. 225–241). New York, NY: Praeger.

Eccles, J. S., Lord, S. E., Roeser, R. W., Barber, B. L., & Jozefowicz, D. M. H. (1997). The association of school transitions in early adolescence with developmental trajectories through high school. In J. Schulenberg, J. Maggs, & K. Hurrelmann (Eds.), *Health risks and developmental transitions during adolescence* (pp. 283–320). New York, NY: Cambridge University Press.

Eccles, J. S., & Midgley, C. (1989). Stage/environment fit: Developmentally appropriate classrooms for early adolescents. In R. E. Ames & C. Ames (Eds.) *Research on motivation in education* (Vol. 3, pp. 139–186). San Diego, CA: Academic Press.

Eccles, J. S., Midgley, C., Wigfield, A., Buchanan, C. M., Reuman, D., Flanagan, C., & Mac Iver, D. (1993). Development during adolescence: The impact of stage-environment fit on young adolescents' experiences in schools and families. *American Psychologist, 48,* 90–101.

Eccles, J. S., & Roeser, R. W. (1999). School and community influences on human development. In M. H. Bornstein & M. E. Lamb (Eds.), *Developmental psychology: An advanced textbook* (4th ed., pp. 503–554). Mahwah, NJ: Erlbaum.

Eccles, J., Wigfield, A., Harold, R. D., & Blumenfeld, P. (1993). Age and gender differences in children's self- and task perceptions during elementary school. *Child Development, 64,* 830–847.

Eckenrode, J., Laird, M., & Doris, J. (1993). School performance and disciplinary problems among abused and neglected children. *Developmental Psychology, 29,* 53–62.

Eddleman, K. A., Malone, F. D., Sullivan, L., Dukes, K., Berkowitz, R. L., Kharbutli, Y., for the First and Second Trimester Evaluation of Risk (FASTER) Trial Research Consortium. (2006). Pregnancy loss rates after midtrimester amniocentesis. *Obstetrics & Gynecology, 108,* 1067–1072.

Eder, D., & Hallinan, M. T. (1978). Sex differences in children's friendships. *American Sociological Review, 43,* 237–250.

Egan, S. K., & Perry, D. G. (2001). Gender identity: A multidimensional analysis with implications for psychosocial adjustment. *Developmental Psychology, 37,* 451–463.

Egeland, B., Jacobvitz, D., & Papatola, K. (1987). Intergenerational continuity of abuse. In R. J. Gelles & J. B. Lancaster (Eds.), *Child abuse and neglect: Biosocial dimensions* (pp. 255–276). Hawthorne, NY: Aldine de Gruyter.

Egeland, B., Jacobvitz, D., & Sroufe, L. A. (1988). Breaking the cycle of abuse. *Child Development, 59,* 1080–1088.

Egeland, B., & Sroufe, L. A. (1981). Attachment and early maltreatment. *Child Development, 52,* 44–52.

Egley, A., Jr., Howell, J. C., & Moore, J. P. (2010). *Highlights of the 2008 National Youth Gang Survey.* U.S. Department of Justice, Office of Justice Programs. Retrieved July 15, 2010, from http://www.ncjrs.gov/pdffiles1/ojjdp/229249.pdf

Ehrenberg, R. G., Brewer, D. J., Gamoran, A., & Willms, J. D. (2001a). Class size and student achievement. *Psychological Science in the Public Interest, 2,* 1–30.

Ehrenberg, R. G., Brewer, D. J., Gamoran, A., & Willms, J. D. (2001b, November). Does class size matter? *Scientific American, 285,* 79–85.

Eigsti, I.-M., Zayas, V., Mischel, W., Shoda, Y., Ayduk, O., Dadlani, M. B., Davidson, M. C., Aber, J. L., & Casey, B. J. (2006). Predicting cognitive control from preschool to late adolescence and young adulthood. *Psychological Science, 17,* 478–484.

Eimas, P. D., Siqueland, E. R., Jusczyk, P., & Vigorito, J. (1971). Speech perception in infants. *Science, 171,* 303–306.

Einav, S., & Hood, B. M. (2008). Tell-tale eyes: Children's attribution of gaze aversion as a lying cue. *Developmental Psychology, 44,* 1655–1667.

Eisenberg, N. (1986). *Altruistic emotion, cognition, and behavior.* Hillsdale, NJ: Erlbaum.

Eisenberg, N., Boehnke, K., Schuhler, P., & Silbereisen, R. K. (1985). The development of prosocial behavior and cognition in German children. *Journal of Cross-Cultural Psychology, 16,* 69–82.

Eisenberg, N., Carol, G., Murphy, B., & Van Court, P. (1995). Prosocial development in late adolescence: A longitudinal study. *Child Development, 66,* 1179–1197.

Eisenberg, N., Fabes, R. A., Bernzweig, J., Karbon, M., Poulin, R., & Hanish, L. (1993). The relations of emotionality and regulation to preschoolers' social skills and sociometric status. *Child Development, 64,* 1418–1438.

Eisenberg, N., Fabes, R. A., Shepard, S. A., Guthrie, I. K., Murphy, B. C., & Reiser, M. (1999). Parental reactions to children's negative emotions: Longitudinal reactions to the quality of children's social functioning. *Child Development, 70,* 513–534.

Eisenberg, N., Fabes, R. A., Shepard, S. A., Murphy, B. C., Guthrie, I. K., Jones, S., et al. (1997). Contemporaneous and longitudinal prediction of children's social functioning from regulation and emotionality. *Child Development, 68,* 642–664.

Eisenberg, N., Fabes, R. A., & Spinrad, T. L. (2006). Prosocial development. In W. Damon & R. M. Lerner (Editors-in-Chief), & N. Eisenberg (Vol. Ed.), *Handbook of child psychology: Vol. 3, Social, emotional, and personality development* (6th ed., pp. 646–718). Hoboken, NJ: Wiley.

Eisenberg, N., Gershoff, E. T., Fabes, R. A., Shepard, S. A., Cumberland, A. J., Losoya, S. H., et al. (2001). Mother's emotional expressivity and children's behavior problems and social competence: Mediation through children's regulation. *Developmental Psychology, 37,* 475–490.

Eisenberg, N., Hertz-Lazarowitz, R., & Fuchs, I. (1990). Prosocial moral judgment in Israeli kibbutz and city children: A longitudinal study. *Merrill-Palmer Quarterly, 36,* 273–285.

Eisenberg, N., & Lennon, R. (1983). Sex differences in empathy and related capacities. *Psychological Bulletin, 94,* 100–131.

Eisenberg, N., & Miller, P. A. (1987). The relation of empathy to prosocial and related behaviors. *Psychological Bulletin, 101,* 91–119.

Eisenberg, N., & Mussen, P. H. (1989). *The roots of prosocial behavior in children.* Cambridge, UK: Cambridge University Press.

Eisenberg, N., Pidada, S., & Liew, J. (2001). The relations of regulation and negative emotionality to Indonesian children's social functioning. *Child Development, 72,* 1747–1763.

Eisenberg, N., Valiente, C., Morris, A. S., Fabes, R. A., Cumberland, A., Reiser, M., Gershoff, E. T., Shepard, S. A., & Losoya, S. (2003). Longitudinal relations among parental emotional expressivity, children's regulation, and quality of socioemotional functioning. *Developmental Psychology, 39,* 3–19.

Eisenberg, N., Zhou, Q., Losoya, S. H., Fabes, R. A., Shepard, S. A., Murphy, B. C., Reiser, M., Guthrie, I. K., & Cumberland, A. (2003). The relations of parenting, effortful control, and ego control to children's emotional expressivity. *Child Development, 74,* 875–895.

Eisenberg, N., Zhou, Q., Spinrad, T., Valiente, C., Fabes, R. A., & Liew, J. (2005). Relations among positive parenting, children's effortful control, and externalizing problems: A three-wave longitudinal study. *Child Development, 76,* 1055–1071.

Ekman, P. (1972). Universals and cultural differences in facial expressions of emotion. In J. K. Cole (Ed.), *Nebraska symposium on motivation, 1971* (pp. 207–283). Lincoln, NE: University of Nebraska Press.

Ekman, P. (1973). Cross-cultural studies of facial expression. In P. Ekman (Ed.), *Darwin and facial expression* (pp. 169–222). New York, NY: Academic Press.

Elardo, R., Bradley, R. H., & Caldwell, B. M. (1975). The relation of infants' home environments to mental test performance from six to thirty-six months: A longitudinal analysis. *Child Development, 46,* 71–76.

Elardo, R., Bradley, R., & Caldwell, B. M. (1977). A longitudinal study of the relation of infants' home environments to language development at age three. *Child Development, 48,* 595–603.

Eley, T. C. (1997). General genes: A new theme in developmental psychopathology. *Current Directions in Psychological Science, 6,* 90–95.

Elfenbein, H. A., & Ambady, N. (2002). On the universality and cultural specificity of emotion recognition: A meta-analysis. *Psychological Bulletin, 128,* 203–235.

Eliez, S., & Reiss, A. L. (2000). Genetics of childhood disorders: XI Fragile X syndrome. *Journal of the American Academy of Child and Adolescent Psychiatry, 39,* 264–266.

Ellis, B. J. (2004). Timing of pubertal maturation in girls: An integrated life history approach. *Psychological Bulletin, 130,* 920–958.

Ellis, B. J., & Essex, M. J. (2007). Family environments, adrenarche, and sexual maturation: A longitudinal test of a life history model. *Child Development, 78,* 1799–1817.

Else-Quest, N. M., Hyde, J. S., & Linn, M. C. (2010). Cross-national patterns of gender differences in mathematics: A meta-analysis. *Psychological Bulletin, 136,* 103–127.

Emde, R. N., & Koenig, K. L. (1969). Neonatal smiling, frowning and rapid eye movement states. *Journal of the American Academy of Child Psychiatry, 8,* 57–67.

Emde, R. N., Plomin, R., Robinson, J., Corley, R., DeFries, J., Walker, D.W., . . . & Kagan, J. (1992). Temperament, emotion, and cognition at fourteen months: The MacArthur Longitudinal Twin Study. *Child Development, 63,* 1437–1455.

Emery, R. E. (1999a). Changing the rules for determining child custody in divorce cases. *Clinical Psychology: Science and Practice, 6,* 323–327.

Emery, R. E. (1999b). *Marriage, divorce, and children's adjustment* (2nd ed.). Thousand Oaks, CA: Sage.

Emery, R. E., Otto, R. K., & O'Donohue (2005). A critical assessment of child custody evaluations. *Psychological Science in the Public Interest, 6,* 1–29.

Emory, E. K., Schlackman, L. J., & Fiano, K. (1996). Drug-hormone interactions on neurobehavioral responses in human neonates. *Infant Behavior and Development, 19,* 213–220.

Engle, R. W. (2002). Working memory capacity as executive attention. *Current Directions in Psychological Science, 11,* 19–23.

Engle, R. W., Kane, M. J., & Tuholski, S. W. (1999). Individual differences in working memory capacity and what they tell us about controlled attention, general fluid intelligence, and functions of the prefrontal cortex. In A. Miyake & P. Shah (Eds.), *Models of working memory: Mechanisms of active maintenance and executive control* (pp. 102–134). New York, NY: Cambridge University Press.

Enright, A. M., & Prober, C. G. (2004). Herpesviridae infections in newborns: Varicella zoster virus, herpes simplex virus, and cytomegalovirus. *Pediatric Clinics of North America, 51,* 889–908.

Enright, M. K., Rovee-Collier, C. K., Fagen, J. W., & Caniglia, K. (1983). The effects of distributed training on retention of operant conditioning in human infants. *Journal of Experimental Child Psychology, 36,* 512–524.

Ensor, R., & Hughes, C. (2008). Content or connectedness? Mother–child talk and early social understanding. *Child Development, 79,* 201–216.

Entwisle, D. (1995). The role of schools in sustaining early childhood program benefits. *The Future of Children: Long-term Outcomes of Early Childhood Programs, 5,* 133–143.

Epstein, C. J. (2001). Down syndrome (trisomy 21). In C. R. Scriver, A. L. Beaudet, W. S. Sly, & D. Valle (Eds.), *The metabolic and molecular bases of inherited disease* (8th ed., Vol. 1, pp. 1223–1256). New York, NY: McGraw-Hill.

Epstein, J. L. (1983). Examining theories of adolescent friendship. In J. L. Epstein & N. L. Karweit (Eds.), *Friends in school* (pp. 39–61). San Diego, CA: Academic Press.

Erbe, R. W., & Levy, H. L. (2002). Neonatal screening. In D. L. Rimoin, J. M. Connor, R. E. Pyeritz, & B. R. Korf (Eds.), *Emery and Rimoin's priniciples and practice of medical genetics.* (4th ed., Vol. 1, pp. 826–841). London, UK: Churchill Livingston.

Erdley, C. A., Cain, K. M., Loomis, C. C., Dumas-Hines, F., & Dweck, C. S. (1997). Relations among children's social goals, implicit personality theories, and responses to social failure. *Developmental Psychology, 33,* 263–272.

Erhardt, D., & Hinshaw, S. P. (1994). Initial sociometric impressions of attention-deficit hyperactivity disorder and comparison boys: Predictions from social behaviors and from nonbehavioral variables. *Journal of Consulting and Clinical Psychology, 62,* 833–842.

Erickson, M. F., Sroufe, L. A., & Egeland, B. (1985). The relationship between quality of attachment and behavior problems in preschool in a high-risk sample. In I. Bretherton & E. Waters (Eds.), *Growing points of attachment theory and research. Monographs of the Society for Research in Child Development, 50* (1–2, Serial No. 209).

Erikson, E. H. (1950). *Childhood and society.* New York, NY: W. W. Norton.

Eron, L. D., Huesmann, L. R., & Zelli, A. (1991). The role of parental variables in the learning of aggression. In D. J. Pepler & K. H. Rubin (Eds.), *The development and treatment of childhood aggression* (pp. 169–188). Hillsdale, NJ: Erlbaum.

Eskenazi, B., Stapleton, A. L., Kharrazi, M., & Chee, W. Y. (1999). Associations between maternal decaffeinated and caffeinated coffee consumption and fetal growth and gestational duration. *Epidemiology, 10,* 242–249.

Eskritt, M., & Lee, K. (2002). "Remember where you last saw that card": Children's production of external symbols as a memory aid. *Developmental Psychology, 38,* 254–266.

Espy, K. A., & Kaufmann, P. M. (2002). Individual differences in the development of executive function in children: Lessons from the delayed response and A-not-B tasks. In D. L. Molfese & V. J. Molfese (Eds.), *Developmental variations in learning: Applications to social, executive function, language, and reading skills* (pp. 113–137). Mahwah, NJ: Erlbaum.

Ethics Committee of the American Society for Reproductive Medicine. (2004). Informing offspring of their conception by gamete donation. *Fertility and Sterility, 81,* 527–31.

European Collaborative Study. (2001). Fluctuations in symptoms in human immunodeficiency virus-infected children: The first 10 years of life. *Pediatrics, 108,* 116–122.

Evans, G. W. (2004). The environment of childhood poverty. *American Psychologist, 59,* 77–92.

Evans, G. W., & English, K. (2002). The environment of poverty: Multiple stressor exposure, psychophysiological stress, and socioemotional adjustment. *Child Development, 73,* 1238–1248.

Eveleth, P. B., & Tanner, J. M. (1990). *Worldwide variation in human growth* (2nd ed.). Cambridge, UK: Cambridge University Press.

Everman, D. B., & Cassidy, S. B. (2000). Genetics of childhood disorders: 12 Genomic imprinting: Breaking the rules. *Journal of the American Academy of Child and Adolescent Psychiatry, 39,* 386–389.

Fabes, R. A., Eisenberg, N., Hanish, L. D., & Spinrad, T. L. (2001). Preschoolers' spontaneous emotion vocabulary: Relations to likability. *Early Education and Development, 12,* 11–27.

Fabes, R. A., Eisenberg, N., Karbon, M., Troyer, D., & Switzer, G. (1994). The relations of children's emotion regulation to their vicarious emotional responses and comforting behaviors. *Child Development, 65,* 1678–1693.

Fabes, R. A., Eisenberg, N., McCormick, S. E., & Wilson, M. S. (1988). Preschoolers' attributions of the situational determinants of others' naturally occurring emotions. *Developmental Psychology, 24,* 376–385.

Fabes, R. A., Hanish, L. D., Martin, C. L., & Eisenberg, N. (2002). Young children's negative emotionality and social isolation: A latent growth curve analysis. *Merrill Palmer Quarterly, 48,* 284–307.

Fabes, R. A., Leonard, S. A., Kupanoff, K., & Martin, C. L. (2001). Parental coping with children's negative emotions: Relations with children's emotional and social responding. *Child Development, 72,* 907–920.

Fackelmann, K. (1998). It's a girl! Is sex selection the first step to designer children? *Science News, 154,* 350–351.

Fagan, J. F., III. (1974). Infant recognition memory: The effects of length of familiarization and type of discrimination task. *Child Development, 45,* 351–356.

Fagan, J. F., & Holland, C. R. (2002). Equal opportunity and racial differences in IQ. *Intelligence, 30,* 361–387.

Fagan, J. F., & Montie, J. E. (1988). The behavioral assessment of cognitive well-being in the infant. In J. Kavanagh (Ed.), *Understanding mental retardation: Research accomplishments and new frontiers* (pp. 207–221). Baltimore, MD: Paul H. Brookes.

Fagiolini, M., Jensen, C. L., & Champagne, F. A. (2009) Epigenetic influences on brain development and plasticity. *Current Opinion in Neurobiology, 19,* 207–212.

Fagot, B. I. (1977). Consequences of moderate cross-gender behavior in preschool children. *Child Development, 48,* 902–907.

Fagot, B. I. (1978). The influence of sex of child on parental reactions to toddler children. *Child Development, 49,* 459–465.

Fagot, B. I. (1985). Changes in thinking about early sex role development. *Developmental Review, 5,* 83–98.

Fagot, B. I., & Leinbach, M. D. (1987). Socialization of sex roles within the family. In D. B. Carter (Ed.), *Current conceptions of sex roles and sex typing: Theory and research* (pp. 89–100). New York, NY: Praeger.

Fagot, B. I., & Leinbach, M. D. (1995). Gender knowledge in egalitarian and traditional families. *Sex Roles, 32,* 513–526.

Fagot, B. I., Leinbach, M. D., & O'Boyle, C. (1992). Gender labeling, gender stereotyping, and parenting behaviors. *Developmental Psychology, 28,* 225–230.

Falbo, T., & Cooper, C. R. (1980). Young children's time and intellectual ability. *Journal of Genetic Psychology, 173,* 299–300.

Falbo, T., & Polit, D. F. (1986). Quantitative review of the only child literature: Research evidence and theory development. *Psychological Bulletin, 100,* 176–189.

Famularo, R., Fenton, T., Kinscherff, R., Ayoub, C., & Barnum, R. (1994). Maternal and child posttraumatic disorder in cases of child maltreatment. *Child Abuse and Neglect, 18,* 27–36.

Fancher, R. E. (1998). Alfred Binet, general psychologist. In G. A. Kimble & M. Wertheimer (Eds.), *Portraits of pioneers in psychology* (Vol. 3, pp. 67–83). Washington, D. C.: American Psychological Association.

Fangman, J. J., Mark, P. M., Pratt, L., Conway, K. K., Healey, M. L., Oswald, J. W., & Uden, D. L. (1994). Prematurity prevention programs: An analysis of successes and failures. *American Journal of Obstetrics and Gynecology, 170,* 744–750.

Fantz, R. L. (1961, May). The origin of form perception. *Scientific American, 204,* 66–72.

Farmer, T. W., Estell, D. B., Bishop, J. L., O'Neal, K. K., & Cairns, B. D. (2003). Rejected bullies or popular leaders? The social relations of aggressive subtypes of rural African American early adolescents. *Developmental Psychology, 39,* 992–1004.

Farooqi, I. S., & O'Rahilly, S. (2000). Recent advances in the genetics of severe childhood obesity. *Archives of Disease in Childhood, 83,* 31–34.

Farrar, M. J. (1992). Negative evidence and grammatical morpheme acquisition. *Developmental Psychology, 28,* 90–98.

Farrington, D. P. (1991). Childhood aggression and adult violence: Early precursors and later-life outcomes. In D. J. Pepler & K. H. Rubin (Eds.), *The development and treatment of childhood aggression* (pp. 5–29). Hillsdale, NJ: Erlbaum

Farver, J. M., Kim, Y. K., & Lee, Y. (1995). Cultural differences in Korean and Anglo-American preschoolers' social interaction and play behaviors. *Child Development, 66,* 1088–1099.

Farver, J. M., & Shin, Y. L. (1997). Social pretend play in Korean- and Anglo-American preschoolers. *Child Development, 68,* 544–556.

Farver, J. M., & Wimbarti, S. (1995). Paternal participation in toddlers' pretend play. *Social Development, 4,* 17–31.

Farver, J. M., Xu, Y., Eppe, S., Fernandez, A., & Schwartz, D. (2005). Community violence, family conflict, and preschoolers' socioemotional functioning. *Developmental Psychology, 41,* 160–170.

Fausto-Sterling, A. (1992). *Myths of gender: Biological theories about women and men* (2nd ed.). New York, NY: Basic Books.

Fearon, R. P., Bakermans-Kranenburg, M. J., van IJzendoorn, M. H., Lapsley, A., & Roisman, G. I. (2010). The significance of insecure attachment and disorganization in the development of children's externalizing behavior: A meta-analytic study. *Child Development, 81,* 435–456.

Feddes, A. R., Noack, P., & Rutland, A. (2009). Direct and extended friendship effects on minority and majority children's interethnic attitudes: A longitudinal study. *Child Development, 80,* 377–390.

Federman, J. (1998). *National Television Violence Study III.* Thousand Oaks, CA: Sage.

Feigenson, L., Dehaene, S., & Spelke, E. (2004). Core systems of number. *Trends in Cognitive Sciences, 8,* 307–314.

Feinberg, M. E., & Hetherington, E. M. (2000). Sibling differentiation in adolescence: Implications for behavioral genetic theory. *Child Development, 71,* 1512–1524.

Feingold, A. (1988). Cognitive gender differences are disappearing. *American Psychologist, 43,* 95–103.

Feingold, A. (1993). Cognitive gender differences: A developmental perspective. *Sex Roles, 29,* 91–112.

Feingold, A. (1994). Gender differences in personality: A meta-analysis. *Psychological Bulletin, 116,* 429–456.

Feldman, D. (1979). The mysterious case of extreme giftedness. In H. Passow (Ed.), *The gifted and talented* (pp. 335–351). Chicago, IL: University of Chicago Press.

Feldman, H., Goldin-Meadow, S., & Gleitman, L. (1978). Beyond Herodotus: The creation of language by linguistically deprived children. In A. Locke (Ed.), *Action, gesture, and symbol: The emergence of language* (pp. 351–418). New York, NY: Academic Press.

Feldman, P. J., Dunkel-Schetter, C., Sandman, C. A., & Wadhwa, P. D. (2000). Maternal social support predicts birth weight and fetal growth in human pregnancy. *Psychosomatic Medicine, 62,* 715–725.

Felner, R. D., & Adan, A. M. (1988). The School Transitional Environment Project: An ecological intervention and evaluation. In R. H. Price, E. L. Cowan, R. P. Lorion, I. Serrano-Garcia, & J. Ramos-McKay (Eds.), *14 ounces of prevention: A casebook for practitioners* (pp. 111–122). Washington, DC: American Psychological Association.

Felson, R. B. (1993). The (somewhat) social self: How others affect self-appraisals. In J. Suls (Ed.), *Psychological perspectives on the self* (Vol. 4, pp. 1–26). Hillsdale, NJ: Erlbaum.

Fenson, L., Dale, P. S., Reznick, J. S., Bates, E., Thal, D. J., & Pethick, S. J. (1994). Variability in early communicative development. *Monographs of the Society for Research in Child Development, 59* (5, Serial No. 242).

Fergusson, D. M., Lynskey, M., & Horwood, L. J. (1995). The adolescent outcomes of adoption: A 16-year longitudinal study. *Journal of Child Psychology and Psychiatry and Allied Disciplines, 36,* 597–615.

Fernald, A. (1985). Four-month-olds prefer to listen to motherese. *Infant Behavior and Development, 8,* 181–195.

Fernald, A. (1991). Prosody in speech to children: Prelinguistic and linguistic functions. In R. Vasta (Ed.), *Annals of child development* (Vol. 8, pp. 43–80). London, UK: Jessica Kingsley.

Fernald, A., & Mazzie, C. (1991). Prosody and focus in speech to infants and adults. *Developmental Psychology, 27,* 209–221.

Fernald, A., & Morikawa, H. (1993). Common themes and cultural variations in Japanese and American mothers' speech to infants. *Child Development, 64,* 637–656.

Fernald, A., Perfors, A., & Marchman, V. A. (2006). Picking up speed in understanding: Speech processing efficiency and vocabulary growth across the 2nd year. *Developmental Psychology, 42,* 98–116.

Fernald, A., Swingley, D., & Pinto, J. P. (2001). When half a word is enough: Infants can recognize spoken words using partial phonetic information. *Child Development, 72,* 1003–1015.

Ferrier, S., Dunham, P., & Dunham, F. (2000). The confused robot: Two-year-olds' responses to breakdowns in conversation. *Social Development, 9,* 337–347.

Feuerstein, R., Rand, Y., & Rynders, J. (1988). *Don't accept me as I am: Helping "retarded" people to excel.* New York, NY: Plenum.

Field, A. E., Austin, S. B., Taylor, C. B., Malspeis, S., Rosner, B., Rockett, H. R., Gillman, M. W., & Golditz, G. A. (2003). Relation between dieting and weight change among preadolescents and adolescents. *Pediatrics, 112,* 900–906.

Field, A. E., Javaras, K. M., Aneja, P., Kitos, N., Camargo, C. A., Jr., Taylor, C. B., & Laird, N. M. (2008). Family, peer, and media predictors of becoming eating disordered. *Archives of Pediatric & Adolescent Medicine, 162,* 574–579.

Field, T. M. (1977). Effects of early separation, interactive deficits, and experimental manipulations on infant-mother face-to-face interactions. *Child Development, 48,* 763–771.

Field, T. M. (1979). Differential behavior and cardiac responses of 3-month-olds to a mirror and a peer. *Infant Behavior and Development, 2,* 179–184.

Field, T. M. (1995). Infants of depressed mothers. *Infant Behavior and Development, 18,* 1–13.

Field, T. M. (2001). Massage therapy facilitates weight gain in preterm infants. *Current Directions in Psychological Science, 10,* 51–54.

Field, T. M. (1982). Affective displays of high-risk infants during early interactions. In T. Field & A. Fogel (Eds.), *Emotion and early interaction* (pp. 110–125). Hillsdale, NJ: Erlbaum.

Field, T. M., Cohen, D., Garcia, R., & Greenberg, R. (1984). Mother-stranger face discrimination by the newborn. *Infant Behavior and Development, 7, 19–25.*

Field, T. M., Diego, M., & Hernandez-Reif, M. (2007). Massage therapy research. *Developmental Review, 27,* 75–89.

Field, T. M., Fox, N. A., Pickens, J., & Nawrocki, T. (1995). Relative right frontal EEG activation in 3- to 6-month-old infants of "depressed" mothers. *Developmental Psychology, 31,* 358–363.

Field, T. M., Healy, B., Goldstein, S., Perry, S., Bendell, D., Schanberg, S., et al. (1988). Infants of depressed mothers show "depressed" behavior even with nondepressed adults. *Child Development, 59,* 1569–1579.

Field, T. M., Hernandez-Reif, M., Feijo, L., & Freedman, J. (2006). Prenatal, perinatal and neonatal stimulation: A survey of neonatal nurseries. *Infant Behavior and Development, 29,* 24–31.

Field, T. M., Scafidi, F., Pickens, J., Prodromidis, M., Pelaez-Nogueras, M., Torquati, J., et al. (1998). Polydrug-using adolescent mothers and their infants receiving early intervention. *Adolescence, 33,* 117–143.

Field, T. M., Woodson, R., Cohen, D., Greenberg, R., Garcia, R., & Collins, K. (1983). Discrimination and imitation of facial expressions by term and preterm neonates. *Infant Behavior and Development, 6,* 485–489.

Field, T. M., Woodson, R., Greenberg, R., & Cohen, D. (1982). Discrimination and imitation of facial expressions by neonates. *Science, 218,* 179–181.

Fields, R. D. (2008, March). White matter. *Scientific American, 298,* 54–61.

Fillmore, L.W., & Meyer, L. (1992). The curriculum and linguistic minorities. In P. Jackson (Ed.), *Handbook of research on curriculum* (pp. 626–658). New York, NY: Macmillan.

Fine, M. A., Coleman, M., & Ganong, L. H. (1999). A social constructionist multi-method approach to understanding the stepparent role. In E. M. Hetherington (Ed.), *Coping with divorce, single parenting, and remarriage* (pp. 273–294). Mahwah, NJ: Erlbaum.

Finkelhor, D., Turner, H., Ormrod, R., Hamby, S., Kracke, K. (2009). *Children's exposure to violence: A comprehensive national survey.* U.S. Department of Justice, Office of Justice Programs. Retrieved July 19, 2010, from http://www.ncjrs.gov/pdffiles1/ojjdp/227744.pdf

Finn, J. D., & Achilles, C. M. (1990). Answers and questions about class size: A statewide experiment. *American Educational Research Journal, 27,* 557–577.

Finnie, V., & Russell, A. (1988). Preschool children's social status and their mothers' behavior and knowledge in the supervisory role. *Developmental Psychology, 24,* 789–801.

Fischbein, S. (1981). Heredity-environment influences on growth and development during adolescence. In L. Gedda, P. Parisi, & W. E. Nance (Eds.), *Twin research 3: Pt. B. Program in clinical and biological research* (pp. 43–50). New York, NY: Liss.

Fischer, K. W., & Bidell, T. R. (2006). Dynamic development of action and thought. In W. Damon & R. M. Lerner (Editors-in-Chief) & R. M. Lerner (Vol. Ed.), *Handbook of child psychology: Vol. 1. Theoretical models of human development* (6th ed., pp. 313–399). Hoboken, NJ: Wiley.

Fisher, C. B. (1994). Reporting and referring research participants: Ethical challenges for investigators studying children and youth. *Ethics & Behavior, 4,* 87–95.

Fisher, C. B., Higgins D'Alessandro, A., Rau, J. M. B., Kuther, T. L., & Belanger, S. (1996). Referring and reporting research participants at risk: Views from urban adolescents. *Child Development, 67,* 2086–2100.

Fisher, C., Gertner, Y., Scott, R. M., & Yuan, S. (2010). Syntactic bootstrapping. *Wiley Interdisciplinary Reviews: Cognitive Science, 1,* 143–149.

Fishkin, J., Keniston, K., & MacKinnon, C. (1973). Moral reasoning and political ideology. *Journal of Personality and Social Psychology, 27,* 109–119.

Fitzgerald, M. (2005). The development of nociceptive circuits. *Nature Reviews Neuroscience, 6,* 507–520.

Fivush, R. (1997). Event memory in early childhood. In N. Cowan (Ed.), *The development of memory in childhood* (pp. 139–161). East Sussex, UK: Psychology Press.

Fivush, R., Haden, C., & Adam, S. (1995). Structure and coherence of preschoolers' personal narratives over time: Implications for childhood amnesia. *Journal of Experimental Child Psychology, 60,* 32–56.

Fivush, R., & Schwarzmueller, A. (1998). Children remember childhood: Implications for childhood amnesia. *Applied Cognitive Psychology, 12,* 455–473.

Flanagan, C. A. (1990). Change in family work status: Effects on parent-adolescent decision making. *Child Development, 61,* 163–177.

Flavell, J. H. (1978). The development of knowledge about visual perception. In C. B. Keasey (Ed.), *Nebraska symposium on motivation* (Vol. 25, pp. 43–76). Lincoln, NE: University of Nebraska Press.

Flavell, J. H. (1993). Young children's understanding of thinking and consciousness. *Current Directions in Psychological Science, 2,* 40–43.

Flavell, J. H. (1996). Piaget's legacy. *Psychological Science, 7,* 200–203.

Flavell, J. H., Beach, D. H., & Chinsky, J. M. (1966). Spontaneous verbal rehearsal in a memory task as a function of age. *Child Development, 37,* 283–299.

Flavell, J. H., Flavell, E. R., Green, F. L., & Korfmacher, J. E. (1990). Do young children think of television images as pictures or real objects? *Journal of Broadcasting & Electronic Media, 34,* 399–419.

Flavell, J. H., Green, F. L., & Flavell, E. R. (1995). The development of children's knowledge about attentional focus. *Developmental Psychology, 31,* 706–712.

Flavell, J. H., & Green, F. L. (1999). Development of intuitions about the controllability of different mental states. *Cognitive Development, 14,* 133–146.

Flavell, J. H., & Wellman, H. M. (1977). Metamemory. In R. V. Kail & J. W. Hagen (Eds.), *Perspectives on the development of memory and cognition* (pp. 3–33). Hillsdale, NJ: Erlbaum.

Fletcher, A. C., Steinberg, L., & Williams-Wheeler, M. (2004). Parental influences on adolescent problem behavior: Revisiting Stattin and Kerr. *Child Development, 75,* 781–796.

Fletcher-Flinn, C. M., & Thompson, G. B. (2000). Learning to read with underdeveloped phonemic awareness but lexicalized phonological recoding: A case study of a 3-year-old. *Cognition, 74,* 177–208.

Florsheim, P., Tolan, P., & Gorman-Smith, D. (1998). Family relationship, parenting practices, the availability of male family members, and the behavior of inner-city boys in single-mother and two-parent families. *Child Development, 69,* 1437–1447.

Foa, E. B., & Meadows, E. A. (1997). Psychosocial treatments for posttraumatic stress disorder: A critical review. *Annual Review of Psychology, 48,* 449–480.

Fodor, J. A. (1983). *The modularity of mind.* Cambridge, MA: MIT Press.

Fodor, J. A . (1992). A theory of the child's theory of mind. *Cognition, 44,* 283–296.

Fogel, A. (1979). Peer- vs. mother-directed behavior in 1- to 3-month-old infants. *Infant Behavior and Development, 2,* 215–226.

Fogel, A. (1982). Early adult-infant face-to-face interaction: Expectable sequences of behavior. *Journal of Pediatric Psychology, 7,* 1–22.

Foley, D. L., Eaves, L. J., Wormley, B., Silberg, J., Maes, H., Kuhn, J., & Riley, B. (2004). Childhood adversity, monoamine oxidase A genotype, and risk for conduct disorder. *Archives of General Psychiatry, 61,* 721–727.

Fonzi, A., Schneider, B. H., Tani, F., & Tomada, G. (1997). Predicting children's friendship status from their dyadic interaction in structured situations of potential conflict. *Child Development, 68,* 496–506.

Forbes, E. E., Cohn, J. F., Allen, N. B., & Lewinsohn, P. M. (2004). Infant affect during parent-infant interaction at 3 months and 6 months: Differences between mothers and fathers and influence of parent history of depression. *Infancy, 5,* 61–84.

Forehand, R. L., & Long, N. (1988). Outpatient treatment of the acting out child: Procedures, long term follow-up data, and clinical problems. *Advances in Behavior Research and Therapy, 10,* 129–177.

Forehand, R. L., Merchant, M. J., Long, N., & Garai, E. (2010). An examination of parenting the strong-willed child as bibliotherapy for parents. *Behavior Modification, 34,* 57–76.

Forman, D. R., Aksan, N., & Kochanska, G. (2004). Toddlers' responsive imitation predicts preschool-age conscience. *Psychological Science, 15,* 699–704.

Forman, D. R., & Kochanska, G. (2001). Viewing imitation as child responsiveness: A link between teaching and discipline domains of socialization. *Developmental Psychology, 37,* 198–206.

Foster, E. M., & Watkins, S. (2010). The value of reanalysis: TV viewing and attention problems. *Child Development, 81,* 368–375.

Foulon, I., Naessens, A., Foulon, W., Casteels, A., & Gordts, F. (2008). A 10-year prospective study of sensorineural hearing loss in children with congenital cytomegalovirus infection. *Journal of Pediatrics, 153,* 84–88.

Foulon, W., Villena, I., Stray-Pedersen, B., Decoster, A., Lappalainen, M., Pinon, J.-M., . . . & Naessens, A. (1999). Treatment of toxoplasmosis during pregnancy: A multicenter study of impact on fetal transmission and children's sequelae at age 1 year. *American Journal of Obstetrics and Gynecology, 180,* 410–415.

Fowler, M. G., Lampe, M. A., Jamieson, D. J., Kourtis, A. P., & Rogers, M. F. (2007). Reducing the risk of mother-to-child human immunodeficiency virus transmission: Past successes, current progress and challenges, and future directions. *American Journal of Obstetrics and Gynecology, 197,* S3-S9.

Fox, N. A. (1994). Dynamic cerebral processes underlying emotion regulation. In N. A. Fox (Ed.), *The development of emotion regulation: Biological and behavioral considerations. Monographs of the Society for Research in Child Development, 59* (Nos. 2–3, Serial No. 240).

Fox, N. A., & Davidson, R. J. (1986). Psychophysiological measures of emotion: New directions in developmental research. In C. E. Izard & P. B. Read (Eds.), *Measuring emotions in infants and children* (Vol. 2, pp. 13–47). Cambridge, UK: Cambridge University Press.

Fox, N. A., Nichols, K. E., Henderson, H. A., Rubin, K., Schmidt, L., Hamer, D., Ernst, M., & Pine, D. S. (2005). Evidence for a gene-environment interaction in predicting behavioral inhibition in middle childhood. *Psychological Science, 16,* 921–926.

Fox, S. E., Levitt, P., & Nelson, C. A. III. (2010). How the timing and quality of early experience influence the development of brain architecture. *Child Development, 81,* 28–40.

Fraiberg, S. (1977). *Insights from the blind.* New York, NY: Basic Books.

Francis, L. A., Ventura, A. K., Marini, M., & Birch, L. L. (2007). Parent overweight predicts daughters' increase in BMI and disinhibited overeating from 5 to 13 years. *Obesity, 15,* 1544–1553.

Franco, P., Groswasser, J., Hassid, S., Lanquart, J. P., Scaillet, S., & Kahn, A. (1999). Prenatal exposure to cigarette smoking is associated with a decrease in arousal in infants. *Journal of Pediatrics, 135,* 34–38.

Frank, D. A., Augustyn, M., Knight, W. G., Pell, T., & Zuckerman, B. (2001). Growth, development, and behavior in early childhood following prenatal cocaine exposure: A systematic review. *Journal of the American Medical Association, 285,* 1613–1625.

Franklin, A., & Davies, I. R. L. (2004). New evidence for infant colour categories. *British Journal of Development Psychology, 22,* 349–377.

Franklin, J., Denyer, G., Steinbeck, K. S., Caterson, I. D., & Hill, A. J. (2006). Obesity and risk of low self-esteem: A statewide survey of Australian children. *Pediatrics, 118,* 2481–2487.

Fraser, S. (1995). *The bell curve wars: Race, intelligence, and the future of America.* New York, NY: Basic Books.

Frauenglass, M. H., & Diaz, R. M. (1985). Self-regulatory functions of children's private speech: A critical analysis of recent challenges to Vygotsky's theory. *Developmental Psychology, 21,* 357–364.

Frazier, J. A., & Morrison, F. J. (1998). The influence of extended-year schooling on growth of achievement and perceived competence in early elementary school. *Child Development, 69,* 495–517.

Fredricks, J. A., & Eccles, J. S. (2002). Children's competence and value beliefs from childhood through adolescence: Growth trajectories in two male-sex-typed domains. *Developmental Psychology, 38,* 519–533.

Fredriks, A. M., Van Buren, S., Burgmeijer, R. J. F., Meulmeester, J. F., Beuker, R J., Brugman, E., . . . & Wit, J. M. (2000). Continuing positive secular growth change in the Netherlands 1955–1997. *Pediatric Research, 47,* 316–323.

Fredriksen, K., Rhodes, J., Reddy, R., & Way, N. (2004). Sleepless in Chicago: Tracking the effects of adolescent sleep loss during the middle school years. *Child Development, 75,* 84–95.

Freedman, D. (1979). Ethnic differences in babies. *Human Nature, 2,* 26–43.

French, D. C., Eisenberg, N., Vaughn, J., Purwono, U., & Suryanti, T. A. (2008). Religious involvement and the social competence and adjustment of Indonesian Muslim adolescents. *Developmental Psychology, 44,* 597–611.

French, S. E., Seidman, E., Allen, L., & Aber, J. L. (2000). Racial/ethnic identity, congruence with the social context, and the transition to high school. *Journal of Adolescent Research, 15,* 587–602.

French, S. E., Seidman, E., Allen, L., & Aber, J. L. (2006). The development of ethnic identity during adolescence. *Developmental Psychology, 42,* 1–11.

Frey, K. S., & Ruble, D. N. (1987). What children say about classroom performance: Sex and grade differences in perceived competence. *Child Development, 58,* 1066–1078.

Fried, P. A. (2002). Conceptual issues in behavioral teratology and their applications in determining long-term sequelae of prenatal marijuana exposure. *Journal of Child Psychology and Psychiatry, 43,* 81–102.

Friederici, A. D., & Wartenburger, I. (2010). Language and brain. *Wiley Interdisciplinary Reviews: Cognitive Science, 1,* 150–159.

Friedman, J. M., & Hanson, J. W. (2002). Clinical teratology. In D. L. Rimoin, J. M. Connor, R. E. Pyeritz, & B. R. Kork (Eds.), *Emery and Rimoin's principles and practice of medical genetics.* (4th ed., Vol. 1, pp. 1011–1045). London, UK: Churchill Livingston.

Friedman, J. M., & Hanson, J. W. (2007). Clinical teratology. In D. L. Rimoin, J. M., Connor, R. E. Pyreritz, & B. R. Korf (Eds.), *Emery and Rimoin's principles and practice of medical genetics* (5th ed., Vol. 1, pp. 900–930). London, UK: Churchill Livingston.

Friedman, J. M., & Polifka, J. E. (1996). *The effects of drugs on the fetus and nursing infant: A handbook for health care professionals.* Baltimore: Johns Hopkins University Press.

Friedrich, L. K., & Stein, A. H. (1973). Aggressive and prosocial television programs and the natural behavior of preschool children. *Monographs of the Society for Research in Child Development, 38* (4, Serial No. 151).

Friends of the Earth, United Kingdom. (2001). *Pollution and poverty: Breaking the link.* London, UK: Author.

Frith, U., & Happé, F. (1999). Theory of mind and self-consciousness: What is it like to be autistic? *Mind & Language, 14,* 1–22.

Frodi, A. M., & Lamb, M. E. (1980). Child abusers' responses to infant smiles and cries. *Child Development, 51,* 238–241.

Frodi, A. M., Lamb, M. E., Leavitt, L. A., & Donovan, W. L. (1978). Fathers' and mothers' responses to infant smiles and cries. *Infant Behavior and Development, 1,* 187–198.

Frodi, A. M., & Thompson, R. (1985). Infants' affective responses in the strange situation: Effects of prematurity and of quality of attachment. *Child Development, 56,* 1280–1290.

Fuligni, A. J. (1997). The academic achievement of adolescents from immigrant families: The roles of family background, attitudes, and behavior. *Child Development, 68,* 351–363.

Fuligni, A. J., & Eccles, J. S. (1993). Perceived parent-child relationships and early adolescents' orientation toward peers. *Developmental Psychology, 29,* 622–632.

Fuligni, A. J., Eccles, J. S., Barber, B. L., & Clements, P. (2001). Early adolescent peer orientation and adjustment during high school. *Developmental Psychology, 37,* 28–36.

Fuligni, A. J., & Stevenson, H. W. (1995). Time use and mathematics achievement among American, Chinese, and Japanese high school students. *Child Development, 66,* 830–842.

Fuligni, A. J., Witkow, M., & Garcia, C. (2005). Ethnic identity and the academic adjustment of adolescents from Mexican, Chinese, and European backgrounds. *Developmental Psychology, 41,* 799–811.

Fulker, O. W., & Eysenck, H. J. (1979). Nature, nurture and socio-economic status. In H. J. Eysenck (Ed.), *The structure and measurement of intelligence* (pp. 154–175). Berlin: Springer-Verlag.

Furman, W., & Bierman, K. L. (1984). Children's conceptions of friendship: A multimethod study of developmental changes. *Developmental Psychology, 20,* 925–931.

Furman, W., & Buhrmester, D. (1992). Age and sex differences in perceptions of networks of personal relationships. *Child Development, 63,* 103–115.

Furman, W., & Collins, W. A. (2009). Adolescent romantic relationships and experiences. In K. H. Rubin, W. M. Bukowski, & B. Laursen (Eds.), *Handbook of peer interactions, relationships, and groups.* (pp. 341–360). New York, NY: Guilford Press.

Furman, W., & Simon V. A. (2008). Homophily and influence in adolescent romantic relationships. In M. Prinstein & K. A. Dodge (Eds.), *Understanding peer influence in children and adolescents* (pp. 203–224). New York, NY: Guilford.

Furman, W., Somin, V. A., Shaffer, L., & Bouchey, H. A. (2002). Adolescents' working models and styles for relationships with parents, friends, and romantic partners. *Child Development, 73,* 241–255.

Furrow, J. L., King, P. E., & White, K. (2004). Religion and positive youth development: Identity, meaning, and prosocial concerns. *Applied Developmental Science, 8,* 17–26.

Furstenberg, F. F., Jr. (1987). The new extended family: The experience of parents and children after remarriage. In K. Paley & M. Ihinger-Tallman (Eds.), *Remarriage and stepparenting* (pp. 42–61). New York, NY: Guilford Press.

Furstenberg, F. F. Jr. (1994). History and current status of divorce in the United States. *The Future of Children, 4,* 29–43.

Fuson, K. C., & Kwon, Y. (1992). Korean children's understanding of multi-digit addition and subtraction. *Child Development, 63,* 491–506.

Gaddis, A., & Brooks-Gunn, J. (1985). The male experience of pubertal change. *Journal of Youth and Adolescence, 14,* 61–69.

Gagnon, M., & Ladouceur, R. (1992). Behavioral treatment of child stutterers: Replication and extension. *Behavior Therapy, 23,* 113–129.

Galambos, N. L. (2004). Gender and gender role development in adolescence. In R. M. Lerner & L. Steinberg (Eds.), *Handbook of adolescent psychology* (2nd ed., pp. 233–262). Hoboken, NJ: Wiley.

Gallahue, D. L. (1989). *Understanding motor development: Infants, children, adolescents.* Indianapolis, IN: Benchmark Press.

Gallistel, C. R., Brown, A. L., Carey, S., Gelman, R., & Keil, F. C. (1991). Lessons from animal learning for the study of cognitive development. In S. Carey & R. Gelman (Eds.), *The epigenesis of mind: Essays on biology and cognition* (pp. 3–36). Hillsdale, NJ: Erlbaum.

Gallistel, C. R., & Gelman, R. (2005). Mathematical cognition. In K. Holyoak & R. Morrison (Eds.), *The Cambridge handbook of thinking and reasoning* (pp. 559–588). New York, NY: Cambridge University Press.

Galton, F. (1883). *Inquiries into human faculty and its development.* London, UK: Macmillan.

Garcia, M. M., Shaw, D. S., Winslow, E. B., & Yaggi, K. E. (2000). Destructive sibling conflict and the development of conduct problems in young boys. *Developmental Psychology, 36,* 44–53.

Gardner, D., Harris, P. L., Ohmoto, M., & Hamasaki, T. (1988). Japanese children's understanding of the distinction between real and apparent emotion. *International Journal of Behavioral Development, 11,* 203–218.

Gardner, H. (1983). *Frames of mind: The theory of multiple intelligences.* New York, NY: Basic Books.

Gardner, H. (1986). The waning of intelligence tests. In R. J. Sternberg & D. K. Detterman (Eds.), *What is intelligence?* (pp. 73–76). Norwood, NJ: Ablex.

Gardner, M., & Steinberg, L. (2005). Peer influence on risk taking, risk preference, and risky decision making in adolescence and adulthood: An experimental study. *Developmental Psychology, 41,* 625–635.

Gardner, W., & Rogoff, B. (1990). Children's deliberateness of planning according to task circumstances. *Developmental Psychology, 26,* 480–487.

Garon, N., Bryson, S. E., & Smith, I. M. (2008). Executive function in preschoolers: A review using an integrative framework. *Psychological Bulletin, 134,* 31–60.

Gash, H., & Morgan, M. (1993). School-based modifications of children's gender-related beliefs. *Journal of Applied Developmental Psychology, 14,* 277–287.

Gauvain, M., & Perez, S. M. (2008). Mother–child planning and child compliance. *Child Development, 79,* 761–775.

Gavin, L., McKay, A. P., Brown, K., Harrier, S., Ventura, S. J., Kann, L. . . . & Ryan, G. (2009). Sexual and reproductive health of persons aged 10–24 years—United States, 2002–2007. *MMWR, 58(SS06),* 1–58. Retrieved August 29, 2010, from http://www.cdc.gov/mmwr/preview/mmwrhtml/ss5806a1.htm?s_cid=ss5806a1_e

Gazelle, H., & Druhen, M. J. (2009). Anxious solitude and peer exclusion predict social helplessness, upset affect, and vagal regulation in response to behavioral rejection by a friend. *Developmental Psychology, 45,* 1077–1096.

Gazelle, H., & Ladd, G. W. (2003). Anxious solitude and peer exclusion: A diathesis-stress model of internalizing trajectories in childhood. *Child Development, 74,* 257–278.

Ge, X., Best, K. M., Conger, R. D., & Simons, R. L. (1996). Parenting behaviors and the occurrence and co-occurrence of adolescent depressive symptoms and conduct problems. *Developmental Psychology, 32,* 717–731.

Ge, X., Conger, R.D., & Elder, G. H., Jr. (1996). Coming of age too early: Pubertal influences on girls' vulnerability to psychological distress. *Child Development, 67,* 3386–3400.

Ge, X., Kim, I. J., Brody, G. H., Conger, R. D., Simons, R. L. et al. (2003). It's about timing and change: Pubertal transition effects on symptoms of major depression among African American youths. *Developmental Psychology, 39,* 430–439.

Geary, D. C., Bow-Thomas, C. C., Fan, L., & Siegler, R. S. (1993). Even before formal instruction, Chinese children outperform American children in mental addition. *Cognitive Development, 8,* 517–529.

Geldart, S., Maurer, D., & Carney, K. (1999). Effects of the height of the internal features of faces on adult's aesthetic ratings and 5-month-old's looking times. *Perception, 28,* 839–850.

Gelman, R., & Gallistel, C. R. (1978). *The child's understanding of number.* Cambridge, MA: Harvard University Press.

Gelman, R., & Meck, E. (1983). Preschoolers' counting: Principles before skill. *Cognition, 13,* 343–359.

Gelman, R., Spelke, E. S., & Meck, E. (1983). What preschoolers know about animate and inanimate objects. In D. Rogers & J. A. Sloboda (Eds.), *The acquisition of symbolic skills* (pp. 297–326). New York, NY: Plenum.

Gelman, S. A., Coley, J. D., Rosengren, K. S., Hartman, E., & Pappas, A. (1998). Beyond labeling: The role of maternal input in the acquisition of richly structured categories. *Monographs of the Society for Research in Child Development, 63* (1, Serial No. 253).

Gelman, S. A., & Ebeling, K. S. (1998). Shape and representational status in children's early naming. *Cognition, 66,* B35–B47.

Gelman, S. A., Taylor, M. G., & Nguyen, S. P. (2004). Mother-child conversations about gender. *Monographs of the Society for Research in Child Development, 69* (1, Serial no. 275).

Genetics Home Reference (2010a). *Chromosomes.* Retrieved August 19, 2010, from http://ghr.nlm.nih.gov/chromosomes

Genetics Home Reference (2010b). *Genetic conditions.* Retrieved August 19, 2010, from http://ghr.nlm.nih.gov/BrowseConditions

Genetics Home Reference (2010c). *What is a gene?* Retrieved August 19, 2010, from http://ghr.nlm.nih.gov/handbook/basics/gene

Gentile, D. (2009). Pathological video-game use among youth ages 8 to 18: A national study. *Psychological Science, 20,* 594–602.

Gergely, G., & Csibra, G. (2003). Teleological reasoning in infancy: The one-year-olds' naïve theory of rational action. *Trends in Cognitive Sciences, 7,* 287–292.

Gershkoff-Stowe, L. (2001). The course of children's naming errors in early word learning. *Journal of Cognition and Development, 2,* 131–155.

Gershkoff-Stowe, L., & Smith, L. B. (1997). A curvilinear trend in naming errors as a function of early vocabulary growth. *Cognitive Psychology, 34,* 37–71.

Gershoff, E. T. (2002). Corporal punishment by parents and associated child behaviors and experiences: A meta-analytic and theoretical review. *Psychological Bulletin, 128,* 539–579.

Gershoff, E. T., Aber, J. L., Ware, A., & Kotler, J. A. (2010). Exposure to 9/11 among youth and their mothers in New York City: Enduring associations with mental health and sociopolitical attitudes. *Child Development, 81,* 1142–1160.

Gershoff, E. T., Grogan-Kaylor, A., Lansford, J. E., Chang, L., Zelli, A., Deater-Deckard, K., & Dodge, K. A. (2010). Parent discipline practices in an international sample: Associations with child behaviors and moderation by perceived normativeness. *Child Development, 81,* 487–502.

Gervain, J., & Werker, J. F. (2008). How infant speech perception contributes to language acquisition. *Language and Linguistics Compass, 2,* 1149–1170.

Geschwind, M., & Galaburda, A. M. (1987). *Cerebral lateralization.* Cambridge, MA: MIT Press.

Gesell, A., & Thompson, H. (1934). *Infant behavior: Its genesis and growth.* New York, NY: McGraw-Hill.

Gesell, A., & Thompson, H. (1938). *The psychology of early growth.* New York, NY: Macmillan.

Gest, S. D., Rulison, K. L., Davidson, A. L., & Welsh, J. A. (2008). A reputation for success (or failure): The association of peer academic reputation with academic self-concept, effort, and performance across the upper elementary grades. *Developmental Psychology, 44,* 625–636.

Gewirtz, J. L., & Peláez-Nogueras, M. (1992). B. F. Skinner's legacy to human infant behavior and development. *American Psychologist, 47,* 1411–1422.

Gibbs, J. C., Basinger, K. S., Grime, R. L., Snarey, J. R., Graf, S. C., Mullis, R. L., & Millis, A. K. (2007). Moral judgment development across cultures: Revisiting Kohlberg's universality claims. *Developmental Review, 27,* 443–500.

Gibson, E. J. (1969). *Principles of perceptual learning and development.* New York, NY: Appleton.

Gibson, E. J. (1982). The concept of affordances in development: The renascence of functionalism. In W. A. Collins (Ed.), *The Minnesota symposia on child psychology: Vol. 15. The concept of development* (pp. 55–81). Hillsdale, NJ: Erlbaum.

Gibson, E. J. (1988). Exploratory behavior in the development of perceiving, acting, and the acquiring of knowledge. *Annual Review of Psychology, 39,* 1–41.

Gibson, E. J., Gibson, J. J., Pick, A. D., & Osser, H. (1962). A developmental study of the discrimination of letter-like forms. *Journal of Comparative and Physiological Psychology, 55,* 897–906.

Gibson, E. J., & Walker, A. (1984). Development of knowledge of visual-tactual affordances of substance. *Child Development, 55,* 453–460.

Gibson, J. J. (1966). *The senses considered as perceptual systems.* Boston: Houghton Mifflin.

Gibson, J. J. (1979). *The ecological approach to visual perception.* Boston: Houghton Mifflin.

Gibson, M., & Ogbu, J. U. (Eds.). (1991). *Minority status and schooling: A comparative study of immigrant and involuntary minorities.* New York, NY: Garland.

Giedd, J. N., Blumenthal, J., Molloy, E., & Castellanos, F. X. (2001). Brain imaging of attention deficit/hyperactivity disorder. *Annals of the New York Academy of Sciences, 931,* 33–49.

Gilbert, S. F. (2003). *Developmental biology* (7th ed.). Sunderland, MA: Sinauer Associates.

Giles, J. W., Gopnik, A., & Heyman, G. D. (2002). Source monitoring reduces the suggestibility of preschool children. *Psychological Science, 13,* 288–291.

Gilligan, C. (1982). *In a different voice: Psychological theory and women's development.* Cambridge, MA: Harvard University Press.

Gilliom, M., Shaw, D. S., Beck, J. E., Schonberg, M. A., & Lukon, J. L. (2002). Anger regulation in disadvantaged preschool boys: Strategies, antecedents, and the development of self-control. *Developmental Psychology, 38,* 222–235.

Ginsberg, H. P. (1972). *The myth of the deprived child: Poor children's intellect and education.* Englewood Cliffs, NJ: Prentice-Hall.

Ginsburg, H. P., Pappas, S., & Seo, K. H. (2001). Everyday mathematical knowledge: Asking young children what is developmentally appropriate. In S. L. Golbeck (Ed.), *The Rutgers invitational symposium on education series: Psychological perspectives on early childhood education: Reframing dilemmas in research and practice* (pp. 181–219). Mahwah, NJ: Erlbaum.

Giordano, P. C., Manning, W. D., & Longmore, M. A. (2006). Adolescent romantic relationships: An emerging portrait of their nature and developmental significance. In A. C. Crouter & A. Booth (Eds.), *Romance and sex in adolescence and emerging adulthood: Risks and opportunities* (pp. 127–150). Mahwah, NJ: Erlbaum.

Glasgow, K. L., Dornbusch., S. N., Troyer, L., Steinberg, L., & Ritter, P. (1997). Parenting styles, adolescents' attributions, and educational outcomes in nine heterogeneous high schools. *Child Development, 68,* 507–529.

Glass, D. C., Neulinger, J., & Brim, O. G. (1974). Birth order, verbal intelligence, and educational aspiration. *Child Development, 45,* 807–811.

Glassman, M., & Zan, B. (1995). Moral activity and domain theory: An alternative interpretation of research on young children. *Developmental Review, 15,* 434–457.

Gleason, J. B., & Perlmann, R. Y. (1985). Acquiring social variation in speech. In H. Giles & R. N. St. Clair (Eds.), *Recent advances in language, communication, and social psychology* (pp. 86–111). London, UK: Erlbaum.

Gleitman, L. R., Gleitman, H., & Shipley, E. F. (1972). The emergence of the child as grammarian. *Cognition, 1,* 137–164.

Gleitman, L. R., Newport, E. L., & Gleitman, H. (1984). The current status of the motherese hypothesis. *Journal of Child Language, 11,* 43–79.

Glynn, L. M., Wadhwa, P. O., Dunkel-Schetter, C., Chicz-DeMet, A., & Sandman, C. A. (2001). When stress happens matters: Effects of earthquake timing on stress responsivity in pregnancy. *American Journal of Obstetrics & Gynecology, 184,* 637–642.

Gogate, L. J., Bahrick, L. E., & Watson, J. D. (2000). A study of multimodal motherese: The role of temporal synchrony between verbal labels and gestures. *Child Development, 71,* 878–894.

Goldberg, M. C., Maurer, D., & Lewis, T. L. (2001). Developmental changes in attention: The effects of endogenous cueing and of distractors. *Developmental Science, 4,* 209–219.

Goldberg, S. (1979). Premature birth: Consequences for the parent-infant relationship. *American Scientist, 67,* 582–590.

Goldberg, W. A., Greenberger, E., & Nagel, S. K. (1996). Employment and achievement: Mothers' work involvement in relation to children's achievement behaviors and mothers' parenting behaviors. *Child Development, 67,* 1512–1527.

Golden, F. (1998, September 21). Boy? Girl? Up to you. *Time,* pp. 82–83.

Goldenberg, R. L., Clivar, S. P., Cutter, G. R., Hoffman, H. J., Cassady, G., Davis, R. O., & Nelson, K. G. (1991). Black-white differences in newborn anthropometric measurements. *Obstetrics and Gynecology, 78,* 782–788.

Goldfield, B. A., & Reznick, J. S. (1990). Early lexical acquisition: Rate, content, and the vocabulary spurt. *Journal of Child Language, 17,* 171–183.

Goldin-Meadow, S. (2006). Nonverbal communication: The hand's role in talking and thinking. In W. Damon & R. M. Lerner (Editors-in-Chief) & D. M. Kuhn & R. S. Siegler (Vol. Eds.), *Handbook of child psychology. Vol. 2. Cognition, perception, and language* (6th ed., pp. 336–369). Hoboken, NJ: Wiley.

Goldin-Meadow, S., Goodrich, W., Sauer, E., & Iverson, J. (2007). Young children use their hands to tell their mothers what to say. *Developmental Science, 10,* 778–785.

Goldsmith, H. H., & Alansky, J. A. (1987). Maternal and infant temperamental predictors of attachment: A meta-analytic review. *Journal of Consulting and Clinical Psychology, 55,* 805–816.

Goldsmith, H. H., Buss, K. A., & Lemery, K. S. (1997). Toddler and childhood temperament: Expanded content, stronger genetic evidence, new evidence for the importance of environment. *Developmental Psychology, 33,* 891–905.

Goldstein, S., & Brooks, R. B. (Eds.). (2005). *Handbook of resilience in children.* New York, NY: Kluwer Academic/Plenum Publishers.

Goldstein, S. E., Davis-Kean, P. E., & Eccles, J. S. (2005). Parents, peers, and problem behavior: A longitudinal investigation of the impact of relationship perceptions and characteristics on the development of adolescent problem behavior. *Developmental Psychology, 41,* 401–413.

Golier, J., & Yehuda, R. (1998). Neuroendocrine activity and memory-related impairments in posttraumatic stress disorder. *Development and Psychopathology, 10,* 857–869.

Golinkoff, R. M., Harding, C. G., Carlson, V., & Sexton, M. E. (1984). The infant's perception of causal events: The distinction between animate and inanimate objects. In L. L. Lipsitt & C. Rovee-Collier (Eds.), *Advances in infancy research.* (Vol. 3, pp. 145–151). Norwood, NJ: Ablex.

Golombok, S., MacCallum, F., Goodman, E., & Rutter, M. (2002). Families with children conceived by donor insemination: A follow-up at stage twelve. *Child Development, 73,* 952–968.

Golombok, S., MacCallum, F., & Murray, C. (2006). Surrogacy families: Parental functioning, parent-child relationships and children's psychological development at age 2. *Journal of Child Psychology and Psychiatry, 47,* 213–222.

Golombok, S., Perry, B., Burston, A., Murray, C., Mooney-Somers, J., Stevens, M., & Golding, J. (2003). Children with lesbian parents: A community study. *Developmental Psychology, 39,* 20–33.

Golombok, S., Rust, J., Zervoulis, K., Croudace, T., Golding, J., & Hines, M. (2008). Developmental trajectories of sex-typed behavior in boys and girls: A longitudinal general population study of children aged 2.5–8 years. *Child Development, 79,* 1583–1593.

Gonzales, P., Calsyn, C., Jocelyn, L., Mak., Kastberg, D., Arafeh, T., et al. (2000). *Pursuing excellence: Comparisons of international eighth-grade mathematics and science achievement from a U.S. perspective, 1995 and 1999* (N CES 2001 028). Retrieved December 18, 2010 from http://nces.ed.gov/pubsearch/pubsinfo.asp?pubid=2001028

Gonzales, P., Williams, T., Jocelyn, L., Roey, S., Kastberg, D., & Brenwald, S. (2008). *Highlights from TIMSS 2007: Mathematics and Science Achievement of U.S. Fourth- and Eighth-Grade Students in an International Context* (NCES 2009–001 Revised). National Center for Education Statistics, Institute of Education Sciences, U.S. Department of Education. Washington, DC.

Goodnow, J. J. (1988). Children's household work: Its nature and functions. *Psychological Bulletin, 103,* 5–26.

Goodwyn, S. W., & Acredolo, L. P. (1993). Symbolic gestures versus word: Is there a modality advantage for the onset of symbol use? *Child Development, 64,* 688–701.

Gopnik, A. (1996). The post-Piaget era. *Psychological Science, 7,* 221–225.

Gopnik, A., & Meltzoff, A. N. (1986). Relations between semantic and cognitive development in the one-word stage: The specificity hypothesis. *Child Development, 57,* 1040–1053.

Gopnik, A., & Meltzoff, A. N. (1987). The development of categorization in the second year and its relation to other cognitive and linguistic attainments. *Child Development, 58,* 1523–1531.

Gopnik, A., & Meltzoff, A. N. (1992). Categorization and naming: Basic-level sorting in eighteen-month-olds and its relation to language. *Child Development, 63,* 1091–1103.

Gorski, R. A. (1980). Sexual differentiation of the brain. In D. T. Krieger & J. C. Hughes (Eds.), *Neuroendocrinology* (pp. 215–222). New York, NY: Rockefeller University Press.

Gottfried, A. E., Bathurst, K., & Gottfried, A. W. (1994). Role of maternal and dual-earner employment status in children's development. In A. E. Gottfried, & A. W. Gottfried (Eds.), *Redefining families: Implications for children's development* (pp. 55–97). New York, NY: Plenum.

Gottfried, A. E., Gottfried, A. W., & Bathurst, K. (2002). Maternal and dual-earner employment status and parenting. In M. H. Bornstein (Ed.), *Handbook of parenting: Vol. 2. Biology and ecology of parenting* (2nd ed., pp. 207–230). Mahwah, NJ: Erlbaum.

Gottfried, G. M. (1997). Using metaphors as modifiers: Children's production of metaphoric compounds. *Journal of Child Language, 24,* 567–601.

Gottlieb, G. (1991). Experimental canalization of behavioral development: Theory. *Developmental Psychology, 27,* 4–13.

Gottlieb, G. (2007). Probabilistic epigenesis. *Developmental Science, 10,* 1–11.

Gottlieb, G., Wahlsten, D., & Lickliter, R. (2006). The significance of biology for human development: A developmental psychobiological systems view. In W. Damon & R. M. Lerner (Editors-in-Chief) & R. M. Lerner (Vol. Ed.), *Handbook of child psychology: Vol. 1. Theoretical models of human development* (6th ed., pp. 210–257). Hoboken, NJ: Wiley.

Gottman, J. M. (1983). How children become friends. *Monographs of the Society for Research in Child Development, 48* (2, Serial No. 201).

Gottman, J. M., Gonso, J., & Rasmussen, B. (1975). Social interaction, social competence, and friendship in children. *Child Development, 46,* 709–718.

Gottman, J. M., Katz, L. F., & Hooven, C. (1997). *Meta-emotion: How families communicate emotionally.* Mahwah, NJ: Erlbaum.

Gowers, S., & Bryant-Waugh, R. (2004). Management of child and adolescent eating disorders: The current evidence base and future directions. *Journal of Child Psychology and Psychiatry, 45,* 63–83.

Goy, R. (1970). Early hormonal influences on the development of sexual and sex-related behavior. In F. Schmitt, G. Quarton, T. Melnechuck, & G. Adelman (Eds.), *The neurosciences: Second study program* (pp. 196–207). New York, NY: Rockefeller University Press.

Graham, G., Allanson, J. E., & Gerritsen, J. A. (2007). Sex chromosome abnormalities. In D. L. Rimoin, J. M. Connor, R. E. Pyeritz, & B. R. Korf (Eds.), *Emery and Rimoin's principles and practice of medical genetics* (5th ed., Vol. 1, pp. 1038–1057). London, UK: Churchill Livingston.

Graham, J. M. (2006). Tummy time is important. *Clinical Pediatrics, 45,* 119–121.

Graham, S. A., & Poulin-Dubois, D. (1999). Infants' reliance on shape to generalize novel labels to animate and inanimate objects. *Journal of Child Language, 26,* 295–320.

Gralinski, J. H., & Kopp, C. B. (1993). Everyday rules for behavior: Mothers' requests to young children. *Developmental Psychology, 29,* 573–584.

Grantham-McGregor, S., Powell, C., Walker, S., Change, S., & Fletcher, P. (1994). The long-term follow-up of severely malnourished children who participated in an intervention program. *Child Development, 65,* 428–439.

Graves, N. B., & Graves, T. D. (1983). The cultural context of prosocial development: An ecological model. In D. L. Bridgeman (Ed.), *The nature of prosocial development: Interdisciplinary theories and strategies* (pp. 795–824). New York, NY: Academic Press.

Graves, S. B. (1993). Television, the portrayal of African Americans, and the development of children's attitudes. In G. L. Berry & J. K. Asamen (Eds.), *Children and television: Images in a changing sociocultural world* (pp. 179–190). Newbury Park, CA: Sage.

Gray, M., & Steinberg, L. (1999). Unpacking authoritative parenting: Reassessing a multidimensional construct. *Journal of Marriage and the Family, 61,* 574–587.

Gray-Little, B., & Hafdahl, A. R. (2000). Factors influencing racial comparisons of self-esteem: A quantitative review. *Psychological Bulletin, 126,* 26–54.

Greenberg, B. S. (1986). Minorities and the mass media. In J. Bryant & D. Zillman (Eds.), *Perspectives on mass media effects* (pp. 165–188). Hillsdale, NJ: Erlbaum.

Greenberg, B. S., & Brand, J. E. (1994). Minorities and the mass media: 1970s to 1990s. In J. Bryant & D. Zillmann (Eds.), *Media effects: Advances in theory and research* (pp. 273–314). Hillsdale, NJ: Erlbaum.

Greenberg, M. T. (2006). Promoting resilience in children and youth: Preventive interventions and their interface with neuroscience. *Annals of the New York Academy of Science, 1094,* 139–150.

Greenberger, E., & Chen, C. (1996). Perceived family relationships and depressed mood in early and late adolescence: A comparison of European and Asian Americans. *Developmental Psychology, 32,* 707–716.

Greene, M. L., Way, N., & Pahl, K. (2006). Trajectories of perceived adult and peer discrimination among Black, Latino, and Asian American adolescents: Patterns and psychological correlates. *Developmental Psychology, 42,* 218–236.

Greenfield, P. M. (1984). A theory of the teacher in the learning activities of everyday life. In B. Rogoff & J. Lave (Eds.), *Everyday cognition: Its development in social context* (pp. 117–138). Cambridge, MA: Harvard University Press.

Greenfield, P. M. (1994). Video games as cultural artifacts. *Journal of Applied Developmental Psychology, 15,* 3–12.

Greenhoot, A. F., Ornstein, P. A., Gordon, B. N., & Baker-Ward, L. (1999). Acting out the details of a pediatric check-up: The impact of interview condition and behavioral style on children's memory reports. *Child Development, 70,* 363–380.

Greenman, P. S., Schneider, B. H., & Tomada, G. (2009). Stability and change in patterns of peer rejection: Implications for children's academic performance over time. *School Psychology International, 30,* 163–183.

Gregg, V., Gibbs, J. C., & Basinger, K. S. (1994). Patterns of developmental delay in moral judgment by male and female delinquents. *Merrill-Palmer Quarterly, 40,* 538–553.

Greif, E. B., & Gleason, J. B. (1980). Hi, thanks, and goodbye: More routine information. *Language in Society, 9,* 159–166.

Greif, M. L., Kemler Nelson, D. G., Keil, F. C., & Gutierrez, F. (2006). What do children want to know about animals and artifacts? Domain-specific requests for information. *Psychological Science, 17,* 455–459.

Gressens, P. (2000). Mechanisms and disturbances of neuronal migration. *Pediatric Research, 48,* 725–730.

Gressens, P., & Hüppi, P. S. (2007). Are prenatal ultrasounds safe for the developing brain? *Pediatric Research, 61,* 265–266.

Griffiths, L. J., Wolke, D., Page, A. S., & Horwood, J. P. (2006). Obesity and bullying: Different effects for boys and girls. *Archives of Disease in Childhood, 91,* 121–125.

Grimshaw, G. M., Adelstein, A., Bryden, M. P., & MacKinnon, G. E. (1998). First-language acquisition in adolescence: Evidence for a critical period for language development. *Brain and Language, 63,* 237–255.

Grimshaw, G. M., Bryden, M. P., & Finegan, J. K. (1995). Relations between prenatal testosterone and cerebral lateralization in children. *Neuropsychology, 9,* 68–79.

Grolnick, W. S., Bridges, L. J., & Connell, J. P. (1996). Emotion regulation in two-year-olds: Strategies and emotional expression in four contexts. *Child Development, 67,* 928–941.

Grolnick, W. S., Ryan, R. M., & Deci, E. L. (1991). Inner resources for school achievement: Motivational mediators of children's perceptions of their parents. *Journal of Educational Psychology, 83,* 508–517.

Groome, L. J., Swiber, M. J., Atterbury, J. L., Bentz, L. S., & Holland, S. B. (1997). Similarities and differences in behavioral state organization during sleep periods in the perinatal infant before and after birth. *Child Development, 68,* 1–11.

Gross, E. F. (2004). Adolescent Internet use: What we expect, what teens report. *Journal of Applied Developmental Psychology, 25,* 633–649.

Grossman, J. B., & Tierney, J. P. (1998). Does mentoring work? An impact study of the Big Brothers/Big Sisters. *Evaluation Review, 22,* 403–426.

Grossmann, K., Grossmann, K. E., Fremmer-Bombik, E., Kindler, H., Scheurer-Englisch, H., & Zimmermann, P. (2002). The uniqueness of the child-father attachment relationship: Fathers' sensitive and challenging play as a pivotal variable in a 16-year longitudinal study. *Social Development, 11,* 307–331.

Grossmann, K., Grossmann, K. E., Spangler, G., Suess, G., & Unzner, L. (1985). Maternal sensitivity and newborns' orientation responses as related to quality of attachment in northern Germany. In I. Bretherton & E. Waters (Eds.), *Growing points of attachment theory and research. Monographs of the Society for Research in Child Development, 50* (1–2, Serial No. 209).

Grotevant, H. D., & Cooper, C. R. (1986). Individuation in family relationships. *Human Development, 29,* 82–100.

Grusec, J. E. (1982). The socialization of altruism. In N. Eisenberg (Ed.), *The development of prosocial behavior* (pp. 139–164). New York, NY: Academic Press.

Grusec, J. E. (1991). Socializing concern for others in the home. *Developmental Psychology, 27,* 338–342.

Grusec, J. E. (1992). Social learning theory and developmental psychology: The legacies of Robert Sears and Albert Bandura. *Developmental Psychology, 28,* 776–786.

Grusec, J. E., & Goodnow, J. J. (1994). Impact of parental discipline methods on the child's internalization of values: A reconceptualization of current points of view. *Developmental Psychology, 30,* 4–19.

Grusec, J. E., Goodnow, J. J., & Cohen, L. (1996). Household work and the development of concern for others. *Developmental Psychology, 32,* 999–1007.

Grusec, J. E., Hastings, P., & Mammone, N. (1994). Parenting cognitions and relationship schemas. In J. G. Smetana (Ed.), *Beliefs about parenting: Origins and developmental implications* (pp. 5–19). San Francisco, CA: Jossey-Bass.

Grusec, J. E., & Skubiski, L. (1970). Model nurturance, demand characteristics of the modeling experiment, and altruism. *Journal of Personality and Social Psychology, 14,* 352–359.

Grych, J. H., Harold, G. T., & Miles, C. J. (2003). A prospective investigation of appraisals as mediators of the link between interparental conflict and child adjustment. *Child Development, 74,* 1176–1193.

Guerra, B., Lazzarotto, T., Quarta, S., Lanari, M., Bovicelli, L., Nicolosi, A., & Landini, M. P. (2000). Prenatal diagnosis of symptomatic congenital cytomegalovirus infection. *American Journal of Obstetrics and Gynecology, 183,* 476–482.

Guinan, M. E. (1995). Artificial insemination by donor: Safety and secrecy. *Journal of the American Medical Association, 273,* 890–891.

Gunnar, M. R. (1998). Quality of early care and buffering of neuroendocrine stress reactions: Potential effects on the developing brain. *Preventive Medicine, 27,* 208–211.

Gunnar, M. R., Porter, F., Wolf, C., Rigatuso, J., & Larson, M. (1995). Neonatal stress reactivity: Predictions to later emotional development. *Child Development, 66,* 1–13.

Gunnar, M. R., & Van Dulmen, M. H. M. (2007). Behavior problems in postinstitutionalized internationally adopted children. *Development and Psychopathology, 19,* 129–148.

Gunnar, M. R., & White, B. P. (2001). Salivary cortisol measures in infant and child assessment. In L. T. Singer & P. S. Zeskind (Eds.), *Biobehavioral assessment of the infant* (pp. 167–189). New York, NY: Guilford Press.

Gutman, L. M., & Eccles, J. S. (1999). Financial strain, parenting behaviors, and adolescents' achievement: Testing model equivalence between African American and European American single- and two-parent families. *Child Development, 70,* 1464–1476.

Guttentag, R. E. (1987). Memory and aging: Implications for theories of memory development during childhood. *Developmental Review, 5,* 56–82.

Hafner-Eaton, C., & Pearce, L. K. (1994). Birth choices, the law, and medicine: Balancing individual freedoms and protection of the public's health. *Journal of Health Politics, Policy and Law, 19,* 813–835.

Hahn, C.-S., & DiPietro, J. A. (2001). In vitro fertilization and the family: Quality of parenting, family functioning, and child psychosocial adjustment. *Developmental Psychology, 37,* 37–48.

Haight, W. L., Wang, X., Fung, H., Williams, K., & Mintz, J. (1999). Universal, developmental, and variable aspects of young children's play: A cross-cultural comparison of pretending at home. *Child Development, 70,* 1477–1488.

Hainline, L. (1998). The development of basic visual abilities. In A. Slater (Ed.), *Perceptual development: Visual, auditory, and speech perception in infancy* (pp. 5–50). East Sussex, UK: Psychology Press.

Hainline, L., & Riddell, P. M. (2002). Eye alignment and convergence in young infants. In F. Vital-Durand, J. Atkinson, & O. J. Braddick (Eds.), *Infant vision* (pp. 221–247). New York, NY: Oxford University Press.

Haith, M. M. (1997). The development of future thinking as essential for the emergence of skill in planning. In S. L. Friedman & E. K. Scholnick (Eds.), *The developmental psychology of planning: Why, how, and when do we plan?* (pp. 25–42). Mahwah, NJ: Erlbaum.

Haith, M. M. (1998). Who put the cog in cognition? Is rich interpretation too costly? *Infant Behavior and Development, 21,* 167–179.

Hakuta, K. (1999). The debate on bilingual education. *Journal of Developmental & Behavioral Pediatrics, 20,* 36–37.

Hakuta, K., & Diaz, R. M. (1985). The relationship between degree of bilingualism and cognitive ability: A critical discussion and some new longitudinal data. In K. E. Nelson (Ed.), *Children's language* (Vol. 5, pp. 319–344). Hillsdale, NJ: Erlbaum.

Haley, D. W., & Stansbury, K. (2003). Infant stress and parent responsiveness: Regulation of physiology and behavior during still-face and reunion. *Child Development, 74,* 1534–1546.

Halit, H., Csibra, G., Volein, Á., & Johnson, M. H. (2004). Face-sensitive cortical processing in early infancy. *Journal of Child Psychology and Psychiatry and Allied Disciplines, 45,* 1228–1234.

Hall, G. S. (1891). The contents of children's minds on entering school. *Pedagogical Seminary, 1,* 139–173.

Hall, J. A. (1978). Gender effects in decoding nonverbal cues. *Psychological Bulletin, 85,* 845–857.

Hall, J. A. (1984). *Nonverbal sex differences: Communication accuracy and expressive style.* Baltimore, MD: Johns Hopkins University Press.

Hall, J. A., & Halberstadt, A. G. (1986). Smiling and gazing. In J. S. Hyde & M. C. Linn (Eds.), *The psychology of gender: Advances through meta-analysis* (pp. 136–158). Baltimore, MD: Johns Hopkins University Press.

Halpern, C. T., Udry, J. R., Campbell, B., & Suchindran, C. (1999). Effects of body fat on weight concerns, dating, and sexual activity: A longitudinal analysis of black and white adolescent girls. *Developmental Psychology, 35,* 721–736.

Halpern, D. F. (1997). Sex differences in intelligence: Implications for education. *American Psychologist, 52,* 1091–1102.

Hamilton, B. E., Martin, J. A., & Ventura, S. J. (2009, March 18). Births: Preliminary data for 2007. *National Vital Statistics Reports, 57(12).* Retrieved February 17, 2010, from http://www.cdc.gov/nchs/data/nvsr/nvsr57/nvsr57_12.pdf

Hamilton, B. E., Martin, J. A., Ventura, S. J., Sutton, P. D., & Menacker, F. (2005). *Births: Preliminary data for 2004* (National Vital Statistics Reports, Vol. 54, No. 8). Hyattsville, MD: National Center for Health Statistics.

Hamlin, J. K., Hallinan, E. V., & Woodward, A. L. (2008). Do as I do: 7-month-old infants selectively reproduce others' goals. *Developmental Science, 11,* 487–494.

Hamm, K., & Ewen, D. (2006). *From the beginning: Early Head Start children, families, staff, and programs in 2004* (Head Start Series, No. 7). Washington, DC: Center for Law and Social Policy.

Hamprecht, K., Maschmann, J., Müller, D., Dietz, K., Besenthal, I., Goelz, R., Middeldorp, J. M., Speer, C. P., & Jahn, G. (2004). Cytomegalovirus (CMV) inactivation in breast milk: Reassessment of pasteurization and freeze-thawing. *Pediatric Research, 56,* 529–535.

Hampson, E., Rovet, J. F., & Altmann, D. (1998). Spatial reasoning in children with congential adrenal hyperplasia due to 21-hydroxylase deficiency. *Developmental Neuropsychology, 14,* 299–320.

Hamre, B. K., & Pianta, R. C. (2001). Early teacher-child relationships and the trajectory of children's outcomes through eighth grade. *Child Development, 72,* 625–638.

Han, J. J., Leichtman, M. D., & Wang, Q. (1998). Autobiographical memory in Korean, Chinese, and American children. *Developmental Psychology, 34,* 701–713.

Han, W. J. (2004). Nonstandard work schedules and child care decisions: Evidence from the NICHD Study of Early Child Care. *Early Childhood Research Quarterly, 19,* 231–256.

Hand, J. Z., & Sanchez, L. (2000). Badgering or bantering? Gender differences in experience of, and reaction to, sexual harassment among U.S. high school students. *Gender & Society, 14,* 718–746.

Hannon, E., & Trehub, S. E. (2005). Metrical categories in infancy and adulthood. *Psychological Science, 16,* 48–55.

Hansen, M., Bower, C., Milne, E., de Klerk, N., & Kurinczuk, J. J. (2005). Assisted reproductive technologies and the risk of birth defects—A systematic review. *Human Reproduction, 20,* 329–338.

Hanson, J. W. (1986). Teratogen update: Fetal hydantoin effects. *Teratology, 33,* 349–353.

Hanson, J. W. (1997). Human teratology. In D. L. Rimoin, J. M. Connor, & R. E. Pyeritz (Eds.), *Emory and Rimoin's principles and practices of medical genetics* (3rd ed., Vol. 1, pp. 697–724). New York, NY: Churchill Livingstone.

Hareven, T. (1985). Historical changes in the family and the life course: Implications for child development. In A. B. Smuts & J. W. Hagen (Eds.), *History and research in child development. Monographs of the Society for Research in Child Development, 50* (4–5, Serial No. 211).

Hargreaves, D., & Tiggemann, M. (2003). The effect of "thin ideal" television commercials on body dissatisfaction and schema activation during early adolescence. *Journal of Youth and Adolescence, 32,* 367–373.

Harlaar, N., Dale, P. S., & Plomin, R. (2007). From learning to read to reading to learn: Substantial and stable genetic influence. *Child Development, 78,* 116–131.

Harley, K., & Reese, E. (1999). Origins of autobiographical memory. *Developmental Psychology, 35,* 1338–1348.

Harlow, H. F., & Zimmerman, R. R. (1959). Affectional responses in the infant monkey. *Science, 130,* 421–432.

Harman, C., Rothbart, M. K., & Posner, M. I. (1997). Distress and attention interactions in early infancy. *Motivation and Emotion, 21,* 27–43.

Harold, G. T., Fincham, F. D., Osborne, L. N., & Conger, R. D. (1997). Mom and dad are at it again: Adolescent perceptions of marital conflict and adolescent psychological distress. *Developmental Psychology, 33,* 333–350.

Harpin, V., Chellappah, G., & Rutter, N. (1983). Responses of the newborn infant to overheating. *Biology of the Neonate, 44,* 65–75.

Harriman, A. E., & Lukosius, P. A. (1982). On why Wayne Dennis found Hopi children retarded in age at onset of walking. *Perceptual and Motor Skills, 55,* 79–86.

Harris, J. R. (1995). Where is the child's environment? A group socialization theory of development. *Psychological Review, 102,* 458–489.

Harris, P. L. (2005). Conversation, pretense, and theory of mind. In J. W. Astington & J. A. Baird (Eds.), *Why language matters for theory of mind* (pp. 70–83). New York, NY: Oxford University Press.

Harris, P. L. (2006). Social cognition. In W. Damon & R. M. Lerner (Editors-in-Chief) & D. M. Kuhn & R. S. Siegler (Vol. Eds.), *Handbook of child psychology. Vol. 2. Cognition, perception, and language* (6th ed., pp. 811–858). Hoboken, NJ: Wiley.

Harris, P. L., Donnelly, K., Guz, G. R., & Pitt-Watson, R. (1986). Children's understanding of the distinction between real and apparent emotion. *Child Development, 57,* 895–909.

Harris, P. L., Olthof, T., & Meerum Terwogt, M. (1981). Children's knowledge of emotion. *Journal of Child Psychology and Psychiatry, 22,* 247–261.

Harrison, D. M. (2008). Oral sucrose for pain management in infants: Myths and misconceptions. *Journal of Neonatal Nursing, 14,* 39–46.

Harrison, L. J., & Ungerer, J. A. (2002). Maternal employment and infant-mother attachment security at 12 months postpartum. *Developmental Psychology, 38,* 758–773.

Harrison, M. R. (1996). Fetal surgery. *American Journal of Obstetrics and Gynecology, 174,* 1255–1264.

Hart, E. L., Lahey, B. B., Loeber, R., Applegate, B., & Frick, P. J. (1995). Developmental change in attention-deficit hyperactivity disorder in boys: A four-year longitudinal study. *Journal of Abnormal Child Psychology, 23,* 729–749.

Hart, S. N., & Brassard, M. R. (1987). A major threat to children's mental health. *American Psychologist, 42,* 160–165.

Harter, S. (1986a). Cognitive-developmental processes in the integration of concepts about emotions and the self. *Social Cognition, 4,* 119–151.

Harter, S. (1986b). Processes underlying the construct, maintenance and enhancement of the self-concept in children. In J. Suls & A. Greenwald (Eds.), *Psychological perspectives on the self* (Vol. 3, pp. 136–182). Hillsdale, NJ: Erlbaum.

Harter, S. (1987). The determinants and mediational role of global self-worth in children. In J. Suls & A. Greenwald (Eds.), *Psychololgical perspectives on the self* (Vol. 3, pp. 136–182). New York, NY: Wiley.

Harter, S. (1999). *The construction of the self: A developmental perspective.* New York, NY: Guilford Press.

Harter, S. (2006). The self. In W. Damon & R. M. Lerner (Editors-in-Chief) & N. Eisenberg (Vol. Ed.), *Handbook of child psychology: Vol. 3. Social, emotional, and personality development* (6th ed., pp. 505–570). Hoboken, NJ: Wiley.

Harter, S., Marold, D. B., Whitesell, N. R., & Cobbs, G. (1996). A model of the effects of perceived parent and peer support on adolescent false self behavior. *Child Development, 67,* 360–374.

Harter, S., & Monsour, A. (1992). Developmental analysis of conflict caused by opposing attributes in the adolescent self-portrait. *Developmental Psychology, 28,* 251–260.

Harter, S., Waters, P., & Whitesell, N. R. (1998). Relational self-worth: Differences in perceived worth as a person across interpersonal contexts among adolescents. *Child Development, 69,* 756–766.

Harter, S., & Whitesell, N. R. (1989). Developmental changes in children's understanding of single, multiple, and blended emotion concepts. In C. Saarni & P. Harris (Eds.), *Children's understanding of emotion* (pp. 81–116). Cambridge, UK: Cambridge University Press.

Hartshorn, K., Rovee-Collier, C., Gerhardstein, P., Bhatt, R. S., Klein, P. J., Aaron, F., . . . & Wurtzel, N. (1998). Developmental changes in the specificity of memory over the first year of life. *Developmental Psychobiology, 33,* 61–78.

Hartup, W. W. (1996). The company they keep: Friendships and their developmental significance. *Child Development, 67,* 1–13.

Hartup, W. W. (1999). Constraints on peer socialization: Let me count the ways. *Merrill-Palmer Quarterly, 45,* 172–183.

Hartup, W. W., French, D. C., Laursen, B., Johnston, M. K., & Ogawa, J. R. (1993). Conflict and friendship relations in middle childhood: Behavior in a closed field situation. *Child Development, 64,* 445–454.

Hartup, W. W., Laursen, B., Stewart, M. I., & Eastenson, A. (1988). Conflict and the friendship relations of young children. *Child Development, 59,* 1590–1600.

Harvey, E. (1999). Short-term and long-term effects of early parental employment on children of the National Longitudinal Survey of Youth. *Developmental Psychology, 35,* 445–459.

Hasebe, Y., Nucci, L., & Nucci, M. S. (2004). Parental control of the personal domain and adolescent symptoms of psychopathology: A cross-national study in the United States and Japan. *Child Development, 75,* 815–828.

Haselager, G. J. T., Hartup, W. W., van Lieshout, C. F. M., & Riksen-Walraven, J. M. A. (1998). Similarities between friends and nonfriends in middle childhood. *Child Development, 69,* 1198–1208.

Hastings, P. D., & Grusec, J. E. (1998). Parenting goals as organizers of responses to parent-child disagreement. *Developmental Psychology, 34,* 465–479.

Hastings, P. D., Zahn-Waxler, C., Robinson, J., Usher, B., & Bridges, D. (2000). The development of concern for others in children with behavior problems. *Developmental Psychology, 36,* 531–546.

Hatfield, J. S., Ferguson, L. R., & Alpert, R. (1967). Mother-child interaction and the socialization process. *Child Development, 38,* 365–414.

Haubenstricker, J., & Seefeldt, V. (1986). Acquisition of motor skills during childhood. In V. Seefeldt (Ed.), *Physical activity and well-being* (pp. 42–102). Reston, VA: American Alliance for Health, Education, Recreation, and Dance.

Hauck, F. R., & Hunt, C. E. (2000). Sudden infant death syndrome in 2000. *Current Problems in Pediatrics, 30,* 241–261.

Hauck, F. R., Omojokun, O. O., & Siadaty, M. S. (2005). Do pacifiers reduce the risk of sudden infant death syndrome? A meta-analysis. *Pediatrics, 116,* e716–e723.

Hauck, F. R., & Tanabe K. O. (2008). International trends in sudden infant death syndrome: Stabilization of rates requires further action. *Pediatrics, 122,* 660–666.

Havens, P. L., & Waters, M. D. (2004). Management of the infant born to a mother with HIV infection. *Pediatric Clinics of North America, 51,* 909–937.

Hawker, D. J., & Boulton, M. J. (2000). Twenty years' research on peer victimization and psychosocial maladjustment: A meta-analytic review of cross-sectional studies. *Journal of Child Psychology and Psychiatry, 4,* 441–455.

Hawn, P. R., & Harris, L. J. (1983). Hand differences in grasp duration and reaching in two- and five-month-old infants. In G. Young, S. Segalowitz, C. M. Carter, & S. E. Trehub (Eds.), *Manual specialization and the developing brain* (pp. 331–348). New York, NY: Academic Press.

Hay, D. F., Caplan, M., & Nash, A. (2009). The beginning of peer relations. In K. H. Rubin, W. M. Bukowski, & B. Laursen (Eds.), *Handbook of peer interactions, relationships, and groups* (pp. 121–161). New York, NY: Guilford Press.

Hay, D. F., Castle, J., Davies, L., Demetriou, H., & Stimson, C. A. (1999). Prosocial action in very early childhood. *Journal of Child Psychology and Psychiatry, 40,* 905–916.

Hay, D. F., Nash, A., & Pedersen, J. (1983). Interaction between 6-month-old peers. *Child Development, 54,* 557–562.

Hayne, H. (2004). Infant memory development: Implications for childhood amnesia. *Developmental Review, 24,* 33–73.

Hearold, S. (1986). A synthesis of 1043 effects of television on social behavior. In G. A. Comstock (Ed.), *Public communications and behavior* (Vol. 1, pp. 65–133). New York, NY: Academic Press.

Heath, S. B. (1989). Oral and literate traditions among black Americans living in poverty. *American Psychologist, 44,* 367–373.

Hebb, D. O. (1980). *Essay on mind.* Hillsdale, NJ: Erlbaum.

Heckman, J. J., & LaFontaine, P. A. (2010). The American high school graduation rate: Trends and levels. *Review of Economics and Statistics, 92,* 244–262.

Held, R., Birch, E., & Gwiazda, J. (1980). Stereoacuity in human infants. *Proceedings of the National Academy of Sciences of the USA., 77,* 5572–5574.

Helwig, C. C., Zelazo, P. D., & Wilson, M. (2001). Children's judgments of psychological harm in normal and noncanonical situations. *Child Development, 72,* 66–81.

Henderlong, J., & Lepper, M. R. (2002). The effects of praise on children's intrinsic motivation: A review and synthesis. *Psychological Bulletin, 128,* 774–795.

Henderson, A. A. (1994). *A new generation of evidence: The family is critical to student achievement.* Washington, DC: National Committee for Citizens in Education.

Henifin, M. S. (1993). New reproductive technologies: Equity and access to reproductive health care. *Journal of Social Issues, 49,* 61–74.

Hepper, P. G., & Shahidullah, B. S. (1994). Development of fetal hearing. *Archives of Disease in Childhood, 71,* F81–F87.

Hepper, P. G., Wells, D. L., & Lynch, C. (2005). Prenatal thumbsucking is related to postnatal handedness. *Neuropsychologia, 43,* 313–315.

Heraghty, J. L., Hilliard, T. N., Henderson, A. J., & Fleming, P. J. (2008). The physiology of sleep in infants. *Archives of Disease in Childhood, 93,* 982–985.

Herpetz-Dahlmann, B., Müller, B., Herpetz, S., Heussen, N., Hebebrand, J., & Remschmidt, H. (2001). Prospective 10-year follow-up in adolescent anorexia nervosa: Course, outcome, psychiatric comorbidity, and psychosocial adaptation. *Journal of Child Psychology and Psychiatry, 42,* 603–612.

Herrnstein, R. J., & Murray, C. (1994). *The bell curve: Intelligence and class structure in American life.* New York, NY: Free Press.

Hertenstein, M. J. (2002). Touch: Its communicative functions in infancy. *Human Development, 45,* 70–94.

Hertsgaard, L., Gunnar, M., Erickson, M. F., & Nachmias, M. (1996). Adrenocortical responses to the Strange Situation in infants with disorganized/disoriented attachment relationships. *Child Development, 66,* 1100–1106.

Hesse, V., Voigt, M., Sälzler, A., Steinberg, S., Friese, K., Keller, E., Gausche R., & Eisele, R. (2003). Alterations in height, weight, and body mass index of newborns, children, and young adults in eastern Germany after German reunification. *Journal of Pediatrics, 142,* 259–262.

Hetherington, E. M. (1989). Coping with family transitions: Winners, losers, and survivors. *Child Development, 60,* 1–14.

Hetherington, E. M., Cox, M., & Cox, R. (1982). Effects of divorce on parents and children. In M. Lamb (Ed.), *Nontraditional families* (pp. 223–288). Hillsdale, NJ: Erlbaum.

Hetherington, E. M., & Henderson, S. H. (1997). The effects of divorce on fathers and their children. In M. E. Lamb (Ed.), *The role of the father in child development* (pp. 191–211). New York, NY: Wiley.

Hetherington, E. M., Henderson, S. H., & Reiss, D. (1999). Adolescent siblings in stepfamilies: Family functioning and adolescent adjustment. *Monographs of the Society for Research in Child Development, 64* (4, Serial No. 259).

Hetherington, E. M., & Jodl, K. M. (1994). Stepfamilies as settings for child development. In A. Booth & J. Dunn (Eds.), *Stepfamilies: Who benefits? Who does not?* (pp. 55–79). Hillsdale, NJ: Erlbaum.

Hetherington, E. M., & Kelly, J. (2002). *For better or for worse: Divorce reconsidered.* New York, NY: Norton.

Heyman, G. D., & Dweck, C. S. (1998). Children's thinking about traits? Implications for judgments of the self and others. *Child Development, 69,* 391–403.

Heynen, A. J., Yoon, B-J., Liu, C-H., Chung, H. J., Huganir, R. L., & Bear, M. F. (2003). Molecular mechanism for loss of visual cortical responsiveness following brief monocular deprivation. *Nature Neuroscience, 8,* 854–862.

Hilgard, J. R. (1932). Learning and maturation in preschool children. *Journal of Genetic Psychology, 41,* 36–56.

Hill, J. L., Brooks-Gunn, J., & Waldfogel, J. (2003). Sustained effects of high participation in an early intervention for low-birth-weight premature infants. *Developmental Psychology, 39,* 730–744.

Hill, J. P. (1987). Research on adolescents and their families: Past and prospect. In C. E. Irwin (Ed.), *Adolescent social behavior and health.* (pp. 13–31) San Francisco, CA: Jossey-Bass.

Hill, J. P., & Lynch, M. E. (1983). The intensification of gender-related role expectations during early adolescence. In J. Brooks-Gunn & A. C. Petersen (Eds.), *Girls at puberty: Biological and psychosocial perspectives* (pp. 201–228). New York, NY: Academic Press.

Hill, N. E., & Taylor, L. C. (2004). Parental school involvement and children's academic achievement: Pragmatics and issues. *Current Directions in Psychological Science, 13,* 161–164.

Hill, N. E., & Tyson, D. F. (2009). Parental involvement in middle school: A meta-analytic assessment of strategies that promote achievement. *Developmental Psychology, 45,* 740–763.

Hill, S. E., & Flom, F. (2007). 18- and 24-month-olds' discrimination of gender-consistent and inconsistent activities. *Infant Behavior & Development, 30,* 168–173.

Hinde, R. A. (1989). Ethological and relationships approaches. In R. Vasta (Ed.), *Annals of child development: Six theories of child development: Revised formulations and current issues* (Vol. 6, pp. 251–285). Greenwich, CT: JAI Press.

Hinde, R. A., Titmus, G., Easton, D., & Tamplin, A. (1985). Incidence of "friendship" and behavior to strong associates versus non-associates in preschoolers. *Child Development, 56,* 234–245.

Hines, M., Golombok, S., Rust, J., Johnston, K. J., Golding, J., & ALSPAC Study Team. (2002). Testosterone during pregnancy and gender role behavior of preschool children: A longitudinal population study. *Developmental Psychology, 73,* 1678–1687.

Hirsch, B. J., & Rapkin, B. D. (1987). The transition to junior high school: A longitudinal study of self-esteem, psychological symptomatology, school life, and social support. *Child Development, 58,* 1235–1243.

Hirschfeld, L. A., & Gelman, S. A. (1994). Toward a topography of mind: An introduction to domain specificity. In L. A. Hirschfeld & S. A. Gelman (Eds.), *Mapping the mind: Domain specificity in cognition and culture* (pp. 3–35). Oxford, UK: Oxford University Press.

Hobel, C., Goldstein, A., & Barrett, E. S. (2008). Psychosocial stress and pregnancy outcome. *Clinical Obstetrics & Gynecology, 51,* 333–348.

Hock, E., & DeMeis, D. K. (1990). Depression in mothers of infants: The role of maternal employment. *Developmental Psychology, 26,* 285–291.

Hoehl, S., & Striano, T. (2008). Neural processing of eye gaze and threat-related emotional facial expressions in infancy. *Child Development, 79,* 1752–1760.

Hoff, E., & Naigles, L. (2002). How children use input to acquire a lexicon. *Child Development, 73,* 418–433.

Hoff, K. E., Reese-Weber, M., Schneider, W. J., & Stagg, J. W. (2009). The association between high status positions and aggressive behavior in early adolescence. *Journal of School Psychology, 47,* 395–426.

Hoff, T. L. (1992). Psychology in Canada one hundred years ago: James Mark Baldwin at the University of Toronto. *Canadian Psychology, 33,* 683–694.

Hoff-Ginsberg, E. (1986). Function and structure in maternal speech: Their relation to the child's development of syntax. *Developmental Psychology, 22,* 155–163.

Hoff-Ginsberg, E. (1991). Mother-child conversation in different social classes and communicative settings. *Child Development, 62,* 782–796.

Hoffman, L. W. (1979). Maternal employment: 1979. *American Psychologist, 34,* 859–865.

Hoffman, L. W. (1984). Maternal employment and the young child. In M. Perlmutter (Ed.), *The Minnesota symposia on child psychology: Vol. 17. Parent-child interaction and parent-child relations in child development* (pp. 101–127). Hillsdale, NJ: Erlbaum.

Hoffman, L. W., & Kloska, D. D. (1995). Parents' gender-based attitudes toward marital roles and child rearing: Development and validation of new measures. *Sex Roles, 32,* 273–295.

Hoffman, L. W., & Youngblade, L. M. (1999). *Mothers at work: Effects on children's well-being.* New York, NY: Cambridge University Press.

Hoffman, M. L. (1970). Moral development. In P. H. Mussen (Ed.), *Carmichael's manual of child psychology* (Vol. 2, pp. 261–359). New York, NY: Wiley.

Hoffman, M. L. (1975). Altruistic behavior and the parent-child relationship. *Journal of Personality and Social Psychology, 31,* 937–943.

Hoffman, M. L. (1976). Empathy, role-taking, guilt, and the development of altruistic motives. In T. Lickona (Ed.), *Moral development and moral behavior: Theory, research, and social issues* (pp. 124–143). New York, NY: Holt, Rinehart & Winston.

Hoffman, M. L. (1982). Development of prosocial motivation: Empathy and guilt. In N. Eisenberg (Ed.), *The development of prosocial behavior* (pp. 281–313). New York, NY: Academic Press.

Hoffman-Plotkin, D., & Twentyman, C. (1984). A multimodal assessment of behavioral and cognitive deficits in abused and neglected preschoolers. *Child Development, 52,* 13–30.

Hogan, A. M., Pit-ten Gate, I. M., Vargha-Khadem, F., Prengler, M., & Kirkham, F. J. (2006). Physiological correlates of intellectual function in children with sickle cell disease: Hypoxaemia, hyperaemia and brain infarction. *Developmental Science, 9,* 379–387.

Holden, G. W. (1983). Avoiding conflict: Mothers as tacticians in the supermarket. *Child Development, 54,* 233–240.

Hollenbeck, A. R., & Slaby, R. G. (1979). Infant visual and vocal responses to television. *Child Development, 50,* 41–45.

Hollingsworth, L. D. (2003). International adoption among families in the United States: Consideration of social justice. *Social Work, 48,* 209–217.

Hollo, O., Rautava, P., Korhonen, T., Helenius, H., Kero, P., & Sillanpää, M. (2002). Academic achievement of small-for-gestational-age children at age 10 years. *Archives of Pediatric and Adolescent Medicine, 156,* 179–187.

Holmes, J. R., & Holmes-Lonergan, H. A. (2004). The bully in the family: Family influences on bullying. In C. E. Sanders & G. D. Phye (Eds.), *Bullying: Implications for the classroom* (pp. 111–135). San Diego, CA: Elsevier Academic Press.

Holowka, S., & Petitto, L. A. (2002). Left hemisphere cerebral specialization for babies while babbling. *Science,* 297, 1515.

Honora, D. (2003). Urban African American adolescents and school identity. *Urban Education, 38,* 58–76.

Hood, K. E., Draper, P., Crockett, L. J., & Petersen, A. C. (1987). The ontogeny and phylogeny of sex differences in development: A biopsychosocial synthesis. In D. B. Carter (Ed.), *Current conceptions of sex roles and sex typing: Theory and research* (pp. 49–77). New York, NY: Praeger.

Hooper, C. J., Luciana, M., Conklin, H. M., & Yarger, R. S. (2004). Adolescents' performance on the Iowa Gambling Task: Implications for the development of decision making and ventromedial prefrontal cortex. *Developmental Psychology, 40,* 1148–1158.

Hopkins, B., & Westra, T. (1990). Motor development, maternal expectations, and the role of handling. *Infant Behavior and Development, 13,* 117–122.

Hops, H., & Finch, M. (1985). Social competence and skill: A reassessment. In B. H. Schneider, K. H. Rubin, & J. E. Ledingham (Eds.), *Children's peer relations: Issues in assessment and intervention* (pp. 23–39). New York, NY: Springer-Verlag.

Horn, J. L. (1968). Organization of abilities and the development of intelligence. *Psychological Review, 75,* 242–259.

Horn, J. L., & Cattell, R. B. (1967). Refinement and test of the theory of fluid and crystallized ability intelligences. *Journal of Educational Psychology, 57,* 253–270.

Horn, J. M., & Packard, T. (1985). Early identification of learning problems: A meta-analysis. *Journal of Educational Psychology, 77,* 349–360.

Horowitz, F. D. (2000). Child development and the PITS: Simple questions, complex answers, and developmental theory. *Child Development, 71,* 1–10.

Hossain, Z., Field, T., Gonzalez, J., Malphurs, J., Del Valle, C., & Pickens, J. (1994). Infants of "depressed" mothers interact better with their nondepressed fathers. *Infant Mental Health Journal, 15,* 348–357.

Hossain, Z., & Roopnarine, J. L. (1994). African-American fathers' involvement with infants: Relationship to their functioning style, support, education, and income. *Infant Behavior and Development, 17,* 175–184.

Hotz, V. J., McElroy, S.W., & Sanders, S. G. (1997). The costs and consequences of teenage childbearing for mothers. In R. A. Maynard (Ed.), *Kids having kids* (pp. 55–94). Washington, DC: Urban Institute.

Hoven, C. W., Duarte, C. S., Lucas, C. P., Wu, P., Mandell, D. J., Goodwin, R. D., . . . & Susser, E. (2005). Psychopathology among New York City public school children 6 months after September 11. *Archives of General Psychiatry, 62,* 545–552.

Howe, M. L., & Courage, M. L. (1997). The emergence and early development of autobiographical memory. *Psychological Review, 104,* 499–523.

Howes, C. (1987). Peer interaction of young children. *Monographs of the Society for Research in Child Development, 53* (1, Serial No. 217).

Howes, C. (1990). Can age of entry and the quality of childcare predict adjustment in kindergarten? *Developmental Psychology, 26,* 292–303.

Howes, C., Phillips, D. A., & Whitebook, M. (1992). Thresholds of quality: Implications for the social development of children in center-based child care. *Child Development, 63,* 449–460.

Hsu, H.-C., & Fogel, A. (2001). Infant vocal development in a dynamic mother-infant communication system. *Infancy, 2,* 87–109.

Hsu, H-C., & Fogel, A. (2003). Stability and transitions in mother-infant face-to-face communication during the first 6 months: A microhistorical approach. *Developmental Psychology, 39,* 1061–1082.

Huang, Y. T., Spelke, E., & Snedeker, J. (2010). When is four far more than three? Children's generalization of newly acquired number words. *Psychological Science, 21,* 600–606.

Hubbard, J. A. (2001). Emotion expression processes in children's peer interaction: The role of peer rejection, aggression, and gender. *Child Development, 72,* 1426–1438.

Hubbs-Tait, L., Nation, J. R., Krebs, N. F., & Bellinger, D. C. (2005). Neurotoxicants, micronutrients, and social environments: Individual effects on children's development. *Psychological Science in the Public Interest, 6,* 57–121.

Hubel, D. H., & Wiesel, T. N. (1979, September). Brain mechanisms of vision. *Scientific American, 241,* pp. 150–162.

Hudson, J. A. (2006). The development of future time concepts through mother-child conversation. *Merrill-Palmer Quarterly, 52,* 70–95.

Hudson, J. A., & Mayhew, E. M. Y. (2009). The development of memory for recurring events. In M. L. Courage & N. Cowan (Eds.), *The development of memory in infancy and childhood* (2nd ed., pp. 69–91). East Sussex, UK: Psychology Press.

Hudson, J. A., Shapiro, L. R., & Sosa, B. B. (1995). Planning in the real world: Preschool children's scripts and plans for familiar events. *Child Development, 66,* 984–998.

Huebner, A., & Garrod, A. (1991). Moral reasoning in a karmic world. *Human Development, 34,* 341–352.

Huesmann, L. R., Eron, L. D., Klein, R., Brice, P., & Fischer, P. (1983). Mitigating the imitation of aggressive behaviors by changing children's attitudes about media violence. *Journal of Personality and Social Psychology, 44,* 899–910.

Huesmann, L. R., Lagerspetz, K., & Eron, L. D. (1984). Intervening variables and the TV violence-aggression relation: Evidence from two countries. *Developmental Psychology, 20,* 746–775.

Huffman, L. C., Bryan, Y. E., del Carmen, R., Pedersen, F. A., Doussrad-Roosevelt, J. A., & Porges, S. W. (1998). Infant temperament and cardiac vagal tone: Assessments at twelve weeks of age. *Child Development, 69,* 624–635.

Hughes, C., & Russell, J. (1993). Autistic children's difficulty with mental disengagement from an object: Its implications for theories of autism. *Developmental Psychology, 29,* 498–510.

Hughes, D., & Johnson, D. (2001). Correlates of children's experiences of parents' racial socialization behaviors. *Journal of Marriage and the Family, 63,* 981–995.

Hughes, J. M., Bigler, R. S., & Levy, S. R. (2007). Consequences of learning about historical racism among European American and African American children. *Child Development, 78,* 1689–1705.

Huizink, A. C., & Mulder, E. J. H. (2006). Maternal smoking, drinking or cannabis use during pregnancy and neurobehavioral and cognitive functioning in human offspring. *Neuroscience & Biobehavioral Reviews, 30,* 24–41.

Huizink, A. C., Mulder, E. J. H., & Buitelaar, J. K. (2004). Prenatal stress and risk for psychopathology: Specific effects or induction of general susceptibility? *Psychological Bulletin, 130,* 115–142.

Human Genome Management Information System (HGMIS). (2008). *About the Human Genome Project.* Retrieved August 19, 2010, from http://www.ornl.gov/sci/techresources/Human Genome/project/about.shtml

Human Genome Project Information. (2009). *Gene therapy.* Retrieved August 19, 2010, from http://www.ornl.gov/sci/techresources// Human_Genome/medicine/genetherapy.shtml

Hurley, J. C., & Underwood, M. K. (2002). Children's understanding of their research rights before and after debriefing: Informed assent, confidentiality, and stopping participation. *Child Development, 73,* 132–143.

Hurtado, N., Marchman, V. A., & Fernald, A. (2008). Does input influence uptake? Links between maternal talk, processing speed and vocabulary size in Spanish-learning children. *Developmental Science, 11,* F31–F39.

Husain, M., & Kennard, C. (1997). Distractor-dependent frontal neglect. *Neuropsychologia, 35,* 829–841.

Huston, A. C. (1983). Sex typing. In E. M. Hetherington (Ed.), *Handbook of child psychology: Vol. IV. Socialization, personality, and social development* (4th ed., pp. 387–467). New York, NY: Wiley.

Huston, A. C. (1985). The development of sex typing: Themes from recent research. *Developmental Review, 5,* 1–17.

Huston, A. C., & Alvarez, M. M. (1990). The socialization context of gender role development in early adolescence. In R. Montemayor, G. R. Adams, & T. P. Gullota (Eds.), *From childhood to adolescence: A transitional period?* (pp. 156–179). Newbury Park, CA: Sage.

Huston, A. C., & Wright, J. C. (1998). Mass media and children's development. In W. Damon (Series Ed.) & R. Lerner (Vol. Ed.), *Handbook of child psychology: Vol. 4. Child psychology in practice* (5th ed., pp. 999–1058). New York, NY: Wiley.

Huston, A. C., Wright, J. C., Marquis, J., & Green, S. B. (1999). How young children spend their time: Television and other activities. *Developmental Psychology, 35,* 912–925.

Huston, A., Wright, J. C., Rice, M. L., Kerkman, D., & St. Peters, M. (1990). Development of television viewing patterns in early childhood: A longitudinal investigation. *Developmental Psychology, 26,* 409–420.

Huttenlocher, J., Haight, W., Bryk, A., Seltzer, M., & Lyons, T. (1991). Early vocabulary growth: Relation to language input and gender. *Developmental Psychology, 27,* 236–248.

Huttenlocher, J., & Lourenco, S. F. (2007). Coding location in enclosed spaces: Is geometry the principle? *Developmental Science, 10,* 741–746.

Huttenlocher, J., Newcombe, N., & Sandberg, E. H. (1994). The coding of spatial location in young children. *Cognitive Psychology, 27,* 115–148.

Huttenlocher, P. R., & Dabholkar, A. S. (1997). Regional differences in synaptogenesis in human cerebral cortex. *Journal of Comparative Neurology, 387,* 167–187.

Hyde, J. S. (1984). How large are gender differences in aggression? A developmental meta-analysis. *Developmental Psychology, 20,* 722–736.

Hyde, J. S. (1986). Gender differences in aggression. In J. S. Hyde & M. C. Linn (Eds.), *The psychology of gender: Advances through meta-analysis* (pp. 51–66). Baltimore: Johns Hopkins University Press.

Hyde, J. S., Lindberg, S. M., Linn, M. C., Ellis, A. B., & Williams, C. C. (2008). Gender similarities characterize math performance. *Science, 321,* 494–495.

Hyde, J. S., & Linn, M. C. (1988). Gender differences in verbal ability: A meta-analysis. *Psychological Bulletin, 104,* 53–69.

Hymel, S., LeMare, L., Ditner, E., & Woody, E. Z. (1999). Assessing self-concept in children: Variations across self-concept domains. *Merrill-Palmer Quarterly, 45,* 602–623.

Imai, M., Li, L., Haryu, E., Okada, H., Hirsh-Pasek, K., Golinkoff, R. M., & Shigematsu, J. (2008). Novel noun and verb learning in Chinese-, English-, and Japanese-speaking children. *Child Development, 79,* 979–1000.

Inhelder, B., & Piaget, J. (1958). *The growth of logical thinking from childhood to adolescence.* New York, NY: Basic Books.

Isabella, R. A. (1993). Origins of attachment: Maternal interactive behavior across the first year. *Child Development, 64,* 605–621.

Isabella, R. A., Belsky, J., & von Eye, A. (1989). Origins of infant-mother attachment: An examination of interactional synchrony during the infant's first year. *Developmental Psychology, 25,* 12–21.

Isensee, W. (1986, September 3). *The Chronicle of Higher Education,* 33.

Ishii-Kuntz, M. (1994). Paternal involvement and perception toward fathers' roles: A comparison between Japan and the United States. *Journal of Family Issues, 15,* 30–48.

Isley, S. L., O'Neil, R., Clatfelter, D., & Parke, R. D. (1999). Parent and child expressed affect and children's social competence: Modeling direct and indirect pathways. *Developmental Psychology, 35,* 547–560.

Iverson, J. M., & Goldin-Meadow, S. (2001). The resilience of gesture in talk: Gesture in blind speakers and listeners. *Developmental Science, 4,* 416–422.

Iverson, J. M., & Goldin-Meadow, S. (2005). Gesture paves the way for language development. *Psychological Science, 16,* 367–371.

Izard, C., & Ackerman, B. P. (2000). Motivational, organizational, and regulatory functions of discrete emotions. In M. Lewis & J. M. Haviland-Jones (Eds.), *Handbook of emotions* (2nd ed., pp. 253–280). New York, NY: Guilford Press.

Izard, C. E. (1978). On the ontogenesis of emotions and emotion-cognition relationships in infancy. In M. Lewis & L. A. Rosenblum (Eds.), *The development of affect* (pp. 389–413). New York, NY: Plenum Press.

Izard, C. E. (2007). Basic emotions, natural kinds, emotion schemas, and a new paradigm. *Perspectives on Psychological Science, 2,* 260–280.

Izard, C. E., & Dougherty, L. M. (1982). Two complementary systems for measuring facial expressions in infants and children. In C. E. Izard (Ed.), *Measuring emotions in infants and children* (Vol. 1, pp. 97–126). Cambridge, UK: Cambridge University Press.

Izard, C. E., Fantauzzo, C. A., Castle, J. M., Haynes, O. M., Rayias, M. F., & Putnam, P. H. (1995). The ontogeny and significance of infants' facial expressions in the first 9 months of life. *Developmental Psychology, 31,* 997–1013.

Izard, C., Fine, S., Schultz, D., Mostow, A., Ackerman, B., & Youngstrom, E. (2001). Emotion knowledge as a predictor of social behavior and academic competence in children at risk. *Psychological Science, 12,* 18–23.

Izard, C. E., Haynes, O. M., Chisolm, G., & Baak, K. (1991). Emotional determinants of infant-mother attachment. *Child Development, 62,* 906–917.

Izard, C. E., Huebner, R. R., Risser, D., McGinnes, G., & Dougherty, L. (1980). The young infant's ability to produce discrete emotion expressions. *Developmental Psychology, 16,* 132–140.

Jaccard, J., Blanton, H., & Dodge, T. (2005). Peer influences on risk behavior: An analysis of the effects of a close friend. *Developmental Psychology, 41,* 135–147.

Jaccard, J., Dittus, P. J., & Gordon, V. V. (1998). Parent-adolescent congruency in reports of adolescent sexual behavior and in communications about sexual behavior. *Child Development, 69,* 247–261.

Jacklin, C. N. (1989). Female and male: Issues of gender. *American Psychologist, 44,* 127–133.

Jacklin, C. N., DiPietro, J. A., & Maccoby, E. E. (1984). Sex-typing behavior and sex-typing pressure in child/parent interaction. *Archives of Sexual Behavior, 13,* 413–425.

Jacklin, C. N., & Maccoby, E. E. (1978). Social behavior at thirty-three months in same-sex and mixed-sex dyads. *Child Development, 49,* 557–569.

Jackson, J. F. (1993). Human behavioral genetics, Scarr's theory, and her views on interventions: A critical review and commentary on their implications for African American children. *Child Development, 64,* 1318–1332.

Jackson, L. A., von Eye, A., Biocca, F. A., Barbatsis, G., Zhao, Y., & Fitzgerald, H. E. (2006). Does home Internet use influence the academic performance of low-income children? *Developmental Psychology, 42,* 429–435.

Jacobs, J. E., & Klaczynski, P. A. (2002). The development of judgment and decision making during childhood and adolescence. *Current Directions in Psychological Science, 11,* 145–149.

Jacobs, J. E., Lanza, S., Osgood, D. W., Eccles, J. S., & Wigfield, A. (2002). Changes in children's self-competence and values: Gender and domain differences across grades one through twelve. *Child Development, 73,* 509–527.

Jacobs, J. E., & Potenza, M. (1991). The use of judgment heuristics to make social and object decisions: A developmental perspective. *Child Development, 62,* 166–178.

Jacobsen, T., Edelstein, W., & Hofman, V. (1994). A longitudinal study of the relation between representations of attachment in childhood and cognitive functioning in childhood and adolescence. *Developmental Psychology, 30,* 112–124.

Jacobson, J. L., & Jacobson, S. W. (1996). Methodological considerations in behavioral toxicology in infants and children. *Developmental Psychology, 32,* 390–403.

Jacobvitz, R. S., Wood, M. R., & Albin, K. (1991). Cognitive skills and young children's comprehension of television. *Journal of Applied Developmental Psychology, 12,* 219–235.

Jaffee, S. R., Moffitt, T. E., Caspi, A., & Taylor, A. (2003). Life with (or without) father: The benefits of living with two biological parents depend on the father's antisocial behavior. *Child Development, 74,* 109–126.

Jaglom, L. M., & Gardner, H. (1981). The preschool television viewer as anthropologist. In H. Kelly & H. Gardner (Eds.), *New directions in child development: Viewing children through television* (pp. 9–30). San Francisco, CA: Jossey-Bass.

Jakibchuk, Z., & Smeriglio, V. L. (1976). The influence of symbolic modeling on the social behavior of preschool children with low levels of social responsiveness. *Child Development, 47,* 838–841.

James, S. (1978). Effect of listener age and situation on the politeness of children's directives. *Journal of Psycholinguistic Research, 7,* 307–317.

James, W. (1890). *The principles of psychology.* New York, NY: Henry Holt.

James, W. (1892). *Psychology: The briefer course.* New York, NY: Henry Holt.

Jarrett, R. L. (1997). Bringing families back in: Neighborhoods' effects on child development. In J. Brooks-Gunn, G. J. Duncan, & J. L. Aber (Eds.), *Neighborhood poverty: Vol. 2. Policy implications in studying neighborhoods* (pp. 48–64). New York, NY: Russell Sage Foundation.

Jencks, C. (1972). *Inequality: A reassessment of the effect of family and schooling in America.* New York, NY: Basic Books.

Jensen, A. R. (1980). *Bias in mental testing.* New York, NY: Free Press.

Jensen, A. R. (1982). The chronometry of intelligence. In R. J. Sternberg (Ed.), *Advances in the psychology of human intelligence* (Vol. 1, pp. 255–310). Hillsdale, NJ: Erlbaum.

Jensen, L. A. (2008). Through two lenses: A cultural–developmental approach to moral psychology. *Developmental Review, 28,* 289–315.

Jensen, P. S., Arnold, L. E., Swanson, J. M., Vitiello, B., Abikoff, H. B., Greenhill, L. L., . . . & Hur, K. (2007). 3-year follow-up of the NIMH MTA study. *Journal of the American Academy of Child & Adolescent Psychiatry, 46,* 989–1002.

Jipson, J. L., & Gelman, S. A. (2007). Robots and rodents: Children's inferences about living and nonliving kinds. *Child Development, 78,* 1675–1688.

Johnson, D. B., Bruemmer, B., Lund, A. E., Evens, C. C. & Mar, C. M. (2009). Impact of school district sugar-sweetened beverage policies on student beverage exposure and consumption in middle schools. *Journal of Adolescent Health, 45,* S30–S37.

Johnson, J. G., Cohen, P., Kasen, S., & Brook, J. S., (2007). Extensive television viewing and the development of attention and learning difficulties in adolescence. *Archives of Pediatric and Adolescent Medicine, 161,* 480–486.

Johnson, J., & Newport, E. (1989). Critical period effects in second language learning: The influence of maturational state on the acquisition of English as a second language. *Cognitive Psychology, 21,* 60–99.

Johnson, K. A., & Tyler, K. A. (2007). Adolescent sexual onset: An intergenerational analysis. *Journal of Youth and Adolescence, 36,* 939–949.

Johnson, K. E., & Mervis, C. M. (1997). First steps in the emergence of verbal humor: A case study. *Infant Behavior and Development, 20,* 187–196.

Johnson, M. (1991). Infant and toddler sleep: A telephone survey of parents in one community. *Journal of Developmental and Behavioral Pediatrics, 12,* 108–114.

Johnson, M. H. (2005). Subcortical face processing. *Nature Reviews Neuroscience, 6,* 766–786.

Johnson, M. H., Grossmann, T., & Kadosh, K. C. (2009). Mapping functional brain development: Building a social brain through interactive specialization. *Developmental Psychology, 45,* 151–159.

Johnson, S. P. (2004). Development of perceptual completion in infancy. *Psychological Science, 15,* 769–775.

Johnson, S. P., Davidow, J., Hall-Haro, C., & Frank, M. C. (2008). Development of perceptual completion originates in information acquisition. *Developmental Psychology, 44,* 1214–1224.

Johnston, J., Brzezinski, E. J., & Anderman, E. M. (1994). *Taking the measure of Channel One: A three year perspective.* Ann Arbor, MI: University of Michigan, Institute for Social Research.

Jones, D. C. (2004). Image among adolescent girls and boys: A longitudinal study. *Developmental Psychology, 40,* 823–835.

Jones, G. P., & Dembo, M. H. (1989). Age and sex role differences in intimate friendships during childhood and adolescence. *Merrill-Palmer Quarterly, 35,* 445–462.

Jones, H. E. (2006). Drug addiction during pregnancy: Advances in maternal treatment and understanding child outcomes. *Current Directions in Psychological Science, 15,* 126–130.

Jones, K. L., & Smith, D. W. (1973). Recognition of the fetal alcohol syndrome in early infancy. *Lancet, 2,* 999–1001.

Jones, M. C. (1965). Psychological correlates of somatic development. *Child Development, 36,* 899–911.

Jones, S. S. (1996). Imitation or exploration? Young infants' matching of adults' oral gestures. *Child Development, 67,* 1952–1969.

Jones, S. S. (2007). Imitation in infancy: The development of mimicry. *Psychological Science, 18,* 593–599.

Jonkmann, K., Trautwein, U., & Lüdtke, O. (2009). Social dominance in adolescence: The moderating role of the classroom context and behavioral heterogeneity. *Child Development, 80,* 338–355.

Joseph, R. (2000). Fetal brain behavior and cognitive development. *Developmental Review, 20,* 81–98.

Juffer, F., & van IJzendoorn, M. A. (2005). Behavior problems and mental health referrals of international adoptees. *Journal of the American Medical Association, 293,* 2501–2515.

Jusczyk, P. W., Cutler, A., & Redanz, L. (1993). Infants' sensitivity to predominant stress patterns in English. *Child Development, 64,* 675–687.

Jusczyk, P. W., Friederici, A. D., Wessels, J. M. I., Svenkerud, V. Y., & Jusczyk, A. M (1993). Infants' sensitivity to the sound patterns of native language words. *Journal of Memory and Language, 32,* 402–420.

Jusczyk, P. W., & Hohne, E. A. (1997). Infants' memory for spoken words. *Science, 277,* 1984–1986.

Kagan, J. (1981). *The second year: The emergence of self-awareness.* Cambridge, MA: Harvard University Press.

Kagan, J. (1994). *Galen's prophecy: Temperament in human nature.* New York, NY: Basic Books.

Kagan, J., & Fox, N. A. (2006). Biology, culture, and temperamental biases. In W. Damon & R. M. Lerner (Editors-in-Chief) & N. Eisenberg (Vol. Ed.), *Handbook of child psychology: Vol. 3. Social, emotional, and personality development* (6th ed., pp. 167–225). Hoboken, NJ: Wiley.

Kagan, J., Reznick, J. S., & Snidman, N. (1988). Biological basis of childhood shyness. *Science, 240,* 167–171.

Kagan, J., Snidman, N., & Arcus, D. (1993). On the temperamental categories of inhibited and uninhibited children. In K. H. Rubin & J. B. Asendorpf (Eds.), *Social withdrawal, inhibition, and shyness in children* (pp. 19–28). Hillsdale, NJ: Erlbaum.

Kahn, P. H., Jr. (1992). Children's obligatory and discretionary moral judgments. *Child Development, 63,* 416–430.

Kahneman, D. (1973). *Attention and effort.* Englewood Cliffs, NJ: Prentice-Hall.

Kail, R. (1990). *The development of memory in children* (3rd ed.). New York, NY: W. H. Freeman.

Kail, R. (1991a). Development of processing speed in childhood and adolescence. In H. W. Reese (Ed.), *Advances in child development and behavior* (Vol. 23, pp. 151–185). San Diego, CA: Academic Press.

Kail, R. (1991b). Processing time declines exponentially during childhood and adolescence. *Developmental Psychology, 27,* 259–266.

Kail, R. V. (2007). Longitudinal evidence that increases in processing speed and working memory enhance children's reasoning. *Psychological Science, 18,* 312–313.

Kail, R. V., & Ferrer, E. (2007). Processing speed in childhood and adolescence: Longitudinal models for examining change. *Child Development, 78,* 1760–1770.

Kaiser Family Foundation. (2004). *Sex education in America: General public/parents survey.* Washington, DC: Kaiser Family Foundation.

Kaitz, M., Shiri, S., Danziger, S., Hershko, Z., & Eidelman, A. I. (1994). Fathers can also recognize their newborns by touch. *Infant Behavior and Development, 17,* 205–207.

Kajii, T., Kida, M., & Takahashi, K. (1973). The effect of thalidomide intake during 113 human pregnancies. *Teratology, 8,* 163–166.

Kalantari, M., & Vostanis, P. (2010). Behavioural and emotional problems in Iranian children four years after parental death in an earthquake. *International Journal of Social Psychiatry, 6,* 158–168.

Kamins, M. L., & Dweck, C. S. (1999). Person versus process praise and criticism: Implications for contingent self-worth and coping. *Developmental Psychology, 35,* 835–847.

Kannass, K. N., Oakes, L. M., & Shaddy, D. J. (2006). A longitudinal investigation of the development of attention and distractibility. *Journal of Cognition and Development, 7,* 381–409.

Kanner, L. (1943). Autistic disturbances of affective contact. *Nervous Children, 2,* 217–250.

Kaplowitz, P. B. (2008). Link between body fat and the timing of puberty. *Pediatrics, 121,* S208–S217.

Karasik, L. B., Tamis-LeMonda, C. S., Adolph, K. E., & Dimitropoulou, K. A. (2008). How mothers encourage and discourage infants' motor actions. *Infancy, 13,* 366–392.

Karevold, E., Røysamb, E., Ystrom, E., & Mathiesen, K. S. (2009). Predictors and pathways from infancy to symptoms of anxiety and depression in early adolescence. *Developmental Psychology, 45,* 1051–1060.

Karmiloff-Smith, A. (1995). Annotation: The extraordinary cognitive journey from foetus through infancy. *Journal of Child Psychology and Psychiatry, 36,* 1293–1313.

Karraker, K. H., Vogel, D. A., & Lake, M. A. (1995). Parents' gender-stereotyped perceptions of newborns: The eye of the beholder revisited. *Sex Roles, 33,* 687–701.

Karrass, J., & Braungart-Rieker, J. M. (2005). Effects of shared parent-infant book reading on early language acquisition. *Journal of Applied Developmental Psychology, 26,* 133–148.

Kasari, C., Freeman, S., & Paparella, T. (2006). Joint attention and symbolic play in young children with autism: A randomized controlled intervention study. *Journal of Child Psychology and Psychiatry, 47,* 611–620.

Kastens, K. A., & Liben, L. S. (2007). Eliciting self-explanations improves children's performance on a field-based map skills task. *Cognition and Instruction, 25,* 45–74.

Katz, P. A. (1987). Variations in family constellation: Effects on gender schemata. In L. S. Liben & M. L. Signorella (Eds.), *New directions for child development: No. 38. Children's gender schemata* (pp. 39–56). San Francisco, CA: Jossey-Bass.

Katz, P. A., & Kofkin, J. A. (1997). Race, gender, and young children. In S. S. Luthar, J. A. Burack, D. Cicchetti, & J. Weisz (Eds.), *Developmental psychopathology: Perspectives on adjustment, risk, and disorder* (pp. 51–74). New York, NY: Cambridge University Press.

Katz, P. A., & Ksansnak, K. R. (1994). Developmental aspects of gender role flexibility and traditionality in middle childhood and adolescence. *Developmental Psychology, 30,* 272–282.

Kaufman, A. S. (2001). WAIS-III IQs, Horn's theory, and generational changes from young adulthood to old age. *Intelligence, 29,* 131–167.

Kaufman, A. S., Kamphaus, R. W., & Kaufman, N. L. (1985). New directions in intelligence testing: The Kaufman Assessment Battery for Children (K-ABC). In B. B. Wolman (Ed.), *Handbook of intelligence* (pp. 663–698). New York, NY: Wiley.

Kavšek, M. (2009). The perception of subjective contours and neon color spreading figures in young infants. *Attention, Perception, and Psychophysics, 71,* 412–420.

Kavšek, M., Granrud, C. E., & Yonas, A. (2009). Infants' responsiveness to pictorial depth cues in preferential-reaching studies: A meta-analysis. *Infant Behavior and Development, 32,* 245–253.

Keller, M., Edelstein, W., Schmid, C., Fang, F., & Fang, G. (1998). Reasoning about responsibilities and obligations in close relationships: A comparison across two cultures. *Developmental Psychology, 34,* 731–741.

Kelley, M. L., Power, T. G., & Wimbush, D. D. (1992). Determinants of disciplinary practices in low-income black mothers. *Child Development, 63,* 573–582.

Kelley, S. A., Brownell, C. A., & Campbell, S. B. (2000). Mastery motivation and self-evaluative affect in toddlers: Longitudinal relations with maternal behavior. *Child Development, 71,* 1061–1071.

Kellman, P. J. (1996). The origins of object perception. In R. Gelman & T. Au (Eds.), *Perceptual and cognitive development* (pp. 3–48). New York, NY: Academic Press.

Kellman, P. J., & Arterberry, M. E. (2006). Infant visual perception. In W. Damon & R. M. Lerner (Editors-in-Chief) & D. M. Kuhn & R. S. Siegler (Vol. Eds.), *Handbook of child psychology. Vol. 2. Cognition, perception, and language* (6th ed., pp. 109–160). Hoboken, NJ: Wiley.

Kellman, P. J., & Banks, M. S. (1998). Infant visual perception. In W. Damon (Series Ed.) & R. Siegler & D. Kuhn (Vol. Eds.), *Handbook of child psychology: Vol. 2. Cognition, perception, and language* (5th ed., pp. 103–146). New York, NY: Wiley.

Kellman, P. J., & Spelke, E. S. (1983). Perception of partly occluded objects in infancy. *Cognitive Psychology, 15,* 483–524.

Kelly, D. J., Quinn, P. C., Slater, A. M., Lee, K., Ge, L., & Pascalis, O. (2007). The other-race effect develops during infancy: Evidence of perceptual narrowing. *Psychological Science, 18,* 1084–1089.

Kelly, S. (2010). The psychological consequences to adolescents of exposure to gang violence in the community: An integrated review of the literature. *Journal of Child and Adolescent Psychiatric Nursing, 23,* 61–73.

Kendler, K. S., Prescott, C. A. Neale, M. C., & Pedersen, N. L. (1997). Temperance Board registration for alcohol abuse in a national sample of Swedish male twins, born 1902–1949. *Archives of General Psychiatry, 54,* 178–184.

Keogh, J., & Sugden, D. (1985). *Movement skill development.* New York, NY: Macmillan.

Kerestes, M., Youniss, J., & Metz, E. (2004). Longitudinal patterns of religious perspective and civic integration. *Applied Developmental Science, 8,* 39–46.

Kerig, P. K., Cowan, P. A., & Cowan, C. P. (1993). Marital quality and gender differences in parent-child interaction. *Developmental Psychology, 29,* 931–939.

Kerschner, J. E. (2004). Neonatal hearing screening: To do or not to do. *Pediatric Clinics of North America, 51,* 725–736.

Kersten, A. W. (1998). A division of labor between nouns and verbs in the representation of motion. *Journal of Experimental Psychology: General, 127,* 34–54.

Kersten, A. W., & Smith, L. B. (2002). Attention to novel objects during verb learning. *Child Development, 73,* 93–109.

Kesler, S. R., Reiss, A. L., Vohr, B., Watson, C., Schneider, K. C., Katz, K. H., . . . & Ment L. R. (2008). Brain volume reductions within multiple cognitive systems in male preterm children at age twelve. *Journal of Pediatrics, 152,* 513–520.

Kharasch, S., Saxe, G., & Zuckerman, B. (2003). Pain treatment: Opportunities and challenges. *Archives of Pediatrics and Adolescent Medicine, 157,* 1054–1056.

Kieras, J. E., Tobin, R. T., Graziano, W. G., & Rothbart, M. K. (2005). You can't always get what you want: Effortful control and children's responses to undesirable gifts. *Psychological Science, 16,* 391–396.

Kiesner, J., Cadinu, M., Poulin, F., & Bucci, M. (2002). Group identification in early adolescence: Its relation with peer adjustment and its moderator effect on peer influence. *Child Development, 73,* 196–208.

Kiesner, J., & Pastore, M. (2005). Differences in the relations between antisocial behavior and peer acceptance across contexts and across adolescence. *Child Development, 76,* 1278–1293.

Kilbride, H., Castor, C., Hoffman, E., & Fuger, K. L. (2000). Thirty-six month outcome of prenatal cocaine exposure for term or near-term infants: Impact of early case management. *Journal of Developmental and Behavioral Pediatrics, 21,* 19–26.

Killen, M., Pisacane, K., Lee Kim, J., & Ardila Rey, A. (2001). Fairness or stereotypes? Young children's priorities when evaluating group exclusion and inclusion. *Developmental Psychology, 37,* 587–596.

Killen, M., Sinno, S., & Margie, N. G. (2007). Children's experiences and judgments about group exclusion and inclusion. In R. V. Kail (Ed.), *Advances in child development and behavior.* (Vol. 35, pp. 173–218). London, UK: Elsevier.

Killen, M., & Stangor, C. (2001). Children's social reasoning about inclusion and exclusion in gender and race peer group contexts. *Child Development, 72,* 174–186.

Kim, J. E., Hetherington, E. M., & Reiss, D. (1999). Associations among family relationships., antisocial peers, and adolescents' externalizing behaviors: Gender and family type differences. *Child Development, 70,* 1209–1230.

Kim, K. H. S., Relkin, N. R., Lee, K., & Hirsch, J. (1997). Distinct cortical areas associated with native and second languages. *Nature, 388,* 171–174.

Kim, K. J., Conger, R. D., Lorenz, F. O., & Elder, G. H., Jr. (2001). Parent-adolescent reciprocity in negative affect and its relation to early adult social development. *Developmental Psychology, 37,* 775–790.

Kim-Cohen, J., & Gold, A. L. (2009). Measured gene–environment interactions and mechanisms promoting resilient development. *Current Directions in Psychological Science, 18,* 138–142.

Kindermann, T. A. (1993). Natural peer groups as contexts for individual development: The case of children's motivation in school. *Developmental Psychology, 29,* 970–977.

Kindermann, T. A. (1998). Children's development within peer groups: Using composite social maps to identify peer networks and to study their influences. In W. K. Bukowski & A. H. Cillessen (Eds.), *New Directions for Child Development: No. 80. Sociometry then and now: Building on six decades of measuring children's experiences in the peer group* (pp. 55–82). San Francisco, CA: Jossey-Bass.

Kindermann, T. A. (2007). Effects of naturally existing peer groups on changes in academic engagement. *Child Development, 78,* 1186–1203.

Kingery, J. N., Erdley, C. A., Marshall, K. C., Whitaker, K. G., & Reuter, T. R. (2010). Peer experiences of anxious and socially withdrawn youth: An integrative review of the developmental and clinical literature. *Clinical Child and Family Psychology Review, 13,* 91–128.

Kinsfogel, K. M, & Grych, J. H. (2004). Interparental conflict and adolescent dating relationships: Integrating cognitive, emotional, and peer influences. *Journal of Family Psychology, 18,* 505–515.

Kinzler, K. D., Dupoux, E., & Spelke, E. S. (2007). The native language of social cognition. *Proceedings of the National Academy of Sciences, 104,* 12577–12580.

Kirkorian, H. L., Anderson, D. R., & Keen, R. (2008, March). Looking at *Sesame Street*: Age differences in eye movements during video viewing. Poster session presented at the Biannual International Conference on Infant Studies, Vancouver, BC.

Kirkorian, H. L., Pempek, T. A., Murphy, L. A., Schmidt, M. E., & Anderson, D. R. (2009). The impact of background television on parent-child interaction. *Child Development, 80,* 1350–1359.

Kisilevsky, B. S., Hains, S. M. J., Jacquet, A. Y., Granier-Deferre, C., & Lecanuet, J. P. (2004). Maturation of fetal responses to music. *Developmental Science, 7,* 550–559.

Kisilevsky, B. S., Hains, S. M. J., Lee, K., Xid, X., Huang, H., Ye, H. H., Zhang, K., & Wang, Z. (2003). Effects of experience on fetal voice recognition. *Psychological Science, 14,* 220–224.

Kisilevsky, B. S., & Low, J. A. (1998). Human fetal behavior: 100 years of study. *Developmental Review, 18,* 1–29.

Klaczynski, P. A. (2000). Motivated scientific reasoning biases, epistemological beliefs, and theory polarization: A two-process approach to adolescent cognition. *Child Development, 71,* 1347–1366.

Klaczynski, P. A. (2001). Analytic and heuristic processing influences on adolescent reasoning and decision-making. *Child Development, 72,* 844–861.

Klaczynski, P. A. (2004). A dual-process model of adolescent development: Implications for decision making, reasoning, and identity. In R. V. Kail (Ed.), *Advances in child development and behavior* (Vol. 32, pp. 73–123). San Diego, CA: Elsevier.

Klahr, D. (1978). Goal formation, planning, and learning by preschool problem solvers or: "My socks are in the dryer." In R. S. Siegler (Ed.), *Children's thinking: What develops?* (pp. 181–212). Hillsdale, NJ: Erlbaum.

Klahr, D. (1989). Information-processing approaches. In R. Vasta (Ed.), *Annals of child development: Vol 6. Six theories of child development: Revised formulations and current issues* (pp. 133–185). Greenwich, CT: JAI Press.

Klahr, D., Chen, Z., & Toth, E. E. (2001). Cognitive development and science education: Ships that pass in the night or beacons of mutual illumination? In S. M. Carver & D. Klahr (Eds.), *Cognition and instruction: Twenty-five years of progress* (pp. 75–119). Mahwah, NJ: Erlbaum.

Klahr, D., & Dunbar, K. (1988). Dual space search during scientific reasoning. *Cognitive Science, 12,* 1–55.

Klahr, D., Fay, A. L., & Dunbar, K. (1993). Heuristics for scientific experimentation: A developmental study. *Cognitive Psychology, 25,* 111–146.

Klahr, D., & MacWhinney, B. (1998). Information processing. In W. Damon (Series Ed.) & D. Kuhn & R. S. Siegler (Vol. Eds.), *Handbook of child psychology: Vol. 2. Cognition, perception, and language* (5th ed., pp. 631–678). New York, NY: Wiley.

Klahr, D., & Robinson, M. (1981). Formal assessment of problem solving and planning processes in preschool children. *Cognitive Psychology, 13,* 113–148.

Klaus, M., & Kennell, J. (1982). *Parent-infant bonding.* St. Louis: C. V. Mosby.

Klebanov, P. K., Brooks-Gunn, J., & McCormick, M. C. (2001). Maternal coping strategies and emotional distress: Results of an early intervention program for low birth weight young children. *Developmental Psychology, 37,* 654–667.

Klein, P. D. (1997). Multiplying the problems of intelligence by eight: A critique of Gardner's theory. *Canadian Journal of Education, 22,* 377–394.

Kliewer, W., Adams Parrish, K., Taylor, K. W., Jackson, K., Walker, J. M., & Shivy, V. A. (2006). Socialization of coping with community violence: Influences of caregiver coaching, modeling, and family context. *Child Development, 77,* 605–623.

Klima, E. S., & Bellugi, U. (1966). Syntactic regularities in the speech of children. In J. Lyons & R. J. Wales (Eds.), *Psycholinguistic papers: The proceedings of the 1966 Edinburgh conference* (pp. 183–208). Edinburgh: Edinburgh University Press.

Kling, K. C., Hyde, J. S., Showers, C. J., & Buswell, B. N. (1999). Gender differences in self-esteem: A meta-analysis. *Psychological Bulletin, 125,* 470–500.

Klingman, A. (2006). Children and war trauma. In W. Damon & R. M. Lerner (Editors-in-Chief) & K. A. Renninger & I. E. Sigel (Vol. Eds.), *Handbook of child psychology, Vol. 4. Child psychology in practice* (6th ed., pp. 619–652). Hoboken, NJ: Wiley.

Knowles, R. V. (1985). *Genetics, society and decisions.* Columbus, OH: Merrill.

Kobak, R. R., Cole, H. E., Ferenz-Gillies, R., & Fleming, W. S. (1993). Attachment and emotion regulation during mother-teen problem-solving: A control theory analysis. *Child Development, 64,* 231–245.

Kobasigawa, A. (1968). Inhibitory and disinhibitory effects of models on sex-inappropriate behavior in children. *Psychologia, 11,* 86–96.

Kobayashi-Winata, H., & Power, T. G. (1989). Child rearing and compliance: Japanese and American families in Houston. *Journal of Cross-Cultural Psychology, 20,* 333–356.

Koch, R., Hanley, W., Levy, H., Matalon, K., Matalon, R., Rouse, B., et al. (2003). The Maternal Phenylketonuria International Study: 1984–2002. *Pediatrics, 112,* 1523–1529.

Kochanska, G. (1994). Beyond cognition: Expanding the search for the early roots of internalization and conscience. *Developmental Psychology, 30,* 20–22.

Kochanska, G. (1997). Mutually responsive orientation between mothers and their young children: Implications for early socialization. *Child Development, 68,* 94–112.

Kochanska, G., & Aksan, N. (2006). Children's conscience and self-regulation. *Journal of Personality, 74,* 1587–1617.

Kochanska, G., Aksan, N., & Koenig, A. L. (1995). A longitudinal study of the roots of preschoolers' conscience: Committed compliance and emerging internalizations. *Child Development, 66,* 1752–1769.

Kochanska, G., Aksan, N., Knaack, A., & Rhines, H. M. (2004). Maternal parenting and children's conscience: Early security as moderator. *Child Development, 75,* 1229–1242.

Kochanska, G., Casey, R. J., & Fukumoto, A. (1995). Toddlers' sensitivity to standard violation. *Child Development, 66,* 643–656.

Kochanska, G., Coy, K. C., & Murray, K. T. (2001). The development of self-regulation in the first four years of life. *Child Development, 72,* 1091–1111.

Kochanska, G., Gross, J. N., Lin, M.-H., & Nichols, K. E. (2002). Guilt in young children: Development, determinants, and relations with a broader system of standards. *Child Development, 73,* 461–482.

Kochanska, G., & Murray, K. T. (2000). Mother-child responsive orientation and conscience development: From toddler to early school age. *Child Development, 71,* 417–431.

Kochanska, G., Murray, K. T., & Harlan, E. T. (2000). Effortful control in early childhood: Continuity and change, antecedents, and implications for social development. *Developmental Psychology, 36,* 220–232.

Kochanska, G., Murray, K., & Coy, K. C. (1997). Inhibitory control as a contributor to conscience in childhood: From toddler to early school age. *Child Development, 68,* 263–277.

Kochanska, G., Tjebkes, T. L., & Forman, D. R. (1998). Children's emerging regulation of conduct: Restraint, compliance, and internalization from infancy to the second year. *Child Development, 69,* 1378–1389.

Kodituwakku, P. W. (2007). Defining the behavioral phenotype in children with fetal alcohol spectrum disorders: A review. *Neuroscience & Biobehavioral Reviews, 31,* 192–201.

Koff, E., & Rierdan, J. (1995). Preparing girls for menstruation: Recommendations from adolescent girls. *Adolescence, 30,* 795–811.

Kohlberg, L. (1966). A cognitive-developmental analysis of children's sex-role concepts and attitudes. In E. E. Maccoby (Ed.), *The development of sex differences* (pp. 82–173). Stanford, CA: Stanford University Press.

Kohlberg, L. (1969). Stage and sequence: The cognitive-developmental approach to socialization. In D. A. Goslin (Ed.), *The handbook of socialization theory and research* (pp. 347–380). Chicago, IL: Rand McNally.

Kohlberg, L. (1976). Moral stages and moralization: The cognitive developmental approach. In T. Lickona (Ed.), *Moral development and moral behavior: Theory, research, and social issues* (pp. 31–53). New York, NY: Holt, Rinehart & Winston.

Kohlberg, L. (1984). *Essays on moral development, Vol. II: The psychology of moral development.* San Francisco, CA: Harper and Row.

Kohlberg, L. (2008). The development of children's orientations toward a moral order. *Human Development, 51,* 8–20.

Kohlberg, L., & Kramer, R. (1969). Continuities and discontinuities in childhood moral development. *Human Development, 12,* 93–120.

Kokko, K., & Pulkkinen, L. (2000). Aggression in childhood and long-term unemployment in adulthood: A cycle of maladaptation and some protective factors. *Developmental Psychology, 36,* 463–472.

Kopp, C. B. (1987). The growth of self-regulation: Caregivers and children. In N. Eisenberg (Ed.), *Contemporary topics in developmental psychology* (pp. 34–55). New York, NY: Wiley.

Kopp, C. B. (1989). Regulation of distress and negative emotions: A developmental view. *Developmental Psychology, 25,* 343–354.

Korner, A. F. (1972). State as a variable, as obstacle, and mediator of stimulation in infant research. *Merrill-Palmer Quarterly, 18,* 77–94.

Korner, A. F. (1987). Preventive intervention with high-risk newborns: Theoretical, conceptual, and methodological perspectives. In J. D. Osofsky (Ed.), *Handbook of infant development* (2nd ed., pp. 1006–1036.). New York, NY: Wiley.

Kosslyn, S. M., Gazzaniga, M. S., Galaburda, A. M., & Rabin, C. (1999). Hemispheric specialization. In M. J. Zigmond, F. E. Bloom, S. C. Landis, J. L. Roberts, & L. R. Squire (Eds.), *Fundamental neuroscience* (pp. 1521–1542). New York, NY: Academic Press.

Kotelchuk, M. (1976). The infant's relationship to the father: Experimental evidence. In M. E. Lamb (Ed.), *The role of the father in child development* (pp. 329–344). New York, NY: Wiley.

Kotimaa, A. J., Moilanen, I., Taanila, A., Ebeling, H., Smalley, S. L., McGough, J. J., . . . & Jarvelin, M.-R. (2003). Maternal smoking and hyperactivity in 8-year-old children. *Journal of the American Academy of Child and Adolescent Psychiatry, 42,* 826–833.

Kovacs, A. M., & Mehler, J. (2009). Cognitive gains in 7-month-old bilingual infants. *PNAS Proceedings of the National Academy of Sciences of the United States of America, 106,* 6556–6560.

Kovacs, D. M., Parker, J. G., & Hoffman, L. W. (1996). Behavioral, affective, and social correlates of involvement in cross-sex friendship in elementary school. *Child Development, 67,* 2269–2286.

Kovacs, M., Joormann, J., & Gotlib, I. H. (2008). Emotion (dys)regulation and links to depressive disorders. *Child Development Perspectives, 2,* 149–155.

Kovelman, I., Baker, S. A., & Petitto, L. A. (2008). Age of first bilingual language exposure as a new window into bilingual reading development. *Bilingualism: Language and Cognition, 11,* 203–223.

Kowal, A. K., & Kramer, L. (1997). Children's understanding of parental differential treatment. *Child Development, 68,* 113–126.

Kowal, A. K., Krull, J. L., & Kramer, L. (2004). How the differential treatment of siblings is linked with parent-child relationship quality. *Journal of Family Psychology, 18,* 658–665.

Kracke, K., & Hahn, H. (2008). The nature and extent of childhood exposure to violence: What we know, why we don't know more, and why it matters. *Journal of Emotional Abuse, 8,* 29–49.

Kraemer, H. C., Korner, A., Anders, T., Jacklin, C. N., & Dimiceli, S. (1985). Obstetric drugs and infant behavior: A re-evaluation. *Journal of Pediatric Psychology, 10,* 345–353.

Krafchuk, E. E., Tronick, E. Z., & Clifton, R. K. (1983). Behavioral and cardiac responses to sound in preterm infants varying in risk status: A hypothesis of their paradoxical reactivity. In T. Field & A. Sostek (Eds.), *Infants born at risk: Physiological, perceptual, and cognitive processes* (pp. 99–128). New York, NY: Grune & Stratton.

Kramer, A. F., Gonzalez de Sather, J. C. M., & Cassavaugh, N. D. (2005). Development of attentional and oculomotor control. *Developmental Psychology, 41,* 760–772.

Kramer, L., Perozynski, L. A., & Chung, T. (1999). Parental responses to sibling conflict: The effects of development and parent gender. *Child Development, 70,* 1401–1414.

Krauss, R. H., & Glucksberg, S. (1969). The development of communication. *Child Development, 40,* 255–266.

Krcmar, M., Grela, B., & Lin, K. (2007). Can toddlers learn vocabulary from television? An experimental approach. *Media Psychology, 10,* 41–63.

Krebs, D. L., & Van Hesteren, F. (1994). The development of altruism: Toward an integrative model. *Developmental Review, 14,* 103–158.

Kreutzer, M. A., Leonard, S. C., & Flavell, J. H. (1975). An interview study of children's knowledge about memory. *Monographs of the Society for Research in Child Development, 40* (1, Serial No. 159).

Krevans, J., & Gibbs, J. C. (1996). Parents' use of inductive discipline: Relations to children's empathy and prosocial behavior. *Child Development, 67,* 3263–3277.

Kroll, J. (1977). The concept of childhood in the Middle Ages. *Journal of the History of the Behavioral Sciences, 13,* 384–393.

Kronenberg, M. E., Hansel, T. C., Brennan, A. M., Osofsky, H. J., Osofsky, J. D., & Lawrason, B. (2010). Children of Katrina: Lessons learned about post-disaster symptoms and recovery patterns. *Child Development, 81,* 1241–1259.

Krumhansl, C. L., & Jusczyk, P. W. (1990). Infants' perception of phrase structure in music. *Psychological Science, 1,* 70–73.

Kuczaj, S. A., Borys, R. H., & Jones, M. (1989). On the interaction of language and thought: Some thoughts and developmental data. In A. Gellatly, D. Rogers, & J. A. Sloboda (Eds.), *Cognition and social worlds* (pp. 168–189). Oxford: Clarendon Press.

Kuczynski, L., & Kochanska, G. (1995). Function and content of maternal demands: Developmental significance of early demands for competent action. *Child Development, 66,* 616–628.

Kuebli, J., Butler, S., & Fivush, R. (1995). Mother-child talk about past emotions: Relations of maternal language and child gender over time. *Cognition and Emotion, 9,* 265–283.

Kuhl, P. K. (1987). Perception of speech and sound in early infancy. In P. Salapatek & L. Cohen (Eds.), *Handbook of infant perception: From perception to cognition* (Vol. 2, pp. 275–382). Orlando, FL: Academic Press.

Kuhl, P. K., Stevens, E., Hayashi, A., Deguchi, T., Kiritani, S., & Iverson, P. (2006). Infants show a facilitation effect for native language phonetic perception between 6 and 12 months. *Developmental Science, 9,* F13–F22.

Kuhn, D. (2000a). Metacognitive development. *Current Directions in Psychological Science, 9,* 178–181.

Kuhn, D. (2000b). Theory of mind, metacognition, and reasoning: A life-span perspective. In P. Mitchell & K. J. Riggs (Eds.), *Children's reasoning and the mind* (pp. 301–326). Hove, UK: Psychology Press.

Kuhn, D. (2006). Do cognitive changes accompany developments in the adolescent brain? *Perspectives on Psychological Science, 16,* 59–67.

Kuhn, D., & Dean, D., Jr. (2005). Is developing scientific thinking all about learning to control variables? *Psychological Science, 16,* 866–870.

Kuhn, D., Garcia-Mila, M., Zohar, A., & Andersen, C. (1995). Strategies of knowledge acquisition. *Monographs of the Society for Research in Child Development, 60* (No. 4, Serial No. 245).

Kuhn, D., & Pearsall, S. (2000). Developmental origins of scientific thinking. *Journal of Cognition and Development, 1,* 113–129.

Kuhn, D., Schauble, L., & Garcia-Mila, M. (1992). Cross-domain development of scientific reasoning. *Cognition and Instruction, 9,* 285–327.

Kuklinski, M. R., & Weinstein, R. S. (2001). Classroom and developmental differences in a path model of teacher expectancy effects. *Child Development, 72,* 1554–1578.

Kulik, J. A., Kulik, C. C., & Bangert-Drowns, R. L. (1985). Effectiveness of computer-based education in elementary schools. *Computers in Human Behavior, 1,* 59–74.

Kunkel, D. (2001). Children and television advertising. In D. Singer & J. Singer (Eds.) *Handbook of Children and the Media* (pp. 375–394). Thousand Oaks, CA: Sage.

Kurdek, L. A. (1989). Siblings' reactions to parental divorce. *Journal of Divorce, 12,* 203–219.

Kurdek, L. A., Fine, M. A., & Sinclair, R. J. (1995). School adjustment in sixth graders: Parenting transitions, family climate, and peer norm effects. *Child Development, 66,* 430–445.

Lackey, P. N. (1989). Adults' attitudes about assignments of household chores to male and female children. *Sex Roles, 20,* 271–281.

Ladd, G. W. (1983). Social networks of popular, average, and rejected children in school settings. *Merrill-Palmer Quartlerly, 29,* 283–307.

Ladd, G. W. (2005). *Children's peer relations and social competence.* New Haven, CT: Yale University Press.

Ladd, G. W., Birch, S. H., & Buhs, E. S. (1999). Children's social and scholastic lives in kindergarten: Related spheres of influence? *Child Development, 70,* 1373–1400.

Ladd, G. W., & Burgess, K. B. (1999). Charting the relationship trajectories of aggressive, withdrawn, and aggressive/withdrawn children during early grade school. *Child Development, 70,* 910–929.

Ladd, G. W., & Golter, B. S. (1988). Parents' management of preschooler's peer relations: Is it related to children's social competencies? *Developmental Psychology, 24,* 109–117.

Ladd, G. W., & Hart, C. H. (1992). Creating informal play opportunities: Are parents' and preschoolers' initiations related to children's competence with peers? *Developmental Psychology, 28,* 1179–1187.

Ladd, G. W., Herald-Brown, S. L., & Reiser, M. (2008). Does chronic classroom peer rejection predict the development of children's classroom participation during the grade school years? *Child Development, 79,* 1001–1015.

Ladd, G. W., Kochenderfer, B. J., & Coleman, C. C. (1996). Friendship quality as a predictor of young children's early school adjustment. *Child Development, 67,* 1103–1118.

Ladd, G. W., & Price, J. M. (1987). Predicting children's social and school adjustment following the transition from preschool to kindergarten. *Child Development, 58,* 1168–1189.

Ladd, G. W., Price, J. M., & Hart, C. H. (1988). Predicting preschoolers' peer status from their playground behaviors. *Child Development, 59,* 986–992.

LaFontana, K. M., & Cillessen, A. H. N. (1998). The nature of children's stereotypes of popularity. *Social Development, 7,* 301–320.

LaFontana, K. M., & Cillessen, A. H. N. (2002). Children's perceptions of popular and unpopular peers: A multimethod assessment. *Developmental Psychology, 38,* 635–647.

LaFontana, K. M., & Cillessen, A. H. N. (2010). Developmental changes in the priority of perceived status in childhood and adolescence. *Social Development, 19,* 130–147.

Lago, P., Garetti, E., Merazzi, D., Pieragostini, L., Ancora, G., Pirelli, A., Bellieni, C. V., & Pain Study Group of the Italian Society of Neonatology. (2009). Guidelines for procedural pain in the newborn. *Acta Paediatrica, 98,* 932–939.

LaGreca, A. M., & Lopez, N. (1998). Social anxiety among adolescents: Linkages with peer relations and friendships. *Journal of Abnormal Child Psychology, 26,* 83–94.

Lahey, B. B., Hammer, D., Crumrine, P. L., & Forehand, R. L. (1980). Birth order sex interactions in child behavior problems. *Developmental Psychology, 16,* 608–615.

Laible, D. J., & Carlo, G. (2004). The differential relations of maternal and paternal support and control to adolescent social competence, self-worth, and sympathy. *Journal of Adolescent Research, 19,* 759–782.

Laible, D., Panfile, T., & Makariev, D. (2008). The quality and frequency of mother–toddler conflict: Links with attachment and temperament. *Child Development, 79,* 426–443.

Laible, D. J., & Thompson, R. A. (2000). Mother-child discourse, attachment security, shared positive affect, and early conscience development. *Child Development, 71,* 1424–1440.

Laible, D. J., & Thompson, R. A. (2002). Mother-child conflict in the toddler years: Lessons in emotion, morality, and relationships. *Child Development, 73,* 1187–1203.

Lamaze, F. (1970). *Painless childbirth: Psychoprophylactic method.* Chicago, IL: Henry Regnery.

Lamb, M. E. (1981). *The role of the father in child development* (rev. ed.). New York, NY: Wiley.

Lamb, M. E. (1997). The development of father–infant relationships. In M. E. Lamb (Ed.), *The role of the father in child development* (3rd ed., pp. 104–120). New York, NY: Wiley.

Lamb, M. E. (2010). How do fathers influence children's development? Let me count the ways. In M. Lamb (Ed.), *The role of the father in child development* (5th ed., pp. 1–26). Hoboken, NJ: Wiley.

Lamb, M. E., & Ahnert, L. (2006). Nonparental child care: Context, concepts, correlates, and consequences. In W. Damon & R. M. Lerner (Editors-in-Chief) & K. A. Renninger & I. E. Sigel (Vol. Eds.), *Handbook of child psychology: Vol. 4. Child psychology in practice* (6th ed., pp. 950–1016). Hoboken, NJ: Wiley.

Lamb, M. E., Easterbrooks, M. A., & Holden, G. (1980). Reinforcement and punishment among preschoolers: Characteristics and correlates. *Child Development, 51,* 1230–1236.

Lamb, M. E., Pleck, J. H., Charnov, E. L., & Levine, J. A. (1987). A biosocial perspective on paternal behavior and involvement. In J. B. Lancaster, J. Altmann, A. S. Rossi, & L. R. Sherrod (Eds.), *Parenting across the life span: Biosocial dimensions* (pp. 111–142). New York, NY: Aldine de Gruyter.

Lamb, M. E., & Roopnarine, J. L. (1979). Peer influences on sex-role development in preschoolers. *Child Development, 50,* 1219–1222.

Lammer, E. J., Chen, D. T., Hoar, R. M., Agnish, N. D., et al. (1985). Retinoic acid embryopathy. *New England Journal of Medicine, 313,* 837–841.

Lampl, M., Veldhuis, J. D., & Johnson, M. L. (1992). Saltation and stasis: A model of human growth. *Science, 258,* 801–803.

Landhuis, C. E., Poulton, R., Welch, D., & Hancox, R. J. (2007). Does childhood television viewing lead to attention problems in adolescence? Results from a prospective longitudinal study. *Pediatrics, 120,* 532–537.

Landolt, M. A., Nuoffer, J.-M., Steinmann, B., & Superti-Furga, A. (2003). Quality of life and psychologic adjustment in children and adolescents with early treated phenylketonuria can be normal. *Journal of Pediatrics, 140,* 516–521.

Landry, M. L. (2004). Viral infections. In G. H. Burrow, T. P. Duffy, & J. Copel (Eds.), *Medical complications during pregnancy* (6th ed., pp. 347–374). Philadelphia, PA: Saunders.

Lang, C. T., & Iams, J. D. (2009). Goals and strategies for prevention of preterm birth: An obstetric perspective. *Pediatric Clinics of North America, 56,* 537–563.

Langlois, J. H., & Stephan, C. (1981). Beauty and the beast: The role of physical attractiveness in the development of peer relations and social behavior. In S. S. Brehm, S. H. Kassin, & F. X. Gibbons (Eds.), *Developmental social psychology* (pp. 152–168). New York, NY: Oxford University Press.

Laplante, D. P., Barr, R. G., Brunet, A., du Fort, G. G., Meaney, M. L., Saucier, J.-F., Zelazo, P. R., & King, S. (2004). Stress during pregnancy affects general intellectual and language functioning in human toddlers. *Pediatric Research, 56,* 400–410.

Larsen, J. T., To, Y. M., & Fireman, G. (2007). Children's understanding and experience of mixed emotions. *Psychological Science, 18,* 186–191.

Larson, R. W. (2001). How U.S. children and adolescents spend time: What it does (and doesn't) tell us about development. *Current Directions in Psychological Science, 10,* 160–164.

Larson, R. W., & Ham, M. (1993). Stress and "storm and stress" in early adolescence: The relationship of negative events with dysphoric affect. *Developmental Psychology, 29,* 130–140.

Larson, R. W., Moneta, G., Richards, M. H., & Wilson, S. (2002). Continuity, stability, and change in daily emotional experience across adolescence. *Developmental Psychology, 73,* 1151–1165.

Latner, J. D., & Stunkard, A. J. (2003). Getting worse: The stigmatization of obese children. *Obesity Research, 11,* 452–456.

Latz, S., Wolf, A.W., & Lozoff, B. (1999). Cosleeping in context: Sleep practices and problems in young children in Japan and the United States. *Archives of Pediatrics and Adolescent Medicine, 153,* 339–346.

Laursen, B., Bukowski, W. M., Aunola, K., & Nurmi, J. (2007). Friendship moderates prospective associations between social isolation and adjustment problems in young children. *Child Development, 78,* 1395–1404.

Laursen, B., Coy, K. C., & Collins, W. A. (1998). Reconsidering changes in parent-child conflict across adolescence: A meta-analysis. *Child Development, 69,* 817–832.

Laursen, B., & Williams, V. A. (1997). Perceptions of interdependence and closeness in family and peer relationships among adolescents with and without romantic partners. In S. Shulman & W. Andrew Collins (Eds.), *New Directions for Child Development: No. 78. Romantic relationships in adolescence: Developmental perspectives* (pp. 3–20). San Francisco, CA: Jossey-Bass.

Laurson, K. R., Eisenmann, J. C., Welk, G. J., Wickel, E. E., Gentile, D. A., & Walsh, D. A. (2008). Combined influence of physical activity and screen time recommendations on childhood overweight. *Journal of Pediatrics, 153,* 209–214.

Lawson, M. (1980). Development of body build stereotypes, peer ratings, and self-esteem in Australian children. *Journal of Psychology, 104,* 111–118.

Lazar, I., & Darlington, R. (1982). Lasting effects of early education: A report from the Consortium for Longitudinal Studies. *Monographs of the Society for Research in Child Development, 47* (2–3, Serial No. 195).

Leaper, C., & Brown, C. S. (2008). Perceived experiences with sexism among adolescent girls. *Child Development, 79,* 685–704.

Learmonth, A. E., Nadel, L., & Newcombe, N. S. (2002). Children's use of landmarks: Implications for modularity theory. *Psychological Science, 13,* 337–341.

Lebedev, I. N., Ostroverkhova, N. V., Nikitina, T. V., Sukhanova, N. N., & Nazarenko, S. A. (2004). Features of chromosomal abnormalities in spontaneous abortion cell culture failures detected by interphase FISH analysis. *European Journal of Human Genetics, 12,* 513–520.

LeBoyer, F. (1975). *Birth without violence.* New York, NY: Knopf.

Lecanuet, J.-P. (1998). Foetal responses to auditory and speech stimuli. In A. Slater (Ed.), *Perceptual development: Visual, auditory, and speech perception in infancy* (pp. 317–355). East Sussex, UK: Psychology Press.

Leclercq, A., & Majerus, S. (2010). Serial-order short-term memory predicts vocabulary development: Evidence from a longitudinal study. *Developmental Psychology, 46,* 417–427.

Lederberg, A. R., Prezbindowski, A. K., & Spencer, P. E. (2000). Word-learning skills of deaf preschoolers: The development of novel mapping and rapid word-learning strategies. *Child Development, 71,* 1571–1585.

Lee, B. C. P., Kuppusamy, K. G. R., El-Ghazzawy, O., Gordon, R. E., Lin, W., & Haacke, M. (1999). Hemispheric language dominance in children demonstrated by functional magnetic resonance imaging. *Journal of Child Neurology, 14,* 78–82.

Lee, K., Cameron, C. A., Xu, F., Fu, G., & Board, J. (1997). Chinese and Canadian children's evaluations of lying and truth telling: Similarities and differences in the context of pro- and antisocial behavior. *Child Development, 68,* 924–934.

Lee, R. M., & Miller, M. J. (2009). History and psychology of adoptees in Asian America. In N. Tewari & A. N. Alvarez (Eds.), *Asian American psychology* (pp. 337–363). New York, NY: Routledge/Taylor & Francis Group.

Lee, R. M., Seol, K. O., Sung, M., Miller, M. J., & The Minnesota International Adoption Project Team (2010). The behavioral development of Korean children in institutional care and international adoptive families. *Developmental Psychology, 46,* 468–478.

Lee, R. V. (1988). Sexually transmitted infections. In G. N. Burrow & T. F. Ferris (Eds.), *Medical complications during pregnancy (*pp. 389–424). Philadelphia: W. B. Saunders.

Legerstee, M., Anderson, D., & Schaffer, A. (1998). Five- and eight-month-old infants recognize their faces and voices as familiar and social stimuli. *Child Development, 69,* 37–50.

Lehmann, M., & Hasselhorn, M. (2007). Variable memory strategy use in children's adaptive intratask learning behavior: Developmental changes and working memory influences in free recall. *Child Development, 78,* 1068–1082.

Leinbach, M. D., Hort, B. E., & Fagot, B. I. (1997). Bears are for boys: Metaphorical associations in young children's gender stereotypes. *Cognitive Development, 12,* 107–130.

Leman, P. J., & Lam, V. L. (2008). The influence of race and gender on children's conversations and playmate choices. *Child Development, 79,* 1329–1343.

Lemish, D., & Rice, M. (1986). Television as a talking picture book: A prop for language acquisition. *Journal of Child Language, 13,* 251–274.

Lenhart, A., & Madden, M. (2007). *Social networking websites and teens.* Pew Internet and American Life Project. Retrieved December 2, 2010, from http://www.pewinternet.org/Reports/2007/Social-Networking-Websites-and-Teens.aspx

Lenhart, A., Purcell, K., Smith, A., & Zickuhr, K. (2010). *Social media & mobile Internet use among teens and young adults.* Pew Research Center. Downloaded October 18, 2010, from http://pewresearch.org/pubs/1484/social-media-mobile-internet-use-teens-millennials-fewer-blog

Lenneberg, E. (1967). *Biological foundations of language.* New York, NY: Wiley.

Leo, I., & Simion, F. (2009). Newborns' Mooney-face perception. *Infancy, 14,* 641–653.

Leppänin, J. K. M., Moulson, M. C., Vogel-Farley, V. K., & Nelson, C. A. (2007). An ERP study of emotional face processing in the adult and infant brain. *Child Development, 78,* 232–245.

Lepper, M. R., & Gurtner, J. (1989). Children and computers: Approaching the twenty-first century. *American Psychologist, 44,* 170–178.

Lerner, R. M. (2006). Developmental science, developmental systems, and contemporary theories of human development. In W. Damon & R. M. Lerner (Editors-in-Chief) & R. M. Lerner (Vol. Ed.), *Handbook of child psychology: Vol. 1. Theoretical models of human development.* (6th ed., pp. 1–17). Hoboken, NJ: John Wiley & Sons.

Lerner, R. M., Jacobs, F., & Wertlieb, D. (Eds.) (2003). *Handbook of applied developmental science: Promoting positive child, adolescent, and family development through research, policies, and programs.* Thousand Oaks, CA: Sage Publications.

Leslie, A. M. (1994). ToMM, ToBy, and Agency: Core architecture and domain specificity. In L. A. Hirschfield & S. A. Gelman (Eds.), *Mapping the mind: Domain specificity in cognition and culture* (pp. 119–148). Cambridge, UK: Cambridge University Press.

Leslie, A. M., Knobe, J., & Cohen, A. (2006). Acting intentionally and the side-effect effect: Theory of mind and moral judgment. *Psychological Science, 17,* 421–427.

Lesser, G. S., Fifer, F., & Clark, D. H. (1965). Mental abilities of children of different social-class and cultural groups. *Monographs of the Society for Research in Child Development, 30* (4, Serial No. 102).

Lester, B. M., Andreozzi, L., & Appiah, L. (2004, April 20). Substance use during pregnancy: Time for policy to catch up with research. *Harm Reduction Journal, 1*(5). Retrieved from http://www.harmreductionjournal.com/content/1/1/5

Lester, B. M., & Brazelton, T. B. (1982). Cross-cultural assessment of neonatal behavior. In D. Wagner & H.W. Stevenson (Eds.), *Cultural perspectives on child development* (pp. 20–53). San Francisco, CA: W.H. Freeman.

Lester, B. M., Tronick, E. Z., LaGasse, L., Seifer, R., Bauer, C. R., Shankaran, S., . . . & Maza, P. L. (2002). The Maternal Lifestyle Study: Effects of substance exposure during pregnancy on neurodevelopmental outcome in 1-month-old infants. *Pediatrics, 110,* 1182–1192.

LeVay, S., & Hamer, D. H. (1994, May). Evidence for a biological influence in male homosexuality. *Scientific American, 270,* 43–57.

Leventhal, T., & Brooks-Gunn, J. (2000). The neighborhoods they live in: The effects of neighborhood residence on child and adolescent outcomes. *Psychological Bulletin, 126,* 309–337.

Leventhal, T., & Brooks-Gunn, J. (2003). Children and youth in neighborhood contexts. *Current Directions in Psychological Science, 12,* 27–31.

Leventhal, T., & Brooks-Gunn, J. (2004). A randomized study of neighborhood effects on low-income children's education outcomes. *Developmental Psychology, 40,* 488–507.

LeVine, R., Dixon, S., LeVine, S., Richman, A., Leiderman, P. M., Keefer, C. H., & Brazelton, T. B. (1994). *Child care and culture: Lessons from Africa.* New York, NY: Cambridge University Press.

LeVine, R. A. (2007). Ethnographic studies of childhood: A historical overview. *American Anthropologist, 109,* 247–260.

Levine, S. C., Jordan, N. C., & Huttenlocher, J. (1992). Development of calculation abilities in young children. *Journal of Experimental Child Psychology, 53,* 72–103.

Levinson, D. R. (2007). *Enrollment levels in Head Start.* Washington, DC: Department of Health and Human Services.

Levitin, D. J., & Bellugi, U. (1998). Musical abilities in individuals with Williams' syndrome. *Music Perception, 15,* 357–389.

Levitt, M. J., Levitt, J., Bustos, G. L., Crooks, N. A., Santos, J. D., Telan, P., . . . & Milevsky, A. (2005). Patterns of social support in the middle childhood to early adolescent transition: Implications for adjustment. *Social Development, 14,* 398–420.

Levy, Y. (1999). Early metalinguistic competence: Speech monitoring and repair behavior. *Developmental Psychology, 35,* 822–834.

Lew, A. R., Bremner, J. G., & Lefkovitch, L. P. (2000). The development of relational landmark use in six- to twelve-month-old infants in a spatial orientation task. *Child Development, 71,* 1179–1190.

Lewis, M. (1983). On the nature of intelligence: Science or bias? In M. Lewis (Ed.), *Origins of intelligence* (pp. 1–24). New York, NY: Plenum Press.

Lewis, M. (1993). Early socioemotional predictors of cognitive competency at 4 years. *Developmental Psychology, 29,* 1036–1045.

Lewis, M., Alessandri, S., & Sullivan, M. (1992). Differences in shame and pride as a function of children's gender and task difficulty. *Child Development, 63,* 630–638.

Lewis, M., & Carmody, D. P. (2008). Self-representation and brain development. *Developmental Psychology, 44,* 1329–1334.

Lewis, M. D. (2000). The promise of dynamic systems approaches for an integrated account of human development. *Child Development, 71,* 36–45.

Lewis, M. D., Lamm, C., Segalowitz, S. A., Stieben, J., & Zelazo, P. D. (2006). Neurophysiological correlates of emotion regulation in children and adolescents. *Journal of Cognitive Neuroscience, 18,* 1–17.

Lewis, M. D., & Todd, R. M. (2007). The self-regulating brain: Cortical-subcortical feedback and the development of intelligent action. *Cognitive Development, 22,* 406–430.

Lewis, M., & Feiring, C. (1982). Some American families at dinner. In L. M. Laosa & I. E. Sigel (Eds.), *Families as learning environments for children* (pp. 115–145). New York, NY: Plenum Press.

Lewis, M., & Michalson, L. (1983). *Children's emotions and moods: Developmental theory and measurement.* New York, NY: Plenum Press.

Lewis, M., & Ramsay, D. (2002). Cortisol response to embarrassment and shame. *Child Development, 73,* 1034–1045.

Lewis, M., & Ramsay, D. (2004). Development of self-recognition, personal pronoun use, and pretend play during the 2nd year. *Child Development, 75,* 1821–1831.

Lewis, T. L., Maurer, D., & Kay, D. (1978). Newborns' central vision: Whole or hole? *Journal of Experimental Child Psychology, 26,* 193–203.

Lewkowicz, D. J. (2000). The development of intersensory temporal perception: An epigenetic systems/limitations view. *Psychological Bulletin, 126,* 281–308.

Lewkowicz, D. J. (2010). Infant perception of audio-visual speech synchrony. *Developmental Psychology, 46,* 66–77.

Li, J. (2005). Mind or virtue: Western and Chinese beliefs about learning. *Current Directions in Psychological Science, 14,* 190–194.

Li, J. (2006). Self in learning: Chinese adolescents' goals and sense of agency. *Child Development, 77,* 482–501.

Li, Z. H., Connolly J., Jiang, D., Pepler D., & Craig, W. (2010). Adolescent romantic relationships in China and Canada: A cross-national comparison. *International Journal of Behavioral Development, 34,* 113–120.

Liben, L. S. (2003). Beyond point and shoot: Children's developing understanding of photographs as spatial and expressive representations. In R. Kail (Ed.), *Advances in child development and behavior.* (Vol. 31, pp. 1–42). San Diego, CA: Elsevier.

Liben, L. S. (2008). Continuities and discontinuities in children and scholarship. *Child Development, 79,* 1600–1605.

Liben, L. S. (2009). The road to understanding maps. *Current Directions in Psychological Science, 18,* 310–315.

Liben, L. S., & Bigler, R. S. (2002). The developmental course of gender differentiation: Conceptualizing, measuring, and evaluating constructs and pathways. *Monographs of the Society for Research in Child Development, 67* (2, Serial No. 269).

Liben, L. S., & Downs, R. M. (1993). Understanding person-space-map relations: Cartographic and developmental perspectives. *Developmental Psychology, 29,* 739–752.

Lickliter, R., & Bahrick, L. E. (2000). The development of infant intersensory perception: Advantages of a comparative convergent-operations approach. *Psychological Bulletin, 126,* 260–280.

Lickliter, R., & Honeycutt, H. (2003). Developmental dynamics: Toward a biologically plausible evolutionary psychology. *Psychological Bulletin, 120,* 819–835.

Lidz, J., & Gleitman, L. R. (2004). Yes, we still need universal grammar: Reply. *Cognition, 94,* 85–93.

Lieberman, E., & O'Donoghue, C. (2002). Unintended effects of epidural analgesia during labor: A systematic review. *Journal of Obstetrics and Gynecology, 186,* S31–S68.

Liebert, R. M., & Sprafkin, J. (1988). *The early window: Effects of television on children and youth* (3rd ed.). New York, NY: Pergamon Press.

Lien, W., Klezovitch, O., Fernandez, T. E., Delrow, J., & Fasioukhin, V. (2006). E-catenin controls cerebral cortical size by regulating the hedgehog signaling pathway. *Science, 311,* 1609–1612.

Light, S. N., Coan, J. A., Zahn-Waxler, C., Frye, C., Goldsmith, H. H., & Davidson, R. J. (2009). Empathy is associated with dynamic change in prefrontal brain electrical activity during positive emotion in children. *Child Development, 80,* 1210–1231.

Lightfoot, D. (1982). *The language lottery: Toward a biology of grammars.* Cambridge, MA: MIT Press.

Lindsay, E. W., Mize, J., & Pettit, G. S. (1997). Differential play patterns of mothers and fathers of sons and daughters: Implications for children's gender role development. *Sex Roles, 37,* 643–661.

Linebarger, D. L., & Walker, D. (2005). Infants' and toddlers' television viewing and language outcomes. *American Behavioral Scientist, 48,* 624–645.

Linn, M. C., & Petersen, A. C. (1985). Emergence and characterization of sex differences in spatial ability: A meta-analysis. *Child Development, 56,* 1479–1498.

Linn, M. C., & Petersen, A. C. (1986). A meta-analysis of differences in spatial ability: Implications for mathematics and science achievement. In J. S. Hyde & M. C. Linn (Eds.), *The psychology of gender: Advances through meta-analysis* (pp. 67–101). Baltimore: Johns Hopkins University Press.

Linney, J. A., & Seidman, E. N. (1989). The future of schooling. *American Psychologist, 44,* 336–340.

Lips, H. M. (2004). The gender gap in possible selves: Divergence of academic self-views among high school and university students. *Sex Roles, 50,* 357–371.

Lipsitt, L. P. (2003). Crib death: A biobehavioral phenomenon? *Current Directions in Psychological Science, 12,* 164–170.

Lipton, J. S., & Spelke, E. S. (2003). Origins of number sense: Large number discrimination in human infants. *Psychological Science, 14,* 396–401.

Lipton, J. S., & Spelke, E. S. (2006). Preschool children master the logic of number word meanings. *Cognition, 98,* B57–B66.

Little, T. D., & Lopez, D. F. (1997). Regularities in the development of children's causality beliefs about school performance across six sociocultural contexts. *Developmental Psychology, 33,* 165–175.

Littleton, K., & Häkkinen, P. (1999). Learning together: Understanding the processes of computer-based collaborative learning. In P. Dillenbourg (Ed.), *Collaborative learning: Cognitive and computational approaches* (pp. 20–30). New York, NY: Pergamon.

Littschwager, J. C., & Markman, E. M. (1994). Sixteen- and 24-month-olds' use of mutual exclusivity as a default assumption in second-label learning. *Developmental Psychology, 30,* 955–958.

Liu, D., Sabbagh, M. A., Gehring, W. J., & Wellman, H. M. (2009). Neural correlates of children's theory of mind development. *Child Development, 80,* 318–326.

Liu, D., Wellman, H. M., Tardif, T., & Sabbagh, M. A. (2008). Theory of mind development in Chinese children: A meta-analysis of false-belief understanding across cultures and languages. *Developmental Psychology, 44,* 523–531.

Liu, H., Kuhl, P. K., & Tsao, F. (2003). An association between mothers' speech clarity and infants' discrimination skills. *Developmental Science, 6,* F1–F10.

Livingston, G., & Parker, K. (2010). *Since the start of the Great Recession, more children raised by grandparents.* Washington, DC: Pew Research Center.

Lobel, M., & DeLuca, R. S. (2007). Psychosocial sequelae of cesarean delivery: Review and analysis of their causes and implications. *Social Science & Medicine, 64,* 2272–2284.

Lobel, T. E., Bempechat, J., Gewirtz, J. C., Shoken-Tpaz, T., & Bashe, E. (1993). The role of gender-related information and self-endorsement of traits in preadolescents' inferences and judgments. *Child Development, 64,* 1285–1294.

Lobel, T. E., Gruber, R., Govrin, N., & Mashraki-Pedhatzur, S. (2001). Children's gender-related inferences and judgments: A cross-cultural study. *Developmental Psychology, 37,* 839–846.

Locke, J. (1964). Some thoughts concerning education. In P. Gay (Ed.), *John Locke on education.* New York, NY: Teacher's College. (Original work published in 1693.)

Locke, John (1961). *An essay concerning human understanding,* (Originally published in 1690.)

Loe, I. M., Balestrino, M. D., Phelps, R. A., Kurs-Lasky, M., Chaves-Gnecco, D., Paradise, J. L., & Feldman, H. M. (2008). Early histories of school-aged children with attention-deficit/hyperactivity disorder. *Child Development, 79,* 1853–1868.

Loeb, R. C., Horst, L., & Horton, P. J. (1980). Family interaction patterns associated with self-esteem in preadolescent girls and boys. *Merrill-Palmer Quarterly, 26,* 203–217.

Loeber, R., & Hay, D. F. (1997). Key issues in the development of aggression and violence from childhood to early adulthood. *Annual Review of Psychology, 48,* 371–410.

Loehlin, J. C., Lindzey, G., & Spuhler, J. N. (1975). *Racial differences in intelligence.* San Francisco, CA: W.H. Freeman.

Loewenstein, J., & Gentner, D. (2001). Spatial mapping in preschoolers: Close comparisons facilitate far mappings. *Journal of Cognition and Development, 2,* 189–219.

López-Camelo, J. S., Orioli, I. M., da Graça Dutra, M., Nazer-Herrera, J., Rivera, N., Ojeda, M. E., et al. (2005). Reduction of birth prevalence rates of neural tube defects after folic acid fortification in Chile. *American Journal of Medical Genetics, Part A, 135,* 120–125.

Lorch, E. P., Bellack, D. R., & Augsbach, L. H. (1987). Young children's memory for televised stories: Effects of importance. *Child Development, 58,* 453–463.

Lorenz, K. Z. (1966). *On aggression* (M. K. Wilson, Trans.). New York, NY: Harcourt, Brace, & World. (Original work published 1963.)

Love, J. M., Harrison, L. , Sagi-Schwartz, A., van IJzendoorn, M. H., Ross, C., et al. (2003). Child care quality matters: How conclusions may vary with context. *Child Development, 74,* 1021–1033.

Love, J. M., Kisker, E. E., Ross, C., Raikes, H., Constantine, J., et al. (2005). The effectiveness of Early Head Start for 3-year-old children and their parents: Lessons for policy and programs. *Developmental Psychology, 41,* 885–901.

Lu, G. C., Rouse, D. J., DuBard, M., Cliver, S., Kimberlin, D., & Hauth, J. C. (2001). The effect of the increasing prevalence of maternal obesity on prenatal morbidity. *American Journal of Obstetrics and Gynecology, 185,* 845–849.

Lu, H., Su, Y., & Wang, Q. (2008). Talking about others facilitates theory of mind in Chinese preschoolers. *Developmental Psychology, 44,* 1726–1736.

Lubinski, D., Benbow, C. P., Webb, R. M., & Bleske-Rechek, A. (2006). Tracking exceptional human capital over two decades. *Psychological Science, 17,* 194–199.

Lubinski, D., Webb, R. M., Morelock, M. J., & Benbow, C. P. (2001). Top 1 in 10,000: A 10-year follow-up of the profoundly gifted. *Journal of Applied Psychology, 86,* 718–729.

Luciana, M., Conklin, H. M., Hooper, C. J., & Yarger, R. S. (2005). The development of nonverbal working memory and executive control processes in adolescents. *Child Development, 76,* 697–712.

Luecke-Aleksa, D. R., Anderson, D. R., Collins, P. A., & Schmitt, K. L. (1995). Gender constancy and television viewing. *Developmental Psychology, 31,* 773–780.

Lukowski, A. F., Wiebe, S. A., Haight, J. C., DeBoer, T. Nelson, C. A., & Bauer, P. J. (2005). Forming a stable memory representation in the first year of life: Why imitation is more than child's play. *Developmental Science, 8,* 279–298.

Lumeng, J. C., Appugliese, D., Cabral, H. J., Bradley, R. H., & Zuckerman, B. (2006). Neighborhood safety and overweight status in children. *Archives of Pediatric and Adolescent Medicine, 160,* 25–31.

Lumeng, J. C., & Hillman, K. H. (2007). Eating in larger groups increases food consumption. *Archives of Disease in Childhood, 92,* 384–387.

Lummis, M., & Stevenson, H. W. (1990). Gender differences in beliefs and achievement: A cross-cultural study. *Developmental Psychology, 26,* 254–263.

Luna, B., Thulborn, K. R., Munoz, D. P., Merriam, E. P., Garver, K. E., et al. (2001). Maturation of widely distributed brain function subserves cognitive development. *Neuroimage, 13,* 786–793.

Luo, J., & Hu, F. B. (2002). Time trends of obesity in pre-school children in China from 1989 to 1997. *International Journal of Obesity, 26,* 553–558.

Luria, A. R. (1961). *The role of speech in the regulation of normal and abnormal behavior.* New York, NY: Liveright.

Luria, A. R. (1969). Speech and formation of mental processes. In M. Cole & I. Maltzman (Eds.), *A handbook of contemporary Soviet psychology* (pp. 519–541). New York, NY: Basic Books.

Lussier, G., Deater-Deckard, K., Dunn, J., & Davies, L. (2002). Support across two generations: Children's closeness to grandparents following parental divorce and remarriage. *Journal of Family Psychology, 16,* 363–376.

Luster, T., & McAdoo, H. P. (1994). Factors related to the achievement and adjustment of young African American children. *Child Development, 65,* 1080–1094.

Luster, T., & McAdoo, H. P. (1996). Family and child influences on educational attainment: A secondary analysis of the High/Scope Perry Preschool data. *Developmental Psychology, 32,* 26–39.

Luthar, S. S., & Becker, B. E. (2002). Privileged but pressured? A study of affluent youth. *Child Development, 73,* 1593–1610.

Luthar, S. S., Cicchetti, D., & Becker, B. (2000). The construct of resilience: A critical evaluation and guidelines for future work. *Child Development, 71,* 543–562.

Luthar, S. S., & D'Avanzo, K. (1999). Contextual factors in substance use: A study of suburban and inner-city adolescents. *Developmental Psychopathology, 11,* 845–867.

Luthar, S. S., & Latendresse, S. J. (2005). Children of the affluent: Challenges to well-being. *Current Directions in Psychological Science, 14,* 49–53.

Luthar, S. S., & Sexton, C. C. (2004). The high price of affluence. *Advances in Child Development and Behavior, 32,* 125–162.

Lutkenhaus, P., Bullock, M., & Geppert, U. (1987). Toddlers' actions: Knowledge, control, and the self. In F. Halisch & J. Kuhl (Eds.), *Motivation, intention, and volition* (pp. 145–161). Berlin: Springer.

Lykken, D. T., McGue, M. Tellegen, A., & Bouchard, T. J., Jr. (1992). Emergenesis: Genetic traits that may not run in families. *American Psychologist, 47,* 1565–1577.

Lyon, T. D., & Flavell, J. H. (1993). Young children's understanding of forgetting over time. *Child Development, 64,* 789–800.

Lyons-Ruth, K., Alpern, L., & Repacholi, B. (1993). Disorganized infant attachment classification and maternal psychosocial problems as predictors of hostile-aggressive behavior in preschool children. *Child Development, 64,* 572–585.

Lyons-Ruth, K., & Jacobvitz, D. (1999). Attachment disorganization: Unresolved loss, relational violence, and lapses in behavioral and attentional strategies. In J. Cassidy & P. R. Shaver (Eds.), *Handbook of attachment: Theory, research, and clinical applications* (pp. 520–554). New York, NY: Guilford Press.

Lytton, H., & Romney, D. M. (1991). Parents' differential socialization of boys and girls: A meta-analysis. *Psychological Bulletin, 109,* 267–296.

Ma, H. K., & Cheung, C.-K. (1996). A cross-cultural study of moral stage structure in Hong Kong Chinese, English, and Americans. *Journal of Cross-Cultural Psychology, 27,* 700–713.

Macchi Cassia, V., Turati, C., & Simion, F. (2004). Can a nonspecific bias toward top-heavy patterns explain newborns' face preference? *Psychological Science, 15,* 379–383.

Macchi Cassia, V., Valenza, E., Simion, F., & Leo, F. (2008). Congruency as a nonspecific perceptual property contributing to newborns' face preference. *Child Development, 79,* 807–820.

Maccoby, E. E. (1984). Socialization and developmental change. *Child Development, 55,* 317–328.

Maccoby, E. E. (1988). Gender as a social category. *Developmental Psychology, 24,* 755–765.

Maccoby, E. E. (1990). Gender and relationships: A developmental account. *American Psychologist, 45,* 513–520.

Maccoby, E. E. (2002). Gender and group process: A developmental perspective. *Current Directions in Psychological Science, 11,* 54–58.

Maccoby, E. E., & Jacklin, C. N. (1974). *The psychology of sex differences.* Stanford, CA: Stanford University Press.

Maccoby, E. E., & Jacklin, C. N. (1987). Gender segregation in childhood. In H. W. Reese (Ed.), *Advances in child development and behavior* (Vol. 20, pp. 239–287). Orlando, FL: Academic Press.

Maccoby, E. E., & Martin, J. A. (1983). Socialization in the context of the family: Parent-child interaction. In E. M. Hetherington (Ed.), *Handbook of child psychology: Vol. IV. Socialization, personality, and social development* (4th ed., pp. 1–101). New York, NY: Wiley.

MacFarlane, J. A. (1975). Olfaction in the development of social preferences in the human neonate. In M. A. Hofer (Ed.), *Parent-infant interaction* (pp. 103–117). Amsterdam: Elsevier.

Mackay, A. P., & Durana, C. (2008). *Adolescent health in the United States.* Hyattsville, MD: Centers for Disease Control, National Center for Health Statistics.

MacKinnon, C. E. (1988). Influences on sibling relations in families with married and divorced parents. *Journal of Social Issues, 9,* 469–477.

MacKinnon, C. E. (1989). Sibling interactions in married and divorced families: Influence of ordinal position, socioeconomic status, and play context. *Journal of Divorce, 12,* 221–251.

MacKinnon-Lewis, C., Rabiner, D., & Starnes, R. (1999). Predicting boys' social acceptance and aggression: The role of mother-child interactions and boys' beliefs about peers. *Developmental Psychology, 35,* 632–639.

MacLusky, N. J., & Naftolin, F. (1981). Sexual differentiation of the nervous system. *Science, 211,* 1294–1303.

MacWhinney, B. (1998). Models of the emergence of language. *Annual Review of Psychology, 49,* 199–227.

Maffeis, C., Schutz, Y., Zaffanello, M., Piccoli, R., & Pinelli, L. (1994). Elevated energy expenditure and reduced energy intake in obese prepubertal children: Paradox of poor dietary reliability in obesity? *Journal of Pediatrics, 124,* 348–354.

Magnusson, D., Stattin, H., & Allen, V. (1986). Differential maturation among girls and its relations to social adjustment: A longitudinal perspective. In P. B. Baltes, D. L. Featherman, & R. M. Lerner (Eds.), *Life-span development and behavior* (Vol. 7, pp. 136–172). Hillsdale, NJ: Erlbaum.

Mahoney, J. L. (2000). School extracurricular activity participation as a moderator in the development of antisocial behavior patterns. *Child Development, 71,* 502–516.

Mahoney, J. L., & Cairns, R. B. (1997). Do extracurricular activities protect against early school dropout? *Developmental Psychology, 33,* 241–253.

Main, M., Kaplan, N., & Cassidy, J. (1985). Security in infancy, childhood, and adulthood: A move to the level of representation. In I. Bretherton & E. Waters (Eds.), *Growing points of attachment theory and research. Monographs of the Society for Research in Child Development, 50* (1–2, Serial No. 209).

Main, M., & Solomon, J. (1986). Discovery of a disorganized/disoriented attachment pattern. In T. B. Brazelton & M.W. Yogman (Eds.), *Affective development in infancy* (pp. 95–124). Norwood, NJ: Ablex.

Malatesta, C. Z., Culver, C., Tesman, J. R., & Shepard, B. (1989). The development of emotion expression during the first two years of life. *Monographs of the Society for Research in Child Development, 54* (1–2, Serial No. 219).

Malina, R. M. (1980). Biosocial correlates of motor development during infancy and early childhood. In L. S. Greene & F. E. Johnstone (Eds.), *Social and biological predictors of nutritional status, physical growth, and neurological development* (pp. 143–171). New York, NY: Academic Press.

Malone, F. D., Canick, J. A., Ball, R. H., Nyberg, D. A., Comstock, C. H., Bukowski, R., et al. (2005). First-trimester or second-trimester screening, or both, for Down's syndrome. *New England Journal of Medicine, 353,* 2001–2011.

Malti, T., Gummerum, M., Keller, M., & Buchmann, M. (2009). Children's moral motivation, sympathy, and prosocial behavior. *Child Development, 80,* 442–460.

Mandara, J., Gaylord-Harden, N. K., Richards, M. H., & Ragsdale, B. L. (2009). The effects of changes in racial identity and self-esteem on changes in African American adolescents' mental health. *Child Development, 80,* 1660–1675.

Mandler, J. M. (1988). How to build a baby: On the development of an accessible representational system. *Cognitive Development, 3,* 113–136.

Mandler, J. M. (1998). Representation. In W. Damon (Series Ed.) & D. Kuhn & R. S. Siegler (Vol. Eds.), *Handbook of child psychology: Vol. 2. Cognition, perception, and language* (5th ed., pp. 255–308). New York, NY: Wiley.

Mandler, J. M. (2008). On the birth and growth of concepts. *Philosophical Psychology, 21,* 207–230.

Mandler, J. M., Fivush, R., & Reznick, J. S. (1987). The development of contextual categories. *Cognitive Development, 2,* 339–354.

Mangelsdorf, S. C., Plunkett, J. W., Dedrick, C. F., Berlin, M., Meisels, S. J., McHale, J. L., & Dichtellmiller, M. (1996). Attachment security in very low birth weight infants. *Developmental Psychology, 32,* 914–920.

Maratsos, M. P. (1983). Some current issues in the study of the acquisition of grammar. In J. H. Flavell & E. M. Markman (Eds.), *Handbook of child psychology: Vol. III. Cognitive development* (4th ed., pp. 707–786). New York, NY: Wiley.

March of Dimes. (2010a). *Chorionic villus sampling.* Retrieved August 19, 2010, from http://www.marchofdimes.com/professionals/14332_1165.asp

March of Dimes (2010b). *Pregnancy and newborn: Birth defects.* Retrieved August 19, 2010, from http://www.marchofdimes.com/pnhec/4439_1206.asp

Marchman, V. A., & Fernald, A. (2008). Speed of word recognition and vocabulary knowledge in infancy predict cognitive and language outcomes in later childhood. *Developmental Science, 11,* F9–F16.

Marcia, J. E. (1980). Identity in adolescence. In J. Adelson (Ed.), *Handbook of adolescent psychology* (pp. 159–187). New York, NY: Wiley.

Marcia, J. E. (1993). The status of the statuses: Research review. In J. E. Marcia, A. S. Waterman, D. R. Matteson, S. L. Archer, & J. L. Orlofsky (Eds.), *Ego identity: A handbook for psychosocial research* (pp. 22–41). New York, NY: Springer-Verlag.

Marcus, G. F. (1996). Why do children say "breaked"? *Current Directions in Psychological Science, 5,* 81–85.

Marcus, G. F., Pinker, S., Ullman, M., Hollander, M., Rosen, T. J., & Xu, F. (1992). Overregularization in language acquisition. *Monographs of the Society for Research in Child Development, 57* (4 Serial No. 228).

Marcus, G. F., Vijayan, S., Bandi Rao, S., & Vishton, P.M. (1998). Rule learning by seven-month-old infants. *Science, 283,* 77–80.

Mares, M.-L., & Woodard, E. H. (2007). Positive effects of television on children's social interaction: A meta-analysis. In R. W. Press, B. M. Gayle, N. Burrell, M. Allen, & J. Bryant (Eds.), *Mass media effects research: Advances through meta-analysis* (pp. 281–300). Mahwah, NJ: Lawrence Erlbaum Associates Publishers.

Margolin, G., Ramos, M. C., & Guran, E. L. (2010). Earthquakes and children: The role of psychologists with families and communities. *Professional Psychology: Research and Practice, 41,* 1–9.

Markham, J. A., Black, J. E., & Greenough, W. T. (2007). Developmental approaches to the memory process. In Kesner, R. P., & Martinez, J. L., Jr. *Neurobiology of learning and memory* (2nd ed., pp. 57–101). San Diego, CA: Elsevier Academic Press.

Markman, E. M. (1987). How children constrain the possible meanings of words. In U. Neisser (Ed.), *Concepts and conceptual development: Ecological and intellectual factors in categorization* (pp. 255–287). Cambridge, UK: Cambridge University Press.

Markman, E. M. (1990). Constraints children place on word meanings. *Cognitive Science, 14,* 57–77.

Markman, E. M., & Hutchinson, J. E. (1984). Children's sensitivity to constraints on word meaning: Taxonomic versus thematic relations. *Cognitive Psychology, 16,* 1–27.

Markman, E. M., & Wachtel G. F. (1988). Children's use of mutual exclusivity to constrain the meanings of words. *Cognitive Psychology, 20,* 121–157.

Marlier, L., & Schaal, B. (2005). Human newborns prefer human milk: Conspecific milk odor is attractive without postnatal exposure. *Child Development, 76,* 155–168.

Marlier, L., Schaal, B., & Soussignan, R. (1998). Neonatal responsiveness to the odor of amniotic and lacteal fluids: A test of perinatal chemosensory continuity. *Child Development, 69,* 611–623.

Marr, D. B., & Sternberg, R. J. (1987). The role of mental speed in intelligence: A triarchic perspective. In P. A. Vernon (Ed.), *Speed of information-processing and intelligence* (pp. 271–294). Norwood, NJ: Ablex.

Marshall, P. J., & Fox, N. A. (2008). Electrophysiological measures in research on social and emotional development. In L. A. Schmidt & S. Segalowitz (Eds.), *Developmental psychophysiology: Theory, systems, and methods* (pp. 127–149). New York, NY: Cambridge University Press.

Marshall, W. A., & Tanner, J. M. (1986). Puberty. In Falkner & J. M. Tanner (Eds.), *Human Growth,* Vol. 2, p. 196.

Martens, M. A., Wilson, S. J., & Reutens, D. C. (2008). Research review: Williams syndrome: A critical review of the cognitive, behavioral, and neuroanatomical phenotype. *Journal of Child Psychology and Psychiatry, 49,* 576–608.

Martin, C. L. (1991). The role of cognition in understanding gender effects. In H. W. Reese (Ed.), *Advances in child development and behavior* (Vol. 23, pp. 113–149). San Diego, CA: Academic Press.

Martin, C. L. (1995). Stereotypes about children with traditional and nontraditional gender roles. *Sex Roles, 33,* 727–751.

Martin, C. L., Eisenbud, L., & Rose, H. (1995). Children's gender-based reasoning about toys. *Child Development, 66,* 1453–1471.

Martin, C. L., & Fabes, R. A. (2001). The stability and consequences of young children's same-sex peer interactions. *Developmental Psychology, 37,* 431–446.

Martin, C. L., & Halverson, C. F. (1981). A schematic processing model of sex typing and stereotyping in children. *Child Development, 52,* 1119–1134.

Martin, C. L., & Halverson, C. F. (1987). The roles of cognition in sex role acquisition. In D. B. Carter (Ed.), *Current conceptions of sex roles and sex typing: Theory and research* (pp. 123–137). New York, NY: Praeger.

Martin, C. L., & Ruble, D. N. (1997). A developmental perspective of self-construals and sex differences: Comment on Cross and Madson (1997). *Psychological Bulletin, 122,* 45–50.

Martin, C. L., & Ruble, D. N. (2010). Patterns of gender development. *Annual Review of Psychology, 61,* 353–381.

Martin, J. A., Hamilton, B. E., Sutton, P. D., Ventura, S. J., Menacker, F., Kirmeyer, S., & Mathews, T. J. (2009). Births: Final data for 2006. *National Vital Statistics Reports, 57*(7).

Martin, J. A., Kung, H.-C., Mathews, T. J., Hoyert, D. L., Strobino, D. M., Guyer, B., & Sutton, S. R. (2008). Annual summary of vital statistics: 2006. *Pediatrics, 121,* 788–801.

Martin McDermott, J. (2008). The response-monitoring mechanism: Influence of feedback and temperament. *Dissertation Abstracts International: Section B: The Sciences and Engineering, 69(5-B),* p. 3298.

Marvin, R. S. (1977). An ethological-cognitive model for the attenuation of mother-child attachment behavior. In T. M. Alloway, L. Krames, & P. Pliner (Eds.), *Advances in the study of communication and affect: Vol. 3. The development of social attachments* (pp. 25–60). New York, NY: Plenum Press.

Mason, C. A., Cauce, A. M., Gonzales, N., & Hiraga, Y. (1996). Neither too sweet nor too sour: Problem peers, maternal control, and problem behavior in African American adolescents. *Child Development, 67,* 2115–2130.

Masten, A. S., Cutuli, J. J., Herbers, J. E., & Reed, M.-G. J. (2009). Resilience in development. In S. J. Lopez & C. R. Snyder (Eds.), *Oxford handbook of positive psychology* (pp. 117–131). New York, NY: Oxford University Press.

Masterpasqua, F. (2009). Psychology and epigenetics. *Review of General Psychology, 13,* 194–201.

Masur, E. F. (1982). Mothers' responses to infants' object-related gestures: Influences on lexical development. *Journal of Child Language, 9,* 23–30.

Masur, E. F., & Flynn, V. (2008). Infant and mother-infant play and the presence of the television. *Journal of Applied Developmental Psychology, 29,* 76–83.

Matas, L., Arend, R. A., & Sroufe, L. A. (1978). Continuity of adaptation in the second year: The relationship between quality of attachment and later competence. *Child Development, 49,* 547–556.

Matias, R., & Cohn, J. F. (1993). Are max-specified infant facial expressions during face-to-face interaction consistent with differential emotions theory? *Developmental Psychology, 29,* 524–531.

Matsumoto, D., Haan, N., Yabrove, G., Theodorou, P., & Carney, C. C. (1986). Preschoolers' moral actions and emotions in prisoner's dilemma. *Developmental Psychology, 22,* 663–670.

Mattys, S. L., & Jusczyk, P.W. (2001). Do infants segment words or recurring contiguous patterns? *Journal of Experimental Psychology: Human Perception and Performance, 27,* 644–655.

Maurer, D. (1983). The scanning of compound figures by young infants. *Journal of Experimental Child Psychology, 35,* 437–448.

Maurer, D., Lewis, T. L., Brent, H. P., & Levin, A. V. (1999). Rapid improvement in the acuity of infants after visual input. *Science, 286,* 108–110.

May, D. C., Kundert, D. K., & Brent, D. (1995). Does delayed school entry reduce later grade retentions and use of special education services? *Remedial and Special Education, 16,* 288–294.

Mayberry, R. I., & Nicoladis, E. (2000). Gesture reflects language development: Evidence from bilingual children. *Current Directions in Psychological Science, 9,* 192–196.

Mayor, J., & Plunkett, K. (2010). A neurocomputational account of taxonomic responding and fast mapping in early word learning. *Psychological Review, 117,* 1–31.

McArdle, J. J., Ferrer Caja, E., Hamagami, F., & Woodcock, R. W. (2002). Comparative longitudinal structural analyses of the growth and decline of multiple intellectual abilities over the life span. *Developmental Psychology, 38,* 115–142.

McBride, W. G. (1961). Thalidomide and congenital abnormalities. *Lancet, 2,* 1358.

McCall, R. B. (1979). *Infants.* Cambridge, MA: Harvard University Press.

McCarthy, A., & Lee, K. (2009). Children's knowledge of deceptive gaze cues and its relation to actual lying behavior. *Journal of Experimental Child Psychology, 103,* 117–134.

McCartney, K., Harris, M. J., & Bernieri, F. (1990). Growing up and growing apart: A developmental meta-analysis of twin studies. *Psychological Bulletin, 107,* 226–237.

McClelland, D. C. (1973). Testing for competence rather than for "intelligence." *American Psychologist, 28,* 1–14.

McClelland, M. M., Cameron, C. E., Connor, C. M., Farris, C. L., Jewkes, A. M., & Morrison, F. J. (2007). Links between behavioral regulation and preschoolers' literacy, vocabulary, and math skills. *Developmental Psychology, 43,* 947–959.

McClintock, M. K., & Herdt, G. (1996). Rethinking puberty: The development of sexual attraction. *Current Directions in Psychological Science, 5,* 178–183.

McCord, J. (1977). A comparative study of two generations of native Americans. In R. F. Meier (Ed.), *Theory in criminology* (pp. 83–92). Beverly Hills, CA: Sage.

McCormick, M. C., Brooks-Gunn, J., Buka, S. L., Goldman, J., Yu, J., Salganik, M., . . . & Casey, P. H. (2006). Early intervention in low birth weight premature infants: Results at 18 years of age for the Infant Health and Development Program. *Pediatrics, 117,* 771–780.

McCormick, M. C., McCarton, C., Tonascia, J., & Brooks-Gunn, J. (1993). Early educational intervention for very low birth weight infants: Results from the Infant Health and Development Program. *Journal of Pediatrics, 123,* 527–533.

McDermott, S., & Greenberg, B. (1984). Parents, peers and television as determinants of Black children's esteem. In R. Bostrom (Ed.), *Communication yearbook* (Vol. 8, pp. 164–177). Beverly Hills, CA: Sage.

McDonald, M. A., Sigman, M., Espinosa, M. P., & Neumann, C. G. (1994). Impact of temporary food shortage on children and their mothers. *Child Development, 65,* 404–415.

McDowell, D. J., & Parke, R. D. (2009). Parental correlates of children's peer relations: An empirical test of a tripartite model. *Developmental Psychology, 45,* 224–235.

McGhee, P. E. (1979). *Humor: Its origin and development.* San Francisco, CA: W.H. Freeman.

McGinniss, M. J., & Kaback, M. M. (2002). Heterozygote testing and carrier screening. In D. L. Rimoin, J. M., Connor, R. E. Pyeritz, & B. R. Korf (Eds.), *Emery and Rimoin's principles and practice of medical genetics* (4th ed., Vol. 1, pp. 752–762). London, UK: Churchill Livingston.

McGraw, M. B. (1935). *Growth: A study of Johnny and Jimmy.* New York, NY: Appleton-Century-Crofts.

McGraw, M. B. (1939). Swimming behavior of the human infant. *Journal of Pediatrics, 15,* 485–490.

McGue, M. (1999). The behavioral genetics of alcoholism. *Current Directions in Psychological Science,* 8, 109–115.

McGuire, J. (1988). Gender stereotypes of parents with two-year-olds and beliefs about gender differences in behavior. *Sex Roles, 19,* 233–240.

McGuire, K. D., & Weisz, J. R. (1982). Social cognition and behavior correlates of preadolescent chumship. *Child Development, 53,* 1478–1484.

McGuire, P. K., Robertson, D. A. T., David, A. S., Kitson, N., Frackowiak, R. S. J., & Frith, C. D. (1997). Neural correlates of thinking in sign language. *NeuroReport,* 8, 695–697.

McGurk, H., & MacDonald, J. (1976). Hearing lips and seeing voices. *Nature* (London), *264,* 746–748.

McHale, S. M., Crouter, A. C., McGuire, S. A., & Updegraff, K. A. (1995). Congruence between mothers' and fathers' differential treatment of siblings: Links with family relations and children's well-being. *Child Development, 66,* 116–128.

McHale, S. M., Crouter, A. C., & Tucker, C. J. (1999). Family context and gender role socialization in middle childhood: Comparing boys to girls and sisters to brothers. *Child Development, 70,* 990–1004.

McHale, S. M., Crouter, A. C., & Tucker, C. J. (2001). Free-time activities in middle childhood: Links with adjustment in early adolescence. *Child Development, 72,* 1764–1778.

McHale, S. M., Kim, J., Dotterer, A. M., Crouter, A. C., & Booth, A. (2009). The development of gendered interests and personality qualities from middle childhood through adolescence: A biosocial analysis. *Child Development, 80,* 482–495.

McHale, S. M., Kim, J., Whiteman, S., & Crouter, A. C. (2004). Links between sex-typed time use in middle childhood and gender development in early adolescence. *Developmental Psychology, 40,* 868–881.

McHale, S. M., Shanahan, L., Updegraff, K. A., Crouter, A. C., & Booth, A. (2004). Developmental and individual differences in girls' sex-typed activities in middle childhood and adolescence. *Child Development, 75,* 1575–1593.

McHale, S. M., Updegraff, K. A., Jackson-Newsom, J., Tucker, C. J., & Crouter, A. C. (2000). When does parents' differential treatment have negative implications for siblings? *Social Development, 9,* 149–172.

McKenna, J. J., Ball, H. L., & Gettler, L. T. (2007). Mother-infant cosleeping, breastfeeding and sudden infant death syndrome: What biological anthropology has discovered about normal infant sleep and pediatric sleep medicine. *American Journal of Physical Anthropology, Supplement: Yearbook of Physical Anthropology, 134,* 133–161.

McKenna, M. T., & Hu, X. (2007). Recent trends in the incidence and morbidity that are associated with perinatal human immunodeficiency virus infection in the United States. *American Journal of Obstetrics and Gynecology, 197,* S10–S16.

McKey, R. H., Condelli, L., Granson, H., Barrett, B., McConkey, C., & Plantz, M. (1985). *The impact of Head Start on children, families and communities* (Final report of the Head Start Evaluation, Synthesis and Utilization Project). Washington, DC: U.S. Government Printing Office.

McLeod, S., Hughes, J. E., Brown, R., Choi, J., & Maeda, Y. (2005). *Algebra achievement in virtual and traditional schools.* Naperville, IL: Learning Point Associates.

McLoyd, V. C. (1990). The impact of economic hardship on black families and children: Psychological distress, parenting, and socioemotional development. *Child Development, 61,* 311–346.

McLoyd, V. C. (1998). Changing demographics in the American population: Implications for research on minority children and adolescents. In V. C. McLoyd & L. Steinberg (Eds.), *Studying minority adolescents* (pp. 3–28). Mahwah, NJ: Erlbaum.

McLoyd, V. C., Epstein Jayaratne, T., Ceballo, R., & Borquez, J. (1994). Unemployment and work interruption among African American single mothers: Effects on parenting and adolescent socioemotional functioning. *Child Development, 65,* 562–589.

McMahon, R. J., Forehand, R. L., & Foster, S. L. (2003). *Helping the noncompliant child: Family-based treatment for oppositional behavior* (2nd ed.). New York, NY: Guilford Press.

McMahon, R. J., Wells, K. C., & Kotler, J. S. (2006). Conduct problems. In E. J. Mash & R. A. Barkley (Eds.), *Treatment of childhood disorders* (pp. 137–268). New York, NY: Guilford Press.

McNally, S., Eisenberg, N., & Harris, J. D. (1991). Consistency and change in maternal child-rearing practices and values: A longitudinal study. *Child Development, 62,* 190–198.

Mead, G. H. (1934). *Mind, self, and society.* Chicago, IL: University of Chicago Press.

Medin, D. L. (1989). Concepts and conceptual structure. *American Psychologist, 44,* 1469–1481.

Medline Plus (2010a). *Chlamydia infections.* Retrieved August 20, 2010, from http://www.nlm.nih.gov/medlineplus/chlamydiainfections.html

Medline Plus (2010b). *Fragile X syndrome.* Retrieved August 17, 2010, from http://www.nlm.nih.gov/medlineplus/ency/article/001668.htm

Medline Plus (2010c). *Health topics.* Retrieved August 17, 2010, from http://www.nlm.nih.gov/medlineplus/healthtopics.html

Meeus, W., Iedema, J., Helsen, M., & Vollebergh, W. (1999). Patterns of adolescent identity development: Review of literature and longitudinal analyses. *Developmental Review, 19,* 419–461.

Meichenbaum, D. (1977). *Cognitive-behavior modification: An integrative approach.* New York, NY: Plenum Press.

Meins, E. (1998). The effects of security of attachment and maternal attribution of meaning on children's linguistic acquisitional style. *Infant Behavior and Development, 21,* 237–252.

Mejía-Arauz, R., Rogoff, B., & Paradise, R. (2005). Cultural variation in children's observation during a demonstration. *International Journal of Behavioral Development, 29,* 282–291.

Mekos, D., Hetherington, E. M., & Reiss, D. (1996). Sibling differences in problem behavior and parental treatment in nondivorced and remarried families. *Child Development, 67,* 2148–2165.

Meltzoff, A. N. (1995). What infant memory tells us about infantile amnesia: Long-term recall and deferred imitation. *Journal of Experimental Child Psychology, 59,* 497–515.

Meltzoff, A. N., & Moore, M. K. (1999). Persons and representation: Why infant imitation is important for theories of human development. In J. Nadel & G. Butterworth (Eds.), *Imitation in infancy* (pp. 9–35). Cambridge, UK: Cambridge University Press.

Mendle, J., Turkheimer, E., & Emery, R. E. (2007). Detrimental psychological outcomes associated with early pubertal timing in adolescent girls. *Developmental Review, 27,* 151–171.

Mennella, J. A., & Beauchamp, G. K. (1996). The human infant's response to vanilla flavors in mother's milk and formula. *Infant Behavior and Development, 19,* 13–19.

Mennella, J. A., Griffin, C. E., & Beauchamp, G. K. (2004). Flavor programming during infancy. *Pediatrics, 113,* 840–845.

Mennella, J. A., Pepino, M. Y., & Reed, D. R. (2005). Genetic and environmental determinants of bitter perception and sweet preferences. *Pediatrics, 115,* 216–222.

Mervis, C. B. (2003). Williams syndrome: 15 years of psychological research. *Developmental Neuroscience, 23,* 1–12.

Mervis, C. B., & Becerra, A. M. (2007). Language and communicative development in Williams syndrome. *Mental Retardation and Developmental Disabilities Research Reviews, 13,* 3–15.

Messer, D. J. (1981). The identification of names in maternal speech to infants. *Journal of Psycholinguistic Research, 10,* 69–77.

Messer, S. C., & Gross, A. M. (1995) Childhood depression and family interaction: A naturalistic observation study. *Journal of Clinical Child Psychology, 24,* 77–88.

Messinger, D. S., & Fogel, A. (1998). Give and take: The development of conventional infant gestures. *Merrill-Palmer Quarterly, 44,* 566–590.

Messinger, D. S., Fogel, A., & Dickson, K. L. (2001). All smiles are positive, but some smiles are more positive than others. *Developmental Psychology, 37,* 642–653.

Meyer, M., & Fienberg, S. (1992). *Assessing evaluation studies: The case of bilingual education strategies.* Washington, DC: National Academy Press.

Michel, G. F. (1988). A neuropsychological perspective on infant sensorimotor development. In C. Rovee-Collier & L. P. Lipsitt (Eds.), *Advances in infancy research* (Vol. 5, pp. 1–37). Norwood, NJ: Ablex.

Michelson, L., Sugai, D. P., Wood, R. P., & Kazdin, A. E. (1983). *Social skills assessment and training with children.* New York, NY: Plenum Press.

Michelsson, K., Sirvio, P., & Wasz-Hockert, D. (1977). Pain cry in full-term asphyxiated newborn infants correlated with late findings. *Acta Paediatrica Scandinavica, 66,* 611–616.

Milgram, N. A. (1998). Children under stress. In T. H. Ollendick & M. Hersen (Eds.), *Handbook of child psychopathology* (3rd ed., pp. 505–533). New York, NY: Plenum.

Milich, R. (1984). Cross-sectional and longitudinal observations of activity level and sustained attention in a normative sample. *Journal of Abnormal Child Psychology, 12,* 261–275.

Miller, A. L., Volling, B. L., & McElwain, N. L. (2000). Sibling jealousy in a triadic context with mothers and fathers. *Social Development, 9,* 433–457.

Miller, B. C., Benson, B., & Galbraith, K. A. (2001). Family relationships and adolescent pregnancy risk: A research synthesis. *Developmental Review, 21,* 1–38.

Miller, C. A., & Sweatt, J. D. (2007). Covalent modification of DNA regulates memory formation. *Neuron, 53,* 857–869.

Miller, C. F., Lurye, L. E., Zosuls, K. M., & Ruble, D. N. (2009). Accessibility of gender stereotype domains: Developmental and gender differences in children. *Sex Roles, 60,* 870–881.

Miller, G. (2006). New clues to Down syndrome-Alzheimer's link. *ScienceNOW Daily News.* Retrieved August 19, 2010, from http://sciencenow.sciencemag.org/cgi/content/full/2006/706/4

Miller, J. G. (1999). Cultural psychology: Implications for basic psychological theory. *Psychological Science, 10,* 85–91.

Miller, L. T., & Vernon, P. A. (1996). Intelligence, reaction time, and working memory in 4- to 6-year-old children. *Intelligence, 22,* 155–190.

Miller, N. B., Cowan, P. A., Cowan, C. P., Hetherington, E. M., & Clingempeel, W. G. (1993). Externalizing in preschoolers and early adolescents: A cross-study replication of a family model. *Developmental Psychology, 29,* 3–18.

Miller, N., & Maruyama, G. (1976). Ordinal position and peer popularity. *Journal of Personality and Social Psychology, 33,* 123–131.

Miller, P. A., Eisenberg, N., Fabes, R. A., & Shell, R. (1996). Relations of moral reasoning and vicarious emotion to young children's prosocial behavior toward peers and adults. *Developmental Psychology, 32,* 210–219.

Millman, R. P., & Working Group on Sleepiness in Adolescents/Young Adults, AAP Committee on Adolescence. (2005). Excessive sleepiness in adolescents and young adults: Causes, consequences, and treatment strategies. *Pediatrics, 115,* 1774–1786.

Mills, D. L., Coffey-Corina, S., & Neville, H. J. (1997). Language comprehension and cerebral specialization from 13 to 20 months. *Developmental Neuropsychology, 13,* 397–445.

Mills, D. L., Conboy, B., & Paton, C. (2005). Do changes in brain organization reflect shifts in symbolic functioning? In L. Namy (Ed.), *Symbol use and symbolic representation* (pp. 123–153). Mahwah, NJ: Lawrence Erlbaum Associates.

Mills, R. S. L., & Grusec, J. E. (1989). Cognitive, affective, and behavioral consequences of praising altruism. *Merrill-Palmer Quarterly, 35,* 299–326.

Mills, R. S. L., Imm, G. P., Walling, B. R., & Weiler, H. A. (2008). Cortisol reactivity and regulation associated with shame responding in early childhood. *Developmental Psychology, 44,* 1369–1380.

Minuchin, P. P. (1988). Relationships within the family: A systems perspective on development. In R. A. Hinde & J. Stevenson-Hinde (Eds.), *Relationships within families: Mutual influences* (pp. 7–26). Oxford: Clarendon Press.

Minuchin, P. P., & Shapiro, E. K. (1983). The school as a context for social development. In E. M. Hetherington (Ed.), *Handbook of child psychology: Vol. IV. Socialization, personality, and social development* (pp. 197–274). New York, NY: Wiley.

Mischel, W. (1966). A social learning view of sex differences in behavior. In E. E. Maccoby (Ed.), *The development of sex differences* (pp. 56–81). Stanford, CA: Stanford University Press.

Mischel, W., Ebbesen, E. B., & Zeiss, A. R. (1972). Cognitive and attentional mechanisms in delay of gratification. *Journal of Personality and Social Psychology, 21,* 204–218.

Mischel, H. N., & Mischel, W. (1983). The development of children's knowledge of self-control strategies. *Child Development, 54,* 603–619.

Mischel, W., Shoda, Y., & Rodriguez, M. L. (1989). Delay of gratification in children. *Science, 244,* 933–938.

Mitchell, E. A., Blair, P. S., & L'Hoir, M. P. (2006). Should pacifiers be recommended to prevent sudden infant death syndrome? *Pediatrics, 117,* 1755–1758.

Mittendorf, R., Williams, M. A., Berkley, C. S., Lieberman, E., & Monson, R. R. (1993). Predictors of human gestational length. *American Journal of Obstetrics and Gynecology, 168,* 480–484.

Mix, K. S., Levine, S. C., & Huttenlocher, J. (1999). Early fraction calculation ability. *Developmental Psychology, 35,* 164–174.

Miyake, A., Friedman, N. P., Rettinger, D. A., Shah, P., & Hegarty, M. (2001). How are visuospatial working memory, executive functioning, and spatial abilities related? A latent variable analysis. *Journal of Experimental Psychology: General, 130,* 621–640.

Miyake, K., Chen, S., & Campos, J. J. (1985). Infant temperament, mother's mode of interaction, and attachment in Japan: An interim report. In I. Bretherton & E. Waters (Eds.), *Growing points of attachment theory and research. Monographs of the Society for Research in Child Development, 50* (1–2, Serial No. 209).

Moffitt, T. E. (1993). Life-course-persistent and adolescence-limited antisocial behavior: A developmental taxonomy. *Psychological Review, 100,* 674–701.

Moffitt, T. E., Caspi, A., & Rutter, M. (2005). Strategy for investigating interactions between measured genes and measured environment. *Archives of General Psychiatry, 62,* 441–452.

Molcho, M., Craig, W., Due, P., Pickett, W., Harel-Fisch, Y., Overpeck, M., & HBSC Bullying Writing Group (2009). Cross-national time trends in bullying behaviour 1994–2006: Findings from Europe and North America. *International Journal of Public Health, 54 (Supplement 2),* 225–234.

Mondloch, C. J., Lewis, T. L., Budreau, D. R., Maurer, D., Dannemiller, J. L., Stephens, B. R., & Kleiner-Gathercoal, K. A. (1999). Face perception during early infancy. *Psychological Science, 10,* 419–422.

Mondloch, C. J., Maurer, D., & Ahola, S. (2006). Becoming a face expert. *Psychological Science, 17,* 930–924.

Mondloch, C. J., & Thomson, K. (2008). Limitations in 4-year-old children's sensitivity to the spacing among facial features. *Child Development, 79,* 1513–1523.

Monfries, M. M., & Kafer, N. F. (1987). Neglected and rejected children: A social-skills model. *Journal of Psychology, 121,* 401–407.

Montague, D. P. F., & Walker-Andrews, A. S. (2001). Peekaboo: A new look at infants' perception of emotion expressions. *Developmental Psychology, 37,* 826–838.

Monuteaux, M. C., Blacker, D., Biederman, J., Fitzmaurice, G., & Buka, S. L. (2006). Maternal smoking during pregnancy and offspring overt and covert conduct problems: A longitudinal study. *Journal of Child Psychology and Psychiatry, 47,* 883–890.

Moore, C. (2008). The development of gaze following. *Child Development Perspectives, 2,* 66–70.

Moon, C., Cooper, R. P., & Fifer, W. P. (1993). Two-day-olds prefer their native language. *Infant Behavior and Development, 16,* 494–500.

Moore, C., & Corkum, V. (1998). Infant gaze following based on eye direction. *British Journal of Developmental Psychology, 16,* 495–503.

Moore, D. G., Goodwin, J. E., George, R., Axelsson, E. L., & Braddick, F. M. B. (2007). Infants perceive human pointlight displays as solid forms. *Cognition, 104,* 377–396.

Moore, D. S., & Johnson, S. P. (2008). Mental rotation in human infants: A sex difference. *Psychological Science, 19,* 1063–1066.

Moore, G. T., & Lackney, J. A. (1993). School design: Crisis, educational performance, and design patterns. *Children's Environments, 10,* 99–112.

Moore, K. L., & Persaud, T. V. N. (2008). *The developing human: Clinically oriented embryology* (8th ed.). Philadelphia, PA: Saunders.

Moore, K. W., & Varela, E. R. (2009). Correlates of long-term posttraumatic stress symptoms in children following Hurricane Katrina. *Child Psychiatry and Human Development, 41,* 239–250.

Morison, P., & Masten, A. S. (1991). Peer reputation in middle childhood as a predictor of adaptation in adolescence: A seven-year follow-up. *Child Development, 62,* 991–1007.

Morrelli, G., Rogoff, B., Oppenheim, D., & Goldsmith, D. (1992). Cultural variation in infants' sleeping arrangements: Questions of independence. *Developmental Psychology, 28,* 604–613.

Morris, R., & Kratchowill, T. (1983). *Treating children's fears and phobias.* New York, NY: Pergamon Press.

Morrison, F. J., Griffith, E. M., & Alberts, D. M. (1997). Nature-nurture in the classroom: Entrance age, school readiness, and learning in children. *Developmental Psychology, 33,* 254–262.

Morrongiello, B. A. (1984). Auditory temporal pattern perception in 6- and 12-month-old infants. *Developmental Psychology, 20,* 441–448

Morrongiello, B. A., Fenwick, K. D., & Chance, G. (1990). Sound localization acuity in very young infants: An observer-based testing procedure. *Developmental Psychology, 26,* 75–84.

Morrongiello, B. A., Fenwick, K. D., & Chance, G. (1998). Crossmodal learning in newborn infants: Inferences about properties of auditory-visual events. *Infant Behavior and Development, 21,* 543–554.

Moses, L. J., Baldwin, D. A., Rosicky, J. G., & Tidball, G. (2001). Evidence for referential understanding in the emotions domain at twelve and eighteen months. *Child Development, 72,* 718–735.

Moss, E., Rousseau, D., Parent, S., St.-Laurent, D., & Saintonge, J. (1998). Correlates of attachment at school age: Maternal reported stress, mother-child interaction, and behavior problems. *Child Development, 69,* 1390–1405.

Moss, H. A. (1974). Early sex differences and mother-infant interaction. In R. C. Friedman, R. M. Richart, & R. L. Vande Wiele (Eds.), *Sex differences in behavior* (pp. 149–163). New York, NY: Wiley.

Mosteller, F. (1995, Summer/Fall). The Tennessee study of class size in the early school grades. *The Future of Children, 5*(2), pp. 113–127.

Mostow, A. J., Izard, C. E., Fine, A., & Trentacosta, C. J. (2002). Modeling emotional, cognitive, and behavioral predictors of peer acceptance. *Child Development, 73,* 1775–1787.

Moulson, M. C., Westerlund, A., Fox, N. A., Zeanah, C. H., & Nelson, C. A. (2009). The effects of early experience on face recognition: An event-related potential study of institutionalized children in Romania. *Child Development, 80,* 1039–1056.

MTA Cooperative Group (1999). A 14-month randomized clinical trial of treatment strategies for attention-deficit/hyperactivity disorder: Multimodal treatment study of children with ADHD. *Archives of General Psychiatry, 56,* 1073–1086.

Muhle, R., Trentacoste, S. V., & Rapin, I. (2004). The genetics of autism. *Pediatrics, 113,* e472–e486.

Muir, D., & Hains, S. (2004). The U-shaped function for auditory localization. *Journal of Cognition and Development, 5,* 123–130.

Mullen, M. K. (1994). Earliest recollections of childhood: A demographic analysis. *Cognition, 52,* 55–79.

Mullen, M. K., & Yi, S. (1995). The cultural context of talk about the past: Implications for the development of autobiographical memory. *Cognitive Development, 10,* 407–419.

Munakata, Y. (2006). Information processing approaches to development. In W. Damon & R. M. Lerner (Editors-in-Chief) & D. M. Kuhn & R. S. Siegler (Vol. Eds.), *Handbook of child psychology: Vol. 2, Cognition, perception, and language* (6th ed., pp. 426–463). Hoboken, NJ: Wiley.

Mundy, P., & Newell, L. (2007). Attention, joint attention, and social cognition. *Current Directions in Psychological Science, 16,* 269–274.

Munroe, R. H., Shimmin, H. S., & Munroe, R. L. (1984). Gender understanding and sex role preference in four cultures. *Developmental Psychology, 20,* 673–682.

Murray, J. P. (2008). Media violence: The effects are both real and strong. *American Behavioral Scientist, 51,* 1212–1230.

Murray, J. P., Liotti, M., Ingmundson, P. T., Mayberg, H. S., Pu, Y., Zamarripa, F., . . . & Fox, P. T. (2006). Children's brain activations while viewing televised violence revealed by fMRI. *Media Psychology, 8,* 25–37.

Murray, R., & Battista, M. (2009). Managing the risk of childhood overweight and obesity in primary care practice. *Current Problems in Pediatric and Adolescent Health Care. 39,* 146–165.

Musher-Eizenman, D. R., Holub, S. C., Miller, A. B., Goldstein, S., E., & Edwards-Leeper, L. (2004). Body size stigmatization in preschool children: The role of control attributions. *Journal of Pediatric Psychology, 29,* 613–620.

Mussen, P. H., & Jones, M. C. (1957). Self-conceptions, motivations, and interpersonal attitudes of late and early maturing boys. *Child Development, 28,* 243–256.

Mussen, P. H., & Jones, M. C. (1958). The behavior inferred motivations of late and early maturing boys. *Child Development, 29,* 61–67.

Mustanski, B. S., Viken, R. J., Kaprio, J., Pulkkinen, I., & Rose, R. J. (2004). Genetic and environmental influences on pubertal development: Longitudinal data from Finnish twins at ages 11 and 14. *Developmental Psychology, 40,* 1188–1198.

Myers, L. J., & Liben, L. S. (2008). The role of intentionality and iconicity in children's developing comprehension and production of cartographic symbols. *Child Development, 79,* 668–684.

Nachmias, M., Gunnar, M., Mangelsdorf, S., Parritz, R., & Buss, K. (1996). Behavioral inhibition and stress reactivity: Moderating role of attachment security. *Child Development, 67,* 508–522.

Naigles, L. (1990). Children use syntax to learn verb meanings. *Journal of Child Language,* 17, 357–374.

Naito, M., & Miura, H. (2001). Japanese children's numerical competencies: Age- and schooling-related influences on the development of number concepts and addition skills. *Developmental Psychology, 37,* 217–230.

Nakamura, K. (2001). The acquisition of polite language by Japanese children. In K. E. Nelson, A. Aksu-Koc, & C. E. Johnson (Eds.), *Children's language: Developing narrative and discourse competence* (Vol. 10, pp. 93–112). Mahwah, NJ: Erlbaum.

Namy, L. L., & Waxman, S. R. (1998). Words and gestures: Infants' interpretations of different forms of symbolic reference. *Child Development, 69,* 295–308.

Nantel-Vivier, A., Kokko, K., Caprara, G. V., Pastorelli, C., Gerbino, M. G., Paciello, M., Côté, S., Pihl, R. O., Vitaro, F., & Tremblay, R. E. (2009). Prosocial development from childhood to adolescence: A multi-informant perspective with Canadian and Italian longitudinal studies. *Journal of Child Psychology and Psychiatry, 50,* 590–598.

Nathanielsz, P. W. (1996). The timing of birth. *American Scientist, 84,* 562–569.

National Clearinghouse for English Language Acquisition (2010). *Frequently asked questions.* Retrieved September 4, 2010, from: http://www.ncela.gwu.edu/faqs/

National Eye Institute, National Institutes of Health (2008). *Older children can benefit from treatment for childhood's most common eye disorder.* Retrieved March 9, 2010, from http://www.nei.nih.gov/news/pressreleases/041105.asp

National Institute of Allergy and Infectious Diseases (2004). *HIV infection in infants and children.* Retrieved December 18, 2009, from http://www.niaid.nih.gov/factsheets/hivchildren.htm

National Institute of Child Health and Human Development Early Child Care Research Network (2008). Mothers' and fathers' support for child autonomy and early school achievement. *Developmental Psychology, 44,* 895–907.

National Institute of Mental Health (1996). *Attention deficit hyperactivity disorder* (NIH Publication No. 96–3572). Washington, DC: U.S. Government Printing Office.

National Research Council and Institute of Medicine (2002a). *Community programs to promote youth development* (J. Eccles & J. A. Gootman, Eds.). Washington, DC: National Academies Press.

National Research Council and Institute of Medicine (2002b). *Deadly lessons: Understanding lethal school violence* (M. H. Moore, C. V. Petrie, A. A. Braga, & B. L. McLaughlin, Eds.). Washington, DC: National Academies Press.

National Research Council and Institute of Medicine, Committee on Family and Work Policies (2003). *Working families and growing kids: Caring for children and adolescents.* Washington, DC: National Academies Press.

Nazzi, T., Bertoncini, J., & Mehler, J. (1998). Language discrimination by newborns: Towards an understanding of the role of rhythm. *Journal of Experimental Psychology: Human Perception and Performance, 24,* 756–766.

Nazzi, T., & Gopnik, A. (2001). Linguistic and cognitive abilities in infancy: When does language become a tool for categorization? *Cognition, 80,* B11–B20.

Needham, A. (2001). Object recognition and object segregation in 4.5-month-old infants. *Journal of Experimental Child Psychology, 78,* 3–24.

Needham, A., & Baillargeon, R. (1998). Effects of prior experience in 4.5-month-old infant's object segregation. *Infant Behavior and Development, 21,* 121–149.

Needham, A., & Modi, A. (2000). Infant's use of prior experiences with objects in object segregation: Implications for object recognition in infancy. In H. W. Reese (Ed.), *Advances in child development and behavior* (Vol. 27, pp. 100–135). San Diego, CA: Academic Press.

Needleman, H. L., & Bellinger, D. (Eds.) (1994). *Prenatal exposure to toxicants: Developmental consequences.* Baltimore: Johns Hopkins University Press.

Neiderhiser, J. M., Reiss, D., & Hetherington, E. M. (2007). The Nonshared Environment in Adolescent Development (NEAD) project: A longitudinal family study of twins and siblings from adolescence to young adulthood. *Twin Research and Human Genetics, 10,* 74–83.

Neiderhiser, J. M., Reiss, D., Hetherington, E. M., & Plomin, R. (1999). Relationships between parenting and adolescent adjustment over time: Genetic and environmental contributions. *Developmental Psychology, 35,* 680–692.

Neisser, U., Boodoo, G., Bouchard, T. J., Jr., Boykin, A.W., Brody, N., Ceci, S. J., . . . & Urbina, S. (1996). Intelligence: Knowns and unknowns. *American Psychologist, 51,* 77–101.

Nelson, C. A. (1995). The ontogeny of human memory: A cognitive neuroscience perspective. *Developmental Psychology, 31,* 723–738.

Nelson, C. A. (2007). A neurobiological perspective on early human deprivation. *Child Development Perspectives, 1,* 13–18.

Nelson, C. A., de Haan, M., & Thomas, K. M. (2006). *Neuroscience of cognitive development: The role of experience and the developing brain.* Hoboken, NJ: Wiley.

Nelson, C. A., & Monk, C. S. (2001). The use of event-related potentials in the study of cognitive development. From C. A. Nelson & M. Luciano (Eds.), *Handbook of developmental cognitive neuroscience* (pp. 125–136). Cambridge, MA: MIT Press.

Nelson, C. A., Monk, C. S., Lin, J., Carver, L. J., Thomas, K. M., & Truwit, C. L. (2000). Functional neuroanatomy of spatial working memory in children. *Developmental Psychology, 36,* 109–116.

Nelson, C. A., Thomas, K. M., & de Haan, M. (2006). Neural bases of cognitive development. In W. Damon & R. M. Lerner (Editors-in-Chief) & D. M. Kuhn & R. S. Siegler (Vol. Eds.), *Handbook of child psychology: Vol. 2. Cognition, perception, and language* (6th ed., pp. 3–57). Hoboken, NJ: Wiley.

Nelson, K. (1973). Structure and strategy in learning to talk. *Monographs of the Society for Research in Child Development, 38* (1–2, Serial No. 149).

Nelson, K. (1993a). Events, narratives, memory: What develops? In C. A. Nelson (Ed.), *Memory and affect in development. The Minnesota symposia on child psychology* (Vol. 26, pp. 1–24). Hillsdale, NJ: Erlbaum.

Nelson, K. (1993b). The psychological and social origins of autobiographical memory. *Psychological Science, 4,* 7–14.

Nelson, K., & Fivush, R. (2004). The emergence of autobiographical memory: A social cultural developmental theory. *Psychological Review, 111,* 486–511.

Nelson, P. B., Adamson, L. B., & Bakeman, R. (2008). Toddlers' joint engagement experience facilitates preschoolers' acquisition of theory of mind. *Developmental Science, 11,* 847–852.

Neu, M. (1999). Parents' perception of skin-to-skin care with their preterm infants requiring assisted ventilation. *Journal of Obstetric, Gynecologic, and Neonatal Nursing, 28,* 157–164.

Newcomb, A. F., & Bagwell, C. L. (1995). Children's friendship relations: A meta-analytic review. *Psychological Bulletin, 117,* 306–347.

Newcomb, A. F., Bukowski, W. M., & Bagwell, C. L. (1999). Knowing the sounds: Friendship as a developmental context. In W. A. Collins & B. Laursen (Eds.), *Minnesota symposia on child psychology: Vol. 30. Relationships as developmental contexts* (pp. 63–84). Mahwah, NJ: Erlbaum.

Newcombe, N., & Huttenlocher, J. (1992). Children's early ability to solve perspective-taking problems. *Developmental Psychology, 28,* 635–643.

Newcombe, N. S., & Huttenlocher, J. (2006). Development of spatial cognition. In W. Damon & R. M. Lerner (Editors-in-Chief) & D. M. Kuhn & R. S. Siegler (Vol. Eds.), *Handbook of child psychology: Vol. 2, Cognition, perception, and language* (6th ed., pp. 734–776). Hoboken, NJ: Wiley.

Newcombe, N. S., Huttenlocher, J., & Learmonth, A. (2000). Infants' coding of location in continuous space. *Infant Behavior and Development, 22,* 483–510.

Newport, E. L. (1977). Motherese: The speech of mothers to young children. In N. J. Castellan, D. B. Pisoni, & G. Potts (Eds.), *Cognitive theory* (Vol. 2, pp. 177–217). Hillsdale, NJ: Erlbaum.

Newport, E. L. (1990). Maturational constraints on language learning. *Cognitive Science, 14,* 11–28.

Newton, N. (1955). *Maternal emotions.* New York, NY: P. B. Hoeber.

Nguyen, S. P. (2007). Cross-classification and category representation in children's concepts. *Developmental Psychology, 43,* 719–731.

NICHD Early Child Care Research Network (1997). The effects of infant child care on infant-mother attachment security: Results of the NICHD study of early child care. *Child Development, 68,* 860–879.

NICHD Early Child Care Research Network (1998). Relations between family predictors and child outcomes: Are they weaker for children in child care? *Developmental Psychology, 34,* 1119–1128.

NICHD Early Child Care Research Network (2000a). Factors associated with fathers' caregiving activities and sensitivity to young children. *Journal of Family Psychology, 14,* 200–219.

NICHD Early Child Care Research Network (2000b). The relations of child care to cognitive and language development. *Child Development, 71,* 960–980.

NICHD Early Child Care Research Network (2001a). Child care and children's peer interaction at 24 and 36 months: The NICHD study of early child care. *Developmental Psychology, 72,* 1478–1500.

NICHD Early Child Care Research Network (2001b). Child care and family predictors of preschool attachment and stability from infancy. *Developmental Psychology, 37,* 847–862.

NICHD Early Child Care Research Network (2002). Child care structure → Process → Outcome: Direct and indirect effects of child care quality on young children's development. *Psychological Science, 13,* 199–206.

NICHD Early Child Care Research Network (2003a). Does amount of time spent in child care predict socioemotional adjustment during the transition to kindergarten? *Child Development, 74,* 976–1005.

NICHD Early Child Care Research Network (2003b). Does quality of child care affect child outcomes at age 4½? *Developmental Psychology, 39,* 451–469.

NICHD Early Child Care Research Network (2004). Does class size in first grade relate to children's academic and social performance or observed classroom processes? *Developmental Psychology, 40,* 651–664.

NICHD Early Child Care Research Network (2006). Infant-mother attachment: Risk and protection in relation to changing maternal caregiving quality over time. *Developmental Psychology, 42,* 38–58.

Niemiec, R., & Walberg, H. J. (1987). Comparative effects of computer assisted instruction: A synthesis of reviews. *Journal of Educational Computing Research, 3,* 19–37.

Nigg, J. T. (2010). Attention-deficit hyperactivity disorder: Endophenotypes, structure, and etiological pathways. *Current Directions in Psychological Science, 19,* 24–29.

Nikken, P., & Peeters, A. L. (1988). Children's perceptions of television reality. *Journal of Broadcasting and Electronic Media, 32,* 417–423.

Nimkarn, S., & New, M. I. (2010). Congenital adrenal hyperplasia due to 21-hydroxylase deficiency. *Annals of the New York Academy of Sciences, 1192,* 5–11.

Ninio, A., & Bruner, J. S. (1978). The achievement and antecedents of labelling. *Journal of Child Language, 5,* 1–15.

Nix, R. L., Pinderhughes, E. E., Dodge, K. A., Bates, J. E., Pettit, G. S., & McFadyen-Ketchum, S. A. (1999). The relation between mothers' hostile attribution tendencies and children's externalizing problems: The mediating role of mother's harsh discipline practices. *Child Development, 70,* 896–909.

Nolen-Hoeksma, S. (2001). Gender differences in depression. *Current Directions in Psychological Science, 10,* 173–176.

Norbeck, J. S., & Tilden, V. P. (1983). Life stress, social support, and emotional disequilibrium in complications of pregnancy: A prospective, multivariate study. *Journal of Health and Social Behavior, 24,* 30–46.

Northrup, H., & Volcik, K. A. (2000). Spina bifida and neural tube defects. *Current Problems in Pediatrics, 30,* 317–332.

Nucci, L. (2001). *Education in the moral domain.* New York, NY: Cambridge University Press.

Nucci, L. P., & Turiel, E. (1978). Social interactions and the development of social concepts in preschool children. *Child Development, 49,* 400–407.

Nucci, L. P., & Turiel, E. (1993). God's word, religious rules, and their relation to Christian and Jewish children's concepts of morality. *Child Development, 64,* 1475–1491.

Nugent, J. K., Lester, B. M., Greene, S. M., Wieczorek-Doering, D., & O'Mahony, P. (1996). The effects of maternal alcohol consumption and cigarette smoking during pregnancy on acoustic cry analysis. *Child Development, 67,* 1806–1815.

Oakes, L. M., Coppage, D. J., & Dingel, A. (1997). By land or by sea: The role of perceptual similarity in infants' categorization of animals. *Developmental Psychology, 33,* 396–407.

Oakley, D., Murray, M. E., Murtland, T., Hayashi, R., Andersen, H. F., Mayes, F., & Rooks, J. (1996). Comparisons of outcomes of maternity care by obstetricians and certified nurse-midwives. *Obstetrics and Gynecology, 88,* 923–929.

Ochs, E. (1988). *Culture and language development: Language acquisition and language socialization in a Samoan village.* New York, NY: Cambridge University Press.

Ochs, E. (1990). Indexicality and socialization. In J. W. Stigler, R. A. Shweder, & G. Herdt (Eds.), *Cultural psychology* (pp. 287–308). Cambridge, UK: Cambridge University Press.

O'Connor, R. D. (1972). Relative efficacy of modeling, shaping, and the procedures for modification of social withdrawal. *Journal of Abnormal Psychology, 79,* 327–334

O'Connor, T. G. (2005). Attachment disturbances associated with early severe deprivation. In C. S. Carter, L. Ahnert, K. E., Grossmann, S. B. Hrdy, M. E. Lamb, S. W. Porges, & N. Sachser (Eds.), *Attachment and bonding: A new synthesis* (pp. 257–268). Cambridge, MA: MIT Press.

O'Connor, T. G., & Croft, C. M. (2001). A twin study of attachment in preschool children. *Child Development, 72,* 1501–1511.

O'Connor, T. G., Caspi, A., DeFries, J. C., & Plomin, R. (2000). Are associations between parental divorce and children's adjustment genetically mediated? An adoption study. *Developmental Psychology, 36,* 429–437.

O'Connor, T. G., Deater-Deckard, K., Fulker, D., Rutter, M., & Plomin, R. (1998). Genotype-environment correlations in late childhood and early adolescence: Antisocial behavioral problems and coercive parenting. *Developmental Psychology, 34,* 970–981.

O'Neil, R., Parke, R. D., & McDowell, D. J. (2001). Objective and subjective features of children's neighborhoods: Relations to parental regulatory strategies and children's social competence. *Applied Developmental Psychology, 22,* 135–155.

Office of Applied Studies (2005). *Results from the 2004 National Survey on Drug Use and Health: National findings* (DHHS Publication No. SMA 05-4062, NSDUH Series H-28). Rockville, MD: Substance Abuse and Mental Health Services Administration.

Ogbu, J. U. (1974). *The next generation: An ethnography of education in an urban neighborhood.* New York, NY: Academic Press.

Ogden, C., & Carroll, M. (2010). *NCHS Health E-Stat: Prevalence of obesity among children and adolescents: United States, trends 1963–1965 through 2007–2008.* Retrieved August 30, 2010 from http://www.cdc.gov/nchs/data/hestat/obesity_child_07_08/obesity_child_07_08.htm

Ogden, C. L., Carroll, M. D., Curtin, L. R., Lamb, M. M., & Flegal, K. M. (2010). Prevalence of high body mass index in US children and adolescents, 2007–2008. *JAMA, 303,* 242–249.

Ojanen, T., & Perry, D. B. (2007). Relational schemas and the developing self: Perceptions of mother and of self as joint predictors of early adolescent's self-esteem. *Developmental Psychology, 43,* 1474–1483.

Oldershaw, L., Walters, G. C., & Hall, D. K. (1986). Control strategies and noncompliance in abusive mother-child dyads: An observational study. *Child Development, 57,* 722–732.

Olsen, E. M., Petersen, J., Skoygaard, A. M., Weile, B., Jørgensen, T., & Wright, C. M. (2007). Failure to thrive: The prevalence and concurrence of anthropometric criteria in a general infant population. *Archives of Disease in Childhood, 92,* 109–114.

Olson, C. K. (2010). Children's motivations for video game play in the context of normal development. *Review of General Psychology, 14,* 180–187.

Olson, K. R., & Dweck, C. S., (2008). A blueprint for social cognitive development. *Perspectives on Psychological Science, 3,* 193–202.

Olson, S. L., Bayles, K., & Bates, J. E. (1986). Mother-child interaction and children's speech progress: A longitudinal study of the first two years. *Merrill-Palmer Quarterly, 32,* 1–20.

Olthof, T., & Goossens, F. A. (2008). Bullying and the need to belong: Early adolescents' bullying-related behavior and the acceptance they desire and receive from particular classmates. *Social Development, 17,* 24–46.

Olweus, D. (1993b). *Bullying at school: What we know and what we can do.* Oxford, UK: Blackwell.

Olweus, D. (1997). Tackling peer victimization with a school-based intervention program. In D. P. Frye & K. Bjorkqvist (Eds.), *Cultural variation in conflict resolution: Alternatives to violence* (pp. 215–231). Mahwah, NJ: Erlbaum.

Orlebeke, J. F., Knol, D. L., & Verhulst, F. C. (1999). Child behavior problems increased by maternal smoking during pregnancy. *Archives of Environmental Health, 54,* 15–19.

Ornoy, A., Michailevskay, V., Lukashov, I., Barttamburger, R., & Harel, S. (1996). The developmental outcome of children born to heroin-dependent mothers, raised at home or adopted. *Child Abuse & Neglect, 20,* 385–396.

Orton, G. L. (1982). A comparative study of children's worries. *Journal of Psychology, 110,* 153–162.

Osterling, J., & Dawson, G. (1994). Early recognition of children with autism: A study of first birthday home videotapes. *Journal of Autism and Developmental Disorders, 24,* 247–257.

Ottolenghi, C., Uda, M., Crisponi, L., Omari, S., Cao, A., Forabosco, A., & Schlessinger, D. (2007). Determination and stability of sex. *BioEssays, 29,* 15–25.

Ounsted, C., Oppenheimer, R., & Lindsay, J. (1974). Aspects of bonding failure: The psychopathology and psychotherapeutic treatment of families of battered children. *Developmental Medicine and Child Neurology, 16,* 447–452.

Overman, W. H., Bachevalier, J., Schuhmann, E., & McDonough-Ryan, P. (1997). Sexually dimorphic brain-behavior development. In N. Krasnegor, G. R. Lyon, & P. S. Goldman-Rakic (Eds.), *Development of the prefrontal cortex: Evolution, neurobiology, and behavior* (pp. 337–357). Baltimore: Paul H. Brookes.

Overton, W. F. (2006). Developmental psychology: Philosophy, concepts, methodology. In W. Damon & R. M. Lerner (Editors-in-Chief) & R. M. Lerner (Vol. Ed.), *Handbook of child psychology: Vol. 1. Theoretical models of human development* (6th ed., pp. 18–88). Hoboken, NJ: Wiley.

Owen, L., Auty, S., Lewis, C., & Berridge, D. (2007). Children's understanding of advertising: An investigation using verbal and pictorially cued methods. *Infant and Child Development, 16,* 617–628.

Owen, M. T., & Cox, M. J. (1988). Maternal employment and the transition to parenthood. In A. E. Gottfried & A. W. Gottfried (Eds.), *Maternal employment and children's development: Longitudinal research* (pp. 85–120). New York, NY: Plenum Press.

Pak, S. (2004). The biological standard of living in the two Koreas. *Economics and Human Biology, 2,* 511–521.

Palacios, J. (1996). Proverbs as images of children and childrearing. In C. P. Hwang, M. E. Lamb, & I. E. Sigel (Eds.), *Images of childhood* (pp. 75–98). Mahwah, NJ: Erlbaum.

Palincsar, A. S., & Brown, A. L. (1984). Reciprocal teaching of comprehension-fostering and comprehension-monitoring activities. *Cognition and Instruction, 1,* 117–175.

Palincsar, A. S., & Brown, A. L. (1986). Interactive teaching to promote independent learning from text. *The Reading Teacher, 39,* 771–777.

Papoušek, H., Papoušek, M., & Koester, L. S. (1986). Sharing emotionality and sharing knowledge: A microanalytic approach to parent-infant communication. In C. E. Izard & P. B. Read (Eds.), *Measuring emotions in infants and children* (Vol. 2 , pp. 93–123). Cambridge, UK: Cambridge University Press.

Papoušek, M. (1992). Early ontogeny of vocal ommunication in parent-infant interactions. In H. Papoušek, U. Jürgens, & M. Papoušek (Eds.), *Nonverbal vocal communication: Comparative and developmental approaches* (pp. 230–261). Cambridge, UK: Cambridge University Press.

Paris, S. G., & Paris, A. H. (2006). Assessments of early reading. W. Damon & R. M. Lerner (Editors-in-Chief) & K. A. Renninger & I. E. Sigel (Vol. Eds.), *Handbook of child psychology: Vol. 4. Child psychology in practice* (6th ed., pp. 48–74). Hoboken, NJ: Wiley.

Parke, R. D. (1969). Effectiveness of punishment as an interaction of intensity, timing, agent nurturance, and cognitive structuring. *Child Development, 40,* 213–235.

Parke, R. D., & Buriel, R. (2006). Socialization in the family: Ethnic and ecological perspectives. In W. Damon & R. M. Lerner (Editors-in-Chief) & N. Eisenberg (Vol. Eds.), *Handbook of child psychology, Vol. 3. Social, emotional, and personality development* (6th ed., pp. 429–504). Hoboken, NJ: Wiley

Parke, R. D., & Collmer, C. W. (1975). Child abuse: An interdisciplinary analysis. In E. M. Hetherington (Ed.), *Review of child development research* (Vol. 5, pp. 509–590). Chicago, IL: University of Chicago Press.

Parke, R. D., Coltrane, S., Duffy, S., Buriel, R., Dennis, J., Powers, J., French, S., et al. (2004). Economic stress, parenting, and child adjustment in Mexican American and European American families. *Child Development, 75,* 1632–1656.

Parke, R. D., & O'Leary, S. (1976). Father-mother-infant interaction in the newborn period: Some findings, some observations, and some unresolved issues. In K. F. Riegel & J. Meacham (Eds.), *The developing individual in a changing world: Vol. 2. Social and environmental issues* (pp. 653–663). The Hague: Mouton.

Parke, R. D., & Slaby, R. G. (1983). The development of aggression. In E. M. Hetherington (Ed.), *Handbook of child psychology: Vol. IV. Socialization, personality, and social development* (4th ed., pp. 547–641). New York, NY: Wiley.

Parker, J. G., & Asher, S. R. (1987). Peer relations and later personal adjustment: Children at risk? *Psychological Bulletin, 102,* 357–389.

Parker, J. G., & Asher, S. R. (1993). Friendship and friendship quality in middle childhood: Links with peer group acceptance and feelings of loneliness and social dissatisfaction. *Developmental Psychology, 29,* 611–621.

Parker, J. G., & Gottman, J. M. (1989). Social and emotional development in a relational context: Friendship interaction from early childhood to adolescence. In T. M. Berndt & G. W. Ladd (Eds.), *Peer relations in childhood* (pp. 95–131). New York, NY: Wiley.

Parker, J. G., & Seal, J. (1996). Forming, losing, renewing, and replacing friendships: Applying temporal parameters to the assessment of children's friendship experiences. *Child Development, 67,* 2248–2268.

Parkhurst, J. T., & Asher, S. R. (1992). Peer rejection in middle school: Subgroup differences in behavior, loneliness, and interpersonal concerns. *Developmental Psychology, 28,* 231–241.

Parsons, J. E. (1980). Psychosexual neutrality: Is anatomy destiny? In J. E. Parsons (Ed.), *The psychobiology of sex differences and sex roles* (pp. 3–29). New York, NY: Hemisphere.

Parten, M. B. (1932). Social participation among pre-school children. *Journal of Abnormal and Social Psychology, 32,* 243–269.

Pascalis, O., de Haan, M., & Nelson, C. A. (2002). Is face processing species-specific during the first year of life? *Science, 296,* 1321–1323.

Pascalis, O., & Kelly, D. J. (2009). The origins of face processing in humans: Phylogeny and ontogeny. *Perspectives on Psychological Science, 4,* 200–209.

Pascalis, O., Scott, L. S., Kelly, D. J., Shannon, R. W., Nicholson, E., Coleman, M., & Nelson, C. A. (2005). Plasticity of face processing in infancy. *Proceedings of the National Academy of Sciences, USA, 102,* 5297–5300.

Paterson, D. S., Trachtenberg, F. L., Thompson, E. G., Belliveau, R. A., Beggs, A. H., Darnall, R., . . . Kinney, H. C. (2006). Multiple serotonergic brainstem abnormalities in sudden infant death syndrome. *JAMA, 296,* 2124–2132.

Patterson, C. J. (2000). Family relationships of lesbians and gay men. *Journal of Marriage and the Family, 62,* 1052–1069.

Patterson, G. R. (1982). *A social learning approach: Vol. 3. Coercive family process.* Eugene, OR: Castalia.

Patterson, G. R. (1986). Performance models for antisocial boys. *American Psychologist, 41,* 432–444.

Patterson, G. R., & Fleischman, M. J. (1979). Maintenance of treatment effects: Some considerations concerning family systems and follow-up data. *Behavior Therapy, 10,* 168–185.

Patterson, G. R., Littman, R. A., & Bricker, W. (1967). Assertive behavior in children: A step toward a theory of aggression. *Monographs of the Society for Research in Child Development, 32* (5, Serial No. 113).

Patterson, G. R., & Reid, J. B. (1973). Intervention for families of aggressive boys: A replication study. *Behavior Research and Therapy, 11,* 383–394.

Patterson, G. R., Reid, J. B., & Dishion, T. J. (1992). *A social learning approach: IV. Antisocial boys.* Eugene, OR: Castalia.

Patterson, G. R., Reid, J. B., Jones, R. R., & Conger, R. E. (1975). *A social learning approach: Vol. 1. Families with aggressive children.* Eugene, OR: Castalia.

Patterson, M. L., & Werker, J. F. (2003). Two-month-old infants match phonetic information in lips and voice. *Developmental Science, 6,* 191–196.

Pauli, S. A., Berga, S. L., Shang, W., & Session, D. R. (2009). Current status of the approach to assisted reproduction. *Pediatric Clinics of North America, 56,* 467–488.

Paus, T. (2004). Mapping brain maturation and cognitive development during adolescence. *Trends in Cognitive Science, 9,* 60–68.

Paxton, S. J., Eisenberg, M. E., & Neumark-Sztainer, D. (2006). Prospective predictors of body dissatisfaction in adolescent girls and boys: A five-year-longitudinal study. *Developmental Psychology, 42,* 888–899.

Pearce, M. J., Jones, S. M., Schwab-Stone, A. E., & Ruchkin, V. (2003). The protective effects of religiousness and parent involvement on the development of conduct problems among youth exposed to violence. *Child Development, 74,* 1682–1696.

Pederson, D. R., Gleason, K. E., Moran, G., & Bento, S. (1998). Maternal attachment representations, maternal sensitivity, and the infant-mother attachment relationship. *Developmental Psychology, 34,* 925–933.

Peisner-Feinberg, E. S., Burchinal, M., Clifford, R., Culkin, M., Howes, C., Kagan, S., & Yazejian, N. (2001). The relation of preschool childcare quality to children's cognitive and social developmental trajectories through second grade. *Child Development, 72,* 1534–1553.

Peláez-Nogueras, M., Field, T., Gewirtz, J. L., Cigales, M., Gonzalez, A., Sanchez, A., & Richardson, S. C. (1997). The effects of systematic stroking versus tickling and poking on infant behavior. *Journal of Applied Developmental Psychology, 18,* 169–178.

Pellegrini, A. D. (1988). Elementary-school children's rough-and-tumble play and social competence. *Developmental Psychology, 24,* 802–806.

Pellegrini, A. D. (2007). The development and function of rough-and-tumble play in childhood and adolescence: A sexual selection theory perspective. In A. Göncü & S. Gaskins, (Eds.), *Play and development: Evolutionary, sociocultural, and functional perspectives* (pp. 77–98). Mahwah, NJ: Lawrence Erlbaum.

Pellegrini, A. D., & Smith, P. K. (1998). Physical activity play: The nature and function of a neglected aspect of play. *Child Development, 69,* 577–598.

Pellicano, E. (2010). Individual differences in executive function and central coherence predict developmental changes in theory of mind in autism. *Developmental Psychology, 46,* 530–544.

Peltola, M. J., Leppänen, J. M., Palokangas, T., & Hietanen, J. K. (2008). Fearful faces modulate looking duration and attention disengagement in 7-month-old infants. *Developmental Science, 11,* 60–68.

Peltonen, L., & McKusick, V. A. (2001). Dissecting human disease in the postgenomic era. *Science, 291,* 1224–1229.

Pempek, T. A., Kirkorian, H. L., Richards, J. E., Anderson, D. R., Lund, A. F., & Stevens, M. (2010). Video comprehensibility and attention in very young children. *Developmental Psychology, 46,* 1283–1293.

Peña, E. D. (2007). Lost in translation: Methodological considerations in cross-cultural research. *Child Development, 78,* 1255–1264.

Peña, M., Maki, A., Kovacic, D., Dehaene-Lambertz, G., Koizumi, H., Bouquet, F., et al. (2003). Sounds and silence: An optical topography study of language recognition at birth. *Proceedings of the National Academy of Science, 100,* 11702–11705.

Penn, A. A., & Shatz, C. J. (2002). Principles of endogenous and sensory activity-dependent brain development. In H. Langercrantz, M. Hanson, P. Evrard, & C. Rodeck (Eds.), *The newborn brain: Neuroscience and clinical applications* (pp. 204–277). Cambridge, UK: Cambridge University Press.

Pennington, B. F. (1998). Dimensions of executive functions in normal and abnormal development. In N. A. Krasnegor, G. R. Lyon, & P. S. Goldman-Rakic (Eds.), *Development of the prefrontal cortex: Evolution, neurobiology, and behavior* (pp. 265–281). Baltimore, MD: Brookes.

Pennington, B. F., McGrath, L. M., Rosenberg, J., Barnard, H., Smith, S. D., Willcutt, E. G., & Olson, R. K. (2009). Gene X environment interactions in reading disability and attention-deficit/hyperactivity disorder. *Developmental Psychology, 45,* 77–89.

Pennisi, E. (2007). GENETICS: Working the (gene count) numbers: Finally, a firm answer? *Science, 316,* 1113.

Penny, H., & Haddock, G. (2007). Children's stereotypes of overweight children. *British Journal of Developmental Psychology, 25,* 409–418.

Penrose, A., & Takaki, M. (2006). Children's rights in emergencies and disasters. *The Lancet, 367,* 698–699.

Perner, J., & Ruffman, T. (1995). Episodic memory and autonoetic consciousness: Developmental evidence and a theory of childhood amnesia. *Journal of Experimental Child Psychology, 59,* 516–548.

Perozynski, L., & Kramer, L. (1999). Parental beliefs about managing sibling conflict. *Developmental Psychology, 35,* 489–499.

Perry, D. G., & Bussey, K. (1979). The social learning theory of sex differences: Imitation is alive and well. *Journal of Personality and Social Psychology, 37,* 1699–1712.

Persing, J., Hector, J., Swanson, J., Kattwinkel, J., & the Committee on Practice and Ambulatory Medicine. (2003). Prevention and management of positional skull deformities in infants. *Pediatrics, 112,* 199–202.

Petersen, A. C. (1980). Biopsychosocial processes in the development of sex-related differences. In J. Parsons (Ed.), *The psychobiology of sex differences and sex roles* (pp. 31–55). New York, NY: Hemisphere.

Petersen, A. C. (1988). Adolescent development. *Annual Review of Psychology, 39,* 583–607.

Petersen, A. C., Compas, B. E., Brooks-Gunn, J., Stemmler, M., Ey, S., & Grant, K. E. (1993). Depression in adolescence. *American Psychologist, 48,* 155–168.

Peterson, C. A., & Siegal, M. (1999). Representing inner worlds: Theory of mind in autistic, deaf, and normal hearing children. *Psychological Science, 10,* 126–129.

Peterson, C. C., Wellman, H. M., & Liu, D. (2005). Steps in theory-of-mind development for children with deafness or autism. *Child Development, 76,* 502–517.

Peterson, C., & Whalen, N. (2001). Five years later: Children's memory for medical emergencies. *Applied Cognitive Psychology, 15,* S7–S24.

Peterson, R. P., Johnson, D. W., & Johnson, R. T. (1991). Effects of cooperative learning on perceived status of male and female pupils. *Journal of Social Psychology, 131,* 717–735.

Petitto, L. A. (2009). New discoveries from the bilingual brain and mind across the life span: Implications for education. *Mind, Brain, and Education, 3,* 185–197.

Petitto, L. A., Katerelos, M., Levy, B. G., Gauna, K., Tétreault, K., & Ferraro, V. (2001). Bilingual signed and spoken language acquisition from birth: Implications for the mechanisms underlying early bilingual language acquisition. *Journal of Child Language, 28,* 453–496.

Petitto, L. A., & Marentette, P. F. (1991). Babbling in the manual code: Evidence for the ontogeny of language. *Science, 251,* 1493–1496.

Pettit, G. S., Bates, J. E., & Dodge, K. A. (1997). Supportive parenting, ecological context, and children's adjustment: A seven-year longitudinal study. *Child Development, 68,* 908–923.

Pettit, G. S., Bates, J. E., Dodge, K. A., & Meece, D. W. (1999). The impact of after-school peer contact on early adolescent externalizing problems is moderated by parental monitoring, neighborhood safety, and prior adjustment. *Child Development, 70,* 768–778.

Pettit, G. S., Clawson, M. A., Dodge, K. A. & Bates, J. E. (1996). Stability and change in peer-rejected status: The role of child behavior, parenting, and family ecology. *Merrill-Palmer Quarterly, 42,* 267–294.

Pettit, G. S., Dodge, K. A., Bakshi, A., & Coie, J. D. (1990). The emergence of social dominance in young boys' play groups: Developmental differences and behavioral correlates. *Developmental Psychology, 26,* 1017–1025.

Pettit, G. S., Laird, R. D., Dodge, K. A., Bates, J. E., & Criss, M. M. (2001). Antecedents and behavior-problem outcomes of parental monitoring and psychological control in early adolescence. *Child Development, 72,* 583–598.

Phelps, E., & Damon, W. (1989). Problem solving with equals: Peer collaboration as a context for learning mathematics and spatial concepts. *Journal of Educational Psychology, 81,* 639–646.

Phenylketonuria. (2000, October 16–18). Phenylketonuria (PKU): Screening and management. *NIH Consensus Statement, 17,* 1–33.

Phinney, J. S. (1990). Ethnic identity in adolescents and adults: Review of research. *Psychological Bulletin, 108,* 499–514.

Phinney, J. S., Ferguson, D. L., & Tate, J. D. (1997). Intergroup attitudes among ethnic minority adolescents: A causal model. *Child Development, 68,* 955–969.

Phinney, J. S., & Rosenthal, D. A. (1992). Ethnic identity in adolescence: Process, context and outcome. In G. R. Adams, T. P. Gullotta, & R. Montemayor (Eds.), *Adolescent identity formation* (pp. 145–172). Newbury Park, CA: Sage.

Piaget, J. (1929). *The child's conception of the world.* London, UK: Routledge & Kegan Paul.

Piaget, J. (1962). *Play, dreams, and imitation in childhood.* New York, NY: W. W. Norton.

Piaget, J. (1965). *The moral judgment of the child.* New York, NY: Free Press. (Original work published 1932.)

Piaget, J. (1971). *Biology and knowledge: An essay on the relationship between organic regulations and cognitive processes.* Chicago, IL: University of Chicago Press.

Pianta, R. C., Barnett, W. S., Burchinal, M., & Thornburg, K. R. (2010). The effects of preschool education: What we know, how public policy is or is not aligned with the evidence base, and what we need to know. *Psychological Science in the Public Interest, 10,* 49–88.

Pick, A. D. (1965). Improvement of visual and tactual discrimination. *Journal of Experimental Psychology, 69,* 331–339.

Pick, H. L., Jr. (1987). Information and the effects of early perceptual experience. In N. Eisenberg (Ed.), *Contemporary topics in developmental psychology* (pp. 59–76). New York, NY: Wiley.

Pick, H. L., Jr. (1992). Eleanor J. Gibson: Learning to perceive and perceiving to learn. *Developmental Psychology, 28,* 787–794.

Pickens, J. (1994). Perception of auditory-visual distance relations by 5-month-old infants. *Developmental Psychology, 30,* 537–544.

Pickens, J., & Field, T. (1993). Facial expressivity in infants of depressed mothers. *Developmental Psychology, 29,* 986–988.

Pierroutsakos, S. L., & DeLoache, J. S. (2003). Infants' manual exploration of pictorial objects varying in realism. *Infancy, 4,* 141–156.

Pike, A., McGuire, S., Hetherington, E. M., Reiss, D., & Plomin, R. (1996). Family environment and adolescent depressive symptoms and antisocial behavior: A multivariate genetic analysis. *Developmental Psychology, 32,* 590–603.

Pillemer, D. B. (1998). *Momentous events, vivid memories.* Cambridge, MA; Harvard University Press.

Pillemer, D. B., & White, S. H. (1989). Childhood events recalled by children and adults. In H.W. Reese (Ed.), *Advances in child development and behavior* (Vol. 21, pp. 297–340). San Diego, CA: Academic Press.

Pinker, S. (1984). *Language learnability and language development.* Cambridge, MA: Harvard University Press.

Pinker, S. (1987). The bootstrapping problem in language acquisition In B. MacWhinney (Ed.), *Mechanisms of language acquisition* (pp. 399–442). Hillsdale, NJ: Erlbaum.

Pinyerd, B. J. (1992). Assessment of infant growth. *Journal of Pediatric Health Care, 6,* 302–308.

Pipe, M., Gee, S., Wilson, J. C., & Egerton, J. M. (1999). Children's recall 1 or 2 years after an event. *Developmental Psychology, 35,* 781–789.

Pleck, J. (2010). Paternal involvement: Revised conceptualization and theoretical linkages with child outcomes. In M. Lamb (Ed.), *The role of the father in child development* (5th ed., pp. 58–93). Hoboken, NJ: Wiley.

Plomin, R. (1994). The Emmanuel Miller Memorial Lecture 1993: Genetic research and identification of environmental influences. *Journal of Child Psychology and Psychiatry and Allied Disciplines, 35,* 817–834.

Plomin, R., & Davis, O. S. P. (2009). The future of genetics in psychology and psychiatry: Microarrays, genome-wide association, and non-coding RNA. *Journal of Child Psychology and Psychiatry, 50,* 63–71.

Plomin, R., DeFries, J. C., & Fulker, D. (1988). The Colorado Adoption Project. In R. Plomin, J. C. DeFries, & D. Fulker (Eds.), *Nature and nurture during infancy and early childhood* (pp. 37–76). Cambridge, UK: Cambridge University Press.

Plomin, R., DeFries, J. C., McClearn, G. E., & McGuffin, P. (2008). *Behavioral genetics* (5th ed.). New York, NY: Worth.

Plomin, R., & Kovas, Y. (2005). Generalist genes and learning disabilities. *Psychological Bulletin, 131,* 592–617.

Plomin, R., & Schalkwyk, L. C. (2007). Microarrays. *Developmental Science, 10,* 19–23.

Plunkett, K. (1995). Connectionist approaches to language acquisition. In P. Fletcher & B. MacWhinney (Eds.), *The handbook of child language* (pp. 36–72). Oxford, UK: Blackwell.

Plunkett, K., & Marchman, V. A. (1996). Learning from a connectionist model of the acquisition of the English past tense. *Cognition, 61,* 299–308.

Polat, U., Ma-Naim, T., & Spierer, A. (2009). Treatment of children with amblyopia by perceptual learning. *Vision Research, 49,* 2599–2603.

Pollak, S. D., Cicchetti, D., Hornung, K., & Reed, A. (2000). Recognizing emotion in faces: Developmental effects of child abuse and neglect. *Developmental Psychology, 36,* 679–688.

Pollak, S. D., Nelson, C. A., Schlaak, M. F., Roeber, B. J., Wewerka, S. S., Wiik, K. L., . . . & Gunnar, M. R. (2010). Neurodevelopmental effects of early deprivation in postinstitutionalized children. *Child Development, 81,* 224–236.

Pollak, S. D., & Tolley-Schell, S. A. (2003). Selective attention in facial emotion in physically abused children. *Journal of Abnormal Psychology, 112,* 323–338.

Pollitt, E. (1994). Poverty and child development: Relevance of research in developing countries to the United States. *Child Development, 65,* 283–295.

Pollitt, E. (1996). Timing and vulnerability in research on malnutrition and cognition. *Nutrition Reviews, 54,* S49–S55.

Pollitt, E., Gorman, K. S., Engle, P. L., Martorell, R., & Rivera, J. (1993). Early supplementary feeding and cognition. *Monographs of the Society for Research in Child Development, 58* (7, Serial No. 235).

Pomerantz, E. M., Ruble, D. N., Frey, K. S., & Greulich, F. (1995). Meeting goals and confronting conflict: Children's changing perceptions of social comparison. *Child Development, 66,* 723–738.

Pomerantz, E. M., Qin, L., Wang, Q., & Chen, H. (2009). American and Chinese early adolescents' inclusion of their relationships with their parents in their self-construals. *Child Development, 80,* 792–807.

Pomerleau, A., Bolduc, D., Malcuit, G., & Cossette, L. (1990). Pink or blue: Environmental gender stereotypes in the first two years of life. *Sex Roles, 22,* 359–367.

Poole, D. A., & Lindsay, D. S. (2002). Reducing child witnesses' false reports of misinformation from parents. *Journal of Experimental Child Psychology, 81,* 117–140.

Poole, D. A., & White, L. T. (1991). Effects of question repetition on the eyewitness testimony of children and adults. *Developmental Psychology, 27,* 975–986.

Poole, D. A., & White, L. T. (1993). Two years later: Effects of question repetition and retention interval on the eyewitness testimony of children and adults. *Developmental Psychology, 29,* 844–853.

Pope, A. W., & Bierman, K. L. (1999). Predicting adolescent peer problems and antisocial activities: The relative roles of aggression and dysregulation. *Developmental Psychology, 35,* 335–346.

Porges, S. W., Doussard-Roosevelt, J. A., & Maiti, A. K. (1994). Vagal tone and the physiological regulation of emotion. In N. A. Fox (Ed.), *The development of emotion regulation: Biological and behavioral considerations. Monographs of the Society for Research in Child Development, 59* (2–3, Serial No. 240).

Porter, F. L., Grunau, R. E., & Anand, K. J. S. (1999). Long-term effects of pain in infants. *Journal of Developmental and Behavioral Pediatrics, 20,* 253–261.

Porter, R. H., Balogh, R. D., & Makin, J. W. (1988). Olfactory influences on mother-infant interaction. In C. Rovee-Collier & L. P. Lipsitt (Eds.), *Advances in infancy research* (Vol. 5, pp. 39–68). Norwood, NJ: Ablex.

Posada, G., Gao, Y., Wu, F., Posada, R., Tascon, M., Schöelmerich, A., . . . & Synnevaag, B. (1995). The secure-base phenomenon across cultures: Children's behaviors, mothers' preferences, and experts' concepts. In E. Waters, B. E. Vaughn, G. Posada, & K. Kondo-Ikemura (Eds.), *Caregiving, cultural, and cognitive perspectives on secure-base behavior and working models: New growing points of attachment theory and research. Monographs of the Society for Research in Child Development, 60* (Nos. 2–3, Serial No. 244).

Posner, M. I., Rothbart, M. K., & Sheese, B. E. (2007). Attention genes. *Developmental Science, 10,* 24–29.

Post, R. M., & Weiss, S. R. B. (1997). Emergent properties of neural systems: How focal molecular neurobiological alterations can affect behavior. *Development and Psychopathology, 9,* 907–929.

Posthuma, D., & de Geus, E. J. C. (2006). Progress in the molecular genetic study of intelligence. *Current Directions in Psychological Science, 15,* 151–155.

Poulin-Dubois, D., Lepage, A., & Ferland, D. (1996). Infants' concept of animacy. *Cognitive Development, 11,* 19–36.

Poulin-Dubois, D., Serbin, L. A., & Derbyshire, A. (1998). Toddlers' intermodal and verbal knowledge about gender. *Merrill-Palmer Quarterly, 44,* 338–354.

Poulin-Dubois, D., Serbin, L. A., Eichstedt, J. A., Sen, M. G., & Beissel, C. F. (2002). Men don't put on make-up: Toddlers' knowledge of the gender stereotyping of household activities. *Social Development, 11,* 166–181.

Power, T. G., & Chapieski, M. L. (1986). Childrearing and impulse control in toddlers: A naturalistic investigation. *Developmental Psychology, 22,* 271–275.

Powers, S. I., Hauser, S. T., & Kilner, L. A. (1989). Adolescent mental health. *American Psychologist, 44,* 200–208.

Prader, A. (1978). Catch-up growth. *Postgraduate Medical Journal, 54,* 133–146.

Pratt, M. W., Green, D., MacVicar, J., & Bountrogianni, M. (1992). The mathematical parent: Parental scaffolding, parenting style, and learning outcomes in long-division mathematics homework. *Journal of Applied Developmental Psychology, 13,* 17–34.

Preyer, W. (1888–1889). *The mind of the child* (H.W. Brown, Trans.). New York, NY: Appleton. (Original work published in 1882.)

Pride, P. G., Drugan, A., Johnson, M. P., Isada, N. B., & Evans, M. I. (1993). Prenatal diagnosis: Choices women make about pursuing testing and acting on abnormal results. *Clinical Obstetrics and Gynecology, 36,* 496–509.

Proffitt, D. R., & Bertenthal, B. I. (1990). Converging operations revisited: Assessing what infants perceive using discrimination measures. *Perception & Psychophysics, 47,* 1–11.

Puhl, R. M., & Latner, J. D. (2007). Stigma, obesity, and the health of the nation's children. *Psychological Bulletin, 133,* 557–580.

Purcell, P., & Stewart, L. (1990). Dick and Jane in 1989. *Sex Roles, 22,* 177–185.

Putallaz, M. (1987). Maternal behavior and children's sociometric status. *Child Development, 58,* 324–340.

Puzzanchera, M. (2009, April). Juvenile arrests 2007. *Juvenile Justice Bulletin.* US. Department of Justice, Office of Justice Programs. Downloaded September 8, 2010, from http://www.ncjrs.gov/pdffiles1/ojjdp/225344.pdf

Pyers, J. E., & Senghas, A. (2009). Language promotes false-belief understanding: Evidence from learners of a new sign language. *Psychological Science, 20,* 805–812.

Quas, J. A., Molloy, L. C., Melinder, A., Goodman, G. S., D'Mello, M., & Shaaf, J. (2007). Developmental differences in the effects of repeated interviews and interviewer bias on young children's event memory and false reports. *Developmental Psychology, 43,* 823–837.

Quick, Z. L., Robb, M. P., & Woodward, L. J. (2009). Acoustic cry characteristics of infants exposed to methadone during pregnancy. *Acta Paediatrica, 98* (1), 74–79.

QuickStats: Spina Bifida and Anencephaly Rates—United States, 1991, 1995, 2000, and 2005. (2008, January 11). *MMWR Weekly, 57*(1), 15. Retrieved August 23, 2010, from http://www.cdc.gov/mmwr/preview/mmwrhtml/mm5701a7.htm

Quinn, P. C., Eimas, P. D., & Rosenkranz, S. L. (1993). Evidence for representations of perceptually similar natural categories by 3-month-old and 4-month-old infants. *Perception, 22,* 324–340.

Quinn, P. C., & Liben, L. S. (2008). A sex difference in mental rotation in young infants. *Psychological Science, 19,* 1067–1070.

Quinn, P. C., Westerlund, A., & Nelson, C. A. (2006). Neural markers of categorization in 6-month-old infants. *Psychological Science, 17,* 59–66.

Radin, N. (1994). Primary-caregiving fathers in intact families. In A. E. Gottfried & A. W. Gottfried (Eds.), *Redefining families: Implications for children's development* (pp. 11–49). NY: Plenum Press.

Radke-Yarrow, M., & Zahn-Waxler, C. (1984). Roots, motives, and patterns of children's prosocial behavior. In E. Staub, D. Bar-Tel, J. Karylowski, & J. Reykowski (Eds.), *Development and maintenance of prosocial behavior* (pp. 81–99). New York, NY: Plenum Press.

Radziszewska, B., & Rogoff, B. (1988). Influence of adult and peer collaborators on children's planning skills. *Developmental Psychology, 24,* 840–848.

Radziszewska, B., & Rogoff, B. (1991). Children's guided participation in planning imaginary errands with skilled adult or peer partners. *Developmental Psychology, 27,* 381–389.

Raffaelli, M. (1997). Young adolescents' conflicts with siblings and friends. *Journal of Youth and Adolescence, 26,* 539–558.

Rajendran, G., & Mitchell, P. (2007). Cognitive theories of autism. *Developmental Review, 27,* 224–260.

Rakison, D. H., & Oakes, L. M. (2003). *Early category and concept development: Making sense of the blooming, buzzing confusion.* New York, NY: Oxford University Press.

Rakoczy, H., Warneken, F., & Tomasello, M. (2008). The sources of normativity: Young children's awareness of the normative structure of games. *Developmental Psychology, 44,* 875–881.

Rallison, M. L. (1986). *Growth disorders in infants, children, and adolescents.* New York, NY: Wiley.

Ram, A., & Ross, H. S. (2001). Problem-solving, contention, and struggle: How siblings resolve a conflict of interests. *Child Development, 72,* 1710–1722.

Ramey, C. T., Bryant, D. M., Wasik, B. H., Sparling, J. J., Fendt, K. H., & LaVange, L. M. (1992). Infant Health and Development Program for low birth weight, premature infants: Program elements, family participation, and child intelligence. *Pediatrics, 89,* 454–465.

Ramey, C. T., & Campbell, F. A. (1981). Educational intervention for children at risk for mild retardation: A longitudinal analysis. In P. Mittler (Ed.), *Frontiers of knowledge in mental retardation: Vol. 1. Social, educational, and behavioral aspects* (pp. 47–57). Baltimore, MD: University Park Press.

Ramey, C. T., Lee, M. W., & Burchinal, M. R. (1989). Developmental plasticity and predictability: Consequences of ecological change. In M. H. Bornstein & N. A. Krasnegor (Eds.), *Stability and continuity in mental development: Behavioral and biological perspectives* (pp. 217–233). Hillsdale, NJ: Erlbaum.

Ramey, C. T., & Ramey, S. L. (1998). Early intervention and early experience. *American Psychologist, 53,* 109–120.

Ramsey, J. L., Langlois, J. H., & Marti, N. C. (2005). Infant categorization of faces: Ladies first. *Developmental Review, 25,* 212–246.

Rao, N., & Stewart, S. M. (1999). Cultural influences on sharer and recipient behavior: Sharing in Chinese and Indian preschool children. *Journal of Cross-Cultural Psychology, 30,* 219–241.

Rapport, M. D. (1995). Attention-deficit hyperactivity disorder. In M. Hersen & R. T. Ammerman (Eds.), *Advanced abnormal psychology* (pp. 353–373). Hillsdale, NJ: Erlbaum.

Razel, M. (2001). The complex model of television viewing and educational achievement. *Journal of Educational Research,* 94, 371–379.

Reece, E. A., Hobbins, J. C., Mahoney, M. J., & Petrie, R. H. (1995). *Handbook of medicine of the fetus & mother.* Philadelphia: J. B. Lippincott.

Reefhuis, J. Honein, M. A., Schieve, L. A., Correa, A., Hobbs, C. A., Rasmussen, S., & the National Birth Defects Prevention Study (2009). Assisted reproductive technology and major structural birth defects in the United States. *Human Reproduction, 24,* 360–366.

Reese, E. (2002). Social factors in the development of autobiographical memory. *Social Development, 11,* 124–142.

Reese, E., & Fivush, R. (1993). Parental styles for talking about the past. *Developmental Psychology, 29,* 596–606.

Reese, E., Haden, C. A., & Fivush, R. (1993). Mother-child conversations about the past: Relationships of style and memory over time. *Cognitive Development, 8,* 403–430.

Reese, E., & Newcombe, R. (2007). Training mothers in elaborative reminiscing enhances children's autobiographical memory and narrative. *Child Development, 78,* 1153–1170.

Regan, P. C., Durvasula, R., Howell, L., Ureno, O., & Rea, M. (2004). Romance seems to be alive and well during the high school years. *Social Behavior and Personality, 32,* 667–676.

Reisman, J. E. (1987). Touch, motion, and proprioception. In P. Salapatek & L. Cohen (Eds.), *Handbook of infant perception: From sensation to perception* (Vol. 1, pp. 265–303). Orlando, FL: Academic Press.

Reiss, D. F. (2005). The interplay between genotypes and family relationships: Reframing concepts of development and prevention. *Current Directions in Psychological Science, 14,* 139–143.

Reissland, N. (1988). Neonatal imitation in the first hour of life: Observations in rural Nepal. *Developmental Psychology, 24,* 464–469.

Remafedi, G., French, S., Story, M., Resnick, M. D., & Blum, R. (1998). The relationship between suicide risk and sexual orientation: Results of a population-based study. *American Journal of Public Health, 88,* 57–60.

Rende, R. D., Plomin, R., Reiss, D., & Hetherington, E. M. (1993). Genetic and environmental influences on depressive symptomatology in adolescence: Individual differences and extreme scores. *Journal of Child Psychology and Psychiatry and Allied Disciplines, 34,* 1387–1398.

Renninger, K. A. (1992). Individual interest and development: Implications for theory and practice. In K. A. Renninger, S. Hidi, & A. Krapp (Eds.), *The role of interest in learning and development* (pp. 361–395). Hillsdale, NJ: Erlbaum.

Renshaw, P. D. & Brown, P. J. (1993). Loneliness in middle childhood: Concurrent and longitudinal predictors. *Child Development, 64,* 1271–1284.

Resches, M., & Pérez Pereira, M. (2007). Referential communication abilities and theory of mind development in preschool children. *Journal of Child Language, 34,* 21–52.

Resnick, L. B. (1986). The development of mathematical intuition. In M. Perlmutter (Ed.), *Perspectives on intellectual development: The Minnesota symposia on child psychology* (Vol. 19, pp. 159–194). Hillsdale, NJ: Erlbaum.

Resnick, L. B. (1995). Inventing arithmetic: Making children's intuitions work at school. In C. A. Nelson (Ed.), *Basic and applied perspectives on learning, cognition, and development. Minnesota Symposia on Child Psychology* (Vol. 28, pp. 75–101). Mahwah, NJ: Erlbaum.

Resnick, L. B., & Singer, J. A. (1993). Protoquantitative origins of ratio reasoning. In T. P. Carpenter, E. Fennema, & T. A. Romberg (Eds.), *Rational numbers: An integration of research* (pp. 107–130). Hillsdale, NJ: Erlbaum.

Reynolds, A. J., Ou, S., & Topitzes, J. W. (2004). Paths of effects of early childhood intervention on educational attainment and delinquency: A confirmatory analysis of the Chicago Child-Parent Centers. *Child Development, 75,* 1299–1328.

Reynolds, A. J., Temple, J. A., Robertson, D. L., & Mann, E. A. (2001). Long-term effects of an early childhood intervention on educational achievement and juvenile arrest: A 15-year follow-up of low income children in public schools. *Journal of the American Medical Association, 285,* 2339–2346.

Reznick, J. S., & Goldfield, B. A. (1992). Rapid change in lexical development in comprehension and production. *Developmental Psychology, 28,* 406–413.

Rhee, K. E., Lumeng, J. C., Appugliese, D. P., Kaciroti, N., & Bradley, R. H. (2006). Parenting styles and overweight status in first grade. *Pediatrics, 117,* 2047–2054.

Rhee, S., Chang, J., & Rhee, J. (2003). Acculturation, communication patterns, and self-esteem among Asian and Caucasian American adolescents. *Adolescence, 38,* 749–768.

Rheingold, H. L., & Cook, K. V. (1975). The contents of boys' and girls' rooms as an index of parents' behavior. *Child Development, 46,* 459–463.

Rhodes, J. E., Grossman, J. B., & Resch, N. L. (2000). Agents of change: Pathways through which mentoring relationships influence adolescents' academic adjustment. *Child Development, 71,* 1662–1671.

Rice, K. G. (1990). Attachment in adolescence: A narrative and meta-analytic review. *Journal of Youth and Adolescence, 19,* 511–538.

Rice, M. L. (1983). The role of television in language acquisition. *Developmental Review, 3,* 211–224.

Rice, M. L., Huston, A. C., Truglio, R., & Wright, J. (1990). Words from "Sesame Street": Learning vocabulary while viewing. *Developmental Psychology, 26,* 421–428.

Rice, M. L., & Woodsmall, L. (1988). Lessons from television: Children's word learning when viewing. *Child Development, 59,* 420–429.

Richards, H. G., Bear, G. G., Stewart, A. L., & Norman, A. D. (1992). Moral reasoning and classroom conduct: Evidence for a curvilinear relationship. *Merrill-Palmer Quarterly, 38,* 176–190.

Richards, H. G., Frentzen, B., Gerhardt, K. J., McCann, M. E., & Abrams, R. M. (1992). Sound levels in the human uterus. *Obstetrics and Gynecology, 80,* 186–190.

Richards, J. E., & Holley, F. B. (1999). Infant attention and the development of smooth pursuit tracking. *Developmental Psychology, 35,* 856–867.

Richards, J. E., Reynolds, G. D., & Courage, M. L. (2010). The neural basis of infant attention. *Current Directions in Psychological Science, 19,* 41–46.

Richards, M. H., Crowe, P. A., Larson, R., & Swarr, A. (1998). Developmental patterns and gender diff erences in the experience of peer companionship during adolescence. *Child Development, 69,* 154–163.

Richardson, K., & Norgate, S. H. (2006). A critical analysis of IQ studies of adopted children. *Human Development, 49,* 319–335.

Rideout, V. J., & Hamel, E. (2006). *The media family: Electronic media in the lives of infants, toddlers, preschoolers and their parents.* Menlo Park, CA: Henry J. Kaiser Family Foundation.

Rideout, V. J., Vandewater, E. A., & Wartella, E. A. (2003). *Zero to six: Electronic media in the lives of infants, toddlers, and preschoolers.* Menlo Park, CA: Kaiser Family Foundation. Retrieved June 22, 2010, from http://www.kff.org/entmedia/loader.cfm?url=/commonspot/security/getfile.cfm&PageID=22754

Rimoin, D. L., Connor, J. M., Pyeritz, R. E., & Korf, B. R. (2002). Nature and frequency of genetic disease. In D. L. Rimoin, J. M. Connor, R. E. Pyeritz, & B. R. Korf (Eds.), *Emery and Rimoin's priniciples and practice of medical genetics.* (4th ed., Vol. 1, pp. 55–59). London, UK: Churchill Livington.

Rivera-Gaxiola, M., Silva-Pereyra, J., & Kuhl, P. K. (2005). Brain potentials to native and non-native speech contrasts in 7- and 11-month-old American infants. *Developmental Science, 8,* 162–172.

Robb, M. B., Richert, R. A., & Wartella, E. A. (2009). Just a talking book? Word learning from watching baby videos. *British Journal of Developmental Psychology, 27,* 27–45.

Roberts, D. F., & Foehr, U. G. (2004). *Kids and media in America.* New York, NY: Cambridge University Press.

Roberts, D. F., & Foehr, U. G. (2008, Spring). Trends in media use. *The Future of Children, 18* (1), 11–37,

Roberts, D. F., Foehr, U. G., & Rideout, V. (2005). *Generation M: Media in the lives of 8–18-year-olds.* Menlo Park, CA: Kaiser Family Foundation.

Roberts, W., & Strayer, J. (1996). Empathy, emotional expressiveness, and prosocial behavior. *Child Development, 67,* 449–470.

Roberts, Y. H., Mitchell, M. J., Witman, M., & Taffaro, C. (2010). Mental health symptoms in youth affected by Hurricane Katrina. *Professional Psychology: Research and Practice, 41,* 10–18.

Robbins, W. J., Brody, S., Hogan, A. G., Jackson, C. M., & Green, C. W. (Eds.). (1928). *Growth.* New Haven, CT: Yale University Press.

Robins, R. W., & Trzesniewski, K. H. (2005). Self-esteem development across the lifespan (pp. 191–203). *Current Directions in Psychological Science, 14,* 158–162.

Robinson, A., & Clinkenbeard, P. R. (1998). Giftedness: An exceptionality examined. *Annual Review of Psychology, 49,* 117–139.

Robinson, C. C., Anderson, G. T., Porter, C. L., Hart, C. H., & Wouden-Miller, M. (2003). Sequential transition patterns of preschoolers' social interactions during child-initiated play: Is parallel-aware play a bidirectional bridge to other play states? *Early Childhood Research Quarterly, 18,* 3–21.

Robinson, J. L., Kagan, J., Reznick, J. S., & Corley, R. (1992). The heritability of inhibited and uninhibited behavior: A twin study. *Developmental Psychology, 28,* 1030–1037.

Robinson, J. L., Zahn-Waxler, C., & Emde, R. N. (1994). Patterns of development in early empathic behavior: Environmental and child constitutional influences. *Social Development, 3,* 125–145.

Robinson, T. N. (2001). Television viewing and childhood obesity. *Pediatric Clinics of North America, 48,* 1017–1026.

Robinson, T. N., Chang, J. Y., Haydel, K. F., & Killen, J. D. (2001). Overweight concerns and body dissatisfaction among third-grade children: The impacts of ethnicity and socioeconomic status. *Journal of Pediatrics, 138,* 181–187.

Rochat, P. (1993). Hand-mouth coordination in the newborn: Morphology, determinants, and early development of a basic act. In G. J. P. Savelsbergh (Ed.), *The development of coordination in infancy* (pp. 265–288). Amsterdam, The Netherlands: Elsevier.

Rochat, P. (2004). *The infant's world.* Cambridge, MA: Harvard University Press.

Rochat, P. (2009). *Others in mind: Social origins of self-consciousness.* Cambridge, MA: Cambridge University Press.

Rochat, P., & Goubet, N. (1995). Development of sitting and reaching in 5- to 6-month-old infants. *Infant Behavior and Development, 18,* 53–68.

Rochat, P., & Morgan, R. (1995). Spatial determinants in perception of self-produced leg movements by 3- to 5-month-old infants. *Developmental Psychology, 31,* 626–636.

Rochat, P., & Striano, T. (1999). Social-cognitive development in the first year. In P. Rochat (Ed.), *Early social cognition: Understanding in the first months of life* (pp. 3–34). Mahwah, NJ: Erlbaum.

Rochat, P., & Striano, T. (2002). Who's in the mirror? Self-other discrimination in specular images by four- and nine-month-old infants. *Child Development, 73,* 35–46.

Roffwarg, H. P., Muzio, J. N., & Dement, W. C. (1966). Ontogenetic development of the human sleep-dream cycle. *Science, 152,* 604–619.

Rogeness, G. A., & McClure, E. B. (1996). Development and neurotransmitter- environmental interactions. *Development and Psychopathology, 8,* 183–199.

Rogoff, B. (1998). Cognition as a collaborative process. In W. Damon (Series Ed.) & D. Kuhn & R. S. Siegler (Vol. Eds.), *Handbook of child psychology: Vol. 2. Cognition, perception, and language* (5th ed., pp. 679–744). New York, NY: Wiley.

Rogoff, B. (2003). *The cultural nature of human development.* New York, NY: Oxford University Press.

Rogoff, B., Mistry, J., Göncü, A., & Mosier, C. (1993). Guided participation in cultural activity by toddlers and caregivers. *Monographs of the Society for Research in Child Development, 58* (8, Serial No. 236).

Rosch, E., Mervis, C. B., Gray, W. D., Johnson, D. M., & Boyes-Braem, P. (1976). Basic objects in natural categories. *Cognitive Psychology, 8,* 382–439.

Roschelle, J. M., Pea, R. D., Hoadley, C. M., Gordin, D. N., & Means, B. M. (2000, Fall/Winter). Changing how and what children learn in school with computer-based technologies. *Future of Children, 10*(2), 76–101.

Rose, A. J., & Asher, S. R. (1999). Children's goals and strategies in response to conflicts within a friendship. *Developmental Psychology, 35,* 69–79.

Rose, A. J., & Asher, S. R. (2004). Children's strategies and goals in response to help-giving and help-seeking tasks within a friendship. *Child Development, 75,* 749–763.

Rose, A. J., Swenson, L. P., & Waller, E. M. (2004). Overt and relational aggression and perceived popularity: Developmental differences in concurrent and prospective relations. *Developmental Psychology, 40,* 378–387.

Rose, S. A., Feldman, J. F., & Jankowski, J. J. (2001a). Attention and recognition memory in the 1st year of life: A longitudinal study of preterm and full-term infants. *Developmental Psychology, 37,* 135–151.

Rose, S. A., Feldman, J. F., & Jankowski, J. J. (2001b). Visual short-term memory in the first year of life: Capacity and recency effects. *Developmental Psychology, 37,* 539–549.

Rose, S. A., Feldman, J. F., & Jankowski, J. J. (2009). A cognitive approach to the development of early language. *Child Development, 80,* 134–150.

Rose, S. A., Feldman, J. F., Jankowski, J. J., & Van Rossem, R. (2005). Pathways from prematurity and infant abilities to later cognition. *Child Development, 76,* 1172–1184.

Rosen, K. S., & Burke, P. B. (1999). Multiple attachment relationships within families: Mothers and fathers with two young children. *Developmental Psychology, 35,* 436–444.

Rosenberg, K. R., & Trevathen, W. R. (2001, November). The evolution of human birth. *Scientific American, 285,* 72–77.

Rosenkoetter, L. I. (1973). Resistance to temptation: Inhibitory and disinhibitory effects of models. *Developmental Psychology, 8,* 80–84.

Rosenshine, B., & Meister, C. (1994). Reciprocal teaching: A review of research. *Review of Educational Research, 64,* 479–530.

Rosenthal, R., & Jacobson, L. (1968). *Pygmalion in the classroom: Teacher expectation and pupils' intellectual development.* New York, NY: Holt, Rinehart & Winston.

Roseth, C. J., Johnson, D. W., & Johnson, R. T. (2008). Promoting early adolescents' achievement and peer relationships: The effects of cooperation, competition, and individualistic goal structures. *Psychological Bulletin, 134,* 223–246.

Ross, G. S. (1980). Categorization in infancy. *Developmental Psychology, 16,* 391–396.

Ross, H., & Howe, N. (2009). Family influences on children's peer relationships. In K. H. Rubin, W. M. Bukowski, & B. Laursen (Eds.), *Handbook of peer interactions, relationships, and groups* (pp. 508–527). New York, NY: Guilford Press.

Rossman, B. R. (1992). School-age children's perceptions of coping with distress: Strategies for emotion regulation and the moderation of adjustment. *Journal of Child Psychology and Psychiatry, 33,* 1373–1397.

Rothbart, M. K., Ahadi, S. A., & Evans, D. E. (2000). Temperament and personality: Origins and outcomes. *Journal of Personality and Social Psychology, 78,* 122–135.

Rothbart, M. K., Ahadi, S. A., & Hershey, K. L. (1994). Temperament and social behavior in childhood. *Merrill-Palmer Quarterly, 40,* 21–39.

Rothbart, M. K., & Bates, J. E. (2006). Temperament. In W. Damon & R. M. Lerner (Editors-in-Chief) & N. Eisenberg (Vol. Eds.), *Handbook of child psychology, Vol. 3. Social, emotional, and personality development* (6th ed., pp. 99–166). Hoboken, NJ: Wiley.

Rothbart, M. K., Derryberry, D., & Posner, M. I. (1994). A psychobiological approach to the development of temperament. In J. E. Bates & T. D. Wachs (Eds.), *Temperament: Individual differences at the interface of biology and behavior* (pp. 83–116). Washington, DC: American Psychological Association.

Rothbart, M. K., & Hwang, J. (2005). Temperament. In A. J. Elliot, & C. S. Dweck (Eds.), *Handbook of competence & motivation* (pp. 167–184). New York, NY: Guilford Press.

Rothbaum, F., Weisz, J., Pott, M., Miyake, K., & Morelli, G. (2000). Attachment and culture: Security in the United States and Japan. *American Psychologist, 55,* 1093–1104.

Rousseau, J. J. (1895). *Émile: Or, treatise on education* (W. H. Payne, Trans.). New York, NY: Appleton. (Original work published 1762).

Rovee-Collier, C. (1999). The development of infant memory. *Current Directions in Psychological Science, 8,* 80–85.

Rovee-Collier, C., & Hayne, H. (1987). Reactivation of infant memory: Implications for cognitive development. In H. W. Reese (Ed.), *Advances in child development and behavior* (Vol. 20, pp. 185–238). San Diego, CA: Academic Press.

Rovee-Collier, C. K. (1987). Learning and memory in infancy. In J. D. Osofsky (Ed.), *Handbook of infant development* (2nd ed., pp. 98–148). New York, NY: Wiley.

Rovee-Collier, C. K., & Shyi, G. (1992). A functional and cognitive analysis of infant long-term retention. In M. L. Howe, C. J. Brainerd, & V. F. Reyna (Eds.), *Development of long-term retention* (pp. 3–55). New York, NY: Springer-Verlag.

Rovee-Collier, C., Schechter, A., Shyi, G. C. W., & Shields, P. (1992). Perceptual identification of contextual attributes and infant memory retrieval. *Developmental Psychology, 28,* 307–318.

Rowe, D. C., Jacobson, K. C., & Van den Oord, E. J. C. G. (1999). Genetic and environmental influences on vocabulary IQ: Parental education level as moderator. *Child Development, 70,* 1151–1162.

Rubin, K., Fredstrom, B., & Bowker, J. (2008). Future directions in . . . Friendship in childhood and early adolescence. *Social Development, 17,* 1085–1096.

Rubin, K. H., & Asendorpf, J. B. (1993). Social withdrawal, inhibition, and shyness in childhood: Conceptual and definitional issues. In K. H. Rubin & J. B. Asendorpf (Eds.), *Social withdrawal, inhibition, and shyness in childhood* (pp. 3–17). Hillsdale, NJ: Erlbaum.

Rubin, K. H., Bowker, J. C., & Kennedy, A. E. (2009). Avoiding and withdrawing from the peer group. In K. H. Rubin, W. M. Bukowski, & B. Laursen (Eds.), *Handbook of peer interactions, relationships, and groups* (pp. 303–321). New York, NY: Guilford Press.

Rubin, K. H., Bukowski, W., & Parker, J. G. (2006). Peer interactions, relationships, and groups. In W. Damon & R. M. Lerner (Editors-in-Chief) & N. Eisenberg (Ed.), *Handbook of child psychology: Vol. 3. Social,* *emotional, and personality development* (6th ed., pp. 1003–1067). Hoboken, NJ: Wiley.

Rubin, K. H., Coplan, R. J., & Bowker, J. C. (2009). Social withdrawal in childhood. *Annual Review of Psychology, 60,* 141–171.

Rubin, K. H., & Krasnor, L. R. (1986). Social-cognitive and social behavioral perspectives on problem-solving. In M. Perlmutter (Ed.), *The Minnesota symposia on child psychology: Vol. 18. Cognitive perspectives on children's social and behavioral development* (pp. 1–68). Hillsdale, NJ: Erlbaum.

Rubin, K. H., Lynch, D., Coplan, R., Rose-Krasnor, L., & Booth, C. L. (1994). "Birds of a feather . . .": Behavioral concordances and preferential personal attraction in children. *Child Development, 65,* 1778–1785.

Rubin, K. H., Maioni, T. L., & Hornung, M. (1976). Free play behaviors in middle- and lower-class preschoolers: Parten and Piaget revisited. *Child Development, 47,* 414–419.

Rubinowitz, L. S., & Rosenbaum, J. E. (2000). *Crossing the class and color lines: From public housing to white suburbia.* Chicago, IL: University of Chicago Press.

Ruble, D. N. (1987). The acquisition of self-knowledge: A self-socialization perspective. In N. Eisenberg (Ed.), *Contemporary topics in developmental psychology* (pp. 243–270). New York, NY: Wiley.

Ruble, D. N., Boggiano, A. K., Feldman, N. S., & Loebl, J. H. (1980). Developmental analysis of the role of social comparison in self-evaluation. *Developmental Psychology, 16,* 105–115.

Ruble, D. N., & Brooks-Gunn, J. (1982). The experience of menarche. *Child Development, 53,* 1557–1566.

Ruble, D. N., Eisenberg, R., & Higgins, E. T. (1994). Developmental changes in achievement evaluation: Motivational implications of self-other differences. *Child Development, 65,* 1095–1110.

Ruble, D. N., & Flett, G. L. (1988). Conflicting goals in self-evaluative information seeking: Developmental and ability level analyses. *Child Development, 59,* 97–106.

Ruble, D. N., Martin, C. L., & Berenbaum, S. A. (2006). Gender development. In W. Damon & R. M. Lerner (Editors-in-Chief) & N. Eisenberg (Vol. Ed.), *Handbook of child psychology. Vol. 3. Social, emotional, and personality development* (6th ed., pp. 858–932). Hoboken, NJ: Wiley.

Ruble, D. N., Taylor, L. J., Cyphers, L., Greulich, F. K., Lurye, L. E., & Shrout, P. E. (2007). The role of gender constancy in early gender development. *Child Development, 78,* 1121–1136.

Rudolph, K. D., Caldwell, M., & Conley, C. S. (2005). Need for approval and children's well-being. *Child Development, 76,* 309–323.

Rudolph, K. D., & Hammen, C. (1999). Age and gender as determinants of stress exposure, generation, and reactions in youngsters: A transactional perspective. *Child Development, 70,* 660–677.

Rudolph, K. D., Lambert, S. F., Clark, A. G., & Kurlakowsky, K. D. (2001). Negotiating the transition to middle school: The role of self-regulatory processes. *Child Development, 72,* 929–946.

Rudy, D., & Grusec, J. E. (2006). Social cognitive approaches to parenting representations. In O. Mayseless (Ed.), *Parenting representations: Theory, research, and clinical implications* (pp. 79–106). Cambridge, UK: Cambridge University Press.

Ruff, H. A., Capozzoli, M., & Weissberg, R. (1998). Age, individuality, and context as factors in sustained visual attention during the preschool years. *Developmental Psychology, 34,* 454–464.

Ruff, H. A., & Lawson, K. R. (1990). Development of sustained, focused attention in young children during free play. *Developmental Psychology, 26,* 85–93.

Ruff, H. A., & Rothbart, M. K. (1996). *Attention and early development: Themes and variations.* New York, NY: Oxford University Press.

Ruffman, T., Slade, L., & Crowe, E. (2002). The relation between children's and mothers' mental state language and theory-of-mind understanding. *Child Development, 73,* 734–751.

Rushton, J. P. (1975). Generosity in children: Immediate and long-term effects of modeling, preaching, and moral judgment. *Journal of Personality and Social Psychology, 31,* 459–466.

Russell, G., & Russell, A. (1987). Mother-child and father-child relationships in middle childhood. *Child Development, 58,* 1573–1585.

Rutter, M. (1983). School effects on pupil progress: Research findings and policy implications. *Child Development, 54,* 1–29.

Rutter, M. (1986). Meyerian psychobiology, personality development, and the role of life experiences. *American Journal of Psychiatry, 143,* 1077–1087.

Rutter, M. (1990). Psychosocial resilience and protective mechanisms. In J. Rolf, A. S. Masten, D. Cicchetti, K. H. Neuchterlein, & S. Weintraub (Eds.), *Risk and protective factors in the development of psychopathology* (pp. 79–101). New York, NY: Cambridge University Press.

Rutter, M. (1991). Age changes in depressive disorders: Some developmental considerations. In J. Garber & K. A. Dodge (Eds.), *The development of emotion regulation and dysregulation* (pp. 273–300). Cambridge, UK: Cambridge University Press.

Rutter, M. (2006). *Genes and behavior: Nature–nurture interplay explained.* Oxford: Blackwell.

Rutter, M., Beckett, C., Castle, J., Colvert, E., et al., (2009). Effects of profound early institutional deprivation: An overview of findings from a UK longitudinal study of Romanian adoptees. In G. M. Wrobel & E. Neil (Eds.), *International advances in adoption research for practice* (pp. 147–167). West Sussex, UK: Wiley.

Rutter, M., & Garmezy, N. (1983). Developmental psychopathology. In E. M. Hetherington (Ed.), *Handbook of child psychology: Vol. IV. Socialization, personality, and social development* (4th ed., pp. 775–911). New York, NY: Wiley.

Rutter, M., & Madge, N. (1976). *Cycles of disadvantage.* London, UK: Heinemmann.

Rutter, M., Maughan, B., Mortimore, P., Ouston, J., & Smith, A. (1979). *Fifteen thousand hours: Secondary schools and their effects on children.* Cambridge, MA: Harvard University Press.

Rutter, M., Silberg, J., O'Connor, T., & Simonoff, E. (1999a). Genetics and child psychiatry: I. Advances in quantitative and molecular genetics. *Journal of Child Psychology and Psychiatry, 40,* 3–18.

Rutter, M., Silberg, J., O'Connor, T., & Simonoff, E. (1999b). Genetics and child psychiatry: II. Empirical research findings. *Journal of Child Psychology and Psychiatry, 40,* 19–55.

Rutter, M., & Silberg, J. (2002). Gene-environment interplay in relation to emotional and behavioral disturbance. *Annual Review of Psychology, 53,* 463–490.

Ryan, R. M., & Grolnick, W. S. (1986). Origins and pawns in the classroom: Self-report and projective assessments of individual differences in children's perceptions. *Journal of Personality and Social Psychology, 50,* 550–558.

Saarni, C. (1998). Issues of cultural meaningfulness in emotional development. *Developmental Psychology, 34,* 647–652.

Saarni, C. (1999). *The development of emotional competence.* New York, NY: Guilford.

Saarni, C., Campos, J. J., Camras, L. A. & Witherinton, D. (2006). Emotional development: Action, communication, and understanding. In W. Damon & R. M. Lerner (Editors-in-Chief) & N. Eisenberg (Vol. Eds.), *Handbook of child psychology, Vol. 3. Social, emotional, and personality development* (6th ed., pp. 226–299). Hoboken, NJ: Wiley.

Sadker, M. & Sadker, D. (1994). *Failing at fairness: How America's schools cheat girls.* New York, NY: Charles Scribner's Sons.

Sadler, T. M. (2004). *Langman's medical embryology* (9th ed.). Philadelphia, PA: Lippincott Williams & Wilkins.

Saffran, J. R. (2001). Words in a sea of sounds: The output of infant statistical learning. *Cognition, 81,* 149–169.

Saffran, J. R. (2003). Absolute pitch in infancy and adulthood: The role of tonal structure. *Developmental Science, 6,* 35–43.

Saffran, J. R., Aslin, R. N., & Newport, E. (1996). Statistical learning by 8-month-olds. *Science, 274,* 1926–1928.

Saffran, J. R., Loman, M. M., & Robertson, R. R. W. (2000). Infant memory for musical experiences. *Cognition, 77,* B15–B23.

Saffran, J. R., Werker, J. F., & Werner, L. A. (2006). The infant's auditory world: Hearing, speech, and the beginning of language. In W. Damon & R. M. Lerner (Editors-in-Chief) & D. M. Kuhn & R. S. Siegler (Vol. Eds.), *Handbook of child psychology, Vol. 2. Cognition, perception, and language* (6th ed., pp. 58–108). Hoboken, NJ: Wiley.

Sagi, A., Lamb, M. E., Lewkowicz, K. S., Shoham, R., Dvir, R., & Estes, D. (1985). Security of infant-mother, -father, and -metapelet attachments among kibbutz-reared Israeli children. In I. Bretherton & E. Waters (Eds.), *Growing points of attachment theory and research. Monographs of the Society for Research in Child Development, 50* (1–2, Serial No. 209).

Sagi, A., Van IJzendoorn, M. H., Aviezer, O., Donnell, F., & Mayseless, O. (1994). Sleeping out of home in a kibbutz communal arrangement: It makes a difference for mother-child attachment. *Child Development, 65,* 991–1004.

Saigal, S., Stoskopf, B., Streiner, D., Boyle, M., Pinelli, J., Paneth, N., & Goddeeris, J. (2006). Transition of extremely low-birth-weight infants from adolescence to young adulthood: Comparison with normal birth-weight controls. *JAMA, 295,* 667–675.

Sakala, C. (1993). Midwifery care and out-of-hospital birth settings: How do they reduce unnecessary cesarean section births? *Social Science and Medicine, 37,* 1233–1250.

Salapatek, P. (1975). Pattern perception in early infancy. In L. B. Cohen & P. Salapatek (Eds.), *Infant perception: From sensation to cognition* (Vol. 1, pp. 143–248). New York, NY: Academic Press.

Salman, M. S., Sharpe, J. A., Eizenman, M., Lillakas, L., Westall, C., To, T., . . . & Steinbach, M. J. (2006). Saccades in children. *Vision Research, 46,* 1432–1439.

Salmivalli, C. (2010). Bullying and the peer group: A review. *Aggression and Violent Behavior, 15,* 112–120.

Salmivalli, C., & Peets, K. (2009). Bullies, victims, and bully-victim relationships in middle childhood and early adolescence. In K. H. Rubin, W. M. Bukowski, & B. Laursen (Eds.), *Handbook of peer interactions, relationships, and groups* (pp. 322–340). New York, NY: Guilford Press.

Salzinger, S., Feldman, R. S., Hammer, M., & Rosario, M. (1993). The effects of physical abuse on children's social relationships. *Child Development, 64,* 169–187.

Samarapungavan, A. (1992). Children's judgments in theory choice tasks: Scientific rationality in childhood. *Cognition, 45,* 1–32.

Sameroff, A. J. (1972). Learning and adaptation in infancy: A comparison of models. In H. W. Reese (Ed.), *Advances in child development and behavior* (Vol. 7, pp. 170–214). New York, NY: Academic Press.

Sameroff, A. J. (2005). The science of infancy: Academic, social, and political agendas. *Infancy, 7,* 219–242.

Sameroff, A. J. (Ed.) (2009). *The transactional model of development: How children and contexts shape each other.* Washington, DC: American Psychological Association.

Sameroff, A. J., & Chandler, P. J. (1975). Reproductive risk and the continuum of caretaking casualty. In F. D. Horowitz (Ed.), *Review of child development research* (Vol. 4, pp. 187–244). Chicago, IL: University of Chicago Press.

Sampson, R. J., Raudenbush, S. W., & Earls, F. (1997). Neighborhoods and violent crime: A multilevel study of collective efficacy. *Science, 277,* 918–924.

Samuelson, L. K., & Smith, L. B. (2000). Children's attention to rigid and deformable shape in naming and non-naming tasks. *Child Development, 71,* 1555–1570.

Sandberg, D. E., Brook, A. E., & Campos, S. P. (1994). Short stature: A psychosocial burden requiring growth hormone therapy? *Pediatrics, 94,* 832–840.

Sandberg, D. E., Meyer-Bahlburg, H. F., Ehrhardt, A. A., & Yager, T. J. (1993). The prevalence of gender-atypical behavior in elementary school. *Journal of the American Academy of Child and Adolescent Psychiatry, 32,* 306–314.

Sandberg, E. H., & Huttenlocher, J. (2001). Advanced spatial skills and advance planning: Components of 6-year-olds' navigational map use. *Journal of Cognition and Development, 2,* 51–70.

Sanders, C. E., Field, T. M., Diego, M., & Kaplan, M. (2000). The relationship of Internet use to depression and social isolation among adolescents. *Adolescence, 35,* 237–242.

Sann, C., & Streri, A. (2007). Perception of object shape and texture in newborn infants: Evidence from cross-modal tasks. *Developmental Science, 10,* 399–410.

Santrock, J. W., & Sitterle, K. A. (1987). Parent-child relationships in stepmother families. In K. Pasley & M. Ihinger-Tallman (Eds.), *Remarriage and stepparenting: Current research and theory* (pp. 273–299). New York, NY: Guilford Press.

Savin-Williams, R. C. (1980). Dominance hierarchies in groups of middle to late adolescent males. *Journal of Youth and Adolescence, 9,* 75–85.

Sawin, D. B., & Parke, R. D. (1979). The effects of interagent inconsistent discipline on children's aggressive behavior. *Journal of Experimental Child Psychology, 28,* 525–538.

Saxton, M. (1997). The contrast theory of negative input. *Journal of Child Language, 24,* 139–161.

Scaramella, L. V., Conger, R. D., & Simons, R. L. (1999). Parental protective influences and gender-specific increases in adolescent internalizing and externalizing problems. *Journal of Research on Adolescence, 9,* 111–141.

Scaramella, L. V., Conger, R. D., Spoth, R., & Simons, R. L. (2002). Evaluating a social contextual model of delinquency: A cross-study replication. *Child Development, 73,* 175–195.

Scarborough, H. S., & Dobrich, W. (1993). On the efficacy of reading to preschoolers. *Developmental Review, 14,* 245–302.

Scarr, S. (1992). Developmental theories for the 1990s: Development and individual differences. *Child Development, 63,* 1–19.

Scarr, S. (1993). Biological and cultural diversity: The legacy of Darwin for development. *Child Development, 64,* 1333–1353.

Scarr, S., & McCartney, K. (1983). How people make their own environments: A theory of genotype environment effects. *Child Development, 54,* 424–435.

Scarr, S., Webber, P. L., Weinberg, R. A., & Wittig, M. A. (1981). Personality resemblance among adolescents and their parents in biologically related and adoptive families. *Journal of Personality and Social Psychology, 40,* 885–898.

Scarr, S., & Weinberg, R. A. (1976). IQ test performance of black children adopted by white families. *American Psychologist, 31,* 726–739.

Scarr, S., & Weinberg, R. A. (1977). Intellectual similarities within families of both adopted and biological children. *Intelligence, 1,* 170–191.

Scarr, S., & Weinberg, R. A. (1978). The influence of "family background" on intellectual attainment. *American Sociological Review, 43,* 674–692.

Scarr, S., & Weinberg, R. A. (1983). The Minnesota adoption studies: Genetic differences and malleability. *Child Development, 54,* 260–267.

Schachar, R., Mota, V., Logan, G. D., Tannock, R., & Klim, P. (2000). Confirmation of an inhibitory control deficit in attention-deficit/hyperactivity disorder. *Journal of Abnormal Child Psychology, 28,* 227–235.

Schachter, F. F. (1982). Sibling deidentification and split-parent identification: A family tetrad. In M. E. Lamb & B. Sutton-Smith (Eds.), *Sibling relationships: Their nature and significance across the life-span* (pp. 123–151). Hillsdale, NJ: Erlbaum.

Schaffer, H. R., & Emerson, P. E. (1964). The development of social attachments in infancy. *Monographs of the Society for Research in Child Development, 29* (3, Serial No. 94).

Schauble, L. (1996). The development of scientific reasoning in knowledge-rich contexts. *Developmental Psychology, 32,* 102–119.

Scheper-Hughes, N. (1992). *Death without weeping: The violence of everyday life in Brazil.* Berkeley: University of California Press.

Schetter, C. D. (2009). Stress processes in pregnancy and preterm birth. *Current Directions in Psychological Science, 18,* 205–209.

Schieffelin, B. B., & Ochs, E. (1983). A cultural perspective on the transition from prelinguistic to linguistic communication. In R. M. Golinkoff (Ed.), *The transition from prelinguistic to linguistic communication* (pp. 115–131). Hillsdale, NJ: Erlbaum.

Schlegel, A., & Barry, H. III. (1991). *Adolescence: An anthropological inquiry.* New York, NY: Free Press.

Schlinger, H. D., Jr. (1992). Theory in behavior analysis: An application to child development. *American Psychologist, 47,* 1396–1410.

Schmidt, M. E., & Vandewater, E. A. (2008, Spring). Media and attention, cognition, and school achievement. Special issue: Children and electronic media. *The Future of Children, 18*(1), 63–85.

Schmidt, M. K., Pempek, T. A., Kirkorian, H. L., Lund, A. F., & Anderson, D. R. (2008). The impact of background television on very young children. *Child Development, 79,* 1137–1151.

Schmitt, K. L., & Anderson, D. R. (2002). Television and reality: Toddlers' use of visual information from video to guide behavior. *Media Psychology, 4,* 51–76.

Schmitt, K. L., Anderson, D. R., & Collins, P. A. (1999). Form and content: Looking at visual features of television. *Developmental Psychology, 35,* 1156–1167.

Schneider, B. H., Atkinson, L., & Tardif, C. (2001). Child-parent attachment and children's peer relations: A quantitative review. *Developmental Psychology, 37,* 86–100.

Schneider, B. H., & Byrne, B. M. (1985). Children's social skills training: A meta-analysis. In B. H. Schneider, K. H. Rubin, & J. E. Ledingham (Eds.), *Children's peer relations: Issues in assessment and intervention* (pp. 179–192). New York, NY: Springer-Verlag.

Schneider, W. (2000). Research on memory development: Historical trends and current themes. *International Journal of Behavioral Development, 24,* 407–420.

Schneider, W., & Lockl, K. (2002). The development of metacognitive knowledge in children and adolescents. In B. L. Schwartz & T. J. Perfect (Eds.), *Applied metacognition* (pp. 224–260). Cambridge, UK: Cambridge University Press.

Schneider-Rosen, K., Braunwald, K., Carlson, V., & Cicchetti, D. (1985). Current perspectives on attachment theory: Illustrations from the study of maltreated infants. In I. Bretherton & E. Waters (Eds.), *Growing points of attachment theory and research. Monographs of the Society for Research in Child Development, 50* (1–2, Serial No. 209).

Schölmerich, A., Fracasso, M. P., Lamb, M. E., & Broberg, A. (1995). Interactional harmony at 7 and 10 months of age predicts security of attachment as measured by Q-sort ratings. *Social Development, 4,* 62–74.

Schore, A. N. (1994). *Affect regulation and the origin of the self: The neurobiology of emotional development.* Hillsdale, NJ: Erlbaum.

Schore, A. N. (1996). The experience-dependent maturation of a regulatory system in the orbital prefrontal cortex and the origin of developmental psychopathology. *Development and Psychopathology, 8,* 59–87.

Schwartz, D., Dodge, K. A., Pettit, G. S., Bates, J. E., & Conduct Problems Prevention Research Group. (2000). Friendship as a moderating factor in the pathway between early harsh home environment and later victimization in the peer group. *Developmental Psychology, 36,* 646–662.

Schwartz, S. J. (2008). Self and identity in early adolescence: Some reflections and an introduction to the special issue. *The Journal of Early Adolescence, 28,* 5–15.

Schwartz, S. J., Pantin, H., Prado, G., Sullivan, S., & Szapocznik, J. (2005). Family functioning, identity, and problem behavior in Hispanic immigrant early adolescents. *The Journal of Early Adolescence, 25,* 392–420.

Schweinle, A., & Wilcox, T. (2004). Intermodal perception and physical reasoning in young infants. *Infant Behavior and Development, 27,* 246–265.

Schwekendiek, D. (2008). Height and weight differences between North and South Korea. *Journal of Biosocial Sciences, 41,* 51–55.

Schwenck, C., Bjorklund, D. F., & Schneider, W. (2009). Developmental and individual differences in young children's use and maintenance of a selective memory strategy. *Developmental Psychology, 45*(4), 1034–1050.

Schwier, C., van Maanen, C., Carpenter, M., & Tomasello, M. (2006). Rational imitation in 12-month-old infants. *Infancy, 10,* 303–311.

Scott, L. S., Pascalis, O., & Nelson, C. A. (2007). A domain-general theory of the development of perceptual discrimination. *Current Directions in Psychological Science, 16,* 197–201.

Scott, S. (2007). Conduct disorders in children. *British Medical Journal, 334,* 646.

Seaton, E. K., Caldwell, C. H., Sellers, R. M., & Jackson, J. S. (2008). The prevalence of perceived discrimination among African American and Caribbean black youth. *Developmental Psychology, 44,* 1288–1297.

Seaton, E. K., Yip, T., & Sellers, R. M. (2009). A longitudinal examination of racial identity and racial discrimination among African American adolescents. *Child Development, 80,* 406–417.

Sebanc, A. M. (2003). The friendship features of preschool children: Links with prosocial behavior and aggression. *Social Development, 12,* 249–268.

Segall, M. H., Campbell, D. T., & Herskovits, M. J. (1966). *The influence of culture on perception.* New York, NY: Bobbs-Merrill.

Seidman, E., Allen, L., Aber, J. L., Mitchell, C., & Feinman, J. (1994). The impact of school transitions in early adolescence on the self-system and perceived social context of poor urban youth. *Child Development, 65,* 507–522.

Seitz, V., & Apfel, N. H. (1994). Effects of a school for pregnant students on the incidence of low-birthweight deliveries. *Child Development, 65,* 666–676.

Selzer, J. A. (1991). Relationships between fathers and children who live apart: The father's role after separation. *Journal of Marriage and the Family, 53,* 79–101.

Senghas, A., & Coppola, M. (2001). Children creating language: How Nicaraguan Sign Language acquired a spatial grammar. *Psychological Science, 12,* 323–328.

Serbin, L. A., Connor, J. M., & Iler, I. (1979). Sex-stereotyped and nonstereotyped introductions of new toys in the preschool classroom: An observational study of teacher behavior and its effects. *Psychology of Women Quarterly, 4,* 261–265.

Serbin, L. A., O'Leary, K. D., Kent, R. N., & Tonick, I. J. (1973). A comparison of teacher response to the preacademic and problem behavior of boys and girls. *Child Development, 44,* 796–804.

Serbin, L. A., Poulin-Dubois, D., Colburne, K. A., Sen, M. G., & Eichstedt, J. A. (2001). Gender stereotyping in infancy: Visual preferences for and knowledge of gender-stereotyped toys in the second year. *International Journal of Behavioral Development, 25,* 7–15.

Serbin, L. A., Powlishta, K. K., & Gulko, J. (1993). The development of sex typing in middle childhood. *Monographs of the Society for Research in Child Development, 58* (No. 2, Serial No. 232).

Serbin, L. A., Tonick, I. J., & Sternglanz, S. H. (1977). Shaping cooperative cross-sex play. *Child Development, 48,* 924–929.

Seress, L., & Abraham, H. (2008). Pre- and postnatal morphological development of the human hippocampal formation. In C. Nelson & M. Luciana (Eds.), *Handbook of developmental cognitive neuroscience* (2nd ed., pp. 187–212). Cambridge, MA: MIT Press.

Shachar, H., & Sharan, S. (1994). Talking, relating, and achieving: Effects of cooperative learning and whole-class instruction. *Cognition and Instruction, 12,* 313–353.

Shafer, V. L., & Garrido-Nag, K. (2007). The neurodevelopmental basis of language. In E. Hoff & M. Shatz (Eds.), *Blackwell handbook of language development* (pp. 21–45). Malden, MA: Blackwell.

Shaffer, D., Fisher, P., Dulcan, M. K., Davies, M., Piacentini, J., Schwab-Stone, M. E., . . . & Regier, D. A. (1996). The NIMH Diagnostic Interview Schedule for Children Version 2.3 (DISC-2.3): Description, acceptability, prevalence rates, and performance in the MECA Study. Methods for the epidemiology of child and adolescent mental disorders study. *Journal of the American Academy of Child and Adolescent Psychiatry, 35,* 865–877.

Shah, N. R., & Bracken, M. B. (2000). A systematic review and meta-analysis of prospective studies on the association between maternal cigarette smoking and preterm delivery. *American Journal of Obstetrics and Gynecology, 182,* 465–472.

Shahar, S. (1990). *Childhood in the Middle Ages.* London, UK: Routledge.

Shannon, J. D., Tamis-LeMonda, C. S., & Margolin, A. (2005). Father involvement in infancy: Influences of past and current relationships. *Infancy, 8,* 21–41.

Shantz, C. (1983). Social cognition. In J. H. Flavell & E. M. Markman (Eds.), *Handbook of child psychology: Vol. III. Cognitive development* (4th ed., pp. 495–555). New York, NY: Wiley.

Sharma, A. R., McGue, M. K., & Benson, P. L. (1998). The psychological adjustment of United States adopted adolescents and their non-adopted siblings. *Child Development, 69,* 791–802.

Sharon, T. (2005). Made to symbolize: Intentionality and children's early understanding of symbols. *Journal of Cognition and Development, 6,* 163–178.

Sharp, D., Cole, M., & Lave, C. (1979). Education and cognitive development: The evidence from experimental research. *Monographs of the Society for Research in Child Development, 44* (1–2, Serial No. 178).

Shatz, M., & Gelman, R. (1973). The development of communication skills: Modification in the speech of young children as a function of listener. *Monographs of the Society for Research in Child Development, 38* (5, Serial No. 152).

Shaw, E., & Darling, J. (1985). *Strategies of being female.* Brighton, UK: Harvester Press.

Shaw, P., Eckstrand, K., Sharp, W., Blumenthal, J., Lerch, J. P., Greenstein, D., . . . & Rapoport, J. L. (2007). Attention-deficit/hyperactivity disorder is characterized by a delay in cortical maturation. *Proceedings of the National Academy of Sciences, 104,* 19649–19654.

Shenkin, S. D., Starr, J. M., & Deary, I. J. (2004). Birth weight and cognitive ability in childhood: A systematic review. *Psychological Bulletin, 130,* 989–1013.

Shepard, L. A., & Smith, M. L. (1986). Synthesis of research on school readiness and kindergarten retention. *Educational Leadership, 44,* 78–86.

Sherif, M., Harvey, O. J., White, B. J., Hood, W. R., & Sherif, C. W. (1961). *Inter-group conflict and cooperation: The Robber's Cave experiment.* Norman: University of Oklahoma Press.

Shoda, Y., Mischel, W., & Peake, P. K. (1990). Predicting adolescent cognitive and self-regulatory competencies from preschool delay of gratification: Identifying diagnostic conditions. *Developmental Psychology, 26,* 978–986.

Shonk, S. M., & Cicchetti, D. (2001). Maltreatment, competency deficits, and risk for academic and behavioral maladjustment. *Developmental Psychology, 37,* 3–17.

Shore, R. (1997). *Rethinking the brain: New insights into early development.* New York, NY: Families and Work Institute.

Shostak, M. (1981). *Nisa: The life and words of a !Kung woman.* Cambridge, MA: Harvard University Press.

Shulman, L. P., & Elias, S. (2007). Techniques for prenatal diagnosis. In D. L. Rimoin, J. M. Connor, R. E. Pyeritz, & B. R. Korf (Eds.), *Emery and Rimoin's principles and practice of medical genetics* (5th ed., Vol. 1, pp. 679–702). London, UK: Churchill Livingston.

Shwalb, B. J., Shwalb, D. W., & Shoji, J. (1994). Structure and dimensions of maternal perceptions of Japanese infant temperament. *Developmental Psychology, 30,* 131–141.

Shwe, H. I., & Markman, E. M. (1997). Young children's appreciation of the mental impact of their communicative signals. *Developmental Psychology, 33,* 630–636.

Shweder, R. A., Mahapatra, M., & Miller, J. G. (1987). Culture and moral development. In J. Kagan & S. Lamb (Eds.), *The emergence of morality in young children* (pp. 1–83). Chicago, IL: University of Chicago Press.

Shweder, R., Goodnow, J., Hatano, G., LeVine, R., Markus, H., & Miller, P. (2006). The cultural psychology of development: One mind, many mentalities. In W. Damon & R. M. Lerner (Editors-in-Chief) & R. M. Lerner (Vol. Ed.), *Handbook of child psychology: Vol. 1. Theoretical models of human development* (6th ed., pp. 716–792). Hoboken, NJ: Wiley.

Siddiqui, F., & James, D. (2003). Fetal monitoring in type 1 diabetic pregnancies. *Human Development, 72,* 1–13.

Siegler & Alibali, M. W. (2005). *Children's thinking.* Upper Saddle River, NJ: Prentice-Hall.

Siegler, R. S. (1989). Mechanisms of cognitive development. In M. R. Rosenzweig & L.W. Porter (Eds.), *Annual Review of Psychology, 40,* 353–379.

Siegler, R. S. (1994). Cognitive variability: A key to understanding cognitive development. *Current Directions in Psychological Science, 3,* 1–5.

Siegler, R. S. (1996). *Emerging minds: The process of change in children's thinking.* New York, NY: Oxford University Press.

Siegler, R. S. (1997). Concepts and methods for studying cognitive change. In E. Amsel & K. A. Renninger (Eds.), *Change and development: Issues of theory, method, and application* (pp. 77–97). Mahwah, NJ: Erlbaum.

Siegler, R. S. (2003). Implications of cognitive science research for mathematics education. In J. Kilpatrick, W. B. Martin, & D. E. Schifter (Eds.), *A research companion to principles and standards for mathematics* (pp. 219–233). Reston, VA: National Council of Teachers of Mathematics.

Siegler, R. S. (2006). Microgenetic analyses of learning. In W. Damon & R. M. Lerner (Series Eds.) & D. Kuhn & R. S. Siegler (Vol. Eds.), *Handbook of child psychology: Volume 2: Cognition, perception, and language* (6th ed., pp. 464–510). Hoboken, NJ: Wiley.

Siegler, R. S. (2009). Improving the numerical understanding of children from low-income families. *Child Development Perspectives, 3,* 118–124.

Siegler, R. S., & Crowley, K. (1991). The microgenetic method: A direct means for studying cognitive development. *American Psychologist, 46,* 606–620.

Siegler, R. S., & Jenkins, E. (1989). *How children discover new strategies.* Hillsdale, NJ: Erlbaum.

Siegler, R. S., & Richards, D. D. (1982). The development of intelligence. In R. J. Sternberg (Ed.), *Handbook of human intelligence* (pp. 897–971). Cambridge, UK: Cambridge University Press.

Siegler, R. S., & Robinson, M. (1982). The development of numerical understandings. In H. W. Reese & L. P. Lipsitt (Eds.), *Advances in child development and behavior* (Vol. 16, pp. 242–312). New York, NY: Academic Press.

Siegler, R. S., & Shrager, J. (1984). Strategy choices in addition and subtraction: How do children know what to do? In C. Sophian (Ed.), *Origins of cognitive skills* (pp. 229–293). Hillsdale, NJ: Erlbaum.

Siegler, R. S., & Stern, E. (1998). Conscious and unconscious strategy discoveries: A microgenetic analysis. *Journal of Experimental Psychology: General, 127,* 377–397.

Sigelman, C. K., Carr, M. B., & Begley, N. L. (1986). Developmental changes in the influence of sex-role stereotypes on person perception. *Child Study Journal, 16,* 191–205.

Sigman, M., Cohen, S. E., & Beckwith, L. (1997). Why does infant attention predict adolescent intelligence? *Infant Behavior & Development, 20,* 133–140.

Signorella, M. L. (1987). Gender schemata: Individual differences and context effects. In L. S. Liben & M. L. Signorella (Eds.), *New directions for child development: No. 38. Children's gender schemata* (pp. 23–37). San Francisco, CA: Jossey-Bass.

Signorelli, N. (2001). Television's gender role images and contributions to stereotyping: Past, present, future. In D. Singer & J. Singer (Eds.), *Handbook of children and the media* (pp. 341–358). Thousand Oaks, CA: Sage.

Signorelli, N., & Bacue, A. (1999). Recognition and respect: A content analysis of prime-time television characters across three decades. *Sex Roles, 40,* 527–544.

Silberstein, L., Gardner, H., Phelps, E., & Winner, E. (1982). Autumn leaves and old photographs: The development of metaphor preferences. *Journal of Experimental Child Psychology, 34,* 135–150.

Silk, J. S., Steinberg, L., & Morris, A. S. (2003). Adolescents' emotion regulation in daily life: Links to depressive symptoms and problem behavior. *Child Development, 74,* 1869–1880.

Silver, L. M. (1998, September 21). A quandary that isn't: Picking a baby's sex won't lead to disaster. *Time,* p. 83.

Silverman, W. K., LaGreca, A. M., & Wasserstein, S. (1995). What do children worry about? Worries and their relation to anxiety. *Child Development, 66,* 671–686.

Simcock, G., & Hayne, H. (2002). Breaking the barrier? Children fail to translate their preverbal memories into language. *Psychological Science, 13,* 225–231.

Simion, F., Regolin, L., & Bulf, H. (2008). A predisposition for biological motion in the newborn baby. *Proceedings of the National Academy of Science, 105,* 809–813.

Simkin, P. P., & O'Hara, M. (2002). Nonpharmacologic relief of pain during labor: Systematic reviews of five methods. *American Journal of Obstetrics and Gynecology, 186,* S131–S159.

Simmons, R. G., & Blyth, D. A. (1987). *Moving into adolescence: The impact of pubertal change and school context.* Hawthorne, NY: Aldine de Gruyter.

Simmons, R. G., Blyth, D. A., Van Cleave, E. F., & Bush, D. M. (1979). Entry into early adolescence: The impact of school structure, puberty, and early dating on self-esteem. *American Sociological Review, 44,* 948–967.

Simmons, R. G., Burgeson, R., Carlton-Ford, S., & Blyth, D. A. (1987). The impact of cumulative change in early adolescence. *Child Development, 58,* 1220–1234.

Simner, M. L. (1971). Newborn's response to the cry of another infant. *Developmental Psychology, 5,* 136–150.

Simon, T. J., Hespos, S. J., & Rochat, P. (1995). Do infants understand simple arithmetic? A replication of Wynn (1992). *Cognitive Development, 10,* 253–269.

Simon, V. A., Aikins, J. W., & Prinstein, M. J. (2008). Romantic partner selection and socialization during early adolescence. *Child Development, 79,* 1676–1692.

Simons, R. L., Chao, W., Conger, R., & Elder, G. H. (2001). Quality of parenting as a mediator of the effect of childhood defiance on adolescent friendship choices and delinquency. *Journal of Marriage and Family, 63,* 63–79.

Sinclair, D. (1985). *Human growth after birth* (4th ed.). New York, NY: Oxford University Press.

Singer, J. D., Fuller, B., Keiley, M. K., & Wolf, A. (1998). Early child-care selection: Variation by geographic location, maternal characteristics, and family structure. *Developmental Psychology, 34,* 1129–1144.

Singer, L. M., Brodzinsky, D. M., Ramsay, D., Steir, M., & Waters, E. (1985). Mother-infant attachment in adoptive families. *Child Development, 56,* 1543–1551.

Singer, L. T., Arendt, R., Fagan, J., Minnes, S., Salvator, A., Bolek, T., & Becker, M. (1999). Neonatal visual information processing in cocaine-exposed and non-exposed infants. *Infant Behavior and Development, 22,* 1–15.

Singer, L. T., Minnes, S., Short, E., Arendt, R., Farkas, K., Lewis, B., . . . & Kirchner, H. L. (2004). Cognitive outcomes of preschool children with prenatal cocaine exposure. *JAMA, 291,* 2448–2456.

Singer, L. T., Nelson, S., Short, E., Min, M. O., Lewis, B., Russ, S., & Minnes, S. (2008). Prenatal cocaine exposure: Drug and environmental effects at 9 years. *Journal of Pediatrics, 153,* 105–111.

Singh, L. Morgan, J. L., & Best, C. T. (2002). Infants' listening preferences. Baby talk or happy talk? *Infancy, 3,* 365–394.

Singh, L., & Singh, N. C. (2008). The development of articulatory signatures in children. *Developmental Science, 11,* 467–473.

Sininger, Y. S., Doyle, K. J., & Moore, J. K. (1999). The case for early identification of hearing loss in children: Auditory system development, experimental auditory deprivation, and development of speech and hearing. *Pediatric Clinics of North America, 46,* 1–14.

Sireteanu, R. (1999). Switching on the infant brain. *Science, 286,* 59–61.

Skinner, B. F. (1953). *Science and human behavior.* New York, NY: Macmillan.

Skinner, B. F. (1971). *Beyond freedom and dignity.* New York, NY: Knopf.

Skinner, B. F. (1974). *About behaviorism.* New York, NY: Knopf.

Skinner, E. A., & Belmont, M. J. (1993). Motivation in the classroom: Reciprocal effects of teacher behavior and student engagement across the school year. *Journal of Educational Psychology, 85,* 571–581.

Skinner, E. A., Zimmer-Gembeck, M. J., & Connell, J. P. (1998). Individual differences and the development of perceived control. *Monographs of the Society for Research in Child Development, 63* (2–3, Serial No. 254).

Skodak, M., & Skeels, H. M. (1949). A final follow-up study of one hundred adopted children. *Pedagogical Seminary and Journal of Genetic Psychology, 75,* 85–125.

Slaby, R. G., & Frey, K. S. (1975). Development of gender constancy and selective attention to same-sex models. *Child Development, 46,* 849–856.

Slade, A., Belsky, J., Aber, J. L., & Phelps, J. L. (1999). Mothers' representations of their relationships with their toddlers: Links to adult attachment and observed mothering. *Developmental Psychology, 35,* 611–619.

Slater, A., & Quinn, P. C. (2001). Face recognition in the newborn infant. *Infant and Child Development, 10,* 21–24.

Slater, A., Rose, D., & Morison, V. (1984). New-born infants' perception of similarities and differences between two- and three-dimensional stimuli. *British Journal of Developmental Psychology, 3,* 211–220.

Slater, A., Von der Schulenburg, C., Brown, E., Badenoch, M., Butterworth, G., Parsons, S., & Samuels, C. (1998). Newborn infants prefer attractive faces. *Infant Behavior and Development, 21,* 345–354.

Slaughter-Defoe, D. T., Nakagawa, K., Takanishi, R., & Johnson, D. J. (1990). Toward cultural/ecological perspectives on schooling and achievement in African- and Asian-American children. *Child Development, 61,* 363–383.

Slavin, R. E. (1990). *Cooperative learning: Theory, research, and practice.* Englewood Cliffs, NJ: Prentice Hall.

Slomkowski, C., & Manke, B. (2004). Sibling relationships during childhood: Multiple perceptions from multiple perspectives. In R. D. Conger, F. O. Lorenz, & K. A. S. Wickrama (Eds.), *Continuity and change in family relations: Theory, methods, and empirical findings* (pp. 293–318). Mahwah, NJ: Erlbaum.

Sluzenski, J., Newcombe, N. S., & Satlow, E. (2004). Knowing where things are in the second year of life: Implications for hippocampal development. *Journal of Cognitive Neuroscience, 16,* 1443–1451.

Smetana, J. (2002). Culture, autonomy, and personal jurisdiction in adolescent-parent relationships. In R. V. Kail & H. W. Reese (Eds.), *Advances in child development and behavior* (Vol. 29, pp. 52–89). San Diego, CA: Academic Press.

Smetana, J. G. (2008). "It's 10 o'clock: Do you know where your children are?" Recent advances in understanding parental monitoring and adolescents' information management. *Child Development Perspectives, 2,* 19–25.

Smetana, J. G., & Braeges, J. L. (1990). The development of toddlers' moral and conventional judgments. *Merrill-Palmer Quarterly, 36,* 329–346.

Smetana, J. G., Campione-Barr, N., & Daddis, C. (2004). Longitudinal development of family decision making: Defining healthy behavioral autonomy for middle-class African American adolescents. *Child Development, 75,* 1418–1434.

Smetana, J. G., Schlagman, N., & Adams, P. W. (1993). Preschool judgments about hypothetical and actual transgressions. *Child Development, 64,* 202–214.

Smith, A. M., Fried, P. A., Hogan, M. J., & Cameron, I. (2006). Effects of prenatal marijuana on visualspatial working memory: An fMRI study in young adults. *Neurotoxicoglogy and Teratology, 28,* 286–295.

Smith, B. L. (1988). The emergent lexicon from a phonetic perspective. In M. D. Smith & J. L. Locke (Eds.), *The emergent lexicon: The child's development of a linguistic vocabulary* (pp. 75–109). New York, NY: Academic Press.

Smith, L., Fagan, J. F., & Ulvund, S. E. (2002). The relation of recognition memory in infancy and parental socioeconomic status to later intellectual competence. *Intelligence, 30,* 247–259.

Smith, L. B. (1995). Self-organizing processes in learning to learn words: Development is not induction. In C. A. Nelson (Ed.), *Basic and applied perspectives on learning, cognition, and development. The Minnesota symposia in child psychology* (Vol. 28, pp. 1–32). Mahwah, NJ: Erlbaum.

Smith, L. B. (1999). Children's noun learning: How general learning processes make specialized learning mechanisms. In B. MacWhinney (Ed.), *The emergence of language* (pp. 277–303). Mahwah, NJ: Erlbaum.

Smith, L. B. (1999b). Do infants possess innate knowledge structures? The con side. *Developmental Science, 2,* 133–144.

Smith, L. B., & Breazeal, C. (2007). The dynamic lift of developmental process. *Developmental Science, 10,* 61–68.

Smith, L. B., Thelen, E., Titzer, R., & McLin, D. (1999). Knowing in the context of acting: The task dynamics of the A-not-B error. *Psychological Review,* 106, 235–260.

Smith, P. K. (2005). Play: Types and functions in human development. In B. J. Ellis & D. F. Bjorklund (Eds.), *Origins of the social mind* (pp. 271–291). New York, NY: Guilford Press.

Smith, P., Perrin, S., Yule, W., & Rabe-Hesketh, S. (2001). War exposure and maternal reactions in the psychological adjustment of children from Bosnia-Hercegovina. *Journal of Child Psychology and Psychiatry, 42,* 395–404.

Smith, R. (1999, March). The timing of birth. *Scientific American, 280,* 68–75.

Snarey, J. R. (1985). Cross-cultural universality of social-moral development: A critical review of Kohlbergian research. *Psychological Bulletin, 97,* 202–232.

Snedeker, J., Geren, J., & Shafto, C. L. (2007). Starting over: International adoption as a natural experiment in language development. *Psychological Science, 18,* 79–87.

Snell, E. K., Adam, E. K., & Duncan, G. J. (2007). Sleep and the body mass index and overweight status of children and adolescents. *Child Development, 78,* 309–323.

Snow, C. E. (1977). The development of conversation between babies and mothers. *Journal of Child Language, 4,* 1–22.

Snow, C. E. (1984). Parent-child interaction and the development of communicative ability. In R. L. Schiefelbusch & J. Pickar (Eds.), *The acquisition of communicative competence* (pp. 69–107). Baltimore: University Park Press.

Snow, C. E. (1987). Relevance of the notion of a critical period to language acquisition. In M. H. Bornstein (Ed.), *Sensitive periods in development* (pp. 183–209). Hillsdale, NJ: Erlbaum.

Snow, C. E. (1993). Families as social contexts for literacy development. In C. Daiute (Ed.), *The development of literacy through social interaction. New Directions for Child Development. No. 61* (pp. 11–24). San Francisco, CA: Jossey-Bass.

Snyder, J., Reid, J., & Patterson, G. (2003). A social learning model of child and adolescent antisocial behavior. In B. B. Lahey, T. E. Moffitt, & A. Caspi (Eds.), *Causes of conduct disorder and juvenile delinquency* (pp. 27–48). New York, NY: Guilford.

Sobal, J., & Stunkard, A. J. (1989). Socioeconomic status and obesity: A review of the literature. *Psychological Bulletin, 105,* 260–275.

Society for Research in Child Development (2007). *Ethical standards for research with children.* Retrieved November 6, 2009, from http://www.srcd.org/index.php?option=com_content&task=view&id=68&Itemid=499

Society for Research in Child Development (2010). *History.* Retrieved 11 August 2010 from http://www.srcd.org/index.php?option=com_content&task=view&id=71&Itemid=495

Sodian, B., Zaitchik, D., & Carey, S. (1991). Young children's differentiation of hypothetical beliefs from evidence. *Child Development, 62,* 753–766.

Soenens, B., Vansteenkiste, M., Luyckx, K., & Goossens, L. (2006). Parenting and adolescent problem behavior: An integrated model with adolescent self-disclosure and perceived parental knowledge as intervening variables. *Developmental Psychology, 42,* 305–318.

Sokol, R. J., Delaney-Black, V., & Nordstrom, B. (2003). Fetal alcohol spectrum disorder. *JAMA, 290,* 2996–2999.

Soley, G., & Hannon, E. E. (2010). Infants prefer the musical meter of their own culture: A cross-cultural comparison. *Developmental Psychology, 46,* 286–292.

Sommerville, J. A., Woodward, A. L., & Needham, A. (2005). Action experience alters 3-month-old infants' perception of others' actions. *Cognition, 96,* B1–B11.

Sophian, C. (2007). *The origins of mathematical knowledge in childhood.* New York, NY: Erlbaum.

Sophian, C., Garyantes, D., & Chang, C. (1997). When three is less than two: Early developments in children's understanding of fractional quantities. *Developmental Psychology, 33,* 731–744.

Sorce, J. F., Emde, R. N., Campos, J., & Klinnert, M. D. (1985). Maternal emotional signaling: Its effect on the visual cliff behavior of 1-year-olds. *Developmental Psychology, 21,* 195–200.

South, S. T., Chen, Z., & Brothman, A. R. (2008). Genomic medicine in prenatal diagnosis. *Clinical Obstetrics & Gynecology, 51,* 62–73.

Southwick, S. M., Yehuda, R., & Charney, D. S. (1997). Neurobiological alterations in PTSD: Review of the clinical literature. In C. S. Fullerton & R. J. Ursano (Eds.), *Posttraumatic stress disorder: Acute and long-term responses to trauma and disaster* (pp. 241–266). Washington, DC: American Psychiatric Press.

Spear, L. P. (2000). The adolescent brain and age-related behavioral manifestations. *Neuroscience and Biobehavioral Reviews, 24,* 417–463.

Spear, L. P. (2003). Neurodevelopment during adolescence. In D. Cicchetti & E. F. Walker (Eds.), *Neurodevelopmental mechanisms in psychopathology* (pp. 62–83). Cambridge, UK: Cambridge University Press.

Spearman, C. (1904). "General intelligence," objectively determined and measured. *American Journal of Psychology, 15,* 72–101.

Spehr, M., Gisselmann, G., Poplawski, A., Riffell, J. A., Wetzel, C. H., Zimmer, R. K., & Hatt, H. (2003). Identification of a testicular odorant receptor mediating human sperm chemotaxis, *Science, 299,* 2054–2058.

Spelke, E., Breinlinger, K., Macomber, J., & Jacobson, K. (1992). Origins of knowledge. *Psychological Review, 99,* 605–632.

Spelke, E., & Hespos, S. (2001). Continuity, competence, and the object concept. In E. Dupoux (Ed.), *Language, brain, and cognitive development: Essays in honor of Jacques Mehler* (pp. 325–340). Cambridge, MA: MIT Press.

Spelke, E. S. (1976). Infants' intermodal perception of events. *Cognitive Psychology, 8,* 553–560.

Spelke, E. S., & Kinzler, K. D. (2007). Core knowledge. *Developmental Science, 10,* 89–96.

Spelke, E. S., & Owsley, C. J. (1979). Intermodal exploration and knowledge in infancy. *Infant Behavior and Development, 2,* 13–27.

Spence, I., & Feng, J. (2010). Video games and spatial cognition. *Review of General Psychology, 14,* 92–104.

Spence, M. J., & Freeman, M. S. (1996). Newborn infants prefer the maternal low-pass filtered voice, but not the maternal whispered voice. *Infant Behavior and Development, 19,* 199–212.

Spencer, J. P., Blumberg, M. S., McMurray, B., Robinson, S. R., Samuelson, L. K., & Tomblin, J. B. (2009). Short arms and talking eggs: Why we should no longer abide the nativist-empiricist debate. *Child Development Perspectives, 3,* 79–87.

Spencer, J. P., Smith, L. B., & Thelen, E. (2001). Tests of a dynamic systems account of the A-not-B error: The influence of prior experience on the spatial memory abilities of two-year-olds. *Child Development, 72,* 1327–1346.

Spencer, J. P., Vereijken, B., Diedrich, F. J., & Thelen, E. (2000). Posture and the emergence of manual skills. *Developmental Science, 3,* 216–233.

Spencer, M. B. (2006). Phenomenology and ecological systems theory: Development of diverse groups. In W. Damon & R. M. Lerner (Editors-in-Chief) & R. M. Lerner (Vol. Ed.), *Handbook of child psychology. Vol. 1. Theoretical models of human development* (6th ed., pp. 829–893). Hoboken, NJ: Wiley Publishers.

Spinrad, T. L., Eisenberg, N., Harris, H., Hanish, L., Fabes, R. A., et al. (2004). The relation of children's everyday nonsocial peer play behavior to their emotionality, regulation, and social functioning. *Developmental Psychology, 40,* 67–80.

Spitz, H. H. (1986). *The raising of intelligence.* Hillsdale, NJ: Erlbaum.

Spitz, H. H. (1999). Attempts to raise intelligence. In M. Anderson (Ed.), *The development of intelligence* (pp. 275–293). Hove, UK: Psychology Press.

Spitz, R. (1946). Anaclitic depression. *Psychoanalytic Study of the Child, 2,* 313–342.

Spohr, H.-L., Willms, J., & Steinhausen, H.-C. (2007). Fetal alcohol spectrum disorders in young adulthood. *Journal of Pediatrics, 150,* 175–179.

Spörer, N., Brunstein, J. C., & Kieschke, U. (2009). Improving students' reading comprehension skills: Effects of strategy instruction and reciprocal teaching. *Learning and Instruction, 19,* 272–286.

Sprauve, M. E. (1996) Substance abuse and HIV in pregnancy. *Clinical Obstetrics and Gynecology, 39,* 316–332.

Spreen, O., Risser, A. H., & Edgell, D. (1995). *Developmental neuropsychology.* New York, NY: Oxford University Press.

SRI/AIR (2002). *Targeted literature review of major constructs and their components: Evaluating the national school district and network grants program.* Palo Alto, CA: Authors.

Sroufe, L. A., Egeland, B., Carlson, E., & Collins, W. A. (2005). Placing early attachment experiences in developmental context. In K. E. Grossmann, K. Grossmann, & E. Waters (Eds.), *Attachment from infancy to adulthood* (pp. 48–70). New York, NY: Guilford Press.

Stams, G. J. M., Juffer, F., & van IJzendoorn, M. H. (2002). Maternal sensitivity, infant attachment, and temperament in early childhood predict adjustment in middle childhood: The case of adopted children and their biologically unrelated parents. *Developmental Psychology, 38,* 806–821.

Stansbury, K., & Gunnar, M. R. (1994). Adrenocortical activity and emotion regulation. In N. A. Fox (Ed.), *The development of emotion regulation: Biological and behavioral considerations. Monographs of the Society for Research in Child Development, 59* (2–3, Serial No. 240).

Stanwood, G. D., & Levitt, P. (2001). The effects of cocaine on the developing nervous system. In C. A. Nelson & M. Luciana (Eds.), *Handbook of developmental cognitive neuroscience* (pp. 519–536). Cambridge, MA: MIT Press.

Statistics Canada (2009). *Visible minority population, by age group* (2006 Census). Retrieved November 6, 2009, from http://www40.statcan.ca/l01/cst01/demo50a-eng.htm

Steele, C. D., Wapner, R. J., Smith, J. B., Haynes, M. K., & Jackson, L. G. (1996). Prenatal diagnosis using fetal cells isolated from maternal peripheral blood: A review. *Clinical Obstetrics and Gynecology, 39,* 801–813.

Steele, C. M., & Aronson, J. (1995). Stereotype threat and the intellectual test performance of African Americans. *Journal of Personality and Social Psychology, 69,* 797–811.

Stein, J. H., & Reiser, L. W. (1994). A study of white middle-class adolescent boys' responses to "semenarche" (the first ejaculation). *Journal of Youth and Adolescence, 23,* 373–384.

Stein, N. (1995). Sexual harassment in the school: The public performance of gendered violence. *Harvard Educational Review, 65,* 145–162.

Stein, N. (2007). Gender-based violence in schools. In R. C. Davis, A. J. Lurigio, & S. Herman (Eds.), *Victims of crime* (3rd ed., pp. 201–210). Thousand Oaks, CA: Sage.

Steinberg, L. (1981). Transformations in family relations at puberty. *Developmental Psychology, 17,* 833–840.

Steinberg, L. (1996). *Beyond the classroom: Why school reform has failed and what parents need to do.* New York, NY: Simon & Schuster.

Steinberg, L. (2001). We know some things: Adolescent-parent relationships in retrospect and prospect. *Journal of Research on Adolescence, 11,* 1–19.

Steinberg, L., Dornbusch, S. M., & Brown, B. B. (1992). Ethnic differences in adolescent achievement: An ecological perspective. *American Psychologist, 47,* 723–729.

Steinberg, L., Elmen, J. D., & Mounts, N. S. (1989). Authoritative parenting, psychosocial maturity, and academic success among adolescents. *Child Development, 60,* 1424–1436.

Steinberg, L., Lamborn, S. D., Darling, N., Mounts, N. S., & Dornbusch, S. (1994). Over-time changes in adjustment and competence among adolescents from authoritative, authoritarian, indulgent, and neglectful families. *Child Development, 65,* 754–770.

Steinberg, L., Lamborn, S. D., Dornbusch, S. M., & Darling, N. (1992). Impact of parenting practices on adolescent achievement: Authoritative parenting, school involvement, and encouragement to succeed. *Child Development, 63,* 1266–1281.

Steiner, J. E. (1979). Human facial expressions in response to taste and smell stimulation. In H. W. Reese & L. P. Lipsitt (Eds.), *Advances in child development and behavior* (Vol. 13, pp. 257–295). New York, NY: Academic Press.

Stephens, B. E., & Vohr, B. R. (2009). Neurodevelopmental outcome of the premature infant. *Pediatric Clinics of North America, 56,* 631–646.

Stern, D. N. (1974). The goal and structure of mother-infant play. *Journal of the American Academy of Child Psychiatry, 13,* 402–421.

Sternberg & J. E. Davidson (Eds.), *Conceptions of giftedness* (pp. 223–243).

Sternberg, K. J., Lamb, M. E., Greenbaum, C., Cichetti, D., Dawud, S., Cortes, R. M., et al. (1993). Effects of domestic violence on children's behavior problems and depression. *Developmental Psychology, 29,* 44–52.

Sternberg, R. J. (1981). A componential theory of intellectual giftedness. *Gifted Child Quarterly, 25,* 86–93.

Sternberg, R. J. (1982). *Intelligence applied.* New York, NY: Harcourt.

Sternberg, R. J. (1985). *Beyond IQ: A triarchic theory of human intelligence.* Cambridge, UK: Cambridge University Press.

Sternberg, R. J. (1986). Triarchic theory of intellectual giftedness. In R. J. Sternberg & J. E. Davidson (Eds.), *Conceptions of giftedness* (pp. 223–243). Cambridge, UK: Cambridge University Press.

Sternberg, R. J. (1995). Testing common sense. *American Psychologist, 50,* 912–927.

Sternberg, R. J. (1998). Applying the triarchic theory of human intelligence in the classroom. In R. J. Sternberg & W. M. Williams (Eds.), *Intelligence, instruction, and assessment: Theory into practice* (pp. 1–15). Mahwah, NJ: Erlbaum.

Sternberg, R. J. (2001). Successful intelligence: Understanding what Spearman had rather than what he studied. In J. M. Collis & S. Messick (Eds.), *Intelligence and personality: Bridging the gap in theory and measurement* (pp. 347–373). Mahwah, NJ: Erlbaum.

Sternberg, R. J., Conway, B. E., Ketron, J. L., & Bernstein, M. (1981). People's conceptions of intelligence. *Journal of Personality and Social Psychology, 41,* 37–55.

Sternberg, R. J., & Frensch, P. A. (1993). Mechanisms of transfer. In D. K. Detterman & R. J. Sternberg (Eds.), *Transfer on trial: Intelligence, cognition, and instruction* (pp. 25–38). Norwood, NJ: Ablex.

Sternberg, R. J., & Kaufman, J. C. (1998). Human abilities. *Annual Review of Psychology, 49,* 479–502.

Stetsenko, A., Little, T. D., Oettingen, G., & Baltes, P. B. (1995). Agency, control, and means-ends beliefs about school performance in Moscow children: How similar are they to beliefs of Western children? *Developmental Psychology, 31,* 285–299.

Stevenson-Hinde, J., & Shouldice, A. (1995). Maternal interactions and self-reports related to attachment classifications at 4.5 years. *Child Development, 66,* 583–596.

Stevenson, H. W., Chen, C., & Lee, S. (1993). Mathematics achievement of Chinese, Japanese, and American children: Ten years later. *Science, 259,* 53–58.

Stevenson, H. W., Lee, S., & Stigler, J. W. (1986). Mathematics achievement of Chinese, Japanese, and American children. *Science, 231,* 693–699.

Stevenson, H. W., Stigler, J. W., Lee, S., Lucker, G. W., Kitamura, S., & Hsu, C. (1985). Cognitive performance and academic achievement of Japanese, Chinese, and American children. *Child Development, 56,* 718–734.

Stevenson, J., Asherson, P., Hay, D., Levy, F., Swanson, J., Thapar, A., & Willcutt, E. (2005). Characterizing the ADHD phenotype for genetic studies. *Developmental Science, 8,* 115–121.

Stice, E., Presnell, K., & Bearman, S. K. (2001). Relation of early menarche to depression, eating disorders, substance abuse, and comorbid psychopathology among adolescent girls. *Developmental Psychology, 37,* 608–619.

Stice, E., Shaw, H., & Marti, C. N. (2006). A meta-analytic review of obesity prevention programs for children and adolescents: The skinny on interventions that work. *Psychological Bulletin, 132,* 667–691.

Stifter, C. A., Fox, N. A., & Porges, S. W. (1989). Facial expressivity and vagal tone in five- and ten-month-old infants. *Infant Behavior and Development, 12,* 127–137.

Stifter, C. A., Spinrad, T. L., & Braungart-Rieker, J. M. (1999). Toward a developmental model of child compliance: The role of emotion regulation in infancy. *Child Development, 70,* 21–32.

Stigler, J. W., Lee, S., & Stevenson, H. W. (1987). Mathematics classrooms in Japan, Taiwan, and the United States. *Child Development, 58,* 1272–1285.

Stigler, J. W., Smith, S., & Mao, L.-W. (1985). The self-perception of competence by Chinese children. *Child Development, 56,* 1259–1270.

Stiles, J. (2008). *The fundamentals of brain development: Integrating nature and nurture.* Cambridge, MA: Harvard University Press.

Stiles, J. (2009). On genes, brains, and behavior: Why should developmental psychologists care about brain development? *Child Development Perspectives, 3,* 196–2002.

Stipek, D., Recchia, S., & McClintic, S. (1992). Self-evaluation in young children. *Monographs of the Society for Research in Child Development, 57* (1, Serial No. 226).

Stoel-Gammon, C., & Otomo, K. (1986). Babbling development of hearing-impaired and normally hearing subjects. *Journal of Speech and Hearing Disorders, 51,* 33–41.

Stolberg, A. L., & Anker, J. M. (1984). Cognitive and behavioral changes in children resulting from parental divorce and consequent environmental changes. *Journal of Divorce, 8,* 184–197.

Stormshak, E. A., Bellanti, C. J., Bierman, K. L., & the Conduct Problems Prevention Group. (1996). The quality of sibling relationships and the development of social competence and behavioral control in aggressive children. *Developmental Psychology, 32,* 79–89.

Story, M., Sallis, J. F., & Orleans, C. T. (2009). Adolescent obesity: Towards evidence-based policy and environmental solutions. *Journal of Adolescent Health, 45,* S1–S5.

Strasburger, V. C. (1993). Children, adolescents, and the media: Five crucial issues. *Adolescent Medicine: State of the Art Review, 4,* 479–493.

Strasburger, V. C (2001). Children and TV advertising: Nowhere to run, nowhere to hide. *Journal of Developmental & Behavioral Pediatrics, 22,* 185–187.

Straus, M. A., & Donnelly, D. A. (1993). Corporal punishment of adolescents by American parents. *Youth and Society, 24,* 419–442.

Straus, M. A., & Stewart, J. H. (1999). Corporal punishment by American parents: National data on prevalence, chronicity, severity, and duration, in relation to child and family characteristics. *Clinical Child and Family Psychology Review, 2,* 55–70.

Streissguth, A. P., Barr, H. M., Bookstein, F. L., Sampson, P. D., & Olson, H. C. (1999). The long-term neurocognitive consequences of prenatal alcohol exposure: A 14-year study. *Psychological Science, 10,* 186–190.

Streissguth, A. P., Bookstein, F. L., Sampson, P. D., & Barr, H. M. (1995). Attention: Prenatal alcohol and continuities of vigilence and attentional problems from 4 through 14 years. *Development and Psychopathology, 7,* 419–446.

Streissguth, A. P., Sampson, P. D., Barr, H. M., Bookstein, F. L., & Olson, H. C. (1994). The effects of prenatal exposure to alcohol and tobacco: Contributions from the Seattle Longitudinal Prospective Study and implications for public policy. In H. L. Needleman & D. Bellinger (Eds.), *Prenatal exposure to toxicants: Developmental consequences* (pp. 148–183). Baltimore: Johns Hopkins University Press.

Streissguth, A. P., Treder, R., Barr, H. M., Shepard, T., Bleyer, A., & Martin, D. (1984). Prenatal aspirin and offspring IQ in a large group. *Teratology, 29,* 59A–60A.

Striegel-Moore, R. H., & Bulik, C. M. (2007). Risk factors for eating disorders. *American Psychologist, 62,* 181–198.

Stroud, L. R., Paster, R. L., Goodwin, M. S., Shenassa, E., Buka, S., Niaura, R., Rosenblith, J. F., & Lipsitt, L. P. (2009). Maternal smoking during pregnancy and neonatal behavior: A large-scale community study. *Pediatrics, 123,* e842–e848.

Strough, J., & Berg, C. A. (2000). Goals as a mediator of gender differences in high-affiliation dyadic conversations. *Developmental Psychology, 36,* 117–125.

Suarez-Orozco, C., & Suarez-Orozco, M. (1996). *Transformations: Migration, family life and achievement motivation among Latino adolescents.* Palo Alto, CA: Stanford University Press.

Subrahmanyam, K., & Greenfield, P. (2008). Online communication and adolescent relationships. *The Future of Children, 18*(1), 119–146.

Subrahmanyam, K., Greenfield, P., Kraut, R., & Gross, E. (2001). The impact of computer use on children's and adolescents' development. *Journal of Applied Developmental Psychology, 22,* 7–30.

Subrahmanyam, K., & Greenfield, P. M. (1994). Effect of video game practice on spatial skills in girls and boys. *Journal of Applied Developmental Psychology, 15,* 13–32.

Subrahmanyam, K., Smahel, D., & Greenfield, P. (2006). Connecting developmental constructions to the Internet: Identity presentation and sexual exploration in online teen chat rooms. *Developmental Psychology, 42,* 395–406.

Substance Abuse and Mental Health Services Administration (2009). *Results from the 2008 National Survey on Drug Use and Health: National findings.* Office of Applied Studies, NSDUH Series H-36, HHS Publication No. SMA 09-4434. Rockville, MD.

Sugarman, S. (1982). Developmental change in early representational intelligence: Evidence from spatial classification strategies and related verbal expressions. *Cognitive Psychology, 14,* 410–449.

Sugarman, S. (1983). *Children's early thought: Developments in classification.* New York, NY: Cambridge University Press.

Sullivan, H. S. (1953). *The interpersonal theory of psychiatry.* New York, NY: W. W. Norton.

Sullivan, S. A., & Birch, L. L. (1990). Pass the sugar, pass the salt: Experience dictates preference. *Developmental Psychology, 26,* 546–551.

Sun, L. C., & Roopnarine, J. L. (1996). Mother-infant, father-infant interaction and involvement in childcare and household labor among Taiwanese families. *Infant Behavior and Development, 19,* 121–129.

Sund, A. M., Larsson, B., & Wichstrøm, L. (2003). Psychosocial correlates of depressive symptoms among 12–14-year-old Norwegian adolescents. *Journal of Child Psychology and Psychiatry, 44,* 588–597.

Super, C. M. (1976). Environmental effects on motor development: The case of "African infant precocity." *Developmental Medicine and Child Neurology, 18,* 561–567.

Super, C. M., & Harkness, S. (1982). The infant's niche in rural Kenya and metropolitan America. In L. Adler (Ed.), *Cross-cultural research at issue* (pp. 247–255). New York, NY: Academic Press.

Super, C. M., & Harkness, S. (1997). The cultural structuring of child development. In J. W. Berry (Ed.), *Handbook of cross-cultural psychology: Vol. 2. Basic processes and human development* (2nd ed., pp. 1–39). Boston: Allyn & Bacon.

Suskind, D. L. (2009). Nutritional deficiencies during normal growth. *Pediatric Clinics of North America, 56,* 1035–1053.

Sutton-Smith, B., & Rosenberg, B. G. (1970). *The sibling.* New York, NY: Holt, Rinehart & Winston.

Swain, I. U., Zelazo, P. R., & Clifton, R. K. (1993). Newborn infants' memory for speech sounds retained over 24 hours. *Developmental Psychology, 29,* 312–323.

Symington, A. J., & Pinelli, J. (2006). Developmental care for promoting development and preventing morbidity in preterm infants. *Cochrane Database of Systematic Reviews,* Issue 2. Art. No.: CD001814. DOI: 10.1002/14651858.CD001814.pub2.

Szechter, L. E., & Liben, L. S. (2007). Children's aesthetic understanding of photographic art and the quality of art-related parent-child interactions. *Child Development, 78,* 879–894.

Taga, K. A., Markey, C. N., & Friedman, H. S. (2006). A longitudinal investigation of associations between boys' pubertal timing and adult behavioral health and well-being. *Journal of Youth and Adolescence, 35,* 401–412.

Tager-Flusberg, H. (2007). Evaluating the theory-of-mind hypothesis of autism. *Current Directions in Psychological Science, 16,* 311–315.

Tager-Flusberg, H., & Zukowski, A. (2009). Putting words together: Morphology and syntax in the preschool years. In J. B. Gleason & N. B. Ratner (Eds.), *The development of language.* (7th ed., pp. 139–191). Boston: Pearson Allyn & Bacon.

Takahashi, K. (1990). Are the key assumptions of the Strange Situation procedure universal? A view from Japanese research. *Human Development, 33,* 23–30.

Takei, W. (2001). How do deaf infants attain first signs? *Developmental Science, 4,* 71–78.

Talwar, V., & Lee, K. (2008). Social and cognitive correlates of children's lying behavior. *Child Development, 79,* 866–881.

Tam, C. W. Y., & Stokes, S. F. (2001). Form and function of negation in early developmental Cantonese. *Journal of Child Language, 28,* 373–391.

Tamis-LeMonda, C. S., Bornstein, M. H., & Baumwell, L. (2001). Maternal responsiveness and children's achievement of language milestones. *Child Development, 72,* 748–767.

Tanner, J. M. (1978). *Fetus into man: Physical growth from conception to maturity.* Cambridge, MA: Harvard University Press.

Tappin, D., Ecob, R., & Brooke, H. (2005). Bedsharing, roomsharing and sudden infant death syndrome in Scotland. *Journal of Pediatrics, 147,* 32–37.

Taras, H. L., Sallis, J. F., Patterson, T. L., Nader, P. R., & Nelson, J. A. (1989). Television's influence on children's diet and physical activity. *Journal of Developmental and Behavioral Pediatrics, 10,* 176–180.

Tardif, T. (1996). Nouns are not always learned before verbs: Evidence from Mandarin speakers' early vocabularies. *Developmental Psychology, 32,* 492–504.

Tardif, T., Fletcher, P., Liang, W., Zhang, Z., Kaciroti, N., & Marchman, V. A. (2008). Baby's first 10 words. *Developmental Psychology, 44,* 929–938.

Tardif, T., Gelman, S. A., & Xu, F. (1999). Putting the "noun bias" in context: A comparison of English and Mandarin. *Child Development, 70,* 620–635.

Task Force on Sudden Infant Death Syndrome (2005) The changing concept of sudden infant death syndrome: Diagnostic coding shifts, controversies regarding the sleeping environment, and new variables to consider in reducing risk. *Pediatrics 116,* 1245–1255.

Taumoepeau, M., & Ruffman, T. (2008). Stepping stones to others' minds: Maternal talk relates to child mental state language and emotion understanding at 15, 24, and 33 months. *Child Development, 79,* 284–302.

Taveras, E. M., Rifas-Shiman, S. L., Oken, E., Gunderson, E. P., & Gillman, M. W. (2008). Short sleep duration in infancy and risk of childhood overweight. *Archives of Pediatric & Adolescent Medicine, 162,* 305–311.

Taylor, R. D. (1996). Adolescents' perceptions of kinship support and family management practices: Association with adolescent adjustment in African American families. *Developmental Psychology, 32,* 687–695.

Tenenbaum, H. R., & Leaper, C. (2002). Are parents' gender schemas related to their children's gender-related cognitions? A meta-analysis. *Developmental Psychology, 38,* 615–630.

Teratology Society. (2005). *Teratology primer.* Reston, VA: Author.

Terman, L. M. (1925). *Genetic studies of genius: Vol. 1. Mental and physical traits of a thousand gifted children.* Stanford, CA: Stanford University Press.

Terman, L. M. (1954). The discovery and encouragement of exceptional talent. *American Psychologist, 9,* 221–238.

Terman, L. M., & Oden, M. H. (1959). *Genetic studies of genius: Vol. 4. The gifted group at midlife.* Stanford, CA: Stanford University Press.

Terrance, C., Logan, A., & Peters, D. (2004). Perceptions of peer sexual harassment among high school students. *Sex Roles, 51,* 479–490.

Terranova, A. M., Boxer, P., & Morris, A. S. (2009). Changes in children's peer interactions following a natural disaster: How predisaster bullying and victimization rates changed following Hurricane Katrina. *Psychology in the Schools, 46,* 333–347.

Tessier, R., Cristo, M. B., Velez, S., Giron, M., Nadeau, L., Figueroa de Calume, Z., . . . & Charpak, N. (2003). Kangaroo mother care: A method for protecting high-risk low-birth-weight and premature infants against developmental delay. *Infant Behavior & Development, 26,* 384–397.

Teti, D. M., & Gelfand, D. M. (1991). Behavioral competence among mothers of infants in the first year: The mediational role of maternal self-efficacy. *Child Development, 62,* 918–929.

Teti, D. M., Gelfand, D. M., Messinger, D. S., & Isabella, R. (1995). Maternal depression and the quality of early attachment: An examination of infants, preschoolers, and their mothers. *Developmental Psychology, 31,* 364–376.

Teti, D. M., Sakin, J. W., Kucera, E., & Corns, K. M. (1996). And baby makes four: Predictors of attachment security among preschool age firstborns during the transition to siblinghood. *Child Development, 67,* 579–596.

Thabet, A. A., & Vostanis, P. (2000). Posttraumatic stress disorder reactions in children of war: A longitudinal study. *Child Abuse & Neglect, 24,* 291–298.

Tharp, R. G. (1989). Psychocultural variables and constants: Effects on teaching and learning in schools. *American Psychologist, 44,* 349–359.

Thelen, E. (1996). The improvising infant: Learning about learning to move. In M. R. Merrens & G. G. Brannigan (Eds.), *The developmental psychologists: Research adventures across the life span* (pp. 21–36). New York, NY: McGraw-Hill.

Thelen, E., & Smith, L. B. (1994). *A dynamic systems approach to the development of cognition and action.* Cambridge, MA: MIT Press.

Thelen, E., & Smith, L. B. (2006). Dynamic systems theories. In W. Damon & R. M. Lerner (Editors-in-Chief) & R. M. Lerner (Vol. Ed.), *Handbook of child psychology: Vol. 1. Theoretical models of human development* (6th ed., pp. 258–312). Hoboken, NJ: Wiley.

Thelen, E., & Ulrich, B. D. (1991). Hidden skills: A dynamic systems analysis of treadmill stepping during the first year. *Monographs of the Society for Research in Child Development, 56* (1, Serial No. 223).

Theokas, C., & Bloch, M. (2006). Out-of-school time is critical for children: Who participates in programs? *Research-to-Results Fact Sheet, 20.* Washington, DC: Child Trends.

Theunissen, N. C. M., Kamp, G. A., Koopman, H. M., Zwinderman, K. A., Vogels, T., & Wit, J.-M. (2002). Quality of life and self-esteem in children treated for idiopathic short stature. *Journal of Pediatrics, 140,* 507–515.

Thierry, K. L., & Spence, M. J. (2002). Source-monitoring training facilitates preschoolers' eyewitness memory performance. *Developmental Psychology, 38,* 428–437.

Thiessen, E. D., Hill, E. A., & Saffran, J. R. (2005). Infant-directed speech facilitates word segmentation. *Infancy, 7,* 53–71.

Thomaes, S., Reijntes, A., Orobrio de Castro, B., Bushman, B. J., Poorthuis, A., & Telch, M. J. (2010). I like me if you like me: On the interpersonal modulation and regulation of preadolescents' stated self-esteem. *Child Development, 81,* 811–825.

Thoman, A. (1993). Obligation and option in the premature nursery. *Developmental Review, 13,* 1–30.

Thomas, D. G., & Lykins, M. S. (1995). Event-related potential measures of 24-hour retention in 5-month-old infants. *Developmental Psychology, 31,* 946–957.

Thomas, M. S. C., & Johnson, M. H. (2008). New advances in understanding sensitive periods in brain development. *Current Directions in Psychological Science, 17,* 1–5.

Thomas, M. S. C., & Karmiloff-Smith, A. (2007). Modeling typical and atypical cognitive development: Computational constraints on mechanisms of change. In U. Goswami (Ed.), *Handbook of childhood cognitive development* (pp. 575–599). Malden, MA: Blackwell.

Thompson, C. (1982). Cortical activity in behavioural development. In J. W. T. Dickerson & H. McGurk (Eds.), *Brain and behavioural development* (pp. 131–167). London, UK: Surrey University Press.

Thompson, R. A. (1990). Vulnerability in research: A developmental perspective on risk research. *Child Development, 61,* 1–16.

Thompson, R. A. (1994). Emotion regulation: A theme in search of definition. In N. A. Fox (Ed.), *The development of emotion regulation. Monographs of the Society for Research in Child Development, 59* (Nos. 2–3, Serial No. 240).

Thompson, R. A. (1996). Attachment and emotional development: From clinic to research to policy. In M. R. Merrens & G. G. Brannigan (Eds.), *The developmental psychologists: Research adventures across the life span* (pp. 69–87). New York, NY: McGraw-Hill.

Thompson, R. A. (2006). The development of the person: Social understanding, relationships, conscience, self. In W. Damon & R. M. Lerner (Editors-in-Chief) & N. Eisneberg (Vol. Ed.), *Handbook of child psychology: Vol. 3. Social, emotional, and personality development* (6th ed., pp. 24–98). Hoboken, NJ: Wiley.

Thompson, R. A., & Nelson, C. A. (2001). Developmental science and the media: Early brain development. *American Psychologist, 56,* 5–15.

Thornton, S. (1999). Creating the conditions for cognitive change: The interaction between task structures and specific strategies. *Child Development, 70,* 588–603.

Thurstone, L. L. (1938). *Primary mental abilities.* Chicago, IL: University of Chicago Press.

Tieger, T. (1980). On the biological basis of sex differences in aggression. *Child Development, 51,* 943–963.

Tietjen, A. M. (1986). Prosocial moral reasoning among children and adults in a Papua New Guinea society. *Developmental Psychology, 22,* 861–868.

Tinbergen, N. (1951). *The study of instinct.* London, UK: Oxford University Press.

Tincoff, R., & Jusczyk, P.W. (1999). Some beginnings of word comprehension in 6-month-olds. *Psychological Science, 10,* 172–175.

Toda, S., & Fogel, A. (1993). Infant response to the still-face situation at 3 and 6 months. *Developmental Psychology, 29,* 532–538.

Tolmie, J. L. (2002). Down syndrome and other autosomal trisomies. In D. L. Rimoin, J. M. Connor, R. E. Pyeritz, & B. R. Korf (Eds.), *Emery and Rimoin's priniciples and practice of medical genetics.* (4th ed., Vol. 1, pp. 1129–1183). London, UK: Churchill Livingston.

Tolmie, J. L., & MacFadyen, U. (2007). Down syndrome and other autosomal trisomies. In D. L. Rimoin, J. M., Connor, R. E. Pyeritz, & B. R. Korf (Eds.), *Emery and Rimoin's principles and practice of medical genetics* (5th ed., Vol. 1, pp. 1015–1037). London, UK: Churchill Livingston.

Tolson, J. M., & Urberg, K. A. (1993). Similarity between adolescent best friends. *Journal of Adolescent Research, 8,* 274–288.

Tomasello, M. (2000). Do young children have adult syntactic competence? *Cognition, 74,* 209–253.

Tomasello, M., Akhtar, N., Dodson, K., & Rekau, L. (1997). Differential productivity in young children's use of nouns and verbs. *Journal of Child Language, 24,* 373–387.

Tomasello, M., & Brooks, P. (1998). Young children's earliest transitive and intransitive constructions. *Cognitive Linguistics, 8,* 375–395.

Tomasello, M., & Brooks, P. J. (1999). Early syntactic development: A construction grammar approach. In M. Barrett (Ed.), *The development of language* (pp. 161–190). Hove, UK: Psychology Press.

Tomasello, M., Carpenter, M., Call, J., Beline, T., & Moll, H. (2005). Understanding and sharing intentions: The origins of cultural cognition. *Brain and Behavioral Sciences, 28,* 675–735.

Tomasello, M., Conti-Ramsden, G., & Ewert, B. (1990). Young children's conversations with their mothers and fathers: Differences in breakdown and repair. *Journal of Child Language, 17,* 115–130.

Tomasello, M., & Farrar, M. J. (1986). Joint attention and early language. *Child Development, 57,* 1454–1463.

Tomasello, M., Strosberg, R., & Akhtar, N. (1996). Eighteen-month-old children learn words in non-ostensive contexts. *Journal of Child Language, 23,* 157–176.

Touwen, B. C. L. (1974). The neurological development of the infant. In J. A. Davis & J. Dobbing (Eds.), *Scientific foundations of paediatrics* (pp. 615–625). Philadelphia: W.B. Saunders.

Trainor, L. J. (1996). Infant preferences for infant-directed versus noninfant-directed play songs and lullabies. *Infant Behavior and Development,* 19, 83–92.

Trainor, L. J., & Heinmiller, B. M. (1998). The development of evaluative responses to music: Infants prefer to listen to consonance over dissonance. *Infant Behavior and Development, 21,* 77–88.

Trehub, S. E., Bull, D., & Thorpe, L. A. (1984). Infants' perception of melodies: The role of melodic contour. *Child Development, 55,* 821–830.

Trehub, S. E., & Hannon, E. E. (2006). Infant music perception: Domain-general or domain-specific mechanisms? *Cognition, 100,* 73–99.

Trehub, S. E., Thorpe, L. A., & Morrongiello, B. A. (1985). Infants' perception of melodies: Changes in a single tone. *Infant Behavior and Development, 8,* 213–223.

Trehub, S. E., & Trainor, L. J. (1998). Singing to infants: Lullabies and play songs. *Advances in Infancy Research, 12,* 43–77.

Treiber, F., & Wilcox, S. (1980). Perception of a "subjective" contour by infants. *Child Development, 51,* 915–917.

Trevathen, W. R. (1987). *Human birth: An evolutionary perspective.* New York, NY: Aldine de Gruyter.

Trickett, P. K., & Susman, E. J. (1988). Parental perceptions of child-rearing practices in physically abusive and nonabusive families. *Developmental Psychology, 24,* 270–276.

Tronick, E. Z. (1987). The Neonatal Behavioral Assessment Scale as a biomarker of the effects of environmental agents on the newborn. *Environmental Health Perspectives, 74,* 185–189.

Tronick, E. Z. (2003). Emotions and emotional communication in infants. In J. Raphael-Leff, (Ed.), *Parent-infant psychodynamics: Wild things, mirrors and ghosts* (pp. 35–53). London, UK: Whirr.

Tronick, E. Z., Als, H., Adamson, L., Wise, S., & Brazelton, T. B. (1978). The infant's response to entrapment between contradictory messages in face-to-face interaction. *Journal of the American Academy of Child Psychiatry, 17,* 1–13.

Tronick, E. Z., & Cohn, J. F. (1989). Infant-mother face-to-face interaction: Age and gender differences in coordination and the occurrence of miscoordination. *Child Development, 60,* 85–92.

Tronick, E. Z., Messinger, D. S., Weinberg, M. K., Lester, B. M., LaGasse, L., Seifer, R., . . . & Liu, J. (2005). Cocaine exposure is associated with subtle compromises of infants' and mothers' social emotional behavior and dyadic features of their interaction in the face-to-face still-face paradigm. *Developmental Psychology, 41,* 711–722.

Tronick, E. Z., Ricks, M., & Cohn, J. F. (1982). Maternal and infant affective exchange: Patterns of adaptation. In T. Field & A. Fogel (Eds.), *Emotion and early interaction* (pp. 83–100). Hillsdale, NJ: Erlbaum.

Troseth, G. L. (2003). TV guide: Two-year-old children learn to use video as a source of information. *Developmental Psychology, 39,* 140–150.

Troseth, G. L. (2010). Is it life or is it Memorex? Video as a representation of reality. *Developmental Review, 30,* 155–175.

Troseth, G. L., & DeLoache, J. S. (1998). The medium can obscure the message: Young children's understanding of video. *Child Development, 69,* 950–965.

Tröster, H., & Brambring, M. (1993). Early motor development in blind infants. *Journal of Applied Developmental Psychology, 14,* 83–106.

True, M. M., Pisani, L., & Oumar, F. (2001). Infant-mother attachment among the Dogon of Mali. *Child Development, 72,* 1451–1466.

Trzesniewski, K. H., Donnellan, M. B., Moffitt, T. E., Robins, R. W., Poulton, R., & Caspi, A. (2006). Low self-esteem during adolescence predicts poor health, criminal behavior, and limited economic prospects during adulthood. *Developmental Psychology, 42,* 381–390.

Tucker, D. M. (1981). Lateral brain function, emotion, and conceptualization. *Psychological Bulletin, 89,* 19–46.

Tucker, G. R., & d'Anglejan, A. (1972). An approach to bilingual education: The St. Lambert experiment. In M. Swain (Ed.), *Bilingual schooling: Some experiences in Canada and the United States* (pp. 15–21). Ontario: Ontario Institute for Studies in Education.

Turati, C. (2004). Why faces are not special to newborns: An alternative account of the face preference. *Current Directions in Psychological Science, 13,* 5–8.

Turati, C., Bulf, H., & Simion, F. (2008). Newborns' face recognition over changes in viewpoint. *Cognition, 106,* 1300–1321.

Turiel, E. (2006). The development of morality. In W. Damon & R. M. Lerner (Editors-in-Chief) & N. Eisenberg (Vol. Ed.), *Handbook of child psychology: Vol. 3. Social, emotional, and personality development* (6th ed., pp. 789–857). Hoboken, NJ: Wiley.

Turiel, E., & Wainryb, C. (1994). Social reasoning and the varieties of social experiences in cultural contexts. In H. Reese (Ed.), *Advances in child development and behavior* (Vol. 25, pp. 289–326). San Diego, CA: Academic Press.

Turkheimer, E., Goldsmith, H. H., & Gottesman, I. I. (1995). Commentary. *Human Development, 38,* 142–153.

Turner, R. A., Irwin, C. E., & Millstein, S. G. (1991). Family structure, family processes, and experimenting with substances during adolescence. *Journal of Research on Adolescence, 1,* 93–106.

Twenge, J. M., & Crocker, J. (2002). Race and self-esteem: Meta-analyses comparing Whites, Blacks, Hispanics, Asians, and American Indians and comment on Gray-Little and Hafdahl (2000). *Psychological Bulletin, 128,* 371–408.

Twyman, A., Friedman, A., & Spetch, M. L. (2007). Penetrating the geometric module: Catalyzing children's use of landmarks. *Developmental Psychology, 43,* 1523–1530.

Ullian, E. M., Sapperstein, S. K., Christopherson, K. S., & Barres, B. A. (2001). Control of synapse number by glia. *Science, 291,* 657–661.

Ulph, F., Betts, P., Mulligan, J., & Stratford, R. J. (2004). Personality functioning: The influence of stature. *Archives of Disease in Childhood, 89,* 17–21.

Underwood, L. E. (1991, March/April). Normal adolescent growth and development. *Nutrition Today,* pp. 11–16.

Underwood, M. K., Schockner, A. E., & Hurley, J. C. (2001). Children's responses to same- and other-gender peers: An experimental investigation with 8-, 10-, and 12-year-olds. *Developmental Psychology, 37,* 362–372.

UNICEF (2002). *The State of the World's Children 2002.* Retrieved November 27, 2002, from http://www.unicef.org/sowc02/

UNICEF (2003). *Social monitor 2003. Innocenti Social Monitors. Florence, Italy: UNICEF Innocent Research Centre.* Retrieved July 21, 2010, from http://www.unicef-irc.org/publications/pdf/monitor03/monitor2003.pdf

UNICEF (2009). *Tracking progress on child and maternal nutrition.* New York, NY: United Nations Children's Fund.

United Nations (2010). *Population and vital statistics report* (Series A, Vol. LXII, No. 1). New York, NY: United Nations.

University of Rochester Medical Center (2010). *Fetal blood sampling.* Retrieved August 19, 2010, from http://www.urmc.rochester.edu/encyclopedia/content.cfm?pageid=P02447

Updegraff, K. A., McHale, S. M., & Crouter, A. C. (1996). Gender roles in marriage: What do they mean for girls' and boys' school achievement? *Journal of Youth and Adolescence, 25,* 73–88.

Urberg, K. A., Degirmencioglu, S. M., Tolson, J. M., & Halliday-Scher, K. (1995). The structure of adolescent peer networks. *Developmental Psychology, 31,* 540–547.

U.S. Census Bureau (2008). *Children characteristics.* Retrieved November 6, 2009, from http://factfinder.census.gov/servlet/STTable?_bm=y&qr_name=ACS_2009_5YR_G00_S0901&-geo_id=01000US&-ds_name=ACS_2009_5YR_G00_

U.S. Census Bureau (2010a). *America's families and living arrangements.* Retrieved September 15, 2010, from http://www.census.gov/population/www/socdemo/hh-fam/cps2009.html

U.S. Census Bureau (2010b). *Fertility of American women current population survey—June 2006.* Retrieved September 15, 2010, from http://www.census.gov/population/www/socdemo/fertility/cps2006.html

U.S. Census Bureau (2010c). *Labor force participation rates for wives, husband present by age of own youngest child.* Retrieved December 21, 2010, from http://www.census.gov/compendia/statab/2010/tables/10s0586.pdf

U.S. Census Bureau (2010d). *Who's minding the kids? Child care arrangements: Spring 2005/Summer 2006.* Retrieved September 23, 2010, from: http://www.census.gov/prod/2010pubs/p70-121.pdf

U.S. Department of Education (1993). *National excellence: A case for developing America's talent.* Washington, DC: Office of Educational Research and Improvement.

U.S. Department of Health and Human Services, Health Resources and Services Administration (2003). *U.S. teens in our world.* Rockville, MD: U.S. Department of Health and Human Services. Retrieved August 30, 2010, from http://mchb.hrsa.gov/mchirc/_pubs/us_teens/main_pages/ch_2.htm

U.S. Department of Health and Human Services (2004a). *The health consequences of smoking: A report of the Surgeon General—2004.* Atlanta, Georgia, Centers for Disease Control and Prevention, Office on Smoking and Health.

U.S. Department of Health and Human Services (2004b). *What you need to know about mercury in fish and shellfish.* Retrieved August 23, 2010, from http://www.fda.gov/food/foodsafety/product-specificinformation/seafood/foodbornepathogenscontaminants/methylmercury/ucm115662.htm

U.S. Department of Health and Human Services (2006). *Results from the 2005 National Survey on Drug Use and Health: National findings.* Retrieved August 23, 2010, from http://oas.samhsa.gov/NSDUH/2k5NSDUH/2k5results.htm#2.7

U.S. Department of Health and Human Services. Administration for Children and Families, Administration on Children, Youth and Families, Children's Bureau (2010). *Child maltreatment 2008.* Available from: http://www.acf.hhs.gov/programs/cb/pubs/cm08/cm08.pdf

Uttal, D. H., Gregg, V. H., Tan, L. S., Chamberlin, M. H., & Sines, A. (2001). Connecting the dots: Children's use of a systematic figure to facilitate mapping and search. *Developmental Psychology, 37,* 338–350.

Uttal, D. H., & Wellman, H. M. (1989). Young children's representation of spatial information acquired from maps. *Developmental Psychology, 25,* 128–138.

Vaish, A., Carpenter, M., & Tomasello, M. (2009). Sympathy through affective perspective taking and its relation to prosocial behavior in toddlers. *Developmental Psychology, 45,* 534–543.

Vaish, A., Grossmann, T., & Woodward, A. (2008). Not all emotions are created equal: The negativity bias in social-emotional development. *Psychological Bulletin, 134,* 383–403.

Valdez-Menchaca, M. C., & Whitehurst, G. J. (1992). Accelerating language development through picture book reading: A systematic extension to Mexican day care. *Developmental Psychology, 28,* 1106–1114.

Valenza, E., Leo, I., Gava, L., & Simion, F. (2006). Perceptual completion in newborn human infants. *Child Development, 77,* 1810–1821.

Valeski, T. N., & Stipek, D. J. (2001). Young children's feelings about school. *Child Development, 72,* 1198–1213.

Valian, V. (1986). Syntactic categories in the speech of young children. *Developmental Psychology, 22,* 562–579.

Valk, A. (2000). Ethnic identity, ethnic attitudes, self-esteem, and esteem toward others among Estonian and Russian adolescents. *Journal of Adolescent Research, 15,* 637–651.

Valkenburg, P. M., & Peter, J. (2007). Preadolescents' and adolescents' online communication and their closeness to friends. *Developmental Psychology, 43,* 267–277.

Valkenburg, P. M., & Peter, J. (2009). Social consequences of the Internet for adolescents: A decade of research. *Current Directions in Psychological Science, 18,* 1–5.

Valsiner, J. (2006). Developmental epistemology and implications for methodology. In W. Damon & R. M. Lerner (Editors-in-Chief) & R. M. Lerner (Vol. Ed.), *Handbook of child psychology: Vol. 1. Theoretical models of human development* (6th ed., pp. 166–209). Hoboken, NJ: Wiley.

Van Balen, F. (1998). Development of IVF children. *Developmental Review, 18,* 30–46.

Vandell, D. L., Belsky, J., Burchinal, M., Steinberg, L., & Vandergrift, N. (2010). Do effects of early child care extend to age 15 years? Results from the NICHD Study of Early Child Care and Youth Development. *Child Development, 81,* 737–756.

Vandell, D. L., & Mueller, E. C. (1980). Peer play and friendships during the first two years. In H. C. Foot, A. J. Chapman, & J. R. Smith (Eds.), *Friendship and social relations in children* (pp. 181–208). New York, NY: Wiley.

Vandell, D. L., & Ramanan, J. (1992). Effects of early and recent maternal employment on children from low-income families. *Child Development, 63,* 938–949.

Vandell, D. L., Wilson, K. S., & Buchanan, N. R. (1980). Peer interaction in the first year of life: An examination of its structure, content, and sensitivity to toys. *Child Development, 51,* 481–488.

Vandenberg, S. G., & Vogler, G. P. (1985). Genetic determinants of intelligence. In B. B. Wolman (Ed.), *Handbook of intelligence: Theories, research and applications* (pp. 3–57). New York, NY: Wiley.

van den Boom, D. C. (1994). The influence of temperament and mothering on attachment and exploration: An experimental manipulation of sensitive responsiveness among lower-class mothers with irritable infants. *Child Development, 65,* 1457–1477.

van den Boom, D. C. (1995). Do first-year intervention effects endure? Follow-up during toddlerhood of a sample of Dutch irritable infants. *Child Development, 66,* 1798–1816.

van den Boom, D. C., & Hoeksma, J. B. (1994). The effects of infant irritability on mother-infant interaction: A growth-curve analysis. *Developmental Psychology, 30,* 581–590.

van den Eijnden, R. J. J. M., Meerker, G.-J., Vermulst, A. A., Spijkerman, R., & Engels, R. C. M. E. (2008). Online communication, compulsive Internet use, and psychosocial well-being among adolescents: A longitudinal study. *Developmental Psychology, 44,* 655–665.

van Doesum, K. T. M., Riksen-Walraven, J. M., Hosman, C. M. H., & Hoefnagels, C. (2008). A randomized controlled trial of a home-visiting intervention aimed at preventing relationship problems in depressed mothers and their infants. *Child Development, 79,* 547–561.

Vange, L. M. (1992). Infant Health and Development Program for low birth weight, premature infants: Program elements, family participation, and child intelligence. *Pediatrics, 89,* 454–465.

Van IJzendoorn, M. H. (1995). Adult attachment representations, parental responsiveness and infant attachment: A meta-analysis on the predictive validity of the Adult Attachment Interview. *Psychological Bulletin, 117,* 387–403.

van IJzendoorn, M. H., Moran, G., Belsky, J., Pederson, D., Bakermans Kranenburg, M. J., & Kneppers, K. (2000). The similarity of siblings' attachments to their mother. *Child Development, 71,* 1086–1098.

van IJzendoorn, M. H., & Sagi, A. (1999). Cross-cultural patterns of attachment. In J. Cassidy & P. R. Shaver (Eds.), *Handbook of attachment: Theory, research, and clinical applications* (pp. 713–734). New York, NY: Guilford Press.

Vannatta, K., Gartstein, M. A., Zeller, M., & Noll, R. B. (2009). Peer acceptance and social behavior during childhood and adolescence: How important are appearance, athleticism, and academic competence? *International Journal of Behavioral Development, 33,* 303–311.

Van Rooy, C., Stough, C., Pipingas, A., Hocking, C., & Silberstein, R. B. (2001). Spatial working memory and intelligence: Biological correlates. *Intelligence, 29,* 275–292.

Varni, J. W. (1983). *Clinical behavioral pediatrics: An interdisciplinary biobehavioral approach.* New York, NY: Pergamon Press.

Vasilyeva, M., Waterfall, H., & Huttenlocher, J. (2008). Emergence of syntax: Commonalities and differences across children. *Developmental Science, 11,* 84–97.

Vaughn, B. E., Kopp, C. B., & Krakow, J. B. (1984). The emergence and consolidation of self-control from eighteen to thirty months of age: Normative trends and individual differences. *Child Development, 55,* 990–1004.

Vaughn, B. E., Taraldson, B., Crichton, L., & Egeland, B. (1980). Relationships between neonatal behavioral organization and infant behavior during the first year of life. *Infant Behavior and Development, 3,* 78–89.

Veenstra, R., Lindenberg, S., Zijlstra, B. J. H., De Winter, A. F., Verhulst, F. C., & Ormel, J. (2007). The dyadic nature of bullying and victimization: Testing a dual-perspective theory. *Child Development, 78,* 1843–1854.

Vernon, P. A. (1983). Speed of information processing and general intelligence. *Intelligence, 7,* 53–70.

Verschueren, K., & Marcoen, A. (1999). Representation of self and socio-emotional competence in kindergartners: Differential and combined effects of attachment to mothers and fathers. *Child Development, 70,* 183–201.

Vicari, S. (2006). Motor development and neuropsychological patterns in persons with Down Syndrome. *Behavior Genetics, 36,* 355–364.

Vihman, M. M. (1998). Early phonological disorders. In J. E. Bernthal & N. W. Bankson (Eds.), *Articulation and phonological development* (4th ed., pp. 63–110). Boston: Allyn & Bacon.

Volkova, A., Trehub, S. E., & Schellenberg, E. G. (2006). Infants' memory for musical performances. *Developmental Science, 9,* 583–589.

Volling, B. L., MacKinnon-Lewis, C., Rabiner, D., & Baradaran, L. P. (1993). Children's social competence and sociometric status: Further exploration of aggression, social withdrawal, and peer rejection. *Development and Psychopathology, 5,* 459–483.

von Hofsten, C., & Rosander, K. (1997). Development of smooth pursuit tracking in young infants. *Vision Research, 37,* 1799–1810.

Vorhees, C. V. (1986). Principles of behavioral teratology. In E. P. Riley & C. V. Vorhees (Eds.), *Handbook of behavioral teratology* (pp. 23–48). New York, NY: Plenum Press.

Vouloumanos, A., & Werker, J. F. (2004). Tuned to the signal: The privileged status of speech for young infants. *Developmental Science, 7,* 270–276.

Vouloumanos, A., & Werker, J. F. (2007). Listening to language at birth: Evidence for a bias for speech in neonates. *Developmental Science, 10,* 159–171.

Vouloumanos, A., & Werker, J. F. (2009). Infants' learning of novel words in a stochastic environment. *Developmental Psychology, 45,* 1611–1617.

Voyer, D., Voyer, S., & Bryden, M. P. (1995). Magnitude of sex differences in spatial abilities: A meta-analysis and consideration of critical variables. *Psychological Bulletin, 117,* 250–270.

Vuchinich, S., Hetherington, E. M., Vuchinich, R. A., & Clingempeel, W. G. (1991). Parent-child interaction and gender differences in early adolescents' adaptation to stepfamilies. *Developmental Psychology, 27,* 618–626.

Vuilleumier, P. (2005). How brains beware: Neural mechanisms of emotional attention. *Trends in Cognitive Sciences, 9,* 585–594.

Vurpillot, E. (1968). The development of scanning strategies and their relation to visual differentiation. *Journal of Experimental Child Psychology, 6,* 632–650.

Vurpillot, E., & Ball, W. A. (1979). The concept of identity and children's selective attention. In G. A. Hale & M. Lewis (Eds.), *Attention and cognitive development* (pp. 23–42). New York, NY: Plenum Press.

Vuyk, R. (1981). *Overview and critique of Piaget's genetic epistemology 1965–1980* (Vols. 1 & 2). New York, NY: Academic Press.

Vygotsky, L. S. (1962). *Thought and language* (E. Hanfmann & G. Vakar, Trans.). Cambridge, MA: MIT Press.

Vygotsky, L. S. (1978). *Mind in society: The development of higher psychological processes.* Cambridge, MA: Harvard University Press.

Waber, D. P. (1976). Sex differences in cognition: A function of maturation rate? *Science, 192,* 572–574.

Wachs, T. D., & Combs, T. T. (1995). The domains of infant mastery motivation. In R. H. McTurk & G. A. Morgan (Eds.), *Mastery motivation: Origins, conceptualizations, and applications* (pp. 147–164). Norwood, NJ: Ablex.

Waddington, C. H. (1971). Concepts of development. In E. Tobach, L. R. Aronson, & E. Shaw (Eds.), *The biopsychology of development* (pp. 17–23). San Diego, CA: Academic Press.

Wager, T. D., Barrett, L. F., Bliss-Moreau, E., Lindquist, K. A., Duncan, S., Kober, H., Joseph, J., et al. (2008). The neuroimaging of emotion. In M. Lewis, J. M. Haviland-Jones, & L. F. Barrett (Eds.), *Handbook of emotions* (3rd ed., pp. 249–271). New York, NY: Guilford.

Wagner, L. (2001). Aspectual influences on early tense comprehension. *Journal of Child Language, 28,* 661–681.

Wagner, M. E., Schubert, H. J. P., & Schubert, D. S. P. (1985). Family size effects: A review. *Journal of Genetic Psychology, 146,* 65–78.

Wagner, M. M. (1995, Summer/Fall). Outcomes for youths with serious emotional disturbance in secondary school and early adulthood. *The Future of Children, 5*(2), pp. 90–112.

Wagner, M. M., Blackorby, J., & Hebbeler, K. (1993). *Beyond the report card: The multiple dimensions of secondary school performance of students with disabilities: A report from the National Longitudinal Transition Study of Special Education Students.* Menlo Park, CA: SRI International.

Wahlstrom, K. (2002). Changing times: Findings from the first longitudinal study of later high school start times. *NASSP Bulletin, 86,* 3–21.

Wainright, J. L., & Patterson, C. J. (2008). Peer relations among adolescents with female same-sex parents. *Developmental Psychology, 44,* 117–126.

Wainright, J. L., Russell, S. T., & Patterson, C. J. (2004). Psychosocial adjustment, school outcomes, and romantic relationships of adolescents with same-sex parents. *Child Development, 75,* 1886–1898.

Wainryb, C., Shaw, L. A., Laupa, M., & Smith, K. R. (2001). Children's, adolescents', and young adults' thinking about different types of disagreements. *Developmental Psychology, 37,* 373–386.

Walden, T. A., & Smith, M. C. (1997). Emotion regulation. *Motivation and Emotion, 21,* 7–25.

Walk, R. D. (1968). Monocular compared to binocular depth perception in human infants. *Science, 162,* 473–475.

Walker-Andrews, A. S., Bahrick, L. E., Raglioni, S. S., & Diaz, I. (1991). Infant's bimodal perception of gender. *Ecological Psychology, 3,* 55–75.

Walker, E. F. (2002). Adolescent neurodevelopment and psychopathology. *Current Directions in Psychological Science, 11,* 24–28.

Walker, L. J., Hennig, K. H., & Krettenauer, T. (2000). Parent and peer contexts for children's moral reasoning development. *Child Development, 71,* 1033–1048.

Walker, L. J. (1984). Sex differences in the development of moral reasoning: A critical review. *Child Development, 55,* 677–691.

Walker, L. J. (1989). A longitudinal study of moral reasoning. *Child Development, 60,* 157–166.

Walker, L. J. (1996). Is one sex morally superior? In M. R. Merrens & G. G. Brannigan (Eds.), *The developmental psychologists: Research adventures across the life span* (pp. 172–186). New York, NY: McGraw-Hill.

Wallerstein, J. S., Corbin, S. B., & Lewis, J. M. (1988). Children of divorce: A ten-year study. In E. M. Hetherington & J. Arasteh (Eds.), *Impact of divorce, single-parenting, and stepparenting on children* (pp. 198–214). Hillsdale, NJ: Erlbaum.

Wallerstein, J. S., & Kelly, J. B. (1980). *Surviving the breakup: How children and parents cope with divorce.* New York, NY: Basic Books.

Walsh, B. T., & Devlin, M. J. (1998). Eating disorders: Progress and problems. *Science, 280,* 1387–1390.

Wang, Q. (2004). The emergence of cultural self-constructs: Autobiographical memory and self-description in European American and Chinese children. *Developmental Psychology, 40,* 3–15.

Wang, Q. (2006a). Earliest recollections of self and others in European American and Taiwanese young adults. *Psychological Science, 17,* 708–714.

Wang, Q. (2006b). Relations of maternal style and child self-concept to autobiographical memories in Chinese, Chinese immigrant, and European American 3-year-olds. *Child Development, 77,* 1794–1809.

Wang, Q., Pomerantz, E. M., & Chen, H. (2007). The role of parents' control in early adolescents' psychological functioning: A longitudinal investigation in the United States and China. *Child Development, 78,* 1592–1610.

Wang, Y., & Lobstein, T. (2006). Worldwide trends in childhood overweight and obesity. *International Journal of Pediatric Obesity, 1,* 11–25.

Ward, L. M. (2004). Wading through stereotypes: Positive and negative associations between media use and black adolescents' conceptions of self. *Developmental Psychology, 40,* 284–294.

Ward, S., Reale, G., & Levinson, D. (1972). Children's perceptions, explanations, and judgments of television advertising. In E. A. Rubenstein, G. A. Comstock, & J. P. Murray (Eds.), *Television and social behavior: Vol. 4. Television in day-to-day life: Patterns of use* (pp. 468–490). Washington, DC: U.S. Government Printing Office.

Wark, G. R., & Krebs, D. L. (1996). Gender and dilemma differences in real-life moral judgment. *Developmental Psychology, 32,* 220–230.

Warkany, J., & Schraffenberger, E. (1947). Congenital malformations induced in rats by roentgen rays. *American Journal of Roentgenology and Radium Therapy, 57,* 455–463.

Warneken, F., & Tomasello, M. (2008). Extrinsic rewards undermine altruistic tendencies in 20-month-olds. *Developmental Psychology, 44,* 1785–1788.

Warren, S. L., Huston, L., Egeland, B., & Sroufe, L. A. (1997). Child and adolescent anxiety disorders and early attachment. *Journal of the American Academy of Child and Adolescent Psychiatry, 36,* 637–644.

Wass, T. S., Persutte, W. H., & Hobbins, J. C. (2001). The impact of prenatal alcohol exposure on frontal cortex development in utero. *American Journal of Obstetrics and Gynecology, 185,* 737–742.

Waterhouse, L., Fein, D., & Modahl, C. (1996). Neurofunctional mechanisms in autism. *Psychological Review, 103,* 457–489.

Waters, E., & Deane, K. E. (1985). Defining and assessing individual differences in attachment relationships: Q-methodology and the organization of behavior in infancy and early childhood. In I. Bretherton & E. Waters (Eds.), *Growing points of attachment theory and research. Monographs of the Society for Research in Child Development, 50* (1–2, Serial No. 209).

Waters, E., Wippman, J., & Sroufe, L. A. (1979). Attachment, positive affect, and competence in the peer group: Two studies in construct validation. *Child Development, 50,* 821–829.

Watson, A. C., Nixon, C. L., Wilson, A., & Capage, L. (1999). Social interaction skills and theory of mind in young children. *Developmental Psychology, 35,* 386–391.

Watson, J. B. (1930). *Behaviorism.* New York, NY: W. W. Norton.

Watson, J. S. (1971). Cognitive-perceptual development in infancy: Settings for the seventies. *Merrill-Palmer Quarterly, 17,* 139–152.

Watson, J. S., & Ramey, C. T. (1972). Reactions to response-contingent stimulation in early infancy. *Merrill-Palmer Quarterly, 18,* 219–227.

Watson, R., Gemin, B., Ryna, J., & Wicks, M. (2009). *Keeping pace with K-12 online learning.* Retrieved May 13, 2010, from http://www.kpk12.com/downloads/KeepingPace09-fullreport.pdf

Waxman, S. R., & Booth, A. E. (2000). Principles that are invoked in the acquisition of words, but not facts. *Cognition, 77,* B33–B43.

Weber-Fox, C. M., & Neville, H. J. (1996). Maturational contraints on functional specializations for language processing: ERP and behavioral evidence in bilingual speakers. *Journal of Cognitive Neuroscience, 8,* 231–256.

Weinberg, M. K., & Tronick, E. Z. (1994). Beyond the face: An empirical study of infant affective configurations of facial, vocal, gestural, and regulatory behaviors. *Child Development, 65,* 1503–1515.

Weinberg, M. K., Tronick, E. Z., Cohn, J. F., & Olson, K. L. (1999). Gender differences in emotional expressivity and self-regulation during early infancy. *Developmental Psychology, 35,* 175–188.

Weinberger, S. E., & Weiss, S. T. (1988). Pulmonary diseases. In G. N. Burrow & T. F. Ferris (Eds.), *Medical complications of pregnancy* (3rd ed., pp. 448–484). Philadelphia: W. B. Saunders.

Weiner, B., & Handel, S. J. (1985). A cognition-emotion-action sequence: Anticipated emotional consequences of causal attributions and reported communication strategy. *Developmental Psychology, 21,* 102–107.

Weinfield, N. S., Ogawa, J. R., & Sroufe, L. A. (1997). Early attachment as a pathway to adolescent peer competence. *Journal of Research on Adolescence, 7,* 241–265.

Weis, R., & Cerankosky, B. C. (2010). Effects of video-game ownership on young boys' academic and behavioral functioning: A randomized, controlled study. *Psychological Science, 21,* 463–470.

Weisner, T. S. (1996). Why ethnography should be the most important method in the study of human development. In A. C. R. Jessor & R. A. Shweder (Eds.), *Ethnography and human development* (pp. 305–324). Chicago, IL: University of Chicago Press.

Weiss, L. H., & Schwarz, J. C. (1996). The relationship between parenting types and older adolescents' personality, academic achievement, adjustment, and substance abuse. *Child Development, 67,* 2101–2114.

Weitzman, L. J. (1985). *The divorce revolution: The unexpected social and economic consequences for women and children in America.* New York, NY: Free Press.

Weitzman, M., Gortmaker, S., & Sobol, A. (1992). Maternal smoking and behavior problems of children. *Pediatrics, 90,* 342–349.

Welch-Ross, M. K., & Schmidt, C. R. (1996). Gender-schema development and children's constructive story memory: Evidence for a developmental model. *Child Development, 67,* 820–835.

Wellman, H. M. (1977). The early development of intentional memory. *Human Development, 20,* 86–101.

Wellman, H. M. (1990). *The child's theory of mind.* Cambridge, MA: MIT Press.

Wellman, H. M., Cross, D., & Watson, J. (2001). Meta-analysis of theory of mind development: The truth about false belief. *Child Development, 72,* 655–684.

Wellman, H. M., & Estes, D. (1986). Early understanding of mental entities: A reexamination of childhood realism. *Child Development, 57,* 910–923.

Wellman, H. M., & Hickling, A. K. (1994). The mind's "I": Children's conception of the mind as an active agent. *Child Development, 65,* 1564–1580.

Wellman, H. M., & Lempers, J. D. (1977). The naturalistic communicative abilities of two-year-olds. *Child Development, 48,* 1052–1057.

Wellman, H. M., & Liu, D. (2004). Scaling of theory-of-mind tasks. *Child Development, 75,* 523–541.

Welsh, M. C. (2002). Developmental and clinical variations in executive functions. In D. L. Molfese & V. J. Molfese (Eds.), *Developmental variations in learning: Applications to social, executive function, language, and reading skills* (pp. 139–185). Mahwah, NJ: Erlbaum.

Wenglinsky, H. (1998). *Does it compute? The relationship between educational technology and student achievement in mathematics.* Princeton, NJ: Educational Testing Service.

Wentzel, K. R. (2002). Are effective teachers like good parents? Teaching styles and student adjustment in early adolescence. *Child Development, 73,* 287–301.

Wentzel, K. R. (2009). Peers and academic functioning at school. In K. H. Rubin, W. M. Bukowski, & B. Laursen (Eds.), *Handbook of peer interactions, relationships, and groups* (pp. 531–547). New York, NY: Guilford Press.

Werker, J. F. (1989). Becoming a native listener. *American Scientist, 77,* 54–59.

Werker, J. F., & Desjardins, R. N. (1995). Listening to speech in the 1st year of life: Experiential influences on phoneme perception. *Current Directions in Psychological Science, 4,* 76–81.

Werker, J. F., & Lalonde, C. E. (1988). Cross-language speech perception: Initial capabilities and developmental change. *Developmental Psychology, 24,* 672–683.

Werker, J. F., & Tees, R. C. (2005). Speech perception as a window for understanding plasticity and commitment of language systems of the brain. *Developmental Psychobiology, 46,* 233–251

Werler, M., Mitchell, A. A., Hernandez-Diaz, S., & Honein, M. A., and the National Birth Defects Prevention Study. (2005). Use of over-the-counter medication during pregnancy. *American Journal of Obstetrics and Gynecology, 193,* 771–777.

Werner, E. (2005). Resilience research: Past, present, and future. In Peters, R. D., Leadbeater, B., & McMahon, R. J. (Eds.) *Resilience in children, families, and communities: Linking context to practice and policy* (pp. 3–11). New York, NY: Kluwer Academic/Plenum.

Werner, E. E. (1972). Infants around the world: Cross-cultural studies of psychomotor development from birth to two years. *Journal of Cross-Cultural Psychology, 3,* 111–134.

Wertsch, J. V. (1985). *Vygotsky and the social formation of mind.* Cambridge, MA: Harvard University Press.

Wertsch, J. V., & Tulviste, P. (1992). L. S. Vygotsky and contemporary developmental psychology. *Developmental Psychology, 28,* 548–557.

Wertz, D. C., & Fletcher, J. C. (1993). Feminist criticism of prenatal diagnosis: A response. *Clinical Obstetrics and Gynecology, 36,* 541–567.

Wertz, D. C., & Fletcher, J. C. (1998). Ethical and social issues in prenatal sex selection: A survey of geneticists in 37 nations. *Social Science & Medicine, 46,* 255–273.

West, T. A., & Bauer, P. J. (1999). Assumptions of infantile amnesia: Are there differences between early and later memories? *Memory, 7,* 257–278.

Wexler, K. (1982). A principle theory for language acquisition. In E. Wanner & L. Gleitman (Eds.), *Language acquisition: The state of the art* (pp. 288–315). Cambridge: Cambridge University Press.

Whalen, C. K., Jamner, L. D., Henker, B., Delfino, R. J., & Lozano, J. M. (2002). The ADHD Spectrum and everyday life: Experience sampling of adolescent moods, activities, smoking, and drinking. *Child Development, 73,* 209–227.

Whalen, R. E. (1984). Multiple actions of steroids and their antagonists. *Archives of Sexual Behavior, 13,* 497–502.

Wheatley, T., Milleville, S. C., & Martin, A. (2007). Understanding animate objects: Distinct roles for the social network and mirror system. *Psychological Science, 18,* 469–474.

Wheeler, P. G., Bresnahan, K., Shephard, B. A., Lau, J., & Balk, E. M. (2004). Short stature and functional impairment: A systematic review. *Archives of Pediatrics and Adolescent Medicine, 158,* 236–243.

Whitaker, R. C., & Orzol, S. M. (2006). Obesity among US urban preschool children relationships to race, ethnicity, and socioeconomic status. *Archives of Pediatric and Adolescent Medicine, 160,* 578–584.

White, R. W. (1959). Motivation reconsidered: The concept of competence. *Psychological Review, 66,* 297–333.

Whitehouse, A. J., & Bishop, D. V. (2008). Do children with autism 'switch off' to speech sounds? An investigation using event-related potentials. *Developmental Science, 11,* 516–524.

Whitehurst, G. J., Arnold, D. S., Epstein, J. N., Angell, A. L., Smith, M., & Fischel, J. E. (1994). A picture book reading intervention in day care and home for children from low-income families. *Developmental Psychology, 30,* 679–689.

Whiting, B. B., & Edwards, C. P. (1988). *Children of different worlds.* Cambridge, MA: Harvard University Press.

Whiting, B. B., & Whiting, J. W. M. (1975). *Children of six cultures: A psychocultural analysis.* Cambridge, MA: Harvard University Press.

Whitlock, J. L., Powers, J. L., & Eckenrode, J. (2006). The virtual cutting edge: The Internet and adolescent self-injury. *Developmental Psychology, 42,* 407–417.

Whitman, T. L., Borkowski, J. G., Keogh, D., & Weed, K. (2001). *Interwoven lives: Adolescent mothers and their children.* Mahweh, NJ: Erlbaum.

Wichstrøm, L. (1999). The emergence of gender difference in depressed mood during adolescence: The role of intensified gender socialization. *Developmental Psychology, 35,* 232–245.

Widaman, K. F. (2009). Phenylketonuria in children and mothers: Genes, environments, behavior. *Current Directions in Psychological Science, 18,* 48–52.

Widom, C. S. (1989). The cycle of violence. *Science, 244,* 160–166.

Wilkins-Haug, L. (2008). Assisted reproductive technology, Congenital malformations, and epigenetic disease. *Clinical Obstetrics & Gynecology, 51,* 96–105.

Willatts, P. (1990). Development of problem-solving strategies in infancy. In D. F. Bjorklund (Ed.), *Children's strategies: Contemporary views of cognitive development* (pp. 23–66). Hillsdale, NJ: Erlbaum.

Williams, J. E., & Best, D. L. (1982). *Measuring sex stereotypes: A thirty nation study.* Beverly Hills, CA: Sage.

Williams, J. M., & Currie, C. (2000). Self-esteem and physical development in early adolescence: Pubertal timing and body image. *Journal of Early Adolescence, 20,* 120–149.

Williams, S. T., Ontai, L. L., & Mastergeorge, A. M. (2010). The development of peer interaction in infancy: Exploring the dyadic processes. *Social Development, 19,* 348–368.

Williamson, R. A., Meltzoff, A. N., & Markman, E. M. (2008). Prior experience and perceived efficacy influence 3-year-olds' imitation. *Developmental Psychology, 44,* 275–285.

Willig, A. C., & Ramirez, J. D. (1993). The evaluation of bilingual education. In M. B. Arias & U. Casanova (Eds.), *Bilingual education: Politics, practice, research* (pp. 65–87). Chicago, IL: National Society for the Study of Education.

Willinger, M., Ko, C.-W., Hoffman, H. J., Kessler, R. C., & Corwin, M. J. (2003). Trends in infant bed sharing in the United States, 1993–2000: The National Infant Sleep Position Study. *Archives of Pediatrics & Adolescent Medicine, 157,* 43–49.

Willoughby, T. (2008). A short-term longitudinal study of Internet and computer game use by adolescent boys and girls: Prevalence, frequency of use, and psychosocial predictors. *Developmental Psychology, 44,* 195–204.

Wilson, A. E., Smith, M. D., & Ross, H. D. (2003). The nature and effects of children's lies. *Social Development, 12,* 21–45.

Wilson, B. J. (2008, Spring). Media and children's aggression, fear, and altruism. Special issue: Children and electronic media. *The Future of Children, 18*(1), 87–118.

Wilson, B. J., & Weiss, A. J. (1992). Developmental differences in children's reactions to a toy advertisement linked to a toy-based cartoon. *Journal of Broadcasting and Electronic Media, 36,* 371–394.

Wilson, J. G. (1977). Current status of teratology: General principles and mechanisms derived from animal studies. In J. G. Wilson & F. C. Fraser (Eds.), *Handbook of teratology: Vol. 1. General principles and etiology* (pp. 47–74). New York, NY: Plenum Press.

Wilson, M. N. (1986). The black extended family: An analytical consideration. *Developmental Psychology, 22,* 246–258.

Wimmer, H., & Perner, J. (1983). Beliefs about beliefs: Representation and constraining function of wrong beliefs in young children's understanding of deception. *Cognition, 13,* 103–128.

Winner, E. (1979). New names for old things: The emergence of metaphoric language. *Journal of Child Language, 6,* 469–491.

Winner, E. (1996). *Gifted children: Myths and realities.* New York, NY: Basic Books.

Winner, E. (1997). Exceptionally high intelligence and schooling. *American Psychologist, 52,* 1070–1081.

Winner, E. (2000). The origins and ends of giftedness. *American Psychologist, 55,* 159–169.

Winsler, A., Diaz, R. M., Atencio, D. J., McCarthy, E. M., & Chabay, L. A. (2000). Verbal self-regulation over time in preschool children at risk for attention and behavior problems. *Journal of Child Psychology and Psychiatry, 41,* 875–886.

Winsler, A., & Naglieri, J. (2003). Overt and covert verbal problem-solving strategies: Developmental trends in use, awareness, and relations with task performance in children aged 5 to 17. *Child Development, 74,* 659–678.

Winstead, B. A. (1986). Sex differences in same-sex friendships. In V. J. Derlaga & B. A. Winstead (Eds.), *Friendship and social interaction* (pp. 81–99). New York, NY: Springer-Verlag.

Wolchik, S. A., West, S. G., Westover, S., Sandler, I. N., Martin, A., Lustig, J., et al. (2002). The children of divorce parenting intervention: Outcome evaluation of an empirically based program. In T. A. Revenson & A. R. D'Augelli (Eds.), *A quarter century of community psychology: Readings from the American Journal of Community Psychology* (pp. 409–444). New York, NY: Kluwer Academic/Plenum Publishers.

Wolf, T. M. (1973). Effects of live modeled sex-inappropriate play behavior in a naturalistic setting. *Developmental Psychology, 9,* 120–123.

Wolfe, D. A. (1985). Child-abusive parents: An empirical review and analysis. *Psychological Bulletin, 97,* 462–482.

Wolfe, D. A., Fairbank, J., Kelly, J. A., & Bradlyn, A. S. (1983). Child abusive parents' physiological responses to stressful and non-stressful behavior in children. *Behavioral Assessment, 5,* 363–371.

Wolff, P. H. (1969). The natural history of crying and other vocalizations in early infancy. In B. Foss (Ed.), *Determinants of infant behavior* (Vol. 4, pp. 81–109). London, UK: Methuen.

Wolff, P. H. (1987). *The development of behavioral states and the expression of emotions in early infancy.* Chicago, IL: University of Chicago Press.

Wolfner, G. D., & Gelles, R. J. (1993). A profile of violence toward children: A national study. *Child Abuse and Neglect, 17,* 197–212.

Wolfson, A. R., & Carskadon, M. A. (1998). Sleep schedules and daytime functioning in adolescents. *Child Development, 69,* 875–887.

Wong, C. A., Eccles, J. S., & Sameroff, A. (2003). The influence of ethnic discrimination and ethnic identity on African American adolescents' school and socioemotional adjustment. *Journal of Personality, 71,* 1197–1232.

Wood, J. N., Kouider, S., & Carey, S. (2009). Acquisition of singular-plural morphology. *Developmental Psychology, 45,* 202–206.

Wood, J. N., & Spelke, E. S. (2005). Infants' enumeration of actions: Numerical discrimination and its signature limits. *Developmental Science, 8,* 173–181.

Woodward, A. L. (1998). Infants selectively encode the goal object of an actor's reach. *Cognition, 69,* 1–34.

Woodward, A. L. (2009). Infants' grasp of others' intentions. *Current Directions in Psychological Science, 18,* 53–57.

Woodward, S. A., McManis, M. H., Kagan, J., Deldin, P., Snidman, N., Lewis, M., & Kahn, V. (2001). Infant temperament and the brainstem auditory evoked response in later childhood. *Developmental Psychology, 37,* 533–538.

Woolfe, T., Want, S. C., & Siegal, M. (2002). Signposts to development: Theory of mind in deaf children. *Child Development, 73,* 768–778.

Woolley, M. E., & Grogan-Kaylor, A. (2006). Protective family factors in the context of neighborhood: Promoting positive school outcomes. *Family Relations, 55,* 93–104.

Worobey, J. (1985). A review of Brazelton-based interventions to enhance parent-infant interaction. *Journal of Reproductive and Infant Psychology, 3,* 64–73.

Wright, J. C., Huston, A. C., Murphy, K. C., St. Peters, M., Piñon, M., Scantlin, R., & Kotler, J. (2001). The relations of early television viewing to school readiness and vocabulary of children from low-income families: The Early Window Project. *Child Development, 72,* 1347–1366.

Wright, J. C., Huston, A. C., Reitz, A. L., & Piemyat, S. (1994). Young children's perceptions of television reality: Determinants and developmental differences. *Developmental Psychology, 30,* 229–239.

Wright, J. C., Murphy, K. C., St. Peters, M., Piñon, M., Scantlin, R., & Kotler, J. (2001). The relations of early television viewing to school readiness and vocabulary of children from low-income families: The Early Window Project. *Child Development, 72,* 1347–1366.

Wright, M. O., & Masten, A. S. (2005). Resilience processes in development. In S. Goldstein & R. B. Brooks (Eds.), *Handbook of resilience in children* (pp. 17–37). New York, NY: Klewar/Plenum.

Wyman, E., Rakoczy, H., & Tomasello, M. (2009). Young children understand multiple pretend identities in their object play. *British Journal of Developmental Psychology, 27,* 385–404.

Wynn, K. (1992). Addition and subtraction by human infants. *Nature, 358,* 749–750.

Wynn, K. (1998). Psychological foundations of number: Numerical competence in human infants. *Trends in Cognitive Science, 2,* 296–303.

Xu, F., & Spelke, E. S. (2000). Large number discrimination in 6-month-olds. *Cognition, 74,* B1–B11.

Xu, J., Kochanek, K. D., & Tejada-Vera, B. (2009, August 19). Deaths: Preliminary data for 2007. *National Vital Statistics Reports, 58(1)* Retrieved August 30, 2010, from http://www.cdc.gov/nchs/data/nvsr/nvsr58/nvsr58_01.pdf

Xu, Y., Farver, J. A. M., & Zhang, Z. (2009). Temperament, harsh and indulgent parenting, and Chinese children's proactive and reactive aggression. *Child Development, 80,* 244–258.

Yale, M. E., Messinger, D. S., Cobo-Lewis, A. B., Oller, D. K., & Eilers, R. E. (1999). An event-based analysis of the coordination of early child vocalizations and facial actions. *Developmental Psychology, 35,* 505–513.

Yarrow, L. J., Goodwin, M. S., Manheimer, H., & Milowe, I. D. (1973). Infancy experiences and cognitive and personality development at 10 years. In L. J. Stone, H. T. Smith, & L. B. Murphy (Eds.), *The competent infant: Research and commentary* (pp. 1274–1281). New York, NY: Basic Books.

Yee, D. K., & Eccles, J. S. (1988). Parent perceptions and attributions for children's math achievement. *Sex Roles, 19,* 317–333.

Yendovitskaya, T. V. (1971). Development of attention. In A. V. Zaporozhets & D. B. Elkonin (Eds.), *The psychology of preschool children* (pp. 65–88). Cambridge, MA: MIT Press.

Yogman, M. W. (1982). Observations on the father-infant relationship. In S. H. Cath, A. R. Gurwitt, & J. M. Ross (Eds.), *Father and child: Developmental and clinical perspectives* (pp. 101–122). Boston: Little, Brown.

Yonas, A., & Owsley, C. (1987). Development of visual space perception. In P. Salapatek & L. Cohen (Eds.), *Handbook of infant perception: From perception to cognition* (Vol. 2, pp. 79–122). Orlando, FL: Academic Press.

Yoon, J. M. D., & Johnson, S. C. (2009). Biological motion displays elicit social behavior in 12-month-olds. *Child Development, 80,* 1069–1075.

Yoon, P. W., Olney, R. S., Khoury, M. J., Sappenfield, W. M., Chavez, G. F., & Taylor, D. (1997). Contribution of birth defects and genetic diseases to pediatric hospitalizations. *Archives of Pediatrics & Adolescent Medicine, 151,* 1096–1103.

Young, M. H., Miller, B. C., Norton, M. C., & Hill, E. J. (1995). The effect of parental supportive behaviors on life satisfaction of adolescent offspring. *Journal of Marriage and Family, 57,* 813–822.

Young, S. K., Fox, N. A., & Zahn-Waxler, C. (1999). The relations between temperament and empathy in 2-year-olds. *Developmental Psychology, 35,* 1189–1197.

Younger, A., Gentile, C., & Burgess, K. (1993). Children's perceptions of social withdrawal: Changes across age. In K. H. Rubin & J. B. Asendorpf (Eds.), *Social withdrawal, inhibition, and shyness in childhood* (pp. 215–235). Hillsdale, NJ: Erlbaum.

Yule, W. (1998). Posttraumatic stress disorder in children and its treatment. In T. W. Miller (Ed.), *Children of trauma: Stressful life events and their effects on children and adolescents* (pp. 219–243). Madison, CT: International Universities Press.

Yunger, J. L., Carver, P. R., & Perry, D. G. (2004). Does gender identity influence children's psychological well-being? *Developmental Psychology, 40,* 572–582.

Zagon, I. S., & McLaughlin, P. J. (1984). An overview of the neurobehavioral sequelae of perinatal opiod exposure. In J. Yanai (Ed.), *Neurobehavioral teratology* (pp. 197–234). New York, NY: Elsevier.

Zahn-Waxler, C., Cole, P. M., & Barrett, K. C. (1991). Guilt and empathy: Sex differences and implications for the development of depression. In J. Garber & K. Dodge (Eds.), *The development of emotion regulation and dysregulation* (pp. 243–272). New York, NY: Cambridge University Press.

Zahn-Waxler, C., Friedman, S. L., & Cummings, E. M. (1983). Children's emotions and behaviors in response to infants' cries. *Child Development, 54,* 1522–1528.

Zahn-Waxler, C., Radke-Yarrow, M., Wagner, E., & Chapman, M. (1992). Development of concern for others. *Developmental Psychology, 28,* 126–136.

Zajonc, R. B., Markus, H., & Markus, G. B. (1979). The birth order puzzle. *Journal of Personality and Social Psychology, 37,* 1325–1341.

Zaslow, M. J., Dion, M. R., Morrison, D. R., Weinfield, N., Ogawa, J., & Tabors, P. (1999). Protective factors in the development of preschool-age children of young mothers receiving welfare. In E. M. Hetherington (Ed.), *Coping with divorce, single parenting, and remarriage* (pp. 193–223). Mahwah, NJ: Erlbaum.

Zeanah, C. H., Smyke, A. T., Koga, S. F., Carlson, E., & The Bucharest Early Intervention Project (2005). Attachment in institutionalized and community children in Romania. *Child Development, 76,* 1015–1028.

Zebrowitz, L. A., Kendall-Tackett, K., & Fafel, J. (1991). The influence of children's facial maturity on parental expectations and punishments. *Journal of Experimental Child Psychology, 52,* 221–238.

Zee, P. C., & Turek, F. W. (2006). Sleep and health everywhere and in both directions. *Archives of Internal Medicine, 166,* 686–1688.

Zelazo, N. A., Zelazo, P. R., Cohen, K. M., & Zelazo, P. D. (1993). Specificity of practice effects on elementary neuromotor patterns. *Developmental Psychology, 29,* 686–691.

Zelazo, P. D., & Frye, D. (1998). Cognitive complexity and control: II. The development of executive function in childhood. *Current Directions in Psychological Science, 7,* 121–125.

Zelazo, P. D., Helwig, C. C. & Lau, A. (1996). Intention, act, and outcome in behavioral prediction and moral judgment. *Child Development, 67,* 2478–2492.

Zelazo, P. R. (1983). The development of walking: New findings and old assumptions. *Journal of Motor Behavior, 15,* 99–137.

Zelazo, P. R. (1998). McGraw and the development of unaided walking. *Developmental Review, 18,* 449–471.

Zeskind, P. S. (1981). Behavioral dimensions and cry sounds of infants of differential fetal growth. *Infant Behavior and Development, 4,* 297–306.

Zhou, Q., Eisenberg, N., Losoya, S. H., Fabes, R. A., Reiser, M., Guthrie, I. K., et al. (2002). The relations of parental warmth and positive expressiveness to children's empathy-related responding and social functioning: A longitudinal study. *Developmental Psychology, 73,* 893–915.

Zhou, Q., Eisenberg, N., Wang, Y., & Reiser, M. (2004). Chinese children's effortful control and dispositional anger/frustration: Relations to parenting styles and children's social functioning. *Developmental Psychology, 40,* 352–366.

Zhou, Q., Lengua, L. J., & Wang, Y. (2009). The relations of temperament reactivity and effortful control to children's adjustment problems in China and the United States. *Developmental Psychology, 45,* 724–739.

Zhu, J. L., Madsen, K. M., Vestergaard, M., Olesen, A. V., Basso, O., & Olsen, J. (2005). Paternal age and congenital malformations. *Human Reproduction, 20,* 3173–3177.

Ziegert, D. I., Kistner, J. A., Castro, R., & Robertson, B. (2001). Longitudinal study of young children's responses to challenging achievement situations. *Child Development, 72,* 609–624.

Zigler, E. (1967). Familial mental retardation: A continuing dilemma. *Science, 155,* 292–298.

Zill, N. (1988). Behavior, achievement, and health problems among children in stepfamilies: Findings from a national survey of child health. In E. M. Hetherington & J. D. Arasteh (Eds.), *Impact of divorce, single-parenting, and stepparenting on children* (pp. 325–368). Hillsdale, NJ: Erlbaum.

Zill, N. (1994). Understanding why children in stepfamilies have more learning and behavior problems than children in nuclear families. In A. Booth & J. Dunn (Eds.), *Stepfamilies: Who benefits? Who does not?* (pp. 97–106). Hillsdale, NJ: Erlbaum.

Zill, N., Morrison, D. R., & Coiro, M. J. (1993). Long-term effects of parental divorce on parent-child relationships, adjustment, and achievement in young adulthood. *Journal of Family Psychology, 7,* 1–13.

Zosuls, K. M., Ruble, D. N., Tamis-LeMonda, C. S., Shrout, P. E., Bornstein, M. H., & Greulich, F. K. (2009). The acquisition of gender labels in infancy: Implications for gender-typed play. *Developmental Psychology, 45,* 688–701.

Zucker, K. J., & Bradley, S. J. (2000). Gender identity disorder. In C. H. Zeanah, Jr. (Ed.), *Handbook of infant mental health* (2nd ed., pp. 412–424). New York, NY: Guilford Press.

Zuckerman, B., & Bresnahan, K. (1991). Developmental and behavioral consequences of prenatal drug and alcohol exposure. *Pediatric Clinics of North America, 38,* 1387–1406.

Zukow-Goldring, P. (2002). Sibling caregiving. In M. H. Bornstein (Ed.), *Handbook of parenting: Vol. 3. Being and becoming a parent* (pp. 253–286). Mahwah, NY: Erlbaum.

Name Index

Subject Index

Note: *f* indicates additional figures; *t* indicates additional tables

PREVIEW

Extensive updates

accurately reflect major advances and current understanding

More than 1,000 new references drawn from the literature provide an up-to-date portrait of contemporary research in child development. In addition, the chapters on cognition, social cognition, and achievement have been significantly revised and reorganized. Turn to this book's Preface (starting on page xiv) for details about all of the new research and topics discussed in this edition.

▶ Chapter 8, "Cognition," now covers traditional theories of cognitive development as well as concept development, attention, and most aspects of memory.

2. *Organize information so that transfers are more likely to occur.* Classroom presentations should have an obvious organizational structure and should be connected to information students already have. Such an approach would provide students with a framework that would enhance understanding and learning. Sternberg and Frensch (1993) add that teachers rarely begin lessons with a discussion of why the information is important in students' lives (i.e., where it fits in their personal scheme of things), but to enhance learning, they should.
3. *Help students see the general features that are common across different content areas to be learned and that are specific to a given lesson.* Sternberg and Frensch (1993) describe a personal experience in learning Spanish in which the general features of the language were explicitly pointed out. At the same time, pronunciations and vocabulary that were unique to a given region or country were also highlighted for students. Learning should proceed more efficiently under circumstances in which common themes and exceptions to those themes are deliberately highlighted.
4. *Test students on their ability to apply what they have learned to new situations rather than on their ability to recall specific pieces of information.* This approach would establish in students a "mental set" for the idea that they will have to engage in transfer—that this is an important expectation of them.

All of these pointers have a common aim: to make students aware of transfer as an explicit goal of learning. In a sense, the preceding suggestions ask teachers and students to be more "metacognitive" about the learning process, to overtly and frequently discuss and reflect on how transfer might be promoted. The more teachers incorporate this goal into their daily classroom instruction, according to these researchers, the more likely students will learn in the truest sense of the word.

Teachers can use several techniques to facilitate transfer in the classroom. Transfer is one of the most important goals of formal instruction in school.

The Executive Function

Numerous times in this chapter, we have mentioned that, with development, children are better able to control their cognitive processing. As children develop, they become better able to analyze the tasks they face, size up their own capabilities, deploy and modify strategies, inhibit certain behaviors if they have to, and monitor the effectiveness of their approaches. The control of cognitive processing is also very important in problem solving, which, as we saw in this chapter, can involve complex tasks such as planning and transfer. Researchers have begun to turn their attention to understanding the role and development of this **executive function**, the portion of the information-processing system that coordinates various component processes in order to achieve some goal (Welsh, 2002). The development of executive function probably starts in the preschool years with the improvements in the attention system we described earlier in this chapter (Garon, Bryson, & Smith, 2008). In the school years and adolescence, children improve in their ability to inhibit their behavioral tendencies, regulate the information they hold in working memory, and finally, shift between the demands of one complex task to another (Best, Miller, & Jones, 2009).

Neuropsychological studies of children who have experienced brain damage indicate that executive function skills

executive function Portion of the information-processing system that coordinates various component processes in order to achieve some goal.

Understanding Others' Goals and Intentions

Suppose a six-month-old infant watches someone reach for a ball or teddy bear. How does she construe this event, as a series of perceptual moments devoid of any deeper social meaning or as a goal-directed act in which the person *intends* to reach for an object? Amanda Woodward (1998) attempted to answer just this question in a study that capitalized on the information provided by the visual habituation technique. Figure 9.2 shows the sequence of activities in this experiment. First, during habituation trials, infants repeatedly saw a hand reaching for one of two toys, in this case, the ball. Then, during the test trials, they were shown the same hand-reaching action, but aimed at a new toy—the teddy bear (the "new object")—or a hand reaching in a new location for the ball again (the "new side"). Infants showed greater looking times to the "new object" scenario, indicating that they found the change in target, as opposed to the change in location, to represent something new. Woodward and others interpret this result as indicating that, throughout the experiment, infants were paying attention to the "intent" of the person reaching: to obtain the ball. Bolstering this interpretation is the finding that this pattern of looking did not occur when the reaching was done by a mechanical claw; in this case, infants looked about the same amount of time at the two test situations. That is, looking based on the actor's intent was specific to conditions where the reaching was done by a human being.

Some researchers believe that the infant's ability to understand goals and intentions in others is yet another example of innately endowed knowledge that has an adaptive function for the growing infant (Biro & Leslie, 2007; Gergely & Csibra, 2003). On the other side of the debate are those who claim that infants' own experiences with goal-directed actions create the conditions for understanding intentional behaviors in others. Consider the "sticky mitten" experiment, for example. Here, three-month-old infants (who typically would not respond to intentions in others) had their hands covered with a Velcro mitten that could help them reach for and grab a teddy bear and a ball. After slightly

Infants and young children often rely on the emotional cues expressed by caregivers to interpret new or strange events. Is this animal an object to be approached or feared? The caregiver's positive emotional expression suggests that the former is the appropri...

Figure 9.2

Understanding Actors' Goals

Six-month-old infants were habituated to a hand reaching for a particular object, in this case, the ball. During test trials, they showed greater looking toward the hand reaching for a new object, suggesting that that they were attending to the intent of the actor who was reaching ("get the ball") rather than the position of the reach. *Source:* Adapted from Henderson, A. M. E., Gerson, S., & Woodward, A. L. (May, 2008). The birth of social intelligence. *Zero to Three*, 13–19.

Habituation

New Object

New Side

◀ Chapter 9, "Social Cognition," now focuses on summarizing the remarkable growth in research concerned with how the infant, child, and adolescent orient to the social world and understand psychological states and groups. It also covers the many influences on cognitive development that originate in and are fostered by social contexts.

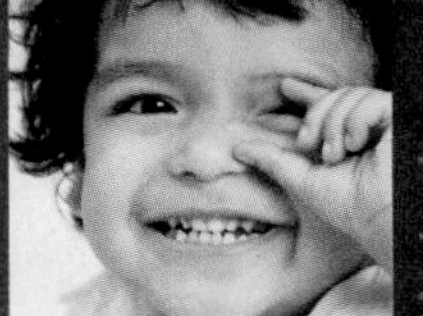

With organizing themes, current research, and practical real-world insights, this new edition gives students the keys to understanding child development

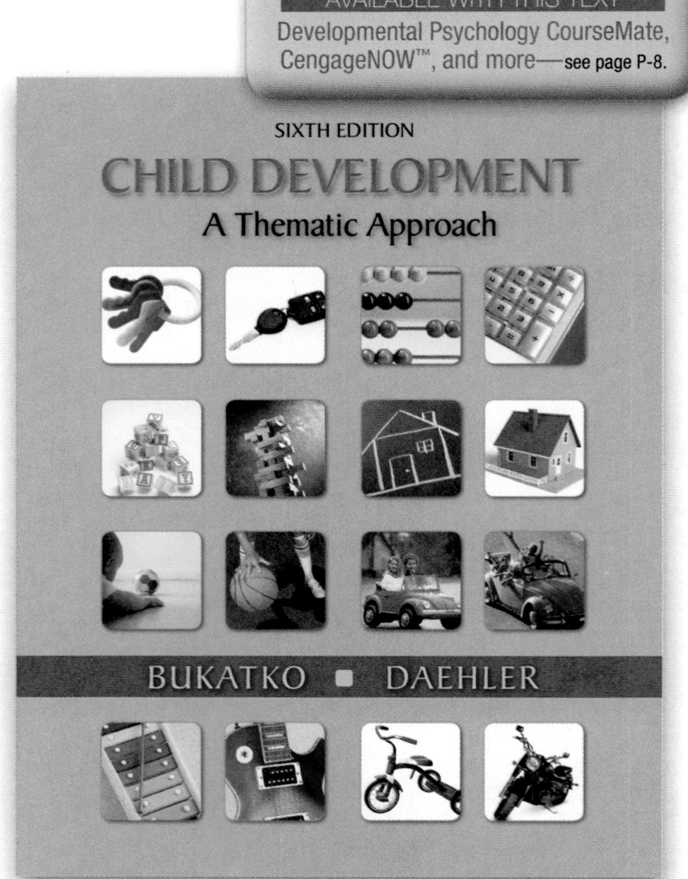

AVAILABLE WITH THIS TEXT
Developmental Psychology CourseMate, CengageNOW™, and more—see page P-8.
SIXTH EDITION
CHILD DEVELOPMENT
A Thematic Approach
BUKATKO ■ DAEHLER

Through five editions this comprehensive, topically organized text has helped students absorb the vast amounts of information about child development while also conveying the most important aspects of the process—and offering a meaningful picture of the child as a whole. Drawing on themes that replay themselves throughout the course of development, the authors help students make sense of myriad facts and research findings. New features encourage students to become more adept at thinking critically, an increasingly important skill in our digital information age. Throughout, numerous examples and real-world vignettes help students appreciate the ramifications of theory and research for applied issues such as parenting practices, education, and social policy for children, which are ultimately concerns for us all.

Highlights of the Sixth Edition

- Up-to-date research and insights in child and adolescent development (pages P-2 and P-3)
- Integrated themes that help students grasp the material (page P-4)
- Practical application of research in parenting and education (page P-5)
- New features to spark critical thinking (page P-6)
- Visual chronologies that encapsulate chapter concepts (page P-7)
- A complete teaching and learning package (page P-8)

Maps

CloseUps

ON THE ROAD WITH FODOR'S

A trip takes you out of yourself. Concerns of life at home disappear, driven away by more immediate thoughts—about, say, what marvels will beguile the next day, or where you'll have dinner. That's where Fodor's comes in. We make sure that you know all your options, so that you don't miss something that's just around the next bend. Because the best memories of your trip might well have nothing to do with what you came to the Carolinas and Georgia to see, we guide you to sights large and small all over the region. You might set out to immerse yourself in the charms of Charleston, but back at home you find yourself unable to forget a perfect day spent on Sapelo Island. With Fodor's at your side, serendipitous discoveries are never far away.

Our success in showing you every corner of the Carolinas and Georgia is a credit to our extraordinary writers. Although there's no substitute for travel advice from a good friend who knows your style, our contributors are the next best thing—the kind of people you would poll for travel advice if you knew them.

Melissa Bigner, a native southerner and Charleston resident, has covered the South in general and the Lowcountry region in particular as a staff writer and editor for *Southern Living, Southern Accents,* and *Charleston* magazines. As a freelancer, her stories have appeared in several national magazines; currently she's at work on a book for the Discovery Channel. Melissa writes from the top corner of an 1850s classic Southern manse, a shabby chic perch hugged by an ancient magnolia, with a view of the Ashley River. She says her best ideas come compliments of the local waters—rowing around the Battery, walking the beaches of Sullivan's Island, or kayaking the Edisto's blackwaters.

Freelance journalist **Deborah Geering** has lived in the Atlanta area since 1994. During eight years at *The Atlanta Journal-Constitution,* she worked the night city desk; ran a suburban bureau; oversaw weekly sections on the arts, TV, and shopping; edited portions of the home-and-garden, food, and travel sections; and contributed at one time or another to every daily section in the newspaper. Since going freelance in 2001, she has interviewed entertainers, politicians, and business leaders; reviewed classical music concerts and haunted houses; compiled local "best" lists ranging from roller coasters to places to kiss; and generally kept readers of several national and regional publications informed of Atlanta goings-on.

Tampa native and former long-time expatriate **Jody Jenkins** has traveled far and wide, writing on everything from the wars in the former Yugoslavia to the travel highlights of his hometown, Savannah. His work has appeared in *Travel & Leisure, Hemispheres, The Spectator, Frank, Foreward, The Guardian,* and numerous other newspapers and magazines.

A wrong turn as a teenager outside Florence on the way to a family beach vacation was freelance writer **Katie McElveen's** first experience exploring South Carolina. Twenty-five years later, she hasn't stopped, although she now travels with a map. From her home base in Columbia, Katie has shared her discoveries with locals and visitors alike through her work in such magazines as *South Carolina Smiles, Sandlapper,* and *Southern Living.*

Asheville native and former New Orleans newspaper editor **Lan Sluder** has written a half dozen books, including travel guides to Belize and the coast of the Carolinas and Georgia. His articles have appeared in *Caribbean Travel & Life,* the *Chicago Tribune,* the *Charlotte Observer, The New York Times,* Canada's *Globe & Mail,* and other publications around the world. He's also contributed to other Fodor's guides, including *Fodor's Belize & Guatemala.* Lan's home base is a mountain farm near Asheville settled by his forebears in the early 1800s.

Lisa H. Towle, an author and award-winning writer, remains fascinated by the diversity of her home state, North Carolina—a place she grew to appreciate after living away for many years. Because she can't decide what part of the Old North State she likes best, she lives in the middle, giving herself equal access in all directions. Lisa is president of the Society of Professional Journalists' chapter in the Triangle area and has contributed to numerous Fodor's guides. Her work has also appeared in national, regional and local publications, including *Time* magazine, *Money* magazine, *The New York Times,* and *North Carolina* magazine.

Doug Wyatt began his journalism career with the *Nashville Tennessean,* where he reviewed concerts and edited the book review section. In the early '90s he transplanted to Savannah, where he went to work for the *Morning News,* spending his last six years there (before going freelance) as the arts editor, editor the weekly book review section, and author of allegedly humorous columns. Doug has also written six plays that have been staged across the Southeast.

ABOUT THIS BOOK

	There's no doubt that the best source for travel advice is a like-minded friend who's just been where you're headed. But with or without that friend, you'll have a better trip with a Fodor's guide in hand. Once you've learned to find your way around its pages, you'll be in great shape to find your way around your destination.
SELECTION	Our goal is to cover the best properties, sights, and activities in their category, as well as the most interesting communities to visit. We make a point of including local food lovers' hot spots as well as neighborhood options, and we avoid all that's touristy unless it's really worth your time. You can go on the assumption that everything you read about in this book is recommended wholeheartedly by our writers and editors. Flip to **On the Road with Fodor's** to learn more about who they are. It goes without saying that no property mentioned in the book has paid to be included.
RATINGS	Orange stars denote sights and properties that our editors and writers consider the very best in the area covered by the entire book. These, the best of the best, are listed in the **Fodor's Choice** section in the front of the book. Use the index to find complete descriptions. Black stars highlight the sights and properties we deem **Highly Recommended,** the don't-miss sights within any region. In cities, sights pinpointed with numbered map bullets in the margins tend to be more important than those without bullets.
SPECIAL SPOTS	**Pleasures & Pastimes** focuses on types of experiences that reveal the spirit of the destination. Watch for **Off the Beaten Path** sights. Some are out of the way, some are quirky, and all are worth your while. If the munchies hit while you're exploring, look for **Need a Break?** suggestions.
TIME IT RIGHT	Wondering when to go? Check **On the Calendar** up front and chapters' **Timing** sections for weather and crowd overviews and best times to visit.
SEE IT ALL	Use Fodor's exclusive **Great Itineraries** as a model for your trip. (For a good overview of the entire destination, or mix regional itineraries from several chapters.) In cities, **Good Walks** guide you to important sights in each neighborhood; ⚑ indicates the starting points of walks and itineraries in the text and on the map.
BUDGET WELL	Hotel and restaurant price categories from **¢ to $$$$** are defined in the opening pages of each chapter—expect to find a balanced selection for every budget. For attractions, we always give standard adult admission fees; reductions are sometimes available for children, students, and senior citizens.
BASIC INFO	**Smart Travel Tips** lists travel essentials for the entire area covered by the book; city- and region-specific basics end each chapter. To find

the best way to get around, see the transportation section; see individual modes of travel ("By Car," "By Train") for details. We assume you'll check Web sites or call for particulars.

ON THE MAPS	Maps throughout the book show you what's where and help you find your way around. Black and orange numbered bullets in the text correlate to bullets on maps.
BACKGROUND	In general, we give background information within the chapters in the course of explaining sights as well as in CloseUp boxes found throughout the book.
FIND IT FAST	Within the book, chapters are arranged in a roughly north-to-south direction. Chapters are divided into smaller regions, within which towns are covered in logical geographical order; attractive routes and interesting places between towns are flagged as En Route.
DON'T FORGET	Restaurants are open for lunch and dinner daily unless we state otherwise; we mention dress only when there's a specific requirement and reservations only when they're essential or not accepted—it's always best to book ahead. Hotels have private baths, phones, TVs, and air-conditioning unless otherwise indicated. We always list facilities but not whether you'll be charged extra to use them, so when pricing accommodations, find out what's included.

SYMBOLS

Many Listings

- ★ Fodor's Choice
- ★ Highly recommended
- ✉ Physical address
- ✥ Directions
- Mailing address
- ☎ Telephone
- Fax
- On the Web
- E-mail
- Admission fee
- ⏲ Open/closed times
- Start of walk/itinerary
- Ⓜ Metro stations
- Credit cards

Outdoors

- Camping

Hotels & Restaurants

- Hotel
- Number of rooms
- Facilities
- Meal plans
- ✕ Restaurant
- Reservations
- Dress code
- Smoking
- BYOB
- Hotel with restaurant that warrants a visit

Other

- Family-friendly
- Contact information
- ⇨ See also
- Branch address
- ☞ Take note

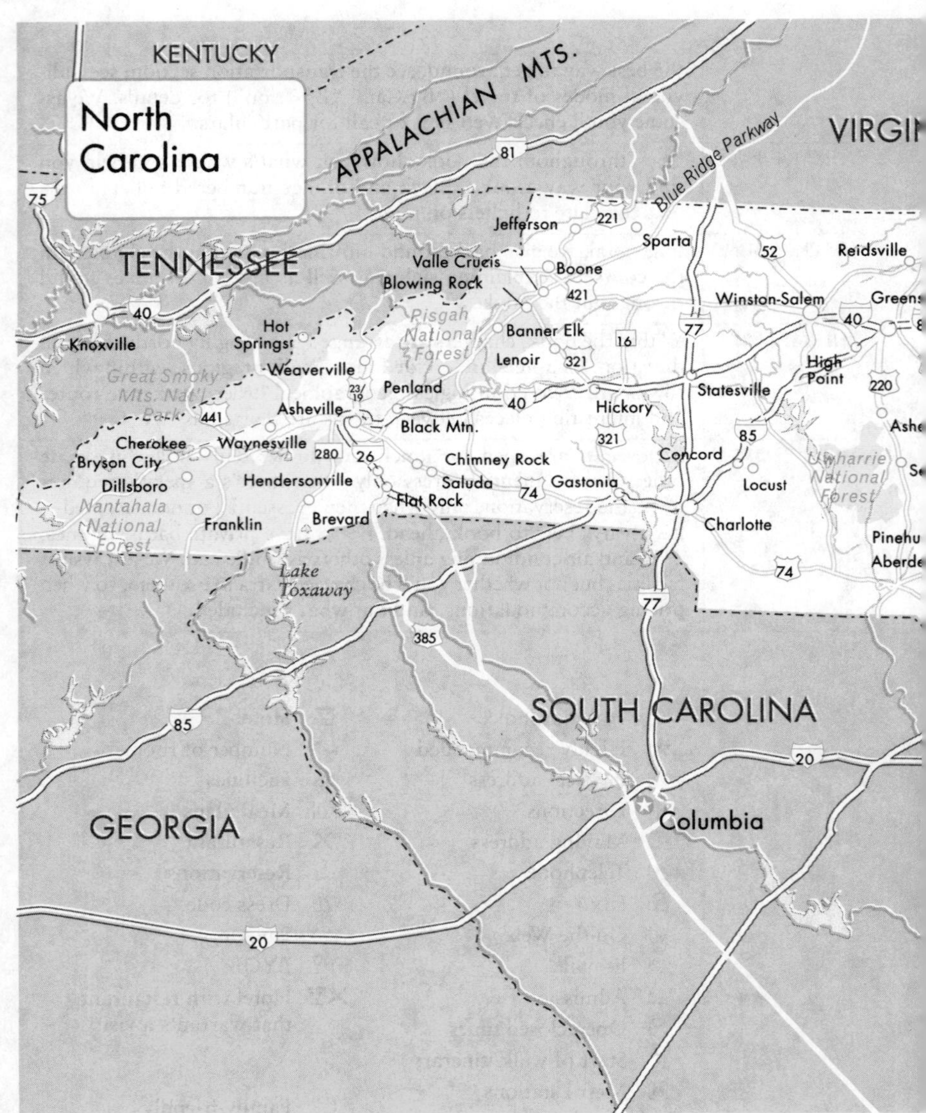

KENTUCKY
North Carolina
APPALACHIAN MTS.
81
Blue Ridge Parkway
VIRGI
75
TENNESSEE
Jefferson
221
Sparta
52
Reidsville
Valle Crucis
Boone
Blowing Rock
421
Winston-Salem
Greens
40
Knoxville
Pisgah National Forest
Hot Springs
Banner Elk
16
77
40
Weaverville
Lenoir
321
High Point
Great Smoky Mts. Nat'l Park
23/19
Penland
Statesville
220
441
Asheville
40
Hickory
Black Mtn.
Ashe
Cherokee
Waynesville
321
85
Bryson City
280
26
Chimney Rock
Concord
Uwharrie National Forest
Dillsboro
Hendersonville
Saluda
74
Gastonia
Locust
Flat Rock
Nantahala National Forest
Franklin
Brevard
Charlotte
Lake Toxaway
74
77
385
SOUTH CAROLINA
85
20
Columbia
GEORGIA
20

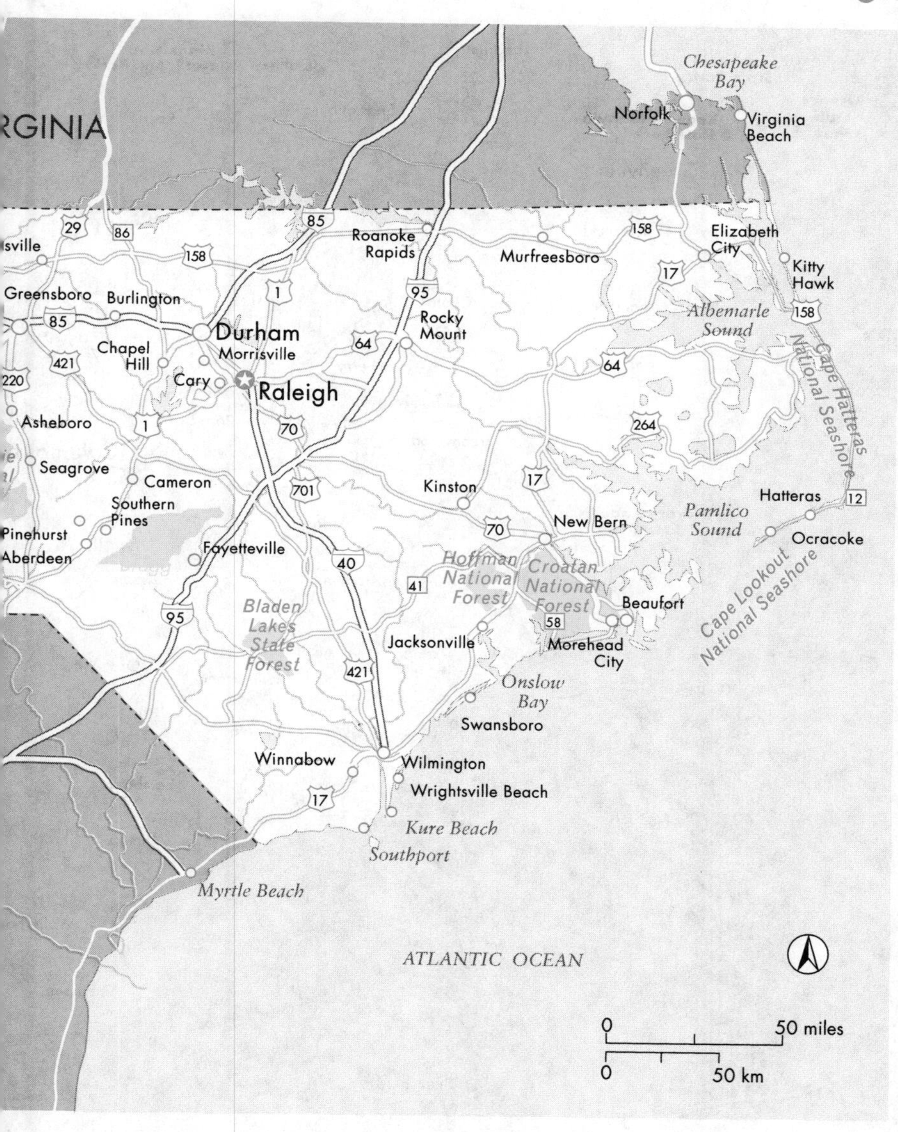

RGINIA
Chesapeake Bay
Norfolk
Virginia Beach
Elizabeth City
Kitty Hawk
Roanoke Rapids
Murfreesboro
sville
Greensboro
Burlington
Durham
Morrisville
Chapel Hill
Cary
Raleigh
Rocky Mount
Albemarle Sound
Cape Hatteras National Seashore
Asheboro
Seagrove
Cameron
Southern Pines
Pinehurst
Aberdeen
Fayetteville
Kinston
New Bern
Hatteras
Pamlico Sound
Ocracoke
Hoffman National Forest
Croatan National Forest
Beaufort
Morehead City
Cape Lookout National Seashore
Bladen Lakes State Forest
Jacksonville
Onslow Bay
Swansboro
Winnabow
Wilmington
Wrightsville Beach
Kure Beach
Southport
Myrtle Beach
ATLANTIC OCEAN
29
86
85
158
1
95
17
64
421
220
70
264
701
40
41
58
12
0
50 miles
0
50 km

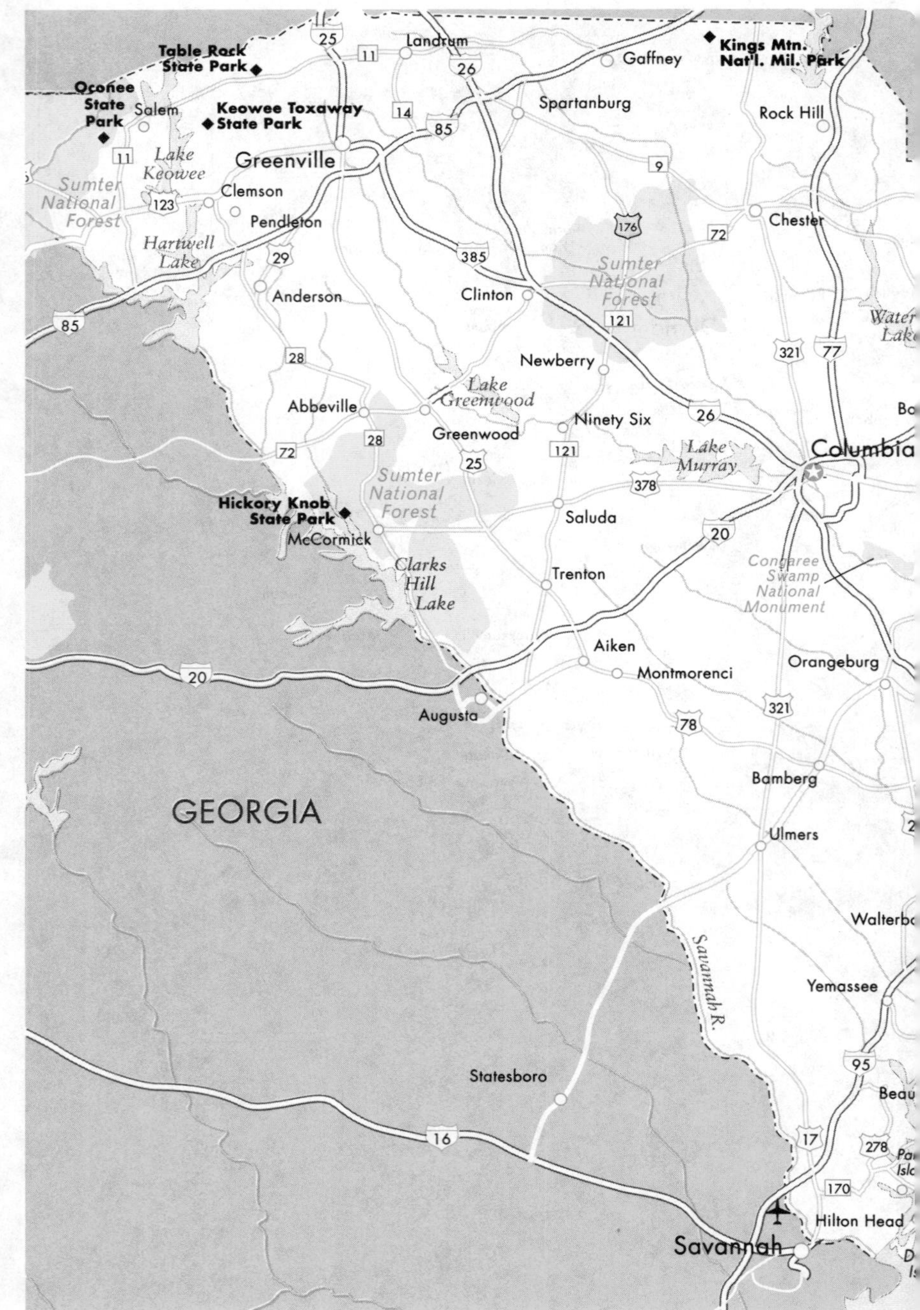
Table Rock State Park
Oconee State Park
Salem
Keowee Toxaway State Park
Landrum
Gaffney
Kings Mtn. Nat'l. Mil. Park
Spartanburg
Rock Hill
Lake Keowee
Greenville
Sumter National Forest
Clemson
Pendleton
Chester
Hartwell Lake
Anderson
Clinton
Sumter National Forest
Water Lake
Newberry
Lake Greenwood
Abbeville
Ninety Six
Greenwood
Lake Murray
Columbia
Sumter National Forest
Hickory Knob State Park
McCormick
Saluda
Congaree Swamp National Monument
Clarks Hill Lake
Trenton
Aiken
Montmorenci
Orangeburg
Augusta
Bamberg
GEORGIA
Ulmers
Walterbo
Savannah R.
Yemassee
Statesboro
Beau
Hilton Head
Savannah

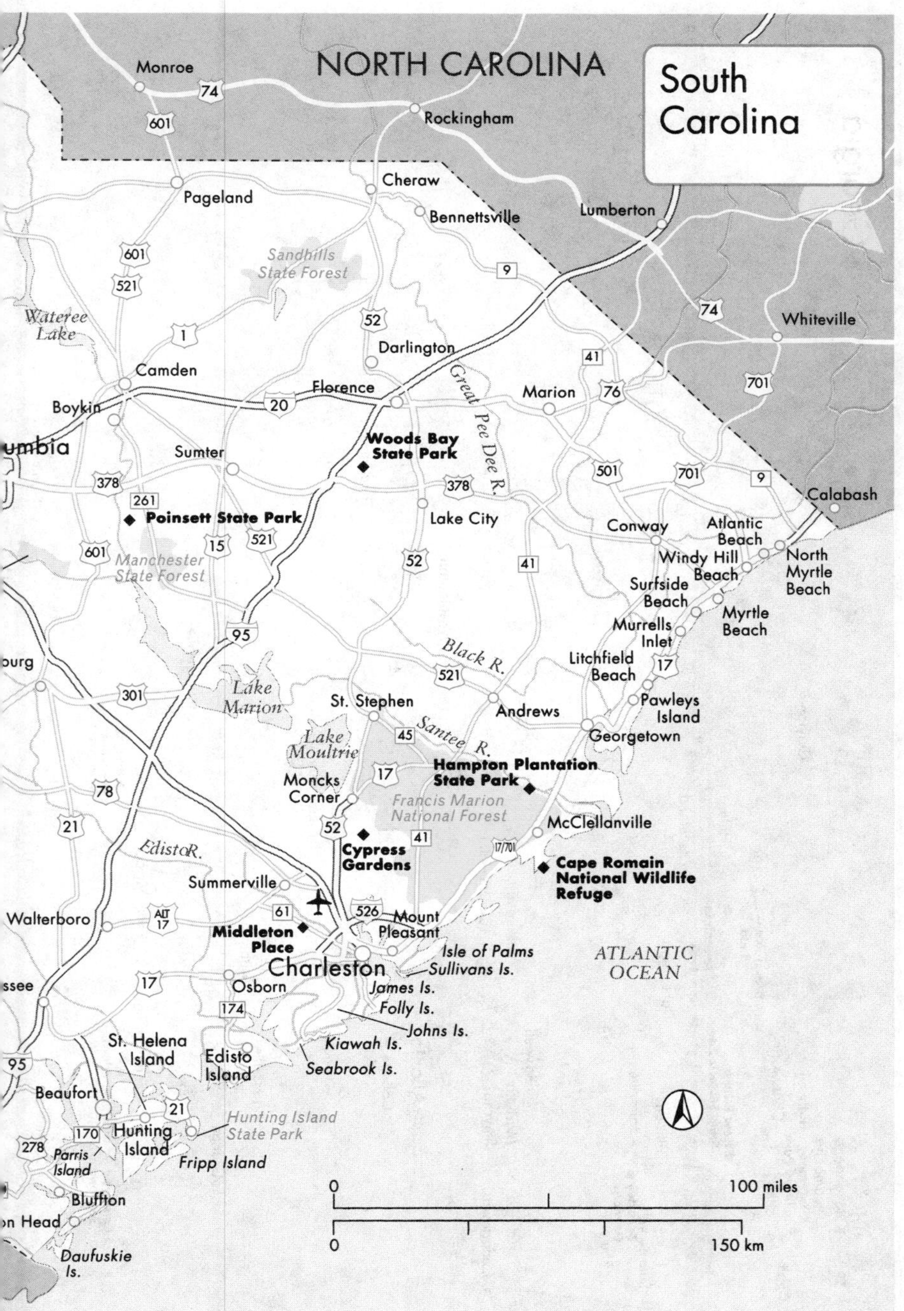
South Carolina
NORTH CAROLINA
Monroe
Rockingham
Cheraw
Pageland
Bennettsville
Lumberton
Sandhills State Forest
Wateree Lake
Whiteville
Darlington
Camden
Florence
Marion
Boykin
Great Pee Dee R.
Woods Bay State Park
Sumter
Columbia
Calabash
Poinsett State Park
Lake City
Conway
Atlantic Beach
Windy Hill Beach
North Myrtle Beach
Manchester State Forest
Surfside Beach
Myrtle Beach
Murrells Inlet
Black R.
Litchfield Beach
Lake Marion
St. Stephen
Andrews
Pawleys Island
Santee R.
Georgetown
Lake Moultrie
Moncks Corner
Hampton Plantation State Park
Francis Marion National Forest
McClellanville
Edisto R.
Cypress Gardens
Cape Romain National Wildlife Refuge
Summerville
Walterboro
Middleton Place
Mount Pleasant
Isle of Palms
Charleston
Sullivans Is.
ATLANTIC OCEAN
Osborn
James Is.
Folly Is.
Johns Is.
St. Helena Island
Edisto Island
Kiawah Is.
Seabrook Is.
Beaufort
Hunting Island
Hunting Island State Park
Parris Island
Fripp Island
Bluffton
Daufuskie Is.
0
100 miles
0
150 km

Georgia

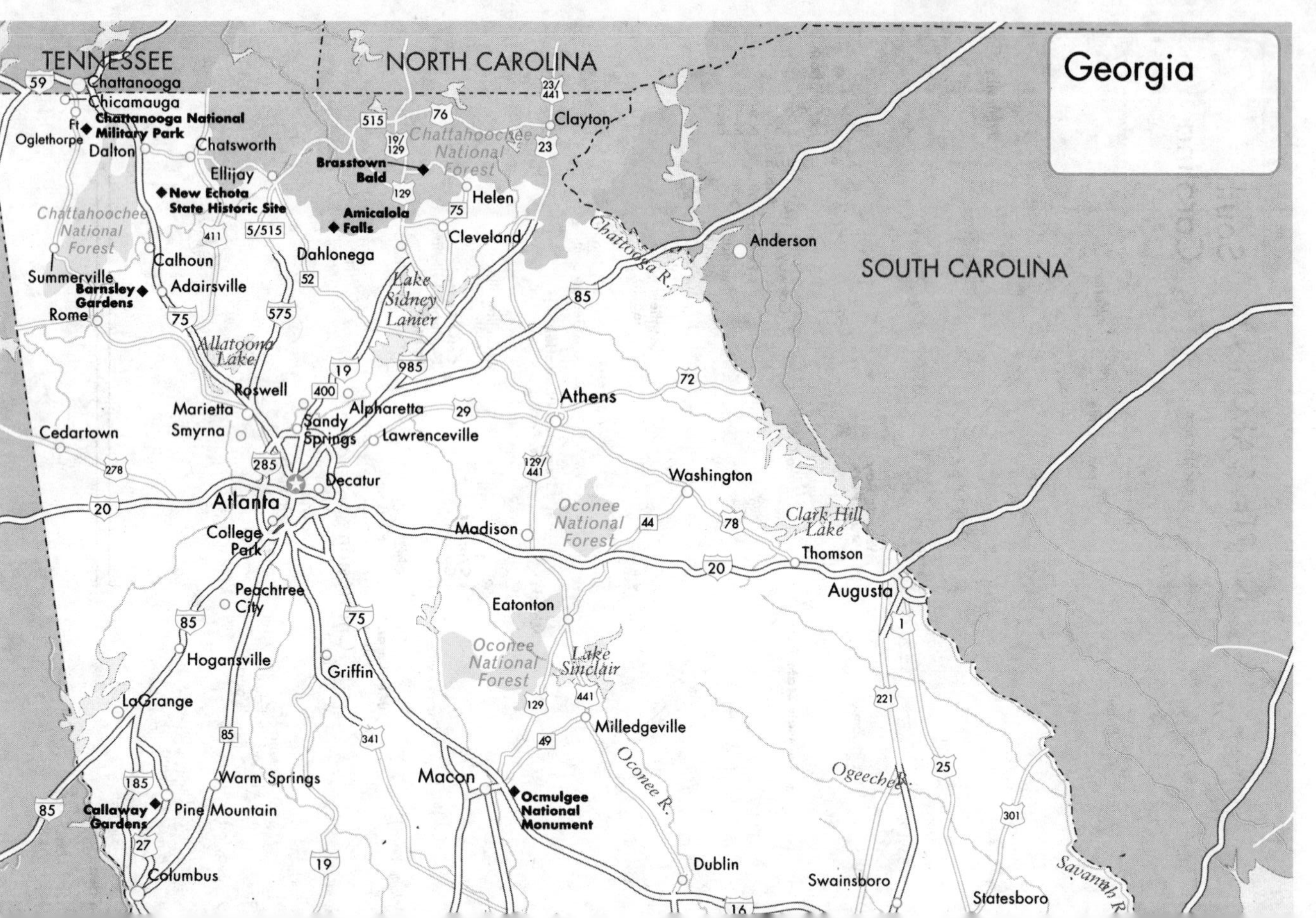

TENNESSEE
NORTH CAROLINA
SOUTH CAROLINA
Chattanooga
Chicamauga
Chattanooga National Military Park
Ft Oglethorpe
Dalton
Chatsworth
Ellijay
New Echota State Historic Site
Chattahoochee National Forest
Calhoun
Summerville
Barnsley Gardens
Adairsville
Rome
Brasstown Bald
Amicalola Falls
Dahlonega
Clayton
Helen
Cleveland
Lake Sidney Lanier
Allatoona Lake
Roswell
Marietta
Smyrna
Alpharetta
Sandy Springs
Lawrenceville
Cedartown
Decatur
Atlanta
College Park
Peachtree City
Hogansville
LaGrange
Griffin
Warm Springs
Pine Mountain
Callaway Gardens
Columbus
Macon
Ocmulgee National Monument
Athens
Madison
Oconee National Forest
Eatonton
Lake Sinclair
Milledgeville
Oconee R.
Dublin
Washington
Clark Hill Lake
Thomson
Augusta
Anderson
Chattooga R.
Ogeechee R.
Swainsboro
Statesboro
Savannah R.
59
515
76
19/129
23/441
23
129
75
411
5/515
52
575
19
400
985
85
29
72
285
278
20
129/441
44
78
341
441
49
221
1
25
301
185
27
16

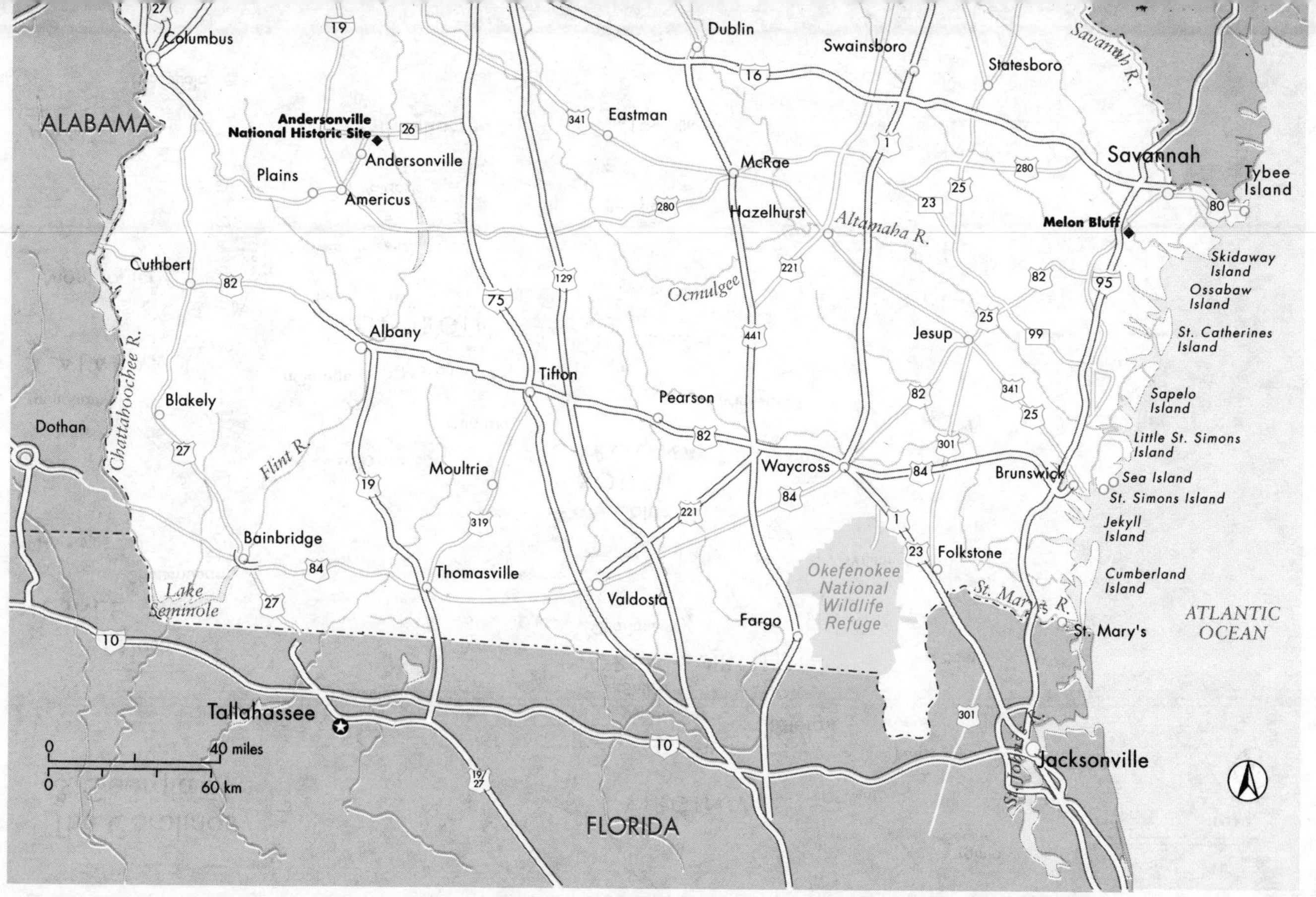
Columbus
Dublin
Swainsboro
Statesboro
Savannah R.
ALABAMA
Andersonville National Historic Site
Eastman
Andersonville
McRae
Savannah
Tybee Island
Plains
Americus
Hazelhurst
Altamaha R.
Melon Bluff
Cuthbert
Skidaway Island
Ocmulgee
Ossabaw Island
Albany
Jesup
St. Catherines Island
Chattahoochee R.
Tifton
Blakely
Pearson
Sapelo Island
Dothan
Flint R.
Little St. Simons Island
Moultrie
Waycross
Brunswick
Sea Island
St. Simons Island
Jekyll Island
Bainbridge
Folkstone
Thomasville
Okefenokee National Wildlife Refuge
Cumberland Island
Lake Seminole
Valdosta
St. Marys R.
ATLANTIC OCEAN
Fargo
St. Mary's
Tallahassee
St. Johns R.
Jacksonville
0
40 miles
0
60 km
FLORIDA
27
19
16
341
26
1
280
25
23
80
221
82
95
129
75
441
99
341
301
84
319
10
19/27

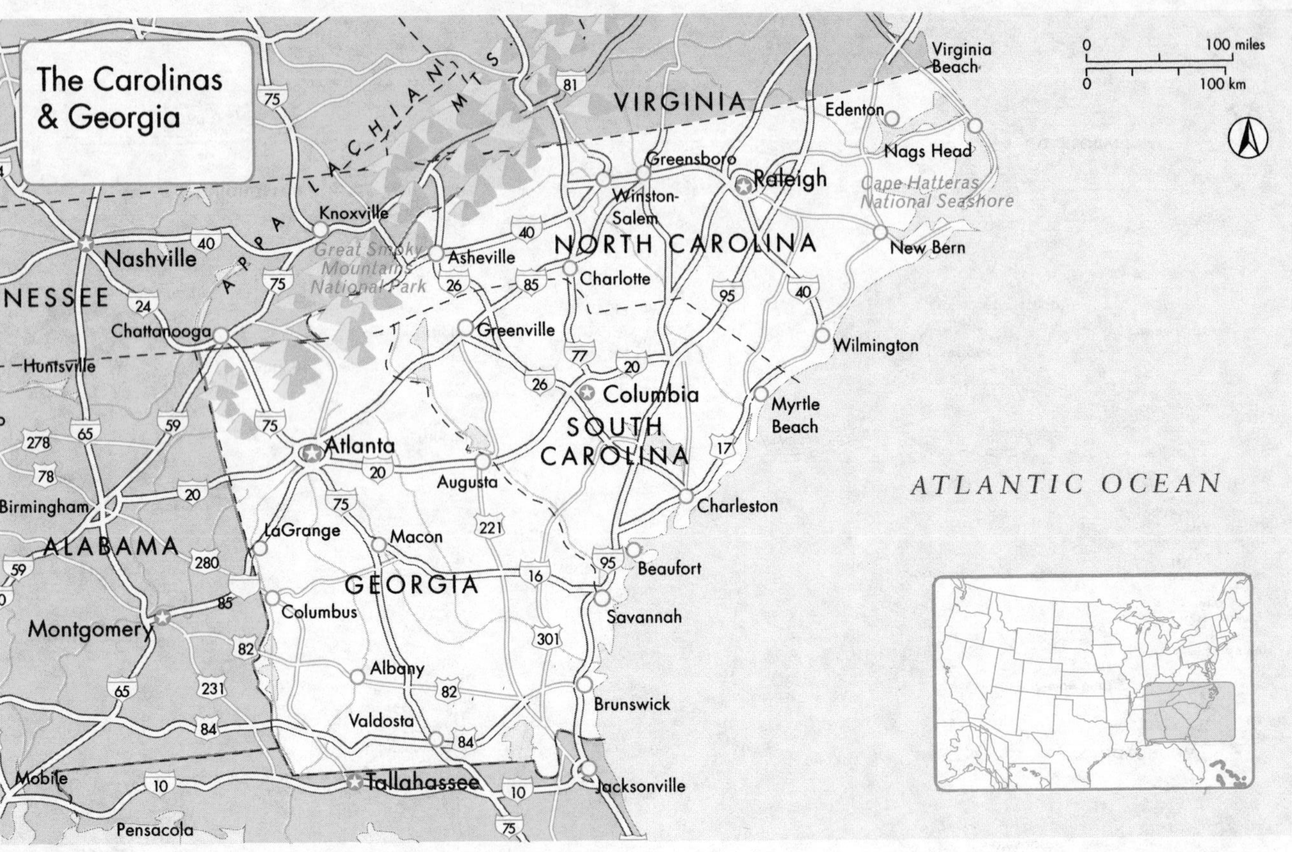
The Carolinas
& Georgia
0
100 miles
0
100 km
VIRGINIA
NORTH CAROLINA
SOUTH
CAROLINA
GEORGIA
ALABAMA
NESSEE
APPALACHIAN MTS
ATLANTIC OCEAN
Virginia
Beach
Edenton
Nags Head
Cape Hatteras
National Seashore
Greensboro
Raleigh
Winston-
Salem
New Bern
Knoxville
Great Smoky
Mountains
National Park
Asheville
Nashville
Charlotte
Chattanooga
Greenville
Wilmington
Huntsville
Columbia
Myrtle
Beach
Atlanta
Augusta
Charleston
Birmingham
LaGrange
Macon
Beaufort
Columbus
Savannah
Montgomery
Albany
Brunswick
Valdosta
Mobile
Tallahassee
Jacksonville
Pensacola
75
81
40
24
26
85
95
77
20
59
65
278
78
17
221
280
16
301
82
231
84
10

WHAT'S WHERE

1 The North Carolina Coast

The Gulf Stream and sunny skies warm North Carolina's 300-mi-long coast most of the year. Despite the similarity in climate, each coastal community has managed to maintain its own personality. At the northern tip of the coast is the thin band of barrier islands known as the Outer Banks, where you can find solitude surrounded by 900 square mi of water, pristine shores, sea oats, and giant sand dunes. Boating, scuba diving, and fishing are the main pastimes in the busy port town of Morehead City, along Central Coast. History lives in genteel, sailing-happy New Bern, a small river city. The old port city of Wilmington, on the Cape Fear River, is home to the University of North Carolina–Wilmington and is the coast's largest city.

2 The Sandhills & the Piedmont

Old South and New South intersect in North Carolina's Piedmont, now more urban and suburban than rural and divided into three main groupings: Metropolitan Charlotte, the Triad (shorthand for Greensboro, Winston-Salem, and High Point), and the Triangle (Raleigh, Durham, and Chapel Hill). Sophisticated shopping, dining, and cultural experiences are readily and widely available here, especially around the bustling I–40/85 corridor, which can pretty much directly get you to anywhere you want to go in the region. Still, you come to know the area's soul most intimately when you explore its peaceful country roads that lead to gristmills, gold mines, and general stores. While the population centers in the Piedmont and Sandhills are vibrant, none are gritty, excessively noisy, or oversized. Their strengths—world-class museums, professional sporting venues, historic sites, and outdoor recreation (including golf, golf, and more golf)—are nurtured by a temperate climate, which allows for year-round activity. It is in the spring and fall, though, that the region really shines.

3 The North Carolina Mountains

Home to the highest mountains in eastern America and with more than 1.5 million acres of stupendous and protected scenery in the Great Smoky Mountains National Park and the Nantahala and Pisgah national forests, western North Carolina offers endless opportunities for outdoor fun and adventure, whether it's exploring one of the region's hundreds of waterfalls, kayaking white-water rapids, camping in the wilderness, climbing Mt. Mitchell (the tallest mountain east of the Rockies), or just picnicking in a quiet cove. One of North America's most scenic roads, the Blue Ridge Parkway, winds for 252 mi among North Carolina's majestic peaks and peaceful valleys. More urbane pleasures also await: in Asheville, a prominent mountain resort city for over a century, you'll find edgy art galleries, sophisticated cafés, the biggest collection of Art Deco architecture outside Miami, and the largest home in America, Biltmore House, with its 250 rooms and an 8,000-acre backyard.

4 Myrtle Beach & the Grand Strand

South Carolina's Grand Strand, a 60-mi-long stretch of white sand beach and tidal marsh, begins (or ends, depending on what direction you're traveling) with the tiny town of Little River, and culminates in historic Georgetown, once America's rice-growing capital. Sandwiched between these two towns is the carnival-like atmosphere of Myrtle Beach, with its water and amusement parks, concert venues and theme shopping centers. Myrtle Beach may be the biggest show on the Strand, but there are other pleasures as well: the quiet refuge of Pawleys Island; historic plantation homes; Brookgreen Gardens, the oldest sculpture garden in the United States; and more than 120 golf courses. As diverse as the area is, water is the blue ribbon that ties it together. There's the Atlantic, of course, easily accessible nearly anywhere on the Strand, but there are also quiet creeks for canoeing, and marshes for crabbing and shrimping. These also offer a unique perspective of the area's history, providing views both of plantation houses not open to the public and of the remnants of rice growing operations, as well as giving you a glimpse of alligators, turtles, otters, and other wildlife that populate the region.

5 Charleston

Long considered South Carolina's crown jewel, Charleston anchors the Lowcountry (the local term for the state's marsh wetlands and coastline) in high style. The harbor town's rich past, dating back to 1670, is vividly evident in residents' everyday lives: they walk to work on cobblestone streets, live in antebellum mansions, and picnic come festival time at the vast plantations in the shadows of old "big houses." African- and Caribbean-born Gullah accents can still be heard among the African-American population, and everyday cuisine includes numerous Old South dishes. Although it's steeped in history, Charleston is very much a town of today. Here you can soak up modern and classical arts (opera, improv, dance, music, theater) during the international Spoleto USA festival each summer, feast at the country's leading Southern nouveau restaurants, and shop for everything from museum-quality paintings and antiques to the chicest fashions from Kate Spade and Mahnolo. Outdoors lovers are challenged to conquer all of Charleston's outlying beaches and marshes.

6 Hilton Head & the Lowcountry

The coastal lowland plains that stretch south of Charleston to the Georgia border just above Savannah are some of the most beautiful landscapes in all of South Carolina. Take U.S. 17 south from Charleston and you pass small towns and scores of slouchy vegetable stands; you wind through coastal forests with ancient live oaks forming tunnels overhead; and you drive alongside wide-open marshes that stretch their golden-green pelts out to the horizon. There are large tracts of pristine wilderness and raw beaches, although development is encroaching. There are also strollable coastal fishing villages with quaint waterfront areas and antebellum homes. Farther south, Hilton Head, once plantation country, is dominated by world-class megaresorts, vacation homes, championship golf courses, tennis courts, and water-sports facilities. Some 2.4 million visitors head to the island each year to take advantage of what's on offer.

7 The South Carolina Midlands & Upstate

Radiating north and west, the regions surrounding Columbia contain both the highest point and exact center of the state, as well as the towns that hold the state record for highest and lowest temperatures. Fresh water is in abundance here, from the murky swamps, wide rivers, and large lakes of the Midlands to the waterfalls, rapids, and cold mountain lakes of Upstate. The flat lands to the east and west of Columbia have their own claims to fame, with Camden and Aiken noted as national equestrian centers, and small towns such as Greenwood and Abbeville developing coordinated programs that make it easy to follow and experience the Civil and Revolutionary War history of the region.

8 Savannah

Savannah—Georgia's oldest city and its third largest, following Atlanta and Columbus—is, like its sister city Charleston to the north, one of the "crown jewels" of the eastern seaboard. A vigorous and well-organized historic zoning effort has preserved the inner town much as it was in the days before and immediately following the Civil War. The city has 1,400 restored or reconstructed buildings dating from the time of its founding. Warehouses still line the banks of the Savannah River, where oceangoing vessels haul cargo upstream for unloading.

9 The Coastal Isles & the Okefenokee

On Georgia's barrier islands, running down the Atlantic coast from Savannah to the Florida border, the diverse flora and fauna have long been a lure for nature lovers. Until recently large segments of the coast were in private hands, and as a result much of the region remains as it was when the first Europeans set eyes on it 450 years ago. The marshes, wetlands, and waterways teem with birds and other wildlife, and they're ideal for exploring by kayak or canoe. Area golf courses are designed to make the most of the islands' rare beauty. There are also numerous archaeological and historical sights, and Sapelo Island is home to a unique and rapidly disappearing community of descendants of African slaves. Owing to their beauty and isolation, the coastal islands have been a favorite getaway of the rich and famous for more than a hundred years. Though no longer exclusively enclaves of the well-heeled, they still bear the marks of wealth with magnificent resorts and mansions. Inland is the wild and mysterious Okefenokee Swamp, one of the nation's largest freshwater marsh- and swamplands

10 Southwest Georgia

This quiet, rural segment of Georgia has felt the impact of two U.S. presidents: Franklin Delano Roosevelt, who died at his summer home of Warm Springs in 1945, and Jimmy Carter, a Plains native who returned there after his term in office to become one of the nation's most accomplished ex-presidents, engaging in philanthropic and diplomatic work that earned him a Nobel peace prize. The brutality of the Civil War is tangible at Andersonville, the huge Confederate prison, while more modern military equipment is on display at the Fort Benning National Infantry Museum near Columbus.

11 Atlanta

The town that began as the end of the Western & Atlantic rail line has evolved into the largest city in Georgia and the gateway to the Southeast. Residents take pride in Atlanta's role in the Civil War and the civil rights movement as well as its vestiges of Southern charm, but they are just as quick to promote it as an up-and-coming global city. Transplants from other regions of the country and the world have prompted a boom in restaurants, shops, and cultural attractions; the growing population has brought new life to many intown neighborhoods in addition to contributing to the metro area's infamous traffic. Preparation for the 1996 Olympics sparked an era of improvement that has yet to slow, adding to the city landscape parks and plazas, wide sidewalks and tree-lined streets, outdoor concerts and cultural festivals.

12 Central Georgia

Central Georgia—stretching from Augusta and Athens to Macon—lies at the heart of the Old South. Sure enough, you'll find plenty of white-columned mansions and sleepy, shady verandas, evoking a romanticized past. Along the way, too, you'll run across lots of that fabled Southern hospitality. The pace picks up in Athens, the home of the University of Georgia; the homeplace '80s rock groundbreakers REM and the B-52's still throbs at night.

13 North Georgia

North Georgia is a region of natural wonder, quaint mountain towns, and rich local history. Less than two hours from Atlanta are the waterfalls and lakes of the southern Blue Ridge mountains; charming small towns like Blue Ridge and Ellijay; Dahlonega, the site of the first gold rush in America; and the re-created Bavarian schmaltz of Helen. In the northwest part of the state, you can walk the hallowed ground of Chickamauga, the site of one of the bloodiest battles in the Civil War, and visit the one-time capital of the Cherokee Nation, New Echota.

WHEN TO GO

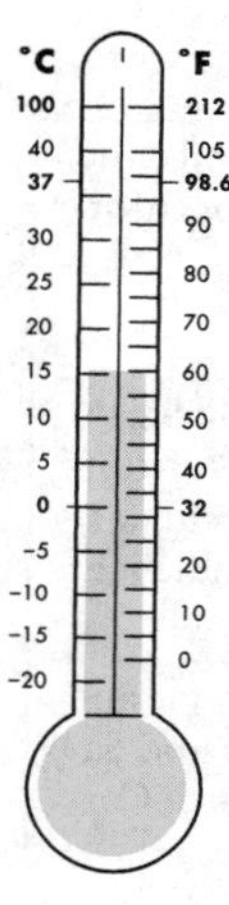

Spring is probably the most attractive season in this part of the United States. Throughout the region the blooming of cherry blossoms is followed by azaleas, dogwoods, and camellias from April into May, with apple blossoms blooming in May. Summer can be hot and humid in many areas, but temperatures will be cooler along the coast or in the mountains. Folk, crafts, art, and music festivals tend to take place in summer, as do sports events. State and local fairs are held mainly in August and September, although there are a few as early as the first part of July and as late as October. Fall can be a delight, with spectacular foliage, particularly in the mountains. The region is large, so conditions vary; *see* the individual chapters for more information.

Climate

In winter, temperatures generally average in the low 40s inland, in the 60s by the shore. Summer temperatures, modified by mountains in some areas, by water in others, range from the high 70s to the mid-80s and now and then the low 90s.

Forecasts **Weather Channel** **www.weather.com.**

The following are average daily maximum and minimum temperatures for key cities.

ATLANTA, GEORGIA

Jan.	52F	11C	May	79F	26C	Sept.	83F	28C
	36	2		61	16		65	18
Feb.	54F	12C	June	86F	30C	Oct.	72F	22C
	38	3		67	19		54	12
Mar.	63F	17C	July	88F	31C	Nov.	61F	16C
	43	6		70	21		43	6
Apr.	72F	22C	Aug.	86F	30C	Dec.	52F	11C
	52	11		70	21		38	3

RALEIGH, NORTH CAROLINA

Jan.	50F	10C	May	78F	26C	Sept.	81F	27C
	29	– 2		55	13		60	16
Feb.	52F	11C	June	85F	29C	Oct.	71F	22C
	30	– 1		62	17		47	8
Mar.	61F	16C	July	88F	31C	Nov.	61F	16C
	37	3		67	19		38	3
Apr.	72F	22C	Aug.	87F	31C	Dec.	52F	11C
	46	8		66	18		30	– 1

CHARLESTON, SOUTH CAROLINA

Jan.	59F	15C	May	81F	27C	Sept.	84F	29C
	41	6		64	18		69	21
Feb.	60F	16C	June	86F	30C	Oct.	76F	24C
	43	7		71	22		59	15
Mar.	66F	19C	July	88F	31C	Nov.	67F	19C
	49	9		74	23		49	9
Apr.	73F	23C	Aug.	88F	31C	Dec.	59F	11C
	56	13		73	23		42	6

ON THE CALENDAR

The Carolinas and Georgia hold plenty of delightful festivals and special events throughout the year. Call local or state visitor information offices for details.

WINTER

December	Highlights among regional **Christmas** celebrations include Old Salem Christmas, which re-creates a Moravian Christmas in Winston-Salem, North Carolina. The annual Festival of Trees in Atlanta features specially decorated trees, and Savannah glows with candlelight tours of the Historic District.
January	**New Year's** events include the Peach Bowl, played in Atlanta, and First Night festivals held in the downtown areas of Athens and Savannah in Georgia; Asheville, Charlotte, and Raleigh in North Carolina; and Charleston and Greenville in South Carolina. **Martin Luther King Jr. Week** is celebrated in Atlanta with lectures, exhibits, and rallies.
February	In North Carolina, Asheville hosts the annual **Arts and Crafts Show** at the Grove Park Inn. Chapel Hill stages the **Carolina Jazz Festival,** usually at the end of the month. The **Memorial Health Tybee Marathon and Half Marathon** runs through Savannah.

SPRING

March	Spring is celebrated with a **cherry-blossom festival** in Macon, Georgia, and **SpringFest** on Hilton Head Island, South Carolina. The Old South comes alive: **antebellum mansion and garden tours** are given in Charleston and Beaufort, South Carolina. A **Revolutionary War battle** is reenacted on the anniversary of the Battle of Guilford Courthouse (on the 15th of the month) in Greensboro, North Carolina. **St. Patrick's Day** in Savannah is one of the nation's largest celebrations of the day. Aiken, South Carolina, has its own horse-racing **Triple Crown,** including Thoroughbred trials, harness races, and steeplechases.
April	**Spring festivals** abound, including dogwood festivals in Atlanta, Georgia, and Fayetteville, North Carolina. The Biltmore Estate in Asheville hosts the **Festival of Flowers,** a breathtaking display with more than 50,000 tulips, hundreds of varieties of azaleas, and dogwood and cherry trees. In Wilkesboro, North Carolina, **MerleFest** is a celebration of the late musician Merle Watson; the highlight is Merle's father Doc Watson's renowned bluegrass picking. The **World Grits Festival** is held near Charleston in St. George, South Carolina. More than 25,000 people participate in the **Cooper River Bridge Run and Walk,** in Charleston. The **Masters Golf Tournament** in Augusta, Georgia, attracts top pros and thousands of spectators.

May	Over Memorial Day weekend, Anderson, South Carolina, hosts Pontiac GMC's Freedom Weekend Aloft, the second-largest hot-air balloon rally in the country. In South Carolina, Beaufort's Gullah Festival highlights the fine arts, customs, language, and dress of Lowcountry African-Americans. The annual Hang Gliding Spectacular takes place in Nags Head, North Carolina. Spoleto Festival USA, in Charleston, South Carolina, is one of the world's biggest arts festivals; Piccolo Spoleto, running concurrently, showcases local and regional talent.
SUMMER	
June	Popular arts festivals such as the juried Virginia-Highland Summerfest flourish throughout Atlanta. June is the time for the renowned American Dance Festival in Durham, North Carolina. In Greenwood, South Carolina, the Festival of Flowers has been going strong since 1967. Summer gets under way at the Sun Fun Festival at Myrtle Beach.
July	Independence Day celebrations are annual traditions around the South. Clog and figure dancing are part of the Shindig on the Green, in Asheville. The annual Highland Games & Gathering of the Scottish Clans is held on Grandfather Mountain near Linville, North Carolina.
August	The Georgia Mountain Fair, a mountain crafts and music extravaganza, is held in Hiawassee. August music festivals include a Beach Music Festival on Jekyll Island, Georgia, and the annual Mountain Dance and Folk Festival, in Asheville.
FALL	
September	In Georgia, Stone Mountain Park, near Atlanta, is the site of the Yellow Daisy Festival, celebrating this flower and also arts and crafts. North Carolina holds an Apple Festival in Hendersonville. The Candlelight Tour of Houses and Gardens is held in Charleston during September and October.
October	The Big Pig Jig in Vienna, Georgia, celebrates the glories of authentic Southern barbecue. A parade of pigs marks the Lexington Barbecue Festival, in North Carolina. The annual Highland Games, a celebration of Scottish heritage, is held at Stone Mountain Park in Georgia. The annual Woolly Worm Festival takes place in Banner Elk, North Carolina. The South Carolina State Fair is a Columbia highlight. Oktoberfest is celebrated in Helen, Georgia, and in Walhalla, South Carolina. Savannah also hosts an Oktoberfest, with dozens of artisans from around the region selling everything from jewelry to stained glass. The "ghost capital of the world"—Georgetown, South Carolina—stages a Ghost Tour.
November	Christmas preparations include the Mistletoe Market in Albany, Georgia. Autumn food festivals include the Catfish Festival in Society Hill, South Carolina, and the Chitlin' Strut, in Salley, South Carolina.

PLEASURES & PASTIMES

Dining

Time was when "dinner" in the South meant the midday meal—the principal meal of the day—and the lighter evening meal was known as "supper." But no more. Now, dinner is the last meal of the day, and grits aren't just for breakfast anymore. In fact, dishes such as chili grits and shrimp with cheese grits are popping up as entrées on the states' most sophisticated menus. And it's not just in major cities that you'll find upscale cuisine. In Blowing Rock, a small resort town in the mountains of North Carolina, one chef regularly whips up wild creations such as grilled ostrich with vegetable tortilla lasagna and smoked apple ketchup. Purists can take heart, however, as there's still plenty of down-home cookin' to be had—country ham and fried chicken, biscuits and corn bread, collard and turnip greens—and South Carolina's Lowcountry kitchens continue to ooze with she-crab soup, stuffed oysters, and pecan pie. Barbecue, which in the South is only a noun, never a verb, is served in a stunning number of ways, the meat (usually pork) dressed in everything from vinegar and red pepper to sweet mustard.

History

Long before 16th-century explorers Giovanni da Verrazano and Hernando de Soto came calling on what is today the Carolinas and Georgia, the land was occupied by indigenous peoples of many tribes. The history of one of the mightiest, the Cherokee, is chronicled in the state-of-the-art Museum of the Cherokee Indian, in Cherokee, North Carolina, under the shadow of the Great Smoky Mountains. Farther south, the Charleston Museum, founded in 1773 as the first public museum in the United States, still welcomes visitors. Across the region, colonial history comes alive at Revolutionary War sites—at Kings Mountain National Military Park, in Upcountry South Carolina, for example, and in Guilford Courthouse National Military Park, in Greensboro, North Carolina. In 1799 America's first gold rush got its start east of Charlotte; the Reed Gold Mine State Historic Site marks the spot. In Georgia, meanwhile, Savannah stands as testimony to the antebellum era, as do many of the towns lining U.S. 441, such as Madison and Milledgeville and, just to the south, Macon. The entire Confederate treasury, last seen at Chennault Plantation, in Lincolnton, Georgia, remains nowhere to be found, though rumor has it the gold is hidden somewhere on the grounds. A century after the Civil War, the South was the center of another wrenching conflict: the civil rights movement. Landmarks and memorials of the campaign, including Martin Luther King Jr.'s Ebenezer Baptist Church in Atlanta, can be found across the region.

Music

Travel along the coast of the Carolinas and Georgia during the summer months, and you'll hear the strains of beach music, sanctified oldies such as "Under the Boardwalk," by the Drifters. The focal point of this music is a dance ritual, the shag. South Carolina's Myrtle Beach, site of a huge annual festival celebrating beach music and the shag, also has a large number of country venues. Out of clubs and bars in the region's college towns have come scores of alternative rock bands and many national headliners, including R.E.M. and Hootie and the Blowfish. For bluegrass head to the mountains of North Carolina; for classical try Charleston's Spoleto Festival USA; and if you want a little of everything, sidle up to the listening stations in the Georgia Music Hall of Fame, in Macon. It honors the amazing number of music industry leaders and artists who hail from the state—from Toni Braxton, James Brown, and Ray Charles to Al Green, Isaac Hayes, and Lena Horne.

Outdoor Activities & Sports

Though the Carolinas and Georgia have professional baseball, basketball, football, and hockey teams, college sports—especially football and basketball—elicit the most fiery loyalty. School colors don't matter when it comes to fishing and boating, though, and Southerners do a lot of both. There are huge bays and sounds here, natural and man-made lakes, the Atlantic Ocean and Intracoastal Waterway, as well as rivers for white-water rafting and flat-water canoeing. If beaches are your passion, take your pick: the windswept shores of North Carolina's Outer Banks, the bustling resorts at South Carolina's Myrtle Beach, or Georgia's lush barrier islands. The myriad courses of Southern Pines and Pinehurst in North Carolina's Sandhills are a golfer's fantasy. The region's mountains, from the Blue Ridge to the Great Smokies, have well-marked hiking trails, including parts of the Appalachian Trail, to take you away from everyday bustle. But if it's sound and motion you crave, then that most Southern of sports, stock car racing (NASCAR), is just the ticket.

FODOR'S CHOICE

Fodor's Choice ★

The sights, restaurants, hotels, and other travel experiences on these pages are our writers' and editors' top picks—our Fodor's Choices. They're the best of their type in the Carolinas and Georgia—not to be missed and always worth your time. In the destination chapters that follow, you will find all the details.

LODGING

$$$$	**The Carolina,** Pinehurst, North Carolina Sandhills. The Southern comforts are found in abundance here: elegant accomodations, rocker-lined verandas, fabulous golf, and a not-so-traditional first-rate spa.
$$$$	**Grove Park Inn,** Asheville, North Carolina Mountains. This is everything a big mountain resort hotel should be, all granite and oak, with lobby fireplaces so big you could park in them, a world-class spa, a superb golf course, and, lounging in the halls of the original 1913 section, the spirit of F. Scott Fitzgerald.
$$$$	**The Lodge at Sea Island Golf Club,** St. Simons Island, Georgia Coastal Isles. This small resort done in the style of an English country manor is one of America's top golfing destinations.
$$$$	**Ritz-Carlton, Buckhead,** Atlanta. With reproduction antiques in the rooms, an elegant but welcoming lounge, and one of the best restaurants in the city, there's little not to like about this stopover for the rich and famous.
$$$$	**Rothschild-Pound House Inn,** Columbus, Southwest Georgia. Few B&Bs have the 19th-century pedigee found here—or the old-time charm to go with it.
$$$$	**Wentworth Mansion,** Charleston. Off the beaten tourist path but still within easy strolling range of the major points of interest, this is the place to experience luxe living Charleston style, with grand suites, tall ceilings, antiques everywhere. A stay here translates to being king or queen for a day.
$$$$	**The Willcox,** Aiken, South Carolina Midlands. Rocking on a large front porch supported by monumental white columns, taking a carriage ride through the woods: staying at this luxury inn adds up to a near perfect Southern fantasy.
$$$–$$$$	**First Colony Inn,** Nags Head, North Carolina Coast. All the details are attended to at this landmark in with ocean views.
$$–$$$$	**Litchfield Beach and Golf Resort,** Litchfield Beach, the Grand Strand. Stay on the ocean, on the marsh, or in between at this beautifully manicured, sprawling family resort that has its own fishing ponds and walking/biking trails in addition to pools and tennis courts.

¢–$$	**Amicalola Falls Lodge,** Dahlonega, North Georgia. A remarkable mountain lodge located in a state park, with budget-stretching motel prices.

RESTAURANTS

$$$$	**Bacchanalia,** Atlanta. The best place in Atlanta for a leisurely, special-occasion dinner, Bacchanalia has items like crab fritters and wood-grilled prime tenderloin of beef on its ever-changing, prix-fixe American menu.
$$$$	**Elizabeth on 37th,** Savannah. The setting—the hardwood floors and spacious rooms of an elegant Savannah mansion on 37th Street—is sumptuous. Thanks to prize-winning chef Elizabeth Terry, the food's even better.
$$$$	**Gabrielle's,** Asheville, North Carolina Mountains. Even on your first visit here you'll be greeted by your name, offered a drink, and invited to stroll the heirloom gardens while your table is being readied.
$$$$	**Magnolia Grill,** Durham, North Carolina Piedmont. All the proof you need that fresh, contemporary food doesn't have to forsake Southern roots.
$$$$	**Windmill Point,** Nags Head, North Carolina Coast. The decor and service are of a bygone era at this classy seafood restaurant.
$$$–$$$$	**Louis's at Pawleys,** Pawleys Island, the Grand Strand. After 13 years in Charleston, Chef Louis Osteen and his signature sophisticated Southern fare that includes crab and bacon stuffed trout, shrimp and grits, crab cakes and house-smoked pork barbecue is back, with the elegant yet casual Louis's.
$$$–$$$$	**McCrady's,** Charleston. The absolute finest of sophisticated Southern cuisine is served on white linen, pairing Charleston charm and local flavors.
$$–$$$$	**Garibaldi's Cafe,** Columbia, South Carolina Midlands. The name may be Italian, but the nightly seafood specials, always creative and always good, are what pack in the crowds.
$$–$$$$	**Nance's Creekfront Restaurant and Oyster Roast,** Murrells Inlet, the Grand Strand. It's all about the seafood at this utilitarian restaurant that's home to gorgeous views of the creek, baskets of piping hot hush puppies, and steampots brimming with fresh local oysters.
$$–$$$	**The Cottage,** Carolina Beach, North Carolina Coast. An early 20th century bugalow makes a comfortable, understated setting for exceptional cuisine.
$$–$$$	**Dillard House Restaurant,** Dillard, North Georgia. All-you-can-eat helpings of regional favorites like fried chicken and ham are served at this quintessentially Southern restaurant.

$$—$$$ **The Wreck of the Richard and Charlene,** Charleston. The fried seafood bounty served up at this creekside favorite is the best in town, with an impeccable view of the shrimp trawlers.

$–$$ **Mert's Heart and Soul,** Charlotte, North Carolina Piedmont. The definition of comfort food, served in suitable quantities.

¢–$ **Po' Pigs Bo-B-Q,** Edisto, Hilton Head. Fans drive for hours to eat the fantastic pork barbecue here, that and the fried okra, squash casserole, and hash on the side.

HOMES OF DISTINCTION

Biltmore Estate, Asheville, North Carolina Mountains. The largest home in America, with its 250 rooms, 12 square mi of land, formal gardens, winery, and stables, is more than you could possibly expect.

Little White House Historic Site/FDR Memorial Museum, Warm Springs, Southwest Georgia. Franklin Roosevelt turned this cottage into the Southern annex of the White House and breathed his last breath here.

Owens-Thomas House and Museum, Savannah. From 1816 to 1819, the English architect William Jay built Savannah's first Regency mansion. Today it's one of Savannah's architectural jewels.

Thomas Wolfe Memorial, Asheville, North Carolina Mountains. Reopened in 2004 after a $2.4 million restoration following an ugly case of arson, "Dixieland," the boarding house where Wolfe grew up, now looks so wonderful that Ashevillians are hoping the author will finally come home again.

MUSEUMS

Atlanta Cyclorama & Civil War Museum, Atlanta. Before there were movie screens, there were cycloramas—360°, panoramic paintings. The one at this museum depicts the Civil War's Battle of Atlanta.

EdVenture Children's Museum, Columbia, South Carolina Midlands. The largest children's museum in the Southeast has loads of hands-on exhibits, including Eddie, a 40-foot-tall, climbable boy.

Mint Museum of Craft + Design, Charlotte, North Carolina Piedmont. The line between art and craft is wiped away at this shrine to contemporary American crafts.

NATURE

Cape Hatteras National Seashore, North Carolina Coast. Come here to feel the grandeur and raw power of the Atlantic.

Cumberland Island, Georgia Coastal Isles. This unspoiled spit of land is home to everything from egrets to armadillos; wild horses roam the beaches.

Edisto Beach State Park, Edisto, South Carolina Lowcountry. Three miles of undeveloped beaches and waterfront campsites and nearby cabins make this quiet preserve seem otherworldly in a state whose sandy strips are becoming more and more crowded.

Mountain Bridge Wilderness Area, Greenville, South Carolina Upstate. Hike over suspension bridges, past waterfalls and spectacular views, on the more than 50 mi of hiking trails contained within 10,000 acres of forest wilderness area.

Sea Pines Resort, Hilton Head. Nature is in refined form at the first of Hilton Head's planned resort communities, which set the tone for such development in the Southeast. It includes a fantastic nature preserve, award-winning golf courses, and a luxury boutique hotel near Hilton Head's lighthouse.

PARKS & GARDENS

Brookgreen Gardens, Pawleys Island, the Grand Strand. Follow a 200-year old oak alley onto this 300-acre scuplture garden (there are more than 550 magnificent works by hundreds of American artists on display) and wildlife preserve that's also home to horses, otters, and alligators.

Centennial Olympic Park, Atlanta. With free lunchtime and evening concert series, occasional festivals, and a fountain that practically compels people to run through its dancing waters, this 21-acre park built for the 1996 Olympics has become a city anchor.

Middleton Place, Charleston. The perfectly preserved plantation grounds, with their terraced lawns, butterfly lakes, and maze of smaller gardens, made up the first truly landscaped estate in the country; outdoor programs and much more let you explore to the fullest.

The State Botanical Gardens of Georgia, Athens, Central Georgia, Over 300 acres are filled with aromatic gardens, woodland paths, and a massive conservatory.

TOWNS & VILLAGES

Bluffton, Hilton Head. Established in 1852, this still-quaint, well-preserved town swathed in plankboard sidewalks was a summertime haven for area planters; now it provides a glimpse of small town life and is full of shops and restaurants.

Cataloochee Cove, Great Smoky Mountains National Park, North Carolina Mountains. This true ghost town, remote and eerie and beautiful, is also for the first time in 150 years home to elk.

Dahlonega, North Georgia. Everybody's favorite little mountain town is in the heart of the north Georgia mountains. Its main square is filled with shops, and gold is in them thar hills nearby.

WALKING THROUGH HISTORY

Battery, Charleston. Walk in postcard perfection as you stroll the most photographed part of Charleston, the High Battery boardwalk, with its backdrop of stately mansions, an expansive view of the harbor, and a majestic live oak park.

Chickamauga & Chattanooga National Military Park, Fort Ogelthorpe, North Georgia. More than 34,000 soldiers took their last breath on this 9,000-acre park area, in one of the bloodiest battles of the Civil War.

Old Salem, Winston-Salem, North Carolina Piedmont. This re-created Moravian village is one of the nation's most authentic and well-documented colonial sites.

Tryon Palace, New Bern, North Carolina Coast. History comes to life at this reconstructed colonial capitol with costumed guides.

SMART TRAVEL TIPS

Finding out about your destination before you leave home means you won't squander time organizing everyday minutiae once you've arrived. You'll be more streetwise when you hit the ground as well, better prepared to explore the aspects of the Carolinas and Georgia that drew you here in the first place. The organizations in this section can provide information to supplement this guide; contact them for up-to-the-minute details, and consult the A to Z sections that end each chapter for facts on the various topics as they relate to the different regions. Happy landings!

AIR TRAVEL

BOOKING

When you book, look for nonstop flights and remember that "direct" flights stop at least once. Try to avoid connecting flights, which require a change of plane. Two airlines may operate a connecting flight jointly, so ask whether your airline operates every segment of the trip; you may find that the carrier you prefer flies you only part of the way. To find more booking tips and to check prices and make online flight reservations, log on to www.fodors.com.

CARRIERS

US Airways offers the greatest number of flights by far into the Charlotte-Douglas International Airport in North Carolina, as one of its hubs is located here. US Airways Express has service between many North Carolina airports as well as those in South Carolina. Hartsfield-Jackson International Airport in Atlanta is the major hub of Delta Airlines, which is headquartered in the city.

Major Airlines **American** ☎ 800/433-7300 🌐 www.aa.com. **Continental** ☎ 800/525-0280 🌐 www.continental.com. **Delta** ☎ 800/221-1212 🌐 www.delta.com. **Northwest Airlines/KLM** ☎ 800/225-2525 🌐 www.nwa.com. **United** ☎ 800/241-6522 🌐 www.united.com. **US Airways/US Airways Express** ☎ 800/428-4322 🌐 www.usairways.com.

Smaller Airlines **Air Canada** ☎ 800/776-3000 🌐 www.aircanada.com. **AirTran** ☎ 770/994-8258 or 800/247-8726 🌐 www.airtran.com. **American Eagle**

☎ 800/433-7300 ⊕ www.aa.com. **Atlantic Southeast/Delta Connection** ☎ 800/221-1212 or 800/282-3424 ⊕ www.delta.com. **ComAir** ☎ 800/221-1212 ⊕ www.comair.com. **Continental Express** ☎ 800/525-0280 ⊕ www.continental.com. **Eastwind** ☎ 888/327-8946. **Kiwi** ☎ 800/538-5494. **Midwest Express** ☎ 800/452-2022 ⊕ www.midwestairlines.com. **Northwest Airlink** ☎ 800/225-2525 ⊕ www.nwairlink.com. **Southwest** ☎ 800/435-9792 ⊕ www.southwest.com. **Spirit** ☎ 800/772-7117 ⊕ www.spiritair.com. **TW Express** ☎ 800/221-2000.
From the U.K. **American** ☎ 0345/789-789 ⊕ www.americanairlines.co.uk. **British Airways** ☎ 0345/222-111 ⊕ www.ba.com. **Delta** ☎ 0800/414-767 ⊕ www.delta.com.

CHECK-IN & BOARDING

Always **find out your carrier's check-in policy.** Plan to arrive at the airport about two hours before your scheduled departure time for domestic flights and 2½ to 3 hours if you're coming from abroad. You may need to arrive earlier if you're flying from one of the busier airports or during peak air-traffic times. Note also that construction is common in the vicinity of the larger airports, which are seemingly always expanding, so be prepared to budget in extra driving time before your departure.

To avoid delays at airport-security checkpoints, try not to wear any metal. Jewelry, belt and other buckles, steel-toe shoes, barrettes, and underwire bras are among the items that can set off detectors.

Assuming that not everyone with a ticket will show up, airlines routinely overbook planes. When everyone does, airlines ask for volunteers to give up their seats. In return, these volunteers usually get a several-hundred-dollar flight voucher, which can be used toward the purchase of another ticket, and are rebooked on the next flight out. If there are not enough volunteers, the airline must choose who will be denied boarding. The first to get bumped are passengers who checked in late and those flying on discounted tickets, so get to the gate and check in as early as possible, especially during peak periods.

Always **bring a government-issued photo ID** to the airport; even when it's not required, a passport is best.

CUTTING COSTS

The least expensive airfares to the Carolinas and Georgia are usually priced for round-trip travel and must be purchased in advance. Airlines generally allow you to change your return date for a fee; most low-fare tickets, however, are nonrefundable. It's smart to call a number of airlines and check the Internet; when you are quoted a good price, book it on the spot—the same fare may not be available the next day, or even the next hour. Always check different routings and look into using alternate airports. Also, price off-peak flights, which may be significantly less expensive than others. Travel agents, especially low-fare specialists (⇨ Discounts & Deals), are helpful.

Consolidators are another good source. They buy tickets for scheduled flights at reduced rates from the airlines, then sell them at prices that beat the best fare available directly from the airlines. (Many also offer reduced car-rental and hotel rates.) Sometimes you can even get your money back if you need to return the ticket. Carefully read the fine print detailing penalties for changes and cancellations, purchase the ticket with a credit card, and confirm your consolidator reservation with the airline.

Consolidators **AirlineConsolidator.com** ☎ 888/468-5385 ⊕ www.airlineconsolidator.com, for international tickets. **Best Fares** ☎ 800/880-1234 or 800/576-8255 ⊕ www.bestfares.com; $59.90 annual membership. **Cheap Tickets** ☎ 800/377-1000 or 800/652-4327 ⊕ www.cheaptickets.com. **Expedia** ☎ 404/728-8787 or 800/397-3342 ⊕ www.expedia.com. **Hotwire** ☎ 920/330-9418 or 866/468-9473 ⊕ www.hotwire.com. **Now Voyager Travel** ✉ 45 W. 21st St., Suite 5A, New York, NY 10010 ☎ 212/459-1616 📠 212/243-2711 ⊕ www.nowvoyagertravel.com. **Onetravel.com** ⊕ www.onetravel.com. **Orbitz** ☎ 888/656-4546 ⊕ www.orbitz.com. **Priceline.com** ⊕ www.priceline.com. **Travelocity** ☎ 888/709-5983, 877/282-2925 in Canada, 0870/876-3876 in U.K. ⊕ www.travelocity.com.

ENJOYING THE FLIGHT

State your seat preference when purchasing your ticket, and then repeat it when you confirm and when you check in. For more legroom, you can request one of the few emergency-aisle seats at check-in if you're capable of moving obstacles comparable in weight to an airplane exit door (usually between 35 pounds and 60 pounds)—a Federal Aviation Administration requirement of passengers in these seats. Seats behind a bulkhead also offer more legroom, but they don't have underseat storage. Don't sit in the row in front of the emergency aisle or in front of a bulkhead, where seats may not recline.

Ask the airline whether a snack or meal is served on the flight. If you have dietary concerns, request special meals when booking. These can be vegetarian, low-cholesterol, or kosher, for example. It's a good idea to pack some healthful snacks and a small (plastic) bottle of water in your carry-on bag. On long flights, try to maintain a normal routine, to help fight jet lag. At night, get some sleep. By day, eat light meals, drink water (not alcohol), and **move around the cabin** to stretch your legs. For additional jet-lag tips consult *Fodor's FYI: Travel Fit & Healthy* (available at bookstores everywhere).

FLYING TIMES

Flying time to Atlanta is 2½ hours from New York, 2 hours from Chicago, 4½ hours from Los Angeles, 2 hours from Dallas, and 9 hours from London. By plane, Charlotte is an hour northeast of Atlanta, Raleigh 75 minutes northeast, Wilmington 1¾ hours east, and Charleston, Hilton Head, and Savannah an hour east–southeast.

HOW TO COMPLAIN

If your baggage goes astray or your flight goes awry, complain right away. Most carriers require that you **file a claim immediately.** The Aviation Consumer Protection Division of the Department of Transportation publishes *Fly-Rights,* which discusses airlines and consumer issues and is available on-line. You can also find articles and information on mytravelrights.com, the Web site of the nonprofit Consumer Travel Rights Center.

Airline Complaints **Aviation Consumer Protection Division** ✉ U.S. Department of Transportation, Office of Aviation Enforcement and Proceedings, C-75, Room 4107, 400 7th St. SW, Washington, DC 20590 ☎ 202/366-2220 🌐 airconsumer.ost.dot.gov. **Federal Aviation Administration Consumer Hotline** ✉ For inquiries: FAA, 800 Independence Ave. SW, Washington, DC 20591 ☎ 800/322-7873 🌐 www.faa.gov.

RECONFIRMING

Check the status of your flight before you leave for the airport. You can do this on your carrier's Web site, by linking to a flight-status checker (many Web booking services offer these), or by calling your carrier or travel agent.

AIRPORTS

The sheer competition and wealth of connections at Atlanta's Hartsfield-Jackson International Airport (ATL), the world's busiest passenger airport, make it a convenient choice. From here you can get to any place in the region or beyond, but you're going to have to tackle crowds whether you're waiting for food, a security check, or the underground train to ferry you to another concourse. That said, things move at a reasonably steady pace so long as you allow yourself a couple of extra hours prior to boarding time.

North Carolina's Charlotte-Douglas International Airport (CLT), near the border of North Carolina and South Carolina, is a US Airways hub and portal to western North Carolina as well as upstate South Carolina, which also has the much smaller but user-friendly Greenville Spartanburg International Airport (GSP). Although not as vast as Hartsfield, Charlotte-Douglas is large, and its people-moving systems work well. In the center of the state, right off I–40, is Raleigh-Durham International Airport (RDU), which seems to be in a constant state of expansion; it's a prime gateway into central and eastern North Carolina and the Triangle area (Raleigh, Durham, and Chapel Hill).

Those who live in the western reaches of the Triangle are just as likely to use the Piedmont Triad International Airport (GSO), located at the convergence of four interstates in North Carolina. It primarily serves the Triad area—Greensboro,

Winston-Salem, and High Point—as well as some cities in southwestern Virginia.

For the most part, fares tend to be lower at the region's major airports, but you can sometimes find good deals at smaller airports such as South Carolina's Charleston International (CHS) and Georgia's Savannah/Hilton Head International (SAV). However, these attractive airports are somewhat off the beaten path for any place but their immediate environs. Additionally, it can be difficult to find direct flights to the smaller airports in the Carolinas and Georgia if you're flying in from outside the region.

Airport Information **Charlotte-Douglas International Airport** ✉ 5501 Josh Birmingham Pkwy., Charlotte ☎ 704/359-4000 🌐 www.flycdia.com. **Charleston International Airport** ✉ 5500 International Blvd. ☎ 843/767-7000. **Greenville Spartanburg International Airport** ✉ 2000 GSP Dr., Greer, SC ☎ 864/877-7426 🌐 www.gspairport.com. **Hartsfield-Jackson International Airport** ✉ 6000 N. Terminal Pkwy., Atlanta ☎ 404/530-6600 or 800/897-1910 🌐 www.atlanta-airport.com. **Piedmont Triad International Airport** ✉ 6415 Bryan Blvd., Greensboro ☎ 336/665-5600 🌐 www.flyfrompti.com. **Raleigh-Durham International Airport** ✉ 1600 Terminal Blvd., Morrisville ☎ 919/840-2100 🌐 www.rdu.com. **Savannah/Hilton Head International Airport** ✉ 400 Airways Ave. ☎ 912/964-0514 🌐 www.savannahairport.com.

BIKE TRAVEL

Throughout coastal Georgia, South Carolina, and North Carolina, hills are few and the scenery remarkable. You can find extensive, in many cases marked, bike routes throughout North Carolina's Outer Banks, around Savannah and Georgia's coastal islands, and throughout greater Charleston and coastal South Carolina's Lowcountry. Serious enthusiasts, especially mountain bikers, might take to the more precipitous parts of North Carolina and Georgia, which are the Great Smoky Mountains and north Georgia mountains, respectively.

There are dozens of local bike clubs throughout the area, and they generally welcome visitors. To reach one of these groups, which can provide detailed advice on local routes and rental shops, contact the local tourist board or visit the appropriate tourism Web site (⇨ Web sites), many of which have information on or links to area cycling resources. Many tourist boards also distribute bike maps.

Delorme's *Atlas & Gazeteer* state maps, usually available in local bike shops and drug stores, contain lots of topographic detail useful for bike riders. The Division of Bicycle and Pedestrian Transportation, part of North Carolina's Department of Transportation, can provide maps of scenic biking routes in the state.

Bike Maps **DeLorme** ✉ 2 DeLorme Dr., Yarmouth, ME 04096 ☎ 800/561-5105 🌐 www.delorme.com. **Division of Bicycle and Pedestrian Transportation** ✉ 1552 Mail Service Center, Raleigh, NC 27699 ☎ 919/733-2804 🌐 www.ncdot.org/transit/bicycle/maps/maps_highways.html.

BUSINESS HOURS

Banks and post offices are usually open weekdays from 9 to 5 and frequently Saturday morning.

MUSEUMS & SIGHTS

Museums typically operate Tuesday through Saturday from 10 to 5, and Sunday from 1 to 5. Most museums and state-run sights are closed Monday.

SHOPS

Shops in urban and suburban areas, particularly in indoor and strip malls, typically open at 9 or 10 Monday through Saturday and stay open until anywhere from 6 PM to 10 PM on weekdays and Saturday; they frequently don't open until noon or later on Sunday, and close at 5 or 6. Many supermarkets in urban and larger suburban communities are 24-hour operations and often contain pharmacies and banks with extended hours.

BUS TRAVEL

Regional bus service, provided by joint agreement between Greyhound and Trailways, is abundant throughout the Carolinas and Georgia. It's a handy and affordable means of getting around; if it's a simple matter of getting from one city to another and you've got a bit of time on your hands, consider this option. Buses sometimes make frequent stops, which may delay you but may also provide you the chance to see parts of the region you might not otherwise. For a comparison of different ways of getting around the region, *see* Transportation Around the Carolinas and Georgia.

CUTTING COSTS

Greyhound's North America Discovery Pass allows unlimited travel in the United States within any 7-, 10-, 15-, 21-, 30-, 45-, or 60-day period ($199–$549, depending on length of the pass). Greyhound's similar International Ameripass (for non–U.S. residents only) offers 4- to 60-day passes for $135–$494. Greyhound also has senior citizen, children's, and student discounts.

Bus Information **Greyhound/Trailways** ☎ 800/231-2222 🌐 www.greyhound.com.

CAMERAS & PHOTOGRAPHY

With mountains that are the highest east of the Mississippi, hundreds of miles of coastline, and countless gardens and historic homes, the Carolinas and Georgia have enough picture-perfect scenes to keep camera-toters happy. South Carolina's Lowcountry, consisting of Charleston, Colleton, and Dorchester counties, has photo-op sites of the oldest settlements in the state as well as its major rivers. In Georgia, the tree-shaded squares of Savannah, Civil War forts, and the elaborate Callaway Gardens in Pine Mountain practically beg to be photographed. North Carolina's quaint fishing villages are timeless, and along the Blue Ridge Parkway the vistas are breathtakingly dramatic. The parkway has numerous overlooks that seem to have been constructed with photographers in mind; mist and low-hanging clouds, however, often don't lift until late morning or early afternoon. Note that many museums prohibit photography of their exhibits. The *Kodak Guide to Shooting Great Travel Pictures* (available at bookstores everywhere) is loaded with tips.

Photo Help **Kodak Information Center** ☎ 800/242-2424 🌐 www.kodak.com.

EQUIPMENT PRECAUTIONS

Sea spray, sand, and summer heat and humidity are prime considerations for photographers in this region. If you leave an air-conditioned car or building and step into muggy air, expect it to take a few minutes for condensation on your camera's lens to clear. **Don't pack film or equipment in checked luggage,** where it is much more susceptible to damage. X-ray machines used to view checked luggage are extremely powerful and therefore are likely to ruin your film. Try to ask for hand inspection of film, which becomes clouded after repeated exposure to airport X-ray machines, and keep videotapes and computer disks away from metal detectors. Always keep film, tape, and computer disks out of the sun. Carry an extra supply of batteries, and be prepared to turn on your camera, camcorder, or laptop to prove to airport security personnel that the device is real.

CAR RENTAL

Rates vary from city to city but are generally lowest in destinations with busy airports, where there's the greatest competition. Below are sample rates, for both economy- and luxury-car rentals, quoted by the most popular agencies in two major cities (note that unlimited mileage is nearly always included). These rates are typical of those found in larger cities in the Carolinas and Georgia, but specials and deals may be available based on dates of travel and length of contract. It's important to **reserve a car well in advance of your expected arrival.**

In Atlanta daily rates range from about $37 to $52 for an economy car to $76–$100 for a luxury car; weekly rates range from $190 to $285 for an economy car to $390–$530 for a luxury car. Atlanta has an additional 7% sales tax, and at the airport location an 11% concession recoupment fee and a 3% airport excise tax are also added.

In Raleigh daily rates range from about $28 to $44 for an economy car to $66–$88 for a luxury car; weekly rates range from $140 to $205 for an economy car to $350–$440 for a luxury car. Raleigh has an additional 8% sales tax and a 5% local transportation tax, and at the airport a 10% concession recoupment fee is also added.

Major Agencies **Alamo** ☎ 800/327-9633 🌐 www.alamo.com. **Avis** ☎ 800/331-1212, 800/879-2847 or 800/272-5871 in Canada, 0870/606-0100 in U.K., 02/9353-9000 in Australia, 09/526-2847 in New Zealand 🌐 www.avis.com. **Budget** ☎ 800/527-0700, 0870/156-5656 in U.K. 🌐 www.budget.com. **Dollar** ☎ 800/800-4000, 0800/085-4578 in U.K. 🌐 www.dollar.com. **Hertz** ☎ 800/654-3131, 800/263-0600 in Canada, 0870/844-8844 in U.K., 02/9669-2444 in Australia, 09/256-8690 in New Zealand 🌐 www.hertz.com. **National Car Rental** ☎ 800/227-7368, 0870/600-6666 in U.K. 🌐 www.nationalcar.com.

CUTTING COSTS

Some off-airport locations offer lower rates, and their lots are only minutes from the terminal via complimentary shuttle. Also ask whether certain frequent-flyer, American Automobile Association (AAA), corporate, or other such promotions are accepted and whether the rates might be lower the day before or after you had originally intended to travel.

In some cases you can find that the same agency offers a region's cheapest luxury car rates but priciest economy cars, or that the cheapest agency in one city may have high rates in another. It pays to check around. Also, although an economy car is almost always your cheapest option, agencies sometimes offer upgrade specials that cost only a dollar or two more per day. Think carefully about how much and where you'll be using the car before choosing among economy, compact, standard, luxury, and premium; it may be worth the extra few dollars per day for a more substantial vehicle if you're traveling long distances, driving up into the mountains or over rugged terrain, traveling with more than a couple of passengers, or using the car extensively.

For a good deal, book through a travel agent who will shop around. Also, price local car-rental companies—whose prices may be lower still, although their service and maintenance may not be as good as those of major rental agencies. Armada has seven locations in Georgia and specializes in vans and SUVs. Triangle Rent A Car has multiple locations in North Carolina and South Carolina.

Also research rates on the Internet. Consolidators that specialize in air travel can offer good rates on cars as well (⇨ Air Travel). Remember to ask about required deposits, cancellation penalties, and drop-off charges if you're planning to pick up the car in one city and leave it in another. If you're traveling during a holiday period, also make sure that a confirmed reservation guarantees you a car.

Local Agencies **Armada** ☎ 770/416-7996 🌐 www.armadavans.com. **Triangle Rent A Car** ☎ 919/840-3400 at Raleigh-Durham International airport 🌐 www.trianglerentacar.com.

INSURANCE

When driving a rented car you are generally responsible for any damage to or loss of the vehicle. You also may be liable for any property damage or personal injury that you may cause while driving. Before you rent, see what coverage you already have under the terms of your personal auto-insurance policy and credit cards.

For about $9 to $25 a day, rental companies sell protection, known as a collision- or loss-damage waiver (CDW or LDW), that eliminates your liability for damage to the car; it's always optional and should never be automatically added to your bill.In most states you don't need a CDW if you have personal auto insurance or other liability insurance.However, **make sure you have enough coverage to pay for the car.** If you do not have auto insurance or an umbrella policy that covers damage to third parties, purchasing liability insurance and a CDW or LDW is highly recommended.

REQUIREMENTS & RESTRICTIONS

In the Carolinas and Georgia you must be 21 to rent a car, and rates may be higher if you're under 25.

SURCHARGES

Before you pick up a car in one city and leave it in another, ask about drop-off charges or one-way service fees, which can be substantial. Also inquire about early-return policies; some rental agencies charge extra if you return the car before the time specified in your contract while others give you a refund for the days not used. To avoid a hefty refueling fee, fill the tank just before you turn in the car, but be aware that gas stations near the rental outlet may overcharge. It's almost never a deal to buy the tank of gas that's in the car when you rent it; the understanding is that you'll return it empty, but some fuel usually remains. Surcharges may apply if you're under 25 or if you take the car outside the area approved by the rental agency. You'll pay extra for child seats (about $8 a day), which are compulsory for children under six, and usually for additional drivers (up to $25 a day, depending on location).

CAR TRAVEL

A car is your most practical and economical means of traveling around the Carolinas and Georgia. Atlanta, Savannah, Charleston, Myrtle Beach, and Asheville can also be explored fairly easily on foot or by using public transit and cabs, but a car is helpful to reach many of the most intriguing nearby museums, parks, restaurants, and lodgings.

Although you'll make the best time traveling along the South's extensive network of interstate highways, keep in mind that U.S. and state highways offer some delightful scenery and the opportunity to stumble on funky roadside diners, leafy state parks, and historic town squares. Although the area is rural, it's still densely populated, so you'll rarely drive for more than 20 or 30 mi—even on local roads—without passing roadside services, such as gas stations, restaurants, and ATMs.

Among the most scenic highways in the Carolinas and Georgia are **U.S. 78,** running east–west across Georgia; **U.S. 25, 19, 74,** and **64,** traveling through the Great Smoky Mountains of western North Carolina; **U.S. 17** from Brunswick, Georgia, along the coast through South Carolina and North Carolina; and the **Blue Ridge Parkway** from the eastern fringes of the Great Smoky Mountains through western North Carolina into Virginia.

For a comparison of different ways of getting around the region, *see* Transportation Around the Carolinas and Georgia.

RULES OF THE ROAD

State lawmakers set speed limits, even for federal interstate highways. Limits vary from state to state and from rural to urban areas, so **check posted speeds frequently.**

Always strap children under age 6 or under 40 pounds (regardless of age) into approved child-safety seats. Children must wear seat belts regardless of where they're seated.

Unless otherwise indicated, you may turn right at a red light after stopping if there's no oncoming traffic. When in doubt, wait for the green. In Atlanta, Columbia, Charlotte, and the Triangle and Triad cities of North Carolina be alert for one-way streets, "no left turn" intersections, and blocks closed to car traffic.

Currently there are no restrictions against the use of radar detectors or handheld cell phones while driving in the Carolinas and Georgia. Lane restrictions (such as for high-occupancy vehicles) are rare but do exist on some major arteries such as those through Atlanta.

CHILDREN IN THE CAROLINAS & GEORGIA

Most of the Carolinas and Georgia is ideal for travel with kids. This is an enjoyable part of the country for family road trips, and things are relatively affordable—you'll have no problem finding inexpensive kid-friendly hotels and family-style restaurants. The numerous antiques-filled bed-and-breakfasts and inns that punctuate the landscape are less suitable for kids; some of them flat-out refuse to accommodate children. Also, some of the quieter and more rural parts of the region—although exuding history—lack child-oriented attractions.

If you are renting a car, don't forget to arrange for a car seat when you reserve. For general advice about traveling with children, consult *Fodor's FYI: Travel with Your Baby* (available in bookstores everywhere).

FLYING

If your children are two or older, ask about children's airfares. As a general rule, infants under two not occupying a seat fly at greatly reduced fares or even for free. But if you want to guarantee a seat for an infant, you have to pay full fare. Consider flying during off-peak days and times; most airlines will grant an infant a seat without a ticket if there are available seats.

Experts agree that it's a good idea to use safety seats aloft for children weighing less than 40 pounds. Airlines set their own policies: if you use a safety seat, U.S. carriers usually require that the child be ticketed, even if he or she is young enough to ride free, because the seats must be strapped into regular seats. And even if you pay the full adult fare for the seat, it may be worth it, especially on longer trips. Do **check your airline's policy about using safety seats during takeoff and landing.** Safety seats are not allowed everywhere in the plane, so get your seat assignments as early as possible.

When reserving, request children's meals or a freestanding bassinet (not available at all airlines) if you need them. But note that bulkhead seats, where you must sit to use the bassinet, may lack an overhead bin or storage space on the floor.

LODGING

Most hotels in the Carolinas and Georgia allow children under a certain age to stay in their parents' room at no extra charge, but others charge for them as extra adults; be sure to **find out the cutoff age for children's discounts.**

SIGHTS & ATTRACTIONS

Places that are especially appealing to children are indicated by a rubber-duckie icon (🦆) in the margin.

CONSUMER PROTECTION

Whether you're shopping for gifts or purchasing travel services, **pay with a major credit card** whenever possible, so you can cancel payment or get reimbursed if there's a problem (and you can provide documentation). If you're doing business with a particular company for the first time, contact your local Better Business Bureau and the attorney general's offices in your state and (for U.S. businesses) the company's home state as well. Have any complaints been filed? Finally, if you're buying a package or tour, always consider travel insurance that includes default coverage (⇨ Insurance).

BBBs Council of Better Business Bureaus ✉ 4200 Wilson Blvd., Suite 800, Arlington, VA 22203 ☎ 703/276–0100 📠 703/525–8277 🌐 www.bbb.org.

CUSTOMS & DUTIES

IN AUSTRALIA

Australian residents who are 18 or older may bring home A$400 worth of souvenirs and gifts (including jewelry), 250 cigarettes or 250 grams of cigars or other tobacco products, and 1,125 ml of alcohol (including wine, beer, and spirits). Residents under 18 may bring back A$200 worth of goods. Members of the same family traveling together may pool their allowances. Prohibited items include meat products. Seeds, plants, and fruits need to be declared upon arrival.

Australian Customs Service 📫 Regional Director, Box 8, Sydney, NSW 2001 ☎ 02/9213–2000 or 1300/363263, 02/9364–7222 or 1800/020–504 quarantine-inquiry line 📠 02/9213–4043 🌐 www.customs.gov.au.

IN CANADA

Canadian residents who have been out of Canada for at least seven days may bring in C$750 worth of goods duty-free. If you've been away fewer than seven days but more than 48 hours, the duty-free allowance drops to C$200. If your trip lasts 24 to 48 hours, the allowance is C$50. You may not pool allowances with family members. Goods claimed under the C$750 exemption may follow you by mail; those claimed under the lesser exemptions must accompany you. Alcohol and tobacco products may be included in the seven-day and 48-hour exemptions but not in the 24-hour exemption. If you meet the age requirements of the province or territory through which you reenter Canada, you may bring in, duty-free, 1.5 liters of wine *or* 1.14 liters (40 imperial ounces) of liquor *or* 24 12-ounce cans or bottles of beer or ale. Also, if you meet the local age requirement for tobacco products, you may bring in, duty-free, 200 cigarettes and 50 cigars. Check ahead of time with the Canada Customs and Revenue Agency or the Department of Agriculture for policies regarding meat products, seeds, plants, and fruits.

You may send an unlimited number of gifts (only one gift per recipient, however) worth up to C$60 each duty-free to Canada. Label the package UNSOLICITED GIFT—VALUE UNDER $60. Alcohol and tobacco are excluded.

Canada Customs and Revenue Agency ✉ 2265 St. Laurent Blvd., Ottawa, Ontario K1G 4K3 ☎ 800/461-9999 in Canada, 204/983-3500, 506/636-5064 🌐 www.ccra.gc.ca.

IN NEW ZEALAND

All homeward-bound residents may bring back NZ$700 worth of souvenirs and gifts; passengers may not pool their allowances, and children can claim only the concession on goods intended for their own use. For those 17 or older, the duty-free allowance also includes 4.5 liters of wine or beer; one 1,125-ml bottle of spirits; and either 200 cigarettes, 250 grams of tobacco, 50 cigars, *or* a combination of the three up to 250 grams. Meat products, seeds, plants, and fruits must be declared upon arrival to the Agricultural Services Department.

New Zealand Customs ✉ Head office: The Customhouse, 17-21 Whitmore St., Box 2218, Wellington ☎ 09/300-5399 or 0800/428-786 🌐 www.customs.govt.nz.

IN THE U.K.

From countries outside the European Union, including the U.S., you may bring home, duty-free, 200 cigarettes, 50 cigars, 100 cigarillos, or 250 grams of tobacco; 1 liter of spirits or 2 liters of fortified or sparkling wine or liqueurs; 2 liters of still table wine; 60 ml of perfume; 250 ml of toilet water; plus £145 worth of other goods, including gifts and souvenirs. Prohibited items include meat and dairy products, seeds, plants, and fruits.

HM Customs and Excise ✉ Portcullis House, 21 Cowbridge Rd. E, Cardiff CF11 9SS ☎ 0845/010-9000 or 0208/929-0152 advice service, 0208/929-6731 or 0208/910-3602 complaints 🌐 www.hmce.gov.uk.

DISABILITIES & ACCESSIBILITY

The Carolinas and Georgia rank on a par with the rest of America in terms of accessibility for people with disabilities or special needs. A drawback is the abundance of historic accommodations, restaurants, and attractions with narrow staircases, doorways, and small rooms that fail to conform to the Americans with Disabilities Act (ADA) guidelines. Increasingly, however, businesses throughout the region—especially those in densely populated areas—are changing to improve accessibility.

LODGING

Despite the Americans with Disabilities Act, the definition of accessibility seems to differ from hotel to hotel. Some properties may be accessible by ADA standards for people with mobility problems but not for people with hearing or vision impairments, for example.

If you have mobility problems, ask for the lowest floor on which accessible services are offered. If you have a hearing impairment, check whether the hotel has devices to alert you visually to the ring of the telephone, a knock at the door, and a fire/emergency alarm. Some hotels provide these devices without charge. Discuss your needs with hotel personnel if this equipment isn't available, so that a staff member can personally alert you in the event of an emergency.

If you're bringing a guide dog, get authorization ahead of time and write down the name of the person with whom you spoke.

RESERVATIONS

When discussing accessibility with an operator or reservations agent, ask hard questions. Are there any stairs, inside *or* out? Are there grab bars next to the toilet *and* in the shower/tub? How wide is the doorway to the room? To the bathroom? For the most extensive facilities meeting the latest legal specifications, opt for newer accommodations. If you reserve through a toll-free number, consider also calling the hotel's local number to confirm the information from the central reservations office. Get confirmation in writing when you can.

TRANSPORTATION

Complaints **Aviation Consumer Protection Division** (⇨ Air Travel) for airline-related problems. **Departmental Office of Civil Rights** ✉ For general inquiries, U.S. Department of Transportation, S-30, 400 7th St. SW, Room 10215, Washington, DC 20590 ☎ 202/366-4648 📠 202/366-9371 🌐 www.dot.gov/ost/docr/index.htm. **Disability Rights Section** ✉ NYAV, U.S. Department of Justice, Civil Rights Division, 950 Pennsylvania Ave. NW, Washington, DC 20530 ☎ ADA information line 202/514-0301, 800/514-0301, 202/514-0383 TTY, 800/514-0383 TTY 🌐 www.ada.gov. **U.S. Department of Transportation Hotline** ☎ For disability-related air-travel problems, 800/778-4838 or 800/455-9880 TTY.

TRAVEL AGENCIES

In the United States, the Americans with Disabilities Act requires that travel firms serve the needs of all travelers. Some agencies specialize in working with people with disabilities.

Travelers with Mobility Problems **Access Adventures/B. Roberts Travel** ✉ 206 Chestnut Ridge Rd., Scottsville, NY 14624 ☎ 585/889-9096 🌐 www.brobertstravel.com ✉ dltravel@prodigy.net, run by a former physical-rehabilitation counselor. **Accessible Vans of America** ✉ 9 Spielman Rd., Fairfield, NJ 07004 ☎ 877/282-8267, 888/282-8267, 973/808-9709 reservations 📠 973/808-9713 🌐 www.accessiblevans.com. **Flying Wheels Travel** ✉ 143 W. Bridge St., Box 382, Owatonna, MN 55060 ☎ 507/451-5005 📠 507/451-1685 🌐 www.flyingwheelstravel.com.

DISCOUNTS & DEALS

Be a smart shopper and compare all your options before making decisions. A plane ticket bought with a promotional coupon from travel clubs, coupon books, and direct-mail offers or purchased on the Internet may not be cheaper than the least expensive fare from a discount ticket agency. And always keep in mind that what you get is just as important as what you save.

DISCOUNT RESERVATIONS

To save money, look into discount reservations services with Web sites and toll-free numbers, which use their buying power to get a better price on hotels, airline tickets (⇨ Air Travel), even car rentals. When booking a room, always **call the hotel's local toll-free number** (if one is available) rather than the central reservations number—you'll often get a better price. Always ask about special packages or corporate rates.

Airline Tickets **Air 4 Less** ☎ 800/AIR4LESS; low-fare specialist.

Hotel Rooms **Accommodations Express** ☎ 800/444-7666 or 800/277-1064 🌐 www.acex.net. **Hotels.com** ☎ 800/246-8357 🌐 www.hotels.com. **Quikbook** ☎ 800/789-9887 🌐 www.quikbook.com. **Steigenberger Reservation Service** ☎ 800/223-5652 🌐 www.srs-worldhotels.com. **Turbotrip.com** ☎ 800/473-7829 🌐 www.turbotrip.com.

PACKAGE DEALS

Don't confuse packages and guided tours. When you buy a package, you travel on your own, just as though you had planned the trip yourself. Fly–drive packages, which combine airfare and car rental, are often a good deal. In cities, ask the local visitor's bureau about hotel and local transportation packages that include tickets to major museum exhibits or other special events.

EATING & DRINKING

The increase of international flavors in the region reflects the tastes and backgrounds of the people who have flooded into the Carolinas and Georgia over the past couple of decades. Bagels are as common nowadays as biscuits, and, especially in urban areas, it can be harder to find country cooking than a plate of hummus. For the most part, though, you can still find plenty of traditional Southern staples—barbecue, fried chicken, greens, and the like.

Outside of the many resort areas along the coast and in the mountains, dining costs in the region are often lower than those in the North.

The restaurants we list are the cream of the crop in each price category. Properties indicated by ✕🏨 are lodging establishments whose restaurant warrants a special trip.

MEALTIMES

The Southern tradition of Sunday dinner—traditionally a midday meal (with a small "supper" eaten in the evening)—has morphed to some degree, at least in urban areas, to Sunday brunch. For many this brunch immediately follows midmorning church services, so be advised that restaurants will often be very busy through the middle of the day. In smaller towns, many restaurants are closed on Sunday. Unless otherwise noted, the restaurants listed in this guide are open daily for lunch and dinner.

RESERVATIONS & DRESS

For the most part, dining tends to be informal; a coat and tie are rarely required, and you'll be safe almost anywhere if you show up in business-casual clothes. We mention dress only when men are required to wear a jacket or a jacket and tie.

Reservations are always a good idea; we mention them only when they're essential or not accepted. Book as far ahead as you can, and reconfirm as soon as you arrive. (Large parties should always call ahead to check the reservations policy.)

WINE, BEER & SPIRITS

Blue laws, legislation forbidding labor and sales on Sunday, have a long history in this region, dating to the 1600s. Although many communities, including major urban areas and resort towns, have dropped the bans, these laws are still observed in more rural areas, particularly with regard to alcohol sales. Additionally, there are entire counties in the Carolinas and Georgia that prohibit the sale of alcoholic beverages in restaurants, although some establishments allow you to bring your own alcohol. In North Carolina, bottled distilled spirits are only sold through state-run "ABC" (Alcoholic Beverage Control) outlets; beer and wine, however, are available in most grocery and convenience stores.

GAY & LESBIAN TRAVEL

Attitudes about gays and lesbians tend toward the disapproving in some parts of the South, especially outside urban areas. On the whole, however, despite a reputation for conservative-minded residents, this part of the country is no more hostile or dangerous for lesbians and gays—traveling solo or together—than the rest of America. It's prudent, however, to show an awareness of your surroundings and exercise a degree of discretion whenever you venture into unfamiliar territory.

There are several major newspapers serving the gay and lesbian community throughout the Carolinas and Georgia, notably *Southern Voice,* based in Atlanta, plus a host of smaller local papers in the Carolinas. The gay nightlife and social scenes in Atlanta rival those of virtually any comparably sized cities in the North, and there are also thriving gay communities of varying sizes in Savannah, Charlotte, Charleston, Raleigh-Durham, and Columbia. With a much lower profile than most cities with large gay populations, Asheville is something of a well-kept secret; it has sizable lesbian and gay communities and a high number of gay-friendly businesses and accommodations.

For details about the gay and lesbian scene, consult *Fodor's Gay Guide to the USA* (available in bookstores everywhere).

Gay- & Lesbian-Friendly Travel Agencies **Different Roads Travel** ✉ 8383 Wilshire Blvd., Suite 520, Beverly Hills, CA 90211 ☎ 323/651-5557 or 800/429-8747 (Ext. 14 for both) 📠 323/651-5454 ✉ lgernert@tzell.com. **Kennedy Travel** ✉ 130 W. 42nd St., Suite 401, New York, NY 10036 ☎ 212/840-8659 or 800/237-7433 📠 212/730-2269 🌐 www.kennedytravel.com. **Now, Voyager** ✉ 4406 18th St., San Francisco, CA 94114 ☎ 415/626-1169 or 800/255-6951 📠 415/626-8626 🌐 www.nowvoyager.com. **Skylink Travel and Tour/Flying Dutchmen Travel** ✉ 1455 N. Dutton Ave., Suite A, Santa Rosa, CA 95401 ☎ 707/546-9888 or 800/225-5759 📠 707/636-0951, serving lesbian travelers.

INSURANCE

The most useful travel-insurance plan is a comprehensive policy that includes coverage for trip cancellation and interruption, default, trip delay, and medical expenses (with a waiver for preexisting conditions).

Without insurance you'll lose all or most of your money if you cancel your trip, regardless of the reason. Default insurance covers you if your tour operator, airline, or cruise line goes out of business—the chances of which have been increasing. Trip-delay covers expenses that arise because of bad weather or mechanical delays. Study the fine print when comparing policies.

U.K. residents can buy a travel-insurance policy valid for most vacations taken during the year in which it's purchased (but check preexisting-condition coverage).

Always **buy travel policies directly from the insurance company**; if you buy them from a cruise line, airline, or tour operator that goes out of business you probably won't be covered for the agency or operator's default, a major risk. Before making any purchase, review your existing health and home-owner's policies to find what they cover away from home.

Travel Insurers In the U.S.: **Access America** ✉ 2805 N. Parham Rd., Richmond, VA 23294 ☎ 800/284-8300 🖷 804/673-1491 or 800/346-9265 🌐 www.accessamerica.com. **Travel Guard International** ✉ 1145 Clark St., Stevens Point, WI 54481 ☎ 715/345-0505 or 800/826-1300 🖷 800/955-8785 🌐 www.travelguard.com.

FOR INTERNATIONAL TRAVELERS

For information on customs restrictions, *see* Customs & Duties.

CAR RENTAL

When picking up a rental car, non-U.S. residents need a reservation voucher for any prepaid reservations that were made in the traveler's home country, a passport, a driver's license, and a travel policy that covers each driver.

CAR TRAVEL

In the Carolinas and Georgia gasoline prices range from $1.45 to $1.90 a gallon at this writing. Stations are plentiful; nearly all are self-serve, and you can usually pay at the pump with a credit card. Most stay open late (24 hours along large highways and in big cities), except in rural areas, where Sunday hours are limited and where you may drive long stretches without a refueling opportunity. Highways are well paved. Interstate highways—limited-access multilane highways whose numbers are prefixed by "I–"—are the fastest routes. Interstates with three-digit numbers encircle or intersect urban areas, which may have other limited-access expressways, freeways, and parkways as well. Tolls may be levied on limited-access highways. So-called U.S. highways and state highways are not necessarily limited access, but many have several lanes.

Along larger highways roadside stops with restrooms, fast-food restaurants, and sundries stores are well spaced. State police and tow trucks patrol major highways and lend assistance. If your car breaks down on an interstate, pull onto the shoulder and wait for help, or have your passengers wait while you walk to an emergency phone. If you carry a cell phone, dial *55, noting your location on the small green roadside mileage markers.

Driving in the United States is on the right. Be sure to **obey speed limits** posted along roads and highways. Watch for lower limits in small towns and on back roads. Georgia and the Carolinas require front-seat passengers to wear seat belts. On weekdays between 6 AM and 10 AM and again between 4 PM and 7 PM **expect heavy traffic,** especially in big cities like Atlanta, Charlotte, Greensboro, Raleigh, and Durham. To encourage carpooling, some freeways have special lanes for what are designated high-occupancy vehicles (HOV)—cars carrying more than one passenger.

Bookstores, gas stations, convenience stores, and rest stops sell maps ($3–$5) and multiregion road atlases ($10 and up).

CONSULATES & EMBASSIES

Australia **Australian Embassy** ✉ 1601 Massachusetts Ave. NW, Washington, DC 20036 ☎ 202/797-3000.

Canada **Canadian Embassy** ✉ 501 Pennsylvania Ave. NW, Washington, DC 20001 ☎ 202/682-1740.

New Zealand **New Zealand Embassy** ✉ 37 Observatory Circle NW, Washington, DC 20008 ☎ 202/328-4800.

United Kingdom **British Embassy** ✉ 19 Observatory Circle NW, Washington, DC 20008 ☎ 202/588-7800.

CURRENCY

The dollar is the basic unit of U.S. currency. It has 100 cents. Coins are the copper penny (1¢); the silvery nickel (5¢), dime (10¢), quarter (25¢), and half-dollar (50¢); and the golden $1 coin, replacing a now-rare silver dollar. Bills are denominated $1, $5, $10, $20, $50, and $100, all mostly green and identical in size; designs and background tints vary. In addition, you may come across a $2 bill, but the chances are slim. The exchange rate at this writing is US$1.78 per British pound, $1.37 per euro, $0.79 per Canadian dollar, $0.72 per Australian dollar, and $0.67 per New Zealand dollar.

ELECTRICITY

The U.S. standard is AC, 110 volts/60 cycles. Plugs have two flat pins set parallel to each other.

EMERGENCIES

For police, fire, or ambulance, **dial 911** (0 in rural areas).

INSURANCE

Britons and Australians need extra medical coverage when traveling overseas.

Insurance Information In the U.K.: **Association of British Insurers** ✉ 51 Gresham St., London EC2V 7HQ ☎ 020/7600–3333 📠 020/7696–8999 🌐 www.abi.org.uk. In Australia: **Insurance Council of Australia** ✉ Insurance Enquiries and Complaints, Level 12, Box 561, Collins St. W, Melbourne, VIC 8007 ☎ 1300/780808 or 03/9629–4109 📠 03/9621–2060 🌐 www.iecltd.com.au. In Canada: **RBC Insurance** ✉ 6880 Financial Dr., Mississauga, Ontario L5N 7Y5 ☎ 800/668–4342 or 905/816–2400 📠 905/813–4704 🌐 www.rbcinsurance.com. In New Zealand: **Insurance Council of New Zealand** ✉ Level 7, 111–115 Customhouse Quay, Box 474, Wellington ☎ 04/472–5230 📠 04/473–3011 🌐 www.icnz.org.nz.

MAIL & SHIPPING

You can buy stamps and aerograms and send letters and parcels in post offices. Stamp-dispensing machines can occasionally be found in airports, bus and train stations, office buildings, drugstores, and the like. You can also deposit mail in the stout, dark blue, steel bins at strategic locations everywhere and in the mail chutes of large buildings; pickup schedules are posted. You can deposit packages at public collection boxes as long as the parcels are affixed with proper postage and weigh less than one pound. Packages weighing one or more pounds must be taken to a post office or handed to a postal carrier.

For mail sent within the United States, you need a 37¢ stamp for first-class letters weighing up to 1 ounce (23¢ for each additional ounce) and 23¢ for postcards. You pay 80¢ for 1-ounce airmail letters and 70¢ for airmail postcards to most countries; to Canada and Mexico, you need a 60¢ stamp for a 1-ounce letter and 50¢ for a postcard. An aerogram—a single sheet of lightweight blue paper that folds into its own envelope, stamped for overseas airmail—costs 70¢.

To receive mail on the road, have it sent c/o General Delivery at your destination's main post office (use the correct five-digit ZIP code). You must pick up mail in person within 30 days and show a driver's license or passport.

PASSPORTS & VISAS

When traveling internationally, carry your passport even if you don't need one (it's always the best form of ID) and **make two photocopies of the data page** (one for someone at home and another for you, carried separately from your passport). If you lose your passport, promptly call the nearest embassy or consulate and the local police.

Visitor visas aren't necessary for Canadian or European Union citizens, or for citizens of Australia who are staying fewer than 90 days.

Australian Citizens **Passports Australia** ☎ 131–232 🌐 www.passports.gov.au. **United States Consulate General** ✉ MLC Centre, Level 59, 19–29 Martin Pl., Sydney, NSW 2000 ☎ 02/9373–9200, 1902/941–641 fee-based visa-inquiry line 🌐 usembassy-australia.state.gov/sydney.

Canadian Citizens **Passport Office** ✉ To mail in applications: 200 Promenade du Portage, Hull, Québec J8X 4B7 ☎ 819/994–3500, 800/567–6868, 866/255–7655 TTY 🌐 www.ppt.gc.ca.

New Zealand Citizens **New Zealand Passports Office** ✉ For applications and information, Level 3,

Boulcott House, 47 Boulcott St., Wellington ☎ 0800/ 22-5050 or 04/474-8100 🌐 www.passports.govt.nz. **Embassy of the United States** ✉ 29 Fitzherbert Terr., Thorndon, Wellington ☎ 04/462-6000 🌐 usembassy.org.nz. **U.S. Consulate General** ✉ Citibank Bldg., 3rd fl., 23 Customs St. E, Auckland ☎ 09/303-2724 🌐 usembassy.org.nz.

U.K. Citizens **U.K. Passport Service** ☎ 0870/ 521-0410 🌐 www.passport.gov.uk. **American Consulate General** ✉ Danesfort House, 223 Stranmillis Rd., Belfast, Northern Ireland BT9 5GR ☎ 028/9032-8239 📠 028/9024-8482 🌐 usembassy.org.uk. **American Embassy** ✉ For visa and immigration information or to submit a visa application via mail (enclose an SASE), Consular Information Unit, 24 Grosvenor Sq., London W1 1AE ☎ 09055/444-546 for visa information (per-minute charges), 0207/499-9000 main switchboard 🌐 usembassy.org.uk.

TELEPHONES

All U.S. telephone numbers consist of a three-digit area code and a seven-digit local number. Within many local calling areas, you dial only the seven-digit number. Within some area codes, you must dial "1" first for calls outside the local area. To call between area-code regions, dial "1" then all 10 digits; the same goes for calls to numbers prefixed by "800," "888," "866," and "877"—all toll free. For calls to numbers preceded by "900" you must pay—usually dearly.

For international calls, dial "011" followed by the country code and the local number. For help, dial "0" and ask for an overseas operator. The country code is 61 for Australia, 64 for New Zealand, 44 for the United Kingdom. Calling Canada is the same as calling within the United States. Most local phone books list country codes and U.S. area codes. The country code for the United States is 1.

For operator assistance, dial "0." To obtain someone's phone number, call directory assistance at 555–1212 or occasionally 411 (free at many public phones). To have the person you're calling foot the bill, phone collect: dial "0" instead of "1" before the 10-digit number.

At pay phones, instructions often are posted. Usually you insert coins in a slot (usually 25¢–50¢ for local calls) and wait for a steady tone before dialing. When you call long-distance, the operator tells you how much to insert; prepaid phone cards, widely available in various denominations, are easier. Call the number on the back, punch in the card's personal identification number when prompted, then dial your number.

LODGING

With the exception of Atlanta, Savannah, Charleston, and Charlotte, most lodging rates in the region fall at or below the national average. They do vary a great deal seasonally, however—coastal areas as well as the Great Smoky Mountains tend to have significantly higher rates in summer. All major chains are well represented in this part of the country, both in cities and suburbs, and interstates are lined with inexpensive to moderate chains. It's not uncommon to find clean but extremely basic discount chains offering double rooms for as little as $25 to $40 nightly along the busiest highways.

In cities and some large towns you might want to forgo a modern hotel in favor of a historic property—there are dozens of fine old hotels, many of them fully restored and quite a few offering better rates than chain properties with comparable amenities and nothing like the style.

The lodgings listed are the cream of the crop in each price category. Properties indicated by ✕🏨 are lodging establishments whose restaurant warrants a special trip. Facilities that are available are listed—but not any extra costs associated with those facilities. When pricing accommodations, **always ask what's included and what costs extra.**

Hotels with the designation **BP** (for Breakfast Plan) at the end of their listing include breakfast in their rate; offerings can range from modest continental breakfasts to lavish spreads. Those designated **EP** (European Plan) have no meals included; **MAP** (Modified American Plan) means you get breakfast and dinner; **FAP** (Full American Plan) includes all meals.

APARTMENT & HOUSE RENTALS

If you want a home base that's roomy enough for a family and comes with cooking facilities, consider a furnished rental. These can save you money, especially if you're traveling with a group. Home-exchange directories sometimes list rentals as well as exchanges.

The far-flung resort-oriented areas of the Carolinas and Georgia are rife with rental properties of all kinds—ranging from efficiency apartments to luxury homes. These are either built by developers specifically for the tourist trade or are privately owned and rented by families for a portion of the year. Most often these properties, whether corporately or individually owned, are professionally managed; such businesses have become an industry unto themselves in the region.

Flannery Fork Rentals rents cabins in the high country of North Carolina. Homestead Log Cabins properties are in the Pine Mountain area of Georgia. Intracoastal Realty has long-term as well as off-season rentals on the Cape Fear coast. Midgett Realty handles Hatteras Island properties on North Carolina's Outer Banks. Island Realty focuses on the Charleston and Isle of Palms area in South Carolina. Tybee Island Realty handles properties on the tiny Georgia island of the same name.

International Agents **Hideaways International** ✉ 767 Islington St., Portsmouth, NH 03801 ☎ 603/430-4433 or 800/843-4433 ⎙ 603/430-4444 🌐 www.hideaways.com; annual membership $145. **Vacation Home Rentals Worldwide** ✉ 235 Kensington Ave., Norwood, NJ 07648 ☎ 201/767-9393 or 800/633-3284 ⎙ 201/767-5510 🌐 www.vhrww.com.

Local Agents **Flannery Fork Rentals** ✉ 232 Flannery Fork Farms Rd., Blowing Rock, NC 28605 ☎ 828/262-1908 🌐 www.flanneryfork.com. **Homestead Log Cabins** ✉ Box 311, Warm Springs, GA 31830 ☎ 706/663-4951 or 866/652-2246 🌐 www.homesteadcabins.com. **Intracoastal Realty** ✉ 605 Causeway Dr., Wrightsville Beach, NC 28480 ☎ 910/256-3780 or 800/346-2463 🌐 www.intracoastalrentals.com. **Island Realty** ✉ 1304 Palm Blvd., Isle of Palms, SC 29451 ☎ 843/886-8144 or 800/707-6421 🌐 www.islandrealty.com. **Midgett Realty** ✉ Box 250, Hatteras, NC 27943 ☎ 252/986-2841 or 800/527-2903 ⎙ 252/986-2745 🌐 www.midgettrealty.com. **Tybee Island Realty** ✉ 1016 1st St., Tybee Island, GA 31328 ☎ 912/786-7070 or 800/379-2298 🌐 www.tybeeislandrealty.com.

BED & BREAKFASTS

Historic B&Bs and inns are found in just about every region in the Carolinas and Georgia and include quite a few former plantation houses and lavish Southern estates. In many rural or less touristy areas, B&Bs offer an affordable and homey alternative to chain properties, but in tourism-dependent destinations you can expect to pay, for a historic inn, about the same as or more than for a full-service hotel. Many of the South's finest restaurants are also found in country inns.

CAMPING

The Carolinas and Georgia are popular for RV and tent camping, with facilities throughout the area, especially in state and national parks. For more information on parks and other campgrounds, contact the state tourism offices (⇨ Visitor Information).

HOME EXCHANGES

If you would like to exchange your home for someone else's, join a home-exchange organization, which will send you its updated listings of available exchanges for a year and will include your own listing in at least one of them. It's up to you to make specific arrangements.

Exchange Clubs **HomeLink International** 📫 Box 47747, Tampa, FL 33647 ☎ 813/975-9825 or 800/638-3841 ⎙ 813/910-8144 🌐 www.homelink.org; $110 yearly for a listing, online access, and catalog; $70 without catalog. **Intervac U.S.** ✉ 30 Corte San Fernando, Tiburon, CA 94920 ☎ 800/756-4663 ⎙ 415/435-7440 🌐 www.intervacus.com; $125 yearly for a listing, online access, and a catalog; $65 without catalog.

HOSTELS

No matter what your age, you can save on lodging costs by staying at hostels. In some 4,500 locations in more than 70 countries around the world, Hostelling International (HI), the umbrella group for a number of national youth-hostel associations, offers single-sex, dorm-style beds and, at many hostels, rooms for couples and family accommodations. Membership in any HI national hostel association, open to travelers of all ages, allows you to stay in HI-affiliated hostels at member rates; one-year membership is about $28 for adults (C$35 for a two-year minimum membership in Canada, £14 in the U.K., A$52 in Australia, and NZ$40 in New Zealand); hostels charge about $10–$30 per night. Members have priority if the hostel is full; they're also eligible for discounts around the world, even on rail and bus travel in some countries.

Organizations **Hostelling International–Canada** ✉ 205 Catherine St., Suite 400, Ottawa, Ontario K2P 1C3 ☎ 613/237-7884 or 800/663-5777 ☎ 613/237-7868 🌐 www.hihostels.ca. **Hostelling International–USA** ✉ 8401 Colesville Rd., Suite 600, Silver Spring, MD 20910 ☎ 301/495-1240 ☎ 301/495-6697 🌐 www.hiusa.org. **YHA Australia** ✉ 422 Kent St., Sydney, NSW 2001 ☎ 02/9261-1111 ☎ 02/9261-1969 🌐 www.yha.com.au. **YHA England and Wales** ✉ Trevelyan House, Dimple Rd., Matlock, Derbyshire DE4 3YH, U.K. ☎ 0870/870-8808, 0870/ 770-8868, or 0162/959-2600 ☎ 0870/770-6127 🌐 www.yha.org.uk. **YHA New Zealand** ✉ Level 1, Moorhouse City, 166 Moorhouse Ave., Box 436, Christchurch ☎ 03/379-9970 or 0800/278-299 ☎ 03/365-4476 🌐 www.yha.org.nz.

HOTELS

In summer, hotel rooms in coastal areas and the mountains are very difficult to find, unless you book months in advance. Lodging in North Carolina's Triad area is especially hard to come by during the twice-yearly international furniture shows: in April and October, all rooms are booked within a 30-mi radius of the show's location in High Point.

All hotels listed in this book have private baths unless otherwise noted.

Toll-Free Numbers **Adam's Mark** ☎ 800/444-2326 🌐 www.adamsmark.com. **Baymont Inns** ☎ 800/428-3438 or 866/999-1111 🌐 www.baymontinns.com. **Best Western** ☎ 800/528-1234 🌐 www.bestwestern.com. **Choice** ☎ 800/424-6423 🌐 www.choicehotels.com. **Clarion** ☎ 800/424-6423 🌐 www.choicehotels.com. **Comfort Inn** ☎ 800/424-6423 🌐 www.choicehotels.com. **Days Inn** ☎ 800/325-2525 🌐 www.daysinn.com. **Doubletree Hotels** ☎ 800/222-8733 🌐 www.doubletree.com. **Embassy Suites** ☎ 800/362-2779 🌐 www.embassysuites.com. **Fairfield Inn** ☎ 800/228-2800 🌐 www.marriott.com. **Four Seasons** ☎ 800/332-3442 🌐 www.fourseasons.com. **Hilton** ☎ 800/445-8667 🌐 www.hilton.com. **Holiday Inn** ☎ 800/465-4329 🌐 www.ichotelsgroup.com. **Howard Johnson** ☎ 800/446-4656 🌐 www.hojo.com. **Hyatt Hotels & Resorts** ☎ 800/233-1234 🌐 www.hyatt.com. **La Quinta** ☎ 800/531-5900 🌐 www.lq.com. **Marriott** ☎ 800/228-9290 🌐 www.marriott.com. **Omni** ☎ 800/843-6664 🌐 www.omnihotels.com. **Quality Inn** ☎ 800/424-6423 🌐 www.choicehotels.com. **Radisson** ☎ 800/333-3333 🌐 www.radisson.com. **Ramada** ☎ 800/228-2828, 800/854-7854 international reservations 🌐 www.ramada.com or www.ramadahotels.com. **Renaissance Hotels & Resorts** ☎ 800/468-3571 🌐 www.renaissancehotels.com/. **Ritz-Carlton** ☎ 800/241-3333 🌐 www.ritzcarlton.com. **Sheraton** ☎ 800/325-3535 🌐 www.starwood.com/sheraton. **Westin Hotels & Resorts** ☎ 800/228-3000 🌐 www.starwood.com/westin. **Wyndham Hotels & Resorts** ☎ 800/822-4200 🌐 www.wyndham.com.

MOTELS

Toll-Free Numbers **Budget Hosts Inns** ☎ 800/283-4678. **Econo Lodge** ☎ 800/553-2666 🌐 www.econolodge.com. **Friendship Inns** ☎ 800/453-4511. **Motel 6** ☎ 800/466-8356 🌐 www.motel6.com. **Rodeway** ☎ 800/228-2000 🌐 www.rodeway.com. **Super 8** ☎ 800/848-8888 🌐 www.super8.com.

MEDIA

NEWSPAPERS & MAGAZINES

There's no major regional newspaper that serves the area, but the *Atlanta Journal-Constitution* (🌐 www.ajc.com) is the most influential daily in the state of Georgia, and the *State* (🌐 www.thestate.com) newspaper out of Columbia is widely respected in South Carolina. Widely circulated dailies in North Carolina include the *News & Observer* (🌐 www.news-observer.com), headquartered in Raleigh, and the *Charlotte Observer* (🌐 www.charlotte.com). Just about every city with a population of greater than 40,000 or 50,000 also publishes its own daily paper.

Most major cities have very good alternative newsweeklies with useful Web sites and information on area dining, arts, and sightseeing—these are usually free and found in restaurants, coffeehouses, bookstores, tourism offices, hotel lobbies, and some nightclubs. Of particular note are Atlanta's weekly *Creative Loafing* (🌐 www.cln.com), which has a separate edition for Charlotte, and Raleigh-Durham's weekly *Independent*.

The monthly features magazine *Southern Living* (🌐 www.southernliving.com) gives a nice sense of travel, food, and lifestyle issues relevant to the region. Local lifestyles magazines serve Asheville, Atlanta, Charleston, Charlotte, Macon, Raleigh, Savannah, and several other cities. These publications have colorful stories and dining and entertainment coverage; they're worth picking up prior to your visit, especially if you're planning an extended stay; virtually all of these have useful Web sites, too.

RADIO & TELEVISION

All the major television and radio networks have local affiliates and channels throughout the Carolinas and Georgia, and the CNN empire is based in Atlanta.

MONEY MATTERS

As with most of America, credit and debit cards are accepted at the vast majority of shops, sit-down restaurants, and accommodations in the Carolinas and Georgia. Common exceptions include small, independent stores and B&Bs in more rural areas.

Although the cost of living remains fairly low in most parts of the South, travel-related costs (such as dining, lodging, museums, and transportation) have become increasingly steep in Atlanta over the years and can also be dear in resort communities throughout the Carolinas and Georgia.

Prices throughout this guide are given for adults. Substantially reduced fees are almost always available for children, students, and senior citizens. For information on taxes, *see* Taxes.

ATMS

Banks—as well as convenience stores, groceries, and even nightclubs—with ATMs are easy to find in just about every community. They are generally reliable and well-stocked. Muggings at ATMs, though rare, do occur, usually in urban centers in the evening hours; take standard safety precautions such as avoiding remote or poorly lighted machines.

CREDIT CARDS

Throughout this guide, the following abbreviations are used: **AE,** American Express; **D,** Discover; **DC,** Diners Club; **MC,** MasterCard; and **V,** Visa.

Reporting Lost Cards **American Express** ☎ 800/992–3404. **Diners Club** ☎ 800/234–6377. **Discover** ☎ 800/347–2683. **MasterCard** ☎ 800/622–7747. **Visa** ☎ 800/847–2911.

NATIONAL & STATE PARKS

National and state parks abound in the Carolinas and Georgia and have lots of visitor facilities, including campgrounds, picnic grounds, hiking trails, boating, and ranger programs. State forests are usually somewhat less developed. For more information contact the state tourism offices (⇨ Visitor Information).

Look into discount passes to save money on park entrance fees. For $50, the National Parks Pass admits you (and any passengers in your private vehicle) to all national parks, monuments, and recreation areas, as well as other sites run by the National Park Service, for a year. (In parks that charge per person, the pass admits you, your spouse and children, and your parents, when you arrive together.) Camping and parking are extra. The $15 Golden Eagle Pass, a hologram you affix to your National Parks Pass, functions as an upgrade, granting entry to all sites run by the NPS, the U.S. Fish and Wildlife Service, the U.S. Forest Service, and the Bureau of Land Management. The upgrade, which expires with the parks pass, is sold by most national-park, Fish-and-Wildlife, and BLM fee stations. A major percentage of the proceeds from pass sales funds National Parks projects.

Both the Golden Age Passport ($10), for U.S. citizens or permanent residents who are 62 and older, and the Golden Access Passport (free), for persons with disabilities, entitle holders (and any passengers in their private vehicles) to lifetime free entry to all national parks, plus 50% off fees for the use of many park facilities and services. (The discount doesn't always apply to companions.) To obtain them, you must show proof of age and of U.S. citizenship or permanent residency—such as a U.S. passport, driver's license, or birth certificate—and, if requesting Golden Access, proof of disability. The Golden Age and Golden Access passes are available only at NPS-run sites that charge an entrance fee. The National Parks Pass is also available by mail and via the Internet.

National Park Foundation ✉ 11 Dupont Circle NW, 6th fl., Washington, DC 20036 ☎ 202/238-4200 🌐 www.nationalparks.org. **National Park Service** ✉ National Park Service/Department of Interior, 1849 C St. NW, Washington, DC 20240 ☎ 202/208-6843 🌐 www.nps.gov. **National Parks Conservation Association** ✉ 1300 19th St. NW, Suite 300, Washington, DC 20036 ☎ 202/223-6722 🌐 www.npca.org.

Passes by Mail & Online **National Park Foundation** 🌐 www.nationalparks.org. **National Parks Pass** National Park Foundation ✉ Box 34108, Washington, DC 20043 ☎ 888/467-2757 🌐 www.nationalparks.org; include a check or money order payable to the National Park Service, plus $3.95 for shipping and handling (allow 8 to 13 business days from date of receipt for pass delivery), or call for passes.

PACKING

The Carolinas and Georgia are hot and humid in summer and sunny and mild in winter. Smart but casual attire works fine almost everywhere you go, with a few exceptions requiring more formal dress, most of them in Atlanta and selected resorts. For colder months pack a lightweight coat, slacks, and sweaters; you'll need heavier clothing in some mountainous areas, where cold, damp weather prevails and snow is not unusual. Keeping summer's humidity in mind, **pack absorbent natural fabrics that breathe;** bring an umbrella, but leave the plastic raincoat at home. You'll want a jacket or sweater for summer evenings and for too-cool air-conditioning. And **don't forget insect repellent.**

In your carry-on luggage, pack an extra pair of eyeglasses or contact lenses and enough of any medication you take to last a few days longer than the entire trip. You may also ask your doctor to write a spare prescription using the drug's generic name, as brand names may vary from country to country. In luggage to be checked, **never pack prescription drugs, valuables, or undeveloped film.** And don't forget to carry with you the addresses of offices that handle refunds of lost traveler's checks. Check *Fodor's How to Pack* (available at online retailers and bookstores everywhere) for more tips.

To avoid customs and security delays, carry medications in their original packaging. Don't pack any sharp objects in your carry-on luggage, including knives of any size or material, scissors, nail clippers, and corkscrews, or anything else that might arouse suspicion.

To avoid having your checked luggage chosen for hand inspection, don't cram bags full. The U.S. Transportation Security Administration suggests packing shoes on top and placing personal items you don't want touched in clear plastic bags.

CHECKING LUGGAGE

You're allowed to carry aboard one bag and one personal article, such as a purse or a laptop computer. Make sure what you carry on fits under your seat or in the overhead bin. Get to the gate early so you can board as soon as possible, before the overhead bins fill up.

Baggage allowances vary by carrier, destination, and ticket class. On international flights, you're usually allowed to check two bags weighing up to 70 pounds (32 kilograms) each, although a few airlines allow checked bags of up to 88 pounds (40 kilograms) in first class. Some international carriers don't allow more than 66 pounds (30 kilograms) per bag in business class and 44 pounds (20 kilograms) in economy. On domestic flights, the limit is usually 50 to 70 pounds (23 to 32 kilograms) per bag. In general, carry-on bags shouldn't exceed 40 pounds (18 kilograms). Expect to pay a fee for baggage that exceeds weight limits. Most airlines won't accept bags that weigh more than 100 pounds (45 kilograms) on domestic or international flights. Check baggage restrictions with your carrier before you pack.

Airline liability for baggage is limited to $2,500 per person on flights within the United States. On international flights it amounts to $9.07 per pound or $20 per kilogram for checked baggage (roughly $545 per 60-pound bag), with a maximum of $634.90 per piece, and $400 per passenger for unchecked baggage. You can buy additional coverage at check-in for about $10 per $1,000 of coverage, but it often excludes a rather extensive list of items, shown on your airline ticket.

Before departure, itemize your bags' contents and their worth, and label the bags with your name, address, and phone number. (If you use your home address, cover it so potential thieves can't see it readily.) Include a label inside each bag and **pack a copy of your itinerary.** At check-in, make sure each bag is correctly tagged with the destination airport's three-letter code. Because some checked bags will be opened for hand inspection, the U.S. Transportation Security Administration recommends that you leave luggage unlocked or use the plastic locks offered at check-in. TSA screeners place an inspection notice inside searched bags, which are re-sealed with a special lock.

If your bag has been searched and contents are missing or damaged, file a claim with the TSA Consumer Response Center as soon as possible. If your bags arrive damaged or fail to arrive at all, file a written report with the airline before leaving the airport.

Complaints **U.S. Transportation Security Administration Contact Center** ☎ 866/289-9673 ⊕ www.tsa.gov.

SENIOR-CITIZEN TRAVEL

To qualify for age-related discounts, mention your senior-citizen status up front when booking hotel reservations (not when checking out) and before you're seated in restaurants (not when paying the bill). Be sure to have identification on hand. When renting a car, ask about promotional car-rental discounts, which can be cheaper than senior-citizen rates.

Educational Programs **Elderhostel** ✉ 11 Ave. de Lafayette, Boston, MA 02111-1746 ☎ 877/426-8056, 978/323-4141 international callers, 877/426-2167 TTY 🖷 877/426-2166 ⊕ www.elderhostel.org.

SHOPPING

Beyond the suburban malls, which are usually anchored by national and/or regional department stores, boutiques and galleries can be found both in the larger cities and throughout the resort areas. Recognizing the changing demographics of the market, northern institutions such as Tiffany & Co. have established shops here. And thanks to the temperate climate, outdoor arts-and-crafts festivals abound. On most Saturday mornings bargain hunters can find deals in the ubiquitous flea markets and garage sales.

KEY DESTINATIONS

People travel from afar to furniture outlets in High Point and Hickory, North Carolina. The dozens of potters clustered around the North Carolina town of Seagrove, in the Sandhills, produce artistic and functional jugs, bowls, mugs, and more. South Carolina's textile industry continues to thrive, producing oceans of fabric sold in retail outlets dotted across the central and upper portions of the state. Chamblee Antique Row, near Atlanta, has more than 500,000 square feet of antiques and collectibles.

SMART SOUVENIRS

"Face jugs," whimsical pottery pitchers that incorporate caricature-like faces designed to ward off evil spirits, can be found at many of the roadside potteries in the Seagrove area of North Carolina, as well as in some city gift shops. Prices vary—anywhere from less than $100 to several hundred dollars—depending on the artist and the size. In South Carolina, particularly in the Lowcountry, sweetgrass baskets, woven using a technique carried over by African slaves, are both beautiful and utilitarian. The many designs, ranging from small baskets to clothes hampers, typically cost from $10 to $100. In a three-story pavilion adjacent to Underground Atlanta is the World of Coca-Cola, an homage to the drink invented here. Lots of fun Coca-Cola–related souvenirs in all price ranges are sold at the gift shop here.

SIGHTSEEING GUIDES

In many of the popular coastal areas, sightseeing tours on watercraft—from catamarans to gigantic speedboats—are offered by individual operators and well-organized companies. The narration typically includes a good dose of both local and natural history. This region is also rich in historic districts and sites, and the guided tours offered at most usually provide a good orientation to each area. Horse-and-buggy, walking, and even ghost tours are staples of the many antebellum towns, such as Charleston. In the Blue Ridge town of Helen, Georgia, a re-created alpine village, the buggy tour comes with a history of the area, which is linked to the Cherokee.

STUDENTS IN THE CAROLINAS & GEORGIA

Student discounts are common in the many college towns in this region.

IDs & Services **STA Travel** ✉ 10 Downing St., New York, NY 10014 ☎ 212/627-3111, 800/777-0112 24-hr service center 🖷 212/627-3387 🌐 www.sta.com. **Travel Cuts** ✉ 187 College St., Toronto, Ontario M5T 1P7, Canada ☎ 800/592-2887 in U.S., 416/979-2406 or 866/246-9762 in Canada 🖷 416/979-8167 🌐 www.travelcuts.com.

TIME

Georgia and the Carolinas fall in the eastern standard time (EST) zone, which is the same as New York and Florida, making it three hours ahead of California.

TIPPING

In group-tour situations—boat excursions along the coast, for example—the crew will split whatever is left in a communal tip jar; a couple of dollars is appropriate. Museum and tour guides are generally either volunteers or on staff, and therefore don't expect tips. Taxi fares can be rounded up by a couple of dollars or 15%, and restaurant tips for servers and bartenders range from 10% to 20%, depending on price and service; gratuities are often included in the bill for large parties. Hairdressers, barbers, and masseuses usually receive a gratuity of 10% to 20%.

Hotel chambermaids should be tipped $1–$3 a night for inexpensive and moderate hotels and up to $5 a night per guest for high-end properties. A concierge typically receives anywhere from $5 to $25, depending on the favor requested. Room-service waiters get 10% to 15% (look to see if it's already included on the bill), and $1–$2 per bag is customary for bellhops, porters, and skycaps. Tips aren't necessary, though they're still accepted, if the hotel includes a service fee in its package price—ask about this in advance.

TOURS & PACKAGES

Because everything is prearranged on a prepackaged tour or independent vacation, you spend less time planning—and often get it all at a good price.

BOOKING WITH AN AGENT

Travel agents are excellent resources. But it's a good idea to collect brochures from several agencies, as some agents' suggestions may be influenced by relationships with tour and package firms that reward them for volume sales. If you have a special interest, find an agent with expertise in that area; the American Society of Travel Agents (ASTA; ⇨ Travel Agencies) has a database of specialists worldwide. You can log on to the group's Web site to find an ASTA travel agent in your neighborhood.

Make sure your travel agent knows the accommodations and other services of the place being recommended. Ask about the hotel's location, room size, beds, and whether it has a pool, room service, or programs for children, if you care about these. Has your agent been there in person or sent others whom you can contact?

Do some homework on your own, too: local tourism boards can provide information about lesser-known and small-niche operators, some of which may sell only direct.

BUYER BEWARE

Each year consumers are stranded or lose their money when tour operators—even large ones with excellent reputations—go out of business. So check out the operator. Ask several travel agents about its reputation, and try to **book with a company that has a consumer-protection program.** (Look for information in the company's brochure.) In the United States, members of the United States Tour Operators Association are required to set aside funds ($1 million) to help eligible customers cover payments and travel arrangements in the event that the company defaults. It's also a good idea to choose a company that participates in the American Society of Travel Agents' Tour Operator Program; ASTA will act as mediator in any disputes between you and your tour operator.

Remember that the more your package or tour includes, the better you can predict the ultimate cost of your vacation. Make sure you know exactly what is covered, and beware of hidden costs. Are taxes, tips, and transfers included? Entertainment and excursions? These can add up.

Tour-Operator Recommendations **American Society of Travel Agents** (⇨ Travel Agencies). **National Tour Association** (NTA) ✉ 546 E. Main St., Lexington, KY 40508 ☎ 859/226-4444 or 800/682-8886 🖷 859/226-4404 🌐 www.ntaonline.com. **United States Tour Operators Association** (USTOA) ✉ 275 Madison Ave., Suite 2014, New York, NY 10016 ☎ 212/599-6599 🖷 212/599-6744 🌐 www.ustoa.com.

TRAIN TRAVEL

Several Amtrak routes pass through the Carolinas and Georgia; however, many areas are not served by train, and those cities that do have service usually only have one or two arrivals and departures each day. Major cities served include Atlanta and Savannah in Georgia; Charlotte, Durham, Greensboro, Raleigh, and Winston-Salem in North Carolina; and Columbia, Charleston, Greenville, and Hilton Head in South Carolina. For a comparison of different ways of getting around the region, *see* Transportation Around the Carolinas and Georgia.

CUTTING COSTS

Amtrak offers different kinds of rail passes that allow for travel within certain regions, including a set number of stops, at a significant savings over the standard posted fare. Also available is a North American Rail Pass that grants you unlimited travel in the United States and Canada within any 30-day period ($674 peak, $475 off-peak). For non–U.S. residents only, Amtrak has several kinds of USA Rail Passes, offering unlimited travel for 15–30 days. Amtrak also has senior citizen, children's, disability, and student discounts, as well as occasional deals that allow a second or third accompanying passenger to travel for half price or even free.

Train Information **Amtrak** ☎ 800/872-7245 🌐 www.amtrak.com.

TRANSPORTATION AROUND THE CAROLINAS & GEORGIA

Although a car is your best bet for traveling around the region, it's worth considering several strategies for getting about conveniently and economically.

If you're planning to spend more than several days and visit more than a couple of cities, you might consider driving your own car rather than flying in and renting one—especially if you live anywhere within 500 mi of the region (i.e., the mid-Atlantic states, the Midwest, or elsewhere in the South) and you're traveling with three or more in your group.

If you don't have your car and you're planning to visit more than one city in the region, check to see what airfares are available between some smaller cities—very often airlines offer specials for popular shorter routes like Atlanta to Savannah or Charlotte to Hilton Head.

If you're trying to save money, you have a fair amount of time, and you're interested in taking in the landscape without having to drive, consider getting around via bus—Greyhound/Trailways (⇨ Bus Travel) has frequent, regular, inexpensive service to virtually every city in the region. Some routes, such as those near the coastal areas and over the mountainous interior section, can be quite breathtaking. A bit less practical is relying on train travel (⇨ Train Travel), as Amtrak's coverage within the region is a bit spotty, and round-trip fares are sometimes substantially higher than bus fares for comparable routes—occasionally even more than the corresponding air fares.

TRAVEL AGENCIES

A good travel agent puts your needs first. Look for an agency that has been in business at least five years, emphasizes customer service, and has someone on staff who specializes in your destination. In addition, **make sure the agency belongs to a professional trade organization.** The American Society of Travel Agents (ASTA)—the largest and most influential in the field with more than 20,000 members in some 140 countries—maintains and enforces a strict code of ethics and will step in to help mediate any agent-client disputes involving ASTA members if necessary. ASTA (whose motto is "Without a travel agent, you're on your own") also maintains a Web site that includes a directory of agents. (If a travel agency is also acting as your tour operator, *see* Buyer Beware *in* Tours & Packages.)

Local Agent Referrals **American Society of Travel Agents** (ASTA) ✉ 1101 King St., Suite 200, Alexandria, VA 22314 ☎ 703/739-2782, 800/965-2782 24-hr hotline 📠 703/684-8319 🌐 www.astanet.com. **Association of British Travel Agents** ✉ 68-71 Newman St., London W1T 3AH ☎ 020/7637-2444 📠 020/7637-0713 🌐 www.abta.com. **Association of Canadian Travel Agencies** ✉ 130 Albert St., Suite 1705, Ottawa, Ontario K1P 5G4 ☎ 613/237-3657 📠 613/237-7052 🌐 www.acta.ca. **Australian Federation of Travel Agents** ✉ Level 3, 309 Pitt St., Sydney, NSW 2000 ☎ 02/9264-3299 or 1300/363-416 📠 02/9264-1085 🌐 www.afta.com.au. **Travel Agents' Association of New Zealand** ✉ Level 5, Tourism and Travel House, 79 Boulcott St., Box 1888, Wellington 6001 ☎ 04/499-0104 📠 04/499-0786 🌐 www.taanz.org.nz.

VISITOR INFORMATION

Learn more about foreign destinations by checking government-issued travel advisories and country information. For a broader picture, consider information from more than one country.

Tourist Information **Georgia Department of Industry, Trade and Tourism** ✉ 285 Peachtree Center Ave., N.E. Marquis Tower II, Suite 1100, Atlanta, GA 30303 ☎ 404/656-3553 or 800/847-4842 📠 404/651-9462 🌐 www.georgia.org. **North Carolina Travel and Tourism Division** ✉ 301 N. Wilmington St., Raleigh, NC 27601 ☎ 919/715-5900 or 800/847-4862 📠 919/733-2616 🌐 www.visitnc.com. **South Carolina Department of Parks, Recreation, and Tourism** ✉ 1205 Pendleton St., Suite 106, Columbia, SC 29201 ☎ 803/734-0122 or 888/727-6453 📠 803/734-0138 🌐 www.travelsc.com.

Government Advisories **Australian Department of Foreign Affairs and Trade** ☎ 300/139-281 travel advice, 02/6261-1299 Consular Travel Advice Faxback Service 🌐 www.dfat.gov.au. **Consular Affairs Bureau of Canada** ☎ 800/267-6788 or 613/944-6788 🌐 www.voyage.gc.ca. **New Zealand Ministry of Foreign Affairs and Trade** ☎ 04/439-8000 🌐 www.mft.govt.nz. **U.K. Foreign and Commonwealth Office** ✉ Travel Advice Unit, Consular Division, Old Admiralty Bldg., London SW1A 2PA ☎ 0870/606-0290 or 020/7008-1500 🌐 www.fco.gov.uk/travel.

WEB SITES

Do check out the World Wide Web when planning your trip. You'll find everything from weather forecasts to virtual tours of famous cities. Be sure to visit Fodors.com (🌐 www.fodors.com), a complete travel-planning site. You can research prices and book plane tickets, hotel rooms, rental cars, vacation packages, and more. In addition, you can post your pressing questions in the Travel Talk section. Other planning tools include a currency converter and weather reports, and there are loads of links to travel resources.

For more information on events in the Carolinas and Georgia, try visiting the Web sites of major newspapers and alternative newsweeklies in the area (⇨ Media). Also take a look at the Web sites listed for regional and local tourism offices in the A to Z sections throughout each chapter.

THE NORTH CAROLINA COAST

1

By Lisa H. Towle

NORTH CAROLINA'S 300-PLUS MILES OF COASTLINE are fronted by a continuous series of fragile barrier islands. Broad rivers lead inland from the sounds, along which port cities have grown. Lighthouses, dunes, and vacation homes (often built by out-of-staters) dot the water's edge. The coast is generally divided into three broad sections that include islands, shoreline, and coastal plains: the Outer Banks (Corolla south through Ocracoke, including Roanoke Island), the Crystal Coast (Core and Bogue Banks, Beaufort, Morehead City, and the inland river town of New Bern), and the greater Cape Fear region (Wrightsville Beach through the Brunswick County islands, including Wilmington).

The Outer Banks, a chain of barrier islands in the Atlantic, forms a giant sandbar south of the Virginia border. Addresses here are commonly noted by mile markers, not building numbers. The picturesque Albemarle area, on the mainland, parallels a portion of the Outer Banks. New Bern is a bit farther inland on the Central Coast and has sights that provide a close-up look at America during the Revolutionary and Civil Wars. Wilmington, on the Cape Fear River, is home to the University of North Carolina–Wilmington and is the coast's largest city. It has fine restaurants and museums. Surrounding it are golf courses, white-sand beaches, and resort hotels, which have been voted some of the best in the nation by various sources.

Whereas once the coast closed up shop after the summer season ended, the entire area, home to two national seashores (Cape Hatteras and Cape Lookout), is now considered a year-round destination. You can explore museums; spend the day swimming, hang gliding, windsurfing, or kayaking; or stop in restaurants with fresh seafood and increasingly innovative chefs after you've spent the day shopping at retail outlets. Whether you're seeking peace or adventure, you can find it on the coast.

Exploring the North Carolina Coast

The relative isolation, which helps to preserve the beauty of this area, also restricts the ways to access it and slows travel along its length. Route 12, with the help of the Hatteras Inlet ferry, travels the entire length of the Outer Banks, but to get to it you must either cross bridges from the mainland on U.S. 158 (from the north) or U.S. 64 (from the west) or take ferries from Swan Quarter or Cedar Island after long mainland drives farther south. Many of the islands and banks of the Crystal Coast and Cape Fear regions are traversed by state routes or U.S. highways, but there's no continuous path along the entire coastline. U.S. 70 is the main route into the Crystal Coast from the west, and Wilmington is the terminus of I–40. The main north–south highway through the Cape Fear region is U.S. 17, which skirts the broadest parts of the rivers and intersects east–west roads as it drops from Virginia to South Carolina.

About the Restaurants

Raw bars serve oysters and clams on the half shell; seafood houses sell fresh crabs (soft shells in the early summer season) and whatever local catch—tuna, wahoo, mahimahi, mackerel, shrimp—has been hauled in that day. This is after all the coast. Increasingly, though, highly trained

GREAT ITINERARIES

Numbers in the text correspond to numbers in the margin and on the Outer Banks, Central & Cape Fear coasts, and Wilmington maps.

If you have 3 days

Start a tour of the Outer Banks by driving north on Route 12 from the mainland to the **Northern Beaches** 1 ; on your first morning in Corolla, visit the Currituck Beach Lighthouse and the Whalehead Club. After lunch head south through Kitty Hawk and stop at the Wright Brothers National Memorial in Kill Devils Hill, or at Jockey's Ridge State Park in **Nags Head** 2. Spend that night on **Roanoke Island** 3, where on Day 2 you visit the lush Elizabethan Gardens, the Fort Raleigh National Historic Site, and the North Carolina Aquarium. On Day 3, leave Roanoke and spend the day along the Cape Hatteras National Seashore visiting sights on **Hatteras Island** 4 in the morning, such as the Chicamacomico Lifesaving Station and the iconic Cape Hatteras Lighthouse. Take the ferry to **Ocracoke Island** 5 for the afternoon, where you can stop by the Ocracoke Pony Pen on your way south to the Ocracoke Lighthouse.

If you have 5 days

Given two more days, follow the three-day itinerary above and then after overnighting on **Ocracoke Island** 5, catch an early run of the ferry to Cedar Island, which takes about 2 ¼ hours plying Pamlico Sound. From Cedar Island, follow Route 12 south to U.S. 70, which winds through the area known as down east, and gets you to the picturesque old town of **Beaufort** 6. After lunch, visit the Beaufort Historic Site and explore the historic district and waterfront by double-decker bus or on foot, saving some time for the North Carolina Maritime Museum. This area easily deserves adding an additional day, which would allow time for the History Place in **Morehead City** 7 and Fort Macon State Park at the east end of the Bogue Banks (an excellent place for some beach time, too). If you choose to depart, continue west on U.S. 70 to the river town of **New Bern** 8. Here the grand Tryon Palace and related old buildings can easily fill your last day. Many fine B&Bs are available as lodging.

If you have 7 days

If you have a full week or more, extend the five-day itinerary to include the Cape Fear coast. From **New Bern** 8, follow U.S. 17 south past forests and Marine bases to the port city of **Wilmington** 9–15 for nights six and seven. The charming and historic riverfront downtown has shops and museums, like the Zebulon Latimer House. Take a quick trip across the river to the USS *North Carolina* Battleship Memorial, where you can learn what life was really like on these immense machines. The lush, subtropical Wilmington area also has arboretums, parks, and gardens to explore. On Day 7 you can take a day-trip south from the city on U.S. 421 to the Fort Fisher State Historic Site and the North Carolina Aquarium at Fort Fisher in **Kure Beach** 17 or further on by ferry to the history and antiques of **Southport** 18. Instead of going back to Wilmington for the night, you could reserve ahead and stay at the private Bald Head Island Resort.

chefs are settling in the region and diversifying menus. Fish dishes—broiled, fried, grilled, or steamed—are listed alongside entrées fusing Asian flavors and traditional Southern ingredients such as black-eyed peas.

As the region's tourist season has grown so have the waiting times at many restaurants, especially during the summer months and festival periods. Many places on the coast don't accept reservations. Restaurant hours are frequently reduced or curtailed in winter, and some restaurants in the remote beach communities close entirely for a month or more. Although some of the more upscale, up-price restaurants may require a tie or at least a collared shirt, casual dress (shorts and polo shirts) is acceptable in the majority of area restaurants.

WHAT IT COSTS

$$$$	$$$	$$	$	¢
over $22	$16–$22	$11–$16	$7–$11	under $7

Prices are for a main course at dinner, excluding sales tax of 7%–7.5%.

About the Hotels

Hundreds upon hundreds of rental properties are scattered among the towns on the seashore. There are still some small beach cottages to be had; increasingly, however, it's the so-called McMansions—built by out-of-towners in search of a vacation home for part of the year and hefty rental income the other—that are available. These multistory houses can sleep anywhere from 12 to 20 people (family groups rent them for reunions) and often have ocean views, swimming pools, fire places, and game rooms in addition to the standard kitchen, laundry room, and satellite or cable TV. Rates run about $800–$1,000 a week in summer. Another option are the motels and hotels clustered up and down the Outer Banks.

If you're visiting Wilmington and the Cape Fear Coast, or New Bern, Morehead City, and the Central ("Crystal") Coast, the choices are condos, resorts overlooking water—whether it be rivers, sounds, or the ocean—and hotels and motels. Chains hotels have outlets here, but there are a surprising number of small, older, family-run lodgings as well. You're not going to get turn-down service or a minibar, but for the budget conscious in search of a clean bed and bathroom, TV and coffeemaker, the local motels are a great deal. You might also consider one of the many in-town bed-and-breakfasts. Most are filled with antiques; many have hosts glad to offer concierge-type services. When planning your trip, always ask about special packages (price breaks on multiple night stays) and off-season rates.

WHAT IT COSTS

$$$$	$$$	$$	$	¢
over $220	$160–$220	$110–$160	$70–$110	under $70

Prices are for two people in a standard double room in high season, excluding service charges and 7%–13% tax.

Beaches Residents treasure the North Carolina Coast's unique geological and biological resources and state law forbids any man-made structures, such as seawalls, that inhibit the ebb and flow of nature along the 300-mi coastline (thus keeping beaches as wide and unspoiled as possible). The concept of private beaches is foreign to North Carolinians, all of whom know where to find the access points to their favorite piece of the coast. The southernmost waterways, preserves, and conservatories, along the South Brunswick Island chain, have remained in near-pristine condition and are some of the most environmentally diverse in the state, while the more northern parts of the coast—the Outer Banks, home to Cape Hatteras, the nation's first national seashore—have the tallest natural sand dunes on all of the eastern seaboard. Fort Macon State Park, on the Central Coast, across from Morehead City, combines a history lesson with a swimming spot.

Shell Collecting A sunrise walk on a North Carolina beach has a wealth of shells, treasures from the sea for those willing to get up early. The coast is home to as many as 1,000 species of mollusks, the outer coverings or skeletons of which are commonly called seashells. There's no single best place to find these shells. Collectors point to the more isolated areas—Cape Hatteras National Seashore, Ocracoke Island, Cape Lookout National Seashore, Shackleford Banks, Hammocks Beach State Park near Bogue Sound, and the inlets near Wrightsville Beach—as prime hunting ground. You can find shells here year-round, but early spring after a storm or during hurricane season are particularly good times for shelling. And if you really want to narrow down the prime shelling time, head out one hour before or one hour after low tide.

Carolina Bays They are mysterious natural wonders—the great, thumb-shape freshwater lakes that dot the flat coastal plain like so many shallow bowls rimmed with white sand. Theories abound as to their prehistoric origins. One hypothesis is that peat fires hollowed out depressions, which subsequently filled with rainwater. Another supposes that gigantic meteors were responsible for the basins, some of which are in forested areas, although others are in boggier spots. They're called Carolina bays: "Carolina" because both North Carolina and South Carolina have them and "bay" because bayberry trees are almost always nearby. Uniting them further is an untamed yet tranquil beauty. Examples of these interesting geographical anomalies: Lake Phelps, 56 mi east of Nags Head; Lake Mattamuskeet, 44 mi northeast of Ocracoke Village; and White Lake, 58 mi northwest of Wilmington.

Timing

North Carolina's coast shines in spring (April and May) and fall (September and October), when the weather is most temperate and the water reasonably warm. Traveling during these times you can avoid the long lines and higher prices associated with peak tourist season. Typically, room rates are lower prior to Memorial Day and after Labor

Day. If you do want a summer rental, it's best to make arrangements by March when there are still a fair number of options available. During holiday periods, such as July 4, two- or three-night minimum stays are common.

THE OUTER BANKS

North Carolina's Outer Banks stretch from the Virginia state line south to Cape Lookout. Think of the OBX (a shorthand used on popular bumper stickers) as a series of stepping stones in the Atlantic Ocean. Throughout history the treacherous waters surrounding these islands have been the nemesis of shipping, gaining them the nickname "the graveyard of the Atlantic." A network of lighthouses and lifesaving stations, which grew around the need to protect seagoing craft, attracts curious travelers, just as the many submerged wrecks attract scuba divers. The islands' coves and inlets, which provided privacy to pirates—the notorious Blackbeard lived and died here—now give refuge to anglers, bird-watchers, and sun bathers.

The region is divided into four coastal sections: the Northern Beaches, beginning with Corolla, followed by Roanoke Island, Hatteras Island, and then Ocracoke Island. For many years the Outer Banks remained isolated, with only a few hardy families making their livings by fishing. Today the islands are linked by bridges and ferries and much of the area is included in the Cape Hatteras and Cape Lookout national seashores. The largest towns are also the most colorfully named: Kitty Hawk, Kill Devil Hills, Nags Head, and Manteo. Vacation rentals here are omnipresent—there are about 12,000 weekly rental cottages available on the Outer Banks. Times may have changed, but fishing still prevails: about 40 million pounds of fish are caught here annually—making it a $27 million industry. Flounder and crab alone account for half the haul; the rest includes bluefish, dolphin, mussels, clams, mackerel, marlin, shark, tuna, and shrimp. Many locals still use crab pots to process their catch in the backyards, and it's not unusual to see a fisherman arrive at a restaurant with fresh crab and ask the chef to cook it.

You can travel the region from the south end by taking a car ferry to Ocracoke Island or, as in the following route, from the north end. Driving the 120-mi stretch of Route 12 from Corolla to Ocracoke can be managed in a day, but be sure to allow plenty of time in summer to wait for the ferry connecting the islands and for exploring the undeveloped beaches, historic lighthouses, and small beach communities stretched along the national seashores. Mile markers (MM) indicate addresses for sites where there aren't many buildings. Sudden squalls frequently blow up on the Outer Banks in summer. Be aware that during major storms and hurricanes the roads and bridges become clogged with traffic following the blue-and-white evacuation signs.

Northern Beaches

❶ *Corolla: 91 mi south of Norfolk, VA, via U.S. 17, U.S. 158, and Rte. 12; 230 mi east of Raleigh via U.S. 64, U.S. 17, and Rte. 12. Duck: 16*

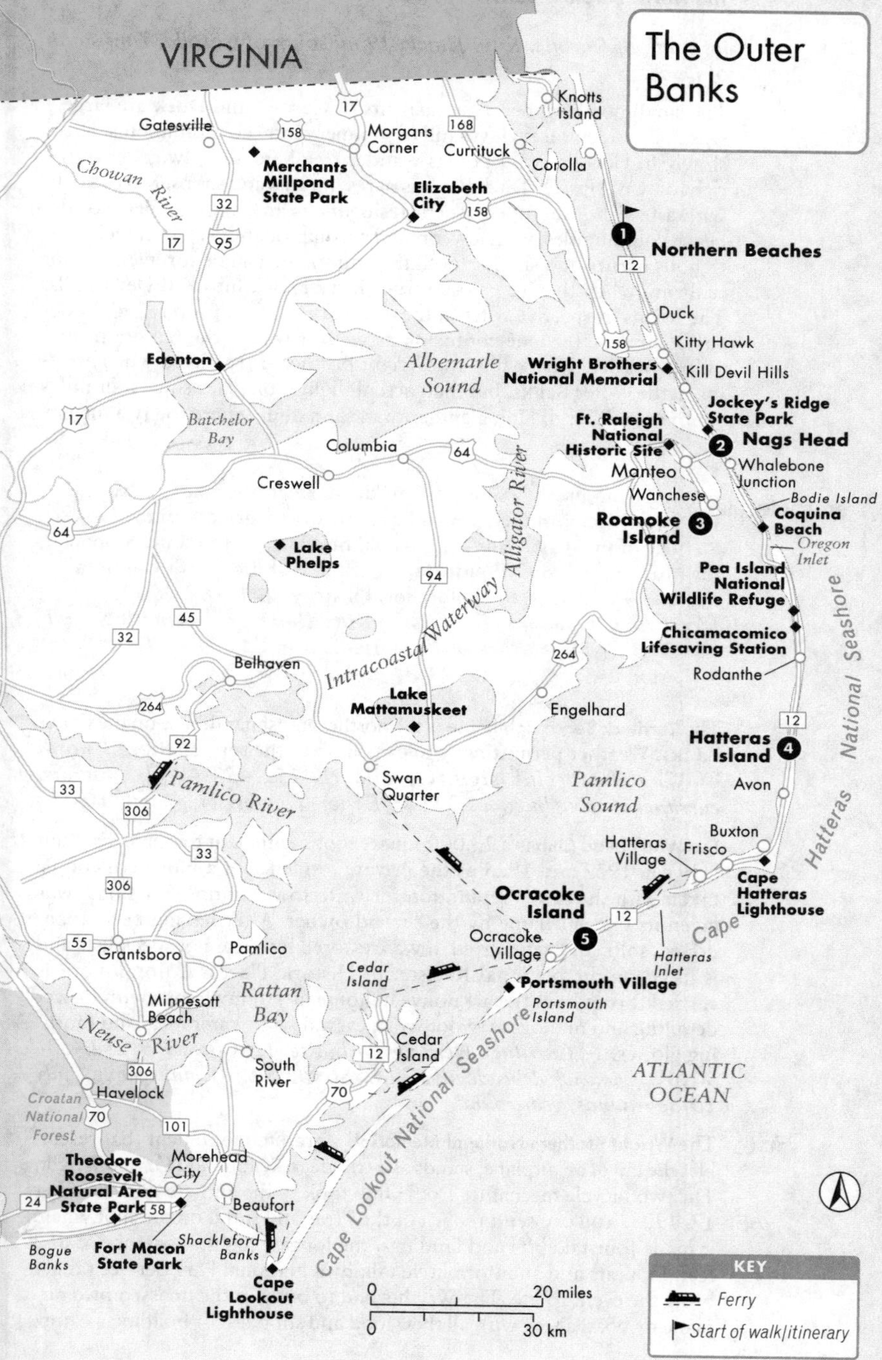

The Outer Banks
VIRGINIA
Knotts Island
Gatesville
Morgans Corner
Currituck
Corolla
Chowan River
Merchants Millpond State Park
Elizabeth City
Northern Beaches
Duck
Kitty Hawk
Edenton
Albemarle Sound
Wright Brothers National Memorial
Kill Devil Hills
Jockey's Ridge State Park
Batchelor Bay
Ft. Raleigh National Historic Site
Nags Head
Columbia
Manteo
Whalebone Junction
Creswell
Wanchese
Bodie Island
Roanoke Island
Coquina Beach
Oregon Inlet
Lake Phelps
Alligator River
Pea Island National Wildlife Refuge
Intracoastal Waterway
Chicamacomico Lifesaving Station
Belhaven
Rodanthe
Lake Mattamuskeet
Engelhard
Hatteras Island
Swan Quarter
Pamlico Sound
Avon
Pamlico River
Cape Hatteras National Seashore
Buxton
Hatteras Village
Frisco
Cape Hatteras Lighthouse
Ocracoke Island
Ocracoke Village
Hatteras Inlet
Grantsboro
Pamlico
Cedar Island
Portsmouth Village
Portsmouth Island
Rattan Bay
Minnesott Beach
Neuse River
South River
Cedar Island
ATLANTIC OCEAN
Havelock
Croatan National Forest
Cape Lookout National Seashore
Theodore Roosevelt Natural Area State Park
Morehead City
Beaufort
Fort Macon State Park
Shackleford Banks
Bogue Banks
Cape Lookout Lighthouse
0
20 miles
0
30 km
KEY
Ferry
Start of walk/itinerary

mi south of Corolla. Kitty Hawk: 19 mi south of Corolla, 7 mi south of Duck.

The small northern beach settlements of Corolla and Duck are largely seasonal residential enclaves full of summer rental condominiums. Drive slowly in Corolla: wild ponies wander free here and always have the right of way. Upscale Duck has lots of restaurants and shops. Kitty Hawk, with a few thousand permanent residents, is among the quieter of the beach communities, with fewer rental accommodations. Given their contiguous nature and similar look, the uninitiated can be forgiven for not realizing when they've crossed from Kitty Hawk into Kill Devil Hills. The towns' respective roles in the drama of the first powered flight occasionally create some confusion as well. It was in the remote fishing village of Kitty Hawk that the Wright brothers first stayed when arriving at the Outer Banks, but their actual flight took place some four miles south on Kill Devil Hill, a gargantuan sand dune where today a memorial stands.

en route

Driving from Norfolk, Virginia, to the northern beaches on U.S. 17, you pass **Elizabeth City,** which has a historic district with the largest number of pre–Civil War commercial buildings in the state. Stop at the **Museum of the Albemarle,** an affiliate of the North Carolina Museum of History, to explore local history. ✉ *1116 U.S. 17, Elizabeth City, 50 mi northwest of Kitty Hawk on Albemarle Sound* ☎ *252/335–1453* 🌐 *www.albemarle-nc.com* 🎫 *Free* ⏲ *Tues.–Sat. 9–5, Sun. 2–5.*

The **Currituck Beach Lighthouse** is the northernmost lighthouse on the Outer Banks. Weather permitting, you can climb to the top. ✉ *Rte. 12, north of Whalehead club sign, Corolla* ☎ *252/453-4939* 🌐 *www.currituckbeachlight.com* 🎫 *$6* ⏲ *Easter–Thanksgiving, daily 10–5.*

The Whalehead Club is a 23,000 square foot monument to opulence. Built between 1922 and 1925 as the private residence of a Northern couple taken with the area's reputation for waterfowl hunting, the home was given its current name by the second owner. After having been abandoned, sold, and vandalized, it was restored by a team of specialists and is listed on the National Register of Historic Places. A floral motif is carried throughout the art nouveau home in Tiffany lamps with flower detailing and mahogany woodwork carved with water lilies and morning glories. ✉ *Currituck Heritage Park, Rte. 12, Corolla* ☎ *252/453–9040* 🌐 *www.whaleheadclub.com* 🎫 *$6* ⏲ *Easter–Thanksgiving, daily 10–5; grounds, year-round.*

★ The **Wright Brothers National Memorial,** a granite monument that resembles the tail of an airplane, stands as a tribute to Wilbur and Orville Wright. The two bicycle mechanics from Ohio took to the air here on December 17, 1903. You can see a replica of the *Flyer* and stand on the spot where it made four takeoffs and landings, the longest flight a distance of 852 feet. Exhibits and an informative talk by a National Park Service ranger bring the event to life. The Wrights had to bring in the unassembled airplane by boat, along with all their food and supplies for building a camp.

CloseUp

FIRST IN FLIGHT

DECEMBER 17, 1903, was a cold and windy day on the Outer Banks, but Wilbur and Orville Wright took little notice. The slightly built brothers from Ohio were undertaking an excellent adventure. With Orville at the controls, Wilbur running alongside, and the men of the nearby Lifesaving Service stations acting as ground crew, the fragile Wright Flyer lifted off from the dunes of Kill Devil Hills and flew 120 feet in 12 seconds.

John Daniels, an Outer Banker, photographed the instant the world forever changed: a heavier-than-air machine was used to achieve controlled, sustained flight with a pilot aboard. To prove that they were not accidental aviators, the Wrights made three more powered flights that day. Wilbur took his turn, flying 195 feet in a little over 15 seconds. Finally, it was Wilbur's chance again. In a 59-second period he took the first airplane 852 feet.

In fact, everything about the start of modern aeronautical science was very intentional. Wilbur and Orville began experimenting in 1899 with their first kite and achieved their goals in 1905, when they built a truly practical airplane. What happened in between, with their work in Kill Devil Hills, helped them solve the problems of mechanical flight, lift, propulsion, and control that had vexed scientists for hundreds of years.

It was the ideal combination of wind and sand and privacy that brought Wilbur and Orville to the then-remote corner of North Carolina. Their success is honored at the Wright Brothers National Memorial in Kill Devil Hills.

They made four trips to the site, beginning in 1900. The First Flight is commemorated annually. ✉ *U.S. 158 between MM 7 and MM 8, Kill Devil Hills, 5 mi south of Kitty Hawk* ☎ *252/441–7430* 🌐 *www.nps.gov* 🎫 *$3* ⏲ *Sept.–May, daily 9–5; June–Aug., daily 9–6.*

off the beaten path

MERCHANTS MILLPOND STATE PARK – A 200-year-old, man-made millpond and an ancient swamp combine to form one of the state's rarest ecosystems. Cypress and gum trees, hung with Spanish moss, reach out of the still, dark waters that are ideal for canoeing. Rent a canoe or go fishing or hiking. Camp sites are also available. The park is on the mainland, 80 mi northwest of Kitty Hawk. ✉ *71 U.S. 158, Gatesville* ☎ *252/357–1191* 🎫 *Free* ⏲ *June–Aug., daily 8 AM–9 PM; Sept., Apr., and May, daily 8–8; Oct. and Mar., daily 8–7; Nov.–Feb., daily 8–6.*

Where to Stay & Eat

$$$$ ✕ **Elizabeth's Cafe & Winery.** Choose to eat in the French country dining room or in the stone grotto: this small bistro evokes big-time romance even though it's in a shopping center. À la carte and fixed menus change constantly to reflect the day's market purchases, whether it's rack of lamb, Angus beef tenderloin, or the freshest vegetables for the Vegetarian du Jour dish. The restaurant's wine list has been written about in the *Wine Spectator,* and the associated wine gallery has more than 1,600 bottles for sale. ✉ *Scarborough Lane Shoppes, Rte. 12, Duck* ☎ *252/261–6145* ✍ *Reservations essential* 💳 *AE, D, DC, MC, V* ⊙ *No lunch.*

$$$$ ✕ **Nicoletta's Italian Cafe.** White linen tablecloths, flowers, and a view of the Currituck Beach Lighthouse mean atmosphere with a capital A here. There's open-air dining on the porch. Nicoletta's is known for fresh seafood and southern Italian pasta dishes. Off-season hours may vary. ✉ *Corolla Light Village Shops, Rte. 12, Corolla* ☎ *252/453–4004* 💳 *MC, V* ⊙ *No lunch.*

$$$–$$$$ ✕ **Blue Point Bar & Grill.** This upscale spot with an enclosed porch overlooking Currituck Sound is as busy as a diner and as boldly colored—with a red, black, and chrome interior—but both the service and the menu are decidedly uptown. The menu mixes Southern style with local seafood, including the ever-popular she-crab soup, a thick and rich concoction made with cream, sherry, herbs, Old Bay seasoning, and, of course, female crab. Brunch is served Sunday. ✉ *1240 Duck Rd., Duck* ☎ *252/261–8090* ✍ *Reservations essential* 💳 *AE, D, MC, V.*

$$$ ✕ **Duck News Café.** The sunset scene from the deck at day's end is something to behold here, on the sound side of Route 12. Inside the small café the scene is bustling, casual, and family-friendly. The menu is heavy on seafood—even the kid's menu lists fried clam strips. But you can also get pasta, prime rib, and Parmesan chicken. ✉ *1564 Duck Rd., Rte. 12, Duck* ☎ *252/255–0773* 💳 *MC, V* ⊙ *Closed Nov.–Mar.*

★ $$$$ ✕🏨 **The Sanderling Resort & Spa.** A remote beach, 5 mi north of Duck, is a fine place to be pampered, go swimming, play tennis, or walk through Pine Island Sanctuary. This resort has three inn buildings—Main Inn, North Inn, and South Inn—plus villas, all with the mellow look of old Nags Head. Whirling ceiling fans, wicker furniture, and bright tones make the rooms casual and summery. The formal, dinner-only Left Bank restaurant ($$$) has wide views of Currituck Sound. Crab cakes, roast duckling, or fricassee of shrimp may be on the seasonal menu. Lifesaving Station ($$$), in a 1899 lifesaving station, serves breakfast, lunch, and dinner. ✉ *1461 Duck Rd., Duck 27949* ☎ *252/261–4111 or 800/701–4111* 📠 *252/261–1638* 🌐 *www.sanderlinginn.com* ⇨ *88 rooms, 29 efficiencies, 4 villas* 👍 *2 restaurants, room service, some in-room hot tubs, some kitchenettes, microwaves, minibars, some refrigerators, some in-room VCRs, golf privileges, 2 tennis courts, pool, health club, hot tub, spa, fishing, bicycles, hiking, racquetball, squash, bar, library, shop, meeting room* 💳 *AE, D, MC, V* 🍽 *BP.*

$$$–$$$$ 🏨 **The Inn at Corolla Light.** The inn is a part of the Corolla Light Resort and sits along Currituck Sound, about 10 mi from Duck. The ocean, ¼ mi away, is easily accessed via bikes or open-air trolley service. Even the smaller rooms feel big thanks to the generous use of richly toned fabrics, large beds, and windows with views of the garden, pool, or sound. A special treat are the off-road tours for the inn's guests to the secluded spot where the area's wild horses are now confined. ✉ *1066 Ocean Trail, Corolla 27927* ☎ *252/453–3340 or 800/215–0772* 📠 *252/453–6947*

www.corolla-inn.com *43 rooms* *Restaurant, some kitchenettes, refrigerators, in-room VCRs, golf privileges, 9 tennis courts, pool, wading pool, health club, hot tub, beach, boating, jet skiing, fishing, bicycles, hiking, racquetball, volleyball, fishing, video game room, shops; no smoking* *D, MC, V* *BP.*

$$–$$$ **Advice 5¢.** A roof with varied pitches and eaves tops this contemporary steely blue-gray beach house with white trim and multipane windows rising from the sandy dunes. Although the name is lighthearted, Advice 5¢ is very serious about guest care. Beds in each room are dressed with crisp, colorful linens. All rooms have private decks, ceiling fans, and baths stocked with thick cotton towels. You have use of the tennis courts, swimming pool, and the beach access at Sea Pines, a nearby resort. From the North Beach area you can easily walk to downtown shops and restaurants. *111 Scarborough La., Duck 27949* *252/255–1050 or 800/238–4235* *www.advice5.com* *4 rooms, 1 suite* *Dining room, fans, some in-room hot tubs; no room phones, no TV in some rooms, no smoking* *MC, V* *Closed Dec.–Feb.* *BP.*

Cape Hatteras National Seashore

Fodor'sChoice ★ *Extends from Nags Head, 70 mi south.*

Unspoiled beaches that are part of Cape Hatteras National Seashore stretch from south Nags Head to Ocracoke Inlet across three narrow islands: Bodie, Hatteras, and Ocracoke. The islands are linked by Route 12 and the Hatteras Inlet ferry. This coastal area is ideal for swimming, surfing, windsurfing, diving, boating, and other water activities. It's easy to find your own slice of beach as you drive south down Route 12, but park only in designated areas. If you want to swim, beware of strong tides and currents—there are no lifeguard stations. Fishing piers are in Rodanthe, Avon, and Frisco.

Nags Head

❷ *9 mi south of Kitty Hawk.*

Nags Head got its name because Outer Bankers would tie lanterns around the heads of their horses to lure merchant ships onto the shoals hoping for shipwrecks and profits from the cargo that washed ashore (or which they brought ashore when they pirateered the boats). The town lies between the Atlantic Ocean and Pamlico Sound, along and between U.S. 158 (known as "the bypass") and Route 12 ("the beach road"). The bypass is very heavily trafficked in the high season, but the entire area is commercialized. On the upside, there are plenty of restaurants, motels, hotels, shops, and entertainment. Vacation rentals are a big industry here. Shingled older homes have wraparound porches. There are small and dated cottages, and increasingly, sprawling new homes—with lots of bells and whistles—that can house several families at a time.

Nags Head has 11 mi of beach with 33 public access points from Route 12, all with parking and some with restrooms and showers. The first North Carolina Historic Shipwreck Site, the **USS *Huron,*** lies in 20 feet of water off the Nags Head Pier and is a favorite with scuba divers. ✣ *Offshore between MM 11 and 12.*

Jockey's Ridge State Park has 400 acres that encompass the tallest sand dune in the East (about 88 feet), although it has lost some 22 feet since the 1930s thanks to the million visitors a year who carry sand away on their persons. Walk along the 384-foot boardwalk from the visitor center to the edge of the dune. The climb to the top is a challenge; nevertheless, it's a popular spot for hang gliding, kite flying, and sand boarding. You can also explore an estuary and several trails through the park. In summer join the free Sunset on the Ridge program: watch the sun disappear while you sit on the dunes and learn about their local legends and history. Covered footwear is a wise choice here, as the loose sand gets quite hot in the summer months. ✉ *U.S. 158, MM 12* ☎ *252/441–7132* 🌐 *www.ils.unc.edu/parkproject* 🎫 *Free* ⏲ *Daily 8–sunset.*

The **Tanger Outlet Center** mall has two dozen stores selling designer clothes, shoes, casual attire, books, sunglasses, and more. ✉ *U.S. 158, MM 16* ☎ *252/441–5634* 🌐 *www.tangeroutlet.com* ⏲ *Sept.–May, Mon.–Sat. 9–9, Sun. 11–6; June–Aug, Mon.–Sat. 9 AM–10 PM, Sun. 11–6.*

Coquina Beach, in the Cape Hatteras National Seashore, is considered by locals to be the loveliest beach in the Outer Banks. The wide-beam ribs of the shipwreck *Laura Barnes* rest in the dunes here. Free parking, showers, and picnic shelters are available. ✉ *Off Rte. 12, MM 26, 8 mi south of U.S. 158.*

off the beaten path

LAKE PHELPS – At 16,600 acres, Lake Phelps (✉ 2252 Lake Shore Rd., Creswell, 56 mi east of Nags Head via I–64 ☎ 252/797–4475), a part of Pettigrew State Park, is a Carolina Bay that has long been considered a treasure by boaters and anglers. But in the mid-1980s, researchers, who believe the lake to be 38,000 years old, began to prize it for other reasons: discovered underneath the sand in the beautifully clear water were ancient American Indian artifacts, including 30 dugout canoes.

Sports & the Outdoors

Bert's Surf Shop (✉ U.S. 158, MM 11 ☎ 252/441–1939) rents surfboards, gives private lessons, and runs three- and five-day surf school programs; it also has a retail shop.

Kitty Hawk Kites (✉ U.S. 158, MM 13 ☎ 800/334–4777 🌐 www.kittyhawk.com) is the oldest (and biggest) hang-gliding school on the East Coast. It also sells wind toys and gives kite surfing lessons.

Kitty Hawk Sports (✉ U.S. 158, MM 12 ☎ 252/441–6800 🌐 www.khsports.com), a retail branch of Kitty Hawk Water Sports, rents kayaks, gives surf and kayaking lessons, and leads waterborne ecotours.

Kitty Hawk Water Sports (✉ U.S. 158, MM 16.5 ☎ 252/441–2756 🌐 www.khsports.com), the oldest water-sports outfitter in the area, hooks you up to go sailing, windsurfing, parasailing, jet skiing, kite boarding, and kayaking.

Nags Head Golf Links (✉ 5615 S. Seachase Dr., off Rte. 12, MM 15 ☎ 252/441–8074 or 800/851–9404) has a par-71, 18-hole course with ocean views.

Outer Banks Dive Center (✉ 3917 S. Croatan Hwy. ☎ 252/449–8349 🌐 www.obxdive.com) has equipment rental, diving instruction, guided offshore charters, and leads off-the-beach dives to shipwrecks.

Where to Stay & Eat

$$$$ Fodor'sChoice ★ ✕ **Windmill Point.** The menu changes here, but you can always count on the signature seafood trio: a choice of any combination of three fish. You can have it lightly poached or grilled, and topped with roasted red pepper and capers, or shredded cucumber and dill, or a pineapple salsa. Brunch is served daily from 10 to 3:30. The restaurant has stunning views of the sound at sunset, eye-catching memorabilia from the luxury liner SS *United States,* and, yes, a real windmill. It's a reproduction of the German-style windmills used in the area a century ago. ✉ *U.S. 158, MM 16.5* ☎ *252/441–1535* ▭ *AE, D, DC, MC, V.*

$$$–$$$$ ✕ **Penguin Isle Soundside Grill & Bar.** The views from Penguin Isle's main dining room and gazebo dining room on Roanoke Sound are panoramic and seductive. The decor is muted as if not to detract from what you're seeing or tasting. Though especially busy in summer, the dining experience here is never uncomfortable, as tables are well spaced. On the dinner menu there's a little of everything: beef tenderloin, yellowfin tuna with sea scallops, wild mushroom fettuccine with sautéed vegetables and feta cheese, as well as options for the kids. ✉ *U.S. 158, MM 16* ☎ *252/441–2637* ▭ *AE, D, MC, V* ⊙ *Closed Jan. and Feb.*

★ **$$–$$$$** ✕ **Owens' Restaurant.** Inside an old Nags Head–style clapboard cottage, this old-fashioned coastal restaurant has been in the same family and location since 1946. Stick with the seafood or chops, at which they excel. Miss O's crab cakes are ever-popular, as is the filet mignon topped with lump crabmeat and asparagus béarnaise sauce. Pecan-encrusted sea scallops are plump and tender. The 16-layer lemon and chocolate cakes are delicious. In summer arrive early and expect to wait. The brass-and-glass Station Keeper's Lounge has entertainment. ✉ *U.S. 158, MM 17* ☎ *252/441–7309* ⛵ *Reservations not accepted* ▭ *AE, D, MC, V* ⊙ *Closed Jan. and Feb. No lunch.*

$$–$$$ ✕ **Basnight's Lone Cedar Café.** This is the stomping ground for Marc Basnight, for years North Carolina's most powerful state senator, and his family. Every one of Lone Cedar's long wooden tables has a view of the water. The restaurant is proud to have its own fish-cleaning facility, so they can serve the freshest seafood possible. Beef, chicken, pork, and pastas are also on the menu. The dining room is very relaxed, very casual. ✉ *Nags Head–Manteo Causeway, 7623 S. Virginia Dare Trail* ☎ *252/441–5405* ⛵ *Reservations not accepted* ▭ *D, MC, V* ⊙ *Closed Jan.*

$$–$$$ ✕ **Pier House Restaurant.** A sign above the entrance reads THE HAPPIEST PEOPLE IN THE WORLD PASS THROUGH THIS DOOR. It might be true considering the spectacular over-ocean views, the friendly service, and the tremendous selection of fresh seafood. The restaurant is literally *on* the crooked, rickety Nags Head Fishing Pier. If you catch and clean your own fish, the chef will cook it to your liking. Hours are from 7 AM until

9 PM. At breakfast and lunch ($–$$) you can have entrées like seafood omelets and crab cakes, or sandwiches such as burgers and grilled cheese. ✉ *U.S. 158, MM 12* ☎ *252/441–4200* ✍ *Reservations not accepted* ▭ *AE, D, MC, V* ⊙ *Closed Thanksgiving–Easter. No dinner Oct.–Easter.*

$$–$$$ ✕ **RV's.** If fiery red sunsets and spicy marinated tuna entice you, head to RV's. It's where locals come to eat, drink, and take in serene views of Roanoke Sound. Portions of everything—from clam chowder to barbecued shrimp to piquant crab cakes and tuna—are huge. You can also get steak, ribs, and chicken. The marvelous turtle cake is a dieter's nightmare, with chocolate, pecans, and caramel. There's a little pier outside and an attached indoor-outdoor gazebo where you can get a drink. The causeway is between Nags Head and Roanoke Island. ✉ *Nags Head–Manteo Causeway, MM 16.5* ☎ *252/441–4963* ✍ *Reservations not accepted* ▭ *MC, V* ⊙ *Closed Dec. and Jan.*

$–$$ ✕ **Don Gato's.** You can't miss the bright-orange building with a surfer on the roof. The interior's bright yellows, reds, and blues are equally intense, but it's the food that holds your attention. The chef draws inspiration from Mexico's Oaxaca region. There's lots of seafood; grilled tuna burritos and shrimp sautéed with onion and cilantro in a garlic sauce are favorites. Mexican beers and made-to-order margaritas get the evening flowing. ✉ *Route 12, MM 11.5* ☎ *252/441–9330* ▭ *MC, V.*

¢–$ ✕ **Sam & Omie's.** This no-nonsense niche is named after two fishermen who were father and son, and it's the oldest restaurant in the Outer Banks. Fishing illustrations hang on the walls, and Merle Haggard plays in the background. It's open daily 7–7, serving every imaginable kind of seafood, and then some. Try the fine marinated tuna steak, Cajun tuna bites, or frothy crab-and-asparagus soup. The chef has been using the same recipe for the she-crab soup for 22 years; locals love it. Diehard fans claim that Sam & Omie's serves the best oysters on the beach. Dress is beach-casual. ✉ *U.S. 158, MM 16.5* ☎ *252/441–7366* ✍ *Reservations not accepted* ▭ *D, MC, V.*

$$$–$$$$ **Fodor's Choice ★** **First Colony Inn.** Stand on the verandas that encircle this old, three-story, cedar-shingle inn and admire the ocean views. Two rooms have wet bars, kitchenettes, and whirlpool baths; others have four-poster or canopy beds, handcrafted armoires, and English antiques. All rooms contain extras, such as heated towel bars. The story of this landmark's near demolition, its rescue, and the move to the present site is told in framed photographs, letters, and news accounts lining the sunny dining room. In fall and winter First Colony hosts birding weekends in collaboration with the North Carolina chapter of the Nature Conservancy. ✉ *6720 S. Virginia Dare Trail, 27959* ☎ *252/441–2343 or 800/368–9390* 🖷 *252/441–9234* 🌐 *www.firstcolonyinn.com* *26 rooms* *Dining room, picnic area, some in-room hot tubs, some kitchenettes, microwaves, refrigerators, pool, croquet, library, business services; no smoking* ▭ *AE, D, MC, V* *BP.*

$–$$$ **The Nags Head Inn.** Being an independent property, not a chain, is not the only thing that makes this motel stand out—the blocky, white stucco exterior with blue accents is in sharp contrast with the cottages that surround it, too. The five-story hotel has basic, tidy rooms right on the beach.

Ask for an oceanside room to get a balcony. Nags Head Inn is especially family-friendly: kids under 12 stay free and cribs and cots are available for $10 extra. ✉ *Rte. 12, MM 14, 27959* ☎ *252/441–0454 or 800/327–8881* 🌐 *www.nagsheadinn.com* *100 rooms* *Refrigerators, cable TV, indoor-outdoor pool, hot tub, no-smoking rooms* *AE, D, MC, V* *Closed late Nov.–Dec.* *EP.*

Roanoke Island

3 *10 mi southwest of Nags Head.*

On a hot July day in 1587, 117 men, women, and children left their boat and set foot on Roanoke Island to make the first permanent English settlement in the New World. Three years later they disappeared without a trace, leaving a mystery that continues to intrigue historians. Much of the 12-mi-long island remains wild. Of the island's two towns, Wanchese is the fishing village, and Manteo is more tourist-oriented, with sights related to the island's history, as well as an aquarium. You get to the island by taking U.S. 64/264 from U.S. 158.

A history, educational, and cultural arts complex, **Roanoke Island Festival Park** sits on the waterfront in Manteo. Costumed interpreters conduct tours of the 69-foot ship, *Elizabeth II,* a re-creation of a 16th-century vessel—except when it's on educational voyages. The complex also has an interactive museum, a fossil pit, plays, concerts, arts-and-crafts exhibitions, and special programs. ✉ *Waterfront, off Budleigh St., Manteo* ☎ *252/475–1500, 252/475–1506 for event hotline* 🌐 *www.roanokeisland.com* *$8* *Mar., Nov. and Dec., daily 10–5; Apr.–Oct., daily 9–7.*

★ The lush **Elizabethan Gardens** are a re-creation of 16th-century English gardens, established as an elaborate memorial to the first English colonists. Walk through the brick and wrought-iron entrance to see antique statuary, wildflowers, rose gardens, a sunken garden and more, all impeccably maintained by the Garden Club of North Carolina. The gate house, designed in the style of a 16th-century orangery, serves as a reception center and gift shop. Many weddings are held in one tranquil garden or another. ✉ *1411 National Park Dr., 3 mi north of downtown Manteo* ☎ *252/473–3234* 🌐 *www.elizabethangardens.org* *$5* *Mid-Sept.–May, daily 9–5; June–early Sept., daily 9–8.*

Fort Raleigh National Historic Site is a restoration of the original 1585 earthworks that mark the beginning of English colonial history in America. Be sure to see the orientation film and then take a guided tour of the fort. A nature trail leads to an outlook over Roanoke Sound. Native American and Civil War history is also preserved here. Fort Raleigh is where the outdoor symphonic drama *The Lost Colony* plays out; it's adjacent to the Elizabethan Gardens. ✉ *National Park Dr., off U.S. 64/264, 3 mi north of downtown Manteo* ☎ *252/473–5772* 🌐 *www.nps.gov* *Free* *Sept.–May, daily 9–5; June–Aug., daily 9–6.*

★ The ***The Lost Colony,*** begun in 1937, is the country's first and longest-running outdoor drama. Staged at the Waterside Amphitheater at Fort

Raleigh National Historic Site, it reenacts the story of the first colonists, who settled here in 1587 and then disappeared. Reservations are essential. ✉ *1409 U.S. 64/264* ☎ *252/473–3414 or 800/488–5012* 🌐 *www.thelostcolony.org* 🎫 *$16* ⏲ *Performances Memorial Day–mid-Aug., Mon.–Sat. at 8:30 PM.*

The **North Carolina Aquarium at Roanoke Island,** overlooking Croatan Sound, occupies 68,000 square feet of space. There are touch tanks and a shoreline boardwalk with observation decks. *The Graveyard of the Atlantic* is the centerpiece exhibit. It's a 285,000-gallon ocean tank containing the re-created remains of the USS *Monitor,* sunk off Hatteras Island. The aquarium hosts a slew of activities and field trips, from feeding fish to learning about medicinal aquatic plants to kids' workshops. ✉ *374 Airport Rd., off U.S. 64, 3 mi northeast of Manteo* ☎ *252/473–3493 for aquarium, 252/473–3494 for educational programs* 🌐 *www.ncaquariums.com* 🎫 *$7* ⏲ *Daily 9–5.*

off the beaten path

EDENTON – As North Carolina's first permanent settlement and the colony's first capital, Edenton is rich with history. Originally incorporated in 1715 with the name Towne on Queen Anne's Creek, it was renamed Edenton seven years later in honor of Governor Charles Eden. A fine collection of 18th-, 19th-, and early-20th-century buildings, mostly clustered in the downtown historic district near the waterfront, have been well taken care of by the town's 5,000 residents. The calm, scenic town sits on the north side of the Albemarle Sound, off U.S. 64 and Route 32, 65 mi west and north of Manteo. Edenton is one of 32 historic, cultural, and natural sites, across 15 northeastern counties, on the state's self-guided Historic Albemarle Tour, pointed out by prominent road markers.

Stop by the **Edenton Visitor Center** (✉ 108 N. Broad St., Edenton ☎ 252/482–2637) to hear tales about the colonists, including those about the women of the Edenton Tea Party, who fought for liberty. An inexpensive pamphlet serves as a guide on a 1½-mi walking tour. Guided tours of the historic district are available—and are recommended.

Historic Albemarle Tour, Inc. (✉ 1 Harding Sq., Washington ☎ 252/974–2950 or 800/734–1117 🌐 www.historicalbemarletour.com) runs guided tours of Edenton itself and publishes a brochure on self-guided tours of the Albemarle region.

Sports & the Outdoors

Oregon Inlet Fishing Center (✉ Rte. 12, north end of Oregon Inlet Bridge ☎ 252/441–6301 or 800/272–5199) is a full-service marina that leads fishing excursions and has all supplies for the experienced fisherman and for vacationers.

Pirates Cove Yacht Club and Marina (✉ 2000 Sailfish Dr., Manteo ☎ 252/473–3906 or 800/367–4728) has a deep-water, charter dock. Internet access is available in the shipstore.

Carolina Outdoors (✉ 307 Queen Elizabeth, Manteo ☎ 252/334–4777, 252/441–4124 for reservations 🌐 www.kittyhawk.com), part of Kitty Hawk Kites, operates sea-kayaking ecotours along the banks of the villages Duck and Manteo (in the latter's downtown area) and through wildlife refuges, islands, and even a maritime forest. You can also rent kayaks here.

Where to Stay & Eat

$$–$$$$ ✕ **Weeping Radish Brewery and Restaurant.** This rambling two-story, Bavarian-style restaurant and microbrewery is known for its traditional German cuisine. The beer is superb. The annual Oktoberfest, held the weekend after Labor Day, showcases German and blues bands. Brewery tours are given on request, free of charge. There's also a gift shop, outdoor beer garden, and children's playground. ✉ *623 U.S. 64, Manteo* ☎ *252/473–1157* 🌐 *www.weepingradish.com* ▭ *D, MC, V.*

$–$$ ✕ **Big Al's.** With its soda fountain and grill, '50s decor, Coca-Cola memorabilia, game room, and dance floor, this is a fun place to come. Burgers, blue-plate specials, and local seafood dominate the menu. Kid-size meals are available as well. Breakfast is served off the menu year-round, and there's an all-you-can-eat breakfast buffet mornings from June to August. ✉ *100 Patty La., U.S. 64/264, Manteo* ☎ *252/473–5570* ▭ *MC, V.*

$–$$ ✕ **Full Moon Café.** Colorful stained-glass panels hang in the large front windows making a wonderfully cheerful bistro. The herbed hummus with roasted pita is fantastic, as are the crab cakes. Other choices include salads, veggie wraps, quesadillas, Cuban-style enchiladas, Lowcountry shrimp and grits, burgers of all kinds, and a dozen innovative and hearty sandwiches. Light eaters beware: even the Waldorf salad comes with a million pecans and apples; expect lots of cheese on any dish that includes it. The café also serves specialty cocktails and maintains a thoughtfully selected wine list. ✉ *306 Queen Elizabeth Ave., Manteo* ☎ *252/473–6666* ▭ *AE, D, DC, MC, V.*

¢ ✕ **Magnolia Grille.** Freddy and Pam Ortega, cheerful New York transplants, run the immensely popular restaurant on Mateo's downtown waterfront. The place is hopping, even at breakfast; lunch gets the overflow from nearby Festival Park. Do like the locals do: get takeout and savor your sandwich by the waterfront. Choose anything from lean, char-grilled chili cheeseburgers to deli sandwiches, quesadillas, salads, and hearty chicken dishes. Quirkier options include spicy shrimp jammers (battered, filled with jalapeño cheese, and fried) or the specials, such as fried oyster sandwiches or burgers topped with crabmeat. ✉ *408 Queen Elizabeth St., Manteo* ☎ *252/475–9877* ▭ *AE, D, MC, V* ⏲ *No dinner Sun. and Mon.*

★ $$–$$$ ✕🏨 **Tranquil House Inn.** This charming 19th-century-style inn sits waterfront, a few steps from shops, restaurants, and the Roanoke Island Festival Park. The mood of the individually decorated rooms is cozy, marked by handmade comforters, Oriental rugs, and hardwood floors. Complimentary wine and cheese are served in the evening. The popular restaurant, 1587 ($$$), is known for its chop-house-style cuts and inventive entrées: Asian salmon, char-grilled duck breast with black mission fig and dried cherry spiked bordelaise, and Rockfish fillet with a cornmeal crust. 📫 *405 Queen Elizabeth Ave., Box 2045, Manteo 27954* ☎ *252/473–1404 or 800/458–7069* 📠 *252/473–1526* *www.1587.com* *25 rooms* *Restaurant, bicycles, business services, meeting room, no-smoking rooms* *AE, D, MC, V* *BP.*

$$ **Island House of Wanchese.** Roy and Jeanne Green purchased the circa-1900 house in 1991 and updated it, turning it into a B&B, but they retained the original wood flooring and wavy glass windows. The wraparound porch is screened in so you can sit and catch the breeze without interference from bugs. Rooms are decorated with antiques, hope chests, and handmade quilts. The resident innkeepers provide evening turn-down service, complimentary beach chairs and beach towels, a freezer for your catch, and a full breakfast. *104 Old Wharf Rd., Wanchese 27981* *252/473–5619* *252/473–6163* *www.islandhouse-bb.com* *4 rooms, 1 suite* *No kids, no smoking* *AE, D, MC, V* *BP.*

$ **Scarborough Inn.** Two stories of wraparound porches surround the Scarborough, which is modeled after a turn-of-the-20th-century inn. Outside each room are benches and rocking chairs; inside, each is decorated differently, with family heirlooms as well as modern conveniences, like coffeemakers. Room refrigerators come stocked with enough items for a small Continental breakfast. The property is within walking distance of popular shops and restaurants and about 3 mi from the beach. *524 U.S. 64/264, Manteo 27954* *252/473–3979* *www.scarborough-inn.com* *12 rooms* *Microwaves, refrigerators, cable TV, bicycles, no-smoking rooms* *AE, D, DC, MC, V* *BP.*

Shopping

Manteo Booksellers (105 Sir Walter Raleigh St., Manteo 252/473–1221 or 866/473–1222) stocks an admirable collection of books on local attractions, cuisine, history, nature, and related fiction. Local author readings are frequent. The children's section is quite large, too.

Opened in 1967, the **Christmas Shop & Island Gallery** (621 S. U.S. 64, Manteo 252/473–2838 or 800/470–2838) has become an Outer Banks legend in its own time. The majority of the 36 rooms are devoted to the winter holiday, but the store has expanded to include Halloween, artwork by more than 200 regional artists and craftspeople, and an old-time general store.

Hatteras Island

4 *15 mi south of Nags Head.*

The Herbert C. Bonner Bridge arches for 3 mi over Oregon Inlet and carries traffic to Hatteras Island, known as the "blue marlin capital of the world." The island, a 33-mi-long ribbon of sand, juts out into the Atlantic Ocean; at its most distant point (Cape Hatteras), Hatteras is 25 mi from the mainland. About 85% of the island belongs to Cape Hatteras National Seashore, and the remainder is privately owned in seven small, quaint villages strung along Route 12, the island's fragile lifeline to points north. The island narrows considerably and the pace of life slows the farther south you go.

Off Route 12 in Buxton are the remnants of a radio tower that broadcast the first radio waves. In 1902 a man named Reginald Fessenden transmitted musical notes via signal between this tower and one on

TO THE LIGHTHOUSE

SOONER OR LATER *while visiting the coast you come within sight of one of North Carolina's lighthouses—the "mighty seven." These beacons, often used as a symbol for the state, have one by one been transferred to the National Park Service or nonprofit organizations.*

They are, in order from north to south: Currituck Beach Lighthouse (162 feet, 1875) was the last major lighthouse constructed along the Outer Banks. The unpainted redbrick tower is open for climbing. Bodie Island Lighthouse (165 feet, 1872) is covered in broad, horizontal alternating black-and-white stripes. Cape Hatteras Lighthouse is famous as America's tallest lighthouse (198 feet, 1868), and for having been relocated 2,900 feet to the southwest in 1999. The tower's distinctive black-and-white spiral pattern is perhaps the most recognizable of all, and is open for climbing again. Ocracoke Lighthouse (76 feet, 1817), rebuilt after a fire in 1823, is the oldest North Carolina lighthouse still in continuous service and the second oldest lighthouse in the United States in continuous service. The exterior is coated with cement and whitewashed with boiled, glued-on rice.

Cape Lookout Lighthouse (150 feet, 1859) is painted with distinctive black-and-white diamonds—black facing North and South, white facing East and West. You can climb the tower only with a reservation. Bald Head Island Lighthouse (90 feet, 1817), "Old Baldy," is south of Southport, and has a plain weathered gray tower that can be climbed. Far to the south, Oak Island Lighthouse (169 feet, 1958) is the lighthouse built most recently in the United States. The completely cylindrical tower has three broad horizontal stripes—black, white, and gray.

Roanoke Island, thus becoming the first person to prove that music could be heard over the air without wires.

Pea Island National Wildlife Refuge is made up of more than 5,000 acres of marsh on the Atlantic flyway. To bird-watchers' delight more than 265 species are sighted regularly from the observation platforms and spotting scopes, including endangered peregrine falcons and piping plovers. A visitor center on Route 12 has an informational display and maps of the two trails. Remember to douse yourself in bug spray, especially in spring. Guided canoe tours are available for a fee. ✉ *Pea Island Refuge Headquarters, Rte. 12, 5 mi south of Oregon Inlet* ☎ *252/987–1118* 🌐 *http://peaisland.fws.gov* 🎟 *Free* 🕒 *May–Sept., daily 9–4; Oct.–Apr., Thurs.–Sun. 9–4.*

The restored 1911 **Chicamacomico Lifesaving Station** is now a museum that tells the story of the brave people who manned 24 stations that once lined the Outer Banks. These were the precursors to today's Coast Guard, with staff who rescued people and animals from sea craft in distress. Living-history reenactments are performed June through August. ✉ *Off Rte. 12, Rodanthe* ☎ *252/987–1552* 🌐 *www.chicamacomico.org* 🎟 *Free* 🕒 *Apr.–Oct., Tues.–Sat. 9–5.*

Cape Hatteras Lighthouse was the first lighthouse built in the region, authorized by Congress in 1794 to help prevent shipwrecks. At 208 feet it's the tallest brick lighthouse in the world, and it's painted with distinctive black-and-white spirals. Endangered by the sea, in 1999 the lighthouse was actually picked up and moved 2,900 feet inland to its present location. It's now the Hatteras Island Visitor Center. In summer the principal keeper's quarters are open for viewing and you can climb up in the lighthouse. Offshore lie the remains of the USS *Monitor,* a Confederate ironclad ship that sank in 1862. ✉ *Off Rte. 12, 30 mi south of Rodanthe, near Buxton* ☎ *252/995–4474* 🌐 *www.nps.gov* 🎫 *Visitor center and keeper's quarters free, lighthouse tower $6* ⏲ *Visitor center and keeper's quarters daily 9–5; lighthouse tower Memorial Day–Labor Day, daily 10–6; Apr.–Memorial Day, Labor Day–mid-Oct., daily 10–2.*

A nationally recognized collection of Native American artifacts fills the **Frisco Native American Museum & Natural History Center.** Galleries display native art from across the United States as well as relics from the first inhabitants of Hatteras Island. The museum has been designated as a North Carolina Environmental Education Center. Several acres of nature trails wind through a maritime forest and a pavilion overlooking a salt marsh on-site. ✉ *Rte. 12, Frisco* ☎ *252/995–4440* 🌐 *www.nativeamericanmuseum.org* 🎫 *$2* ⏲ *Tues.–Sun. 11–5.*

Where to Eat

$$$$ ✕ **Breakwater.** Fat Daddy crab cakes, rolled in potato chips then fried and served on pineapple jalapeño salsa, and oyster stew with grits are two of the more creative, signature dishes here. You also get more standard seafood options, such as shrimp fried or broiled with white wine and butter. The restaurant sits atop Oden's Dock. Given the casual nature of life here, Breakwater stands out with tables dressed in white linen. The dining room is a bit small, but waiting for a table in comfortable chairs on the deck overlooking Pamlico Sound is not a chore. ✉ *Waterfront, Rte. 12, Hatteras Village* ☎ *252/986–2733* ▭ *AE, D, MC, V* ⏲ *Closed Sun.*

$$–$$$ ✕ **Channel Bass.** Mounted fish on the walls are evidence of the owner's fishing prowess, and a nautical theme carries through to the menu, which lists fish caught in the sound and in the ocean. The Hatteras chowder has a deep and hearty flavor. Meat eaters might try the steak, chicken, or ribs. The hush puppies come from an old family recipe and both salad dressings and pies are homemade. Channel Bass is north of Hatteras Village, on the canal side of the main road. It's popular with residents of Hatteras as well as veteran visitors and boaters. ✉ *Rte. 12, Hatteras Village* ☎ *252/986–2250* ✍ *Reservations not accepted* ▭ *D, MC, V* ⏲ *Closed Dec.–Feb. and Sun. No lunch.*

$$–$$$ ✕ **Tides.** South of the entrance for the Cape Hatteras Lighthouse, this place is popular for its good service, well-prepared food, and homey manner. In addition to offering the usual seafood, the menu has chicken and ham. It's also a popular breakfast spot. ✉ *Rte. 12, Buxton* ☎ *252/995–5988* ▭ *MC, V* ⏲ *Closed Dec.–early Apr. No lunch.*

Where to Stay

$ **Sea Gull.** The mid-size, tidy, family-run and family-friendly motel, which opened in the 1950s, has weathered several hurricanes over the years. The cottages, on both the soundside and oceanside, are raised (protecting them from the water), roomy (each sleeps up to six people), and have decks and washers and dryers. It's a popular place with surf and deep-sea anglers—in fact, a fish-cleaning table is available for guest use. From here you have quick access to the Ocracoke ferry and Cape Hatteras Lighthouse. ✉ *Rte. 12, Hatteras Village 27943* ☎ *252/986–2550* 🌐 *www.seagullhatteras.com* *45 rooms, 2 cottages* *Picnic area, some kitchens, cable TV, pool, beach, fishing, laundry facilities, no-smoking rooms* *D, MC, V* *EP.*

Ocracoke Island

5 *Ocracoke Village: 20 mi southwest of Hatteras Village.*

For a long time, Ocracoke Island was cut off from the world. According to some marine geologists, the formation of Ocracoke began about 17,000 years ago, and wind erosion ultimately disconnected it from the mainland. Many believe that some of the early European explorers who made landfall here left behind their horses, and that these are the ancestors of the island's "wild ponies" (now penned). Pirates found shelter in Ocracoke's dense maritime forest and behind its dunes in the 18th century. Sailors and commercial fishermen have been a steady presence on the island, but it was the start of ferry service in the 1950s that really opened Ocracoke to the outside world. The year-round population numbers about 800. Although the island remains a destination for people seeking peace and quiet, it's hard to find during the summer season when tourists and boaters swamp all 16 mi of the place. A village of shops, motels, and restaurants surrounds Silver Lake Harbor, where the pirate Blackbeard met his death in 1718. About 90% of Ocracoke Island is part of Cape Hatteras National Seashore; the island is on the eastern flyway for many migrating land and water birds. A free ferry leaves hourly from Hatteras Island and arrives 40 minutes later; other ferries connect with the mainland at Swan Quarter (2½ hours) and at Cedar Island (15 minutes).

Ocracoke Island **beaches** are among the least populated and most beautiful on the Cape Hatteras National Seashore. Four public access areas have parking as well as off-road vehicle access. ✉ *Off Rte. 12.*

Look out from the **Ocracoke Pony Pen** observation platform at the descendants of horses that roamed wild before the island came under the jurisdiction of Cape Hatteras National Seashore. The park service took over management of the ponies in the 1960s and has helped maintain the population. All the animals you see today were born in captivity and are fed and kept at a farm you can view. There's some disagreement as to whether the first horses on the island were (a) Spanish mustangs that survived shipwrecks or (b) horses that came ashore with the original Sir Walter Raleigh expedition. ✉ *Rte. 12, 6 mi southwest of the Hatteras-Ocracoke ferry landing.*

Ocracoke Village Visitor Center and Museum, run by the local preservation society, contains photographs and artifacts illustrating the island's lifestyle and history. The National Park Service office is nearby. ✉ *Off Rte. 12 Silver Lake Rd., beside the Cedar Island ferry dock, Ocracoke Village* ☎ *252/928–7375* 🌐 *www.ocracokepreservation.org* 🎫 *Free* ⏲ *June–Aug., weekdays 10–5, weekends 11–4; Easter–May and Sept.–Nov., Mon.–Sat. 11–4.*

The **Ocracoke Lighthouse,** the oldest continuously operating lighthouse on the eastern seaboard, is unfortunately not open to the public, but it's a photographer's dream. ✉ *Off Rte. 12, Live Oak Rd., Ocracoke Village.*

On May 11, 1942, the HMS *Bedfordshire,* an armed British trawler on loan to the United States, was torpedoed by a German U-boat and sank with all hands lost off the coast of Ocracoke Island. Four crew members were found and buried on Ocracoke; two of them remain unidentified. Each year the Queen of England remembers this loss by sending a British flag, via a personal envoy, to the tiny, well-tended **British Cemetery** surrounded by a white picket fence. ✉ *Off Rte. 12, British Cemetery Rd., Ocracoke Village* ☎ *252/926–9171.*

off the beaten path

LAKE MATTAMUSKEET – The largest of the Carolina bays is Hyde County's Lake Mattamuskeet. Despite attempts to drain it for farmland and mine it for peat, it is the centerpiece of a wildlife refuge that echoes with the calls of trumpeter swans in the winter and shorebirds in the summer. ✉ *38 Mattamuskeet Rd., Swan Quarter, 2 ½-hr ferry ride and 15-min drive from Ocracoke Island* ☎ *252/926–9171.*

Where to Stay & Eat

$$$–$$$$ ✕ **The Pelican.** This 19th-century harborfront home in a grove of twisted oak trees has a patio next to an outdoor bar: a lot of people take a seat here and don't leave for a long while. Jumbo shrimp, stuffed with cream cheese and jalapeño peppers, and lump crab cakes are two of the most requested food items. "Shrimp Hour," which is really two hours every day (3–5), draws crowds because large steamed shrimp sell for 15¢ each. The Pelican also serves breakfast—cereal, egg dishes, and corned beef hash—until 11 AM. Acoustic music plays weekends. ✉ *Rte. 12, Ocracoke Village* ☎ *252/928–7431* 💳 *AE, D, MC, V.*

$$$ ✕ **Back Porch Restaurant.** Seafood is the star here, naturally, but there are some notable beef and chicken dishes, including a stir fry with seasonal vegetables. A consistently pleasant dining experience comes in part from a menu that changes seasonally in order to feature the freshest available ingredients. The wine list is respectable and you have the choice of enjoying your meal indoors or on a screened porch. No smoking is allowed anywhere. ✉ *110 Back Rd., Ocracoke Village* ☎ *252/928–6401* 💳 *MC, V* 🚭 *No smoking* ⏲ *No lunch.*

$ ✕🏨 **Island Inn and Dining Room.** The white clapboard inn, built as a private lodge back in 1901, shows its age a bit but is full of Outer Banks character. The rooms in the modern wing are good for families. The large rooms in the Crow's Nest, on the third floor, have the most architectural interest—they have cathedral ceilings and look out over the island. The restaurant ($–$$) is known for its oyster omelet, crab cakes, and hush puppies. *Lighthouse Rd. and Rte. 12, Box 9, 27960 252/928–4351, 877/456–3466 for inn, 252/928–7821 for dining room 252/928–4352 www.ocracokeislandinn.com 35 rooms, 4 villas Restaurant, cable TV, pool, lobby lounge, airport shuttle; no smoking AE, MC, V BP.*

$ **Sand Dollar Motel.** Owner Roger Garrish, an Ocracoke native, is a great source of island information. The Sand Dollar is small and unassuming, but well-run. Rooms have either a king-, a queen-, or two double-size beds. A garden and a walkway to a secluded swimming pool are amenities that give this motel a sense of privacy. It's on a quiet residential street two blocks from Route 12 and the village center. *70 Sand Dollar Rd., 27960 252/928–5571 or 866/928–5571 12 rooms, 1 cottage Some kitchens, microwaves, refrigerators, cable TV, pool, no-smoking rooms MC, V Closed Dec.–Mar. BP.*

Cape Lookout National Seashore

Southwest of Ocracoke Island via Cedar Island.

Extending for 55 mi from Portsmouth Island to Shackleford Banks, Cape Lookout National Seashore includes 28,400 acres of uninhabited land and marsh. The remote, sandy islands are linked to the mainland by private ferries. Loggerhead sea turtles, which have been placed on the federal list of threatened and endangered species, nest here. To the south, wild ponies roam Shackleford Banks. Four-wheel-drive vehicles are allowed on the beach, and primitive camping is allowed. There are primitive cabins (with and without electricity, no linens or utensils) with bunkbeds. Ferry service is available from Harkers Island to the Cape Lookout Lighthouse area, from Davis to Shingle Point, from Atlantic to an area north of Drum Inlet, and from Ocracoke Village to Portsmouth Village. The Cape Lookout Visitor Center is on Harkers Island, at the end of U.S. 70 East, near the ferry terminal. *252/728–2250 for visitor center, 252/729–2791 and 252/225–4261 for cabins Park free, ferry ride $10–$30 Visitor center daily, 8:30–4:30.*

Portsmouth Village was inhabited from 1753 until the early 1970s. At its peak in 1860, the village had 505 permanent residents. Buildings of that period which are open to the public include the schoolhouse, post office, general store, church, and life saving station. There's also a visitor center with varying hours, and a cemetery. The walking trails on the approximately 250 acres of this village archaeological site can be difficult due to standing water, sandy soil, and during the summer months, a voluminous number of mosquitoes. Public restrooms and water fountains are not abundant. *Portsmouth Island Free Visitor center and buildings Apr.–Nov.*

While the National Park Service works to restore the 1859 **Cape Lookout Lighthouse,** with its white-and-black diamond markings (a project that will take years), the beacon continues to function as a navigational aid. A small museum inside the visitor center on Harkers Island tells the story of the lighthouse from its first incarnation in 1812. From there you must take a ferry to get to the lighthouse. The tower is open only on specific dates, by reservation. For 2005, climbing dates are March 12 (reservations open March 1), June 18 (reservations open June 1), August 6 (reservations open July 18), and November 5 (reservations open October 17). Reservations open at 9 AM and often are booked up in two hours. This system was developed because the climbs have proved to be extraordinarily popular. ✉ *Lighthouse, Core Banks; visitor center, U.S. 70 E, Harkers Island* ☎ *252/728–2250 for information, 252/728–5766 for lighthouse climb reservations only* 🎫 *Free* ⏲ *Visitor center daily 8:30–4:30.*

THE CENTRAL COAST & NEW BERN

Carteret County, with nearly 80 mi of ocean coastline, is known as the Central, or Crystal, Coast. It's composed of the south-facing beaches along the barrier island Bogue Banks (Atlantic Beach, Pine Knoll Shores, Indian Beach, Salter Path, and Emerald Isle), three mainland townships (Morehead City, Beaufort, and Newport), and a series of small, unincorporated "down-east" communities traversed by a portion of U.S. 70, designated a Scenic Byway.

Neighboring Craven County—which contains New Bern, a good chunk of the 157,000-acre Croatan National Forest, and Cherry Point, the world's largest Marine Corps air station—is by turns genteel and historic, modern and commercialized, rural and wild. Golfers, boaters, and a growing number of retirees find the area a haven.

Beaufort

❻ *20 mi west of Harkers Island–Cape Lookout ferry; 150 mi southeast of Raleigh.*

There's a feeling of having stepped back in time in the small seaport with a bustling boardwalk; residents take great pride in the city's restored public buildings and homes—and in their homes' histories, which sometimes include tales of sea captains and pirates. The third-oldest town in North Carolina, Beaufort was named for Henry Somerset, duke of Beaufort, and it's hard to miss the English influence here: the streets, at least those in the historic district, are named after British royalty and colonial leaders.

Today the town still has a strong connection with the sea and everything from motorized dinghies to sail boats to fabulous yachts from around the world anchor here. Boat rides of all types—dolphin watches, dinner cruises, party cruises, scenic harbor tours—are available for a fee. Waterfront restaurants and shops await those either coming or going or just happily marking time. Also on the harbor is the private Duke University Marine Laboratory, with the National Science Foundation's huge research vessel, the *Cape Hatteras,* moored out back.

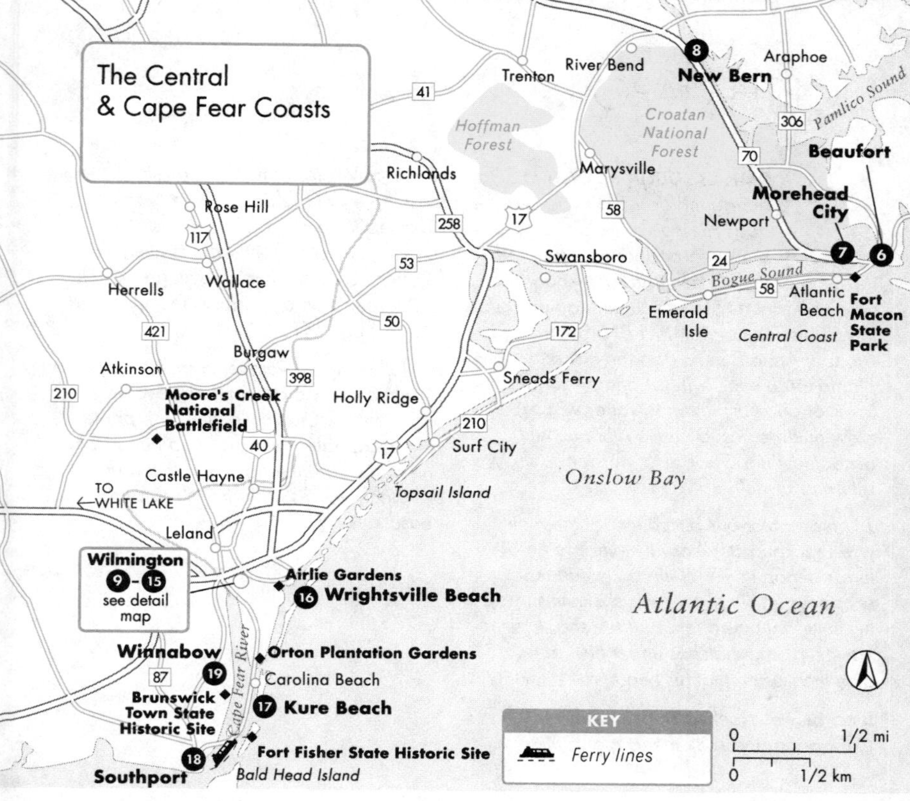

Note: this Beaufort (pronounced BOW-fort) is not to be confused with another old, but much larger Beaufort (pronounced BUE-fert) across the border in South Carolina.

The **Beaufort Historic Site,** in the center of town, consists of restored buildings dating from 1767 to 1859, including the **Carteret County Courthouse** and the **Apothecary Shop** and **Doctor's Office.** Don't miss the **Old Burying Grounds** (1731), where Otway Burns, a privateer in the War of 1812, is buried under his ship's cannon; a nine-year-old girl who died at sea is buried in a rum keg; and an English soldier saluting the king is buried upright in his grave. The required tours, either on an English-style double-decker bus or by guided walk, depart from the visitor center. ✉ *130 Turner St.* ☎ *252/728–5225* 🌐 *www.historicbeaufort.com* 🎫 *Bus tour $6, bus and walking tour $10* ⏲ *Easter–Nov., Mon.–Sat. 9:30–5, Sun. 1:30–4; Dec.–Feb., Mon.–Sat. 10–4, Sun. 1:30–4.*

North Carolina Maritime Museum documents the state's seafaring history. An exhibit about the infamous pirate Blackbeard includes the discovery of his flagship near Beaufort Inlet. The associate **Watercrafts Center,** across the street, leads boat-building classes, and its education staff also provides year-round programs, including trips to the marsh and barrier islands. ✉ *315 Front St.* ☎ *252/728–7317* 🌐 *www.ah.dcr.state.nc.*

CloseUp

NORTH CAROLINA'S PIRATES

N **ORTH CAROLINA'S COAST** *was a magnet for marauding sea dogs during the golden age of piracy, a period that spanned the 17th and 18th centuries. Among those who visited was Stede Bonnet, captured in the Cape Fear region in 1718 but able to escape; Anne Bonny, daughter of a plantation owner, wife of one pirate and lover of another; Charles Vane, whose crew mutinied; and Paul Williams, who accepted King George I's pardon, only to return to piracy.*

The most notorious buccaneer of them all was Blackbeard, whose two-year reign of terror began in 1716: he cultivated fear by strapping on six pistols and six knives, tying his luxuriant beard into pigtails and, legend has it, lighting matches under his hat to give the illusion that his head was smoking.

Blackbeard attacked ships in the Caribbean and settlements along the coasts of Virginia and the Carolinas. At least three of his ships sank in North Carolina's waters; archaeologists are studying artifacts from what is likely the flagship, Queen Anne's Revenge, which ran aground on a sandbar near Beaufort Inlet in May 1718.

The following November a seafaring posse caught Blackbeard in one his favorite playgrounds, Ocracoke Inlet. The pirate was decapitated and his head hung from one of the conquering ships. Still sought are Blackbeard's other lost ships and his treasure.

us 🎫 *Free* ⏲ *Museum weekdays 9–5, Sat. 10–5, Sun. 1–5; Center Tues.–Fri. 9–5, Sat. 10–5, Sun. 1–5.*

Where to Stay & Eat

$$$–$$$$ ✕ **Blue Moon Bistro.** Chef Kyle Swain, a Beaufort native, returned home to put into use the lessons he learned apprenticing at some of North Carolina's top caliber restaurants. He pairs classical French technique with creative presentation: for example, oysters are lightly fried in curry-infused batter and served in a martini glass with a piquant Thai-style sauce. Though the emphasis is on local seafood, meat and vegetarian dishes can be had. Made-from-scratch ice creams top the dessert list. The restaurant occupies the 175-year-old Dill House, which has been dressed up with oak woodwork, wainscoting, and suns and moons made of pressed tin. ✉ *119 Queen St.* ☎ *252/728–5800* ✍ *Reservations essential* 💳 *D, MC, V* ⏲ *Closed Sun. and Mon. No lunch.*

$$–$$$ ✕ **Clawson's 1905 Restaurant and Pub.** Housed in what was a general store in the early 1900s, Clawson's is stuffed with memorabilia. It gets very crowded in summer, so arrive early for both lunch and dinner. Hearty food such as ribs, steaks, pasta, and local seafood are part of the attraction. Fishtowne Java, the associated coffee bar, opens at 7 AM. ✉ *425 Front St.* ☎ *252/728–2133* ▭ *D, MC, V* ⊙ *Closed Sept.–Apr. and Sun.*

$$$ ✕ **The Spouter Inn.** Dining at a shaded table on the Spouter's deck overlooking Beaufort Harbor and Taylor's Creek is one of life's treats. Boats glide by, you see a wild horse or two on Carrot Island just across the way, and a waiter appears with a cool drink and plate of shrimp—caught that day—sitting on a bed of pasta. The prime rib and steak are popular alternatives to seafood; the banana cream crêpe may make you forget all other desserts for a while. Sunday brunch choices include quiche, steak and eggs, and omelets. There's indoor seating as well. ✉ *218 Front St.* ☎ *252/728–5190* ▭ *AE, MC, V* ⊙ *Closed Mon. and Labor Day–Memorial Day.*

$–$$ ✕ **The Net House.** Once upon a time, the Net House, a long, low-slung building with few windows, was just that—a place where fishing nets were made, repaired, and stored. Today, it's people, not fishing gear, occupying every corner of the building, which is divided into dining rooms with walls of weathered pine. People spill onto the sidewalk waiting to get into this family-owned restaurant to sample house specialties such as steamed shellfish and lightly battered and fried seafood. Locals tout the broiled grouper Dijon and key lime pie for good reason. Call in the off-season to make sure it's open; hours vary. ✉ *133 Turner St.* ☎ *252/728–2002* *Reservations not accepted* ▭ *MC, V.*

★ **$–$$** **The Cedars by the Sea.** Two side-by-side homes (circa 1768 and 1851) and a private cottage make up this romantic B&B in the historic district, near the waterfront. Rooms reflect an eye for detail; they combine contemporary and antique furnishings from the owners' world travels, and many have fireplaces, four-poster beds, and original art. Space has been put to good use to create surprisingly large shower stalls and bathrooms. There's a small wine bar in the registration area. Every morning, a full breakfast is served buffet style in the dining room. The gardens are a favorite spot for wedding receptions. ✉ *305 Front St., 28516* ☎ *252/728–7036 or 800/732–7036* 🖷 *252/728–1685* 🌐 *www.cedarsinn.com* *10 rooms* *Dining room, cable TV, Internet; no kids under 10, no smoking* ▭ *AE, D, MC, V* 🍴 *BP.*

$$ **Pecan Tree Inn.** Local lore has it that when the late-1860s building with gingerbread trim was converted from a Masonic Lodge and school house to a private home, it was the first in Beaufort to have gas lighting, indoor plumbing, and a telephone. Today technological amenities include wireless Internet access and cable television. Innkeepers Dave and Allison DuBuisson haven't forgotten, however, the things that make for gracious living. Rooms have lush floral fabrics and rugs, as well as antiques. Fresh-baked bread and pastries are part of every breakfast. A large flower-and-herb garden provides something for the senses year-round. ✉ *116 Queen St., 28516* ☎ *252/728–6733 or 800/728–7871* 🌐 *www.pecantree.com* *7 rooms* *Dining room, cable TV, Internet; no kids under 10, no smoking* ▭ *AE, D, MC, V* 🍴 *BP.*

$ **Captain's Quarters Bed & Biscuit.** Richard (Capt. Dick) and Ruby (Miss Ruby) Collins, and their daughter Polly, welcome guests with an enthusiasm that is as genuine as their passion for Beaufort and Carteret

County, an area Dick first came to know during his years as a Navy pilot in World War II. Each morning, along with a weather report, the Captain serves breakfast, which includes fresh biscuits his wife and daughter make from an old family recipe. Antiques, most of them family heirlooms, fill the 19th-century home that the family restored. Reading material and reading lights are just two of the thoughtful touches they added. ✉ *315 Ann St., 28516* ☎ *252/728–7711 or 800/659–7111* 🌐 *www.captainsquarters.us* *3 rooms, 2 with bath* *Dining room, ceiling fans; no room phones, no room TVs, no kids under 10, no smoking* *MC, V* *BP.*

Morehead City

❼ *3 mi west of Beaufort via U.S. 70.*

The thriving commercial waterfront at Morehead City comes alive with restaurants, shops, and galleries in old buildings. This is a state port and a large charter fishing fleet anchors here. It's also home to sizeable marine research facilities for the National Oceanic and Atmospheric Administration, the University of North Carolina at Chapel Hill, and North Carolina State University. Arendell Street (U.S. 70) is Morehead's main drag. Running parallel to the waterfront, it and some side streets contain the Fish Walk, a series of colorful sculptures in clay relief depicting indigenous fish and other types of sea life. Outside the city, you can fish, swim, picnic, and hike at Fort Macon State Park. Route 58 passes through all of the beach communities on the Bogue Banks, a barrier island across Bogue Sound from Morehead City. There are a number of popular family beaches, including Atlantic Beach and Emerald Isle. Points of public access along the shoreline are marked by orange-and-blue signs. Lifeguards monitor some of the beaches.

North Carolina Seafood Festival is much anticipated and heavily attended; it celebrates the central coast's heritage the first weekend in October. There are arts-and-crafts vendors as well as food, live entertainment, cruises, rides, sand castle building, and a blessing of the fleet. ✉ *Waterfront, 907-B Arendell St.* ☎ *252/726–6273* 🌐 *www.ncseafoodfestival.org.*

The History Place has a large artifact collection, which reflects the history of Carteret County and the Cape Lookout region, from Native American through modern times. There's also a gift shop and a public research library, with a notable genealogy collection. ✉ *1008 Arendell St.* ☎ *252/247–7533* 🌐 *www.crystalcoast.com/ccmuseum/* *Free* *Tues.–Sat. 10–4.*

★ The centerpiece of **Fort Macon State Park** is the pentagon-shape fortress built in 1834 that was used first to protect the coast against foreign invaders and later, during the Civil War, against the Yankees. You can explore on your own or take a guided tour. But that's not all there is to this 365-acre park set in a maritime forest: there are picnicking areas and hiking trails, and a mile-long beachfront has a large bathhouse and refreshments. Follow the boardwalk over the dunes to the beach, which, due to strong currents, has lifeguards on duty June through Labor Day from 10 to 5:45. A bathhouse locker costs $4. ✉ *East end of Rte.*

58, Bogue Banks, Atlantic Beach, 3 mi south of Morehead City ☎ *252/726–3775* 🌐 *http://ils.unc.edu/parkproject* 💵 *Free* 🕑 *Nov.–Feb., daily 8–6; Mar. and Oct., daily 8–7; Apr., May, and Sept., daily 8–8; June–Aug., daily 8–9.*

The **North Carolina Aquarium at Pine Knoll Shores,** closed for renovation and expansion, is scheduled to reopen in 2006. ☎ *252/247–2003* ✉ *U.S. 58, Atlantic Beach* 🌐 *www.ncaquariums.com.*

Sports & the Outdoors

Two wreck sites popular for scuba diving are the *Schurz,* sunk in World War I, and the *Papoose,* a World War II tanker inhabited by docile sand sharks. **Olympus Dive Center** (✉ 713 Shephard St. ☎ 252/726–9432 🌐 www.olympusdiving.com) has five dive boats and has full- and half-day charters, equipment rental, and lessons.

Where to Stay & Eat

$$$–$$$$ ✕ **Stardust.** Chef-owners Ashley and Ralph McGee worked in New Orleans restaurants, and the cooking reflects that background—even the shrimp-and-grits has a kick. Sauces, spices, and Southern ingredients (black-eyed peas, green tomato chow chow) are used liberally. Veggies come straight from local farmers' markets and the seafood is fresh off the boat. A former Coca-Cola bottling plant, a simple waterfront building with white siding and maroon and silver trim and awning, houses the Stardust. Inside, a bar takes up most of the downstairs; an upstairs balcony seating area has a mural of the waterfront. ✉ *714 Shepard St.* ☎ *252/726–0080* 💳 *AE, D, MC, V* 🕑 *Closed Sun. and Mon. No lunch.*

$$–$$$ ✕ **Finz.** Come as you are to this bar and grill (in a 1929 Gulf Oil Corp. warehouse) on the waterfront: informality is the keyword and a second-story deck has particularly nice views. Children are welcome, though at night, especially in summer, things can get loud. Most of the menu items are simply prepared and filling. There are soups and salads, sandwiches and burgers. A few pasta and beef dishes are thrown in for good measure. This Finz has a sister by the same name in nearby Beaufort. ✉ *105 S. 7th St.* ☎ *252/726–5502* 💳 *D, MC, V.*

★ **$$–$$$** ✕ **Sanitary Fish Market & Restaurant.** In 1938, when the Sanitary was founded, many fish houses were ill kept. The owners wanted to signal that theirs was different; clean, simple, and generous are still the bywords at this waterfront place where diners sit at long wooden tables. It can get busy (waits of an hour) and noisy (the restaurant seats 600), but people from around the world gush about the seafood. Have it prepared almost any way you want it—steamed, fried, grilled, or broiled. The two-course Deluxe Shore dinner has, among other things, shrimp, oysters, crabs, and tuna. Hush puppies and cole slaw come with every meal. ✉ *501 Evans St.* ☎ *252/247–3111* 🌐 *www.sanitaryfishmarket.com* 💳 *D, MC, V* 🕑 *Closed Dec. and Jan.*

$–$$ ✕ **Bistro by the Sea.** An atrium in the bar is decorated as a grape arbor, which says a lot about the importance of wines to the dining experience here. The stonework and stucco exterior hint at the Mediterranean style within, but the cuisine defies any particular theme. Beef, chicken, and seafood all share space on the menu—favorites include stir-fry chicken with rice and wontons; and capellini tossed with pesto, fresh scallops, and vegetables, which are always garden fresh. The service is consistently friendly. There are also a piano bar and cigar lounge. ✉ *4301 Arendell St.* ☎ *252/247–2777* ▭ *MC, V* ⊗ *Closed Sun. and Mon. in Jan. No lunch.*

$$ **Best Western Buccaneer.** The inn sits beside the Morehead Plaza shopping center, a 10-minute drive from Atlantic Beach. Rooms are attractive and comfortable. Some of the rooms with king beds also have jetted tubs. ✉ *2806 Arendell St., 28557* ☎ *252/726–3115 or 800/682–4982* 🖷 *252/726–3864* 🌐 *www.bestwestern.com* *91 rooms* *Restaurant, refrigerators, in-room data ports, some in-room hot tubs, cable TV, pool, exercise equipment, bar, business services, meeting room, no-smoking rooms* ▭ *AE, D, DC, MC, V* *BP.*

$$ **Windjammer Inn.** If your desire is easy access to the ocean, this is the place for you. What you get here is straightforward—a comfortable, large room with a private balcony and ocean view. The five-story glass elevator sets the inn apart from typical beach lodging. There's a two-night minimum stay on summer weekends. ✉ *Salter Path Rd. in Pine Knoll Shores, Atlantic Beach 28512* ☎ *252/247–7123 or 800/233–6466* 🖷 *252/247–0133* 🌐 *www.windjammerinn.com* *46 rooms* *Some in-room hot tubs, microwaves, refrigerators, cable TV, pool, beach, no-smoking rooms* ▭ *AE, D, MC, V* *EP.*

Shopping

Owners Doug and Jane Wolfe have assembled a large selection of books at **Dee Gee's Gifts and Books** (✉ 508 Evans St. ☎ 252/726–3314 or 800/333–4377), focused on local and regional authors. Gifts for sale include nautical charts. A landmark for several generations, Dee's is across the street from another Morehead City landmark, the Sanitary restaurant.

New Bern

❽ *36 mi northeast of Morehead City via U.S. 70.*

The pace is quiet and slow in New Bern, the second-oldest town in North Carolina. Settled in 1710 by Swiss and German colonists and named for Bern, Switzerland, the city has a heraldic Swiss black bear symbol that is everywhere. New Bern, the state capital from the period of English rule until immediately after the revolution, is where North Carolina's first newspaper was printed and Pepsi-Cola was invented. History is taken seriously here; the town has more than 150 sites included in the National Register of Historic Places.

Sailors and sunseekers enjoy the area, as the Neuse and Trent rivers are perfect for such activities as waterskiing and crabbing. The historic downtown area is filled with shops, many of them selling antiques.

Fodor's Choice ★ The reconstructed **Tryon Palace,** an elegant Georgian building, was the colonial capitol and the home of Royal Governor William Tryon during the 1770s. It was rebuilt according to architectural drawings of the original palace and furnished with English and American antiques corresponding to Governor Tryon's inventory. An audiovisual orientation prepares you for a tour of the house led by costumed guides. In summer actors deliver monologues reenacting a day in the life of ordinary citizens and the governor. The stately **John Wright Stanly House** (circa 1783), the **George W. Dixon House** (circa 1826), the **Robert Hay House** (circa 1805), and the **New Bern Academy** (circa 1809) are all part of the 13-acre Tryon Palace complex. You can stroll through the 18th-century formal gardens afterwards. ✉ *610 Pollock St.* ☎ *252/514–4900* *Self-guided tours $8; tours of garden, kitchen, office, and stables $8; tour of all bldgs. and gardens $15* ⏲ *Mon.–Sat. 9–5, Sun. 1–5.*

Where to Stay & Eat

$$–$$$ ✕ **Captain Ratty's.** The storefront restaurant is draped in fish netting and colorful pennants listing the names of patrons' boats. Sandwiches, tortilla wraps among them, are popular lunch items; seafood and steaks are the prime choices for evening meals. The price of oysters depends on whether you do the shucking or have the Ratty's staff do it for you. Live entertainment on weekend evenings draws a crowd. ✉ *202 Middle St.* ☎ *252/633–2088* ▭ *MC, V.*

$$–$$$ ✕ **The Chelsea.** This two-story restored 1912 structure, originally the second drugstore of the pharmacist who invented Pepsi-Cola, retains some fine architectural details, such as its tin ceiling. It's a magnet for weekenders, who look forward to selecting from sandwiches (wrapped, pita, and burgers), large salads, and entrées such as shrimp and grits. The bar is well stocked, and Pepsi products are, as might be expected, the nonalcoholic drinks of choice. ✉ *335 Middle St.* ☎ *252/637–5469* ▭ *AE, D, DC, MC, V.*

$$–$$$ ✕ **The Flame.** The considerate staff at this dark, woodsy steak house with furnishings vaguely reminiscent of the Victorian era, helps make dinners special. Steak, lobster, grilled shrimp, and teriyaki chicken are all good bets. Sunday brunch is popular. ✉ *2303 Neuse Blvd.* ☎ *252/633–0262* ▭ *AE, D, DC, MC, V* ⏲ *No dinner Sun. No lunch Mon.–Sat.*

¢–$ ✕ **Pollock Street Deli.** Good-size crowds gather in the tiny rooms of this historic district colonial house—and at its sidewalk tables—for classic deli treats and Sunday brunch. The chicken salad is a winner. Service can be leisurely but it's also friendly. ✉ *208 Pollock St.* ☎ *252/637–2480* ▭ *AE, MC, V* ⏲ *No dinner Sun.*

$$ **Sheraton New Bern Hotel and Marina.** At the confluence of the Neuse and Trent rivers, this Sheraton—with marina facilities—is actually two properties in one. A hotel has guest rooms overlooking the Trent River, and rooms at the inn have either waterfront or city views. ✉ *100 Middle St., 28560* ☎ *252/638–3585 or 888/625–5144* 🖷 *252/638–8112* 🌐 *www.newbernsheraton.com* *150 rooms, 22 suites* *Restaurant, room service, cable TV, pool, exercise equipment, marina, 2 bars, concierge, business services, meeting room, airport shuttle, no-smoking rooms* ▭ *AE, D, DC, MC, V* *EP.*

$ **Bridge Pointe Hotel & Marina.** Standard motel-like rooms have above-average views of the rivers on the east side of the city. Ducks reside in the on-site pond and you can park your boat at the hotel's dock. The Bridge Pointe is on the Trent River, across the bridge from the historic section of New Bern. ✉ *101 Howell Rd., 28562* ☎ *252/636–3637 or 877/283–7713* 🖷 *252/637–5028* 🌐 *www.bridgepointehotel.com* *116* *rooms* ♿ *Restaurant, microwaves, refrigerator, cable TV, pool, marina, lounge, laundry service, Internet, business services, meeting rooms, no-smoking rooms* ▭ *AE, D, DC, MC, V* 🍴 *EP.*

$ **Hanna House.** Camille and Joe Klotz moved here from "up North" and renovated the Rudolph Ulrich House (circa 1896), incorporating the latest in plumbing and bath fixtures into antique-filled rooms. In so doing, they made a home not just for themselves but for other visitors to this river city. Regulars return again and again to the small B&B, where lush robes hang in closets. Breakfast is served at the time of your preference, and may include eggs Florentine with hollandaise sauce, apple pancakes, or poached grey trout in remoulade sauce. ✉ *218 Pollock St., 28560* ☎ *252/635–3209 or 866/830–4371* 🌐 *www.hannahousenc.net* *3 rooms* ♿ *Dining room; no room phones, no room TVs, no smoking* ▭ *MC, V* 🍴 *BP.*

$ **Harmony House Inn.** This old home has a curious past: at one point, two brothers sawed the house in half, and built double hallways, stairs and a dividing wall. Today the property is back together, joined by a set of double front doors. Here you can sleep in spacious rooms that lodged Yankee soldiers during the Civil War. Crafty wreaths, quilts, and embroidery complement the mix of antiques and reproductions in guest rooms. White and dessert wines are served in the evening. ✉ *215 Pollock St., 28560* ☎ *252/636–3810 or 800/636–3113* 🖷 *252/636–3810* 🌐 *www.harmonyhouseinn.com* *10 rooms* ♿ *Dining room, fans, some in-room hot tubs, cable TV, shop, business services, airport shuttle; no smoking* ▭ *AE, D, MC, V* 🍴 *BP.*

$ **New Berne House.** Owner Barbara Pappas turned the three floors of a 1922 brick house into a tasteful, albeit eclectic, showcase for her collections. Breakfast is served on vintage dishes, books fill built-in shelves, art covers the walls, and a funky set of hats hang on the second-floor landing rack. A third-floor bedroom has a brass bed that was once owned by U.S. Senator Barry Goldwater. Pappas, soft-spoken and genial, keeps a refrigerator stocked with drinks. Her popular mystery weekends (advance reservations a must) involve scavenging the town's nearby historic district for clues. ✉ *709 Broad St., 28560* ☎ *252/636–2250 or 866/782–8266* 🌐 *www.newbernehouse.com* *7 rooms* ♿ *Bicycles, library, piano; no room phones, no room TVs, no smoking* ▭ *MC, V* 🍴 *BP.*

WILMINGTON & THE CAPE FEAR COAST

The greater Cape Fear region stretches from Topsail Island north of Wilmington south to Southport. A role in early-American history and a nearness to water are factors that unite the region. Cape Fear River begins in North Carolina's Piedmont and empties into the Atlantic Ocean about 30 mi south of downtown Wilmington. First settled in 1729, Wilmington is one of two deepwater ports in the state. It also has one of the largest historic districts, containing 300 blocks, and a picturesque riverfront, listed on the National Register of Historic Places. EUE/Screen Gems Studios, the largest full-service motion picture facility in the United States east of California, is headquartered in Wilmington. Since

1984, this studio has been involved in 300 film, television, and commercial productions, many of them shot in the Cape Fear area.

Miles and miles of sand stretch northward to the Outer Banks and southward to South Carolina. The beaches offer activities from fishing to sunbathing to scuba diving, and the towns here have a choice of accommodations. Approximately 100 points of public access along the shoreline are marked by orange-and-blue signs. South of Wilmington, there are three distinct island communities that are an easy day-trip: Wrightsville Beach, Kure (pronounced "cure-ee") Beach, and Carolina Beach. Southport, which sits along the west side of the Cape Fear River's mouth, was founded in 1792. With its revitalized waterfront, shaded streets, grand homes, antiques shops, and year-round golf, it oozes charm. Such is the personality of the region that it has something for artists, sportspeople, history buffs, naturalists, shoppers, and sunbathers alike. Filmmakers, too.

Wilmington

89 mi southwest of New Bern via U.S. 17 and 117; 130 mi south of Raleigh via I–40.

The city's long history, including its part in the American Revolution and its role as the main port of the Confederacy, is revealed in sights downtown and in the surrounding area. Chandler's Wharf, the Cotton Exchange, and Water Street Market are old buildings now used as shopping and entertainment centers. *Henrietta II,* a paddle wheeler similar to those that plied the waters of the Cape Fear River, has been put into service as a tourist vessel. Wilmington, also a college town, has special annual events such as the Azalea Festival, North Carolina Jazz Festival, Christmas candlelight tours, and fishing tournaments.

Doing justice to all the sights and experiences offered by this scenic, old city requires several days. The downtown historic district of Wilmington, along the riverfront, is very walkable. As you move away from this immediate area, however, a car becomes necessary for visits to places like the Louise Wells Cameron Art Museum, Airlie Gardens, and the USS *North Carolina* Battleship Memorial. In summer the major thoroughfare can be fairly busy, so allow more time than the distance would indicate. Route 132, the main north–south road through town, continues south where I–40 leaves off. U.S. 76 runs from downtown east to Wrightsville Beach; U.S. 421 goes south to Carolina and Kure beaches.

a good tour

A fine place to start exploring downtown Wilmington is at the **Cape Fear Museum** 9, where you can learn about the history of the entire Cape Fear region. Walk along Market Street toward the waterfront and then south past 3rd Street to the restored colonial period **Burgwin-Wright Museum House** 10, which you can tour. Return to 3rd Street to get to the **Zebulon Latimer House** 11, where you can take a tour of the home and obtain information from the Lower Cape Fear Historical Society. Go east on Orange Street to the Riverfront and the restaurants and shops of **Chandler's Wharf** 12. From here you can turn upriver (right) and in a

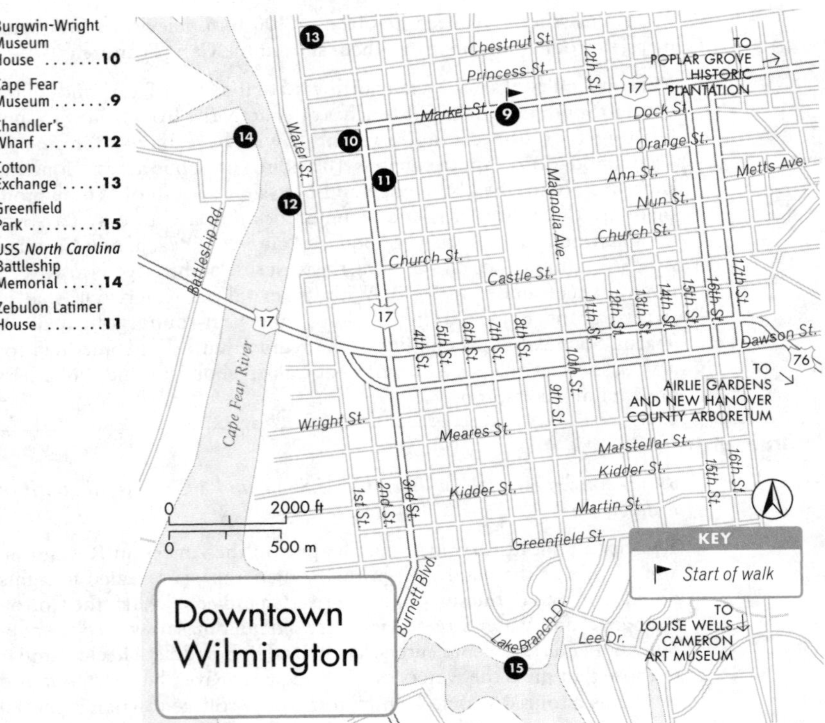

few blocks reach the **Cotton Exchange** 13, an impressive re-use of an old building as a shopping complex.

Although the **USS *North Carolina* Battleship Memorial** 14 is visible across the water from anywhere on the riverfront, to visit it you need a car. Drive south on 3rd Street for several blocks until you can turn right on U.S. 17/74/76, which crosses the river on a high bridge. Look for signs directing you to the right, where the memorial is a bit north on U.S. 421. If you'd prefer, instead of crossing the river, continue driving south on 3rd Street for several more blocks to find signs directing you into **Greenfield Park** 15, which is magnificent in spring when azaleas and dogwood trees are in bloom.

TIMING Take time during your walk to admire the architecture along the way. If you decide to visit the house museums, this walk could easily fill up a day. If you want to explore the battleship or Greenfield Park instead, each is worth at least a couple of hours.

What to See

★ **Airlie Gardens.** Designed first as a European-style garden showcasing plants in all four seasons, Airlie has suffered its share of hurricane damage since it was built in the early 1900s, but has come back each time and is now owned by New Hanover County. There are 67 acres in this lush Southern garden—azaleas, magnolias, and camellias abound—as well as two freshwater lakes that attract waterfowl. The greatest specimen of them all is the gargantuan 450-year-old Airlie Oak. The last tickets for the day are sold one hour before closing. ✉ *300 Airlie Rd., Midtown, 8 mi east of downtown via U.S. 76* ☎ *910/798–7700* 🌐 *www.airliegardens.org* 🎟 *$8* ⏲ *Tues.–Sat. 9–5, Sun. 11–5.*

10 **Burgwin-Wright Museum House.** The house General Cornwallis used as his headquarters in April of 1781 was built in 1770, on the foundations of a jail. After a fine, furnished restoration, this colonial gentleman's town house was turned into a museum that includes seven distinct period gardens. One Saturday a month you can see open-hearth cooking demonstrations. ✉ *224 Market St., Downtown* ☎ *910/762–0570* 🎟 *$7* ⏲ *Tues.–Sat. 10–4.*

9 **Cape Fear Museum.** Trace the natural, cultural, and social history of the lower Cape Fear region from its beginnings to the present. One exhibit follows the youth of one of Wilmington's most famous native sons, basketball superstar Michael Jordan. ✉ *814 Market St., Downtown* ☎ *910/341–7413* 🌐 *www.capefearmuseum.com* 🎟 *$5* ⏲ *Early Sept.–late May, Tues.–Sat. 9–5, Sun. 1–5; late May–early Sept., daily 9–5.*

Cape Fear Tours. Take a driving tour of the Wilmington Historic District, the mansions, and the beaches for about $20 per hour. ✉ *8112 Sidbury Rd., Downtown* ☎ *910/686–7744.*

12 **Chandler's Wharf.** Cobblestone streets and a renovated 19th-century pier along the Cape Fear River are part of the intrigue of this shopping and dining complex that anchors downtown Wilmington. ✉ *225 S. Water St., Downtown.*

13 **Cotton Exchange.** In an area along the Cape Fear River that has flourished as a trading center since pre–Civil War days stands a shopping mall in a rambling restored cotton warehouse. There are also several restaurants on-site. Note that only some of the shops are open on Sunday. ✉ *321 N. Front St., Downtown* ☎ *910/343–9896* 🌐 *www.shopcottonexchange.com* ⏲ *Mon.–Sat. 10–5:30, Sun. 1–5.*

15 **Greenfield Park.** Come here for picnic spots, bike paths, nature trails, and canoe and paddleboat rentals on a 150-acre lake bordered by cypress trees laden with Spanish moss. In April the park is ablaze with azaleas. ✉ *S. 3rd St. (U.S. 421), 1 mi south of downtown, South Metro* ☎ *910/341–7852* 🎟 *Free* ⏲ *Daily dawn–dusk.*

Louise Wells Cameron Art Museum. The museum, formerly known as the St. John's Museum of Art, is dedicated to the art of North Carolina from the 18th to the 20th centuries. Its permanent collection, contained in a sleek 42,000-square-foot facility, includes originals by Mary Cassatt, master potter Ben Owen, and folk artist Clyde Jones. On the 10-acre grounds are restored Confederate defense mounds built during a battle in the waning days of the Civil War. Forks restaurant serves lunch Tuesday through Saturday and has a jazz brunch on Sunday. ✉ *3201 S. 17th St., South Metro, 4 mi south of downtown* ☎ *910/395–5999* 🌐 *www.cameronartmuseum.com* 🎟 *$7* ⏲ *Tues.–Sat. 10–5, Sun. 10:30–4.*

New Hanover County Arboretum. Lose yourself in more than 33 natural exhibits, among 100 varieties of shade-loving camellias. There are magnolia and patio gardens, a salt-spray garden, and a children's garden with a maze. ✉ *6206 Oleander Dr., Midtown, 6 mi east of downtown via U.S. 76* ☎ *910/452–6393* 🌐 *www.arboretumnhc.org* *Free* *Daily dawn–dusk.*

Poplar Grove Historic Plantation. Tour the 1850 Greek Revival manor house and its outbuildings. You can also see crafts demonstrations, shop in the country store, and pet the farm animals. ✉ *10200 U.S. 17, North Metro, 9 mi northeast of downtown* ☎ *910/686–9518* 🌐 *www.poplargrove.com* *Guided tours $7* *Feb.–Dec., Mon.–Sat. 9–5, Sun. noon–5.*

off the beaten path

MOORE'S CREEK NATIONAL BATTLEFIELD – American patriots defeated the Loyalists on this site in 1776. An interpretive trail lines the battlefield and there are exhibits in the visitor center. The 85-acre park is also a wildlife habitat. ✉ *200 Moore's Creek Rd., Currie, 20 mi northwest of Wilmington on Rte. 210* ☎ *910/283–5591* 🌐 *www.nps.gov* *Free* *Daily 9–5.*

14 **USS *North Carolina* Battleship Memorial.** Take a self-guided tour of a ship that participated in every major naval offensive in the Pacific during World War II. Exploring the floating city, with living quarters, a post office, chapel, laundry, and even an ice-cream shop, takes about two hours. A 10-minute orientation film is shown throughout the day, and you can rent narrated tours on cassette. Warning: a climb down into the ship's interior is not for the claustrophobic. The ship can be reached by car or by taking the river taxi from Riverfront Park, Memorial Day through Labor Day, at a cost of $2 per person. ✉ *Junction of U.S. 74/76 and U.S. 17 and 421, west bank of Cape Fear River, Downtown* ☎ *910/251–5797* 🌐 *www.battleshipnc.com* *$9* *Mid-May–mid-Sept., daily 8–8; mid-Sept.–mid-May, daily 8–5.*

11 **Zebulon Latimer House.** Built in 1852 in the Italianate style, this home museum is a reminder of opulent antebellum living. The Lower Cape Fear Historical Society is based here; it leads guided walking tours of the downtown historic district that depart from the house on Wednesday and Saturday mornings at 10. ✉ *126 S. 3rd St., Downtown* ☎ *910/762–0492* 🌐 *www.latimerhouse.org* *$7* *Weekdays 10–4, Sat. noon–5.*

off the beaten path

WHITE LAKE – The white, sandy bottom at this Carolina bay in Bladen County is clearly visible. A clean appearance, plus the shaded summer cottages that rim its shore and the public boat ramp and dock, have helped fuel this bay's reputation as the "nation's safest beach." ✉ *1879 Lake Dr., White Lake, 58 mi northwest of Wilmington via U.S. 74 and Rte. 87* ☎ *910/862–4800.*

Sports & the Outdoors

From April through December, **Cape Fear Riverboats, Inc.** (✉ Near the Hilton, 301 N. Water St., Downtown ☎ 910/343–1611 or 800/676–

0162) runs cruises aboard a stern-wheel riverboat, the *Henrietta III,* which departs from Riverfront Park. The cost is $18–$33.

Wrecks such as the World War II tanker *John D. Gill* make for exciting scuba diving off the Cape Fear Coast; **Aquatic Safaris** (✉ 5751–4 Oleander Dr., Wilmington ☎ 910/392–4386) leads trips to see them and rents scuba equipment.

Where to Eat

$$$–$$$$ ✕ **Caprice Bistro.** White lace curtains at the windows, tables dressed in white paper, and plain white plates serve as an unobtrusive backdrop for the food here, which is all French, all the time. Chef Thierry is proud of his "solid bistro cooking"—onion soup, *pommes frites* (fries) served with aioli, classic steak *au poivre* (with pepper), and crisped duck confit. The wine list has American labels as well as French. Although there's no smoking allowed downstairs, you can smoke upstairs in the art-filled sofa bar, which stays open until 2 AM. ✉ *10 Market St., Downtown* ☎ *910/815–0810* ▭ *AE, D, MC, V* ⊙ *No lunch.*

$$$–$$$$ ✕ **Pilot House.** You can dine indoors at tables with linen tablecloths secured by vases of fresh flowers or outdoors overlooking the Cape Fear River on Chandler's Wharf. The Pilot House is known for its pastas, fresh vegetables, and seafood, such as backfin crabcakes and Carolina seafood bisque, with clams, shrimp, fish, and scallops. Sunday brunch, which starts at 11:30, is popular. ✉ *2 Ann St., Downtown* ☎ *910/343–0200* ▭ *AE, D, DC, MC, V.*

$$–$$$ ✕ **Water Street Restaurant and Sidewalk Café.** A restored two-story brick waterfront warehouse dating from 1835 holds an eclectic restaurant and outdoor café. Enjoy Greek, Mexican, and Middle Eastern dishes, as well as salads, pitas, burgers, and pasta. Seafood chowder is made daily on the premises. ✉ *5 Water St., Downtown* ☎ *910/343–0042* ▭ *AE, MC, V.*

$–$$ ✕ **Caffé Phoenix.** First there's the scene: an old, glass-front building (a former dry goods store), high ceilings, an interior balcony, recorded classical or jazz music playing, area artists' work on the walls. Then comes the service: friendly, attentive. Finally the food: eclectic (Mediterranean, Italian, French, Spanish), in generous portions. The salads—think pear, fennel and walnuts—and daily specials are especially inventive. Because of the number of wines, coffees, and homemade desserts, the café draws a large after-hours crowd. On Sunday mornings a line forms for brunch with Bloody Marys, thick-cut French toast, eggs, and lunch selections. ✉ *9 S. Front St., Downtown* ☎ *910/343–1395* ▭ *AE, D, DC, MC, V.*

$–$$ ✕ **K-38 Baja Grill.** A popular surfers' side road in Baja, Mexico, the K-38 road leads to ideal waves—and the K-38 menu heavily references Baja culinary traditions. You won't find Americanized Mexican fare here; instead, sample tricolor corn tortillas with shrimp, scallops, and crab with cheese and roasted garlic cream, tortilla lasagna, and chicken breast baked with artichokes, sun-dried tomatoes, green-chili pesto, and goat cheese cream. Rice, grilled vegetables, and fresh fruit accompany many dishes. This restaurant is especially popular with people in their twenties. ✉ *5410 Oleander Dr., Midtown* ☎ *910/395–6040* ▭ *AE, D, MC, V.*

Where to Stay

★ **$$–$$$$** **The Wilmingtonian.** Members of the entertainment industry often frequent the Wilmingtonian. Luxurious suites each have a different theme—classic movies, nautical heritage, country French, and so on. The Cupola Suite, in the 1841 de Rosset House, is great fun: decorated in soothing blue and cream, it has a spiral staircase leading to a sitting room with views of the city's rooftops. Rooms are spread throughout five buildings set in gardens, including in an antebellum home and a convent. Many have gas fireplaces and large whirlpool tubs. Staying here you get dining privileges at the City Club, a private restaurant. *101 S. 2nd St., Downtown, 28401 910/343–1800 or 800/525–0909 910/251–1149 www.thewilmingtonian.com 40 suites Restaurant, room service, in-room data ports, some in-room hot tubs, some kitchens, microwaves, refrigerators, cable TV, in-room VCRs, library, laundry facilities, Internet, business services, meeting rooms, some pets allowed; no kids under 12, no smoking AE, D, DC, MC, V BP.*

$$$ **Hilton-Riverside.** Overlooking the Cape Fear River on one side and the city on the other, the spacious Hilton is one of the most convenient places to stay in town. The lobby is plush; guest rooms are traditional, with dark woods and autumn colors. Rollicking parties are held poolside on summer weekends. *301 N. Water St., Downtown, 28401 910/763–5900 or 800/445–8667 910/763–0038 www.wilmingtonhilton.com 263 rooms, 11 suites Restaurant, in-room data ports, cable TV with movies and video games, pool, gym, dock, bar, shop, concierge floor, business services, meeting room, airport shuttle, no-smoking rooms AE, D, DC, MC, V EP.*

$$–$$$ **Catherine's Inn.** This two-story Italianate home, built in 1883 in what is now a historic district overlooking the Cape Fear River, is a B&B with hardwood floors, a sunken garden, four-poster and canopy beds, and phones in each room. Many items were collected by the innkeepers over the years. Coffee is delivered to your door every morning. This is the only inn in the area with a direct river view. *410 S. Front St., Downtown, 28401 910/251–0863 or 800/476–0723 910/772–9550 www.catherinesinn.com 5 rooms Dining room, library; no room TVs, no smoking MC, V BP.*

$$ **Hampton Inn.** This moderately priced chain motel is 3 mi from downtown and 6 mi from Wrightsville Beach. Perks include in-room coffeemakers and free local calls. King Study rooms have a sofa that folds out into a bed, and a desk. *5107 Market St., Midtown, 28403 910/395–5045 or 800/426–7866 910/799–1974 www.hampton-inn.com 118 rooms In-room data ports, cable TV, pool, exercise equipment, laundry service, business services, meeting room, no-smoking rooms AE, D, DC, MC, V BP.*

Nightlife & the Arts

The city has its own symphony orchestra, oratorio society, civic ballet, and concert association. The North Carolina Symphony makes four appearances here each year. The old riverfront area, with its restaurants and nightclubs, strolling couples and horse-drawn carriages, really jumps on weekend nights.

The **North Carolina Jazz Festival** (☎ 910/962–3500 or 800/732–3643) plays out for three days in February in venues around town, with world famous musicians performing in different styles (swing and Dixieland, for example).

Cape Fear Festival (☎ 910/350–8822 ⊕ www.capefearblues.com), held four days in July, culminates in an all-day blues jam at Battleship Park. There are also concerts in nightclubs and on paddle wheelers, and festival parties and workshops.

Thalian Hall Center for the Performing Arts (✉ 310 Chestnut St., Downtown ☎ 910/343–3664 or 800/523–2820 ⊕ www.thalianhall.com), a restored opera house built between 1855 and 1858, hosts more than 250 theater, dance, and musical performances each year. Theatrical productions are staged by the Thalian Association, Opera House Productions, and Tapestry Players.

Charley Brownz (✉ 21 S. Front St., Downtown ☎ 910/245–9499) has nightly musical entertainment that ranges from reggae and rock to karaoke and DJ dance music.

Wrightsville Beach

16 *12 mi east of Wilmington.*

Wrightsville Beach is a small, quiet island community that's very family oriented. It has a number of fine restaurants, and beaches good for swimming, boating, and surfing.

Where to Stay & Eat

$$–$$$ ✕ **Oceanic Restaurant and Grill.** Thanks to three floors of seating with large windows all over, you have a panoramic view of the Atlantic for miles around—a great backdrop for the fresh seafood, steaks, and chicken. Dinner on the pier at sunset is a treat. ✉ *703 S. Lumina St.* ☎ *910/256–5551* ▭ *AE, MC, V.*

★ ¢ ✕ **Causeway Cafe.** Sipping coffee supplied by the efficient staff, patrons waiting on the wide front porch to be seated contemplate what to order this time—Malted pancakes? Eggs Benedict? A country ham sandwich? Cinnamon-raisin-sourdough french toast? Shrimp and grits? Cereal and fruit? Greek omelet? Though it has a perfectly respectable lunch menu, breakfast is what packs 'em in at the Causeway, which is less than ¼ mi from the Intracoastal Waterway bridge separating Wilmington from Wrightsville Beach Island. ✉ *114 Causeway Dr.* ☎ *910/256–3730* ✍ *Reservations not accepted* ▭ *No credit cards* ⊙ *No dinner.*

$$$–$$$$ ✕🏨 **Blockade Runner Resort Hotel and Conference Center.** East, the hotel's restaurant ($$$–$$$$, reservations essential), attracts crowds with its weekend buffets and jazz brunch on Sunday. Guest rooms at the ocean-side resort complex are done in bright colors and overlook either the Intracoastal Waterway or, for a higher price, the ocean. Service can be uneven, especially at the height of the season, but the hotel's beachfront location and guaranteed parking keep them coming back. Spa privileges and summer children's programs are bonuses. A two-night minimum is required weekends March through October. ✉ *275 Waynick Blvd.,*

28480 ☎ 910/256–2251 or 800/541–1161 🖷 910/256–5502 🌐 www.blockade-runner.com ⇆ 147 rooms, 3 suites ♂ Restaurant, refrigerators, indoor-outdoor pool, health club, beach, boating, parasailing, bicycles, volleyball, bar, children's programs (ages 5–12), business services, meeting room, airport shuttle, no-smoking rooms ▭ AE, D, DC, MC, V 🍴 EP.

Kure Beach

17 *17 mi southwest of Wrightsville Beach; 21 mi southwest of Wilmington via U.S. 421.*

A resort community, Kure Beach contains Fort Fisher State Historic Site and one of North Carolina's three aquariums. In some places twisted live oaks still grow behind the dunes. The community has miles of beaches; public access points are marked by orange-and-blue signs.

Fort Fisher State Historic Site marks one of the South's largest and most important earthworks fortifications from the Civil War. A reconstructed battery, Civil War relics, and artifacts from sunken blockade-runners are on-site. The fort is part of the Fort Fisher Recreation Area, with 4 mi of undeveloped beach. ✉ *U.S. 421, Kure Beach* ☎ *910/458–5538* 🎫 *Free* ⏲ *Apr.–Oct., Mon.–Sat. 9–5, Sun. 1–5; Nov.–Mar., Tues.–Sat. 10–4, Sun. 1–4.*

The oceanfront **North Carolina Aquarium at Fort Fisher** is the largest of North Carolina's three aquariums. Its 235,000 gallon salt water tank is home to sharks, stingrays, moray eels, and other fish from nearby waters. Twice a day, scuba divers enter the multistory tank and answer questions from the onlookers. The Waters of the Cape Fear exhibit follows the river from the Piedmont to the Atlantic. Among the other 20 tanks and streams, there's a touch tank, a tank with glowing jellyfish, and alligator and turtle ponds. ✉ *900 Loggerhead Rd., off U.S. 421, Kure Beach* ☎ *866/301–3476* 🌐 *www.ncaquariums.com* 🎫 *$7* ⏲ *Daily 9–5.*

Carolina Beach, a town established in 1857, has a boardwalk with a Ferris wheel and an arcade. Bars and marinas line a lively central business district. Fishing is a major activity and anglers can test their skill on the pier, in the surf, and on deep-sea charter excursions. You can also take a nightly party cruise. And, of course, there's the beach. ✥ *3 mi northeast of Kure Beach via U.S. 421.*

Where to Stay & Eat

$$–$$$ ✕ **Big Daddy's.** You can't miss this place—the huge sign outside sits next to the only stoplight in town. Inside, the enormity continues: three noisy, dimly lighted dining areas seat nearly 500 people. And the menu is substantial, with more than 40 items. Although some chicken, steak, and prime rib are listed, seafood stars. It comes prepared almost any way you could want it, and portions are large. The gift shop at the entrance, which sells beach kitsch and candy, is a magnet for children. ✉ *202 K Ave., Kure Beach* ☎ *910/458–8622* ▭ *AE, D, MC, V* ⏲ *Closed late Nov.–Feb.*

$$–$$$ **Fodor'sChoice ★** ✕ **The Cottage.** Cypress shingles complement yellow trim on Carolina Beach's oldest bungalow (1916); an updated interior, with a series of small dining rooms, is spare but not monastic—wood-plank floors, white walls, Japanese-style screens, and uncovered tables. The Cottage is a refuge of calm, and has some of the best dining around. Specialties such as Fish in Foil and salmon cooked on a cedar plank, served with lemon caper butter, all involve seafood. The black-eyed pea cakes are seasoned to perfection and given some zing thanks to a drizzle of citrus sauce. For dessert, don't pass on the key lime pie. ✉ *1 N. Lake Park Blvd., Carolina Beach* ☎ *910/458–4383* ▭ *AE, D, MC, V* ⊗ *Closed Sun.*

$$$ **The Ocean Princess Inn.** Two brightly painted (magenta and sea-green), two-story buildings with white porches sit among palm trees and the remnants of a maritime forest. Each room has different furniture and colors: the effect is sometimes bold and tailored, sometimes muted and romantic. Local artists' work hangs on the walls, adding another bright note. The attentive staff will gladly provide directions or arrange with the company contracted to set up chairs and umbrellas for guests at the beach across the street. ✉ *824 Ft. Fisher Blvd. S., Kure Beach 28449* ☎ *910/458–6712 or 800/762–4863* ⊕ *www.oceanprincessinn.com* *10 rooms, 2 villas* *Dining room, some kitchens, cable TV, pool, some in-room hot tubs, outdoor hot tub, bicycles, croquet, library, piano, some laundry facilities, no-smoking rooms; no room phones* ▭ *MC, V* *BP.*

$$–$$$ **Docksider Inn.** The nautical theme is no surprise given that this hotel is yards from the beach. The inn is furnished in light-color beach-type furniture accented with marine art and artifacts, including a set of 1930s British Admiralty signal flags. Bright bedspreads with flowers and fish give the rooms something of a tropical feel. Owners Kip and Maureen Darling have another property a block away on Atlantic Avenue. The five contemporary luxury suites of Darlings by the Sea are for adults only. Each has an expansive ocean view, custom drapes, bed skirting, and cabinetry. There are whirlpools for two and wet bars. ✉ *202 Fort Fisher Blvd. (U.S. 421), Kure Beach 28449* ☎ *910/458–4200 or 800/383–8111* *910/458–6468* ⊕ *www.docksiderinn.com* *34 rooms* *Some kitchens, pool, outdoor hot tub, beach, no-smoking rooms* ▭ *AE, D, MC, V* *Darlings By the Sea* ✉ *329 Atlantic Ave., Kure Beach, 28445* ☎ *800/383–8111* *910/458–6468* ⊕ *www.darlingsbythesea.com* *5 rooms* *In-room hot tubs, gym, beach, no-smoking room* ▭ *AE, D, MC, V* *EP.*

Southport

18 *10 mi southwest of Kure Beach via U.S. 421 and ferry; 30 mi south of Wilmington via Rte. 133.*

This small town, which sits quietly at the mouth of the Cape Fear River, is listed on the National Register of Historic Places. An increasingly desirable retirement spot, Southport retains its village charm and character. Stately and distinctive homes, antiques stores, gift shops, and restaurants line streets that veer to accommodate ancient oak trees. The town, portrayed in Robert Ruark's novel *The Old Man and the Boy,* is

CloseUp

OPERATION BUMBLEBEE

TOPSAIL (PRONOUNCED *TOP-SUHL*) *was the first barrier island south of Bogue Inlet subject to commercial development. But before there was commerce, and definitely before there were tourists, there was a secret.*

The island, 26-mi long and only about ½-mi wide, is home to eight evenly spaced, reinforced-concrete towers. These lookouts are all that's left of Operation Bumblebee, a U.S. Navy rocket program that was the precursor to NASA. In the 1940s, Topsail, an isolated place that had experienced some military buildup during World War II, was selected as the top-secret site for the development and testing of defense missiles—the granddaddies of supersonic missiles.

These first rockets were put together in the large Assembly Building; they were then transferred via underground tunnels to a seaside launching pad that presently serves as a patio at the Jolly Roger Motel. Observers stationed in either the concrete watchtowers or safer underground bunkers would track the flight of the guided missiles and measure their speed. Between 1947 and 1948, some 200 two-stage rockets blasted out over the ocean. The experiments made Topsail as significant to jet flight as Kitty Hawk was to propeller flight.

Ultimately, salt air, humidity, and increased traffic within the 20-mi firing range did the project in. Many of the buildings and much of the equipment associated with the operation were donated or sold, and two years after the military moved out, Topsail Island had its first incorporated town, Surf City. You can find out more about Operation Bumblebee at the **Missiles & More Museum.** ✉ 720 Channel Blvd., off Rte. 50, Topsail Beach ☎ 910/328–8663 🎫 Free ⏲ Apr.–mid-Oct., Mon., Tues., and Thurs.–Sat. 2–4.

---

ideal for walking; it's also popular with moviemakers—*Crimes of the Heart* was filmed here.

If you're approaching the town from Kure Beach and Fort Fisher via U.S. 421, the **Southport–Fort Fisher Ferry,** a state-operated car ferry, provides a river ride between Old Federal Point at the tip of the spit and the mainland. Old Baldy Lighthouse, on Bald Head Island, is seen en route, as well as the Oak Island Lighthouse and the ruins of the Price's Creek Lighthouse—in fact, this is the only point in the United States where you can see three lighthouses at the same time. It's best to arrive early (30 minutes before ferry departure), as it's first-come, first-served. *☎ 910/458–3329 or 800/293–3779 🎫 $3 per car ⏲ Ferries run mid-Mar.–mid-Nov., daily every 45 min 6:15 AM–9:15 PM; mid-Nov.–mid-Mar., daily every 1½ hrs 6:15 AM–4:45 PM.*

Where to Stay & Eat

¢ ✕ **Trolly Stop.** An institution in the Cape Fear region (there are also locations in Wrightsville Beach, Carolina Beach, and Wilmington), this long, narrow hot dog joint is known for a unique selection of dogs, all with their own names. The North Carolina comes with chili, slaw, and mustard and the Surfer Dog is topped with bacon bits and cheese. Those who are more health conscious can get vegetarian and fat-free dogs. A pickle costs a quarter more. Sweet Italian sausage, drinks, and ice cream are also on the menu. ✉ *111 S. Howe St.* ☎ *910/457–7017* ▭ *No credit cards.*

★ **$$–$$$** **Bald Head Island Resort.** Reached by ferry from Southport, this private, self-contained, carless community complete with grocery store and restaurants has bleached-wood buildings and shingle cottages. Accommodations include fully equipped rental condos, villas, cottages, and B&Bs; a two-night minimum stay is required. You can explore the semitropical island on foot, by bicycle, or in a golf cart. Climb to the top of the lighthouse, watch the loggerhead turtles, or take a guided tour through the maritime forest. The ferry costs $15 per person round-trip and runs on the hour, 8–6 (except noon on weekdays). Advance reservations are necessary for the ferry and resort. ✉ *Bald Head Island, 28461* ☎ *910/457–5000, 800/432–7368, 910/457–5003 for ferry reservations* 🖷 *910/457–9232* 🌐 *www.baldheadisland.com* *195 condos, villas, and cottages; 25 rooms in 2 B&Bs* *5 restaurants, grocery, some kitchens, 18-hole golf course, 4 tennis courts, pool, boating, fishing, bicycles, croquet, babysitting, concierge, business services, no-smoking rooms* ▭ *AE, DC, MC, V* 🍴 *EP.*

Winnabow

⓳ *12 mi north of Southport; 18 mi southwest of Wilmington via U.S. 17.*

On your way along Route 133 between Southport and Wilmington, Winnabow is more of a crossroads than a town to visit; but there are gardens and a historic site, both near the Cape Fear River, worth seeing.

★ The house at **Orton Plantation Gardens** is not open to the public, but the 20 acres of beautiful, comprehensive gardens are great for strolling. The former rice plantation holds magnolias, ancient oaks, and all kinds of ornamental plants; the grounds are also a refuge for waterfowl. Thirty-five movies have had scenes shot here. ✉ *9149 Orton Rd. SE, off Rte. 133* ☎ *910/371–6851* 🌐 *www.ortongardens.com* *$9* ⏲ *Mar.–Aug., daily 8–6; Sept.–Nov., daily 10–5.*

At **Brunswick Town State Historic Site** you can explore the excavations of a colonial town; see Fort Anderson, a Civil War earthworks fort; and have a picnic. Special events include reenactments of Civil War encampments. ✉ *8884 St. Phillips Rd., off Rte. 133* ☎ *910/371–6613* *Free* ⏲ *Apr.–Oct., Mon.–Sat. 9–5, Sun. 1–5; Nov.–Mar., Tues.–Sat. 10–4, Sun. 1–4.*

THE NORTH CAROLINA COAST A TO Z

To research prices, get advice from other travelers, and book travel arrangements, visit www.fodors.com.

AIR TRAVEL

Outer Banks Airways provides charter service between the Dare County Regional Airport and major cities along the East Coast, as does Flightline Aviation, which flies into the First Flight depot, at the Wright Memorial in Kill Devil Hill. US Airways Express and Midway fly into Craven County Regional Airport in New Bern. US Airways, Atlantic Southeast Airlines, and Midway serve the Wilmington International Airport.

Carriers **Atlantic Southeast Airlines** ☎ 800/221-1212 🌐 www.flyasa.com. **Flightline Aviation** ☎ 800/916-3226 🌐 www.flightlineair.com. **Midway** ☎ 800/446-1392 🌐 www.midwayair.com. **Outer Banks Airways** ☎ 252/441-7677. **US Airways Express** ☎ 800/428-4322 🌐 www.usair.com.

AIRPORTS

The closest large, commercial airports to the Outer Banks are Raleigh-Durham, a 5-hour drive, and Norfolk International in Virginia, a 1½-hour drive. Craven County Regional Airport in New Bern has charter service and car rentals available. Wilmington International Airport serves the Cape Fear Coast

Airport Information **Craven County Regional Airport** ✉ U.S. 70, New Bern ☎ 252/638-8591. **Dare County Regional Airport** ✉ 410 Airport Rd., Manteo ☎ 252/473-2600 🌐 www.fly2mqi.com. **Norfolk International** ✉ 2200 Norview Ave. ☎ 757/857-3351 🌐 www.norfolkairport.com. **Wilmington International Airport** ✉ 1740 Airport Blvd. ☎ 910/341-4125 🌐 www.flyilm.com.

TRANSFERS Beach Cabs, based in Nags Head, runs 24-hour service from Norfolk to Ocracoke and towns in between; a ride to the Norfolk airport runs about $140. Coastal Cab serves the Outer Banks—from the southern shores down to Nags Head—and charges you $135 to get to the airport. Coastal Limo, which serves the entire 100 mi stretch of the Outer Banks, is quite a bargain: $68 for one or two people from Nags Head, Kill Devil Hills, or Kitty Hawk to the Norfolk airport. The Outer Banks Limousine Service, headquartered in Kill Devil Hills, serves the entire area and Norfolk International Airport and runs around the clock; getting to the airport costs about $125 from Nags Head.

Beach Cabs ☎ 252/441-2500 or 800/441-2503. **Coastal Cab** ☎ 252/449-8787. **Coastal Limo** ☎ 252/441-2262. **Outer Banks Limousine Service** ☎ 252/261-3133 or 800/828-5466.

BOAT & FERRY TRAVEL

Seagoing folks travel the Intracoastal Waterway through the Outer Banks and the Albemarle region. Boats may dock at nearly 150 marinas, including Elizabeth City, Manteo Waterfront Docks, and National Park Service Silver Lake Marina, in Ocracoke. From Ocracoke there are car ferries to Cedar Island and Swan Quarter on the mainland. You need to reserve the ferry by calling the terminal.

The Intracoastal Waterway provides access to many Central Coast destinations, including Beaufort, Morehead City, and Emerald Isle. Beaufort has plentiful anchorage and more than 35 marinas, including the Beaufort Town Docks and the Morehead City Yacht Basin. New Bern can be reached via the Neuse River from Pamlico Sound. Several marinas are available here, including the Sheraton Grand Marina. You can dock for the day (but not overnight) at the public docks of Union Point Park.

The Wilmington area has public marinas at Carolina Beach State Park and Wrightsville Beach and a number of hotels provide docking facilities for guests. A state-run car ferry connects Fort Fisher, south of Kure

Beach, with Southport on the coast. For information about the state-run ferry system and its schedules and costs, call the North Carolina Department of Transportation's ferry information line.

FARES & SCHEDULES

Boat & Ferry Information **Beaufort Town Docks** ☎ 252/728–2053. **Carolina Beach State Park** ☎ 910/458–7770. **Cedar Island Ferry Terminal** ☎ 252/225–3551 or 800/856–0343. **Elizabeth City** ☎ 252/338–2886. **Manteo Waterfront Docks** ☎ 252/473–3320. **Morehead City Yacht Basin** ☎ 252/726–6862. **National Park Service Silver Lake Marina** ☎ 252/928–5111. **North Carolina Department of Transportation Ferry Information** ☎ 800/293–3779. **Ocracoke Island Ferry Terminal** ☎ 252/928–3841 or 800/345–1665. **Sheraton Grand Marina** ☎ 252/638–3585. **Swan Quarter Ferry Terminal** ☎ 252/926–1111 or 800/773–1094. **Union Point Park** ☎ 252/636–4060. **Wrightsville Beach** ☎ 910/256–6666.

EMERGENCIES

The Healtheast/Outer Banks Medical Center, Beach Medical Care, and Outer Banks hospital all provide around the clock care or emergency services in the Outer Banks region. Carteret General Hospital in Morehead City, and Craven Regional Medical Center in New Bern handle emergencies on the Central Coast. For emergency medical attention in Wilmington contact the Cape Fear Memorial Hospital or the New Hanover Regional Medical Center, a trauma center.

Emergency Services **Ambulance, police** ☎ 911. **Coast Guard** ☎ 910/343–4881.

Hospitals **Beach Medical Care** ✉ 5200 N. Croatan Hwy., MM 1.5, Kitty Hawk ☎ 252/261–4187. **Cape Fear Memorial Hospital** ✉ 5301 Wrightsville Ave. Midtown, Wilmington ☎ 910/452–8100. **Carteret General Hospital** ✉ 3500 Arendell St., Morehead City ☎ 252/247–1616. **Craven Regional Medical Center** ✉ 2300 Neuse Blvd., New Bern ☎ 252/633–8111. **Healtheast/Outer Banks Medical Center** ✉ 2808 S. Croatan Hwy., Nags Head ☎ 252/441–7111. **New Hanover Regional Medical Center** ✉ 2131 S. 17th St., South Metro, Wilmington ☎ 910/343–7000. **Outer Banks Hospital** ✉ 4800 S. Croatan Hwy., Nags Head ☎ 252/449–4500.

LODGING

CAMPING

Camping is permitted in four designated areas along the Cape Hatteras National Seashore. These campgrounds have spaces for tents, trailers, and motor homes. All camping at Cape Lookout National Seashore is primitive, and allowed only from mid-April through mid-October. Be sure to take extra-long tent stakes for sand, and don't forget insect repellent. All sites are available on a first-come, first-served basis, except Ocracoke, where reservations are accepted. For information about private campgrounds contact the Dare County Tourist Bureau.

Cape Hatteras National Seashore ✉ 1401 National Park Dr., Manteo 27954 ☎ 252/473–2111 🌐 www.nps.gov. **Cape Lookout National Seashore** ✉ 131 Charles St., Harkers Island 28531 ☎ 252/728–2250 🌐 www.nps.gov. **Dare County Tourist Bureau** ☎ 252/473–2138 or 800/446–6262 🌐 www.outerbanks.org.

VACATION RENTALS

An increasingly popular choice in lodging is vacation rental, as properties are available to meet almost every taste and budget. Rentals are booked primarily through agencies, and there are scads of them. Midgett Realty, owned and operated by a family that's lived on the Outer Banks for generations, handles hundreds of properties from one end of Hat-

teras Island to the other. Intracoastal Realty, which represents places all along the Cape Feat coast, is another respected option.
Intracoastal Realty 605 Causeway Dr., Wrightsville Beach 28480 910/256-3780 or 800/346-2463 www.intracoastalrentals.com. **Midgett Realty** P.O. Box 250, Hatteras Village 27943 252/986-2841 or 800/527-2903 252/986-2745 www.midgettrealty.com.

SPORTS & THE OUTDOORS

FISHING Fishing, whether surf casting or deep-sea, is wonderful on the Outer Banks and beyond on the North Carolina Coast. You can fish from piers, board a charter boat, or head out in your own craft. You don't need a license for saltwater fishing. For fishing regulations all along the coast, call the North Carolina Division of Marine Fisheries.

The Atlantic Beach King Mackerel Tournament is held on the Central Coast in September, and one of the largest and oldest sportfishing contests, the Big Rock Blue Marlin Tournament, is held in June. Fishing piers are mostly on Bogue Banks and are closed in winter. Dozens of charter boats operate year-round. In New Bern bass-fishing tournaments are popular.

Four major fishing tournaments are held in Cape Fear, all with substantial prize money: the Cape Fear Marlin Tournament, the Wrightsville Beach King Mackerel Tournament, the East Coast Open King Mackerel Tournament, and the U.S. Open King Mackerel Tournament.
North Carolina Division of Marine Fisheries 252/726-7021.

TOURS

Kitty Hawk AeroTours leaves from the First Flight Airstrip or from Manteo for Kitty Hawk, Corolla, Cape Hatteras, Ocracoke, Portsmouth Island, and other areas along the Outer Banks. Tours take place from March through Labor Day.
Air Tours **Kitty Hawk AeroTours** Behind Wright Brothers Monument, U.S. 158, MM 8, Kill Devil Hills 252/441-4460.

TRAIN TRAVEL

Amtrak connects to Norfolk, Virginia, about 75 mi to the north of the Outer Banks, but it does not serve the North Carolina Coast.
Train Information **Amtrak** 800/872-7245 www.amtrak.com.

VISITOR INFORMATION

In the Outer Banks, Dare County Tourist Bureau operates three information centers: the Aycock Brown Welcome Center in Kitty Hawk; the smaller, seasonal Hatteras Island Welcome Center near Bodie Island; and the Outer Banks Welcome Center on Roanoke Island, in Manteo.

The National Park Service's group headquarters, at the Fort Raleigh National Historic Site in Manteo, has a 24-hour general information line about Cape Hatteras National Seashore, or you can write the superintendent. The National Park Service at the Cape Lookout National Seashore has information about visiting Cape Lookout.

The Carteret County Tourism Development Bureau operates two visitor centers on the Central coast: one in Morehead City and one on

Route 58 north of the Cameron Langston Bridge to Emerald Isle. Craven County Convention and Visitors Bureau has information about New Bern.

You can find out more about Wilmington and the Cape Fear Coast at the Cape Fear Coast Convention and Visitors Bureau. Southport is part of the area covered by the South Brunswick Islands Chamber of Commerce.

Tourist Information **Aycock Brown Welcome Center** ✉ U.S. 158, MM 1.25, Kitty Hawk 27949 ☎ 252/261-4644. **Cape Fear Coast Convention and Visitors Bureau** ✉ 24 N. 3rd St., Wilmington 28401 ☎ 910/341-4030 or 800/222-4757 🌐 www.cape-fear.nc.us. **Carteret County Tourism Development Bureau** ✉ 3409 Arendell St., Morehead City 28557 ☎ 800/786-6962 ✉ 263 Rte. 58, Swansboro 28584 ☎ 252/393-3100 🌐 www.sunnync.com. **Craven County Convention and Visitors Bureau** ✉ 314 S. Front St., New Bern 28560 ☎ 252/637-9400 or 800/437-5767 🌐 www.visitnewbern.com. **Dare County Tourist Bureau** 📫 704 S. U.S. 64/264, Box 399, Manteo 27954 ☎ 252/473-2138 or 800/446-6262 🌐 www.outerbanks.org. **Hatteras Island Welcome Center** ✉ Rte. 12, Buxton ☎ no phone. **National Park Service, Cape Lookout National Seashore** ✉ 131 Charles St., Harkers Island 28531 ☎ 252/728-2250 🌐 www.nps.gov. **National Park Service's Group Headquarters** ✉ 1401 National Park Dr., Manteo ☎ 252/473-2111 24 hrs 🌐 www.nps.gov. **National Park Service's superintendent** 📫 Rte. 1, Box 675, Manteo 27954. **Outer Banks Welcome Center on Roanoke Island** ✉ 1 Visitors Center Circle, Manteo 27954 ☎ 877/298-4373. **South Brunswick Islands Chamber of Commerce** 📫 4948 Main St., Box 1380, Shalotte 28459 ☎ 910/754-6644 or 800/426-6644 🌐 www.ncbrunswick.com.

THE PIEDMONT & THE SANDHILLS

2

By Lisa H. Towle

LINKING THE COASTAL PLAIN in the eastern third of North Carolina to the mountains in the western third is the Piedmont region in the central third of the state. The elevations here gradually rise from 300 to 1,500 feet above sea level. Gently rolling and well-rounded hills, long low ridges, meandering rivers, and large human-made lakes characterize this area, the most heavily developed region of the state.

Also known as the heartland, this area was once mostly farmland, but development has grown along with the region's major arteries, making the Piedmont a center of commerce, education, government, and manufacturing. For the sake of verbal convenience, North Carolinians group six of the area's urban centers into two threesomes: the Triad and the Triangle. The Triad is short for Greensboro, Winston-Salem, and High Point; the Triangle refers to the shape traced by Raleigh, Durham, and Chapel Hill, in whose center sits Research Triangle Park—a renowned complex of international companies and public and private research facilities. These urban centers have brought world-class museums, shopping, sophisticated restaurants, and professional sporting venues to the region. And one of the beauties of the Piedmont's cities—including Charlotte, which has the state's most dramatic skyline—is that they're characterized by canopies of hardwoods and pines. Beyond the cities, the Piedmont has 15 large state parks best experienced on foot or by water.

Southeast of the Triangle are the widely spread towns of the Sandhills, an area renowned for its golf courses. There are many horse farms here, to be sure, and equestrian activities, tennis, and even cricket tournaments are popular. But golf is king, and picturesque, secluded Pinehurst is the center of the kingdom. No less than the United Kingdom's St. Andrews Links Trust, responsible for the operation and maintenance of the granddaddy of all golf courses, has said, "Of all the great golf centers of the world, there is only one that comes close to sharing the ideals and aspirations of St. Andrews: Pinehurst."

Exploring the Sandhills & the Piedmont

Connecting the Atlantic Ocean in the east to the Appalachians in the west, as well as Virginia to South Carolina, is the Piedmont, North Carolina's prosperous urban and commercial core. Universities and colleges, sprawling medical facilities and scientific think tanks, and banking centers and government complexes call the heartland home. The region's major highways, Interstates 40, 85, and 95, are always crowded. But get on one of the numerous, scenic byways outside any of the three largest metropolitan areas—Charlotte/Mecklenburg County, the Triad (Greensboro, Winston-Salem, High Point), the Triangle (Raleigh, Durham, Chapel Hill)—and the soul of the Piedmont emerges. Leisurely journeys reveal small towns and farms, roadside produce stands, historic sites, inns and B&Bs, parks and forests, and waterways, including the reservoirs of the Pee Dee River. NASCAR races and the potters of Seagrove, whose work is on display in museums around the world, have helped make this region famous.

The Sandhills, a golf-centered region of pine forests rooted in sandy soil, are about 1½ hours southeast of the Triangle. This area is traversed by U.S. 1.

About the Restaurants

In North Carolina's Piedmont cities, risotto and dim sum are as common as grits and corn bread. Ethnic specialties of all kinds are available, as well as contemporary and eclectic-American cuisine. Restaurants in urban areas are now just as likely to carry North Carolina wines as European and California labels. In some smaller towns, however, alcoholic beverages are not served. The Sandhills region, too, has a growing number of sophisticated restaurants. But you can still find plenty of good old-fashioned Southern cooking throughout the region, including fried chicken, Brunswick stew, ham, biscuits, and fruit cobblers. Chopped or sliced pork barbecue is a regional specialty. And it's still customary in most places to offer free endless refills of iced tea (make sure to specify "sweet" or "unsweet") and soda. With a few notable exceptions, dressy casual is about as formal as it gets at any dining establishment.

WHAT IT COSTS

$$$$	$$$	$$	$	¢
over $22	$16–$22	$11–$16	$7–$11	under $7

Prices are for a main course at dinner, excluding sales tax of 7%–7.5%.

About the Hotels

Accommodations in the Piedmont include everything from economy motels to sprawling convention hotels to bed-and-breakfasts in lovely historic districts. Most major chains are represented, and some hotels offer great weekend packages, including theater tickets. During the biannual (April and October) furniture market in High Point, when tens of thousands of people descend on the city, hotel rooms and rental cars are almost impossible to find for miles around. May is the primary graduation time for all of the Triangle's colleges and universities; hotels are booked, in some cases, years in advance.

Most lodging options in the Sandhills fall into the resort category; pricing plans and options are multitudinous and can be confusing. Many of the prices quoted are for golf packages. However, there are some chain motels in Southern Pines and Aberdeen, as well numerous historic B&Bs in the area. The high season for golf, which brings the most expensive lodging rates, is from mid-March to mid-May and again from mid-September to mid-November.

WHAT IT COSTS

$$$$	$$$	$$	$	¢
over $220	$160–$220	$110–$160	$70–$110	under $70

Prices are for two people in a standard double room in high season, excluding service charges and 7%–13% tax.

2

Numbers in the text correspond to numbers in the margin and on the North Carolina Heartland, Downtown Raleigh, Durham, and Charlotte maps.

If you have
3 days

Devote your first two days to an exploration of the Triangle. Begin the first day in **Durham** 13–18 with a stroll through the West Campus of Duke University, with its Gothic Revival architecture. Visit the university's **Sarah P. Duke Gardens** 14, where you can eat a light lunch at the Terrace Café. Next head south via U.S. 15/501 and Franklin Street to the Morehead Planetarium in **Chapel Hill** 19. In this college town you can also visit the campus of the 200-plus-year-old University of North Carolina. Franklin Street, running along the northern edge of the campus, has loads of shopping and dining opportunities. Spend the second day in the state capital, **Raleigh** 1–10, exploring its museums of history, art, and science. On the third day, head south on U.S. 1 toward Moore County and the Sandhills area. You can find antiques shops and wildly painted barns and farm equipment in Cameron, north of **Southern Pines** 38. In Southern Pines and the nearby town of **Pinehurst** 39, enjoy the manicured, green serenity of golf courses and horse farms. If you plan on overnighting here, you can find lodging in either Southern Pines or Pinehurst.

If you have
5 days

Follow the three-day itinerary above and then add the pleasures of the Triad. On your fourth day, travel west from Pinehurst on Route 211 until you connect with I–73/74. This will take you north into Greensboro, from which you should follow I–40 west to **Winston-Salem** 21. Plan to spend the entire day at historic Old Salem, with its restored buildings, museums, and shops. Begin the fifth day by taking a guided tour of Blandwood Mansion in downtown **Greensboro** 20. From there, stroll through Greensboro Cultural Center at Festival Park, where you can also stop for lunch. Then head to **High Point** 22 for the evening. Among the sights you can see here before nightfall is the world's largest chest of drawers.

If you have
7 days

With a week at your disposal, you can do a reasonably full tour of the Piedmont and Sandhills, starting with the five-day itinerary above. On the sixth day head for **Charlotte** 23–37, where you should concentrate on the city center: a walking tour of Uptown, a visit to **Discovery Place** 27, and a stop by the Mint **Museum of Craft + Design** 28. Once you're done here, drive or take a taxi to the funky **North Davidson Arts District** 30, also known as NoDa, where you can browse a gallery or two before lingering over a meal and a drink. If you're feeling adventurous on the seventh day, end your tour with a bang—a visit to **Lowe's Motor Speedway** 37, where you may be able to watch a race or even take a driving lesson. Located nearby are the shops and in some cases museums of various racing teams.

Timing

North Carolina's Piedmont and Sandhills regions shine particularly in the spring (April and May) and fall (September and October), when the weather is most temperate and the trees and flowers burst with color. Because of the high concentration of schools in the Piedmont, graduation season (from the middle to the end of May) is a busy one for restaurants and hotels. This is also true for the furniture-market time in April and October; hotel rooms and dining tables in the Triad are at a premium during this period. In the Sandhills, the high season for golfers is mid-March to mid-May and again from mid-September to mid-November.

THE TRIANGLE

The cities of Raleigh, Durham, and Chapel Hill are known collectively as the Triangle, with Raleigh to the east, Durham to the north, Chapel Hill to the west, and, in the center, Research Triangle Park—a renowned complex of corporations and public and private research facilities set in 6,800 acres of lake-dotted pineland that attracts scientists, academics, and businesspeople from all over the world. Throughout the Triangle, an area that's been characterized as "trees, tees, and PhDs," politics and basketball are always hot topics. The NCAA basketball championship has traded hands among the area's three major universities.

Raleigh

104 mi east of Winston-Salem; 143 mi northeast of Charlotte.

Raleigh is Old South and New South, down-home and upscale, all in one. Named for Sir Walter Raleigh, who established the first English colony on the coast in 1585, it's the state capital and the biggest of the Triangle's three cities. Many of the state's largest and best museums are here, as are North Carolina State University and six other universities and colleges.

a good walk

Downtown the streets are laid out in an orderly grid with the state capitol as the hub. Most downtown Raleigh attractions are state government buildings, historic buildings, and museums and are free to the public. Begin with a walk through the **Oakwood Historic District** 1 ▸. Next, stroll west to Blount Street and the **Executive Mansion** 2, the home of governors since 1891.

Follow Jones Street west past Wilmington Street to visit the **State Legislative Building** 3. Cross Jones Street to Bicentennial Plaza, flanked by the **North Carolina Museum of Natural Sciences** 4, to the west, and the **North Carolina Museum of History** 5, to the east. Continue south across Edenton Street to Capitol Square and the **State Capitol** 6.

Starting just south of the capitol across Morgan Street and continuing for four blocks is the **Fayetteville Street Mall** 7, a pedestrians-only walkway. From the mall walk two blocks east on Hargett Street to **Exploris** 8, a children's museum. One block south is the **City Market** 9, a revital-

Antiquing Whether you are an antiques expert or need a copy of *Antiquing for Dummies,* the beauty of following the antiques trail through the Piedmont is that the journey is as enjoyable as the finds. In Charlotte, the first weekend of the month you can visit the Metrolina Expo, where more than 2,000 antiques and collectibles dealers gather with their wares. If you're on a quest for antiques, it may be worth your while to travel east via I–40 through the bucolic countryside of Iredell and Davidson counties and on to the Triad and Triangle. Start southwest of Winston-Salem at Mocksville and Farmstead Antiques. Continue east on I–40 to downtown Greensboro, where you can visit the antiques shops on South Elm Street and the surrounding area. Next follow I–40 to Raleigh, where antiques stores are clustered on increasingly trendy upper Glenwood Avenue. Still farther east is the small city of Wilson, which with more than 30 antiques shops makes good on its claim to be the largest antiques market on the East Coast.

Golfing In the beginning was Pinehurst, the Sandhills village brought to fame by James Walker Tufts, whose desire to better his health and that of others led to the building of a health resort and ultimately a golf course. The area's topography, pine-scented air, and gentle climate encouraged the creation of more and more courses. Today, there are 70 golf courses within a 40-mi radius of Pinehurst. From Aberdeen to Vass, there's something for every skill level and budget every week of the year. Golfing isn't a way of life for you, you say? You're more spectator than participant? Well, don't be quick to discount the experience of the golf vibe. There's no denying the visceral attraction of the manicured greens, the trees and the lakes, even the architecture of the clubhouses. The elegance and peace you'll find may well be worth the trip.

---

ized area between Blount and Person streets. Just south of the market are the studios and galleries of **Artspace** ⑩, at the corner of Blount and Davie streets.

TIMING You'll need several hours just to hit the sights of this walk and even more time if you're the kind of person who tends to get hooked on museums.

What to See

⑩ **Artspace.** A private, nonprofit visual-arts center adjacent to the Moore Square art district, Artspace offers open studios, exhibits, and galleries. The gift shop showcases the work of the resident artists, who are happy to talk to you about their work. ✉ *201 E. Davie St., Downtown* ☎ *919/821–2787* 🌐 *www.artspacenc.org* 🎟 *Free* ⏲ *Tues.–Sat. 10–6.*

⑨ **City Market.** Specialty shops, art galleries, restaurants, a comedy club, and a small farmers' market make up this revitalized area with cobblestone streets. The free Entertainment Trolley shuttles between the market and other downtown restaurant and nightlife locations from 6:40 PM to 12:40 AM Thursday through Saturday. ✉ *Martin and Blount Sts.*

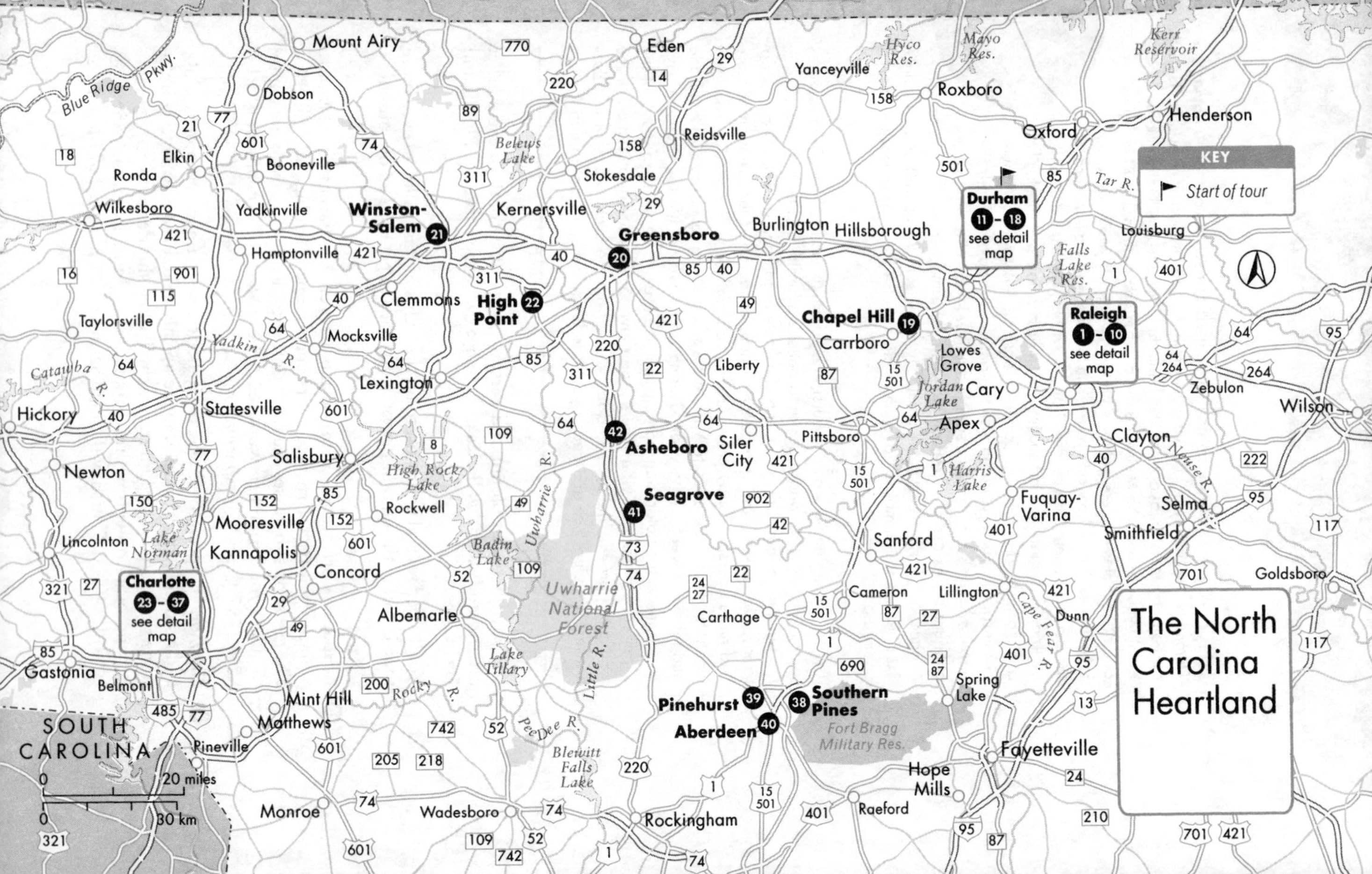
The North Carolina Heartland
KEY
Start of tour
Durham 11-18 see detail map
Raleigh 1-10 see detail map
Charlotte 23-37 see detail map
Chapel Hill 19
Greensboro 20
Winston-Salem 21
High Point 22
Asheboro 42
Seagrove 41
Pinehurst 39
Southern Pines 38
Aberdeen 40
Mount Airy
Eden
Yanceyville
Roxboro
Oxford
Henderson
Louisburg
Dobson
Reidsville
Stokesdale
Kernersville
Burlington
Hillsborough
Elkin
Ronda
Booneville
Wilkesboro
Yadkinville
Hamptonville
Clemmons
Mocksville
Lexington
Taylorsville
Hickory
Statesville
Salisbury
Newton
Mooresville
Kannapolis
Concord
Lincolnton
Rockwell
Albemarle
Gastonia
Belmont
Mint Hill
Matthews
Pineville
Monroe
Wadesboro
Rockingham
Liberty
Siler City
Pittsboro
Carrboro
Lowes Grove
Cary
Apex
Zebulon
Wilson
Clayton
Selma
Smithfield
Goldsboro
Fuquay-Varina
Sanford
Lillington
Dunn
Cameron
Carthage
Spring Lake
Fayetteville
Hope Mills
Raeford
Blue Ridge Pkwy.
Belews Lake
Hyco Res.
Mayo Res.
Kerr Reservoir
Tar R.
Falls Lake Res.
Jordan Lake
Harris Lake
Neuse R.
Cape Fear R.
Yadkin R.
Catawba R.
High Rock Lake
Badin Lake
Uwharrie R.
Uwharrie National Forest
Little R.
Lake Tillary
Rocky R.
Pee Dee R.
Blewitt Falls Lake
Lake Norman
Fort Bragg Military Res.
SOUTH CAROLINA
0 20 miles
0 30 km

at Moore Sq., Downtown ☎ *919/821–1350* 🌐 *www.citymarket.citysearch.com* 🕓 *Most stores Mon.–Sat. 10–5:30; most restaurants Mon.–Sat. 7 AM–1 AM, Sun. 11:30–10.*

2 **Executive Mansion.** Since 1891, this brick Queen Anne cottage–style structure with elaborate gingerbread trim and manicured lawns has been the home of the state's governors. Tour hours vary; check with the Capital Area Visitor Center on Blount Street. ✉ *200 N. Blount St., Downtown* ☎ *919/733–3456* 🌐 *www.ah.dcr.state.nc.us/sections/capitol* 🎟 *Free.*

8 **Exploris.** This 84,000-square-foot architectural showplace (the marble wall is a dazzler) is a learning center that stands apart from most other children's museums. It emphasizes a global perspective, as opposed to specific health and natural science topics. Exhibits explore language, culture, geography, trade, and communications. There's also an IMAX theater. ✉ *201 E. Hargett St., Downtown* ☎ *919/834–4040* 🌐 *www.exploris.org* 🎟 *Exhibits $9.95, exhibits and IMAX theater $13.95* 🕓 *Tues.–Sat. 9–5, Sun. noon–5.*

7 **Fayetteville Street Mall.** Extending from the State Capitol south to the Raleigh Civic and Convention Center, this pedestrian walkway provides entrance to several high-rise office buildings. The shops and restaurants in the area cater to the weekday business crowd.

5 **North Carolina Museum of History.** Founded in 1898, the museum is now in a state-of-the-art facility on Bicentennial Plaza. Artifacts, audiovisual programs, and interactive exhibits bring the state's history to life. Exhibits include the "N. C. Sports Hall of Fame," "N. C. Folklife," and "Militaria, Politics, and Society." ✉ *5 E. Edenton St., Downtown* ☎ *919/715–0200* 🌐 *www.ncmuseumofhistory.org* 🎟 *Free* 🕓 *Tues.–Sat. 9–5, Sun. noon–5.*

★ 4 **North Carolina Museum of Natural Sciences.** At 200,000 square feet, this museum is the largest of its kind in the Southeast. Permanent exhibits and dioramas celebrate the incredible diversity of species in the state's three regions—the coast, piedmont, and mountains. There are enough live animals and insects—including butterflies, hummingbirds, snakes, and a two-toed sloth—to qualify as a small zoo. One signature exhibit contains rare whale skeletons. The pièce de résistance, however, is the "Terror of the South" exhibit, featuring the dinosaur skeleton of "Acro," a giant carnivore that lived in the region 110 million years ago. ✉ *11 W. Jones St., Downtown* ☎ *919/733–7450 or 877/462–8724* 🌐 *www.naturalsciences.org* 🎟 *Free* 🕓 *Mon.–Sat. 9–5, Sun. noon–5.*

1 **Oakwood Historic District.** Several architectural styles—though the Victorian structures are especially notable—can be found in this tree-shaded 19th-century neighborhood. Brochures for self-guided walking tours of the area, which encompasses 20 blocks bordered by Person, Edenton, Franklin, and Watauga/Linden streets, are available at the Capital Area Visitor Center, on Blount Street. Adjacent to historic Oakwood is **Oakwood Cemetery** (✉ 701 Oakwood Ave., Downtown ☎ 919/832–6077). Established in 1869, it's the resting place of 2,800 Confederate soldiers,

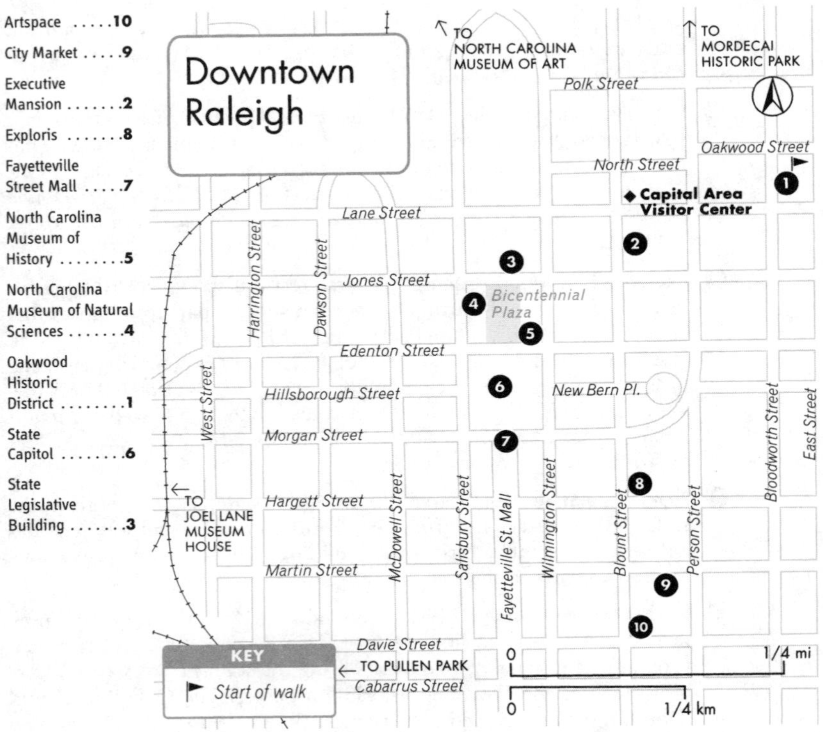

Civil War generals, governors, and numerous U.S. senators. Free maps are available at the cemetery office.

❻ **State Capitol.** This beautifully preserved example of Greek Revival architecture from 1840 once housed all the functions of state government. Today it's part museum, part executive offices. The capitol contains, under the domed rotunda, a copy of Antonio Canova's statue of George Washington depicted as a Roman general with tunic, tight-fitting body armor, and a short cape. ✉ *Capitol Sq., 1 E. Edenton St., Downtown* ☎ *919/733–4994* 🌐 *www.ah.dcr.state.nc.us/sections/capitol* 🎟 *Free* ⏲ *Weekdays 8–5, Sat. 10–4, Sun. 1–4.*

❸ **State Legislative Building.** One block north of the state capitol, this complex hums with lawmakers and lobbyists when the legislature is in session. It's fun to watch from the gallery. A free guided tour is also available through the Capital Area Visitor Center. ✉ *Salisbury and Jones Sts., Downtown* ☎ *919/733–7928* 🌐 *www.ncga.state.nc.us* 🎟 *Free* ⏲ *Weekdays 8–5, Sat. 9–5, Sun. 1–5.*

Other Area Attractions

The city is spread out, so a car is necessary for visits to museums and parks beyond downtown.

off the beaten path

AVA GARDNER MUSEUM – In the hometown of the legendary movie star is this museum with an extensive collection of memorabilia tracing her life from childhood on the farm to Hollywood glory days. It's about 30 mi southeast of Raleigh in downtown Smithfield. *325 E. Market St., Smithfield 919/934–5830 www.avagardner.org $5 Mon.–Sat. 9–5, Sun. 2–5.*

Joel Lane Museum House. Dating to the 1760s, the oldest dwelling in Raleigh was the home of Joel Lane, known as the "father of Raleigh" because he sold the state the property on which the capital city grew. Costumed docents tell the story and show the restored house and beautiful period gardens. *720 W. Hargett St., at St. Mary's St., Downtown 919/833–3431 $3 Mar.–mid-Dec., Tues.–Fri. 10–2, Sat. 1–4.*

Mordecai Historic Park. You can see the Mordecai family's plantation home and other structures, including the house where President Andrew Johnson was born, in 1808. One-hour guided tours begin every hour. You can also board a trolley here for a narrated 45-minute tour of historic Raleigh. *1 Mimosa St., at Wake Forest Rd., Downtown 919/834–4844 Guided house tour $6, trolley tour $8, combo tour $11 Guided house tour Tues.–Sat. 10–3, trolley tour Mar.–Dec., Sat. 11–2.*

★ **North Carolina Museum of Art** (NCMA). The NCMA, on the west side of Raleigh, houses 5,000 years of artistic heritage, including one of the nation's largest collections of Jewish ceremonial art. Other exhibits range from ancient Egyptian times to the present, from the Old World to the New. The museum hosts touring exhibitions of works by such artists as Caravaggio and Rodin. The in-house restaurant, **Blue Ridge,** looks out on mammoth modernistic sculptures that, when viewed from above, spell the words PICTURE THIS. *2110 Blue Ridge Rd., Northwest/Airport 919/839–6262, 919/833–3548 restaurant www.ncartmuseum.org Free Wed.–Sat. 9–5, Sun. 10–5; tours Wed.–Sun. at 1:30.*

Pullen Park. In summer, crowds come to picnic and ride the 1911 Dentzel carousel, the train, and paddleboats. You can swim here in a large, public, indoor aquatic center or outdoor pool, play tennis, explore an arts-and-crafts center, or, if the timing is right, see a play at the Theater in the Park. *520 Ashe Ave., near North Carolina State University, University 919/831–6468 or 919/831–6640 www.raleigh-nc.org/parks&rec/pullenpark.asp Fees vary Apr.–Oct., daily 10–dusk; Mar. and Nov., Fri. and Sat. 10–5, Sun. 1–5.*

Sports & the Outdoors

FISHING Jordan Lake, a 13,900-acre reservoir in Apex, west of Raleigh, is a favorite fishing spot. Others are Lake Wheeler, in Raleigh, and the Falls Lake State Recreation Area, in Wake Forest (north of Raleigh).

GOLF There are 20 golf courses, either public or semiprivate, within a half-hour drive of downtown Raleigh. **Cheviot Hills Golf Course** (7301 Capital Blvd., North Hills 919/850–9983) is a par-71, 18-hole championship course. **Devil's Ridge Golf Club** (5107 Links Land Dr., Holly Springs 919/557–6100), about 15 mi southwest of Raleigh, is a challenging par-72, 18-hole course with large, rolling greens. **Lochmere Golf**

Club (✉ 2511 Kildaire Farm Rd., Cary ☎ 919/851–0611) provides a friendly environment, good value, and a challenge with 18 holes at par 71. A 30-minute drive southeast of Raleigh is the **Neuse Golf Club** (✉ 918 Birkdale Dr., Clayton ☎ 919/550–0550), an attractive par-72, 18-hole course on the banks of the Neuse River.

Where to Stay & Eat

$$$$ ✕ **Angus Barn.** A huge rustic barn houses this famous Raleigh institution. The dimly lighted, always-busy restaurant is known for its steaks, baby-back ribs, prime rib, and fresh seafood, as well as its clubby Wild Turkey Lounge. The astonishing wine-and-beer list is 35 pages long. The oversize desserts are freshly made; on your way out, you can purchase pies at a small store near the front door. Reservations aren't accepted for Saturday dinner. ✉ *U.S. 70W (Glenwood Ave.) near Aviation Pkwy., Northwest/Airport* ☎ *919/781–2444* ▭ *AE, D, DC, MC, V* ⊙ *No lunch.*

$$$$ ✕ **The Cosmopolitan.** Taupe walls, recessed lighting, strategically placed orchids to soften the abstract art: this restaurant a few miles west of Raleigh whispers understated style. Chef-owner John Toler, who named his restaurant for the cocktail, has a lot of fun experimenting with contemporary menus that scream flavors. One of his creations is mahimahi served over red beans, wilted baby spinach, sweet crawfish tails, and andouille. Another is sticky toffee pudding with vanilla chantilly and pecan brittle. ✉ *103 Edinburgh Dr., Cary* ☎ *919/380–1322* ▭ *AE, D, MC, V* ⊙ *Closed Sun. No lunch.*

★ **$$$$** ✕ **Second Empire.** Wood paneling, crown molding and high ceilings, floral arrangements, muted lighting, and well-spaced tables make for a calming and elegant dining experience in a restored historic house. The menu, which changes monthly, has a regional flavor; the food is best described as art on a plate, intricately styled so that colors, textures, and tastes fuse. For an entrée you might get sea-scallop ceviche and baby-snow-pea salsa or marinated porterhouse pork chops with country-style collards and mustard-and-thyme spaetzle. A wood-and-brass tavern on the lower level has a simpler and less expensive menu. ✉ *300 Hillsborough St., Downtown* ☎ *919/829–3663* ▭ *AE, MC, V* ⊙ *Closed Sun. No lunch.*

$$$–$$$$ ✕ **Enoteca Vin.** As the combination French-Italian name indicates, wine takes center stage at this sophisticated, yet unpretentious restaurant. The sleek interior—in the former ice-cream freezer of the old Pine State Creamery—consists of warm maple, stainless steel, exposed brick, and leather club chairs. The eclectic menu emphasizes local (flounder, goat cheese) and seasonal (okra, peaches) organic ingredients, complemented by food-friendly wines from all over the world. There are even wines that can be paired with an ever-changing Sunday brunch menu that might include greens with marinated plum tomatoes, avocado, smoked bacon, and crispy tortillas, or shrimp and cheddar-cheese grits. ✉ *410 Glenwood Ave., Suite 350, Downtown* ☎ *919/834–3070* ▭ *AE, D, MC, V* ⊙ *Closed Mon.*

$$–$$$ ✕ **Irregardless Café.** The contemporary seasonal menu at this café mixes up meat-based and vegetarian dishes: vegetable-stuffed samosas with mango chutney, for example, and beef medallions served with a mushroom-and-pinot-noir sauce. Salads are amply portioned, and the breads,

TAKING YOUR 'CUE

WANT A GUARANTEED *one-word conversation starter in any gathering of North Carolinians? Say "barbecue." John Shelton Reed, a Southerner, a sociologist, and a former director of the Odum Institute for Research in Social Science at the University of North Carolina-Chapel Hill, has called barbecue "the most southern meal of all." But just as there are a myriad of southern accents, there are many types of barbecue. Understanding the distinctions between them is key to understanding a culinary and cultural phenomenon in North Carolina, where barbecue begins with pork (banish all thoughts of beef!) and is not so much a verb as a noun (that is, a dish or an event known as a pig-pickin').*

The state's barbecue tradition, variously linked to the cooking techniques of Native Americans, African slaves, and Scottish-Irish settlers, has been immortalized in song, prose, poetry, and the electronic media. So revered is the moist and tangy meat that it has inspired place names such as Barbecue Presbyterian Church, which rises beside Barbecue Creek in the Piedmont's Harnett County. Everyone from politicians to firefighters to high school bands offer barbecue at fund-raisers, and it's often the featured food at receptions and reunions of all sorts. Versions of it are served in eating establishments ranging from top-drawer to lunch counter, though many argue the most authentic barbecue is found in small-town cinder-block restaurants with on-site smokehouses.

Barbecue even has its own annual festivals. Two of the biggest in North Carolina's heartland are ***Hillsborough Hog Day*** *in June and the* ***Barbecue Festival*** *in Lexington in October. Tens of thousands of lovers of all things porcine (not to mention a good party) attend these blowouts, which feature everything from arts and crafts and live entertainment to sporting events and contests: best-dressed pig, hog hollering, and, of course, barbecue cook-offs.*

And right there is the, ah, meat of the matter: taste. The method of cooking the meat and the ingredients of the sauce that coats it spark a passion that cuts across lines of age, class, and race. One hundred years or more of tradition have dictated that either whole hogs or shoulders be slow-roasted over a wood or charcoal fire to imbue the meat with an appropriate smoky flavor. Over the past few decades, however, an increasing number of barbecuers have switched to cleaner propane flames.

The real fault line, though, is geography. In eastern North Carolina (that's east of I–95), the entire hog is cooked and the meat is "pulled" (off the bone) or coarsely chopped and then heavily seasoned with a vinegar-and-pepper-based sauce. This concoction, whose exact ingredients are jealously guarded by each owner, has a definite kick. West of I–85, the meat, which usually includes just the pork shoulders, can be sliced or chopped. It's then mixed with a somewhat sweeter sauce made of vinegar, ketchup, brown sugar, and perhaps Worcestershire sauce. Serving as a buffer between these two regions is the Research Triangle area, where you'll find both types of barbecue.

Oftentimes, fried or barbecued chicken is available in deference to those who don't eat pork. Either meat can be served with various side dishes, including boiled potatoes, greens such as collards, and Brunswick stew, but some items are essential to a barbecue plate: coleslaw, hush puppies (fried cornmeal, a staple of Southern meals since colonial days), and sweetened iced tea.

No matter where North Carolinians stand on the barbecue debate, both sides agree that the line of good taste has got be drawn somewhere. In this case, it's at the mustardy sauce used in the state just south of the border.

soups, and yogurts are homemade. Live music every night, dancing on Saturday evening, and brunch on Sunday spice things up here, but the blond wood, brightly hued contemporary art, sunlit dining areas, and well-spaced tables all underscore one theme: relaxation. The restaurant is midway between North Carolina State University and downtown. ✉ *901 W. Morgan St., University* ☎ *919/833–8898* ▭ *AE, D, DC, MC, V* ⏲ *No lunch Sat. No dinner Sun.*

$$–$$$ ✕ **Margaux's.** Eclectic is the key word to describe the international cuisine served at this North Raleigh fixture. A blackboard lists the diverse specials, such as red-chili fettuccine with goat cheese, lamb with coconut-curry sauce, or grilled-shrimp-and-crawfish tostada with roasted corn, black beans, and salsa *verde.* A stone fireplace warms the room in winter, and modern sculpture stands and hangs here, there, and everywhere. ✉ *Brennan Station Shopping Center, 8111 Creedmoor Rd., North Hills* ☎ *919/846–9846* ▭ *DC, MC, V.*

$–$$ ✕ **La Shish.** It can take a while to eat in this small storefront café, where the art, recorded music, and grocery items for sale all announce Greek and Lebanese food is served here. That's because everything, with the exception of the spanakopita, is made in-house—even the rosewater-infused lemonade. It's all worth the wait. The husband-and-wife team of Nawwaf and Dayan Said along with a couple of assistants turn out savory marinated kebabs, falafel, plates of hummus drizzled with peppery olive oil, salads, and *shawarmas* (thinly sliced marinated meat), plus such desserts as baklava and tiramisu. ✉ *908 N.E. Maynard Rd., Cary* ☎ *919/388–8330* ▭ *MC, V.*

¢–$ ✕ **Big Ed's City Market Restaurant.** A must for breakfast or lunch, Big Ed's is filled with antique farm implements and the owner's political memorabilia, including pictures of presidential candidates who have stopped at this landmark. Every Saturday morning a Dixieland band plays. Come here for down-home cooking, and make sure you indulge in the biscuits. ✉ *220 Wolfe St., City Market, Downtown* ☎ *919/836–9909* ✍ *Reservations not accepted* ▭ *No credit cards* ⏲ *Closed Sun. No dinner.*

$$$ 🏨 **Raleigh Marriott Crabtree Valley.** Fresh floral arrangements adorn the elegant public rooms of one of the city's most luxurious hotels. Soft colors, Asian floral prints, and dark cherrywood furnishings decorate the guest rooms. You can dine at the Crabtree Grill and at Quinn's, a lounge where light fare and drinks are served daily. ✉ *4500 Marriott Dr., U.S. 70 near Crabtree Valley Mall, University, 27612* ☎ *919/781–7000 or 800/228–9290* 📠 *919/781–3059* 🌐 *www.marriotthotels.com/rdunc* 🛏 *375 rooms, 4 suites* ☝ *Restaurant, in-room data ports, cable TV, indoor-outdoor pool, health club, hot tub, bar, lounge, laundry facilities, laundry service, concierge, business services, meeting room, airport shuttle* ▭ *AE, D, DC, MC, V* 🍽 *EP.*

$$–$$$ 🏨 **William Thomas House.** On the edge of downtown Raleigh a few blocks from the Executive Mansion is this stately but not stuffy Victorian B&B. Rooms, named for family members, are traditionally and elegantly decorated and have oversize windows and 12-foot ceilings. The richly hued common rooms are filled with heirlooms, including a grand piano from 1863, and antique china. ✉ *530 N. Blount St., Downtown, 27604* ☎ *919/755–9400 or 800/653–3466* 📠 *919/755–3966* *www.williamthomashouse.com* *4 rooms* *Fans, in-room data ports, refrigerators, library* *AE, D, DC, MC, V* *BP.*

$–$$$ **The Oakwood Inn.** A lavender lady, this 1871 Victorian B&B, one of the original homes built in what is now the Oakwood Historic District, is listed on the National Register of Historic Places as the Raynor-Stronach House. The individually decorated rooms have working fireplaces and are painted everything from deep red to forest green to creamy yellow. Rosewood antiques fill one room; another has a queen-size sleigh bed as its centerpiece. Afternoon tea is served on the front porch overlooking a yard filled with irises and star magnolias. Dinner and theater packages are available. *411 N. Bloodworth St., Downtown, 27604* *919/832–9712 or 800/267–9712* *919/836–9263* *www.oakwoodinnbb.com* *6 rooms* *In-room data ports, cable TV* *AE, D, MC, V* *BP.*

$$ **Hampton Inn & Suites.** In the southwest corner of Cary, right over the Raleigh line, this hotel is just minutes from the RBC Center (a sports and entertainment arena), the state fairgrounds, and North Carolina State University. Rooms are typical of the chain. You'll need a car to get to restaurants. *111 Hampton Woods La., off I–40, Cary 27607* *919/233–1798 or 800/426–7866* *919/854–1166* *www.hampton-inn.com* *126 rooms* *In-room data ports, kitchenettes, refrigerators, cable TV, pool, exercise equipment, babysitting, laundry service, business services, meeting room* *AE, D, DC, MC, V* *EP.*

$–$$ **North Raleigh Hilton.** This is a favorite spot for corporate meetings. The standard rooms are done in mauve and green, with traditional furniture and prints. Lofton's Cafe is open for breakfast, and the Skybox Grill & Bar has a sports-bar atmosphere. *3415 Wake Forest Rd., North Hills, 27609* *919/872–2323 or 800/445–8667* *919/876–0890* *www.hilton.com* *331 rooms, 7 suites* *Restaurant, room service, cable TV, indoor pool, exercise equipment, 2 bars, Internet, business services, meeting room, airport shuttle* *AE, D, DC, MC, V* *EP.*

CAMPING **Clemmons State Forest** (2411 Old Garner Rd., West Clayton 919/553–5651), near Clayton, has campsites. You can camp at **Jordan Lake** (280 State Park Rd., Apex 919/362–0586), which is between Apex and Pittsboro. The **North Carolina State Fairgrounds** (1025 Blue Ridge Rd. 919/821–7400) allow RV camping only. The 5,439-acre **William B. Umstead State Park** (8801 Glenwood Ave. 919/571–4170), between Raleigh and Durham, has campsites.

Nightlife & the Arts

THE ARTS **Alltel Pavilion at Walnut Creek** (3801 Rock Quarry Rd., Southeast Metro 919/831–6666), known as "the Creek," accommodates 20,000. Headliners appear spring through mid-fall and cover the musical spectrum. This is the most attended amphitheater on the East Coast.

The **BTI Center for the Performing Arts** (1 E. South St., Downtown) is a multivenue complex. The 2,300-seat **Memorial Auditorium** (919/831–6061) is home base for the North Carolina Theatre, which stages productions that have been on Broadway and off-Broadway. The 1,700-seat **Meymandi Concert Hall** (919/733–2750) hosts the North Carolina Symphony. The 600-seat **Fletcher Opera Theater** (919/831–6011) provides a showcase for the nationally acclaimed Carolina Ballet and productions of the Opera Company of North Carolina. The 170-seat **Kennedy Theater** (☎ 919/831–6011) stages shows of smaller, sometimes alternative theater groups.

The **North Carolina State University Arts Programs** (☎ 919/515–1100) include the Center Stage series, host to professional touring productions and world-class artists. All arts program performances are open to the public.

NIGHTLIFE The **Berkeley Café** (✉ 217 W. Martin St., Downtown ☎ 919/821–0777) is one of the hottest gathering places in the Triangle for live music: rock and roll, R&B, and blues. **Cappers** (✉ 4216 Six Forks Rd., North Hills ☎ 919/787–8963), a restaurant and tavern, is *the* spot for jazz and blues. **Charlie Goodnight's Comedy Club** (✉ 861 W. Morgan St., University ☎ 919/828–5233) combines dinner with a night of laughs. Alumni include Jay Leno, Jerry Seinfeld, and Elaine Boosler.

Part restaurant, part music-listening room, part bar, the smoke-free **Six String Café and Music Hall** (✉ MacGregor Village Center, U.S. 64W and U.S. 1S, Cary ☎ 919/469–3667) hosts performances of original acoustic music every night along with some stand-up comedy. **Tir na nog** (✉ 218 S. Blount St., Downtown ☎ 919/833–7795) has Irish entertainers and Murphy's Irish Amber, Guinness, and even whiskey on tap.

Shopping

SHOPPING CENTERS **Cameron Village Shopping Center** (✉ 1900 Cameron St., Downtown), Raleigh's first shopping center, contains specialty shops and boutiques and restaurants. **Prime Outlets** (✉ Exit 284 off I–40, Airport Blvd., Morrisville, between Raleigh and Durham ☎ 919/380–8700) is decidedly un-mall-like with its wooden floors and greenery. The area's only factory outlet center has more than 40 stores, including Off 5th Saks Fifth Avenue and Nine West. Among the shops at **Triangle Town Center** (✉ Capital Blvd. and I–540, North Raleigh ☎ 919/792–2222) are Saks Fifth Avenue, Williams-Sonoma, and Pottery Barn Kids.

ART & ANTIQUES Several antiques shops are clustered on upper Glenwood Avenue. Another good place for antiques is the town of Wilson, about 45 mi east of Raleigh, which has more than 30 antiques shops and claims to be the largest antiques market on the East Coast. Inside the Arts Council building, the **Wilson Visitors Bureau** (✉ 124 Nash St. SW, Wilson ☎ 252/243–8440 or 800/497–7398), closed Sunday, has maps of the town's antiques stores as well as information on the stores' hours, which vary.

At **Artspace** (✉ 201 E. Davie St., Downtown ☎ 919/821–2787) you can visit artists' studios and purchase their works. **Boone** (✉ 2014 U.S. 301 S, Wilson ☎ 252/237–1508), an important fixture of Wilson's antiques scene, is a huge store with thousands of pieces of antique furniture and accessories, including garden and architectural items. The merchandise changes daily at **Carolina Antique Mall** (✉ 1900 Cameron St. ☎ 919/833–8227), in Cameron Village, where 75 dealers stock the floor. **City Market** (✉ Martin and Blount Sts. at Moore Sq., Downtown ☎ 919/821–1350) is a revitalized downtown shopping area with shops and art galleries.

FOOD Open year-round, the 60-acre **State Farmers' Market** (✉ 1201 Agriculture St., Lake Wheeler Rd. and I–40, Southwest Metro ☎ 919/733–7417) includes a garden center, a seafood restaurant, and a down-home restaurant.

Durham

23 mi northwest of Raleigh.

Durham has more than a dozen historic sites, plus three of North Carolina's 22 National Historic Landmarks. Having long since shed its tobacco-town image, Durham is now known as the City of Medicine for the medical and research centers at prestigious Duke University. With more than 20,000 employees, Duke is not only the largest employer in Durham but also one of the largest in the state. Warehouses and mills around the city have been converted to chic shops, offices, and condos.

a good tour

Durham has some areas appropriate for walking, such as Duke University's campus. However, it's best to drive to most places. Start your tour 1½ mi south of downtown, exiting the Durham Freeway (Route 147) at Fayetteville Street, along which you'll find the **North Carolina Central University Art Museum** 11 and the **Hayti Heritage Center** 12.

The next stop is about 3 mi away. Return to the Durham Freeway and continue northwest to the exit at Chapel Hill Street. Follow Chapel Hill west into the West Campus of **Duke University,** which includes the **Duke Chapel** 13 and the **Sarah P. Duke Gardens** 14. Return to Chapel Hill Street and take it past the Durham Freeway to Duke Street and turn left. Head north toward downtown, stopping at **Brightleaf Square** 15. From here it's a short drive north to the **North Carolina Museum of Life and Science** 16. Continue north to reach the **Duke Homestead** 17. Conclude your tour farther north at **West Point on the Eno** 18.

TIMING To really appreciate these sights you should plan on spending a day or more on this tour.

What to See

15 **Brightleaf Square.** Named for the kind of tobacco once manufactured in the old warehouses here, Brightleaf Square, with its flowering courtyard, striking turn-of-the-20th-century architecture, upscale shops, and restaurants, is the shining star of a downtown revitalization effort. The square anchors a larger arts-and-entertainment district, which includes the Carolina Theatre and the Durham Bulls Athletic Park. ✉ *905 W. Main St., Duke University* ☎ *919/682–9229.*

★ 13 **Duke Chapel.** A Gothic-style gem built in the early 1930s, this chapel is the centerpiece of the Duke University campus. It was modeled after England's Canterbury Cathedral and has 77 stained-glass windows and a 210-foot-tall bell tower. ✉ *Chapel Dr., West Campus, Duke University* ☎ *919/684–2572* 🌐 *www.chapel.duke.edu* ⏲ *Aug.–May, daily 8 AM–10 PM; June and July, daily 8–8.*

17 **Duke Homestead.** The Duke family empire began at this homestead, now a State Historic Site, in the 1860s with tobacco. You can tour the

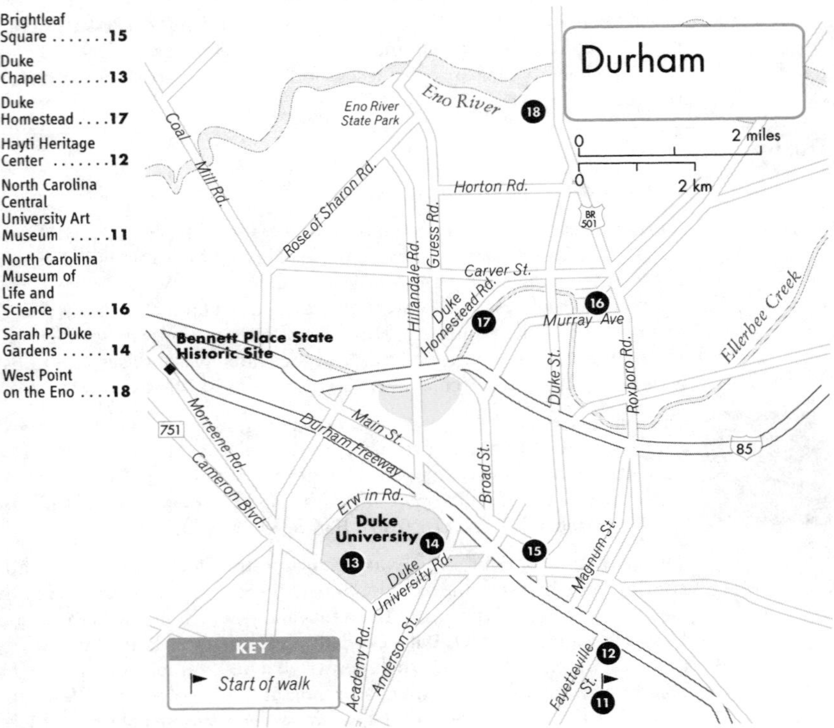

small wood-frame factories, pack house, and curing barn; guides demonstrate early manufacturing processes. The visitor center exhibits early tobacco advertising. ✉ *2828 Duke Homestead Rd., Downtown* ☎ *919/477–5498* 🎫 *Free* 🕓 *Tues.–Sat. 10–4.*

Duke University. A stroll along the wide tree-lined streets of this campus is a lovely way to spend a few hours. In all, the university encompasses 525 acres in the heart of Durham, with Georgian and Gothic Revival architecture. The East Campus, off Broad Street, has Georgian architecture and the **Duke University Museum of Art** (✉ Buchanan Blvd. at Trinity Ave., Duke University ☎ 919/684–5135), which displays African, American, European, and Latin American artwork from various eras. Note that the museum will close after May 2005 but is scheduled to reopen in October 2005 in a new state-of-the-art building (Anderson St. at Campus Dr.) as the Nasher Museum of Art. The West Campus is dominated by ⇨ **Duke Chapel,** on Chapel Drive, and late-Gothic-style buildings. The sprawling medical school is on Erwin Road. A bus system and bike paths connect the campuses. 🌐 *www.duke.edu.*

12 **Hayti Heritage Center.** One of Durham's oldest ecclesiastical structures, St. Joseph's A.M.E. Church, houses this center for African-American art and culture. In addition to exhibitions of traditional and contemporary

art by local, regional, and national artists, the center hosts special events such as the Black Diaspora Film Festival. ✉ *804 Old Fayetteville St., Downtown* ☎ *919/683–1709 or 800/845–9835* ⊕ *www.hayti.org* *Free; fees for special events vary* ⏲ *Weekdays 9–7:30, Sat. 9–3, Sun. hrs vary.*

11 **North Carolina Central University Art Museum.** African-American art is showcased at the nation's first publicly supported liberal arts college (opened in 1910) for African-Americans. The permanent collection includes 19th-century masterpieces and 20th-century works created during the Harlem Renaissance; also on display is artwork by students and local artists. ✉ *1801 Fayetteville St., South/NCCU* ☎ *919/560–6211* ⊕ *www.nccu.edu/artmuseum* *Free* ⏲ *Tues.–Fri. 9–5, Sun. 2–5.*

16 **North Carolina Museum of Life and Science.** Here you can create a tornado, encounter dinosaurs on a prehistoric trail, view NASA artifacts, and ride a train through a wildlife sanctuary. The nature center contains such native North Carolina animals as flying squirrels. The three-story **Magic Wings Butterfly House** has a tropical-butterfly conservatory and includes the Insectarium, where you can see and hear live insects under high magnification and amplification. ✉ *433 Murray Ave., off I–85, Downtown* ☎ *919/220–5429* ⊕ *www.ncmls.org* *Museum $8.50, train ride $1.50* ⏲ *Mon.–Sat. 10–5, Sun. noon–5.*

★ 14 **Sarah P. Duke Gardens.** A wisteria-draped gazebo and a Japanese garden with a lily pond teeming with fat goldfish are some of the highlights of these 55 acres of gardens. More than 5 mi of pathways meander through formal plantings and woodlands. The **Terrace Café** serves lunch Tuesday–Sunday. ✉ *Main entrance on Anderson St., West Campus, Duke University* ☎ *919/684–8861* ⊕ *www.hr.duke.edu/dukegardens* *Free* ⏲ *Daily 8–dusk.*

18 **West Point on the Eno.** Included in a city park on the banks of the Eno River are a 19th-century blacksmith shop, an 1880s home, and a restored mill dating from 1778. It's the site of an annual three-day folklife festival surrounding the Fourth of July; musicians, artists, and craftspeople come from around the region. ✉ *5101 N. Roxboro Rd. (U.S. 501N), North Metro* ☎ *919/471–1623* *Free* ⏲ *Daily 8–sunset; historic buildings weekends only 1–5.*

Where to Stay & Eat

$$$$ Fodor's Choice ★ **Magnolia Grill.** This bistro is consistently one of the area's finest, most innovative places to dine. The food created by chef-owners Ben and Karen Barker is as eye-catching as the art on the walls. On the daily menu, which always maintains a Southern sensibility, you may find spicy green-tomato soup with crab and country ham or striped bass with oyster stew. ✉ *1002 9th St., Downtown* ☎ *919/286–3609* *MC, V* ⏲ *Closed Sun. and Mon. No lunch.*

$$$–$$$$ **Kemp's Seafood House.** Everything about Kemp's is big. The wooden interior was built to resemble a boat hull, and the platters of shrimp, stuffed crab, and flounder are as big as boats. The seafood is cooked in a variety of ways, but the specialty of the house is calabash style, meaning lightly battered and fried, but not greasy. Entrées are meant to be shared, assuming you haven't filled up on hush puppies and tea be-

forehand. Show up early on weekends or be prepared for a lengthy wait. ✉ *115 Page Point Circle, Southeast Metro* ☎ *919/957–7155* *Reservations not accepted* ▭ *AE, D, MC, V.*

$$–$$$$ ✕ **Café Parizäde.** Soft lighting, white tablecloths, and an enclosed courtyard are among the inviting aspects of this Erwin Square bistro. One particularly fine appetizer is fried calamari with jalapeño-tomato salsa; popular entrées include fettuccine with fresh salmon and black-pepper dill cream, sesame pasta with scallops, and roast duck with fresh vegetables. ✉ *2200 W. Main St., Downtown* ☎ *919/286–9712* ▭ *AE, D, DC, MC, V* ⏲ *No lunch weekends.*

$–$$$ ✕ **George's Garage.** This restaurant in the heart of happening 9th Street defies pigeonholing. It's part nouvelle restaurant, part prepared-food market, part bar (sushi and drinks), and part bakery—all in a cavernous, pumped-up room. Fresh fish and Mediterranean fare are specialties, but you can also dine on grilled chicken, pork, lamb, and beef. Live entertainment and dancing make this a popular after-hours hangout, and there's brunch every Sunday. ✉ *737 9th St., Downtown* ☎ *919/286–1431* ▭ *AE, D, DC, MC, V.*

★ **$$$–$$$$** ✕ **Washington Duke Inn & Golf Club.** On the campus of Duke University, this luxurious hotel overlooks a Robert Trent Jones–designed golf course. Rooms evoke the feeling of an English country inn, with floral bedspreads and creamy striped wall coverings. On display in the public rooms are memorabilia belonging to the Duke family, for whom the hotel and university are named. At the quietly sophisticated Fairview restaurant ($$$$), you can dine on poached tiger shrimp and mango cocktail sauce followed by prosciutto-wrapped monkfish with goat-cheese grits. ✉ *3001 Cameron Blvd., Duke University, 27706* ☎ *919/490–0999 or 800/443–3853* 🖷 *919/688–0105* 🌐 *www.washingtondukeinn.com* *164 rooms, 7 suites* *Restaurant, room service, in-room data ports, cable TV, driving range, 18-hole golf course, putting green, 12 tennis courts, pool, health club, bar, laundry service, concierge, business services, meeting room, airport shuttle* ▭ *AE, D, DC, MC, V.*

$$–$$$ **Arrowhead Inn.** Brick chimneys and tall Doric columns distinguish this B&B in an 18th-century white-clapboard farmhouse. Antiques, heritage plants, fireplaces, and a log cabin in the garden create a cozy environment. ✉ *106 Mason Rd., North Metro, 27712* ☎ *919/477–8430 or 800/528–2207* 🖷 *919/471–9538* 🌐 *www.arrowheadinn.com* *9 rooms, 2 suites* *Picnic area, Internet, business services* ▭ *AE, D, DC, MC, V* 🍽 *BP.*

$$ **Blooming Garden Inn.** With its yellow exterior, this B&B is literally and figuratively a bright spot in the Holloway Historic District. Inside, the inn explodes with color and warmth, thanks to exuberant hosts Dolly and Frank Pokrass. Breakfast might be walnut crêpes with ricotta cheese and warm raspberry sauce. A sister B&B, the Victorian Holly House, across the street, accommodates extended stays. ✉ *513 Holloway St., Downtown, 27701* ☎ *919/687–0801 or 888/687–0801* 🖷 *919/688–1401* 🌐 *www.bloominggardeninn.com* *4 rooms, 2 suites* ▭ *AE, D, DC, MC, V* 🍽 *BP.*

$–$$ **Durham Marriott at the Civic Center.** Given this nine-floor hotel's excellent location in the downtown art-and-entertainment district, atop the Durham Civic Center, the rates here are very reasonable. Several fountains run through the lobby entrance, and the rooms are spacious and well appointed. Guests have access to a health club one block away. ✉ *201 Foster St., Downtown, 27701* ☎ *919/768–6000* 🖷 *919/768–6037* 🌐 *www.marriotthotels.com* *185 rooms, 2 suites* *Restaurant, room service, in-room data ports, in-room safes, cable TV, exercise equipment, bar, dry cleaning, laundry service, concierge floor, business services, free parking* 💳 *AE, D, DC, MC, V* 🍽 *EP.*

Nightlife & the Arts

THE ARTS The 1926 beaux arts **Carolina Theatre** (✉ 309 W. Morgan St., Downtown ☎ 919/560–3030) hosts orchestras, operas, dance troupes, and programs for children, as well as the North Carolina Jewish Film Festival (February), the Doubletake Documentary Film Festival (May), and the North Carolina Gay and Lesbian Film Festival (August).

Most of the performances at the internationally known **American Dance Festival** (☎ 919/684–6402), held annually in June and July, take place at the **Page Auditorium** and **Reynolds Theater** (✉ West Campus, Duke University ☎ 919/684–4444). The old **Durham Athletic Park** (428 Morris St., Downtown) and **St. Joseph's Church** (804 Old Fayetteville St., Downtown), at the Hayti Heritage Center, are the venues for the two-day **Bull Durham Blues Festival** (☎ 919/683–1709), presented early each September.

NIGHTLIFE The **James Joyce Irish Pub** (✉ 912 W. Main St., Downtown ☎ 919/683–3022) serves food and drinks to go along with sports on the televisions, including rugby matches and Duke University basketball. Live traditional-Irish music on Friday and Saturday starts at 10 PM.

Shopping

SHOPPING CENTERS **Brightleaf Square** (✉ 905 W. Main St., Downtown ☎ 919/682–9229) is an upscale shopping-and-entertainment complex housed in old tobacco warehouses. Durham's **9th Street** has funky shops and restaurants. The **Streets of Southpoint mall** (✉ 6910 Fayetteville Rd., off I–40, Southeast ☎ 919/572–8808) dominates Durham's shopping scene with its village look, restaurants, movie theater, and trendy stores, including Nordstrom and Restoration Hardware.

CRAFTS **One World Market** (✉ 1918 Perry St., Duke University ☎ 919/286–2457) carries unique, affordable gifts. One goal of the store is to provide increased self-employment for low-income crafters from around the world.

FOOD **Fowler's** (✉ 112 S. Duke St., Downtown ☎ 919/683–2555) stocks exotic spices, wines, fresh meats and seafood, European chocolates, teas and coffees, and more. Customized gift baskets can be shipped all over the country.

Chapel Hill

19 *28 mi northwest of Raleigh, 12 mi southwest of Durham.*

Chapel Hill may be the smallest city in the Triangle, but its reputation as a seat of learning—and of liberalism—looms large. This is the home of the nation's first state university, the University of North Carolina (UNC), opened to students in 1795. Despite the large number of students and retirees here, Chapel Hill retains the feel of a quiet, tree-shaded village.

Morehead Planetarium, where the original Apollo astronauts and many since have trained, is one of the largest in the country. You can learn about the constellations and take in laser-light shows. ✉ *250 E. Franklin St., University* ☎ *919/962–1236, 919/549–6863 for show information* 🌐 *www.moreheadplanetarium.org* 🎫 *$4.75* ⏲ *Mon.–Wed. 12:30–5, Thurs.–Sat. 10–5 and 6:30–9:30, Sun. 12:30–5; call ahead for show times.*

★ **Franklin Street,** in the heart of downtown Chapel Hill, is lined with bookstores, clothing boutiques, restaurants and coffee shops, and a movie theater.

Franklin Street runs along the northern edge of the **University of North Carolina** campus, which is filled with oak-shaded courtyards and stately old buildings. The **Louis Round Wilson Library** (✉ South St., University ☎ 919/962–0114), opened in 1929, houses the largest single collection of state literature in the nation. The library's **North Carolina Collection Gallery** (☎ 919/962–1172) exhibits rare books, photos, and oil portraits. Several historic rooms, such as the Walter Raleigh Room, highlight topics on the state's history.

The university's **Ackland Art Museum** showcases some of the Southeast's strongest collections of art from India, plus Western art, including old-master paintings and sculptures. The museum is now seeking to build its collection of 20th-century modern art. ✉ *Columbia and Franklin Sts., University* ☎ *919/406–9837* 🌐 *www.ackland.org* 🎫 *Free* ⏲ *Wed.–Sat. 10–5, Sun. 1–5.*

The **ArtsCenter** has exhibits, offers classes of all kinds for children, and hosts dance, theater, and music events for adults. ✉ *300G E. Main St., Carrboro, 2 mi west of Chapel Hill* ☎ *919/929–2787* 🌐 *www.artscenterlive.com.*

The **North Carolina Botanical Garden,** south of downtown via U.S. 15/501 Bypass, has the largest collection of native plants in the Southeast. Nature trails wind through a 300-acre piedmont forest. The herb garden and carnivorous-plant collection are impressive. There are frequent plant sales. ✉ *Old Mason Farm Rd., South Metro* ☎ *919/962–0522* 🌐 *www.ncbg.unc.edu* 🎫 *Free* ⏲ *Weekdays 8–5, Sat. 10–6, Sun. 1–6.*

Where to Stay & Eat

$$$$ ✕ **La Residence.** In a historic house with highly polished wood floors, butter-yellow walls, and a minimalist decorating scheme, La Rez, as it's known to locals, produces consistently excellent regional and seasonal foods with a classic French spin. For example, North Carolina mountain trout is wrapped in pancetta and served with lemon beurre blanc and roasted potatoes. The wine list is extensive. The patio off the main dining area resembles a Southern cottage garden; it's heated in winter. ✉ *202 W. Rosemary St., Downtown* ☎ *919/967–2506* 💳 *AE, D, MC, V* ⏲ *No lunch.*

$$–$$$ **Crook's Corner.** This small, often noisy restaurant is an exemplar of Southern chic. The menu, which changes often, highlights regional specialties such as snapper with mint, pecans, and oranges; hot-pepper jelly; crab gumbo; and buttermilk pie. A wall of bamboo and a waterfall fountain make the patio a delightful alfresco experience. Look for the faded pink pig atop the building. *610 W. Franklin St., Downtown 919/929–7643 AE, D, DC, MC, V No lunch.*

$$–$$$ **The Weathervane Café.** Tucked into A Southern Season, an expansive fine-foods shop, the café borrows heavily from the store's inventory for such dishes as maple-mustard-glazed salmon and goat-cheese risotto. There's plenty of comfortable seating around the open kitchen, but the spacious courtyard, filled with plants and fountains, is what people stand in line for, particularly for Sunday brunch: French toast stuffed with mascarpone and strawberries, or poached eggs and crab meat on a buttermilk biscuit with asparagus, hollandaise sauce, and grilled sea scallops. There's live jazz weekday evenings and Sunday 11–2. *Eastgate Shopping Center, 201 S. Estes Dr. (Hwy. 15/501 at University Mall), North Metro 919/929–9466 AE, D, MC, V.*

$–$$ **Mama Dip's Country Kitchen.** Mildred Edna Cotton Council (aka Mama Dip) is just about as well known in this town as another tall, gregarious Chapel Hillian, Michael Jordan. That's because she and her restaurant, which serves authentic home-style Southern meals in a roomy but simple setting, have been on the scene since the early '60s. Everything from chicken and dumplings, ribs, and country ham to fish, beef, salads, a mess of fresh vegetables, and melt-in-your-mouth buttermilk biscuits appear on the lengthy menu. *408 W. Rosemary St., Downtown 919/942–5837 MC, V.*

★ **$$$–$$$$** **Fearrington House.** A member of the prestigious Relais & Châteaux group, this country inn is on a 200-year-old farm that has been remade into a residential community, complete with small shops, resembling a country village. The village mascots, the "Oreo cows" (black on the ends, snow white in the middle), roam the pasture at the entrance. Antiques, English pine, and oversize tubs furnish the inn's modern guest rooms, which overlook a courtyard, gardens, and a pasture. The prix-fixe restaurant ($$$$) serves dressed-up regional food, such as collard-pecan-pesto-stuffed chicken breast with Hoop cheddar grits, for dinner. *2000 Fearrington Village Center, Pittsboro, 8 mi south of Chapel Hill on U.S. 15/501, 27312 919/542–2121 919/542–4202 www.fearringtonhouse.com 29 rooms, 2 suites 2 restaurants, 2 tennis courts, pool, croquet, business services, meeting room AE, MC, V BP.*

$$$ **Siena Hotel.** Sam and Susan Longiotti's love for Siena, Italy, has carried over to their posh European-style hotel. The lobby and rooms have imported carved-wood furniture, along with fabrics and artwork that conjure the Italian Renaissance. The public areas are filled with plush furniture grouped for conversation. Tuscan cuisine is the hallmark of Il Palio Ristorante ($$$–$$$$). You won't be hurried here, which is a good thing because it takes a while just to get through the antipasto while you anticipate entrées such as *filetto di branzino*—prosciutto-wrapped black grouper filled with greens and served in a saffron broth. *1505*

E. Franklin St., North Metro, 27514 ☎ 919/929–4000 or 800/223–7379 🖷 919/968–8527 🌐 www.sienahotel.com ⇨ 68 rooms, 12 suites ♁ Restaurant, picnic area, room service, in-room data ports, in-room VCRs, bar, dry cleaning, laundry service, concierge, business services, meeting room, airport shuttle ▭ AE, DC, MC, V 🍽 BP.

$$–$$$ **Sheraton Chapel Hill.** The look of the guest rooms here differs a bit from other area hotels, as they're done in a modern, Scandinavian style, with fitted bedding and sleek furniture, including work desks. The marble lobby has a clean, spare look as well. Almost all of the rooms overlook pine-dotted grounds. This property, with its outdoor garden, is conveniently located on U.S. 15/501 at the far edge of the University of North Carolina campus; it's easy access to Durham and Raleigh. ✉ *1 Europa Dr., University, 27514 ☎ 919/968–4900 or 800/325–3535 🖷 919/929–8170 🌐 www.sheratonchapelhill.com ⇨ 168 rooms, 4 suites ♁ Restaurant, room service, some in-room data ports, pool, exercise equipment, 2 bars, Internet, business services, meeting rooms, airport shuttle ▭ AE, D, DC, MC, V 🍽 EP.*

Nightlife & the Arts

THE ARTS The **Dean E. Smith Center** (✉ Skipper Bowles Dr., on the UNC campus, University ☎ 919/962–7777) hosts not only UNC men's basketball games but also special events and concerts. The **Playmakers Repertory Company** (✉ Country Club Dr., on the UNC campus, University ☎ 919/962–7529), a nonprofit professional theater company, performs six plays annually (September–May) at the Paul Green Theatre.

NIGHTLIFE The Chapel Hill area is the place to hear live rock and alternative bands. **Cat's Cradle** (✉ 300 E. Main St., Carrboro ☎ 919/967–9053) is smoky and dark and presents entertainment nightly. The **West End Wine Bar** (✉ 450 W. Franklin St., Downtown ☎ 919/967–7599) attracts professionals and postgraduates with its comprehensive wine list (more than 80 vintages by the glass), dinner menu, rooftop patio, and urbane sensibility.

Shopping

SHOPPING CENTERS Minutes from downtown, the lively **Eastgate Shopping Center** (✉ between E. Franklin St. and U.S. 15/501, North Metro) sells everything from antiques to wine. **Fearrington Village,** a planned community 8 mi south of Chapel Hill on U.S. 15/501 in Pittsboro, has upscale shops selling art, garden items, handmade jewelry, and more. **Franklin Street** in Chapel Hill has a wonderful collection of shops, including bookstores, art galleries, crafts shops, and clothing stores.

BOOKS At the independent **McIntyre's Fine Books and Bookends** (✉ Fearrington Village, U.S. 15/501, Pittsboro ☎ 919/542–3030) you can read by the fire in one of the cozy rooms. It has extensive collections of travel and gardening books.

FOOD **A Southern Season** (✉ Eastgate Shopping Center, 201 S. Estes Dr., Hwy. 15/501 at University Mall, North Metro ☎ 919/929–9466 or 800/253–3663) stocks a dazzling variety of cookware, books, wine, and treats, including barbecue sauces, peanuts, and hams. The adjoining Weathervane Café has indoor and outdoor dining.

THE TRIAD

Although they share geography and the major arteries of the region, and claim rich histories as well as institutions of higher learning, the Triad's leading cities have very distinct personalities. Greensboro, to the east, bustles as a center of commerce. Smaller Winston-Salem, to the west, may catch you by surprise with its eclectic arts scene. High Point, to the south, has managed to fuse the simplicity of Quaker forebears with its role as a world-class furniture market.

2

Greensboro

 *96 mi northeast of Charlotte; 26 mi east of Winston-Salem; 58 mi west of Durham.*

With more than 200,000 citizens, Greensboro is the largest population center in the Triad, and thanks to spacious convention facilities, it's an increasingly popular destination for business travelers. Yet this city, named in honor of General Nathanael Greene, a Revolutionary War hero, takes pride in its role in American history and has taken great pains to preserve and showcase the sights of past eras.

Outside of Old Greensborough and the downtown historic district, walking is not a comfortable sightseeing option. To tour the grand historic homes, glimpse monuments to famous native sons and daughters—including former first lady Dolley Madison, journalist Edward R. Murrow, short-story writer O. Henry—or visit one of the many recreation areas, you'll need a car.

Guilford Courthouse National Military Park, the nation's first Revolutionary War park, established in 1917, has monuments, military memorabilia, and more than 200 acres with wooded hiking trails. It memorializes one of the earliest events in the area's recorded history and a pivotal moment in the life of the colonies. On March 15, 1781, the Battle of Guilford Courthouse so weakened British troops that they surrendered seven months later at Yorktown. Today many families use the 3 mi of foot trails. ✉ *2332 New Garden Rd., Northwest Metro* ☎ *336/288–1776* 🌐 *www.nps.gov/guco* 🎟 *Free* ⏲ *Daily 8:30–5.*

Tannenbaum Historic Park, a hands-on history experience near Guilford Courthouse National Military Park, draws you into the life of early settlers. Free guided tours are available, and costumed reenactors are present for special events such as living-history weekends. There are exhibits in the **Colonial Heritage Center** and the restored **1778 Hoskins House,** and a blacksmith shop and barn are also on the property. The park has one of the most outstanding collections of original colonial settlement maps in the country. ✉ *2200 New Garden Rd., Northwest Metro* ☎ *336/545–5315* 🎟 *Free* ⏲ *Tues.–Sat. 9–5.*

You can roam through a dinosaur gallery, learn about gems and minerals, and see the lemurs, snakes, and amphibians at the **Natural Science Center of Greensboro.** A planetarium, a petting zoo, and a herpetarium are also on the premises. ✉ *4301 Lawndale Dr., adjacent to Country*

Park, Northwest Metro ☎ 336/288–3769 Science Center $6, planetarium $2; prices subject to change for special exhibits and events Science Center Mon.–Sat. 9–5, Sun. 12:30–5; petting zoo Mon.–Sat. 10–4:30, Sun. 12:30–4:30.

The **Greensboro Historical Museum,** in a Romanesque 1892 church, has exhibits about Greensboro's own O. Henry and Dolley Madison, as well as one about the Woolworth sit-in, which launched the civil rights movement's struggle to desegregate Southern eating establishments. Behind the museum are the graves of several Revolutionary War soldiers. ✉ *130 Summit Ave., Downtown* ☎ *336/373–2043* *www.greensborohistory.org* *Free* *Tues.–Sat. 10–5, Sun. 2–5.*

Greensboro Cultural Center at Festival Park, an architectural showplace, houses 15 visual- and performing-arts organizations, four art galleries, rehearsal halls, a sculpture garden, a restaurant with outdoor café-style seating, and an outdoor amphitheater. **ArtQuest,** developed by educators and artists, was North Carolina's first permanent interactive children's art gallery. ✉ *200 N. Davie St., Downtown* ☎ *336/373–2712* *Free; ArtQuest $4* *Weekdays 8 AM–10 PM, Sat. 9–5, Sun. 2–5.*

Exhibits and activities at the **Greensboro Children's Museum** are designed for children under 12. They can tour an airplane cockpit with an interactive screen, conduct an orchestra in the music room, or learn about buildings in the construction zone. ✉ *220 N. Church St., Downtown* ☎ *336/574–2898* *www.gcmuseum.com* *$6* *Early Sept.–late May, Tues.–Sat. 9–5, Sun. 1–5; late May–early Sept., Mon.–Sat. 9–5, Sun. 1–5.*

Elm Street, with its turn-of-the-20th-century architecture, is the heart of **Old Greensborough** (✉ 100 block of N. Elm St. to 600 block of S. Elm St., with portions of several other streets, Downtown), which is listed on the National Register of Historic Places. Stop by the offices of **Downtown Greensboro, Inc.** (✉ 122 N. Elm St., Downtown ☎ 336/379–0060) to collect your shopping guide and self-guided tour map.

In Old Greensborough, the elegant **Blandwood Mansion,** home of former governor John Motley Morehead, is considered the prototype of the Italian-villa architecture that swept the country during the mid-19th century. Noted architect Alexander Jackson Davis designed the house, which has a stucco exterior and towers and still contains many of its original furnishings. ✉ *447 W. Washington St., Downtown* ☎ *336/272–5003* *www.blandwood.org* *$5* *Tours Feb.–Dec., Tues.–Sat. 11–2, Sun. 2–5; last tour begins 30 min before closing.*

The **Weatherspoon Art Museum,** on the campus of the University of North Carolina–Greensboro, consists of six galleries and a sculpture courtyard. It is nationally recognized both for its permanent collection, which includes lithographs and bronzes by Henri Matisse, and for its changing exhibitions of 20th-century American art. ✉ *Tate and Spring Garden Sts., University* ☎ *336/334–5770* *web.uncg.edu/wag/root* *Free* *Tues., Wed., and Fri. 10–5, Thurs. 10–9, weekends 1–5.*

off the beaten path

CHARLOTTE HAWKINS BROWN MEMORIAL STATE HISTORIC SITE – On the site of the Palmer Institute, 10 mi east of Greensboro, this memorial honors the African-American woman who founded the school in 1902. Before closing in 1971, this accredited preparatory school for African-Americans was recognized as one of the country's best and had expanded to more than 350 acres of land. A visitor center and a gift shop are on the premises. ✉ *6136 Burlington Rd., Sedalia, off I–85, Exit 135* ☎ *336/449–4846* 🌐 *www.chbfoundation.org* 🎫 *Free* ⏲ *Apr.–Oct., Mon.–Sat. 9–5; Nov.–Mar., weekdays 10–4.*

2

Sports & the Outdoors

GOLF Golfers can choose from among 27 public courses and four driving ranges. **Bryan Park and Golf Club** (✉ 6275 Bryan Park Rd., Browns Summit ☎ 336/375–2200) is a highly regarded 18-hole, par-72 course 6 mi north of Greensboro. The **Grandover Resort/Grandover Golf Club** (✉ 1000 Club Rd., South Metro ☎ 336/294–1800 or 800/472–6301) has two 18-hole, par-72 courses. The **Greensboro National Golf Club** (✉ 330 Niblick Dr., Summerfield ☎ 336/342–1113), 15 minutes north of Greensboro, is an 18-hole, par-72 course.

The PGA's **Greater Greensboro Chrysler Classic** (✉ U.S. 421S, Southeast Metro ☎ 336/379–1570) is held each April at the Forest Oaks Country Club.

HIKING The **Bog Garden** (✉ Hobbs Rd. and Starmount Farms Dr., Northwest Metro ☎ 336/373–2199) has an elevated wooden walkway through a swampy area with more than 8,000 individually labeled trees, shrubs, ferns, and wildflowers. There are walking trails and an exercise course at the 120-acre **Oka T. Hester Park** (✉ 910 Ailanthus St., South Metro ☎ 336/373–2937).

Where to Stay & Eat

$$$–$$$$ ✕ **Gate City Chop House.** This place has a lock on the upscale, everything-is-bigger-here steak house concept in the Triad. The look is masculine and clubby, and portions are geared to large appetites. Beef is the star, but there's plenty of good to say about other menu items, such as the seafood (try the shrimp bisque) and salads. The wine list is respectable. ✉ *106 S. Holden Rd., West Metro* ☎ *336/294–9977* 💳 *AE, D, DC, MC, V* ⏲ *Closed Sun.*

$$–$$$ ✕ **Basil's Trattoria & Wine Bar.** Murals of the Italian countryside adorn some of the walls here. The Tuscan-inspired menu changes regularly; specialties include house-made squid-ink fettuccine with grilled shrimp and seafood in a cream sauce. A jazz trio plays Friday and Saturday. ✉ *1720 Battleground Ave., Northwest Metro* ☎ *336/333–9833* 💳 *AE, D, MC, V.*

$–$$ ✕ **Bianca's.** "Value" is a word that leaps to mind at this restaurant, where Italian-style four- and five-course meals offer a lot of bang for the buck. However, for more than a few people, "*amore*" defines this place best: Bianca's has been rated the most romantic restaurant in several local diners'-choice surveys. Paneled walls painted peach and blue, royal-blue window treatments, tiny white lights, and Italian-theme posters set the mood at this former neighborhood grocery with a bar and outdoor seating. Ample portions of food are set out on Formica-topped tables; the pork chops are particularly popular. The wine list is extensive. ✉ *1901 Spring Garden St., Downtown* ☎ *336/273–8114* ▭ *AE, D, MC, V* ⏲ *No lunch Tues.–Sat.*

$–$$ ✕ **Pho Hien Vuong.** Don't be fooled by the appearance of this storefront restaurant—decorated with only a few items that speak to the owners' Vietnamese and Thai ancestry—in a small, nondescript strip mall: there's nothing unassuming about the food. The flavors and textures of the Vietnamese and Thai dishes are excellent, permeating everything from the hot-and-sour shrimp soup to the vegetable curry to the sliced grilled pork. If you want the food to have extra kick, request it "hot." ✉ *4109-A Spring Garden St., Downtown* ☎ *336/294–5551* ▭ *D, MC, V.*

★ **$$$** **O. Henry Hotel.** This boutique hotel, named for the renowned author who grew up in Greensboro, is privately owned by a small company with a knack for detail and customer service. The furnishings evoke the Arts and Crafts style, with lots of wood, tapestries, and upholstery in warm tones. Particularly nice touches are the oversize rooms, tile bathrooms with standing shower stalls and separate tubs, and bed coverlets that are laundered daily. A complimentary breakfast buffet is served in a sunny pavilion overlooking a small garden. ✉ *624 Green Valley Rd., Northwest Metro, 27408* ☎ *336/854–2000 or 800/965–8259* 🖷 *336/854–2223* 🌐 *www.o.henryhotel.com* *121 rooms, 10 suites* *Restaurant, room service, in-room data ports, in-room safes, microwaves, refrigerators, room TVs with movies, pool, exercise equipment, dry cleaning, laundry service, business services, meeting room, airport shuttle* ▭ *AE, D, DC, MC, V* *BP.*

$$–$$$ **Sheraton Greensboro Hotel at Four Seasons.** Business travelers are the mainstay here, at the state's largest hotel, which is adjacent to the convention center. Accommodations are a notch above standard, and the hotel and its nearby sister property, the Park Lane Hotel, are convenient to major thoroughfares and the Four Seasons Town Centre, a three-story regional mall. ✉ *3121 High Point Rd., West Metro, 27407* ☎ *336/292–9161 or 800/242–6556 for Sheraton, 336/294–4565 for Park Lane* 🖷 *336/292–1407* 🌐 *www.sheratongreensboro.com* *910 rooms, 80 suites* *5 restaurants, room service, in-room data ports, cable TV, pool, wading pool, health club, sauna, racquetball, 4 bars, nightclub, laundry facilities, business services, convention center, meeting rooms, airport shuttle* ▭ *AE, D, DC, MC, V* *EP.*

$$ **Greenwood Bed and Breakfast.** Eclectic antiques, art, and various other collections fill this 1905 craftsman-style home in historic Fisher Park. Owners Bob (a former New Orleans chef) and Dolly (a decorator) Guertin serve a full breakfast at the time of your choosing. Café au lait, French bread, eggs Benedict, and crêpes suzette come with freshly squeezed orange juice and fruit. Desserts are set out in the evening. ✉ *205 N. Park Dr., Downtown, 27401* ☎ *336/274–6350 or 877/374–7067* 🌐 *www.greenwoodbb.com* 🖷 *336/274–9943* *5 rooms* *Pool, meeting room; no room TVs, no kids under 16, no smoking* ▭ *AE, D, DC, MC, V* *BP.*

$ **Biltmore Greensboro Hotel.** The Biltmore, in the heart of the central business district, has an old-world, slightly faded feel, with 16-foot ceilings, a cage elevator, and a lobby with walnut-panel walls and a fireplace. Some guest rooms have Victorian-era or Victorian-reproduction furniture and electric candle sconces. ✉ *111 W. Washington St., Downtown, 27401* ☎ *336/272–3474 or 800/332–0303* 🖷 *336/275–2523* 🌐 *www.biltmorehotelgreensboro.com* *25 rooms, 2 suites* *In-room data ports, minibars, refrigerators, Internet, business services, meeting room, airport shuttle* 💳 *AE, D, DC, MC, V* *BP.*

CAMPING You can rent a cabin or bring a tent to the **Greensboro KOA** (✉ 2300 Montreal Ave., Southeast Metro ☎ 336/274–4143 or 800/562–4143). **Hagan-Stone Park** (✉ 5920 Hagan-Stone Rd., Southeast Metro ☎ 336/674–0472) is a wildlife reserve with hiking, water sports, and other activities. Hookups for trailers and RVs are available.

2

Nightlife & the Arts

The **Broach Theatre** (✉ 520 S. Elm St., Downtown ☎ 336/378–9300) stages professional adult (February–December) and children's (September–May) theater in the Old Greensborough historic district. The **Carolina Theatre** (✉ 310 S. Greene St., Downtown ☎ 336/333–2605), a restored vaudeville venue, serves as one of the city's principal performing-arts centers, showcasing dance, concerts, films, and plays.

The vast **Greensboro Coliseum Complex** (✉ 1921 W. Lee St., West Metro ☎ 336/373–7474, 336/333–7490 for Greensboro Symphony, 336/273–9472 for Greensboro Opera Company) hosts arts and entertainment events throughout the year, as well as professional, college, and amateur sports. The Greensboro Symphony and the Greensboro Opera Company both perform here.

The **Eastern Music Festival** (✉ 200 N. Davie St., Downtown ☎ 336/333–7450 or 877/833–6753), whose guests have included André Watts and Wynton Marsalis, brings six weeks of professional classical music concerts to Greensboro's Guilford College campus in summer.

Shopping

Antiques stores, galleries, cafés, and unique shops line **South Elm Street** and adjacent streets.

More than 75 stores and services constitute the **Burlington Manufacturers Outlet Center** (✉ Exit 145 off I–85, Burlington ☎ 336/227–2872), which makes the area off I–85 near here—about 25 mi east of Greensboro—a trove for bargain hunters.

Replacements, Ltd. (✉ I–85/I–40 at Mt. Hope Church Rd., Exit 132, East Metro ☎ 800/737–5223), the world's largest retailer of discontinued and active china, crystal, flatware, and collectibles, stocks more than 10 million pieces of inventory and 200,000 patterns. The cavernous showroom is open 9–8 daily, and free tours are given.

en route

It's a good thing guides are available to direct visitors through the architectural fantasyland known as **Körner's Folly,** located midway between Greensboro and Winston-Salem. Completed in 1880 by Jule Körner, this highly ornamented, 100-foot-tall bachelor-pad-turned-family-home has three floors of odd rooms, ceilings ranging from 5½ feet to 25 feet high, 15 uniquely designed fireplaces, winding stairways, and cubbyholes. Particularly intriguing are the children's rooms and theater room. ✉ *413 S. Main St., Kernersville* ☎ *336/996–7922* ⊕ *www.kornersfolly.org* 🎟 *$6* ⏲ *Thurs.–Sat. 10–3, Sun. 1–5.*

Winston-Salem

21 *26 mi west of Greensboro; 81 mi north of Charlotte.*

Winston-Salem residents' donations to the arts are among the highest per capita in the nation: the city bills itself as the City of the Arts, and its museums show the benefits of this support. The North Carolina School of the Arts commands international attention. Salem College, the oldest women's college in the country, is here, as is Wake Forest University, where writer Maya Angelou teaches. Old Salem, a restored 18th-century Moravian town within the city, has been a popular attraction since the early 1950s.

Staff at the **Winston-Salem Visitor Center** (✉ 601 N. Cherry St., Downtown ☎ 336/777–3796 or 800/331–7018) can assist with directions and help you make dining and lodging reservations.

Fodor'sChoice ★ Founded in 1766 as a Moravian congregation town and backcountry trading center, **Old Salem** has become one of the nation's most authentic and well-documented colonial sites. At this living-history museum with about 100 reconstructed and original buildings, costumed interpreters re-create household activities and trades common in Salem in the late 18th and early 19th centuries. You can participate in African-American programs that include a stop by the 1861 St. Philip's Church, the state's oldest-standing African-American church. Old Salem also has a toy museum, a children's museum, the 1816 Salem Tavern restaurant, and the Winkler Bakery (don't pass up the Moravian sugar cake). The village is a few blocks from downtown Winston-Salem and near I–40 Business (take the Old Salem/Salem College exit). ✉ *600 S. Main St., Old Salem* ☎ *336/721–7300 or 888/653–7253* ⊕ *www.oldsalem.org* 🎟 *$21, includes admission to Museum of Early Southern Decorative Arts* ⏲ *Mon.–Sat. 8:30–5:30, Sun. 12:30–5:30.*

★ The **Museum of Early Southern Decorative Arts** (MESDA), on the southern edge of Old Salem, is the only museum dedicated to exhibiting and researching the regional decorative arts of the early South. Twenty-four intricately detailed period rooms and seven galleries showcase the furniture, painting, ceramics, and metalware made and used regionally through 1820. The bookstore carries current and hard-to-find books on Southern decorative arts, culture, and history. ✉ *924 S. Main St., Old Salem* ☎ *336/721–7360 or 888/653–7253* ⊕ *www.mesda.org* 🎟 *$21, includes admission to Old Salem* ⏲ *Mon.–Sat. 9:30–5, Sun. 1:30–5.*

The **SciWorks** complex includes a 120-seat planetarium, a 15-acre Environmental Park, and 45,000 square feet of interactive and hands-on exhibits, including the *Coastal Encounters* wet lab. ✉ *400 W. Hanes Mill Rd., North Metro* ☎ *336/767–6730* 🎟 *$8* ⏲ *Weekdays 10–4, Sat. 11–5.*

Historic Bethabara Park, set in a wooded 175-acre wildlife preserve, was the site of the first Moravian settlement (1753) in North Carolina. Bethabara—meaning "house of passage"—was to be temporary until the town of Salem was established, and it did indeed decline after Salem's completion. You can tour restored buildings such as the 1788 congregation house, explore the foundations of the town, or browse the colonial and medicinal gardens. Children love the reconstructed fort from the French and Indian War. Brochures for self-guided walking tours are available year-round at the visitor center. ✉ *2147 Bethabara Rd., University* ☎ *336/924–8191* 🌐 *www.bethabarapark.org* 🎫 *$2* ⏲ *Exhibit buildings Apr.–Nov., Tues.–Fri. 9:30–4:30, weekends 1:30–4:30; guided tours Apr.–Nov. or by appointment.*

Reynolda House Museum of American Art, formerly the home of tobacco magnate Richard Joshua Reynolds and his wife, Katherine, is filled with American paintings, prints, and sculptures by such artists as Thomas Eakins, Frederic Church, and Georgia O'Keeffe. There's also a costume collection, as well as vintage clothing and toys used by the Reynolds children. The museum is next to **Reynolda Village,** a collection of shops, restaurants, and gardens that fill the estate's original outer buildings. ✉ *2250 Reynolda Rd., University* ☎ *336/758–5150 or 888/663–1149* 🌐 *www.reynoldahouse.org* 🎫 *$8* ⏲ *Tues.–Sat. 9:30–4:30, Sun. 1:30–4:30.*

The ever-changing exhibits at the sleek **Southeastern Center for Contemporary Art** (SECCA), near Reynolda House, showcase regional arts and crafts and works by nationally known artists. The Centershop sells many one-of-a-kind pieces. ✉ *750 Marguerite Dr., University* ☎ *336/725–1904* 🌐 *www.secca.org* 🎫 *$5* ⏲ *Tues.–Sat. 10–5, Sun. 2–5; open until 8 the 1st Thurs. every month.*

Ten minutes south of the city, on land once claimed for Queen Elizabeth by Sir Walter Raleigh, is **Tanglewood Park.** The home of the late William and Kate Reynolds is now open to the public for golfing, boating, hiking, fishing, horseback riding, and swimming. The **Tanglewood Festival of Lights,** the largest holiday-lights festival in the Southeast, runs from mid-November to January 2 every year. ✉ *U.S. 158 off I–40, Clemmons* ☎ *336/778–6300* 🌐 *www.forsyth.cc/tanglewood* 🎫 *$2 per car; separate fees for each activity* ⏲ *Daily dawn–dusk.*

Where to Stay & Eat

$$$–$$$$ ✕ **Noble's Grille.** French and Mediterranean flavors are key to the menu, which changes nightly. Typical entrées, grilled or roasted over the omnipresent oak-and-hickory fire, might include Roquefort risotto–stuffed portobello mushroom with roasted polenta or veal sweetbreads with garlic mashed potatoes. The dining room, with tall windows and track lighting, has a view of the grill. ✉ *380 Knollwood St., West Metro* ☎ *336/777–8477* 💳 *AE, DC, MC, V.*

$$$–$$$$ ✕ **Opie's Southbound Grille.** Although housed in a building erected in 1913 as the headquarters for Southbound Railway, this place is anything but old-fashioned. Like the simple and tidy interior with its climate-controlled wine-storage unit, hardwood floors, exposed-brick wall, and large windows, the lunch and dinner menus have contemporary sensibilities. Grilled Norwegian salmon is served with herb-and-Asiago polenta and Asian-cucumber relish, and wild-mushroom ravioli comes with roasted-red-pepper-and-black-olive relish. A tapas option is also available for dinner. ✉ *300 S. Liberty St., Old Salem* ☎ *336/723–0322* ▭ *AE, MC, V* ⏲ *Closed Sun. No lunch Mon. and Sat.*

$$–$$$ ✕ **Old Salem Tavern Dining Room.** The costumed staff happily details the varied lunch and dinner menus, from which you might order traditional Moravian chicken pie or the bratwurst platter. You can also opt for something more innovative, such as fillet of beef with brandied green peppercorns. In the warm months drinks are served under the arbor, and outdoor seating draws diners to the covered back porch. ✉ *736 S. Main St., Old Salem* ☎ *336/748–8585* ▭ *AE, D, MC, V.*

$$–$$$ ✕ **The Vineyards.** Heart-healthy options such as poached-salmon salad are served in this Reynolda Village favorite in what was the boiler room of the Reynolds family estate. The innovative seasonal menu might include pan-seared duck breast with sautéed mushrooms and a bordeaux-and-sun-dried-tomato sauce. The homemade bread pudding is considered the best in town. There's live music Thursday through Saturday. ✉ *120 Reynolda Village Rd., University* ☎ *336/748–0269* ▭ *AE, D, MC, V* ⏲ *Closed Sun.*

¢–$$ ✕ **Grecian Corner.** This restaurant in a small, white, corner building with blue trim has been dishing up gyros and chicken and pork souvlakia since 1970. Patrons, from the physicians at nearby Baptist Hospital to soccer moms, appreciate the friendly service and ample portions of moussaka, spanakopita, and salads. The wine list includes Greek reds and whites. ✉ *1st St. at Cloverdale Ave., Downtown* ☎ *336/722–6937* ▭ *No credit cards.* ⏲ *Closed Sun.*

$$–$$$ **Adam's Mark Winston Plaza Hotel.** The hotel, centrally located off I–40, occupies two towers connected by a skywalk. The East Tower has a traditional look, and the West Tower is a bit sleeker and more contemporary. The Cherry Street Bar, with its smoothly tailored living room, is a great place to relax. ✉ *425 N. Cherry St., Downtown, 27101* ☎ *336/725–3500 or 800/444–2326* 🖷 *336/721–2240* 🌐 *www.adamsmark.com/winstonsalem* *603 rooms, 26 suites* *Restaurant, room service, in-room data ports, room TVs with movies, indoor pool, health club, sauna, steam room, 2 bars, dry cleaning, laundry service, business services, meeting room, parking (fee)* ▭ *AE, D, DC, MC, V* *EP.*

$$–$$$ **Brookstown Inn.** Handmade quilts, two-person tubs, and wine and cheese and freshly baked cookies in the lobby are just a few of the amenities at this inn. The rooms, with their rafters, high ceilings, and brick walls, retain the character of the 1837 textile mill this building once housed. The Graffiti Wall, where young female factory workers left their mark, has been carefully preserved. ✉ *200 Brookstown Ave., Old Salem, 27101* ☎ *336/725–1120 or 800/845–4262* 🖷 *336/773–0147* 🌐 *www.brookstowninn.com* *40 rooms, 31 suites* *In-room data ports, cable TV, exercise equipment, business services, meeting room* ▭ *AE, DC, MC, V* *BP.*

$–$$ **Henry F. Shaffner House.** Accessible to downtown and Old Salem, this B&B is a favorite with business travelers and honeymooners. The rooms

NORTH CAROLINA'S WINERIES

*F**ORCED TO NAME** North Carolina's top agricultural crop, most people would likely respond with tobacco. But in fact, the golden leaf is in decline, and it's grapes that are on the rise—grapes and their glamorous first cousins, wineries.*

There's a fitting historical symmetry here. It's a little-known fact that North Carolina was home to the nation's first cultivated grape and for a while grew more wine grapes than all the other states combined. The earliest written account of the sweet, musky "big white grape" still associated with the state is in the 1524 logbook of Florentine navigator Giovanni da Verrazano, who found the muscadines growing in the Cape Fear River valley. Settlers, who called these grapes "scuppernogs," began making wine from them in the 1700s, and the first commercial vineyard was founded in 1835. At the turn of the 20th century, 25 wineries operated in North Carolina,but the grape presses ground to a halt with the onset of Prohibition.

Today, wineries are making a robust comeback. Grapes are found throughout the state; growers in the Piedmont, a particularly active wine-making area, cultivate traditional European varieties as well as French-American hybrids.

The Yadkin River valley, largely west of Winston-Salem (in Surry, Wilkes, and Yadkin counties and portions of Stokes, Davie, Davidson, and Forsyth counties), has growing conditions similar to the Burgundy region of France. Grapes grown here are used to produce chardonnay, Riesling, cabernet sauvignon, merlot, and syrah. September and October are the prime grape-picking months, but tours and wine-and-cheese tastings are popular year-round. Each winery in the valley works to make the experience a unique one.

*At **Shelton Vineyards** (✉ 286 Cabernet La., Dobson ☎ 336/366–4724 🌐 www.sheltonvineyards.com), the largest family-owned winery in the area, daily tours include a trip to Shelton Cheeses, where the cheeses are made on-site. Based out of a large cabin near Shelton Vineyards is **Black Wolf Vineyards** (✉ 283 Vineyard La., Dobson ☎ 336/374–2532 🌐 www.blackwolfvineyards.com) and its Wolf's Lair Restaurant. The playful symbol for **RagApple Lassie Vineyards and Winery** (✉ 3724 Rockford Rd., Boonville ☎ 336/367–6000 🌐 www.ragapplelassie.com) is a cow sipping a glass of wine while sitting on a crescent moon.*

*Husband-and-wife-team Michael and Amy Helton were inspired to start **Hanover Park Vineyard** (✉ 1927 Courtney-Huntsville Rd., Yadkinville ☎ 336/463–2875 🌐 www.hanoverparkwines.com) after honeymooning in the south of France. Ronda is home to **Windy Gap Vineyards** (✉ 656 Pardue Farm Rd., Ronda ☎ 336/984–3926 🌐 www.windygapwine.com), the smallest winery in the Yadkin River valley. **Raffaldini Vineyards** (✉ 450 Groce Rd., Ronda ☎ 336/835–9463 🌐 www.raffaldini.com) focuses on Italian varietals, reflecting the owners' heritage. **Laurel Gray Vineyards** (✉ 5726 Old Hwy. 21, Hamptonville ☎ 336/468–8463 🌐 www.laurelgray.com) is part of the Swan Creek Wine Trail. The October Harvest Festival is popular at **Westbend Vineyards** (✉ 5394 Williams Rd., Lewisville ☎ 336/945–5032 🌐 www.westbendvineyards.com). **Round Peak Vineyards** (✉ 765 Round Peak Church Rd., Mt. Airy ☎ 336/352–5595 🌐 www.roundpeak.com) produces chardonnay, merlot, and rosé. Each year in early spring, **RayLen Vineyards & Winery** (✉ 3577 U.S. Hwy. 158, Mocksville ☎ 336/998–3100 🌐 www.raylenvineyards.com) hosts a wine festival.*

in the restored English Tudor house are meticulously furnished in 19th-century Victorian elegance. Rates include afternoon tea and evening wine and cheese. ✉ *150 S. Marshall St., Old Salem, 27101* ☎ *336/777–0052 or 800/952–2256* 🖷 *336/777–1188* 🌐 *www.shaffnerhouse.com* *6 rooms, 3 suites* *Restaurant, business services, meeting room* 💳 *AE, MC, V* 🍴 *BP.*

$–$$ **Tanglewood Manor House Bed & Breakfast.** Highlights of this B&B, the former home of a branch of the Reynolds family on the grounds of Tanglewood Park, include crystal chandeliers, a library, a large rock fireplace, and a veranda overlooking the expansive grounds. Antiques and reproductions fill the guest rooms, which are considerately stocked with wine, soft drinks, and bottled water. Guest cottages and a guesthouse are available for rent by the week March–October, or for nightly rental November–February. Admission to the park and swimming pool are included; a fishing license costs extra. Greens fees at park courses are discounted. ✉ *U.S. 158 off I–40, Clemmons 27012* ☎ *336/778–6300* 🖷 *336/778–6379* 🌐 *www.forsyth.cc/tanglewood* *5 rooms, 5 suites, 5 cottages, guesthouse* *Picnic area, refrigerators, cable TV, driving range, 2 18-hole golf courses, pool, wading pool, fishing, horseback riding, playground, meeting room* 💳 *AE, DC, MC, V* 🍴 *BP.*

¢–$ **Comfort Inn–Cloverdale.** Off I–40 Business near downtown and Old Salem, this five-story hotel in the Ardmore neighborhood is near the business and nightlife nexus of Winston-Salem. ✉ *110 Miller St., Downtown, 27103* ☎ *336/721–0220 or 800/228–5150* 🖷 *336/723–2117* 🌐 *www.choicehotels.com* *122 rooms* *Microwaves, refrigerators, cable TV, pool, exercise equipment, sauna, laundry service, meeting room, no-smoking rooms* 💳 *AE, D, DC, MC, V* 🍴 *BP.*

Nightlife & the Arts

THE ARTS Many North Carolina School of the Arts musical and dramatic performances are held at the on-campus **Stevens Center** (✉ 405 W. 4th St., Downtown ☎ 336/721–1945), a restored 1929 movie palace. It's also home to an opera company, theater company, and symphony. The Broadway Preview Series stages first-run productions, with big-name actors, before they move on to Broadway engagements.

Every two years in summer the North Carolina Black Repertory Company hosts the **National Black Theatre Festival** (✉ 610 Coliseum Dr., University ☎ 336/723–2266). This weeklong showcase of African-American talent attracts tens of thousands of people, including a who's who of celebrities. The *New York Times* has hailed this event as "one of the most historic and culturally significant in the history of black theatre and American theatre in general." The next festival is scheduled for early August 2005.

NIGHTLIFE **Burke Street Pub** (✉ 1110 Burke St., West Metro ☎ 336/750–0097), open until 2 AM daily, has music, dancing, games, and sports on the TV; it can get rowdy. In the Adam's Mark Winston Plaza Hotel, the smart, stylish **Cherry Street Bar** (✉ 425 N. Cherry St., Downtown ☎ 336/725–3500) has live entertainment. **Lucky 32** (✉ 109 S. Stratford Rd., University ☎ 336/777–0032), a fine bar adjoining a restaurant, caters to a professional crowd.

Shopping

SHOPPING DISTRICTS The **Art District,** at 6th and Trade streets (just behind the Winston-Salem Visitor Center), has several galleries and arts-and-crafts shops. **Reynolda Village,** near the Reynolda House Museum of American Art, has shops and restaurants. **Stratford Place,** a collection of upscale shops, restaurants, and cafés, is off I–40 Business in the Five Points area, where Country Club, Miller Road, and 1st Street converge.

ANTIQUES **Farmstead Antiques** (✉ 120 Farmstead La., Mocksville ☎ 336/998–3139), housed in a former dairy barn about 20 mi southwest of Winston-Salem, carries antique art, furniture, and decorative objects from the South as well as England and France.

CRAFTS All of the contemporary and traditional crafts at the **Piedmont Craftsmen's Shop and Gallery** (✉ 601 N. Trade St., Downtown ☎ 336/725–1516) are juried. An annual fair is held in November.

High Point

 *18 mi southeast of Winston-Salem; 76 mi northeast of Charlotte; 20 mi southwest of Greensboro.*

Settled by Quakers in the 1700s, High Point was incorporated in 1859. Its name is derived from its former position as the highest point on the railroad between Goldsboro and Charlotte. It's also the childhood home of legendary jazz saxophonist John Coltrane, as well as the 2004 *American Idol* winner, Fantasia Barrino. Today when people think of High Point, they think of furniture. It's here that the twice-a-year (April and October) International Home Furnishings Market, the largest wholesale furniture market in the world (not open to the public), takes place. Tens of thousands of buyers and others associated with the trade "go to market" and in the process lend sophistication to this warm and hospitable city. More than 70 retail outlets here sell furniture and home accessories at bargain prices.

The **High Point Museum/Historical Park,** focusing on Piedmont history and Quaker heritage, includes the 1786 Haley House and a mid-1700s blacksmith shop and weaving house. Exhibits highlight furniture, pottery, communication, transportation, and military artifacts. Tours of the buildings, conducted by costumed staff, are available weekends. The park also serves as base camp for the Guilford Militia Living Historians. ✉ *1859 E. Lexington Ave.* ☎ *336/885–1859* 🌐 *www.highpointmuseum.org* 🎟 *Free* ⏲ *Museum Tues.–Sat. 10–4:30, Sun. 1–4:30; park buildings Sat. 10–4, Sun. 1–4.*

The **Furniture Discovery Center,** in a renovated fabric warehouse downtown, simulates the furniture-design and -manufacturing process. It has a Furniture Hall of Fame and an extensive miniature collection exhibited in room displays. ✉ *101 W. Green Dr.* ☎ *336/887–3876* 🌐 *www.furniturediscovery.org* 🎟 *$5; combination ticket with Angela Peterson Doll and Miniature Museum $8.50* ⏲ *Apr.–Oct., weekdays 10–5, Sat. 9–5, Sun. 1–5; Nov.–Mar., Tues.–Fri. 10–5, Sat. 9–5, Sun. 1–5.*

The **Angela Peterson Doll and Miniature Museum** houses the collection begun by one woman and now including more than 2,500 dolls, costumes, miniatures, and dollhouses. ✉ *101 W. Green Dr.* ☎ *336/885–3655* *$4; combination ticket with Furniture Discovery Center $8.50* ⏲ *Apr.–Oct., weekdays 10–4:30, Sat. 9–4:30, Sun. 1–4:30; Nov.–Mar., Tues.–Sat. 10–4:30, Sun. 1–4:30.*

In the 1920s, a building shaped like an 18th-century chest of drawers was constructed to call attention to High Point as the home-furnishings capital of the world. The **world's largest chest of drawers** (✉ 508 N. Hamilton St.) was renovated in the late 1990s and now houses the offices for the High Point Jaycees, a community organization. The building rises 40 feet high; dangling from a drawer are two 6-foot-long socks meant to symbolize the city's hosiery industry.

off the beaten path

MENDENHALL PLANTATION – A few miles northwest of High Point is this well-preserved example of 19th-century Quaker domestic architecture. The Mendenhalls opposed slavery, and here you can find one of the few surviving false-bottom wagons, used to help slaves escape to freedom on the Underground Railroad. ✉ *603 W. Main St., Jamestown* ☎ *336/454–3819* 🌐 *www.mendenhallplantation.org* *$2* ⏲ *Mid-Apr.–Nov., Tues.–Fri. 11–2, Sat. 1–4, Sun. 2–4.*

Sports & the Outdoors

GOLF There are six public golf courses in High Point: three have 18 holes, and three have 9. Pete Dye designed the notable par-72 course at **Oak Hollow** (✉ 3400 N. Centennial St. ☎ 336/883–3260).

HIKING The 376-acre **Piedmont Environmental Center** (✉ 1220 Penny Rd. ☎ 336/883–8531) has 11 mi of hiking trails adjacent to City Lake Park, with recreational activities and a nature preserve. There's also access to a 6-mi greenway trail.

Where to Stay & Eat

$$–$$$$ ✕ **J. Basul Noble's.** Locals hold this place in high esteem, and it's easy to see why. It's architecturally dramatic, with 10-foot-high pillars, a pyramid-shape glass ceiling, and a river-rock wall. The menu covers all the bases—fish, veal, pork, game, beef, and lamb. You could make a meal out of the fine breads (baked daily on the premises) and desserts. There's live jazz Thursday through Saturday. Reservations are a must during the furniture markets in April and October. ✉ *101 S. Main St.* ☎ *336/889–3354* ▭ *AE, DC, MC, V.*

$$–$$$ ✕ **Ham's.** The original Ham's opened in Greensboro in the early 1930s and offered curb service, kosher meats, and deli takeout. Today this independently owned company has restaurants in several North Carolina cities and towns, and though each is decorated a bit differently, they're all linked by a casual eat-and-play atmosphere especially popular with the college-age crowd. Among the hearty fare are sandwiches, burgers, and wraps, and almost everything comes with homemade chips. The High Point branch is in a shopping center. ✉ *2531 Eastchester Dr.* ☎ *336/887–2434* ▭ *AE, D, MC, V.*

$–$$ **Radisson Hotel High Point.** The central location makes the Radisson a favorite with people coming to town for weekend shopping trips. Guest rooms are standard, but each suite is outfitted with furniture from the different manufacturers represented in the area. ✉ *135 S. Main St., 27260* ☎ *336/889–8888* 🖷 *336/885–2737* 🌐 *www.radisson.com* *239 rooms, 13 suites* *Restaurant, indoor pool, gym, bar, business services, meeting room, airport shuttle, parking (fee)* *AE, D, DC, MC, V* *EP.*

$ **Toad Alley Bed & Bagel.** A wide wraparound porch fronts this three-story, 1924, Victorian-style house in a quiet neighborhood 1 mi north of downtown. Rooms are distinguished by 9-foot ceilings and individual decorating schemes—in one there's a dramatic custom-designed four-poster bed. You can relax while sipping wine by the fireplace or on the front-porch swing. ✉ *1001 Johnson St., 27262* ☎ *336/889–8349 or 800/409–7946* 🖷 *336/886–6646* 🌐 *www.toadalley.com* *6 rooms* *Some refrigerators, in-room VCRs* *MC, V* *BP.*

Nightlife & the Arts

Headquartered in High Point is the **North Carolina Shakespeare Festival** (✉ High Point Theatre, 220 E. Commerce Ave. ☎ 336/887–3001). The professional troupe performs August–October and in December at the High Point Theatre.

Shopping

There are more than 70 retail furniture stores in and around High Point. The 22 stores in the **Atrium Furniture Mall** (✉ 430 S. Main St. ☎ 336/882–5599), closed Sunday, carry items by more than 700 manufacturers of furniture and home accessories.

Solo and group art shows rotate through the three exhibition spaces of the **Theatre Art Galleries** (✉ 220 E. Commerce Ave. ☎ 336/887–2137), based in a wing of the High Point Theatre, in the massive International Home Furniture Center. The galleries are open Tuesday–Saturday noon–5 and Sunday by appointment; they're closed during market weeks in April and October.

CHARLOTTE

Although Charlotte dates from Revolutionary War times (it's named for King George III's wife, Queen Charlotte), its Uptown is distinctively New South, with gleaming skyscrapers and broad streets. Uptown encompasses all of downtown Charlotte, a center of government, commerce, and culture. It also has some fashionable historic neighborhoods that are noted for their architecture and their winding, tree-shaded streets. Public art—such as the sculptures at the four corners of Trade and Tryon streets—is increasingly displayed in the city. Erected at Independence Square, the sculptures symbolize Charlotte's roots and aspirations: a gold miner (commerce), a mill worker (the city's textile heritage), an African-American railroad builder (transportation), and a mother holding her baby aloft (the future). Residents of the Queen City take enormous pride in their home being not only the largest city in the Carolinas but also the second-largest banking center in the nation.

Heavy development has created some typical urban problems. Outdated road systems in this metropolis make traffic a nightmare during rush hour, and virtually all of the city's restaurants are packed on weekends. But the locals' Southern courtesy is contagious, and people still love the laid-back pleasures of jogging, picnicking, and sunning in Freedom Park.

You'll be able to walk around Uptown and the historic Fourth Ward, and buses are adequate for getting around within the city limits. Cars, however, remain the best bet for touring.

Uptown Charlotte

Uptown Charlotte is ideal for walking. The city was laid out in four wards around Independence Square, at Trade and Tryon streets. The Square, as it is known, is the center of the Uptown area.

a good walk

Your first stop should be **Main Street Charlotte** 23, on South Tryon Street, for information on Charlotte and exploring the Fourth Ward. Take a stroll north on Tryon Street and enjoy this revitalized area, noting the outdoor sculptures on the plazas and the creative architecture of some of the newer buildings, including the **Bank of America Corporate Center** 24.

Walk two blocks northwest on Trade Street to the First Presbyterian Church and begin exploring the **Fourth Ward** 25, Charlotte's "old" city. Work your way around to East 7th Street near College Street (just east of Tryon Street), where you'll find the **Levine Museum of the New South** 26, with its interactive exhibits of southern history. Then head south to North Tryon Street just above 6th Street to the wonderful science-and-technology museum **Discovery Place** 27. Finish your walk at the **Mint Museum of Craft + Design** 28, which showcases North Carolina's rich crafts tradition.

TIMING You could easily spend two days touring these areas. Allow an hour to browse through the Bank of America Corporate Center and Founders Hall. You can tour the Fourth Ward in a half day or less. The bulk of your time will likely be spent in Discovery Place and the other museums. Avoid the workday bustle by visiting on the weekend, but note that the museums have limited Sunday hours.

What to See

24 **Bank of America Corporate Center.** One of the city's most striking buildings, this Cesar Pelli–designed structure rises 60 stories to a crownlike top. The main attractions are three monumental lobby frescoes by Ben Long, whose themes are making/building, chaos/creativity, and planning/knowledge. Also in the tower are the **North Carolina Blumenthal Performing Arts Center** and the restaurants, shops, and exhibition space of **Founders Hall.** ✉ *100 N. Tryon St., Uptown.*

★ 27 **Discovery Place.** At Charlotte's premier attraction, the wonderful hands-on **Science Museum** is a priority, but you should also allow at least two hours for the **aquariums**, the three-story **rain forest**, the **Omnimax theater**, and the **Morphis MovieRide Theater**, a motion simulator in a space-age capsule. A ham-radio room, a puppet theater, and a 10-foot

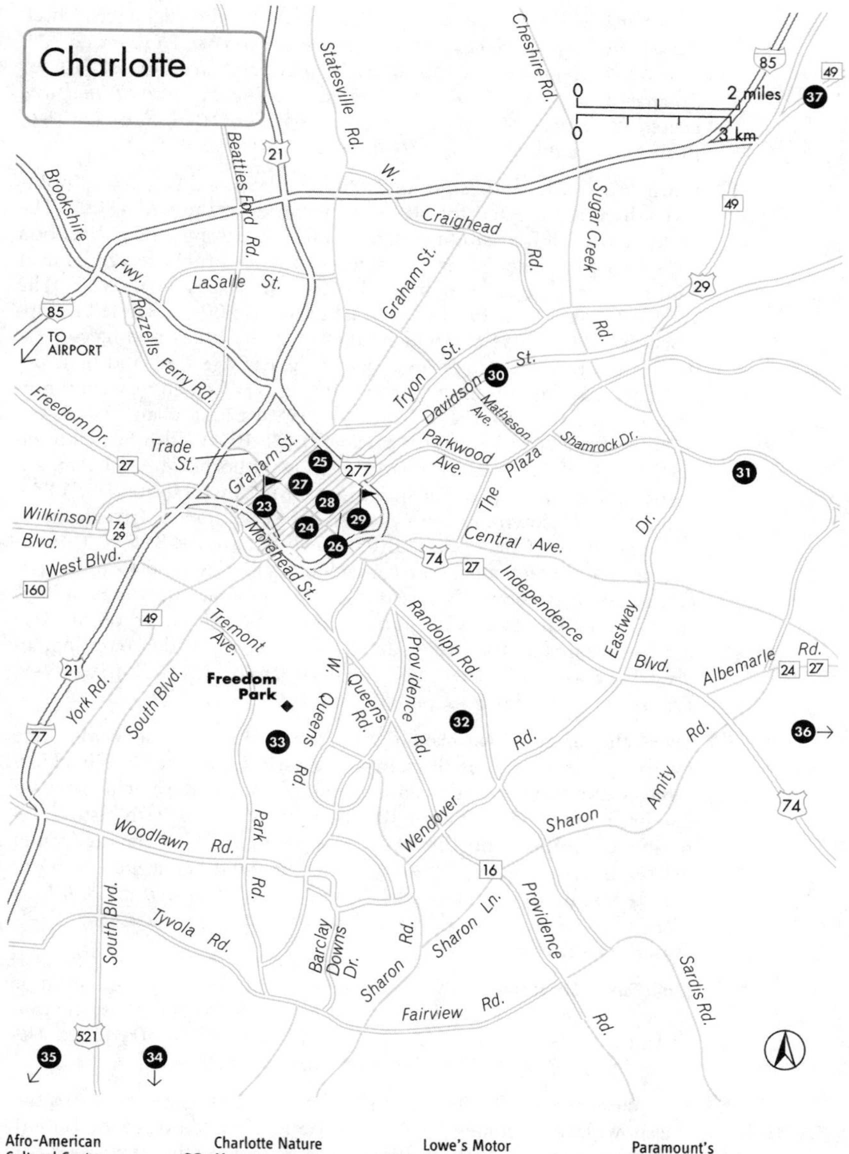

Afro-American Cultural Center **29**

Bank of America Corporate Center **24**

Charlotte Museum of History and Hezekiah Alexander Homesite **31**

Charlotte Nature Museum **33**

Discovery Place **27**

Fourth Ward **25**

James K. Polk Memorial **34**

Levine Museum of the New South **26**

Lowe's Motor Speedway **37**

Main Street Charlotte **23**

Mint Museum of Art **32**

Mint Museum of Craft + Design **28**

North Davidson Arts District (NoDA) **30**

Paramount's Carowinds **35**

Reed Gold Mine State Historic Site **36**

model of an eyeball that you can walk through are other highlights. Check the schedule for special exhibits. ✉ *301 N. Tryon St., Uptown* ☎ *704/372–6261 or 800/935–0553* 🌐 *www.discoveryplace.org* 🎫 *$13 for Science Museum and Omnimax theater, plus $4 for any additional area visited* 🕑 *Labor Day–May, weekdays 9–5, Sat. 10–6, Sun. 12:30–6; June–Labor Day, Mon.–Sat. 10–6, Sun. 12:30–6.*

25 **Fourth Ward.** Charlotte's popular old neighborhood began as a political subsection created for electoral purposes in the mid-1800s. The architecture and sensibility of this quiet, homespun neighborhood provide a glimpse of life in a less hectic time. A brochure available at Main Street Charlotte includes 18 historic places of interest. The Gothic Revival **First Presbyterian Church** (✉ 200 W. Trade St., Uptown ☎ 704/332–5123), which takes up a city block and faces West Trade Street, reflects the prosperity of the early settlers and their descendants. Behind the church is the Old Settlers Cemetery, with tombstones that date from the 1700s. **Fourth Ward Park** is an oasis in the middle of the city. **Alexander Michael's** (✉ 401 W. 9th St., Uptown ☎ 704/332–6789) is a warm and worn neighborhood bar. U.S. president William Taft spent the night in the **McNinch House** (✉ 511 N. Church St., Uptown), now an exclusive, reservations-only restaurant, when he visited Charlotte in 1909. **Spirit Square** (✉ 345 N. College St., Uptown), in a former church, includes galleries, a performing-arts center, and classrooms that used to be the sanctuary for the First Baptist Church. The four-story **public library** (✉ 310 N. Tryon St., Uptown) contains a mural reproducing a Romare Bearden painting, an art gallery, and a children's section; it's open Monday–Thursday 9–9, Friday and Saturday 9–6, and Sunday 1–6.

26 **Levine Museum of the New South.** With its 8,000-square-foot centerpiece exhibit "Cotton Fields to Skyscrapers: Charlotte and the Carolina Piedmont in the New South" as a jumping-off point, the Levine offers a comprehensive interpretation of post–Civil War Southern history. Interactive exhibits and different "environments"—a tenant-farmer house, an African-American hospital, a main-street scene—bring to life the history of the region. ✉ *200 E. 7th St., Uptown* ☎ *704/333–1887* 🌐 *www.museumofthenewsouth.org* 🎫 *$6* 🕑 *Tues.–Sat. 10–5, Sun. noon–5.*

23 **Main Street Charlotte.** At this visitor center you can find information on three self-guided walking tours of the Fourth Ward and a historic tour of Uptown, as well as maps and brochures. ✉ *330 S. Tryon St., Uptown* ☎ *704/331–2700* 🕑 *Weekdays 8:30–5, Sat. 9–3.*

28 **Mint Museum of Craft + Design.** A sister to the Mint Museum of Art, this is a showplace for contemporary studio crafts. In addition to the 16,000-square-foot gallery, with its 40-foot-tall glass wall, the permanent collections of ceramics, glass, fiber, metal, and wood make this one of the country's major crafts museums. You can use your receipt from the crafts museum to enter the Mint Museum of Art free on the same day. ✉ *220 N. Tryon St., Uptown* ☎ *704/337–2000* 🌐 *www.mintmuseum.org* 🎫 *$6* 🕑 *Tues.–Sat. 10–5, Sun. noon–5.*

Fodor's Choice ★

Greater Charlotte

Beyond Uptown and farther afield lie many of Charlotte's most interesting sights, from gardens to museums. You can reach the ones listed below by car or by city bus; for visits elsewhere a car is essential.

a good tour

From Uptown follow 7th Street east and turn north on North Myers Street to visit the galleries of the **Afro-American Cultural Center** 29 ⚑. Backtrack to North Davidson Street, turn right, and continue for just over 2 mi to Matheson Avenue, the start of the **North Davidson Arts District** 30, also known as NoDa. This revived main street of a former mill village—now with a collection of singular galleries, bars, coffeehouses, shops, and artist's residences—extends north to 36th Street. Travel east on 36th Street less than a mile to the Plaza, turn right, go south to Shamrock Drive, and turn left for the **Charlotte Museum of History and Hezekiah Alexander Homesite** 31, where you can see the county's oldest building. Return west on Shamrock Drive to Eastway Drive, which you should follow south until it becomes Wendover Road. Continue 1⅔ mi to Randolph Road and then turn right to reach the **Mint Museum of Art** 32, a wide-ranging collection in a former mint. Finish your tour with a visit to the **Charlotte Nature Museum** 33, next to Freedom Park.

TIMING Within a few miles of each other, these sites can easily be covered over the course of two days.

What to See

⚑ 29 **Afro-American Cultural Center.** In a historic former church, this center, with its galleries and theater, is a showcase for art, music, drama, and dance. ✉ *401 N. Myers St., Uptown* ☎ *704/374–1565* 🌐 *www.aacc-charlotte.org* 🎫 *Free* 🕒 *Tues.–Sat. 10–6, Sun. 1–5.*

31 **Charlotte Museum of History and Hezekiah Alexander Homesite.** The stone house, built in 1774, is the oldest dwelling in the county. Hezekiah Alexander and his wife, Mary, reared 10 children in this house and farmed the land. Seasonal events commemorate the early days. Permanent and rotating exhibits in the museum span 300 years of southern Piedmont history. ✉ *3500 Shamrock Dr., East Charlotte/Merchandise Mart* ☎ *704/568–1774* 🌐 *www.charlottemuseum.org* 🎫 *Museum and homesite, Tues.–Sat. $6; Sun. free* 🕒 *Tues.–Sat. 10–5, Sun. 1–5; tours by costumed docents Tues.–Sun. at 1:15 and 3:15.*

33 **Charlotte Nature Museum.** You'll find a butterfly pavilion, live animals, nature trails, Native American relics, a puppet theater, and hands-on exhibits just for children at this museum affiliated with Discovery Place. ✉ *1658 Sterling Ave., next to Freedom Park, Uptown* ☎ *704/372–0471* 🌐 *www.discoveryplace.org* 🎫 *$4* 🕒 *Weekdays 9–5, Sat. 10–5, Sun. 1–5.*

★ 32 **Mint Museum of Art.** Built in 1836 as a U.S. Mint, this building has served as a home for art since 1936. Among the holdings in its impressive permanent collections are American and European paintings, furniture, and decorative arts; African, pre-Columbian, and Spanish colonial art; porcelain and pottery; and regional crafts and historic costumes. On the day you visit this museum your receipt will entitle you to free admission to downtown's Mint Museum of Craft + Design. *2730 Randolph Rd., East Charlotte/Merchandise Mart 704/337–2000 www.mintmuseum.org $6 Tues. 10–10, Wed.–Sat. 10–5, Sun. noon–5.*

30 **North Davidson Arts District** (NoDa). Historic NoDa is as funky as Uptown is elegant. Creative energy flows through the reclaimed textile mill and mill houses, cottages, and commercial spaces of this north Charlotte neighborhood where you'll find both the kooky and the conformist—artists, musicians, and dancers; street vendors; and restaurateurs—sharing space. The heart of NoDa is the **Neighborhood Theatre** (511 E. 36th St., NoDa 704/358–9298), a converted movie house that seats 700 and presents all manner of performance art. **Center of the Earth** (3204 N. Davidson St., NoDa 704/375–5756) and **Blue Pony Gallery and Press** (3202-A N. Davidson St., NoDa 704/334–9390) are representative of the contemporary art galleries that have made a home here. Adding to the spice of this compact enclave are several notable restaurants and working-class bars. **Cabo Fish Taco** (3201 N. Davidson St., NoDa 704/332–8868) serves vegetarian and seafood dishes, including mango barbecue shrimp, and is known for its large homemade margaritas. **The Smelly Cat Coffeehouse** (514 E. 36th St., NoDa 704/374–9656) is a tiny place with a big choice of coffee, bagels, ice cream, drinks, and pastries. To truly experience NoDa, attend a nighttime Gallery Crawl, held the first and third Friday of every month. The crawls, which run officially from 6 to 9:30, have gained a regional reputation for their informal and entertaining nature. *704/344–8440 www.noda.org.*

Other Area Attractions

Historic sites, a speedway, and a theme park provide plenty to explore beyond the city.

34 **James K. Polk Memorial.** A state historic site south of Charlotte marks the humble 1795 birthplace and childhood home of the 11th U.S. president. Guided tours of the log cabins (replicas of the originals) are available. *308 S. Polk St., Pineville 704/889–7145 Free Tues.–Sat. 9–5.*

37 **Lowe's Motor Speedway.** NASCAR races are held at this state-of-the-art, 167,000-seat facility with a gift shop. "Hot laps" (160 mph) lessons are given at the track through the Richard Petty Driving Experience or Fast Track Driving School. Classes are available year-round, though intermittently. The Speedway Club, an upscale restaurant, is on the premises, as are condominiums above the first turn. The surrounding area includes shops, restaurants, and museums and shrines to various racing teams. *5555 Concord Pkwy. S, Concord, northeast of Charlotte 704/455–3200, 800/455–3267, 704/455–9443 for Richard Petty Driving Experience, 704/455–1700 for Fast Track Driving School www.lowesmotorspeedway.com Prices vary, usually $10–$60 Racing season runs Apr.–Nov.*

35 **Paramount's Carowinds.** A 100-acre amusement park on the South Carolina state line has rides and attractions based on films. Costumed movie and TV characters and actors greet visitors, and the Palladium

THE LOUDEST THING ON WHEELS

For an adrenaline fix there's no beating the speed and brain-rattling roar of NASCAR. Stock car racing, which began in the mountains as a way for moonshiners to elude revenuers, came down into the Piedmont in the 1940s. Driving rules (well, sort of) along with paved tracks were developed, as was a ticket-selling system for the fledgling sport. The first "official" NASCAR race was held in Charlotte in June 1949. Ten years later, the 1½-mi Charlotte Motor Speedway opened. Now known as Lowe's Motor Speedway, it's been at the forefront of many racing innovations. It has also gone somewhat upscale, with an exclusive, country-club-style dining facility called the Speedway Club and year-round condominiums above the first turn. This granddaddy of racing venues also features the Coca-Cola 600, held in May. But before they bring on the derring-do of this longest of races, there are family-oriented events, NASCAR drivers on parade, and even racing classes. Like the fans say: Come early, stay late . . . and remember the earplugs.

stages musical concerts with star entertainers. Rides include a "flying" roller coaster. ✉ *14523 Carowinds Blvd., off I–77 at Carowinds Blvd., South Charlotte/Pineville* ☎ *704/588–2600 or 800/888–4386* 🌐 *www.carowinds.com* *$40* ⏲ *Late Mar.–May and mid-Aug.–early Oct., weekends; June–mid-Aug., daily. Park opens at 10; closing hrs vary.*

36 **Reed Gold Mine State Historic Site.** This area, east of Charlotte in Cabarrus County, is where America's first documented gold rush began, following Conrad Reed's discovery of a 17-pound nugget in 1799. Forty-minute guided underground tours of the gold mine are available, as well as seasonal gold panning, walking trails, and a stamp mill. ✉ *9621 Reed Mine Rd., north of Rte. 24/27, Locust, follow signs beyond town* ☎ *704/721–4653* *Free; gold panning $2 per pan* ⏲ *Apr.–Oct., Tues.–Sat. 9–5; Nov.–Mar., Tues.–Sat. 10–4; call for tour schedules.*

Sports & the Outdoors

Auto Racing

NASCAR races, such as the Coca-Cola 600 (May) and UAW/GM 500 (October), draw huge crowds at the **Lowe's Motor Speedway** (✉ 5555 Concord Pkwy. S, Concord, northeast of Charlotte ☎ 704/455–3200 or 800/455–3267).

Canoeing

Inlets on Lake Norman and Lake Wylie are ideal for canoeing, as are some spots of the Catawba River. The Pee Dee River east of Charlotte and the New River in the mountains offer other options.

Fishing

You can find good fishing in Charlotte's neighboring lakes and streams. A mandatory state license can be bought at local bait-and-tackle shops or over the phone (with a credit card) from the **North Carolina Wildlife Commission** (☎ 919/662–4370).

Golf

There are more than 50 golf courses within a 40-mi drive of Uptown Charlotte. **Highland Creek Golf Club** (✉ 7001 Highland Creek Pkwy., University/Speedway ☎ 704/875–9000), an 18-hole, par-72 course with a driving range, is considered by some to be the best public course in Charlotte. **Larkhaven Golf Club** (✉ 4801 Camp Stewart Rd., East Charlotte/Merchandise Mart ☎ 704/545–4653) is a championship 18-hole, par-72 course with a clubhouse and pro shop. **Paradise Valley Golf Center** (✉ 9309 N. Tryon St., University/Speedway ☎ 704/548–1808) has an 18-hole, all-par-3 course. The **driving range** (✉ 9615 N. Tryon St., University/Speedway ☎ 704/548–8114) is a half mile down the street. **Woodbridge Golf Links** (✉ 922 New Camp Creek Church Rd., Kings Mountain ☎ 704/482–0353), an attractive par-72 course, has 18 holes and a driving range.

Tennis

Tennis courts are available in several Charlotte city parks, including Freedom, Hornet's Nest, Park Road, and Veterans. For details call the **Charlotte Parks and Recreation Department** (☎ 704/336–3854).

Where to Eat

$$$–$$$$ ✕ **Latorre's.** The emphasis at this downtown retreat is on the heat, color, and tastes of Latin America. Art splashed with vibrant shades of mango, lemon, and salmon complement exposed-brick walls and hardwood floors. Live salsa and merengue music is sometimes played. It's the perfect backdrop for the likes of orange-and-cumin-encrusted salmon over black-bean rice cakes, and tender grilled *chimichurri* (a piquant Argentinian herb sauce) flank steak served with tortillas and three salsas. ✉ *118 W. 5th St., Uptown* ☎ *704/377–4448* ▭ *AE, MC, V* ⏲ *Closed Sun.*

$$–$$$$ ✕ **Campania.** Warmth is the byword for this restaurant tucked in a shopping center within a country-club community. Golden textured walls, richly toned wood, lots of candlelight, and genuine Italian music, from opera to contemporary, define the dining room. The food, too, is about as authentic as it gets outside southern Italy. Try the excellent shrimp sautéed in garlic butter and herbs, smoked salmon with a cognac-tomato-cream sauce, or the veal chops. ✉ *6414 Rea Rd., South Park* ☎ *704/541–8505* ▭ *AE, D, MC, V* ⏲ *No dinner Sun.*

$–$$$ ✕ **Providence Café.** The signature purple awnings and trendy furnishings lend atmosphere to the original branch of this lively café. New dishes are introduced every spring and fall, but the menu always includes chicken, beef, seafood, and pasta options. Focaccia is baked daily on the premises. It's a great place for Sunday brunch, and on Wednesday and many Thursday evenings there's live jazz. ✉ *110 Perrin Pl., South Park* ☎ *704/376–2008* ▭ *AE, MC, V.*

★ **$–$$$** ✕ **300 East.** The gentrified, leafy Dilworth neighborhood in which this casual spot resides doesn't lack for older, refurbished houses. Even so, 300 East makes its mark, and not just because of its brightly hued signage, private dining nooks and crannies, and open-air patio. The bold contemporary menu—Thai pork tenderloin with banana-mango salsa and saffron rice, for instance, or penne with duck and lobster—attracts a hip and eclectic bunch. Here, people-watching is as much fun as eating. ✉ *300 East Blvd., South Park* ☎ *704/332–6507* ▭ *AE, D, DC, MC, V.*

$–$$ Fodor's Choice ★ ✕ **Mert's Heart and Soul.** Talk about the New South. Laborers, executives, and arts patrons all make their way to Mert's, named for Myrtle, a favorite customer with a sunny disposition. Owners James and Renee Bezzelle serve large portions of down-home staples such as fried chicken with greens, macaroni and cheese, and corn bread. Lowcountry specialties include shrimp-and-salmon omelets, and red beans and rice. ✉ *214 N. College St., Uptown* ☎ *704/342–4222* ▭ *AE, MC, V* ⊙ *No dinner Mon. and Tues.*

$–$$ ✕ **Thai House.** Fiery pleasures await you here if you're an adventurous diner. Sample from a selection of vegetarian, seafood, and classic Thai dishes—the food has proved so popular here that the owners opened two more branches. The satays (skewers of meat, fish, or poultry with peanut sauce) are mild enough for any taste buds, and you can order many dishes as spicy or mild as you wish. ✉ *3210 N. Sharon Amity Rd., East Charlotte/Merchandise Mart* ☎ *704/532–6868* ▭ *AE, D, DC, MC, V* ✉ *Tower Plaza Shopping Center, 8652 Pineville-Matthews Rd., No. 1000, South Charlotte/Pineville* ☎ *704/542–6300* ▭ *AE, D, DC, MC, V* ✉ *4918 Central Ave., East Charlotte/Merchandise Mart* ☎ *704/535–6716* ▭ *AE, D, DC, MC, V.*

¢–$$ ✕ **Landmark Diner.** This spacious and informal diner in the Eastland Mall neighborhood is a cut above most other inexpensive restaurants, and it's open until 3 AM on weeknights and 24 hours on weekends. The chocolate cream pie and chef's salad with grilled chicken are musts. ✉ *4429 Central Ave., East Charlotte/Merchandise Mart* ☎ *704/532–1153* ✍ *Reservations not accepted* ▭ *AE, DC, MC, V.*

¢–$ ✕ **College Place Restaurant.** Expect simple down-home cooking—and plenty of it—at this large cafeteria and grill close to the convention center. Come for breakfast or lunch (7–3), and know that you'll have to work hard to spend more than $5. Breakfasts in particular are big and include any combination of eggs, pancakes, grits, bacon, and sausage, among other items. Lunch has lots of vegetable choices (12), meats, homemade corn bread, and cobblers, plus a soup-and-salad bar. ✉ *300 S. College St., Uptown* ☎ *704/343–9268* ▭ *No credit cards* ⊙ *Closed weekends. No dinner.*

Where to Stay

$$–$$$ **Adam's Mark.** Within walking distance of the convention center, this is the city's largest convention hotel. The expansive main lobby, with its woodwork and shades of green and gray, feels a bit clubby. Guest rooms are done in blues and plums. Bravo!—its popular signature restaurant, which serves northern Italian cuisine—is known for its singing waiters. ✉ *555 S. McDowell St., Uptown, 28204* ☎ *704/372–4100 or 800/444–2326* 🖷 *704/348–4646* 🌐 *www.adamsmark.com* ⇒ *631 rooms, 21 suites* ♁ *Restaurant, in-room data ports, cable TV, indoor-outdoor pool, health club, sauna, racquetball, bar, dry cleaning, laundry service, concierge, business services, meeting room, airport shuttle, free parking* ▭ *AE, D, DC, MC, V* 🍽 *EP.*

★ $$ **The Park.** Executives, entertainers, sports stars, and heads of state appreciate the privacy and pampering as well as the parklike setting of this hotel on a former estate in the southeast corner of the city. Antique furnishings, polished marble, and art grace the public areas. Guest rooms, with lush fabrics, seem more like a home than a hotel. The hotel is a short drive away from such specialty stores as Tiffany & Co. ✉ *2200 Rexford Rd., South Park, 28211* ☎ *704/364–8220 or 800/334–0331* 🖷 *704/365–4712* 🌐 *www.theparkhotel.com* *184 rooms, 9 suites* *Restaurant, in-room data ports, minibars, cable TV with movies and games, 18-hole golf course, putting green, pool, health club, massage, spa, piano bar, concierge, business services, meeting room, airport shuttle, free parking* 💳 *AE, D, DC, MC, V* 🍽 *EP.*

$–$$ **Hyatt Charlotte at SouthPark.** The focal point of the four-story atrium is a Mexican water fountain surrounded by 25-foot-tall olive trees. Scalini, the restaurant, serves northern Italian cuisine; the Club piano bar is a favorite. The hotel, with contemporary rooms, lies within walking distance of the upscale South Park Mall. ✉ *5501 Carnegie Blvd., South Park, 28209-3462* ☎ *704/554–1234 or 800/233–1234* 🖷 *704/554–8319* 🌐 *www.hyatt.com* *258 rooms, 4 suites* *Restaurant, in-room data ports, cable TV, indoor pool, health club, hot tub, sauna, piano bar, business services, airport shuttle* 💳 *AE, D, DC, MC, V* 🍽 *EP.*

¢–$ **Econo Lodge Lake Norman.** This motel for the budget-minded is north of Charlotte on I–77, within 3 mi of Lake Norman and Davidson College. All rooms have refrigerators and coffeemakers, and a gym is right across the street. ✉ *20740 Torrence Chapel Rd., Cornelius 28031* ☎ *704/892–3500 or 800/848–9751* 🖷 *704/892–6473* 🌐 *www.choicehotels.com* *90 rooms* *Some microwaves, refrigerators, cable TV, pool, Internet, business services, meeting room* 💳 *AE, D, DC, MC, V* 🍽 *BP.*

¢ **Sterling Inn.** This economy option has an upscale sensibility, with large and tasteful rooms with oversize beds and coffeemakers. The inn is near several restaurants, Queens College, and I–77 and I–85. ✉ *242 E. Woodlawn Rd., Airport/Coliseum, 28217* ☎ *704/525–5454* 🖷 *704/525–5637* *100 rooms* *Refrigerators, health club, laundry service, meeting room, airport shuttle, free parking* 💳 *AE, D, DC, MC, V* 🍽 *BP.*

Bed-and-Breakfasts

$$–$$$ **Morehead Inn.** Although it's now a commercial venture catering to corporate clients, this grand colonial revival B&B in the Dilworth neighborhood was once a private estate and still has all the comforts of a beautiful home. Several rooms have four-poster beds. ✉ *1122 E. Morehead St., South Park, 28204* ☎ *704/376–3357 or 888/667–3432* 🖷 *704/335–1110* 🌐 *www.moreheadinn.com* *8 rooms, 2 suites, 1 2-bedroom apartment* *In-room VCRs, meeting room* 💳 *AE, DC, MC, V* 🍽 *BP.*

$$–$$$ **The VanLandingham Estate Inn.** Built in 1913 as a private home in the historic Midwood neighborhood, this inn has earned a spot on the National Register of Historic Places. Period furnishings fill the rooms, which are spread among the main house—a California-style bungalow—and the nearby carriage house. Highlights of the estate include a solarium, library, working orangery, and 4 acres of gardens. ✉ *2010 The Plaza, South Park 28205* ☎ *704/334–8909 or 888/524–2020* 🖷 *704/*

940–8830 🌐 www.vanlandinghamestate.com 9 suites ♿ Some kitchenettes, cable TV, library, concierge, Internet, business services, meeting rooms; no smoking ▭ AE, D, DC, MC, V 🍴 BP.

★ $$ **Homeplace.** A spotless early-20th-century Victorian gem in a residential neighborhood, Homeplace has a wraparound porch, fireplaces, and 10-foot ceilings and is full of antiques and memorabilia. Rooms, with four-poster beds, are country Victorian in style. ✉ *5901 Sardis Rd., South Park, 28270 ☎ 704/365–1936 📠 704/366–2729 🌐 www.bbonline.com/nc/homeplace/ 2 rooms, 1 suite ♿ No kids under 10, no smoking ▭ AE, MC, V 🍴 BP.*

Camping

Lake Norman State Park (✉ Rte. 2, Troutman ☎ 704/528–6350) is ideal for hiking and water sports. Near Charlotte, campsites, fishing, and live animal exhibits can be found at **McDowell Park and Nature Reserve** (✉ 15222 York Rd., South Charlotte/Pineville ☎ 704/588–5224). At the theme park **Paramount's Carowinds** (✉ 14523 Carowinds Blvd., off I–77, South Charlotte/Pineville ☎ 704/588–2600 or 800/888–4386), you can pitch a tent or park a mobile home right next to the roller coasters.

Nightlife & the Arts

The Arts

Charlotte's key venue for performing arts is the **North Carolina Blumenthal Performing Arts Center** (PAC; ✉ 130 N. Tryon St., Uptown ☎ 704/372–1000). It houses several resident companies, including the Charlotte Symphony Orchestra, North Carolina Dance Theatre, Charlotte Repertory Theatre, and Opera Carolina. PAC also presents national tours of Broadway musicals. The **Spirit Square Center for the Arts & Education** (✉ 345 N. College St., Uptown ☎ 704/372–7469) is an interdisciplinary arts center with classes, exhibits, and national acts such as Wynton Marsalis and Jerry Jeff Walker.

Verizon Wireless Amphitheater (✉ 707 Pavilion Blvd., University/Speedway ☎ 704/549–1292) spotlights big-name concerts—Norah Jones, Tim McGraw, Melissa Etheridge—spring through fall. The **Paladium Amphitheater** (✉ 14523 Carowinds Blvd., South Charlotte/Pineville ☎ 704/588–2600 or 800/888–4386), at Paramount's Carowinds, presents stars in concert mid-spring through mid-fall.

Nightlife

The Big Chill (✉ 911 E. Morehead St., South Park ☎ 704/347–4447) is a restaurant with a live house band that plays music primarily from the '40s, '50s, and '60s every Friday and Saturday night. It's best to reserve ahead. **Comedy Zone** (✉ 516 N. College St., Uptown ☎ 704/348–4242) showcases live comedy Tuesday through Saturday night.

Presenting live music nightly, the **Double Door Inn** (✉ 218 E. Independence Blvd., Uptown ☎ 704/376–1446) is a staple of the national blues circuit. Eric Clapton, Junior Walker, and Stevie Ray Vaughn are among the legends who've played this laid-back venue. **Ri Ra** (✉ 208 N. Tryon St., Uptown ☎ 704/333–5554), Gaelic for "uproar" or "a lot of fun," is filled with Irish food, ale, and, on Sunday night, live traditional Irish music. Other musical styles are presented Thursday through Saturday.

Shopping

Charlotte is the largest retail center in the Carolinas. Most stores are in suburban malls; villages and towns in outlying areas have shops selling regional specialties.

Shopping Malls

Carolina Place Mall (✉ 11025 Carolina Place Pkwy., off I–277 at Pineville, South Charlotte/Pineville ☎ 704/543–9300) is the only Charlotte shopping center with five anchors and interstate access. Ask for a visitor discount card at the customer-service center. Destination shopping has been raised to an art form at **Concord Mills** (✉ 8111 Concord Mills Blvd., off I–85, Concord, 10 mi north of downtown Charlotte ☎ 704/979–3000), which sells hundreds of brand names. A Polo Ralph Lauren factory store and an OshKosh B'Gosh branch are here, and there's a rotating schedule of events and entertainment.

SouthPark Mall (✉ 4400 Sharon Rd., South Park ☎ 704/364–4411 or 888/364–4411), in the most affluent section of the city, has high-end stores, including Tiffany & Co., Montblanc, Coach, Eddie Bauer, and Godiva Chocolatier. A concierge provides executive services, gift wrap, and delivery.

Specialty Stores

ANTIQUES The nearby towns of Waxhaw, Pineville, and Matthews are the best places to find antiques. Waxhaw sponsors an antiques fair each February. You can find a good selection of antiques and collectibles at the sprawling **Metrolina Expo** (✉ 7100 N. Statesville Rd., off I–77, North Charlotte/Lake Norman ☎ 704/596–4643 or 800/824–3770) on the first weekend of the month.

BOOKS The **Little Professor Book Center** (✉ Park Road Shopping Center, 4139 Park Rd., South Park ☎ 704/525–9239 ✉ Jetton Village, 19910 N. Cove Rd., North Charlotte/Lake Norman, Cornelius ☎ 704/896–7323) stocks a good selection of contemporary fiction, classics, and children's books.

FOOD & PLANTS The **Charlotte Regional Farmers Market** (✉ 1801 Yorkmount Rd., Airport/Coliseum ☎ 704/357–1269) sells produce, fish, plants, and crafts.

THE SANDHILLS

Because of their sandy soil—they were once Atlantic beaches—the Sandhills weren't of much use to early farmers, most of whom switched to lumbering and making turpentine for a livelihood. Since the turn of the 20th century, however, this area, with its vast pine forests and lakes, has proved ideal for golf, tennis, and horse farms. A panel of experts assembled by *Golf Digest* magazine has named the region one of the top three golfing destinations in the world. First-class resorts are centered around the region's 40 championship golf courses, which have seen their share of PGA tournaments. At this writing, Pinehurst was scheduled to host the prestigious U.S. Open Championship in 2005. Public and private tennis courts abound, and dozens of equestrian events are held each year, including professional steeplechase and harness racing.

The Highland Scots who settled the area left a rich heritage perpetuated through festivals and gatherings. In colonial times English potters were attracted to the rich clay deposits in the soil, and today their descendants and others turn out beautiful wares sold in more than 40 local shops.

2

Southern Pines

 *104 mi east of Charlotte; 71 mi southwest of Raleigh.*

Southern Pines, the center of the Sandhills, is a good place to start your visit to the area.

Sandhills Horticultural Gardens has a wetland area that can be observed from elevated boardwalks. It's part of a 32-acre series of gardens showcasing roses, fruits and vegetables, herbs, conifers, hollies, a formal English garden, pools, and a waterfall. ✉ *2200 Airport Rd., Sandhills Community College campus* ☎ *910/695–3882 or 800/338–3944* 🌐 *www.sandhills.cc.nc.us/lsg/hort.html* 🎫 *Free* ⏲ *Daily sunrise–sunset.*

The 1820 **Shaw House,** typical of the sturdy homes built by the Scottish families who settled the region, serves as headquarters for the Moore County Historical Association. Two other restored cabins, both of which date to the 1700s, were relocated to the grounds here from elsewhere in the area to help illustrate the lives of early settlers. ✉ *S.W. Broad St. and Morganton Rd.* ☎ *910/692–2051* 🎫 *Free* ⏲ *Tues.–Sat. 1–4.*

Weymouth Center, former home of author and publisher James Boyd, hosts numerous concerts and lectures. Boyd, who died in 1944, was visited by many well-known writers; his home served as a cultural center for the area. The North Carolina Literary Hall of Fame is on the 24-acre property, as is a writer-in-residence program, which has hosted more than 600 writers. ✉ *555 E. Connecticut Ave.* ☎ *910/692–6261* 🌐 *www.weymouthcenter.org* 🎫 *Tours $5* ⏲ *Weekdays 10–2; call ahead to arrange tours.*

Weymouth Woods Sandhills Nature Preserve, on the eastern outskirts of town, is a 900-acre wildlife preserve with 4 mi of hiking trails, a beaver pond, and a naturalist on staff. ✉ *1024 N. Fort Bragg Rd., off U.S. 1* ☎ *910/692–2167* 🌐 *ils.unc.edu/parkproject/visit/wewo/home.html* 🎫 *Free* ⏲ *Apr.–Oct., daily 9–7; Nov.–Mar., daily 9–6.*

off the beaten path

CAMERON – The town of Cameron, with a historic district on the National Register of Historic Places, has pockets that haven't changed all that much since the 19th century. This is the place to shop for antiques: approximately 60 antiques dealers operate out of several stores. Most shops are open Tuesday through Saturday 10–5, Sunday 1–5. Another draw is a collection of barns, farm equipment, and tractor-trailers whimsically painted by the Barnstormers, an artists' collective led by David Ellis, a native of Cameron now living in New York City. Most of the murals can be found along Route 24. ✉ *Off U.S. 1, 12 mi north of Southern Pines* ☎ *910/245–7001 for information on antiques shops.*

Where to Stay & Eat

$$$–$$$$ ✕ **Lob Steer Inn.** Salad and dessert bars complement generous broiled seafood and prime-rib dinners at this casual, dimly lighted steak house. ✉ *U.S. 1* ☎ *910/692–3503* ✍ *Reservations essential* ▭ *AE, DC, MC, V* ⏲ *No lunch.*

¢–$ ✕ **Sweet Basil.** This cozy corner café is run by a family whose considerable restaurant expertise shows in the service and the cooking: lots of homemade breads, hefty loaded sandwiches, and lush salads. Special treats are the soups—especially the ginger-carrot and flavorful red-pepper varieties—and decadent desserts. Arrive early to avoid the lunch rush. ✉ *134 N.W. Broad St.* ☎ *910/693–1487* ▭ *MC, V* ⏲ *Closed Sun. No dinner.*

$$$$ **Pine Needles Lodge and Golf Club.** One of the bonuses of staying at this informal resort comprising 11 lodges is the chance to meet Peggy Kirk Bell, a champion golfer and golf instructor. She built the resort with her late husband and continues to help run it. The club has hosted the U.S. Women's Open. The rooms are done in a rustic chalet style; many have exposed beams. *1005 Midland Rd., Box 88, 28387* ☎ *910/692–7111 or 800/747–7272* *910/692–5349* *www.pineneedles-midpines.com* *78 rooms* *Dining room, snack bar, cable TV, driving range, 18-hole golf course, putting green, 2 tennis courts, pool, bicycles, bar, business services, meeting room, airport shuttle* ▭ *AE, MC, V* *FAP.*

$$ **Mid Pines Inn and Golf Club.** This sister resort community to Pine Needles includes a Georgian-style clubhouse and a golf course designed by Donald Ross that has hosted numerous tournaments. The spacious rooms in the 1921 inn are Wedgwood blue, with American antiques or good copies. Jackets are required in the dining room. ✉ *1010 Midland Rd., 28387* ☎ *910/692–2114 or 800/323–2114* *910/692–4615* *www.pineneedles-midpines.com* *112 rooms, 7 villas* *Dining room, snack bar, in-room data ports, cable TV, 18-hole golf course, putting green, 4 tennis courts, pool, gym, bar, recreation room, business services, meeting room, airport shuttle* ▭ *AE, D, DC, MC, V* *FAP.*

Sports & the Outdoors

GOLF There are many excellent 18-hole golf courses here.

Club at Longleaf (✉ 2001 Midland Rd. ☎ 910/692–6100 or 800/889–5323) was built on a former horse farm. The front 9 of the 18-hole, par-71 course play through posts, rails, and turns of the old racetrack.

Mid Pines Golf Club (✉ 1010 Midland Rd. ☎ 910/692–2114 or 800/323–2114) is a golf getaway with a Donald Ross–designed, 18-hole, par-72 course.

Pine Needles Resort (✉ 1005 Midland Rd. ☎ 910/692–7111 or 800/747–7272) has a Donald Ross–designed, 18-hole, par-71 course complemented by practice facilities, grass tennis courts, and an outdoor swimming pool.

Talamore at Pinehurst (✉ 1595 Midland Rd. ☎ 910/692–5884 or 800/552–6292), with its unusual llama caddies, is a par-71 course designed by Rees Jones.

Shopping

Regional authors do readings and signings at the **Country Bookshop** (✉ 140 N.W. Broad St. ☎ 910/692–3211), in the historic downtown district. The store stocks a lot of everything, including children's books and classical and jazz CDs.

2

Pinehurst

39 *6 mi west of Southern Pines.*

Pinehurst, a New England–style village with quiet, shaded streets and immaculately kept homes ranging from rambling Victorians to small cottages, was laid out in the late 1800s in a wagon-wheel design by landscape genius Frederick Law Olmsted. Annie Oakley lived here for a number of years and headed the gun club. Today Pinehurst attracts retirees, tourists, and sports enthusiasts, who come for the renowned golf courses.

The **Tufts Archives** recount the founding of Pinehurst in the letters, pictures, and news clippings, dating from 1895, of James Walker Tufts, who once served as president of the United States Golf Association. Pinehurst owes its origins to Tuft, who chose this area to build a health resort. Golf memorabilia are on display. ✉ *Given Memorial Library, 150 Cherokee Rd.* ☎ *910/295–6022 or 910/295–3642* *Free* *Weekdays 9:30–5, Sat. 9:30–12:30.*

Where to Stay & Eat

$$–$$$ ✕ **Theo's.** Under a brick arch and behind some shops facing Chinquapin Road is a taverna as sunny as the Greek countryside from which owner Elias Dalitsouris hails. Fresh flowers, brightly colored artwork, white vaulted ceilings, lots of windows, and outdoor seating on a garden patio draw diners; the made-from-scratch food, including breads and desserts, keeps them coming back. Salads, pastas, chicken, and beef are served, but the seafood and lamb are the specialties of the house and a real treat. Wash it all down with strong Greek coffee served in traditional small cups. ✉ *140 Chinquapin Rd.* ☎ *910/295–0780* *MC, V* *Closed Sun.*

¢ ✕ **Players Cafe.** This casual spot is *the* place to meet for soups, sandwiches, and pizza. It's in the shop-filled Theater Building in the heart of the village. ✉ *W. Village Green* ☎ *910/295–8873* *Reservations not accepted* *No credit cards* *Closed Sun. No dinner.*

$$$$ Fodor'sChoice ★ ✕ **The Carolina.** In operation since 1901, this stately hotel, the centerpiece of the Pinehurst Resort, has never lost the charm that founder James Tufts intended it to have. Civilized decorum rules in the spacious public rooms and elegantly traditional accommodations, on the rocker-lined wide verandas, and amid the gardens. You can tee off on one of eight signature golf courses or relax in the spa, with warm, dark wood accented by a moss-green-and-cream color scheme. The 45-room Manor Inn has the feel of a B&B; guests have access to all the

resort facilities, including the formal Carolina Dining Room, with a changing eclectic menu. *1 Carolina Vista Dr., Box 4000, 28374 910/295–6811 or 800/487–4653 910/295–8503 www.pinehurst.com 338 rooms, 130 condos 2 restaurants, room service, 8 18-hole golf courses, 24 tennis courts, 5 pools, health club, massage, spa, windsurfing, boating, fishing, bicycles, croquet, bar, children's programs (ages 3–12), concierge, business services, meeting room AE, D, DC, MC, V.*

$$$$ **The Holly.** This historic hotel, affiliated with the Pinehurst Resort, was the first in the village. Molding, lighting, and plumbing fixtures, based on research from local archives, recall the 1890s, the decade of its opening. Luxuries include silk hangers, embroidered robes, and afternoon sandwiches, cookies, and iced tea. A two-night stay is required. The prix-fixe menu at 1895, the bistro-style restaurant, changes seasonally. Inventive dinner entrées may include pinecone-smoked free-range chicken with truffles, tarragon-scented roast tenderloin of veal, and Carolina blue-crab hash. Jackets are required at the restaurant. *Cherokee Rd., 28374 910/295–6811 or 800/487–4653 910/295–8503 www.pinehurst.com 78 rooms, 7 suites Restaurant, room service, golf privileges, pool, croquet, bar, library, concierge, Internet, business services, meeting room AE, DC, MC, V MAP.*

$$$ **Magnolia Inn.** A turn-of-the-20th-century inn, once just a hangout for golfing buddies, has been tastefully decorated with unusual antiques. Most guest rooms are Victorian style with wicker and brass beds; bathrooms have original fixtures such as claw-foot tubs. The inn's dining rooms ($$$$), with their dusty-rose wallpaper and fireplaces, are cozy. The regional menu includes Magnolia duck breast and leg of duck with a pear, sweet-potato, and wild-cherry glaze. There's also an English-style pub. *Magnolia and Chinquapin Rds., Box 818, 28370 910/295–6900 or 800/526–5562 910/215–0858 www.themagnoliainn.com 11 rooms Restaurant, golf privileges, pool, business services AE, MC, V BP.*

$$–$$$ **Pine Crest Inn.** Chintz and mahogany fill the rooms of this slightly faded gem once owned by golfing great Donald Ross. The chefs whip up meals reminiscent of Sunday supper: homemade soups, fresh fish dishes, and the house special, stuffed pork chops. Mr. B's Lounge is one of the liveliest nightspots in town. Guests have golf and tennis privileges at local clubs. *50 Dogwood Rd., Box 879, 28370 910/295–6121 or 800/371–2545 910/295–4880 www.pinecrestinnpinehurst.com 40 rooms Dining room, cable TV, golf privileges, bar AE, D, DC, MC, V MAP.*

Sports & the Outdoors

GOLF ★ **Pinehurst Resort** (1 Carolina Vista Dr. 910/295–6811 or 800/487–4653) has eight 18-hole courses designed by such masters as Donald Ross, including the famed par-72 Number 2. The 18-hole, par-71 **Pit Golf Links** (Rte. 5 910/944–1600 or 800/574–4653) was designed by Dan Maples and sculpted from a 230-acre sand quarry.

HORSEBACK RIDING **McClendon Hills Equestrian Center** (✉ Hwy. 211, West End ☎ 910/673–4971) offers horseback riding, though no children under 8 are allowed. Riding lessons (by appointment) are available.

TENNIS The **Lawn and Tennis Club of North Carolina** (✉ 1 Merrywood ☎ 910/692–7270) has seven courts and a swimming pool. **Pinehurst Resort** (✉ Carolina Vista Dr. ☎ 910/295–6811 or 800/487–4653) is considered one of the best facilities in the country and has clay courts.

Aberdeen

2

40 *5 mi southeast of Pinehurst; 5 mi southwest of Southern Pines.*

Aberdeen, a small town of Scottish ancestry, has a beautifully restored early-20th-century train station and plenty of shops with antiques and collectibles.

The **Bethesda Presbyterian Church,** on Bethesda Road east of town, was founded in 1790. The present wooden structure, which is used for weddings, funerals, and reunions, was built in the 1860s and has preserved its slave gallery as well as exterior bullet holes from a Civil War battle. The cemetery, where many early settlers are buried, is always open.

Malcolm Blue Farm, one of the few remaining examples of the 19th-century Scottish homes that dotted the area, has farm buildings and an old gristmill. A September festival recalls life here in the 1800s. The farm and museum are part of the North Carolina Civil War Theme Trail. ✉ *Bethesda Rd.* ☎ *910/944–7558, 910/944–9483 for museum* 🎫 *Free* 🕒 *Wed.–Sat. 1–4.*

off the beaten path

FORT BRAGG/POPE AIR FORCE BASE – This army–air force duo outside Fayetteville, 45 mi east of Aberdeen via Route 211 and U.S. 401, is one of the world's largest military complexes. **Pope** (☎ 910/394–4183) hosts an open house and air show every other year (the next show is scheduled for May 2005). **Fort Bragg** (☎ 910/907–2026, 910/432–3443 for 82nd Airborn museum 🌐 www.bragg.army.mil), the biggest army post east of the Mississippi, is open year-round. Self-guided tours are available, though security is tight; clearance may take some time, and a photo ID is a must. Guards at the main gate can direct you to maps indicating public-access areas. Free sites include the 82nd Airborne Division War Memorial Museum (open Tuesday–Saturday 10–4:30), which tells the story of this unit, famous from World War I through Desert Storm. ✉ *Off Rte. 24 or the All American Freeway* 🕒 *Some sites closed Mon.*

AIRBORNE AND SPECIAL OPERATIONS MUSEUM – The story of the fabled airborne and special-ops units is told through film and video, interactive displays, walk-through dioramas, and rare artifacts. ✉ *100 Bragg Blvd., Fayetteville* ☎ *910/483–3003* 🌐 *www.asomf.org* 🎫 *Museum free, Vistascope Theater $4, motion simulator $4* 🕒 *Tues.–Sat. 10–5, Sun. noon–5.*

Where to Stay

$ **Inn at Bryant House.** One block east of U.S. 1, this charming downtown B&B, built in 1913, is a home away from home. All rooms are individually decorated; some have canopy beds. The inn has golf packages and arranges tennis and horseback riding. ✉ *214 N. Poplar St., 28315* ☎ *910/944–3300 or 800/453–4019* 🖷 *910/944–8898* 🌐 *www.innatbryanthouse.com* *9 rooms, 7 with bath* *Picnic area, business services* *AE, D, MC, V* *BP.*

Sports & the Outdoors

GOLF **Legacy Golf Links** (✉ U.S. 15/501 ☎ 910/944–8825 or 800/344–8825) has the first American course designed by Jack Nicklaus II (par 72, 18 holes).

Seagrove

★ 41 *40 mi northwest of Aberdeen; 35 mi northwest of Pinehurst.*

Potters, some of whom are carrying on traditions that have been in their families for generations and others who are newer to the art, handcraft mugs, bowls, pitchers, platters, vases, and clay "face jugs" in the Seagrove area. Some of the work of local artisans is exhibited in national museums, including the Smithsonian. More than 90 potteries are scattered along and off Route 705 and U.S. 220. Most shops are open Tuesday through Saturday 10–5. The annual spring kiln opening (mid-April) and Seagrove Pottery Festival (November, the week before Thanksgiving) are always much anticipated events.

★ The **North Carolina Pottery Center,** a museum and educational facility, exhibits pottery from around the state. You can pick up maps of the various studios around the area. ✉ *250 East Ave.* ☎ *336/873–8430* 🌐 *www.ncpotterycenter.com* *$3* *Tues.–Sat. 10–4.*

Asheboro

42 *13 mi north of Seagrove; 23 mi south of Greensboro.*

Asheboro, the seat of Randolph County, sits in the Uwharrie National Forest, which is popular with hikers, bikers, horseback riders, and fisherfolk. At 500 million years old, the Uwharries are the oldest mountain range in North America. This part of the southern Piedmont is a lovely place to view scenery and visit crafts shops.

★ The **North Carolina Zoological Park,** a 1,500-acre home for more than 1,100 animals and 60,000 exotic and tropical plants, was the first zoo in the country designed from the get-go as a natural-habitat facility. The park includes the 300-acre African Pavilion, an aviary, a gorilla habitat, a Sonoran Desert habitat, a 200-acre North American habitat with polar bears and sea lions, and an Australian "walkabout." A tram connects the different areas. ✉ *4401 Zoo Pkwy.* ☎ *336/879–7000 or 800/488–0444* 🌐 *www.nczoo.org* *$10* *Apr.–Sept., daily 9–5; Oct.–Mar., daily 9–4.*

HEARTLAND GARDENS

*N**ORTH CAROLINA'S PIEDMONT** is characterized by low hills canopied by trees. Here, the four seasons tend to merge into one another. The climate is favorable, the hearty soil is mainly loam or clay loam, and people live in floriferous splendor, for gardening is a year-round pleasure. Gardens in North Carolina's heartland are heady stuff. For starters, there are lots of them, and they are diverse in size, style, and plant life. Many offer the charm of surprise, as they can be found in little-known places as well as open but unlikely spaces. From April until the first frost in November, for example, hundreds of varieties of flowers offer dazzling bursts of color along miles and miles of roadway, thanks to an aggressive beautification program by the state's Department of Transportation.*

Garden hopping offers valuable lessons about aesthetics, culture, and persistence. Even if achieving horticultural clarity isn't a top life goal, such visits are still a nice way to while away a day. Herewith, then, is a small sample of the state's signature gardens, regional treasures, and smaller gardens of note:

***Asheboro:** In the Uwharries mountains is the city of Asheboro and the **North Carolina Zoological Park** (✉ 4401 Zoo Pkwy. ☎ 336/879–7000 or 800/488–0444 🌐 www.nczoo.org), home not just to creatures great and small but also botanicals from the Arctic to the tropics.*

***Belmont:** The **Daniel Stowe Botanical Garden** (✉ 6500 S. New Hope Rd., 13 mi west of Charlotte ☎ 704/825–4490 🌐 www.stowegarden.org) is known for its painterly display of colors in a vast perennial garden, wildflower meadow, Canal Garden, and other themed areas.*

***Charlotte:** At the **Wing Haven Garden & Bird Sanctuary** (✉ 248 Ridgewood Ave. ☎ 704/331–0664 🌐 www.winghavengardens.com), 4 acres of formal gardens and natural areas in one of the city's most exclusive neighborhoods create a serene environment for feathered visitors and others.*

***Fayetteville:** **Cape Fear Botanical Garden** (✉ 536 N. Eastern Blvd., 45 mi east of Aberdeen ☎ 910/486–0221 🌐 www.capefearbg.org), at the confluence of the Cape Fear River and Cross Creek, consists of old-growth forest, a laboratory for ornamental horticulture, and a heritage garden complete with a re-created 19th-century farmstead.*

***Hillsborough:** In its annual paean to America's best private gardens, the Garden Conservancy has hailed historic Hillsborough's **Chatwood Garden** (✉ 1900 Faucette Mill Rd., 12 mi north of Chapel Hill ☎ 919/644–0791), with its camellia collections, walled rose garden, woodland area, and heritage fruit-and-vegetable garden. Tours are by reservation only for groups of five or more.*

***Raleigh:** **JC Raulston Arboretum at North Carolina State University** (✉ 4415 Beryl Rd. ☎ 919/515–3132 🌐 www.ncsu.edu/jcraulstonarboretum) is primarily a working, research, and teaching garden; it has the most diverse collection of hardy temperate-zone plants in the southeastern United States, a white garden, a 450-foot-long perennial border, and more. In Raleigh, on the grounds of CBS-affiliate **WRAL-TV** (✉ 2619 Western Blvd.), is a free public garden whose myriad azalea varieties, dogwoods, and bedding plants serve as a backdrop for many a spring wedding.*

***Wilson:** Sculptural art and more than 1,100 rose plants consisting of 170 different varieties are the heart and soul of the fragrant **Wilson Rose Garden** (✉ 1800 Herring Ave., 45 mi east of Raleigh ☎ 252/399–2261 🌐 www.wilsonrosegarden.com), which blooms mid-April through October.*

THE PIEDMONT & THE SANDHILLS A TO Z

To research prices, get advice from other travelers, and book travel arrangements, visit www.fodors.com.

AIRPORTS

Charlotte-Douglas International Airport is west of Charlotte off I–85. Most major airlines serve the facility.

Moore County Airport, based in the Southern Pines community of the Sandhills, serves only private aircraft.

Just west of Greensboro, the Piedmont Triad International Airport is off Route 68 north from I–40; it's served by AirTran, American Eagle, Continental, Delta, Northwest, United, and US Airways.

The Raleigh-Durham International Airport, off I–40 between the two cities, is served by most major airlines. It takes about 20 minutes to get to any of the three cities in the Triangle from the airport.

Airport Information **Charlotte-Douglas International Airport** ✉ 5501 Josh Birmingham Blvd., Airport/Coliseum, Charlotte ☎ 704/359–4013 ⊕ www.charlotteairport.com. **Moore County Airport** ✉ Rte. 22, Southern Pines ☎ 910/692–3212. **Piedmont Triad International Airport** ✉ 6451 Bryan Blvd., Greensboro ☎ 336/665–5666 ⊕ www.ptia.org. **Raleigh-Durham International Airport** ✉ 1600 Terminal Blvd., Morrisville ☎ 919/840–2123 ⊕ www.rdu.com.

TRANSFERS From Charlotte-Douglas International, taxis charge a set fee to designated zones. From the airport to most destinations in Charlotte the cost is $15–$20 (plus $2 for each additional passenger). Airport vans are approximately $8 per person to Uptown. By car take the Billy Graham Parkway, then Wilkinson Boulevard (U.S. 74) east to I–277, which leads to the heart of Uptown.

Taxi service to and from Piedmont Triad International Airport is provided by Airport Express and other tour, charter, limousine, and cab services, including the Golden Eagle Cab Company and Piedmont Executive Transportation.

RDU Airport Taxi Service provides taxi service from Raleigh-Durham International Airport.

Taxis & Shuttles **Airport Express** ☎ 800/934–8779. **Golden Eagle Cab Company** ☎ 336/724–6481. **Piedmont Executive Transportation** ☎ 336/723–2179. **RDU Airport Taxi Service** ☎ 919/840–7277.

CAR TRAVEL

U.S. 1 runs north–south through the Sandhills and the Triangle and is the recommended route from the Raleigh-Durham area, a distance of about 70 mi.

Charlotte is a transportation hub; I–77 comes in from Columbia, South Carolina, to the south, and then continues north to Virginia, intersecting I–40 on the way. I–85 arrives from Greenville, South Carolina, to the southwest, and then goes northeast to meet I–40 between Winston-

Salem and the Triangle. From the Triangle I–85 continues northeast and merges with I–95 in Petersburg, Virginia.

Greensboro and Winston-Salem are on I–40, which runs east–west through North Carolina. From the east I–40 and I–85 combine coming into the Triad, but in Greensboro, I–85 splits off to go southwest to Charlotte. High Point is off a business bypass of I–85 southwest of Greensboro.

U.S. 1 runs north–south through the Triangle and links to I–85 going northeast. U.S. 64, which makes an east–west traverse across the Triangle, continues eastward all the way to the Outer Banks. I–95 runs northeast–southwest to the east of the Triangle and the Sandhills, crossing U.S. 64 and I–40 from Virginia to South Carolina.

2

EMERGENCIES

For minor emergencies go to one of the many urgent-care centers in Raleigh, Cary, Durham, or Chapel Hill.

Emergency Services **Ambulance, fire, police** ☎ 911.

Hospitals **Carolinas Medical Center** ✉ 1001 Blythe Blvd., South Park, Charlotte ☎ 704/355-2000. **FirstHealth Moore Regional Hospital** ✉ 155 Memorial Dr., Pinehurst ☎ 910/215-1000. **Presbyterian Hospital** ✉ 200 Hawthorne La., East Charlotte/Merchandise Mart, Charlotte ☎ 704/384-2273. **University Hospital** ✉ 8800 N. Tryon St., University/Speedway, Charlotte ☎ 704/548-6000.

Late-Night Pharmacies **Eckerd Drug Store** ✉ Lake Boone Shopping Center, Wycliff Rd., Raleigh ☎ 919/781-4070. **Eckerd Drugs** ✉ Park Road Shopping Center, South Park, Charlotte ☎ 704/523-3031 ✉ 3740 E. Independence Blvd., East Charlotte/Merchandise Mart, Charlotte ☎ 704/536-3600 ✉ 3527 Hillsborough Rd., Durham ☎ 919/383-5591. **Wal-Mart pharmacy** ✉ 6600 Glenwood Ave., Raleigh ☎ 919/783-9693.

TAXIS

In Charlotte, Crown Cab and Yellow Cab have taxis and airport vans. University Towncar caters to business travelers. You won't pay more for the company's flat rate than you would for a cab ride.

Dozens of taxi companies, including City Taxi, Orange Cab and RDU Airport Taxi Service, serve the Triangle; fares are calculated by the mile.

Taxi Companies **Central Piedmont Transportation** ✉ Winston-Salem ☎ 336/668-9808 or 866/796-5466. **City Taxi** ✉ Raleigh ☎ 919/832-1489. **Crown Cab** ✉ Charlotte ☎ 704/334-6666. **Orange Cab** ✉ Durham ☎ 919/682-6111. **RDU Airport Taxi Service** ✉ Raleigh-Durham International Airport ☎ 919/840-7277. **University Towncar** ✉ Charlotte ☎ 704/553-2424 or 888/553-2424. **Yellow Cab** ✉ Charlotte ☎ 704/332-6161.

TOURS

The Capital Area Visitor Center in Raleigh offers maps, brochures, and free guided and self-guided tours of government buildings; it's open weekdays 8–5, Saturday 10–4, and Sunday 1–4.

The *Catawba Belle* and the *Catawba Queen* paddle wheelers give dinner cruises and tours on Lake Norman, near Charlotte. Reservations are essential.

The Historic Chapel Hill/UNC Trolley Tour is given Wednesday 2–3, mid-April to mid-November. Departure is from the Horace Williams House, and the fare is $5; call for reservations.

Fees & Schedules **Capital Area Visitor Center** ✉ 301 N. Blount St., Raleigh ☎ 919/733-3456. ***Catawba Belle* and *Catawba Queen*** ✉ Rte. 150, Exit 36, North Charlotte/Lake Norman, Mooresville ☎ 704/663-2628. **Historic Chapel Hill/UNC Trolley Tour** ✉ Horace Williams House, 610 E. Rosemary St., Downtown, Chapel Hill ☎ 919/942-7818.

TRAIN TRAVEL

Both southbound and northbound Amtrak trains, one daily in each direction, stop in Southern Pines. From Charlotte, there's daily service to Washington, D.C., Atlanta, and points beyond, as well as daily service to the Triangle cities of Raleigh, Durham, and Cary (near Raleigh). The in-state *Piedmont* connects nine cities between Raleigh and Charlotte each day. Amtrak also serves Greensboro and High Point in the Triad.

Train Information **Amtrak** ☎ 800/872-7245 ⊕ www.amtrak.com.

VISITOR INFORMATION

The Durham Bullhorn provides 24-hour recorded information on events and activities in Durham. For details on local events in the Sandhills, call the Events Hot Line.

Tourist Information **Chapel Hill/Orange County Visitors Bureau** ✉ 501 W. Franklin St., Suite 104, Chapel Hill 27516 ☎ 919/968-2060 or 888/968-2060 ⊕ www.chocvb.org. **Downtown Chapel Hill Welcome Center** ✉ Old Post Office Bldg., 179 E. Franklin St. ☎ 919/929-9700. **Durham Convention and Visitors Bureau** ✉ 101 E. Morgan St., 27701 ☎ 919/687-0288 or 800/446-8604 ⊕ www.dcvb.durham.nc.us. **Durham Bullhorn** ☎ 919/688-2855 or 800/772-2855. **Events Hot Line** ☎ 910/692-1600. **Greater Raleigh Convention and Visitors Bureau** ✉ Bank of America Bldg., 421 Fayetteville St. Mall, Suite 1505, 27601 ☎ 919/834-5900 or 800/849-8499 ⊕ www.raleighcvb.org. **Greensboro Area Convention and Visitors Bureau** ✉ 317 S. Greene St., 27401 ☎ 336/274-2282 or 800/344-2282 ⊕ www.greensboronc.org. **High Point Convention and Visitors Bureau** ✉ 300 S. Main St., 27260 ☎ 336/884-5255 or 800/720-5255 ⊕ www.highpoint.org. **Moore County Parks and Recreation Department (The Sandhills)** ☎ 910/947-2504 ⊕ www.co.moore.nc.us. **Pinehurst Area Convention and Visitors Bureau** ✉ 1480 U.S. 15/501, Box 2270, Southern Pines 28388 ☎ 910/692-3330 or 800/346-5362 ⊕ www.homeofgolf.com. **Visit Charlotte/Main Street Charlotte** ✉ 330 S. Tryon St., Uptown, 28202 ☎ 704/331-2700 or 800/231-4636 ⊕ www.charlottecvb.org. **Winston-Salem Convention and Visitors Bureau** Box 1409, 27102 ☎ 336/728-4200 or 866/728-4200 Visitor center, ✉ 601 N. Cherry St. ☎ 336/777-3796 ⊕ www.visitwinstonsalem.com.

THE NORTH CAROLINA MOUNTAINS

3

By Lan Sluder **THE MAJESTIC PEAKS,** meadows, balds, and valleys of the Appalachian, Blue Ridge, and Great Smoky mountains epitomize the western corner of North Carolina. The Great Smoky Mountains National Park, national forests, handmade-crafts centers, Asheville's eclectic and sophisticated pleasures, the astonishing Biltmore Estate, and the Blue Ridge Parkway are the area's main draws, providing prime opportunities for shopping, skiing, hiking, bicycling, camping, fishing, canoeing, and just taking in the views.

The city of Asheville is one of the stops on the counterculture trail and a center of the New Age movement, as well as being a popular retirement area. Its restaurants regularly make the TV food show circuit. Thanks to their monied seasonal residents and long histories as resorts, even smaller towns like Highlands, Cashiers, Flat Rock, and Hendersonville are surprisingly sophisticated, boasting restaurants with daring chefs and professional summer theater. In the High Country, where summer temperatures are as much as 15 degrees cooler than in the flatlands, and where snow skiing is a major draw in the winter, affluent retirees and hip young entrepreneurs bring a panache to even the most rural enclaves.

Some of the most important arts and culture movements of the 20th century, including abstract impressionist painting and the Beat movement, had roots just east of Asheville, at Black Mountain College, where in the 1930s and 1940s the notables included famed artists Josef Albers, Willem de Kooning, and Robert Motherwell, dancemeisters John Cage and Merce Cunningham, thinker Buckminster Fuller, architect Walter Gropius, and writers Charles Olson and Paul Goodman.

Exploring the North Carolina Mountains

For sightseeing purposes, western North Carolina can be divided into four areas: Asheville, for decades a retreat for the wealthy and famous and now home to a vibrant mix of artists, relocatees and retirees, hippies, and proud natives, all reveling in the revitalized downtown and hot dining, music and art scenes; the North Carolina portion of the Great Smoky Mountains National Park, together with the towns and areas that border the park; the northern mountains, known as the High Country (Blowing Rock, Boone, Banner Elk and other high-altitude towns), with the highest average elevation and the tallest mountain (Mt. Mitchell) in Eastern America; and, finally, the southern mountains, including areas to the south and west of Asheville, such as Hendersonville, Brevard, and the chic summer enclaves of Lake Toxaway, Cashiers, and Highlands.

Spanning much of western North Carolina is the Blue Ridge Parkway. The parkway, ranked as one of the most beautiful drives in North America, winds across parts of all these areas except the Great Smoky Mountains National Park itself; the parkway terminates near the entrance of the Great Smokies.

Seeing western North Carolina almost certainly requires a car. Bus transportation, other than tour buses, is limited except in Asheville and

Numbers in the text correspond to numbers in the margin and on the North Carolina mountains and Asheville maps.

If you have
3 days

You'll find the most to do and see in the shortest time in and around **Asheville** 1–15. Plan to stay there, visiting the major attractions including the Biltmore Estate and the Thomas Wolfe Memorial. You can make day trips to towns and points of interest in the Southern Mountains nearby, including **Hendersonville** 30 and **Flat Rock** 31. Don't miss a drive on the **Blue Ridge Parkway** 24, either south toward **Cherokee** 19 or north to Mt. Mitchell. If you don't mind spending a little more time on the road, you can reach the **Great Smoky Mountains National Park** 18 on a day trip, as it's only 55 mi from Asheville to the Cherokee entrance of the park via I–40 and U.S.19, or about 90 mi via the Blue Ridge Parkway.

3

If you have
5 days

With five days, you can expand your explorations of the **Great Smoky Mountains National Park** 18. Spend three days (as outlined above) in and around **Asheville** 1–15. Then drive to **Bryson City** 20, **Cherokee** 19, or **Waynesville** 23 and spend two nights in one of those towns near the park. Alternatively, if you would rather explore the High Country instead of the Great Smokies, drive to **Blowing Rock** 25 or **Boone** 26 and spend two nights there, visiting **Valle Crucis** 27, **Banner Elk** 28, Grandfather Mountain, and other spots.

If you have
7 days

With seven days, you can take in the highlights of three of the four regions of North Carolina mountains, or even all four—Asheville, the High Country, the Great Smokies, and the small towns of the Southern Mountains. However, to see all these areas in depth requires even longer, 14 to 21 days, or more. First, follow the three-day itinerary above, staying in **Asheville** 1–15. From Asheville, drive to the Smokies for two days, staying overnight in **Cherokee** 19, **Bryson City** 20, or **Waynesville** 23. Then, visit some of the towns in the Southern Mountains south and west of Asheville, perhaps staying in **Brevard** 33, **Cashiers** 34, or **Highlands** 35 for one or two days. Finally, if time permits, drive northwest and visit the High Country for a couple of days, staying in **Blowing Rock** 25, **Boone** 26, or **Banner Elk** 28.

---

a few other towns. Train travel, except on tourist trains such as the Great Smoky Mountains Railroad between Dillsboro and Bryson City, isn't an option. When traveling by car, don't overplan your routes. Try getting lost once in a while. Some of the most rewarding sights—an old mountain cemetery, a country store—aren't on any map or in any guidebook, including this one.

Although the distances involved are not huge—from the tip of western North Carolina near Murphy to the mountain foothills at Morganton is only about 165 mi by road—it's not practical to try to see the entire area from a single base. Aside from Interstate 40 and 26 and a few other highways, most roads in the region are winding two-lanes, and it takes longer than you'd expect to get from A to B. On some roads, such as the scenic Blue Ridge Parkway, which winds 252 mi through the mountains in the region, you'll be lucky to average 30 mph, even though the speed limit is 45, given the twisting roads, the steep grades, and the many stops you'll make to admire the views.

Unlike the rough, jagged Rockies, the Carolina mountains are gentle green giants, smoothed and molded by eons of geological time. These are some of the oldest mountains on earth, dating back about 480 million years. Still, 125 peaks in the region rise to at least 5,000 feet, and 43 are more than 6,000 feet. Getting to the top of these peaks and back down safely will test your driving skills and the condition of your car's brakes.

About the Restaurants

You can still get tradional mountain food, served family-style, at places like Dan'l Boone Inn in Boone and Pisgah View Ranch in Candler, near Asheville. Increasingly, though, mountain cooks are offering more sophisticated fare. Chefs, trained at Asheville-Buncombe Technical College's culinary program, and in Charleston, New York, and even Paris, are creating innovative dishes. At many places, especially in Asheville, the emphasis is on "slow food"—locally grown ingredients, often organic. You can find nearly every world cuisine somewhere in the region, from Thai to Jamaican to Salvadoran.

WHAT IT COSTS

$$$$	**$$$**	**$$**	**$**	**¢**
over $22	$16–$22	$11–$16	$7–$11	under $7

Prices are for a main course at dinner, excluding sales tax of 6%.

About the Hotels

Around the mountains, at least in the larger cities and towns such as Asheville, Hendersonville, and Boone, you can find the usual chain motels and hotels: Hampton Inn, Best Western, Holiday Inn, Comfort Inn, Fairfield Inn, Red Roof, Residence Inn, and others. For more of a local flavor, look at the many mountain lodges and country inns, some with just a few rooms with simple comforts, others with upmarket amenities like tennis courts, golf courses, and spas. The mountains also have a few large resorts, with all the offerings of a grand hotel, of which the Grove Park Inn in Asheville is the prime example.

There are plenty of bed-and-breakfasts, too. Asheville alone has more than a dozen. Another option, especially good for families, is a cabin rental. These come in several varieties, from a single small cabin built and rented for extra income by a local resident, to cabin and cottage colonies with 5, 10, or more units to rent. Typically these rent by the week, or with two-, three-, or four-day minimum stays. Especially around ski resorts in the High Country, condos are available. Western North Carolina is also camping country, with hundreds of campgrounds ranging from primitive campsites in remote areas of the Smokies to full-service RV camps.

Arts & Crafts Asheville, sometimes called "the Santa Fe of the South," has an arts-and-crafts community that rivals those in much larger cities. Galleries are seemingly on every corner. Around internationally known crafts centers such as Penland School, workshops have sprung up of talented craftspeople; many are open to the public.

Mountain Highs If you're eager to escape concrete and heat, and to experience some of the most stupendous scenery this side of Switzerland, western North Carolina will have you out of your car and dancing for joy. Around nearly every country bend is a photograph waiting to be taken—a gray weathered barn or corn crib, a log cabin with a wisp of wood fire smoke tailing up to the sky, a flash of orange flame azalea, or a tangled stand of rhododendron in a medley of green, white, and purple, or an overlook view that stretches 20 mi into the brilliant distance. The Great Smokies alone have more kinds of trees and plants than all of Europe. Wildlife is abundant almost everywhere. Rarely will you drive a lonely mountain road without seeing a flock of wild turkeys crossing the lane, a fat groundhog munching grass at the edge of the road, white-tailed deer, pheasants, and quail, or, if you're lucky, even a black bear pulling berries. In the Cataloochee area of the Smokies, elk have been reintroduced and are making a comeback.

WHAT IT COSTS

$$$$	$$$	$$	$	¢
over $220	$160–$220	$110–$160	$70–$110	under $70

Prices are for two people in a standard double room in high season, excluding service charges and 11% tax.

Timing

Western North Carolina is a four-season destination, and that's more than a chamber of commerce slogan. Dates for high season, when hotel demand is strongest and rates are highest, vary from hotel to hotel, but generally it's from Memorial Day in late May through early November, at the end of the fall color season. Mid-June to mid-August draws a lot of families, since kids are out of school. Around ski resorts, winter, especially January and February, is prime time; elsewhere, these winter months are dead, and some hotels are closed.

Everywhere, peak demand for hotels is October, leaf-watching season; on weekends during the second through fourth weeks of the month, usually prime color time, nearly every hotel in the mountains is 100% booked. For these weekends, book as far ahead as you can, and never arrive without advance reservations. At other times, booking a week or two in advance is usually okay, although the top resorts can be full almost any time.

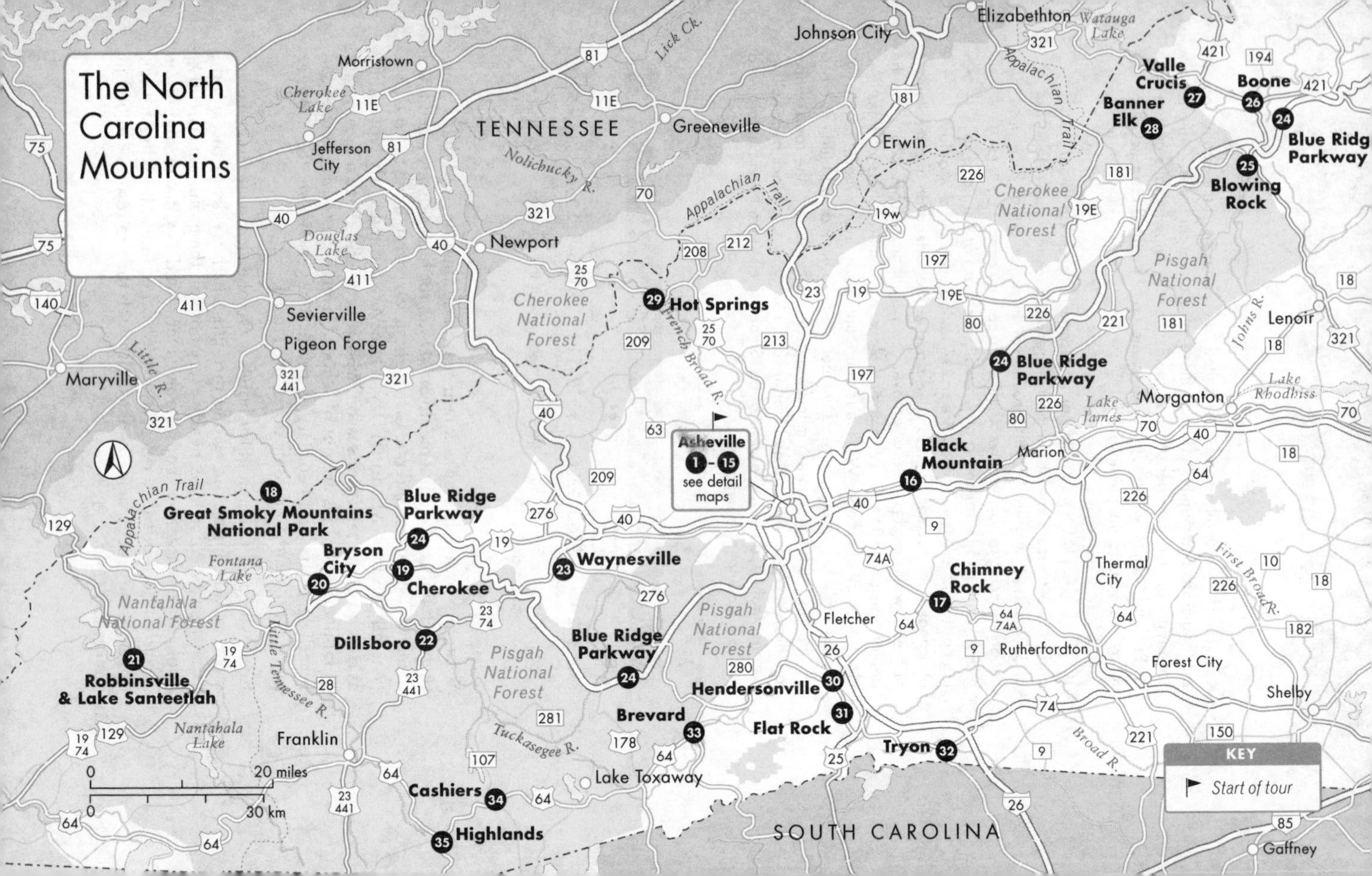

The North Carolina Mountains
TENNESSEE
SOUTH CAROLINA
Johnson City
Elizabethton
Watauga Lake
Morristown
Cherokee Lake
Jefferson City
Greeneville
Erwin
Nolichucky R.
Lick Ck.
Appalachian Trail
Newport
Douglas Lake
Sevierville
Pigeon Forge
Maryville
Little R.
Cherokee National Forest
Pisgah National Forest
Nantahala National Forest
29 Hot Springs
French Broad R.
Asheville
1 - 15 see detail maps
Valle Crucis 27
Banner Elk 28
Boone 26
24 Blue Ridge Parkway
25 Blowing Rock
Lenoir
Johns R.
Lake Rhodhiss
Morganton
Lake James
Marion
Black Mountain 16
Chimney Rock 17
Thermal City
First Broad R.
Rutherfordton
Forest City
Shelby
Broad R.
Fletcher
Hendersonville 30
Flat Rock 31
Tryon 32
Brevard 33
Lake Toxaway
Tuckasegee R.
23 Waynesville
Blue Ridge Parkway 24
18 Great Smoky Mountains National Park
Fontana Lake
Bryson City 20
19 Cherokee
Dillsboro 22
21 Robbinsville & Lake Santeetlah
Nantahala Lake
Little Tennessee R.
Franklin
Cashiers 34
35 Highlands
Gaffney
0 20 miles
0 30 km
KEY
Start of tour

Spring is a wonderful time to visit the mountains, as there are plenty of hotel rooms at bargain rates, the weather is pleasantly moderate, and native flowers are in bloom.

ASHEVILLE

Asheville is the hippest city in the South. At least that's the claim of Asheville's fans, who are legion. Visitors flock to Asheville to experience the arts and culture scene, which rivals that of Santa Fe, and to experience the city's blossoming downtown, with its myriad restaurants, coffeehouses, museums, galleries, bookstores, antiques shops, and boutiques.

Named "the best place to live" by many books and magazines, Asheville is also the destination for retirees escaping the cold North, or of "halfbacks," those who moved to Florida but who are now coming half the way back to the North. Old downtown buildings have been converted to upmarket condos for these affluent retirees, and new housing developments are springing up south, east, and west of town. As a result of this influx, Asheville has a much more cosmopolitan population than most cities of its size (70,000 people in the city, 385,000 in the metro area), and also real estate prices that are the highest in North Carolina and similar to Atlanta's.

Asheville has a diversity you won't find in many cities in the South. Gays and lesbians run many businesses downtown, and *Rolling Stone* magazine's claim that Asheville is "the freak capital of America" reflects the fact that the area has drawn many aging hippies and young alternative-lifestyle seekers.

The city really comes alive at night, with the restaurants, sidewalk cafés, and coffeehouses luring locals and visitors alike. Especially on warm summer weekends, Pack Square, Haywood Street, Wall Street, and Battery Park Avenue are busy until well after midnight.

Exploring Asheville

A city of neighborhoods, Asheville rewards careful exploration, especially on foot. You can break up your sightseeing with stops at the more than 50 restaurants in downtown alone, and at any of hundreds of unique shops.

Downtown Asheville has the largest extant collection of art deco buildings outside of Miami Beach, most notably the S&W Cafeteria (1929), Asheville City Hall (1928), First Baptist Church (1927), and Asheville High School (1929). It's also known for its architecture in other styles: Battery Park Hotel (1924) is neo-Georgian; the Flatiron Building (1924) is neoclassical; the Basilica of St. Lawrence (1912) is Spanish baroque; and Pack Place, formerly known as Old Pack Library (1925), is in the Italian Renaissance style.

North Asheville, the historic Montford section (home to about a dozen bed-and-breakfast inns), and the Grove Park neighborhood all have fine Victorian-era homes, including many remarkable Queen Anne houses.

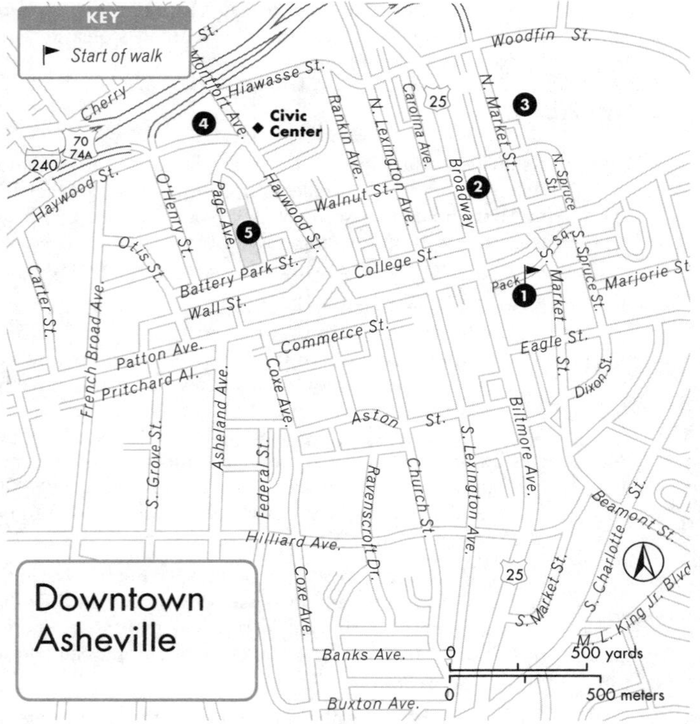

Biltmore Village, across from the entrance to the Biltmore Estate, was constructed at the time that Biltmore House was being built, and is now predominantly an area of retail boutiques and galleries. The River District, along the French Broad River, is an up-and-coming arts area, with many studios and lofts. Across the river, West Asheville has suddenly become the hottest part of the city, with its main artery, Haywood Road, sporting new restaurants, edgy stores, and popular clubs.

Each of these neighborhoods can be explored on foot, but to get from one to another, except between downtown and the Montford section, you need a car, or you can go by taxi or by city bus.

a good tour

At a minimum, you need three full days to see Asheville. Downtown is most profitably explored on foot, but to discover the outer reaches of the city and the sights in the rural areas of Buncombe County, you'll want to drive.

Dedicate at least a morning to downtown. Start your walking tour at **Pack Place Education, Arts & Science Center** 1 in the heart of town. From there, walk north on Broadway to **Black Mountain College Museum** 2, then two blocks east to the **Thomas Wolfe Memorial** 3, the famed author's childhood home. Walk west to the **Basilica of St. Lawrence** 4, and end your downtown exploration at **Grove Arcade Public Market** ⑤, where you can relax with a cold drink, a snack, or a meal.

After touring downtown, hop in your car and head for North Asheville, where you can visit the **Riverside Cemetery** ⑥, the **Botanical Gardens at Asheville** ⑦, and the **Grove Park Inn** ⑧. Next, drive out to the **Vance Birthplace** ⑨. If you have kids with you, finish the day by heading east to the **WNC Nature Center** ⑩.

To do them justice, you should devote a full day to the **Biltmore Estate** ⑪ and **Biltmore Village** ⑫. Take another day to drive to southwest Asheville's **Smith-McDowell House Museum** ⑬ and the nearby **WNC Farmers Market** ⑭ and **North Carolina Arboretum** ⑮ to the west.

What to See

Asheville Urban Trail. This 1.7-mi walk developed by the City of Asheville has about 30 "stations," with plaques marking places of historical or architectural interest. The self-guided tour begins at Pack Place Education, Arts & Science Center. To enhance your experience, you can rent an audio guide at the Asheville Art Museum, which is part of the Pack Place complex. From April to November, guided group tours are usually scheduled at 10 and 3 on Saturday, weather permitting. ✉ *2 S. Pack Sq., at Pack Place (Asheville Art Museum)* ☎ *828/258–0710* 🌐 *www.urbantrails.net* 🎫 *Audio guide $5, tour $5.*

❹ **Basilica of St. Lawrence.** A collaboration of Biltmore House head architect Richard Sharp Smith and the Spanish engineer-architect Rafael Gustavin, this elaborate Catholic basilica was completed in 1908. It follows a Spanish Renaissance design, rendered in brick and polychrome tile, and has a large, self-supporting dome with Catalan-style vaulting. ✉ *97 Haywood St., Downtown* ☎ *828/252–6042* 🎫 *Free* ⏲ *Weekdays 9–4.*

⓫ **Biltmore Estate.** Built in the 1890s as the private home of George Vanderbilt, the astonishing 250-room French Renaissance château is America's largest private residence. (Some of Vanderbilt's descendants still live here, but the bulk of the home and grounds are open to visitors.) Richard Morris Hunt designed it, and Frederick Law Olmsted landscaped the original 125,000-acre estate (now 8,000 acres), which faces Biltmore Village. It took 1,000 workers five years to complete the gargantuan project. On view are the priceless antiques and art collected by the Vanderbilts, along with 75 acres of gardens and formally landscaped grounds. You can also see the state-of-the-art winery and take candlelight tours of the house at Christmastime. The historic horse stables are also open to the public. Allow a full day to tour the house and grounds. ✉ *Exit 50 off I–40, South Metro* ☎ *828/255–1700 or 800/624–1575* 🌐 *www.biltmore.com* 🎫 *$39* ⏲ *Jan.–Mar., daily 9–4; Apr.–Dec., daily 8:30–5.*

Fodor's Choice ★

⓬ **Biltmore Village.** Across from the Biltmore Estate, Biltmore Village is a highly walkable collection of restored English village–style houses, now mostly shops and galleries. Of particular note is **All Souls Cathedral,** one of the most beautiful churches in America. It was designed by

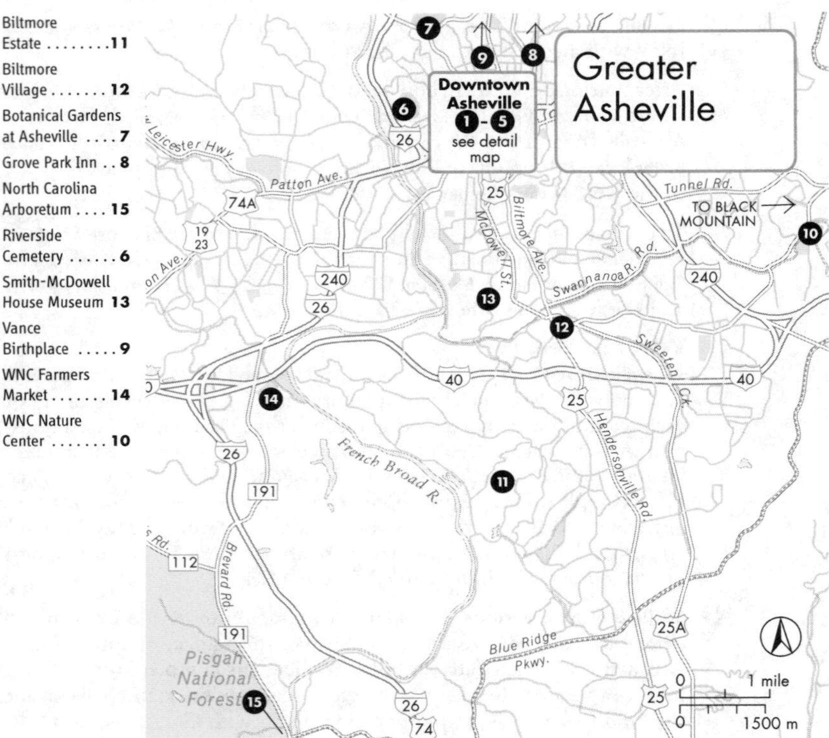

Richard Morris Hunt following the traditional Norman cross plan and opened in 1896. ✉ *3 Angle St., South Metro* ☎ *828/274–2681* 🎫 *Free* ⏲ *Daily, hrs vary.*

❷ **Black Mountain College Museum & Arts Center.** Famed Black Mountain College (1933–56), 16 mi east of Asheville, was important in the development of several groundbreaking 20th-century art, dance, and literary movements. A museum and gallery dedicated to the history of the radical college occupies a small space in downtown Asheville. It puts on occasional exhibits and publishes material about the college. Call ahead to find out what's currently happening. ✉ *54 Broadway, Downtown* ☎ *828/299–9306* 🌐 *www.blackmountaincollege.org* ⏲ *Thurs.–Sat. noon–4.*

❼ **Botanical Gardens at Asheville.** Adjoining the University of North Carolina at Asheville campus, this 10-acre site has walking trails and displays of native plants, including a bog with carnivorous plants such as Venus's-flytraps, pitcher plants, and sundew. ✉ *151 Weaver Blvd., at Broadway, 2 mi north of downtown Asheville, North Metro* ☎ *828/252–5190* 🌐 *www.ashevillebotanicalgardens.org* 🎫 *Free* ⏲ *Daily dawn–dusk.*

5 **Grove Arcade Public Market.** When it opened in 1929, the Grove Arcade was trumpeted as "the most elegant building in America" by its builder, W. E. Grove, the man also responsible for the Grove Park Inn. With the coming of the Great Depression and World War II, the Grove Arcade evolved into a dowdy government building. In late 2002, its polished limestone elegance was restored, and it reopened as a public market patterned in some ways after Pike Place Market in Seattle. The market covers a full city block and has about 50 locally owned stores and restaurants, along with apartments and office space. The building is an architectural wonder, with gargoyles galore, and well worth a visit even if you don't shop or dine here. ✉ *1 Page Ave., Downtown* ☎ *828/252–7799* 🌐 *www.grovearcade.com* 🎫 *Free* ⏲ *Daily 10–6; store hrs vary.*

★ 8 **Grove Park Inn.** This large resort overlooking Asheville is well worth a visit even if you don't stay here. The oldest section was built in 1913 using huge, locally mined granite stones, some weighing 10,000 pounds. Inside there's the largest collection of Arts and Crafts furniture in the world, as well as two small but interesting museums: the North Carolina Homespun Museum, which tells the story of a training school established by the Vanderbilt family (of Biltmore Estate fame) to revive interest in native crafts, and the Estes-Winn Memorial Automobile Museum, which has a collection of antique cars. ✉ *290 Macon Ave., North Metro* ☎ *800/438–5800 or 828/252-2711* 🌐 *www.groveparkinn.com* 🎫 *Free* ⏲ *Hotel daily 24 hrs; Homespun Museum and Estes-Winn Automobile Museum Apr.–Dec., Mon.–Sat 10–5, Sun. 1–5.*

★ 15 **North Carolina Arboretum.** Part of the original Biltmore Estate, these 426 acres completed Frederick Law Olmsted's dream of creating a world-class arboretum in the western part of North Carolina. Highlights include southern Appalachian flora in stunning settings, such as the Blue Ridge Quilt Garden, with bedding plants arranged in patterns reminiscent of Appalachian quilts. An extensive network of trails is available for walking or mountain biking. ✉ *100 Frederick Law Olmsted Way, 10 mi southwest of downtown Asheville, at Blue Ridge Pkwy., near I–26 and I–40, South Metro* ☎ *828/665–2492* 🌐 *www.ncarboretum.org* 🎫 *$6 per car parking fee; free Tues.* ⏲ *Visitor education center Mon.–Sat. 9–5, Sun. noon–5; gardens and grounds daily 8–7.*

1 **Pack Place Education, Arts & Science Center.** This 92,000-square-foot complex in downtown Asheville houses the **Asheville Art Museum, Colburn Earth Science Museum, Health Adventure,** and **Diana Wortham Theatre.** The **YMI Cultural Center,** also maintained by Pack Place, and focusing on the history of African-Americans in western North Carolina, is across the street. The Health Adventure has 11 galleries with hands-on exhibits, all of interest to children. The Asheville Art Museum stages major exhibits several times a year, with some highlighting regional artists. The Colburn Earth Science Museum displays local gems and minerals. ✉ *2 S. Pack Sq., Downtown* ☎ *828/257–4500* 🌐 *www.packplace.org* 🎫 *Art museum $6, earth science museum $4, other museums $5 each, all museums $16* ⏲ *Tues.–Sat. 10–5, Sun. 1–5.*

6 **Riverside Cemetery.** Authors Thomas Wolfe and O. Henry are buried here, along with about 13,000 others, including some of Asheville's most prominent citizens. The 87-acre cemetery, overlooking the French Broad River in the historic Montford area, has flower gardens and ancient oaks and poplars. ✉ *Birch St. off Pearson Dr., North Metro* ☎ *828/258–8480.*

13 **Smith-McDowell House Museum.** This is the oldest surviving house in Asheville, dating from 1840. The grounds were designed by Frederick Law Olmsted in 1900. The interior has much of the house's original Greek Revival woodwork, and restored rooms date from 1840 to 1900. Exhibits in the gallery focus on Asheville's early history. ✉ *283 Victoria Rd., Metro East* ☎ *828/253–9231* 🌐 *www.wnchistory.org* *$5* ⏲ *Tues.–Sat. 10–4, Sun. 1–4.*

3 **Thomas Wolfe Memorial.** Asheville's most famous son, novelist Thomas Wolfe, grew up in a 29-room Queen Anne–style home that his mother ran as a boardinghouse. The house, a state historic site, was badly damaged in a 1998 fire (a still-unsolved case of arson); it reopened in mid-2004 following a painstaking $2.4 million renovation. Though about one-fourth of the furniture and artifacts were lost in the fire, the house—memorialized as "Dixieland" in Wolfe's novel *Look Homeward, Angel*—has been restored to its original 1916 condition, including a light canary yellow paint on the exterior. You'll find a visitor center and many displays, and there are guided tours of the house and heirloom gardens. ✉ *52 Market St., Downtown* ☎ *828/253–8304* *$1* ⏲ *Apr.–Oct., Tues.–Sat. 9–5, Sun. 1–5; Nov.–Mar., Tues.–Sat. 9–4, Sun. 1–4.*

Fodor's Choice ★

9 **Vance Birthplace.** A reconstructed pioneer cabin and outbuildings mark the childhood home of Zebulon Vance, three-time governor of North Carolina and United States senator from 1979 to 1994. You can tour the site, which is representative of more prosperous mountain homesteads during the early 19th century. ✉ *911 Reems Creek Rd., 13 mi north of downtown Asheville, North Metro* ☎ *828/645–6706* *Free* ⏲ *Apr.–Oct, Tues.–Sat. 9–5, Sun. 1–5; Nov.–Mar., Tues.–Sat., 9–4, Sun. 1–4.*

14 **WNC Farmers Market.** The highest-volume farmers market in North Carolina is a good place to buy local jams, jellies, honey, and, in season, local fruits and vegetables. A wholesale section below the main retail section (both are open to all) offers produce in bulk. ✉ *570 Brevard Rd., 5 mi southwest of downtown Asheville, off I–40, South Metro* ☎ *828/253–1691* *Free* ⏲ *Apr.–Oct., daily 8–6; Nov.–Mar., daily 8–5.*

10 **WNC Nature Center.** On a 42-acre Natural Heritage site, the WNC Nature Center is one of the region's most popular attractions for kids. It's basically a zoo focusing on animals native to the region, with cougars, bobcats, black bear, white-tailed deer, gray and red wolves, and gray and red foxes in natural-like settings. The center also has an excellent area on native reptiles and amphibians, plus a petting zoo. ✉ *75 Gashes Creek Rd., Metro East* ☎ *828/298–5600* *$5* ⏲ *Daily 10–5.*

Sports & the Outdoors

Golf

Broadmoor (✉ 101 French Broad La., Fletcher ☎ 828/687–1500), 15 mi south of Asheville, is a public Scottish-style links course, playing to 7,111 yards, par 72. **Buncombe County Golf Course** (✉ 226 Fairway Dr. ☎ 828/298–1867), is the par-72, 18-hole public municipal course designed by Donald Ross. **Colony Lake Lure Golf Resort** (✉ 201 Blvd. of the Mountains, Lake Lure ☎ 828/625–2888 or 800/260–1040), 25 mi from Asheville, has two 18-hole, par-72 courses known for their beauty. **Grove Park Inn Resort** (✉ 290 Macon Ave. ☎ 828/252–2711 or 800/438–5800) has a beautiful par-71 course.

Horseback Riding

Cataloochee Ranch (✉ 119 Ranch Rd., Maggie Valley ☎ 828/926–1401 or 800/868–1401) allows riders to explore the property's mile-high vistas on horseback. Trail rides are offered by stables throughout the region between April and November, including **Pisgah View Ranch** (✉ Pisgah View Ranch Rd., Candler ☎ 828/667–9100), where you can gallop through the wooded mountainside.

Llama Treks

Avalon Llama Trek (✉ 310 Wilson Cove Rd., Swannanoa ☎ 828/298–5637) leads llama trips on the lush trails of the Pisgah National Forest. One-day and overnight hikes with llamas carrying your pack through local forests are arranged by **Windsong Llama Treks, Ltd.** (✉ 120 Ferguson Ridge Rd., Clyde ☎ 828/627–6111).

Skiing

In addition to having outstanding skiing, **Cataloochee Resort** (✉ Rte. 1, Maggie Valley ☎ 828/926–0285 or 800/768–0285) hosts lots of different activities for the whole family. **Fairfield-Sapphire Valley** (✉ 4000 U.S. 64W, Sapphire Valley ☎ 828/743–3441 or 800/533–8268) offers basic skiing despite minimal snowfall. **Wolf Laurel** (✉ Rte. 3, Mars Hill ☎ 828/689–4111) has night skiing and excellent snowmaking capabilities.

Where to Eat

$$$$ Fodor's Choice ★ ✕ **Gabrielle's.** From the moment you're met at the door, offered an ice-cold martini, and invited to stroll the lovely Victorian gardens while your table is readied, you suspect that dinner at Gabrielle's is going to be your best dining experience in the mountains—and chances are it will be. The best does come at a price, however. The five-course "grande menu," which changes frequently, is $85, or $120 with paired wines. The somewhat less expensive à la carte menu has items such as sake-marinated seabass and herb-and-pinenut-encrusted salmon. The near-perfect service and the setting in an elegant, art-filled 19th-century cherry-panel space, with piano music in the background, make for a memorable splurge. *✉ 87 Richmond Hill Dr., at Richmond Hill Inn, North Metro ☎ 828/252–7313 or 888/742–4536 Reservations essential ▭ AE, MC, V ⊙ Closed Tues. No lunch.*

★ **$$$–$$$$** ✕ **Zambras.** Sophisticated tapas selections, such as paella, kobe beef, and steamed mussels, many influenced by the cuisine of Mediterranean

Spain, and a wine list featuring unusual Spanish wines and sherries, make this one of the most interesting restaurants in the mountains. Voluptuous Moorish colors and live gypsy music (and belly dancers on weekends) lend an exotic air. ✉ *85 Walnut St., Downtown* ☎ *828/232–1060* ✍ *Reservations essential* ▭ *AE, D, MC, V* ⊙ *No lunch.*

$$–$$$$ ✕ **The Market Place.** Clean lines, neutral colors, and brushed steel mobiles create a sophisticated style here. The food offers refreshing twists on ingredients indigenous to the mountains (such as game and trout) and the South in general. Possible entrées are roasted trout with portobello mushrooms, and tenderloin of pork with a sweet-potato timbale. Iron gates open onto an exterior courtyard and dining patio. ✉ *20 Wall St., Downtown* ☎ *828/252–4162* ✍ *Reservations essential* ▭ *AE, MC, V* ⊙ *Closed Sun. No lunch.*

★ **$$–$$$** ✕ **Bistro 1896.** Recently doubled in size, Bistro 1896 (in a building on Pack Square dating from that year) focuses on seafood but also offers other dishes. Start with oysters on the half shell, so fresh you can smell the salt air, or fried calamari, then jump to herbed salmon or ahi tuna with black-and-white sesame seeds. The bistro look comes from the period photos on the walls and glass-top tables with fresh flowers. On Sunday, there's a brunch with a build-it-yourself Bloody Mary bar. ✉ *7 Pack Sq., Downtown* ☎ *828/251–1300* ▭ *AE, MC, V.*

$$–$$$ ✕ **Vincenzo's.** There are two distinct halves of this pastel-hue *ristorante* on the last brick street remaining in Asheville: a casual trattoria downstairs and a more formal dining room upstairs. The trattoria serves an abbreviated version of the full northern Italian menu. Specialties include filet of beef in a Gorgonzola cream sauce topped with pine nuts and caramelized shallots, and chicken breast with prosciutto, sautéed spinach, and mushrooms, served over fettuccine. The wine list is extensive. Smoking is allowed in the trattoria, where there's live music nightly. ✉ *10 N. Market St., Downtown* ☎ *828/254–4699* ▭ *AE, D, DC, MC, V* ⊙ *No lunch.*

$–$$ ✕ **Asheville Pizza and Brewing Company.** Locally known as the "Brew 'n View," this funky eatery-cum-movie theater is extremely popular. Grab a micro-brew beer and a pizza with portobello mushrooms and fresh spinach, and watch *Star Wars* from the comfort of an old sofa. ✉ *675 Merrimon Ave., North Metro* ☎ *828/254–1281* ▭ *MC, V.*

$–$$ ✕ **Early Girl Eatery.** Named after an early-maturing tomato variety, Early Girl Eatery is casually Southern, with a cheerfully chic twist. A wall of south-facing windows provides wonderful light most of the day. No white tablecloths here: you eat on brown butcher paper. The dinner menu runs to items like grilled duck with collard greens. At breakfast, choose huge stacks of buttermilk pancakes or Creole catfish and stoneground grits. ✉ *8 Wall St. Ave., Downtown* ☎ *828/259–9592* ▭ *MC, V.*

$–$$ ✕ **Laughing Seed Café.** You'll get more than brown rice and beans at this vegetarian eatery, completely redone in mid-2004, with a bold mural on one wall and a bar. The extensive menu ranges from fruit drinks to sandwiches and pizzas to dinner specialties influenced by the flavors of India, China, and Morocco. Fruits and vegetables come from local organic farms during the growing season. Breads are baked daily on premises. There's outdoor dining. ✉ *40 Wall St., Downtown* ☎ *828/252–3445* ▭ *AE, D, MC, V* ⊙ *Closed Tues.*

$–$$ ✕ **Salsa's.** In an expanded space with a slightly retro-hippy look, you'll find spicy and highly creative Mexican and Caribbean fare in huge portions. Fire-roasted pepper tacos, black bean and goat cheese tacos, and plantains stuffed with herbs, meat, and vegetables are among the recommended entrées. Delicious desserts include caramelized mango. ✉ *6 Patton Ave., Downtown* ☎ *828/252–9805* ▭ *AE, D, MC, V* ⊙ *Closed Sun.*

$–$$ ✕ **Tupelo Honey.** Hello, darlin'! This is the place for downhome Southern cooking with an uptown twist. Owner Sharon Schott delivers a lot more than grits, with dishes like sautéed salmon topped with crabcakes with candied ginger cornbread, and free range chicken with mashed sweet potatoes. Breakfast is served anytime. The atmosphere is loud and a little funky. There's a jar of tupelo honey on every table. ✉ *12 College St., Downtown* ☎ *828/255–4863* ▭ *AE, MC, V* ⊙ *Closed Mon. No lunch Fri. and Sat.*

¢–$ ✕ **Delores and José Mexican Restaurant.** Mexico City natives José, Delores, and Mena dish out simple but delicious and inexpensive Mexican lunches for Asheville's fast-growing Mexican community and loyal gringos. The enchilada plate is *bueno,* with the hottest salsa in town on the side. Killer french fries, too. ✉ *521 Haywood Rd., West Asheville* ☎ *828/253–3557* ▭ *No credit cards* ⊙ *Closed Sun. No dinner.*

¢–$ ✕ **Doc Chey's.** "Peace, love, and noodles" is the theme at this outpost of an Atlanta noodle house, with Vietnamese, Thai, Japanese, and Chinese noodle bowls and rice plates served fast, cheap, and tasty. It's always packed. ✉ *37 Biltmore Ave., Downtown* ☎ *828/252–8220* ▭ *AE, MC, V.*

¢–$ ✕ **Sunny Point Café and Bakery.** In a restored storefront in up-and-coming West Asheville, Sunny Point lives up to its name with bright, cheerful decor. It's a good spot for breakfast, where free-range pork sausage shares the menu with granola, herbed potatoes, and some of the biggest biscuits in town. ✉ *626 Haywood Rd., Asheville West* ☎ *828/252–0055* ▭ *MC, V* ⊙ *Closed Sun. and Mon. No dinner.*

¢ ✕ **Old Europe.** The Hungarian owner, Zoltan Vetro, brings a European sensibility to this immensely popular pastry shop. It's usually jammed; at night the crowd spills over to the sidewalk tables, slurping coffee and liqueurs and downing delicious tortes, cakes, and other Europastries. ✉ *18 Battery Park Ave., Downtown* ☎ *828/252–0001* ▭ *MC, V.*

Where to Stay

$$$$ Fodor'sChoice ★ **Grove Park Inn Resort & Spa.** Asheville's premier large resort has an imposing granite edifice that dates from 1913 and panoramic views of the Blue Ridge Mountains. Henry Ford, F. Scott Fitzgerald, and Michael Jordan have stayed here. It is furnished with oak antiques in the Arts and Crafts style, and the lobby fireplaces are as big as cars. Four restaurants offer plenty of choices: Horizons, for example, specializes in game dishes, from ostrich to boar. The spa is one of the finest in the country. ✉ *290 Macon Ave., North Metro, 28804* ☎ *828/252–2711 or 800/438–5800* 🖷 *828/252–6102* 🌐 *www.groveparkinn.com* ⇨ *498 rooms, 12 suites* ♖ *4 restaurants, 18-hole golf course, putting green, 9 tennis courts, indoor pool, health club, hot tub, spa, 3 bars, nightclub, shops, playground, laundry service, concierge, business services, meeting rooms* ▭ *AE, D, DC, MC, V* 🍴 *EP.*

CloseUp

CAFFEINATED ASHEVILLE

Given Asheville's artsy sensibilities, it shouldn't come as a surprise that the city has a flourishing café scene. While Starbucks has made inroads here, you shouldn't come to Asheville without trying at least one of the locally operated coffeehouses, which have become something of a civic claim to fame.

There are about a dozen specialty coffee places to choose from in Asheville, each with its own personality. These are among the best: ***Beanstreets*** *(✉ 3 Broadway Ave. ☎ 828/255–8180) has a funky, urban atmosphere and great Belgian waffles.* ***Gold Hill Espresso and Fine Teas*** *(✉ 64 Haywood St. ☎ 828/254–3800) is refined and jazzy. At* ***Mountain City Coffee Roasters*** *(✉ Grove Arcade ☎ 828/232–9937) the brew is made from locally roasted beans, including some magnificent varietals from North Africa.* ***Malaprop's Café*** *(✉ 55 Haywood St. ☎ 828/254–6734) is associated with a first-rate downtown independent bookstore.*

★ **$$$$** **Inn on Biltmore Estate.** Many people who have in the past come to see the Biltmore mansion have longed to lodge here overnight. In 2001 their wishes were granted when this posh ridge-top property opened. The hotel mimics the look of Biltmore House with natural stone and copper. French manor houses inspired the interior. Nice touches include afternoon tea in the library. The dining room is bookended by large windows with mountain views and a massive fireplace. Menus deftly blend local and international ingredients. ✉ *Biltmore Estate, exit 50 off I–40, South Metro, 28803* ☎ *800/922–0084* 🖷 *828/225–1629* 🌐 *www.biltmore.com/inn* *207 rooms, 9 suites* *Restaurant, room service, golf privileges, pool, health club, hot tub, mountain bikes, hiking, horseback riding, bar, library, shops, concierge, meeting rooms* *AE, D, DC, MC, V* *EP.*

$$$$ **Haywood Park Hotel.** The lobby of this all-suites downtown hotel, once a department store, has golden oak woodwork accented with gleaming brass. The suites are spacious, with baths done in Spanish marble. A continental breakfast is delivered to your room. The Flying Frog Café, with an astonishingly eclectic menu—mixing French, Indian, and German cuisine—is in the hotel. There's a small shopping galleria in the atrium, and a sidewalk café. ✉ *1 Battery Park Ave., Downtown, 28801* ☎ *828/252–2522 or 800/228–2522* 🖷 *828/253–0481* 🌐 *www.haywoodpark.com* *33 suites* *Restaurant, room service, exercise equipment, sauna, bar, shops, laundry service, concierge, business services, meeting rooms* *AE, D, DC, MC, V* *BP.*

★ **$$$$** **Richmond Hill Inn.** Once a private residence, this elegant Victorian mansion is on the National Register of Historic Places. Many rooms in the mansion are furnished with canopy beds, Victorian sofas, and other antiques, while the more modern cottages have contemporary pine poster beds. Although Richmond Hill does not enjoy the panoramic views of Asheville's other top hotels, and the immediate neighborhood is not exactly upscale, the grounds are stunning, with ever-changing gardens. Its restaurant, Gabrielle's, is arguably the best in the region. ✉ *87 Richmond Hill Dr., North Metro, 28806* ☎ *828/252–7313 or 888/742–4536* 🖷 *828/252–8726* 🌐 *www.richmondhillinn.com* *24 rooms, 3 suites, 9 cottages* *Restaurant, croquet, library, business services, meeting rooms* *AE, MC, V* *BP.*

$$$–$$$$ **Albemarle Inn.** Famed Hungarian composer Béla Bartók lived here in the early 1940s, creating his Third Piano Concerto, the "Asheville Concerto." You can stay in his room on the third floor, although Juliet's Chamber, with its private balcony overlooking lovely gardens, may appeal more to modern Romeos. Owners Cathy and Larry Sklar, expat lawyers from Connecticut, have turned this 1907 Greek Revival mansion in a quiet North Asheville residential area into one of the top B&Bs in the region. Gourmet breakfasts are prepared by the inn's chef. ✉ *86 Edgemont Rd., 1 mi north of I–240, North Metro, 28804* ☎ *828/255–0027 or 800/621–7435* 🖷 *828/236–3397* 🌐 *www.albemarleinn.com* *10 rooms, 1 suite* *Cable TV; no kids under 12, no smoking* *D, MC, V* *BP.*

$$$–$$$$ **Black Walnut Inn.** The Biltmore House supervising architect Richard Sharp Smith built this 1899 home in Asheville's Monford section. Today it's a B&B on the National Register of Historic Places. Most of the rooms—all redone in 2004 by owners Peter and Lori White—have working fireplaces. Parts of the 2000 movie *28 Days* were filmed here. (The star, Sandra Bullock, stayed in the Dogwood Room.) ✉ *288 Montford Ave., North Metro, 28801* ☎ *828/254–3878 or 800/381–3878* 🌐 *www.blackwalnut.com* *6 rooms, 1 cottage* *No smoking* *D, MC, V* *BP.*

$$–$$$$ **Pisgah View Ranch.** You have 2,000 acres of mountain land to explore at this countrified dude ranch, a one-of-a-kind place that's been in the same family since 1790. There are 28 comfortable (but far from fancy) cabins and cottages, many with views of mile-high Mt. Pisgah. The ranch has 20 horses to ride, a fishing pond, tennis courts, a big red barn with dance floor and stage, and a log cabin museum. No low-carb meals here—a typical country dinner is fried chicken, sweet potato soufflé, and pickled beans. Rates cover everything except horseback riding. ✉ *70 Pisgah View Ranch Rd., 18 mi west of downtown Asheville, West Metro, 28715* ☎ *828/667–9100 or 866/252–8361* 🌐 *www.pisgahviewranch.com* *48 rooms in 28 cottages* *Restaurant, picnic area, BBQs, kitchens, 2 tennis courts, pool, fishing, hiking, horseback riding, horseshoes, Ping-Pong, shuffleboard, recreation room, laundry facilities, meeting rooms* *AE, D, MC, V* *Closed Dec.–Apr.* *FAP.*

$$–$$$ **Cedar Crest Victorian Inn.** Biltmore craftspeople constructed this beautiful Queen Anne house, with its lead-glass front door and corbeled brick fireplaces, as a private residence in 1891. The lovingly restored guest rooms are furnished with period antiques. You are treated to afternoon tea, evening coffee or chocolate, and a breakfast of fruit, pastry, and coffee. It's better suited to older children than younger ones. ✉ *674 Biltmore Ave., South Metro, 28803* ☎ *828/252–1389 or 800/252–0310* 🖷 *828/252–7667* 🌐 *www.cedarcrestvictorianinn.com* *9 rooms, 3 cottage suites* *Croquet, business services* *AE, D, DC, MC, V* *BP.*

$$–$$$ **The Lion and the Rose.** One of the characters in Thomas Wolfe's *Look Homeward, Angel* lived in this house, an 1898 Queen Anne/Georgian in the historic Montford Park area near downtown. It couldn't have looked any better then than it does now. A special detail is a 6-foot Palladian-style stained glass window at the top of oaks stairs. Innkeepers Jim and Linda Palmer keep the heirloom gardens and five guest rooms looking gorgeous. For the most privacy, choose the Craig-Toms suite, which occupies the entire third floor. *276 Montford Ave., North Metro, 28801 828/255–6546 or 800/546–6988 828/285–9810 www.lion-rose.com 4 rooms, 1 suite No kids under 12, no smoking D, MC, V BP.*

$–$$ **Hampton Inn–Biltmore Square.** You can relax beside the fire in the lobby at this motel off I–26, five mi southwest of downtown. Some guest rooms have whirlpool baths. Cookies and coffee are served every evening. *1 Rocky Ridge Rd., South Metro, 28806 828/667–2022 or 800/426–7866 828/665–9680 www.hampton-inn.com 121 rooms Indoor pool, exercise equipment, sauna, dry cleaning, laundry service, business services, meeting rooms, airport shuttle AE, D, DC, MC, V BP.*

¢–$ **Mountaineer Inn.** A fixture along Tunnel Road, this motel is ever popular with families and others who care less about fanciness than they do about affordable surroundings. A newer addition contains larger rooms. *155 Tunnel Rd., Metro East, 28805 828/254–5331 or 800/255–4080 828/254–5331 79 rooms Pool, business services, meeting rooms AE, D, MC, V BP.*

¢–$ **Red Roof Inn Asheville West.** This is the most affordable of the chain motels in Asheville, with rates regularly under $50 for a double. For that you get clean, standard-issue Red Roof rooms. *16 Crowell Rd., West Metro, 28806 828/667–9803 or 800/733–7663 828/667–9810 109 rooms AE, D, MC, V BP.*

Nightlife & the Arts

The Arts

One of the oldest community theater groups in the country, **Asheville Community Theatre** (35 E. Walnut St., Downtown 828/254–1320) stages professional plays year-round in its own theater building.

As the headquarters of the prestigious craft group, the Southern Highland Craft Guild, as well as a Blue Ridge Parkway visitor center, the **Folk Art Center** (Blue Ridge Parkway MM 382 828/298–7298), regularly puts on exceptional quilt, woodworking, pottery, and other crafts shows and demonstrations.

With professional summer theater that often celebrates mountain culture, **Southern Appalachian Repertory Theatre (SART)** (Owen Hall, Mars Hill College 828/689–1239), produces plays such as William Gregg and Perry Deane Young's *Mountain of Hope,* about the 1835 controversy over whether or not Mt. Mitchell is the highest peak east of the Rockies.

Nightlife

More than a restaurant, more than a movie theater, **Asheville Pizza and Brewing Company**, also called Brew 'n' View (✉ 675 Merrimon Ave. ☎ 828/254–1281), is a wildly popular place to catch a flick while lounging on a sofa, drinking a microbrew, and scarfing a veggie pizza.

The camp decor at **Hairspray** (✉ 38 N. French Broad Ave. ☎ 828/258–2027) will make you feel like you're back in 1961, though the music is contemporary. The crowd is diverse but predominately lesbian.

From the day it opened in 2002, **The Orange Peel Social Aid and Pleasure Club** (✉ 101 Biltmore Ave. ☎ 828/225–5851) instantly became, far and away, the number one nightspot in downtown Asheville, with names like Bob Dylan, Hootie and the Blowfish, and Steve Winwood playing here in an intimate (relatively speaking), smoke-free setting for audiences of up to about 950. For smaller events, it also has a great dance floor, with springy wood slats.

Asheville's best-known gay club, **Scandal's** (✉ 11 Grove St. ☎ 828/252–2838), has a lively dance floor and drag shows on weekends.

In a 1913 downtown building, the jazz and blues club **Tressa's** (✉ 28 Broadway ☎ 828/254–7072) is nominally private, but lets nonmembers in for a nominal cover charge. There's a quieter, no-smoking room upstairs.

In happening West Asheville, the smoke-free **Westville Pub** (✉ 777 Haywood Rd. ☎ 828/225–9782) has about 50 different beers on the menu, and a different band plays nearly every night.

Shopping

Biltmore Village (✉ Hendersonville Rd. ☎ 828/274–5570), across from the Biltmore Estate, is a cluster of specialty shops, restaurants, galleries, and hotels in an early-20th-century-English-hamlet style. You'll find everything from children's books to music, antiques, and wearable art.

Shopping is excellent all over **Downtown Asheville,** with at least 200 stores, including about 30 art galleries and over a dozen antiques shops. Several streets, notably **Biltmore Avenue, Lexington Avenue,** and **Wall Street** are lined with small, independently owned stores.

The **Grove Arcade Public Market** (✉ 1 Page Ave., Downtown ☎ 828/252–7799), one of America's first indoor shopping centers, originally opened in 1929. The remarkable building, which covers an entire city block, was totally redone and reopened in 2002 as a collection of some 50 local specialty shops and restaurants.

Grovewood Gallery at the Homespun Shops (✉ 111 Grovewood Rd. ☎ 828/253–7651), adjacent to the Grove Park Inn and established by Mrs. George Vanderbilt, sells furniture and contemporary and traditionally crafted woven goods made on the premises.

CloseUp

CAROLINA ARTS & CRAFTS

A **CENTURY AGO,** *as young George Vanderbilt prepared to build a retreat in then-bucolic Asheville, he and an architect traveled the French countryside, looking at 16th-century Loire Valley châteaux for inspiration. Craftspeople labored long to create the resulting Biltmore Mansion, including its unlikely gargoyles and grotesques.*

The lesson is, when it comes to arts and crafts in western North Carolina, expect the unexpected. There's much more going on than first meets the eye, and half the fun is in the discovery. Sometimes handmade treasures are found out in the open: more than 85 crafts fairs are held annually throughout the rural 21-county region. The best source of information is The Craft Heritage Trails of Western North Carolina *by Jay Fields and Betty Hurst, widely available in bookstores in the region. It gives details on more than 500 crafts studios, shops, and galleries.*

More than 4,000 people in the region earn part or all of their living from crafts, and many of them can be found "around the bend" and in homes tucked back in forested hollows. They patiently coax form from clay and wood and metal, and they are usually happy to talk about what they do—so explore. Interesting roads that are off the map can lead to workshops.

In the beginning, practical function, rather than notions of folk art, were behind all the quilting, weaving, woodworking, and pottery making. But by the late 19th century missionaries, social workers, and women of means—Frances Goodrich and Edith Vanderbilt among them—began to recognize that these things of day-to-day life contained artistry. The result was economic salvation for a beautiful but isolated and impoverished area.

Today utility and aesthetics have melded. From furnaces in the northwest counties of Mitchell and Yancey comes art glass prized by collectors and dealers worldwide. Many glassblowers have perfected their métier at the prestigious ***Penland School of Crafts,*** *whose courses also include printmaking, wood, surface design, metals, drawing, clay, and fibers. The work of students and graduates is on display in area galleries, including Penland's own extensive shop. Another well-known crafts school is* ***John C. Campbell Folk School,*** *in Brasstown near Murphy in the far western tip of the state.*

Here are several other good places to begin your crafts search:

The largest crafts event in the Southeast is held annually in mid-July and again in October in the Asheville Civic Center: the ***Craft Fair of the Southern Highlands*** *put on by the Southern Highlands Handicraft Guild. At the* ***Balsam Mountain Inn*** *(✉ Off Rte. 23/74, Balsam ☎ 828/456–9498), just off the Blue Ridge Parkway near Waynesville, the work of a number of artisans is tastefully showcased year-round. In the tiny village of Crossnore, in southern Avery County, a rock cottage houses the* ***Crossnore School's Weaving Room*** *(✉ U.S. 221 ☎ 828/733–4660). Favored here are patterns used by the early settlers of the Appalachians; however, in a nod to modernity the ladies spin with easy-care rayon and synthetics as well as with cotton, wool, and linen.On the Cherokee Reservation, in the shadow of the Smoky Mountains, elders pass on to children the secrets of finger weaving, wood carving, and mask and beaded jewelry making. Their work, found in shops such as* ***Medicine Man Crafts*** *(✉ U.S. 441 ☎ 828/497–2202) in downtown Cherokee, is a connective thread to a time predatings the United States by thousands of years.*

SIDE TRIPS FROM ASHEVILLE

Black Mountain

16 *16 mi east of Asheville via I–40.*

Black Mountain is a small town that has played a disproportionately large role in American cultural history, because it is the site of Black Mountain College. For 20 years in the middle of the 20th century, from its founding in 1933 to its closing in 1953, Black Mountain College was one of the world's leading centers for experimental art, literature, architecture, and dance, with a list of faculty and students that reads like a *Who's Who* of American arts and letters.

On a different front, Black Mountain is also the home of evangelist Billy Graham. The Graham organization maintains a training center near Black Mountain, and there are several large church-related conference centers in the area, including Ridgecrest, Montreat and Blue Ridge Assembly. Downtown Black Mountain is small and quaint, with a collection of little shops and several B&Bs.

Originally housed in rented quarters at nearby Blue Ridge Assembly, in 1941 **Black Mountain College** moved across the valley to its own campus at Lake Eden, where it remained until it closed in 1953. The school's buildings were originally designed by the Bauhaus architects Walter Gropius and Marcel Breuer, but at start of World War II the college turned to an American architect, Lawrence Kocher, and several intriguing buildings resulted, including one known as "The Ship," which still stands, with murals by Breuer. Among the students who enrolled at Black Mountain College in the 1940s were Arthur Penn, Kenneth Noland, Robert Rauschenberg, and James Leo Herlihy. Today, the site is a privately owned 550-acre summer camp for boys. While it is usually closed to the public, during the Lake Eden Festival, a music and arts festival in May and October, you can visit the grounds. You can also rent a cabin on the grounds for overnight stays. The Ship building and other campus buildings are viewable from Lake Eden Road. There's a small museum devoted to Black Mountain College in Asheville. ✉ *375 Lake Eden Rd., 5 mi west of Black Mountain* ☎ *828/686–3885.*

Sports & the Outdoors

GOLF Black Mountain doesn't have the plethora of golf courses that some other mountain towns do, but **Black Mountain Golf Course** (✉ Black Mountain ☎ 828/669–2710), a par-72, 6,215-yard public course, boasts the longest par 6 in the country, the 747-yard 17th hole.

Where to Stay & Eat

$–$$$ ✕🏨 **Red Rocker Inn.** A dozen red rocking chairs line the front porch of this inn, located in a quiet residential area two blocks from downtown. Your room may have a golf theme (the Pinehurst Room) or skylights, a fireplace, and a claw-foot tub (the Garrett Room). The restaurant is open to the public for breakfast ($10) and dinner ($20) by reservation.

You'll enjoy heaping portions of Southern food, served by candlelight. ✉ *136 N. Dougherty St., 28711* ☎ *888/669–5991 or 828/669–5991* 🌐 *www.redrockerinn.com* *Restaurant; no smoking* *17 rooms* *MC, V* *BP.*

$$ **Lake Eden Cabin.** This rustic log cabin, which dates from 1814, is on the original Lake Eden site of Black Mountain College. The cabin sleeps up to four, with a queen bed in the loft and a double and single futon downstairs. It has a kitchenette and fireplace, and linens and cooking utensils are provided. Some of the facilities of Camp Rockmont, a Christian summer camp for boys, are usually available to guests. There's a two-night minimum on weekends and at peak periods. ✉ *377 Lake Eden Rd., 28711* ☎ *828/686–5380* *1 cabin* *Kitchenette; no smoking* *MC, V* *EP.*

Shopping

Part authentic small-town hardware store and part gift shop, **Town Hardware & General Store** (✉ 103 W. State St. ☎ 828/669–7723) sells hard-to-find tools like scythes and push plows, along with cast iron cookware, Case knives, and Radio Flyer red wagons.

en route

Running in places beside the Rocky Broad River and then beside Lake Lure, **NC Highway 9,** between Black Mountain and Chimney Rock/Lake Lure, is a scenic but steep mountain road with many hairpin curves not suited for larger vehicles such as RVs.

Chimney Rock

17 *24 mi southeast of Asheville on U.S. 64/74A; 20 mi southeast of Black Mountain.*

Chimney Rock and neighboring Lake Lure—both popular day trips from Asheville—were the dream projects of a single man, Dr. Lucius Morse. In the early 1900s he bought and began developing Chimney Rock, and in the 1926 he dammed the Rocky Broad River to create Lake Lure. The Depression interrupted his plans, but his descendants still own much of this area. While the scenery, particularly when viewed from atop Chimney Rock, is spectacular—several movies have been filmed here—the commercial development along parts of Hickory Nut Gorge is not so appealing.

At privately owned **Chimney Rock Park** an elevator travels through a 26-story shaft of rock for a staggering view of Hickory Nut Gorge and the surrounding mountains. Trails, open year-round, lead to 400-foot Hickory Nut Falls, where the 1992 movie *The Last of the Mohicans* was filmed. The Old Rock Café can prepare picnics to go. ✉ *U.S. 64/74A* ☎ *828/625–9611 or 800/277–9611* 🌐 *www.chimneyrockpark.com* *$14* *May–Oct., daily 8:30–5:30; Nov.–Apr., daily 8:30–4:30.*

Sports & the Outdoors

WATER SPORTS The 1,500-acre **Lake Lure** (✉ U.S. 64/74A ☎ 877/386–4255 or 828/625–1373 🌐 www.lakelure.com) draws the region's water sports enthusiasts: you can rent boats (from kayaks and water bikes to pontoon boats), waterski, swim, and fish. The 1987 movie *Dirty Dancing* was partly filmed at Lake Lure. (The ballroom used in the movie was later destroyed by a fire.)

THE GREAT SMOKY MOUNTAINS NATIONAL PARK & ENVIRONS

At 521,495 acres, the Great Smoky Mountains National Park is one of the great wild areas in the eastern United States. The most visited of all national parks, the Great Smokies gets some ten million visitors each year. Even so, if you get out of your car, you can soon be in a remote cove where your only neighbors are deer and black bears. About half of the park is in North Carolina, with the remainder in Tennessee. (Only the North Carolina section is included in this guide.)

Due to a fortuitous combination of moderate climate and diverse geography, the Great Smoky Mountains National Park is one of the most biologically rich spots on earth. Naturalists think the park contains at least 100,000 different species of plants and animals, although to date only about 10,000 have been identified. More than 1,600 types of wildflowers and more than 140 species of trees flourish in this wildlife sanctuary. Bears are the most famous life form in the park; biologists estimate that about 1,500 black bears live in the Smokies, a density of about two per square mile. For the first time in 150 years, elk now roam the Great Smokies; more than 50 elk were brought to the park in 2001–2002, and elk cows have given birth to calves in the late spring of each year since.

Weather in the park is highly changeable, especially in the spring. On one day it can be a balmy 70°F, and on the next bitterly cold and snowy. By mid-June, haze, heat, and high humidity have arrived. Of course, temperatures vary with elevation. In July, highs at the lower elevations average 88Df"Symbol"děF, but at Clingsmans Dome (elevation 6,643 feet) the average high is 65. In September, a pattern of warm, sunny days and cool nights is established. Winters in the park see some snow, especially at the higher elevations. Newfound Gap gets an average of almost six feet of snow a year. Highway 441 and other park roads are sometimes closed due to snow.

Alas, air pollution is taking a toll on the park. Fifty years ago, from Clingman's Dome on an average day you could see 113 mi. Today, you can only see about 25 mi. The whitish haze you see in the Smokies, especially in the summer, is not in fact what the park was named for. It consists of airborne particles, mostly sulfates from coal-burning power plants as far away as the Ohio Valley, the Gulf Coast, and the Northeast.

Other than camping, the North Carolina side of the park has no accommodations or commercial operations of any kind—no shops, gas stations, or other services. You can take care of such needs at the park's gateway towns—Cherokee, Bryson City, Dillsboro, and Waynesville.

Great Smoky Mountains National Park

18 *Major gateway: Cherokee, 51 mi west of Asheville.*

U.S. Highway 441, also called Newfound Gap Road, is the main road through the park. On the North Carolina side, it runs from Cherokee to Newfound Gap, then continues on down into Tennessee near Gatlinburg. Branching off from U.S. 441, and throughout the park, are secondary roads, most of them unpaved. Also throughout the park are hiking trails, with the level of difficulty ranging from short easy walks to backcountry trips that test veteran mountain hikers. The quality of your experience in the park likely will be in direct relation to how far you are from paved roads and automobiles. The biggest crowds in the park arrive mid-June to mid-August, and all of the month of October, peak fall color season. There are six times as many visitors in the park in July as in January.

Among the regulations of the park: No picking or digging plants. No feeding of wildlife. Pets are not permitted on most park trails. Fishing permits and visitor information are available at ranger stations.

Except at **Le Conte Lodge** (☎ 865/429–5704) on the Tennessee side, which is accessible by trail only, the only accommodations in the park are at ten developed campsites, but these have no showers or RV hookups. Some campsites can be reserved in advance, by contacting the **National Park Service** (☎ 800/365–2267 🌐 http://reservations.nps.gov). Back country camping is also available, but such camping requires a (free) **permit** (☎ 865/436–1231). Admission to the park is free.

A car will only take you so far in the Great Smokies. You can drive the main road, U.S. 441, which traverses the park, and you can also reach several key sights by car, including the Mountain Farm Museum, Mingus Mill, Clingman's Dome, and the "ghost towns" of the Smokies, Cataloochee on the North Carolina side and Cades Cove on the Tennessee side. However, the best of the park is inaccessible by motorized vehicle. The Appalachian Trail runs along the crest of the rugged mountains through the park. Within the park's 800 square mi are 800 mi of trails and more than 600 mi of trout streams. Among the most interesting hikes are seven to waterfalls, including an easy two-miler to three falls at Deep Creek, near Bryson City. Another rewarding walk is the 3.4 mile roundtrip hike from Clingsmans Dome along Forney Ridge Trail. You will see a mountaintop meadow, Andrews Bald, with high-elevation plants including flame azalea and Catawba rhododendron.

Fodor'sChoice ★ One of the most memorable, and eeriest, sites in all of the Smokies is **Cataloochee Cove.** At one time, Cataloochee was a community of more than 1,200 people, in some 200 buildings. After the land was taken over in 1934 for the national park, the community dispersed. While many of the original buildings are now gone, about a dozen houses, cabins and barns, two churches, and other structures have been kept up. You can visit the Palmer Methodist Chapel, a one-room schoolhouse, Beach Grove School, and the Woody and Messer homesteads. it is much like Cades Cove on the Tennessee side, but much less visited. On a quiet day, you can almost hear the ghosts of the former Cataloochee settlers. Elk have been reintroduced around Cataloochee, and the population now is approaching 100, with about 25 elk calves born in 2004. This is the first time in 150 years that the Smokies have had a thriving elk population. You can often see them from the road in the evening and early morning. Cataloochee is the most remote part of the Smokies reachable by car, via a narrow, winding, gravel road. ✉ *Cataloochee Community, via U.S. 276 near Maggie Valley, off Exit 20 of I–40, to Cove Creek Rd.* ☎ *For general park information, 865/436–1200.*

At an elevation of over 6,600 feet, **Clingmans Dome** is one of the highest peaks east of the Rockies, only a few feet shorter than Mt. Mitchell. Walk up a paved, but steep, ½-mi trail to an observation tower offering 360-degree views of the Smokies. ✉ *At the end of Clingmans Dome Rd., 7 mi from U.S. 441* ☎ *For general park information, 865/436–1200.*

For the effort of a two-mile hike, **Deep Creek Waterfalls** will reward you with three pretty waterfalls, Tom Branch, Indian Creek, and Juney Whank. Deep Creek also has a picnic area and campground. ✉ *Trailhead at the end of Deep Creek Rd., near Bryson City entrance to park* ☎ *For general park information, 865/436–1200.*

The **Mingus Mill** is a working, water-powered gristmill. In its time, the late 19th-century, this was the state-of-the-art in grist mills, the two large grist stones powered by a store-bought turbine rather than a hand-built wheel. You can watch the miller make cornmeal, and even buy a pound of it. ✉ *U.S. 441, 2 mi north of Cherokee* ☎ *828/497–1904* ⏲ *Mid-Mar–late Nov.*

The **Mountain Farm Museum** at the Oconaluftee Visitors Center is perhaps the best re-creation anywhere of a mountain farmstead. The nine farm buildings, all dating from around 1900, were moved here from locations within the park. Besides a furnished two-story log cabin, you'll see a barn, apple house, corn crib, smokehouse, chicken coop, and other outbuildings. In season, corn, tomatoes, pole beans, squash, and other mountain crops are grown in the garden. The museum celebrated its 50th year of operation in 2004. ✉ *U.S. 441 at Oconaluftee Visitors Center* ☎ *828/497–1904.*

Cherokee

19 *178 mi east of Charlotte, 51 mi west of Asheville, 2 mi from entrance to Great Smoky Mountains National Park.*

The 56,000-acre Cherokee reservation is known as the Qualla Boundary, and the town of Cherokee is its capital. Truth be told, there are two Cherokees. There's the Cherokee with the sometimes tacky pop culture, designed to appeal to the masses of tourists, many of whom are visiting the nearby Great Smoky Mountains National Park. But there's another Cherokee that's a window onto the rich heritage of the tribe's Eastern Band. Although now relatively small in number—tribal enrollment is 12,500—these Cherokee and their ancestors have been responsible for keeping alive the Cherokee culture. They are the descendants of those

CloseUp

LITERARY MOUNTAIN LIONS

THEY MAY NOT BE ABLE to go home again, but many famous writers have made their homes in the North Carolina mountains. The one most closely associated with the terrain is Thomas Wolfe (1900–1938), author of Look Homeward, Angel, *who was born and buried in Asheville. His contemporary F. Scott Fitzgerald visited Asheville and environs frequently in the 1930s, staying for long periods at the Grove Park Inn and at other hotels in the area. Fitzgerald's wife, Zelda, an author and artist in her own right, died in a 1948 fire at Highland Hospital, then a psychiatric facility in North Asheville.*

William Sydney Porter, who under the pen name O. Henry wrote "The Ransom of Red Chief," "The Gift of the Magi," and many other stories, married into an Asheville-area family and is buried in Asheville at Riverside Cemetery. Carl Sandburg, Pulitzer prize–winning poet and biographer of Lincoln, spent the last 22 years of his life on a farm in Flat Rock. A younger generation of poets, including Jonathan Williams, Robert Creeley, Joel Oppenheimer, Robert Duncan, and Charles Olson, made names for themselves at Black Mountain College, an avant garde hotbed during the 1940s and early 1950s.

More recently, Jan Karon and Sharyn McCrumb have set popular mystery series in the area. Novelist Charles Frazier, born in Asheville in 1950, made Cold Mountain, *in the Shining Rock Wilderness of the Pisgah National Forest, the setting (and the title) for his million-selling Civil War drama. The mountain can be viewed from the Blue Ridge Parkway at mile marker 412. The movie, however, was filmed in Romania.*

who hid in the Great Smoky Mountains to avoid becoming part of the Trail of Tears, the forced removal of the Cherokee Nation to Oklahoma in the 19th century. They are survivors, extremely attached to the hiking, swimming, trout fishing, and natural beauty of their ancestral homeland.

The **Museum of the Cherokee Indian,** with displays and artifacts that cover 12,000 years, is one of the best Native American museums in the United States. Computer-generated images, lasers, specialty lighting, and sound effects help re-create events in the history of the Cherokee: for example, you'll see children stop to play a butter bean game while adults shiver along the snowy Trail of Tears. The museum has an art gallery, a gift shop, and an outdoor living exhibit of Cherokee life in the 15th century. ✉ *U.S. 441 at Drama Rd.* ☎ *828/497–3481* 🌐 *www.cherokeemuseum.org* 🎫 *$8* ⏲ *June–Aug., Mon.–Sat. 9–8, Sun. 9–5; Sept.–May, daily 9–5.*

At the historically accurate, re-created **Oconaluftee Indian Village,** guides in native costumes will lead you through a village of 225 years ago while others demonstrate traditional skills such as weaving, pottery, canoe construction, and hunting techniques. ✉ *U.S. 441 at Drama Rd.* ☎ *828/*

497–2315 ⊕ www.oconalufteevillage.com $13 ⊙ May 15–Oct. 25, daily 9:30–5.

Every mountain county has significant deposits of gems and minerals, and at the **Smoky Mountain Gold and Ruby Mine**, on the Qualla Boundary, you can search for gems such as aquamarines. Children love panning precisely because it can be wet and messy. Here they're guaranteed a find. Gem ore can be purchased, too: gold ore costs $5 per bag. ✉ *U.S. 441N* ☎ *828/497–6574* *$4–$10, depending on the gems* ⊙ *Mar.–Nov., daily 10–6.*

Sports & the Outdoors

FISHING There are 30 mi of regularly stocked trout streams on the **Cherokee Indian Reservation** (☎ 828/497–5201 or 800/438–1601). To fish in tribal water, you need a tribal fishing permit, available at nearly two dozen reservation businesses. The $7 permit is valid for one day and has a creel limit of 100.

HIKING A five-minute hike from the **Mingo Falls Campground** (✉ Big Cove Rd., about 4 mi north of Acquoni Rd.) will reward you with a view of the 200-foot-high Mingo Falls. In the downtown area you can cross the Oconaluftee River on a footbridge to **Oconaluftee Islands Park & Trail** (✉ Off U.S. 441, across from Cherokee Elementary School) and walk a trail around the perimeter of the Island Park, which also has picnic facilities. The flat 1½-mi **Oconaluftee River Trail** begins at the Great Smoky Mountains National Park entrance sign on U.S. 441 (near the entrance to the Blue Ridge Parkway) and ends at the Mountain Farm Museum–Park Visitor Center.

HORSEBACK RIDING Privately operated **Smokemont Stables** (✉ U.S. 441 in Great Smoky Mountains National Park ☎ 828/ 497–2373) offers riding trips in the Smokies from one hour to all day, including a waterfall trip.

Where to Stay & Eat

$$–$$$$ **Harrah's Cherokee Casino Hotel.** The 15-story hotel, which opened in 2002, towers over the mom 'n' pop motels nearby and the casino next door, to which it is umbilically attached via a series of escalators and walkways. The lobby and other public areas incorporate Cherokee traditional art themes. Rooms are large, about 500 square feet, and have 32-inch TVs. For high-rollers, there are suites on the top floor. The Selu Garden Café ($$$) in the hotel and the Seven Sisters restaurant in the casino ($$$–$$$$) are handy after a day of playing the slots. An expansion set for completion in 2005 will double the size of the hotel. ✉ *U.S. 19 at U.S. 441 Business, 28719* ☎ *800/427–7247 or 828/497–7777* ⊕ *www.harrahs.com* *252 rooms, 8 suites* *2 restaurants, indoor pool, recreation room* *AE, D, DC, MC, V* *EP.*

$–$$ **Fairfield Inn & Suites.** Opened in 2003, this three-story chain motel is directly across from Harrah's Casino. ✉ *568 Painttown Rd., 28719* ☎ *828/497–0400* *828/497–4242* ⊕ *www.marriott.com* *96 rooms, 4 suites* *Cable TV, pool, exercise equipment, recreation room, laundry facilities, laundry service, Internet, business services, meeting room, free parking* *AE, D, DC, MC, V* *BP.*

$–$$ **Hampton Inn.** Of the chain lodging around Cherokee, this is the nicest. The two-story motel is a bit away from the casino hustle-bustle but offers a free shuttle there. ✉ *185 Tsalagi Rd., 28719* ☎ *800/426–7866* 🖷 *828/497–3115* 🌐 *www.hamptoninn.com* *67 rooms* *Cable TV, outdoor pool, laundry facilities* 💳 *AE, D, DC, MC, V* *BP.*

$–$$ **Holiday Inn Cherokee.** Guest rooms are standard chain fare, but the staff at this well-equipped, full-service facility is very friendly. The Chestnut Tree restaurant has dinner buffets that are veritable groaning boards, and the native crafts shop, the Hunting Ground, with works by local artists, is a nice touch. ✉ *U.S. 19, 28719* ☎ *828/497–9181 or 800/465–4329* 🖷 *828/497–5973* 🌐 *www.holiday-inn.com* *150 rooms, 4 suites* *Restaurant, indoor pool, wading pool, sauna, recreation room, shop, playground, laundry, business services, meeting room* 💳 *AE, D, DC, MC, V* *EP.*

Nightlife & the Arts

THE ARTS **Unto These Hills Outdoor Drama** (✉ Mountainside Theater on Drama Rd., off U.S. 441N ☎ 828/497–2111 or 866/554–4557 🌐 www.untothesehills.com) is a colorful and well-staged history of the Cherokee from the time of Spanish explorer Hernando de Soto's visit in 1540 to the infamous Trail of Tears. The show runs from mid-June to late August and tickets start at $16.

NIGHTLIFE Owned by the Eastern Bank of the Cherokee, **Harrah's Casino** (✉ U.S. 19 at U.S. 441 Business ☎ 828/497–7777 or 800/427–7247) has more than 3,600 video gaming machines in a casino the size of more than three football fields. Digital blackjack and digital baccarat combine live dealers with digital cards. Big-name stars provide entertainment at the casino, which has a theater seating 1,500. The casino attracts large crowds, and parking space is at a premium. You'll either have to use valet parking ($8) or park for free in a remote lot and wait for a shuttle. In a pinch, park in the Harrah's Cherokee Casino Hotel lot and walk through the hotel. The casino is open 24 hours a day and is alcohol-free.

Shopping

The **Qualla Arts and Crafts Mutual** (✉ U.S. 441 at Drama Rd. ☎ 828/497–3103), across the street from the Museum of the Cherokee Indian, is a cooperative that displays and sells items created by 300 Cherokee craftspeople. The store has a large selection of high-quality baskets, masks, and wood carvings, which can cost hundreds of dollars.

Bryson City

20 *65 mi east of Asheville and 11 mi southwest of Cherokee.*

Bryson City is a little mountain town on the Nantahala River, one of the lesser-known gateways to the Great Smokies. The town's most striking feature is a city hall with a four-sided clock. Since becoming a tourist stop on the Great Smoky Mountains Railroad, the downtown shopping area has been rejuvenated, mostly with T-shirt shops and ice cream stands.

The most popular river in western North Carolina for rafting and kayaking is **Nantahala River,** which races through the scenic Nantahala

Gorge, a 1,600-foot-deep gorge that begins about 13 mi west of Bryson City on U.S. 19. Class III and Class IV rapids (Class V are the most dangerous) make for a thrilling ride. Several outfitters run river trips or rent equipment. At several points along the river you can park your car and watch rafters run the rapids—on a summer day you'll see hundreds of rafts going by. ✉ *U.S. 19, beginning 13 mi west of Bryson City.*

Overly commercial and overpriced, the **Smoky Mountain Model Railroad Museum** nevertheless appeals to kids or anyone with a fond memory of model trains. More than 2,500 model trains are displayed, around a 24-by-45-foot model railroad operating layout. ✉ *100 Greenlee St., near Great Smoky Mountains Railroad Depot* ☎ *828/488–5200 or 866/914–5200* 🌐 *www.smokymtntrains.com* *$8* ⏲ *Mon.–Sat. 8:30–5:30.*

Sports & the Outdoors

GOLF The par-71, 5,987-yard course at semi-private **Smoky Mountain Country Club** (✉ Conley Creek Valley, Box 937, Whittier ☎ 828/4497–4653 or 800/474–0070), has 400 feet of elevation change over the 18 holes, not to mention stunning views of the mountains.

HORSEBACK RIDING Privately owned **Deep Creek Stables** (✉ Deep Creek Picnic Area, near Bryson City entrance to Great Smokies National Park ☎ 828/488–8504) offers trail riding in the Smokies.

RIVER RAFTING & KAYAKING The class act on the Nantahala River is **Nantahala Outdoor Center** (✉ U.S. 19 ☎ 800/232–7238 🌐 www.noc.com), which was founded in 1972 and now has a staff of 600 at the peak of the summer season. It guides more than 30,000 rafters every year on the Nantahala and five other rivers. NOC also rents kayaks, ducks, and other equipment. About 10% of people in guided raft trips on the Nantahala do fall out of the raft sometime on the trip (you'll wear a life vest), so prepare to get wet. The NOC complex on the Nantahala River is virtually a tourist attraction itself, especially for young people, with two restaurants, cabin rentals, and an outdoor store.

Where to Eat & Stay

$$–$$$ ✕ **Nantahala Village Restaurant.** This roomy rock-and-cedar restaurant with front-porch rocking chairs is about 10 mi southwest of Cherokee and is a local favorite. The food isn't fancy, but the choices—trout, chicken, country ham, and even some vegetarian options—are good and filling. Sunday brunch has some surprises, including *huevos rancheros* (tortilla with fried eggs and salsa) and eggs Benedict. ✉ *9400 U.S. 19W, Bryson City* ☎ *828/488–9616 or 800/438–1507* ▭ *MC, V* ⏲ *Closed late Nov.–early Mar.*

¢–$$ ✕ **River's End at Nantahala Outdoor Center.** The casual riverbank setting and high-energy atmosphere at NOC's eatery draws lots of hungry people just returned from an invigorating day of rafting. There are salads, soups, and sandwiches during the day and fancier fixins' in the evening. The chili's a winner. ✉ *U.S. 19/74W* ☎ *828/488–2176* ▭ *MC, V* ⏲ *Closed Nov.–Mar.*

¢–$ ✕ **Everett Street Diner.** A classic small-town restaurant, with friendly service and well-prepared simple dishes made from local ingredients, Everett Street Diner, near the Chamber of Commerce, is where to go to meet the locals. It's open only for breakfast and lunch, except on the fourth Friday of the month, when dinner is served. ✉ *52 Everett St.* ☎ *828/488–0326* 💳 *D, MC, V* ⊙ *Closed Sat. No dinner.*

$$$ ✕🏨 **Hemlock Inn.** This folksy, friendly mountain inn on 50 acres above Bryson city is the kind of place where you can rock, doze, and play Scrabble. Even if you're not a guest at the inn, you can make a reservation for dinner Monday through Saturday and for lunch on Sunday. The fixed-price, all-you-can-eat meals are prepared with regional foods and served family-style on lazy susans at big round tables. ✉ *Galbraith Creek Rd., 1 mi north of U.S. 19, 28713* ☎ *828/488–2885* 📠 *828/488–8985* 🌐 *www.hemlockinn.com* *22 rooms, 3 suites, 3 cottages* *Restaurant, fans, recreation room; no a/c, no room phones, no room TVs* 💳 *D, MC, V* ⊙ *Closed Nov.–mid-Apr.* 🍽 *MAP.*

$$ ✕🏨 **Fryemont Inn.** An institution in Bryson City for eight decades, the Fryemont Inn is on the National Register of Historic Places. The lodge exterior is bark, rooms in the main lodge are paneled in real chestnut, and the lobby has a fireplace big enough for 8-foot logs. If you need more luxury, choose one of the suites with fireplaces and air-conditioning. The restaurant, serving Southern fare, is open to the public for breakfast and dinner. ✉ *Freymont St. Box 459, 28713* ☎ *828/488–2159 or 800/845–4879* 🌐 *www.fryemontinn.com* *37 rooms, 3 suites, 1 cabin* *Restaurant, pool; no a/c in some rooms, no room phones, no TV in some rooms* 💳 *D, MC, V* ⊙ *Main lodge and restaurant closed late Nov.–mid-Apr.* 🍽 *MAP.*

Robbinsville & Lake Santeetlah

21 *98 mi southwest of Asheville, 35 mi southwest of Bryson City.*

If you truly want to get away from everything, head to the area around Robbinsville in the far southwest corner of North Carolina, a little south of the southern edge of the Great Smokies. The town of Robbinsville offers little, but the Snowbird Mountains, Lake Santeetlah, Fontana Lake, the rugged Joyce Kilmer–Slickrock Wilderness, and the Joyce Kilmer Memorial Forest, with its giant virgin poplars and sycamores, definitely are highlights of this part of North Carolina.

Over 29 mi long, **Fontana Lake & Dam** borders the southern edge of the Great Smokies. Unlike most other lakes in the mountains, Fontana has a shoreline that is almost completely undeveloped, since about 90% of its 240 mi are owned by the federal government. Fishing here is excellent, especially for small-mouth bass, muskie, and walleye. On the downside, the Tennessee Valley Authority (TVA) manages the lake for power generation, and at peak visitor period in the fall the lake is drawn down, leaving large areas of mudflats. Fontana Dam, completed in 1944, at 480 feet is the highest dam east of the Rockies. The Appalachian Trail crosses the top of the dam. ✉ *Fontana Dam Visitor Center, off Rte. 28, 3 mi from Fontana Village* ☎ *TVA, 865/632–2101* 🎟 *Free* ⊙ *Visitor center May–Nov., daily 9–7.*

One of the few remaining sections of the original Appalachian forests, **Joyce Kilmer Memorial Forest,** a part of the 17,000-acre Joyce Kilmer–Slickrock Wilderness, has 400-year-old yellow poplars that are as much as 20 feet in circumference, along with huge hemlocks, oaks, sycamores, and other trees. A 2-mi trail takes you through wildflower- and moss-carpeted areas of incredible beauty. It is, of course, named for the early 20th century poet, killed in World War I, who is famous for the lines "I think I shall never see / A poem lovely as a tree." ✉ *15 mi west of Robbinsville, off Cherohala Skyway via Hwy. 143 and Kilmer Rd.* ☎ *Cheoah Ranger District, 828/479–6431* 🎫 *Free.*

Formed in 1928 with the construction of the Santeetlah Dam, **Lake Santeetlah,** meaning "blue waters" in the Cherokee language, has 76 mi of shoreline, with good fishing for crappie, bream, and lake trout. The lake is managed by Alcoa as a hydro-electric project, but most of the land is owned by the federal government, a part of the Nantahala National Forest. ✉ *Cheoah Point Recreation Area, Rte. 1145 off U.S. 129, about 7 mi north of Robinsville* ☎ *Nantahala National Forest, Cheoah Ranger District, 828/479–6431* 🎫 *Free.*

3

off the beaten path

JOHN C. CAMPBELL FOLK SCHOOL – Founded in 1925, the Folk School is a nationally known crafts school on 380 acres in a rural area near Murphy, at the far western tip of the state. Students and resident faculty are involved in woodcarving, ironwork, weaving, woodturning, pottery, furniture-making, glasswork, painting, and basketry. The school's crafts shop has high-quality crafts for sale by about 300 regional and national artists, including many instructors at the school. ✉ *1 Folk School Rd., 7 mi east of Murphy, Brasstown, 28902* ☎ *800/365–5724 or 828/837–2775* ⏲ *Shop Mon.–Sat. 9–5, Sun. 1–5.*

Sports & the Outdoors

BOATING

Boat rentals, including a 65-foot houseboat, are available at **Fontana Marina** (✉ Fontana Village, Fontana Dam ☎ 800/849–2258 or 828/498–2211), open late May–early September. For a fast boating experience, try **Smoky Mountain Jet Boats** (✉ U.S. 74 at Needmore Rd. ☎ 828/488–0522 or 888/900–9091), offering half-hour rides on Fontana Lake for $25 a person.

Where to Stay & Eat

★ $$$–$$$$

✕🏨 **Snowbird Mountain Inn.** When it's 95 degrees and the paperwork is piling up, Snowbird is the kind of mountain lodge you daydream about. The main lodge, built in 1941 and now in the National Register of Historic Places, has two massive stone fireplaces, solid chestnut beams across the ceiling, and beautiful views across the valley. If you run out of things to do, there are 2,500 books in the library. The restaurant serves "rustic" meals like fresh trout with grilled vegetable salsa. Alcoholic beverages are BYOB, as this is a dry county. For more luxury than the lodge rooms offer, choose a king suite in a separate cottage. ✉ *4633 Santeetlah Rd., Robbinsville 28771* ☎ *828/479–3433 or 800/941–9290* 📠 *828/479–3473* 🌐 *www.snowbirdlodge.com* ⇆ *15 rooms, 8 suites in separate cottages* 👍 *Restaurant; no a/c in some rooms, no room phones, no room TVs* 💳 *MC, V* ⏲ *Closed late Nov.–early Apr.* 🍽 *MAP.*

$–$$ **Blue Boar Inn.** On the outside, it looks like a mountain inn for bear and wild boar hunters. Inside, it has been totally redone, with upscale modern furnishings, including air-conditioning and TVs. Each room has a porch. You can kayak or canoe on nearby Lake Santeetlah. A full breakfast is included, and dinner is available at an extra charge. Originally built in 1950 by a Cincinnati beer magnate, today—because the county is legally dry—no alcohol is sold at the lodge. *1283 Blue Boar Rd., Robbinsville 28771 828/479–8126 or 866/479–8126 828/479–2415 www.blueboarinn.com 8 rooms Dining room, refrigerators, pond, boating AE, D, MC, V Closed late Nov.–late Mar. BP.*

Dillsboro

22 *51 mi southwest of Asheville; 13 mi southeast of Cherokee on U.S. 441.*

The tiny town of Dillsboro, in Jackson County, has developed a big reputation for shopping, especially if you like crafts and gift shops. The Great Smoky Mountains Railroad arrivals and departures add to the hustle and bustle of the two-block "downtown," especially in season. Crowds line up to eat country ham at the Jarrett House, an institution in Dillsboro since 1884, across the street from the railway depot.

The popular train rides of the **Great Smoky Mountains Railroad** include five regular excursions from Dillsboro, along with four originating in Bryson City, and several special trips. Diesel-electric or steam locomotives go through Nantahala Gorge or along the Tuckasegee River. Open-sided cars or standard coaches are ideal for picture taking as the mountain scenery glides by. Some rides include a meal: on Friday evenings there's a mystery theater train with dinner, and on Saturday a gourmet dinner train. *119 Front St. 828/586–8811 or 800/872–4681 www.gsmr.com $28–$74.*

Sports & the Outdoors

RIVER TUBING & KAYAKING

On the Tuckaseegee River, much gentler than the Nantahala River, **Tuckaseegee Outfitters** (U.S. 74/441 800/539–5683) offers non-guided trips by tube, raft, and inflatable kayak.

Where to Stay & Eat

$$ **Jarrett House.** The food here may not win any awards for creative cooking, but folks love the mountain trout, country ham with red-eye gravy, and fried chicken at the Jarrett House, in continuous operation since 1884 and now on the National Register of Historic Places. Rooms in this three-story white frame country inn ($), with porches on all three levels, are small and unpretentious, but you can't beat the location right across from Dillsboro's shops and the train depot. *U.S. 441, 28725 828/586–0265 or 800/972–5623 32 rooms No a/c, no room phones, no room TVs No credit cards BP.*

$$$ **Best Western River Escape Inn & Suites.** Many of the rooms at this three-story motel have balconies overlooking the Tuskaseegee River. There's an indoor pool, and some rooms have whirlpool tubs. It's within walking distance of the railroad depot and Dillsboro shops. The "suites" are not true suites, just slightly larger regular rooms. *268*

WBI Dr., off exit 81, Hwy. 23/74, 28725 ☎ 828/586–6060 66 rooms Picnic area, indoor pool, business services AE, D, DC, MC, V BP.

Shopping

A co-op of more than 80 area artisans owns and runs **Dogwood Crafters** (✉ 90 Webster St. ☎ 828/586–2248), where you can purchase pottery, rugs, baskets, and other crafts.

You can see potters throwing pots at **Mountain Pottery** (✉ 152 Front St. ☎ 828/586–9183), where pottery, ceramics, and raku by about 75 different local potters are for sale.

Waynesville

23 *17 mi east of Cherokee on U.S. 19.*

This is where the Blue Ridge Parkway meets the Great Smokies. Pretty, arty Waynesville is the seat of Haywood County. About 40% of the county is occupied by the Great Smoky Mountains National Park, Pisgah National Forest, and the Harmon Den Wildlife Refuge.

The **Museum of North Carolina Handicrafts,** in the Shelton House (circa 1875), has a comprehensive exhibit of 19th-century heritage crafts. *✉ 307 Shelton St. ☎ 828/452–1551 $5 May–Oct., Tues.–Fri. 10–4.*

Cold Mountain, the vivid best-selling novel by Charles Frazier, has made a destination out of the real **Cold Mountain.** About 15 mi from Waynesville in the Shining Rock Wilderness Area of Pisgah National Forest, the 6,030-foot rise had long stood in relative anonymity. But with the success of Frazier's book, people want to see the region that Inman and Ada, the book's Civil War–era protagonists, called home.

There are different ways to experience Cold Mountain. For a view of the splendid mass—or at least of the surrounding area—stop at any of a number of overlooks off the Blue Ridge Parkway. Try the Cold Mountain Parking Overlook, just past mile marker 411.9; the Wagon Road Gap parking area, at mile marker 412.2; or the Waterrock Knob Interpretative Station, at mile marker 451.2. You can climb the mountain, but beware, as the hike to the summit is rather strenuous. No campfires are allowed in Shining Rock, so you'll need a stove if you wish to cook. Inform the **ranger station** (☎ 828/877–3350) if you plan to hike or camp.

The **Lake Junaluska Conference & Retreat Center** is the international headquarters of the World Methodist Council and also headquarters of the southeastern jurisdiction of the United Methodist Church. Besides a large conference center and a collection of inns and guesthouses that can accommodate 2,000 people—some are open to the general public when not in use by delegates—the **World Methodist Museum** has the world's largest collection of items relating to the Wesleyan movement. On the 1,400-acre grounds of the conference center are a 200-acre lake, golf course, and various recreational activities. *✉ 575 Lakeshore Dr., Lake Junaluska, 28745 ☎ 828/456–9432 Free Weekdays 9–5.*

Sports & the Outdoors

FISHING If you want to fly fish for rainbow, brown, or native brook trout, try **Low Fly Shop** (⊠ 15 Woodland Dr. ☎ 828/452–0039), which runs wading and floating trips on area streams and lakes. A full-day wade trip for two with guide costs around $300.

GOLF A public course at the Methodist conference center, **Lake Junaluska Golf Course** (⊠ 19 Golf Course Rd. ☎ 828/456–5777) is short but surprisingly tricky, due to all the trees. At **Waynesville Country Club Inn** (⊠ 300 Country Club Dr. ☎ 828/452–4617), you can play three 9-hole courses in any combination.

Where to Stay & Eat

$$$–$$$$ ✕ **Lomo Grill.** Waynesville's best restaurant combines Mediterranean-style ingredients with the chef-owner's Argentine background, resulting in delicious dishes like Argentine Corvina alla Piccatta, a delicate fish with white wine, olive oil, and capers. Many of the fruits and vegetables used at Lomo Grill, in a 1920s downtown building, are grown in the chef's garden. ⊠ *44 Church St.* ☎ *828/452–5222* ▭ *AE, D, DC, MC, V* ⊙ *No dinner Sun.*

★ **$$$$** **The Swag.** This exquisite, rustic inn sits high atop the Cataloochee Divide overlooking a swag—a deep depression in otherwise high ground. Its 250 wooded acres share a border with Great Smoky Mountains National Park and have access to hiking trails. Guest rooms and cabins were assembled from six authentic log structures transported here. All have exposed beams and wood floors and are furnished with early American crafts. The inn's restaurant won the 2003 NC Gourmet Diners Society award. ⊠ *2300 Swag Rd., 28786* ☎ *828/926–0430 or 800/789–7672* 🖷 *828/926–2036* 🌐 *www.theswag.com* *16 rooms, 3 cabins* *Dining room, pond, massage, sauna, badminton, croquet, racquetball, library, business services; no room TVs* ▭ *AE, D, MC, V* ⊙ *Closed Nov.–Mar.* *FAP.*

$$$–$$$$ **The Yellow House on Plott Creek Road.** Located just outside town, and at 3,000 feet, The Yellow House, a lovely two-story Victorian on a knoll, with surrounding gardens, strives for an impressionist feel, with light, dappling pastoral colors. (Yes, the house is yellow, as is one of the guest rooms.) Most rooms have fireplaces. Innkeepers Steve and Donna Shea are adding three new suites with fireplaces and whirlpool baths. ⊠ *89 Oak View Dr., at Plott Creek Rd., 1 mi west of Waynesville, 28786* ☎ *828/452–0991 or 800/563–1236* 🖷 *828/452–1140* 🌐 *www.theyellowhouse.com* *7 rooms, 3 suites* ▭ *MC, V* *BP.*

Shopping

The **Downtown Waynesville** (⊠ Main St.) shopping area stretches three blocks from the city hall to the Haywood County courthouse, with a number of small boutiques, bookstores, and antique shops.

THE HIGH COUNTRY

The High Country is North Carolina taken to the highest degree. Here you'll find the highest, steepest, coldest, snowiest, windiest, and, some say, friendliest parts of the mountains. The High Country has not only the tallest mountains east of the Rockies, but the highest average elevation in all of Eastern America. With temperatures 10 to 15 degrees cooler than in the foothills and flatlands, even folks from Asheville come to the High Country in the summer to cool down.

Unlike the rest of the mountains, winter is the peak season in much of the High Country. The reason? The white stuff. Towns like Boone, Blowing Rock, and Banner Elk have boomed in the 40 years since the introduction of snowmaking equipment, and the ski resorts of Beach Mountain, Sugar Mountain, and Appalachian Ski Mountain attract skiers, snowboarders, and snowtubers from all over the Southeast. The fiery colors of autumn against the green backdrop of firs also bring carloads of visitors to the High Country, and many come for the cool summers, too. Luxury resorts now dot the valleys and mountaintops, and you can take advantage of many crafts shops, music festivals, and theater offerings.

The Blue Ridge Parkway is highlighted in this section, as this magnificent road enters the High Country from Virginia, but the parkway actually transverses much of western North Carolina, including Asheville and parts of the southern mountains, until it terminates at the entrance of the Great Smoky Mountains National Park.

Blue Ridge Parkway

★ 24 *Entrance 2 mi east of Asheville, off I–40 and at many other points.*

The Blue Ridge Parkway's 252 mi within North Carolina wind down the High Country through Asheville, ending near the entrance of the Great Smoky Mountains National Park. This section describes the highlights of the parkway and includes hotel listings for properties on or immediately adjoining the parkway. However, remember that nearly all the towns and cities along the parkway route offer accommodations, dining, and sightseeing. In particular, look at the listings for Boone, Blowing Rock, Burnsville, Asheville, Waynesville, Brevard, and Cherokee, all of which are near popular entrances to the parkway.

The beautiful **Blue Ridge Parkway** gently winds through mountains and meadows and crosses mountain streams for more than 469 mi on its way from Cherokee, North Carolina, to Waynesboro, Virginia, connecting the Great Smoky Mountains and Shenandoah national parks. With elevations ranging from 649 to 6,047 feet, and with more than 250 scenic lookout points, it is truly one of the most beautiful drives in North America. No commercial vehicles are allowed, and the entire parkway is free of billboards, although in a few places residential or commercial development encroaches close to the road. It is the most scenic route from Asheville to Boone and Blowing Rock, and also from Asheville to Cherokee and the Great Smoky Mountains National Park. The parkway, which has a maximum speed limit of 45 mph, is generally open year-round but often closes during inclement weather. In winter, sections can be closed for weeks at a time due to snow, and even in good weather fog and clouds occasionally can make driving difficult. Maps and information are available at visitor centers along the highway. Mile markers (MMs) identify points of interest and indicate the distance from the parkway's starting point in Virginia. ✉ *Superintendent, Blue Ridge Pkwy., 199 Hemphill Knob Rd., Asheville 28803* ☎ *828/298–0398* 🌐 *www.nps.gov/blri* 🎫 *Free.*

Craggy Gardens at mile marker 364.6, at 5,500–6,000 feet, has some of the parkway's most colorful displays of rhododendrons, usually in June. You can also hike trails and picnic here. ✉ *MM 364.6* ☎ *828/298–0398* 🎫 *Free.*

At **Emerald Village** you can tour an underground mine or dig for gems of your own. ✉ *McKinney Mine Rd. at Blue Ridge Pkwy., MM 334, Little Switzerland* ☎ *828/765–6463 or 877/389–4653* 🌐 *www.emeraldvillage.com* 🎫 *Mine $5, gem bucket $3–$100* ⏲ *May–Oct., weekdays 9–5, weekends 9–6; Apr., daily 10–4.*

The **Folk Art Center** displays and sells authentic mountain crafts made by members of the Southern Highland Craft Guild. Demonstrations are held frequently. This is one of the best places in the region to buy high-quality crafts. ✉ *Blue Ridge Pkwy., MM 382 at Asheville* ☎ *828/298–7928* ⏲ *Jan.–Mar., daily 9–5; Apr.–Dec., daily 9–6.*

Just off the parkway at mile marker 305, **Grandfather Mountain** soars to 6,000 feet and is famous for its Mile-High Swinging Bridge, a 228-foot-long bridge that sways over a 1,000-foot drop into the Linville Valley. The **Natural History Museum** has exhibits on native minerals, flora and fauna, and pioneer life. The annual **Singing on the Mountain,** in June, is an opportunity to hear old-time gospel music and preaching, and the **Highland Games** in July bring together Scottish clans from all over North America for athletic events and Highland dancing. ✉ *Blue Ridge Pkwy. and U.S. 221, Linville* ☎ *828/733–4337 or 800/468–7325* 🌐 *www.grandfather.com* 🎫 *$12* ⏲ *Apr.–mid-Nov., daily 8–dusk; mid-Nov.–Mar., daily 8–5.*

Green spaces along the parkway include **Julian Price Park,** which has hiking, canoeing on a mountain lake, trout fishing, and camping. ✉ *MM 295–MM 298.1.*

Linville Caverns are the only caverns in the Carolinas. They go 2,000 feet beneath Humpback Mountain and have a year-round temperature of 51°F. North of Asheville, exit the parkway at mile marker 317.4 and turn left onto U.S. 221. ✉ *U.S. 221, between Linville and Marion* ☎ *828/756–4171* 🌐 *www.linvillecaverns.com* 🎫 *$5* ⏲ *June–early Sept., daily 9–6; Apr., May, and early Sept.–Oct., daily 9–5; Nov. and Mar., daily 9–4:30; Dec.–Feb., weekends 9–4:30.*

From the **Linville Falls Visitor Center,** a half-mile hike leads to one of North Carolina's most photographed waterfalls. The easy trail winds through evergreens and rhododendrons to overlooks with views of the series of cascades tumbling into Linville Gorge. There are also a campground and a picnic area. ✉ *Rte. 1, MM 316.3, Spruce Pine* ☎ *828/765–1045.*

The **Moses H. Cone Park** has a turn-of-the-20th-century manor house that's now the **Parkway Craft Center.** The center sells fine work by area craftspeople. ✉ *MM 292.7–MM 295.*

Mt. Mitchell State Park includes the highest mountain peak east of the Rockies, Mt. Mitchell at 6,684 feet. The summit was named after Elisha Mitchell, who died from a fall while trying to prove the mountain's true height. At the 1,855-acre park, you can climb an observation tower and get food at a restaurant. Keep an eye on the weather here, as high winds and snow can occur at almost any time, occasionally even in summer. The lowest temperature ever recorded in North Carolina was at Mt. Mitchell on Jan. 21, 1985: -34°F. Clouds obscure the views here for at least parts of eight days out of ten. ✉ *2388 NC Hwy. 128, MM 355, Burnsville* ☎ *828/675–4611* 🎫 *Free.*

3

Mt. Pisgah, at 5,721 feet one of the most easily recognized peaks due to the television tower installed there in the 1950s, has walking trails, an amphitheater where nature programs are given most evenings June–October, a campground, inn, picnic area, and small grocery. The nearby area called **Graveyard Fields** is popular for blueberry picking in July. In 1992, a snowstorm in *May* dropped more than 5 feet of snow here. ✉ *Blue Ridge Pkwy., MM 408.6* ☎ *828/235–8228.*

Museum of North Carolina Minerals at mile marker 331 has hands-on displays about gold, copper, kaolin, and other minerals found nearby. ✉ *MM 331 at U.S. 226* ☎ *828/765–2761* 🎫 *Free* ⏲ *May–Oct., daily 9–5; Nov.–Apr., daily 9–noon and 1–5.*

off the beaten path

PENLAND SCHOOL OF CRAFTS – This world-famous institution about 45 mi northeast of Asheville on a remote mountainside is the oldest and largest school for high-quality mixed-media arts and crafts in North America. It has classes in book and paper making, glassblowing, ceramics, textile arts, and other media. An extraordinary gallery (open mid-Apr.–mid-Dec., Tues.–Sat. 10–5, Sun. 12–5) displays works of faculty and students (some are for sale; call to check hours and winter closing). Classes aren't open to the public, but you can call about a free campus tour. Penland students often hang out at the campus coffeehouse, which has a student art gallery and views of llamas in the field across the street. ✉ *Off Penland Rd. and U.S. 19/23, Penland* ☎ *828/765–2359 for school, 828/765–6211 for gallery and campus tours* 🌐 *www.penland.org.*

Sports & the Outdoors

HIKING More than 100 trails lead off the Blue Ridge Parkway, from easy strolls to strenuous hikes. For more information on parkway trails, contact the **National Park Service Blue Ridge Parkway office** (☎ 828/298–0398 🌐 www.nps.gov/blri). Another good source is *Walking the Blue Ridge: A Guide to the Trails of the Blue Ridge Parkway,* by Leonard Adkins, available at most parkway visitor center gift shops. The **Bluff Mountain Trail,** at Doughton Park (MM 238.5), is a moderately strenuous 7½-mi trail winding through forests, pastures, and valleys, and along the mountainside. Moses H. Cone Park's (MM 292.7) **Figure 8 Trail** is an easy and beautiful trail that the Cone family designed for their morning walks. The ½-mi loop winds through a tunnel of rhododendrons and a hardwood forest. Those who tackle the half-mile, strenuous **Waterrock Knob Trail**

(MM 451.2), near the south end of the parkway, will be rewarded with spectacular views from the 6,400-foot-high Waterrock Knob summit.

ROCK CLIMBING One of the most challenging climbs in the country is the **Linville Gorge** (MM 317), often called "the Grand Canyon of North Carolina." Permits are available from the district forest ranger's office in Nebo (☎ 828/652–2144) or from the Linville Falls Texaco station on U.S. 221.

SKIING **Moses H. Cone Park** (☎ 828/295–7591) is known for its cross-country skiing trails. On the Blue Ridge Parkway, **Roan Mountain** (☎ 615/772–3303), open daily during the winter, is famous for its deep powder. Tours and equipment are available from **High Country Ski Shop** (☎ 828/733–2008), in Pineola on U.S. 221.

Where to Stay & Eat

★ $$$$ **Eseeola Lodge and Restaurant.** Rebuilt in 1936 after a fire, this lakeside lodge, best described as dressed-up rustic, sits 3,800 feet above sea level and is one sure way to beat summer's heat. Golf is a passion here, but the diversions are many. All rooms overlook the manicured grounds and gardens. Rich chestnut paneling and stonework grace the public areas. Entrées at the restaurant may include free-range chicken and rainbow trout; jacket and tie are required at dinner. ✉ *175 Linville Ave., off U.S. 221, Linville 28646* ☎ *828/733–4311 or 800/742–6717* 📠 *828/733–3227* 🌐 *www.eseeola.com* *19 rooms, 5 suites, 1 cottage* *Restaurant, 18-hole golf course, putting green, 8 tennis courts, pool, exercise equipment, boating, fishing, croquet, hiking, bar, children's programs, playground, business services* *MC, V* *Closed late Oct.–mid-May* *MAP.*

$ **Pisgah Inn.** This inn, run by a park service concessionaire, has motel-like rooms of no distinction, but the setting, at almost a mile high right on the parkway, is spectacular. Rooms have small porches or balconies with rocking chairs. Although an inn has been on this site since 1919, the present structure was built in 1964. The restaurant ($$–$$$) has great views to the west and offers mountain trout, along with burgers and other standard fare. ✉ *MM 408, Waynesville 28786* ☎ *828/235–8228* 🌐 *www.pisgahinn.com* *Restaurant, some refrigerators, shops; no a/c* *MC, V* *Closed Nov.–late Mar.* *EP.*

$$–$$$ **Little Switzerland Inn.** Families cozy up in the lobby of this old mountain inn, which dates to 1910, to play Monopoly or just doze over a book. The staff is cheerful, and you have a choice of comfy lodge rooms (without A/C) or bigger, brighter rooms in newer buildings. The Swiss theme is carried through to the Chalet restaurant and the ice cream and sweet shops on the grounds. ✉ *MM 334 at Hwy. 226A, Little Switzerland 28749* ☎ *828/765–2153 or 800/654–4026* 📠 *828/765–0049* 🌐 *www.switzerlandinn.com* *59 rooms, 5 cottages* *Restaurant, 2 tennis courts, pool, shuffleboard, shops, no-smoking rooms; no a/c in some rooms* *MC, V* *Closed Nov.–mid-Apr.* *BP.*

Blowing Rock

25 *86 mi northeast of Asheville, 93 mi west of Winston-Salem.*

Blowing Rock, a draw for mountain visitors since the 1880s, has retained the flavor of a quiet New England village, with stone walls and buildings with wood shakes or bark siding. About 1,000 people are permanent residents of this town at a 4,000-foot elevation, but the population swells each summer. To ensure that the town would remain rural, the community banded together to prohibit large hotels and motels. Blowing Rock is the inspiration for the small town in resident Jan Karon's novels about country life in the fictional town of Mitford. To get here from the Blue Ridge Parkway, take U.S. 221/321 to just north of the entrance to Moses H. Cone Park.

The **Blowing Rock** looms over the Johns River Gorge. If you throw your hat over the sheer precipice, it may blow back to you, should the wind gods be playful. The story goes that a Cherokee man and a Chickasaw maiden fell in love. Torn between his tribe and his love, he jumped from the cliff, but she prayed to the Great Spirit, and he was blown safely back to her. ✉ *Off U.S. 321* ☎ *828/295–7111* 🌐 *www.blowingrock.org* 🎟 *$6* ⏲ *June–Oct., 8–8; Jan.–Mar., 8:30–5; Apr., 8:30–6; May, 8:30–7; Nov., and Dec. 9–5.*

The **Tweetsie Railroad** is a popular Wild West theme park built into the side of a mountain and centered on a steam locomotive beset by robbers. A petting zoo, carnival amusements, gem panning, shows, and concessions, all mostly of interest to young children, are also here. Several of the attractions are at the top of the mountain and can be reached by foot or ski lift. ✉ *U.S. 321/221, off Blue Ridge Pkwy. at MM 291* ☎ *828/264–9061 or 800/526–5740* 🌐 *www.tweetsie-railroad.com* 🎟 *$25* ⏲ *May and mid-Aug.–Oct, Fri.–Sun., 9–6; June–mid-Aug., daily 9–6.*

Sports & the Outdoors

RAFTING You can go white-water rafting on Wilson Creek or the Nolichucky or Wautaga rivers with **High Mountain Expeditions** (✉ Main St., Box 1299 ☎ 828/295–4437 or 800/262–9036).

SKIING There's downhill skiing and snowboarding at **Appalachian Ski Mountain** (✉ 940 Ski Mountain Rd. ☎ 828/295–7828 or 800/322–2373).

Where to Stay & Eat

$$$–$$$$ ✕ **Best Cellar.** Surely this is the only log cabin restaurant in North Carolina with valet parking, an oyster bar, and an extensive wine list. Don't let the rustic cabin fool you—the Best Cellar is among the best restaurants in the High Country and has been since 1976. The menu isn't particularly daring, running to upscale standards like steak au poivre, roast duck, and veal marsala, with seasonal seafood dishes such as softshell crab. The martinis are ice cold and huge, and the seafood appetizer sampler, featuring oysters Rockefeller, crab cakes, boiled shrimp, and other goodies is almost a meal in itself. ✉ *Off U.S. 321 bypass* ☎ *828/295–3466* *Reservations essential* 💳 *AE, MC, V* ⏲ *Closed Sun. No lunch.*

$–$$ ✕ **Canyons.** The long-range view from the deck of Canyons is so dramatic owner Bart Conway, one of the High Country's best-known restaurateurs, put a live minicam on the restaurant's Web site. While oohing over the mountain scenery, or eyeing the funky artwork on the walls inside, you can munch on fresh-made tortilla chips, chimichangas, veggie burritos, or a classic drive-in burger slathered with chili and slaw. On most days, the restaurant is the busiest one in town. There's live entertainment Thursday–Sunday nights and a Sunday brunch. ✉ *Off U.S. 321 bypass* ☎ *828/295–7661* ▭ *AE, D, MC, V.*

$$$$ **Westglow Spa.** If you want get buff, lose weight, and be pampered at a beautiful mountain estate, and if money is no object, Westglow Spa may be your cup of herbal tea. Housed in an elegant 1916 mansion on 20 acres, once the home of 19th-century impressionist painter Elliott Daingerfield, the health resort spares nothing for its few, select guests. The fitness center is packed with the latest workout machines, health gizmos, spa facilities, and an indoor pool with a stunning view of the mountains. Meals, emphasizing low-fat and high-fiber items, are served in the Elliott restaurant in the Manor House. Owner Glynda Valentine leads guests on hikes every morning promptly at 9. *2845 U.S. 221S, 28605* ☎ *828/295–4463 or 800/562–0807* *www.westglow.com* *8 rooms, 2 cottages* *Restaurant, tennis court, indoor pool, fitness classes, hair salon, hot tubs, massage, saunas, spa; no kids under 16, no smoking* ▭ *AE, MC, V* *FAP.*

$$$–$$$$ **Inn at Ragged Gardens.** With a grand stone staircase in the entry hall, colorful gardens, richly toned chestnut paneling, and the chestnut bark siding found on many older homes in the High Country, it's no wonder that this manor-style house in the heart of Blowing Rock gets rave reviews. You're likely to appreciate the attention to detail: the European and American antiques blended with contemporary art and the all-hours butler's pantry. All rooms have fireplaces, and some have private balconies. A two-night minimum is required on weekends. ✉ *203 Sunset Dr., 28605* ☎ *828/295–9703* *www.ragged-gardens.com* *6 rooms, 5 suites* *Dining room, some in-room hot tubs, meeting room; no kids under 13* ▭ *MC, V* *BP.*

$$–$$$ **Chetola Resort.** This inn and condo resort, named for the Cherokee word meaning "haven of rest," grew out of an early-20th-century stone-and-wood lodge. The original building now houses the resort's restaurant and meeting rooms and is adjacent to the 1988 lodge. Many guest rooms in the lodge have private balconies facing either the mountains, a small lake, or both. In late 2004 the resort opened a new section, the Bob Timberlake Lodge. Condominiums are spread among the hills, and the 87-acre property adjoins Moses H. Cone Park, with hiking trails and riding facilities. *N. Main St., Box 17, 28605* ☎ *828/295–5500 or 800/243–8652* *828/295–5529* *www.chetola.com* *37 rooms, 5 suites, 62 condominiums* *2 restaurants, minibars, 5 tennis courts, indoor pool, health club, hot tub, massage, sauna, boating, fishing, bicycles, Ping-Pong, racquetball, piano bar, playground, business services, meeting rooms* ▭ *AE, D, MC, V* *EP.*

$–$$$ **Maple Lodge Bed & Breakfast.** Blowing Rock's oldest continuously operating B&B is just off Main Street. Built in 1946, the inn has a wonderful garden, pine paneling in the foyer and twin parlors, and pine ceilings and woodwork throughout. Some rooms are small, but most can hold a queen-size bed and antique dresser, table, and chair comfortably. The larger rooms on the second floor have fireplaces and four-poster beds. A full breakfast, served in an enclosed porch, includes delicious homemade breads and muffins. There's a two-night minimum many weekends. ✉ *152 Sunset Dr., 28605* ☎ *828/295–3331* 🌐 *www.maplelodge.net* *10 rooms, 1 suite* *Dining room, some refrigerators* *AE, D, MC, V* *BP.*

¢–$$ **Alpine Village Inn.** This motel in the heart of Blowing Rock harks back to a simpler time. Rooms are neat and attractive in a homey way. Owners Rudy and Lynn Cutrera have decorated them with antiques, quilts, even flowers on holidays. Room refrigerators are available, and morning coffee is served. ✉ *297 Sunset Dr., 28605* ☎ *828/295–7206* 🌐 *www.alpine-village-inn.com* *16 rooms* *Some refrigerators* *AE, D, MC, V* *EP.*

$ **Ridgeway Inn.** "Park and stroll" could be the motto of this centrally located inn, clad in dark brown wood shakes and with pleasant grounds sprinkled with flowers. Rooms are spic 'n' span clean; if you need more space, choose one of the two cottages, each with fireplace, whirlpool bath, and kitchen. ✉ *127 Yonahlossee, Box 1086, 28605* ☎ *828/295–7321* *828/295–4498* 🌐 *www.ridgewaymotorinn.com* *Some kitchens, refrigerators* *17 rooms, 2 cottages* *EP.*

Shopping

Classic, high-quality women's clothing goes at outlet sale prices at **Tanner Factory Store** (✉ U.S. 321 bypass ☎ 828/295–7031).

Bolick Pottery (✉ Rte. 8 off U.S. 321, Lenoir ☎ 828/295–3862), 3 mi southeast of Blowing Rock, sells mountain crafts and pottery handcrafted by Glenn and Lula Bolick, fifth-generation potters.

Boone

26 *8 mi north of Blowing Rock.*

Boone, at the convergence of three major highways—U.S. 321, U.S. 421, and Route 105—is a fast-growing college town, home to Appalachian State University and its 14,000 students. Suburban sprawl has arrived, especially along U.S. 321 with its clusters of fast-food restaurants, chain motels, and a small mall, the only enclosed mall in the High Country. Closer to ASU, however, you get more of the college-town vibe, with organic food stores and boutiques. The town was named for frontiersman Daniel Boone, whose family moved to the area when Daniel was 15. Restaurants here serve only wine and beer, not mixed drinks.

On six acres adjacent to the Horn in the West amphitheater, **Daniel Boone Native Gardens** highlights local plants and trees in a setting of quiet beauty. The wrought-iron gate to the gardens was a gift of Daniel Boone VI, a direct descendant of the pioneer. ✉ *651 Horn in the West Dr., ¼ mi off U.S. 321* ☎ *828/264–6390* *$2* *May–Oct., daily 10–6; mid-June–mid-Aug., Tues.–Sun. 10–8.*

The **Appalachian Cultural Museum** at Appalachian State University examines the lives of Native Americans and African-Americans in the High Country, showcases the successes of such mountain residents as stock-car racer Junior Johnson and country singers Lula Belle and Scotty Wiseman, and exhibits a vast collection of antique quilts, fiddles, and handcrafted furniture. ✉ *University Hall Dr. off U.S. 321* ☎ *828/262–3117* 🌐 *www.museum.appstate.edu* 🎟 *$4, free on Tues.* ⏲ *Tues.–Sat. 10–5, Sun. 1–5.*

off the beaten path

BLUE RIDGE MOUNTAINS FRESCOES – In the 1970s North Carolina artist Ben Long and his students painted four luminous big-as-life frescoes in two churches about 45 mi northeast of Boone, in Ashe County, past Blue Ridge Parkway mile marker 258.6. *The Last Supper* is in the Glendale Springs Holy Trinity Church; the others, including *Mary, Great with Child,* are in St. Mary's Episcopal Church at Beaver Creek near West Jefferson. Signs from the parkway lead to the churches. ☎ *336/982–3076* 🎟 *Free.*

Sports & the Outdoors

CANOEING & RAFTING Near Boone and Blowing Rock, the New River, a federally designated Wild and Scenic River (Class I and II rapids) provides excitement for canoeists and rafters, as do the Watauga River, Wilson Creek, and the Toe River. One outfitter is **Wahoo's Adventures** (☎ 828/262–5774 or 800/444–7238).

GOLF The High Country has many challenging courses. **Boone Golf Club** (✉ Fairway Dr. ☎ 828/264–8760) is a good par-71 course for the whole family. **Hound Ears Club** (✉ Rte. 105 ☎ 828/963–4312) has a par-72 18-hole course with great mountain views. **Linville Golf Club** (✉ 83 Roseboro Rd., Linville ☎ 828/733–4363), 17 mi from Boone, has a par-72 Donald Ross–designed course.

Where to Stay & Eat

$$$–$$$$ ✕ **Wildflower Casually Eclectic.** Widely considered the best restaurant in Boone, and possibly in all of the High Country, Wildflower lives up to its name, with a casually eclectic menu featuring unusual combinations of flavors and colors. Chef-owners Brad and Bernadette Kirk create such dishes as duck breast with sweet corn risotto, seared wild salmon with couscous and saffron, and crab cakes with purple sticky rice and pickled cabbage. In 2004, the restaurant moved to a light, airy new space filled with art in the Market Place at King. Wildflower's store next door sells hand-made cheeses, sauces, and other gourmet items. ✉ *Market Place at King, 783 West King St.* ☎ *828/264–3463* 👤 *Reservations essential* 💳 *D, MC, V* ⏲ *Closed Sun. and Mon.*

$$ ✕ **Dan'l Boone Inn Restaurant.** Near Appalachian State University, in a former hospital surrounded by a picket fence and flowers, Dan'l Boone offers old-fashioned food served family style. Warning: the portions of fried chicken, country-style steak, ham, mashed potatoes, scrambled eggs, bacon, and breads (to name a few) are extremely generous. Lunch or dinner, including beverage and dessert, is a bargain at $12.95, and breakfast is $7.95. (You can't get breakfast on weekdays.) There's usually a line waiting to get in. ✉ *130 Hardin St.* ☎ *828/264–8657* 💳 *No credit cards* ⏲ *No lunch weekdays, Nov.–late May.*

¢–$$ ✕ **Red Onion Café.** Perky and pleasant young waitpersons serve the basics—burgers, wraps, pizzas—at this popular college town eatery, but also available are less usual items such as baked salmon and veg-

MOUNTAIN FOOD

Traditional mountain cooking is rib-sticking fare, intended for people who work hard on the farm all day. It dates to a time when the biggest meal of the day was dinner, taken at noon, and the food was heavy on country ham with red eye gravy, pan-fried chicken, and vegetables from the garden such as half runner beans seasoned with fatback, creamed sweet corn, and new potatoes. With it came cat-head biscuits (so called because of their size), fresh-churned butter, sourwood honey (light-color honey from sourwood trees that bloom in late spring), and tall glasses of spring water and buttermilk. Some the more unusual mountain dishes, only rarely available at local restaurants, include ramps (a smelly cousin of the onion) with eggs; baked groundhog; bear meat (prepared as a roast or stew); creases or creasie greens (a salad of wild wintercress); leather-britches (beans dried in the pod and boiled with salt pork); dried-apple pie; and dasquini (dumplings made by the Cherokee from chestnuts).

gie sandwiches and black bean pesto lasagna. Art lines the walls, and in good weather you can sit on the outside deck. ✉ *227 Harden St.* ☎ *828/264–5470* ▭ *AE, D, MC, V.*

$$$$ **Hound Ears Lodge and Club.** This alpine inn, overlooking Grandfather Mountain and a lush golf course designed by George Cobb, offers amenities such as a swimming pool secluded in a natural grotto and comfortable, well-kept rooms dressed in Waverly print fabrics. From April through October the room rate for special packages includes breakfast and dinner. The dining area is open only to guests and members; reservations are required, as are a jacket and tie for dinner. ✉ *328 Shulls Mill Rd., off Rte. 105, 6 mi from Boone, 28605* ☎ *828/963–4321* 📠 *828/963–8030* 🌐 *www.houndears.com* *29 rooms* *Dining room, 18-hole golf course, 8 tennis courts, pool, fishing, business services, meeting rooms* ▭ *AE, MC, V* *EP.*

$$–$$$ **Lovill House Inn.** This restored two-story country farmhouse once housed the law offices of Captain Edward Francis Lovill, a decorated Confederate officer and a founding trustee of what became Appalachian State University. Built in 1875 and featuring unusual details such as wormy chestnut woodwork, the inn occupies 11 wooded acres in a quiet area just west of downtown. On the grounds are a picnic area, gardens, and a stream with a waterfall. Some rooms have antique iron bedsteads or sleigh beds and fireplaces. Every evening owners Scott and Anne Peecook host a social hour. ✉ *404 Old Bristol Rd., 28607* ☎ *828/264–4204 or 800/849–9466* 🌐 *www.lovillhouseinn.com* *6 rooms* *Dining room; no a/c in some rooms, no kids under 12* ▭ *MC, V* *Closed Mar.* *BP.*

$ **Holiday Inn Express.** This is the spiffiest of the chain motels in town (you can also choose from Hampton Inn, Fairfield Inn, Comfort Suites and others). The lobby of the five-story motel features local artwork. The suites have fireplaces and whirlpool baths. ✉ *1943 Blowing Rock Rd. (U.S. 321) 28607* ☎ *828/264–2451* 📠 *828/265–3861* 🌐 *www.*

holidayinn-boone.com ⇆ *124 rooms, 5 suites* ♁ *Pool, exercise equipment, hot tub, laundry facilities, business services, meeting rooms* ▭ *AE, D, MC, V* 🍽 *BP.*

Nightlife & the Arts

Horn in the West, a project of the Southern Appalachian Historical Association, is an outdoor drama that traces the story of the lives of Daniel Boone and other pioneers, as well as the Cherokee, during the American Revolution. ✉ *Amphitheater off U.S. 321* ☎ *828/264–2120* 🎟 *$12* ⏲ *Performances mid-June–mid-Aug., Tues.–Sun. at 8 PM.*

A part of Appalachian State University, and expanded in 2004 with new gallery space and a 135-seat lecture hall, the **Turchin Center for the Visual Arts** (✉ 423 W. King St. ☎ 828/262–3017) is the largest visual arts center in the High Country, with regular exhibitions of regional as well as national and international art.

Shopping

Mast General Store (✉ 630 W. King St. ☎ 828/262–0000), at the Old Boone Mercantile, is a classic general store, updated with gift items, trendy clothes, and barrels of candy.

Valle Crucis

27 *5 mi south of Boone.*

This tiny mountain town has the state's first rural historic district; vintage stores line the downtown streets.

Everything from ribbons and overalls to yard art and cookware is sold in the original **Mast General Store** (✉ Rte. 194 ☎ 828/963–6511). Built in 1882, the store has plank floors worn to a soft sheen and an active old-timey post office. You can take a shopping break by sipping bottled soda pop while sitting in a rocking chair on the store's back porch. For more shopping, an annex is just down the road.

Sports & the Outdoors

GOLF The par-72 **Gauntlet at St. James Plantation** (✉ Rte. 211 ☎ 910/253–3008 or 800/247–4806) lives up to its reputation as a challenging course.

Where to Stay & Eat

$$$–$$$$ ✕ **Mast Farm Inn.** You can turn back the clock and still enjoy modern amenities at this charming pastoral inn, built in the 1800s and now on the National Register of Historic Places. Rooms are in the farmhouse or in log outbuildings. The restaurant uses locally and organically grown vegetables to enhance its innovative uptown menu. Organic gardening demonstrations are held in the inn's gardens. ✉ *2543 Broadstone Rd., Box 704, 28691* ☎ *828/963–5857 or 888/963–5857* 📠 *828/963–6404* 🌐 *www.mastfarminn.com* ⇆ *9 rooms, 6 cottages* ♁ *Restaurant, pond* ▭ *AE, D, MC, V* 🍽 *BP.*

Shopping

If you are looking for a mountain painting, stop by **Gallery Alta Vista** (✉ 2839 Broadstone Rd. ☎ 828/963–5247), which features the work of some 200 artists, many from western North Carolina. If shopping wears you out, you can overnight here, because the gallery is also a bed-and-breakfast.

Banner Elk

28 *6 mi southwest of Valle Crucis, 11 mi southwest of Boone.*

Banner Elk is a popular ski resort town, which bills itself as the "highest town in the East," surrounded by the lofty peaks of Grandfather, Hanging Rock, Beech, and Sugar mountains. The massively ugly condo tower you'll see on top of Little Sugar Mountain (not a part of the Sugar Mountain ski resort) is the only scar on the scenic beauty of the area. At least something good came of the monstrosity—it so outraged local residents that it prompted the passing of a ridge line law preventing such mountaintop development.

Sports & the Outdoors

CANOEING & RAFTING **Edge of the World Outfitters** (✉ Rte. 184 ☎ 828/898–9550 or 800/789–3343) offers white-water rafting, rappelling, canoeing, and snowboarding lessons in the Banner Elk area.

SKIING At 5,506 feet above sea level, **Ski Beech** (✉ Rte. 184, Beech Mountain ☎ 828/387–2011 or 800/438–2093) is the highest resort in the eastern United States. One of the larger resorts in the area, **Sugar Mountain** (✉ Off Rte. 184, Banner Elk ☎ 828/898–4521 or 800/784–2768) has an equipment shop and lessons and tubing for the kids. A higher-end resort, **Hawksnest Golf and Ski Resort** (✉ 1800 Skyland Dr., Seven Devils ☎ 828/963–6561 or 800/822–4295) has full snowmaking capability and challenging slopes. Call for **ski conditions** (☎ 800/962–2322).

Where to Stay & Eat

$$$–$$$$ ✕ **Jackalope's View.** The outside is brought indoors at this restaurant at Archer's Inn, where picture windows upstairs and down look out over the countryside (there's also a dining deck on the lower level). Jackalope classics include Wiener schnitzel and Jamaican jerk shrimp over linguine. The chef also prepares weekly specials, such as duck confit with a raspberry glaze over matchstick vegetables and potatoes. In the summer season there's live music on weekends. ✉ *2489 Beech Mountain Pkwy.* ☎ *828/898–9004* ▭ *D, MC, V* ⊗ *Closed Mon.*

¢–$ ✕ **Captain Crabby's Galley Restaurant.** Conch fritters ($2 a serving), fried shrimp ($2 for six) and New England clam chowder ($4) are tasty specialities at this casual spot where you eat on paper plates at picnic tables. You won't find fresher fish in the High Country. Captain Crabby's shares space with a retail seafood store, and the co-owner, Skipper Olcott, also operates a wholesale seafood business in Jacksonville, Florida. ✉ *Food Lion Shopping Plaza, 3597 Tynecastle Hwy.* ☎ *828/898–9244.*

$–$$$ **Banner Elk Inn Bed & Breakfast and Cottages.** Here, less than ½ mi from Banner Elk's only stoplight, you have the choice of either traditional B&B rooms in a restored 1912 farm house or spacious cottages with kitchens. Even if you opt for one of pewter-gray, newly constructed cottages at the back of the main house, you can get a full B&B breakfast on weekends, or a continental breakfast weekdays. Owner Beverly Lait also offers several vacation rental houses nearby. ✉ *407 Main St. E, 28604*

828/898–6223 or 800/295–7851 www.bannerelkinn.com 6 rooms, 3 cottages Dining room, some kitchens; no a/c in some rooms, no TV in some rooms MC, V BP.

$–$$ **The Inns of Beech Mountain.** These two ski resorts—the Beech Alpen Inn and the Top of Beech Inn—are the closest resorts to the ski slopes of Beech Mountain. Beech Alpen is the more casual of the two. The staff is friendly, and some rooms have fireplaces and balconies. The restaurant at Beech Alpen is open for dinner only. Top of Beech Inn is closed in the spring and summer, except for special events. *700 Beech Mountain Pkwy., 28604 828/387–2252 www.beechalpen.com 48 rooms Restaurant, cable TV AE, D, MC, V BP.*

¢–$ **Smoketree Lodge.** Views of Grandfather Mountain and an in-house art gallery that shows the work of local artists are the highlights of this good-value mountain inn near the ski slopes. The lobby has a massive stone fireplace. All rooms are fully equipped and have kitchenettes; use of the laundry facilities is free. *11914 Rte. 105, 28607 828/963–6505 or 800/422–1880 828/963–7815 www.smoketree-lodge.com 46 rooms Room service, indoor pool, exercise equipment, hot tub, recreation room AE, D, MC, V EP.*

Shopping

For hardware, firewood, a half gallon of milk, locally grown vegetables, pumpkins for Halloween, snowboard and ski rentals, gourmet bird seed, today's *Wall Street Journal,* and just about anything else you need, **Fred's General Mercantile** (501 Beech Mountain Pkwy. 828/387–4838), half general store and half boutique, is the place to go in Banner Elk, and has been for more than 25 years.

Hot Springs

29 *30 mi northwest of Asheville via U.S. 23/19 and U.S. 25/70 past Marshall.*

This little village is a way station for hikers on the Appalachian Trail. Since the early 1800s, Hot Springs, not far from the Tennessee border in Madison County, has attracted visitors seeking relief from real or imagined ailments in its 104°F mineral water. At one time, the town boasted a 350-room hotel, one of the largest in the South, with a dining room seating 600. By the early 20th century, however, fewer people "took the waters," and the town's only remaining hotel burned to the ground. In recent years, thanks to its location beside the French Broad River, Hot Springs has attracted rafters and other visitors seeking a quiet, unpretentious vacation. Don't leave town without meeting the delightful Helen Gosnell, who staffs the visitor information center, in a red caboose on Bridge Street. Helen, a Madison County native who has lived in Hot Springs since 1962, knows everything and everybody in Hot Springs.

The mineral springs at **Hot Springs Resort & Spa** maintain a natural 104°F temperature year-round and for many decades have provided relief for those suffering from various ailments, including rheumatism and pelvic troubles. Today, however, the atmosphere is more like a trailer park than a spa. The water still flows naturally hot, but to experience it you sit in a hot tub like the ones sold at your local building supply store, in a wood shack. It can still be fun, but upscale it's not. Massage therapy is also available. ✉ *315 Bridge St.* ☎ *828/622–7676 or 800/462–0933* 🌐 *www.nchotsprings.com* *$10–$30 per hr, depending on time of day and number of people in tub* ⏲ *Feb.–Nov., daily 9 AM–11 PM; Dec.–Jan., hrs vary, call in advance.*

off the beaten path

MAX PATCH BALD – A bald is a big grassy area at the top of a mountain where no trees grow. How balds come to be is not clearly understood, but it has something to do with the combination of wind, weather and soil conditions. Max Patch Bald, right on the Appalachian Trail, is one of the best examples, and it has been called one of the crown jewels of the trail. At 4,629 feet, on a clear day you can see both Mt. Mitchell and into the Great Smokies. To get here from Hot Springs, go south on NC 209 6.4 mi to Meadow Fork Rd. Continue south for 3.5 mi, mostly on a gravel road. At the top of the mountain, turn right on SR 1182 and go 1.5 mi to Max Patch parking area. From there you go by foot on a pleasant trail; the total walk is less than 1½ mi. ✉ *NC SR 1182.*

Where to Stay & Eat

$$–$$$$ **Mountain Magnolia Inn.** This restored 1868 inn is about all that remains of the grandeur that was once Hot Springs. On a shady and hidden back road beside the French Broad River, the inn sits among well-tended perennial gardens. If you want the best digs, ask for the Walnut Room, with a king bed, small whirlpool bathtub, and balcony overlooking the gardens and the river. The dining room is open to the public for dinner, offering mountain trout, steaks, and other dishes. ✉ *204 Lawson St., Hot Springs 28743* ☎ *828/622–3543* *828/622–9953* 🌐 *www.mountainmagnoliainn.com* *5 rooms, 1 cottage* *Restaurant; no room TVs, no smoking* *AE, MC, V* *BP.*

¢–$ **Bridge Street Café & Inn.** This renovated storefront, circa 1922, is right on the Appalachian Trail and overlooks Spring Creek. Upstairs are simply decorated rooms and two baths filled with antiques. One bathroom has a claw-foot tub. The café ($–$$$) downstairs has a wood-fired oven and grill, from which emerge delicious pizzas. There's live music most Saturdays on the outdoor dining deck. *Bridge St., Box 502, 28743* ☎ *828/622–0002* *828/622–7282* 🌐 *www.bridgestreetcafe.com* *3 rooms with shared bath* *Restaurant; no room TVs, no smoking* *AE, D, MC, V* ⏲ *Inn and restaurant closed Nov.–mid-Mar.; restaurant closed Mon.–Wed.* *BP.*

THE SOUTHERN MOUNTAINS

The Southern Mountains encompass a diverse area in ten North Carolina counties south and west of Asheville. They include the towns of Hendersonville and Flat Rock in Henderson County, and Brevard in Transylvania County. The Southern Mountains also include Cashiers, Highlands, and Lake Toxaway, chic summer enclaves where some lake-front building lots now cost a million dollars.

Hendersonville

30 *23 mi south of Asheville via I–26.*

Hendersonville, with about 11,000 residents, has one of the most engaging and vibrant downtowns of any small city in the South. Historic Main Street, as it's called, extends 10 serpentine blocks, lined with flower boxes and about 40 shops, including many antiques stores. Each year from April through October Main Street has displays of public art. In 2004, the theme was "bearfootin'," with 33 whimsical bear sculptures created by local artists and sponsored by area businesses. Within walking distance of downtown are several bed-and-breakfasts and many restaurants.

The Hendersonville area is North Carolina's main apple-growing area, and some 200 apple orchards dot the rolling hills around town. An Apple Festival attracting some 200,000 people is held each year in August.

The **Holmes Educational State Forest,** a 235-acre state forest, has "talking trees," a fun way for kids to learn about the forests of western North Carolina—just punch a button on a hickory or poplar, and a recording tells you about the tree. ✉ *Crabtree Rd., 9 mi from downtown Hendersonville* ☎ *828/692–0100* *Free* *Mid-Mar.–mid-Nov., Tues.–Fri. 9-5, weekends 11-8.*

The **Historic Johnson Farm,** a 19th-century tobacco farm that is now operated by Henderson County Public Schools, has the original farm house, barn, outbuildings, and a museum with about 1,000 artifacts typical of farm life of the time. ✉ *3346 Haywood Rd., 4 mi north of downtown Hendersonville* ☎ *828/697–4733* *Guided tours $3* *Tues.–Fri. 9–2:30.*

The **Henderson County Curb Market,** which first opened in 1924 and now has about 100 vendors, requires that all sellers be local residents and all items sold must be either hand-made or locally grown. ✉ *Corner of Second Ave. and Church St.* ☎ *828/692–8012* *Apr.–Dec., Tue., Thurs., and Sat. 8–2; Jan.–Mar., Tues. and Sat. 8–2.*

off the beaten path

THOMAS WOLFE'S ANGEL – In his novel *Look Homeward, Angel,* Asheville-born Thomas Wolfe makes many references to an angel statue. The famous angel, in real life carved from Italian marble by Wolfe's father, W. O. Wolfe, stands in Hendersonville's Oakdale Cemetery, marking the graves of a family named Johnson, to whom the senior Wolfe sold the statue. The statue is protected by an iron fence. ✉ *U.S. 64, just west of downtown Hendersonville.*

Sports & the Outdoors

GOLF Among the five golf courses in Hendersonville, the 6,719-yard, par-71, private **Champion Hills Golf Club** (✉ 1 Hagen Dr. ☎ 828/693–3600) is the home course of famed golf course designer Tom Fazio. An enjoyable public course is **Crooked Tree Golf Club** (✉ 764 Crooked Tree Rd. ☎ 828/692–2011), where the clubhouse was once a corporate retreat owned by Warner Bros., the movie company.

Where to Stay & Eat

$$$–$$$$ ✕ **Expressions.** Opened in 1982 by Chef Tom Young, Expressions is one of the region's most consistently dependable places for interesting meals. Located right on Main Street, the interior is understated, with brick walls and wood accents (it can be a bit noisy). At lunch, you can choose a sidewalk table under a green umbrella. The menu changes daily but features items such as smoked mountain trout, lamb with dijon herb sauce, and roast duck breast. ✉ *114 N. Main St.* ☎ *828/693–8516* ▭ *DC, MC, V* ⊙ *Closed Sun.*

$$–$$$ **Claddagh Inn.** Next door to the Waverly Inn, Claddagh (pronounced CLAW-da, Gaelic for "love and friendship") was built around 1888, in the Classic Revival style, as the home of the first mayor of Hendersonville. It has been an inn under various names for almost a century. The 16 rooms on three floors are all decorated and furnished differently, but most have Victorian wallpaper and antique beds. Enjoy a complimentary evening sherry in the library, with its oriental rugs and wood paneling. Tuesdays are free if you're staying at least three days. ✉ *755 N. Main St., 28792* ☎ *828/697–7778 or 800/225–4700* 🌐 *www.claddaghinn.com* *14 rooms, 1 suite* *Dining room; no TV in some rooms* ▭ *AE, D, MC, V* *BP.*

$$ **Waverly Inn.** On a warm afternoon, you'll love to "sit a spell" in a rocking chair on the front porch of Hendersonville's oldest inn. All 14 rooms in the 1898 three-story Victorian, two blocks from downtown, are named after native flowers and shrubs and outfitted with antique furnishings. The Mountain Magnolia suite has a king canopy bed, and the Silverbell room, painted an airy yellow and white, has a four-poster bed and a claw-foot bathtub. ✉ *783 N. Main St., 28792* ☎ *828/698–9193 or 800/537–8195* 🌐 *www.waverlyinn.com* *13 rooms, 1 suite* *No smoking* ▭ *AE, D, DC, MC, V* *BP.*

Nightlife & the Arts

THE ARTS The Skyland Hotel is where Jazz Age novelist F. Scott Fitzgerald stayed when he visited his wife in a mental institution in Asheville, and the building is now the **The Arts Center** (✉ 538 N. Main St. ☎ 828/693–8504), a nonprofit organization that puts on art exhibits and other cultural programs.

NIGHTLIFE While local nightlife is limited, you can hear live music on weekend nights and enjoy one of about 125 types of beer at **Hannah Flanagan's Pub** (✉ 300 N. Main St. ☎ 828/696–1665).

Shopping

If you like to shop, you'll enjoy browsing the 40 shops on **Historic Main Street,** including several antiques stores, a branch of Mast General Store, and local boutiques.

Flat Rock

31 *3 mi south of Hendersonville, 26 mi south of Asheville via I–26.*

Flat Rock has been a summer resort since the early 19th century. It was a favorite of wealthy planters from Charleston, eager to escape the Lowcountry heat. The trip from Charleston to Flat Rock by horse and carriage took as long as two weeks, so you know there must be something here that made the long trek worthwhile.

★ The **Carl Sandburg Home National Historic Site** is the spot to which the poet and Lincoln biographer Carl Sandburg moved with his wife, Lillian, in 1945. Guided tours of their house, Connemara, where Sandburg's papers still lie scattered on his desk, are given by the National Park Service. In summer the productions *The World of Carl Sandburg* and *Rootabaga Stories* are presented at the amphitheater. Kids enjoy a walk around the grounds of the farm, which still maintains descendants of the Sandburg family goats. ✉ *1928 Little River Rd.* ☎ *828/693–4178* 🌐 *www.nps.gov/carl* *$3* *Daily 9–5.*

The **Flat Rock Playhouse** has a high reputation for summer stock theater. The season runs from May to mid-December. ✉ *2661 Greenville Hwy.* ☎ *828/693–0731* 🌐 *www.flatrockplayhouse.org.*

Tryon

32 *30 mi southeast of Asheville, 19 mi southeast of Flat Rock.*

Tryon is western North Carolina's horse country—not as in trail horse rides, but as in riding to the hounds. The annual mid-April running of the **Blockhouse Steeplechase Races** attracts big crowds to this little town, which is just ½ mi from the South Carolina state line. For information about the race, contact the **Tryon Riding & Hunt Club** (✉ 1 Depot St. ☎ 828/859–6109 or 800/438–3681 🌐 www.trhcevents.com). The equally tiny nearby town of Saluda is famous for its steep railroad grade up Saluda mountain.

Where to Stay & Eat

$$–$$$ **Pine Crest Inn.** A former hunt club, this is *the* place to stay and dine in Tryon. Built in 1906 and first used as a lodging in 1917, the inn was visited by Hemingway and Fitzgerald and is now on the National Register of Historic Places. The Fox and Hounds bar will put you in mind of a weekend at an English country home. The restaurant ($$$–$$$$) is noted for its flawless service. It has won *Wine Spectator* magazine's Excellence award for many years, and the local wine society meets here weekly. ✉ *895 Pine Crest La., 28782* ☎ *828/859–9135* *828/859–9135* 🌐 *www.pinecrestinn.com* *23 rooms, 7 suites* *Restaurant, some in-room hot tubs, business services, meeting rooms* *AE, D, MC, V* *BP.*

Brevard

33 *40 mi southwest of Asheville on Rte. 280.*

With its friendly, highly walkable downtown, Brevard is Mayberry RFD transported to the Pisgah National Forest. In fact, a popular toy store in town is called O. P. Taylor's—get it?

Brevard residents go nuts over the white squirrels which dart around the town's parks. These aren't albinos, but a variation of the eastern gray squirrel. The white squirrels are thought to have come originally from Hawaii by way of Florida; they possibly were released in Brevard by a visitor in the 1950s. Whatever the truth, today Brevard capitalizes on it by holding a White Squirrel Festival in late May.

Of perhaps wider interest is Brevard's claim as the gateway to the "Land of Waterfalls." The area boasts at least 250 waterfalls, the largest of which are Whitewater Falls, 400 feet high, and the privately owned Slatton Falls, 600 feet high.

About 45% of Transylvania County, where Brevard is located—sorry, no vampires here—is a part of the Pisgah National Forest. In the Brevard area are more than 15 summer camps for boys and girls.

The oldest frame house in western North Carolina, the **Allison-Deaver House** was built in the early 1800s, and has been renovated and expanded several times. ✉ *N.C. Hwy. 280, Pisgah Forest, near Forest Gate Shopping Center* ☎ *828/884–5137* 🎫 *Donations accepted* ⏲ *Apr.–Oct., Fri. and Sat. 10–4, Sun. 1–4.*

★ Nearby Pisgah National Forest has the **Cradle of Forestry in America National Historic Site,** the home of the first forestry school in the U.S., with a 1-mi interpretive trail, the school's original log buildings and a visitor center with many hands-on exhibits of interest to kids. The road from Brevard to the Cradle of Foresty, a scenic byway, continues on to connect with the Blue Ridge Parkway near Mt. Pisgah. ✉ *1001 Pisgah Hwy., U.S. 276* ☎ *828/884–5823* 🌐 *www.cradleofforestry.com* 🎫 *$5.*

The newest addition to nature sites near Brevard is **DuPont State Forest,** which was established in 1996 and expanded in 2000. You'll find 10,400 acres with four waterfalls and 80 mi of old dirt roads to explore, with ideal conditions for biking or horseback riding. ✉ *U.S. 64 and Little River Rd.* ☎ *828/877–6527* 🌐 *www.dupontforest.com* 🎫 *Free.*

Near the road and easy to get to, **Looking Glass Falls** is a classic, with water cascading 60 feet into a clear pool. ✉ *Pisgah National Forest, north of Brevard, off U.S. 276* 🎫 *Free.*

At the **Pisgah Center for Wildlife Education** the fish hatchery produces more than 400,000 brown, rainbow, and native brook trout each year for release in local streams. You can see the fish up close in tanks called raceways and even feed them (approved trout feed is sold for a quarter). There's also a small visitor center with information about the life cycle of trout and an educational nature trail. ✉ *Rte. 475 off U.S. 276 in Pisgah National Forest* ☎ *828/877–4423* 🎫 *Free.*

At **Sliding Rock** in summer you can skid 60 feet on a natural water slide. Wear old jeans and tennis shoes and bring a towel. ✉ *Pisgah National Forest, north of Brevard, off U.S. 276* ☎ *828/877–3265* 🎫 *$3 per car* ⏲ *Late May–early Sept., daily 10–5:30.*

off the beaten path

ALUMINUM CHRISTMAS TREE MUSEUM – One more piece of evidence in the case that there's a museum for everything, this installation features those tacky aluminum trees from the 1950s and '60s. Among the tackiest: the Elvis tree and the Tammy Faye Bakker tree. The museum, open annually from Thanksgiving to New Year's, is the creation of Brevard resident Stephen Paul Jackson. The venue varies from year-to-year. In 2003, the museum was at Kris Klassics store, 36 W. Main St. If you are in the area around Christmas, for time and place check with the Brevard Chamber of Commerce/ Visitors Information Center ✉ *35 W. Main St.* ☎ *828/883–3700.*

Sports & the Outdoors

CANOEING AND KAYAKING Self-guided kayak, canoe, and tube trips on the French Broad River are offered by **Headwaters Outfitters** (✉ U.S. 64 and NC 215, Rosman ☎ 828/877-3106).

FISHING Catch rainbow, brown, or brook trout on the Davidson River, named one of the top 100 trout streams in the U.S. by Trout Unlimited. **Davidson River Outfitters** (✉ 26 Pisgah Forest Hwy. ☎ 828/877–4181) arranges trips and also has a fly fishing school and a fly shop.

GOLF **Etowah Valley Country Club and Golf Lodge** (✉ U.S. 64, Etowah ☎ 828/891–7141 or 800/451–8174), has three very different (one par-72, two par-73) 18-hole courses and offers good package deals.

SKATEBOARDING Western North Carolina's largest indoor skateboard, skating, and BMX biking facility is **Zero Gravity Skatepark** (✉ 1800 Old Hendersonville Hwy. ☎ 828/862–6700), with fun boxes, ramps, launch boxes, ledges, roll-ins, and a pyramid and bowl.

Where to Stay & Eat

$$–$$$ ✕ **Hobnob.** You can hobnob with old and new friends at this casual spot in a colorfully painted house near downtown. The owners, who formerly ran a restaurant in Charleston, have brought a Lowcountry edge to dining in Brevard, with dishes like Carolina crabcake with lobster sauce and seafood lasagna. ✉ *226 Main St.* ☎ *828/966–4662* ▭ *AE, MC, V.*

¢ ✕ **Cardinal Drive-In.** The cheeseburgers are just fair and the onion rings are like fried cardboard, but this is an authentic piece of Americana—a real drive-in, with car hops and everything. ✉ *7328 S. Broad St.* ☎ *828/884–7085* ▭ *No credit cards.*

$$ **The Inn at Brevard.** Built in 1885 as a private home, this white, two-story inn with stately entrance columns sits on a shady corner three blocks from downtown Brevard. With old photos and art on the walls, some by the Irish portrait painter Eileen Fabian, and mix-and-match antique furniture, it may remind you of your grandmom's house, but the overall effect is homey and comfortable. A motel-like annex next door has 10 rooms with knotty pine paneling. Guests staying here have access to the privately owned Slatton waterfalls adjoining Pisgah National Forest. ✉ *410 E. Main St., 28712* ☎ *828/884–2105* *828/885–7996* *www.innatbrevard.8m.com* *14 rooms, 2 with shared bath, 1 suite* *Restaurant* ▭ *AE, DC, MC, V* *Closed Dec.–early Apr.* *BP.*

$–$$ **Hampton Inn.** This standard-issue three-story Hampton Inn has 80 recently renovated rooms, all with broadband WI-FI. It's in a suburban area next to a Wal-Mart, 3 mi from downtown and less than 1 mi from the entrance to Pisgah National Forest. ✉ *800 Forest Gate Center, 28768* ☎ *828/883–4800* *828/877–5884* *www.hamptoninn.com*

80 rooms Pool, meeting rooms, laundry services, Internet AE, D, DC, MC, V BP.

$–$$ **The Red House Inn.** One of the oldest houses in Brevard, the Red House Inn was built in 1851 as a trading post and later served as a court house, tavern, post office, and school. Now it is an unpretentious but pleasant B&B four blocks from the center of town. There are four rooms in the main house and an efficiency cottage. The common area has a working fireplace. *412 W. Probart St., 28712 828/884–9349 4 rooms, 2 with shared bath, 1 cottage Some refrigerators; no TV in some rooms MC, V BP.*

3

Nightlife & the Arts

THE ARTS The nationally known **Brevard Music Center** (828/884–2011 www.brevardmusic.org) has a seven-week music festival each summer, with about 80 concerts from mid-June to early August.

As unlikely as it may be, Brevard is home to a cowboy museum, the **Jim Bob Tinsley Museum and Research Center** (20 W. Jordan St. 828/884–2347), dedicated to the life and interests of this Brevard native, a musicologist and author of 10 books who played with Gene Autry. There are displays of art by Frederick Remington, Western memorabilia, and much more.

en route

If you're a waterfall fanatic, take the **"Waterfall Highway"** (U.S. 64W) toward Highlands, and you'll pass many falls including Hickory Nut Falls near Chimney Rock, and Bridal Veil Falls near Cashiers, among others.

Lake Toxaway

40 mi southwest of Asheville.

A century ago a group called the Lake Toxaway Company created a 640-acre lake in the high mountains between Brevard and Cashiers. Nearby, a grand 500-room hotel built with the finest materials, providing the most modern conveniences and serving European cuisine, attracted many of the country's elite. That hotel is long gone, but the scenic area, which some still call "America's Switzerland," has a number of fine resorts and some of the priciest real estate in the North Carolina mountains.

Those who love nature, even if you're just looking at it from the road, will enjoy being in this mountain wilderness. And those who think shopping is a sport will appreciate the upscale stores in the area, many specializing in antiques and regional arts and crafts.

Where to Stay

$$$$ **Earthshine Mountain Lodge.** You can have as much solitude or adventure as you want at this spacious cedar log cabin with stone fireplaces. The lodge, which sits on 70 acres midway between Brevard and Cashiers on a ridge that adjoins the Pisgah National Forest, offers horseback riding, hiking, fishing, and even an opportunity to gather berries, feed the goats, pan for gems, take guided trail rides, and try the 30-foot climb-

ing wall or zip line. In the evening families gather around an open fire to sing songs, square dance, and exchange stories. This is a BYOB establishment. ✉ *Golden Rd., 28747* ☎ *828/862–4207* 🌐 *www.earthshinemtnlodge.com* *10 rooms* *Dining room, fishing, hiking, horseback riding, babysitting, children's programs (ages 6 and up), meeting rooms; no room TVs* *D, MC, V* *FAP.*

$$$$ **Greystone Inn.** In 1915 Savannah resident Lucy Molz built a second home on Lake Toxaway. Today the six-level Swiss-style mansion is an inn listed on the National Register of Historic Places. Guest rooms have antiques or period reproductions, and suites that border the lake of this mountain resort are modern. Rates include breakfast and dinner, afternoon tea and cake, and cocktails. The inn is open weekends only January through March. ✉ *Greystone La., 28747* ☎ *828/966–4700 or 800/824–5766* *828/862–5689* 🌐 *www.greystoneinn.com* *33 rooms* *Dining room, in-room VCRs, golf privileges, putting green, 5 tennis courts, pool, lake, massage, spa, dock, waterskiing, fishing, children's programs, business services* *AE, MC, V* *MAP.*

Cashiers

34 *74 mi southwest of Asheville via U.S. 74 and NC 107, 14 mi west of Lake Toxaway.*

As you approach Cashiers (locally pronounced CASH-ers), you begin to see BMW, Mercedes, and Lexus automobiles crowding the narrow and winding roads. It's amply evident that people with second (or third or fourth) homes in Cashiers and nearby Glenville and Highlands have money.

Cashiers is not a quite a town. Until recently, it was just a crossroads, with a store or two, a summer getaway for wealthy South Carolinians escaping the heat. But with the building of many exclusive gated developments, the Cashiers area, at a cool 3,500 foot elevation, is seeing new restaurants, lodges, and golf courses open seemingly every month.

Whiteside Mountain is one of the highest continuous cliffs in the East. The sheer cliffs of white granite rise up to 750 feet, overlooking the Chattooga River in the Nantahala National Forest. The cliffs are popular with climbers. ✉ *Whiteside Mountain Rd., 4.6 mi from Cashiers on U.S. 64* ☎ *828/586–2155* *Closed to climbers Jan.–Jul.*

Sports & the Outdoors

GOLF At the golf course at the **High Hampton Inn & Country Club** (✉ 1525 NC 107S ☎ 828/743–2411) is a par-71, 6,012-yard George Cobb design, with an 8th hole *Golf Digest* has featured as one of America's finest holes. The newest course in the Cashiers area, a par-71, 6,699-yard semi-private course designed by Tom Jackson, **Highlands Cove** (✉ U.S. 64 ☎ 828/526–4185) has an elevated Highlands side and a flatter Cove side. Perched at 4,500 feet, **Trillium Links** (✉ 975 New Trillium Way ☎ 828/743–4251), a public course built in 1998, plays to 6,505 yards at par 71.

Where to Stay & Eat

$$–$$$$ ✕ **The Orchard.** Widely considered the best restaurant in the Cashiers area, The Orchard, in a cozy house with brown wood shakes, puts a Southern twist on traditional American dishes. Trout is served three ways. ✉ *NC 107S* ☎ *828/743–7614* ⊙ *Closed Mon. No lunch.*

$$$–$$$$ **High Hampton Inn & Country Club.** On the front lawn of this old inn are some of the most ancient trees in the region, including a giant fraser fir that is a national champion. Many of the buildings are bark-covered, and inside the main building, rebuilt in 1932 after a fire, you'll find rare wormy chestnut. Coats and ties are required for dinner, but otherwise the atmosphere is more down-home than country club. ✉ *1525 NC 107S, Cashiers 28717* ☎ *828/743–2411 or 800/334–2551* 📠 *828/743–5991* 🌐 *www.highhamptoninn.com* *117 rooms, 16 cottages* *Restaurant, some kitchens, 18-hole golf course, 6 tennis courts, lake, exercise equipment, boating, fishing, hiking, shops, laundry service, meeting rooms; no smoking* 💳 *AE, D, DC, MC, V* ⊙ *Closed mid-Nov.–mid-Apr.* 🍽 *FAP.*

$$–$$$$ **Innisfree Victorian Inn.** On a hill above Lake Glenville, you can indulge your literary, or romantic, fantasies in the Bronte Suite or one of the other garden-house rooms named after writers. And a fine fantasy it would be, with a four-poster bed and a glassed-in fireplace so you can see the fire from either the comfy bed or the two-person tub. The main inn has a wraparound veranda, an observatory, and an octagonal dining room. ✉ *NC 107N, Glenville 28736* ☎ *828/743–2946* 🌐 *www.innisfreeinn.com* *10 rooms* *Some refrigerators, pond; no TV in some rooms, no kids, no smoking* 💳 *AE, D, MC, V* 🍽 *BP.*

Highlands

35 *85 mi southwest of Asheville; 11 mi south of Cashiers on U.S. 64.*

Highlands is a tony small town of around 900 people, but the surrounding area swells to 10,000 or more in the summer and fall, when those with summer homes here flock back, like wealthy sparrows of Capistrano. Once Highlands billed itself as the highest town in the East, but it relinquished the title when Banner Elk and other tiny communities a little higher up in the High Country were incorporated as towns. Still, at 4,118 feet it is usually cool and pleasant when even Asheville gets hot. The town's five-block downtown is, not surprisingly given the local demographics, lined with upscale shops, antique stores, and coffeehouses.

West of Highlands via U.S. 64 toward Franklin, the **Cullasaja Gorge** (Cul-lah-SAY-jah) is an 8-mi gorge passing Lake Sequoyah and several waterfalls, including **Bridal Veil Falls** and the 200-foot **Cullasaja Falls.** ✉ *U.S. 64.*

In the center of downtown Highlands, the **Highlands Botanical Garden,** run by Western Carolina University, is a 30-acre biological reserve of native plants. There's also a small nature museum, open seasonally. ✉ *265 Sixth St.* ☎ *828/526–2602* *Free.*

Where to Stay & Eat

$$$$ ✕ **On the Verandah.** You'll enjoy views of Lake Sequoyah from the big windows of this former speakeasy. The owner has a collection of more than 1,300 hot sauces, any of which you can sample. The menu is long and varied, and many dishes are infused with Asian or Caribbean flavors. There's live piano music nightly. ✉ *1536 Franklin Rd.* ☎ *828/526–2338* ▭ *D, MC, V* ⊙ *Closed Dec.–mid-Mar. No lunch Mon.–Sat.*

$$–$$$$ ✕ **Ristorante Paoletti.** At this storefront restaurant on Main Street you are taken care of in a style that's more Italian-provincial than nouveau-riche. The menu includes a lengthy section of freshmade pastas, along with veal and seafood. The wine list includes more than 800 selections. ✉ *440 Main St.* ☎ *828/526–4906* ▭ *AE, MC, V* ⊙ *Closed Jan. and Feb. No lunch.*

$$–$$$ **Highlands Suites Hotel.** If you want to be in the heart of downtown Highlands but prefer all the modern amenities, consider this upscale spot on Main Street. It offers spacious suites, each with a full kitchen, whirlpool bath, and a living area that converts into a second bedroom by pulling out the queen sofa. Each suite has two TVs and two phones; some have fireplaces. ✉ *200 Main St., 28741* ☎ *828/526–4502 or 877/553–3761* *828/526–4840* ⊕ *www.mountainhighinn.com* *28 suites* *In-room hot tubs, kitchens, minibars, refrigerators, in-room VCRs* ▭ *AE, D, MC, V.*

The Arts

The well-respected **Highlands Playhouse** (✉ Oak St. ☎ 828/526–2695), an equity theater, puts on four or five productions each summer.

Shopping

Highlands is known for its upscales antique stores, which total at least a dozen.

The nightly antiques auctions from June through October at **Scudder's Gallery** (✉ 352 Main St. ☎ 828/526–4111), a high-end antiques dealer and estate liquidator established in 1925, are a form of local entertainment.

Since 1963, **Elephants Foot Antiques** (✉ U.S. 64 at Foreman Rd. ☎ 828/526/5451) has sold decorative furniture, antique lamps and other antiques.

en route

Many mountain roads can be described as steep and winding, but **U.S. 64 to Franklin** takes a special prize, though the frustrations of driving it are rewarded by beautiful scenery in the Cullasaja Gorge and the many waterfalls along the way.

THE NORTH CAROLINA MOUNTAINS A TO Z

To research prices, get advice from other travelers, and book travel arrangements, visit www.fodors.com.

AIR TRAVEL

Asheville Regional Airport (AVL), one of the most pleasant and modern airports in the South, is served by ASA/Delta Connection, Comair/

Delta Connection, Continental Express, Northwest, and US Airways Express. There are nonstop flights to Atlanta, Charlotte, Cincinnati, Detroit, Houston, Neward, New York LaGuardia, and Raleigh-Durham. US Airways Express serves the Hickory Airport (HKY), about 40 mi from Blowing Rock.

Airport Information **Asheville Regional Airport** ☒ 708 Airport Rd., Fletcher ☎ 828/684-2226 ⊕ www.flyavl.com. **Hickory Airport** ☒ U.S. 321 ☎ 828/323-7408.

Carriers **ASA/Delta Connection** ☎ 800/221-1212 ⊕ www.delta.com. **Comair/Delta Connection** ☎ 800/221-1212 ⊕ www.comair.com. **Continental Express** ☎ 800/523-3273 ⊕ www.continental.com. **Northwest** ☎ 800/225-2525 ⊕ www.nwa.com. **US Airways Express** ☎ 800/428-4322 ⊕ www.usair.com.

3

CAMPING

You can camp at the five developed, or "frontcountry," campgrounds in the North Carolina part of Great Smoky Mountains National Park; one of these, Smokemont, accepts reservations through the National Park Service Reservation Service. The remaining four campgrounds—Balsam Mountain, Big Creek, Cataloochee, and Deep Creek—are first-come, first-served only. All frontcountry camping in the park is primitive by design.

The Pisgah National Forest has 10 developed campgrounds, with a total of 484 campsites, and the Nantahala National Forest has 12 campgrounds with a total of 182 campsites. In addition, camping is permitted at designated points along roads in these national forests. Camping is also permitted in some state and local parks. The mountains also have numerous privately operated campgrounds and RV parks.

Great Smoky Mountains National Park Headquarters ☒ 107 Park Headquarters Rd., Gatlinburg, TN 37738 ☎ 865/436-1230, 865/436-1231 for inquiries about backcountry camping ⊕ www.gsmnp.com. **National Park Service Reservation Service** ☎ 800/365-2267 ⊕ www.reserveusa.com.

CAR TRAVEL

I–40 runs east-west through Asheville. I–26 runs from Charleston, South Carolina, to Asheville and, partly on a temporary route, continues northwest into Tennessee. I–240 forms a perimeter around the city. U.S. 19/23 is a major north and west route. The Blue Ridge Parkway runs northeast from Great Smoky Mountains National Park to Shenandoah National Park in Virginia, passing Cherokee, Asheville, and the High Country. U.S. 221 runs north to the Virginia border through Blowing Rock and Boone and intersects I–40 at Marion. U.S. 321 intersects I–40 at Hickory and heads to Blowing Rock and Boone.

EMERGENCIES

Dial 911 for police and ambulance service everywhere but the Cherokee Reservation, where the police and the EMS can be reached at the numbers listed below.

Doctors & Dentists **Mission St. Joseph's** ☒ 509 Biltmore Ave., Asheville ☎ 828/213-1111. **Watauga Medical Center** ☒ 336 Deerfield Rd., Boone ☎ 828/262-4100.

Emergency Services **Ambulance, police** ☎ 911. **Cherokee Reservation Police and EMS** ☎ 828/497-4131 for police, 828/497-6402 for EMS.

Hospitals **Mission St. Joseph's** ✉ 509 Biltmore Ave., Asheville ☎ 828/213–1111. **Pardee Hospital** ✉ 800 N. Justice St., Hendersonville ☎ 828/696-1000. **Blowing Rock Hospital** ✉ 416 Chestnut Dr., Blowing Rock ☎ 828/295–3136. **Cannon Memorial Hospital** ✉ 805 Shawneehaw Ave., Banner Elk ☎ 828/898–5111. **Wautauga Medical Center** ✉ 336 Deerfield Rd., Boone ☎ 828/262–4100.

TOURS

If you don't care to walk or drive around downtown Asheville, an alternative way to hit high spots is the Asheville Historic Trolley Tour, which costs $16. Call to make arrangements.

Asheville Historic Trolley Tours ☎ 888/667–3600.

VISITOR INFORMATION

In Asheville, the Asheville Convention and Visitors Bureau will answer questions and provide maps. The Cherokee Visitors Center provides information on the reservation. North Carolina High Country Host is a complete information center for the High Country counties of Watauga, Ashe, and Avery. Smoky Mountain Host of North Carolina has information about the state's seven westernmost counties.

Tourist Information **Asheville Convention and Visitors Bureau** 151 Haywood St., Box 1010, 28802 ☎ 828/258–6102 or 800/257–1300 www.ashevillechamber.org. **Cherokee Visitors Center** ✉ U.S. 441 Business ☎ 828/497–9195 or 800/438–1601 www.cherokee-nc.com. **North Carolina High Country Host** ✉ 1701 Blowing Rock Rd., Boone 28607 ☎ 828/264–1299 or 800/438–7500 www.visitboonenc.com. **Smoky Mountain Host of NC** ✉ 4437 Georgia Rd., Franklin 28734 ☎ 828/369–9606 or 800/432–4678 www.visitsmokies.org.

MYRTLE BEACH & THE GRAND STRAND

4

SHOP TILL YOU DROP
at Broadway on the Beach ⇨ *p.178*

RAMBLE AMONG THE REMINGTONS
at Brookgreen Gardens ⇨ *p.182*

EAT OYSTERS FRESH OFF THE BOAT
at Nance's Creekfront Restaurant ⇨ *p.184*

RENT A CONDO FOR THE WHOLE FAMILY
at Litchfield Beach and Golf Resort ⇨ *p.186*

TAKE A KAYAK THROUGH THE TIDELANDS
on a guided tour out of Georgetown ⇨ *p.189*

By Katie McElveen

THE LIVELY, FAMILY-ORIENTED GRAND STRAND, a booming resort area along the South Carolina coast, is one of the eastern seaboard's megavacation centers. The main attraction, of course, is the broad, beckoning beach—60 mi of white sand, stretching from the North Carolina border south to Georgetown, with Myrtle Beach at the hub. People come to the Strand for all of the traditional beach-going pleasures: shell hunting, fishing, swimming, sunbathing, sailing, surfing, jogging, and strolling. Most of the sand is packed hard, so that at low tide you can explore for miles on a bicycle. Away from the water, golfers have more than 120 courses to choose from, designed by the likes of Arnold Palmer, Robert Trent Jones, Jack Nicklaus, and Tom and George Fazio. There are also excellent seafood restaurants; giant shopping malls and factory outlets; amusement parks, water slides, and arcades; a dozen shipwrecks for divers to explore; campgrounds, most of them on the beach; plus antique-car and wax museums, an aquarium, the world's largest outdoor sculpture garden, an antique German band organ and merry-go-round, and a museum dedicated entirely to rice. The Strand has also emerged as a major center for country music, with an expanding number of theaters. When it comes to diversions, you could hardly be better served.

Myrtle Beach is the center of activity on the Grand Strand; its year-round population of 23,000 explodes to about 450,000 in summer, and as a result it alone accounts for about 40% of South Carolina's tourism revenue. Here you'll find the amusement parks and other children's activities that make the area so popular with families, as well as most of the nightlife that keeps parents and teenagers alike entertained. As Myrtle Beach's reputation as a family-friendly destination has grown, so have the size, sophistication, and number of activities available. Water and amusement parks are huge, well maintained, and offer name-brand attractions such as a NASCAR SpeedPark and an IMAX Discovery Theater. Immense live-performance theaters offer everything from Vegas-style reviews to a reenactment of the Civil War (on horseback no less).

The communities to the north of Myrtle Beach—Little River and North Myrtle Beach among others—are more residential and lack the glitz of their neighbor. On the South Strand the family retreats of Surfside Beach and Garden City offer more summer homes and condominiums, as well as small boardwalks and old-timey arcades, miniature golf, and snow cone stands. Farther south, Murrells Inlet was once a pirates' haven (Blackbeard is said to have landed here) and is now a center for seafood restaurants, boat, Jet Ski and kayak rentals, and fishing and sightseeing charters. A boardwalk lets you wander along the marsh from one of Murrells' famed seafood restaurants and outdoor bars to another.

Although they've been discovered by travelers, the beaches and towns of Litchfield and Pawleys Island (one of the East Coast's oldest resorts), remain free of the whirlwind activity of Myrtle Beach. Instead, they're the domain of families renting the homes and condominiums along the water. At night, in deference to the loggerhead sea turtles who nest in the dunes, the only light along these coastal areas comes from the flashlights of beachcombers—most often couples walking hand in hand.

Numbers in the text correspond to numbers in the margin and on the Grand Strand map.

If you have **3 days**

Begin your visit at **Myrtle Beach** 1 ►. Whether you choose to stay in the north end or the south end, spend your first morning getting your bearings with a Carolina Safari Jeep Tour. Afterward, poke around Myrtle Beach's Broadway at the Beach, where you'll find shops, an IMAX theater, and an aquarium; you can have lunch here, too. In the evening, take in a show at the House of Blues or one of the many theaters nearby. Start your second day with a bike ride on the beach—early, before the heat of the day sets in—then drive to the South Strand and wander through **Georgetown** 5 and Brookgreen Gardens, just beyond **Murrells Inlet** 3. On your last day, hit the outlet stores after breakfast, then check out the Strip's many shops, arcades, and museums.

If you have **5 days**

If you're going to be around for more than a couple of days, it makes sense to stay at one of the many cottages, condos, and villas available for rent. You're likely to get a bigger bang for the buck, and having kitchen facilities can be convenient and economical. As the week progresses, lines at the attractions of **Myrtle Beach** 1 get longer, so it's a good idea to plan your visits to such places earlier in the week rather than later. With that in mind, spend your first morning in the area visiting an attraction. The NASCAR SpeedPark makes for a quick joyride, or you can shoot through the tunnels at Myrtle Waves WaterPark. In the afternoon, get on a bike and ride up and down the beach, a fun activity that you can't do everywhere. (In the heat of the summer, consider reversing the schedule and biking in the morning.) Spend the morning of your second day on the water off the South Strand, either on a fishing expedition, a boat tour, or a charter sailboat. Browse the afternoon away at the shops and museums that line Front Street in **Georgetown** 5. Stay for dinner, or drive to **Murrells Inlet** 3 and eat overlooking the marsh.

After breakfast do some outlet shopping, then spend the rest of your third day in the carnival that is Myrtle Beach's Strip, where you can reminisce with a game of skeeball and a spin on the Ferris wheel. Plan to spend your fourth day back in the South Strand. Start out taking a kayak tour or the jeep tour of Hobcaw Barony, north of Georgetown. After lunch, wander through the sculpture gardens of Brookgreen, or take part in one of the tours of the gardens' wildlife preserve. Your ticket is good for reentry all week, so if you're taken with the place you can return later. For your final day, let your mood be your guide: a Carolina Safari Jeep Tour, a visit to Alligator Adventure, a final romp at Broadway at the Beach, and a day lounging on the beach are all good options.

Historic Georgetown forms the southern tip of the Grand Strand. A hub of rice and indigo plantations, Georgetown was settled by the Spanish in 1526, making it the state's third-oldest city, after Charleston and Beaufort. During the mid-19th century, almost half the rice consumed in the United States was grown here. The work required to create the rice plantations—clearing thousands of muddy, alligator-filled acres by hand—has been compared to building the Egyptian pyramids. After the Civil War, many of the plantations became winter homes and hunting clubs for wealthy Northerners. One of these, Hobcaw Barony, was Bernard Baruch's home and saw a number of visiting dignitaries, including Winston Churchill and Franklin Roosevelt. Today, this large tract of land is a museum and research facility. Front Street, the central roadway, is filled with antiques shops, museums, bed-and-breakfasts, and small restaurants.

Exploring Myrtle Beach & the Grand Strand

The Grand Strand's main drag is north-south-running U.S. Highway 17, which has the Atlantic Ocean to one side and the Intracoastal Waterway to the other. Between Murrells Inlet and the north end of Myrtle Beach, the road splits into U.S. 17 Bypass and U.S. 17 Business. Be sure to take note of whether an establishment is on Business 17 or the bypass when getting directions—confusing the two could lead to hours of frustration. Another potential cause for confusion: the north end of Myrtle Beach is a distinctly different place than the town of North Myrtle Beach.

U.S. 17 takes you through most of the cultures that exist on the Grand Strand, from the quiet homes of North Myrtle Beach to the hopping family resorts of Myrtle Beach to the pristine marshes of Murrells Inlet and beyond. Traffic, particularly in summer, can be quite heavy on U.S. 17 (both the business and bypass routes). It's wise to hit the road as early in the day as possible during high season, which is roughly May through mid-September.

About the Restaurants

Not surprisingly, the Grand Strand specializes in seafood. For many years the restaurant scene was dominated by uninspired fried-fish buffets, where the emphasis was decidedly on quantity over quality. Today such establishments remain, but thanks to the Strand's increasing number of year-round residents and visitors, there are a surprising number of excellent restaurants (seafood and otherwise) in all price ranges.

In summer, waits at some of the moderately priced restaurants—even for breakfast—can be an hour or more. A hotel room or condo with kitchen facilities can be a blessing, allowing you to save time and money by preparing some of your own meals.

WHAT IT COSTS

$$$$	$$$	$$	$	¢
over $22	$16–$22	$11–$16	$7–$11	under $7

Prices are for a main course at dinner, excluding sales tax of 7.5%.

About the Hotels

Although high-rise condominiums have replaced many of the smaller, locally owned motels along Myrtle Beach's Ocean Boulevard, there's still

Beaches All of the Grand Strand's beaches are family oriented, and most are public. The widest expanses are in North Myrtle Beach, where at low tide the sand stretches as far as 650 feet from the dunes to the water. If you want to combine your sunning with nightlife and amusement-park attractions, head for Myrtle Beach, the Strand's longtime hub. You get a quieter day in the sun at the South Strand communities of Surfside Beach and Garden City.

Family Fun The Myrtle Beach area makes every effort to keep families entertained. Traditional vacation amusements, from miniature golf to water parks to variety shows, are here in abundance, often in their most over-the-top, modernized guises. Take a stroll along Ocean Boulevard in the height of summer and you can't avoid being caught up in the carnival-like atmosphere. For a more mellow experience, head to the southern reaches of the Strand, where families often rent condos by the week, break out their favorite books and board games, and unwind. The beauty of the Grand Strand is that you can have the best of both worlds, following a day of high-octane activities with a day of sweet idleness.

Golf Wherever you are on the Grand Strand, you won't be far from a golf course. Whether you're a hacker or a scratch player, you can find a place to tee up that suits your style. Many courses skillfully incorporate the surrounding water; some are designed by the game's most famous names, from Jack Nicklaus to Pete Dye.

---

a wide variety of accommodations on the Strand, including beachside camping, motels, luxury hotels, resort communities, and rental houses (mostly available by the week). Generally, smaller properties won't have restaurants (except for the occasional coffee shop), but just about every option, with the exception of houses, has a pool. Many hotel rooms, particularly in Myrtle Beach, come with kitchenettes. Golf, outlet shopping, and other activities attract almost as many visitors as the beach does, which means that going inland doesn't guarantee a lower room rate. Since many people return again and again to the same property, some options, particularly beach houses, need to be reserved months in advance for summer stays. Rates can vary considerably depending on the time of year and how long you plan to stay. Many hotels offer packages that include discounts at local restaurants and entertainment venues.

WHAT IT COSTS

$$$$	$$$	$$	$	¢
over $220	$160–$220	$110–$160	$70–$110	under $70

Prices are for two people in a standard double room in high season, excluding service charges and 10% tax.

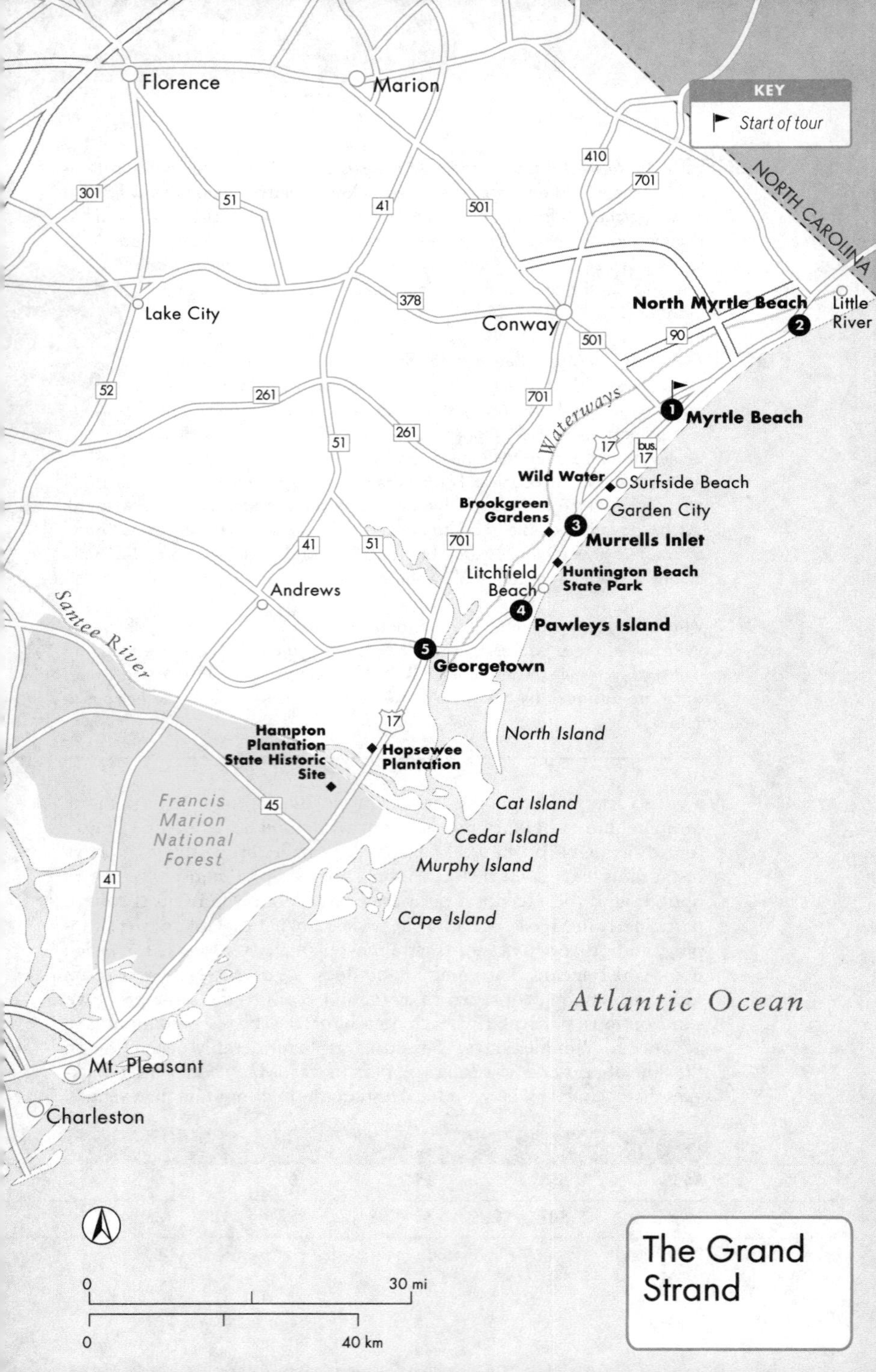

KEY
Start of tour
Florence
Marion
Lake City
Conway
North Myrtle Beach
Little River
NORTH CAROLINA
Waterways
Myrtle Beach
Wild Water
Surfside Beach
Brookgreen Gardens
Garden City
Murrells Inlet
Huntington Beach State Park
Litchfield Beach
Pawleys Island
Andrews
Santee River
Georgetown
North Island
Hampton Plantation State Historic Site
Hopsewee Plantation
Cat Island
Cedar Island
Murphy Island
Cape Island
Francis Marion National Forest
Atlantic Ocean
Mt. Pleasant
Charleston
301
51
41
501
410
701
378
90
52
261
17
bus. 17
45
0
30 mi
40 km
The Grand Strand

Timing

The Grand Strand was developed as a summer resort, and with its gorgeous beaches, flowering tropical plants, and generally good—if warm—weather, it continues to shine during the height of the season. That said, the fall and spring shoulder seasons may be even more pleasant. Warm temperatures usually continue to allow for beach activities, but the humidity drops and the heat of summer has passed. It's less crowded, but only marginally so, as empty-nesters, young families, and others not tied to a school schedule come in droves to take advantage of fine weather. Prices, too, are only slightly lower, and reservations, particularly at the larger properties that often host conventions, should be made several weeks out.

Winter—November through February—isn't usually thought of as a time to visit the beach, but the region can be quite pleasant. While there are certainly cold days here and there, for the most part golfers, tennis players, and other outdoor enthusiasts can enjoy their pursuits during these months—at rock-bottom prices.

THE MYRTLE BEACH AREA

Myrtle Beach was a late bloomer. Until 1901 it didn't even have an official name; that year the first hotel went up, and oceanfront lots were selling for $25. Today, more than 13 million people a year visit the region, and no wonder: lodging, restaurants, shopping, and entertainment choices are varied and plentiful. The 120 golf courses in the area add to the appeal.

Myrtle Beach has a reputation as a frenzied strip of all-you-can-eat buffets, T-shirt shops, and bars. The reputation isn't completely unwarranted, but this side of Myrtle Beach's character is generally limited to parts of Ocean Boulevard (the "strip"), Kings Highway, and Restaurant Row (sometimes called the Galleria area). Some blocks may be a bit seedy, but the pedestrian-friendly strip is generally safe and clean (though at night the sidewalks can be crowded with the young bar crowd). Attractions such as the Pavillion and Ripley's Haunted Adventure can add a dose of fun to your afternoon on the strip.

There are a number of entertainment centers in Myrtle Beach that combine food, shopping, activities, and lodging in one massive complex. These places are well planned and offer a menu of options so large—think movies, miniature golf, theme park–like amusements and rides, retail centers full of national chains, live and IMAX theaters—that a weekend might not be enough to experience everything. The flip side is that you don't get much in the way of local atmosphere; you might even forget you're at the beach. The crowd at these complexes is a mix of families and singles, mostly local professionals who, like the visitors, enjoy the upbeat environment.

What may come as a surprise is that it's also not terribly difficult to spend a quiet vacation here, dining in sophisticated spots after spending the day on relatively uncrowded beaches. Myrtle Beach State Park, for instance, is a bastion of peace and quiet, as are the beaches adjacent to the residential areas of Myrtle Beach at either end of the strip.

Myrtle Beach

❶ *94 mi northeast of Charleston via U.S. 17, 138 mi east of Columbia via U.S. 76 to U.S. 378 to U.S. 501.*

Myrtle Beach, with its high-rises and hyperdevelopment, is the nerve center of the Grand Strand and one of the major seaside destinations on the east coast. Visitors are drawn here for the swirl of classic vacation activity, from beaches to arcades to live music shows.

To capture the flavor of the place, start at the Myrtle Beach Pavilion Amusement Park and stroll north on Ocean Boulevard. Here's where you'll find an eclectic assortment of gift and novelty shops, a wax museum, and a museum of oddities. When you've had your fill, turn east and make your way back onto the beach amid the sunbathers, kite-fliers, and kids building sand castles.

Myrtle Beach Pavilion Amusement Park has thrill and children's rides, a log flume, South Carolina's largest wooden roller coaster, video games, a teen nightclub, specialty shops, a NASCAR simulator, antique cars, and sidewalk cafés, as well as an oceanfront arcade. It's a bit like going to a state fair that runs all summer long. There's no admission charge to enter the park. Operating hours can vary, so it's worthwhile to call before visiting. ✉ *9th Ave. N and Ocean Blvd., The Strip* ☎ *843/913–5200* 🌐 *www.mbpavilion.com* 🎟 *Fees vary for individual attractions; 1-day unlimited access to most rides $25.75* ⏲ *June–mid-Aug., daily 1 PM–midnight; Mid-Mar.–May and mid-Aug.–Sept., weekdays 6 PM–10 PM, Sat. 1–10, Sun. 1–8.*

At **NASCAR SpeedPark** you can drive on seven different NASCAR-replica tracks. The cars vary in their sophistication and speed; to use the most advanced track you need to be a licensed driver. The 26-acre facility also has racing memorabilia, an arcade, and miniature golf. ✉ *U.S. 17 Bypass and 21st Ave. N, at Broadway at the Beach, Central Myrtle Beach* ☎ *843/918–8725* 🌐 *www.nascarspeedpark.com* 🎟 *$21.95 unlimited day pass or $5 each ride* ⏲ *Mar.–Oct., weekdays 5 PM–midnight, weekends noon–midnight; hrs vary, so call to confirm.*

Convincing vampires and other costumed characters will taunt and entice you to come inside **Ripley's Haunted Adventure,** a fun, creepy haunted house. Once you're inside, high-tech animation and other special effects keep the scream factor high. ✉ *915 N. Ocean Blvd., The Strip* ☎ *843/916–4240* 🌐 *www.ripleys.com/haunted/myrtle.html* 🎟 *$10* ⏲ *June–Aug., daily 9 AM–2 AM; late Feb.–May and Sept.–mid-Oct., daily 9 AM–11 PM.*

Ripley's Aquarium has an underwater tunnel exhibit longer than a football field and exotic marine creatures on display, from poisonous lionfish to moray eels to an octopus. Children can examine horseshoe crabs and eels in touch tanks. ✉ *Broadway at the Beach, U.S. 17 Bypass between 21st Ave. N and 29th Ave. N, Central Myrtle Beach* ☎ *843/916–*

0888 or 800/734–8888 ⊕ www.ripleysaquarium.com $16.95 ⏲ Sun.–Thurs. 9 AM–10 PM, Fri. and Sat. 9 AM–11 PM.

About 9 mi south of Myrtle Beach, **Wild Water** has 25 water-oriented rides and activities, along with go-karts and minigolf. If your children are old enough to navigate the park on their own, spend a few minutes at the adults-only lounge pool, where you can sit immersed in Jacuzzi-like bubbles. ✉ *910 U.S. 17S, Surfside Beach* ☎ *843/238–3787* ⊕ *www.wild-water.com* *$21.95, $13.98 after 3 PM* ⏲ *Late May–early Sept., daily 10–7.*

Myrtle Waves is South Carolina's largest water park. You can shoot through twisty chutes, swim in the Ocean in Motion Wave Pool, float the day away on an inner tube on the LayZee River, or ride a boogie board on the Racer River. There's beach volleyball, too, for when you've had enough water. ✉ *U.S. 17 Bypass and 10th Ave. N, South End* ☎ *843/448–1026 or 800/524–9283* ⊕ *www.myrtlewaves.com* *$23.95 for full day, $15.95 after 3 PM* ⏲ *Early May–early Sept., daily 10–6.*

The medieval-themed **Dragon's Lair Fantasy Golf** miniature golf course is well maintained and well lit—and it has a 30-foot-tall fire-breathing dragon. The course has no steps, making it perfect for strollers and wheelchairs. ✉ *Broadway at the Beach, U.S. 17 Bypass between 21st Ave. N and 29th Ave. N* ☎ *843/444–3215* *$7* ⏲ *Daily 10–10.*

On **Carolina Safari Jeep Tours** you visit everything from a plantation house to an alligator-laden salt marsh to an 18th-century church. Along the way you learn fun facts, scary ghost stories, and fascinating history, told from a script that keeps even history-phobes entertained. The 3 ½-hour tour, which includes some walking, provides a surprisingly complete overview of the region and beautiful views of the Grand Strand's varied ecosystem. To take part, call to make a reservation; you'll be picked up at your hotel in a Jeep that seats about a dozen people. ✉ *725 Seaboard Ave. Unit E* ☎ *843/497–5330* ⊕ *www.carolinasafari.com* *$30* ⏲ *Arrange tour times when making reservation.*

Sports & the Outdoors

BEACHES After a $60-million renourishment program, the beaches of Myrtle Beach are broader than ever, with plenty of room for playing beach games and jogging. A side benefit of the widening project is that the new sand, brought in from the depths of the Atlantic, is full of interesting shells. Be aware while you collect the shells to resist any temptation to pick the sea oats that sway from the tops of the sand dunes: these fragile-looking plants serve to anchor the dunes, and there are stiff, strictly enforced fines and penalties for disturbing them.

Regardless of whether you're staying on the beach, you shouldn't have too much trouble getting to a spot of sand. There are nearly 150 public beach access points in the city, all marked with signs. Most have ample parking and "shower towers" for cleaning up; few have restroom facilities.

Since much of Myrtle Beach's coastline is dominated by high-rise hotels, there are plenty of places to get lunch or a cool drink without having to get back in your car. Many of these hotels also rent beach chairs, boogie boards, and other accessories. Some also have nets set up for games of beach volleyball.

Dogs, kayaks, and surfboards are limited on many beaches from May through September. Be sure to read the ordinances posted at each access point for details.

For a more out-of-the-way experience, head south of Myrtle Beach to **Myrtle Beach State Park.** There you can swim in the ocean, hike on a nature trail, and fish in the surf or from a pier. You can also camp, but you need to book in advance. ✉ *U.S. 17, 3 mi south of Myrtle Beach* ☎ *843/238–5325* *$3, $4.50 to fish off pier, no license required.*

FISHING The Gulf Stream makes fishing usually good from early spring through December. Anglers can fish from 10 piers and jetties for amberjack, sea trout, and king mackerel. Surfcasters may snare bluefish, whiting, flounder, pompano, and channel bass. In the South Strand, salt marshes, inlets, and tidal creeks yield flounder, blues, croakers, spots, shrimp, clams, oysters, and blue crabs.

The annual **Grand Strand Fishing Rodeo** (☎ 843/626–7444 Apr.–Oct.) holds a fish-of-the-month contest, with prizes for the largest catch of a designated species. There's no registration fee; entrants must take their catch to designated weigh stations for consideration.

GOLF Many of the Grand Strand's more than 100 courses are championship layouts; most are public. **Tee Times Central** (☎ 843/347–4653 or 800/344–5590) makes it easy to book tee times at nearly all the Strand's courses, or you can book them yourself, either by calling or, for some courses, going online.

Two of Myrtle Beach's courses are particularly notable: built in the 1920s, **Pine Lakes** (✉ 5603 Woodside Ave. ☎ 843/315–7700 🌐 www.pinelakes.com) is considered the granddaddy of Strand courses. During the spring, you can get mimosas on the 10th tee; in winter they serve clam chowder. Pine Lakes is a terrific walking course. Former home to the Senior PGA Tour, the Tom Fazio-designed **Tournament Players Club at Myrtle Beach** (✉ 1189 TPC Blvd., Murrells Inlet ☎ 888/742–8721 🌐 www.tpc.com) is a challenging journey through the salt marshes.

A bit less demanding, but still interesting, thanks to surprising changes in elevation, **The Witch** (✉ 1900 Hwy. 44, East Conway ☎ 843/448–1300 🌐 www.mysticalgolf.com) is built on wetlands and contains nearly 4,000 feet of bridges. Known for its top-notch condition, regardless of the season, **Arrowhead** (✉ 1201 Burcale Rd. ☎ 800/236–3243 🌐 www.arrowheadcc.com) is the only Raymond Floyd–designed course in the region. Several of the 27 holes run along the intracoastal waterway. If you're lucky, you might spot dolphins cavorting in the smooth water.

There are a few bargains on the Myrtle Beach golfing scene. One is **Indigo Creek** (✉ 9480 Indigo Creek Dr., Murrells Inlet ☎ 800/718–1830 🌐 www.indigocreekgolfclub.com), which is cut through forests of huge oaks and pines. Built on the site of an old airbase, **Whispering Pines** (✉ U.S.

17 Business and 22nd Ave. S ☎ 843/918–2305 🌐 www.mbteetime.com) is recognized as an Audubon Cooperative Sanctuary.

SCUBA DIVING In summer, many warm-water tropical fish travel to the area from the Gulf Stream. Off the coast of Little River, near the North Carolina border, rock and coral ledges teem with coral, sea fans, sponges, reef fish, anemones, urchins, and crabs. Several outlying shipwrecks are flush with schools of spadefish, amberjack, grouper, barracuda, and even the occasional octopus and loggerhead turtle.

Instruction and equipment rentals, as well as an indoor dive tank, are available in the Sports Corner shopping center from **New Horizons Dive and Travel** (✉ 515 U.S. 501, Suite A, The Strip ☎ 843/839–1932).

TENNIS There are more than 200 courts on the Grand Strand. Facilities include hotel and resort courts, as well as free municipal courts in Myrtle Beach, North Myrtle Beach, and Surfside Beach.

Prestwick Tennis and Swim Club (✉ 1375 McMaster Dr. ☎ 843/828–1000) offers court time, rental equipment, and instruction; courts are lighted for nighttime play. **Grande Dunes Tennis** (✉ U.S. 17 Bypass at Grande Dunes Blvd. ☎ 843/449–4486) is a full fitness facility with 10 Har-Tru courts, five of which are lighted; the club also offers private and group lessons.

WATER SPORTS Hobie Cats, Jet Skis, Windsurfers, and sailboats are available for rent at **Downwind Sails** (✉ Ocean Blvd. at 29th Ave. S, South End ☎ 843/448–7245); they also have banana boat rides (where you're towed in a long, yellow inflatable raft) and parasailing. **Ocean Watersports** (✉ 4th Ave. S and the beach, next to Family Kingdom amusement park, The Strip ☎ 843/445–7777) rents water-sports equipment.

Where to Stay & Eat

★ $$$–$$$$ ✕ **Collectors Cafe.** A successful restaurant, art gallery, and coffeehouse rolled into one, this unpretentiously arty spot has bright, funky paintings and tile work covering its walls and tabletops. The cuisine is among the most inventive in the area. Try the grilled tuna with Indian spices, served with Cuban black bean sauce and mango salsa—it's a far cry from standard Myrtle Beach fish-house fare. ✉ *7726 N. Kings Hwy., North End* ☎ *843/449–9370* ▭ *AE, D, MC, V* ⏲ *Closed Sun. No lunch.*

$$$–$$$$ ✕ **Thoroughbreds.** For a special night out, or to fulfill a red meat craving, Thoroughbreds, with its dark wood, leather banquettes, and top-notch meat, is a romantic escape from the whirlwind of Myrtle Beach. Fish selections are fresh and well prepared, but steaks, pork chops, and rack of lamb steal the show. There's a great wine list, too. ✉ *9706 N. Kings Hwy.* ☎ *843/497–2636* ✍ *Reservations essential* ▭ *AE, D, MC, V* ⏲ *No lunch.*

$$–$$$ ✕ **Sea Captain's House.** At this picturesque restaurant with a nautical theme, the best seats are in the windowed porch room, which overlooks the ocean. The fireplace in the wood-panel dining room inside is warmly welcoming on cool off-season evenings. Menu highlights include Low-country crab casserole and avocado-seafood salad. The breads and desserts are baked on the premises. ✉ *3000 N. Ocean Blvd., The Strip* ☎ *843/448–8082* ▭ *AE, D, MC, V.*

CloseUp

FABULOUS FISH, SMOKIN' BARBECUE

With ocean on one side and tidal marsh and rivers on the other, the Grand Strand isn't at a loss for fresh seafood. Local shrimp, oysters, and fish, particularly grouper, are good bets, as is she-crab soup, a creamy bisquelike creation served with a cruet of sherry on the side. Don't drink the sherry—add a splash to the soup, along with a dash of hot sauce.

Barbecue is a ubiquitous Southern cuisine that's well represented on the Strand. Keep in mind that in these parts "barbecue" doesn't mean something cooked on the backyard grill. It's meat (most often pork) that's been smoked and then slathered with a spicy sauce, usually with a vinegar, a tomato, or a mustard base. Grits are a trademark side dish, served at breakfast and again at dinner, when they're usually gussied up with cream, cheese, butter, or all three. The beverage of choice is often iced tea; the uninitiated should be aware that, unless you want yours sweet enough to melt your teeth, you need to ask for it "unsweet."

$$–$$$ ✕ **Villa Katrina's Mexican Café.** The spinach-and-chicken burritos, fish tacos, sangria, and award-winning margaritas are all sure bets here, and as a bonus, nothing on the menu—not even the tortilla chips—is fried. The hacienda-like mirrored space is particularly appealing at night. ✉ *7731 N. Kings Hwy., in Northwoods shopping center, North End* ☎ *843/497–2572* ▭ *MC, V* ⏲ *Closed Sun. No lunch Mon.*

★ **$$–$$$** ✕ **Villa Romana.** It's all about family at Villa Romana, where Mama Lucia comes in early to make the gnocchi and sticks around to greet customers. It's hard to resist filling up on the stracciatella soup, bruschetta, salad, and rolls (perhaps the best on the Strand) that accompany every meal, but try. The gnocchi is a perfect foil for any of the homemade sauces, and the veal absolut (sautéed veal in a sauce of cream, mushrooms, and vodka) is a specialty. ✉ *707 S. Kings Hwy.* ☎ *843/448–4990* ✍ *Reservations essential* ▭ *AE, D, MC, V* ⏲ *No lunch.*

$–$$$ ✕ **Key West Grill.** Known for its Caribbean flair and daily fish specials, such as cashew-crusted red snapper, Key West Grill has a fun, beachy vibe, but the food is well-crafted and well-presented. There are large entrées such as the mojito grilled pork chop, as well as less substantial choices such as burgers and salads with grilled fish. Call about early-bird and bar specials: you'll get a good deal, and arriving early lessens the likelihood of having to wait for a table. ✉ *Broadway at the Beach, U.S. 17 Bypass between 21st Ave. N and 29th Ave. N* ☎ *843/444–3663* ✍ *Reservations not accepted* ▭ *AE, D, MC, V.*

¢–$ ✕ **Southern Market.** Part restaurant, part food emporium, Southern Market features seven food stations that serve everything from pancakes in the morning to salmon with brandied peppercorn gravy at dinner. Everything is available to go, or take your tray and eat in the dining room or the outdoor courtyard. The market's butcher case is packed with prime meat, free-range poultry, and fresh seafood for cooking at home. The wine selection is extensive, and the cakes, pies, and brownies are made on-site. ✉ *959 Lake Arrowhead Rd.* ☎ *843/497–4901* ♣ *Reservations not accepted* ▭ *AE, D, MC, V.*

¢ ✕ **Croissants Bakery & Café.** The lunch crowd loves this spot, which has an on-site bakery. Black-and-white tile floors, café tables, checked tablecloths, and glass pastry cases filled with sweets create an appetizing feel to the place. Try the chicken or broccoli salads, a Reuben or Monte Cristo sandwich, or one of the pasta specials, and save room for the peanut butter cheesecake. ✉ *504A 27th Ave. N, The Strip* ☎ *843/448–2253* ▭ *D, MC, V* ⊙ *Closed Sun. No dinner.*

¢ ✕ **Dagwood's Deli.** Dagwood and Blondie could split one of the masterful sandwiches at Dagwood's Deli. There are the usual suspect—ham, turkey, and the like—but you won't regret trying one of the more distinctive creations, such as blackened mahimahi with homemade pineapple salsa, or the Gamecock, a grilled chicken breast covered with bacon, provolone, and ranch dressing. Salads and burgers round out the menu, and they deliver (for $1) to most of Myrtle Beach. Dagwood's is open until six on Friday and Saturday, so you can duck in on those days for an early dinner. (On other days they close at four.) ✉ *400 11th Ave. N* ☎ *843/448–0100* ♣ *Reservations not accepted* ▭ *MC, V* ⊙ *Closed Sun. No dinner.*

$$$–$$$$ ▣ **Hampton Inn and Suites Oceanfront.** This property combines the reliability of an established hotel chain with the joys of a beach resort. Rooms have balconies and a cheerful style; all have ocean views. There's a lazy river—a pool with a moving current—that carries swimmers along its course. ✉ *1803 S. Ocean Blvd., South End, 29577* ☎ *843/946–6400 or 877/946–6400* ⎙ *843/946–0031* ⊕ *www.hamptoninnoceanfront.com* ⇨ *80 rooms, 36 suites* ♁ *Cable TV, microwaves, refrigerators, 3 pools (1 indoor), gym, hot tub, business services, meeting rooms* ▭ *AE, D, DC, MC, V* 🍽 *BP.*

$$$–$$$$ ▣ **Kingston Plantation.** This complex includes two hotels, as well as restaurants, shops, and one- to three-bedroom condominiums, situated on 145 acres of ocean-side woodlands. One hotel, an Embassy Suites, has guest rooms with bleached-wood furnishings and kitchenettes. The other, a Hilton, has a more classic decor and no kitchen facilities. The villas and condos are privately owned, but you can reserve one through the central booking number and Web site. Although these options are decorated to the taste of their owners, they all have the same standard amenities such as sheets and towels, and kitchen equipment. Beachgoing is enhanced by a beach club with bathrooms, water fountains, and parking. ✉ *9800 Lake Dr., North End, 29572* ☎ *843/449–0006 or 800/876–0010* ⎙ *843/497–1110* ⊕ *www.kingstonplantation.com* ⇨ *600 rooms and suites, 510 villas and condos* ♁ *3 restaurants, tennis courts, 8 pools, fitness classes, health club, sauna, racquetball, golf privileges* ▭ *AE, D, MC, V* 🍽 *BP.*

★ **$$$–$$$$** ▣ **Myrtle Beach Marriott Resort at Grande Dunes.** Entering this plantation-chic high-rise resort, with its airy wicker furniture, giant palms, and mahogany details, will take you away from the hubbub of Myrtle Beach and straight to a tropical locale. Green-and-gold guest rooms have plush carpet that makes them quiet and serene, perfect for watching the waves break on the beach. The spa, which offers a full range of treatments, is top notch, and the health club has well-maintained, state-of-the-art machines. The golf and tennis clubs are both on-site, as is a marina with charters and Jet Ski, boat, and kayak rentals. ✉ *8400 Costa Verde Dr., 29572* ☎ *843/449–8880* 🖷 *843/449–8669* 🌐 *www.myrtlebeachmarriott.com* *400 rooms* *Restaurant, snack bar, 3 pools (1 indoor), marina, golf, tennis, business center, cable TV, room service, refrigerator* 💳 *AE, D, MC, V* *EP.*

$$–$$$ **Breakers Resort Hotel.** The rooms in this four-tower oceanfront hotel are airy and spacious, with contemporary furnishings. Most have kitchenettes and Murphy beds; the Paradise Tower has one-, two- and three-bedroom suites. There are several pools, a lazy river, and a pirate-ship facade that kids can swim in and around. The hotel is within walking distance of the Pavilion. *2006 N. Ocean Blvd., Box 485, 29578* ☎ *843/444–4444 or 800/845–0688* 🖷 *843/626–5001* 🌐 *www.breakers.com* *204 rooms, 186 suites* *2 restaurants, room service, refrigerators, 3 pools, gym, outdoor hot tubs, saunas, lounge, video game room, children's programs (ages 4–10), laundry service* 💳 *AE, D, DC, MC, V* *EP.*

$$–$$$ **Radisson Plaza Hotel Myrtle Beach.** With its round, glass-encased tower, cantilevered lobby windows, sweeping staircases and curved balconies, Myrtle Beach's newest Radisson is a stylish addition to the landscape. Although the blond-wood-appointed rooms have an airy feel, the atmosphere is more that of an urban hotel than a beach one: amenities include Starbucks coffee and super-luxe bedding rather than microwaves or a children's program. The hotel is connected to the Myrtle Beach Convention Center. ✉ *2101 N. Oak St., 29578* ☎ *843/918–5000* 🖷 *843/918–5011* 🌐 *www.radisson.com/myrtlebeachsc* *392 rooms, 10 suites* *Indoor pool, beach, airport shuttle* 💳 *AE, D, MC, V* *EP.*

$$ **Sheraton Myrtle Beach Resort.** All rooms and suites here have a fresh, contemporary look. Oceanfront Lounge, highlighted by tropical colors and rattan furnishings, is a lively evening gathering spot. There are a lazy river (artificial stream) and an arcade nearby. ✉ *2701 S. Ocean Blvd., South End, 29577* ☎ *843/448–2518 or 800/992–1055* 🖷 *843/449–1879* 🌐 *www.sheratonresort.com* *211 rooms, 8 suites* *Restaurant, indoor pool, health club, cable TV, children's program (ages 5–12)* 💳 *AE, D, DC, MC, V* *EP.*

$–$$ **Cabana Shores Hotel.** Although the Cabana Shores is across Ocean Boulevard from the beach, thanks to the area's designation as a "cabana district" there are no buildings across the street and the beach is blissfully quiet and uncrowded. The spacious rooms have dark-wood furniture, balconies, and full kitchens; larger rooms have two balconies. Behind the hotel is a lovely old residential neighborhood that's great for strolling. ✉ *5701 N. Ocean Blvd., 29577* ☎ *843/449–6441 or 800/277–7562* 🖷 *843/449–6441* 🌐 *www.cabanashores.com* *72 rooms* *Pool, cable TV* 💳 *AE, D, MC, V* *EP.*

$–$$ **Driftwood on the Oceanfront.** Under the same ownership for more than 65 years, the Driftwood is one of the few remaining small, independent hotels in Myrtle Beach. Its well-maintained facilities and reasonable rates are especially popular with families. Some rooms are on the oceanfront, and all are decorated in sea, sky, or earth tones. ✉ *1600 N. Ocean Blvd., Box 275, 29578* ☎ *843/448–1544 or 800/942–3456* 🖷 *843/448–2917* *www.driftwoodlodge.com* *90 rooms* *Microwaves, refrigerators, cable TV, 2 pools, shuffleboard, laundry facilities* *AE, D, MC, V* *EP.*

$–$$ **The Mariner.** This Caribbean-inspired inn is across the street from the ocean, in a location shaded by live oak trees and situated among winding brick walkways and lush, hummingbird-friendly gardens. The nautical-theme rooms are a bit dated, but they aren't shabby, and most open onto a porch. Guests are invited to the complimentary Tuesday night grill dinner. Dogs are welcome (for a $9 fee), and on Thursday there's a canine social. *7003 N. Ocean Blvd., 29572* *843/449–5281 or 800/213–0392* *843/692–2641* *www.myrtlebeachmariner.com* *33 rooms* *BBQs, refrigerators, cable TV, 2 pools, tennis court, shuffleboard, Ping-Pong, some pets allowed, no-smoking rooms* *AE, D, MC, V* *BP.*

$–$$ **Seashore Motel.** With its funky aqua-and-white-stripe awnings and pale stucco exterior, the Seashore Motel looks more Miami than Myrtle Beach. Inside, the clean rooms are decorated in blue tones and with cheerful cottage furniture. Oceanfront rooms have balconies, and larger rooms have kitchenettes. One of the nicest things about this hotel is its location a block away from an amusement park and the Strand's only oceanfront waterpark. *107 S. Ocean Blvd., 29577* *843/448–3700 or 800/826–5810* *www.myrtlebeachinns.com* *51 rooms* *Pool, game room, laundry facilities* *AE, D, MC, V* *EP.*

$ **Chesterfield Inn.** A remnant from the past, this oceanfront brick inn, hidden beneath the towers of Myrtle Beach's glitzier hotels, has been in operation for more than a half century. The rooms in the original building are plain and a bit worn, but many people prefer them to those in the newer wing because of their old beach-hotel charm. Although the rooms don't have balconies, and only end rooms have an ocean view, the wide back porch is a delightful gathering spot. *700 N. Ocean Blvd., The Strip, 29578* *843/448–3177or 866/213–9534* *843/626–4736* *www.chesterfieldinnmb.com* *63 rooms* *Restaurant, some kitchenettes, pool, shuffleboard* *AE, D, DC, MC, V* *EP.*

$ **Serendipity Inn.** This cozy Spanish-villa-style inn is about 300 yards from the beach. Though the layout is much like a hotel, each guest room is decorated in a different way, most with four-poster beds and antique chests in pine or mahogany. There's also a colorful pool area dotted with hanging flowers and a trickling fountain. A breakfast of homemade coffee cake, hardboiled eggs, yogurt, cereal, and fruit is served in the wicker-appointed garden room. *407 71st Ave. N, North End, 29572* *843/449–5268 or 800/762–3229* *www.serendipityinn.com* *12 rooms, 2 suites* *Some kitchenettes, refrigerators, pool, outdoor hot tub, Ping-Pong, shuffleboard; no room phones* *MC, V* *BP.*

Nightlife & the Arts

CLUBS & LOUNGES

Clubs offer varying fare, including beach music, the Grand Strand's unique '50s-style sound. Some clubs and resorts have sophisticated live entertainment in summer. Some hotels and resorts also have piano bars or lounges with easy-listening music.

South Carolina's only Hard Rock Cafe, Planet Hollywood, and NASCAR Cafe are just a few of the hot spots in **Broadway at the Beach** (U.S. 17

Bypass between 21st and 29th Aves. N, The Strip ☎ 843/444–3200), which also has shopping. In the evenings, dueling piano players compete to perform the most outlandish versions of audience requests at **Crocodile Rocks** (✉ Broadway at the Beach, U.S. 17 Bypass between 21st and 29th Aves. N, The Strip ☎ 843/444–2096); singing along is part of the fun. The shag (South Carolina's state dance) is popular at **Studebaker's** (✉ 2000 N. Kings Hwy., The Strip ☎ 843/448–9747 or 843/626–3855).

FILM The **IMAX Discovery Theater** (✉ Broadway at the Beach, U.S. 17 Bypass between 21st and 29th Aves. N, The Strip ☎ 843/448–4629) shows educational films on a six-story-high screen.

MUSIC & LIVE SHOWS Live acts, and country-and-western shows in particular, are a big draw in Myrtle Beach. There are many family-oriented shows to choose from.

Carolina Opry (✉ 82nd Ave. N, North End ☎ 843/238–8888 or 800/843–6779) is a family-oriented variety show featuring country, light rock, show tunes, and gospel. At **Dolly Parton's Dixie Stampede** (✉ 8901B U.S. 17 Business, North End ☎ 843/497–9700 or 800/843–6779) dinner theater, actors on horseback—dozens of them—recreate Civil War cavalry battles. **Legends in Concert** (✉ 301 U.S. 17 Business, Surfside Beach ☎ 843/238–7827 or 800/843–6779) has high-energy shows by impersonators of Little Richard, Elvis, Cher, and the Blues Brothers. The elegant **Palace Theater** (✉ Broadway at the Beach, U.S. 17 Bypass between 21st and 29th Aves. N, The Strip ☎ 843/448–0588 or 800/905–4228) hosts Broadway shows such as *Les Miserables* and *Stomp* and headliner performances by the likes of Jerry Seinfeld and the Marshall Tucker Band. Watch knights on horseback battle for their kingdom, followed by a real jousting tournament, at **Medieval Times Dinner & Tournament** (✉ 2904 Fantasy Way ☎ 888/935–6878 🌐 www.medievaltimes.com).

PERFORMING ARTS Theater productions, concerts, art exhibits, and other cultural events are regularly offered at the **Myrtle Beach Convention Center** (✉ Oak and 21st Ave. N, The Strip ☎ 843/448–7166).

Shopping

For recreational shopping, Myrtle Beach's main attraction is **Broadway at the Beach** (✉ U.S. 17 Bypass between 21st Ave. N and 29th Ave. N). Over 100 shops include everything from high-end apparel to Harley Davidson-themed gifts.

DISCOUNT OUTLETS The **Tanger 501 Outlet Center** (✉ U.S. 501, Waccamaw Pottery Area ☎ 843/236–5100) is a large outlet center with Gap, Nike, Polo, and Off 5th (a division of Saks Fifth Avenue). **Tanger 17 Outlet Center** (✉ 10785 Kings Rd., at U.S. 17, North End ☎ 843/449–0491) has 75 factory outlet stores, including Polo and Old Navy.

North Myrtle Beach

❷ *5 mi north of Myrtle Beach via U.S. 17.*

North Myrtle Beach, best known as the site where the shag, South Carolina's state dance, originated, is made up of the beach towns of Cherry

Grove, Crescent Beach, Windy Hill, and Ocean Drive. Entering North Myrtle Beach from the south on U.S. 17, you'll see Barefoot Landing, a huge shopping and entertainment complex that sits on the Intracoastal Waterway. As you make your way east toward the ocean, then north on Ocean Boulevard South, high-rises will give way to small motels, then to single beach houses, many of which are available for rent. This end of the strand marks the end of a large peninsula, and there are lots of little islands, creeks, and marshes between the ocean and the Intracoastal to explore by kayak or canoe.

★ **Alligator Adventure** has interactive reptile shows, including an alligator-feeding demonstration. Boardwalks lead through marshes and swamps on the 15-acre property, where you'll see wildlife of the wetlands, including a pair of rare white albino alligators; Utan, the largest known crocodile in captivity; giant Galápagos tortoises; and all manner of other reptiles, including boas, pythons, and anacondas. Unusual plants and exotic birds also thrive here. ✉ *U.S. 17 at Barefoot Landing* ☎ *843/361–0789* 📠 *843/361–0742* 🌐 *www.alligatoradventure.com* *$13.95* ⏲ *Daily 10–9.*

Hawaiian Rumble is the crown jewel of Myrtle Beach miniature golf. The course hosts championship tournaments, and is best known for its smoking volcano, which rumbles and belches fire at timed intervals. ✉ *3210 33rd Ave. S, at U.S. 17* ☎ *843/272–7812* *$9 all day (9–5), $7 per round after 5 PM* ⏲ *Mar.–Dec., daily 9 AM–11 PM.*

Myrtle Beach Grand Prix Family Thrill Park is a hot spot for would-be auto racers. You can navigate courses in ¾-scale Formula 1 race cars, go-karts, and bumper boats, and there's a kids' park with mini-go-karts and self-guided kids' cars. To drive the Formula 1 cars (which can reach speeds up to 55 mph), you need to have a driver's license. ✉ *3201 U.S. 17* ☎ *843/272–7770* ✉ *Windy Hill, 3900 U.S. 17S, North End* ☎ *843/272–7770* 🌐 *www.mbgrandprix.com* *$29.98 unlimited rides, individual rides $3–$6 each* ⏲ *Mar.–Oct., daily 1–11.*

Sports & the Outdoors

FISHING The **Cherry Grove Fishing Pier** (✉ 3500 N. Ocean Blvd. ☎ 843/249–1625) has a two-story observation deck and reaches 985 feet into the ocean, making it the place to catch pompano, bluefish, mackerel, and other fish. You can rent tackle and buy bait at the pier. For full- and half-day deep-sea fishing excursions, contact the **Hurricane Fishing Fleet** (✉ River Rd., Calabash waterfront ☎ 843/249–3571). They also conduct a dolphin adventure cruise using a working shrimp boat.

GOLF In Cherry Grove Beach you'll find the much-touted 18-hole, par-72 **Tidewater Golf Club** (✉ 1400 Tidewater Dr. ☎ 866/639–6962 🌐 www.myrtlebeachgolftrips.com), one of only two courses in the area with ocean views. A 2002 renovation restored the greens to tournament condition and speed; the high bluffs are reminiscent of Pebble Beach.

The four 18-hole championship courses at **Barefoot Resort and Golf** (✉ 4980 Barefoot Resort Bridge Rd. ☎ 843/390–7999) were designed by Tom Fazio, Davis Love III, Pete Dye, and Greg Norman and have proven to be new favorites of Grand Strand golfers. Notable details include a replica of plantation ruins on the Love course and only 60 acres of mowable grass on the Norman course.

WATER SPORTS You can rent your own pontoon boats or Jet Skis at **Myrtle Beach Water Sports, Inc.** (✉ 4495 Mineola Ave. ☎ 843/280–7777), or let them take you parasailing. Learn to scuba dive, take a dive trip, or just rent equipment at **Coastal Scuba** (✉ 1501 U.S. 17S ☎ 800/249–9388 or 843/361–3323 🌐 www.coastalscuba.com), which is PADI-certified.

Where to Stay & Eat

★ $$$–$$$$ ✕ **Greg Norman's Australian Grille.** Overlooking the Intracoastal Waterway, this large restaurant in Barefoot Landing has leather booths, Australian aboriginal art on the walls, an extensive wine list, and a classy bar area. The menu features grilled meats, and many of the selections have an Asian flair. (The Austalian theme comes through more strongly in the decor, and the Greg Norman merchandise for sale, than in the food.) Highlights are the lobster dumplings, miso-marinated sea bass, and habanero-rubbed tenderloin. ✉ *4930 U.S. 17S* ☎ *843/361–0000* *Reservations essential* *AE, D, MC, V* *No lunch.*

$$$–$$$$ ✕ **Rockefellers Raw Bar.** Yes it's a raw bar—and a good one, with a bounty of fresh seafood—but don't sell the cooked items short at this small, casual locals' joint. The oysters Rockefeller, with their splash of Pernod and fresh spinach, are the real deal, and the iron pot of steamed mussels, clams, scallops, and other goodies is a terrific version of a Lowcountry staple. ✉ *3613 U.S. 17S,* ☎ *843/361–9677* *Reservations not accepted* *AE, D, MC, V.*

$–$$$ ✕ **White Point Seafood.** Get your fried-fish fix without the guilt: White Point's signature flounder (there are other fish available every day) is nearly grease-free, and comes from local waters to boot. Homemade cole slaw and hushpuppies round out the meal. You can also get fish grilled or broiled, salads, and sandwiches. ✉ *3303A U.S. 17S,* ☎ *843/272–6732* *Reservations not accepted* *AE, D, MC, V* *Closed Jan. and Feb. No lunch.*

¢ ✕ **Rick's Cafe.** Join Rick and his wife at this coffee shop on the ground floor of the Bahama Sands motel for tasty eggs, burgers, and salads. If you're really hungry, consider tackling Ernie's Breakfast in a Bowl, filled with the South's four food groups (grits, cheese, eggs, and bacon). At lunch, the Redneck Burger—topped with chili and slaw—is another deliciously daunting meal that will have you reaching for the napkins. ✉ *1321 S. Ocean Blvd.* ☎ *843/272–5131* *Reservations not accepted* *No credit cards* *Closed Sun. No dinner.*

$–$$ **Best Western Ocean Sands.** One of the few fairly small, family-owned properties left in North Myrtle Beach, the Ocean Sands has some nice touches that make it a good choice for families, including full kitchens in every room and large suites with true separate bedrooms. Although it's not luxurious, it's clean and breezy, and all rooms have balconies. The exercise room is very small, with just a treadmill and stair climber. ✉ *1525 S. Ocean Blvd., 29582* ☎ *843/272–6101 or 800/588–3570* *843/272–7908* 🌐 *www.oceansands.com* *80 rooms, 36 suites* *Kitchens, 3 pools (1 indoor), no-smoking rooms* *AE, D, MC, V* *BP.*

LIGHTS OUT FOR SEA TURTLES!

You'll notice that many of the Strand's beachfront resorts keep the lights turned down low on the ocean side. This may add to the romance of a night-time stroll along the sand, but the primary beneficiaries of the darkness aren't humans . . . they're turtles.

Loggerhead sea turtles have been nesting on the beaches of the Grand Strand for thousands of years. (Seeing one of these often-giant reptiles come ashore to lay eggs in the sand is a rare thrill.) Today, loggerheads are a threatened species, so it's important to cut down on obstacles to their breeding.

That's where the darkness comes in. After a 60-day incubation period, the baby turtles hatch and begin to crawl toward the ocean. But bright lights confuse their navigation systems, causing them to head toward the light instead of the water—and making them easy prey for sand crabs and sea birds. Keeping lights to a minimum allows the baby turtles to heed their instincts and make it to the ocean.

Nightlife & the Arts

CLUBS & LOUNGES Sassy and saucy, but with live music that ranges from R&B to classic rock to beach favorites, **Dick's Last Resort** (✉ Barefoot Landing, 4700 U.S. 17S ☎ 843/272–7794) is big and loud, but the beer is cold.

You can dance the shag (the state dance) at **Duck's** (✉ 229 Main St. ☎ 843/249–3858). **Sandals** (✉ 500 Shore Dr. ☎ 843/449–6461) is an intimate lounge with live entertainment.

MUSIC & LIVE SHOWS Live acts, and country-and-western shows in particular, are a big draw on the Grand Strand. Music lovers have many family-oriented shows to choose from. The 2,250-seat **Alabama Theater** (✉ Barefoot Landing, 4750 U.S. 17S ☎ 843/272–1111) has a regular variety show with a wonderful patriotic closing; the theater also hosts different guest music and comedy artists during the year. The **House of Blues** (✉ Barefoot Landing, 4640 U.S. 17S ☎ 843/272–3000 for tickets) showcases big names and up-and-coming talent in blues, rock, jazz, country, and R&B on stages in its Southern-style restaurant and patio as well as in its 2,000-seat concert hall. The gospel brunch is a great deal. The **Tribute Theater** (✉ 701 Main St., North Myrtle Beach ☎ 800/313–6685 for tickets) embraces the idea that imitation is the sincerest form of flattery. Shows here feature talented impersonators re-creating performances of pop music's biggest stars. Each production runs for six to eight months and usually features a particular music era. Featured "stars" have included Cher, Frank Sinatra, Tina Turner and Shania Twain.

Shopping

MALLS **Barefoot Landing** (✉ 4898 S. Kings Hwy. ☎ 843/272–8349), built over marshland along the Intracoastal Waterway, has over 100 specialty shops, along with numerous entertainment activities. Shops include many mall standards, such as Sunglass Hut, Chico's, and Thomas Kinkead Gallery. There are several gift shops, jewelry stores, and even a bakery for dogs. Among the 13 outlets within the complex are Birkenstock and Izod.

SPECIALTY STORES Beach music lovers have been finding their long-lost favorites at **Judy's House of Oldies** (✉ 300 Main St. ☎ 843/249–8649), for years. Find classics on cassette and CD at this small but packed-to-the-gills music emporium.

THE SOUTHERN GRAND STRAND

Unlike the more developed area to the north, the southern end of the Grand Strand—Murrells Inlet, Litchfield, Pawleys Island, and Georgetown—has a barefoot, laid-back vibe that perfectly suits its small restaurants, shops, galleries, and outdoor outfitters. And what this part of the Strand lacks in glitz, it more than makes up for in natural beauty. The beaches are wide and empty enough for bike riding, bocci ball, and surf fishing. Spanish moss hangs gracefully from tree branches overlooking salt marshes alive with herons, egrets, and shrimp. Several large preserves, parks, and nature centers make it easy to observe the alligators, wild boar, deer, otter, and rare plants that inhabit the wild land between the ocean and the rivers, and there are a number of 18th- and 19th-century plantation houses and churches to explore.

Murrells Inlet

❸ *15 mi south of Myrtle Beach on U.S. 17.*

Murrells Inlet, a fishing village with some popular seafood restaurants, is a perfect place to rent a fishing boat or join an excursion. A notable garden and state park provide other diversions from the beach.

What to See

Fodor's Choice ★ Just beyond *The Fighting Stallions,* the Anna Hyatt Huntington sculpture alongside U.S. 17, lies **Brookgreen Gardens,** one of the Grand Strand's most magnificent hidden treasures. Here, in the oldest and largest sculpture garden in the United States, are more than 550 examples of figurative American sculpture by such artists as Frederic Remington and Daniel Chester French. Each is carefully set within garden rooms and outdoor galleries graced by sprawling live oak trees, colorful flowers, and peaceful ponds. The gardens are lush and full in spring and summer, and in winter they can be equally compelling, with splashes of color from winter-blooming shrubs set off against the stark surroundings.

The 9,000-acre property was originally a winter home for industrialist Archer Huntington and his wife Anna Hyatt Huntington. Within two years they decided instead to open it to the public as a sculpture garden and wildlife sanctuary. Today, more than 70 years later, their legacy endures as a center for not only American art but Lowcountry culture and nature preservation as well. You'll find here a wildlife park, an aviary, a cypress swamp, nature trails, and an education center. Several tours, including a boat tour of tidal creeks and a Jeep excursion into the preserve, leave from Brookgreen. ✉ *West of U.S. 17, 3 mi south of Murrells Inlet* ☎ *843/237–4218 or 800/849–1931* 🌐 *www.brookgreen.*

GHOSTS OF THE GRAND STRAND

SPEND ANY TIME *on the Grand Strand and you'll likely hear about two of the area's eeriest residents: Alice Flagg and the Gray Man.*

Alice Flagg was the teenage sister of the wealthy owner of the Hermitage, a rice plantation near Murrells Inlet. She was sent by her family to boarding school in Charleston to keep her away from a boy who'd captured her heart. The young lovers managed to see each other on the sly and soon became secretly engaged. Alice wore her engagement ring around her neck, hidden next to her heart. She came down with a high fever and returned to the Hermitage, where she died with the name of her fiancé on her lips. Her brother discovered the ring and, in a rage, threw it in the marsh.

Although she was buried at the Hermitage, her body was later moved to the cemetery at All Saints Church near Pawleys Island, where it now rests under a marble slab bearing only the name "Alice." For many years, her ghost was seen wandering the marsh near the house, looking for the ring. Her spirit, it is said, can be summoned by walking around the grave backward 13 times.

The Gray Man, according to most renditions of his story, was a young man who, while rushing to see his sweetheart, was thrown from his horse and died. After his funeral, his love took to walking along the beach each night. One evening, she was approached by a ghostly version of her lover. "Leave the island at once," he warned. "You are in great danger." She heeded the warning, and later that day a hurricane struck. Ever since, the Gray Man has delivered storm warnings to island residents, most famously before Hurricane Hugo hit in September 1989.

com 🎫 *$12* ⏲ *June–Sept., Wed.–Fri. 9:30–9:00, Sat.–Tues. 9:30–5; Oct.–May, daily 9:30–5.*

Huntington Beach State Park, the 2,500-acre former estate of Archer and Anna Huntington, lies east of U.S. 17, across from the couple's Brookgreen Gardens. The park's focal point is **Atalaya** (circa 1933), their Moorish-style 30-room home, which is open to visitors. In addition to the splendid beach, there are nature trails, fishing, an interpretive center, and an education center with fresh- and saltwater aquariums and a loggerhead sea turtle nesting habitat. There are also picnic areas, a playground, concessions, and a campground. ✉ *East of U.S. 17, 3 mi south of Murrells Inlet* ☎ *843/237–4440* 🌐 *www.southcarolinaparks.com* 🎫 *$5* ⏲ *mid-Mar.–Oct., daily 6 AM–10 PM; Nov.–mid-Mar., daily 6–6.*

Sports & the Outdoors

BOATING **Capt. Dick's** (✉ U.S. 17 Business ☎ 843/651–3676) runs half- and full-day fishing and sightseeing trips. You can also rent boats and kayaks and go parasailing. The evening ghost story cruise is scary fun.

Where to Eat

★ $$–$$$$ ✕ **Lee's Inlet Kitchen.** They're closed at lunchtime, on Sunday, and in winter; they don't take reservations or have a view, but nobody fries up a mess of seafood like Lee's. Even the biggest eaters will get their fill when they order the Shore Dinner: fried or broiled flounder, shrimp, oysters, scallops, deviled crab, and lobster, along with a shrimp cocktail, clam chowder, hush puppies, fries, and cole slaw. Sure, you can get your fish broiled or grilled, but why mess with deep-fried perfection? ✉ *4660 U.S. 17 Business* ☎ *843/651–2881* *Reservations not accepted* *AE, MC, V* *Closed Sun., Dec., and Jan. No lunch.*

$$–$$$$ Fodor's Choice ★ ✕ **Nance's Creekfront Restaurant.** You can smell the brine and Old Bay seasoning the minute you leave your car and head toward the front door of Nance's. There's not much atmosphere, but that's okay. Oysters, the small local ones that taste of saltwater and seaweed, are the specialty, available raw or steamed in an iron pot and served with butter. There are other selections on the menu, but it's really all about the oysters—and the 10-layer chocolate cake, made specially for Nance's by a local baker. ✉ *4883 U.S. 17 Business* ☎ *843/651–2696* *Reservations not accepted* *D, MC, V* *No lunch.*

★ **$–$$$** ✕ **Bovine's Wood-Fired Specialties.** What started as a meat-lovers-only restaurant has quietly morphed into a local favorite not just for delicious mesquite-grilled beef, lamb, pork, and fish, but also for superb crisp-crusted pizzas, baked in an imported brick oven and topped with a creative assortment of toppings. Add to that a terrific view of Murrells Inlet and Surfside Beach in the distance, and a sleek, modern decor, and Bovine's is a nice change from the usual waterfront establishment. ✉ *3979 U.S. 17 Business* ☎ *843/651–2888* *Reservations essential* *AE, D, MC, V* *No lunch.*

$–$$ ✕ **Inlet Crab House.** Locals love this weathered pink crab shack for its attitude-free atmosphere as well as its unfussy food. Oyster stew and fish chowder are specialties, simple and good, while the odd crab pizza dip is surprisingly tasty. Fresh fish, burgers, salads, and spicy boiled shrimp round out the menu. ✉ *3572 U.S. 17 Business* ☎ *843/651–8452* *Reservations not accepted* *AE, D, MC, V* *Closed Sun; Nov.–Mar., call ahead to confirm hrs.*

Nightlife

You can have a drink, watch boats come back from a day of fishing, and enjoy the evening breeze on the deck at **Captain Dave's Dockside** (✉ 4037 U.S. 17 Business ☎ 843/651–5880), where there's live music most nights during the summer. Strewn with party lights and offering live bands every night, the **Gazebo at the Hot Fish Club** (✉ 4911 U.S. 17 Business ☎ 843/357–9175) is a happening spot with a great view.

Pawleys Island

❹ *10 mi south of Murrells Inlet via U.S. 17.*

About 4 mi long and ½ mi wide, this island, sometimes referred to as "arrogantly shabby," began as a resort before the Civil War, when wealthy planters and their families summered here. It's mostly made up of weathered old summer cottages nestled in groves of oleander and oak trees. You can watch the famous Pawleys Island hammocks being made and bicycle around admiring the beach houses, many dating to the early 1800s. Golf and tennis are nearby.

Sports & the Outdoors

GOLF The **Litchfield Beach and Golf Resort** (✉ U.S. 17S, Litchfield Beach ☎ 843/237–3000 or 800/845–1897) is a popular 18-hole course. **Pawleys Plantation Golf & Country Club** (✉ U.S. 17S ☎ 843/237–8497 or 800/367–9959) is a Jack Nicklaus–designed course; several holes play along saltwater marshes. **Litchfield Country Club** (✉ U.S. 17S ☎ 843/237–3411) is a mature, old-style course with tight fairways and moss-laden oaks. The **River Club** (✉ U.S. 17S ☎ 843/626–9069) has water on 14 of its holes. **Willbrook** (✉ U.S. 17S ☎ 843/247–4900) is on a former rice plantation and winds past historical markers, a slave cemetery, and a tobacco shack. The live oak alley and wonderful greens help make the **Heritage Club** (✉ 478 Heritage Dr. ☎ 800/530–1875 🌐 www.legendsgolf.com) one of the South Strand's top courses, and its fees are lower than courses of similar difficulty and condition.

Where to Stay & Eat

★ **$$$–$$$$** ✕ **Frank's.** This local favorite serves dishes that give traditional cooking methods and ingredients a new twist. In a former 1930s grocery store with wood floors, framed French posters, and cozy fireside seating, diners indulge in large portions of fish, seafood, beef, and lamb cooked over an oak-burning grill. The local grouper with mustard-bacon butter, served with a side of stone-ground grits, is a star on the menu. Behind Frank's is the casual (but still pricey) Outback, a lush candlelit garden with a huge stone fireplace. The steak with Clemson blue cheese is a standout, as is the daily cobbler. Enjoy an after-dinner drink and admire the massive oak tree that sits in the middle of Outback's bar. ✉ *10434 U.S. 17* ☎ *843/237–3030* *Reservations essential* ▭ *D, MC, V* ⊙ *Closed Sun. No lunch.*

$$$–$$$$ Fodor's Choice ★ ✕ **Louis's at Pawleys.** A perfectionist to the core, chef Louis Osteen creates delicious renditions of traditional dishes such as crab cakes, barbecued shrimp, and lobster bisque, and he's not afraid to try his hand at more inventive dishes, such as crab-and-bacon-stuffed trout. Whatever you order, the food sings. For a casual night, have dinner outside on the deck at the Fish Camp. On Sunday, stop by for a lunch of fried chicken with all the fixings. ✉ *10880 U.S. 17* ☎ *843/237–8757* *Reservations essential* ▭ *AE, D, MC, V.*

$$–$$$ ✕ **Pawleys Island Tavern.** This little eatery has terrific crab cakes, hickory-smoked barbecue, roasted chicken, and pizza (they deliver). Summer weekend nights tiki torches outside blaze and live music rocks the place. ✉ *The Island Shops, U.S. 17* ☎ *843/237–8465* ▭ *AE, MC, V* ⊙ *Closed Mon.*

$–$$$ ✕ **Hog Heaven.** Part barbecue joint, part raw bar (after 5), Hog Heaven's wonderful smoky aroma perfumes U.S. 17 for miles. Pulled pork barbecue has the tang of vinegar, but mostly the taste of long hours in the pit. Although sandwiches are available, the buffet, which includes Southern delicacies such as fried chicken, greens, and sweet potato casserole, makes it a meal. In the evening, try the seafood tray, an assortment of shellfish steamed to order and served piping hot. ✉ *7147 U.S. 17* ☎ *843/237–7444* *Reservations not accepted* ▭ *MC, V* ⊙ *Closed Sun.–Tues.*

¢ ✕ **Landolphi's.** This Italian pastry shop and restaurant, fourth-generation-owned, has excellent coffee, hearty hoagies, pizzas, homemade sorbet, and delicious and authentic pastries, including cannoli and *pasticciotti* (a rich pastry). There's both counter and table service. ✉ *9305 Ocean Hwy.* ☎ *843/237–7900* ▭ *AE, MC, V* ⊗ *Closed Sun. No dinner Mon.–Wed.*

¢ ✕ **Sam's Corner.** Some people call Sam's Corner a dive, but most folks think of it as the best place on the Strand for a hot dog. Deep fried and covered in the traditional South Carolina style with chili and cole slaw, these dogs are legendary. Try them with a side of onion rings and sweet tea or a super-cold beer. ✉ *12036 U.S. 17* ☎ *843/235–3741* ✍ *Reservations not accepted* ▭ *No credit cards* ✉ *Other locations, 101 Atlantic Ave., Garden City; 7718 N. Kings Hwy., Myrtle Beach.*

$$$–$$$$ ✕▣ **Litchfield Plantation.** Period furnishings adorn four spacious suites of this impeccably restored 1750 rice-plantation manor house–turned–country inn, and all of the rooms are lovely, with rich fabrics and views of lakes, woods, or creeks. Use of a beach-house club a short drive away is part of the package, as is a full breakfast at the elegant Carriage House Club; guests also have golf privileges at eight nearby courses. The resort is approximately 2 mi south of Brookgreen Gardens on U.S. 17 (turn right at the Litchfield Country Club entrance and follow the signs). ✉ *Kings River Rd., Box 290, 29585* ☎ *843/237–9121 or 800/869–1410* 🖷 *843/237–8558* 🌐 *www.litchfieldplantation.com* ⇨ *35 rooms, 4 suites, 9 2- and 3-bedroom cottages* 👍 *Restaurant, 2 tennis courts, pool, library, concierge* ▭ *AE, D, DC, MC, V* 🍴 *BP.*

$$–$$$$ Fodor's Choice ★ ▣ **Litchfield Beach and Golf Resort.** This beautifully landscaped 4,500-acre resort runs along both sides of U.S. 17. The almost 2-mi stretch of oceanfront accommodations ranges from condos to the 160-room Litchfield Inn, which has standard motel rooms; other options, such as high-rise condos, duplexes, and even Charleston-style beach houses, overlook fairways, lakes, or the marsh. All accommodations are grouped into miniresorts, each with its own pool and tennis courts. A bike trail connects them all and also winds to the large lake, which has a small fishing dock and a couple of resident alligators. There's a one-week minimum for oceanfront rentals during June, July, and August, except at the Inn, where the minimum is three nights. ✉ *U.S. 17, 2 mi north of Pawleys Island, Litchfield Beach, 29585* ☎ *843/237–3000 or 800/845–1897* 🖷 *843/237–4282* 🌐 *www.litchfieldbeach.com* ⇨ *140 rooms, 216 suites, 200 condominiums, cottages, and villas* 👍 *2 restaurants, 3 18-hole golf courses, 26 tennis courts, 18 pools (2 indoor), health club, bicycles, business center* ▭ *AE, D, MC, V* 🍴 *EP.*

$$–$$$ ▣ **Sea View Inn.** A "barefoot paradise," Sea View is a no-frills beachside boardinghouse (there are no TVs or in-room phones) with long porches. Rooms in the main inn, with views of the ocean or marsh, have half baths; showers are down the hall and outside. Cottage rooms are marshside and have air-conditioning. Three meals, served family style—with grits, gumbo, crab salad, pecan pie, and oyster pie—make this an unbeatable deal. There's a two-night minimum stay during May and September and a one-week minimum from June through August. ✉ *414 Myrtle Ave., 29585* ☎ *843/237–4253* 🖷 *843/237–*

7909 🌐 www.seaviewinn.com ⇨ 20 rooms, 1 cottage ♨ Dining room; no a/c in some rooms, no phones, no TV ▭ No credit cards ⏲ Closed Nov.–Mar. 🍴 FAP.

¢–$ **Pawleys Island Hampton Inn.** Ongoing upgrades keep this hotel in tip-top condition. Like most Hampton Inns, the property offers a wide array of amenities and is clean and well maintained. The beach at Pawleys is a 10-minute drive away. ✉ *150 Willbrook Blvd., 29585 ☎ 843/235–3000 📠 843/235–2099 🌐 www.pawleysislandhamptoninn.com ⇨ 66 rooms ♨ Pool, cable TV, health club ▭ AE, D, MC, V 🍴 BP.*

The Arts

Pawleys Island comes alive each September during the **Pawleys Island Festival of Music & Art** (📫 Box 1975, 29585 ☎ 843/237–4774 🌐 www.pawleysmusic.org), which brings national and local artists together for a month of concerts, exhibitions, and readings. Past performers have included David Sanborn and Delbert McClinton.

Shopping

Lighthearted and colorful, **Cuz-I Gotta Have It** (✉ 11195 U.S. 17 ☎ 843/235–6491) is a folk-art gallery that represents a number of well-known local and gullah artists. Browse through the collection of paintings, sculpture, furniture and clothing, or take part in one of the gallery's workshops.

The **Hammock Shops at Pawleys Island** (✉ 10880 Ocean Hwy. ☎ 843/237–8448) is a complex of two dozen boutiques, gift shops, and restaurants built with old beams, timber, and ballast brick. Outside the Original Hammock Shop, in the Hammock Weavers' Pavilion, craftspeople demonstrate the 19th-century art of weaving the famous cotton-rope Pawleys Island hammocks. Also look for jewelry, toys, antiques, and designer fashions.

Georgetown

❺ *13 mi south of Pawleys Island via U.S. 17.*

Founded on Winyah Bay in 1729, Georgetown became the center of America's colonial rice empire. A rich plantation culture developed on a scale comparable to Charleston's, and the historic district, which can be walked in a couple of hours, is among the prettiest in the state. Today oceangoing vessels still come to Georgetown's busy port, and the **Harborwalk,** the restored waterfront, hums with activity.

What to See

The graceful market and meeting building in the heart of Georgetown, topped by an 1842 clock and tower, has been converted into the ☺ **Rice Museum,** with maps, tools, dioramas, and, at the museum's Prevost Gallery next door, the Brown's Ferry river freighter, which is the oldest American-built water-going vessel still in existence. The museum gift shop has an interesting selection of local pine needle baskets, African dolls, and art (including baskets made from whole cloves), and carries South Carolina rice and honey. ✉ *Front and Screven Sts. ☎ 843/546–7423 🎫 $5 ⏲ Mon.–Sat. 10–4:30.*

Prince George Winyah Episcopal Church (named after King George II) still serves the parish established in 1721. It was built in 1737 with bricks brought from England. ✉ *Broad and Highmarket Sts., Georgetown* ☎ *843/546–4358* 🎫 *Donation suggested* ⏲ *Mar.–Oct., weekdays 11:30–4:30.*

Overlooking the Sampit River from a bluff is the **Kaminsky House Museum** (circa 1769). It's especially notable for its collections of regional antiques and furnishings, its Chippendale and Duncan Phyfe furniture, Royal Doulton vases, and silver. ✉ *1003 Front St.* ☎ *843/546–7706* 🎫 *$5* ⏲ *Mon.–Sat. 10–4, Sun. 1–4.*

Hobcaw Barony Visitors Center is at the entrance of Hobcaw Barony, on the vast estate of the late Wall Street financier Bernard M. Baruch; Franklin D. Roosevelt and Winston Churchill came here to confer with him. A small interpretive center has exhibits on coastal ecology and history, with special emphasis on the Baruch family. There are aquariums, touch tanks, and video presentations; you can also take a guided three-hour tour of the 17,500-acre wildlife refuge Tuesday, Wednesday, and Friday morning and Thursday afternoon. ✉ *On U.S. 17, 2 mi north of Georgetown* ☎ *843/546–4623* 🌐 *www.hobcawbarony.com* 🎫 *Visitors center free, tours $15* ⏲ *Weekdays 10–5; reservations necessary for tour.*

Hopsewee Plantation, surrounded by moss-draped live oaks, magnolias, and tree-size camellias, overlooks the North Santee River. The circa-1740 mansion has a fine Georgian staircase and hand-carved lighted-candle moldings. ✉ *U.S. 17, 12 mi south of Georgetown* ☎ *843/546–7891 or 800/648–0478* 🌐 *www.hopsewee.com* 🎫 *Mansion $10; grounds $5 per car; parking fees apply toward tour* ⏲ *Mansion Mar.–Nov., weekdays 10–4:30; Dec.–Feb., Thurs. and Fri 10–4:30, or by appointment. Grounds, including nature trail, daily dawn–dusk.*

Hampton Plantation State Historic Site preserves the home of Archibald Rutledge, poet laureate of South Carolina for 39 years until his death in 1973. The 18th-century plantation house is a fine example of a Lowcountry mansion. The exterior has been restored; cutaway sections in the finely crafted interior show the changes made through the centuries. The grounds are landscaped, and there are picnic areas. ✉ *Off U.S. 17, at edge of Francis Marion National Forest, 16 mi south of Georgetown* ☎ *843/546–9361* 🎫 *Mansion $4, grounds free* ⏲ *Mansion June–Aug., daily 11–4; Sept.–May, Thurs.–Mon. 11–4. Grounds Thurs.–Mon. 9–6.*

Sports & the Outdoors

BOATING Cruise past abandoned rice plantations and hear stories about the belles who lived there with Captain Rod of **Lowcountry Plantation Tours** (✉ Front St. Harborwalk ☎ 843/477–0287); other tours include a lighthouse expedition and a ghost stories cruise. Feel the spray on your face as you explore Winyah Bay aboard a 40-foot yacht with Captain Dave of **Wallace Sailing Charters** (✉ 607 Front St. ☎ 843/902–6999). Each trip is limited to six passengers, so it feels like you're touring on a private yacht.

CANOEING & KAYAKING ★ **Black River Outdoor Center and Expeditions** (✉ 21 Garden Ave., U.S. 701 ☎ 843/546–4840 🌐 www.blackriveroutdoors.com) offers naturalist-guided canoe and kayak day and evening tours (including moonlight tours) of the tidelands of Georgetown. Part of what makes these trips fun is that the guides are well versed not just in the wildlife, but in local lore. Tours take kayakers past settings such as Drunken Jack's (the island that supposedly holds Blackbeard's booty), and Chicora Wood plantation, where dikes and trunk gates mark canals dug by slaves to facilitate rice growing in the area. It's said that digging the canals required as much manual labor as Egypt's pyramids. Black River also rents and sells equipment.

GOLF The premier course in the Georgetown area is the 18-hole, par-73 **Wedgefield Plantation** (✉ 129 Club House La., off U.S. 701 ☎ 843/448–2124 or 843/546–8587). The 18-hole, par-70 **Winyah Bay Golf Club** (✉ 336 Golf Dr. ☎ 877/527–7765) is a popular option with some challenging water holes.

4

Where to Stay & Eat

★ **$$$–$$$$** ✕ **Rice Paddy.** At lunch, locals flock to this Lowcountry restaurant for the shrimp and bacon quesadilla and the creative salads and sandwiches. Dinner in the Victorian building, with windows overlooking Front Street, is more relaxed. Grilled local tuna with a ginger-soy glaze is a winner, as are the crab cakes, which you can get uncooked to go. ✉ *732 Front St.* ☎ *843/546–2021* *Reservations essential* *AE, MC, V* *Closed Sun.*

$$–$$$ ✕ **River Room.** This restaurant on the Sampit River specializes in chargrilled fish, Cajun fried oysters, seafood pastas, and steaks. For lunch you can have shrimp and grits or your choice of sandwiches and salads. The dining room has river views from most tables. It's especially romantic at night, when the oil lamps and brass fixtures cast a warm glow on the dark wood and brick interior of the early-20th-century building. ✉ *801 Front St.* ☎ *843/527–4110* *Reservations not accepted* *AE, MC, V* *Closed Sun.*

$–$$$ ✕ **Dogwood Cafe.** The menu is large and varied at this casual eatery housed in one of Georgetown's old riverfront buildings. Share appetizers like bacon-wrapped shrimp and fried green tomatoes—they're the real thing—or, on Thursday, Frogmore Stew, a Lowcountry dish composed of layers of shrimp, corn, smoked sausage, and potatoes that have been boiled together in a big pot. The best seats are on the rustic back deck that overlooks the river. ✉ *713 Front St.* ☎ *843/545–7777* *AE, D, MC, V* *Closed Sun.*

¢–$$ ✕ **Kudzu Bakery.** Come here for the justifiably famous Key-lime pie and red velvet cake, both of which are available whole or by the slice, and can be eaten in the bakery's garden. Kudzu is also a great source for ready-to-cook specialties such as cheese biscuits, macaroni and cheese, and quiche. In addition you'll find fresh bread, deli items, and a terrific selection of wines. ✉ *714 Front St.* ☎ *843/546–1847* *MC, V* *Closed Sun. No dinner.*

¢–$ ✕ **Thomas Cafe.** There's great fried chicken, homemade biscuits, and pie at this lunch counter, not to mention grits, eggs, country ham, and other breakfast favorites served every day but Sunday (when the café opens at 11 AM instead of 7. Join the regulars at the counter, or sit in one of the booths or café tables in the 1920s storefront building. ✉ *714 Front St.* ☎ *843/546–7776* 💳 *MC, V* ⊗ *No dinner.*

$$$$ **Lodge at Lofton Landing.** To stay here you must rent this entire lodge, a modern facility overlooking the marshland of Cape Romain National Wildlife Refuge. It sleeps eight and has a furnished kitchen, a wraparound porch, and a dock for fishing and crabbing. ✉ *8889 U.S. 17, about 22 mi south of Georgetown, McClellanville 29458* ☎ *843/720–7332* 📠 *843/856–8468* *1 lodge with 3 rooms* *Boating, fishing* 💳 *AE, D, DC, MC, V* 🍽 *EP.*

$$–$$$ **Harbor House Bed and Breakfast.** Watch the shrimp boats come into the harbor from the front porch of Georgetown's only waterfront bed-and-breakfast; if you're lucky, innkeeper Meg Tarbox will turn some of the catch into shrimp and grits for breakfast. All four rooms (named for ships that have docked at Georgetown) have water views, as well as decades-old heart-pine floors and family antiques. Refreshments in the afternoon include more of those shrimp, this time in the family's locally famous dip. ✉ *15 Cannon St., 29440* ☎ *843/546–6532 or 877/511–0101* 📠 *843/546–0014* 🌐 *www.harborhousebb.com* *4 rooms* *Bicycles* 💳 *MC, V* ⊗ *Closed mid-Dec.–mid-Feb.* 🍽 *BP.*

Shopping

You'll find hand-carved wooden bowls and trays as well as an assortment of dishes and kitchen tools at **Kudzu Mercantile** (✉ 932 Front St. ☎ 843/546–0040). The cookbook selection is also good.

MYRTLE BEACH & THE GRAND STRAND A TO Z

To research prices, get advice from other travelers, and book travel arrangements, visit www.fodors.com.

AIRPORTS

The Myrtle Beach International Airport is served by AirTran, Continental, COMAIR, Delta's regional carrier Atlantic Southeast, Hooters Air, Northwest, PanAm, Spirit, Vanguard, US Airways, and Vacation Express.

Airport Information **Myrtle Beach International Airport** ✉ 1100 Jetport Rd. ☎ 843/448–1580.

BOAT & FERRY TRAVEL

Boaters traveling the Intracoastal Waterway may dock at Hague Marina, Harbor Gate, and Marlin Quay.

Boat & Ferry Information **Hague Marina** ✉ Myrtle Beach ☎ 843/293–2141. **Harbor Gate** ✉ North Myrtle Beach ☎ 843/249–8888. **Marlin Quay** ✉ Murrells Inlet ☎ 843/651–4444.

CAR TRAVEL

Midway between New York and Miami, the Grand Strand isn't connected directly by any interstate highways but is within an hour's drive of I–95, I–20, I–26, and I–40. U.S. 17 is the major north–south coastal route through the Strand.

EMERGENCIES

Both the Grand Strand Regional Medical Center and Georgetown Memorial Hospital have emergency rooms open 24 hours a day. The Grand Strand Regional Medical Center has the only pharmacy in the area open all night.

Emergency Services **Ambulance, fire, police** ☎ 911.

Hospitals **Georgetown Memorial Hospital** ✉ 606 Black River Rd., Georgetown ☎ 843/527-7000. **Grand Strand Regional Medical Center** ✉ 809 82nd Pkwy., off U.S. 17, Myrtle Beach ☎ 843/692-1000.

24-Hour Pharmacies **Grand Strand Regional Medical Center Pharmacy** ✉ 809 82nd Pkwy., off U.S. 17, Myrtle Beach ☎ 843/692-1000.

4

LODGING

With more than 60,000 rooms, cottages, villas, and high-rise units available along the Grand Strand, it's seldom difficult to find a place to stay, and discounting is rampant.

APARTMENT & VILLA RENTALS

For the free directory *Where to Stay and Play,* contact the Myrtle Beach Area Convention Bureau. For Pawleys Island and Litchfield Beach, try Pawleys Island Realty.

Local Agents **Myrtle Beach Area Convention Bureau** ☎ 843/448-1629 or 800/356-3016 **Pawleys Island Realty** ☎ 843/237-4257 or 800/937-7352.

TAXIS

Taxi service in Myrtle Beach is provided by Coastal Cab Service.

Taxi Companies **Coastal Cab Service** ☎ 843/448-4444.

TOURS

Palmetto Tour & Travel and Leisure Time Unlimited/Gray Line, both in Myrtle Beach, offer tour packages and guide services.

Fees & Schedules **Georgetown County Chamber of Commerce and Information Center** ☎ 843/546-8436 or 800/777-7705. **Swamp Fox II Tours** ☎ 843/527-6469. **Leisure Time Unlimited/Gray Line** ☎ 843/448-9483. **Miss Nell's "Real South" Tours** ☎ 843/546-3975. **Palmetto Tour & Travel** ☎ 843/626-2660.

VISITOR INFORMATION

Tourist Information **Georgetown County Chamber of Commerce and Information Center** 1001 Front St., Box 1776, Georgetown 29442 ☎ 843/546-8436 www.georgetownchamber.com. **Murrells Inlet 2007** Box 1357, Murrells Inlet 29576 ☎ 843/357-2007 www.murrellsinletsc.com. **Myrtle Beach Area Chamber of Commerce and Information Center** 1200 N. Oak St., Box 2115, Myrtle Beach 29578 ☎ 843/626-7444 or 800/356-3016 www.myrtlebeachinfo.com. **Pawleys Island Chamber of Commerce** U.S. 17, Box 569, Pawleys Island 29585 ☎ 843/237-1921.

CHARLESTON

5

TRACE THE ORIGINS OF THE CIVIL WAR
at Fort Sumter National Monument ⇨ *p.199*

TAKE IN THE CITY'S FINEST VIEWS
along the High Battery boardwalk ⇨ *p.203*

MINGLE WITH THE PEACOCKS
on the grounds of Middleton Place ⇨ *p.208*

TASTE GREAT LOWCOUNTRY FARE
at Slightly North of Broad ⇨ *p.220*

SLEEP LIKE A SOUTHERN ARISTOCRAT
at the grand Wentworth Mansion ⇨ *p.228*

By Melissa Bigner

AT FIRST GLIMPSE, Charleston looks like an 18th-century etching come to life. The spires and steeples of more than 180 churches punctuate her low skyline, and tourists ride in horse-pulled carriages that pass grandiose, centuries-old mansions and antique gardens brimming with heirloom plants. First settled in 1670, immigrants flocked here initially for religious freedom and later for prosperity (compliments of the rice, indigo, and cotton plantation industries).

Preserved through the poverty following the Civil War, and natural disasters like fires, earthquakes, and hurricanes, many of Charleston's earliest public and private architecture still stands. And thanks to a rigorous preservation movement and strict Board of Architectural Review, the city's new structures blend with the old ones. In many cases, recycling is the name of the game—antique handmade bricks literally lay the foundation for new homes. But while locals do live—on some literal levels—in the past, the city is very much a town of today.

Take the internationally heralded Spoleto Festival, for instance. For two weeks every summer, arts patrons from around the world come to enjoy local and international concerts, dance performances, operas, improv shows, and plays at venues citywide. Day in and out, diners can feast at upscale Southern restaurants, shoppers can look for museum-quality paintings and antiques, and outdoor adventurers can explore all Charleston's outlying beaches, parks, and marshes.

EXPLORING CHARLESTON

The heart of the city is on a peninsula, sometimes just called "downtown" by the nearly 100,000 residents who populate the area. Walking Charleston's peninsula is the best way to get to know the city. The main downtown historic district is roughly bounded by Calhoun Street to the north, the Cooper River to the east, the Battery to the south, and Lockwood Boulevard to the west. More than 2,000 historic homes and buildings occupy this fairly compact area divided into South of Broad (Street) and North of Broad. King Street, the main shopping street in town, cuts through Broad Street, and the most trafficked tourist area ends a few blocks south of the Crosstown, where U.S. 17 cuts across Upper King. Downtown you can explore most areas by foot. Otherwise, bikes, pedicab rickshaws, and abs are the best way to get around, as the bus and shuttle system has been in flux for years, street parking is irksome, and tickets are given freely.

Beyond downtown, the Ashley River hugs the west side of the peninsula, and the region on the far shore is called West Ashley. The Cooper River runs along the east side of the peninsula, with Mount Pleasant on the opposite side and the Charleston Harbor in between. Last, there are outlying sea islands (James, Folly Beach, Johns, Kiawah, Isle of Palms, Sullivan's), with their own appealing attractions. Everything that entails crossing the bridges is best explored by car.

North of Broad

Large tracts of available land made the area North of Broad ideal for suburban plantations during the early 1800s. A century later, the peninsula had been built out, and today the area is a vibrant mix of residential neighborhoods and commercial clusters, with verdant parks scattered throughout. Though there are a number of majestic homes and prerevolutionary buildings in this area (including the oldest public building in the city, the Old Powder Magazine), the main draw is the area's collection of stores, museums, restaurants, and historic churches.

As you explore, note that the farther north you travel (up King Street in particular), the newer and more commercial development becomes. While pretty much anywhere on the peninsula is considered prime real estate these days, the farther south you go, the more expensive the homes become. In times past, Broad Street was considered the cutoff point for the most coveted addresses. Those living in the area Slightly North of Broad were called mere "SNOBs," while their neighbors South of Broad were nicknamed "SOBs."

Numbers in the text correspond to numbers in the margin and on the Charleston map.

a good walk

Before you begin walking, drop by the **Visitor Information Center** 1 on Meeting Street for an overview of the city and a map. The **Charleston Museum** 2, across the street, has a large decorative arts collection worth seeing. Afterward, turn right on Ann Street and right again on Elizabeth Street to tour the palatial **Aiken-Rhett House** 3. South on Elizabeth Street, and right on John Street, is the **Joseph Manigault House** 4, another impressive house museum dating to the early 1800s. Continue on John Street to reach the **Children's Museum of the Lowcountry** 5. Return to Meeting Street and walk south, passing the **Old Citadel Building** 6, now an Embassy Suites.

If you take a left on Calhoun Street, a half block down is the **Emanuel African Methodist Episcopal Church** 7, where slave rebellion leader Denmark Vesey was a member. If you turn right, you pass the Francis Marion Hotel (in the 1920s the highest building in the Carolinas) and can continue two blocks west to St. Philip Street, where a left turn puts you on the romantic campus of the **College of Charleston** 8, where you can stroll under the many moss-draped trees. Turn southwest (right) on George Street and jog north on Coming before continuing west (left) five blocks on Bull Street to get to the **Avery Research Center for African-American History and Culture** 9, where generations of freed blacks were trained as teachers after the Civil War.

Retrace your steps back past the college to King Street, Charleston's main shopping thoroughfare, and turn right; turn left on Hasell Street to see **Kahal Kadosh Beth Elohim Reform Temple** 10, a Greek Revival building. Across the street is **St. Mary's Catholic Church** 11. Follow King south and turn left on Market Street. Classy **Charleston Place** 12 has a graceful hotel and cluster of shops. You can browse from one end to the other, exiting on King Street. Keep walking down Meeting Street to the **Mar-**

If you have
3 days

The best way to get acquainted with Charleston is to take a carriage ride, especially those that take you through the South of Broad neighborhood. After the ride, carriage companies drop you off near the Old City Market in the North of Broad, in the Market area, where you can wander looking for souvenirs. Head to lunch and then hoof it to the Battery and White Point Gardens; take time for a house tour or two at mansions such as the Nathaniel Russell House and the Heyward-Washington House. Spend the night in the historic district, and on Day 2 drive to the magnificent plantations in West Ashley; you might tour Middleton Place, Drayton Hall, or Magnolia Gardens. Return downtown for the night, and spend Day 3 shopping for antiques, seersucker suits, and one-of-a-kind jewelry on Lower King Street. Break for lunch and wander down toward Broad Street again, stopping to peek inside the churches and graveyards. Finish the day on a bench at Waterfront Park before heading to a sumptuous dinner.

If you have
5 days

Follow the three-day tour above, then on Day 4 make your first stop the South Carolina Aquarium, near Upper King, which overlooks Charleston Harbor. From there take the harbor ferry to Fort Sumter National Monument to see where the Civil War began, or tour the waterfront on one of the other boat tours that depart from the Maritime Center. On Day 5 drive across the Cooper River into Mount Pleasant and visit Patriots Point, the Old Village neighborhood, and Fort Moultrie on Sullivan's Island. After lunch on Middle Street drive to one of the beaches, maybe to the Isle of Palms, to wind down. Return to Charleston after catching the sunset.

If you have
7 days

After finishing the five-day itinerary, spend Day 6 outdoors. You might take a short road trip over the Ashley River from downtown to Folly Beach County Park. Bring a picnic lunch and fish off the pier, walk through the forest, or surf from the beach. Or you could head north instead, and explore Bull Island and the Cape Romain Wildlife Refuge. Spend the night back in Charleston, and finish your tour of the area by heading northwest to Moncks Corner for a tour through Mepkin Abbey, or a canoe trip through Cypress Gardens, which is sure to impress all ages.

---

ket Hall 13 and the bustling **Old City Market** 14. Now is a good time for a carriage tour; many depart from here.

South on Stone Street and right on Cumberland Street, is the **Old Powder Magazine** 15. To the left as you face the building, you can catch a glimpse of the steeple of **St. Philip's (Episcopal) Church** 16, famous in the city's skyline; it's around the corner on Church Street. Continue west on Cumberland, and turn left down Market Street for **Gibbes Museum of Art** 17, with its spectacular stained-glass dome. Across the street is the **Circular Congregational Church** 18. Two blocks west, on quiet Archdale Street, you can wander through **St. John's Lutheran Church** 19 and the peaceful graveyard of the **Unitarian Church** 20. Turn left on Queen Street at the bottom of Archdale and walk three blocks to Meeting Street, where you turn right on picturesque Church Street to get to the **Dock Street Theatre** 21 and the **French Protestant (Huguenot) Church** 22 across the street. You might detour east here, down Queen Street and along Vendue Range to **Waterfront Park** 23, to relax in a bench swing overlooking beautiful river views, dramatic fountains, and a fishing pier.

You can stop at the park or go north by pedicab to the **South Carolina Aquarium** 24. Next door at the Fort Sumter Liberty Square Visitor Education Center, part of the **Fort Sumter National Monument** 25, you can catch a boat to the historic Fort Sumter out in Charleston Harbor.

TIMING Set aside from two to four hours for the walk alone, depending on your pace. Add extra time for stops at museums. Most house-museum tours last about 40 minutes. A trip to the aquarium can add two or so hours, as will a trip to Fort Sumter. If you want to tour both of the latter sites, you may wish to split the trip into two half-days. Charleston rickshaws (bicycle-power, two seat cabs) take you anywhere downtown for $6, which can ease the trip.

What to See

3 **Aiken-Rhett House.** This stately 1819 mansion still has its original wallpaper, paint colors, and some of its furnishings. The kitchen, slave quarters, and work yard are much as they were when the original occupants lived here, making this one of the most complete examples of urban slave life of the period. Confederate general P. G. T. Beauregard made his headquarters here during his 1864 Civil War defense of Charleston. ✉ *48 Elizabeth St., Upper King* ☎ *843/723–1159* 🌐 *www.historiccharleston.org* 🎫 *$8; combination ticket with Nathaniel Russell House $14* ⏲ *Mon.–Sat. 10–5, Sun. 2–5.*

9 **Avery Research Center for African-American History and Culture.** This center, part museum and part archives, was once a school for freed slaves. Collections include slavery artifacts (manacles, bills of sale, slave badges), old manuscripts, and African artifacts with ties to Lowcountry slaves. A riveting mural chronicles the Middle Passage—the journey slaves made from Africa to Charleston's shores. The free tours include a brief film. Although it's a short, five-block walk from the Cistern quad, Avery Research Center is affiliated with the College of Charleston. ✉ *125 Bull St., College of Charleston* ☎ *843/953–7609* 🌐 *www.cofc.edu* 🎫 *Free* ⏲ *Weekdays noon–5, mornings by appointment.*

★ 2 **Charleston Museum.** Founded in 1773, the country's oldest museum is now housed in a contemporary complex. The museum's decorative arts holdings and its permanent Civil War exhibit are extraordinary. There are more than 500,000 items in the collection. In addition to displaying Charleston silver, fashions, toys, snuffboxes, and the like, there are exhibits relating to natural history, archaeology, and ornithology. The 1803, federal-style ⇨ **Joseph Manigault House,** owned by the Charleston Museum, is across the street. George Washington once slept at the 1772 ⇨ **Heyward-Washington House,** which is seven blocks southeast of its parent, the Charleston Museum. ✉ *360 Meeting St., Upper King* ☎ *843/722–2996* 🌐 *www.charlestonmuseum.org* 🎫 *$9; museum and houses $18; 2 of 3 sights $12* ⏲ *Mon.–Sat. 9–5, Sun. 1–5.*

5

Beach Bound Historic homes might be what brings you to the city the first time, but it's the area's beautiful beaches, mysterious marshlands, and all those winding rivers that will beckon you back. Celebrate the outdoors Charlestonian-style and hit the beaches at Sullivan's Island, Folly Beach, Isle of Palms, Kiawah, or Seabrook Island while you're here. You could take an eco-tour to a nature preserve like Bull Island, or kayak past one-time rice plantations eye-level with the gators. In no time, you're sure to find the smell of pluff mud endearing.

The Living Past The past—good and bad—is very much a part of Charleston's present-day life. House museum tour guides tell stories about the Civil War cannon balls still stuck in attic floors; walking tours include house-by-house gossip and point out the sites of former slave auctions and horrific morgues. The first shots of the Civil War were fired just off the Battery at Fort Sumter, and there are plenty of Civil War sights to see in the area. Outside of downtown, there are rice plantations, and a way of life gone-by, to explore. Small festivals throughout the year focus on different aspects of history and the Fall Candlelight Tour of Homes lets you inside old homes that are not generally open to the public. So take a boat, bus, or walking tour and you're likely to learn as much as you've ever wanted to know about this city's colorful past.

Walking the Streets The best way to get to know old Charleston is by foot: walking along its streets, venturing down quaint alleyways, peeking into gardens, and simply gawking at everything along the way. A general walking tour that covers the area at least from the Old City Market south to the Battery and White Point Gardens provides a good overview, or if you have a specific interest you might choose a theme tour. Once you have the lay of the land, break out on your own to marvel at the grand mansions and overflowing window boxes. From Waterfront Park you might be able to watch carousing dolphins or racing sailboats. Don't expect to be alone on your walks though; strolling through town is a long-standing local custom not just reserved for visitors.

★ ⓬ **Charleston Place.** The city's chief world-class hotel, an Orient-Express property, is flanked by a gallery of upscale boutiques and specialty shops for you to explore. Afterward, wander into the luxe lobby and head to the lounge where you can sip cocktails or take tea in high style. The finest public restrooms are downstairs by the shoe-shine station. Entrances for the garage and reception area are on Hasell Street between Meeting and King streets. ✉ *130 Market St., Market area* ☎ *843/722–4900.*

★ ☺ ❺ **Children's Museum of the Lowcountry.** Daily art projects and other exhibits promote hands-on science, culture, and creativity for toddlers up to 12-year-olds. Kids can climb on a replica of a local shrimp boat, play in exhibits that show how water evaporates from and returns to the Lowcountry, wander the inner workings of a medieval castle, and more. This

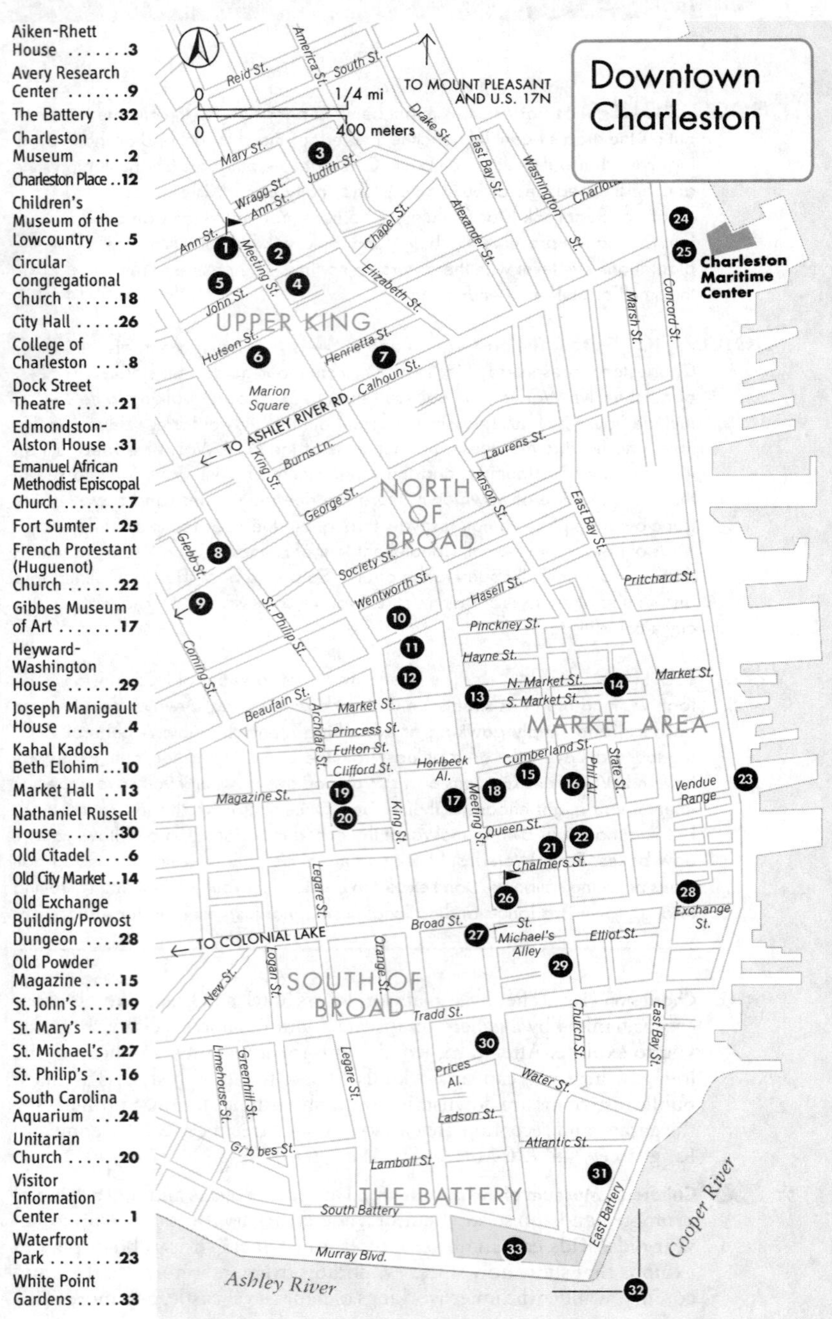
Aiken-Rhett House 3
Avery Research Center 9
The Battery ..32
Charleston Museum 2
Charleston Place ..12
Children's Museum of the Lowcountry ...5
Circular Congregational Church 18
City Hall 26
College of Charleston 8
Dock Street Theatre 21
Edmondston-Alston House .31
Emanuel African Methodist Episcopal Church 7
Fort Sumter ..25
French Protestant (Huguenot) Church 22
Gibbes Museum of Art 17
Heyward-Washington House 29
Joseph Manigault House 4
Kahal Kadosh Beth Elohim ...10
Market Hall ..13
Nathaniel Russell House 30
Old Citadel 6
Old City Market ..14
Old Exchange Building/Provost Dungeon 28
Old Powder Magazine 15
St. John's 19
St. Mary's 11
St. Michael's .27
St. Philip's ...16
South Carolina Aquarium ...24
Unitarian Church 20
Visitor Information Center 1
Waterfront Park 23
White Point Gardens 33
Downtown Charleston
0
1/4 mi
0
400 meters
TO MOUNT PLEASANT AND U.S. 17N
Charleston Maritime Center
UPPER KING
NORTH OF BROAD
MARKET AREA
SOUTH OF BROAD
THE BATTERY
TO ASHLEY RIVER RD.
TO COLONIAL LAKE
Marion Square
Ashley River
Cooper River
Reid St.
America St.
South St.
Drake St.
East Bay St.
Washington St.
Charlotte
Mary St.
Judith St.
Wragg St.
Ann St.
Chapel St.
Alexander St.
Meeting St.
John St.
Elizabeth St.
Marsh St.
Concord St.
Hutson St.
Henrietta St.
Calhoun St.
Laurens St.
King St.
Burns Ln.
George St.
Anson St.
Glebb St.
Society St.
Pritchard St.
Wentworth St.
Hasell St.
St. Philip St.
Pinckney St.
Coming St.
Hayne St.
N. Market St.
Market St.
S. Market St.
Beaufain St.
Archdale St.
Princess St.
Fulton St.
Clifford St.
Horlbeck Al.
Cumberland St.
Phil Al.
State St.
Vendue Range
Magazine St.
Queen St.
Chalmers St.
Legare St.
Exchange St.
Broad St.
St. Michael's Alley
Elliot St.
Logan St.
Orange St.
New St.
Tradd St.
Church St.
Limehouse St.
Greenhill St.
Prices Al.
Water St.
Ladson St.
Gibbes St.
Atlantic St.
Lamboll St.
South Battery
East Battery
Murray Blvd.

top-notch museum opened in 2004. ✉ *25 Ann St., Upper King* ☎ *843/853–8962* 🌐 *www.explorecml.org* 🎟 *$5* ⏲ *Tues.–Sat. 10–5, Sun. 1–5.*

need a break? Refresh with an icy treat at **Paolo's Gelato Italiano** (✉ 41 John St., Upper King ☎ 843/577–0099). Flavors include chocolates, fruits and florals, and Italian traditions.

18 **Circular Congregational Church.** The first church building erected on this site by Protestants in the 1680s gave bustling Meeting Street its name. The present-day Romanesque structure (1890) is configured on a Greek-cross plan and has rounded corners and a beamed, vaulted ceiling that are especially breathtaking when seen from inside. Explore the graveyard, the oldest in the city, with records dating to 1696. ✉ *150 Meeting St., Market area* ☎ *843/577–6400* 🌐 *www.circularchurch.org.*

8 **College of Charleston.** Randolph Hall (1828)—a gorgeous building with columns, designed by Philadelphia architect William Strickland—anchors the central Cistern area of the college. Majestic oaks envelop the Cistern's lush green quad, where graduation ceremonies and concerts take place. The college was founded in 1770. Scenes from *Cold Mountain* were filmed here. ✉ *St. Philip and George Sts., College of Charleston* 🌐 *www.cofc.edu.*

21 **Dock Street Theatre.** A 1936 WPA project merged the site's original Georgian playhouse with the remains of its Old Planter's Hotel (circa 1809). The active theater, draped in red-velvet curtains and bearing wonderful woodwork, welcomes you to look around when shows are not under way. ✉ *135 Church St., Market area* ☎ *843/720–3968* 🌐 *www.charlestonstage.com* 🎟 *Free* ⏲ *Weekdays 10–4.*

7 **Emanuel African Methodist Episcopal Church.** Home of the South's oldest AME congregation, the church had its beginnings in 1818. Authorities closed it in 1822 when they suspected freedman Denmark Vesey used the sanctuary to plan a massive slave uprising. The church reopened on the present site after the Civil War ended, in 1865. ✉ *110 Calhoun St., Upper King* ☎ *843/722–2561* 🎟 *Donations accepted* ⏲ *Daily 9–4.*

22 **French Protestant (Huguenot) Church.** The tiny Gothic-style church is the only one in the country still using the original Huguenot liturgy. A special spring service is delivered in French. Services are held at 10:30 Sunday. ✉ *136 Church St., Market area* ☎ *843/722–4385* 🌐 *www.frenchhuguenotchurch.org* ⏲ *Mid-Mar.–mid-June and mid-Sept.–mid-Nov., Mon.–Thurs. 10–4, Fri. 10–1.*

★ 25 **Fort Sumter National Monument.** On a man-made island in Charleston Harbor Confederate forces fired the first shot of the Civil War on April 12, 1861. After a 34-hour bombardment, Union forces surrendered and Confederate troops occupied Sumter, which became a symbol of Southern resistance. The Confederacy held the fort, despite almost continual bombardment, for nearly four years; when it was finally evacuated, the place was a heap of rubble. Today, the National Park Service oversees the Fort Sumter National Monument complex. *Park offices* ✉ *1214 Middle St., Sullivan's Island* ☎ *843/883–3124* 🌐 *www.nps.gov/fosu* ⏲ *Week-*

days 7:30–5:30..The **Fort Sumter Liberty Square Visitor Center,** next to the South Carolina Aquarium, contains exhibits on the Civil War. This is one of the departure points for ferries headed to Fort Sumter itself. ✉ *340 Concord St., Upper King* ☎ *843/883–3123* 🎫 *Free* 🕘 *Daily 8:30–5.*Rangers conduct guided tours of the restored **Fort Sumter,** which includes a museum with historical displays. Tours begin at 9:30, noon, and 2:30 from March through November and at 11 and 2:30 from December through February, with some variation during Christmastime. To access the island the fort occupies, you have to take a ferry; boats depart from Liberty Square Visitor Center and from across Cooper's River Bridges at Patriot's Point in Mount Pleasant. ✉ *Charleston Harbor* ☎ *843/577–0242, 843/881–7337, or 800/789–3678 for Fort Sumter Tours Inc.* 🌐 *www.fortsumtertours.com* 🎫 *Fort free; $12 ferry ride* 🕘 *Apr.–early Sept., daily 10–5:30; early Sept.–Mar., daily 10–4.*

17 **Gibbes Museum of Art.** The collections of American art include notable 18th- and 19th-century portraits of Carolinians. There are Lowcountry-theme exhibits and touring shows. Don't miss the miniatures—shadow boxes set in dark-panel walls are intricately decorated with miniature fabrics and furnishing. ✉ *135 Meeting St., Market area* ☎ *843/722–2706* 🌐 *www.gibbesmuseum.org* 🎫 *$7* 🕘 *Tues.–Sat. 10–5, Sun. 1–5.*

need a break?

Take a break and enjoy a Southern breakfast or a sandwich lunch at **Joseph's** (✉ 129 Meeting St., Market area ☎ 843/958–8500), next door to the Gibbes Museum. Slip into the tiny back courtyard for alfresco dining.

4 **Joseph Manigault House.** A National Historic Landmark and an outstanding example of federal architecture, this home was designed by Charleston architect Gabriel Manigault in 1803 and is noted for its carved-wood mantels, elaborate plasterwork, and garden "folly." Furnishings are antiques from France, England, and Charleston; the pieces of rare tricolor Wedgwood are noteworthy. ✉ *350 Meeting St., Upper King* ☎ *843/722–2996* 🌐 *www.charlestonmuseum.org* 🎫 *$8; combination ticket with Charleston Museum $14, with museum and Heyward-Washington House $18* 🕘 *Mon.–Sat. 10–5, Sun. 1–5.*

10 **Kahal Kadosh Beth Elohim Reform Temple.** Considered one of the nation's finest examples of Greek Revival architecture, this temple was built in 1840 to replace an earlier one. The original was the birthplace of American reform Judaism in 1824 and was destroyed by fire. Tours are conducted six days a week. ✉ *90 Hasell St., Market area* ☎ *843/723–1090* 🌐 *www.kkbe.org* 🎫 *Free* 🕘 *Weekdays 10–noon, Sun. 12:30–3:45.*

13 **Market Hall.** Built in 1841, this imposing landmark was modeled after the Temple of Nike in Athens. The hall contains the **Confederate Museum,** in which the United Daughters of the Confederacy preserve and display flags, uniforms, swords, and other Civil War memorabilia. ✉ *188 Meeting St., Market area* ☎ *843/723–1541* 🎫 *$5* 🕘 *Tues.–Sat. 11–3:30.*

6 **Old Citadel Building.** A fortresslike building on Marion Square was the first home of the Citadel (the Carolina Military College) and once

housed troops and arms. This 1822 structure is now the Embassy Suites Historic Charleston. The present-day Citadel is in Hampton Park on the Ashley River. ✉ *341 Meeting St., Upper King* ☎ *843/723–6900.*

14 Old City Market. This area is often called the Slave Market because it's where house slaves once shopped for produce and fish. Today stalls are lined with restaurants and shops selling children's toys, Charleston souvenirs, crafts, leather goods, and more. Local "basket ladies" weave and sell sweet-grass, pine-straw, and palmetto-leaf baskets—a craft passed down through generations from their West African ancestors. ✉ *North and South Market Sts. between Meeting and E. Bay Sts., Market area* ⏲ *Daily 9–dusk.*

15 Old Powder Magazine. Built in 1713, the oldest public building in South Carolina is the only one that remains from the time of the Lords Proprietors. The city's volatile—and precious—gun powder was kept here during the Revolutionary War. The building was designed to implode if detonated (and thus save Charleston). It is not open to the public. ✉ *79 Cumberland St., Market area.*

19 St. John's Lutheran Church. This Greek Revival church with delicate wrought-iron gates was completed in 1817 for a congregation that was established in 1742. Its most noteworthy leader, Dr. John Bachman, served as preacher 1815–74 and was known for ministering to local African-Americans and for collaborating on two books with naturalist—and friend—John James Audubon. ✉ *5 Clifford St., Market area* ☎ *843/723–2426* 🌐 *www.stjohnscharleston.org.*

11 St. Mary's Catholic Church. Beautiful stained glass, wall paintings, and an interesting cemetery tucked between stone walls are highlights of the earliest Roman Catholic church in the Carolinas and Georgia. The white-pillar structure was constructed in 1839. ✉ *95 Hasell St., Market area* ☎ *843/722–7696* ⏲ *By appointment.*

16 St. Philip's (Episcopal) Church. The namesake of Church Street, this graceful late-Georgian building is the second on its site: the congregation's first building burned down in 1835 and was rebuilt in 1838. During the Civil War, the steeple was a target for shelling; one Sunday a shell exploded in the church yard—the minister continued his sermon. Afterward, the congregation gathered elsewhere for the duration of the war. Notable Charlestonians (like John C. Calhoun) can be found in the graveyard, which flanks the church and continues across the street. ✉ *146 Church St., Market area* ☎ *843/722–7734* 🌐 *www.stphilipschurchsc.org* ⏲ *Church, weekdays 9–11 and 1–4; cemetery, daily 9–4.*

★ **24 South Carolina Aquarium.** The 380,000-gallon Great Ocean Tank has the tallest aquarium window in North America. Exhibits display more than 10,000 living organisms, representing more than 500 species. You travel through the five major regions of the Southeast Appalachian Watershed as found in South Carolina: the Blue Ridge Mountains, the Piedmont, the coastal plain, the coast, and the ocean. Little ones can pet stingrays at one touch tank and horseshoe crabs and conchs at another. ✉ *100 Aquarium Wharf, Upper King* ☎ *843/720–1990 or 800/722–6455*

🌐 *www.scaquarium.org* 🎫 *$15* ⏲ *Mid-Apr.–mid-Aug., Mon.–Sat. 9–5, Sun. noon–5; mid-Aug.–mid-Apr., Mon.–Sat. 9–4, Sun. noon–4.*

20 **Unitarian Church.** Completed in 1787, this church was remodeled in the mid-19th century using plans inspired by the Chapel of Henry VII in Westminster Abbey. The Gothic fan-tracery ceiling was added during that renovation. An entrance to the church grounds is at 161½–163 King Street and leads to a secluded, overgrown Victorian-style graveyard that invites contemplation. Sunday service is at 11 AM. ✉ *8 Archdale St., Market area* ☎ *843/723–4617* 🎫 *Free* ⏲ *Sanctuary Fri. and Sat. 10–1, graveyard daily 9–5.*

1 **Visitor Information Center.** The center's 20-minute film *Forever Charleston* is a fine introduction to the city. A $34.95 Charleston Heritage Passport, sold here, allows admission to the Gibbes Museum of Art, Nathaniel Russell House, Edmondston-Alston House, Aiken-Rhett House, Drayton Hall, and Middleton Place. The film starts on the half hour. Garage parking is $1 per hour. ✉ *375 Meeting St., Upper King* ☎ *843/853–8000 or 800/868–8118* 🌐 *www.charlestoncvb.com.* 🎫 *Center free, film $2.50* ⏲ *Mar.–Oct., daily 8:30–5:30; Nov.–Feb., daily 8:30–5.*

★ 23 **Waterfront Park.** Enjoy the fishing pier's porch-style swings, rest in the bench-filled gardens that overlook Charleston Harbor, or stroll the waterside jogging path of this relaxing park. You can even douse yourself in a water sculpture fountain to get refreshed on hot summer days. The park is at the foot of Vendue Range, along the east side of Charleston Harbor and Cooper River. ✉ *Prioleau St., Market area* ☎ *843/724–7321* 🎫 *Free* ⏲ *Daily 6 AM–midnight.*

City Gallery at Waterfront Park is an expansive, open venue that affords fantastic views of the Harbor and fountain. Regional, national, and international artists are shown here. ✉ *34 Prioleau St., Market area* ☎ *843/958–6484* 🎫 *Free* ⏲ *Tues.–Fri. 11–6, weekends noon–5.*

need a break?

Climb to the upper deck of the **Rooftop Restaurant and Bar at Vendue Inn** (✉ 23 Vendue Range, Market area ☎ 843/577–7970 or 800/845–7900) for a great view of the harbor and Waterfront Park, and to relax with drinks and appetizers.

The Battery & South of Broad

Locals have long joked that just off the Battery (at Battery Street and Murray Boulevard), the Ashley and Cooper rivers join to form the Atlantic Ocean. Such a lofty proclamation speaks volumes about the area's rakish flair. To take in their pride and joy, head to the point of the downtown peninsula. Here, handsome mansions surrounded by elaborate gardens greet incoming boats and passersby. The look is reminiscent of the West Indies with good reason: before coming to the Carolinas in the late 17th century, many early British colonists had first settled on Barbados and other Caribbean isles where homes with high ceilings and broad porches (or piazzas) at each level caught the sea breezes. Charleston's single houses (single-room wide, two- to four-story homes built with a shallow profile toward the street) emerged for the same reason—to take advantage of any cool wind.

The heavily residential area south of Broad Street and west of the Battery brims with beautiful private homes, most of which bear plaques with a short written description of the property's history. Mind your manners, but feel free to peek through iron gates and fences at the verdant displays in elaborate gardens. Although an open gate once signified guests were welcome to venture inside, that time has mostly passed, but you never know when an invitation to look around from a friendly owner-gardener might come your way. Several of the city's lavish house museums call this famously affluent neighborhood home.

Numbers in the text correspond to numbers in the margin and on the Charleston map.

a good walk

Begin your walk at the northeast corner of Meeting and Broad streets, where the **City Hall** 26 has some historical displays and portraits. **St. Michael's Episcopal Church** 27, the city's oldest surviving church, is across the street in St. Michael's Alley. Two blocks east down Broad Street is the **Old Exchange Building & Provost Dungeon** 28, which held prisoners during the American Revolution. From there turn south on East Bay Street and then west on Trodd Street to get to **Heyward-Washington House** 29 on Church Street. Next to it is picturesque Cabbage Row, the inspiration for Catfish Row in *Porgy and Bess*. The **Nathaniel Russell House** 30 is farther west on Trodd and south on Meeting Street; it has a beautiful free garden, terrific house tour docents, and a well-stocked gift shop. Follow Water Street to East Battery to reach **Edmondston-Alston House** 31. The house overlooks Charleston's famous **Battery** 32 and Charleston Harbor. A park bench in the shade of **White Point Gardens** 33, so named because of the bleached whiteness of oyster shells left here by Native Americans, makes a splendid spot for a rest with a view.

TIMING Plan to spend at least two to four hours doing this walk, depending on your pace and which house tours you go on. Wear good walking shoes, because the sidewalks, Battery promenade, and brick streets are very uneven. Take a bottle of water, or sip from the fountains in White Point Gardens, for there are practically no shops in this area off Broad Street. In spring and summer the gardens are in full glory. And in winter and fall the homes dress in their holiday finest. Twilight strolls year-round create a Dickenslike experience, with homes lit from within showing off cozy scene after scene.

What to See

32 **Battery.** From the intersection of Water Street and East Battery you can look east of the sea wall and promenade toward the city's grandest, most photographed mansions; look west for views of Charleston Harbor and Fort Sumter. Walk south along East Battery to White Point Gardens, where the street curves and becomes Murray Boulevard. This is where the Ashley and Cooper rivers meet. ✉ *East Bay St. and Murray Blvd., South of Broad.*

Fodor's Choice ★

26 **City Hall.** The intersection of Meeting and Broad streets is known as the Four Corners of Law, representing the laws of nation, state, city, and church. On the northeast corner is the graceful, pale pink City Hall, dating from 1801. The second-floor council chambers double as a museum whose curator will explain the historical displays and portraits, including John Trumbull's 1791 satirical portrait of George Washington and Samuel F. B. Morse's likeness of James Monroe. ✉ *80 Broad St., South of Broad* ☎ *843/577–6970 or 843/724–3799* 🎫 *Free* ⏲ *Weekdays 8:30–5.*

off the beaten path

COLONIAL LAKE – Joggers, walkers, and folks looking for a tranquillity in the city, flock to this small man-made lake that rises and lowers with the tides. A wide sidewalk circles the lake and there are plentiful trees and benches. Neighboring is a public park with tennis courts, a playground, and basketball court. In the late 19th century, Colonial Common (as the area was then called) was a popular gathering place for Victorian Charleston. ✉ *Ashley and Rutledge Aves. to the east and west, Broad and Beaufain Sts. to the north and south, South of Broad* ☎ *843/724–7327.*

31 **Edmondston-Alston House.** First built in 1825 in late-federal style, the Edmondston-Alston House was transformed into the imposing Greek Revival structure you see today during the 1840s. Tours of the home—furnished with antiques, portraits, Piranesi prints, silver, and fine china—are informative and in-depth. The home commands an excellent view of Charleston Harbor. ✉ *21 E. Battery, South of Broad* ☎ *843/722–7171* 🌐 *www.middletonplace.org* 🎫 *$10; combination ticket with Middleton Place $36* ⏲ *Tues.–Sat. 10–4:30, Sun. and Mon. 1:30–4:30.*

29 **Heyward-Washington House.** The area where rice planter Daniel Heyward built his home (1772) is believed to have been the inspiration for DuBose Heyward's book *Porgy,* and resulting folk opera *Porgy and Bess.* Once a mix of tenements and mansions known as Cabbage Row, the neighborhood is central to Charleston's African-American history. And the home has a history of its own: President George Washington stayed in the house during his 1791 visit. The fine period furnishings include those made by local craftsmen such as Thomas Elfe. The Holmes Bookcase (circa 1780) is one of the finest remaining American furniture pieces of its era because of its excellent condition and superb craftsmanship. Pay attention to the restored 18th-century kitchen, as it's the only one like it in Charleston open to the public. ⇨ **Charleston Museum** owns and runs the house museum. ✉ *87 Church St., South of Broad* ☎ *843/722–2996* 🌐 *www.charlestonmuseum.org* 🎫 *$8; combination ticket with Charleston Museum $14, with museum and Joseph Manigault House $18* ⏲ *Mon.–Sat. 10–5, Sun. 1–5.*

★ 30 **Nathaniel Russell House.** One of the nation's finest examples of Adam-style architecture, the Nathaniel Russell House was built in 1808. The interior is distinguished by its ornate detailing, its lavish period furnishings, and the "free flying" circular staircase that spirals three stories with no visible support. The garden is well worth a stroll. ✉ *51 Meeting St., South of Broad* ☎ *843/724–8481* 🌐 *www.historiccharleston.org* 🎟 *$8; garden free; combination ticket with Aiken-Rhett House $14* ⏲ *Mon.–Sat. 10–5, Sun. 2–5.*

28 **Old Exchange Building & Provost Dungeon.** Originally a customs house with a waterside entrance, this building was used by the British to house prisoners during the Revolutionary War. Today costumed guides and robotic mannequins brings the revolutionary era to life. ✉ *122 E. Bay St., South of Broad* ☎ *843/727–2165* 🌐 *www.oldexchange.com* 🎟 *$8* ⏲ *Daily 9–5.*

27 **St. Michael's Episcopal Church.** The first cornerstone of St. Michael's was set in place in 1752, making it Charleston's oldest surviving church. Through the years other elements were added: the steeple clock and bells (1764); the organ (1768); the font (1771); and the altar (1892). The pulpit—original to the church—was designed to maximize natural acoustics. ✉ *14 St. Michael's Alley, South of Broad* ☎ *843/723–0603* 🌐 *www.stmichaelschurch.net* ⏲ *Weekdays 9–4:30, Sat. 9–noon.*

need a break?

On your way down Broad Street toward Church Street, duck into the dark-panel, tin-ceiling **Blind Tiger Pub** (✉ 38 Broad St., South of Broad ☎ 843/577–0088) for a beer and a snack, or sit on the patio out back.

★ 33 **White Point Gardens.** Pirates once hung from gallows here; now it's a serene park, with a bandstand, Charleston benches—small wood-slat benches with cast-iron sides—and views of the harbor and Fort Sumter. Children love to climb on the replica cannon and pile of cannonballs. ✉ *Murray Blvd. and E. Battery, South of Broad* ☎ *843/724–7327* ⏲ *Weekdays 9–5, Sat. 9–noon.*

Mount Pleasant & Vicinity

East of Charleston across the Cooper River Bridge, via U.S. 17N, is the town of Mount Pleasant, named not for a mountain or a hill but for a plantation in England from which some of the area's settlers hailed. In its Old Village neighborhood are antebellum homes and a sleepy, old-time town center with a drugstore where patrons sidle up to the soda fountain and lunch counter for egg salad sandwiches and floats. Along Shem Creek, where the local fishing fleet brings in the daily catch, several seafood restaurants serve the area's freshest (and most deftly fried) seafood. Other attractions in the area include military and maritime museums, plantations, and, farther north, the Cape Romain National Wildlife Refuge.

a good tour

Driving is the name of the game in Mount Pleasant, as area attractions are spread out among suburban housing and commercial strip developments. Naval and military history buffs might choose to visit the ships at the large maritime museum, **Patriots Point** to the right on Coleman Boulevard after you cross the Cooper River Bridge from Charleston. Continue along Coleman Boulevard, past boat-lined docks and restaurants at Shem Creek; a nice detour is a drive through the **Old Village** neighborhood, right at Whilden Street. Return to Coleman Boulevard and head to Sullivan's Island; follow the signs to **Fort Moultrie,** where one of the first successful battles of the Revolutionary War was fought.

If you want to explore plantation history, drive out U.S. 17N to **Boone Hall Plantation** (8 mi), tour the home, and pass under its famous Avenue of Oaks. **Charles Pinckney National Historic Site,** across Long Point Road, has a tour that examines the role of slaves on a plantation. Bring a picnic and rent bikes to the north at **Palmetto Islands County Park,** along Boone Hall Creek; bring a swimsuit for Splash Island, a small water park.

Nature lovers can travel the 35-mi drive north to take a ferry ride and visit Bull Island, part of the **Cape Romain National Wildlife Refuge,** one of the nation's most pristine wildlife areas.

TIMING Plan to explore Mount Pleasant & Vicinity sights independently or combine a couple of sights in one side-trip. You need three days to see all the attractions here; with one day or less, you'll need to narrow your choices.

What to See

★ **Boone Hall Plantation and Garden.** A ½-mi drive through a live oak alley draped in Spanish moss introduces you to the still-operating plantation, the oldest of its kind in the country. Tour the 1935 mansion, the butterfly pavilion, the heirloom rose garden, and nine antebellum-era brick slave cabins. Stroll along the winding river, tackle the fields to pick your own strawberries and more, or dine in Serena's Kitchen, the on-site restaurant that serves Southern fare. *North and South, Queen,* and Nicholas Sparks' *The Notebook* were filmed here. ✉ *1235 Long Point Rd., off U.S. 17N, Mount Pleasant, 11 mi east of Charleston* ☎ *843/884–4371* 🌐 *www.boonehallplantation.com* 🎫 *$14.50* ⏲ *Apr.–early Sept., Mon.–Sat. 8:30–6:30, Sun. 1–5; early Sept.–Mar., Mon.–Sat. 9–5, Sun. 1–4.*

off the beaten path

BASKET LADIES – Drive along U.S. 17N, through and beyond Mount Pleasant to find the basket ladies set up at rickety roadside stands, weaving sweet-grass, pine-straw, and palmetto-leaf baskets. Baskets typically cost less on this stretch than in downtown Charleston, but remember you're buying a nearly lost art. Each purchase supports the artisans, who are becoming fewer and fewer each year as the sweet grass harvest becomes less and less plentiful.

Cape Romain National Wildlife Refuge. A grouping of barrier islands and salt marshes, this 60,000-acre refuge is one of the most outstanding in the country. The **Sewee Visitor & Environmental Education Center** has information and exhibits on the refuge, trails, and rescued or breeding live birds of prey and red wolves. From here you can take a ferry to Bull Island ($30) for a day visit. The island is a nearly untouched wilderness; the beach here, strewn with bleached driftwood, is nicknamed Boneyard Beach. ✉ *5821 U.S. 17N, Awendaw* ☎ *843/928–3368* 🌐 *http://capromain.fws.gov* 🎫 *Free* ⏲ *Tues.–Sun. 9–5.*

Charles Pinckney National Historic Site. Across the street from Boone Hall Plantation, this is the only protected remnant of the country estate of Charles Pinckney, drafter and signer of the Constitution. A self-guided tour focuses on African-American farm life, including the plantation owner–slave relationship. You can also tour an 1820s tidewater cottage. ✉ *1254 Long Point Rd., off U.S. 17N, Mount Pleasant* ☎ *843/881–5516* 🖷 *843/881–7070* 🌐 *www.nps.gov* 🎟 *Free* 🕒 *Daily 9–5.*

Fort Moultrie National Monument. Here Colonel William Moultrie's South Carolinians repelled a British assault in one of the first Patriot victories of the Revolutionary War. Completed in 1809, this is the third fort on this site at **Sullivan's Island,** reached on Route 703 off U.S. 17N (10 mi southeast of Charleston). A 20-minute film tells the history of the fort. Self-guided tours and interpretive signs fill out the experience. ✉ *1214 Middle St., Sullivan's Island* ☎ *843/883–3123* 🌐 *www.nps.gov* 🎟 *$3* 🕒 *Daily 9–5.*

Old Village. This neighborhood is distinguished by white-picket-fenced colonial cottages, antebellum manses, tiny neighborhood churches, and restored (or new) waterfront homes with pricetags in the millions. It's a lovely area to stroll or bike. The Blessing of the Fleet seafood festival takes place each April at Alhambra Hall and Park, on Middle Street, which is a top picnic spot year-round. ✣ *Bounded by Church Street to the west, water to the east, Shem Creek to the South, and Alhambra Park to the North.*

Palmetto Islands County Park. On this 943-acre park, there's a Big Toy playground, a 2-acre pond, paved trails, an observation tower, and marsh boardwalks. Splash Island ($7) is a small water park on-site. You can rent bicycles and paddleboats. ✉ *Long Point Rd., ½ mi past Boone Hall Plantation, off U.S. 17N, Mount Pleasant* ☎ *843/884–0832* 🌐 *www.ccprc.com* 🎟 *$2* 🕒 *Apr., Sept., and Oct., daily 9–6; May–Aug., daily 9–7; Nov.–Feb., daily 10–5; Mar., daily 10–6.*

★ **Patriots Point.** Tour actual naval vessels at the world's largest naval and maritime museum, which also houses the Congressional Medal of Honor Museum. Ships berthed here include the aircraft carrier USS *Yorktown,* the World War II submarine USS *Clamagore,* the destroyer USS *Laffey,* and the Coast Guard cutter *Ingham,* responsible for sinking a U-boat during World War II. A Vietnam exhibit showcases naval air and watercraft used in the war, and includes artifacts from North and South Vietnam. ✉ *Foot of Cooper River Bridge, Mount Pleasant* ☎ *843/884–2727* 🌐 *www.patriotspoint.org* 🎟 *$13* 🕒 *Apr.–Sept., daily 9–7:30; Oct.–Mar., daily 9–6:30.*

Sullivan's Island. Spend the day relaxing on the beach or bicycling throughout Sullivan's Island, a residential community of early-20th-century beach houses. ⇨ **Fort Moultrie** sits at the northern end of the island. ✉ *Rte. 703 off U.S. 17N, 8 mi southeast of Charleston.*

West of the Ashley River

Ashley River Road, Route 61, begins a few miles northwest of downtown Charleston, over the Ashley River Bridge. Sights are spread out along the way and those who love history, old homes, and gardens may need several days to explore places like the Charles Towne Landing village museum, Drayton Hall, Middleton Place, and Magnolia Plantation and Gardens. Spring is a peak time for the flowers, although the gardens are in bloom throughout the year.

What to See

★ **Charles Towne Landing State Historic Site.** Commemorating the site of the original 1670 Charleston settlement, this park on Route 171 has a reconstructed village and fortifications, English park gardens with bicycle trails and walkways, and a replica 17th-century vessel moored in the creek. In the animal park native species roam freely—among them alligators, bison, pumas, bears, and wolves. Bicycle rentals are available. The park has begun a $5 million renovation that includes a comprehensive archaeological dig and a new visitor center–museum. ✉ *1500 Old Towne Rd. (Rte. 171), off Rte. 61, West Ashley, 3 mi northwest of downtown Charleston* ☎ *843/852–4200* 🌐 *www.southcarolinaparks.com* *$5* *Daily 8:30–5.*

★ **Drayton Hall.** Considered the nation's finest example of unspoiled Georgian-Palladian architecture, this mansion is the only plantation house on the Ashley River to have survived the Civil War. A National Trust historic site, built between 1738 and 1742, it's an invaluable lesson in history as well as in architecture. Drayton Hall has been left unfurnished to highlight the original plaster moldings, opulent hand-carved woodwork, and other ornamental details. Watch *Connections,* a media presentation that details the conditions under which slaves were brought from Africa. You can also see copies of documents that recorded the buying and selling of local plantation slaves. Tours depart on the hour. ✉ *3380 Ashley River Rd., West Ashley, 9 mi northwest of downtown Charleston* ☎ *843/769–2600* 🌐 *www.draytonhall.org* *$12* *Mar.–Oct., daily 10–4; Nov.–Feb., daily 10–3.*

Magnolia Plantation and Gardens. The extensive informal garden, begun in 1685, has evolved into an overflowing collection of plants that bloom year-round, including a vast array of azaleas and camellias. You can take a nature tram ($7) or a nature boat ($7) for an overall tour. Rent a canoe ($7 per hour) to paddle through the 125-acre Waterfowl Refuge, or explore the 30-acre Audubon Swamp Garden ($5) along boardwalks and bridges. You can walk or rent bikes ($7 per hour) to traverse the more than 500 acres of wildlife trails. The grounds also hold a petting zoo and a miniature-horse ranch. The original house was burned down during the Civil War. You can tour ($7) the current plantation house (mid-1800s), which was moved here from Summerville after the war. The home was taken apart, floated down the Ashley River, reassembled, and completed after four years. ✉ *3550 Ashley River Rd., north of Drayton Hall, West Ashley, 13 mi northwest of downtown Charleston* ☎ *843/571–1266 or 800/367–3517* 🌐 *www.magnoliaplantation.com* *Grounds $13* *Daily 8–5:30.*

Fodor's Choice ★ **Middleton Place.** Blooms of all seasons form floral *allées* (alleys) along terraced lawns, and around ornamental lakes shaped like butterfly wings. Much of the year, the landscaped gardens, begun in 1741, are ablaze with camellia, magnolia, azalea, and rose blossoms. A large part of the mansion was destroyed during the Civil War, but the south wing has been restored and houses impressive collections of silver, furniture, paintings, and historic documents. In the stable yard craftspeople use authentic tools and equipment to demonstrate spinning, blacksmith work, and other domestic skills from the plantation era. Farm animals, peacocks, and other creatures roam freely. The Middleton Place restaurant serves Lowcountry specialties for lunch daily; the gift shop carries local arts, crafts, and souvenirs; and the garden shop sells rare seedlings of plants found on the grounds. You can sign up for kayak, bike, wagon, or horseback tours, and you can stay overnight at the modern, Danish-style inn, with its floor-to-ceiling windows that splendidly frame the Ashley River (access to the gardens is included in the room price). ✉ *4300 Ashley River Rd., 4 mi north of Magnolia Plantation, West Ashley, 17 mi northwest of downtown Charleston* ☎ *843/556–6020 or 800/782–3608* 🌐 *www.middletonplace.org* 🎫 *Grounds $20; house tour $10 extra* ⏲ *Grounds daily 9–5; house tours Tues.–Sun. 10–4:30, Mon. noon–4:30.*

off the beaten path

ANGEL OAK – This magnificent live oak is believed to be more than 1,400 years old. Its massive branches slope gently, reaching armlike to the ground, and create 17,000 square feet of shade. Angel Oak, named for the plantation that was here, was once a gathering point for area slaves. ✉ *3688 Angel Oak Rd., off Rte. 700, Johns Island, 12 mi southwest of Charleston* ☎ *843/559–3496* 🎫 *Free* ⏲ *Mon.–Sat. 9–5.*

CAW CAW INTERPRETIVE CENTER – Eight miles of historical, interpretive trails, including a 1,200-foot marsh boardwalk, spread out across the 650-acre cypress swamp park that was once a part of a 1700s rice plantation. The information on rice cultivation is especially detailed. Gullah storytelling, African-American music and craft demonstrations, discussions of the vital role slaves played in the rice fields are part of the 900 programs the center sponsors annually. ✉ *5200 Savannah Hwy. (U.S. 17), Ravenel, 15 mi west of Charleston* ☎ *843/889–8898* 🌐 *www.ccprc.com* 🎫 *$4* ⏲ *Wed.–Fri. 9–3, weekends 9–5.*

SPORTS & THE OUTDOORS

Beaches

The Charleston area's mild climate generally is conducive to swimming from April through October. All public and private beaches are family-oriented, with a choice of water sports, sunbathing, shelling, fishing, or quiet moonlight strolling. The resort hotels on the islands east of Charleston claim much of the oceanfront as private beach. Public beaches, run by the Charleston County Parks & Recreation Commission, generally have lifeguards in season, snack bars, restrooms and dressing areas, outdoor showers, umbrella and chair rental, and large parking lots.

CloseUp

CHARLESTON PRESERVED

IT'S EASY TO THINK CHARLESTON *is a neverland, sweetly arrested in pastel perfection. But look at Civil War–era images of the Battery mansions on East Bay Street, one of the most photographed areas in town today, and you see the surrounding homes disfigured with crippling battle scars. Because of the poverty that followed the Civil War, on the whole locals simply couldn't afford to build anew from the late 1860s through the latter part of the 20th century, so they did what they could to put the homes they had back together.*

In the 1920s it was community activism that rescued the old homes from being destroyed. According to Jonathan Poston, author of Buildings of Charleston, *the preservation movement began when an Esso gas station was slated to take the place of the Joseph Manigault House. Citizens formed the Society for the Preservation of Old Dwellings (the first such group in the nation) and saved what's now a popular house museum. By 1931 Charleston's City Council had created the Board of Architectural Review (BAR), and designated the historic district protected from unrestrained development—two more national firsts. The Historic Charleston Foundation was established in 1947, and preservation is now second-nature (by law).*

As you explore, look for Charleston single houses: a single room–wide, these houses were built with the narrow end streetside and multistory south or southwestern porches to catch prevailing breezes. Single houses are thought to have one of the most naturally efficient designs for air circulation. Shaded by overhangs, cool air seeps into open windows on the porch (often called a piazza), and moves throughout the house. Look at the northern wall of a single house (the wall that faces a neighbor's garden and piazza), and you see few windows original to the structure. That's a tipping of the hat to privacy, a little urban built-in gentility.

Note the many "carriage houses" around town. While a handful actually housed horses and carriages, most were urban slave quarters or kitchen houses, originally set apart from the main houses for social or safety reasons. Many have been converted into guest quarters, B&Bs, or posh rental units.

Another popular home design was the freedman's cottage. Similar to a Charleston single house with its north–south orientation, southwestern side porch, and false streetfront "front" door, these homes are on one floor and usually have a relatively open plan.

You see numerous architectural vestiges along Charleston's preserved streets. Many houses have plaques detailing their history, and others have Carolopolis Awards given for fine restoration work. Old fire insurance plaques are more rare; they denote the company that insured the home and that would extinguish the flames if a fire broke out. Notice the bolt heads and washers that dot house facades along the Battery; some are in the shape of circles or stars, and others are capped with lion heads. These were added after the earthquake of 1886; they straightened sagging houses when tightened via a crank under the floorboards.

The streetside slabs of marble or stone are horse mounts, and boot scrapes are set in the sidewalk beside the front doors of many homes. Note the iron spikes that line the tops of some residential gates, doors, walls, and windows. Serving the same purpose as razor wire atop prison fences, most of these cheveux de frise *(French for frizzy hair) were added after a thwarted 1822 slave rebellion, to deter break-in—or escape.*

The public **Kiawah Beachwalker Park,** on the west end of Kiawah Island (which is otherwise a private resort), has about 500 feet of deep beach. ✉ *Beachwalker Dr., Kiawah Island, 28 mi southwest of Charleston* ☎ *843/768–2395 or 843/768–4386* 🎫 *$5 per car* ⏲ *Apr. and Oct., weekends 10–6; Mar., weekends 10–5; May–Aug., daily 10–7; Sept., daily 10–6.*

Trees, palmettos, and other natural foliage cover the interior, and there's a river that winds through **Folly Beach County Park.** The beach is more than six football fields long. ✉ *1100 W. Ashley Ave., off U.S. 17, Folly Island, 12 mi southwest of Charleston* ☎ *843/588–2426 or 843/768–4386* 🎫 *$5 per car* ⏲ *Apr., Sept., and Oct., daily 10–6; May–Aug., daily 9–7; Nov.–Mar., daily 10–5.*

Play beach volleyball or rent a raft at the 600-foot-long beach in the **Isle of Palms County Park.** ✉ *1 14th Ave., Isle of Palms, Mount Pleasant* ☎ *843/886–3863 or 843/768–4386* 🎫 *$5 per car* ⏲ *May–Aug., daily 9–7; Apr., Sept., and Oct., daily 10–6; Nov.–Mar., daily 10–5.*

Biking

The historic district is ideal for bicycling as long as you stay off the main, busy roads; many city parks have biking trails. Palmetto Islands County Park also has trails. You can rent bikes at the **Bicycle Shoppe** (✉ 280 Meeting St., Market area ☎ 843/722–8168 ✉ 1539 Johnnie Dodds Blvd., Mount Pleasant ☎ 843/884–7433). **Sea Island Cycle** (✉ 4053 Rhett Ave., North Charleston ☎ 843/747–2453) rents bikes and delivers to area islands.

Alligator Bike (✉ 1823 Paulette Dr., Johns Island ☎ 843/559–8200) will deliver to Kiawah and Seabrook islands. **Island Bike and Surf Shop** (✉ 3665 Bohicket Rd., Kiawah Island ☎ 843/768–1158) rents bikes and surfboards.

Fishing

Deep-sea fishing charters cost about $1,400 for 12 hours for a boatload of anglers, though rates drop for shorter trips. Fly-fishing guides generally charge between $300 and $400 for two people for a half-day.

Landlubbing anglers can rent gear ($8–$10) and cast a line at **Folly Beach County Park** (✉ 101 E. Arctic Ave., Folly Beach ☎ 843/795–3474 or 843/795–4386) fishing pier, which is more than 1,000 feet long.

Fly-fishers looking for a native guide do best calling **Captain Richard Stuhr** (✉ 547 Sanders Farm La., North Charleston ☎ 843/881–3179 🌐 www.captstuhr.com); he'll haul his boat to you.

March through October is the time to be fishing for yellowfin tuna in open waters on the 54-foot boat of **Aut-top-Sea Charters** (✉ Shem Creek docks, Mount Pleasant ☎ 843/454–0312 🌐 www.aut-top-sea.com). **Palmetto Charters** (✉ 224 Patriots Point Rd., Mount Pleasant ☎ 843/849–6004 🌐 www.palmettocharters.com) has guided trips that go offshore, and others that are closer inland. **Bohicket Yacht Charters** (✉ 1880 Andell Bluff Blvd., Seabrook Island ☎ 843/768–7294 🌐 www.bohicketboat.com) has half- and full-day charters on 24- to 48-foot boats. They also have dolphin-watching and dinner cruises.

Golf

One of the most appealing aspects of golfing in the Charleston area is the relaxing pace. With fewer golfers playing the courses than in golf destinations like Hilton Head, more choice starting times are available. Nonguests may play on a space-available basis at private island resorts, such as Kiawah Island, Seabrook Island, and Wild Dunes. Top private and public area courses listed here tend to be 18-hole, par-72. To find out about golf vacation packages in the area, contact **Charleston Golf Inc.** (☎ 800/774–4444 🌐 www.charlestongolfinc.com).

Tom Fazio designed the Links and the Harbor courses at **Wild Dunes Resort** (✉ 10001 Back Bay Dr., Isle of Palms, 18 mi east of Charleston ☎ 843/886–2180 ✉ 5881 Palmetto Dr., Isle of Palms ☎ 843/886–2301). **Seabrook Island Resort** (✉ Seabrook Island Rd., Seabrook Island, 24 mi southwest of Charleston ☎ 843/768–2529) has two championship courses: Crooked Oaks, by Robert Trent Jones Sr., and Ocean Winds, by Willard Byrd. The prestigious **Ocean Course** (✉ 1000 Ocean Course Dr., Kiawah Island, 28 mi southwest of Charleston ☎ 843/768–7272), designed by Pete Dye, was the site of the 1991 Ryder Cup. Of the three championship courses at **Kiawah Island Resort** (✉ 12 Kiawah Beach Dr., Kiawah Island, 28 mi southwest of Charleston), Gary Player designed Marsh Point; Tom Fazio designed Osprey Point; and Jack Nicklaus designed Turtle Point.

The public **Charleston Municipal Golf Course** (✉ 2110 Maybank Hwy., James Island, 5 mi southwest of Charleston ☎ 843/795–6517) is a walker-friendly course. **Patriots Point** (✉ 1 Patriots Point Rd., Mount Pleasant, 6 mi east of Charleston ☎ 843/881–0042) has a partly covered driving range and spectacular harbor views. **Shadowmoss Golf Club** (✉ 20 Dunvegan Dr., West Ashley, 12 mi northwest of Charleston ☎ 843/556–8251) is a well-marked, forgiving course with one of the best finishing holes in the area.

Charleston National Country Club (✉ 1360 National Dr., Mount Pleasant, 14 mi east of Charleston ☎ 843/884–7799) is well maintained and tends to be quiet on weekdays. The **Dunes West Golf Club** (✉ 3535 Wando Plantation Way, Mount Pleasant, 17 mi northwest of Charleston ☎ 843/856–9000) has great marshland views and lots of modulation on the greens. **Links at Stono Ferry** (✉ 4812 Stono Links Dr., Hollywood, 21 mi west of Charleston ☎ 843/763–1817) is a popular public course with great rates.

Horseback Riding

M & M Farms (✉ 1859 Hoover Rd., Huger, 29 mi north of Charleston ☎ 843/336–4886 🌐 www.mmfarms.com) leads guided trail rides into Francis Marion National Forest. **Seabrook Island Equestrian Center** (✉ Seabrook Island Rd., Seabrook Island, 24 mi southwest of Charleston ☎ 843/768–7541) is open to the public and has trail rides on the beach and through maritime forests. There are also pony rides for kids.

Kayaking

Kayak through marsh rivers and to outlying islands with **Coastal Expeditions** (✉ 514B Mill St., Mount Pleasant ☎ 843/884–7684). You can rent kayaks from **Middleton Place Plantation** (✉ 4300 Ashley River Rd., West Ashley ☎ 843/556–6020) and glide along the Ashley River.

Sailing

To hire a sailing charter, contact **AquaSafaris** (✉ Patriots Point Marina, Mount Pleasant ☎ 843/886–8133 🌐 www.aqua-safaris.com). To learn how to command a sailboat on your own, enlist with **Ocean Sailing Academy** (✉ 24 Patriots Point Rd., Mt. Pleasant ☎ 843/971–0700 🌐 www.oceansail.com).

Scuba Diving

Experienced divers can explore the **Cooper River Underwater Heritage Diving Trail,** upriver from Charleston. The 2-mi-long trail has six submerged sites, including ships that date to the Revolutionary War. Charters will run you out to the starting point. **Charleston Scuba** (✉ 335 Savannah Hwy., West Ashley ☎ 843/763–3483 🌐 www.charlestonscuba.com) has maps, rentals, excursion information, and charters trips to the Cooper River Trail.

Tennis

You can play for free at neighborhood courts, including several across the street from Colonial Lake and at the Isle of Palms Recreation Center on the Isle of Palms. Courts on the big island resort properties outside Charleston are generally open to the public. **Charleston Tennis Center** (✉ 19 Farmfield Ave., West Ashley ☎ 843/724–7402) is a city facility with lots of courts and locker rooms. **Maybank Tennis Center** (✉ 1880 Houghton Dr., James Island ☎ 843/406–8814) has lights on its six courts. The women's tennis Family Circle Cup takes place in April at the **Family Circle Tennis Center** (✉ 161 Seven Farms Dr., Daniel Island ☎ 843/534–2400). The 17 courts (13 clay, 4 hard) all have lights and are open to the public.

Water Sports

Motorized and nonmotorized watersport equipment is available for rent at the large island resorts surrounding Charleston. Kitesurfing is the latest intense watersport to hit local shores. Rent gear and take lessons from **AIR** (✉ 735 Coleman Blvd., Mount Pleasant ☎ 843/388–9300). **Halfmoon Outfitters** (✉ 425 Coleman Blvd., Mount Pleasant ☎ 843/881–9472) gives kite surfing lessons and sells and rents gear.

The longtime pros at **McKevlin's Surf Shop** (✉ 8 Center St., Folly Beach ☎ 843/588–2247) can teach you what you need to know about regular surfing at Folly Beach County Park.

WHERE TO EAT

Eating is a serious pastime in Charleston—for residents and visitors alike. You can dine at nationally renowned white-linen-and-crystal establishments serving the best of Southern nouveau, or if you prefer, a paired-down waterfront shack with some of the best fried grits south of the Mason-Dixon line. Big-name chefs in the area, including Bob Waggoner of Charleston Grill, Bob Carter of Peninsula Grill, Ken Vedrinkski of Sienna, Michael Kramer of McCrady's, Frank Lee of Slightly North of Broad, and Mike Lata of FIG, have earned reputations for their prowess in serving regional fare with a worldly flair. There are scores of unexpected places downtown, including French bistros and corner gourmet markets. If alfresco dining suits you best, aim for one of the many restaurant courtyards tucked away throughout the city, or you could do as the locals do, and forego the tables and grab takeout for a picnic at Waterfront Park, Marion Square, or White Point Gardens. Upscale corner groceries are common downtown.

Reservations are a good idea for dinner year-round, especially on weekends, as there is almost no off-season for tourism. Tables are especially hard to come by during the Southeastern Wildlife Expo (President's Day weekend in February) and the Spoleto Festival (late May to mid-June). The overall dress code is relaxed: unless noted below, casual khakis and an oxford or polo for men, casual slacks (or a skirt), top, and sandals for women work for any place you might pull up a chair.

Prices

A gastro tour here can get expensive. You might try several of the small plates that many establishments now serve as an option to keep costs down. In general, prices downtown are higher than those in restaurants over the bridges and on the islands.

WHAT IT COSTS

$$$$	$$$	$$	$	¢
over $22	$16–$22	$11–$16	$7–$11	under $7

Restaurant prices are for a main course at dinner, excluding sales tax of 7%–8%.

American–Casual

¢–$ ✕ **Lilies Gourmet Deli.** Stop into this fresh and friendly salad-and sandwich-café while shopping the middle King Street area. Try a wrap with spicy sweet potatoes, plum tomatoes, carrots, roasted red peppers, and spiced carrot spread on a jalapeño tortilla, or one with chicken breast, cherries, toasted walnuts, and blue cheese on a spinach tortilla. Prosciutto, Brie, Havarti, pesto, and pecan mayo are special options on the build-your-own sandwich menu. Smashed bananas and peanut butter drizzled with honey on a toasted bagel is just one of the breakfast options. ✉ *41B George St., College of Charleston* ☎ *843/722–6877* ▭ *AE, D, MC, V* ⏲ *Closed Sun. No dinner.*

¢ ✕ **Jack's.** Juicy burgers and just-right fries attract locals to Jack's no-frills, dinerlike place. Try the cheese-steak subs, the fat Reubens, and at breakfast, the made-from-scratch biscuits. The restaurant is one block off King Street's busiest shopping area. ✉ *41 George St., College of Charleston* ☎ *843/723–5237* ▭ *V, MC* ⏲ *Closed weekends. No dinner.*

¢ ✕ **Ye Olde Fashioned Ice Cream and Café.** Where else can you find a BLT with 10 slices of bacon or a triple-decker grilled-cheese sandwich? For dessert, dive into some of the city's largest, most gooped-up sundaes. There's both booth and counter service. Expect a line at the drive-through on summer nights. ✉ *474 Savannah Hwy. (U.S. 17S), West Ashley* ☎ *843/766–4854* ▭ *AE, D, MC, V.*

Contemporary

$$$$ ✕ **Circa 1886.** If you've got an occasion for champagne cocktails and foie gras, celebrate at this formal, conducive-to-conversation dining room in a carriage house behind the Wentworth Mansion. Crabmeat is the central ingredient in a signature soufflé, and fried green tomatoes offset the spices used on the grilled shrimp. Don't miss the crunchy sweet potatoes. ✉ *149 Wentworth St., Market area* ☎ *843/853–7828* *Reservations essential* ▭ *AE, D, DC, MC, V* ⊙ *No lunch.*

$$$$ ✕ **Robert's of Charleston.** Owner Robert is both a classically trained chef and a singer who belts out renditions of Broadway tunes in the intimate dining room. The set menu changes, but might include a mousse made from scallops, duck with grilled vegetables, and beef tenderloin with a red wine sauce, paired with accompanying wines. The restaurant is a family-run affair, which puts a warm spin on the experience; they'll even open additional nights on request. ✉ *182 E. Bay St., Market area* ☎ *843/577–7565* *Reservations essential* ▭ *D, MC, V* ⊙ *Closed Sun.–Wed. No lunch.*

$$$–$$$$ ✕ **Cypress.** From the owners of Magnolias and Blossom comes a sleek restaurant in a renovated 1834 brick-wall building. Large, rust-color leather booths, a ceiling with light sculptures that change color, and a "wine wall" of 5,000 bottles under glass, keep it contemporary. Sample the wines, but also try salads like the fabulous arugula with Gorgonzola, pecans, and apples. The green-tea–smoked duck is a good entrée choice. The fillet, cooked over hickory, comes with a Madeira wine sauce and a house-made soft cheese with herbs. ✉ *167 E. Bay St., Market area* ☎ *843/727–0111* *Reservations essential* ▭ *AE, DC, MC, V* ⊙ *No lunch.*

$$$–$$$$ Fodor'sChoice ★ ✕ **McCrady's.** Locals rave over this 1778 tavern restaurant, with exposed beam ceilings and brick arches, tucked into a brick alleyway. Dishes are national caliber in look and taste: potato gnocchi, tuna tartare, grouper with a creamy leek sauce and truffle oil, and a rack of lamb flavored with thyme and other herbs, for example. Chocolate martinis for two appeal to those with a sweet tooth. The encyclopedia-size wine list birthed the adjoining McCrady's Wine Bar, a more casual rendition of the restaurant that sells the same amazing vinos, plus appetizers. ✉ *2 Unity Alley, Market area* ☎ *843/577–0025* *Reservations essential* ▭ *AE, MC, V* ⊙ *No lunch.*

★ $$$–$$$$ ✕ **Peninsula Grill.** Eighteenth century–style portraits hang on walls covered in olive-green velvet. You sit beneath black-iron chandeliers feasting on appetizers such as tarts filled with salmon, grouper, and shrimp and entrées like Carolina quail with pecan-cornbread stuffing. The rack of lamb is covered in a benne (African sesame) seed crust. ✉ *112 N. Market St., Market area* ☎ *843/723–0700* *Reservations essential* *Jacket required* ▭ *AE, D, DC, MC, V* ⊙ *No lunch.*

★ $$$ ✕ **FIG.** Spend an evening at FIG for local, fresh-off-the-farm ingredients cooked with unfussy, flavorful finesse. The menu changes daily but heavy-rotation favorites include appetizers like fresh-dug Hakurei turnips

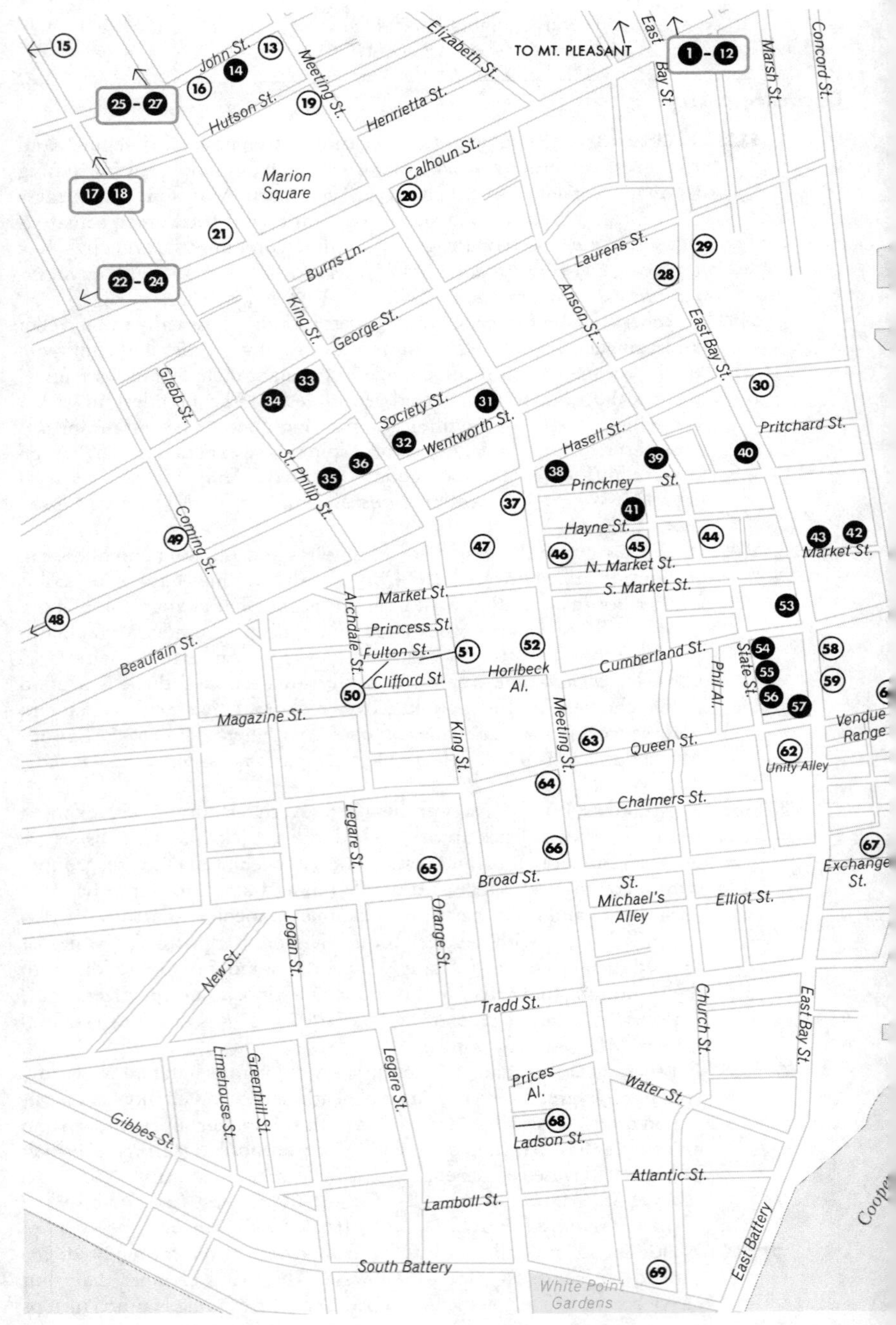
TO MT. PLEASANT
Elizabeth St.
John St.
Hutson St.
Meeting St.
Henrietta St.
Calhoun St.
Marion Square
East Bay St.
Marsh St.
Concord St.
Burns Ln.
Laurens St.
King St.
George St.
Anson St.
East Bay St.
Glebb St.
Society St.
Wentworth St.
Pritchard St.
Hasell St.
Pinckney St.
St. Philip St.
Hayne St.
Coming St.
Market St.
N. Market St.
S. Market St.
Market St.
Archdale St.
Princess St.
Fulton St.
Clifford St.
Beaufain St.
Horlbeck Al.
Cumberland St.
State St.
Phil Al.
Vendue Range
Magazine St.
King St.
Meeting St.
Queen St.
Unity Alley
Chalmers St.
Legare St.
Exchange St.
Broad St.
St. Michael's Alley
Elliot St.
Orange St.
Logan St.
New St.
Tradd St.
Church St.
East Bay St.
Limehouse St.
Greenhill St.
Legare St.
Prices Al.
Water St.
Gibbes St.
Ladson St.
Atlantic St.
Lamboll St.
East Battery
South Battery
White Point Gardens

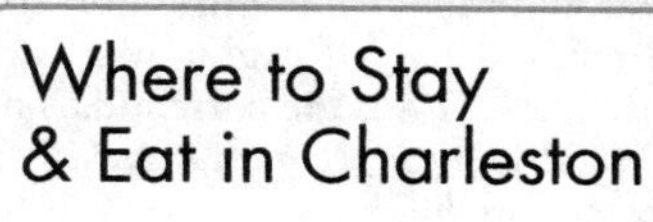

0 1/4 mile
0 400 meters

60
61
per River

KEY
3 *Hotels*
1 *Restaurants*

Restaurants

- Andolini's Pizza **36**
- Anson **44**
- Blossom **55**
- Boathouse Restaurant **1,2**
- Boulevard Diner **3**
- Carolina's **67**
- Charleson Grill **47**
- Circa 1886 ...... **48**
- Coast **14**
- Coco's **4**
- Cru Café **40**
- Cypress **56**
- Doe's Pita Plus **29**
- FIG **38**
- Fulton Five **50**
- Gaulart and Maliclet Café **66**
- Grill 225 ...... **53**
- Gullah Cuisine **5**
- Hank's Seafood **41**
- High Cotton **54**
- Hominy Grill **15**
- Il Cortile del Re **51**
- J. Bistro **6**
- Jack's **34**
- Jestine's Kitchen **31**
- Juanita Greenberg's Nacho Royale **17**
- Lillies Gourmet Deli **33**
- Magnolias **57**
- McCrady's **62**
- Peninsula Grill **46**
- Pita King **18**
- Robert's of Charleston **59**
- Sermet's Corner **32**
- Sienna **12**
- Slightly North of Broad **58**
- Sticky Fingers **37**
- 39 Rue de Jean **16**
- Union Hall **43**
- Vintage Restaurant & Wine Bar **42**
- The Wreck of the Richard and Charlene **7**
- Ye Olde Fashioned Ice Cream and Café **22**
- Yo Burrito **35**
- Zinc Bistro and Bar **11**

Hotels

- Andrew Pickney Inn **39**
- Ansonborough Inn **30**
- Cannonboro Inn and Ashley Inn **25**
- Charleston Place **47**
- Charleston's Historic Hostel & Inn **26**
- Doubletree Guest Suites Historic Charleston **45**
- 1837 Bed and Breakfast and Tea Room **49**
- Elliott House Inn **63**
- Embassy Suites Historic Charleston **19**
- Francis Marion Hotel **21**
- Hampton Inn-Historic District **11**
- Harbor View Inn **60**
- Hayne House **68**
- Holiday Inn Historic District **20**
- John Rutledge House Inn **65**
- Kiawah Island Golf Resort **23**
- Market Pavilion Hotel **53**
- Meeting Street Inn **52**
- Mills House Hotel **64**
- Not So Hostel **27**
- Old Village Post House **8**
- Phoebe Pember House **28**
- Planters Inn **46**
- Red Roof Inn Mount Pleasant **9**
- Seabrook Island Resort **24**
- Two Meeting Street **69**
- Vendue Inn **61**
- Wentworth Mansion **48**
- Wild Dunes **10**

with soft butter and sea salt, sides like beets roasted in sherry vinegar, and entrées like pork shank with limas and yellow corn grits, and scallops pan-seared and served on roasted and puréed cauliflower with pancetta. The bar scene is urbane and lively. This is the current darling of the city's hip dining-out crowd. ✉ *232 Meeting St., Market area* ☎ *843/805–5900* ▭ *AE, D, DC, MC, V* ⊙ *No lunch.*

$$–$$$ ✕ **Vintage Restaurant & Wine Bar.** A husband-and-wife team infuse this restaurant with their gentle hospitality. Expect low-key lighting—and fellow patrons—but high-impact food with a Provençal tinge. Try the filet mignon tartar and entrées like scallops with sweet peas, shallots, and bacon. The duck confit is served on wilted cabbage, with cherries. Eighty-plus by-the-glass choices make for an impressive wine list. ✉ *14 N. Market St., Market area* ☎ *843/577–0090* ▭ *AE, D, MC, V* ▭ *No lunch.*

$$ ✕ **Cru Café.** In a cheery, yellow, Charleston single house, Cru is a hidden treat. Locals come for the laid-back, down-to-earth dining room and the inventive menu. Chinese chicken salad translates to pulled meat on top of thin slices of cabbage, carrots, peppers, white radish, and red onions in a ginger dressing—fried wontons on the side. Fried chicken breasts are topped with poblano peppers and mozzarella, served with potatoes au gratin. Steaks (fish and red meat) come with sauces such as green peppercorn, port wine, pear sherry, honey chipotle, and horseradish cream. Small plate options work well for small appetites. ✉ *18 Pinckney St., Market area* ☎ *843/534–2434* ▭ *AE, D, DC, MC, V.*

$$ ✕ **Sermet's Corner.** Colorful, bold artwork by chef Sermet Aslan decorates the walls of this lively eatery. The Mediterranean menu has *panini* (grilled Italian sandwiches), seafood, flavorful pastas, and healthful options. The poached pear salad and lavender pork are favorites. Sermet's Corner is in the midst of the King Street shopping district. ✉ *276 King St., Market area* ☎ *843/853–7775* ▭ *AE, MC, V.*

French

$$$–$$$$ ✕ **Zinc Bistro and Bar.** Patriots Point's youngest headliner, Zinc, has brought high-style, high-end dining to Mount Pleasant. Chic, dark-wood millwork and a zinc-topped bar help create a bistro style. The covered deck, with occasional live jazz and a bustling happy-hour scene, is *the* place to take in waterfront Charleston and the bridges. Menu stars include roast chicken with gruyere-cheese orzo and grouper encased in brioche, served with baby spinach. Those with a sweet tooth rave about the dessert that combines the tastes of chocolate mousse and peanut butter with a side of peanut brittle and bananas. ✉ *28-A Bridgeside Blvd., Mount Pleasant* ☎ *843/216–9330* ✍ *Reservations essential* ▭ *AE, D, DC, MC, V.*

$$–$$$ ✕ **39 Rue de Jean.** In classy French style—gleaming wood, white-papered tables, and booths—Charleston's trendy set wines and dines until late (1 AM, except Sunday) on wonderful mussels, steak frites, scallops St. Jacques, and even sushi. Those seeking quiet should ask for the back room or dine outside on the terrace; this long-standing gathering place tends to be noisy up front. ✉ *39 John St., Upper King* ☎ *843/722–8881* ✍ *Reservations essential* ▭ *AE, D, DC, MC, V.*

$$ ✕ **Coco's.** A nondescript strip mall hosts this gem of an authentic French bistro, complete with crowded tables and an imported chef–owner. Make the trip over the bridge for homemade duck paté, escargot with garlic butter, rabbit in a red wine mushroom sauce, and pan-fried flounder in brown butter. Prices are less inflated here than food of the same caliber on the downtown Charleston peninsula. ✉ *863 Houston Northcutt Blvd., Mount Pleasant* ☎ *843/881–4949* ▭ *AE, MC, V* ⊙ *Closed Sun.*

$–$$ ✕ **Gaulart and Maliclet Café.** Eat at community-style tables for breakfast, lunch, snacks, and dinner; Thursday night fondues are a favorite. Choose from breads and pastries, soups, salads and sandwiches. Nightly specials, such as seafood Normandy and chicken sesame, round out the menu. A carafe of their specially blended coffee goes well with a slice of the subtly sweet chocolate mousse cake. ✉ *98 Broad St., South of Broad* ☎ *843/577–9797* ▭ *AE, D, MC, V* ⊙ *Closed Sun. No dinner Mon.*

Italian

$$$–$$$$ ✕ **Sienna.** Sumptuous meals here have all the flavor and flair befitting the five-star chef-owner, Ken Vedrinkski—but without the five-star pomp. Service is top-caliber yet surprisingly down-to-earth at this restaurant opened in 2004. Start with a Caesar salad with fresh anchovies or roasted local quail breast complemented by a fruit reduction tinged with peach and cherries. The halibut entrée comes with homemade shrimp-and-crab–stuffed tortellini in a sauce flavored with truffles. You might finish with artisanal cheeses, crispy pineapple turnovers, or rosemary vanilla granita. Well worth the drive over the bridges, it's the best of downtown dining, minus the crowding and price markups. ✉ *901 Island Park Dr., Daniel Island* ☎ *843/881–9211* ▭ *AE, MC, V* ⊙ *No lunch.*

$$$–$$$$ ✕ **Union Hall.** Look for favorite Italian ingredients in terrific contemporary combinations here: grouper is served atop a red-currant-and-pinenut stew; gnocchi pairs with lobster; and a duck breast rests on charred corn. The see-and-be-seen bar, bustling dining room, and open kitchen, draw a crowd that revels in high energy. ✉ *16 N. Market St., Market area* ☎ *843/377–1090* ▭ *AE, MC, V* ⊙ *No lunch.*

$$–$$$ ✕ **Fulton Five.** There are 15 tables in this romantic restaurant with chartreuse walls and antique brass accents. In warm weather, you can opt for a seat on the second-floor terrace. Either way, the northern Italian specialties are worth savoring. Mushroom risotto with sweet corn accompanies the beef surrounded by porcini mushrooms and topped with a caper-tomato sauce. Crabmeat and tarragon-laced butter flavor the spinach gnocchi. Fulton Five is in the antique district near King Street. ✉ *5 Fulton St., Market area* ☎ *843/853–5555* ✍ *Reservations essential* ▭ *AE, DC, MC, V* ⊙ *Closed Sun. and late Aug.–1st wk Sept. No lunch.*

$$–$$$ ✕ **Il Cortile del Re.** Great wines, hearty soups and pastas, and fresh cheeses and breads make this a slice of Tuscany. An expansion added streetfront views, a swank bar that's popular with locals, and more tables for all. The cozy back room and hidden courtyard rank high for privacy. ✉ *193 King St., Market area* ☎ *843/853–1888* ▭ *MC, V* ⊙ *Closed Sun. No lunch Sun.–Wed.*

Kosher

$–$$ ✕ **Pita King.** The renderings of typical Middle Eastern dishes—falafel, hummus, and *shawarma* (a type of gyro)—are uncommonly good at the only fully Kosher establishment in Charleston. The baba ghanoush (eggplant dip), the side of red cabbage, and the Israeli salad are worth a try. Order your stuffed pita to go and take the short walk to the nearby Marion Square for a picnic in the park. ✉ *437 King St., Upper King* ☎ *843/722–1977* ▭ *AE, D, MC, V* ⊙ *Closed Sat. and Jewish holidays.*

Lowcountry & Southern

$$$$ ✕ **Carolina's.** Hidden on a quiet side street between East Bay Street and Waterfront Park, this long-time staple occupies a former wharf building. Crew Carolina (owners of the Boathouse Restaurant group) bought, overhauled and reopened Carolina's in March 2004. Smartened-up decor includes banquettes and some walls done in red velvet. Well-known Lowcountry flavors still reign: avocado salsa with black-eyed pea cakes; shrimp-paste and green-tomato grits next to fried quail; and sweet potato–covered flounder spiced up with green apples. ✉ *10 Exchange St., South of Broad* ☎ *843/724–3800* ✍ *Reservations essential* ▭ *D, MC, V* ⊙ *No lunch.*

★ **$$$$** ✕ **Slightly North of Broad.** This former warehouse with brick-and-stucco walls and high ceilings has a shared chef's table that looks directly into the exposed kitchen (great for single diners). The Maverick Grits (with scallops, shrimp, ham and smoked sausage) are Lowcountry dining defined. Chef Frank Lee's other creations include barbecued tuna with fried oysters. You can order many of the items as either a small plate or as a main course. The wine list is long, and moderately priced. ✉ *192 E. Bay St., Market area* ☎ *843/723–3424* ▭ *AE, D, DC, MC, V* ⊙ *No lunch weekends.*

$$$–$$$$ ✕ **Anson.** Nearly a dozen French windows afford views of passing horse-drawn carriages from the softly lit, gilt-trim dining room. Here you can sample Southern specialties like shrimp and grits, oysters fried in corn bread, and barbecued grouper. The she-crab soup is some of the best around. ✉ *12 Anson St., Market area* ☎ *843/577–0551* ▭ *AE, D, DC, MC, V* ⊙ *No lunch.*

★ **$$$–$$$$** ✕ **Charleston Grill.** Club chairs, dark paneling—and the jazz played nightly—create a comfortable and elegant home for Bob Waggoner's ground-breaking New South cuisine. The down-to-earth chef's dishes are made with local organic and heirloom ingredients. Collards from Wadmalaw Island are cooked with pigs' feet in amber beer; the Charleston Grill's version of Frogmore Stew uses homemade sausage. It's not your typical hotel restaurant experience. ✉ *Charleston Place Hotel, 224 King St., Market area* ☎ *843/577–4522* ✍ *Reservations essential* ▭ *AE, D, DC, MC, V.*

$$$–$$$$ ✕ **High Cotton.** Lazily spinning fans, palm trees, and brick walls make you feel like you're on a plantation. You can feast on spit-roasted and grilled meats and fish. Weeknight specials are great deals; and weekend brunch is the place in town for mimosas and Bloody Marys. The chocolate soufflé with blackberry sauce and the praline soufflé are fabulous;

LOWCOUNTRY CUISINE

COLONIAL SETTLERS TO CHARLES TOWNE *found maritime forests, winding rivers, and vast marshes along a flat coastal plain, which came to be called the Lowcountry. This expansive backyard provided a cornucopia of sustenance—seafood, game, and produce—and the recipes French and English settlers brought from their homeland were altered to match the ingredients found here. After slaves were brought in from the West Indies and West Africa to work the rice fields, the Gullah language—a rollicking creole of English with African words and accents—and culture developed. Because blacks and whites were in such close proximity (slaves outnumbered whites for generations), the two groups' languages, accents, and cuisines melded. The mix of continental recipes and African flavors, made by using the harvest of the region, became known as Lowcountry cooking.*

Rice, rice, and more rice is ever-present in Lowcountry dishes, including pilau, *also spelled* purlieu *(both pronounced pur-low), which is a pilaf—rice cooked in meat or vegetable broth. Salty-sweet shrimp and grits is on menus of every price category in Charleston. You can buy creamy she-crab soup in restaurants and stores. Other essential dishes are Hoppin' John (rice and beans), and Frogmore Stew (with shrimp, sausage, and corn). Okra, eggplant, hominy (cooked grits), tomatoes, butterbeans, benne seeds, ham, shrimp, fish, and game are all part of the regional cuisine. Southern favorites like fried green tomatoes, fried fish and oysters, bacon-wrapped shad roe, and stuffed quail are popular here, too. But Charleston cuisine is not all about things past; true to the spirit of Lowcountry cooking, town chefs continue to innovate and create using the local harvest of farm-fresh heirloom vegetables and seafood caught daily just offshore.*

live jazz further sweetens the scene. ✉ *199 E. Bay St., Market area* ☎ *843/724–3815* ✍ *Reservations essential* ▭ *AE, D, DC, MC, V* ⊙ *No lunch weekdays.*

$$$–$$$$ ✕ **Magnolias.** The theme here is evident in the vivid paintings of Magnolia blossoms that adorn the walls and in the magnolia trees growing in window wells, as well as in the name. Southern-inspired cuisine includes appetizers like a chicken-and-greens egg roll and fried shrimp that is battered with local Palmetto Beer—horseradish gives it a kick. Brunch is served Sunday. ✉ *185 E. Bay St., Market area* ☎ *843/577–7771* ✍ *Reservations essential* ▭ *AE, DC, MC, V.*

$$–$$$ ✕ **Blossom.** Revamped in 2004, and owned by the same people as Magnolias and Cypress, Blossom specializes in Southern-style seafood. You can see the wood-burning oven where they make the pizzas ($10) from the dining room. Exposed white rafters and linenless tables keep the upscale place casual, and outside dining provides a view of St. Philip's majestic spire. ✉ *171 E. Bay St., Market area* ☎ *843/772–9200* ▭ *AE, DC, MC, V* ⊙ *No dinner Mon.*

★ **$$–$$$** ✕ **Gullah Cuisine.** Chef-owner Charlotte Jenkins cooks up a mean lunch buffet, stocked with fried chicken, fried and fresh vegetables (collard greens with ham, crispy okra, and more), and macaroni pie. But it's the Gullah dishes (from an African-American culture and language that traces back to the African rice coast and Lowcountry plantations) that make her place truly unique. The Gullah rice—red rice with chicken, sausage, shrimp, vegetables—and the gator tails are both delightful lessons in regional taste. Don't hesitate to take the trip across the bridge to this no-frills, side-of-the-highway restaurant. ✉ *1717 U.S. 17N, Mount Pleasant, 9 mi northeast of Charleston* ☎ *843/881–9076* ▭ *AE, MC, V* ⊙ *Closed Sun.*

$$–$$$ ✕ **J. Bistro.** Funky steel cutouts liven up outside and inside walls, and quirky lights hang low over tables. A varied list of appetizers and small plates makes this a great place to graze. Choose from steamed lobster wontons, grouper with crabmeat and a champagne cream sauce, and catfish in a pecan crust with grits. ✉ *819 Coleman Blvd., Mount Pleasant, 9 mi southeast of Charleston* ☎ *843/971–7778* ✍ *Reservations essential* ▭ *AE, MC, V* ⊙ *Closed Mon. No lunch Tues.–Sat.*

$–$$$ ✕ **Hominy Grill.** The young chef's Southern upbringing shows in dishes from the vegetable plate (squash casserole, collard greens, black-eyed pea cakes with guacamole, and mushroom hominy) to the pimiento cheese sandwich and the turkey club with homemade french fries. The avocado and *wehani* (a clay-color brown variety) rice salad with grilled vegetables is a refreshing, don't-miss summer item. Leave room for the excellent buttermilk pie or bread pudding. This breezy café has a whitewashed wood floor, a pressed-tin ceiling, and chalkboard specials. Breakfast is served daily. ✉ *207 Rutledge Ave., Upper King* ☎ *843/937–0930* ▭ *AE, MC, V* ⊙ *No dinner Sun.*

$–$$$ ✕ **Sticky Fingers.** Have your barbecue ribs with your choice of five different sauces or preparations here: wet or dry, with honey-, habanero-, or whisky-base sauces. Portions are generous; this casual, family-friendly restaurant is always action-packed. Sticky Fingers, a Southeastern chain, has three local outlets. ✉ *235 Meeting St., Market area* ☎ *843/853–7427 or 800/671–5966* ✉ *341 Johnnie Dodds Blvd., Mount Pleasant* ☎ *843/856–9840* ✉ *1200 N. Main St., Summerville* ☎ *843/875–7969* ▭ *AE, DC, MC, V.*

$–$$ ✕ **Boulevard Diner.** There are no frills at this counter-and-booth diner where the service is attentive and the food soulfully prepared. Among the winners: the daily variety of homemade veggies, the fried eggplant-and-blue-cheese sandwich, and the Cajun meat loaf and chili. You can also eat breakfast at the Boulevard. ✉ *409 W. Coleman Blvd., Mount Pleasant* ☎ *843/216–2611* ▭ *MC, V* ⊙ *Closed Sun.*

★ ¢–$$ ✕ **Jestine's Kitchen.** Enjoy dishes made from passed-down family recipes—like sweet chicken with limas—at the last of the true down-home, blue-plate Southern restaurants in the historic district. This casual eatery is known for its fried everything: chicken, okra, shrimp, pork chops, green tomatoes, and more. The cola cake and coconut cream pie are divine. ✉ *251 Meeting St., Upper King* ☎ *843/722–7224* ▭ *MC, V* ⊙ *Closed Mon.*

Middle Eastern

¢ ✕ **Doe's Pita Plus.** Residents working downtown crowd in at lunchtime in particular. Among the best-sellers: chicken salad stuffed in a pita, Greek or avocado salad, pita chips, hummus, meat pies, and tabbouleh. There's a simple grouping of tables and chairs inside, as well as some outdoor seating, but many take out. ✉ *334 E. Bay St., Market area* ☎ *843/577–3179* ▭ *AE* ⏲ *No dinner weekends.*

Pizza

¢ ✕ **Andolini's Pizza.** A college joint and cheap date spot, Andolini's is a class-A cool dive. The twenty- to thirtysomething crowd hides out in tall booths or on the patio out back. The dough and sauce are homemade daily, and the cheese is freshly grated. Toppings include the expected, plus banana peppers, anchovies, feta, garlic, jalapeños, and extra-tasty Italian sausage. A whole pie costs between $12 and $20, for a specialty pizza. ✉ *82 Wentworth St., College of Charleston* ☎ *843/722–7437* ▭ *AE, D, MC, V.*

Seafood

$$$–$$$$ ✕ **Boathouse Restaurant.** Large portions of fresh seafood at reasonable prices make both Charleston-area locations wildly popular. The shrimp hush puppies with spicy mayonnaise, grilled fish with specialty sauces, and lightly battered fried shrimp and oysters are irresistible. Entrées come with mashed potatoes, grits, collard greens, or blue-cheese coleslaw. The original Isle of Palms location is right on the water. Brunch is served Sunday. ✉ *101 Palm Blvd., Isle of Palms, 11 mi east of Charleston* ☎ *843/886–8000* ✉ *549 E. Bay St., Upper King* ☎ *843/577–7171* ✍ *Reservations essential* ▭ *AE, DC, MC, V* ⏲ *No lunch Mon.–Sat.*

$$–$$$$ ✕ **Coast.** Tucked away off a little alley in a restored warehouse, Coast has pared-down trappings like exposed brick and wood floors. Fried fare and heavy sauces are on the menu, but lighter dishes such as the fish tacos and ceviche make it a standout. The best choices include fish and lobster grilled over oak, and served with pineapple-chili salsa, a white-wine-and-lemon sauce, or garlic butter, among other options. ✉ *39D John St., Upper King* ☎ *843/722–8838* ▭ *AE, D, DC, MC, V* ⏲ *No lunch.*

$$–$$$$ ✕ **Hank's Seafood.** A lively spot with a popular bar and community dining area flanked by paper-topped private tables, Hank's is an upscale fish house. Seafood platters come with sweet-potato fries and coleslaw. Fishes include grouper, snapper, and tuna. That location off the Old Market, and the fact it's sister restaurant to the fancy-pants Peninsula Grill, makes the place noteworthy. ✉ *Church and Hayne Sts., Market area* ☎ *843/723–3474* ▭ *AE, D, DC, MC, V* ⏲ *Closed Mon. No lunch.*

$$–$$$ Fodor'sChoice ★ ✕ **The Wreck of the Richard and Charlene.** Waterfront and full of wacky characters, they weren't kidding with the name—expect a shabby, candlelit, screened-in porch and small dining area with a view of the shrimp boats on Shem Creek. Here Southern tradition is served on a plate: boiled peanuts, fried shrimp, stone crab claws, deviled crab, and oyster platters. The seaside-joint charm and fresh-off-the-dock bounty are the best in the Charleston area. ✉ *106 Haddrell St., Mount Pleasant* ☎ *843/884–0052* ✍ *Reservations not accepted* ▭ *No credit cards* ⏲ *No lunch.*

Steak

$$$$ ✕ **Grill 225.** Expect hefty portions and upscale renderings of steak house favorites, such as Kobe beef tartare and burgers, at Charleston's top grill. Prosciutto and provolone fill the veal rib chop; applewood-smoked bacon wraps around the filet mignon stuffed with blue cheese. Wood floors, white linens, and red-velvet upholstery add to the elegance. Grill 225 is inside the top-end Market Pavilion Hotel. ✉ *225 East Bay St., Market area* ☎ *843/266–4222* ▭ *AE, D, DC, MC, V.*

Tex-Mex

¢–$ ✕ **Juanita Greenberg's Nacho Royale.** Fast and fresh are the priorities here. Order a brick-size, one-plus pound burrito, or try the *pico de gallo* (coarsely chopped salsa) and meat quesadillas, with double meat as an option. Wash down the Royale Nachos (steak, pico, black beans, black olives, jalapeños, lettuce and cheese) with a Mexican soda. ✉ *439 King St., Upper King* ☎ *843/723–6224* ▭ *AE, D, MC, V.*

¢–$ ✕ **Yo Burrito.** Kick back at a students' favorite a block off King Street, at the fringe of the College of Charleston area. Funky art, cement floors, tall community tables with mile-high bar stools, a salsa bar, a tequila bar, and cheap beer-and-taco specials create the appeal. Request your quesadilla or burrito with fresh shrimp, pulled pork, mahimahi, chicken, or vegetables and top it off with the tastiest guacamole around. ✉ *86 Wentworth St., College of Charleston* ☎ *843/853–3287* ▭ *AE, D, MC, V.*

WHERE TO STAY

In a city known for its old homes, bed-and-breakfasts appear in nearly every residential block of the greater historic district. Upscale business hotels are also in the heart of downtown; the Market area and South of Broad are the prime locations. Chain hotels line the busy, car-trafficked areas (like Meeting and East Bay streets). In addition, there are quite a few chains near the hospitals on Lockwood Boulevard, which are a short ride from the city's main points of interest. Look for backpacker hostels south of the Crosstown (U.S. 17). Resort properties are southeast of Charleston on the islands across Cooper's River Bridge.

Prices

Charleston's downtown lodging establishments have three seasons: high season (fall and spring); mid-season (summer, June to August); and low season (late fall through mid-March). Prices drop significantly during the short low season, except during holidays. Resort high season is summer; rates drop for weekly stays and during off-season. To save money, try booking your room online, staying outside of downtown, or visiting from Sunday to Wednesday. Always try the B&Bs, as they tend to be more flexible and can negotiate prices. Smaller inns and B&Bs often have packages that might help as well. Reservations are essential during Spoleto, the Spring Festival of Homes, and the Southeastern Wildlife Expo.

WHAT IT COSTS				
$$$$	$$$	$$	$	¢
over $220	$160–$220	$110–$160	$70–$110	under $,

Hotel prices are for two people in a standard double room in high season, exclu ing service charges and 12% tax.

Hotels & Motels

★ $$$$ **Charleston Place.** Even casual passersby enjoy gazing up at the handblown Moreno glass chandelier in the hotel's open lobby, clicking across the Italian marble floor, and admiring the antiques from Sotheby's. A gallery of upscale shops and top-of-the-line restaurants complete the ground floor. Rooms are furnished with period reproductions, such as two-poster beds, but they also have modern necessities like fax machines. The impeccable service is what you would expect from an Orient-Express property. A day spa is on-site. ✉ *130 Market St., Market area, 29401* ☎ *843/722–4900 or 800/611–5545* 📠 *843/724–7215* 🌐 *www.charlestonplacehotel.com* *400 rooms, 42 suites* *2 restaurants, room service, in-room fax, minibars, cable TV with movies, 2 tennis courts, indoor pool, health club, hot tub, spa, bar, lobby lounge, dry cleaning, concierge, concierge floor, business services, convention center, parking (fee), no-smoking rooms* 💳 *AE, D, DC, MC, V* *EP.*

$$$$ **Market Pavilion Hotel.** The melee of one of the busiest corners in the city vanishes as soon as the uniformed bell man opens the lobby door to dark, wood-panel walls, antique furniture, and chandeliers hung from high ceilings. Get used to being pampered—butlers and babysitters are quick at hand. Room amenities include aristocratic French-style chaises, direct phone lines, marble baths with phones, padded hangers in the closet, and thick terry robes. Take a dip in the rooftop pool, or sip a cocktail at the rooftop bar overlooking the city. Even Charleston's top place for steaks, Grill 225, is here. ✉ *225 East Bay St., Market area, 29401* ☎ *843/723–0500 or 877/440–2250* 📠 *843/723–4320* 🌐 *www.marketpavilion.com* *61 rooms, 9 suites* *Restaurant, café, in-room fax, cable TV, pool, bar, babysitting, dry cleaning, concierge, concierge floor, Internet, travel services, parking (fee); no smoking* 💳 *AE, D, DC, MC, V* *EP.*

$$$–$$$$ **Embassy Suites Historic Charleston.** The courtyard of the Old Citadel military school where cadets once marched is now an atrium with skylights, stone floors, armchairs, palm trees, and a fountain. The restored brick walls of the breakfast room and some guest rooms in this contemporary hotel contain original gun ports, reminders that the 1822 building was originally a fortification. Teak and mahogany furniture, safari motifs, and sisal carpeting recall the British colonial era. Breakfast and evening refreshments are complimentary. ✉ *341 Meeting St., Upper King, 29403* ☎ *843/723–6900 or 800/362–2779* 📠 *843/723–6938* 🌐 *www.embassysuites.com* *153 suites* *Restaurant, room service, some in-room hot tubs, kitchenettes, cable TV with movies and video games, pool, gym, outdoor hot tubs, lounge, shop, babysitting, laundry facili-*

ties, business services, meeting rooms, parking (fee), no-smoking rooms ▭ *AE, D, DC, MC, V* 🍽 *BP.*

$$$–$$$$ **HarbourView Inn.** Ask for a room facing the harbor and you could open your French doors to look out at the fountain in Waterfront Park, and the bay beyond. Calming earth tones and rattan soothe and relax; high ceilings, four-poster beds, and sea-grass rugs complete the Lowcountry look. Some of the rooms are in a former 19th-century shipping warehouse with exposed brick walls, plantation shutters, and whirlpool tubs; others have fireplaces. Afternoon wine and cheese, evening milk and cookies, and turn-down service are included. ✉ *2 Vendue Range, Market area, 29401* ☎ *843/853–8439 or 888/853–8439* 📠 *843/853–4034* 🌐 *www.harbourviewcharleston.com* *52 rooms* *In-room data ports, some in-room hot tubs, some minibars, cable TV, concierge, Internet, business services, parking (fee), no-smoking rooms* ▭ *AE, D, DC, MC, V* 🍽 *BP.*

$$$–$$$$ **Mills House Hotel.** A reconstruction of an old hostelry on its original site in the historic district, Mills House is a Holiday Inn property. The rooms are small and a bit standard, but the lobby does have antiques, and there's a lounge with live entertainment and a nice dining room. The prime location makes up for any potential shortcomings. ✉ *115 Meeting St., Market area, 29401* ☎ *843/577–2400 or 800/874–9600* 📠 *843/722–0623* 🌐 *www.millshouse.com* *199 rooms, 16 suites* *Restaurant, room service, cable TV, pool, bar, lounge, laundry services, concierge, concierge floor, Internet, business services, meeting rooms, parking (fee), no-smoking rooms* ▭ *AE, D, DC, MC, V* 🍽 *EP.*

$$–$$$$ **Doubletree Guest Suites Historic Charleston.** This one-time bank wears a restored entrance portico from 1874. Fountains bubble in the three interior garden courtyards. Go for one of the spacious suites; all have 18th-century reproductions and canopy beds, wet bars, microwave ovens, and refrigerators. ✉ *181 Church St., Market area, 29401* ☎ *843/577–2644 or 877/408–8733* 📠 *843/577–2697* 🌐 *www.doubletree.com* *182 suites* *Some microwaves, some refrigerators, cable TV with movies, gym, lounge, shop, laundry facilities, business services, meeting room, parking (fee), no-smoking rooms* ▭ *AE, D, DC, MC, V* 🍽 *EP.*

★ $$$ **Hampton Inn–Historic District.** Hardwood floors and a fireplace in the lobby of what was once a 1800s warehouse help elevate this chain hotel a bit above the standard. Spindle posts on the headboards give guest rooms a little personality, and there's a courtyard garden. The little perks of a chain—coffeemakers in your room, free coffee and newspaper in the lobby—are here, too. ✉ *373 Meeting St., Upper King, 29403* ☎ *843/723–4000 or 800/426–7866* 📠 *843/722–3725* 🌐 *www.hamptoninn.com* *166 rooms, 5 suites* *In-room data ports, some microwaves, some refrigerators, cable TV with movies, pool, babysitting, laundry facilities, concierge, Internet, business services, meeting rooms, travel services, parking (fee), no-smoking rooms* ▭ *AE, D, DC, MC, V* 🍽 *BP.*

$$–$$$ **Andrew Pinckney Inn.** A small boutique hotel in a handful of restored buildings, the Andrew Pinckney Inn tends to be off the tourist radar, even though the location is great. Simple furnishings include upholstered couches and basic wood headboards (value rooms have no seating area).

The town houses have two stories, 1½ bathrooms, a whirlpool tub, and kitchenettes. Try the heavy continental breakfast on the rooftop terrace and take in the sunrise over the soon-to-be hopping historic district. Solid service makes up for the lack of a full-scale lobby. Ask for rooms away from the street if quiet concerns you. ✉ *40 Pinckney St., Market area, 29401* ☎ *843/937–8800 or 800/505–8983* 📠 *843/937–8810* 🌐 *www.andrewpinckneyinn.com* *37 rooms, 3 town houses, 1 suite* *Dining room, in-room data ports, some in-room hot tubs, some kitchenettes, laundry service, concierge, parking (fee); no smoking* 💳 *AE, MC, V* 🍽 *BP.*

★ **$$–$$$** **Francis Marion Hotel.** Wrought-iron railings, crown moldings, and decorative plasterwork speak of the elegance of 1924, when the Francis Marion was the largest hotel in the Carolinas. Bountiful throw pillows, and billowy curtains add to the softness of the guest rooms, many of which have views of Marion Square and the harbor. Lowcountry cuisine can be had at Swamp Fox restaurant, where live jazz is played on weekends. Indulge in some self-care at the full-service day spa. ✉ *387 King St., Upper King, 29403* ☎ *843/722–0600 or 877/756–2121* 📠 *843/723–4633* 🌐 *www.francismarioncharleston.com* *193 rooms, 34 suites* *Restaurant, coffee shop, room service, in-room data ports, cable TV, gym, spa, lounge, shop, concierge, Internet, business services, meeting rooms, parking (fee), no-smoking rooms* 💳 *AE, D, DC, MC, V* 🍽 *EP.*

$$–$$$ **Meeting Street Inn.** The 1874, salmon-color single house—with second- and third-story porches—originally contained a tavern on the ground floor. Rooms overlook a lovely courtyard with fountains and gardens; many have have hardwood floors and oriental rugs. Four-poster or canopy beds, chair rails, and bright pattern wallpaper (turquoise floral, scarlet red with medallions) create a period feel. ✉ *173 Meeting St., Market area, 29401* ☎ *843/723–1882 or 800/842–8022* 📠 *843/577–0851* 🌐 *www.meetingstreetinn.com* *56 rooms* *Some refrigerators, cable TV, outdoor hot tub, bar* 💳 *AE, D, DC, MC, V* 🍽 *BP.*

$–$$ **Holiday Inn Historic District.** This hotel draws loyal repeat guests because of its location—a block from the Gaillard Municipal Auditorium and within walking distance of many must-see spots. Rooms are pretty traditional with medium wood tone armoires, headboards, coffee and side tables. The fabrics on the upholstered chairs, bed linens, and draperies are hotel floral. Suites have a separate bedroom. ✉ *125 Calhoun St., Upper King, 29401* ☎ *843/805–7900 or 877/805–7900* 📠 *843/805–7700* 🌐 *www.charlestonhotel.com* *122 rooms, 4 suites* *Restaurant, in-room data ports, cable TV, pool, bar, concierge, concierge floor, Internet, business services, meeting rooms, parking (fee), no-smoking rooms* 💳 *AE, D, DC, MC, V* 🍽 *BP.*

¢–$ **Red Roof Inn Mount Pleasant.** Take advantage of the motel at the foot of the Cooper River Bridge in Mt. Pleasant, about 10 minutes from historic Charleston, for its bargain rates. Rooms have two double beds, or one king. Deluxe rooms have small refrigerators and microwaves. ✉ *301 Johnnie Dodds Blvd., Mount Pleasant 29464* ☎ *843/884–1411 or 800/843–7663* 📠 *843/971–0726* 🌐 *www.redroof.com* *124 rooms* *Some microwaves, some refrigerators, cable TV, pool, laundry facilities, business services, meeting rooms, some pets allowed, no-smoking rooms* 💳 *AE, D, DC, MC, V* 🍽 *EP.*

Inns, B&Bs & Guesthouses

★ $$$$ **John Rutledge House Inn.** One of the framers of the U.S. Constitution, John Routledge, constructed the 1763 mansion that has become a luxurious inn. Solid painted walls—in forest green and buttercream yellow—in several rooms complement the canopy fabrics on the four-poster beds. Parquet floors sit beneath 14-foot ceilings adorned with plaster moldings. Rooms are in either the mansion or in two carriage houses; some have fireplaces. Newspapers come straight to your room. Enjoy afternoon tea or port and sherry in the lounge–ballroom; breakfast pastries and breads can be served in the courtyard if you prefer sitting outside. ✉ *116 Broad St., South of Broad, 29401* ☎ *843/723–7999 or 800/476–9741* 📠 *843/720–2615* 🌐 *www.charminginns.com* *16 rooms, 2 suites* *Refrigerators, some hot tubs, business services, no-smoking rooms* 💳 *AE, D, DC, MC, V* *BP.*

$$$$ **Planters Inn.** Part of the upscale Relais & Châteaux group, Planters Inn, a stately, small, in-town hotel, lives up to the exclusive reputation. High-ceiling rooms and suites are beautifully appointed with mahogany four-poster beds, and marble baths. Audubon prints hint of Lowcountry life. Twenty-one of the rooms have modest piazzas that overlook the intimate garden courtyard. Also of note, ⇨ **Peninsula Grill** is among the state's best dining rooms. ✉ *112 N. Market St., Market area, 29401* ☎ *843/722–2345 or 800/845–7082* 📠 *843/577–2125* 🌐 *www.plantersinn.com* *56 rooms, 6 suites* *Restaurant, room service, in-room data ports, some in-room hot tubs, in-room safes, concierge, business services, meeting room, parking (fee), no-smoking floors* 💳 *AE, D, DC, MC, V* *EP.*

$$$$ Fodor'sChoice ★ **Wentworth Mansion.** The city's hoi polloi find rest at this grand brick mansion (circa 1886) originally built as an opulent private home. Hand-carved marble and wood fireplaces, brass and crystal chandeliers, and antiques and Second Empire reproductions add to the dignified grace. Spacious guest rooms have rich fabrics, detailed inset wood paneling or trim, seating areas, and oversize, whirlpool tubs. King-size beds are turned down nightly. The breakfast buffet, afternoon lemonade or sherry, and evening wine and cheese are complimentary. Circa 1886, the restaurant in the former carriage house, is the perfect spot for a special-occasion meal. ✉ *149 Wentworth St., College of Charleston, 29403* ☎ *843/853–1886 or 888/466–1886* 📠 *843/720–5290* 🌐 *www.wentworthmansion.com* *21 rooms* *Restaurant, in-room data ports, in-room hot tubs, cable TV, lounge, concierge, meeting rooms, free parking; no smoking* 💳 *AE, D, DC, MC, V* *BP.*

$$$–$$$$ **Ansonborough Inn.** Formerly a stationer's shipping warehouse dating from the early 1900s, the building's original architectural details have been emphasized by leaving brick walls exposed and designing around the grand heart-pine beams and wood ceilings. Oil painting of hunting dogs and scene of the sea hang above clubby leather chairs and sofas. Evening wine and cheese on a rooftop terrace helps make this inn a standout, as does the friendly, professional staff. ✉ *21 Hasell St., Market area, 29401* ☎ *843/723–1655 or 800/522–2073* 📠 *843/527–6888* 🌐 *www.ansonboroughinn.com* *37 suites* *Bar, in-room data ports, in-room*

safes, microwaves, refrigerators, business services, meeting room, parking (fee); no smoking ▭ *AE, MC, V* 🍴 *BP.*

$$$–$$$$ **Hayne House.** Old furnishings combine with a fresh, light spirit at Hayne House. Rooms have federal antiques and other heirlooms from the proprietors' families set against cheery corals, cornflower blues, and lime green, among other colors. Two guest rooms are in the main house; the other four rooms and suites are in the kitchen house or the connection between. The narrow stairways, colonial brickwork and chimney are typical of 1755 when the house was built. Ask about discounted rooms off season. ✉ *30 King St., South of Broad, 29401* ☎ *843/577–2633* 🖷 *843/577–5906* 🌐 *www.haynehouse.com* *3 rooms, 3 suites* *Dining room; no room phones, no room TVs, no smoking* ▭ *MC, V* 🍴 *BP.*

★ **$$$–$$$$** **Two Meeting Street.** As pretty as a wedding cake, and just as romantic, this white Queen Anne mansion has overhanging bays, colonnades, balustrades, and a turret. While rocking on the front porch you can look through soaring arches to see White Point Gardens and the Ashley River. Tiffany windows, carved English oak paneling, and a chandelier from the former Czechoslovakia dress up the public spaces. Two guest rooms have balconies and working fireplaces; all have lace or Victorian florals. Expect to be treated to afternoon high tea. This is one of the most recognizable homes on the Battery, and a favorite spot for celebs and honeymooners. ✉ *2 Meeting St., South of Broad, 29401* ☎ *843/723–7322* 🌐 *www.twomeetingstreet.com* *9 rooms* *Dining room, concierge; no room phones, no kids under 12, no smoking* ▭ *No credit cards* 🍴 *BP.*

$$$ **Cannonboro Inn and Ashley Inn.** B&B sisters and neighbors on the edge of the historic district share many similarities. At both expect a full breakfast with main dishes like fruit waffles or French toast served on a wide porch overlooking a garden, tea and treats in the afternoon, and free use of bicycles. Rooms have antiques suitable to the era of the houses (circa 1853 and 1839 respectively). But the pinkish Ashley Inn has a two-bedroom carriage house with kitchen that you can rent out, while the grey Cannonboro does not. ✉ *Cannonboro, 184 Ashley Ave., Medical University of South Carolina, 29403* ☎ *843/723–8572 or 800/235–8039* 🖷 *843/723–8007* 🌐 *www.charleston-sc-inns.com* *7 rooms, 1 suite* *Dining room, cable TV, bicycles, business services, free parking; no kids under 10, no smoking* ▭ *AE, D, DC, MC, V* 🍴 *BP* ✉ *Ashley, 201 Ashley Ave., Medical University of South Carolina, 29403* ☎ *843/723–1848 or 800/581–6658* 🖷 *843/579–9080* 🌐 *www.charleston-sc-inns.com* *7 rooms, 1 suite, 1 house* *Dining room, some kitchenettes, cable TV, bicycles, business services, free parking; no room phones, no kids under 10, no smoking* ▭ *AE, D, DC, MC, V* 🍴 *BP.*

$$$ **Vendue Inn.** The inn's rooftop restaurant and bar has sweeping harbor views because the waterfront is so close (though room views are obstructed by a condo building). Two mid-1800s warehouses across the street from each other have been transformed into guest rooms and suites with a variety of antiques. Bathrobes are provided, and full buffet breakfast, afternoon wine and cheese, and evening milk and cookies are complimentary. ✉ *19 Vendue Range, Market area, 29401* ☎ *843/577–7970 or 800/845–7900* 🌐 *www.vendueinn.com* *31 rooms, 35 suites*

Restaurant, in-room data ports, some in-room hot tubs, some in-room safes, cable TV, bicycles, bar, business services, meeting room; no smoking *AE, D, DC, MC, V* *BP.*

$$–$$$ **1837 Bed and Breakfast and Tea Room.** An extremely hospitable staff helps you get a sense of what it'd be like to really live in one of Charleston's beloved old homes. Antique, lace-canopy beds fill much of the guest rooms, which are in the main and in the carriage house. A delicious breakfast includes homemade breads and hot entrées such as sausage pie or ham frittatas. *126 Wentworth St., Market area, 29401* *843/723–7166 or 877/723–1837* *843/722–7179* *www.1837bb.com* *8 rooms, 1 suite* *Refrigerators; no room phones* *AE, D, MC, V* *BP.*

$$–$$$ **Elliott House Inn.** Listen to the chimes of St. Michael's Episcopal Church as you sip wine in the courtyard of this lovely old inn in the heart of the historic district. You can then retreat to a cozy room with period furniture, including canopied four-posters and Oriental carpets. *78 Queen St., Market area, 29401* *843/723–1855 or 800/729–1855* *843/722–1567* *www.elliotthouseinn.com* *24 rooms* *Hot tub, bicycles; no kids, no smoking* *AE, D, MC, V* *BP.*

$$–$$$ **Old Village Post House.** Once a grocery, a community supper club, and more, the latest reincarnation of the white wooden building anchoring Mount Pleasant's historic district is as a restaurant–tavern–inn. Rooms are small, but first-rate. Neutral linens and wall coverings offset dark wood furnishings that feel right at home in a building with roots in the 1880s. The Post House is run by the group behind downtown restaurants Slightly North of Broad and High Cotton, so the muffins and pastries at breakfast and the food in the restaurant are excellent. Staying here you're within walking distance to Charleston harbor and Shem Creek shrimp docks. *101 Pitt St., Mount Pleasant 29464, 6 mi east of Charleston* *843/388–8935* *843/388–8937* *www.oldvillageposthouse.com* *6 rooms* *Restaurant, dining room, fans, some in-room hot tubs, cable TV, bar, free parking; no smoking* *AE, D, DC, MC, V* *BP.*

$$–$$$ **Phoebe Pember House.** The 1807 property has two separate guesthouses: a carriage house with two guest rooms upstairs and a living room, dining room, kitchenette, and garden downstairs; and a coach house with individual rooms. Cheerful colors (cranberry, sunshine yellow, and sky blue) brighten beds and walls. The vibrant artwork is done by Charleston artists. An associated studio provides women's workshops and yoga classes. The inn is off a busy street, but the piazza is cocooned by a walled garden overlooking Charleston's port. *26 Society St., Market area, 29401* *843/722–4186* *843/722–0557* *www.phoebepemberhouse.com* *6 rooms* *Massage, fitness classes, free parking; no smoking* *AE, MC, V* *BP.*

¢ **Not So Hostel.** Several 1840s-era buildings, including a Charleston single house, make up the Not So Hostel hostel. The laid-back-but-professional management style helps attract many European backpackers. A platform out back provides a place for camping. Grits and waffles for breakfast, a wild vegetable garden you can plunder—and prices that put the rest of the city's lodging to shame—make this a great place to stay if you can handle a little peeling paint, a bit of clutter, an ungentrified urban neighborhood, and cats. Linens, a locker (bring a lock), and Internet access are free. ✉ *156 Spring St., Medical University of South Carolina, 29403* ☎ *843/722–8383* 🌐 *www.notsohostel.com* *24 dorm beds, 4 rooms without bath* *Dining room, bicycles, recreation room, laundry facilities, Internet, airport shuttle, free parking; no room phones, no room TVs, no smoking* *No credit cards* *BP.*

¢ **Charleston's Historic Hostel & Inn.** A lively green-and-purple shuttered Charleston single house turned hostel is painted in crisp Caribbean colors inside, too—pinks for the women's dorm room, blues for the men's, and greens and yellows for the fully stocked, free-to-use kitchen. The effect is a cheerful one, and with house rules neatly posted here and there, it's as organized as hosteling gets. There are three bunk beds per room, and one private double. You can rock on the porch, nap in the hammock, or gather in the yard for a Sunday cookout. Rent a bike and ride the easy distance to the College of Charleston area. Movies are shown nightly and linens and towels are included. ✉ *194 St. Philip St., Medical University of South Carolina, 29403* ☎ *843/478–1446* 🌐 *www.charlestonhostel.com* *12 dorm beds, 1 room without bath* *BBQs, bicycles, recreation room, laundry facilities, Internet, free parking; no room phones, no room TVs* *MC, V* *BP.*

Resorts

$$$$ **Wild Dunes.** This top-notch 1,600-acre resort on the Isle of Palms has cheerfully colored one- to six-bedroom villas and homes for rent, plus the elegant plantation-style Boardwalk Inn. Rental locations range from oceanfront (Ocean Point is the most secluded) to courtside to marshside. The inn sits among a cluster of villas and shops, and is steps off the beach; many guest rooms have balconies and overlook the ocean. You have a long list of recreational options here including Tom Fazio golf courses and nationally ranked tennis programs; packages are available. Nearby is a yacht harbor on the Intracoastal Waterway. ✉ *Palm Blvd. at 41st Ave., Isle of Palms* *Box 20575, Charleston 29413* ☎ *843/886–6000 or 888/845–8926* *843/886–2916* 🌐 *www.wilddunes.com* *430 units, 93 rooms* *3 restaurants, ice-cream parlor, pizzeria, snack bar, fans, some in-room hot tubs, some minibars, cable TV, 2 18-hole golf courses, 17 tennis courts, 4 pools, health club, boating, fishing, bicycles, volleyball, lounge, video game room, children's programs (ages 3–12), concierge, Internet, meeting rooms, airport shuttle, no-smoking rooms* *AE, D, DC, MC, V* *EP.*

$$$–$$$$ **Kiawah Island Golf Resort.** Choose from one- to four-bedroom villas and three- to seven-bedroom private homes in two luxurious resort villages on 10,000 wooded and oceanfront acres. Or opt to stay at the Sanctuary at Kiawah Island, a 255-room, luxury waterfront hotel and spa, which opened in August 2004. The rooms' West-Indies style is evident in subtle palm prints, bed posts carved with an impressionistic pineapple pattern, and some plantation ceilings with exposed planks painted white. Along with the 10 mi of island beaches, recreational options include kayak and surf board rental, nature tours, and arts and crafts classes.

⊠ 12 Kiawah Beach Dr., Kiawah Island 29455 ☎ 843/768–2121 or 800/654–2924 🖷 843/768–6099 🌐 www.kiawahresort.com ⇨ 255 rooms, 600 villas and homes ♖ 10 restaurants, some room service, some in-room safes, some kitchens, some minibars, cable TV, some in-room VCRs, 5 18-hole golf courses, 28 tennis courts, pro shop, 4 pools, wading pool, health club, spa, beach, boating, fishing, bicycles, lounge, shops, children's programs (ages 3–12), concierge, concierge floor, Internet, business services, convention center, parking (fee), no-smoking rooms ▭ AE, D, DC, MC, V 🍽 EP.

$$$–$$$$ **Seabrook Island Resort.** About 200 completely equipped one- to six-bedroom villas, cottages, and beach houses occupy this property (the number varies according to how many homeowners sign up for the rental program). The resort is noted for its natural beaches, secluded wooded areas, and abundance of wildlife—look for bobcats and white-tail deer. The Beach Club and Island House are centers for dining and leisure activities. Bohicket Marina Village, the hub of activity around the island, has restaurants, pizza and sub shops, plus scuba diving, deep-sea- and inshore-fishing charters. You can rent small boats, kayaks, fishing rods, crab traps, and beach chairs and umbrellas. *⊠ 3772 Seabrook Island Rd., Seabrook Island 29455 ☎ 843/768–1000 or 800/845–2475 🖷 843/768–7524 🌐 www.discoverseabrook.com ⇨ 200 units ♖ 3 restaurants, café, kitchens, cable TV, some in-room VCRs, 2 18-hole golf courses, 15 tennis courts, 2 pools, wading pool, fitness classes, gym, massage, beach, boating, fishing, bicycles, basketball, billiards, horseback riding, Ping-Pong, volleyball, 3 bars, recreation room, video game room, shops, babysitting, children's programs (ages 4–17), playground, no-smoking rooms ▭ AE, D, DC, MC, V 🍽 EP.*

NIGHTLIFE & THE ARTS

The Arts

Concerts

Charleston Concert Association (☎ 843/722–7667 for tickets 🌐 www.charlestonconcerts.com) brings national and international symphony, ballet, opera, and jazz performances to Gaillard Municipal Auditorium, October through April. Bluegrass, blues, country, singer–songwriter musicians and more grace the stage at the **Charleston Music Hall** (⊠ 37 John St., Upper King ☎ 843/853–2252 🌐 www.charlestonmusichall.com). The **Charleston Symphony Orchestra** (☎ 843/723–7528 🌐 www.charlestonsymphony.com) season runs from October through April, with a master works series, pops series, chamber series, family-oriented series, and holiday concerts. **Monday Night Recital Series** (⊠ Simon Center for the Arts, 54 St. Philip St., College of Charleston ☎ 843/953–8228 🌐 www.cofc.edu) takes place at the College of Charleston, admission is just $5.

Dance

Anonymity Dance Company (☎ 843/886–6104), a modern dance troupe, performs throughout the city. The **Charleston Ballet Theatre** (⊠ 477 King St., Upper King ☎ 843/723–7334 🌐 www.charlestonballet.com) performs everything from classical to contemporary dance at locations around the city. The **Robert Ivey Ballet Company** (☎ 843/556–1343 🌐 www.cofc.edu), a semiprofessional company that includes College of Charleston students, puts on a fall and spring program of jazz, classical, and modern dance at the Sottile Theater.

Festivals

The **Fall Candlelight Tours of Homes and Gardens** (☎ 843/722–4630 🌐 www.preservationsociety.org), sponsored by the Preservation Society of Charleston in September and October, provides an inside look at Charleston's private buildings and gardens.

More than 100 private homes, gardens, and historic churches are open to the public for tours during the **Festival of Houses and Gardens** (☎ 843/722–3405 🌐 www.historiccharleston.org), held during March and April each year, sponsored by the Historic Charleston Foundation. There are also symphony galas in stately drawing rooms, plantation oyster roasts, and candlelight tours.

The **MOJA Arts Festival** (☎ 843/724–7305 🌐 www.mojafestival.com), which takes place during the last week of September and first week of October, celebrates the rich heritage of the African continent and Caribbean influences on African-American culture. It includes theater, dance, and music performances, art shows, films, lectures, and tours of the historic district.

Piccolo Spoleto (☎ 843/724–7305 🌐 www.piccolospoleto.org) is the spirited companion festival of Spoleto Festival USA, showcasing the best in local and regional talent from every artistic discipline. There are about 300 events—from jazz performances to puppet shows and expansive art shows in Marion Square—from mid-May through early June, and many of the best performances are free.

The **Southeastern Wildlife Exposition** (☎ 843/723–1748 or 800/221–5273 🌐 www.sewe.com) in mid-February is one of Charleston's biggest annual events, with find art by renowned wildlife artists, live animal demonstrations, an oyster roast, and galas.

Spoleto USA (☎ 843/722–2764 🌐 www.spoletousa.org), founded by the composer Gian Carlo Menotti in 1977, is a world-famous celebration of the arts and Charleston's premiere cultural event. From late May to early June, the city teems with events from sunup to well past sundown. Concert halls, theaters, parks, churches, streets, and gardens become the stage for opera, dance, theater, symphonic and chamber music, jazz, and the visual arts.

Film

Scoot to the bar downstairs at intermission at the **American Theater** (✉ 446 King St., Upper King ☎ 843/722–3456), a 1940s venue, for everything from wine and beer to wings and popcorn. Each plush chair in the two state-of-the-art movie theaters has its own fold-out tray table. The **IMAX Theater** (✉ 360 Concord St., Upper King ☎ 843/725–4629) is next to the South Carolina Aquarium.

CloseUp

SPOLETO USA

EVERY YEAR from late May to early June, all of Charleston is a stage thanks to ***Spoleto USA*** *(☎ 843/722–2764 ⊕ www.spoletousa.org). The 17-day festival plays out nearly everywhere you turn: under the oaks of the College of Charleston's Cistern; on the stage of the Dock Street Theatre; in the cells of the 1850s Old City Jail; on the lawns of the Waterfront Park, Marion Square, and Hampton Park; and in area schools, libraries, and music halls. It all culminates with an orchestral concert and fireworks finale on the plantation grounds of Middleton Place, where attendees set up elaborate picnics.*

More than 100 performances by 30-plus national and international acts ensure that there's no shortage of options—from improv to Shakespeare, from rap to chamber music, from ballet to salsa. Artists include the traditional and the cutting edge—which was what Pulitzer-prize winning composer Gian Carlo Minotti had in mind when, in 1977, he initiated the festival as a complement to his opera-heavy Italian festival. He chose Charleston because of its European looks, and because its residents love the arts—and any cause for celebration.

As if Spoleto itself weren't enough, in 1979 the City of Charleston started ***Piccolo Spoleto*** *(☎ 843/724–7305 ⊕ www.piccolospoleto.com) held during the same time period. Local performers stage affordable events for mass audiences. Although Spoleto tickets range from $10 to $75, Piccolo Spoleto (literally, "little Spoleto") rates tend to stay below $20, and some events are free. To sort out what to see, go online for schedules and tickets. Be sure to book rooms months in advance (rates are high during this time), and make dinner reservations well ahead of your arrival.*

Theater

Charleston Stage Company performs at the **Dock Street Theatre** (✉ 135 Church St., Market area ☎ 843/965–4032). The Footlight Players regularly perform fun plays and musicals at the **Footlight Players Theatre** (✉ 20 Queen St., Market area ☎ 843/722–4487). **Theatre 99** puts on improv comedy shows at the (✉ American Theater, 446 King St., Upper King ☎ 843/722–3456, 843/853–6687 for tickets).

Venues

Gaillard Municipal Auditorium (✉ 77 Calhoun St., Upper King ☎ 843/577–7400) hosts symphony and ballet companies, as well as numerous festival events. The box office is open weekdays from 10 to 6.

Dance, symphony, and theater productions are among those staged at the **North Charleston Performing Art Center** (✉ 5001 Coliseum Dr., North Charleston ☎ 843/529–5050 ⊕ www.coliseumpac.com).

Performances by the College of Charleston's theater department and musical recitals are presented during the school year at the **Simons Center for the Arts** (✉ 54 St. Phillips St., College of Charleston ☎ 843/953–5604).

The chamber series by the Charleston Symphony takes place at the **Sottile Theater** (✉ 44 George St., Market area ☎ 843/953–6340), as do performances by area ballet companies and Spoleto Festival events.

Nightlife

Bars & Breweries

Charlie's Little Bar (✉ 141 E. Bay St., Market area ☎ 843/723–6242), above Saracen Restaurant, is intimate, cozy, and popular with a local, low-key crowd. **Club Habana** (✉ 177 Meeting St., Market area ☎ 843/853–5900 or 843/853–5008) is a chic wood-panel martini bar (open late) with a cigar shop downstairs. **Southend Brewery** (✉ 161 E. Bay St., Market area ☎ 843/853–4677) has a lively bar and beer brewed on the premises; try the wood-oven pizzas.

Drinks and appetizers, with a view, draw young professionals to the covered rooftop at the **Terrace on Marion Square** (✉ 145 Calhoun St., Market area ☎ 843/937–0314). **Vickery's Bar & Grill** (✉ 139 Calhoun St., Market area ☎ 843/723–1558 ✉ 1313 Shrimp Boat La., Mount Pleasant ☎ 843/849–6770) is a festive nightspot with an outdoor patio and good late-night food.

Pool tables and sports on the TVs—-plus 20 on-tap beers—make **Charleston Beer Works** (✉ 468 King St., Upper King ☎ 843/577–5885) a favorite of students and other of-age youth. A list of 100 bottled beers and 30-plus TVs make **King Street Grille** (✉ 304 King St., Upper King ☎ 843/723–5464) a destination for those who like the game loud.

Late-night, alternative bands and cheap "mystery beers" make **Cumberland's** (✉ 301 King St., Market Area ☎ 843/577-9469) the favorite of college kids and laid-back locals.

Dance Clubs

Pop, hip-hop, and songs from the '70s and '80s, alternate with a throbbing dance beat from DJ Amos at **213 Top of the Bay** (✉ 213C E. Bay St., Market area ☎843/722–1311), a lively and lighthearted part of downtown's single scene. Dance music is the backdrop for the serious, stylish see-and-be-seen scene at the **City Bar** (✉ 5 Faber St., Market area ☎ 843/577–7383). Dance to funky '70s music Wednesday through Saturday at **Trio Club** (✉ 139 Calhoun St., Upper King ☎ 843/965–5333); Thursday means live Latin tunes.

Dinner Cruises

Reservations for all evening cruises are essential. For dinner theater and other specialty trips, cruise the harbor on the ***Charleston Belle*** (☎ 843/344–4483 🌐 www.charlestonharbortours.com). Dine and dance the night away aboard the luxury yacht ***Spirit of Carolina*** (☎ 843/881–7337 🌐 www.spiritlinecruises.com).

Jazz Clubs

The elegant **Charleston Grill** (✉ 224 King St., Market area ☎ 843/577–4522), in Charleston Place hotel, has live jazz and dinner nightly. Make a reservation. At **Mistral Restaurant** (✉ 99 S. Market St., Market area ☎ 843/722–5709) there's a regular Dixieland jazz band Monday through

Saturday, and a four-piece jazz band on Sunday. **The Swamp Fox** (✉ Francis Marion Hotel, 387 King St., Upper King ☎ 843/722–0600 or 877/756–2121) has a jazz pianist playing Thursday through Saturday.

Live Music

Listen to authentic Irish music at **Tommy Condon's Irish Pub & Restaurant** (✉ 15 Beaufain St., Market area ☎ 843/577–5300). **Best Friend Lounge** (✉ Mills House Hotel, 115 Meeting St., Market area ☎ 843/577–2400) has a guitarist playing on weekends. At the **Lobby Lounge** (✉ Charleston Pl., 205 Meeting St., Market area ☎ 843/722–4900) afternoon high tea or cocktails are accompanied by piano or classical guitar. The cavernous **Music Farm** (✉ 32 Ann St., Upper King ☎ 843/853–3276), in a renovated train station, showcases live national and local rock, techno, and alternative bands popular with college students and those 10-years-graduated.

JB Pivot's Beach Club (✉ 1662 Savannah Hwy., West Ashley ☎ 843/571–3668) is no-frills, with live South Carolina beach music and shag or swing dancing lessons Tuesday through Thursday. It's across the river from downtown Charleston. **Bert's Bar** (✉ 2209 Middle St., Sullivan's Island ☎ 843/883–3924), a true beach-bum neighborhood hangout, has live music on weekends on Sullivan's Island. The **Windjammer** (✉ 1000 Ocean Blvd., Isle of Palms ☎ 843/886–8596), on the Isle of Palms, is an oceanfront bar with live local and national rock Thursday through Sunday.

SHOPPING

Shopping Districts

The Market area is a complex of specialty shops and restaurants centered around the **Old City Market** (✉ E. Bay and Market Sts., Market area), a covered flea mart. Sweet-grass basket weavers "sew" their creations here, and you can buy the resulting wares. **Shops at Charleston Place** (✉ 130 Market St., Market area) is home to Gucci, Caché, Benetton, Godiva, Limited Express, Brookstone, and more. **King Street** is the major shopping street in town. Lower King (from Broad to Market streets) is high-end antiques central. Middle King (from Market to Calhoun streets) is a mix of national chains like Banana Republic and Pottery Barn and local boutiques. Upper King (from Calhoun Street to Cannon street) is the up-and-coming area where fashionistas search out one-of-a-kind deals. From May until September a festive **farmers' market** (✉ King St. at Calhoun St., Market area) takes place Saturday mornings (8–1) at Marion Square.

Antiques

Birlant & Co. (✉ 191 King St., Lower King ☎ 843/722–3842) mostly carries 18th- and 19th-century English antiques, but keep your eye out for a Charleston Battery bench. **Livingstons' Antiques** (✉ 163 King St., Lower King ☎ 843/723–9697 ✉ 2137 Savannah Hwy., West Ashley ☎ 843/556–6162) deals in 18th- and 19th-century English and continental furniture, clocks, and bric-a-brac. The branch west of the Ashley River is the largest. **Period Antiques** (✉ 194 King St., Lower King ☎ 843/723–2724) carries 18th- and 19th-century pieces. **Petterson Antiques** (✉ 201 King St., Lower King ☎ 843/723–5714) sells curious objets d'art, books, furniture, porcelain, and glass.

English Rose Antiques (✉ 436 King St., Upper King ☎ 843/722–7939) has country-style accessories at some of the best prices on the Peninsula. **King Street Antique Mall** (✉ 495 King St., Upper King, ☎ 843/723–2211) is part flea-market finds and part true-antiques store.

On James Island, a 10-minute drive from downtown, **Carolopolis Antiques** (✉ 2000 Wappoo Dr., James Island ☎ 843/795–7724) has good bargains on country antiques, many of which are bought by downtown stores. On U.S. 17 in Mount Pleasant, **Hungryneck Mall** (✉ 401 Johnnie Dodds Blvd., Mount Pleasant ☎ 843/849–1744) has more than 60 antiques dealers hawking sterling silver, oak and mahogany furnishings, linens, and Civil War memorabilia. **Page's Thieves Market** (✉ 1460 Ben Sawyer Blvd., Mount Pleasant ☎ 843/884–9672) has furniture, glassware, and occasional auctions.

Art & Crafts Galleries

Serious art collectors head to **Ann Long Fine Art** (✉ 12 State St., Market area ☎ 843/577–0447) for neoclassical and modern works. **Blink** (✉ 62B Queen St., Market area ☎ 843/577–5688) has regionally and locally produced paintings, photos, pottery, jewelry, and garden art. **Charleston Crafts** (✉ 87 Hasell St., Market area ☎ 843/723–2938) has a fine selection of pottery, quilts, weavings, sculptures, and jewelry fashioned mostly by local artists. The **Gallery Chuma** (✉ 43 John St., Market area ☎ 843/722–8224) sells African-American artwork and locally made, elaborate Sunday hats.

Nina Liu and Friends (✉ 24 State St., Market area ☎ 843/722–2724) sells contemporary art objects including pottery, handblown glass, jewelry, and photographs. **One of a Kind** (✉ 164 Church St., Market area ☎ 843/534–1774) is filled with the works of more than 300 artists (35 local ones). **Pink House Gallery** (✉ 17 Chalmers St., Market area ☎ 843/723–3608), inside the oldest stone house in the city, has prints and paintings of traditional Charleston scenes done by local artists. Be sure to go up to the third floor to get a look at the small, 17th-century living quarters. **Charleston Renaissance Gallery** (✉ 103 Church St., South of Broad ☎ 843/723–0025) carries museum-quality Southern art.

Books

The **Preservation Society of Charleston** (✉ King and Queen Sts., Market area ☎ 843/722–4630) carries books and tapes of historic and local interest, sweet-grass baskets, prints, and posters. Buy picture books of Charleston homes, gardens, and food at **Waldenbooks** (✉ 120 Market St., Market area ☎ 843/853–1736).

Antique collectible books fill the shelves of **Charleston Rare Book Company** (✉ 66 Church St., South of Broad ☎ 843/723–3330). Look for out-of-print and rare books (on Southern topics and beyond) at **Boomer's Books & Collectibles** (✉ 420 King St., Upper King ☎ 843/722–2666).

Clothing

Charleston's and London's own **Ben Silver** (✉ 149 King St., Market area ☎ 843/577–4556), premier purveyor of blazer buttons, has more than 800 designs, including college and British regimental motifs. He also sells British neckties, embroidered polo shirts, and blazers. **Bob Ellis Shoes** (✉ 332 King St., Market area ☎ 843/722–2515) sells shoes from Dolce & Gabbana, Prada, and Mahnolo. **Christian Michi** (✉ 220 King St., Market area ☎ 843/723–0575) carries chi-chi women's clothing and accessories. Shop **Copper Penny** (✉ 311 King St., Market area ☎ 843/723–2999) for chic, trendy dresses. **MooRoo Handbags** (✉ 316 King St., Market area ☎ 843/724–1081) is popular with Hollywood's A-Listers. **nula** (✉ 320 King St., Market area ☎ 843/853–6566) sells hipster wear.

Need a ballgown? **Berlins** (✉ 114 King St., South of Broad ☎ 843/723–5591) is your place. **Magar Hatworks** (✉ 557 ½ King St., Upper King ☎ 843/577–7740) sells hand-crafted hats.

Gifts

ESD (✉ 314 King St., Market area ☎ 843/577–6272) is a top local interior design firm; its King Street shop sells coffee-table books, jewelry, gifts, pillows and more. Look for cool kitchen gear at **fred** (✉ 237 King St., Market area ☎ 843/723–5699). **Indigo** (✉ 4 Vendue Range, Market area ☎ 843/723–2983) stocks funky home and garden accessories, knickknacks, and stationery. Magnets, cards, ornaments, books, fresh flowers, and home furnishings—for all budgets—are at **Metropolitan Deluxe** (✉ 164 Market St., Market area ☎ 843/722–0436). Artsy and hip baby gear, house-warming gifts, jewelry, books, and even office supplies make the mundane fun at **Worthwhile** (✉ 268 King St., Market area ☎ 843/723–4418).

dwelling (✉ 474 King St., Upper King ☎ 843/723–9699) sells modern accessories and furniture. **Charleston Collections** (✉ 625 Skylark Dr., West Ashley ☎ 843/556–8911) has Charleston chimes, Rainbow Row prints, Charleston rice spoons and rice steamers, and more.

Foodstuffs

Charleston Candy Kitchen (✉ 32A N. Market St., Market area ☎ 843/723–4626) sells fudge made on-site, Charleston chews, and benne seed (an African sesame seed) wafers; check out the gift tins. The downtown, 24-hour **Harris Teeter** (✉ 290 East Bay St., Market area ☎ 843/722–6821) has Charleston foodstuffs and other groceries. Make time to stop at **Market Street Sweets** (✉ 100 N. Market St., Market area ☎ 843/722–1397) for their melt-in-your-mouth pralines and fudge, along with other candies. Try their terrific samples.

Get Charleston foods, including benne seed wafers, pepper jelly, she-crab soup, and pickled okra, at area grocery stores like **Piggly Wiggly**

(✉ 1501 U.S. 17N, Mount Pleasant ☎ 843/881–7921 ✉ IOP Connector, Mount Pleasant ☎ 843/881–8939).

Bull Street Gourmet (✉ 60 Bull St., College of Charleston ☎ 843/720–8992) sells upscale picnic fare made fresh daily, and has great deals on wine.

Kennedy's Bakery and Market (✉ 60 Calhoun St., Upper King ☎ 843/723–2026) sells wine and cheeses, plus fresh-baked breads, muffins, and scones.

Period Reproductions

Historic Charleston Reproductions (✉ 105 Broad St., South of Broad ☎ 843/723–8292) has superb replicas of Charleston furniture and accessories, all authorized by the Historic Charleston Foundation. Royalties from sales contribute to restoration projects. At the **Old Charleston Joggling Board Co.** (✉ 652 King St., Upper King ☎ 843/723–4331), these Lowcountry oddities (on which people bounce) can be purchased.**Carolina Lanterns** (✉ 917 Houston Northcutt Blvd., Mount Pleasant ☎ 843/881–4170 🌐 www.carolinalanterns.com) sells gas lanterns based on designs from downtown's historic district.

SIDE TRIPS FROM CHARLESTON

Gardens, parks, and the charming town of Summerville are good reasons to travel a bit farther afield for day trips.

Moncks Corner

30 mi northwest of Charleston on U.S. 52.

This town is a gateway to a number of attractions in Santee Cooper Country. Named for the two rivers that form a 171,000-acre basin, the area brims with outdoor pleasures centered on the basin and nearby Lakes Marion and Moultrie.

Explore the inky swamp waters of **Cypress Gardens** in a complimentary flat-bottom boat; walk along paths lined with moss-draped cypress trees, azaleas, camellias, daffodils, wisteria, and dogwood; and marvel at the clouds of butterflies in the butterfly house. The swamp garden was created from what was once the freshwater reserve of the vast Dean Hall rice plantation. It's about 24 mi north of Charleston via U.S. 52, between Goose Creek and Moncks Corner. ✉ *3030 Cypress Gardens Rd.* ☎ *843/553–0515* 🌐 *www.cypressgardens.org* 🎫 *$9* 🕒 *Daily 9–4.*

Mepkin Abbey is an active Trappist monastery overlooking the Cooper River. The site was the former plantation home of Henry Laurens and, later, of publisher Henry Luce and wife Clare Boothe Luce. You can tour the gardens and abbey or even stay here on a retreat—one- to six-night stays are open to anyone, including married couples, willing to observe the rules of the abbey (reservations are required and donations are greatly appreciated). The gift shop carries items the monks have produced—soaps, honey, crafts, and sweets—and eggs farmed on the premises. Tours leave at 11:30 and 3. ✉ *1098 Mepkin Abbey Rd., off Dr. Evans Rd., 8 mi southeast of Moncks Corner via Rte. 402* ☎ *843/761–8509* 🌐 *www.mepkinabbey.org* *Grounds free; guided tours $5* *Tues.–Fri. and Sun. 9–4:30, Sat. 9–4.*

On the banks of the Old Santee Canal is the **Old Santee Canal Park,** which you can explore on foot or by canoe. The park includes a 19th-century plantation house and an interpretive center. The on-site Berkeley Museum focuses on cultural and natural history. ✉ *900 Stony Landing Rd., off Rembert C. Dennis Blvd.* ☎ *843/899–5200* 🌐 *www.oldsanteecanalpark.org* *$3* *Daily 9–5.*

Francis Marion National Forest consists of 250,000 acres of swamps, vast oaks and pines, and little lakes thought to have been formed by falling meteors. It's a good place for picnicking, hiking, camping, horseback riding, boating, and swimming. ✉ *U.S. 52, 35 mi north of Charleston* ☎ *843/336–3248* *Free* *Daily 9–4:30.*

Lakes Moultrie and Marion attract anglers after bream, crappie, catfish, and several kinds of bass. Supplies, camps, guides, rentals, and accommodations abound in the areas around the lakes. *Lake Moultrie, 2 mi northwest of Moncks Corner, off Rte. 6; Lake Marion, 20 mi northwest of Moncks Corner, off Rte. 6.*

For more information about area lakes and facilities, contact **Santee Cooper Counties Promotion Commission & Visitors Center** *9302 Old Hwy. 6, Drawer 40, Santee 29142* ☎ *803/854–2131, 800/227–8510 outside SC* 🌐 *www.santeecoopercountry.org.*

Where to Stay

$$–$$$ **Rice Hope Plantation.** A former 285-acre rice plantation outside Moncks Corner, this inn overlooks the Cooper River, and is on 11 acres of live oaks and gardens designed by landscape architect Loutrell Briggs. Antiques and reproductions fill the home and there are five working fireplaces. Guest rooms have wood floors and some four-poster beds; the suite has a porch overlooking the river. ✉ *206 Rice Hope Dr., 29461* ☎ *843/849–9000 or 800/569–4038* 🌐 *www.ricehope.com* *4 rooms, 1 suite* *Tennis court, boating, fishing, basketball; no smoking* *AE, MC, V* *BP.*

Summerville

25 mi northwest of Charleston via I–26 and Rte. 165.

Victorian homes, many of which are listed on the National Register of Historic Places, line the public park. Colorful gardens brimming with camellias, azaleas, and wisteria abound. Downtown and residential streets curve around tall pines, as a local ordinance prohibits cutting them down. Visit for a stroll in the park, or to go antiquing on the downtown shopping square. Summerville was originally built by wealthy planters.

For more information about Summerville, stop by the **Greater Summerville/Dorchester County Chamber of Commerce and Visitor Center** (402 N. Main St., Box 670, 29484 ☎ 843/873–2931).

Where to Stay & Eat

★ $$$$ ✕ **Woodlands Resort and Inn.** People drive from Charleston for superb meals ($$$$) at this luxury inn, part of the prestigious Relais & Châteaux group. Entrées have delicate sauces and subtle touches, like the beef filet kissed by Madeira. Other options might include crab cakes in a potato crust, or lobster. Four- or five-course menus with wine are available. Although the inn, built in 1906 as a winter home, backs up to a suburb today, it's still a first-rate getaway. Some rooms have fireplaces, whirlpool or claw-foot tubs, and heated towel racks. Rates include a split of wine at arrival and afternoon tea. ✉ *125 Parsons Rd., 29483* ☎ *843/875–2600 or 800/774–9999* 📠 *843/875–2603* 🌐 *www.woodlandsinn.com* *10 rooms, 9 suites* *Restaurant, room service, in-room data ports, some in-room hot tubs, in-room safes, in-room VCRs, 2 tennis courts, pool, bicycles, croquet, lounge, meeting rooms, some pets allowed, no-smoking rooms* 💳 *AE, D, DC, MC, V.*

5

CHARLESTON A TO Z

To research prices, get advice from other travelers, and book travel arrangements, visit www.fodors.com.

AIRPORTS

Charleston International Airport on I–26, 12 mi west of downtown, is served by Continental, Delta, Independence Air (to Washington Dulles), United Express, Northwest, and US Airways.

Airport Information **Charleston International Airport** ✉ 5500 International Blvd., North Charleston ☎ 843/767-1100.

TRANSFERS Several shuttle and cab companies service the airport. It costs about $19–$22 to travel downtown by taxi; to Mount Pleasant, $23–$35. Fares are approximately $1.65 per mi. Airport Ground Transportation arranges shuttles, which cost $10 per person to the downtown area. Some hotels provide shuttle service.

Airport Ground Transportation ☎ 843/767-1100. **Harvie's Taxi Limo Service** ☎ 843/709-4276. **Lee's Limousine** ☎ 843/797-0041. **Mitch Limo Service and Transportation** ☎ 843/270-6902 or 843/270-7774.

BOAT TRAVEL

Boaters—many traveling the Intracoastal Waterway—dock at Ashley Marina and City Marina, in Charleston Harbor, or at Wild Dunes Yacht Harbor, on the Isle of Palms.

Ashley Marina ✉ Lockwood Blvd., Medical University of South Carolina ☎ 843/722-1996. **City Marina** ✉ Lockwood Blvd., Medical University of South Carolina ☎ 843/723-5098. **Wild Dunes Yacht Harbor** ✉ Pine Blvd., Isle of Palms ☎ 843/886-5100.

BUS TRAVEL

Greyhound serves Charleston and Moncks Corner.

Charleston Bus Station ✉ 3610 Dorcester Rd., North Charleston ☎ 843/744-4247. **Greyhound** ☎ 800/231-2222 🌐 www.greyhound.com.

CAR TRAVEL

I–26 traverses the state from northwest to southeast and terminates at Charleston. U.S. 17, the coast road, passes through Charleston. I–526, also called the Mark Clark Expressway, runs primarily east–west, connecting the West Ashley area to Mount Pleasant.

EMERGENCIES

Medical University of South Carolina (MUSC) Hospital and Roper Hospital have 24-hour emergency rooms.

Emergency Services **Ambulance, police** ☎ 911.

Hospitals **MUSC Hospital** ✉ 169 Ashley Ave., Medical University of South Carolina ☎ 843/792-2300. **Roper Hospital** ✉ 316 Calhoun St., Upper King ☎ 843/724-2000.

Late-Night Pharmacy **Eckerds** ✉ 261 Calhoun St., Upper King ☎ 843/805-6022.

LODGING

APARTMENT & VILLA RENTALS

For historic home rentals in Charleston, contact Ann Green Property Management. For condo and house rentals on Kiawah Island, Sullivan's Island, and the Isle of Palms—some with private pools and tennis courts—contact Great Beach Vacations.

Local Agents **Ann Green Property Management** ✉ 18 Fulton St., Market area, 29401 ☎ 843/720-5881. **Great Beach Vacations** ✉ 1517 Palm Blvd., Isle of Palms 29451 ☎ 843/886-9704.

BED-AND-BREAKFASTS

To find rooms in homes, cottages, and carriage houses, contact Historic Charleston Bed and Breakfast.

Reservation Services **Historic Charleston Bed and Breakfast** ✉ 60 Broad St., South of Broad, 29401 ☎ 843/722-6606.

TAXIS

Fares within the city average $3–$4 per trip. Companies include Safety Cab and Yellow Cab.

Charleston Rickshaw Company will take you anywhere in the historic district on one of their pedicabs for $6–$12. Cabs stand near Charleston place in the daytime; call for pickup 5 PM to 3 AM daily.

Taxi Companies **Charleston Rickshaw Company** ✉ 21 George St., Market area ☎ 843/723-5685. **Safety Cab** ☎ 843/722-4066.

SIGHTSEEING TOURS

AIR TOURS

Flying High Over Charleston provides aerial tours.

Flying High Over Charleston ✉ Mercury Air Center, W. Aviation Ave., off 1-26 ☎ 843/569-6148 🌐 http://flyinghighovercharleston.com.

BOAT TOURS

Charleston Harbor Tours gives history and specialty boat tours. Spiritline Cruises has harbor tours, dinner trips, and it runs the ferry to Fort Sumter. Sandlapper Tours has boat tours focused on harbor history, coastal wildlife, and ghostly lore.

Charleston Harbor Tours ✉ 196 Concord St., Market area ☎ 843/722-1691 🌐 www.charlestonharbortours.com. **Sandlapper Tours** ✉ Charleston Maritime Center, Concord St., Market area ☎ 843/849-8687 🌐 www.sandlappertours.com. **Spiritline Cruises** ✉ 360 Concord St, Market area ☎ 843/881-7337 or 800/789-3678 🌐 www.spiritlinecruises.com.

BUS TOURS Adventure Sightseeing does motor-coach tours of the historic district. Associated Guides of Historic Charleston pairs local tour guides with visiting bus groups. Doin' the Charleston, a van tour, combines its narration with audiovisuals and makes a stop at the Battery. Sites and Insights is another van tour that covers downtown and nearby sea islands. Gullah Tours is fluent in the Gullah language, and stops at local sights significant to the African-American culture. Chai Y'All shares stories and sights of Jewish interest. Most bus tours leave from near the visitor information center, though special arrangements can be made. Call for reservations.

Adventure Sightseeing ☎ 843/762-0088 or 800/722-5394 🌐 http://touringcharleston.com. **Associated Guides of Historic Charleston** ☎ 843/724-6419 🌐 www.historiccharleston.org. **Chai Y'All** ☎ 843/556-0664. **Doin' the Charleston** ☎ 843/763-1233 or 800/647-4487 🌐 www.dointhecharlestontours.com. **Gullah Tours** ☎ 843/763-7551 🌐 www.gullahtours.com. **Sites and Insights** ☎ 843/762-0051 🌐 www.sitesandinsightstours.com.

CARRIAGE TOURS Carriage tours are a great way to see Charleston. Lowcountry Carriage Co., Old South Carriage Company, and Palmetto Carriage Tours run horse- and mule-drawn carriage tours of the historic district, some conducted by guides in Confederate uniforms, that each last about one hour. They have a set itinerary and cover one of four zones in the historic district; once the carriages have picked up passengers the drivers draw from a lottery to decide which zone each carriage will cover. Carriage companies queue up at North Market and Anson streets; plan on touring before 5 PM to see the residential section.

Lowcountry Carriage Co. ☎ 843/577-0042. **Old South Carriage Company** ☎ 843/723-9712. **Palmetto Carriage Tours** ☎ 843/723-8145.

ECOTOURS Barrier Island Ecotours, at the Isle of Palms Marina, runs three-hour pontoon-boat tours to a barrier island, sunset tours, crabbing and fishing expeditions. Coastal Expeditions has half-day and full-day naturalist-led kayak tours down historic rivers. Charleston Explorers leads educational boat ecotours for school classes and other groups. June through August, seats are available to the public.

Barrier Island Ecotours ✉ Off U.S. 17, Isle of Palms ☎ 843/886-5000 🌐 www.nature-tours.com. **Coastal Expeditions** ✉ 514 B Mill St., Mount Pleasant ☎ 843/884-7684 🌐 www.coastalexpeditions.com. **The Charleston Explorer** ✉ Charleston Maritime Center, off Calhoun St. ☎ 843/723-5656 🌐 http://charlestonexplorers.org.

PRIVATE GUIDES To hire a private guide for the city and outlying plantations, contact Charleston's Finest Historic Tours or Janice Kahn, who has been doing customized tours for more than 30 years.

Charleston's Finest Historic Tours ☎ 843/577-3311. **Janice Kahn** ☎ 843/556-0664.

WALKING TOURS General and theme—area home, garden, Civil War, slavery, women's history—walking tours are given by Charleston Strolls and the Original Charleston Walks. Cobblestone Tours and Tours of Charleston have walks that explore the supernatural side of town. Anna's House and Garden Walking Tour focuses on architectural and botanical delights. Military history buffs should consider Jack Thompson's Civil War Walking Tour. Call for reservations.

Anna's House and Garden Walking Tour ✉ 61 Queen St., Market area ☎ 843/577-5931 🌐 www.ghostwalk.net. **Charleston Strolls** ✉ Charleston Place, 130 Market St., Market area ☎ 843/766-2080 🌐 www.charlestonstrolls.com. **Cobblestone Tours** ✉ 40 N. Market St., Market area ☎ 843/568-3315 🌐 www.cobblestonewalkingtours.com. **Tours of Charleston** ✉ Waterfront Park, Prioleau St., Market area ☎ 843/723-1670 or 800/854-1670. **Jack Thompson's Civil War Walking Tour** ✉ The Mills House Hotel, 115 Meeting Street, Market Area ☎ 843/722-7033. **Original Charleston Walks** ✉ 58½ Broad St., South of Broad ☎ 843/577-3800 or 800/729-3420.

TRAIN TRAVEL

Train Information **Amtrak** ✉ 4565 Gaynor Ave., North Charleston ☎ 843/744-8264 or 800/872-7245 🌐 www.amtrak.com.

VISITOR INFORMATION

The Charleston Area Convention & Visitors Bureau runs the Charleston Visitor Center, which also has information on Kiawah Island, Seabrook Island, Mount Pleasant, North Charleston, Edisto Island, Summerville, and the Isle of Palms. You can pick up a schedule of events at the visitor center or at area hotels, inns, and restaurants. The Historic Charleston Foundation and the Preservation Society of Charleston have information on house tours.

Tourist Information **Charleston Visitor Center** ✉ 375 Meeting St., Upper King 📫 423 King St., 29403 ☎ 843/853-8000 or 800/868-8118 🌐 www.charlestoncvb.com. **Historic Charleston Foundation** 📫 Box 1120, 29402 ☎ 843/723-1623 🌐 www.historiccharleston.org. **Preservation Society of Charleston** 📫 Box 521, 29402 ☎ 843/722-4630 🌐 www.preservationsociety.org.

HILTON HEAD & THE LOWCOUNTRY

6

SEE THE ARTSY SIDE OF HILTON HEAD
at the village of Bluffton ⇨*p.251*

GOLF FROM DAWN TILL DUSK
on 24 championship courses ⇨*p.254*

GET ALL THE SOUTHERN COMFORTS
at the Inn at Harbor Town ⇨*p.258*

FIND THE PERFECT SEASHELL
at Edisto Beach State Park ⇨*p.267*

SAMPLE THREE KINDS OF SAUCE
at smokin' good Po' Pigs Bo-B-Q ⇨*p.267*

By Melissa Bigner

ACTION-PACKED HILTON HEAD ISLAND anchors the southern tip of South Carolina's coastline and attracts 2.4 million visitors each year. This half-tame, half-wild area is home to more than 24 world-class golf courses and even more resorts, hotels, and top restaurants. Still, it's been managed development thanks to building restrictions that aim to marry progress with environmental protection. North of Hilton Head, the coastal landscape is peppered with quiet small towns and flanked by rural sea islands. Beaufort is a hidden gem, a graceful antebellum waterfront town with a compact historic district. Many of the 18th- and 19th-century mansions have been converted to bed-and-breakfasts and Bay Street is lined with locally owned shops and restaurants. Continuing north, midway between Beaufort and Charleston is Edisto Island, where you can comb the beach for shells and camp out on the mostly barren Edisto Beach State Park, or rent the modest waterfront cottages that have been in the same families for generations.

Archaeological evidence shows Native American tribes inhabited the Lowcountry area as far back as 4,000 BC. In 1514 the Spanish first landed at Port Royal (later Beaufort), starting the competition for ownership rights of the deep port areas on either side of the Port Royal Sound. The fighting raged among European explorers, including the French, Scots, and British, and between native tribes of Cherokees, Catawbas, and Yemasee, with alliances changing as quickly as the surrounding sea island tides. By 1663, the British had established a stronghold. That same year a British sea captain exploring the area for a syndicate of planters named 42-square-mi Hilton Head island, a dense wilderness of maritime forests ruled by majestic live oaks drenched in Spanish moss, after himself.

In the 1700s, planters came and tamed the land, clearing great swaths of land for plantations that grew rice, indigo, and cotton. Beaufort first became a town in 1710, and quickly grew into one of the wealthiest cities of its size in the country, thanks to its cash crops and shipping. Hilton Head and Edisto remained mainly agrarian areas with large plantations. The plantation lifestyle continued until the Civil War, when nearby Port Royal was taken in 1861 in the largest naval assault on American soil to date.

After the war subsided, Hilton Head proper, like other parts of the Lowcountry, was parceled out to the freed slaves who had once worked its fields. For nearly a century, the area was the heart of Gullah (African-American) culture; speaking the slave-created Gullah language, inhabitants survived by farming and fishing, and locals further perfected Lowcountry cuisine by cooking up what the land and sea supplied. Life was less than ideal, however, as poverty was widespread. Then in the 1950s, Charles Fraser, whose family once owned a local plantation, spearheaded the resort movement on the southernmost tip of Hilton Head with his Sea Pines Resort. Something of a revolutionary, his goal was to stimulate growth while still protecting the environment. His master planning of the community and resort set the tone for the island and the region's development. Today no building is more than five stories tall, resort roads wind around native trees and twist around alligator-

Numbers in the text correspond to numbers in the margin and on the Hilton Head & the Lowcountry map.

If you have 3 days

Three days in the area translates to outdoor fun, shopping, and a history lesson or two in the **Hilton Head** 1–4 area. Start the trip by getting settled into your lodging, and getting a feel for the property, especially if it's a resort. No matter where you stay, spend your first day on the beach or hitting the links, as both give you time for R&R and show off the gorgeous island landscape. Day 2, head to the **Coastal Discovery Museum** 1 and sign up for a historical tour of the area to learn what the place was like before it was a vacation central. Next, head south to the **Sea Pines Resort** 3 to explore the (tamed) wild side of the island at Sea Pines Forest Preserve, then finish the day checking out the shops and restaurants of Harbour Town; be sure to peek up at the lighthouse. Day 3, drive over to **Bluffton** 4 to see the quaint 1850s town and wander through quirky, locally owned shops or stop at the outlet malls.

6

If you have 5 days

After you've spent your first three days in the Hilton Head area, head north to **Beaufort** 5. (The ride along U.S. 17 or 170 is a pretty one, so don't rush.) The heart of this town is its historic district, which has the feel of a sweet and sleepy fishing village. After taking a carriage ride, wander Bay Street's shops and restaurants and spend two nights here in an antebellum B&B. Upon awakening, take a day trip to Hunting Island State Park, where you can explore the more than 5,000-acre wilderness spread, or go on a nature tour of the A.C.E. Basin rivers and marshes. If there's time, head to the Penn Center on St. Helena Island.

If you have 7 days

After following the five-day itinerary, it's time to hit the road on Day 6 and drive north to **Edisto** 6. Stop by Po' Pigs Bo-B-Q for the barbecue buffet (or get some to go), then head to Edisto Beach, where you can pitch a tent or rent a rustic cabin. Fall asleep listening to the surf crash nearby, and continue the beach playfest the next day. That night, stop by the Old Post Office for a meal that is all finesse. Spend the next day enjoying the beach and the outdoors; don't forget to make time for a hike.

---

filled lagoons, and light and sign pollution is prohibited. Much of the region's draw remains the serene environment, casual pace, and residents' affinity for the good life.

Exploring Hilton Head & the Lowcountry

Hilton Head is just north of the South Carolina–Georgia border. It's so close to Savannah, in fact, that they share the same airport. This part of the state is best explored by car, as its points of interest spread over a flat coastal plain that is a mix of wooded areas, marshes, and sea islands, the latter of which are sometimes accessible only by boat or ferry. Take U.S. 170 and 17 to get from one key spot (Hilton Head, Beaufort, and Edisto) to another. It's a pretty drive that winds through small towns and over old bridges. Charleston is at the northern end of the region.

About the Restaurants

Given the proximity to the Atlantic and surrounding small farms, most locally owned restaurant menus are still heavily influenced by the catch of the day and seasonal field harvests. As the Lowcountry area becomes more standardized, like the rest of the world, its restaurant scene reflects that fact. Especially in Hilton Head, there are numerous national chain restaurants and hoity-toity, high-end spots in addition to the down-home holes-in-the-wall. For the most part, restaurants are open weekdays from 11 AM to 9 PM, (until 10 on weekends), and many on Hilton Head offer early-bird discounted meals (up to $10 off), served from 5 to 5:45.

WHAT IT COSTS

$$$$	$$$	$$	$	¢
over $22	$16–$22	$11–$16	$7–$11	under $7

Prices are for a main course at dinner, excluding sales tax of 6%.

About the Hotels

Hilton Head is known as one of the best vacation spots on the East Coast, and its hotels are a testimony to the reputation. The island is covered in resorts and hotels, or you can rent beachfront- or golf-course-view villas, cottages, and mansions. Here, and on private islands, expect the most modern conveniences and world-class service at the priciest places. Clean, updated rooms and friendly staff are everywhere—even at lower-rate establishments—this is the South, after all. Staying in cooler months, for extended periods of time, and commuting from nearby Bluffton, can mean better deals.

While the resorts are spreading northward, they become fewer and farther between as you go up U.S. 17, until you reach the greater Charleston area. In between there's Beaufort, where there are B&Bs to fit a variety of budgets. You can often get price breaks if you call ahead when things are slow, or if you stay midweek. The offerings in Edisto are bare-bones beach cabins or modest family cottages; if you want more pampering, stay in Beaufort and make the short drive to Edisto area attractions.

The region's high season lasts from spring through summer (May through August), plus holiday and festival weekends. Of all the lower Lowcountry region, Hilton Head is the most demanding in which to score a good deal, or even a good room—unless you plan ahead. The choicest locations are booked a year to six months in advance almost year-round, but booking agencies can help you make room reservations.

WHAT IT COSTS

$$$$	$$$	$$	$	¢
over $220	$160–$220	$110–$160	$70–$110	under $70

Prices are for two people in a standard double room in high season, excluding service charges and 10% tax.

Natural Attractions The wild—and not so wild—parts of the Lowcountry are filled with palmettos, giant live oaks, and loads of lagoons, populated with alligators, herons, kingfishers, and the like. No visit to the area would be complete without at least a half day exploring the nature preserves. On Hilton Head you can choose from the Sea Pines Forrest Preserve or the Audubon-Newhall Preserve. Near Beaufort, Hunting Island State Park has more than 5,000 acres to explore and you can camp out at Edisto Island State Park. In the Beaufort and Edisto area, kayak, canoe, and other boat tours of the A.C.E. Basin are one of the best ways to see the marshes, rivers, and critters up close and personal.

Golfing Views World-class—highly picturesque—golf courses are a main reason many people vacation in far southeastern South Carolina. In and around Hilton Head Island alone there are more than 24 championship courses. The Arthur Hill course at Palmetto Dunes resort is known for its alligator sightings. Old South Golf Links overlooks marshland and the Intercoastal Waterway. The Ocean course at Sea Pines Resort is on the south side of the island, facing open water. Each megaresort has several courses to choose among; so it's hard to go wrong no matter what view you get.

Lowcountry Fare Sit down for a meal and go local; aim for shrimp and grits, pork barbecue flavored with sweet mustard, Frogmore Stew (with corn, shrimp, and sausage), spicy rice, sausage, and seafood dishes, plus fresh vegetables seasoned with pork. Sample superb Southern dishes like fried green tomatoes and comforting soul food like butter beans and ham. As you work your way up or down U.S. 17, don't miss the vegetable stands for peach chutneys, strawberry jam, pickled melon rinds, and even homemade pork crackling. The common thread that unites food particular to this area is that it's fresh fare, locally raised or harvested, prepared with a respectful nod to the past.

Shopping Residents drive from small towns all over the southern part of the state to Bluffton—to go shopping. The outlets there are deal-central, with large, well-known national stores represented. After you've found the bargain of the century, head into the historic district to look for purchases that are more one-of-a-kind. The streets are lined with funky boutiques and antiques stores. Farther north in the antebellum town of Beaufort, are more unique shops and little boutiques.

Timing

The high season follows typical beach-town cycles, with May through August and holidays year-round being the busiest and most costly. However, as local guides will tell you, thanks to the Lowcountry's mostly moderate temperatures year-round, tourists are ever-present. Spring is the most glorious time to visit, especially in Beaufort, as the historic district is awash in blooming azaleas, wisteria, and jasmine.

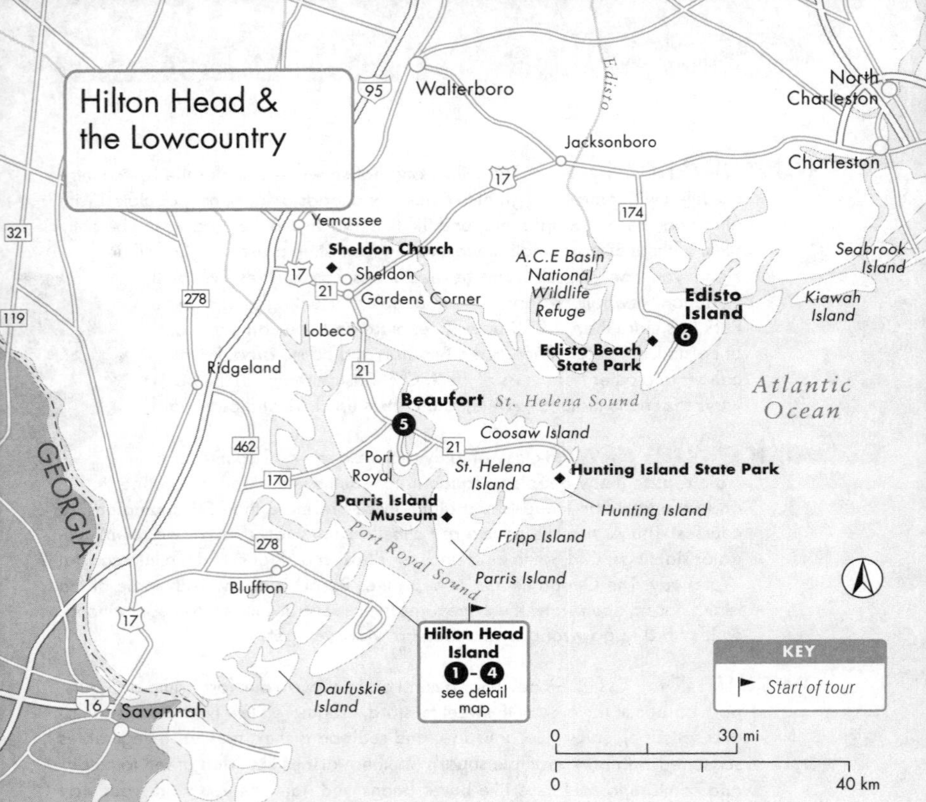

HILTON HEAD ISLAND

No matter how many golf courses pepper its landscape, Hilton Head will always be a semitropical barrier island. That means the 12 mi of beaches are lined with towering pines, palmetto trees, and wind-sculpted live oaks; the interior is a blend of oak and pine woodlands and meandering lagoons. Rental villas, lavish private houses, and luxury hotels line the coast as well.

Since the 1950s, resorts like Sea Pines, Palmetto Dunes, and Port Royal have sprung up all over. Although the gated resorts are private residential communities, many have public restaurants, marinas, shopping areas, and recreational facilities. All are secured, and cannot be toured unless arrangements are made at the visitor office near the main gate of each plantation. Hilton Head prides itself on strict laws that keep light and sign pollution to a minimum; but the lack of neon and street lights also makes it difficult to find your way at night, so be sure to get good directions.

Exploring Hilton Head Island

Driving Hilton Head by car or tour bus is the only way to get around. Off Interstate 95, take Exit 8 onto U.S. 278, which leads you through

Bluffton and then onto Hilton Head proper. A 5¾-mi Cross Island Parkway toll bridge ($1) is just off 278, and makes it easy to bypass traffic and reach the south end of the island, where most of the resort areas and hotels are. Know that U.S. 278 can slow to a standstill at rush hour and during holiday weekends, and the signs are so discreet that it's easy to get lost without explicit directions. The island is divided into the North End, Mid-Island, and South End.

a good tour

Hilton Head is a destination vacation spot because of its golf courses and beaches; many visitors move from their rooms to the water or links, to restaurants, and back again. To explore farther, drive first to the **Coastal Discovery Museum** 1 ⚑ at the Chamber of Commerce's Welcome Center. There you can get activity calendars and comprehensive maps, plus you can sign up for tours that focus on themes such as Native American, African-American, plantation, and colonial life. Next, head south on the Cross Island Parkway, which turns into Palmetto Bay Road. Turn off at signs for the **Audubon-Newhall Preserve** 2 to learn more about local flora. Continue south to the **Sea Pines Resort** 3 where you can tour 605 acres of managed wilderness at the Sea Pines Forest Preserve. Another option would be to drive the 6 mi to the **Bluffton** 4 historic district. You can do all of the above in a day, or stretch it out over several.

What to See

2 **Audubon-Newhall Preserve,** in the south, is 50 acres of pristine forest, where native plant life is tagged and identified. There are trails, a self-guided tour, and seasonal plant walks. ✉ *Palmetto Bay Rd., near southern base of Cross Island Pkwy, South End* ☎ *843/842–9246* 🌐 *www.hiltonheadaudubon.org* 🎟 *Free* ⏲ *Daily dawn–dusk.*

4 **Bluffton.** Tucked away from the bustle of Hilton Head's resorts, charming Bluffton village has several old homes and churches, a growing artists' colony, and oak-lined streets dripping with moss. You could grab Southern-style picnic food and head to the boat dock at the end of Pritchard Street or the boat landing at Brighton Beach for great views. There are great little shops around, too. ✉ *Route 46, 8 mi northwest on U.S. 278.*

Fodor's Choice ★

⚑ 1 **Coastal Discovery Museum.** Here you find two types of permanent exhibits—depicting Native American island life and sea island biodiversity—along with various temporary displays. The museum also sponsors historical and natural history tours of Native American sites, forts, and plantations as well as kayak trips, turtle watches, cruises, birding, and visits to wildlife preserves. ✉ *100 William Hilton Pkwy., North End* ☎ *843/689–6767* 🌐 *www.coastaldiscovery.org* 🎟 *Free* ⏲ *Mon.–Sat. 9–5, Sun. 10–3.*

Palmetto Dunes Resort. This complex is home to the renowned Rod Laver Tennis Center, a good stretch of beach, three golf courses, and several oceanfront rental villa complexes. The oceanfront Hilton Head Marriott Beach & Golf Resort an the Hilton Resort are also on this property. ✉ *Queens Folly Rd. at U.S. 278, Mid-Island* ☎ *800/845–8160* 🌐 *www.palmettodunesresort.com.*

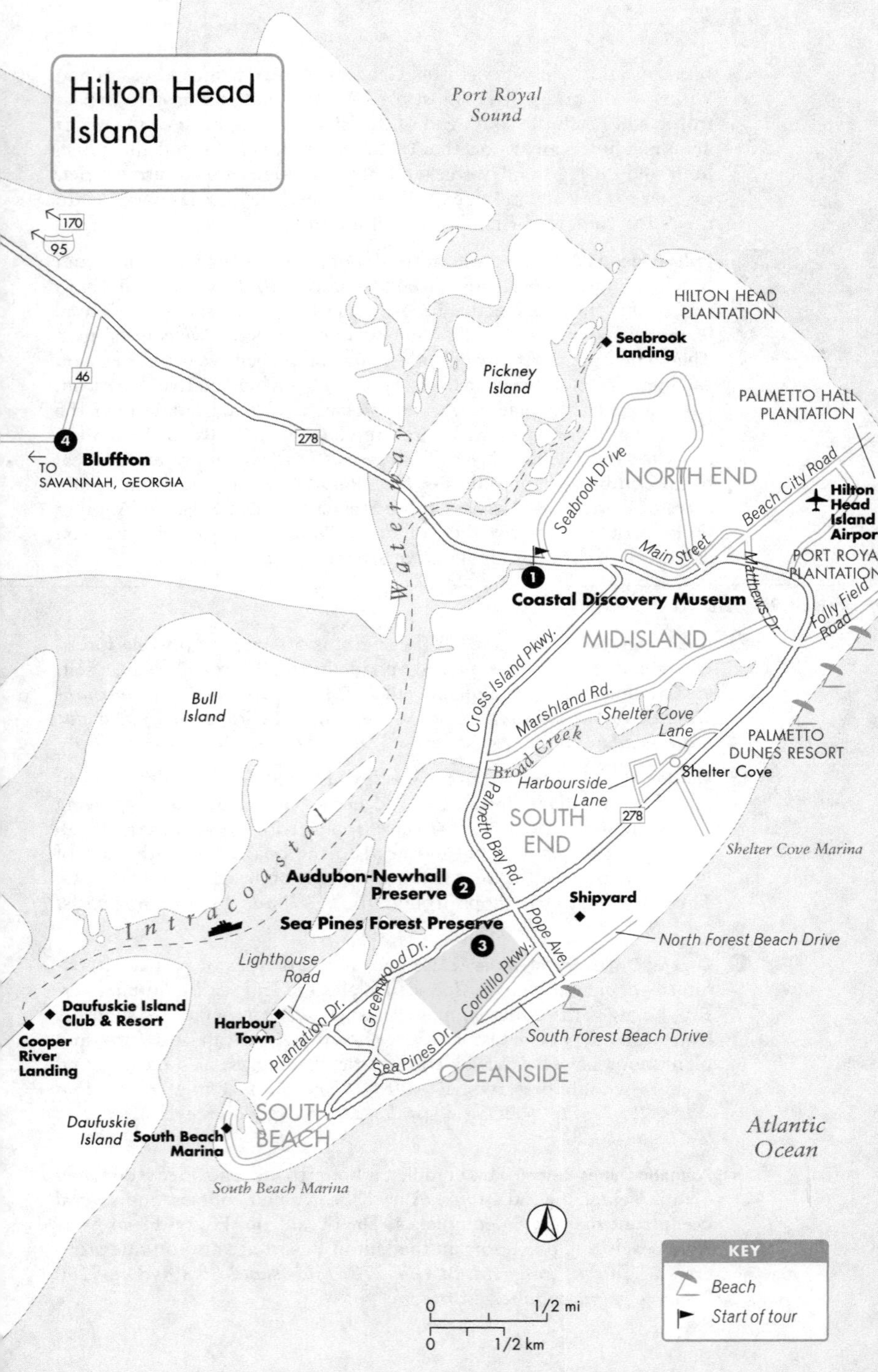

Hilton Head Island
Port Royal Sound
170
95
46
278
4 Bluffton
TO SAVANNAH, GEORGIA
Pickney Island
Seabrook Landing
HILTON HEAD PLANTATION
PALMETTO HALL PLANTATION
Seabrook Drive
NORTH END
Beach City Road
Hilton Head Island Airport
Main Street
Matthews Dr.
PORT ROYAL PLANTATION
1 Coastal Discovery Museum
Folly Field Road
MID-ISLAND
Cross Island Pkwy.
Marshland Rd.
Shelter Cove Lane
Broad Creek
Bull Island
PALMETTO DUNES RESORT
Shelter Cove
Harbourside Lane
Palmetto Bay Rd.
SOUTH END
Shelter Cove Marina
Intracoastal Waterway
Audubon-Newhall Preserve 2
Shipyard
Sea Pines Forest Preserve 3
Pope Ave.
North Forest Beach Drive
Lighthouse Road
Greenwood Dr.
Cordillo Pkwy.
Daufuskie Island Club & Resort
Cooper River Landing
Harbour Town
Plantation Dr.
South Forest Beach Drive
Sea Pines Dr.
OCEANSIDE
SOUTH BEACH
Daufuskie Island
South Beach Marina
Atlantic Ocean
South Beach Marina
0 1/2 mi
0 1/2 km
KEY
Beach
Start of tour

Port Royal Plantation. The main draws here are the posh Westin Resort, which is on the beach, three PGA-championship golf courses, Port Royal racquet club, with 16 tennis courts. ✉ *2 Grasslawn Ave., Mid-Island* ☎ *843/681–4000* 🌐 *www.westinhiltonhead.com.*

3 **Sea Pines Forest Preserve.** At this 605-acre public wilderness tract, walking trails take you past a stocked fishing pond, waterfowl pond, and a 3,400-year-old Indian shell ring. Both guided and self-guided tours of the preserve are available. Pick up the extensive activity guide at the Sea Pines Welcome Center to take advantage of goings-on—moonlight hayrides through the preserve, Gullah storytelling around evening campfires, and alligator- and bird-watching boat tours. The preserve is part of the Plantation grounds at ⇨ **Sea Pines Resort.** It's closed during the MCI Heritage golf tournament in April. ✉ *Off U.S. 278, Sea Pines Resort, South End* ☎ *843/363–4530* 🌐 *www.seapines.com* 🎟 *$5 per car for nonguests* ⏲ *Daily dawn–dusk.*

Fodor's Choice ★ **Sea Pines Resort.** The oldest and best known of Hilton Head's resort developments, or plantations, occupies 4,500 thickly wooded acres with three golf courses, a fine beach, tennis clubs, stables, and shopping plazas. The focus of Sea Pines is **Harbour Town,** a charming marina, with a luxury boutique hotel, shops, restaurants, some condominiums, and the landmark Hilton Head Lighthouse. The Crowne Plaza Hilton Head Beach Island Resort is the oceanfront centerpiece of **Shipyard,** which also has villa condominiums, three 9-hole golf courses, a tennis club, and a small beach club. There are luxurious houses and villas facing the ocean and the golf courses. You can arrange a guided resort tour. Also on-site is the ⇨ **Sea Pines Forest Preserve.** ✉ *Off U.S. 278, South End* ☎ *843/363–4530* 🌐 *www.seapines.com* 🎟 *$5 per car for nonguests.*

off the beaten path

DAUFUSKIE ISLAND – From Hilton Head you can take a 45-minute ferry ride to nearby Daufuskie Island, the setting for Pat Conroy's novel *The Water Is Wide,* which was made into the movie *Conrack.* A few descendants of former slaves live on small farms here, among remnants of churches, homes, and schools—all reminders of antebellum times. Once on the island, you can rent a golf cart or take guided tours that include sights such as a two-hundred-year-old cemetery, the Haig Point Lighthouse, former slave quarters, and a local winery, plus pre-arranged meals.

Staying at the **DAUFUSKIE ISLAND CLUB & RESORT** (✉ Embarkation Center, 421 Squire Pope Rd., North End ☎ 843/341–4820 or 800/648–6778 🌐 www.daufuskieresort.com) —with an oceanfront inn, cottages, golf courses, tennis, spa, pools, water sports, and several restaurants—is a wonderful getaway.

Calibogue Cruises (✉ Broad Creek Marina, 164B Palmetto Bay Rd., Mid-Island ☎ 843/342–8687 🌐 www.freeport-marina.com) has several Daufuskie tour options, including guided tours with lunch and gospel music performances starting at $40. **Vagabond Cruises**

(⊠ Harbour Town Marina, South End ☎ 843/785–2662 🌐 www.vagabondcruise.com) conducts daytime boat rides in conjunction with tours led by the local historical society, as well as candle-lit cemetery tours. Prices start at $28.

Sports & the Outdoors

Beaches

Although resort beach access is reserved for guests and residents, there are four public entrances to Hilton Head's 12 mi of ocean beach. The two main parking spots are off U.S. 278 at Coligny Circle in the South End, near the Holiday Inn, and on Folly Field Road, Mid-Island. Both have changing facilities. South of Folly Field Road, Mid-Island along U.S. 278, Bradley Beach Road and Singleton Road lead to beaches where parking space is limited.

Biking

There are more than 40 mi of public paths that crisscross Hilton Head island (many in the resorts), and pedaling is popular along the firmly packed beach. Bicycles can be rented at most hotels and resorts. You can also rent bicycles from the **Hilton Head Bicycle Company** (⊠ 112 Arrow Rd., South End ☎ 843/686–6888). **South Beach Cycles** (⊠ Sea Pines Resort, off U.S. 278, South End ☎ 843/671–2453) rents bikes, helmets, tandems, and adult tricycles. **Outside Hilton Head** (⊠ Sea Pines Resort, off U.S. 278, South Beach Marina, South End ☎ 843/671–2643 or 800/686–6996 ⊠ Shelter Cove La., at U.S. 278, Mid-Island ☎ 843/686–6996 or 800/686–6996 🌐 www.outsidehiltonhead.com) rents bikes and Rollerblades.

Canoeing & Kayaking

Outside Hilton Head (⊠ Sea Pines Resort, off U.S. 278, South Beach Marina, South End ⊠ Shelter Cove La., at U.S. 278, Mid-Island ☎ 843/686–6996 or 800/686–6996 🌐 www.outsidehiltonhead.com) is an ecologically sensitive company that rents canoes and kayaks; it also runs nature tours.

Fishing

Local marinas offer inshore and deep-sea fishing charters. Each year a bill-fishing tournament and two king mackerel tournaments attract anglers.

On Hilton Head you can pick oysters, dig for clams, or cast for shrimp; supplies are available at the **Shelter Cove Harbour** (⊠ Palmetto Dunes, Shelter Cove La., at U.S. 278, Mid-Island ☎ 843/842–7001).

Golf

Hilton Head is nicknamed "Golf Island" for good reason: the island itself has 24 championship courses (most semi-private, with public access allowed) and the outlying area has 16 more. The **Island West Golf Course** (⊠ U.S. 278, 8 mi northwest of Hilton Head Island, Bluffton ☎ 843/689–6660) is an 18-hole course. **Old South Golf Links** (⊠ U.S. 278, 1 mi northwest of bridge to Hilton Head island, Bluffton ☎ 843/785–5353) has scenic holes with marshland and Intracoastal Waterway views. **Palmetto Dunes Resort** (⊠ Off Queens Folly Rd. at U.S. 278, Mid-

Island ☎ 843/785–1138) has two 18-hole courses: the Arthur Hills has an old lighthouse (and lots of alligator sightings) and there are permanent junior tees at the Robert Trent Jones course. **Port Royal** (✉ Grass Lawn Ave., North End ☎ 843/689–5600) has three 18-hole courses, all on Bermuda grass. **Ocean Course at Sea Pines** (✉ 100 North Sea Pines Dr., South End ☎ 843/842–8484) is a championship course with narrow fairways and water on all but four holes. **Harbour Town Golf Links at Sea Pines** (✉ Sea Pines Resort, off U.S. 278, 11 Lighthouse La., South End ☎ 843/671–2448 or 800/955–8337) hosts the MCI Heritage tournament every spring.

6

Horseback Riding

Lawton Stables (✉ Sea Pines Resort, Plantation, off U.S. 278, South End ☎ 843/671–2586) gives horseback riding lessons and pony rides, in addition to having horseback tours through the Seapine Forest Preserve.

Summer Camp

On Hilton Head Island all major hotels offer summer youth activities; some have full-scale youth programs. The **Island Recreation Center** runs a summer camp that visiting youngsters can join. ✉ *Hilton Head Island Recreation Association, Wilborn Rd., Box 22593, North End, Hilton Head Island 29925* ☎ *843/681–7273* 🌐 *www.islandreccenter.org* ⏲ *Weekdays mid-June–late Aug.*

Tennis

There are more than 300 courts on Hilton Head. **Port Royal** (✉ 15 Wimbledon Ct., North End ☎ 843/686–8803) has 16 courts, including two grass. **Sea Pines Racquet Club** (✉ Sea Pines Resort, off U.S. 278, 32 Greenwood Dr., South End ☎ 843/363–4495) has 23 courts, instructional programs and a pro shop. **Shipyard** (✉ Off U.S. 278, Shipyard Dr., next to Crowne Plaza Resort, Mid-Island ☎ 843/686–8804) has clay courts and hard courts, a few of which are lighted. **Palmetto Dunes Resort** (✉ 6 Trent Jones La., Mid-Island ☎ 843/785–1152) welcomes nonguests. **Van der Meer Tennis Center** (✉ Shipyard Plantation, 19 deAllyon Rd., Mid-Island ☎ 843/785–8388) is highly rated and is recognized for tennis instruction. Four of its 28 courts are covered.

Where to Eat

$$$–$$$$ ✕ **Old Fort Pub.** Tucked away on a quiet site overlooking the sweeping marshlands of the Intracoastal Waterway and beside the Civil War ruins of Fort Mitchell, this romantic restaurant has almost panoramic views. It specializes in such dishes as grilled scallops, duck confit, crab cakes, and fresh fish. The wine list is extensive, and there's outdoor seating plus a third-floor porch for toasting the sunset. Sunday brunch is also a good bet. ✉ *65 Skull Creek Dr., North End* ☎ *843/681–2386* 💳 *AE, D, DC, MC, V* ⏲ *No lunch.*

$$$–$$$$ ✕ **Redfish.** The "naked" catch of the day—seafood grilled with olive oil, lime, and garlic—stands out here; it's a welcome change from the fried fare at many other local spots. Caribbean flavors pervade the rest of the menu in dishes such as red trout with Boursin cheese grits; *tasso* (a spicy cured ham) in a cream sauce spiked with amaretto, Tabasco, and Worcestershire; and Dominican braised pork, roasted with bananas, chilis, and coconut. Although the commercial strip location isn't inspired, the lively crowd sitting amid candlelight, subdued artwork, dark furniture, and white linens more than makes up for the shortcoming. ✉ *8 Archer Rd., South End* ☎ *843/686–3388* ▭ *AE, D, MC, V.*

$$–$$$$ ✕ **Brick Oven Café.** Velvet drapes, chandeliers, booths, and '40s lounge-style entertainment—on top of good, reasonably priced food served late—make this the trendy place to be. It's a refreshingly quirky joint on an island that is more luxe than funky and the menu is equally eclectic: appetizers include sweet potato and lobster cakes, shrimp and pork spring rolls; entrées are wood-fired pizzas, stir-fry, roasted veggie sandwiches, and grilled veal meatloaf. Plus, the wine list has a nice variety. ✉ *Park Plaza, Greenwood Dr., South End* ☎ *843/686–2233* ✍ *Reservations essential* ▭ *AE, D, DC, MC, V* ⊙ *No lunch.*

¢–$$ ✕ **Mi Tierra.** At this friendly Mexican restaurant, freshness is the key to tasty fare like ceviche fish tacos. Next door, Baja Tacos—run by the same people—is a simple taco stand with counter service, café tables, and a condiments bar with fresh, fresh salsas and relishes. ✉ *160 Fairfield Sq., North End* ☎ *843/342–3409* ▭ *MC, V.*

¢–$ ✕ **Kenny B's French Quarter Café.** Surrounded by Mardi Gras memorabilia, Kenny serves jambalaya, po' boys, muffaletta sandwiches, and gumbo against a wall mural of Bourbon Street. A local favorite, this café—in a strip mall—is open from morning until 9 PM. At the Sunday buffet brunch you can get chicory coffee, beignets, and Cajun omelettes. ✉ *70 Pope Ave., Bi-Lo Circle, Mid-Island* ☎ *843/785–3315* ▭ *AE, D, MC, V* ⊙ *Closed Mon.*

¢ ✕ **Signe's Heaven Bound Bakery & Café.** Mornings find locals rolling in for the deep-dish French toast, Signe's breakfast polenta, and whole wheat waffles. Smart patrons come back for a light lunch (gourmet salads and loaded hot and cold sandwiches) or order the beach bag to go ($10 for a cold sandwich, pasta or fresh fruit, chips, a drink, and cookie). Don't miss the amazing cookies, melt-in-your mouth cakes, and rave-worthy breads—from Italian *ciabatta* (sourdough) to Squaw Bread (rye sweetened with local honey). ✉ *93 Arrow Rd., South End* ☎ *843/785–9118* ▭ *AE, D, MC, V* ⊙ *Closed Sun. No dinner.*

Where to Stay

In addition to stand-alone hotels, elaborate resorts have hotels and condominiums (sometimes with rentals), and there are houses and villas to rent.

Hilton Head Accommodations and Golf Line (✉ 20 Pope Ave., South End ☎ 800/444–4772 ☎🖷 843/686–6662 🌐 www.hiltonheadusa.com) books both hotels and tee times. **Island Rentals** (✉ 3 Pensacola Pl., unit 3A, South End ☎ 800/845–6134 ☎🖷 843/785–3813 🌐 www.irhhi.com) brokers oceanfront, ocean-oriented, and golf-oriented home, condo and villa rentals, as well as providing concierge service. **The Vacation Company** (✉ U.S. 278 and Arrow Rd., South End ☎ 843/785–9050 or 800/845–7018 🖷 843/686–3255 🌐 www.vacationcompany.com) represents almost every hotel, motel, and rental agency on the island.

★ $$$$ **Disney's Hilton Head Island Resort.** Disney's typical cheery colors and designs create a look that is part Southern and part Adirondack getaway. The villas here have fully furnished dining, living, and sleeping areas, as well as porches with rocking chairs and picnic tables. Many have marsh or marina views. The smallest is a studio villa, the largest has three bedrooms, four baths, and sleeping space for 12. The resort has a fishing pier and a lively beach club a mile from the accommodations (shuttle service provided) with a pool, a snack bar, and decorative fountains. Guests have golf and tennis privileges at neighboring Palmetto Dunes. ✉ *22 Harbourside La., Mid-Island, 29928* ☎ *843/341–4100 or 407/939–7540* 📠 *843/341–4130* 🌐 *www.dvcmagic.com* *102 units* *2 snack bars, fans, some in-room hot tubs, kitchens, golf privileges, miniature golf, 2 pools, gym, outdoor hot tub, dock, boating, marina, fishing, bicycles, billiards, horseshoes, Ping-Pong, shuffleboard, recreation room, video game room, children's programs (ages 3–16), playground, laundry service, no-smoking rooms* 💳 *AE, MC, V* 🍽 *EP.*

$$$$ **Hilton Head Marriott Beach & Golf Resort.** Marriot's standard rooms get a tropical twist in this palm-enveloped, beachfront location: sunny yellow-and-green floral fabrics and cherrywood furnishings are part of the peppy decor. All guest rooms have private balconies, desk areas, and down comforters. You can lounge by the seaside pool to take in the ocean view. ✉ *1 Hotel Circle, South End, 29928* ☎ *843/686–8400* 📠 *843/686–8450* 🌐 *www.hiltonheadmarriott.com* *476 rooms, 36 suites* *Restaurant, café, pizzeria, room service, some kitchens, some minibars, driving range, 3 18-hole golf courses, putting green, 26 tennis courts, 2 pools (1 indoor), gym, 2 hot tubs (1 indoor), beach, bicycles, bar, piano bar, shop, babysitting, children's programs (ages 3–12), concierge, business services, meeting rooms, no-smoking rooms* 💳 *AE, D, DC, MC, V* 🍽 *EP.*

$$$–$$$$ **Crowne Plaza Hilton Head Island Beach Resort.** This oceanfront resort is a member of the upscale Intercontinental Hotel Group, and is appropriately resplendent, glimmering with brass railings and accents, and shiny wood floors and trim. Decorated in a nautical theme and set in a luxuriant garden, the Crowne Plaza has access to all the amenities of Shipyard Plantation. ✉ *130 Shipyard Dr., Mid-Island, 29928* ☎ *843/842–2400 or 800/334–1881* 📠 *843/785–8463* 🌐 *www.crowneplazaresort.com* *331 rooms, 9 suites* *2 restaurants, snack bar, room service, minibars, 3 18-hole golf courses, 3 pools (1 indoor), health club, hot tub, bicycles, lounge, children's programs (ages 3–12), business services, meeting room, no-smoking rooms* 💳 *AE, D, DC, MC, V* 🍽 *EP.*

$$$–$$$$ **Hilton Oceanfront Resort.** There's a Caribbean sensibility to this five-story chain hotel, located mid-island. The grounds are beautifully landscaped with deciduous and evergreen bushes, as well as beach-front palms. All the rooms face the ocean and are decorated with upscale wood furniture, such as carved armoires. Warm colors like red accent neutral beiges and creams in the linens and upholstery. ✉ *23 Ocean La., Mid-Island,* *Box 6165, 29938* ☎ *843/842–8000 or 800/845–8001* 📠 *843/842–4988* 🌐 *www.hiltonheadhilton.com* *303 rooms, 20 suites* *2 restaurants, kitchenettes, 3 18-hole golf courses, 2 pools, health club, hot tub,*

sauna, boating, fishing, bicycles, Ping-Pong, volleyball, lounge, children's programs (ages 5–12), no-smoking rooms ▭ *AE, D, DC, MC, V* 🍽 *EP.*

$$$–$$$$ **Holiday Inn Oceanfront Resort.** A handsome high-rise motor hotel, this property is on one of the busiest stretches of the island's beaches—the South End—and is within walking distance of shops and restaurants. The rooms are spacious and furnished in a contemporary style; golf and tennis packages are available. The outdoor Tiki Hut lounge, a poolside bar, is hugely popular. ✉ *S. Forest Beach Dr., South End* 📫 *Box 5728, 29938* ☎ *843/785–5126 or 800/423–9897* 📠 *843/785–6678* 🌐 *www.hihiltonhead.com* 🛏 *201 rooms* 👍 *Restaurant, snack bar, pool, wading pool, gym, bicycles, volleyball, lounge, children's programs (ages 3–12), meeting rooms, no-smoking rooms* ▭ *AE, D, DC, MC, V* 🍽 *EP.*

$$$–$$$$ **Main Street Inn.** Classical gardens, shuttered doors, an elegant, narrow pool, and elaborate ironwork make this inn reminiscent of an Italianate villa. Luxury abounds inside, too, in the antique furnishings and the heart-pine floors covered in Turkish and sisal rugs. Guest rooms have velvet and silk brocade linens, feather duvets, and porcelain and brass sinks. The elaborate European-style breakfast includes imported meats, cheeses, quiches, breads, and pastries. Evening cocktails are served at the mahogany bar and the turn-down service is nightly. ✉ *2200 Main St., North End, 29926* ☎ *843/681–3001 or 800/471–3001* 📠 *843/681–5541* 🌐 *www.mainstreetinn.com* 🛏 *33 rooms* 👍 *Dining room, some in-room hot tubs, pool, hot tub, bar; no smoking* ▭ *AE, MC, V* 🍽 *BP.*

★ $$$ **The Inn at Harbor Town.** The most buzzworthy of Hilton Head's properties is this small boutique hotel with a British accent. A proper staff, clad in kilts, pamper you with a dose of Southern charm. Butlers and concierges are on hand 24 hours, the Inn's kitchen delivers around the clock, and turn-down service is nightly. The spacious guest rooms have a neutral palette and Lowcountry art. The attention to detail includes cotton Frette sheets and lighted makeup mirrors. Harbor Town Grill serves some of the best steak and seafood on the island. The Inn is part of the quaint Harbor Town Village at the Sea Pines Resort. ✉ *Lighthouse La., off U.S. 278, South End, 29926* ☎ *843/785–3333 or 888/807–6873* 🌐 *www.seapines.com* 🛏 *60 rooms* 👍 *Restaurant, room service, refrigerators, 3 18-hole golf courses, 4 tennis courts, bicycles, laundry service, concierge, no-smoking rooms* ▭ *AE, D, DC, MC, V* 🍽 *EP.*

★ $$$ **Westin Resort, Hilton Head Island.** The lush oceanfront landscape of the Westin lies on the island's quietest, least inhabited stretch. A 2004, $3.3 million renovation has made it all the more fabulous. Guest rooms come with all-white, 250-thread-count sheets, five pillows, and down comforters. Leather desk chairs, fold-out sofas, and comfy lounge chairs were added, as well as new carpet and lighting. Rooms, most with ocean views and balconies, have crown molding and, because of the rich colors and comfortable wicker and contemporary furniture, it seems somewhat residential. The resort also has 100 two- and three-bedroom villas, each with a kitchen, VCR, and washer-dryer. ✉ *2 Grass Lawn Ave., North End, 29928* ☎ *843/681–4000 or 800/228–3000* 📠 *843/681–1087* 🌐 *www.westin.com* 🛏 *412 rooms, 29 suites* 👍 *3 restaurants, in-room data ports, driving range, 3 18-hole golf courses, 16 tennis courts, pro shop, 2 pools (1 indoor), wading pool, health club, massage, out-*

door hot tub, beach, bicycles, children's programs (ages 4–12), concierge, concierge floor, Internet, business services, meeting rooms, no-smoking rooms ▭ *AE, D, DC, MC, V* 🍴 *EP.*

$$ **Hampton Inn.** A short drive from the public beaches, this inn is clean, nicely landscaped, and sheltered from the noise and traffic, making it popular with business and leisure travelers alike. Rooms have one king or two double beds; some double rooms have refrigerators and microwaves; some king rooms have sleeper sofas. A friendly staff keeps customers coming back year after year. ✉ *1 Dillon Rd., Mid-Island, 29926* ☎ *843/681–7900* 📠 *843/681–4330* 🌐 *www.hampton-inn.com* *124 rooms* *Some microwaves, some refrigerators, pool, no-smoking rooms* ▭ *AE, D, DC, MC, V* 🍴 *BP.*

¢–$ **Red Roof Inn.** This two-story lodging with exterior halls is popular with families because of low rates (with kids under 18 free of charge) and rules that permit one small pet per room. Some of the clean and functional rooms have microwaves and refrigerators. The motel is just a short drive from the public beaches. ✉ *5 Regency Pkwy., Mid-Island, 29928* ☎ *843/686–6808 or 800/733–7663* 📠 *843/842–3352* 🌐 *www.redroof.com* *111 rooms* *In-room data ports, some microwaves, some refrigerators, pool, some pets allowed, no-smoking rooms* ▭ *AE, D, DC, MC, V* 🍴 *BP.*

Nightlife & the Arts

The Arts

In warm weather free outdoor concerts are held at Harbour Town and Shelter Cove Harbour; at the latter fireworks light up the night Tuesdays from June to August.

Concerts, plays, films, art shows, sporting events, food fairs, and mini-tournaments make up Hilton Head's **Spring and Winter Fests** (☎ 843/686–4944 or 800/424–3387), which runs from January through March. The **Native Islander Gullah Celebration** (☎ 843/689–9314 🌐 www.gullahcelebration.com) takes place in February and showcases Gullah life through arts, crafts, food, music, and plays. **Bravo!** (☎ 800/523–3373) is a hotline that details local arts events.

The **Arts Center of Coastal Carolina** (✉ Shelter Cove La., Mid-Island ☎ 843/686–3945 🌐 www.artscenter-hhi.org) has an art gallery, a theater that stages plays, musicals, concerts and dance programs, and a theater program for youth. The Hallelujah Singers, Gullah performers, appear regularly here.

Nightlife

Bars, like everything else in Hilton Head, are often in strip malls. Try the **Ryder's** (✉ 4 Target Rd., South End ☎ 843/842–6683) for live music. **Hilton Head Brewing Co.** (✉ Hilton Head Plaza, Greenwood Dr., South End ☎ 843/785–2739) has late-night disco every Wednesday, live bands on Friday, and karaoke on Saturday. The **Lodge** (✉ Hilton Head Plaza, Greenwood Dr., South End ☎ 843/842–8966) has pool tables and roaring fires in the stone fireplaces in season. **Monkey Business** (✉ Park Plaza, Greenwood Dr., South End ☎ 843/686–3545) is a dance club popular with young professionals. In summer Monday is teen night and Friday is live beach music night. **Salty Dog Café** (✉ South Beach Marina, off U.S. 278, South End ☎ 843/671–2233) has a great dockside happy hour, ice-cream shop for kids, and live music at the Sea Pines Resort.

Turtle's (✉ 2 Grass Lawn Ave., North End ☎ 843/681–7009), an oceanfront lounge at the Westin Resort, has informal entertainment every night. **Regatta** (✉ 23 Ocean La., Mid-Island ☎ 843/341–8080), a sophisticated oceanfront nightspot in the Palmetto Dunes Resort, has live beach and jazz music nightly. **Tiki Hut** (✉ S. Forest Beach Dr., South End ☎ 843/785–5126), a locally popular beachside bar at the Holiday Inn Oceanfront Resort, has live music during the high season.

Shopping

Art Galleries

The **Red Piano Art Gallery** (✉ 220 Cordillo Pkwy., Mid-Island ☎ 843/785–2318) showcases 19th- and 20th-century works by regional and national contemporary artists.

Jewelry

The **Bird's Nest** (✉ Coligny Plaza, Coligny Circle and N. Forest Beach Dr., South End ☎ 843/785–3737) sells locally made shell and sand-dollar jewelry, plus island-theme charms. The **Goldsmith Shop** (✉ 3 Lagoon Rd., Mid-Island ☎ 843/785–2538) carries classic jewelry and island charms.

Nature

The **Audubon Nature Store** (✉ The Village at Wexford, U.S 278, MM 10.5, Mid-Island ☎ 843/785–4311) has items with a nature theme. **Outside Hilton Head** (✉ The Plaza at Shelter Cove, U.S. 278 at Palmetto Dunes, Mid-Island ☎ 843/686–6996 or 800/686–6996) sells Pawleys Island hammocks (handwoven, cotton-rope hammoks first made in the late 1800s on an island between Charleston and Myrtle Beach), swings, and other items that have an emphasis on nature and gardening.

Malls & Outlets

Tanger Outlet Factory Stores 1 & 2 (✉ U.S. 278 at island gateway, Bluffton ☎ 843/837–4339 or 888/746–7333 🌐 www.tangeroutlet.com) has more than 80 clothing and housewares outlets, including J. Crew, Banana Republic, Brooks Brothers, Harry & David, and Coach. The enclosed **Mall at Shelter Cove** (✉ U.S. 278, ½ mi north of Palmetto Dunes Resort, Mid-Island ☎ 843/686–3090 🌐 www.mallatsheltercove.com) has Saks Fifth Avenue, Williams-Sonoma, and fast-food options.

THE LOWCOUNTRY

The stretch of coastline between Hilton Head and Charleston is one of the most scenic parts of South Carolina, and is still a mostly underdeveloped blend of small towns, winding country roads, and gorgeous wilderness that turns into pristine beachfront before ending at the Atlantic. Here, especially along U.S. 17, look for roadside stands that sell boiled peanuts and homemade jams and jellies, and small-time shrimpers selling their catch out of coolers. Listen, too, for Gullah-tinged accents among the African-American natives—the sound is simply beautiful and rollicking. Along the way, there are a few noteworthy stops, Beaufort being one. For the record, locals will tell you that the beau in Beaufort is fittingly pronounced as in "beautiful." Scoot past the newer suburban sprawl on U.S. 21 to get to the historic district that hugs the waterfront. Antebellum homes have been converted into inns and a lively main street area thrives with shops and restaurants. It's an easy walking town that feels Southern to the core. North of Beaufort is rural Edisto Island and the rustic Edisto Beach, where you can camp out, collect shells, and dolphin-watch. This portion of the coast—between Edisto and Beaufort—is an outdoors-lovers' paradise, and outfitter groups can set you up in canoes, kayaks, and boats to explore as natives have for centuries.

Beaufort

5 *38 mi north of Hilton Head via U.S. 278 and Rte. 170; 70 mi southwest of Charleston via U.S. 17 and U.S. 21.*

Charming homes and churches from Beaufort's prosperous antebellum days as a cotton center grace this old town on Port Royal Island. Although it's unusual for the private homes in the historic district of Old Point to be open to visitors, some may be included in the annual Fall House Tour in mid-October, and the Spring Tour of Homes and Gardens, March through May. Come here on a day trip from Hilton Head, Savannah, or Charleston, or to spend a quiet weekend at a B&B, shopping and strolling the historic district. A truly Southern town, its charms have lured moviemakers here to film favorites such as *The Big Chill* and *The Prince of Tides*. Author Pat Conroy calls the place home and has waxed poetic about the area in some of his bestselling books, including *The Water Is Wide*.

The **Greater Beaufort Chamber of Commerce** can provide more information about house-tour schedules. The Gullah Festival, which takes place Memorial Day weekend, celebrates Lowcountry and West African culture. ✉ *1006 Carteret St.* ☎ *843/524–5400* 🌐 *www.beaufortsc.org.*

John Mark Verdier House Museum, built in the federal style, has been restored and furnished as it would have been between its construction in 1805 and the visit of Lafayette in 1825. It was the headquarters for Union forces during the Civil War. ✉ *801 Bay St.* ☎ *843/379–6335* 🎟 *$4* ⏲ *Mon.–Sat. 10–3:30.*

Built in 1795 and remodeled in 1852, the Gothic-style building that was the home of the Beaufort Volunteer Artillery now houses the **Beaufort Museum & Arsenal.** Prehistoric relics, native pottery, and Revolutionary War and Civil War exhibits are on display. ✉ *713 Craven St.* ☎ *843/379–3331* 🎟 *$3* ⏲ *Mon.–Sat. 11–4.*

St. Helena's Episcopal Church (1724) was turned into a hospital during the Civil War, and gravestones were brought inside to serve as operating tables. ✉ *505 Church St.* ☎ *843/522–1712* ⏲ *Tues.–Fri. 10–4, Sat. 10–1.*

Henry C. Chambers Waterfront Park, off Bay Street in old town Beaufort, is a great place to survey the scene. Barbra Streisand filmed *Prince of Tides* here. Its seven landscaped acres along the Beaufort River, part of the Intracoastal Waterway, include a seawall promenade, a crafts market, gardens, and a marina. Some events of the popular mid-July Beaufort Water Festival, as well as a seasonal farmers' market (April through August, Saturday 8 to noon) and the Beaufort Shrimp Festival in October take place here.

St. Helena Island, 9 mi southeast of Beaufort via U.S. 21, is the site of the Penn Center Historic District. Established in the middle of the Civil War, Penn Center was the South's first school for freed slaves; today it provides community services and has cottages for rent.

The **York W. Bailey Museum** (formerly a clinic) has displays on the Penn Center and on the heritage of Sea Island blacks. These islands are where Gullah, a musical language that combines English and African languages, developed. ✉ *Martin Luther King Jr. Blvd., St. Helena Island* ☎ *843/838–2432* 🎫 *$4* ⏲ *Mon.–Sat. 11–4.*

★ **Ibile Indigo House** is a studio for indigo processing and dyeing. A king crop during South Carolina's plantation days, indigo brought wealth to the Lowcountry and became closely enmeshed in Gullah culture. At this studio, you can buy indigo-dye cloth and clothes, and take lessons in crafting your own midnight-blue designs. ✉ *27 Penn Circle E, St. Helena Island* ☎ *843/838–3884* 🌐 *www.ibileindigo.com* ⏲ *Mon.–Sat. 8–6.*

★ Secluded **Hunting Island State Park** has nature trails and about 3 mi of public beaches—some dramatically and beautifully eroding. The 1,120-foot-long fishing pier is among the longest on the East Coast. You can climb the 181 steps of the **Hunting Island Lighthouse** (built in 1859 and abandoned in 1933) for sweeping views. The park is 18 mi southeast of Beaufort via U.S. 21; write for cabin and camping reservations. ✉ *1775 Sea Island Pkwy., off St. Helena Island, Hunting Island* ☎ *843/838–2011* 🌐 *www.huntingisland.com* 🎫 *$3; lighthouse additional 50¢* ⏲ *Apr.–Oct., daily 6 AM–9 PM; Nov.–Mar., daily 6–6. Lighthouse daily 10–5.*

On Route 802, 10 mi south of Beaufort, at **Parris Island** you can observe U.S. Marine Corps recruits training and drive through the base on your own. There's a replica of the Iwo Jima flag-raising monument on the base. The **Parris Island Museum** exhibits uniforms, photographs, and weapons chronicling military history since 1562, when the French Huguenots built a fort on St. Helena. ✉ *Off Rte. 802, 111 Panama St.* ☎ *843/228–2951* 🎫 *Free* ⏲ *Daily 10–4:30.*

Sports & the Outdoors

BIKING Beaufort is great for bicycling. Rentals are available from **Lowcountry Bicycles** (✉ 102 Sea Island Pkwy. ☎ 843/524–9585).

CANOE & BOAT TOURS Beaufort's on the Intracoastal Waterway and the greater Beaufort area is where the Ashepoo, Combahee, and Edisto rivers form the A.C.E. Basin, a vast wilderness of marshes and tidal estuaries loaded with history. The

THE WORLD OF GULLAH

IN THE LOWCOUNTRY, *Gullah refers to several things: language, people, and a culture. Gullah (the word itself is believed to be a version of Angola), an English-based dialect rooted in African languages, is the unique language of the African-Americans of the Sea Islands of South Carolina and Georgia. More than 300 years old (developed beginning in the 1700s), this rhythmic language has survived, in part, because of the geographic isolation of the people who speak it; most locally born African-Americans of the area can understand, if not speak, Gullah.*

Descended from thousands of slaves who were imported by planters in the Carolinas during the 18th century, the Gullah people have maintained not only their dialect but also their heritage. Much of Gullah culture traces back to the African rice-coast culture and survives today in the art forms and skills, including sweet-grass basket making, of Sea Islanders. During the colonial period, when rice was king, Africans from the West African rice kingdoms drew high premiums as slaves. Those with basket-making skills were extremely valuable because baskets were needed for agricultural and household use. Still made by hand, sweet-grass baskets are intricate coils of a marsh grass with a sweet, haylike aroma. Other Gullah art forms include hand-carved bateaus and gourds and in hand-tied nets used to catch shrimp.

Nowhere is Gullah culture more evident than in the foods of the region. Rice appears at nearly every meal—Africans taught planters how to grow rice and how to cook and serve it as well. Lowcountry dishes use okra, peanuts, benne (the African word for sesame seeds), field peas, and hot peppers. Gullah food reflects the bounty of the islands: shrimp, crabs, oysters, fish, and such vegetables as greens, tomatoes, and corn.

Many dishes are prepared in one pot, a method similar to the stew-pot cooking of West Africa. Frogmore combines shrimp, potatoes, sausage, and corn. Hoppin' John—a mixture of rice and field peas traditionally served on New Year's Day—is similar to rice and pigeon peas, a mainstay in West Africa.

Praise houses—one-room churches—were introduced by plantation owners, who thought Christianity would keep slaves docile. An unintended result was one of the backbones of Gullah culture: plantation melodies. These songs live on in performances by groups including the Hallelujah Singers, Sea Island Singers, Mt. Zion Spiritual Singers, and Ron and Natalie Daise, all of whom perform regularly in Charleston and Beaufort.

On St. Helena Island, near Beaufort, Penn Center is the unofficial Gullah headquarters, preserving the culture and developing opportunities for Gullahs. In 1852 the first school for freed slaves was established at Penn Center, and later Dr. Martin Luther King Jr. and the Southern Christian Leadership Council regularly met at the site to organize civil rights activities. You can delve into the culture further at the York W. Bailey Museum, also on the island.

On St. Helena, many Gullahs still go shrimping with hand-tied nets, harvest oysters, and grow their own vegetables. Nearby on Daufuskie Island, as well as on Edisto, Wadmalaw, and Johns islands near Charleston, you can find Gullah communities as well. A famous Gullah proverb says: If oonuh ent kno weh oonuh dah gwine, oonuh should kno weh oonuh come f'um. *Translation: If you don't know where you're going, you should know where you come from.*

best way to explore former rice plantations and the rest of the area is by kayak, canoe, or boat.

For tours in the immediate Beaufort Intracoastal area, in Hunting Park, and for sea kayaking, try **Beaufort Kayak Tours** (✉ 2709 Oaklawn St. ☎ 843/525–0810 🌐 www.beaufortkayaktours.com).

A.C.E. Basin Tours (✉ 1 Coosaw River Dr. Coosaw Island, 10 mi northeast of Beaufort ☎ 843/521–3099 🌐 www.acebasintours.com) might be the best bet for the very young, or anyone with limited mobility as they operate a 38-foot pontoon boat tour. **A.C.E. Basin Adventures** (✉ U.S. 17, Jacksonboro, 38 mi northeast of Beaufort ☎ 843/844–2514 🌐 www.outpostmoes.com) leads kayak, powerboat, and driving tours.

GOLF Most golf courses are about a 10- to 20-minute drive from Beaufort. The 18-hole **Cat Island Golf Club** (✉ 8 Waveland Ave., Port Royal, 6 mi southwest of Beaufort ☎ 843/524–0300) is challenging and beautiful. **Dataw Island** (✉ Dataw Club Rd., off U.S. 21, Dataw Island, 6 mi east of Beaufort ☎ 843/838–8250), has two 18-hole, par-72 courses.Try the 27 holes designed by Tom Fazio at **Callawassie Island Club** (✉ Rte. 170, Callawassie Island, 17 mi southwest of Beaufort ☎ 800/221–8431).

Where to Stay & Eat

$$$–$$$$ ✕ **Emily's.** Crowds here linger over $8 tapas that include chicken spring rolls, lamb chops, and crab wontons. Long, narrow, and wood-paneled, Emily's is a lively restaurant and bar that serves until 11 PM. It's definitely *not* a no-smoking haven. ✉ *906 Port Republic St.* ☎ *843/522–1866* 💳 *AE, MC, V* ⊗ *Closed Sun. No lunch.*

$$$–$$$$ ✕ **Saltus River Grill.** The hippest eatery in Beaufort won over local epicureans with its cool look (subdued lighting, mod booths, dark-wood bartop and accents), terrific location (on the town's version of Main Street), patio (with a view the Intracoastal Waterway), and solid Southern nouveau menu. Try the fresh Carolina rice-and-shrimp *pilau* (southern-stlye pilaf), which is flavored with herbs, fava beans, lemon zest, celery, onions, twice-smoked bacon, garlic, and shallots. A seafood stew has clams, mussels, and lobster with saffron, tomatoes, sweet onions, andouille sausage, and grilled focaccia. ✉ *802 Bay St.* ☎ *843/379–3474* 💳 *AE, D, MC, V.*

$$–$$$$ ✕ **11th Street Dockside.** The succulent fried oysters, shrimp, and fish here are some of the best around. Other seafood specialties are the steamed seafood pot and, by request only, Frogmore stew (with shrimp, potatoes, sausage, and corn). It's all served in a classic wharf-side environment, where you can eat on a screened porch, and there are water views from nearly every table. ✉ *1699 11th St. W, Port Royal, 6 mi southwest of Beaufort* ☎ *843/524–7433* 💳 *AE, D, DC, MC, V* ⊗ *No lunch.*

$ ✕ **Shrimp Shack.** On the way to Hunting Island, stop here, as locals have for 20 years—for shrimp burgers, sweet-potato fries, and sweet tea. Dinner is served only until 8 PM. ✉ *1929 Sea Island Pkwy., St. Helena, 18 mi southeast of Beaufort* ☎ *843/838–2962* 💳 *No credit cards* ⊗ *Closed Sun.*

¢ Blackstone's. Locals flock to this bustling family restaurant for the signature shrimp-and-cheese stoneground grits, for omelets fat with fresh veggies and local seafood, and for breakfast all day long. Hot and cold deli sandwiches are made to order. Service is down-home and the decor resembles an everything-goes flea market: if you have to wait on weekends, there's always something to look at. *205 Scott St. 843/524–4330 843/524–4330 AE, D, MC, V No dinner.*

$$–$$$$ **Beaufort Inn and Restaurant.** This peach-color 1897 Victorian inn, with its many gables and porches, has a superb restaurant ($$$–$$$$) with two mahogany-panel dining rooms, porch dining, and a wine bar. Among the classy seafood dishes are crispy flounder with yucca chips and tuna sashimi in peanut sauce. Guest rooms are decorated with period reproductions, tasteful fabrics, and comfortable chairs. All have pine floors; several have fireplaces and four-poster beds. *809 Port Republic St., 29901 843/521–9000 843/521–9500 www.beaufortinn.com 21 rooms Restaurant; no kids under 8, no smoking AE, D, MC, V BP.*

★ $$$–$$$$ **Rhett House Inn.** Art and antiques abound in a circa 1820 home turned storybook inn. Look for the little luxuries—down pillows and duvets, a CD player in each room, and fresh flowers. Breakfast, afternoon tea, evening hors d'oeuvres, and dessert are included in the rate. Visiting celebrities have included Barbra Streisand, Jeff Bridges, and Dennis Quaid. The remodeled house across the street has eight more rooms, each of which has a gas fireplace, a whirlpool bath, a private entrance, and a porch. *1009 Craven St., 29902 843/524–9030 843/524–1310 www.rhetthouseinn.com 16 rooms, 1 suite Dining room, some in-room hot tubs, bicycles; no kids under 5, no smoking AE, D, MC, V BP.*

$$$ **Cuthbert House Inn.** The owners have filled this 1790 home with 18th- and 19th-century heirlooms; it retains the original federal fireplaces and crown and rope molding. Guest rooms are elegant yet comfortable, with Oriental rugs on pine floors, commanding beds, quilts, and books. The inn looks out on the bay waters. *1203 Bay St., 29902 843/521–1315 or 800/327–9275 843/521–1314 www.cuthberthouseinn.com 5 rooms, 2 suites In-room dataports, some in-room hot tubs, some refrigerators, bicycles; no kids under 12, no smoking AE, D, MC, V BP.*

$$–$$$ **Craven Street Inn.** Clean, Pottery-Barn style welcomes you, with warm olive and neutral tones, hand-crafted cabinets, wreaths, and baskets. The spacious guest rooms in the 1870 main house have pine floors, high ceilings, and fireplaces; those in the 1920s cottages are small, but cozy and comfortable. Breakfast might be stuffed French toast or a ham-and-cheese omelet with homemade crumpets. *1103 Craven St., 29902 843/522–1668 or 888/522–0250 843/522–9975 www.thecravenstreetinn.com 7 rooms, 2 suites AE, D, MC, V BP.*

★ $$–$$$ **Fripp Island Resort.** An exclusive resort encompasses the entire Fripp island, making it guests-only. The more than 200 rental villas and cottages (two- and three-bedroom) are contemporary in style. There's a pavilion with shops, restaurants, and a marina. During peak season (June to

August) a four-night minimum is required; off-peak there's a two-night minimum. ✉ *1 Tarpon Blvd., Fripp Island 29920, 19 mi south of Beaufort* ☎ *843/838–3535 or 877/374–7748* 📠 *843/838–9079* 🌐 *www.frippislandresort.com* *240 units* *5 restaurants, 2 18-hole golf courses, 10 tennis courts, 4 pools, boating, bicycles, children's programs (ages 3–12); no smoking* ▭ *AE, D, DC, MC, V* 🍽 *EP.*

$$ **Best Western Sea Island Inn.** At this well-maintained but standard motel in the downtown historic district, you are within walking distance of shops, restaurants, and the waterfront area. Basic rooms have two doubles or king beds. Cookies and coffee are available 24 hours. ✉ *1015 Bay St.* 📫 *Box 532, 29901* ☎ *843/522–2090 or 800/528–1234* 📠 *843/521–4858* 🌐 *www.sea-island-inn.com* *43 rooms* *Refrigerators, pool, gym, no-smoking rooms* ▭ *AE, D, DC, MC, V* 🍽 *BP.*

¢ **Howard Johnson.** Rooms are spacious and have desks, many have views of the river and marsh, and the price is right. This clean and cheerfully staffed hotel sits on the edge of the marsh a few miles from the historic district. ✉ *3651 Trask Pkwy. (U.S. 21), 29902* ☎ *843/524–6020 or 800/528–1234* 📠 *843/521–4858* 🌐 *www.hojo.com* *62 rooms* *Microwaves, refrigerators, pool, no-smoking rooms* ▭ *AE, D, DC, MC, V* 🍽 *BP.*

Nightlife & the Arts

The **Hallelujah Singers** (✉ Office, Tabernacle Church, 806 Elizabeth St. ☎ 843/379–3594 for schedule), Gullah performers, sing at Lowcountry venues.**Plum's** (✉ 904½ Bay St. ☎ 843/525–1946) is the local hot spot for dinner on the porch, late drinks at the bar, and relaxed mingling.

Shopping

ART GALLERIES On canvas and sculpture as well as on bits of tin roofing, rugs, frames, and furniture, the colorful designs of Suzanne and Eric Longo decorate their **Longo Gallery** (✉ 901 Bay St. ☎ 843/522–8933). The **Rhett Gallery** (✉ 901 Bay St. ☎ 843/524–3339) sells Lowcountry art by members of the Rhett family and antique maps and prints, including Audubons.

Quirky Southern and folk art, beads, and pottery fill the 3,500-square-foot 1940s farmers' market building that is **Red Piano Too Art Gallery** (✉ 870 Sea Island Pkwy., St. Helena, 18 mi southeast of Beaufort ☎ 843/838–2241) on St. Helena Island.

GIFTS The **Craftseller** (✉ 818 Bay St. ☎ 843/525–6104) displays jewelry and other items by Southern craftspeople.

In charming little Walterboro, the **SC Artisans Center** (✉ 334 Wichmann St., Walterboro, 48 mi north of Beaufort ☎ 843/549–0011) carries the works of more than 200 South Carolina artists, with pottery, glass, folk art, furniture, quilts and metalwork for sale. Most Saturdays there are craft demonstrations. Find funky and elegant gifts (jewelry, house accessories, knickknacks) at **Lulu Burgess** (✉ 917 Bay St., Walterboro, 48 mi north of Beaufort ☎ 843/524–5858).

OUTFITTERS Orvis fans find the favorite outdoor and fishing gear at **Bay Street Outfitters** (✉ 815 Bay St. ☎ 843/524–5250). **Bay Street Outfitters** (✉ 1307

Boundary St. ☎ 843/379–4327) also sells top outdoor gear to help you best explore the nearby A.C.E. Basin.

en route

The ruins of **Sheldon Church,** built in 1753, make an interesting stop if you're driving from Beaufort to Edisto Island. The church burned down in 1779 and again in 1865. Only the brick walls and columns remain beside the old cemetery. The place is lovely—it's dripping with moss—and has become a favorite spot for people to get married. Get here from Beaufort on U.S. 21; it's about 1 mi west of Gardens Corner. *18 mi northwest of Beaufort.*

6

Edisto Island

6 *62 mi northeast of Beaufort via U.S. 17 and Rte. 174; 44 mi southwest of Charleston via U.S. 17 and Rte. 174.*

On rural Edisto (pronounced *ed*-is-toh) Island, magnificent stands of age-old oaks festooned with Spanish moss border quiet streams and side roads; wild turkeys may still be spotted on open grasslands and amid palmetto palms. The small "downtown" beachfront is a mix of public beach access spots, restaurants, and old, shabby-chic beach homes that are a far cry from the palatial villas rented out on the resort islands. The outlying Edisto Beach State Park is a pristine wilderness and camper's delight.

Fodor'sChoice ★ **Edisto Beach State Park** covers 1,255 acres and includes marshland and tidal rivers, a 1½-mi-long beachfront, towering palmettos, and a lush maritime forest with a 3½-mi trail running through it. The one-time CCC project park has the best shelling on public property in the Lowcountry. Overnight options include rustic furnished cabins by the marsh and campsites by the ocean (although severe erosion is limiting availability). Luxury resort development has begun to encroach around the edges of the park. ✉ *Route 174, off U.S. 17* ☎ *843/869–2156* 🌐 *www.discoversouthcarolina.com* *$3* *Early Apr.–late Oct., 8 AM–10 PM; Late Oct.–early Apr., 8–6.*

Where to Stay & Eat

★ $$$–$$$$ ✕ **Old Post Office.** On par with Charleston and Savannah kitchens—but with none of their big-city pretense—the Old Post Office is the best restaurant in this sleepy part of the state. The house specialty is shrimp and grits and, well, *anything* else with grits. Also try the "fussed-over" pork chop or the firecracker flounder, served with locally grown greens and vegetables, and fresh-baked bread. ✉ *1442 Rte. 174* ☎ *843/869–2339* *MC, V* *Closed Sun.; Oct.–May, Mon. No lunch.*

¢–$ Fodor'sChoice ★ ✕ **Po' Pigs Bo-B-Q.** Step inside the super-casual restaurant for pork barbecue that has national gourmet magazines and South Carolinians alike driving long distances to clamor up to the buffet. Sample the different 'que sauces (sweet mustard, tomato, and vinegar) and wash it all down with a tall glass of sweet tea. Don't miss down-home sides like squash casserole, hash, pork skins, limas and ham, and red rice. This is the real thing. The blink-and-you-miss-it location is on the tail end of a gas station along an undeveloped Edisto road. ✉ *2410 Rte. 174* ☎ *843/869–9003* ▭ *No credit cards* ⊗ *Closed Sun.–Tues.*

$$–$$$$ **Fairfield Ocean Ridge Resort.** Looking for resort amenities in a get-away-from-it-all escape? You've found it here. Well-furnished one- to five-bedroom villas and homes have contemporary furnishings. Although none of the accommodations are right on the beach, most are just a short walk away from it. (Be sure to ask where yours are.) A trolley transports you to the resort's beach shelter. *1 King Cotton Rd., Box 27, 29438* ☎ *843/869–2561 or 800/845–8500* *843/869–2384* *www.efairfield.com* *100 units* *Restaurant, 18-hole golf course, miniature golf, 4 tennis courts, pool, wading pool, beach, boating, fishing, bicycles, hiking, lounge, no-smoking rooms* ▭ *AE, D, MC, V* *EP.*

¢–$$$$ **The Atwood Agency.** Dying to pretend you're a property owner in Edisto? Rent out a family-owned cottage from the Atwood Agency. Their list of properties include single-bedroom condos ($400 per week) to six-bedroom homes ($2,000 per week), and run the gamut from old to new houses, near-beach to beachfront. All kitchens are stocked with appliances and dishes, but you need to bring your own bed linens. Three-day minimum stays are required. ✉ *495 Rte. 174, 29438* ☎ *843/869–2151* *www.atwoodagency.com* *BBQs, kitchens, cable TV* ▭ *MC, V* *EP.*

Edisto Beach State Park. Primitive camp sites include access to privies and picnic table areas; regular sites have concrete pads, water and electricity, grills, and picnic tables. The two-bedroom furnished cottages have heat and air-conditioning, screened-in porches, carpeting and wood-panel walls. There's a two-night minimum stay for the cabins. ✉ *Route 174, off U.S. 17* *8377 State Cabin Rd., 29438* ☎ *843/869–2156* *www.discoversouthcarolina.com* *89 sites, 5 cabins* *Sites $10–$23, cabins $65–$156* *Full hookups, partial hookups (electric and water), dump station, drinking water, showers, grills, picnic tables, public telephone, general store, play area* ▭ *D, MC, V.*

HILTON HEAD & THE LOWCOUNTRY A TO Z

To research prices, get advice from other travelers, and book travel arrangements, visit www.fodors.com.

AIRPORTS

Hilton Head Island Airport is served by US Airways Express. Most travelers use the Savannah/Hilton Head International Airport, about an hour from Hilton Head, which is served by AirTran, ComAir, Continental Express, Delta, Northwest, United Express, and US Airways.

Airport Information **Hilton Head Island Airport** ☎ 843/689–5400. **Savannah/Hilton Head International Airport** ✉ 400 Airways Ave., Savannah, GA ☎ 912/964–0514.

BOAT TRAVEL

Hilton Head is accessible via the Intracoastal Waterway, with docking available at Harbour Town Yacht Basin, Hilton Head Boathouse, and Shelter Cove Harbour.

Boat Information **Harbour Yacht Basin** ☎ 843/671–2704. **Hilton Head Boathouse** ☎ 843/681–2628. **Shelter Cove Harbor** ☎ 843/842–7001.

CAR TRAVEL

Hilton Head Island is 40 mi east of I–95 (Exit 28 off I–95S, Exit 5 off I–95N). If you're heading to the south end of the island, your best bet to save time and avoid traffic is to take the Toll Expressway ($1 each way). Beaufort is 25 mi east of I–95, on U.S. 21.

EMERGENCIES

Emergency medical service is available at the Hilton Head Medical Center and Clinics. CVS is open until 10 PM.

Emergency Services **Ambulance, fire, police** ☎ 911.

Hospitals **Hilton Head Regional Medical Center and Clinics** ✉ Hospital Center Blvd., Mid-Island, Hilton Head ☎ 843/681-6122.

Late-Night Pharmacies **CVS** ✉ 10 Pope Ave., South End, Hilton Head ☎ 843/785-7786.

TAXIS

Lowcountry Taxi and Limousine Service and Yellow Cab provide service in Hilton Head. Other options include At Your Service and Lowcountry Adventures. In Beaufort, Point Tours and Yellow Cab provide service.

Taxi Companies **At Your Service** ☎ 843/837-3783. **Greyline Lowcountry Adventures** ☎ 843/681-8212. **Point Tours** ☎ 843/522-3576. **Yellow Cab** ☎ 843/686-6666 in Hilton Head, 843/522-1121 in Beaufort.

TOURS

Hilton Head's Adventure Cruises hosts dinner, sightseeing, and murder-mystery cruises. Several companies, including H20 Sports and Lowcountry Nature Tours in Hilton Head, run dolphin sightseeing and environmental trips. Low Country Nature Tours has tours of Hilton Head, Beaufort, and Charleston.

Carolina Buggy Tours show you Beaufort's historic district by horse-drawn carriage. Gullah 'n' Geechie Mahn Tours lead tours throughout Beaufort and the outlying sea islands like St. Helena, with a focus on African-American traditions and culture. Costumed guides sing and act out history during walking tours by the Spirit of Old Beaufort tour group. Call the Greater Beaufort Chamber of Commerce to find out about self-guided walking or driving tours of Beaufort.

Boat Tours **Adventure Cruises** ✉ Shelter Cove Marina, 9 Shelter Cove La., Mid-Island, Hilton Head ☎ 843/785-4558 🌐 www.hiltonheadisland.com. **H20 Sports** ✉ Harbour Town Marina, 149 Lighthouse Rd., South End, Hilton Head ☎ 843/363-2628 🌐 www.h2osportsonline.com. **Low Country Nature Tours** ✉ Shelter Cover Harbour, Shelter Cove La., Mid-Island, Hilton Head ☎ 843/683-0187 🌐 www.lowcountrynaturetours.com.

Beaufort City Tours **Carolina Buggy Tours** ✉ 901 Port Republic St., Beaufort ☎ 843/525-1300 🌐 www.carolinabuggytours.com. **Greater Beaufort Chamber of Commerce** ✉ 1006 Carteret St., Beaufort ☎ 843/524-5400 🌐 www.beaufortsc.org. **Gullah 'n' Geechie Mahn Tours** ✉ 671 Sea Island Pkwy., Beaufort ☎ 843/838-7516. **Spirit of Old Beaufort** ✉ 103 West St., Beaufort ☎ 843/525-0459 🌐 www.thespiritofoldbeaufort.com.

VISITOR INFORMATION

For information on Edisto, call the Edisto Island Chamber of Commerce. The Greater Beaufort Chamber of Commerce has information about Beaufort and the surrounding area. In Hilton Head your best bet for local information is to stop by the Welcome Center, on the island side of the bridge that connects Hilton Head to Bluffton.

Tourist Information **Edisto Island Chamber of Commerce** 430 Rte. 174, Box 206, Edisto Island 29438 843/869-3867 or 888/333-2781 www.edistochamber.com. **Greater Beaufort Chamber of Commerce** 1006 Carteret St., Box 910, Beaufort 29901 843/524-5400 www.beaufortsc.org. **Welcome Center of Hilton Head** 100 William Hilton Pkwy., 29938 800/523-3373 www.hiltonheadisland.org.

THE MIDLANDS & UPSTATE

7

By Katie McElveen

SOUTH CAROLINA'S MIDLANDS, between the coastal Lowcountry and the mountains, is a varied region of swamps and flowing rivers, fertile farmland—perfect for horse raising—and hardwood and pine forests. Lakes have wonderful fishing, and the many state parks are popular for hiking, swimming, and camping. Small, old towns with mansions turned bed-and-breakfasts are common, and the many public gardens provide islands of color during most of the year. At the center of the region is the state capital, Columbia, an engaging contemporary city enveloping cherished historic elements. You can dive into lively arts and dining scenes and also tour mansion museums. Just outside of town, Congaree Swamp National Park has the largest intact tract of old-growth floodplain forest in North America. Aiken, the center of South Carolina's thoroughbred country, is where champions Sea Hero and Pleasant Colony were trained. Towns such as Abbeville and Camden preserve and interpret the past, with old house museums, history re-creations, and museum exhibits.

The Upstate of South Carolina is a land of waterfalls and wide vistas, cool pine forests and fast rapids. Camping, hiking, white-water rafting and kayaking are less than an hour from downtown Greenville and just a paddle's-throw from the small hamlets that are scattered about. Greenville itself, artsy and refined, is a modern southern city with a thriving downtown full of trendy restaurants, boutiques, and galleries. Cinderella-cousin Spartanburg is also up and coming, thanks to an influx of high-level manufacturers such as BMW and Michelin and the rising popularity of area colleges.

Exploring the Midlands & Upstate

South Carolina's Midlands and Upstate regions are well endowed with highways: from Columbia, I–26 heads toward the mountains, northwest, to Spartanburg. Greenville, just west of Spartanburg, is the gateway to dozens of tidy mountain towns. I–20 will take you from Columbia east to Camden or southwest through Aiken and on to Atlanta. I–77 runs north toward Charlotte, and is an easy connector to I–85 in North Carolina, but it also cuts through I–26 and I–20, giving fairly direct cross-region access. Less direct, but providing pretty views, which range from peach orchards to mountain outcroppings (along with plenty of stops for local fruits and vegetables), is the two-lane Cherokee Foothills Scenic Highway (Route 11), which follows an old Cherokee Indian path in the northwestern corner of the state.

To get a true sense of the geographic diversity of this huge area—there are sand hills, rich farmland and mountains within a two-hour drive—you'll need a car and a full tank of gas. But bring good walking shoes, or hiking boots, so you can take advantage of the many trails, paths, and parks—some quite wild—that wind through the region.

About the Restaurants

Most of the smaller towns have at least one dining choice that might surprise you with its take on sophisticated fare (filet mignon with pimento cheese, anyone?). Larger cities such as Columbia, Greenville, and Spartanburg have both upscale foodie haunts and ultracasual grits-and-

Numbers in the text correspond to numbers in the margin and on the Midlands & Upstate map.

If you have 3 days — Start your trip with two nights in **Greenville** 6; make sure to tour the vast collection of rare religious paintings and icons at the Bob Jones University Museum & Gallery and to stroll past the shops, restaurants, and other sights along Main Street. There are numerous state parks and lakes northwest of Greenville, so you might make a day trip to go hiking, swimming, or fishing. Day 3 drive south to **Pendleton** 7, where you can see the Village Green and visit the nearby South Carolina State Botanical Garden, where—in addition to hundreds of varieties of plants, there are two old houses to tour, and a geology museum on site. Spend the night at an area inn like Liberty Hall, rocking away your worries on a wide front porch.

If you have 5 days — Follow the three-day itinerary and then on Day 4 drive to **Columbia** 1, where you spend two nights. You could tour the State House (be sure to note the bronze stars that mark places where the building was hit by cannonballs during the Civil War), shop along Devine Street, and have several good meals during this time.

If you have 7 days — After you've completed the five-day itinerary, leave **Columbia** 1 for **Camden** 2; shop for antiques and visit the Historic Camden Revolutionary War Site or stop in nearby Boykin to watch brooms being made at the General Store. You can spend the night at one of the B&B's in Camden, or drive back to Columbia. Horse lovers, or anyone who wants to live like royalty for a night (at The Wilcox), should drive to **Aiken** 3 the next day. Another option would be to head to **Abbeville** 5, where you can tour historic homes such as the Burt-Stark House and have lunch at the Village Grille.

---

greens joints. Many local restaurants serve "meat and three," which is your choice of a meat main and three side dishes. Macaroni and cheese, rice and gravy, mashed potatoes, and Jell-o are popular sides. Barbecue and other down-home Southern specialties are sometimes served buffet-style. Thanks to the rich farmland in the area, fresh fruits and vegetables are easy to come by in restaurants and at roadside stands. Mexican food is usually a good bet because many of the farm workers have emigrated to South Carolina from Mexico, bringing their cooking skills with them. Plan ahead: many places close on Sunday.

WHAT IT COSTS

$$$$	$$$	$$	$	¢
over $22	$16–$22	$11–$16	$7–$11	under $7

Prices are for a main course at dinner, excluding sales tax of 5%–8%.

About the Hotels

Your best bet, particularly if you're interested in hearing more than the textbook version of the history of whatever town you're in, is to stay in an area inn or B&B. These establishments tend to be owned and occupied by engaging locals who want to raise their families in the area where they grew up, or by couples from the North who have retired. Either way, count on just a handful of rooms, family favorites for breakfast and, if you're lucky, a garden for wandering and a restored town square just steps away. What you gain in charm, however, you may have to give up in convenience. If you want to be close to lots of dining options, and have an on-site workout room and cable television, you might opt for one of the chain motels that flourish in this part of South Carolina.

State parks offer an alternative: some, like Hickory Knob and Devils Fork, have cottages available; most have camping facilities, both primitive and with hookups. If you're interested in renting one of the cottages, you need to reserve at least a year in advance. Rooms in hotels are usually easy to reserve, unless there's a major event such as horse races in Aiken and Camden or big football games at USC's Williams-Brice Stadium or Clemson's Death Valley.

WHAT IT COSTS

$$$$	$$$	$$	$	¢
over $220	$160–$220	$110–$160	$70–$110	under $70

Prices are for two people in a standard double room in high season, excluding service charges and 5%–8% tax.

Timing

Central South Carolina comes alive in spring, beginning in early March, when the azaleas, dogwoods, wisteria, and jasmine turn normal landscapes into fairylands of pink, white, and purple shaded by a canopy of pines. Days are bright and sunny, humidity is remarkable in its absence and cool night breezes blow heady floral scents around and around. Late May through September can be oppressive, particularly in the Midlands where neither an ocean breeze nor cool mountain air are around to take the edge off; people do spend a lot of time outside and, as a result, parks, lakes and trails are usually quite busy—although not uncomfortably crowded. Despite the heat, festivals celebrating everything from peaches to okra are held in summer. Fall will bring the state fair in Columbia, SEC and ACC football to the University of South Carolina and Clemson University, rich yellows and reds of the changing trees in the mountains and a number of art and music festivals. Come Christmastime, nearly every town puts out its holiday best with candlelight tours, winter garden shows, and other holiday festivities.

COLUMBIA & THE MIDLANDS

The wide swath of land that comprises the Midlands may have only one large city—the state capital, Columbia—but its profusion of small and

Wild Rivers The Chattooga River, along the northwestern South Carolina–Georgia border has both gentle stretches and wild, Calss V-plus rapids. The Saluda is another wild river you can raft or canoe; outfitters run trips of different degrees of difficulty that conquer the Class III and IV rapids. The slower Congaree has a gentler pace and you might consider just renting a canoe and paddling along. Outfitters run rafting trips at both the expert and the beginner levels.

Botanical Bliss Gardens are taken seriously here. South Carolina State Botanical Garden is an obvious must-see, noteworthy for the rare collection of nature-based sculptures (don't miss Sittin' Pretty, Patrick Dougherty's castle made entirely of saplings), which fuse art into the landscape seamlessly. Visit the Gardens of Park Seed Co., outside Greenville, to see the company's experimental gardens with the newest flowers, shrubs, vegetables, and ornamentals. Swan Lake Iris Garden, has thousands of irises that bloom in what was once a swamp, and is also the only public park in the country that hosts all eight swan species. In Columbia, 70 acres along the Saluda River make up the Riverbanks Zoo and Garden, a botanical wonderland that includes a shade garden, moonlight garden, and a garden devoted just to roses.

Falling Water The craggy mountains that give the Upstate its wondrous views and cool temperatures give visitors yet another reason to explore this undulating region: waterfalls. And thanks to higher than average rainfall, the abrupt ending of the 2,000-foot Blue Ridge escarpment and a series of creeks and rivers cut into the granite cliffs, more than 50 of these captivating wonders are concentrated into a fairly small area. Best of all, of the 25 that are on public lands, a handful can be viewed after a short stroll down a flat path. Lower Whitewater Falls, 200 feet tall, cascades into Lake Jocassee at Devils Fork State Park, northwest of Greenville. Twin Falls is close to the road outside of Greenville. Issaqueena Falls, named after an Indian princess in love with an Englishman, is outside Pendleton. The short trail to King Falls, outside of Pendleton, is especially pretty in spring when the flowers are blooming.

---

medium-size towns makes this area a patchwork quilt of history and activity.

Columbia

❶ *112 mi northwest of Charleston via I–26, 101 mi southeast of Greenville via I–385 and I–26.*

Old as Columbia may be, trendy and collegiate neighborhoods have given the city a bit of an edge. The symphony, two professional ballet companies, several theaters that stage live—and often locally written—productions, and a number of engaging museums keep culture alive. The city is a sprawling blend of modern office blocks, suburban neighborhoods, and the occasional antebellum home. Here, too, is the expan-

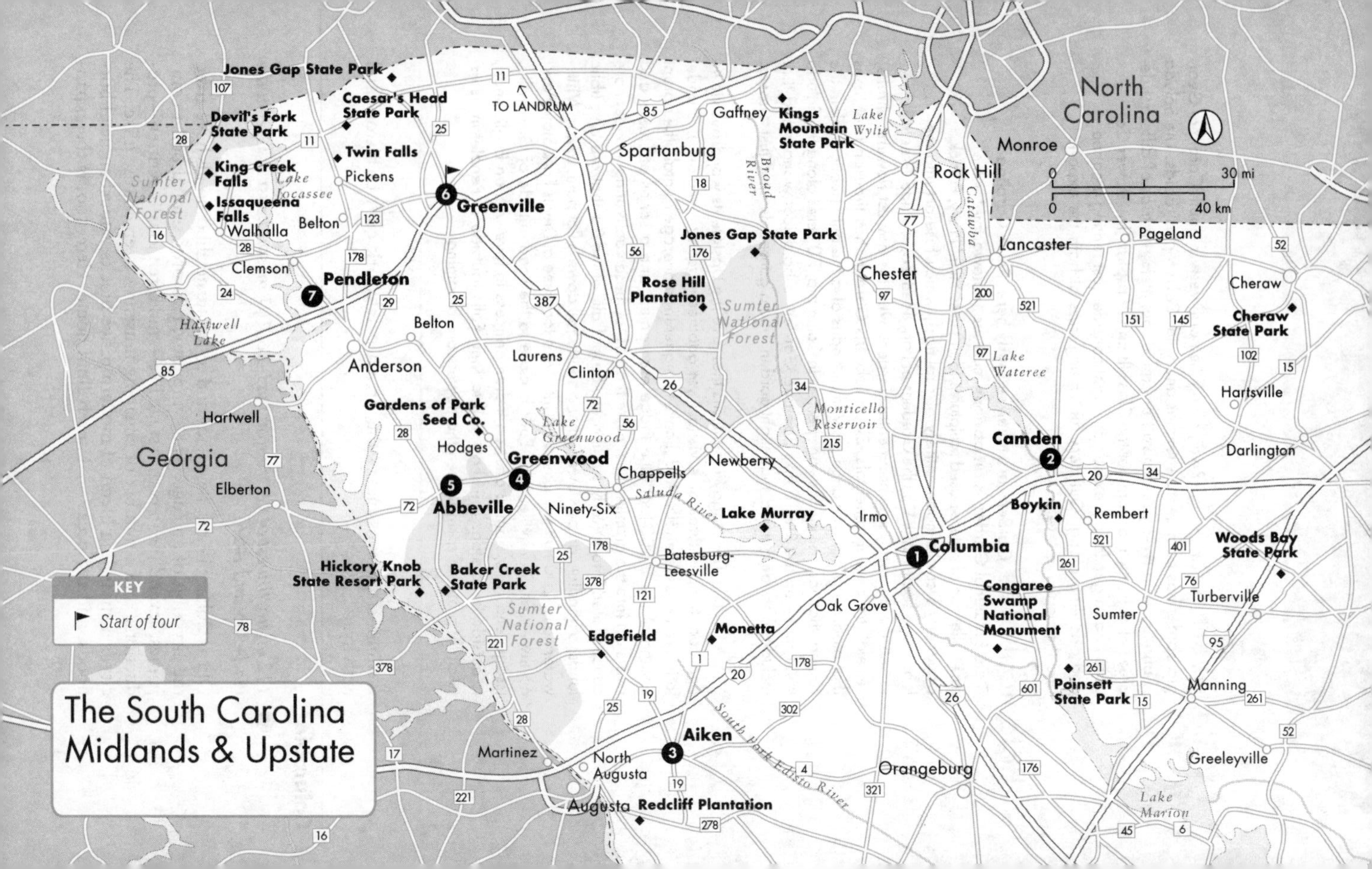
The South Carolina Midlands & Upstate
KEY
Start of tour
North Carolina
Georgia
0 30 mi
0 40 km
1 Columbia
2 Camden
3 Aiken
4 Greenwood
5 Abbeville
6 Greenville
7 Pendleton
Jones Gap State Park
Caesar's Head State Park
Devil's Fork State Park
Twin Falls
King Creek Falls
Issaqueena Falls
Kings Mountain State Park
Rose Hill Plantation
Gardens of Park Seed Co.
Lake Murray
Hickory Knob State Resort Park
Baker Creek State Park
Edgefield
Monetta
Redcliff Plantation
Boykin
Congaree Swamp National Monument
Poinsett State Park
Woods Bay State Park
Cheraw State Park
TO LANDRUM
Monroe
Rock Hill
Gaffney
Spartanburg
Pickens
Walhalla
Belton
Clemson
Anderson
Laurens
Clinton
Hodges
Hartwell
Elberton
Chester
Lancaster
Pageland
Cheraw
Hartsville
Darlington
Rembert
Sumter
Turberville
Manning
Greeleyville
Newberry
Chappells
Ninety-Six
Irmo
Batesburg-Leesville
Oak Grove
Orangeburg
North Augusta
Augusta
Martinez
Lake Wylie
Broad River
Catawba
Lake Jocassee
Sumter National Forest
Hartwell Lake
Lake Greenwood
Saluda River
Monticello Reservoir
Lake Wateree
South Fork Edisto River
Lake Marion

sive main campus of the University of South Carolina. Out of town, 550-acre Lake Murray is full of pontoon boats and Jet Skis, and Congaree Swamp National Park is waiting to be explored.

In 1786 South Carolina's capital was moved from Charleston to Columbia, along the banks of the Congaree River. One of the nation's first planned cities, Columbia has streets that are among the widest in America because it was then thought that stagnant air in narrow streets fostered the spread of malaria. The city soon grew into a center of political, commercial, cultural, and social activity, but in early 1865 General William Tecumseh Sherman invaded South Carolina and incinerated two-thirds of Columbia. A few homes, public buildings, and historic sights were spared. The First Baptist Church, where secession was declared, still stands because a janitor directed Sherman's troops to a Presbyterian church when they asked for directions.

Smack in the center of town, the State House anchors downtown's Main Street area. The Vista, an old warehouse area that's been restored with shops, galleries, and apartments, starts about a block west of the State House and continues to the banks of the Congaree River. The University of South Carolina's sprawling campus radiates southeast to Five Points, a lively area that's considered almost an extension of the campus. Devine Street, at the center of the Shandon neighborhood, travels east from Five Points.

Stop by the museum shop of the **Historic Columbia Foundation** to get maps of walking and driving tours of historic districts. You must buy tickets here to tour four old Columbia houses ($5 each): the Robert Mills House (on-site), the Hampton-Preston Mansion, the Mann-Simons Cottage, and the Woodrow Wilson Boyhood Home. ✉ *Robert Mills House, 1616 Blanding St., Main Street area* ☎ *803/252–1770* 🌐 *www.historiccolumbia.org* 🎟 *Free* ⏲ *Tues.–Sat. 10–3, Sun. 1–4.*

The **Hampton-Preston Mansion,** dating from 1818, is filled with lavish furnishings collected by three generations of two influential families. Buy a ticket for a tour at theHistoric Columbia Foundation in the Robert Mills House. ✉ *1615 Blanding St., Main Street area* ☎ *803/252–1770* 🎟 *$5* ⏲ *Tues.–Sat. 10–3, Sun. 1–4.*

The classic, columned 1823 **Robert Mills House** was named for its architect, who later designed the Washington Monument. It has opulent Regency furniture, marble mantels, and spacious grounds. ✉ *1616 Blanding St., Main Street area* ☎ *803/252–1770* 🎟 *$5* ⏲ *Tues.–Sat. 10–3, Sun. 1–4.*

The **Mann-Simons Cottage** was the home of Celia Mann, one of only 200 free African-Americans in Columbia in the mid-1800s. Buy a ticket for a tour at the Historic Columbia Foundation in the Robert Mills House. ✉ *1403 Richland St., Main Street area* ☎ *803/252–1770* 🎟 *$5* ⏲ *Tues.–Sat. 10–3, Sun. 1–4.*

The **Woodrow Wilson Boyhood Home** displays the gaslights, arched doorways, and ornate furnishings of the Victorian period. Buy a ticket for a tour at the Historic Columbia Foundation in the Robert Mills House.

✉ *1705 Hampton St., Main Street area* ☎ *803/252–1770* 🎫 *$5* ⏲ *Tues.–Sat. 10–3, Sun. 1–4.*

Columbia Museum of Art contains art from the Kress Foundation collection of Renaissance and baroque treasures, sculpture, decorative arts, including art glass, and European and American paintings, including a Monet and a Botticelli; there are also changing exhibitions. ✉ *Main and Hampton Sts., Main Street area* ☎ *803/799–2810* 🌐 *www.columbiamuseum.org* 🎫 *$5* ⏲ *Wed.–Thurs. and Sat. 10–5, Fri. 10–9, Sun. 1–5.*

Fodor's Choice ★

With more than 67,000 square feet for climbing, exploring, painting, playing, building—oh, and learning, too, **EdVenture Children's Museum** is a full day of hands-on fun. Eddie, a 40-foot-tall statue of a boy that can be climbed on and in by children and adults, stands as the museum centerpiece. Each of eight galleries has a theme, such as Body Works, World of Work, and Mission Imagination. Older children might like to anchor a newscast and take home a tape for their efforts, and participate in science experiments; the younger set might want go to the Bone Zone to meet a talking skeleton or climb aboard a real fire truck. ✉ *211 Gervais St., Vista* ☎ *803/779–3100* 🌐 *www.edventure.org* 🎫 *$7.95* ⏲ *Tues.–Sat. 9–5, Sun. noon–5.*

Exhibits in the refurbished textile mill that is the **South Carolina State Museum** explore the state's natural history, archaeology, historical development, and South Carolinians' technological and artistic accomplishments. An iron gate made for the museum by Phillip Simmons, the "dean of Charleston blacksmiths," is on display, as is the surfboard that biochemist Kary Mullis was riding when he heard he'd won the Nobel prize. A display on African-American astronauts is dedicated to native son Dr. Ronald McNair, who died aboard the space shuttle *Challenger.* In the Stringer Discovery Center, an interactive display, children can check out microorganisms under a microscope and climb trees to observe the animals that live in the branches. Other exhibit subjects include a reproduction of the Confederate submarine the *Hunley,* and the state's cotton industry and slavery. ✉ *301 Gervais St., Vista* ☎ *803/898–4921* 🌐 *www.museum.state.sc.us* 🎫 *$5* ⏲ *Tues.–Sat. 10–5, Sun. 1–5.*

★ Six bronze stars on the western wall of the **State House** mark where direct hits were made by General Sherman's cannons. The capitol building, started in 1851 and completed in 1907, is made of native blue granite in the Italian Renaissance style. The interior is richly appointed with brass, marble, mahogany, and artwork. Guided tours are available by reservations. ✉ *Main and Gervais Sts., Main Street area* ☎ *803/734–2430* 🎫 *Free* ⏲ *Weekdays 9–5, Sat. 10–5, 1st Sun. of month 1–5.*

Make sure it's dark out when you drive by **Tunnelvision,** a glowing optical illusion painted on the wall of the Federal Land Bank Building by local artist Blue Sky. Next to it is Sky's bigger-than-life silver "busted" Fire Hydrant, a working fountain. ✉ *Taylor and Marion Sts., Main Street area.*

A highlight of the sprawling **University of South Carolina** is its original campus—the scenic, tree-lined **Horseshoe**—dating to 1801. Two-hour guided walking tours leave from the visitor center. Although the tours are geared to prospective students, the public is welcome. Reservations are essential. *Visitor's Center* ✉ *Bull St. at Pendleton St., USC Campus* ☎ *800/922–9755* 🌐 *www.sc.edu.*

Explore the special collections on state history and genealogy at the **South Caroliniana Library,** established in 1840. ✉ *Sumter St., USC Campus* ☎ *803/777–3131* ⏲ *Weekdays 9–5, Sat 9–1.*

The **McKissick Museum** has geology, gemstone, and folklife exhibits, as well as a fine display of silver. ✉ *Sumter St., USC Campus* ☎ *803/777–7251* 🎟 *Free* ⏲ *Weekdays 8:30–5, Sat. 11–3.*

Riverfront Park and Historic Columbia Canal, where the Broad and Saluda rivers form the Congaree River, was created around the city's original waterworks and hydroelectric plant. Interpretive markers describe the area's plant and animal life and tell the history of the buildings. ✉ *312 Laurel St., Vista* ☎ *803/733–8613* 🎟 *Free* ⏲ *Daily dawn–dusk.*

★ **Riverbanks Zoological Park and Botanical Garden** contains more than 2,000 animals and birds, some endangered, in natural habitats. Walk along pathways and through landscaped gardens to see sea lions, polar bears, Siberian tigers, and black rhinos. Koalas are the latest addition. The South American primate collection has won international acclaim, and the park is noted for its success in breeding endangered and fragile species. The Aquarium–Reptile Complex has South Carolina, desert, tropical, and marine specimens. At the Bird Pavilion you can view birds and wildlife under a safarilike tent. You can ride the carousel and also take a tram over the Saluda River to the 70-acre botanical gardens on the west bank. (A new entrance in West Columbia, off Highway 378, takes you directly to the botanical gardens.) A forested section with walking trails has spectacular views of the river and passes Civil War ruins. ✉ *I–126 and U.S. 76, at Greystone Riverbanks exit, West Columbia* ☎ *803/779–8717* 🌐 *www.riverbanks.org* 🎟 *$8.75* ⏲ *Apr.–Oct., weekdays 9–6; Nov.–Mar., daily 9–5.*

The **Fort Jackson Museum,** on the grounds of a U.S. army training center, displays heavy equipment from the two world wars and has exhibits on the history of the fort from 1917 to the present. ✉ *Bldg. 4442, Jackson Blvd., East Columbia* ☎ *803/751–7419* 🎟 *Free* ⏲ *Weekdays 9–4.*

The 41-mi-long **Lake Murray** has swimming, boating, picnicking, and superb fishing. There are many marinas and campgrounds in the area. The lake is off I–26, 15 mi west of Columbia. ✉ *Capital City–Lake Murray Country Visitors Center, 2184 N. Lake Dr., Lake Murray* ☎ *803/781–5940 or 866/785–3935* 🌐 *www.scjewel.com.*

★ The alluvial floodplain, bordered by high bluffs, at the 22,200-acre **Congaree Swamp National Park** contains many old-growth bottomland hardwoods (the oldest and largest trees east of the Mississippi River). The water and trees are beautifully eerie. Hiking and canoe trails line the park, which is full of wildlife, such as otters, deer and woodpeckers, as well as the occasional wild boar. Guided nature walks are held the first and second Saturday of each month at 9:30 AM. When darkness falls, join park naturalists for a hike deep into the forest in search of owls and other nighttime wildlife Friday nights in September and October. Call for reservations. ✉ *Off Rte. 48, Old Bluff Rd., Hopkins, 20 mi southeast of Columbia* ☎ *803/776–4396* 🌐 *www.nps.gov* 🎫 *Free* ⏲ *Visitor center, daily 8:30–5.*

Sports & the Outdoors

CANOEING & KAYAKING The Saluda River near Columbia has challenging Class III and Class IV rapids for kayaking and canoeing. Saluda access is out of town in Gardendale and Saluda Shoals Park as well as at the Riverbanks Zoo (you must pay Zoo admission). The Broad and the Saluda rivers meet in the center of town to become the calmer Congaree River. There's public access for the Congaree behind EdVenture on Senate Street at the Senate Street Landing.

You can rent canoes or sign up for any of several different guided river or swamp expeditions at the **River Runner Outdoor Center** (✉ 905 Gervais St., Vista ☎ 803/771–0353). Guided Saluda and Congaree river (Saluda has rapids, Congaree is calm) trips and swamp canoeing excursions can be arranged, as can canoe rentals, at **Adventure Carolina** (✉ 1107 State St., Cayce, 4 mi southwest of Columbia ☎ 803/796–4505), which is just outside Columbia. Canoe and kayak rentals are available at **Saluda Shoals Park** (✉ 5605 Bush River Rd., Irmo, 12 mi northwest of Columbia ☎ 803/772–1228).

Self-guided canoe trails traverse **Congaree Swamp National Park** (✉ Off Rte. 48, Old Bluff Rd., Hopkins ☎ 803/776–4396), 20 mi southeast of Columbia.

HIKING **Congaree Swamp National Park** (✉ Off Rte. 48, Old Bluff Rd., Hopkins, 20 mi southeast of Columbia ☎ 803/776–4396) has 22 mi of trails and a ¾-mi boardwalk for people with disabilities. Guided nature walks leave Saturday at 9:30 AM.

Where to Stay & Eat

$$–$$$$ Fodor's Choice ★ ✕ **Garibaldi's.** Although the name is Italian, locals flock here for the creative fish dishes that might include grouper with a brandy and peppercorn cream sauce, or tilapia atop a hash of bacon, corn, and potatoes. The house specialty (quite delicious) is a whole flounder served with a tangy apricot glaze. Creative dinner salads make interesting starters and the ice cream in an almond basket makes a crunchy-smooth finale to a meal. ✉ *2013 Greene St., Five Points* ☎ *803/771–8888* ✍ *Reservations essential* 💳 *AE, D, MC, V* ⏲ *No lunch.*

$$–$$$ ✕ **Blue Marlin.** With polished wood, lines of booths, and an oceanic mural over the bar, this restaurant speaks of bygone years—fitting for an eatery that was once a train station. Seafood and pasta dishes include tilapia with shrimp and crabmeat sauce, lobster ravioli, and a basic lobster or fish fillet. All main dishes are served with steaming collard greens and grits. Fruit cobblers come topped with liqueur-laced whipped cream. ✉ *1200 Lincoln St., Vista* ☎ *803/799–3838* ✍ *Reservations not accepted* 💳 *AE, D, MC, V.*

MIDLANDS BARBECUE

Barbecue in the Midlands, like elsewhere in the Carolinas and Georgia, means pork (or on rare occasion, chicken), roasted all day over an open fire and basted with sauce, not cooked on a grill. What makes Midlands barbecue distinctive is the sauce, which has a mustard base, rather than the vinegar or tomato commonly used elsewhere. The result is a flavor that's pungent but not spicy, and meat that lacks the red tint often associated with Southern barbecue. (Some places serve a variety of sauces, so you can do a taste test and see what you think of the native style.)

To go with your barbecue, side dishes usually include macaroni and cheese, collard greens, and coleslaw. The drink of choice is iced tea, served highly sweetened unless you request otherwise. Do give it a try: the flavor is smooth and round, and it will help you keep your eyes open during a langorous summer afternoon. If your sweet tooth isn't satisfied, order up cobbler or cream pie for dessert.

★ **$$–$$$** ✕ **Mr. Friendly's New Southern Cafe.** Who knew that barbecue sauce could be the base for such tasty salad dressing or that lowly pimiento cheese could elevate a fillet to near perfection? That kind of creative thinking is what makes Mr. Friendly's such a treasure; the ever-changing wine-by-the-glass menu that's pulled from an eclectic list is another. ✉ *2001 A Greene St., Five Points* ☎ *803/254–7828* ✍ *Reservations not accepted* ▭ *AE, D, MC, V* ⏲ *No lunch weekends.*

$ ✕ **Little Pigs Barbecue.** Grab a plate, get in the buffet line and load up on barbecue (pork), fried chicken, ribs, and fried fish, along with fixings such as collards, cole slaw, and macaroni and cheese. Since Little Pigs uses mustard-, tomato-, and vinegar-base barbecue sauces, you can sample all three and pick your favorite. ✉ *4927 Alpine Rd., Northeast Columbia* ☎ *803/788–8238* ✍ *Reservations not accepted* ▭ *No credit cards* ⏲ *Closed Mon. No dinner Wed.*

¢–$ ✕ **The Gourmet Shop.** Sit in a black-and-white French-inspired café where mirrors and art prints decorate the walls. The Gourmet Shop has long been serving wonderful coffee and sandwiches. The chicken salad, potato salad, and the tomato, feta, and basil salad are all super. Next door, the shop sells food to go (great for picnics), wine, and fancy food items. ✉ *724 Saluda Ave., Five Points* ☎ *803/799–9463* ✍ *Reservations not accepted* ▭ *AE, MC, V* ⏲ *No dinner Sun.*

¢–$ ✕ **Mediterranean Tea Room.** The tabbouleh, Greek salad, and kebabs are fresh and flavorful, served in a small and friendly restaurant. Specialties such as eggplant pita pizza and broiled shrimp with feta cheese are a nice change of pace. ✉ *2601 Devine St., Shandon* ☎ *803/799–3118* ✍ *Reservations not accepted* ▭ *AE, D, MC, V* ⏲ *Closed Sun.*

$$–$$$ 🏨 **Embassy Suites Hotel Columbia–Greystone.** In the spacious seven story atrium lobby—with skylights, fountains, pool, and live plants—you can enjoy your complimentary breakfast and evening cocktails. All rooms are suites that come with sleeper sofas in the living room. The staff, which caters mainly to a business clientele, works hard to please.

✉ 200 Stoneridge Dr., St. Andrews, 29210 ☎ 803/252–8700 or 800/362–2779 🖷 803/256–8749 ⊕ www.embassysuites.com ⇨ 214 suites ♢ Restaurant, microwaves, refrigerators, cable TV, indoor pool, gym, hot tub, lounge, recreation room, business services, meeting rooms, no-smoking rooms ▭ AE, D, DC, MC, V 🍴 BP.

$$–$$$ **Hampton Inn Downtown Historic District.** This classy chain is within walking distance of restaurants and nightlife in the Vista neighborhood. Blond-color wood furnishings are comfortable, though standard. The hotel's staff provides attentive service. *✉ 822 Gervais St., Vista, 29201 ☎ 803/231–2000 🖷 803/231–2868 ⊕ www.hamptoninncolumbia.com ⇨ 122 rooms ♢ Dining room, some in-room hot tubs, some microwaves, some refrigerators, cable TV, pool, gym, Internet, no-smoking rooms ▭ AE, D, DC, MC, V 🍴 BP.*

$$ **Claussen's Inn.** A bakery warehouse has been converted into an attractive small hotel with the rooms arranged around the lobby. The rooms in this eclectic inn are generally traditional, but each has its own personality: bright red or blue walls, for instance. Some have antique brass or iron beds, others have wooden four-posters. Generally they have floral or print fabrics and desk areas. Eight loft suites have downstairs sitting rooms furnished in period reproductions, spiral staircases, and four-poster beds upstairs. *✉ 2003 Greene St., Five Points, 29205 ☎ 803/765–0440 or 800/622–3382 🖷 803/799–7924 ⊕ www.bbonline.com/sc/claussens ⇨ 21 rooms, 8 suites ♢ Hot tub, meeting room; no smoking ▭ AE, D, MC, V 🍴 BP.*

$$ **The Whitney Hotel.** Because they were originally built as condos, the large rooms in the Whitney have full kitchens, dining rooms, bedrooms with doors and, in the two- and three-bedroom models, two full baths. Traditional wood and upholstered furnishings include formal desks and wingback chairs. Set among the trees in residential Shandon, from the hotel you can stroll to dinner and window shop for trendy clothes, housewares, and shoes; there are even two grocery stores around the corner. Access to an off-site health club is provided. *✉ 700 Woodrow St., Shandon, 29205 ☎ 803/252–0845 🖷 803/771–0495 ⊕ www.whitneyhotel.com ⇨ 74 suites ♢ Dining room, in-room data ports, kitchens, cable TV, pool, business services, meeting room, airport shuttle, no-smoking rooms ▭ AE, D, DC, MC, V 🍴 BP.*

$–$$ **Clarion Town House.** Thanks to a separate entrance for meeting rooms, the rather innlike lobby of this busy chain hotel is never too crowded. Rooms are large and decorated in traditional furnishings with soothing greens and blues; there are coffeemakers, and in the suites there are microwaves and refrigerators. You can opt for a Jacuzzi tub. *✉ 1615 Gervais St., Downtown, 29201 ☎ 803/771–8711 🖷 803/252–9347 ⊕ www.clariontownhouse.com ⇨ 142 rooms, 21 suites ♢ Cable TV, some in-room hot tubs, some microwaves, some refrigerators, pool, gym, meeting rooms, no-smoking rooms ▭ AE, D, MC, V 🍴 EP.*

$ **Comfort Suites.** A short drive down the access road from a mall, shopping center, and cinema complex, the Comfort Suites is off I–26 just west of downtown Columbia. Rooms are clean and as you'd expect from this chain; the exercise room and indoor pool are nice added benefits. *✉ 750 Saturn Pkwy., Exit 103, Harbison, 29212 ☎ 803/407–*

4444 or 800/426–6423 ☎ 803/407–4500 ⊕ www.comfortinn.com ⇨ 82 suites ♁ Dining room, microwaves, refrigerators, cable TV, pool, gym, Internet, no-smoking rooms ▭ AE, D, MC, V ⚇ BP.

Nightlife & the Arts

THE ARTS The **Cultural Council of Richland and Lexington Counties** (☎ 803/799–3115 ⊕ www.getcultured.org) provides information by phone or on their Web site about local cultural events including the ballet and symphony. The **Colonial Center** (✉ 801 Lincoln St., Vista ☎ 803/576–9200 ⊕ www.carolinacenter.net) is the largest arena in the state and hosts major entertainment events as well as University of South Carolina basketball games. **Trustus** (✉ 520 Lady St., Vista ☎ 803/254–9732 ⊕ www.trustus.org) is a local professional theater group.

Koger Center for the Arts (✉ Assembly St., USC Campus ☎ 803/777–7500 ⊕ http://koger.sc.edu/) presents national and international theater, ballet, and musical groups, as well as individual performers. The **Town Theatre** (✉ 1012 Sumter St., USC Campus ☎ 803/799–2510 ⊕ www.towntheater.org), founded in 1919, stages six plays a year from September to late May, plus a special summer show. The **Workshop Theatre of South Carolina** (✉ 1136 Bull St., USC Campus ☎ 803/799–4876 ⊕ www.towntheatre.com) produces a number of plays.

NIGHTLIFE In the hopping Vista neighborhood, the **Art Bar** (✉ 1211 Park St., Vista ☎ 803/254–4792) is funky, with splash-painted walls, lighted lunch boxes, and world music for dancing. **Willy's Restaurant & Grill** (✉ 1200B Lincoln St., Vista ☎ 803/799–3111), in a former train station waiting room, has live music (bluegrass, rock, country) and an outdoor patio.

★ Jazz is king at **Mac's on Main** (✉ 1710 Main St., Main Street area ☎ 803/929–0037), where local groups often jam into the night. If you're more into rock, **Hunter-Gatherer Brewery & Alehouse** (✉ 900 Main St., USC Campus ☎ 803/748–0540), has it on tap most nights, along with an excellent selection of beers, some made in-house. **Goatfeathers** (✉ 2017 Devine St., Five Points ☎ 803/256–3325 or 803/256–8133) is a bohemian bar–café that's popular with university and law-school students, and it also appeals to late-night coffee and dessert seekers.

Shopping

Many of Columbia's antiques outlets, boutique shops, and restaurants are in the ever-growing Vista neighborhood around Huger and Gervais streets, between the state house and the river. A number of intriguing shops and cafés are in Five Points, around Blossom at Harden streets, as well as along Devine Street in the Shandon neighborhood to the east. There are also antiques shops across the river on Meeting and State streets in West Columbia.

Old Mill Antique Mall (✉ 310 State St., West Columbia ☎ 803/796–4229) has items from many dealers, including furniture, glassware, jewelry, and books.

The **State Farmers' Market** (✉ Bluff Rd., USC Campus ☎ 803/737–4664) is one of the 10 largest in the country. Fresh vegetables, along with flowers, plants, seafood, and more, are sold weekdays 6 AM–9 PM and Sunday 1–6.

Camden

❷ *35 mi northeast of Columbia via I–20.*

A town with a horsey history and grand Southern colonial homes, charming Camden has never paved some of its roads for the sake of the hooves that regularly trot over them. The Carolina Cup and Colonial Cup are run here and in addition to the horse races, champagne tailgate parties are thrown using elegant crystal and china.

Camden is South Carolina's oldest inland town, dating from 1732. British general Lord Cornwallis established a garrison here during the Revolutionary War and burned most of Camden before evacuating it. A center of textile trade from the late 19th century through the 1940s, Camden blossomed when it became a refuge for Northerners escaping the cold winters. Because General Sherman spared the town during the Civil War, most of its antebellum homes still stand.

National Steeplechase Museum contains the largest collection of racing memorabilia in the U.S. (A steeplechase is a horse race over open land that has been set up with obstacles.) The Equisizer, a training machine used by jockeys for practice, let's you experience the race from the jockey's perspective; don't stay on too long, unless you want to feel the race all day. ✉ *200 Knights Hill Rd.* ☎ *800/780–8117* 🌐 *www.carolina-cup.org* 🎫 *Free* ⏲ *Sept.–May, daily 10–5, other months by appointment.*

The **Historic Camden Revolutionary War Site** puts emphasis on the period surrounding the British occupation of 1780. Several structures dot the site, including the 1789 **Craven House** and the **Blacksmith Shed.** The **Kershaw House**, a reconstruction of the circa-1770 home of Camden's founder, Joseph Kershaw, also served as Cornwallis's headquarters; it's furnished with period pieces. A nature trail, fortifications, powder magazine, picnic area, and crafts shop are also here. Guided tours are available by prearrangement. ✉ *U.S. 521, 1½ mi north of I–20* ☎ *803/432–9841* 🌐 *www.historic-camden.org* 🎫 *$5, grounds free* ⏲ *Tues.–Sat. 10–5, Sun. 1–5.*

off the beaten path

HISTORIC BOYKIN – This 19th-century agricultural community, on the National Register of Historic Places, was centered around the now restored and working grist mill. Buy freshly ground grits or cornmeal from the Boykin Mill General Store, which has floor-to-ceiling shelves. Step inside Broom Place, a restored 1740 slave house, to see and shop for brooms being handmade on late-19th-century equipment. You can also visit the 1820s Swift Creek Baptist Church and the original mill by appointment. The Mill Pond Restaurant occupies three buildings in the village. ✉ *Off U.S. 521, Rte. 261 and Boykin Mill Rd., 10 mi south of Camden* ☎ *803/425–0933* 🎫 *Free* ⏲ *Broom Place weekdays 10–5, Sat. 10:30–2; General Store Mon.–Sat. 9–3.*

Sports & the Outdoors

EQUESTRIAN EVENTS You're likely to see Thoroughbreds working out most mornings October through April at the **Springdale Race Course** (✉ 200 Knights Hill Rd. ☎ 803/432–6513 🌐 www.carolina-cup.org). Camden puts on two steeplechase events here: the Carolina Cup, in late March or early April; and the Colonial Cup, in November.

Where to Stay & Eat

★ **$$$–$$$$** ✕ **Mill Pond Restaurant.** You can dine alfresco overlooking the sprawling millpond, close enough to see pond life, or inside a trio of old buildings where you can ponder the stories the ancient heart-pine floors could tell. The wood paneling was reclaimed from the Boykin Tractor Shed after it was destroyed by Hurricane Hugo. The more casual side of the restaurant has a vintage saloon-style bar, which, in its first life, was the soda fountain at Zemps, a drug store in Camden. Perfectly fried cornmeal-crust oysters, and crab cakes with shrimp tartar sauce, are among the modern interpretations of Southern cuisine served here. Save room for homemade fruit cobbler with ice cream. ✉ *84 Boykin Mill Rd., Boykin, 10 mi south of Camden* ☎ *803/425–8825* ▭ *AE, MC, V* ⊙ *Closed Sun. and Mon. No lunch.*

$–$$ ✕ **Lucy's Food & Spirits.** Sit at the immense wooden bar or at café tables in a high-ceiling, brick-wall, turn-of-the-20th-century building. Try the veal Lucy with portobello mushrooms, the pear and endive salad, or, for lunch, the curried-chicken salad. ✉ *1034 Broad St.* ☎ *803/432–9096* ▭ *AE, D, MC, V* ⊙ *Closed Sun. and Mon. No lunch Tues.*

$–$$ ✕ **The Pearl.** A former school teacher, Ms. Pearl is famous for cooking country food like collards, pork chops, catfish, fried chicken, and banana pudding. A meat-and-two (lunch) or -three (dinner) comes with salad and beverage. Do like the locals and save the sweet-potato soufflé for dessert. Each room has a theme: for example, the Pearl Room has framed pearl necklaces on the wall. ✉ *707 DeKalb St.* ☎ *803/713–8009* ▭ *AE, MC, V.*

★ **$–$$** ✕ **Greenleaf Inn of Camden.** The 1890 McLean house serves as the main inn, with four rooms on the second floor above the restaurant; the nearby Joshua Reynolds (circa 1805) house has six more rooms. Furnishings are classic Victorian, with some four-poster beds, and all bathrooms are modern. Rooms in the main inn are more spacious, those in the separate house more private. In the elegant-yet-approachable restaurant ($$–$$$), high ceilings and elaborate tiled fireplaces set the tone inside and there's patio dining outside. Try the wonderful crispy whole flounder, or seafood lasagna; lunches come with homemade potato chips. ✉ *1308 Broad St., 29020* ☎ *803/425–1806 or 800/437–5874* 📠 *803/425–5853* 🌐 *www.greenleafinncamden.com* *10 rooms* *Restaurant; no smoking* ▭ *AE, D, MC, V* 🍽 *BP.*

$ **Candlelight Inn.** What it lacks in size—there are only three rooms—the Candlelight Inn makes up for in style, particularly the 2-acre garden that's on fire with azaleas in spring and shaded year-round by ancient live oaks. Breakfast is a special treat: everything is homemade, including the strawberry syrup that accompanies the Hawaiian French toast. ✉ *1904 Broad St., 29020* ☎ *803/424–1057* 🌐 *www.bbonline.*

com/sc/candlelight/ ⇨ *2 rooms, 1 suite* ♁ *No room phones, no smoking* ▭ *AE, D, MC, V* 🍽 *BP.*

$ **Fairfield Inn.** Sometimes you need the conveniences of a chain hotel like this one: coffeemakers, hair dryers, free high-speed Internet access, and large workspaces. Suites have refrigerators and microwaves. There's also an exercise room and a pool. ✉ *220 Wall St., 29020* ☎ *803/425–1010* 🖷 *803/425–4006* 🌐 *www.marriott.com* ⇨ *48 rooms, 18 suites* ♁ *Dining room, cable TV, in-room data ports, some microwaves, some refrigerators, pool, gym, no-smoking rooms* ▭ *AE, D, MC, V* 🍽 *BP.*

Shopping

Camden is known for its antiques shopping, with the heart of the antiques and arts district along Broad Street, as well as on the neighboring Rutledge, DeKalb and Market streets.

Aiken

❸ *100 mi southwest of Sumter via U.S. 378/76 to I–20 to U.S. 1, 56 mi southwest of Columbia via I–20 and U.S. 1.*

This is Thoroughbred Country, and Aiken first earned its fame in the 1890s, when wealthy Northerners wintering here built stately mansions and entertained one another with horse shows, hunts, and lavish parties. Many up-to-60-room homes stand as a testament to this era of opulence. The town is still a center for all kinds of outdoor activity, including the equestrian events of the Triple Crown, as well as tennis and golf.

The area's horse farms have produced many national champions, which are commemorated at the **Aiken Thoroughbred Hall of Fame** with exhibitions of horse-related decorations, paintings, and sculptures, plus racing silks and trophies. The Hall of Fame is on the grounds of the 14-acre **Hopeland Gardens,** where you can wind along paths, past quiet terraces and reflecting pools. There's a Touch and Scent Trail with Braille plaques. Open-air free concerts and plays are presented on Monday evening May through August. ✉ *Dupree Pl. and Whiskey Rd.* ☎ *803/642–7630* 🎟 *Free* ⏲ *Museum Oct.–May, Tues.–Sun. 2–5; grounds daily dawn–dusk.*

The **Aiken County Historical Museum,** in one wing of an 1860 estate, is devoted to early-regional culture. It has Native American artifacts, firearms, an authentically furnished 1808 log cabin, a schoolhouse, and a miniature circus display. ✉ *433 Newberry St. SW* ☎ *803/642–2015* 🎟 *Donations suggested* ⏲ *Tues.–Fri. 9:30–4:30, weekends 2–5.*

Aiken surrounds **Hitchcock Woods,** 2,000 acres of Southern forest with hiking trails and bridal paths. Three times the size of New York's Central Park, it's the largest urban forest in the country and is listed on the National Register of Historic Places. ✣ *Enter from junction of Clark Rd. and Whitney Dr., Berrie Rd., and Dibble Rd.*

Home to James Hammond, who is credited with being first to declare that "Cotton is King," **Redcliff Plantation** remained in the family until 1975 when it was willed to the state. The 10,000-square-foot mansion (which sits on 400 acres) remains just as it was, down to the 19th-century books on the carved shelves. Slave quarters still contain bedding

EDGEFIELD STONEWARE

POTTERY FROM South Carolina's Edgefield district was once considered a necessity in plantation kitchens. Pieces were sold locally, and they also made their way along trade routes to Columbia, Charleston, and beyond. Today Edgefield stoneware has become a prized item for collectors of Southern folk art.

By the early 1800s, thanks to soil rich in minerals and the development of a unique alkaline glaze, the Edgefield district in west-central South Carolina had become a center for pottery manufacture. Vessels ranging in size from one-half to 30 gallons were used for a variety of kitchen jobs, such as pickling, churning butter, and carrying water.

As Edgefield's potters, most of them slaves, became experienced in their craft, many began to decorate their jugs and jars with flowers, architectural motifs, and, sometimes, scenes from their lives. Less often, they produced "face vessels," with faces sculpted into the surface. The white Kaolin clay used for the teeth and eyes give these rare pieces a striking appearance.

But Edgefield is best known for the 20- to 30-gallon jugs created by Dave, a literate slave. He signed and dated his pieces, and occasionally he decorated them with verses that are a window into his world: "I wonder where is all my relations / Friendship to all and every nation"; "Dave belongs to Mr. Miles / where the oven bakes and the pot biles."

Dave, who later took the surname Drake, produced some 40,000 pieces in his lifetime. Only 28, however, are inscribed with verse, making them extremely valuable: some have sold for upward of $40,000 and several are in major museum collections.

pallets and other coarse furnishings. Once you've toured the house (starting at 1, 2, or 3 PM), be sure to explore the grounds on the 2-mi-long trail. Be warned: the house has no central heat or air conditioning. ✉ *181 Redcliff Rd., Beech Island, 15 mi southwest of Aiken* 🎫 *$2* ⏲ *Thurs.–Mon. 9–5.*

Stephen Ferrell has an extensive collection of Edgefield pottery on display at his shop, **Old Edgefield Pottery.** Ferrell, like his father, is an accomplished potter in his own right, steeped in the Edgefield tradition. His work is on display and for sale as well. ✉ *230 Simpkins St., Edgefield, 20 mi northwest of Aiken* ☎ *803/637–2060* ⏲ *Tues.–Sat. 10–5.*

Sports & the Outdoors

EQUESTRIAN EVENTS

In Aiken, polo matches are played at **Whitney Field** (✉ 200 Mead Dr., off Whiskey Rd. [U.S. 19] ☎ 803/648–7874) Sunday at 3, September through November and March through July.

Three weekends in late March and early April are set aside for the famed **Triple Crown** (✉ Horse district, off Whiskey Rd. [U.S. 19] ☎ 803/641–1111), which includes thoroughbred trials of promising yearlings, a steeplechase, and harness races by young horses making their debut.

Where to Stay & Eat

$$$–$$$$ ✕ **Linda's Bistro.** Chef Linda Rooney elevates traditional European favorites, turning out excellent mushroom-Gruyère tarts, risotto with roasted mushrooms and Asiago cheese, and steak and frites. Main courses come with a salad, a vegetable, and potatoes. Rum-coconut-cream bread pudding is a favorite for dessert. It's all served in an open, café-like environment. ✉ *210 The Alley* ☎ *803/648–4853* ▭ *AE, D, DC, MC, V* ⊙ *Closed Sun. and Mon. No lunch.*

$$–$$$ ✕ **Malia's.** Locals love this busy contemporary restaurant, with dim lighting and dark fabrics that convey a cool class. Grilled chicken salad might be a menu staple, but here, thanks to the addition of seasonal fruit and greens, it seems new again. At dinner, creative international-influence cuisine includes lamb soup with curry, veal with shiitake mushrooms and a brandy sauce—and the lighter baked ham, Brie, and portobello mushroom sandwich. ✉ *120 Laurens St.* ☎ *803/643–3086* ▭ *D, MC, V* ⊙ *No lunch weekends. No dinner Sun.–Tues.*

¢–$ ✕ **New Moon Cafe.** The coffee beans at New Moon Cafe are roasted right next door. Here you can pair Aiken's best coffee with freshly baked muffins and sweet rolls, wraps and salads, and homemade soups (the black bean and crab bisque are particularly good). ✉ *116 Laurens St.* ☎ *803/643–7088* ✍ *Reservations not accepted* ▭ *No credit cards* ⊙ *No dinner.*

¢–$ ✕ **Track Kitchen.** The who's who of Aiken's horsey set eat here most mornings, feasting on the heavy and hearty cooking of Carol and Pockets Curtis. The small dining room is unpretentious, with walls of mint-green cinder block and simple Formica counters. ✉ *420 Mead Ave.* ☎ *803/641–9628* ▭ *No credit cards* ⊙ *Closed May–Sept. No dinner.*

$$$$ **The Willcox.** Winston Churchill, Franklin D. Roosevelt, and the Astors have slept at this grand, 19th-century inn. Massive stone fireplaces, rosewood trim, heart-pine floors, and antiques grace the lobby. Guest rooms and suites contain upscale furniture with classic lines, like the sleek, dark-stain, four-poster beds. Choose to soak in the extra-deep tub, or relax beside your fireplace. A bottle of lavender linen spray sits bedside and a CD player awaits your music selection. All meals, spirits, and activities such as skeet, and carriage rides through Hitchcock Woods, are included. Here you can pretend, at least for one night, that you're a Vanderbilt. ✉ *100 Colleton Ave., 29801* ☎ *803/648–1898 or 877/648–2200* 🖷 *803/643–0971* 🌐 *www.thewillcox.com* *7 rooms, 15 suites* *Dining room, room service, spa, lobby lounge, some pets allowed; no smoking* ▭ *AE, D, DC, MC, V* ⊙ *Closed mid-May—mid-Sept.* *FAP.*

Fodor's Choice ★

$ **Briar Patch.** You can learn plenty about both the Old and New South from the knowledgeable innkeepers of this terrific B&B, which was formerly tack rooms in Aiken's stable district. You get two choices—either the frilly room with French provincial furniture or the less dramatic one with pine antiques and a weather vane. ✉ *544 Magnolia La. SE, 29801* ☎ *803/649–2010* 🌐 *www.bbonline.com/sc/briar* *2 rooms* *Dining room, tennis court; no room phones, no smoking* ▭ *No credit cards* *BP.*

Greenwood

4 *10 mi east of Greenwood on Rte. 248, 75 mi west of Columbia via U.S. 378 and U.S. 178.*

Founded by Irish settlers in 1802, Greenwood received its name from the site's gently rolling landscape and dense forests. Andrew Johnson, the 17th U.S. president, operated a tailor shop at Courthouse Square before migrating to East Tennessee. Anglers, swimmers, and boaters head for nearby Lake Greenwood's 200-mi shore. Two sections of Sumter National Forest are nearby.

★ **Gardens of Park Seed Co.,** one of the nation's largest seed supply houses, maintains colorful experimental gardens and greenhouses 6 mi north of Greenwood. The flower beds are especially vivid mid-June through July. Seeds and bulbs are for sale in the company store. The **South Carolina Festival of Flowers**—with a performing-artist contest, a beauty pageant, private house and garden tours, and live entertainment—is held at Park's headquarters annually at the end of June. ✉ *Rte. 25, off U.S. 178, Hodges* ☎ *864/941–4213 or 800/845–3369* 🌐 *www.parkseeds.com* *Free* ⏲ *Gardens daily dawn–dusk; store Mon.–Sat. 9–5.*

Where to Stay & Eat

$$–$$$ ✕ **Regan's.** When Regan Marshall decided to open a restaurant he wanted to make it personal, so he asked friends to donate items that they'd like displayed. Looking at the results, including a poster-size photo of Kramer from the Seinfeld show, makes for an interesting few minutes before you sit down to eat. A lunch favorite is the daily fresh salad (usually homemade tuna or chicken on greens); for dinner, chicken crepês with tarragon cream sauce are good, as is the seafood chowder served on weekends. The strawberry cream cheese pie tastes like a delicious milk shake you eat with a fork. ✉ *328 Main St.* ☎ *864/388–0565* *AE, MC, V* ⏲ *Closed Sun. No dinner Mon. No lunch Sat.*

$ **Inn on the Square.** This inn was fashioned out of a warehouse in the heart of town. Simple, solid color carpets and linens brighten spacious guest rooms furnished with 18th-century reproductions, four-poster beds, and writing desks. Also note thoughtful touches such as turndown service and complimentary morning newspapers. ✉ *104 Court St., 29648* ☎ *864/223–4488 or 800/231–9109* *864/223–7067* 🌐 *www.innonthesquare.us* *48 rooms* *2 restaurants, room service, cable TV, pool, lounge, business services, meeting rooms, no-smoking rooms* *AE, D, DC, MC, V* *BP.*

Abbeville

★ 5 *14 mi west of Greenwood on Rte. 72, 102 mi west of Columbia.*

Abbeville may well be one of inland South Carolina's most satisfying lesser-known towns. An appealing historic district includes the old business areas, early churches, and residential areas. What was called the "Southern cause" by supporters of the Confederacy was born and died here: it's where the first organized secession meeting was held and where, on May 2, 1865, Confederate president Jefferson Davis officially disbanded the defeated armies of the South in the last meeting of his war council.

The **Abbeville Welcome Center** (✉ 107 Court Sq. ☎ 864/366–4600) has on display a series of paintings by Wilbur Kurtz, a respected authority on pre–Civil War life in the early to mid-20th century. Kurtz, a consultant on the movies *Gone With the Wind* and *Song of the South,* also painted the Battle of Atlanta murals on the Atlanta Cyclorama. The oversize Abbeville paintings depict five Civil War scenes including the first secession meeting (John C. Calhoun is from the area) and Jefferson Davis's final Council of War meeting. They have been completely restored and are quite mesmerizing because of their size and detail.

In 1865 the Confederate council met at the **Burt-Stark House** (1820) and Jefferson Davis disbanded the Confederate Armies, effectively ending the Civil War. The house was a private residence until 1971 when Mary Stark Davis died. She willed the house to the city, with a provision that states nothing can be added or removed from the house. It's filled with lovely antiques, carved wood surfaces, and old family photos. Her clothing is still in the dresser drawers. ✉ *306 N. Main St.* ☎ *864/459–4297 or 864/459–2181* *$3* ⏲ *Sept.–May, Fri. and Sat. 1–5 and by appointment; June–Aug., Tues.–Sat. 1–5 and by appointment.*

Where to Stay & Eat

★ **$–$$$** ✕ **Village Grille.** Many locals frequent the Village Grille because of the herb rotisserie chicken, but the ribs, the fillet with blue cheese and portobello mushrooms, and the cordial-laced desserts are just as good a reason to come. Antique mirrors hang on pomegranate-color walls below high ceilings. The feeling here is trendy yet easygoing; the staff bend over backward to please. ✉ *114 Trinity St.* ☎ *864/366–2500* *AE, D, MC, V* ⏲ *Closed Sun. and Mon.*

¢–$ ✕ **Yoder's Dutch Kitchen.** Try some authentic Pennsylvania Dutch home cooking in this unassuming South Carolina redbrick building. There's a lunch buffet and evening smorgasbord with fried chicken, stuffed cabbage, Dutch meat loaf, breaded veal Parmesan, and plenty of vegetables. Shoofly pie, Dutch bread, and apple butter can be purchased to go. ✉ *Rte. 72, east of downtown* ☎ *864/459–5556* *No credit cards* ⏲ *Closed Sun.–Tues. No dinner Wed.*

$ **Belmont Inn.** Because of the theater-dining-and-lodging packages, the Belmont Inn is a popular overnight stop for opera-house goers. The redbrick building with colonnade was built in the 1900s in a Spanish style. Guest rooms are spacious, with high ceilings, pine floors, and colonial-look furniture. The restaurant is open only on weekends when a show is playing at the opera house. ✉ *104 E. Pickens St., 29620* ☎ *864/459–9625 or 877/459–8118* *www.belmontinn.net* *25 rooms* *Restaurant, in-room data ports, cable TV, business services, meeting rooms, no-smoking rooms* *AE, D, DC, MC, V* *BP.*

THE UPCOUNTRY

The Upcountry, in the northwest corner of the state, has long been a favorite for family vacations because of its temperate climate and natural beauty. The abundant lakes and waterfalls and several state parks (including Caesar's Head, Keowee-Toxaway, Oconee, Table Rock, and the Chattooga National Wild and Scenic River) provide all manner of recreational activities. Beautiful anytime, the 130-mi Cherokee Foothills Scenic Highway (Route 11), which goes through the Blue Ridge Mountains, is especially delightful in spring (when the peach trees are in bloom) and autumn.

Greenville is growing fast and attracting lots of industry, much of it textile-related, in keeping with the area's history. Clemson, home of Clemson University and the "Orange Wave," is pretty much a university town. Pendleton, just a few miles away, has one of the nation's largest historic districts. With its village green, surrounded by shops and restaurants, it's a lovely step back in time. The comfortable communities of Spartanburg and Anderson are beginning to rejuvenate their downtown areas.

Greenville

6 *58 mi south of Greenville on Rte. 20, 100 mi northwest of Columbia via I–26 and I–385.*

Once known for its textile and other manufacturing plants, Greenville has reinvented itself as a trendy and sophisticated city able to support a surprising number of innovative restaurants, imaginative galleries, and upscale boutiques along a tree-lined Main Street that passes a stunning natural waterfall. Anchored by two performance centers, the city's business district is alive and well into most evenings with couples and families enjoying the energy of this revitalized southern city. In fact, downtown development has been so successful that more and more young professionals are moving downtown and creating interesting living spaces from old warehouses and retail establishments.

★ The renowned international collection of religious art at **Bob Jones University Museum & Gallery** includes works by Botticelli, Rembrandt, Rubens, and van Dyck. Note that children younger than six are not permitted. ✉ *Bob Jones University, 1700 Wade Hampton Blvd.* ☎ *864/242–5100* 🌐 *www.bjumg.org* 🎟 *$5, free Sun.* ⏲ *Tues.–Sun. 2–5.*

Housed in an innovative modern building, the **Greenville County Museum of Art** displays American works dating from the colonial era. Works by Paul Jenkins, Jamie Wyeth, Jasper Johns, and noted Southern artists are on exhibit. ✉ *420 College St.* ☎ *864/271–7570* 🌐 *www.greenvillemuseum.org* 🎟 *Free* ⏲ *Tues.–Sat. 10–5, Sun. 1–5.*

Fodor's Choice ★ There are more than 50 mi of hiking trails within **Mountain Bridge Wilderness Area,** 30 mi north of Greenville, which encompasses two state parks. The trail leading to 420-foot-tall Raven Cliff Falls can be accessed 1 mi north of the main entrance to **Caesar's Head State Park;** along the way there are spectacular views of river gorges and pine-covered mountains. Cross Matthews Creek on a suspension bridge; the view of the falls is worth the terror of knowing you're held in the air by nothing but wire. Register at Park Headquarters before you head out on the trail. Near the headquarters are Table Rock and Devil's Kitchen, a geological phenomenon that stays cool even in the heat of summer. ✉ *8155 U.S. 276, Cleveland* ☎ *864/836–6115* 🌐 *www.discoversouthcarolina.com* 🎫 *$2* ⏲ *Daily 9–9 during daylight savings time; daily 9–6 rest of yr.*

Famous for the Rim of the Gap trail, which has views of Rainbow Falls, **Jones Gap State Park** is 6 mi east of U.S. 276 on Jones Gap Road. Access several trails from the Park Headquarters, or pick up a map and drive to one of the many well-marked trailheads. Be sure to pick up your trail map and register before venturing into the wilderness, as some of the trails are quite long and strenuous. ✉ *Jones Gap Rd., 6 mi east off U.S. 276, Marionetta* ☎ *864/836–3647* 🌐 *www.discoversouthcarolina.com* 🎫 *$2* ⏲ *Daily 9–9 during daylight savings time; daily 9–6 rest of yr.*

off the beaten path

SYMMES CHAPEL PRETTY PLACE – Built into a mountain, this outdoor chapel that's part of Camp Greenville has stunning views of valleys and mountains in the distance not too far from Caesar's Head State Park. The chapel is closed to the public on weekends; call for other scheduled closings or to book it for a wedding. ✉ *U.S. 276, Brevard, NC, 45 mi north of Greenville* ☎ *864/836–5785* 🎫 *Free* ⏲ *Grounds daily dawn–dusk, chapel weekdays dawn–dusk.*

Devils Fork State Park, on Lake Jocassee, has luxurious villas and camping facilities, hiking, boating, and fishing. Lower Whitewater Falls plunges more than 200 feet over huge boulders to splash into the lake waters. The falls can be viewed from an overlook or from a boat on the lake. ✉ *Jocassee Lake Rd., off Rte. 11, north of Salem, 45 mi northwest of Greenville* ☎ *864/944–2639* 🌐 *www.discoversouthcarolina.com* 🎫 *$2* ⏲ *Daily 9–9 during daylight savings time; daily 9–6 rest of yr.*

Sports & the Outdoors

South Carolinians sometimes prefer Upcountry golf courses to those on the coast, as they're less crowded and enjoy a slightly cooler climate. The area's rolling hills provide an added challenge.

Links O'Tryon (✉ 11250 New Cut Rd., Campobello ☎ 864/468–4995) is an 18-hole course with stunning views of the Blue Ridge Mountains and fieldstone bridges and walls in the Tom Jackson–design layout. **Rock at Jocassee** (✉ 171 Sliding Rock Rd., Pickens ☎ 864/878–2030) is a mountain course with many water hazards; its signature hole has a waterfall view.

Where to Stay & Eat

$$$–$$$$ ✕ **Augusta Grill.** Depending on what's in season, and on the whims of the chef, menu selections change daily. Seafood and beef with French-influence sauces are typical. The crab cake special on Wednesday night packs the house. Lunch service is brisk. There's an attached martini bar, too. ✉ *1818 Augusta St.* ☎ *864/242–0316* 💳 *AE, D, MC, V* ⏲ *Closed Sun. No lunch Sat.*

$$$–$$$$ ✕ **Soby's New South Cuisine.** The decorator palette of plums and golds is a stunning contrast to the original brick and wood that was uncovered during the renovation of this 19th-century cotton exchange building. Although the menu changes seasonally, perennial favorites such as a layered appetizer of fried green tomatoes and jalapeño pimiento cheese, shrimp and locally ground grits and the famous mind-numbing white-chocolate banana-cream pie are always available. ✉ *207 S. Main St.* ☎ *864/232–7007* ▭ *AE, MC, V* ⊙ *Closed Sun. No lunch.*

¢–$$ ✕ **Stax's Omega Diner.** This contemporary diner has both booths and a half-circle counter with stools. The menu lists a little of everything: bacon and eggs, burgers, souvlaki, Greek-style chicken, shrimp, and grits. It's all good, and it's open almost around-the-clock (closed 2 AM–6:30 AM weekdays, 3 AM–6:30 AM weekends). ✉ *72 Orchard Park Dr.* ☎ *864/297–6639* ▭ *AE, DC, MC, V.*

¢–$ ✕ **Two Chefs Delicatessen.** Mix and match from the deli's selection of delicious homemade sandwiches and salads. Try the roasted potato salad, Asian chicken salad, dried-cranberry-and-grilled-chicken salad or pepper-crusted turkey on rosemary sourdough. There are a lot of tempting desserts, too, including apple brandy cake, flourless chocolate cake, and fruit tarts, so the place is often packed. There's a second, to-go location on the east side. ✉ *104 S. Main St., Suite 105* ☎ *864/370–9336* ✉ *Two Chefs To Go,* ✉ *29 Pelham Rd.* ☎ *864/284–9970* ▭ *MC, V* ⊙ *Closed Sun. No dinner Sat.*

¢ ✕ **Meador's Sandwich Shop.** Join generations of Greenville families who've been raised on Meador's "Vardry" burgers, big fat hamburgers named for Greenville founding father Vardry McBee. Try one topped with blue cheese made up the road at Clemson University. The pimiento cheese and BLT sandwiches are popular, too. ✉ *15 Conestee Ave.* ☎ *864/233–6854* ✉ *123 S. Main St.* ☎ *864/235–9993* ▭ *AE, MC, V* ⊙ *No dinner.*

★ $$$$ ✕ **La Bastide.** About 19 mi northwest (30 minutes) of Greenville in the sloping Piedmont hills, a French provincial–style inn—with surrounding vineyard—emulates a French countryside experience. Rooms have European linens, French antiques and reproductions, elaborate wrought iron chandeliers, gas fireplaces, and hillside views. French country cuisine, such as duck with blood-orange sauce, and fine wine are served at the restaurant ($$$–$$$$). A weeknight special pairs a double room and dinner for two ($299). Guests have access to golf at a nearby country club. ✉ *10 Road of Vines, Travelers Rest 29690* ☎ *864/836–8463 or 877/836–8463* 📠 *864/836–4820* 🌐 *www.labastide.com* *12 rooms, 2 suites* *Restaurant, some in-room hot tubs, golf privileges, croquet, no-smoking rooms* ▭ *AE, D, DC, MC, V* *BP.*

$$ ✕ **Phoenix–Greenville's Inn.** Ask for a room overlooking the courtyard gardens and pool at this accommodating Southern inn with plantation shutters. The graceful spindles of the four-poster beds are painted or stained according to the room's decor (white, mahogany, cherry). Chef Don Hiers cooks at the Palms Restaurant ($$–$$$$), one of Greenville's best. Sophisticated fare includes the signature hot smoked Atlantic salmon with ginger and soy, and roast rack of lamb with wild mushrooms, lentils, and fennel. ✉ *246 N. Pleasantburg Dr., 29607* ☎ *800/257–3529*

864/233–4651 www.phoenixgreenvillesinn.com 181 rooms, 3 suites Restaurant, in-room data ports, pool, lounge, pub, business services, meeting rooms, no-smoking rooms AE, D, DC, MC, V BP.

$–$$ **Hyatt Regency Hotel.** This upscale chain offering's best asset is its location in the midst of the revitalized downtown of shops and restaurants. Rooms come with one king or queen bed or two doubles. Make sure you ask for a room overlooking the palm-filled atrium, which are far better than those without views. *220 N. Main St., 29601 864/235–1234 or 800/633–7313 864/232–7584 www.hyatt.com 330 rooms Restaurant, room service, cable TV, pool, health club, lounge, airport shuttle, no-smoking rooms AE, D, DC, MC, V EP.*

$–$$ **Westin Poinsett Hotel.** A 1925, 12-story hotel has been brought back to life by Westin. In the public spaces, intricate moldings adorn the many columns, ironwork rails and chandeliers are apparent throughout, and decorative plasterwork has been restored. The large guest rooms have down comforters, marble baths, and high ceilings. *120 S. Main St., 29601 864/421–9700 864/421–9719 www.westin.com 181 rooms, 9 suites Restaurant, coffee shop, room service, in-room safes, cable TV, health club, lounge, concierge, Internet, business services, meeting rooms, no-smoking rooms AE, D, DC, MC, V EP.*

Pendleton

7 *30 mi southwest of Greenville via U.S. 123.*

Walk among the interesting architecture of Pendleton's historic district, just a few miles from Clemson University. The Farmers Hall (1826) was originally built to be a courthouse. The Square, a district of restaurants and shops, faces the Village Green. Keep your eyes peeled for Richard Burnside, a self-taught folk artist whose paintings decorate several House of Blues locations. Burnside, who has lived in Pendleton since the 1980s, paints at various locations around the square.

The **South Carolina State Botanical Garden,** on the Clemson University campus, holds more than 2,000 varieties of plants on more than 295 acres, including wildflower, fern, and bog gardens. Niche gardens, and there are 20 of them, include a winter (February) blooming camellia garden, and a wildflower meadow buzzing with bees and hummingbirds. Some garden sculptures are buildings made totally from living trees. The **Fran Hanson Discovery Center** has information on regional history and cultural heritage, and a hands-on learning station on natural history, a microscope with a big-screen monitor, and a talking animated raccoon. *102 Garden Trail, Clemson, 4 mi northwest of Pendleton 864/656–3405 www.clemson.edu/scbg Free Daily dawn–dusk.*

Issaqueena Falls is said to be named for Issaqueena, an Indian princess in love with an Englishman. Rather than face the wrath of her angry tribe, she's said to have leapt off the edge of the 100-foot falls. There the legend takes a twist: it is said Issaqueena actually jumped to a hidden ledge, reunited with her lover and the two escaped to live happily ever after. One of the most popular of the state's waterfalls, Issaqueena

BOILED WHAT?

Wondering about the hand-lettered signs advertising "Hot Boiled Peanuts" on display in nearly every gas station, convenience store, and roadside stand? Hot boiled peanuts are exactly that: raw peanuts simmered in brine—often in a crock pot—for long periods. The result is a slightly slippery, but never slimy, treat. Boiled peanuts are eaten just like roasted peanuts, but the texture is more akin to a canned bean than a nut, and napkins are an absolute necessity.

Route 11, in the Upstate area, has a lot of roadside stands, and most sell boiled peanuts in addition to farm products. Shriners and other local charities sometimes sell boiled peanuts straight from the pot in the parking lots of big chain discount stores like Wal-Mart to raise money. Go ahead, give 'em a try; you might just find these salty morsels addictive.

7

can be reached via a trail that, although only ¼ mi long, is fairly steep. ✉ *Stumphouse Tunnel Park, off Rte. 28, 7 mi outside Wahalla, 28 mi northwest of Pendleton* ☎ *864/638–4343* 🎫 *Free* ⏲ *Daily 10–5.*

off the beaten path

CHATTOOGA NATIONAL WILD AND SCENIC RIVER – Designated as a Wild and Scenic River by Congress in 1974, the Chattooga River can test the skills of even the most experienced rafters with Class V–plus runs that have names like "Crack-in-the-Rock," "Corkscrew," and "Sock-Em Dog" (which includes a stomach-sinking 7-foot drop). Commercial rafting outfitters, including **Nantahala Outdoor Center** (☎ 864/647–9014 or 800/232–7238 🌐 www.noc.com), **Southeastern Expeditions** (☎ 800/868–7238 🌐 www.southeasternexpeditions.com), and **Wildwater Ltd.** (☎ 864/647–9587 or 800/451–9972 🌐 www.wildwaterrafting.com), also run shorter, more gentle rides (Class II and below) that are appropriate for senior citizens and children as young as eight years old—they even bring lunch. The river is on the border of South Carolina and Georgia, about 38 mi northeast of Pendleton via U.S. 76 or Rte. 28, and is part of Sumter National Forest on the Carolina side.

KING CREEK FALLS – Take the Chattooga Trail in Sumter National Forest to see 70 feet of rushing water that enters a pool in a half-moon, raising a glorious spray. A tiny sand beach makes the banks a nice place to spend an afternoon. The hike is about a ½ mi each way. *Sumter National Forest* ✉ *Burrells Ford Rd., off Rte 28 and Rte. 107.*

Where to Stay & Eat

$–$$$ ✕ **Sullivan's Metropolitan Grill.** Housed in a 19th-century building that was most recently a hardware store, Sullivan's interior is almost as interesting as its Mediterranean-influence food. Massive plaster columns stand above heart-pine floors and elaborate moldings decorate the room. Foodwise, duck is the star here. Save room for owner Sabra Nickas's decidedly non-Med desserts that include huge wedges of peanut butter pie, slabs of homemade cake, and even homemade cookies. ✉ *208 S. Main St., Anderson, 8 mi south of Pendleton* ☎ *864/226–8945* *Reservations essential* ▭ *AE, D, MC, V* ⊗ *Closed Sun. No lunch Sat.*

$ **Liberty Hall Inn.** A country inn in the middle of town: on-site owners have decorated the 1840s building with family heirlooms and antiques such as tall, carved, darkwood-headboards set dramatically against red walls. Breakfast is a choice of yogurt parfait or French toast. The restaurant, Café Leisure ($$–$$$), displays intensely colorful art on red walls and serves dishes such as grilled Cornish hen with Madeira mushroom sauce to panfried sea bass with cucumber-dill sauce. ✉ *621 S. Mechanic St., 29670* ☎ *800/643–7944* *864/646–7500* 🌐 *www.bbonline.com/sc/liberty* *7 rooms* *Restaurant; no smoking* ▭ *AE, D, MC, V* *BP.*

$ **Rocky Retreat.** A red tin roof tops the 1849 Boone-Douthit house that was once a summer home of the family that owned Charleston's Boone Hall Plantation. The B&B that has taken up residence was named for the large granite boulders that jut out of the nearby mountains. Rooms have original heart-pine floors, antiques, claw-foot tubs, and working fireplaces. Breakfast, prepared by innkeeper Jim Ligon, is hearty and delicious. ✉ *1000 Milwee Creek Rd., 29670* ☎ *864/225–3494* 🌐 *www.bbonline.com/sc/rockyretreat* *3 rooms* *No room phones, no room TVs, no children under 10, no smoking* ▭ *MC, V* *BP.*

THE MIDLANDS & UPSTATE A TO Z

To research prices, get advice from other travelers, and book travel arrangements, visit www.fodors.com.

AIRPORTS

Columbia Metropolitan Airport, 10 mi west of downtown Columbia, is served by ASA/DeltaConnection, ComAir, Continental, Delta, Independence, Northwest, United Express, and US Airways/Express. Greenville-Spartanburg Airport, off I–85 between the two cities, is served by American Eagle, ASA/DeltaConnection, ComAir, Continental, Delta, Independence, Northwest, United Express, and US Airways/Express.

Airport Information **Columbia Metropolitan Airport** ✉ 3000 Aviation Way, Airport ☎ 803/822–5000 🌐 www.columbiaairport.com. **Greenville-Spartanburg Airport** ✉ 2000 G.S.P. Dr. ☎ 864/867–7426 🌐 www.gsairport.com.

CAR TRAVEL

I–77 leads into Columbia from the north, I–26 runs through north–south, and I–20 east–west. I–85 provides access to Greenville, Spartanburg, Pendleton, and Anderson. I–26 runs from Charleston through Columbia to the Upcountry, connecting with I–385 into Greenville. Car rental by all the national chains is available at the airports in Columbia and Greenville.

EMERGENCIES

Emergency-room services are available at Palmetto Health Richland. Kroger Sav-on has a pharmacy open 24 hours; other regional locations are open until 9.

Emergency Services **Ambulance, fire, police** ☎ 911.

Hospitals **Palmetto Health Richland** ✉ 5 Richland Medical Park, Columbia ☎ 803/434-7000.

24-Hour Pharmacies **Kroger Sav-On** ✉ 7467 Woodrow St., Irmo ☎ 803/732-0426.

VISITOR INFORMATION

Tourist Information **Capital City/Lake Murray Country Visitors Center** ✉ 2184 N. Lake Dr., Irmo 29063 ☎ 803/781-5940 or 866/785-3935 ⊕ www.scjewel.com. **Columbia Metropolitan Convention and Visitors Bureau** ✉ 900 Assembly St., Columbia 29201 ☎ 803/545-0000 or 800/264-4884 ⊕ www.columbiacvb.com. **Discover Upcountry Carolina Association** 📫 Box 3116, Greenville 29602 ☎ 864/233-2690 or 800/849-4766 ⊕ www.theupcountry.com. **Greater Abbeville Chamber of Commerce** ✉ 107 Court Sq., Abbeville 29620 ☎ 864/366-4600 ⊕ www.abbevillescchamber.com. **Greater Aiken Chamber of Commerce** 📫 121 Richland Ave. E, Box 892, Aiken 29802 ☎ 803/641-1111 ⊕ www.aikenchamber.net. **Greater Cheraw Chamber of Commerce** ✉ 221 Market St., 29520 ☎ 843/537-8425 or 888/537-0014 ⊕ www.cheraw.com. **Greater Greenville Convention and Visitors Bureau** 📫 206 S. Main St., Box 10527, 29603 ☎ 864/421-0000 or 800/351-7180 ⊕ www.greatergreenville.com. **Greater Sumter Convention & Visitors Bureau** ✉ 822 W. Liberty St., Sumter 29150 ☎ 803/436-2640 or 800/688-4748 ⊕ www.sumter-sc.com. **Kershaw County Chamber of Commerce** 📫 607 S. Broad St., Box 605, Camden 29020 ☎ 803/432-2525 or 800/968-4037 ⊕ www.camden-sc.org. **Ninety Six Chamber of Commerce** 📫 112 N. Cambridge St., Box 8, 29666 ☎ 864/543-2900. **Spartanburg Convention and Visitors Bureau** ✉ 298 Magnolia St., 29306 ☎ 864/594-5050 or 800/374-8326 ⊕ www.visitspartanburg.com.

SAVANNAH

8

TOUR A REGENCY–STYLE MASTERPIECE,
the Owens-Thomas House ⇨ *p.307*

SEPARATE FACT FROM FICTION
on a Good & Evil walking tour ⇨ *p.309*

VISIT A PIECE OF CIVIL WAR HISTORY
outside of town at Fort Pulaski ⇨ *p.311*

DIG INTO SOME SOPHISTICATED GRITS
from elegant Elizabeth on 37th ⇨ *p.314*

COZY UP TO A BEDROOM FIREPLACE
at the Green Palm Inn B&B ⇨ *p.320*

Updated by Doug Wyatt

GENERAL JAMES OGLETHORPE, Savannah's founder, set sail for England in 1743, never to return. His last instructions, it's said, were, "Don't change a thing until I get back." That local joke holds more than a bit of truth. Savannah's elegant mansions, dripping Spanish moss, and sticky summer heat can make the city seem sleepy and stubbornly resistant to change. Which is exactly why many folks like the place.

Savannah, Georgia's oldest city, began its modern history on February 12, 1733, when Oglethorpe and 120 colonists arrived at Yamacraw Bluff on the Savannah River to found the 13th and last of the British colonies. As the port city grew, more settlers from England and Ireland arrived, joined by Scottish Highlanders, French Huguenots, Germans, Austrian Salzburgers, Sephardic and Ashkenazic Jews, Moravians, Italians, Swiss, Welsh, and Greeks.

In 1793 Eli Whitney of Connecticut, who was tutoring on a plantation near Savannah, invented a mechanized means of "ginning" seeds from cotton bolls. Cotton soon became king, and Savannah, already a busy seaport, flourished under its reign. Waterfront warehouses were filled with "white gold," and brokers trading in the Savannah Cotton Exchange set world prices. The white gold brought in hard currency; the city prospered.

General William Tecumseh Sherman's army rampaged across Georgia in 1864, setting fire to railroads, munitions factories, bridges, and just about anything else between them and the sea. Rather than see the city torched, Savannahians surrendered to the approaching Yankees.

As the cotton market declined in the early 20th century, the city's economy collapsed. For decades, Savannah's historic buildings languished; many were razed or allowed to decay. Cobwebs replaced cotton in the dilapidated riverfront warehouses. The tide turned in the 1950s, when residents began a concerted effort—which continues to this day—to restore and preserve the city's architectural heritage.

That link to the past is Savannah's main draw for travelers: the 2½-square-mi Historic District is the nation's largest. But Savannah's attraction also lies in its people, who give Southern charm their own special twist. As John Berendt's wildly popular book *Midnight in the Garden of Good and Evil* amply demonstrates, eccentricities can flourish in this hothouse environment.

EXPLORING SAVANNAH

The Historic District

Georgia's founder, General James Oglethorpe, laid out the city on a perfect grid. The Historic District is neatly hemmed in by the Savannah River, Gaston Street, East Street, and Martin Luther King Jr. Boulevard. Streets are arrow-straight, public squares of varying sizes are tucked into the grid at precise intervals, and each block is sliced in half by narrow, often unpaved streets. Bull Street, anchored on the north by City Hall and the south by Forsyth Park, charges down the center of the grid and maneuvers around the five public squares that stand in its way.

Numbers in the text correspond to numbers in the margin and on the Savannah Historic District map.

You can cover historic Savannah on foot, but to save time and energy, you might want to drive part of this tour. Start at the **Savannah Visitors Center** 1, on Martin Luther King Jr. Boulevard. In the same building, the **Savannah History Museum** 2 is an ideal introduction to the city's history. There's public parking next to the center and museum.

Exit the parking lot and turn left (north), walking or driving two short blocks and one very long one on Martin Luther King Jr. Boulevard to the **Scarborough House** 3, which contains the Ships of the Sea Museum. Cross Martin Luther King Jr. Boulevard and continue two blocks east on West Congress Street, past Franklin Square to **City Market** 4. Skirting around Franklin Square north on Montgomery Street, go two blocks to West Bay Street and turn right.

From this point continue east on West Bay Street four blocks to Bull Street. On your left you'll see **City Hall** 5. Continue east along West Bay Street (which now becomes East Bay Street) to **Factors Walk** 6, which lies south of River Street and the Savannah River. If you're driving, leave your car here to continue on foot (be sure to choose long-term parking, as the short-term meters are monitored vigilantly). Step down from Factors Walk toward the river and visit **Riverfront Plaza** 7, which is best seen on foot.

At this point, if you're driving, you'll probably want to get back in your car to continue the tour. Return to East Bay Street and head west two long blocks back to Bull Street. Walk four blocks south on Bull Street to **Wright Square** 8; then turn right (west) and go two blocks to Telfair Square, where you can stop at the **Telfair Mansion and Art Museum** 9. Stroll around Telfair Square and then continue east on West York Street back toward Wright Square, and turn right on Bull Street, heading two blocks south to the **Juliette Gordon Low Birthplace/Girl Scout National Center** 10. Two more short blocks south from the Low House on Bull Street, and you'll reach **Chippewa Square** 11. Continue south on Bull Street to the Gothic Revival **Green-Meldrim House** 12. Next, walk four blocks south on Bull Street to **Monterey Square** 13. Proceed two blocks farther south from Monterey Square to **Forsyth Park** 14, the divide between East and West Gaston streets.

From the park walk east on East Gaston Street and go one block to Abercorn Street; then turn left (north) on Abercorn Street to Calhoun Square and note the **Wesley Monumental Church** 15. Continue north on Abercorn four blocks to Lafayette Square and view the **Andrew Low House** 16. Northeast of Lafayette Square looms the **Cathedral of St. John the Baptist** 17, on East Harris Street. Two blocks north, at the intersection of Abercorn and East Oglethorpe streets, is the huge **Colonial Park Cemetery** 18. Proceeding two blocks north on Abercorn Street from the cemetery takes you to Oglethorpe Square; across from the square is the **Owens-Thomas House and Museum** 19. From the house walk east on East President Street two blocks to Columbia Square. Northwest of the square on East State Street stands the **Isaiah Davenport House** 20. From here continue north

Numbers in the text correspond to numbers in the margin and on the Savannah map.

If you have 3 days

Any trip to Savannah should include a walking tour of the Historic District. Though it's possible to take in most of the district in a day (see the Good Walk above), you might be more comfortable, particularly in the summer heat, devoting two days to your wanderings. A good way to divide your days might be to spend one in the area closest to the river, taking in such sights as the Savannah History Museum, the First African Baptist Church, Factor's Walk, and the Telfair Museum. On the second day, tour the southern part of the district, including Forsyth Park, the Andrew Low House, the Green-Meldrim House, Monterey Square, and the Cathedral of St. John the Baptist. On a third day, why not go to the beach? Tybee Island, roughly a 20-minute drive from downtown, is largely unchanged over the last few decades. You'll find a wide, pleasant public beach. Once you're back downtown, River Street, down by the Savannah River, is worth a visit for its shops and restaurants.

If you have 4 days

Follow the three-day itinerary above, then try a side trip across the Savannah River into South Carolina. Beaufort is a classy seaside town with rows of elegant historical homes. Nearby Hilton Head offers high-end shopping, a fine beach, and countless courses to tempt golfers. Outside of Beaufort, Hunting Island State Park is one of the state's most popular attractions, with a pristine beach, a historic lighthouse, and camping areas.

If you have 5 days

Follow the four-day itinerary above, then take a look at coastal Georgia, south of Savannah. In an easy day's drive, you can visit sleepy, oak-shaded towns like Midway and Darien, surrounded by historic sites like Fort McAllister, Fort Morris, and the colonial town site of Sunbury. Numerous important incidents during the Revolutionary War occurred in the region. About an hour and a half south of Savannah is Jekyll Island, where you can find a nice public beach. The island's historic district was the playground for the 19th-century's plutocratic elite, the Astors, Vanderbilts, Pulitzers, and Morgans among them.

---

up Habersham Street to **Emmet Park** 21, a splendid park to relax in at the end of your tour.

TIMING This is a long but comfortable walk, as Savannah has no taxing hills. Allow a full day to see everything along this route, especially if you plan to read all the historic markers and explore the sights thoroughly, stopping for tours. Driving around the squares can be slow—but you can drive the entire route in two hours, a pace that allows for some stopping along the way. Allow extra time if you want to linger in Riverfront Plaza for a half hour or so.

What to See

16 **Andrew Low House.** This residence was built in 1848 for Andrew Low, a native of Scotland and one of Savannah's merchant princes. The home

later belonged to his son William, who married Juliette Gordon. After her husband's death, she founded the Girl Scouts in this house on March 12, 1912. The house has 19th-century antiques, stunning silver, and some of the finest ornamental ironwork in Savannah. ✉ *329 Abercorn St., Historic District* ☎ *912/233–6854* 🎫 *$7* ⏲ *Mon.–Wed., Fri., and Sat. 10–4, Sun. noon–3:30.*

Beach Institute African-American Cultural Center. Works by African-American artists from the Savannah area and around the country are on display in this building, which once housed the first school for African-American children in Savannah, established in 1867. On permanent exhibit are more than 230 wood carvings by folk artist Ulysses Davis. ✉ *502 E. Harris St., Historic District* ☎ *912/234–8000* 🌐 *www.kingtisdell.org* 🎫 *$4* ⏲ *Tues.–Sat. noon–5.*

17 **Cathedral of St. John the Baptist.** Soaring over the city, this French Gothic–style cathedral, with pointed arches and free-flowing traceries, is the seat of the diocese of Savannah. It was founded in 1799 by the first French colonists to arrive in Savannah. Fire destroyed the early structures; the present cathedral dates from 1874. ✉ *222 E. Harris St., Historic District* ☎ *912/233–4709* ⏲ *Weekdays 9–5.*

11 **Chippewa Square.** Daniel Chester French's imposing bronze statue of General James Edward Oglethorpe, founder of Savannah and Georgia, anchors the square. Also note the **Savannah Theatre,** on Bull Street, which claims to be the oldest continuously operated theater site in North America. ✉ *Bull St. between Hull and Perry Sts., Historic District.*

5 **City Hall.** Built in 1905 on the site of the Old City Exchange (1799–1904), this imposing structure anchors Bay Street. Notice the bench commemorating Oglethorpe's landing on February 12, 1733. ✉ *1 Bay St., Historic District* ☎ *912/651–6410* ⏲ *Weekdays 8–5.*

4 **City Market.** Alas, the original 1870s City Market was razed years ago to make way for a dreary-looking parking garage. Next to the garage you'll find this popular pedestrian-only area that encompasses galleries, nightclubs, restaurants, and shops. ✉ *Between Franklin Sq. and Johnson Sq. on W. St. Julian St., Historic District.*

★ 18 **Colonial Park Cemetery.** The park is the final resting place for Savannahians who died between 1750 and 1853. You may want to stroll the shaded pathways and read some of the old tombstone inscriptions. There are several historical plaques, one of which marks the grave of Button Gwinnett, a signer of the Declaration of Independence. ✉ *Oglethorpe and Abercorn Sts., Historic District.*

Columbia Square. When Savannah was a walled city (1757–90), Bethesda Gate (one of six) was here. The square was laid out in 1799. ✉ *Habersham St. between E. State and E. York Sts., Historic District.*

21 **Emmet Park.** The lovely tree-shaded park is named for Robert Emmet, a late-18th-century Irish patriot and orator. ✉ *Borders E. Bay St., Historic District.*

Good & Evil Nothing has brought Savannah more acclaim (or notoriety) than John Berendt's *Midnight in the Garden of Good and Evil,* published in 1994. A nonfiction account of a notorious 1980s shooting, the book brings to life such Savannah sites as Monterey Square, Mercer House, and Bonaventure Cemetery. Some old-timers rue the day the book was published, but for curious outsiders it remains great fun to read the story, then gaze on the sites where the events transpired.

Restored Dignity In 1955 news that the exquisite Isaiah Davenport House (324 E. State St.) was to be destroyed prompted seven outraged ladies to raise money to buy the house. They saved it the day before the wrecking ball was to swing. Thus was born the Historic Savannah Foundation, the organization responsible for the restoration of downtown Savannah, where more than 1,000 restored buildings form the Historic District. Their beauty is what makes Savannah one of the country's top cities for walking tours. Many of the buildings are open to the public during the annual tour of homes.

St. Patrick's Day Savannah may be steeped in tradition, but that doesn't mean it's staid. Locals have their enthusiasms, including, perhaps most notably, St. Patrick's Day. Each March 17, the city holds a massive, boisterous celebration second only to New York's, with everything in town turning green—including the scrambled eggs and grits.

---

6 **Factors Walk.** A network of iron walkways connects Bay Street with the multistory buildings that rise up from the river level, and iron stairways descend from Bay Street to Factors Walk. Cobblestone ramps lead pedestrians down to River Street. (These are serious cobblestones, so wear comfortable shoes.) ✉ *Bay St. to Factors Walk, Historic District.*

14 **Forsyth Park.** The park forms the southern border of Bull Street. On its 20 acres are a glorious white fountain dating to 1858, Confederate and Spanish-American War memorials, and the Fragrant Garden for the Blind, a project of Savannah garden clubs. There are tennis courts and a tree-shaded jogging path. Outdoor plays and concerts often take place here. At the northwest corner of the park, in **Hodgson Hall**, a 19th-century Italianate–Greek Revival building, you'll find the **Georgia Historical Society,** which shows selections from its collection of artifacts and manuscripts. ✉ *501 Whitaker St., Historic District* ☎ *912/651–2128* 🌐 *www.georgiahistory.com* ⏲ *Tues.–Sat. 10–5.*

★ 12 **Green-Meldrim House.** Designed by New York architect John Norris and built in 1850 for cotton merchant Charles Green, this Gothic Revival mansion cost $90,000 to build—a princely sum back then. The house was bought in 1892 by Judge Peter Meldrim, whose heirs sold it to **St. John's Episcopal Church** to use as a parish house. General Sherman lived here after taking the city in 1864. Sitting on **Madison Square,** the house

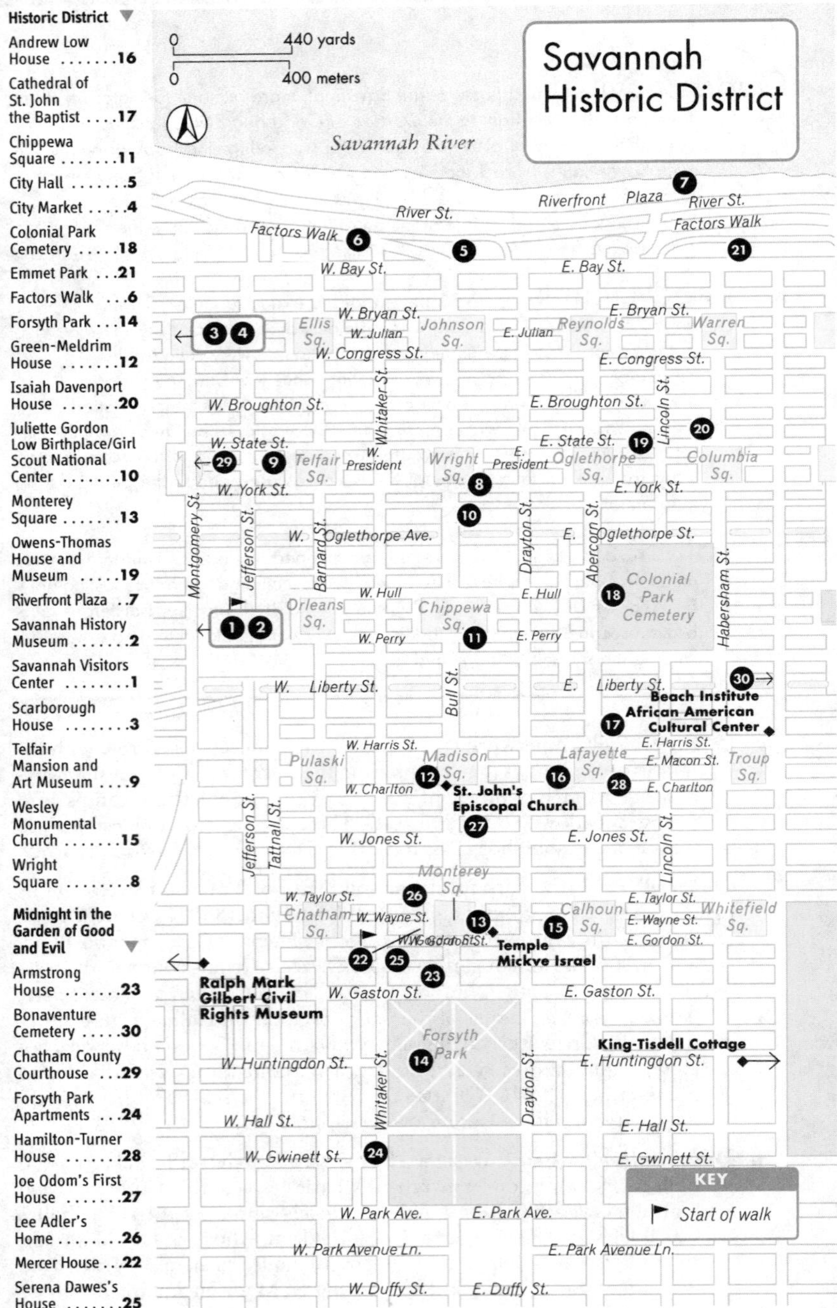
Historic District
Andrew Low House 16
Cathedral of St. John the Baptist 17
Chippewa Square 11
City Hall 5
City Market 4
Colonial Park Cemetery 18
Emmet Park ...21
Factors Walk ...6
Forsyth Park ...14
Green-Meldrim House 12
Isaiah Davenport House 20
Juliette Gordon Low Birthplace/Girl Scout National Center 10
Monterey Square 13
Owens-Thomas House and Museum 19
Riverfront Plaza ..7
Savannah History Museum 2
Savannah Visitors Center 1
Scarborough House 3
Telfair Mansion and Art Museum 9
Wesley Monumental Church 15
Wright Square 8
Midnight in the Garden of Good and Evil
Armstrong House 23
Bonaventure Cemetery 30
Chatham County Courthouse ...29
Forsyth Park Apartments ...24
Hamilton-Turner House 28
Joe Odom's First House 27
Lee Adler's Home 26
Mercer House ...22
Serena Dawes's House 25
Savannah Historic District
0 440 yards
0 400 meters
Savannah River
Riverfront Plaza
River St.
Factors Walk
E. Bay St.
W. Bay St.
W. Bryan St.
E. Bryan St.
Ellis Sq.
Johnson Sq.
Reynolds Sq.
Warren Sq.
W. Julian
E. Julian
W. Congress St.
E. Congress St.
W. Broughton St.
E. Broughton St.
W. State St.
E. State St.
Telfair Sq.
Wright Sq.
Oglethorpe Sq.
Columbia Sq.
W. President
E. President
W. York St.
E. York St.
W. Oglethorpe Ave.
E. Oglethorpe St.
Colonial Park Cemetery
W. Hull
E. Hull
Orleans Sq.
Chippewa Sq.
W. Perry
E. Perry
W. Liberty St.
E. Liberty St.
Beach Institute African American Cultural Center
W. Harris St.
E. Harris St.
Pulaski Sq.
Madison Sq.
Lafayette Sq.
Troup Sq.
E. Macon St.
W. Charlton
E. Charlton
St. John's Episcopal Church
W. Jones St.
E. Jones St.
Monterey Sq.
W. Taylor St.
E. Taylor St.
Chatham Sq.
W. Wayne St.
E. Wayne St.
Calhoun Sq.
Whitefield Sq.
E. Gordon St.
Temple Mickve Israel
Ralph Mark Gilbert Civil Rights Museum
W. Gaston St.
E. Gaston St.
Forsyth Park
King-Tisdell Cottage
W. Huntingdon St.
E. Huntingdon St.
W. Hall St.
E. Hall St.
W. Gwinett St.
E. Gwinett St.
W. Park Ave.
E. Park Ave.
W. Park Avenue Ln.
E. Park Avenue Ln.
W. Duffy St.
E. Duffy St.
Montgomery St.
Jefferson St.
Barnard St.
Whitaker St.
Bull St.
Drayton St.
Abercorn St.
Lincoln St.
Habersham St.
Tattnall St.
KEY
Start of walk

has such Gothic features as a crenellated roof, oriels, and an external gallery with filigree ironwork. Inside are mantels of Carrara marble, carved black-walnut woodwork, and doorknobs and hinges of either silver plate or porcelain. ⊠ *1 W. Macon St., Historic District* ☎ *912/233–3845* 🎫 *$5* ⏲ *Tues., Thurs., and Fri. 10–4, Sat. 10–1. Closed last 2 wks of Jan. and 2 wks before Easter.*

★ 20 **Isaiah Davenport House.** The proposed demolition of this historic Savannah structure galvanized the city's residents into action to save their treasured buildings. Semicircular stairs with wrought-iron trim lead to the recessed doorway of the redbrick federal mansion that master builder Isaiah Davenport built for himself between 1815 and 1820. Three dormered windows poke through the sloping roof of the stately house, and the interior has polished hardwood floors, fine woodwork and plasterwork, and a soaring elliptical staircase. Furnishings, from the 1820s, are Hepplewhite, Chippendale, and Sheraton. ⊠ *324 E. State St., Historic District* ☎ *912/236–8097* ⊕ *www.davenportsavga.com* 🎫 *$7* ⏲ *Mon.–Sat. 10–4, Sun. 1–4.*

Johnson Square. The oldest of James Oglethorpe's original 24 squares was laid out in 1733 and named for South Carolina governor Robert Johnson. A monument marks the grave of Nathanael Greene, a hero of the Revolutionary War. The square was once a popular gathering place: Savannahians came here to welcome President Monroe in 1819, to greet the Marquis de Lafayette in 1825, and to cheer for Georgia's secession in 1861. ⊠ *Bull St. between Bryan and Congress Sts., Historic District.*

10 **Juliette Gordon Low Birthplace/Girl Scout National Center.** This majestic Regency town house, attributed to William Jay (built 1818–21), was designated in 1965 as Savannah's first National Historic Landmark. "Daisy" Low, founder of the Girl Scouts, was born here in 1860, and the house is now owned and operated by the Girl Scouts of America. Mrs. Low's paintings and other artwork are on display in the house, restored to the style of 1886, the year of Mrs. Low's marriage. ⊠ *142 Bull St., Historic District* ☎ *912/233–4501* ⊕ *www.girlscouts.org/birthplace* 🎫 *$7* ⏲ *Mon., Tues., and Thurs.–Sat. 10–4, Sun. 12:30–4:30.*

Lafayette Square. Named for the Marquis de Lafayette, the square contains a graceful three-tier fountain donated by the Georgia chapter of the Colonial Dames of America. ⊠ *Abercorn St. between E. Harris and E. Charlton Sts., Historic District.*

Madison Square. A statue on the square, laid out in 1839 and named for President James Madison, depicts Sergeant William Jasper hoisting a flag and is a tribute to his bravery during the Siege of Savannah. Though mortally wounded, Jasper rescued the colors of his regiment in the assault on the British lines. ⊠ *Bull St. between W. Harris and W. Charlton Sts., Historic District.*

13 **Monterey Square.** Commemorating the victory of General Zachary Taylor's forces in Monterrey, Mexico, in 1846, this is the fifth and southernmost of Bull Street's squares. A monument honors General Casimir Pulaski, the Polish nobleman who lost his life in the Siege of Savannah

CloseUp

FAMOUS FACES IN SAVANNAH

NOTORIETY IN SAVANNAH DIDN'T BEGIN *with* Midnight in the Garden of Good and Evil. *Long before the days of the Lady Chablis, interesting people were doing interesting things in this city. Here's a sampling of the figures who have etched themselves into Savannah's collective memory—one local who went on to do great things, and three out-of-towners who made an impression.*

Actor Robert Mitchum (1917–97) gave one of his finest performances as a psychotic ex-convict out to exact revenge on the lawyer who put him away (Gregory Peck) in 1961's Cape Fear, *which was filmed in and around Savannah (and later remade by Martin Scorcese, with Robert DeNiro in the Mitchum role). The shooting wasn't Mitchum's first visit to the city. In 1934, as a wayward 17-year-old, he roamed across America; while panhandling in Savannah, he was arrested on the charges of vagrancy and begging. He ended up doing labor on a chain gang; six days after he was jailed, he escaped. When he returned 27 years later as an established star, his earlier visit—and transgressions—were never mentioned by the adoring local press.*

The fiction writer Flannery O'Connor (1925–64) spent the first 13 years of her life in Savannah. A devout Catholic from her earliest years, she was a regular presence at services held in the Cathedral of St. John the Baptist. For the rest of her life O'Connor would make a farm near the central Georgia town of Milledgeville her home. From that unlikely spot she raised peacocks and developed into one of the most distinct voices in American literature. Her novels Wise Blood *and* The Violent Bear It Away *amply convey her unique take on the Southern Gothic style, but her greatest achievement is found in her short stories, published in the collections* A Good Man is Hard to Find *and* Everything That Rises Must Converge. *She died of lupus at the age of 39.*

James L. Pierpont wrote the Christmas classic "Jingle Bells" in Savannah—at least that's what locals will tell you. A native of Medford, Massachusetts, Pierpont (1822–93) became music director of Savannah's Unitarian church in the 1850s. In 1857, he obtained a copyright for "The One Horse Open Sleigh"—what commonly came to be known as "Jingle Bells." In the 1980s, tempers boiled when Medford claimed that Pierpont had written the song in their city, not in Savannah. The dispute has never been resolved: today, both cities have erected historical markers that claim the song as their own.

John Wesley (1703–91), known today as the founder of Methodism, had some rough times in Savannah. Long interested in the British colonies, he arrived in the city in 1735, and once there it wasn't long before he met the 18-year-old Sophia Hopkey. A romance developed. But Wesley, already in his thirties, wasn't prepared to commit to marriage. Sophia soon found another suitor, William Williamson. The apparently jealous Wesley eventually charged her with neglect of public church services and refused to allow her to participate in communion. Sophia's uncle, Thomas Causton, Savannah's chief magistrate, charged Wesley with defamation, claiming the defendant was unfit to be a minister. Wesley, found guilty on some of the counts, fled to England. By the time he died, at 88, he had become one of the towering figures in religious history.

during the Revolutionary War. Also on the square is Temple Mickve Israel. ✉ *Bull St. between Taylor and Gordon Sts., Historic District.*

19 **Owens-Thomas House and Museum.** English architect William Jay's first
Fodor's Choice ★ Regency mansion in Savannah is widely considered the country's finest example of that architectural style. Built in 1816–19, the English house was constructed mostly with local materials. Of particular note are the curving walls of the house, Greek-inspired ornamental molding, half-moon arches, stained-glass panels, and Duncan Phyfe furniture. The carriage house includes rare urban slave quarters and a gift shop. ✉ *124 Abercorn St., Historic District* ☎ *912/233–9743* 🌐 *www.telfair.org* 🎫 *$8* ⏲ *Mon. noon–5, Tues.–Sat. 10–5, Sun. 1–5.*

8

off the beaten path

RALPH MARK GILBERT CIVIL RIGHTS MUSEUM – In Savannah's Historic District, this history museum has a series of 15 exhibits on segregation, from emancipation through the civil rights movement. The role of black and white Savannahians in ending segregation in their city is detailed in these exhibits, largely derived from archival photographs. The museum also has touring exhibits. ✉ *460 Martin Luther King Jr. Blvd., Historic District* ☎ *912/231–8900* 📠 *912/234–2577* 🎫 *$4* ⏲ *Mon.–Sat. 9–5.*

Reynolds Square. John Wesley, who preached in Savannah and wrote the first English hymnal in the city in 1736, is remembered here. A monument to the founder of the Methodist Church is shaded by greenery and surrounded by park benches. The **Olde Pink House** (✉ 23 Abercorn St.), built in 1771, is one of the oldest buildings in town. Now a restaurant, the porticoed pink-stucco Georgian mansion has been a private home, a bank, and headquarters for a Yankee general during the Civil War. ✉ *Abercorn St. between E. Bryant and E. Congress Sts., Historic District.*

7 **Riverfront Plaza.** Here you can watch a parade of freighters and pug-nose tugs; youngsters can play in the tugboat-shape sandboxes. River Street is the main venue for many of the city's celebrations, including the First Saturday festivals, when flea marketers, artists, and artisans display their wares and musicians entertain the crowds. ✉ *River St. between Abercorn and Barnard St., Historic District.*

2 **Savannah History Museum.** This museum in a restored railway station is an excellent introduction to the city. Exhibits range from old locomotives to a tribute to Savannah-born songwriter Johnny Mercer. Built on the **site of the Siege of Savannah,** it marks the spot where in 1779 the colonial forces, led by Polish count Casimir Pulaski, laid siege to Savannah in an attempt to retake the city from the redcoats. They were beaten back, and Pulaski was killed while leading a cavalry charge against the British. The dead lie underneath the building. ✉ *303 Martin Luther King Jr. Blvd., Historic District* ☎ *912/238–1779* 🌐 *www.chsgeorgia.org/shm/home.htm* 🎫 *$4* ⏲ *Daily 9–5.*

1 **Savannah Visitors Center.** Come here for free maps and brochures, friendly advice, and an audiovisual overview of the city. The starting point for

a number of guided tours, the center is in a big 1860 redbrick building with high ceilings and sweeping arches. It was the old Central of Georgia railway station. The parking lot is a good spot to leave your car while you explore the Historic District. ✉ *301 Martin Luther King Jr. Blvd., Historic District* ☎ *912/944–0455* 🌐 *www.savannahvisit.com* ⏲ *Weekdays 8:30–5, weekends 9–5.*

★ ❸ **Scarborough House.** This exuberant Greek Revival mansion, built during the 1819 cotton boom for Savannah merchant prince William Scarborough, was designed by English architect William Jay. Scarborough was a major investor in the steamship *Savannah*. The house has a Doric portico capped by one of Jay's characteristic half-moon windows. Four massive Doric columns form a peristyle in the atrium entrance hall. Inside is the **Ships of the Sea Museum,** with displays of ship models, including steamships, and a nuclear-power ship. ✉ *41 Martin Luther King Jr. Blvd., Historic District* ☎ *912/232–1511* 🌐 *www.shipsofthesea.org* 🎫 *$7* ⏲ *Tues.–Sun. 10–5.*

❾ **Telfair Mansion and Art Museum.** The oldest public art museum in the Southeast was designed by William Jay in 1819 for Alexander Telfair and sits across the street from **Telfair Square.** Within its marble rooms are American, French, and Dutch impressionist paintings; German tonalist paintings; a large collection of works by Kahlil Gibran; plaster casts of the Elgin Marbles, the Venus de Milo, and the Laocoön, among other classical sculptures; and some of the Telfair family furnishings, including a Duncan Phyfe sideboard and Savannah-made silver. ✉ *121 Barnard St., Historic District* ☎ *912/232–1177* 🌐 *www.telfair.org* 🎫 *$8* ⏲ *Mon. noon–5, Tues.–Sat. 10–5, Sun. 1–5.*

Temple Mickve Israel. A Gothic Revival synagogue on Monterey Square houses the third-oldest Jewish congregation in the United States; its founding members settled in town five months after the establishment of Savannah in 1733. The synagogue's collection includes documents and letters (some from George Washington, James Madison, and Thomas Jefferson) pertaining to early Jewish life in Savannah and Georgia. ✉ *20 E. Gordon St., Historic District* ☎ *912/233–1547* 🌐 *www.mickveisrael.org* ⏲ *Weekdays 10–noon and 2–4.*

⓯ **Wesley Monumental Church.** This Gothic Revival–style church memorializing the founders of Methodism is patterned after Queen's Kerk in Amsterdam. It dates from 1868 and is particularly noted for its magnificent stained-glass windows. ✉ *429 Abercorn St., Historic District* ☎ *912/232–0191* ⏲ *By appointment only.*

❽ **Wright Square.** Named for James Wright, Georgia's last colonial governor, this square has an elaborate monument in its center that honors William Washington Gordon, founder of the Central of Georgia Railroad. A slab of granite from Stone Mountain adorns the grave of Tomo-Chi-Chi, the Yamacraw chief who befriended General Oglethorpe and the colonists. ✉ *Bull St. between W. State and W. York Sts., Historic District.*

Midnight in the Garden of Good & Evil

Town gossips can give you the best introduction to a city, and as author John Berendt discovered, Savannah's not short on them. In his 1994 best-seller, *Midnight in the Garden of Good and Evil,* Berendt shares the juiciest of tales imparted to him during the eight years he spent here wining and dining with Savannah's high society and dancing with her Grand Empress, drag queen the Lady Chablis, among others. By the time he left, there had been a scandalous homicide and several trials: the wealthy Jim Williams was accused of killing his assistant and sometime lover, Danny Hansford.

Before you set out, find a copy of the book, pour yourself a cool drink, and enter an eccentric world of cutthroat killers and society backstabbers, voodoo witches, and garden-club ladies. Then head over to the Historic District to follow the characters' steps. By the end of this walking tour, you'll be hard-pressed to find the line between Berendt's creative nonfiction and Savannah's reality. Note: unless otherwise indicated, the sights on this tour are not open to the public.

a good walk

Begin at the southwest corner of Monterey Square, site of the **Mercer House** 22, whose construction was begun by songwriter Johnny Mercer's great-grandfather just before the Civil War. Two blocks south on Bull Street is the **Armstrong House** 23, an earlier residence of Jim Williams, the main character in the book. Walk south through Forsyth Park to the corner of Park Avenue and Whitaker Street. The **Forsyth Park Apartments** 24, where author John Berendt lived, are on the southwest corner of Forsyth Park. Then turn back north through the park. At the midpoint of the park's northern edge, turn north up Bull Street in the direction of Monterey Square. Turn left on West Gordon Street off Bull Street and walk toward the corner of West Gordon Street and Whitaker Street, where you can reach **Serena Dawes's House** 25. Next, cross West Gordon Street, walk north on Bull Street in front of Mercer House, cross Wayne Street, and you find that the first house on the left facing Bull Street at Wayne Street is **Lee Adler's Home** 26, which sits across from Monterey Square's northwest corner. Continue walking north on Bull Street and take a right (east) on East Jones Street. **Joe Odom's first house** 27 is the third house on the left before Drayton Street.

Continue on East Jones Street to Abercorn Street and turn left (north), walking two blocks on Abercorn Street to East Charlton Street and the **Hamilton-Turner House** 28, now a B&B inn. Then swing around Lafayette Square to East Harris Street, and take it about six blocks west to Pulaski Square at Barnard Street; turn right (north) on Barnard Street through Orleans Square and continue north to Telfair Square. On foot, you may elect to head west down West York Street to find the **Chatham County Courthouse** 29, scene of all those trials, two blocks away. Finally, take either Whitaker Street or Abercorn Street south to Victory Drive and turn left. Go through Thunderbolt to Whatley Avenue, and turn left again. Whatley Avenue leads directly to Bonaventure Road, which curves in both directions; bear left, and on your right about a quarter mile up the road is **Bonaventure Cemetery** 30.

TIMING Allow a leisurely two hours to walk the main points of the tour, plus another hour to visit the cemetery.

What to See

23 **Armstrong House.** Antiques dealer Jim Williams lived and worked in this residence before purchasing the Mercer House. On a late-afternoon walk past the mansion, Berendt met Mr. Simon Glover, an 86-year-old singer and porter for the law firm of Bouhan, Williams, and Levy, occupants of the building. Glover confided that he earned a weekly $10 for walking the deceased dogs of a former partner of the firm up and down Bull Street. Baffled? So was the author. Behind the house's cast-iron gates are the offices of Frank Siler, Jim Williams's attorney, who doubles as keeper of Uga, the Georgia Bulldog mascot. ⊠ *447 Bull St., Historic District.*

30 **Bonaventure Cemetery.** A cemetery east of downtown is the final resting place for Danny Hansford. The haunting female tombstone figure from the book's cover has been removed to protect surrounding graves from sightseers. The figure is now on display at the Telfair Mansion. ⊠ *330 Bonaventure Rd., Eastside* ☎ *912/651–6843.*

29 **Chatham County Courthouse.** The courthouse was the scene of three of Williams's murder trials, which took place over the course of about eight years. An underground tunnel leads from the courthouse to the jail where Williams was held in a cell that was modified to allow him to conduct his antiques business. ⊠ *133 Montgomery St., Historic District.*

24 **Forsyth Park Apartments.** Here was Berendt's second home in Savannah; from his fourth-floor rooms he pieced together the majority of the book. While parking his newly acquired 1973 Pontiac Grand Prix outside these apartments, Berendt met the Lady Chablis coming out of her nearby doctor's office, freshly feminine from a new round of hormone shots. ⊠ *Whitaker and Gwinnett Sts., Historic District.*

28 **Hamilton-Turner House.** After one too many of Joe Odom's deals went sour, Mandy Nichols, his fourth fiancée-in-waiting, left him and took over his third residence, a Second Empire–style mansion dating from 1873. Mandy filled it with 17th- and 18th-century antiques and transformed it into a successful museum through which she led tour groups. The elegant towering hulk is at the southeast corner of Lafayette Square. The house was sold in the late 1990s and has since become the elegant Hamilton-Turner Inn. ⊠ *330 Abercorn St., Historic District.*

27 **Joe Odom's first house.** At this stucco town house, Odom, a combination tax lawyer, real-estate broker, and piano player, hosted a 24-hour stream of visitors. The author met Odom through Mandy Nichols, a former Miss Big Beautiful Woman, who stopped by to borrow ice one time after the power had been cut off, a frequent occurrence. ⊠ *16 E. Jones St., Historic District.*

26 **Lee Adler's Home.** Just north of the Mercer House, in half of the double town house facing West Wayne Street, Lee Adler, the adversary of Jim Williams, runs his business of restoring historic Savannah properties. Adler's howling dogs drove Williams to his pipe organ, where he churned

out a deafening version of César Franck's *Pièce Heroïque*. Later, Adler stuck reelection signs in his front lawn, showing his support for the district attorney who prosecuted Williams three times before he was finally found not guilty. ✉ *425 Bull St., Historic District.*

22 **Mercer House.** This redbrick Italianate mansion on the southwest corner of Monterey Square became Jim Williams's Taj Mahal; here he ran a world-class antiques dealership and held *the* Christmas party of the season; here also Danny Hansford, his sometime house partner, succumbed to gunshot wounds. Williams himself died here of a heart attack in 1990, near the very spot where Hansford fell. Today his sister lives quietly among the remnants of his Fabergé collection and his Joshua Reynolds paintings, in rooms lighted by Waterford crystal chandeliers. ✉ *429 Bull St., Historic District.*

25 **Serena Dawes's House.** Near the intersection of West Gordon and Bull streets, this house was owned by Helen Driscoll, also known as Serena Dawes. A high-profile beauty in the 1930s and '40s, she married into a Pennsylvania steel family. After her husband accidentally and fatally shot himself in the head, she retired here, in her hometown. Dawes, Berendt writes, "spent most of her day in bed, holding court, drinking martinis and pink ladies, playing with her white toy poodle, Lulu." Chief among Serena's gentlemen callers was Luther Driggers, rumored to possess a poison strong enough to wipe out the entire city. ✉ *17 W. Gordon St., Historic District.*

Other Area Attractions

Ebenezer. When the Salzburgers arrived in Savannah in 1734, Oglethorpe sent them up the Savannah River to establish a settlement. The first effort was assailed by disease, and they sought his permission to move to better ground. Denied, they moved anyway and established Ebenezer. Here, they engaged in silkworm production and, in 1769, built the Jerusalem Church, which still stands. After the revolution, the silkworm operation never resumed, and the town faded into history. Descendants of these Protestant religious refugees have preserved the church and assembled a few of the remaining buildings, moving them to this site from other locations. Be sure to follow Route 275 to its end and see Ebenezer Landing, where the Salzburgers came ashore. ✉ *Ebenezer Rd., Rte. 21–Rte. 275, Rincon, 25 mi north of Savannah.*

Old Fort Jackson. About 2 mi east of Broad Street via President Street, you'll see a sign for the fort, which is 3 mi from the city. Purchased in 1808 by the federal government, this is the oldest standing fort in Georgia. It was garrisoned in 1812 and was the Confederate headquarters of the river batteries. The brick edifice is surrounded by a tidal moat, and there are 13 exhibit areas. Battle reenactments, blacksmithing demonstrations, and programs of 19th-century music are among the fort's activities for tour groups. ✉ *1 Ft. Jackson Rd., Fort Jackson* ☎ *912/232–3945* 🌐 *www.chsgeorgia.org/jackson/home.htm* 🎟 *$4* ⏲ *Daily 9–5.*

★ **Fort Pulaski National Monument.** Named for Casimir Pulaski, a Polish count and Revolutionary War hero, this must-see sight for Civil War buffs was built on Cockspur Island between 1829 and 1847. Robert E. Lee's first assignment after graduating from West Point was as an engineer here. During the Civil War the fort fell, on April 11, 1862, after a mere 30 hours of bombardment by newfangled rifled cannons. The restored fortification, operated by the National Park Service, has moats, drawbridges, massive ramparts, and towering walls. The park has trails and picnic areas. It's 14 mi east of downtown Savannah; you'll see the entrance on your left just before U.S. 80 reaches Tybee Island. ✉ *U.S. 80, Fort Pulaski* ☎ *912/786–5787* 🌐 *www.nps.gov/fopu* 🎫 *$3* ⏲ *Daily 9–7.*

Melon Bluff. On a centuries-old 3,000-acre plantation that has been in one family since 1735, Melon Bluff includes a nature center and facilities for canoeing, kayaking, bird-watching, hiking, and other outdoor activities. You can camp here or stay at one of the three B&B inns ($$–$$$): Palmyra Plantation, an 1850s cottage; the Ripley Farmhouse, a classic rural house with a tin-covered roof; and an old barn, renovated to contain nine guest rooms. From Melon Bluff you can visit nearby **Seabrook Village,** a small but growing cluster of rural buildings from an African-American historic community; **Old Sunbury,** whose port made it a viable competitor to Savannah until the Revolutionary War ended its heyday; **Fort Morris,** which protected Savannah during the revolution; and **Midway,** an 18th-century village with a house museum and period cemetery. To reach Melon Bluff, take I–95 south from Savannah (about 30 mi) to Exit 76 (Midway/Sunbury), turn left, and go east for 3 mi. The other sites mentioned here are all within a short drive. ✉ *2999 Islands Hwy., Midway* ☎ *912/884–5779 or 888/246–8188* 📠 *912/884–3046* 🌐 *www.melonbluff.com.*

Mighty Eighth Air Force Heritage Museum. The famous World War II squadron the Mighty Eighth Air Force was formed in Savannah in January 1942 and shipped out to the United Kingdom. Flying Royal Air Force aircraft, the Mighty Eighth became the largest air force of the period. Exhibits at this museum begin with the prelude to World War II and the rise of Adolf Hitler and continue through Desert Storm. You can see vintage aircraft, fly a simulated bombing mission with a B-17 crew, test your skills as a waist gunner, and view interviews with courageous World War II vets. The museum also has three theaters, an art gallery, a 1940s-era English pub, a 7,000-volume library, archives, memorial garden, chapel, and museum store. ✉ *175 Bourne Ave., I–95, Exit 102, to U.S. 80, Pooler,14 mi west of Savannah* ☎ *912/748–8888* 🌐 *www.mightyeighth.org* 🎫 *$8* ⏲ *Daily 9–5.*

Skidaway Marine Science Complex. On the grounds of the former Modena Plantation, Skidaway has a 14-panel, 12,000-gallon aquarium with marine and plant life of the continental shelf. Other exhibits highlight coastal archaeology and fossils of the Georgia coast. Nature trails overlook marsh and water. ✉ *30 Ocean Science Circle, Skidaway Island, 8 mi south of Savannah* ☎ *912/598–2496* 🎫 *$2* ⏲ *Weekdays 9–4, Sat. noon–5.*

Tybee Island. *Tybee* is an Indian word meaning "salt." The Yamacraw Indians came to this island in the Atlantic Ocean to hunt and fish, and legend has it that pirates buried their treasure here. The island is about

SAVANNAH'S NO-HILLS WORKOUT

SAVANNAH IS TABLE FLAT—*bad news indeed for any mountaineers who find themselves in coastal Georgia, but a relief for many bicyclists. One favorite spot for local bikers is the Savannah Wildlife Refuge, where alligators (not that you should poke at them with a stick, but they're really about as dangerous as furniture) bask alongside the trail. Another possibility is Rails-to-Trails, a 3-mi route that starts a mile east of the Bull River Bridge on Highway 80 and ends at the entrance to Fort Pulaski. Tom Triplett Park, east of town on U.S. 80, offers three bike loops—3.5 mi, 5 mi, and 6.3 mi. Though much of downtown is fairly unfriendly to bikers, several of the suburbs—Windsor Forest, Ardsley Park, the Isle of Hope—are fine for riding relatively free of traffic hassles.*

That same flat terrain makes Savannah popular with runners (though the city's sizzling summer temperatures make light-color clothing and liquids, plenty of them, life-saving necessities). Many local runners enjoy the wide, shady sidewalks of Forsyth Park; others venture to Daffin Park (on Victory Drive, between Bee Road and Waters Ave). Lake Mayer, on the city's Southside, offers a nice 1.41-mi loop. Tybee Island has a white-sand beach that is hard packed and relatively debris-free, making it a favorite with runners. The area's most challenging run is by far its steepest—the bridge crossing over into South Carolina. The bridge run, particularly for runners accustomed to the region's horizontal landscape, can mean a particularly painful 5 mi.

5 mi long and 2 mi wide, with seafood restaurants, chain motels, condos, and shops—most of which sprang up during the 1950s and haven't changed much since. The entire expanse of white sand is divided into a number of public beaches, where you can shell and crab, charter fishing boats, and swim. It's 18 mi east of Savannah; take Victory Drive (U.S. 80), sometimes called Tybee Road, onto the island. On your way here stop by Fort Jackson and Fort Pulaski National Monument. Nearby, the misnamed Little Tybee Island, actually larger than Tybee Island, is entirely undeveloped. Contact **Tybee Island Convention and Visitors Bureau** (📭 Box 491, Tybee Island 31328 ☎ 800/868–2322 🌐 www.tybeevisit.com).

SPORTS & THE OUTDOORS

Boating

At the **Bull River Yacht Club Marina** (✉ 8005 Old Tybee Rd., Tybee Island ☎ 912/897–7300), you can arrange a dolphin tour, a deep-sea fishing expedition, or a jaunt through the coastal islands. **Lake Mayer Park** (✉ Montgomery Crossroads Rd. and Sallie Mood Dr., Cresthill ☎ 912/652–6780) has paddleboats, sailing, and canoeing, as well as an in-line skating and hockey facility. **Saltwater Charters** (✉ 111 Wickersham Dr., Skidaway Island ☎ 912/598–1814) provides packages ranging from two-hour sightseeing tours to 13-hour deep-sea fishing expeditions. Water taxis to the coastal islands are also available. Public boat ramps are found at **Bell's on the River** (✉ 12500 Apache Ave., off Abercorn St., Windward ☎ 912/920–1113), on the Forest River. **Savannah Islands Expressway** (✉ Adjacent to Frank W. Spencer Park, Skidaway Island ☎ 912/231–8222) offers boat ramps on the Wilmington River. **Savannah Marina** (✉ Thunderbolt) provides ramps on the Wilmington River.

Golf

Bacon Park (✉ 1 Shorty Cooper Dr., Southside ☎ 912/354–2625) is a public facility with 27 holes of golf and a lighted driving range. **Henderson Golf Club** (✉ 1 Al Henderson Dr., at I–95, Exit 94 to Rte. 204, Southside ☎ 912/920–4653) is an 18-hole, par-71 course about 15 mi from downtown Savannah. The **Mary Calder Golf Course** (✉ W. Lathrop Ave., West Chatham ☎ 912/238–7100) is par 35 for its 9 holes.

Tennis

Bacon Park (✉ 6262 Skidaway Rd., Southside ☎ 912/351–3850) has 16 lighted asphalt courts. Fees are $3 per person, and you can reserve courts in advance. **Forsyth Park** (✉ Drayton St. and Park Ave., Historic District ☎ 912/652–6780) contains four lighted courts available until about 10 PM; there's no charge to use them. **Lake Mayer Park** (✉ Montgomery Crossroads Rd. and Sallie Mood Dr., Southside ☎ 912/652–6780) has eight asphalt lighted courts available at no charge and open 8 AM–10 PM; until 11 PM May–September.

WHERE TO EAT

Savannah has excellent seafood restaurants, though locals also have a passion for spicy barbecued meats. The Historic District yields culinary treasures, especially along River Street. Several of the city's restaurants—such as Elizabeth on 37th, 45 South, the Olde Pink House, and Sapphire Grill—have been beacons that have drawn members of the culinary upper crust to the region for decades. From there they explored and discovered that such divine dining isn't isolated to Savannah's Historic District, as nearby Thunderbolt, Skidaway, Tybee, and Wilmington islands also have a collection of remarkable restaurants.

WHAT IT COSTS

$$$$	$$$	$$	$	¢
over $22	$16–$22	$11–$16	$7–$11	under $7

Restaurant prices are for a main course at dinner, excluding sales tax of 6%.

$$$$ Fodor'sChoice ★ ✕ **Elizabeth on 37th.** Regional specialties are the hallmark at this acclaimed restaurant that goes so far as to credit local produce suppliers on its menu. Chef Elizabeth Terry manages to make dishes such as Maryland crab cakes and a plate of roasted shiitake and oyster mushrooms sit comfortably beside Southern-fried grits and country ham. The extravagant

Savannah cream cake is the way to finish your meal in this elegant turn-of-the-20th-century mansion with hardwood floors and spacious rooms. ✉ *105 E. 37th St., Victorian District* ☎ *912/236–5547* *Reservations essential* *AE, D, DC, MC, V* *No lunch.*

$$$$ **Sapphire Grill.** Savannah's young and restless pack this trendy haunt nightly. Chef Chris Nason focuses his seasonal menus on local ingredients, such as Georgia white shrimp, crab, and fish. Vegetarians will delight in his elegant vegetable presentations—perhaps including roasted sweet onions, spicy peppers, wild mushrooms, or roasted shallots. Chocoholics, try the delicious, potent chocolate flan. ✉ *110 W. Congress St., Historic District* ☎ *912/443–9962* *Reservations essential* *AE, D, DC, MC, V* *No lunch.*

$$$–$$$$ **Belford's Steak and Seafood.** In the heart of City Market, Belford's is great for brunch on Sunday, when so many of the downtown venues are closed. A complimentary glass of sparkling wine arrives at your table when you place your order. Brunch entrées include egg dishes, such as smoked salmon Florentine and crab frittatas. The lunch and dinner menus focus on seafood, including Georgia pecan grouper and Lowcountry shrimp and grits. ✉ *315 W. St. Julian St., Historic District* ☎ *912/233–2626* *AE, D, DC, MC, V.*

★ **$$$–$$$$** **Bistro Savannah.** High ceilings, burnished heart-pine floors, and gray-brick walls lined with local art contribute to the bistro qualities of this spot by City Market. The menu has such specialties as seared beef tenderloin with shiitakes, scallions, corn pancakes and horseradish sauce, and shrimp and *tasso* (seasoned cured pork) on stone-ground grits. Another treat is the crispy roasted duck. ✉ *309 W. Congress St., Historic District* ☎ *912/233–6266* *AE, MC, V* *No lunch.*

★ **$$$–$$$$** **45 South.** This popular eatery is small and stylish, with a contemporary mauve-and-green interior. The game-heavy menu often includes a confit of tender rabbit with morels and mashed potatoes. ✉ *20 E. Broad St., Victorian District* ☎ *912/233–1881* *Reservations essential* *AE, D, DC, MC, V* *Closed Sun. No lunch.*

$$$–$$$$ **Georges' of Tybee.** Tybee's first upscale restaurant has a romantic setting, with a warmly lit interior, a lovely stone fireplace, and dark rose-painted walls. Duck liver and frisée salad, and Thai-barbecued Muscovy duck breast are popular choices on the menu. Lobster, crab, and four-cheese ravioli with carrots, snow peas, and arugula, in a saffron-cream sauce, is also outstanding. ✉ *1105 E. U.S. 80, Tybee Island* ☎ *912/786–9730* *AE, MC, V* *Closed Mon. No lunch.*

$$$–$$$$ **Il Pasticcio.** Sicilian Pino Venetico turned this former department store into his dream restaurant—a bistro-style place gleaming with steel, glass, and tile. The menu changes frequently, but fresh pasta dishes are a constant, and excellent desserts include a superior tiramisu. The scene is lively and hip—which on a good night can add to the fun, but on a bad one can mean service with an attitude. While you're there, check out the second-floor art gallery. ✉ *2 E. Broughton St., Historic District* ☎ *912/231–8888* *AE, D, DC, MC, V* *No lunch.*

$$$–$$$$ **Olde Pink House.** This brick Georgian mansion was built in 1771 for James Habersham, one of the wealthiest Americans of his time, and the old-time atmosphere comes through in the original Georgia pine floors

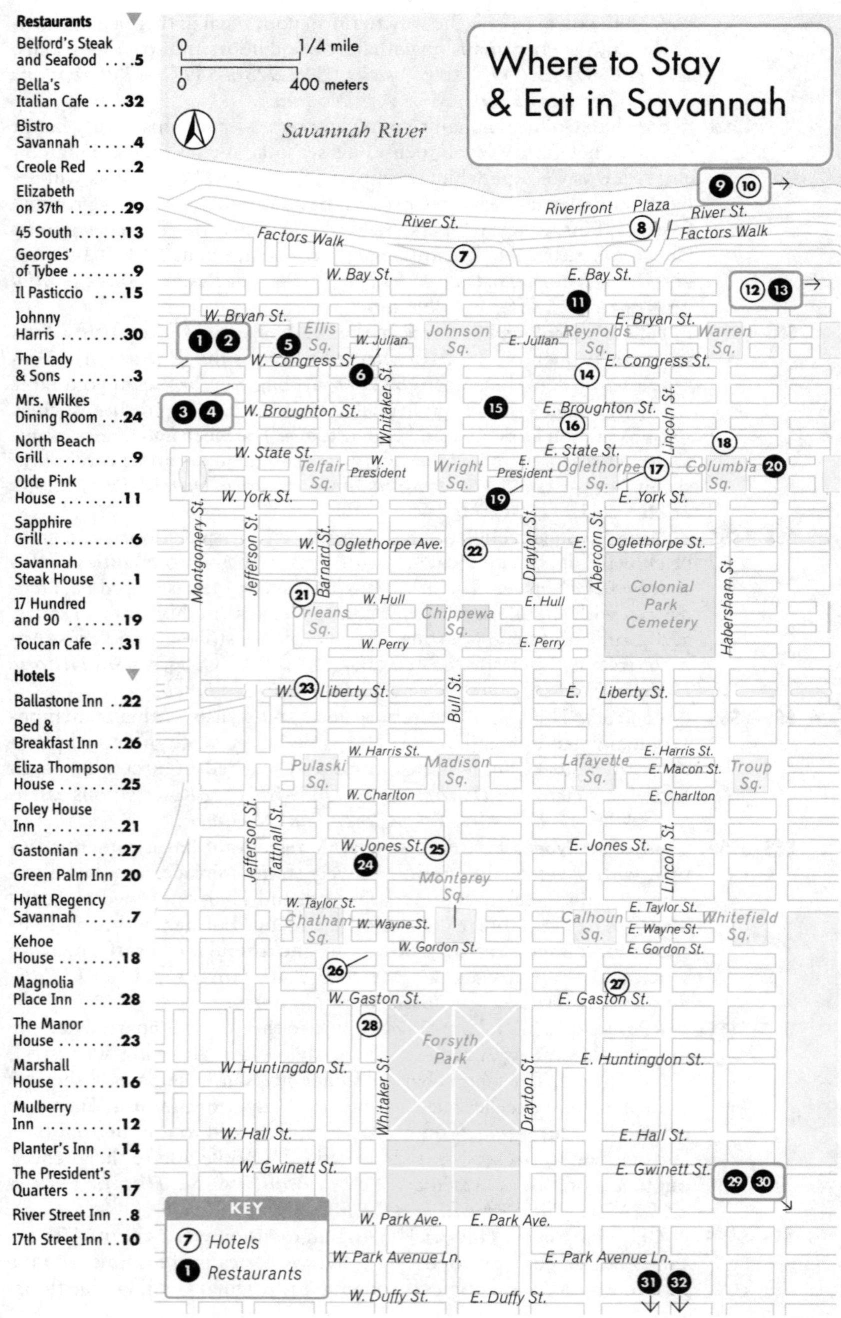
Where to Stay & Eat in Savannah
Restaurants
Belford's Steak and Seafood 5
Bella's Italian Cafe 32
Bistro Savannah 4
Creole Red 2
Elizabeth on 37th 29
45 South 13
Georges' of Tybee 9
Il Pasticcio 15
Johnny Harris 30
The Lady & Sons 3
Mrs. Wilkes Dining Room . . .24
North Beach Grill 9
Olde Pink House 11
Sapphire Grill 6
Savannah Steak House 1
17 Hundred and 90 19
Toucan Cafe . . .31
Hotels
Ballastone Inn . .22
Bed & Breakfast Inn . .26
Eliza Thompson House 25
Foley House Inn 21
Gastonian 27
Green Palm Inn 20
Hyatt Regency Savannah 7
Kehoe House 18
Magnolia Place Inn 28
The Manor House 23
Marshall House 16
Mulberry Inn 12
Planter's Inn . . .14
The President's Quarters 17
River Street Inn . .8
17th Street Inn . .10
0 1/4 mile
0 400 meters
Savannah River
Riverfront Plaza
River St.
Factors Walk
W. Bay St.
E. Bay St.
W. Bryan St.
E. Bryan St.
Ellis Sq.
W. Julian
Johnson Sq.
E. Julian
Reynolds Sq.
Warren Sq.
W. Congress St.
E. Congress St.
W. Broughton St.
E. Broughton St.
W. State St.
E. State St.
Telfair Sq.
W. President
Wright Sq.
E. President
Oglethorpe Sq.
Columbia Sq.
W. York St.
E. York St.
W. Oglethorpe Ave.
E. Oglethorpe St.
Colonial Park Cemetery
W. Hull
E. Hull
Orleans Sq.
Chippewa Sq.
W. Perry
E. Perry
W. Liberty St.
E. Liberty St.
W. Harris St.
E. Harris St.
E. Macon St.
Pulaski Sq.
Madison Sq.
Lafayette Sq.
Troup Sq.
W. Charlton
E. Charlton
W. Jones St.
E. Jones St.
Monterey Sq.
W. Taylor St.
E. Taylor St.
Chatham Sq.
W. Wayne St.
E. Wayne St.
Calhoun Sq.
Whitefield Sq.
W. Gordon St.
E. Gordon St.
W. Gaston St.
E. Gaston St.
Forsyth Park
W. Huntingdon St.
E. Huntingdon St.
W. Hall St.
E. Hall St.
W. Gwinett St.
E. Gwinett St.
W. Park Ave.
E. Park Ave.
W. Park Avenue Ln.
E. Park Avenue Ln.
W. Duffy St.
E. Duffy St.
Montgomery St.
Jefferson St.
Barnard St.
Whitaker St.
Bull St.
Drayton St.
Abercorn St.
Lincoln St.
Habersham St.
Tattnall St.
KEY
Hotels
Restaurants

of the tavern, the Venetian chandeliers, and the 18th-century English antiques. The she-crab soup is a light but flavorful version of a Low-country specialty. Regional ingredients find their way into many of the dishes, including the black grouper stuffed with blue crab and served with a Vidalia onion sauce. ✉ *23 Abercorn St., Historic District* ☎ *912/232–4286* ▭ *AE, MC, V* ⏲ *No lunch.*

$$$–$$$$ ✕ **Savannah Steak House.** This art-filled, dashing restaurant with a striking collage on its ceiling has made an impressive splash in Savannah dining circles. The menu offers a tremendously varied number of inventive delicacies. Traditionalists might stick with the hefty rib-eye steak, but if you're game for something more exotic, consider "wild" entrées like ostrich fillet, wild-boar chili, and antelope medallions. ✉ *423 W. Congress St., Historic District* ☎ *912/232–0092* ▭ *AE, MC, V* ⏲ *Closed Sun.*

★ **$$$–$$$$** ✕ **17 Hundred and 90.** Chef Deborah Noelk keeps a creative kitchen in this restaurant—in a rustic structure dating to colonial days, tucked in among ancient oaks dripping with Spanish moss. Entrées include pan-seared veal medallions with artichoke hearts and capers in a lemon butter; roasted half duckling with a port wine lingonberry sauce; and local shrimp stuffed with scallops and crabmeat and served with a lemon beurre blanc sauce. There's a ghost story to go with dinner, so make sure the waiter fills you in. ✉ *307 E. Presidents St., Historic District* ☎ *912/231–8888* ▭ *AE, D, DC, MC, V* ⏲ *No lunch weekends.*

$$$ ✕ **The Lady & Sons.** Expect to take your place in line, along with locals, here. Everyone patiently waits to attack the buffet, which is stocked for both lunch and dinner with such specials as moist, crispy fried chicken; the best baked spaghetti in the South; green beans cooked with ham and potatoes; tender, sweet creamed corn; and homemade lemonade. Owner Paula H. Deen's cookbook includes recipes for the most popular dishes. ✉ *102 W. Congress St., Historic District* ☎ *912/233–2600* ▭ *AE, D, MC, V* ⏲ *No dinner Sun.*

★ **$$–$$$** ✕ **Toucan Cafe.** This colorful café is well worth a trip a bit off the beaten path to Savannah's Southside. It's a favorite for Savannahians entertaining out-of-town visitors; no one, it seems, leaves unsatisified. The menu defines the term "eclectic," with plenty of appealing options for both vegetarians and meat-eaters, including Indian veggie samosas with curried broccoli, Jamaican jerk chicken, and rib-eye steaks. ✉ *531 Stephenson Ave., Southside* ☎ *912/352–2233* ▭ *AE, D, MC, V* ⏲ *Closed Sun.*

$$ ✕ **Johnny Harris.** What started as a small roadside stand in 1924 has grown into one of the city's mainstays, with a menu that includes steaks, fried chicken, seafood, and meats spiced with the restaurant's famous tomato-and-mustard sauce. The lamb barbecue is a treat, and their sauces are now so famous that they bottle them for take-home and shipping. There's live music Friday and Saturday night, except on the first Saturday night of the month, when there's dancing. ✉ *1651 E. Victory Dr., Eastside* ☎ *912/354–7810* ▭ *AE, D, DC, MC, V* ⏲ *Closed Sun.*

★ **$$** ✕ **Mrs. Wilkes' Dining Room.** Folks line up for a culinary orgy of fine Southern food, served family style at big tables. For breakfast there are eggs, sausage, piping hot biscuits, and grits. At lunch try fried or roast chicken, collard greens, okra, mashed potatoes, and corn bread. ✉ *107 W. Jones St., Historic District* ☎ *912/232–5997* ✍ *Reservations not accepted* ▭ *No credit cards* ⊙ *Closed Jan. and weekends. No dinner.*

$$ ✕ **North Beach Grill.** The tiny kitchen of this casual beachfront restaurant on Tybee Island serves up a taste of the Caribbean. The jerk-rubbed fish tacos with fruit salsa—which you'll be hard-pressed to find prepared right in the South—are wonderful. You can come in a swimsuit for lunch, but throw on something casual for dinner. ✉ *41A Meddin Dr., Tybee Island* ☎ *912/786–9003* ✍ *Reservations not accepted* ▭ *D, MC, V* ⊙ *Closed weekdays Dec. and Jan.*

★ $–$$ ✕ **Bella's Italian Cafe.** From its unpretentious spot in a Midtown shopping center, Bella's serves up simple, wildly popular fare, including scampi, ziti, and particularly delicious gnocchi. Desserts are also standout versions of classics, such as Italian wedding cake, tiramisu, cannoli. The genial, hospitable service makes this a perfect place to relax over a glass of wine. ✉ *4408 Habersham St., Midtown* ☎ *912/354–4005* ✍ *Reservations not accepted* ▭ *AE, D, DC, MC, V* ⊙ *No lunch weekends.*

$ ✕ **Creole Red.** This jaunty little no-frills storefront café is patronized with great enthusiasm by locals. Everybody seems to love the delicious and inexpensive Louisiana specialties, from fresh crawfish étouffée to deviled crabs, served with warmth and aplomb by the friendly proprietor and staff. ✉ *409 W. Congress St., Historic District* ☎ *912/234–6690* ▭ *MC, V.*

WHERE TO STAY

Although Savannah has its share of chain hotels and motels, the city's most distinctive lodgings are the more than two dozen historic inns, guest houses, and B&Bs gracing the Historic District.

If the term *historic inn* brings to mind images of roughing it in shabby-genteel mansions with antiquated plumbing, you're in for a surprise. Most of these inns are in mansions with the requisite high ceilings, spacious rooms, and ornate carved millwork. And most do have canopy, four-poster, or Victorian brass beds. But amid all the antique surroundings, there's modern luxury: enormous baths, many with whirlpools or hot tubs; film libraries for in-room VCRs; and turndown service with a chocolate, a praline, even a discreet brandy on your nightstand. Continental breakfast and afternoon refreshments are often included in the rate. Special seasons and holidays, such as St. Patrick's Day, push prices up a bit. On the other hand, weekdays and the off-season can yield excellent bargains.

WHAT IT COSTS

$$$$	$$$	$$	$	¢
over $220	$160–$220	$110–$160	$70–$110	under $70

Hotel prices are for two people in a standard double room in high season, excluding service charges and 12% tax.

Inns & Guesthouses

★ $$$$ **Gastonian.** Guest rooms at this inn, built in 1868, have working fireplaces and antiques from the Georgian and Regency periods; most also have whirlpool tubs or Japanese soak tubs. The Caracalla Suite is named for the oversize whirlpool tub built in front of the fireplace. At breakfast you can find such specialty items as ginger pancakes. Afternoon tea, evening cordials, and complimentary wine are other treats. ✉ *220 E. Gaston St., Historic District, 31401* ☎ *912/232–2869 or 800/322–6603* 📠 *912/232–0710* 🌐 *www.gastonian.com* *14 rooms, 3 suites* *Internet* *AE, D, MC, V* *BP.*

★ $$$–$$$$ **Ballastone Inn.** This sumptuous inn occupies an 1838 mansion that once served as a bordello. Rooms are handsomely furnished, with luxurious linens on canopy beds, antiques and fine reproductions, and a collection of original framed prints from *Harper's* scattered throughout. On the garden level rooms are small and cozy, with exposed brick walls, beam ceilings, and, in some cases, windows at eye level with the lush courtyard. Most rooms have working gas fireplaces, and three have whirlpool tubs. Afternoon tea and free passes to a nearby health club are included. ✉ *14 E. Oglethorpe Ave., Historic District, 31401* ☎ *912/236–1484 or 800/822–4553* 📠 *912/236–4626* 🌐 *www.ballastone.com* *14 rooms, 3 suites* *In-room VCRs, bicycles* *AE, MC, V* *BP.*

$$$–$$$$ **Eliza Thompson House.** Eliza Thompson was a socially prominent widow when she built her fine town house around 1847; today the lovely Victorian edifice is one of the oldest B&Bs in Savannah. A peaceful garden courtyard provides a quiet respite. The rooms are lavishly decorated, with marble baths, rare antiques, plush bedding, and other designer accents. Continental breakfast and complimentary afternoon wine and cheese are served in the parlor or on the patio, which has a fine Ivan Bailey sculpture. ✉ *5 W. Jones St., Historic District, 31401* ☎ *912/236–3620 or 800/348–9378* 📠 *912/238–1920* 🌐 *www.elizathompsonhouse.com* *25 rooms* *Cable TV* *MC, V* *BP.*

★ $$$–$$$$ **Foley House Inn.** Two town houses, built 50 years apart, form this elegant inn. Proprietor Phillip Jenkins often entertains during the evening wine-and-dessert service—he plays lively numbers on the baby grand piano in the parlor. Most rooms have antiques and reproductions; five rooms have whirlpool tubs. A carriage house to the rear of the property has less expensive rooms. ✉ *14 W. Hull St., Historic District, 31401* ☎ *912/232–6622 or 800/647–3708* 📠 *912/231–1218* 🌐 *www.foleyinn.com* *17 rooms, 2 suites* *In-room VCRs* *AE, MC, V* *BP.*

$$$–$$$$ **Kehoe House.** A fabulously appointed 1890s B&B, the Victorian Kehoe House has brass-and-marble chandeliers, a courtyard garden, and a music room. On the main floor a double parlor holds two fireplaces and sweeps the eye upward with its 14-foot ceilings. Rates include access to the Downtown Athletic Club. ✉ *123 Habersham St., Historic District, 31401* ☎ *912/232–1020 or 800/820–1020* 📠 *912/231–0208* 🌐 *www.kehoehouse.com* *13 rooms, 2 suites* *Meeting room* *AE, D, DC, MC, V* *BP.*

★ $$$–$$$$ **Magnolia Place Inn.** Looking out directly across breathtaking Forsyth Park, this opulent 1878 inn dazzles. There are regal antiques, prints, and porcelain from around the world—you'd expect one of Savannah's wealthy old cotton merchants to occupy such a mansion. Many rooms have Jacuzzis and fireplaces. With expansive verandas, lush terraces, and soaring ceilings, the Magnolia Place Inn typifies Savannah's golden era. *503 Whitaker St., Historic District, 31401 912/236–7674 or 800/238–7674 912/231–1218 www.magnoliaplaceinn.com 13 rooms, 3 suites, 2 town houses In-room VCRs, Internet AE, MC, V BP.*

★ $$–$$$ **The Manor House.** Built for the Lewis Byrd family in the 1830s, this majestic historic structure housed Union officers during General Sherman's Civil War march to the sea. All rooms are suites with a master bedroom and a separate cozy sitting area. The Manor House also oversees three additional properties off-site from the main inn: a gorgeous, antiques-filled loft suite on Factors Walk overlooking the historic Savannah waterfront; a large historic town house complete with formal dining room on Broughton Street; and a magnificent, two-bedroom oceanfront town house with two sprawling private decks on Tybee Island. *201 W. Liberty St., Historic District, 31401 912/233–9597 or 800/462–3595 www.manorhouse-savannah.com 8 suites Some in-room hot tubs, in-room VCRs AE, D, DC, MC, V BP.*

★ $$–$$$ **The President's Quarters.** You'll be impressed even before you enter this lovely inn, which has an exterior courtyard so beautiful and inviting it has become a popular wedding-reception spot. Each room in this classic Savannah inn, fashioned out of a pair of meticulously restored 1860s town houses, is named for an American president. Some rooms have four-poster beds, working fireplaces, and private balconies. Expect to be greeted with wine and fruit, and a complimentary afternoon tea will tempt you with sweet cakes. Turndown service includes a glass of port or sherry. There are also rooms in an adjacent town house. *225 E. President St., Historic District, 31401 912/233–1600 or 800/233–1776 912/238–0849 www.presidentsquarters.com 11 rooms, 8 suites Some hot tubs D, DC, MC, V BP.*

$–$$ **Bed & Breakfast Inn.** So called, the owner claims, because it was the first such property to open in Savannah more than 20 years ago, the inn is a restored 1853 federal-style row house on historic Gordon Row near Chatham Square. The courtyard garden is a lovely cluster of potted tropical flowers surrounding an inviting koi pond. A sweeping renovation has added private baths to all the rooms but managed to keep many elements of the original charm, such as beamed ceilings and exposed-brick walls; only the Garden Suite has a full kitchen. Afternoon pastries, lemonade, coffee, and tea are served. *117 W. Gordon St., Historic District, 31401 912/238–0518 912/233–2537 www.savannahbnb.com 15 rooms AE, D, MC, V BP.*

★ $–$$ **Green Palm Inn.** This inn is a pleasing little discovery. Originally built in 1897 but renovated top to bottom by owners Jack Moore and Rick Ellison, it's now a B&B. The elegant furnishings were inspired by Savannah's British colonial heritage; some rooms have fireplaces. A separate cottage has two bedrooms, a fireplace, and a lush garden with a marble wading pool. ✉ *548 E. President St., Historic District, 31401* ☎ *912/447–8901 or 888/606–9510* 📠 *912/236–4626* 🌐 *www.greenpalminn.com* *5 suites, 1 cottage* *Fans, cable TV* *AE, MC, V* *BP.*

$–$$ **17th Street Inn.** You're steps from the beach at this Tybee Island inn dating from 1920. The front deck, adorned with plants, palms, and swings, is a gathering place where you can chat, sip wine, and enjoy breakfast. The inn's rooms each offer a queen bed, efficiency kitchen, private bath, and private entrance. A continental breakfast is served each morning. *12 17th St., Box 114, Tybee Island 31328* ☎ *912/786–0607 or 888/909–0607* 📠 *912/786–0602* 🌐 *www.tybeeinn.com* *8 rooms, 1 condo* *Kitchenettes* *AE, D, MC, V* *BP.*

8

Hotels & Motels

$$$$ **Hyatt Regency Savannah.** You won't precisely get the feel of old Savannah here, despite the location in the Historic District: the seven-story structure, built in 1981, has a modern feel, with a towering atrium and glass elevators. Rooms have contemporary furnishings, marble baths, and balconies overlooking either the atrium or the Savannah River. MD's Lounge is an appealing spot to have a drink and watch the river traffic drift by. Windows, the hotel's restaurant, serves a fine Sunday buffet. ✉ *2 W. Bay St., Historic District, 31401* ☎ *912/238–1234 or 800/233–1234* 📠 *912/944–3673* 🌐 *www.savannah.hyatt.com* *325 rooms, 22 suites* *Restaurant, indoor pool, health club, bar, lounge, business services, meeting rooms* *AE, D, MC, V* *EP.*

★ **$$$** **Mulberry Inn.** This Holiday Inn–managed property is ensconced in an 1860s livery stable that later became a cotton warehouse and then a Coca-Cola bottling plant. Gleaming heart-pine floors and antiques, including a handsome English grandfather clock and an exquisitely carved Victorian mantel, make it unique. The café is a notch nicer than most other Holiday Inn restaurants. An executive wing, at the back of the hotel, is geared to business travelers. ✉ *601 E. Bay St., Historic District, 31401* ☎ *912/238–1200 or 800/465–4329* 📠 *912/236–2184* 🌐 *www.savannahhotel.com* *145 rooms, 24 suites* *Restaurant, café, some microwaves, some refrigerators, some in-room VCRs, outdoor pool, outdoor hot tub, bar, Internet, meeting room* *AE, D, DC, MC, V* *EP.*

★ **$$$** **Planters Inn.** Formerly the John Wesley Hotel, this inn is housed in a structure built in 1812, and though it retains the regal tone of that golden age, it still offers all the intimate comforts you would expect from an upscale inn. The inn's 60 guest rooms are all decorated in the finest fabrics and Baker furnishings (a 1920s design style named for the Dutch immigrant cabinetmaker). According to lore, a (good) ghost inhabits the hotel, floating through the hallways and straightening skewed paintings hanging in the hallway. ✉ *29 Abercorn St., Historic District, 31401* ☎ *912/232–5678* 📠 *912/236–2184* 🌐 *www.plantersinnsavannah.com* *60 rooms* *Cable TV, hot tubs* *AE, D, DC, MC, V* *EP.*

$$–$$$ **Marshall House.** This restored hotel, with original pine floors, woodwork, and bricks, caters to business travelers while providing the intimacy of a B&B. Different spaces reflect different parts of Savannah's history, from its founding to the Civil War. Artwork is mostly by local artists. You can listen to live jazz on weekends in the hotel lounge. Guests get free passes to a downtown health club. ✉ *123 E. Broughton St., Historic District, 31401* ☎ *912/644–7896 or 800/589–6304* 🖷 *912/234–3334* 🌐 *www.marshallhouse.com* *65 rooms, 3 suites* *Restaurant, lounge, meeting room* 💳 *AE, D, MC, V* 🍽 *EP.*

$$–$$$ **River Street Inn.** The interior of this 1817 converted warehouse is so lavish that it's hard to believe the five-story building once stood vacant in a state of disrepair. Today the 86 guest rooms are filled with antiques and reproductions from the era of King Cotton. French-style balconies overlook both River Street and Bay Street. One floor has charming souvenir and gift shops. ✉ *124 E. Bay St., Historic District, 31401* ☎ *912/234–6400 or 800/253–4229* 🖷 *912/234–1478* 🌐 *www.riverstreetinn.com* *86 rooms* *2 restaurants, billiards, 3 bars, shops, business services, meeting rooms* 💳 *AE, D, DC, MC, V* 🍽 *EP.*

NIGHTLIFE & THE ARTS

Savannah's nightlife reflects the city's laid-back personality. Some clubs have live reggae, hard rock, and other contemporary music, but most stick to traditional blues, jazz, and piano-bar vocalists. After-dark merrymakers usually head for watering holes on Riverfront Plaza or the south side.

Bars & Nightclubs

The **Bar Bar** (✉ 219 W. St. Julian St., Historic District ☎ 912/231–1910), a neighborhood hangout, has pool tables, games, and a varied beer selection. Once a month at **Club One Jefferson** (✉ 1 Jefferson St., Historic District ☎ 912/232–0200), a gay bar, the Lady Chablis bumps and grinds her way down the catwalk, lip-synching disco tunes in a shimmer of sequin and satin gowns; the cover is $5. **Kevin Barry's Irish Pub** (✉ 114 W. River St., Historic District ☎ 912/233–9626) has a friendly vibe, a full menu until 1 AM, and traditional Irish music from Wednesday to Sunday; it's *the* place to be on St. Patrick's Day. The rest of the year there's a mix of tourists and locals of all ages. Go to **M. D.'s Lounge** (✉ 2 W. Bay St., Historic District ☎ 912/238–1234) if you have a classy nightcap in mind. The bar is literally perched above the Savannah River and surrounded by windows big enough to be glass walls. **Stogies** (✉ 112 W. Congress St., Historic District ☎ 912/233–4277) has its own humidor where patrons buy expensive cigars. It's a fun spot if you can take the smoke.

Coffeehouses

Thanks to a substantial student population, the city has sprouted coffeehouses as if they were spring flowers. **Christy's Espresso Delights** (✉ 7400 Abercorn St., Highland Park ☎ 912/356–3566) is a full-service espresso café with a wonderful selection of fine desserts and a light-lunch menu. The **Express** (✉ 39 Barnard St., Historic District ☎ 912/

233–4683) is a warm, unassuming bakery and café that serves specialty coffees along with decadent desserts and tasty snacks. **Gallery Espresso** (✉ 6 E. Liberty St., Historic District ☎ 912/233–5348) is a combined coffee haunt and art enclave, with gallery shows; it stays open late.

Jazz & Blues Clubs

Bayou Café and Blues Bar (✉ 14 N. Abercorn St., at River St., Historic District ☎ 912/233–6414) has acoustic music during the week and the Bayou Blues Band on the weekend. There's also Cajun food. **Cafe Loco** (✉ 1 Old Hwy. 80, Tybee Island ☎ 912/786–7810), a few miles outside Savannah, showcases local blues and acoustics acts.

8

Music Festivals

The **Savannah Music Festival** (🌐 www.savannahmusicfestival.org), held each March, offers a rich, blend of world-class blues, jazz, classical, rock, and zydeco. The **Savannah Jazz Festival** (🌐 www.coastaljazz.com) is a free event held each September in Forsyth Park featuring artists from around the region. For four days in October, the free **Savannah Folk Music Festival** (🌐 www.savannahfolk.org) becomes the city's main musical attraction.

SHOPPING

Find your own Lowcountry treasures among a bevy of handcrafted wares—handmade quilts and baskets; wreaths made from Chinese tallow trees and Spanish moss; preserves, jams, and jellies. The favorite Savannah snack, and a popular gift item, is the benne wafer. It's about the size of a quarter and comes in different flavors. Savannah has a wide collection of colorful businesses—revitalization is no longer a goal but an accomplishment. Antiques malls and junk emporiums beckon you with their colorful storefronts and eclectic offerings, as do the many specialty shops and bookstores clustered along the moss-embossed streets.

Shopping Districts

City Market (✉ W. St. Julian St. between Ellis and Franklin Sqs., Historic District) has sidewalk cafés, jazz haunts, shops, and art galleries. **Riverfront Plaza/River Street** (✉ Historic District) is nine blocks of shops in renovated waterfront warehouses where you can find everything from popcorn to pottery.

Specialty Shops

Antiques

Arthur Smith Antiques (✉ 402 Bull St., Historic District ☎ 912/236–9701) has four floors showcasing 18th- and 19th-century European furniture, porcelain, rugs, and paintings.

Art Galleries

Compass Prints, Inc./Ray Ellis Gallery (✉ 205 W. Congress St., Historic District ☎ 912/234–3537) sells original artwork, prints, and books by internationally acclaimed artist Ray Ellis. **Gallery Espresso** (✉ 6 E. Lib-

CloseUp

THE MYSTIQUE OF SPANISH MOSS

Spanish moss—the silky, snakelike garlands that drape over the branches of live oaks—has come to symbolize the languorous sensibilities of the Deep South. A relative of the pineapple, the moisture-loving plant requires an average year-round humidity of 70 percent, and thus thrives in subtropical climates—including Georgia's coastal regions.

Contrary to popular belief, Spanish moss is not a parasite; it's an epiphyte, or "air plant," taking water and nutrients from the air and photosynthesizing in the same manner as soil-bound plants. It reproduces using tiny flowers. When water is scarce, it turns gray, and when the rains come it takes on a greenish hue. The old saying "Good night, sleep tight, don't let the bed bugs bite," is thought to come from the past practice of stuffing mattresses with Spanish moss, which often harbored the biting menaces commonly known as chiggers.

erty St., Historic District ☎ 912/233–5348) has a new show every two weeks focusing on work by local artists. A true coffeehouse, it stays open until the wee hours. **Gallery 209** (✉ 209 E. River St., Historic District ☎ 912/236–4583) is a co-op gallery, with paintings, watercolors, pottery, jewelry, batik, stained glass, weavings, and sculptures by local artists. **Off the Wall** (✉ 206 W. Broughton St., Historic District ☎ 912/233–8840) exhibits artists from everywhere, including Savannah. **Savannah College of Art and Design** (✉ 516 Abercorn St., Historic District ☎ 912/525–5200), a private art college, has restored at least 40 historic buildings in the city, including 12 galleries. Work by faculty and students is often for sale, and touring exhibitions are frequently in the on-campus galleries. Stop by Exhibit A, Pinnacle Gallery, and the West Bank Gallery, and ask about other student galleries. Garden for the Arts has an amphitheater and shows performance art.

Benne Wafers

Byrd Cookie Company & Gourmet Marketplace (✉ 6700 Waters Ave., Highland Park ☎ 912/355–1716), founded in 1924, is the best place to get benne wafers, the trademark Savannah cookies. They're also sold in numerous gift shops around town.

Books

E. Shaver Booksellers (✉ 326 Bull St., Historic District ☎ 912/234–7257) is the source for 17th- and 18th-century maps and new books on regional subjects; the shop occupies 12 rooms. **V. & J. Duncan** (✉ 12 E. Taylor St., Historic District ☎ 912/232–0338) specializes in antique maps, prints, and books.

Country Crafts

Charlotte's Corner (✉ 1 W. Liberty St., Historic District ☎ 912/233–8061) carries expensive and moderately priced Savannah souvenirs, children's clothes and toys, and beachwear.

SAVANNAH A TO Z

To research prices, get advice from other travelers, and book travel arrangements, visit www.fodors.com.

AIR TRAVEL TO & FROM SAVANNAH

CARRIERS Savannah is served by AirTran Airways, Continental Express, Northwest Airlink, Delta, United Express, and US Airways/Express for domestic flights.

AIRPORTS & TRANSFERS

Savannah International Airport is 18 mi west of downtown. Despite the name, international flights are nonexistent. The foreign trade zone, a locus for importing, constitutes the "international" aspect.

Airport Information **Savannah International Airport** ✉ 400 Airways Ave., West Chatham ☎ 912/964-0514 🌐 www.savannahairport.com.

AIRPORT TRANSFERS B&B Shuttle has service from the airport to Savannah and the surrounding region. The trip downtown takes 15 minutes, and the fare is $16 one-way, $31 round-trip for one person.

Taxi service is an easy way to get from the airport to downtown; try AAA Adam Cab Incorporated and Yellow Cab Company; the one-way fare is about $20, plus $5 for each addition person. By car take I–95 south to I–16 east into downtown Savannah.

Taxis & Shuttles **AAA Adam Cab Incorporated** ☎ 912/927-7466. **McCall's Limousine Service** ☎ 912/964-1411. **Yellow Cab Company** ☎ 912/236-1133.

BUS TRAVEL TO & FROM SAVANNAH

Bus Information **Greyhound/Trailways** ✉ 610 W. Oglethorpe Ave., Downtown ☎ 912/233-8186 or 800/231-2222.

BUS TRAVEL WITHIN SAVANNAH

Chatham Area Transit (CAT) operates buses in Savannah and Chatham County Monday through Saturday from 6 AM to 11 PM, Sunday from 9 to 7. Some lines may stop running earlier or may not run on Sunday. The CAT Shuttle operates throughout the Historic District and is free of charge. For other Savannah buses, the fare is $1.

Bus Information **Chatham Area Transit** ☎ 912/233-5767 🌐 www.catchacat.org.

CAR TRAVEL

I–95 slices north–south along the eastern seaboard, intersecting 10 mi west of town with east–west I–16, which dead-ends in downtown Savannah. U.S. 17, the Coastal Highway, also runs north–south through town. U.S. 80, which connects the Atlantic to the Pacific, is another east–west route through Savannah.

EMERGENCIES

Candler Hospital and Memorial Health University Medical Center are the area hospitals with 24-hour emergency rooms.

Emergency Services **Ambulance, police** ☎ 911.

Hospitals **Candler Hospital** ✉ 5353 Reynolds St., Kensington Park ☎ 912/692-6000. **Memorial Health University Medical Center** ✉ 4700 Waters Ave., Fairfield ☎ 912/350-8000.

24-Hour Pharmacies **CVS Pharmacy** ✉ Medical Arts Shopping Center, 4725 Waters Ave., Fairfield ☎ 912/355-7111.

TAXIS

AAA Adam Cab Co. is a reliable 24-hour taxi service. Calling ahead for reservations could yield a flat rate. Yellow Cab Company is another dependable taxi service. Standard taxi fare is $1.50 a mile.

Taxi Companies **AAA Adam Cab Co.** ☎ 912/927-7466. **Yellow Cab Company** ☎ 912/236-1133.

TOURS

HISTORIC DISTRICT TOURS

Beach Institute African-American Cultural Center is headquarters for the Negro Heritage Trail Tour. A knowledgeable guide traces the city's more than 250 years of black history. Tours, which begin at the Savannah Visitors Center, are at 1 and 3 and cost $15.

Carriage Tours of Savannah takes you through the Historic District by day or by night at a 19th-century clip-clop pace, with coachmen spinning tales and telling ghost stories along the way. A romantic evening tour in a private carriage costs $85; regular tours are a more modest $19 per person.

Garden Club of Savannah runs spring tours of private gardens tucked behind old brick walls and wrought-iron gates. It costs $30 and finishes with tea at the Green-Meldrim House.

Old Town Trolley Tours has narrated 90-minute tours traversing the Historic District. Trolleys stop at 13 designated stops every half hour daily 9–4:30; you can hop on and off as you please. The cost is $18–$22.

Fees & Schedules **Beach Institute African-American Cultural Center** ☎ 912/234-8000. **Carriage Tours of Savannah** ☎ 912/236-6756. **Garden Club of Savannah** ☎ 912/238-0248. **Old Town Trolley Tours** ☎ 912/233-0083.

SPECIAL-INTEREST TOURS

Historic Savannah Foundation, a preservation organization, leads tours of the Historic District and the Lowcountry. Preservation, *Midnight in the Garden of Good and Evil,* the Golden Isles, group, and private tours also are available. In addition, the foundation leads specialty excursions to the fishing village of Thunderbolt; the Isle of Hope, with its stately mansions lining Bluff Drive; the much-photographed Bonaventure Cemetery, on the banks of the Wilmington River; and Wormsloe Plantation Site, with its mile-long avenue of arching oaks. Fees for the specialty tours start at $75 per hour, with a two-hour minimum for a private group of up to five people.

Square Routes provides customized strolls and private driving tours that wend through the Historic District and other parts of the Lowcountry. In-town tours focus on the city's architecture and gardens, and specialized tours include the *Midnight in the Garden of Good and Evil* walk. Tours usually last two hours and start at $35 per person, with a minimum of two people per tour.

Fees & Schedules **Historic Savannah Foundation** ☎ 912/234-4088 or 800/627-5030. **Square Routes** ☎ 912/232-6866 or 800/868-6867.

WALKING TOURS Much of the downtown Historic District can easily be explored on foot. Its grid shape makes getting around a breeze, and you'll find any number of places to stop and rest.

A Ghost Talk Ghost Walk tour should send chills down your spine during an easy 1-mi jaunt through the old colonial city. Tours, lasting an hour and a half, leave from the middle of Reynolds Square, at the John Wesley Memorial. Call for dates, times, and reservations; the cost is $10.

Savannah-by-Foot's Creepy Crawl Haunted Pub Tour is a favorite. According to the true believers, there are so many ghosts in Savannah they're actually divided into subcategories. On this tour, charismatic guide and storyteller Greg Proffit specializes in those ghosts that haunt taverns only, regaling you with tales from secret subbasements discovered to house skeletal remains, possessed gum-ball machines, and animated water faucets. Tours traditionally depart from the Six Pence Pub, where a ghost named Larry likes to fling open the bathroom doors, but routes can vary, so call for departure times and locations; the cost is $15.

Fees & Schedules **A Ghost Talk Ghost Walk Tour** ✉ Reynolds Sq., Congress and Abercorn Sts., Historic District ☎ 912/233-3896. **Savannah-By-Foot's Creepy Crawl Haunted Pub Tour** ☎ 912/398-3833. **Six Pence Pub** ✉ 245 Bull St., Historic District.

VISITOR INFORMATION

Tourist Information **Savannah Area Convention & Visitors Bureau** ✉ 101 E. Bay St., Historic District, 31401 ☎ 912/644-6401 or 877/728-2662 🖷 912/944-0468 🌐 www.savcvb.com.

THE COASTAL ISLES & THE OKEFENOKEE

9

GET TO KNOW GEECHEE CULTURE
at Hog Hammock on Sapelo Island ⇨*p.335*

TRY YOUR HAND AT CRABBING
off the pier at St. Simons Island ⇨*p.339*

TEE OFF AT A WORD-CLASS RESORT,
the Lodge at Sea Island Golf Club ⇨*p.342*

SEE THE WILD HORSES ROAM
on Cumberland Island's beaches ⇨*p.349*

GRIN BACK AT THE GATORS
of the Okefenokee Wildlife Refuge ⇨*p.353*

By Jody Jenkins **GEORGIA'S COASTAL ISLES** are a string of lush barrier islands meandering down the Atlantic coast from Savannah to the Florida border. Notable for their subtropical beauty and abundant wildlife, the isles also strike a unique balance between some of the wealthiest communities in the country and some of the most jealously protected preserves found anywhere. Nearly side by side with bustling vacation playgrounds you can find loggerhead sea turtles, dolphins, manatees, and extremely rare right whales, which nest only off the Georgia coast.

The Golden Isles—St. Simons Island, Little St. Simons Island, Sea Island, and Jekyll Island—are the most developed of the coastal isles and have everything for the vacationer. While Little St. Simons Island and Sea Island cater primarily to the wealthy looking to get away from it all, St. Simons Island and Jekyll Island are diverse havens with something for everyone from beach bums to family vacationers to the suit-and-tie crowd. Though it has only a few hundred full-time residents, Sea Island is one of the wealthiest zip codes in America. Except for Little St. Simons, the Golden Isles are connected to the mainland by bridges around Brunswick and are the only coastal isles accessible by car. Little St. Simons, a private island with accommodations for a limited number of overnight guests and day trippers, is accessible by private launch from the northern end of St. Simons.

Sapelo Island and the Cumberland Island National Seashore can only be reached by ferry from Meridian and St. Marys, respectively. Generally unmarred by development, these remote islands with their near-pristine ecology are alluring for anyone seeking an authentic getaway. Both are excellent for camping, with sites ranging from primitive to (relatively) sophisticated. Noncamping accommodations are limited and require booking well in advance. Miles of untouched beaches, forests of gnarly live oak draped with Spanish moss, swamps and marshlands teeming with birds and wildlife combine to make these islands unique. The best way to visit them is on either public or private guided tours.

The Okefenokee National Wildlife Refuge, 60 mi inland from St. Marys near Folkston, is one of the largest wetlands in the United States. Spread over 700 square mi of southeastern Georgia and northeastern Florida, the swamp is a treasure trove of flora and fauna that naturalist William Bartram called a "terrestrial paradise" when he visited in the 1770s. From towering cypress swamps to alligator- and snake-infested waters to prairielike grasslands, the Okefenokee is a mosaic of ecosystems, much of which has never been visited by humans.

Exploring the Coastal Isles & the Okefenokee

Visiting the region is easiest by car, particularly Sapelo and the Okefenokee, because many of the outer reaches of Georgia are remote places with little in the way of transportation options. Touring by bicycle is an option for most of the region, but note that the ferries at Sapelo and Cumberland do not allow bicycles on board.

Coastal Georgia is a complex jigsaw wending its way from the ocean and tidal marshes inland along the intricate network of rivers. U.S. 17, the old coastal highway, gives you a taste of the slower, more rural South. But because of the subtropical climate, the lush forests tend to be dense along the mainland and there are few opportunities to glimpse the broad vistas of salt marsh and islands. To truly appreciate the mystique of Georgia's coastal salt marshes and islands, make the 40-minute ferry crossing from Meridian to Sapelo Island.

The Okefenokee National Wildlife Refuge is a mysterious world where, as a glance at a map will indicate, all roads suddenly disappear. This large, interior wetland is navigable only by boat, and it can be confusing and intimidating to the uninitiated. None of the individual parks within the area give a sense of the total Okefenokee experience—each has its own distinct natural features. Choose the park that best aligns with your interests and begin there.

About the Restaurants

Restaurants range from fish camps—normally rustic dockside affairs connected to marinas where the food is basic but good, plentiful, and reasonably priced—to the more upscale eateries that tend to spawn around the larger towns. A series of restaurants has sprung up in the Golden Isles and Brunswick that are defying the stereotype that equates beach vacations with fast food. And though there's still room for growth, the area now has several menus gaining not only local but nationwide attention. The rising tide of quality has begun to lift all boats.

"Family style" is a dining method you're likely to encounter in this part of the world. It's a traditional, "pass-the-peas-please" approach whereby diners, both from your group and sometimes others as well, sit together at large tables with courses already set out for you to serve yourself at will.

WHAT IT COSTS

$$$$	$$$	$$	$	¢
over $22	$16–$22	$11–$16	$7–$11	under $7

Prices are for a main course at dinner, excluding sales tax of 6%.

About the Hotels

Hotels range from Victorian mansions to Spanish-style B&Bs to some of the most luxurious hotel–spa accommodations found anywhere. Outside the Golden Isles and Brunswick, some towns have only a few places to stay the night, so if you plan on visiting, book as far in advance as possible. Most hotels offer the full range of guest services but, as a matter of philosophy, many B&Bs do not provide televisions or telephones in the rooms. When that's the case, you'll find them in the common areas.

Lodging prices quoted here may be much lower during nonpeak seasons, and specials are often available during the week in high season.

Numbers in the text correspond to numbers in the margin and on the Georgia Coast map.

If you have 3 days

Begin with a visit to **Sapelo Island** 1, reached from Meridian by a 45-minute ferry ride through Doboy Sound, past the shell banks and small islands made from ships' ballast stones. Take a private tour of the island and visit the Chocolate Plantation and the Reynolds mansion. Then head for Hog Hammock, a community of descendants of slaves that is slowly disappearing. Have a cold beer with Julius Bailey in the Trough, the only bar in town. Then head out to the nearly deserted beaches, where you might see someone digging in the sand for conch or, offshore, the silhouettes of shrimpers plying their timeless trade.

On Day 2, head south and stop at the Hofwyl-Broadfield Plantation, just beyond Darien, where you'll get an appreciation of the massive investment in time, money, and sweat a rice plantation required. About 30 minutes farther south on U.S. 17 you'll come to Brunswick. Cross the towering Sidney Lanier Bridge, look out at the endless stretches of salt marsh. Take the causeway to **Jekyll Island** 5 and tour the historic district. Contemplate the kind of wealth that could build the mansions here and then call them winter "cottages."

On Day 3, head down to Folkston and the **Suwannee Canal Recreation Area** 7, the eastern entrance to the Okefenokee National Wildlife Refuge. Book a tour and glide through a world of primitive beauty. If you have your tent with you and you've made arrangements, camp in the park for the night, or hop in the car and head 8 mi back up to Folkston. If you choose the second option, after dinner head down Main Street to Tower and spend some time watching the trains pass by at the Folkston Funnel.

If you have 5 days

Follow the three-day itinerary, but after Sapelo and Jekyll, head over to **Little St. Simons** 3 for a day to visit a world that combines the rustic with the pampered. The cost to visit here—either for the day or overnight—is substantial, but if you're going to splurge in one place, this should be it. Drive to the Hampton River Club Marina and take the private launch for a 15-minute ride on rivers and creeks winding through the salt marshes. The boat lets you off at the dock of the Lodge on Little St. Simons Island, a turn-of-the-20th century hunting compound. You'll have an unspoiled, 7-mi-long subtropical barrier island practically all to yourself; there are abundant activities, from horseback riding to kayaking to birding with a naturalist.

After Little St. Simons, stop on your way south to have a look at Fort Frederica National Monument, which in its heyday in the 1740s was the most elaborate fortification built by the British in North America. Then follow the itinerary for Folkston and the Suwannee Canal Recreation Area. On your final day take the 1½ hour trip to St. Marys and catch the 11:45 ferry to **Cumberland Island** 6. Spend the afternoon wandering the peaceful beaches before saying good-bye to Georgia's barrier island beauty and returning to the mainland.

WHAT IT COSTS				
$$$$	$$$	$$	$	¢
over $220	$160–$220	$110–$160	$70–$110	under $70

Prices are for two people in a standard double room in high season, excluding service charges and 12% tax.

Timing

Early spring and late fall are ideal for visiting the coastal isles and the Okefenokee. By February, temperatures often reach into the 70s, while nights remain cool and even chilly, which keeps the bugs at bay. Because of the high demand to visit these areas before the bugs arrive and after they depart, you should book ferry reservations to Sapelo Island and Cumberland Island National Seashore months in advance in spring and fall: without a reservation, you risk having to wait days for a cancellation. If you plan to stay in the immediate vicinity of St. Marys or Meridian, the docking points for the Cumberland and Sapelo ferries, or Folkston, the gateway to the Okefenokee, it's advisable to book rooms for these areas well in advance for spring as accommodations are scarce and the demand is high. The Cumberland Island ferry accepts reservations six months in advance. If you go during the warmer months, always remember to bring water because these areas generally offer minimal services.

By May, deerflies and mosquitoes swarm the coast and islands in abundance. Don't underestimate their impact: During peak times in some areas they are so thick they sound like hail hitting your car. And though many localities spray, it's imperative to have a good repellent handy, especially when traveling to outlying areas. Despite the subtropical heat and humidity, summer is busy and you can count on crowds flocking to the beaches, so you'll want to make reservations at least a couple of months in advance. The season lasts until Labor Day, but you can still count on many travelers making weekend getaways until October or late November, when the weather begins to turn cooler.

THE COASTAL ISLES

Each of the six coastal isles described in this chapter offers a different experience. Sapelo, Little St. Simons, and Cumberland are the least developed and most ecologically intact of all the islands. With their broad range of wildlife and pristine, little-used beaches, they're perfect if you want a real getaway. Visiting these isles requires some advance planning: they're only accessible by ferry or private launch, and Cumberland and Sapelo have very limited services. Brunswick and most of the Golden Isles are more complete vacation destinations, with a broad range of lodging, dining, and entertainment options. Though they're more developed and more easily accessible, they still offer the best of what Georgia's coastal isles are all about: natural beauty, beaches, and a slower pace of life.

Canoeing & Kayaking Among coastal Georgia's greatest treasures, kayakers and canoeists have found, are its rivers, marshes, and barrier islands. You can spend tantalizingly slow, sunlit afternoons on the Altamaha River, drifting down toward the sea. On Cumberland Island, feral horses run among towering sand dunes. All along the twisting, endlessly fascinating coast, there are spots where you can drop your boat in the water and, within minutes, find yourself paddling past a crimson sunset or splashing dolphins.

Fish & More The local table of Georgia's coastal isles is, not surprisingly, flavored by the sea. Many restaurants pride themselves on carrying only local seafood, and you can taste the freshness. There are shrimp and oysters in abundance, the blue crab is as good as it gets, and fried catfish is a perennial favorite. The region's two most famous dishes—staples on many local menus—are the Lowcountry boil and Brunswick stew. Lowcountry boil is a blend of shrimp, corn, potatoes, and sausage cooked in a broth; Brunswick stew—named for the town where it was invented—is a slow-simmered blend of corn, potatoes, tomatoes, butter beans, chicken, pork, and beef, traditionally cooked in a cast iron pot over an open wood fire.

Salt Marshes Perhaps nothing so marks the geography of Georgia's coast as the vast, teeming expanses of salt marsh. An estimated 400,000 acres of it stretches from Savannah in the north to St. Marys on the Florida border. The marshes are vital to the continued health of the coast. They filter and clean tidal and inland water, and they're one of the most productive ecosystems on earth, providing food, nutrients, and shelter to numerous species—most notably shrimp, crab, and wild birds. The green-and-brown tealike hue of the water along much of the Georgia coast is a result of the marshes' decaying plant matter steeping in the constant shifting of tides.

Sapelo Island

1 *8 mi northeast of Darien.*

The fourth largest of Georgia's coastal isles—and bigger than Bermuda—Sapelo Island is a unique community in North America; it's home to the Geechee, direct descendants of African slaves who speak a creole of English and various African languages. This rapidly dwindling community maintains many traditional African practices, including sweetgrass basket making and the use of herbal medicines the recipes for which have been passed down for generations. It is also a nearly pristine barrier island with miles of undeveloped beaches and abundant wildlife. To take the 40-minute ferry ride from Meridian on the mainland through the expanse of salt marshes to Sapelo Island is to enter a world seemingly forgotten by time.

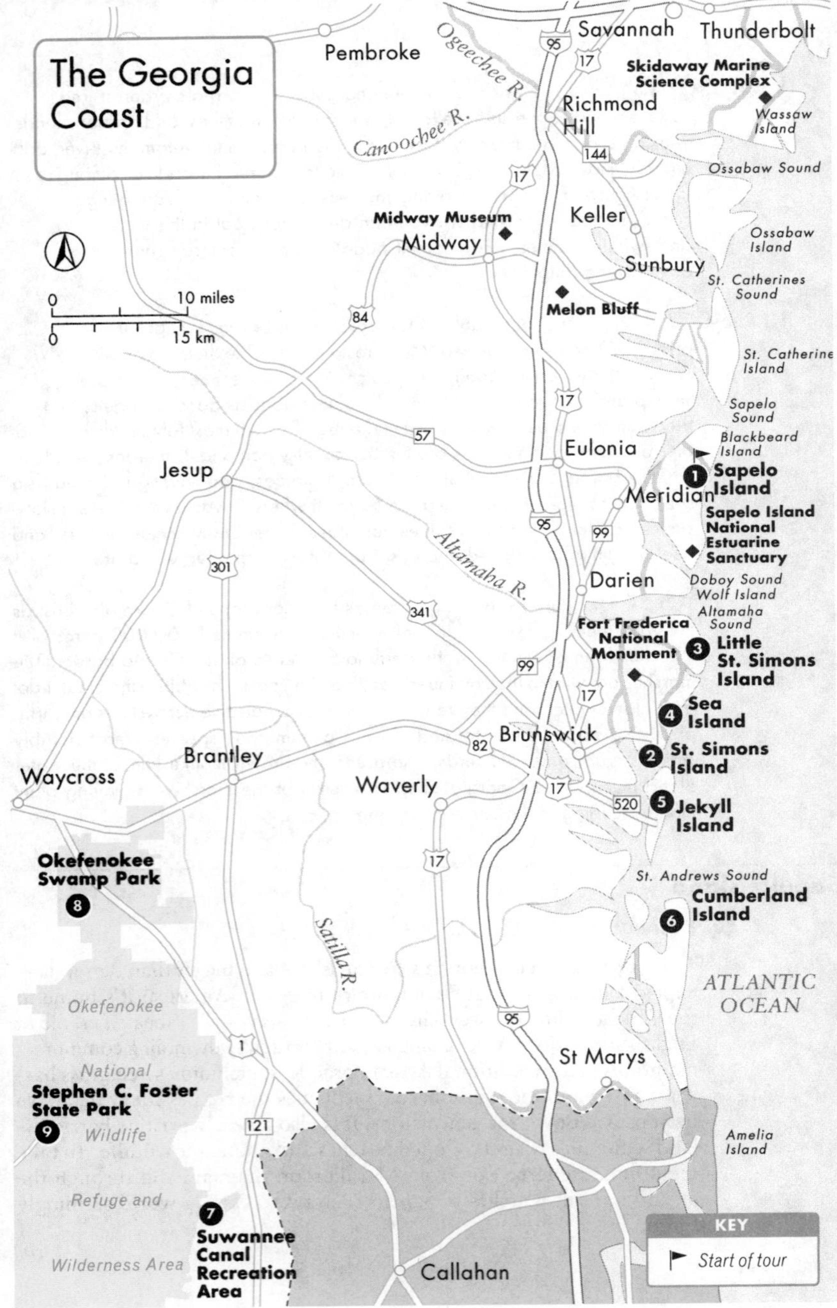

The Georgia Coast
Savannah
Thunderbolt
Pembroke
Ogeechee R.
Skidaway Marine Science Complex
Richmond Hill
Wassaw Island
Canoochee R.
Ossabaw Sound
Midway Museum
Keller
Midway
Ossabaw Island
Sunbury
St. Catherines Sound
Melon Bluff
0
10 miles
0
15 km
St. Catherine Island
Sapelo Sound
Blackbeard Island
Eulonia
Jesup
Sapelo Island
Meridian
Sapelo Island National Estuarine Sanctuary
Altamaha R.
Darien
Doboy Sound
Wolf Island
Altamaha Sound
Fort Frederica National Monument
Little St. Simons Island
Sea Island
Brunswick
St. Simons Island
Brantley
Waycross
Waverly
Jekyll Island
Okefenokee Swamp Park
St. Andrews Sound
Cumberland Island
Satilla R.
ATLANTIC OCEAN
Okefenokee National Wildlife Refuge and Wilderness Area
St Marys
Stephen C. Foster State Park
Amelia Island
Suwannee Canal Recreation Area
Callahan
KEY
Start of tour

A TABBY OF A DIFFERENT STRIPE

To most of the English-speaking world, the word tabby brings to mind dapple-coated cats, but along the coast of Georgia and South Carolina it means something else entirely. Here, tabby is a traditional building material, commonly used in the 17th and 18th centuries and still employed to give a regional signature to modern-day structures.

Tabby is made from sand, oyster shells, and lime. Originally, the lime was leeched out of oyster shells by burning them; today all but the most diehard traditionalists simply use packaged lime, which is mixed with shells, sand, and water to make a cement. At one time entire structures were made from tabby, but now it's most commonly used as a facing, like stucco, and is distinguishable by the shell fragments clearly visible in the finished product. The origins of tabby are disputed. The prevailing theories are either that it came from African culture via the slave trade, or that it was the creation of Spanish settlers.

You can explore many historical periods and natural environments here, but facilities on the island are limited. Note that you can't simply walk up to the dock and catch the ferry—you need to have a reservation for a tour, a campsite, or one of the island's lodgings (or have prearranged plans to stay with island residents). Bring insect repellent, especially in summer, and leave your pets at home. You can rent a bicycle on the island, but you cannot bring a bicycle on the ferry.

Start your visit at the **Sapelo Island Visitor Center,** located in Meridian on the mainland near the Sapelo Island ferry docks. Here you'll see exhibits on the island's history, culture, and ecology, and you can purchase tickets for a round-trip ferry ride and bus tour of the island. The sights that make up the bus tour vary depending on the day of the week but always included are the marsh, the sand dune ecosystem, and the wildlife management area. On Friday and Saturday the tour includes the 80-foot **Sapelo Lighthouse,** built in 1820, a symbol of the cotton and lumber industry once based out of Darien, a prominent shipping center of the time. To see the island's **Reynolds Mansion,** schedule your tour for Wednesday. To get to the visitor center and Meridian Ferry Dock from downtown Darien, go north on Route 99 for 8 mi, following signs for the Sapelo Island National Estuarine Research Reserve. Turn right onto Landing Road at the Elm Grove Baptist Church in Meridian. The visitor center is about a ½ mi down the road. ✉ *Rte. 1, Box 1500 Meridian* ☎ *912/437–3224, 912/485–2300 for group tours, 912/485–2299 for camping reservations* 🌐 *www.sapelonerr.org.*

Hog Hammock Community is one the few remaining sites on the south Atlantic coast where ethnic African-American culture from the slave era has been preserved. The "Salt Water Geechee," Georgia's sea island equivalent to the Gullah, are descendants of slaves who worked the island's plantations during the 19th century. Hog Hammock's 40 residents are the last members of a disappearing culture with its own distinct language and customs. **The Spirit of Sapelo Tours** (✉ Box 7, Sapelo Island, 31327 ☎ 912/485–2170) provides private guided bus tours led by an island native who discusses island life, culture, and history. **Sapelo Culture Day** (☎ 912/485–2197 🌐 www.sapeloislandgeorgia.org.), a celebration of Geechee folklore, music, food, handcrafts, and art takes place in Hog Hammock every year on the third weekend in October. Reservations are required.

Sports & the Outdoors

CANOEING & KAYAKING The Altamaha River, the largest undammed river on the east coast, runs inland from near Darien. You can take expeditions along it with **Altamaha Outpost's Coastal Adventures** (✉ 112 Witcher Rd., Carlton ☎ 912/437–6010), which rents equipment and conducts guided trips from the waterfront in Darien. With them you can explore tidal swamps, marshlands, and Queen and Sapelo islands.

Where to Stay & Eat

$$–$$$ ✕ **Mudcat Charlie's.** This tabby-and-wood restaurant on the Altamaha River sits right in the middle of the Two Way Fish Camp and is a favorite haunt of locals from nearby Darien. The restaurant overlooks the boats moored in the marina, and the seafood is local. Crab stew, fried oysters, and shrimp are the specialties, and the peach and apple pies are made in-house. For a decadent dessert, try the Fanny Kemble, a blend of brandy, Kahlua, Amaretto, ice cream, and chocolate syrup; it's as thick as a sweltering summer's night. It's 1 mi south of Darien on U.S. 17, just after the third bridge. Look for the Two Way Fish Camp sign. *✉ 250 Ricefield Way ☎ 912/261–0055 💳 AE, D, MC, V.*

$–$$$ ✕ **Skipper's Fish Camp.** You'll find this upscale take on the fish camp theme at the foot of Skipper's dock on the Darien River, where the working shrimp boats moor. It has a beautiful courtyard pond that uses water from the river and an open-air oyster bar. Popular menu items include Georgia white shrimp, ribs, and fried flounder. There's usually a wait on the weekends, so get there early. At the southern end of Darien, turn right at Broad just before the river bridge, then take the first left down to the docks. *✉ 85 Scriven St. ☎ 912/437–3474 ✍ Reservations not accepted 💳 AE, D, MC, V.*

¢–$$ ✕ **The Tabby Cottage.** There are lots of novelties—from sweetgrass baskets to roadkill jewelry—prominently displayed at this tabby souvenir shop in Hog Hammock, but the main attraction is the small dining area in the corner. There Nancy and Ceaser Banks work their magic with fresh local shrimp, smothered pork chops, and slow-cooked, open-pit ribs. The secrets of Sapelo cooking are on full display here, and the "killer bread pudding" is as advertised. The old Wurlitzer jukebox by the bathrooms has everything from James Brown to Marvin Gaye to Harold Melvin and the Blue Notes—and it's still just a quarter. *✉ 400 E. Autobahn, Hog Hammock ☎ 912/485–2199 ⊗ Closed Sun. and Mon. No dinner.*

$–$$ 🏨 **The Blue Heron Inn.** Bill Chamberlain's airy, Spanish-style home sits on the edge of the marsh and is only minutes from the ferry at the Sapelo Island Visitors Center. The downstairs dining and living areas have an open, Mediterranean feel, with a large, rustic fireplace and a sweeping view of the marsh. Guest rooms are simply decorated with colorful quilts;

THE NILE OF THE EAST COAST

The Altamaha River is a national treasure. Formed by the confluence of the Ocmulgee and Oconee rivers near Hazelhurst, it's the longest undammed river and the second largest watershed in the eastern United States, covering almost 15,000 square mi. After running its 137-mi course, it spills into the Altamaha Sound, between Sapelo Island and Little St. Simons, at a rate of 100,000 gallons every second, or more than three trillion gallons a year—a flow comparable to Egypt's Nile.

The Altamaha's greatest value lies in the 170,000 acres of river swamps that shoulder the length of its course, serving as refuge to at least 130 endangered plants and animals, including several freshwater mussels found nowhere else in the world. The swamps are also incubators for life-giving organic matter such as leaves, twigs, and other detritus. Spring floods flush this matter downstream, where it's trapped by the salt marshes that stretch between the mouth of the river and Georgia's barrier islands. This natural fertilizer feeds marsh grasses, which in turn feed fungi and phytoplankton, and so on up the food chain.

most have four-poster beds, and all have a view of the marsh. The proprietor, an Athens native, provides drinks and hors d'oeuvres on the third-floor terrace overlooking the Doboy Sound every evening, and his breakfast specialties include lime French toast and shrimp omelets. ⊠ *1 Blue Heron La., Meridian 31319* ☎🖷 *912/437–4304* 🌐 *www.blueheroninngacoast.com* *4 rooms, 1 with bath, 1 apartment* *No room TVs, no phones* *MC, V* *BP.*

$–$$ **Open Gates.** Built by a timber baron in 1876, this two-story, white-frame house on Darien's Vernon Square is filled with antiques and Victorian atmosphere. Innkeepers Kelly and Jeff Spratt hold masters degrees in biology and arrange guided tours of the Altamaha River and surrounding area. A full Southern breakfast and evening cocktails are included in your stay. ⊠ *301 Franklin St., Box 662, Darien 31305* ☎ *912/437–6985* 🖷 *912/882–9427* 🌐 *www.opengatesbnb.com* *5 rooms, 3 with bath* *Pool, library; no room TVs* *MC, V* *BP.*

¢ **The Wallow Lodge.** Cornelia Walker Bailey's memoir of life growing up Geechee on Sapelo, *God, Dr. Buzzard, and the Bolito Man,* has made her a folk hero and focused awareness on the disappearing communities of descendants of African slaves. A stay at Bailey's Wallow Lodge offers a chance to experience the island's distinct culture. Each room is decorated in what Bailey describes as "Sapelo Period" style, with furniture and memorabilia from residents of the island. Cotton chenille, a tradition on Sapelo, and quilted spreads cover the beds. The lodge has a communal kitchen. Unless you make prior arrangements for meals, you must bring your own supplies from the mainland. ⊠ *Box 34, Sapelo Island (1 Main Rd.) 31327* ☎ *912/485–2206* 🖷 *912/485–2174* 🌐 *www.gacoast.com/geecheetours.html* *6 rooms, 2 with shared bath* *No room TVs, no room phones* *No credit cards* *EP.*

Comyam's Campground. The name of Hog Hammock's only campground comes from the Geechee word meaning "come here." And the marsh-side view is just for backpackers coming for a more rustic taste of the island life. *Flush toilets, showers* *30 sites* *Box 7, Sapelo Island (Tom's Hole), 31327* *912/485–2170* *912/485–2174* *comyams£yahoo.com* *$10 per person per day, does not include ferry* *Reservations essential.*

Nightlife

It seems appropriate that the only watering hole in Hog Hammock is named **The Trough** (Box 34 [1 Main Rd.] 912/485–2206). It's a small, bare bones, belly-up-to-the-bar establishment, but owner Julius Bailey serves his beer ice cold, and there's usually a good conversation going on. It's next to the Wallow Lodge (operated by Julius's wife, Cornelia), right "downtown."

en route

Rice, not cotton, dominated Georgia's coast in the antebellum years, and the **Hofwyl-Broadfield Plantation** is the last remaining example of a way of life that fueled an agricultural empire. The main farmhouse, in use since the 1850s when the original house burned, is now a museum with family heirlooms accrued over five generations, including extensive collections of silver and Cantonese china. A guide gives an insightful talk on rural plantation life. Though grown over, some of the original dikeworks and rice fields remain, as do some of the slave quarters. A brief film at the visitor center complements exhibits on rice technology and cultivation, and links to Sierra Leone, from where many slaves were taken because of their expertise in growing rice. *555 U.S. 17N, 4 mi south of Darien* *912/264–7333* *htttp//gastateparks.org/info/hofwyl* *$4* *Tues.–Sat. 9–5, Sun. 2–5:30.*

St. Simons Island

2 *22 mi south of Darien, 4 mi east of Brunswick.*

St. Simons may be the Golden Isles' most developed vacation destination: here you can swim and sun, golf, hike, fish, ride horseback, tour historic sites, and feast on local seafood at more than 50 restaurants. (It's also a great place to bike and jog, particularly on the southern end, where there's an extensive network of trails.) Despite the development, the island has managed to maintain some of the slow-paced Southern atmosphere that made it such draw in the first place. Upscale resorts and the restaurants are here for the asking, but this island the size of Manhattan has only 20,000 year-round residents, so you can still get away from it all without a struggle. Even down in the village, the center of much of St. Simons' activity along Mallory Street, there are unpaved roads and quiet back alleys of chalky white sand that seem like something out of the past.

In the village area, at the more developed south end of the island, you can find shops, several restaurants, pubs, and a popular public pier. For $18 a quaint **"trolley"** (912/638–8954) takes you on a 1½-hour guided tour of the island, leaving from near the pier at 11 and 1 in high season and at 11 in winter.

Named after St. Simons slave Neptune Small, **Neptune Park** (✉ 550 Beachview Dr. ☎ 912/638–0305), on the island's south end in the village, has picnic tables, a children's play park, miniature golf, and beach access. The Casino swimming pool ($4 per person), is open each summer near the St. Simons Lighthouse. Bathrooms are available in the library beside the visitor center.

St. Simons Lighthouse, one of only five surviving lighthouses in Georgia, has become a symbol of the island. It's been in use since 1872; a predecessor was blown up to prevent its capture by Union troops in the Civil War. The **Museum of Coastal History,** occupying two stories of the lightkeeper's cottage, has period furniture and a gallery with photo displays illustrating the significance of shipbuilding on St. Simons, the history of the lighthouse, and the life of James Gould, the first lighthouse keeper. The second floor keeper's quarters contain a parlor, kitchen and two bedrooms furnished with period pieces, including beds with rope mattress suspension. ✉ *101 12th St.* ☎ *912/638–4666* *www.saintsimonslighthouse.org* *$5* *Mon.–Sat. 10–5, Sun. 1:30–5.*

At the north end of the island is the **Fort Frederica National Monument,** the ruins of a fort built by English troops in the mid-1730s to protect the southern flank of the new Georgia colony against a Spanish invasion from Florida. At its peak in the 1740s, it was the most elaborate British fortification in North America. Around the fort are the foundations of homes and shops and the partial ruins of the tabby barracks and magazine. Start your visit at the National Park Service Visitors Center, which has a film and displays. ✉ *Off Frederica Rd. near Christ Episcopal Church* ☎ *912/638–3639* *www.nps.gov/fofr* *$5 per car* *Daily 9–5.*

The white-frame, Gothic-style **Christ Episcopal Church** was built by shipwrights and consecrated in 1886 following an earlier structure's desecration by Union troops. It's surrounded by live oaks, dogwoods, and azaleas. The interior has beautiful stained-glass windows, and several of the pews were handmade by slaves. ✉ *6329 Frederica Rd.* ☎ *912/638–8683* *Donations suggested* *Weekdays 2–5.*

off the beaten path

EBO LANDING – In May 1803, an "Igbo" chief and his West African tribesmen became Geechee folk legends when they "walked back to Africa," drowning en masse rather than submitting to a life of slavery. Captured in what is modern-day Nigeria, the tribesmen disembarked their slave ship and headed straight into Dunbar Creek, chanting a hymn. Though the site is now private property, it can be seen from the road. From the F. J. Torras Causeway, take the first left on Sea Island Road, the first road on St. Simons. After Hawkins Island Drive, look left (north) just before crossing the small bridge at Dunbar Creek. The landing is at the bend in the creek.

Sports & the Outdoors

CRABBING & FISHING

There's no simpler fun for the kids than to grab a crab basket or fishing pole and head to St. Simons Island Pier next to Neptune Park. **St. Simons Island Bait and Tackle** (✉ 121 Mallory St. ☎ 912/634–1888) is near the foot of the pier and is open 364½ days a year. Owners Mike and Trish

Wooten have everything from crabbing and fishing gear to snacks and cold drinks. They also sell one-day, weekly, and yearly licenses.

CYCLING St. Simons has an extensive network of bicycle trails, and you can ride on the beach as well. **Ocean Motion** (✉ 1300 Ocean Blvd. ☎ 912/638–5225 or 800/669–5215) rents bikes for the entire family, from trail bikes to beach bikes to seats for infants. At **Wheel Fun** (✉ 532 Ocean Blvd., just off the intersection with Mallory St. ☎ 912/634–0606) you can rent anything from multispeed bikes to double surreys with bimini tops that look like antique cars and carry four people.

GOLF The top-flight golf facilities at the Lodge at Sea Pines are available only to members and guests of the Lodge and the Cloister, but St. Simons has two other high-quality courses open to the general public. **The Hampton Club** (✉ 100 Tabbystone, St. ☎ 912/634–0255 🌐 www.hamptonclub.com), at the north end of St. Simons on the site of an 18th-century cotton, rice, and indigo plantation, is a *Golf Digest* "Places to Play" four-star winner. The par-72 course designed by Joe Lee is set amid towering oaks, salt marshes, and lagoons. **Sea Palms Golf and Tennis Resort** (✉ 5445 Frederica Rd. ☎ 912/638–3351 or 800/841–6268 🌐 www.seapalms.com) set on a former cotton plantation, offers 27 holes of golf and a driving range.

KAYAKING & SAILING After an instructional clinic, head off to explore the marsh creeks, coastal waters, and beaches with **Ocean Motion** (✉ 1300 Ocean Blvd. ☎ 912/638–5225 or 800/669–5215), which has been giving kayaking tours of St. Simons for more than 20 years. If sailing is your thing, try **Barry's Beach Service** (✉ 420 Arnold Rd. ☎ 912/638–8053 or 800/669–5215) for Hobie Cat rentals and lessons in front of the King and Prince Beach and Golf Resort on Arnold Road. Barry's also has boogie boards and beach funcycles.

SCUBA DIVING Gray's Reef, off Sapelo island, is one of only 12 National Marine Sanctuaries, home to Loggerhead turtles, and part of the northern right whale breeding grounds, all of which make it an attractive place for diving. **Island Dive Center** (✉ 101 Marina Dr., in the Golden Isles Marina on the F. J. Torras Causeway ☎ 912/638–6590 or 800/940–3483) is the place to go for scuba and snorkeling instruction, equipment rental, and charter trips. They also have Jet Skis for rent.

Where to Stay & Eat

★ $$$–$$$$ ✕ **CARGO Portside Grill.** This superb bistro beside the port in Brunswick has a menu that reads like a foodie's wish list, with succulent coastal fare from many ports. All of it is creatively presented by owner–chef Alix Kenagy, formerly of Atlanta's Indigo Coastal Grill. From the sesame catfish to the pasta Veracruz with grilled chicken, smoked tomatoes, poblano peppers, and caramelized onions in a chipotle cream sauce, it's all good here. ✉ *1423 Newcastle St., Brunswick 31520* ☎ *912/267–7330* 💳 *AE, MC, V* ⊗ *Closed Sun. and Mon.*

★ $$$–$$$$ ✕ **Halyards.** When you ask St. Simons restaurateurs which is their pick for the island's best, Halyards gets a nod nearly every time. This polished, elegant restaurant with a laid-back attitude makes everything but the bread and ketchup in house. Chef–owner Dave Snyder's devotion to quality has earned a faithful following of discerning locals and was a favorite haunt of the foreign delegations during the G-8. Headliners are the seared, sushi-grade tuna with a plum wine reduction and the tenderloin. But who could resist chorizo-cheddar grits? There's also a tasting menu with four sample dishes paired with select wines. A winner of Wine Spectator's Award of Excellence, the restaurant serves 200 mostly American wines. Seven servers are sommeliers, so if you don't know, just ask. And there's a kids' menu. ✉ *600 Sea Island Rd., in the Shops At Sea Island shopping center, intersection of Sea Island and Frederica roads* ☎ *912/638–9100* *Reservations essential* *Casual* ▭ *AE, D, MC, V* ⊙ *No lunch.*

$$–$$$$ ✕ **Bennie's Red Barn.** The steaks are cut fresh daily and cooked over an oak fire in this barn of a restaurant that has been serving St. Simons for 50 years. Though there's room for 200 people, it feels just like family with the checkered tablecloths and the big open fireplace. There's also fresh local seafood. The pies are homemade. And there's music next door at Ziggy Mahoney's Thursday–Saturday. ✉ *5514 Frederica Rd.* ☎ *912/638–2844* ⊕ *www.benniesredbarn.com* ▭ *AE, D, MC, V* ⊙ *No lunch.*

$$–$$$$ ✕ **Georgia Sea Grill.** Tucked away behind the kiosks on Mallory Street, this cool and cozy restaurant is popular for its quality seafood and eclectic dishes. Standouts include tender shrimp au gratin, as well as fresh seafood prepared six different ways. Nightly specials are prepared personally by the chef–owners. ✉ *310B Mallory St.* ☎ *912/638–1197* ▭ *AE, D, MC, V* ⊙ *Closed Sun. and Mon. No lunch.*

$$–$$$ ✕ **TwoCan Cafe.** Ken and Kimberly McCord's original idea was an eatery small enough for just two to run. But nothing succeeds like success and their café has morphed into a teeming, casually elegant restaurant with room for 70. The menu features everything from a delicious sauteed crab melt—a TwoCan original—to Ken's special platter of steak and shrimp or oysters. There's live jazz on the weekends. Look for the white- and brown-stripe awning at the north end of Newcastle Street, across the F. J. Torras Causeway in Brunswick. ✉ *1514 Newcastle St., Brunswick 31520* ☎ *912/280–0899* ▭ *MC, V* ⊙ *Closed Sun.*

$–$$$ ✕ **Gnat's Landing.** There's more than a little bit of Margaritaville in this Key West–style bungalow catering to the flip-flop crowd. Seafood is their specialty with a gumbo that's outta sight. Besides being the strangest item on the menu, the fried dill pickle is also the most popular. And, of course, there's the "$8,000 margarita," which is about how much owner Robert Bostock spent in travel and ingredients coming up with the recipe. There's live music Sunday nights and once a year there's "Gnatfest," a party blowout with live bands for all those pesky regulars. ✉ *310 Redfern Village* ☎ *912/638–7378* ▭ *AE, D, MC, V.*

$–$$ ✕ **The Beachcomber Bar and Grill.** No shoes, no shirt, no problem in this small, rustic eatery where the walls are covered with reed mats and the barbecue smokes away on a cooker right beside the front door. Touting themselves as the "onliest Bar-B-Que joint on the island," the Beachcomber has everything from sandwiches to pulled pork, ribs, and brisket by the pound. ✉ *319 Arnold Rd., near Ocean Motion* ☎ *912/634–5699* ▭ *AE, MC, V.*

$ ✕ **Reynolds Street Deli and Cafe.** Choose from one of the 18 deli salad selections made in-house and go sit under the 125-year-old live oak out on the deck. This little red deli across the F. J. Torras Causeway in Brunswick is a laid-back, eat-in, or take-out spot with everything from a roasted barley salad to Southwest pasta with chipotle pepper to chicken piccata with grilled asparagus. Owners Suzanne and Rodney Scaglione offer two- and three-item samplers and nightly dinner specials. ✉ *1402 Reynolds St., Brunswick 31520* ☎ *912/261–2082* ▭ *D, MC, V* ⏲ *Closed Sun.*

¢–$ ✕ **Rafters Blues Club, Restaurant and Raw Bar.** If you're looking for cheap, delicious food and a raucous good time, this is your place. Revelers sit at long picnic tables and heartily partake of the offerings from the prodigious bar and the equally generous kitchen. The restaurant serves ocean fare such as "U-Crak-'em" oysters, baked mussels, and a "sea-style" shrimp quesadilla with caramelized papaya, lime, and molasses. Rafters is open late and presents live entertainment Wednesday through Saturday. ✉ *315½ Mallory St.* ☎ *912/634–9755* ▭ *AE, D, MC, V* ⏲ *Closed Sun.*

$$$$ **Fodor'sChoice** ★ **The Lodge at Sea Island Golf Club.** Simply put, this small resort overlooking the sea is one of the top golf destinations in the country. It has the feel of an elegant English country manor, with exposed ceiling beams, walls covered with tapestries, hardwood floors softened by oriental rugs, and your own private butler, on call 24 hours a day. Dashingly decorated rooms and suites have water or golf-course views, and there are four stellar restaurants. The lodge serves as the clubhouse for the Sea Island Golf Club (though the name is misleading—all of the facilities are on St. Simons Island). Seaside, the first of three courses here, was inspired by St. Andrews in Scotland and has breathtaking panoramas of coastal Georgia. ✉ *St. Simons Island 31522* ☎ *912/638–3611 or 866/465–3563* 🌐 *www.golflodge.com* *40 rooms, 2 suites* *4 restaurants, in-room VCRs, 3 18-hole golf courses, tennis court, pool, spa, hot tub, bar, lounge, Internet, meeting room, children's programs (ages 3–19)* ▭ *AE, D, DC, MC, V* *EP.*

$$$–$$$$ **King and Prince Beach and Golf Resort.** This beachfront property is a cushy retreat with spacious guest rooms and luxurious two- and three-bedroom villas. Guests get golf privileges at the Hampton Club at the Hampton Plantation on St. Simons. The villas are owned by private individuals, so the total number available for rent varies from time to time. ✉ *201 Arnold Rd., 31522* ☎ *912/638–3631 or 800/342–0212* *912/634–1720* 🌐 *www.kingandprince.com* *146 rooms, 2 suites, 41 villas* *2 restaurants, golf privileges, 2 tennis courts, 5 pools (1 indoor), 3 hot tubs, bicycles, bar, lounge, Internet* ▭ *AE, D, MC, V* *EP.*

$$$–$$$$ **Sea Palms Golf and Tennis Resort.** If you're looking for an active getaway, this contemporary complex could be the place for you—it has golf, tennis, a fitness center loaded with state-of-the-art equipment, a beach club, sand-pit volleyball, horseshoes, and bicycling. The guest rooms, touted to be the largest standard rooms in the Golden Isles, have balconies with views of the Marshes of Glynn and the golf course; the furnishings are somewhat unimaginative. Guests have beach club privileges. ✉ *5445 Frederica Rd., 31522* ☎ *912/638–3351 or 800/841–6268*

912/634–8029 *www.seapalms.com* *112 rooms, 23 suites, 11 villas* *2 restaurants, 27-hole golf course, 3 tennis courts, 2 pools, health club, bicycles, volleyball, bar, conference center* *AE, DC, MC, V* *EP.*

$–$$$ **St. Simons Inn.** This Spanish-style inn sits in a prime spot by the lighthouse, only minutes by foot from the village and the beaches. Rooms are basic but clean and comfortable. Suites have whirlpools, and apartments are fully equipped. There's a two-night minimum during high season. Discounts are available for longer stays. *609 Beachview Dr., 31522* *912/638–1101* *912/638–0943* *www.stsimonsinn.com* *34 rooms, 6 suites, 8 apartments* *Pool, microwaves, refrigerators* *AE, D, DC, MC, V* *BP.*

$ **Holiday Inn Express.** With brightly decorated rooms at great prices, this no-smoking facility is an attractive option in this price category. The King Executive rooms have sofas and desks. *Plantation Village, 299 Main St., 31522* *912/634–2175 or 800/787–4666* *912/634–2174* *www.holidayinnexpressssi.com/index.html* *60 rooms* *Cable TV, pool, bicycles, laundry service, meeting room* *AE, D, MC, V* *BP.*

Little St. Simons Island

3 *10–15 min by ferry from the Hampton River Club Marina on St. Simons Island.*

Little St. Simons is 15 minutes by boat from St. Simons, but in character it's a world apart. The entire island is a privately owned resort; there are no telephones and no televisions, and the only habitation, a rustic former hunting lodge on the riverfront with a small guest compound, is so at home with its surroundings that deer graze there in the open. "Luxury" on Little St. Simons means having the time and space to relax and get in tune with the rhythms of nature.

The island's forests and marshes are inhabited by deer, armadillos, raccoons, gators, otters, and more than 200 species of birds. As a guest at the resort, you can take part in guided activities, including tours, horseback rides, canoe trips, and fly-fishing lessons, most for no additional charge. You're also free to walk the 7 mi of undisturbed beaches, swim in the mild surf, fish from the dock, and seine for shrimp and crab in the marshes.

From June through September, up to 10 nonguests per day may visit the island for a fee of $100, which includes the ferry to the island, a tour by truck, lunch at the lodge, and a beach walk. Contact the Lodge on Little St. Simons Island for more information.

Where to Stay

★ $$$$ **Lodge on Little St. Simons Island.** Privacy and simplicity are the star attractions at this rustic island lodge with a capacity of only 30 guests. Staying here is a package deal: you get three meals a day, use of all equipment and facilities, and drinks at the cocktail hour. The friendly, attentive staff includes three full-time naturalists who lead nature talks and tours. Meals, taken family style, feature platters heaped with fresh fish and homemade breads and pies. Transportation from St. Simons Island is also part of the package. *Box 21078, 31522* *912/638–7472 or*

888/733–5774 🖷 912/634–1811 🌐 www.littlestsimonsisland.com 14 rooms, 1 suite Restaurant, pool, beach, boating, fishing, bicycles, horseback riding; no phones, no room TVs AE, D, MC, V FAP.

Sea Island

❹ *5 mi northeast of St. Simons Island.*

Tiny Sea Island—with a full-time population of less than 200—is one of the nation's wealthiest communities, and over the years it's played host to presidents, kings, and counts. (It's not surprising that the island's biggest export is political contributions.) Established by Howard Coffin, the wealthy Detroit auto pioneer who also owned Sapelo Island, Sea Island has been the domain of the well-heeled since 1928. The hub of activity is the Cloister Hotel, which the island's residents use as a country club. Despite the island's air of exclusivity, you can simply drive across the causeway from St. Simons to admire the hotel's beautifully planted grounds and drive past the mansions lining Sea Island Drive. For rentals, contact **Sea Island Cottage Rentals** (Box 30351, 31561 ☎ 912/638–5112 or 800/732–4752 🖷 912/638–5824).

Where to Stay

★ $$$$ **The Cloister.** The Cloister undeniably lives up to its celebrity status as a grand coastal resort. You can get a spacious, comfortably appointed room or suite in the Spanish Mediterranean–style hotel designed by Florida architect Addison Mizner, or stay in the property's more recently built Ocean Houses, which have dramatic suites connected by lavish house parlors with fireplaces and staffed bars. The state-of-the-art spa at the Cloister is in a beautiful building all its own. You also get access to the nearby Sea Island Golf Course. ✉ *Sea Island 31561* ☎ *912/638–3611 or 800/732–4752* 🖷 *912/638–5823* 🌐 *www.cloister.com* *212 rooms, 32 suites 4 restaurants, cable TV, 3 18-hole golf courses, 18 tennis courts, 2 pools, health club, spa, bicycles, bar, 2 lounges, children's programs (ages 3–19), business services, airport shuttle AE, D, DC, MC, V FAP.*

en route

Head south toward Jekyll Island on U.S. 17; you cross over the longest spanning bridge in the state, the soaring **Sidney Lanier Bridge,** which rises 185 feet into the air. It's fittingly named for the Macon native and poet who penned *The Marshes of Glynn,* considered a masterpiece of 19th-century American poetry. It was inspired by the breathtaking vistas of the salt marshes surrounding Brunswick, St. Simons, and Jekyll islands.

Jekyll Island

❺ *18 mi south of St. Simons Island, 90 mi south of Savannah.*

For 56 winters, between 1886 and 1942, America's rich and famous faithfully came south to Jekyll Island. Through the Gilded Age, World War I, the Roaring '20s, and the Great Depression, Vanderbilts and Rockefellers, Morgans and Astors, Macys, Pulitzers, and Goodyears shuttered their 5th Avenue castles and retreated to elegant "cottages" on their wild Georgia island. It's been said that when the island's distinguished winter residents were all "in," a sixth of the world's wealth was represented. Early in World War II the millionaires departed for the last time. In 1947 the state of Georgia purchased the entire island for the bargain price of $675,000.

Jekyll Island is still a 7½-mi playground but is no longer restricted to the rich and famous. A water park, picnic grounds, and facilities for golf, tennis, fishing, biking, and jogging are all open to the public. One side of the island is lined by nearly 10 mi of hard-packed Atlantic beaches; the other by the Intracoastal Waterway and picturesque salt marshes. Deer and wild turkeys inhabit interior forests of pine, magnolia, and moss-veiled live oaks. Egrets, pelicans, herons, and sandpipers skim the gentle surf. Jekyll's clean, mostly uncommercialized public beaches are free and open year-round. Bathhouses with restrooms, changing areas, and showers are open at regular intervals along the beach. Beachwear, suntan lotion, rafts, snacks, and drinks are available at the Jekyll Shopping Center, facing the beach at Beachview Drive. Visitors must pay a parking fee of $3 per entry at the island toll gate. The money is used to support conservation of the island's natural and cultural resources.

The **Jekyll Island History Center** gives tram tours of the Jekyll Island National Historic Landmark District. Tours originate at the museum's visitor center on Stable Road four times a day. Tours at 11 and 2 include two millionaires' residences in the 240-acre historic district. Faith Chapel, illuminated by Tiffany stained-glass windows, is open for meditation daily 2–4. ✉ *100 Stable Rd., I–95, Exit 29* ☎ *912/635–2762 or 912/635–4036* 📠 *912/635–4004* 🌐 *www.jekyllisland.com* 🎫 *$10 (tours at 10 and 4), $17.50 (tours at 11 and 2)* ⏲ *Daily 9–5; tours daily, 10, 11, 2 and 4.*

off the beaten path

DRIFTWOOD BEACH – If you've ever wondered about the effects of erosion on barrier islands, head at low tide to this oceanfront boneyard on North Beach, where live oaks and pines are being consumed by the sea at an alarming rate. The snarl of trunks and limbs and the dramatic, massive root systems of upturned trees are an eerie and intriguing tableau of nature's slow and steady power. It's been estimated that nearly 1,000 feet of Jekyll's beach have been lost since the early 1900s. ✣ *Head to the far north of Jekyll on Beachview Dr. to large curve where the road turns inland. When the ocean is visible through the forest to your right, pull over and take one of the many trails through the trees to the beach.*

Sports & the Outdoors

CYCLING The best way to see Jekyll is by bicycle: a long, paved trail running right along the beach, and there's an extensive network of paths throughout the island. **Jekyll Island Mini Golf and Bike Rentals** (✉ N. Beachview Dr. at Shell Rd. ☎ 912/635–2648) has a wide selection, from the surrey pedal cars, which can hold four people, to lay-down cycles, to the more traditional bikes. **Wheel Fun** (✉ 60 S. Oceanview Dr. ☎ 912/635–9801) sits right in front of the Days Inn and is easy to get to from Jekyll's southern beachfront.

FISHING With 40 years of experience in local waters, Captain Vernon Reynolds of **Coastal Expeditions** (✉ Jekyll Harbor Marina ☎ 912/265–0392 🌐 www.coastalcharterfishing.com) provides half-day and full-day trips in-shore and offshore for fishing, dolphin-watching, and sightseeing. Aside from his ample angling skills, Larry Crews of **Offshore Charters** (✉ Jekyll Island Marina ☎ 912/270–7474 or 912/265–7529 🌐 www.offshore-charters.com) also offers his services as captain to tie the knot for anyone who's already landed the big one.

GOLF The **Jekyll Island Golf Club** (✉ 322 Capt. Wylly Rd. ☎ 912/635–2368) has 63 holes, including three 18-hole, par-72 courses, and a clubhouse. Greens fees are $35, good all day, and carts are $16 per person per course. The 9-hole, par-36 **Historic Oceanside Nine** (✉ N. Beachview Dr. ☎ 912/635–2170) is where Jekyll Island millionaires used to play. Greens fees are $22, and carts are $7.25 for every 9 holes.

HORSEBACK RIDING Take a sunset ride through the Maritime forest along the North Beach with **Victoria's Carriages and Trail Rides** (✉ 100 Stable Rd., in stables at Jekyll Island History Center ☎ 912/635–9500). Morning and afternoon rides include visits to the salt marsh and Driftwood Beach, a boneyard of live oaks and pine trees being reclaimed by the sea. Rides leave from the Clam Creek picnic area across from the Jekyll Island Campground.

NATURE CENTER The **Tidelands Nature Center,** a 4H program sponsored by the University of Georgia, has summer classes for kids and adults on everything from loggerhead sea turtles to live oaks to beach ecology. You can learn how the maritime forest evolves or get a lesson in seining and netting. There are guided nature walks, kayak tours, and canoe and paddleboat rentals. The center also has touch tanks and exhibits on coastal ecology. ✉ *100 Riverview Dr.* ☎ *912/635–5032* 🌐 *www.tidelands4h.org/* *$1 for exhibit* ⏲ *Mar.–Oct., Mon.–Sat. 9–4, Sun 10–2; Nov.–Feb., weekdays 9–4, Sat. 10–2.*

TENNIS The **Jekyll Island Tennis Center** (✉ 400 Capt. Wylly Rd. ☎ 912/635–3154 🌐 www.gate.net/~jitc) has 13 clay courts, with seven lighted for nighttime play. The facility hosts six USTA-sanctioned tournaments throughout the year and provides summer camps for juniors. Courts cost $16 per hour daily 9 AM–10 PM. Reservations for lighted courts are required and must be made prior to 6 PM the day of play.

WATER PARK **Summer Waves** is an 11-acre park using more than a million gallons of water in its 18,000-square-foot wave pool, water slides, children's activity pool with two slides, and circular river for tubing and rafting. Inner tubes and life vests are provided at no extra charge. ✉ *210 S. Riverview Dr.* ☎ *912/635–2074* 🌐 *www.summerwaves.com* *$16.95* ⏲ *Late May–early Sept., Sun.–Thurs. 10–6, Sat. 10–8; hrs vary at beginning and end of season.*

Where to Stay & Eat

★ $$$$ ✕ **Grand Dining Room.** The colonnaded Grand Dining Room of the Jekyll Island Club maintains a tradition of fine dining first established in the 19th century. The huge fireplace, views of the pool, and sparkling silver and crystal all contribute to the sense of old-style elegance. Signature dishes are the pecan-crusted grouper and the filet mignon, but the menu includes local seafood and regional dishes such as Southern fried quail salad. The wine cellar has its own label pinot noir and chardonnay, made by Mountain View Vineyards. ✉ *371 Riverview Dr.* ☎ *912/635–2600* *Reservations essential* *Jacket required* *AE, D, DC, MC, V.*

$$$–$$$$ ✕ **Courtyard at Crane.** When it was built in 1917, the Crane cottage—actually an elegant Italianate villa—was the most expensive winter home on Jekyll Island. Now, as part of the Jekyll Island Club Hotel, the Courtyard at Crane offers casual alfresco dining. The menu focuses on creative salads and entrées inspired by the kitchens of the Napa–Sonoma Valley wine country. You might sample the Mediterranean shrimp salad with mixed greens, green olives, and fresh basil dribbled with lemon juice and olive oil; or lobster fettuccine with a champagne cream sauce. ✉ *375 Riverview Dr., Jekyll Island Club Hotel* ☎ *912/635–2600* *AE, D, DC, MC, V* *No dinner Fri. and Sat.*

$$–$$$ ✕ **Latitude 31.** Right on the Jekyll Island Club Wharf, in the middle of the historic district, Latitude 31 wins the prize for best location. The menu has everything from Oysters Rockefeller to seafood crêpes to bourbon peach- and pecan-glazed pork tenderloin. There's also a kids' menu. ✉ *Jekyll Island Club Wharf* ☎ *912/635–3800* *D, MC, V* *Closed Mon.*

$–$$$ ✕ **The Rah Bar.** A tiny swamp shack raw bar right on the end of the Jekyll Island Club Wharf (connected to Latitude 31), the Rah Bar is the place for a hands-on experience. It's elbow-to-elbow dining (unless you eat at the tables outside on the wharf) with "rah" oysters, "crawdaddies," and "u peel 'em" shrimp. As you eat, you look out on the shrimp boats and the beautiful salt marsh sunsets. ✉ *Jekyll Island Club Wharf* ☎ *912/635–3800* *D, MC, V* *Closed Mon.*

$$ ✕ **SeaJay's Waterfront Cafe & Pub.** A casual tavern overlooking the Jekyll Harbor Marina, SeaJay's serves delicious, inexpensive seafood, including a crab chowder that locals love. This is also the home of the wildly popular Lowcountry boil buffet: an all-you-can-eat feast of local shrimp, corn on the cob, smoked sausage, and new potatoes. There's live music Thursday through Saturday night. ✉ *1 Harbor Point Rd., Jekyll Harbor Marina, 31527* ☎ *912/635–3200* *AE, D, MC, V.*

★ $$$–$$$$ **Jekyll Island Club Hotel.** This sprawling 1886 resort, the focal point of which is a four-story clubhouse, has wraparound verandas and Queen Anne–style towers and turrets. Rooms, suites, apartments, and cottages are decorated with mahogany beds, armoires, and plush sofas and chairs. Two beautifully restored former "millionaires' cottages"—the Crane and the Cherokee—add 23 elegant guest rooms to this gracefully groomed compound. The B&B packages are a great deal. ✉ *371 Riverview Dr., 31527* ☎ *912/635–2600 or 800/535–9547* *912/635–2818* *www.jekyllclub.com* *138 rooms, 19 suites* *3 restaurants,* *cable TV, in-room VCRs, pool, bicycles, croquet, bar, lounge, Internet, meeting room* ▭ *AE, D, DC, MC, V* 🍽 *EP.*

★ $$–$$$ **Beachview Club.** Grand old oak trees shade the grounds of this luxury, all-suites lodging. Rooms are either on the oceanfront or have a partial ocean view; some rooms are equipped with hot tubs and gas fireplaces. Efficiencies have either one king-size or two double beds, a desk, and a kitchenette. The interior design reflects an understated island theme, and the unique meeting room in the Bell Tower accommodates up to 35 people for business events. Higher-end suites have full kitchens. ✉ *721 N. Beachview Dr., 31527* ☎ *912/635–2256 or 800/299–2228* 🖷 *912/635–3770* 🌐 *www.beachviewclub.com* *38 rooms, 6 suites* *Some kitchenettes, microwaves, pool, hot tub, bar, bicycles, Internet, meeting room* ▭ *AE, D, DC, MC, V* 🍽 *EP.*

$$–$$$ **Buccaneer Beach Resort.** If you want to be far from the crowds of the historic district, try this resort where most of the 200-plus rooms and suites have private balconies overlooking the ocean on Jekyll Island's southern shore. Accommodations include one-, two- and three-bedroom suites. Golf and honeymoon packages are available. ✉ *85 S. Beachview Dr., 31527* ☎ *912/635–2261* 🖷 *912/635–3230* 🌐 *www.buccaneerbeachresort.com* *200 rooms, 6 suites* *Restaurant, pool, hot tub, tennis court, playground, fitness center, shuffleboard, bicycles, 2 bars, meeting rooms* ▭ *AE, D, DC, MC, V* 🍽 *EP.*

$$–$$$ **Jekyll Inn.** The buildings of this oceanfront inn are spread across 15 verdant acres. Popular with families, the inn accommodates children under 17 free when they stay with parents or grandparents. Packages include summer family-focused arrangements and romantic getaways. The restaurant offers basic, hearty fare. ✉ *975 N. Beachview Dr., 31527* ☎ *912/635–2531 or 800/736–1046* 🖷 *912/635–2332* 🌐 *www.jekyllinn.com* *262 rooms, 76 villas* *Restaurant, refrigerators, pool, volleyball, spa, 2 bars, lobby lounge, children's programs, playground, laundry service, meeting room* ▭ *AE, D, DC, MC, V* 🍽 *EP.*

$ **Holiday Inn Beach Resort.** Concealed amid the dunes and live oaks of Jekyll's southern oceanfront, this moderately priced resort hotel has a private beach and a boardwalk that winds through the palms and native flora. Each room has a balcony; none have ocean views, but the beach is only a short walk away. Golf packages include your choice of nine area courses. ✉ *200 S. Beachview Dr., 31527* ☎ *912/635–3311 or 800/753–5955* 🖷 *912/635–3919* 🌐 *www.holiday-inn.com/jekyllislga* *198 rooms, 6 suites* *Restaurant, 2 tennis courts, pool, health club, bicycles, bar, lobby lounge, playground, some pets allowed* ▭ *AE, D, DC, MC, V* 🍽 *EP.*

Jekyll Island Campground. At the northern end of Jekyll across from the entrance to the fishing pier, this campground with more than 200 sites can accommodate everything from backpackers looking for primitive sites to RVs needing full hookups. Pets are welcome but there's a $2 fee. *Flush toilets, dump station, running water, guest laundry, showers, electricity, public telephone* ✉ *1197 Riverview Dr., 31527* ☎ *912/635–3021 or 866/658–3021* 🌐 *www.jekyllisland.com* ▭ *AE, MC, V* *$29–$36.*

RENTALS Jekyll's more than 200 rental cottages and condos are handled by **Jekyll Realty** (Box 13096, 31527 912/635–3301 or 888/333–5055 912/635–3303 www.jekyll-island.com). **Parker-Kaufman Realty** (Box 13126, 31527 912/635–2512 or 888/453–5955 912/635–2190 www.parker-kaufman.com/jekyll) handles one- to six bedroom rentals.

Cumberland Island

6 Fodor's Choice ★ *47 mi south of Jekyll Island, 115 mi south of Savannah to St. Marys via I–95, 45 min by ferry from St. Marys.*

Cumberland, the largest of Georgia's coastal isles, is a national treasure. The 18-mi spit of land off the coast of St. Marys is a nearly unspoiled sanctuary of marshes, dunes, beaches, forests, lakes and ponds. And while it has a long history of human habitation, it remains much as nature created it: a dense, lacework canopy of live oak shades sand roads and foot trails through thick undergrowths of palmetto. Wild horses roam freely on pristine beaches. Waterways are homes for gators, sea turtles, otters, snowy egrets, great blue herons, ibises, wood storks, and more than 300 other species of birds. In the forests are armadillos, wild horses, deer, raccoons, and an assortment of reptiles.

In the 16th century, the Spanish established a mission and a garrison, San Pedro de Mocama, on the southern end of the island. But development didn't begin in earnest until the wake of the American Revolution, with timbering operations for shipbuilding, particularly construction of warships for the early U.S. naval fleet. Cotton, rice, and indigo plantations were also established. In 1818, Revolutionary War hero Gen. "Lighthorse" Harry Lee, father of Robert E. Lee, died and was buried near the Dungeness estate of Gen. Nathaniel Greene. Though his body was later moved to Virginia to be interred beside his son, the gravestone remains. During the 1880s the family of Thomas Carnegie (brother of industrialist Andrew) built several lavish homes here. In the 1950s, the National Park Service named Cumberland Island and Cape Cod as the most significant natural areas on the Atlantic and Gulf coasts. And in 1972, in response to attempts to develop the island by Hilton Head developer Charles Fraser, Congress passed a bill establishing the island as a national seashore. Today most of the island is part of the national park system.

Though the **Cumberland Island National Seashore** is open to the public, the only public access to the island is via the *Cumberland Queen*, a reservations-only, 146-passenger ferry based near the National Park Service Information Center at St. Marys. Ferry bookings are heavy in summer. Cancellations and no-shows often make last-minute space available, but don't rely on it. You can make reservations up to six months in advance.

From the park-service docks at the island's south end, you can follow wooded nature trails, swim and sun on 18 mi of undeveloped beaches, go fishing and bird-watching, and view the ruins of Thomas Carnegie's great estate, **Dungeness.** You can also join history and nature walks led by park-service rangers. Bear in mind that summers are hot and humid and that you must bring everything you need, including your own food,

CloseUp

GEORGIA'S BLACK REPUBLIC

A **FTER CAPTURING SAVANNAH** *in December 1864, General William Tecumseh Sherman read the Emancipation Proclamation at the Second African Baptist Church and issued his now famous Field Order Number No. 15, giving freed slaves 40 acres and a mule. The field order set aside a swath of land reaching 30 mi inland from Charleston to northern Florida (roughly the area east of I–95), including the coastal islands, for an independent state of freed slaves.*

Under the administration of General Rufus Saxton and his assistant, Tunis G. Campbell, a black New Jersey native who represented McIntosh County as a state senator, a black republic was established with St. Catherines Island as its capital. Hundreds of former slaves were relocated to St. Catherines and Sapelo islands, where they set about cultivating the land. In 1865 Campbell established himself as virtual king, controlling a legislature, a court, and a 275-man army. Whites called Campbell "the most feared man in Georgia."

Congress repealed Sherman's directive and replaced General Saxton with General Davis Tillison, who was sympathetic to the interests of former plantation owners, and in 1867 Federal troops drove Campbell off St. Catherines and into McIntosh County, where he continued to exert his power. In 1876 he was convicted of falsely imprisoning a white citizen and sentenced, at the age of 63, to work on a chain gang. After being freed, he left Georgia for good and settled in Boston, where he died in 1891. Every year on the fourth Saturday in June, the town of Darien holds a festival in Campbell's honor.

---

soft drinks, sunscreen, and insect repellent. There's no public transportation on the island. *Cumberland Island National Seashore, Box 806, St. Marys 31558 ☎ 912/882–4335 or 888/817–3421 912/673–7747 www.nps.gov/cuis Round-trip ferry $12, day pass $4, annual pass $20 Mar.–Nov., ferry departure from St. Marys daily, 9 AM and 11:45 AM, from Cumberland 10:15 AM and 4:45 PM; Mar.–Sept., Wed.–Sat. additional departure from Cumberland 2:45; Dec.–Feb., Thurs.–Sun., ferry departure from St. Marys 9 AM and 11:45 AM, from Cumberland 10:15 AM and 4:45 PM.*

off the beaten path

THE FIRST AFRICAN BAPTIST CHURCH – This small, one-room church on the north end of Cumberland Island is where John F. Kennedy Jr. and Carolyn Bessette were married on Sept. 21, 1996. Constructed of whitewashed logs, it's simply adorned with a cross made of sticks tied together with string and 11 hand-made pews seating 40 people. It was built in 1937 to replace a cruder 1893 structure used by former slaves from the High Point–Half Moon Bluff community. The Kennedy–Bessette wedding party stayed at the Greyfield Inn, built on the south end of the island in 1900 by the Carnegie family. *North end of Cumberland near Half Moon Bluff.*

Sports & the Outdoors

KAYAKING Whether you're a novice or skilled paddler, **Up The Creek** (✉ 111 Osborne St., St. Marys ☎ 912/882–0911) can guide you on kayak tours through some of Georgia and Florida's most scenic waters. Classes include navigation, tides and currents, and kayak surfing and racing. Trips include Yulee, the St. Marys River, and the Cumberland Sound. The sunset dinner paddle includes a meal at Borrell Creek Restaurant overlooking the marsh.

WATER PARK If the heat has you and the kids are itching to get wet, head to the **St. Marys Aquatic Center** (✉ 301 Herb Bauer Dr., St. Marys ☎ 912/673–8118 🌐 www.ci.st-marys.ga.us/aquatic.htm), a full-service water park where you can get an inner tube and relax floating down the Continuous River or corkscrew yourself silly sliding down the Orange Crush.

Where to Stay & Eat

ISLAND ★ $$$$ **Greyfield Inn.** Once described as a "Tara by the sea," this turn-of-the-20th-century Carnegie family home is Cumberland Island's only accommodation. Built in 1900 for Lucy Ricketson, Thomas and Lucy Carnegie's daughter, the inn is filled with period antiques, family portraits, and original furniture that evoke the rustic elegance of a bygone era. And with a 1,000-acre private compound, it offers a solitude that seems a thing of the past as well. Prices include all meals, transportation, tours led by a naturalist, and bikes. Nonguests can dine here, too. ✉ *8 N. 2nd St., Box 900, Fernandina Beach, FL 32035-0900* ☎ *904/261–6408 or 888/243–9238* 🖷 *904/321–0666* 🌐 *www.greyfieldinn.com* *16 rooms, 4 suites* *Restaurant, bicycles, bar; no TV, no room phones* 💳 *D, MC, V* *FAP.*

MAINLAND $–$$$ **Lang's Marina Restaurant.** Everything's made from scratch at this popular waterside restaurant, including the desserts. And the seafood comes fresh from the owner's boats. You can order shrimp, scallops, or oysters, or opt for the Captain's Platter and get some of everything. Fish is available fried, grilled, or blackened. ✉ *307 W. St. Marys St., near the waterfront park, St. Marys* ☎ *912/882–4432* 💳 *MC, V* *Closed Sun. and Mon. No dinner Tues. No lunch Sat.*

$–$$$ **Seagle's.** Sitting on the corner of St. Marys and Osborne streets, Seagle's has the best view around—a 180-degree panorama of downtown and the St. Marys River. In the kitchen, chef Oliver Farlin likes things with a bit of a twist, so he serves his Lowcountry boil with a spicy lobster sauce over grits. There's a Friday night seafood buffet featuring jambalaya, crab legs, and broiled scallops. And the Saturday night chef's table has all-you-can-eat dungeness and snow crab. For dessert don't miss the "death by chocolate." ✉ *100 W. St. Marys St., near the Cumberland Island ferry office, St. Marys* ☎ *912/882–4187* 💳 *AE, D, DC, MC, V* *Closed Mon. and Tues.*

$–$$ **The Williams' Saint Marys Seafood and Steak House.** Don't let the tabby-and-porthole decor fool you. In a region full of seafood restaurants, this one's full of locals for a reason. The food is fresh, well made, and plentiful, and the price rarely gets so right. The menu includes frogs' legs and gator tail for the more adventurous. ✉ *1837 Osborne Rd., St. Marys* ☎ *912/882–6875* 💳 *MC, V.*

$$–$$$ **Spencer House Inn.** At this pink Victorian inn, built in 1872, some rooms have expansive balconies that overlook the neatly tended grounds, and some have antique claw-foot bathtubs. Innkeepers Mike and Mary Neff will prepare picnic lunches if you ask. The inn is a perfect base for touring the St. Marys and Cumberland Island area. *200 Osborne St., St. Marys 31558 912/882–1872 or 888/840–1872 912/882–9427 www.spencerhouseinn.com 14 rooms, 1 suite AE, D, MC, V BP.*

¢ **Cumberland Island Inn and Suites.** Children under 18 stay free at this moderately priced hotel on Osborne Road, 3 mi from the St. Marys waterfront. The spacious suites have complete kitchens, large refrigerators, sleeper sofas, executive work desks with ergonomic chairs, and free high-speed Internet access. Some suites feature Jacuzzis. *2710 Osborne Rd., St. Marys 31558 912/882–6250 or 800/768–6250 912/882–4471 www.cumberlandislandinn.com 79 rooms, 39 suites Restaurant, in-room data ports, microwaves, refrigerators, pool, bar AE, D, MC, V BP.*

¢ **Riverview Hotel.** This circa 1916 tabby hotel has an airy, Dodge City atmosphere that's straight out of the Old West. Among the features are a double veranda, mounted deer heads on the wall, an old camera collection in a glass case, and antique, high-backed typewriters on display. It's across from the Cumberland Island Ferry office, flanked on one side by Seagle's Restaurant and on the other by Seagle's Saloon. With its very reasonable rates, it's something of an econo-resort right on the St. Marys waterfront. *105 Osborne St., St. Marys 31558 912/882–3242 www.stmaryswelcome.com 18 rooms Restaurant, cable TV, bar AE, D, DC, MC, V BP.*

Nightlife

The closer you get to borders, the more pronounced allegiances become. A case in point is **Seagle's Saloon and Patio Bar** (105 Osborne St., St. Marys 912/822–1807), a little watering hole not far from the Florida state line, that's festooned with University of Georgia Bulldog memorabilia. Bawdy bartender Cindy Deen is a local legend who keeps the customers entertained.

en route

On your way back from Cumberland Island, stop in at the **St. Marys Submarine Museum** (102 W. St. Marys St., across from the Cumberland Island Ferry office 912/882–2782 http://stmaryssubmuseum.com). This small, fascinating museum is a natural in a town that owes much of its existence to the nearby Kings Bay Naval Base, home of the Atlantic Trident fleet. The museum has an extensive collection of photos and artifacts, including uniforms, flags, scale models, designs, sonar consoles, hatches, working steering positions, and a working periscope that looks out into the St. Marys River. Other features are a deep-sea diver's suit, a display honoring eight submariners who have won the Medal of Honor, dioramas, and a library.

OKEFENOKEE NATIONAL WILDLIFE REFUGE

Larger than all of Georgia's barrier islands combined, the Okefenokee National Wildlife Refuge covers 730 square mi of southeastern Georgia and spills over into northeastern Florida. From the air, all roads and almost all traces of human development seem to disappear into this vast, seemingly impenetrable landscape, the largest intact freshwater wetlands in the contiguous United States. The rivers, lakes, forests, prairies, and swamps all teem with seen and unseen life: alligators, otters, bobcats, raccoons, opossums, white-tailed deer, turtles, bald eagles, red-tailed hawks, egrets, muskrats, herons, cranes, red-cockaded woodpeckers, and black bears all make their home here. The term *swamp* hardly does the Okefenokee justice. It's the largest peat-producing bog in the United States, with numerous and varied landscapes, including aquatic prairies, towering virgin cypress, sandy pine islands, and lush subtropical hammocks.

During the last Ice Age, 10,000 years ago, this area was part of the ocean flow. As the ocean receded, a dune line formed, which acted as a dam, forming today's refuge. The Seminole Indians named the area "Land of the Quivering Earth." And if you have the good fortune to walk one of the many bogs, you can find the earth does indeed quiver like Jell-o in a bowl.

There are three gateways to the refuge: an eastern entrance at the U.S. Fish and Wildlife Service headquarters in the Suwannee Canal Recreation Area, near Folkston; a northern entrance at the Okefenokee Swamp Park near Waycross; and a western entrance at Stephen C. Foster State Park, outside the town of Fargo. Visiting here can feel frustrating, because none of the parks encompass everything the refuge has to offer; you need to determine what your highest priorities are and pick your gateway on that basis. The best way to see the Okefenokee up close is to take a day trip from whichever gateway you choose. You can take an overnight canoeing-camping trip into the interior, but be aware that access is restricted by permit. Plan your visit between September and April to avoid the biting insects that emerge in May, especially in the dense interior.

Suwannee Canal Recreation Area

❼ *8 mi southwest of Folkston via Rte. 121.*

The east entrance of the Okefenokee near Folkston offers access into the core of the refuge by way of the man-made Suwannee Canal. The most extensive open areas in the park—Chesser, Grand, and Mizell Prairies—branch off the canal and contain small natural lakes and gator holes. The prairies are excellent spots for sport fishing and birding, and it's possible to take one- and two-hour guided boat tours of the area at the Okefenokee Adventures concession, near the visitor center. The concession also has equipment rentals and food at the Camp Cornelia Cafe. The visitor center has a film, exhibits, and a mechanized mannequin that tells stories about life in the Okefenokee (which sounds hokey but

CloseUp

TRAIN-SPOTTING, SOUTHERN STYLE

The town of Folkston is best known as a gateway to the Okefenokee, but it also has a growing reputation as a hot spot for train aficionados. As many as 60 trains a day pass through the "Folkston Funnel," a double track that serves as the main artery for traffic in and out of Florida; just to the north, in Waycross, is the largest rail yard in the southeast.

The Funnel—located on Tower Street, just off Main—is decidedly spectator-friendly: it has a covered track-side viewing platform equipped with ceiling fans, a scanner to monitor radio traffic between trains, bathrooms, picnic tables, a grill, and lights that flood the tracks for nighttime viewing. The Folkston chamber of commerce has even put together a Web page (www.folkston.com/trains/trains.htm) for train watchers. Park yourself on the platform and you're likely to see trains carrying everything from automobiles to grain to orange juice. Several Amtrak passenger trains pass daily as well, including the Autotrain.

is surprisingly informative). A boardwalk takes you over the water to a 50-foot observation tower. Hikers, bicyclists, and private motor vehicles are welcome on the Swamp Island Drive; several interpretive walking trails may be taken along the way. Picnicking is permitted. *Refuge headquarters Rte. 2, Box 3330, Folkston 31537 912/496–7836 okefenokee.fws.gov $5 per car; 1-hr tours $12.50; 2-hr tours $20.50 Refuge Mar.–Oct., daily ½ hr before sunrise–7:30 PM; Nov.–Feb., daily ½ hr before sunrise–5:30 PM.*

Sports & the Outdoors

CANOEING & CAMPING Wilderness canoeing and camping in the Okefenokee's interior are allowed by reserved permit only (for which there's a $10 fee per person per day). Permits are difficult to come by, especially in the cooler seasons. Reservations can be made only by phone. You need to call **refuge headquarters** (912/496–3331 Weekdays 7 AM–10 AM) within two months of your desired starting date to make a reservation. Guided overnight canoe trips can be arranged by **Okefenokee Adventures** (Rte. 2, Box 3325, Folkston 31537 912/496–7156 www.okefenokeeadventures.com).

Where to Stay & Eat

$$–$$$ **The Vickery House Bistro.** This cozy bungalow is adding a little flair to the downtown Folkston scene as one of the area's few options for fine dining—and the only place in town with a liquor license. Almost everything is made in house, from the blue cheese bacon puffs to the Old South crab cakes. For dessert try the butter pecan cheese cake. *108 S. 1st St. 912/496–7942 or 800/337–5436 AE, D, MC, V Closed Sun. and Mon. No dinner Tues.–Thur. No lunch Sat.*

¢–$ **Okefenokee Restaurant.** Everything's home-cooked at this half-century-old local institution, and from the fried shrimp to the fried whole catfish, it's all good. They open early for breakfast and have a daily lunch buffet from 11 to 2, which includes a drink for just $7. *103 S. 2nd St., Folkston 31537 912/496–3263 D, MC, V Closed Sun.*

$$–$$$ **The Inn at Folkston.** Eight miles from the Suwannee Canal Recreation Area entrance to the Okefenokee, the Inn at Folkston is a minirefuge with a huge front veranda, hot tub, porch swings, and rocking chairs. This beautifully restored, craftsman-style inn is filled with antiques, and each room is uniquely decorated. The romantic Lighthouse Room has a king-size bed, a fireplace, and a screened-in porch; the Oriental Room has an Asian theme. Ask about midweek business rates. ✉ *509 W. Main St., Folkston 31537* ☎ *912/496–6256 or 888/509–6246* 🌐 *www.innatfolkston.com* *4 rooms* *Hot tub, library, Internet; no room TVs, no smoking* *AE, D, MC, V* *BP.*

$–$$ **The Folkston House.** This white, two-story B&B built in 1900 has elegantly furnished rooms with antiques and period furniture. Each evening homemade refreshments are served in the parlor and in the morning there's a full Southern breakfast in the Victorian dining room or outside on the dining porch. ✉ *802 Kingsland Dr., Folkston 31537* ☎ *912/496–3455 or 877/312–6726* 🌐 *www.folkstonhouse.com* *6 rooms* *No phones in some rooms, no TV in some rooms, no smoking* *AE, D, MC, V* *BP.*

¢–$ **Western Motel.** Though nondescript, this clean, moderately priced hotel is a good base for visiting the Okefenokee. The rooms are spacious, and there are executive suites and a Jacuzzi suite. ✉ *1207 S. 2nd St., Folkston 31537* ☎ *912/496–4711* *912/496–2075* *30 rooms, 3 suites* *In-room data ports, pool, no-smoking rooms* *AE, D, DC, MC, V* *BP.*

Okefenokee Swamp Park

8 *8 mi south of Waycross via U.S. 1.*

This park serves as the northern entrance to the Okefenokee National Wildlife Refuge, offering easy access as well as exhibits and orientation programs good for the entire family. The park has a 1⅓-mi nature trail, observation areas, wilderness walkways, an outdoor museum of pioneer life, and boat tours into the swamp that reveal its unique ecology. A boardwalk and 90-foot tower are excellent places to glimpse cruising gators and birds. A 1½-mi train tour (included in the admission price) passes by a Seminole village and stops at Pioneer Island, a re-created pioneer homestead, for a 30-minute walking tour. ✉ *5700 Okefenokee Swamp Park Rd., Waycross* ☎ *912/283–0583* *912/283–0023* 🌐 *www.okeswamp.com* *$12, plus $4–$8 for boat tours* *Daily 9–5:30.*

Where to Stay & Eat

$$–$$$ ✕ **Pond View Downtown.** Though the pond is long gone, everything else is just as it should be in one of the more elegant dining options in Waycross. This restaurant in the historic district has 18-foot ceilings, hardwood floors, and white table cloths, and the food makes some interesting variations on a Southern theme: there's a catfish fillet with a cream pecan sauce, and the crab cakes are excellent. For dessert, try the bread pudding with rum butterscotch sauce. ✉ *311 Pendleton St., Waycross* ☎ *912/283–9300 or 866/582–5149* *AE, MC, V* *Closed Sun. and Mon. No lunch.*

$$ **Pond View Inn.** Sara and David Rollison's small B&B is just upstairs from their Pond View Restaurant and has a similar elegance. There's a sense of refinement in these double rooms with views of the downtown historic district. Rooms feature queen beds, private baths, and Jacuzzis. Dinner from the restaurant downstairs is also available in the rooms. *311 Pendleton St., Waycross 31501* *912/283–9300 or 866/582–5149* *www.bbonline.com/ga/pondview/index.html* *4 rooms* *No smoking* *AE, MC, V* *BP.*

$ **Holiday Inn Waycross.** What makes this chain hotel stand out is its bargain package deal: for $74 you get a double room and two adult admissions to the Okefenokee Swamp Park ($24 value), including the boat ride, train ride, and attractions. *1725 Memorial Drive, 31501* *912/283–4490 or 800/465–4329* *912/283–4490* *www.ichotelsgroup.com* *142 rooms, 9 suites* *Putting green, pool, exercise equipment, lounge, bar, laundry, car rental, some pets allowed (fee)* *AE, D, DC, MC, V* *BP.*

Laura S. Walker State Park. One of the few state parks named for a woman, this 600-acre park honors a Waycross teacher who championed conservation. The park, 9 mi northeast of the Okefenokee Swamp Park, has campsites with electrical and water hookups. Be sure to pick up food and supplies on the way. Boating and skiing are permitted on the 120-acre lake, and there's an 18-hole golf course. Rustic cabins cost $20 per night, plus $2 parking. *5653 Laura Walker Rd., Waycross 31503* *912/287–4900 or 800/864–7275* *http://gastateparks.org/info/lwalker* *44 tent, trailer, RV campsites; group campsite sleeps 142* *Picnic area, pool, fishing, playground* *$17–$21.*

Stephen C. Foster State Park

9 *18 mi northeast of Fargo via Rte. 177.*

Named for the songwriter who penned *Swanee River,* this 80-acre island park is the southwestern entrance to the Okefenokee National Wildlife Refuge and offers trips to the headwaters of the Suwannee River, Billy's Island—site of an ancient Indian village—and a turn-of-the-20th-century town built to support logging efforts in the swamp. The park is home to hundreds of species of birds and a large cypress-and-black-gum forest, a majestic backdrop for one of the thickest growths of vegetation in the southeastern United States. Park naturalists lead boat tours and recount a wealth of Okefenokee lore while you observe alligators, birds, and native trees and plants. You may also take a self-guided excursion in a rental canoe or a motorized flat-bottom boat. Campsites and cabins are available. *Rte. 1, Box 131, Fargo 31631* *912/637–5274* *http://gastateparks.org/info/scfoster* *$5 per vehicle for National Wildlife Refuge* *Mar.–mid-Sept., daily 6:30 AM–8:30 PM; mid-Sept.–Feb., daily 7 AM–7 PM.*

off the beaten path

SUWANNEE RIVER VISITORS CENTER – A high-definition film and exhibits on swamp, river, and timbering history are part of the fare at this visitor center in Fargo. There are also animal exhibits featuring black bears, bobcats, otters, snakes, fish and birds. The 7,000-square-foot facility is ecofriendly, employing solar-powered fans, composting toilets that use no water, decking made from recycled plastic, insulation from recycled newspapers, and a retaining wall made from recycled dashboards and electrical cables. Boating is available. ✉ *124 Suwannee River Dr. at U.S. 441 bridge over Suwannee River, near Fargo* ☎ *912/637–5274* 🌐 *http://gastateparks.org/info/scfoster* *Free* ⏲ *Wed.–Sun. 9–5.*

Where to Stay

Stephen C. Foster State Park. The park has sites for all types of camping as well as basically equipped, two-bedroom cottages that can sleep up to eight. Be aware that the gates of the park are closed between sunset and sunrise—there's no traffic in and out for campers, so you need to stock up on supplies before the sun goes down. You can book sites and cabins up to 11 months in advance. *Rte. 1, Box 131, Fargo 31631* ☎ *912/637–5274 or 800/864–7275* 🌐 *http://gastateparks.org/info/scfoster* *66 tent, trailer and RV sites, pioneer camping, 9 cottages* *$15–$90.*

THE COASTAL ISLES & THE OKEFENOKEE A TO Z

To research prices, get advice from other travelers, and book travel arrangements, visit www.fodors.com

AIR TRAVEL

AIRPORTS The coastal isles are served by the Brunswick Golden Isles Airport, 6 mi north of Brunswick, and the McKinnon St. Simons Airport on St. Simons Island. McKinnon accommodates light aircraft and private planes.

Airport Information **The Brunswick Golden Isles Airport** ✉ 500 Connole St. ☎ 912/265-2070 🌐 www.glynncountyairports.com. **McKinnon St. Simons Island Airport** ✉ Off Demere Rd. ☎ 912/628-8617.

CARRIERS The Brunswick Golden Isles Airport is served by Delta affiliate Atlantic Southeast Airlines (ASA), with four daily flights from Atlanta.

Airlines & Contacts **Atlantic Southeast Airlines** ☎ 800/282-3424.

BOAT & FERRY TRAVEL

Cumberland Island, Sapelo Island, and Little St. Simons are accessible only by ferry or private launch. The *Cumberland Queen* serves Cumberland Island and the *Anne Marie* serves Sapelo Island. The Lodge on Little St. Simons Island operates a private launch that is available only to overnight or day-trip guests by prior arrangement.

Boat & Ferry Information **Anne Marie** Sapelo Island Visitors Center, Rte. 1 Box 1500, Darien 31305 ☎ 912/437-3224 or 912/485-2300 🌐 www.sapelonerr.org. **Cumberland Queen** ☞ Cumberland Island National Seashore Box 806, St. Marys, 31558 ☎ 912/882-4335 or 888/817-342 912/673-7747 🌐 www.nps.gov/cuis. **The Lodge on Little St. Simons Island** Box 21078, Little St. Simons Island 31522 ☎ 912/638-7472 or 888/733-5774 912/634-1811 🌐 www.littlestsimonsisland.com.

CAR TRAVEL

From Brunswick take the Jekyll Island Causeway ($3 per car) to Jekyll Island and the Torras Causeway to St. Simons and Sea Island. You can get by without a car on Jekyll Island and Sea Island, but you'll need one on St. Simons. You cannot bring a car to Cumberland Island, Little St. Simons, or Sapelo.

Car Rental Information **Avis Rental Car** ✉ Brunswick Golden Isles Airport ☎ 912/267-0326 ✉ St. Simons ☎ 912/638-2232 ⊕ www.avis.com. **Hertz Rental Car** ✉ Brunswick Golden Isles Airport ☎ 912/265-3645 or 800/654-3131 ✉ McKinnon St. Simons Island Airport ☎ 912/638-2522 ⊕ www.hertz.com.

VISITOR INFORMATION

The Brunswick and the Golden Isles Visitors Center provides helpful information on all of the Golden Isles. For camping, tour, ferry and other information and reservations contact the Georgia State Parks Department.

Tourist Information **Brunswick and the Golden Isles Visitors Center** ✉ 2000 Glynn Ave., Brunswick 31520 ☎ 912/264-5337 or 800/933-2627 ⊕ www.bgivb.com. **Georgia State Parks** ☎ 800/864-7275 for reservations, 770/398-7275 within metro Atlanta, 404/656-3530 for general park information ⊕ www.gastateparks.org.

SOUTHWEST GEORGIA

10

VISIT FDR'S "LITTLE WHITE HOUSE"
in the village of Warm Springs ⇨*p.365*

PIG OUT IN COLUMBUS,
the world pit-barbecue capital ⇨*p.368*

SETTLE INTO A COTTAGE
at Callaway Gardens Resort ⇨*p.367*

SENSE THE CIVIL WAR'S TRAGIC TOLL
at the Andersonville Historic Site ⇨*p.373*

SOAK UP THE TARA-STYLE GRANDEUR
at Pebble Hill Plantation ⇨*p.376*

By Jody Jenkins **THE ROLLING AGRICULTURAL LANDSCAPES** of a slower, older South, where things remain much the same as they were for generations, can be found within a couple of hours' drive of Atlanta's high-rise bustle. Here, scattered along a vast coastal plain that covers much of the southern part of the state, small towns evoke a time when the world was a simpler place where people lived close to the land and life was measured on a personal scale. In southwest Georgia, peanuts, corn, tobacco, and cotton are the lifeblood of the local economies, and you're as likely to see a tractor on a country road as a car.

People here live far from the hassles of modernity—the daily grind of traffic jams and suburban sprawl. The accents are slow and seductive. Small towns and petite country hamlets beckon with their charming town squares and elegant bed-and-breakfasts. In southwest Georgia the inclination simply to relax is contagious—it can saturate you slowly but completely, like syrup on a stack of pancakes.

Despite the quiet pace of life here, this is the land of such greats as President Jimmy Carter, writers Erskine Caldwell and Carson McCullers, singers "Ma" Rainey and Otis Redding, and baseball-legend Jackie Robinson. For a time even Franklin Delano Roosevelt was drawn here; he returned again and again for the healing mineral waters of Warm Springs. Columbus was the birthplace of Coca-Cola, the first product ever to gain truly international fame. And Habitat for Humanity, an international nonprofit organization that builds low-income housing, was also born and is still based here, in Americus.

Exploring Southwest Georgia

Because of the long distances involved, the best way to see southwest Georgia is by car. Between Cordele and Archery, you can opt out of driving duties and hop a ride on the SAM Shortline—a great way to see the countryside.

This chapter takes you southwest through Pine Mountain—more accurately foothills than true mountains—and Warm Springs, down to Columbus, and southeast to the Americus and Plains area. This last area consists of rolling farmland dotted with dairies, large pecan groves, and corn, peanut, and cotton fields. Farther south the rolling farmland gives way to the broad open stretches of cotton country en route to Tifton and Thomasville.

About the Restaurants

Columbus has gained renown as the pit-barbecue capital of the world, and indeed this region of Georgia does lovely things by slow-cooking pork over green oak. Barbecue joints in the area, such as Columbus's own Country's On Broad, are homey, hands-on affairs that specialize in lots of high-quality country-style cooking at relatively low prices.

There are numerous other dining options as well. Though you won't find the same culinary range as in urban areas, there are plenty of small surprises in the most unexpected of places. The Windsor, a grand Victorian resort hotel in the small town of Americus, and Liam's, in Thomasville, are both known for their updated versions of Southern cui-

Numbers in the text correspond to numbers in the margin and on the Southwest Georgia map.

If you have 3 days

Start in **Warm Springs** 1 at the Little White House Historic Site/FDR Memorial Museum, where Franklin D. Roosevelt stayed during his visits here. Pick up provisions for a picnic and head south on Route 85 and west on Route 190 to Dowdell's Knob, President Roosevelt's favorite picnic spot, overlooking the Pine Mountain Valley Community. After lunch go horseback riding with Roosevelt Stables in the Franklin D. Roosevelt State Park. Overnight in **Pine Mountain** 2. Start your second day off at the Callaway Gardens Resort and Preserve, where you can visit one of the largest free-flight butterfly conservatories in North America. If you're feeling adventurous, head southeast to the Flint River Outdoor Center to test your skills in a canoe or kayak. Drive to **Columbus** 3, the pit-barbecue capital of the world, and stop in at Country's On Broad to taste some of the city's finest. Take a walking tour of Heritage Corner and see the Pemberton House, the birthplace of Coca-Cola; follow this up with a peek at the house of blues singer Gertrude "Ma" Rainey. On the third day, stop by the Port Columbus National Civil War Naval Museum, where you can walk the decks of reconstructed warships, before heading out to **Plains** 4. Spend the rest of the morning at the Jimmy Carter National Historic Site, which includes the railroad depot where the former president launched his bid for the White House. Then visit the farm where Carter grew up during the Depression. Finish your visit at Koinonia, a utopian farming commune (call ahead to arrange lunch and a tour).

If you have 5 days

Follow the three-day itinerary above and on the fourth day, drive north on Route 49 through the rolling countryside to **Americus** 5 and the nearby Andersonville National Historic Site, the remains of the infamous Confederate prisoner-of-war penitentiary. Continue north on Route 49 and east on Route 26 below Oglethorpe. About 3 mi past Montezuma you start to notice small green signs on the mailboxes containing biblical quotes: you're in Mennonite country now. Stop in at Yoder's Deitsch Haus for a hearty meal, followed by a visit to the bakery next door. Settle in for the drive south to **Thomasville** 7, where you can spend the night. The next day visit the Pebble Hill Plantation and the Lapham-Patterson House, a fascinating Victorian home with 45 exit doors.

---

sine. Elsewhere you can often encounter traditional cuisine with a twist, including fried green tomatoes with feta, yam purée, and various kinds of dressed-up grits.

WHAT IT COSTS

$$$$	$$$	$$	$	¢
over $22	$16–$22	$11–$16	$7–$11	under $7

Prices are for a main course at dinner, excluding sales tax of 6%.

About the Hotels

Lodging in the area runs the gamut from elegant four-star properties to low-profile but unique B&Bs to reliable and inexpensive chain hotels. RV parks and campgrounds are also available.

WHAT IT COSTS				
$$$$	$$$	$$	$	¢
over $220	$160–$220	$110–$160	$70–$110	under $70

Prices are for two people in a standard double room in high season, excluding service charges and 12% tax.

Timing

Because many of the towns in the region are off the beaten path, crowds are rarely a problem, though spring (which comes early) and fall (which comes late) are the most popular seasons. If you're not fond of the heat, March–May and September–December are the best times to visit. During this time, book well in advance for the more popular hotels and B&Bs in Pine Mountain, Warm Springs, and Thomasville.

Though it requires a certain amount of resilience to visit in summer, there's something quintessentially Southern about the heat that shapes the psychology of the region and makes it an interesting time to visit. Roadside stands are filled with fruits and vegetables, trucks heavily laden with watermelons traverse the back roads, and the song of the cicadas pulses day and night. In some areas in summer you can find off-season deals on hotel accommodations. By June, summer is already in full swing, and in late July and early August the days can be hot and humid, with temperatures reaching into the high 90s and low 100s. Dress accordingly, and bring plenty of sunscreen.

WESTERN FOOTHILLS & FARMLAND

You won't be able to visit this slice of Georgia without feeling the influence of two generations of American presidents, Franklin Roosevelt and Jimmy Carter. About a hundred miles south of Atlanta, near the Alabama border, Pine Mountain and Warm Springs retain vestiges of their earlier identities as rural retreats. Americus and Plains are two more towns seemingly cut from the pages of the past; not far from Amicus is Andersonville, site of the Civil Wars most notorious prison. In the center of the region is Columbus, Georgia's second-largest city and home to America's largest military complex, Fort Benning.

Warm Springs

1 *27 mi southeast of LaGrange via U.S. 27, Rte. 18, and Rte. 194.*

Renowned for centuries for the supposed healing properties of its thermal waters, Warm Springs is where the Creek Indians brought their wounded warriors when all other treatments had failed. In the early 1920s, news spread that a young Columbus native and polio victim, Louis Joseph, had made a dramatic recovery after extensive therapy in the springs. Word

Barbecue Completely unrelated to grilling, barbecue in this part of the world means pork—shoulder, ribs, or even whole hogs—slow-roasted over logs of green blackjack oak and hickory, placed deep down in a brick or earth pit. Known as the pit-barbecue capital of the world, Columbus in particular is a good place to sample this treat. Barbecue comes "chipped," or chopped up; "sliced," with slabs or wedge cuts; as "plates," which usually means with Brunswick stew and/or cole slaw on the side; or as sandwiches, on a hamburger bun. Sauces range from the tomato-based red, which is sweeter, to the mustard-based yellow sauce, which usually has a zip to it.

The Presidential Legacy In still-tangible ways, two presidents cast long shadows over southwest Georgia. Franklin Roosevelt, the son of privilege, came to Warm Springs dozens of times during the last 20 years of his life to exercise his polio-ridden body in the mineral waters. Moved by the poverty and struggles of his neighbors, Roosevelt helped form many of the New Deal programs that revolutionized life in the rural South. One, the Rural Electrification Administration, literally brought the light to another president-to-be, Jimmy Carter, who as a young boy grew up on a 360-acre Depression-era farm only hours from Warm Springs. Today you can visit the places where these presidents lived (and still live, in Jimmy Carter's case): the Little White House Historic Site/FDR Memorial Museum in Warm Springs, and the Jimmy Carter National Historic Site in Plains.

Rural Landscapes From the broad, flat reaches of the southern coastal plain to the rolling countryside farther north near Americus and Plains, southwest Georgia seems one limitless ocean of agriculture and farmlands. Small towns appear adrift against the vast, open stretches of peanuts, cotton, and tobacco that surround them, persisting against the relentless heat. Towering pecan groves suddenly transform a sweltering tongue of road into a shadowy corridor. Great round bales of hay lay haphazardly coiled in the fields like champagne corks from some celestial celebration. Out on the horizon an old clapboard shack or tobacco barn sags against the evening sky, begging the question of its own history. There's a slow, monotonous patience in these landscapes that invites consideration and meandering. And at times the vacancy seem to pulse like the song of the cicadas that fills the summer air.

---

reached Franklin Delano Roosevelt (1882–1945), who had contracted polio, and a 20-year relationship began between him and this remote mountain village, where he built a cottage for his visits that came to be known as the Little White House. Roosevelt's experiences here led to the effort to eradicate polio around the world through the founding of the March of Dimes, and his encounters with his poor rural neighbors fueled ideas for his Depression-era New Deal recovery programs. After Roosevelt's death, the town fell on hard times, but an influx of crafts and antiques shops in the 1980s has revitalized Warm Springs somewhat.

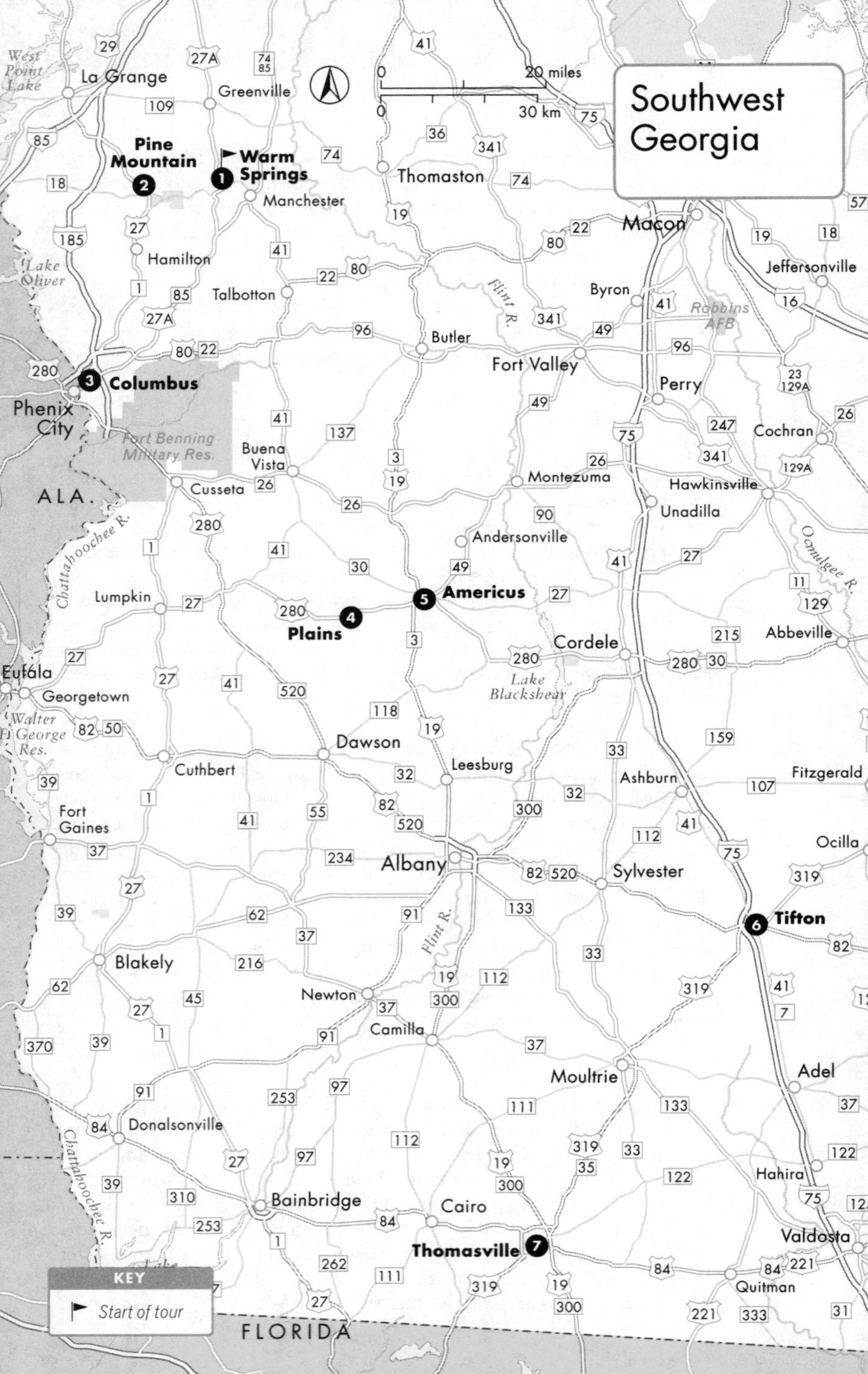

Southwest Georgia
0
20 miles
0
30 km
Warm Springs
Pine Mountain
Columbus
Plains
Americus
Tifton
Thomasville
La Grange
West Point Lake
Greenville
Manchester
Thomaston
Macon
Hamilton
Lake Oliver
Talbotton
Byron
Robbins AFB
Jeffersonville
Butler
Fort Valley
Perry
Phenix City
Fort Benning Military Res.
Buena Vista
Cusseta
Cochran
Montezuma
Hawkinsville
Unadilla
ALA.
Chattahoochee R.
Flint R.
Ocmulgee R.
Andersonville
Lumpkin
Cordele
Abbeville
Lake Blackshear
Eufala
Georgetown
Walter F. George Res.
Dawson
Cuthbert
Leesburg
Ashburn
Fitzgerald
Fort Gaines
Albany
Sylvester
Ocilla
Blakely
Newton
Camilla
Moultrie
Adel
Donalsonville
Hahira
Bainbridge
Cairo
Valdosta
Quitman
FLORIDA
KEY
Start of tour

Fodor's Choice ★ The **Little White House Historic Site/FDR Memorial Museum**, at the south end of town, contains the modest three-bedroom cottage in which Roosevelt stayed during his visits here. The cottage, built in 1932, remains much as it did the day he died here (while having his portrait painted) and includes the wheelchair Roosevelt designed from a kitchen chair. The unfinished portrait is on display along with the 48-star American flag that flew over the grounds when Roosevelt died. The FDR Memorial Museum includes an interesting short film narrated by Walter Cronkite, exhibits detailing Roosevelt's life and New Deal programs, and some of Roosevelt's personal effects, such as his 1938 Ford, complete with the full hand controls he designed. Admission here allows you to also visit the nearby pools where Roosevelt took his therapy. ✉ *401 Little White House Rd.* ☎ *706/655–5870* 🌐 *www.fdr-littlewhitehouse.org* *$5* ⏲ *Daily 9–4:45.*

Where to Stay

$–$$ **Grand Wisteria Plantation.** Built circa 1832, this elegant neoclassical plantation home 9 mi north of Warm Springs is listed on the National Register of Historic Places. You're free to wander the 13-acre grounds, on which deer, rabbits, and turkeys roam. Mahogany period pieces, Victorian settees, sleigh beds, and claw-foot tubs fill the rooms. Candlelight dinners and bistro baskets are available by request, and there are weekend packages and seasonal specials. ✉ *15380 Roosevelt Hwy./Alt. 27, Box 397, Greenville 30222* ☎ *706/672–0072* 🌐 *www.grandwisteria.com* *5 rooms* *Some in-room DVDs, hot tubs, library; no TV in some rooms, no kids under 16* *MC, V* *BP.*

¢–$ **Hotel Warm Springs Bed & Breakfast Inn.** Right in downtown Warm Springs, this old hotel has plenty of character and is a great bargain. The guest rooms have oak furniture and 12-foot ceilings with crown molding. Prices are even cheaper if you opt not to have breakfast, though this means you'll miss out on the "Southern breakfast feast," complete with cheese grits. ✉ *47 Broad St., 31830* ☎ *706/655–2114 or 800/366–7616* 🌐 *www.hotelwarmspringsbb.org* *13 rooms* *Cable TV* *AE, D, MC, V* *BP.*

Pine Mountain

❷ *14 mi west of Warm Springs via Rte. 18 and Rte. 194.*

Pine Mountain Ridge is the last foothill of the Appalachian chain, and the town of Pine Mountain rests at the same elevation of Atlanta, making it generally cooler than the surrounding communities. The flora and fauna here reflect the town's Appalachian connections. Most visitors are lured by the surrounding area's large-scale attractions—such as Callaway Gardens Resort and Preserve—and are then pleasantly surprised that the small-town berg has a folksy, inviting downtown square. Antiques figure prominently in the area economy and shops abound in the town center.

No mere tourist curiosity, **Kimbrough Brothers General Store** is the real thing: a fourth-generation working general store, housed in the oldest building (late 19th century) in Pine Mountain. Clothes, shoes, hats, farm and garden implements, rockers, spurs, and just about anything else you can think of are all sold here under one roof. There's even a potbellied stove where you can warm yourself when the weather turns cold. ✉ *44 Main St.* ☎ *706/663–2528* ⏲ *Weekdays 8–6.*

Just south of the village lies the area's main draw: **Callaway Gardens Resort and Preserve,** a 14,000-acre, nonprofit, family-style golf and tennis resort with elaborate gardens. This botanical wonderland was developed in the 1930s by textile magnate Cason J. Callaway and his wife Virginia, who were determined to breathe new life into the area's dormant cotton fields. With more than 1,000 varieties, the **Day Butterfly Center** is one of the largest free-flight conservatories in North America. **Mountain Creek Lake** is well stocked with largemouth bass and bream. ✉ *U.S. 27* ☎ *706/225–5292 or 800/225–5292* 🌐 *www.callawaygardens.com* 🎫 *$14; free to overnight guests* ⏲ *Daily 9–5.*

At the **Wild Animal Safari,** a few miles northwest of town, you can either drive yourself or ride a bus through a 500-acre animal preserve. You may not believe you're still in Georgia: camels, llamas, antelopes, and hundreds of other exotic animals traipse around freely, often coming close to vehicles. An added plus is the **Old McDonald's Farm,** a petting zoo with jovial monkeys and writhing-reptile pits. ✉ *1300 Oak Grove Rd.* ☎ *706/663–8744 or 800/367–2751* 🌐 *www.animalsafari.com* 🎫 *$13.95* ⏲ *Mar. and Apr., daily 10–6:30; May–Labor Day, daily 10–7:30; Labor Day–Feb., daily 10–5:30; call to confirm hrs and tour-bus schedule.*

Sports & the Outdoors

CANOEING & KAYAKING

About 45 minutes from Pine Mountain between Thomaston and Columbus is the **Flint River Outdoor Center** (✉ 4429 Woodland Rd., Rte. 36 at the Flint River, Thomaston ☎ 706/647–2633 🌐 www.flintriverfun.com), with 5 mi of river courses where you can test your skills in everything from a float tube to kayaks running Class II rapids. The more daring can try Yellow Jacket Shoals, the Flint's only Class III/IV run—rumored to have destroyed more canoes than any other rapids in the Southeast.

HORSEBACK RIDING

The mountain terrain makes the Pine Mountain area an interesting place for horseback riding. **Roosevelt Stables** (✉ 1063 Group Camp Rd. ☎ 706/628–7463 or 877/696–4613), in Franklin D. Roosevelt State Park, has 25 mi of trails and offers everything from one-hour rides to overnight trips complete with cowboy breakfasts.

Where to Stay & Eat

$$–$$$$ ✕ **Carriage & Horses.** International cuisine is served in this Victorian house just north of town and overlooking the horse pastures of Grey Eagle Farm. The eclectic menu includes escargot, alligator with lemon sauce, seared Alaskan salmon, quail with garlic mashed potatoes, and filet mignon in a wine reduction. The restaurant is locally renowned for its sunset dining, and there's frequently live music. ✉ *607 Butts Mill Rd.* ☎ *706/663–4777* ✍ *Reservations essential* 💳 *AE, D, MC, V* ⏲ *Closed Mon. No dinner Tues.*

★ $–$$ **Callaway Gardens Resort and Preserve.** With 14,000 acres of landscaped and wild grounds and countless shops and restaurants, this sprawling resort dwarfs many nearby towns. Accommodations range from fairly basic motel-style guest rooms to fully furnished cottages and villas, all of them with lovely panoramic vistas and verdant garden settings. A 10-mi paved bike trail meanders through the property. There's great fishing in 13 stocked ponds, and the golf courses are famously impressive. Various meal and recreation packages are available. ✉ *U.S. 27, 31822* ☎ *706/663–2281 or 800/225–5292* 🖷 *706/663–5090* 🌐 *www.callawaygardens.com* *749 units, 10 suites, 155 cottages, 57 villas* *4 restaurants, 2 cafés, kitchenettes, cable TV, 2 18-hole golf courses, miniature golf, 10 tennis courts, lake, health club, beach, waterskiing, fishing, bicycles, Ping-Pong, racquetball, volleyball, 2 bars, lounge, shops* 💳 *AE, D, MC, V* *EP.*

$–$$ **Chipley Murrah House B&B.** One mile from the Callaway Gardens entrance and near downtown Pine Mountain, this lavish inn occupies a high-style Queen Anne Victorian dating to 1895. A favorite perch in this period-decorated house is the wraparound porch, decked out with rockers, swings, and wicker chairs. Hardwood floors, 12-foot ceilings, and decorative molding are among the beautifully preserved original details. In addition to the guest rooms there are two cottages, one with two bedrooms and one with three bedrooms. ✉ *207 W. Harris St., Box 1154, 31822-1154* ☎ *706/663–9801 or 888/782–0797* 🌐 *www.chipleymurrah.com* *4 rooms, 2 cottages* 💳 *AE, MC, V* ⏲ *Closed Jan.* *BP.*

$ **Days Inn.** There are no surprises at this old standby, but it's clean and close to downtown Pine Mountain and area attractions. Check the Web site for significantly cheaper specials. ✉ *368 S. Main Ave., Box 1570, 31822* ☎ *706/663–2121 or 800/325–2525* 🖷 *706/663–2169* 🌐 *www.daysinn.com* *40 rooms* *Microwaves, refrigerators, cable TV, pool, some pets allowed (fee)* 💳 *AE, D, MC, V* *BP.*

CAMPING ¢–$ **Pine Mountain Campground.** A favorite pick of *Where to Retire* magazine, this large, well-kept campground just north of town has everything from tent sites to full RV hookups to cabins. "Megasites" are paved sites with patios, grills, and fences for privacy. You can swim in the pool and play miniature golf, volleyball, and horseshoes. Pets on a leash are welcome. ✉ *8804 Hamilton Rd./U.S. 27, 31822–4711* ☎ *706/663–4329* 🌐 *www.camppinemountain.com* *75 sites* *Flush toilets, full hookups, partial hookups (water and electric), dump station, drinking water, guest laundry, showers, grill, public telephone, general store, play area, swimming (pool)* *Full hookups $23, partial hookups $21, tent sites $19, cabins $75* 💳 *MC, V.*

Shopping

Downtown Pine Mountain is flush with antiques stores, and **Chanticleer** (✉ 141 Main St. ☎ 706/663–7878), specializing in French-country and English-cottage styles, sits right in the middle of it all. The **Pine Mountain Antique Mall** (✉ 230 S. Main St. ☎ 706/663–8165 or 800/613–9072), open daily, has several vendors under one roof. **Sweet Home Antiques** (✉ 149 Main St. ☎ 706/663–7776) carries Southern primitive art and Oriental rugs.

Columbus

❸ *35 mi south of Pine Mountain via U.S. 27.*

Today one of Georgia's largest cities, Columbus literally rose from the ashes of the Civil War to become a major industrial force in the state. Chartered in 1827 along the falls of the Chattahoochee River as a "trading town," Columbus harnessed the energy of the river to power looms and spinning machines for the growing textile industry being fed by surrounding cotton fields. Because of its location at the head of the Chattahoochee, the town quickly became a prominent inland shipping port, and by the start of the Civil War, it was the largest manufacturing center south of Richmond. The town was second only to Richmond in supplying uniforms, weapons, and other goods to the Confederate army, making Columbus a prime target for Union troops. But because of its distance from the battle lines, it wasn't until April 16, 1865—a week after the war had ended at Appomattox—that the 13,000 cavalrymen known as "Wilson's Raiders" attacked Columbus and nearby West Point and burned all the war industries to the ground. The textile mills soon recovered, however, and grew to a prominence that dwarfed their prewar significance. Textiles still play a major role in the Columbus economy.

Today, Columbus is perhaps best known as the home of Fort Benning, the largest infantry-training center in the world; it's also the site of Columbus College's Schwob School of Music, one of the finest music schools in the South. A project to rejuvenate the downtown area has included the renovation of old manufacturing and ironworks buildings and the creation of the 12-mi Riverwalk to highlight the city's river origins; this linear park along the Chattahoochee is ideal for jogging, strolling, biking, and rollerblading.

Heritage Corner consists of several historic buildings that you can visit via a guided walking tour given by the Historic Columbus Foundation, headquartered in an 1870 building. Among these buildings is the 1840 four-room **Pemberton House,** home to Columbus native John Pemberton (1831–88), the pharmacist who created Coca-Cola. Other structures here include the one-room early-19th-century **log cabin** that is said to be the oldest extant structure in Muscogee County, the 1828 federal-style **Walker-Peters-Langdon House,** and the 1840s **Woodruff Farm House.** ✉ *708 Broadway* ☎ *706/323–7979 or 706/322–0756* 🎟 *Tours $5 per person, 2-person minimum* ⏲ *Tours daily at 2.*

The child of minstrel-show performers, blues singer Gertrude Pridgett (1886–1939), more famously known as "Ma" Rainey, the "mother of the blues," toured in tent shows, levee camps, and cabarets throughout the South and Midwest. She recorded more than 100 songs and entertained with the greats, including Louis Armstrong, Bessie Smith, and Tommy Dorsey. She's buried in **Porterdale Cemetery,** an extension of an old slave cemetery, on 10th Avenue. The **Ma Rainey house** (✉ 805 5th Ave. 🌐 www.gawomen.org/honorees/raineyg.htm), listed on the National Register of Historic Places, can be viewed from the exterior only. The house is listed with other black-heritage sites on a self-guided-tour brochure available at the **Convention and Visitors Bureau** (✉ 900 Front Ave. ☎ 800/999–1613 for brochure).

Military buffs and anybody else with an interest in the nation's Civil War past should make it a point to visit the **Port Columbus National Civil War Naval Museum,** which has been lauded for its interactive approach and high-tech exhibits. This is one of the nation's most innovative Civil War museums, heavily focused on the Confederate navy and its influence on the U.S. navy's subsequent development. You can walk the decks of partially reconstructed Civil War ships, and get a glimpse of what combat was like in a full-scale replica of the CSS *Albermarle,* an ironclad combat simulator. ✉ *1002 Victory Dr.* ☎ *706/327–9798* 🌐 *www.portcolumbus.org* *$4.50* *Daily 9–5.*

Columbus State University's **Coca-Cola Space Science Center,** part of the Riverwalk, houses a planetarium, an observatory, a replica of an Apollo space capsule, a space shuttle, and other space-related exhibits. ✉ *701 Front Ave.* ☎ *706/649–1470* 🌐 *www.ccssc.org* *Free; planetarium show $4* *Tues.–Thurs. 10–4, Fri. 10–5, Sat. 11:30–6, Sun. 1:30–4.*

★ One of the city's most notable attractions, the **Columbus Museum** is the state's largest art and history museum and one of the largest in the Southeast. Collections focus heavily on American art ranging from colonial portraiture to the Ashcan School to provocative contemporary works. Other exhibits concentrate on science and the history of the Chattahoochee Valley. A branch of the Columbus Museum, the **Columbus Museum Uptown** (✉ 1004 Broadway, Suite 101 ☎ 706/221–7580) hosts changing exhibits of contemporary arts and crafts in all media. Classes and workshops are also available. This branch is open Tuesday–Saturday noon–8. ✉ *1251 Wynnton Rd.* ☎ *706/649–0713* 🌐 *www.columbusmuseum.com* *Free* *Tues., Wed., Fri., and Sat. 10–5, Thurs. 10–9, Sun. 1–5.*

The **Smith-McCullers House Museum** was the childhood home of novelist and short-story-writer Carson McCullers (1917–67), who lived here from 1925 to 1944. Among her best-known works are *The Heart Is a Lonely Hunter* and *Reflections in a Golden Eye*. The house is now the site of Columbus State University's Carson McCullers Center for Writers and Musicians, but tours are available by appointment. ✉ *1519 Stark Ave.* ☎ *706/568–2054* 🌐 *www.mccullerscenter.org* *Free* *Tours by appointment.*

off the beaten path

NATIONAL INFANTRY MUSEUM – It requires some effort to get here, but if you're a military buff it's worth the trouble. Exhibits in this four-story museum include weaponry, uniforms, and equipment of all kinds, and they examine the history of the U.S. infantry. Among the items displayed are Civil War–era dominoes, a gas mask for a horse, a prisoner-of-war uniform, and a Springfield rifle from World War I. Also here are a 100-seat theater, a gallery of military art, and a gift shop. To get to the museum take I–185 south to the Victory Drive exit. ✉ *Baltzell St., Bldg. 396, Fort Benning, 6 mi south of Columbus* ☎ *706/545–6762* 🌐 *www.benningmwr.com/museum.cfm* *Free* *Weekdays 10–4:30, weekends 12:30–4:30.*

Where to Stay & Eat

$$–$$$$ ✕ **Olive Branch Cafe.** The menu of this dapper downtown eatery reflects heavy Italian influences, with chicken *rollatini* (rolled in prosciutto), lasagna, and pasta primavera. The influence of other cuisines is apparent in the surf and turf, tropical crab cakes, and a center-cut pork chop wrapped in apple-smoked bacon and served with a key-lime-mango chutney. ✉ *1032 Broadway* ☎ *706/322–7410* 💳 *AE, MC, V* ⊙ *Closed Sun. No lunch.*

$–$$ ✕ **Buckhead Grill.** This upscale American grill is touted as one of the best-value restaurants in Georgia. Beef plays a prominent role on the menu, with Kansas City sirloin and Caribbean rib eye as headliners; Monday is steak night. Seafood is also done well here, in such entrées as grilled salmon marinated in a mouthwatering, house-made teriyaki sauce. The wine list is said to be the most extensive in Columbus. You can dine inside or on the patio. ✉ *5010 Armour Rd.* ☎ *706/571–9995* 💳 *AE, D, DC, MC, V* ⊙ *No lunch.*

★ ¢–$$ ✕ **Country's On Broad.** In a land where barbecue reigns supreme, Country's does it not only with taste but with a certain style as well. You can eat inside the restaurant, a converted bus terminal decorated with '50s flair, or sit at a table inside the 1946 bus-turned-diner. The barbecue, cooked over hickory and oak, includes not only pork, but also chicken, beef, turkey, ribs, and brisket; buttermilk fried chicken is also on the menu. Besides the two sides and bread, the plates come with a selection of four sauces of varying heats. There are also options for kids and a semi-low-calorie menu. A couple of other branches are around town. ✉ *1329 Broadway* ☎ *706/596–8910* 🌐 *www.countrysbarbecue.com* 💳 *MC, V.*

¢ ✕ **Fountain City Coffee.** This bustling little coffee shop in the heart of downtown has everything for the coffee hound, including a low-carb latte. Signature drinks include a "mint mocha," a "blackberry Viennese latte," and a "mimosa mocha" (chocolate and orange); smoothies are also served here. Breakfast *panini* (grilled sandwiches) are served in the morning, and the lunch menu includes soups, salads, sandwiches, tapas, and other snacks. The pastries are wonderful, and the cheesecakes are the best around. Occasionally there's live music. ✉ *1007 Broadway* ☎ *706/494–6659* 💳 *AE, MC, V.*

$$–$$$$ Fodor'sChoice ★ **Rothschild-Pound House Inn.** If pedigree is any indication of quality, then it's no wonder that this B&B has garnered praise of all sorts. Set in an 1870 Second Empire Victorian home with a sweeping veranda, the inn is an elegant reminder of old Columbus, with four-poster mahogany beds, hardwood floors, and period antiques. Original artwork by owner Garry Pound decorates the walls. Occupying the entire front of the second floor of the main house, the Golden Suite has windows on two sides, a separate sitting room, a balcony with rocking chairs, and a Jacuzzi. Guests have access to a nearby health club. ✉ *201 7th St., 31901* ☎ *706/322–4075 or 800/585–4075* 📠 *706/494–8156* 🌐 *www.thepoundhouseinn.com* *16 rooms, 4 cottages* *Refrigerators, cable TV, in-room VCRs, Internet* 💳 *AE, D, MC, V* *BP.*

$–$$$ **Gates House Inn.** Highlights of this exquisitely restored property, which actually consists of two inns, include lush gardens and beautifully appointed interiors straight out of a Victorian novel. Gates Inn West is an 1880 twin-chimney colonial revival decorated with Oriental rugs and antiques. In warm weather you can breakfast on the front porch. Rooms in the Gates Inn East, with its bamboo-furniture-furnished screened porch, are decorated according to such themes as Versailles and Mardi Gras. The extravagant breakfast at either inn might include homemade sourdough bread and brown-sugar, cinnamon, and pecan French toast. Guests have access to a nearby health club. ✉ *800 Broadway, 31901* ☎ *706/324–6464 or 800/891–3187* 🖷 *706/324–2070* 🌐 *www.gateshouse.com* *10 rooms* *Cable TV, in-room DVD/VCR players, bicycles, free parking* ▭ *AE, MC, V* 🍴 *BP.*

$$ **Wyndham Columbus.** On the site of a vast 1860s complex of warehouses, factories, mills, and a Confederate arsenal, this hotel is a key component of the Columbus Ironworks Convention and Trade Center just across the street. Rooms are simple but tasteful, and many overlook the Riverwalk park. With a terrific location between Broadway's Victorian district and the Riverwalk, and a reliable restaurant (Pemberton's), the Wyndham is a focal point of the city's downtown revival. ✉ *800 Front Ave., 31901* ☎ *706/324–1800 or 800/996–3426* 🖷 *706/576–4413* 🌐 *www.wyndham.com* *177 rooms, 4 suites* *Restaurant, in-room data ports, minibars, cable TV, pool, health club, bar, lounge, laundry service, Internet, meeting rooms, free parking, no-smoking rooms* ▭ *AE, D, DC, MC, V* 🍴 *EP.*

$ **Country Inn and Suites.** This is a reliable chain property that's ideal if you're staying for more than a few days. The rooms and suites—decorated in a country style, with gingham fabrics and grapevine wreaths on the walls—are spacious, and all have coffeemakers and other helpful amenities. ✉ *1720 Fountain Ct., 31904–1604* ☎ *706/660–1880 or 800/456–4000* 🖷 *706/243–3473* 🌐 *www.countryinns.com* *62 rooms, 13 suites* *Microwaves, refrigerators, cable TV, pool, gym, free parking* ▭ *AE, D, DC, MC, V* 🍴 *BP.*

Nightlife & the Arts

The 2,000-seat **RiverCenter for the Performing Arts** (✉ 900 Broadway ☎ 706/256–3600, 888/332–5200 for tickets), home to the Columbus Symphony Orchestra, the third oldest orchestra in the country, always has something interesting on tap. The center has hosted the likes of Itzhak Perlman, the Moscow Boys Choir, Bobby McFerrin, and Al Green, and has featured such Broadway shows as *Fiddler On the Roof* and *Miss Saigon*.

Since its opening in 1871, the **Springer Opera House** (✉ 103 10th St. ☎ 706/324–1100, 706/324–5714 for tours), a National Historic Landmark, has been known as one of the finest opera houses in the South. The theater hosts musicals, dramas, and regional talent.

Plains

4 *55 mi southeast of Columbus via U.S. 27 and U.S. 280.*

This rural farming town—originally named the Plains of Dura after the biblical story of Shadrach, Meshach, and Abednego—is the birthplace and current home of former president Jimmy Carter and his wife Rosalynn. The Carters still live in a ranch-style brick house on the edge of town—the only home they have ever owned. Although it's the hub of a thriving farming community, the one-street downtown paralleling the railroad tracks resembles a 1930s movie set.

Each September the town comes alive with the **Plains Peanut Festival,** which includes a parade, live entertainment, arts and crafts, food vendors, and races. The annual softball game pitting President Carter and Secret Service agents against alumni from Plains High School is always a festival highlight.

★ At the **Jimmy Carter National Historic Site** you can still see the late-1880s **railroad depot** that housed his 1976 presidential campaign headquarters; in January 1977, the "Peanut Special," an 18-car train filled with supporters, departed from here for Carter's inauguration in Washington. The vintage phones here play recordings of Carter discussing his grassroots run for the White House. A couple of miles outside of town on the Old Plains Highway is the 360-acre **Jimmy Carter Boyhood Farm,** where the Carter family grew cotton, peanuts, and corn; it has been restored to its original appearance before electricity was introduced. Period furniture fills the house, and the battery-powered radio plays Carter's reminiscences of growing up on a Depression-era farm. **Plains High School,** in which the Carters were educated, is now a museum and the headquarters of the historic site. You can visit these places and tour the town by picking up a self-guided tour book at the visitor center or the high school. ✉ *Plains High School, 300 N. Bond St.* ☎ *229/824–4104* 🌐 *www.nps.gov/jica* 🎫 *Free* 🕒 *Daily 9–5.*

When he's in town, President Carter still teaches Sunday school at the **Maranatha Baptist Church** (✉ 148 Rte. 45 ☎ 229/824–7896 🌐 www.sowega.net/~alcrump/maranatha/), about ½ mi past Plains High School on Buena Vista Road. Area visitor centers keep current listings of Carter's scheduled church appearances, and you can get updates on the church's Web site. If you plan to come to hear him teach, book accommodations well in advance as they fill up quickly once his schedule is announced. Sunday school classes begin at 10, but the church opens at 8:30; arrive early if you want to get a spot.

Where to Stay

$–$$ **Plains Historic Inn.** Each spacious room of this inn, in a turn-of-the-20th-century furniture store directly above the Antiques Mall on Main Street, is decorated to reflect the aesthetics of a particular decade between the 1920s and the 1980s. The street-side rooms have a view across Main Street, where Billy Carter's old gas station still sits along with the railroad depot from which President Carter ran his bid for the White House. The inn books up fast when President Carter is teaching Sunday school and during the Peanut Festival. ✉ *106 Main St., Box 314, 31780* ☎ *229/824–4517* 📠 *229/824–4529* 🌐 *www.plainsgeorgia.com/Plains_Inn.htm* *6 rooms, 1 suite* *Cable TV; no smoking* 💳 *AE, D, MC, V* 🍽 *BP.*

Americus

5 *11 mi east of Plains via U.S. 280.*

Founded in 1832, Americus is the only city in the United States named for explorer Amerigo Vespucci (1454–1512). At one time this was one of the largest cities in Georgia and a major center of cotton production. At the turn of the 20th century, Americus was popular as a winter retreat for Northerners fleeing the cold. The four-story Windsor Hotel, a sprawling 1892 Victorian structure that takes up a city block, dominates the downtown business district and is a testament to the town's heyday as a resort. Its dazzling turrets, towers, and verandas are a dramatic and elegant reminder of the city's prestigious past.

Today Americus is best known as the site of the international headquarters of **Habitat for Humanity,** an organization dedicated to building decent, affordable housing for low-income families around the world. You can tour the headquarters and watch videos discussing the group's work. A few blocks farther west on West Church Street is **Habitat's Global Village & Discovery Center,** which examines different housing conditions around the world and the scope of Habitat's mission. You can make compressed-earth blocks or try your hand at roof tiles, just like Habitat builders in Africa and Asia. ✉ *121 Habitat St.* ☎ *229/924–6935 or 800/422–4828* 🌐 *www.habitat.org* 🎫 *Headquarters free, $5 suggested donation for Global Village* ⏲ *Headquarters Tues.–Sat. 8–5, Global Village Mon.–Sat. 9–5, Sun. 1–5.*

★ About 10 mi northeast of Americus via Route 49, you can visit a solemn reminder of the Civil War's tragic toll, the **Andersonville National Historic Site,** which looms menacingly over the rural countryside with barred windows and jutting towers. This infamous prisoner-of-war penitentiary is the nation's only POW museum. Photographs, artifacts, and high-tech exhibits detail not just the plight of Civil War prisoners, but also prison life and conditions affecting all of America's 800,000 POWs since the Revolutionary War. Some 13,000 Union prisoners died—mostly from disease, neglect, and malnutrition—at Andersonville during its 14-month tenure at the tail of the war. At the conclusion of the Civil War, the Swiss-born commandant of Andersonville, Captain Henry R. Wirz, believed by some to be a scapegoat, became the only person executed for war crimes. Wirz refused a pardon promised if he implicated Confederate president Jefferson Davis and was hanged on November 10, 1865. ✉ *496 Cemetery Rd., Andersonville* ☎ *229/924–0343* 🌐 *www.nps.gov/ande/index.htm* 🎫 *Free* ⏲ *Daily 8:30–5.*

Where to Stay & Eat

¢ ✕ **Java Jaay.** Step back in time into a 1950s-style soda shop that serves the best cup of joe around. Old movie posters of films like *Man on a Tightrope* cover the walls, and the marble tops glisten. You can order mochas, smoothies, sandwiches, pastries, bagels, and more. It's near Habitat's Global Village & Discovery Center. ✉ *308 W. Lamar St.* ☎ *229/928–5918* ⏲ *Closed Sun. No dinner.* 💳 *MC, V.*

★ $ **Windsor Hotel.** This ornate jewel of a hotel has garnered awards from the National Trust for Historic Preservation. Built in 1892, it's a monument to Victorian architecture and remains one of the South's best showcases of American heritage. All of the rooms have 12-foot ceilings, and the circular Carter Presidential Suite takes up an entire floor of the hotel's tallest tower. The elegant Grand Dining Room ($$–$$$$, no dinner Sunday) serves a varied menu with a focus on Southern food: corn chowder, crab cakes, quail in an orange-cream sauce, and pecan-crusted or bourbon-glazed salmon. ✉ *125 W. Lamar St., 31709* ☎ *229/924–1555 or 888/297–9567* 📠 *229/928–0533* 🌐 *www.windsor-americus.com* *53 rooms, 4 suites* *Restaurant, fans, spa, bar* *AE, D, DC, MC, V.*

$–$$ **The 1906 Pathway Inn.** Though Tara-esque in size and style, this Greek Revival inn has reasonable rates. Antiques fill the rooms, which are named for historic figures connected to the region, such as Roosevelt and Lindbergh. A sprawling veranda with rockers and a swing wraps around the house. The sumptuous candlelight breakfasts include everything from pancakes and waffles to French toast stuffed with peaches or cream cheese. Check the Web site for specials. ✉ *501 S. Lee St., 31709* ☎ *229/928–2078 or 800/889–1466* 📠 *229/928–2078* 🌐 *www.1906pathwayinn.com* *5 rooms* *In-room VCRs* *AE, D, MC, V* *BP.*

$ **The White House Farm Bed & Breakfast.** On a 250-acre dairy farm in the heart of the Mennonite community sits this comfortable, two-story wood-frame house. It was built in the early 1950s in a construction "frolic," a Mennonite tradition of sharing labor to save money and foster a sense of community. Lovely quilts decorate the simple rooms. The full breakfast might include such treats as raspberry-stuffed French toast cooked with homemade bread, grits, eggs, and ham. ✉ *1679 Mennonite Church Rd., Montezuma 31603* ☎ *478/472–7942 or 478/957–6363* 🌐 *www.whitehousefarmbnb.com* *3 rooms* *No room phones, no room TVs* *MC, V* *BP.*

THE SOUTHWEST CORNER

Tifton and Thomasville are the highlights of Georgia's southwest corner. Both are often cited among the nation's most appealing small towns, thanks to inviting town squares, shaded glens, and an easygoing air; you can also find some fine country inns here.

Tifton

❻ *72 mi southeast of Americus via U.S. 280 and I–75; 183 mi south of Atlanta via I–75.*

In 1872 Henry Harding Tift, a Connecticut Yankee, set up a lumbering operation that grew into the present-day town (Tifton and the nearby town of Fitzgerald share the distinction of having been founded by Northerners). Tifton derived its wealth chiefly from tobacco farming. The old downtown (Main Street between 4th and 9th streets) dates to the 1940s and includes an art deco movie house. Norman Crampton ranked Tifton 54th in his noted book *The 100 Best Small Towns in America.*

Agrirama is the site of the town's Tourist Information Center and the Georgia Living History Museum, which depicts life in 19th-century rural Georgia. Agrirama consists of a traditional farm community from the 1870s, an 1890s progressive farmstead, an industrial-sites complex, and a rural town. Among the 35 restored period structures are traditional houses, a forge, a turpentine still, a gristmill, and a cotton gin. Costumed interpretive guides lead you through the 95-acre site. A logging train takes you through the woods to the village, where you can stroll the main street and visit the feed and seed store, the print shop, the drugstore, and the original Victorian home of Henry Harding Tift. ✉ *1493 Whiddon Mill Rd., I–75 at Exit 63B* ☎ *229/386–3344 or 800/767–1875* 🌐 *www.agrirama.com* *$7* *Tues.–Sat. 9–5.*

A 1900 Romanesque brick church sparkling with stained glass houses the **Tifton Museum of Arts & Heritage.** Exhibits of varied media are held year-round. ✉ *285 Love Ave.* ☎ *229/382–3600* *Free* *Tues.–Fri. 1–5.*

off the beaten path

JEFFERSON DAVIS MEMORIAL HISTORIC SITE – A small museum filled with flags, uniforms, weapons, and other Civil War items sits near the wooded site where Confederate president Jefferson Davis was captured by Federal troops nearly a month after Lee's surrender at Appomattox. A spur worn by Davis at the time of his capture as well as posters advertising the reward for his capture are on display, and there's an interesting short film. It's about 15 minutes north of Tifton on Route 125. ✉ *338 Jeff Davis Park Rd., Fitzgerald* ☎ *229/831–2335* 🌐 *www.gastateparks.org/info/jeffd/* *$2.50* *Tues.–Sat. 9–5, Sun. 2–5:30.*

Where to Stay & Eat

$$–$$$ ✕ **Bergeron's Downtown.** This popular Cajun restaurant and late-night haunt is right in the middle of Main Street, but the entrance is actually around the corner on 1st Street. And the dining rooms are tucked away in the labyrinthine corridors of the second floor of the old Myon Hotel. Just follow the signs to owner Hersall Bergeron's Cajun hideaway, where he serves the likes of crawfish bisque, étouffée, gumbo, and red beans and rice. ✉ *128 1st St., Suite 229* ☎ *229/388–0075 or 229/388–0077* *AE, MC, V* *Closed Sun. No lunch Sat.*

$ ✕ **Pit Stop Bar-B-Que & Grill.** In addition to barbecue pork, you have a choice of beef, chicken, or turkey dishes, plus Brunswick stew, baked beans, corn on the cob, and cobbler and banana pudding. Locals swear by Pit Stop's "awesome potato," a baked potato stuffed with pork, layered with cheese, and served with cole slaw on the side. It's a meal in itself. ✉ *1112 W. 8th St., across from Agrirama* ☎ *229/387–0888* *AE, D, MC, V.*

$ **Hummingbird's Perch Bed and Breakfast.** Innkeeper Francis Wilson has created a diverting retreat with this American traditional–style inn just 5 mi north of downtown Tifton. Thirteen acres of peaceful grounds, including a pond, surround the house. Wilson serves a full Southern-style spread for breakfast. ✉ *305 Adams Rd., I–75 to Exit 69, Chula 31733* ☎🖷 *229/382–5431* *3 rooms, 1 with bath* *Pond; no room phones* *No credit cards* *BP.*

Thomasville

❼ *55 mi south of Tifton via U.S. 319; 236 mi south of Atlanta via I–75 and U.S. 319; 38 mi north of Tallahassee, FL, via U.S. 319.*

The early fortunes of this appealing small town in the Tallahassee Red Hills paralleled the rise and fall of the antebellum cotton plantations that lined the region's famed "Plantation Trace." Following the Civil War, thousands of Union prisoners who had been evacuated from the nearby Andersonville prison to Thomasville brought home stories of the curative effects of the balsam breezes of the pine-scented air. These stories fueled the second boom in the region's fortunes, during which Northerners fleeing the cold wintered here. The wealthier among them built elegant estates in an around the town.

Although Thomasville's golden era has long since ended and there's little left of the old-growth forests that brought winter vacationers south, the distinct pine-scented air remains, as does the Victorian elegance of the town's heyday. Thomasville retains the rich atmosphere of a bygone era and the stately vestiges of a once-posh resort, but without the crowds. Known as the "City of Roses," it draws thousands of visitors each spring to its annual Rose Festival (the fourth weekend in April). And during the Victorian Christmas, locals turn out in period costumes to enjoy horse-drawn carriage rides, caroling, and street theater.

One of Thomasville's more interesting sights is the **Lapham–Patterson House,** built by Chicago shoe manufacturer Charles W. Lapham. At the time of its construction in 1884, the three-story Victorian house was state-of-the-art, with gas lighting and indoor plumbing with hot and cold running water. Each room was built with at least five or six walls. But the most curious feature of this unusual house is that Lapham, who had witnessed the Great Chicago Fire of 1871, had 45 exit doors installed because of his fear of being trapped in a burning house. The house is now a National Historic Landmark because of its unique architectural features. ✉ *626 N. Dawson St.* ☎ *229/225–4004* 🌐 *www.gastateparks.org/info/lapham/* *$4* ⏲ *Tues.–Sat. 9–5, Sun. 2–5:30.*

The **Birdsong Nature Center** encompasses 565 acres of lush fields, forests, swamps, and butterfly gardens, plus miles of walking trails. It's a wondrous haven for birds and scores of other native wildlife. Nature programs are offered year-round. ✉ *2106 Meridian Rd.* ☎ *229/377–4408 or 800/953–2473* 🌐 *www.freenet.tlh.fl.us/birdsong* *$5* ⏲ *Wed., Fri., and Sat. 9–5, Sun. 1–5.*

★ For a glimpse of the grandeur of Southern life Tara-style, visit **Pebble Hill Plantation,** listed on the National Register of Historic Places and the only plantation in the area open to the public. Pebble Hill dates to 1825,

KING COTTON'S ROYAL COMEBACK

S**UCH WAS GEORGIA'S PREEMINENCE** *in world cotton production at the turn of the 20th century that the international market price was set at the Cotton Exchange in Savannah. And the huge antebellum plantations of southwest Georgia in areas such as Plantation Trace around Thomasville—which in their heyday required an estimated 20,000 slaves to operate—were major players in the engine driving the state's economic prosperity.*

For more than 100 years, from the first time it was planted in Georgia in 1733 until the beginning of the Civil War, cotton was the most commercially successful crop in the state. Its tolerance to drought made it ideally suited to the state's climate, and its soft fibers were in high demand throughout the United States and England. But because the seeds had to be separated from the lint by hand, production was slow and laborious and output was limited. Slavery was actually on the decline in Georgia until 1793, when a young Yale graduate named Eli Whitney (1765–1825) came to Savannah's Mulberry Grove Plantation as a tutor to the children of Revolutionary War hero Nathaniel Greene. After watching the difficulty workers were having separating the seeds from the cotton, he invented a simple machine of two cylinders with combs rotating in opposite directions. The "gin," as he called it (short for engine), could do the work of 50 people and revolutionized the cotton industry. So significant was its immediate impact on the U.S. economy that President George Washington personally signed the patent issued to Whitney. The gin unleashed the industry's massive potential, requiring large amounts of cheap labor to expand production, and thus firmly set Georgia's place among the slave-holding states.

After the industry's devastation during the Civil War, cotton found new life, thanks in large part to a man named Levi Strauss, who had produced denim clothes for miners during the 1849–60 California gold rush. The growing demand for Strauss's rugged work clothes fueled an explosion in cotton production, and within 15 years of the end of the Civil War, the state recorded its first million-bale harvest.

But in 1900 a new problem arose: the boll weevil came to the United States via Mexico and quickly undermined cotton production with its voracious appetite for young cotton bolls. The weevil is credited as one of the major causes of the onset of the economic depression that spread throughout the South and sent mass migrations of laborers to the North. Though cotton production was at an all-time low in Georgia by 1978, in 1987 the state began a boll weevil eradication program that has all but wiped out the threat. And the result is that today Georgia is once again one of the top cotton producers in the nation.

Cotton, sometimes called "white gold," was planted in 95 of Georgia's 159 counties in 2002. Typically between 1.25 and 1.5 million acres of cotton are planted in Georgia each year, supporting more than 40,000 jobs in the state in farming, ginning, merchandising, warehousing, cottonseed-oil milling, and textile milling. Aside from the lint, which is used for fabric, cottonseed is crushed to make oil used in shortening, margarine, cooking oil, and salad dressing. Cottonseed meal and hulls are used to make feed for livestock. Cellulose from cottonseed linters is used in the production of ice cream, paper currency, photo paper, plastics, mattresses, and coverings for auto cushions. And the remaining stalks and leaves are plowed back into the earth to enrich the soil.

although most of the original house was destroyed in a fire in the 1930s. Highlights of the current two-story main house include a dramatic horseshoe-shape entryway, a wraparound terrace on the upper floor, and an elegant sunroom decorated with a wildlife motif. Surrounding the house are 34 acres of immaculately maintained grounds that include gardens, a walking path festooned with confederate jasmine, a log-cabin school, a fire station, a carriage house, kennels, and a hospital for the plantation's more than 100 dogs (prized dogs were buried with full funerals, including a minister). The sprawling dairy-and-horse-stable complex resembles an English village. Grab a cup of lemonade from the large thermos under the oak tree opposite the Plantation Store—it's compliments of the house. ✉ *5 mi south of Thomasville on U.S. 319, just past the Melhana Plantation on right* ☎ *229/226–2344* 🌐 *www.pebblehill.com* 🎫 *Grounds $3, house tour $7* ⏲ *Oct.–Aug., Tues.–Sat. 10–5, Sun. 1–5; last tour at 4.*

Where to Stay & Eat

$$$–$$$$ ✕ **Liam's Restaurant.** With a flair for the unexpected, this bistro turns out a rotating seasonal menu with such updated Southern dishes as Jamaican pork loin with sweet red-onion marmalade, and duck with yam purée and cane-syrup reduction. Liam's also serves cheeses from the local Sweet Grass Dairy. Wine is not on the menu, but you're free to bring your own bottle. An open kitchen, garden dining, and paintings by local artists create a cozy dining room. ✉ *109 E. Jackson St.* ☎ *229/226–9944* 💳 *MC, V* ⏲ *Closed Sun. and Mon. No dinner Tues. and Wed.*

$$–$$$ ✕ **Mom and Dad's Italian Restaurant.** That's definitely oregano in the air you smell on entering Mom and Dad's—but also expect to hear a Southern drawl wafting overhead. These go together perfectly at this restaurant, a great place for Italian food made with rich cheeses and thick red tomato sauce. The garlic bread is served warm and strong enough to turn your breath into a blowtorch. ✉ *1800 Smith Ave.* ☎ *229/226–6265* 💳 *MC, V* ⏲ *Closed Sun. and Mon. No lunch.*

$–$$ ✕ **George & Louie's.** The fresh Gulf seafood served at this airy Key West–style restaurant is as good as you can find anywhere. Try the broiled shrimp, cooked in olive oil with a smattering of fresh garlic; fresh mullet dinner; or combination platter with homemade deviled crab, shrimp, oysters, scallops, and flounder for one, two, or three people. The fried green tomatoes sprinkled with feta are cooked to perfection, and the burgers are a local favorite. Vintage music from the '40s plays on the sound system, and there's outdoor dining under umbrellas. ✉ *217 Remington Ave.* ☎ *229/226–1218* 💳 *No credit cards* ⏲ *Closed Sun.*

$$$$ ✕🏨 **Melhana Grand Plantation Resort.** The grounds of this sprawling 50-acre plantation—listed on the National Register of Historic Places—are dotted with dozens of buildings, shade trees, gardens, bridal paths, and trails. Most rooms are massive, with gorgeous four-poster beds and antique writing desks. A highlight here is Melhana's Chapin Dining Room (jacket requested, reservations required, no lunch). The Southern meals here—including the likes of Atlantic salmon with a black-bean-and-tomato

ragout, and sea scallops with succotash and chipotle—are every bit as exquisite as the surroundings in which they are served. ✉ *301 Showboat La., 31792* ☎ *229/226–2290 or 888/920–3030* 🖷 *229/226–4585* 🌐 *www.melhana.com* *38 rooms, 17 suites, 2 cottages* *Restaurant, cable TV, tennis court, indoor pool, health club, spa, horseback riding, bar, library, concierge* 💳 *AE, D, DC, MC, V* *BP.*

★ **$$$–$$$$** **1884 Paxton House Inn.** Each room is unique in this immaculate property, a stately blue Victorian mansion with a wraparound veranda. Antiques and period reproductions decorate the public spaces and guest rooms. Thoughtful details include Egyptian-cotton bath towels, goose-down pillows, evening turndown service, and homemade cranberry, orange, or blueberry bread for breakfast. Accommodations are spread among the main inn, a pool house, a garden cottage, and a carriage house. Afternoon tea and lemonade socials are part of the fun of this inn in the downtown historic district. ✉ *445 Remington Ave., 31792* ☎ *229/226–5197* 🖷 *229/226–9903* 🌐 *www.1884paxtonhouseinn.com* *9 rooms* *Fans, in-room data ports, in-room DVD/VCR players, pool, hot tubs; no kids under 12* 💳 *AE, MC, V* *BP.*

SOUTHWEST GEORGIA A TO Z

To research prices, get advice from other travelers, and book travel arrangements, visit www.fodors.com

CAR TRAVEL

A car is the best way to tour this part of Georgia. I–75 runs north–south through the eastern edge of the region and connects to several U.S. and state highways that traverse the area. I–85 runs southwest through LaGrange and Columbus.

EMERGENCIES

Emergency Services **Ambulance, fire, police** ☎ 911.

Hospitals **Baptist Meriwether Hospital** ✉ 5995 Spring St., Warm Springs ☎ 706/655–3331 🌐 www.gbhcs.org. **Columbus Doctors Hospital** ✉ 616 19th St., Columbus ☎ 706/494–4262 🌐 www.doctorshospital.net. **John D. Archibold Memorial Hospital** ✉ 915 Gordon St., Thomasville ☎ 229/228–2000 🌐 www.archbold.org. **Sumter Regional Hospital** ✉ 100 Wheatley Dr., Americus ☎ 229/924–6011 🌐 www.sumterregional.org.

TRAIN TRAVEL

A great means of seeing the countryside, the SAM Shortline Southwest Georgia Excursion Train originates in Cordele and runs west through the Georgia Veteran's State Park; Leslie, home of the Georgia Rural Telephone Museum; Americus; Plains; and Archery. You can get on or off at any of the stations, stop over for the night, and take the train again the next morning (check the schedule to be sure there's a train running the next day).

SAM Shortline Southwest Georgia Excursion Train ✉ 105 E. 9th Ave., Box 845, Cordele 31010 ☎ 229/276–0755 or 877/427–2457 🌐 www.samshortline.com.

VISITOR INFORMATION

Tourist Information **Americus-Sumter County Welcome Center** ✉ Windsor Hotel, 125 W. Lamar St., Box 275, Americus 31709 ☎ 229/928-6059 or 888/278-6837. **Columbus Convention and Visitors Bureau** ✉ 900 Front Ave., 31901 ☎ 706/322-3181 or 800/999-1613 🌐 www.visitcolumbusga.com. **LaGrange-Troup County Chamber of Commerce** ✉ 111 Bull St., Box 636, LaGrange 30241-0636 ☎ 706/884-8671 🌐 www.lagrangechamber.com. **Pine Mountain Welcome Center** ✉ 101 E. Broad St., Pine Mountain 31822 ☎ 706/663-4000 or 800/441-3502 🌐 www.pinemountain.org. **Plains Welcome Center** ✉ 1763 U.S. 280, Plains 31780 ☎ 229/824-7477 🌐 www.plainsgeorgia.com. **Thomasville Welcome Center** ✉ 401 S. Broad St., Thomasville 31792 ☎ 229/228-7977 or 866/577-3600 🌐 www.thomasvillega.com. **Tifton-Tift County Tourism Association** ✉ 1439 Whiddon Mill Rd., Box Q, Tifton 31793 ☎ 229/386-3848 🌐 www.tiftontourism.com. **Warm Springs Welcome Center** ✉ 1 Broad St., Warm Springs 31830 ☎ 706/655-3322 or 800/337-1927 🌐 www.warmspringsga.com/warmsprings.asp.

ATLANTA

11

DASH THROUGH THE FOUNTAINS
of Centennial Olympic Park ⇨ *p.388*

SEE THE 1800S' ANSWER TO IMAX
at the Atlanta Cyclorama ⇨ *p.388*

LEARN ABOUT A CIVIL RIGHTS GIANT
at the M. L. King Jr. birth home ⇨ *p.395*

CELEBRATE A SPECIAL OCCASION
at classy Bacchanalia restaurant ⇨ *p.411*

DO THE "PEACHTREE SHUFFLE"
in pursuit of Atlanta nightlife ⇨ *p.431*

By Deborah Geering

THOUGH STEEPED IN HISTORY and centered in America's South, Atlanta is far too ambitious to settle for a description like "charming Southern city." Founded in 1837 as the end of the Western & Atlantic railroad line, the city has been trying to get somewhere ever since.

Atlanta has a long history of trying to re-create itself: it was first named Marthasville in honor of the then-governor's daughter, nicknamed Terminus for its rail location, and then changed soon after to Atlanta, the feminine of Atlantic—as in the railroad. The city's rallying cry these days is to become a "global city," known throughout the world as one of the most attractive and prosperous urban communities. So far, so good.

Still a transportation hub, the city now serves the world through busy Hartsfield-Jackson Atlanta International Airport. Direct flights to Europe, South America, and Asia have made metro Atlanta easily accessible to the more than 1,600 international businesses that operate here and the more than 50 countries that have representation in the city through consulates, trade offices, and chambers of commerce. Atlanta has emerged as a banking center and is the world headquarters for such Fortune 500 companies as Home Depot, Coca-Cola, United Parcel Service, BellSouth, and SunTrust Banks.

Since 1990 Atlanta has experienced unprecedented growth. The official city population remains steady, at about 430,000, but the 10-county metro population grew about 50%, from 2.5 million in 1990 to 3.7 million in 2003. A good measure of this growth is the ever-changing downtown skyline, along with skyscrapers constructed in the Midtown, Buckhead, and outer perimeter (fringing I–285, especially to the north) business districts. Residents, however, are less likely to measure the city's growth by skyscrapers than by the increase in traffic jams and crowds, higher prices, and the ever-burgeoning subdivisions that continue to push urban sprawl farther and farther into surrounding rural areas.

Perhaps more important to the people who live and visit Atlanta is its character, which has evolved as the city has grown. Transplanted Northerners and those from elsewhere account for more than half the population and have undeniably affected the mood of the city, as well as the mix of accents of its people. Irish immigrants played a major role in the city's early history, along with Germans and Austrians; the Hungarian-born Rich brothers founded Atlanta's principal department store (now called Rich's-Macy's). Since the 1980s, Atlanta has seen spirited growth in its Asian and Latin-American communities. Related restaurants, shops, and institutions have become part of the city's texture.

"The city too busy to hate," Atlanta has a strong link to the civil rights movement. It was the home of Dr. Martin Luther King Jr. Dr. King's widow, Coretta Scott King, is still involved with the King Center, which she founded after her husband's assassination in 1968. The center is at the heart of the Sweet Auburn historic district, once the home of Atlanta's first black millionaire, Alonzo Herndon, and now a carefully restored and preserved neighborhood that seeks to tell the story of African-American segregation and success.

If you have 3 days

Begin your visit downtown with a couple of Atlanta icons: Coca-Cola and CNN. You can learn the history of Atlanta's favorite beverage by walking though the World of Coca-Cola Pavilion. Stop for a snack or a little window shopping at Underground Atlanta, and then walk west on Marietta Street to CNN Center (reservations for tours must be made 24 hours in advance). Grab lunch at CNN Center and then stroll through Centennial Olympic Park. If you have young children, spend the afternoon at Imagine It! The Children's Museum of Atlanta. Older kids and adults may want to take a taxi to Grant Park to visit the Atlanta Cyclorama & Civil War Museum and Zoo Atlanta.

Devote your second day to the Martin Luther King Jr. National Historic District. Start at the visitor center, at 450 Auburn Avenue, where you can sign up for a tour of the Martin Luther King Jr. Birth Home; then head over to the Sweet Auburn Curb Market. Spend the rest of the day exploring the historic district's museums and historic buildings, including King's tomb and the African-American Panoramic Experience.

On the third day, explore Midtown. Start the day with a visit to the Atlanta Botanical Garden at Piedmont Park. The park itself is a wonderful place to get some exercise or to just relax under a tree. After lunch, head east to Peachtree Street and the High, one of the nation's top art museums. In the evening, you might want to catch a concert or play at Woodruff Arts Center.

If you have 5 days

Follow the three-day itinerary above. On the fourth day, head to Buckhead for some history and shopping. In addition to its fine exhibits, the Atlanta History Center also has carefully tended grounds landscaped with native plants. A block away, shops of all kinds line Peachtree and its side streets. To the north are Phipps Plaza and Lenox Square, two of the most famous malls in the Southeast. On your fifth day, explore some of Atlanta's great neighborhoods. Start at Emory University's Michael C. Carlos Museum or the Fernbank Museum of Natural History. Next drive to Virginia-Highland, which is rich in art galleries, boutiques, and restaurants. A mile or two to the southeast is Little Five Points, the city's most bohemian neighborhood. For a night of beer and rock and roll, head to East Atlanta. If you prefer a quieter evening, visit downtown Decatur for dinner, a stroll, and maybe a free concert at the gazebo behind the Decatur Historical Courthouse.

If you have 7 days

Follow the five-day itinerary above, and then dedicate your last two days to the kids—or the kid in you. On your way out east to Stone Mountain Park, be sure to stop by Your DeKalb Farmers Market for a danish and other goodies. You can easily spend a day at the park. Hike or take the cable car to the top of the mountain, and if the Lasershow Spectacular is playing that night, stick around for it. Spend your final day at the Six Flags Over Georgia amusement park, or drive to Kennesaw to visit the Kennesaw Mountain National Battlefield and the Southern Museum of Civil War and Locomotive History.

The traditional South—which in romantic versions consists of lacy moss dangling from tree limbs, thick sugary Southern drawls, a leisurely pace, and luxurious antebellum mansions—rarely reveals itself here. Even before the Civil War, the columned house was a rarity—and prior to the construction boom of the 1850s, houses of any kind were rare. The frenetic pace of rebuilding that characterized the period after the Civil War continues unabated. Still viewed by die-hard Southerners as the heart of the Old Confederacy, Atlanta has become the best example of the New South, a fast-paced modern city proud of its heritage.

EXPLORING ATLANTA

The greater Atlanta area embraces five counties. The city of Atlanta is primarily in Fulton and DeKalb counties, with its southern end and the airport in Clayton County. Outside I–285, which encircles the city, Cobb and Gwinnett counties, to the northwest and northeast, respectively, are experiencing much of Atlanta's population increase.

Atlanta's lack of a grid system confuses many drivers, even locals. Some streets change their names along the same stretch of road, including the city's most famous thoroughfare, Peachtree Street, which follows a mountain ridge from downtown to suburban Norcross, outside I–285: it becomes Peachtree Road after crossing I–85 and then splits into Peachtree Industrial Boulevard beyond the Buckhead neighborhood and the original Peachtree Road, which heads into Chamblee. Adding to the confusion, dozens of other streets in the metropolitan area use "Peachtree" in their names. Before setting out anywhere, get the complete street address of your destination, including landmarks, cross streets, or other guideposts, as street numbers and even street signs are often difficult to find.

Atlanta proper has three major regions—downtown, Midtown, and Buckhead—as well as several smaller commercial districts and intown neighborhoods. Atlanta's downtown is filled with government staffers and office workers by day, but at night the visiting conventioneers—and, as city improvements take hold, metro residents—come out to play. Midtown and Buckhead are the best places to go for dinner, nightclubs, and shows, but some intown neighborhoods like Virginia-Highland and Little Five Points have unique characters that merit exploration.

The city's public transportation system, the Metropolitan Atlanta Rapid Transit Authority (MARTA), operates bus and rail networks in Fulton and DeKalb counties. The two major rail lines, which run east–west and north–south (there's a northern spur, so consult a map before you jump on board), extend roughly to the edges of I–285. A few of the neighboring counties also operate bus and shuttle services. MARTA is best for traveling to and from the airport and within downtown, Midtown, and Buckhead; if you plan to venture beyond those regions, you should call for cabs or rent a car.

Numbers in the text correspond to numbers in the margin and on the Downtown Atlanta & Sweet Auburn and Atlanta neighborhoods maps.

Rooting for the Home Team Atlantans love their sports teams, especially the Braves. Several years of postseason success for the National League baseball team has made it hard to distinguish the fair-weather fans from the die-hards. Football has gained popularity here, too, ever since Home Depot cofounder Arthur Blank bought the Falcons, cranked up the promotions, and reduced some ticket prices at the Georgia Dome. Professional basketball (the Hawks) and hockey (the Thrashers) are played at Philips Arena.

Nightlife If you like to stay out late, you've come to the right place. Neighborhoods all over the city have great places to stop for a drink and some live music, whether it be blues, jazz, acoustic, or local rock and roll. Most of the clubs are concentrated in Buckhead, making it a good place to start the evening. In this trendy part of town, you'll find hip-hop, R&B, Top 40, and a few jazz spots. Midtown also has all sorts of clubs, although it's especially popular among the city's gay population.

History Having played a crucial role in the Civil War and the civil rights movement, Atlanta and the surrounding areas are packed with interesting historical sights and museums. The Atlanta History Center provides a good introduction to the city's story. The well-preserved Sweet Auburn historic district was the home of Dr. Martin Luther King Jr. and many of the city's other African-American leaders. Within the Atlanta Cyclorama & Civil War Museum are a panoramic painting depicting the Battle of Atlanta, and a Civil War locomotive. The Kennesaw Mountain National Battlefield looks much as it did at the time of the Civil War. And the Fernbank Museum of Natural History will take you even farther back in Georgia's history: back to the time of the formation of the planet.

Eclectic Cuisine From Southern-style comfort eateries to upscale establishments catering to the expense-account crowd, Atlanta, the sixth-largest restaurant market in the nation, has something for everyone. Some of the most interesting dining can be credited to the city's diverse immigrant population, which has introduced cuisines from Africa, Asia, and the Middle East, as well as Europe and Latin America. Few roads in America better illustrate the concept of the melting pot than Buford Highway, north of Atlanta, which is dotted with signs advertising restaurants in Chinese, Korean, Vietnamese, Spanish, and other languages.

Downtown Atlanta

Downtown Atlanta clusters around the hub known as Five Points. Here you'll find the MARTA station that intersects the north–south and east–west transit lines. On the surface Five Points is formed by the intersection of Peachtree Street with Marietta, Broad, and Forsyth streets.

a good walk

This walk branches in three directions, which are most efficiently managed by taking MARTA trains to get quickly from one spot to the next. The valiant will, of course, prefer to go it on foot. Starting at **Woodruff Park** ①, proceed north on Peachtree Street, noting Atlanta's **Flatiron Building** ② on the west side of Peachtree and the **Candler Building** ③ on the east side of the street. Nearby on Peachtree Street at John Wesley Dobbs Avenue is the modern **Georgia-Pacific Center** ④, and across from it is **Margaret Mitchell Square** ⑤. Continuing north on Peachtree Street, note the sprawling **Peachtree Center** ⑥ complex, which includes the small but worthwhile **Atlanta International Museum of Art and Design** ⑦. Walk east on Baker Street one block to Courtland Street; head north on Courtland until you reach Ralph McGill Boulevard, and go one block east to the corner of Piedmont Avenue. Here you can find an open-air folk-art exhibition known as **Folk Art Park** ⑧.

Return to Peachtree Center and take the subway one stop to the **Five Points MARTA Station** ⑨, from which you can walk north on Peachtree Street to the **William-Oliver Building** ⑩. (From Folk Art Park you can also follow Ralph McGill Boulevard west to Peachtree and retrace your steps south to the William-Oliver Building.) From here go east on Edgewood Avenue, and just ahead you'll see the **Hurt Building** ⑪, a rare Atlanta example of Chicago-style architecture. Around the corner on Marietta Street at Broad Street is the handsome **J. Mack Robinson College of Business** ⑫, formerly the Bank of America Building. Nearby is the **Statue of Henry Grady** ⑬, right across from the building now housing the newspaper he founded, the ***Atlanta Journal-Constitution*** ⑭. North on Marietta Street, at Techwood Drive, is **Centennial Olympic Park** ⑮, which hosts concerts and special events. At the north end of the park is **Imagine It! The Children's Museum of Atlanta** ⑯. The south end of the park holds the **CNN Center** ⑰, which you may tour (by advance reservation). At the rear of the center is the **Georgia Dome** ⑱.

At the CNN Center/Georgia Dome station, take MARTA one stop back to the Five Points station and exit at the sign for **Underground Atlanta** ⑲. After having a rest and a restorative snack in its food court, wander the maze of subterranean streets here and leave through the Central Avenue exit of Underground Atlanta, bearing slightly south toward the **Georgia Railroad Freight Depot** ⑳. Across the plaza from the depot is the **World of Coca-Cola Pavilion** ㉑, with fun memorabilia on display. Across Martin Luther King Jr. Drive at Central Avenue is the **Shrine of the Immaculate Conception** ㉒, one of many historic churches still operating in downtown. Just south of the church are the neo-Gothic **City Hall** ㉓, with a modern addition housing a permanent art collection, on Mitchell Street, and the Renaissance-style **Georgia State Capitol** ㉔, on Washington Street.

TIMING This walk requires at least a day, assuming you don't spend much time at any one location. If you plan to walk at a more leisurely pace, finish the first day at Centennial Olympic Park, and allow another half day for the rest of the walk. If you plan tours of the CNN Center and World of Coca-Cola Pavilion, plus some time for the kids at Imagine It!, you'll need an additional full day or more. The terrain is fairly level and not too taxing.

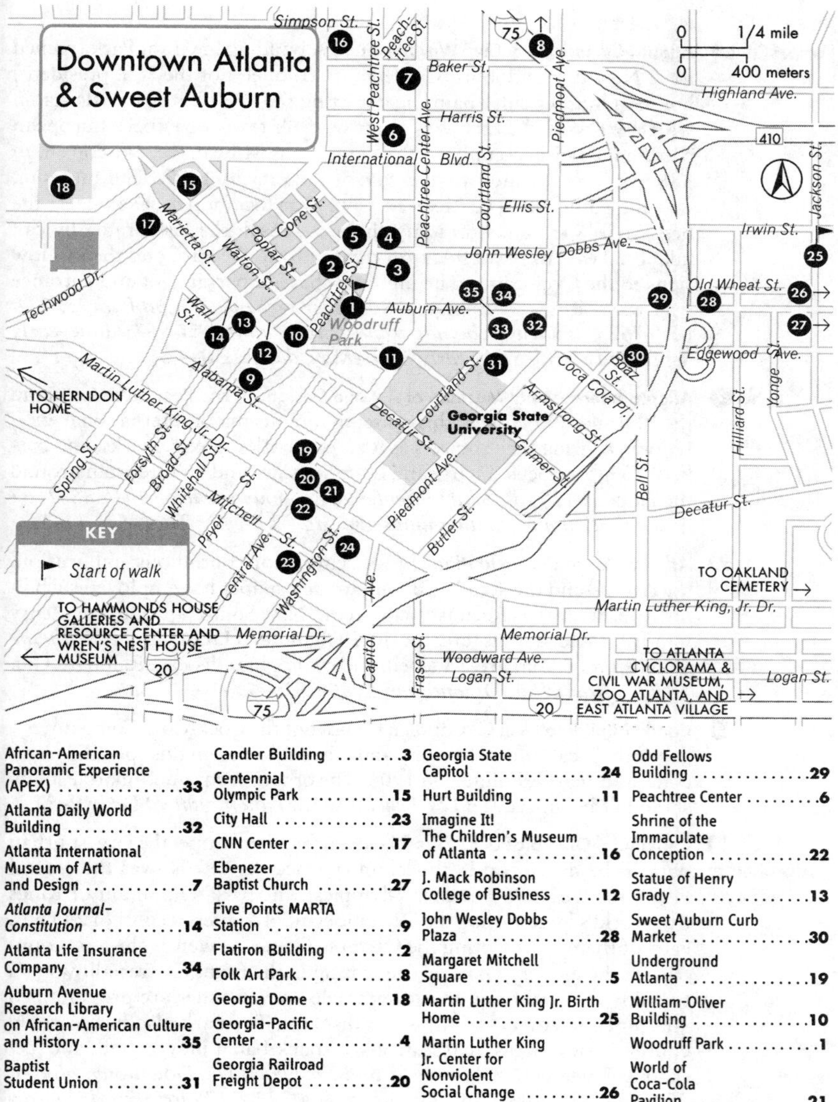

African-American Panoramic Experience (APEX) **33**
Atlanta Daily World Building **32**
Atlanta International Museum of Art and Design **7**
Atlanta Journal-Constitution **14**
Atlanta Life Insurance Company **34**
Auburn Avenue Research Library on African-American Culture and History **35**
Baptist Student Union **31**
Candler Building **3**
Centennial Olympic Park **15**
City Hall **23**
CNN Center **17**
Ebenezer Baptist Church **27**
Five Points MARTA Station **9**
Flatiron Building **2**
Folk Art Park **8**
Georgia Dome **18**
Georgia-Pacific Center **4**
Georgia Railroad Freight Depot **20**
Georgia State Capitol **24**
Hurt Building **11**
Imagine It! The Children's Museum of Atlanta **16**
J. Mack Robinson College of Business **12**
John Wesley Dobbs Plaza **28**
Margaret Mitchell Square **5**
Martin Luther King Jr. Birth Home **25**
Martin Luther King Jr. Center for Nonviolent Social Change **26**
Odd Fellows Building **29**
Peachtree Center **6**
Shrine of the Immaculate Conception **22**
Statue of Henry Grady **13**
Sweet Auburn Curb Market **30**
Underground Atlanta **19**
William-Oliver Building **10**
Woodruff Park **1**
World of Coca-Cola Pavilion **21**

What to See

Fodor's Choice ★ **Atlanta Cyclorama & Civil War Museum.** A building in Grant Park (named for a New England–born Confederate colonel, not the U.S. president) houses a huge circular painting depicting the 1864 Battle of Atlanta, in which 90% of the city was destroyed. A team of expert European panorama artists completed the painting in Milwaukee, Wisconsin, in 1887; it was donated to the city of Atlanta in 1897. The museum, which also houses The Texas, a Civil War locomotive, has one of the best Civil War bookstores anywhere. To reach the Cyclorama by car, take I–20 east to Exit 59A, turn right onto Boulevard, and then follow signs to the Cyclorama. The museum shares a parking lot and entrance walkway with Zoo Atlanta. ✉ *800 Cherokee Ave., Grant Park* ☎ *404/658–7625* 🌐 *www.webguide.com/cyclorama.html* 🎫 *$6* ⏲ *June–early Sept., daily 9:30–5:30; early Sept.–May, daily 9:30–4:30.*

★ 7 **Atlanta International Museum of Art and Design.** In the Peachtree Center in the Marquis Two Tower, this museum mounts major international exhibitions covering such subjects as textiles, puzzles, boxes, masks, and baskets. Exhibits focus on arts and crafts, design, and culture from around the globe. ✉ *285 Peachtree Center Ave., Downtown* ☎ *404/688–2467* 🌐 *www.atlantainternationalmuseum.org* 🎫 *Free* ⏲ *Tues.–Sat. 11–5.*

14 ***Atlanta Journal-Constitution.*** In its century of continuous publication, the city's—and the state's—dominant newspaper has employed such illustrious writers as Reconstruction-era "New South"–proponent Henry Grady, Uncle Remus–creator Joel Chandler Harris, *Gone With the Wind*–author Margaret Mitchell, and civil rights advocate Ralph McGill. ✉ *72 Marietta St., Downtown* ☎ *404/526–5151.*

3 **Candler Building.** Asa G. Candler, founder of the Coca-Cola Company, engaged the local firm of Murphy and Stewart to design this splendid terra-cotta-and-marble building in 1906. The ornate bronze-and-marble lobby shouldn't be missed. ✉ *127 Peachtree St., Downtown* ⏲ *Daily 9–5.*

15 Fodor's Choice ★ **Centennial Olympic Park.** This 21-acre urban landscape, the largest urban park to be developed in this country since the 1970s, was the central venue for the 1996 Summer Olympics. The park's Fountain of Rings (the world's largest using the Olympic symbol) centers a court of 24 flags, each of them representing the Olympic Games as well as the host countries of the modern Games. The seating in the fountain area allows you to enjoy the water and music spectacle—seven tunes are programmed and timed to coincide with water displays. The park also has seasonal concert series, occasional festivals, a snack bar, a playground, and ice-skating in winter. ✉ *Marietta St. and Techwood Dr., Downtown* ☎ *404/223–4412 for administration office, 404/222–7275 for recorded information* 🌐 *www.centennialpark.com* ⏲ *Daily 7 AM–11 PM.*

23 **City Hall.** When the fancy 14-story neo-Gothic building, designed by Atlanta architect G. Lloyd Preacher, was erected in 1929, critics dubbed it the "Painted Lady of Mitchell Street." The newer wing, with its five-story glass atrium and beautiful marble entryway, houses a splendid permanent collection of art. ✉ *68 Mitchell St., Downtown* ☎ *404/330–6000* ⏲ *Weekdays 8:30–5.*

★ 17 **CNN Center.** The home of Cable News Network occupies all 14 floors of this dramatic structure on the edge of downtown. The 50-minute CNN studio tour offers a behind-the-scenes glimpse of the control room, news rooms, and broadcast studios. Tours are not open to children under the age of four. Reservations are required 24 hours in advance and are held with a credit card. ✉ *1 CNN Center, Downtown* ☎ *404/827–2300* 🌐 *www.cnn.com/studiotour* 🎫 *Tour $10* ⏲ *Daily 9–5.*

off the beaten path

EAST ATLANTA VILLAGE – This earthy outpost of edgy-cool shops and restaurants evolved thanks to a group of proprietors with dreams much bigger than their bank accounts: spurning the high rents of fancier parts of town, they set up businesses in this then-blighted but beautiful ruin of a neighborhood 4 mi southeast of downtown. Soon artists and trendoids came to soak up the ensuing creative atmosphere. Years later East Atlanta, which is centered at Flat Shoals and Glenwood avenues, just southeast of Moreland Avenue at I–20, ranks among the hippest neighborhoods in metro Atlanta. The majestic homes have almost all been renovated, and what remains unrestored seems simply to romanticize the area's hint of "fashionable" danger. Check out the delightfully funky gift shop **Traders** (✉ 485-B Flat Shoals Ave., East Atlanta ☎ 404/522–3006).

9 **Five Points MARTA Station.** Even if you're driving everywhere, it's worth visiting the busiest public-transit rail station in the city, bustling with people. On the practical side, this MARTA station serves Underground Atlanta (via a tunnel below Peachtree Street), nearby Woodruff Park, and numerous businesses; the station is at the crossroads of MARTA's east–west and north–south lines. Outside the station, on the corner of Peachtree and Alabama streets, stands an old-fashioned gas streetlight with a marker proclaiming it the **Eternal Flame of the Confederacy.** ✉ *Peachtree and Alabama Sts., Downtown.*

2 **Flatiron Building.** The English-American Building, as it was originally known, was designed by Bradford Gilbert. Similar to the famous New York City Flatiron Building, built in the early 1900s, this 11-story building dates from 1897 and is the city's oldest high-rise. ✉ *74 Peachtree St., Downtown.* ⏲ *Weekdays 8:15–5:30.*

8 **Folk Art Park.** Revitalizing an ignored part of the city, this park pays homage to an important American art form by gathering works that reflect the diverse styles of the country's (especially Southern) folk art. Works by more than a dozen artists are on display, among them Harold Rittenberry, Howard Finster, and Eddie Owens Martin. Martin's brightly painted totems and snake-top walls replicate portions of Pasaquan, the legendary visionary environment that Martin created at his farm near Columbus, Georgia. ✉ *Ralph McGill Blvd. at Courtland St., Baker St., and Piedmont Ave., Midtown.*

18 **Georgia Dome.** This arena accommodates 71,250 spectators with good visibility from every seat; it's the site of Atlanta Falcons football games and other sporting events, conventions, and trade shows. The white, plum, and turquoise 1.6 million-square-foot facility is crowned with the world's

largest cable-supported oval, giving the roof a circus-tent top. ✉ *1 Georgia Dome Dr., Downtown* ☎ *404/223–8687* 🌐 *www.gadome.com* 🎟 *Tour $2* ⏲ *Tours Tues.–Sat. every hr 10–3, events schedule permitting; call to confirm tours are available.*

4 **Georgia-Pacific Center.** The towering, 52-story structure occupies the site of the old Loew's Grand Theatre, where *Gone With the Wind* premiered in 1939. From certain angles the red-marble high-rise appears to be flat against the sky. The **High Museum of Art Folk Art and Photography Galleries** (✉ Georgia-Pacific Center, 133 Peachtree St. NE, gallery entrance on 30 John Wesley Dobbs Ave., Downtown ☎ 404/577–6940 for information) are inside. ✉ *133 Peachtree St., at John Wesley Dobbs Ave., Downtown* 🌐 *www.high.org* 🎟 *Free* ⏲ *Mon.–Sat. 10–5, 1st Thurs. of month 10–8.*

20 **Georgia Railroad Freight Depot.** After downtown's oldest extant building was constructed in 1869 to replace the one torched by Sherman's troops in 1864, it burned again in 1935 and was rebuilt in its present form. It's now used by several downtown companies as a banquet hall and for special events. It can be viewed only by appointment. ✉ *65 Martin Luther King Jr. Dr., Downtown* ☎ *404/656–3850.*

★ 24 **Georgia State Capitol.** The capitol, a Renaissance-style edifice, was dedicated on July 4, 1889. The gold leaf on its dome was mined in nearby Dahlonega. Inside, the **Georgia Capitol Museum** houses exhibits on the history of the capitol building. On the grounds, state historical markers commemorate the 1864 Battle of Atlanta, which destroyed 90% of the city. Statues memorialize a 19th-century Georgia governor and his wife (Joseph and Elizabeth Brown), a Confederate general (John B. Gordon), and a former senator (Richard B. Russell). Former governor and president Jimmy Carter is depicted with his sleeves rolled up, a man at work. ✉ *Capitol Sq., Downtown* ☎ *404/656–2844* 🌐 *www.sos.state.ga.us* ⏲ *Museum weekdays 8–5:30; guided tours weekdays at 10, 11, 1, and 2; during legislative session, Jan.–Mar., the first 2 tours operate at 9:30 and 10:30.*

off the beaten path

HAMMONDS HOUSE GALLERIES AND RESOURCE CENTER – Dr. Otis Thrash Hammonds donated his handsome Eastlake Victorian house and his fine collection of Victorian furniture and paintings to Fulton County as an art gallery and resource center. The permanent and visiting exhibitions are devoted chiefly to works by African-American artists, although art from anywhere in the African-influenced world can be a focus. ✉ *503 Peeples St., West End* ☎ *404/752–8730* 🌐 *www.hammondshouse.org* 🎟 *$2* ⏲ *Tues.–Fri. 10–6, weekends 1–5.*

HERNDON HOME – Alonzo Herndon (1858–1927) emerged from slavery and founded both a chain of successful barbershops and the **Atlanta Life Insurance Company.** He traveled extensively and influenced the cultural life around Atlanta's traditionally black colleges. Alonzo's son, Norris, created a foundation to preserve the handsome beaux arts home as a museum and heritage center.

✉ *587 University Pl., near Morris Brown College, Vine City* ☎ *404/581–9813* 🌐 *www.herndonhome.org* 🎫 *$5* ⏲ *Tues.–Sat. 10–4; tours every hr.*

11 **Hurt Building.** Named for Atlanta developer Joel Hurt, this restored 1913 Chicago-style high-rise, with its intricate grillwork and sweeping marble staircase, has a lower level of shops and art galleries. The excellent City Grill restaurant is at the top of the sweeping staircase. ✉ *50 Hurt Plaza, Downtown.*

★ **16** **Imagine It! The Children's Museum of Atlanta.** In this colorful and joyfully noisy museum geared toward children ages two to eight, kids can build sand castles, watch themselves perform on closed-circuit TV, and operate a giant ball-moving machine. At this writing, the Georgia Aquarium was scheduled to open here in spring 2005, followed by a new World of Coca-Cola complex in 2006. Opened in 2003, the museum was the first anchor built to help revitalize property surrounding Centennial Olympic Park. ✉ *275 Centennial Olympic Park Dr. NW, Downtown* ☎ *404/659–5437* 🌐 *www.childrensmuseumatl.org* 🎫 *$11* ⏲ *Daily 10–5.*

12 **J. Mack Robinson College of Business.** Atlanta architect Phillip Trammel Shutze designed this handsome, 14-story, 1901 edifice, originally known as the Empire Building, in the Chicago style. In 1929 Shutze refashioned the first three floors, bestowing on them a decidedly Renaissance look. This was one of the city's first steel-frame structures, but during the renovation Shutze resheathed the base with masonry. The edifice is also known as the Bank of America Building, the NationsBank Building, the Citizens & Southern National Bank Building, and the Atlanta Trust Company Building. ✉ *35 Broad St., Downtown.*

5 **Margaret Mitchell Square.** A cascading waterfall and columned sculpture are highlights of this park named for one of Atlanta's most famous authors, whose masterpiece is *Gone With the Wind.* ✉ *Peachtree St. at Forsyth St. NW, Downtown.*

6 **Peachtree Center.** John Portman designed this skyscraper complex, built between 1960 and 1992, which contains shops, offices, and restaurants. Across the street, connected to Peachtree Center by skywalks, is the massive **AmericasMart-Atlanta** wholesale market. Two additional Portman creations, the **Atlanta Marriott Marquis** and the **Hyatt Regency Atlanta** hotels, are also connected to the center by skywalks. A MARTA stop is available at Peachtree Center. ✉ *230 Peachtree Center Ave., Downtown* ☎ *404/654–1296* 🌐 *www.peachtreecenter.com.*

22 **Shrine of the Immaculate Conception.** During the Battle of Atlanta, Thomas O'Reilly, the church's pastor, persuaded Union forces to spare his church and several others around the city. That 1848 structure was then replaced by this much grander building, whose cornerstone was laid in 1869. O'Reilly, a native of Ireland, was interred in the basement of the church. The church was nearly lost to fire in 1982 but has been exquisitely restored. To view the church you must contact the rectory for an appointment. ✉ *48 Martin Luther King Jr. Dr., at Central Ave., Downtown* ☎ *404/521–1866* ⏲ *By appointment only.*

13 **Statue of Henry Grady.** New York artist Alexander Doyle's bronze sculpture honors the post–Civil War editor of the *Atlanta Constitution* and early advocate of the so-called New South. Much about Grady is reminiscent of Ted Turner, the contemporary Atlanta media mogul. The memorial was raised in 1891, after Grady's untimely death at age 39. ✉ *Marietta and Forsyth Sts., Downtown.*

19 **Underground Atlanta.** This six-block entertainment and shopping district, dotted with historic markers, was created from the web of underground brick streets, ornamental building facades, and tunnels that fell into disuse in 1929, when the city built viaducts over the train tracks. Merchants then moved their storefronts to the new viaduct level, leaving the original street level for storage. Today the district houses restaurants, clubs, art galleries, shopping emporiums, and a food court, making it a good stop on a walking tour. ✉ *50 Upper Alabama St., Downtown* ☎ *404/523–2311* 🌐 *www.underground-atlanta.com.*

10 **William-Oliver Building.** Walk through the lobby of this art deco gem and admire the ceiling mural, brass grills, and elevator doors. Originally an office building named for developer Thomas Healey's grandsons, William and Oliver, it has been renovated for luxury downtown residences; the structure won a prestigious award for historic preservation from the Atlanta Urban Design Commission. ✉ *32 Peachtree St., Downtown.*

1 **Woodruff Park.** This triangular park named for the city's great philanthropist, Robert W. Woodruff, the late Coca-Cola magnate, fills during lunchtime on weekdays with executives, street preachers, politicians, Georgia State University students, and homeless people. Nearby restaurants catering to the office crowd make it an easy place to enjoy a take-out lunch. ✉ *Bordered by Edgewood and Peachtree Sts., Downtown.*

21 **World of Coca-Cola Pavilion.** At this three-story, $15 million special-exhibit facility, you can sip samples of 38 Coca-Cola Company products from around the world and study memorabilia from more than a century's worth of corporate archives. Everything Coca-Cola, the gift shop, sells everything from refrigerator magnets to evening bags. ✉ *55 Martin Luther King Jr. Dr., Downtown* ☎ *770/578–4325 Ext. 1465* 🌐 *www.woccatlanta.com* *$7* ⏲ *June–Aug., Mon.–Sat. 9–6, Sun. 11–5; Sept.–May, Mon.–Sat. 9–5, Sun. 11–5.*

off the beaten path

WREN'S NEST HOUSE MUSEUM – Joel Chandler Harris, author of the Uncle Remus tales, lived in this rambling cottage in Atlanta's West End from 1881 until his death in 1908. Forty years later Walt Disney filmed *Song of the South,* based on Harris's stories, on the property. ✉ *1050 Ralph David Abernathy Blvd., West End* ☎ *404/753–7735* 🌐 *www.cr.nps.gov/nr/travel/atlanta/har.htm* *$7* ⏲ *Tues.–Sat. 10–2:30.*

Zoo Atlanta. This zoo has nearly 1,000 animals living in naturalistic habitats, such as the Ford African Rain Forest, Flamingo Plaza, Masai Mara (re-created plains of Kenya), and Sumatran tiger exhibits. The gorillas are always hits, as are the giant pandas: two precocious bears named

Yang Yang and Lun Lun. To reach the zoo by car, take I–20 east to Exit 59A and turn right on Boulevard. Follow the signs to the zoo, which is right near the Atlanta Cyclorama & Civil War Museum. ✉ *800 Cherokee Ave., Grant Park* ☎ *404/624–5600* 🌐 *www.zooatlanta.org* 🎫 *$16.50* ⏲ *Daily 9:30–4:30.*

Sweet Auburn

Between 1890 and 1930 the historic Sweet Auburn district was Atlanta's most active and prosperous center of black business, entertainment, and political life. Following the Depression, the area went into an economic decline that lasted until the 1980s, when the residential area where civil rights leader Reverend Martin Luther King Jr. (1929–68) was born, raised, and later returned to live was declared a National Historic District.

a good walk

Start your walk in the Martin Luther King Jr. National Historic District, the heart of Sweet Auburn, where you can get a sense of what the civil rights movement and its principal leader were all about. First visit the **Martin Luther King Jr. Birth Home** 25 ⚑, on Auburn Avenue, and on the next block west, the **Martin Luther King Jr. Center for Nonviolent Social Change** 26, where Dr. King is entombed. Next stop at the nearby **Ebenezer Baptist Church** 27, at 407 Auburn Avenue, where Dr. King preached along with his grandfather, father, and brother (note that the church may be closed for renovation during your visit). Proceed a few blocks west on Auburn Avenue to near the I–75/85 overpass to enjoy the **John Wesley Dobbs Plaza** 28, a good place to take a breather. The **Odd Fellows Building** 29, on the other side of Auburn Avenue just after you walk under the expressway, is a handsome structure. At this point, go south on Bell Street one block to Edgewood Avenue to visit the **Sweet Auburn Curb Market** 30. Walk three blocks west on Edgewood Avenue, and you'll reach the **Baptist Student Union** 31, a fine example of Victorian architecture. Returning north to Auburn Avenue, you can see the **Atlanta Daily World Building** 32 and next to it the **African-American Panoramic Experience (APEX)** 33. Continue down Auburn Avenue just a few steps and enter the lobby of the **Atlanta Life Insurance Company** 34 to view its fabulous art collection. Across the street is the final stop on this tour, the **Auburn Avenue Research Library on African-American Culture and History** 35.

TIMING This is a leisurely walk along level sidewalks, with shops and historic sites along the way. If you stop for tours, you can fill an entire day. If you simply stroll and look, the walk should take an hour or two.

What to See

★ 33 **African-American Panoramic Experience (APEX).** The museum's quarterly exhibits chronicle the history of black people in America. Videos illustrate the history of Sweet Auburn, the name bestowed on Auburn Avenue by businessman John Wesley Dobbs, who fostered business development for African-Americans on this street. ✉ *135 Auburn Ave., Sweet Auburn* ☎ *404/521–2739* 🌐 *www.apexmuseum.org* 🎫 *$4* ⏲ *June–Aug. and Feb., Tues.–Sat. 10–5, Sun. 1–5; Sept.–Jan. and Mar.–May, Tues.–Sat. 10–5.*

CloseUp

DIVIDING HIGHWAYS

IN A CAR-CRAZY TOWN *like Atlanta, it's probably not surprising that roads define and even divide the city in so many ways. Many of the baffling, sudden name changes of Atlanta's roads have their roots in Jim Crow. After the Civil War, with the city essentially split into a white north half and a black south half during Reconstruction, white residents lobbied to have street names changed so they would not have to share addresses with black residents. At the east–west divider streets of North and Ponce de Leon avenues, north–south streets change names: Boulevard to Monroe, Moreland to Briarcliff, even Highland to North Highland.*

A more modern, and less sinister, dividing road is the I–285 highway bypass, aptly nicknamed "The Perimeter." The Perimeter serves as a cultural divider between the metro area's "two kinds" of people: those who live Inside the Perimeter (ITP'ers) and those who live Outside the Perimeter (OTP'ers). ITP'ers fancy themselves the hip intowners who support the arts, take advantage of the city's nightlife, and generally live more ecofriendly, short-commute lives. OTP'ers consider themselves genteel family folk who live the good life with better schools, less crime, and larger house lots.

Neither description would stand up in court, of course. Just like in any city, there are pockets of crime here and there, outstanding schools here and there, and great restaurants and cultural institutions sprinkled throughout. But everyone who lives in metro Atlanta knows which part of town is best: it's whichever side of the Perimeter they live on.

32 **Atlanta Daily World Building.** This simple two-story brick building, banded with a white frieze of lion heads, was constructed in the early 1900s; since 1945 it has housed one of the nation's oldest black newspapers (it's no longer a daily, however). Alexis Scott, publisher and CEO, is the granddaughter of William A. Scott II, who founded the paper in 1928. ✉ *145 Auburn Ave., Sweet Auburn* ☎ *404/659–1110* 🌐 *www.atlantadailyworld.com.*

34 **Atlanta Life Insurance Company.** The landmark enterprise founded by Alonzo Herndon, a former slave, was in modest quarters at 148 Auburn Avenue until this modern complex at No. 100 was opened in 1980. The lobby holds an exhibition of art by black artists from the United States and Africa. ✉ *100 Auburn Ave., Sweet Auburn* ☎ *404/659–2100* ⏲ *Weekdays 8–5.*

35 **Auburn Avenue Research Library on African-American Culture and History.** An extension of the Atlanta-Fulton Public Library system, this unit houses a noncirculating library with about 35,000 volumes devoted to African-American subjects. Special exhibits, programs, and tours are free to the public. The archives division contains art and artifacts, ephemera, transcribed oral histories, pamphlets, prints, rare periodicals, rare books,

manuscript collections, photographs, and memorabilia. ✉ *101 Auburn Ave., Sweet Auburn* ☎ *404/730–4001* 🌐 *http://aarl.af.public.lib.ga.us* 🕒 *Mon.–Thurs. 10–8, Fri.–Sun. noon–6.*

31 **Baptist Student Union.** This restored Victorian building adjacent to the Georgia State University campus once contained the Coca-Cola Company's first bottling plant. ✉ *125 Edgewood Ave., Sweet Auburn* ☎ *404/659–8726* 🌐 *www.gsu.edu/~wwwbsu.*

★ 27 **Ebenezer Baptist Church.** A Gothic Revival–style building completed in 1922, the church came to be known as the spiritual center of the civil rights movement after Martin Luther King Jr. won the Nobel peace prize in 1964. Members of the King family preached at the church for three generations, and Dr. King's funeral was held here. A tour of the church includes an audiotape outlining the history of the building. The congregation itself now occupies the building across the street. A federally funded restoration project is set for January 2005–January 2006, during which time the church will be closed; call ahead before visiting. ✉ *407 Auburn Ave., Sweet Auburn* ☎ *404/688–7263* 🎫 *Free* 🕒 *Tours mid-June–mid-Aug., Mon.–Sat. 9–6, Sun. 1–6; mid-Aug.–mid-June, Mon.–Sat. 9–5, Sun. 1–5; scheduled to be closed for restoration Jan. 2005–Jan. 2006.*

28 **John Wesley Dobbs Plaza.** John Wesley Dobbs was an important civic leader whose legacy includes coining the name "Sweet Auburn" for Atlanta's black business and residential neighborhood. The plaza, which was built for the 1996 Olympic Games, has a life mask of Dobbs himself; children playing in the plaza can view the street through the mask's eyes. ✉ *Auburn Ave. adjacent to I–75/85 overpass, Sweet Auburn.*

★ ⚑ 25 **Martin Luther King Jr. Birth Home.** This modest Queen Anne–style historic home is managed by the National Park Service, which also has a visitor center across the street from the Martin Luther King Jr. Center for Nonviolent Social Change. The visitor center contains an outstanding multimedia exhibit focused on the civil rights movement and Dr. King's role in it. To sign up for tours, go to the **Visitor Center** (✉ 450 Auburn Ave., Sweet Auburn). ✉ *501 Auburn Ave., Sweet Auburn* ☎ *404/331–6922* 🌐 *www.nps.gov/malu/* 🎫 *Free* 🕒 *Guided ½-hr tours daily 10–5.*

26 **Martin Luther King Jr. Center for Nonviolent Social Change.** The Martin Luther King Jr. National Historic District occupies several blocks on Auburn Avenue, a few blocks east of Peachtree Street in the black business and residential community of Sweet Auburn. Martin Luther King Jr. was born here in 1929; after his assassination in 1968, his widow, Coretta Scott King, established this center, which exhibits such personal items as King's Nobel peace prize, bible, and tape recorder, along with memorabilia and photos chronicling the civil rights movement. In the courtyard in front of Freedom Hall, on a circular brick pad in the middle of the rectangular Meditation Pool, is Dr. King's white-marble tomb; the inscription reads; FREE AT LAST! Nearby, an eternal flame burns. A chapel of all faiths sits at one end of the reflecting pool. ✉ *449 Auburn Ave., Sweet Auburn* ☎ *404/524–1956* 🌐 *www.thekingcenter.org* 🎫 *Free* 🕒 *Daily 9–5.*

off the beaten path

OAKLAND CEMETERY – Established in 1850 in the Victorian style, Atlanta's oldest cemetery was designed to serve as a public park as well as a burial ground. Some of the 70,000 permanent residents include six governors, five Confederate generals, novelist Margaret Mitchell, and golfing great Bobby Jones. You can bring a picnic here or take a tour conducted by the preservation-foundation volunteers. The King Center MARTA stop on the east–west line also serves the cemetery. ✉ *248 Oakland Ave., Sweet Auburn* ☎ *404/688–2107* 🌐 *www.oaklandcemetery.com* ⏲ *Tours May–Sept., Sat. at 10, 2, and 7, Sun. at 2; Mar., Apr., and Oct.–Dec., Sat. at 10 and 2, Sun. at 2. Call ahead to verify tour times and topics.*

29 **Odd Fellows Building.** The Georgia Chapter of the Grand United Order of Odd Fellows was a trade and social organization for African-Americans. In 1912 the membership erected this handsome Romanesque revival–style building housing meeting rooms, a theater, commercial spaces, and a community center. Terra-cotta figures adorn the splendid entrance. Now handsomely restored, the building houses offices. ✉ *250 Auburn Ave., Sweet Auburn* ☎ *404/525–5027* ⏲ *Weekdays 9–5.*

30 **Sweet Auburn Curb Market.** The market, an institution on Edgewood Avenue since 1923, sells vegetables, fish, flowers, prepared foods, and meat. Individual stalls are operated by separate owners, making this a true public market. Don't miss the splendid totemic sculptures by Atlanta artist Carl Joe Williams. The pieces were placed as part of Atlanta's Olympic art program. ✉ *209 Edgewood Ave., Sweet Auburn* ☎ *404/659–1665* ⏲ *Mon.–Thurs. 8–6, Fri. and Sat. 8–7.*

Midtown

Just north of downtown lies this thriving area, a hippie hangout in the late '60s and '70s that now houses a large segment of the city's gay population, along with young families, young professionals, artists, and musicians. Formerly in decline, Midtown has evolved into one of the city's most interesting and sought-after neighborhoods. Confirming its other facet as one of the city's most burgeoning business centers, its gleaming office towers now define a skyline that nearly rivals that of downtown, and the renovated mansions and bungalows in its residential section have made it a city showcase.

a good drive

Start your visit on Peachtree Street at the 1929 **Fox Theatre** 36 ⚑ and, across the street, the **Georgian Terrace** 37, a luxury suites hotel. From Peachtree Street circle around the block, turning right onto 3rd Street; turn right on Juniper Street, continue two blocks, and turn right onto North Avenue. Turn right again onto Peachtree Street to view the **Bank of America Plaza Tower** 38. Continuing up Peachtree Street to Peachtree Place (one block south of 10th Street), you'll find the **Margaret Mitchell House and Museum** 39, the restored building where the Pulitzer prize–winning author lived while completing *Gone With the Wind.* Across the street to the north is the **Federal Reserve Bank** 40. Walk west two blocks on 10th Street, turn right onto West Peachtree Street, and continue north to its intersection with 14th Street, where you'll see Philip Johnson's distinctive One Atlantic Center. Turn left onto 18th Street to reach the **Center for Puppetry Arts** 41 and **William Breman Jewish Heritage Museum** 42. Take 18th Street east back to Peachtree Street, turn left, and continue on to the **Woodruff Arts Center** 43, which includes the modern structure of the **High Museum of Art** 44. From this point travel two blocks north on Peachtree Street to the **Museum of Contemporary Art of Georgia** 45 and **Rhodes Memorial Hall** 46. From here take Beverly Road east off Peachtree Street for about ¼ mi to Montgomery Ferry Drive; turn a quick dogleg left, then right, continuing on Beverly to Park Lane, and then turn right onto Park Lane and drive about a ¼ mi to where it intersects the Prado. Here, these two streets dead-end onto Piedmont Avenue, where you'll enter the **Atlanta Botanical Garden** 47, which adjoins **Piedmont Park** 48, bounded by Piedmont Avenue, 10th Street, and Westminster Drive.

TIMING This drive is best accomplished between midmorning (about 9:30) and midafternoon (3:30) to avoid rush-hour traffic. Give yourself between four and five hours to visit all the sights. Each place has parking no more than a few steps away, and often it's free.

What to See

★ 47 **Atlanta Botanical Garden.** Occupying 30 acres inside Piedmont Park, the grounds contain 15 acres of display gardens, including a serene Japanese garden; a 15-acre hardwood forest with walking trails; the Fuqua Conservatory, which has unusual and threatened flora from tropical and desert climates; and the Fuqua Orchid Center, with displays of tropical and high-elevation flowers. A permanent exhibit within the conservatory of tiny, brightly colored poison-dart frogs is popular, especially with children. ✉ *1345 Piedmont Ave., at the Prado, Midtown* ☎ *404/876–5859* 🌐 *www.atlantabotanicalgarden.org* *$12* *Apr.–Sept., Tues.–Sun. 9–7; Oct.–Mar., Tues.–Sun. 9–5.*

38 **Bank of America Plaza Tower.** At 1,023 feet, this is the South's tallest building, erected in 1992. The skyscraper's graceful birdcage roof is easily visible from the interstate. The elegant marble central lobby is worth a glimpse. ✉ *600 Peachtree St., Midtown.*

★ 41 **Center for Puppetry Arts.** At this interactive museum you can see puppets from around the world and attend puppet-making workshops. Elaborate performances, which include original dramatic works and classics adapted for the museum theater, are presented by professional puppeteers—youngsters and adults alike are spellbound. In particular, the popular Christmas performance of *The Velveteen Rabbit* is a truly magical experience. ✉ *1404 Spring St., at 18th St., Midtown* ☎ *404/873–3391* 🌐 *www.puppet.org* *$5; special exhibits and programs extra* *Mon.–Sat. 9–5, Sun. 11–5.*

40 **Federal Reserve Bank.** The exhibits within this grand, monetary museum explain the story of money as a medium of exchange and the history of the U.S. banking system. Items displayed include rare coins, uncut sheets of money, and a gold bar. The self-guided tour includes a video, *The Fed Today.* ✉ *1000 Peachtree St., Midtown* ☎ *404/498–8777* 🌐 *www.frbatlanta.org* *Free* *Weekdays 9–4.*

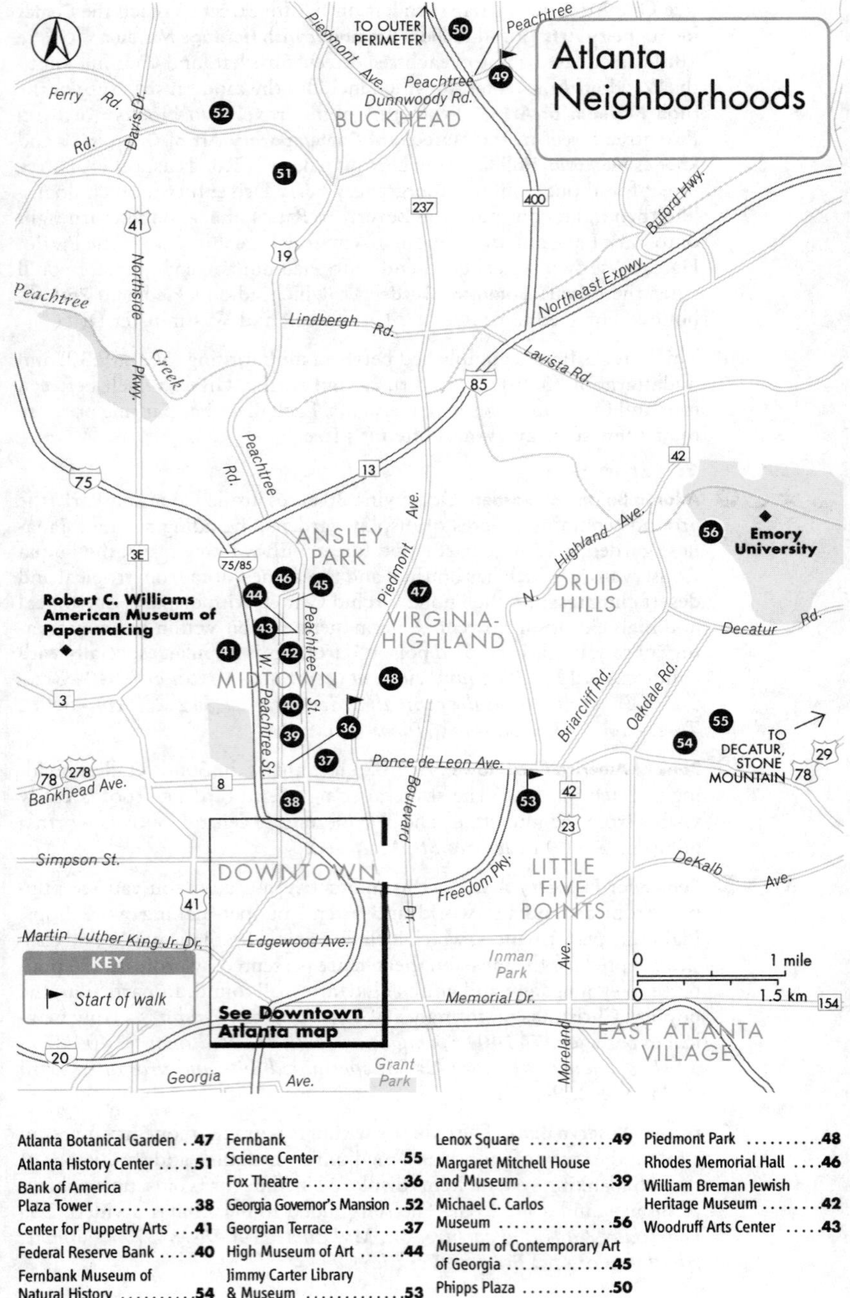

Atlanta Botanical Garden . . .47
Atlanta History Center 51
Bank of America Plaza Tower 38
Center for Puppetry Arts . . .41
Federal Reserve Bank 40
Fernbank Museum of Natural History 54
Fernbank Science Center 55
Fox Theatre 36
Georgia Governor's Mansion . .52
Georgian Terrace 37
High Museum of Art 44
Jimmy Carter Library & Museum 53
Lenox Square 49
Margaret Mitchell House and Museum 39
Michael C. Carlos Museum 56
Museum of Contemporary Art of Georgia 45
Phipps Plaza 50
Piedmont Park 48
Rhodes Memorial Hall 46
William Breman Jewish Heritage Museum 42
Woodruff Arts Center 43

★ 36 **Fox Theatre.** One of a dwindling number of vintage movie palaces in the nation, the Fox was built in 1929 in a fabulous Moorish-Egyptian style to be the headquarters of the Shriners Club. The interior's crowning glory is its ceiling, complete with moving clouds and twinkling stars above Alhambra-like minarets. Threatened by demolition in the 1970s, the Fox was saved from the wrecker's ball by concerted civic action and is still a prime venue for musicals, rock concerts, dance performances, and film festivals. *660 Peachtree St., Midtown 404/881–2100, 404/876–2041 for Atlanta Preservation Center www.foxtheatre.org Tour, conducted by Atlanta Preservation Center, $10 Tours Mon., Wed., and Thurs. at 10, Sat. at 10 and 11.*

11

37 **Georgian Terrace.** Built in 1911 as a fine beaux arts–style hotel, the Georgian Terrace, designed by William L. Stoddart, housed the stars of the film *Gone With the Wind* when it premiered at the nearby Loew's Theater (now demolished) in 1939. President Calvin Coolidge also slept here. Stars of the Metropolitan Opera stayed at the hotel when the Met used to make its annual trek to Atlanta, and according to locals, Enrico Caruso routinely serenaded passersby from its balconies. Renovated with style and historic sensitivity, the building is now a luxury hotel. *459 Peachtree St., Midtown 404/897–1991 www.thegeorgianterrace.com.*

★ 44 **High Museum of Art.** The permanent holdings of this high-tech museum focus on American and African art and decorative arts. The Uhry Print Collection contains works by French impressionists and other European artists. In 1991 the American Institute of Architects listed the sleek structure, designed by Richard Meier and built in 1983, among the 10 best works of American architecture of the '80s. At this writing an expansion designed by Renzo Piano was set to open in spring 2005. *Woodruff Arts Center, 1280 Peachtree St., MARTA Arts Center station, Midtown 404/733–4400, 404/733–4444 recorded information www.high.org $10, varies for special events Tues.–Sat. 10–5, Sun. noon–5; hrs often extended for special exhibits and programs.*

39 **Margaret Mitchell House and Museum.** Although the author of *Gone With the Wind* detested the turn-of-the-20th-century apartment house (she called it "the Dump") in which she lived when she wrote her masterpiece, determined volunteers got backing to restore the house and open it to the public. To many Atlantans, the Margaret Mitchell House is a lightning rod, symbolizing the conflict between promoting the city's heritage and respecting its varied roots. The house has been gutted by arsonists twice, in 1995 and 1996, the second time within days of a major restoration. Although Mitchell (1900–49) is the city's most famous author, her fame derived from writing a book that includes stereotypes of African-Americans that many find offensive. Others point out that before her tragically early death, Mitchell secretly helped to fund medical-school scholarships to Morehouse College for scores of African-American college students. Both supporters and critics of the house hold their views passionately. The visitor center exhibits photographs, archival material, and personal possessions, including her original typewriter. *990 Peachtree St., at Peachtree Pl., Midtown 404/249–7015 www.gwtw.org $12 Daily 9:30–5.*

CloseUp

IN SEARCH OF TARA

GONE WITH THE WIND enthusiasts like to say that no book other than the Bible has sold more copies worldwide than the novel about a scrappy Southern gal desperately trying to hold on to her family home during the Civil War. But fans who come to Atlanta, where Margaret Mitchell lived when she wrote the book, are often disappointed to discover that Scarlett O'Hara's beloved plantation, Tara, was no more real than Scarlett herself.

You're not going to find Tara here, but that doesn't mean that you can't have a good time looking. Several local businesses, promoters, and Gone With the Wind fans will happily help you find your own little piece of antebellum romance. And if nothing else, you are sure to stumble across some real history in the process: the people, places, and events that inspired Mitchell's work.

In Atlanta, "the Dump," the Midtown apartment house in which Margaret Mitchell and her husband, John Marsh, lived when Mitchell wrote the novel, has been rebuilt and is now called the Margaret Mitchell House and Museum; the visitor center here contains photographs and some of Mitchell's personal effects. Also in Atlanta is Mitchell's grave, at the Oakland Cemetery in Sweet Auburn. Several Confederate generals and other historic figures are also buried in this Victorian-style cemetery-park dating to 1850.

Clayton County, approximately 15 mi south of Atlanta, promotes itself as the "Legendary Land of Gone With the Wind," since much of the novel was set here. The ***Clayton County Convention and Visitor's Bureau*** *(✉ 104 N. Main St., Jonesboro 30236 ☎ 770/478–4800 🌐 www.visitscarlett.com) highlights several sights and activities related to the book and film, including a Gone With the Wind tour (☎ 770/477–8864). Clayton County's* ***Road to Tara Museum*** *(✉ 104 N. Main St., Jonesboro ☎ 770/478–4800) houses props and reproduction costumes from the movie. For some true Civil War history, visit the* ***Patrick R. Cleburne Confederate Memorial Cemetery*** *(✉ McDonough and Johnson Sts., Jonesboro): this is the resting place of hundreds of Confederate soldiers who died during the 1864 Battle of Jonesboro. The* ***Stately Oaks Historic Home & Plantation Community*** *(✉ 100 Carriage Dr., at Jodeco Rd., Jonesboro ☎ 770/473–0197) isn't Tara, but it can reveal what life was like on a real plantation home. Costumed guides lead tours through the 1839 Greek Revival main house and several outbuildings.*

In Barnesville, about 50 mi south of Atlanta, is the ***Tarleton Oaks Bed & Breakfast*** *(✉ 643 Greenwood St., Barnesville ☎ 770/358–4989 🌐 www.tarleton-oaks.com), owned by Gone With the Wind cast member Fred Crane, who delivered the film's opening lines as suitor Brent Tarleton. The B&B plays up the Gone With the Wind theme with a Hall of Stars Museum, which houses costumes, photographs, and the stars' personal memorabilia from the film. The refurbished circa-1849 building served as a Confederate headquarters and hospital during the war and is on the National Register of Historic Places.*

Just a few miles north of Atlanta, the ***Marietta Gone With the Wind Museum: Scarlett on the Square*** *(✉ 18 Whitlock Ave., Marietta ☎ 770/794–5576 🌐 www.gwtwmarietta.com) houses book and movie memorabilia, including a gown worn by Vivian Leigh as Scarlett O'Hara in the film and copies of the book printed in several different languages. A display here is dedicated to the movie's African-American cast members.*

45 **Museum of Contemporary Art of Georgia.** Georgian visual artists are showcased in this office-building lobby formerly occupied by a restaurant. More than 250 paintings, photographs, sculptures, and other works are part of the permanent collection. ✉ *1447 Peachtree St., Midtown* ☎ *404/881–1109* 🌐 *www.mocaga.org* 🎫 *Free* 🕐 *Tues.–Sat. 10–5.*

48 **Piedmont Park.** The city's outdoor recreation center, this park, founded in the late 19th century, is a major venue for special events. Tennis courts, a swimming pool, and paths for walking, jogging, and rollerblading are part of the attraction, but many retreat to the park's great lawn for picnics with a smashing view of the Midtown skyline. Each April the park hosts the popular Dogwood Festival. ✉ *Piedmont Ave. between 10th St. and Monroe Dr., Midtown* 🌐 *www.piedmontpark.org.*

46 **Rhodes Memorial Hall.** This former residence, now headquarters of the **Georgia Trust for Historic Preservation,** is one of the finest works of Atlanta architect Willis F. Denny II. It was built at the northern edge of the city in 1904 for Amos Giles Rhodes, the wealthy founder of a Southern furniture chain. The stained-glass windows in the hall depict the rise and fall of the Confederacy. ✉ *1516 Peachtree St., Midtown* ☎ *404/881–9980* 🌐 *www.georgiatrust.org* 🎫 *$5; $8 for Sunday behind-the-scenes tour* 🕐 *Weekdays 11–4, Sun. noon–3.*

Robert C. Williams American Museum of Papermaking. More than 10,000 tools, machines, papers, and watermarks, plus manuscripts and books, trace the history of papermaking from its origins. The museum is housed at the Georgia Institute of Technology's Institute of Paper Science and Technology. ✉ *500 10th St. NW, Midtown* ☎ *404/894–7840* 🌐 *www.ipst.gatech.edu/amp/index.html* 🎫 *Free* 🕐 *Weekdays 9–5.*

42 **William Breman Jewish Heritage Museum.** The history of the Jewish community in Atlanta is told through a permanent exhibit called "Creating Community." Other exhibits document the Holocaust and the immigrant experience in America. ✉ *1440 Spring St., Midtown* ☎ *678/222–3700* 🌐 *www.thebreman.org* 🎫 *$6* 🕐 *Mon.–Thurs. 10–5, Fri. 10–3, Sun. 1–5.*

43 **Woodruff Arts Center.** The center includes the world-renowned **Atlanta Symphony Orchestra,** the **High Museum of Art,** and the **Alliance Theatre,** plus the nearby **14th Street Playhouse,** which has several repertory companies. Both theaters present contemporary dramas, classics, and frequent world premieres. Next door, the center is building Symphony Center, scheduled to open in 2008. ✉ *1280 Peachtree St., Midtown* ☎ *404/733–4200* 🌐 *www.woodruffcenter.org.*

Buckhead

Many of Atlanta's trendy restaurants, music clubs, chic shops, and hip art galleries are concentrated in this neighborhood. Atlanta's sprawl doesn't lend itself to walking between major neighborhoods, so take a car or MARTA to reach Buckhead. Finding a parking spot on the weekends and at night can be a real headache, and waits of two hours or more are common in the hottest restaurants.

a good drive

Begin this drive at the intersection of two splendid shopping malls. The older and larger of the two is **Lenox Square** 49, at 3393 Peachtree Road. Across the street are the elegant shops of **Phipps Plaza** 50. Leaving Phipps Plaza, exit onto Peachtree Road and turn right (south), traveling about ⅓ mi to West Paces Ferry Road. Turn right and proceed to the **Atlanta History Center** 51. After visiting the center drive west about ½ mi along West Paces Ferry Road to reach the **Georgia Governor's Mansion** 52.

A 4-mi drive north along Peachtree-Dunwoody Road takes you by some of the city's most impressive residential dwellings and leads you straight to the popular Perimeter Mall, a sprawling "shop-opolis" bolstered with nearby megastores and home-design outlets. Its location is at the northern crest of I–285, the freeway circling the city in an approximate 10-mi radius, thus delineating the inner and outer perimeters of metro Atlanta. Loosely speaking, the Perimeter area, which is most heavily focused along this northern section of I–285, has become one of the nation's fastest-growing "edge cities," complete with hundreds of trendy restaurants, office towers, mostly business-oriented hotels, and condo and housing subdivisions galore.

TIMING Simply driving the distance around the sights, looking briefly at each one, will consume, generally, no more than 30 minutes. Allot several hours if you want to shop or tour the Atlanta History Center and Georgia Governor's Mansion. And give yourself at least another two hours if you wish to explore the Perimeter area north of Buckhead—a section that's plagued by heavy traffic much of the time.

What to See

★ 51 **Atlanta History Center.** Life in Atlanta, the South, and the military are the focus of this museum, which also highlights materials native to Georgia, with a floor of heart pine and polished Stone Mountain granite. Displays are provocative, juxtaposing *Gone With the Wind* romanticism with the grim reality of Ku Klux Klan racism. Also on the 33-acre site are the elegant 1928 **Swan House**; the **Tullie Smith Farm;** with a two-story plantation plain house (1840s); and **McElreath Hall,** an exhibition space for artifacts from Atlanta's history. The grounds are landscaped with native plants. ✉ *130 W. Paces Ferry Rd., Buckhead* ☎ *404/814–4000* 🌐 *www.atlantahistorycenter.com* 🎟 *$12* ⏲ *Mon.–Sat. 10–5:30, Sun. noon–5:30.*

52 **Georgia Governor's Mansion.** This 24,000-square-foot 1967 Greek revival mansion contains 30 rooms and sits on 18 acres that originally belonged to the Robert Maddox family (no relation to Georgia governor Lester Maddox, who was its first occupant). Federal-period antiques fill the public rooms. ✉ *391 W. Paces Ferry Rd., Buckhead* ☎ *404/261–1858* 🌐 *www.gov.state.ga.us/about_mansion.shtml* ⏲ *Free guided tours Tues.–Thurs. 10–11:30.*

49 **Lenox Square.** Local shoppers come for the more than 250 stores and several good restaurants at this mall. ✉ *3393 Peachtree Rd., Buckhead* ☎ *404/233–6767* 🌐 *www.lenoxsquare.com.*

50 **Phipps Plaza.** The mall is one of Atlanta's premier shopping areas, with upscale chain stores, specialty shops, and restaurants. It also includes a

14-screen movie theater. ✉ *3500 Peachtree Rd., Buckhead* ☎ *404/262–0992 or 800/810–7700* 🌐 *www.phippsplaza.com.*

Virginia-Highland & the Emory Area

Restaurants and art galleries are the backbone of Virginia-Highland/Morningside, northeast of Midtown. Like Midtown, this residential area was down-at-the-heels in the 1970s. Reclaimed by writers, artists, and a few visionary developers, Virginia-Highland (and its bordering Morningside neighborhood, to the north) today offers intriguing shopping and delightful walking. Nightlife hums here as well. To the east, the Emory University area is studded with enviable mansions and expansive landscaping.

a good drive

This tour meanders through some residential areas, such as Druid Hills, the location for the film *Driving Miss Daisy,* by local playwright Alfred Uhry. The neighborhood was designed by the firm of Frederick Law Olmsted, which also designed New York's Central Park. Begin at the **Jimmy Carter Library & Museum** 53 ⚑, the central attraction in a subneighborhood called Poncey Highland (because it lies south of Ponce de Leon Avenue along Highland Avenue). The presidential center is bounded by Freedom Parkway, which splits and encircles the facility. To reach it from downtown, drive on Ralph McGill Boulevard about 1 mi east of I–75/85 (Exit 248C) to where the boulevard intersects with Freedom Parkway.

From the center take a left, drive only one short block on Highland Avenue to Ponce de Leon Avenue, and turn right (east), continuing for 1 mi to Clifton Road; take a left onto Clifton Road and almost immediately enter the driveway for the **Fernbank Museum of Natural History** 54. On the east end of this extensive forest and recreational, educational preserve lies the **Fernbank Science Center** 55. After visiting the science center, return to the Fernbank Museum, turn right onto Clifton Road, and head north to the campus of Emory University to visit the **Michael C. Carlos Museum** 56, an exquisite contemporary structure.

TIMING You can drive this tour in about 15 minutes without stops. If you spend a few hours at each sight, it can easily take a full day.

What to See

★ 54 **Fernbank Museum of Natural History.** One of the largest natural history museums south of the Smithsonian Institution in Washington, D.C., holds a permanent exhibit, "A Walk Through Time in Georgia." You can meander through 15 galleries to explore the earth's natural history, or watch a film on the natural world in the on-site IMAX theater. The café, with an exquisite view of the forest, serves great food. ✉ *767 Clifton Rd., Emory* ☎ *404/929–6300* 🌐 *www.fernbank.edu/museum/* *Museum $12, IMAX $10, combination ticket $17* ⏲ *Museum Mon.–Sat. 10–5, Sun. noon–5; IMAX Mon.–Thurs. 10–5, Fri. 10–10, Sat. 10–5, Sun. noon–5.*

55 **Fernbank Science Center.** The museum focuses on geology, space exploration, and ecology. In addition to the exhibit hall, the center also has a planetarium, a space observatory, the 65-acre Fernbank Forest, and a public rose garden. ✉ *156 Heaton Park Dr., Emory* ☎ *678/874–7102*

⊕ *http://fsc.fernbank.edu/* 🎫 *Museum free, planetarium shows $4* ⏲ *Mon. 8:30–5, Tues.–Fri. 8:30 AM–10 PM, Sat. 10–5, Sun. 1–5; planetarium shows Tues. and Thurs. at 8 PM, Wed. and Fri. at 3 and 8, weekends at 3.*

off the beaten path

INMAN PARK AND LITTLE FIVE POINTS – Since this once-grand neighborhood about 4 mi east of downtown was laid out by famous developer Joel Hurt in 1889, the area has faded and flourished a number of times, which explains the vast gaps in opulence evident in much of the architecture here. Huge, ornate Victorian mansions sit next to humble shotgun shacks. But no matter the exact address or style of home—be it modest or massive—all of Inman Park now commands considerable cachet among all types, from young families to empty-nesters to gays and lesbians. Here you'll also find the delightfully countercultural Little Five Points section, ground zero for Atlanta funk. Though many of the storefronts here where Moreland, Euclid, and McLendon avenues intersect defy description, all are delightful. Check out the fascinating **Junkman's Daughter,** a funky-junky department store (✉ 464 Moreland Ave. NE, Inman Park ☎ 404/577–3188). The **Clothing Warehouse** (✉ 420 Moreland Ave., Inman Park ☎ 404/524–5070) is one of the many colorful vintage-clothing stores here. **A Capella Books** (✉ 1133 Euclid Ave. NE, Inman Park ☎ 404/681–5128) stocks some 25,000 new and out-of-print titles.

★ ⚑ 53 **Jimmy Carter Library & Museum.** This complex occupies the site where Union general William T. Sherman orchestrated the Battle of Atlanta (1864). The museum and archives detail the political career of former president Jimmy Carter. The Carter Center, which shares the campus but is not open to the public, focuses on conflict resolution and human rights issues. It sponsors foreign-affairs conferences and projects on such matters as the world food supply. Outside, the Japanese-style garden is a serene spot to unwind. ✉ *441 Freedom Pkwy., Virginia-Highland* ☎ *404/865–7100* ⊕ *www.jimmycarterlibrary.org* 🎫 *$7* ⏲ *Mon.–Sat. 9–4:45, Sun. noon–4:45.*

★ 🦆 56 **Michael C. Carlos Museum.** Housing a permanent collection of more than 16,000 objects, this excellent museum designed by renowned American architect Michael Graves exhibits artifacts from Egypt, Greece, Rome, the Near East, the Americas, and Africa. European and American prints and drawings cover the Middle Ages through the 20th century. The gift shop sells rare art books, jewelry, and art-focused items for children. The museum's Caffé Antico is a good lunch spot. ✉ *Emory University, 571 S. Kilgo St., Emory* ☎ *404/727–4282* ⊕ *http://carlos.emory.edu/* 🎫 *Suggested donation $5* ⏲ *Tues., Wed., Fri., and Sat. 10–5, Thurs. 10–9, Sun. noon–5.*

Other Area Attractions

It's essential to drive to most of these venues, so plan your visits with Atlanta's notorious rush hours in mind.

Château Élan. This inn, built in the style of a 16th-century French château, has Georgia's best-known winery, ensconced in 2,400 rolling acres about an hour north of downtown Atlanta. Château Élan is also a complete resort: European luxury blends with Southern hospitality at the 274-room inn and spa with private villas, golf courses, and an equestrian center. *100 Rue Charlemagne, Braselton, I–85 to GA 211, Exit 126 (Chestnut Mountain/Winder) 800/233–9463 770/271–6005 www.chateauelan.com Winery tours and tastings free Wine market daily 10–9. Tours weekdays at 11, 12:30, 2, 3:30, Sat. hourly 11–5, Sun. hourly noon–4.*

Chattahoochee Nature Center. Birds and animals in their natural habitats may be seen from nature trails and a boardwalk winding through 124 acres of woodlands and wetlands. A gift shop, indoor exhibits, birds-of-prey aviaries, and a picnic area are on the property. *9135 Willeo Rd., Roswell 770/992–2055 www.chattnaturecenter.com $3 Mon.–Sat. 9–5, Sun. noon–5.*

Decatur Historical Courthouse. Known as the Old Courthouse on the Square, this charming building was constructed in 1823 and now houses the DeKalb History Center. It's right in the midst of the shops, coffee-houses, and cafés of Decatur's quaint main square. Free concerts are sometimes held in the gazebo behind the Old Courthouse. Downtown Decatur has its own stop on MARTA's east–west rail line. *101 E. Court Sq., Decatur, Ponce de Leon Ave., east 8 mi to Decatur Sq. at Clairmont Ave. 404/373–1088 404/373–8287 www.dekalbhistory.org Free Weekdays 9–4.*

★ **Kennesaw Mountain National Battlefield.** A must for Civil War buffs, this 2,884-acre park with 16 mi of hiking trails was the site of several crucial battles in June 1864. The visitor center contains a small museum with exhibits of Civil War weapons, uniforms, and other items recovered from the battlefield. A 10-minute slide presentation explains the battles. *Old U.S. 41 and Stilesboro Rd., look for signs on I–75N, Kennesaw 770/427–4686 www.nps.gov/kemo Free Daily 7:30–8.*

Six Flags Over Georgia. Atlanta's major theme park, with eight sections, heart-stopping roller coasters, and water rides (best saved for last so you won't be damp all day), is a child's ideal playground. The Superman Ultimate Flight roller coaster lets you "fly" headfirst through loops and dives at up to 60 mph. The park also has well-staged musical revues, concerts by top-name artists, and other performances. Take MARTA's west line to the Hamilton Homes station and then the Six Flags bus. *I–20W at 7561 Six Flags Pkwy., Austell 770/739–3400 www.sixflags.com All-inclusive 1-day pass $42.99, parking $10 or $12, depending on the lot June–Aug., daily 10 AM–11 PM; Mar.–May, Sept., and Oct., weekends from 10, closing times vary.*

Southern Museum of Civil War and Locomotive History. The General, the locomotive stolen by Union forces from the Confederates during the Civil War's "Great Locomotive Chase," is the star attraction at this museum affiliated with the Smithsonian Institution. Other permanent exhibits illustrate how railroads were used to ship troops, weapons, and supplies during the war; the role railroads played in rebuilding the South after the war is also examined here. The museum is about 25 mi north of downtown Atlanta off I–75, and about 4 mi north of Kennesaw Mountain National Battlefield. ✉ *2829 Cherokee St., Kennesaw* ☎ *770/427–2117* 🌐 *www.southernmuseum.org* 🎟 *$7.50* ⏲ *Mon.–Sat. 9:30–5, Sun. noon–5.*

★ **Stone Mountain Park.** At this 3,200-acre, privately managed state park 15 mi east of Atlanta you'll find the largest exposed granite outcropping on earth. The Confederate Memorial on the north face of the 825-foot-high domed mountain is the world's largest sculpture, measuring 90 feet by 190 feet. The park has a cable car to the mountaintop, a steam locomotive ride around the mountain's base, an antebellum plantation, a swimming beach, golf courses, a campground, a hotel, a resort, a wildlife preserve, restaurants, and two Civil War museums. Summer nights are capped with the spectacular **Lasershow Spectacular,** an outdoor light display set to music and projected onto the side of Stone Mountain—attendance is a rite of passage for new Atlantans. Annual events such as the Yellow Daisy Festival and the Scottish Highland Games are popular in the fall. Crossroads, an entertainment complex with an 1870s-Southern-town theme, offers costumed interpreters and a "4-D" movie theater. ✉ *U.S. 78E (Stone Mountain Pkwy.), Stone Mountain* ☎ *770/498–5600* 🌐 *www.stonemountainpark.com* 🎟 *$7 per car; annual pass $30; day pass to all attractions $19; some attractions are free* ⏲ *Daily 6 AM–midnight; Lasershow Spectacular nightly after sunset in summer, Sat. night after sunset in spring and fall; call for exact schedule.*

★ **Your DeKalb Farmers Market.** This sprawling warehouse store 9 mi east of Atlanta may not be a true farmers' market, but it's truly a market experience to remember. Rows of bins of produce from around the world are perhaps the biggest attraction: root vegetables from Africa, greens from Asia, wines from South America, cheeses from Europe. The store also has one of the largest seafood departments in the country (a few species still swimming) and sizable meat, deli, beer–wine, and import sections. People-watching and chaos (the floor is the size of two football fields) are part of the fun. Staffers wear name tags listing the languages they speak. The reasonably priced cafeteria sells freshly prepared vegetables and dishes ranging from lasagna to goat stew. The market is accessible by MARTA bus from the Avondale rail station. ✉ *3000 E. Ponce de Leon Ave., Decatur* ☎ *404/377–6400* 🌐 *www.dekalbfarmersmarket.com* ⏲ *Daily 9–9.*

SPORTS & THE OUTDOORS

At almost any time of the year, in parks, private clubs, and neighborhoods throughout the city, you'll find Atlantans pursuing everything from tennis to soccer to rollerblading. The magazine ***Atlanta Sports & Fitness*** (☎ 404/843–2257), available free at many health clubs and sports and outdoors stores, is a good link to Atlanta's athletic community. Pick up ***Georgia Athlete*** at gyms and sports stores if you need a guide to individual sporting events.

Baseball

Atlanta's most beloved team, Major League Baseball's **Atlanta Braves** (✉ Turner Field, I–75/85, Exit 246 [Fulton St.]; I–20, westbound Exit 58A [Capitol Ave.], eastbound Exit 56B [Windsor St./Spring St.], Downtown ☎ 404/522–7630), play in Turner Field, formerly the Olympic Stadium.

Basketball

The **Atlanta Hawks** (✉ Philips Arena, 1 Philips Dr., Downtown ☎ 404/827–3800 or 404/827–3865) had a proud moment in '96 when then-coach Lenny Wilkens was selected to head the U.S. Olympic men's basketball team in Atlanta. The purchase of the team in 2004 by a group of investors called Atlanta Spirit, LLC, has sparked hopes of future glory on the court.

Biking & Rollerblading

Closed to traffic, **Piedmont Park** (✉ Piedmont Ave. between 10th St. and Monroe Ave., Midtown) is popular for rollerblading, biking, dog-walking, and other recreational activities. **Skate Escape** (✉ 1086 Piedmont Ave., across from Piedmont Park, Midtown ☎ 404/892–1292) rents bikes and skates.

Part of the Atlanta–DeKalb trail system, the **Stone Mountain/Atlanta Greenway trail** is a mostly paved, off-road path that follows Ponce de Leon Avenue east of the city into Stone Mountain Park. A good place to start is at Your DeKalb Farmer's Market (3000 E. Ponce de Leon Ave., Decatur), as it has extensive parking; from here head east toward Stone Mountain. It's about 17 mi round-trip to the park gates and back; a circle around the park adds another 5 mi. Another paved, shorter portion of the trail goes by the Jimmy Carter Library & Museum.

Football

The **Atlanta Falcons** (✉ Georgia Dome, 1 Georgia Dome Dr., Downtown ☎ 770/965–3115), enjoyed a surge of popularity beginning in 2002, when the team's new owner, Home Depot cofounder Arthur Blank, restructured ticket pricing and poured energy into promoting the team. Season tickets sold out in a matter of minutes in 2003 and were expected to do the same in 2004 and 2005.

Georgia Force (✉ The Arena at Gwinnett Center, 6400 Sugarloaf Pkwy., Duluth ☎ 770/813–7610) is part of the Arena Football League, whose season runs February–May.

Golf

Golf is enormously popular here, as the numerous courses attest. The only public course within sight of downtown Atlanta is the **Bobby Jones Golf Course** (✉ 384 Woodward Way, Buckhead ☎ 404/355–1009), named after the famed golfer and Atlanta native and occupying a portion of the site of the Civil War's Battle of Peachtree Creek. Despite having some of the city's worst fairways and greens, the immensely popular 18-hole, par-71 course is always crowded. The 18-hole, par-71 **North Fulton Golf Course** (✉ 216 W. Wieuca Rd., Buckhead ☎ 404/255–0723) has one of the best layouts in the area. It's at Chastain Park, within the I–285 perimeter.

Stone Mountain Park (✉ U.S. 78E [Stone Mountain Pkwy.], Stone Mountain ☎ 770/465–3278) has two courses. Stonemont, an 18-hole, par-72 course with several challenging and scenic holes, is the better of the two. The other course, Lakemont, is also 18-hole, par 72.

Hockey

The National Hockey League's young **Atlanta Thrashers** (✉ Philips Arena, 1 Philips Dr., Downtown ☎ 404/827–5300), named for the state bird, the brown thrasher, debuted during the 1999–2000 season. The team is backed by Atlanta Spirit, LLC, which also owns the Atlanta Hawks basketball team and the operating rights to Philips Arena.

The **Gwinnett Gladiators** (✉ The Arena at Gwinnett Center, 6400 Sugarloaf Pkwy., Duluth ☎ 770/497–5100), a farm team for the Atlanta Thrashers, play in the ECHL; 2003–2004 was their inaugural season. Games are played October–April.

Jogging & Running

Chattahoochee National Recreation Area (✉ 1978 Island Ford Pkwy. ☎ 678/538–1200) contains different parcels of land that lie in 16 separate units spread along the banks of the Chattahoochee River, much of which has been protected from development. The area is crisscrossed by 70 mi of trails.

Tennis

Bitsy Grant Tennis Center (✉ 2125 Northside Dr., Buckhead ☎ 404/609–7193), named for one of Atlanta's most well-known players, is the area's best public facility, with 13 clay courts (6 of which are lighted) and 10 lighted hard courts. Charges per person per hour are $2.50 for the hard courts, $4.50 for the clay courts. The courts close around 8, and the clubhouse closes at 9.

Piedmont Park (✉ Piedmont Ave. between 10th St. and Monroe Dr., Midtown ☎ 404/853–3461), Atlanta's most popular park, has 12 lighted hard courts. Access the tennis center from Park Drive off Monroe Drive; even though the sign says DO NOT ENTER, the security guard will show you the parking lot. The courts are always open, but the staff keeps specific hours (weekdays 9–9, weekends 9:30–6). The costs are $2.50 per person per hour before 6 PM and $3 after 6 PM.

WHERE TO EAT

Atlanta has sophisticated kitchens run by world-class chefs, myriad ethnic restaurants, and classic Southern establishments serving such regional favorites as fried chicken, fried catfish, and okra. There's no shortage of urban chic in the dining scene, but traditional Southern fare—including Cajun and creole, country-style and plantation cuisine, coastal and mountain dishes—thrives.

The local taste for things sweet and fried holds true for restaurants serving traditional Southern food. Tea in the South comes iced and sweet; if you want hot tea, specify hot. Desserts in the region are legendary. Catch the flavor of the South at breakfast and lunch in modest establishments that serve only these meals. Reserve evenings for culinary exploration, including some of the new restaurants that present traditional ingredients and dishes in fresh ways. The influx of Asian immigrants makes Atlanta the perfect city to sample Thai, Vietnamese, Korean, Japanese, Indian and authentic Chinese cuisines.

Most restaurants will accept you just as you are; dress codes are extremely rare in this casual city. But that come-as-you-are attitude can work against patrons on busy nights; many popular restaurants operate on a first-come, first-served basis on weekends, accepting only limited reservations. Waits at some hot dining spots can exceed an hour, especially if you arrive after 7 PM.

11

Prices

Dining in Atlanta and its suburbs can be quite expensive. Fortunately, many of the more expensive restaurants offer early-bird weeknight specials and prix-fixe menus. Ask when you call to make reservations.

A dining option that has become very popular in recent years are counter-service restaurants. These usually casual restaurants require guests to place their order at a counter, which cuts staffing expenses. In general, the food quality remains quite high, and the food is still brought to the table by servers. Many local restaurant names operate under this system, including Fellini's Pizza, Willy's California-Style Burritos and Moe's Southwest Grill, as well as Figo Pasta and Taqueria del Sol.

WHAT IT COSTS

$$$$	$$$	$$	$	¢
over $22	$16–$22	$11–$16	$7–$11	under $7

Restaurant prices are for a main course at dinner, excluding sales tax of 6%–8%.

Downtown

American/Casual

$–$$$$ ✕ **Ted's Montana Grill.** It has another state's name and it's a chain, but Atlantans still feel a sense of ownership for this burger joint specializing in bison meat. Chicken, beef, and trout also play a role on the menu. Ceiling fans and wood accents add to the rustic decor. The "Ted" in question is CNN founder Ted Turner, who has left a significant mark on this city. ✉ *133 Luckie St., Downtown* ☎ *404/521–9796* ✍ *Reservations not accepted* ▭ *AE, D, DC, MC, V.*

$–$$$ ✕ **Max Lager's American Grill & Brewery.** Line up a tasting of the house brews—the pale ale and brown ale are tops—and then order the Gulf Coast gumbo, the "Maximum" T-bone (an 18-ounce steak), or one of the popular specialty pizzas. The pub also brews its own root and ginger beers. This lively brewpub near the city's major high-rise buildings is hopping after business hours. ✉ *320 Peachtree St., Downtown* ☎ *404/525–4400* ▭ *AE, D, DC, MC, V.*

Barbecue

¢–$ ✕ **ACE Barbecue Barn.** Delicious ribs and chopped rib tips, baked chicken and dressing, and sweet-potato pie are the draws at this slightly worn down-home restaurant. It's near the Martin Luther King Jr. Center. ✉ *30 Bell St. NE, Sweet Auburn* ☎ *404/659–6630* *Reservations not accepted* ▭ *No credit cards* ⏲ *Closed Tues.*

Contemporary

★ $$$–$$$$ ✕ **Food Studio.** No less stylish for being a piece of a former plow factory, the restaurant gleams with high-tech and industrial touches. From the same group that made South City Kitchen a success, Studio is known for innovative American food—but has added a few more traditional dishes, such as New York strip steak with blue-cheese mashed potatoes. Desserts range from the parfaitlike frozen lemon-basil bombe to chocolate-dipped cheesecake. ✉ *887 W. Marietta St., Studio K-102, King Plow Arts Center, Downtown* ☎ *404/815–6677* *Reservations essential* ▭ *AE, DC, MC, V* ⏲ *No lunch.*

Eclectic

$$$–$$$$ ✕ **Luxe.** A 50-foot-long granite-topped bar and a giant fireplace salvaged from Georgia's first governor's mansion are the centerpieces at this contemporary-style spot popular with businesspeople. At lunch, the burgers are made with Kobe beef and the grilled-cheese sandwiches have cured salmon; at dinner, classics like rack of lamb are updated with pea ravioli and trout is stuffed with serrano peppers. ✉ *89 Park Pl., Downtown* ☎ *404/389–0800* ▭ *AE, MC, V* ⏲ *Closed Sun. No lunch Sat.*

Pizza

¢–$ ✕ **Rosa's Pizza.** It takes a bit of courage to shout out your order in front of the long line that snakes back and forth in the entryway of this New York–style pizza joint. But regulars—mostly downtown office workers—are used to the routine and will even gently prod newcomers when it's their turn to speak up. The two-slice special—one topping per slice plus a drink, for $4.99—is always a good choice, as are the handmade calzones. Note that Rosa's is only open until 6 PM and is closed weekends. ✉ *62 Broad St. NW, Downtown* ☎ *404/521–2596* ▭ *No credit cards* ⏲ *Closed weekends.*

Southern

$$$$ ✕ **Atlanta Grill.** With an outdoor veranda overlooking Peachtree Street, this restaurant in the Ritz-Carlton, Atlanta, has taken dining in the hotel from formal to casual. Chef Matthew Swickerath makes the most of Southern ingredients such as Carolina trout and Sweet Grass Dairy cheeses. Signature dishes include grilled pork porterhouse and shrimp and grits. ✉ *181 Peachtree St., Downtown* ☎ *404/221–6550* ▭ *AE, D, DC, MC, V.*

★ $$–$$$$ ✕ **City Grill.** This is the poshest power-lunch spot in Atlanta and has made the most of its grand location in the elegantly renovated historic Hurt Building. An impressive wine list accompanies the equally impressive menu, which includes hickory-grilled meats and seasonal-berry shortcake. ✉ *50 Hurt Plaza, Downtown* ☎ *404/524–2489* ▭ *AE, D, DC, MC, V* ⏲ *Closed Sun. No lunch Sat.*

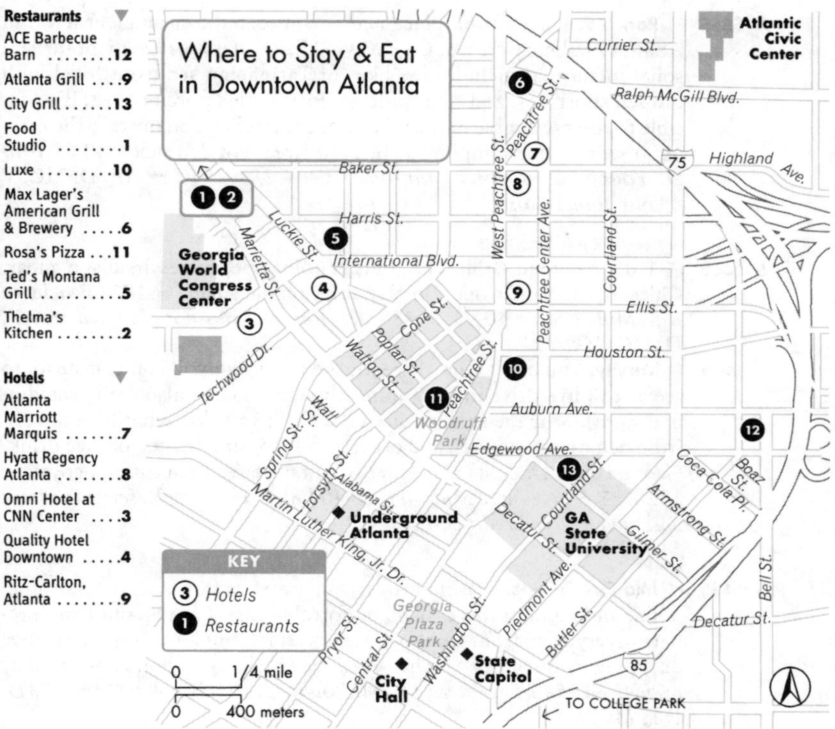

¢–$ ✕ **Thelma's Kitchen.** After losing her original location to the construction of Centennial Olympic Park, Thelma Grundy moved her operation down the road to the street level of the Roxy Hotel. The new location, brighter, spiffier, and more cheerful than the earlier spot, serves okra pancakes, fried catfish, "cold" slaw, and macaroni and cheese, all of which are among the best in town. Thelma's desserts are stellar. ✉ *768 Marietta St. NW, Downtown* ☎ *404/688–5855* ✍ *Reservations not accepted* ▭ *No credit cards* ⏲ *Closed weekends. No dinner.*

Midtown

American

$$$$ ✕ **Bacchanalia.** Often listed as Atlanta's best restaurant, Bacchanalia has been a special-occasion destination for locals since its opening in Buckhead in 1993. Chef-owners Anne Quatrano and Clifford Harrison helped pioneer the transformation of an intown industrial neighborhood west of Midtown by relocating the restaurant there in 2000. Items on the changing, prix-fixe menu could include crab fritters, wood-grilled prime tenderloin of beef, a cheese course, and warm Valrhona-chocolate cake. The prix-fixe lunch includes three courses for $35. ✉ *1198 Howell Mill Rd., West Midtown* ☎ *404/365–0410 Ext. 22* ✍ *Reservations essential* ▭ *AE, DC, MC, V* ⏲ *Closed Sun. No lunch Mon. and Tues.*

Fodor's Choice ★

★ $$$$ ✕ **Park 75.** It's a swank place and is considered a prominent jewel in Atlanta's culinary crown. Chef Kevin Hickey has created a vibrant seasonal menu that includes the likes of Tasmanian sea trout filled with braised short ribs, and Angus filet mignon with a porcini crust. It's possible to reserve a table in the middle of the kitchen and observe the master at work while sampling a constant stream of delicacies. ✉ *75 14th St., Four Seasons Hotel, Midtown* ☎ *404/253–3840* ▭ *AE, D, MC, V* ⊙ *No dinner Sun.*

American/Casual

$–$$$$ ✕ **Ted's Montana Grill.** This burger joint specializes in bison meat. Chicken, beef, and trout also play a role on the menu. ✉ *1874 Peachtree Rd., Midtown* ☎ *404/355–3897* ✍ *Reservations not accepted* ▭ *AE, D, DC, MC, V.*

¢–$ ✕ **Varsity.** You don't come here for the fine food: you come, instead, to see a real, live drive-in restaurant (though you can also eat in the dining room), hear the servers shout "What'll ya have, what'll ya have?" from behind the counter, and order a chili dog and frosted orange drink. Georgia Tech students and other Atlantans have been eating here since 1928. ✉ *61 N. Ave., Midtown* ☎ *404/881–1706* ✍ *Reservations not accepted* ▭ *No credit cards.*

Café

$$$–$$$$ ✕ **Mid City Cuisine.** Seasonal American brasserie fare is served morning, noon, and night in this coolly comfortable café. Chef Shaun Doty prepares everything from gumbo to steak tartare, but locals especially love dropping by on Sunday night, when the special is all-you-can-eat fancy pizzas. ✉ *1545 Peachtree St., Midtown* ☎ *404/888–8700* ▭ *AE, D, DC, MC, V.*

Contemporary

$$–$$$ ✕ **One Midtown Kitchen.** An unassuming warehouse entrance down a Piedmont Park side street leads to a seductively lighted, industrial-chic restaurant. The dining room is energetic but can be loud; the back porch, on the other hand, is quieter and offers a serene view of the park and skyline. Small plates like the wood-roasted pizza and garden sampler are outstanding, as is the price-tiered wine list. Order a glass or bottle, choose several plates for the table, and share. ✉ *559 Dutch Valley Rd., Midtown* ☎ *404/892–4111* ▭ *AE, MC, V* ⊙ *No lunch.*

Continental

$$$–$$$$ ✕ **The Abbey.** A former church houses this restaurant established in 1968; stained-glass windows and waiters dressed as Franciscan monks reinforce the headiness. Dishes range from a venison chop to butter-poached lobster with vanilla and Jerusalem artichokes. Finish your meal with goat-cheese cake with brandied apricots or triple-chocolate mousse. ✉ *163 Ponce de Leon Ave., Midtown* ☎ *404/876–8532* ▭ *AE, D, DC, MC, V* ⊙ *No lunch.*

Eclectic

¢–$$ ✕ **Flying Biscuit.** Big hits at this branch of Flying Biscuit are the big, fluffy biscuits with spicy apple butter, egg dishes, turkey sausage, and bean cakes with tomatillo salsa. ✉ *1001 Piedmont Ave., Midtown* ☎ *404/874–8887* ✍ *Reservations not accepted* ▭ *AE, D, MC, V.*

Italian

$$–$$$$ ✕ **Veni Vidi Vici.** Gleaming wood, contemporary styling, and an outdoor boccie court and dining patio create the perfect environment for an indulgent Italian meal. Start with *piatti piccoli* (savory appetizers) before moving on to one of the following: mushroom risotto, linguine with white clam sauce, or the excellent osso buco. Gnocchi with Gorgonzola is another favorite, as are the fragrant rotisserie meats. ✉ *41 14th St., Midtown* ☎ *404/875–8424* ▭ *AE, D, DC, MC, V* ⏲ *No lunch weekends.*

$–$$ ✕ **Figo Pasta.** High-quality counter-service restaurants like this Italian one have changed the face (it's smiling) of Atlanta dining. In exchange for standing in a short line and paying up front, you can still be served excellent food at a reasonable price. That's the concept behind Figo, which keeps it simple with some pastas and sauces, a few salads, and a few desserts. ✉ *1210 Howell Mill Rd., West Midtown* ☎ *404/351–3700* ✍ *Reservations not accepted* ▭ *MC, V* ⏲ *Closed Sun.* ✉ *1170 Collier Rd., West Midtown* ☎ *404/351–9667* ✍ *Reservations not accepted* ▭ *MC, V* ⏲ *No lunch weekends.*

Japanese

★ ¢–$$ ✕ **Ru-San's.** With sushi chefs who holler greetings, servers who encourage diners to engage in beer-chugging contests, loud music, and a boisterous clientele, this storefront sushi joint feels more like a party than a restaurant. Locals love the extensive menu, which includes tempura and vegetarian offerings in addition to sushi, and the casual environment. ✉ *1529 Piedmont Rd. NE, Midtown* ☎ *404/875–7042* ▭ *AE, D, MC, V.*

Mexican

$–$$$ ✕ **Zocalo.** People come to the inviting open-air patio of this restaurant—warmed in the frigid winter months by giant heaters—for the best Mexican food in town. Order the guacamole, prepared tableside, as a starter for dishes like chicken breast simmered in a thick mole or shrimp sautéed in chipotle salsa. The bar has an excellent selection of epicurean tequilas. ✉ *187 10th St., Midtown* ☎ *404/249–7576* ✍ *Reservations not accepted* ▭ *AE, D, DC, MC, V.*

Pan-Asian

¢–$ ✕ **Doc Chey's Noodle House.** Claim your fair share of bench space at the usually crowded rows of tables, smile at the folks crammed in next to you, and then dig in to the big bowls of flavorful soups, noodles, and rice dishes. Entrées such as noodles and eggplant with tomato-ginger sauce, and *massaman* curry (Thai curry) over rice come with your choice of chicken, tofu, shrimp, or salmon. ✉ *1424 N. Highland Ave., Virginia-Highland* ☎ *404/888–0777* ✍ *Reservations not accepted* ▭ *AE, D, MC, V* ⏲ *No lunch Mon.* ✉ *1556 N. Decatur Rd., Emory* ☎ *404/378–8188* ✍ *Reservations not accepted* ▭ *AE, D, MC, V* ⏲ *No lunch Sun.*

Southern

$$–$$$$ ✕ **South City Kitchen.** The culinary traditions of South Carolina's Lowcountry inspire the cooking at this cheerful restaurant. This is the place

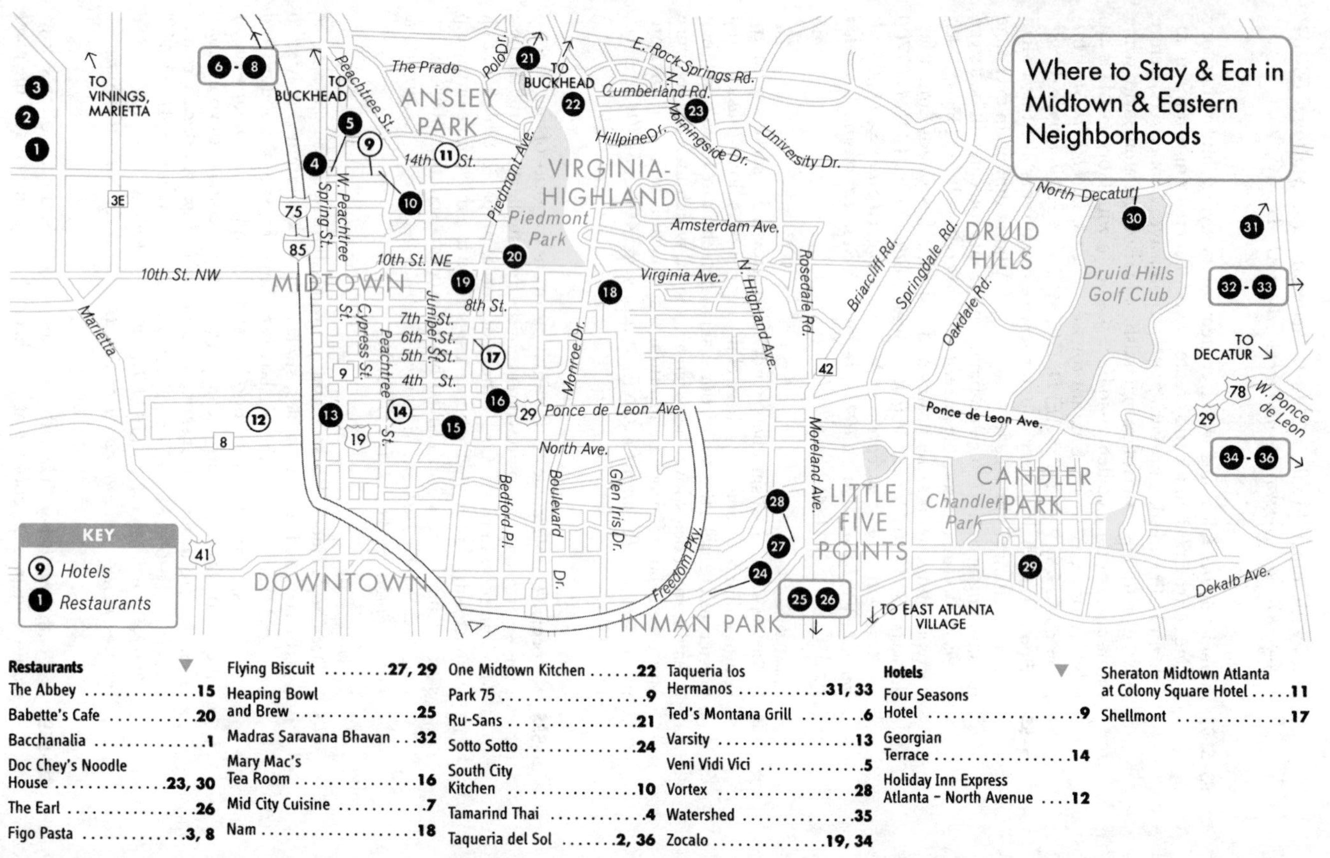

Restaurants

The Abbey 15
Babette's Cafe 20
Bacchanalia 1
Doc Chey's Noodle House 23, 30
The Earl 26
Figo Pasta 3, 8
Flying Biscuit 27, 29
Heaping Bowl and Brew 25
Madras Saravana Bhavan ... 32
Mary Mac's Tea Room 16
Mid City Cuisine 7
Nam 18
One Midtown Kitchen 22
Park 75 9
Ru-Sans 21
Sotto Sotto 24
South City Kitchen 10
Tamarind Thai 4
Taqueria del Sol 2, 36
Taqueria los Hermanos 31, 33
Ted's Montana Grill 6
Varsity 13
Veni Vidi Vici 5
Vortex 28
Watershed 35
Zocalo 19, 34

Hotels

Four Seasons Hotel 9
Georgian Terrace 14
Holiday Inn Express Atlanta – North Avenue 12
Sheraton Midtown Atlanta at Colony Square Hotel 11
Shellmont 17

to get fried green tomatoes with goat cheese, she-crab soup, or buttermilk fried chicken. The chef prepares catfish in many intriguing ways. Crab hash, served with poached eggs and chive hollandaise, is a classic. Don't miss the chocolate pecan pie. Within walking distance of the Woodruff Arts Center, the spare, art-filled restaurant attracts a hip crowd. ✉ *1144 Crescent Ave., Midtown* ☎ *404/873–7358* ▭ *AE, DC, MC, V.*

$–$$$ ✕ **Mary Mac's Tea Room.** Local celebrities and ordinary folk line up for the country-fried steak, fried chicken, and fresh vegetables. Here, in the Southern tradition, waitresses will call you "honey" and pat your arm to assure you that everything's all right. It's a great way to experience Southern food and hospitality all at once. ✉ *224 Ponce de Leon Ave., Midtown* ☎ *404/876–1800* ▭ *AE, MC, V.*

Tex-Mex

★ ¢–$ ✕ **Taqueria del Sol.** Don't let the long lines outside at this hip, Tex-Mex, counter-service eatery discourage you. They move quickly, and you'll soon be rewarded with a full bar, a wide selection of tacos and enchiladas, unusual sides like spicy collard greens and jalapeño cole slaw, and a fabulous salsa trio. ✉ *1200-B Howell Mill Rd., West Midtown* ☎ *404/352–5811* ✍ *Reservations not accepted* ▭ *AE, MC, V* ⊙ *Closed Sun. No dinner Mon.*

Thai

$–$$$ ✕ **Tamarind Thai.** All that is good about Thai flavors—clean lime, fresh basil, hot peppers, and cooling coconut, all tempered with smoky fish sauces—is even better at this standout restaurant known for excellent service. Note that parking is limited in the area; you may end up having to make a mad dash across multilane 14th Street. ✉ *80 14th St., Midtown* ☎ *404/873–4888* ▭ *AE, MC, V* ⊙ *No lunch weekends.*

Vietnamese

★ $–$$$ ✕ **Nam.** After elevating Atlanta sushi restaurants with their upscale MF Sushibar, brothers Alex and Chris Kinjo opened this stylish tribute to their mother's homeland, Vietnam, in 2003. Gauzy curtains separate dining tables in the small room, and sleek servers whisk by dressed in black and red. Crab-and-asparagus soup is packed with lump meat. Rich caramelized onions add mouthwatering depth to spicy clay-pot catfish. ✉ *931 Monroe Dr., Suite A-101, Midtown* ☎ *404/541–9997* ▭ *AE, D, DC, MC, V* ⊙ *No lunch weekends.*

Inman Park, Candler Park & East Atlanta Village

American

¢–$ ✕ **Vortex.** Talk about a funky design: you enter this restaurant through the mouth of a massive, spiral-eyed skull. The restaurant's motto, printed on waitstaff T-shirts, is IT'S NEVER TOO LATE TO START WASTING YOUR LIFE. But beyond the shenanigans are tasty delights, particularly the hefty burgers. A little-known perk is the bar's amazingly extensive selection of top-shelf liquor, consistently voted "Best in Atlanta" by the city's namesake magazine. ✉ *438 Moreland Ave., Little Five Points* ☎ *404/688–1828* ▭ *AE, D, DC, MC, V.*

CloseUp

SOUTHERN FLAVORS

GEORGIA IS AN EXCELLENT PLACE *to sample Southern food. In Atlanta and Savannah you'll find restaurants that serve the finest traditional cuisine, as well as more innovative cooking. Remember that Southern food varies widely across the region and even within states. Nothing reflects this more than barbecue, and few culinary differences produce as many passionate opinions. Taste as you travel, and add to the debate.*

Locals in Georgia and Mississippi generally prefer tomato-based sauces on ribs or chopped meat—but variations abound. In North Carolina barbecue is chopped pork piled on a bun with hand-cut coleslaw on top. Sauces range from vinegar and pepper (and little else) to Lexington style, with some tomato in the mix. And North Carolinians serve hush puppies (deep-fried ball-shape cornmeal fritters) with barbecue, which, for them, does not generally include ribs. For the rest of the South, the hush puppy is reserved for fried fish, whether fin or shell.

In South Carolina mustard-based barbecue sauces are widely savored, whether on chopped meat or on ribs. In eastern Alabama (and the Florida Panhandle), you'll find a unique white sauce for barbecue. Memphis-style 'cue is famous for its dry rub, although there's also a "wet" style, in which the same spices, moistened, are rubbed on the ribs. In parts of Tennessee, barbecued mutton is traditional.

Prior to the Depression, there were two sorts of cooking in the South—country food and the elegant plantation fare drawn from French and English models. More recent country cooking blends European, African, and Native American styles and has come to be the defining Southern cuisine in most people's minds. But in the past many an elegant table was set with European-based dishes, especially along the coasts.

Gumbo, the spicy soup that is so clearly from this region, is a more apt metaphor for the South's demographics than the term melting pot *because the word* gumbo *reflects all that comes to the Southern table (and to Southern culture) from its people. The term is West African, from* ngombo, *which meant "okra" in that part of the world. And what would gumbo be without okra? But gumbo is also French: a proper gumbo is based on a* roux, *a sauté of fat and flour cooked to the color of peanut butter. The cook might sauté vegetables for a gumbo, making a kind of* sofrito, *a legacy from the Spanish settlers in the lower part of Louisiana. Using sassafras or filé powder to thicken gumbo is a legacy of Southern Native Americans.*

One defining ingredient in Southern cooking is corn—another Native American legacy. Parch the corn with lye, which swells the grains, and you get hominy. Grind the corn, white or yellow, and you have grits. Sift the grits, and you have cornmeal for making corn bread, fluffy spoon bread, corn pone, hoecakes, hush puppies, johnnycake (or Native American "journey" cake). Ferment the grain, and you get corn whiskey, also known as white lightning or moonshine (and arguably like Southern grappa).

When traveling in Georgia and the rest of the South, you'll find the area's diversity on its tables. Many of the region's chefs use the traditional ingredients to craft "new" Southern dishes as a way of restoring that sense of elegant dining to the region's cuisine. Others wouldn't get near that sort of style, preferring to do the original dishes proud. Take your pick: either way you'll dine divinely.

American/Casual

¢–$$$ ✕ **The Earl.** A scrappy yet delightful first stop on the East Atlanta bar scene, the Earl has a hearty menu of classic pub food, as well as a few entrées that are more innovative, such as jerk tuna. Don't let the comically eclectic interior fool you: the food is surprisingly substantial and well prepared. There's a casual stage in the corner, too—this is one of the city's favorite rock venues. ✉ *488 Flat Shoals Ave., East Atlanta Village, East Atlanta* ☎ *404/522–3950* ▭ *AE, D, MC, V* ⊙ *No lunch Mon.*

Eclectic

¢–$$ ✕ **Flying Biscuit.** There's an hour-long wait on weekends for the big, fluffy biscuits and spicy apple butter. Other huge hits at this garage-sale-decorated spot include egg dishes, turkey sausage, and bean cakes with tomatillo salsa. Fancier dinners include roasted chicken, mozzarella and Parmesan cheese, spinach, and caramelized onions in puff pastry. ✉ *1655 McLendon Ave., Candler Park* ☎ *404/687–8888* ✍ *Reservations not accepted* ▭ *AE, D, MC, V.*

¢–$ ✕ **Heaping Bowl and Brew.** Trendoids and scenesters from all over town are devoted to this eatery in ultrahip East Atlanta Village. As the name suggests, many of the meals—spaghetti, pierogi, stir-fried vegetables, Southwestern-style chicken—come in big bowls. ✉ *469 Flat Shoals Ave., East Atlanta Village, East Atlanta* ☎ *404/523–8030* ▭ *AE, MC, V.*

Continental

$$–$$$$ ✕ **Babette's Cafe.** Sunny yellow walls and back-porch seating add to the homey charm of this renovated bungalow. The restaurant, which describes its cuisine as European country, offers such seasonal dishes as halibut with potato-leek gratin and veal piccata. If the mushroom tortellini, served with a buttery sage sauce, is available, order it: it's out of this world. ✉ *573 N. Highland Ave., Inman Park* ☎ *404/523–9121* ▭ *AE, D, DC, MC, V* ⊙ *Closed Mon. No lunch.*

Italian

★ $$–$$$$ ✕ **Sotto Sotto.** Atlanta's hot spot close to downtown has an adventurous take on Italian cuisine. The former commercial space hops with young, hip patrons dining on wood-roasted duck breast with polenta and 12-year-old balsamic vinegar, spaghetti with sun-dried mullet roe, and utterly perfect *panna cotta* (custard). ✉ *313 N. Highland Ave., Inman Park* ☎ *404/523–6678* ▭ *AE, DC, MC, V* ⊙ *Closed Sun. No lunch.*

Buckhead

American

★ $$$–$$$$ ✕ **Woodfire Grill.** Chef Michael Tuohy carefully selects every ingredient on his daily rotating menu, from the organic greens tucked under chèvre-stuffed fried squash blossoms to the Kobe sirloin ground in-house into top-shelf burgers. Opened in 2002, this restaurant has quickly gained a reputation as one of the city's finest. ✉ *1782 Cheshire Bridge Rd. NE, Buckhead* ☎ *404/347–9055* ▭ *AE, D, DC, MC, V* ⊙ *Closed Sun. No lunch.*

American/Casual

¢–$ ✕ **Varsity.** You don't come here for the fine food: you come, instead, to see a real, live drive-in restaurant, hear the servers shout "What'll ya have, what'll ya have?," and order a chili dog and frosted orange drink. ✉ *1085 Lindbergh Dr., Buckhead* ☎ *404/261–8843* *Reservations not accepted* *No credit cards.*

Contemporary

★ $$$$ ✕ **Seeger's.** Celebrated chef Guenter Seeger, formerly at the Dining Room in the Ritz-Carlton, presides over this sophisticated, sleek place. Some find it a bit noisy, but after the first fragrant, flavorful bite you'll likely forget about the volume. The smoked salmon with horseradish cream and the five-spice squab with date chutney are outstanding. Local inspirations include sweet-onion tarts with pecan sauce. In season, you can indulge in an entire menu based on truffles. It's prix fixe only, here. ✉ *111 W. Paces Ferry Rd., Buckhead* ☎ *404/846–9779* *Jacket required* *AE, DC, MC, V* *Closed Sun. No lunch.*

★ $$$–$$$$ ✕ **Aria.** Chef Gerry Klaskala is known for making masterful entrées of rustic heartiness that also appeal to the epicurean palate. His signature talent is best captured by his love of "slow foods"—braises, stews, steaks, and chops cooked over a roll-top French grill. This makes for very weighty plates, but Klaskala lovingly flavors every ounce. For example, pork shoulder is presented with a delicious balsamic reduction and Gorgonzola polenta. Don't miss renowned pastry chef Kathryn King's mouth-watering dessert menu, including Valrhona-chocolate-cream pie with Drambuie sauce. ✉ *490 E. Paces Ferry Rd., Buckhead* ☎ *404/233–7673* *Reservations essential* *AE, D, DC, MC, V* *Closed Sun. No lunch.*

$$$–$$$$ ✕ **Canoe.** This popular spot on the banks of the Chattahoochee River brims with appreciative patrons nearly all day. In nice weather the outdoor dining spaces allow the best view of the river. The restaurant has built a national reputation based on such dishes as sage-roasted pheasant with blackberry-encrusted conserve, seared Georgia mountain trout with braised Vidalia onions, and slow-roasted Carolina rabbit. Sunday brunch is superb. ✉ *4199 Paces Ferry Rd. NW, Buckhead* ☎ *770/432–2663* *AE, D, DC, MC, V.*

★ $$$–$$$$ ✕ **Joël.** Chef Joël Antunes, former executive chef at the heralded Dining Room in the Ritz-Carlton, Buckhead, spices up this chic French brasserie with Mediterranean and Asian influences. Sample entrées on the rotating menu include sautéed veal sweetbreads with gnocchi romaine, seared scallops with leek confit, and duck breast with a sauce made of pears, oranges, and coriander. ✉ *3290 Northside Pkwy., Berkeley Park* ☎ *404/233–3500* *Reservations essential* *AE, D, DC, MC, V* *Closed Sun. No lunch Sat.–Mon.*

Continental

$$$$ ✕ **Dining Room, Ritz-Carlton, Buckhead.** If you like the style of an old gentlemen's club, you'll appreciate this elegant, restrained room, with formal hunt scenes on the walls, romantic lighting, and generously spaced tables. Chef Bruno Menard ensures a delectable daily assortment of creative options on the pricey, continental, prix-fixe menu. Specialties have

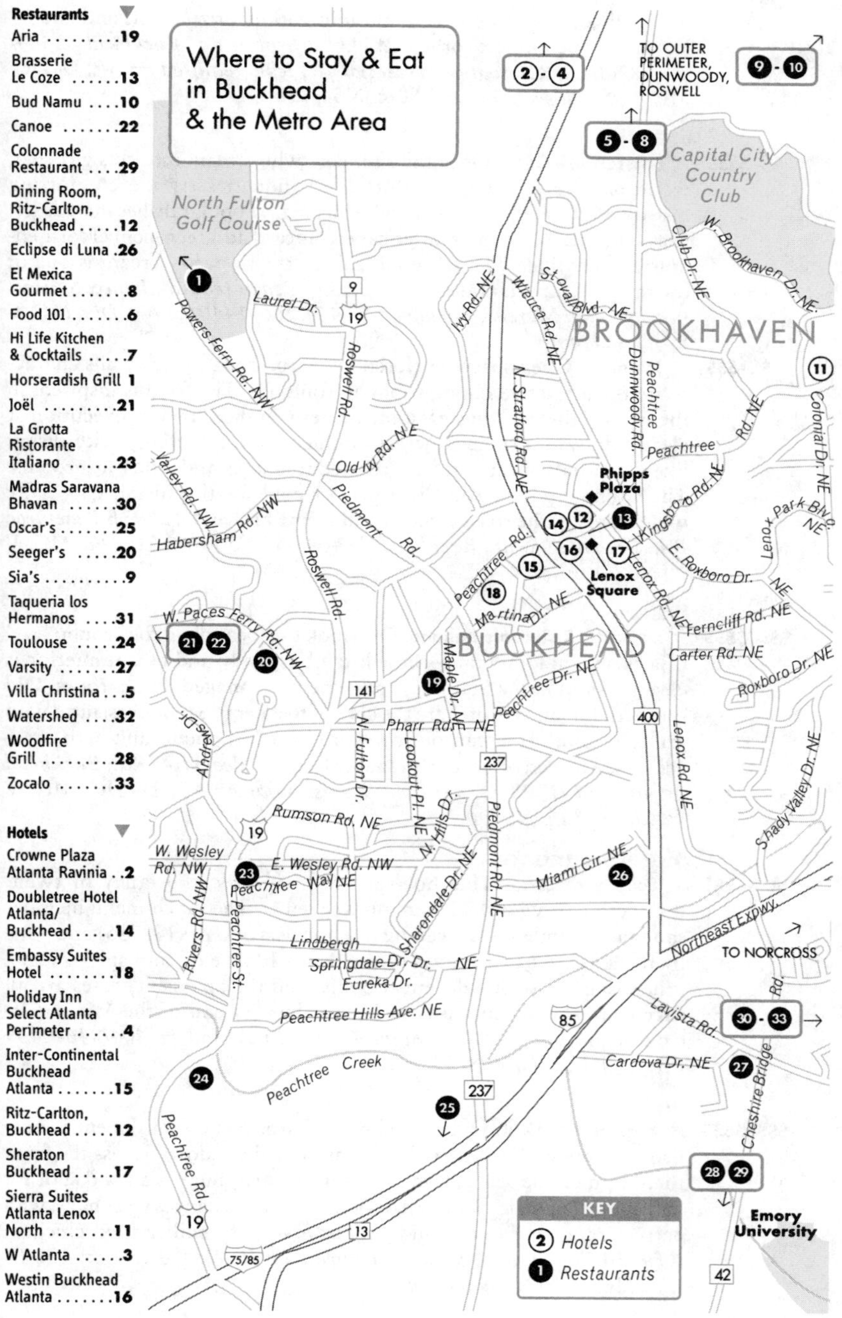
Where to Stay & Eat in Buckhead & the Metro Area
Restaurants
Aria 19
Brasserie Le Coze 13
Bud Namu 10
Canoe 22
Colonnade Restaurant 29
Dining Room, Ritz-Carlton, Buckhead 12
Eclipse di Luna .26
El Mexica Gourmet 8
Food 101 6
Hi Life Kitchen & Cocktails 7
Horseradish Grill 1
Joël 21
La Grotta Ristorante Italiano 23
Madras Saravana Bhavan 30
Oscar's 25
Seeger's 20
Sia's 9
Taqueria los Hermanos 31
Toulouse 24
Varsity 27
Villa Christina . . .5
Watershed 32
Woodfire Grill 28
Zocalo 33
Hotels
Crowne Plaza Atlanta Ravinia . .2
Doubletree Hotel Atlanta/ Buckhead 14
Embassy Suites Hotel 18
Holiday Inn Select Atlanta Perimeter 4
Inter-Continental Buckhead Atlanta 15
Ritz-Carlton, Buckhead 12
Sheraton Buckhead 17
Sierra Suites Atlanta Lenox North 11
W Atlanta 3
Westin Buckhead Atlanta 16
TO OUTER PERIMETER, DUNWOODY, ROSWELL
Capital City Country Club
North Fulton Golf Course
BROOKHAVEN
BUCKHEAD
Phipps Plaza
Lenox Square
TO NORCROSS
Emory University
KEY
Hotels
Restaurants
Powers Ferry Rd. NW
Laurel Dr.
Roswell Rd.
Ivy Rd. NE
Wieuca Rd. NE
Stovall Blvd. NE
Dunnwoody Rd.
Peachtree
Club Dr. NE
W. Brookhaven Dr. NE
N. Stratford Rd. NE
Colonial Dr. NE
Old Ivy Rd. NE
Piedmont Rd.
Valley Rd. NW
Habersham Rd. NW
Peachtree Rd.
Kingsboro Rd. NE
Lenox Park Blvd. NE
E. Roxboro Dr.
Lenox Rd. NE
Martina Dr. NE
W. Paces Ferry Rd. NW
Ferncliff Rd. NE
Carter Rd. NE
Maple Dr. NE
Peachtree Dr. NE
Roxboro Dr. NE
Pharr Rd. NE
N. Fulton Dr.
Lookout Pl. NE
Andrews Dr.
Shady Valley Dr. NE
Rumson Rd. NE
N. Hills Dr.
Piedmont Rd. NE
W. Wesley Rd. NW
E. Wesley Rd. NW
Peachtree Way NE
Sharondale Dr. NE
Miami Cir. NE
Rivers Rd. NW
Peachtree St.
Lindbergh
Springdale Dr.
Eureka Dr.
Northeast Expwy.
Lavista Rd.
Peachtree Hills Ave. NE
Cardova Dr. NE
Peachtree Creek
Cheshire Bridge Rd.
Peachtree Rd.
9
19
141
400
237
85
13
75/85
42

included cocoa-bean-coated lamb loin with chorizo crust, and chocolate tart with chocolate sorbet. ✉ *3434 Peachtree Rd., Buckhead* ☎ *404/237–2700* *Reservations essential* *Jacket required* ▭ *AE, D, DC, MC, V* ⏲ *Closed Sun. and Mon. No lunch.*

French

$$–$$$$ ✕ **Brasserie Le Coze.** Once the shoppers who stream into this glowing, wood-panel space with comfortable banquettes try the comforting bistro-style fare, they forget they're in a mall. Popular dishes include the roasted skate in brown-butter-caper sauce, and green-peppercorn-encrusted beef fillet. The seasonal-fruit tart with pastry cream is one of the many extravagant desserts. ✉ *3393 Peachtree Rd., Lenox Square, near Neiman Marcus, Buckhead* ☎ *404/266–1440* ▭ *AE, DC, MC, V* ⏲ *Closed Sun.*

$$–$$$ ✕ **Toulouse.** Open spaces enclosed by warm, rough-brick walls characterize the attractive dining room at Toulouse. The food is inspired, in theory, by the cooking of southwestern France, but in execution it clearly draws on some American influences—particularly with dishes like the buffalo meat loaf with roasted tomatoes and wild mushrooms. The country potato soup is a perfect cold-weather meal. Especially wonderful are the roast chicken and crème brûlée. ✉ *2293B Peachtree Rd., Peachtree Walk, Buckhead* ☎ *404/351–9533* ▭ *AE, DC, MC, V* ⏲ *No lunch.*

Italian

$$$–$$$$ ✕ **La Grotta Ristorante Italiano.** Overlook the location in the ground level of a posh condominium—though the burgundy-and-cream interior is elegant—and know that this is an expertly managed dining room. Old northern Italian favorites are the core of the menu. Savor prosciutto with grilled pears and mascarpone cheese followed by potato-and-herb gnocchi tossed in a crawfish cream sauce. ✉ *2637 Peachtree Rd., Buckhead* ☎ *404/231–1368* *Reservations essential* ▭ *AE, D, DC, MC, V* ⏲ *Closed Sun. No lunch.*

Mediterranean

★ $–$$$ ✕ **Eclipse di Luna.** This hot spot has captured the fancy of twentysomethings, who flock here on weekends. The lunch menu includes sandwiches and salads; evening fare consists of tapas ($3–$5) and wine by the glass. *Patatas bravas* (potatoes with olive oil and spicy sauce), grilled salmon with wild mushrooms, and the Spanish cheeses are all excellent. The restaurant is tucked at the very end of the Miami Circle design center. ✉ *764 Miami Circle, Buckhead* ☎ *404/846–0449* ▭ *AE, DC, MC, V* ⏲ *Closed Mon.*

Southern

$$$–$$$$ ✕ **Horseradish Grill.** Once a red horse barn, this establishment is now painted gray with white trim and has arched windows across the front that brighten the space. It may be a little noisy, but it's a good spot for authentic, if upscale, Southern dishes. The menu changes seasonally, with entrées ranging from autumn venison stew to skillet-fried chicken. ✉ *4320 Powers Ferry Rd., Buckhead* ☎ *404/255–7277* ▭ *AE, D, DC, MC, V* ⏲ *No lunch Sat.*

$–$$$ ✕ **Colonnade Restaurant.** For traditional Southern food—fried chicken, ham steak, and turkey and dressing—insiders head to Colonnade, an Atlanta institution since 1927. The interior, with patterned carpeting and red banquettes, is a classic version of a 1950s restaurant. ✉ *1879 Cheshire Bridge Rd., Buckhead* ☎ *404/874–5642* ⚠ *Reservations not accepted* ▭ *No credit cards* ⊙ *No lunch Mon. and Tues.*

Metro Atlanta

American

$–$$$$ ✕ **Hi Life Kitchen & Cocktails.** This hip restaurant 20 mi northeast of downtown Atlanta presents an eclectic menu of American favorites, but devotees swear by the Lobster Menu, a heaping plate of lobster prepared three ways—chilled, steamed, and poached. The design is trendy upscale, with light-wood and wrought-iron accents. ✉ *3380 Holcomb Bridge Rd., Norcross* ☎ *770/409–0101* ▭ *AE, DC, MC, V* ⊙ *No lunch weekends.*

Contemporary

★ **$$$–$$$$** ✕ **Oscar's.** This friendly, upscale bistro near the Atlanta airport continues to wow both locals and big-city types who don't mind venturing 10 mi south of downtown. Behind the prosaic facade of a former pawn shop, you'll discover a dazzling interior of peppermint-stripe lights, mod tableware, and light-wood furnishings. The inventive, seasonal menu emphasizes carefully balanced flavors, such as English pea soup with rosemary cream and prosciutto bits, or venison with watercress and apple marmalade. ✉ *3725 Main St., College Park* ☎ *404/766–9688* ▭ *AE, MC, V* ⊙ *Closed Sun. No lunch weekends.*

$$$–$$$$ ✕ **Sia's.** "Creative American" is how this sleek suburban restaurant describes its contemporary cuisine, which includes such entrées as ginger seared salmon and cranberry grilled lamb chops. A cozy bar tucked away from the open circular dining room is a nice place to stop for drinks, too. ✉ *10305 Medlock Bridge Rd., Duluth* ☎ *770/497–9727* ▭ *AE, D, DC, MC, V* ⊙ *Closed Sun. No lunch weekends.*

$$–$$$$ ✕ **Food 101.** This was a smash hit as soon as it opened, and no wonder, given the gut-filling comfort food—lamb shank with braised vegetables, for example, or meat loaf with mashed potatoes, gravy, and string beans. Wine drinkers especially love this place for its selection of 50 American wines by the glass. ✉ *4969 Roswell Rd., #200, 6 mi north of Atlanta, Sandy Springs* ☎ *404/497–9700* ▭ *AE, D, MC, V* ⊙ *No lunch Sat.*

Indian

★ **¢–$** ✕ **Madras Saravana Bhavan.** This outstanding South Indian vegetarian restaurant is almost always packed with Indian families and other diners happily devouring huge *dosai* (rice- or lentil-flour crêpes rolled and filled with vegetables), curries, and *thalis* (sample platters). Service is friendly and helpful, especially for the uninitiated. The restaurant is hidden in a rundown shopping center on the outskirts of Decatur. ✉ *2179 Lawrenceville Hwy., Decatur* ☎ *404/636–4400* ⚠ *Reservations not accepted* ▭ *AE, D, MC, V.*

Italian

$$ ✕ **Villa Christina.** Look no farther for elegant Italian food with a twist. You enter down a lighted path resplendent with gardens, a waterfall, and a stone bridge. The dining room doubles as an art gallery, with two murals depicting a glorious Tuscan landscape. From the kitchen comes seared wild striped sea bass on a bed of spinach, and grilled Tuscan veal chops with a sweet-onion brûlée of Parma ham. The house specialty, Christina's seafood *cioppino,* is a medley of succulent shellfish swimming in a saffron-tomato stew. ✉ *4000 Perimeter Summit Blvd., 14 mi north of Atlanta, Dunwoody* ☎ *404/303–0133* ▭ *AE, D, DC, MC, V* ⏲ *Closed Sun. No lunch Sat.*

Korean

$–$$ ✕ **Bud Namu.** City foodies drive 25 mi into the suburbs and Korean-Americans come from far-away counties for this Korean restaurant's clay-wrapped roasted duck, and stuffed pumpkin (with sticky rice, plums, chestnuts, and pine nuts), both of which must be ordered at least a few hours—and on weekends a few days—in advance. Friendly, helpful service enhances the experience. ✉ *3585 Peachtree Industrial Blvd., Duluth* ☎ *770/622–8983* ▭ *AE, MC, V.*

Mexican

$–$$$ ✕ **Zocalo.** Order the guacamole, prepared tableside, as a starter for dishes like chicken breast simmered in a thick mole or shrimp sautéed in chipotle salsa. Reservations are not accepted weekends. ✉ *123 E. Court Sq., Decatur* ☎ *404/270–9450* ▭ *AE, D, DC, MC, V.*

$–$$ ✕ **Taqueria los Hermanos.** At this tiny storefront restaurant in a shopping center, the Ballasteros brothers serve marinated-pork tacos, delicate chiles rellenos, and, occasionally, their mother's handmade tamales. Don't leave without tasting the *tres leches* ("three-milk") cake. ✉ *Killian Hills Crossing shopping center, 4760 Lawrenceville Hwy., 18 mi northeast of Atlanta, Lilburn* ☎ *678/380–3727* ▭ *AE, D, MC, V* ⏲ *No lunch weekends* ✉ *4418 Hugh Howell Rd., 10 mi east of Atlanta, Tucker* ☎ *678/937–0660* ▭ *AE, D, MC, V* ⏲ *No lunch weekends.*

¢–$$ ✕ **El Mexica Gourmet.** The authentic fare produced by the El Mexica kitchen illustrates that Mexican cuisine is not all tacos and enchiladas—though if that's what you're up for, you'll find plenty of that here, too. Alongside those Mexican staples dig into specialties like *carne tampiquena* (charbroiled steak smothered with sautéed onions and peppers) and red snapper Veracruz (panfried with a fresh tomato sauce). ✉ *11060 Alpharetta Hwy., Suite 172, behind Applebee's, 20 mi north of Atlanta, Roswell* ☎ *770/594–8674* ▭ *AE, MC, V.*

Southern

★ **$$–$$$$** ✕ **Watershed.** Indigo Girl Emily Saliers and three of her friends launched this casual restaurant–cum–gift shop in a converted gas station. Chef Scott Peacock, coauthor of *The Gift of Southern Cooking,* specializes in elegant takes on classic Southern fare: the planet's best shrimp salad, homemade pimento cheese with sharp cheddar and egg, roasted or fried chicken served with grits, an outstanding chocolate cake, and Georgia pecan tart with a scrumptious shortbread crust. Also an *enoteca* (wine bar), Watershed sells wine both retail in bottles and by the glass at the comfy bar. When she's not in the recording studio, Saliers makes a fine sommelier and loves to talk about wine. ✉ *406 W. Ponce de Leon Ave., 6 mi east of Atlanta, Decatur* ☎ *404/378–4900* ▭ *AE, MC, V* ⊙ *No dinner Sun.*

Tex-Mex

★ ¢–$ ✕ **Taqueria del Sol.** The lines move quickly at this Tex-Mex counter-service eatery serving a wide selection of tacos and enchiladas, unusual sides like spicy collard greens and jalapeño cole slaw, and a fabulous salsa trio. ✉ *359 W. Ponce de Leon Ave., Decatur* ☎ *404/377–7668* ✍ *Reservations not accepted* ▭ *AE, MC, V* ⊙ *Closed Sun. No dinner Mon.*

11

WHERE TO STAY

One of America's most popular convention destinations, Atlanta offers plenty of variety in terms of lodgings. More than 76,000 rooms are in metro Atlanta, with about 12,000 downtown, close to the Georgia World Congress Center, Atlanta Civic Center, Atlanta Merchandise Mart, and Philips Arena. Other clusters are in Buckhead, in the north I–285 perimeter, and around Hartsfield-Jackson Atlanta International Airport.

Prices

Atlanta lodging facilities basically have two seasons: summer and convention (conventions are generally held year-round, though there are fewer in summer). Some downtown hotels offer special rates between the biggest conventions, and summertime deals are common throughout the city.

WHAT IT COSTS

$$$$	$$$	$$	$	¢
over $220	$160–$220	$110–$160	$70–$110	under $70

Hotel prices are for two people in a standard double room in high season, excluding service charges and 6%–8% sales tax, plus a 7% bed tax.

Downtown

★ $$$$ **Ritz-Carlton, Atlanta.** Traditional afternoon tea—served in the intimate, sunken lobby beneath an 18th-century chandelier—sets the mood. Notice the 17th-century Flemish tapestry when you enter from Peachtree Street. Some of the most luxurious guest rooms are decorated with marble writing tables, plump sofas, four-poster beds, and white-marble bathrooms. The Atlanta Grill is one of downtown's few outdoor dining spots. ✉ *181 Peachtree St., opposite Peachtree Center MARTA, Downtown, 30303* ☎ *404/659–0400 or 800/241–3333* 🖷 *404/688–0400* 🌐 *www.ritzcarlton.com* *441 rooms, 13 suites* *Restaurant, cable TV, bar, laundry service, Internet, business services, parking (fee)* ▭ *AE, D, DC, MC, V* *EP.*

$$$–$$$$ **Omni Hotel at CNN Center.** Adjacent to the home of the Cable News Network is this sleek hotel with a 600-room tower. The ultramodern,

marble main lobby overlooks Centennial Olympic Park with floor-to-ceiling windows. Creams, browns, and rich red accents decorate the rooms and complement the mahogany furniture. ✉ *100 CNN Center, by Omni MARTA, Downtown, 30305* ☎ *404/659–0000 or 800/843–6664* 🖷 *404/525–5050* 🌐 *www.omnihotels.com* *1,036 rooms, 31 suites* *2 restaurants, cable TV, pool, health club, spa, lobby lounge, Internet, business services, meeting rooms, parking (fee)* *AE, D, DC, MC, V* *EP.*

$$–$$$$ **Atlanta Marriott Marquis.** Immense and coolly contemporary, the building seems to go up forever as you stand under the lobby's huge fabric sculpture that hangs from the skylighted roof 47 stories above. Guest rooms, which open onto this atrium, are decorated in dark greens and neutral shades. Live plants and fresh flowers fill the major suites, two of which have grand pianos and ornamental fireplaces. You don't even have to walk outside to reach the Peachtree Center MARTA station; it's connected via an office building. ✉ *265 Peachtree Center Ave., Downtown, 30303* ☎ *404/521–0000 or 800/932–2198* 🖷 *404/586–6299* 🌐 *www.marriott.com* *1,675 rooms, 69 suites* *4 restaurants, cable TV, indoor-outdoor pool, health club, 2 bars, business services, Internet, meeting rooms, parking (fee)* *AE, D, DC, MC, V* *EP.*

$$–$$$$ **Hyatt Regency Atlanta.** Constructed in 1967, this was architect John Portman's first atrium-centered building, and it became the model for his other hotels, including the San Francisco Embarcadero and the Atlanta Marriott Marquis. From the exterior the most notable feature is the space-age blue dome, which houses a revolving cocktail lounge, crowning the structure. Inside is Portman's trademark spectacular 22-story skylighted atrium, with exposed-glass elevators zipping up and down. Expect the careful service and quality facilities typical of Hyatt hotels. ✉ *265 Peachtree St., connected by skywalk to Peachtree Center, Downtown, 30303* ☎ *404/577–1234 or 800/233–1234* 🖷 *404/460–6544* 🌐 *www.hyatt.com* *1,202 rooms, 58 suites* *3 restaurants, cable TV, pool, health club, lobby lounge, Internet, business services, meeting rooms, parking (fee)* *AE, D, DC, MC, V* *EP.*

¢–$$ **Quality Hotel Downtown.** This quiet, older downtown hotel two blocks off Peachtree Street is priced reasonably for its location; this, along with the hotel's proximity to the Georgia World Congress Center and the show marts, makes the hotel popular during conventions. Note that prices go up when conventions are in town. Sofas and a grand piano fill the marble lobby, and teal and navy decorate the modest-size rooms. ✉ *89 Luckie St., Downtown, 30303* ☎ *404/524–7991 or 888/729–7705* 🖷 *404/524–0672* 🌐 *www.qualityinn.com* *75 rooms* *Cable TV, parking (fee)* *AE, D, DC, MC, V* *BP.*

Midtown

★ $$$$ **Four Seasons Hotel.** From the lobby a sweeping staircase leads up to a refined but welcoming bar and to Park 75, the hotel's American-chic dining establishment. Rose-hue marble creates a warm feeling in the public spaces and lounges. Amenities abound throughout: marble bathrooms with extra-large soaking tubs, lemon or celadon color schemes, comfy mattresses, and brass chandeliers. The hotel prides itself on its immensely courteous staff—it's considered scandalous if a phone call to reception exceeds two rings before it's answered. Stewards and other staff members are on hand the moment you need their help. ✉ *75 14th St., Midtown, 30309* ☎ *404/881–9898 or 800/819–5053* 📠 *404/873–4692* 🌐 *www.fourseasons.com* *226 rooms, 18 suites* *Restaurant, in-room data ports, cable TV, pool, health club, spa, bar, Internet, business services, meeting rooms, parking (fee)* 💳 *AE, D, DC, MC, V* *EP.*

$$$–$$$$ **Sheraton Midtown Atlanta Hotel at Colony Square.** The Sheraton's theatrical lobby, with sweeping staircases and overhanging balconies, opens onto the bright, open mall of Colony Square, a complex of office, residential, and retail buildings. Rooms are modern, with muted tones; those on higher floors have city views. The hotel is two blocks from MARTA's Arts Center station and two blocks from the Woodruff Arts Center and High Museum of Art. Note that the parking garage is a bit of a maze. ✉ *188 14th St., Midtown, 30361* ☎ *404/892–6000 or 800/422–7895* 📠 *404/872–9192* 🌐 *www.starwood.com* *467 rooms, 32 suites* *Restaurant, cable TV, pool, lobby lounge, Internet, meeting rooms, parking (fee), some pets allowed* 💳 *AE, D, DC, MC, V* *EP.*

$$–$$$$ **Shellmont.** Designed in 1891 by Massachusetts-born, Atlanta-reared architect Walter T. Downing, Shellmont is on the National Register of Historic Places and is a City of Atlanta Landmark Building. The house, which is named for the shell motif that adorns it, has antique stained, leaded, and beveled glass, enhanced by artfully carved woodwork and charming stencils. American-made Victorian-style antiques fill the guest rooms, which also have CD players and data ports on the phones. There are gym facilities nearby. ✉ *821 Piedmont Ave., Midtown, 30306* ☎ *404/872–9290* 📠 *404/872–5379* 🌐 *www.shellmont.com* *5 rooms, 2 suites, 1 carriage house* *In-room data ports, in-room VCRs* 💳 *AE, D, DC, MC, V* *BP.*

$–$$$ **Georgian Terrace.** Enrico Caruso and the Metropolitan Opera stars once lodged in this fine 1911 hotel across the street from the Fox Theatre. From its beginning the hotel has housed the rich and famous, but it fell into disrepair for a few decades; it has been renovated several times and is now on the National Register of Historic Places. The tiled, columned lobby is striking, and breathtaking terraces traverse the exterior, making it a popular wedding-reception venue. All units are suites, most with washer-dryers; they are pastel and plush, providing competent if not luxurious comfort. ✉ *659 Peachtree St., Midtown, 30308* ☎ *404/897–1991* 📠 *404/724–9116* 🌐 *www.thegeorgianterrace.com* *319 suites* *Restaurant, some kitchens, some kitchenettes, cable TV, pool, health club, Internet, business services, convention center, meeting rooms, parking (fee)* 💳 *AE, D, DC, MC, V* *EP.*

$$ **Holiday Inn Express Atlanta–North Avenue.** Across the street from the Georgia Institute of Technology is this no-frills but comfortable establishment. Forest-green and cranberry accents, floral bedspreads, and striped curtains spice up the neutral decor. ✉ *244 North Ave., Midtown, 30313* ☎ *404/881–0881* 📠 *404/874–8838* 🌐 *www.holiday-inn.com* *108 rooms, 2 suites* *In-room data ports, cable TV, laundry service, business services, free parking* 💳 *AE, D, DC, MC, V* *BP.*

Buckhead & Outer Perimeter

★ **$$$$** **Inter-Continental Buckhead Atlanta.** Marble bathrooms with separate soaking tubs and glass showers, 300-thread-count Egyptian-cotton linens, Web-based TV, plush bathrobes and slippers, and twice-daily housekeeping are some of the highlights of the traditional-style rooms in this hotel, the flagship for the Atlanta-based Inter-Continental Hotels Group. Bar XO has outdoor terrace seating overlooking Peachtree. ✉ *3315 Peachtree Rd. NE, Buckhead, 30326* ☎ *404/946–9000 or 800/327–0200* 🖷 *770/604–5305* 🌐 *www.ichotelsgroup.com/buckhead* *401 rooms, 21 suites* *Restaurant, cable TV, pool, health club, spa, bar, lounge, shop, Internet, business services, meeting rooms, parking (fee)* *AE, D, DC, MC, V* *EP.*

$$$$ Fodor's Choice ★ **Ritz-Carlton, Buckhead.** Decorated with 18th- and 19th-century antiques and art, this is an elegant gem of a hotel and a regular stopover for visiting celebrities. The richly paneled Lobby Lounge is a respite for shoppers from nearby Lenox Square mall and Phipps Plaza; afternoon tea and cocktails are popular here. The Dining Room is one of the city's finest restaurants, and many of the area's top chefs have passed through its kitchen doors. The spacious rooms are furnished with traditional reproductions and have luxurious white-marble baths. ✉ *3434 Peachtree Rd., Buckhead, 30326* ☎ *404/237–2700 or 800/241–3333* 🖷 *404/239–0078* 🌐 *www.ritzcarlton.com* *524 rooms, 29 suites* *3 restaurants, cable TV, pool, health club, spa, hot tub, bar, parking (fee)* *AE, D, DC, MC, V* *EP.*

$$$–$$$$ **Crowne Plaza Atlanta Ravinia.** If you're visiting one of the many businesses in Atlanta's Perimeter Center, about a 10-minute drive north of Buckhead, you can't beat the convenience of this hotel and conference center in the 45-acre Ravinia complex. A lushly landscaped atrium lobby echoes the surrounding wooded property. All rooms are furnished opulently and have hair dryers and upscale bath amenities. ✉ *4435 Ashford-Dunwoody Rd., Dunwoody 30346* ☎ *770/395–7700 or 800/227–6963* 🖷 *770/392–9503* 🌐 *www.crowneplaza.com* *473 rooms, 22 suites* *3 restaurants, in-room data ports, cable TV, tennis court, indoor pool, gym, hot tub, lounge, laundry service, Internet, business services, meeting rooms, free parking* *AE, D, DC, MC, V* *EP.*

$$$–$$$$ **Westin Buckhead Atlanta.** Behind the chic glass-and-white-tile exterior with curved walls of this hotel overlooking Lenox Square are Biedermeier-style interiors. When Westin took over the former Swissôtel in January 2004, it made a few changes, including installing its signature beds and showerheads in the guest quarters and updating the carpeting and furniture in the sweeping two-level lobby. The Palm restaurant is noted for its steaks. ✉ *3391 Peachtree Rd., Buckhead, 30326* ☎ *404/365–0065 or 800/228–3000* 🖷 *404/365–8787* 🌐 *www.westin.com/buckhead* *349 rooms, 16 suites* *Restaurant, cable TV, pool, health club, spa, bar, Internet, business services, parking (fee), some pets allowed* *AE, D, DC, MC, V* *EP.*

$$–$$$ **Embassy Suites Hotel.** Just blocks from the Phipps Plaza and Lenox Square malls is this modern high-rise with different kinds of suites—from deluxe presidential (with wet bars) to more basic sleeping-and-sitting-room combinations. All of the suites open onto a 16-story sunlighted atrium towering above the lobby. Rates include afternoon cocktails. ✉ *3285 Peachtree Rd., Buckhead, 30305* ☎ *404/261–7733 or 800/362–2779* 🖷 *404/261–6857* 🌐 *www.embassysuites.com* *317 suites* *Restaurant, cable TV, indoor-outdoor pool, gym, Internet, parking (fee)* *AE, D, DC, MC, V* *BP.*

$$–$$$ **Sheraton Buckhead.** This modern, eight-floor hotel has the advantage of being right across from the Lenox Square mall. Contemporary furnishings fill the rooms; some have a desk and chair, others sofas. All are equipped with amenities such as hair dryers, coffeemakers, and irons and ironing boards. ✉ *3405 Lenox Rd., Buckhead, 30326* ☎ *404/261–9250 or 800/325–3535* 🖷 *404/848–7391* 🌐 *www.sheraton.com/buckhead* *362 rooms, 7 suites* *Restaurant, cable TV, pool, gym, bar, Internet, business services, parking (fee), some pets allowed* *AE, D, DC, MC, V* *EP.*

★ **$$–$$$** **W Atlanta.** An ultrachic member of the W hotel chain, this Perimeter property makes good on its promise to pamper business travelers. Guest rooms are sweepingly large, with oversize wet bars and all the comforts of home—assuming your home is a dazzling showcase of impeccable taste. In your room you'll find a lush terry robe and a coffeemaker complete with the hotel's own brand of specialty coffee. Baths are outfitted with high-end-salon toiletries. ✉ *111 Perimeter Center W, Dunwoody 30346* ☎ *770/396–6800 or 877/946–8357* 🖷 *770/394–4805* 🌐 *www.starwood.com/whotels* *252 rooms, 23 suites* *Restaurant, cable TV, pool, gym, hot tub, sauna, lounge, Internet, free parking* *AE, D, DC, MC, V* *EP.*

$–$$$ **Doubletree Hotel Atlanta/Buckhead.** If the complimentary fresh-baked chocolate-chip cookies that welcome you don't convince you to stay here, maybe the spacious rooms and reasonable rates—given the excellent location—will. The hotel offers complimentary transportation within 3 mi of the hotel and is adjacent to the Buckhead MARTA station. ✉ *3342 Peachtree Rd., Buckhead, 30326* ☎ *404/231–1234 or 800/222–8733* 🖷 *404/231–5236* 🌐 *www.doubletree.com* *230 rooms, 1 suite* *Restaurant, cable TV, indoor pool, health club, Internet, business services, meeting rooms, parking (fee)* *AE, D, DC, MC, V* *EP.*

$–$$ **Holiday Inn Select Atlanta Perimeter.** If frills come second to comfort and familiarity, consider this hotel—which generally caters to the briefcase set—with a superb location in the Perimeter business district. Rooms are reliably appointed with coffeemakers, hair dryers, and desks. ✉ *4386 Chamblee-Dunwoody Rd., Dunwoody 30341* ☎ *770/457–6363 or 800/465–4329* 🖷 *770/936–9592* 🌐 *www.hiselect.com/atl-perimeter* *250 rooms, 2 suites* *Restaurant, cable TV, pool, gym, lounge, laundry service, Internet, business services, meeting rooms, free parking, some pets allowed* *AE, D, DC, MC, V* *EP.*

$–$$ **Sierra Suites Atlanta Lenox North.** The next-door grocery store is handy at this comfortable hotel with a kitchenette (no ovens) in each open studio suite. Earthy tones contribute to the homey feel. The property is 1 mi north of Lenox Square and across the street from the Brookhaven MARTA station. ✉ *3967 Peachtree Rd., Brookhaven 30319* ☎ *404/237–9100 or 800/474–3772* 🖷 *404/237–0055* 🌐 *www.*

sierrasuites.com ⇨ *91 suites* ♁ *In-room data ports, cable TV, kitchenettes, pool, gym, laundry service, free parking, some pets allowed* ▭ *AE, D, DC, MC, V* 🍴 *BP.*

NIGHTLIFE & THE ARTS

The Arts

For the most complete schedule of cultural events, check the *Atlanta Journal-Constitution*'s Thursday "Access Atlanta" section. The city's lively and free alternative newsweekly *Creative Loafing* also has cultural and entertainment listings.

AtlanTIX Ticket Services (☎ 678/318–1400), at the visitor center at Underground Atlanta, is a good ticket outlet. **Ticketmaster** (☎ 404/249–6400 or 800/326–4000 ⊕ www.ticketmaster.com) handles tickets for Fox Theatre, Atlanta Civic Center, Philips Arena, and other venues.

Concerts

The **Atlanta Symphony Orchestra (ASO),** under the musical direction of Robert Spano, has more than 21 Grammy awards to its credit. It performs the fall–spring subscription series in the 1,800-seat Symphony Hall at **Woodruff Arts Center** (✉ 1280 Peachtree St., Midtown ☎ 404/733–5000). In summer the orchestra regularly plays with big-name popular and country artists in the outdoor **Chastain Park Amphitheatre** (✉ 4469 Stella Dr., Buckhead ☎ 404/233–2227 or 404/733–5000).

Emory University (✉ Arts at Emory box office, Schwartz Center for the Performing Arts, 1700 N. Decatur Rd., Emory ☎ 404/727–5050 📠 404/727–6421), an idyllic suburban campus, has four venues where internationally renowned guest artists and faculty and student groups perform. Expect quality music from various ensembles, including woodwind, brass, jazz, and vocal.

Georgia State University (✉ Art and Music Bldg., Peachtree Center Ave. and Gilmer St., Downtown ☎ 404/651–4636 or 404/651–3676) sponsors many concerts (about 80%) that are free and open to the public. Performances by faculty, student, and local groups and guest artists focus on jazz and classical music. The entrance is on Gilmer Street, and there's free parking at the corner of Edgewood and Peachtree Center avenues. The **Rialto Center for the Performing Arts** (✉ 80 Forsyth St., Downtown ☎ 404/651–4727 ⊕ www.rialtocenter.org), an old movie theater the university turned into a performance venue, hosts concerts.

Dance

The **Atlanta Ballet** (✉ 1400 W. Peachtree St., Midtown ☎ 404/873–5811 ⊕ www.atlantaballet.com), founded in 1929, is the country's oldest continuously operating ballet company. It has been internationally recognized for its productions of classical and contemporary works. Artistic director John McFall has choreographed such dance greats as Mikhail Baryshnikov and Cynthia Gregory; only the third director in the company's history, McFall brings a constant stream of innovative ideas and vision to the group. Performances are usually at the Fox Theatre but sometimes take place elsewhere.

Festivals

The **Atlanta Jazz Festival** (☎ 404/817–6815 for Atlanta Bureau of Cultural Affairs 🖷 404/817–6976 ⊕ www.atlantafestivals.com), held Memorial Day weekend, gathers the best local, national, and international musicians to give mostly free concerts at Atlanta's Piedmont Park.

Music Midtown (⊕ www.musicmidtown.com), founded in 1994 with mostly local acts, has evolved into one of the biggest and most diverse music festivals in the country. Over the course of three days in April or May and for about $50, festivalgoers can see about 100 acts representing several musical genres. The temporary festival grounds cover about 40 acres from Midtown to downtown.

The **National Black Arts Festival** (✉ 659 Auburn Ave., Sweet Auburn ☎ 404/730–7315 ⊕ www.nbaf.org), celebrating literature, dance, visual arts, theater, film, and music in venues throughout the city, is held the third week in July. Maya Angelou, Cicely Tyson, Harry Belafonte, Spike Lee, Tito Puente, and Wynton Marsalis have appeared at past events. Prices for performances, exhibits, and lectures vary.

Opera

The **Atlanta Opera** (✉ 728 W. Peachtree St., Midtown ☎ 404/881–8885 or 800/356–7372 ⊕ www.atlantaopera.org) usually mounts four main-stage productions each year from spring through fall at the Boisfeuillet Jones Atlanta Civic Center. Major roles are performed by national and international guest artists; the chorus and orchestra come from the local community.

Performance Venues

Boisfeuillet Jones Atlanta Civic Center (✉ 395 Piedmont Ave., Midtown ☎ 404/523–6275), christened after the improbably named Atlanta philanthropist, presents touring Broadway musicals, pop concerts, dance performances, and opera.

Chastain Park Amphitheatre (✉ 4469 Stella Dr. NW, Buckhead ☎ 404/233–2227 or 404/733–5000), home to Atlanta Symphony Orchestra's summer series and other pop concerts, feels more like an outdoor nightclub than a typical performance venue. Pack a picnic, bring a blanket if you've snagged some of the sparse and less-expensive lawn seats, and prepare to listen to your favorite performers over the clink of dishes and the low chatter of dinner conversation.

The **Coca-Cola Roxy** (✉ 3110 Roswell Rd., Buckhead ☎ 404/233–7699) was once a theater, so its sloped floors make for an ideal concert hall. Shows range from comedy to rock, jazz, and R&B.

Ferst Center for the Performing Arts (✉ 349 Ferst Dr., Georgia Tech ☎ 404/894–9600), at the Georgia Institute of Technology, hosts performances that run the gamut from classical and jazz to dance and theater. There's ample free parking.

Fox Theatre (✉ 660 Peachtree St., Midtown ☎ 404/881–2100), a dramatic faux-Moorish theater, is the principal venue for touring Broadway shows and national productions, as well as the home of the Atlanta Ballet.

Gwinnett Center (✉ 6400 Sugarloaf Pkwy., Duluth ☎ 770/813–7500 or 800/224–6422), 30 mi north of downtown Atlanta, houses the 700-seat Performing Arts Center and the 13,000-seat Arena. The Arena hosts national touring acts as well as Georgia Force Arena Football and Gwinnett Gladiators minor-league hockey games.

HiFi Buys Amphitheatre (✉ 2002 Lakewood Way, Downtown ☎ 404/443–5090), 4 mi south of downtown Atlanta, draws national popular music acts all summer. There's seating for up to 19,000 in reserved areas and on its sloped lawn.

Mable House Amphitheatre (✉ 5239 Floyd Rd., Mableton ☎ 770/819–7765), a 2,000-seat venue 6 mi west of downtown Atlanta, stages classical, pop, jazz, and country music.

With a seating capacity of 21,000 and its giant "Atlanta" archway, **Philips Arena** (✉ 1 Philips Dr., Downtown ☎ 404/878–3000) is the major venue downtown. In addition to hosting the biggest acts, it's also the home arena for the Atlanta Hawks NBA team and the Atlanta Thrashers NHL team.

Rialto Center for the Performing Arts (✉ 80 Forsyth St., Downtown ☎ 404/651–4727 🌐 www.rialtocenter.org), developed by Georgia State University in a beautifully renovated and restructured former movie theater, shows film, theater, and dance, as well as musical performances by local and international performers.

★ **Spivey Hall** (✉ 5900 N. Lee St., Morrow ☎ 770/961–3683 🌐 www.spiveyhall.org) is a gleaming, modern, acoustically magnificent performance center at Clayton College and State University, 15 mi south of Atlanta in Morrow. The hall is considered one of the country's finest concert venues. Internationally renowned musicians perform everything from chamber music to jazz.

Tabernacle (✉ 152 Luckie St., Downtown ☎ 404/659–9022) began its postchurch life as a House of Blues venue during the 1996 Olympics. Now it hosts top acts of all genres in an intimate setting. Seating is limited; the main floor of the former sanctuary is standing-room only.

Variety Playhouse (✉ 1099 Euclid Ave., Little Five Points, Inman Park ☎ 404/521–1786), a former movie theater, is one of the cultural anchors of the hip Little Five Points neighborhood. Its denizens don't don fancy frocks to listen to rock, bluegrass and country, blues, reggae, folk, jazz, and pop.

Woodruff Arts Center (✉ 1280 Peachtree St., Midtown ☎ 404/733–4200) houses the Alliance Theatre and the Atlanta Symphony Orchestra.

Theater

Check local newspaper listings for information on the outstanding companies in Atlanta and its suburbs.

Actor's Express (✉ 887 W. Marietta St., Downtown ☎ 404/607–7469 for Actor's Express, 404/885–9933 for King Plow Arts Center 🌐 www.actors-express.com), an acclaimed theater group, presents an eclectic selection of classic and cutting-edge productions in the 150-seat theater of the King Plow Arts Center, a stylish artists' complex hailed by local critics as a showplace of industrial chic. For an evening of dining and theater, plan dinner at the Food Studio, at the King Plow Arts Center.

Alliance Theatre (✉ 1280 Peachtree St., Midtown ☎ 404/733–5000 🌐 www.alliancetheatre.org), Atlanta's premier professional theater, presents everything from Shakespeare to the latest Broadway and off-Broadway hits. It's in the Woodruff Arts Center.

The **Atlanta Shakespeare Company** (✉ 499 Peachtree St., Midtown ☎ 404/874–5299 🌐 www.shakespearetavern.com) stages plays by the Bard and his peers, as well as by contemporary dramatists, at the New American Shakespeare Tavern. Performances vary in quality but are always fun. The Elizabethan-style playhouse is a tavern, so alcohol and pub-style food are available.

14th Street Playhouse (✉ 173 14th St., Midtown ☎ 404/733–4750) is part of the Woodruff Arts Center. The house has three theaters—a 400-seat main stage, a 200-seat second stage, and a 90-seat third stage—which are rented for special productions. Resident companies include Art Within, Atlanta Classical Theatre, and Theatre Gael. Musicals, plays, and sometimes opera are presented.

★ The **Georgia Shakespeare Festival** (✉ 4484 Peachtree Rd., Buckhead ☎ 404/264–0020 🌐 www.gashakespeare.org), a June–November Atlanta tradition since 1986, brings plays by the Bard and other enduring authors to the 509-seat Conant Performing Arts Center, on the campus of Oglethorpe University.

Horizon Theatre Co. (✉ 1083 Austin Ave., Little Five Points, Inman Park ☎ 404/584–7450), a professional troupe established in 1983, produces premieres of provocative and entertaining contemporary plays in its 185-seat theater.

Nightlife

Atlanta has long been known for having more bars than churches, and in the South that's an oddity. The pursuit of entertainment—from Midtown to Buckhead—is known as the "Peachtree shuffle." Atlanta's vibrant nightlife includes everything from coffeehouses to sports bars, from country line dancing to high-energy dance clubs.

Most bars and clubs are open nightly, often until 2 AM or 4 AM. Those with live entertainment usually charge a cover.

Acoustic

Eddie's Attic (✉ 515B N. McDonough St., Decatur ☎ 404/377–4976) is a good spot for catching local and some national acoustic, folk, pop, and country-music acts. It has a full bar and restaurant and is right near the Decatur MARTA station. Covers range from $6 to $15.

Bars

The **Beluga Martini Bar** (✉ 3115 Piedmont Rd., Buckhead ☎ 404/869–1090) serves caviar, smoked salmon, champagne by the glass, and other light fare in an intimate, comfortable space with live music.

You can't get a Budweiser or Coors at the **Brick Store Pub** (✉ 125 E. Court Sq., Decatur ☎ 404/687–0990), but you can choose from about 80 other bottled and draft brews, along with some very good burgers, salads, and sandwiches. The interior is cavelike but comfortable.

If you want to feel like a local—a loud, too-cool-for-school local—stop by the **Euclid Avenue Yacht Club** (✉ 1136 Euclid Ave. NE, Little Five Points, Inman Park ☎ 404/688–2582). Everyone's welcome at this neighborhood dive with the ironically preppy name—college kids, punkers, motorcycle riders, and corporate types—but it's where the guys who are staying out way later than their wives allow always end up.

For Irish fun, food, beer, and music (both live and on CD), head to **Irish Bred Pub & Grill** (✉ 94 Upper Pryor St., Downtown ☎ 404/524–5722). The food ranges from *boxty* (potato pancakes with savory fillings) to Irish stew made with lamb, cottage pie, and whiskey trifle.

Limerick Junction (✉ 822 N. Highland Ave., Virginia-Highland ☎ 404/874–7147), a lively Irish pub, showcases singers from the large Atlanta community that ably render traditional Irish music, as well as performers from the old sod itself. It has a rollicking, good-time feeling about it. Parking is dreadful, so consider a cab. A small cover may be charged.

Manuel's Tavern (✉ 602 N. Highland Ave., Virginia-Highland ☎ 404/525–3447) is a neighborhood saloon where families, politicians, writers, students, and professionals gather to brainstorm and partake of the tavern's menu of pleasantly upscale pub food. When the Atlanta Braves play, the crowd gathers around the wide-screen TVs.

Vortex (✉ 878 Peachtree St., Midtown ☎ 404/875–1667) has a friendly style, knowledgeable bartenders, live bands, and hearty pub fare, making it a local favorite.

Comedy

In the Startime Entertainment complex in Roswell, 20 mi north of downtown Atlanta, is **Funny Farm** (✉ 608 Holcomb Bridge Rd., Roswell ☎ 770/817–4242). Admission is usually $13.50, plus a two-item minimum from the menu or bar.

Punchline (✉ 280 Hilderbrand Dr., Balconies Shopping Center, Sandy Springs ☎ 404/252–5233), Atlanta's oldest comedy club, books major national acts. The small club is popular, so you need a reservation. Cover charges vary and can be upward of $20 for some acts, but it's usually worth it.

Country

The 44,000-square-foot **Cowboys Concert Hall** (✉ 1750 N. Roberts Rd., Kennesaw ☎ 770/426–5006) attracts national talent twice monthly on Friday. On Wednesday, Thursday, Friday, and Sunday, line-dancing and couple-dancing lessons are taught. The cover is $7—more if an unusually high-profile act is slated.

Billing itself as the nation's largest country-music dance club and concert hall, **Wild Bill's** (⊠ 2075 Market St., Duluth ☎ 678/473–1000) has room for 5,000 dancin', drinkin', partyin' cowpokes. The cover is $8–$10 on dance nights and $17–$33 for concerts.

Dance

Compound (⊠ 1008 Brady Ave., West Atlanta ☎ 404/472–4621) opened in spring 2004 in warehouses converted into an elegant club with Asian touches. It reaches out to Atlanta's diverse scene with themed nights, including gay, Latin, and "Dirty Tokyo"; call ahead for the theme schedule.

Havana Club (⊠ 247 Buckhead Ave., Buckhead ☎ 404/869–8484) offers free salsa lessons on Thursday so patrons will be ready for the live Latin music on Friday and Saturday.

To make it through the door at **Tongue & Groove** (⊠ 3055 Peachtree Rd., Buckhead ☎ 404/261–2325), you must dress up—long dresses for women and jackets for men. Live music—sometimes rock, sometimes salsa—alternates with recorded tunes. The light-fare menu is as chic as the sense of style here. Covers range from $4 to $10, depending on the program.

The dress code at **Vision Night Club & Lounge** (⊠ 1068 Peachtree St., Midtown ☎ 404/874–4460)—no athletic gear in general, no T-shirts on Friday—ensures that visitors dress to impress. The music is hip-hop, disco, and R&B, and the dance floor is huge. The cover charge is $10–$20.

Gay & Lesbian

Most of the city's many lesbian and gay clubs are in Midtown, but a few can be found in Buckhead and the suburbs.

Backstreet (⊠ 845 Peachtree St., Midtown ☎ 404/873–1986), though it draws men and women of all affinities, has been Midtown's mainstay gay club for nearly two decades. Downstairs is the dance floor with recorded music; upstairs is Charlie Brown's Cabaret, with female impersonators. Because the club is open 24 hours, membership is required; quarterly memberships cost $10, entitling cardholders to free admission Sunday–Thursday and $5 covers Friday and Saturday.

Bulldog's (⊠ 893 Peachtree St., Midtown ☎ 404/872–3025), open since 1978, is the place for guys to cruise, dance, and relax. Music theme nights range from hip-hop to Latin. The cover is $3–$5.

Burkhart's (⊠ 1492 F Piedmont Rd., Ansley Square Shopping Center, Midtown ☎ 404/872–4403) caters to a male clientele with pool, lots of karaoke, and the occasional drag show. It's more of a hang-out bar than a dance club. There's no cover.

Hoedowns (⊠ 931 Monroe Dr., Midtown ☎ 404/876–0001) is where gays and lesbians go to two-step to country music. Free dance lessons are offered Tuesday, Wednesday, Thursday, and Saturday, and there's never a cover charge.

Jazz & Blues

Blind Willie's (✉ 828 N. Highland Ave., Virginia-Highland ☎ 404/873–2583) showcases New Orleans and Chicago-style blues that send crowds into a frenzy. Cajun and zydeco are also on the agenda from time to time. The name honors Blind Willie McTell, a native of Thomson, Georgia; his original compositions include "Statesboro Blues," made popular by the Macon, Georgia–based Allman Brothers. Cover charges run $3–$10.

Churchill Grounds (✉ 660 Peachtree St., Midtown ☎ 404/876–3030) celebrates the art of jazz music with weekly jam sessions and great local and national acts. Cover charges range from $5 to $10 per set.

Dante's Down the Hatch (✉ 3380 Peachtree Rd., Buckhead ☎ 404/266–1600) is popular for its music and sultry sensibility. Most nights music is provided by a jazz trio, which conjures silky-smooth tunes in the "hold" of a make-believe sailing ship.

Fuzzy's Place (✉ 2015 N. Druid Hills Rd., Druid Hills ☎ 404/321–6166), a crowded smoke-filled neighborhood bar, begins the day by serving lunch to the denizens of nearby office buildings. By night it's a restaurant with a surprisingly sophisticated menu, sports bar, and blues room. The finest local talent holds forth on the stage, including the venerable Francine Reed, one of Atlanta's favorite entertainers. There's usually no cover.

Sambuca Jazz Cafe (✉ 3102 Piedmont Rd., Buckhead ☎ 404/237–5299), with decent dining, a lively bar, and good live jazz, attracts a trendy young set.

Rock

Echo Lounge (✉ 551 Flat Shoals Ave. SE, East Atlanta ☎ 404/681–3600) is a popular stop for local garage bands and touring groups. Covers range from $7 to $20.

Masquerade (✉ 695 North Ave., Virginia-Highland ☎ 404/577–8178) is a grunge hangout with everything from industrial and techno to disco and swing. The mix of people reflects the club's three separate spaces, dubbed Heaven, Hell, and Purgatory. Basic bar food is available. The cover is $8–$30.

Smith's Olde Bar (✉ 1578 Piedmont Ave., Ansley Park ☎ 404/875–1522) schedules different kinds of talent, both local and regional, in its acoustically fine performance space. Food is available in the downstairs restaurant. Covers vary depending on the act but are usually $5–$15.

Star Community Bar (✉ 437 Moreland Ave., Inman Park ☎ 404/681–9018) is highly recommended for those who enjoy garage bands and rockabilly. Bands play almost nightly, with covers varying depending on the act. The bar in this former bank space is fully equipped, and an all-Elvis jukebox and an Elvis shrine in the vault must be seen to be believed.

10 High Club (✉ 816 N. Highland Ave., Virginia-Highland ☎ 404/873–3607), in the basement of the Dark Horse Tavern, hosts local and touring bands that are guaranteed to be loud in this close, brick-walled space. Covers rarely exceed $10.

SHOPPING

Atlanta's department stores, specialty shops, large enclosed malls, and antiques markets draw shoppers from across the Southeast. Most stores are open Monday–Saturday 10–9, Sunday noon–6. Many downtown stores close Sunday. The sales tax is 7% in the city of Atlanta and Fulton County and 6%–7% in the suburbs.

11

Shopping Neighborhoods

Buckhead, a commercial district with many specialty shops and strip malls, is no minor shopping destination. At Peachtree Plaza, at the intersection of Peachtree Road and Mathieson Drive, you'll find Beverly Bremer Silver Shop, devoted to fine antique silver, and Irish Crystal Co., offering fine cut glass and linens. Down Maple Drive off Peachtree Road is Yesteryear, dealing in antique books; it's next to the Maple Street Guitars store. Boutiques, gift shops, and some fine restaurants line Grandview Avenue (off Peachtree Road), and another similar collection runs down East Shadowlawn Avenue. East Village Square (Buckhead Avenue and Bolling Way) has art galleries and restaurants. Andrews Square, on East Andrews Drive, is a good conglomeration of shops, eateries, nightspots, and galleries. Next to it, Cates Center has similar stores.

Decatur Square, a quaint town quad with a sophisticated, artistic vibe, is teeming with interesting specialty shops and delectable coffeehouses and cafés. Lively downtown Decatur, 8 mi east of Midtown Atlanta, is one of the metro area's favorite spots for sidewalk strolling and window-shopping.

Little Five Points (✉ Moreland and Euclid Aves., Inman Park) attracts "junking" addicts, who find happiness in Atlanta's version of Greenwich Village, characterized by vintage-clothing stores, art galleries, used-record and -book shops, and some stores that defy description.

Virginia-Highland is a wonderful urban neighborhood for window-shopping, thanks to its art galleries, restaurants, fashionable boutiques, antiques shops, and bookstores. Parking can be tricky in the evenings, so if you go late in the day, take a cab or be prepared to park down a side street and walk a few blocks.

Shopping Centers

Brookwood Square (✉ 2140 Peachtree Rd., Buckhead) is an arrangement of unusual shops, including the Pickles and Ice Cream maternity shop and Park Avenue Kids.

Lenox Square (✉ 3393 Peachtree Rd., Buckhead ☎ 404/233–6767), one of Atlanta's oldest and most popular shopping centers, has branches of Neiman Marcus, Bloomingdale's, Crate & Barrel, and Rich's-Macy's looming next to specialty shops such as Cartier and Mori (luggage and travel gifts). You'll do better at one of the several good restaurants here—even for a quick meal—than at the food court.

Peachtree Center Mall (✉ 231 Peachtree St., Downtown ☎ 404/524–3787) does steady business. Stores here are chiefly specialty shops, such as International Records, the Architectural Book Center, Touch of Georgia gift shop, and the Atlanta International Museum gift shop.

Perimeter Mall (✉ 4400 Ashford-Dunwoody Rd., Dunwoody), known for upscale family shopping, has Nordstrom, Williams-Sonoma, and Bebe, as well as branches of Rich's-Macy's and Bloomingdale's and a food court.

Phipps Plaza (✉ 3500 Peachtree Rd., Buckhead ☎ 404/262–0992 or 800/810–7700) has branches of Tiffany & Co., Saks Fifth Avenue, the Birmingham-based Parisian, Ann Taylor, Gucci, and Abercrombie & Fitch alongside such shops as Niketown and Teavana.

Underground Atlanta (✉ 50 Upper Alabama St., Downtown ☎ 404/523–2311) has galleries such as African Pride, with objets d'art from Africa; specialty shops, including Hats Under Atlanta; and Habersham Winery, a tasting room for Georgia wines. The food court is great for a quick bite, or you might want to visit Lombardi's, a downtown power-lunch staple, for a nice sit-down lunch.

Outlets

The interstate highways leading to Atlanta have discount malls similar to those found throughout the country. About 60 mi north of the city on I–85 at Exit 149 is a huge cluster of outlets in the town of Commerce. **Discover Mills Mall** (✉ 5900 Sugarloaf Pkwy., I–85 at Rte. 120, Lawrenceville ☎ 678/847–5000), 25 mi northeast of downtown Atlanta, has bargain stores like Off 5th Saks Fifth Avenue and Last Call Neiman Marcus. Also here are a large sporting-goods store and a skating park. **North Georgia Premium Outlets** (✉ 800 Rte. 400, at Dawson Forest Rd., Dawsonville ☎ 706/216–3609) is worth the 45 minutes it takes to get here from Atlanta's northern perimeter. This shopping center has more than 140 stores, including Williams-Sonoma for cookware; OshKosh, a clothing store for children; Music for a Song, dealing in discount CDs and tapes; and numerous designer outlet shops not found in most malls.

Specialty Shops

ANTIQUES & DECORATIVE ARTS

Buckhead has several antiques shops, most of them along or near Peachtree Road; expect rare goods and high prices here. Venture into Virginia-Highland and nearby suburban towns to find all sorts of treasures.

Bennett Street (🌐 www.buckhead.net/bennettstreet) in Buckhead has antiques shops, home-decor stores such as John Overton Oriental Rugs, and art galleries, including the Bennett Street Gallery. The Stalls on Bennett Street is a good antiques market. With Fratelli di Napoli (2101B Tula St., 404/351–1533), a good restaurant, nearby, it's easy to spend an entire day here.

Chamblee Antique Row (☎ 404/606–3367 for Chamblee Antique Dealers Association 🌐 www.antiquerow.com) is a browser's delight. At Peachtree Road and Broad Street in the suburban town of Chamblee, it's just north of Buckhead and about 10 mi north of downtown.

Miami Circle, off Piedmont Road, is an upscale enclave for antiques and decorative-arts lovers. Drop in for a snack at Eclipse di Luna (☎ 404/846–0449).

20th Century Antiques (✉ 1044 N. Highland Ave., Virginia-Highland ☎ 404/892–2065) carries lots of memorabilia.

2300 Peachtree Road (✉ North of Piedmont Hospital, near Peachtree Hills intersection, Buckhead) is one of Buckhead's most stylish complexes. It has more than 25 antiques shops, art galleries, and enough home-furnishing stores to fill multiple mansions.

ART GALLERIES The city bursts with art galleries—some well established, others new, some conservative, others cutting edge. For more information on the Atlanta art-gallery scene, including openings and location maps, consult ***Museums & Galleries*** (☎ 770/992–7808), a magazine distributed free at welcome centers and select area galleries.

Fay Gold Gallery (✉ 764 Miami Circle, Buckhead ☎ 404/233–3843) displays works by nationally renowned contemporary artists.

Jackson Fine Art Gallery (✉ 3115 E. Shadowlawn Ave., Buckhead ☎ 404/233–3739) exhibits fine art photography.

Marcia Wood Gallery (✉ 263 Walker St., Castleberry Hill ☎ 404/827–0030) shows exquisite original paintings by such notable artists as Drew Galloway.

Modern Primitive (✉ 1393 N. Highland Ave., Virginia-Highland ☎ 404/892–0556) has a fascinating assembly of folk and visionary art from around the state and the region.

Vespermann Gallery (✉ 309 E. Paces Ferry Rd., Buckhead ☎ 404/266–0102) carries lovely handblown glass objects.

FOOD **East 48th St. Market** (✉ 2462 Jett Ferry Rd., at Mt. Vernon Rd., Williams at Dunwoody Shopping Center, Dunwoody ☎ 770/392–1499) sells Italian deli meats, fabulous breads, cheeses, and Italian prepared foods.

Shop at **Eatzi's Market & Bakery** (✉ 3221 Peachtree Rd., Buckhead ☎ 404/237–2266) for prepared foods, imported cheeses, great breads, and fine wines.

Star Provisions (✉ 1198 Howell Mill Rd., West Midtown ☎ 404/365–0410) is a chef's dream, with fine cookware, gadgets, and tableware for sale, plus top-of-the-line cheeses, meats, and baked goods.

The health-wise can take comfort at **Whole Foods Market** (✉ 2111 Briarcliff Rd., Druid Hills ☎ 404/634–7800), with a dizzying amount of additive- and pesticide-free foods and baked goods.

Your DeKalb Farmers Market (✉ 3000 E. Ponce de Leon Ave., Decatur ☎ 404/377–6400) has 175,000 square feet of exotic fruits, cheeses, seafood, sausages, breads, and delicacies from around the world. The cafeteria-style buffet, with a selection of earthy and delicious hot foods and salads, is alone worth the trip.

ATLANTA A TO Z

To research prices, get advice from other travelers, and book travel arrangements, visit www.fodors.com.

AIR TRAVEL

Atlanta is served by more than 80 airlines, including AirTran, America West, American, Atlantic Southeast Airlines, Continental, Delta, JetBlue, Midway, Midwest Express, Northwest, United, and US Airways, as well as many regional and international carriers.

AIRPORTS

Hartsfield-Jackson Atlanta International Airport is 13 mi south of downtown.

Airport Information **Hartsfield-Jackson Atlanta International Airport** ✉ 6000 N. Terminal Pkwy., Hapeville ☎ 404/530-6600 or 800/897-1910 ⊕ www.atlanta-airport.com.

TRANSFERS Atlanta Airport Superior Shuttle vans run daily every 15 minutes between 6 AM and 11:30 PM to Perimeter Center. The cost is $25 one-way, $40 round-trip.

Atlanta Link operates vans every 15 minutes to downtown, Midtown, and the Buckhead–Lenox area. The downtown trip—$16 one-way, $28 round-trip—takes about 20 minutes and stops at major hotels. Vans to Midtown cost $18 one-way, $32 round-trip; vans to the Buckhead–Lenox area cost $20 one-way, $36 round-trip.

Airport Metro Shuttle operates shuttles round-the-clock and serves the entire region.

If your luggage is light, take MARTA high-speed trains between the airport and downtown and other locations. Trains operate 5 AM–1 AM weekdays and 6 AM–12:30 AM weekends. The trip downtown takes about 15 minutes to the Five Points station, and the fare is $1.75.

From the airport to downtown the taxi fare is $25 for one person, $26 for two, and $30 for three, including tax. From the airport to Buckhead, the fare is $35 for one, $36 for two, and $39 for three people. Buckhead Safety Cab and Checker Cab offer 24-hour service.

Taxis & Shuttles **Airport-taxi information** ☎ 404/530-6698. **Atlanta Airport Superior Shuttle** ☎ 404/766-5312. **Atlanta Link** ☎ 404/524-3400 ⊕ www.theatlantalink.com. **Airport Metro Shuttle** ☎ 404/766-6666. **Buckhead Safety Cab** ☎ 404/233-1152. **Checker Cab** ☎ 404/351-1111. **MARTA** ☎ 404/848-4711.

BUS TRAVEL TO & FROM ATLANTA

Amtrak operates its Thruway bus service daily from Montgomery and Mobile, Alabama, to Atlanta's Brookwood Station. Other Thruway buses go from the station to Macon and Columbus, Georgia, and to Chattanooga and Nashville, Tennessee. Greyhound Bus Lines provides transportation from numerous points in the country to downtown Atlanta and Hartsfield-Jackson Atlanta International Airport.

Bus Information **Amtrak** ✉ 1688 Peachtree St., Buckhead ☎ 404/881-3060 or 800/872-7245 🌐 www.amtrak.com. **Greyhound Bus Lines** ✉ 232 Forsyth St., Downtown ☎ 404/584-1728 or 800/231-2222 🌐 www.greyhound.com.

BUS TRAVEL WITHIN ATLANTA

MARTA, with a fleet of about 700 buses, operates 125 routes covering 1,100 mi. The fare is $1.75, and exact change is required. Weekly and monthly TransCards, available at MARTA stations and Rides Stores, give you a slight discount. Service is very limited outside the perimeter set by I–285, except for a few areas in Clayton, DeKalb, and Fulton counties.

Bus Information **MARTA** ☎ 404/848-4711 🌐 www.itsmarta.com.

CAR RENTAL

If you plan to venture beyond the neighborhoods served by a MARTA train stop, you may want to rent a car, as bus service is somewhat limited. Many national agencies have branch offices all over the city, in addition to counter service at Hartsfield-Jackson Atlanta International Airport; the numbers listed below are for airport branches.

Agencies **Avis** ☎ 404/530-2725. **Budget** ☎ 404/530-3000. **Hertz** ☎ 404/530-2925. **National/Alamo** ☎ 404/530-2800.

CAR TRAVEL

The city is encircled by I–285. Three interstates also crisscross Atlanta: I–85, running northeast–southwest from Virginia to Alabama; I–75, running north–south from Michigan to Florida; and I–20, running east–west from South Carolina to Texas.

TRAFFIC Some refer to Atlanta as the Los Angeles of the South because driving is virtually the only way to get to most parts of the city. Although the congestion hasn't quite caught up to that of Los Angeles, Atlantans have grown accustomed to frequent delays at rush hour—the morning and late-afternoon commuting periods seem to get longer every year. Beware: the South as a whole may be laid-back, but Atlanta drivers are not; they tend to drive faster than drivers in other Southern cities.

EMERGENCIES

For 24-hour emergency rooms contact Atlanta Medical Center, Grady Memorial Hospital, Northside Hospital, and Piedmont Hospital.

Emergency Services **Ambulance, fire, police** ☎ 911.

Hospitals **Atlanta Medical Center** ✉ 303 Parkway Dr., Downtown ☎ 404/265-4000. **Grady Memorial Hospital** ✉ 80 Butler St., Downtown ☎ 404/616-4307. **Northside Hospital** ✉ 1000 Johnson Ferry Rd., Dunwoody ☎ 404/851-8000. **Piedmont Hospital** ✉ 1968 Peachtree Rd., Buckhead ☎ 404/605-5000.

24-Hour Pharmacies **CVS** ✉ 1943 Peachtree Rd., Buckhead ☎ 404/351-7629 ✉ 1554 N. Decatur Rd., Decatur ☎ 404/373-4192 ✉ 2350 Cheshire Bridge Rd., Buckhead ☎ 404/486-7289.

LODGING

BED-AND-BREAKFASTS Bed & Breakfast Online can provide detailed cyber-brochures on inns in Atlanta and the surrounding area.

Reservation Information **Bed & Breakfast Online** Box 829, Madison, TN 37116 www.bbonline.com/ga 615/868-1946.

SIGHTSEEING TOURS

BUS TOURS Gray Line of Atlanta has an "Atlanta Past and Present" tour ($40, 3½ hours) and an "All Around Atlanta" tour ($45, four hours).

Fees & Schedules **Gray Line of Atlanta** 770/449-1806 or 800/593-1818 770/249-9397.

WALKING TOURS The Atlanta Preservation Center runs several walking tours of historic areas and neighborhoods for $10 each; tours usually last one to two hours. Especially noteworthy are tours of Sweet Auburn, the neighborhood associated with Martin Luther King Jr. and other leaders of Atlanta's African-American community; Druid Hills, the verdant, genteel neighborhood where *Driving Miss Daisy* was filmed; and the Fox Theatre, the elaborate 1920s picture palace.

Fees & Schedules **Atlanta Preservation Center** 404/688-3353, 404/688-3350 for tour hotline www.preserveatlanta.com.

SUBWAY TRAVEL

MARTA has clean and safe rapid-rail subway trains with somewhat limited routes that link downtown with many major landmarks. The system's two main lines cross at the Five Points station downtown. Weekend passes, weekly and monthly TransCards, and information on public transportation are available at Rides Stores, open weekdays 7–7 and Saturday 8:30–5; Rides Stores are at the airport, Five Points Station, the headquarters building by Lindbergh station, and Lenox Station. You can also buy passes at Kroger and Publix groceries. Obtain free transfers, needed for some bus routes, by pressing a button on the subway turnstile or requesting one from the driver.

FARES & SCHEDULES Trains run 5 AM–2 AM, and large, free parking lots are at most stations beyond downtown. Tokens ($1.75 each) can be bought from machines outside each station.

Subway Information **MARTA** 404/848-4711 www.itsmarta.com.

TAXIS

Taxi service in Atlanta can be uneven. Drivers often lack correct change, so be prepared either to charge your fare (many accept credit cards) or insist that the driver obtain change. Drivers can also appear as befuddled as you may be by Atlanta's notoriously winding streets, so if your destination is something other than a major hotel or popular sight, come with directions.

Taxi fares cost $2 on entry, plus 25¢ for each additional ⅐ mi, $1 per extra passenger, and $18 per hour of waiting time. If you stay within the Downtown Convention Zone, the Midtown Zone, or the Buckhead Zone, a flat rate of $6 for one person plus $1 per additional passenger will be charged for any destination.

You generally need to call ahead for a cab; Atlanta is not a cab-hailing sort of town. Buckhead Safety Cab and Checker Cab offer 24-hour service.

Taxi Companies **Buckhead Safety Cab** ☎ 404/233-1152. **Checker Cab** ☎ 404/351-1111.

TRAIN TRAVEL

Amtrak operates the *Crescent* train, with daily service to Atlanta's Brookwood Station from New York; Philadelphia; Washington, D.C.; Baltimore; Charlotte, North Carolina; Greenville, South Carolina; and New Orleans.

Train Information **Amtrak** ✉ 1688 Peachtree St., Buckhead ☎ 404/881-3060 or 800/872-7245 ⊕ www.amtrak.com.

VISITOR INFORMATION

The Atlanta Convention & Visitors Bureau (ACVB), which can provide information on Atlanta and the outlying area, has several visitor information centers in Atlanta: Hartsfield-Jackson Atlanta International Airport, in the atrium of the main ticketing terminal; Underground Atlanta; Georgia World Congress Center; and Lenox Square mall.

Tourist Information **Atlanta Convention & Visitors Bureau** ✉ 233 Peachtree St., Suite 100, Downtown, 30303 ☎ 404/222-6688 ⊕ www.atlanta.net ✉ Underground Atlanta, 65 Upper Alabama St., Downtown ✉ Georgia World Congress Center, 285 International Blvd., Downtown ☎ 404/223-4000 ⊕ www.gwcc.com ✉ Lenox Square, 3393 Peachtree Rd., Buckhead ☎ 404/266-1398.

CENTRAL GEORGIA

12

HEAR BROTHER RAY AND THE B-52S
at the Georgia Music Hall of Fame ⇨p.444

REST IN RUSTIC ELEGANCE
at Henderson Village resort ⇨p.446

TRAVEL BACK IN TIME
along the Antebellum Trail ⇨p.447

VISIT THE BIRTHPLACE OF BR'ER RABBIT
at Eatonton's Uncle Remus Museum ⇨p.449

STOP AND SMELL THE ROSES
at the State Botanical Gardens ⇨p.450

Updated by Doug Wyatt

LOOKING FOR MISS SCARLETT? Tool down U.S. 441—the Antebellum Trail—and you can catch more than a whiff of the Old South as you make your way toward Macon. Madison, spared from General Sherman's wrath as he rampaged toward the sea in 1864, offers charming antebellum and Victorian architecture. Eatonton, 20 mi down the highway, also has its share of stately historic houses, but your attention will really be arrested by the statue of the giant rabbit on the courthouse lawn. It's part of the town's tribute to favorite son Joel Chandler Harris, creator of Br'er Rabbit and Uncle Remus.

If possible, make it to Macon in March, when the city's cherry trees are in full, spectacular flower. The annual festival celebrating the trees is a blast. And you can rock year-round at Macon's Georgia Music Hall of Fame, paying tribute to the state's musicians who have contributed so much to America's musical culture. Ray Charles, James Brown, the Allman Brothers Band, Chet Atkins, and Otis Redding are but a few of the legends honored in the hall.

In Athens, you can find remnants of antebellum Georgia, but the home of the University of Georgia also pulses with college life. The birthplace of REM and the B-52s, Athens still has a thriving entertainment scene.

Exploring Central Georgia

Athens, Macon, and Augusta form, roughly, a triangle. The best way to catch the region's flavor is to head from Athens down U.S. 441 toward Macon. You'll pass through smaller towns such as Milledgeville and Eatonton. Washington, the first city chartered in honor of the first president, lies on U.S. 78, 38 mi east of Athens. Continue along U.S. 78 and hit I–20 to get to Augusta.

About the Restaurants

Central Georgia isn't the first place to look for haute cuisine—even haute Southern cuisine—but there are plenty of opportunities eat simply and well at reasonable prices. Things get spiced up a bit in Athens, which presents the greatest variety of choices.

WHAT IT COSTS

$$$$	$$$	$$	$	¢
over $22	$16–$22	$11–$16	$7–$11	under $7

Prices are for a main course at dinner, excluding sales tax of 5%–7%.

About the Hotels

The most attractive lodging options here tend to have been around for a long time—the structures, at least, often date from the 19th century. At such places—most commonly B&Bs, but sometimes larger inns—you're likely to find big porches with rocking chairs and bedrooms decorated with antiques. If that's more Southern charm than you're after, you can choose from a smattering of chain hotels.

WHAT IT COSTS				
$$$$	$$$	$$	$	¢
over $220	$160–$220	$110–$160	$70–$110	under $70

Prices are for two people in a standard double room in high season, excluding service charges and 11%–13% tax.

MACON & THE ANTEBELLUM TRAIL

Macon

1 *32 mi southwest of Milledgeville via U.S. 441 to Rte. 49; 85 mi southeast of Atlanta via I–75.*

At the state's geographic center, Macon, founded in 1823, has more than 100,000 flowering cherry trees, which it celebrates each March with a knockout festival. Its antebellum and Victorian homes are among the state's best preserved.

★ Among the city's many sites is the **Georgia Music Hall of Fame,** located in Macon as a tribute to the city's extensive contribution to American music. The museum recognizes the Georgians who have helped to define America's musical culture. Among the honorees are Ray Charles, James Brown, the Allman Brothers Band, Chet Atkins, REM, and the B-52s. Exhibits also celebrate classical musicians, including Robert Shaw, the late director of the Atlanta Symphony Orchestra; opera singers Jessye Norman and James Melton; and violinist Robert McDuffie. *✉ 200 Martin Luther King Jr. Blvd. ☎ 478/750–8555 or 888/427–6257 🌐 www.gamusichall.com 🎫 $8 ⏲ Mon.–Sat. 9–5, Sun. 1–5.*

The **Georgia Sports Hall of Fame,** with its old-style ticket booths, has the look and feel of an old ballpark. Exhibits honor sports at all levels, from prep and college teams to professional. *✉ 301 Cherry St. ☎ 478/752–1585 🌐 www.gshf.org 🎫 $8 ⏲ Mon.–Sat. 9–5, Sun. 1–5.*

★ The unique **Hay House,** designed by the New York firm T. Thomas & Son, is a study in fine Italianate architecture prior to the Civil War. The marvelous stained-glass windows and many technological advances, including indoor plumbing, make a tour worthwhile. *✉ 934 Georgia Ave. ☎ 478/742–8155 🌐 www.georgiatrust.org/historic_sites/hay_house.htm 🎫 $6 ⏲ Mon.–Sat. 10–5, Sun. 1–5.*

African-American entrepreneur Charles H. Douglass built the **Douglass Theatre** in 1921. Great American musicians have performed here, among them Bessie Smith, Ma Rainey, Cab Calloway, Duke Ellington, and locals Little Richard and Otis Redding. It's currently a venue for movies, plays, and other performances. You can take a guided tour of the building. *✉ 355 Martin Luther King Jr. Blvd. ☎ 478/742–2000 🌐 www.douglasstheatre.org ⏲ Tues.–Sat. 9–5.*

The **Macon Museum of Arts and Sciences and Mark Smith Planetarium** displays everything from a whale skeleton to fine art. Discovery House,

Numbers in the text correspond to numbers in the margin and on the Central Georgia map.

If you have 3 days

Athens 4 makes a good starting point. There's usually something going on around town, especially when the University of Georgia is in session. Fans of REM, the B-52s, and their heirs can find a still lively club scene in Athens. If you favor things a bit slower, check out the city's quieter, more traditional side. The Athens Welcome Center is a great place to find out about the area's historic homes. The next morning, head down U.S. 441, the "Antebellum Trail." Madison, about 30 mi down the road, offers restaurants, antiques shops, and some exquisite historical architecture spared from the ravages of General Sherman. Another 20 mi or so down the way, **Eatonton** 3 offers similar antebellum treasures—and you must see the statue of the giant rabbit by the courthouse. Kids will enjoy the Uncle Remus Museum. **Milledgeville** 2, another 20 mi on, might be a good place to spend the night. Check out the Governor's Mansion there, an 1838 Greek Revival mansion that served as headquarters for the reviled Sherman during the war. On your third day, drive into **Macon** 1, about 30 mi southwest of Milledgeville. The Georgia Music Hall of Fame is a must, and kids should enjoy the interactive exhibits at the Macon Museum of Arts and Sciences. The Hay House is a nice stop for the historically inclined.

If you have 5 days

Start your trip in **Athens** 4. The next morning, head southeast down U.S. 78 toward **Washington** 5. There you can find historic buildings, some dating to the American Revolution, cafés, and antiques shops. **Augusta** 6, about 55 mi down the road, should make a nice stop for your second night; while you're there, try a leisurely stroll along the Riverwalk, next to the Savannah River. The next morning, head out on I–20, west to U.S. 441, then head south toward **Eatonton** 3 and **Milledgeville** 2. Stop in either place on your third night. On your fourth day, wend your way down toward **Macon** 1, where you can fruitfully occupy you on your fourth night and fifth day.

---

an interactive exhibit for children, is modeled after an artist's garret. *4182 Forsyth Rd. 478/477–3232 www.masmacon.com $7 Mon. 9–8, Tues.–Sat. 9–5, Sun. 1–5.*

Just 3 mi east of downtown Macon is the **Ocmulgee National Monument,** a significant archaeological site. It was occupied for more than 10,000 years; at its peak, between AD 900 and AD 1100, it was populated by the Mississippian peoples. There are a reconstructed earth lodge and displays of pottery, effigies, and jewelry of copper and shells discovered in the burial mound. *1207 Emery Hwy., take U.S. 80 east 478/752–8257 www.nps.gov/ocmu Free Daily 9–5.*

★ The **Tubman African American Museum** honors the former slave who led more than 300 people to freedom as one of the conductors of the Underground Railroad. A mural depicts several centuries of black culture. The museum also has an African artifacts gallery. ✉ *340 Walnut St.* ☎ *478/743–8544* 🌐 *www.tubmanmuseum.com* *$5* ⏲ *Mon.–Sat. 9–5, Sun. 2–5.*

off the beaten path

THE OCONEE NATIONAL FOREST – The Oconee National Forest, about half way between Macon and Athens, Georgia, was established by the government to reclaim farm land ruined by erosion. The park offers hiking and camping; the region also includes several lakes suitable for motorboats. ☎ *770/536–0541* 🌐 *www.fs.fed.us/conf/welcome.htm.*

MUSEUM OF AVIATION – This museum at Robins Air Force Base has an extraordinary collection of 90 vintage aircraft including a MiG, an SR-71 (Blackbird), a U2, and assorted other flying machines from past campaigns. From Macon take I–75 south to Exit 146 (Centerville/Warner Robins), and turn left onto Watson Boulevard, 7 mi to Route 247/U.S. 129, then right for 2 mi. ✉ *Rte. 247/U.S. 129 at Russell Pkwy., Warner Robins, 20 mi south of Macon* ☎ *478/926–6870* 🌐 *www.museumofaviation.org* *Free; film $2* ⏲ *Daily 9–5.*

Where to Stay & Eat

★ $$$–$$$$ **Henderson Village.** At this resort, 38 mi south of Macon, you can find stunning 19th- and early-20th-century Southern homes clustered around a green. Guest rooms have a rustic-style elegance, with fine antiques and access to inviting wraparound porches; suites are even nicer, with fireplaces and whirlpool tubs. Buttermilk-yellow walls add warmth to the fine 1838 Langston House restaurant, which is perfect for a meal of Southern-style turbot and pan-seared beef fillet. ✉ *125 S. Langston Circle, Perry 31069* ☎ *478/988–8696 or 888/615–9722* *912/988–9009* 🌐 *www.hendersonvillage.com* *19 rooms, 5 suites* *Restaurant, in-room VCRs, pool, hot tub, fishing, hiking, horseback riding, bar, library, meeting rooms* *AE, MC, V* *BP.*

$$$–$$$$ **1842 Inn.** With its grand white-pillared front porch and period antiques, this inn offers a true taste of antebellum grandeur, and it's easy to see why this place is considered to be one of America's top inns. The rooms have an aristocratic flair, with plush coverlets and embroidered pillows. There are also loveseats, ornate window stoops, and tile fireplaces, as well as period antiques and heirloom-quality accessories. In the morning you can eat breakfast in your room, in one of the parlors, or in the gorgeous courtyard. It's an easy walk to downtown and the historic district. ✉ *353 College St., 31201* ☎ *800/336–1842* *478/741–1842* 🌐 *www.the1842inn.com* *21 rooms, 1 guest house* *Cable TV, hot tub, laundry service, Internet* *AE, DC, MC, V* *BP.*

Milledgeville

❷ *20 mi south of Eatonton on U.S. 441.*

Locals believe ghosts haunt what remains of the antebellum homes in Milledgeville. Laid out as the state capital of Georgia in 1803 (a title it

The Antebellum Trail

The antebellum South, filtered through the romanticized gauze of *Gone With the Wind,* evokes graciousness, gentility, and a code of honor demanding that dashing gentlemen named Beauregard or Jeb escort young ladies to the cotillion and cheerfully slaughter each other in nonsensical duels. More acute observers, cutting through all the magnolias and moonlight, remind us that the white-column mansions were built with the sweat of slaves. Bearing such harsh historical realities in mind, travelers can still appreciate the historical architecture of central Georgia. The Antebellum Trail, designated a state trail in 1985, links the historical communities of Athens, Watkinsville, Madison, Eatonton, Milledgeville, Old Clinton, and Macon, all rich in architecture that somehow escaped the malevolent attention of General Sherman. Along the trail, you can find such sights as Macon's Hay House (rumored to harbor Confederate gold in a secret room), Madison's elegant oak-lined streets, and the old Governor's mansion in Milledgeville.

Music Cities

Central Georgia has two towns with outsize significance in the world of popular music. Macon is the home to Georgia Music Hall of Fame, which honors the state's greats—of which there are many, from Ray Charles to Jessye Norman to Macon's own Little Richard. Athens burst on the scene as a hotbed of alternative rock in the 1980s, led by REM and the B-52s. The town's cutting edge hasn't dulled: in clubs throughout town, the music scene continues to be lively.

---

held until Atlanta assumed the role in 1868), the town was not as fortunate as Madison in escaping being torched during the Civil War. Sherman's troops stormed through with a vengeance after the general heard hardship stories from Union soldiers who had escaped from a prisoner-of-war camp in nearby Andersonville.

The 1838 Greek Revival **Old Governor's Mansion** became Sherman's headquarters during the war. His soldiers are said to have tossed government documents out of the windows and fueled their fires with Confederate money. Guided tours of the building, now a museum home, are given daily. ✉ *120 S. Clark St.* ☎ *478/453–4545* 🎫 *$5* ⏲ *Mon.–Sat. 10–4, Sun. 2–4.*

On West Hancock Street is the Georgia College and State University campus. One of its most famous students was novelist and short-story writer Flannery O'Connor, author of such acclaimed novels as *Wise Blood* and *The Violent Bear It Away.* O'Connor did most of her writing at the family farm, Andalusia, just north of Milledgeville on U.S. 441. The **Flannery O'Connor Room,** inside the **Ina Russell Library,** has many of the author's handwritten manuscripts on display. It also contains O'Connor's typewriter and some of her furniture. ✉ *231 W. Hancock St.* ☎ *478/445–4047* 🎫 *Free* ⏲ *Weekdays 9–4.*

Where to Stay & Eat

$–$$ ✕ **Brewers Downtown Café.** Pocketed nicely in a historic building, this warmly decorated restaurant specializes in Californian–Mediterranean fare with such entrées as braised mussels and steak prepared Tuscan-style. ✉ *138 W. Hancock St.* ☎ *478/452–5966* ▭ *AE, D, MC, V* ⊙ *Closed Sun.*

$–$$ ✕ **The Brick.** This bar-restaurant has a comfortable, worn-at-the-elbows appeal—which is all-important when you're about to consume massive pizzas with tasty toppings like feta cheese and spinach. The menu also has salads and calzones. ✉ *136 W. Hancock St.* ☎ *478/452–0089* ▭ *AE, D, MC, V* ⊙ *Closed Sun.*

$–$$ 🏨 **Antebellum Inn.** Each room in this pre–Civil War mansion has beautiful period antiques. The Southern breakfasts are fabulous. Proprietress Dianne Johnson is a bird lover, and you'll get a kick out of all the birds and woodland creatures that flock to her gardens in the morning, attracted to the many decorative feeders. ✉ *200 N. Columbia St., 31061* ☎ *478/453–3993* 🌐 *www.antebelluminn.com* 🛏 *5 rooms* ♨ *Pool* ▭ *AE, MC, V* 🍽 *BP.*

Eatonton

3 *22 mi south of Madison on U.S. 129/441.*

Right in the middle of the Antebellum Trail, Eatonton is a historical trove of houses that still retain the rare Southern antebellum architecture that survived Sherman's torches. But this isn't the only source of pride for this idyllic town. Take a look at the courthouse lawn; it's not your imagination—that really is a giant statue of a rabbit.

★ Eatonton is the birthplace of celebrated novelist Joel Chandler Harris, of Br'er Rabbit and Uncle Remus fame. The **Uncle Remus Museum,** built from authentic slave cabins, houses countless carvings, paintings, and other artwork depicting the characters made famous by the imaginative author. It's on the grounds of a park. ✉ *Turner Park, U.S. 441* ☎ *706/485–6856* 🌐 *www.uncleremus.com/museum.html* *50¢* ⏲ *Wed.–Mon. 10–5.*

The **Eatonton-Putnam Chamber of Commerce** (✉ 105 Sumter St. ☎ 706/485–7701) provides printed maps detailing landmarks from the upbringing of Eatonton native Alice Walker, who won the Pulitzer prize for her novel *The Color Purple*. It also has information on the many fine examples of antebellum architecture in Eatonton, including descriptions and photographs of the town's prize antebellum mansions, and a walking tour of Victorian antebellum homes.

Where to Stay

$$ **Crockett House.** With its aromatic gardens, majestic wraparound porch, and in-room fireplaces, this B&B in a restored 1895 Victorian home is perfect for a romantic getaway. Make sure to get a room with an old-fashioned claw-foot bathtub. All rooms have working fireplaces. ✉ *671 Madison Rd., 31024* ☎ *706/485–2248* *5 rooms* *AE, MC, V* *BP.*

Athens

4 *70 mi east of Atlanta via I–85 north to Rte. 316.*

Athens, an artistic jewel of the American South, is known as a breeding ground for such famed rock groups as the B-52s and REM. Because of this distinction, creative types from all over the country flock to its trendy streets in hopes of becoming, or catching a glimpse of, the next big act to take the world by storm. At the center of this artistic melee is the University of Georgia (UGA). With more than 28,000 students, UGA is an influential ingredient in the Athens mix, giving the quaint but compact city a distinct flavor that falls somewhere between a misty Southern enclave, a rollicking college town, and a smoky, jazz club–studded alleyway. It truly is a fascinating blend of Mayberry R.F.D. and MTV. The effect is as irresistible as it is authentic.

Although the streets bustle at night with students taking in the coffeehouse and concert life, Athens's quieter side also flourishes. The streets are lined with many gorgeous old homes, some of which are open to the public. Most prominent among them is the **Athens Welcome Center**

(✉ 280 E. Dougherty St. ☎ 706/353–1820 🌐 www.visitathensga.com), in the town's oldest surviving residence, the 1820 Church-Waddel-Brumby House. Athens has several splendid Greek Revival buildings, including the **university chapel,** on campus, built in 1832. The **university president's house** (✉ 570 Prince Ave.), on campus, was built in the late 1850s. The **Taylor-Grady House** (✉ 634 Prince Ave.) was constructed in 1844. The 1844 **Franklin House** (✉ 480 E. Broad St.) has been restored and reopened as an office building.

Fodor'sChoice ★ Just outside the Athens city limits is the **State Botanical Gardens of Georgia,** a tranquil, 313-acre wonderland of aromatic gardens and woodland paths. It has a massive conservatory overlooking the International Garden that functions as a welcome foyer and houses an art gallery, gift shop, and café. ✉ *2450 S. Milledge Ave., off U.S. 129/441* ☎ *706/542–1244* 🌐 *www.uga.edu/botgarden* 🎫 *Free* ⊙ *Grounds Apr.–Sept., weekdays 8–8; Oct.–Mar., weekdays 8–6. Visitor center Tues.–Sat. 9–4:30, Sun. 11:30–4:30.*

Where to Stay & Eat

$$–$$$$ ✕ **Harry Bissett's.** Get primed to taste the offerings at one of the best restaurants in Athens, where you can expect sumptuous Cajun recipes straight from the streets of New Orleans. Nosh on oysters on the half shell at the raw bar while waiting for a table (if it's the weekend, expect to wait a while). Popular main dishes include amberjack Thibodaux (broiled fresh fillet smothered in crawfish étouffée) and chicken Rochambeau (a terrine of chicken breast, béarnaise sauce, shaved ham, and wine sauce). ✉ *279 E. Broad St.* ☎ *706/353–7065* ▭ *AE, D, MC, V* ⊙ *No lunch Mon.*

$–$$$ ✕ **East–West Bistro.** This popular bistro—one of the busiest spots downtown—has a bar, formal dining upstairs, and casual dining downstairs. The most interesting selections downstairs are the small plates that allow you to sample cuisines from around the world—from wasabi-crusted tilapia to salmon in rice paper. Specials include sautéed corvina (sea bass) topped with macadamia-nut kimchi, and spinach- and Swiss cheese–stuffed flank steak. The quieter upstairs room serves a more expensive classic Italian menu. ✉ *351 E. Broad St.* ☎ *706/546–9378* ▭ *AE, D, MC, V.*

$–$$$ ✕ **Last Resort Grill.** This is a pleasant place to unwind—especially in the restaurant's cheery sidewalk café section. The cuisine is a cross between Tex-Mex and California, with items such as salmon and black-bean quesadillas, and grilled shiitake mushrooms and feta cheese tossed with pasta. ✉ *174 W. Clayton St.* ☎ *706/549–0810* ▭ *AE, D, MC, V.*

$ ✕ **Weaver D's Fine Foods.** Besides serving some of the best soul food in Athens–Clarke County, this place represents a piece of musical history: REM was so inspired by Weaver D's service motto, "Automatic for the People," that the band named its 1992 album after it. The cooks specialize in hearty home-style meals—fish and chicken, barbecued pork, meat loaf, and steak with gravy. All entrées come with vegetables picked fresh from the garden. ✉ *1016 E. Broad St.* ☎ *706/353–7797* ▭ *No credit cards.*

$$–$$$ **Magnolia Terrace.** This B&B is housed in a 1912 mansion right in the middle of the historic district. Each room is decorated with a mishmash of antiques. The rooms are warmly appointed with individual care, favoring rich, stately hues, such as burnt orange and velvet red. Some are carpeted with intricate Persian rugs, and others have large claw-foot tubs. Many have working fireplaces. *288 Hill St., 30601 706/548–3860 706/369–3439 www.bbonline.com/ga/magnoliaterrace/ 8 rooms, 1 suite AE, D, MC, V BP.*

$$ **Nicholson House.** This 19th-century house, on 6 acres of an 18th-century land grant originally deeded to William Few, one of Georgia's two signers of the U.S. Constitution, literally is a two-over-two log house. Later additions and changes hide this original structure beneath a 1947 colonial revival exterior. The inn has a wide front veranda with rocking chairs. Rooms are decorated in rich colors, and furnishings are a mix of antiques and good reproductions. *6295 Jefferson Rd., 30607 706/353–2200 706/353–7799 www.bbonline.com/ga/nicholson 7 rooms, 2 suites AE, D, MC, V BP.*

¢ **Best Western Colonial Inn.** A half mile from the UGA campus, it's a favorite among relatives who come to attend graduation. Don't expect to be blown away by the architectural design, as the hotel building itself, like the rooms it offers, is basic. Rooms, however, are quite comfortable, with thick flowery bedspreads; each room comes equipped with a coffeemaker. Excellent freshly baked cookies are offered every afternoon. Directly across the street is the Varsity Drive-In, where hungry students feast on smothered hot dogs and heaps of fries. *170 N. Milledge Ave., 30607 706/546–7311 or 800/528–1234 706/546–7959 www.bestwestern.com 69 rooms Some microwaves, some refrigerators, pool AE, D, DC, MC, V EP.*

EAST TO AUGUSTA

Washington

5 *38 mi east of Athens via U.S. 78; 100 mi east of Atlanta via I–20 to Exit 154; 100 mi northeast of Macon via U.S. 129 to I–20 to Rte. 47.*

Washington, the first city chartered in honor of the country's first president, is a living museum of Southern culture. Brick buildings, some of which date to the American Revolution, line the lively downtown area, which bustles with people visiting shops, cafés, and antiques shops. Residents live and work downtown, giving Washington a little-city appeal that distinguishes it from most other small Southern towns. The Confederate treasury was moved here from Richmond in 1865, and soon afterward the half-million dollars in gold vanished. This mysterious event has been the inspiration for numerous treasure hunts, as many like to believe the gold is still buried somewhere in Wilkes County.

The **Washington Historical Museum** (308 E. Robert Toombs Ave. 706/678–2105) houses a collection of Civil War relics, including the camp chest of Jefferson Davis. The **Robert Toombs House** (216 E. Robert Toombs Ave. 706/678–2226) is furnished with 19th-century antiques, some of which are the personal items of the former U.S. senator for which it is named, who served as secretary of state for the Confederacy during part of the Civil War.

Be sure to stop by historic **Callaway Plantation,** 4 mi west of downtown. Here, at a site dating to 1785, you can experience the closest thing to an operating plantation. Among a cluster of buildings on the estate you can find a blacksmith's house, schoolhouse, and weaving house. An ancient family cemetery is also fun to explore. During the second week of both April and October the estate comes alive with Civil War reenactments and activities such as butter-churning and quilting demonstrations. ✉ *U.S. 78* ☎ *706/678–7060* *$4* ⏲ *Tues.–Sat. 10–5, Sun. 2–5.*

Where to Stay & Eat

$–$$$ ✕ **Another Thyme Café.** This eating establishment has at least three things going for it: homemade breads and desserts (including pecan pie), location (right on the square in downtown Washington), and excellent salads and sandwiches (try the grilled vegetables on focaccia). Dinner runs slightly more upscale but stays regional with fried green tomatoes, sweet-potato chips, and fried seafood. ✉ *5 E. Public Sq.* ☎ *706/678–1672* ▭ *AE, D, MC, V* ⏲ *Closed Sun. No dinner Sun.–Thurs.*

$–$$ **Maynard's Manor.** Fireplaces in the main house warm the public spaces of this 1820 Classic Revival structure. You might find it fun to join the others who gather in the library and parlor for conversation and light refreshments. The day begins with coffee, tea, and juice in the main hall at 7 AM, followed by a full breakfast in the morning rooms. In the evening there's a dessert service conducted in the parlor, where a buffet of homemade sweets beckons. The proprietors make sure you return to turned-down bedding once you retire to your room for the evening. ✉ *219 E. Robert Toombs Ave., 30673* ☎ *706/678–4303* 🌐 *www.kudcom.com/maynard* *6 rooms, 1 suite* *Lounge, library* ▭ *MC, V* *BP.*

Augusta

❻ *55 mi east of Washington via U.S. 78 and I–20; 150 mi east of Atlanta via I–20; 70 mi southwest of Columbia, SC, via I–20.*

Although Augusta escaped the ravages of Union troops during the Civil War, nature itself was not so kind. On a crossing of the Savannah River, the town was flooded many times before modern-day city planning redirected the water into a collection of small lakes and creeks. Now the current is so mild that citizens gather to send bathtub toys downstream every year in the annual Rubber Duck Race.

Augusta is Georgia's third-oldest city, founded in 1736 by James Edward Oglethorpe, who founded Savannah in 1733. The city was named for Augusta, Princess of Wales, wife of Frederick Louis, Prince of Wales. Augusta served as Georgia's capital from 1785 to 1795.

The well-maintained paths of **Riverwalk** (between 5th and 10th streets) curve along the Savannah River and are the perfect place for a leisurely stroll. **Olde Town,** lying along Telfair and Greene streets, is a restored neighborhood of Victorian homes. The 1845 tree-lined **Augusta Canal** is another pleasant place for a walk. Many antebellum and Victorian homes of interest are spread throughout the city.

Meadow Garden was the home of George Walton, one of Georgia's three signers of the Declaration of Independence and, at age 26, its youngest signer. It has been documented as Augusta's oldest extant residence. ✉ *1320 Independence Dr.* ☎ *706/724–4174* 🎫 *$3* ⏲ *Weekdays 10–4, weekends by appointment.*

The **Morris Museum of Southern Art** has a splendid collection of Southern art, from early landscapes, antebellum portraits, and Civil War art, through neo-impressionism and modern contemporary art. ✉ *Riverfront Center, 1 10th St., 2nd fl.* ☎ *706/724–7501* 🌐 *www.themorris.org* 🎫 *$3, free on Sun.* ⏲ *Tues.–Sat. 10–5, Sun. noon–5.*

Children love the National Science Center's **Fort Discovery,** an interactive museum with a moonwalk simulator, a bike on square wheels, a hot-air balloon, and a little car propelled by magnets. ✉ *1 7th St.* ☎ *706/821–0200 or 800/325–5445* 🌐 *www.nationalsciencecenter.org/fortdiscovery* 🎫 *$8* ⏲ *Tues.–Sat. 10–5.*

Where to Stay & Eat

$$$–$$$$ ✕ **La Maison on Telfair.** Augusta's finest restaurant, operated by chef-owner Heinz Sowinski, presents a classic menu of game, sweetbreads, and, with a nod to the chef's heritage, Wiener schnitzel. The experience is enhanced by the quiet and elegant style here. ✉ *404 Telfair St.* ☎ *706/722–4805* 💳 *AE, D, DC, MC, V* ⏲ *Closed Sun. No lunch.*

$ **Partridge Inn.** A National Trust Historic hotel, this restored inn sits at the gateway to Summerville, a hilltop neighborhood of summer homes dating to 1800. There's a splendid view of downtown Augusta from the roof. Rooms are elegant, and have double-line cordless phones and high-speed Internet lines. The hotel's exterior has 12 common balconies and a breathtaking upper veranda accented with shaded architectural porticos over wood-plank flooring, creating a truly lustrous reprieve for a quick coffee and newspaper read. There's also videoconferencing for those who can't bear to be out of sight of their business partners. ✉ *2110 Walton Way, 30904* ☎ *706/737–8888 or 800/476–6888* 📠 *706/731–0826* 🌐 *www.partridgeinn.com* *133 rooms, 26 suites* *Restaurant, some kitchens, pool, gym, bar, lounge, concierge floor, Internet, meeting room* 💳 *AE, D, DC, MC, V* *BP.*

Sports & the Outdoors

In early April Augusta hosts the much-celebrated annual **Masters Tournament** (🌐 www.masters.org), one of pro golf's most distinguished events. Tickets for actual tournament play are not available to the general public, but you can try to get tickets for one of the practice rounds earlier in the week—which, for golf addicts, is still hugely entertaining. Tickets are awarded on a lottery basis; write to the Masters Tournament Practice Rounds office Box 2047, Augusta, GA 30903 by July 15 of the year preceding the tournament.

CENTRAL GEORGIA A TO Z

To research prices, get advice from other travelers, and book travel arrangements, visit www.fodors.com

AIRPORTS

Athens Ben Epps Airport is served by US Airways. Augusta Regional Airport is served by Continental, Delta, and US Airways Express. Middle Georgia Regional Airport is served by Atlantic Southeast Airlines.

Airport Information **Athens Ben Epps Airport** ✉ 1010 Ben Epps Dr. ☎ 706/613-3420 🌐 www.athensairport.net. **Augusta Regional Airport** ✉ 1501 Aviation Way ☎ 706/798-3236. **Middle Georgia Regional Airport** ✉ 1000 Terminal Dr., Rte. 247 at I-75 ☎ 478/788-3760.

BUS TRAVEL

Greyhound Bus Lines serves Athens, Augusta, Macon, Madison, Milledgeville, and Washington.

FARES & SCHEDULES

Bus Information **Greyhound Bus Lines** ☎ 800/231-2222 🌐 www.greyhound.com.

CAR TRAVEL

U.S. 441, known as the Antebellum Trail, runs north–south, merging with U.S. 129 for a stretch and connecting Athens, Madison, Eatonton, and Milledgeville. Macon is on Route 49, which splits from U.S. 441 at Milledgeville. Washington lies at the intersection of U.S. 78, running east from Athens to Thomson, and Route 44, running south to Eatonton. I–20 runs east from Atlanta to Augusta, which is about 93 mi east of U.S. 441.

EMERGENCIES

Emergency Services **Ambulance, police** ☎ 911.

Hospitals **Doctors Hospital** ✉ 3651 Wheeler Rd., Augusta ☎ 706/651-3232. **Medical Center** ✉ 1199 Prince Ave., Athens ☎ 706/549-9977. **Macon Northside Hospital** ✉ 400 Charter Blvd., Macon ☎ 478/757-8200.

24-Hour Pharmacies **CVS** ✉ 1271 Gray Hwy., Macon ☎ 478/743-6979 or 912/743-8936.

LODGING

BED-AND-BREAKFASTS

Bed & Breakfast Online has detailed cyberbrochures on inns in Atlanta and surrounding areas.

Reservation Information **Bed & Breakfast Online** Box 829, Madison, TN 37116 🌐 www.bbonline.com/ga ☎ 615/868-1946.

TAXIS

Augusta Cab Company provides transportation throughout Augusta-Richmond County. There's a $1.75 initial charge, plus $1.50 per mi.

Your Cab Company is a reliable, 24-hour taxi service in Athens. Rates, based on a grid of designated area zones, start at $3. The fare to downtown from the airport costs $6.

Taxi Companies **Augusta Cab Company** ☎ 706/724-3543. **Your Cab Company** ☎ 706/546-5844.

TOURS

The Augusta Cotton Exchange conducts free tours of its historic brick building, with exhibits from its past as an arbiter of cotton prices. It also has Saturday van tours throughout the historic district of Augusta; the fee is $10 per person.

Classic City Tours conducts daily walking tours starting from the steps of the Athens Welcome Center at 2 PM. The 1½-hour tour takes participants through the city's antebellum neighborhoods. The fee is $10 per person ($8 per person for groups of 10 or more).

Tour Operators **Augusta Cotton Exchange** ☎706/724-4067. **Classic City Tours** ☎706/208-8687.

VISITOR INFORMATION

Georgia Welcome Center provides maps and brochures about prominent historical and recreational sites around the state.

Tourist Information **Athens Convention and Visitors Bureau** ✉ 300 N. Thomas St., 30601 ☎ 706/357-4430 or 800/653-0603 📠 706/549-5636 🌐 www.visitathensga.com. **Eatonton-Putnam Chamber of Commerce** ✉105 Sumter St., Eatonton 31024 ☎706/485-7701 🌐 www.eatonton.com. **Georgia Welcome Center** 📫 Box 211090, Martinez 30917 ☎ 706/737-1446. **Macon-Bibb County Convention and Visitors Bureau** ✉ 200 Cherry St., Macon 31201 ☎478/743-3401 or 800/768-3401 🌐 www.maconga.org. **Madison/Morgan County Chamber of Commerce** ✉ 115 E. Jefferson St., Madison 30605 ☎ 706/342-4454 🌐 www.madisonga.org. **Milledgeville Convention and Visitors Bureau** ✉ 200 W. Hancock St., 31061 ☎ 478/452-4687 🌐 www.milledgevillecvb.com. **Washington-Wilkes Chamber of Commerce** 📫 104 E. Liberty St., Box 661, Washington 30673 ☎ 706/678-2013 🌐 www.washingtonga.org.

NORTH GEORGIA

13

By Lan Sluder

AS AN ANTIDOTE to city life, nothing beats the clear skies, cascading waterfalls, and tranquil town squares of north Georgia. Within less than a half-day's drive from Atlanta, you can find yourself in the middle of a refreshing cluster of old Southern towns and nature sites that pepper the northern region of the state—the heart of lower Appalachia.

Mostly rural and lightly populated, north Georgia is home to one of the largest national forest areas in the East, the 750,000-acre Chattahoochee National Forest. About 15% of the Chattahoochee is designated as wilderness, and of this, the 37,000-acre Cohutta Wilderness is the largest national forest wilderness area in the Southeast. Several bold rivers, including the Chattahoochee, Oconee, Toccoa, and Chattooga, cut across the region, and Rabun, Burton, Nottley, and Chatuge lakes offer boating and fishing. All over north Georgia are small but enticing state parks, most with cabins for rent and inexpensive camp sites.

In Dahlonega, Cleveland, Blue Ridge, Helen, Clayton, and Ellijay, north and northeast of Atlanta, you can find shops selling handmade quilts, folk-art pottery, antiques, and loads of Grandma's chowchow in gingham-capped mason jars. These towns also offer plenty of activities—you can descend into a gold mine, explore a re-created Alpine village, or go apple picking. To the northwest are two of Georgia's most important historic sites: New Echota State Historic Site and the Chickamauga & Chattanooga National Military Park. And whether your preference is rustic or romantic, there are plenty of B&Bs, lodges, motels, and campgrounds to accommodate you.

Sandwiched between dynamic Atlanta and the dramatic western North Carolina mountains, north Georgia remains relatively undiscovered. Yours may be the only car at a scenic overlook, and you may be the only customer in an antiques shop—all the better for enjoying a quiet moment or finding a bargain. North Georgia lodgings usually only fill up on summer weekends and in October, when leaf colors are at their peak.

Exploring North Georgia

North Georgia is comprised of two fairly distinct areas: the northwest, with modest rolling hills at the edge of the Cumberland Plateau; and the north Georgia mountains, a part of the Blue Ridge Mountains, ranging from a modest 1,000 feet to Brasstown Bald, the highest peak in Georgia at 4,784 feet.

This is a region of small towns, connected by a web of country roads. Public transit is almost nonexistent; you'll need a car to explore. No single main highway gets you to all the points of interest. You'll have to study your maps carefully, and you'll likely end up doubling back here and there. Most of the secondary roads are lightly trafficked, but in the more mountainous areas you can face steep grades with sometimes treacherous curves.

Interstate 75 bisects northwest Georgia, running from Atlanta to Chattanooga, Tennessee. I–575 branches off from I–75, becoming U.S. highways 5, 515, and 76, winding up to the low mountains around Ellijay and Blue Ridge. State roads also branch off I–75 to the small towns in the northwestern part of the state and to the Chickamauga & Chattanooga National Military Park.

Traveling to the north Georgia mountains from Atlanta, you have two options. One is going north on U.S. 19 to Dahlonega, and from there to Cleveland and Helen, and then on, via GA 75, to Hiawassee, connecting with U.S. 76 there. The other route is I–985 toward Gainesville; I–985 (also GA 365) becomes U.S. 441, continuing up to Clayton and then to North Carolina and eventually into the Great Smoky Mountains National Park. If the mountains and lakes of Georgia are your main interests, U.S. 76 traverses most of them. This road covers a long arc from Clayton in the northeast to the towns of Hiawassee, Young Harris, Blairsville, Blue Ridge, and Ellijay. From Blairsville west and south it's mainly a four-lane divided road; in the other direction U.S. 76 is a two-lane or three-lane road. Dahlonega, Helen, and several of the Georgia state parks are contained within that arc, but you'll have to take side roads to reach them. The Cohutta Wilderness can be reached via GA 52, west out of Ellijay.

About the Restaurants

You can find far more fast food than four-star dining in north Georgia. Krystal, which was founded in 1932 across the Tennessee line in Chattanooga, has a number of outlets in northwest Georgia, serving distinctive small square burgers light on the beef and heavy on the onions. Small towns may have local diners where the menu runs to chopped beef and chicken pot pie. Here and there you can find a hotel dining room or independent restaurant with local specialties such as mountain trout. At a few country-style eateries, of which the Dillard House Restaurant near Clayton is a prime example, you'll be served heaping plates of ham, fried chicken, and other Southern dishes.

In season you can do well to buy local fruits and vegetables and have a picnic. Wonderful peaches and strawberries are available in early summer, followed by cantaloupe and watermelon season. Around Ellijay and Blue Ridge, apples are the major local crop, ripe in late summer and fall.

WHAT IT COSTS

$$$$	$$$	$$	$	¢
over $22	$16–$22	$11–$16	$7–$11	under $7

Prices are for a main course at dinner, excluding sales tax of 5%–7%.

About the Hotels

Motels, both chain and independents, are found along I–75 and in the 'burbs and small towns of north Georgia. You're not confined to motels, however; in some towns you can find 19th-century homes transformed into small inns or B&Bs.

In the mountains are several popular lodges, although the number and quality of inns and lodges in the north Georgia mountains doesn't stand

Numbers in the text correspond to numbers in the margin and on the North Georgia map.

If you have 3 days

Start your north Georgia visit in the heart of the Georgia mountains, with a night in the charming town of **Dahlonega** 1 where you can stay in comfort and visit the authentic Consolidated Gold Mine and the Gold Museum. Then, drive to Amicalola Falls State Park and stay at a lodge there. Explore parts of the Chattahoochee National Forest in the Amicalola. Finally, drive to **Helen** 2 for a look at a faux Bavarian village. If you need more fresh air, Smithgalls and Unicoi state parks are nearby, and both have lodges and campgrounds.

If you have 5 days

Follow the three-day itinerary above. On the fourth day, if you are a history buff, drive to northwest Georgia and stay in the **Chickamauga &Chattanooga National Military Park** 9 area. Visit the park and **New Echota** 7, one-time capital of the Cherokee Nation. On the fifth day, visit Cloudland Canyon and Lookout Mountain, or **Rome** 8. Alternatively, if you prefer the mountains, on the fourth day drive to **Clayton** 3 and stay in that area. Don't miss Tallulah Gorge and Black Rock Mountain state parks.

If you have 7 days

If you have a full week, follow the three-day itinerary above, visiting **Dahlonega** 1 and **Helen** 2. Then, drive to **Clayton** 3 and stay overnight in that area or along the shores of Lake Rabun. The next day, drive U.S. 76 to **Hiawassee** 4. Visit Brasstown Bald, the highest mountain in Georgia, and Lake Chatuge. Then, spend the night in the **Blue Ridge** 5 area, taking a trip on the Blue Ridge Scenic Railway. End your trip in northwest Georgia, staying in the **Chickimauga** 9 area, visiting Chickamauga and **New Echota** 7. If you have the time, visit **Rome** 8 and the unusual geological formations of far northwestern Georgia.

---

up to competition in the neighboring North Carolina mountains. Of special note in north Georgia are the accommodations at state parks, with attractively priced rustic cabins in scenic settings and, in several cases (such as the Lodge at Smithgall Woods and the Amicalola Falls Lodge), gorgeous mountain lodges are run by the state, and at bargain prices to boot. Private owners also offer cabins and cottages for rent, usually by the week. Local chambers of commerce and visitor bureaus usually maintain lists of these cabin rentals.

WHAT IT COSTS

$$$$	$$$	$$	$	¢
over $220	$160–$220	$110–$160	$70–$110	under $70

Prices are for two people in a standard double room in high season, excluding service charges and 11%–13% tax.

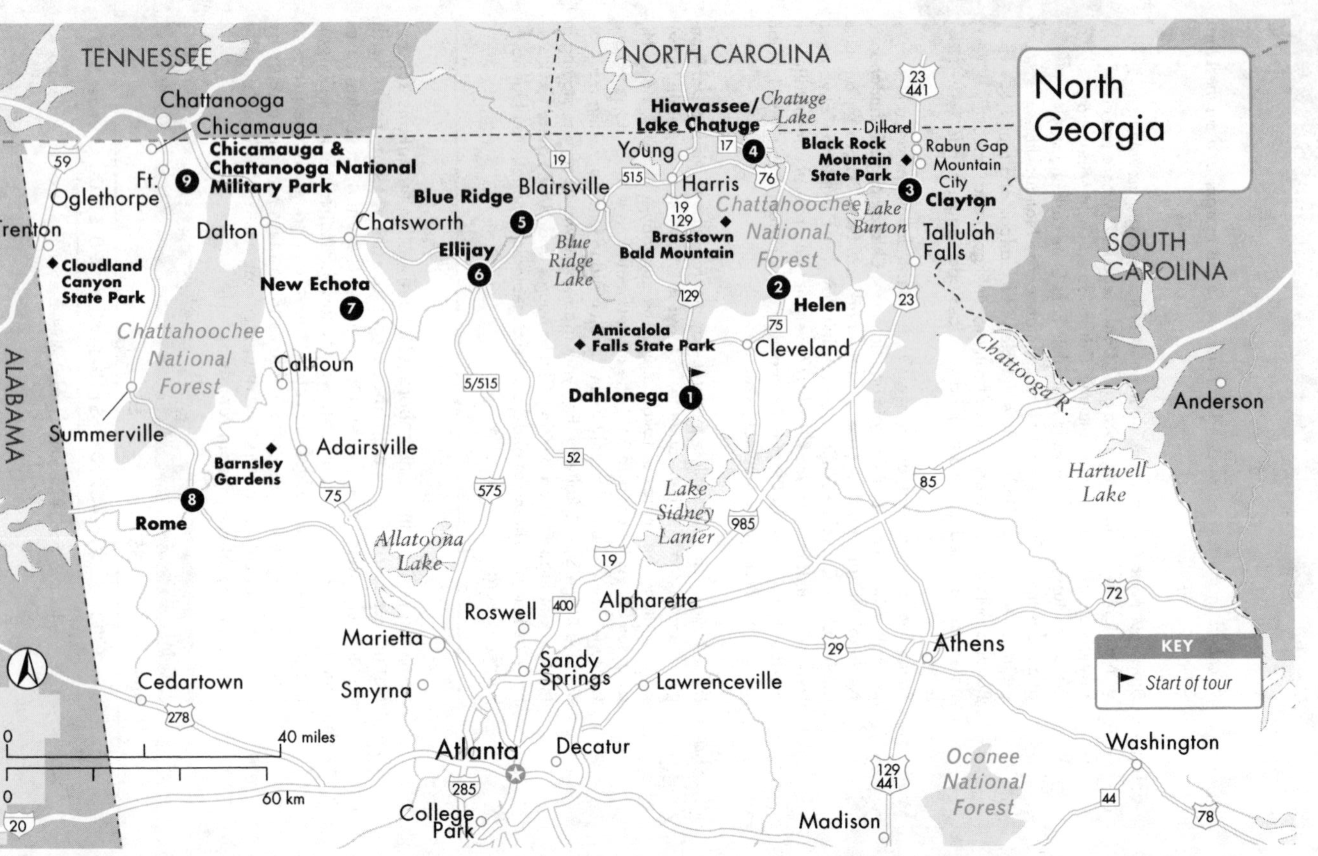

North Georgia
TENNESSEE
NORTH CAROLINA
SOUTH CAROLINA
ALABAMA
Chattanooga
Chicamauga
Chicamauga & Chattanooga National Military Park
Ft. Oglethorpe
Trenton
Cloudland Canyon State Park
Dalton
Chatsworth
Blue Ridge
Ellijay
Blairsville
Young
Harris
Hiawassee/Lake Chatuge
Chatuge Lake
Dillard
Black Rock Mountain State Park
Rabun Gap
Mountain City
Clayton
Lake Burton
Tallulah Falls
Chattahoochee National Forest
Brasstown Bald Mountain
Blue Ridge Lake
Helen
New Echota
Amicalola Falls State Park
Cleveland
Chattooga R.
Anderson
Dahlonega
Calhoun
Summerville
Adairsville
Barnsley Gardens
Rome
Hartwell Lake
Lake Sidney Lanier
Allatoona Lake
Roswell
Alpharetta
Marietta
Sandy Springs
Athens
KEY
Start of tour
Cedartown
Smyrna
Lawrenceville
0
40 miles
0
60 km
Atlanta
Decatur
Washington
Oconee National Forest
College Park
Madison

Timing

Summer and fall are prime times for travel. Weekends are far busier than weekdays, since many of the visitors to this region come up from nearby Atlanta to beat the heat. For the mountains, the ideal time is October and early November, when fall color is at its peak. Don't arrive at this time of year without reservations.

Most of the festivals take place in late summer and early fall. These include the Georgia Mountain Fair in Hiawassee in late July–early August; the Georgia Apple Festival in Ellijay and the Gold Rush Days in Dahlonega, in October; the Sorghum Festival in Blairsville in October; and the Oktoberfest in Helen, which now stretches from mid-September to early November.

THE NORTH GEORGIA MOUNTAINS

To most Georgians, "north Georgia" means the northeast and north central mountains and foothills—from Clayton and Dillard in the east to Hiawassee and Lake Chatuge in the north, and Blue Ridge and Ellijay and the Cohutta Wilderness to the west. Dahlonega, Helen, and several state parks—Black Rock Mountain, Moccasin Creek, Unicoi, Vogel, and Amicalola Falls—are contained within the broad arc of this scenic mountain region.

Dahlonega

1 Fodor's Choice ★

65 mi northeast of Atlanta via GA 400 and U.S. 19/GA 60 or via I–985, U.S. 23/441 and GA 60.

Hoards of fortune seekers stormed the town of Dahlonega (pronounced Dah-LON-eh-gah), in the 1820s after the discovery of gold in the hills nearby. The town's name comes from the Cherokee word for "precious yellow metal." But the boom didn't last long. By 1849 miners were starting to seek riches elsewhere. In fact, the famous call "There's gold in them thar hills!" originated as an enticement to miners in the Georgia mountains to keep their minds away from the lure of the gold rush out West. It worked for a while, but government price fixing eventually made gold mining unprofitable, and by the early 1920s Dahlonega's mining operations had halted completely.

Many former mining settlements became ghost towns, but not Dahlonega. Today it thrives as a rustic country outpost with an irresistible town square rife with country stores, art galleries, coffeehouses, gem shops, old small-town businesses, and even a sophisticated restaurant or two. Many of the 19th- and early-20th-century buildings in Dahlonega have been restored, and you can spend an enjoyable afternoon on a walking tour around town. The gold mines are still here, but are open mainly for show.

Gold Rush Days, a festival celebrating the first gold rush in 1828, attracts about 200,000 weekend visitors to this town of 3,700 people. The festival is always held the third weekend in October.

The **Gold Museum,** on the main square, has coins, tools, and a 5½-ounce nugget on display. The courthouse is the oldest public building in north Georgia, and if you look closely at the bricks that form the building's foundation, you'll notice a sprinkling of gold dust in their formation. Along with the exhibits, the museum has a short film celebrating the region's history through interviews with Appalachian old-timers. ✉ *Public Sq.* ☎ *706/864–2257* 🌐 *www.dahlonega.org* 🎫 *$3* ⏲ *Mon.–Sat. 9–5, Sun. 10–5.*

You can't miss the shiny gold steeple of **Price Memorial Hall,** the site of the U.S. Branch Mint before it burned down in 1878. (A U.S. Mint operated in this modest boomtown from 1838 to 1861—it closed and was later destroyed by fire, but the foundation remained intact.) Price Memorial Hall is now part of North Georgia College & State University. The steeple, erected in 1879, was originally covered with Dahlonega gold, but when it was regilded in 2000 local gold was not available. ✉ *W. Main St.* ☎ *706/864–1400* 🌐 *www.ngcsu.edu* ⏲ *Daily dawn–dusk.*

★ 👶 At **Consolidated Gold Mine** you can take guided tours of a real mine, last worked in the early 1980s. With 5 mi of underground tunnels, Consolidated is said to be the largest gold mine east of the Mississippi. You enter the mine (which has been reconstructed for safety), pass through a breathtaking stone passage, and then begin a descent of 120 feet into the mine's geological wonders. Guides, most of them actual miners, expound on historical mining techniques and give demonstrations of tools, such as the "widowmaker," a drill that kicks up mining dust and caused lung disease in many miners. After the tour, you're invited to pan for gold, prospector-style, from a long wooden sluice. ✉ *185 Consolidated Rd.* ☎ *706/864–8473* 🌐 *www.consolidatedgoldmine.com* 🎫 *$11* ⏲ *Daily 10–5.*

👶 The largest collection of kangaroos outside Australia is at the **Kangaroo Conservation Center,** an 87-acre wildlife park. This working farm is no zoo; the center has more than 200 red and gray 'roos, along with other wildlife, like wallabies, East African crowned cranes, and Australian wood ducks. You can go on a guided tour by truck, then walk through a "field of kangaroos." Admission by advance reservation only; minimum age for admission is 8 years ✉ *222 Bailey-Waters Rd., 15 mi from Dahlonega via GA 52, Dawsonville* ☎ *706/265–6100* 🎫 *$24.95.*

In the Dahlonega area you can find the largest concentration of **wineries** in Georgia. The most interesting include: **Wolf Mountain Vineyards** (✉ 180 Wolf Mountain Trail, 5 mi north of Dahlonega ☎ 706/867–9862 🌐 www.wolfmountainvineyards.com), a 25-acre vineyard on a ridgetop with hillside plantings of Cabernet Sauvignon, Syrah, Mourvedre, and Touriga Nacional. The winery has a collection of early winemaking artifacts. Call for tour information. **Three Sisters Vineyards** (✉ 439 Vineyard Way, 8 mi northeast of Dahlonega ☎ 706/865–9463 🌐 www.threesistersvineyards.com ⏲ Thurs.–Sat. 11–6, Sun. 1–6), on 184 acres, has 13 acres of plantings including Cabernet Franc, Merlot, Cabernet Sauvignon, Pinot Noir, Pinot Blanc, and Chardonnay, along with American varietals such as Cynthiana-Norton. **Frogtown Cellars** (✉ 3300 Damascus Church Rd., 6 mi northeast from Dahlonega ☎ 706/865–

0687 🌐 www.frogtownwine.com) is a 50-acre vineyard and winery featuring an atypical underground, gravity-flow winemaking facility on three floors. It uses gravity in place of pumps, with wine crush on the first level, fermentation on the second, and storage in wine barrels on the third and lowest level. Call for tour information and seasonal hours.

off the beaten path

AMICALOLA FALLS – This is claimed to be the highest waterfall east of the Mississippi, with waters plunging an eye-popping 729 feet through a cluster of seven cascades. The surrounding 1,021-acre state park is dotted with scenic campsites and cottages strategically situated near a network of nature trails, picnic sites, and fishing streams. The southern starting point of the 2,150-mi Appalachian Trail begins at Springer Mountain near Amicalola Falls. ✉ *Off GA 52, 18 mi west of Dahlonega, Dawsonville* ☎ *706/265–8888* 🌐 *www.ngeorgia.com/parks/amicalola.html* *Parking $2* ⏲ *Daily 7 AM–10 PM.*

13

Sports & the Outdoors

Appalachian Outfitters (✉ 1236 Golden Ave. ☎ 800/426–7177) provides equipment and maps for self-guided canoeing and kayaking expeditions on the Chestatee River. River trails begin at its outpost in town and extend to GA 400.

Where to Stay & Eat

$$–$$$$ ✕ **The Oar House.** Despite being housed in a rustic green building in the woods near the Chestatee River, this fine dining option brings a bit of Atlanta urbanity to Dahlonega. You can sit on the open-air patio decks while you have oysters on the half shell, shrimp scampi, or rack of New Zealand lamb. ✉ *3072 E. GA 52, 3½ mi from Dahlonega at MM 18* ☎ *706/864–9938* ▭ *AE, MC, V* ⏲ *Closed Sun.*

$$–$$$ ✕ **Smith House.** This is one of the most popular dining destinations in the north Georgia mountains. Heaping platters of all-you-can-eat family-style meals challenge the stamina of the tables and your stomach. Potatoes, fried chicken, peas, cobbler—you name a Southern dish, and it's probably offered here. The restaurant is mostly below ground, beneath the main house, which is a hotel. ✉ *84 S. Chestatee St.* ☎ *706/867–7000 or 800/852–9577* 🌐 *www.smithhouse.com* ▭ *AE, D, MC, V* ⏲ *Closed Mon.*

$–$$$ **Lily Creek Lodge.** This eclectic-looking B&B appears slightly Bavarian on the outside, and some of the rooms echo Venice, Morocco, and Argentina with their decor. The lodge sits on 7 acres and has a pool and outdoor hot tub. Breakfast includes cheese biscuits, granola, and fresh fruits, and port is served in the gathering room in the evening. ✉ *2608 Auraria Rd., 30533* ☎ *706/864–6848 or 888/844–2694* 🌐 *www.lilycreeklodge.com* *10 rooms, 3 suites* *Some kitchens, pool, boccie* ▭ *AE, MC, V* *BP.*

$–$$ **Worley Homestead.** This pristine B&B occupies an 1845 mansion with two garden courtyards. Everyone sits family-style at the large, formally set dining room table; breakfast includes caramelized French toast, casseroles, ham, sausage, and cheese grits. Often on weekend evenings the proprietors arrange a wine table with cheese and crackers in the entry

CloseUp

SWEET SORGHUM

IF YOU'VE EVER TASTED HOT BISCUITS *with fresh butter and sorghum syrup, you've come as close to heaven as you can get on this earth. At least, that's what country people in north Georgia say.*

Sorghum syrup has a sweet yet delicate flavor, not like regular molasses. Good sorghum syrup has a rich amber color, with just a hint of green, and when you mix it with farm butter and put it on a hot biscuit—made from White Lily flour, and only White Lily—there's nothing like it.

Sorghum syrup is the end product of sorghum cane, a cereal grass that in the field looks something like corn, and which probably came from Africa originally. Creating this sweet elixir is expensive and time-consuming so making sorghum syrup is a dying art. According to the University of Georgia, the cost of growing a single acre of sorghum cane is about $800, and takes 45 hours or more of a farmer's time.

At the end of the summer the cane stalks have to be harvested and pressed in a cane mill, often using horse power, to extract the cane juice.

In September or October local farms will slowly boil the fragrant cane juice in big copper pans, over wood fires. It takes 20 gallons of cane juice to make two gallons of sorghum syrup. This is a job that requires patience, skill, and practice. It takes about three hours to reduce the cane syrup to the right consistency and color. It has to be an amber color, not too green, and not burned. Connoisseurs of sorghum syrup know the real thing when they taste it. It may cost $8 or $10 a quart in a country store, but it's worth it.

foyer. Rooms are beautifully furnished, and three have wood-burning fireplaces. The B&B is within walking distance of the Dahlonega town square. ✉ *410 W. Main St., 30533* ☎ *706/864–7002 or 800/348–8094* ⊕ *www.bbonline.com/ga/worley* *7 rooms* ▭ *MC, V* *BP.*

¢–$$ **Fodor's Choice ★** **Amicalola Falls Lodge.** One of the most appealing mountain lodges in Georgia is part of the state park system. As you sit beside a large stone fireplace in the glass-walled lobby, you'll have panoramic views over the mountains. The rooms aren't fancy but you can pay far less than at a private country inn. The park also has 14 cottages for rent and a restaurant serving buffet meals. ✉ *418 Amicalola Falls State Park Rd., 20 mi west of Dahlonega via GA 52, Dawsonville 30534* ☎ *706/265–8888 or 800/573–9656* *706/265–4575* ⊕ *www.amicalolafalls.com* *53 rooms, 4 suites, 14 cottages* *Restaurant, cable TV, meeting rooms* ▭ *MC, V* *MAP.*

$ **Len Foote Hike Inn.** No cell phones, beepers or radios allowed! If you really want to get away from civilization and feel up to a 4½ mi hike of moderate difficulty (2 to 4 hours each way), this backcountry pack-it-in-and-pack-it-out inn at Amicalola State Park could be for you. While the inn has electric lights, there are no electrical outlets, and the showers and bathrooms are in a separate bathhouse. Rustic wood-paneled rooms each have two bunk beds and meals are served family-style. In order to have time to hike to the lodge, you *must* check in no later than 2 PM at the Amicalola Falls State Park visitor center. ✉ *240 Amicalola Falls State Park Rd., 20 mi west of Dahlonega via GA 52, Dawsonville 30534* ☎ *706/265–8888 or 800/573–9656* 📠 *706/265–4575* 🌐 *www.hike-inn.com* *20 rooms without bath* *Dining room; no A/C, no room phones; no pets* 💳 *MC, V* 🍽 *MAP.*

Helen

❷ *13 mi north of Cleveland via GA 75.*

When Helen was founded at the turn of the 20th century, it was a simple little lumber outpost. By the 1960s it was in danger of turning into a ghost town because of a logging bust. Local business leaders came up with a plan to save the town: they transformed the tiny village of 300 into a theme town, and "Alpine Helen," population 2,307, was born. Today businesses along Helen's central streets sport a distinctive German facade, giving you, at least initially, the impression that you've stumbled on a Bavarian vista in the middle of Appalachia. (There's also a scattering of Swiss, Belgian, Danish, Dutch, and Scandinavian facades.) There's no shortage of beer halls, restaurants serving imitation German food, steepled roofs, flowering window boxes, and billboards written in a vaguely Teutonic script. As phony as it all is, the effect can be contagious, making you feel as if you've walked into a fairy tale.

On weekends in summer and fall, Helen's streets approach a traffic gridlock, and parking (most lots in town charge $2 or $3 a day) is at a premium. Despite the ersatz Alpine theme, Helen's elevation of a mere 1,440 feet means it can get swelteringly hot in the summer. To cool off, consider a tube trip down the Chattahoochee or head to more authentic country towns like Dahlonega in the nearby Blue Ridge Mountains.

Chattahoochee National Forest covers about ¾-million acres of land in north Georgia. It's named after the Chattahoochee River, whose headwaters are in the north Georgia mountains. The area was created piecemeal, beginning in 1907, from bits and pieces of often environmentally degraded and abused land, and was officially established in 1936. About 15% of the Chattahoochee is wilderness. The national forest supports an estimated 500 species of fish and wildlife, including more than 600 black bears, 30,000 white-tailed deer, and 6,000 wild turkeys. In 1959, 96,000 acres of land in middle Georgia were added, and the combined forests are called the Chattahoochee-Oconee National Forests and total more than 865,000 acres. ✉ *1755 Cleveland Hwy. Gainesville 30501* ☎ *770/297–3000.*

At the **Nora Mill Granary,** the original 1,500-pound, 48-inch millstones from 1876 are still in working order. The grist mill, on the banks of the Chattahoochee River, utilizes a 100-foot sluice to feed 19th-century turbines. Grain is hauled to the mill in a vintage 1941 Chevrolet dump truck. A gift shop next door sells cornmeal, grits, and other staples ground on the premises. ✉ *7107 S. Main St.* ☎ *800/927–2375* 🌐 *www.noramill.com.*

off the beaten path

BRASSTOWN BALD – The highest mountain in Georgia, at 4,784 feet, rises in the heart of the Chattahoochee National Forest. Expect a dramatic vantage from which you can view four states—Tennessee, North Carolina, South Carolina, and Georgia. Bushels of wildflowers in the spring and autumn make this a fragrant sojourn as well. ✉ *1881 GA 515, 18 mi northwest of Helen via GA 17 and GA 180* ☎ *706/896–2556 or 706/745–6928* *Parking $3, shuttle to mountain $2* ⏲ *Daily 10–6.*

Sports & the Outdoors

TUBING "Tube the Hootch" with **Cool River Tubing** (✉ 590 Edelweiss Strasse ☎ 706/878–4078 or 800/896–4595 ⏲ Late May–early Sept.), which shuttles you on a bus upriver to begin the float back to town. You can choose a short (1½ hrs) or long (2½ hrs) float trip. Prices are $5 for a single trip of either length or $9 all day. Cool River also operates a waterslide. A combination all-day ticket for tubing and waterslide is $10.

Where to Stay & Eat

$$–$$$$ ✕ **Hofbrauhaus Inn.** This beer hall, which shares its name with a famous counterpart in Munich, welcomes a convivial and lively bunch, especially during Oktoberfest. The menu is saturated with hearty German-style food, including schnitzel and *bratkartoffeln* (fried potatoes), but none of it very good, despite its popularity among those who want to eat the "local" cuisine. There are also plenty of options for other international fare, including Hungarian goulash and broiled African lobster tails. ✉ *1 Main St.* ☎ *706/878–2248* ▭ *D, MC, V.*

$$–$$$$ ✕ **Nacoochee Grill.** Beef, chicken, and fish grilled on a live fire are the focus at this casual restaurant set in a cottage in Nacoochee Village, just outside town. A chowder made of roasted corn, trout and salmon is a specialty. Venison stew, delicious with a side of smashed horseradish potatoes; crabcakes; and pies made from local fruit, are available seasonally. ✉ *7277 S. Main St.* ☎ *706/969–8090* ▭ *AE, D, DC, MC, V.*

$–$$ ✕ **Farmer's Market Café.** This cheerfully decorated eatery has hearty, reasonably priced American fare—seafood, sandwiches, salads, and vegetable plates. ✉ *63 Chattahoochee St.* ☎ *706/878–3705* ▭ *AE, D, DC, MC, V.*

★ **$$$$** **The Lodge at Smithgall Woods.** As part of a 5,600-acre heritage preserve park run by the state of Georgia, the lodge, set in old growth hardwoods, consists of five separate cottages. The centerpiece is a two-story, four-bedroom cabin constructed of Montana lodge-pole pine. Meals, featuring locally grown vegetables and local specialties like mountain trout, are included in the rates. The state park has some of the best trout streams in Georgia, and the lodge is often used as an executive retreat by Atlanta businesspeople. Guests can book an individual room, a cottage (3 to 5 rooms), or the entire lodge. ✉ *61 Tsalaki Trail, 30545* ☎ *706/878–3087 or 800/318–5248* *706/878–0301* 🌐 *www.smithgallwoods.com* *14 rooms in 5 cottages* *Dining room, kitchens, fishing, hiking* ▭ *AE, D, MC, V* *FAP.*

¢–$$ **Country Inn & Suites.** This is the best of the chain motels in Helen. The faux-Bavarian motif carries only to the front door, and inside you'll find a lobby with hardwood floors and fireplace, a modern heated swimming pool, and well-maintained guestrooms. ✉ 877 s Strasse, 30545 ☎ 706/878–9000 or 800/458–4000 📠 706/878–7878 🌐 www.countryinns.com/helenga 47 rooms, 16 suites Indoor pool, exercise equipment, laundry facilities AE, D, DC, MC, V BP.

¢–$$ **The Lodge at Unicoi.** Choose either the comfortable mountain lodge, with 100 attractive lodge rooms, or a one-, two-, or three-bedroom cottage (some with a fireplace), at this state-run accommodation. You can fish, canoe, or swim in the 53-acre lake, play tennis, hike on 12 mi of trails, or take part in educational and nature events led by park rangers. In summer and fall reservations are essential and can be made up to 11 months in advance. ✉ *GA 356, 30545, 4 mi from Helen via GA 356* ☎ *706/878–2201 or 800/573–9659* 📠 *706/878–1897* 🌐 *www.unicoilodge.com* *100 rooms, 30 cottages* *Dining room, some kitchens, 4 tennis courts, lake, fishing, hiking, meeting rooms* *AE, D, MC, V* *EP.*

en route

Beginning and ending in Helen, the **Russell-Brasstown Scenic Byway** is a 41-mi loop through some of the most dramatic mountain scenery in northeastern Georgia. Start the counterclockwise drive from GA 17/75 north from Helen, turning left on GA 180 to GA 348, and then connecting with GA 17A back to Helen. The loop passes the Raven Cliff Wilderness, the headwaters of the Chattahoochee River, a section of the Appalachian Trail, and goes near the state parks of Vogel, Unicoi, and Smithgall Woods, and Brassy Bald mountain.

Clayton

❸ *35 mi northeast of Helen via GA 356, GA 197, and U.S. 76; 106 mi northeast of Atlanta via I–85, I–985, and U.S. 23/441; 95 mi southwest of Asheville, NC, via I–40 and U.S. 23/441.*

The town of Clayton, otherwise of little interest to visitors, is a gateway to north Georgia's mountains. It makes a good base to explore Tallulah Gorge State Park and its falls, and Black Rock Mountain State Park. A short drive northwest on U.S. 76 will take you to several of the region's most appealing lakes, including Rabun and Chatuge.

★ **Tallulah Gorge State Park** is home to a 2 mi-long, 1,000-foot-deep canyon, one of the deepest in the country. In the late 1800s this 2,689-acre park was one of the most-visited destinations in the Southeast, with 17 hotels to house tourists who came to see the roaring falls on the Tallulah River. Then, in 1912, to provide electric power, the "Niagara of the South" was dammed, and the falls dried up, along with the tourism. Today the state of Georgia has designated more than 20 mi of the state park as walking and mountain biking trails. There's also an interpretive center, a 63-acre lake with a beach, a picnic shelter, and 50 tent and RV sites. Permits (limited to 100 a day) are required to hike down into the gorge, which can be dangerous for inexperienced hikers. ✉ *U.S. 441, Tallulah Falls* ☎ *706/754–7970, 706/754–7979 for camping reservations* 🌐 *www.gastateparks.org/info/tallulah* *$4 parking fee* *Daily 8 AM–dusk.*

The **Foxfire Museum** is a collection of 20 log cabins, some authentic, assembled to re-create Appalachian life before the days of electricity and running water. The drive to the museum, up a steep, narrow road lined with junk cars and mobile homes, displays a bit of modern-day Appalachia. The nonprofit foundation behind Foxfire, established in 1966, has published a dozen Foxfire books on traditional Appalachian life, the most recent in late 2004. ✉ *Foxfire La., off Cross St., ½ mi from U.S. 441, Mountain City* ☎ *706/746–5828* 🎫 *$5* ⏲ *Weekdays 9–4.*

★ The **Chattooga River** was the first river in the Southeast to be designated a Wild and Scenic River by Congress. It begins in the Whitesides Mountains of North Carolina and forms the border between Georgia and South Carolina. With Class II to Class V rapids, the Chattooga is popular for white-water rafting, especially in spring and summer when water levels are highest. Movie buffs should note that this was one of the locations for the movie *Deliverance*. ✣ *From Clayton drive east 7 mi on U.S. 76 to the Hwy. 76 Bridge at the Georgia-South Carolina state line.*

Lake Rabun was built in 1915, the first of six lakes in the state built by Georgia Railway and Power Co. It covers only 834 acres, but its small size is misleading as its narrow fingers dart through mountain valleys. Lightly visited by tourists and populated with weekend cabins and old boat houses, it has a low-key charm. The lake offers boating and fishing, and there's a small beach at Rabun Beach Recreation Area at the east end of the lake. ✉ *West of U.S. 23/441 via Old Hwy. 441S. and Burton Lake Rd., 2½ mi southwest of Clayton* 🌐 *www.lakerabun.com.*

Another of the six lakes built by Georgia Railway and Power Co., the 2,700-acre **Lake Burton** is in the Chattahoochee National Forest. On the lake, at GA 197, is the **Lake Burton Fish Hatchery**, inside Moccasin Creek State Park. It has trout raceways (used to raise trout from fingerlings), and a kids-only trout fishing pool. ✉ *Off U.S. 76, west of Clayton, Clarkesville* ☎ *706/947–3194* 🎫 *$2 parking fee.*

★ At over 3,600 feet, **Black Rock Mountain State Park** is the highest state park in Georgia. Named for the black gneiss rock visible on cliffs in the area, the 1,738-acre park has 10 mi of trails, a 17-acre lake, 64 camp and RV sites, and 10 cottages. ✉ *Black Rock Mountain Pkwy., off U.S. 441, 3 mi northwest of Clayton, Mountain City* ☎ *706/746–2141, 800/864–7275 for camping and cottage reservations* 🌐 *www.gastateparks.org/info/blackrock/* 🎫 *$2 parking fee* ⏲ *Daily 7 AM–10 PM.*

Sports & the Outdoors

WHITE-WATER RAFTING

The North Carolina-based **Nantahala Outdoor Center** (✉ Chattooga Ridge Rd., 13 mi from Clayton off U.S. 76 ☎ 800/232–7238), the largest rafting company in the region, runs part-day, daylong, and overnight white-water rafting trips on the Chattooga River, for $50 to $230 per person. **Southeastern Expeditions** (✉ 7350 U.S. 76E ☎ 800/868–7328) has similar lengths and prices for its trips.

Where to Stay & Eat

★ $$–$$$$ **Glen-Ella Springs Country Inn.** This restored old hotel has a rustic charm, peaceful location, and fine food emphasizing regional specialties, such as trout pecan, pickled shrimp, and Lowcountry shrimp on grits. Rooms have no TVs but plenty of reading material, and they open onto common porches with rocking chairs. The splendid grounds invite hiking and exploring. The restaurant ($$–$$$$) has been showcased in many books, including *Great Cooking with Country Inn Chefs*, by Gail Greco. You have to BYOB. *1789 Bear Gap Rd., Clarkesville 30523 706/754–7295 or 877/456–7527 706/754–1560 www.glenella.com 12 rooms, 4 suites Restaurant, pool, hiking, meeting rooms; no room TVs AE, MC, V BP.*

¢–$$ Fodor's Choice ★ **Dillard House.** An inviting cluster of cottages and motel-style rooms, this establishment sits on a plateau near the North Carolina border. The extremely popular Dillard House Restaurant ($$–$$$), which was expanded in 2004, serves all-you-can-eat platters of Southern favorites such as country ham, fried chicken, barbecue, corn on the cob, and cabbage casserole. Breakfast is a gut buster. Some rooms have vistas of the Blue Ridge Mountains, stone fireplaces, or interior French doors, and many open onto a large front porch with rocking-chairs. *768 Franklin St., Dillard 30537 706/746–5348 or 800/541–0671 706/746–3680 www.dillardhouse.com 75 rooms, 25 chalets, 4 cottages, 6 suites Restaurant, some kitchens, some refrigerators, cable TV, 2 tennis courts, hot tub, horseback riding AE, D, DC, MC, V.*

$ **Lake Rabun Hotel.** Set in shady hemlocks across the road from Lake Rabun, this rustic hotel has rough-hewn wood paneling, a fieldstone fireplace, furniture handmade from mountain laurel and rhododendron, quilts on the beds, and very little to do except canoe, fish, or swim in the lake. The inn, built in 1922, is truly a throwback to an earlier time, so avoid it if you need modern amenities like TV and a private bath in every room. *35 Andrea La., Lakemont 30552 706/782–4946 www.lakerabunhotel.com 16 rooms, some with shared bath Restaurant, bar; no a/c, no room TVs AE, D, MC, V BP.*

Shopping

Clayton has more junk shops and flea markets than art galleries, but **Main Street Gallery** (641 Main St. 706/782–2440), one of the state's best sources for folk art, carries works by regional artists, including Sarah Rakes, O. L. Samuels, John DiSanza, Jay Schuette, and Jimmy Lee Sudduth. Quality local arts and crafts items are offered at **Georgia Heritage Center for the Arts** (U.S. 441 706/754–5989), which also has a branch at Clarkesville.

en route

From Clayton, **U.S. Highway 76** rambles west through rural areas and by lakes and small towns like Hiawassee, Young Harris, Blairsville, Blue Ridge, and Ellijay. Although not always scenic, the road makes for a pleasant drive, and the light traffic (except on weekends in peak summer and fall periods), is a plus. Beyond Blairsville, the two- and three-lane road becomes a divided highway of near-interstate quality.

Hiawassee/Lake Chatuge

❹ *26 mi northwest of Clayton, via U.S. 76; 21 mi north of Helen via GA 17 and 180.*

The little town of Hiawassee, population 750, and nearby Young Harris, population 600, are located near the largest lake in north Georgia, Lake Chatuge, and the tallest mountain in the state, Brasstown Bald. The lake has excellent boating and other water-themed recreation. Appealing mountain resorts are nearby as well. A half hour's drive will take you to Brasstown Bald, where temperatures even on the hottest summer day rarely rise above the low 80s. The Georgia Mountain Fair, held annually in July, has a permanent location on the shores of Lake Chatuge. A number of festivals are held at the fairgrounds every year, including the Rhododendron and Bluegrass festivals in May and the Fall Festival and State Fiddler's Convention in October. The Georgia Mountain Fair claims to be the "Country Music Capital of Georgia."

★ **Brasstown Bald,** in the Chattahoochee National Forest, reaches 4,784 feet, the highest point in Georgia. Below the Bald is Georgia's only cloud forest, an area of lichen-covered trees often kept wet by clouds and fog. From the observation platform at the top of the Bald on a clear day you can see Georgia, North Carolina, South Carolina, and Tennessee. A paved but steep ½-mi trail leads from the parking lot (where there are restrooms and a picnic area) to the visitor center, which has exhibits and interpretative programs. You also can ride a bus ($2) to the visitor center. ✉ *GA 180 Spur, 18 mi southwest of Hiawassee via U.S. 76, GA 75, GA 180, and GA 180 Spur* ☎ *706/896–2556* 🎫 *$3 parking fee* 🕒 *Late May–Oct., daily 10–6; Nov.–late May, weekends 10–6, depending on weather.*

Hamilton Rhododendron Gardens, on the grounds of the Georgia Mountain Fair at Lake Chatuge, display more than 3,000 rhododendrons, native azaleas, and other unique plants, including the rare yellow azalea developed by the garden's founder, Fred Hamilton. The best time to see the rhododendrons and azaleas in bloom is April to June. ✉ *Georgia Mountain Fairgrounds, Hiawassee* ☎ *706/896–4191* 🎫 *Free* 🕒 *Daily, 24 hrs.*

Where to Stay

★ **$$$–$$$$** ✕ **Brasstown Valley Resort.** For upscale, lodge-style accommodations, this resort is a great option. The rooms are comfortable and spacious, in an elegant but rustic style. Some have fireplaces and balconies overlooking the valley. The stone fireplace in the lobby is an impressive 70 feet high. The resort also features a variety of sports activities. ✉ *6321 U.S. 76, Young Harris 30582* ☎ *706/379–9900 or 800/201–3205* 📠 *706/379–4615* 🌐 *www.brasstownvalley.com* *102 rooms, 32 cottages, 5 suites* *Restaurant, cable TV, 18-hole golf course, 4 tennis courts, pool, health club, hot tub, sauna, hiking, bar, convention center* 💳 *AE, D, DC, MC, V* 🍽 *BP.*

$–$$$ **Fieldstone Inn.** Many of the beautifully appointed rooms in this lodge are decorated with cherry-wood furniture and have a gorgeous view of Lake Chatuge. You can relax in the lobby before a towering fieldstone fireplace and admire the landscape from the floor-to-ceiling window that faces the lake. A nearby marina has boat rentals, including pontoons, paddleboats, houseboats, sailboats, and kayaks. Sizable discounts are available in winter. ✉ *3499 U.S. 76, at Georgia Mountains Fairgrounds, Hiawassee 30546* ☎ *706/896–2262 or 888/834–4409* 🖷 *706/896–4128* 🌐 *www.fieldstoneinn.com* *62 rooms, 4 suites* *Restaurant, tennis court, pool, exercise equipment, boating, marina, convention center* 💳 *AE, D, DC, MC, V* *BP.*

Blue Ridge

13

❺ *39 mi southwest of Hiawassee via U.S. 76/GA 515; 66 mi west of Clayton via U.S. 76/GA 515; 53 mi northwest of Dahlonega via GA 52 and GA 515; 93 mi north of Atlanta via I–75, I–575 and GA 5/515*

Blue Ridge, population 1,200, is one of the most pleasant small mountain towns in north Georgia. After you've shopped for antiques or crafts at Blue Ridge's many small shops, you can ride the revived Blue Ridge Scenic Railway to McCaysville, a town at the Tennessee line, and then back through the mountains.

The **Blue Ridge Scenic Railway** makes a 3½ hour, 26-mi round-trip along the Toccoa River, including a stop in McCaysville, Georgia. The train, which has open and Pullman cars and is pulled by diesel engines, is staffed with friendly volunteer hosts. The ticket office, now on the National Register of Historic Places, dates from 1905 and was originally the depot of the L&N Railroad. ✉ *241 Depot St.* ☎ *706/632–9833 or 800/934–1898* 🌐 *www.brscenic.com* *$22–$28* *Mid-Mar.–mid-Dec. Call for schedules.*

The **Swan Drive-In Theater** originally opened in 1955 and is one of only four drive-in movie theaters still operating in Georgia. You can take in a movie under the stars and fill up on corn dogs, tater wedges, and popcorn from the concession stand. Window speakers have been replaced by the movie sounds broadcast to your car radio. The name of the drive-in comes from the swans in the ponds of England that the owner admired during World War II. ✉ *651 Summit St.* ☎ *706/632–5235.*

Ellijay

❻ *84 mi west of Clayton via U.S. 76; 37 mi northwest of Dahlonega via GA 52; 80 mi north of Atlanta via I–75, I–575, and GA 5/515.*

Billed as "Georgia's apple capital," Ellijay is also popular among antiques aficionados. The town, on the site of what had been a Cherokee village called Elatseyi (meaning "place of green things"), has a colorful cluster of crafts shops, antiques markets, and art galleries.

The most popular time to visit Ellijay is in fall, when roadside stands brimming with delicious ripe apples dot the landscape. The annual Georgia Apple Festival takes place in mid-October. In addition to showcasing the many manifestations of the crisp fruit—apple butter, apple pie, apple cider, and so on—the festival offers a host of arts and crafts shows.

Pick your own apples (usually August–early November) at the 80-acre **Hillcrest Orchards.** Feast on homemade jellies, jams, breads, and doughnuts at the farm's market and bakery. Also on the orchard's premises are a petting zoo, a small museum, and a picnic area. On some September weekends (dates vary), the Apple Pickin' Jubilee features live music, wagon rides, and other activities. ✉ *9696 GA 52* ☎ *706/273–3838* 🌐 *www.hillcrestorchards.net* *$5 for special events including Apple Pickin' Jubilee; $3 for petting zoo* ⏲ *Daily 9-6.*

The 3,500-acre **Fort Mountain State Park** has a 17-acre lake with sandy beach, horseback riding (for a fee), 14 mi of hiking trails, and 30 mi of mountain biking trails ($2 trail fee for biking). The gem of the park is a mysterious wall of rock, 855 feet long, thought to have been built by Native Americans around 500 AD Tent and RV sites ($20–$22) and rental cottages ($80–$120) are also on-site. ✉ *181 Fort Mountain Park Rd., Chatworth* ☎ *706/695–2621* *Free* ⏲ *Daily 7 AM–10 PM.*

Sports & the Outdoors

There are plenty of options for fishing, canoeing, and kayaking on the Cartecay River, which runs through town. **Mountaintown Outdoor Expeditions** (✉ GA 52 ☎ 706/635–2524) arranges outdoor adventures for people of all skill levels.

Where to Stay

$$$ **Whitepath Lodge.** From nearly every room you get panoramic vistas of the tranquil north Georgia mountains. The main lodge has eight suites, each with two bedrooms, three baths, and a fully equipped kitchen. The neighboring Shenandoah Lodge has six two-floor suites with fireplaces and multilevel decks overlooking the woods. If you're a sports enthusiast, you'll be happy with all the recreational activities nearby—18-hole golf courses, mountain biking, horseback riding, tubing, seasonal whitewater rafting, boating, canoeing, kayaking, and fishing. ✉ *987 Shenandoah Dr., Ellijay 30540* ☎ *706/276–7199* 🌐 *www.whitepathlodge.com* *14 suites* *Restaurant, some kitchens, tennis court, pool, basketball, hiking, meeting rooms* *AE, D, DC, MC, V* *EP.*

$–$$ **Cohutta Lodge.** Set on 150 acres atop Fort Mountain near the Cohutta Wilderness, the views from this lodge are resplendent. Reopened under new management in 2003, the lodge's faux log-cabin exterior and sometimes less-than-eager service may not be perfect, but the location makes up for it. Outdoor activities can be arranged through the hotel. ✉ *500 Cochise Trail, off GA 52, Chatsworth 30705* ☎ *706/695–9601* *706/695–0913* 🌐 *www.cohuttalodge.com* *52 rooms, 3 suites, 1 cabin* *Restaurant, indoor pool, 2 tennis courts, hiking, horseback riding, meeting rooms* *AE, D, MC, V* *EP.*

¢–$$ **Best Western Mountain View Inn.** New in 2003, this two-story motel sits on a hilltop above East Ellijay. It lacks atmosphere, but the rooms sport cheerful decor with bedspreads in bright primary colors. Some rooms indeed have mountain views. The suites are just oversized rooms with a sitting area, not true suites, but they have two TVs. ✉ *43 Coosawattee Dr., East Ellijay 30539* ☎ *706/515–1500 or 866/515–4515* 🌐 *www.bwmountainviewinn.com* *52 rooms* *Indoor pool, hot tub, Internet* *AE, D, DC, MC, V* *BP.*

Shopping

Mountain Treasures (✉ 511 GA 52 ☎ 706/635–5590) sells mountain home furnishings with a comfortable lodge motif. **Ellijay Antiques Mall** (✉ 66 N. Main St. ☎ 706/276–7622) is a fun collective that spans 7,000 square feet, with everything from clocks to ceramic curios.

en route

From Ellijay, GA 52 west to Chatsworth and the Chief Vann historic site, passing Fort Mountain State Park, has some very scenic sections. Likewise, the same road going southeast to Dahlonega has beautiful mountain vistas.

THE NORTHWEST

Northwest Georgia remains partly in the shadow of the troubled history of the Cherokee Indians, driven from their verdant homes in Georgia and North Carolina on the Trail of Tears to dusty Oklahoma. There are also ghosts of the Civil War, notably the bloody battle of Chicamauga. You can explore this sad history at New Echota, once the capital of the Cherokee Nation, and at the Chicamauga and Chattanooga National Military Park. Northwest Georgia lies along the Cumberland Plateau, with its flat-topped sandstone mountains. Most of the Cumberland Plateau is in neighboring Alabama and Tennessee, but Cloudland Canyon and Lookout Mountain are Georgia's.

New Echota

7 *71 mi northwest of Atlanta via I–75 north to GA 225; 41 mi southwest of Ellijay via U.S. 76 to GA 136.*

From 1825 to 1838 New Echota was the capital of the Cherokee Nation, whose constitution was patterned after that of the United States. The town was named in honor of Chota, a Cherokee town in present-day Tennessee. There was a council house, a printing office, a Supreme Court building, and the *Cherokee Phoenix*, a newspaper, the first established (in 1826) by Native Americans, that utilized the 86-character alphabet developed by Sequoyah, who spent 12 years developing the written Cherokee language despite having no formal education. He is the only known person in history to have single-handedly created a written language.

The Treaty of 1835, signed in New Echota by a small group of Cherokee leaders who had decided it was futile to resist the U.S. plan to remove them from their lands, relinquished Cherokee claims to lands east of the Mississippi. Most Cherokees considered the treaty fraudulent. A few years later 7,000 federal and state troops began removing Cherokee from their homes in Georgia, North Carolina, and Tennessee and put them in stockades, including one in New Echota. The Cherokee were then forced to travel west to Oklahoma, along what is known as the "Trail of Tears," as some 4,000 died along the way. After reaching Oklahoma in 1839, the three principal signers of the Treaty of 1835 were assassinated by Cherokee who considered them traitors.

CloseUp

CAN YOU SPEAK MOUNTAIN?

THESE DAYS, MOST PEOPLE IN THE MOUNTAINS *of north Georgia speak the same version of English everyone else speaks. Television, radio, and compulsory education have diluted the diversity of the local patois.*

But even today, the farther back to the "head of the holler" (the starting point of a cove in the mountains) you're "a-likely" to go, the more you will hear the old-timey English of the Blue Ridge mountains. The accents aren't a product of ignorance and their speakers are no "hillbillies." The mountain dialect is a result of the geographic isolation of descendants of the English and Scotch-Irish who moved to the mountains several centuries ago. In fact, the accents and cadences of their language echo the old English of Shakespeare's time.

Here are a few translations of some mountain expressions you may hear in north Georgia:

Airish: *cool, as in, "It's airish tonight."*

Boomer: *a red squirrel, common in the higher mountains.*

Dope: *a soft drink or soda, as in, "I'm goin' to buy me a dope to drink."*

Poke: *a paper bag.*

Her'n and his'n: *hers and his; these possessive forms go back to the Middle Ages.*

Hit: *it, as in, "Hit don't make no difference."*

Waspers and mud dabbers: *wasps.*

Whar and thar: *where and there; relics of common Scots usage.*

Following the removal of the Cherokee, New Echota reverted to farmland. Some buildings here have been entirely reconstructed, and some originals have simply been restored, but there is no town there today. When visiting New Echota and the Chief Vann House, you can stay in Calhoun, the nearest town to New Echota, or in Dalton, Rome, Chickamauga, or even in Chattanooga.

A small museum and a collection of reconstructed and restored buildings at **New Echota State Historic Site** detail the site's history. ✉ *1211 Chatsworth Hwy., GA 225, 1 mi east of I–75 near Calhoun* ☎ *706/624–1321* 🌐 *www.georgiastateparks.org* 🎫 *$3.50* ⏲ *Tues.–Sat. 9–5, Sun. 2–5:30.*

The beautifully restored, three-story brick **Chief Vann House** was commissioned in 1804 by a leader of the Cherokee Nation. Moravian artisans helped construct the intricately carved interior mantles and other woodwork. Of mixed Scottish and Cherokee parentage, Chief James Vann owned numerous slaves who also worked on the construction of the house. His son, Cherokee statesman Joseph Vann, lived in the house until he was evicted by the Georgia Militia in 1835, and forced to move to Cherokee Territory, in what is now Oklahoma. ✉ *82 GA 225 at GA 52,*

Chatsworth, 20 mi northeast of New Echota ☎ *706/695–2598* 💵 *$3* ⏲ *Tues.–Sat. 9–5, Sun. 2–5:30.*

Rome

8 *23 mi southwest of Calhoun via GA 53; 62 mi southwest of Chatsworth via GA 52, I–75 and GA 53; 70 mi northwest of Atlanta via I–75, U.S. 411 and U.S. 27.*

Like its much larger Italian namesake, Rome, Georgia, population 35,000, is built on seven hills. Indeed, a bronze replica of the Capitoline Wolf on which Romulus and Remus suckled, can be seen in downtown Rome, in front of City Hall. The statue was a 1929 gift from the government of Italy.

Rome was an important transportation center during the Civil War, but since then has become better known as the site of a remarkable college, Berry College, where generations of rural Georgians have earned higher educations.

The **Oak Hill and the Martha Berry Museum** has exhibits telling the story of Martha Berry (1866–1942) and the college that bears her name. Founded by Berry in 1902 as a public school for enterprising but poor rural Georgians, Berry College is now considered the largest college campus in America, sitting on a 28,000-acre campus. "Education combines the head, heart, and hands," Berry said, and the school continues its founder's policies of low tuition and a work-study program so that first-generation college students can afford to attend. You can also tour Berry's estate, Oak Hill, with its five gardens, originally designed 1927–33. ✉ *Veterans Memorial Hwy. at U.S. 27* ☎ *706/291–1883 or 800/220–5504* 🌐 *www.berry.edu* 💵 *$5* ⏲ *Mon.–Sat. 10–5.*

Featuring Native American artifacts, art work, and other displays, the **Chieftains Museum,** on the banks of the Oostanaula River, is housed in an 18th-century white clapboard plantation house, the former home of Major Ridge, a Cherokee tribal leader. ✉ *501 Riverside Pkwy. NE* ☎ *706/291–9494* 💵 *$3* ⏲ *Tues.–Fri. 9–3, Sat. 10–4.*

Where to Stay & Eat

$$–$$$ ✕ **La Scala.** Piero Barba from Capri, Italy, established this outpost of Italian cooking in 1996. The menu is dominated by classic dishes: osso buco, braciola, seafood, and pasta. The wine list, which Barba claims is the largest in north Georgia, includes French, American, and Italian wines. ✉ *413 Broad St.* ☎ *706/238–9000* 💳 *AE, D, DC, MC, V* ⏲ *Closed Sun. No lunch.*

★ **$–$$** 🏨 **Claremont House.** This beautifully restored 1890s Victorian inn has huge rooms with 14-foot ceilings and furnished with period antiques. Breakfast is sumptuous, featuring stuffed French toast among its delicious options. ✉ *906 E. 2nd Ave., 30161* ☎ *706/291–0900 or 800/254–4797* 📠 *706/232–9865* 🌐 *www.bbonline.com/ga/claremont/* 🛏 *4 rooms, 1 cottage* ♿ *Internet* 💳 *AE, D, MC, V* 🍽 *BP.*

$ 🏨 **Hampton Inn.** Set on a hill on the east side of Rome, this chain motel has the usual Hampton Inn amenities. It's clean and comfortable. ✉ *21*

Chateau Dr., off U.S. 411, 30161 ☎ 706/232–9551 or 800/426–7866 📠 706/232–5272 🌐 www.hamptoninn.com 60 rooms, 4 suites Refrigerators, pool, exercise equipment AE, D, DC, MC, V BP.

Chickamauga & Chattanooga National Military Park

9 *110 mi northwest of Atlanta via I–75 and GA 2; 42 mi north of New*
Fodor'sChoice *Echota State Historic Site via I–75; 12 mi south of Chattanooga, TN,*
★ *via U.S. 27.*

This site, established in 1890 as the nation's first military park, was the scene of one of the Civil War's bloodiest battles: 34,624 killed and wounded in September 1863. Though the Confederates won the battle at Chickamauga, the Union army retained control of Chattanooga. The normally thick cedar groves and foliage covering Chickamauga were trampled and, according to eyewitness accounts, trees were so shot up that a sweet cedar smell mingled with the blood of fallen soldiers.

Some areas around the park now suffer from suburban sprawl, but the 9,000-acre park itself is made up of serene fields and islands of trees. Monuments, battlements, and weapons adorn the roads that traverse the park, with markers explaining the action.

The excellent **Chickamauga Battlefield Visitor Center** has reproduction memorabilia, books, a large collection of antique military rifles, and a film on the battle. There's a 7-mi self-guided auto tour through the park, and mid-June to September you can join a free, 90-minute auto tour through the park, led by a park ranger, each in your own vehicles. *✉ Fort Oglethorpe, 1 mi south of intersection of GA 2 and U.S. 27 ☎ 706/866–9241 🌐 www.nps.gov/chch Free Daily 8–4:45.*

The **Walker County Regional Heritage & Model Train Museum,** in a former railroad depot, has a fascinating hodgepodge of items from the attics and garages of Chickamauga residents. You'll see everything from Civil War and World War I artifacts to 1950s lawn mowers and HO-gauge model trains. *✉ 100 Gordon St., Chickamauga ☎ 706/375–4488 Donations accepted Mon.–Sat. 10–4.*

off the beaten path

CLOUDLAND CANYON STATE PARK – At this 2,515-acre park, you can see firsthand the unusual geology of this remote part of northwestern Georgia. Hike down the canyon, which drops 1,100 feet from the rim, and you're literally walking down millions of years of geologic time. If you make it all the way to the bottom—the trail totals 4.5 mi—you'll be rewarded with sights of two waterfalls. *✉ 122 Cloudland Canyon Park Rd., Rising Fawn ☎ 706/657–4050 Free Daily 7 AM–10 PM.*

Where to Stay

$–$$ **Gordon-Lee Mansion.** To capture the feeling of the Civil War era, stay overnight at this antebellum Greek Revival brick mansion, which served as a field hospital during the battle at Chickamauga. Four bedrooms are in the main house, where breakfast is served. Or you can stay in the 1900 log house, formerly Congressman Gordon Lee's office, and have the run of two bedrooms, a living room with fireplace, and a full kitchen where you prepare your own breakfast. ✉ *217 Cove Rd., Chickamauga 30707* ☎ *706/375–4728 or 800/487–4728* 🖷 *706/375–9499* 🌐 *www.gordonleemansion.com* *4 rooms, 1 cottage* *AE, MC, V* *BP.*

NORTH GEORGIA A TO Z

To research prices, get advice from other travelers, and book travel arrangements, visit www.fodors.com

13

CAR TRAVEL

U.S. 19 runs north–south, passing through Dahlonega and up into the north Georgia mountains. U.S. 129 runs northwest from Athens, passing through Cleveland and subsequently merging with U.S. 19. GA 75 stems off U.S. 129 and goes through Helen and up into the mountains. U.S. 23/441 runs north through Clayton; U.S. 76 runs west from Clayton to Dalton, merging for a stretch with GA 5/515. GA 52 runs along the edge of the Blue Ridge Mountains, passing through Ellijay. I–75 is the major artery in the northwesternmost part of the state and passes near the New Echota State Historic Site and the Chickamauga and Chattanooga National Military Park.

EMERGENCIES

Emergency Services **Ambulance, police** ☎ 911.

Hospitals **Laurelwood/Blairsville Hospital** ✉ 214 Hospital Circle, Blairsville ☎ 706/745-8641. **Northwest Georgia Regional Hospital** ✉ 400 Redmond Rd., Rome ☎ 706/295-6246.

Pharmacies **CVS** ✉ 220 Old Orchard Sq., Ellijay ☎ 706/635-2538 ✉ 40 GA 515, Blairsville ☎ 706/745-9601 ✉ U.S. 441 ☎ 706/782-2722.

SPORTS & THE OUTDOORS

FISHING Upper Hi Fly Fishing and Outfitters offers personalized guided trout and fly-fishing trips in the southern Appalachian Mountains. It also operates a full-service fly-fishing shop with state-of-the-art equipment. In Helen, Unicoi Outfitters offers fly-fishing classes and guided fishing trips.

Upper Hi Fly Fishing and Outfitters ✉ Hiawassee ☎ 706/896-9075 🌐 www.upper-hi-fly.com. **Unicoi Outfitters** ✉ 7280 S. Main St., Helen ☎ 706/878-3083.

HIKING All of the Georgia state parks in north Georgia offer excellent hiking opportunities. Black Rock Mountain State Park has 10 mi of hiking trails; Fort Mountain, 14 mi; Tallulah Gorge State Park, 30 mi; Unicoi, 12 mi; and Vogel, 17 mi. Most state parks in north Georgia also have picnic sites and campgrounds, and some have fishing lakes, trout streams, and horseback riding. About ¾-million acres of forest land are in the Chattahoochee National Forest, which covers large areas of north Georgia. And the Appalachian Trail's southernmost point is in north Georgia, at Springer Mountain, near Amicalola Falls State Park.

Black Rock Mountain State Park ✉ Black Rock Mountain Pkwy., Drawer A, Mountain City 30562 ☎ 706/746-2141 🌐 www.gastateparks.org/info/blackrock/. **Fort Mountain State Park** ✉ 181 Fort Mountain Park Rd., Chatsworth 30705 ☎ 706/695-2621 🌐 www.gastateparks.org/info/fortmt/. **Tallulah Gorge State Park** ✉ U.S. 441 (Box 248), Tallulah Falls 30573 ☎ 706/754-7970 🌐 www.gastateparks.org/info/tallulah/. **Unicoi State**

Park ⊠ 1788 GA 356 (Box 849), Helen 30545 ☎ 706/878-3983 ⊕ www.gastateparks.org/info/unicoi/. **Vogel State Park** ⊠ 7485 Vogel State Park Rd., Blairsville 30512 ☎ 706/745-2628 ⊕ www.gastateparks.org/info/vogel/.

VISITOR INFORMATION

Tourist Information **Alpine Helen–White County Convention and Visitors Bureau** Box 730, Helen 30545 ☎ 706/878-2181 or 800/858-8027 ⊕ www.helenga.org. **Blairsville/Union County Chamber of Commerce** ⊠ 385 Blue Ridge Hwy., Blairsville 30512 ☎ 706/745-5789 ⊕ www.blairsvillechamber.com. **Dahlonega-Lumpkin Chamber of Commerce** ⊠ 13 Park St. S, Dahlonega 30533 ☎ 706/864-3513 or 800/231-5543 706/864-7917 ⊕ www.dahlonega.org. **Dalton–Whitfield County Convention and Visitors Bureau** ⊠ 2211 Dug Gap Battle Rd., Dalton 30720 ☎ 706/270-9960 or 800/331-3258 706/278-5811 ⊕ www.daltoncvb.com. **Fannin County Chamber of Commerce** ⊠ 3990 Appalachian Hwy., Blue Ridge 30513 ☎ 706/632-5680 or 800/899-6867 ⊕ www.blueridgemountains.com. **Gilmer County Chamber of Commerce** ⊠ 5 Westside Sq., Ellijay 30540 ☎ 706/635-7400 ⊕ www.gilmerchamber.com. **Helen Welcome Center** 726 Bruckenstrasse, Box 730, 30545 ☎ 706/878-2181 or 800/858-8027 706/878-4032 ⊕ www.helenga.com. **Rabun County Welcome Center** Box 750 232 U.S. 441N, Clayton 30525 ☎ 706/782-5113 ⊕ www.gamountains.com. **Greater Rome Convention and Visitors Bureau** Box 5823, Rome 30162 ☎ 706/295-5576 or 800/444-1834 ⊕ www.romegeorgia.org.**Towns County Chamber of Commerce** 1411 Fuller Circle, Young Harris 30582 ☎ 706/896-4966. **White County Chamber of Commerce** ⊠ 122 N. Main St., Cleveland 30528 ☎ 706/865-5356 ⊕ www.whitecountychamber.org.

INDEX

G

W

Y

Z